MACMILLAN
COMPENDIUM

AMERICA AT WAR

MACMILLAN

COMPENDIUM

AMERICA AT WAR

SELECTED ARTICLES FROM THE
THREE-VOLUME
Encyclopedia of the American Military

MACMILLAN LIBRARY REFERENCE USA

New York

Macmillan Library Reference USA
1633 Broadway
New York, NY 10019

Manufactured in the United States of America

Printing number
1 2 3 4 5 6 7 8 9 10

Library of Congress Cataloging-in-Publication Data

America at war : selected articles from the three-volume
Encyclopedia of the American military.
p. cm. — (Macmillan compendium)
"Biographies . . . were gleaned from various Macmillan and Scribner encyclopedias"—Pref.
Includes index.
Summary: Presents America's wartime history from the Revolution to the Persian Gulf. Includes biographies of military personnel and information on treaties.
ISBN 0-02-865061-1 (alk. paper)
1. United States—History, Military. 2. United States—Armed Forces—Biography. [1. United States—History, Military. 2. United States—Armed Forces—Biography.] I. Encyclopedia of the American military. II. Series.
E181.A39 1998
355′.0092′273—dc21
[B] 98-41961
CIP
AC

This paper meets the requirements of ANSI/NISO Z39.48-1992 (Permanence of Paper).

Contents

Part 1 – America's Wars

Part 2 – The Armed Forces

Part 3 – America's Military Leaders

Appendices

Preface

ORIGINS

This single-volume reference work is garnered and assembled from the award-winning three-volume *Encyclopedia of the American Military*, originally published in 1994 by Charles Scribner's Sons. The *Encyclopedia of the American Military* was lauded by the *Wilson Library Bulletin* for thoroughly explaining the United States military history "in the context of the society it serves, the institutions it protects, and the legal limits within which it must operate." Foremost among the encyclopedia's accolades was the honor of being named an American Library Association Outstanding Reference Source for 1994 and a *Library Journal* outstanding reference source for 1994.

The Encyclopedia of the American Military was originally edited by John E. Jessup, Dean of the American Military University and former president of the United States Commission on Military History. Many other noted historians, experts, and professors contributed to the original multivolume set, and selected efforts are presented in this volume. (For complete author information, please consult the multivolume encyclopedia.) From such peerage comes this single-volume encyclopedia describing America's wartime history from colonial times to the 1990s, as well as the history of America's military leaders and the five branches of America's armed services.

It is no simple editorial task to take the 2,255 pages of the multivolume work and publish a 1,000-page version; our editors, therefore, selected the most relevant articles with complete bibliographies and cross-references, and presented them as whole, uncut selections. Biographies in *America at War* were gleaned from various Macmillan and Scribner encyclopedias, including the *Encyclopedia of the Confederacy*, the *Encyclopedia of African American History*, and the *Encyclopedia of the American West*. Thus, this volume is an overview of the evolution of America's wartime history. The Macmillan Compendium *America at War* is the concise, one-source reference for discussion, clarification, definition, research, and elucidation for readers interested in every aspect of America's wartime history.

FEATURES

To add visual appeal and enhance the usefulness of the volume, the page format was designed to include the following helpful features.

- Call-out quotations: These relevant, provocative quotations are highlighted to promote reader interest and exploration.
- Cross-references: Appearing within articles, cross-references will encourage further research.
- Photographs: Chosen to complement the text, the photographs are selected to further engage the reader.
- Index: A thorough index provides thousands of additional points of entry into the work.

Macmillan Library Reference

Timeline

A chronology of the events in American military history can provide a listing of any or all skirmishes, battles, campaigns, and wars and pinpoint key events within the military itself, such as structure reorganizations or reductions and increases in troop strength. The purpose of this timeline, which includes horizontal columns for both American military history and general American history, is to present a flow of American history that illustrates the often overlapping and inseparable signal events in different areas of American history. It also attempts, in addition to providing many dates, names, and places in American history, to demonstrate that the wars and campaigns and changes and developments within the military have had a profound effect on the political, economic, and social fabric of the nation—from Columbus' first voyage to the New World to the early clashes of cultures between the native Americans and white settlers to the 1992 presidential campaign of Bill Clinton.

The column headed "American Military History," while not including every military event in the *Encyclopedia,* does give the reader a thorough listing of the wars and key battles and conflicts, both on North American soil and abroad, and the significant events within the military itself. The entries under "General American History" include those events that portend or immediately follow the military events listed or are directly related to those events; they will remind readers of how diverse the American historical experience has been and highlight some interesting coincidences and commingling of events. For the periods preceding the election of George Washington as president in 1788, the "Key Figures" column includes only those names from the General American History and American Military History columns; from Presidents Washington to Clinton, the names of the significant administration leaders are included.

— SHEILA A. DAY AND LOUISE B. KETZ

Timeline, 1492–1640

PRINCIPAL EXPLORERS (SPONSORING COUNTRY)

Bering, Vitus (Russia)
Cabot, John and Sebastian (England)
Cartier, Jacques (France)
Columbus, Christopher (Spain)
Coronado, Francisco Vásquez de (Spain)
Drake, Sir Francis (England)
Hennepin, Louis (France)
Hudson, Henry (England)
Jolliet, Louis (France)
La Salle, René-Robert Cavelier de (France)
Marquette, Jacques (France)
Menéndez de Avilés, Pedro (Spain)
Oñate, Juan de (Spain)
Ponce de León, Juan (Spain)
Raleigh, Sir Walter (England)
Verrazano, Giovanni da (France)

GENERAL AMERICAN HISTORY

1492–1504 Columbus makes 4 voyages to New World: arrives in Bahamas (12 Oct. 1492), discovers Cuba and Haiti; discovers (1493–1496) Puerto Rico, Dominica, and Jamaica; sights South America (1498); reaches central America (31 July 1502).

1497–1498 Cabots make 2 voyages to New World: sail possibly as far south as Chesapeake Bay along North American coast.

1507 Martin Waldseemüller proposes naming New World "America," after Amerigo Vespucci.

1513 Ponce de León explores Florida coast.

1524 Verrazano reaches New York Harbor.

1534–1535 Cartier makes 2 voyages to New World: travels up St. Lawrence to Quebec (Sept. 1535) and Montreal.

1538 Gerhardus Mercator uses "America" and "North America" on maps for the first time.

1542 Coronado leads expedition from New Mexico to Texas, Oklahoma, and eastern Kansas.

c. 1560 Seneca, Cayuga, Oneida, Onondaga, and Mohawk form the League of the Iroquois aimed at peace between the tribes.

1562–1564 Huguenots settle Port Royal and Fort Carolina, Fla.

1565 Menéndez de Avilés founds St. Augustine, Fla. (28 Aug.).

1577–1580 Drake circumnavigates world, anchors at San Francisco Bay (17 June 1579).

1584–1585 Raleigh discovers Virginia; establishes colony on Roanoke Island.

1587 Raleigh's 2nd colony established on Roanoke (22 July); first English child born in America, Virginia Dare (18 Aug.).

1598 Spanish settlement of Southwest begins in New Mexico by Oñate.

1606 Virginia Co. of London and Virginia Co. of Plymouth formed to settle northeast.

1607 Popham and Gorges colonize in Maine; Jamestown established (24 May) in Virginia.

1609 Hudson explores Hudson River.

AMERICAN MILITARY HISTORY

1565 Spanish capture Fort Carolina (17–19 Sept.), rename it San Mateo, and build forts and blockhouses.

Spanish establish fort at Santa Elena, Fla.

1568 French recapture San Mateo (12 Apr.).

1586 Drake destroys St. Augustine and loots Santa Elena.

KEY COLONIAL FIGURES

Adams, Samuel
Andros, Sir Edmund
Argall, Sir Samuel
Bacon, Nathaniel
Baltimore, Lords, Cecilius and Charles Calvert
Berkeley, Sir William
Block, Adriaen
Braddock, Edward
Byrd, William
Carteret, Philip
Claiborne, William
Coode, John
Culpeper, Thomas, Lord
Dale, Sir Thomas
Davenport, John
Dieskau, Ludwig August
Dinwiddie, Robert
Forbes, John
Franklin, Benjamin
Frontenac, Comte de, Louis de Buade
Gorges, Sir Ferdinando
Henry, Patrick
Hutchinson, Anne
Johnson, Sir William
Joseph, William
Kieft, Willem
Leisler, Jacob
Le Moyne, Charles
Mason, John
Minuit, Peter
Morton, Thomas
Nicolls, Richard
Oglethorpe, James
Penn, William
Phips, Sir William
Popham, George
Sloughter, Henry
Smith, John
Standish, Miles
Stuyvesant, Peter
Sullivan, John
Underhill, John
Washington, George
Williams, Roger
Winthrop, John

GENERAL AMERICAN HISTORY

1619	General assembly meets in Jamestown, 1st colonial legislature in New World; 1st slaves (20 blacks) arrive in Jamestown.
1620	Estimated colonial population: 2,499
	Pilgrims voyage to Plymouth; Mayflower Compact signed (21 Nov.), a preliminary plan of government; Standish hired as military leader.
1621	Privy Council orders exports from colonies, has customs paid in England (21 Oct.).
1624	New Netherland founded; Virginia becomes royal colony (24 May); colony established on Cape Ann, Mass.
1625	New Amsterdam founded (July) on Manhattan Island, N.Y.
1626	Minuit purchases Manhattan from Indians for 60 guilders of trade goods.
1629	Dutch States General creates Charter of Freedoms and Exemptions for patroon system of land ownership in America.
1629–1630	Winthrop leads 900 colonists to Massachusetts; Cambridge Agreement signed by Puritans (5 Sept.); colonies established at Boston, Charlestown, Medford, Watertown, Dorchester, and Roxbury.
1634	First colonists in Maryland (26 Mar.); English Commission for Foreign Plantations established to oversee trade and colonies (28 Apr.).
1636	Williams founds Providence, R.I. (June); Moses His Judicials, earliest compilation of New England legislation, presented to Massachusetts general court; Harvard College founded (28 Oct.).
1636–1638	Antinomian Controversy: Hutchinson tried for sedition (Nov.) and banished.
1638	Davenport founds New Haven, Conn.; New Sweden Co. settles on Delaware (Mar.), builds Fort Christina (Wilmington).
1639	Fundamental Orders of Connecticut, 1st constitution in colonies; 1st post office authorized in Massachusetts.
1640	Estimated colonial population: 27,947.

AMERICAN MILITARY HISTORY

1607	Capt. Smith of Jamestown captured then freed by Powhatan (Dec.).
1608	Capt. Smith elected president of Virginia council and institutes compulsory work program.
1611	Laws Divine, Morall, and Martiall imposed by Dale in Virginia to quell internal disorder; forts and system of stockades built.
1613	Block arrives in Manhattan; Fort Nassau (later Fort Orange) built by Dutch on Hudson River.
	Capt. Argall destroys French settlements at Bay of Fundy.
1619	Defensive alliance between Wampanoag, led by Squanto, and Pilgrims at Strawberry Hill, Mass.
1622	1st Tidewater War: 1st Indian massacre in New World, led by Opechancanough at Jamestown (22 Mar.); 25% of Virginia's population killed.
1628	Standish dispatched to destroy Morton's settlement at Mount Wollaston (June).
1633	Fort Good Hope (Hartford) established on Connecticut River.
1635	Claiborne of Virginia and Lord Baltimore of Maryland clash over Kent Island; Crown rules against Claiborne (4 Apr. 1638).
1636	First veterans pensions awarded, to wounded soldiers by Plymouth Colony.
	National Guard originates with the Old North, South, and East regiments of colonial militia in Massachusetts Bay.
1636–1637	Pequot War; reprisals against Pequot for murder of traders, led by Mason of Connecticut and Underhill of Massachusetts, aided by several hundred Indian allies.
1637–1645	Dutch Wars in New York, brought on by brutal Indian policy of colonial director Kieft.
1638	Ancient and Honorable Artillery Company created in Boston.

Timeline, 1641–1691

KEY REVOLUTIONARY WAR FIGURES

Adams, Samuel
Allen, Ethan
André, John
Arnold, Benedict
Barry, John
Burgoyne, John
Butler, John
Carleton, Sir Guy
Clark, George Rogers
Clinton, Sir Henry
Conway, Thomas
Cornwallis, Charles
Dawes, William
De Kalb, Baron Johann
Estaing, Jean Baptiste, Comte d'
Gage, Thomas
Grasse, François, Comte de
Graves, Thomas
Green, Nathanael
Hale, Nathan
Henry, Patrick
Herkimer, Nicholas
Hopkins, Esek
Howe, Sir William
Jefferson, Thomas
Jones, John Paul
Kościuszko, Tadeusz
Lafayette, Marie-Joseph de Motier de
Lee, Charles
Montgomery, Richard
Moultrie, William
North, Frederick, Lord
Paine, Thomas
Revere, Paul
Rochambeau, Comte de
St. Clair, Arthur
St. Leger, Barry
Stark, John
Townshend, Charles
Ward, Artemus
Washington, George
Wayne, Anthony

GENERAL AMERICAN HISTORY

1641 Massachusetts Body of Liberties enacted.

1643 United Colonies of New England (New England Confederation) formed (19 May), with representatives from Massachusetts, Plymouth, Connecticut, and New Haven; guarantees territorial integrity of colonies with commissioners empowered to make war.

1646 Breuckelen (Brooklyn), N.Y., settled.

1647 Rhode Island drafts constitution calling for separation of church and state.

1650 Treaty of Hartford settles boundary disputes between Dutch and New England Confederation.

1651 Massachusetts imprisons and expels Quakers.

1652 Massachusetts mints "pine-tree" shilling; Maine joined to Massachusetts Bay.

1653 Settlers from Virginia found Albemarle Colony in Carolinas.

1660 Basic Navigation Act passed in England to protect and regulate colonial trade.

1662 Connecticut receives royal charter (3 May).

1663 Rhode Island granted royal charter (18 July), including guarantee of religious freedom.

1663–1664 Cape Fear River settlements made in Carolinas.

1665 New Haven annexed to Connecticut (5 Jan.); Concessions and Agreements issued by Berkeley and Carteret to encourage settlement of New Jersey.

1669 John Locke draws up Fundamental Constitutions of Carolina.

1670 Charles Town (Charleston), S.C., settled.

1673 Marquette and Jolliet leave Mackinac to explore Mississippi Valley (17 May).

AMERICAN MILITARY HISTORY

1641 Algonquin War, provoked by colonial expansion on Manhattan and Staten Island.

1642–1653 Iroquois War: Five Nations of the Iroquois, armed by the Dutch, attack the Huron in Canada and several French forts; Iroquois and French sign treaty (5 Nov. 1653).

1644–1646 2nd Tidewater War: Indian uprising in Virginia by Opechananough (18 Mar.) suppressed; 500 settlers killed.

1646 First American battle cruiser commissioned by Connecticut colonies to patrol Long Island Sound against Dutch.

1649 Civil War begins in Virginia.

1650–1655 Religious war in Maryland between Catholics and Puritans.

1652–1654 1st Anglo-Dutch War: dispute over Long Island boundaries.

1655 Stuyvesant retakes Fort Casimir (Newcastle, Del.) from Swedes, ending Swedish rule in America.

1664–1667 2nd Anglo-Dutch War: British Col. Nicolls confiscates all Dutch West India Co. property; Stuyvesant surrenders New Netherland to Nicolls; New Amsterdam renamed New York; Fort Orange surrenders to British and renamed Albany; Peace of Breda (21 July 1667).

1665 Iroquois War revived; Iroquois ally with English in hostilities against French.

1671 Coosa Indians near Charles Town in Carolinas defeated and enslaved; first experiment with Indian slavery.

1672–1674 3rd Anglo-Dutch War: Dutch naval and land forces reoccupy New York; restored to England by Treaty of Westminster (19 Feb. 1674).

GENERAL AMERICAN HISTORY

1676 East Jersey and West Jersey created by Quinpartite Deed (11 July).

1679 Hennepin discovers Niagara Falls.

1680 New Hampshire separates from Mass. by royal commission (Sept.); French colonial empire organized from Quebec to mouth of Mississippi.

1681 Penn receives charter (14 Mar.) for Pennsylvania.

1682 La Salle claims Louisiana territory for France and takes possession of Mississippi Valley; Delaware granted to Penn; Penn issues first Frame of Government (5 May).

1683 Quakers settle Germantown, Pa.; New York Charter of Liberties adopted; Mennonites (1st German settlers) arrive in Philadelphia (Oct.).

1684 Stuart's Town at Port Royal in Carolinas settled by Scotch Covenanters; Massachusetts charter annulled (21 June) for failure to enforce Navigation Acts.

1686 Dominion of New England established (Dec.) by Massachusetts, Plymouth, Rhode Island, Connecticut, New Hampshire, and Maine, for administration of colonies under Andros.

1688 New York and New Jersey join Dominion of New England; Carolinas divide into North and South Carolina.

AMERICAN MILITARY HISTORY

1675 Joint forces of Marylanders and Virginians fail to destroy Susquehannock Indians who committed atrocities at Piscataway Creek (27 Sept.).

1675–1676 King Philip's War: Hostilities between New England Confederation and Narragansett, Wampanoag, Mohegan, and other Indians, resulting in colonial victory in Great Swamp Fight (19 Dec. 1675) and ending with death of Philip (Metacomet) and more than 600 colonists and 3000 Indians.

1676 Bacon's Rebellion: Bacon leads a force of 500 into Jamestown to claim seat in House of Burgesses (23 June); forces Berkeley's troops out of Jamestown (18 Sept.); burns Jamestown next day.

1677–1679 Culpeper's Rebellion: insurrection by Culpeper and other Albemarle residents; acting Gov. Miller imprisoned with insurrectionists administering affair; Culpeper acquitted of treason charge.

1680 Westo War between Westo Indians and British along Savannah River.

1680–1696 Pueblo destroy missions and drive Spanish from New Mexico.

1684–1689 Renewed Iroquois hostilities against Huron; 200 slaughtered at Lachine (Aug.) in St. Lawrence Valley.

1686 Le Moyne captures English James Bay posts in Hudson Bay.

Treaty of Whitehall: France and England agree that despite wars in Europe, "a true and firm peace and neutrality shall continue in America."

1689 Andros ousted in armed uprising in Boston (18 Apr.).

Revolution in Virginia.

Revolution in Maryland led by Coode; Gov. Joseph surrenders assembly (1 Aug.).

1689–1691 Leisler's Rebellion: Capt. Leisler seizes Fort James (31 May 1689) and southern New York City (May–June 1689); surrenders to new governor, Col. Sloughter (30 Mar. 1691).

Timeline, 1689–1768

GENERAL AMERICAN HISTORY

1696	Board of Trade and Plantations established in England to oversee colonial affairs (abolished 1782).
1701	Pennsylvania Charter of Liberties enacted (8 Nov.); Detroit founded.
1702	East and West Jerseys united as royal colony (26 Apr.).
1703	Delaware separates from Pennsylvania.
1704	*Boston News-Letter,* 1st regular newspaper in America, starts weekly publication.
1715	Maryland restored to Baltimores as proprietary colony.
1718	New Orleans, La., established by Le Moyne.
1720	Estimated colonial population: 474,388.
	French establish Louisbourg in Canada; build Fort Niagara to secure Lower Great Lakes and as base against Iroquois.
1721	South Carolina made a royal colony.
1722	League of Six Nations created; Iroquois agree not to cross Potomac or Blue Ridge.
1729	Albemarle, N.C., becomes royal colony (25 July); Baltimore founded; Franklin publishes *Pennsylvania Gazette.*
1733	Oglethorpe founds Savannah, Ga. (12 Feb.); British Molasses Act prohibits American trade with French West Indies.
1735	French settle at Vincennes, Ind.; John Peter Zenger acquitted of libel in New York in trial for freedom of the press.
1737	Byrd founds Richmond, Va.
1740	Bering discovers Alaska and Aleutians.

AMERICAN MILITARY HISTORY

1689–1697	King william's War (1st Anglo-French War): Comte de Frontenac with Indian allies raids Schenectady, N.Y.; Salmon Falls, N.H.; Falmouth, Maine (1690), and attacks the Iroquois (1693–1696); Massachusetts troops under Phips seize Port Royal (1690), which is recaptured by French (1691); Treaty of Ryswick (30 Sept. 1697) restores *status quo antebellum* in colonies.
1702–1713	Queen Anne's War (2nd Anglo-French War): Carolina colonists and Indian allies burn St. Augustine (Dec. 1702); Abnaki and French raid New England settlements, including Deerfield, Mass.; Treaty of Utrecht (11 Apr. 1713) cedes Newfoundland, Acadia, and Hudson Bay to British, and French retain Cape Breton and St. Lawrence islands.
1711–1713	Tuscarora War: 200 North Carolinians massacred by Tuscarora, who are later defeated.
1715–1716	Yamassee War: Yamassee and Lower Creek of South Carolina, incensed over encroachments on their land, kill 90 traders and their families near Port Royal; Yamassee driven into Florida.
1718	French and Spanish clash in Florida and Texas.
1720	French establish Fort Niagara to secure lower Great Lakes and as a base against Iroquois.
1724–1725	Dummer's War: Boundary dispute between Abnaki and Maine and Vermont settlers; whites defeat superior Indian forces (23 Aug., 19 May) and kill Jesuit missionary Sebastian Rasle.
1725	British build Fort Oswego on Lake Ontario.
1733–1739	Oglethorpe builds forts on Georgia's southern frontier; makes peace with interior tribes, especially the Creek.
1739–1742	War of Jenkins' Ear; Great Britain declares war on Spain over Florida boundaries and commercial treaties (19 Oct. 1739) and is aided by Indian allies; besieged St. Augustine (May-July 1740); Spanish counterattack crushed at St. Simon's Island in Battle of Bloody Swamp (1742).
1740	First American Regiment formed, 36 companies of 100 men each from 9 colonies.
1744–1748	King George's War: French attack Annapolis Royal (1744), repulsed by British; New Englanders capture Louisbourg (15 June 1745); Peace of Aix-la-Chapelle grants mutual restoration of conquests.

GENERAL AMERICAN HISTORY

1749 Ohio Co.chartered.

1754 Georgia becomes royal colony; Albany Congress of 7 colonies meets (19 June–10 July); Franklin submits Plan of Union of all colonies; plan rejected by colonists and home government.

1760 Estimated colonial population: 1,610,000.

1761 Writs of Assistance (search warrants) issued to Massachusetts customs officers.

1762 Secret Treaty of Fontainebleau (3 Nov.) cedes to Spain New Orleans and all French territory west of Mississippi (Louisiana).

1763 Treaty of Paris (10 Feb.)—France cedes all of Canada and lands east of Mississippi (except New Orleans) to Britain, Cuba returned to Spain in exchange for Floridas; British Proclamation of 1763 (7 Oct.) to regulate settlement of North America and conciliate Indians.

1764 1st permanent settlement at St. Louis, Mo.; British pass Currency Act prohibiting issue of legal-tender currency in colonies; Sugar Act passed to raise money in colonies for the Crown; Boston town meeting (24 May) denounces taxation without representation; nonimportation of British goods begins.

1765 Stamp Act passed (22 Mar.), 1st direct tax on British colonies; Quartering Act passed (24 Mar.); Sons of Liberty formed to protest Stamp Act; Stamp Act Congress meets (7–25 Oct.), delegates from 7 colonies issue Declaration of Rights and Grievances.

1766 Stamp Act repealed (18 Mar.); Declaratory Act (18 Mar.) asserts British right to make laws binding on colonies.

1767 Townshend Acts passed by Parliament, requiring colonies to pay import duties on tea, glass, oil, lead, paper; New York assembly suspended for nonsupport of Quartering Act; Charles Mason and Jeremiah Dixon complete survey of Pennsylvania boundary with Delaware, Maryland, and West Virginia.

1768 Massachusetts assembly dissolved for not collecting taxes; Adams writes Massachusetts Circular Letter informing other 12 colonies of Massachusetts actions against Townshend Acts (11 Feb.).

AMERICAN MILITARY HISTORY

1752 French begin move into Ohio Valley; attack trading post at Pickawillany and kill defenders; establish Fort Presque Island (Erie, Pa.).

1753 French build Fort Le Boeuf at portage to French Creek in Ohio Valley.

1753–1754 Gov. Dinwiddie of Virginia dispatches Lt. Col. Washington to Ohio Valley to ascertain French intentions; Washington reports (Jan. 1754) French can be removed only by force.

1754–1763 French and Indian War: Hostilities open with repulse of Washington and a party of 150 at Great Meadows (Fort Necessity); British ally with Iroquois League, French ally with Delaware, Shawnee, Wyandot, and smaller tribes.

1755 Bay of Fundy Expedition: British capture Forts St. John and Beausejour (June).

Battle of the Wilderness (9 July): Gen. Braddock, commander of British forces in America, defeated and killed by 900 French and Indians.

Battle of Lake George (8 Sept.): Johnson defeats Baron Dieskau's force of 1400 French and Indians.

Royal Americans, a 4-battalion regiment of light infantry, established by British War Office.

1757 British capture Louisbourg (26 July) and Fort Frontenac (27 Aug.).

1758 For Duquesne taken by Forbes and Washington (25 Nov.).

1759 Fort Niagara (25 July), Ticonderoga (26 July), and Crown Point (31 July) fall to British; Quebec surrenders (18 Sept.).

1760 Canada surrendered to British (8 Sept.)

1763 Paxton Boys kill 20 peaceful Indians in Pennsylvania (Dec.) because assembly failed to provide frontier security.

1763–1766 Pontiac's War: Indians of Great Lakes region battle British, including unsuccessful siege of Detroit.

1766 New York citizens and British clash over Quartering Act (11 Aug.).

GENERAL AMERICAN HISTORY

1769 Virginia assembly dissolved (17 May); Virginia Resolves and Association (16–18 May) passed, resolutions denouncing British taxation and a nonimportation agreement.

1770 Townshend Acts, except for tea duty, repealed (12 Apr.); Quartering Act allowed to expire; Boston Massacre (5 Apr.), in which British soldiers fire into mob, killing 5.

1772 Adams forms Committees of Correspondence in Massachusetts (Nov.).

1773 British Tea Act passed (27 Apr.), allowing East India Co. to cut prices and undersell colonial competition; Boston Tea Party (16 Dec.), Bostonians disguised as Indians dump 342 chests of East India Co. tea in Boston Harbor; Virginia appoints Committee of Correspondence.

1774 Quebec Act passed (20 May) to secure loyalty of Canada to Britain, extends boundaries of Canada to northern Ohio; Coercion (Intolerable) Acts imposed on Massachusetts in reprisal for Boston Tea Party (Mar.–June)—Boston Port Act, Massachusetts Government Act, Act for Administration of Justice, and Quartering Act; 1st Continental Congress meets in Philadelphia (5 Sept.–26 Oct.)—56 delegates form 12 colonies (Georgia does not attend) adopt Declaration of Rights, 10 resolutions on rights of colonists, and create Continental Association to bind colonies in nonimportation, nonexportation, and nonconsumption agreement against Britain.

1775 Lord North's conciliation plan passes (27 Feb.), eliminating all but regulatory taxes on colonies; New England Restraining Act passed (27 Feb.), forbidding New England to trade with any nation but Britain and British West Indies; Henry delivers "liberty or death" speech to Virginia burgesses (23 Mar.); 2nd Continental Congress (10 May–2 Aug.) adopts Olive Branch Petition (5 July) setting forth grievances and hope for harmony, rejects North's conciliation plan (31 July); George III rejects Olive Branch petition and proclaims colonies in open rebellion (23 Aug.); Congress reconvenes (12 Sept.) with all 13 colonies; Committee of Secret Correspondence appoints 3 commissioners to contact foreign nations for support (29 Nov.); royal proclamation closes American colonies to all commerce (effective 1 Mar. 1776).

AMERICAN MILITARY HISTORY

1769–1772 Yankee-Pennamite Wars: Clashes in Wyoming Valley, Pa., between Connecticut and Pennsylvania settlers and Pennamite Indians; Connecticuters gain possession of region.

1770 Battle of Golden Hill (19 Jan.): New York City Sons of Liberty clash with 60 British troops.

1771 Battle of Alamance (16 May); 2000 North Carolina Regulators rise up against British rule; suppressed by 1200 militia.

1772 Customs schooner *Gaspée* runs aground (9 June) near Providence, R.I., and set afire by merchants.

1774 Dunmore's War: Gov. John Murray, Earl of Dunmore, sends a force of Virginia militia to suppress Shawnee uprising on Virginia-Kentucky frontier.

1774 Band of colonials led by Sullivan carries off arms and gunpowder from Fort William and Mary in Portsmouth, N.H. (14 Dec.).

1775 Lexington and Concord (19 Apr.): Revere and Dawes alert Lexington and Concord of massing of British troops (18–19 Apr.); 700 British troops under Gen. Gage meet 70 minutemen on Lexington Common, Mass., and kill 8; proceed to Concord, killing 14, then return to Boston.

Massachusetts Provincial Congress authorizes raising of 13,600 militia, who begin siege of Boston under Maj. Gen. Ward.

Capture of Fort Ticonderoga (10 May): Col. Arnold and Allen and his Green Mountain Boys surprise the fort's garrison; nearby Crown Point also taken (12 May).

Congress (14–15 June) accepts forces besieging Boston as the Continental army; creates a committee to draft rules for government of the army; votes to raise 6 rifle companies; appoints Washington commander in chief.

Battle of Bunker Hill (17 June): 2000 British under Maj. Gen. Howe overtake 2000 militia under Col. Prescott but suffer heavy casualties.

Congress authorizes Continental navy (13 Oct.); authorizes fitting out of 4 ships (30 Oct.); names Hopkins commodore; resolves to raise 2 battalions of marines (10 Nov.).

GENERAL AMERICAN HISTORY

1776 Paine calls for independence of colonies in *Common Sense* (9 Jan.); Congress votes on independence resolution (2 July); Jefferson drafts Declaration of Independence, approved 4 July; Congress appoints 3 commissioners to negotiate treaties with foreign nations (26 Sept.); Congress flees for Baltimore (12 Dec.).

AMERICAN MILITARY HISTORY

1775 *cont'd* Brig. Gen. Montgomery takes St. John's garrison (2 Nov.) and Montreal (13 Nov.) in Canada.

Arnold and Montgomery repulsed at Quebec by 1800-man garrison (31 Dec.), with Arnold wounded and Montgomery killed.

British hire 29,000 German mercenaries for war in North America.

1775–1776 Dunmore defeated by a mixed force of 900 Virginians and North Carolinians at Great Bridge, Va. (11 Dec.); relands at Norfolk (1 Jan.) and burns much of the city.

1775–1783 The American War for Independence

1776 Battle of Moore's Creek Bridge (27 Feb.): Loyalists crushed near Wilmington, N.C.

Gen. Howe evacuates troops and ships from Boston (17 Mar.).

Louis XVI of France authorizes (2 May) supplying munitions to Americans; Charles II of Spain follows suit.

Battle of Three Rivers (7 June): Americans defeated and forced to retreat from Canada.

Battle of Sullivan's Island (28 June): British Gen. Clinton's squadron and troops defeated by troops under Gen. Lee and Col. Moultrie.

Battle of Long Island (27 Aug.): Gen. Howe, in command of 23,000 British and 9000 German troops, defeats Continental forces and takes Gen. Sullivan prisoner.

Washington retreats to Harlem Heights in New York (15–16 Sept.) and British occupy city.

300 buildings destroyed by fire in New York City (21 Sept.).

Hale executed as an American spy in New York City (22 Sept.).

Battle of Valcour Island (11 Oct.): Sir Carleton and Arnold's flotillas meet near Lake Champlain; most of the American flotilla destroyed.

Battle of White Plains (28 Oct.): Gen. Howe engages Washington in sharp battle; Washington slips away.

GENERAL AMERICAN HISTORY

1777 Congress reconvenes in Philadelphia (12 Mar.); Committee of Secret Correspondence reconstituted as Committee for Foreign Affairs (17 Apr.); Congress adopts "Stars and Stripes" flag (14 June); Congress flees to Pennsylvania (Sept.); Conway Cabal (Sept.–Dec.) fails to replace Washington with Gen. Gates; Articles of Confederation adopted (15 Nov.).

AMERICAN MILITARY HISTORY

1776 *cont'd* Fort Washington, N.Y., capitulates to British (16 Nov.).

Washington and Greene retreat through New Jersey (18 Nov.–20 Dec.) and cross into Pennsylvania.

Gen. Cornwallis assaults Fort Lee, N.J. (19 Nov.); Gen. Greene forced to evacuate and abandon supplies.

Washington crosses back into New Jersey (25 Dec.) and takes Hessian garrison at Trenton next morning.

1777 Battle of Princeton (3 Jan.): Washington's troops force Cornwallis from the field in New Jersey.

Marquis de Lafayette of France and Baron de Kalb arrive (27 July); commissioned major generals in Continental army; Kościuszko of Poland made colonel of engineers (18 Oct.).

Battle of Brandywine Creek (11 Sept.): 18,000 British and Hessian troops force Washington's 11,000 to retire toward Philadelphia; Howe occupies Philadelphia (26 Sept.).

Battle of Germantown (4 Oct.): Defeat of Americans by Cornwallis, forcing retreat to Valley Forge as winter quarters (mid-Dec.).

Battle of Paoli (21 Sept.): Gen. Wayne routed by British.

St. Clair abandons Fort Ticonderoga to Burgoyne (6 July).

Fort Standwix besieged and taken (3–22 Aug.) by British Col. St. Leger and Hessian troops.

Battle of Oriskany (6 Aug.): Gen. Herkimer ambushed by Indians and Tories in New York.

Battle of Bennington (16 Aug.): Gen. Stark's 2600 Continentals destroy a British force of 800 in Vermont.

Battle of Freemans' Farm (19 Sept.): Gen. Burgoyne repulsed in New York by Americans, with 600 casualties.

Battle of Bemis Heights (7 Oct.): Arnold drives back Burgoyne and British; Burgoyne surrenders to Americans (17 Oct.).

GENERAL AMERICAN HISTORY

1778 2 treaties of alliance and commerce signed with France (6 Feb.).

1779 Convention of Aranjuez (12 Apr.) between France and Spain provides for Spain to enter American Revolution; Spain declares war on Britain (21 June) but does not recognize U.S. independence.

1780 Catherine the Great of Russia declares armed neutrality (28 Feb.); British Maj. André captured (23 Sept.) after meeting with Arnold, who gave André papers to aid British taking of West Point; Arnold flees to British warship (25 Sept.).

AMERICAN MILITARY HISTORY

1778 Capt. Jones raids Whitehaven, England (23 Apr.), and captures British sloop *Drake* (24 Apr.).

Battle of Monmouth (28 June): Gen. Lee attacks British force in New Jersey; reinforced by Washington, drives back Clinton's attack.

Settlers massacred by Indians and Loyalists known as Butler's Rangers at Wyoming Valley (3 July) and Cherry Valley, N.Y. (11 Nov.).

Clark captures Kaskaskia (4 July) from Loyalists and Indians.

French fleet under Comte d'Estaing arrives off Newport, R.I. (29 July); a storm scatters British and French fleets (11 Aug.).

British troops crush militia in Savannah, Ga. (29 Dec.), and occupy town.

1779 British seize Augusta, Ga. (29 Jan.).

British capture and set fire to Portsmouth and Norfolk, Va. (10 May).

British capture Stony Point and Verplanck's Point in New York (1 June); Stony Point recaptured (15 July).

British driven from New Jersey (19 Aug.).

Loyalists and Indian allies defeated at Newtown, N.Y. (29 Aug.).

Bonhomme Richard-Serapis fight (23 Sept.): Jones replies to request for surrender, "I have not yet begun to fight," and defeats *Serapis*.

Joint French-American operation fails to retake Savannah (Sept.-Oct.).

1780 British take Charleston, S.C. (Feb.).

5000 French troops with strong naval escort arrive at Newport, R.I. (11 July).

Battle of Camden (16 Aug.): American troops overwhelmed in South Carolina.

Battle of King's Mountain (7 Oct.): 900 Carolina frontiersmen defeat British riflemen.

Mutiny of American troops at Morristown, N.J., curbed by Pennsylvania troops (25 May).

Timeline, 1781–1798

GENERAL AMERICAN HISTORY

1781 Articles of Confederation ratified (1 Mar.).

1782 British House of Commons votes against further prosecution of war in America (27 Feb.); authorizes Crown to make peace (5 Mar.); peace negotiations between Great Britain and U.S. open in Paris (12 Apr.), begin formally (27 Sept.); Preliminary Articles of Peace signed (30 Nov.) to go into effect when Britain concludes war with France and Spain.

1783 Great Britain proclaims cessation of hostilities (4 Feb.); 3 definitive treaties of peace signed between Great Britain and the U.S., France, and Spain (3 Sept.).

1784 Jefferson's land ordinance report for temporary government in the West (23 Apr.); New York City made temporary capital of U.S. (23 Dec.); Spain closes Mississippi River to U.S. trade.

1785 John Adams appointed minister to Great Britain (24 Feb.), Jefferson to France (10 Mar.).

1786 Morocco signs treaty with U.S. for unmolested trade in Mediterranean; Annapolis Convention held (11–14 Sept.), 12 delegates from 5 states resolve that all states meet in May 1787 to revise Articles of Confederation.

1787 Constitution Convention opens in Philadelphia (25 May); Virginia Plan (29 May) and New Jersey Plan (15 June) for union put before convention; Northwest Ordinance enacted (13 July) for government of territory north of Ohio River.

1788 New Hampshire becomes requisite 9th state to ratify U.S. Constitution (21 June).

AMERICAN MILITARY HISTORY

1781 Pennsylvania (1 Jan.) and New Jersey (20 Jan.) divisions mutiny; order restored after concessions and several executions.

Capt. Barry returns from France on *Alliance*, forces 2 British privateers to surrender (2 Apr.), and forces surrender of 2 British men-of-war (29 May).

Cornwallis campaigns in Virginia (May-Aug.); lands in Yorktown (1 Aug.).

Washington and Rochambeau agree (21 May) on joint French-American attack on New York.

Yorktown Campaign (30 Aug.–19 Oct.): Comte de Grasse and French fleet arrive off Yorktown; British Adm. Graves withdraws after 3 days to New York; siege of Yorktown with joint French-American troops begins (28 Sept.); Cornwallis, unable to escape, negotiates for surrender (17 Oct.): British forces lay down arms (19 Oct.).

Washington marches to New York (Oct.).

1783 Newburgh Addresses (10, 12 Mar.): anonymous letters from Continental army officers pressing for assurances of payments for services and pensions.

Loyalists (26 Apr.) and British troops (25 Nov.) evacuate New York City.

Society of the Cincinnati formed (May) by officers of Continental army, with hereditary membership.

Continental army disbands (13 June) after congressional vote to furlough army (26 May).

1784 2nd Yankee-Pennamite War (May-July): uneasy truce halts fighting in Wyoming Valley, leading to settlement in Pennsylvania's favor.

1786–1787 Shays's Rebellion: debt-ridden farmers in Massachusetts block seating of courts in various towns; insurgents led by Daniel Shays in Springfield avoid clash with military (26 Sept. 1786); attack on Springfield arsenal repulsed (26 Jan. 1786); rebellion collapses (Feb.).

PRESIDENT AND KEY LEADERS, TERM OF OFFICE

George Washington, *president,* 1789–1797

John Adams, *vice president,* 1789–1797
Thomas Jefferson, *secretary of state,* 1790–1793
Edmund Randolph, *secretary of state,* 1794–1795
Timothy Pickering, *secretary of state,* 1795–1797
Alexander Hamilton, *secretary of Treasury,* 1789–1795
Oliver Wolcott, *secretary of Treasury,* 1795–1797
Henry Knox, *secretary of war,* 1789–1794
Timothy Pickering, *secretary of war,* 1795–1796
James McHenry, *secretary of war,* 1796–1797
Edmund Randolph *attorney general,* 1789–1794
William Bradford, *attorney general,* 1794–1795
Charles Lee *attorney general,* 1795–1797
John Jay, *chief justice,* 1789–1795

John Adams, *president,* 1797–1801

Thomas Jefferson, *vice president,* 1797–1801
Timothy Pickering, *secretary of state,* 1797–1800
John Marshall, *secretary of state,* 1800–1801
Oliver Wolcott, *secretary of Treasury,* 1797–1800
Samuel Dexter, *secretary of Treasury,* 1801
James McHenry, *secretary of war,* 1797–1800
Samuel Dexter, *secretary of war,* 1800–1801
Charles Lee, *attorney general,* 1797–1801
Benjamin Stoddert, *secretary of navy,* 1798–1801

GENERAL AMERICAN HISTORY

1789 1st session of Congress convenes (4 Mar.); Washington inaugurated (30 Apr.); Federal Judiciary Act (24 Sept.) creates Supreme Court.

1790 Congress authorizes 1st U.S. census (Mar.); population, 3,929,625; locates projected federal capital on Potomac (10 July) and federal government assumes state revolutionary war debts (4 Aug.).

1791 Bank of the U.S. created (25 Feb.); Whiskey Tax passed (3 Mar.); Bill of Rights added to Constitution (15 Dec.).

1792 Washington and John Adams reelected (5 Dec.).

1793 Washington issues Neutrality Proclamation (22 Apr.), warning Americans to avoid aiding either France or Great Britain in their war.

1794 Barbary states begin preying on American shipping; Neutrality Act (5 June) forbids enlisting in service of a foreign nation or fitting out foreign armed vessels.

1795 Yazoo Land Fraud between Georgia legislators and 4 land companies for present-day Alabama and Mississippi; Pinckney's Treaty (27 Oct.) with Spain gives U.S. free navigation of Mississippi.

1796 Washington's Farewell Address (17 Sept.) warns against U.S. involvement in foreign disputes; Adams and Jefferson elected president and vice president (7 Dec.).

1797–1798 XYZ Affair: 3 commissioners sent to France to negotiate commerce and amity treaty; Adams discloses to Congress (3 Apr. 1798) refusal of French Foreign Affairs Secretary Talleyrand to receive commissioners unless a loan was granted France and a bribe paid.

1798 Alien and Sedition Acts: Naturalization Act (18 June), Alien Act (6 July), Alien Enemies Act (6 July), and Sedition Act (14 July) impose severe restrictions on aliens.

AMERICAN MILITARY HISTORY

1789 Department of War created (7 Aug.).

Congress adopts First American Regiment (Sept.).

1790 Total authorized armed forces: 1,216.

Congress authorizes construction of ten vessels for the Revenue Marine (later Coast Guard).

Harmar's Expedition (Oct.): punitive expedition by Brig. Gen. Josiah Harmar against Maumee Indians in Ohio Valley; the militia flee and the few regulars are slaughtered.

St. Clair's defeat (4 Nov.): army of 1400 under Gen. Arthur St. Clair routed on the Ohio frontier by Indians, who kill 900.

1791 Militia Act passed (8 May), authorizing state enrollment of able bodied free white men between 18 and 45 and a larger army, the Legion of the United States.

1793 Gen. Anthony Wayne marches army to Ohio; builds Fort Greenville and Fort Recovery (Dec.), the latter on the site of St. Clair's defeat.

1794 Congress votes to create four arsenals; Springfield, Mass., arsenal completed.

Naval Act authorizes construction of six frigates.

The first *United States,* 44-gun frigate, launched (10 May).

Battle of Fallen Timbers (20 Aug.): Wayne's troops overwhelm 800 Maumee.

Whiskey Rebellion: protest by farmers objecting to whiskey tax; halted by militia of New Jersey, Pennsylvania, Virginia, and Massachusetts—the first use of militia as a federal force.

1796 Legion of the United States abolished and army reorganized into 2 light dragoon companies and 4 infantry regiments. Harpers Ferry, Va., arsenal completed.

1798 Congress creates Provisional Army to be raised in the event of war and empowers president to accept volunteer companies into federal service; authorizes raising of New Army of 12 infantry regiments and 6 troops of dragoons.

Department of the Navy created (3 May).

Timeline, 1798–1814

PRESIDENT AND KEY LEADERS, TERM OF OFFICE

Thomas Jefferson, *president,* 1801–1809

Aaron Burr, *vice president,* 1801–1805
George Clinton, *vice president,* 1805–1809
James Madison, *secretary of state,* 1801–1809
Samuel Dexter, *secretary of Treasury,* 1801
Albert Gallatin, *secretary of Treasury,* 1801–1809
Levi Lincoln, *attorney general,* 1801–1804
John Breckenridge, *attorney general,* 1805–1806
Caesar A. Rodney, *attorney general,* 1807–1809
Henry Dearborn, *secretary of war,* 1801–1809
Benjamin Stoddert, *secretary of navy,* 1801
Robert Smith, *secretary of navy,* 1801–1809
John Marshall, *chief justice,* 1801–1835

James Madison, *president,* 1809–1817

George Clinton, *vice president,* 1809–1812
Elbridge Gerry, *vice president,* 1813–1814
Robert Smith, *secretary of state,* 1809–1811
James Monroe, *secretary of state,* 1811–1817
Albert Gallatin, *secretary of Treasury,* 1809–1814
George W. Campbell, *secretary of Treasury,* 1814
Alexander Dallas, *secretary of Treasury,* 1814–1816
William H. Crawford, *secretary of Treasury,* 1816–1817
Caesar A. Rodney, *attorney general,* 1809–1811
William Pinkney, *attorney general,* 1811–1814
Richard Rush, *attorney general,* 1814–1817
William Eustis, *secretary of war,* 1809–1812
John Armstrong, *secretary of war,* 1813–1814
James Monroe, *secretary of war,* 1814–1815
William H. Crawford, *secretary of war,* 1815–1816
Paul Hamilton, *secretary of navy,* 1809–1812
William Jones, *secretary of navy,* 1813–1814
Benjamin Crowninshield, *secretary of navy,* 1814–1817

GENERAL AMERICAN HISTORY

1798–1799 Kentucky (16 Nov. 1798, 22 Nov. 1799) and Virginia (24 Dec. 1798) resolutions protest Alien and Sedition acts as unconstitutional and advocate state sovereignty.

1799 Logan Act (30 Jan.) prohibits correspondence with enemy foreign nations.

1800 U.S. population: 5,308,483

Harrison Land Act (10 May) facilitates individual land purchases; Congress convenes in Washington for 1st time (17 Nov.); secret Treaty of San Ildefonso cedes Louisiana to France (1 Oct.).

1801 Jefferson inaugurated (4 Mar.) in Washington, D.C.

1803 U.S. purchases Louisiana (828,000 sq. miles) from France (2 May) for $15 million.

1805 *Essex* decision by British admiralty destroys principle of broken voyage; British begin seizing U.S. ships carrying French and Spanish goods; impressment by British ships is increased.

1806–1807 Burr Conspiracy: Gen. James Wilkinson warns Jefferson of Burr's expedition to allegedly build a western empire from Spanish territories; Burr arrested (19 Feb. 1807) and acquitted of treason (1 Sept.).

1807 Non-Importation Act (14 Dec.) put into effect against Britain; Robert Fulton's *Clermont* inaugurates commercial steam navigation; Embargo Act (22 Dec.) forbids U.S. ships to leave for foreign countries.

1808 Importation of slaves forbidden (1 Jan.); Madison elected president (7 Dec.).

1809 Non-Intercourse Act (1 Mar.) bans trade with Great Britain and France; Embargo Act repealed.

1810 Rambouillet Decree signed by Napoleon, ordering seizure of U.S. shipping in French ports; Macon's Bill No. 2 passes (1 May) to supplant Non-Intercourse Act; West Florida annexed (27 Oct.).

1811 Secret act passed (15 Jan.) authorizing president to take possession of East Florida.

AMERICAN MILITARY HISTORY

1798–1800 Quasi-War with France: undeclared war with France begins with French seizure of American merchantmen; U.S. navy of 3 ships enlarged to 54; U.S. victorious in all 4 naval engagements; peace concluded by Convention of 1800 (30 Sept.).

1799 Fries's Rebellion: armed resistance by Pennsylvania farmers led by John Fries to protest federal tax on land and houses; put down by federal troops.

1801–1805 Tripolitan War: Tripoli declares war on U.S. (14 May 1801); Commodore Edward Preble dispatched (1803) with naval force to blockade Tripoli; Lt. Stephen Decatur captures and destroys *Philadelphia,* a U.S. frigate captured by Tripolitans (16 Feb. 1804); William Eaton, U.S. consul, leads a small force from Libya to Tripoli, capturing fortress at Derna (1805); peace treaty signed (4 June).

1802 Military Peace Establishment Act (16 Mar.) establishes U.S. Military Academy (opens at West Point, N.Y., 4 July) and Corps of Engineers and reduces army to 3000 men.

1803–1806 U.S. Army officers Meriwether Lewis and William Clark explore the Far West.

1805–1807 Lt. Zebulon Pike dispatched by Gen. Wilkinson to explore sources of Mississippi (1805–1806) and Colorado and New Mexico (1806–1807).

1807 U.S. frigate *Chesapeake* attacked by British frigate *Leopard* (22 June) with 3 Americans killed and 4 alleged British deserters removed; Jefferson orders small gunboats built to patrol U.S. coast against British and French warships.

1808 Jefferson increases size of army to control smuggling into Canada.

1811 "Little Belt" Affair (16 May): U.S. frigate *President* sinks British gunboat *Little Belt.*

Battle of Tippecanoe (7 Nov.): Indians under Tecumseh fight William Henry Harrison's forces near Vincennes, Ind., who defeat Indians and burn their capital, Prophetstown.

PRESIDENT AND KEY LEADERS, TERM OF OFFICE	GENERAL AMERICAN HISTORY		AMERICAN MILITARY HISTORY	
	1812	Congress enacts embargo on Great Britain (4 Apr.); president authorized to raise 100,000 militia for 3 months; Congress authorizes 1st issue of war bonds valued at $11 million (Mar.); Madison elected president (2 Dec.) for 2nd term.	1812	East Florida "Patriot" Revolution (Mar.): Gen. George Mathews captures San Marcos fortress and organizes government.
	1813	Lord Castlereagh's proposal for peace negotiations reaches Washington (4 Nov.).	1812–1815	The War of 1812: U.S. declares war on Great Britain (18 June) over freedom of the seas, impressment of seamen, and blockade of U.S. ports.
			1812	British capture Fort Mackinac (17 July) and massacre garrison at Fort Dearborn (15 Aug.).
				Gen. William Hull surrenders Detroit (16 Aug.) to British.
				Battle of Queenston Heights (13 Oct.): Maj. Gen. Stephen Van Rensselaer's force captured in failed invasion of Canada.
				United States under Capt. Stephen Decatur captures *Macedonian* (25 Oct.).
				Militia forces under Maj. Gen. Henry Dearborn refuse to advance into Canada (19 Nov.).
				USS *Constitution* demolishes British frigate *Guerrière* (19 Aug.) and *Java* (29 Dec.).
			1813	British blockade of Chesapeake and Delaware Bays (26 Dec. 1812) extended to mouth of Mississippi (26 May).
				Raisin River Massacre (22 Jan.): British kill or capture 900 Americans at Frenchtown in Ohio.
				Americans repel British in Battles of Fort Meigs (1–9 May), Fort George (27 May), Sackets Harbor (28–29 May), Fort Stephenson (2 Aug), Lake Erie (10 Sept.), Thames River (5 Oct.), Chateaugay (25 Oct.), and Chrysler's Farm (10 Nov.).
				USS *Hornet* captures HMS *Peacock* (24 Feb.); HMS *Shannon* takes USS *Chesapeake* (1 June) commanded by Capt. James Lawrence ("Don't give up the ship"); HMS *Pelican* sinks the USS *Argus* (14 Aug.); USS *Enterprise* captures HMS *Boxer* (5 Sept.).
			1813–1814	Creek War: Gen. Andrew Jackson campaigns against Creek Indians of Alabama and Georgia, including Battle of Horseshoe Band (27 Mar.); Treaty of Fort Jackson (9 Aug. 1814) cedes 20 million acres of Indian lands.
				Warship *Essex* under Capt. David Porter inflicts $6 million loss to British whaling in South Pacific.

Timeline, 1814–1840

PRESIDENT AND KEY LEADERS, TERM OF OFFICE

James Monroe, *president,* 1817–1825

Daniel D. Tompkins, *vice president,* 1817–1825
John Quincy Adams, *secretary of state,* 1817–1825
William H. Crawford, *secretary of Treasury,* 1817–1825
Richard Rush, *attorney general,* 1817
William Wirt, *attorney general,* 1817–1825
John C. Calhoun, *secretary of war,* 1817–1825
Benjamin Crowninshield, *secretary of navy,* 1817–1818
Smith Thompson, *secretary of navy,* 1818–1823
Samuel L. Southard, *secretary of navy,* 1823–1825

John Quincy Adams, *president,* 1825–1829

John C. Calhoun, *vice president,* 1825–1829
Henry Clay, *secretary of state,* 1825–1829
Richard Rush, *secretary of Treasury,* 1825–1829
William Wirt, *attorney general,* 1825–1829
James Barbour, *secretary of war,* 1825–1828
Peter B. Porter, *secretary of war,* 1828–1829
Samuel L. Southard, *secretary of navy,* 1825–1829

GENERAL AMERICAN HISTORY

1814 Treaty of Ghent (24 Dec.): ends War of 1812, U.S. rights to Newfoundland fisheries acknowledged, boundary commissions established.

1814–1815 Hartford Convention (15 Dec.–5 Jan.): 26 New England delegates hold secret sessions to consider a convention to revise U.S. Constitution concerning states' rights in national emergencies.

1816 2nd Bank of United States established (10 Apr.); Monroe elected president (4 Dec.).

1817 Rush-Bagot Agreement: an exchange of notes between U.S. and Great Britain (28–29 Apr.) agreeing to limit naval power on the Great Lakes.

1818 Convention of 1818 (20 Oct.): U.S. citizens given fishing rights off Newfoundland; establishes Northwest boundary.

1819 Panic of 1819: severe depression in which banks suspend specie payments and much western property turned over to Bank of the U.S.; Adams-Onís Treaty (22 Feb.): Spain cedes Florida to U.S. along with claims to Pacific Northwest; *McCullough* v. *Maryland* (4 Wheaton 316): Supreme Court interprets implied powers of Congress.

1820 U.S. population: 9,638,453

Missouri Compromise (3 Mar.): Maine admitted to union as free state, Missouri with no restrictions on slavery.

1821 William Becknell outlines Santa Fe Trail; Monroe inaugurated for 2nd term (5 Mar.).

1822 Bill signed by Monroe recognizing Latin American republics (4 May).

1823 Monroe doctrine (2 Dec.): laid down principle that European governments could not establish new colonies in Western Hemisphere and interference in hemisphere internal affairs would be considered an act of aggression.

1824 Henry Clay coins term "American system" (30–31 Mar.), hoping to check decline of U.S. industry through internal improvements and creation of a home market; Adams elected president (1 Dec.).

1824–1825 Russia relinquishes claims to territory in Pacific Northwest.

1825 Indian removal adopted as policy.

AMERICAN MILITARY HISTORY

1814 British successes at Lacolle Mill (30 Mar.), Bladensburg (24 Aug.), Fort McHenry (13–14 Sept.).

American victories in Battles of Chippewa (5 July), Lundy's Lane (25 July), Fort Erie (2 Aug.–1 Sept.), Lake Champlain (11 Sept.), Plattsburgh (11 Sept.), and Baltimore (12–14 Sept).

USS *Wasp* sinks HMS *Avon* (1 Sept.) and disappears.

1815 Battle of New Orleans (8 Jan.): British soundly defeated by Gen. Jackson's forces.

USS *President* surrenders to British (14 Jan.); USS *Constitution* fights off HMS *Cyane* and *Levant* (20 Feb.); USS *Hornet* defeats HMS *Penguin* (23 Mar.).

War with Algiers: Capt. Stephen Decatur sails to Algiers in retaliation for Algerian interference with U.S. shipping; captures frigate *Mashuda* (17 June) and negotiates treaty with dey of Algiers (28 June).

Congress orders gunboat flotilla sold (27 Feb.) and fixes army strength at 10,000 and creates General Staff (3 Mar.).

1817–1818 1st Seminole War: following Indian raids in Florida, U.S. forces destroy Indian villages, breaking all Indian resistance by Apr. 1818.

1820 Maj. Stephen H. Long's army expedition sets out (6 June) to explore region between Missouri River and Rocky Mountains.

1820 Jackson's Military Road completed from Florence, Ala., to New Orleans and Gulf of Mexico.

1824 General Survey Act authorizes use of military engineers for transportation improvements.

PRESIDENT AND KEY LEADERS, TERM OF OFFICE

Andrew Jackson, *president*, 1829–1837

John C. Calhoun, *vice president*, 1829–1832
Martin Van Buren, *vice president*, 1833–1837
Martin Van Buren, *secretary of state*, 1829–1831
Edward Livingston, *secretary of state*, 1831–1833
Louis McLane, *secretary of state*, 1833–1834
John Forsyth, *secretary of state*, 1834–1837
Samuel D. Ingham, *secretary of Treasury*, 1829–1831
Louis McLane, *secretary of Treasury*, 1831–1833
William J. Duane, *secretary of Treasury*, 1833
Roger B. Taney, *secretary of Treasury*, 1833
Levi Woodbury, *secretary of Treasury*, 1834–1837
John M. Berrien, *attorney general*, 1829–1831
Roger B. Taney, *attorney general*, 1831–1833
Benjamin F. Butler, *attorney general*, 1833–1837
John H. Eaton, *secretary of war*, 1829–1831
Lewis Cass, *secretary of war*, 1831–1836
Benjamin F. Butler, *secretary of war*, 1837
John Branch, *secretary of navy*, 1829–1831
Levi Woodbury, *secretary of navy*, 1831–1834
Mahlon Dickerson, *secretary of navy*, 1834–1837
Roger B. Taney, *chief justice*, 1836–1864

Martin Van Buren, *president*, 1837–1841

Richard M. Johnson, *vice president*, 1837–1841
John Forsyth, *secretary of state*, 1837–1841
Levi Woodbury, *secretary of Treasury*, 1837–1841
Benjamin F. Butler, *attorney general*, 1837–1838
Felix Grundy, *attorney general*, 1838–1839
Henry D. Gilpin, *attorney general*, 1840–1841
Joel R. Poinsett, *secretary of war*, 1837–1841
Mahlon Dickerson, *secretary of navy*, 1837–1838
James K. Paulding, *secretary of navy*, 1838–1841

GENERAL AMERICAN HISTORY

1826 Treaty of Washington: Creek Indians cede lands in Georgia and are removed beyond Mississippi (1827–1829).

1828 Jackson elected president (3 Dec.); Tariff of Abominations passed (19 May); South Carolina Resolves adopted (19 Dec.) declaring Tariff of Abominations unjust and unconstitutional.

1829 Jackson inaugurated president (4 Mar.); Kitchen Cabinet, a small group of unofficial advisers, established by Jackson.

1830 U.S. population: 12,866,020

Webster-Hayne Debate (19–27 Jan.) on interpretation of Constitution; Indian removal act passed (28 May), calling for resettlement of Indians west of Mississippi.

1831 *Cherokee Nation* v. *Georgia* (5 Peters 1): appeal to Supreme Court by Cherokee to prevent Georgia from enforcing its laws in Cherokee nation, in which court rules Cherokee were not U.S. citizens or a foreign nation and the court lacked jurisdiction; Nat Turner's Rebellion (13–23 Aug.): insurrection by 100 blacks in Virginia, with 55 whites killed, and 20 blacks executed; French spoliation claims (4 July) made by U.S. citizens for losses sustained by French blockade of England.

1832 Bill to renew Bank of United States vetoed (10 July); South Carolina Nullification Ordinance (24 Nov.) nullifies tariffs acts of 1828 and 1832; Jackson issues proclamation (10 Dec.) asserting supremacy of federal government; Jackson reelected for 2nd term (5 Dec.).

1833 Force Bill (2 Mar.) and compromise tariff passed; South Carolina suspends ordinance of nullification (15 Mar.).

1834 Bureau of Indian Affairs established (June) in War Department.

1836 Van Buren elected president (7 Dec.).

1837 Jackson recognizes Republic of Texas (3 Mar.), following congressional resolutions (July 1836); Panic of 1837 begins with suspension of specie payments by New York banks (May).

1838 Trail of Tears: forced journey of Cherokee from Georgia to Oklahoma, in which 4000 Indians die.

1840 U.S. population: 17,069,453

AMERICAN MILITARY HISTORY

1827 Supreme Court rules that president has final authority to call out the militia (*Martin* v. *Mott*).

1830 Army abolishes daily liquor ration.

1832 Black Hawk War: Sac and Fox Indians in Illinois and Wisconsin under Black Hawk attack white settlements and are defeated at Battle of Bad Axe (3 Aug.).

1st U.S. armed intervention in Asia at Quallah Battoo, Sumatra, to avenge attack on U.S. merchant vessel; 100 Sumatrans killed and town burned.

1833 Force Act (2 Mar.) authorizes president to use army and navy to collect customs duty; forts in South Carolina put on alert (29 Oct.).

1835–1836 Texas Revolution: Texas settlers revolt against Mexican rule, defeated at the siege of the Alamo (23 Feb.–6 Mar. 1836); massacred at Goliad (27 Mar.), vanquished the Mexican army in Battle of San Jacinto (21 Apr.) under Sam Houston.

1835–1842 2nd Seminole War: Indians under Osceola devastate Florida; U.S. troops reduce number of Indians to 300 by 1842.

1837–1838 William Lyon Mackenzie launches rebellion in Upper Canada (Nov.), flees to United States; Canadian troops invade U.S. territory in pursuit and seize the steamer *Caroline* (29 Dec.) and kill an American merchant; U.S. militia placed along Canadian frontier under Gen. Winfield Scott; Mackenzie surrenders (13 Jan. 1838).

1838–1839 Aroostook War; undeclared and bloodless war with England over Maine's boundaries; 10,000 U.S. troops camp along Aroostook River.

1838–1842 Wilkes Exploring Expedition: Lt. Charles Wilkes commands six ships to chart and survey Pacific islands, Northwest coast, and Antarctica.

1839 Helderberg War: New York State militia put down farmers rioting against leasehold system.

Timeline, 1840–1856

PRESIDENT AND KEY LEADERS, TERM OF OFFICE

William Henry Harrison, *president*, 1841

John Tyler, *president*, 1841–1845

John Tyler, *vice president*, 1841
Daniel Webster, *secretary of state*, 1841–1843
Abel P. Upshur, *secretary of state*, 1843–1844
John C. Calhoun, *secretary of state*, 1844–1845
Thomas Ewing, *secretary of Treasury*, 1841
Walter Forward, *secretary of Treasury*, 1841–1843
John C. Spencer, *secretary of Treasury*, 1843–1844
George M. Bibb, *secretary of Treasury*, 1844–1845
John J. Crittenden, *attorney general*, 1841
Hugh S. Legare, *attorney general*, 1841–1843
John Nelson, *attorney general*, 1843–1845
John Bell, *secretary of war*, 1841
John C. Spencer, *secretary of war*, 1841–1843
James M. Porter, *secretary of war*, 1843–1844
William Wilkins, *secretary of war*, 1844–1845
George E. Badger, *secretary of navy*, 1841
Abel P. Upshur, *secretary of navy*, 1841–1843
David Henshaw, *secretary of navy*, 1843–1844
Thomas W. Gilmer, *secretary of navy*, 1844
John Y. Mason, *secretary of navy*, 1844–1845

James Knox Polk, *president*, 1845–1849

George M. Dallas, *vice president*, 1845–1849
John C. Calhoun, *secretary of state*, 1845
James Buchanan, *secretary of state*, 1845–1849
Robert J. Walker, *secretary of Treasury*, 1845–1849
John Y. Mason, *attorney general*, 1845
Nathan Clifford, *attorney general*, 1846–1848
Isaac Toucey, *attorney general*, 1848–1849
William L. March, *secretary of war*, 1845–1849
George Bancroft, *secretary of navy*, 1845
John Y. Mason, *secretary of navy*, 1845–1849

GENERAL AMERICAN HISTORY

1840–1841 McLeod Case: Alexander McLeod, Canadian sheriff, arrested for involvement in *Caroline* affair and tried despite British demand for his release; congressional act of 1842 provides for removal of accused aliens from state courts to federal courts.

1841 Harrison inaugurated president (4 Mar.), dies in office (4 Apr.), Tyler becomes president.

1842 Webster-Ashburton Treaty (9 Aug.): settles northeastern boundary dispute with England.

1844 Texas annexation treaty signed (12 Apr.); Treaty of Wanghia (3 July) opens 5 Chinese ports to U.S. ships.

1844–1846 Mormon War: disorders between Mormons in Nauvoo, Ill., and non-Mormon neighbors; Mormons depart for Utah.

1846 Treaty with Great Britain passes Senate (18 June) and establishes Oregon boundary.

1848 Gold discovered in California (24 Jan.), gold rush begins; Treaty of Guadalupe Hidalgo (2 Feb.): Mexico cedes claims to Texas, California, Arizona, New Mexico, Utah, and Nevada and sets U.S.-Mexico boundary at Rio Grande; Taylor elected president (4 Dec.).

AMERICAN MILITARY HISTORY

1841–1842 Dorr's Rebellion: President Tyler offers military assistance to Rhode Island governor against malcontents under Thomas W. Dorr, protesting suffrage limitations; state militia quells rebellion.

1844 *Princeton* Disaster (28 Feb.): 12-inch gun aboard the 1st warship driven by a screw propeller blows up, killing secretaries of state and navy and several congressmen.

1845 United States Naval Academy established at Annapolis, Md.

1846–1848 The Mexican War: United States declares war (11 May); orders Gen. Zachary Taylor to Rio Grande (28 May) to defend Texas; ends with Mexico ceding all rights to Texas and U.S. purchase of New Mexico and California.

1846 American victories in Texas in Battles of Palo Alto (8 May) and Resaca de la Palma (9 May).

Bear Flag Revolt (10 June–5 July): California settlers revolt against Mexican rule.

Naval Expedition to California (7 July–17 Aug.): Commodore John D. Sloat sends naval force ashore at Monterey (7 July); Capt. John Charles Frémont forms California Battalion (24 July); Commodore Robert F. Stockton declares U.S. annexation of California (17 Aug.).

1846 Brig. Gen. Stephen W. Kearney proclaims New Mexico part of United States (15 Aug.).

U.S. troops defeat Mexican forces at Battles of Monterrey (21–23 Sept.), San Pasqual (6 Dec.), and El Brazito (25 Dec.).

1847 U.S. forces victorious in Mexican battles of San Gabriel (8–9 Jan.), Buena Vista (22–23 Feb.), the Sacramento (28 Feb.); capture Veracruz (29 Mar.); defeat Mexicans in battles of Cerro Gordo (18 Apr.), Contreras (19–20 Aug.), Churubusco (20 Aug.), Molino del Rey (8 Sept.), and Chapultepec (13 Sept.); capture Mexico City (13–14 Sept.).

1847–1850 Cayuse War: Cayuse destroy mission of Marcus Whitman in southeastern Washington, killing 14, including Whitman; military expedition forces surrender of 5 Cayuse (1850) who are tried and hanged.

1848 U.S. forces evacuate Mexico City (12 June) and Veracruz (2 Aug.).

PRESIDENT AND KEY LEADERS, TERM OF OFFICE

Zachary Taylor, *president,* 1849–1850

Millard Fillmore, *president,* 1850–1853

Millard Fillmore, *vice president,* 1849–1850
James Buchanan, *secretary of state,* 1849
John M. Clayton, *secretary of state,* 1849–1850
Daniel Webster, *secretary of state,* 1850–1852
Edward Everett, *secretary of state,* 1852–1853
William M. Meredith, *secretary of Treasury,* 1849–1850
Thomas Corwin, *secretary of Treasury,* 1850–1853
Reverdy Johnson, *attorney general,* 1849–1850
John J. Crittenden, *attorney general,* 1850–1853
George W. Crawford, *secretary of war,* 1849–1850
Charles M. Conrad, *secretary of war,* 1850–1853
William B. Preston, *secretary of navy,* 1849–1850
William A. Graham, *secretary of navy,* 1850–1852
John P. Kennedy, *secretary of navy,* 1852–1853
Thomas Ewing, *secretary of interior,* 1849–1850
Thomas M. T. McKennan, *secretary of interior,* 1850
Alexander H. H. Stuart, *secretary of interior,* 1850–1853

Franklin Pierce, *president,* 1853–1857

William Rufus King, *vice president,* 1853
William L. Marcy, *secretary of state,* 1853–1857
James Guthrie, *secretary of Treasury,* 1853–1857
Caleb Cushing, *attorney general,* 1853–1857
Jefferson Davis, *secretary of war,* 1853–1857
James C. Dobbin, *secretary of navy,* 1853–1857
Robert McClelland, *secretary of interior,* 1853–1857

GENERAL AMERICAN HISTORY

1849 Department of Interior established (3 Mar.).

1850 U.S. population: 23,191,876

Clayton-Bulwer Treaty (19 Apr.) calls for joint U.S.-British control of a canal across Central American isthmus; Nashville Convention (10 June) affirms legality of slavery by southern states; Fillmore becomes president on death of Taylor (9 July); Compromise of 1850 (Sept.): 5 statutes admitting California as a free state, Texas and New Mexico with no restrictions, and including Fugitive Slave Act (18 Sept.), placing fugitive slave cases under federal jurisdiction.

1851 *Uncle Tom's Cabin* by Harriet Beecher Stowe published (20 Mar.).

1850–1851 López Filibustering Expeditions: 2 failed armed attempts by Cuban revolutionists and American annexationists to free Cuba from Spain.

1853 Gadsden Purchase (30 Dec.): settles boundary question with Mexico for $10 million.

1854 Kansas-Nebraska Act passed (30 May) permitting local option on slavery and repealing Missouri Compromise; Canadian Reciprocity Treaty (5 June) opens U.S. markets to Canada and grants U.S. fishing rights.

1856 Buchanan elected president (4 Nov.).

AMERICAN MILITARY HISTORY

1854 Commodore Matthew C. Perry signs Treaty of Kanagawa (31 Mar.) with Japan, opening Japanese ports to United States.

1855–1857 Walker's Filibustering Expeditions: 2 attempts by William Walker to establish himself as head of government of Nicaragua; surrenders both times (May, November 1857) to U.S. Navy.

1855–1858 3rd Seminole War: Brig. Gen. William S. Harney subdues Billy Bowlegs and other Seminole warriors.

1856 Kansas Civil War (21 May–15 Sept.): between proslavery and antislavery forces; Lawrence sacked (21 May); John Brown carries out Pottawatomie Massacre (24–25 May); proslavery militia called out (25 Aug.); federal troops intercept Border Ruffians marching on Lawrence, bringing temporary peace.

Timeline, 1857–1867

PRESIDENT AND KEY LEADERS, TERM OF OFFICE

James Buchanan, *president,* 1857–1861

John C. Breckinridge, *vice president,* 1857–1861
William L. March, *secretary of state,* 1857
Lewis Cass, *secretary of state,* 1857–1860
Jeremiah S. Black, *secretary of state,* 1860–1861
Howell Cobb, *secretary of Treasury,* 1857–1860
Philip F. Thomas, *secretary of Treasury,* 1860–1861
John A. Dix, *secretary of Treasury,* 1861
Jeremiah S. Black, *attorney general,* 1857–1860
Edwin M. Stanton, *attorney general,* 1860–1861
John B. Floyd, *secretary of war,* 1857–1860
Joseph Holt, *secretary of war,* 1861
Isaac Toucey, *secretary of navy,* 1857–1861
Jacob Thompson, *secretary of interior,* 1857–1861

Abraham Lincoln, *president,* 1861–1865

Hannibal Hamlin, *vice president,* 1861–1865
Andrew Johnson, *vice president,* 1865
Jeremiah S. Black, *secretary of state,* 1861
William H. Seward, *secretary of state,* 1861–1865
Salmon P. Chase, *secretary of Treasury,* 1861–1864
William P. Fessenden, *secretary of Treasury,* 1864–1865
Hugh McCulloch, *secretary of Treasury,* 1865
Edward Bates, *attorney general,* 1861–1864
James Speed, *attorney general,* 1864–1865
Simon Cameron, *secretary of war,* 1861–1862
Edwin M. Stanton, *secretary of war,* 1862–1865
Gideon Welles, *secretary of navy,* 1861–1865
Caleb B. Smith, *secretary of the interior,* 1861–1862
John P. Usher, *secretary of interior,* 1863–1865
Salmon P. Chase, *chief justice,* 1864–1873

GENERAL AMERICAN HISTORY

1857 Dred Scott Case (6 Mar.): Supreme Court rules slaves are not U.S. citizens and cannot sue in federal courts; Panic of 1857 follow boom after Mexican War.

1858 Lincoln delivers "House Divided" speech (16 June); Lincoln-Douglas Debates (21 Aug.–15 Oct.).

1859 Comstock Lode of silver deposits discovered in Virginia City, Nev.

1860 U.S. population: 31,443,321

Davis Resolutions (2 Feb.): Jefferson Davis introduces in Senate slavery resolutions; Lincoln delivers Cooper Union speech (27 Feb.) on extension of slavery and popular sovereignty doctrine; Lincoln elected president (6 Nov.); South Carolina secedes from the Union (20 Dec.).

1861 Confederate States of America formed at Montgomery, Ala. (8 Feb.), and adopts constitution; Congress institutes income tax; Committee on Conduct of the War established (20 Dec.).

1862 Homestead Act enacted (20 May), providing for citizens to acquire 160 acres of public land.

AMERICAN MILITARY HISTORY

1857–1858 Mormon Expedition: U.S. Army campaign under Col. Albert S. Johnston to subdue Mormons refusing to obey federal laws.

1859 John Brown's Raid (16–18 Oct.): Brown seizes Harpers Ferry, Va., armory; captured by marine force under Col. Robert E. Lee; hanged for treason (2 Dec.).

1861–1865 The American Civil War: war begins with Confederate firing on Fort Sumter, S.C. (12 Apr.), and surrender of fort; ends with Confederate surrender to Union forces at Appomattox Courthouse (9 Apr.).

1861 Confederate President Jefferson Davis calls for 60,200 volunteers (9 Mar.–16 Apr.); Lincoln calls for 75,000 three-month militia (15 Apr.), then Congress approves authority to raise 500,000 three-year volunteers (4 July).

Virginia militiamen force garrison at Harpers Ferry arsenal to flee (18 Apr.) and capture Norfolk Navy Yard and the *Merrimack* (21 Apr.); Massachusetts militia arrives in Washington (19 Apr.) and saves capital from being taken.

First Battle of Bull Run, Va. (21 July): Confederate troops defeat Union forces; Port Royal, S.C., captured (7 Nov.) by Union.

Trent Affair (8 Nov.–25 Dec.): Union Capt. Charles Wilkes stops the *Trent* off Cuba and arrests 2 Confederate diplomats bound for London and Paris; war with England averted by Lincoln's ordering release of the men.

1862 Union victories at Mill Springs, Ky. (19–20 Jan.), Fort Donelson (16 Feb.), Nashville (25 Feb.), Glorieta Pass, N.Mex. (28 Mar.); New Orleans captured (26 Apr.); rebel troops defeated at Shiloh, Miss. (6–7 Apr.), Seven Pines, Va. (31 May–1 June), Antietam, Md. (17 Sept.).

Confederate victories in the Shenandoah Valley (23 Mar.–9 June), 2nd Bull Run (29–30 Aug.), and Fredericksburg, Va. (13 Dec.).

Sioux Uprising in Minnesota (18 Aug.–23 Sept.): Little Crow's warriors defeated by Col. Henry H. Schley's troops.

PRESIDENT AND KEY LEADERS, TERM OF OFFICE

Andrew Johnson, *president,* 1865–1869

William H. Seward, *secretary of state,* 1865–1869
Hugh McCulloch, *secretary of Treasury,* 1865–1869
James Speed, *attorney general,* 1865–1866
Henry Stanbery, *attorney general,* 1866–1868
William M. Evarts, *attorney general,* 1868–1869
Edwin M. Stanton, *secretary of war,* 1865–1868
John M. Schofield, *secretary of war,* 1868–1869
Gideon Welles, *secretary of navy,* 1865–1869
John P. Usher, *secretary of interior,* 1865
James Harlan, *secretary of interior,* 1865–1866
Orville H. Browning, *secretary of interior,* 1866–1869

GENERAL AMERICAN HISTORY

1863 Emancipation Proclamation (1 Jan.) grants freedom to slaves in rebelling states; antidraft riots in New York City (13–16 July).

1865 Lincoln assassinated (14 Apr.) by John Wilkes Booth; Johnson becomes president; Reconstruction Proclamation (29 May–13 July) grants amnesty to Confederates who took oath of allegiance; Freedmen's Bureau established (24 Nov.); 13th Amendment ratified (18 Dec.) abolishing slavery; Ku Klux Klan established in Pulaski, Tenn.

1866 Supplementary Reconstruction Acts passed (23 Mar., 19 July), providing for registration of all qualified voters; U.S. agrees to purchase Alaska from Russia for $7.2 million (29 Mar.); Civil Rights Act (9 Apr.) bestows citizenship on blacks; 14th Amendment submitted to states (16 June) for ratification, defines national citizenship, ratification necessary for states to be readmitted to Union; Patrons of Husbandry (Grangers) formed (4 Dec.) to promote agricultural interests.

AMERICAN MILITARY HISTORY

1863 Union victories at Murfreesboro, Tenn. (31 Dec. 1862–3 Jan. 1863), Vicksburg, Miss. (22 May–4 July), Gettysburg, Pa. (1–3 July), Chickamauga, Tenn. (19–20 Sept.), and Chattanooga (23–25 Nov.).

Confederate victory at Chancellorsville, Va. (2–4 May), but Gen. Jackson killed.

1st national conscription act passed (3 Mar.).

Congressional Medal of Honor 1st awarded by army (25 Mar.) and navy (3 Apr.).

1864 Ulysses S. Grant is named commander of all Union forces (9 Mar.).

Union victories in Wilderness battle (5–6 May), William T. Sherman's Atlanta campaign (7 May–2 Sept.) and march to the sea (14 Nov.–2 Dec.), Nashville (15–16 Dec.), and Savannah (22 Dec.).

Confederate victories in Virginia at Spotsylvania (8–12 May), Cold Harbor (1–3 June), and Petersburg (15–18 June), and Jubal Early's raids (2–13 July) in Maryland.

Sand Creek Massacre (29 Nov.): Colorado militiamen kill one-third of a band of Cheyenne, mostly women and children.

1865 Union captures Fort Fisher, N.C. (15 Jan.); Sherman drives through Carolinas (16 Jan.–21 Mar.); Petersburg and Richmond, Va., abandoned (2 Apr.).

Confederate Gen. Robert E. Lee surrenders to Gen. Grant at Appomattox Courthouse (9 Apr.); Gen. J. E. Johnston surrenders 32,000 troops to Sherman at Durham Station, N.C. (26 Apr.); last rebel troops surrender in New Orleans (26 May).

1866 Grand Army of the Republic formed (6 Apr.), an association for Union veterans; last member dies in 1956.

Congress authorizes (July) peacetime army strength of 54,302, including 4 black infantry regiments (later 2, 1869) and 2 black cavalry regiments.

1867 1st Reconstruction Act (2 Mar.) divides South into 5 military districts subject to martial law and under military commanders. William T. Sherman's *Infantry Tactics* published and adopted by the War Department.

Timeline, 1868–1884

PRESIDENT AND KEY LEADERS, TERM OF OFFICE

Ulysses Simpson Grant, *president,* 1869–1877

Schuyler Colfax, *vice president,* 1869–1873
Henry Wilson, *vice president,* 1873–1875
Elihu B. Washburne, *secretary of state,* 1869
Hamilton Fish, *secretary of state,* 1869–1877
George S. Boutwell, *secretary of Treasury,* 1869–1873
William A. Richardson, *secretary of Treasury,* 1873–1874
Benjamin H. Bristow, *secretary of Treasury,* 1874–1876
Lot M. Morrill, *secretary of Treasury,* 1876–1877
Ebenezer R. Hoar, *attorney general,* 1869–1879
Amos T. Akerman, *attorney general,* 1870–1871
George H. Williams, *attorney general,* 1871–1875
Edwards Pierrepoint, *attorney general,* 1875–1876
Alphonso Taft, *attorney general,* 1876–1877
John A. Rawlins, *secretary of war,* 1869
William T. Sherman, *secretary of war,* 1869
William W. Belknap, *secretary of war,* 1869–1876
Adolph E. Borie, *secretary of navy,* 1869
George M. Robeson, *secretary of navy,* 1869–1877
Jacob D. Cox, *secretary of interior,* 1869–1870
Columbus Delano, *secretary of interior,* 1870–1875
Zachariah Chandler, *secretary of interior,* 1875–1877
Morrison R. Waite, *chief justice,* 1874–1888

GENERAL AMERICAN HISTORY

1868 Impeachment trial of Johnson (24 Feb.–26 May): president impeached for removal of Stanton as secretary of war as violation of Tenure of Office Act (2 Mar. 1867), president acquitted; first federal 8-hour workday enacted; Grant elected president (3 Nov.).

1869 First transcontinental rail route completed; Black Friday (24 Sept.), an attempt by James Fisk, Jay Gould, and others to corner the U.S. gold supply.

1870 U.S. population: 39,818,449

15th Amendment ratified (30 Mar.), stating no citizen can be denied right to vote because of race, color, or previous condition of servitude.

1871 Enforcement Acts provide federal election law (28 Feb.) and enforcement of 14th Amendment (20 Apr.); Indian Appropriation Act decrees the federal government would not enter into any further Indian treaties; Civil Service Commission established (3 Mar.); Ku Klux Klan Act (20 Apr.) to enforce 14th and 15th amendments and permit president to declare martial law; Treaty of Washington (8 May) between U.S. and Britain lays down rules of maritime neutrality and submits Alabama Claims to arbitration (settled 14 Sept. 1872); Chicago Fire (8 Oct.) destroys 17,500 buildings and $200 million in property loss, plus 200–300 dead.

1872 Grant reelected (5 Nov.).

1873 Panic of 1873 in which 5000 businesses fail; Coinage Act (12 Feb.) establishes gold standard.

1875 Whiskey Ring conspiracy of revenue officials to defraud government of internal revenue tax.

1876 Alexander Graham Bell patents the telephone; Secretary of War Belknap impeached for receiving bribes for sale of Indian posts; Hayes elected president despite Samuel Tilden's majority popular vote.

AMERICAN MILITARY HISTORY

1868 Georgia returned to military rule after expelling black members from legislature; federal troops compel state to restore members to gain readmission to Union (15 July 1870).

1868 *Ex Parte Milligan* (4 Wallace 2): Supreme Court declares unconstitutional the use of martial law in theaters of war when civil courts are in operation.

1869 Adm. David D. Porter orders all navy vessels fitted out with sails and requires commanders to justify any steam power.

1870 U.S. Navy reduced from Civil War peak of 700 ships to 52.

1871 War with Korea: punitive expedition of four navy steamships against 1866 murder of a merchant ship crew; shore batteries fire on ships (1 June); 250 enemy killed in battle (11 June); treaty secured in 1882.

1871–1886 Apache Wars: begin with Camp Grant, Ariz., Massacre (30 Apr.) by Tucson citizens; series of repeated raids take place under Geronimo and Victorio (killed 1880); wars end with Geronimo's surrender (1886).

1872–1873 Modoc War: Cavalry try to return Modoc and their leader, Capt. Jack (Kintpuash), back to Oregon reservation; more than 1000 soldiers needed to pursue and capture 75 warriors and 150 women and children; Capt. Jack hanged and Modoc exiled to Indian Territory.

1873 Army adopts single-shot, breech-loading, black-powder Springfield rifle.

United States Naval Institute established.

1876 Black Hills War: discovery of gold in South Dakota leads to encroachment on Sioux lands; Gen. George Crook mounts three-pronged invasion of Indian country (June); Col. George A. Custer and 264 soldiers of 7th Cavalry killed at Little Bighorn (25 June); renewed army offenses quell further Indian attacks.

United States Coast Guard Academy founded (31 July) at New London, Conn.

Authorized maximum strength of army: 27,442.

PRESIDENT AND KEY LEADERS, TERM OF OFFICE

Rutherford Birchard Hayes, *president*, 1877–1881

William A. Wheeler, *vice president*, 1877–1881
Hamilton Fish, *secretary of state*, 1877
William M. Evarts, *secretary of state*, 1877–1881
John Sherman, *secretary of Treasury*, 1877–1881
Charles Devans, *attorney general*, 1877–1881
George W. McCrary, *secretary of war*, 1877–1879
Alexander Ramsey, *secretary of war*, 1879–1881
Richard W. Thompson, *secretary of navy*, 1877–1880
Nathan Goff, *secretary of navy*, 1881
Carl Schurz, *secretary of interior*, 1877–1881

James Abram Garfield, *president*, 1881

Chester Alan Arthur, *president*, 1881–1885

Chester Alan Arthur, *vice president*, 1881
William M. Evarts, *secretary of state*, 1881
James G. Blaine, *secretary of state*, 1881
Frederick Frelinghuysen, *secretary of state*, 1881–1885
William Windom, *secretary of Treasury*, 1881
Charles J. Folger, *secretary of Treasury*, 1881–1884
Walter Q. Gresham, *secretary of Treasury*, 1884
Hugh McCulloch, *secretary of Treasury*, 1884–1885
I. Wayne MacVeagh, *attorney general*, 1881
Benjamin H. Brewster, *attorney general*, 1881–1885
Robert T. Lincoln, *secretary of war*, 1881–1885
William H. Hunt, *secretary of navy*, 1881–1882
William E. Chandler, *secretary of navy*, 1882–1885
Samuel J. Kirkwood, *secretary of interior*, 1881–1882
Henry M. Teller, *secretary of interior*, 1882–1885

GENERAL AMERICAN HISTORY

1877 Thomas Edison patents the phonograph; Reconstruction ends in the South.

1880 U.S. population: 50,155,783

Garfield elected president (2 Nov.); Treaty with China (17 Nov.) limits immigration of Chinese laborers.

1881 Garfield assassinated (2 July) by Charles J. Guiteau; Arthur becomes president (20 Sept.).

1883 Pendleton Act (16 Jan.) establishes Civil Service Commission and competitive examinations.

1884 Cleveland elected president (4 Nov.).

AMERICAN MILITARY HISTORY

1877 Railroad strike begins (17 July) on Baltimore & Ohio and spreads across nation; federal troops sent in to restore order at Martinsburg, W.Va., after strikers repulsed militia, and at Pittsburgh, Pa.; National Guard kills a total of 100 strikers.

Nez Perce War; Gen. O. O. Howard moves against the previously peaceful Nez Perce in Idaho, Washington, and Oregon, after some settlers were killed; Chief Joseph leads skillful retreat toward Canada but forced to surrender (15 Oct.); 300 warriors opposed more than 5000 troops moving more than 1000 miles in four months.

1878 Bannock War: Bannock attack settlers in Idaho; pursued by Gen. Howard, suffer heavy losses, and drift back to Fort Hall Reservation.

Military Service Institution established.

Treaty with Samoa (17 Jan.) gives U.S. right to establish a naval station.

1882 Commodore Robert W. Shufeldt negotiates 1st treaty between a Western nation and Korea.

Office of Naval Intelligence created.

1883 Naval Appropriations Act authorizes building of 3 steel cruisers and one dispatch boat and creates Gun Foundry Board.

1884 Naval War College established at Newport, R.I. (6 Oct.).

Timeline, 1885–1900

PRESIDENT AND KEY LEADERS, TERM OF OFFICE

Stephen Grover Cleveland, *president,* 1885–1889

Thomas A. Hendrick, *vice president,* 1885
Frederick Frelinghuysen, *secretary of state,* 1885
Thomas F. Bayard, *secretary of state,* 1885–1889
Daniel Manning, *secretary of Treasury,* 1885–1887
Charles S. Fairchild, *secretary of Treasury,* 1887–1889
Augustus Garland, *attorney general,* 1885–1889
William C. Endicott, *secretary of war,* 1885–1889
William C. Whitney, *secretary of navy,* 1885–1889
Lucius Q. C. Lamar, *secretary of interior,* 1885–1888
William F. Vilas, *secretary of interior,* 1888–1889
Norman J. Colman, *secretary of agriculture,* 1889
Melville W. Fuller, *chief justice,* 1888–1910

Benjamin Harrison, *president,* 1889–1893

Levi P. Morton, *vice president,* 1889–1893
Thomas F. Bayard, *secretary of state,* 1889
James G. Blaine, *secretary of state,* 1889–1892
John W. Foster, *secretary of state,* 1892–1893
William Windom, *secretary of Treasury,* 1889–1891
Charles Foster, *secretary of Treasury,* 1891–1893
William H. H. Miller, *attorney general,* 1889–1893
Redfield Proctor, *secretary of war,* 1889–1891
Stephen B. Elkins, *secretary of war,* 1891–1893
John W. Noble, *secretary of interior,* 1889–1893
Jeremiah M. Rusk, *secretary of agriculture,* 1889–1893

GENERAL AMERICAN HISTORY

1886 Presidential Succession Act (19 Jan.) delineates line of succession to presidency; Haymarket Riot erupts (4 May) in Chicago, a protest for 8-hour workday, with 7 killed and 70 injured.

1887 Interstate Commerce Act (4 Feb.) gives federal government right to regulate transportation and business extending beyond state lines.

1888 Harrison elected president (6 Nov.).

1889 1st Oklahoma land run (22 Apr.) by 50,000.

1890 U.S. population: 62,947,714

Sherman Antitrust Act (2 July) declares restraint of trade illegal.

1892 Cleveland elected president (8 Nov.).

AMERICAN MILITARY HISTORY

1885 War Department creates Military Information Division, forerunner of army intelligence organizations.

Fortifications Appropriation Act creates Endicott Board to investigate coastal defenses.

1886 Endicott Board proposes massive fortress program of $27 million.

1887 Hawaiian government grants United States use of Pearl Harbor as a fueling and naval repair station; Cleveland vetoes veterans pension bills and approves order for return of captured Confederate flags to South (7–15 June).

1888 Congress creates Army Board of Ordnance and Fortifications to test weapons.

Massachusetts establishes 1st naval militia.

1890 Messiah War: an outgrowth of Ghost Dance excitement among the Sioux in the Badlands, S.Dak.; Gen. Nelson A. Miles apprehends Sitting Bull, who is killed resisting arrest (15 Dec.); principal band of hostile Indians under Big Foot, camped at Wounded Knee Creek, surrender, but are massacred (28 Dec.); final fight between Indians and U.S. Army.

The Influence of Sea Power upon History, 1660–1783 by Alfred Thayer Mahan published; Dependent Pension Act (27 June) grants pensions to veterans of Union forces.

Army adopts Krag-Jörgensen smokeless-powder repeating rifle.

1891 Uss *Charleston* pursues Chilean rebel vessels off San Diego, which gives rise to mob attack in Chile on sailors ashore from the U.S. cruiser *Baltimore,* killing 2.

1892 State militia break up Homestead Steelworkers Strike (12 July); martial law declared in Coeur d'Alene silver mines in Idaho after violence between striking miners and strike breakers.

PRESIDENT AND KEY LEADERS, TERM OF OFFICE

Stephen Grover Cleveland, *president,* 1893–1897

Adlai E. Stevenson, *vice president,* 1893–1897
Walter Q. Gresham, *secretary of state,* 1893–1895
Richard Olney, *secretary of state,* 1895–1897
John G. Carlisle, *secretary of Treasury,* 1893–1897
Richard Olney, *attorney general,* 1893–1895
Judson Harmon, *attorney general,* 1895–1897
Daniel S. Lamont, *secretary of war,* 1893–1897
Hilary A. Herbert, *secretary of navy,* 1893–1897
Hoke Smith, *secretary of interior,* 1893–1896
David R. Francis, *secretary of interior,* 1896–1897
J. Sterling Morton, *secretary of agriculture,* 1893–1897

William McKinley, *president,* 1897–1901

Garret Augustus Hobart, *vice president,* 1897–1899
Theodore Roosevelt, *vice president,* 1901
Richard Olney, *secretary of state,* 1897
John Sherman, *secretary of state,* 1897–1898
William R. Day, *secretary of state,* 1898
John M. Hay, *secretary of state,* 1898–1901
Lyman J. Gage, *secretary of Treasury,* 1897–1901
Joseph McKenna, *attorney general,* 1897–1898
John W. Griggs, *attorney general,* 1898–1901
Philander C. Knox, *attorney general,* 1901
Russel A. Alger, *secretary of war,* 1897–1899
Elihu Root, *secretary of war,* 1899–1901
John D. Long, *secretary of navy,* 1897–1902
Cornelius N. Bliss, *secretary of interior,* 1897–1898
Ethan A. Hitchcock, *secretary of interior,* 1898–1901
James Wilson, *secretary of agriculture,* 1897–1901

GENERAL AMERICAN HISTORY

1893 Panic of 1893 with failure of 4000 banks and 14,000 commercial businesses; Diplomatic Appropriation Act (Mar.) creates rank of ambassador; Thomas Francis Bayard appointed U.S. ambassador to Great Britain (Apr.).

1894 Coxey's Army: 500 unemployed men led by Jacob Coxey march to Washington D.C., (30 Apr.), seeking public works relief program; disbanded after Coxey's arrest for trespassing; Pullman Strike (11 May–20 July): 4000 members of American Railway Union strike Pullman Palace Car Company and defy blanket injunction prohibiting interference with trains, quelled by federal troops; Edison's kinetoscope has first public showing in New York City.

1896 *Plessy* v. *Ferguson* (163 U.S. 537) upholds validity of separate but equal facilities for races; McKinley elected president (3 Nov.).

1899 1st Hague Conference (18 May–29 July): establishes Permanent Court of Arbitration; Open Door Policy enunciated affirming U.S. commercial and industrial rights in China.

1900 U.S. population: 75,994,575.

McKinley reelected (6 Nov.); Samoan Partition Treaty (2 Dec.): islands divided between Germany, Great Britain, and U.S.

AMERICAN MILITARY HISTORY

1893 U.S. marines land in Hawaii and aid revolutionary committee of safety in overthrowing monarchy.

1897 German General Staff publishes survey of world military forces, excludes United States Army.

1898 Spanish-American War: U.S. battleship *Maine* explodes in Havana harbor, Cuba (15 Feb.); U.S. declares (25 Apr.) independence of Cuba and that state of war existed with Spain since 21 Apr.; U.S. victories in Battle of Manila Bay and Philippines (1 May) and Manila falls (13 Aug.); Battle of Santiago, Cuba, defeats Spanish fleet (3 July) and Santiago surrenders (17 July); Treaty of Paris (10 Dec.) establishes independence of Cuba, cedes Puerto Rico and Guam to U.S., and U.S. purchases Philippines for $20 million.

Leech Lake Uprising: Chippewa in Minnesota resist apprehension and successfully battle soldiers from Fort Snelling (5 Oct.).

1899–1902 Philippine Insurrection: Filipino revolutionaries battle troops of U.S. military government; Gen. Arthur MacArthur captures thousands (Nov. 1900); Gen. Frederick S. Funston captures leader Emilio Aguinaldo (Mar. 1901); revolutionaries surrender (1902).

1900 Boxer Rebellion: antiforeign uprising in China by secret society of Boxers (June); begin siege of legations in Peking (17 June); U.S., Great Britain, Russia, Germany, France, and Japan lead relief expedition of 5000 troops, raise siege (14 Aug.).

Timeline, 1901–1912

PRESIDENT AND KEY LEADERS, TERM OF OFFICE

Theodore Roosevelt, *president,* 1901–1909

Charles W. Fairbanks, *vice president,* 1905–1909

John M. Hay, *secretary of state,* 1901–1905

Elihu Root, *secretary of state,* 1905–1909

Robert Bacon, *secretary of state,* 1909

Lyman J. Gage, *secretary of Treasury,* 1901–1902

Leslie M. Shaw, *secretary of Treasury,* 1902–1907

George B. Cortelyou, *secretary of Treasury,* 1907–1909

Philander C. Knox, *attorney general,* 1901–1904

William H. Moody, *attorney general,* 1904–1906

Charles J. Bonaparte, *secretary of navy,* 1905–1906

Victor H. Metcalf, *secretary of navy,* 1906–1908

Truman H. Newberry, *secretary of navy,* 1908–1909

Ethan A. Hitchcock, *secretary of interior,* 1901–1907

James R. Garfield, *secretary of interior,* 1907–1909

James Wilson, *secretary of agriculture,* 1901–1909

George B. Cortelyou, *secretary of commerce and labor,* 1903–1904

Victor H. Metcalf, *secretary of commerce and labor,* 1904–1906

Oscar S. Straus, *secretary of commerce and labor,* 1906–1909

GENERAL AMERICAN HISTORY

1901 Platt amendment adopted (2 Mar.), outlining U.S.-Cuban relations and agreements, repealed (29 May 1934).

McKinley assassinated (6 Sept.) by Leon Czolgosz; Roosevelt becomes president (14 Sept.).

1902 Reclamation Act (June) authorizes president to retain public lands as part of public domain and to construct irrigation works in western states.

1903 Hay-Bunau-Varilla Treaty (13 Nov.) provides for construction and operation of canal in Panama.

1904 Theodore Roosevelt elected president (8 Nov.); Roosevelt Corollary to Monroe Doctrine pronounced (6 Dec.) to prevent intervention in Latin America by European creditors.

1905 Taft-Katsura Memorandum (29 July): U.S.-Japanese cooperation agreement for "maintenance of peace in Far East."

1906 Algeciras Conference (16 Jan.): U.S. obtains privileged position in Morocco; San Francisco earthquake and fire (18–21 Apr.) kills 700.

1907 Gentlemen's Agreement (24 Feb.): U.S. and Japan agree to exclude further Japanese laborers from emigrating to U.S.; Panic of 1907; 2nd Hague Peace Conference (15 June–18 Oct.).

1908 Henry Ford introduces Model T (1 Oct.); Taft elected president (3 Nov.).

1908–1909 Root Arbitration Treaties: 25 bilateral pacts, obligating parties to arbitrate differences of legal nature or interpretation of a treaty.

AMERICAN MILITARY HISTORY

1901 Army War College founded (27 Nov.).

1903 Militia Act of 1903 (Dick Act) passes (14 Feb.), establishing General Staff.

U.S. warships stand by to protect U.S. interests as Panama revolts against Colombia; Panama independence recognized (6 Nov.).

1907 Panama Canal project placed under secretary of war with Col. George W. Goethals of Army Corps of Engineers in charge.

Signal Corps creates Aeronautical Division.

1907–1909 Great White Fleet Cruise: in a demonstration of U.S. strength, 16 battleships begin to sail around the world (Dec. 16), visiting China, Australia, and Japan; return to U.S. (22 Feb. 1909).

PRESIDENT AND KEY LEADERS, TERM OF OFFICE

William Howard Taft, *president,* 1909–1913

James S. Sherman, *vice president,* 1909–1912
Robert Bacon, *secretary of state,* 1909
Philander C. Knox, *secretary of state,* 1909–1913
Franklin MacVeagh, *secretary of Treasury,* 1909–1913
George W. Wickersham, *attorney general,* 1909–1913
Jacob W. Dickinson, *secretary of war,* 1909–1911
Henry L. Stimson, *secretary of war,* 1911–1913
George L. von Meyer, *secretary of navy,* 1909–1913
Richard A. Ballinger, *secretary of interior,* 1909–1911
Walter L. Fisher, *secretary of interior,* 1911–1913
James Wilson, *secretary of agriculture,* 1911–1913
Charles Nagel, *secretary of commerce and labor,* 1909–1913
Edward D. White, *chief justice,* 1910–1921

GENERAL AMERICAN HISTORY

1909 Robert E. Peary reaches North Pole (6 Apr.); awarded rank of admiral (1911).

1910 U.S. population: 91,972,266.

Mann-Elkins Act (18 June) places telephone, telegraph, cable, and wireless companies under Interstate Commerce Commission jurisdiction.

1912 Lodge Corollary (2 Aug.), 1st application of Monroe doctrine to Asian nation, prevents Japanese purchase of land in Baja California; Wilson elected president (5 Nov.).

AMERICAN MILITARY HISTORY

1911 Plattsburgh Movement of summer military training camps begins.

1912 Marines arrive in Nicaragua (14 Aug.) to support Adolfo Díaz government; token force withdraws in 1925, last marines leave 1933.

Congress creates Quartermaster Department.

Timeline, 1913–1923

PRESIDENT AND KEY LEADERS, TERM OF OFFICE

Woodrow Wilson, *president*, 1913–1921

Thomas R. Marshall, *vice president*, 1913–1921
Philander C. Knox, *secretary of state*, 1913
William Jennings Bryan, *secretary of state*, 1913–1915
Robert Lansing, *secretary of state*, 1915–1920
Bainbridge Colby, *secretary of state*, 1920–1921
William G. McAdoo, *secretary of Treasury*, 1913–1918
Carter Glass, *secretary of Treasury*, 1918–1920
David F. Houston, *secretary of Treasury*, 1920–1921
James C. McReynolds, *attorney general*, 1913–1914
Thomas W. Gregory, *attorney general*, 1914–1919
A. Mitchell Palmer, *attorney general*, 1919–1921
Lindley M. Garrison, *secretary of war*, 1913–1916
Newton D. Baker, *secretary of war*, 1916–1921
Josephus Daniels, *secretary of navy*, 1913–1921
Franklin K. Lane, *secretary of interior*, 1913–1920
John B. Payne, *secretary of interior*, 1920–1921
David F. Houston, *secretary of agriculture*, 1913–1920
Edwin T. Meredith, *secretary of agriculture*, 1920–1921
William C. Redfield, *secretary of commerce*, 1913–1919
Joshua W. Alexander, *secretary of commerce*, 1919–1921
William B. Wilson, *secretary of labor*, 1913–1921

GENERAL AMERICAN HISTORY

1913 Federal Reserve System established (23 Dec.).

1914 Wilson proclaims U.S. neutrality in European war (4 Aug.); Panama Canal opened (15 Aug.).

1915 *Lusitania* sinks (7 May) with loss of 128 Americans after attack by German submarine; 1st transcontinental telephone conversation (25 Jan.).

1916 British steamer *Sussex* attacked by German submarine (24 Mar.), and two Americans injured; treaty signed for purchase of Danish West Indies (4 Aug.); Wilson reelected (7 Nov.).

1917 Wilson's "Peace without victory" speech (22 Jan.); Germany informs U.S. of resumption of unrestricted submarine warfare (31 Jan.); Wilson severs diplomatic relations with Germany (3 Feb.); Zimmerman note of German guarantees to Mexico published (1 Mar.); U.S. declares war on Germany (6 Apr.); federal government takes over railroads (26 Dec.).

1918 Wilson's 14 Points (8 Jan.) state U.S. terms of peace with Germany; Sedition Act (16 May) provides heavy penalties of hindering war effort; war ends (11 Nov.).

1919 Eighteenth Amendment (Prohibition) ratified (19 Jan.); 1st transatlantic flight by navy seaplane (8–27 May).

1920 U.S. population: 105,710,620

Red Scare: 2700 Communists arrested (Jan.–May); Senate refuses to ratify Versailles Treaty (19 Mar.); Merchant Marine Act (5 June) repeals emergency war legislation on shipping and reorganizes U.S. Shipping Board.

Nineteenth Amendment gives right to vote to women (20 Aug.); Harding elected president (2 Nov.).

AMERICAN MILITARY HISTORY

1913 1st Aero Squadron formed.

1914 U.S. marines arrested at Tampico, Mexico (9 Apr.), while nation is under martial law; U.S. forces bombard Veracruz and occupy city (21 Apr.).

1915 U.S. marines occupy Haiti after civil war (28 July); treaty signed by Haitian senate (16 Sept.) makes island nation virtual U.S. protectorate; troops withdraw 1934.

1916 National Defense Act (3 June) increases size of army, National Guard, establishes ROTC; Naval Act provides for construction of 10 battleships, 16 cruisers, 50 destroyers, 72 submarines.

Resistance in Dominican Republic to U.S. customs receivership leads to martial law (29 Nov.) with government headed by U.S. navy officer; receivership continues until 1924.

1916–1917 Punitive Expedition into Mexico: Mexican bandit Pancho Villa raids Columbus, N.Mex., killing 18; Brig. Gen. John J. Pershing leads 11,000 U.S. troops into Mexico; unable to capture Villa, troops withdraw (5 Feb.).

1917 Selective Service Act passes (18 May) providing for registration and classification for military service.

War Industries Board established (28 July)

1917–1918 World War I: war declared on Germany (6 Apr.); American Expeditionary Forces begin to arrive in France (26 June) under Gen. Pershing. Major battles and offensives (1918): Belleau Wood (6 June–1 July), Aisne-Marne (18 July–6 Aug.), Somme (6 Aug.–11 Nov.), Oisne-Aisne (18 Aug.–11 Nov.), Ypres-Lys (19 Aug.–11 Nov.), St. Mihiel salient (12–16 Sept.), Meuse-Argonne (26 Sept.–11 Nov.); armistice declared (11 Nov. 1918).

1918–1920 Siberian Expedition: U.S. and other Allied troops move to Vladivostok, Murmansk, and Archangel to protect war supplies during Russian Revolution.

1919 Boston Police Strike (9 Sept.): Boston militia restores order, entire Massachusetts militia called out by Gov. Calvin Coolidge.

PRESIDENT AND KEY LEADERS, TERM OF OFFICE

Warren Gamaliel Harding, *president,* 1921–1923

Calvin Coolidge, *vice president,* 1921–1923
Charles Evans Hughes, *secretary of state,* 1921–1923
Andrew W. Mellon, *secretary of Treasury,* 1921–1923
Harry M. Daugherty, *attorney general,* 1921–1923
John W. Weeks, *secretary of war,* 1921–1923
Edwin Denby, *secretary of navy,* 1921–1923
Albert B. Fall, *secretary of interior,* 1921–1923
Hubert Work, *secretary of interior,* 1923
Henry C. Wallace, *secretary of agriculture,* 1921–1923
Herbert C. Hoover, *secretary of commerce,* 1921–1923
James. J. Davis, *secretary of labor,* 1921–1923
William Howard Taft, *chief justice,* 1921–1930

GENERAL AMERICAN HISTORY

1922–1923 2nd Central American Conference (4 Dec.–7 Feb.) settles issues between Nicaragua and Honduras.

AMERICAN MILITARY HISTORY

1921 1st trans-Pacific submarine cruise takes 7 months; Veterans Bureau established as independent unit (9 Aug.).

1921–1922 Washington Naval Conference (12 Nov.–6 Feb.): to deal with arms race and Pacific security; Five-Power Naval Treaty puts 10-year holiday on ship construction and fixes ship tonnage ratio; submarine use restricted during war and poison gas outlawed.

1922 Joint Army-Navy Munitions Board created.

Timeline, 1923–1932

PRESIDENT AND KEY LEADERS, TERM OF OFFICE

John Calvin Coolidge, *president,* 1923–1929

Charles G. Daws, *vice president,* 1925–1929
Charles Evans Hughes, *secretary of state,* 1923–1929
Frank B. Kellogg, *secretary of state,* 1925–1929
Andrew W. Mellon, *secretary of Treasury,* 1923–1929
Harry M. Daugherty, *attorney general,* 1923–1924
Harlan Fiske Stone, *attorney general,* 1924–1925
John G. Sargent, *attorney general,* 1925–1929
John W. Weeks, *secretary of war,* 1923–1925
Dwight F. Davis, *secretary of war,* 1925–1929
Edwin Denby, *secretary of navy,* 1923–1924
Curtis D. Wilbur, *secretary of navy,* 1924–1929
Hubert Work, *secretary of interior,* 1923–1928
Roy O. West, *secretary of interior,* 1928–1929
Henry C. Wallace, *secretary of agriculture,* 1923–1924
Howard M. Gore, *secretary of agriculture,* 1924–1925
William M. Jardine, *secretary of agriculture,* 1925–1929
Herbert C. Hoover, *secretary of commerce,* 1923–1928
William F. Whiting, *secretary of commerce,* 1928–1929
James J. Davis, *secretary of labor,* 1923–1929

GENERAL AMERICAN HISTORY

1923 Harding dies (2 Aug.); Coolidge sworn in as president (3 Aug.).

1924 Snyder Act (2 June) declares all U.S. Indians citizens; Coolidge elected president (4 Nov.).

1925 1st national congress of the Ku Klux Klan in Washington, D.C. (8 Aug.).

1926 Civilian Aviation Act (2 Nov.) establishes bureau in Dept. of Commerce to map airways and provide flying regulations.

1927 Charles A. Lindbergh makes first solo nonstop transatlantic flight (20–21 May), from New York to Paris.

1928 Merchant Marine (Jones-White) Act (22 May) passes to encourage private shipping; Kellogg-Briand Pact signed (27 Aug.) by 15 nations, renouncing war as an instrument of national policy; Hoover elected president (6 Nov.).

AMERICAN MILITARY HISTORY

1923 Teapot Dome Oil Scandal: corruption unearthed by Senate investigation over illegal leases of naval oil reserves at Teapot Dome, Wyo., and Elk Hills, Calif.

1924 World War Adjusted Compensation Act (Soldiers Bonus Act) passes (19 May), providing payment of adjusted compensation comparable to civilian pay.

Occupation of Dominican Republic ends (July).

Federal government starts paying National Guardsmen for weekly drills.

1925 Gen. Billy Mitchell Trial (28 Oct.–17 Dec.): Mitchell of Army Air Service found guilty of conduct prejudicial to good order and military discipline because of his comments and actions about the army command concerning air power.

1926 Robert H. Goddard tests world's first liquid-fuel rocket (16 Mar.).

Congress passes (2 July) Air Corps Act, creating Army Air Corps.

Air Commerce Act passes (2 Nov.).

Commander Richard E. Byrd circles North Pole in plane (9 May).

1927 100 marines land in China (5 Mar.) to protect U.S. property during civil war.

PRESIDENT AND KEY LEADERS, TERM OF OFFICE

Herbert Clark Hoover, *president,* 1929–1933

Charles Curtis, *vice president,* 1929–1933
Frank B. Kellogg, *secretary of state,* 1929
Henry L. Stimson, *secretary of state,* 1929–1933
Andrew W. Mellon, *secretary of Treasury,* 1929–1932
Ogden L. Mills, *secretary of Treasury,* 1932–1933
William D. Mitchell, *attorney general,* 1929–1933
James W. Good, *secretary of war,* 1929
Patrick J. Hurley, *secretary of war,* 1929–1933
Charles F. Adams, *secretary of navy,* 1929–1933
Ray L. Wilbur, *secretary of interior,* 1929–1933
Arthur M. Hyde, *secretary of agriculture,* 1929–1933
Robert P. Lamont, *secretary of commerce,* 1929–1932
Roy D. Chapin, *secretary of commerce,* 1932–1933
James J. Davis, *secretary of labor,* 1929–1930
William N. Doak, *secretary of labor,* 1930–1933
Charles Evans Hughes, *chief justice,* 1930–1941

GENERAL AMERICAN HISTORY

1929 Panic of 1929 results from stock market crash (29 Oct.).

1930 U.S. population: 122,775,046

"Star-Spangled Banner" becomes national anthem (3 Mar.); Smoot-Hawley Tariff (June) raises duties to prohibitive level on 890 articles.

1932 Reconstruction Finance Corp. established (2 Feb.) with $2 billion to advance loans to failing banks, building and loan societies, and insurance companies; Roosevelt elected president (8 Nov.).

AMERICAN MILITARY HISTORY

1930 London Naval Treaty (22 Apr.) signed by U.S., Great Britain, Italy, France, and Japan.

1931 Congress passes (27 Feb.) veterans bonus over Hoover's veto.

1932 Bonus March on Washington (May–July): 15,000 World War I veterans seek economic relief from Congress; driven away by U.S. tanks, infantry, and cavalry.

Timeline, 1933–1944

PRESIDENT AND KEY LEADERS, TERM OF OFFICE

Franklin Delano Roosevelt, *president*, 1933–1945

John Nance Garner, *vice president*, 1933–1941
Henry A. Wallace, *vice president*, 1941–1945
Harry S. Truman, *vice president*, 1945
Cordell Hull, *secretary of state*, 1933–1944
Edward R. Stettinius, *secretary of state*, 1944–1945
William H. Woodin, *secretary of Treasury*, 1933
Henry Morgenthau, Jr., *secretary of Treasury*, 1934–1945
Homer S. Cummings, *attorney general*, 1933–1939
Frank Murphy, *attorney general*, 1939–1940
Robert H. Jackson, *attorney general*, 1940–1941
Francis Biddle, *attorney general*, 1941–1945
Harry H. Woodring, *secretary of war*, 1936–1940
Henry L. Stimson, *secretary of war*, 1940–1945
Claude A. Swanson, *secretary of navy*, 1933–1939
Charles Edison, *secretary of navy*, 1940
Frank Knox, *secretary of navy*, 1940–1944
James V. Forrestal, *secretary of navy*, 1944–1945
Harold L. Ickes, *secretary of interior*, 1933–1945
Henry A. Wallace, *secretary of agriculture*, 1933–1940
Claude R. Wickard, *secretary of agriculture*, 1940–1945
Daniel C. Roper, *secretary of commerce*, 1933–1938
Harry L. Hopkins, *secretary of commerce*, 1938–1940
Jesse Jones, *secretary of commerce*, 1940–1945
Henry A. Wallace, *secretary of commerce*, 1945
Frances Perkins, *secretary of labor*, 1933–1945
Harlan Fiske Stone, *chief justice*, 1941–1946

GENERAL AMERICAN HISTORY

1933 Good Neighbor Policy announced (4 Mar.) by Roosevelt to improve relations with Latin America; Roosevelt launches New Deal (9 Mar.) legislation: Emergency Banking Relief Act (9 Mar.), Civilian Conservation Corps (31 Mar.), Agricultural Adjustment Act (12 May), Federal Emergency Relief Act (12 May), Tennessee Valley Authority (18 May), Federal Securities Act (27 May), National Industrial Recovery Act (16 June), Civil Works Administration (8 Nov.); U.S. comes off gold standard (30 Apr.); U.S. recognizes USSR (16 Nov.); Prohibition ends (5 Dec.).

1934 Export-Import Bank established (2 Feb.); Securities and Exchange Act passes (6 June); Federal Communications Commission established (19 June).

1935 2nd New Deal announced by Roosevelt (4 Jan.), program of social reform: Soil Conservation Act (27 Apr.), Works Progress Administration (11 May), National Labor Relations Act (5 July), Social Security Act (14 Aug.), Public Utilities Act (28 Aug.).

1936 Roosevelt signs 2nd neutrality bill (29 Feb.), banning loans to countries at war; Merchant Marine Act (26 June) creates U.S. Maritime Commission.

1937 Neutrality Act (1 May) prohibits export of arms and ammunition to belligerent nations and the use of U.S. ships for carrying munitions and war materials into belligerent zones; Amelia Earhart lost on round-the-world flight (2 July).

1938 House Committee to Investigate Un-American Activities formed (26 May); Civil Aeronautics Act passed (23 June), establishes Civil Aeronautics Authority to supervise non-military air transport; Fair Labor Standards (Wages and Hours) Act passes (25 June).

1939 Defense appropriations (Apr.): Roosevelt signs $549 million for defense appropriation, Congress approves $300 million for aircraft; U.S. proclaims neutrality (5 Sept.); Roosevelt declares limited national emergency (8 Sept.); Neutrality Act of 1939 passes (4 Nov.) authorizing "cash and carry" sale of arms to belligerents.

AMERICAN MILITARY HISTORY

1933 Air Corps adopts Norden bombsight.

U.S. troops withdraw from Nicaragua (6 Aug.).

1934 Air Corps carries airmail.

Vincent-Tramell Naval Parity Act (27 Mar.) authorizes navy to build 100 warships.

Nye Munitions Investigation Committee (12 Apr.) appointed by Senate investigates arms makers during World War I.

National Guard Act makes Guard part of army in war or national emergency (15 June).

U.S. troops withdraw from Haiti (6 Aug.).

1935 Patman Bonus Bill for cash payments to World War I veterans vetoed (22 May).

1936 Adjusted Compensation Act (24 Jan.) for World War I veterans provides payments of 9-year interest-bearing bonds—$1,500 million distributed to 3 million veterans.

1937 *Panay* Incident (12 Dec.): U.S. gunboat sunk by Japanese engaged in war with China; Japan apologizes.

1938 Vinson Naval Expansion Act (17 May) authorizes expansion of two-ocean navy beyond treaty limits and 3000 naval aircraft.

PRESIDENT AND KEY LEADERS, TERM OF OFFICE

GENERAL AMERICAN HISTORY

1940 U.S. population: 131,669,275

National Defense Research Committee established (15 June) with Vannevar Bush as chairman; Pittman Resolution (16 June) authorizes sale of munitions to Western Hemisphere nations; Alien Registration (Smith) Act (28 June) requires registration and fingerprinting of aliens; Permanent Joint Board on Defense created by U.S. and Canada (18 Aug.); embargo on exports of scrap iron and steel to non-Western Hemisphere nations except Great Britain (26 Sept.); Roosevelt reelected for record 3rd term (5 Nov.); Office of Production Management established (20 Dec.); Roosevelt calls for production effort to make U.S. "arsenal of democracy" (29 Dec.).

1941 Lend-Lease bill passes (11 Mar.), for lending goods and services to democratic countries in return for services; secret U.S.-British talks in Washington (27 Jan.–29 Mar.) produce war plan ABC-1 and set "Germany first" priority in event of war with Germany and Japan; U.S.-Danish agreement to defend Greenland in exchange for defense installation rights (9. Apr.); Roosevelt declares unlimited national emergency (27 May); German and Italian consulates ordered closed (6 June); Office of Scientific Research and Development established (28 June); Japanese assets in U.S. frozen (26 July); Atlantic Charter formulated (14 Aug.) by Roosevelt and Churchill outlining war aims.

1941–1945 World War II: Japanese attack Pearl Harbor (7 Dec.); U.S. declares war on Japan (8 Dec.) and Germany (11 Dec.); Germany surrenders (7 May 1945); atomic bombs exploded over Japan (6, 9 Aug.); Japan surrenders (15 Aug.).

1942 U.S. signs UN Declaration (1 Jan.); Roosevelt orders (19 Feb.) relocation of Japanese-Americans to interior internment camps; 1st Moscow Conference (12–15 Aug.): U.S., Soviet Union, and Great Britain decide not to open 2nd front in Europe.

1943 Casablanca Conference (14–24 Jan.): Roosevelt and Churchill decide that war would be fought to "unconditional surrender"; 1st Cairo Conference (22–26 Nov.): Roosevelt and Churchill confer with Chiang Kai-shek regarding war in Far East.

1944 Bretton Woods Conference (1–22 July) establishes International Monetary Fund; Dumbarton Oaks Conference (21 Aug.–7 Oct.) establishes basis for UN Charter.

AMERICAN MILITARY HISTORY

1940 War Department releases (3 June) to Great Britain surplus or outdated stocks of arms, munitions, and aircraft.

Congress authorizes induction of National Guard into federal service (27 Aug.).

U.S. gives 50 overage destroyers to Great Britain (3 Sept.) in exchange for 99-year leases on naval and air bases.

Congress enacts (16 Sept.) Selective Training and Service Act, first peacetime program of compulsory service.

1941 U.S. lands forces in Iceland (7 July).

Philippine armed forces nationalized and MacArthur made commander in chief of U.S. forces in Far East (26 July).

Early Atlantic warfare: USS destroyer *Greer* attacked (4 Sept.); Roosevelt gives navy "shoot on sight" order (11 Sept.); destroyers *Kearney* (17 Oct.) and *Reuben James* (30 Oct.) attacked by German subs.

Japanese Attack (7 Dec.) on Pearl Harbor cripples Pacific fleet, 19 ships sunk or damaged, 2300 dead; Japanese also strike in Philippines and Guam.

1942 Major Pacific battles: Bataan-Corregidor (2 Jan.–6 May), Battle of Coral Sea (7–8 May), Battle of Midway (3–6 June), Guadalcanal (7 Aug.–9 Feb. 1943).

Major European and Mediterranean battles: North Africa (23 Oct.–24 Dec.).

Manhattan Project to develop atomic bomb placed under command of Leslie R. Groves (31 Aug.).

1943 Pacific: Battle of Bismarck Sea (2–3 Mar.); Tarawa and Makin (21–24 Nov.).

Europe and Mediterranean: African war ends (13 May); invasion of Sicily (10 July–17 Aug.).

U.S. Merchant Marine Academy dedicated (30 Sept.) at Kings Point, N.Y.

1944 GI Bill of Rights (Servicemen's Readjustment Act) enacted, providing aid for veterans hospitals, college benefits, and purchase of houses, farms and businesses.

Pacific: Burma Campaign (17 May–3 Aug.); Philippines (19 June–23 Feb. 1945).

Operation Overlord (D-Day)—massive Allied landings (6 June) on Normandy beaches; Battle of Germany (12 Sept.–3 Dec.); Battle of the Bulge (16–26 Dec.).

Timeline, 1945–1958

PRESIDENT AND KEY LEADERS, TERM OF OFFICE

Harry S. Truman, *president,* 1945–1953

Alben W. Barkley, *vice president,* 1949–1953
Edward R. Stettinius, Jr., *secretary of state,* 1945
James F. Byrnes, *secretary of state,* 1945–1947
George C. Marshall, *secretary of state,* 1947–1949
Dean Acheson, *secretary of state,* 1949–1953
Frederick M. Vinson, *secretary of Treasury,* 1945–1946
John W. Snyder, *secretary of Treasury,* 1946–1953
Thomas C. Clark, *attorney general,* 1945–1949
J. Howard McGrath, *attorney general,* 1949–1952
James P. McGranery, *attorney general,* 1952–1953
Henry L. Stimson, *secretary of war,* 1945
Robert P. Patterson, *secretary of war,* 1945–1947
Kenneth C. Royall, *secretary of war,* 1947
James V. Forrestal, *secretary of defense,* 1947–1949
Louis A. Johnson, *secretary of defense,* 1949–1950
George C. Marshall, *secretary of defense,* 1950–1951
Robert A. Lovett, *secretary of defense,* 1951–1953
James V. Forrestal, *secretary of navy,* 1945–1947
Harold L. Ickes, *secretary of interior,* 1945–1946
Julius A. Krug, *secretary of interior,* 1946–1949
Oscar L. Chapman, *secretary of interior,* 1949–1953
Claude R. Wickard, *secretary of agriculture,* 1945
Clinton P. Anderson, *secretary of agriculture,* 1945–1948
Charles F. Brannan, *secretary of agriculture,* 1948–1953
Henry A. Wallace, *secretary of commerce,* 1945–1946
W. Averell Harriman, *secretary of commerce,* 1946–1948
Charles Sawyer, *secretary of commerce,* 1948–1953
Lewis B. Scwellenbach, *secretary of labor,* 1945–1948
Maurice J. Tobin, *secretary of labor,* 1948–1953
Omar N. Bradley, *chairman, Joint Chiefs,* 1949–1953
Fred Moore Vinson, *chief justice,* 1946–1953

GENERAL AMERICAN HISTORY

1945 Yalta Conference (4–11 Feb.), Roosevelt, Churchill, and Stalin plan defeat of Germany; United Nations Conference (25 Apr.–26 June) in San Francisco drafts UN Charter; Roosevelt dies (12 Apr.); Truman becomes president; European Advisory Commission (5 June) establishes German occupation zones; Potsdam Conference (17 July–2 Aug.), Truman, Stalin, and Churchill plan final defeat of Germany.

1946 Atomic bomb tests at Bikini Atoll in Pacific (1 July); Philippines given independence (4 July); Atomic Energy Act (1 Aug.) passes control of atomic energy activities to new Atomic Energy Commission.

1947 Truman Doctrine (12 Mar.), 1st U.S. attempt to contain communism; aid to Greece and Turkey approved (22 May); Marshall plan proposed (5 June) to aid Europe in postwar economic recovery.

1948 Truman signs Foreign Assistance Act for European Recovery Program (2 Apr.); Truman reelected president (2 Nov.).

1948–1949 Berlin Airlift and Berlin Blockade: USSR blockades Berlin's Allied sectors (1 Apr.); British and U.S. planes' aerial supply operation sustains West Berliners; blockade lifted (12 May 1949).

1949 North Atlantic Treaty Organization established (24 Aug.) by U.S. and Canada and 10 European nations.

1950 U.S. population: 150,697,361

U.S. recalls (14 Jan.) consular officials from China after consulate general seized in Peking; H-bomb production authorized (31 Jan.); Truman orders air force and navy to Korea following invasion of south by North Korea (25 June).

1951 Julius and Ethel Rosenberg found guilty (29 Mar.) as spies and sentenced to death.

1952 Truman seizes steel mills (8 Apr.) to prevent strike; seizure ruled unconstitutional (2 June); Eisenhower elected president (4 Nov.).

AMERICAN MILITARY HISTORY

1945 Berlin falls (2 May); Germans surrender (7 May).

Pacific: Iwo Jima (19 Feb.–17 Mar.); Okinawa (1 Apr.–21 June); atomic bombs dropped on Hiroshima (6 Aug.) and Nagasaki (9 Aug.); U.S. forces enter Korea to displace Japanese (8 Sept.).

1945–1949 International Military Tribunals try war criminals at Nuremburg, Germany (20 Nov. 1945–1 Oct. 1946), and Japan (3 June 1946–12 Nov. 1948); special tribunals convene in Japan through 1949 for trials.

1947 National Security Act passes (26 July) to unify armed services under Department of Defense and establishes National Security Council and Central Intelligence Agency.

United States Air Force established (18 Sept.) as an independent service under National Military Establishment.

1948 Selective Service Act signed (24 June), providing for registration of all men between 18 and 25.

Truman orders equality in the armed services (30 July).

1949 U.S. troops withdraw from Korea (29 June), leaving 500 military advisers.

1950–1953 Korean War: North Koreans cross 38th parallel into South Korea (25 June); UN command in Korea formed (7 July) with Gen. MacArthur designated commander (8 July); amphibious Inchon landing (15 Sept.) leads to recapture of capital, Seoul (26 Sept.); Communist Chinese intervene on North Korean side (Nov.); MacArthur removed by Truman over strategy disagreements (11 Apr. 1951); armistice negotiations begin (10 July 1951); hostilities halted 26 July 1953.

1950 35 military advisers sent to South Vietnam (27 June), U.S. agrees to provide military and economic aid to non-Communist government.

Army seizes railroads (27 Aug.) to prevent strike.

1952 Korean War GI Bill of Rights (16 July) provides veterans with educational benefits, housing, business, and home-loan guarantees, benefits similar to those for World War II veterans.

PRESIDENT AND KEY LEADERS, TERM OF OFFICE

Dwight David Eisenhower, *president*, 1953–1961

Richard M. Nixon, *vice president*, 1953–1961
John Foster Dulles, *secretary of state*, 1953–1959
Christian A. Herter, *secretary of state*, 1959–1961
George M. Humphrey, *secretary of Treasury*, 1953–1957
Robert B. Anderson, *secretary of Treasury*, 1957–1961
Herbert Brownell, *attorney general*, 1953–1957
William P. Rogers, *attorney general*, 1958–1961
Charles E. Wilson, *secretary of defense*, 1953–1957
Neil H. McElroy, *secretary of defense*, 1957–1959
Thomas S. Gates, *secretary of defense*, 1959–1961
Douglas McKay, *secretary of interior*, 1953–1956
Frederick A. Seaton, *secretary of interior*, 1956–1961
Ezra Taft Benson, *secretary of agriculture*, 1953–1956
Sinclair Weeks, *secretary of commerce*, 1953–1958
Lewis L. Strauss, *secretary of commerce*, 1958
Frederick H. Mueller, *secretary of commerce*, 1959–1961
Martin P. Durkin, *secretary of labor*, 1953
James P. Mitchell, *secretary of labor*, 1953–1961
Arthur W. Radford, *chairman, Joint Chiefs*, 1953–1957
Nathan F. Twining, *chairman, Joint Chiefs*, 1957–1960
Lyman L. Lemnitzer, *chairman, Joint Chiefs*, 1960–1961
Earl Warren, *chief justice*, 1953–1969

GENERAL AMERICAN HISTORY

1954 *Brown* v. *Board of Education of Topeka, Kansas*, bans racial segregation (17 May); Southeast Asia Treaty Organization formed (8 Sept.) by 8 nations.

1955 Supreme Court orders desegregation "with all deliberate speed" (31 May); black boycott of Montgomery, Ala., bus system (1 Dec.).

1956 1st transatlantic cable in operation (25 Sept.).

1957 Civil Rights Act (9 Sept.): 1st since Reconstruction, establishes Civil Rights Commission; Soviets launch Sputnik I (4 Oct.) and II (3 Nov.); first artificial satellites.

AMERICAN MILITARY HISTORY

1954 Dulles articulates (12 Jan.) "massive retaliation" doctrine against direct Soviet attack to be carried out by Strategic Air Command.

Nautilus, 1st atomic powered submarine, launched (21 Jan.).

U.S. Air Force Academy authorized (1 Apr.).

McCarthy-Army Hearings (22 Apr.–17 June): investigation by Sen. Joseph McCarthy into charges army was lax in ferreting out Communist spies and army countercharges that McCarthy used influence to obtain special treatment for Pvt. David Schine; final report clears army and McCarthy.

"DEW" (distant early warning) line established (27 Sept.) across continent north of U.S.-Canadian border.

1955 Military advisers dispatched to South Vietnam to train army (23 Feb.).

U.S. 7th Fleet helps Nationalist Chinese evacuate 25,000 troops and 17,000 civilians from China (Feb.).

U.S. ends occupation of West Germany (5 May).

1957 Arkansas National Guard called in (4 Sept.) to bar black students from integrating Little Rock High School; federal court orders Guardsmen removed; federal troops—1000 U.S. paratroopers—sent in (24 Sept.) and Arkansas National Guard put under federal command.

1958 Army launches first U.S. satellite (31 Jan.) into orbit named Explorer I.

5000 marines from 6th Fleet sent into Lebanon (15 July) to protect Lebanese government; U.S. forces reach 15,000 but are withdrawn (25 Oct.).

Defense Reorganization Act (6 Aug.) affirms control of secretary of defense over armed services.

7th fleet begins to furnish naval escort (Sept.) to Chinese Nationalists fleeing Quemoy.

National Defense Education Act (2 Sept.) provides $295 million for college student loans.

Timeline, 1959–1968

PRESIDENT AND KEY LEADERS, TERM OF OFFICE

John Fitzgerald Kennedy, *president,* 1961–1963

Lyndon B. Johnson, *vice president,* 1961–1963
Dean Rusk, *secretary of state,* 1961–1963
C. Douglas Dillon, *secretary of Treasury,* 1961–1963
Robert F. Kennedy, *attorney general,* 1961–1963
Robert S. McNamara, *secretary of defense,* 1961–1963
Stewart L. Udall, *secretary of interior,* 1961–1963
Orville L. Freeman, *secretary of agriculture,* 1961–1963
Luther H. Hodges, *secretary of commerce,* 1961–1963
Arthur J. Goldberg, *secretary of labor,* 1961–1962
W. Willard Wirtz, *secretary of labor,* 1962–1963
Maxwell D. Taylor, *chairman, Joint Chiefs,* 1962–1963

GENERAL AMERICAN HISTORY

1959 Alaska (3 Jan.) and Hawaii (21 Aug.) admitted as states; St. Lawrence Seaway opens (25 Apr.).

1960 Congress approves voting rights act (21 Apr.) and civil rights act (6 May); Kennedy elected president (8 Nov.).

1961 Bay of Pigs Invasion (17 Apr.): failed CIA-backed invasion of Cuba by Cuban exiles; Commander Alan B. Shepard in 1st U.S. manned suborbital space flight (5 May).

1962 Lt. Col. John Glenn is 1st American in orbit (20 Feb.); 1st U.S. communications satellite launched (July); Cuban Missile Crisis—buildup of Soviet missiles in Cuba revealed (22 Oct.), Cuba quarantined, USSR removes missiles.

AMERICAN MILITARY HISTORY

1959 George Washington, 1st U.S. ballistic missile, launched (9 June).

Veterans Pension Act (29 Aug.) revised benefits for needy veterans for nonservice disabilities.

Eisenhower orders U.S. naval units to patrol Central American waters (17 Nov.).

1960 U.S. U-2 reconnaissance plane downed over USSR; pilot Gary Powers found guilty of espionage (19 Aug.); released (10 Feb. 1962) in exchange for Russian spy Rudolf Abel.

Reconnaissance plane shot down over USSR; 2 surviving airmen released 25 Jan. 1961.

1961 Eisenhower gives farewell address (17 Jan.) and warns of military-industrial complex.

1962 Kennedy orders 5000 troops to Thailand (May) to bolster Laotian government.

Federal troops and Mississippi National Guard assist in admitting black student James Meredith into University of Mississippi (30 Sept.–10 Oct.).

Cuban Missile Crisis (22 Oct.–20 Nov.): Kennedy orders naval and air quarantine on offensive missiles going to Cuba and directs armed forces to "prepare for any eventuality."

PRESIDENT AND KEY LEADERS, TERM OF OFFICE

Lyndon Baines Johnson, *president,* 1963–1969

Hubert H. Humphrey, *vice president,* 1965–1969

Dean Rusk, *secretary of state,* 1963–1969

C. Douglas Dillon, *secretary of Treasury,* 1963–1965

Henry H. Fowler, *secretary of Treasury,* 1965–1968

Joseph W. Barr, *secretary of Treasury,* 1968–1969

Robert F. Kennedy, *attorney general,* 1963–1964

Nicholas B. de Katzenbach, *attorney general,* 1965–1966

Ramsey Clark, *attorney general,* 1967–1969

Robert S. McNamara, *secretary of defense,* 1963–1968

Clark M. Clifford, *secretary of defense,* 1968–1969

Stewart L. Udall, *secretary of interior,* 1963–1969

Orville L. Freeman, *secretary of agriculture,* 1963–1969

Luther H. Hodges, *secretary of commerce,* 1963–1965

John T. Conner, *secretary of commerce,* 1964–1967

Alexander B. Trowbridge, *secretary of commerce,* 1967–1968

C. R. Smith, *secretary of commerce,* 1968–1969

W. Willard Wirtz, *secretary of labor,* 1963–1969

Alan S. Boyd, *secretary of transportation,* 1966–1969

Earle G. Wheeler, *chairman, Joint Chiefs,* 1964–1969

GENERAL AMERICAN HISTORY

1963 U.S., USSR, and Great Britain agree (25 July) on nuclear test ban treaty, barring all but underground tests; 200,000 people demonstrate for equal rights for blacks in Washington (28 Aug.); hot-line communications installed between Moscow and White House (30 Aug.); South Vietnam Pres. Diem assassinated (2 Nov.); Kennedy assassinated in Dallas by Lee Harvey Oswald (22 Nov.); Johnson becomes president.

1964 Panamanian riots lead to severing of diplomatic relations with U.S. (9 Jan.) and U.S. offers to negotiate new canal treaty (18 Dec.); Civil Rights Act (29 June) bans all discrimination; War on Poverty bill passes (11 Aug.); Warren Commission report (27 Sept.) concludes Oswald was lone assassin of Kennedy; Johnson elected president (3 Nov.).

1965 Johnson orders continuous bombing of North Vietnam (Feb.); Voting Rights Act (6 Aug.).

1967 Riots by blacks (July) put down by federal troops and National Guardsmen.

1968 Martin Luther King, Jr., assassinated (4 Apr.) by James Earl Ray; Sen. Robert F. Kennedy assassinated (5 June) by Sirhan Sirhan; Richard Nixon elected president (5 Nov.).

AMERICAN MILITARY HISTORY

1964 U.S. military assistance in the form of planes and 105 military personnel sent to Congo (13 Aug.); U.S. military aids in rescue of hostages from rebels (24 Nov.).

1964–1973 Vietnam War: 2 destroyers attacked by North Vietnam (Aug.); Congress authorizes Johnson to "repel any armed attack" in Gulf of Tonkin Resolution (7 Aug.); 8 military advisers killed at Pleiku (7 Feb. 1965); reprisal air bombing of North Vietnam escalates attacks; buildup of military units begins (8 Mar.); U.S. forces increase through 1968; Tet Offensive (30 Jan. 1968) by North Vietnamese; U.S. bombing halted (31 Oct. 1968); peace talks open in Paris (10 May 1968); My Lai massacre by U.S. troops reported (16 Nov. 1969); troops cross into Cambodia to find North Vietnamese sanctuaries (30 Apr. 1970); massive bombing of North Vietnam (Dec. 1971); North Vietnamese attack in force across demilitarized zone (30 Mar. 1972) and U.S. bombs Hanoi and Haiphong (15 Apr.); cease-fire effective 28 Jan. 1973.

1965 400 marines land in Dominican Republic at start of civil war (28 Apr.), increase to 22,000 (17 May); troops withdrawn 1966.

1966 Veterans Educational Benefits granted for all who served on active duty after 1955 for 180 days. (3 Mar.).

1967 U.S. troops in Vietnam number 475,000 by year's end.

1968 USS *Pueblo* (23 Jan.) seized as spy ship in North Korean waters with 83 crew members, who are imprisoned; crew released (22 Dec.).

Timeline, 1969–1976

PRESIDENT AND KEY LEADERS, TERM OF OFFICE

Richard Milhaus Nixon, *president,* 1969–1974

Spiro T. Agnew, *vice president,* 1969–1973
Gerald R. Ford, *vice president,* 1973–1974
William P. Rogers, *secretary of state,* 1969–1973
Henry A. Kissinger, *secretary of state,* 1973–1974
David M. Kennedy, *secretary of Treasury,* 1969–1971
John B. Connally, *secretary of Treasury,* 1971–1972
George P. Shultz, *secretary of Treasury,* 1972–1974
John N. Mitchell, *attorney general,* 1969–1972
Richard G. Kleindienst, *attorney general,* 1972–1973
Elliot L. Richardson, *attorney general,* 1973
William B. Saxbe, *attorney general,* 1974
Melvin R. Laird, *secretary of defense,* 1969–1973
Elliot L. Richardson, *secretary of defense,* 1973
James R. Schlesinger, *secretary of defense,* 1973–1974
Walter J. Hickel, *secretary of interior,* 1969–1970
Rogers C. B. Morton, *secretary of interior,* 1971–1974
Clifford M. Hardin, *secretary of agriculture,* 1969–1971
Earl L. Butz, *secretary of agriculture,* 1971–1974
Maurice H. Stans, *secretary of commerce,* 1969–1972
Peter G. Peterson, *secretary of commerce,* 1972–1973
Frederick B. Dent, *secretary of commerce,* 1973–1974
George P. Shultz, *secretary of labor,* 1969–1970
James D. Hodgson, *secretary of labor,* 1970–1973
Peter J. Brennan, *secretary of labor,* 1973–1974
John A. Volpe, *secretary of transportation,* 1969–1973
Claude S. Brinegar, *secretary of transportation,* 1973–1974
Thomas H. Moorer, *chairman, Joint Chiefs,* 1970–1974
Warren E. Burger, *chief justice,* 1969–1986

GENERAL AMERICAN HISTORY

1969 Apollo 11 astronauts, Neil A. Armstrong and Edwin E. Aldrin, Jr., take man's first walk on the moon (20 July).

1971 Voting age lowered to 18 (30 June); Communist China takes seat in UN (25 Oct.), Nationalist China ousted.

1972 Pres. Nixon visits Peking (21 Feb.); Nixon visits Moscow (22 May), 1st for a U.S. president; Watergate break-in of Democratic National Party Headquarters (17 June); Nixon reelected (7 Nov.).

1973 China and U.S. agree (22 Feb.) to establish liaison offices in each country; Vice President Agnew resigns (10 Oct.), pleading no contest to tax evasion charges; Gerald Ford becomes 1st appointed vice president (12 Oct.); ban by Middle East oil nations on exports to U.S. (19–22 Oct., lifted 18 Mar. 1974).

AMERICAN MILITARY HISTORY

1970 National Guardsmen kill 4 students at Kent State University, Ohio (4 May), following burning of ROTC building.

1971 Lt. William L. Calley convicted (29 Mar.) of premeditated murder of 22 South Vietnamese at My Lai (16 Mar. 1968).

Classified Pentagon Papers, history of U.S. involvement in Vietnam, published in *New York Times* (13 June).

1973 Military draft ends (27 Jan.).

U.S. officially ceases bombing of Cambodia (14 Aug.).

War Powers Act passes (7 Nov.) and sets 60-day limit on presidential commitment of troops unless Congress authorizes continued action.

PRESIDENT AND KEY LEADERS, TERM OF OFFICE

Gerald Rudolph Ford, *president,* 1974–1977

Nelson A. Rockefeller, *vice president,* 1974–1977

Henry Kissinger, *secretary of state,* 1974–1977

William E. Simon, *secretary of Treasury,* 1974–1977

William B. Saxbe, *attorney general,* 1974–1975

Edward H. Levi, *attorney general,* 1975–1977

James R. Schlesinger, *secretary of defense,* 1975

Donald H. Rumsfeld, *secretary of defense,* 1975–1977

Rogers C. B. Morton, *secretary of interior,* 1974–1975

Stanley K. Hathaway, *secretary of interior,* 1975

Thomas S. Kleppe, *secretary of interior,* 1975–1977

Earl L. Butz, *secretary of agriculture,* 1974–1976

John A. Knebel, *secretary of agriculture,* 1976–1977

Frederick B. Dent, *secretary of commerce,* 1974–1975

Rogers C. B. Morton, *secretary of commerce,* 1975

Elliot L. Richardson, *secretary of commerce,* 1975–1977

Peter J. Brennan, *secretary of labor,* 1974–1975

John T. Dunlop, *secretary of labor,* 1975–1976

William J. Usery, *secretary of labor,* 1976–1977

Claude S. Brinegar, *secretary of transportation,* 1975–1977

George S. Brown, *chairman, Joint Chiefs,* 1974–1977

GENERAL AMERICAN HISTORY

1974 House Judiciary Committee recommends 3 articles of impeachment against Nixon (24–30 July), approved by Congress; Nixon resigns (9 Aug.); Ford becomes president (9 Aug.); Nixon pardoned (8 Sept.).

1975 U.S. civilians evacuated from Saigon (29 Apr.), Communists overrun country; Rockefeller Commission reveals (10 June) illegal CIA operations.

1976 United States celebrates bicentennial (4 July); Viking II lands on Mars (3 Sept.); President Ford escapes 2 assassination attempts (5, 22 Sept.); Carter elected president.

AMERICAN MILITARY HISTORY

1975 *Mayaguez* Incident (15 May): merchant ship is rescued from Cambodians by U.S. Navy and marines.

Timeline, 1977–1987

PRESIDENT AND KEY LEADERS, TERM OF OFFICE

James Earl Carter, *president,* 1977–1981

Walter F. Mondale, *vice president,* 1977–1981
Cyrus R. Vance, *secretary of state,* 1977–1980
Edmund S. Muskie, *secretary of state,* 1980–1981
W. Michael Blumenthal, *secretary of Treasury,* 1977–1979
G. William Miller, *secretary of Treasury,* 1979–1981
Griffin B. Bell, *attorney general,* 1977–1979
Benjamin R. Civiletti, *attorney general,* 1979–1981
Harold Brown, *secretary of defense,* 1977–1981
Bob S. Bergland, *secretary of agriculture,* 1977–1981
Cecil D. Andrus, *secretary of interior,* 1977–1981
Juanita M. Kreps, *secretary of commerce,* 1977–1979
Philip M. Klutznick, *secretary of commerce,* 1979–1981
F. Ray Marshall, *secretary of labor,* 1977–1981
Brock Adams, *secretary of transportation,* 1977–1979
Neil E. Goldschmidt, *secretary of transportation,* 1979–1981
James R. Schlesinger, *secretary of energy,* 1977–1979
Charles W. Duncan, *secretary of energy,* 1979–1981
David C. Jones, *chairman, Joint Chiefs,* 1978–1981

Ronald Wilson Reagan, *president,* 1981–1989

George Bush, *vice president,* 1981–1989
Alexander M. Haig, *secretary of state,* 1981–1982
George P. Shultz, *secretary of state,* 1982–1989
Donald T. Regan, *secretary of Treasury,* 1981–1985
James A. Baker, *secretary of Treasury,* 1985–1988

cont'd

GENERAL AMERICAN HISTORY

1977 Dept. of Energy created (4 Aug.); Carter pardons approximately 10,000 Vietnam draft evaders.

1978 Congress votes (18 Apr.) to turn over Panama Canal to Panama in 1999; Humphrey-Hawkins Full Employment Act (15 Oct.) sets goals for reducing unemployment.

1979 Nuclear reactor accident at Three Mile Island, Pa. (28 Mar.); 63 Americans taken hostage at U.S. embassy in Tehran, Iran (4 Nov.).

1980 U.S. retaliates against Soviet invasion of Afghanistan by grain embargos (4 Jan.); Reagan elected president (4 Nov.).

1981 American hostages released in Iran (20 Jan.); space shuttle Columbia sent into space, the 1st reusable spacecraft (12 Apr.); largest tax cut in nation's history passes (29 July); federal air traffic controllers strike (3 Aug.) and are dismissed by Reagan (5 Aug.).

1982 Equal Rights Amendment defeated after 10 years without sufficient ratifications.

AMERICAN MILITARY HISTORY

1980 Military mission fails (24 Apr.) in attempt to rescue American hostages in Iran; 8 killed and 5 wounded.

1983 U.S. peacekeeping force in Lebanon attacked at marine headquarters by truck bomb (23 Oct.); 241 marines and sailors killed.

Operation Urgent Fury (25 Oct.): rescue mission of U.S. medical students by marines and rangers and against Marxist regime in Grenada.

PRESIDENT AND KEY LEADERS, TERM OF OFFICE	GENERAL AMERICAN HISTORY	AMERICAN MILITARY HISTORY
Reagan administration *cont'd*		
Nicholas F. Brady, *secretary of Treasury,* 1988–1989 William French Smith, *attorney general,* 1981–1985 Edwin Meese, *attorney general,* 1985–1988 Richard L. Thornburgh, *attorney general,* 1988–1989 Caspar W. Weinberger, *secretary of defense,* 1981–1987 Frank C. Carlucci, *secretary of defense,* 1987–1989 James G. Watt, *secretary of interior,* 1981–1983 William P. Clark, *secretary of interior,* 1983–1985 Donald P. Hodel, *secretary of interior,* 1985–1989 John R. Block, *secretary of agriculture,* 1981–1986 Richard E. Lyng, *secretary of agriculture,* 1986–1989 Malcolm Baldrige, *secretary of commerce,* 1981–1987 C. William Verity, *secretary of commerce,* 1987–1989 Raymond J. Donovan, *secretary of labor,* 1981–1985 William E. Brock, *secretary of labor,* 1985–1987 Ann D. McLaughlin, *secretary of labor,* 1987–1989 Andrew L. Lewis, *secretary of transportation,* 1981–1983 Elizabeth H. Dole, *secretary of transportation,* 1983–1987 James H. Burnley, *secretary of transportation,* 1987–1989 James B. Edwards, *secretary of energy,* 1981–1982 Donald P. Hodel, *secretary of energy,* 1983–1985 John S. Herrington, *secretary of energy,* 1985–1989 John W. Vessey, *chairman, Joint Chiefs,* 1982–1985 William J. Cowe, *chairman, Joint Chiefs,* 1985–1989 William H. Rehnquist, *chief justice,* 1986–	1984 U.S. government found negligent (10 May) in aboveground testing of nuclear weapons, 1951–1962; Geraldine Ferraro chosen as Democratic vice presidential candidate; Reagan reelected president (6 Nov.). 1985 $1.5 million appropriated (Mar.) for development of MX missile; hijackers seize Italian cruise ship (7 Oct.) *Achille Lauro.* 1986 Space shuttle Challenger explodes (28 Jan.) shortly after takeoff, killing 7 aboard; Congress passes comprehensive Tax Reform Law (Sept.); U.S. and USSR reach agreement on worldwide ban of medium-range missiles (18 Sept.); Iran-Contra scandal emerges (3 Nov.). 1987 1st trillion-dollar U.S. budget; Wall Street crashes (19 Oct.); U.S. and USSR agree on dismantling of some missiles.	1984 U.S. marines removed from Beirut and put on U.S. ships offshore (26 Feb.). Vietnam veterans settle lawsuit (7 May) with chemical companies for disabilities caused by Agent Orange. 1985 Navy F-14s force down plane (11 Oct.) carrying hijackers of *Achille Lauro* cruise ship (7 Oct.); plane lands in Sicily. 1986 U.S. war planes strike Libya (14 Apr.) in retaliation for Libyan bombing of a West Berlin disco (5 Apr.). Jerry A. Whitworth, former navy radioman, convicted as spy (24 July). 1987 37 sailors killed (27 May) aboard USS *Stark* by Iraqi missile in Persian Gulf; *Stark*'s officer found negligent (14 June). Congressional hearings into Iran-Contra scandal (July): Colonel Oliver North and Admiral John Poindexter involved in sale of arms to Iran and use of profits to support rebels in Nicaragua.

Timeline, 1988–1997

PRESIDENT AND KEY LEADERS, TERM OF OFFICE

George Herbert Walker Bush, *president,* 1989–1993

J. Danforth Quayle, *vice president,* 1989–1993
James A. Baker, *secretary of state,* 1989–1993
Nicholas F. Brady, *secretary of Treasury,* 1989–1993
Richard Thornburgh, *attorney general,* 1989–1993
Richard Cheney, *secretary of defense,* 1989–1993
Manuel Lujan, *secretary of interior,* 1989–1993
Clayton, K. Yeutter, *secretary of agriculture,* 1989–1993
Robert A. Mosbacher, *secretary of commerce,* 1989–1993
Elizabeth H. Dole, *secretary of labor,* 1989–1991
Lynn Martin, *secretary of labor,* 1991–1993
Samuel K. Skinner, *secretary of transportation,* 1989–1993
Edward J. Derwinski, *secretary of veterans affairs,* 1989–1993
Colin L. Powell, *chairman, Joint Chiefs,* 1989–1993

GENERAL AMERICAN HISTORY

1988 Gen. Manuel Noriega indicted in Florida (4 Feb.) for drug trafficking; more than a million illegal aliens apply (4 May) for amnesty; Bush elected president (8 Nov.).

1989 Largest oil spill in U.S. history (24 Mar.) from the *Exxon Valdez* in Prince Edward Sound; legislation passed (9 Aug.) to rescue savings and loan industry.

1990 Clean Air Act (15 Nov.), comprehensive plan to reduce 50% of annual level of emissions.

1992 Bill Clinton elected president.

AMERICAN MILITARY HISTORY

1988 USS *Vincennes* mistakenly fires a missile on Iranian commercial airliner (3 July), killing 300.

1989 Col. Oliver North convicted of obstruction of Congress in Iran-Contra scandal (4 May).

Army Gen. Colin Powell nominated (10 Aug.) to serve as chairman of Joint Chiefs of Staff, the 1st black to hold post.

Operation Just Cause (20 Dec.–3 Jan. 1990): 20,000 U.S. troops land in Panama to apprehend General Manuel Noriega for drug trafficking, to secure Panama Canal, and to defend democracy in Panama.

1990–1991 Gulf War: Iraq invades Kuwait (2 Aug.); UN coalition forces including 450,000 U.S. troops under Gen. H. Norman Schwarzkopf begin Operation Desert Shield (6 Aug.) to protect Saudi Arabia from invasion by Iraq; aerial bombing (Operation Desert Storm) begins (17 Jan. 1991); coalition defeats Iraq with ground war (24–27 Feb.); Iraq accepts UN cease-fire terms (3 Mar.).

1992 Last U.S. forces withdraw from Philippines (24 Nov.).

Democratic candidate Bill Clinton campaigns for the presidency with a platform that includes lifting the ban on homosexuals in the military.

PRESIDENT AND KEY LEADERS, TERM OF OFFICE

William Jefferson Clinton, *president,* 1993

Albert A. Gore, Jr., *vice president,* 1993
Warren M. Christopher, *secretary of state,* 1993–1997
Madeleine Albright, *secretary of state,* 1997
Lloyd Bentsen, *secretary of Treasury,* 1993–1995
Robert E. Rubin, *secretary of Treasury,* 1995
Janet Reno, *attorney general,* 1993
Les Aspin, *secretary of defense,* 1993–1994
William Perry, *secretary of defense,* 1994–1997
William Cohen, *secretary of defense,* 1997
Bruce Babbitt, *secretary of interior,* 1993
Mike Espy, *secretary of agriculture,* 1993–1995
Dan Glickman, *secretary of agriculture,* 1995
Ronald H. Brown, *secretary of commerce,* 1993–1996
Mickey Cantor, *secretary of commerce,* 1996–1997
William Daley, *secretary of commerce,* 1997
Robert B. Reich, *secretary of labor,* 1993–1997
Alexis Herman, *secretary of labor,* 1997
Federico F. Peña, *secretary of transportation,* 1993–1997
Rodney Slater, *secretary of transportation,* 1997
Hazel R. O'Leary, *secretary of energy,* 1993
Jesse Brown, *secretary of veterans affairs,* 1993
Federico F. Peña, *secretary of energy,* 1997
Colin L. Powell, *chairman, Joint Chiefs,* 1993
John Shalikashvili, *chairman, Joint Chiefs,* 1993–1997

GENERAL AMERICAN HISTORY

AMERICAN MILITARY HISTORY

1992–1993 U.S. troops go to Somalia as part of a coalition of military forces from several countries to help restore order and deliver food during a period of unrest and famine in the country.

1994–1995 U.S. Army sends troops to Haiti in September 1994 to help restore a democratic government. Most troops leave Haiti by March 1995.

1995 The United States sends about 20,000 troops to Bosnia to join a NATO peacekeeping force there.

PART 1
America's Wars

The Colonial Period

Military preparedness and armed conflict were a pervasive part of the American colonial experience. Of the more than 160 years between the founding of Jamestown and the outbreak of the American Revolution, at least one-third were marked by warfare of one kind or another. The reasons for so much deadly strife are numerous and complex, but were essentially the result of intrusive colonialization in the seventeenth century by rival European nations contending for the advantages and opportunities of the New World. All of these ambitious colonizers faced the threat of potentially hostile native Americans who often welcomed European trade but deeply resented European domination, especially when it undermined traditional Indian culture and deprived the Indians of extensive tracts of land needed for sustaining their traditional way of life.

Ambitious colonizers faced the threat of hostile native Americans who welcomed European trade but resented European domination.

Each European colonizing nation claimed exclusive right to certain loosely defined areas by virtue of first discovery, ignoring the fact that native Americans had preceded them and were already well established in those regions (see map). Spain claimed Florida as an outpost of the vast Spanish Empire in Mexico, Central America, and South America. France established small trading settlements in Acadia (later renamed Nova Scotia) and the valley of the Saint Lawrence River. The Dutch developed a commercial colony on Manhattan Island and settlements in the Hudson Valley. As for the English, they established toeholds at a number of points along the Atlantic coast from the Chesapeake region north to New England. During most of the seventeenth century, all of these European colonies, despite their typically grandiose territorial claims, were quite localized and sparsely populated, with the consequence that they had little incentive and less means for attacking each other.

Compared with western Europe, where the settlers originated, the territories on the other side of the Atlantic Ocean were vast and, for the most part, heavily forested. At any considerable distance inland, the terrain was at first a total mystery, dark and foreboding. Travel was easiest by sea, either along the coast or by way of the numerous rivers flowing into the ocean. These rivers originated in the watershed of the extensive Appalachian Mountains, a great barrier consisting of many parallel ranges extending from northern New England all the way down to Georgia. The French were fortunate in the fact that the Saint Lawrence River, bypassing these mountains, led directly to the easternmost of the Great Lakes, thus affording a gateway to the entire Mississippi Valley. Likewise, those Europeans who occupied the Hudson Valley had potential access to the Great Lakes by way of the Mohawk River, a rather difficult route that was not exploited at first. Another important geographical feature is the chain of rivers and lakes constituting a natural route running north and south between the upper Hudson and Saint Lawrence rivers. This Lake George–Lake Champlain corridor was to be repeatedly a highway for contending French and British military forces and their Indian allies.

In the fiery struggle for dominance in North America, the native Americans often fought bravely and well, sustained the greatest numbers of casualties, and were the heaviest losers. It is believed that when English colonization of eastern North America began early in the seventeenth century, the Indian population east of the Mississippi numbered no more than about three hundred thousand. European diseases, previously unknown in the New World, were already eating away at the Indian population.

Native Americans were organized in tribes (sometimes called "nations" by the colonists), and each tribe was composed of a number of distinct village groups scattered over the extensive but usually well-defined tribal territory. Villages and tribes were governed by councils of chiefs or sachems often endowed with only limited authority, except in a consensual way, but fully capable of shaping internal affairs and negotiating for intertribal agreements. European observers were inclined to perceive a greater degree of centralized authority among the Indians than was actually the case.

By European standards the Indians were a primitive people, although marvelously skilled in meeting the often harsh demands of their natural environment. They built dwellings, hunted and fished productively, and raised nutritious crops. They crafted domestic utensils, suitable clothing, items of personal adornment, and effective weapons such as the bow and arrow. They traded with other tribes, sometimes over great distances. They knew the wilderness well and traveled extensively either on foot or by canoe. They also speculated about the world of nature and the meaning of life.

Some of the tribes had joined together in confederacies, the most influential and important being the League of the Iroquois, which was composed of five (later six) tribes occupying the region between the upper Hudson River and Lake Ontario. This region was of strategic importance because of its location between areas claimed and being colonized by the French and the Dutch (see map), the latter soon to be succeeded by the English. Therefore, the Iroquois were in a position to dominate the major routes for exploration and trade between the northern colonies and the vast interior of North America.

Some tribes were more warlike than others, but very few escaped conflict altogether, even before the arrival of the Europeans. Indian warfare often took the form of private feuding that was personal, small-scale, and relatively brief, but public and official warfare certainly was not unknown. Occasionally, some of the better-led and better-organized tribes were able to mount and sustain fairly extensive organized operations. In general, Indian military operations depended heavily on the element of surprise and tended to be brief rather than protracted. In these conflicts the bow and arrow proved quite effective, as did the spear, club, and tomahawk or hatchet. Once the Indians had acquired firearms by trading with Europeans, they became skilled in the use of those weapons as well.

The English were mentally prepared to be militarily ruthless, even while hoping for a congenial relationship with their Indian neighbors.

Naturally, native Americans were committed to protecting their own best interests as effectively as they could, which more than any other consideration shaped their attitude toward the white colonizers. Many Indians actually welcomed the arrival of Europeans who could provide much-desired items of European manufacture in exchange for peltry and furs. Sometimes, too, armed colonists were viewed as potential protectors against a hostile neighboring tribe. Any Indians who had had a previous bad experience with whites, however, were likely to show hostility toward any new arrivals. Such hostility, with flights of arrows, was the actual experience of the first English groups to arrive at Chesapeake Bay in 1607 and Cape Cod in 1620.

The English were hardly surprised by Indian hostility. They came to America expecting to have to defend themselves and had made appropriate preparations. Prominent among the early colonial leaders were professional soldiers, such as Captain John Smith and Captain Miles Standish, who readily assumed responsibility for military action as required. The colonists also brought with them a well-developed military tradition shaped by a long experience of continental and domestic warfare, together with the imposition of English rule in Ireland. Hence, they were mentally prepared to be militarily ruthless if necessary, even while hoping for a mutually congenial relationship with their Indian neighbors.

English equipment for defense or attack included swords, polearms, small cannon, and body armor, together with the long-barreled, muzzle-loading, smoothbore musket that fired a molded leaden ball. Throughout the colonial period, except in the earliest decades, the firing mechanism for the musket was a flintlock by which, when the trigger was pulled, a piece of flint was made to strike against a steel plate, dropping a spark into the propelling charge. Such a gun, slow and complicated to load and unreliable in wet weather, was effective only at short range, perhaps less than 100 yards.

European soldiers were trained to march and fight in close formation, delivering volley fire on command, which often worked well amidst the smoke and confusion of an open battlefield, but required intensive training and discipline. Moreover, as colonial commanders soon discovered, marching and fighting in close formation was easier said than done in dense woods and swamps, the favorite battle sites of Indian warriors, who chose not to stand out in the open.

The early American concept of defense was deeply rooted in the English experience. Lacking a standing professional army, England had developed a national system of trainbands—local military companies consisting of men drafted from the local populace who were required to be ready for mobilization whenever needed. Periodic training under officers appointed by the Crown was compulsory. Thus, required maintenance of arms, obligatory enrollment, and compulsory service were practices viewed as normal by the English people, and when they migrated to the American colonies, they brought with them this well-established tradition. Colonial leaders saw such a system as essential for security and hastened to make the necessary arrangements, well aware that little or no military assistance could be expected from the distant homeland.

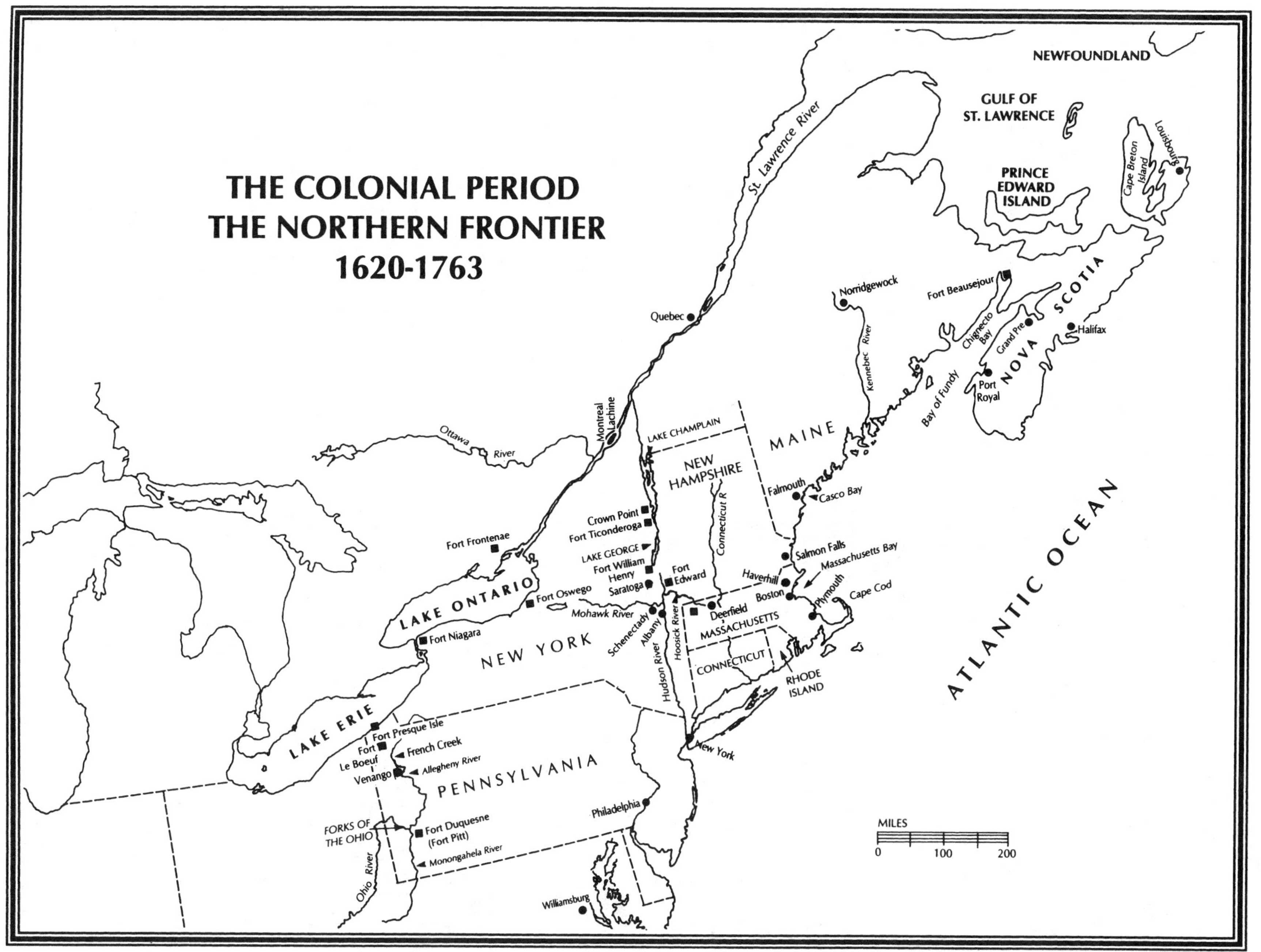
THE COLONIAL PERIOD
THE NORTHERN FRONTIER
1620-1763
NEWFOUNDLAND
GULF OF ST. LAWRENCE
PRINCE EDWARD ISLAND
Cape Breton Island
Louisbourg
St. Lawrence River
Quebec
Norridgewock
Fort Beausejour
Chignecto Bay
Grand Pre
NOVA SCOTIA
Halifax
Kennebec River
Bay of Fundy
Port Royal
Montreal
Lachine
Ottawa River
LAKE CHAMPLAIN
MAINE
NEW HAMPSHIRE
Falmouth
Casco Bay
Connecticut R.
Crown Point
Fort Ticonderoga
Fort Frontenae
LAKE GEORGE
Fort William Henry
Saratoga
Fort Edward
Salmon Falls
Massachusetts Bay
Haverhill
Boston
Plymouth
Cape Cod
ATLANTIC OCEAN
LAKE ONTARIO
Fort Oswego
Mohawk River
Schenectady
Albany
Hoosick River
Deerfield
MASSACHUSETTS
Fort Niagara
NEW YORK
Hudson River
CONNECTICUT
RHODE ISLAND
LAKE ERIE
Fort Presque Isle
Fort Le Boeuf
French Creek
Allegheny River
Venango
New York
PENNSYLVANIA
Philadelphia
FORKS OF THE OHIO
Fort Duquesne (Fort Pitt)
Monongahela River
Ohio River
Williamsburg
MILES
0
100
200

Basic to the American system was the concept that all citizens had an obligation to contribute to the defense of the community. For adult males this meant enrollment and service in the militia. As early as 1621 the Pilgrim colony of Plymouth, at that time no more than a tiny village, began building a rudimentary militia system. Virginia, having become a royal colony in 1624, did the same, as did the Puritan colony of Massachusetts Bay in 1631. By 1635 each of these English colonies had established a system of military training for all qualified male inhabitants, largely derived from the system in England but modified to meet the capabilities and needs of infant states in a remote wilderness. As new colonies were founded, they too made similar arrangements. Among the English colonies, the notable exception was Pennsylvania, founded and long dominated by pacifistic Quakers who wanted no part of military preparedness.

Typically, the age span for compulsory training was sixteen to sixty, which meant that during the course of his lifetime a man gained considerable experience, at least in the basics. Men engaged in certain occupations might be exempted by law, among them judges, sheriffs, and clergymen. Generally, all members of the militia were required to own and maintain specified weapons, ammunition, and other personal equipment. In addition, the colonial government undertook to maintain supplies of gunpowder in convenient storehouses. All such rules and arrangements, of course, were subject to revision by the legislature, and colonial records reveal frequent tinkering with the system, sometimes as a response to political pressure, but not infrequently as an adaptation to special local needs, the peculiar conditions of the American environment, or new developments in military science. Americans were learning by experience.

The basic militia unit was the company, comprised of local men under training by local leaders, which included a captain assisted by a lieutenant, an ensign, and several noncommissioned officers. In the New England colonies, at times, the commissioned officers might be elected by the members of the company; elsewhere they were appointees of the governor, who, in most colonies, was denominated commander in chief. Some colonies also had mounted troops as part of the militia. Eventually, as colonies grew and established more and more settlements, they found it advantageous to organize their numerous local companies into one or more regiments, each headed by a colonel. It must be emphasized that to a very large degree the colonial militia mirrored the economic and social stratification of colonial society. Farmers and laborers marched in the ranks, the most able or experienced among them aspiring to become corporals or sergeants. The commissioned officers were almost always drawn from the upper echelons of local society. Thus, the militia tended to reinforce the existing pattern of class and place.

It is also important to note that from the very beginning the military was held in subordination to civil authority. Indeed, as all members of the militia were actually civilians on temporary duty, civil authority permeated and dominated the military structure, which provided a firm foundation for the eventual establishment of an important constitutional safeguard of civil liberty.

Training day was the centerpiece of military activity. Each company was required by law to assemble for drill a specified number of days per year in its own locale (except for the occasional regimental musters). The purpose was to make sure that all members were available, to inspect their equipment, and to provide them with basic military training. These local mobilizations often took on the character of communal fetes, with old men, women, and children taking a welcome break from their normal routine to watch the militiamen. At times, one suspects, authority was hard put to maintain a proper degree of order and military discipline, but the training was the best available under the circumstances. From the captain down to the greenest private, the men learned the rudiments of soldiering.

In times of sudden emergency, a company of militia might be hastily assembled for local defense. More commonly, however, the militia served as a pool of trained manpower for the colony as a whole. If, for example, the colonial government resolved to send a military expedition against some enemy, it would draw quotas of men from each of the companies, assemble them at some convenient location, and organize them into an expeditionary structure under specially appointed officers. Thus, each company remained at home essentially intact to continue training and to defend the local area. When the expedition was over, the survivors were sent home to rejoin their local units.

There was a firm tradition in England that a trainband could not be ordered to serve outside its own county except in an instance of actual invasion. This popularly cherished restriction was readily transplanted to America, where it quickly took root. It became a general understanding, sometimes backed by actual legislation, that the militia was not to be sent beyond the borders of its own colony without its own consent. As long as individual colonies were able to limit their attention to their own military needs that was not a great problem, but once colonial security became a matter of intercolonial concern, as it soon did, that firmly rooted tradition would become a frustrating handicap for colonial leaders.

EARLY CONFLICTS WITH NATIVE AMERICANS

The seventeenth century was punctuated with a number of deadly conflicts between native Americans and European colonists, conflicts caused by mutual suspicion or mistreatment and, above all, by colonial encroachment and domination. Complicating the situation was the fact that neither the Indians nor the colonists could stand united. Tribes groping uncertainly for their own best interests either tried to remain neutral or aligned themselves with one of the contending sides. English colonies tended to be jealous of each other, sometimes stinting economic or military aid needed by a neighbor under attack, and there was no help from England. The colonies were on their own.

In 1622, virtually without warning, the resentful Indians in Virginia made a concerted attack upon the most exposed settlements, slaughtering approximately 25 percent of the total population. This violent uprising, eventually repressed by the settlers, made a lasting impression upon other colonists as far north as Plymouth, leaving the perception that all Indians were potentially treacherous and murderous. In 1644 Virginia again experienced a horrifying massacre by local Indians but with the same result—total victory for the English.

The sachem of the Wampanoag tribe in Plymouth Colony, known as Metacomet or King Philip, had long smoldered under English arrogance and dominance.

In the meantime, Puritan New England had been having its own warfare experience. After the Pequot tribe began challenging the security of new settlements in the Connecticut Valley, in 1637 the colonies of Connecticut and Massachusetts Bay sent out a joint expedition reinforced with Mohegan and Narraganset Indians to chastise the offending tribe. The commander of the expedition, Captain John Mason, was determined to teach the Pequot—and all other tribes in New England—an unforgettable lesson. Accordingly, after managing to arrive at the main Pequot village without being detected, Mason had his men surround the place and set it on fire. As terrified Indians ran into the open, they were gunned down indiscriminately. During subsequent weeks colonial troops relentlessly pursued all Pequot fugitives, in effect destroying the tribe as a viable entity.

The Dutch of New Netherland on the Hudson River showed an equal lack of restraint. Trouble there began when a local tribe failed to hand over an Indian accused of murdering a colonist. The authorities readily resorted to armed force, igniting a war that lasted from 1642 until 1645, with the Indians, as usual, suffering defeat. Dutch triumph, however, did not portend a great future for New Netherland. In 1664 the colony surrendered to a small fleet of English warships, becoming the new English colony of New York. This important transformation, coupled with the Treaty of Madrid (1670), in which Spain finally acknowledged the right of England to colonize as far south as Carolina, meant that England now possessed a solid block of coastal territory from Carolina north to New England. By 1675 the colonial population in that area probably totaled more than 125,000.

Another Indian war erupted in Virginia in 1675. As was so often the case, it began with private violence followed by escalating reprisals that led in turn to deadly warfare. Groups of enraged Indians attacked isolated settlements along the Virginia frontier, slaughtering inhabitants and terrorizing the survivors. The royal governor of the colony, Sir William Berkeley, adopted a defensive posture, relying on a chain of crude forts and parties of mounted rangers to ward off further attacks. This policy failed to satisfy the endangered frontier settlers, who saw both justification and material gain in a vigorous offensive that would crush Indian power. In 1676, when Berkeley stuck to his plan, the frontiersmen took matters into their own hands and turned for leadership to a young planter named Nathaniel Bacon.

Bacon led his armed followers on a series of forays into the wilderness, killing Indians and plundering their villages with little regard for whether or not the victims were hostile, neutral, or even friendly. The rough frontiersmen also showed little reverence for traditional military tactics, relying instead on improvisation and sheer audacity. Berkeley considered Bacon and his men to be rebels against his authority, with the result that the Indian war also became a civil war, in which Bacon burned Jamestown to prevent its use by the governor as a base. A little over a month later, Bacon died of dysentery. Berkeley regained effective control of the colony and its Indians. By the time an expeditionary force of more than a thousand regular soldiers had arrived from England early in 1677, there was no more fighting to be done.

Of all the seventeenth-century Indian wars, none was for contemporaries more destructive than King Philip's War, which ravaged New England from 1675 to 1677.

The Puritan leaders of the New England colonies sincerely believed that they had a divine mandate to survive in the wilderness, planting the seeds of biblical and English law and, insofar as possible, converting the native inhabitants from "paganism" and "savagery" to Christianity and civility. To have any chance of succeeding they had to exert effective control over all inhabitants, including neighboring Indians. They intended to treat these Indians justly, in accordance with accepted principles of English jurisprudence, but the proud and self-reliant Indians were not always willing to submit. Worse yet, many ambitious English settlers, having only contempt for the seemingly primitive Indians, developed a growing appetite for Indian territory that could be made immensely profitable.

The sachem of the Wampanoag tribe in Plymouth Colony, known as Metacomet or King Philip, had long smoldered under English arrogance and dominance. In 1675 some of his ardent young warriors began looting English property. The colonists retaliated, and hostilities quickly escalated into full-scale war. Plymouth called for aid from its partners in the New England Confederation, Connecticut and Massachusetts, with the result that all three colonies became involved in what proved to be a rapidly spreading conflict. Philip and his immediate followers managed to escape from the first trap set for them by the colonial forces consisting of men from the militia. Additional tribes were drawn quickly into the conflict, some in support of the Wampanoag, others preferring to remain attached to the English.

With the rapid spread of the war, all isolated frontier communities lay open to surprise attack. For defense, heavy reliance was placed on the ancient concept of the stronghold, a fortified refuge for all members of the community when threatened with enemy action. In the New England forest, this might be a palisaded blockhouse or fort. Quite commonly, however, it was merely a designated dwelling that had been fortified as effectively as possible. General retreat to a stronghold meant the abandonment of all other buildings and possessions to Indian depredation and almost unbearable overcrowding in the place of refuge. Because many raids occurred without warning, there might be great difficulty in summoning help from other communities. Furthermore, the Indians proved very skillful in the art of the ambush, with the consequence that any colonial military force venturing to pursue ran the risk of sudden disaster. Under these circumstances, the Puritan colonies suffered grievous losses during the early stages of King Philip's War.

Most feared of all the local tribes were the Narraganset of Rhode Island, who were clinging to a tenuous neutrality. When that tribe failed to fulfill certain stip-

King Philip's War. When warriors of the Wampanoag tribe in Plymouth Colony, led by Metacomet or King Philip, began looting English property in 1675, the colonists retaliated. Hostilities soon escalated into a full-scale war between colonists and native Americans that lasted for more than two years. (Library of Congress/Corbis)

ulations laid down by the English, the latter mounted a heavy preemptive strike in December 1675, using more than a thousand well-armed troops, including friendly Indians. Although this force suffered heavy casualties in assaulting the principal Narraganset stronghold deep in a Rhode Island swamp, it was able to destroy the entire village and its large supply of food and to kill many of the Indians and disperse the others. Thereafter, the surviving Narraganset were in the war up to the hilt.

Two factors began to work powerfully against the Indians. One was the growing ability of strong English forces, ably served by friendly Indian scouts, to advance through the wilderness, which enabled the English to attack Indian villages and destroy crops and caches of food, thereby subjecting the enemy to starvation. The other factor was the enmity of the Mohawk tribe of New York, the easternmost member of the League of the Iroquois, toward the New England Indians, resulting in further heavy losses for the latter.

During the first half of 1676 the hostile Indians fought desperately and enjoyed some successes, but their strength was waning. A notable example of how well the colonists were learning from hard experience was the independent company of English and Indian volunteers commanded by Captain Benjamin Church of Plymouth Colony. Church was one of the first American military leaders to develop a style of combat based upon both European practice and American experience, shaped to the conditions of the wilderness environment. Keeping his men well-spaced and on the alert, Church proved eminently successful in trapping and defeating enemy groups. In August his volunteer company trapped and killed Philip, a coup made possible through information provided by a defector. With that stroke the war quickly ended in southern New England. Farther north, conflict persisted for some months longer, finally ending in 1677.

Colonial America was, in sum, a laboratory of wilderness warfare where weapons and techniques were tested with rigor.

King Philip's War was a true catastrophe. A large number of colonists had either lost their lives or become impoverished through loss of property. The outermost frontier had been driven back many miles. While the English had the resources to recover from such losses, the Indians did not. Those tribes that had been hostile were irrevocably ruined and made subject to English control. Even the friendly tribes that had provided vital assistance to the colonial forces were rendered largely impotent and submissive.

Colonial America was, in sum, a laboratory of wilderness warfare where weapons and techniques were tested with rigor. When success was achieved, it usually was by an intelligent combination of tried-and-true basics and imaginative improvisation. These early conflicts between Indians and Europeans also seem to have created and solidified a tragic pattern for future encounters along more distant frontiers. Such warfare was to be characterized by cruelty and unrestrained violence on both sides, followed by ruthless suppression of the defeated native Americans. The suppression usually included confinement to a specified area or reservation, a system of control that had its origin in English America when Virginia defeated its hostile Indians in 1646. Thirty years later New England followed suit, but only after selling many of its defeated Indians into the horrors of West Indian slavery.

KING WILLIAM'S WAR AND QUEEN ANNE'S WAR

The year 1689 marked the beginning of a fateful period in North America, because in that year the first of a series of four international wars began, the last of which did not end until 1763. All were deadly armed conflicts involving the colonies belonging to England, France, and, in most instances, Spain. The first three of these wars broke out in Europe, with the colonies joining in to fulfill their imperial obligations and, even more so, to further their own interests. In contrast, the last and greatest of these conflicts began in a remote corner of the American wilderness as a consequence of rival colonial ambitions, eventually involving the respective mother countries to a degree that none had foreseen.

These wars were not glorious adventures or noble crusades, as depicted in some histories, nor were they fought primarily for abstract ideals, such as liberty, justice, or religion, although contemporary leaders generally liked to cast them in such a light. A more realistic interpretation would place heavy emphasis on such considerations as commercial gain, territorial security, land hunger, and an advantage in relations with important groups of native Americans in order to profit from the fur trade. Eventually the struggles would determine whether French culture or British culture, in terms of government, language, and religion, would prevail in the eastern part of what was to become the United States. Therefore, the contemporary rationale was, after all, not so wide of the mark.

Over and over again the English colonies, prompted by selfish and parochial considerations, and even the personal antipathies of their leaders, revealed an astonishing lack of unity. Each colony, it seemed, sought to contribute as little manpower and funds to the common war effort as it decently could, while lusting to harvest the best fruits of victory. When directly threatened by enemy forces, a colony might even refuse to send any of its troops to participate in a more general campaign. Such attitudes, of course, were intensely frustrating to both British and American leaders striving to carry on extensive intercolonial operations.

The colonial wars occurred during a period when the number of black slaves in the colonies was increasing quite rapidly. In many colonies blacks were barred from military activity but could be assigned to the hard labor involved in building fortifications and cutting roads through the wilderness, not a slight contribution. On the other hand, many blacks dwelling in areas open to attack served and suffered along with their masters and neighbors. Some, too, were seamen serving on merchant vessels, always a dangerous occupation but especially so in times of international conflict.

A much larger and critically important role was played by the thousands of native Americans who always, whether by choice or unavoidable circumstances, were caught up in the colonial wars. Patterns of colonial influence, assistance, and trade with the various tribes had developed during the seventeenth century in such a way that most groups of Indians within contact range had become attached as clients to one colony or another, all the while struggling to preserve some remnant of autonomy. The French had dominant influence among the Indians of Acadia, northern New England, and the Great Lakes, while the English enjoyed a profitable commercial relationship with the strategically located tribes of the League of the Iroquois. Similarly, Spanish Florida exerted a strong influence on the Indians of the adjacent Gulf of Mexico region. Client tribes understandably looked to their white patrons for support against any threatening foes, whether European or Indian. Likewise, colonies hoped that the Indians with whom they maintained a special relationship would become valuable allies in time of war.

As with the colonists, the Indians had both able and inept leaders. Some were prone to subordinate tribal interests to personal advantages, while others were skillful diplomats and persons of integrity. The Iroquois are perhaps the prime example of an important and powerful group striving to survive by all available means, including alliances and diplomacy, trade, combat, and the extension of influence among other tribes both near and far. The intricate and delicate web of Indian-colonist relationships was subject to almost constant unraveling and reknitting, especially at times of intense international rivalries.

The great disparities in population among the contending imperial territories also exerted a strong influence on the course and outcome of the colonial wars. In 1689 Florida was weakly held by fewer than two thousand Spaniards, most of them clustered at Saint Augustine. New France (Canada) was home to perhaps twelve thousand inhabitants. In contrast, the English colonists outnumbered the Spanish and French by more than ten to one. Moreover, the disparity would increase over time with awesome rapidity as a result of a high birth rate and massive immigration. Population was not the only significant difference. Both Florida and New France were governed by autocratic royal regimes that left no room for democratic participation, whereas the English colonies varied considerably in their governmental arrangements, with all encouraging or at least tolerating to some degree a meaningful element of representation for persons of property. The economy of the English area was also much more diversified than that of either Florida or New France, with correspondingly greater resilience in difficult economic times.

Despite some examples of occasional mutual chivalry or mere decency in the actual campaigning, in general these wars were quite nasty. All participants anticipated plunder, which for the Indians meant not only goods but prisoners who might later be tortured and killed or held for ransom. The massacre of disarmed or disabled opponents, not sparing even helpless noncombatants, was all too common. English colonial governments offered bounties for enemy scalps, and, as a result, some bold frontiersmen went hunting for Indians, being none too particular in distinguishing between friend and foe. The French became notoriously adept at combining fierce Indian warriors with equally fierce woodsmen (coureurs de bois) for the purpose of raiding isolated English settlements. Almost invariably the leaders of such groups were French, and the raids were aimed at carefully selected targets, the ultimate purpose being to terrorize the inhabitants and cause the collapse of the English frontier. Surprise was of the essence. A successful attack meant burned dwellings and barns, mutilated livestock, and slaughtered inhabitants (except for those who were spared and herded off as prisoners). With retaliation and counterretaliation, fear and hatred burgeoned on both sides.

King William's War began in Europe, where it became known as the War of the League of Augsburg, the principal opponents being England and France. Hostilities quickly crossed the Altantic Ocean when the Iroquois, closely tied to New York by the fur trade and

LAKE MICHIGAN
LAKE HURON
LAKE ERIE
Detroit
Fort Presque Isle
French Creek
Venango
PENNSYLVANIA
Allegheny River
Fort Duquesne
(Fort Pitt)
FORKS OF
THE OHIO
New
York
Philadelphia
Pickawillanee
Miami River
Fort Necessity
Great Meadows
Williamsburg
Jamestown
VIRGINIA
Chesapeake
Bay
Ohio
River
Cumberland
River
APPALACHIAN MOUNTAINS
Neuse River
New Bern
NORTH
CAROLINA
Tennessee
River
Mississippi
River
SOUTH
CAROLINA
Savannah River
Charleston
Yazoo River
Tombigbee
River
GEORGIA
Altamaha River
Savannah
Fort Toulouse
ATLANTIC
OCEAN
Alabama River
Frederica
Mobile
Suwanee
River
St. Augustine
New Orleans
GULF OF MEXICO
FLORIDA
THE COLONIAL PERIOD
THE SOUTHERN FRONTIER
1607-1763
MILES
0
100
200

deeply resentful of French incursions, seized the opportunity to make a devastating raid on the village of Lachine, seven miles from Montreal. Indeed, much of the fighting and ravaging in this war was done by Indians aligned with either the English or the French, which meant danger and destruction for the distraught colonists living precariously in exposed frontier areas. There simply was no way to protect all the scattered villages and farms, and, because neither England nor France was willing to provide any appreciable military support, the colonies were left to carry on the war in accordance with their own capabilities. New France did have the advantage of some regular troops already stationed there, but the far more numerous English had to rely almost entirely on their own militias.

Colonial governments offered bounties for enemy scalps, and, as a result, some bold frontiersmen went hunting for Indians, being none too particular in distinguishing between friend and foe.

In 1690 the governor of New France, Louis de Buade, Comte de Frontenac, dispatched three raiding parties of French and Indians to attack English frontier settlements. One of these groups surprised Schenectady, New York (9 February), killing many of the inhabitants and taking a number of prisoners. Nearly every house in the village was burned to the ground. A second group did much the same to Salmon Falls in New Hampshire (18 March). The third target, Falmouth, Maine, on the shore of Casco Bay, fell on 20 May. This series of successful and devastating assaults terrorized the northern frontier.

In the meantime, New England and New York were laying plans for a major offensive operation designed to cut the heart out of New France. The principal objective was to seize control of the Saint Lawrence Valley by capturing Quebec, the administrative center of the French colony. Consulting their maps, the planners could see that the most promising way to achieve that difficult objective was by a pincer movement, with one force advancing northward from Albany, New York, through the Champlain corridor while a seaborne army sailed from Boston to ascend the Saint Lawrence River. This pincer plan, first formulated in 1690, was to become the prototype for all major offensives against the heartland of New France for the remainder of the colonial period.

As frequently happens in war, the difficulties were underestimated. The Albany force had to make its way through 150 miles of wilderness, a task requiring substantial Iroquois support, which was not forthcoming, apparently because of smallpox among the tribes. An adequate number of watercraft for carrying troops and supplies were also not available. Therefore, the Albany arm of the pincer had to be withdrawn. Prior to this discouraging failure, a fleet of leased merchant vessels carrying hundreds of New England soldiers had sortied bravely from Boston en route to the treacherous Saint Lawrence. In command was Sir William Phips, a New Englander well known for his seizure of Port Royal in Acadia on 11 May. After a long delay, Phips and his motley fleet arrived before Quebec, but Frontenac, freed from concern over the Albany force, was ready for them. The New England army was put ashore some distance below the town and began skirmishing with the French defenders. Before long it became clear that the natural and man-made defenses of Quebec were more than adequate, and the army withdrew hastily. The humiliated Phips took his fleet back to Boston.

After this stunning failure both sides resorted to the familiar and more feasible raiding of isolated frontier settlements, always with the invaluable assistance of allied Indians. The dream of conquering New France had evaporated for the time being.

England and France finally brought hostilities to an inconclusive end on 30 September 1697 by signing the Treaty of Ryswick. There had been no clear victor either in Europe or America. Thus, no one was really satisfied with the outcome after so much expenditure of lives and money, least of all the Iroquois, who suffered heavy losses in the fighting against the French and their Indian allies. In fact, it seemed to the Iroquois that their English friends, while quarreling among themselves, were quite happy to let them do most of the hard fighting. Greatly weakened and deeply disillusioned, the Iroquois began maneuvering toward a position of neutrality that might enable them to retain the advantages of their special relationship with New York while avoiding involvement in future Anglo-French hostilities. From this time on, the Five Nations were a divided people, some of them pro-English and others pro-French. This shifting, unstable condition was alarming to all English expansionists, who remained convinced that the traditional Anglo-Iroquois relationship was essential for English predominance in the West.

During the next few years, the French resumed their bold advance into the remote interior. Having already established a fortified trading post, Fort Frontenac, where Lake Ontario empties into the Saint Lawrence River, and another at Niagara that dominated the portage between Lake Ontario and Lake Erie, in 1701 they erected a fort at Detroit to control passage between Lake Erie and Lake Huron. Such fortified outposts enabled French officials, fur traders, and missionaries to exert effective influence on the surrounding tribes. Far to the south, on the Gulf coast east of the mouth of the Mississippi River, the French established a post at Biloxi in 1699, the beginning of strong French influence in the lower Mississippi Valley.

Painfully aware of these advances, the English began to perceive what appeared to be an ambitious French program for gaining control of a vast arc of territory extending all the way from the Saint Lawrence through the Great Lakes and down the Mississippi Valley to the Gulf of Mexico. If successful, the French not only would be able to dominate all the tribes in that region, thereby taking over the fur trade of the interior while binding those tribes to the cause of French imperialism, but they would also confine the English colonies to the narrow coastal strip east of the Appalachian Mountains. One may well doubt that the French rulers had formulated such a program at this early date, and even if they had, New France simply lacked the resources to carry it out. Nevertheless, the mere contemplation of such encirclement caused great concern among the English.

Because King William's War had settled nothing, an early resumption of hostilities was almost inevitable. It came in May 1702 with the outbreak of Queen Anne's War (known in Europe as the War of the Spanish Succession), again pitting England against France. This time, however, Spain was allied with France, which meant that in North America both the southern and northern frontiers would become active theaters. As before, the Indians also became involved. During the early stages of the war none of the mother countries gave any substantial assistance to their contending colonies. This war, like the last, was in origin and purpose basically a European and oceanic conflict.

From the outset the expansionists of South Carolina were eager to destroy Spanish influence among neighboring Indians, a goal best achieved by the conquest of Florida, whose only strong point was at Saint Augustine on the east coast of the peninsula. In the first year of the war Governor James Moore of South Carolina led a small expeditionary force of English colonists and Indians against Saint Augustine. Learning of their approach, the Spaniards and Indians in that town withdrew into the nearby fort, permitting Moore to begin a systematic siege that went on for nearly seven weeks. Eventually he was forced to acknowledge that he lacked the strength to overcome Spanish resistance and withdrew.

Early in 1704 Moore led another expedition against the Spaniards, which included about fifty colonists and one thousand friendly Indians, this time deep into the Apalachee country in western Florida, an area dotted with Spanish missions among the Apalachee Indians. Moore went on a rampage, exacting tribute, gathering plunder, sacking villages, torturing and killing both Indians and Spaniards. He returned to South Carolina with about fourteen hundred Indian prisoners, many of whom were destined for slavery. As a result of these destructive assaults, Spanish influence among the tribes was seriously undermined, a process that continued as the Indians began to discover the advantages of trading with the Carolinians. In 1706 a combined force of French and Spaniards threatened Charleston but were repulsed.

While these actions were occurring in the south, the northern frontier also was a stage for violence. As in King William's War, New France made effective use of Indian raiding parties to attack and devastate New England frontier settlements. In February 1704 the Massachusetts town of Deerfield, west of the Connecticut River, fell victim to such a raid. Dwellings were burned, defenders slaughtered, and survivors herded into the northern forest as prisoners. A similar fate befell the Massachusetts town of Haverhill in 1708.

New England did not accept such blows without retaliation. In 1704 a waterborne expedition led by Benjamin Church advanced up the coast of Maine, picking off hostile Indians wherever they could be found. In June Church arrived at the French farming village of Minas on the eastern arm of the Bay of Fundy, whereupon the English demonstrated that they too could burn and destroy.

Seemingly, neither New France nor New England had the resources to plan and carry out a major strategic advance that would inflict a decisive defeat on the enemy. This situation was especially true of New France, whose small, widely dispersed population was no match for the numerous English. The latter, on the other hand, remembered well Phips's failure at Quebec and were determined not to undertake such a risky venture again without strong backing from the mother country.

French and Indian raids along the New England frontier aggravated intercolonial tensions between New England and New York, because New York, intent on furthering its advantage in the fur trade, was clinging to a precarious neutrality. The French and their Indian allies valued that neutrality and were careful not to disturb it, which meant that the New York frontier was not subjected to the kind of attacks that was causing such fear and suffering in New England. Suspicious New Englanders were led to surmise that the Yorkers actually were finding ways to profit from New England's losses. As for the Iroquois, they carefully pursued their own policy of neutrality.

In 1709 England first became actively involved in the North American theater, which forced New York to abandon its policy of neutrality. The Iroquois reluctantly followed suit. All this came about because New England merchant Samuel Vetch was able to persuade the English government of the great benefits to be realized through the conquest of New France. Accordingly, England promised to send warships and regular troops for a joint operation with colonial forces. The plan adopted was almost a duplicate of that attempted in 1690, the critical difference being the active leadership and participation of royal regular forces, who presumably had the discipline, equipment, and skill required for success.

Acting with unusual enthusiasm and promptness, the northern colonies began the costly task of assembling troops and supplies at both Albany and Boston while awaiting the arrival of the fleet from England. The summer passed without a glimpse of any English troops, except those of the four independent companies of regulars already stationed in New York. Finally, in October Boston received official notification that the operation had been cancelled in London, which was a bitter disappointment.

In 1711 Great Britain took up with greater enthusiasm and commitment the "glorious enterprise" of capturing Quebec.

Great Britain tried again in 1710, this time actually dispatching six warships and a regiment of marines. Again the colonies cooperated, but long delays in preparation rendered a major campaign against Quebec infeasible, so an easier target was substituted—the weakly defended Port Royal in Acadia. Command of the army of about nineteen hundred colonists and marines was given to Colonel Francis Nicholson, who had both extensive civil and military American experience. His second-in-command was Vetch. The French defenders of Port Royal, no match for the overwhelming British force, put up a token resistance and then surrendered in October. As a result, Port Royal was renamed Annapolis Royal, and Acadia became the new British colony of Nova Scotia.

In 1711 Great Britain took up with greater enthusiasm and commitment the "glorious enterprise" of capturing Quebec, again relying upon the pincer plan. Late in June a powerful fleet of warships and transports commanded by Rear Admiral Sir Hovenden Walker, carrying seven regiments of soldiers and a battalion of marines, arrived at Boston. Overall command of the operation belonged to Walker, an officer of mediocre talents. The participating colonies were already far along in their own preparations for the raising of substantial forces for both the Albany and the Boston wings, with Nicholson designated to command the former. The prospects seemed bright.

Walker, however, discovered that the colonists with whom he had to deal were motivated not so much by selfless patriotism as by self-interest. With preparations for the expedition continuing at a frantic pace, New England merchants raised the prices they charged the British for supplies, New England pilots tried to avoid the unwelcome task of navigating the British ships up the treacherous Saint Lawrence, and New England householders concealed British deserters. This unhappy situation at Boston extended over a period of several weeks and caused severe friction between colonists and regulars, fixing in the minds of the regulars a most unflattering image of the stubborn, money-grubbing New Englanders.

At last, on 30 July 1711, the fleet and army, substantially reinforced with New England ships and men, sailed for the Saint Lawrence. The armada consisted of eleven warships escorting sixty transports and auxiliary vessels carrying twelve thousand sailors, soldiers, and Indians. At Albany Nicholson commanded more than two thousand additional soldiers and Indians, including Iroquois warriors. This was the largest military operation in North America up to that time. The governor of New France had fewer than twenty-five hundred French soldiers, together with some allied Indians, with which to oppose the British pincers now reaching for Quebec.

Once in the Saint Lawrence River, Walker's fleet began to encounter serious difficulties. Fog and unfamiliar currents made navigation uncertain. During the night of 23 August, lookouts were startled to see breakers ahead, and seven of the loaded transports and another vessel foundered on the rocks. Nearly nine hundred people, most of them British regulars and seamen, perished in the disaster. Walker still had a very powerful force under his command, but his self-confidence, which had long been eroding in contemplation of the difficulties and dangers ahead, collapsed altogether. In consultation with his senior officers he decided to turn back; accordingly, the provincial ships and troops were sent home. In the meantime, Nicholson and his men had been slowly pushing northward through the wilderness toward Montreal. About four weeks after Walker's disaster in the Saint Lawrence, word of what had happened and the subsequent decision to cancel the operation reached Nicholson. There was nothing for him to do but to call off his troops. New France was saved.

The southern frontier had remained relatively quiet since 1703, during which time the Carolina traders and expansionists continued their activities in such a way as to cause mounting resentment among the affected tribes. Especially incensed were the Tuscarora of North Carolina, an Iroquoian-speaking tribe distantly related to the Five Nations. In 1711 the Tuscarora struck back in fury, surprising and killing a number of frontier settlers. North Carolina was too weak to deal with the crisis alone, and the more populous colony of South Carolina, seeing its own interests threatened, sent Colonel John Barnwell with a force of about thirty Carolinians and nearly five hundred allied Indians to suppress the Tuscarora. By despoiling Tuscarora villages along the upper Neuse River, Barnwell was able to impose a peace in 1712.

Before long, however, there was a renewed outbreak of Indian violence, stimulating South Carolina to send an even larger expedition up into the neighboring colony. During a vicious, three-day fight in March 1713 at a fortified Indian village northwest of New Bern, the Carolinians killed hundreds of Tuscarora. After burning down the fort, they imposed a hard peace. Unable to see a good future for themselves in their home territory, the beaten Tuscarora began a slow migration northward, eventually being received as kinsmen by the League of the Iroquois, which thereafter was known as the Six Nations. In the wake of the Tuscarora War, the southern frontier was the scene of renewed and aggressive white expansionism.

The ill-fated Walker expedition of 1711 and the defeat of the Tuscarora in 1712–1713 were the last major American military activities in Queen Anne's War. By this time the belligerent powers in Europe were nearing exhaustion from the long and costly struggle. Neither side had been able to achieve decisive superiority, and both badly needed peace and recuperation. Great Britain did hold some advantage in the military equation, however, so that France and Spain were induced to make substantial concessions as the price for avoiding prolonged warfare. This was worked out over a period of months by diplomats from the several nations meeting at the Dutch town of Utrecht. The treaties they signed are known collectively as the Peace of Utrecht, concluded in 1713.

The French found it necessary to yield important territory in North America. While retaining Canada, the new colony of Louisiana in the lower Mississippi Valley, Prince Edward Island, and the strategically situated Cape Breton Island at the southern entrance to the Gulf of Saint Lawrence, France relinquished to Great Britain the territory bordering Hudson Bay, the great island of Newfoundland, and the region known as Acadia, the boundaries of which remained ambiguous, even as the peninsula became the British colony of Nova Scotia. No longer would this area, so close to New England, serve as a base for French privateers operating against British colonial shipping. The southeast, on the other hand, remained undisturbed. Spain continued to hold Florida, while France resumed the development of Louisiana, which meant continuing international rivalry for the trade and allegiance of the southeastern tribes, just as similar intense rivalry persisted along the northern frontier. The murky issue of whether or not the League of the Iroquois had a special binding relationship with the British government, as the latter had long insisted, or remained free to prefer a closer relationship with New France, also remained clouded. Thus, there was ample room for future trouble and conflict in the colonial world.

During a vicious, three-day fight in March 1713 at an Indian village near New Bern, Carolinian colonists killed hundreds of Tuscarora.

INTERWAR INTERLUDE (1714–1738)

The next twenty-five years were a time of uneasy peace in North America, broken by occasional localized violence. Great Britain, France, and Spain, drained by the previous two wars, were striving to regain equilibrium and strength, a necessarily slow process. For these old and now-weary rivals, a period of international stability seemed preferable to further military adventures. Their respective colonies tended to follow the same prudent policy.

By this time the discrepancies in colonial population were increasing at an alarming rate. It has been estimated that in 1713, the year of the Peace of Utrecht, the Spanish colony of Florida still had a white population of only about two thousand, while the French population of New France, concentrated mainly in the Saint Lawrence Valley, numbered approximately eighteen thousand. The British mainland colonies, in contrast, were home to about 375,000 black and white inhabitants, a population that would continue to increase even more rapidly during the postwar interlude. By the end of this brief period, the British colonial population had reached almost nine hundred thousand, the result of continuing large-scale immigration from both Europe and Africa. Increasingly, too, this population included people of diverse European origins, including Germans, Irish, and the so-called Scotch-Irish or Ulster Scots. Spain counted Florida as a very unimportant segment of its vast American empire and did virtually nothing to encourage growth. France demonstrated somewhat more concern for Canada and Louisiana, but found no effective way to promote emigration by productive French settlers. The British colonies grew rapidly because their forms of government, their policy of openness and toleration, and readily available land did provide genuine opportunities for the hard-pressed underclasses of western Europe.

Despite the sparse population available in New France and Louisiana, however, the political leaders of those two colonies actively promoted territorial expansion, both for the potential profits of increasing trade with the tribes of the interior and to forestall the British, whose rapidly increasing numbers of land-hungry farmers were moving inexorably westward toward the Appalachian barrier. With such competitive expansionism under way after 1713, the irregular zone of wilderness serving as a buffer between areas of actual British, French, and Spanish settlement was shrinking. The situation was complicated by the fact that the international boundaries in North America were loosely defined and strenuously disputed, with territorial claims wildly overlapping, all of which made for instability and potential trouble along these remote frontiers. The expansionists, both British and French, found themselves operating in a very fluid situation, where the temptation to grab and hold was almost irresistible.

French determination was shown in 1717 with the establishment of Fort Toulouse two hundred miles up the Alabama River from Mobile, an advance intended to ward off the aggressive traders from South Carolina. In 1718 the French founded a settlement at New Orleans, some distance above the mouth of the Mississippi River. Far to the north on the Atlantic coast, they began construction in 1720 of an elaborate fortress at Louisbourg on Cape Breton Island to offset the new British power in Nova Scotia. Louisbourg, with its excellent harbor, was to become an important military and naval base. Recognizing the strategic importance of the Champlain corridor, in 1731 the French began building a fort at Crown Point near the southern end of Lake Champlain and less than sixty miles above the bend of the Hudson River.

Such territorial advances were very much a part of the international competition for advantageous alliances with the Indians. The expansionists knew that the loss of key Indian alliances, such as that with the Six Nations, could be fatal in the tough competition for empire, especially in the pivotal fur trade. Indians who trapped fur-bearing animals and prepared the peltry for market had become dependent upon the European manufactured goods that they received in exchange. Many also had become addicted to the liquor provided by white traders. For reasons having to do with technology, transport, and distribution, the British traders were able to undersell their French competitors, pleasing their Indian clients with better quality at lower prices. Thus, many tribes tended to be drawn into the British orbit. The French enjoyed a somewhat counterbalancing advantage because the Indians had become aware that the French traders were not followed by a horde of land-hungry farmers eager to occupy Indian territory and cut down the forest that sustained the Indian way of life.

The Iroquois remained divided. Frustrated in their relations with both the British and the French, shrewd leaders of the Six Nations found ways to expand their influence over other tribes farther south and west, thereby developing an effective power in the very region where Anglo-French rivalry later would come to focus. In the southeast, well beyond the influence of the Six Nations, two powerful tribes vied for advantage. The Cherokee inhabited the mountainous area east of the Tennessee River, well situated for trade with Virginia and the Carolinas. Their principal rivals were the Creek, who lived between the upper Suwannee and Alabama rivers athwart the trading paths of the deep South. All of these Indians were competitors for the advantages of trade with the various colonies.

The Yamassee were a smaller tribe occupying the area below Charleston, South Carolina. Thus situated, they traded regularly with the Carolinians while also maintaining some contact with Spaniards and the Creek. Often abused by rough South Carolina traders, and perhaps instigated by the Spaniards or even the French, in April 1715 the Yamassee suddenly began killing all English traders within reach. Before long the aroused warriors were threatening Charleston itself. The colonial militia quickly rallied for the defense of the colony, while the Creek nation joined the Yamassee in the attack. Before being repulsed, the fiery wave actually came within about twelve miles of the capital. That winter the Cherokee threw their support to the colonial side, a good example of division among Indians that always weakened their resistance to English expansion. It was not until 1728, when a South Carolina expedition defeated a remnant of the hostile Indians not far from Saint Augustine, that the bloody fighting of the Yamassee War finally ceased. Thereafter, the Creek adopted a policy much like that pursued by the Iroquois, seeking advantage and security by remaining neutral and, whenever possible, playing one European colony against its rivals.

The greatest immediate threat to New England frontiersmen during this period were the so-called Eastern Indians, consisting of various groups dwelling in the wilderness of Maine and strongly influenced by French Catholic priests who maintained missions in their midst. New Englanders, who traded regularly with these Indians, considered them completely unreliable in their wavering between the English and the French. The Eastern Indians were alarmed and angered by the new tide of land-seeking pioneers pushing northward after 1713. Their anger sometimes erupted in isolated acts of violence that in turn alarmed and angered New Englanders.

Finally, Massachusetts had had enough of Indian depredations and again resorted to military coercion. Attention came to focus on the mission village of Norridgewock in Maine, situated on the bank of the Kennebec River some seventy-five miles inland. The Jesuit priest Sébastian Rasles had been working devotedly for many years as spiritual mentor to the local Indians, but the New Englanders were convinced that he and other missionaries also were active in promoting Indian hostility toward the Protestant English. Thus, Dummer's War, as the conflict is known, like so much of the Anglo-French warfare in North America, became something of a crusade.

In 1724 the British decided to arrest Rasles as a trespasser on territory under British jurisdiction, ignoring the fact that France still claimed jurisdiction as far south as the Kennebec River. An expedition commanded by Captain Johnson Harmon of York, Maine, advanced up the Kennebec undetected and invested Norridgewock. Attacking vigorously, the British overwhelmed the surprised Indians, killing many within the village itself and slaying others who tried to escape by swimming across the river. After scalping the victims and burning down the village, Harmon and his men withdrew victorious. Rasles was among those slain in this bloody fight. After this incident, the Eastern Indians were less aggressive and the British patrols increasingly successful. New France did not actively intervene. By 1727 the chastened Indians, yearning for a resumption of normal trade with the New Englanders, had abandoned the path of open hostility.

It was shortly after this that the Yamassee below South Carolina also were brought to heel, and in 1730 seven prominent tribal leaders of the Cherokee signed a treaty of friendship with the British. Thus, both the northern and the southern frontiers enjoyed a time of relative peace. During this period a few ardent British imperialists in London, among them former army officer James Oglethorpe, brought to reality their scheme for advancing British interests in the "debatable land" between Spanish Florida and the British settlements in South Carolina. In 1732 these men obtained a royal charter designating them trustees for a new proprietary colony to be known as Georgia. Extending from the Savannah River down to the Altamaha (territory originally assigned to Carolina), this new colony was to serve as a military buffer protecting the Carolinas from Spanish and French intrusion. Actual settlement was begun by Oglethorpe in February 1733 with the founding of Savannah. Fortunately for the colonists, the local Indians did not oppose this new venture.

The aggressive Oglethorpe then undertook a systematic program of fort-building south of the Altamaha, alarming the Spanish governor, who saw Saint Augustine again being threatened despite the fact of international peace. In the meantime, enterprising British traders were penetrating deep into the interior, bringing along liquor and other enticing goods and enjoying considerable success in weaning the Creek and other southeastern Indians away from their former allegiances to the Spaniards or the French. In 1737 Oglethorpe, commissioned a general in the British army, was given command of all forces in Georgia and South Carolina, including a regiment of regulars newly brought to Georgia. These developments left no doubt that Great Britain was now determined to uphold its imperial interests, at least on the southern end of its North American block of colonies.

THE WAR OF THE 1740s

A persistent maritime dispute propelled Great Britain and Spain into a new war in October 1739, a conflict known as the War of Jenkins' Ear, expanded in 1740 to include other European powers in the War of the Austrian Succession. The North American colonies were involved from the outset. It was not until 1744, however, that Great Britain and France went to war against each other. Thereafter, the conflict became known in the British colonies as King George's War, the reigning monarch being George II. Collectively, the struggles from 1739 to 1748 can be called the War of the 1740s.

As in all previous colonial wars, European considerations were paramount, the concerns and needs of the respective American colonies secondary or less, which meant that military support from each of the warring mother countries generally was grudging and inadequate. Also, as in earlier conflicts, naval power was a significant factor in the outcome, while extensive privateering took a heavy toll of colonial commerce.

General Oglethorpe saw this war as an opportunity to wrest Florida from the Spaniards. Having gained a pledge of friendship from the Creek, in 1740 he put together a joint Georgia–South Carolina expeditionary force of regulars, colonists, Cherokee, Chickasaw, and Creek, with the advantage of a cooperating squadron from the Royal Navy. The latter clamped a blockade on Saint Augustine, while the expedition made its approach from the north, occupied siege positions, and began bombarding the fort. Governor Manuel de Montiano, an experienced soldier, believed that he could hold out against the British if he could be resupplied from the major Spanish base at Havana. To prevent that, Oglethorpe counted on his blockading squadron. Beginning in June, the bombardment of the fort continued day after day without inflicting fatal damage. As time passed, the morale of the besieging force began eroding dangerously. There was quarreling between the Georgians and Carolinians, while Oglethorpe and increasing numbers of his troops were being weakened by fever.

In all colonial wars, European considerations were paramount, the concerns and needs of the respective American colonies secondary or less.

When Spanish supply ships arrived off the coast and managed to slip into the harbor despite the Royal Navy, Montiano was given the boost he needed to continue resistance almost indefinitely. Oglethorpe recognized that for him the game was up, and he simply called off the unsuccessful siege and brought his frustrated and weary soldiers home. In the aftermath of this humiliating defeat, the governments of Georgia and South Carolina fell into mutual recrimination, further illustrating the perennial British problem of intercolonial rivalry. Oglethorpe and his British troops assumed a defensive posture while awaiting further developments.

While this rather minor operation played itself out in Florida, a much more ambitious military venture was being planned by the British government in London. The intention was to strike a major blow at vital Spanish positions on the rim of the Caribbean in order to disrupt the flow of metallic wealth from Spanish colonies to the Iberian mainland and, if possible, appropriate a rich portion of that wealth. To achieve this goal, a very powerful military-naval expedition was to be assembled at the British base of Port Royal in Jamaica. A variety of men were attracted to the venture by the prospect of sharing in the plunder. For everyone involved—officers, sailors, soldiers—it seemed a quick if dangerous way of acquiring wealth.

The American mainland colonies, prompted by London, hastened to raise a large regiment of thirty-six hundred volunteers. Upon arrival in Jamaica late in 1740, this regiment came under British command as an integral part of the expeditionary force. Eventually, the army included a number of regular regiments as well as the Americans, all under the command of General Thomas Wentworth. The large fleet of fighting ships and transports was commanded by Admiral Edward Vernon. Typically, there were long delays while these forces assembled and prepared themselves, and tropical disease began taking its inevitable toll. Moreover, some of the American troops were drafted by the British against their will and assigned to duty aboard ships of the Royal Navy, where they were subjected to serious abuse.

The designated objective of the operation was the major Spanish base of Cartagena on the northern coast of South America east of Panama, a point of assembly for Spanish treasure fleets and presumably a storehouse of wealth. Departing from Port Royal early in 1741, the British armada sailed to the vicinity of Cartagena and succeeded in landing the troops. Not being much valued as soldiers, the Americans were assigned tasks as laborers in the service of the British army. Skirmishing with the Spanish defenders began some distance from the base and proved indecisive. At the same time, tropical fever again made its presence felt among the troops. Vernon and Wentworth realized that they were incapable of capturing the Spanish base and ordered the army back on board.

Another long delay followed while the British commanders tried to decide what to do next. During this period of inactivity, disease spread throughout the crowded ships, and sailors and soldiers perished by the dozens. In short, the massive Cartagena expedition was a monumental failure. The pitiful remnant of colonial soldiers who eventually arrived back on the North American mainland were left with extremely negative impressions of British contempt, harshness, and ineptitude, memories not soon forgotten. The Cartagena expedition left a legacy of antipathy between British professional military men and American colonists that would be ripe for renewal in many subsequent joint operations.

The Spaniards, in the meantime, thought they saw a way of eliminating the persistent British threat to the security of weakly held Florida. In 1742 a seaborne striking force was assembled at Saint Augustine, under the command of Montiano, its mission to proceed northward up the coast to attack Georgia and South Carolina. The sparse population of Georgia gave reason to anticipate easy success there, once Oglethorpe's regiment of regulars had been overcome. After that, the plan was to continue on to South Carolina and foment a revolt among the numerous black slaves of the tidewater area, thereby creating such chaos and violence that the colony would be incapable of any effective defense.

In early July the Spanish expedition landed at the southern end of Saint Simon Island on the coast of Georgia, easily brushing aside the opposition. Their immediate objective was the fortified garrison of Frederica, only a few miles north of the beachhead. Spanish probes in that direction produced some skirmishing, with Indians involved on both sides. Apparently the invaders were able to advance to within a mile or two of Frederica before being driven back. Then a detachment of fierce Highlanders from Oglethorpe's regiment surprised a sizable body of Spanish troops along the narrow route leading back to the landing place. Wielding their sharp, two-edged claymores, the Scots drove the Spaniards into the adjacent swamp, where many were slaughtered. The Battle of Bloody Marsh was a decisive victory for Oglethorpe and seriously undermined Spanish morale. After some further inconclusive activity, Montiano decided to withdraw and returned to Saint Augustine without bothering South Carolina.

Up to this point in the war of seaborne expeditionary forces, the advantage seemed to have remained with the defense. The reasons are not difficult to discover. In addition to the debilitating effects of disease were the extremely difficult problems of coordinating the movements of sailing vessels, providing essential supplies where and when needed, and controlling scattered units operating on unfamiliar terrain. By the beginning of 1744 the war along the southern frontier had become a stalemate.

The situation changed drastically for North America after France declared war against Great Britain in March 1744, because the northern frontier again became a theater of fierce conflict. British fur traders, land speculators, and pioneering farmers saw their future threatened by the renewal of Franco-Indian raiding activity from Maine to the upper Hudson Valley. In all the areas exposed to this threat, there were clear signs of wavering confidence, a jolting halt in the hitherto dynamic surge of British expansionism.

Inevitably, too, the role of the Six Nations became a nagging problem for the British and an enticing opportunity for the French. The tribes themselves were seriously divided among pro-British, pro-neutrality, and pro-French factions, and the various tribal leaders tried desperately to find the safest path through a morass of contending imperial interests. Every imperalist, whether British or French, recognized the critical importance of these confederated tribes because of their strategic location and their influence over other tribes farther west. Neither side in the war could be confident of unwavering Indian support, nor could the Indians afford to trust their European patrons. It was truly a bog of quicksand for all involved.

The tribes of the Six Nations were seriously divided among pro-British, pro-neutrality, and pro-French factions.

The French fort at Crown Point on the western shore of Lake Champlain was well situated to serve as a place of assembly and departure for Franco-Indian raiding parties targeted against British frontier outposts and settlements. One such expedition, consisting of more than 520 French and Indians led by Lieutenant Paul Marin, began a stealthy advance toward the upper Hudson in November 1745. Taking great care to avoid detection by Indians allied with the British, they arrived in the vicinity of the small and unsuspecting farming village of Saratoga, only about thirty miles north of Albany. Achieving complete surprise, Marin's raiders struck hard and quickly gained total control of the village. After plundering the dwellings and rounding up more than a hundred terrified prisoners, the French set the place afire and then headed for Crown Point with their captives. The following year another similar party forced the surrender of Fort Massachusetts, a small New England outpost on the Hoosick River twenty-five miles east of Albany. The worst fears of the British seemed well founded—the frontier was again collapsing.

In the disputed area north of the Kennebec River, the Eastern Indians, under strong French influence, became active again in 1746, attacking isolated and weakly defended settlements. All along the exposed frontier settlers found themselves in a most precarious situation. As always, the government was slow to provide any military assistance. Many lives were lost and much valuable property was destroyed by a kind of warfare against which it proved nearly impossible to protect a thinly scattered population.

French hardihood and skill were once again well demonstrated in the depths of the winter of 1746–1747 in northern Nova Scotia. Between the French base at Beaubassin and the British-occupied settlement of Grand

Pré lay more than a hundred miles of wintry terrain. Grand Pré was garrisoned by about five hundred Massachusetts soldiers under the command of Colonel Arthur Noble. A French attack force led by Antoine Coulon de Villiers, equipped with snowshoes and dragging their supplies on sledges, made its way toward Grand Pré, acquiring some Acadian and Indian recruits en route. Achieving complete surprise because of the seeming impossibility of their long approach, these tough raiders fell upon the British defenders with ferocity, killing Noble and many others. The survivors surrendered and were permitted to withdraw to Annapolis Royal, sixty-five miles to the southwest.

All of these events had some impact on the course of King George's War in North America, but for New England in particular the most important campaign took place in 1745. The French fortress town of Louisbourg on the rugged coast of Cape Breton Island, although not a direct and immediate menace to New England itself, was in many ways a powerful threat to New England interests. Its well-protected harbor served as a base and haven for French naval vessels and privateers preying upon New England fishing boats and merchant vessels. French influence emanated from Louisbourg to undermine British authority in Nova Scotia, not only with the local Indians but also the French Acadian peasants who had remained after the British conquest. As long as Louisbourg remained in French hands, neither the sea-lanes nor adjacent British territory were secure.

New England merchants were quite familiar with Louisbourg because in peacetime that port was a busy center for Anglo-French trade. The merchants knew that the narrow channel leading into the harbor was guarded by a strong fort situated on a rocky islet at the entrance, as well as by the Grand Battery on the shore directly facing the entrance. The town of Louisbourg, constructed on the western side of the entrance behind the Island Battery, was a flourishing fishing and mercantile community with dwellings, shops, and warehouses. On the land side the town was completely protected by a series of fortified bastions connected by a high earthen wall faced with stone. There was a citadel within that was the quarters of the governor and barracks for the garrison of nearly six hundred French and Swiss professional soldiers. Governor Louis Du Chambon knew that the morale of his troops was not the best, but he believed that his well-placed artillery could prevent any attacking fleet from forcing its way into the harbor.

Governor William Shirley of Massachusetts, an ambitious imperialist eager to enhance his fortune and prestige by undercutting the French, came to believe that Louisbourg was not impregnable. By January 1745 Shirley was envisioning a large intercolonial expedition with substantial support from the Royal Navy, charged with the mission of wresting Louisbourg from the French. The somewhat skeptical Massachusetts legislature finally gave its approval to Shirley's proposal, London was duly notified, and the other colonies as far south as Pennsylvania were solicited for support. Only New Hampshire and Connecticut were fully supportive, although Rhode Island did contribute an armed sloop and New York sent some much-needed cannon. Nearly everyone realized that this venture against such a well-fortified position was a gigantic gamble; if it did succeed the payoff could be enormous.

Command of the intercolonial army to be raised was given to William Pepperrell, the commander of the Maine militia (at that time Maine was under Massachusetts jurisdiction). Given Pepperrell's widespread popularity and the prospect of plunder at Louisbourg, New Englanders enlisted briskly, apparently convinced that this would not be another Cartagena. Thousands of volunteers began converging on Boston, where they found quantities of supplies and a motley fleet of colonial ships. Although this was an amateur army led by an amateur general, it was an army determined to win the prize. Altogether more than three thousand New Englanders responded to Pepperrell's call. These troops were conveyed to the advance staging base at Canso for the completion of final preparations. There they were joined by a squadron from the Royal Navy under the command of Commodore Peter Warren, who immediately reinforced the tight blockade of the enemy base.

Late in April the expeditionary force sailed for Louisbourg, and on the last day of the month established a beachhead on the shore of Gabarus Bay some distance west of the fortress, which completely surprised Du Chambon, who had assumed that any assault would have to come through the well-guarded entrance to the harbor. With great difficulty Pepperrell's men dragged their artillery across intervening swampy terrain to establish siege lines within range of the massive walls. In addition, they acquired many other cannon after the French abandoned the Grand Battery. A highly destructive bombardment of Louisbourg began, while the British and American blockading ships prevented desperately needed supplies and reinforcements from reaching the defenders. Pepperrell's artillery not only made good progress in breaching the walls and silencing some of the French cannon, but also inflicted severe damage on the many buildings within those walls, to the terror of the civilian inhabitants. Du Chambon's supply of gunpowder diminished at an alarming rate.

The New Englanders tried and failed to capture the Island Battery, taking very heavy losses in an amphibious attempt, but when they succeeded in mounting some cannon at Lighthouse Point on the eastern side of the entrance, the Island Battery became virtually untenable. The bombardment of Louisbourg itself continued day after day, while the terrified women and children cowered in fortified casemates. Altogether some nine thousand solid cannonballs and six hundred explosive shells rained down on the hapless town.

In general, Pepperrell and Warren maintained a fairly cordial relationship and cooperated remarkably well, although there were clear signs of tension. Warren was a professional officer and a very ambitious one, who was fully aware of Pepperrell's lack of experience in major military operations. As time passed, Warren became impatient with the slow progress of the siege and began pressing Pepperrell, who resented such prompting from the sea. By mid-June the two men had agreed on a plan for a joint simultaneous assault, the army to rush the battered walls while the navy forced its way into the harbor. This dramatic consummation was forestalled by Du Chambon's prudent capitulation.

The surrender of mighty Louisbourg caused rejoicing in the colonies and in England as well. New England gloried in its remarkable achievement, perhaps forgetting that such a success could not have been achieved without the active involvement of the Royal Navy in preventing the reinforcement of Louisbourg by sea. Adding to the provincial satisfaction was the generosity of Great Britain in reimbursing the colonies for their expenses. Soon, however, the victorious troops at Louisbourg found mounting reasons for complaint. For one thing, the terms of surrender granted to the French precluded the plundering that the New Englanders had assumed would be their reward. The French inhabitants were allowed to take their personal possessions with them when they departed. Moreover, instead of being sent home to receive the adulation of family and friends, the troops were detained indefinitely to garrison a badly shattered town. In fact, they found themselves spending a very unpleasant winter in Louisbourg, with many dying from disease. All in all, it was an unhappy ending to an amazingly successful military operation.

The war in Europe had been a long, indecisive struggle, and by 1748 both sides were ready for a cessation of hostilities. In October of that year a treaty of peace was signed at the ancient town of Aix-la-Chapelle. For North America this meant the mutual restoration of captured territory, with the result that the unstable southern frontier remained as it was, while in the north, Cape Breton Island, including Louisbourg, reverted to France. Most New Englanders were outraged by this provision, which seemed to cast away so callously what they had won so gloriously. Great Britain had sacrificed Louisbourg in order to regain some lost territory on the coast of India, a clear indication of how far the conflict had spread and how little consideration the British government gave to colonial interests. The Treaty of Aix-la-Chapelle did almost nothing to resolve such long-standing issues as Indian relations and international boundaries in North America that were so threatening to peace and stability.

Both Britain and France knew the strengths and weaknesses of the other, and each envisioned the other as a scheming aggressor bent on ending the game by winning all.

Spain, despite its retention of Florida, no longer was a serious competitor for dominance above the Gulf of Mexico, which left Great Britain and France as the two chief rivals in the mid-eighteenth century. Each country knew the strengths and weaknesses of the other, and each envisioned the other as a scheming aggressor bent on ending the game by winning all. Any probe or thrust by one side caused instant suspicion by the other, who tended to view the advance as a step toward conquest. Indeed, there was a great temptation to make advances because the disputed areas between the respective frontiers of British and French settlement were largely vacant except for native Americans, whose interests and rights seldom survived the dynamism of imperial ambitions. By this time, too, the rival colonial societies had become so firmly rooted and formed that the conflict was showing signs of becoming total, an irrepressible contest between two quite different systems of government and two widely differing cultures.

The international rivalry for dominance in the fur trade of the Mississippi Valley was becoming more intense. Pennsylvania traders managed to establish a regular base for business in the Indian village of Pickawillanee on the Miami River, 250 miles west of the Appalachian barrier. Their presence had the effect of promoting British influence and prestige throughout the entire region until June 1752, when a war party of pro-French Indians attacked and destroyed Pickawillanee. After that, British trade and influence in the remote interior began to decline markedly. The advantage now appeared to be shifting toward New France.

During this same period attention was becoming sharply focused on the geographical area known as the Forks of the Ohio, where the Allegheny and Monongahela rivers joined to form the Ohio River, which then flowed on into the Mississippi. The Forks was the most direct route connecting the French zone of interest around Lake Erie to their colony of Louisiana. If the French succeeded in preempting that corridor of communication, at the same time drawing all the tribes of the region into their trading orbit, the very heart of the trans-Appalachian West would become forbidden territory for the British. There were four principal contenders for control of the Forks area—the Six Nations, New France, Pennsylvania, and Virginia—the latter two basing their respective claims on the terms of conflicting royal charters, but none of the claimants was firmly planted on the scene and none exercised actual control.

A number of politically influential Virginians had joined forces with some prominent Englishmen to form the Ohio Company of Virginia, whose purpose was to expropriate and exploit a large portion of the area in dispute. Obtaining a royal charter in 1749, the company began advancing a plan for establishing British settlements in the area as an effective way of forestalling the French. It was a private, profit-making scheme with important imperial implications. At the time, Pennsylvania had nothing to match it. The French, however, were not caught napping. By 1753 the new governor of New France, the Marquis Duquesne de Menneville, was ready to make good the extensive claim of his colony. He dispatched a military expedition to Lake Erie with orders to construct a chain of wilderness forts south to the Forks and beyond, which would bind the Indians to the French interest while making it impossible for the British to maintain their influence west of the Appalachians, or so Duquesne hoped.

The French constructed Fort Presque Isle on the present site of Erie, Pennsylvania, and a second, Fort Le Boeuf, near French Creek, a tributary of the Allegheny River. They also appropriated a former British trading post at Venango on the shore of the Allegheny, but the French were unable to proceed further and had to leave the Forks area as vacant as before.

Governor Robert Dinwiddie of Virginia watched these developments with deep apprehension, as did all other investors in the Ohio Company. Somehow, the French "invasion" of Virginia territory had to be stopped, probably by military force, but first it was necessary to try diplomacy. George Washington, then a twenty-one-year-old officer in the Virginia militia, was sent by Dinwiddie to demand that the French withdraw. When the commander of Fort Le Boeuf heard what Washington had to say, he politely declined to obey, pointing out that he took his orders from Quebec.

THE FRENCH AND INDIAN WAR

Although in the spring of 1754 Great Britain and France were officially at peace, the Ohio Company of Virginia sent a party to construct a fortified post at the Forks of the Ohio, hoping to forestall the French. Governor Dinwiddie dispatched a hastily raised force of armed frontiersmen to protect the laborers, and George Washington raised another company to help defend the contested area. Before long a powerful French expedition arrived at the Forks, forcing the Virginians to abandon their work and withdraw altogether, whereupon the French began building Fort Duquesne at the strategic site. This development, in turn, impelled the Indians of the area to begin shifting their support toward the French. In May Washington led his force of about 150 men to Great Meadows, fifty miles southeast of the Forks. Then, learning from friendly Indians the location of a French scouting party, he proceeded to attack and defeat his opponents, killing their commander in the process. Thus began the French and Indian War, which blended into the Seven Years' War fought in Europe and elsewhere from 1756 to 1763.

Hastily withdrawing to Great Meadows, Washington erected there a crude palisade called Fort Necessity. He also received some reinforcements, including an independent company of British regulars, but they were not enough to prevent defeat when a more powerful force of French and Indians from Fort Duquesne arrived on the scene. After many hours of unequal musketry, the British were forced to capitulate on the evening of 3 July, after which they dragged themselves miserably back across the mountains, leaving the transmontane West to the victorious French. In the meantime, a congress of delegates from seven of the British colonies, meeting at Albany, had accomplished very little either in promoting intercolonial cooperation or in propping up the badly sagging Anglo-Iroquois alliance.

Neither Great Britain nor France wanted war at this time, for both were striving to recover from the War of the Austrian Succession while contending with difficult internal problems and continental concerns. It was their fractious American colonies, greedily contending for tribal alliances, the Indian trade, and western territory, that were leading them down a slippery slope. Despite the much larger population of the British colonies (about 1.5 million) and their highly diversified economy, New France (possibly 55,000 inhabitants) seemed to have gained a distinct advantage through its bold military occupation of the Great Lakes area, the upper Ohio Valley, and the lower Mississippi, leaving to the British only the coastal strip east of the Appalachian

Mountains. Encirclement seemed to be virtually an accomplished fact in 1754, but the French were spread dangerously thin along that extensive arc, their strongest positions being at Louisbourg, Quebec, Montreal, Fort Frontenac, Toronto, Fort Niagara, Detroit, Crown Point on Lake Champlain, and Fort Duquesne at the Forks of the Ohio.

At the same time, the Indians of the region were confronted by a cruel dilemma. They had become heavily dependent upon trade with the British colonies, which were able to provide them with superior trade goods, including guns and ammunition, at lower prices than those of the French. With the French becoming dominant militarily throughout so much of the interior, however, the Indians could not afford to offend them by continuing to deal with the British. Naturally, no tribe wanted to be on the losing side of the next big Anglo-French conflict. Therefore, even the Iroquois and the many remote interior tribes over which the Iroquois exerted considerable influence were beginning to edge away from the British connection, a trend seen as ominous by British imperialists.

After learning of these developments, the British government realized that the Americans lacked the necessary military resources and skills to effectively counter the French threat. Accordingly, the momentous decision was made to dispatch General Edward Braddock with the Forty-fourth and Forty-eighth regiments of foot plus a train of artillery, all to be conveyed to Virginia by a squadron of the Royal Navy. Not to be outdone, the French government sent a number of its own regular regiments under the command of the General Ludwig August Dieskau. The infusions of large numbers of professional troops marked the beginning of a significant intensification of the struggle for domination in North America, even as the two contending nations continued high-level negotiations to avert impending war.

Braddock, after arriving in Virginia, convened a conference of colonial leaders in April 1755 to coordinate operations. It was decided that the regulars already stationed in Nova Scotia, reinforced by New England provincial troops, would seize control of the isthmus of Chignecto. A provincial army under William Johnson of New York, now designated sole superintendent of the Six Nations, would capture the French base at Crown Point. A third expedition, commanded by Governor William Shirley of Massachusetts, who was appointed second-in-command under Braddock of all British forces, would proceed against Fort Niagara. Braddock himself would lead a large combined army of regulars and provincials across the mountains to seize Fort Duquesne, after which he would move northward to help bring the other operations to a victorious conclusion, expelling the French. It was a most ambitious plan, liberally ladled with optimism.

The first success came early. In mid-June, after a brief siege by two thousand New Englanders and some British regulars, Fort Beausejour at the head of the Bay of Fundy surrendered to the British. Two days later a similar result was achieved at Fort Gaspereau on the north shore of the isthmus. Chignecto was now fully under British control, greatly enhancing the security of Nova Scotia—except for the continued presence of the Acadians, who were viewed as potential subversives. To solve that problem the British resorted to an exceedingly harsh expedient. In 1755 they forcibly deported about seven thousand Acadians, shipping them off as homeless refugees to British colonies as far south as Georgia, burning their dwellings and barns. New Englanders, who coveted this rich farming area, gloated at what in retrospect must be accounted an atrocity.

By 9 July Braddock's army was approaching Fort Duquesne when it suddenly encountered a scouting force of about 250 French and 650 Indians.

Braddock had a much more difficult task. From the outset he encountered frustrating difficulties in gaining the needed cooperation of the various colonies involved, obtaining adequate numbers of Indian scouts, and assembling the essential transport for the bulky supplies required by his army of twenty-two hundred regulars and provincials. His progress through the wilderness was necessarily slow, because a wagon road had to be constructed to move the artillery and supplies. Although a blunt and somewhat opinionated officer who placed little value on the advice of provincial leaders, Braddock did appreciate the danger of ambush and systematically took reasonable precautions.

By 9 July the advance section of Braddock's army was approaching Fort Duquesne when it suddenly encountered a strong scouting force of about 250 French and 650 Indians. Quickly occupying advantageous positions along both flanks of the startled and confused British column, the enemy poured in such effective fire that all British attempts to rally and respond proved futile. Suffering extremely heavy losses, the British eventually succumbed to panic and began a precipitous retreat, leaving their dead and much of their equipment on the field. Braddock himself was mortally wounded. Thus, the hopeful attempt to regain control of the Forks was a staggering failure.

At about this same time the separate provincial expeditions under Johnson and Shirley, totaling nearly five thousand men, were assembling and making their preparations in the Albany-Schenectady area. In the latter part of July they went their separate ways, Johnson northward to the southern end of Lake George, Shirley westward to Fort Oswego at the southeastern entrance to Lake Ontario. There were more delays because both commanders kept their men at work building defensive fortifications before advancing toward their assigned targets.

In the meantime, Dieskau led a strong force of fifteen hundred French regulars, Canadians, and Indians southward from Crown Point to forestall the dilatory Johnson. On 8 September this force attacked Johnson's camp only to be badly mauled and repulsed by musketry and close-range artillery fire. Dieskau himself was wounded and captured, and his surviving troops fled back to Crown Point. Soon the French were busy constructing a new fort at Ticonderoga, eleven miles south of Crown Point, where the portage route from Lake George meets Lake Champlain. As for Shirley, he judged it imprudent to proceed beyond Oswego so late in the year, and, like Johnson, failed to gain his objective.

It had been confidently anticipated, both in England and the colonies, that the British operation plan for 1755 would succeed because of overwhelming strength, perhaps even without sparking a new war with France. The totally unexpected defeat of Braddock near Fort Duquesne simply stunned the optimists. The subsequent failures of Johnson and Shirley only added to the widespread gloom, although some Americans did try to discern more than a little glory in Johnson's victory over Dieskau. Above all, the ineptitude and rout of Braddock's regulars caused many Americans to reassess their awe of the British army. Perhaps, after all, the regulars were not very effective fighters in the American wilderness; indeed, perhaps experienced provincial soldiers actually were superior when fighting on home ground. This intriguing thought was to become fairly widespread in the colonies, with significance for the future.

Some British leaders began to recognize the need for greater military adaptation to American conditions. In 1756 Parliament ordered that a new regiment of regulars be recruited in the colonies, to be known as the Royal Americans, a regiment that was to become especially proficient in wilderness warfare. That same year Robert Rogers, a New Hampshire frontiersman, began organizing and training his own corps of rangers, a group of tough, woods-wise fighters who soon would prove invaluable to the British when operating in conjunction with regular units. Some British line officers broadened their professional experience by actually serving with ranger units. The British army in North America also began developing its own light infantry within the regular regiments, units especially equipped and trained for forest warfare.

In the spring of 1756, Dieskau's successor, the Marquis Louis Joseph de Montcalm, was sent to Canada with two fresh regiments of regulars. Montcalm, an able and experienced soldier, proceeded to Fort Frontenac on Lake Ontario, where he stood ready to unleash a strong expeditionary force. On the British side, Shirley was succeeded as commander in chief by John Campbell, Earl of Loudoun, an experienced professional officer. Loudoun was preceded to America by Major General James Abercromby, who assumed command until Loudoun arrived in July.

In Europe during that same spring the so-called Diplomatic Revolution was effected, producing a new alignment of the major powers— Britain and Prussia versus France and Austria. Spain, unable to reverse its long decline, prudently remained neutral. On 17 May 1756 Great Britain declared war on France, the official beginning of a world war that had been under way in North America for nearly two years, and that would see the opposing forces at grips in Europe, the Mediterranean, the West Indies, India, and on the high seas.

Long before Shirley was aware that he was being replaced, he had made elaborate plans for the campaign of 1756. Consequently, by the time Loudoun arrived and assumed full responsibility, a large force of provincial soldiers under Major General John Winslow of Massachusetts was based at Fort Edward forty-five miles north of Albany, while another force consisting of both regulars and provincials under Colonel James Mercer was in position at Fort Oswego. There was no time for Loudoun to alter the situation in any significant way. Winslow balked at the prospect of British regulars joining his expedition and managed to stave off that unwelcome development, but he gained nothing against the French.

The aggressive Montcalm, in the meantime, brought his troops southward, bombarded Fort Oswego on 14 August, and forced its surrender. After thoroughly demolishing that important British gateway to the Great Lakes, the French army withdrew to Montreal, taking with them about sixteen hundred prisoners, ending the campaigning in 1756 and leaving Loudoun much to ponder and correct. Farther south, in Pennsylvania, Maryland, Virginia, and the Carolinas, the British frontier had been ravaged by war parties of pro-French Indians.

During the winter of 1756–1757 the Saint Lawrence River remained frozen for months, preventing the arrival of much-needed reinforcements and supplies from France. Canada was locked in ice. With food in short supply and growing scarcer, the governor of Canada, Pierre de Rigaud, Marquis de Vaudreuil, and General Montcalm, together with their shivering troops and the few thousand inhabitants of New France, waited out the slow weeks while contemplating the coming year.

Loudoun made a bold decision for 1757. He would redeem all previous British disasters by capturing Louisbourg and then advancing up the Saint Lawrence to take Quebec. The plan was made theoretically feasible by the availability of not only a large number of colonial troops and vessels but also several regiments of British regulars and numerous ships of the Royal Navy. It would be a far more potent force than the one that brought Louisbourg low in 1745. The staging base was to be Halifax in Nova Scotia, where Loudoun assembled his great expedition, spending precious weeks in July and August drilling his troops and making final preparations. The French had gotten wind of all this and were hastening to build up their naval strength at Louisbourg. They were so successful that after Loudoun's scouting ships had finished counting the masts in Louisbourg harbor, the British commander decided that he simply did not have the strength to capture that great French base and cancelled the operation.

Montcalm's Indians fell upon a column of British prisoners, killing some and leading others into wilderness captivity.

In the meantime, Montcalm had not been idle. His chosen target for 1757 was Fort William Henry, the advance British base at the southern end of Lake George. With overwhelming strength the French, taking their departure from Ticonderoga, advanced southward down Lake George in early August. Arriving at their destination, they began a siege that ended on 9 August with the surrender of the British garrison. The following day some of Montcalm's Indians fell upon a column of British prisoners, killing some and leading others into wilderness captivity, a shocking atrocity that mortified the European general. After razing the captured fort, the victorious French troops then withdrew to their base on Lake Champlain. Thus, 1757, like the three preceding years of conflict, had produced little but discouragement and loss for the British.

In that same year, however, a strong, consistent hand was applied to the shaping of British strategy. Functioning as secretary of state in a divided government, William Pitt gained effective control over the entire British war effort. Unlike the king and many politicians in London who saw the European theater as the most important, Pitt had a vision of victory achieved by defeating the French in America and India. Through his determination and drive, the allocation of British military and naval resources began a significant shift toward the American theater. Pitt also was able to persuade Parliament that it would be wise to encourage the Americans by promising to subsidize a large part of colonial participation in future campaigns. Thus, beginning in 1758 the Americans would see even more ships of the Royal Navy, regiments of British regulars, and British money. All this, in turn, made the habitual and often unrelenting stinginess of the provincial legislatures in helping fund military endeavors seem even more unpatriotic.

After the failures of 1757, Pitt was convinced that new commanders were needed in the American theater. Somewhat reluctantly, he acquiesced in the king's choice of Abercromby as Loudoun's successor. More important, Pitt disregarded the old seniority system by appointing unusually promising subordinate commanders, notably John Forbes and Jeffrey Amherst. Pitt also saw clearly that the ultimate goal must be the capture of Quebec and Montreal, key centers of government and commerce, whose fall would mean the demise of New France. In planning for the campaigning of 1758, Pitt took pains to ensure that enough ships, supplies, and manpower would be available when and where needed, with regular forces playing the major roles. The British very definitely were about to go on the offensive. In contrast, the French, increasingly outnumbered and woefully deficient in material resources, had no choice but to adopt a more defensive strategy, trying desperately to hold on to the territory they controlled. The tide of war, it seemed, might at last be turning.

Three major operations were set in motion for 1758. Abercromby was to lead a large expedition northward from Albany to seize the French bastions on Lake Champlain. Amherst was to conduct an elaborate amphibious assault upon Louisbourg. Forbes was to advance with a powerful force of regulars and provincials westward from Philadelphia to capture Fort Duquesne and gain effective control of the Forks area. Subsequent advances by all three expeditions would then be made into the heartland of Canada. The French again led by Montcalm, waited courageously but nervously.

Abercromby, commanding a force of more than six thousand regulars and almost as many provincials, failed miserably, losing many of his most valuable troops in a futile assault on the outer defenses at Ticonderoga, whereupon he withdrew. Quite the opposite occurred at Louisbourg. After a successful landing of thousands of troops several miles west of the great fortress, Amherst began a systematic siege that was far more disciplined and professional than the one carried on by Pepperrell in 1745. Prominent among Amherst's brigade commanders was Brigadier General James Wolfe, an ardent professional officer whose talent had already been noted by Pitt. Decisive in the outcome was the fact that the British outnumbered the French by nearly four to one, had ample artillery, and were effectively served by the thirty-nine blockading ships of the Royal Navy. But it was no pushover. The siege had been under way for more than six weeks when Louisbourg finally surrendered on 27 July. Later, British engineers systematically and thoroughly demolished the fallen French fortress.

Montcalm feared that Abercromby might make a second attempt to seize Ticonderoga and dared not shift his troops away from Lake Champlain, which meant that other vulnerable outposts, such as Fort Frontenac, remained understrength. In August Colonel John Bradstreet at the head of a force of more than three thousand men, mostly provincials, departed from the ruins of Fort Oswego in a large fleet of bateaus and landed near Fort Frontenac. The French garrison found itself outnumbered by more than twenty to one, but held off the attackers for about twenty-four hours before surrendering on 27 August. Had the victorious Bradstreet decided to station a strong garrison of his own at Fort Frontenac, the British would have controlled Lake Ontario, cutting the lines of communication between Montreal and the West. They also would have had an advance base for their intended drive down the Saint Lawrence River to Montreal. Instead, Bradstreet's army satisfied itself with plundering and then demolishing the French installations before returning to home territory.

For British imperialists, 1759 was to be the year of great opportunity in North America, bringing to a decisive climax the dream of conquering Canada.

While Amherst was tasting victory and Abercromby defeat in 1758, Forbes was experiencing great difficulties farther south. He had arrived at Philadelphia in April only to be confronted with a tangle of frustrating administrative problems. The elected assemblies of Maryland and Pennsylvania, pursuing their own political objectives, seemed strangely uncooperative. Ordinary citizens likewise were intent on protecting their own interests. It was only by a combination of cajolery and threats that Forbes was able to hire the large numbers of wagons and horses needed to supply his army of sixteen hundred regulars, including four companies of the Royal Americans under Colonel Henry Bouquet, twenty-seven hundred Pennsylvania provincials under Colonel John Armstrong, and twenty-six hundred Virginia provincials commanded by Colonel George Washington. Forbes found the provincial troops to be poorly disciplined and generally unkempt. There was even a political struggle between Virginia and Pennsylvania over the route to be chosen for approaching the Forks. By the end of July Pennsylvania had won that battle, with Forbes preferring the more direct route westward instead of Braddock's old road. In advancing westward Forbes was very careful and deliberate, constructing fortified supply depots at convenient intervals and cutting new roads as needed, all of which took much time.

In October Forbes delayed his advance further in order not to interfere with important negotiations between the government of Pennsylvania and more than five hundred Indians from fifteen tribes, including the Iroquois. This momentous conference, held at the town of Easton, was Pennsylvania's attempt to detach the Delaware and other interior tribes from the French in the upper Ohio Valley. With the British now willing to make some territorial concessions and the Iroquois leadership cooperative, the Treaty of Easton proved a success. The marked shift in the attitude of these Indians could only be helpful to Forbes as he drew nearer to Fort Duquesne. In fact, shortly after the Easton Conference many of the Ohio Valley Indians who had been allied with the French moved away from the fort, leaving the French garrison considerably weakened.

In November, with the approach of winter, Forbes knew that he must hurry or else give up. Accordingly, he detached an advance force of about twenty-five hundred men to push forward rapidly. On 24 November Indian scouts reported that Fort Duquesne had been burned and abandoned. The next evening the advance force arrived on the scene to find that the fort and village were indeed in ruins and the French gone. For the first time since 1754, the strategic Forks of the Ohio was under effective British control. It soon became certain that the tribes in that entire region were abandoning their hostility toward the British as they watched the collapse of French power.

For British imperialists, led by Pitt, 1759 was to be the year of great opportunity in North America, bringing to a decisive climax the dream of conquering Canada. Deprived of much of their Indian support and hard pressed for reinforcements and supplies, the French defenders clearly were facing disaster. Pitt now had the commanders and the trained manpower required for the job, although the victorious Forbes had died. Supreme command was given to Amherst, whose new challenge was to lead a large army of regulars and provincials from the upper Hudson to the Saint Lawrence. Wolfe was to take a second large army, mostly regulars, up the Saint Lawrence with full naval support. The two armies were to converge and cut the heart out of New France. A letter written by Amherst concerning these plans fell into French hands, giving Montcalm a fairly clear picture of British intentions.

Amherst decided to advance northward to Lake Champlain, capture Ticonderoga and Crown Point, and then continue on toward Montreal and join up with Wolfe. He also dispatched a sizable force of regulars and provincials to Oswego with the mission of taking Niagara, a task that was accomplished before the end of July. Amherst's own army of more than eleven thousand men, trained in forest tactics, headed up Lake George on 21 July in four long parallel columns of boats and a large raft carrying the artillery. At Ticonderoga, Amherst began a siege, and after several days the French blew up their main magazine on 26 July and escaped to Crown Point. Scouts were sent north to assess the situation and returned with the astonishing news that the fort at Crown Point also had been abandoned. The British readily occupied the place on 4 August. At this point Amherst became infected with caution, setting his

The Battle of Quebec. In September 1759, General James Wolfe and the British army attacked Quebec city, which was defended by French troops under the command of the Marquis de Montcalm (on horse). The British were victorious, but both Montcalm and Wolfe were killed. (Corbis/Bettmann)

men to work on time-consuming tasks, such as fortification and the construction of two small naval vessels.

In the meantime, Wolfe's armada had ascended the Saint Lawrence successfully and arrived before Quebec in June. The extreme difficulty in gaining access to the fortified town because of two rivers on the downriver side and steep cliffs on the upriver side quickly became painfully clear. Placing his artillery on the opposite shore, Wolfe began bombarding the town with devastating effect. He also tried landing operations below Quebec, without any significant success. Vaudreuil and Montcalm sat secure, apparently prepared to endure the bombardment until the British tired of the game and departed. Time, it seemed, was on their side.

After weeks of frustration, Wolfe discovered an obscure path leading from the shore a short distance above the town to the top of the cliffs and became convinced that this route could give his army access to the relatively flat and open Plains of Abraham just outside the town wall. By slipping his transports upriver past the town and then bringing his landing force downriver in small boats under cover of darkness, Wolfe was able to achieve his immediate objective. The gamble paid off handsomely. On the morning of 13 September the French were amazed to see long lines of British regulars in battle array on the Plains of Abraham, a place supposedly inaccessible from the river. Imagination and daring had won the first round.

Up to this point in the war, as far as North America was concerned, much of the fighting had been carried on in wilderness style. Now, on the open Plains of Abraham, European-style warfare was to have its day. While waiting to see what the French would do, Wolfe had his men lie down on the ground in ranks. Before long, a surging army of French regulars and provincial troops, led by Montcalm on horseback, emerged from the town and began forming up for battle. The British soldiers now sprang to their feet and waited, muskets ready. On each side the numbers were roughly equal, fewer than five thousand.

There was some preliminary skirmishing, after which Montcalm's courageous troops began advancing directly toward the British lines. Not until they were very close did the disciplined British regulars open fire. They delivered one devastating volley and then another, shredding the French formation. Then, without pause, they charged forward with bayonets at the ready, routing the French survivors and driving them back into the town. Montcalm, mortally wounded, went with his men in shattering defeat. The British victory, however, was not achieved without cost. Hundreds of British soldiers lay wounded and about sixty were dead, including Wolfe.

Vaudreuil and a large number of French troops managed to withdraw from the vicinity of Quebec, circling wide around the victorious British to take positions between them and Montreal. Quebec surrendered on 18 September and the British army marched in, there to endure the coming winter. A month later Amherst, learning of Wolfe's victory and death, prudently decided to terminate his own efforts.

During the ensuing winter the British army in Quebec, now under the command of General James Murray, suffered great hardship because of the cold. By April 1760 Murray had fewer than four thousand effectives to defend Quebec against a much larger French force not far distant. On the 28th of that month, when the British ventured outside to prepare defenses, they were severely mauled, and thereafter were closely besieged until relieved by the timely arrival of ships of the Royal Navy. The French still held Montreal under Governor Vaudreuil.

With Quebec now securely in British hands there could be little doubt as to what the remainder of 1760 would bring. Indian defection from the French cause was continuing as British officials offered the enticement of peace, security, and a thriving trade; Vaudreuil could no longer count on massive Indian support in the last-ditch defense of the Canadian heartland. That summer three powerful British armies began converging on poorly defended Montreal. The first, consisting of twenty-five hundred troops under Murray, began pushing upriver from Quebec in a flotilla of boats. The second, led by Lieutenant Colonel William Haviland, advanced northward from Crown Point, aided by effective harassing attacks on French settlements by Rogers' Rangers. The third and most powerful was commanded by Amherst himself, a force of ten thousand men descending the Saint Lawrence River from Lake Ontario. All three armies reached their objective during the first week of September. Montreal was confronted with an overwhelming force.

Vaudreuil saw that resistance would be futile, with the needless sacrifice of many lives. Therefore, on 8 September he and Amherst completed negotiations and agreed upon articles of capitulation providing for the end of all French military resistance throughout Canada. In effect, Canada was out of the war, releasing the British colonies from the age-old threat of raids and conquest. The transition to British military control was made with little difficulty, marking the demise of a vast colony that a few thousand Frenchmen had been courageously building and defending for a century and a half.

Even though the southern colonies were not directly involved in the climactic campaigning against the

French, they did not escape serious violence. Beginning in 1758 there had been increasing tension between some of the Cherokee and the frontier people of the Carolinas, leading eventually to killings. By early 1760, as Amherst was planning for the drive against Montreal, the situation along the Carolina frontier had become so critical that Amherst felt obliged to send down Colonel Archibald Montgomery with thirteen hundred regulars to suppress the hostile Indians. After burning some Cherokee villages, Montgomery returned to the north, leaving the problem unresolved. In 1761 Amherst sent another expedition, led by Lieutenant Colonel James Grant. Like Montgomery before him, Grant rampaged through the Cherokee country, destroying at least fifteen villages. By August the chastened Indians were ready for negotiations, which resulted in a treaty ending the Cherokee War in December 1761.

Naval warfare in the Caribbean had been carried on sporadically for years, much of it by well-armed privateers preying on enemy merchantmen, but fleets and expeditions also were sometimes active. During the early months of 1759 a British expedition forced the surrender of the French sugar island of Guadeloupe. Two years later the island of Dominica came under British control. In 1762 a British fleet and landing force conquered the French island of Martinique. Saint Lucia, Grenada, and Saint Vincent also were handily pocketed. By this time hitherto-neutral Spain had been drawn into the war alongside France, even as the long, debilitating Seven Years' War was drawing to a close.

Diplomats from Great Britain, France, and Spain assembled at Paris in 1762 to negotiate for a much-needed peace. Preliminary articles were signed in November, the final terms in the form of the Treaty of Paris three months later. These terms affected America in very significant ways with an impact whose force has continued to the present day. In the Caribbean the various islands were reassigned: Spain recovered Cuba, which had been taken by a British expedition; France regained Guadeloupe and Martinique plus two lesser islands; Great Britain retained Dominica, Grenada, Saint Vincent, and Tobago. In North America, France ceded to Great Britain not only all of Canada, Cape Breton Island, and Prince Edward Island, but also all of Louisiana east of the Mississippi River excepting New Orleans. Great Britain also took Spanish Florida, while Spain gained New Orleans and all French territorial claims west of the Mississippi. Thus, France lost everything it had owned or claimed in North America except for two small islands, Saint Pierre and Miquelon, off the south coast of Newfoundland for use as fishing bases. Great Britain had emerged victorious, mistress of a large and dynamic empire of which the colonies in North America, old and new, were a most important part.

WAR AND COLONIAL SOCIETY

During all of the colonial period, preparation for war, and the all-too-frequent military conflicts in which the British colonists became involved, had significant and often severely damaging effects on colonial life and society. Disruption of the economy, almost always a serious side effect of warfare, affected nearly everyone. Whenever large numbers of civilians were called into military service, the loss of labor was detrimental to agriculture, fisheries, industry, and the merchant marine. Many colonial wives and children worked desperately to keep farms or shops productive while husbands and older sons were away campaigning. Most Americans at that time lived by farming, often on small, laboriously worked tracts of land that afforded little more than a marginal existence subject to the vagaries of climate and weather. Adequate labor was a crucial element, especially during the two seasons of planting and harvest. These pressing demands often actually shaped the timing and length of military operations; if not taken into consideration by military planners and commanders, the result was likely to be a high rate of desertion.

Many colonial wives and children worked desperately to keep farms or shops productive while husbands and older sons were away campaigning.

Colonists residing in areas vulnerable to enemy incursion lived in daily fear of deadly violence, never knowing when they might suddenly hear the terrible sounds of a ruthless raid. When the danger became unbearable, these people would simply abandon their hard-won property to become homeless refugees living from hand to mouth, unless they were able to gain the hospitality of charitable relatives or acquaintances in safer places. Husbands and sons serving in the army generally received at best minimal material support from their colonial governments while facing the prospect of death by enemy action or, more commonly, disease. Thousands died tragically, far from home, and any death benefits later provided by the government to next of kin were likely to be small indeed.

Provincial governments were confronted during wartime by extraordinary expenses that could only be dealt with by three undesirable expedients: borrowing, higher taxation, and the printing of paper currency. Higher taxation imposed a financial strain on nearly every person and was politically unpopular, although often essential. The printing of large quantities of paper money was a tempting alternative seized on by more than one desperate colony, but the consequence was inevitable. As the volume of money in circulation increased, its value declined; the result was inflation, which, like higher taxes, hurt nearly everyone.

The presence of British regular forces was sometimes a welcome stimulus for the local economy, because the regulars came supplied with hard currency that they used to buy large quantities of provisions and other supplies required for extensive military operations. Such a situation gave provincial merchants an irresistible chance to make extraordinary profits by raising prices. The almost insatiable demands of the military, in turn, created an abnormal shortage of consumer goods. Again, the effect was inflationary for all inhabitants, and when the regulars had departed, the local economy would be thrown into reverse, with equally disruptive and painful effects.

Wartime hazards on the high seas also had a heavy impact on costs. Merchant seamen, contemplating the increased dangers of a calling that was hazardous enough in peacetime, naturally were inclined to dicker for higher wages. At the same time and for the same reason, the cost increased for maritime insurance covering ships and cargos. Loaded ships sometimes had to spend many days in port awaiting convoy or were otherwise delayed by wartime conditions. All these circumstances proved costly to the shipowners and merchants, who passed the burden on to the consumer. Ordinary people experienced financial hardship as they strained to meet the demands of inflation and taxation.

Some people, on the other hand, did find ways to profit from wartime conditions. They were often men with the right political connections, able to gain advance knowledge of new developments that they could turn to good account. Merchants sometimes lost heavily if they made a wrong guess, but more often scored major economic gains through luck or shrewdness. Many were in a position to take advantage of abnormal shortages, not scrupling to profiteer by raising prices. Others (or, indeed, the same ones) actually engaged in clandestine trade with enemy ports, typically in the West Indies. This, too, could be highly profitable. To both English and American government officials this common colonial practice seemed unpatriotic if not actually treasonable, but all attempts failed to stamp out the unlawful traffic.

Fur traders and land speculators always were prominent among those seeking profit from war. Those who succeeded best in that regard did so because they had the great advantage of position or intimacy with men of position. Many were themselves provincial governors, councillors, assemblymen, and military officers. Their shaping of policy and operations could be heavily influenced by their economic aspirations. Some of these men were both greedy and unscrupulous, taking the fullest possible advantage of their influence and power in order to acquire access to land and trade, with little regard for equity or legality. Seldom did they hesitate to take unfair advantage of the native Americans in particular, employing the tactics of deception or intimidation, with little or no regard for Indian rights or well-being. As a consequence of the colonial wars, native Americans suffered severe losses in population, land, and, perhaps most lasting and serious of all, self-esteem. Their tragic role as second-class citizens had begun.

In times of peace the various British colonies often were at odds with each other over boundaries, Indian relations, and other divisive issues. What is worse, they tended to persist in such rivalry even in time of war. This persistent habit often puzzled and frustrated British military commanders, who found their critical missions seriously hampered by intercolonial bickering. Selfish interests prompted individual colonies to hold back funds, manpower, and supplies needed for the overall war effort. In the colonial world a sense of common obligation and mutual responsibility proved slow to develop. To ardent imperialists, this could only be perceived as strangely perverse and unpatriotic.

There also were serious internal tensions within the colonies that affected the war effort. Two related struggles were of major importance—one between civil and military authority, the other between the executive and legislative branches of government. Central to these struggles was the fact that the provincial governor was both the chief civil official of the colony and also the commander in chief of its militia. Again and again in times of war, elected legislatures found ways to diminish the governor's control of military policy and practice. Whatever success they enjoyed came as a result of their effective control of financial appropriations, commonly called the power of the purse. Using their ability to withhold funds, these elected representatives managed to extract significant concessions from the governor by the threat of refusing to appropriate funds required for the war effort. The techniques that evolved in this process, to the embarrassment of both executive and military authority, represent a clear foreshadowing of the later revolutionary crisis.

THE ROAD TO REVOLUTION

The colonial wars had brought major contingents of British regular forces into the colonies in addition to the small garrisons stationed there. In the various and sometimes extensive campaigns of those wars, large numbers of hastily raised provincial troops had operated in close conjunction with the regulars, often under the direct or indirect command of regular officers. When not actually campaigning, the British regulars generally were encamped or quartered in close proximity to areas of civilian habitation. As provincial troops and colonists found themselves rubbing shoulders with imported professional soldiers and sailors, often under difficult conditions, Anglo-American friction was almost inevitable.

Officers in the British army were prone to view the general run of colonists with whom they came in contact as crude, uncultivated outlanders.

Nearly all of the commissioned officers in the British army had their origins in the aristocracy or the highest levels of the middle class. As such, they were prone to view the general run of colonists with whom they came in contact as crude, uncultivated outlanders. They scorned provincial troops in particular because of their all-too-obvious military deficiencies and slack discipline in contrast to the highly trained and strictly disciplined regulars under their immediate command. Undervaluing the Americans' long experience of Indian warfare, together with the earnest dedication of most of the provincial officers, the British were slow to adapt their own military practices to the peculiar, often extraordinarily difficult conditions prevailing in the North American wilderness, while dwelling upon the apparent sloppiness and unreliability of the provincials. Their contempt for the Americans, born of mounting exasperation in dealing with them under trying circumstances, became readily visible to all and left its sting.

The colonists, whether civilians or soldiers, naturally resented the self-satisfied superiority displayed by the regulars in their midst, all the more so because of its partial validity. To some degree Americans of that era did have an inferiority complex that they often relieved by highlighting the perceived faults of the regulars—snobbery, impiety, immorality, and brutish disregard of civil rights.

While British commanders were infuriated by the apparent lack of patriotism displayed by the colonists, as evidenced by the reluctance of provincial legislatures to appropriate ample funds in support of military operations, and the equally stubborn reluctance of their constituents to make any personal financial sacrifices in the common cause, Americans in general were inclined to resent the heavy demands made upon their resources. To make matters worse, American profiteering in the face of urgent military necessity had become notorious. It seemed to the British that the colonists were showing an incomprehensible lack of gratitude toward their rescuers and defenders. Inevitably, this negative impression traveled eastward across the ocean to emerge in Parliament itself as well as the royal chambers. Therefore, it is hardly surprising that Americans gained little praise or respect.

Prominent among the divisive issues was the problem of finding adequate quarters for regular troops stationed in or near provincial towns, such as Boston, Albany, New York, Philadelphia, and Charleston. In such urban centers military barracks were either nonexistent or insufficient for housing large numbers of soldiers. Consequently, the military commanders usually insisted that local authorities take whatever steps were necessary in order to make other buildings available. It seemed a reasonable request, but the local inhabitants generally resented and sometimes tried to resist having to open up their barns, sheds, and warehouses to a soldiery widely viewed as destructive and immoral. Most of all, the colonists feared being forced to take British troops into their own homes, an extreme expedient invoked only under the most pressing of circumstances. Indeed, forced quartering of troops in dwellings was considered by Americans a serious violation of civil rights guaranteed by the British Constitution.

Equally divisive, especially in coastal communities, was the Royal Navy's brutal practice of impressing seamen to help man the king's ships. All American merchant seamen were vulnerable, with the consequence that when the press gangs were active, seamen went into hiding. The danger of impressment inevitably caused a scarcity of hands for operating colonial shipping, with higher wages and increased costs. Moreover, the press gangs from the Royal Navy sometimes were none too particular about whom they seized, taking married landsmen as well as seamen. These notorious sweeps in colonial seaports aroused bitter resentment, occasionally leading to destructive rioting. In justification, British naval officers charged that deserters often were welcomed and concealed by the colonists.

Thus, although the Americans were glad to have British regular forces protecting them from their enemies, the necessary commingling of regulars and provincials created an ominous atmosphere of mutual dislike and distrust. Added to that was a growing American suspicion that the king's forces might readily be transformed from defenders into oppressors, an iron fist raised against colonial resistance to royal authority.

The demise of French power in 1760 opened the way for the colonists to resume their westward advance across the Appalachian Mountains, in the process further exploiting and dominating the Indian tribes. Widespread Indian resentment finally exploded with shocking violence in 1763. In May of that year, Pontiac, a chief of the Ottawa, suddenly began a close siege of the fort at Detroit, which was garrisoned by British regulars. The Indian uprising quickly spread from tribe to tribe across a wide area of the upper West. Soon at least eight major groups of Indians were involved, and before the end of June, eight British frontier forts had fallen, their defenders either slain or held in captivity. Among the major posts only Detroit and Fort Pitt, the latter an important British post at the Forks of the Ohio, still held out. To all appearances, the great gains achieved in defeating the French were about to dissolve, a disaster that the British commander in chief, Lord Jeffrey Amherst, was determined to prevent.

Massachusetts proved to be the most stubbornly resistant of the colonies and Boston by far the most unruly of urban centers.

In the recent struggle against the French and their Indian allies, Colonel Henry Bouquet of the Royal American Regiment was among those few British regulars who fully absorbed the lessons of defeat and learned well the techniques of wilderness warfare. Under orders from Amherst, Bouquet led a small expedition comprised mostly of regular troops to relieve Fort Pitt. On 5 August 1763, when this force was only about twenty-six miles from its objective, it was attacked by hostile Indians who quickly surrounded the furiously fighting troops. Refusing to panic, the British held fast throughout that night. The next morning Bouquet skillfully sucked in and then defeated the Indians by feigning a retreat, using his well-trained companies of light infantry to deliver the fatal blow. After the Battle of Bushy Run, as this encounter became known, Bouquet continued on his way and relieved the fort.

Detroit also was holding out. By October Indian confidence had passed its peak and was declining rapidly. Eventually, Pontiac himself brought the long siege of Detroit to an end, although he was not yet ready to admit that his cause was dead. That the cause was in fact dying, however, became more evident in 1764, as tribe after tribe met with British authorities and accepted terms. Finally, in July 1766 even the persistent Ottawa chief was brought to submission. Pontiac's uprising was over, and the British once again were in unchallenged control of the West.

In the following years the provincial militia almost never engaged in actual combat. A brief but notable exception was the Battle of Alamance Creek on 16 May 1771, the climax of a campaign of civil disobedience in the Carolinas. During the late 1760s people living in the frontier areas of North Carolina were becoming increasingly frustrated and angry because of serious abuses in local and colonial government. Eventually their anger erupted in violence that posed a threat to constituted authority. In the spring of 1771, as the frontiersmen (known as Regulators) took up arms, Governor William Tryon called out the militia. At Alamance Creek a well-armed force of more than a thousand militiamen confronted a body of ill-prepared and poorly organized Regulators nearly twice that size. Discipline, organization, and effective weaponry won the day for the militia, which readily defeated and scattered the opposition, thereby ending the threat to governmental authority. American frontiersmen, it seems, were not always the traditionally assumed great fighters.

In 1763 the royal government in London made two fateful decisions concerning the North American colonies. First, in order to maintain peace with the Indians in the newly acquired West, fifteen battalions of regular troops, approximately seven thousand men, were to be retained as a permanent garrison in North America. For the most part these troops were to be stationed at various posts along a vast arc extending from Halifax through the Saint Lawrence Valley and the Great Lakes, down through the trans-Appalachian West, then curving eastward to end at Saint Augustine in Florida. In other words, most of them would garrison remote western outposts, leaving the coastal area from New England down to Georgia, with the exception of army headquarters at New York, largely devoid of troops. Second, in order to aid the overburdened British treasury, saddled as it was with the enormous cost of the Seven Years' War and the elevated cost of maintaining and defending royal government in the colonies, those colonies were to be made to yield substantial revenue through more effective taxation. The existence of a standing army in North America, along with the British determination to tax the colonies, created conditions from which ultimately sprang the American Revolution.

After the suppression of Pontiac's War, there seemed to be less of a need for large numbers of regular troops in the remote West, while American resistance to the various attempts at taxation, such as the Stamp Act and the Townshend duties, showed the advantage of having adequate military forces in the East to uphold royal authority. Consequently, beginning in 1768 there occurred a significant shift of forces from the frontier to the coastal area, notably to such urban centers as New

York and Philadelphia. This, in turn, meant intensified friction between local inhabitants and unwelcome British troops, despite the best efforts of responsible commanders to prevent provocations and confrontations.

Massachusetts proved to be the most stubbornly resistant of the colonies and Boston by far the most unruly of urban centers, although other colonies and towns were far from placidly compliant. In order to protect and uphold royal authority in the Bay Colony, substantial numbers of regulars were dispatched to Boston, where they found themselves scorned by the populace. The Boston Massacre of 5 March 1770, in which five civilians were killed by soldiers on guard duty, and the audacious Boston Tea Party of 16 December 1773 in outright defiance of royal tax collectors, revealed only too clearly the deadly seriousness of the mounting crisis. Great Britain's answer was more repression and more troops.

By the end of 1774 the Boston garrison consisted of nine regiments plus elements of two others, trying to hold down the lid on a furiously boiling pot. In the adjacent countryside not actually occupied by the army, the patriot resistance movement thrived and even began making preparations for armed conflict. The provincial militia, many of whose older members had gained much practical experience in the colonial wars while taking the measure of the British army, provided a ready basis. Volunteers from the local companies were organized as minutemen, pledging themselves to be available as ready-armed soldiers on very short notice.

At the time, General Thomas Gage, an experienced officer in the British army who had been present at Braddock's defeat and had fought throughout the French and Indian War, was serving as both royal governor and commander in chief, with headquarters in Boston. On 14 April 1775 Gage received instructions

The Boston Massacre of 5 March 1770, in which five civilians were killed by British soldiers on guard duty, revealed only too clearly the deadly seriousness of the mounting crisis. (National Archives/chromolithograph by John Bufford)

from London requiring him to take more decisive action in repressing the incipient rebellion. Accordingly, he secretly ordered a large detachment from the garrison to invade the countryside, not for the purpose of fighting but to destroy the patriot party's accumulated store of weapons and munitions. The secret could not be kept. Riding well ahead of that expedition, Paul Revere and William Dawes warned every farm and village on the route that the redcoats were coming. Church bells began ringing and the minutemen began assembling, weapons in hand. As a result, when the head of the marching column of British troops approached the village green at Lexington in the early light of 19 April, there stood waiting for them a double line of about seventy apprehensive but determined minutemen. The deadly violence that erupted almost immediately, together with the subsequent battle at the north bridge in Concord, saw the opening shots of the American War for Independence.

BIBLIOGRAPHY

Guides to Further Reading

Carp, E. Wayne. "Early American Military History: A Review of Recent Work." *Virginia Magazine of History and Biography* 94 (July 1986).

Higginbotham, Don. "The Early American Way of War: Reconnaissance and Appraisal." *William and Mary Quarterly* 44 (April 1987).

Higham, Robin, ed. *A Guide to the Sources of United States Military History* (1975).

Higham, Robin, and Donald Mrozek, eds. *A Guide to the Sources of United States History, Supplement I* (1981), *Supplement II* (1986).

Relations with Indians

Aquila, Richard. *The Iroquois Restoration: Iroquois Diplomacy on the Colonial Frontier, 1701–1754* (1983).

Bannon, John Francis. *The Spanish Borderlands Frontier, 1513–1821* (1970).

Eccles, W. J. *The Canadian Frontier, 1534–1760* (1969; rev. 1983).

Eid, Leroy V. " 'National' War Among Indians of Northeastern North America." *Canadian Review of American Studies* 16 (Summer 1985).

Hirsch, Adam J. "The Collision of Military Cultures in Seventeenth-Century New England." *Journal of American History* 74 (March 1988).

Jacobs, Wilbur R. *Wilderness Politics and Indian Gifts: The Northern Colonial Frontier, 1748–1763* (1966).

———. *Dispossessing the American Indian: Indians and Whites on the Colonial Frontier* (1972).

Jennings, Francis. *The Invasion of America: Indians, Colonialism, and the Cant of Conquest* (1975).

———. *The Ambiguous Iroquois Empire: The Covenant Chain Confederation of Indian Tribes with English Colonies from Its Beginnings to the Lancaster Treaty of 1744* (1984).

———. *Empire of Fortune: Crowns, Colonies, and Tribes in the Seven Years' War in America* (1988).

Johnson, Richard R. "The Search for a Usable Indian: An Aspect of the Defense of Colonial New England." *Journal of American History* 64 (December 1977).

Leach, Douglas Edward. *The Northern Colonial Frontier, 1607–1763* (1966).

Richter, Daniel K., and James H. Merrill, eds., *Beyond the Covenant Chain: The Iroquois and Their Neighbors in Indian North America, 1600–1800* (1987).

Robinson, W. Stitt. *The Southern Colonial Frontier, 1607–1763* (1979).

Sheehan, Bernard W. "Indian-White Relations in Early America: A Review Essay." *William and Mary Quarterly* 26 (April 1969).

Slotkin, Richard. *Regeneration through Violence: The Mythology of the American Frontier, 1600–1860* (1973).

Sosin, Jack M. *The Revolutionary Frontier, 1763–1783* (1967).

Trelease, Allen W. *Indian Affairs in Colonial New York: The Seventeenth Century* (1960).

Vaughan, Alden T. *New England Frontier: Puritans and Indians, 1620–1675* (1965, rev. 1979).

Military Equipment, Organization, and Practice

Beattie, Daniel J. "The Adaptation of the British Army to Wilderness Warfare, 1755–1763." In *Adapting to Conditions: War and Society in the Eighteenth Century*, edited by Maarten Ultee (1986).

Breen, T. H. "English Origins and New World Developments: The Case of the Covenanted Militia in Seventeenth-Century Massachusetts." *Past & Present* 57 (November 1972).

Brown, M. L. *Firearms in Colonial America: The Impact on History and Technology, 1492–1792* (1980).

Cress, Lawrence Delbert. *Citizens in Arms: The Army and the Militia in American Society to the War of 1812* (1982).

Frey, Sylvia R. *The British Soldier in America: A Social History of Military Life in the Revolutionary Period* (1981).

Fortescue, John W. *A History of the British Army* (1889–1930).

Hamilton, Edward Pierce. "Colonial Warfare in North America." *Proceedings of the Massachusetts Historical Society* 80 (1969).

Houlding, J. A. *Fit for Service: The Training of the British Army, 1715–1795* (1981).

Mahon, John K. "Anglo-American Methods of Indian Warfare, 1676–1794." *Mississippi Valley Historical Review* 45 (September 1958).

Morton, Louis, "The Origins of American Military Policy." *Military Affairs* 22 (Summer 1958).

Peterson, Harold L. *Arms and Armor in Colonial America, 1526–1783* (1956).

Selesky, Harold E. *War and Society in Colonial Connecticut* (1990).

Shea, William L. *The Virginia Militia in the Seventeenth Century* (1983).

Shy, John W. "A New Look at Colonial Militia." *William and Mary Quarterly* 20 (April 1963).

Campaigns and Wars

Alden, John Richard. *John Stuart and the Southern Colonial Frontier: A Study of Indian Relations, War, Trade, and Land Problems in the Southern Wilderness, 1754–1775* (1944).

Anderson, Fred. *A People's Army: Massachusetts Soldiers and Society in the Seven Years' War* (1984).

Dederer, John Morgan. *War in America to 1775: Before Yankee Doodle* (1990).

De Forest, Louis Effingham, ed. *Louisbourg Journals, 1745* (1932).

Ferling, John E. *A Wilderness of Miseries: War and Warriors in Early America* (1980).

Frégault, Guy. *Canada: The War of the Conquest* (1969).
Gipson, Lawrence H. *The British Empire Before the American Revolution* (1936–1970).
Graham, Gerald S. *Empire of the North Atlantic: The Maritime Struggle for North America* (1950).
Graham, Gerald S., ed. *The Walker Expedition to Quebec, 1711* (1953).
Greene, Jack P. "The Seven Years' War and the American Revolution: The Causal Relationship Reconsidered." *Journal of Imperial and Commonwealth History* 8 (January 1980).
Hamilton, Edward P. *The French and Indian Wars: The Story of Battles and Forts in the Wilderness* (1962).
Higginbotham, Don. *George Washington and the American Military Tradition* (1985).
James, Alfred P., and Charles M. Stotz. "Drums in the Forest." *Western Pennsylvania Historical Magazine* 41 (Autumn 1958).
Knox, John. *An Historical Journal of the Campaigns in North America, for the Years 1757, 1758, 1759, and 1760* (1769, rev. 1914–1916).
Kopperman, Paul E. *Braddock at the Monongahela* (1977).
Lanning, John Tate. *The Diplomatic History of Georgia: A Study of the Epoch of Jenkins' Ear* (1936).
Leach, Douglas Edward. *Flintlock and Tomahawk: New England in King Philip's War* (1958, repr. 1966).
———. *Arms for Empire: A Military History of the British Colonies in North America, 1607–1763* (1973).
———*Roots of Conflict: British Armed Forces and Colonial Americans, 1677–1763* (1986).
Lloyd, Christopher. *The Capture of Quebec* (1959).
Mante, Thomas. *The History of the Late War in North-America, and the Islands of the West-Indies, Including the Campaigns of MDCCLXIII and MDCCLXIV Against His Majesty's Indian Enemies* (1772).
Millets Allan R., and Peter Maslowski. *For the Common Defense: A Military History of the United States of America* (1984).
Morgan, Gwenda. "Virginia and the French and Indian War: A Case Study of the War's Effects on Imperial Relations." *Virginia Magazine of History and Biography* 81 (January 1973).
Nicolai, Martin L. "A Different Kind of Courage: The French Military and the Canadian Irregular Soldier during the Seven Years' War." *Canadian Historical Review* 70 (March 1989).
O'Meara, Walter. *Guns at the Forks* (1965).
Pargellis, Stanley ed. *Military Affairs in North America, 1748–1765: Selected Documents from the Cumberland Papers in Windsor Castle* (1936).
Parkman, Francis. *France and England in North America,* (1865–1892).
Pease, Theodore Calvin, ed. *Anglo-French Boundary Disputes in the West, 1749–1763* (1936).
Peckham, Howard H. "Speculations on the Colonial Wars." *William and Mary Quarterly* 17 (October 1960).
———. *The Colonial Wars, 1689–1762* (1964).
Pencak, William. *War, Politics, & Revolution in Provincial Massachusetts* (1981).
Rawlyk, G. A. *Yankees at Louisbourg* (1967).
Rogers, Alan. *Empire and Liberty: American Resistance to British Authority, 1755–1763* (1974).
Rogers, Robert. *Journals* (1765, repr. 1961).
Samuel, Sigmund, ed. *The Seven Years' War in Canada, 1756–1763* (1934).
Savelle, Max. *The Diplomatic History of the Canadian Boundary, 1749–1763* (1940).
———. *The Origins of American Diplomacy: The International History of Angloamerica, 1492–1763* (1967).
Shy, John, *Toward Lexington: The Role of the British Army in the Coming of the American Revolution* (1965).
———. "Armed Force in Colonial North America: New Spain, New France, and Anglo-America." In *Against All Enemies: Interpretations of American Military History from Colonial Times to the Present,* edited by Kenneth J. Hagan and William R. Roberts (1986).
Stacey, C. P. *Quebec, 1759: The Siege and the Battle* (1959).
Stout, Neil R. *The Royal Navy in America, 1760–1775: A Study of Enforcement of British Colonial Policy in the Era of the American Revolution* (1973).
Swanson, Carl E. "American Privateering and Imperial Warfare, 1739–1748." *William and Mary Quarterly* 42 (July 1985).
Titus, James. *The Old Dominion at War: Society, Politics, and Warfare in Late Colonial Virginia* (1991).
Webb, Stephen Saunders. *The Governors-General: The English Army and the Definition of the Empire, 1569–1681* (1979).
———. *1676: The End of American Independence* (1985).
Wiener, Frederick B. *Civilians Under Military Justice: The British Practice Since 1689 Especially in North America* (1967).

— DOUGLAS EDWARD LEACH

The War of the Revolution

The end of the French and Indian War in America (1754–1763) and the Seven Years' War in Europe (1756–1763) shifted the international balance of power heavily in favor of Great Britain. By the terms of the Treaty of Paris, which the belligerents ratified in February 1763, France gave up title to virtually all of its territory in North America. French Canada and its lucrative fur trade now belonged to Great Britain. To regain Cuba, Spain turned over the Floridas to the British, who also maintained firm control of their valuable West Indian sugar islands. The British likewise strengthened their hold on the subcontinent of India, a preserve of the London-based East India Company. With a formidable navy able to protect its interests and impose its will around the globe, Great Britain had become the preeminent power among the nations of the world.

In North America, the fall of New France removed a huge psychological and physical weight from the minds and shoulders of the colonists. Freedom from the constant worry of French or French-led Indian attacks, as well as dreams of continued westward expansion and new trading ties within the empire, all excited the American colonists. Great Britain, however, had nearly doubled its national debt—up from £75 to £137 million—to finance the war effort. Conventional wisdom among the ministers of King George III was that the Americans had benefited most from this huge expenditure. These British leaders wanted something in return, most specifically an enhanced commitment from the colonists in paying for the ongoing costs of imperial administration of the colonies.

The first sixty years of the eighteenth century have been called the "era of salutary neglect."

The king's advisers expected something else as well—greater obedience to the imperial will. The first sixty years of the eighteenth century have been called the "era of salutary neglect," a time during which the home government allowed the colonists (or "provincials," as the British called them) to manage their own internal affairs as long as they conformed to the navigation laws governing imperial trade. For various reasons, permissive feelings quickly gave out during the Seven Years' War. Among other matters, imperial officials received regular reports about colonists who were trading with the enemy, even in war goods. The ministers also worried about the expense of continual wars with the Indian populace, should the expansive colonists be given full access to territory beyond the Appalachian Mountains. By 1763 the home government had decided to exercise more direct control over its North American colonies. The decision to do so provoked the crisis in relations that resulted in the War of the Revolution, which is also called the War for American Independence, the American Revolution, and the revolutionary war.

"THE SWEETS OF LIBERTY!": EVENTS LEADING TO THE WAR

British attempts to levy a variety of taxes, such as the Stamp Act of 1765 and the Townshend Duties Act of 1767, and to enforce long-ignored customs duties with backing from the Royal Navy angered the colonists, as did the Proclamation of 1763, which confined westward expansion to the headwaters of rivers flowing into the Atlantic Ocean. In the midst of a population boom, land-hungry Americans, whose numbers reached 1.6 million in 1760, were anxious to develop the fertile region beyond the mountains. The Crown, however, declared the trans-Appalachian West a huge Indian preserve.

Therefore, the colonists believed that Great Britain was not acting responsibly but tyrannically, especially that the taxes imposed by Parliament, a legislative body in which no colonist sat, were illegal and oppressive. Likewise, they appreciated that the regular force—on paper up to ten thousand troops—Great Britain kept in place after the Seven Years' War was not for their protection, but to serve as a roadblock to westward expansion. Worse yet, the British army was a potential vehicle of repression, a very real threat to their liberties and freedom.

These overt philosophical and political concerns highlighted a serious underlying problem between the English parent nation and the colonies. As the British empire emerged, it was as much an economic venture as anything else. Home government leaders presumed that the colonists existed to stimulate the economy of Great Britain by supplying raw materials and purchasing finished products. They never considered American provincials to be coequal partners in the imperial en-

On 23 September 1779, Captain John Paul Jones (bottom right) boarded and captured the British frigate HMS Serapis *in one of the most famous naval battles of the Revolutionary War. When the British demanded Jones's surrender, he reportedly shouted, "I have not yet begun to fight." (National Archives/engraving from a painting by Alonzo Chappel)*

terprise; rather, they classified them as subordinate constituents, or second-class citizens.

Imperial leaders clung doggedly to their attitudes of provincial inferiority, despite the reality of what was happening in British North America three thousand miles away. To survive the colonists had long since proved themselves self-reliant, which in turn bred strong feelings of self-assurance. By the 1760s they wanted recognition for their contributions to making the British empire the most powerful in the world. After all, the provinces had become valuable because of their travail, so valuable, as one leading colonist wrote, that Great Britain "could not long subsist as an independent kingdom" had it experienced "the loss of her colonies" to France and Spain during the late war.

General James Wolfe referred to the colonists as "the dirtiest, most contemptible, cowardly dogs that you can conceive."

In expressing their self-confidence, Americans were asking to be treated with the same respect as subjects back in Great Britain. Their resentment came to the fore whenever home officials reminded them of their provincial status, which was particularly true when the colonists fought alongside British regulars in the imperial wars that occurred from 1689 to 1763. They had to defer to the judgment of British military officers who quite often had no idea how to fight in the American wilderness. What the colonists saw was that English ways and leaders were not always correct. When they dared to question, what they experienced were attitudes of contempt, so pithily summarized by General James Wolfe when he referred to the provincials under his command before Quebec as "the dirtiest, most contemptible, cowardly dogs that you can conceive."

To their disappointment, the colonists found at the end of the French and Indian War that the old pejorative attitudes were still in place, especially with home government leaders now demanding greater obedience than ever before. In response, they defied and resisted the new imperial legislation. They turned to economic boycotts and crowd actions in rendering the Stamp Act impotent, and they shunned statements from Parliament about the political supremacy of that body. Perhaps even more significant, British actions fostered a spirit of intercolonial cooperation that had heretofore not existed.

Prior to the Stamp Act, attempts at intercolonial accord (the Albany Convention and Plan of 1754 and several treaties with Indians) had only worked briefly, but for the most part mutual distrust between the American provinces was the watchword. The Stamp Act changed this pattern. Crowd protests and the destruction of property owned by designated stamp distributors occurred in almost all of the colonies because the act affected every province and every colonist. Even after Parliament rescinded the Act in 1766, like-minded Americans began corresponding. What may be described as a loosely organized infrastructure evolved. Organized in 1765, Boston's Sons of Liberty and their principal leader, Samuel Adams, were in the forefront of the burgeoning intercolonial movement. Such was the spirit of unrest caused by the Stamp Act that events began to assume a life of their own.

In 1768 British customs officials sought to impose duties on smuggled goods brought to Boston on John Hancock's vessel *Liberty*. The Sons of Liberty intervened and a riot broke out. With most British troops scattered elsewhere, two regiments of British regulars had to be dispatched from England to restore order. Here was the long arm of tyranny that worried colonists had long feared. As one exclaimed: "Good God! What can be worse to a people who have tasted the sweets of liberty! Things have come to an unhappy crisis." These words proved prophetic, especially after a small detachment of regulars fired into a crowd menacing them before the Boston Customs House on 5 March 1770. The so-called Boston Massacre resulted in the shooting deaths of five local inhabitants, the first martyrs, as outraged Americans perceived matters, in defying the evil designs of an increasingly tyrannical parent state.

Farther south this spirit of unrest manifested itself in different ways. In South Carolina the struggle for power between coastal planters and backcountry farmers led to a series of skirmishes. In 1768 North Carolina backcountry people, demanding an end to lawlessness, formed themselves into a self-policing force and called themselves "Regulators." Their growing power resulted in a confrontation with the militia loyal to the royal government. After fighting at Alamance Creek in 1771, the Regulators were broken up, but unrest and violence continued to plague the colonies.

With ever-mounting vigilance, the colonists kept on guard against any assaults on their fundamental rights. In 1765 Parliament amended the Mutiny Act, adding a supplement called the Quartering Act. As in England, the act allowed military commanders to place, or "quarter," troops in local homes—at fair rental rates—when barracks were absent. When put into effect in America, this practice led to additional rioting. In New York City during 1770 at the Battle of Golden Hill, redcoated British regulars ("Lobsterbacks") put down a riot with bayonets and birdshot, wounding thirty to forty colonists. Breaking the law in the interest of liberty became increasingly acceptable. For example, in 1772 the British customs vessel *Gaspée,* adept at capturing smugglers, ran aground in the waters of Rhode Island. Local patriots boarded the ship and burned it.

Alleged British transgressions created the need for more efficient intercolonial organization, and the colonists started to form committees of correspondence. These committees opened lines of communication among the provinces and kept Americans in even the most rural hamlets aware of events. After the outbreak of hostilities, citizen groups formed committees of safety, which managed the local militia, kept the spirit of rebellion alive, and harassed and evicted neighbors still loyal to the Crown.

In the meantime, committees of correspondence played a vital role in organizing ongoing resistance, particularly after May 1773, when Parliament passed the Tea Act. Part of the idea was to get the colonists to purchase East India Company tea, with the Townshend duty of three pence per pound attached to the price. On 16 December Bostonians showed their contempt for this plan by dumping £10,000 worth of East India tea into the harbor. Such open defiance convinced the king and Parliament that the colonists, particularly those in New England, had to be brought under control.

The home government responded in March and May 1774 with the Coercive Acts, which among other matters closed the port of Boston until local citizens paid for losses from the Tea Party and put the Massachusetts government under the authority of an all-powerful governor. When the Crown selected General Thomas Gage, commander in chief of British military forces in North America, to serve as the new Massachusetts governor, the colonists again shouted tyranny. Twelve colonies expressed their unity through the meeting of the First Continental Congress (5 September to 26 October) in Philadelphia, which advised the Americans to prepare for armed resistance to protect their lives, liberties, and property. Even as they did so, Lord Frederick North, the king's chief minister, stated, "The die is now cast, the colonies must either submit or triumph." The stage was set for a military showdown.

THE AMERICAN WAY OF WAR

The American way of war represented the system that society and government imposed on its military forces during the revolutionary war, that is, the basic attitudes, ideas, myths, practices, and traditions regarding war, the military, and military leadership that evolved in American society from colonial times. Briefly summarized, there were three principal influences—geographic, philosophic, and religious—none mutually exclusive and all with varying influences upon the others.

Geographically, North America offered colonists conditions and opponents unlike any faced in Europe. The Atlantic Ocean was a giant moat, precluding the necessity for a large regular, or, in the parlance of the times, standing, army or navy. To the colonists, regular or professional armed forces were expensive, wasteful, and potentially menacing to the liberties of a people fearful of tyranny. Philosophically, from the earliest colonial times, Americans loathed standing armies and anything that smacked of militarism. A regular army controlled by one man (Caesarism) or a small coterie of officers (Praetorianism) could usurp public liberty. Therefore, the colonists had opted for a military comprised of citizen-soldiers or militia—full-time citizens and part-time soldiers. The ruling colonial polity, which also controlled the purse strings, appointed the commander, thus ensuring subordination of the military to the civil government.

In peace the militia system worked well, but in war it did not provide for a well-trained, stable source of disciplined soldiers. During the revolutionary war George Washington and other military leaders decried the militia system, and reforms extending enlistments for service in the Continental army to three years or the length of the war only partially solved the problem. What Washington wanted were real soldiers. Time, training, and experience gave him the hard-core veterans he needed to fight and prevail over Britain's highly disciplined professionals.

The crusader impulse of Americans, born of religious fervor and fear of massacres in the seventeenth century, was adequate for raising companies to fight Indians or to control rebellious slaves. Expressed in terms of patriotism, it brought many citizens into the ranks at the outset of the Revolution, but this patriotic ardor was short-lived. Only peer pressure, esprit de corps, personal loyalty to certain officers, enlistment bounties, and promises of regular pay, decent food and clothing, and free land at war's end kept a barely adequate number of patriots, most of them in some way destitute, serving in the Continental army's rank and file for the duration of the war.

AMERICAN AND BRITISH STRATEGY: 1775–1783

Grand strategy may be defined as the general design of a nation, the overarching historical theme governing the geopolitical goals and policies of a country during peace and war. Great Britain's grand strategy—before, during, and after the War of the Revolution—centered on its ancient rivalry with France. The American war, although important, was more of a sideshow to the main event. It was another round in what some have called the second Hundred Years' War, a seemingly endless contest between the rival European powers and their allies that finally ended in 1815 with the defeat of Napoleon at Waterloo.

Losing thirteen of the North American seaboard colonies had the potential to hurt the British empire in a variety of ways. It would have been catastrophic if the French and other Europeans interceded on the rebel side and captured Canada, India, and especially England's productive West Indian sugar islands. To avoid French intervention, Britain's specific strategy was, initially, to snuff out the colonial rebellion as quickly as possible militarily or by any other means.

British strategy for 1776 involved sending massive forces to America to overawe the rebels while at the same time offering terms for a peaceful accord. If the latter failed, this great military force would carry out its mission, using New York City as the primary base for operations. The idea was to regain control of the Hudson River–Lake Champlain corridor running north to Canada before sweeping eastward to break the will of rebellion in New England, the initial hotbed of American resistance.

Military movements would also act as a beacon light to gain active support from what the king's ministers presumed was a large but cowed loyalist population. The belief that thousands of Americans remained loyal to the Crown was central to all British strategy. After all, if most colonists were pro-rebel, pro-independence, and anti-George III, then the war made no sense. The British understood that trying to reconquer thirteen colonies without strong loyalist backing was militarily impossible, politically unfeasible, and economically senseless. Therefore, some sort of settlement, such as granting Americans commonwealth status or limited independence, would be much wiser than fighting a costly war.

Following the entry of France into the war in early 1778, British strategy underwent serious modification. The French now became a major focus of attention. Military operations in the rebellious colonies became

On 16 December 1773, a group of Bostonians disguised as Indians showed their contempt for a British tax on tea by dumping £10,000 worth of East India tea into Boston Harbor. Such open defiance convinced King Richard III that the colonists had to be brought under control. (National Archives/lithograph by Sarony and Major)

secondary or tertiary to defense of the homeland and revenue-producing areas of the empire. In 1779–1780, limited military successes in the American South caused British leaders to attempt to employ that elusive loyalist majority while utilizing as few British troops as possible. A British army would be the cutting tool, but pacification and civil governance fell upon the loyalists. This southern strategy came extremely close to succeeding but ultimately failed.

After the Declaration of Independence in 1776, everything changed.

As for American strategies, grand or otherwise, initially they were of a reactive nature. Military leaders tried to counter expected British operations, sometimes successfully, sometimes not. After the Declaration of Independence in 1776, everything changed. Americans now had a grand strategy—defense of their self-proclaimed republic and their political liberties. For an actual military strategy, Washington realized after the failure of the New York campaign of 1776 that he could not hold every city and square inch of America without a fleet capable of gaining tactical ascendancy over the Royal Navy. As long as British forces remained near America's extensive coastline, the Royal Navy would ensure their mobility and supply. Frittering away his small army in a series of doomed defensive stands made little sense. The fate of his army and that of the Revolution, Washington keenly understood, were inextricably bound together; he had to keep his army alive and active in the field if the Revolution was to succeed.

Having a Continental force, however small, that was capable of continuing the fight governed Washington's thinking. Cities, even the capital at Philadelphia, could fall, but on the shoulders of his tiny army rested the hopes and dreams of American independence. Thus was born Washington's decision to "protract the war," to "avoid a General Action, or put anything to the Risque, unless compelled by a necessity, into which we ought never to be drawn." Washington would trade space for time with the goal of outlasting the British.

Because British land forces depended on the Royal Navy for supplies and protection, the farther one drew their armies inland, the more British supply lines and columns would be susceptible to disruption. Washington's approach represented much more than a simple war of attrition; it was the timeless strategy of the weak against the strong. Time would allow rebel officers and soldiers to harden into skilled military veterans. Time might see the entrance of France—and even Spain and the Netherlands—into the war on the American side. A protracted war also conjured up all sorts of internal points of stress in Britain; as early as 1776 a strong opposition was developing in Parliament.

Later in the war, after the British began serious operations in the South, one of Washington's most talented lieutenants, General Nathanael Greene, took the basic strategy of his mentor and turned it into an art form. Without winning a single battle, Greene, a master of the operational art, helped ensure conditions that saw the British lose an army at Yorktown.

INTERNATIONAL DIPLOMATIC REALITIES

American foreign policy during the War for Independence had three interconnected objectives: to gain recognition for the United States as a legitimate nation; to find sources of badly needed financial support and military supplies; and to have a powerful European nation, preferably France, intervene militarily on the side of the rebels. The amateur diplomats America sent abroad to carry out these objectives—Benjamin Franklin, Arthur Lee, Silas Deane, Ralph Izard in Paris; John Adams in Amsterdam; and John Jay in Madrid, among others—succeeded admirably. On the surface, this spoke well for their efforts, even when remembering that the aspirant republic was little more than a pawn in an ongoing contest of wills among the most powerful nations of Europe.

France felt extreme humiliation over the loss of its North American empire. Even in 1775, the new French foreign minister, Charles Gravier, Comte de Vergennes, burned with a hatred of England and a desire for revenge. Even before a shooting war started, Vergennes perceived an opportunity to strike a blow against his hated foe. Under the courtier and playwright Pierre Augustin, Caron de Beaumarchais, the French established a bogus trading firm, Roderigue Hortalez et Cie., to funnel military supplies to the colonies. Such vital French aid helped keep American forces in the field during the early part of the war.

The Americans also desired full diplomatic recognition. Following the Saratoga campaign, the French government in February 1778 recognized the United States and forged a military and trading alliance with the new nation. Much of this success has been attributed to Franklin's wooing of the French populace, but at its heart, the ministers of Louis XVI had much less interest in promoting a republican form of government than in striking a major blow against their English enemies. Along with Catherine II of Russia, Vergennes played a major role in establishing the League of Armed Neutrality of 1780, which Denmark and Sweden joined immediately, followed by Portugal, the Netherlands, Prussia, Austria, and the Two Sicilies within the next two years. Great Britain had tipped the European scales of power too heavily in its favor by the 1760s; to correct the imbalance, Europe as a whole offered virtually no support in putting down the American rebellion.

Because of these circumstances, British foreign policy was primarily reactive. The ministry sought to disrupt the forging of any accords by American diplomats. The British organized a very effective secret service operation, and agents followed Americans throughout Europe, rifling through their papers and getting vital information to London long before it reached Philadelphia. The wily British even penetrated the American legation in Paris through its secretary, Edward Bancroft, who was a British agent. Learning of the French alliance from Bancroft long before word got to Congress, the British dispatched a commission led by the head of their secret service, Frederick Howard, Lord Carlisle, and his chief administrator, Sir William Eden, to offer a peace settlement to the rebels. With the French alliance, however, the war was going well for the Americans in the spring of 1778. Nothing came of this effort.

COMPETING NAVAL FORCES

In many respects, the War of the Revolution was very much a series of naval encounters. Major British campaign successes can be directly linked to the superiority of the Royal Navy. Because of its naval supremacy the British landed vast numbers of troops whenever they wished in the face of little American resistance. The Royal Navy also had to protect the long British supply line that stretched three thousand miles across the Atlantic. With few exceptions, rebel sailors could do little more than snipe at the British giant until the French fleet arrived in American waters.

For the average seaman, life aboard an English warship was tantamount to slavery, except that most slaves received better treatment.

Simply put, the Royal Navy from 1775 to 1783 was the finest navy in the world. No matter what noteworthy naval leaders the Americans produced and what sailing ships they built, they could never match the British fleets, but neither could the French, Spanish, or Dutch fleets or any combination of these navies.

The Royal Navy was not without its shortcomings. In 1775 it was living in the glory of past wars. Its ships were aging, literally rotting away, and many of its admirals were in their dotage and better off in retirement than at sea. Renewed warfare soon disclosed these problems. Young officers who participated in campaigns either against the Americans, such as Sir Edward Pellew at Valcour Island, or the French, such as Horatio Nelson in the West Indies, gained valuable experience after 1775, which allowed them to play dominant roles in the wars of the French Revolution and Napoleonic wars.

For the average seaman, life aboard an English warship was tantamount to slavery, except that most slaves received better treatment. The "jolly jack tar" of legend, sipping his tot of rum and singing "Hearts of Oak," certainly existed, but, as with every American soldier being perceived as a coonskin-capped sharpshooter, these scenes were few and far between. "Rum, bum, and the lash," as Sir Winston Churchill was fond of saying, ensured the iron discipline demanded in both war and peace by a captain of an eighteenth-century ship-of-the-line that had sixty to one hundred mounted cannons. Any such battleship had more firepower than any army that fought in the Revolution. To sail such a vessel twenty yards or less alongside another and fire broadside after broadside into an opponent while accepting the same in return, to force barefoot men to climb 150 feet up swaying masts and onto slippery ropes to unfurl sails, to do this and more required sailors of indomitable will.

Most naval officers were not cruel men, but only rigid discipline over their crew members could assure some prospect of survival in naval encounters. In matters of discipline, British naval officers were little different from their American cousins. Shirking of duty simply did not work at sea. American officers had to be as strong-willed as their British counterparts, because they faced the same conditions.

Many Americans went to sea on privateering ships, which were merchant and fishing vessels converted to warships by bringing artillery aboard. They became master fighters in a guerrilla war at sea. Operating under the aegis of the Continental Congress, privateers fought for their country and themselves. They targeted primarily enemy supply ships, because they could keep significant portions of their captured loot as pay. It was dangerous employment, and many privateersmen finished the war languishing in British prisons. Because it was also lucrative work, American naval captains, such as Joshua Barney and John Paul Jones, found themselves chronically short of experienced seamen.

As many as two thousand privateering vessels entered the war by 1783, and they took at least six hundred British prizes (the American navy captured about two hundred enemy vessels). The privateersmen were so effective that they forced the British, who were dependent upon a seaborne supply system, to reinstitute time-consuming convoys that required additional naval escort forces. The effect was to weaken any attempted blockade of American port towns and make it possible for patriot ships to roam far and wide in search of war matériel to sustain the rebellion on land.

Man for man and ship for ship, the tiny patriot navy comported itself well during the war. The largest American ships were frigates, carrying between twenty and forty guns. The Americans never had a ship-of-the-line. John Paul Jones ("I have not yet begun to fight"), best remembered for commanding the *Bonhomme Richard* against the British frigate HMS *Serapis* off the English coast in September 1779, had taken the war into the British Isles, raiding along the coast of Scotland. Despite such dramatic encounters, the Continental navy was never able to negate the superior fleet strength of the Royal Navy in either its home waters or near America.

With the intervention of the French in 1778, the naval war took on a new dimension. A planned French invasion of England almost caught the Royal Navy napping. Only poor weather and supply shortages ended what might have been a disaster for the British. French amphibious operations in the West Indies, the Franco-Spanish siege of Gibraltar, and even French naval operations in and about India turned the War of the Revolution into a worldwide conflict and taxed the outer limits of the strength of the Royal Navy. Later, in the closing months of the war, the Royal Navy exerted its supremacy over the French in the West Indies. For one brief moment in 1781, however, the French gained tactical ascendancy off the Virginia Capes, a key factor in the victory at Yorktown.

THE MAKEUP OF LAND FORCES

During the revolutionary war the basic tactical infantry unit was the battalion or regiment, usually one and the same in both the American and British armies. Battalions were composed of a field-grade commander, either a colonel or lieutenant colonel, several unassigned junior officer aides, and eight to ten companies of varying size (at full strength a company might have sixty to one hundred privates). Each company had a captain in command, seconded by two or more lieutenants and ensigns, and several noncommissioned officers. Even though captains were the ranking company-grade officers, sergeants managed daily assignments, including such matters as drill.

In the regular British army, the battalion or regiment was more than a military designation. It was home for the soldiers, and their brother soldiers were their family. British soldiers enlisted (or were enlisted by having a recruiting sergeant ply them with liquor and press the "king's gold" into their hands) for up to twenty years or more. Many down-and-outers chose the army over prison or the gallows, but by the years of the revolutionary war quite a few British soldiers were victims of the unstable economy in Great Britain.

Officers, on the other hand, were invariably gentlemen with political connections and peerages, in some cases the younger sons of nobility. They purchased commissions and learned their trade on the job, because there was little in the way of formal military education. A few officers advanced on meritorious performance, but purchase was the standard means of gaining promotion. Officers, of course, could resign by selling their commissions at any time, and those who survived until retirement received half-pay pensions for life.

Americans had no such system of enlistment in place, and republican ideology forbade anything that smacked of an officer caste. Until 1777 patriots enlisted to serve in the ranks for up to one full campaign season; after that, recruiters demanded enlistment terms for three years or the length of the war, a reform Washington loudly called for when his army all but disintegrated during 1776. Foot soldiers elected their company-grade officers, but this system, like purchase in the British army, somehow worked out as if all had been appointed—some officers turned out well, others less so.

Death in combat was often preferable to being wounded; large lead musket balls caused devastating wounds, and, save for amputation, surgeons could do little.

Life in the ranks, just as it was for sailors aboard ship, consisted of monotonous weeks full of basic camp routines—constant drill and duty, pitiful food, rare moments when paid if paid at all, and harsh, even brutal discipline—interspersed with moments of sheer terror in combat. In the British army, up to sixty soldiers per regiment were allowed to have their wives and families accompany them, and in the Continental army the ratio was two-thirds. Women "on the ration" performed auxiliary service, from cooking and washing to caring for the sick and wounded and scavenging the enemy dead after battle.

Death in combat was often preferable to being wounded; large caliber lead musket balls caused devastating wounds, and, save for amputation, surgeons of either army could do little for the wounded. As ineffective as the treatment was of battle wounds, most deaths in both armies came from camp diseases. The American rebels often inoculated themselves against smallpox, but typhus, yellow fever, malaria, and dozens of other diseases swept through their camps, killing an estimated ten thousand soldiers.

In the British army, Englishmen were in the minority. Many troops came from Ireland, Scotland, and Wales. There was also a German contingent, some thirty thousand mercenaries over half of whom came from Hesse-Cassel in Germany. Many loyalists also organized regiments, but British officers rarely used them effectively. English officers simply could not get over their condescending attitudes toward the fighting prowess of American provincials. British officers, by comparison, were with rare exception predominantly English.

At the outset of the war, American rank-and-filers had a middle-class character. After the campaign debacle of 1776, propertied citizens rarely performed long-term regular service but did on occasion come out for short-term militia duty. Meantime, economically destitute and nonfree persons increasingly filled Washington's ranks. Many post-1776 Continentals were young, landless, poverty-stricken males whose families, when they had families, were also in desperate economic straits. Some criminals opted for Continental service rather than face the hangman's noose or the lash. In time, captured British regulars and even Germans joined the ranks, as did indentured servants and black slaves who served as substitutes for their masters. On rare occasions women engaged in combat, such as the legendary heroine Molly Pitcher, whose real name was Mary Ludwig Hays McCauley, an impoverished domestic servant before the war who helped fire a cannon

On rare occasions women engaged in combat. The legendary Molly Pitcher (whose real name was Mary Ludwig Hays McCauley), a domestic servant, helped fire a cannon at the Battle of Monmouth in June 1778. (National Archives/engraving from a painting by Alonzo Chappel)

at the Battle of Monmouth in June 1778. Field-grade and general-grade officers invariably were men of substantial means before the war. Over time, then, the Continental army took on more of the caste character of the regular British army.

WEAPONS AND TACTICS

To a large measure, weapons dictated doctrine and tactics. In the War of the Revolution, this meant that on both land and sea the closer one was to the enemy and the faster one could fire, the better one's chance of success. The weapons—artillery and muskets—employed by all the combatants were pretty much the same. They were single-shot, black powder–fired weapons; the smoke from this powder quickly enshrouded the combatants, obscuring movement on both sides.

The basic infantry weapon was a smoothbore, muzzleloading, flintlock musket that fired a very heavy .69 to .80 caliber round (by comparison, a modern M-16 fires a .223 caliber round). Standing four and a half to five feet (depending upon make and model) and topped with a wicked eighteen-inch socket bayonet, the smoothbore musket made a formidable weapon for close-order fighting, because it was notoriously inaccurate beyond fifty yards.

According to contemporary European field manuals and doctrine, an infantry battalion stood in three lines, loaded, shouldered their weapons, then, on command, the first line fired one unaimed volley at the approaching enemy. The first line then kneeled to reload while the second line fired, and so on. In the British army a soldier was trained to fire three rounds per minute. Multiplied by three lines, this meant that an advancing detachment had to withstand nine rounds per minute at extremely close range. If the attackers could fire first or withstand the first volley, they could then close with bayonets.

European doctrine specifically forbade aiming at an individual target; the objective was to fire concentrated volley after volley downrange. Because weapons were so inaccurate and it was assumed that soldiers were too untrustworthy to aim and fire at will, officers and sergeants (noncommissioned officers) directed every step in each volley of fire. To load and shoot required upward of twenty specific steps, and to do so on a smoky battlefield while splattered with gore and in the face of a fierce enemy required almost inhuman discipline. Such situations were the reason why it took some two to six years of training to turn a civilian into a regular soldier. Americans, more accustomed to shooting game for the dinner table, were prone to aim at their targets, which helped their accuracy, but lessened the concentrated force of their volleys. Either way, aimed or unaimed, being hit by a round, over one ounce of lead, had a nasty effect on the human body.

American folklore has enshrined the legendary sharpshooting rifleman as the hero of the Revolution. Riflemen such as those commanded by Daniel Morgan of Virginia were very effective skirmishers and snipers, but their "Pennsylvania" or "Kentucky" long rifles required careful loading that took up to one minute, totally unsuitable for the volley line. (A rifle had grooves cut inside the barrel, imparting spin to the fired projectile, which enhanced its accuracy and range; a smoothbore was easier to load but lacked the rifling.) In the hands of a skilled riflemen targets up to three hundred yards could be struck and killed. Riflemen were deployed ahead of the major battle lines as skirmishers to snipe at opposing officers and artillerymen. When opposing lines started to close, skirmishers pulled back.

The British and French employed standard issue infantry weapons (the British Brown Bess musket remained the regulation piece through Waterloo), while Americans had a hodgepodge of infantry weapons. Rebel soldiers came to battle with every weapon imaginable, which created all sorts of problems in resupply.

As for artillery, both on land and at sea, cast-iron and bronze cannons ranging from 3- to 32-pounders were in common use (the nomenclature refers to the weight of the ball fired). On land the larger cannons were primarily employed only in sieges—they were simply too heavy for the battlefield. Artillery units employed canister (cans filled with musket balls) for close-in infantry support. At sea carronades and other enormous cannons capable of firing heavy iron balls dictated operational strategy. Tactics usually consisted of trying to gain the wind advantage (wind coming from behind the ship, pushing it forward), before closing on enemy vessels to fire thunderous broadsides. A broadside involved every cannon on one side of a warship firing at virtually the same time, an awesome amount of firepower at short range. Ship-shaking broadsides cast up huge splinters even as marines fired at or tossed grenades at opposing crews. The smoke and noise were horrendous. Casualties were extremely high in such actions, and contemporary reports that the scuppers (deck drains) ran red with blood were commonplace.

MILITARY OPERATIONS: 1775

Hostilities between British regulars and the colonists broke out in Massachusetts during April 1775, in what became a year of many surprises. The British sought to restore order with the troops on hand, but this police action failed. By the end of the year, one patriot army had a British force bottled up in Boston, and another was hammering at the gates of Quebec. The king's min-

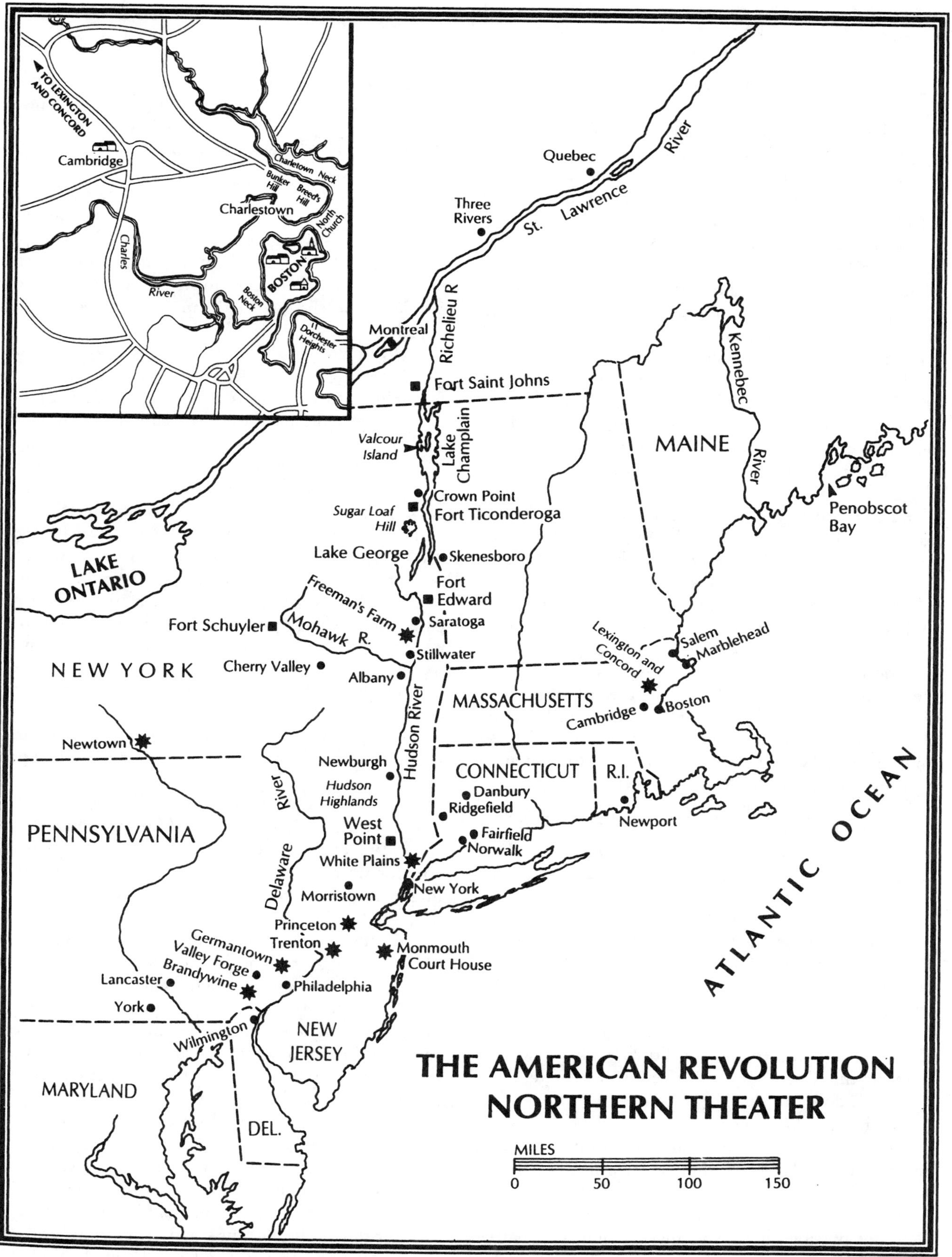
THE AMERICAN REVOLUTION
NORTHERN THEATER
TO LEXINGTON AND CONCORD
Cambridge
Charlestown Neck
Bunker Hill
Breed's Hill
Charlestown
North Church
Charles
River
BOSTON
Boston Neck
Dorchester Heights
Quebec
St. Lawrence
River
Three Rivers
Montreal
Richelieu R
Fort Saint Johns
Kennebec
River
MAINE
Valcour Island
Lake Champlain
Crown Point
Fort Ticonderoga
Sugar Loaf Hill
Penobscot Bay
Lake George
Skenesboro
LAKE ONTARIO
Fort Edward
Freeman's Farm
Saratoga
Fort Schuyler
Mohawk R.
Stillwater
NEW YORK
Cherry Valley
Albany
Lexington and Concord
Salem
Marblehead
MASSACHUSETTS
Cambridge
Boston
Newtown
Hudson River
Newburgh
CONNECTICUT
R.I.
Hudson Highlands
Danbury
Ridgefield
Newport
River
PENNSYLVANIA
West Point
Fairfield
Norwalk
Delaware
White Plains
Morristown
New York
ATLANTIC OCEAN
Princeton
Trenton
Monmouth Court House
Germantown
Valley Forge
Brandywine
Lancaster
Philadelphia
York
Wilmington
NEW JERSEY
MARYLAND
DEL.
MILES
0
50
100
150

isters began to realize that they had a real war on their hands. Secretary for American Affairs Lord George Sackville Germain took the lead in formulating a strategy to bring the rebellion to a speedy resolution in 1776 before other powers, such as France, could use the imperial rift to undermine Britain's imperial dominance in world affairs.

LEXINGTON AND CONCORD: THE WAR BEGINS. In February 1775, the king and Parliament declared Massachusetts to be in open rebellion. This action gave General Thomas Gage all the power he needed to enforce British laws, even if that amounted to shooting down colonists arbitrarily. If his regulars could crush the Massachusetts rebels quickly, potential troublemakers in other colonies would take pause.

Even before the home government announced its declaration, a nervous Gage futilely tried to stamp out the brushfire of armed resistance that was flaring in New England. During the winter of 1774–1775 New England colonists began to drill in militia companies and to accumulate arms and gunpowder, some seizing military stores from under the noses of the British. Angry patriots also terrorized loyal inhabitants and drove some of them to the protection of Boston with coats of tar and feathers. Later historians have accused Gage of a lack of ruthlessness because, in part, he had an American-born wife. In considering the size of his force (fewer than four thousand) and the breadth of his mission, a more forceful policy only would have hastened the outbreak of hostilities. Unlike most of his British counterparts, Gage had some respect for the potential fighting prowess of the Americans.

"Fire if you have the courage, but I doubt it."

General Gage responded to the incendiary activities of the rebels by fortifying Boston Neck in September 1774. He also ordered out raiding parties that met with varying measures of success—one abortive raid on Salem in February 1775 came close to starting the war. During this search-and-destroy mission one resident, Sarah Tarrant, earned Barbara Fritchie–like honors by taunting the British soldiers, "Fire if you have the courage, but I doubt it."

In mid-April Gage received "secret orders" from London that directed him to take immediate military action against "a rude Rabble without plan, without concert, and without conduct." Hoping to avoid bloodshed, the general was to arrest the principal incendiaries. If that were not possible, he was to make a dramatic martial statement by using his troops against a populace "unprepared to encounter with a regular force." The home government simply assumed that mere provincials would never stand up to massed British arms.

Through their network of informers, Boston patriots received word of these orders even before they were read by Gage. Notable local leaders, such as Samuel Adams and John Hancock, quickly fled into the interior to avoid arrest, but Gage was not without his own spies. He learned that Concord, twenty miles northwest of Boston, was a supply depot for rebel arms and gunpowder. With orders now in hand, he decided to strike quickly.

Unfortunately for Gage, his troops could not move quickly enough, especially with rebel watchers posted throughout the city. On 16 April, popular leader Joseph Warren ordered Paul Revere, a well-known silversmith and patriot courier, to be ready to warn the countryside. Revere set up his now-famous signal:—if British troops marched down the Boston Neck or rowed across the back bay, a patriot in the Old North Church would flash lantern warnings, "one if by land, two if by sea." All of Gage's elaborate plans for secrecy went for naught, and late on the evening of 18 April Revere and William Dawes galloped off. Even as the British prepared for the raid, minutemen, militiamen, and ordinary citizens were removing their muskets and fowling pieces from their mantles.

Considering British opinion of American military abilities, the seven hundred men Gage sent to Lexington and Concord under Lieutenant Colonel Francis Smith seemed ample. Gage, however, a veteran of Braddock's march, knew the value of reinforcements; and he wisely had Sir Hugh Percy standing by with a reserve force of eleven hundred men. In several Massachusetts villages, Americans convened on town greens, repaired to taverns for warmth and courage, and waited to see what might happen. When Smith sent six companies under Major John Pitcairn into Lexington on 19 April, they found only seventy rebels milling about on the green. Ordered to disperse and lay down their arms, the patriots began moving off when someone, no doubt accidentally, fired a weapon. In an instant the British regulars unloaded a volley at the Americans from forty yards, optimum range for a Brown Bess. Eight Americans lay dead and ten wounded in the opening encounter of the War of the Revolution.

Pitcairn's column moved on to Concord, five miles farther down the road, where it met up with Smith and where they destroyed some weapons and powder. Some buildings were ignited, and the British opened fire on several companies of assembled patriot militia near the North Bridge. The patriots stood their ground and even drove back the surprised regulars, who left behind three dead comrades. Smith then withdrew. The return march turned into a bloodbath. Sniping from behind trees, firing while standing beside the road, firing until they ran out of ammunition, hundreds, perhaps thousands of colonists shot up the British column. Without the appearance of Percy's relief force, the slaughter might have been worse. As it was, the British suffered 273 casualties, compared to ninety-five for the Americans, before finding shelter inside Charlestown Neck under the protective guns of the Royal Navy. Within two weeks, at least ten thousand New Englanders had made camp around Boston, creating something the world had rarely seen before—a totally spontaneous armed insurrection.

When the Second Continental Congress first gathered in early May, the delegates had to deal with these unforeseen circumstances. The rebel leaders of Massachusetts were unable to provide for the thousands of armed patriots, so they turned to what was the only intercolonial legislative body available—the Congress. Barely united over sending protestations to the king, the delegates, now cast in the mold of a national government, had to come to grips with an ever-growing rebellion, for the uprising had spread beyond Massachusetts.

On 10 May, Benedict Arnold of Connecticut and Ethan Allen and his Green Mountain Boys from the Hampshire Grants (modern Vermont) crossed into New York and captured strategically important Fort Ticonderoga on Lake Champlain. Another local Hampshireman, Seth Warner, secured Crown Point, twelve miles north of Ticonderoga, on 12 May, and Arnold captured Saint Johns in Canada on 16 May. Suddenly the traditional invasion route into Canada was wide open, which spurred the notion that Quebec should become the fourteenth colony to join the rebellion.

WASHINGTON TAKES COMMAND AND BUNKER HILL. Congress reeled from all these events. Many in the coalition—for Congress was indeed a coalition of thirteen individual entities—thought the British

The Battle of Lexington on 19 April 1775 was the opening encounter of the Revolutionary War. No one knows who fired the first shot, which caused British soldiers to unload a volley at seventy American minutemen, killing eight and wounding ten of them. (National Archives/drawing from engraving by Amos Doolittle)

overbearing, but to rise in actual rebellion against the king was unthinkable. More cautious delegates raised many questions, such as whether they should give back Ticonderoga. Others disagreed, stating that they would rather die than sacrifice American rights. Moving deliberately, Congress set about organizing itself for directing armed resistance. On 14 June 1775, the delegates took the first step by adopting the citizen's army before Boston as their own, and the next day they named George Washington commander in chief of the "army of the United Colonies."

Trying to instill and maintain discipline in a gathering of independent-minded folk who elected company-level officers proved no simple matter.

A wealthy Virginia planter and gentleman of renown, Washington had as much prior military experience as any native-born American, having seen extensive service both as a regimental commander and a gentleman-volunteer during the French and Indian War. In the latter capacity, he had accompanied Edward Braddock on his ill-fated march toward Fort Duquesne in 1755. There he exhibited great personal courage and leadership. While attending Congress Washington did not hurt his chances for selection by wearing his uniform. His appointment would also help draw southerners into what was still a New England–based war. A large man for his time, standing more than six feet tall and weighing about 220 pounds, Washington clearly had command presence. He would need every scrap of it when he reached his army in early July.

The situation facing the new general was certainly unusual, if not wholly unique. Here was a commander with neither a trained army nor funds to maintain it, and even the government he represented was unrecognized as legitimate, either among the world's nations or even among the colonies themselves. The colonists had little hard money, no credit, few arms, and almost no munitions. Although there were plenty of colonial ships, establishing a seaborne force capable of challenging the Royal Navy was beyond colonial means. "The sword of war," Washington later wrote, "was forged on the anvil of necessity."

While Washington prepared to assume command, events moved on as if they had a life of their own. British reinforcements arrived in Boston along with three generals who would play major roles in the upcoming drama—William Howe, Henry Clinton, and John Burgoyne. On the evening of 16 June, sixteen hundred patriots under the command of Colonel William Prescott and others crossed the narrow neck leading to Charlestown Peninsula across the harbor from Boston and threw up crude fortifications atop Breed's Hill (Bunker Hill, behind Breed's, crawled with unarmed patriots). Instead of launching an amphibious operation cutting across the narrow Charlestown Neck and cutting off the rebels, Gage, at Howe's urging, decided upon a frontal assault on the patriot position on Breed's Hill. Showing disdain for the colonists was part of the plan; Howe was sure they would flee from any advancing British battle line.

On the afternoon of 17 June, a brutally hot day and under the eyes of all of Boston, Howe sent his twenty-four hundred troops directly against the rebels. Dressed as if on parade with their heavy red woolen coats and white breeches, carrying 80-pound packs, the British regulars advanced up Breed's Hill with fixed bayonets. Armed with shotguns, smoothbore muskets, and a wide variety of other weapons, the colonists nervously waited until the British were upon them. Then, when they could "see the whites of the regulars' eyes," they fired a massive volley that shattered the British lines. The redcoat advance halted, took another volley, and then broke, the men running down the hill. Another assault met the same fate. Finally, on the third try, with the colonists running out of ammunition, the brave and angry British succeeded in pushing, not driving, their opponents from the hill. Howe won the field, but the Battle of Bunker Hill was a pyrrhic victory. The Americans lost 411 killed and wounded, but British casualties numbered 1,054, representing 40 percent of Howe's command. The bloodiest battle of the war, Bunker Hill hardly proved the vast superiority of massed British arms.

Washington did not arrive at his Cambridge headquarters until early July. He assumed command in the name of Congress, replacing General Artemas Ward of the Massachusetts militia. His first task was to organize, feed, and arm his New England army, which soon would be supplemented by the addition of riflemen from Virginia (under Daniel Morgan) and Pennsylvania. Keeping men in camp proved a chronic problem. Americans were quick to go to war and proved to be excellent fighters when ably led, but they were equally quick to return home immediately after a battle or when their terms of enlistment (running from three months to a year) were complete. Such were the ideological proscriptions against maintaining a regular or standing army, and it was not until 1777 that Congress allowed the enlisting of soldiers for the length of the war. Even then, obtaining enough troops was a constant bane for the commander in chief throughout the war.

The siege of Boston was one of despair and hard work for Washington. Twice his army all but dissolved and had to be rebuilt. In January 1776, for example, the number of American troops present and fit for duty numbered fewer than six thousand, less than the British force in Boston. Trying to instill and maintain discipline in a gathering of independent-minded folk who elected company-level officers proved no simple matter. Because of biblical injunctions and congressional mandate, Washington was only allowed to flog troublemakers with thirty-nine lashes. Food was scarce, arms were few, except for some captured by privateers ("Washington's Navy"), and gunpowder was measured in grains. Great numbers left camp for these reasons.

Many of the senior officers had little military experience, but there were bright spots. During the winter of 1775–1776, Boston bookseller and self-taught artillerist Henry Knox suggested that he could bring the cannons captured at Fort Ticonderoga to Boston. It was a heroic travail, and by midwinter Washington had guns covering most British positions. Other amateur officers also proved helpful, such as Nathanael Greene, a former private in the Kent (Rhode Island) militia. Like Knox, Greene was a military buff who read widely but who had no actual military experience.

Two ex-British officers with substantial experience were Horatio Gates and Charles Lee. Gates knew administration and as adjutant general was initially a great help to Washington. Lee, who also had served in Poland as a major general, was a fount of knowledge, but his eccentric ways, massive ego, caustic tongue, and constant intriguing for higher command made him a disruptive influence. Ranked second only to Washington among American generals, Lee believed himself more suited to the higher post.

THE INVASION OF CANADA. While trying to solve these myriad problems, Washington helped organize the attempted conquest of what many hoped would become the fourteenth colony—the province of Quebec in Canada. The invasion was to be a two-pronged

The Battle of Bunker Hill on 17 June 1775 proved the bloodiest battle of the war. The British were victorious but suffered 1,054 casualties. The Americans lost 411 killed or wounded. (National Archives/engraving from a painting by John Trumbull)

movement. Brigadier General Richard Montgomery, another former British officer living in New York who had cast his lot with the rebels, led one force from Saint Johns, capturing Montreal in mid-November. Montgomery was to then join with the other prong, commanded by Colonel Benedict Arnold, and lay siege to Quebec, because whoever held Quebec and Montreal had Canada under control.

A Connecticut merchant, apothecary, and ship's captain, Arnold was a natural leader of men. His epic autumn journey (12 September to 14 November) up Maine's Kennebec River to Quebec was a death-defying adventure. Faint-hearted subordinates who dropped out with their commands left him with only about 675 troops when he emerged from the wilderness outside Quebec still determined to succeed.

Once united with Montgomery's force in early December, the two officers found Quebec's fortifications too strong for their puny artillery. This situation and the fast-approaching expiration of their soldiers' terms of service forced them to gamble on an assault. Early on New Year's Eve 1775, under the cover of darkness and a heavy snowstorm, they sent their men against Quebec. Unluckily, a round killed Montgomery and another seriously wounded Arnold. What veteran troops might have accomplished proved impossible for inexperienced recruits. The Americans lost nearly five hundred, including more than four hundred taken prisoner, many of the latter group being Virginia riflemen under Morgan.

Lexington and Concord, Bunker Hill, and the expedition against Canada were the main actions of 1775, but hostilities flared throughout the colonies. Along the coast, British naval supremacy made its weight felt, subjecting several New England, New York, and Virginia towns to bombardment. Instead of striking terror into American hearts, these attacks hardened patriot resolve and won more converts to the rebel cause. At sea, despite losses, American privateers snapped up a number of British supply ships, bringing badly needed war matériel to Washington's army.

Even as Washington sought to keep soldiers in camp and Arnold nursed his mangled leg outside Quebec's walls, the British were drawing up elaborate plans for the coming campaign. Now fully serious about the spreading war, they intended to overawe the Americans and snuff out the flame of rebellion. They almost succeeded in 1776.

MILITARY OPERATIONS: 1776

Americans declared their independence in 1776 and then almost lost it on the battlefield. The British developed what they believed was a winning strategy. As soon as the ice melted, a reinforced army under Governor Guy Carleton of Canada would move up Lake Champlain, retake Crown Point and Ticonderoga, and then capture Albany. Another force would sail from Ireland to join with North Carolinians still loyal to the Crown to take back that colony, and then, supported by a fleet, either move south to capture South Carolina or sail north to New York. New York City would be the linchpin to British campaign of 1776. Howe, who had replaced Gage as commander in chief, would sail to New York early in the summer and use it as his base of operations. Howe was to link up with Carleton by moving up the Hudson River valley, thereby cutting off New England from the rest of the colonies or, if the opportunity presented itself, pursue and destroy Washington's army.

The Americans, on the other hand, after driving the British from Boston, had little that passed as a strategy. Lacking a naval force and not having a well-trained army, all they could do was keep the Revolution alive by reacting to British movements.

THE SOUTH. Deposed royal governors in the South reported home to Lord Germain that their region contained an untapped reservoir of loyal Americans anxious to fight for the king. There was some truth to this. For example, many Scottish veterans of the Jacobite Rising of the '45 that had ended with the 1746 defeat at Culloden had sworn allegiance to the Crown and migrated to North Carolina. British officers contacted them in late 1775 and worked out a plan. In February a fleet under Admiral Marriot Arbuthnot would appear offshore carrying a large army commanded by General Henry Clinton. Their arrival would signal a counter-rebellion. After restoring the royal standard to North Carolina, the combined force might then try to bring either South Carolina or Virginia back into the British fold.

The plan failed. In February Arbuthnot's fleet lay stalled in Cork, Ireland, unable to sail in the face of turbulent winds. Nevertheless, the Scots and other loyalists in North Carolina strapped on their claymores and rose up. Unexpectedly, patriot militia rallied under Colonel Richard Caswell and overwhelmed twelve hundred at the Battle of Moore's Creek Bridge on 27 February. Almost all of the loyalist force was captured.

Moore's Creek Bridge was a minor battle with far-reaching implications. When Clinton finally arrived in May, he found the loyalists in hiding. Searching for a new objective, he and Arbuthnot moved on Charleston, South Carolina. Because of their delay in sailing, the harbor's defenses had been shored up under the direction of General Charles Lee. When the British attacked on 28 June, South Carolinians commanded by Colonel

William Moultrie gave a good account of themselves. At Sullivan's Island, Clinton's troops suffered more than two hundred casualties to thirty-two for the Americans, and the British lost several ships. Squabbling over who was to blame for the fiasco, Clinton and Arbuthnot sailed to New York to join Howe.

The second result of Moore's Creek Bridge was that it curbed organized loyalist enthusiasm in the Carolinas for quite some time; future British attempts to stir up a loyalist counterrebellion would be met with some skepticism. Third, except for some raiding along the Georgia–East Florida boundary, the failed attack on Charleston ended British military operations in the South until late 1778. Many loyalists suffered mightily under patriot hands, and when the British finally did develop their southern strategy, they found the loyalists unorganized and more interested in gaining revenge against patriot neighbors than restoring royal government.

THE NORTHERN THEATER. Matters were less sanguine for patriots in the far North. Despite his heroics on the Kennebec and at Quebec, Benedict Arnold lacked the troop strength and material resources to maintain a hold on Canada. Congress promoted him to brigadier general but named less talented men to direct the war effort in Canada. Once the British relief force started arriving at Quebec in early May 1776, the outgunned and outmanned Americans had to accept defeat and retreat. Serious rebel setbacks included a rebel encounter at the Cedars, southwest of Montreal, in mid-May, where a British-Indian force captured nearly four hundred Americans, and at Three Rivers in early June, where the patriots lost another three hundred troops.

By the end of June, the Americans had retreated up Lake Champlain to Crown Point and Ticonderoga, giving up all that Montgomery and Arnold had won the previous year. Patriot officers at Ticonderoga spent as much time bickering over who was at fault for the Canadian fiasco as they did preparing for the imminent British invasion. Appointed by Congress as overall commander of the Continental army's Northern Department, General Philip Schuyler spent most of his time in Albany, gathering supplies and reinforcements. (Washington was commander in chief of the entire Continental army, but he wisely delegated authority to departmental commanders in the field. Thus, for Schuyler and other independent and theater commanders, Washington acted more in an advisory capacity than as commander.) Command of Ticonderoga fell upon Horatio Gates, who was anxious to supplant Schuyler as head of the Northern Department. Arnold worked closely with the former British officer in preparing to stop the expected British advance.

The key was to retain Lake Champlain and Ticonderoga. Lake Champlain and the connecting Lake George formed a natural north-south corridor for invading Canada or, conversely, striking southward to Albany and the Hudson Valley. Arnold directed the construction of a fleet, including highly maneuverable row galleys with lateen sails, to challenge the British invaders. Since there was no road running through the dense wilderness bordering Lake Champlain, the British built their own fleet, even disassembling a frigate and portaging it over the Richelieu rapids to Saint Johns, where it was reconstructed. Schuyler and Arnold sent out pleas for shipbuilders, and all sorts of nautical supplies wound their way north. This work took most of the summer.

Benedict Arnold's leadership created the impression that patriots, no matter how bad the odds, would resist until death.

When the patriot fleet was ready, Arnold, a skilled mariner, sailed northward to meet the enemy. Off Valcour Island on 11 October, he fought a valiant but doomed action before making a miraculous escape under cover of darkness. The British gave chase, and Arnold eventually lost most of his vessels. Some American officers castigated him for destroying the fleet, but the farseeing Arnold's efforts achieved his strategic objective—delay. He had traded space and ships to gain precious time. By his leadership he also created the impression that patriots, no matter how bad the odds, would resist until death. To be sure, the British now controlled the lake, but Arnold's show of unremitting courage caused Carleton to pause at Crown Point, declare the season too late to conduct a siege of Ticonderoga, and abandon any notion of making an incursion all the way to Albany, an invasion that would have to wait until 1777.

TRIUMPH AT BOSTON. Over the winter of 1775–1776, Washington thought of and then discarded a variety of plans, including attacking Boston over the ice when the harbor was frozen over. The arrival of Knox and his cannons heralded a new phase in the campaign. Overlooking Boston peninsula from the south were low hills known as Dorchester Heights. Artillery strategically positioned on the heights could threaten any British position in Boston, but getting the cannons in place in the face of British batteries and the Royal Navy

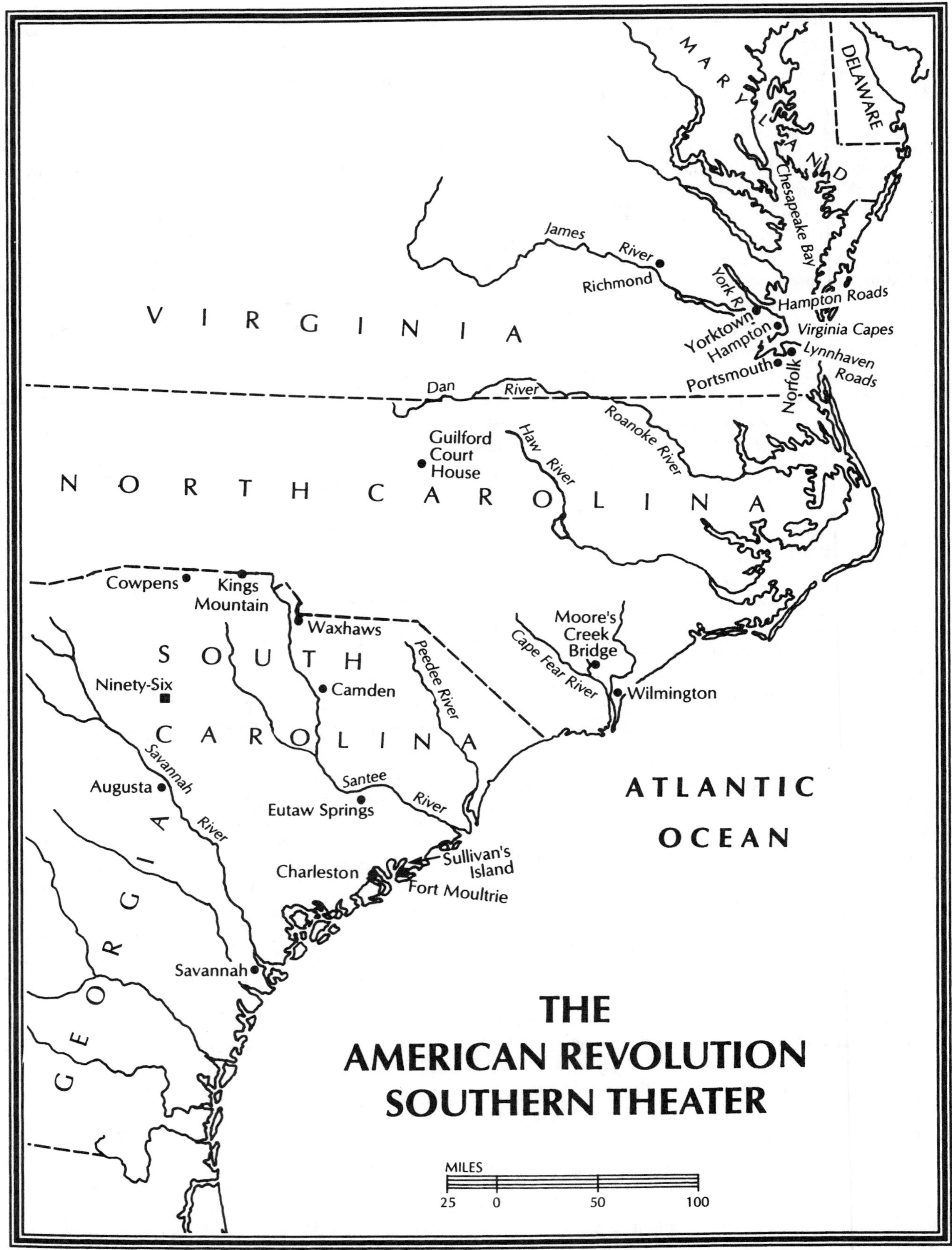
MARYLAND
DELAWARE
Chesapeake Bay
James
River
Richmond
York R.
Hampton Roads
Virginia Capes
Yorktown
Hampton
Portsmouth
Norfolk
Lynnhaven
Roads
VIRGINIA
Dan
River
Roanoke River
Haw
River
Guilford
Court
House
NORTH CAROLINA
Cowpens
Kings
Mountain
Waxhaws
Moore's
Creek
Bridge
Cape Fear River
Wilmington
SOUTH
Ninety-Six
Camden
Peedee River
CAROLINA
Augusta
Savannah
River
Santee
River
Eutaw Springs
ATLANTIC
OCEAN
Sullivan's
Island
Charleston
Fort Moultrie
GEORGIA
Savannah
THE
AMERICAN REVOLUTION
SOUTHERN THEATER
MILES
25
0
50
100

would be most difficult. Washington developed a rather sophisticated plan. Rebel forces would create a diversion, then, under the cover of darkness, other troops would place gabions (straw baskets filled with soil) on the heights to form ready-made field fortifications and protection for the artillery. The ruse worked, and on 4 March three thousand troops under General John Thomas occupied Dorchester Heights.

Rebel artillery now made Howe's position untenable. He planned an amphibious assault, but a fortuitous storm wrecked the effort. At this point the British commander had little choice but to vacate Boston. To forestall a damaging cannonade during the evacuation, Howe threatened to burn the city. Washington allowed the British to sail away unscathed on 17 March, taking on board some thousand loyalists who sailed with Howe's fleet to Halifax, Nova Scotia. Boston was again free.

Howe would have abandoned Boston anyway, according to Germain's strategy, but Washington could not be sure where the British general would strike next. After allowing his troops a day or so of celebration, he gambled by marching them toward New York City. It was there, the American commander believed, by process of elimination, that the British would strike next.

A NEW NATION IS BORN. As Washington's troops tramped through Rhode Island and Connecticut to New York, momentous events were transpiring in Philadelphia—a new nation was coming to life. Throughout 1775, despite the ongoing armed conflict, many members of Congress and Americans from all walks of life hoped for a reconciliation of differences with the home government. If only George III would intercede on their behalf, grievances could be resolved. Many colonists stubbornly refused to acknowledge the king's role in threatening them with tyranny, and others did not wish to make an irrevocable break with England.

By spring 1776 it was obvious that no ministerial leader, not even George III, would redress American complaints. The word "independence," not surprisingly, increasingly grew in use. In June Congress voted to draft a declaration declaring the thirteen colonies free and independent states. A young red haired lawyer from Virginia, Thomas Jefferson, prepared a document that the delegates accepted with little debate and few revisions. In the Declaration of Independence, adopted by unanimous vote on 4 July, the signers stated for the world to read that they had no choice but to separate from Great Britain. The king had overstepped the legal, moral, and natural bounds that tied him to the people, as evidenced by the long "train of abuses" denoting his actions.

The declaration had important military implications. First, by stating that Americans were not questioning the right of the king to rule but that he—not they—had broken with his subjects, they showed the world, and especially France, that kings as a whole were fine but George III was a tyrant. France was already being wooed to supply arms and munitions, and a blatantly antiroyal statement would have gained congressional emissaries few friends at the court of King Louis XVI.

Second, the declaration claimed legitimacy for the former colonies, and, thus, Congress, by asserting independence before the whole world. By the act of revolution the Americans were transforming themselves into a new nation, which is one reason why later that summer in New York Washington refused a letter from Howe addressed to him as a civilian; he would accept such communications only as commander of the Continental army. Legitimization also meant that Americans would abide by the rules of war, and they would demand equal treatment from the British. Now, captured American soldiers and sailors expected to be accorded the rights of prisoners of war, not those of rebels subject to treason under English law and hanging.

Third, but not least, for the troops in the field the declaration forever altered a rebellion *cum* revolution into a war to defend their new nation. The amorphous idea of liberty had been transmuted into something hard and real—a nation—in which every soldier and every citizen had a share in its defense. When the Declaration of Independence was read to Washington's troops in mid-July, they cheered. Their huzzahs originated from feelings of patriotism, but the shouting also bolstered their own confidence. Even as they listened, a forest of Royal Navy masts in New York harbor grew larger every day.

PATRIOT DISASTER IN NEW YORK. Soon after Washington arrived in New York City, he came to understand that it was indefensible for an army without naval support. There were simply too many bays, beaches, and other landing areas accessible to the Royal Navy to defend, even if the American forces were huge and well-trained, which they were not. Nonetheless, Congress and Washington's generals dictated that he should try with his already limited strength of nineteen thousand effectives.

The British arrived and kept arriving throughout July and August, eventually totaling over thirty thousand troops (they also had thirteen thousand sailors in the vicinity). It was the largest amphibious operation the world had ever seen and would not be exceeded until the allied invasion of North Africa in 1942. Many of these troops were German mercenaries, hired by the British to flesh out their own small army. Traditionally the English always preferred to have others—Scots, Irish, American loyalists, or Germans—do their fighting for them. Originally, Lord North's ministry tried to hire Russians, but Catherine II vetoed that plan. Therefore, British agents went to Hesse-Cassel, Hesse-Hanau, and several other German states where they paid by the head for troops. The practice of hiring mercenaries was not at all unusual in the eighteenth century.

William Howe's brother, Admiral Richard, Lord Howe, known as "Black Dick" because of his swarthy complexion, commanded the Royal Navy in New York, which arrived on 12 July. The Howe brothers were members of the Parliamentary opposition that sought a peaceful, nonmilitary solution to the imbroglio. North and Germain knew this, but they chose William and "Black Dick" to lead the primary British forces in battle, which may explain why the brothers were also given another, seemingly contradictory role to play. In one last chance to avoid a fatal confrontation, the Howes came forth as peace commissioners, charged with getting Americans to renounce their rebellion. These contradictory roles—warmakers and peacemakers—seemingly had much to do with the way the Howes conducted the campaign.

Washington divided his army and positioned his primary force on Long Island, a disposition that, in retrospect, was a blunder. Had the Howes stationed war vessels in the East River between the village of Brooklyn and Manhattan Island, they could have cut off the avenue of retreat. Washington knew that his position was vulnerable, so he secured every available boat in the area and kept close watch on the British fleet and the wind. If the wind shifted and Howe's fleet lifted anchor preparatory to advancing upriver, he would know in a matter of minutes. In the meantime, Washington deployed his troops along a narrow band of hills with his right anchored on the shore, but his left flank was in the air (not abutted against a natural obstacle such as a river). He and his generals hoped that the British would repeat their Bunker Hill tactics and attempt a frontal assault on entrenched patriot positions.

Legend has the polite Lord Howe being stopped by a patriotic American lady who invited him in for tea.

William Howe, who had led troops at Breed's Hill on the third and final assault, vowed never again to repeat his error in directly attacking Americans behind fortifications. Under such circumstances even veteran European troops could be shot to pieces by a rabble of farmers and clerks emboldened behind stone walls. Landing at Gravesend, Long Island, on 22 August, Howe ordered a demonstration in the patriots' front to fix their attention while sending his principal column on a long night march around the barely guarded American left flank. On 27 August, he rolled up the American left flank and sent his own left crashing against the American right. Caught in a vise, the seven thousand vastly outnumbered Americans fell back in chaos to Brooklyn Heights (the British incurred 367 casualties to Washington's two hundred killed and more than one thousand captured).

A vigorous pursuit might have gained Howe complete victory, but two matters intervened. On the American right, about one thousand Maryland and Delaware troops under Lord Stirling (a pretender to Scottish nobility—his real name was William Alexander) forgot that they were untrained. They resisted the British regulars and Hessians so vigorously that by their heroism they allowed the rest of the army to get behind the earthworks on Brooklyn Heights. Second, Howe called a halt to the pursuit. Why he did so remains unclear. Perhaps Howe, the peacemaker not warmaker, saw an opportunity to bag the overextended rebel force without additional bloodshed. Whatever the reason, Washington called upon John Glover and his mariners from Marblehead, Massachusetts, to row his troops and equipment to Manhattan under the cover of fog and darkness on 29 August. It was an epic withdrawal as well as an embarrassing retreat. As one of the few remaining boats pulled away from Long Island, a lieutenant noted a tall, cloaked man stepping into the last boat. It was General Washington, who never again deployed his army in so potentially a disastrous position.

Howe just could not seem to get himself moving. Approximately thirteen thousand British troops were ferried up the East River and landed at Kips Bay with little opposition on 15 September. Great numbers of patriot troops were still on the southwest side of Manhattan, and a brisk cross-island march by Howe could have nabbed nearly half the American army. Legend has the polite Howe being stopped by a patriotic American lady who invited him in for tea. For whatever reason, Howe again failed to mount a vigorous pursuit, and the patriots tumbled behind earthworks on Harlem Heights.

The next day, however, the desultory British advance ran into a hornet's nest on the site of modern Central Park. As the British advanced up Manhattan on 16 September, they encountered rebel resistance. A brisk skirmish ensued. More British and German troops came up, and the Americans began to fall back. Washington ordered in reinforcements, which bolstered the line, then a sudden American attack forced Howe's troops, including the famed Scottish 42nd Black Watch Regiment, into a full-scale retreat. Washington broke off the action when additional British reinforcements appeared. To be sure, the engagement was little more than a firefight with some sixty American and 170 British casualties, but such modest success temporarily buoyed flagging American morale.

Still unwilling to confront entrenched Americans, Howe used his naval superiority to make several additional landings northeast of New York City. Outflanked, Washington marched his troops northward toward White Plains. Howe pursued in desultory fashion, and on 28 October the two armies clashed there. In an indecisive engagement, the British suffered more than three hundred casualties to half that number for the Americans.

Well before the White Plains encounter, the American commander had decided upon a new plan of action, employing the textbook strategy known as a war of posts. In period terminology, it meant developing a series of mutually supporting strong points with an army of observation (maneuver) rushing to whichever fort needed assistance. The sole remaining American presence on Manhattan was Fort Washington. Along with Fort Lee, directly across the Hudson River from Fort Washington on the New Jersey Palisades, the guns of Fort Washington were to prevent the British from sailing up the Hudson (or the Great River as it was also known). Back in July, however, two British naval vessels had braved the combined batteries of the forts and run past them with little damage.

After White Plains, Howe took advantage of Washington's textbook strategy, which stressed the importance of leaving a fortress in the enemy's rear. Displaying uncharacterisic operational energy, he wheeled about and quick-marched his army to lay siege to Fort Washington. Washington considered withdrawing his troops from the fort, but General Nathanael Greene assured him that it could be held. Greene was wrong. After only

The Battle of Long Island. The British forced the Americans from New York's Long Island on 27 August 1776. More than 200 of General Washington's troops were killed and 1,000 more were captured in the Battle of Long Island. (National Archives/engraving from a painting by Alonzo Chappel)

a one-day siege and battle, Fort Washinqton surrendered on 16 November. Howe lost almost four hundred troops, but the American casualties were enormous, totaling more than three thousand, including 2,858 captured, along with the loss of invaluable artillery, munitions, and supplies.

With Manhattan and the lower Hudson River now totally in British hands, Howe unleashed General Charles Cornwallis in pursuit of Washington's disorganized and shrinking army in New Jersey. Washington could do little but fall back and hope for better tidings.

"THE TIMES THAT TRY MEN'S SOULS." The series of patriot setbacks in and around New York City caused Washington to rethink his strategy. He abandoned the war of posts for a "war on posts." He decided to protract the war, avoiding general actions unless he had an optimum chance for success. When Lord Cornwallis captured Fort Lee on 20 November, Washington withdrew before him. Washington would lure the enemy after him, and, when the time was ripe and the enemy least expected it, he would, in his words, move decisively "to beat them up."

In this strategy Washington was influenced by the writings of such great eighteenth-century military writers and leaders as Field Marshal de Saxe of France and King Frederick the Great of Prussia. Reduced to its essence, their belief was that military leaders should not engage in set-piece battles unless they had done everything possible to ensure victory. The key was to maneuver or avoid the enemy until a force was ready to strike on a battlefield of its own choosing. Washington had allowed the British to control the initiative, thereby dictating the course of combat. He had waged conventional, European-style warfare near a coast controlled by the Royal Navy against a foe long-skilled in such operations. Thus, he had played directly into British hands. By withdrawing inland and using the vast land mass of America, Washington, who was learning the art of war by making war, would force the enemy to fight on his terms. The question was whether his army could survive long enough to utilize this strategy.

As the frozen, hungry Continental soldiers marched, they could be tracked easily by their bloody footprints in the snow.

After the Battle of White Plains, Washington left some eight thousand troops under Major General Charles Lee to guard the all-important Hudson Highlands. The Highlands were of great strategic interest to both sides. The primary American logistical network ran northeast-southwest from New England to Pennsylvania directly through them. Patriot control of the Highlands meant that New York was always under constant threat. At Fishkill, Peekskill, Newburgh, and West Point, the rebels maintained major depots (or magazines), funneling supplies to the armies of both Washington and Schuyler. Because the Americans experienced shortages in almost everything needed to keep and maintain an army in the field, any disruption of this slender thread of a supply network could have starved the rebel armies. West Point, in particular, was a key geographic location for control of the Hudson River, and the patriots placed strong fortifications there. Lee was left to guard the Highlands, but if Howe pursued Washington, then he was to rejoin the main army.

As Washington's army retreated across New Jersey with Cornwallis in pursuit, it almost ceased to exist. Rampant disease and desertion took the greatest toll. By the time Washington reached the Delaware River in early December, those troops who were still with him were in desperate shape. Whatever uniforms and clothing they possessed were little more than tatters, and most swaddled themselves in blankets and whatever else they could find to ward off the bitter cold. (The War of the Revolution was fought during what modern meteorologists call the Little Ice Age, which did not end until around 1850.) Some had little to wear other than blankets, and many had no shoes, wrapping their cracked and frostbitten feet in rags. As these frozen, hungry Continentals marched, they could be tracked easily by their bloody footprints in the snow. These were truly, as pamphleteer Thomas Paine wrote, "the times that try men's souls."

Little assistance was to be found in New jersey. Local militia units failed to rally, and much of the population acted as if it were nonaligned or loyalist. Washington kept close control of his troops as they retreated; he did not allow the pillaging of Americans, even suspected loyalists. The British and Hessians, by comparison, were used to fighting in European wars where looting and raping represented a soldier's rewards for facing death in battle. New Jersey loyalists welcomed Cornwallis' troops, only to discover that their liberators were hardly benefactors. Loyalist chickens and pigs were as tasty as patriot animals, and most British officers, who condescendingly dismissed provincials as rabble, winked at the sexual abuse of women. Failure to control their troops (and Indian allies) in friendly regions helped undermine the British effort to win back the hearts and minds of Americans throughout the war. Unwise British pacification measures ultimately spurred thousands of

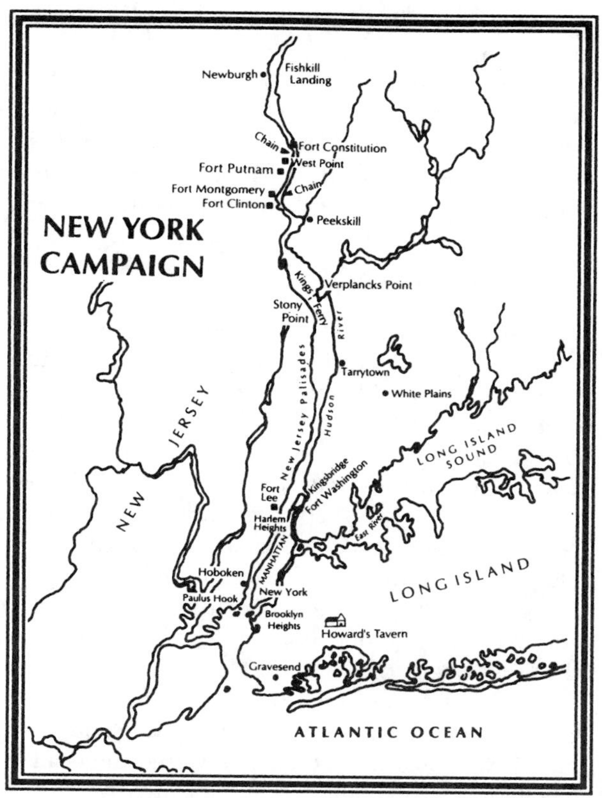

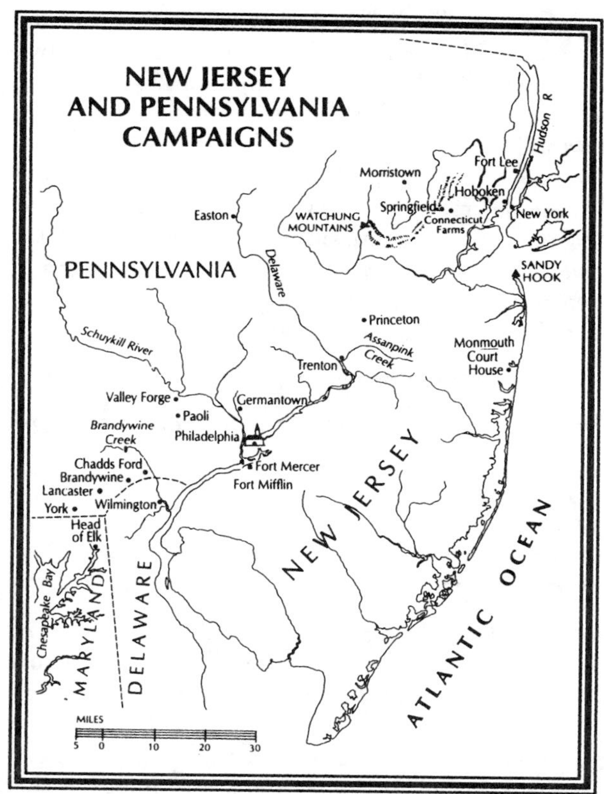

neutrals—and even some loyalists—to accept, however reluctantly, the patriot cause.

In retreat, Washington continually called upon Lee to rejoin the main army, but the former British officer, at first, ignored these orders. When he finally began to march, he moved slowly. Personal rather than military reasons explained Lee's reluctance. Believing that it was only a matter of time before the British captured or annihilated Washington's force, he hoped that Congress would name him to overall command. In official correspondence, Washington was circumspect, but privately he found Lee's behavior insufferable and close to treasonous. For the moment, however, Lee dropped from the picture when British cavalry captured him taking a late breakfast at a New Jersey tavern away from his troops. For Americans who did not know of his perfidy, this was another major blow.

Washington crossed the icy Delaware on 11 December, bringing every available boat with him, and set up a defensive line along the Pennsylvania bank. When Howe arrived at the Delaware, he halted the pursuit. He now went over to a war of posts strategy, detaching his troops into winter quarters across New Jersey. He could have pushed the remains of Washington's army aside and captured Philadelphia, but eighteenth-century doctrine advised against winter campaigning. It was better to have the soldiery snug and rested at the opening of the next campaign season. Spring would come soon enough to destroy the remaining patriot force and put an end to the rebellion. Leaving Cornwallis in command with an army of observation, Howe returned to the comforts of New York City.

TRENTON AND PRINCETON: RENEWAL. Across the Delaware, Washington despaired. On 18 December he wrote to his brother: "I think the game will be pretty well up." Washington's army was all but dissolved, most troops only waiting until their enlistments expired on 1 January 1777, and patriot morale was reaching low ebb throughout the states. Now was the time for Washington to put into effect the offensive side of his operational strategy, to "move to beat them up." In his attack on Trenton, both his lack of experience and bold leadership may be discerned. His plan of attack called for multiple assaults on several British outposts, a plan much too sophisticated for even the best-trained officers and soldiers to execute completely, particularly in such inclement weather. At the same time, Washington chose to act decisively during a critical hour.

On Christmas evening, John Glover's mariners rowed Washington's main force of twenty-four hundred through the icy floes of the Delaware. The commander then marched his band to Trenton in a blinding snowstorm, arriving early on the morning of 26 December. Hoping the Hessians there under Colonel Johann Rall would still be feeling the effects of too much liquor from Christmas celebrating, Washington sent four columns of troops storming into the town. The stunned Germans put up little resistance. The patriots suffered twelve casualties but captured nearly one thousand of the enemy. Not wishing to be trapped on the Jersey side of the river, Washington then retreated.

The patriots were faring poorly when a large man on a white horse rode into the midst of the fray, rallied them, and led them in the attack.

Back in Pennsylvania, patriot officers literally begged their troops to reenlist, and, cheered by their victory and from personal loyalty to Washington and other officers, many agreed. While the pleas for reenlistment went on, the American commander recrossed the Delaware again on 30 December, hoping to inflict further damage on British outposts. Accepting the challenge, Cornwallis rushed forward toward Trenton and engaged in an artillery duel across Assunpink Creek on 2 January. The next morning, the British general believed, he would finish off the rebel force. When daylight broke, the Americans were gone. Washington left a skeleton detachment to keep the campfires burning, and, with artillery wheels muffled by rags, he marched off toward Princeton, near which Washington's men skirmished sharply with British troops marching to join Cornwallis. The patriots were faring poorly when a large man on a white horse rode into the midst of the fray, rallied them, and led them in the attack. Under Washington's fearless leadership, the British broke and fled. The Battle of Princeton was another rebel victory.

Fooled by the ruse de guerre of the Americans, an outraged Cornwallis gave pursuit, but Washington was already gone. He led his army northward to an excellent defensive position at Morristown behind the Watchung Mountains. For the British the damage was already done. In little more than a week, Washington had turned a seemingly overwhelming series of British triumphs on their head. In the history of military affairs, Trenton and Princeton rank only as skirmishes, little more than raids, not battles. The value of these victories, however, multiplied geometrically. Most important, Washington had stolen the initiative from the British, who pulled back their outposts, thereby abandoning much of New Jersey to the rebels. Instead of being poised for the offensive, the minions of Sir William Howe, who gained his knighthood as a reward for his victory on Long Island, spent the winter huddled in defensive positions fearful of attack. For committed rebels, by comparison, the flame of revolution, nearly extinguished during 1776, was still flickering.

MILITARY OPERATIONS: 1777

The engagements at Trenton and Princeton have been described as a key turning point of the war, but their true benefits would only be realized in the following campaign. In 1777 the British initiated another powerful effort to defeat the rebels. By European standards, Lord Germain's overall strategy was sound: General John Burgoyne, who replaced Carleton as commander of the army in Canada, was to drive through the Champlain corridor and into the Hudson Valley, aiming at Albany,; the British fleet, operating out of New York and Newport, Rhode Island, would continue raiding the New England coast; and Howe was to push up the Hudson Valley and link up with Burgoyne's force. The broad objective was to cut off New England from the other rebellious states, thereby severing the head of the rebellion and allowing the natural divisiveness of the provincials to break apart the rest of the rebel confederation. From a strictly military perspective, British control of the Hudson would shut off a major source of patriot supplies and manpower, perhaps forcing Washington to engage in a decisive battle in which British discipline and firepower would surely destroy his force.

The plan, however, began to go awry immediately. Howe decided to capture Philadelphia, the rebel capital. Occupying an enemy capital usually brought about a cessation in hostilities in Europe, but certainly not in America where the loss of the rebel "capital" meant little to a people barely united under the banner of a new nation. Far more important were patriot diplomatic efforts, which began to pay dividends. France, at first covertly, then more openly, had started to supply war matériel. These goods helped sustain the patriot force that entrapped Burgoyne at Saratoga, a crucial event in setting the stage for French diplomatic recognition and world war.

THE NEW JERSEY—NEW YORK THEATER. Camping at Morristown for the winter did not stop rebel military operations. In dozens of small-scale actions, Americans continued to carry the war to the British and their loyalist supporters in New Jersey. This was guerrilla warfare, employing the Duke of Wellington's early-nineteenth-century term, but in the late eighteenth century it went by the French name petit guerre, or partisan war. Forming into small to midsize units, the patriots employed hit-and-run tactics and raided British outposts, captured couriers, and attacked foraging parties. Along the Hudson, the British used their naval superiority to launch raids against American magazines at Peekskill and other towns, known as cutting out expeditions.

On occasion, some raids were not that small, such as the major raid conducted by the British under Colonel William Tryon against Danbury, Connecticut, in late April. Tryon's troops burned the town and a patriot supply center, but on the way back to the shore came under attack near Ridgefield by local militiamen led by Benedict Arnold, who was home on leave, heard about the raid, and rushed to the fray.

Washington had little opportunity to train troops in his winter cantonment, because with the expiration of enlistments he again had to rebuild his army nearly from scratch while in the field. At Morristown his troop strength dwindled to below three thousand. By May

Washington crossed the icy Delaware River on 11 December 1776 and set up a defensive line along the Pennsylvania bank. On Christmas evening, John Glover's mariners rowed 2,400 Americans back across the Delaware, where they marched to Trenton and stormed the city. (National Archives/painting by Emanuel Leutze)

1777 his meager following was back up to ten thousand, with 7,363 present and fit for duty, the latter figure representing about one-third of the troop strength immediately available to Howe.

Because of such severe manpower shortages that winter, it was fortunate for the Americans that Howe remained in hibernation until early June. At that point, the British general initiated some probing actions in central New Jersey, some of which became sharp firefights. Howe hoped that he could lure Washington away from his strong defensive line along the first Watchung Mountain and inflict an injurious if not backbreaking defeat on the Continental force before moving on Philadelphia. Washington shrewdly ignored the bait. In late June, Howe gave up, abandoned New Jersey (and thousands of loyalists), loaded fifteen thousand troops aboard ship, and prepared to approach Philadelphia by sea.

Washington was able to follow much of what occurred within the British camp because he assiduously cultivated a strong intelligence network. Intelligence-gathering was crucially important. Even though Washington had little money in camp, he always found a few gold coins to pay his agents. A fellow Virginian, Henry "Light Horse Harry" Lee, was Washington's go-between for all but a very few top secret agents.

Thus, Washington knew something was afoot in Howe's camp, and that Philadelphia, in all likelihood, was his target. Because Howe appeared to be letting the 1777 campaign season pass without action, and from dire necessity, Washington sent a few of his best units up the Hudson to bolster Schuyler's army, then Gates's Northern Department army. Howe continued to delay, his soldiers sweating aboard their airless transports, before sailing on 23 July. He dawdled off Sandy Hook for some days, then disappeared over the horizon. The still-strong garrison, at New York, amounting to seventy-three hundred under General Clinton, plus the weakness of the patriots, preempted an attack on the city.

Depending upon which report of Howe's purported movements reached his desk, Washington shifted his camps back and forth in northern New Jersey, because he had to maintain contact with the Hudson River should Howe suddenly strike northward toward Albany. Intelligence reports kept pointing toward Philadelphia as Howe's ultimate destination. Then, in mid-August, rebels sighted Howe's transports off the Virginia capes. Sir William was ignoring the British invasion from Canada; he was sailing up the Chesapeake toward Philadelphia. Washington moved to meet him.

THE FALL OF THE GIBRALTAR OF THE NORTH. British General John Burgoyne's campaign to split the rebellious colonies down the Hudson Valley got off to a colorful start. "Gentleman Johnny," so named by his troops in the Seven Years' War for his relatively mild discipline, launched his "splendid regatta" upon Lake Champlain in mid-June amid a flurry of bagpipes and bands. The lake fairly glimmered with reflections from the gold-laced officers, redcoated British, green-jacketed Hessians, kilted Scots, and the many hues of the war-painted Indians as Burgoyne's invasion fleet, approaching eight thousand strong, moved south toward Ticonderoga. All the splendor would be the high point of a campaign that ended with the commanding general's name being turned into a verb—therefore, to be "burgoyned" was to be surrounded and forced to surrender.

Lake Champlain glimmered with reflections from the gold-laced officers, redcoated British, green-jacketed Hessians, kilted Scots, and the many hues of the war-painted Indians.

The general strategic plan agreed to by Burgoyne and Germain in early 1777 was for Carleton and thirty-five hundred troops to remain in Canada. Burgoyne and his troops would retake Crown Point and Ticonderoga, cross over to the Hudson, and then capture Albany, where Burgoyne would put himself under the command of Howe, who, it was supposed, would come upriver. As part of the plan, a second force under Lieutenant Colonel Barry Saint Leger, numbering about two thousand British and loyalists troops and Indian allies, would create unrest among the settlers in the Mohawk Valley before moving in on Albany from the west.

On the defense, the Americans were in sorry shape. Getting no support or leadership from Congress, Schuyler, despite having had all winter and spring to prepare, could barely scrape together enough men to man Ticonderoga and its outer works. In direct command at Ticonderoga was General Arthur Saint Clair of Pennsylvania. He had only about twenty-one hundred Continentals and militiamen, and these troops had little training or battle experience. Saint Clair was in an impossible position, and the arrival of an additional nine hundred fresh militia in late June only compounded his problems, because he was running short on food and supplies.

Ticonderoga, aptly misnamed the "Gibraltar of America," fell early on 6 July but with a speed that surprised everyone. Overlooking the fort to the southwest was

Sugar Hill with no fortifications. Surveying that sharply rising promontory the day before, General William Phillips, Burgoyne's artillery chief and second in command, declared that "where a goat can go a man can go, and where a man can go he can drag a gun." Phillips ordered the placement of artillery on Sugar Hill's summit, soon renamed Mount Defiance. The prospect of artillery fire raining down on patriot defenders forced the patriots to abandon Ticonderoga. In the long run, the decision to retreat proved correct, since Saint Clair was able to save most of his troops from capture or annihilation. The fall of Ticonderoga raised British and loyalist spirits (King George reportedly danced in glee) and the upper Hudson Valley now lay open to a supremely overconfident Burgoyne.

THE INVASION SOURS: FORT SCHUYLER AND BENNINGTON. Fortunately for the American cause, Burgoyne, like Sir William Howe, was not especially vigorous in pursuit. Having raised the rebel standard at Fort Edward on the east bank of the upper Hudson River, Schuyler sent out desperate pleas for troops. He also ordered one thousand militiamen armed with axes to lay waste to the forest in Burgoyne's front. These patriots felled huge trees in crisscross patterns, rolled boulders into fording points on creeks, destroyed bridges, and dug trenches out of marshes overflowing from unusually heavy rains in order to flood low-lying points along the rough trail. The damage wrought was so heavy that it took the British army twenty-two days to claw its way through twenty-four miles of rugged terrain from Skenesborough to Fort Edward. It was not until 29 July that Burgoyne reached the burned-out remains of that fort, where he now elected to wait for the arrival of his artillery pieces and other heavy equipment being shipped southward over Lake George.

At Fort Edward Burgoyne still had nearly fifty miles to go before reaching Albany, but he was two hundred miles from his main base of supplies at Montreal. If he moved swiftly, supplies could be secured near Albany, but Burgoyne procrastinated. In Europe, Burgoyne would have requisitioned (a polite term for stealing) food and forage from the local populace for his troops and animals. Northern New York was sparsely populated, and Schuyler's men had stripped bare the mostly abandoned farmsteads. Even though Burgoyne was close to his objective, shortages forced him to send foraging parties farther and farther afield. This led to serious trouble near Bennington, Vermont.

At the same time, other aspects of the invasion plan were malfunctioning. Most obviously, General Howe, having found enough ambiguity in Germain's orders to forgo moving up the Hudson, was heading for the Chesapeake and Philadelphia. Sir William left Clinton in command of New York, and Clinton did not think he had enough troops to protect this important base, much less to assist Burgoyne in any significant way.

Saint Leger, leading the western prong of the British invasion, was also having his difficulties. By 2 August he had arrived outside of Fort Schuyler (previously known as Fort Stanwix) at the upper end of the Mohawk Valley. Saint Leger expected the dilapidated old fort to be garrisoned only by a few militiamen. His intelligence reports were wrong; the fort had been strengthened and defending it were 750 Americans ably led by Colonel Peter Gansevoort and Lieutenant Colonel Marinus Willett, two outstanding officers.

Not wanting to risk heavy casualties, Saint Leger lay siege to the fort. In the meantime, a local patriot militia officer, General Nicholas Herkimer, rallied eight hundred men and boys to march up the valley to relieve Fort Schuyler. Saint Leger sent four hundred Indians under the Mohawk chief Joseph Brant (Thayendanegea), and loyalist troops, including Colonel John Butler's Tory Rangers and Sir John Johnson's Royal Greens, to ambush this column. The Americans blundered into the trap at Oriskany on 6 August, suffering 150 casualties, including Herkimer.

When news of the slaughter at Oriskany reached Schuyler, now camped at Stillwater, he detached Benedict Arnold with eight hundred Continentals to relieve Fort Schuyler. Seeking to gain time, Arnold sent a local man trusted by the Indians to spread tales that his relief column was much larger than its actual size. The Indians, bolted away, already disheartened by the loss of several warriors at Oriskany and the lack of loot and scalps promised by Saint Leger, who could do little but retreat. Arnold joyously received that news in a message from Gansevoort on 23 August. Burgoyne's diversionary force had ceased to exist.

On the whole, Britain's Indian allies during Burgoyne's campaign were not very useful beyond serving as instruments of terror. They also played a significant role in creating one of the great myths of the Revolution. Moving ahead of Burgoyne's march, several Indians happened across a young woman named Jane McCrea near Fort Edward on 27 July. They killed and scalped her. Myth has it that McCrea's death so infuriated New Englanders that thousands of militiamen marched to Saratoga, where they defeated Burgoyne. Her brutal murder did cause some anger, but McCrea was a loyalist sympathizer engaged to an officer in Burgoyne's army, hardly an identity to evoke much sympathy. Further, so many settlers had been slaughtered over the years by Indian raiding parties that yet another death was unlikely to sour such a turnout. The presence of Burgoyne's army and the threat it posed to New England was reason enough.

About the same time that the McCrea story was spreading, Burgoyne's German commander, General Friedrich Adolph von Riedesel, suggested a raid to replenish the army's dragoon mounts and draft animals.

Moving ahead of Burgoyne's march, several Indians happened across a young woman named Jane McCrea near Fort Edward on 27 July. They killed and scalped her.

Burgoyne turned it into a major expedition to rally loyalists to the king's standard, sending eight hundred troops under Lieutenant Colonel Friedrich Baum—a poor choice because he could not speak English. At Bennington, on 14 August, Baum ran into General John Stark and fifteen hundred Continentals and militia. Baum's Indians fled, and Stark, who refused to serve under Continentals officers whom Congress had promoted over his head, brilliantly crushed his opponent two days later. Stark then turned his attention to a relief column under Lieutenant Colonel Heinrich von Breymann, defeating it in short order. At the cost of about eighty Americans killed and wounded, Burgoyne lost more than two hundred killed and another seven hundred captured.

SARATOGA. Bennington was a significant blow in a campaign that was no longer going according to Burgoyne's plan. As the British force inched closer to the major American position at Bemis Heights in Stillwater, New York, twenty-four miles south of Fort Edward on the west bank of the Hudson, its numbers shrank every day. Not only was there attrition from normal camp wastage (desertion, disease) and from constant sniping by Americans, but Burgoyne had to leave troops at Ticonderoga and Fort Edward to protect his supply route. Losing more than nine hundred on his best Hessian troops at Bennington reduced his army even further to about six thousand effectives as of 13 September, when he finally crossed the Hudson on a bridge of boats near Saratoga (now Schuylerville). Still believing Clinton would come to his aid, he cut his supply line in crossing over the Hudson.

Waiting for Burgoyne was a growing American force under a new commander, Horatio Gates. New Englanders in Congress had long wanted Schulyer's removal in favor of Gates, and the loss of Ticonderoga finally gave them that opportunity. Gates proudly took command on 19 August. Hearing that Burgoyne was about to cross the Hudson, Gates moved his men five miles north of Stillwater to defensive positions laid out by Benedict Arnold and Polish engineer Thaddeus Kosciusko at Bemis Heights. On 19 September Burgoyne divided his troops into three independent columns and advanced on the American lines. Arnold brought the Americans forward, and the battle opened at long range with Daniel Morgan's riflemen shooting down British officers. At Freeman's Farm the armies clashed, and the Americans held their own. The British suffered six hundred casualties and the Americans half that number.

Burgoyne continued to wait for Clinton, but his troops were growing short of supplies while the Americans gained new strength daily. Gates was content to sit behind his Bemis Heights fortifications while Arnold chafed over the lack of activity. On 7 October Burgoyne launched his second assault, really a reconnaissance in force. Led by Morgan, Henry Dearborn, Enoch Poor, and others, the Americans fought well. The battle had reached a critical point when up rode Arnold. He and Gates had quarreled after the first Battle of Freeman's Farm over many things, including Gates's lack of aggressiveness. Gates relieved Arnold of his command, but, urged by pro-Schuyler officers, he remained near American headquarters. When word came that the Americans were at a stalemate, Arnold rode with fury to the front, rallied the troops, and led them in a brilliant assault on the enemy. With Arnold in the van, they stormed and captured a British redoubt that anchored the enemy line. In the midst of this encounter, Arnold received another serious wound, shot in the same leg injured at Quebec. The second Battle of Freeman's Farm was a great patriot triumph, with the British losing another six hundred troops to 130 for the Americans. It also marked the beginning of the end for Burgoyne's army.

Clinton, in the meantime, was at last working his way up the Hudson. On 6 October he captured Fort Clinton and Fort Montgomery south of West Point, inflicting 250 casualties on the Americans under Israel Putnam while losing an equal number himself. Clinton's diversionary effort was feeble at best, and on 17 October Burgoyne formally surrendered his entire army to Gates, a general who had hardly drawn a whiff of gunpowder during the two battles. His name joined Burgoyne's on the surrender document, and his New England friends quickly lauded him as the "hero of Saratoga," a title that more properly belonged to Arnold, whose subsequent treason resulted in the deprecation of his indomitable role in entrapping Burgoyne's army.

BRANDYWINE CREEK. Sir William Howe chose not to sail directly up the Delaware River, since strategically placed American forts on the river south of Philadelphia could prevent or seriously hinder any operations of the Royal Navy. These forts would have to be reduced from the land, not river, side. Sailing up Chesapeake Bay instead, the British landed with no resistance at Head of Elk, (Maryland), about fifty miles southwest of Philadelphia. After spending several days letting his men and horses adapt to being on land, Howe advanced toward the rebel capital.

News that Howe's armada was rounding the Virginia capes set Washington's troops in motion. To bolster the sagging morale of its citizens and Congress, the American commander marched his army through Philadelphia on 24 August, then set up camp near Wilmington, Delaware. Several skirmishes occurred as the two forces jockeyed for position.

For political as well as military reasons, Washington could not allow the British to march unhindered into Philadelphia. Howe's force was moving farther inland, away from any naval support and stretching its supply line. An American victory had the potential to cause a British retreat. Washington deployed his troops along Brandywine Creek, centering his line at Chadds Ford. With his right somewhat in the air, Washington, recalling Howe's flanking movement on Long Island, had patrols posted to warn of any enemy attempt to envelop his line. Howe also remembered Long Island and Bunker Hill. On 11 September, he sent Baron Wilhelm von Knyphausen with five thousand troops against Chadds Ford as a demonstration. His main stroke came from

Surrender at Saratoga. British General John Burgoyne found himself surrounded by American troops on 17 October 1777 at Saratoga; he was forced to surrender his entire army to American General Horatio Gates. (National Archives/painting by John Trumbull)

Cornwallis, who started his seventy-five hundred soldiers on a wide, seventeen-mile flanking movement that would take them beyond the American right and into the very rear of Washington's army.

Washington and his generals had learned a great deal about waging war since Long Island, but the infrastructure of their army (for example, staff and field intelligence) remained undernourished and weak. Knyphausen drove back the patriot light infantry in his front, and then he and the Americans exchanged desultory artillery fire across Chadds Ford. Around midday, reports began arriving at Washington's headquarters that a large number of enemy troops and artillery were marching far to his right. Washington suspected that Howe had divided his columns. A full-scale assault by the concentrated American army might destroy Knyphausen's wing. The attack across the ford was being readied when General John Sullivan sent a note suggesting that the suspicious force could well be late-arriving militia. Fearful that he was facing the bulk of Howe's army instead of a wing, Washington cancelled the attack.

Around one o'clock in the afternoon a local farmer reported directly to Washington that the rebel army was nearly surrounded. Others confirmed the same. The American commander rushed up forces to strengthen his exposed flank. Washington's reinforcements picked good defensive positions but when Sullivan arrived on the scene he countermanded their orders and shifted their deployment.The British attacked in the midst of these changes.

Washington arrived just as the rebel line was breaking. He shored it up as best he could, but the British pressure was great. Some rebels were beginning to fall back when up rushed General George Weedon's Virginia division, having covered four miles in forty-five minutes. Weedon's panting men formed a line, opened it to let their retreating comrades through, then fired volley after volley into the advancing British. With Knyphausen pushing across Chadds Ford, Washington withdrew his army in relatively good order. Of the eleven thousand American troops engaged at Brandywine Creek, at least six hundred were killed or wounded with an additional three hundred or more taken prisoner. Of Howe's thirteen thousand men, about ninety were killed and another 450 wounded.

For the most part, the Americans fought extremely well, but this battle illustrated problems that plagued the rebels throughout the early years of the war. As a surveyor, Washington understood the importance of knowing the overall lay of the land, but neither he nor his leading generals fully understood how to take full advantage of battlefield terrain. In time they would learn how to gather and utilize solid tactical intelligence brought to them by such cavalry officers as Henry Lee. For the time being, however, British superiority in battlefield management gave them a large advantage.

STRIKING A COUNTERBLOW: GERMANTOWN. Following the battle and retreat from the Brandywine, Washington regrouped. It also helped that Howe, as was his fashion, failed to pursue. Howe sent a force to capture Wilmington and then evacuated his wounded to that location where the fleet, having left Head of Elk, was due to appear. As for Washington, he remained determined to resist and sought a battle on a field of his choice. He had to do something, he reasoned, because morale was plummeting and his total manpower had dropped to six thousand effectives. On 16 September at Warren Tavern near Philadelphia, the two armies readied for battle when a heavy rain soaked the ammunition of the Americans, so Washington withdrew behind the Schuylkill River.

Now British operational and tactical superiority showed itself. Washington marched his ragged, hungry army back and forth across the countryside in an effort to gain an advantage over the enemy. The disciplined, well-organized British gave no opening. On 19 September, Congress, realizing there was little hope of saving the capital, abandoned Philadelphia. The delegates soon relocated to Lancaster and then York, Pennsylvania. On 26 September, Cornwallis led a British column into Philadelphia, while Howe and the rest of his army set up camp in nearby Germantown.

The British had finally taken Philadelphia, certainly a comfortable location for winter quarters, but Howe had not finished off the rebel army. Further, he had paid a horrible price for capturing Philadelphia—the loss of Burgoyne's army. British generals may have been better than their American counterparts in operations and tactics, but Howe demonstrated their greatest weakness—the inability to execute a strategic plan with the potential to break the back of the rebels.

On 20 September, Wayne's force camped at Paoli.

Led by General Sir Charles Grey, the British

launched a surprise attack using only their bayonets.

It was a slaughter.

None of this was yet clear when the Americans suffered another setback in the early morning hours of 21 September. As Washington maneuvered, he left behind

General Anthony Wayne's division of fifteen hundred to harass the enemy. On the evening of 20 September, Wayne's force camped at Paoli. Led by General Sir Charles Grey, the British launched a surprise attack using only their bayonets, earning Grey the nickname "No-Flint." It was a slaughter. Six British soldiers were killed and twenty-two wounded to Wayne's two hundred killed, one hundred wounded, and almost another one hundred captured. The Paoli massacre only further dampened patriot morale.

More determined than ever, Washington refused to back off and give up the fight. Gaining twenty-five hundred reinforcements from the Hudson Highlands, he could count on nearly eight thousand Continentals and three thousand militia in early October. Demonstrating a level of boldness lacking in his opponent, he decided on an attack on Germantown, where Howe had stationed nine thousand regulars, hoping to catch the overconfident British off guard. Washington's plan of attack was something of a repeat of his highly successful Trenton operation—four converging columns striking simultaneously at dawn. Strategic initiative, however, did not translate into sound operational planning. Involving thousands rather than hundred of troops, the plan proved too complex, plus the vagaries of war interceded, in this case an impenetrable fog.

Washington worked throughout the evening of 3 October to move his columns into position. The battle began at first light. The dense fog initially assisted the attackers, who stormed into the British camps and sent them fleeing. A dramatic turnabout victory seemed possible, but this time, unlike Trenton, Washington would not achieve his campaign-saving triumph. The fog started to hamper American pursuit operations. When a company of British soldiers barricaded themselves in a brick house, Henry Knox tried to reduce that stronghold rather than leaving a small unit to tie down these troops. The effect was to slow one part of the advance. In the heavy fog two rebel columns collided and incurred casualties from friendly fire before becoming disentangled. The British rallied and began driving forward. With each column alone and feeling the weight of the British counterattack, panic set in, but instead of running, many American units simply about-faced and marched from the battlefield. The patriots lost about 650 casualties and another four hundred were captured, while the British suffered 550 killed and wounded.

In a roundabout way, the American defeat at Germantown functioned to boost patriot morale. What Howe had hoped would be a quick and easy campaign to capture Philadelphia and destroy Washington's army was taking too long a time and costing the British hundreds of casualties. Although severely battered, the main rebel army was still in the field, a true point of despair for Howe as well as political leaders back in England, who had seen a sensible campaign strategy go completely awry through mismanagement in America and who now wondered whether there was any way to win the Revolution. All of this became clear with the loss of Burgoyne's army on 17 October.

In the meantime, Howe gained another tactical triumph. He abandoned Germantown in mid-October and concentrated his efforts on reducing the river forts below Philadelphia. He had to do so in order to reestablish a convenient supply line with the British fleet. After heated exchanges, Fort Mifflin on the Pennsylvania side fell on 16 November, and the defense of Fort Mercer on the Jersey side became untenable five days later. The Royal Navy now controlled the lower Delaware and had access to Philadelphia, but in reducing the forts the British again suffered heavy casualties. These were troops that could not be easily replaced once the French formally entered the war in 1778.

VALLEY FORGE. Washington led his eleven thousand exhausted soldiers into Valley Forge, twenty miles northwest of Philadelphia, on 19 December. The troops were in desperate shape. "Unless some great and capital change takes place," explained the commander in chief, "this Army must inevitably . . . starve, dissolve, or disperse." The most pressing problem was the need for basic supplies. Even as the soldiers constructed rude huts, they had virtually no food or drink. Firecake, flour cooked in water, represented the common meal, the kind of food that turned human "Guts . . . to pasteboard," according to one officer. Even before the New Year soldiers could be heard chanting, "No meat, no bread, no soldier!"

Under the ineffective management of General Thomas Mifflin of Pennsylvania, the Continental supply system had broken down. The problem only began to correct itself after wealthy Connecticut merchant Jeremiah Wadsworth took over the commissary department and Nathanael Greene accepted the quartermaster generalship. These staff changes were little solace to soldiers who were virtually naked and in some cases starving to death. Even as late as February 1778, about four thousand troops were unfit for duty because they lacked such essentials as shoes, clothing, and blankets.

Not surprisingly, death was a daily occurrence at Valley Forge. About one-fourth of Washington's total troop strength perished that winter, succumbing to malnutrition, typhus, and smallpox, among other diseases. Local civilians did not seem to care. They wanted nothing to do with rapidly depreciating Continental dollars, but they did not mind selling rotten meat and old, moth-infested clothing and blankets to the army, basically the goods the British would not take with their gold and silver. Out of desperation, Washington started to allow occasional requisitioning—looting is a more accurate term—of basic supplies from local citizens, especially those known to be trading with the British. He had no other choice, since his ill-clad, hungry soldiers were deserting at an alarming rate. If he was to have an army that he could put in the field after the winter season, he had to violate his own sensibilities about always treating local civilians with respect.

Fortunately, the Valley Forge winter was not the harshest in terms of frigid weather; that dubious honor befell the winter encampment of 1779–1780 at Jockey Hollow near Morristown, New Jersey. Relatively mild weather plus an early shad run on the Schuylkill River saved many lives but did not eliminate the bitterness welling up in thousands of officers and soldiers who could not understand why patriot civilians were so indifferent to their needs.

Even before Valley Forge, restive officers had became vocal in demanding postwar pensions, as well as salable commissions and pensions for the widows of officers who gave their lives to the cause of liberty. During the winter Washington wrote Congress on behalf of the officers, but the delegates rejected these demands as unrepublican. They wanted no professional officer caste, as existed in Europe, but in May 1778 they approved half-pay pensions for seven years and a bonus of eighty dollars for each soldier who continued service. Congress did so to assure that an army existed for the 1778 campaign, but the delegates did not take the pension promise very seriously.

"Heaven has been determined to save your Country; or a weak General and bad Councelors would have ruind it."

Driven from Philadelphia, Congress provided weak, ineffective civilian leadership that winter. Characteristic was its decision to name General Thomas Conway, a foreign adventurer in the Continental officer corps, to the post of inspector general. Conway arrived at Valley Forge ready to assume his duties in training the troops, but Washington and his family of staff officers would have nothing to do with a man whom they thought was at the heart of an intrigue, known as the Conway Cabal, to supplant Washington at the head of the army with the "hero of Saratoga," Horatio Gates.

Conway had written Gates the previous autumn: "Heaven has been determined to save your Country; or a weak General and bad Councelors would have ruind it." When Washington and his staff found out about Conway's comments, they assumed the worst. Historians have argued that there really was not much of a plot to replace Washington, but the commander in chief believed there was, and he was not going to let the likes of Conway get a foothold at Valley Forge for his political enemies, among whom Washington numbered a few leaders in Congress.

Out of this small tempest came good fortune. Baron Friedrich Wilhelm von Steuben, a pretended Prussian nobleman, had presented himself to Congress and offered to serve as a volunteer in the Continental army. Steuben traveled to Valley Forge and sought out Washington, who gave him a chance to train a model company of troops. Since he spoke little English, the baron used his vibrant personality along with grunts and universal swear words to convey the essentials of drill. The soldiers and officers, whom he insisted had to lead in the training, loved Steuben and his methods of instruction. There can be no doubt that a better-trained army emerged at the end of the Valley Forge encampment. As for Steuben, he received a general's commission and the position of inspector general.

More than anything else, the signing of two treaties of alliance with France in February 1778 cheered the soldiery at Valley Forge. They thoroughly enjoyed the official celebration in early May. Besides having all rank and filers participate in a *feu de joie* of musketry, Washington permitted each an extra gill of rum that day. Not only had they survived the winter and received better training than ever before, but they also had gained a powerful European ally. The British thus had the most to be downcast about at the end of the Valley Forge winter, not the Americans.

MILITARY OPERATIONS: 1778

The Franco-American alliance had a dramatic impact on Britain's approach to the war. Rather than continuing to concentrate its military strength against the erstwhile colonists in North America, the new theme was dispersal of manpower—to protect the homeland and especially valuable holdings in the West Indies as well as other points around the globe. The initial indication came in June 1778 when Sir Henry Clinton, who replaced a discredited Sir William Howe as Britain's North American commander, received orders from Lord Germain. Clinton was to vacate Philadelphia, retreat to New York City, and prepare to furnish regulars for defense elsewhere, particularly the West Indies. Germain's directive curtailed any major British offensive for the year. With his reinvigorated army, Washington gave chase across New Jersey and nearly scored a major victory at Monmouth Court House. The American commander then chose to hover outside New York, longing for the opportunity to engage in combined operations with the French and strike a mortal blow against Clinton's depleted forces.

MONMOUTH COURT HOUSE. With vessels in short supply, Clinton decided to march his ten thousand troops, along with camp followers, loyalists, and considerable baggage, across New Jersey to New York. On 18 June he evacuated Philadelphia. Washington immediately broke camp and ordered his light cavalry and local militiamen to throw obstructions in the British path. Somewhat unsure of his strategy, the commander hoped to loop a net around Clinton's force. On 24 June, Washington called a council of war and asked his generals how best to inflict a serious wound, perhaps even bag his prey without putting his own army at grave risk.

The recently exchanged Major General Charles Lee, having missed the hardening of the patriot soldiery during the 1777 campaign and the Valley Forge winter, vigorously objected to Washington's desire to attack; Americans stood little chance against British professionals, Lee sneered, as if time had stood still while he was an enemy prisoner. What resulted was a compromise plan that pleased no one—the detachment of fifteen hundred troops to shadow Clinton while the main American army followed behind.

Washington then learned that Clinton's path was taking him through Monmouth Court House in New Jersey. He decided to strengthen the detachment, raising its numbers to four thousand with the idea of striking at Clinton's rear. Washington wanted the Marquis de Lafayette to lead the force, but protocol dictated that he first offer the post to Lee, his second-ranking general. Lee disdainfully turned down the assignment, then reversed himself when he learned that Washington would entrust the command to the much younger and less experienced Lafayette.

Clinton, in the meantime, pushed his wool-coated, heavily laden column toward Monmouth Court House, but with the temperature soaring to nearly one hundred degrees, some died from heat exhaustion along the route. On 27 June, Washington ordered Lee, now reinforced to five thousand troops, to attack. Early the next morning, on what turned out to be an equally sweltering day, Lee, having failed to reconnoiter the enemy, moved his troops forward but with no apparent plan of attack. In response, Clinton ordered his rear guard to confront the Americans. As the patriots maneuvered for position, they became confused and pulled back, either on their own or under Lee's orders. Lee then led all of his men in an orderly retreat—not a regrouping. It now appeared that Clinton would escape unscathed.

At this point, all was in confusion in the rebel ranks, at least until Washington arrived to find Lee's exhausted men heading to the rear. Washington confronted his subordinate, and whether he "swore that day till the leaves shook on the trees" was irrelevant. He did upbraid Lee, then relieved him of command. The truculent Lee would later demand a court-martial to clear his name, but he was convicted of disobeying orders and of showing lack of respect for his commander in chief, which effectively ended his controversial military career.

Washington confronted Lee, and whether he "swore that day till the leaves shook on the trees" was irrelevant. He relieved him of command.

With the rebels in retreat, Clinton saw an opportunity to strike a telling blow. Sending his wagon train northward, he launched a major attack. Washington quickly formed a patchwork defensive line. His soldiers fought well, despite the oppressive heat. Steuben's training had indeed paid off. As dusk closed on the battlefield, Washington tried to organize a counterattack, but total exhaustion and thirst stymied the assault. Early the next morning, Clinton's troops stole off. By 30 June, they were at Sandy Hook, waiting to be ferried to safety in New York City.

British casualties at Monmouth amounted to more than 250 dead and well over three hundred wounded and missing; rebel losses were slightly less. Tactically the battle was a draw, but it demonstrated that the remodeled Continental army could now hold its own against the king's regulars. This point was not lost on Clinton, who avoided further large-scale engagements with Washington. The British commander kept arguing in letters home that he could not risk a showdown engagement without new increments of troops, which the ministry repeatedly refused him. Thus, Monmouth Court House was the last major battle in the northern theater during the war.

From this point forward, Washington concentrated his energies on trying to devise a plan to drive the British from New York City. It seemed as if the opportunity was immediately at hand when a French fleet under Charles, Comte d'Estaing, appeared off Sandy Hook just a few days after British vessels had moved Clinton's force safely across New York bay. Without a plan of joint operations and with d'Estaing fretting about safely crossing the sand bar at the bay's entrance, nothing resulted from these potentially fortuitous circumstances. Washington never obtained his longed-for opportunity to challenge the British on Manhattan.

BUNGLED FRANCO-AMERICAN OPERATIONS AT NEWPORT. On 22 July, d'Estaing sailed for Rhode Island, where an American force under General John Sullivan was trying to dislodge some three thousand British troops. The British had originally taken Newport late in 1776 to secure a second strong naval base. With the French fleet on its way, Washington sent reinforcements eastward and called for an outpouring of militia support. Sullivan assembled ten thousand troops and carefully coordinated his battle plan with d'Estaing. At first everything went well. The French fleet penetrated into the bay, driving several English ships on the rocks. Sullivan, in the meantime, started advancing from Providence toward Newport. On 9 August a British fleet under "Black Dick" Howe came over the horizon. Abandoning the patriot land force, which included French troops, d'Estaing sailed out to engage Howe. A sudden, violent storm on 11 August did serious damage to both fleets, and Howe soon sailed back to New York with his outnumbered vessels.

D'Estaing returned to the bay, but he only wanted to embark previously landed troops. He informed Sullivan that he was going to Boston to refit. Sullivan was apoplectic. His force had made great strides in advancing toward the British, but his entreaties and those of Lafayette fell on deaf ears. Seeing the French fleet depart, the militia also decided to leave. Sullivan had no choice but to withdraw, at which point the British commander, General Robert Pigot, was quick to pursue what remained of the patriot force. At the northern end of the island a violent little battle took place, during which the Americans fought well and drove back the British on 29 August before making an orderly retreat. Pigot's troops sustained 260 casualties, as compared to about 210 for the patriots. Newport, with its fine anchorage, remained in British hands, and the first joint Franco-American venture proved to be something of an embarrassment.

THE BRITISH RECAPTURE SAVANNAH. In late 1778 the war in the South began heating up, an important harbinger of future events. Lieutenant Colonel Archibald Campbell and thirty-five hundred troops sailed from New York in late November with naval escort under Admiral Sir Hyde Parker. On 23 December, the small assault force arrived at the mouth of the Savannah River. Assisted by General Augustine Prevost, who moved up from East Florida, Campbell drove back American General Robert Howe's mixed Continental and militia unit. On 29 December Campbell launched a demonstration attack against the American front, holding them in place, while a local black guided the British through swamps and around the American right flank. Forced from their strong defensive positions, the patriots retreated across a treacherous swamp where many drowned. Eighty-three Americans were killed and more than 450 were captured. At the cost of only twenty-six casualties, Campbell and Prevost had resecured Savannah for the British.

MILITARY OPERATIONS: 1779

The year began with additional American losses in the South. Georgia fell into British hands, and a joint Franco-American effort to liberate that state was an unmitigated disaster. In the north, the British, for the most part, remained inert. Washington stayed poised for action but was unable to gather enough troop strength for an assault. The ongoing petit guerre continued without respite, as demonstrated by successful rebel raids on Stony Point and Paulus Hook. On their own, Massachusetts patriots tried to drive the British from what is now modern Maine, but they failed miserably. Only in the West did the Americans score victories of lasting consequence. These triumphs came at the expense of native Americans allied with the British and helped open western New York and the Ohio country to white settlement after the revolutionary war.

THE SOUTH. Except for sporadic outbursts of guerrilla warfare, the revolutionary war in the South had not seen a major action since Clinton's attempt to take Charleston in June 1776. When Savannah fell, everything changed. In early 1780 General Prevost moved against rebel resisters in Georgia, and soon that former colony was again a royal province. Mounted militia under rebel partisan Colonel Andrew Pickens carried off some successful raids, but nothing stopped the British from advancing into South Carolina. General Prevost made an attempt on Charleston in May but backed off in the face of stout resistance. Oppressive summer heat and outbreaks of malaria and yellow fever caused a virtual suspension of operations during the summer.

In the meantime, Comte d'Estaing had refitted his fleet at Boston and sailed to the West Indies, promising to return the next year. Washington remained anxious to conduct joint operations against New York City, but d'Estaing decided to focus on the South. In early September he arrived unexpectedly in Charleston with thirty-three ships and almost forty-five hundred troops. He and General Benjamin Lincoln, the Continental army's commander, in the South, decided to strike at Savannah. Moving into position later that month, the allies had the opportunity to achieve a notable victory.

When General Prevost refused to surrender his heavily outnumbered force, d'Estaing decided on a formal siege. A few days later, however, the admiral started to grow nervous. His captains had him worried about the damage that could be done to his fleet by potentially turbulent autumn weather, including hurricanes. Likewise, his sailors were succumbing to scurvy at an estimated rate of thirty-five per day.

D'Estaing informed Lincoln of his desire to attack the British fortifications. The ill-fated assault came on 9 October. An American flanking party got lost in the swamps and proved useless. South Carolinians, some under a feisty little officer named Francis Marion, took one British redoubt, but that was the high point. Unsupported, the Carolinians fell back in the face of a fierce British counterattack. The French fared little better, marching their columns directly into strong enemy fire, and d'Estaing was wounded. The brave Continental dragoon leader General Casimir Pulaski, a Polish nobleman who had fought at Brandywine and Germantown, foolishly led his cavalry against the well-entrenched enemy and received a mortal wound. The British sustained about 150 casualties, as compared to nearly nine hundred for the allies, in what was truly an inglorious day for combined operations.

The French returned to their ships and sailed away for France in late October. Lincoln could do little more than retreat to Charleston. D'Estaing had disappointed the Americans three times—off Sandy Hook, at Newport, and now at Savannah. These failures help to account for the lack of popular enthusiasm when word reached America that Spain had also decided to join the allied coalition.

THE NORTH. Little combat occurred in the New England states after Burgoyne's surrender. General William Tryon, former New York royal governor, led raiding expeditions against coastal Connecticut communities, burning Norwalk and Fairfield, and other towns, which occasionally received harassing fire from passing British warships. In addition, the British had fortified a

Attack on Savannah. The British captured Savannah on 29 December 1778. In October 1779, American General Benjamin Lincoln, allied with French Admiral d'Estaing, attacked Savannah in an ill-fated attempt to drive the British from the city. (National Archives/illustration by A. I. Keller)

post on Penobscot Bay in the Massachusetts province of Maine to cut timber for masts. In the summer of 1779, the state decided to drive away the British. Two thousand militia boarded ships under Commodore Dudley Saltonstall. For two weeks the commodore bombarded the enemy post, but these efforts were ineffective. Then, on 14 August, a British squadron sailed into the bay. Reboarding the militia, Saltonstall fled up the Penobscot River, where the citizen-soldiers debarked and fled. Completely trapped, Saltonstall set his ships afire as the expedition ended in disaster. Having used a portion of its merchant fleet as transports, Massachusetts lost about $7 million on the venture, which left the government in virtually bankruptcy.

Farther south, finances—or, rather, the lack of them—hurt Washington's efforts to challenge Clinton. The commander struggled to keep enough troops in the field in the absence of pay and basic supplies. Washington did the best with what few resources he had and put as much pressure on the British as possible, as witnessed by two major raids that helped keep patriot morale from completely collapsing.

By 1778 Henry Hamilton had earned the name "Hair Buyer" because of the British willingness to pay for scalps.

On 1 June, after sallying up the Hudson, a British force captured the American post at Verplancks Point, forcing the rebels to abandon their position at Stony Point across the river. After sending out "Light Horse Harry" Lee to ascertain whether Stony Point could be retaken, Washington called upon Anthony Wayne, the victim of the surprise attack at Paoli, to lead a late night bayonet assault. The plan worked flawlessly, and early on 16 July Wayne's light infantry force scored a major victory, retaking Stony Point and capturing nearly 475 enemy troops (plus more than 130 killed and wounded) at the cost of one hundred casualties. Two months later, Washington approved another operation, Henry Lee's daring foray in which on 19 August he attacked and temporarily captured a British outpost on Paulus Hook, New Jersey.

Such raids helped keep the indecisive Clinton on guard and inactive in the southern New York theater. Worried about his limited troop strength, the British commander doubted that he could afford to conduct a war of attrition against Washington. He did continue to authorize coastal raids, and as the chilling temperatures of autumn swept over New York, he focused his energies on capitalizing on British successes in the South.

PATRIOT VICTORIES IN THE WEST. Sporadic British and Indian forays along the frontier were a source of much bloodshed during the revolutionary war. The rebels did retaliate, and in 1779 they gained noteworthy victories. In the areas of Kentucky and western Virginia, the Indian allies of Henry Hamilton, based in Detroit as a lieutenant governor of the Quebec government, had regularly sponsored guerrilla-like raids in which Indians scalped and killed those few whites who were brave enough to risk settlement in the trans-Appalachian West. By 1778 Hamilton had earned the name "Hair Buyer" because of the British willingness to pay for scalps.

Virginia Governor Patrick Henry listened to the entreaties of young George Rogers Clark, who had been imploring him to go on the offensive against the Indians. The plan was to protect such areas as Kentucky by striking north of the Ohio River, particularly in the Indiana-Illinois country. Clark and his 175 rangers marched overland to the old French settlements of Kaskaskia, Cahokia, and Vincennes. Clark convinced the inhabitants to recognize the political authority of Virginia, and he also intimidated the local Indians into making promises of peace.

When "Hair Buyer" Hamilton heard about Clark's expedition, he rallied 230 troops, including seventy Indians, and marched for Vincennes in October 1778, where he reestablished royal authority. Clark, who was with the main body of his rangers at Kaskaskia, accepted the challenge. Trudging through torrential winter rains in February 1779, the determined frontiersmen reached Vincennes before the end of the month. Then, in full view of the small stockade, Clark brought forward four Indians, who when captured had white scalps tied to their belts. He next ordered his troops to tomahawk the Indians to death, shouting that the same fate would befall anyone captured in the fort. Hamilton quickly surrendered with his force.

Although Clark's rangers were too few to control the entire region, their dramatic capture of Hamilton and his followers at Vincennes so impressed warlike local Indians that their raids became much more infrequent after February 1779—at least until thousands of white settlers started pouring into the region after the Revolution. Equally important, Clark's exploits became a basis for American claims to the huge territory known as the Old Northwest during the peace negotiations with the British that commenced in 1782.

The New York–Pennsylvania frontier was also a hot spot for bloody raids. Although some of the powerful

Clark's march against the Vincennes. In February 1779, Colonel George Rogers Clark (center) led a body of rangers though torrential rains and floods toward Vincennes, an Indiana settlement under British control. (National Archives/painting by Ezra Winter)

tribes in the Iroquois confederacy of Six Nations sought neutrality or sided with the Americans, many joined the British as allies, usually with Chief Joseph Brant in the lead. Fort Niagara in western New York was their staging point, and they engaged in destructive raids in concert with the loyalist rangers under Major John Butler and his son, Walter. In 1777 they fought at Oriskany (6 October), and in 1778 they massacred settlers (3 July) in the Wyoming Valley region of Pennsylvania and in Cherry Valley (11 November) near the Mohawk River.

At the urging of the Continental Congress, Washington ordered John Sullivan to organize a punitive expedition. Sullivan gathered a force of three thousand Continentals at Easton, Pennsylvania, during May 1779, then headed westward toward the Wyoming Valley. Finding no signs of his prey, Sullivan turned northward in July and marched his troops into the heart of the Iroquois country. On 29 August they tangled with Brant's Indians and John Butler's rangers at Newtown, New York. Facing possible extinction, Brant and Butler finally retreated, leaving western New York open to Sullivan's force.

During September the Continentals pursued a scorched-earth strategy. They systematically destroyed crops and ransacked and burned at least forty-one Indian villages. The devastation was so great that hundreds of Iroquois, unable to get adequate supplies from the British, starved to death during the next winter. Sullivan's expedition all but destroyed the capacity of Brant and Butler to keep terrorizing the New York–Pennsylvania frontier. Even more significant, the Six Nations never regained the strength to keep control of central and western New York. Like other native Americans, they would be swept westward in the postwar rush of land-hungry white speculators and settlers to claim yet more territory.

MILITARY OPERATIONS: 1780

The Revolution reached its low point for the Americans in 1780. Even though fifty-five hundred French troops under Jean Baptiste de Vimeur, the Comte de Rochambeau, landed in Rhode Island during July, Washington could not convince his ally to conduct joint operations against New York. Rochambeau believed that without tactical naval support and superiority, any such effort would fail miserably. About all the American commander had to cheer about in 1780 were small-scale victories at Connecticut Farms (6 June) and Springfield (23 June) in New Jersey, when the British made an uninspired attempt to carry the war back into that state.

Washington's determination to go on the offensive was a reflection of his fears about the possible disintegration of his army. Among what Alexander Hamilton referred to as "symptoms of a most alarming nature" were such basic problems as lack of pay, decent food, clothing, and what officers and soldiers alike perceived as civilian indifference toward the army's pitiful circumstances.

What pay there was came in the form of Continental dollars, now so worthless that a private's wages for four months, complained a despondent officer, "will not procure his wretched wife and children a single bushel of wheat." Congress attempted to refinance its currency in the spring of 1780, but the effort failed. Restive soldiers rose in mutinies, the most dramatic coming in January 1781 when first the Pennsylvania and then the New Jersey lines revolted. Delicate negotiations and, in the case of the Jerseyites, brute force, got these troops back under control while Washington struggled to maintain a military presence in the field.

The officers were also in a foul mood. They spoke openly of civilian ingratitude. They complained that citizens were prospering at home while they sacrificed their own self-interest by continuing to engage in long-term military service. In 1779 General Alexander McDougall of New York asked: "Can the Country expect Spartan Virtue in her army, while the people are wallowing in all the luxury of Rome in her declining State?" He thought the "consequence is obvious." In July 1780 Washington's angry senior officers sent a belligerent remonstrance to Congress in which they threatened to resign en masse unless the delegates guaranteed them, at a minimum, half-pay pensions for life. As before, Congress balked. Not only did that body lack a fixed source of revenue, but civil leaders continued to worry about the creation of a privileged military caste in a republican society.

Events beyond the control of Congress forced that body to concede the demands of the officers. In September, General Benedict Arnold, after plotting with Clinton's adjutant, Major John André, to turn the crucial West Point defenses over to the British, renounced the American cause. Over the years Arnold had grown bitter. Despite a brilliant military record, Congress had treated him shabbily with respect to promotions. As did other ranking officers, Arnold had dissipated much of his personal fortune in support of the war, but the delegates had refused to settle his military accounts on something akin to a fair basis. As a former fervent rebel who no longer thought the cause worth saving, he was openly lamenting in the summer of 1780 "that our army is permitted to starve in a land of plenty."

Arnold's treason infuriated the civilian populace, but their wrath—they labeled him as the greatest villain in the American experience—did not carry over into a new rush of enlistments. Washington's troop resources continued to dwindle during the fall of 1780, partially caused by the need to send Continentals southward into North Carolina and South Carolina where the British were mounting a major campaign. The rebels had lost Charleston in May 1780, and then they took a second beating at Camden in August. Grim news from the South in combination with Arnold's treason forced Congress to concede on officers' pensions in October, provided a source was found for funding. The delegates did so out of dire necessity. They worried about other ranking officers going over to the British standard, and they had to have a command structure in place to deal with enemy forces.

REVAMPED BRITISH STRATEGY AND THE TAKING OF CHARLESTON. With British troops spread more thinly across the globe, Lord Germain and other home leaders resurrected earlier reports from royal governors regarding widespread loyalist sentiments in the South. Seeing loyal Americans as a substitute source of strength in the face of troop shortages, the king's ministers put together a strategy that had a substantial body of regulars initially reconquering a particular southern region, then drawing upon loyalists to restore royal government and maintain military order, especially in breaking up lingering bands of rebel partisans. Once pacification was under way, the regular force would move into yet another region and begin the process anew. By attrition, the entire South would return to royal authority and, in time, become a vast staging area for subduing the north.

Reconquering Georgia in 1779 and holding it against a combined Franco-American force seemed to prove the merits of the British southern strategy. The next logical step was to capture Charleston, the major southern port town and a logical naval and supply base in support of inland operations. Leaving General Knyphausen in command of ten thousand troops in New York City, Clinton loaded eighty-seven hundred soldiers aboard ships—the flotilla of ninety transport vessels and ten warships also carried five thousand sailors and marines—and set sail for Charleston.

The British invasion fleet cleared Sandy Hook on 26 December 1779. Violent storms blew the fleet all over the Atlantic, but Clinton finally had enough troops in place to begin his campaign against Charleston by mid-February 1780. The commander of the Southern Department, Benjamin Lincoln, worked feverishly to block Clinton's advances. He commanded thirty-six hundred troops, less than half of whom were Continentals. He would be reinforced by another 750 Virginia Continentals led by General William Woodford.

Clinton moved slowly against the city, initiating a formal siege. Naval vessels under Admiral Arbuthnot ran the gauntlet of Charleston's harbor defenses, and Cornwallis swept away all rebel resistance in the surrounding areas. British raiding parties under Lieutenant Colonel Banastre Tarleton and Major Patrick Ferguson ranged deeper into South Carolina with the objective of cutting off all sources of aid.

Lincoln wanted to pull his troops out of Charleston, sacrificing it to save his army as Washington advised, but the town fathers begged him to stay. When the British noose tightened and he could not withdraw, the leading citizens then reproached him for the suffering his stand brought upon the city. Ringed by the British lines, running out of ammunition and food, Lincoln found himself with no other choice but surrender, which he did in formal ceremonies with regimental colors cased on 12 May. The fall of Charleston was a second major building block in successfully executing the British southern strategy.

"Tarleton's quarter" became a phrase among patriots for massacring surrendered foes.

An ironic indication that all was not yet lost for the Americans came later that month on 29 May at Waxhaw Creek near the North Carolina border. Tarleton's light dragoons stumbled onto four hundred Virginia Continentals under Colonel Abraham Buford who had not made it to Charleston in time and were marching home. In the ensuing action, the patriots fared poorly and sought to surrender (or "quarter"). Just then Tarleton's horse took a tumble. Seeing their leader go down infuriated the loyalist horsemen, who slaughtered the surrendering Americans with their sabers, killing and wounding more than 260. "Tarleton's quarter" became a phrase among patriots for massacring surrendered foes and helped reignite rebel partisan resistance that was never successfully overcome by the British.

Before returning to New York, Clinton set up a series of posts to control the South Carolina backcountry, and he issued a pardon to all who had borne arms against the Crown. Many patriots believed that the war was over and came in under this armistice to take the prescribed oath of loyalty. Then, as Clinton departed, leaving Cornwallis in charge of operations, he altered the conditions of parole. Not only would parolees have to swear not to take up arms against the British, but they would now have to fight for them. Disgusted by what they considered British duplicity, many parolees re-

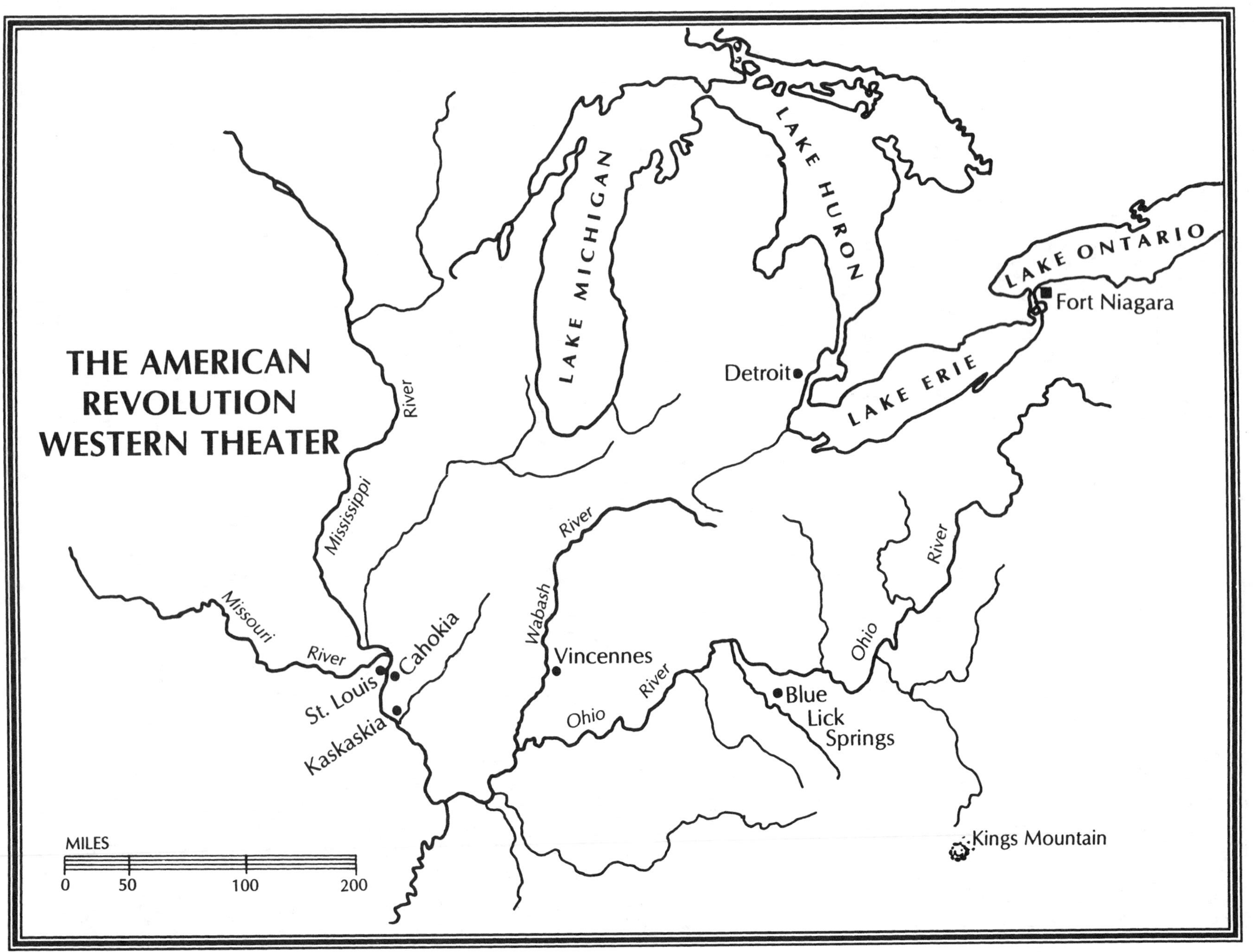

THE AMERICAN
REVOLUTION
WESTERN THEATER
LAKE MICHIGAN
LAKE HURON
LAKE ONTARIO
Fort Niagara
Detroit
LAKE ERIE
River
Mississippi
River
Wabash
River
Missouri
River
Cahokia
St. Louis
Kaskaskia
Vincennes
Ohio
River
Blue
Lick
Springs
Ohio
River
Kings Mountain
MILES
0
50
100
200

nounced their oaths, returned to the field, and engaged in what became a particularly nasty guerrilla war. They joined the partisan bands of such leaders as Francis Marion, Andrew Pickens, and Thomas Sumter, men who intimately knew the terrain, including the best places for ambushes and the most secretive swamps for hideouts.

Loyalist guerrillas, in turn, now spurred on by the presence of the British army, sought revenge for years of brutal treatment at the hands of rebel partisans. The result was a bitter, violent civil war between former friends and even among families with quarter rarely asked for or given.

ANOTHER REBEL DEBACLE: CAMDEN. Bereft of a commander in the South, Congress turned to General Horatio Gates, so long a favorite of the New Englanders, and ordered him to North Carolina to pull together what troops there were into a Continental force. Washington would have preferred Nathanael Greene, but Congress had unbounded confidence in Gates, who gladly took the assignment and soon assembled an army of three thousand, consisting of half-trained militia and veteran Maryland and Delaware Continentals under Baron Johann de Kalb, a pretended German nobleman of great martial talent.

Taking hardly a moment to train his soldiers, Gates incautiously marched southward in search of the enemy, moving toward Camden, South Carolina, supposedly a lightly garrisoned British outpost. What the new southern commander did not know was that Cornwallis was rushing toward him from Charleston with hundreds of troops. Before dawn on 16 August the two armies squared off for battle just north of Camden. Making a colossal error, Gates placed all of his militia on one flank and his Continentals under de Kalb on the other. Cornwallis sent his best veterans against the inexperienced militiamen, who quickly broke and ran. Gates himself soon fled, riding more than sixty miles northward before the day was through. As a demonstration of horsemanship, quipped Alexander Hamilton, it did "admirable credit to the activity of a man at his time of life. But it disgraces the general and the soldier."

The tough British and loyalist troops next turned their attention to the Continentals. Rallying around the massive de Kalb, these veterans fought like demons until their leader, bleeding from eleven wounds, fell dead. They then broke in what became a rout. The British suffered 324 casualties to well over one thousand for the Americans. Not only had a second Continental force been taken out of the war in a space of four months, but North Carolina now lay wide open to advances from Cornwallis.

KINGS MOUNTAIN. Throwing aside caution, an exuberant Cornwallis decided to rally the loyalists of North Carolina. He appreciated that the pacification of South Carolina would never be complete as long as the rebels could use North Carolina as a sanctuary to refit and resupply. Cornwallis sent Major Patrick Ferguson and his loyalist troops into the South Carolina backcountry, near the North Carolina and Tennessee borders, while he moved into the central part of the state.

Ferguson believed in aggressive counterinsurgency methods, and he threatened those in his path with destruction. Frontiersmen from over the mountains (in what is now modern east Tennessee) took umbrage at his actions and bragging. They gathered under several officers, tracked Ferguson and his men down, and on 7 October surrounded them atop Kings Mountain in northern South Carolina. Armed with long rifles and shouting "Remember Buford" and "no quarter," the frontiersmen poured a torrent of fire on the enemy, pulling back each time when Ferguson's soldiers counterattacked, then driving them back up the mountain. Before the battle was over, they had killed Ferguson and about 150 of his men, wounded 160, and captured all but a handful of the remaining 700 troops.

The frontiersmen were not trained soldiers, rather partisans who summarily hanged nine captured loyalists after giving gallows reprieves to many others. Cornwallis, in the meantime, quit North Carolina to regroup while news of Kings Mountain curbed loyalist enthusiasm for joining his army. What the enraged frontiersmen had effected was a turning point victory for rebel fortunes in the South.

The army that Nathanael Greene found in North Carolina was in terrible condition, lacking everything. Some Virginia militia were nearly naked and Greene sent them home.

GREENE ASSUMES THE SOUTHERN COMMAND. With Gates in open disrepute, Congress asked Washington to name a Southern Department commander. He selected the person he originally wanted—Nathanael Greene. Prior to the war, Greene's only military experience came from service as a militia private and from studying works on the art of war. His wartime experiences, both as a line commander and as quartermaster general, prepared him well for the type of innovative warfare he would have to conduct in the

South. The essence of Greene's task, as he wrote, was "making bricks without straw."

The army that Greene found in North Carolina was in terrible condition, lacking everything. Some Virginia militia were nearly naked and Greene sent them home. He did have a solid, although limited, nucleus of veterans upon which to build. Among them were Maryland and Delaware Continentals who had survived Camden, William Washington's (George's distant relative) Continental cavalry, the old rifleman Daniel Morgan, and, from Washington's army, Henry Lee and his legion, a three hundred-man mixed cavalry and infantry force specifically created by Washington to make the most of Lee's unique partisan talents. Greene could not take time to clothe and reorder his small assemblage of troops, since even as he took command, Cornwallis was ready to move again. The players were now set for what would become a year of decision.

MILITARY OPERATIONS: 1781

Initially, the year 1781 promised to be even worse for the rebel military establishment than 1780. In the north, Washington had to contend with serious mutinies by the Pennsylvania and New Jersey Continental lines as the new year began. The American commander met with Rochambeau several times and they established a good rapport. Ever persistent, Washington pursued his plans for an assault against Clinton until an opportunity for a major victory presented itself at Yorktown, Virginia. In the South, the situation faced by Greene was grim at best. Except for some pesky guerrillas, Cornwallis controlled Georgia and South Carolina.

More generally, the war, now entering its seventh year, appeared destined to go on until one side or the other grew too weary to continue. In early 1781 it looked as if the Americans might be the first to give up. By the end of the year, the land war in North America was all but over. South Carolina and Georgia had patriot governments. British troops huddled in New York, Charleston, and a few other coastal enclaves. As the British band played during the surrender at Yorktown in October, the world had rather quickly been turned upside down.

GREENE'S UNORTHODOXY IN THE SOUTH. Upon taking command, Greene decided to do something that flew in the face of conventional military wisdom. Rather than keeping his troops concentrated, he divided his already small army in the face of a powerful enemy. He sent Daniel Morgan and eight hundred of his best Continentals, Washington's cavalry, and assorted militia into western South Carolina. Morgan's mission was to rally patriot inhabitants and threaten the British post at Augusta, Georgia. Next, Greene established cordial relations with the Carolina partisans, making them integral to his plans. To this end, the day after Henry Lee and his legion arrived, Greene dispatched them to the South Carolina coast to operate in conjunction with Francis Marion, raiding and threatening British posts outside of Charleston. Matching Lee's highly mobile, disciplined regulars with Marion's hard-fighting irregulars was a master stroke.

The end result was that Greene had stolen the initiative from Cornwallis. If Cornwallis advanced on Morgan, Greene would join with Marion and Lee in threatening the British line of communications and possibly even Charleston. If Cornwallis moved against Greene or Marion and Lee, Morgan was free to liberate Augusta and other backcountry British posts. Greene, well-schooled by Washington, knew that he was fighting a nonlinear war—a war without a front—and that for military and political reasons, as well as to preserve some semblance of morale, he could not afford a direct confrontation with Cornwallis.

Cornwallis responded in early January by dividing his own force. He sent Banastre Tarleton and eleven hundred mixed British and loyalist cavalry and infantry column after Morgan. Morgan understood the skittishness of poorly trained militiamen and knew how to get the most of their limited abilities. Receiving word that Tarleton was advancing rapidly toward him, he carefully selected his battlefield, picking the open fields at Hannah's Cowpens in northwestern South Carolina. First, he sent out some riflemen, then, contrary to conventional wisdom, he placed his militia in two lines well in advance of his other troops. After the sharpshooters fired and fell back, all Morgan wanted from the militia, he said, was two volleys. Then they could turn and run behind his next line, which consisted of veteran Maryland and Delaware Continentals under Colonel John Eager Howard. For a reserve, he kept Washington's cavalry and some mounted militia.

Tarleton thundered forward, saw lines of ragged militia to his front, and immediately launched his weary force in an attack at around 7 A.M. on 17 January. The patriot militia did as told, firing two solid volleys before retreating. Momentarily stunned but seeing the militia fleeing, the British rallied and charged. Disciplined fire from the Continental line stopped their forward movement, at which point the Continentals counterattacked even as Washington's cavalry swept down on their flanks, enveloping the British. Only Tarleton and some horsemen escaped. Morgan's soldiers killed or wounded about 340 British troops and captured another six hundred, while the rebel force suffered twelve dead and sixty wounded.

Not resting on the laurels of victory, Morgan began withdrawing his force to the northeast, putting several rivers between him and the pursuers that were sure to follow. A furious Cornwallis, pausing only to burn his supply wagons, then quick-marched his army after Morgan.

Once informed of Morgan's master stroke at Cowpens, Greene recalled Lee from the coast, set his army in motion to the north, and then rushed to join Morgan. Thus began the race to the Dan River, which loosely formed the North Carolina–Virginia border. Once across, Greene was safe but Cornwallis drove his troops hard. Lee's dragoons formed the rear guard, and they fought a series of running skirmishes with the forward troops of British General Charles O'Hara. Rain-swollen rivers, bitter February weather, and viscous Carolina mud hindered both Greene's ragged, hungry force and the enemy. The pace was such that Cornwallis' troops were coming to look like those whom they pursued. Finally, having reached the north shore of the Dan, Greene's army rested briefly.

Having failed to bag his prey, a frustrated and sick Cornwallis sought to rally the loyalists of North Carolina. Greene quickly sent Lee and Andrew Pickens back across the Dan to disrupt the British design. The uniforms of Lee's legion closely resembled those of Tarleton's, and on 25 February near the Haw River four hundred loyalists under Colonel John Pyle mistook Lee's men for Tarleton's. It proved a costly error. Infiltrating the loyalists, Lee's column suddenly turned on them and cut them down with their sabers. Against one dead American, the loyalists lost ninety killed, dozens more wounded, and the entire command dispersed. After "Pyle's hacking party," Cornwallis attracted few loyalist recruits.

Greene suffered more than 260 casualties at Guilford Courthouse, excluding one thousand militia that never stopped running.

Cornwallis was isolated deep in North Carolina, bereft of supplies and far from the Royal Navy. As for Greene, now reinforced by a large increment of local militia, he sensed an opportunity to destroy his opponent or, at worst, inflict a serious blow. Although Morgan's rheumatism had forced him to return home, Greene sought to emulate the tactics of the "Old Wagoner" at the Cowpens. Having moved back into central North Carolina, he aligned his forty-three hundred troops at Guilford Courthouse in three lines—riflemen up front, then militia, and then a line of Continentals with mounted horsemen under Lee and Washington on either flank.

Cornwallis, again in hot pursuit, brought up his army of two thousand, made his dispositions, then launched his assault early on the afternoon of 15 March. The American first line executed its mission, but as it retreated, some of the new militia gave way and ran. The Continentals stood strong, counterattacking. Both lines closed and engaged in vicious hand-to-hand combat. Cornwallis ordered canister fired into the swarm of fighting men, killing friend and foe alike. Greene may have been able to sweep the field with one last charge, but remembering Washington's admonition never to risk his whole army, he ordered a retreat. Greene suffered more than 260 casualties at Guilford Courthouse, excluding one thousand militia that never stopped running, and Cornwallis lost fully one-third of his force. The British held the field, but Cornwallis' position was even more desperate than before the battle. Worn down and baffled by a rebel force that refused to be beaten, Cornwallis led his greatly reduced army to the coast and the Royal Navy. Greene started after him, but Lee suggested that the Americans return to South Carolina. Greene agreed.

A reinforced Cornwallis considered returning to South Carolina, but the thought of again chasing after Greene and the guerrillas changed his mind. Benedict Arnold and other British raiders were having some success in Virginia. If Cornwallis joined with them, perhaps Virginia could be knocked out of the war. Abandoning the British southern strategy, he moved north that April.

Greene dispatched Lee to rejoin Marion, and the taciturn South Carolinian and the Virginia patrician set about reducing several British strong points—once by constructing a makeshift tower to shoot down into a fort and another time by shooting fire arrows. Colonel Francis Hastings, Lord Rawdon, left behind by Cornwallis to defend British posts in South Carolina and Georgia, kept his troops marching about the countryside. When Greene laid siege to Fort Ninety-Six (22 May–19 June), deep in the South Carolina backcountry, Rawdon quick-marched to its relief. Greene withdrew, but Rawdon burned the fort. He could not keep the British perimeter from shrinking in the face of relentless American strikes.

Greene, Lee, Pickens, Marion, and others kept hammering away at the enemy in both South Carolina and Georgia. In early September a British force of nearly two thousand under Lieutenant Colonel Alexander Stewart rested at Eutaw Springs on the Santee River.

Greene, whose strength was twenty-two hundred, launched a surprise attack on 8 September and nearly won the field. His hungry troops broke ranks among the British tents to eat and loot, giving their adversary a chance to rally in what was a hard-fought battle with heavy casualties on both sides. Having seriously damaged the enemy, Greene withdrew, giving Stewart a technical victory. The bold attack at Eutaw Springs, however, forced the British into their lines at Charleston.

In a few short months, without winning one battlefield victory, Greene had reduced the British presence in the Carolinas and Georgia to Charleston, Savannah, and a few tiny coastal enclaves. Reinforced that autumn by Anthony Wayne's Pennsylvanians from Washington's army, Greene would bring additional pressure on the remaining British posts and reinstitute patriot political control. Employing mobility in action, flexibility of thought, and making full use of what little troop strength he had available, Greene proved to be a rare talent and brilliant military commander.

COMBINED OPERATIONS PREVAIL: YORKTOWN. The full benefits of Greene's campaigning were not yet clear when Washington and Rochambeau met on 21 May to discuss possible joint operations. Washington again pushed for a drive against New York City, but then Rochambeau informed him that a large fleet under Admiral François Joseph de Grasse was heading for the West Indies and then to North America for possible joint operations. Rochambeau favored moving against the growing British force in Virginia, but Washington persisted in his own plan, pointing toward midsummer as an optimal time for an assault. The American commander, however, had to concede in July that

Siege of Yorktown. In late September 1781, a combined French and American force of about 16,700 soldiers and sailors laid siege to British forces at Yorktown. (National Archives/engraving from a painting by Condor)

his troops were not yet ready to strike, and he despaired when Clinton received a reinforcement of twenty-five hundred Hessians in early August, bringing the British manpower total to fifteen thousand. Even counting the French troops, Washington lacked the strength for a direct attack and the equipment for a formal siege.

On 14 August, Washington received word that de Grasse was on his way north to the Chesapeake with thirty warships and three thousand soldiers. The French admiral promised to remain there for two months. The news thrilled the American commander, because Cornwallis, after repeated skirmishes with a much smaller Continental and militia force under the Marquis de Lafayette, was setting up a defensive base at Yorktown. Clinton, who was furious with Cornwallis for having forsaken the Carolinas and the southern strategy, had ordered Cornwallis to occupy the town. He intended to pick up the British force, now numbering eighty-five hundred with loyalists, by sea and transport them north for further operations. If the French fleet could block off British naval access to Chesapeake Bay and Washington and Rochambeau could surround Cornwallis on land, then the allies might yet enjoy a decisive victory before the campaign season was over.

Washington immediately shifted his strategic view from New York southward. He and Rochambeau worked out a plan of march, including feints to hold Clinton in New York. Clinton also knew about de Grasse, but he believed Cornwallis safe because Admiral Sir George Rodney was shadowing the French fleet with one of his own. Lafayette hovered about in Virginia, staying out of harm's way, but keeping some pressure on the enemy, even as the allies marched south at a rapid pace. At Head of Elk, most of the troops embarked on every available vessel and sailed down the bay to the Virginia peninsula formed by the York and James rivers. Washington briefly stopped at Mount Vernon (his first visit home since leaving in 1775), and then caught up with his troops as they moved toward Yorktown.

Cornwallis, having been "burgoyned," felt too indisposed to attend the surrender ceremonies.

As promised, de Grasse's fleet appeared off the Virginia Capes on 26 August. Within a few days, the admiral began disembarking three thousand troops, who joined Lafayette. Luckily, another British fleet under Admiral Sir Samuel Hood had stopped by the bay on 23 August. Not finding the French there, Hood continued on to New York. If he had remained, he could have contested the landing of French troops, and quite possibly the combined fleets of Hood and Rodney could have defeated de Grasse. As it was, Rodney appeared off the capes alone, and on 5 September de Grasse sailed out to engage him.

The Battle of Virginia Capes virtually assured the capture of Cornwallis. De Grasse did not win a resounding victory, but he drove off the British and gained tactical superiority on the Chesapeake. On land the Americans (fifty-seven hundred Continentals and thirty-two hundred militia) and French (seventy-eight hundred troops) organized themselves for a formal siege. Yorktown was not set up to withstand such a siege, but Cornwallis had built up strong defenses. Still, he wrote Clinton on 23 September, "If you cannot relieve me very soon, you must be prepared to hear the Worst."

The allies first captured British outposts, and then they began digging parallel trenches, bringing their artillery closer and closer to British positions. Heavy cannonading began on 9 October. Five evenings later they overran Cornwallis' advanced redoubts nine and ten. With supplies becoming scarce and smallpox breaking out, Cornwallis tried to ferry some troops across the York River on the evening of 16 October, but a sudden squall ruined this operation. On the following morning, the allies began their most intensive bombardment yet. More than one hundred artillery pieces were in action. At midmorning, a British drummer boy stood atop the British fortifications and beat parley. The guns gradually fell silent as a British officer emerged carrying a white flag.

Despite earlier failures, combined Franco-American operations had at last scored a knockout victory, proving how valuable the French alliance was to the American martial effort. During the siege of Yorktown, the British had suffered 596 casualties to 340 for the allies, and 8,081 enemy troops formally gave up their arms on the sunny autumn afternoon of 19 October. Cornwallis, having been "burgoyned," felt too indisposed to attend the surrender ceremonies.

An exasperated Clinton had fumed and browbeaten his naval counterparts to get a relief expedition to Cornwallis on time. It finally arrived off the capes on 26 October, seven days too late. Washington tried to get de Grasse to operate with him and Greene against Charleston and Savannah, but de Grasse departed for the West Indies. Washington dispatched two thousand troops to reinforce Greene before marching back to the vicinity of New York. Rochambeau remained in Virginia, then moved his force to Newport and returned to France.

WAR AND PEACE, 1782–1783

Regardless of common lore, Yorktown was not completely responsible for Britain's decision to terminate the conflict. When Lord North read the official report of Cornwallis' defeat in late November, he received the news "as he would have taken a ball in the breast." Repeatedly he stated to those in his company, "Oh, God! it is all over!" The problem in the chief minister's mind was Yorktown in the context of so many dangerous threats to valuable British interests around the globe.

In many ways the British military problem in late 1781 was one of overextension. Much of Europe had ganged up on the mighty empire. The American rebels had gained formidable allies in the French, Spanish, and Dutch. (The British declared war on the Netherlands in December 1780 as an excuse to attack Dutch trading vessels and West Indian islands, such as Saint Eustatius. A British fleet under Admiral Rodney captured this center of contraband trade in February 1781.) Even though the British still had thirty thousand soldiers deployed in North America at the end of 1781, it looked as if the empire might be slowly bled to death. Spanish troops under Bernardo de Gálvez had captured British holdings along the Gulf coast, including the large British garrison in Pensacola, Florida, in May 1781. There were losses in India and other parts of the West Indies, and Lord North expected a combined Franco-Spanish assault on Gibraltar. Getting out of the war was a matter of reducing global losses as much as acknowledging the heavy blow taken at Yorktown.

Parliament saw the same pattern. When that body convened in March 1782, the House of Commons proclaimed that any English subject advocating a continuation of the war would be considered an enemy of Britain. Lords North and Germain soon resigned, and a new, short-lived ministry pursued a peace settlement. On 30 November 1782, British and American diplomats—Benjamin Franklin, John Adams, and John Jay were the prime negotiators—signed preliminary peace accords, later ratified in a more general peace settlement at Paris on 3 September 1783.

The terms were favorable for the Americans. Not only did the British recognize American independence,

Surrender at Yorktown. On 19 October 1781, a British officer emerged from the fortifications at Yorktown carrying a white flag. General Washington scored a major victory as General Cornwallis and 8,081 British troops formally gave up their arms. (National Archives/painting by John Trumbull)

but they gave the erstwhile colonists all territory running west to the Mississippi River. In a separate provision, Britain returned East Florida and West Florida to the Spanish, thus temporarily establishing 31 degrees north latitude as the southern boundary of the United States.

The terms might have even been more generous and possibly even included Canada had the war not swung back in Britain's favor during 1782. In a bloody Caribbean naval engagement, the battle off Saints Passage in April 1782, Admiral Rodney's fleet had thrashed de Grasse's naval force, and even captured the French admiral. By autumn British defenders had driven off the Franco-Spanish expeditionary force besieging Gibraltar. Even without Canada, the Americans had gotten the most that could be expected. Through war and peace, they had established a broad base upon which to construct the new American republic.

Even as the American peace commissioners conducted negotiations, sporadic outbursts of combat continued in North America. The internecine local war between patriots and loyalists continued to claim victims in the South. The situation only improved after loyalists began migrating elsewhere, including Britain, Canada, and the Bahamas. A bloody fight also occurred during 1782, when Daniel Boone and some 180 militiamen attacked loyalist-led natives at Blue Lick Springs in Kentucky. The Americans experienced ninety-seven casualties, as compared to seventeen Indians. Regular British and patriot forces, on the other hand, effectively avoided major combat after 1781.

Indeed, the most pressing problem for Washington in 1782–1783 was keeping his restive and angry long-term officers and soldiers under control while waiting for news of a final peace settlement. At Newburgh, New York, the army's last cantonment, Washington's officers grew particularly indignant about back pay and postwar pensions. In December 1782 they sent a menacing petition to Congress stating that "any further experiments on their patience may have fatal effects." The officers were threatening to keep the army under arms until Congress and the states gave them their financial due. Some even talked openly of a military takeover of the central government.

Washington defused the crisis on 15 March 1783 when he met with his assembled officers at Newburgh and enjoined them to remember why they had gone to war in the first place. He startled them when he put on eyeglasses to read a letter. This was the first time he had worn glasses in public. Hearing them murmur, he calmly said: "Gentleman, you must pardon me. I have grown gray in your service and now find myself growing blind." What he had stated was that they had all sacrificed, that they should never want to threaten the ideals for which they had fought and end up with military tyranny in government—little different than the perceived system of imperial tyranny over which they had revolted in the first place.

By challenging his officers at Newburgh, Washington helped enshrine the principle of civil supremacy over military authority as an essential precept of human freedom in any true republic. Despite its grievances, the Continental army did lay down its arms and formally disbanded during the autumn of 1783. On 4 December, after the last British troop transport ships debarked from New York City, Washington met with his officers for the last time and said farewell in a tearful scene at Fraunces Tavern. In another lugubrious ceremony on 23 December, he surrendered his commission and sword to the Continental Congress at Annapolis, Maryland. The former commander in chief then rode for Mount Vernon with the satisfaction of knowing that he and thousands of others had overcome incredible obstacles in winning the War of the Revolution, thereby assuring a successful beginning to a new nation called the United States of America.

BIBLIOGRAPHY

General Studies

Anderson, Fred. *A People's Army: Massachusetts Soldiers and Society in the Seven Years' War* (1984).

Cress, Lawrence Delbert. *Citizens in Arms: The Army and the Militia in American Society in the War of 1812* (1982).

Christie, Ian R. *Wars and Revolutions: Britain, 1760–1815* (1982).

Dederer, John Morgan. *War in America to 1775: Before Yankee Doodle* (1990).

Ferling, John. *A Wilderness of Miseries: War and Warriors in Early America* (1980).

Higginbotham, Don. *The War of American Independence: Military Attitudes, Policies, and Practice, 1763–1789* (1971).

Leach, Douglas Edward. *Roots of Conflict: British Armed Forces and Colonial Americans, 1677–1763* (1986).

Mackesy, Piers. *The War for America, 1775–1783* (1964).

Martin, James Kirby. *In the Course of Human Events: An Interpretive Exploration of the American Revolution* (1979).

Martin, James Kirby, and Mark Edward Lender. *A Respectable Army: The Military Origins of the Republic, 1763–1789* (1982).

Middlekauff, Robert. *The Glorious Cause: The American Revolution, 1763–1789* (1982).

Palmer, R. R. *The Age of the Democratic Revolution: A Political History of Europe and America, 1760–1800* (1959–1964).

Robson, Eric. *The American Revolution in Its Political and Military Aspects, 1763–1783* (1955).

Royster, Charles. *A Revolutionary People at War: The Continental Army and American Character, 1775–1783* (1979).

Shy, John W. *Toward Lexington: The Role of the British Army in the Coming of the American Revolution* (1965).

———. *A People Numerous and Armed: Reflections on the Military Struggle for American Independence* (1976).

Wallace, Willard W. *Appeal to Arms: A Military History of the American Revolution* (1951).

Ward, Christopher. *The War of the Revolution,* ed. by John Richard Alden (1952).

Armies, Generals, and Soldiers

Billias, George A., ed. *George Washington's Generals* (1964).

———. *George Washington's Opponents: British Generals and Admirals in the American Revolution* (1969).

Bowler, Arthur. *Logistics and the Failure of the British Army in America, 1775–1783* (1975).

Bowman, Larry G. *Captive Americans: Prisoners During the American Revolution* (1976).

Carp, E. Wayne. *To Starve the Army at Pleasure: Continental Army Administration and American Political Culture. 1775–1783* (1984).

Ferling, John C., ed. *The World Turned Upside Down: The American Victory in the War of Independence* (1988).

Frey, Sylvia R. *The British Soldier in America: A Social History of Military Life in the Revolutionary Period* (1981).

Gerlach, Don R. *Proud Patriot: Philip Schuyler and the War of Independence, 1775–1783* (1987).

Gruber, Ira D. *The Howe Brothers and the American Revolution* (1972).

Higginbotham, Don., ed. *Reconsiderations on the Revolutionary War* (1978).

———. *George Washington and the American Military Tradition* (1985).

Hoffman, Ronald, and Peter J. Albert, eds. *Arms and Independence: The Military Character of the American Revolution* (1984).

Houlding, J. A. *Fit for Service: The Training of the British Army, 1715–1795* (1981).

Kohn, Richard H. "The Inside History of the Newburgh Conspiracy: America and the Coup d'Etat." *William and Mary Quarterly,* 3d series, 27 (1970): 187–220.

Mintz, Max M. *The Generals of Saratoga: John Burgoyne and Horatio Gates* (1990).

Nelson, Paul David. *General Horatio Gates: A Biography* (1976).

Palmer, Dave R. *The Way of the Fox: American Strategy in the War for America, 1775–1783* (1975).

Rankin, Hugh F. *The North Carolina Continentals* (1971).

Rogers, H. C. B. *The British Army of the Eighteenth Century* (1977).

Rossie, Jonathan Gregory. *The Politics of Command in the American Revolution* (1975).

Smith, Paul H. *Loyalists and Redcoats: A Study in British Revolutionary Policy* (1964).

Naval Affairs and International Diplomacy

Bemis, Samuel Flagg. *The Diplomacy of the American Revolution,* rev. ed. (1957).

Dull, Jonathan R. *The French Navy and American Independence: A Study of Arms and Diplomacy, 1774–1787* (1975).

———. *A Diplomatic History of the American Revolution* (1985).

Fowler, William M., Jr. *Rebels Under Sail: The American Navy During the Revolution* (1976).

Hoffman, Ronald, and Peter J. Albert, eds. *Diplomacy and Revolution: The Franco-American Alliance of 1778* (1981).

———. *Peace and the Peacemakers: The Treaty of 1783* (1986).

Mahan, Alfred T. *The Major Operations of the Navies in the War of American Independence* (1913).

Morris, Richard B. *The Peacemakers: The Great Powers and American Independence* (1965).

Nordholt, Jan Willem Schulte. *The Dutch Republic and American Independence* (1982).

Stinchcombe, William C. *The American Revolution and the French Alliance* (1969).

Syrett, David. *Shipping and the American War, 1775–1783: A Study of Transport Organization* (1970).

Tilley, John A. *The British Navy and the American Revolution* (1987).

Regional Studies

Buel, Richard, Jr. *Dear Liberty: Connecticut's Mobilization for the Revolutionary War* (1980).

Dederer, John Morgan. *Making Bricks Without Straw: Nathanael Greene's Southern Campaigns and Mao Tse-Tung's Mobile War* (1983).

Gross, Robert A. *The Minutemen and Their World* (1976).

Higgins, W. Robert, ed. *The Revolutionary War in the South: Power, Conflict, and Leadership* (1979).

Hoffman, Ronald, Thad W. Tate, and Peter J. Albert, eds. *An Uncivil War: The Southern Backcountry During the American Revolution* (1985).

Sosin, Jack M. *The Revolutionary Frontier, 1763–1783* (1967).

Leiby, Adrian. *The Revolutionary War in the Hackensack Valley: The Jersey Dutch and the Neutral Ground, 1775–1783* (1962).

Weigley, Russel F. *The Partisan War: The South Carolina Campaign of 1780–1782* (1970).

Reference Works

Boatner, Mark M., III, ed. *Encyclopedia of the American Revolution,* rev. ed. (1974).

Blanco, Richard L., ed. *The War of the American Revolution: A Selected Annotated Bibliography of Published Sources* (1984).

Commager, Henry S., and Richard B. Morris, eds. *The Spirit of 'Seventy-Six: The Story of the American Revolution as Told by Participants* (1958; rev. ed. 1975).

Dann, John C., ed. *The Revolution Remembered: Eyewitness Accounts of the War for Independence* (1980).

Gephart, Ronald M., comp. *Revolutionary America: 1763–1789* (1984).

Higginbotham, Don. "The Early American Way of War: Reconnaissance and Appraisal." *William and Mary Quarterly,* 3d series, 44 (1987): 230–273.

Higham, Robin, ed. *A Guide to the Sources in U.S. Military History* (1975).

Higham, Robin, and Donald J. Mrozek, eds. *A Guide to the Sources in U.S. Military History, Supplement I* (1981), *Supplement II* (1986), *Supplement III* (1991).

Nelson, Paul David. "British Conduct of the American Revolutionary War: A Review of Interpretations." *Journal of American History* 65 (1978): 623–653.

Peckham, Howard H., ed. *The Toll of Independence: Engagements and Battle Casualties of the American Revolution* (1974).

Scheer, George F., and Hugh F. Rankin, eds. *Rebels and Redcoats* (1957).

Shy, John W., comp. *The American Revolution* (1973).

Wright, Robert K., Jr. *The Continental Army* (1984).

— JAMES KIRBY MARTIN
JOHN MORGAN DEDERER

The Early National Period

ARTICLES OF CONFEDERATION

Vigorous participation in the American Revolution by France in 1781 moved the would-be United States closer to independence. Significant changes in the American administration of the war effort also moved the new nation closer to the goal. Belatedly, Congress created executive offices not staffed by its own members, thus enhancing efficiency. It founded the position of secretary at war, and on 30 October appointed General Benjamin Lincoln to the post. Earlier it had appointed Robert Morris to be superintendent of finance. That fall, by dint of his power as the richest man in the United States, Morris was able to pay the troops a month's wages in specie, the first the soldiers had received in years. John C. Miller (1948) writes, "Largely through Morris' exertions the American Army was held together and enabled to fight a successful campaign." In September 1781 Congress imposed another burden on Morris, making him the agent of marine, and, as such, he efficiently handled naval affairs until the end of the war.

Major combat ended with the Yorktown campaign on 19 October 1781. During 1782, as sources of funds dried up, supporting the army became increasingly difficult. It now seems a miracle that the United States could sign a treaty of peace with Great Britain on 30 November. Equally miraculous was the ability to survive the year 1783. Trade was sluggish, the government of the confederation insolvent. It owed $6 million in overdue pay to soldiers, a dangerous sort of debt to be in, and it lacked sufficient income to pay current expenses. British troops remained in New York and in the posts that controlled the fur trade along the Canadian border.

"A Standing Army, however necessary it may be at some times, is always a danger to the liberties of the people."

Notwithstanding that armed conflict had won independence, with peace about to break out, there was strong sentiment against the military. The fear of mutiny by unpaid soldiers was a contributing factor as was the traditional fear of standing military forces. Samuel Adams expressed that fear, inherited from the English experience, in 1776: "A Standing Army, however necessary it may be at some times, is always a danger to the liberties of the people."

In 1783 General George Washington turned his attention to what the American military establishment should be in peacetime. He agreed that the new nation could not maintain a standing army without "great oppression of the people." He also believed that the United States was too poor to support one. Early in 1783 he wrote to several of his generals—Henry Knox, Baron Friedrich Wilhelm von Steuben, Timothy Pickering, William Heath, Edward Hand, and Israel Putnam—requesting their ideas on the proper establishment of an army. He told them that the protection of the country would have to depend on a respectable, well-established militia, a belief that rested on the time-honored principle that every able-bodied male citizen owed a personal and property obligation to defend the government.

The generals and others considered Washington's ideas and responded to him with their own. They agreed that the primary reliance could not be on a regular army, but that there had to be a small force of twenty-six hundred to four thousand men. If war came this professional force would become the body upon which units of militiamen could rally. First to rally would be a select corps drawn from younger citizen-soldiers who would have armed themselves and undergone rigorous training. It was essential that the militias of the several states receive identical training in order to be interchangeable if they were called on to fight. The respondents also stressed the need for military academies, government arsenals, and for public ownership of some factories producing arms and ammunition.

Washington sent the bundle of opinions and his own on 2 May 1783 to Alexander Hamilton, chairman of the congressional Committee on Military Affairs. Hamilton's committee considered the proposals during May and June, but having no funds took no action.

Meanwhile, at Washington's headquarters in Newburgh, New York, there was far less concern for the peacetime establishment than for back pay and promised pensions. Major General Alexander McDougall, Colonel John Brooks, and Colonel Mathias Ogden, three men with distinguished war records, carried a list of officers' demands to Congress, but learned only that that body, having no money, could do nothing for them. A movement grew at Newburgh to hold the army together and force Congress to somehow settle their accounts.

Robert Morris, Gouverneur Morris, and Hamilton, though not directly implicated in the growing conspiracy at Newburgh, indirectly encouraged the officers to press their demands so that a strong central government, able to pay civilian, military, and foreign creditors, might take shape. In March at Newburgh, Major John Armstrong, Jr., on the staff of Major General Horatio Gates, circulated two unsigned addresses urging officers and men to hold together until given justice. Armstrong and Brigadier General James Wilkinson called upon Gates to chair a meeting to decide on the specific steps to be taken.

Gates, who was born in England, had served in the British army and been badly wounded during General Edward Braddock's disastrous defeat on 9 July 1755 at the Battle of the Wilderness. He spent the next fifteen years in England, returning to the colonies three years before the Revolution. Embued with republican ideas, he joined the cause of American independence, and because of his command experience, rare among native-born Americans, he received a commission as major general in the Continental army. His greatest moment came from the defeat of General John Burgoyne's army in October 1777. Convinced that his abilities had been underrated, he agreed to head the cabal.

"Gentlemen, you will permit me to put on my spectacles, for I have not only grown gray, but almost blind, in the service of my country."

Without informing Washington, the conspirators set 11 March 1783 as the day to hold their pivotal meeting. Washington found out about the meeting, attended it, and asked to speak. What he said touched some of the disaffected officers almost to tears: "Gentlemen, you will permit me to put on my spectacles, for I have not only grown gray, but almost blind, in the service of my country." With this beginning he flatly stated to the group that what they proposed to do, to hold the army intact to intimidate Congress, would destroy what all of them had fought to preserve. Following his talk the threat ended, the closest to military coercion that civil control of the military has experienced in the United States.

Although the menace appeared to have diminished, on 22 March 1783 Congress voted five years full pay to officers. It acknowledged at the same time the obligation to make up arrears of pay, but truthfully stated that it could not satisfy their just claims.

Knox and other general officers, uncertain of the future despite the good intentions of Congress, founded the Society of the Cincinnati in the spring of 1783. Only officers who had served three years in the revolutionary army or were in the army at the end of hostilities were eligible to join, and none but the elder sons of those officers could enter in the future. The organization appeared to such public figures as John Adams, Samuel Adams, John Jay, and Thomas Jefferson to be an attempt to found an American aristocracy, based on military service. To placate the opposition, the founders of the society announced that they would change their constitution, but they never did. Before long, however, concern about the society declined and it continues to exist.

Also in the spring of 1783, there were still about twelve thousand men in Washington's northern army. Every day the debt that Congress owed these soldiers increased, but to discharge them without pay might cause armed revolt. The only solution that Congress could devise was to authorize Washington on 26 May to furlough the troops at his discretion. On 2 June 1783 the general told the men that they could accept a furlough if they chose, with a small payment against what they were owed. Robert Morris raised money by drawing drafts on Dutch and other European creditors, but when the creditors delayed honoring the drafts, on 13 June most of the members of the northern army opted to go home with promissory notes for pay. Only two regiments and fourteen separate companies of infantry waited to be furloughed.

Elsewhere, army troops were not as accommodating. On 21 June 1783, 280 new recruits of the Pennsylvania line surrounded Independence Hall, where Congress was meeting. For three hours they held the delegates hostage, until the congressmen summoned the courage to march out in a body, successfully passing through the encircling lines. There were no injuries, but Congress hurried out of Philadelphia to convene in Princeton, New Jersey. Congress had expected the Pennsylvania militia to defend them, but the state could not stir any of its units into action. Later, the city of Philadelphia offered inducements to woo Congress back, but it did not return while the Confederation lasted. From Princeton, Congress went to Annapolis, Maryland, and Trenton, New Jersey, holding alternate sessions in the two locations. Citizens who followed public affairs worried about the total absence of any military force to defend the government.

In September 1783 the War of the Revolution was brought to a formal conclusion. Representatives signed the treaty in Paris on 3 September. England recognized the independence of the United States and its title to an enormous tract of land extending westward to the Mississippi River. The Indians, scattered thinly over that land, were not parties to the treaty. The Floridas reverted to Spain.

As soon as the conflict legally ended, erstwhile belligerents turned away from war. On 12 November Benjamin Lincoln resigned as secretary of war. On 25 November the last British detachment on the eastern seaboard shipped out of New York City, and a detachment of American troops marched in. Two days before Christmas, Washington appeared before twenty members of Congress, sitting at the statehouse in Annapolis, and resigned his commission. He said, "Having now finished the work assigned me, I retire from the great theater of action; and bidding an affectionate farewell to this august body, under whose orders I have so long acted, I here offer my commissions." Washington had indeed acted under the orders of the Congress, even when he was urged by supporters to assume full authority, and in so doing he had established the precedent for civil control of the military.

Washington left Knox in command of the army, most of it in New York, but about fourteen hundred Continentals were camped near Charleston, South Carolina. Knox was instructed to discharge all but five hundred infantrymen and one hundred artillerists, even though Congress had no funds to pay even these remaining six hundred. Because no secretary of war had been appointed following Lincoln's resignation, Joseph Carleton, an able and conscientious public servant, carried on army business. The small needs of the vanishing navy were taken care of by Agent of Marine Robert Morris.

Congress was divided into confederationists, who wanted sovereignty to remain with the states, and nationalists, who believed that the United States could not survive without a more centralized government. Often neither persuasion could press its case because of the lack of a quorum, and when there was a quorum, it had almost no funds to work with. The states were too poor to pay their quotas into the treasury, although negligible sums trickled in from the sale of the ships of the Continental navy and the last two were not sold until 1785.

One of the regiments of the six hundred Continentals retained was from Massachusetts. The enlisted men in it received $8.33⅓ per month, nearly twice the $4.25 that was the standard rate. The nation and the states desperately needed to be free of this expense, and there were also political reasons for discharging the Massachusetts regiment. If the British evacuated the posts along the Canadian border, as they had agreed to do in the Treaty of Paris, the Massachusetts men would garrison those posts. New York was unwilling to permit that because New York wanted to control those important points in the fur trade. New Englanders, including those of Massachusetts, wanted to discharge the Continentals because they were convinced that the militia, such as they had, could defend the nation without the help of professionals. Although delegates from the middle and southern states opposed the discharge, on 2 June 1784 Congress voted to release all but eighty men, fifty-five to guard the stores at West Point, New York, and twenty-five to garrison Fort Pitt, Pennsylvania.

The next day, Congress created a new army, free of the stigmas attached to the Continentals. Its seven hundred men came from the militias of four states: 260 from Pennsylvania; 165 from New York; 165 from Connecticut; and 110 from New Jersey. Pennsylvania was authorized to appoint the commanding officer, and it chose Josiah Harmar, who had been born in Philadelphia, had been well-educated in Quaker schools, and was brought up among well-to-do people. At the start of the Revolution he was appointed a captain, but at the war's end he was colonel by brevet. He delivered the peace treaty to France, and when he returned was commissioned a lieutenant colonel on 12 August 1784, which made him the senior officer in the Confederation's diminutive army. Harmar's regiment, the First American Regiment, could not be considered a standing army because the men were enrolled for only one year. Nor was it militia, because the standard tour of duty for militia was three months. New England accepted this hybrid force, while delegates of the southern and middle states put up with it as better than no force at all.

New York did not trouble to raise its quota of troops in 1784; Connecticut and New Jersey assembled theirs too late to be useful in that year. The Pennsylvanians, in contrast, were available, and a detachment accompanied commissioners to Fort McIntosh for talks with the Indians. Soldiers were an essential part of the panoply drawn together for negotiating with Indians. At Fort McIntosh on 21 January 1785 representatives of Wyandot, Delaware, Chippewa, and Ottawa tribes agreed to relinguish much of what is now the state of Ohio. On 25 January the Wyandot and Delaware deeded to Pennsylvania previously claimed lands.

Earlier New York did find some soldiers to be present at Fort Stanwix, where the white agent spoke harshly to the Onondaga, Mohawk, Seneca, Oneida, Cayuga, and Tuscarora. "You are a subdued people," he told them. "We are at peace with all but you. . . . When we offer you peace in moderate terms we do it in magnanimity and mercy." On 22 October 1784 those Iroqois tribes gave up their claims to all land in Pennsylvania and ceded a small tract in New York.

Even though the war was over, military expenses accounted for 44 percent of the Confederation's operating costs ($187,000 out of $485,000). At the close of 1785, the government owed the men of Harmar's regiment $4,000 in unpaid wages. Expenses would have been higher had the British evacuated the forts in compliance with the terms of the peace treaty: Oswegatchie on the Saint Lawrence River; Oswego at the foot of Lake Ontario; Niagara, where the Niagara River enters Lake Ontario; Pointe au Fer at the mouth of the Richelieu River; and Mackinac at the straits between Lake Huron and Lake Michigan. Americans were convinced that the British incited the Indians against them from these posts.

In the southeast Spanish officials openly incited the Indians against the United States, having persuaded the Creek, Choctaw, and Chickasaw nations to put themselves under Spain's protection, excluding traders from all other countries. Because the United States and Spain were disputing the ownership of parts of West Florida, Spanish officials closed the Mississippi River to American commerce, an action that constituted a grave threat to the territorial integrity of the union, because twenty-five thousand dwellers west of the Allegheny Mountains depended on the river to carry their goods to market. If the United States could not guarantee the flow of that commerce, the settlers in the southwest might consider aligning with Spain.

After the United States separated from England, the Barbary states—Algiers, Morocco, Tripoli, and Tunis—

Washington resigning his commission. Two days before Christmas in 1783, Washington appeared before Congress at the statehouse in Annapolis and resigned his commission as head of the U.S. Army. (National Archives)

began to harass American merchantmen in the Mediterranean Sea. These North African principalities financed themselves on tribute exacted from nations whose merchant ships traded in the area and on ransom paid for captured and enslaved sailors. The United States made a cheap settlement with Morocco on 28 June 1786, a tribute of $10,000, but the other three pirate states continued to be troublesome. John Adams, minister to England and a lifelong supporter of naval power, held that there was no choice but to pay tribute, following the example of some of the great European powers. In contrast, Thomas Jefferson, minister to France, abhorred the payment of tribute and urged Congress to immediately begin building a navy, but because of a lack of funds, naval building did not begin.

Even without funds, the Confederation government in the spring of 1785 achieved two of the enduring accomplishments of its tenure. In April it turned the hybrid First American Regiment into the parent unit of the regular United States Army. It took the same regiment with the same commander and as many of the enlisted men as would reenlist and enrolled them for three years. During a three-year tour of duty, competent officers could make professionals out of the men of the regiment. Whereas in 1784 there had been an acrimonious debate over the creation of the regiment for just one year, in 1785 a three-year term was accepted almost casually. Rufus King said of this action, "A little firmness, and a great deal said about candor and harmony brought the measure to adoption without much difficulty." The firmness was exerted by those persons who were sure that the new nation had to have at least a small standing army. Whatever the candor was that King referred to, it probably did not include an admission of the determination of some men to bring a regular force into being.

The only tangible asset of the Confederation government was the vast unoccupied land (save for Indians) west of the Allegheny mountains, which would have to be surveyed in order to turn this asset into operating funds. The need for a survey brought about the second lasting achievement of the Confederation government. In May 1785 it established the rectangular system of surveying, which has made the transfer of land simple by laying a uniform grid across most of America. The First American Regiment was assigned to protect the surveyors of the initial Seven Ranges, to drive white settlers off the land guaranteed to the Indians, and to expel them from unsold public lands. The futility of attempting to curb the land hunger of people whose ancestors in Europe had never been able to own a piece of the earth soon became evident. Detachments of soldiers evicted families and burned their shacks, but the evicted returned and rebuilt. In a petition to Congress, one group wrote, "All mankind, agreeable to every constitution formed in America, have an undoubted right to pass into every vacant country," but Ensign John Armstrong classified some of the squatters as "Banditti whose actions are a disgrace to human nature."

The only tangible asset of the Confederation government was the vast unoccupied land (save for Indians) west of the Allegheny mountains.

Veterans of the Continental army had a keen interest in the activities of the First American Regiment because some of the western lands had been promised to them as partial payment for past-due pay. Old friends asked Harmar to identify the best tracts of land. The Ohio Company of Associates, organized by former officers, outstripped all other speculators. It contracted with the Treasury Board to purchase 1,781,760 acres for $1 million with an option to buy five million more acres. The regiment was indispensable to the Ohio Company for protection, and when it built Fort Harmar near the west side of the mouth of the Muskingum River, the Ohio Company erected the city of Marietta nearby to enjoy the security provided by Fort Harmar.

Although the First American Regiment was too small by far to carry out all its assigned duties, it became the most conspicuous symbol on the frontier of the political union of the states.

During 1785 and 1786 commodity prices fell by 30 percent, and farm wages declined to forty cents a day. Conditions were particularly acute in Massachusetts, which suffered from the loss of trade with the West Indies, now closed by Great Britain to American ships. English merchants more than before pressed Americans for payment of their obligations. Creditors resorted increasingly to court action and foreclosures multiplied on farmland. For debtors the horror of debtors prison drew closer.

The government of Massachusetts, controlled by merchant interests, raised taxes and demanded that they be paid in specie. As early as 1782 crowds of farmers forced a county court to close, thus preventing foreclosure processes. Farmers wanted an issue of paper money, but merchant interests defeated them. Semiorganized bodies of farmers throughout the state increased their interference with the sitting of the courts in 1786. Governor James Bowdoin called upon Congress for help and it responded with an appropriation of $530,000 to

Fort Mackinac
NORTHWEST TERRITORY
LAKE MICHIGAN
INDIANA TERRITORY
LAKE HURON
St. Lawrence River
LAKE ONTARIO
Oswego
Fort Stanwix
Niagara
NEW YORK
Niagara River
Newburgh
West Point
LAKE ERIE
Fort Miami
Maumee River
Fallen Timbers
SEVEN RANGES
Fort McIntosh
River
PENNSYLVANIA
New York
Tippecanoe River
Blue Jackets Town
HARMAR'S DEFEAT
OHIO
Muskingum
Fort Pitt
Carlisle
Philadelphia
NEW JERSEY
BATTLE OF TIPPECANOE
Fort Recovery
ST. CLAIR'S DEFEAT
Fort Greenville
Fort Harmar
Marietta
MARYLAND
Annapolis
DELAWARE
Mississippi
River
Fort Washington
River
Ohio
River
Yorktown
VIRGINIA
Vincennes
River
Richmond
St. Louis
KENTUCKY
Hampton Roads
Wabash
Ohio
NATCHEZ TRACE
NORTH CAROLINA
TENNESSEE
River
SOUTH CAROLINA
Charleston
NATCHEZ TRACE
GEORGIA
Mississippi
ATLANTIC
OCEAN
Fort Stoddert
WEST FLORIDA
LOUISIANA
SPANISH EAST FLORIDA
New Orleans
GULF OF MEXICO
THE EARLY NATIONAL PERIOD
1783-1811
MILES
0
100
200

suppress the insurrections, but because it could not raise that money, no help came from the Confederation government. Thrown upon its own resources, Massachusetts appointed Benjamin Lincoln to raise and command a force. Lincoln, one of Massachusetts' elite, procured an initial $20,000 from wealthy merchants, hired an army of forty-four hundred unemployed men, and moved against the insurgents, now known as Shaysites, named for Daniel Shays, a farmer and revolutionary war officer who actually never made any pretension toward leading the rebellion. Enough Massachusetts militia supported Lincoln to defeat the Shaysites early in 1787. The victors also had artillery, which was a factor in winning, and they had the military skill of Lincoln. There were close to one hundred casualties among the rebels, four times those of the Massachusetts troops. Two of the rebellious yeomen were hanged, but Shays escaped to Vermont, which was open territory, and was eventually pardoned.

Agrarian unrest was not confined to Massachusetts, but it was squelched in the other New England states, except for Rhode Island, which calmed the unrest by issuing paper money, as did North Carolina, New York, and Georgia. Shays's Rebellion, although confined to Massachusetts, had nationwide significance. Property interests learned that there was no central authority strong enough to control internal disorder and protect property. Shays's Rebellion moved the nation away from the Confederation and toward a more centralized polity.

Inadequate though the government of the Articles of Confederation was, it left lasting legacies. It had established an efficient decimal system of money; created a permanent peacetime army; enacted the Ordinance of 1785, which overlaid all of the nation with the rectangular grid for surveying, except for the thirteen original colonies and, later, Maine, Vermont, Kentucky, Tennessee, West Virginia, and Texas; provided in that same ordinance one square mile from each township of thirty-six square miles for the advancement of education; and enacted the Northwest Ordinance of 1787, which provided a system through which unorganized territories could in time enter the union as coequal members with other states. Finally, it had held the rickety union together.

THE U.S. CONSTITUTION

Although nine states agreed to meet at Annapolis in September 1786 to try to settle problems of commerce, only New York, Pennsylvania, Delaware, New Jersey, and Virginia sent delegates, and they could not take the necessary action. Informally, therefore, a group of nationalists led by Alexander Hamilton, James Madison, and John Dickinson issued a call for a convention to revise the Articles of Confederation. One by one, almost reluctantly, the states appointed delegates, and the sessions began in Philadelphia on 25 May and ended on 17 September 1787. During those nine weeks, the members did not revise the articles, but instead created a new constitution.

In the sessions, confederationists struggled against centralization and the augmented military power that went with it. Delegates from the small states tried every parliamentary device to prevent the creation of a peacetime standing army. Failing in this, they attempted to limit its size. When Elbridge Gerry, a delegate from Massachusetts, proposed a figure of two thousand to three thousand men, Washington, as presiding officer supposed to keep silent, loudly whispered that they must not forget also to place a cap on the size of enemy forces. The delegates, whether influenced by Washington or not, defeated Gerry's motion, leaving Congress free to keep a peacetime army of any size that it chose. Less than half of the delegates joined in the debate on the military, so the provisions dealing with the army and navy were approved on 27 August 1787.

The ingrained fear of a standing army found limited expression in the proposed document. Congress could make no appropriation for the army to be applied for longer than two years. The framers placed no such restriction on the navy. They made provision for the militia, one reason being that it should serve as a counterweight to the regular force.

Charles Pinckney of South Carolina proposed a clause that stated, "the military shall always be subordinate to the Civil power." It provoked no debate.

The delegates took for granted civil control of the military. On 20 August 1787 Charles Pinckney of South Carolina proposed a clause that stated, "the military shall always be subordinate to the Civil power." It provoked no debate. It would appear that the delegates assumed civilian control to be assured through the common law and through long-standing practice. As a result, civil control is implicit rather than explicit in the U.S. Constitution.

Experience with monarchy had kept the delegates from giving the ultimate military power to the executive. They placed it instead with Congress, which alone can raise and support armies, provide and maintain a navy, decide how manpower may be procured for the armed services, procure individuals for military service without having to consult a state, and declare war. Congress alone can levy taxes, incur debts, and pay indebtedness. The Senate has to agree to all appointments of civil and military officers made by the president. Last, the delegates made a sweeping grant to Congress, "To make all Laws which shall be necessary and proper for carrying into Execution the foregoing Powers, and all other Powers vested by this Constitution in the Government of the United States."

The president, a civil officer, had no counterpart in the Articles of Confederation. Under the Constitution he is the commander in chief of the national forces and of the militia when called into federal service. Because the Constitution does not enumerate the powers of a commander in chief, strong presidents have construed those powers to be very great, dangerously so from the viewpoint of skeptics of the military.

Under the Articles of Confederation, control of the militia wholly resided with the several states, which were enjoined to keep their citizen-soldiers well-drilled and supplied and to store military supplies for issue in emergencies. No such charge entered the Constitution, nor were the states left in exclusive control of the militia. Congress received the power to organize, arm, and discipline it, reserving to the states the right to officer and train it. This lean wording has produced many a controversy between the states and federal government over the years because it is not clear what is included in the power to organize, to arm, and to discipline citizen-soldiers, nor what is the difference between disciplining and training.

Although some members of the convention believed that the states might have to use their militia to defend themselves against the federal government, they specified the situations under which the United States could summon militia for its own use. Congress received authority to call the militia into federal service for three defensive purposes—to execute the laws of the union, suppress insurrections, and repel invasions. This wording also has sometimes set states against the federal government. The earliest instance occurred at the start of the War of 1812, when the president called on Massachusetts and Connecticut to provide militia for the federal government to use to repel invasion. The two governors replied that they considered the call to be unconstitutional, as they saw no invasion to repel. The beginning of hostilities that led to the Civil War produced a similar but more emphatic disagreement. When President Abraham Lincoln called on the governors of southern states for militia to suppress insurrection, the governors indignantly denied his right to make the call.

When the framers finished their substitute for the Articles of Confederation, they sent it to Congress to forward to the states, which were to call special conventions to ratify or reject it. Delaware was first to ratify the Constitution, on 7 December 1787. Opponents of a strong central government saw that the proposed Constitution endowed the center implicitly with great military power. For this and other reasons they fought ratification fiercely. In Virginia, Patrick Henry, in one of his greatests bursts of oratory, prevented approval for twenty-three days, speaking continuously for seven hours during a single day. He predicted armed despotism, as did Elbridge Gerry in the Massachusetts convention. Luther Martin of Maryland argued that dividing power over the militia between the states and the federal government threatened the survival of the states.

Alexander Hamilton, arguing brilliantly before an anti-Constitution convention in New York, contended that foreign threats to the new nation made concentration of military power essential. He pointed out that the British still held the posts in the Old Northwest, from which they could control the Indian tribes, while Spain remained a menace in the south, and the West Indies were certain to be basing points for invasion of the United States. In the end, on 26 July 1788, the delegates to the New York Convention ratified the document, thirty to twenty-seven. North Carolina and Rhode Island did not enter the union until after the new government was in operation.

Amendment II reads: "A well regulated Militia, being necessary to the security of a free State, the right of the people to keep and bear Arms, shall not be infringed."

More than one of the states had ratified on the basis of the promise that a bill of rights would be added to the document. James Madison, to fulfill this promise, regularly brought before the Congress a set of amendments. Finally, Congress passed them on to the states, and on 15 December 1791 enough states ratified ten amendments to make them a part of the Constitution. Amendment V exempts persons in the armed services accused of capital or infamous crimes from the grand jury process, as it does the militia when in actual service in time of war or public danger. Amendment II reads as follows: "A well regulated Militia, being necessary to the security of a free State, the right of the people to keep and bear Arms, shall not be infringed." This amendment has been the constitutional basis for a great deal of litigation. The issue before the courts has usually been whether or not the right to keep and bear arms stems from the needs of the militia or whether it is a basic right possessed by all free individuals.

Sixteen days after the Constitutional Convention finished its work, Congress resolved to enlarge slightly the regular army. The reaction of the Indians of the Northwest to white encroachment was the reason for this legislation. The increase consisted of two companies of artillery, which, added to the two in existence, were to form a battalion. Despite the designation, the battalion was furnished no cannon and was trained as "red legged" infantry. At the end of the era of the Articles of Confederation, the army had a strength of 840 enlisted men and forty-six officers, organized as one regiment of infantry and one battalion of artillery, functioning as infantry.

ERA OF THE FEDERALISTS

Electors unanimously chose George Washington to be the first president under the U.S. Constitution, and he took office in New York City on 30 April 1789. Although the new government was designed and controlled by American conservatives, the hereditary rulers in Europe saw it as a radical and dangerous innovation. They believed that this upstart republic lacked the stamina to survive and that some provocation from them would bring it to an end.

English agents in America were inciting the Indians against the United States in the north, Spanish agents in the south. Although Great Britain had ceded the land west to the Mississippi River to the new nation, some of its governing elements hoped to see the Old Northwest, between the Ohio and Mississippi rivers, become hunting grounds for the Indians, a buffer between the United States and Canada. Whether the result of foreign agitation or not, depredations on the western frontier increased. District Judge Harry Innes of Kentucky estimated that from 1783 to 1790 Indians killed at least fifteen hundred people in his state or traveling to it and destroyed twenty thousand horses and vast quantities of property. One of the first priorities of the new federal government was to control the Indians or risk losing the frontier areas to Great Britain or Spain.

The First Congress passed an act on 11 September 1789 creating the Department of the Treasury, which had far more power than Superintendent of Finance Robert Morris during the Revolution. Alexander Hamilton became the first secretary. On 12 September Congress confirmed Henry Knox as secretary of war, the War Department having been set up on 7 August. Thomas Jefferson assumed the duties of secretary of state on 22 March 1790. These three men and the president dominated the shaping of the American military. Hamilton believed, almost with religious fervor, in a strong peacetime army, and Knox supported him. Jefferson had written to James Monroe on 11 August 1786, "Every rational citizen must wish to see an effective instrument of coercion. . . . A naval force can never endanger our liberties nor occasion bloodshed; a land force would do both." He drew comfort from the belief that the United States would not be plagued with a standing army because it lacked the social dregs from which standing armies were recruited. Jefferson had called in 1786 for the building of a navy while minister to France, and he continued to do so, but he left the cabinet before legislation to revive the navy was passed. In 1793, while still in Washington's cabinet, he opposed the proposal by the president for the founding of a military academy. He argued that such an institution was unconstitutional, but nine years later, when president himself, he authorized the establishment of the United States Military Academy.

Jefferson left the cabinet in 1793, because he could no longer appear to endorse the policies of the administration, devised in the main by Hamilton. The advocates of a strong central government, controlled by an elite, had grouped behind Hamilton's financial program into a political party, the Federalist party. Jefferson, and others of a similar mind, fearful of what to them was excessive centralization and dangerous elitism, had drawn together as Jeffersonian Republicans. Contrary to the hopes of the framers, antagonistic political parties had formed.

The French Revolution further intensified the differences between the two parties. The Federalists saw in that revolution a disastrous release of an inherent savagery of man and a bloody slaughter of innocent people. The French Revolution, they believed, threatened orderly government and so did the Jeffersonian Republican party.

The Republican view of the French Revolution was entirely the opposite. It was seen as releasing the oppressed strata of society that had been ground down by elites throughout history. The bloodshed was a small price to pay for this epochal liberation. Republicans further believed that Federalist policies were returning the nation to colonial status under England. In doing so, they were abandoning France, without which the colonies could never have won independence. All this made the Federalists traitorous in Republican eyes. Party hostility has never been fiercer, never more uncompromising than during the 1790s, when the new nation was being formed.

There was also continuous tension between the parties on military matters. Republicans were convinced that what the Federalists wanted to establish were true European-style standing forces, but, whatever the Federalists wanted, what they actually were doing did not appear very dangerous. Congress took over the diminutive army of the Confederation on 29 September 1789, the last day of its first session. Of the 840 enlisted men authorized for the army, only 672 were actually in service, and these men were owed $150,000 in back pay.

WASHINGTON'S INDIAN WARS. In 1790 the government under the Constitution engaged in its first test of military strength. Complaints and pleas for protection were pouring in from the region north of the Ohio River, and Washington's administration chose to concentrate its limited strength in that region. In April the president persuaded Congress to authorize 376 additional soldiers, but times were relatively prosperous, providing work for men at higher pay than the two dollars a month they could draw as enlisted men in the army. As a result, new men entered the service too slowly to take part in the initial campaign against the tribes of the Old Northwest.

Josiah Harmar had been breveted brigadier general in 1787 and in that grade commanded the U.S. Army of 1,216 enlisted men and an estimated fifty officers. He also led the government's first punitive expedition. Because there were eight Indian tribes scattered in the Old Northwest, there was no one point at which to strike all of them. The object of Harmar's expedition was to destroy villages and food supplies, thus demonstrating the power of the United States. Arthur Saint Clair, governor of the Northwest Territory, which was established by Congress in 1787, traveled widely in the area and to the seat of government to gather supplies and support for Harmar's advance.

One column of 330 men, commanded by Major John F. Hamtramck, marched westward out of Vincennes toward the Wea and Kickapoo towns on 30 September 1790. Several days out it became necessary to cut the food ration. At this point the militia officers with Hamtramck refused to continue the march on half rations, whereupon the major decided that he had no choice but to return to Vincennes.

Harmar himself led 1,453 men out of Fort Washington (present-day Cincinnati) late in September northward toward the Shawnee and Delaware towns on the Maumee River. Three hundred and twenty men were from the First American Regiment, the balance were militia from Kentucky. Although Kentucky was vulnerable to Indian raids by the tribes across the Ohio River, the militia it sent to Harmar was poorly armed and generally poor quality soldiers, one reason being that Major General Charles Scott of Kentucky had developed a strong aversion to Harmar, refusing therefore to serve with him or to aid.

The Kentuckians destroyed villages and crops, but grew careless and began to straggle, which enabled the Indians to trap them in an ambush and severely punish them.

By 13 October, Harmar's force was about one hundred miles north of Fort Washington. The force had burned deserted villages and destroyed standing crops, but had encountered no serious brushes with the foe. The Maumee villages were still two days' march to the north, and the colonels of the Kentucky contingent implored the general to let them take troops and make the march. Against his better judgment, Harmar agree to divide his force, and the Kentuckians moved out with a company of regulars. They destroyed villages and crops, but grew careless and began to straggle, which enabled the Indians to trap them in an ambush and severely punish them. Their losses were so severe that Harmar felt obliged to retreat toward Fort Washington, which he reached on 3 November.

As a result of the expedition, seventy-five regulars were killed and five were wounded, 108 Kentuckians were killed and twenty-eight wounded. Writing from Fort Washington, Harmar reported that his men had burned five villages and destroyed twenty thousand bushels of corn. He wrote of his campaign as a victory and blamed the militia for his excessive losses. Federalist Fisher Ames, who had a mistrust of militia and a preference for regulars, as did other Federalists, stated that by using political influence, the Kentuckians had pressured their way into Harmar's force not to fight Indians, but to draw two-thirds of a dollar a day of federal money. As for the Indians, the fight had convinced them that they could defeat any American force, and they increased their pressure on the settlements.

Statements such as that made by Ames infuriated Kentuckians. Charles Scott went into action to prove them wrong. Born in Virginia, he had been with General Edward Braddock in 1755. During the Revolution he had commanded Virginia regiments as a colonel, then in April 1777 was commissioned a brigadier general in the Continental army. Although captured by the British at Charleston in May 1780 and kept out of action for the rest of the war, he was made brevet major general in September 1783. He was an influential person and able to persuade Congress to finance a campaign waged by Kentuckians. In the spring of 1791 he raised 750 Kentucky mounted volunteers. Mounted and with a train of pack mules, the volunteers could draw twenty dollars a month from the federal treasury instead of the three dollars a day for service on foot. Scott crossed the Ohio River and for thirty days in May ravaged the Wea and Kickapoo villages. During August Colonel James Wilkinson, also a Kentucky officer, repeated Scott's performance. The two expeditions proved to Kentuckians that they were more effective Indian fighters than U.S. regulars. Meanwhile, Harmar's claim of victory had not convinced the administration, and he demanded a court of inquiry. Belatedly, it met on 15 September 1791 and pronounced him free of any blame.

To hold the west in the union, the federal government had to launch a second campaign and do it soon. Washington chose Governor Saint Clair to command it and to replace Harmar as commanding general of the army. Saint Clair, born in Scotland, had received a sound education and studied medicine for a time. He inherited a substantial sum from his mother and with part of it bought a commission as ensign in the 60th Foot Regiment. He came with the regiment to America in 1757 and took part in important actions during the French and Indian War. He resigned his commission in 1762 and settled in western Pennsylvania. His wife brought with her a substantial dowry, which he used to buy great tracts of land in the western country. He sided with the Americans in the Revolution and by 1777 attained the rank of major general in the Continental army. When the war was over, he became a staunch Federalist and served in the Confederation Congress. As a Federalist, a wealthy man, an elitist, and one set apart on the frontier by his superior education, he was not much loved in the Northwest Territory, but the Congress commissioned him governor of the territory on 5 October 1787. Saint Clair held two government posts, governor and major general, and drew two salaries.

To make certain that this time the army would overcome the Indians, Congress constituted a second regiment of infantry of 912 enlisted men and forty-three officers. In addition, it provided for recruiting two thousand levies, who were to volunteer for six months and serve under officers appointed by the president. These men were supposed to eliminate the public mistrust of regulars on the one hand and the shortcomings of militia on the other. Once the Office of Quartermaster General was revived, $312,000 was appropriated for Saint Clair's offensive.

The prestige of Washington, Hamilton, and Knox carried the provisions for Saint Clair's campaign through Congress, but not without opposition. Any increase in the military under the Federalists was opposed by the Republicans. Senator William Maclay of Pennsylvania believed that Knox was fomenting an Indian war primarily to build up the federal military power. Texas, in part made necessary by the costs of preparing to fight Indians, raised up desperate opposition. The passage in March 1791 of Hamilton's excise tax on whiskey was especially obnoxious. Westerners brought against it an indignation akin to the colonials' feelings against the Stamp Act twenty-six years earlier.

The administration was in fact trying to field an expedition strong enough to defeat the small but combined tribes of the Old Northwest. Events nullified the preparations. Because the westerners, most of them Republicans, detested Saint Clair as governor and his militant federalism, few of them would work with him willingly. Major General Scott at first refused to serve with Saint Clair. Also, it took several months to raise the levies. William Duer, under contract to provide food, diverted some of the money for provisions into land speculation, neglecting this contract.

Because of these problems, Saint Clair could not move his column until October. An army needed grazing for its horses and mules, on which movement depended, but by October the grass was either frosted or soon would be. The tardy force consisted of 625 regulars, 1,675 levies, and 470 militiamen, three types of soldiers that had no experience working together and were suspicious of each other. Because Saint Clair had not been able to hire guides, his army groped its way by compass. Moreover, he had scant knowledge of the foe toward which he was fumbling and little idea of where they were. In contrast, the coalition of Indian tribes—Delaware, Wyandot, Ottawa, Kickapoo, Chippewa, and Potawatami—well led by Little Turtle of the Miamis, had known where Harmar's army was at all times.

Although winter was drawing close, Saint Clair halted about every twenty-five miles to build a fort, and between forts axmen had to hack a road through primeval forest wide enough for the cannon and wagons. Regular soldiers, as well-skilled with the ax as with the musket, were not supplied enough axes by the quartermaster to make maximum progress. Saint Clair, fifty years old, was so ill that he had to be carried in a litter slung between two horses.

At daybreak, the time when Indians were most likely to attack, on 4 November 1791, Saint Clair's troops were lined up, but instead of being kept under arms, they were dismissed to prepare for the march. Some of the officers knew that the forest was alive with Indians, but the information had not reached the general. Once the soldiers had fallen out, the Indians attacked. The militia had unwisely been bivouacked apart from the main camp, and the attackers drove them in confusion to and through the other camp, disrupting the attempt to form a line of battle. In a short time the Indians had encircled their foe and fired from cover into a shrinking center. Events went so swiftly that only 1,440 of the 2,700 soldiers were able to engage the enemy. Six hundred and thirty men died in the fight, and about 275 others were wounded. In proportion to the size of the force, this was the army's severest loss before Bataan and Corregidor, 150 years later. Only twice thereafter did the North American Indians so completely defeat a U.S. military operation—the annihilation of Major Francis L. Dade's small column of 112 in December 1835 during the Second Seminole War and George A. Custer's command at the Battle of Little Bighorn in June 1876.

Saint Clair's defeat was a staggering blow to the federal government. It almost broke the thin tie that held the frontier to the union. If the federal government, not very popular anyway, could not control the Indians, frontiersmen asked, what was it good for? Congress immediately requested the papers relating to the campaign from the president. Washington submitted the documents, and with them the legislators began the first congressional inquiry into the conduct of business by the executive branch. Although a court of inquiry cleared Saint Clair of blame, it was obvious that neither he nor the military system had been equal to the task. Saint Clair resigned from the army and returned to his duties as territorial governor, and it took all of Washington's prestige to persuade Congress to appropriate funds to undo the damage.

Anthony Wayne was a dandy, vain, and sometimes a hard drinker, but he was also an ardent competitor, determined to succeed.

The president made a careful and lengthy canvass of the revolutionary war commanders. None perfectly fitted the need, but in 1792 he recommended Anthony Wayne to the Senate as commander of the army. This was a difficult but wise choice. On 3 January 1776, Congress had appointed Wayne, who had no military experience, colonel of the Chester County Regiment of Pennsylvania in the Continental army. He became a brigadier general on 21 February 1777, in command of the Pennsylvania Line. He served in most of the major actions of Washington's northern army and was transferred in 1781 to take part in the southern campaigns. He retired as a brevet major general late in 1783 and reentered military service only when called by Washington on 5 March 1792 as major general and commanding general of the U.S. Army. As a person he was a dandy, vain, and sometimes a hard drinker, but he was also an ardent competitor, determined to succeed. It was ironic that Saint Clair, whom he replaced, had been his arch enemy in the officer corps during and after the Revolution. James Wilkinson, also one of Wayne's antagonists, was made a brigadier general and Wayne's second in command. During the Indian campaign of 1793–1795, Wilkinson did all he could clandestinely to undermine Wayne's position.

On 5 March 1792 Congress constituted three additional regiments of infantry and four troops of dragoons, adding horse soldiers for the first time since the Revolution. These new units became part of the army, now entirely reorganized, following the recommendations of Baron von Steuben, as the Legion of the United States, composed of four sublegions, each containing infantry, riflemen, and artillery. There were now 5,120 enlisted men in the regular establishment, nearly two and one-half times the highest previously authorized total.

Secretary of the Treasury Hamilton had all contracting for food for Wayne's legion transferred from the War Department to the Treasury. He was sure that he could correct some of the flaws revealed by the previous Indian campaigns, but the practice of relying on private contractors to keep an army fed in the wilderness was not satisfactory, even when handled by as skilled an administrator as Hamilton. The offices of Paymaster and Quartermaster General remained unchanged.

The legion was targeted at the small tribes north of the Ohio River and south of the Great Lakes. These could field at best about five thousand warriors. South of the Ohio, however, the Creek, Cherokee, Chickasaw, and Choctaw had an estimated fourteen thousand fighting men. They had remained quiet while Harmar and Saint Clair sought to overcome the northern tribes. The arrival of a new Spanish governor at New Orleans in 1791, Baron Francisco Luis Hector de Carondelet, threatened to end that quiet. Carondelet encouraged the southern tribes to form a confederation and attack American settlements, and his agitation produced assaults on Watauga and Cumberland settlements in Tennessee.

Frontier dwellers south of the Ohio River asked for federal assistance and resented the lack of it. In the entire area of the four large tribes there were only 264 regular soldiers. Moreover, the government had not been able to oblige Spain to open the mouth of the Mississippi River to American products. Some leaders in the southern backcountry considered following the example of the State of Franklin, which was established in 1784 as a new commonwealth, following the cession of its land to the federal government by North Carolina, in order to protect itself against the Indians.

Washington's administration hoped to settle disputes peacefully if possible with the Indians, both north and south. While negotiations proceeded, Wayne had time to train the legion. A skillful organizer and trainer, he had another advantage over his unsuccessful predecessors—the several forts in the line of his advance that had been built by Saint Clair. During the balance of 1792 and until the autumn of 1793, he trained his troops strenuously, emphasizing individual marksmanship, and waited impatiently to be released to move northward. He was committed to his mission because he regarded the Indians as savages who had to be pushed aside by force.

While the legion trained and waited, other significant domestic events were shaping the future of the American military. Recommendations had been before the Congress since 1790 to pass acts implementing the militia clauses of the Constitution. These acts had been delayed to make time for action on the public debt, the admission of Vermont and Kentucky as states, creation of the Bank of the United States, and passage of an excise tax and the Post Office Act. Finally, on 8 May 1792 Congress passed the Uniform Militia Act, prescribing organization and standards and requiring every able-bodied man aged eighteen to forty-five to provide himself with a good firearm and accountrements. It imposed no penalties, however, for failure to do so, either against states or individuals, because no law could possibly pass Congress that gave the federal government power to coerce a state. The states held the power to regulate individuals, and some states did provide fines and imprisonment for individual violations of the federal act. Because the states organized as they pleased, their militia systems were too diverse in weapons and training to be formed into a common force for federal use. In summary, the act placed control of the militias entirely with the states. Therefore, the militia could not become the primary reserve behind the regulars that was hoped for by Washington, Hamilton, Knox, and other nationalists.

During the 1790s events in Europe also were shaping the American military future. The French revolutionaries executed their king in 1793, after which the crowned rulers of Europe combined to conquer France and end regicide. The wars that followed turned into struggles of peoples, altering for all time the nature of warfare. Nations employed mass armies and deployed behind them their entire economies. The western world was passing from an era of limited war into one of total war.

Conflict in Europe increased the demand for American goods, and from 1789 to 1797 exports tripled and imports quadrupled. To continue to enjoy the resultant profits, the United States had to keep itself clear of the fracas across the Atlantic. Accordingly, Washington issued the Neutrality Proclamation on 22 April 1793. The rights of neutrals were ill-defined, however, and both Great Britain and France were determined to keep them narrow. Neither belligerent was willing to permit American goods to flow freely to the other.

The risks of shippers carrying goods across the Atlantic were very high, but the profits induced U.S. merchants to take them. British and French navies and privateers took hundreds of U.S. ships as prizes. What galled especially was the British practice of impressing men from American ships to fill out shortages in their own crews. Great Britain did not honor the process of naturalization and impressed any sailor who had been born in one of the British Isles.

Booming U.S. shipping was under attack not only from England and France, but also by Algiers, Tripoli, and Tunis, which had been harassing American commerce ever since independence. Washington's administration fended them off as well as it could by irregular purchases of protection in the form of tribute. Without a navy, it had no choice, but it took steps to avoid future humiliation. On 27 March 1794, Congress, by a margin of two votes, authorized the building of six frigates. To broaden support for a navy, Knox shrewdly scattered contracts to build the frigates up and down the Atlantic Coast, but the first of these warships was not ready for use until 1797.

France threw the French West Indies open to U.S. trade in 1793, but the British captured those islands. Because grain from the United States was so necessary to France, French warships escorted convoys of grain ships across the Atlantic. British Admiral Richard Howe assailed the escorting French naval vessels on 1 June 1794 and won a decisive victory, gravely weakening the power of France at sea, but this particular U.S. grain fleet managed to reach French ports safely.

When negotiations with the Indians of the Old Northwest finally broke down, Washington, realizing that the frontier issue now had to be settled by force, directed Anthony Wayne on 11 September 1793 to advance northward with the legion. Wayne marched slowly but without resistance. A swarm of scouts led the columns, which marched and bivouacked so securely that they could not be taken by surprise. The legion camped on Christmas Day on Saint Clair's battleground. Human bones lay so thickly that men had to push them aside to pitch their tents. The next day they interred the remains with ceremony. The soldiers, being skilled axmen, quickly erected a sturdy fort named Fort Recovery. They armed the fort with four of Saint Clair's artillery pieces located by William May, one of Wayne's scouts, and by Christopher Miller, a white boy who had been captured years before and brought up by the Shawnee.

When spring arrived Wayne put his force in motion again, advancing ten or twelve miles a day. His supply line became dangerously extended. Seeing this weakness, more than a thousand Shawnee and Ottawa attacked a train of 360 packhorses moving slowly north from Fort Recovery on 30 June 1794. They inflicted forty casualties at a loss to themselves of only three, but, made reckless by their success, they attempted to storm the fort, a mistake rarely committed by Indians because they lacked artillery. British officers accompanying the Indians considered this a turning point in the campaign. Losses in the two-day unsuccessful storming effort, together with ever-present hunger, opened up divisions among the tribes and disputes as to which warriors should lead.

Sir Guy Carleton, Lord Dorchester, governor general of Canada, just returned from England, ordered that a fort be built at the rapids of the Maumee River, deep in U.S. territory. He told the Indians that England would soon be at war with the United States and would fight for its Indian allies as well as for itself. Meanwhile, however, his government could not feed those hungry allies. The warriors had to scatter into the forest to hunt in order to feed themselves and their families.

Blue Jacket selected a position in an area known as Fallen Timbers. Wayne, well-served by spies and scouts, knew they were there and that they were underfed.

Miami, Delaware, Wyandot, Shawnee, Ottawa, Kickapoo, Chippewa, and Potawatamie, almost sixteen hundred in all, gathered close to the newly built British Fort Miami on the Maumee. Some wanted to fight the legion, while others advocated talks. Little Turtle of the Miami opposed fighting, but Blue Jacket, a Shawnee leader, demanded the use of force. Blue Jacket prevailed, and he selected a position just above the fort, in an area known as Fallen Timbers. Wayne, well-served by spies and scouts, knew they were there and that they were underfed. He waited for three days to let hunger and suspense weaken them. When he ordered the assault on 20 August 1794, a very hot day, many of the Indians, not having eaten in three days, were elsewhere hunting. The infantry, relying solely on bayonets, a weapon much feared by the Indians, attacked from the front; dismounted dragoons sought the flanks in order to encircle the enemy. The Indian defense collapsed into a rout, opening the way for the legion to go to the very walls of Fort Miami. Wayne directed a march around the picketwork, defying the defenders, and destroyed all installations outside the palisade. The British neither sallied from the fort nor opened it to let in their Indian allies. Wayne taunted the garrison but was careful to do nothing that might drive England into warring on the United States. He had averted war, loosened the hold of Great Britain on the Old Northwest, and convinced the tribes of the Northwest that they must give up their allegiance to Great Britain and transfer it to the United States.

Despite the policy of the Washington administration to deal peacefully with the Indian tribes south of the Ohio River, fighting did break out. John Sevier was a central figure in the territory of Tennessee. He had lived all his life on the southwestern frontier and had performed heroically at the Battle of Kings Mountain on 7 October 1780, where frontiersmen pitted themselves against conventionally trained British regulars. Sevier was not strongly influenced by orders or even suggestions from the national administration. When bloody incidents reached a level unacceptable to him in 1793, he raised a force of Tennessee volunteers from scratch, led a foray against the Indians, and with his usual success weakened Indian fighting strength. The next year James Robertson, major general of the militia of the Territory South of the Ohio River, ignoring the warning of the governor of the territory, raised a volunteer detachment and attacked the Cherokee and some Creek. Although both Sevier and Robertson had flouted federal Indian policy, they had the temerity to apply for funds to pay their men. Several years later, the United States paid those volunteers.

HEIGHTENING PARTY TENSIONS. The small U.S. Army was stretched to the limit, giving the Federalist administration the opportunity to enlarge it piecemeal. The need for engineer officers became conspicuous when four new arsenals were to be built and it was necessary to hire French engineers to supervise the work. Therefore, on 7 May 1794, Congress voted to form the Corps of Artillerists and Engineers, to contain four battalions. Each of the battalions would have eight cadets attached, providing a steady influx of trained engineer officers. The administration chose all the cadets from Federalist families.

Hamilton's financial program, the central activity around which the Federalist party had formed, contained an excise tax on whiskey that was enacted on 3 March 1791. The farmers in western Pennsylvania grew wheat, distilled it into whiskey, and stored it in huge casks that could be easily rolled to nearby rivers for shipment. Whiskey was their best source of income, the tax on it a discrimination. Those who hated this tax argued that Hamilton had created it mainly to provide a test of the federal government's power to enforce its laws. Western Pennsylvanians were so thoroughly riled that they attacked some revenue agents and destroyed property. Hamilton argued that the government had to use force to establish its authority. Washington agreed, but was not willing to use the small regular army, not only because it was preoccupied with the northwestern tribes, but also because it would appear to Jeffersonian Republicans to be an agent of arbitrary power, projected from the center into the states.

The alternative was to summon militia under the constitutional provision that gave Congress the power to use militia to suppress insurrection. On 7 August 1794 the president called for 5,200 militiamen from Pennsylvania, 2,300 from Maryland, 2,100 from New Jersey, and 3,300 from Virginia, totaling 12,900. It was necessary to draft militiamen in Virginia and Maryland and riots resulted. Western Pennsylvanians, declaring that they were willing to die for their county, would not march against their own people. Militia from Pennsylvania had to be drawn from Philadelphia and the eastern seaboard. Early in October the militia was assembled and Washington himself was present to see some of them off at Carlisle, Pennsylvania. Henry Lee of Virginia was in command, but Hamilton himself was along as the president's personal representative. Hamilton was in an element he loved—military—and involved in a cause that would establish beyond doubt the power of the federal government. The march westward was arduous; the weather was bad and the roads muddy. The troops destroyed or appropriated some personal property and treated a few individuals roughly, but took no lives. Once the militiamen reached the western counties, the Whiskey Rebellion faded and the ringleaders tried to hide. The easterners rounded up some of those leaders and brought them eastward tied to the tails of the horses of mounted men. Republicans, viewing this triumphal procession, thought they were seeing the use of military force to suppress dissenting opinion. Two of the insurrectionists were charged with treason, convicted, and condemned to death, but were later pardoned by Washington. The whiskey tax continued to be collected until repealed in Thomas Jefferson's administration.

Meanwhile, Washington's original cabinet of remarkable men had already begun to disintegrate. Jefferson resigned at the end of 1793. Once the Northwest Indians were subdued and the Whiskey Rebellion quelled, Knox felt he could leave honorably, which he did in 1794. He had served nearly ten years, a longer tenure than any other secretary of war. Hamilton resigned in January 1795.

By the beginning of Washington's second term, cabinet posts had lost much of their prestige, and the president had trouble filling the positions. To succeed Jefferson as secretary of state, he chose a Virginia planter and longtime friend, Edmund Randolph, who had served as attorney general since 1789. Randolph had strongly supported separation from England, and from 1786 to 1788 he had been governor of Virginia. He charged most of the troubles of the postwar era to the "turbulence and follies of democracy."

Timothy Pickering replaced Henry Knox in the War Department. He was a graduate of Harvard and a practitioner of law in Massachusetts. He was also a key figure in the state militia and became knowledgeable enough to write a booklet at the start of the Revolution on how to train militia. During the Revolution he was adjutant general of the army in 1777–1778, served on the Board of War from 1778 to 1780, and was quartermaster general from 1780 to 1783. Randolph resigned on 19 August 1795 under suspicion of corruption, and Pickering became acting secretary of state and then secretary in December. Oliver Wolcott, Jr., a member of a powerful Connecticut family, succeeded Hamilton at the Treasury on 2 February 1795. Trained as a lawyer, he had gained financial experience as an auditor and then as comptroller in the Treasury Department.

When Pickering moved to the State Department, Washington asked three men to be secretary of war, all of whom turned him down. His fourth choice, James McHenry, accepted the position and took office on 27 January 1796. He was born in Ireland, migrating to the colonies in 1771. He studied medicine with Benjamin Rush and was a surgeon during the Revolution. He was captured, exchanged, and became General Washington's personal secretary in 1778. He was the least capable of the appointees, but like the other cabinet members, was a dedicated Federalist.

Under the Calling Forth Act of 1792, Congress had delegated some of its power to call militia into the service of the United States to the president. In case of invasion or the threat of it, he could issue a call to any state militia officer without having to go through the governor, but if the use of the militia was to enforce the laws, the federal judge would have to certify the existence of such a need. This act was to expire in 1795, hence Congress renewed it on 28 February 1795 with the one alteration that a federal judge no longer need be involved.

Dissension between Federalists and Republicans intensified during Washington's last two years as president, but it did not prevent the administration from certain specific accomplishments. One of these was the settlement of dangerous differences with Spain through Pinckney's Treaty (also known as the Treaty of San Lorenzo), signed on 27 October 1795. This agreement fixed the northern boundary of Florida at the thirty-fist parallel, included a pledge from Spain not to incite the Florida Indians to raid across the border, and, above all, gave Americans free navigation of the Mississippi River. Thereafter, for a time, Spain seemed less of a threat to American security.

In the Great Lakes region, the British at long last began to evacuate the posts that they had agreed to give up in the Treaty of Paris of 1783. They left the last one on 11 September 1796. Wayne's victory at Fallen Timbers in 1794 had forced this withdrawal. Another consequence of Fallen Timbers was the Treaty of Greenville, signed 3 August 1795. At Greenville the Wyandot, Delaware, Chippewa, and Ottawa reaffirmed what they had transferred in 1785 at Fort McIntosh, adding to it more land, and the Miami, Potawatamie, Shawnee, and Piankashaw agreed to transfer to the United States about two-thirds of Ohio and a slice of Indiana. In 1796 Indian commissioner Benjamin Hawkins reached an accord with the Creek, the Treaty of Coleraine, which kept them peaceful for a few years.

Peace appeared to be breaking out and with it came a determination to reduce the army. Whereas Washington had created the legion by executive order, Congress dissolved it on 30 May 1796. Thereafter, the U.S. Army consisted of four regiments of infantry, two companies of light dragoons, and the Corps of Artillerists and Engineers, totaling 3,126 enlisted men and an estimated two hundred officers. Just before he left office, Washington interceded to prevent Congress from deleting the horse soldiers. The 1796 act and the distribution of troops following it established the prototype to which the land forces would return after every war in the nineteenth century—a small army, scattered widely in isolated frontier posts, artillery and engineers for coastal defense, and a tiny cavalry component.

Brigadier General Wilkinson, always an intriguer, had gradually won many officers to support him against Wayne, who became aware of Wilkinson's machinations and prepared to confront him to heal the rift in the officer crops. The confrontation never took place because Wayne died on 15 December 1796, which made Wilkinson the ranking officer in the U.S. Army. His actions had always been devious. He had been part of the Conway Cabal, which in 1777, in the midst of the War for Independence, had tried to replace General Washington with Horatio Gates. He had been involved in the attempt to keep the army at Newburgh in 1783 as a threat to Congress. Various contemporary observers had suspected that he received payment from Spain for information but none could prove it. It was not until the scholar Herbert E. Bolton found evidence in the Mexican Archives in the twentieth century that it was established that Wilkinson, beginning in 1787, had been receiving $2,000 a year in gold. Although the information that Wilkinson transmitted to Spain benefited him, it did little harm to the United States, and scant good to Spain.

In November 1796 the United States signed Jay's Treaty with Great Britain, enabling American traders to reenter the stream of commerce in which they had prospered before the Revolution. The Republic of France was at this time governed by the Directory, a group of opportunists made aggressive by French victories. They declared that Jay's Treaty hurt France and was a violation of the alliance of 1778, through which France had enabled the colonies to become independent. Accordingly, they ordered French vessels to seize more American ships presumed to be engaged in trade with England. About five thousand U.S. merchant ships were endangered at sea by both England and France.

When the American Revolution removed the United States from British naval protection, the pirates of the Barbary states began to prey on U.S. vessels.

At the same time, four dictatorships lined the coast of North Africa—Algiers, Morocco, Tripoli, and Tunis. Their revenue came from highjacking the ships of other nations, confiscating their cargoes, and enslaving the crews to hold for ransom. When the American Revolution removed the United States from British naval protection, the Barbary states began to prey on U.S.

vessels, which, in effect, produced an undeclared war with the pirate states.

In 1795 Washington's government signed a humiliating treaty with Algiers. In return for promises not to molest U.S. shipping in the Mediterranean and the adjacent Atlantic, the United States agreed to pay the Dey of Algiers $525,000 tribute and ransom money for American sailors in Algerian dungeons, to contribute large quantities of naval stores, and to deliver one complete frigate. Because the frigates authorized in 1794 were not ready, no other course seemed open than protection money and goods, although one frigate was delivered in 1798.

In 1796 the sultan of Morocco entered into an acceptable treaty with the United States, and thereafter U.S. policy centered on trying to get each of the other Barbary States to agree to such a treaty. An accommodation of sorts was reached with Tripoli in 1796 and Tunis and the new sultan of Morocco in 1797. Although humiliating demands continued, the U.S. administrations considered payment of tribute cheaper than war. Under the policy of paying tribute, the pride of naval officers was taxed to its limits. For example, William Bainbridge, commanding the *George Washington,* was obliged to carry lumber, coffee, sugar, and other tribute in his warship to the Dey of Algiers. The dey then demanded that Bainbridge take aboard a zoo of animals, one hundred slaves, and a miscellany of other cargo and deliver them to the Grand Seignor in Constantinople, who was his suzerain and who had never heard of the United States. Because refusing to comply meant war, Bainbridge completed that mission in 1800.

THE PRESIDENCY OF JOHN ADAMS. When George Washington announced that he would step down at the end of two terms, Vice-president John Adams became the Federalist candidate, although part of the Federalist party would not support Adams. Thomas Jefferson, the leading Republican, became vice-president.

Even though extreme Federalists considered war with France essential to purge the country of bloody radicalism, the new president sought peacefully to settle differences with France. Adams appointed Charles Cotesworth Pinckney U.S. minister to France, but the Directory refused to meet with him in December 1796. Adams then appointed a commission consisting of Pinckney, John Marshall, and Elbridge Gerry to try for peaceful settlement. In October 1797 the directory refused to meet officially with these commissioners without prior agreement to a very large loan to France and a bribe to the French agents, known in U.S. history as X, Y, and Z. Their insulting demands nullified the intentions of Adams and increased tension between the two nations.

Throughout his long public life Adams had always championed a navy adequate to protect American commerce. When he took office he had little naval power to work with, only three unfinished frigates, the *United States, Constellation,* and *Constitution,* all without crews, and a list of ship captains. French depredations goaded Congress on 15 April 1798 to appropriate $950,000 to enlarge and improve the navy. The following year it voted $1 million to construct six seventy-four-gun ships-of-the-line, six sloops, and some auxiliary vessels. If the frigates were completed and the ships-of-the-line constructed, the United States would have a navy that the European powers would have to take into account, the sort of navy Vice-president Jefferson and his Republican associates opposed as certain to involve the nation in Europe's imbroglios.

French spoliation of U.S. commerce in the Caribbean and the XYZ Affair brought the United States, despite the effects of Adams, into undeclared war at sea in 1798. Congress reversed the shipbuilding plans; all six of the frigates authorized in 1794 were to be finished. These ships were stronger than French and British ships of the same rating, because there was a gangway along both sides, which not only added strength to the hull, but also served as a second gundeck. Because of that second deck, the *Constellation,* as an example, was rated at thirty-six guns, but actually mounted forty-eight.

In January 1798 the French government decreed that any neutral ship carrying British goods was subject to confiscation. To cope with the undeclared Quasi-War with France, Congress on 30 April 1798 established the Navy Department. President Adams could not persuade George Cabot, his first choice, to be secretary, but Benjamin Stoddert accepted reluctantly. The salary of $3,000 a year was not an inducement. Stoddert, a Marylander, had seen two years of action during the Revolution in a Pennsylvania militia company, serving as captain. In the fall of 1779 he became secretary of the Board of War, which position he filled efficiently until 1781. After the war he prospered as a merchant in Georgetown, Maryland, and invested his profits in land, some of which he sold to the United States for the new seat of government, the District of Columbia. His good sense and willingness to accept moderate profits prevented wasteful speculation. Stoddert knew shipping, but had never been a seaman.

He took over the purchase, building, and providing of ships from Secretary of the Treasury Wolcott. In 1790 Hamilton had established a seagoing revenue service in the Treasury Department and with it the supervision of naval building. An act of 1 July 1797 authorized the president to use revenue cutters in naval service, and by the end of 1798 nine of the twenty-one operational ships in the navy were cutters. They were outgunned, outsized, and outmanned even by French privateers, but a second generation of cutters was quickly constructed. These were fine vessels, on average fifty-eight feet long and twenty feet wide, carrying ten to sixteen brass guns, four and six pounders. They were made very sharp for speed. Stoddert formally took control of seven of the new cutters on 10 October 1798, but one by one released them back to the Treasury as the naval vessels came into service. He kept three of them until the end of the Quasi-War. From 1798 to 1801 cutters captured twenty-six French merchantmen and recaptured ten Americans.

Stoddert proved to be an able administrator. With only eighteen people in the Navy Department, he supervised the addition of fifty-four fighting ships to the fleet and commissioned 365 privateers. Since there was no commissioned chief in the navy, he corresponded with every ship captain, including the revenue cutters. Under him the number of sailors expanded to six thousand, officers to seven hundred. When Congress reconstituted the Marine Corps in July 1798, Stoddert took over the eleven hundred marines. The expansion of the navy during the Quasi-War showed that Stoddert had true ability; it also revealed the remarkable capacity of the new nation to shift rapidly from peace to war.

French privateers took a heavy toll of U.S. merchant ships in the Caribbean Sea despite all that the growing U.S. Navy could do and despite the superiority of the American frigates. On 9 February 1799 the *Constellation,* with Thomas Truxtun commanding, engaged *L'Insurgente,* a frigate of about equal strength, and forced it to surrender. During the next year Truxtun armed his ship with carronades—short, light guns capable of smashing heavy balls into enemy vessels at close range. Using carronades for the first time on an American warship, he crippled the *Vengeance* despite its heavier broadsides on 1–2 February 1800. This fight severely damaged both ships and decimated the crews, but neither captain surrendered.

Secretary Stoddert had to use his utmost tact in handling the captains. He tried to follow established lists of seniority, which were sacrosanct to the captains. The two captains at the top of the roster presented the first problem. One of them was not up to command because of age, the other because of temperament. Stoddert skillfully placed them out of the way without wounding either's pride. The next three seniors were Silas Talbot, Richard Dale, and Truxtun, not one of them willing to be subordinate to either of the other two. Dale took himself out of contention, and Stoddert used his finest diplomacy to keep Talbot and Truxtun from resigning.

Because their tasks were very difficult, captains were worth special handling. They were responsible for completing construction of the ships assigned to them and for rigging and equipping them, hence, their ships differed widely in spread of sail, rigging, hull design, and weight of guns. They had to find their own guns, scarce at first and mostly imported from England, but by 1800 American foundries were adding to the supply. Captains also had to recruit their own crews, and no one shared the responsibilities with them. Naval officer David Porter described a captain's solitariness:

> A man of war is a petty kingdom governed by a petty despot. The little tyrant, strutting his few fathoms of scoured plank, dare not unbend, lest he should lose the appearance of respect from his inferiors which their fears inspire. He has therefore no society, no smile, no courtesies for or from anyone. He stands alone, without the friendship or sympathy of one on board, a solitary being in the midst of the ocean.

Great Britain, seeing that the United States was warring at sea with its own enemy, strongly supported U.S. vessels in the Caribbean. Its ports there were open to them and they were supplied by British depots in the islands. This cooperation was never formalized in writing, but the British ships did as much indirectly to guard the coasts of the United States as American ships did directly. Moreover, friendly contact with the British fleet gave the U.S. Navy its basic signal system, some maneuvers in formation, and a start toward true professionalism. In the midst of cooperation, however, British captains continued to practice impressment. One of them even boarded the U.S. twenty-gun *Baltimore* and removed fifty-five of the crew, although only five were retained. For permitting this indignity without a fight, Captain Isaac Phillips was dismissed from the navy.

Everything that happened in the military services produced a reaction in U.S. party politics. A small group of Republicans, led by Abraham Albert Gallatin, contested every bill that enlarged the army or navy or increased their costs, because he believed that naval expansion inevitably resulted in imperialism. Along with other dedicated Republicans, he was sure that the Federalists improved on every employment of the military to make standing forces permanent, which they believed would end in economic ruin.

The costs of the Quasi-War with France obliged the Federalist administration to try to increase its revenues. In July 1798 it imposed a direct tax levied by the federal government on land, houses, and slaves. Hated by Republicans as a dangerous invasion into state jurisdiction, the direct tax produced a small insurrection the following year.

Citizens in Northhampton, Montgomery, and Bucks counties in Pennsylvania refused to allow the tax appraisers on their properties. Jacob Fries, an auctioneer, assumed leadership, giving the skirmish the name Fries's Rebellion. President Adams, reacting swiftly to this challenge, made a brigadier general of the Pennsylvania militia the same grade in the U.S. Army and called upon Pennsylvania and New Jersey for militia. In addition, unlike President Washington during the Whiskey Rebellion, Adams sent five hundred regulars into the insurgent counties and the rebellion was put down. Fries was tried for treason and sentenced to be hanged, but was pardoned by President Adams.

The Federalist party reached its peak in 1798. In July Congress passed a sedition act that made it a crime even to speak slightingly of federal officials. That act and the Enemy Aliens Acts (thought to have been aimed at Swiss-born Gallatin) suggested to Republicans that the Federalist administration meant to suppress the political opposition. Their concern was increased by the creation by Congress of the Provisional Army, authorized to have up to forty-one thousand men. This adjunct to the old army was not for suppression of the political opposition, but for fighting in Europe. The ultra-Federalists (known also as High Federalists) wanted full-scale, declared war against France, believing war to be the only way to wipe out the subversive radicalism injected into the world by the French Revolution. President Adams saw no need for the new army, but felt obliged to accept it in order to hold the party together. If Washington would command it, the Provisional Army might be sensibly controlled, but Washington accepted command reluctantly and the rank of lieutenant general only on condition that Hamilton, commissioned a major general, could organize the force. By this time Adams and Hamilton were bitter enemies, but once again the president felt he had to make the appointment. Hamilton and Pinckney selected the officers, taking care that all of them were Federalists. Gallatin, meanwhile, stated publicly that the entire Provisional Army was unconstitutional.

Many men, including the president, were fearful of an army controlled by Hamilton, but in reality that army did not materialize. It never had more than thirty-four hundred men in it, and members of the regular army were reluctant to cross over for fear of being dropped if the new army was discontinued.

President Adams, without consulting either the cabinet or the party, in February 1799 sent the nomination

Constellation *versus* L'Insurgente. *On 9 February 1799, the* Constellation, *with Thomas Truxtun commanding, engaged* L'Insurgent, *a French frigate of about equal strength, and forced it to surrender. (National Archives/drawing by William Bainbridge)*

of William Vans Murray as peace emissary to the Senate. High Federalists were so enraged that they prepared to block the appointment. Adams then let them know that if they did so, he would resign and turn the presidency over to arch-Republican Jefferson. This threat forced the Senate to agree to the nomination if the president would appoint two additional peace commissioners. Adams accepted this condition; Chief Justice Oliver Ellsworth and William R. Davie, former governor of North Carolina, joined Murray and sailed away to negotiate a peaceful settlement to the undeclared hostilities with the French minister of foreign affairs, Charles Maurice de Tallyrand-Périgord. The French government had let it be known that it would receive them.

On 5 May 1800 Adams called Secretary of War McHenry aside at a state dinner, dressed him down, and demanded his resignation.

While the commissioners negotiated, Adams made a full break with the right wing of his party. He had known throughout his term that his cabinet, held over from Washington's second term, had looked more toward Hamilton in New York than to him. For a proud man this was hard to bear, and on 5 May 1800 he called Secretary of War McHenry aside at a state dinner, dressed him down, and demanded his resignation. Pickering, too, had to go.

On 30 September 1800 the three American commissioners entered into a convention with France. France abrogated the alliance of 1778, but refused any compensation for the 1,853 documented cases of spoliation, which had cost American merchants an estimated $12 million. (A century later the U.S. government itself paid this amount to private creditors.) More important, the Convention of 1800 ended the undeclared war. French ships stopped preying on U.S. merchantmen in the Caribbean, while the danger of warfare on land, if it had ever existed, faded away. The officers and men of the Provisional Army were discharged with three months pay.

American sailors had been killed and wounded when the *Constellation* engaged *L'Insurgente* and the *Vengeance*, but aside from these actions, casualties in the undeclared war had been limited. The French captured only one U.S. war vessel, the *Retaliation*, which they took in 1798 and lost to the U.S. Navy the following year. *L'Insurgente* was repaired and recommissioned the *Insurgent* in the American service, sent to sea in 1800, and never heard from again. Similarly, the *Pickering*, a revenue cutter with fourteen guns, also sailed outward and disappeared.

In 1801 the federal government spent $10 million, 70 percent of which was applied against the public debt and its interest. Most of the remaining 30 percent was consumed by the army and the navy. America had paid a high price for military action. Hamilton, bitter over the loss of his chance to control an army and with it save the nation, bent his energies to defeat Adams for a second term as president. Federalists, disgruntled by the Convention of 1800, combined with Republicans to defeat Adams and to elect Jefferson.

ERA OF THE JEFFERSONIAN REPUBLICANS

JEFFERSON: ARMY AND NAVY. Considering the ferocity of party feeling and the conviction by both parties that its opponent was unfit to govern, the transfer of power without violence in 1801 was proof of the durability of the United States. President Jefferson did not disturb the institutions established by the Federalists. He believed, however, in practicing less government. He strongly mistrusted standing military forces and abhorred the public debt that he had inherited from the previous administrations. The internal taxes levied by the Federalist administrations were unacceptable and he instituted the repeal of the whiskey tax.

Jeffersonians saw no contradiction between strict economy and national security. Neither Canada to the north nor Spain to the south presented an immediate menace, and three thousand miles of ocean seemed an adequate moat to fend off the ever-warring European nations. Added security would come from a consistent, nonaggressive U.S. policy. The navy could safely be kept small. As for the Indians, local forces could handle them.

Jeffersonian military theory included heavy reliance on citizens, acting temporarily as soldiers and sailors, to defend the country. The nation would never tolerate regular forces on land and water large enough to defend twenty-five hundred miles of coastline and about as much Indian-threatened frontier. The male citizens, organized as militia, could be relied on to fend off the first blows of an attacker until troops with longer enlistments could be raised, trained, and hurried into action. It would take only a few weeks, this line of reasoning went, to convert citizens into soldiers, except for artillery and engineers. There was no thought of stopping an attack at sea because a peaceful policy would make oceanic aggression unlikely. If war did come, privateers could do at sea what the militia did ashore.

In the army that Jefferson inherited, 95 percent of the officers were Federalists. Considering the hostility between the parties, highlighted during the election, the president was not sure he could rely on those officers. Jefferson appointed Henry Dearborn as secretary of war, and he and Dearborn began systematically to put some Republicanism into the officer corps. Like his predecessor, James McHenry, Dearborn was a medical doctor who had practiced in New Hampshire, but he did not serve in the Revolution as a surgeon. He became a line officer, serving in the thick of the conflict—Bunker Hill, Quebec, the campaign against John Burgoyne, Valley Forge, Monmouth, John Sullivan's campaign against the Indians, and Yorktown. He was a lieutenant colonel when the war ended.

Although there was no pool of Republican officers to draw from, Jefferson began to create one by building upon the corps of engineers that John Adams had placed at West Point. An act of 16 March 1802 provided for seven officers and ten cadets at West Point to be the cadre for a military academy. Dearborn chose cadets who were, or could become, Republicans. The act of 1802 was the statutory basis for the United States Military Academy, but the great importance of the academy resided in the future. It did not achieve stature until after 1817, but no one in that time period imagined the power it would exert in U.S. military affairs later in the nineteenth century and after.

Most of the nation's colleges were Federalist with a curriculum based on the classics. President Jefferson wanted the academy to break away from the classics and offer courses in science, which would give the graduates a better opportunity to apply their knowledge more directly for the benefit of society. Another function of the academy would be to produce graduates who would spread military knowledge throughout the militia system. Jefferson's reforms in the long run built a middle-class officer corps, one which offered no threat to the government. By the time he left office, Jefferson had reversed the party affiliation of the officers from 95 percent Federalist to 89 percent Republican.

The administration inherited Brigadier General James Wilkinson as the senior officer of the army, and it continued to receive allegations that he was in the pay of Spain. Wilkinson remained what he had always been, a conspirator, feuding with other officers, and had developed strong political connections, such as that with Congressman (later Senator) Samuel Smith of Maryland. A feud with Wade Hampton sharply split the officer corps, but one way or another, Wilkinson controlled many key officers of the army.

The Peacetime Establishment Act of 17 March 1802 called for deep cuts in the military. Secretary Dearborn studied carefully what existed in order to determine what to delete. Neither he nor the president sought the advice of General Wilkinson or any other commissioned officer. Dearborn even handled the details of army administration. Purchasing agents needed his approval for any expenditure exceeding fifty dollars.

The authorized size of the army was reduced from fifty-four hundred men to thirty-two hundred, but since actual strength in 1802 was only thirty-five hundred, the cut came to three hundred. The number of officers in actual service declined from 230 to 162. The organization required by the reduction consisted of twenty companies of infantry in two regiments and twenty companies of artillery in one regiment of five battalions. No horse troops were authorized.

There was no longer a quartermaster department; its duties were assigned to three civilian agents, who were not controlled by the military. The paymaster handled clothing. These changes in supply reduced both efficiency and costs. The reduction cut total army appropriations from $2,093,000 in 1801 down to $680,000 in 1803.

Secretary of the Navy Robert Smith was the president's fifth choice for that position. His brother, Samuel Smith, legislator from Maryland, was a powerful figure in the Republican party. Their relationship was useful to the administration. Robert Smith and Secretary of the Treasury Gallatin did not get along well, because Smith made demands on the Treasury for naval purposes which invariably Gallatin protested against. Smith was also a blunt man, who sometimes ruffled the sensibilities of the navy's captains. He remained at this post throughout both of Jefferson's administrations.

Smith began to reduce the ambitious beginnings made by the Federalists. He stopped work on the six seventy-four-gun ships-of-the-line and halted building on lands that former Secretary of the Navy Stoddert had bought for naval yards near four major ports.

The Pasha of Tripoli, however, halted the reduction of naval expenses. As early as 1784, Jefferson had argued for war rather than tribute for the Barbary states. Against such weak opponents, force was his preferred policy. Accordingly, when Tripoli, dissatisfied with the tribute from the United States, declared war on 2 April 1801, the secretary of the navy sent out a squadron under Commodore Richard Morris that accomplished little until Commodore Edward Preble arrived to relieve Morris in the spring of 1803. Preble controlled six warships plus auxiliary vessels. He took into service six U.S.-built gunboats loaned by King Ferdinand and IV of Naples.

Preble decided to reduce the heavily walled city of Tripoli by naval action. On 3 August 1803 he sent the *Constitution*, three brigs, three schooners, two bomb vessels, and six gunboats, manned by 1,060 men, against the city. The attempt did not force a capitulation, and action continued in the Mediterranean Sea and the harbor. On 31 October the thirty-six-gun *Philadelphia*, pursuing a vessel into the harbor, grounded on an uncharted reef, and the ship was immediately surrounded by small craft, their crews looking for a chance to board the frigate. It was further menaced by being within range of the guns of the fort.

Captain William Bainbridge, in command of the *Philadelphia*, had entered the navy from the merchant marine during the Quasi-War with France. It had been his misfortune to lose the *Retaliation*, the only U.S. war vessel lost during that war. Known in the navy as a fierce fighter, in this case he decided to surrender, a decision that haunted him for the rest of his life. While in Tripolitan service the *Philadelphia* was a deadly menace to Preble's squadron. Accordingly, Bainbridge authorized Lieutenant Stephen Decatur to try to enter the harbor and burn the ship. This very dangerous mission was a sentimental one for Decatur because the *Philadelphia* had been paid for by the citizens of his home town, for which it was named, and because his father had commanded it during the Quasi-War. No American ship could penetrate the harbor, so Decatur captained a captured Tripolitan ketch, the *Intrepid.* He put the carefully picked volunteers, about seventy-five of them, in the hold, and on 16 February 1804 was able to enter the harbor, draw close to the big ship, and even receive a line extended to bring them alongside. Only then did the Tripolitan crew see that the sailors scrambling out of the hold and onto the *Philadelphia* were Americans. Without firing a shot the boarders quickly overran the ship, set it on fire, and narrowly escaped the resultant explosions. This daring feat brought Decatur, age twenty-five, immediate promotion to captain and made him the unchallenged hero of the Tripolitan War.

Stephen Decatur (center) was the unchallenged hero of the Tripolitan War, a war noted for hand-to-hand combat without quarter. (National Archives/engraving after Alonzo Chappel)

When word reached Preble that he was soon to be superseded, he initiated a series of three naval attacks on the city of Tripoli, but all were repulsed. The city was too heavily fortified and too heavily gunned to be reduced by naval action alone. Commodore Samuel Barron arrived on 9 September 1804 to replace Preble, who was disappointed keenly by being relieved just when he felt that he could be victorious. Barron accomplished little and was relieved in the spring of 1805 by Commodore John Rogers.

William Eaton, formerly a captain in the U.S. Army and now naval agent to the Barbary states, organized a commando party to move by land against the rear of the city. Joined by the disaffected brother of the pasha and aided by the navy, Eaton moved toward the rear of Tripoli from 8 March to 25 April 1805. Just when Eaton believed that he was able to enter the city, the Navy Department ordered him home. By this time, however, the pasha, eager to end the conflict, accepted $60,000 in ransom for American prisoners and agreed to peace on 4 June 1805.

Thus ended the Tripolitan War, notable for hand-to-hand fighting without quarter. For example, when Stephen Decatur learned that a Tripolitan captain had killed his brother James after James had surrendered, he pursued the captain's vessel, boarded it, and, at all hazard, carved his way to the captain and killed him in a sword fight. The war also provided the stirring phrase "to the shores of Tripoli" for the Marine Corps hymn and demonstrated that the Republican administration was willing to use force if force seemed the best tool to carry out national purposes.

Once relieved of the heavy costs of war, the Jeffersonians returned to reducing the navy. The driving reductionist was Gallatin, secretary of the Treasury for fourteen years, the longest tenure of any Treasury secretary. Gallatin, who was Swiss-born, never overcame a very broad accent, and when elected to the U.S. Senate in 1793, the senators ousted him as a member because he had not been a U.S. citizen for the mandatory nine years. Gallatin believed that the first duty of the Republican administration was to pay off the heavy public debt, which he considered to be as much a danger to the nation as any foreign foe. He never ceased to oppose a substantial peacetime navy. To operate a frigate for one year, he pointed out, cost half as much as the original cost of its construction. Commerce, he said, could take care of itself, but on this point he did not have the support of the president, although Jefferson did concur with him on the need to reduce naval expenditures.

The first step was to cut funds for the offensive instruments of the navy, the frigates and brigs. Only two frigates were in service late in 1807, with two others ready if needed and three more nearly so. Jefferson himself had drawn up plans for sheltered dry docks for frigates, but Congress had refused to fund them. Of five brigs, three were in service and one ready. The Marine Corps dropped to four hundred, the number of captains from twenty-eight to fifteen, lieutenants from 110 to fifty-six, while the whole number of enlisted sailors fell below one thousand. Naval appropriations, which had been $3 million in 1801, dropped to $1 million in 1803.

Jefferson's administration is notorious for its reliance on gunboats, vessels designed to operate in shoal water, guarding the home coast and harbors. It authorized the building of 276 gunboats during 1805–1807 and actually built 176. Secretary of the Navy Smith ensured support for the gunboat policy by awarding contracts to build them all along the eastern coast, on the Gulf coast, and even up the western rivers. One was built at Cincinnati, Ohio, another at Eddyville, Kentucky. They varied in length from sixty to seventy-three feet and were about seventeen feet wide. Whereas frigates carried thirty-eight to fifty-four guns, gunboats mounted only one or two heavy ones. Their crews, twenty-five to forty-five men, were one-tenth those of frigates. Jefferson believed that local militia could man the gunboats in peacetime and at low cost hold the enemy offshore if attacked without warning. Although not built for ocean service, six of the gunboats, somewhat modified, crossed the Atlantic to take part in the Tripolitan War.

LAND AND SEA FRONTIERS. From 1801 to 1803, there was a hiatus in the war in Europe that had begun in 1793. During this peace Napoleon Bonaparte secretly forced the Spanish rulers to return the huge area west of the Mississippi River to France. When Jefferson learned of this, he recognized it as a grave threat to the security of the United States. Had Napoleon's original plans carried, it certainly would have meant danger. He intended to occupy the island of Hispaniola (Santo Domingo) as a base, cross to New Orleans, and reestablish France in America, from which it had been expelled in 1763. His plan failed in Hispaniola, and after that failure he lost all interest in Louisiana except as a source of money to resume waging war. From this situation emerged the dazzling opportunity for the United States to purchase Louisiana. Although the boundaries were not sharply defined, this transaction added at least 828,000 square miles to the nation by a treaty of cession dated 30 April 1803.

When Stephen Decatur learned that a Tripolitan captain had killed his brother, he pursued the captain's vessel, boarded it, carved his way to the captain, and killed him.

Resistance by Spanish and French nationals to being absorbed by the United States seemed likely and would have to be controlled by military means. Jefferson put through Congress a bill to call a detachment of eighty thousand militiamen, to be raised by the states on a quota basis, to be held in readiness. When the Federalists had called for volunteers from the militia, they had given the power of appointment of officers to the president, but in this Republican detachment, the states appointed the officers.

The president sent two representatives to receive the formal transfer of Louisiana from Spain. One of them was General Wilkinson, who took with him three companies of regulars, but the transfer on 20 December was perfectly peaceful. Detachments of regulars began to occupy a few of the key forts that the French and Spanish had built in the Mississippi valley.

When in 1805 that portion of the Louisiana Purchase north of thirty-three degrees north latitude was organized as the Territory of Louisiana, the president appointed Wilkinson governor, making him senior officer in the U.S. Army and at the same time a civil official. The major military decisions, however, emanated from Washington, D.C., without the advice or even the knowledge of the senior military officer.

White men had never explored and most had never seen much of the thousands of acres that the United States had bought in 1803, and President Jefferson turned to army officers to explore the regions. For the first expedition, he picked Captain Meriwether Lewis, who not only had a sound classical education, but was an expert woodsman. Lewis had been with the Virginia militia detachment involved in the Whiskey Rebellion and enjoyed military life well enough to enter the regular army as an ensign on 1 May 1795. Immediately after becoming president, Jefferson asked Lewis to be his private secretary, a position he accepted and in that capacity lived in the White House for two years. When assigned the role of explorer, he asked that he share the command with William Clark, under whom he had served in the Legion of the United States and who had left the army in 1796.

The present secured $2,500 from Congress to start the exploration. Lewis and Clark enrolled nine Kentucky woodsmen and fourteen soldiers chosen from among the hundreds of volunteers of the regular army. Adding one slave, they set out from Saint Louis on 14 May 1804 and disappeared, returning to their starting point on 23 September 1806. The information they gathered on their expedition made possible the future opening of the western country.

General Wilkinson, on his own authority, sent out a second official exploring party. Lieutenant Zebulon Montgomery Pike, with a sergeant, two corporals, and seventeen privates, started on 9 August 1805 to explore the Mississippi River to its source, returning on 30 April 1806. Two and a half months later, with another small military detachment, Pike set off to explore the southwest region. The Spanish captured him for encroaching on their territory and took him and his party to Chihauhau in Mexico. They released him unharmed but stripped of his records of observations, and he returned two weeks short of a year from his start. His was the last of the successful official explorations of that era. Traders and trappers, in pursuit of profit, took over pathfinding.

The Peace of Amiens, which had enabled the Jefferson administration to buy Louisiana and had begun on 1 October 1801, ended in May 1803. Resumption of the war in Europe made U.S. seaborne commerce both exceedingly profitable and exceedingly hazardous. From May 1803 to 1807, England seized at least 528 American merchantmen, France no less than 389. As in the 1790s, the United States tried to persuade France and England to respect an interpretation of neutral rights lenient enough to permit U.S. trade to garner generous profits, but both belligerents denied the plea and imposed an increasingly intricate web of restrictions.

Just off Hampton Roads on 22 June 1807, the British frigate *Leopard* hailed the U.S. frigate *Chesapeake*, demanding that it receive British officers on board to search for deserters. The *Chesapeake* was on its way to deliver dispatches to the government of France, and its captain, Samuel Barron, had not prepared his ship for combat or even mounted his guns. He refused this gross violation of sovereignty, whereupon the *Leopard* fired four broadsides, killing three Americans and wounding eighteen. A search party boarded the *Chesapeake* and took off four deserters. Only once before, during the *Baltimore* incident in 1798, had an English captain presumed to board and search an American warship. In that case the American captain had been dismissed from the service. Barron, however, was suspended from duty for five years without pay. Actually, he never served at sea again. The *Chesapeake-Leopard* incident so outraged Americans that President Jefferson could easily have led the nation into war. Had he called Congress into special session, conflict would almost certainly have resulted, but he refrained from that call.

Federalists, who controlled most of the endangered shipping, opposed going to war. Despite impressment and seizure of U.S. ships at sea, profits remained high. Federalist owners urged the administration to comply with the restrictions and to keep ships away from French ports. Such a policy was unacceptable to Republicans, who were unwilling to favor England in the European conflict.

By mid-summer 1807, the secretary of the navy had withdrawn the squadron from the Mediterranean Sea. There were two purposes for this move—to keep the ships clear of incidents that might bring on war and to concentrate the U.S. Navy near home.

DRIFT TOWARD WAR. During 1806 and 1807 the administration tried to build up the combat power of the citizen soldiery. Jefferson asked Congress to classify the militia, that is to put young men in a special class to receive vigorous training and to be called first in case of war. Congress turned down this classification because it would disarrange the traditional militia system. Instead, on 24 February 1807, it authorized the president to raise thirty thousand citizen-soldiers to be on call for two years and obligated to serve one year if enrolled. They were not militia, but the states could appoint the officers. This body of volunteers, small because few men volunteered, had scant training.

Jefferson asked Congress to classify the militia, that is to put young men in a special class to receive vigorous training and to be called first in case of war.

The violation of sovereignty by the *Leopard* demanded a strong response, but, as the president saw it, not war, because Jefferson knew how ill-prepared the country was for hostilities. The tool he chose was an embargo, because he believed that England could not get along without American goods. His control of Congress was so thorough that he pushed through the strenuous alternative to war in one day, 22 December 1807. The embargo forbad U.S. ships to leave port without explicit federal permission; no ships could carry goods to or from Great Britain. Besides coercing Great Britain into concessions, the embargo was intended to keep American ships off the high seas and out of trouble.

The Embargo of 1807 proved to be nearly as heavy a strain on the U.S. economy as war. In the past Jefferson had condemned the use of regular forces as constabulary, but to enforce the embargo, he was obliged to employ all military instruments. He could do so by reason of a very un-Jeffersonian law that he had to drive through Congress on 3 March 1807. The law authorized the president to use the regular army and navy in any situation in which he could call forth and use militia. Gunboats took position off the principal ports, such as Portsmouth, New Hampshire, and Boston and New York, and the companies of the army near navigable water detained shipping. Harbor authorities were delegated and used the power to call militia.

The embargo had hardly begun to operate when Jefferson confused the Republicans by asking Congress to increase the regular army, which induced a bitter debate. Some debaters restated the Old Republican belief in the militia as the bulwark of the nation. They enumerated societies that had lost their liberties because of standing armies, but Jefferson's hold on the party was so strong that on 12 April 1808 Congress agreed to add five regiments of infantry, one of rifles, one of light artillery, and one of dragoons.

The enlargement was a milestone; it tripled the authorized size of the army from 3,068 to 9,311 enlisted men and 327 officers. The new rifle regiment was the first since the dissolution of the Legion of the United States and was valuable because Americans were pioneers in the military use of rifles. It placed light artillery in the U.S. Army because the war in Europe had shown the importance of cannon that were truly mobile. Last, it reintroduced horse troops.

The president's request for this enlargement made it plain that he knew war was inevitable if the embargo failed to bring England to terms. As with the Provisional Army of the Federalist era, much of the enlargement never materialized; the total army remained close to three thousand men below authorized strength. Regular officers did not want to transfer into the new regiments lest they be lopped off in the future. Many of the new officers were appointed because they were Republicans and were without special military qualifications. Because the command of the added regiments was exercised by the new officers, with little help from those who had been in the service, the recruits received scanty training.

The light artillery, a promising innovation, proved too expensive for the Republicans. All but one of the companies were armed and trained as infantry. One company was for a time true flying artillery, that is it could move at horse-speeds because every crewman, officer, or enlisted man either rode a horse or rode the caissons. In 1809, however, the flying company lost its horses because they were too expensive to feed. A compensatory gain was made in the artillery, although not toward lightness. Brass cannon were made of tin and copper, procured from foreign sources; therefore, Secretary Dearborn began to accept some iron guns.

The enlargement of the military extended to the coasts and to the navy. Congress appropriated $1 million to build forts on the coasts, a sum within $166,000 of equaling the money spent for the same purpose during the previous fifteen years. The number of authorized midshipmen increased from 150 to 450, sailors from 1,425 to 5,025. All of the frigates were readied for sea service.

The year 1807 was critical in the life of the republic. There was the *Chesapeake-Leopard* fiasco, the imposition of the embargo, and serious friction on the western frontier. Spain assessed heavy duties on U.S. goods passing through Spanish Florida, penalizing westerners and inclining them toward war. In 1807 the British, after an interval of eleven years, began once more to incite the Indians near the Canadian border. Two Shawnee brothers, Tecumseh and Tenskwatawa, the latter known as the Shawnee Prophet, attempted to form a confederation of tribes strong enough to halt white encroachments. They began among the tribes of the Old Northwest—Miami, Delaware, Wyandot, Ottawa, Kickapoo, Chippewa, Potawatamie, and their own Shawnee. With a select band of warriors, skilled in ceremonial appeal, Tecumseh went south to also enlist the Creek, Cherokee, Choctaw, and Chickamauga in the Carolinas, Alabama, and Georgia. The effort produced no alliance, but while it went on, it produced fear among the white population.

An added source of tension in the southwest was the arrival of Aaron Burr. The vice-president during Jefferson's first term, in 1804 Burr had killed Alexander Hamilton in a duel, which ended Burr's political career. Jefferson thoroughly detested him and was convinced that he was in the southwest on a treasonous mission, to separate the western states from the United States. The president knew that Burr had opened communication with General Wilkinson, and for a time was not sure that he could rely on the army to hunt down Burr. By this time the administration had ceased to correspond with Wilkinson, except when absolutely necessary, but the general waxed vociferous in denouncing the alleged traitor. Captain Edmund Pendleton Gaines, commanding at Fort Stoddert in Alabama, arrested Burr on 19 February 1807. Gaines took his prisoner to Richmond, Virginia, to be tried for treason. The U.S. Circuit Court, presided over by anti-Jeffersonian Chief Justice John Marshall, acquitted Burr. The outcome was an anathema to President Jefferson, who was convinced of Burr's guilt.

Government-owned trading posts ran on the supposition that ample supplies, traded honestly and without liquor, would bring peaceful relations with the Indians.

Wilkinson went to Washington to dispel the cloud on his reputation as a co-conspirator with Burr. He stayed on in 1808 because Congress was enlarging the army, and he lobbied to be promoted to major general, but Congress did not create that post; instead it provided for two additional brigadier generals. The president appointed Peter Gansevoort to one of the new posts to satisfy the powerful New York segment of the Republican party, and Wade Hampton of South Carolina to please southern Republicans. Hampton was one of the implacable foes Wilkinson had made among the officers through his continuous conniving.

When Wilkinson returned to Louisiana early in 1809, he moved 2,036 soldiers to a camp below New Orleans. It was in some way to his advantage to have them there, but the place was malarious and fatal for 834 of the men. The general stood trial for this loss, which exceeded many a battle, but was found innocent of any wrongdoing.

Part of Jefferson's system to end the Federalist character of the army was to involve it in useful nonmilitary projects. One consequence was that the army became the major roadbuilder on the frontiers. Much of the initial roadbuilding occurred outward from New Orleans. The most ambitious project was to convert the Natchez Trace into a wagon road. Authorized by Congress in 1806, the Natchez Trace, and other roads built by soldiers, in a short time began to carry all sorts of traffic.

The War Department, which handled Indian affairs, slowly multiplied the western posts. Garrisons were usually a company or less. Since 1795 government-owned trading posts, referred to as factors or the Indian factory system, had been operating close to major forts. They ran on the supposition that ample supplies, traded honestly and without liquor, would bring peaceful relations with the Indians. To support a policy of peace through trade, Congress in 1806 created the Office of Superintendent of Indian Trade within the War Department. The government trading posts or factories increased to eight.

The ambitious flurry of preparations for defense stimulated by the *Leopard*'s attack on the *Chesapeake* dwindled by early 1809. The last important defensive act for three and one-half years went into effect on 31 January 1809. It provided for fitting out four of the frigates, but restricted them and their sisters ships to cruising in American waters. Old Republican John Randolph proposed seriously in the House of Representatives that, since ocean trade was ruined, there was no longer a need for a navy and that it should be dismantled.

Jefferson's substitute for war, the embargo, had by 1809 devastated U.S. commerce at sea, but British goods flowed almost unrestrained across the Canadian border. A future soldier of great distinction, Jacob Brown, became wealthy from this illegal trade, as did many other reputable citizens. As exports fell from $108.3 million in 1807 to $22.4 million in 1808, New England shippers grew more embittered toward the Republicans. All the military instruments were overtaxed trying to enforce the law. Moreover, the embargo had not forced England to give up impressment of sailors. By this time Jefferson knew that his attempt at economic coercion was a failure, and he lifted it, as one of the last acts of his presidency, on 1 March 1809 with the Non-Intercourse Act. After fourteen months of unsuccessful operation, his substitute for war had in fact turned into a step toward war.

James Madison, Jefferson's choice to succeed him, became president on 4 March 1809. He did little to alter the military posture, instituting some nonintercourse measures that also did not push England away from its course. Madison's choices to head the military departments were primarily political. William Eustis of Massachusetts, secretary of war, was acceptable to the New England wing of the Republican party. It was a coincidence, not a matter of policy, that he was a doctor, following his predecessors, Dearborn and McHenry. Eustis had served in the Revolution as a surgeon. Madison picked Paul Hamilton, a planter from South Carolina, for secretary of the navy. He had served with guerrilla chiefs Thomas Sumter and Francis Marion and had been governor of South Carolina from 1804 to 1806. Both men had to be replaced when war began in 1812.

According to Republican doctrine, the militia was the bulwark of land defense, indispensable in war, which seemed to be drawing closer and closer, but the administrations of Jefferson and Madison did little to strengthen it. Five territories had entered the union, none of them with reliable militia systems. In the established states, Congress took the position that the militia was adequate as it stood. A House committee in 1810 recorded that the system would work if the states made it work, that is, it was a state responsibility. Because it was intimately linked to state sovereignty, states' rights advocates did not want the federal government tinkering with the militia.

Congress passed a very important law relating to the militia on 23 April 1808. It appropriated $200,000 to be spent each year on arming the citizen-soldiers. This was no more than a token, because it had been estimated in 1792 that $42 million would be required to equip the militia properly. The $200,000 would not even arm the young men coming of military age each year. Still, the act was significant because it tightened the relationship of the federal government to the several state militias.

Jefferson and Madison tried harder than their predecessors to learn the true strength of the militias. The states had failed to send the reports to the president required by the Uniform Militia Act of 1792 until Jefferson demanded those reports. From what he received, he compiled the first comprehensive statistics ever drawn together on the organized citizen-soldiery. The report showed 525,000 men enrolled, most of them in infantry. Forty percent of the artillery was in Massachusetts. Although the 1792 act set the number of enlisted men in a regiment at 770, Rhode Island had regiments of 400, South Carolina of 850. In Tennessee, Ohio, and Mississippi, all close to hostile Indians, the reports showed only four firearms per ten militiamen. Obviously, the several militias were not interchangeable enough to function as a first line reserve to enter federal service.

The Republican administrations were at their most effective in coping with the federal debt. Managed by Gallatin, the debt dropped 30 percent in ten years, thereby, as he and the president believed, increasing national security. Jefferson avoided internal taxes by increasing import duties. Both he and Gallatin considered it morally wrong for one generation to incur debts that burdened later generations.

Once the embargo had failed, the possibility of war increased. Jefferson considered war a tool to be used if the national interest required it, but he and President Madison were unwilling to believe that it could not be avoided, even at the last minute. Preparations fell short of what would be needed. The enlargements in 1808 of the forces and the monies appropriated were slow in producing results. Critics ridiculed the gunboats as useless to protect commerce and totally incapable of preventing strangulation of the country by blockade. Also, the military departments were not staffed to handle war. The secretary of the navy, for example, with only three clerks, was overburdened even in peacetime. Because there was no commissioned head of the navy, the secretary had to maintain communication with every ship. One burden was partially lifted from the department by civilian agents who bought naval supplies, but under this arrangement the professional users had little control of what was purchased and delivered.

The army establishment, although bigger than the navy, was no more efficient. Here, too, the secretary had no professional chief to work through, so he had to correspond with the regiments and higher units, and sometimes even with the captains of companies. Like the navy, there were three civilian agents who bought supplies, but the lines of control were confused because the president appointed their subordinates. A field commander could never be sure that his troops would have the supplies they needed, especially food.

Tecumseh had ordered delay, but had worked the warriors into a frenzy, promising them that no bullet could harm them.

After the demise of the embargo, the hostility of the Old Republicans to standing forces came forward and stayed until the fall of 1811. It made no headway, however, against the drift toward war. By 1812 British captains had impressed six thousand sailors from American ships. Nevertheless, the seaboard interests, still earning high profits, urged for peace. Farther west, however, a war spirit predominated. Throughout the Indian country, relentless violence enraged the frontiersmen. Tecumseh, who wore a red coat with a brigadier's insignia, convinced westerners that England was causing their miseries.

Accordingly, General William Henry Harrison, governor of Indiana Territory, asked permission to engage the Indians. Harrison came from a distinguished Virginia family and had studied to be a doctor with Benjamin Rush, a career he gave up to become an ensign in the army. He was aide-de-camp to Wayne during the

Fallen Timbers campaign. He resigned from the army in June 1798 and received the Indian appointment in May 1800. Harrison started northward from Vincennes on 25 September 1811, with one thousand men, three hundred of whom were regulars from the Fourth Infantry Regiment (the lineage of which is now held by the Fifth Infantry Regiment). Harrison copied Wayne's march formation to avoid being ambushed. A single movement could bring the men into battle line, and each man slept at night with armament beside him, opposite his place in the line.

Tecumseh was still traveling among the southern Indians, trying to perfect a coalition of tribes. Harrison knew this and warned the Shawnee Prophet that he would advance against them if they continued to be hostile. Seen through Harrison's eyes, they defied his warning, and he advanced and bivouacked two miles from Prophet's Town, established in 1808. The reduced numbers of the northwestern Indians showed at Prophet's Town, between 550 and 700 warriors representing nine tribes—Kickapoo, Wyandot, Potawatamie, Piankashaw Shawnee, Muco, Huron, Ottawa, Chippewa, and Winnebago. Tecumseh had ordered delay, but the Prophet had worked the warriors into a frenzy, promising them that no bullet could harm them.

In darkness at 4 A.M. on 7 November 1811, the warriors of this tenuous coalition, fanatical but not well-coordinated, attacked the soldiers' camp. There was fierce hand-to-hand fighting until daylight, when the attackers drew back. Harrison then ordered counterattacks on both flanks, inflicting heavy losses. The attackers killed sixty-six soldiers and wounded 122. Indian losses were high, but not recorded.

This fight, known as the Battle of Tippecanoe because it was close to the Tippecanoe River, had several important consequences. Harrison became a national

Battle of Tippecanoe. On 11 November 1811, Indian forces under the command of the Prophet attacked U.S. troops commanded by William Henry Harrison. News of the battle confirmed public suspicions that the British were encouraging Indian raids on the United States. (Corbis-Bettmann)

hero. It reduced the fighting power of the Indians of the Old Northwest, but at the same time pushed them into alliance with England. It focused the attention of the westerners on the British as inciters of the Indians, and thus as enemies. Western congressmen and senators leaned toward war with England.

With war looming, public figures waxed bombastic about annexing Canada, but did little to prepare to do so. Far to the south, however, some annexing was taking place. In October 1810, basing the right to do so on the Louisiana Purchase, President Madison proclaimed West Florida from the Isle of Orleans to the Perdido River to be part of the United States. A few troops occupied the new territory, but only as far as the Pearl River. Forces in the area were too scanty to occupy onward to the Perdido. Colonel Richard Sparks, commander at Fort Stoddert, just across the thirty-first parallel from Spanish Florida, managed to keep his supply route up the Mobile River open, offering to use force if Spain tried to interdict it.

In East Florida a group of Americans residing there wanted to be free of Spain and absorbed by the United States and induced a scattering of military actions. Madison's administration encouraged Major General George Mathews of the Georgia militia to support the East Floridians and generate a public request from them to be taken into the United States. The administration's relationship to Mathews was secret, but troops of the regular army went into Florida and took position near Saint Augustine early in 1812. Although the naval commander off the southeastern coast had no instructions, he was finally persuaded to position two gunboats off Amelia Island. The East Florida scheme died because of the approach of war with England and the fear of a second war with Spain. Secretary of State James Monroe disavowed Mathews' activities, asserting that he had exceeded his instructions. The secretary of the navy pulled out all naval vessels hovering off Spanish East Florida, but the army detachment remained in Spanish territory, publicly disavowed by secretly supported, engaging in some fights with Indians as late as 1813.

Although conflict loomed, Congress, without realizing it, damaged the nation's ability to finance war. Unless Congress renewed its charter, the Bank of the United States would go out of business in March 1811. Gallatin urged renewal, but many Republican legislators, lifelong despisers of Hamilton's financial program, of which the bank was one of the centerpieces, opposed renewal. The vote in the senate on 4 March 1811 was a tie. Vice-president DeWitt Clinton voted not to renew the charter. Actual liquidation required time, but slowly it contracted the already short supply of currency by $5 million and exported $7 million of essential specie to foreign stockholders. It also deprived the government of its most most reliable source of loans and of its agent for transferring funds from one part of the country to another.

Secretary Gallatin offered the administration a preview of the taxes that would be required in the event of war. Customs duties would have to be increased 100 percent. There would be excise taxes, detested by Republicans, on salt, spirits, and carriages. The administration would also need to reenact that unique direct tax, proportioned among the states by population on land, buildings, and slaves, which the Republicans had denounced when the Federalists originated it in 1798.

The prospect horrified Old Republican John Randolph, who said that the United States could not possibly go to war without embracing every evil that Republicans had accused the Federalists of advocating—a huge army, paper money, high taxes, and a swarm of new federal officers.

Regardless of the cost and the lack of adequate military preparation, President Madison sent a message to Congress on 1 June 1812 excoriating Great Britain for continuing to impress American sailors, violating U.S. waters, maintaining illegal blockades, and inciting Indians to murder and pillage. Madison did not request war, but the invitation to Congress to declare war was unmistakable. Accordingly, Congress passed the declaration of war on 18 June 1812.

BIBLIOGRAPHY

Ambrose, Stephen E. *Duty, Honor, Country: A History of West Point* (1966).

Ammon, Harry. *James Monroe* (1971).

Baldwin, Leland D. *Whiskey Rebels* (1939).

Bernhard, Winfred E. A. *Fisher Ames, Federalist and Statesman* (1965).

Billias, George A. *Elbridge Gerry* (1976).

Bond, Beverly W. *The Civilization of the Old Northwest, 1788–1812* (1934).

Bradford, James C., ed. *Command Under Sail: Makers of the American Naval Tradition* (1985).

Burt, Alfred L. *The United States, Great Britain, and British North America from the Revolution to the Establishment of Peace after the War of 1812* (1940).

Carter, Harvey Lewis. *The Life and Times of Little Turtle* (1987).

Cassell, Frank A. *Merchant Congressman in the Young Republic: Samuel Smith of Maryland, 1752–1839* (1971).

Clarfield, Gerard H. *Timothy Pickering and the American Republic* (1980).

Coffman, Edward M. *The Old Army* (1986).

Combs, Jerald A. *The Jay Treaty* (1970).

Crackel, Theodore J. *Mr. Jefferson's Army* (1987).

Cress, Lawrence D. *Citizens in Arms: The Army and the Militia in American Society to the War of 1812* (1982).

Cunliffe, Marcus. *Soldiers and Civilians: The Martial Spirit in America, 1775–1865* (1968).

Dauer, Manning J. *The Adams Federalists* (1953).

Davis, William W. H. *The Fries Rebellion, 1798–1799* (1899).

De Conde, Alexander. *The Quasi-War* (1966).

———. *This Affair of Louisiana* (1976).
Driver, Carl S. *John Sevier, Pioneer of the Old Southwest* (1932).
Edmunds, Russell David. *Tecumseh and the Quest for Indian Leadership* (1984).
Ekirch, Arthur A., Jr. *The Civilian and the Military* (1956).
Elliott, Charles W. *Winfield Scott* (1937).
Ferguson, Elmer James, ed. *National Unity on Trial, 1781–1816* (1970).
Ferguson, Eugene S. *Truxton of the Constellation* (1956).
Fowler, William M., Jr. *Jack Tars and Commodores: The American Navy, 1783–1815* (1984).
Goetzmann, William H. *Army Exploration in the American West, 1803–1863* (1959).
Guthman, William H. *March to Massacre: A History of the First Seven Years of the United States Army, 1784–1791* (1974).
Guttridge, Leonard F., and Jay D. Smith. *The Commodores: The United States Navy in the Age of Sail* (1969).
Heinl, Robert D. *Soldiers of the Sea: The United States Marine Corps, 1775–1962* (1962).
Heitman, Francis B. *Historical Register and Dictionary of the United States Army, 1789–1903* (1903).
Jacobs, James Ripley. *Tarnished Warrior: Major-General James Wilkinson* (1938).
———. *The Beginning of the United States Army, 1783–1812* (1947).
Jennings, Walter W. *The American Embargo, 1807–1809* (1921).
Jensen, Merrill. *The New Nation, 1781–1789* (1950).
Kemble, Charles Robert. *The Image of the Army Officer in America* (1973).
Ketcham, Ralph L. *James Madison* (1971).
Knox, Dudley W. *A History of the United States Navy* (1936).
Kohn, Richard H. *Eagle and Sword: The Federalists and the Creation of the Military Establishment in America, 1783–1802* (1975).
Kurtz, Stephen G. *The Presidency of John Adams* (1957).
Langley, Harold D. *Social Reform in the United States Navy, 1798–1862* (1967).
Long, David F. *Ready to Hazard: A Biography of Commodore William Bainbridge, 1774–1833* (1981).
McDonald, Forrest. *The Presidency of George Washington* (1974).
McKee, Christopher. *Edward Preble: A Naval Biography, 1761–1807* (1972).
Mahon John K. *History of the Militia and the National Guard* (1983).
Martin, James K., and Mark E. Lender. *A Respectable Army: The Military Origins of the Republic, 1763–1789* (1982).
Matthews, Thomas E. *General James Robertson, Father of Tennessee* (1934).
Miller, John C. *Triumph of Freedom, 1775–1783* (1945).
———. *Alexander Hamilton* (1959).
———. *The Federalist Era, 1789–1801* (1960).
Nelson, Paul David. *General Horatio Gates* (1976).
———. *Anthony Wayne, Soldier of the Early Republic* (1985).
Palmer, Michael A. *Stoddert's War: Naval Operations During the Quasi-War with France, 1798–1801* (1987).
Parmet, Herbert S., and Marie B. Hecht. *Aaron Burr* (1967).
Patrick, Rembert W. *Florida Fiasco: Rampant Rebels on the Georgia-Florida Border, 1810–1815* (1954).
Peterson, Merrill D. *Thomas Jefferson and the New Nation* (1970).
Prucha, Francis Paul. *American Indian Policy in the Formative Years, 1790–1834* (1962).
Risjord, Norman K. *The Old Republicans: Southern Conservatism in the Age of Jefferson* (1965).
Silver, James W. *Edmund Pendleton Gaines, Frontier General* (1949).
Slaughter, Thomas P. *The Whiskey Rebellion* (1986).
Smelser, Marshall. *The Congress Founds the Navy, 1787–1798* (1959).
Smith, James Morton. *Freedom's Fetters: The Alien and Sedition Laws and American Civil Liberties* (1956).
Stagg, John C. A. *Mr. Madison's War: Politics, Diplomacy and Warfare . . . 1783–1830* (1983).
Stinchcombe, William. *The XYZ Affair* (1980).
Stuart, Reginald C. *War and American Thought: From the Revolution to the Monroe Doctrine* (1982).
Sword, Wiley. *President Washington's Indian War (1985).*
Symonds, Craig L. *Navalists and Antinavalists: The Naval Policy Debate in the United States, 1785–1827* (1980).
Tucker, Glenn. *Dawn Like Thunder: The Barbary Wars and the Birth of the United States Navy* (1963).
Weigley, Russell. *History of the U.S. Army* (1967).
White, Leonard D. *The Federalists* (1948).
———. *The Jeffersonians* (1951).
Zahniser, Marvin R. *Charles Cotesworth Pinckney, Founding Father* (1967).

— JOHN K. MAHON

The War of 1812 and Postwar Expansion

The War of 1812 has frequently been mythically portrayed as a stout contest in which outnumbered United States forces fought valiantly against British regulars and their Indian allies, suffered early setbacks, and finally won a gallant victory that validated national institutions and presaged the growth and expansion of the young Republic. This assessment, preached to students over many generations, has taught some of the wrong lessons. In 1812, Congress declared a war that the nation was unprepared to fight, and, in many actions, U.S. forces outnumbered the British enemy but still failed to win decisively. The final outcome was a stalemate that resulted in a fortuitous negotiated peace for the nearly bankrupt and divided nation. The results of the war also demonstrated that the nation's founders and their successors had seriously miscalculated the efficacy of American military institutions as they had evolved in the years 1783–1812.

ANGLO-AMERICAN RELATIONS

The United States went to war in June 1812 because Great Britain had violated U.S. sovereignty in ways that suggested that the new nation was still a colonial entity, subject to imperial whim. By May 1812 a consensus had developed in Congress that suggested there was no alternative to war if national honor were to be maintained. When the Jeffersonian Republicans came to power in 1801, tensions between Great Britain and the United States had gradually increased while diplomatic relations worsened, despite the strenuous efforts of U.S. statesmen to seek a resolution of the differences that separated the two countries.

The issues that divided the United States and Great Britain came into sharper focus after 1805. The Napoleonic wars in Europe had created great opportunities as well as great dangers for the U.S. Republic. Beginning with the Treaty of Paris of 1783, which ended the American Revolution, the overseas trade of U.S. merchants had grown steadily, taking over markets formerly serviced by Great Britain. After the outbreak of the War of the First Coalition, pitting France against Austria, Prussia, and Sardinia in 1792 and England, Holland, and Spain in 1793, the United States remained neutral and its citizens endeavored to trade with both sides. Exports from the United States had averaged $20 million annually from 1790 to 1792. Thereafter, the trend was sharply upward, reaching $94 million in 1801 and a high of $108 million in 1807. Imports followed the same trend, rising from $23 million in 1790 to $110 million in 1801. After a brief contraction, they surged again to a new high of $138.5 million in 1807. This situation became increasingly difficult, as both France and England objected to this trade as not being "neutral." U.S. merchant ships were in danger of being halted on the high seas, boarded, inspected, and, if their papers revealed trade with the opposing power, seized and confiscated. From 1803 until the issuance of the British Orders in Council of 1807, the British seized 528 American ships, while France seized 206 from 1803 until France issued the Berlin Decree in 1806. In England influential essayists pointed out the folly of allowing the United States to supersede the former mother country in trade with the West Indies and Canada.

A seaman on board an American vessel who could not prove his U.S. origins risked being seized and virtually enslaved on board a British warship for years.

At the same time, commanders of British warships patrolling the Atlantic, short of seamen in their own ships, pressed American merchant seamen into service. When boarding a U.S. ship for inspection, British officers frequently demanded a muster of the ship's crew in order to search for deserters. Without doubt, some American merchantmen had signed on British deserters, but the majority of men taken were naturalized U.S. citizens who had been born in the British Isles or colonies. The British, however, did not recognize changes in citizenship. A man born a British subject always owed service and allegiance to the Crown. Thus, a seaman on board an American vessel who could not prove his U.S. origins risked being seized and virtually enslaved on board a British warship for years. Similarly, the British press gangs in English ports were infamous for carrying away to sea any able-bodied men found in their way. This practice, called impressment in the American popular press, grew to be a detested evil.

In December 1806, with tensions increasing between Great Britain and the United States, President Thomas Jefferson sought grounds for amicable settlement of grievances through a new treaty, negotiated by James Monroe and William Pinkney. Its principal aims were to obtain the end of impressment of U.S. seamen; the restoration of the West Indian trade, which Great Britain had forbidden; and to obtain payments of indemnities for ship seizures made after 1805. When the two diplomats faced British intransigence, however, they yielded on some points and failed to follow their instructions on the issue of impressment. When they returned with the treaty in early 1807, Jefferson refused to submit it to the Senate for ratification.

Following this diplomatic fiasco, Jefferson had to cope with the most serious threat to peace since his assumption of the presidency. In 1807, Captain Salusbury Humphreys, commander of the British frigate *Leopard*, knowing in advance that Commodore James Barron's flagship *Chesapeake* carried British deserters among its crew, followed the *Chesapeake* to sea from Hampton Roads, Virginia, on 21 June. The following day, when several miles out, Humphreys signaled the *Chesapeake* to heave to. The British boarding officer demanded that Barron have the crew mustered, which the commodore refused to do, and minutes later the *Leopard* opened fire on the unprepared U.S. frigate. Barron ordered the colors struck and submitted to the British, who mustered the crew of the *Chesapeake* and took off four men, claiming them to be British subjects and deserters. Humphreys refused to accept Barron's sword and allowed him to proceed back into port, a disgraced man in a wounded and disgraced ship. This outrageous act incensed the American populace and President Jefferson could have gone to war immediately, but he was content merely to proclaim the British warships unwelcome visitors in U.S. ports. He did not believe the time had come for hostilities and was wedded to the concept of economic warfare.

Jefferson's method of extracting concessions from the British would henceforth be that of withholding trading privileges. Thus, the Embargo Act of 1807 and various nonimportation acts were intended to damage the British economy in the midst of its war against France. The effects, Jefferson hoped, would persuade England that it needed U.S. trade more than it needed impressed seamen or confiscated cargoes, but Jefferson's efforts failed. British officials viewed his attempts at economic coercion as the efforts of a weak nation that did not have the will or the resources to commit to war. In effect, the president had failed to understand the nature of the balance of power in Europe and the degree to which British policy reacted to French actions, not those of the United States.

THE ANGLO-FRENCH WAR AGAINST NEUTRAL TRADE

The government of Napoleon Bonaparte took advantage of the U.S. situation. The U.S. embargo of British goods placed the United States in the position of being a French ally while not having any of the advantages of such a position. Indeed, Napoleon's restrictive decrees increased the danger of U.S. ships being taken by the French navy and others. Such was his Berlin Decree of 21 November 1806, which placed the British Isles under blockade, forbidding commerce with them and authorizing the confiscation of ships suspected of trading with the British. Retaliation came in the form of the British Orders in Council of November 1807, forbidding trade with France and its allies. Responding with his Milan Decree on 17 December, Napoleon declared that even vessels that were searched by the British or that obeyed the Orders in Council were subject to seizure. On 17 April 1808, with the Bayonne Decree, Napoleon authorized confiscation of any U.S. ship in European harbors, arguing that he was helping enforce the U.S. embargo act. Despite these offensive measures, President Jefferson took no effective action to oppose the French. He had hoped that France would force Spain to cede the Floridas to the United States in gratitude for his anti-British posture. Fearing Great Britain more than France, Jefferson played the French card but was ultimately to be disappointed.

President James Madison also felt the sting of French duplicity. On 1 May 1810, Congress enacted Macon's Bill No. 2, a law that ended commercial restrictions against the belligerents but also provided a lure. If either France or Britain removed their restrictions on U.S. trade and the other did not, the U.S. government would reimpose its nonimportation policy against the recalcitrant nation. On hearing that Congress had passed Macon's Bill No. 2, Napoleon ordered his foreign Minister, the Duc de Cadore, to inform U.S. Ambassador John Armstrong that France would revoke the Berlin and Milan decrees if the United States would renew nonintercourse against Great Britain. Contrarily, Napoleon also ordered the sequestration of U.S. vessels that had called at French ports in 1809–1810. The Duc de Cadore, however, wrote Madison that the decrees had already been revoked, and the United States halted commerce with Great Britain and opened trade with France. The letter of the Duc de Cadore became well-known

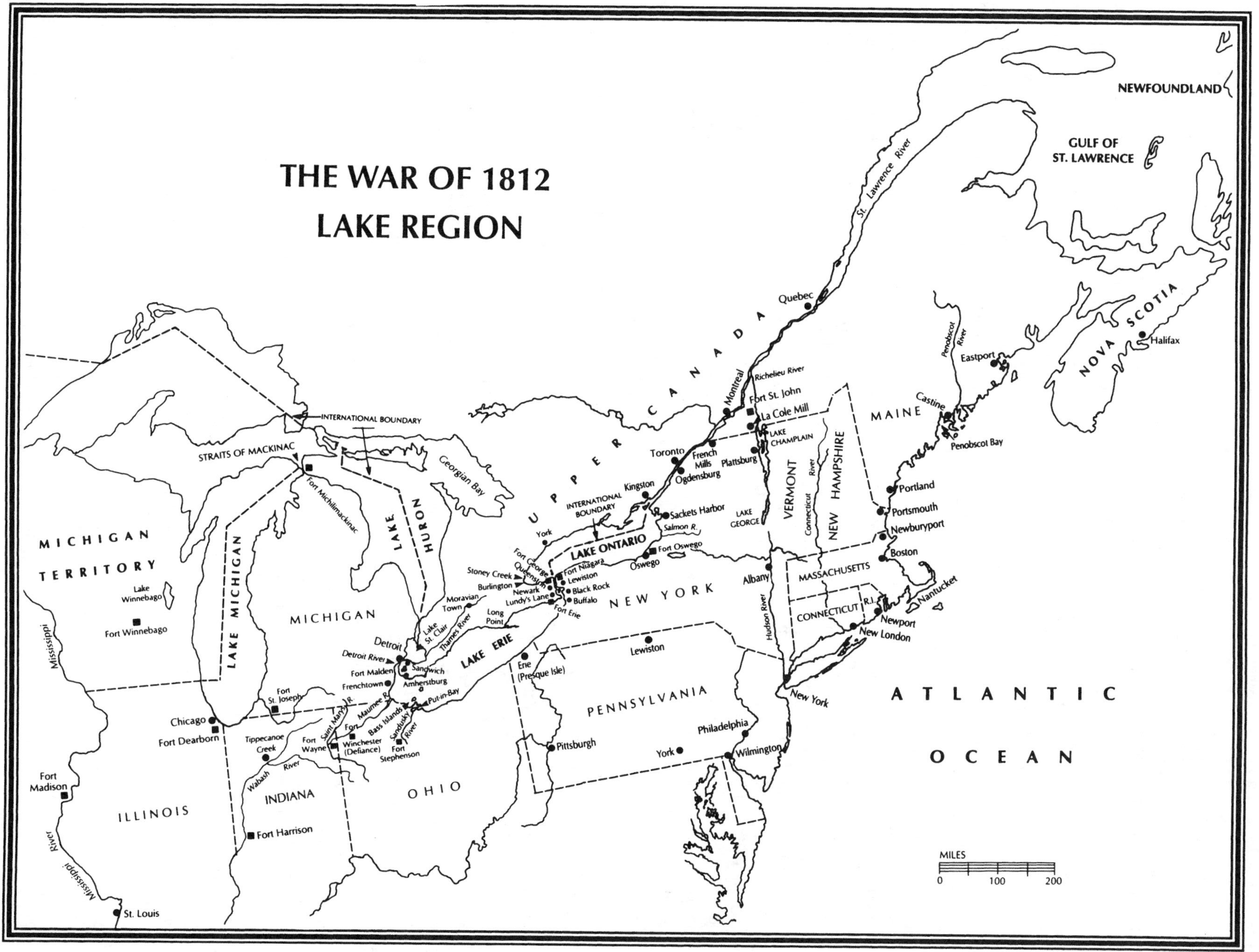
THE WAR OF 1812
LAKE REGION
NEWFOUNDLAND
GULF OF ST. LAWRENCE
St. Lawrence River
Quebec
NOVA SCOTIA
Halifax
Penobscot River
Eastport
Castine
Penobscot Bay
MAINE
Portland
Portsmouth
Newburyport
Boston
Nantucket
R.I.
Newport
New London
MASSACHUSETTS
CONNECTICUT
NEW HAMPSHIRE
Connecticut River
VERMONT
LAKE CHAMPLAIN
LAKE GEORGE
Hudson River
Albany
New York
ATLANTIC
OCEAN
MILES
0
100
200
UPPER CANADA
Montreal
Richelieu River
Fort St. John
La Cole Mill
Plattsburg
French Mills
Ogdensburg
Toronto
Kingston
Sackets Harbor
Salmon R.
Fort Oswego
Oswego
INTERNATIONAL BOUNDARY
LAKE ONTARIO
York
Fort George
Queenston
Fort Niagara
Lewiston
Black Rock
Buffalo
Fort Erie
Stoney Creek
Burlington
Newark
Lundy's Lane
NEW YORK
Lewiston
Erie (Presque Isle)
PENNSYLVANIA
Pittsburgh
Philadelphia
York
Wilmington
Moravian Town
Thames River
Long Point
Lake St. Clair
LAKE ERIE
Detroit
Detroit River
Fort Malden
Sandwich
Amherstburg
Frenchtown
Put-in-Bay
Maumee R.
Bass Islands
Sandusky River
Fort Stephenson
Fort Winchester (Defiance)
Saint Marys R.
Fort Wayne
OHIO
Georgian Bay
LAKE HURON
INTERNATIONAL BOUNDARY
STRAITS OF MACKINAC
Fort Michilimackinac
MICHIGAN
LAKE MICHIGAN
Fort St. Joseph
Chicago
Fort Dearborn
Tippecanoe Creek
Wabash River
INDIANA
Fort Harrison
ILLINOIS
Fort Madison
Mississippi River
St. Louis
Mississippi
MICHIGAN TERRITORY
Lake Winnebago
Fort Winnebago

as the document that duped Madison and his foreign policy officials, the second Republican administration to fail in an attempt to play the French against the British.

In 1811, the mood of the American people and their government vacillated between fear and boastful posturing.

During almost ten years of attempted economic coercion and failed diplomatic efforts, two U.S. presidents experienced the frustrations and embarrassments that prepared the way for war as the ultimate remedy for the loss of U.S. ships, cargoes, and seamen and wounded national honor. Following the passage of Macon's Bill No. 2 and the Cadore letter episode, an increasing number of Americans felt that war was the only remaining path by which U.S. interests and national honor could be protected. In 1811, Congress finally contemplated preparation for war, while the mood of the American people and their government vacillated between fear and boastful posturing.

THE *LITTLE BELT* AFFAIR

Another event that helped precipitate the War of 1812 was the *Little Belt* affair. Several of the U.S. frigates that had served in the Barbary Wars had been laid up to save the cost of paying their crews and the continual repairs required by ships on active duty. Only a few ships were left to enforce the embargo and to protect U.S. shipping. Tensions increased when President Madison prohibited trade with Great Britain under Macon's Bill No. 2. To prepare the navy for the possibility of action, Secretary of the Navy Paul Hamilton issued a general order reminding naval personnel of the *Chesapeake-Leopard* affair and calling on them "to be prepared and determined at every hazard to vindicate the injured honour of our Navy and revive the drooping spirit of the Nation." The secretary established two small squadrons to patrol the coast from Norfolk, Virginia, northward.

In May 1811, having spent winter quarters in New London, Connecticut, Commodore John Rodgers was visiting his family in Havre de Grace, Maryland, when he received orders to sail immediately for New York in his forty-four-gun frigate, the *President.* The Navy Department had received news that a British frigate, believed to be the *Guerrière,* was interrupting merchant shipping off New York. Within a day, Rodgers was under way from Annapolis, and on 16 May he sighted the sails of a strange British warship that stood toward him and then fled. Believing the ship to be the *Guerrière,* Rodgers pursued it into the night and finally overhauled his opponent. When he did not receive a satisfactory answer to his hail and the British ship fired on his vessel, Rodgers answered with a damaging broadside. The firing from both ships continued for forty-five minutes. At daybreak it was discovered that the British ship was the *Little Belt,* a single-decked corvette and much smaller warship then the *Guerrière,* although it had the same square-sailed, three-masted rig. The *Little Belt* lost thirty-two killed and wounded; only one man was wounded on the *President.* Commodore Rodgers was embarrased at having taken on such an inferior opponent, but in a night action, when it was difficult to determine the scale of his opponent, he had decided to act if his opponent were a large frigate. Commander Arthur Bingham of the *Little Belt,* however, stated that Rodgers was spoiling for a fight and would have taken on any size frigate. Rodgers requested a court of inquiry and was acquitted of any wrongdoing in the affair because the evidence showed that the British ship had fired first. This bloody incident indicates that the small U.S. Navy was tuned to a fighting pitch and would not avoid an opportunity to avenge the *Chesapeake* affair of 1807. When British diplomats asked for reparations on the *Little Belt* affair, Secretary of State James Monroe responded that nothing could be done until U.S. demands for the *Chesapeake* were satisfied.

THE WAR HAWK CONGRESS

Adding kindling to the fire, six months later another incident stirred Anglo-American hostility. On 7 November 1811, at Tippecanoe Creek in Indiana Territory, about one thousand U.S. militiamen led by General William Henry Harrison were attacked by an Indian confederacy led by Tecumseh and his brother, known as the Prophet. Almost one-fifth of Harrison's force was killed or wounded. Suspecting the British in Canada had inspired the Indians, western settlers began to urge the United States to attack Canada to halt Indian raids, to seize control of the fur trade, and possibly to acquire new lands. These "war hawks" and their representatives in Congress, Henry Clay, Langdon Cheves, John C. Calhoun, and Peter B. Porter, were the leading supporters of the Madison administration's policy to resort to force if Great Britain would not respect U.S. nationhood.

When Congress returned to Washington in the fall of 1811, it was generally agreed that the methods adopted by the United States to obtain cooperation from Great Britain had been found wanting. President Madison, with the astute assistance of Secretary of State

Monroe, communicated frequently, if informally, with congressional leaders about the prospects for peace and war. It was through Monroe in November 1811 that the Senate Foreign Relations Committee heard the administration's support for declaring war in the spring of 1812, unless an "honorable peace" was at hand. When in March 1812 Congressman Porter of New York asked Monroe about the president's sentiments on whether an embargo should be enacted preparatory to war, Monroe replied that "without an accommodation with Great Britain Congress ought to declare war before adjourning."

The war hawks in Congress urged and obtained passage of a ninety-day embargo in mid-April, as a signal to merchants that they should halt foreign trade and keep their ships in port. Some congressmen, however, voted because they thought it might serve as another negotiating instrument, while others saw it as a renewal of economic coercion. Its immediate effect was opposite to congressional intent because U.S. shippers rushed their ships to sea as a last opportunity to trade with England. Freight rates jumped by 20 percent and ships were loaded in record time. About 140 ships cleared New York harbor alone. The result was that a large part of the U.S. merchant marine was still at sea when the United States declared war on Great Britain.

THE SITUATION IN ENGLAND

Ironically, as events propelled the U.S. Congress to consider seriously the declaration of war against Great Britain, events in England were slowly moving in a direction that might have made war unnecessary. The two principal complaints of the United States against the Crown were confiscation of U.S. merchant ships by virtue of the Orders in Council and the impressment of seamen. If Great Britain could have been persuaded to eliminate even one of these odious practices and could communicate the news of it to the United States before the end of the congressional session, the War of 1812 might not have occurred at all. There had been a movement for repeal of the Orders in Council for some years in Parliament, but the pro-American lobby was too weak to have much influence until 1811. British industry was undergoing a serious depression during 1809–1811, although U.S. attempts to bring economic hardship by withholding trade had had little direct effect.

The parliamentary opposition to royal policy, led by Alexander Baring and Henry Brougham, was probably most outspoken in 1809, but the parliamentary majority scorned the weak U.S. foreign policy that could not enforce its own will. The principal weakness of the British Orders in Council was that they were inequitably enforced. In addition, there were legal loopholes, such as the license system. U.S. trade with England's continental enemy, France, actually was legal, if one bought a license from British officials in Canada and the Caribbean to trade in goods that would likely end up in enemy hands. It has been estimated that during 1809–1812, between fifteen thousand and twenty thousand licenses were issued per year, to shippers who wished to trade with the Continent. Prime Minister Spencer Perceval, long a proponent of the Orders in Council, yielded to the steady drumbeat of growing opposition in March 1812 and instructed Foreign Minister Castlereagh to offer the United States the withdrawal of the orders in exchange for reopening trade with Great Britain. At the same time, debates within Parliament went forward over a possible repeal of the orders. On 9 May, Jonathan Russell, the U.S. minister to Great Britain, wrote that for the first time he sensed a sincere change of mood, a "softening of temper" as he put it, among British politicians. Fate, however, took a hand just as events seemed to be working toward rapprochement with the United States. James Bellingham, a man with a grudge against the ministry but who had nothing to do with the Orders in Council, fatally shot Prime Minister Perceval as he entered the House of Commons on 11 May. The resulting chaos paralyzed the British government for nearly a month. Repeal of the Orders in Council was by then a foregone conclusion, but this was not known in the United States, where Congress was under the impression that support for the Orders in Council was as strong as ever.

The president threw down the gauntlet on 1 June 1812. In a closely argued message to Congress, he asked its members to choose between peace and war. He cited the many provocations that Great Britain had shown the United States, particularly the maritime issues of ship seizure, confiscation of cargoes, and impressment of seamen. Congress went into secret session and on 17 June delivered a verdict. The following day Madison declared a state of war with Great Britain.

THE MILITARY CAMPAIGNS OF 1812

The United States opened the war with a plan for an overland campaign against Canada that some thought would be successful without encountering significant resistance. The objective was not to conquer Canada, but to hold important parts hostage until Great Britain agreed to concessions. Without adequate time to raise, equip, and train an army, only seven thousand U.S. regulars were available, although thirty-five thousand were authorized by law. President Madison could also call on fifty thousand volunteers, and, theoretically, 100,000 state militiamen were available, but opposition to the war in New England prevented the use of the best of these units. With these potential resources and the knowledge that the British had few regular troops stationed in Canada, many Americans believed that the enemy's defenses would collapse at the first signs of invasion and that Great Britain, with a greater war to fight in Europe, would soon see the wisdom of making concessions in North America. These were grave misjudgments.

In March 1812, Secretary of War William Eustis had ordered Major General Henry Dearborn to prepare a plan for a comprehensive attack on Canada. Dearborn's plan, which was ready by early April, involved a three-pronged offensive along the extensive border with Canada to be implemented by three small armies consisting of a nucleus of regular army troops, supplemented by militia and volunteers. On the right of the American line, General Dearborn, an aging veteran of the Revolution, would gather an army at Greenbush, near Albany, New York, with the objective of an attack on Montreal. In the center of the line, Major General Stephen van Rensselaer of the New York militia prepared to launch his troops across the Niagara River to capture Fort Erie and Fort George. On the left, General William Hull, another aging revolutionary war veteran, would march at the head of a force of two thousand men, comprised of regular army and Michigan and Ohio militia and volunteers. With this miniature army, Hull proposed to capture Sandwich, Fort Malden, and Amherstburg, the principal outposts of British military and naval strength in Upper Canada. One key to the success of the plan was rapid execution. The troops would have to consolidate their victories before the British recovered from the first shock and sent reinforcements from Europe. Another key to success was naval control of the Great Lakes, which had been postulated earlier by General Hull, but there was not enough time to build a fleet before the beginning of land operations. The absence of U.S. naval squadrons on Lakes Erie and Ontario would be a determining factor in the failure of the U.S. invasion.

News of the declaration of war traveled rapidly, reaching places in Canada even before couriers could bring official notification to U.S. armies in the field. Governor General Sir George Prevost was in overall command in Canada, with Major General Isaac Brock commanding Upper Canada and Lieutenant General Sir John C. Sherbrooke commanding in Nova Scotia. The British regulars at their disposal numbered no more than six thousand and were thinly stretched from the Atlantic provinces to Lake Superior. Most of the soldiers who were posted to Canada were those deemed unfit for service in Europe.

In addition to these regulars were the few hundred Canadian "fencibles," men who had been recruited in Canada for North American service only. There was also the local militia, of whom it was estimated there were sixty thousand in Lower Canada and perhaps eleven thousand in Upper Canada, although many of the latter were deemed unreliable because they had immigrated from the United States. The problem with militia was that a call-up would disrupt local agriculture and the system of supply for the army. From the outset of the war, General Prevost's main concern was to protect Quebec, but General Brock, the more active of the two, understood that unless the Americans could be resisted in Upper Canada, everything west of Kingston, Ontario, might be lost to invaders.

HULL ATTEMPTS TO INVADE CANADA. The first news of war arrived in Montreal on 24 June, at Fort George on 25 June, at Amherstberg on 28 June, and at Kingston on 3 July. General Hull, who was already in motion with his troops, marching toward Detroit, did not receive the news until later. He decided to send his heavy baggage, official papers, and sick soldiers to Detroit on a chartered schooner, but it was captured by the brig *General Hunter* on 2 July. Soon thereafter, General Brock learned the contents of Hull's official orders. Armed with this vital intelligence, Brock set in motion the few troops at his disposal, three hundred officers and men of the Royal Artillery, Forty-first Regiment of Foot, and Royal Newfoundland Fencibles, supplemented by four hundred Indians under Tecumseh. Hull crossed the Detroit River into British territory on 12 July and issued a proclamation, promising emanicipation from "tyranny and oppression." He suggested that British subjects not oppose him; if they did, "the horrors and calamities of war will Stalk before you." Hull's force had not been large to begin with, and he had begun to lose troops as soon as he invaded Canada, because the militia was not obligated to fight on foreign soil. Still, the Canadians were dubious that Brock's force could hold out, and this discouraged their militia from turning out.

General Hull suggested that British subjects not oppose him; if they did, "the horrors and calamities of war will Stalk before you."

At this juncture, Brock was encouraged by the sudden good news that the U.S. outpost at Michilimackinac had fallen on 17 July. On 26 June, Brock had sent orders that the British garrison at Fort Saint Joseph on the Saint Marys River should attack the Americans on Mackinac Island. Captain Charles Roberts embarked about six hundred men, mostly Sioux, Winnebago, and Menominee Indians, some Ottawa and Ojibwa fur traders and a few soldiers, in the North West Company's schooner *Caledonia.* On 17 July they arrived at a height above Michilimackinac, a log fort, displayed a cannon, and received the surrender of Lieutenant Porter Hanks and his sixty-one U.S. infantry regulars without a fight.

This good news reached Brock in York, Ontario, on 29 July, and with this change of fortune, volunteers began to join Brock's ranks. This same news depressed the vacillating General Hull, who could not make up his mind whether to attack Fort Malden or not, Ultimately, he abandoned the project and withdrew back across the river to Detroit. At the same time, he ordered the garrison at Fort Dearborn to abandon their post near the present site of Chicago. Hull proposed to withdraw south to the Maumee River but was met with adamant arguments from officers of his Ohio regiments. Meanwhile, a force of British regulars, Canadian militia, and Indians ambushed a U.S. supply train that was approaching Detroit near Maguaga.

Brock arrived at Amherstburg by boat from Long Point and quickly devised an attack on Hull's position. Brock made the most of the psychological warfare, and on 15 August he sent a flag of truce demanding Hull's immediate surrender and suggested that once the attack began, the Indians would be beyond his control. On that night Brock crossed the Detroit River and deployed seven hundred regulars and militia and six hundred Indians of mixed tribes without opposition. As soon as Brock's artillery was in position and sent a shell into Hull's fort, the U.S. general called for a truce and capitulated. With his officers in a mutinous condition and troops melting away, Hull was terrified of what might happen to the women and children within the fort should things go wrong.

By the articles of surrender, the American volunteers were paroled, but Hull and his regulars were sent to Quebec as prisoners of war. Hull's brig, the *Adams,* was taken into the Provincial Marine, renamed the *Detroit,* and later would figure in naval events on Lake Erie. Hull had unknowingly set in motion a second military tragedy. On 15 August a group of Potawatomi Indians, without British supervision, massacred most of the small group of fifty-four regulars, twelve militia, nine women, and eighteen children as they withdrew from Fort Dearborn, in accordance with Hull's orders. The British had, by swift, shrewd strokes, undermined the U.S. invasion, won the loyalty of the region's Indians, and regained control of the Old Northwest.

The U.S. strategy had begun to collapse before the summer was half over. At Albany, on the right of the American line, Major General Dearborn's force was not ready to approach the Canadian boundary. Dearborn, although a veteran of the Continental army, was no longer a man of good health or great energy. By age sixty-one, he had enjoyed a distinguished political career, having served as secretary of war under President Jefferson and later as collector of taxes for the port of Boston. Secretary of War Eustis appointed Dearborn to head the army of the Northern Department, despite his being at an advanced age for a field commander. Eustis' orders had not indicated any great urgency, having instructed Dearborn to "arrange for the defence of the seacoast" before reporting to Albany. When Dearborn did arrive on 28 July, he found but twelve hundred men awaiting him, without organization, training, or equipment.

No sooner had Dearborn started to train this disorganized body than he was startled by the arrival of British Colonel Edward Baynes at his headquarters, under a flag of truce. Baynes carried a message from Prevost. Owing to the arrival of a ship with news of Parliament's repeal of the Orders in Council, the former British minister to the United States was seeking to negotiate a peace. Although Dearborn lacked authority to agree to an armistice, he did send orders to officers to confine themselves to defensive measures, which would be in effect until he received positive instructions from Washington. As Dearborn's preparations had some distance to go, he welcomed the opportunity to slow the pace of military operations in his theater. Prevost, likewise, saw that he could strengthen his defenses during the pause. Baynes's mission also returned to Canada, having gathered intelligence of Dearborn's weaknesses and of U.S. political dissension over the war.

THE ATTACK ON QUEENSTON HEIGHTS. Prevost's instructions at Niagara had also been heeded by Major General Roger Shaeffe, who made a similar agreement with his opponent, except that Van Rensselaer also demanded that no reinforcements could be sent higher than Fort Erie nor could troops be moved to the westward without four days notice, to which Shaeffe agreed. When the news of the cease-fire reached Washington, President Madison lost no time in repudiating Dearborn's action. The British had only repealed the Orders in Council conditionally and had not agreed to cease the impressment of U.S. seamen. At this stage, with Hull defeated, Madison could not have agreed to the British maneuver without severe political embarrassment. Dearborn notified Prevost that the cease-fire was at an end. The hostilities were resumed on 4 September.

The scene of military action soon shifted to Niagara where on 29 September, General Alexander Smyth brought 1,650 regulars to reinforce Van Rensselaer's force of forty-five hundred regulars and militia. Dearborn had put Smyth in charge of the regulars because Dearborn was in command of the army intended for Montreal and Niagara was a full three hundred miles distant from Albany. Dearborn rightly saw that he could not by himself conduct both campaigns. Smyth and Van Rensselaer were not destined to cooperate harmoniously. Although Smyth lacked military experience, he belonged to the regular army and was not about to take orders from a New York State militia general. Van Rensselaer was planning an assault that would involve crossing the swift Niagara River below the falls and scaling the steep Queenston Heights. Smyth preferred to attack above the falls where the river flowed more gradually and the river banks were lower. On 13 October, Van Rensselaer launched his attack against Queenston without Smyth's collaboration. One company of the U.S. Thirteenth Infantry Regiment led by Captain John E. Wool discovered a path up the heights and emerged at the top, 350 feet above the river. In the surprise and confusion, General Brock was killed attempting to rally the Forty-ninth Foot and Lincoln militia, and soon thereafter his aide-de-camp, Lieutenant Colonel John Macdonell, met the same fate. In the succeeding firefight, Wool was wounded and Lieutenant Colonel Winfield Scott took command. The Americans held out until British reinforcements arrived under the command of Shaeffe, supplemented by three hundred Iroquois. The Americans, trapped with their backs to the precipice and the river below, surrendered to Shaeffe. On hearing the news, on 24 October Van Rensselaer sent his resignation to Dearborn, who then placed Smyth in command of the entire U.S. force on the Niagara.

General Smyth was a Virginian of immense ego and little military experience who issued pompous calls to arms and then delayed in executing planned assaults.

General Smyth was a Virginian of immense ego and little military experience who issued pompous calls to arms and then delayed in executing planned assaults. He had set in motion an assault against Fort Erie, opposite Black Rock (Buffalo), near the head of the Niagara River. His troops were a mixture of too few regulars and many undisciplined New York and Pennsylvania militia. On 28 November two advance units succeeded in crossing the Niagara to prepare the way for an invasion force of three thousand, but flawed execution allowed the British to counterattack. With only part of his force embarked, Smyth called off the attack. On 30 November he ordered another attack but again called it off, much to the disgust of stalwart officers, such as Brigadier General Porter of the New York militia, who accused Smyth of cowardice and fought him in a harmless duel over the incident. In all, there was much activity with little result, men wounded and killed from the lack of organized planning, and desertion from the service because of the lack of good leadership. The War Department censured Smyth's conduct of the campaign and his involvement in New York political squabbles. The failure at Niagara brought demoralization and disintegration to the army in that quarter. When the troops went into winter quarters, they numbered barely twenty-six hundred.

THE FAILED ATTACK ON MONTREAL. The third prong of the invasion of Canada was to be General Dearborn's thrust at Montreal. In the summer of 1912, Dearborn was a man overwhelmed by his responsibilities. When called to command at Albany, Dearborn delayed departure from Boston because of the strong resistance he encountered there in attempting to raise troops. The New England Federalists were overwhelmingly against the war, which was reflected in the opposition of most New England governors to contributing their militia to the campaign. This weakened the position of the federal government because President Madison did not feel he had the means of coercing the cooperation of the New England governors.

When Dearborn at last began his march northward on 8 November to join General Joseph Bloomfield at Plattsburgh, he expected to find five thousand regulars and forty-five hundred militia ready for action. He was disappointed to find that the total force awaiting him was about five thousand, that many were ill, and that the militia were already opposed to crossing the border. Dearborn realized that he lacked the forces to capture Montreal but decided to invade and occupy a base in Canada from which he could launch later operations. He crossed the border on 19 November and fought a skirmish with a Canadian militia and Indian force led by Lieutenant Colonel Charles Michel de Salaberry at La Cole Mill. The Americans withdrew in confusion after having fired on their own men. Dearborn discharged militia and volunteers and set up winter camp near Plattsburgh. Dearborn's attack accomplished nothing, but when compared to Hull, Van Rensselaer, and Smyth, he had lost but little. For this reason, Dearborn was not immediately disgraced, although he did ask to be relieved of his command. Madison did not grant his request, and Dearborn remained in charge of the army's field operations until well into the 1813 campaign.

THE NAVAL CAMPAIGN OF 1812

While U.S. armies were preparing for their invasion of Canada, the navy was readying its ships for war. From 4 April, when President Madison approved the ninety-day embargo, until 18 June, when war was declared against Great Britain, naval commanders went on alert preparing to face the Royal Navy, the world's largest naval force. At the outset, the United States Navy had sixteen vessels in commission, excluding gunboats. These ostensibly faced a huge British navy that included six hundred warships of all types, actively employed, not counting 250 ships under construction and refitting. The British Admiralty, however, had stationed only a handful of ships along the North American coast because of worldwide demands on their naval resources. The ongoing war against Napoleonic France and its allies required deployment of British ships to protect communications in the English Channel and the North Sea, at Gibraltar and off French ports in the Mediterranean, and on convoy to the Caribbean and the Indian Ocean. The North American station, meanwhile, was patrolled by one ship of the line, the *Africa,* sixty-four guns, and two dozen smaller vessels, mainly frigates, corvettes, and brigs of less force, and they were scattered between Halifax and Bermuda.

Secretary of the Navy Paul Hamilton and the four clerks who were his administrative staff in Washington suddenly faced a crushing burden of work, issuing orders, authorizing expenditures, and providing logistical support to ship commanders at navy yards all along the Atlantic coast. As increased demands were placed upon senior commanders in various shore stations, there were desperate shortages of men and material and incomplete states of readiness for most of the vessels under their command. The navy was only partially prepared for war by mid-June 1812, especially at southern stations, such as Wilmington and Charleston, but the cruising squadrons were at sea and ready to meet ships of at least equal strength. For the U.S. Navy, the first months of the war were marked by many more successes than defeats. These events provided the public with a welcome antidote to the bitter disappointments resulting from U.S. military defeats in the northwest from Detroit to Niagara.

Most of the navy's cruising vessels had been ordered to rendezvous at Staten Island, below New York, to await the outbreak of war. Commodore John Rodgers, the senior naval captain, had advocated the concentration of all available ships in one squadron under his command. He expected that this strategy would force the British to concentrate their own ships in order to not lose them singly should Rodgers' squadron overtake them. He expected to operate primarily against British commerce in the sea-lanes they normally sailed, between South America and the British Isles or in the lanes used by East Indiamen. Any frigates or small vessels not in the squadron would be at liberty to operate in the North Atlantic, harassing ships trading between England and Canada.

Rodgers' squadron sailed from New York on 21 June, three days after the declaration of war. The squadron included Rodgers' own command, the frigate *President,* forty-four guns; the frigate *United States,* forty-four guns, commanded by Captain Stephen Decatur; the frigate *Congress,* thirty-eight guns, commanded by Captain John Smith; the brig Hornet, eighteen guns, commanded by Master Commandant James Lawrence; and the brig *Argus,* sixteen guns, commanded by Master Commandant Arthur Sinclair. Their cruise was disappointing from the viewpoint of prizes. Rodgers nearly overtook the British frigate *Belvidera,* but it escaped in the ensuing fight. For the rest of the cruise, which lasted more than two months, Rodgers' squadron captured only seven British ships. Nevertheless, the strategic purpose of sailing in strength was well served. The British ships based on Halifax were also obliged to concentrate in squadron on the chance of meeting with Rodgers, which effectively prevented the British from blockading the northern U.S. ports. Consequently, a great many U.S. merchantmen were able to return safely from Europe at the beginning of the war.

Captain Isaac Hull and his frigate *Constitution* had originally been intended for Rodgers' squadron, but the ship had been held up by an extensive refitting and was still engaged in shakedown cruises in Chesapeake Bay when Rodgers sailed from New York. When Hull finally departed the Chesapeake on 12 July, he was hoping to rendezvous with Rodgers. He had not heard that Rodgers' ships were now far to the northeast in pursuit of a convoy of merchant ships en route to England. Hull shaped his course for New York and five days later was off Egg Harbor, New Jersey, when he sighted a cluster of four ships near shore and another rapidly approaching from the northeast. When he was unable to obtain an identification, he presumed that all five were enemy ships. Hull turned away and the British squadron pursued him for the next two days until he was able to escape because of superior seamanship and some lucky breaks in the weather.

Hull then made for Boston, hoping to obtain new sailing orders because he had missed the rendezvous with Rodgers. To his dismay, there were no new orders at Boston, so he took the initiative of cruising to the northeast, hoping to find British merchantmen off Nova Scotia or Newfoundland. It was in these latitudes that the *Constitution* captured a number of merchantmen and on 19 August engaged the British frigate *Guerrière.* After two hours of approach and maneuvering for position, the battle commenced with exchanges of broadsides. As the *Constitution* was a larger, better-handled, and more heavily armed ship, the *Guerrière* soon was so damaged as to be unmanageable. Captain Sir James Richard Dacres struck his colors and surrendered his ship. This was the first of a series of naval battles won by the U.S. Navy in a war that many had expected the Royal Navy to dominate from the beginning.

Two days before chasing Captain Hull, the British squadron under the command of Commodore Philip Broke had captured their first U.S. naval prize, the brig *Nautilus,* commanded by Lieutenant William M. Crane, as it was outward bound from New York. Ironically, Crane was attempting to deliver letters from Secretary Hamilton to Commodore Rodgers warning him about the presence of the British squadron. Crane and his men were taken to Halifax and held as prisoners of war under Vice Admiral Herbert Sawyer who commanded the North American station. Several American privateers were also taken by the smaller British vessels operating in the Bay of Fundy and the waters outside Nova Scotia.

In June, Commodore Rodgers reported that Captain David Porter's *Essex,* thirty-two guns (carronades), was reported as needing new spars and a careening to clean its hull. Instead of sailing with Rodgers, Porter delivered his ship to the New York Navy Yard for an emergency overhaul. Within three weeks, Commodore Isaac Chauncey's shipyard workers and Porter's crew had done their work, and Porter sailed in early July on a remarkably successful cruise. The *Essex* captured nine

On 19 August 1812, Captain Isaac Hull and his frigate Constitution *(left) engaged the British frigate* Guerriere. *The was the first of a series of naval battles won by the U.S. Navy in a war that many had expected the Royal Navy to dominate. (National Archives/artwork by Thomas Birch)*

ships, including the British brig *Alert,* sixteen guns, on 14 August. This was an easy victory for Porter, as the *Essex* carried much heavier armament. Porter's success proved embarrassing, because at one point he was carrying five hundred prisoners. He finally sent them into Saint John's, Newfoundland, in a flag-of-truce ship called a cartel. This was an unorthodox procedure because prisoners were usually sent to central point where a U.S. commissioner kept strict records of who was captured and arranged for their systematic parole and exchange. Frequently, however, commanding officers became overburdened with prisoners, who could become a danger to their ships, outnumbering the crew and consuming large amounts of water and rations. Porter hoped that his cartel would be permitted to leave Saint John's with an equal number of Americans to be taken to New York in exchange. The British were unwilling to do so, because they had gained an unauthorized return of their own men without a reciprocal sacrifice of their prisoners.

As normal trade was virtually impossible during a maritime war, many merchants fitted out their trading ships as privateers or letters of marque.

Hundreds of American privateers put to sea in July 1812, as a result of the passage of the "Act concerning Letters of Marque, Prizes and Prize Goods on June 26, 1812." This law laid out the strict procedures required of privateer owners and captains, the records they had to keep, and the penalties that would be meted out in case of violation. Seamen on board privateers were subject to the same punishments as seamen enlisted in public ships of war. On the other hand, privateersmen could reap greater benefits than any navy seamen in the capturing of prizes. As normal trade was virtually impossible during a maritime war, many merchants fitted out their trading ships as privateers or letters of marque, trading vessels carrying guns for self-defense and for seeking targets of opportunity. One of the most successful privateers of the summer of 1812 was the Baltimore schooner *Rossie,* commanded by Joshua Barney. Departing on a cruise on 11 July, the *Rossie* had captured eighteen vessels off Nova Scotia and Newfoundland by 30 August. Barney put in to Newport, Rhode Island, resupplied his ship, and put out again on 7 September. When he returned to Baltimore on 22 October, Barney had taken a total of 3,698 tons of shipping worth $1.5 million, and 217 British prisoners—a highly successful cruise. There were many privateers who did not do as well. A total of twenty-four American privateers were captured by British warships on the Halifax station between 1 July and 25 August 1812.

For the remainder of the year, U.S. Navy commanders adopted a new cruising pattern. Instead of cruising in a large combined squadron, the ships were divided initially into small squadrons, each made up of a heavy frigate, a light frigate, and a brig. This stratagem had been recommended in May by Commodore Decatur and was seconded in September by Commodore Rodgers. The ships would sortie in squadron and then separate for individual cruises with the objective of deceiving enemy ships and persuading them to cruise in squadron strength. If the British followed the desired scheme, it would allow more U.S. merchantmen to reach home ports without passing through a blockade.

The ships would be distributed as follows with seniority deciding which ships would be associated. The *President* would sail with the *Congress* and the sloop of war *Wasp,* eighteen guns and commanded by Master Commandant Jacob Jones. The *Constitution,* forty-four guns, Captain William Bainbridge, was to go with the *Essex* and the sloop of war *Hornet.* The *United States* would be accompanied by the *Chesapeake,* thirty-eight guns, Captain Samuel Evans, and the brig *Argus.*

These groupings were an ideal that never came to be. In each squadron one ship was delayed in preparations and did not sail with its consorts. On 8, October Commodore Rodgers made an impressive departure from Boston in the *President,* with the *Congress, United States,* and *Argus* in company. Four days later, the *United States* and *Argus* separated from the *President.* The *Wasp,* unable to rendezvous with Rodgers, sailed from the Delaware River on 13 October, and five days later discovered a British convoy escorted by the sloop-of-war *Frolic* (twenty-two guns). He engaged and defeated it in a sharp contest, but then had the misfortune to be captured while repairing battle damage a few hours later by the ship of the line *Poictiers,* (seventy-four guns). Porter sailed separately in the *Essex,* intending to rendezvous with Bainbridge and Lawrence at the island of Fernando de Noronha off Brazil. Porter missed the rendezvous by only a few days and, having discretionary orders, decided to carry the war to the Pacific, where for a year he had a relatively free hand. The *Chesapeake* did not depart Boston until 12 December, two months after Rodgers' squadron and cruised alone for two months, taking several prizes before returning to Boston in March 1813.

The most successful of the fall cruises were those of Commodores Bainbridge and Decatur. In mid-October, Decatur was sailing off the island of Madeira when he encountered the new British frigate *Macedonian,* thirty-eight guns, under the command of Captain John S. Carden. On 25 October, after a battle of two hours, Carden struck his colors. Decatur put a prize crew on board and escorted his capture to Newport. At the end of December, Bainbridge was cruising off the Brazilian coast near Bahia on the *Constitution* when he engaged the British frigate *Java,* thirty-eight guns, commanded by Captain Henry Lambert, carrying Lieutenant General Thomas Hislop and his staff en route to India. Bainbridge repeated Isaac Hull's feat by wreaking such havoc on board the *Java* that he was obliged to burn it at sea. Captain Lambert died within hours of the end of battle

One of the last events stemming from the fall cruises of the U.S. Navy was the exploit of Master Commandant Lawrence of the sloop of war *Hornet.* In late December, after parting company with Bainbridge's *Constitution* off the coast of Brazil, Lawrence headed northwest toward the Guianas in search of merchantmen returning to Great Britain. Instead, on 24 February 1813, he discovered the handsome British brig *Peacock,* eighteen guns, commanded by Captain William Peake, sailing off British Guiana, and brought the brig to action. The duel ended in a little over a quarter of an hour, with the *Peacock*'s gun crews all killed or wounded and the hull settling. Captain Peake died of a cannon shot and his senior lieutenant waved his hat as a signal of surrender because the gaff and ensign had been shot away. This apparently easy victory was not a happenstance, for Lawrence had constantly drilled his men at gunnery while the British captain took more pride in the appearance of his vessel than in his crew's training. When Lawrence returned with his prisoners, this feat was hailed as further evidence of U.S. naval invincibility.

These U.S. victories stunned the lords commissioners of the British Admiralty as much as they delighted the

The eighteen-gun sloop-of-war Wasp *(right), commanded by Jacob Jones, engaged and defeated the British twenty-two gun* Frolic *on 18 October 1812. (National Archives/engraving by F. Kearney)*

U.S. government, which was starving for want of good news. Following the summer successes of Hull, Porter, and Jones, the good work of Decatur and Bainbridge seemed too good to be true. When Lawrence returned in March with the news that the *Hornet* had defeated and sunk the *Peacock* it seemed as though the navy's luck had come to stay. The ultimate affect of these maritime feats was to sting the British into reinforcing their squadrons on the North American Station, to extend the blockade, and to order that, henceforth, no British warship without an escort should accept battle with a U.S. frigate.

Although Canada loomed large among the military objectives of the Madison administration, nothing had been done to prepare naval forces for action on the borders of the United States and Canada. From Lake Superior to Lake Ontario, the United States possessed but one commissioned warship constructed for the purpose, the sixteen-gun brig *Oneida,* based at Sackets Harbor, New York. Farther east, Lake Champlain held an exceedingly important strategic position, but likewise little effort and money had been expended to defend or exploit that position. No land campaign around or beyond these lakes could succeed without first achieving naval superiority. Without population centers and local industries that could support an extensive campaign, invasion forces lacking command of the northern lakes would find their communications and supply lines at risk. For both the United States and Great Britain, the logistical side of the lakes campaigns posed an unending series of problems.

The armed vessels that patrolled the northern lakes from Canadian bases belonged not to the Royal Navy but to the Provincial Marine, a transportation service under the qartermaster general branch of the British army. At the beginning of the war, the officers in charge of these vessels were elderly, the vessels needed repairs, and they lacked effective armament. On Lake Ontario, the gun vessels at their disposal were the corvette *Royal George,* twenty-two guns, the brig *Earl of Moira,* fourteen guns, and the schooner *Duke of Gloucester,* ten guns. On Lake Erie were the corvette *Queen Charlotte,* sixteen guns, and the schooner *General Hunter,* six guns. Soon to be added to these was the brig *Adams,* captured by the Provincial Marine when General William Hull made his advance on Detroit, and renamed the *Detroit.* This vessel remained part of the Provincial Marine's Lake Erie flotilla until October 1812, when a U.S. naval contingent recaptured it in a raid off Fort Erie.

The first naval action on Lake Ontario was precipitated by the arrival of the *Royal George, Earl of Moira, Prince Regent,* and *Duke of Gloucester* off Sackets Harbor on 19 July, which were to cut out the *Oneida* and shell U.S. fortifications. Lieutenant Melancthon Woolsey, commander of the *Oneida,* found himself outgunned, anchored his vessel, and offloaded his guns to supplement those of a nearby battery. The British squadron was beaten off with a sharp exchange of cannonfire. In this affair, Woolsey had taken on board local militiamen who had volunteered to serve as marines. In his next move, Woolsey sent a small force, including the armed schooner *Julia,* under the command of Lieutenant Henry Wells, down the Saint Lawrence to Ogdensburg, where he hoped to seek out and destroy the *Earl of Moira* and *Duke of Gloucester,* which were at anchor off Prescott on the Canadian side. These two vessels threatened several unarmed U.S. merchant schooners that were moored across the river at Ogdensburg. After a cannon duel on 21 July, the British vessels retired to safety. Woolsey's prompt action in sending Wells probably saved the schooners from capture or destruction. When Prevost and Dearborn declared their armed truce in August, the Americans brought these schooners safely upriver and into the Sackets Harbor naval base. Most of them later became part of the U.S. Navy Lake Ontario squadron.

The U.S. naval policy regarding the northern lakes began to develop after the news of General William Hull's defeat at Detroit arrived in Washington in late August. It then became clear that future military operations in that region would require control of the lakes. Secretary Hamilton ordered Commodore Chauncey to transfer from his post as commandant of the New York Navy Yard to Sackets Harbor, where he would assume the command of Lakes Ontario and Erie. In that capacity, Chauncey was given wide discretion in purchasing, chartering, or building vessels suitable for fighting the enemy. From the amply supplied New York Navy Yard, Chauncey was authorized to bring shipwrights, caulkers, riggers, sailmakers, and other skilled labor, as well as all the sailors and marines he might require. The New York naval agent, John Bullus, would provide additional needed commodities. Hamilton emphasized to Chauncey that the naval station at Buffalo (Black Rock) on Lake Erie should receive as much attention as the Sackets Harbor base.

In less than a month, Chauncey accomplished a logistical miracle in transporting the tons of naval stores and ordnance and hundreds of men that were required for building an entire squadron at the eastern end of Lake Ontario, an almost virgin wilderness, hundreds of miles from established settlements and decent roads. While Chauncey was preparing this feat, Daniel Dobbins, a veteran lake mariner from Erie (Presque Isle), Pennsylvania, visited Washington in the fall with valuable intelligence on British naval resources in that area.

Hamilton responded immediately to his recommendations about commencing a squadron at Erie, appointing Dobbins a sailing master in the navy and providing him with plans for building a gunboat. As events would prove, Dobbins' intuition was correct, but he received little material assistance until after the first of the year.

Woolsey had purchased for the navy a corvette named Madison *that was capable of mounting twenty-four 32-pound carronades.*

At Sackets Harbor, Chauncey's shipwrights and carpenters immediately set to work altering several commercial schooners that Lieutenant Woolsey had purchased for the navy and commenced construction of the twenty-four-gun corvette named *Madison.* This new ship was launched on 26 November and was capable of mounting twenty-four 32-pound carronades, having been built in the remarkably short time of forty-five days. By early November, Chauncey was in command of a small squadron comprised of the brig *Oneida* and nine armed schooners. In his first sortie, Chauncey sailed with seven vessels, including the *Oneida,* with a total of forty guns and 430 men, including marines. Chauncey's first mission was an attack on the British naval base at Kingston, about forty miles directly across the lake from Sackets Harbor. On 9 November, Chauncey's squadron discovered the *Royal George* in Kingston channel and chased it into the harbor, exchanging cannon fire with both the ship and shore batteries for almost two hours. Unable to close the enemy ship because of the shore batteries and fighting a wind that threatened to drive them deeper into Kingston harbor, Chauncey withdrew, having damaged the *Royal George* and captured two small schooners. Chauncey's fleet lost one man killed and three wounded in the affair. He sailed for Sackets Harbor, having demonstrated his willingness to fight. The Provincial Marine offered no further provocations, leaving Chauncey dominant on Lake Ontario for the remainder of the sailing season.

In the meantime, a naval event of some importance had taken place at Niagara. A U.S. raiding party led by naval Lieutenant Jesse D. Elliott had captured two British armed vessels near Fort Erie. On 7 September, Chauncey had sent Elliott, his second-in-command, to Buffalo for the purpose of organizing the shipbuilding activity on Lake Erie. When Elliott arrived in mid-September, General Van Rensselaer referred him to Brigadier General Porter, who was more knowledgeable about the navigation of Lake Erie. Porter, who was in charge of building vessels for the army, also agreed to build four for the navy according to Elliott's specifications. Elliott then turned his attention to preparing construction of barracks and a magazine for the new naval station at Black Rock. When Dobbins wrote to Elliott asking for instructions about building the gunboats at Erie, Elliott gave him no satisfaction, stating that there was not enough depth of water at Erie to float the vessels. The better-informed Dobbins persisted, however, and when Chauncey visited Erie in January 1813, he encouraged Dobbins to proceed and ordered the shipwrights Adam and Noah Brown to Erie to hasten the construction of the squadron.

In early October, Elliott observed that two brigs of the Provincial Marine, the *Detroit* and *Caledonia,* had recently arrived and were anchored off Fort Erie in a vulnerable position. He gathered a force of mixed regular soldiers and sailors in two boats and seized the brigs in the early morning hours of 9 October. He made off with them in light air but was unable to get both safely out of cannon shot. The *Detroit,* unable to maneuver in light air and swift current, grounded within gunshot of the Canadian shore. There was a stiff contest for control but the Americans finally burned it, thus denying its use to the British. The *Caledonia,* which was loaded with furs and pork intended for Amherstberg, and armed with four 12-pounders and two-hundred muskets, reached the U.S. shore and was a valuable prize. Elliott's daring and successful attack attracted the attention of the press and stimulated his army colleagues to action, resulting in the assault on Queenston Heights on 11 October. While not affecting the military struggle at Niagara in 1812, the absence of both brigs would prove to be a palpable liability to the British in the Battle of Lake Erie in September 1813.

NEW LEADERSHIP FOR A LONGER WAR

The military and naval events of the first year of the War of 1812 brought several realizations. It signified to U.S. military and civilian authorities the beginning of a long and costly struggle for which the nation was ill-equipped in the areas of experience, leadership, training, and matériel. There would have to be a rapid improvement in the number and quality of available officers and enlisted men in the army in order to recover from the setbacks on all fronts in the summer and fall. While the navy experienced exhilarating victories in its few battle-tested frigates, some realized that the main tests were still to come, when Great Britain would send reinforcements from its huge navy. The first order of business in the opinion of knowledgeable congressmen was to place more competent men in the top military and naval posts.

As soon as President Madison gained reelection in November 1812, he focused his attention on finding replacements for his secretaries of war and navy. Eustis had shown his inability to cope with the burgeoning responsibilities of war by focusing on details instead of the larger problems of leadership and policy. After considerable debate, Madison settled on John Armstrong, an imperfect, ambitious, arrogant former Continental army soldier-turned-diplomat. As a young officer, he had been an author of the Newburgh Addresses in 1783, posing a challenge to constituted authority. Possessing political and administrative skills, he was selected by President Jefferson as ambassador to France (1804–1810). Madison finally selected Armstrong instead of James Monroe, who wanted the job, for secretary of war because he needed a fellow Republican from New York State who knew the military officers and the politicians where the bulk of the army was stationed.

For secretary of the navy, Madison selected William Jones, a naval veteran of the revolutionary war, former merchant ship captain, and banker from Philadelphia to replace Hamilton, whose modest administrative abilities had been overwhelmed by a propensity for drink. Both Jones and Armstrong assumed their offices in January 1813, as early as practicable in a time of national emergency. Planning for the spring campaigns was yet to be accomplished and the new leaders needed time to adjust to their manifold duties. The appointment of Jones received the plaudits of professional navy men who knew him as a seafaring man of great administrative ability. One of Jones's earliest official acts on arriving in Washington was to dismiss Chief Clerk Charles Goldsborough, who had served in the secretariat since its creation in 1798. Goldsborough, although experienced, had fallen into easy ways under Secretary Hamilton, who was not a stern supervisor. This position was a critical one for the Navy Department because the chief clerk was the primary administrator for the Office of the Secretary of the Navy. Goldsborough's replacement was Benjamin Homans, who had been recommended to Jones by Vice President Eldbridge Gerry and Secretary of State Monroe as a solid Republican, an experienced merchant ship commander, and a competent bureaucrat who had served as the secretary of the Commonwealth of Massachusetts. Homans was a highly competent chief clerk, keeping the job from 1813 until shortly before his death in 1823.

Fortunately for Jones, the Navy Department was running on the momentum born of the small, competent bureaucracy that Hamilton and his predecessors had nurtured as well as an extremely competent group of senior officers. The successes of the late months of 1812 were evidence of this, and the early months of 1813 showed signs that this would continue. There was, however, another matter to consider that would affect the navy's development for years to come, a major naval construction bill that had finally been authorized in December 1812.

Despite the Navy Department's earlier requests for new construction, Congress had refused to do more than repair ships in service. After the first signs of success and the increasing likelihood that the British would reinforce their ocean squadrons, Congress was more willing to listen. In mid-November 1812, Burwell Bassett, chairman of the Naval Committee of the House of Representatives, had received a detailed proposal from Secretary Hamilton, accompanied by a persuasive letter from Captain Charles Stewart, who argued for the construction of four seventy-four-gun ships of the line and six frigates of forty-four guns each. After a month of argument, Congress passed the act, and it was signed into law by President Madison on 2 January 1813. Another act passed by Congress, but which was signed later, authorized the navy to build six additional smaller vessels and to decommission many gunboats.

The navy commenced construction of the ships of the line, the *Washington, Independence,* and *Franklin,* at Portsmouth, Boston, and Philadelphia, respectively. They were the largest ships of the navy and most difficult to build, and although their construction started in 1813, none was ready for sea before the war came to end in 1815. The frigates *Guerrière, Java,* and *Columbia* were to be constructed at Philadelphia, Baltimore, and Washington, respectively. Of the six sloops planned, the *Columbia* would eventually be built at Washington, while the *Erie* and *Ontario* were constructed at Baltimore. Three other sloops of war, *Wasp, Peacock,* and *Frolic,* were scheduled for construction at Newburyport (Massachusetts), New York, and Boston, respectively. Paradoxically, only the last three sloops would be completed in time to see action in the War of 1812. The other vessels became the nucleus of the postwar navy, seeing action for the first time in the Tripolitan War in 1815.

Knowing that new construction would take many months if not years, Secretary Jones improvised, bringing into the lists, by purchase or charter, merchantmen that could be rapidly converted into warships and privateers on the Atlantic seaboard. These included the brigs *Vixen* (fourteen guns) and *Rattlesnake* (fourteen guns) and the schooners *Carolina* (fifteen guns) and *Nonsuch* (thirteen guns). In addition, the navy took over the Revenue Service schooner cutters *Surveyor, Active,*

Jefferson, Mercury, Vigilant, Gallatin, Madison, Eagle, and *Commodore Hull.* Thus, the navy expanded rapidly with smaller vessels rather than larger ones, and the ability of the United States to contend with the enemy ships of the line did not improve, but the new vessels enhanced the navy's capacity to take unarmed British merchantmen.

Of the ships that were under the navy secretary's more immediate control, two became trapped in Chesapeake Bay for almost the duration of the war. The frigate *Constellation,* needing expensive repairs at the outset, had been sent into a shipyard at Baltimore and was still undergoing construction in the fall of 1812. Its commanding officer, Charles Stewart, took great pains to see that it was ready for sea. In December 1812, while heading down the bay from Baltimore, he paused at Annapolis to complain that the ship's ironwork, gunpowder, and cordage were in poor condition. While this was occurring, the British were reinforcing their blockading squadrons. Unfortunately for Stewart, the enemy's frigates made their appearance in the lower Chesapeake during the same week that he arrived at Norfolk. Anchored off Lynnhaven Roads, these ships were a powerful obstacle to the *Constellation*'s escape. Stewart anticipated the British tactics, knowing they had hopes of cutting his ship out of Norfolk. He lightened ship and had it towed up the Elizabeth River, where enemy boats could not reach it without running the gauntlet of gunboats, batteries, and forts that ringed the city. Despite all the steps Stewart took in undertaking to challenge and deceive the enemy, the *Constellation* was fated to remain a blockaded vessel until the end of the war. In mid-1813 the Navy Department found him a replacement, and he was posted to the *Constitution.*

The *Adams* was another vessel that needed repairs badly and it was refitted at the Washington Navy Yard. When completed in late 1813, it was a flush-deck corvette, heavily armed with twenty-six 18-pounder Columbiads and one long 12-pounder cannon. Its commanding officer, Captain Charles Morris, sailed frequently down the Potomac to test the blockade and obtain intelligence on British movements in the bay. When not actively cruising, Morris enjoyed the life of the Maryland capital and became firm friends with established figures of government. He finally slipped through the blockade in January 1814 and headed northward toward an unhappy destiny in Penobscot Bay on the Maine coast.

THE CAMPAIGNS OF 1813

Just as the navy was reaping rewards in the Atlantic, the army was marching to regain territory lost in the Detroit campaign. To improve his luck, in September 1812 President Madison had appointed Governor William Henry Harrison of the Indiana territory a brigadier general and commander in chief of the northwestern army. Harrison placed this force, numbering ten thousand men, under the immediate command of a regular army officer, Brigadier General James Winchester. Harrison's overall plan was to send three columns of troops toward Detroit. Winchester was to protect the left flank, Harrison's own center column would march directly north from Ohio, and the right wing would bring artillery along the Upper Sandusky River. The three would converge at the rapids of the Maumee River before launching a combined northward offensive. The U.S. forces moved into Indian territory in September and October, reinforcing Fort Harrison and Fort Madison on the upper Mississippi, relieving Fort Wayne in northeastern Indiana, and rebuilding Fort Defiance on the Maumee, renaming it Fort Winchester. The Indians offered little opposition, having deserted villages ahead of the advancing Americans, but they scouted the margins of the army's progress, taking an occasional scalp and starting prairie fires. Harrison's Ohio and Kentucky troops were enthusiastic but raw, untrained, and poorly equipped as the cold autumn rains began, spreading sickness and bringing discontent into their camps. Harrison, who at one point had predicted retaking Detroit before mid-December, altered his schedule. He would wait until the margins of Lake Erie were frozen and march toward Detroit across the ice. The winter set in early, making life miserable.

Harrison chose to wait until the margins of Lake Erie were frozen so his troops could march toward Detroit across the ice.

Harrison, although prone to suspending operations, sent orders to Winchester to continue his march toward the rapids of the Maumee. Shortly thereafter, Harrison changed his mind and recalled Winchester, but the message arrived too late. When Winchester arrived at the rapids on 10 January, he received news from Frenchtown on the Raisin River that a small British and Indian force was approaching from the north. A delegation of citizens from Frenchtown pleaded with Winchester to bring his army to defend their settlement. At that moment, Harrison's force was sixty-five miles away and Winchester's men wanted food and fighting, both of which they were likely to find at Frenchtown. Instead of waiting for reinforcment, Winchester held a council with his officers and decided to go to the aid of Frenchtown. When Harrison heard of Winchester's advance on 18 January, he became alarmed at the risk taken and hastened his own march. Winchester had sent Lieutenant Colonel William Lewis ahead with 660 Kentuckians to make contact with Frenchtown. On 18 January, after a difficult skirmish, Lewis' men took possession of the town, but they were in an exposed position, facing an enemy that had withdrawn but was unbeaten. When Winchester arrived, he met Lewis' troops, who, although victorious, were fatigued and weakened by overindulgence in food and drink provided by a grateful community. These troops were in no condition to mount a defense. In the meantime, the British commandant at Amherstburg, Lieutenant Colonel Henry A. Proctor, sent reinforcements to counterattack at Frenchtown before Harrison's reinforcements could arrive. Despite knowledge that the British were capable of returning, Winchester's men failed to maintain an alert and were surprised when firing began at dawn on 22 January.

The British, aided by Wyandot and Potawatomi Indians, attacked the Americans, whose backs were against the river. Demoralized and disorganized, the Americans could not make an effective defense. Winchester was captured, others were shot and scalped, and the balance surrendered after Colonel Proctor offered security. Winchester lost two hundred Kentucky troops dead or wounded and seven hundred as prisoners of war. Proctor then withdrew to nurse his own wounded and left the prisoners with no guards but Indians who soon were drunk and unrestrained. These Indians fell on thirty or so wounded and killed them, scalping and stripping the corpses. These actions soon became known as the Raisin River Massacre, and grief and anger spread among Kentucky families when the news arrived that many of their young men who had marched gloriously to war were no more. "Remember the River Raisin" became a rallying cry for the second year of the war. Throughout the American Northwest, Colonel Proctor's name was inevitably linked with the dishonor of his failed promise and inability to control his Indian allies. General Harrison's winter offensive was at an end, and his plea for further troops was refused by the governors of Ohio and Kentucky.

When Secretary of War Armstrong arrived in Washington in February, he urged a new campaign in the East, using as its focal point a joint army-navy attack on Kingston, Ontario. If this succeeded, the U.S. force would attack York, the capital of Upper Canada, and Fort George, and Upper Canada would be soon be the hostage of the United States. The way would then be clear to proceed against Montreal. President Madison adopted this strategy, but it was soon modified on receipt of exaggerated intelligence reports from General Dearborn and Commodore Chauncey that the British were reinforcing Kingston. Fearing their forces would be outgunned, the two commanders recommended that the objectives be reversed, with York and Fort George becoming the first targets of attack. Kingston could be assaulted later without fear of British reinforcements from the West, because the U.S. Navy would be in control of Lake Ontario.

THE LAKE ONTARIO CAMPAIGN. Chauncey and Dearborn began their preparations for an amphibious expedition in March 1813, to be ready to sail as soon as the lake ice broke up. For an immediate on-scene commander, Dearborn selected Brigadier General Zebulon M. Pike, who had already made his reputation in exploration of the American West. Although the lake was usually open by early April, the breakup did not occur until 18 April. To ready his vessels, mostly schooners, Chauncey took extraordinary measures, practically emptying the New York Navy Yard of its supplies and craftsmen. His need for seamen virtually immobilized several naval vessels at New York harbor. Chauncey had received an offer in January from a master commandant stationed in Newport to join him on the lakes with more than a hundred seamen from the seacoast. Chauncey immediately accepted this offer of service from Oliver Hazard Perry, who was known to him because of his service in the Mediterranean eight years earlier. When Perry arrived in March, Chauncey sent him to take command of the vessels being assembled by Lieutenant Elliott at Black Rock and Erie. Elliott, now superseded, returned to Sackets Harbor to act as Chauncey's second-in-command on Lake Ontario.

When the Americans were nearly within gunshot, the British fired their magazine, which erupted in an enormous explosion and a cascade of rocks.

Pike and his seventeen hundred troops boarded the fourteen vessels of the navy squadron to await the moment of sailing. During this time, cold wind and rains swept their anchorage at Sackets Harbor, bringing illness to the troops even before they departed. Dearborn was so anxious to get under way, he requested that Chauncey order out the squadron in the face of a gathering storm. The weather worsened and Chauncey ordered the expedition back to harbor. With damage and spirits repaired, the squadron sailed again for York on

25 April. The British commander at York, Major General Shaeffe, had seven hundred regulars and about one hundred Indians, little more than half the strength of the invasion forces. They put up a defense at first, with batteries firing at the U.S. ships and landing parties. A stiff breeze from the east blew the landing boats out of range, and they landed where they could, reassembled, and marched toward the fort. When the Americans were nearly within gunshot, the British fired their magazine, which erupted in an enormous explosion and a cascade of rocks, one of which fatally wounded General Pike. Dearborn took direct command of the troops and moved into the town of York as Shaeffe and his troops withdrew. The U.S. troops burned the public buildings, including the parliament building, the governor's residence, barracks, and any supplies they could not take with them. The most important result from the naval point of view was the burning of a nearly completed twenty-four-gun ship and the capture of its cannon. Another valuable prize was the ten-gun brig *Gloucester,* which Chauncey sent back to Sackets Harbor. Among the naval stores destroyed were those destined for the naval base at Amherstburg at the western end of Lake Erie. The lack of these supplies delayed the completion of the British squadron at a critical time, just before the Battle of Lake Erie.

Meanwhile, the British had succeeded in sending additional military and naval assistance to the beleaguered governor general, Lieutenant General Prevost. In late October 1812, Prevost had warned the British government of U.S. naval preparations and asked that he be sent experienced naval officers. At the same time, he also ordered construction of warships at Kingston and Amherstburg. With the usual delay of communications, naval assistance was not on the way until March 1813, with a small number of seamen and officers coming from Admiral John Warren's command at Halifax, the rest being sent directly from England under the command of Captain Sir James L. Yeo, who received orders to bring four hundred officers and seamen and take command of the lakes navy. The British Admiralty also instructed Yeo that his role would be defensive in nature and that he would be subordinate to Prevost in preserving the Canadian colony. In the event, Yeo expended most of his resources on the Lake Ontario squadron, and there was little left over for the Lake Erie and Lake Champlain contingents.

SACKETS HARBOR AND FORT GEORGE. When Yeo arrived at Kingston on 15 May, he learned of the setback at York and immediately proposed taking advantage of the absence of the U.S. fleet by sending an amphibious force to attack their base at Sackets Harbor. The British force departed under the command of General Prevost and was in position to attack Sackets Harbor on 28 May, but he delayed the attack one entire day against Yeo's advice. The Americans, anticipating the attack, gathered in the militia and made other defensive arrangements. Major General Jacob Brown of the New York militia arrived to take charge of the defense. On the next day, Brown's forces repelled the raid, killing forty-eight, wounding 211, and taking sixteen prisoners of war. Although the defeated British withdrew, their attack had not been without damage on the American side. A U.S. naval officer burned some naval stores and set fire to the nearly completed corvette *General Pike,* thinking the day was lost and that he was preventing the enemy from capturing the vessel. Ultimately, this deprived Chauncey of his strongest vessel for several weeks while the damage was repaired. The most damaging result of the British attack, however, was to undermine Chauncey's confidence in the safety of his base. Kingston was less than one day's sail from Sackets Harbor, while Chauncey had been operating more than one hundred miles to the west at York and Fort George. In the future, he became more cautious about leaving his base when Yeo's vessels were at or near Kingston. In so doing, he occasionally withheld assistance from U.S. troops at the western end of the lake who needed Chauncey's ships to cut supply and communications lines between the British commanders and the enemy units fighting on the Niagara peninsula.

As Prevost and Yeo launched their raid, Dearborn and Chauncey were executing the second phase of their operation, an amphibious attack on 27 May on Fort George on the Canadian side of the Niagara River. The Americans carried out a carefully laid joint plan that included the construction of troop-carrying barges, the towing of the barges by warships, shore bombardment, and an attack upon a defended shoreline. Dearborn appointed Lieutenant Colonel Winfeld Scott to lead the four thousand assault troops, while Chauncey had the assistance of Master Commandant Perry, who had hastened from Black Rock to participate in the battle. Perry worked closely with Scott in coordinating the assault and supervised naval gunfire in support of the landing parties. As a result, about two thousand British troops retreated as the Americans landed, and Fort George was soon in U.S. hands. General John Vincent, commanding the British army at Niagara, ordered a withdrawal westward toward Burlington from their exposed positions at Forts Erie and Chippewa.

With Fort Erie in American hands, the U.S. Navy schooners that had been pinned down earlier at Black Rock could be worked out of the Niagara River and into Lake Erie. When Perry arrived at Lake Erie on 27 March to take charge of the shipbuilding effort, he found the two brigs and other vessels under construction were behind schedule and lacking necessary equipment. He traveled to Pittsburgh to expedite the ordering and arrival of equipment and munitions. He took steps to ensure the protection of the shipyard against possible raids from Long Point across the lake, where enemy vessels were frozen in the ice. In May three schooners were ready for launching but the brigs were still incomplete. At that moment, Perry's work was interrupted by the call from Chauncey at Niagara. After the landing at Fort George, Perry and Elliott remained two weeks at Black Rock, struggling to move five vessels, including the brig *Caledonia* and the schooners *Ohio, Amelia, Sommers,* and *Trippe,* from their winter quarters into the Niagara River. He finally brought them, without enemy interference, to Lake Erie on 18 June and added them to his flotilla. For the next two months. he would be preoccupied by two problems—the final fitting out of these vessels and the lack of a sufficient number of experienced officers and seamen.

The U.S. Army's capture of Fort George was the high point of the Niagara campaign. After that, the U.S. forces faced reversals resulting both from a lack of experienced leadership and a failure of nerve. Instead of keeping constant pressure on the retreating British troops, Generals William Winder and John Chandler moved cautiously westward, allowing the British to regroup and counterattack. Both Winder and Chandler were captured during such an event at their encampment at Stoney Creek on 6 June.

General Dearborn, unable to continue in command because of ill health, placed General Morgan Lewis in

Winfield Scott and 4,000 assault troops stormed Fort George near the Niagara River on 27 May 1813. Oliver Hazard Perry supervised naval gunfire in support of the landing parties. The battle forced the British to withdraw west toward Burlington. (National Archives/engraving by Alonzo Chappel)

charge, as the British advanced to recapture their earlier positions. Lewis ordered a withdrawal from Forts Erie and Chippewa, anchoring his defense on Fort George. A U.S. force of about five hundred cavalry and infantry commanded by Lieutenant Colonel C. G. Boerstler moved out of Fort George on 23 June to attack a British post at Beaver Dams, west of Queenston Mountain, but intelligence of this move resulted in an attack the next day by Caughnawaga and Mohawk Indians and Boerstler's surrender after a three-hour battle. By this time, the War Department sensed that Dearborn had outlived his usefulness and would have to be replaced.

The man whom Madison and Armstrong chose to replace Dearborn was not a great improvement, for they selected an aging revolutionary war veteran with a tainted reputation. Lieutenant General James Wilkinson had for many years been associated with the defense of the Louisiana Territory. Suspected of double-dealing with Aaron Burr and with the Spanish in Florida, he had managed to restore his faltering reputation by leading a U.S. expedition to expel the Spanish from Mobile, Alabama, in May 1813.

By the time Wilkinson arrived at Sackets Harbor, he was in ill-health and his reputation for corruption had preceded him. Despite his more than twenty years in the army, Wilkinson was an unfortunate choice to command a demoralized force on the northern frontier. Since the capture of Fort George, the army had been weakened by poor leadership, bad food, disease, and defeat. The results were reflected in desertions and officer resignations at Niagara. The general would have had an enormous task even under ordinary circumstances. Secretary of War Armstrong brought up questions during cabinet discussions in early August, in which he proposed that the army shift its objectives from Niagara to Kingston, the Saint Lawrence, and Montreal. He also announced his intention to travel northward to supervise the army's activities. Many in the army realized that before the army could move safely, the navy would have to weaken or eliminate the Royal Navy's interference on Lake Ontario. In order for this to happen, Commodore Chauncey's squadron would have to defeat soundly the British squadron.

THE STRUGGLE FOR LAKE ONTARIO. In the summer campaign of 1813, Chauncey and Yeo thrust, parried, and feinted, each attempting to gain the upper hand without risking the loss of their entire squadron, but the weather or other circumstances withheld victory from both sides. In determining who controlled Lake Ontario, major factors were the number of vessels and guns that could be brought to bear. Chauncey had in his squadron the brig *Oneida,* sixteen guns; the corvette *Madison,* twenty-four guns; eleven schooners purchased in 1812 with three or four guns apiece; the newly constructed schooner *Lady of the Lake,* five guns; and the corvette *General Pike,* twenty-eight guns. Still under construction was the schooner *Sylph,* ten guns, not completed until 18 August. Yeo's vessels were the sloops of war *Wolfe,* twenty-three guns; *Royal George,* twenty-one guns; and the brigs *Earl of Moira,* fourteen guns; *Prince Regent,* sixteen guns; *Sydney Smith,* twelve guns; and *Lord Melville,* fourteen guns. Behind the growth of these squadrons was the enormous logistical effort of each side that manifested itself in a shipbuilding contest on the opposing shores of the lakes.

Chauncey's new flagship was the *General Pike,* ready for sea in mid-July. The commodore wasted no more time and led his entire squadron to the western end of the lake. He took on board Colonel Scott and some troops at Niagara and, failing to find Yeo's squadron, paid another visit to York on 31 July. The town was virtually defenseless, having not recovered from the raid of 25 April. Chauncey's force landed and destroyed eleven barges, five cannon, and a quantity of flour. He departed after burning the barracks and carrying off some ammunition. In doing so, Chauncey again harmed the British Lake Erie squadron, which depended on provisions that were transported by water and often were stored at York.

The schooners Hamilton *and* Scourge *capsized and sank in a sudden midnight squall on the evening of 8 August with the loss of many men.*

In early August, Chauncey suffered two setbacks featuring the loss of four vessels. First, the schooners *Hamilton* and *Scourge* capsized and sank in a sudden midnight squall on the evening of 8 August with the loss of many men. Two days later, during a squadron engagement, the schooners *Julia* and *Growler* were captured when they either ignored or misunderstood a signal to tack and sail toward the squadron instead of away from it. The two schooners sailed toward the Canadian shore, then they put about and tried to run the gauntlet among the pursuing enemy, whose gunfire cut down their rigging before they could escape. For Chauncey, these four vessels represented a significant proportion of his squadron. In two days, he lost four of his eleven schooners, 160 men, and twenty-three guns. The first two were lost by poor seamanship and the latter by faulty communications and improper tactics. These losses numerically shifted the control of the lake to

Commodore Yeo, but Chauncey still had the more powerful ships and this showed to advantage in their next engagement.

The two squadrons finally met off York on 28 September in what might have been the deciding battle of Lake Ontario. The opposing vessels were at sufficiently close quarters for the British to use their carronades, while the Americans had both long- and short-range guns. The *General Pike* damaged the *Wolfe* severely and might have captured it had Chauncey cast off the schooners his ships were towing, and if Captain William Mulcaster had not brought the *Royal George* between the two flagships and covered his commodore's retreat. A chase ensued with the Americans pursuing, but not overtaking, the British squadron, which took refuge under batteries in Burlington Bay. Unwilling to risk his vessels on a fortified lee shore, Chauncey withdrew to try his luck another day. For the remainder of the season, the U.S. squadron dominated the lake and protected the army's movements, a critical situation that Armstrong and Wilkinson had anxiously awaited.

THE ATTEMPT ON MONTREAL. In October, as the U.S. fleet conducted Wilkinson's army from Niagara to Sackets Harbor, Armstrong and Wilkinson planned the army's next move, either a descent of the Saint Lawrence River or an attack on Kingston. When Chauncey joined them, he voted for Kingston as the target, but ultimately, Armstrong ordered only a feint at Kingston and a passage downriver to a point where they would rendezvous with the troops of Major General Wade Hampton. The ultimate objective was Montreal, the control of which would determine the future of Canada. Armstrong ordered General Hampton to march northward from Plattsburgh to join Wilkinson just short of the city. If all went well, they would assault Montreal together.

All, however, did not go well. Hampton's force of four thousand began its march into Canada on 21 September but was soon discouraged by the lack of drinking water on the line of march. He retired into U.S. territory, marched westward to the Chateauguay River, and entered Canada and marched northward again, generally following the Chateauguay toward its confluence with the Saint Lawrence. After a month of such maneuvering, the Canadian militia, led by Lieutenant Colonel De Salaberry, met Hampton's army at a ford on the Chateauguay on 25 October. Although Hampton's men far outnumbered the militia, the Americans were ignorant of the terrain and became lost and confused by their situation. A small skirmish ensued, wherein the American casualties were fifty and the Canadians twenty-five. With these minuscule losses, the Battle of the Chateauguay was at an end. The Canadian defenders had won the day at little cost, because Hampton's army then turned about and marched to Plattsburgh. The Canadian militia properly won their laurels, and Hampton fully earned his disgrace for a pathetic performance at arms.

Wilkinson's army put forth a greater effort but it was no less poorly handled and had a similar result. Starting their descent of the Saint Lawrence too late in the season to be assured of clement weather, Wilkinson entered the river with seven thousand men in barges on 5 November. The initial stage of his voyage was covered by Chauncey's squadron, although he did not succeed in preventing British gunboats from entering the river. Captain Mulcaster once again performed well, eluding Chauncey's ships and passing downriver to harass the rearguard of Wilkinson's flotilla.

The British and Canadian land forces, called a "corps of observation," followed Wilkinson's progress on the left bank. Recognizing the need to confront those forces in order to maintain his force in good order, Wilkinson landed his army at a point called Chrysler's Field, where a smaller Canadian force of about eight-hundred joined battle on 11 November with about two thousands Americans under the command of General John P. Boyd. While this battle was more than skirmish, its result showed the poor quality of training and leadership of the men under Wilkinson's control. Boyd's troops suffered more than four hundred killed, wounded, or captured, whereas British casualties numbered somewhat less than two hundred. Wilkinson, who had been ill to begin with, now became despondent, especially after hearing that Hampton would not make the planned rendezvous. He then ordered his troops into winter quarters at French Mills on the Salmon River. These men were to have a miserable winter, lacking proper clothes, bedding, and medical supplies. Armstrong's two-pronged attack on Montreal was a truly unwise adventure, poorly planned and badly timed.

THE STRUGGLE FOR THE WEST. From a military perspective, the brightest accomplishment of the United States in 1813 took place at the western end of Lake Erie. The cooperation of Commodore Perry and General Harrison in defeating the British forces in September and October demonstrated a fine example of what could be achieved with careful planning and energetic collaboration. Harrison had successfully withstood the British and Indian siege of Fort Meigs during late April and early May. When the siege was lifted, thanks to the arrival of reinforcements from Kentucky, General Proctor withdrew his men, who, in any event, wanted to return to their farms.

In the meantime, the British base at Fort Malden and Amherstburg was suffering from lack of supplies, and

Proctor hoped to keep his men busy in campaigns on the south side of the lake while living off the land. On 1–2 August, he attempted an assault on Fort Stephenson on the Sandusky, but Major George Croghan, who was in charge of the defense of the fort, ignored Harrison's order to retreat and repelled the British assault. During July, Commodore Perry was anxiously working to complete his largest vessels, the twenty-gun brigs *Lawrence* and *Niagara*, and to move them over the bar into Lake Erie to join the other vessels, the small brig *Caledonia*; the schooners *Ariel, Scorpion, Somers, Porcupine, Tigress, Ohio,* and *Amelia*; and the sloop *Trippe.* By the second week of August, Perry's squadron was clear of the harbor and became a definite threat to British control of Lake Erie. Captain Robert Barclay had failed to keep a close watch over Perry's preparations and missed a chance to attack the U.S. vessels when the most dangerous were still virtually landlocked in Misery Bay.

At the British naval base in early September, Proctor and Barclay were in desperate straits as they realized the Americans were tightening the blockade of Amherstburg. Proctor realized that he could not supply either his army or the hundreds of dependent Indian families without water transport. As long as Perry controlled the lake, Barclay's ships could not escort and protect supply convoys from Fort Erie. Without seamen, Barclay could not sail his ships, and Commodore Yeo withheld men from Barclay just as Chauncey had withheld them from Perry. The best hands were kept on Lake Ontario to man the larger squadrons.

THE BATTLES OF LAKE ERIE AND THE THAMES. Barclay finally, reluctantly, sailed with his ships undermanned and outnumbered as compared with Perry's squadron. The naval contest for control of Lake Erie erupted on 10 September, a day of light breezes in which Perry's squadron seized the weather gauge outside of the Bass Islands near Put-In Bay. The battle lasted a full two hours and was accompanied by some notable events. The two battle lines joined slowly and the lead U.S. ship, Perry's flagship *Lawrence,* attacked and took the brunt of the firing from the two strongest of Barclay's ships, the *Detroit* and *Queen Charlotte.* The *Lawrence* gave as good as it got, although by the end of the battle it was nearly destroyed. Its two opponents were also in very poor shape, with both commanding officers and their seconds-in-command either dead or wounded. At that moment, Perry decided to continue the battle from Master Commandant Elliott's *Niagara,* as Elliott had held *Niagara* in its assigned position in the line of battle, despite the flagship's precarious position. This behavior became a matter of much controversy in the aftermath, some of the survivors alleging that Elliott deliberately held position in order to be able to win the laurels after Perry failed or fell in battle.

The Lawrence *gave as good as it got, although by the end of the battle it was nearly destroyed.*

Perry was completely within his rights to shift his flag to Elliott's command and to send Elliott on other duty, which he immediately did, to bring the smaller vessels into the line of battle. With this, Perry sailed the *Niagara* directly where it could do the most damage to the largest British ships. Within minutes, Barclay's flagship had struck its colors, and the others soon followed their commodore's example. It is another remarkable aspect of this battle that, with the exception of U.S. Marine Lieutenant John Brooks and his unit of thirty-four men from Sackets Harbor, most of the marines on board Perry's vessels were drawn from the Pennsylvania and Ohio volunteers in Harrison's army under the command of Captain Henry Brevoort, who acted as Elliott's captain of marines on the *Niagara.*

The result of this bloody naval battle was the complete capitulation of the British naval squadron on Lake Erie and the rapid change of fortunes of Harrison's army, which now could move at will across the water to engage Proctor's army in western Ontario. With the help of Perry's vessels, the western army moved north up the Detroit River to Lake Saint Clair and then eastward along the Thames River to Moravian Town, where Proctor and Tecumseh made a stand.

In the Battle of the Thames on 5 October, Proctor formed his regulars of the Forty-first Regiment of Foot across the main road while Tecumseh's Indians took position in a swamp to his right and faced the approaching Americans. Harrison sent his Kentucky cavalry through the poorly defended British positions. While the British were surrendering after weak opposition the Americans turned toward the swamp and had a stiff fight during which Tecumseh and many of his followers were killed. In the final result, eighteen British were killed and about six hundred were captured, as compared with seven Americans killed and twenty-two wounded.

With the battle won, Harrison withdrew most of his army and sailed with Perry for Buffalo. Meanwhile, General Proctor and the remnants of his army straggled overland to join Major General John Vincent's Army of the Centre at Burlington. Harrison's army virtually dissolved following his victory. The small corps of regulars was brought by sea to Sackets Harbor to guard Chauncey's naval base, as the rest of the army had departed with Wilkinson on his ill-fated Saint Lawrence expedition. The Americans virtually abandoned the Niagara peninsula when the New York militia's enlistment expired, and even the Brigadier General John McClure's small garrison of regulars remaining in Fort George departed that post for Fort Niagara in early December, but not before they needlessly burned the small Canadian town of Newark on 10 December.

This deed became an excuse for revenge as Canadian and British troops under Lieutenant General George Gordon Drummond and Major General Phineas Riall moved into Fort George. Within days, a British unit commanded by Lieutenant Colonel John Murray moved across the Niagara River and rapidly took control of the U.S. side, surprising the sentries and rushing Fort Niagara, which the British held for the remainder of the war. Another group under Riall's command burned Lewiston, Black Rock, and Buffalo; destroyed four armed schooners; and burned U.S. supply depots, meeting scarcely any resistance. The lack of U.S. troops and leaders capable of occupying and defending captured enemy territory made a mockery of earlier sacrifices in taking the ground. The entire situation reflects poorly on the U.S. "strategists" who advised making war in the first place.

SETBACKS ON LAKE CHAMPLAIN. The Colonel John Murray who captured Fort Niagara was the same intrepid soldier who had made life miserable for the U.S. military posted at Lake Champlain the previous summer. When the U.S. campaign against Canada began, the military and naval forces stationed on that lake were negligible. Lieutenant Sidney Smith had been posted to Vergennes, Vermont, where he was in charge of two seven-gun sloops in poor condition. As soon as it was evident that the Lake Champlain station would have to be strengthened, Secretary Hamilton ordered a

The Battle of Lake Erie on 10 September 1813 resulted in the complete capitulation of the British naval squadron on Lake Erie. After Commodore Oliver Hazard Perry's flagship, the Lawrence*, was disabled, he and his men rowed to the* Niagara *to continue the battle. (National Archive/ engraving by Phillibrown after W. H. Powell)*

senior lieutenant, Thomas Macdonough, from a gunboat command at Portland, Maine, to take charge of the Lake Champlain station. He superseded Lieutenant Smith and reported to Brigadier General Joseph Bloomfield, a former and future governor of New Jersey, who had under his control four sloops that Dearborn ordered transferred to the navy.

Macdonough placed only three of these sloops in commission. These were the *President,* eight guns; *Growler,* seven guns; and *Eagle,* seven guns. In addition, there were two nondescript gunboats that carried one 12-pounder each. He designated three other sloops to be used as transports. Meanwhile, at Isle aux Noix in the Richelieu River, the British began to arm three sloops, three gunboats, and a schooner. In the first naval action on Lake Champlain, Macdonough's men came out second best. In early June 1813, Macdonough sent Smith in charge of the *Growler* and *Eagle* to patrol the northern part of lake. Smith exceeded his orders, however, and entered the Richelieu River, where he found himself unable to escape a galling fire from both banks and three enemy gunboats, having both wind and current against him. After a two-hour battle, Smith surrendered both vessels.

The British decided to take advantage of Macdonough's weakened condition by raiding U.S. bases. Colonel James Murray got under way on 13 July with one thousand troops in transports, escorted by Captain Thomas Everard, commanding the captured gunboats *Growler* and *Eagle,* now renamed *Chubb* and *Finch.* They landed at Plattsburgh, destroyed the blockhouse, barracks, and stores there and at Saranac. Murray sent smaller detachments to destroy supply depots at Swanton and Burlington, Vermont. Finding the Burlington garrison of three thousand regulars and volunteers too strong to attack, they returned to Isle aux Noix with four commercial lake vessels as prizes. Murray's raid set back Macdonough's preparations by several months, so that it was not until November 1813 that the U.S. squadron was again ready to contest control of the lake.

BRITISH RESURGENCE ON THE HIGH SEAS. In the wake of unexpected U.S. frigate victories, the British Admiralty took steps to reinforce its blockade of major estuaries and ports in early 1813 and to mount a land campaign in the middle Atlantic region that might relieve pressure on Canada. The earliest effects of this new strategy were felt in the spring of the year. The appearance of British ships on station at Lynnhaven Roads in Chesapeake Bay provided a sign of things to come. The frigate *Constellation* was unable to escape the bay under these circumstances, and many merchantmen and privateers were similarly threatened.

In May, Captain James Lawrence was given command of the frigate *Chesapeake,* thirty-eight guns, at Boston where it was preparing for a cruise. The British blockaded at Boston as they did off Montauk Point, Long Island. Montauk was strategically located to prevent egress from Long Island Sound, one of the two approaches to New York. A blockade at Montauk also cut off access to three major New England seaports—Providence, Newport, and New London. At this same moment, Commodore Stephen Decatur was in New York, preparing for a cruise in the *United States,* with the *Macedonian* (Captain Jacob Jones) and *Hornet* (Master Commandant James Biddle). Decatur attempted to sail from Sandy Hook but turned back after sighting the blockading squadron and decided to try the Long Island Sound passage. On 1 June, thinking the British squadron was busily engaged off Sandy Hook, Decatur set sail for Montauk but sighted a strong squadron off Block Island, reversed course, and headed for New London, where the *United States* and *Macedonian* remained for the duration of the war; the *Hornet* managed to slip through the blockade the following year.

Lawrence's final command was,

"Fight her till she sinks and don't give up the ship."

Paradoxically, Lawrence also attempted to break out in the *Chesapeake* on 1 June, but in doing so accepted a virtual challenge from the British frigate *Shannon,* thirty-eight guns and commanded by Captain Sir Philip Vere Broke. The two ships were equally matched in size and armament, but Broke's crew were experienced and well-trained, as opposed to that of Lawrence, many of whom had just transferred from other ships and had not trained as a unit. As Lawrence came into action, he gallantly gave away a maneuvering advantage in order to initiate a fair fight. In so doing, he lost his ship and his life in a bloody, fifteen-minute duel just outside of Massachusetts Bay. Lawrence's final command was, "Fight her till she sinks and don't give up the ship." It was an inglorious first of June when four American ships were effectively put out of action, the *Chesapeake* forever and Decatur's squadron for almost the duration of the war.

Captain William Henry Allen's brig *Argus,* ten guns, became one of the more celebrated navy vessels when it took the war to the British Isles in the summer of 1813. Following a passage to L'Orient in the Bay of Biscay, Allen attacked British shipping in the English Channel, cruised along the coast of Cornwall, raided in the Shannon River, and entered St. George's Channel between England and Ireland. In all, Allen captured and destroyed or ransomed nineteen vessels. At dawn on 14 August, the British sloop *Pelican*, under captain John Fordyce Maples, bore down on the *Argus* and began a spirited forty-five-minute battle that ended in the surrender of the *Argus* and the death of Allen. On Allen's behalf, he was short of men, having sent them off as prize crews, but this was a calculated risk that did not pay off.

A high-seas fight that showed both Americans and British at their best was that of the American brig *Enterprise,* sixteen guns, and the British brig *Boxer,* fourteen guns, which took place off the Maine coast near Portland on 5 September 1813. Lieutenant William Burrows was patrolling the Maine coast to protect coastal merchantmen when he found the *Boxer,* commanded by Lieutenant Samuel Blyth, at anchor inside Penguin Point. The ensuing battle was hard fought, bringing the death of both commanding officers early in the battle. The surviving lieutenants took over and continued the fight for three-quarters of an hour. The *Boxer* fought until it could no longer be maneuvered with its rigging and spars shot away. Burrows and Blyth were buried side by side in the Portland cemetery with military honors.

THE PACIFIC: THE ESSEX ON THE RAMPAGE. Captain David Porter, having thrice missed rendezvous with Commodore Bainbridge, implemented discretionary orders and sailed the thirty-two-gun frigate *Essex* around Cape Horn to Chile late in 1812. During the voyage, on 12 December he captured the British mail packet *Nocton,* which was carrying £10,000. He sent the *Nocton* to the United States as a prize, but it was intercepted and recaptured by the British *Belvidera.* Arriving at Valparaiso in March 1813, Porter soon became embroiled in the Chilean revolution against the Spanish Bonapartists, who were attempting to wrest Spanish America from the Bourbon viceroys. The Chilenos provided Porter with welcome assistance in reprovisioning his ship. Completing the process within days, Porter sailed for the British whaling grounds, stating that "I have as complete power in the Pacific as the whole British navy can have in the Atlantic." Until Porter's arrival on the west coast of South America, there were no British warships anywhere in the eastern Pacific, an extremely advantageous situation, and Porter soon made his presence felt. Within a few days, he took the Peruvian privateer *Nereyda,* which had been plundering Yankee whaling ships. He had to be careful not to offend the Peruvian viceroy who was being courted by the English and was theoretically neutral in the War of 1812.

From Valparaiso and Lima, Porter sailed for the Galapagos Islands, using them as a base from April until October. During this time he captured twelve British whaling ships and lengthened his stay by living off their provisions and the fresh fruit available in the islands. The value of these prizes to the English was estimated to have been in the millions of pounds. Porter put one of these prizes, the British privateer *Georgiana,* under the command of Lieutenant John Downes in order to capture even more prizes. Among the junior officers taking part was Porter's foster son, David Glasgow Farragut, who would become the U.S. Navy's first admiral during the Civil War. Porter continued to enlarge his squadron by arming the prize *Atlantic* with twenty guns and renaming it *Essex Junior.* The *Greenwich* was converted to use as a store ship and placed under the command of Marine Lieutenant John Gamble, who led the marine guards of the *Essex.* Porter was so short of officers he appointed Chaplain David P. Adams as prize master.

Because the condition of the *Essex* had deteriorated during its lengthy cruise, in October Porter determined to overhaul the ship in the Marquesas Islands, some three thousand miles distant and where the British might not search and the crew could enjoy shore leave. Porter brought his squadron to anchor at Nuku Hiva and immediately set to work, while attempting to stave off involvement in the continuing wars of the island population. By December 1813, Porter's men had completed their refitting of the *Essex,* but by that date, the British Admiralty was implementing a plan to destroy a U.S. fort and trading post at Astoria on the Columbia River and had received news of Porter's exploits. HMS *Phoebe,* commanded by Captain James Hillyar, escorted the store ship *Isaac Todd* to Rio de Janeiro, where Rear Admiral Manley Dixon added the sloops of war *Cherub* and *Racoon* to Hillyar's command to ensure success if he met up with *Essex.*

THE CHESAPEAKE CAMPAIGN. In an effort to divert U.S. troops from the Canadian front, British attacks on Chesapeake Bay became an integral part of their strategy to hold off the United States until sufficient forces could be sent from Europe. The idea had merit as Chesapeake Bay was a vulnerable trade and communications link and was close enough to the nation's capital to have caused worry among the nation's politicians. The British Adimiralty provided Admiral John B. Warren with an expeditionary force of twenty-four hundred men, including two battalions of Royal Marines, three hundred infantry from Bermuda, and three hundred French chasseurs who were prisoners of war used as British troops. Colonel Sir Thomas Sydney Beckwith commanded this force while Rear Admiral Sir George Cockburn was sent to augment Warren's block-

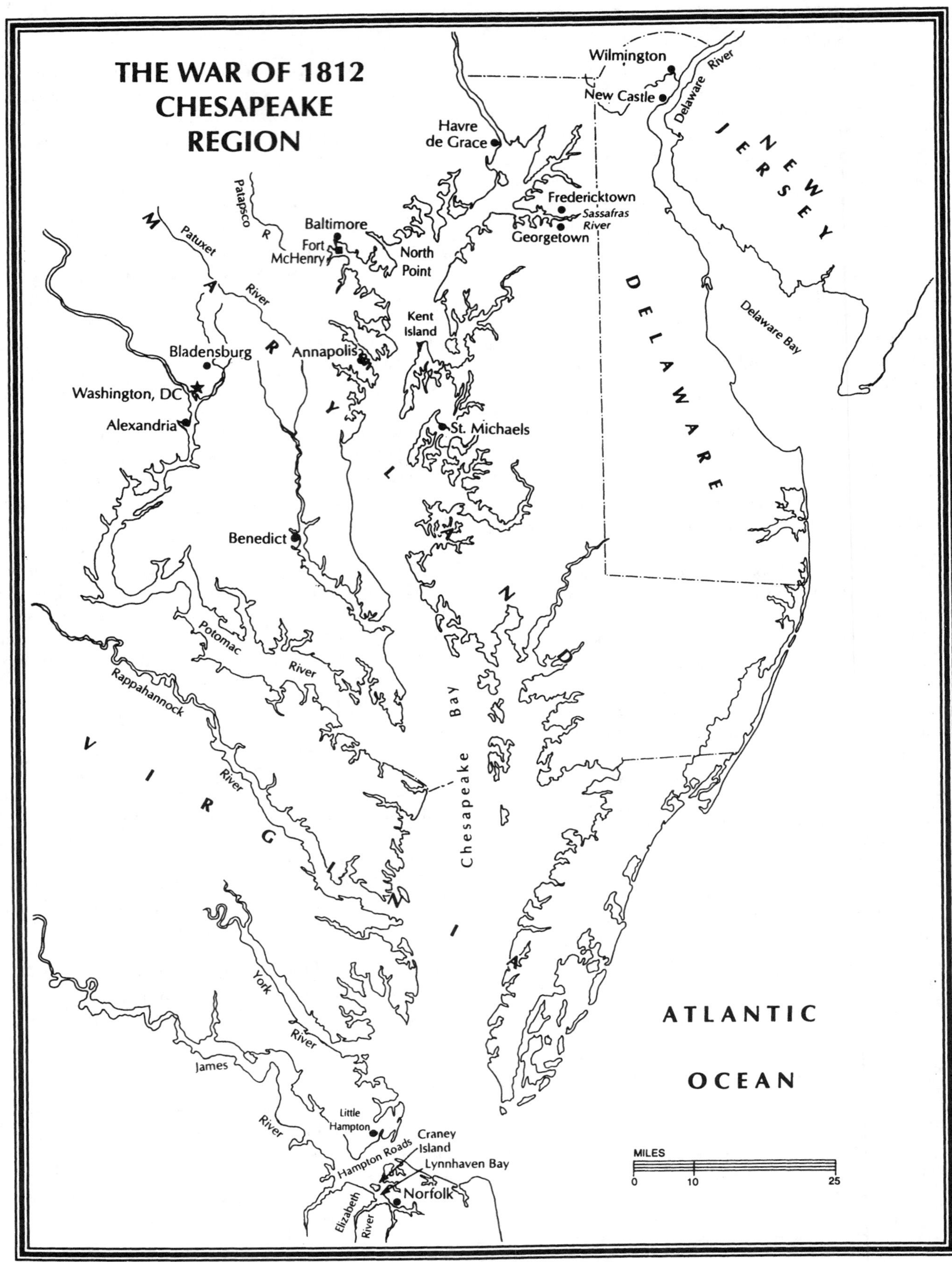
THE WAR OF 1812
CHESAPEAKE
REGION
Wilmington
New Castle
Delaware River
NEW JERSEY
Havre
de Grace
Fredericktown
Sassafras
River
Georgetown
Patapsco
R
Baltimore
Fort
McHenry
North
Point
MARYLAND
Patuxent
River
Kent
Island
DELAWARE
Delaware Bay
Bladensburg
Annapolis
Washington, DC
Alexandria
St. Michaels
Benedict
Potomac
River
Rappahannock
River
VIRGINIA
Chesapeake
Bay
York
River
James
River
Little
Hampton
Craney
Island
Hampton Roads
Lynnhaven Bay
Norfolk
Elizabeth
River
ATLANTIC
OCEAN
MILES
0
10
25

ading force and provide mobility for the land troops. Warren ordered Cockburn to blockade Chesapeake and Delaware bays; capture and destroy shipping in the James, York, Rappahannock, and Potomac Rivers; and in general to punish the Americans.

Cockburn arrived off Lynnhaven Roads in March 1813 and was joined by Admiral Warren from Bermuda two weeks later. In April, Cockburn launched an amphibious raiding expedition that extended as far north as Havre de Grace in Maryland, reaching up the broadest estuaries, raiding plantations, and destroying any communities that dared to offer opposition. During this entire operation, Cockburn faced no serious military opposition, although there was sharp resistance from revenue cutters and Baltimore privateers. The only land forces available were the Virginia and Maryland militias that turned out bravely, although they were usually outnumbered. The best example of this was the Virginia militia's fierce defense of Norfolk on 22 June, when the militia artillery, the gunboat flotilla, and gun crews from the blockaded frigate *Constellation* repelled a British boat raid on the Elizabeth River from Warren's squadron at little cost to the United States and considerable embarrassment for the attackers. Cockburn and Beckwith took their revenge several days later in a savage raid on Little Hampton, near Newport News. It was at this battle that the French chasseurs ran amok, raping and killing innocent civilians. So upset were the British commanders at this breach of discipline that the French were not used again and were shipped back to their English prison camps.

As for maritime defense, there was little at hand save three gunboat squadrons at Norfolk under the command of Captain John Cassin, a division of four privateers temporarily placed under the command of Captain Charles Gordon at Baltimore, and the frigate *Adams,* commanded by Captain Charles Morris. During the summer of 1813, Secretary of the Navy Jones adopted the ideas of revolutionary naval veteran Joshua Barney to build a flotilla of well-armed sailing barges to defend Chesapeake Bay. He was to be given an independent command and to find his seamen among the unemployed seafarers of the bay. As it required time for construction and recruitment, the Chesapeake flotilla did not appear until 1814.

After the Little Hampton attack, the British again worked their way northward in Chesapeake Bay. They reconnoitered but did not attack Annapolis or Baltimore, although the inhabitants of those cities were fearful and prepared for the worst. The British landed on and occupied Kent Island in August and probed the rivers of the eastern shore for points of resistance. The Maryland militia made a creditable stand at Saint Michaels on the Miles River in an artillery action during which the British naval patrol retreated. In September, with his troops and sailors plagued by the heat and sickness, Cockburn withdrew the fleet from Kent Island to the southern reaches of the bay and left for Bermuda. Captain Robert Barrie was left to maintain the blockade in HMS *Dragon,* seventy-four guns, in charge of some frigates, brigs, and schooners. Despite his best efforts, some Baltimore privateers slipped through the blockade on the autumn northerlies.

In a savage raid on Little Hampton, near Newport News, French chasseurs ran amok, raping and killing innocent civilians.

For thousands of citizens in the middle Atlantic states, and particularly those living in tidewater Maryland and Virginia, the events of 1813 brought fear, threats, loss and destruction of property, imprisonment on British vessels, and death for some if, in the path of the enemy, they chose to stand and fight or were unable to escape. British vessels tested the defenses of the bay and up the Potomac. By mid-July, the alarm had spread to Washington, as the British had intended, to "embarrass the enemy in the measures for the further invasion of Canada."

The British withdrew but had learned much that would be useful in the next campaign season—the weakness of the U.S. defenses, the wealth of the area to be plundered, a knowledge of navigation of the rivers of the Chesapeske, and how easy it would be to stage a raid in depth toward the national capital. The officials of Madison's administration might also have taken a lesson from these factors—the strength of its opponent, its seaborne mobility, the vulnerability of the Chesapeake region to such attacks, and the likelihood that, if the war lasted another year, the British would return with a more strategic objective.

THE WAR IN THE SOUTH. While dramatic and tragic events were taking place on the Great Lakes and high seas, the War of 1812 was seemingly quiescent in the south, and yet there were subtle linkages to the northern events that soon bore fruit. On the New Orleans station, naval Captain John Shaw fretted because his requests for funds and seamen were ignored or diminished by the Navy Department. Shaw sensed that one day the British could make a serious incursion through New Orleans into the Mississippi River valley, and he knew that the defenses of the region were vulnerable. U.S. forces acting jointly had seized Fort Charlotte at Mobile, Alabama, from the Spanish in May 1813, extending U.S. control of formerly Spanish territory from Baton Rouge, Louisiana, eastward to the Apalachicola River. This acquisition was made with the acquiesence of President Madison and Congress, even though the United States technically was not at war with Spain.

Gradual incursions into the lands of Creek Indians in Georgia and Alabama provoked the more radical leaders, known as the Red Sticks, into open warfare against white settlers in August 1813, just forty-five miles north of Mobile at Fort Mims, where one thousand Creek led by William Weatherford (Red Eagle) attacked four hundred settlers who had gathered for protection. The result was nearly 250 dead and many more wounded and mutilated. The nearest effective militia was that of Tennessee, under the command of Major General Andrew Jackson, aided by Major Generals John Cocke and John Coffee. As these forces moved into Creek territory, they fell on the Indians at Tallishatchee and Talladega in Alabama early in November 1813. A force of 950 Georgia militia led by Brigadier General John Floyd marched in from the east and attacked a Creek village near Autossee on 29 November. These attacks killed more than 750 Creek in one month.

In early 1814, the Creek had become desperate and fought with great skill and energy, forcing Jackson, Floyd, and others into a retreat until reinforcements came. Strengthened by the arrival of the U.S. Thirty-ninth Regiment and the addition of some friendly Creek and Cherokee, Jackson's troops went forward again and made a devastating attack on a Creek fortification at Horseshoe Bend on the Tallapoosa River on 27 March. This campaign broke the main Creek resistance and on 9 August they were forced to cede over half their lands to the United States in the Treaty of Fort Jackson. As his reward Jackson was appointed a brigadier general in the U.S. Army, with a brevet rank of major general in charge of the Seventh Military District, based in Mobile. This fortuitously placed Jackson as the senior general in command of the Gulf Coast at a time when the British had set in motion a plan to invade the South from the sea.

BRITISH STRATEGY IN 1814

As the third campaign season of the war opened, major events in Europe conspired to enhance Great Britain's force structure in North America. Napoleon's invasion of Russia had collapsed and the allied coalition armies ultimately forced his abdication in April 1814. With this event, Great Britain began to redeploy some of its naval and military forces to North America to transform what had been defensive warfare into a strategic offensive. The sending of troops to Prevost in Canada would allow him to destroy the U.S. naval base at Sackets Harbor, retain Fort Niagara, regain Detroit, and to establish a buffer zone as insurance against future U.S. aggression. Prevost's orders also required him to destroy the U.S. naval establishment on Lake Champlain, a vulnerable route into the northeastern United States.

For the Chesapeake Bay, the Crown sent a new commander and fresh orders. Admiral Warren was replaced by the more aggressive Admiral Alexander Cochrane, whose principal subordinates would be the redoutable Rear Admiral Cockburn and Major General Robert Ross, who had fought in the Peninsular Campaign under the Duke of Wellington. Prevost had written to Cochrane asking that he take revenge, in his area, for the spiteful acts of U.S. forces in the north, principally the destruction at York and Newark in 1813. Cochrane, concurring, had decided that there would be three principal targets—Alexandria, Washington, and Baltimore.

Finally, a major invasion effort would be made at New Orleans by the forces of Cochrane after they had hit their Chesapeake objectives. The Gulf Coast had been the object of speculation by British strategists since the beginning of the war, but most of Great Britain's resources had been committed to the war in Europe. If successful at New Orleans, they could interrupt and control the trade of the Mississippi River valley and bedevil the western movement of the United States in company with Spain, a recent ally in the wars against France. At the very least, New Orleans could be held hostage against the good behavior of the U.S. government. These considerations were uppermost in the thinking of the Earl Bathurst, the principal adviser on military policy for the prince regent, when he ordered the dispatch of military and naval reinforcements to North America in the spring of 1814.

THE BLOCKADE OF NEW ENGLAND. As part of a tougher British policy in dealing with the United States, Admiral Cochrane intended that their former leniency in dealing with the New England states be ended. In place of that policy, he declared on 25 April 1814 that New England would be henceforth blockaded in a "rigorous and effective manner." Beyond this, an offensive strategy was implemented, calling for raids on ports deemed dangerous or deserving of punishment. For example, a raid conducted eight miles up the Connecticut River on 7 April had destroyed twenty-seven vessels valued at $150,000. Cochrane then canceled the trading licenses that had usually been awarded to merchants engaged in the illicit coastal trade between New England and New Brunswick. On 6 June, the Earl

Bathurst issued further orders to Lieutenant General John C. Sherbrooke, governor of New Brunswick and Nova Scotia, to occupy much of the district of Maine to ensure an uninterrupted communication between Halifax and Quebec.

Captain Thomas Hardy had landed troops, occupied Moose Island, and given the inhabitants seven days to take an oath of allegiance to King George III.

In August, Sherbrooke sent an expedition to Moose Island in Passamaquoddy Bay. The town of Eastport had long been a base of operations for smugglers with Canada. In July, Captain Thomas Hardy and his military counterpart, Lieutenant Colonel Andrew Pilkington, had landed troops, occupied the island, and given the inhabitants seven days to take an oath of allegiance to King George III. Farther south, ships from Hardy's squadron were sending raiding parties into Buzzards Bay, Massachusetts, where they attacked a cotton factory. The HMS *Bulwark* sent another boat raid to burn vessels at the mouth of the Saco River in Maine.

Hardy sailed his squadron from Maine into Long Island Sound and took station off Stonington, Connecticut. The British suspected that this town harbored the manufacturers of floating mines known as "Fulton's torpedoes," which were occasionally launched against blockaders in the sound. On 9 August, Hardy's flagship *Ramillies,* along with the *Pactolus, Dispatch,* and *Terror,* attempted to destroy the town by shore bombardment, giving the inhabitants only one hour to evacuate their homes and shops. The men sent their women and children away and then set to work hauling a battery into place. The pacifistic Yankees showed their mettle. During a bombardment exchange of three days, the British squadron suffered more casualties than the town.

On the other hand, the island of Nantucket, thirty miles from the mainland, was totally isolated from Massachusetts, as was Block Island from the government of Rhode Island, and both were forced to capitulate and sign articles of neutrality in order to receive supplies of wood, and they were then given permission to fish to fend off starvation. Nantucketers were also instructed not to pay taxes to the United States; in exchange, the British agreed that Nantucket citizens imprisoned in Dartmoor would be released.

In late August the British moved troops into the Penobscot River, extending their territorial claims to that boundary. The operation was conducted by Rear Admiral Edward Griffith, aided by General Sherbrooke with twenty-five hundred troops lately released from service in Spain and southern France. During the first three days of September, the British captured the rude fort at Castine, the town of Belfast, and Hampden. At Hampden the British encountered the sloop of war *Adams,* commanded by Captain Charles Morris, who found himself trapped in Penobscot Bay when the British squadron appeared. Morris took his ship as far upstream as possible and then removed its guns to set up a shore battery. The British sent a boat attack to destroy the ship, but Morris and his men did their work for them, not wanting their ship to fall into enemy hands. On 12 September, British troops marched into Machias, brushing aside a garrison of U.S. soldiers, and the town was taken without opposition.

Shortly thereafter, Rear Admiral Griffith reported that all of Maine between Passamaquoddy Bay and the Penobscot River was under their control. This was nothing but the truth, for the United States had no naval force to defend the coast and few troops to defend the inland areas, at least in Maine. In large part, of course, this resulted from the attitude of New Englanders toward the war. Unwilling to attack Canada when called upon, or to defend other parts of the United States when they were needed, New Englanders were largely unable also to defend themselves when the threat materialized, and the federal government was by then in no condition to assist.

THE CAMPAIGNS OF 1814

NIAGARA AND LAKE ONTARIO. Even when the shooting died away during winter of 1813–1814 on the Great Lakes, the shipbuilding contest continued. Both the United States and Great Britain recognized that dominance on the lakes ensured victory on land. The British gained the upper hand in this contest during the winter of 1813–1814. Commodore Yeo had pressed forward the construction of larger warships, naming them *Prince Regent,* fifty-eight guns, and *Princess Charlotte,* forty-four guns. He now had eight vessels, armed with 208 guns, manned by 1,620 seamen. In addition, he renamed the rest of his Lake Ontario squadron, perhaps as a way of confusing the enemy. Yeo's squadron was ready for sea before that of Chauncey. In order to interrupt or halt Chauncey's preparations, Yeo and General Drummond made an amphibious thrust at the naval depot at Oswego on the southern side of the lake.

Commodore Chauncey's naval preparations had been seriously delayed by difficulties in transporting supplies to Sackets Harbor. The winter had been unusually mild, and without the accustomed snow and ice, guns and other heavy equipment had to be drawn slowly over muddy roads or diverted by water routes to Oswego where they awaited transport by lake barge to Sackets Harbor. This accumulation of supplies made Oswego an inviting target. The British arrived with nine hundred troops and launched their attack on 6 May. The U.S. defenders, with but three-hundred men, put up a short resistance and then retreated. The attackers burned barracks and provisions and brought away several heavy guns, losing eighteen killed and seventy-four wounded. The Americans lost six killed and thirty-eight wounded. For all their efforts, however, the British had not done their worst. The major U.S. depot was twelve miles away, at Oswego Falls, and it was not touched.

Chauncey ordered the supplies to be moved despite the risk of them falling into British hands. In late May a barge convoy moved a cargo of guns, cables, and shot along the shore and halted at Big Sandy Creek. One barge was captured by Yeo, who determined to obtain the the rest. He sent a boat attack under Captain Stephen Popham with two hundred seamen and marines into the Big Sandy. As they moved upstream, they were ambushed on 30 May by a company of riflemen and Oneida Indians. Captain Popham was captured with his entire unit, suffering eighteen killed and fifty wounded, a serious setback for Commodore Yeo, who could ill afford to lose naval personnel.

Riall had been expecting the U.S. troops to weaken and run as soon as confronted with a show of force. This did not happen.

Meanwhile, Chauncey's shipwrights were completing the construction of four new vessels, the frigates *Superior,* fifty-eight guns, and *Mohawk,* forty-two guns, and the brigs *Jefferson* and *Jones,* both twenty-two guns. These vessels gave Chauncey eight purpose-built vessels, equal in number to Yeo's, but larger and carrying more armament. In order to provide seamen and guns for the lakes, the Navy Department was obliged to remove them from ships on the seacoast, such as the frigates *Congress* and *Macedonian,* which were unable to get to sea because of the blockade. Chauncey had hoped to complete his preparations by 1 July, in order to assist the army's operations across the Niagara River. Unfortunately, at just that time, the commodore became ill of lake fever, and the squadron remained at Sackets Harbor another three weeks, even though it was urgently needed at Fort Niagara.

At the War Department, Secretary of War Armstrong finally removed the aging revolutionary war veterans Dearborn and Wilkinson from command. In their places, Armstrong put Major General George Izard in charge at Plattsburgh and appointed Major General Jacob Brown to command at Sackets Harbor, seconded by Brigadier General Edmund P. Gaines. The War Department sent Brigadier General Winfield Scott to Buffalo to commence the training of troops for the summer campaign. Secretary Armstrong, unfortunately, had no use for his only successful general, William Henry Harrison, objecting to his political ambitions and non-regular army status. Feeling unappreciated, with his troops sent elsewhere, Harrison resigned from command of Military District No. 8, his place being given to Andrew Jackson, whose volunteer status and ambitions were similar but less threatening.

As in 1813, Armstrong wavered on the question of whether to attack Kingston, Montreal, or Niagara, and allowed his subordinates sufficient scope to make this strategic decision for him. General Brown and Commodore Chauncey argued that Kingston was too strong for them and that another attempt at Niagara might succeed where it had failed the previous year. At the same time, Madison's cabinet approved a naval expedition from Lake Erie into Lake Huron under the command of Captain Arthur Sinclair, with the objective of recapturing Mackinac Island and preventing resurrection of the British-Indian alliance in the Northwest. The U.S. plan for 1814, finally approved on 7 June, envisaged that General Brown would lead five thousand regulars and three thousand volunteers in an attack on Fort Erie, capturing other outposts on the Niagara peninsula and then concentrating on Burlington and York.

The Americans set their plan in motion on 3 July, with two brigades crossing the Niagara River near Fort Erie, Scott landing below Erie and Brigadier General Eleazar Ripley above. Their Indian allies penetrated to the rear of the fort and within hours, the two companies of redcoats holding Fort Erie surrendered. Scott's brigade marched northward the next day toward the Chippewa River, where he found five companies of General Phineas Riall's Royal Scots encamped on the far side. Between General Scott and the British lay a flat plain divided by a narrow water course named Street's Creek. On 5 July, Scott deployed his battalions and ordered an advance just as Riall decided to attack over the Street's Creek bridge and into the plain beyond. Riall had been expecting the U.S. troops to weaken and run as soon as confronted with a show of force. This did not happen and the British met a withering fire from muskets and artillery, losing 148 killed and 321 wounded, compared to 48 Americans killed and 227 wounded. Scott's months of training had instilled discipline under fire, and the Americans held their ground. Riall's oft-quoted remark on that occasion, "Those are regulars, by God," was taken by Americans as a compliment, for it showed how far their battlefield behavior had improved. (In another tradition-making incident, the battle-dress worn by Scott's troops was of gray cloth, because the blue commonly used for U.S. uniforms was not available. In honor of this occasion, gray became the uniform color adopted for West Point cadets.)

Riall retreated from Chippewa to Fort George, while Scott, now with General Brown present, moved forward to occupy Queenston Heights and await reinforcements. At this point, the Americans were aware that the British were rushing reinforcements by water to Fort George, and Brown believed that Commodore Chauncey had promised to send his squadron to cut off these reinforcements and to use the long guns of the fleet against the forts. Chauncey, however, had not moved from Sackets Harbor, even though Brown expected him to appear.

When no help arrived, Brown ordered a withdrawal to Chippewa to reprovision before advancing to Burlington. An advanced guard of one thousand British regulars marched under Lieutenant Colonel Thomas Pearson to Lundy's Lane, about a mile from the Portage Road near Niagara Falls. General Riall soon followed with another fifteen hundred and an artillery battery. General Drummond arrived at Fort George with troops from York and immediately sent a regiment to support Riall.

General Scott, late on the afternoon of 25 July, moved up with his brigade from Chippewa to Lundy's Lane, where he quickly attacked a force about equal in strength to his own. He had driven back the British left and stormed the battery when Drummond's troops arrived to stiffen the enemy's opposition. A fierce and confusing battle then raged into the night. Brigades led by Ripley and Colonel Peter Porter came to Scott's assistance while hand-to-hand battles showed a grim determination on both sides. General officers on both sides were wounded, Riall and Drummond for the British and Brown and Scott for the Americans. Brigadier General Ripley took over battlefield command for the Americans. The drawn battle ended in mutual disen-

In early July 1814, General Winfield Scott (on horse) and his army advanced on five companies of British troops encamped near the Chippewa River. The British were forced to retreat and the Americans moved forward to occupy Queenstown Heights. (National Archives/engraving after F. O. C. Darley)

gagement that night, but Ripley withdrew the next day, leaving the field to Drummond, who could then claim a tactical victory. The American casualties were 171 killed, 572 wounded, and 110 missing; the British suffered 84 killed, 559 wounded, and 42 taken prisoner.

General Brown now ordered that U.S. troops defend Fort Erie as a foothold on the British side of the Niagara. Ripley, who had argued for a return to the U.S. side, was returned to the command of his brigade, and Brigadier General Gaines came from Sackets Harbor to take command at Fort Erie until Brown and Scott could recover from their wounds. Drummond moved his troops to invest Fort Erie but refrained from attacking until heavy guns could be brought up.

Meanwhile, his health recovered and ships in full readiness, Commodore Chauncey had finally sailed from Sackets Harbor and, on 5 August, established a blockade of Fort Niagara at the river's mouth. Had Chauncey arrived two weeks earlier, he might have prevented British reinforcments arriving from York and Burlington with a very different result for the Americans at Lundy's Lane. Nevertheless, although deprived of resupply, Drummond ordered an attack on the strongly defended position at Fort Erie. The Americans not only held out but inflicted heavy casualties on the British during an assault on 15 August. Still, Drummond maintained a siege on Fort Erie until Brown, who had reassumed command when Gaines was wounded, ordered a sortie on 17 September to destroy enemy gun emplacements. This attack surprised the besiegers, spiked their guns, and destroyed their ammunition. Drummond ordered his troops to fall back on Chippewa and, because there was no American pursuit, the Niagara campaign of 1814 ended without much change in the positions of the opponents. The British still held Fort Niagara, but the Americans had gained Fort Erie by dint of considerable sacrifice. Yet even this was of no enduring usefulness, because on 5 November, Major General Izard blew up the fort and crossed the Niagara to the American side.

THE WAR IN THE NORTHWEST. In two minor operations in the Northwest, the Americans were repulsed, on Lake Huron and at Prairie du Chien, Wisconsin.

In the westernmost military action of the War of 1812, a U.S. force of three hundred men, led by Governor William Clark of the Missouri Territory, made their way up the Mississippi River to probe the fur-trading territory controlled by Winnebago and Sioux Indians. Clark's force seized the island of Prairie du Chien and proceeded to kill some of the Winnebago leaders. The British Commandant at Mackinac, Lieutenant Colonel Robert McDouall, decided that he had to send a retaliatory expedition to Prairie du Chien if the British were to retain the loyalty of their Indian allies. Relying on the leadership of William McKay, a Northwest Company employee, McDouall sent off a force of Michigan fencibles, Canadian voyageurs, and Sioux, Winnebago, Menominee, and Chippewa Indians. When the British-Indian force arrived, it outnumbered Clark's although his fort was defended by a gunboat. After a brief standoff on 17–19 July, a deal was struck providing for surrender and parole for the Americans.

Captain Sinclair had sailed in early June from Lake Erie with the brigs *Saint Lawrence* and *Niagara,* the schooners *Tigress* and *Scorpion,* and two smaller gunboats with the mission of recapturing Fort Mackinac at the head of Lake Huron. Sinclair took with him seven hundred troops led by Lieutenant Colonel Croghan, who had led the defense of Fort Stephenson. Sinclair's attempted assault on Mackinac on 26 July did not succeed because he and Croghan failed to appreciate the terrain of Michilimackinac Island and underestimated the abilities of its defenders. Lieutenant Colonel McDouall hit Croghan's force just after they landed and pushed them to the water's edge, inflicting thirteen dead and fifty-one wounded. Sinclair withdrew to seek other targets that could undermine his enemy. Sailing into Georgian Bay on 14 August, Sinclair attacked a blockhouse at the mouth of the Nottawasaga River and destroyed the supply sloop *Nancy* that was the fragile link between Mackinac and Montreal. This accomplished, Sinclair sailed for Lake Erie, leaving his schooners to blockade Mackinac Island until the autumn gales would drive them from the lake. To his later embarrassment, Sinclair learned that in September the British captured his schooners, using a night boat attack to storm the *Tigress* and then taking it to approach and capture the unsuspecting *Scorpion.*

Another American expedition moved up the Mississippi River in September 1814. Led by Major Zachary Taylor, this force of three hundred intended to attack Indians assembled near the confluence of the Rock River with the Mississippi. Taylor soon discovered that he was opposed by more than a thousand Indians and a small 3-pounder cannon sent by the British to Prairie du Chien. After Taylor's boat expedition came under fire he retreated to the mouth of the Des Moines River, burned a fort there, and descended the Mississippi to St. Louis.

THE BATTLE FOR LAKE CHAMPLAIN AND PLATTSBURGH. At the time Drummond was pressing the siege of Fort Erie, another, considerably larger British force was on the verge of invading U.S. territory several hundred miles to the east. The Lake Champlain

Valley, a valuable and vulnerable waterway, led directly south to Lake George and the Hudson River. A successful British effort at Lake Champlain could have led to distressing events for the United States. Governor General Prevost received sizable reinforcements from Europe during the spring and summer months of 1814. Some of the Duke of Wellington's leading generals accompanied the troops. Prevost selected Major General Francis de Rottenberg as overall commander of the army, while the brigades were commanded by Major Generals Manley Power, Thomas Brisbane, and Frederick Robinson. Both Prevost and Rottenberg, although experienced in Canadian-American warfare, were far less battle-seasoned than the European veterans.

Prevost ordered his army of more than ten thousand to march southward toward New York State in late August. The troops crossed the boundary on 1 September and surged ahead, almost impervious to the defensive annoyances such as the U.S. militia directed at them. Within five days, they were on the outskirts of Plattsburgh. The U.S. defenders were now led by Brigadier General Alexander Macomb, who withdrew south of the Saranac River that divided the town.

On 10 August, Secretary of War Armstrong had ordered the previous commander, Major General Izard, to move westward with four thousand regulars toward the Saint Lawrence to threaten British communications with Niagara. This order appeared incomprehensible to those on the scene, but even after Armstrong was informed of the situation, he refused to change his mind. In part, this may have been caused by his preoccupation with Admiral Cochrane's impending attack on Washington, D.C., although even this excuse is difficult to credit. Izard had been extremely reluctant to remove this force from Plattsburgh because he was aware of the buildup of forces south of Montreal. Because no countermanding orders arrived, Izard marched out on 29 August for Sackets Harbor. He left behind only fifteen hundred in Macomb's command to defend Plattsburgh.

Prevost, on the verge of attacking across the Saranac, postponed the thrust on 6 September for two reasons. He did not know the location of the U.S. defenses, and he did not want to move without first being assured that the British naval commander, Captain George Downie, had control of the lake. At this point, Prevost pressured Downie to attack Macdonough's squadron, although Downie was barely ready. The mood was reminiscent of Proctor's goading of Barclay on Lake Erie. Downie had engaged in the same type of shipbuilding contest with Macdonough that had determined the pace of fighting on Lake Ontario. Downie's squadron numbered sixteen vessels, although most of them were humble indeed. His strongest vessels were the frigate *Confiance,* thirty-eight guns; the brig *Linnet,* sixteen guns; and the sloops *Chubb* and *Finch,* both eleven guns. These were supported by twelve gunboats, each mounting two guns, a long gun and a carronade.

Macdonough's squadron was made up of the corvette *Saratoga,* twenty-six guns; the brig *Eagle,* twenty guns; the schooner *Ticonderoga,* seventeen guns; and the sloop *Preble,* seven guns. He was supported by six row galleys of two guns, and four row galleys with one gun each. Macdonough's shipbuilding effort was greatly aided by Noah and Adam Brown and their carpenters from Erie, Pennsylvania. Following the Battle of Lake Erie, with Henry Eckford's men still needed at Sackets Harbor, Secretary of the Navy Jones had transferred the Browns and their men to Vergennes, Vermont, where most of the shipbuilding took place.

General Macomb marched and countermarched his troops to make them seem double their number and sent deceptive messages indicating reinforcements were on the way.

Sensing that battle was imminent, Macdonough brought his squadron into Plattsburgh Bay, under Macomb's protecting guns and anchored so that Downie's squadron had to enter the bay and fight on Macdonough's terms. The Americans also attached spring lines to their anchor cables and dropped kedge anchors in order to be able to turn ship in the absence of wind when the time came. Prevost's impatient prodding finally brought Downie's squadron into Plattsburgh Bay on 11 September, expecting that Prevost would start his attack simultaneously. This was an empty promise, because Prevost's artillery was not yet in position. With the battle joined, superior U.S. gunnery and the act of turning on the spring lines of the ships to bring fresh batteries to bear won the day for Macdonough. Commodore Downie was killed early in the action, but the battle continued for more than two hours. Finally, the other British commanders followed Captain Daniel Pring's example in surrendering to Macdonough on board the *Saratoga.*

General Macomb had prepared for the worst by using every method in the defender's book. He made the most of his few men, welcomed volunteers from Vermont, camouflaged roads, marched and countermarched his troops to make them seem double their number, sent deceptive messages indicating reinforcements were on the way, and burned houses to clear fields of fire. Perhaps no one was more surprised than Macomb when he observed the British division suddenly abandon the siege when news of Macdonough's victory became known. The much-disappointed British campaigners were ordered to turn in their tracks and return to Montreal. Prevost, a cautious man to begin with, had decided that he could not possibly risk his army and his reputation if he did not control Lake Champlain with its supply and communications links to Canada.

At Plattsburgh, Macomb and Macdonough had won a strategic defensive victory. Prevost's thrust was potentially the most dangerous of the war, as it could have divided New York State, put New England under British control, and held New York City hostage. As it was, the British failure at Plattsburgh was the best news of 1814 for war-weary Americans. It gave heart to a discouraged nation and jeopardized the British temporizing at the Ghent peace conference.

THE BURNING OF WASHINGTON

The most disheartening event of 1814 for most Americans was the embarrassment of learning that the national capital had been for a short time in enemy hands, that the president and his cabinet had fled, and that the defenders of the region had totally failed to prevent a British army from marching all the way from the Patuxent River to Bladensburg, Maryland. The portents of this astounding event were, however, evident in the British summer campaign of 1813.

The blockading ships at Hampton Roads still kept the frigate *Constellation* at bay, but they had not been fully vigilant. Captain Morris' frigate *Adams* had managed to slip past the British on 18 January 1814 and escape into the Atlantic after more than a year of trying. A long cruise took Morris to the coast of Africa and then into the North Atlantic, but he captured only a few prizes, running often into tightly escorted convoys. He ended his voyage in the Penobscot River, defending his ship against a boat attack.

Expecting the British to return to their amphibious raids, the Navy Department had authorized Commodore Barney to build and fit out a flotilla of gunboats for the defense of Chesapeake Bay. These were mainly row galleys carrying from twenty to forty men with one or two long guns as a battery. The sloop *Scorpion* served as Barney's flotilla flagship. The most successful work of the flotilla was Barney's defensive action in Saint Leonard's Creek on 1 June 1814. The *Scorpion* and fourteen galleys chased the British schooner *Saint Lawrence* and seven ship's boats off the mouth of the Patuxent River until the *Dragon* came up and chased Barney's boats into the Patuxent. As other British vessels joined, Barney withdrew up Saint Leonard's Creek. A cat-and-mouse game ensued for three days until a battery of two long 18-pounders, commanded by U.S. Army Colonel Decius Wadsworth and marine Colonel Samuel Miller, drove off the frigates *Loire* and *Narcissus,* allowing the flotilla to escape.

Shortly thereafter, the British began their long-planned attack on Washington, Alexandria, and Baltimore, cities they had bypassed the previous year. Cochrane ordered Major General Ross and Rear Admiral Cockburn to move five thousand troops by barge up the Patuxent as far as Nottingham, then to march on Washington. Meanwhile, he sent a naval expedition up the Potomac led by Captain James Alexander Gordon in the *Seahorse,* in company with the frigate *Euryalus*; the bomb-ships *Devastation, Aetna,* and *Meteor*; and the rocket-launcher *Erebus.* The British landed at Benedict, Maryland, on 19 August and commenced their march on Washington the next day. Barney blew up his flotilla in the Upper Patuxent on 22 August as the British arrived at Nottingham. To reach Washington, the British had to cross the Eastern Branch of the Potomac (Anacostia River), but the navy yard bridge had been destroyed. They marched north to Bladensburg, where they found the U.S. militia making a stand. As soon as the British made a show of their determination to cross the river, the Maryland and District of Columbia militia began a retreat across country that has been ridiculed as the "Bladensburg Races." Barney gained everlasting fame as the commander of the one unit that stood and fought—four hundred sailors and marines from his Potomac flotilla, assisted by officers and men from the Marine Barracks at 8th and I Streets in Washington.

Ross's troops overwhelmed the defenders in the Battle of Bladensburg on 24 August and quickly marched the few miles to Washington, where they burned many public buildings, including the Capitol, the White House, and any other building from which there was opposition. Captain Thomas Tingey, commandant of the Washington Navy Yard, burned his own establishment rather than see it fall into enemy hands. Among the victims of this patriotic conflagration were the old frigates *New York* and *Boston,* as well as the just-completed *Columbia* and *Argus.* The British expedition left a day later, almost as quickly as it had come, recalled by Admiral Cochrane, who was ignorant of the ease of their overwhelming success. Captain Gordon's squadron ascended the Potomac to Alexandria, where they forced that city to open its storehouses by spreading fear of total destruction if the citizens did not peaceably comply. The Virginia militia and some notably unemployed U.S. Navy officers, namely Commodores John Rodgers, David Porter, and Oliver Hazard Perry, harassed the squadron's departure with fire rafts and bombardment from shore batteries, but without significantly damaging Gordon's ships.

Cochrane met at Baltimore a well-thought-out defense supported by citizens committed to the survival, not just of themselves, but of their community.

Cochrane's final target in the Chesapeake Bay was Baltimore, the city that produced the many privateers that so bedeviled British commerce on the high seas. Baltimore was a wealthy commercial city in 1814, capable of producing a hefty ransom, an attractive lure for old seadogs Cochrane and Cockburn whose personal fortunes owed much to prize money earned by the captains and squadrons in their control. When Cochrane's Chesapeake fleet had retrieved its Washington and Alexandria expeditions, he made for Baltimore. He met at Baltimore the kind of defense other cities could have made, a well-thought-out plan supported by citizens committed to the survival, not just of themselves, but of their collective community. Maryland militia General Samuel Smith, aided by regular army and navy officers, met the British at every point with determined resistance.

When General Ross and Rear Admiral Cockburn landed on North Point, twelve miles from Baltimore, trenches and earthworks had already been prepared and troops deployed to obstruct their progress. Ships were sunk in the channel of the Patapsco River approaches to Baltimore and shore batteries were manned and ready to contest access to the river. Admiral Cochrane had begun to have second thoughts about attempting Baltimore, but Cockburn and Ross were hot for action. Ross's troops, numbering thirty-five hundred effectives, landed on 12 September and began their march toward the city. Even before they did so, Smith ordered Brigadier General John Stricker to advance along North Point with thirty-two hundred men and artillery. On the morning of 12 September, Ross was in the advance guard when it met with Stricker's skirmishers. Ross fell, fatally wounded, on receiving a musket ball in his chest. Colonel Arthur Brooke, his second-in-command, took over and brought up reinforcements. After a firefight, the Marylanders retreated to take up defensive positions in front of the Baltimore defense lines.

On the next day, Colonel Brooke advanced again but then paused and called for support from the fleet so that he could storm the entrenchments. The fleet came up as close to Fort McHenry as it could and commenced a twenty-four-hour bombardment. The fort's defenses held and the defenders produced a dangerous and accurate counterfire. The Americans kept up a stiff resistance from another defensive position, Fort Covington on the Patapsco, which prevented the British from encircling Fort McHenry from their left. It was at this time that Francis Scott Key, who had visited Cochrane's fleet to ask for the release of an American doctor from the fleet, wrote his verses on the "Star Spangled Banner," the huge U.S. flag that flew from Fort McHenry throughout the evening's bombardment. On the morning of 14 September, the British withdrew from their positions on North Point and rejoined the fleet, and Cochrane ordered his fleet to sail down the bay.

Americans viewed the defense of Baltimore as a victory against a larger, more mobile, and more powerful enemy. Certainly they had every right to think so, even though there had not been a true test of strength. Despite the successes at Washington and Alexandria, U.S. defensive victories at Baltimore and Plattsburgh, together with the stalemate on the Niagara, indicated that even with infusions of officers, men, and ships from Europe, the British were unable to muster the overwhelming strength that would be needed to win a convincing victory in the United States.

THE ATTACK ON NEW ORLEANS

With British and U.S. commissioners negotiating at Ghent, Belgium, since the summer of 1814, and this process being affected by war news, for good or ill, British plans for a final effort to win the war on land and in the conference room went forward. The Earl of Bathurst had previously given approval for an effort at New Orleans, Louisiana, although it remained for the on-scene commander to work out the details. Admiral Cochrane urged the British Admiralty in June 1814 to provide three thousand troops, which he would land at Mobile. From there, he would enlist allies from disaffected French, Spaniards, and Creek Indians. He intended to march from Mobile to Baton Rouge and from there to New Orleans, but he also requested shallow draft boats for navigation in the Mississippi Sounds. Cochrane had begun to make his arrangements by sending the frigates *Orpheus* and *Shelburne* to the Gulf Coast, where they were to open communications with the Creek. He also sent Major Edward Nicholls of the Royal Marines to take a party of one hundred marines and firearms and an artillery piece to train the Indians and to encourage slaves to flee from plantations to British protection.

These plans had been set in motion in August, when Cochrane received the admiralty's final approval. He was to use General Ross's troops, as well as 2,130 additional men sailing directly from Europe. These would be sent to Jamaica, to arrive about the middle of November. After Ross's death at Baltimore, the Earl of Bathurst gave command of the New Orleans troops to Major General Edward Pakenham, brother-in-law of the Duke of Wellington, although Cochrane was still in overall command of the expedition. It was notable that Rear Admiral Cockburn was not designated to take part in the expedition; rather, he was to create a diversion on the Georgia—South Carolina coast. As an admiral, Cockburn made a fine marine and amphibious warfare was his forte. Relegation to a minor coastal diversion when a major attack was being launched at New Orleans indicated Cochrane's displeasure at Cockburn's aggressive use of the men at his disposal. Although it is difficult to identify precisely the source of Cochrane's discontent, it may have been the death of General Ross, who usually found Cockburn's arguments convincing.

The activities of Nicholls and other British agents in arming and organizing the Indians of the Gulf Coast rapidly became known to General Jackson in Alabama and U.S. military and naval officials in New Orleans. In late August, Jackson began to summon assistance from regional governors and to warn governor William Claiborne of Louisiana to take steps for strengthening his defenses at New Orleans. In particular, Fort Bowyer at the mouth of Mobile Bay needed strengthening. Jackson sent Major William Lawrence to Fort Bowyer to make it ready. No sooner had he done so than on 12 September a squadron of four British corvettes—*Hermes,* twenty-two guns; *Carron,* twenty guns; *Childers,* eighteen guns; and *Sophia,* eighteen guns—arrived from Pensacola and proceeded to open fire. The *Hermes* anchor cable was shot away and the ship grounded on a sandbar. Unable to maneuver, the ship was quickly disabled by cannon fire from the fort. The crew abandoned and blew it up that evening. The squadron withdrew, having suffered a severe setback that would ultimately affect Cochrane's invasion plans, which eliminated the possibility that he could seize control of the coast and march from Mobile to New Orleans.

In another gambit, the British attempted to win over the pirates at Lake Barataria, a bayou hiding place for Jean Lafitte's pirates and privateers who were preying on Spanish shipping while flying the colors of the newly created republics in South America. Captain Nicholas Lockyer of the *Sophia* attempted to strike a bargain in September, offering land and colonist status if they would assist the British in attacking New Orleans. Lafitte spurned the offer and reported it to the U.S. authorities. Nevertheless, sensing a weakness at that place, Master Commandant Daniel T. Patterson attacked and destroyed the Barataria encampment on 11 September.

The Battle of New Orleans. British forces attacked New Orleans on 8 January 1815, two weeks after the Treaty of Ghent was signed. The advancing British columns never made it past General Andrew Jackson's line of artillery. (National Archives/engraving from a sketch by Latour)

Despite this action, Lafitte and his men ended up supporting Jackson.

The suspicion that the British were planning a major attack on the Gulf Coast was strongly felt among U.S. naval officers assigned to the New Orleans station. Captain John Shaw, on being relieved by Captain Patterson in late 1813, shared this view with his young successor. Patterson, in September, wrote a now-famous letter to Jackson in which he predicted the route the British would take in assaulting the city. Ultimately, Cochrane's flotilla arrived from Jamaica at the chain of islands east of Lake Borgne from which it launched the attack, through a pass blockaded by U.S. naval gunboats.

The defense of Pass Christian by Lieutenant Thomas Catesby Jones on 14 December was one of the major reasons that Jackson was able to rescue New Orleans from its predicament. With Jones's gunboats blocking the shortest route to New Orleans, Cochrane's fleet delayed its preparations in order to send a flotilla of forty-five barges and 980 men against the U.S. gunboats. The battle was hard-fought, with severe losses sustained on the British side, but their overwhelming numbers carried the day. All of Jones's vessels were captured, but they had held up the British progress toward New Orleans by seven to ten days, allowing Jackson more time to set up the defenses on the Mississippi. Once in control of the pass and Lake Borgne, the British had to plan their descent on the city. They decided to proceed to Pea Island, where they established a temporary camp while more men were brought from the fleet. The troops were ferried laboriously across fifty miles of water in shallow-draft barges and gunboats.

General Jackson, meanwhile, had arrived in New Orleans in early December and immediately made a tour of inspection. He soon identified the weaknesses of his position and commenced to set up defense lines. It was not until 21 December that the British began to move their troops from Pea Island to the bayoux, penetrating the Villere plantation on 23 December and establishing themselves on a line perpendicular to the river about seven miles below the city. Jackson attacked immediately on the 23rd, at night, with more than two thousand men, including nine hundred regulars, 550 mounted infantry under General Coffee, and 650 Louisiana and Mississippi militiamen, and supported by the U.S. Navy schooner *Carolina,* fourteen guns, commanded by Master Commandant John Henley. The *Carolina* sprayed grapeshot on the British troops who were bivouacked on the flood plain below the levee. The British still lacked artillery and were unable to respond.

The enemy's position was constantly improving as more and more men and munitions were brought in from Cochrane's fleet. General Pakenham arrived to take field command on 26 December, and by the next day, the British had set up a battery that fired hot shot at the *Carolina* and finally blew it up. The *Carolina*'s gun crews were transferred to land artillery opposing the British left and continued to work in Jackson's line. Another U.S. naval vessel, the corvette *Louisiana,* mounting sixteen 24-pounders, escaped injury and continued to serve well on the river, sending hundreds of rounds into the British flank for the remainder of the battle. By this time, Jackson's line across the plain was fully defended, and it was obvious to Pakenham that he required more 18- and 24-pounder artillery. They experienced great difficulty in bringing such heavy pieces of ordnance and ammunition in by small boats through swampy terrain.

The British attempted to win over the pirates at Lake Barataria, a bayou hiding place for Jean Lafitte's pirates and privateers who were preying on Spanish shipping.

Pakenham received more reinforcements in the person of major General John Lambert's troops, who arrived on 6 January 1815. By this time, Pakenham's engineers had conceived a plan of outflanking Jackson's line by cutting through the levee and pushing boats and supplies across the Mississippi to the right bank. If this position were secured, Colonel William Thornton would take his men and charge the unprotected battery on Jackson's right, threatening his line with enfilade gunfire. With this plan, the principal Battle of New Orleans commenced on 8 January, with Pakenham ordering a frontal assault in a swirling fog.

It was a plan born of desperation at the optimum time in a worst-case situation for the invader. Jackson's defenses could only have gotten stronger, while the British were in a poorly chosen site that was vulnerable and difficult to reinforce and resupply. Major General Sir Samuel Gibbs led a column of twenty-two hundred men against the left of Jackson's line, which was defended by General William Carroll heading the Tennessee and Kentucky militia. At the same time, British Major General John Keane, commanding a column of twelve hundred men, attacked on the right. Major General Lambert was to hold twelve hundred men in reserve.

Gibbs's column marched through swirling mist and fog into the unrelenting fire of a battery of 18-pounders while being raked by other batteries firing solid shot and grape. The British advance halted and reformed under the most difficult conditions, but when just under the U.S. guns, General Gibbs was badly wounded. Pakenham, perceiving the troops faltering, rode up to rally them and was mortally wounded as well. Even Lambert's reserve was committed and advanced but faltered under the hail of lead. General Keane, advancing on the levee, reached a small battery, but his men were then open to a tremendous rifle and cannon fire from Jackson's right. They arrived at a deep ditch before the U.S. line, were driven back, and General Keane fell, to be carried from the field. Most of his men were captured, wounded, or killed. Meanwhile, Thornton's men had succeeded in crossing the river and moved forward on the right bank, overrunning a battery manned by naval personnel. They posed a serious threat to Jackson, who sent troops back to New Orleans to cross the river and drive them back. Lambert, however, was in no mood to continue the battle, having lost many senior officers, hundreds of men dead, and more than twelve hundred wounded in the main attack. He saw it would be folly to continue with such losses and soon withdrew his men to the fleet.

It was a plan born of desperation at the optimum time in a worst-case situation.

The struggle of 7–8 January climaxed the Battle of New Orleans, although it was fought two weeks after the Treaty of Ghent was signed and before news of the agreement reached the United States. While this was the last land battle of the war, several sea battles remained to be fought. It took five months before all the far-flung British and U.S. naval units learned of the "peace of Christmas."

FINAL NAVAL ACTIONS

Although several of the U.S. Navy's frigates and smaller fighting vessels were effectively blockaded during 1814–1815, others were able to slip through the Royal Navy's cordon and seek out targets in Great Britain's large merchant fleet. Among the more notable naval events of this period were the cruises of the frigate *Constitution,* the end of the *Essex* saga, the exploits of the sloop of war *Wasp,* and the cruise of the sloop of war *Peacock.* At the same time, the United States lost the frigate *President,* the sloop of war *Frolic,* the brig *Rattlesnake,* and the brig *Syren.* Privateers still sailed from U.S. ports and some achieved notable success, including the schooner *General Armstrong,* the brig *Prince de Neufchâtel,* and the brig *Chasseur.*

When the *Constitution* arrived in Boston on 27 March 1813, after its engagement with the *Java* the previous December, it entered a period of repair and refitting, not sailing again until 1 January 1814. Now under the command of Captain Charles Stewart, it headed south for Barbados and the coast of South America. During this cruise, it captured the schooner *Pictou* (14 February) and several merchant ships off the Guianas. On its return in April, it had a narrow escape while approaching Massachusetts Bay. The two British blockading ships were the *Tenedos* and *Junon,* both thirty-eight guns, working closely together. Attempting to prevent the *Constitution* from entering Boston harbor, they crowded on sail, but Stewart reckoned his chances of getting to that port were poor, so he altered course for Marblehead and entered the narrow, fortified channel, just ahead of his pursuers. The British ships withdrew, not wanting to risk their ships in confined waters. The *Constitution* sailed unmolested for Boston some days later but did not sortie again until 17 December, after it was reported that the three blockading frigates were off station. The *Constitution* sailed for Europe, visited the Bay of Biscay and Portuguese waters, and was searching for prizes off the Madeira Islands when it encountered the frigate *Cyane,* thirty-four guns, and the corvette *Levant,* twenty-one guns, on 20 February. Stewart demonstrated excellent tactics and seamanship, defeating these two ships in a single night action. Proceeding with his two prizes to the Cape Verde Islands, Stewart discovered a British frigate squadron made up of the *Acasta,* forty guns; *Leander,* fifty guns; and *Newcastle,* fifty guns. They gave chase but he escaped with the *Cyane* and brought it to the United States. The pursuing squadron overtook and recaptured the *Levant.*

Commodore David Porter's *Essex* was overtaken in February 1814 at Valparaiso by Captain James Hillyar's British squadron of the *Phoebe* and the *Cherub.* Porter's prize *Essex Junior* was present, and, hoping to allow it to escape, on 28 March he took the *Essex* out to challenge Hillyar, who was blockading the port. As he was doing so, a squall struck and carried away his main topmast. In this crippled condition, Porter attempted to reenter Valparaiso, but the wind would not permit it, and he anchored in a small harbor three miles from Valparaiso, half a mile from shore. Momentarily, he hoped that the British would observe Chilean neutrality and refrain from attacking until his own vessel was repaired and could accept battle in international waters. At this vulnerable moment, Hillyar brought down the *Phoebe* and *Cherub* and opened fire on the *Essex* with

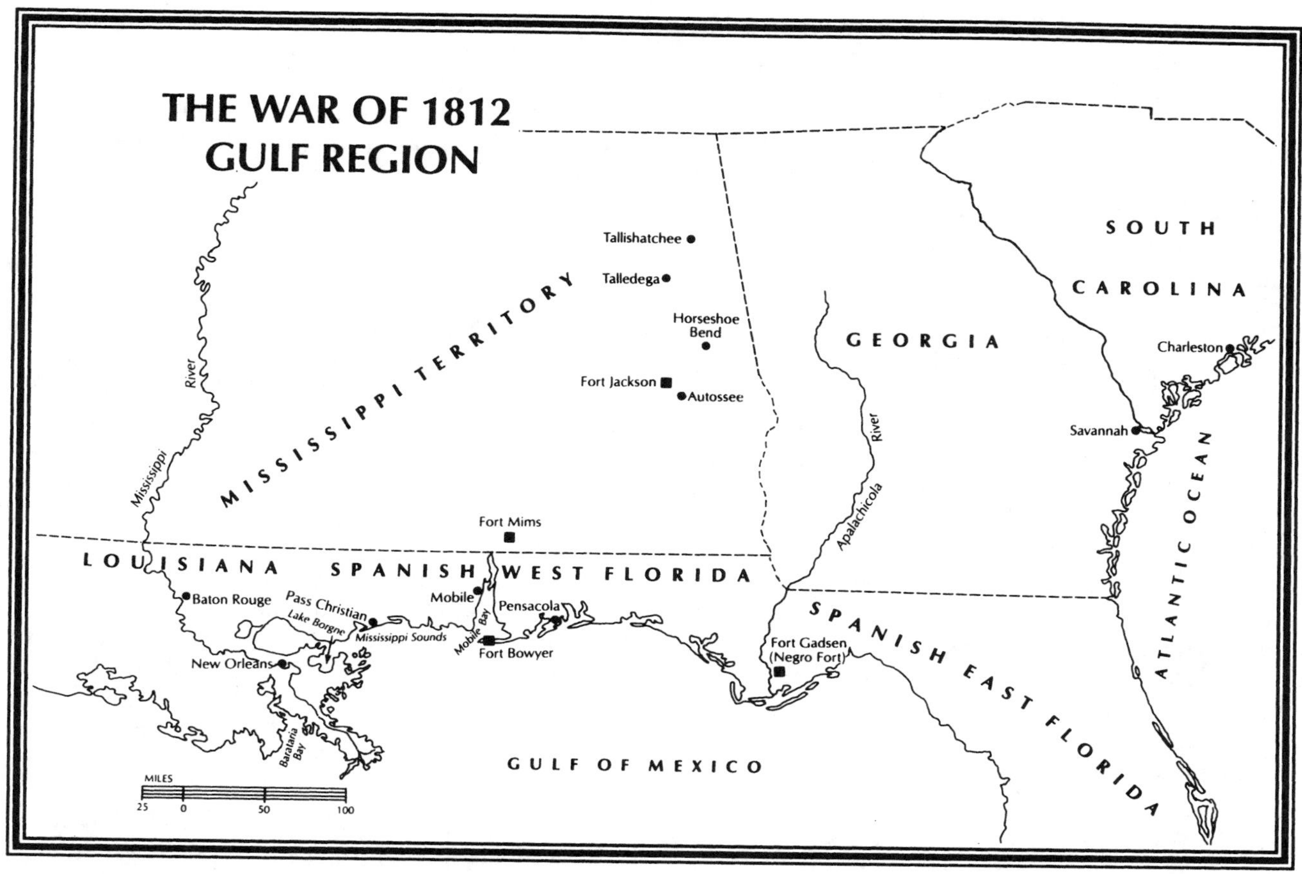

their long guns. Porter was at a double disadvantage—his ship was equipped with carronades and only three long 12-pounders, and he could not maneuver to get out of range of Hillyar's long 18-pounders. Nevertheless, Porter did inflict some damage on his opponent before striking his flag, having suffered terrible carnage. Hillyar paroled Porter and his crew and allowed them to sail for home in the *Essex Junior*. Porter and his men reached New York in July, and he traveled to Baltimore and Washington in time to oppose Captain Gordon's raid on Alexandria, participating in the shelling of the British squadron as it dropped down the Potomac.

One of the most successful younger naval captains of the war was North Carolinian Johnston Blakely, who took command of the new sloop of war *Wasp,* twenty-two guns, and set out from Portsmouth, New Hampshire, on 1 May 1814. It sailed directly for the heart of English shipping, the English Channel, where it terrorized the trade, taking and burning many ships. On 28 June, Blakely fought, boarded, and captured the brig *Reindeer,* eighteen guns. After putting into Lorient for a refit, Blakeley took the *Wasp* to sea again on 27 August and attacked a Gibraltar-bound convoy on 1 September. He overtook one of the escorts, the brig *Avon*, eighteen guns, and defeated it in a running battle in which both brigs received damage. The last that was heard of the *Wasp* was that it halted and boarded the Swedish brig *Adonis* on 9 October and removed U.S. Navy Lieutenant Decatur McKnight and the master's mate, both survivors of the *Essex*'s last battle, whom the British had sent to England from Brazil. Blakeley and all his men were lost at sea when a vicious storm overtook and capsized the *Wasp* in late October.

The *Peacock*, twenty-two guns, was one of the newer sloops of war completed by Noah and Adam Brown at New York in late 1813. Command was given to Captain Lewis Warrington, who had previously served on the frigate *Congress.* The *Peacock* sailed from New York on 12 March, and on 29 April overtook a British convoy en route to Bermuda, escorted by the brig *Epervier,* eighteen guns, carrying $118,000 in specie. Warrington got the better of his opponent in a one-hour battle. When the *Peacock*'s crew boarded the *Epervier,* it was very nearly in sinking condition. They made temporary repairs, and Warrington escorted his prize to Savannah, which not only earned him good prize money but was considered such a fine vessel that it was purchased into the U.S. Navy.

Warrington sailed again in June, reaching out to the Grand Banks, the Azores, and the Irish Channel, capturing many prizes and disrupting trade north of Ireland. He returned to the United States via the Spanish coast and Barbados, having captured fourteen merchantmen. During the *Peacock*'s last cruise there occurred what may be considered one of the last battles of the War of 1812. Warrington was assigned to accompany a squadron comprised of Commodore Decatur's *President,* Captain Biddle's *Hornet,* and the brig *Tom Bowline* with the mission of cruising in the East Indies. The *Tom Bowline* was essentially a store ship, carrying spares of every description that would be needed on a long cruise in waters rimmed by British colonies. Warrington sailed on 22 January 1815, only a week after a British squadron captured the *President* while Decatur was trying to slip through their New York blockade. Well into the south Atlantic, Biddle's *Hornet* fought and captured the brig *Penguin,* eighteen guns, which was searching for a U.S. privateer that had been hounding homeward-bound Indiamen off the Cape of Good Hope. Warrington sent the *Tom Bowline* into Rio de Janeiro as a cartel with the British prisoners.

Blakeley and all his men were lost at sea when a vicious storm overtook and capsized the Wasp *in late October.*

After waiting in vain for the *President*'s arrival at the island of Tristan da Cunha, the *Peacock* and *Hornet* continued toward the Indian Ocean. A month later they chased and were chased in turn by the *Cornwallis,* a seventy-four-gun ship of the line. The *Hornet* was the slower of the two U.S. vessels and was soon in danger of being overtaken. Jettisoning all guns, boats, and spare tackle, Biddle managed to escape his fate and returned to New York in June. Meanwhile, the *Peacock* sailed on to the East Indies, where Warrington reaped a harvest, capturing four large Indiamen, and entered the Sunda Strait.

On 30 June 1815, Warrington encountered the East India Company's brig *Nautilus,* fourteen guns, off Fort Anjier. Warrington was, until that time, ignorant that peace had been declared. The commanding officer of the *Nautilus,* Lieutenant Charles Boyce, had been fully apprised of this fact. He hailed Warrington and asked if he had heard the news, whereupon Warrington denied it, suspecting this was a ruse to avoid combat. He demanded that Boyce strike his colors, and when he refused, the *Peacock* fired two broadsides into the *Nautilus,* after which Boyce hauled down his ensign. This perhaps avoidable duel marked the final battle of the War of 1812, fought six months after the signing of the Treaty of Ghent.

SIGNIFICANCE OF THE WAR OF 1812

The War of 1812 was a costly one for a young nation. The United States forces had raised about 200,000 land troops—57,000 regulars, 10,000 volunteers, 3,000 rangers, more than 100,000 militia, and 20,000 who served in the navy and marines. In battle casualties, the United States suffered 2,260 killed and 4,505 wounded. There were also non-battle deaths, from disease and accidents, numbering about 17,000, which was about two and one-half times as many as were wounded or killed in battle.

The War of 1812 marked a turning point in the history of the Republic. It concluded twenty-five years of troubled diplomacy and domestic political strife, and ushered in the "era of good feelings." Although the war marked the downfall of the Federalist party, it paradoxically vindicated many federalist policies that were later adopted by Republican administrations. The war weakened the resistance of the Indians in the Old Northwest and the Southeast, paving the way for expansion. The passions unleashed by the war strengthened the Anglophobia that had germinated before the American Revolution. By the same token, the war also inspired the Canadian nationalism that emerged from a successful defensive campaign that, from the British view, was caused by aggressive U.S. imperialism. For many years the British policy in Canada was driven by a need to be prepared should another conflict arise with their American cousins.

Americans felt humiliated over their lack of preparedness and the failed land campaigns of 1812 and 1813. These sentiments stimulated military reform, including the creation of a larger standing army and an enlargement of the War Department. Similarly, Congress authorized an increase of naval strength because, although the navy had performed well, there had been many embarrassments, primarily because the Navy Department lacked the funds to build ships of the line that could overwhelm the British blockading squadrons. Finally, the positive events of the war stimulated U.S. national pride and fed an expansionist spirit that was to dominate nineteenth-century America.

POSTWAR EXPANSIONISM

In the immediate aftermath of the War of 1812, there were many wounds that needed binding. The recent unpleasantness with Great Britain led inevitably to diplomatic discussions on how to effect disarmament along the border between the United States and Canada, which led to the Rush-Bagot Agreement of 1817 for neutral disarmament on the Great Lakes and demilitarization of the border. Great Britain and the United States would, thenceforth, have but one vessel each on Lake Champlain and Lake Ontario and two on the Upper Lakes, none exceeding 100 tons or carrying more than one long 18-pounder. Therefore, most of the naval vessels, including the huge incomplete ships of the line that were under construction in 1814–1815, were allowed to decay where they lay. Most sank, although some were dismantled for their fittings.

The most serious lingering problems were the Spanish claims to the Floridas and the Pacific Northwest. Spain's military strength in North America had steadily deteriorated since the American Revolution. The Spanish Crown's primary concern since the Latin American independence movement broke out in 1810 was to crush the rebellions in its former colonies. This was virtually impossible until British armies expelled Napoleon's forces from Spain and the Congress of Vienna gave its blessing for the return of King Ferdinand VII to the Bourbon throne in 1815.

From that moment, the Spanish redoubled their efforts to suppress the revolutionary outbreaks that had occurred throughout Latin America. This was made doubly difficult because of Great Britain's advocacy of free trade and its desire to penetrate Latin American markets. The British were not inclined to assist Spain when it was in their interest to see the Spanish empire crumble. Thus, the United States could effectively coerce Spain without fearing European retaliation.

The progress of the U.S. takeover in the Floridas had begun with a U.S.-inspired rebellion in Spanish-held Baton Rouge in 1810. It continued in 1813 with General Wilkinson's expulsion of the Spanish from Fort Charlotte at Mobile. The Spanish military retreated to Pensacola, on the Apalachicola River, sixty miles east of the boundary between U.S. and Spanish territory. With the defeat and expulsion of the Creek Indians by Jackson and others in 1814, the way was clear for the settlement of West Florida by U.S. citizens. The pretext for further military action was the existence of the "Negro Fort" on the Apalachicola, where about three hundred escaped slaves and forty Seminole Indians were living, posing a threat to would-be settlers in the U.S.-claimed western lands by occasionally raiding settlements in Georgia and then retreating into Spanish territory, where they claimed Spanish protection.

As military commandant of the Southern District, Major General Jackson believed he had President Monroe's tacit permission to invade and expel the Spanish. The War Department had ordered General Gaines to construct Fort Scott near the mouth of the Flint River north of the Florida border. Gaines next launched an expedition and destroyed the Negro Fort, killing about 270 persons. On 6 January 1818, Jackson wrote a letter to President Monroe and Secretary of War John C. Calhoun, requesting written authorization to take the Floridas. It did not arrive, but when no order was issued not to take such action, Jackson went into motion. He marched his troops into Florida on 22 January, seizing St. Marks (7 April) and Pensacola (24 May). On 2 June, Jackson informed President Monroe that the Seminole War was at an end.

With the defeat and expulsion of the Creek Indians by Jackson and others in 1814, the way was clear for the settlement of West Florida by U.S. citizens.

As Jackson was attaining his objectives, Secretary of State John Quincy Adams was engaged in negotiations with Spanish minister Luis de Onís in an attempt to resolve the Florida question. When challenged on this issue, the United States accused Spain of aiding and abetting the Indian raids into U.S. territory and claimed the United States was acting in self-defense. Although Jackson's military moves were not officially sanctioned and there was criticism of his actions in Congress, he was not punished. Jackson's demonstrated military strength supported the government's hand and made it possible to obtain a more far-reaching settlement than Monroe had expected.

Ultimately, in the Adams-Onís Treaty, 22 February 1819, the posts that Jackson seized were returned to Spain, but Spain then yielded all claims to West Florida and ceded East Florida to the United States. In exchange, the United States renounced any claims it might have to Texas and undertook to pay the claims of U.S. citizens against Spain, up to a limit of $5 million. The treaty also defined more clearly the western limits of the Louisiana Purchase, proceeding from the Gulf of Mexico along the courses of the Sabine, Red, and Arkansas rivers to the forty-second parallel, and from there to the Pacific Ocean. The two governments exchanged ratifications of this important treaty on 22 February 1821. Again, Jackson's assertive use of military force obtained the most favorable conditions for negotiations that clarified the legal claim of the United States to the Floridas and the Pacific Northwest, at least with respect to Spain. This was, in effect, an invitation for Americans to migrate and settle in the Deep South and trans-Mississippi Northwest.

BIBLIOGRAPHY

Adams, Henry. *History of the United States of America,* 9 vols. (1889–1891).

Berton, Pierre. *The Invasion of Canada, 1812–1813* (1980).

———. *Flames Across the Border: The Canadian-American Tragedy, 1813–1814* (1981).

Brant, Irving. *James Madison: The President, 1809–1812* (1956).

———. *James Madison: Commander in Chief, 1812–1836* (1961).

Brown, Roger Hamilton. *Republic in Peril: 1812* (1964).

Brown, Wilburt S. *The Amphibious Campaign for West Florida and Louisiana, 1814–1815: A Critical Review of Strategy and Tactics at New Orleans* (1969).

Chapelle, Howard. *The History of the American Sailing Navy: The Ships and Their Development* (1949).

Coles, Harry Lewis. *The War of 1812* (1965).

Cooper, James Fenimore. *The History of the Navy of the United States of America,* 2 vols. (1839).

Cress, Lawrence D. *Citizens in Arms: The Army and the Militia in American Society to the War of 1812* (1982).

Cruikshank, E. A., ed. *Documentary History of the Campaign upon the Niagara Frontier,* 9 vols. (1896–1908).

Dudley, William S., and Michael J. Crawford, eds. *The Naval War of 1812: A Documentary History,* 2 vols. (1985–1992).

Douglas, W. A. B. "The Anatomy of Naval Incompetence: The Provincial Marine in Defense of Upper Canada Before 1813." *Ontario History* 81 (March 1979): 3–24.

Egan, Clifford L. *Neither Peace Nor War: Franco-American Relations, 1803–1812* (1983).

Everest, Allan Seymour. *The War of 1812 in the Champlain Valley* (1981).

Forester, C. S. *The Age of Fighting Sail: The Story of the Naval War of 1812* (1956).

Frederickson, John G., comp. *Free Trade and Sailors Rights: A Bibliography of the War of 1812* (1985).

Garitee, Jerome R. *The Republic's Private Navy: The American Privateering Business as Practiced by Baltimore During the War of 1812* (1977).

Giddings, Joshua. *The Exiles of Florida* (1858).

Goldsborough, Charles W. *The United States Naval Chronicle* (1824).

Hagan, Kenneth J. *This People's Navy: The Making of American Sea Power* (1991).

Hatzenbuehler, Ronald L., and Robert L. Ivie. *Congress Declares War: Rhetoric, Leadership, and Partisanship in the Early Republic* (1983).

Hickey, Donald R. *The War of 1812: A Forgotten Conflict* (1989).

Higham, Robin, et al., eds. *A Guide to the Sources of United States Military History* (1975, 1981, 1986).

Hitsman, J. Mackay. *The Incredible War of 1812: A Military History* (1966).

Horsman, Reginald. *The War of 1812* (1969).

Jacobs, James R. *Tarnished Warrior: Major General James Wilkinson* (1938).

James, William. *A Full and Correct Account of the Chief Naval Occurrences of the Late War between Great Britain and the United States of America* (1817).

Kaplan, Lawrence S. *Entangling Alliances with None: American Foreign Policy in the Age of Jefferson* (1987).

Kohn, Richard. *Eagle and Sword: The Federalists and the Creation of the Military Establishment in America, 1783–1802* (1975).

Long, David Foster. *Gold Braid and Foreign Relations: Diplomatic Activities of U.S. Naval Officers, 1798–1883* (1988).

Lossing, Benson John. *Pictorial Field Book of the War of 1812* (1869).

Mahon, John K. *The War of 1812* (1972).

Malone, Dumas. *Jefferson and His Time,* vol. 5, *The Sage of Monticello* (1981).

McKee, Christopher. *A Gentlemanly and Honorable Profession: The Creation of the U.S. Naval Officer Corps, 1794–1815* (1991).

Mahan, Alfred Thayer. *Sea Power and Its Relations to the War of 1812,* 2 vols. (1905).

Maloney, Linda M. *The Captain from Connecticut: The Life and Naval Times of Isaac Hull* (1986).

Millett, Allan R. *Semper Fidelis: The History of the United States Marine Corps* (1981).

Owsley, Frank Lawrence. *Struggle for the Gulf Borderlands: The Creek War and the Battle for New Orleans, 1812–1815* (1981).

Pack, James A. *The Man Who Burned the White House: Admiral Sir George Cockburn, 1772–1853* (1987).

Patrick, Rembert Wallace. *Florida Fiasco: Rampant Rebels on the Florida Border, 1810–1815* (1954).

Perkins, Bradford. *Prologue to War: England and the United States, 1805–1812* (1961).

———. *Castlereagh and Adams: England and the United States, 1812–1823* (1964).

Remini, Robert V. *The Life of Andrew Jackson* (1988).

Risch, Erna. *Quartermaster Support of the Army: A History of the Corps, 1775–1939* (1962).

Roosevelt, Theodore. *The Naval War of 1812* (1882, repr. 1968).

Rosenberg, Max. *The Building of Perry's Fleet* (1950).

Skaggs, David Curtis. "Joint Operations During the Detroit–Lake Erie Campaign, 1813." In *New Interpretations in Naval History: Selected Papers from the Eighth Naval History Symposium,* edited by William R. Cogar.

Skeen, Carl Edward. *John Armstrong, Jr., 1758–1843* (1981).

Smith, Dwight L. *The War of 1812: An Annotated Bibliography* (1985).

Spivak, Burton. *Jefferson's English Crisis: Commerce, Embargo, and the Republican Revolution* (1979).

Stagg, J. C. A. *Mr. Madison's War: Politics, Diplomacy, and Welfare in the Early Republic, 1783–1830* (1983).

Stanley, George F. G. *The War of 1812: Land Operations* (1983).

Symonds, Craig L. *Navalists and Antinavalists: The Naval Policy Debate in the United States, 1785–1827* (1980).

Tucker, Glenn. *Poltroons and Patriots: A Popular Account of the War of 1812,* 2 vols. (1954).

Weigley, Russell F. *The American Way of War: A History of United States Military Strategy and Policy* (1973).

Wood, William C. H., ed. *Select British Documents of the Canadian War of 1812,* 4 vols. (1920).

Zaslow, Morris, ed. *The Defended Border: Upper Canada and the War of 1812* (1964).

— WILLIAM S. DUDLEY

The War with Mexico

On 18 April 1846 Mexican President Mariano Paredes y Arrillaga wrote a blunt order to the commander of his Army of the North, General Pedro de Ampudia: "At the present time I suppose you to be at the head of our valiant army, either fighting already or preparing for the operations of the campaign. . . . It is indispensable that hostilities be commenced, yourself taking the initiative against the enemy." Five days later, long before his letter to Ampudia could have been taken from Mexico City to Matamoros and a reply received, President Paredes issued a proclamation declaring "defensive war" against the United States.

The following day, 24 April, Ampudia was replaced as commander of the Army of the North by General Mariano Arista, a militant, who immediately issued orders for sixteen hundred cavalry to cross the Rio Grande and attack U.S. forces on the north side of the river. That same afternoon part of this cavalry detachment came upon Captain Seth B. Thornton and sixty-three American dragoons, who were investigating a report of a large-scale Mexican crossing of the river onto Texas soil. Following intensive skirmishing, in which sixteen Americans were killed or wounded, Thornton was forced to surrender.

Thus began a war that would redraw political boundaries, bring dramatic change to the officer corps of the U.S. Army and U.S. Navy, produce lingering hatreds between neighboring nations, and generate an endless argument in assessing blame for causing the conflict.

CAUSES OF THE WAR

The order from President Paredes to commence hostilities was a result of a deep political division that had developed in Mexico after it won its independence from Spain in 1821. The two major parties in Mexico were the Centralists and the Federalists, the former wanting a strong national government, with appointed state and local officials, and the latter a federal republic similar to the United States. In 1822 the Centralists had installed an emperor, Agustín de Iturbide, only to see him quickly ousted and replaced by a Federalist regime, inaugurated under the Mexican constitution of 1824. That regime lasted, albeit with several revolutions, until 1835, when Antonio López de Santa Anna, president since 1833, overthrew the constitution and installed himself as a Centralist dictator, causing Texas and six other Mexican states to revolt. Santa Anna lost power after he was captured by Texans at the Battle of San Jacinto in April 1836.

Federalism returned to power in Mexico in 1842 with the election of a constituent assembly that restored the constitution of 1824, and Santa Anna again became president, only to dissolve the assembly in 1843 and reinstall himself as a Centralist dictator. Revolution began anew in 1844 with Federalist José Joaquin Herrera installed as president in December and Santa Anna forced into exile in Cuba. It was at this juncture that the question of Texas became a major issue while the Centralists fought to regain power.

On 2 March 1836 the Texas rebels, both American and Mexican, declared their independence and created an interim government for the Republic of Texas.

Texas had been a province in the Spanish viceroyalty of New Spain and then had been joined with Coahuila to form the state of Coahuila-Texas under the Mexican constitution of 1824. The previous year colonists had been allowed to settle in Texas from the United States and elsewhere, and by 1835 about thirty thousand Americans had moved into the province. Santa Anna's overthrow of the 1824 constitution caused Texas, along with six other Mexican states, to rise in rebellion to restore federalism. On 2 March 1836 the Texas rebels, both American and Mexican, declared their independence and created an interim government for the Republic of Texas. This independence was ratified on 21 April 1836 at the Battle of San Jacinto, where General Sam Houston and a force of 783 Texans defeated Santa Anna and a Mexican force of about fifteen hundred. The Mexican dictator was captured in the uniform of a private soldier and quickly signed the Treaties of Velasco, which recognized Texas independence and ordered Mexican troops to withdraw south of the Rio Grande.

Texas subsequently maintained its status as a republic for almost ten years, but it clearly preferred annexation to the United States. On 28 February 1845 the U.S. Congress adopted a joint resolution calling for the annexation of Texas as a state, and on 1 March President John Tyler signed it.

On 6 March the Mexican ambassador to the United States, Juan Nepomuceno Almonte, a Centralist not yet recalled following the overthrow of Santa Anna's dictatorship in December 1844, demanded his passport and stormed out of Washington. He asserted that the annexation of Texas was tantamount to a declaration of war. In reality, his action was intended to embarrass the new Federalist regime in Mexico City and to inflame Mexican patriotism. His declaration was popular in Mexico and became a rallying cry for Centralist opposition to Herrera and the Federalists.

Moreover, Federalist support waned when it became known that Herrera had indicated he would receive a minister plenipotentiary from the United States. In October 1845, amid Centralist cries for war to preserve the spurious Mexican claim to Texas, the Mexican congress met in secret session and approved a declaration that it would receive a representative from the United States "with full powers to settle the present dispute." President James K. Polk then named John Slidell to negotiate with the Herrera government. Slidell was given instructions to settle not only the dispute over Texas but also several other points of disagreement between the two nations, including the claims question.

During the continuing political unrest south of the Rio Grande, many U.S. citizens had filed claims against both state and national governments in Mexico for property taken or destroyed. During his eight years in office, President Andrew Jackson made repeated attempts to have these claims paid, leading to the severing of diplomatic relations between the two countries in 1836.

In 1839 Powhatan Ellis reopened the U.S. embassy in Mexico City (after France had attacked Mexico in 1838 to recover what was owned by its citizens, and British gunboats had forced payment of claims to British subjects). Early in 1840 the United States and Mexico agreed to binding arbitration of the U.S. claims. Delegates from the two countries met, with Baron Roenne of Prussia acting as umpire. After months of haggling, the baron adjourned the session in disgust early in 1842. Of the $11 million in claims, $7 million was discussed, $2 million was awarded, and $5 million was tabled. By this time Santa Anna was back in power and, short on money, refused to pay these claims. Arbitration was scheduled to begin anew in 1843, but broke down after three of twenty payments were made on the earlier settlement.

Another issue that Slidell was empowered to negotiate was that of California. By 1845 California was virtually independent of Mexico. The British consul there wrote that separation was inevitable, while the French minister to Mexico asserted that it was a moot question whether Great Britain or the United States would get the Pacific Coast territory. In 1845 the United States was negotiating with England over the boundary between Oregon and Canada, and British intrigue was evident in California. Polk instructed Thomas O. Larkin, the U.S. consul at Monterey, California, to support any movement for separation from Mexico. Polk also had Lieutenant John Charles Frémont and a detachment of sixty-two armed men stationed just north of the forty-second parallel in Oregon awaiting developments in California.

In short, Polk was protecting U.S. interests in California, which was reflected in his instructions to Slidell to attempt to purchase California from Mexico. The minister plenipotentiary was empowered to accept the Nueces River as the southern boundary of Texas if Mexico would agree to a prompt settlement of the claims; to assume payment by the United States of the claims of its citizens if Mexico would accept the Rio Grande as far north as El Paso del Norte as the boundary; to pay $5 million if Mexico would cede New Mexico to the United States; to pay an additional $5 million for northern California; and to give as much as $25 million for all of California to San Diego.

During the months in which Herrera agreed to receive U.S. minister and Polk dispatched Slidell, the annexation of Texas moved forward rapidly. In October 1845 the voters of the Lone Star Republic agreed to the terms of the joint congressional resolution of annexation and elected a convention, which drafted a state constitution. After Congress approved this constitution, Polk signed the Texas Admission Act on 29 December 1845, making Texas the twenty-eighth state in the Union.

Earlier in December Slidell arrived in Mexico City to be informed that Herrera would not receive a minister from the United States until Texas was returned to Mexico. By this point the Centralists had so inflamed Mexican public opinion that no government in Mexico could even negotiate with the United States. On 14 December Paredes raised the standard of revolt by proclaiming that Herrera repeatedly had kept the Mexican army from attacking the Americans in Texas. On the same day that Polk signed the Texas Admission Act, Paredes was able to enter Mexico City and take power without firing a shot. A revolutionary junta named him president and rewarded Almonte with appointment as secretary of war. It also reiterated an intention to make war on the United States to recover Texas—indeed, it was claimed that a state of war already existed between the two countries.

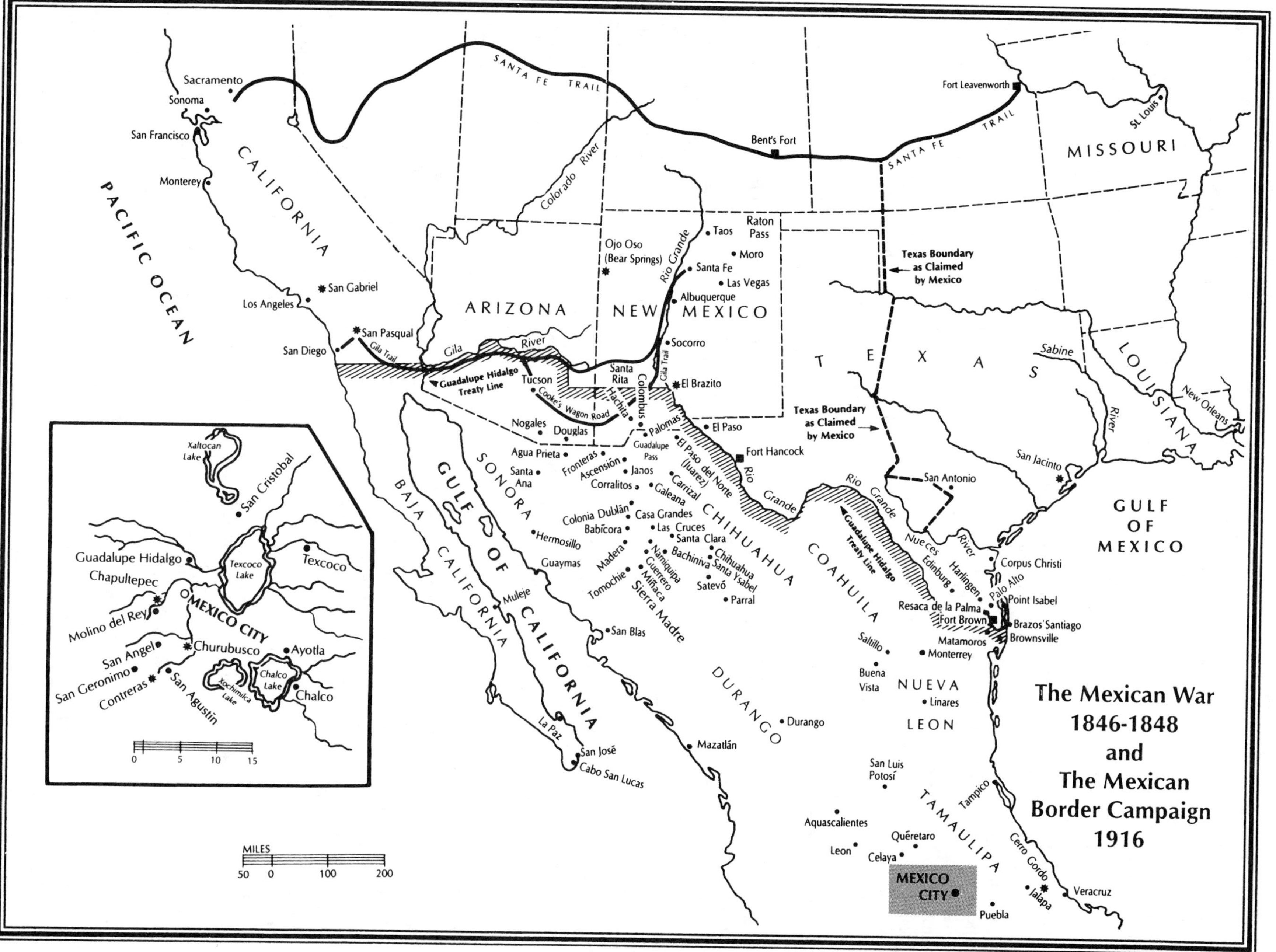
The Mexican War
1846-1848
and
The Mexican
Border Campaign
1916
MISSOURI
St. Louis
LOUISIANA
New Orleans
GULF
OF
MEXICO
Sabine
River
TEXAS
San Jacinto
San Antonio
Corpus Christi
Palo Alto
Point Isabel
Brazos Santiago
Brownsville
Fort Brown
Resaca de la Palma
Matamoros
Harlingen
Edinburg
Nueces
River
Rio Grande
Texas Boundary as Claimed by Mexico
Texas Boundary as Claimed by Mexico
Fort Leavenworth
SANTA FE TRAIL
Bent's Fort
SANTA FE TRAIL
Raton Pass
Taos
Moro
Las Vegas
Santa Fe
Albuquerque
NEW MEXICO
Socorro
El Brazito
El Paso
Fort Hancock
Rio Grande
Gila Trail
Ojo Oso (Bear Springs)
Rio Grande
Colorado River
Santa Rita
Hachita
Columbus
Palomas
Guadalupe Pass
El Paso del Norte (Juarez)
ARIZONA
Gila
River
Tucson
Cooke's Wagon Road
Nogales
Douglas
Guadalupe Hidalgo Treaty Line
Guadalupe Hidalgo Treaty Line
CALIFORNIA
Sacramento
Sonoma
San Francisco
Monterey
Los Angeles
San Gabriel
San Pasqual
Gila Trail
San Diego
PACIFIC OCEAN
BAJA CALIFORNIA
GULF OF CALIFORNIA
Muleje
La Paz
San José
Cabo San Lucas
SONORA
Agua Prieta
Santa Ana
Fronteras
Ascensión
Corralitos
Janos
Carrizal
Galeana
Colonia Dublán
Casa Grandes
Babícora
Las Cruces
Santa Clara
Bachiniva
Namiquipa
Guerrero
Miñaca
Madera
Tomochic
Hermosillo
Guaymas
CHIHUAHUA
Chihuahua
Santa Ysabel
Satevó
Parral
Sierra Madre
San Blas
COAHUILA
Saltillo
Buena Vista
Monterrey
NUEVA LEON
Linares
DURANGO
Durango
Mazatlán
TAMAULIPA
Tampico
San Luis Potosí
Aquascalientes
Leon
Celaya
Quêretaro
MEXICO CITY
Puebla
Jalapa
Cerro Gordo
Veracruz
MILES
50
0
100
200
Xaltocan Lake
San Cristobal
Texcoco
Texcoco Lake
MEXICO CITY
Ayotla
Chalco
Chalco Lake
Xochimilca Lake
Churubusco
San Agustin
Guadalupe Hidalgo
Chapultepec
Molino del Rey
San Angel
San Geronimo
Contreras
0
5
10
15

The new Centralist president began mobilizing his forces for a war that he and his cabinet members fervently believed would be won by Mexico. They expected aid from Great Britain in the event of war because of the U.S.-British quarrel over Oregon. They also had convinced themselves that France likewise would send aid to Mexico.

Most foreign military observers assured Paredes and his Centralist ministers that the Mexican regular army was superior to U.S. troops, because it was more than four times larger, well-armed, well-disciplined, and experienced. Lewis Pakenham, the British minister to Mexico, declared it would be impossible for U.S. troops to defeat Mexican soldiers on their own territory. Because the U.S. army was so small, the bulk of its fighting would have to be done by volunteers, and it was axiomatic among military observers that regulars could defeat volunteers in any contest of arms.

In addition, Mexican Centralist leaders counted on their side geography and political divisiveness in the United States. Should U.S. troops invade Mexico, they would find themselves in a thinly populated desert, a land of vast distances, barren mountains, and ever-lengthening supply lines, where they would be cut to pieces by guerrilla warfare and local resistance.

Paredes assured his fellow countrymen that he would see the Eagle and Serpent of Mexico flying over the White House in Washington before he would negotiate anything.

Just as important were the political divisions that Almonte and other observers reported in the United States. The former ambassador to the United States assured Paredes that U.S. northern abolitionists would not support the war, that internal conflict would destroy American morale, and that Indians in the American Southwest and slaves in the South would rise up to join the Mexican army when it invaded and marched toward Washington, D.C.

For all these reasons President Paredes assured his fellow countrymen that he would see the Eagle and Serpent of Mexico flying over the White House in Washington before he would negotiate anything. Privately he believed that at the first news of a victory in the north, his countrymen would rise up and proclaim him king of Mexico.

Thus, it was not a dispute over the southern boundary of Texas—the Nueces or the Rio Grande—that led to the outbreak of hostilities between the United States and Mexico. No Mexican politician ever asserted that the Nueces was the boundary; rather they were unanimous in claiming that the Sabine River (the present boundary between Texas and Louisiana) was the true boundary. Nor was the war caused by any American feelings of Manifest Destiny—a belief that the Divine Being intended for the United States to extend its rule over all of North America. The war was also not a result of a conflict of cultures.

The conflict began in 1846 because President Paredes and his Centralist advisers wanted a war—in fact, deliberately provoked a war—to achieve their goals. The accusations that Polk plotted war in order to acquire New Mexico and California were the inventions of Whigs bent on winning victory in the election of 1848.

TAYLOR'S CAMPAIGN

When President Polk learned of the deteriorating political condition in Mexico and that Slidell's mission had been rejected, he ordered Brevet Major General Zachary Taylor to move to the mouth of the Rio Grande to protect American interests.

"Old Rough and Ready," as Taylor was known, was commander of the Department of the Southwest. On 28 May 1845 he had been ordered by Polk to repel any Mexican effort to invade Texas and had moved from Louisiana to the mouth of the Nueces River (the site of present-day Corpus Christi). He next moved to the mouth of the Rio Grande, where he arrived with four thousand men on 23 March 1846, and established a depot at Point Isabel, where his supplies could land by ship from New Orleans. Named Fort Polk after the president, it was fortified by hastily constructed earthen breastworks. Taylor also had his troops erect Fort Texas, another earthen fortification, some thirty miles inland and opposite the Mexican town of Matamoros.

Second in command to sixty-two-year-old Taylor was Brigadier General William J. Worth, ten years younger and with an appetite for alcohol and bad decisions. Other high officers included colonels William G. Belknap, David E. Twiggs, and William Whistler and Lieutenant Colonel James S. McIntosh. All were more than fifty years old and, as one journalist wrote, "prepared to fight in 1846. . . . as [the] army had fought in 1812." Among the junior officers at the mouth of the Rio Grande were Ulysses S. Grant, then a lieutenant of infantry, and Ephraim Kirby Smith, an infantry captain and brother of Civil War General Edmund Kirby Smith.

When Taylor received word that Captain Thornton's dragoons had been attacked on 24–25 April, he had 3,880 troops, of whom about five hundred were disabled with amebic dysentery, diarrhea, yellow fever, and a host of other diseases arising from the unsanitary conditions at Fort Polk, Fort Texas, and other encampments.

Across the river in Mexico was forty-four-year-old General Mariano Arista. He arrived at Matamoros on 24 April 1846 to take command of the Army of the North, which consisted of more than eight thousand soldiers. Some of the elements of the Army of the North were crack units, such as the Tampico veterans, the Second Light Infantry, the Fourth and Tenth infantries, and General Anastasio Torrejón's lancers; these were all experienced men who had demonstrated competence in battle, veterans of discipline and courage. Arista's troops also included, however, poorly trained and equipped raw conscripts and convict soldiers who lacked experience and were prepared to desert at the first opportunity. Arista's subordinate officers included generals Torrejón, Luis Noriega, and José María García and Colonel José López Uraga.

The first commander of the Army of the North had been General Francisco Mejía, a twenty-four-year-old political appointee filled with bombast and self-importance. When he did not attack Taylor's army on the north side of the Rio Grande, after an order dated 4 April from President Paredes, he was replaced by General Ampudia. The new commander of Mexican forces at Matamoros ordered Taylor to withdraw as far north as the Nueces River and told all American civilians to leave Matamoros because a state of war existed. Ampudia, however, like Mejía, did not take the initiative, and on 24 April he was superseded by General Arista. It was Arista who at last ordered troops north of the Rio Grande, attacking Captain Thornton and his dragoons.

Meanwhile, on 23 April President Paredes had issued a curious proclamation: "At the time Mr. Slidell presented himself [in Mexico] the troops of the United States occupied our territory [Texas]. . . . Hostilities then have been commenced by the United States of the north. . . . I solemnly announce that I do not declare war on the United States. . . . From this day commences a defensive war."

President Polk, after learning of the ambush on Captain Thornton, sent a message to Congress on 11 May to ask for recognition that a state of war existed between the United States and Mexico and for authority to raise fifty thousand twelve-month volunteers, stating that "American blood had been shed upon American soil." That same day the House of Representatives passed the bill by a vote of 174 to 14, and the next day the Senate concurred by a vote of 40 to 2. Every vote against the declaration of war was cast by a Whig, and all of them northerners. Angry abolitionists in the Senate were able to delay temporarily an appropriations bill of $10 million for the war, charging that the war was being promoted to acquire more slave territory, but on 13 May the bill went to Polk for his signature. A Mexican congress assembled by President Paredes on 1 July voted a declaration of "offensive war," a declaration made public five days later.

"American blood had been shed upon American soil."

These political actions were unknown to the U.S. troops at the mouth of the Rio Grande. On 1–2 May, General Taylor, who had advanced to a point opposite Matamoros to establish Fort Texas, left five hundred men there and returned to Point Isabel. At 3:00 P.M. on 7 May he began marching back to Fort Texas with supplies and two 18-pound siege guns. The next day, at about noon, he and his estimated twenty-two hundred effectives were confronted at Palo Alto by Arista and about six thousand Mexican troops, the entire Army of the North having crossed the Rio Grande. Despite the advice of his officers, Taylor placed his sixteen batteries of artillery in the center of his formation and his infantry on the flanks; his 932 artillerymen were regulars, and he felt he could depend on them.

Stand firm the artillery did, cutting the Mexican army to pieces with explosives and canister, as well as fighting occasionally as infantry. The cannon fire was so devastating that huge holes appeared in the Mexican ranks. After an hour Arista ordered Torrejón's lancers to charge the American right, with the intent of taking the supply wagons. Colonel Twiggs and the Fifth Infantry, drawn up in a square, met the Mexican charge, which was in column not line. The lancers were repulsed, and repulsed again when they charged a second time.

When the two U.S. 18-pounders, under command of Lieutenant William Churchill, opened fire with grape and canister, the Mexicans several times tried to charge and halt the devastation. They were repulsed each time, however, and by 7:00 that evening the Americans were preparing to charge when darkness intervened. A count that evening showed nine American dead and forty-seven wounded; Arista later reported 250 dead or wounded.

The light of day on 9 May revealed that the Mexican army had retreated. Despite a vote of seven to three by his senior officers to entrench and wait, Taylor ordered an advance. The Mexicans, he learned, had retreated seven miles toward the Rio Grande until they had entered a thick woods and found Resaca de la Palma, an ancient channel of the Rio Grande. There Arista had implanted his artillery and scattered his troops along both sides of the road.

When U.S. scouts determined the Mexican location, Taylor advanced with seventeen hundred men. After several skirmishes, Taylor ordered Colonel Belknap and the Eighth Infantry to capture the Mexican artillery, saying, "Take those guns, and by God keep them." With fiendish yells the infantry charged, captured the guns, and held them, thereby demoralizing Arista's force.

Seeing his artillery lost, Arista fled to the Rio Grande and crossed. His soldiers followed as fast as possible, dropping weapons, supplies, and clothing in their haste. By the time they reached the river, they were in total panic, believing that the Americans were following with their deadly artillery. Most crowded into boats for the crossing, some of which overturned, while other soldiers tried to swim, resulting in the death of many men by drowning. Resaca de la Palma was another decided American victory, because Arista's army had dwindled to four thousand when it finally regrouped.

Taylor made no attempt to cross the Rio Grande immediately, choosing instead to regroup and resupply. He then began preparations to invade Mexican territory. Arista, meanwhile, found himself with scant funds, panicky troops, and little ammunition. On 17 May he requested an armistice from Taylor, only to have the American general reply, "I must have Matamoros even if I am forced to batter the entire town." His terms were blunt: "The city must capitulate; all property must be surrendered; then and only then may the Mexican army march out and retire." A reply was demanded by 3:00 P.M. on 17 May.

Told by his officers that Matamoros was indefensible, Arista fled the city, leaving behind his wounded and part of his supplies. The next day a delegation of leading citizens from Matamoros called on Taylor to ask for terms. Taylor responded that the Americans would respect persons and property. When the Mexicans agreed,

The Battle of Resaca de la Palma. On 9 May 1846, General Zachary Taylor and his troops attacked General Mariano Arista's unit at Resaca de la Palma. Many Mexican soldiers drowned in the Rio Grande as they fled the advancing American army. (National Archives/lithograph by James Baillie)

Taylor's troops crossed the river, entered without opposition what had been called Fort Paredes, and raised the Stars and Stripes as they sang "Yankee Doodle."

Arista's army, fleeing southward, was in almost total panic. His route to Linares was lined with dead animals and soldiers who had dropped out in exhaustion and despair. Arista arrived in Linares with 2,638 troops and made his report, placing himself in as favorable a light as possible after the disasters at the mouth of the Rio Grande. Because of drought in northern Mexico that summer, the Army of the North soon moved on to Monterrey, the nearest major city.

In Mexico City the Centralists were stunned at the news from the north, because they had been predicting a quick victory over the Americans. When confidence plummeted, President Paredes blamed Arista for the defeat and replaced him with General Mejía.

The reaction in the United States to news of Taylor's victories was soaring confidence and hordes of young men seeking to fill the quota for volunteers in each state. A call for twenty-eight hundred men in Tennessee saw a response by thirty thousand, some of the disappointed trying to buy a billet. In Maine the Aroostook County boys sang gaily as they marched off to war, while in Connecticut there were twice as many volunteers as needed. Texans were especially enthusiastic during the war, seeing an opportunity to strike once again at the nation from which they had fought for their independence. Texas Governor James Pinckney Henderson took a leave of absence to accept a commission as a colonel and fight. Taylor was the great hero of the hour, Congress voting him two gold medals, while Whigs talked of running him for president in 1848.

There was little rejoicing for the U.S. army in Matamoros, as more and more volunteers swarmed to the city. Young officers, trained at West Point, cursed Taylor as inept, bumbling, old, and foolish, saying he was incapable of using the information given him by Texas Ranger scouting companies. The enlisted men were bivouacked in poorly planned locations, drinking brackish water and sweating out fevers as they watched many of their companions die of disease. Out of boredom they flocked to the gambling halls, cantinas, and brothels for entertainment.

Still the volunteers came, many of them signing up for only three or six months. Taylor sent some of them home, but by 1 August he had almost twenty thousand men under his command. At last Taylor decided to move his army inland, in part to get away from the fleshpots of Matamoros and in part to press the war.

Captain Ben McCulloch and a company of Texas Rangers scouted the route toward Monterrey, where the Mexican Army of the North was rebuilding. The move from Matamoros began on 6–7 July toward a place known as Camargo, forty miles up the Rio Grande from Matamoros and in the general direction of Monterrey. Taylor and his staff arrived there by steamer on 8 August.

"I have seen more suffering since I came out here than I could have imagined to exist."

Camargo proved a place of death for fifteen hundred Americans, because of heat, poor sanitation, and diseases brought from Matamoros. Lieutenant George B. McClellan wrote of the encampment at Camargo, "I have seen more suffering since I came out here than I could have imagined to exist. It really is awful. I allude to the suffering of the volunteers. They literally die like dogs." Lew Wallace, a volunteer from Indiana, commented, "I cannot recall another instance of a command so wantonly neglected and so brutally mislocated."

The march to Monterrey began on 19 August in two parallel (later converging) columns consisting of two divisions of regulars and one division of volunteers, a total of 6,640 men. Commanding the regulars were Major General Worth and Brigadier General Twiggs, while the volunteers served under Brevet Major General William O. Butler, a Kentucky lawyer. There was little Mexican opposition to this march, the Texas Rangers enthusiastically clearing the route.

Unknown to the Americans, Monterrey was heavily defended. Command of the Army of the North had passed from Mejía to the far more formidable General Ampudia, who awaited Taylor with ten thousand soldiers. Monterrey, located on the north bank of the Rio Santa Catarina, was a natural fortress with mountains on the south and west and forts on the north and northeast. To the west of the city, atop Independence Hill, was the strongly fortified Bishop's Palace. Ampudia believed he could hold off Taylor and his army.

The fight for Monterrey on 21–24 September was sharp and bitter, but Texas Rangers turned the tide of battle by storming the Bishop's Palace and other fortresses on high ground. U.S. artillerists then turned their pieces on the city while the infantry moved into town on 23 September for house-to-house fighting. The next day Ampudia sent an emissary under a flag of truce to ask for an armistice. Colonel Jefferson Davis, commanding a regiment of Mississippi volunteers, along with General Worth and Colonel Henderson, negotiated an agreement that allowed the Mexican army to retire with their sidearms and accoutrements, along with six pieces of artillery. The agreement also stipulated that U.S. troops would not advance farther into Mexico for eight weeks. Ampudia and the Mexican troops withdrew on 25 September, after which Taylor and his army raised the U.S. flag. The supposedly impregnable city of Monterrey had been taken with a loss of eight hundred Americans killed and wounded.

Taylor's troops gave food and water to the Mexican wounded on the field of battle, while Taylor and Wool hugged each other with relief.

News of Taylor's latest victory caused celebrations in the United States, but not everyone was happy. Because of increasing talk among Whigs of running Taylor for the presidency, many Democrats criticized the terms of the armistice granted at Monterrey. President Polk declared, "In agreeing to this armistice General Taylor violated his express orders." Late in November he wrote in his diary, "I am now satisfied that he is . . . wholly unqualified for the command he holds." Therefore, on 26 January 1847 he issued orders for Taylor to remain in Monterrey and to dispatch four-fifths of his troops to accompany General Winfield Scott, who was to invade Mexico at Veracruz. Taylor and his remaining men were to remain on the defensive.

When Ampudia led the remains of the Army of the North south from Monterrey, he retreated all the way to San Luis Potosí, arriving in that city in mid-October. He learned that the army had been renamed the Army of Liberation and that he had been replaced as commander by General Santa Anna. When the war broke out, Santa Anna used diplomatic channels from his exile in Cuba to promise a quick end to the war on U.S. terms if he was allowed to return to Mexico. Issued a safe-conduct pass through the U.S. naval blockade of the Mexican coast by Polk, Santa Anna reached Mexico City on 14 September. Three days later José Mariano Salas, acting president after Paredes had been deposed, named Santa Anna commander of the Army of Liberation.

As always, Santa Anna proved efficient at raising men, and soon he had twenty thousand troops. When his scouts intercepted a letter from Winfield Scott to Zachary Taylor ordering Taylor to send all but six thousand of his men to the coast for embarkation, Santa Anna decided to go north to fight Taylor. He knew that the U.S. troops would consist mainly of volunteers and that they would be largely untrained. With visions of a quick victory and the Mexican presidency that would follow, Santa Anna marched his army north, his promises to make peace forgotten.

Meanwhile, Taylor chose to ignore Polk's order to remain on the defensive. On 8 November 1846 he ordered General Worth to begin a march to Saltillo, seventy-five miles southwest of Monterrey. His daring was made possible by the arrival of fourteen hundred fresh troops under the command of Brigadier General John E. Wool. Learning that Santa Anna was advancing toward him, Taylor and his troops took up a defensive position just south of Saltillo on the road to San Luis Potosí. At this encampment he had 4,759 men, of whom only two squadrons of cavalry and three batteries of artillery were regulars, a total of 476 men.

When Santa Anna approached on 21 February 1847, Taylor withdrew his troops to the hacienda of Buena Vista, seven miles south of Saltillo. On the morning of 22 February, Santa Anna sent a note to Taylor demanding an unconditional surrender, stating, "You are surrounded by twenty thousand men, and cannot in any human probability avoid suffering a rout." He also gave Taylor just one hour to reply. Old Rough and Ready's response was brief: "In reply to your note . . . summoning me to surrender my forces at discretion, I beg leave to say that I decline acceding to your request."

Santa Anna hurried to start the battle despite the poor condition of his men, who had been rushed north with little chance for rest or hot food. On the first day of battle, repeated Mexican charges failed to breach the U.S. lines, thanks mainly to withering artillery fire directed by Captain John Paul Jones O'Brien. Shortly after darkness Santa Anna brought forward the San Patricio Battalion, a small unit composed of American deserters, mainly Irish-Catholics, who were fighting on the Mexican side. That night a cold, drizzling rain fell, and both sides got little sleep because of repeated rumors of attack.

The second day of fighting saw the Mexicans again halted in their attacks by withering artillery fire. At a critical juncture in the battle, Colonel Davis and the Mississippi volunteers charged and turned the Mexicans back. When the Mexicans regrouped and came forward again, the Illinois infantry charged into them; among their dead were Colonel John J. Hardin and Lieutenant Colonel Henry Clay (son of the politician). When this charge faltered, Captain O'Brien and the artillery again turned the tide of battle, opening holes in the Mexican lines with grape and canister. By nightfall the center of the Mexican line had collapsed, and the Americans were advancing.

During the night of 23–24 February, Taylor counseled with his generals. His casualties that day had been 673 killed and wounded, and General Wool and other top aides advised a retreat. At about 3:00 A.M. on 24 February, however, about four hundred men and two 18-pound guns arrived from Saltillo, and Taylor decided to continue the fight.

To Taylor's delight, the light of day revealed that Santa Anna had quit the field of battle. Twice the Mexican army seemingly had victory within its grasp after brave charges, and twice it had been routed by deadly artillery fire. Santa Anna's men were without food and exhausted, their ammunition largely expended. Realizing his men could not fight again, the Mexican general had ordered a retreat, the wounded to be left behind. What started as an orderly retreat became a rout as conscripts fled the scene of death. Men discarded weapons and fled into the hills. By the time the Army of Liberation returned to San Luis Potosí, there were nine thousand men unaccounted for.

Taylor's troops gave food and water to the Mexican wounded on the field of battle, while Taylor and Wool hugged each other with relief. Taylor wrote to his brother, "The great loss on both sides . . . has deprived me of everything like pleasure." He remained in northern Mexico through most of 1847, after Congress voted him yet another gold medal, while President Polk criticized his actions. Late in 1847 he returned to the United States expecting both Whigs and Democrats to nominate him for the presidency and election by near acclamation.

NEW MEXICO AND CHIHUAHUA

While Taylor was winning his stunning victories in northern Mexico, a second major U.S. offensive was taking place in the Southwest. New Mexico east of the Rio Grande had been claimed by Texas prior to the outbreak of war, a claim with little legitimacy. Santa Fe traders, however, had shown the commercial value of this Mexican state, and President Polk was determined to have it. There was no great national patriotism in New Mexico, and its citizens had received little protection from Indian raids, taxes were exorbitantly high, and government was arbitrary. Thus, Polk's move to take New Mexico was strategically sound.

On 13 May 1846, shortly after the U.S. declaration of war, the president called on the governor of Missouri

The Storming of Monterrey. The fight for the supposedly impregnable city of Monterrey on 21–24 September 1846 was sharp and bitter, but Texas Rangers turned the tide of battle by storming the Bishop's Palace and other fortresses on high ground. (National Archives/lithograph by Kelloggs & Thayer)

to raise eight companies of dragoons and two companies of light artillery for the conquest of New Mexico. Command of this Army of New Mexico was given to Colonel Stephen Watts Kearny, commander of the Third Military Department in 1846. Recruiting proved easy, and the First Regiment of Missouri Mounted Volunteers, 856 men, was soon filled to capacity. Elected commander of this unit was Alexander W. Doniphan, who was given the rank of colonel. Other units, including the 1st Dragoons of the regular army, brought Kearny's total strength to 1,658. After twenty days of drill, the move toward Santa Fe began on 5 June. A month later, on 5 July, the first units reached Council Grove, where a halt was called for the men to rest before beginning the five hundred-mile trek to Bent's Fort (in present-day southeast Colorado), at which point the first elements arrived on 22 July.

Accompanying the soldiers west from Missouri was a wagon train of 414 vehicles belonging to civilian traders anxious to do business in Santa Fe and another one hundred wagons loaded with provisions and supplies for the soldiers, along with eight hundred cattle for food.

At Bent's Fort, Kearny allowed his weary men to rest from the hardships of the trail. Informants had brought him word that New Mexico Governor Manuel Armijo had called twenty-five hundred men to defend Santa Fe and that another army was assembling at Taos, making a total enemy force of more than three thousand. These troops, however, mainly were raw recruits with little inclination to fight, but thanks to geography they stood a real chance of victory. A short distance east of Santa Fe was Apache Canyon, a narrow mountain pass through which the Americans would have to pass in order to reach Santa Fe. A handful of loyal Mexicans, even those with few military skills, could hold off Kearny's army until heat, hunger, and thirst forced their retreat or surrender.

As Kearny pondered his options, a wagon arrived on 27 July bringing James Wiley Magoffin, a Santa Fe trader who spoke fluent Spanish and was a friend of Governor Armijo. He brought Kearny letters from President Polk and Secretary of War William L. Marcy, which instructed Kearny to allow Magoffin to go ahead of the Army of the West to negotiate with Governor Armijo.

A man of cunning and greed, Armijo, said Magoffin, was not courageous. In fact, one of the New Mexican governor's favorite sayings was, "It is better to be thought brave than to be so." In short, he might be persuaded to surrender the province without a shot being fired.

After conferring with Magoffin, Kearny announced that he would protect the property of all New Mexicans who did not resist the U.S. occupation and that New Mexicans would have full civil and religious freedom. On 31 July, Magoffin departed ahead of Kearny's army for Santa Fe accompanied by twelve dragoons under the command of Captain Philip St. George Cooke. On 1–2 August, Kearny's army left Bent's Fort to march south through Raton Pass and enter New Mexico.

Magoffin was hospitably received in Santa Fe on 12 August by Armijo, who soon was persuaded that resistance was useless. Some reports indicate the method of persuasion was a satchel filled with gold brought by Magoffin from Washington. The governor never stated his intentions. The military commander in New Mexico, Colonel Diego Archuleta, was told that the Americans intended to take only that part of the province east of the Rio Grande and that an enterprising officer might make himself governor of that part of the province west of the river. The conference adjourned on a cordial note. The next morning, 13 August, Magoffin prepared a sealed packet for Kearny, which Captain Cooke set out to deliver.

Meanwhile, Kearny and the Army of the West had been making its way south, arriving at Las Vegas on 15 August, just after a courier arrived with dispatches from Washington and Kearny's commission as a brigadier general, with date of rank from 30 June. Kearny proclaimed that New Mexico was part of the United States and to the assembled citizens of Las Vegas promised them freedom of religion and security of property. Everyone then was administered an oath of allegiance to the United States.

The next day, 16 August, just west of Las Vegas, Kearny received Magoffin's report from Captain Cooke. Whatever its content, Kearny continued his march westward. Armijo, meanwhile, did lead his army from Santa Fe to Apache Canyon, taking up a position there on 16 August. The next morning, however, he ordered his troops home, spiked eight cannon and hid them in the woods, and fled south to the neighboring Mexican state of Chihuahua. That afternoon the U.S. army reached Apache Canyon and were able to march through it the next morning without opposition.

On 18 August, in a driving rain, Kearny read General Order Thirteen to his troops, which declared New Mexico east of the Rio Grande annexed to the United States as part of Texas and ordered the soldiers to respect persons and property in New Mexico. That evening the army entered Santa Fe without firing a shot. The U.S. flag was raised in the central plaza on a makeshift flagpole accompanied by a salute of thirteen shots from a howitzer.

The next morning, 19 August, Kearny issued a formal proclamation to the people of New Mexico from the plaza in Santa Fe. In this he declared himself governor of the province, which was declared part of the United States. He then administered an oath of loyalty to local officials, whom he left in office. Three days later another proclamation announced that all of New Mexico had been annexed. Subsequently, he issued a code of laws (known as the Kearny Code), and a territorial constitution was drafted. William Bent was named acting governor along with a slate of civil officials.

This work done, Kearny then divided his command into four parts. A significant portion of the troops, under the command of Colonel Sterling Price, would remain in New Mexico as an army of occupation. Kearny personally would lead three hundred dragoons to California to conquer that province, while Colonel Doniphan and his Missouri Mounted Volunteers were to subdue troublesome Indians in New Mexico, particularly the Navajo, then march southward to Chihuahua City, after which they were to move east to link up with General Taylor's force.

The fourth part of the Army of the West consisted of a curious sidelight to the war with Mexico. On 25 September, after Kearny had departed Santa Fe for California, word reached him of the arrival in Santa Fe of a special unit of troops, which consisted of about five hundred Mormons, members of the Church of Jesus Christ of Latter-Day Saints, who had been enlisted into the U.S. Army at the request of their leader, Brigham Young. Their pay would go directly to the church to help finance the epic trek of the Mormons from Illinois to Utah. These men, known as the Mormon Battalion, had followed Kearny down the Santa Fe Trail and were in that city awaiting orders. Kearny decided that the Mormon Battalion should follow him to California, blazing a wagon road on the way. At Kearny's orders, Colonel Cooke took command of this unique battalion.

The units under Kearny, Doniphan, and Cooke had just departed Santa Fe when trouble began. Price's troops, unhappy at being left behind for garrison duty, began drinking, gambling, and cursing the local population. By 1 December Colonel Archuleta found willing recruits for an uprising to reclaim the province for Mexico. The conspirators gathered arms and ammunition in secret, planning an uprising for 19 December, then postponed it to Christmas Eve. U.S. authorities learned of the uprising, however, and arrested some of the conspirators, whereupon Archuleta and others fled to Chihuahua. On 5 January 1847 Governor Bent issued a proclamation describing what had transpired and asked the people to remain loyal.

Thinking all danger past, Bent went to Taos to visit his family. On 19 January the rebellion finally began under the leadership of Pablo Montoya, a self-styled "Santa Anna of the North," and Tomasito, an Indian; most of their followers were from Taos Pueblo, along with some Mexican sympathizers. On the first day of the uprising, Governor Bent was killed and scalped, as were five other men, while seven more Americans were killed at Turley's Mill and a similar number at the town of Mora.

Colonel Price heard of the outbreak on 20 January and quickly gathered a force to crush the rebels. Marching 279 men north through bitter cold, he met fifteen hundred insurgents at La Canada on 24 January and won a decisive victory. Five days later Price won another battle against six hundred to seven hundred Mexicans and Indians. On 3 February he entered Taos to find the remaining seven hundred rebels had taken refuge inside Taos Pueblo, which was stormed in a battle in which seven of Price's force were killed and approximately 150 rebels died. The fifteen ringleaders of the revolt, including Montoya, were tried by a makeshift court and hanged, bringing an end to the New Mexican uprising.

Subsisting on half rations, Doniphan's men nevertheless managed to march about fifty miles a day.

Doniphan's Missouri Mounted Volunteers, meanwhile, set out in October 1846 to negotiate a peace treaty with the Navajo, who had raided in New Mexico for centuries. Marching west in three columns that converged at Ojo Oso (Bear Springs, near present-day Gallup), these volunteers had not been paid, they had no supply train, and they were without winter clothing. Despite snowstorms, typhoid fever, and other problems, they made their rendezvous, and on 21–22 November, Doniphan conferred with Navajo leaders at Ojo Oso. On 26 November, Doniphan held another conference, this one with Zuni leaders. His message to the leaders of both tribes was the same—New Mexico had become part of the United States, the Indians were to cease raiding on pain of severe punishment, and they should learn to trade. He persuaded both the Navajo and Zuni to sign treaties with the United States.

His task with the Indians concluded, Doniphan on 1 December began moving his men down the Rio Grande to fulfill the remaining part of his orders. His ragged army was accompanied by 315 wagons of traders anxious to penetrate Chihuahua. George Ruxton, an English observer, commented that the Missouri Mounted Volunteers did not look like an army, saying they sat about in the evening "playing cards, and swearing and cursing, even at the officers." Doniphan dressed in ragged clothing, pitched his own tent, cooked his own meals, and swore like the rest of the men.

Subsisting on half rations, Doniphan's men nevertheless managed to march about fifty miles a day. As they approached El Paso del Norte (present-day Juárez, Mexico), they learned that a Mexican force of about five hundred men and one two-pound howitzer were waiting for them about thirty miles north of El Paso at El Brazito. On 25 December their commander, Brevet Lieutenant Colonel Juan Ponce de León, sent a lieutenant forward under a flag of truce to demand Doniphan's surrender or else his force would charge and annihilate the Missourians. Doniphan calmly replied, "Charge and be damned!"

When Ponce de León ordered his men forward, the Missourians patiently waited, then opened fire with devastating result. The enemy soon was in disorganized retreat. Seven Americans were slightly wounded, while Ponce de León had lost approximately one hundred men and his howitzer. The fleeing Mexican force did not halt at El Paso, but chose to continue southward to Chihuahua City. A delegation of leading citizens from El Paso then invited Doniphan into town, where his men soon were feasting to make up for the lost rations, drinking the strong local brew, and fighting the town's men for the affections of their women.

It was in El Paso that Doniphan learned of the uprising at Santa Fe, which, if successful, would cut him off from supplies and a route of retreat. He also learned that the Mexicans three hundred miles to the south at Chihuahua City were preparing a stout defense if he advanced. Without waiting to learn the fate of Price and his men, he chose to march south. The advance began on 8 February 1847 with 924 effectives and approximately three hundred wagons driven by traders. This march was one of great hardship—cold nights, hot days, storms that battered tents, shortages of food and water, and even a grass fire.

At Chihuahua City a confident Mexican force of twelve hundred cavalry and fifteen hundred infantry, all well-armed, along with one thousand ranch workers armed with lances and machetes, awaited Doniphan. Breastworks were erected fifteen miles north of town on the south bank of the Sacramento River, and ten cannon, ranging from 4- to 9-pounders, were in place. Commanding these troops was Brigadier General José Antonio de Heredia with Governor Angel Trías Alvarez as his second. Before the battle commenced, Brigadier General Pedro García Condé, a professional soldier and diplomat, arrived on the scene. Because of their superior numbers, an entrenched position, ten cannon, and good leadership, morale was high among the Mexican troops.

The Missourians and their entourage of traders approached the Sacramento River on the morning of 28 February 1847. Viewing the Mexican defenses, Doniphan chose to execute a flanking movement, ordering his men to turn right and then cross downriver, bringing them against the Mexicans from a not-so-stoutly-defended position. This maneuver was executed despite the hardship of steep river banks, even by the traders and their wagons.

About 3:00 that afternoon both sides opened fire with their artillery, the Americans using solid and chain shot, their shells demoralizing the Mexican lancers who charged. The Mexican artillery was using locally made gunpowder, which proved so inferior that their shots reached the American lines only on the bounce, easily seen and dodged. After this opening artillery duel, Doniphan called for a charge that quickly breached the Mexican lines. By 5:00 the shooting was almost over. A count of casualties showed four Americans dead and eight wounded, while the Mexicans had lost three hundred killed and another three hundred wounded. Governor Trías and General Heredia fled toward Mexico City, and the next morning, 1 March, Doniphan and his men entered Chihuahua City unopposed.

Within a few weeks almost 30 percent of the Missourians were on the sick list, many with venereal disease, the rest with diarrhea and assorted fevers. The small scouting party Doniphan sent east found General Taylor at Saltillo, and on 23 April the scouts returned to Chihuahua City with orders for Doniphan to join the larger American force to the southeast.

In late April the Missourians began a march in two sections, arriving at Saltillo on 21 May in ragged condition. After a brief rest, they marched on to Monterrey and then to the mouth of the Rio Grande. There they boarded ship for New Orleans, where they were taken aboard steamboats for a return to Saint Louis to be mustered out of service—and to be paid for the first time since they had volunteered. They had marched six thousand miles, had fought and won two major battles, had promoted trade and commerce, and had helped conquer and annex New Mexico to the United States, all without uniforms, government supplies, commissary, or paymaster.

THE PACIFIC COAST

Before the war with Mexico began, President Polk had taken steps to protect U.S. interests in California. On 17 October 1845, to offset British and French intrigues there, he had appointed Thomas O. Larkin, U.S. consul at Monterey, a confidential agent in the province. Larkin was told to work against any transfer of ownership to France or England. Polk's instructions had been communicated by Secretary of State James Buchanan and were very clear: "Whilst the President will make no effort and use no influence to induce California to become one of the free and independent States of this Union, yet if the people should desire to unite their destiny with ours, they would be received as brethren, whenever this can be done without affording Mexico just cause of complaint." The U.S. policy, Secretary Buchanan wrote, was to "let events take their course, unless an attempt should be made to transfer them [Californians] without their consent either to Great Britain or France. This they ought to resist."

Polk also had taken precautions to see that U.S. aid was readily available should the Californians rise up in rebellion in order to join the United States or if force was needed to prevent a transfer to British ownership. In 1845 Polk had sent an officer of the Corps of Topographical Engineers, Captain John Charles Frémont, west with a party of sixty-two soldiers ostensibly on a mapping expedition. Guided by the scout Kit Carson, Frémont had arrived in California late in 1845 only to be ordered out of the province. Early in 1846 he and his soldiers were encamped near Klamath Lake on the California-Oregon border, obviously waiting to intervene at a moment's notice.

Also ready to intervene was the Pacific Squadron of the U.S. Navy. The navy at this time was deployed in two squadrons, the Home Squadron, operating in the Atlantic and the Gulf of Mexico, and the Pacific Squadron. The West Coast squadron consisted of two seventy-gun warships and six lesser vessels and was under the command of Commodore John D. Sloat. Taking command on 18 November 1845, Sloat remained in the harbor at Mazatlán waiting for orders.

Such was the situation in the spring of 1846 when U.S. Marine Corps Lieutenant Archibald Gillespie was sent by Polk with secret instructions, some written, some oral, for Sloat, Larkin, and Frémont. Traveling under the guise of a Boston company's commercial agent, Gillespie set out late in 1845 and made his way to Veracruz, thence overland to Mazatlán, where he found Sloat and elements of the Pacific Squadron. The orders Sloat received from Gillespie were to cruise within striking distance of Monterey and to avoid aggression, but he was to seize and hold the ports of California on first word of an outbreak of war with Mexico.

Sailing on to Monterey, Gillespie next met with Larkin, after which he set out overland to find Frémont. He found him on 9 May 1846, the same day that Taylor's troops were rejoicing after their victory at Resaca de la Palma. Gillespie later said the oral orders he transmitted from the president to Frémont were "to watch over the interests of the United States, and counteract the influence of any foreign agents who might be in the country with objects prejudicial to the United States."

Frémont's response to Gillespie's arrival was immediate. He resigned his commission in the army and set out for California, sending Gillespie to rendezvous with a U.S. warship at San Francisco to procure arms and supplies for the insurgents Frémont intended to raise. At the town of Sonoma on 14 June, a group of U.S. civilians who had moved to California earlier, led by Ezekiel Merritt and William B. Ide, seized a store of arms and ammunition, devised a flag decorated with the Lone Star of Texas and a grizzly bear, and began what came to be known as the Bear Flag Revolt.

Frémont assumed command of the Bear Flag Revolt, seized the ungarrisoned fort at San Francisco, and spiked its guns.

On hearing of this declaration, the military commander governing the northern portion of the province, General José Castro, sent men north to disperse the revolutionists. A brief skirmish on 24 June, called the Battle of Olompali, forced the Mexicans to retreat. It was then that Frémont assumed command of the Bear Flag Revolt, seized the ungarrisoned fort at San Francisco, and spiked its guns. On 5 July he formally organized the California Battalion with himself as commander and Gillespie as his adjutant.

At this juncture Commodore Sloat and the U.S. Navy intervened. Arriving at Monterey on 2 July aboard the *Savannah,* Sloat counseled with Larkin. On 6 July he sent Captain John B. Montgomery and the *Portsmouth* to take San Francisco, and the next day ordered Captain William Mervine ashore at Monterey with 165 sailors and eight-five marines. After the U.S. flag was raised over the customshouse on 9 July, Mervine read Sloat's proclamation, which stated that California henceforth "was a portion of the United States" and that its residents were U.S. citizens who would be protected in their religion and property. Castro and his adherents fled southward to Los Angeles to link up with California Governor Pío Pico.

On 16 July, British Admiral Sir George E. Seymour arrived at Monterey aboard the eighty-gun *Collingwood.* A week later he sailed away, reporting to his superiors that there was nothing he could do. His presence and the content of his message clearly indicated that British designs on California had been thwarted by the measures taken by Polk.

At this juncture Commodore Robert Field Stockton arrived in California, and on 23 July he officially assumed command of the Pacific Squadron, replacing Sloat. That same day he enrolled the California Battalion as a volunteer force in the U.S. Army, naming Frémont its major and Gillespie its captain. He then loaded Frémont and the volunteers aboard the *Cyane* and sent them to San Diego to attack Castro, Governor Pico, and loyalist Mexican forces from the rear. With Frémont in command at San Diego and advancing toward Los Angeles and with another U.S. force coming from San Pedro, landed there by the navy, Castro and Pico realized that they had lost. On 10 August they fled southeastward to Sonora, thereby ending all Mexican resistance.

On 17 August, Stockton issued another proclamation, this one declaring all of California to be under martial law. He divided the province into two parts with Frémont at Monterey in charge of the northern half and Gillespie administering the southern portion. Kit Carson was sent overland to Washington, D.C., with dispatches reporting all that had transpired.

On 6 October at the New Mexican village of Socorro, sixty miles south of Albuquerque, Carson met General Kearny and his three hundred dragoons bound for California. On learning of the conquest of California, Kearny sent two hundred dragoons back to Santa Fe and proceeded westward with one hundred men guided by Carson, whom he persuaded to accompany him. His intent was to go to California and assume control over the new U.S. territory, believing he needed only a token force.

Passing the ancient copper mines at Santa Rita and crossing the Continental Divide, this column marched to the headwaters of the Gila River, which they followed to the Colorado River. Near the junction of the Gila and Colorado on 22 November, Kearny learned that a counterrevolution was under way in California under the leadership of José María Flores.

These Mexican patriots had driven Gillespie out of Los Angeles in September and soon had control of the entire southern part of the province except for San Diego and San Pedro, which were under the protection of guns aboard U.S. naval vessels. The exultant Mexicans then convened a legislative body in Los Angeles to name Flores governor and commanding general and to declare martial law.

The army of this body met Kearny's dragoons at San Pasqual on 6 December, thirty-five miles northeast of San Diego, under the command of Captain Andrés Pico, brother of the departed governor. Incredibly, the U.S. soldiers had allowed their powder to get wet and their horses were jaded. Nevertheless, Kearny ordered a charge. Pico's men used lances with deadly precision to kill eighteen Americans and wound a similar number. That evening Carson and Lieutenant Edward Fitzgerald Beale slipped through the enemy lines, reached San Diego, and informed Commodore Stockton of Kearny's plight. Stockton sent two hundred marines, which enabled Kearny to break out of his encirclement on 10 December and to reach San Diego two days later.

The combined forces at San Diego marched out as a land force on 29 December with Stockton commanding and Kearny as executive officer. They met Governor Flores and a force of 450 Mexicans on 8 January 1847 at Bartolo Ford on the San Gabriel River (twelve miles from Los Angeles). After brief skirmishing that day and the next, Flores fled to Mexico, and U.S. forces once again victoriously entered Los Angeles. Frémont, advanced to the rank of brevet lieutenant colonel, came south from Sacramento and on 13 January received the surrender of Andrés Pico and the remaining insurgents, signing the Treaty of Cahuenga. The war for California was over, but the battle to govern it had just begun.

Stockton's orders from the Navy Department concerning the government of California were vague, but he interpreted them broadly and named Frémont governor of the territory before departing. Kearny's orders from the War Department were not vague; he had been told to take and govern California, and he refused to recognize Frémont's appointment. The headstrong, politically ambitious Frémont refused to relinquish the governor's office despite repeated orders from Kearny to do so.

When orders came from Washington on 7 March 1847 upholding Kearny's claim, he arrested Frémont, charged him with mutiny and insubordination, and sent him to Washington for court-martial. The court found Frémont guilty on 31 January 1848 and sentenced him to dismissal from the army. President Polk approved the verdict but remitted the penalty, whereupon Frémont in anger resigned his commission. He returned to California, where he acquired a large land grant, and in 1850 became a senator when California entered the Union.

While these events were unfolding, the Mormon Battalion was opening a wagon road from New Mexico to California. Departing Santa Fe on 19 October 1846, this battalion came down the Rio Grande to a point below Socorro, then turned to the southwest to Playas Lake and followed an ancient Spanish-Mexican road to Janos, Chihuahua. From there the column turned westward to the valley of the Santa Cruz River, then went north down this river toward Tucson, which it entered unopposed on 18 December. Continuing north to the Gila, the Mormons then went down this stream to Yuma Crossing and California soil. Crossing the final mountain range, the coastal sierra, the Mormons suffered mightily before reaching San Diego on 29 January 1847. In his final report Cooke wrote, "Marching half naked and half fed, and living upon wild animals, we have discovered and made a road of great value to our country." Indeed they had, for Cooke's Wagon Road, later called the Gila Trail, would become a principal route to the gold fields for the forty-niners.

"Marching half naked and half fed, and living upon wild animals, we have discovered and made a road of great value to our country."

The Pacific Squadron did more than merely assist in the conquest of California. It also blockaded Guaymas, Sonora, the major Mexican port in the Gulf of California. On 22 January 1847, before Stockton could take further measures, he was replaced by Commodore William Branford Shubrick, who exercised command from January to March of 1847 and from 19 July 1847 to the end of the war. When he arrived in California, Shubrick found that the Pacific Squadron consisted of seven warships and two supply vessels. He supplemented the squadron by commandeering commercial ships, whose owners subsequently filed exorbitant claims for their services. Between March and July 1847 the Pacific Squadron was commanded by Commodore James Biddle.

On Commodore Biddle's orders, Commander John B. Montgomery sailed the *Portsmouth* to San José, at the tip of Baja California, and a landing party of 140 men occupied the city on 30 March 1847. Another landing party went ashore unopposed at Cabo San Lucas, and a third party took the port of La Paz on 14 April. The mainland ports of Guaymas and San Blas were blockaded despite inclement weather, and that fall they and Mazatlán were occupied by landing parties, as was Muleje in Baja California. The only battle occurred at Guaymas, when troops came ashore on 17 October. At Mazatlán on 10 November the twelve hundred Mexican soldiers in the city at first threatened to fight, but when Shubrick sent 750 men ashore, the Mexicans withdrew without firing a shot.

In almost two years of warfare (July 1846 to May 1848), the Pacific Squadron was a decisive factor on the West Coast of North America. Shubrick's final report to the secretary of the navy proudly noted his men had occupied twelve Mexican Pacific port cities and had destroyed or confiscated forty enemy ships, mostly coastal vessels. He had accomplished this with never more than ten naval vessels at his command, and his men had collected sufficient customs duties in those port cities to offset the cost of his operations.

GULF COAST OPERATIONS

The Home Squadron of the U.S. Navy, with a supply depot at Pensacola, Florida, numbered seven steamers, three frigates, six sloops, one schooner, five brigs, seven gunboats, and four bomb vessels. The largest was the fifty-gun *Raritan.* Commanding the Home Squadron at the outbreak of hostilities was Commodore David Conner. His first task was to blockade Mexican Gulf ports in order to prevent the arrival of arms and munitions from Europe, to wage war on any privateers that might try to operate out of Mexico, and to support General Taylor. Despite the fact that the mouth of the Rio Grande was nine hundred miles from Pensacola, ships of the Home Squadron actively aided Taylor, even contributing five hundred sailors and marines for combat and continuously landing supplies for Taylor's troops at Point Isabel during 1846 and 1847.

To make the blockade truly effective, Conner knew he had to occupy the principal Mexican ports. Moreover, if these ports were captured, his men could collect the customs duties and use the money to buy supplies for his fleet. Thus, on 8 June 1846 a naval expedition attacked Tampico, which was taken on 10 November. On 23 October, Conner's second-in-command, Captain Matthew C. Perry, occupied Frontera, a port at the mouth of the Tabasco River and an important source of cattle. In addition, Conner was effective in obtaining the neutrality of the Mexican state of Yucatán. Conner sent Perry with four ships to occupy the major port of Carmen in this state, which was accomplished on 2 December.

Conner's most important service, however, was transporting Major General Scott and more than twelve thousand soldiers to land at Veracruz in February 1847. President Polk ordered this invasion as much because of politics as for reasons of military strategy. By late 1847 Zachary Taylor had become so popular that the president decided to order him to halt at Monterrey and to send most of his regular troops for an invasion of Mexico at Veracruz. The officer chosen to head this new effort was Scott, the commanding general of the army.

On 18 November 1846 Polk gave his orders to "Old Fuss and Feathers," as the troops called Scott, who since the outbreak of hostilities had argued that Mexico could be conquered only by the occupation of its capital. Moreover, he said this could not be done by invading across the northern deserts, but rather would have to follow the route of Hernando Cortes in his conquest of the Aztecs—a thrust from Veracruz to Mexico City. Polk's orders to Scott, delivered through Secretary of War William L. Marcy on 23 November, were purposefully vague: "The President, several days since, communicated in person to you his orders to repair to Mexico, to take the command of the forces there assembled, and particularly to organize and set on foot an expedition to operate on the Gulf coast, if, on arriving at the theater of action, you shall deem it practicable." Responsibility for any failure clearly would fall on the general, not the president.

Shortly after Scott sailed for New Orleans and then to Brazos Santiago at the mouth of the Rio Grande, intrigues began in Washington to name Senator Thomas Hart Benton a lieutenant general, thereby having him outrank Major General Scott. Congress refused to approve this, but President Polk satisfied his partisan feelings by refusing to give Scott adequate financial and logistic support for the campaign.

The army of invasion was delayed at Brazos Santiago because the president failed to order the necessary transport vessels. When the ships did arrive, most were sailing vessels despite Polk's promise to Scott that all would be steam-powered. The army finally embarked the second week in February 1847 and paused briefly at Tampico on 19–20 February. While at Tampico, Scott issued General Order No. 20 (later reissued at Veracruz, Puebla, and Mexico City), which was designed to prevent atrocities. It said that soldiers committing what would have been civil crimes at home would be punished in military courts. In effect, the order meant Scott had established martial law in all areas occupied by U.S. troops.

Scott arrived on 7 March at Antón Lizardo, an anchorage thirty miles south of Veracruz that was to be the staging area for the invasion. Scott faced a need for haste, for the heat of late spring would mark the beginning of the deadly yellow fever season. Knowing Veracruz to be heavily defended, Scott conferred with his generals about a course of action. The fortress of San Juan de Ulúa in the harbor was formidable, and it was known that there were more than three hundred serviceable cannon and mortars in the city pointing seaward to defend it against naval invasion. His staff advised a frontal assault, one certain to win public admiration for heroics, but Scott feared that such an assault would so decimate his ranks that he would have insufficient troops to continue to the interior of Mexico. He also could not rely on a siege to accomplish his purpose because the port could be reprovisioned from the interior.

His decision was daring. He would put ashore his 12,803 men, along with horses, cannon, and supplies, by amphibious landing at the beach of Collado, three miles southeast of Veracruz, thereby bypassing San Juan de Ulúa and the other defenses by attacking Veracruz from the undefended rear. Scott and Commodore Conner devised an elaborate flag system of communication between the army and the fleet of approximately one hundred ships, and at sunrise on 9 March the operation began, the first amphibious landing in U.S. history. Using sixty-seven whale boats that transported sixty to eighty men each, the first wave of forty-five hundred men went ashore at 6:00 P.M., and by 10:00 more than ten thousand men had been landed along with their equipment and supplies. The entire operation took only sixteen hours and was completed without a casualty. The following day the remaining men and equipment were brought ashore, and by 15 March Veracruz was surrounded by land and blockaded by sea. On 21 March, just as the battle was about to be joined, Conner was succeeded as commodore of the Home Squadron by Perry. He loaned Scott some of his siege guns, which were manned by navy crews after being hauled ashore and wrestled into position.

After Scott went through the formality of asking the commander of Veracruz to surrender, the siege began on 22 March with a roar of cannon from both land and Perry's fleet. On 27 March, Scott halted the shelling to inform the Mexican commander, General Juan Morales, that if he did not surrender by 6:00 the following morning, the town would be stormed. Morales saw no reason to fight and on 28 March signed articles of capitulation. The Mexicans were allowed the honors of war—soldiers were paroled on oath not to fight again and persons and property were to be respected. Scott had taken the city with only nineteen Americans killed and sixty-three wounded in skirmishing. On 29 March, Conner sailed for Washington with dispatches telling of this astonishing victory.

Armies invading Mexico usually paused long enough at Veracruz for yellow fever to decimate their ranks.

In Mexico City news of the defeat caused little panic, because, in the past, armies invading Mexico usually paused long enough at Veracruz for yellow fever to decimate their ranks. Scott, however, wasted no time. Buying supplies from Mexican merchants, who preferred

U.S. Treasury drafts to the confiscation methods of Mexican officials, he sent Brigadier General Twiggs and the First Division marching inland on 8 April, soon followed by most of the remainder of his force, a total of eighty-five hundred men. Only a small garrison was left behind to hold Veracruz. The remainder of the army brought ashore at Veracruz were volunteers whose term of service had expired and they were sent home. As Scott marched inland, he was plagued constantly by problems of supply and manpower, because President Polk was slow to send either to support the campaign of the Whig general.

POLITICAL MANEUVERING

In the United States both Democrats and Whigs were seeking in every way to gain political advantage from the conflict. Polk's war message to Congress in May 1846 had triggered the outbreak of this bickering. The Whig-abolitionist position was that the Texas Revolution had been the result of a conspiracy among southern slaveowners to steal Texas from Mexico, that Polk's order moving Taylor from the mouth of the Nueces River to the mouth of the Rio Grande was a provocation, and that southern Democrats were promoting the war in order to gain additional slave territory, especially California.

The charge that the Nueces was the real boundary received the most Whig-abolitionist play. Most abolitionists were forced to admit that the Texas Revolution and annexation were accomplished facts, and the California question was intertwined in the Oregon boundary dispute then under negotiation with England. The claim that the Nueces was the true boundary of Texas, however, was made entirely in the United States, because the Mexican position was that all of Texas belonged to Mexico and that the Sabine River was the boundary. Despite these charges, the war bill passed, and the response in all parts of the United States was enthusiastic. There was continuing Whig-abolitionist opposition that was vocal but not violent, but the overwhelming majority of Americans supported Polk and the war.

The abolitionists found a champion in Congressman David Wilmot of Pennsylvania. Elected in 1844 as a Polk Democrat, he nevertheless introduced an amendment to a $2 million war appropriation bill in August 1846 providing that no slavery should ever exist in any territory acquired as a result of negotiations or war with Mexico. Debate on the amendment was especially bitter, raising questions of constitutionality that would not be resolved until the end of the Civil War. The Wilmot Proviso caused a split in both the Whig and Democratic parties, nearly 40 percent of Democrats voting for it in the House and 30 percent of the Whigs voting against it. The bill was passed in the House and went to the Senate, which adjourned without voting on it, but the Wilmot Proviso did not die. When reintroduced in the next session of Congress, beginning in December 1846, it passed the House by a vote of 115 to 106, but it failed in the Senate by a vote of 31 to 21, with splits in both parties and heated debate. The proviso had delayed a much-needed war appropriation by six months, and it continued to be introduced as an amendment to dozens of bills. Abraham Lincoln, then serving in the House of Representatives, later said he voted for the Wilmot Proviso at least forty times.

In the bitter off-year election of 1846, Whigs won control of the House of Representatives, and they smelled victory in the upcoming presidential election of 1848. Despite their opposition to any extension of slavery as a result of the war, northern Whigs joined their southern brethren in talking openly of nominating a military hero—someone such as Taylor or Scott—as their candidate for the presidency, which created great difficulty for Polk and the Democrats. They wanted to win the war, but neither Scott nor Taylor could be allowed to develop a heroic public image. Thus, neither general ever got the political and logistical support he deserved, especially Scott. Because Taylor had been the early hero of the war, Polk had ordered him to halt in northern Mexico and had taken most of his troops from him, giving command of the invasion at Veracruz to Scott.

Moreover, there were various peace movements in the United States creating some opposition to the war, including such organizations as the Non-Resistant Peace Society founded by abolitionist William Lloyd Garrison and others. These peace groups denounced Polk and his administration and demanded an end to war. Among religious sects, the most unwavering opposition came from Quakers, Unitarians, and Congregationalists. Because these denominations were strongest in New England, it was from there that they harangued the president and deluged the public with antiwar propaganda.

Because of such opposition, as well as political considerations Polk repeatedly tried to negotiate a peace treaty with Mexico. In May 1846 he asked Bishop John Joseph Hughes of New York to influence the Catholic church in Mexico to help in restoring peace. In July 1846, Secretary of State Buchanan sent dispatches to Mexico suggesting negotiations for peace, but these were rejected. Other efforts also came to naught.

Following the off-year elections in November 1846, in which the Whigs gained control of the House, and because of the vocal minority of peace advocates in the United States, Polk decided on a major peace initiative.

He appointed Nicholas P. Trist, chief clerk in the State Department, to secretly accompany Scott to Mexico. Carrying a variety of proposals for ending the war with him, Trist slipped out of Washington on 16 April 1847 for New Orleans and then went by ship to Veracruz, arriving on 6 May. From Veracruz he was to make his way to Scott's headquarters and accompany the army as it marched inland to Mexico City.

In Mexico the opposition to war was far more vocal, leading to continued political instability. After they provoked an outbreak of hostilities, Paredes and his advisers found that their hopes for aid from England and France had been ill-founded. After the defeats at Palo Alto and Resaca de la Palma, public opinion welled up against the regime. Various Mexican commanders resorted to pamphlets to "explain" their actions, and Arista was arrested and later court-martialed.

When Taylor crossed the Rio Grande and took Matamoros in April 1846, Paredes was confronted with a separatist movement and by Federalist plots. In northern Mexico there had been separatist efforts since 1835 and the Texas Revolution. In 1839 Federalists had organized the Republic of the Rio Grande (immediately south of Texas), which failed to win independence. As early as September 1845 Taylor was receiving messages from Federalists in Tamaulipas, Nuevo León, and Coahuila, saying that if war broke out these states would support the United States. Moreover, most of Taylor's supplies came from Mexican merchants anxious to take drafts on the U.S. Treasury. While Taylor was in northern Mexico, there was also talk of rebellion against the Centralist regime throughout the region. Most local citizens never gave outright military cooperation to the Americans, but there was little overt opposition.

Another area of separatist sympathies was in Yucatán, whose citizens had rebelled against centralism in 1839 and had declared their independence from Mexico in 1842. Because of its geographical isolation from the rest of Mexico, no Mexican attempt to reconquer this area had been made when war broke out. In November 1846 the Mexican government offered concessions to Yucatán if it would rejoin the nation, whereupon U.S. naval forces occupied key ports in that state. In January 1847 insurgents in Yucatán again declared independence and even sent a delegation to Washington to discuss annexation to the United States with Secretary of State Buchanan. The idea was rejected, but the hostility in Yucatán to centralism was another factor in weakening the Mexican war effort.

Following Taylor's victories on the Rio Grande, in July 1846 Paredes was faced with several uprisings in central Mexico, some of them Federalist, some personally directed against him. From Havana, Cuba, came word that Santa Anna was opposed to the monarchical tendencies of Paredes, causing Almonte to swing his allegiance to Santa Anna. Moreover, Gómez Farías, leader of a radical group of Federalists, began planning a coup. On 28 July Paredes announced that he was leaving Mexico City to take personal command of the army, but stayed in hiding in the city. His de facto resignation allowed the reins of government to fall to Vice-president Nicolas Bravo.

On 3 August, Bravo proclaimed the restoration of constitutional government, but that same day the garrison at Veracruz pronounced in favor of Santa Anna. The next day in Mexico City the commander of local troops, General Salas, also announced for Santa Anna, and on 6 August Bravo resigned. On 22 August, Salas, guided by Farías and Federalists, announced the restoration of the constitution of 1824. It was at this juncture that Santa Anna returned to Mexico, passing through the U.S. naval blockade after assuring the Polk administration that if allowed to do so he would conclude an immediate peace. Landing at Veracruz on 16 August, he declared his support of federalism and the constitution of 1824. Shortly afterward he assumed command of the Army of Liberation and began raising troops for it, eventually doing battle with Taylor at Buena Vista in February 1847.

Under the restored constitution, elections were held in November for delegates to a congress that was to name a new president. The man selected on 22 December 1846 was Farías, who took office two days later. He found an empty treasury, despite the millions of pesos that had been raised for the war effort by Paredes. There were so many charges of widespread corruption that efforts to levy new taxes and float new loans proved futile. Santa Anna's Buena Vista campaign was financed by a forced loan.

The only institution with wealth in Mexico was the Catholic church, and on 11 January 1847 the Mexican congress passed a law authorizing the president to use church lands as collateral for a loan, if lenders could be found, and to sell church lands if the president could not borrow. Priests were threatened with excommunication if they implemented the law, and opposition to the Federalist anticlerical policy snowballed. The militia of Mexico City turned against the regime, as did regular army units shortly afterward. By the end of February 1847 Farías was no longer able to govern and was forced from power.

At this opportune moment, Santa Anna returned from the disaster of Buena Vista to find everyone welcoming him as a potential savior of Mexico. On 23 March he formally assumed the presidency with a vote of thanks from congress for his "victory" at Buena Vista.

Milking two million pesos from the church in return for an annulment of the laws of 11 January, Santa Anna then marched east from Mexico City to confront Scott, who in early April had begun marching inland from Veracruz.

SCOTT'S DECISIVE CAMPAIGN

Santa Anna's chosen site for a battle with the invading Americans was Cerro Gordo, one of those places that nature seemingly created for a defensive army. Just east of the little village of Plan del Rio, the road wound upward six to seven miles through a rocky defile from the hot and malarial coastal plain to the cool inland plateau. On the way up, the road passed between steep hills, from whose tops artillery could stop an invading army with both direct and cross fire. It was here that Santa Anna located his army, his reserves at the rear, thirty-five of his artillery pieces atop the high ground and others at strategic points, and his fifty-six hundred regulars and more than six thousand national guardsmen from the capital manning the high ground. He was confident that he and his men would win the victory that had eluded him at Buena Vista. Morale was high as they waited.

Cerro Gordo was one of those places that nature seemingly created for a defensive army.

On the morning of 12 April 1847 Scott's advance unit of twenty-six hundred men commanded by General Twiggs began climbing through the gorge. Fortunately for them the Mexican artillery opened fire too soon, and they withdrew to safety. Twiggs, however, was prepared to order a charge the next morning, but his staff persuaded him to wait. Scott and additional soldiers arrived the next day—to the cheers of Twiggs's nervous soldiers—and that afternoon all were joined by General Worth and another sixteen hundred men, bringing the total U.S. force to eighty-five hundred.

Rather than order a suicidal charge into the Mexican guns, Scott sent two engineering officers into the ravines of each side, Captain Robert E. Lee and Lieutenant George H. Derby. They found a trail that bypassed the road, a difficult task because it was overgrown with cactus and chaparral, and up this trail were hauled by hand the heavy 24-pound howitzers.

Scott's major attack came on the morning of 18 April, as Americans stormed the summit and, using bayonets, pistols, and muskets as clubs, drove off the Mexicans and raised the U.S. flag. Just as Santa Anna was about to rally a counterattack, Brigadier General James Shield and three hundred men, who had circled the Mexican camp, attacked them from the rear, which threw the Mexicans into panic, and they fled, amid cries of "Everyone for himself." By 10:00 A.M. the battle was over, Santa Anna and his staff fleeing westward over the road to Mexico City. A final count of casualties showed sixty-four American dead and 353 wounded. Mexican casualties were estimated at between one thousand and twelve hundred, and another three thousand had been captured along with forty-three cannon and some four thousand small arms.

Scott could not mount an effective pursuit because he had too few cavalry, but his infantry and artillerymen advanced despite having rations for only two days in their knapsacks. The fleeing Mexicans were pursued to within four miles of Jalapa, the next village along the road to Mexico City, but the Mexican army did not halt there or at the next village, La Hoya, choosing instead to fall back toward Puebla.

Scott's soldiers entered Jalapa the morning of 19 April to an absence of hostility. In fact, the church bells were rung as if in celebration. Fortunately for his troops, Scott was able to buy supplies from Mexican merchants, because nothing was coming from the United States. It was at Jalapa that U.S. troops began to suffer terribly because of the climate. In the hot, low country, many had discarded blankets and heavy clothing. Now in the mountains, they shivered at night and many fell ill. Scott tried to send the sick back to Veracruz, but those who went found it ravaged by yellow fever. On 4 June, Scott reported to Secretary of War Marcy that he had one thousand bedridden at Veracruz and another one thousand ill at Jalapa.

Another problem Scott faced the farther he marched into the interior was keeping the road open to Veracruz. Mexican irregulars committed atrocities on stragglers and attacked supply trains, couriers, and small detachments. Scott's answer was to assign Captain Samuel H. Walker, a former Texas Ranger and designer of the six-shooter that bore his name, the Walker-Colt, to patrol the road. A regiment of Texas Rangers sent by President Polk and the secretary of war was also on patrol. Commanded by Texas Ranger Captain John Coffee Hays, these rangers did their task with such ferocity that Mexicans soon were referring to them as *los Tejanos sangrietes* ("those bloody Texans"). When the rangers once brought in a prisoner, a soldier noted in his diary that this was considered "one of the seven wonders."

While at Jalapa, Scott sent General Worth and a division after the retreating Mexicans. Worth pursued them as far as Perote Castle, once a fortified position on the Veracruz–Mexico City road, but in use as a prison prior to the war. Worth found fifty cannon, five hundred muskets, and twenty-five thousand rounds of cannon and musket shot in the castle. He halted to await further orders.

Scott's position at this time was precarious. Food, clothing, and ammunition were in short supply, and he knew he could expect little help from Polk. Moreover, many of the enlistments of his volunteers were ending around the middle of June. When his pleas for them to reinlist failed, he sent them to the coast for shipment home, leaving him with 7,113 men. He continued his advance the first week in May, after issuing a proclamation to the Mexican people, in which he praised the valor of Mexican soldiers and blamed their defeats on generals who had lived "in idleness." He noted that his troops had given fair treatment to churches and clergy.

Santa Anna, meanwhile, had retreated to Puebla, arriving there on 11 May, and began trying to raise another army. He was facing a sullen population that finally realized that Buena Vista had been a defeat. He did manage to raise a force that he claimed numbered four thousand, but that was much nearer to twenty-five hundred. Unknown to him, however, the clergy and leading citizens in Puebla did not want a battle to take place there. They had heard that when Scott arrived in a town, the hated Mexican taxes were abolished, that the U.S. troops respected persons and property, that religion and churches were left alone, and that Scott

The Attack on Churubusco. As General Scott's troops advanced toward Mexico City, Santa Anna and his soldiers took refuge at the convent of Churubusco. On 20 August 1847, an American battery stormed the convent, reducing Santa Anna's army by a third and capturing thirty-two Mexican cannons. (National Archives/engraving by Phillibrown after Alonzo Chappel)

paid for supplies with valid drafts drawn on the U.S. treasury. Therefore, they sent word to the advancing Americans that the city would be open to them.

Santa Anna did his utmost, seizing horses, conscripting men, and forcing loans, but when Worth and General John Anthony Quitman approached with a U.S. force, the Mexican leader was able to make only a token attack with about two thousand men. Seeing many of his men desert under cover of battle, Santa Anna fled toward Mexico City. Worth and Quitman entered Puebla unopposed on the morning of 15 May.

At Puebla, Scott was able to provision his troops from the countryside, as well as to purchase clothing and shoes for them from merchants in the city. Had it not been for Mexicans who hated their own government and were willing to trade with the Americans, Scott would have been forced to withdraw. Moreover, Scott chose to wait at Puebla until volunteers began arriving from the United States. By 3 July he had 8,061 effectives and 2,215 sick at Puebla. On 6 August twenty-five hundred men arrived from Veracruz under command of Brigadier General Franklin Pierce, by which time Scott's army had grown to almost fourteen thousand (of whom twenty-five hundred were ill and another six hundred convalescent and unable to perform their duties).

As Scott waited in Puebla, confusion reigned in Mexico City. Plan followed plan for defense of the city, and orders went out to the Mexican states for a loan of twenty million pesos, which never was delivered. The states were also sent quotas to bring thirty-two thousand men to the capital's defense, but few responded. Santa Anna arrived into this troubled situation on 19 May with three thousand men. The next day he announced that, despite his wishes to the contrary, he would assume the presidency. He tried to win popular support by announcing freedom of the press, but when bitter attacks resulted he announced his resignation, only to retract it on 2 June, suspend freedom of the press, and lock up his political opponents. He had become a virtual dictator with little popular support.

With great energy, however, Santa Anna set about preparing his defenses. Cannon were cast from melted bells, arms were confiscated from private citizens, gunpowder was manufactured, and bullets were molded. He united the three thousand men he had brought with him with the two thousand regulars and eight thousand militia in the capital. This army was augmented by all the able-bodied men he could conscript, bringing his force to twenty-five thousand. His strategy was to concentrate his troops to defend the city en masse. The perimeter would be rimmed with fortifications guarded by militia, while regulars would rush to any threatened point. General Juan Alvarez, commanding the Army of the South outside the city, was ordered to move behind Scott and harass his advance and destroy him when he retreated.

The president-general ordered outlying villages emptied, laborers were conscripted, and the prisons emptied. All the men were used to dig gun emplacements, parapets, breastworks, and trenches to be filled with water, which Santa Anna decreed must be completed in just eight days. By 9 August all was in readiness, and Santa Anna issued a proclamation designed to increase morale: "Blinded by pride the enemy have set out for the capital. For this, Mexicans, I congratulate myself and you."

Meanwhile in England, the Duke of Wellington was following Scott's campaign closely, and he commented to his junior officers, "Scott is lost. He cannot capture the city and he cannot fall back upon his base."

On 7 August, Scott began his advance from Puebla, with Twiggs's division in the lead and other units following, a total of 10,738 men and officers. The road crested at 10,500 feet about thirty-six miles outside Mexico City and before them lay the beautiful valley of Mexico, unconquered by a foreign army since Cortes had defeated the Aztecs in 1519–1521. On 9 August the advance halted at Ayotla, fifteen miles outside the capital. Scott looked at his maps and listened to the reports of his scouts on the fortifications ahead.

After three days of slogging through "mud, mud, mud," the main body of Scott's force arrived at the village of San Agustín.

Scott's decision was to avoid the bulk of Santa Anna's defenses by swinging most of his army to the south around Lake Chalco through unguarded wastelands, cold lava flows called *pedregals,* which the Mexicans thought impassable. The route the Americans followed had been scouted by engineering officers Lee and Pierre G. T. Beauregard. After three days of slogging through "mud, mud, mud," the main body of Scott's force arrived on 18 August at the village of San Agustín, ten miles to the south of Mexico City, but they could not tarry long. They had only four days of rations on hand.

When Santa Anna realized what Scott was doing, he rushed troops to take up a position between San Agustín and Mexico City under the command of General Gabriel Valencia. Morale was slipping among the Mexican troops, however, because of Scott's surprise march to the south.

At San Agustín on 19 August the U.S. commander divided his force, leaving Worth and Quitman, along with his artillery and baggage, while he and the remainder of the troops continued through the cold lava flows and wastelands to the village of Padierna, where light American guns commanded by John B. Magruder, Jesse Lee Remo, and Thomas Jonathan Jackson were silenced by Mexican artillery, which included several 68-pounders. The village was eventually taken, however, thanks to the outstanding courage of charging American troops.

Padierna was immediately north of Contreras, where Valencia's troops awaited the Americans, and it was just south of the village of San Geronimo where Santa Anna had arrived with a force that, in effect, caught the Americans in the middle. That night of 19 August a violent storm hit, during which Santa Anna's troops withdrew north to San Angel. The Americans then slipped out of their camp at 3:00 A.M. on 20 August and three hours later attacked the unprepared Valencia from behind. The Battle of Contreras lasted only seventeen minutes and caused approximately seven hundred Mexican casualties. The remainder fled in panic toward the capital and were joined by Santa Anna's soldiers. Brigadier General James Shield, waiting on the road to San Angel, captured eight hundred Mexicans, including four generals. U.S. losses amounted to sixty dead and wounded.

Santa Anna rallied what men he could, falling back to the convent of Churubusco and declaring Valencia a traitor to be shot on sight. He then ordered General Manuel Rincón and former President Pedro María Anaya to hold the convent against the Americans. They had almost the remainder of Santa Anna's forces outside Mexico City for this effort, including two hundred members of the San Patricio Battalion, lrish-Catholic deserters from the American army fighting for Mexico. Churubusco was a natural fortress with stout walls, a parapeted roof, breastworks to the south and west, and a ditch twenty feet wide filled four feet deep with water.

Expecting no stiff resistance, Scott ordered his two columns to converge at Churubusco, one coming from its victory at Contreras, the other from San Agustín, where it had waited with artillery and baggage. Arriving at Churubusco, the Americans were allowed to advance until they were in musket range before both they and Mexican cannon opened fire. For a time the American advance halted almost in panic, but individual and unit courage asserted itself and the Americans moved forward. Lieutenant Richard Stoddert Ewell had two horses killed under him, while others were less fortunate and were killed. First Lieutenant James Longstreet was adjutant of the Eighth Infantry that day, while Second Lieutenant Winfield Scott Hancock charged with the Sixth Infantry. Finally, the parapet of the convent was breached by a battery of artillery commanded by Captain James Duncan and the Americans swarmed inside.

When the shooting halted, a count of Mexican losses showed 4,297 killed or wounded and 2,637 prisoners, among whom were eight generals, two of them former presidents of the republic. Additional thousands of Mexican troops had deserted, bringing Santa Anna's total loss to more than a third of his entire army. Thirty-two Mexican cannon were captured and added to the U.S. batteries. American losses that day were 133 killed, 865 wounded, and 40 missing. One of Scott's first orders, after the cheering for him had stopped, was to execute the captured members of the San Patricio Battalion.

Next, he wrote a note calling for a peaceful surrender of Mexico City, to which Mexican officials responded with a request for an armistice. On 24 August Quitman and Twiggs met with General Mora y Villamil and agreed to an armistice while a peace treaty was drafted. Scott used these days to reprovision his army through purchases from Mexican merchants in the capital city and the surrounding area. Santa Anna likewise used the truce to augment his army by conscription and to strengthen his defenses of the city.

Santa Anna bragged that the U.S. agreement to an armistice was the result of a Mexican victory, and thus Mexican demands during peace talks were unrealistic. The Mexican congress arrogantly resolved that no peace treaty would be considered until all U.S. forces were withdrawn from Mexican soil and Mexico had been indemnified for the entire cost of the war. On 6 September the Mexican commissioners offered to accept the annexation of Texas if the United States paid for the territory, which was to have the Nueces as its southern boundary. These demands were so outrageous that Scott declared the armistice at an end on 7 September.

The next day Santa Anna assumed command of a large Mexican force in the vicinity of the castle of Chapultepec. Half a mile away were stone buildings a quarter of a mile long known as El Molino del Rey (the King's Mill). Spies had said that this was a foundry where bells were being melted to cast cannon that reportedly were stored five hundred yards away in a powder magazine known as Casa Mata.

On 8 September, General Worth moved forward to take these two sites. After only a brief cannonade he ordered five hundred men forward in a charge, because

Worth had a fondness for the bayonet. Despite heavy losses in bloody fighting, the mill and powder magazine were taken, only to find no evidence of cannon-casting. U.S. losses in the Battle of Molino del Rey were 117 killed and 658 wounded, along with 18 missing, out of a total of 3,447 engaged. Mexican casualties were estimated at twenty-seven hundred. Ethan Allen Hitchcock echoed the sentiments of several U.S. officers when he wrote in his diary that this battle had been "a sad mistake."

On 11 September, Scott counseled with his staff about his next move, stating he preferred to attack Mexico City through its western gate, which would require taking the castle of Chapultepec. Lee and all engineering officers except one argued for an attack through the southern gate. The other engineering officer, Beauregard, along with Twiggs and Riley, preferred the western route. After all had expressed an opinion, Scott concluded, "Gentlemen, we will attack by the western gate." Quitman and General Gideon J. Pillow took troops to make a feint at the eastern gate as a diversion, then abandoned that position during the night of 12 September.

The Mexican fortification of Chapultepec had gone forward since May 1847 despite shortages of money and supplies. Rising two hundred feet above the plain and protected by steep cliffs on its northern and eastern faces, Chapultepec was a formidable obstacle. The approach to it on its southern side was steep and ended at a fifteen-foot wall; on the west the Americans would have to advance up a steep, rough hillside strewn with land mines into the face of fire from troops atop a steep masonry wall. Chapultepec originally had been built as the summer palace for viceroys of New Spain, but by 1846 was the home of the Military Academy of Mexico. Inside were a hundred cadets and 240 regular troops

The Attack on Chapultepec. Approximately 1,800 Mexican troops were either killed, wounded, or captured when the U.S. Army stormed the hilltop fortification at Chapultepec in September 1847. (National Archives/painting by J. Duthie after H. Bellings)

along with the crews of twelve guns; six hundred infantry and artillerymen guarded the outworks, and another four thousand soldiers were on the causeways close to the eastern side of the castle hill. Commanding these men was General Nicolas Bravo.

The U.S. artillery assembled to bombard Chapultepec was formidable, consisting of 8-, 12-, 16-, and 24-pounders as well as howitzers and mortars, which opened fire on the morning of 12 September and continued throughout the day with demoralizing effect on the Mexicans. Bravo sent a request to Santa Anna for reinforcements, but was told these would be sent only at a critical moment.

On the morning of 13 September, the American bombardment commenced anew at 5:30, then halted at 8:00 as Pillow and Twiggs advanced with infantry. Ninety minutes later the battle was over, Bravo surrendering his sword when Santa Anna failed to send him reinforcements. U.S. casualties numbered slightly under five hundred, while the Mexicans had eighteen hundred dead, wounded, and captured.

After this victory Scott did not hesitate. He sent Quitman's division hurrying across the Belén causeway into the city. Santa Anna, half mad with fury, tried to rally resistance, but demoralized Mexican troops would not stand. By 1:20 P.M. the U.S. flag was flying inside the city walls, and Worth's troops were crossing the Veronica causeway. That night, despite having approximately twelve thousand men, Santa Anna decided his cause was lost. At 1:00 A.M. on the morning of 14 September he ordered Mexico City evacuated, saying Mexican honor had been satisfied. He took what troops he could muster north with him to the town of Guadalupe Hidalgo. Just after dawn on 14 September, Quitman marched troops into the grand plaza of Mexico City and raised the U.S. flag.

Scott's next act was to organize some kind of government, because looting broke out in parts of the city. General Quitman was named governor of the city, and troops and Texas Rangers began patrolling. These men had to be severe, for Scott had only a small army in a city of 180,000 people. So effectively did the U.S. troops and Texas Rangers restore order in Mexico City that a delegation of leading Mexican citizens asked Scott to become dictator of the nation. He refused.

In the weeks immediately after Mexico City surrendered, Scott faced anxious moments. He had only six thousand effective troops, and along every road into the city there were guerrilla bands, little more than bandits but a threat to couriers, small detachments, and supply trains. By mid-December 1847, however, replacements began arriving and Scott's force increased to more than thirteen thousand, but these new men fell victim to the same diseases that had riddled U.S. troops earlier.

Among those who died of camp fever was Edward Webster, son of the great Massachusetts orator Daniel Webster. Some of those who came to be part of the army of occupation were good men, such as young West Point graduates Ambrose E. Burnside and John Gibbon, but many of the newly arrived soldiers were ready for any opportunity to plunder and desert.

For a brief time there was no real Mexican government.

Scott tried to find duties that would keep these men busy. From December 1847 to the following May, for example, his soldiers levied assessments in various cities and collected the customs duties to make Mexico pay for the costs of the war. His men were able to collect about $3 million to defray part of the $23 million the war actually cost the United States.

For a brief time there was no real Mexican government. On 22 September Santa Anna resigned the presidency and retired to his plantation, but two weeks later, he had raised an army of four thousand, with which he attacked the U.S. garrison at Puebla. He believed a victory there would cause the Mexican people to rise up and proclaim him dictator. Defeated at Puebla on 9 October, he quit the war and departed the country with an escort of U.S. soldiers to protect him from Texans who remembered him from the massacres he had inflicted during the Texas Revolution.

In London, the Duke of Wellington, after reading the details of Scott's invasion and conquest of Mexico, urged young English officers to study the details, saying "His [Scott's] campaign was unsurpassed in military annals. He is the greatest living soldier." Unfortunately for Scott, the Democratic administration in Washington did not want a military hero, especially one who was a Whig.

THE TREATY OF GUADALUPE HIDALGO

The Mexican congress, which met in Querétaro on 11 November 1847, elected Anaya the acting president. He, in turn, formed a cabinet that included Manuel de Peña y Peña as minister of foreign affairs. There were some Centralists in Querétaro that favored a continuation of war, but Anaya was a moderate and a realist. Therefore, negotiations for a peace treaty with the United States began on 15 November. The Mexican commissioners were José Bernardo Cuoto, Miguel

Atristán, Manuel Rincón, and Luís Gonzaga Cuevas. Negotiating for the United States was Nicholas Trist.

Trist had hardly begun serious negotiations when an order arrived from Washington on 16 November recalling him, along with a rebuke for his prolonged quarrels with Scott during the march toward Mexico City. By this time he and Scott had patched over their dispute and become friends. Nevertheless, the recall order left him without any authority to negotiate, and he packed his bags to return to the United States.

At this juncture he was asked to stay and negotiate by the British ambassador and by Scott, both of whom realized that the collapse of peace talks would be followed by the collapse of Mexican government itself. Trist knew that if he stayed and negotiated, he could prepare a treaty that would include most of what he had been instructed to obtain—Texas with the Rio Grande as the boundary and a cession of New Mexico and California in return for a cash indemnity. He decided to stay, and on 2 January 1848 he met the Mexican commissioners in Mexico City and began secret negotiations.

The haggling was endless and tediously slow and Anaya's term as acting president expired, whereupon Peña y Peña assumed the mantle of chief executive. At last the two sides settled on the Rio Grande as the boundary of Texas, in return for which the United States would assume the claims owed U.S. citizens. New Mexico and California would become part of the United States in return for $15 million. On 2 February the treaty was signed at the suburb of Guadalupe Hidalgo and sent by swift courier to Washington for the president's consideration.

A week after the Treaty of Guadalupe Hidalgo was signed, Scott learned that President Polk intended to bring him before a court of inquiry for his conduct during the late war. This situation was a result of the president playing partisan politics and because of the ambitions and jealousies of some of Scott's staff, particularly Worth and Pillow. Following the battles of Contreras and Chapultepec, Pillow's reports had been so self-glorifying that Scott asked him to modify them. Pillow did so, but there soon appeared in U.S. newspapers letters under the pen names "Leonidas" and "Veritas," heaping praise on Pillow. One letter laughably stated that Pillow belonged "in the first rank of American generals." A former law partner of President Polk and a political general, Pillow had been responsible for some of the greatest blunders of Scott's campaign.

Old Fuss and Feathers responded with a general order dated 12 November 1847 that the authors of these letters were guilty of "despicable self puffings" and demanded to know if the letters were meant to demean his own contributions. General Worth, feeling himself the object of this general order, accused Scott of conduct unbecoming an officer, whereupon Scott placed Worth, Pillow, and Colonel James Duncan under arrest and asked Washington that they be court-martialed. Duncan had admitted writing one of the letters in question, a violation of army regulations.

On receiving notification of these arrests, the President concluded that Pillow was being persecuted because he was a Democrat and that the charges against Worth and Duncan were unwarranted. He wrote that these charges came "more by the vanity and tyrannical temper of General Scott, and his want of prudence and common sense, than from any other cause." After discussing the matter with his cabinet, Polk ordered that Major General William O. Butler, a veteran of the Battle of New Orleans, as well as a Democrat, should take command in Mexico City; that Pillow, Worth, and Duncan should be released from arrest; and that Scott should face a court of inquiry in Mexico City. As for Trist, whom the president in January had learned was negotiating with the Mexicans despite the order recalling him, he concluded that the State Department clerk was staying at Scott's "insistence and dictation" and that General Butler was to order him home.

The court of inquiry met in Mexico City on 14 March 1848, but nothing came of it. Worth asked that his charges against Scott be withdrawn, and Scott decided he would not press his charges against Pillow. Moreover, many of the witnesses already had departed for the United States, making any full inquiry difficult. Pillow, however, insisted that the charges be examined, because he believed his friend in the White House would not let him be convicted. Lee, Hitchcock, and Longstreet, among other junior officers, testified to the extravagance of Pillow's claims.

The court adjourned on 21 April to return to the United States to take additional testimony. Scott, leaving Mexico the next day, returned to a vote of thanks from Congress and its request that the president have a gold medal struck for him. He did attend the further session of the court of inquiry when it met at Frederick, Maryland, to hear testimony from Quitman, Twiggs, and others, and on 1 July it delivered its report. It found that Pillow had exaggerated his own importance, but recommended no punishment for him. President Polk promptly approved the court's findings and, realizing that Scott was a great hero to most Americans, invited him and his wife to the White House for dinner.

Trist's treaty arrived at the White House on the evening of 19 February, just seventeen days after it was dated at Guadalupe Hidalgo. The next day, a Sunday, Polk met with his cabinet to discuss the agreement, whose negotiator, Trist, he wanted "severely punished" if some legal means could be found. Polk wrote that Trist was "arrogant, impudent, and very insulting."

The Treaty of Guadalupe Hidalgo presented Polk with difficulty. By the time the treaty was concluded, there was a growing movement in the United States to annex all of Mexico or, at least, several additional north Mexican states. Some proponents of this all-of-Mexico movement were idealistic, arguing that it would be beneficial to Mexicans to have a stable, republican government extended over them. Others were covetous of the mines of Guanajuato and northern Mexico, while yet others wanted an opportunity to grab huge landed estates. There were also many Protestant ministers who thought they might make millions of converts from Catholicism. This movement gained momentum in direct proportion to news of Scott's victories, and by late 1847–early 1848 the stance of the Polk administration toward Mexico was hardening.

Then Trist's treaty arrived. The State Department clerk had overlooked (or conveniently forgotten) some of his instructions. He had not gotten agreement for a U.S. canal across the Isthmus of Tehuantepec. He had not obtained a favorable railroad route to the West Coast by way of the Gila Valley, instead agreeing that no railroad along this route could be built save by mutual consent of both nations. Nor was there a U.S. outlet to the Gulf of California, and, contrary to orders, he had agreed to recognize land grants made in the ceded territory after the declaration of war in 1846. Finally, he had agreed both to an indemnity of $15 million to Mexico and to the assumption of claims against Mexico by private U.S. citizens.

Despite these drawbacks, however, Polk found the treaty to be worth serious consideration. It had been made with only the pretense of an existing government in Mexico and to reject it would mean a long and bloody battle to conquer all of the rest of that nation. The treaty did, however, contain most of what Polk originally had demanded: the Rio Grande was to be the boundary of Texas; New Mexico and California would become part of the United States in return for only

Just after dawn on 14 September 1847, General John Quitman (front) led his troops into the grand plaza of Mexico City and raised the U.S. flag. (National Archives/painting by Sgt. Tom Lovell)

$15 million rather than the $30 million the Mexicans wanted; and the claims issue was settled at long last (at the expense of U.S. taxpayers).

On 21 February, Polk told his cabinet that he would submit the Treaty of Guadalupe Hidalgo to the Senate. He said it was the best that could be obtained without additional fighting, and he believed the Congress would not vote more men and money for that. The only cabinet member to speak against the treaty was Secretary of State Buchanan.

The treaty met a storm of criticism in the Senate. For some it took too much land, for others too little. Abolitionists were against it because they felt it would add probable slave territory to the country. Reflection, however brought a realization that the alternative was a continuation of war, and on 10 March the Senate gave its consent, thirty-eight to fourteen.

As for the negotiator of the treaty, Trist was arrested in Mexico on 17 March 1848 and escorted under guard out of Mexico. He was never brought to trial, although his job in the State Department was forfeited. The expenses he had incurred on his mission and his salary for that period of time were not paid until 1874, shortly before his death.

There was also discontent in Mexico over ratification of this treaty. There was an outburst of indignation everywhere when the terms of the agreement became known, and there appeared dozens of vituperative pamphlets. Peña y Peña and the peace advocates, however, argued that this agreement saved Mexico's honor. The country had not been forced to beg for peace terms, and the $15 million it was to receive in return for the ceded territory, already lost to Mexico, would restore the country to fiscal solvency. New elections were held, a new congress convened, and what one historian called a "quorum of shaking legislators" ratified the treaty.

At 6:00 on the morning of 12 June 1848, the U.S. flag was replaced by the Mexican tricolor above the National Palace in Mexico City.

A formal exchange of ratifications of the treaty took place at Querétaro on 30 May 1846. At that time the Mexican secretary of state and relations, Luís de la Rosa, asked that the U.S. army of occupation remain in Mexico City until Mexican authorities could take precautions to avoid disorders. At 6:00 on the morning of 12 June 1848, the U.S. flag was replaced by the Mexican tricolor above the National Palace in Mexico City, and that same day U.S. troops began withdrawing from Veracruz. The signed copy of the treaty was returned to Washington and delivered to President Polk on the morning of 4 July, and he ordered the secretary of state to proclaim it on that anniversary of the Declaration of Independence.

RESULTS OF THE WAR

The number of casualties in the war with Mexico made it the deadliest conflict in U.S. history in terms of the total deaths per thousands who served per year. Of the 100,182 soldiers, sailors, and marines who participated, 1,548 were killed in action, but another 10,970 died from disease and various other complications—a mortality rate of 110 per 1,000 per annum (as compared with the Civil War rate of 85 and the World War II rate of 30). Moreover, additional thousands died as a result of diseases contracted in Mexico in the months and years after the war. J. J. Oswandel, a veteran of the conflict, wrote in 1885, "After the close of war we returned . . . with a disease contracted in a strange climate, which, in a few years after the war had taken from their homes more than half of those who returned."

Other results of the war were numerous. It made the United States a Pacific power. It led to a Whig victory in the election of 1848, as Zachary Taylor was swept into office over Democrat Lewis Cass. It brought a renewal of intense debate with regard to slavery in the territories, leading to the Compromise of 1850—which, in turn, would lead to the doctrine of squatter sovereignty, the Dred Scott decision, Bleeding Kansas, John Brown's raid, the formation of the Republican party, the election of Abraham Lincoln, and the Civil War. In that bloody "Brother's War," many of the officers who commanded had won their spurs on the field of battle in the conflict with Mexico.

BIBLIOGRAPHY

Alcaraz, Ramón, et al. *The Other Side,* trans. by Albert C. Ramsey (1850).

Bauer, Karl Jack. *Surfboats and Horse Marines: U.S. Naval Operations in the Mexican War* (1969).

Bill, Alfred Hoyt. *Rehearsal for Conflict: The War With Mexico* (1947).

Brooks, Nathan C. *A Complete History of the Mexican War* (1849).

Chidsey, Donald Barr. *The War with Mexico* (1968).

Clarke, Dwight L. *Stephen Watts Kearny: Soldier of the West* (1961).

Connor, Seymour V., and Odie B. Faulk. *North America Divided: The Mexican War, 1846–1848* (1971).

Cooke, Philip St. George. *The Conquest of New Mexico and California* (1878).

Dufour, Charles L. *The Mexican War: A Compact History* (1968).

Dyer, Brainerd. *Zachary Talor* (1946).

Elliott, Charles Winslow. *Winfield Scott: The Soldier and the Man* (1937).

Faulk, Odie B., and Joseph A. Stout, Jr., eds. *The Mexican War: Changing Interpretations* (1973).

Fuller, John D. P. *The Movement for the Acquisition of All Mexico, 1846–1848* (1936).

Furber, George C. *The Twelve Months Volunteer, or, Journal of a Private in the Tennesse Regiment . . .* (1848).

George, Isaac. *Heroes and Incidents of the Mexican War* (1982).

Greer, James K. *Colonel Jack Hays* (rev. 1974).

Hamilton, Holman. *Zachary Taylor: Soldier of the Republic* (1941).

Hammond, George P., ed. *The Treaty of Guadalupe Hidalgo, February Second, 1848* (1949).

Henry, Robert Selph. *The Story of the Mexican War* (1950).

Hitchcock, Ethan Allen. *Fifty Years in Camp and Field,* ed. by William A. Croffut (1909).

Hughes, John Taylor. *Doniphan's Expedition* (1848).

Jenkins, John Stilwell. *History of the War Between the United States and Mexico* (1848).

Johannsen, Robert W. *To the Halls of the Montezumas: The Mexican War in the American Imagination* (1985).

Lavender, David. *Climax at Buena Vista: The American Campaigns in Northeastern Mexico, 1846–47* (1966).

Lawson, Don. *The United States in the Mexican War* (1976).

McAfee, Ward, and J. Cordell Robinson, eds. *Origins of the Mexican War,* 2 vols. (1982).

Merk, Frederick. *The Monroe Doctrine and American Expansionism, 1843–1849* (1966).

Morrison, Chaplain W. *Democratic Politics and Sectionalism: The Wilmot Proviso Controversy* (1967).

Myers, William S., ed. *The Mexican War Diary of General George B. McClellan* (1917).

Nevins, Allan, *Frémont: Pathmarker of the West* (1939).

Nevin, David. *The Mexican War* (1978).

Nichols, Edward J. *Zach Taylor's Little Army* (1963).

Oswandel, J. Jacob. *Notes of the Mexican War* (1885).

Pletcher, David M. *The Diplomacy of Annexation: Texas, Oregon, and the Mexican War* (1973).

Price, Glenn W. *Origins of the War With Mexico* (1967).

Quaife, Milo M., ed. *The Diary of James K. Polk, During His Presidency, 1845 to 1849,* 4 vols. (1910).

Ripley, Robert S. *The War With Mexico,* 2 vols. (1849).

Rippy, James Fred. *The United States and Mexico* (rev. 1931).

Schroeder, John H. *Mr. Polk's War* (1973).

Sellers, Charles G. *James K. Polk: Continentalist: 1843–1846* (1966).

Singletary, Otis A. *The Mexican War* (1960).

Smith, Justin H. *The War With Mexico,* 2 vols. (1919).

Stephenson, Nathaniel W. *Texas and the Mexican War: A Chronicle of the Winning of the Southwest* (1919).

Villa-Amor, Manuel. *Biografia del General Santa-Anna* (1847, rev. 1857).

Weems, John Edward. *To Conquer a Peace: The War Between the United States and Mexico* (1974).

Weinberg, Albert K. *Manifest Destiny: A Study of Nationalist Expansionism in American History* (1935).

— ODIE B. FAULK

Expansion and the Plains Indian Wars

For most Americans, the war with Mexico (1846–1848) reaffirmed the supremacy of the traditional military system of the nation. A small regular army, agreed President James K. Polk and Congress, could in times of war be supplemented by state militias and volunteers. These citizen-soldiers had indeed performed well in the recent conflict. Thus, while the Treaties of Guadalupe-Hidalgo and Buchanan-Pakenham, which secured Texas, New Mexico, California, and Oregon, had increased the total area of the United States by 50 percent, the military establishment of the nation would remain relatively stable. A small standing army was still sufficient to defend national security at minimal cost.

Indeed, a large permanent military would remain an anathema to most Americans throughout the latter half of the nineteenth century. Fears that a regular army might threaten the democratic Republic and the desire to limit the power of the federal government dominated discussions concerning the size of the military. Protected by the Atlantic and Pacific oceans to the east and west, and with Mexico and British Canada posing minimal threats to the south and north, the United States had little reason to fear a surprise invasion. The navy would discourage enemy raids and harass any major amphibious assaults, the army would patrol the frontiers and garrison coastal defenses, and state militias and assembled volunteers would overwhelm any intruders.

These assumptions would not be seriously challenged until the Spanish-American War, but the new territorial acquisitions would call into question the traditional frontier defensive policies. Earlier military and political officials had assumed that Indians could be removed to lands undesirable to white settlers. Several eastern tribes had thus been moved to the Indian Territory, on the fringes of what many still believed to be the Great American Desert. To separate these and other Indians from whites, small army detachments had garrisoned a line of forts established well in advance of American settlements. According to such designs, reserve forces, concentrated at inner posts, such as Jefferson Barracks, Missouri, were to use military roads and water transportation to converge upon any threat.

The new land acquisitions, however, shattered these assumptions. Texas, with its long heritage of white-Indian violence, retained state control over its public lands. In an age of limited federal budgets, this would severely restrict the U.S. government's military efforts in the Lone Star State. Elsewhere, the central government could build posts and establish Indian reservations at minimal cost. In Texas, however, such tracts would have to be leased or purchased from the state.

The new Pacific outposts also presented a problem because settlers would no longer follow the neat east-to-west progression envisioned by earlier defensive schemes. More significant were the astonishing numbers involved in this disorderly migration. Fewer than twenty thousand Americans lived in Oregon and California before 1848; the discovery of gold at Sutter's Mill that year unleashed a massive overland emigration that numbered at least 250,000 by 1860. Thousands more came by sea, boosting the population of California to nearly 380,000. Another sixty-four thousand lived in Washington and Oregon, with Utah boasting about forty thousand residents by 1860. These new arrivals needed protection, thus necessitating more military posts in the Far West.

To reduce commissary and transportation costs at the far-flung western outposts, Secretary of War Charles M. Conrad ordered each garrison to plant a post garden in 1851.

Economy in all things dominated the status of the antebellum army. To cut expenses troops were hired out on extra duty (at between twenty and forty cents per day) as construction workers, rather than hire civilians to build the frontier posts necessary for continued expansion. Because the War Department could not afford to purchase extra ammunition and gunpowder, target practice for regular troops was not conducted on a regular basis. To reduce commissary and transportation costs at the far-flung western outposts, Secretary of War Charles M. Conrad ordered each garrison to plant a post garden in 1851. In an effort to improve mobility

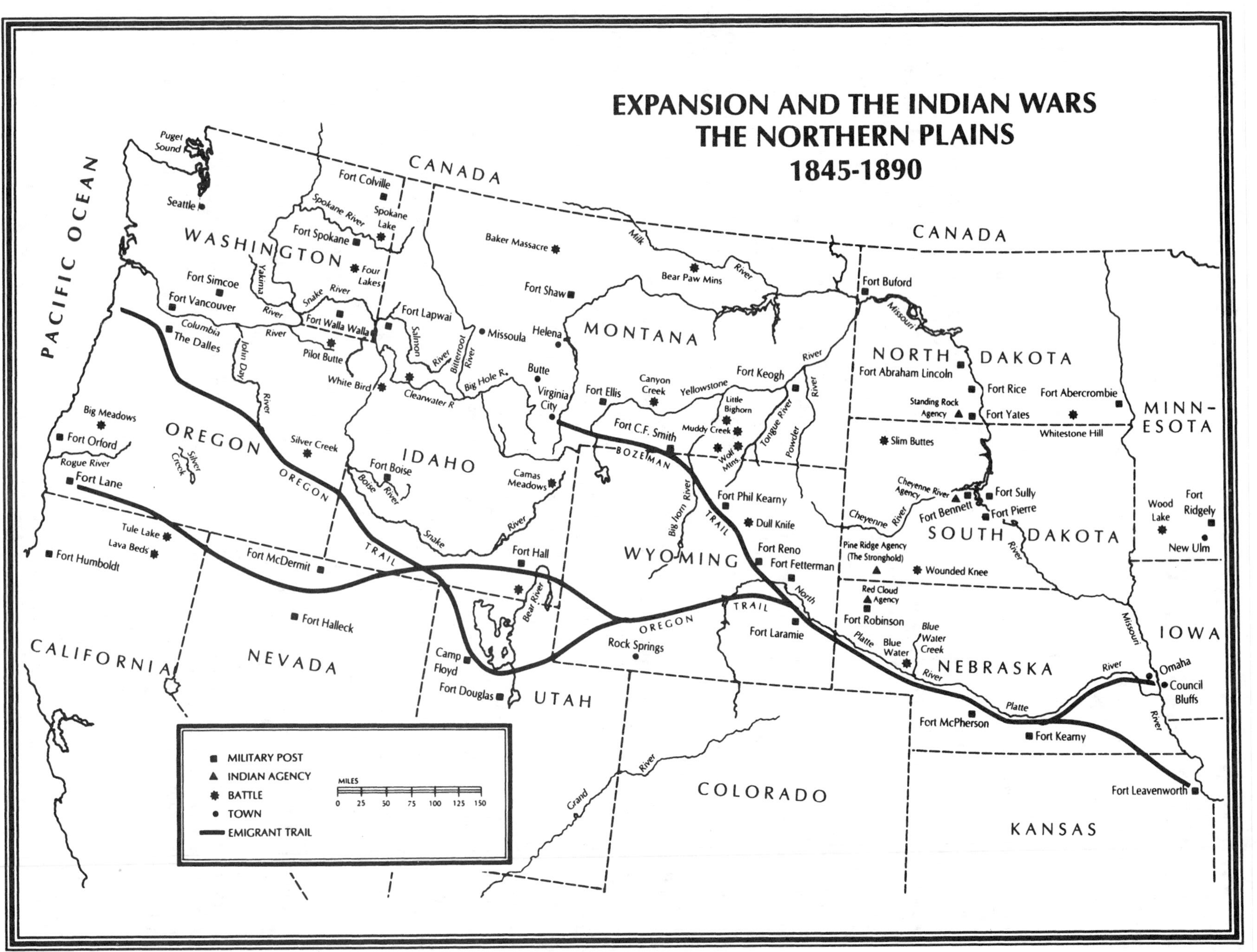
EXPANSION AND THE INDIAN WARS
THE NORTHERN PLAINS
1845-1890
PACIFIC OCEAN
CANADA
CANADA
WASHINGTON
OREGON
CALIFORNIA
NEVADA
IDAHO
MONTANA
WYOMING
UTAH
COLORADO
NORTH DAKOTA
SOUTH DAKOTA
NEBRASKA
KANSAS
MINN-ESOTA
IOWA
Puget Sound
Seattle
Fort Colville
Spokane River
Spokane Lake
Fort Spokane
Four Lakes
Fort Simcoe
Yakima
Fort Vancouver
Columbia River
The Dalles
Snake River
Fort Walla Walla
Fort Lapwai
Salmon River
Bitterroot River
Pilot Butte
John Day River
White Bird
Clearwater R
Big Hole R.
Missoula
Baker Massacre
Fort Shaw
Milk River
Bear Paw Mtns
Helena
Butte
Virginia City
Fort Ellis
Canyon Creek
Yellowstone
Fort Keogh
Little Bighorn
Muddy Creek
Wolf Mtns
Tongue River
Powder River
Fort C.F. Smith
BOZEMAN TRAIL
Big Horn River
Fort Phil Kearny
Dull Knife
Fort Reno
Fort Fetterman
North Platte River
Fort Laramie
OREGON TRAIL
Rock Springs
Big Meadows
Fort Orford
Rogue River
Fort Lane
Silver Creek
Silver Creek
Fort Boise
Boise River
Snake River
Camas Meadows
Fort Hall
Bear River
Tule Lake
Lava Beds
Fort Humboldt
Fort McDermit
Fort Halleck
Camp Floyd
Fort Douglas
Grand River
Fort Buford
Missouri
Fort Abraham Lincoln
Standing Rock Agency
Fort Rice
Fort Yates
Fort Abercrombie
Whitestone Hill
Slim Buttes
Cheyenne River Agency
Cheyenne River
Fort Bennett
Fort Sully
Fort Pierre
Pine Ridge Agency (The Stronghold)
Wounded Knee
Red Cloud Agency
Fort Robinson
Blue Water Creek
Blue Water
Platte River
Fort McPherson
Fort Kearny
Missouri River
Omaha
Council Bluffs
Wood Lake
Fort Ridgely
New Ulm
Fort Leavenworth
MILITARY POST
INDIAN AGENCY
BATTLE
TOWN
EMIGRANT TRAIL
MILES
0 25 50 75 100 125 150

at low cost, several experiments in mounting infantry on horses and mules, all of which proved unsuccessful, were conducted during the 1850s.

The need to reduce expenditures also influenced larger policy decisions. On the advice of Lieutenant Colonel Edwin V. ("Bull") Sumner, Secretary Conrad estimated the annual military expenses in New Mexico to be nearly one-half the real estate value of the territory. Rather than continue the tenuous defense of the region, Conrad proposed that the government buy up all the property of every citizen in New Mexico. With the non-Indian population thus removed, the army might also be withdrawn. According to Conrad, the change would rid the military of a tremendous burden, allow the army to reinforce more valuable areas, and save money.

Although Conrad's proposal was soon forgotten, skyrocketing expenses especially affected the Quartermaster's Department. Before the mid-1840s, all military posts had been accessible by water, but with the recent expansion, many inland forts could only be reached by wagon. The effects were painfully obvious. In 1845 the annual costs to the army to transport men and supplies had been $130,000; in 1851, the cost exceeded two million dollars, with further increases in the coming years. Money that might have been spent on training or recruitment was instead devoted to transportation.

Financial limitations often delayed deployment of new weapons to the frontiers. In 1855 the army adopted a new .58-caliber rifle-musket, a nine-pound weapon that boasted a new primer system and used the recently developed minié balls, replacing the 1842 percussion musket. The War Department also adopted several models of Colt repeating pistols. Those troops equipped with such weapons posed formidable challenges to the Indians, whose bows, arrows, and muskets could match neither the range nor the accuracy of the newer firearms. Army inspectors in the late 1850s frequently bemoaned the fact that soldiers at western posts had not yet received these more modern tools of war and had rarely if ever taken target practice.

In addition to garrisoning the coastal fortifications and attempting to quell violence along the frontiers, the army was also responsible for a wide array of nonmilitary tasks. The regulars had long been pressed into service in building and improving military roads, and the years after 1848 would not alter this practice. With transportation costs so high, it was not surprising that the army took a particularly keen interest in the developing railroad system. As early as 1838, General Edmund P. Gaines presented a detailed plan for frontier defense that featured an extensive system of railroads, to be constructed by soldiers during peacetime.

Military officials continued to study means of reducing transportation costs. In addition to roads and railroads, some urged a massive system of river improvements. Some observers, such as Quartermaster General Thomas S. Jesup, speculated that the Rio Grande might be transformed into a waterway to supply posts in west Texas and New Mexico.

Secretary of War Jefferson Davis sponsored a program to replace army mules and oxen with camels.

Most of these antebellum river improvements failed, and other officials suggested more esoteric plans. Secretary of War Jefferson Davis sponsored a program to replace army mules and oxen with camels. More than seventy of the ungainly beasts were imported to the Southwest, and, in a series of tests, they proved their ability to carry larger loads at lower costs than more traditional work animals. Their handlers, however, found it nearly impossible to deal with the acute halitosis and voluminous sneezing of the camels, plus their fierceness during rutting season. The camels lost their most powerful advocate when Davis resigned as secretary of war, and they were largely forgotten amidst the growing sectional crisis of the late 1850s.

In a more general sense, the army had long recognized the importance of western emigration. By facilitating the expansion of the frontiers, the military might also secure a few friends in Congress or the executive branch. Carrying the brunt of this work was the Corps of Topographical Engineers, reorganized in 1838 under the leadership of Colonel John J. Abert. John C. Frémont, a brash young topographical officer who had married the daughter of Senator Thomas Hart Benton, led three western expeditions that helped bring the corps, and Frémont himself, wide popular acclaim.

Other engineers provided useful services during the war with Mexico, but the heyday of the Corps of Topographical Engineers came in the late 1840s and 1850s. Eager young officers, most full of the dreams that would conquer a continent, helped map the vast expanses of west Texas and the Mexican cession. The corps took a special interest in railroads, and when Congress authorized Secretary of War Davis to survey rail routes to the Pacific Ocean, he assigned many of its best officers to his newly established Bureau of Explorations and Surveys. In 1854 army officers headed scientific parties that examined four potential routes along the forty-eighth, thirty-eighth, thirty-fifth, and thirty-second parallels. Each team reported enthusiastically about its survey, but Davis, a Mississippian, threw his weight behind the southernmost route. Whatever the merits of that survey, however, sectional rivalries quickly combined to block congressional support for any transcontinental railroad.

The army also committed significant resources to check civil disturbances in Kansas and Utah. To restore peace between proslavery and antislavery forces in Kansas, most of the First Cavalry Regiment was deployed to that bloody territory in 1856. Fear of Mormon hegemony led Secretary of War John B. Floyd to dispatch Colonel Albert Sidney Johnston, two infantry regiments, the Second Dragoons, and a battery of artillery into Utah in late 1857. The Mormons initially readied to resist the army, and their extensive defenses and scorched-earth strategy would have cost Johnston's column dearly if some skillful last-minute diplomacy had not brought peace. Upon occupying Utah in June 1858, Johnston was able to support emigrant trains bound for Oregon and California, but these distractions hindered the army's efforts against the Indians of the American West.

Violent encounters with Indians increased during the first half of the 1800s as land-hungry white settlers moved farther and farther west. This poster, dating from about 1800, warns settlers of the Indian threat. (Library of Congress/Corbis)

Only grudgingly did Congress recognize the added responsibilities and importance of the army in westward expansion. The volunteers who had swelled the ranks during the war against Mexico were quickly disbanded—by 1849 only 10,744 officers and men were in uniform, a figure roughly equivalent to that of the previous decade. The army was then reconstituted to include eight infantry, two dragoon, and four artillery regiments, as well as the Regiment of Mounted Riflemen, which had been created in 1846. The mounted and infantry units each included ten companies, the artillery twelve. An act of 1850 increased the army by authorizing companies stationed on the frontier to expand to seventy-four privates each. A captain, assisted by two lieutenants and assorted noncommissioned personnel, headed each unit. Regimental staffs included one colonel, one lieutenant colonel, two majors, two sergeants, and a few musicians. Two officers, drawn from the line companies, served as regimental adjutant and quartermaster.

Plagued by chronic shortages in recruiting and rapid turnover, the army never reached these authorized unit levels. A survey in 1853 showed that of the 13,821 men allowed by law, only 10,417 were actually in uniform. Slightly more than eight thousand men were assigned to the fifty-four western posts, but fewer than seven thousand were actually present at those forts. Desertion rates were about 15 percent per year, while another 12 percent of the men died or were discharged annually.

The survey also found that the western forts boasted an average garrison of 128, but even this figure was inflated, because sickness, extra duty assignments, and recruiting details further stripped available forces. A typical army inspector's assessment was that made in 1860 of Fort Davis, Texas, a strategic post guarding the road between El Paso and San Antonio. One company of the Eighth Infantry garrisoned the fort, but the commanding officer and an escort were away on court-martial duty. A lieutenant and twenty-two enlisted men were on detached service at nearby Fort Quitman. Another officer was temporarily at San Antonio, thus leaving Fort Davis with one commissioned officer, one sergeant, two corporals, twenty-six privates, and a musician. Of those present, seven privates were in confinement and another ten enlisted men were assigned to extra duty, leaving a total disposable force of one officer and twelve men—hardly enough to strike fear into the hearts of the region's Indian tribes.

As a U.S. senator, Jefferson Davis, also a West Point graduate and Mexican War veteran, supported the increase of 1850 and was well aware of the army's dilemma. Appointed secretary of war by Franklin Pierce in 1853, he proved to be one of the most effective champions of the regular military establishment during the antebellum years. Davis pressed hard for another increase, pointing out that the army had expanded by fewer than three thousand men in forty-five years, during which time the population of the nation had grown by eighteen million and the territories by a million square miles. Dispersed in tiny pockets across the vast frontiers, Davis argued, the army's obvious weakness invited Indian attacks. In 1855 he convinced Congress to raise two new infantry and two new cavalry regiments, thus bringing the strength of the regular army to nearly sixteen thousand men.

The officers who comprised the backbone of this force remained a mixed lot. An increasing number—73 percent by the mid-1850s—were graduates of the U.S. Military Academy. Many were well-read and most had won recognition for their gallantry in action during the war with Mexico. The mid-level ranks bulged with men who would rise to greatness in the coming years. Lieutenant Philip H. Sheridan served with the First and Fourth Infantry regiments in Texas and Oregon. Lieutenant Colonel Robert E. Lee helped patrol the frontiers with the Second Cavalry, as did fifteen other men who would become general officers during the Civil War.

Other commissioned personnel, however, left much to be desired. Lieutenant George Crook, who became one of the premier Indian fighters after the Civil War, described the typical post commanders of the 1850s as "petty tyrants" whose long years of frontier isolation narrowed "their habits and minds . . . down to their surroundings." One young lieutenant found in Major John S. Simonsen, a veteran of the War of 1812, "a simple, but kind old fellow . . . deficient in reason, cramped in his understanding and warped in his judgment." Monotony, low pay, poor food, and decrepit housing drove many to drink. Others left the army, including such future Civil War leaders as William T. Sherman, Ulysses S. Grant, and Thomas E. Jackson, disgusted with not only their miserable living conditions but also the slow rate of promotion that resulted from the refusal of Congress to set mandatory retirement ages.

Enlisted personnel reflected equally diverse elements of American society. Official regulations provided that prospective recruits be white males between the ages of eighteen and thirty-five, speak English, and be at least five feet four and a half inches tall. Commissioned personnel complained that many of their soldiers failed to meet even these minimal requirements; indeed, except in times of extreme economic distress (such as the depression of 1857–1859), enlisted life offered few attractions. Immigrants thus dominated the ranks, with Ireland and Germany providing the largest share of recruits.

Most Indians had scant regard for the strange laws of the United States and little appreciation for the determination of Americans to dominate the West.

The army made little effort to develop tactical doctrine applicable to Indian warfare before the Civil War. *The Elements of Military Art and Science* by Henry W. Halleck, first published in 1846, became a staple military primer, but included little notice of nontraditional conflicts. Contemporary tactical manuals, including *Infantry Tactics* (1855) by Captain William J. Hardee and *Cavalry Tactics* (officially adopted in 1861) by Colonel Philip St. George Cooke also concentrated on European-style warfare.

West Point offered little assistance. Mathematics and sciences, rather than tactics and strategy, comprised the bulk of the curriculum. The most celebrated course at the academy, an offering by Professor Dennis Hart Mahan on military and civil engineering and the science of war, briefly emphasized the use of superior firepower and the employment of Indians to fight Indians, but spoke little to the subject of fighting indigenous peoples.

Zealous officers might pick up bits and pieces from more popular accounts, namely Cooke's *Scenes and Adventures in the Army: or, Romance of Military Life.* A few colleagues probably knew something of the report by Captain George B. McClellan on his tour of the Crimean War, in which he suggested that the U.S. Army develop a light cavalry designed to combat western Indians. McClellan's report was relegated to an obscure government document and failed to attract a wide audience.

In fact, conflicts between commanding General Winfield Scott and Secretary of War Davis seemed to take precedence over discussions of strategy and tactics. Scott, a pompous, punctilious man who nonetheless possessed great military talent, saw his position as being independent from the secretary's authority. Several years before Davis even took the cabinet post, Scott declared his independence by moving his offices to New York. Equally proud and difficult, Davis sought to control his testy subordinate, but failing in this, he simply acted without bothering to consult General Scott.

THE ARMY AND THE INDIANS, 1848–1861

With all of its distractions and problems, the United States Army remained a formidable fighting force, with, if emergencies arose, a nearly inexhaustible pool of volunteer reserves. Reasonably well-disciplined and representing a nation determined to fulfill what it believed to be its manifest destiny—expansion to the Pacific Ocean—the regular military faced about 360,000 Indians in the trans–Mississippi West. Approximately eighty-four-thousand of these belonged to the Five Civilized Tribes of the Indian Territory, and another seventy-five thousand roamed what had once been the Louisiana Territory. An estimated twenty-five thousand Indians lived in Texas, with a similar number in the Oregon Country. One hundred and fifty thousand probably inhabited the areas recently secured from Mexico. Most of these Indians had scant regard for the strange laws of the United States and little appreciation for the determination of Americans to dominate the West.

White citizens bent on extermination launched a series of campaigns; two companies at Fort Lane scrambled to protect those Indians who still sought peace.

Bent on encouraging white expansion into the West, the U.S. government nonetheless hoped to avoid warfare. In an effort to improve relations with the tribes, the Indian Bureau was separated from the War Department and incorporated into the newly created Home Department (later the Department of the Interior) in 1849. Civilians, it was hoped, would be more successful than the military had been in negotiating treaties and removing Indians to areas not desired by whites.

Access to the newly acquired regions had to be guaranteed. Therefore, Indian ownership to lands suitable for white development, argued the government, had to be extinguished. Because the tribes were thought to represent inferior cultures, it was believed that they could be removed in the name of progress. Once placed on reservations, the Indians would, in theory, be protected from the evil effects of white society, taught the blessings of Christian civilization, and transformed into thrifty farmers. It was determined that treaties had to be concluded with the various tribes, and although some effort should be made to do so peacefully, the army was seen as a legitimate tool in the work of Indian removal.

THE PACIFIC NORTHWEST. U.S. troops made a less than auspicious entry into the Pacific Northwest, where the murders of Reverend Marcus Whitman, his wife, and a dozen others by Cayuse Indians disrupted the uneasy peace in 1847. Counterstrikes by Oregon volunteers the following year failed, and as late as October 1849, only six companies of regulars were present for duty in the region. Lieutenant Colonel William W. Loring, the one-armed commander of the Eleventh Department (merged with the Tenth Department to form the Pacific Division in 1851), was almost immediately faced with the en masse desertion of a third of his troops to the burgeoning mining camps of southern Oregon and northern California. The newly arrived Regiment of Mounted Riflemen, which was to have comprised the bulk of Loring's command, was broken up in 1851, to the delight of a civilian populace because its ill-disciplined actions had terrorized rather than protected.

Violent encounters with the Indians increased as gold-hungry whites poured into the mountains along the California-Oregon boundary line. In keeping with standard practice, the army established a line of forts designed to keep the two groups apart while government negotiators attempted to convince the tribes to move to reservations to the east. Logistical and manpower shortages limited the regulars, however, as ill-disciplined volunteers took it upon themsevles to rid the country of Indians. In 1853 a series of treaties carved out temporary reservations in the Rogue River area, but neither whites nor Indians respected the official lines of separation. The arrival of fiery Brigadier General John E. Wool to the Department of the Pacific in 1854 exacerbated the civil-military tensions, because Wool blamed the troubles squarely on the antics of local volunteers. His efforts to protect a few of the Indians only incurred the wrath of the settlers.

In October 1855, full-scale war broke out in the Rogue River valley. Oregon volunteers initiated the bloodletting with attacks against three Indian camps. About five hundred Rogue, Shasta, Scoton, Klamath, Grave Creek, Umpqua, and Cow Creek Indians retaliated with a quick strike before fleeing to the mountains. White citizens bent on extermination launched a series of campaigns; two companies of beleaguered regulars at Fort Lane scrambled to protect those Indians who still sought peace, at the same time assisting efforts against those tribes that had joined the hostilities.

In the spring of 1856, Wool was determined to crush the Rogue River uprising. Columns from Forts Humboldt, Lane, and Orford converged against those tribes deemed hostile; further expeditions of Oregon volunteers, along with a sharp action with the regulars at the Battle of Big Meadows (28 May 1856), convinced the Indians to surrender. Twelve hundred persons were eventually removed from the southern Oregon–northern California coastal regions.

Even more formidable military opponents awaited the army east of the mountains. The proud Nez Perce roamed the Columbia and Snake rivers. In the valleys drained by the Snake River resided the Yakima, Klikitat, Palouse, Umatilla, and Walla Walla tribes. To the north lived the Spokane, Coeur d'Alene, Pend d'Oreilles, and Flatheads. These tribes, most of whom owned considerable horse herds, lived seminomadic lives, exchanging the fisheries of the spring and fall for the mountain berries and roots of the summer harvest. Long familiar

A delegation of government agents pose with Indian representatives on the White House grounds in Washington D.C. in 1876. (National Archives)

with the traders of Hudson's Bay Company, they had acquired firearms, but were often split between progressive factions that espoused Christianity and more conservative groups that followed traditional beliefs.

In 1855 government agents initiated a determined effort to place these people on defined reservations. Isaac I. Stevens, governor of Washington Territory, led the campaign. A West Point graduate and confirmed supporter of a transcontinental railroad, Stevens wanted clear title to the Pacific Northwest from the Indians. A few tribes signed treaties, even as gold discoveries near Fort Colville, along the border with British Canada, led to another torrent of intruders across the Cascade Mountains and up the Columbia River. Sparked by the leadership of Kamaiakin, other Indians determined to resist the encroachments. Major Gabriel J. Rains sought to overawe the tribes with a demonstration of force in the fall of 1855, but hundreds of angry warriors checked the three companies sent to do the job. A mixed column of regulars and territorial militia that penetrated the Yakima River country in the closing months of 1855 only drove more tribes into the opposing camp, as did a subsequent volunteer sweep through the Walla Walla Valley.

As General Wool feuded with Governor Stevens over the incendiary actions of the volunteers, Colonel George Wright and the Ninth Infantry poured into the Pacific Northwest. The regulars cleared the Puget Sound region of Indians in the spring of 1856. Meanwhile, Wright pushed into the Yakima country and, in a bloodless campaign that satisfied neither whites nor Indians, concluded an uneasy peace. From the newly established Fort Simcoe and Fort Walla Walla, the army maintained a semblance of order until spring 1858, when Spokane, Coeur d'Alene, and Palouse warriors nearly annihilated three companies of dragoons near Spokane Lake.

Wool, whose order closing eastern Washington to white settlement had irritated many, had been transferred to a quieter eastern station in 1857. His replacement, Colonel Newman S. Clarke, was determined to crush all Indian resistance and thus expedite new westward migration. Major Robert S. Garnett would push out from Fort Simcoe while Wright marched north from Fort Walla Walla. Garnett struck a camp of Yakima and forced their surrender, but Wright, a superb tactician and regimental commander, inflicted even more telling blows. With two mountain howitzers and nearly six hundred men, many of whom carried the new model 1855 Springfield .58-caliber rifled muskets, Wright dealt the Indians a pair of stinging defeats at the Battles of Four Lakes (1 September 1858) and Spokane River (5 September). The regulars reported only one man wounded in the unequal duels, while the Indians, whose muskets could not match the ranges of the new rifles in these conventional battles, were routed with heavy losses. Wright ordered several Indian leaders hung, and the remaining tribes were forced to accept the Stevens treaties of 1855.

THE ARMY IN TEXAS. Texas posed unique problems for the U.S. Army. Its enormous size brought huge transportation costs and made communication between scattered frontier stations extremely difficult. The long border with Mexico presented innumerable opportunities for Indian raiders, petty thieves, and revolutionaries to escape pursuers by crossing the Rio Grande. The thousands of California-bound immigrants also demanded protection and forced the army to extend its defenses far past existing non-Indian settlements. The Treaty of Guadalupe-Hidalgo had also obliged the U.S. government to prevent incursions into Mexico from the American side. Not to be forgotten was the Lone Star republic's virulent expansionism and anti-Indian policies, which left the remaining indigenous people determined to fight for their tribal lands.

General George Mercer Brooke began establishing a string of forts across central Texas in the late 1840s and early 1850s. He also proposed a three-pronged offensive against the Plains tribes, but the chronic shortage of manpower precluded such a move. With Brooke's death, Brevet Major General Persifor Smith succeeded to department command in 1851. By the mid-1850s, Smith's soldiers had erected another line of federal posts. According to theory, mounted troops would man the inner line and chase down enemy intruders; at the same time, infantry garrisons at the outer posts would cut off Indian retreat onto the Great Plains.

In practice, this plan left much to be desired. The regulars were too few, the distances too great, and the Indian raiders too crafty to fall victim to the army's traps. Texans howled for action and derided the regulars, particularly the infantry. Although another chain of posts was established along the road between San Antonio and El Paso during the mid-1850s, Texans made little effort to hide their displeasure with the federal government. Only locally raised and mounted rangers, argued the Texans, could effectively combat the mobile warriors of the southern Plains.

Secretary of War Davis dispatched the crack Second Cavalry Regiment to Texas, but also urged state officials to set aside public lands for Indian reservations. Reluctantly, the state established two reserves along the upper Brazos River in 1854; continued violence and loud protests by Texas congressmen, however, led the federal government to abort the experiment five years later. A similar project west of the Pecos River never got off the ground.

Far more satisfactory to Texans were a series of military operations during the late 1850s. A contingent of Texas Rangers led by Captain John S. ("Rip") Ford struck first. Operating independently of the regulars, Ford's Rangers, aided by one hundred Indian auxiliaries, splashed across the Red River in the early spring of 1858. At the Battle of Antelope Hills (11 May), the Texans routed several hundred Comanche. Rather than overawing the tribesmen, however, the action inspired bitter retaliatory raids. With the entire Second Cavalry Regiment conveniently gathered at Fort Belknap (orders to transfer the horse soldiers to Kansas had only recently been cancelled), Brigadier General David E. Twiggs, having assumed command of the Department of Texas in May 1857, opted for another offensive.

To lead the campaign, Twiggs selected Brevet Major Earl Van Dorn, a battle-hardened combat veteran of wars against Mexico and the Florida Seminole. With four troops of cavalrymen and several dozen Indian auxiliaries from the short-lived Brazos Reservation, Van Dorn left Fort Belknap on 15 September 1858. Establishing their base in the southwest corner of Indian Territory, the command received word that Buffalo Hump and his Comanche were encamped at Rush Spring. A series of forced marches allowed Van Dorn to approach the enemy unnoticed. Taking advantage of his surprise, the major led three companies directly into the village while the fourth company and the Indian allies went after the horses just after daybreak on 1 October. Four soldiers were killed and twelve others, including Van Dorn and the leader of the auxiliaries, were wounded in the swirling melee. Enemy losses were much heavier—fifty-eight dead, 120 lodges burned, three hundred horses captured, and irreplaceable winter supplies lost to the soldiers.

In strictly military terms, Rush Spring had been a complete success for the U.S. military. The aftermath of the battle, however, dramatically symbolized the western dilemma of the army. Unknown to Van Dorn, several Comanche chiefs had concluded a treaty six weeks before the fight. Buffalo Hump had freely admitted that he intended to lead raids into Texas that summer, but the federal government's actions—extending one hand of friendship while using the other as a mailed fist—had seemed no less duplicitous.

The Comanche reacted vigorously, launching raid after raid onto the northern Texas frontiers. Van Dorn's victory at Crooked Creek the following year (13 May 1859) almost completely annihilated an entire Comanche village of nearly one hundred inhabitants, but did no more than the Battle of Rush Spring to bring peace. Troopers from Kansas, New Mexico, and Fort Cobb, Indian Territory, swept the southern Plains again in 1860, but only seemed to further antagonize the tribes.

The army also erected a series of military posts in New Mexico. With the transfer of Sumner, Brigadier General John Garland took command of the Department of the West and initiated several offensive thrusts during the mid-1850s. The Jicarilla Apache were humbled by late 1854; although the Mescalero Apache dodged several army columns, they too accepted a reservation in south central New Mexico when confronted by three hundred infantrymen commanded by Lieutenant Colonel Dixon Miles. After three months of hard campaigning, mixed volunteer-regular columns led by Colonel Thomas T. Fauntleroy and trapper Cerán St. Vrain defeated the Ute in spring 1855.

THE ARMY IN NEW MEXICO. Despite these efforts, other Indians continued to harass non-Indian emigrants and settlers in New Mexico and Arizona. Colonel Benjamin L. E. Bonneville surprised a large camp of Coyotero Apache along the Gila River on 27 June 1857, killing or wounding nearly forty warriors and taking forty-five women and children captive. Brevet Lieutenant Colonel William Hoffman's seven infantry companies were enough to impress the Mohave, who had earlier driven back a large emigrant party, to sue for peace in 1859.

Lured by gifts and promises of future annuities, few chiefs realized that they had promised to allow the U.S. government to build military posts across their tribal homelands.

The more numerous Navaho proved more resilient. Several military thrusts into their homelands produced a temporary truce in late December 1858, but open warfare again erupted thirteen months later. In an unusually bold move, several hundred Navaho warriors attacked Fort Defiance in April 1860. The garrison held, and reinforcements raced to New Mexico. Three army columns pushed west from Fort Defiance into Arizona. Failing to secure a decisive victory, the troops nonetheless inflicted great damage upon the Navaho herds and crops. The onset of the secession crisis in 1860–1861, however, prevented local commanders from implementing the subsequent winter campaign envisioned by Washington officials.

THE GREAT PLAINS. The War Department had long analyzed the military problems associated with expansion into the Great Plains. During the 1830s Secretaries of War Lewis Cass and Joel R. Poinsett had based their plans for western defense on the idea of a permanent Indian frontier. As settlers streamed west, however, it became evident that static defense was impracticable. Small dragoon expeditions thus began to comb the vast lands west of the Mississippi River during the late 1830s. Hoping that a show of force might overawe the Plains tribes before violence against white overlanders became commonplace, Colonel Stephen Watts Kearny led five companies of horsemen from Fort Leavenworth, Kansas, to the Rocky Mountains in 1845. Similarly, Congress attempted to protect emigrants on the Oregon Trail by creating the Regiment of Mounted Riflemen the following year.

Kearny's mounted force had met representatives of several tribes in its 2,200-mile roundtrip journey. Convinced that this display of American military might have impressed the Indians, Kearny argued that periodic mounted columns might dispel the need for permanent military posts in the Great Plains. During the war against Mexico, regular and volunteer columns continued to patrol the Santa Fe and Oregon trails. Notably, however, one of the most vocal leaders of these battalions, William Gilpin, had concluded that key strategic positions must be occupied if the migrants were to be protected. At the urging of Adjutant General Roger Jones and Secretary of War George W. Crawford, troops erected Fort Atkinson (1950) and Fort Union (1851) to guard the Santa Fe Trail. Colonel Loring had already begun the process on the route to Oregon, establishing Fort Kearny (1846) and garrisoning older trading posts at Forts Laramie, Hall, and Vancouver.

Several government officials questioned the reversion to a fixed-post strategy. Indian agent Thomas Fitzpatrick joined commanding General Scott and Colonel Fauntleroy in advocating the abandonment of the costly, manpower-intensive forts in favor of roving columns launched from a strategic base, a concept also supported by Quartermaster General Jesup. Fort Riley, established in 1853 near the junction of the Kansas and Republican rivers, was intended to replace Forts Leavenworth, Scott, Atkinson, Kearny, and Laramie, but abandoning military posts proved politically unpalatable to western congressmen, who saw each site as an uncommonly good source of patronage and federal contracts. The small forts also served as helpful way stations for travelers and stimulated settlement, and the army dared not antagonize its western supporters.

Diplomacy, it was hoped, might substitute for immediate military action. Chiefs of the northern tribes signed treaties with Indian Bureau agents at Fort Laramie in 1851; two years later, negotiations with southern tribes resulted in similar pacts at the Fort Atkinson

The U.S. Army erected a series of military posts in New Mexico to deal with uncooperative Apache and Navaho. In this photograph, the U.S. 6th Cavalry trains at Fort Bayard, New Mexico, during the 1880s. (National Archives)

conferences. Lured by gifts and promises of future annuities, few chiefs realized that they had promised to end their intertribal feuds and to allow the U.S. government to build overland trails and military posts across their tribal homelands.

However earnest the supplications of the diplomats might have been, good intentions could not hide the clear and present danger on the Great Plains. The white intruders, convinced of their own moral and cultural righteousness, made little effort to understand the tribal ways of the indigenous peoples. Equally sure of their own superiority, the Indians failed to comprehend the zeal with which the newcomers approached the American West. With garrisons at many of the Plains forts reduced to a single company, tensions increased when a Miniconjou Sioux fired a shot at a soldier outside Fort Laramie in June 1853. Only a year out of West Point and anxious to make his mark in the army, Lieutenant Hugh Fleming and a squad of twenty-three men attempted to arrest the wayward marksman. The soldiers killed six Indians but failed to bring back their captive.

With the Sioux still in an ugly mood the following year, Brevet Second Lieutenant John L. Grattan, fresh out of West Point and still awaiting his permanent appointment, determined to show the Sioux the supremacy of white military techniques. Backed by two howitzers, Grattan, an interpreter, two NCOs, and twenty-seven privates, moved into a Brulé Sioux village and demanded that a young warrior accused of slaughtering a stray cow be given up. Enraged at the defiance of the Indians, Grattan unlimbered the cannons and fired. The shells went high and the Indians swarmed over the outnumbered soldiers. One mortally wounded regular struggled back to Fort Laramie to report the events.

The Plains Wars had begun. Secretary of War Davis recalled Brevet Brigadier General William S. Harney, veteran of the Black Hawk, Seminole, and Mexican wars, from leave in Paris to direct the army's response. At the head of six hundred men as he rode out of Fort Kearny in August 1855, Harney determined to strike first and negotiate later. "By God, I'm for battle—no peace," roared the colonel. Discovering a Brulé camp of two hundred and fifty persons in western Nebraska along Blue Water Creek, Harney took his infantry straight at the Indian lodges and sent four troops of mounted men to hit the enemy rear. The soldiers routed the Sioux, killing or capturing well over half of the village's inhabitants.

Harney then pushed north into the Dakotas, wintering along the Missouri River at the dilapidated old fur trading post of Fort Pierre. The following spring, the colonel received promises of peace from seven Sioux tribes. Although the Senate refused to ratify the soldier-chief's treaties, the Indians of the upper Missouri had been cowed for nearly a decade.

To the south, several violent incidents in 1856 between the Cheyenne and whites convinced both sides to take to the warpath the following year. With a semblance of order having been restored among proslavery and abolitionist factions in Kansas, Colonel Sumner's First Cavalry Regiment spearheaded the thrust from Fort Leavenworth. After nearly two months of campaigning, Sumner encountered three hundred mounted Cheyenne on 29 July 1857. With their left flank resting comfortably on the Solomon Fork of the Kansas River and their spirits buoyed by the assurances of a medicine man that the enemy's bullets had been rendered harmless, the warriors braced for battle. Sumner deployed his own forces, of roughly equal size. Both sides thundered forward on a collision course; the colonel, to the surprise of his own command, ordered his men to sling their carbines and draw sabers.

The medicine man's magic had no power over the flashing swords. The Cheyenne hesitated, then broke. Savage individual combats followed as the cavalry horses galloped after the fleeing ponies. Although Sumner reported only nine Indians killed (his own wounded included the dashing young cavalier J. E. B. Stuart), the Battle of the Solomon was a dramatic psychological victory for the cavalry. During the following winter, the Cheyenne, whose lands had been violated and whose battlefield supremacy had been challenged, remained quiet despite the intrusions of prospectors heading toward new mining camps west of Denver.

THE CIVIL WAR

The secession of eleven southern states and the onset of the Civil War had a dramatic effect upon the American West. Three hundred and thirteen officers, including such stalwart Indian fighters as Lee, Stuart, Van Dorn, and John Bell Hood, resigned their commissions and joined the ranks of the Confederacy. The vast majority of enlisted men, however, remained loyal to the Union. Most of the regulars marched east to confront the rebellion, to be replaced by state and territorial volunteers. The exodus of the southern states, which had often opposed the creation of new governments in the West, allowed Congress to create several new territories—Colorado, Dakota, and Nevada in 1861 (with Nevada securing statehood in 1864), Idaho and Arizona in 1863, and Montana in 1864.

The Civil War wreaked havoc on the Texas frontiers. The withdrawal of federal forces left the state vulnerable to attack by Indians whose cultural proclivities toward warfare had been fired by motives of revenge. As thousands of Texans joined Confederate armies in Virginia, Tennessee, and Arkansas, Texas officials scraped together a few mounted regiments for frontier duty. These poorly supplied units, however, could not protect every western settlement. Texans living in exposed counties often banded together to erect crude defensive stockades for self-protection, but the Battle of Dove Creek (8 January 1865), in which fourteen hundred migratory Kickapoo routed a 370-man ranger force led by Captain Henry Fossett, seemed indicative of the crisis.

Wartime mobilization did allow white expansionists to secure major gains in New Mexico. After driving back a Confederate invasion force in 1862, federal troops there turned their attention to the Indians. The Department of New Mexico commander, Colonel James Henry Carleton, an autocratic professional who determined to make no concessions with any Indians, found in frontiersman Christopher ("Kit") Carson an ideal man for his uncompromising policies. Most of the Mescalero Apache were removed to the Bosque Redondo Reservation. After dodging Carson's columns for nearly nine months in 1863–1864, the Navaho also succumbed to reservation life. Carson also struck a large Kiowa village on 25 November 1864; in a fiercely fought engagement with the Kiowa and a nearby Comanche camp, Carson destroyed the lodges and with artillery support from two howitzers managed to escape with his own force largely intact. Only in Arizona, where the Yavapai and Chiricahua Apache continued to harass would-be miners who flocked to the mining camps of southern Arizona, were Carleton's legions unable to force a temporary peace.

In Brigadier General Wright's Department of the Pacific, volunteer forces managed to preserve the long communication lines through California, Oregon, Nevada, and Utah. On 27 January 1863, California troops under Colonel Patrick E. Connor won a signal victory by storming Bear Hunter's fortified Shoshone village, located along the Bear River in southeastern Idaho. More than two hundred Shoshone were killed in the bloody assault, which cost nearly seventy California casualties. Nearly three months later, another column scattered two hundred Ute at Spanish Fork Canyon, Utah (15 April 1863). The remaining Shoshone, Ute, Bannock, and Gosiute quickly made peace. Other campaigns in northern California, southern Oregon, and central Nevada also proved largely successful.

Conditions to the north deteriorated badly during the Civil War. In Minnesota, Little Crow's Santee Sioux had long suffered at the hands of white intruders. Repeated delays in annual annuities and chronic food shortages created a tempest that boiled over in August 1862. A two-day bloodletting left four hundred whites dead. Assaults on Fort Ridgely and New Ulm, however, were repulsed with severe loss. An attempted ambush of Colonel Henry H. Sibley's Minnesota volunteers at Wood Lake (23 September 1862) also failed, with about two thousand Sioux subsequently turning themselves in. The most belligerent fled west, with Sibley inflicting heavy casualties upon an informal Sioux coalition in a summer campaign in 1863. A second volunteer column from Nebraska and Iowa, headed by the experienced Brigadier General Alfred Sully, drove into present-day North Dakota. At the Battle of Whitestone Hill (3 September 1863), Sully's legions killed over three hundred Sioux and captured another two hundred and fifty women and children.

Violence also spread to the central Plains, where the expeditionary columns of 1860 had failed to encounter significant resistance. Although the overland and emigrant mail routes had been subjected to some harassment, most tribes remained relatively tolerant of the intruders during the early stages of the Civil War. Colorado officials, such as district commander Colonel John M. Chivington, however, feared a major Indian uprising, and launched a series of probing actions in spring 1864. The Plains tribes struck back against the trails with a savage fury, leading to another flurry of volunteer expeditions that cost a great deal of money and energy but failed to locate many Indians.

Disregarding the U.S. flag that flew over Black Kettle's tepee, the Colorado volunteers swept through the village, slaughtering two hundred Indians.

As winter approached peace factions regained the initiative among several tribes. Led by Black Kettle, some Cheyenne and Arapaho opened negotiations with government officials, but Chivington declared all Indians to be hostile, and attacked Black Kettle's village near Sand Creek, Colorado, on 28 November 1864. Disregarding the U.S. flag that flew over Black Kettle's tepee, the Colorado volunteers swept through the village, slaughtering two hundred Indians, two-thirds of whom were women and children.

Ripples from the Sand Creek massacre swept the Plains. More than fifteen hundred Cheyenne, Oglala, Brulé, and Arapaho warriors gathered to launch a wave of attacks through the Platte and Powder River valleys. To deal with the crisis, Lieutenant General Grant created a large new command, the Division of the Missouri, which would consolidate the entire Plains regions into a single administrative unit. To command the new division, Grant selected Major General John Pope, a failure against the Confederates but still considered by fellow officers a solid Indian fighter. Pope immediately began planning a major offensive, which some speculated might include twelve thousand men.

Originally slated to begin in April 1865, supply foul-ups, contract problems, and a new peace initiative coming from Senator James R. Doolittle's congressional committee on Indian relations delayed Pope's offensive until the summer. In the meantime, the Indian coalition had ambushed a small escort just outside the Platte Bridge Station in central Wyoming. On 26 July the Indians, at the cost of sixty killed and more than one hundred wounded, finally succeeded in destroying an approaching wagon train. To the south, because most of the Plains tribes were opting for peace, one projected offensive was abandoned by the army.

Three columns, commanded by Brigadier General Connor, finally pushed out from Omaha and Fort Laramie in July and early August. Collectively totaling twenty-five hundred soldiers, the expeditions scoured the Powder River region for two months. An early blizzard, the rugged terrain, and poor army leadership, however, combined to largely thwart the effort. Another eight hundred men under Sully pushed up the Missouri River into the northern Dakotas, but once again produced few tangible results. At a cost of well over $20 million, the summer campaigns of 1865 had killed no more than one hundred Indians.

THE POST–CIVIL WAR ARMY

In May 1865 the combined armies of the United States had numbered more than one million men. Swift demobilization followed the defeat of the Confederacy, as the volunteers were mustered out and the regulars slowly returned to the frontiers. In July 1866 Congress cut the peacetime army to 54,302; further reductions in 1869, 1870, and 1874 trimmed the maximum authorized regular force to just over twenty-seven thousand. The reconstituted army would include ten cavalry, twenty-five infantry, and five artillery regiments. In partial recognition of the service provided by black volunteers during the Civil War, two cavalry (the Ninth and Tenth) and two infantry (the Twenty-fourth and Twenty-fifth) regiments would be comprised of black enlisted personnel. Black officers, however, remained virtually unknown during the postbellum years, with the first black graduate of West Point, Lieutenant Henry O. Flipper, court-martialed for dubious cause in 1882.

Although even the force of twenty-seven thousand represented an increase over the antebellum military, the growing national population and continued westward expansion would have made the army's task extremely difficult, and circumstances were less than ideal. From 10 to 15 percent of the soldiers guarded the arsenals and coastal defenses of the east, and were as such unavailable for service against the Indians. In 1885 a special board headed by Secretary of War William C. Endicott recommended major improvements in the seaboard defenses. Congress refused to fund all the proposals, but further attention was nonetheless paid to such defensive needs in the wake of the Endicott plan.

From 1865 to 1877, Reconstruction drained even more manpower. Federal forces occupied the South immediately after the war, but their powers and authority remained unclear until the Reconstruction Act of 1867, which carved the unreconstructed states into five military districts. In that year duties involved nearly 40 percent of the army, and even as late as 1876, about 15 percent of the regulars were stationed in the South. The army's efforts to supervise the new governments and to guarantee the rights of freedmen proved immensely unpopular among white southerners. Congressional Democrats also challenged the military's activist role, and the resurgence of the Democrats would not augur well for advocates of a stronger military establishment in following years.

Although the Civil War had confirmed the supremacy of the federal government, lawmakers generally proved reluctant to assert this authority, particularly after the end of Reconstruction. The number of federal agencies thus remained small. Rather than creating new offices to handle emerging problems, Congress and the executive branch continued to rely upon the U.S. Army, which seemed to many politicians a convenient alternative to new bureaucracy. As such, the regulars undertook a variety of quasi-military responsibilities in the late nineteenth century.

These duties encompassed a wide array of tasks. Civilian scientists and explorers in the American West required military escorts. In addition, under the direction of the Signal Service and Corps of Engineers, the army conducted extensive surveys and observations of its own throughout the period. The United States Weather Bureau, for example, was created in 1870 from one branch of the Signal Service. Likewise, the army served as official custodian of the Yellowstone, Yosemite, General Grant, and Sequoia national parks during the 1880s and 1890s. Squads of cavalry policed these natural wonders, protecting wildlife and suppressing vandalism by careless tourists. In the absence of federal relief agencies, troops distributed food, blankets, and shoes to civilians rendered destitute by natural disaster. Similarly, when a fire destroyed much of Chicago in 1871, four companies of regulars were called in to help restore order to the city.

The army also took an active role in quelling the internal disorders of the late nineteenth century. Nearly four thousand soldiers participated in the government's efforts to reopen the railroads during the strikes of 1877. Federal troops occupied Seattle, Washington; Omaha, Nebraska; and Rock Springs, Wyoming, during a wave of anti-Chinese riots during the 1880s. In 1894 nearly two-thirds of the army stood poised to intervene against domestic unrest; in Chicago, General Nelson A. Miles used his troops to assist railroad management during the Pullman strikes. Still fearful of the power of the Mormons in Utah, the government also dispatched troops into Deseret on several occasions.

The diversion of so many troops away from duties along the Indian frontiers posed major hurdles. Civilian demands for protection against Indian attack or for offensive campaigns against tribes deemed hostile could not always be met while quasi-military responsibilities siphoned off available units. The army remained committed to national expansion, but limited manpower made it impossible to garrison every area and prevented the military from opening simultaneous offensives throughout the West.

Problems of organization and administration, doctrine, and politics added to the dilemma. As had been the case before the Civil War, the military divided the American West into a series of districts, departments, and divisions, including the Division of the Missouri (generally encompassing Texas, New Mexico, and the lands drained by the Missouri River and its tributaries) and the Division of the Pacific (the Pacific coast plus Arizona), which were the prime commands for Indian duty. The commands were organized largely for convenience, with the number of divisions usually equal to the number of two-star generals. Brigadier generals typically handled the departments, with periodic administrative changes being tailored to fit personnel rather than military necessity.

In theory, the secretary of war, after consultation with the president, would set general policy for the commanding general, who would then lend his military expertise in refining and issuing more detailed instructions to division commanders, who would add their own endorsements in forwarding orders to the respective department chiefs. Had everyone followed proper military procedure, had the respective authorities of the secretary of war and commanding general been clearly delineated, and had the separation of responsibilities between staff

U.S. soldiers watched Shoshone Indians dance at Fort Washakie, Wyoming, in 1892. After fighting in the 1860s, the Shoshone tribe made peace with white settlers. Shoshone Chief Washakie, (left, pointing) provided the army with scouts and warriors. (National Archives)

and line officers been clear, the system might have worked reasonably well.

The post–Civil War military establishment, however, benefited from none of these routine procedures or definitions in authority. The long-standing dispute between war secretaries and commanding generals grew worse, the latter position remaining ill-defined, even though it was held by such tested Civil War veterans as William T. Sherman (1869–1883), Philip H. Sheridan (1883–1888), John M. Schofield (1888–1895), and Nelson A. Miles (1895–1903). Of these individuals, only Schofield, who had briefly served as secretary of war from 1868 to 1869, opted not to challenge the secretary's authority. Disgusted with his rivalry with Secretary William W. Belknap, Sherman transferred the offices of the commanding general to Saint Louis in 1874. For the next two years, during which some of the largest campaigns against Indians took place, the senior general was virtually removed from discussions regarding his troops. Belknap's subsequent resignation to avoid charges of selling post sutlerships allowed Sherman to return to Washington, D.C., but the fundamental problem remained unresolved. Sheridan subsequently tested, without success, Secretary of War Robert T. Lincoln; Miles would later confront Elihu Root, who responded by abolishing the commanding general's office altogether.

Controversies between staff and line officers also divided the army. The brigadier generals in command of the War Department's ten staff bureaus after the Civil War (Adjutant General's Office, Inspector General's Department, Judge-Advocate General's Office, Quartermaster Department, Subsistence Department, Ordnance Department, Corps of Engineers, Medical Department, Signal Bureau, and Pay Department) controlled their petty fiefdoms with virtual impunity. Staff personnel, often protected by strong political alliances, controlled logistics and weapons development. Line officers, jealous of the influence and privileges of their rivals, demanded a system of rotation between staff and line positions. Staff officers, they charged, had grown soft and cared little for the welfare of men in the field and in combat.

Confusion over proper doctrine against Indians also hampered the army. Few officers showed much interest in questions of strategy; those who did concerned themselves almost entirely with issues related to traditional, European-style foes. Those who hoped to reform the U.S. military system found a limited audience during the nineteenth century. The most notable reformer, Emory Upton, compiled a manuscript, "The Military Policy of the United States," which eventually served as an important guide for Secretary Root, who led a major renaissance in organizational thinking after the war against Spain. Upton's work, however, contained little of interest to those fighting Indians, and although compiled before his death in 1881, was not published until 1904. Although a few commissioned personnel supported new postgraduate educational programs, the typical officer continued to scorn the proverbial schoolbook soldier.

In the absence of formal doctrine, experience and tradition provided a few generally accepted means of dealing with Indians and assisting expansion. Fixed posts, as had been the case before the Civil War, again provided the basis for these efforts. Railroad and telegraph lines also continued to receive the army's close attention. Decisive results could only be obtained, argued military leaders, through offensive action, but the army faced a cruel dilemma, because mounted warriors from the military societies of the Plains tribes comprised a growing percentage of those Indians deemed hostile by the federal government. Forcing these skilled tribesmen to fight posed a major problem. Horses were too expensive to maintain in the field, thus prohibiting the military from mounting all of its soldiers, and the sheer vastness of the American West made it difficult for even the most determined columns to track down their foes.

Only the most perceptive officers learned to overcome these obstacles. To increase mobility, the regulars often abandoned their wagons in favor of the more ambulatory mules. Miles, one of the ablest of the Indian fighters, mounted his Fifth Infantry Regiment on captured ponies and even managed to deploy light mountain howitzers. More widespread was the employment of Indian auxiliaries, essential in tracking and defeating their brethren declared hostile by federal authorities. Converging columns also proved their worth, at tactical as well as strategic levels. By threatening Indian villages from several directions, such columns often forced the warriors to stand and fight under unfavorable tactical conditions.

Political hurdles severely hindered military effectiveness. "The army," wrote Sherman in 1873, "has no 'policy' about Indians or anything else. It has no voice in Congress, but accepts the laws as enacted." Following Sherman's apolitical lead, the army neglected to mount an effective lobbying campaign, a failure that contrasted starkly with the determined efforts of the navy during the period to enlist public and congressional support for modern warships. Private traders, contractors, and local interests thus weighed more immediately in the minds of most congressmen than did the nation's army. With Civil War veterans offering eloquent testimony to the effectiveness of volunteers, the traditional fears of a standing military establishment detracted from efforts to build a larger regular force. The army's political weakness was perhaps nowhere better demonstrated than in June 1877, when a congressional impasse over appropriations left officers without pay for nearly five months.

"The army," wrote Sherman in 1873, "has no 'policy' about Indians or anything else. It has no voice in Congress, but accepts the laws as enacted."

Conflicts with other governmental agencies and civilian reformers further complicated the task of the War Department. Few tribes respected the artificial boundaries with Mexico and Canada, and the army demanded permission to pursue Indians accused of depredations across these lines. International cooperation, argued officers on the scene, was also necessary. To secure these ends, the army depended upon the State Department, whose agents viewed the military effort against Indians as only one part of a much broader range of international relations. Thus, securing a reciprocal crossing agreement with Mexico (such agreements were concluded in 1880 and 1882) remained only a secondary goal of the State Department's diplomacy.

The Department of Interior proved even more recalcitrant. The essential problem remained the same as before the Civil War—the military jurisdiction of the army did not extend to the reservations, which were administered by a branch of the Interior Department, the Bureau of Indian Affairs. Military men claimed that Indians committed depredations off their reservations, then fled back to the reserves for safety just ahead of their army pursuers. Emphasizing the corruption that infected many Indian Bureau agencies, the army also asserted that its officers could better distribute supplies and administer justice on the reservations than the political hacks who had received government jobs by virtue of their personal connections. All Indian affairs, claimed nearly every general officer, should be consolidated under the aegis of the Department of War.

Interior Department officials denied such accusations. Army officers trained in the arts of war could scarcely be qualified to initiate peaceful efforts with the tribes, which required men who espoused Christian morality. Transferring Indian affairs to the War Department, argued Interior officials, would merely legitimize a large standing army and threaten democratic institutions. Most of the self-styled "Indian reformers" of the period—well-meaning if somewhat paternalistic individuals, such as Indian Rights Association secretary Herbert Welsh, Episcopal clergyman Henry B. Whipple, Secretary of the Interior Carl Schurz, and Senator Henry L. Dawes—also opposed the transfer to the War Department. Congressional challenges to the existing system therefore failed, leaving in their wake a legacy of tense relations and mistrust between the War and Interior departments.

THE WARS AGAINST THE INDIANS, 1865–1891

In November 1865, General Sherman, inexperienced in handling Indian affairs, predicted that the return of the regulars would quickly overwhelm the Indians. Although Sherman had demonstrated his leadership abilities during the Civil War, he and many fellow veterans, who had served some time on the frontier, did not have much command experience in the West. In a futile gesture to defend westward emigrants immediately after the war, Sherman suggested that commanders at Forts Ridgely (Minnesota), Abercrombie (North Dakota), Kearny (Nebraska), and Riley and Larned (Kansas) organize travelers into groups that each included at least thirty armed men.

THE BOZEMAN TRAIL. Such stopgap measures could hardly be expected to bring peace to the frontier. Slowed by the Civil War, western migration would increase dramatically after 1865. New problems arose as the overlanders threatened the traditional hunting grounds of the proud Plains Indians. Relations were particularly tense in Wyoming and Montana along the recently opened Bozeman Trail, which offered the shortest route to the Montana gold fields near Virginia City, Butte, and Helena. In 1866 Fort Reno, Wyoming, was reoccupied and Forts Phil Kearny, Wyoming, and C. F. Smith, Nebraska, were established to guard the Bozeman Trail.

Colonel Henry B. Carrington, a patient, literate individual who had spent most of the Civil War behind a desk, commanded the isolated garrison at Fort Phil Kearny. Junior officers chafed under Carrington's inactivity, and, when one of the post's woodgathering parties was attacked on 21 December, Brevet Lieutenant Colonel William J. Fetterman was selected to lead an eighty-man relief force. Decoyed into a superbly laid ambush, Fetterman's command was annihilated and the entire region rendered unsafe for all but the strongest patrols. Paralyzed by the crisis, Carrington was transferred to a quieter position in Colorado. Heavy snows delayed a retaliatory strike until the following February.

As commander of the crucial Division of the Missouri, Sherman was working on more general plans for the Great Plains. The federal government he believed needed to establish an Indian-free belt between the Arkansas and Platte rivers, which would allow unimpeded continued construction of the Kansas Pacific and Union Pacific railroads, which were vital to western expansion. The southern tribes, in Sherman's view, had to be kept east of Fort Union, New Mexico, and the Sioux restricted to an area west of the Missouri River and east of the Bozeman Trail. Expecting reinforcements to bolster his division, Sherman hoped to launch major offensives in spring 1867. The Fetterman massacre only stiffened his resolve. "We must act with vindictive earnestness against the Sioux," he reported, "even to their extermination, men, women, and children".

However exaggerated such a statement (Sherman's subsequent actions suggest that he never advocated complete physical extermination), his bombastic rhetoric certainly confirmed suspicions of military inhumanity. The Senate refused to transfer the Indian Bureau to the War Department. Indeed, President Andrew Johnson dispatched a new peace commission to speak with the Sioux. Rather than the offensives promised by Sherman, the army was thus relegated to a defensive posture on the northern Plains even as the number of raids increased against the Bozeman Trail. In 1867 detachments from Forts C. F. Smith and Phil Kearny turned back determined attacks by the Sioux and northern Cheyenne in the Hayfield (1 August) and Wagon Box (2 August) fights, respectively, while other soldiers erected several forts on the outskirts of the Sioux country.

THE SOUTHERN PLAINS. The diplomatic initiatives in the north did not deter a major campaign to the south. Winfield Scott Hancock, an able Civil War veteran who later made a determined bid for the presidency, led a column that eventually totaled fourteen hundred men out of Fort Riley in April 1867. Cursory discussions convinced Hancock that the Indians had opted for war; he burned a large Cheyenne and Sioux village near Pawnee Fork, Kansas, and detached Lieutenant Colonel George Armstrong Custer on a wildly unsuccessful pursuit of the warriors. Although Sherman credited the Hancock expedition with having broken up a massive coalition, the regulars had not brought peace to the region. Peace commissioners blamed the campaign for having ruined their efforts, and Kansans and Nebraskans felt the wrath of angry Indian attacks throughout the summer.

Congress responded by forming another commission, which included three generals—Sherman, Alfred H. Terry, and retired Brigadier General Harney—among its seven members. Meetings with a variety of Indian delegations confirmed the civilian majority's belief that the government should adopt a more pacific policy. Treaties signed at Medicine Lodge Creek, Kansas, in 1867 established two large reservations in western Indian territory for the Cheyenne, Arapaho, Kiowa, and Comanche. The agreements reached at Fort Laramie, Wyoming, in 1868 defined another large reserve for the Sioux in western South Dakota. Extensive hunting privileges were also promised, and the army agreed to abandon its posts along the Bozeman Trail. In both sets of agreements, the Indians relinquished most of their other rights off the reservations in return for government annuities.

Although conducted with the full support of President Grant, Sherman was certain the new peace policy would fail. Indeed, fiercely independent southern Plains warriors continued to launch raids while Congress delayed funding the Indian appropriations. Therefore, the army began patroling Kansas, Nebraska, and Colorado more actively in August 1868. Skirmishing culminated in the Battle of Beecher Island (17–25 September), during which Brevet Colonel George A. Forsyth and a company of fifty volunteer scouts fended off a week-long Oglala Sioux and Cheyenne siege along the Arikara River.

Sherman concluded that major offensive actions were needed. To oversee the campaigns, he selected Sheridan, a pugnacious battler whose temperament had nearly prevented him from graduating from West Point and who had been an unrelenting campaigner against the Cascade and Yakima Indians during the mid-1850s. Brilliant service during the Civil War had culminated in his masterly conquest of the Shenandoah Valley in 1864–1865 and catapulted him to the rank of major general. After the close of the war, however, his heavy-handed rule of Texas and Louisiana had antagonized President Andrew Johnson, who transferred him from Reconstruction duties to the Department of the Missouri in 1868. When Sherman took the office of commanding general the following year, Sheridan stepped up to command the Division of the Missouri. Sheridan's willingness to make enemy noncombatants feel the hard hand of war, his insensitive view of Indians, and a determination to protect white expansion ideally suited him to Sherman's purposes.

As army columns scoured the region between the Red and Republican rivers, the peace commission reconvened in early October 1868. The absence of Senator John Henderson and the subsequent appointment of Brigadier General Christopher C. Augur gave the military a working majority on the commission. Seizing this opportunity to dictate government policy, the generals sharply increased the authority of the army, thus enabling Sheridan and Sherman to put their offensives into motion. All the Indians who wanted peace were instructed to gather near Fort Cobb, Oklahoma, under the loose protective custody of Colonel William B. Hazen. Those who did not report to Hazen were declared hostile and subject to attacks timed to coincide with the onset of winter.

Three colunns took the field in November 1868. Major Andrew W. Evans led over five hundred men out of Fort Bascom, New Mexico, eastward down the South Canadian River. From Fort Lyon, Colorado, Major Eugene A. Carr commanded a slightly larger force that pushed south and east toward the Red River. From a new base at Camp Supply in Indian Territory, Sheridan accompanied a third column, which boasted a strong infantry escort and most of Lieutenant Colonel Custer's Seventh Cavalry Regiment. It was hoped that the cold weather would restrict Indian movement and that the convergence of Evans and Carr would force the enemy to retreat into the jaws of the heavy column spearheaded by Custer's cavalry.

Custer indeed struck first. Upon locating a large Indian village along the Washita River, he ordered a dawn assault on 27 November. Eager to recoup his fortunes (he had been court-martialed for having left his command during a reckless visit to his wife during the Hancock campaign of 1867), the lack of information as to the dispositions of the enemy did not deter the ambitious officer. Custer assumed that his Seventh Cavalry could defeat any opposition. Dividing his command into four detachments in an effort to trap the entire camp, Custer thundered into the village as surprised inhabitants rushed from their lodges.

Although the delayed arrival of two of the columns allowed many of the Indians to escape, Custer's men enjoyed complete surprise. Pockets of resistance were eliminated as Custer gained control of the village within ten minutes. To the east, however, Major Joel H. Elliott's battalion had encountered an unforeseen enemy.

General William T. Sherman and commissioners negotiated with Indian Chiefs at Fort Laramie in 1867–1868. The Fort Laramie Treaty defined a large reservation for the Sioux in western South Dakota. (National Archives)

Elliott and his nineteen men were never heard from again as hundreds of fresh warriors from camps Custer had not yet found ringed the original Indian encampment. Still ignorant of Elliott's whereabouts, Custer, after destroying the Indian lodges and winter stores and slaughtering the captured pony herd, pulled back toward Camp Supply.

The army's victory at the Washita was full of irony. The village had been that of Black Kettle, the Cheyenne chief who had barely escaped from the disaster at Sand Creek. Seeking peace, Black Kettle had attempted to gain succor with Hazen earlier in the month, but the chief's followers had not been without blame, as witnessed in the four white captives and assorted wartime spoils found in the village. Custer emerged an even more controversial figure. Supporters pointed out that he had destroyed an Indian village and inflicted more than one hundred casualties, while his critics emphasized his willingness to depart the field without determining Elliott's fate and to the high number of Indian noncombatants killed in the action.

The army kept up the pressure all winter. Colonel Benjamin Grierson's black Tenth Cavalry began constructing strategic Fort Sill along the eastern face of the Wichita Mountains. In December, Evans razed a Comanche camp at Soldier Spring, in the southwestern corner of the Indian Territory. Casualties were light, but the soldiers once again burned the invaluable winter stores of their foes. Thousands of southern Cheyenne, Kiowa, and Comanche turned themselves in as the winter took its cruel toll. After briefly pausing to refit their strike forces, Custer, Evans, and Carr continued to comb suspected Indian haunts through the early spring. In a final fling, Carr destroyed an encampment of Cheyenne Dog Soldiers at Summit Springs, Colorado, on 11 July 1869.

By striking at the homes of their foes, the army had forced the Indians to fight on less than favorable terms during the campaigns of 1868–1869. Although the battles had not always been decisive, the ceaseless pressure had shattered Indian morale. The tribes could no longer rely on their traditional winter security blanket. Of course, the cold weather campaigns also displayed critical army weaknesses. Severe supply shortages plagued every army column, and hundreds of horses and mules died of exposure and starvation. Several officers had displayed neither the skill nor the determination to track down and engage their foes. The effort to distinguish peaceful and hostile Indians had not worked, and Sheridan never forgave Hazen for having promised safe haven to so many Indians. (The two had clashed earlier over their respective roles in the Battle of Missionary Ridge during the Civil War.)

THE PACIFIC NORTHWEST. Violence also disrupted non-Indian expansion into the Pacific Northwest. Gold discoveries in the Boise Basin region of southwestern Idaho had attracted thousands of prospectors during the Civil War. Placer yields in eastern Oregon also drew large migrant populations. Others headed east for Helena and Virginia City in Montana. The Snake River Paiute vigorously resisted these encroachments, and desultory campaigns by state and territorial volunteers failed to clear the region of its native inhabitants.

For expansion to continue unabated, it fell to the bewhiskered Lieutenant Colonel Crook to defeat the northern Paiute. A stubborn campaigner, Crook's legendary feats of stamina were rivaled only by his determination to fulfill every promise he made to his Indian foes. Using pack mules to bring up supplies, Crook also took great pains to enlist qualified scouts, many of whom were recruited from the nearby Shoshone. For twenty-one months his command engaged in forty battles and skirmishes with the Paiute, who finally gave up the cause by summer 1868.

Events in Montana the following winter gave the army less cause for self-congratulation. Mountain Chief's band of Piegan Indians had harassed white intruders for several years. Tired of the clamor for action, Sheridan urged a winter strike and suggested Brevet Colonel Eugene M. Baker as an excellent man to do the job. "Tell Baker to strike them hard," concluded Sheridan. Eager to comply, Baker found a Piegan camp near the Big Bend of the Marias River in mid-January 1870.

Three hundred Piegan captives were turned loose to face the winter blizzards without their belongings, which had been destroyed by the soldiers.

At dawn on the twenty-third, the regulars swept through the surprised village with a vengeance; official army figures state that fifty-three of the 173 Indians reported killed had been women and children. Another three hundred captives were turned loose to face the winter blizzards without their belongings, which had been destroyed by the soldiers. The Piegan had not been followers of Mountain Chief; instead, they adhered to the peaceful leadership of Heavy Runner, who had been killed early in the slaughter.

THE ARMY AND THE PEACE POLICY. Eager to cut military spending and appalled by reports of the Baker massacre, Congress determined to rein in the

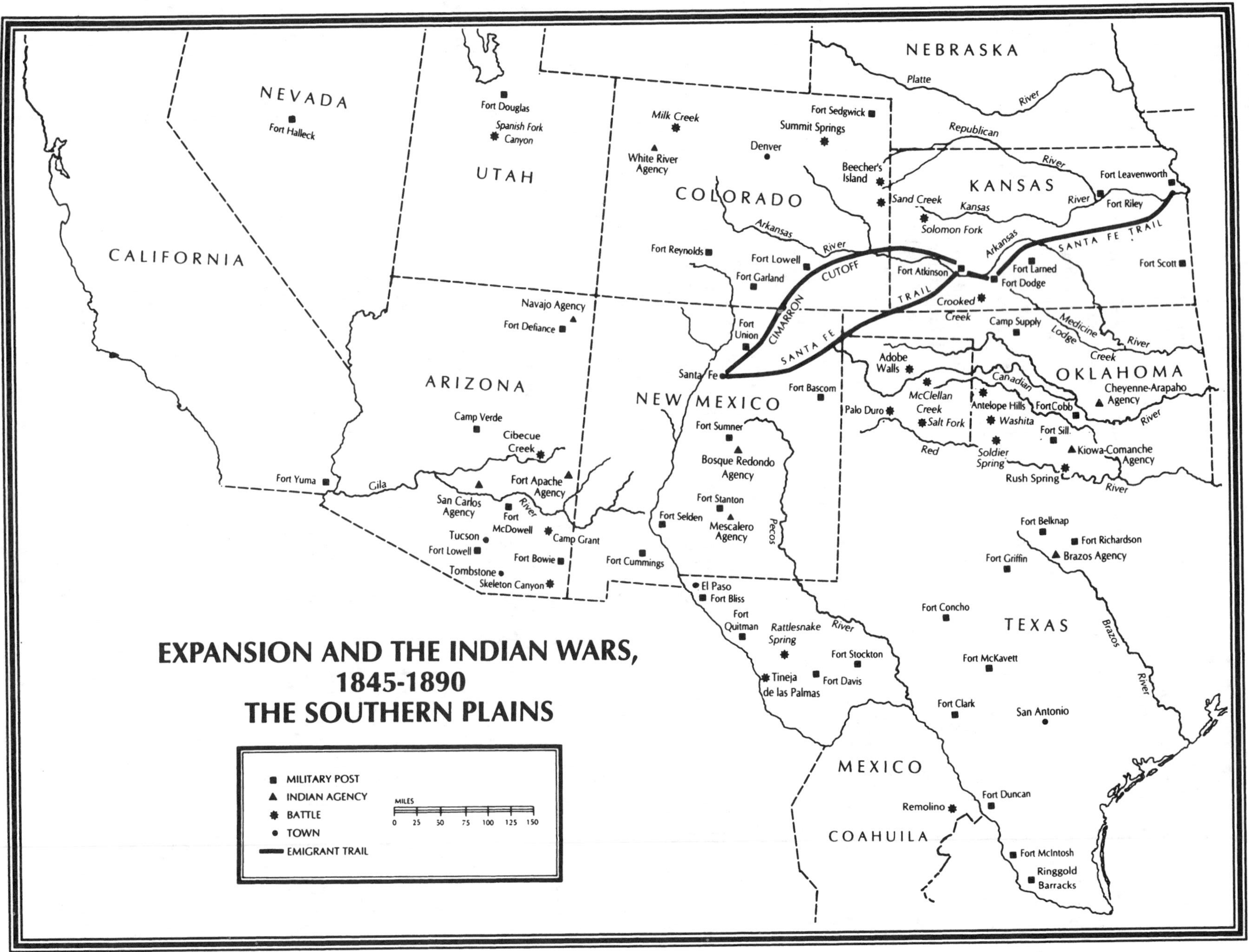
EXPANSION AND THE INDIAN WARS, 1845-1890
THE SOUTHERN PLAINS
MILITARY POST
INDIAN AGENCY
BATTLE
TOWN
EMIGRANT TRAIL
MILES
0 25 50 75 100 125 150
NEBRASKA
KANSAS
OKLAHOMA
COLORADO
NEW MEXICO
TEXAS
UTAH
ARIZONA
NEVADA
CALIFORNIA
MEXICO
COAHUILA
SANTA FE TRAIL
CIMARRON CUTOFF
SANTA FE TRAIL
Platte
River
Republican
River
Kansas
River
Solomon Fork
Arkansas
River
Medicine Lodge Creek
River
Crooked Creek
Canadian
River
Washita
Red
River
McClellan Creek
Brazos
River
Pecos
River
Gila
River
Fort Leavenworth
Fort Riley
Fort Scott
Fort Larned
Fort Dodge
Fort Atkinson
Camp Supply
Cheyenne-Arapaho Agency
Fort Cobb
Fort Sill
Kiowa-Comanche Agency
Rush Spring
Antelope Hills
Washita
Soldier Spring
Salt Fork
Adobe Walls
Palo Duro
Sand Creek
Beecher's Island
Fort Sedgwick
Summit Springs
Denver
Fort Lowell
Fort Garland
Fort Union
Santa Fe
Fort Bascom
Fort Reynolds
Milk Creek
White River Agency
Fort Sumner
Bosque Redondo Agency
Fort Stanton
Mescalero Agency
Fort Selden
Fort Cummings
El Paso
Fort Bliss
Fort Quitman
Rattlesnake Spring
Tineja de las Palmas
Fort Stockton
Fort Davis
Fort Belknap
Fort Richardson
Brazos Agency
Fort Griffin
Fort Concho
Fort McKavett
Fort Clark
San Antonio
Fort Duncan
Remolino
Fort McIntosh
Ringgold Barracks
Fort Douglas
Spanish Fork Canyon
Navajo Agency
Fort Defiance
Camp Verde
Cibecue Creek
Fort Apache Agency
Camp Grant
Fort McDowell
Fort Bowie
Skeleton Canyon
Tombstone
Tucson
Fort Lowell
San Carlos Agency
Fort Yuma
Fort Halleck

army. Expansion had to continue but the peace policy of newly elected President Grant needed a chance to succeed. The Indians would become self-sufficient, argued the reformers, by adopting agriculture on the reservations. Christian virtue and forgiveness would replace the sword in dictating Indian policy. Because the army needed to secure Interior Department permission before entering the reservations, a ten-man board of commissioners was created to advise the secretary of the interior. Church groups would send dedicated agents to the reservations to help the tribes achieve the white man's version of civilization.

Reformers concentrated their efforts on the Great Plains, where the peace policy had halted army offensives. In Arizona, however, the regulars continued to strike various Apache bands whose defiance of government authority threatened non-Indian settlers and travelers. The terrain and sparse population of the territory rendered impossible defense of each ranch, mining camp, settlement, and overland party. In response to a chorus of demands for action, the War Department carved out a separate Department of Arizona in April 1870.

Officers stationed in the region decried Apache culture and urged that they be allowed to stamp out all Indian resistance, but implementing such harsh policies demanded more effort than many were willing to give. The first head of the Department of Arizona, Colonel George Stoneman, for example, found no solace in the stark physical isolation of the Far Southwest and set up headquarters near Los Angeles, California. Desultory campaigns in the winter of 1870–1871 pleased few Arizonans, who demanded that the Indians be removed to make room for white immigrants. As usual, special criticisms were reserved for the infantrymen, whose immobility often relegated them to garrison duty.

Intense pressure from western politicians led President Grant to transfer the able Crook to command the department. Before he arrived, however, a group of Tucson vigilantes, joined by a contingent of Papago Indians, slaughtered at least eighty-five Apache at Camp Grant, Arizona. The hue and cry raised by eastern reformers to the Camp Grant massacre forced Crook to delay his offensives until peace delegations were given another chance. Crook publicly supported such initiatives, but privately he believed that he should be allowed to "conquer a lasting peace" in Arizona.

Although more than five thousand Apache and Yavapai accepted terms and government rations, the violence continued. Indian raiders killed forty-four persons between September 1871 and September 1872, with more than five hundred head of livestock reported stolen. An impatient Crook received permission to take the offensive in late 1872. Encouraging subordinates to study the terrain and the people with whom they were dealing, he signed up swarms of Indian auxiliaries to scout for and fight with his regulars. His remorseless columns swept through suspected enemy haunts, forcing most of the Indians onto reservations by the close of 1873.

A far different scenario disrupted the peace policy in Oregon. The Modoc had ceded their lands along the northern California–southern Oregon boundary in 1864, but now chafed under reservation life in which they were dominated by the more numerous Klamath. Kintpuash (Captain Jack) led about seventy warriors and their families back to their Lost River homelands; by 1871, white settlers in the area demanded that the military remove the Modoc back to their reservation.

An attack on Kintpuash's village the following year forced the issue. The Modoc, although badly outnumbered by army forces (which eventually totaled nearly one thousand men), retreated into the lava beds south of Tule Lake and set up virtually impregnable defenses. Clumsy attempts to storm the natural stronghold having failed, Brigadier General Edward R. S. Canby was authorized to seek a peaceful settlement. Militants within the Modoc camp, presumably buoyed by what some considered a sign of government weakness, demanded that Kintpuash kill the peace commissioners in a desperate attempt to secure a reservation at Lost River.

On 11 April 1873, Canby and three delegates met with Modoc leaders in a tent between the two lines. Jack drew a pistol and murdered Canby, the only regular army general to be killed by Indians during the long history of Indian-white conflicts in the United States. Two of the other commissioners also fell dead, with the third severely wounded. Subsequent efforts to close the siege again reflected poorly on the army, with a strong reconnaissance commanded by Captain Evan Thomas nearly annihilated on 26 April.

Only with the arrival of Colonel Jefferson C. Davis did the shaken regulars regain the initiative. Some of the Modoc began surrendering in May, with Kintpuash and his family, at the behest of deserters from his own tribe, giving up in early June. Kintpuash and three advisers were hung by order of a military court-martial; 155 of his followers were escorted to Indian Territory that October. The campaign painted a dismal picture of army tactics. Well-led, determined Modoc warriors had enjoyed superb positions, but poor marksmanship and timid leadership had plagued the regular attackers. Junior officers seemed incapable even of properly deploying a skirmish line. Concluded one blunt critic, "Those men don't know how to fight Indians."

In Texas western travelers and non-Indian frontier settlers were voicing bitter complaints about Indian depredations. Delayed by the Civil War, thousands poured into north central and southwestern Texas during the late 1860s and the 1870s. Others headed to New Mexico, Arizona, and California via the roads across the trans-Pecos. Immediately following the Civil War, the regulars were more closely involved with Reconstruction than western expansion. By the late 1860s, however, the army had reoccupied its frontier posts and stepped up its patrols.

Kickapoo, Lipan, and Mescalero Apache raiders had long terrorized settlers along both sides of the Rio Grande. U.S. Army officers demanded permission to cross the border into Mexico, but officials of that nation remained reluctant to authorize such military excursions. Still chafing under the dictates of Grant's peace policy, division commander Sheridan searched for some means of eliminating the Indian threats. Colonel Ranald S. Mackenzie and his Fourth Cavalry Regiment were transferred to the Texas borderlands in early 1873; his fine Civil War record and good relationship with President Grant augured well for those who hoped for decisive action.

Texans did not have to wait long. Sheridan visited Mackenzie at Fort Clark in April 1873. Verbally assuring the young colonel of presidential support, he encouraged Mackenzie to take any steps necessary to bring peace to the borderlands. Mackenzie drilled his men for several weeks before implementing Sheridan's suggestions. On 17 May 1873, a squad of hand-picked scouts guided nearly four hundred regulars across the Rio Grande. Burning three Indian villages near Remolino, Mexico, they splashed back across the river two days later. Several smaller border crossings followed that summer, although the international furor resulting from the Remolino raid convinced Sheridan to rein in his eager subordinate.

Violence on the southern Plains soon shifted attention away from Mackenzie's raid and called into question the entire peace policy. Although the region's major tribes were still drawing rations from their respective agencies, raids into Kansas and Texas intensified as memories faded of the winter campaigns of 1868–1869. The danger posed by these attacks was made abundantly clear in May 1871, when, during an inspection tour of north Texas, General Sherman and a small escort narrowly escaped a Kiowa war party outside Fort Richardson, Texas. Satank, Satanta, and Big Tree, among the most outspoken of the Indian war leaders, were arrested soon thereafter.

Satank later died while trying to escape; a Texas jury sentenced Satanta and Big Tree to death, only to have their sentences commuted to life imprisonment by Governor Edmund J. Davis. As the two Indians whiled away their hours in a Huntsville prison, army columns crisscrossed the Llano Estacado (Staked Plain) in the summer of 1872. On 29 September, Mackenzie routed a Comanche village near McClellan Creek, killing fifty Indians and taking another 124 captive. Officials still hoped, however, that a final gesture of diplomacy might convince the Indians to lay down their arms. In a move designed to end the raids against Texas, Satanta, Big Tree, and the Comanche prisoners were freed in fall 1873.

THE RED RIVER WAR. Instead of bringing peace, the act prompted a series of Kiowa and Comanche raids into Texas. Infuriated by what they considered to be the gullibility of the Christian agents and the corruption of the Interior Department, army officers demanded the opportunity to take the field. Only by disarming and dismounting the tribes, argued military men, could western expansion be freed from the threat of Indian attack. Sheridan drew up plans for a winter offensive in 1873–1874, only to be rebuffed by a hesitant Department of the Interior. Indian attacks continued the following year, culminating in an unsuccessful assault on a camp of buffalo hunters at Adobe Walls, Texas, in June 1874. On 18 July Secretary of the Interior Columbus Delano gave the army permission to enter the reservations.

Having anticipated Delano's decision, Sheridan had already encouraged his key department commanders, Augur (Department of Texas) and Pope (Department of the Missouri) to draw up plans for an offensive. Augur did so, but Pope remained reluctant, arguing instead that the army should wait until the onset of winter to launch its columns. Premature attacks, maintained Pope, would only waste the cavalry and that it would be better to wait until the timing was right and do the job properly.

But Sheridan held firm. The army had to move immediately, he believed, or it would risk having the Interior Department retract its decision to allow troops to enter the reservations. As such, sketchy plans for a late summer offensive slowly materialized despite Pope's objections. As division commander, Sheridan took little direct role except as cheerleader and chief logistical officer. "I will not sketch out any plan of operations for your cavalry," he told Pope on 22 July, "leaving you to exercise your good judgment in this respect." Pope and Augur could thus organize their efforts as they saw fit, a policy that gave wide latitude for flexibility and initiative, but that discouraged efforts to coordinate the various columns. To further complicate planning, Sherman, in his flight from Secretary of War Belknap, had recently transferred his headquarters to Saint Louis, thereby removing him from any effective role in the upcoming campaign.

Augur and Pope also opted to give their field commanders optimum freedom of action. From the Department of the Missouri, Pope organized columns under Colonel Nelson A. Miles and Major William R. Price. Miles was to move south from Fort Dodge, Kansas, then operate west of the Wichita Mountains, attacking hostile Indians wherever they might be located. He should not, suggested Pope, be bound by any more specific guidelines. Price was to march down the Canadian River from Fort Bascom, New Mexico, then link up with Miles. Again, however, Pope cautioned his subordinate to fit his actions to the circumstances as they presented themselves.

Augur braced his forces for a similar effort. Mackenzie and the veteran Fourth Cavalry, recently transferred from the borderlands to Fort Concho, would spearhead the thrust. Other forces, commanded by Lieutenant Colonels George Buell, John W. Davidson, and Thomas H. Neill, would operate north of Mackenzie. Davidson and Neill, assigned to separate friendly from hostile Indians at Fort Sill and the Darlington Agency, respectively, had particularly difficult assignments. Other than warning his commanders that the campaign would be prolonged, Augur declined to issue detailed instructions, relying chiefly upon the abilities of Mackenzie as a combat leader.

Skirmishing began in August as Davidson unsuccessfully tried to disarm the Kiowa and Comanche near Fort Sill. Some five thousand southern Cheyenne, Comanche, and Kiowa, about one-quarter of them warriors, fled the reservations in confusion. Price, Miles, Mackenzie, Buell, and Davidson had also taken the field, collectively mounting about two thousand men capable of offensive action. Moving south of the Canadian River through the drought-ravaged southern Plains, Miles struck a strong Cheyenne force near the Salt Fork of the Red River on 30 August. In a running battle, he drove the Indians back in disrepair, only to see his pursuit ended by supply shortages. Raids against his rearguard areas nearly annihilated several detached escorts, even as Price's forces linked up with the main body.

Davidson and Buell set forth from Fort Sill in September, encountering little organized resistance at the onset. More determined was Mackenzie, who had established a supply depot on the upper Brazos River. His 471-strong force threw back a night assault on 26 September, then hurried ahead to Palo Duro Canyon, where Tonkawa scouts had located a large camp of Cheyenne, Kiowa, and Comanche. At daybreak of 28 September, Mackenzie's veterans scrambled down the canyon slopes. Warning shots fired by sleepy Indian pickets enabled most of the inhabitants to flee, but the soldiers seized the lodges and ponies left behind in the rush to freedom. Mackenzie's troopers burned the camp, and the following day his men replaced their jaded mounts, then slaughtered the remainder of the herd.

The army maintained the pressure through the fall. Buell burned two Indian villages, collectively numbering more than five hundred lodges, on 11–12 October. A detachment from Miles' main force led by Lieutenant Frank D. Baldwin dealt a Cheyenne camp another stinging blow near McClellan Creek on 8 November. The onset of winter forced Davidson, Buell, and Mackenzie to break up their expeditions in December, but Miles remained indefatigable despite the icy blizzards. At the head of three companies, the colonel set out in early January 1875 on a final drive through the headwaters of the Red River.

The New York Tribune *noted, "If there is gold in the Black Hills, no army on earth can keep the adventurous men of the west out of them."*

Although combat casualties had been relatively light, the Red River campaigns had taken a severe toll among the Indians. Shorn of their mobility by the forageless winter, the destruction of so many ponies, and the relentless pursuits of the army, tattered bands had started to turn themselves in the previous October. Most of those remaining out surrendered in the early spring of 1875. A final group of four hundred Comanches came in as late as 2 June.

The regulars had also suffered, because of the army's dependence upon private contractors for logistical support, particularly the transportation of supplies from depots to the field columns. The failure to establish unity of command also hampered their efforts. Sheridan had designed the general plan, but then concerned himself largely with trying to resolve the supply morass. Troops from two departments (Texas and Missouri), therefore, struck out with only vague notions of where their comrades might be. Critics also speculated that the competition between Miles and Mackenzie had needlessly endangered the lives of their men, for each of these able but ambitious leaders had failed to cooperate as well as might have been expected.

THE GREAT SIOUX WAR. The Red River War, in leaving behind a defeated, demoralized Plains peoples, had shattered the peace policy in the south. With the full support of the military, the government had opted to back the interests of those who sought western development over the objections of the earlier inhabitants of the region. Blatant expansionism would more directly end the brief peace initiatives on the northern Plains. The Fort Laramie Treaties had left to the Sioux a huge reservation comprising much of western South Dakota, but large numbers of Sioux, northern Arapaho, and northern Cheyenne, proud of their independent heritage, continued to deny government sovereignty. The tense situation was exacerbated by the seemingly inexorable advance of the Northern Pacific Railroad, which by the early 1870s neared the Yellowstone River valley.

As railroad parties approached lands that the Sioux considered theirs (the recent treaties were unclear as to whether the Indian cessions extended as far as the Yellowstone), Indian resistance grew more apparent. Military escorts accompanied railroad surveying parties in 1871 and 1872. Mounting pressure led to an even larger army effort the following year; Colonel David S. Stanley, fifteen hundred troops, and four hundred civilians comprised the 1873 summer expedition. Near the mouth of the Tongue River, several hundred warriors engaged detachments of Stanley's command led by Custer on 4 August. Another sharp skirmish occurred a week later.

Although the Northern Pacific was thrown into bankruptcy by the panic of 1873, rumors of rich mineral deposits heightened interest in the Black Hills. The army also wanted to establish a large new military post in the region. To investigate both possibilities, Custer mounted another strong expeditionary force in the summer of 1874. Nearly one hundred wagons, three Gatling guns, one cannon, a military band, four scientists, and a photographer accompanied the two companies of infantrymen and ten troops of horse soldiers as they wound their way through western Dakota and the Black Hills.

Custer was able to find a good location for a fort. His reports also stressed the potential economic value of the region's hunting, lumbering, and grazing areas. Although the lieutenant colonel played down the mineral prospects, thousands of prospectors seized upon more inflated press reports and began rushing to the Black Hills. The *New York Tribune* noted, "If there is gold in the Black Hills, no army on earth can keep the adventurous men of the west out of them." The army was sincere if ineffective in preventing the onslaught of white trespassers onto the Great Sioux Reservation.

To have attempted to check white expansion would have been incongruent with army policy. In early November 1875, Sheridan and Crook joined President Grant and Interior Department officials in determining to end the efforts to block trespassers and to force the Indians to sign new treaties. Declaring that diplomacy had failed, on 1 February 1876, Secretary of the Interior Zachariah Chandler authorized the War Department to send the army in against the Sioux and the northern Cheyenne.

The military scrambled to take advantage of the diplomatic opening, with hastily formulated plans that month calling for a two-pronged invasion of the Black Hills. From the Department of the Platte, Colonel Joseph J. Reynolds led nearly nine hundred men out of Fort Fetterman, Wyoming, on 1 March. Crook accompanied the column in an observer's role. To the east and from the Department of Dakota, General Terry prepared to mount an expedition from Fort Abraham Lincoln. Although the troops were to come from different departments, Sheridan, whose Division of the Missouri encompassed both regions, declined to coordinate movements.

Winter snows forced Terry to abandon the campaign even before it began. Reynolds and Crook were slightly more persistent, but retired after less than a month in the field. The latter force had managed to capture one pony herd, only to see the Indians recapture their animals in a night raid. Acknowledging the failure of the winter campaign, Sheridan ordered his subordinates to try again when weather and supplies permitted. As usual, the general declined to outline specific campaign plans; he did, however, assure his field commanders of "the impossibility of any large numbers of Indians keeping together as a hostile body for even one week."

On 30 March, Colonel John Gibbon and 450 men left Fort Ellis, Montana, pushing through the remaining snows to the Yellowstone River valley. Terry led a larger column, spearheaded by Custer and the Seventh Cavalry, out of Fort Lincoln on 17 May. Crook rejoined the chase from Fort Fetterman twelve days later. Bitter experience led each officer to agree with Sheridan's claim about potential opposition. Finding the enemy, and then forcing that enemy to fight, had traditionally been the most difficult challenge on the western Plains.

Crook fought the campaign's first engagement. On 17 June, his column met determined resistance at the Battle of Rosebud Creek. Claiming victory, Crook nonetheless fell back to his field depot to await reinforcements. Terry in the meantime was still struggling to locate the enemy. Suspecting that a large Indian camp lay along the Little Bighorn River, Terry dispatched Custer and the Seventh to drive up the Rosebud and approach the enemy from the south. Gibbon would block any retreat to the north. Mindful of the need for flexibility, Terry's orders were vague, as was customary during such campaigns.

Early on 25 June, Custer's Indian scouts verified Terry's suspicions about an Indian presence along the Little Bighorn. Fearful that the Sioux and northern Cheyenne would retreat unscathed and certain that the enemy must be aware of his regiment, Custer pushed his tired troopers ahead. Replicating his tactics of nearly eight years ago at the Washita, he divided his forces. Three companies under the acerbic yet talented Captain Frederick Benteen would screen the advance to the south. Major Marcus A. Reno took three more companies to hit the village; Custer and five companies would complete the pincer movement against the enemy, about whose dispositions he still knew little.

But Custer's luck had run out. Contrary to Sheridan's prediction, the northern Cheyenne, a few Arapaho, and five Sioux tribal circles—Sans Arc, Miniconjou, Hunkpapa, Blackfoot, and Oglala—had stayed together this summer. Numerical estimates vary wildly, from a conservative guess of ten thousand to as many as fifteen thousand Indians with between fifteen hundred and four thousand warriors. Ably led by men such as Crazy Horse, Sitting Bull, Gall, Lame Deer, and Hump, the Sioux and northern Cheyenne, their confidence buoyed by the recent action against Crook, began swarming from their lodges to attack the intruders.

Reno's troopers were checked well short of the village. With great difficulty Reno managed to withdraw across the Little Bighorn, where he hung on until joined by Benteen. The Indians kept up the pressure against Reno's men through the following evening, killing forty-seven soldiers and wounding another fifty-three. Custer suffered an even worse fate—all 215 of his men fell, after a spirited defense, among the broken, grassy ridges north of the huge Indian encampment.

Terry and Gibbon came up on 27 June. Shocked by the carnage on the Custer battlefield, they withdrew to the mouth of the Rosebud to refit and await reinforcements, which brought Terry's combined command up

The Black Hills Expedition confirmed the location of gold in the Indian territories. The expedition included these columns of cavalry, artillery, and wagons, which crossed the plains of the Dakota Territory under the command of George A. Custer in 1874. (National Archives)

to seventeen hundred men. Crook, his force now boasting nearly two thousand men and a large pack train, rejoined the campaign on 5 August. He blundered into Terry five days later near the Rosebud. Still shaken by the defeats of the early summer, Terry and Crook unified their command as they drove eastward toward the Powder River. Morale sunk ever lower as the leadership's temerity became more obvious; in late August, the two columns again went their separate ways.

Miles and the Fifth Infantry had been among the reinforcements bound for Terry. Anxious to leave the joint column, which he believed too large to find any Indians, Miles had jumped at the opportunity to take his regiment north to hold the Yellowstone River against a possible Indian flight toward Canada. In early September a thoroughly baffled Terry broke up his remaining command, but instructed Miles to occupy the Yellowstone through the winter. Crook continued the pursuit, and on 9 September fought an extended skirmish at Slim Buttes, South Dakota, but even Crook retired back to Fort Fetterman without having beaten his Sioux antagonists.

The military braced for a long war. In a cruel preventive measure, reservation peoples at the Red Cloud, Standing Rock, and Cheyenne River agencies were disarmed and dismounted. The burden of the campaigning now fell to two colonels, both relative newcomers to the northern Plains. Colonel Miles, with five hundred infantrymen of his Fifth Regiment and two companies of the Twenty-second, had established his base on the mouth of the Tongue River, from which he patrolled the Yellowstone fords. Heavy Montana snows failed to deter his probes, which drove off all Indian attempts to interdict his supply lines. On 7 January 1877 Miles captured a number of Cheyenne women and children, then fended off attacks by Crazy Horse's Sioux and the Cheyenne that night and the following day at the Battle of Wolf Mountain.

Colonel Mackenzie had also been transferred north, where he joined another massive command that Crook led out from Fort Fetterman into central Wyoming on 14 November. Mackenzie's cavalrymen and Indian auxiliaries hit Dull Knife's Cheyenne village, consisting of nearly two hundred lodges, eleven days later. Savage fighting ensued as the Cheyenne withdrew, leaving twenty-five dead; government casualties numbered thirty-two soldiers and scouts. Mackenzie reproached himself for not pursuing the Cheyenne, but his troops, in capturing five hundred ponies and destroying the village and the winter stores, had in fact dealt the Indians another harsh blow.

In the spring of 1878, large numbers of Sioux and northern Cheyenne began turning themselves in to military authorities. By April about three thousand had come in at the Red Cloud, Spotted Tail, and Cheyenne River agencies. Another three hundred Cheyenne surrendered at the Tongue River cantonment; on 6 May Crazy Horse led most of the Oglala into the Red Cloud Agency. Miles whipped Lame Deer's band at the Little Muddy Creek on 7 May. Scattered remnants of the northern Plains peoples gave up during the summer, although Sitting Bull and a few hundred followers fled into Canada.

Large new army posts throughout the region symbolized the determination of the government to occupy the high Plains. Tension remained high among the Indians who had surrendered. Crazy Horse was killed in captivity and the northern Cheyenne were allowed to return to their homelands only after desperate escape attempts from the Indian Territory. Miles continued to patrol the Canadian border, with a sharp engagement at Milk River, Montana, on 17 July 1879. After numerous defections, Sitting Bull finally turned himself in at Fort Buford, North Dakota in July 1781.

THE NEZ PERCE CAMPAIGN. As the wars against the Sioux continued, the army was also called upon to expedite white expansion into the Wallowa Valley in Oregon, where the Nez Perce had attempted to coexist with their new neighbors. In 1877, however, the government determined that the Indians must be removed in order to preempt future violence. Leading the mission was Brigadier General Oliver O. Howard, a battle-scarred veteran of the Civil War and Reconstruction. Chief Joseph and his followers opted instead to make their way to the Salmon River, where they hoped to join a group of fellow tribesmen. Wayward warriors killed several whites en route, and Captain David Perry set out with a hundred troopers and a swarm of volunteers from Fort Lapwai to defend the settlers. At White Bird Canyon, Idaho, however, the Nez Perce repulsed Perry with heavy casualties on 17 June.

Commanding the Department of the Columbia, Howard assembled four hundred men and set out after Joseph. Another botched effort to negotiate with Looking Glass and his followers, who as yet remained neutral, only convinced this group to join Joseph. After a tortuous march, Howard caught his foes near the Clearwater River on 11 July. The battle again reflected poorly on the regulars as the Indians escaped to the northeast in good order.

Howard reorganized his command and rejoined the pursuit after a three-week delay, but it seemed unlikely that his column of infantry, cavalry, Bannock scouts, and civilian packers could catch Joseph's people. From Missoula, Colonel Gibbon prepared to cut off the Nez Perce escape. Assembling 161 regulars and forty-five volunteers, he pushed down the Bitterroot Valley and surprised the Indians near the mouth of the Big Hole River on 9 August 1877. Once again, the Nez Perce proved resourceful fighters, quickly recovering from the initial shock to dominate the battlefield. Indian sharpshooters pinned down the troops as their families made good their escape. One-third of Gibbon's men had fallen casualty, while eighty-nine Nez Perce, many of them women and children slain during the first onslaught, also littered the field.

One-third of Gibbon's men had fallen casualty, while eighty-nine Nez Perce, many of them women and children slain during the first onslaught, also littered the field.

Howard and a small escort joined Gibbon's bloodied command two days later. They resumed the chase only after messages from General Sherman and Colonel Miles, who had been alerted at Tongue River about Joseph's eastern flight into Montana, goaded a dispirited Howard into action. As Miles took the field, the Nez Perce continued to confound his fellow officers, on 13 September escaping efforts by Colonel Samuel D. Sturgis to block the Yellowstone Valley passes at the Battle of Canyon Creek. Miles, however, proved to be of sterner stuff. The tired Nez Perce slowed enough as they neared the Canadian border for Miles to jump their camp near the Bear Paw Mountains on the morning of 30 September.

Stiff resistance forced Miles to call off the attack after suffering sixty casualties, but his soldiers and hired Sioux and Cheyenne auxiliaries had seized most of the Nez Perce ponies and settled in for a siege. Miles ignored rumors that Sitting Bull was coming to spring the trap as the winter snows continued. Howard, accompanied by a small escort, arrived on 4 October. The constant skirmishing and winter snows had taken their toll upon the Nez Perce, and about four hundred men, women, and children joined Joseph in surrendering the following day. "I will fight no more forever," pledged the chief. Canadian officers later reported that about three hundred Nez Perce had escaped to Canada.

THE BANNOCK, SHEEPEATER, AND UTE CAMPAIGNS. Embarrassed during the campaigns against the Nez Perce, General Howard redeemed himself the following year. In spring 1878 the Bannock Indians of Idaho, Oregon, and Nevada found that the livestock of white farmers and ranchers had nearly devastated their favored Camas Prairie, a site rich in camas roots and tribal tradition. To check the plundering that followed, Howard organized three columns to converge upon the Bannock, estimated to have amassed 450 warriors. Captain Reuben F. Bernard struck the first blow, surprising an Indian village at Silver Creek, Oregon, and capturing most of the Bannock supplies on 23 June.

Howard himself took up the pursuit as the chase wound through the tangled ravines of the John Day River. On 8 July a strike force, again led by Bernard, bested the coalition at Pilot Butte. Displaying tactical skills rarely equaled during the long wars against the Indians, Bernard's cavalrymen drove the well-placed warriors from the field. The pursuit resumed thereafter, with the Bannock still unable to shake the army columns. By now, expeditionary forces led by Colonel Frank Wheaton and Miles had also taken the field, blocking escape routes and cementing the collapse of the coalition.

In the summer of 1879, about thirty Sheepeater Indians and their families led another prolonged chase, this time through the Salmon River Mountains of Idaho. Pursuit teams scoured the rugged ranges for three months, with a small detachment led by Lieutenant Edward S. Farrow forcing the surrender of the Sheepeater in early October. In the same year there was an uprising among the Ute at the White River Agency, Colorado, where the tribe had resisted the demands of agent Nathan C. Meeker that his charges give up their culture for the ways of the white man. After he was assaulted by an Indian, he called upon the army to enforce his new order. The Ute checked the first column, led by Major Thomas T. Thornburgh, in a bloody encounter near Milk Creek on 29 September. Thornburgh himself was killed during the action. On the same day other Ute attacked the agency, killing Meeker and seven others. The Ute then extended the violence to nearby settlements along White Creek. The army rushed in reinforcements, and only the determined intercession of Secretary of the Interior Schurz averted a full-scale war. Still threatening to resist any further encroachments, the Ute eventually gave up and accepted a new reservation.

THE FAR SOUTHWEST. Wars against the Indians also continued in the Far Southwest, but the army had sometimes been less enthusiastic about guaranteeing white expansion in that region. During the 1850s, Lieutenant Colonel Sumner and Secretary of War Conrad had urged the nation to sell rather than defend the arid regions of New Mexico and Arizona. Two decades later, commanding General Sherman seemed to espouse a similar policy. "The occupation of Arizona by Whites I am satisfied was premature and the cost of maintaining troops there is all out of proportion to the result," he concluded in 1870. Like his predecessors, the general saw the region as an inhospitable desert that should be abandoned by the army and left to the Indians.

The near-annihilation of Colonel Carr's two troops of Sixth Cavalrymen at Cibicu Creek, Arizona, by Chiricahua and Warm Spring's Apache suggested the need for new leadership.

Political pressure had forced a reluctant Sherman to allow the transfer of Crook to the Department of Arizona in 1872. Crook exploited his unusual familiarity with the ways of the Apache to enforce a peace upon most of the region by the mid-1870s. His replacement, Colonel August V. Kautz, proved less able to balance the competition between military, interior, and political officials for jurisdiction over the Indian reservations, which had become a profitable source of federal contracts. The army's top brass, however, reasoned that demands for offensive action in regions better suited to white development required their best field commanders. If the theory held true, even mediocre talents like Kautz and Colonel Orlando B. Willcox could do little to hinder the prospects of this forlorn region.

Contrary to army prognostications, however, the 1870s brought much economic development to the Far Southwest. The Tombstone silver strike and increasing capital investments in the copper mines of the region lured settlers and entrepreneurs alike. Construction of the Santa Fe and Southern Pacific railroads added further luster. By 1880 Arizona and New Mexico boasted a collective population of 160,000 people. Even Sherman was convinced that the recent years had transformed the prospects of the region.

New army policy accompanied the new appreciation for the Far Southwest. The top officials concluded that efforts to stamp out Indian resistance had to be intensified. Victorio, the dynamic Warm Springs Apache, broke from the Mescalero Agency in 1879, followed by a number of his fellow tribesmen and a smattering of Mescalero and Chiricahua. With nearly one hundred and fifty warriors, Victorio avoided Mexican and U.S. soldiers as he skipped back and forth across the international boundary. To reduce the threat, troops from New Mexico and Texas disarmed the reservation Mescalero in April 1880. Efforts to track down the recalcitrant Victorio having failed, Colonel Grierson suggested a new tactic—by holding the strategic water holes of the dry trans-Pecos region, the army could save itself the wear and tear of the fruitless desert treks and drive Victorio from Texas.

Victorio acted as Grierson had expected and tangled with army detachments at Tinaja de las Palmas (30 July) and Rattlesnake Springs (6 August). The Indians fell back into Mexico in some confusion. Colonels Carr and Buell pushed across the border under agreement that allowed reciprocal crossings in hot pursuit of hostile Indians. A strong column of Mexican soldiers under Colonel Joaquin Terrazas eventually dealt the Indians a crushing blow, with Victorio dying during the fighting.

Even these blows, however, failed to bring about a peaceful solution to problems stemming from white expansion. On 30 August, the near-annihilation of Colonel Carr's two troops of Sixth Cavalrymen at Cibicu Creek, Arizona, by Chiricahua and Warm Spring's Apache suggested the need for new leadership. Mackenzie seemed a perfect candidate to inject new life into the dispirited southwestern garrisons. Slated for command of the Department of New Mexico, Mackenzie's outbursts of insanity led military officials instead to spirit him away to a New York asylum. Consistent with the new importance attributed to the region, Crook was returned to Arizona in 1882.

Crook implemented what he hoped to be a comprehensive policy based on a rigorous adherence to treaty promises. Officers replaced civilian agents at several reservations; scores of Apache scouts were hired to assist the government. Those Indians who resisted the reservation system were subjects for intense campaigning, but small bands led by Geronimo, Chato, and other raiders continued to elude government forces and wreak terror upon the non-Indian citizens of Sonora, Chihuahua, Arizona, and New Mexico. Crook led a force of forty-five regulars and nearly two hundred scouts deep into the Sierra Madre in May 1883. After a series of exhausting marches and skirmishes, success seemed imminent that June, when most of the leading warriors agreed to turn themselves in.

A brief peace followed as various Apache bands drifted in to the San Carlos Reservation, but Geronimo and about ninety followers (including forty-two men) again broke from the reservation in May 1885. To recapture the fugitives, Crook deployed three thousand men to occupy key water holes, patrol the Sierra Madre, and protect the Southern Pacific Railroad. Grueling chases into Mexico, keyed by Captains Emmet Crawford and Wirt Davis and Indian scouts, finally located Geronimo's camp about two hundred miles into Mexico in January 1886, but just as Crawford secured a

Geromino was a Chiricahua Apache warrior who led attacks on settlers and soldiers in Mexico and the southwestern United States during the 1870s and 1880s. (National Archives)

meeting with Geronimo, a strong force of Mexican militia struck the soldiers, killing Crawford and forcing the expedition back into the United States.

Stunned by Crawford's death but convinced that Geronimo and the others wanted to talk, Crook arranged a meeting just south of the border two months later. Tired of the struggle, Geronimo, Nachez, and Chihuahua agreed to surrender if allowed to make their own way back to Fort Bowie. Overjoyed, Crook hastened back with the news, only to learn that Geronimo, twenty men, and thirteen women made yet another break on the way north. Sheridan, who upon Sherman's retirement had assumed the office of commanding general in 1883, had long questioned Crook's reliance upon Indian scouts and quickly accepted his subordinate's request for a transfer.

Nelson Miles replaced Crook as commander of the Department of Arizona in April 1886. A frustratingly ambitious yet inordinately talented combat leader, Miles assured Sheridan that he would change Crook's tactics. Heliograph stations would improve communications, regulars would replace the Apache scouts, and no preliminary discussions with the Indians would be sanctioned. An ineffective summer campaign by the regulars, guided by less able scouts recruited from other tribes, led Miles to quietly reintroduce Crook's methods. It thus came as little surprise to experienced southwestern hands that Lieutenant Charles B. Gatewood, one of Crook's favorites, made the first significant contact with Geronimo in August.

Miles had adopted one innovation that would prove crucial to the negotiations. He had recently orchestrated the removal of the reservation Chiricahua (including many of the same scouts who had formerly worked for Crook) from Arizona to Florida. Stunned by the enforced transfer of their fellow tribesmen, Geronimo and his followers surrendered to Miles at Skeleton Canyon, Arizona, on 4 September. War Department orders that these people be held in Arizona for civil trial arrived too late to be implemented, and the fugitive bands were packed off to Florida. The confusing denouement, however, embarrassed Miles before government officials and led many to question whether the general had made unauthorized guarantees to secure Geronimo's surrender.

THE GHOST DANCE. Isolated incidents would keep soldiers in Arizona, New Mexico, and Texas on edge for years to come, but the next major encounter with Indians broke out on the northern Plains, scene of relative peace during the 1880s. The effects of white expansion in the region were clearly apparent among the Indians. Relegated to their reservations and stripped of their pride, many Plains peoples had grown dispirited during the late 1880s. The decline of the buffalo, years of drought, and the ravages of disease accelerated their physical decline. Cuts in promised annuities and the surrender of nearly half of their reservation by the Sioux Act of 1889 had taken a heavy toll.

The spread of the Ghost Dance among the Indians seemed to fire forgotten hopes. Initially propagated as a peaceful movement by the prophet Wovoka, many Sioux accepted a more violent version of the movement that promised the destruction of the white people. Interior Department agents, spooked by visions of this Indian millennium, called for army assistance in November 1890. Recently promoted to head the Division of the Missouri, Miles tried to contain the outbreak by sending strong garrisons to the most excited agencies in South Dakota and Nebraska. A plan to arrest Sitting Bull at Standing Rock in December was botched; his death at the hands of Indian police sent to capture him only hastened the panicky flight from the reserves.

Reinforcements poured into western South Dakota and northern Nebraska. Many Oglala and Brulé Sioux took refuge in a defensible plateau north of the Pine Ridge Reservation, known as the Stronghold. Three hundred and ten Miniconjou, led by the respected Big Foot and joined by about forty Hunkpapa from Grand River, had also fled from their reservation on the Cheyenne River and were by late December heading toward Pine Ridge. Eluding Lieutenant Colonel Sumner, Big Foot's people were caught by another army column on 28 December. That night, Colonel James W. Forsyth arrived at the camp near Wounded Knee Creek with orders to disarm the tribes. Both the Indians and the troopers of Forsyth's regiment—ironically, the Seventh Cavalry, so ignominously defeated fourteen and a half years ago along the banks of the Little Bighorn—spent a tense wintry night.

Disarming 120 warriors without violence would have tested the most grizzled Indian campaigner. Forsyth, although a competent staffer, had never faced the tribes in battle. He had at his disposal five hundred soldiers and four Hotchkiss cannon, but only 110 of his troops were in direct contact with the warriors. A scuffle broke out and the firing became general. Men, women, and children alternately fought back and fled for cover as the troops poured volley after volley into the melee. Twenty-five soldiers lay dead, with another thirty-nine wounded; Indian losses were more than 150 dead and about fifty wounded.

The bloody carnage at Wounded Knee nearly precipitated a general conflict. On 30 December, Forsyth again blundered, allowing his command to stumble into an ambush near the Drexel Mission. Several troops of black cavalrymen rode in to save Forsyth's command from an embarrassing situation. Only the cool direction of the campaign by Miles and the overwhelming numerical superiority of the thirty-five hundred government forces (those fighting men declared "hostile" probably numbered less than one thousand) prevented an even greater calamity.

The Wounded Knee campaign would be the last major conflict associated with the Indian wars of the nineteenth century, but the army remained attuned to potential Indian difficulties throughout much of the West for years. Only with the onset of the Spanish-American War in 1898 and the retirement of Miles as commanding general in 1903 did the United States Army truly recognize that its service as a frontier constabulary had ended.

THE ARMY AND WESTERN EXPANSION

Frederick Jackson Turner pronounced the American frontier to be closed in his essay "The Significance of the American Frontier in American History," which he read at the 1893 meeting of the American Historical Association. The essay argued that the uniqueness of the American character was explained through the frontier experience and would dominate historical thought in the United States for nearly a half century. Turner's much-debated work largely ignored the army; only belatedly have historians come to recognize the multifaceted role of the military in the nation's westward march.

Few military officials of the nineteenth century doubted the cause of expansion. Winfield Scott, commanding general from 1841 to 1861, triggered the territorial expansion of 1848 by capturing Mexico City. Secretary of War Jefferson Davis worked hard to conquer the newly acquired lands of the Far West, spurring efforts to increase the size of the army, supporting the Gadsden Purchase, and sponsoring the railroad explorations of the mid-1850s. After the Civil War, commanding Generals Sherman (1869–1883), Sheridan (1884–1888), John M. Schofield (1888–1895), and Miles (1895–1903) all championed the rights of white settlers to occupy huge portions of the trans-Mississippi West.

After years of campaigning, the army ultimately established its military supremacy over the Indians. Of course, civilian activities greatly assisted this process. Most important were the millions of settlers themselves; by occupying vast regions of the West, these immigrants significantly reduced the amount of land available to the native tribes. Hunters and sportsmen furthered the ultimate success of the United States government. Their

Big Foot, a respected Sioux leader, was killed during fighting between Indians and the U.S. Army near Wounded Knee Creek in South Dakota in 1890. In this photograph, Big Foot's dead body lies frozen on the battlefield. (National Archives)

destruction of the great buffalo herds severely weakened the Plains peoples. The railroads were also crucial in facilitating this westward push. As Sherman noted in his last annual report, "The recent completion of the last of the four great transcontinental lines of railway has settled forever the Indian question."

Thus, only when analyzed in conjunction with civilian activities can the army's role in the westward expansion of the United States be properly assessed, but the multipurpose army of the nineteenth century was more than a military force. Its forts attracted entrepreneurs, encouraged settlement, and at least indirectly supplied the buffalo hunters; its escorts guarded railroad construction and overland wagon trails; and its officers espoused an optimistic view of the western environment that helped attract the millions of immigrants.

Few in the army espoused physical extermination of the Indians. At the same time, however, most military leaders accepted the racism and paternalism that accentuated white approaches to the native peoples of the late nineteenth-century frontiers. The reservation system, therefore, is in part an army legacy, just as are the cities, towns, and dramatic history of the American West.

BIBLIOGRAPHY

General Histories

Clendenen, Clarence C. *Blood on the Border: The United States Army and the Mexican Irregulars* (1969).

Coffman, Edward M. *The Old Army: A Portrait of the American Army in Peacetime, 1784–1898 (1986).*

Dunlay, Thomas W. *Wolves for the Blue Soldiers: Indian Scouts and Auxiliaries with the United States Army, 1860–1890 (1982).*

Ellis, Richard N. "The Humanitarian Generals." *Western Historical Quarterly* 3 (1972).

Frazer, Robert W. *Forts of the West: Military Forts and Presidios, and Posts Commonly Called Forts, West of the Mississippi River to 1898* (1965).

Hutchins, James S. "Mounted Riflemen: The Real Role of Cavalry in the Indian Wars." In *Probing the American West: Papers from the Santa Fe Conference on the History of Western America,* edited by Kenneth Ross Toole et al. (1962).

Hutton, Paul A. "The Indians' Last Stand: A Review Essay." *New Mexico Historical Review* 59 (1984).

Leckie, William H. *The Military Conquest of the Southern Plains* (1963).

Myres, Sandra L. "Romance and Reality on the American Frontier: Views of Army Wives." *Western Historical Quarterly* 13 (1982).

Russell, Don. "How Many Indians Were Killed? White Man Versus Red Man: The Facts and the Legend." *American West* 10 (July 1973).

Smith, Sherry L., "A Window on Themselves: Perceptions of Indians by Military Officers and Their Wives." *New Mexico Historical Review* 64 (1989).

Tate, James P. ed. *The American Military on the Frontier: The Proceedings of the 7th Military History Symposium* (1978).

Tate, Michael L. "The Multi-purpose Army on the Frontier: A Call for Further Research." In *The American West: Essays in Honor of W. Eugene Hollon,* edited by Ronald Lora (1980).

Utley, Robert M. *The Indian Frontier of the American West, 1846–1890* (1984).

Wade, Arthur P. "The Military Command Structure:. The Great Plains, 1853–1891." *Journal of the West* 15 (1976).

Wooster, Robert. " 'A Difficult and Forlorn Country': The Military Looks at the American Southwest, 1850–1890." *Arizona and the West* 28 (1986).

Antebellum and Civil War Years

Bender, Averam. "The Soldier in the Far West, 1848–1860." *Pacific Historical Review* 8 (1939).

———. *The March of Empire: Frontier Defense in the Southwest, 1848–1860* (1952).

Bischoff, William N. "The Yakima Indian War, 1855–1856: A Problem in Research." *Pacific Northwest Quarterly* 41 (1950).

Goetzmann, William H. *Army Exploration in the American West, 1803–1863* (1959).

Prucha, Francis Paul. *Broadax and Bayonet: The Role of the United States Army in the Development of the Northwest, 1815–1860* (1953).

Sievers, Michael A. "Sands of Sand Creek Historiography." *Colorado Magazine* 49 (1972).

Skelton, William B. "Army Officers' Attitudes Toward Indians, 1830–1860." *Pacific Northwest Quarterly* 67 (1976).

Thompson, Gerald. *The Army and the Navajo* (1976).

Trafzer, Clifford E. *The Kit Carson Campaign: The Last Great Navajo War* (1982).

Utley, Robert M. *Frontiersmen in Blue: The United States Army and the Indian, 1848–1865* (1967).

Wooster, Robert. "Military Strategy in the Southwest, 1848–1860." *Military History of Texas and the Southwest* 15 (1979).

Biographies

Athearn, Robert G. *William Tecumseh Sherman and the Settlement of the West* (1956).

Hutton, Paul A. *Phil Sheridan and His Army* (1985).

Hutton, Paul A., ed. *Soldiers West: Biographies from the Military Frontier* (1987).

King, James T. "George Crook: Indian Fighter and Humanitarian." *Arizona and the West* 9 (1967).

Kroeker, Marvin E. *Great Plains Command: William B. Hazen in the Frontier West* (1976).

Smith, Sherry L. *Sagebrush Soldier: Private William Earl Smith's View of the Sioux War of 1876* (1989).

Utley, Robert M. *Cavalier in Buckskin: George Armstrong Custer and the Western Military Frontier* (1988).

Young, Otis E. The *West of Philip St. George Cooke, 1809–1895* (1955).

The Post–Civil War Years

Fite, Gilbert. "The United States Army and Relief to Pioneer Settlers, 1874–1875." *Military Affairs* 29 (1965).

Gates, John M. "The Alleged Isolation of U.S. Army Officers in the Late 19th Century." *Parameters* 10 (1980).

Gray, John S. *Centennial Campaign: The Sioux War of 1876* (1976).

Greene, Jerome A. *Slim Buttes, 1876: An Episode of the Great Sioux War* (1982).

Haley, James L. *The Buffalo War: The History of the Red River Indian Uprising of 1874* (1976).

Hedren, Paul L. *Fort Laramie in 1876: Chronicle of a Frontier Post at War* (1988).
Jackson, Donald D. *Custer's Gold: The United States Cavalry Expedition of 1874* (1966).
Josephy, Alvin M. *The Nez Perce Indians and the Opening of the Northwest* (1965).
Leckie, William H. *The Buffalo Soldiers: A Narrative of the Negro Cavalry in the West* (1967).
Miller, Darlis A. *Soldiers and Settlers: Military Supply in the Southwest, 1861–1885* (1989).
Rickey, Don. *Forty Miles a Day on Beans and Hay: The Enlisted Soldier Fighting the Indian Wars* (1963).
Thompson, Erwin N. *Modoc War: Its Military History and Topography* (1971).
Utley, Robert M. *The Last Days of the Sioux Nation* (1963).
———. *Frontier Regulars: The United States Army and the Indian, 1866–1891* (1973).
Wooster, Robert. *The Military and United States Indian Policy, 1865–1903* (1988).
———. "The Army and the Politics of Expansion: Texas and the Southwestern Borderlands, 1870–1886." *Southwestern Historical Quarterly* 93 (1989).

— ROBERT WOOSTER

The Civil War

THE COMING OF WAR

What caused the Civil War is a question that both puzzles and fascinates and answers are as numerous as questioners. North and South were split over slavery, economic systems, and ways of life, and each had different ideas about democracy and freedom. It seemed that by the election of 1860 the United States had nearly ruptured already, so angry were the words heard in Congress and read in the daily press. Aggressive northern pursuit of progress caused some of the problem. Burgeoning with money and people, the North rushed into the Industrial Age almost as a reward for good Yankee business sense. All sections of the nation except the agrarian South followed in pursuit of the power of wealth. The South had lagged woefully in the traces of the plantation system, in the thrall of slavery, and shackled to the land. And the South nagged at northern consciences.

Democracy, progress, and the graces come from money all blessed by the land of the "free and the brave." But what about slavery? The "peculiar institution," which persisted from colonial times, had a place in the U.S. Constitution and spread with the Cotton Kingdom. Slaves worked in gangs, in teams, and sometimes alongside their masters and were the labor source in the South. Because they were essential to the agrarian way, the South adapted a society around slavery, and as abolitionism grew in the American conscience to the focus of all reform, the South stood at bay.

Democracy, progress, and the graces come from money all blessed by the land of the "free and the brave." But what about slavery?

Increasingly through the nineteenth century, the cotton states turned away from the future; their citizens looked backward toward a calmer, slower time. Not a great proportion of them owned slaves, and according to 1860 figures, from a total southern population of 9,103,332, some 365,000 owners held 3,953,696 slaves. Even small owners, certainly in their own eyes, were part of the elite planter class—the class that set the tone of southern life—but many of the elite were uneasy with their social order and freeing slaves was not uncommon. There were 132,760 free blacks in the cotton states.

As abolition rhetoric rose, Southerners felt threatened, isolated, and resentful and turned from guilt to pride in slavery. Politicians began to speak of slavery's "positive good" and point to plantation paternalism as superior to the sweatshop exploitation of northern labor. Some planters boasted of the idyllic southern way of life and railed against the crass materialism they saw tarnishing existence north of Mason and Dixon's Line. Both sections looked at each other's stereotypes and saw evil, although neither North nor South cared about what was going on in the other section. Prejudices were fully made up, and by election time in 1860, two belligerents stared in anger across American ballot boxes. The splintering of the Democratic party during the campaign wrecked the last national political organization and made way for the triumph of the sectional Republicans and their presidential candidate, Illinois lawyer Abraham Lincoln.

Lincoln's election ignited secession sentiment. Southerners saw him as the embodiment of "black republicanism," a man determined to end slavery in the south. His debates with Democrat Stephen A. Douglas during the 1858 Illinois senatorial campaign seemed to confirm his antislavery views and his studied ambiguity during the 1860 presidential campaign to justify the worst suspicions. South Carolina adopted an ordinance of secession on 20 December 1860. A combination of admiration for the Palmetto State's dedication and fear of the possible economic and social policies of Lincoln spurred secession conventions across the south. Mississippi seceded on 9 January 1861, followed by Florida on the 10th, Alabama on the 11th, Georgia on the 19th, and Louisiana on the 26th. Texas submitted its secession ordinance to voters on 23 February, but the state had withdrawn from the Union on 1 February.

As moderates were crowded out by zealots, secession had its own momentum and eliminated the fence sitters; many people who doubted the wisdom of disunion went with their native states. Most Unionists in the South shared the view that loyalty lay with the closest government and that the Union had second claim on their patriotism. Those straggling few who remained steadfast to the United States would soon be the "Tories" of the southland and would suffer like their earlier counterparts.

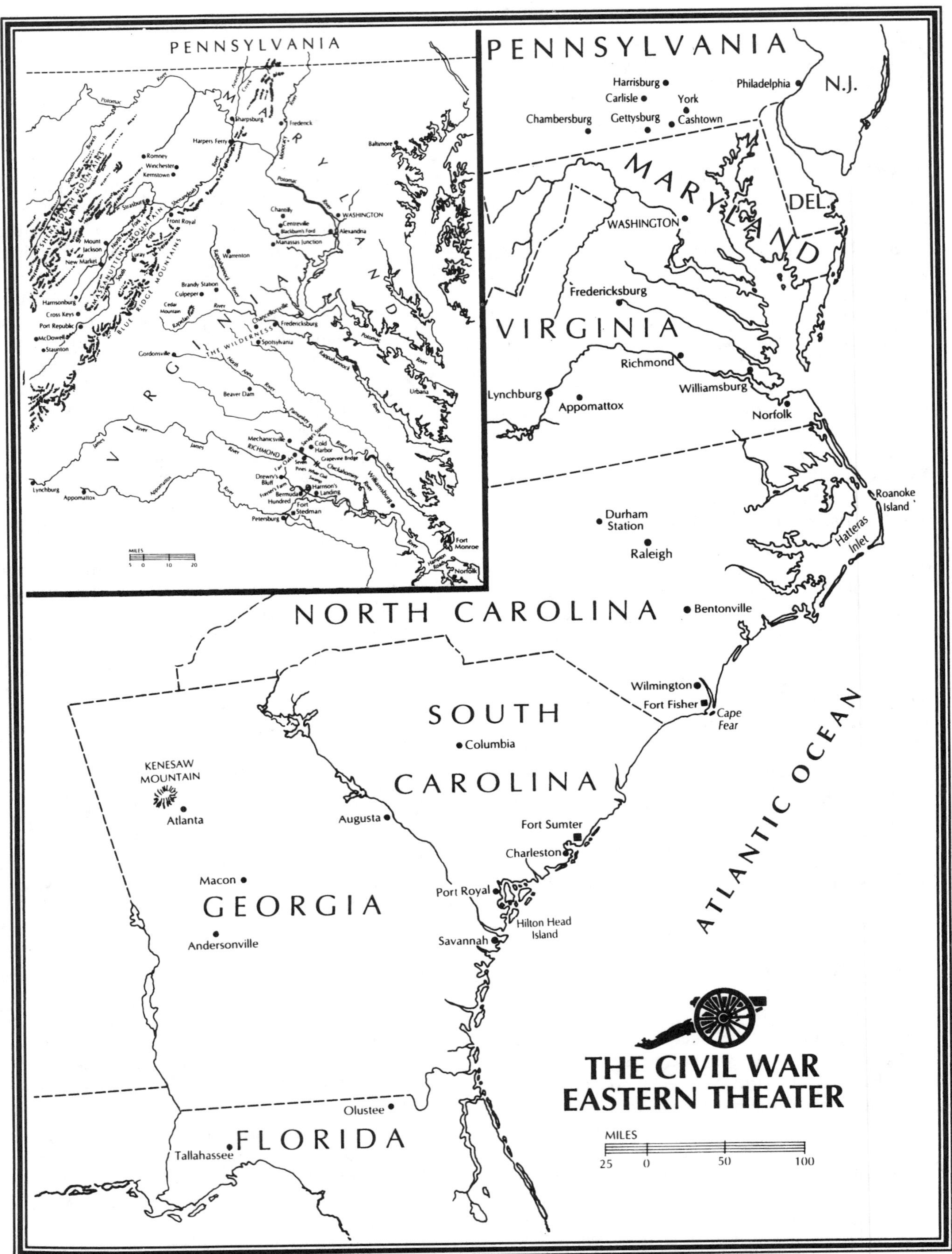

PENNSYLVANIA
MARYLAND
VIRGINIA
Sharpsburg
Frederick
Harpers Ferry
Baltimore
Romney
Winchester
Kernstown
Strasburg
Front Royal
WASHINGTON
Alexandria
Chantilly
Centreville
Blackburn's Ford
Manassas Junction
Warrenton
Mount Jackson
New Market
Luray
MASSANUTTEN MOUNTAIN
BLUE RIDGE MOUNTAINS
SHENANDOAH MOUNTAIN
Harrisonburg
Cross Keys
Port Republic
McDowell
Staunton
Brandy Station
Culpeper
Cedar Mountain
Chancellorsville
Fredericksburg
Spotsylvania
THE WILDERNESS
Gordonsville
Beaver Dam
Urbana
Mechanicsville
RICHMOND
Cold Harbor
Grapevine Bridge
Drewry's Bluff
Bermuda Hundred
Harrison's Landing
Fort Stedman
Petersburg
Williamsburg
Lynchburg
Appomattox
Fort Monroe
Norfolk
MILES
5 0 10 20
PENNSYLVANIA
Harrisburg
Carlisle
York
Philadelphia
N.J.
Chambersburg
Gettysburg
Cashtown
MARYLAND
DEL.
WASHINGTON
Fredericksburg
VIRGINIA
Richmond
Lynchburg
Appomattox
Williamsburg
Norfolk
Roanoke Island
Durham Station
Raleigh
Hatteras Inlet
NORTH CAROLINA
Bentonville
Wilmington
Fort Fisher
Cape Fear
SOUTH CAROLINA
Columbia
KENESAW MOUNTAIN
Atlanta
Augusta
Fort Sumter
Charleston
Macon
GEORGIA
Port Royal
Hilton Head Island
Andersonville
Savannah
ATLANTIC OCEAN
THE CIVIL WAR EASTERN THEATER
MILES
25 0 50 100
Olustee
Tallahassee
FLORIDA

Leaders of the seceded states congregated at Montgomery, Alabama, on 4 February 1861, to form a government. Despite the wash of independence across the South, there was general agreement that a new confederation would have to be formed to face the Union and that the new government would have to be a good deal stronger than the one created under the Articles of Confederation. Delegates to Montgomery were not all "fire-eaters" (southern proslavery extremists) and a sense of moderation tinged their doings in convention. They were, they thought, the legitimate inheritors of traditional strains of American political freedom, and they wanted to show that the nation they were creating came more in evolution than revolution. They adopted a provisional constitution that resembled the United States document in everything save the fact that the new congress would be unicameral and worked to perfect a permanent constitution that would be better than the U.S. model. Drafted in a few days, the Confederate Constitution did show such wisdoms as the item veto and six-year terms for the president and vice-president.

Montgomery's delegates decided on a name for their nation that conformed to conservative views of states' rights—the Confederate States of America. For national leaders, they selected Alexander H. Stephens of Georgia as vice-president, and Jefferson Davis of Mississippi as president. Stephens, a well-known Unionist, dragged his feet toward secession and represented the "Tory" minority. Davis, a long-time U.S. senator (1847–1851, 1857–1861), held John C. Calhoun's mantle as national spokesman for the South. A states' righter and defender of slavery, Davis nonetheless took a cautious stand on secession and quit his senate seat with high hopes and great fears for the Confederacy.

Davis seemed almost the embodiment of the southland he so loved. A tall man with a chiseled, ascetic face ravaged by neuralgia that clouded one eye, he had graciousness blended with the reserve of the severely shy. Warm and winning in person, he showed a chilly public exterior. A devoted Confederate patriot, he found the petty bickering of many Southerners unfathomable. For him, patriotism had no limits and he had a zealot's stout heart and short patience. Nevertheless, he was the best man the South could call to fashion independence. Davis knew far better than most fellow Southrons the fragility of his new country. Long political experience gave him perspective on the economic anomalies of an agrarian state in an industrializing world; experience as secretary of war (1853–1857) in President Franklin Pierce's administration gave him acute awareness of the Confederacy's military weaknesses. In his inaugural address on 18 February 1861, he put forth the best hope for a collection of new "'republics" flushed with the bravado of independence. He hoped for peaceful separation from the Union, but expected war, and tried to brace Southerners for a long and costly conflict.

As Abraham Lincoln stood on the Capitol's steps and gave his own inaugural on 4 March 1861, he shared some of Davis' qualms. His trip to Washington from Springfield, Illinois, had been awkward. Detective Allan Pinkerton warned of southern plotters everywhere, kept the president-elect's travel plans secret, and ushered him covertly into the capital near dawn on Saturday, 23 February 1861. Nine crowded days before the inauguration gave Lincoln a measure of the confusion facing the Union. A peace convention wrangled over proposals to save the United States, Congress wrestled with various amendments, and waves of office-seekers filled the Willard Hotel lobby for a word with the incoming president. Lincoln shuffled candidates for his cabinet, listened to varying views on how to save the country, and perhaps realized fully the reality of the crisis he had casually called "artificial." Everyone wondered what the mysterious Illinoisan would do; rumors preceded him and they ran from admiration to derision. Since the election he had kept quiet and ambiguous counsel. Washington, D.C., saw a tall, plain, and ungainly rustic, thin in political experience, rich in western jokes, and altogether out of place at a crossroads of history.

Impressions shifted after the inauguration on 4 March. He did not, said Lincoln, have any intent to interfere with slavery where it existed, would not object to the proposed constitutional amendment forbidding federal interference, and supported enforcement of the Fugitive Slave Act of 1850. He also assured Southerners that he would be lenient in administering the government and would not put "obnoxious strangers" in the South to enforce the laws. The South, he argued, had no real grievances—differences could be settled by the next election—but the Union was "perpetual," and "the central idea of secession is the essence of anarchy." Nor could the states physically separate—trade and political relations would continue. Would legal separation make anything easier? Let passions cool, he urged. "If the Almighty Ruler of nations, with his eternal truth and justice, be on your side of the North, or on yours of the South, that truth and that justice, will surely prevail by the judgment of this great tribunal of the American people." Responsibility for trouble would be clear. "In *your* hands, my dissatisfied fellow countrymen, and not in *mine,* is the momentous issue of civil war. The government will not assail *you.* You can have no conflict, without being yourselves the aggressors. *You* have no oath registered in Heaven to destroy the government, while *I* shall have the most solemn one to 'preserve, protect and defend' it."

Memories caught some poetry in his heart as he made an emotional call for caution. "I am loath to close. We are not enemies, but friends. We must not be enemies. Though passion may have strained, it must not break our bonds of affection. The mystic chords of memory, streching [*sic*] from every battlefield and patriot grave, to every living heart and hearthstone, all over this broad land, will yet swell the chorus of the Union, when again touched, as surely they will be, by the better angels of our nature." Lincoln's address rewards careful study. In this one speech, he proclaimed a policy of preserving the Union, focused on slavery as the evil in dispute, and fixed any war guilt on the South. In addition, he had tried to put America's crisis in a rational frame of legal reference and put it in terms of political reason. Reason, however, ran differently in this crisis time, as words played tricks in meaning and symbols stood for facts.

Consequently, reaction to Lincoln's inaugural address ran according to prejudice. To radicals, North and South, it sounded either too weak or too strong. Some border-state moderates liked it and for a time the border stood firm, but many in the North found scant leadership in what they heard. To sober southern readers, however, the inaugural came as a declaration of war. Although Lincoln might allow interruptions in local administration, he would keep the forts and other properties of the Union, a fact that negated Confederate sovereignty.

Both sides prepared for war. Rationally, the South had no chance in a war against the North and the statistics were chilling (see chart "Comparison of North and South"). Although the South boasted its cotton culture and lead in cottage industry, the North had a large lead in cash crops from improved farmland. The South manufactured only 3 percent of all arms produced in the United States, and in 1861 could count only $27 million in specie. The South's chances looked grimmer still in a counting of military manpower. The Confederacy had about 1 million men ready for service in 1861, and the North, about 3.5 million. Slaves were not expected to be used, save for personal service and labor, but slave numbers were important to both sides.

After the war, some critics argued that southern leaders ignored all the odds in a vain attempt for glory. Convenient as this charge is to believers in the cynical theory of history, it ignores the cause of independence, the South's strategic position, and especially cotton and courage, two tangibles of value.

President Davis and his cabinet—men of greater substance than most accounts allow—agreed from the beginning that cotton would be the Confederacy's best fulcrum for success. Most of the industrial nations, particularly Great Britain and France, supported large textile industries that relied heavily on southern cotton. Foreign recognition and intervention might come in direct response to the need for "King Cotton." Although Davis and his advisers counted the odds against the South realistically, they did not ignore the rising tide of rebel sentiment that spurred a new patriotic zeal.

Lincoln followed his inaugural with a cautious attitude toward two United States forts. Fort Sumter, an old coastal bastion athwart Charleston Harbor, South Carolina, was held by a small U.S. garrison that had moved into the fort in December 1860. Fort Pickens, in Florida's Pensacola Harbor, had been garrisoned in January 1861. Both were old, designed for forgotten sieges from the sea, and of dubious military value. Suddenly, however, they had awesome symbolic power, because they stood as Union anchors against secession tides, especially Fort Sumter. Southern authorities wanted Sumter most of all, because of its threat to international commerce, and demanded its evacuation.

COMPARISON OF NORTH AND SOUTH

	North	South
Number of states	23	11
Population	22,000,000	9,000,000*
Cities over 100,000 population	8	1 (New Orleans)
Cities over 50,000 population	7	1
Railroad mileage	22,000	9,000
Annual shipping tonnage**	13,654,925	737,901
Horses	4,417,130	1,698,328
Mules	328,890	800,663
Industrial establishments	110,274	18,026
Industrial workers	1,300,000	110,000
Annual product	$1,754,650,000	$145,350,000

* Including 3.5 million slaves

** June 1860 to June 1861

Several members of Lincoln's cabinet thought Sumter too hard to hold and a risk beyond its worth. They also believed that there might be a chance to trade off Sumter if Pickens were held. Lincoln groped toward a policy to uphold federal honor and reduce southern fears. Southern concern made these forts useful tokens in an opening game of wits. Davis sent three commissioners to treat with Lincoln's government about peaceful separation and about public property scattered across the Confederacy, especially the forts. Maneuvering to win northern support for a war to coerce southern loyalty, Lincoln cannily avoided Davis's emissaries. He let his shrewd secretary of state, William H. Seward, deal with them in varying guises of cooperation.

"We are not enemies, but friends. We must not be enemies. Though passion may have strained, it must not break our bonds of affection."

Frustration tinged Confederate cabinet meetings as reports arrived of Seward's delaying tactics. Davis, however, began to learn that diplomacy can be a system of deceit and came to suspect that the forts might be pawns in a game to push the South into firing the first shot. Aware of uncertain northern opinion, Davis also knew that the Confederacy could not boast full independence unless at least Fort Sumter flew the new rebel banner. How long could the South wait? On 6 April, Seward told the southern commissioners that the United States would defend its property only when attacked, and on that same day a messenger from Lincoln informed Governor Francis Pickens of South Carolina that Fort Sumter would be resupplied, but reinforced only in case of resistance.

Rumors of a large relief expedition moving toward Charleston in early April caused serious war jitters. After anguished cabinet consultation, Davis authorized action. Secretary of War Leroy P. Walker telegraphed the Confederate commander in Charleston, General Pierre G. T. Beauregard, that once he knew Sumter would be resupplied, "you will at once demand its evacuation, and if this is refused proceed, in such manner as you may determine, to reduce it." Beauregard worked to complete and garrison the works and batteries surrounding Fort Sumter. On 11 April a small boat under a white flag took three men out to Sumter. They carried a message to Major Robert Anderson, commanding the fort, demanding evacuation. After long talks with his officers, Anderson refused, but said that he would be starved out in a few days. Beauregard reported this to Montgomery and was told that the Confederate government did not "desire needlessly to bombard Fort Sumter," and that, if Anderson would say when he would quit the fort without a fight, "you are authorized thus to avoid the effusion of blood." Anderson, informed of the new terms, replied that he would leave at noon on the 15th unless he received reinforcements or new orders. The southern negotiators rejected this reply and announced that firing would begin in an hour. At 4:30 A.M. on 12 April 1861, one of Beauregard's guns signaled the start of the Civil War.

Surrender of the fort on the 13th triggered swift northern reaction. Lincoln carefully crafted a call for seventy-five thousand volunteers to put down the insurrection, which had the effect of a declaration of war and fixed the nature of the conflict—Southerners had rebelled, hence their new "confederacy" did not exist. Lincoln knew that Northerners might lag to coerce the South but would flock to save the Union. He also knew that the call for men would force the border states to make some decisions. Lincoln hoped, too, that defining the coming conflict as a rebellion would prevent foreign recognition of the Confederacy, which would mean a southern victory. Queen Victoria's proclamation of neutrality on 13 May comforted Lincoln and Seward, but her concession of Confederate belligerency angered them, because belligerency gave legality to southern armies, ships, and commissions and was just a step short of full recognition.

Although technicalities tinged some border state withdrawals, Lincoln's proclamation of insurrection and call for volunteers pushed Virginia out of the Union on 17 April, Arkansas on 6 May, Tennessee on 7 May, and North Carolina on 20 May. Later critics would see Lincoln's proclamation of insurrection as a great mistake, one that lost him the best chance to save the Union short of war. While some border state governors were rejecting the Union call for men, Davis issued a proclamation calling 100,000 men into Confederate service, and, when the Confederate Provisional Congress convened on 29 April, he requested more money to prosecute the war and to organize the War and Navy departments.

By the end of April 1861, nothing seemed the same. War had come—a war to run beyond all bounds of reckoning and all previous American experience. Small armies led by individual generals operating in isolation were gone forever. North and South edged toward the first war of the industrial revolution, the first modern war of machines—not just the traditional machines of conflict, such as artillery and digging tools and wagons, but such new machines as rolling mills, railroads, ironclad warships, rapid-fire guns, torpedoes, chemical agents, workable submarines, balloons, telegraphs, battlefield semaphore signals, massed fire, and sophisticated trenches. It would be a total war of peoples, nations, and resources that smashed traditions as it forged a new power in the world.

BEGINNING OF THE WAR

North and South began with the same ideas of war. Because the South rejected revolution, it followed federal military precedents. Both sides faced problems of handling vast numbers of recruits; of supplying, training, and organizing them into armies; and, most urgently, of providing competent officers. The North had an army in being, and therefore faced an apparently easy problem of expansion, but the South faced vexing issues of creating a national war machine from fragmented state efforts.

Northern military preparations were the responsibility of Simon Cameron, a canny Pennsylvania politico and the new secretary of war. A crafty dealer and maneuverer, he had no art for War Department bureaucracy. Uncertain, equivocating, and a slow decider, Cameron added confusion to red tape. Fortunately, he had good professional officers heading the small national army of the Union.

General Winfield Scott, veteran of the War of 1812 and hero of the Mexican War whose experience weighed against his age (seventy-five) and lent wisdom to his portents, served as general in chief of the army. He grasped quickly that expanding existing offices, bureaus, and army units would be much more difficult than expected and sought highly competent men to head various departments. He put western Virginia, a highly pro-Union section, under command of the dashing, young Major General George Brinton McClellan, who proceeded to wage an extremely effective campaign with a relatively small army that preserved his area for the North and defeated several Confederate forces.

Lincoln and Scott offered the vital position of commanding the main Union army to Colonel Robert E. Lee of Virginia, a judicious soldier whose commands had included the illustrious Second Cavalry and who boasted wide engineering experience. Lee pondered the offer, but resigned his U.S. commission because he could not war against his native Virginia. Scott considered several other officers, in various department commands, as he looked for someone else to take charge of

Fort Sumter, which stands on an island in Charleston Harbor, South Carolina, was held by a small U.S. garrison until 12 April 1861, when Confederate troops fired on the fort and captured it. Fort Sumter is shown here in 1861 under a Confederate flag. (National Archives)

the large federal army gathering near Washington, D.C. On 28 May 1861, Brigadier General (soon to be Major General) Irvin McDowell received command of the Department of Northeastern Virginia, which included the troops mustering at Alexandria and in the Union capital and the major federal army. A competent professional, McDowell's experience suffered the limitations of long service in a small U.S. army, but he quickly showed ability as an organizer.

As recruits gathered around Washington, McDowell and his staff struggled to use regulars to mold volunteers and militiamen into soldiers and fashion an army from an amalgam of enthusiasts. This difficult task was complicated by a growing demand to attack the rebels. President Lincoln, not yet a patient paragon, also demanded action. McDowell, still learning his job and his army, wisely delayed advancing into Virginia until strength, training, and prudence allowed. Problems abounded. Not only did receiving and training men occupy every day, but logistical tangles confused everything. The Eleventh Massachusetts Infantry had twenty-five wagons for the baggage of 950 men—a fairly typical ratio. Thousands of horses and mules had to be tended and distributed. Rifles, ammunition, cannon, wagons, harness, uniforms, shoes—all the staff of armies—had to be sorted, inventoried, and issued. Field hospitals were new and untested and the number of doctors too few. Officers were usually as raw and untrained as their men. Everywhere McDowell looked, chaos roiled his camps.

Gradually a kind of order arrived. Streets could be seen amidst the sea of tents; men marched in semblance of formations; artillery batteries took shape; and cavalry galloped without undue damage. Unlikely as it seemed, McDowell's army came into being, a huge force of nearly thirty-five thousand men. Lincoln pressed for action because further delay might cool Yankee ardor. At a cabinet meeting on 29 June, McDowell revealed his plan to attack Confederate positions at Manassas, Virginia. At that meeting, General Scott proposed his Anaconda Plan, an expedition down the Mississippi River to cut the Confederacy in two and make possible a squeezing operation around the coast and interior borders of the eastern seceded states. The cabinet and Lincoln decided to deal first with the Virginia rebels.

Lincoln understood the need for a grand strategic plan, but political pressure focused his eye toward the enemy capital, which had moved from Montgomery to Richmond, Virginia, on 29 May. On 16 July, McDowell's army moved west from the Potomac toward Centreville and Manassas in response to the rising cry of "On to Richmond" and to open the summer campaign of 1861. His columns were long, at first somewhat confused, and made scarcely six miles that first day, but he had advanced, and the North writhed in justifiable excitement because scattered military operations along the Potomac boundary of Virginia and in Missouri and Kentucky had gone the North's way. A few reverses in the Far West could be glossed over in the wash of success.

In the meantime, successes were being claimed by the South. As secession continued in the border areas and in some of the Indian nations, boundaries and resources expanded. Much pro-Confederate sentiment persisted in Missouri, and that state's plight stood stark and clear during rioting in St. Louis in May and in the removal of the state government to the southwestern corner of the state. When the Confederate capital shifted to Richmond, it marked the addition of a good deal more than territory or industrial strength. The ancient ambience of the Old Dominion gave a special imprimatur to the reseated Confederate government.

The Eleventh Massachusetts Infantry had twenty-five wagons for the baggage of 950 men—a fairly typical ratio.

Shifting the government moved the focus of the Confederacy and also the war. Virginia's exposed position demanded some Confederate commitment. With the government came trainloads of recruits from the deeper South to pass through Richmond and muster near Manassas, some thirty miles southwest of Washington. Thousands of variously garbed and eager troops went through the new capital on the way to join the army commanded by the hero of Fort Sumter, Brigadier General Beauregard.

News of McDowell's advance brought a quick call for help to the army around Manassas. Westward, in the Shenandoah Valley of Virginia, Brigadier General Joseph E. Johnston, with about twelve thousand men, had been holding the area near Harpers Ferry and was ordered to move rapidly to aid Beauregard. In the first strategic use of railroads in the war, Johnston began to move his army on 18 July, and his leading elements reached Manassas on the 19th, in time for the approaching battle. By that time, Beauregard had about thirty-thousand men in his Army of the Potomac.

On the 18th, McDowell's men had probed Beauregard's right flank and became embroiled in unexpected action at Blackburn's Ford. They were repulsed and that shifted McDowell's attention to the Confederate left. He prepared to throw some thirteen thousand men against the northwestern end of Beauregard's line early on the morning of 21 July. As it happened, that section of front would be lightly held, because Beauregard planned to attack McDowell's left at roughly the same time, and had both plans carried, the armies might well have switched position. Beauregard's boldness came with Johnston's arrival. With about thirty-five thousand rebels on the field, an attack seemed feasible. The Battle of Bull Run or Manassas (the federals named battles after the nearest body of water; the Confederates, after the nearest town or community), was about to start.

"There is Jackson standing like a stone wall.

Let us determine to die here, and we will conquer.

Follow me."

A mix-up in orders delayed the southern attack and by mid-morning on the 21st, McDowell's flanking force struck a small Confederate brigade near Sudley Springs Ford and began to move eastward toward Beauregard's bunched legions. Unchecked, this advance would sweep up the whole Confederate line in a rolling defeat. Beauregard's grandiose plans awry, he and Johnston devoted themselves to a defensive battle. As the main battle unfolded, they fed reinforcements to their left, especially the Virginia brigade commanded by Brigadier General Thomas J. Jackson, a somber and devout former professor of artillery tactics at the Virginia Military Institute. While the thin Confederate flank guard grudgingly retreated in front of the Union attack, Jackson's brigade anchored a growing force atop the Henry House hill. Around 2 A.M., McDowell launched a heavy drive against the hill. As Confederates retired, Brigadier General Barnard E. Bee of South Carolina saw Jackson's line and rallied his retreating men with immortal last words: "There is Jackson standing like a stone wall. Let us determine to die here, and we will conquer. Follow me."

McDowell's men were repulsed but surged forward again and again. By 4 A.M., both sides were exhausted. The timely arrival of Confederate reinforcements finally turned the Union right. McDowell's men halted, withdrew, and then stampeded toward Centreville. As the rout gathered momentum, all kinds of flotsam were swept in its wake, including a group of Union congressmen and ladies who had come out to watch the "Bull Run races." Confederate cavalry nudged the retreaters, but confusion in gray ranks impeded proper pursuit. The victors were stunned by success, and many survivors wandered over the field looking for comrades, some to pilfer from the dead, others simply to bask in living. The costs of the Battle of Bull Run were high: Union losses amounted to some twenty-eight hundred killed, wounded, and captured; Confederate casualties came to about nineteen hundred.

News of the battle was received differently in the North and the South. Richmond basked in expected triumph, its citizens wrapped in winners' rectitude. Washington huddled in gloomy fear, Lincoln shocked by the disarmed and dispirited rabble that thronged the streets. These different reactions were measures of the attitudes toward the prosecution of the war. Southerners were confirmed in confidence and knew that one rebel soldier could whip ten Yankees. Northerners suddenly knew the seriousness of the war and the toughness of the rebels. In the aftermath, the South relaxed and the North girded.

Small operations continued in the remaining summer weeks. President Davis reorganized his army's command by appointing eight generals on 31 August; since the appointees took their rank on different dates, jealousies were instant. The South still boasted about Manassas, but Yankee incursions around Confederate coasts and borders were disturbing. By the end of the year, the war's writ ran for the Union.

Confederate morale sagged as Port Royal in South Carolina fell on 7 November, when Hilton Head Island passed to the Yankees on the 8th, and especially when Roanoke Island off North Carolina was lost on 8 February 1862. These losses, most particularly Roanoke, seemed to be the fruits of a piecemeal strategy, weak leadership, or indefensible stupidity. They crowned a winter of bleak discoveries: railroad weaknesses that compounded the rustic backwardness of highway development across the South; financial errors that robbed the South of monetary confidence; logistical problems almost beyond belief and made worse by the blockade of southern ports announced by Lincoln back on 19 April 1861; and strategical errors that called presidential wisdom into question. Instead of concentrating smaller numbers of Confederate troops for the strategic offensive, Davis had scattered soldiers in a doomed attempt to hold the entire borderline of the Confederacy. There were not enough men to do this, proved by steady losses of important coastal areas. Davis confessed his error but explained that strategic weakness forced boundary bravado. Men and supplies were inadequate to taking the offensive. By the time he took the oath of office as the permanent president of the Confederacy on 22 February 1862, he had already developed a strategy for the war—the offensive-defensive—just the kind of plan that the weaker side needed to husband scarce resources until a chance came for decisive concentration at a vital

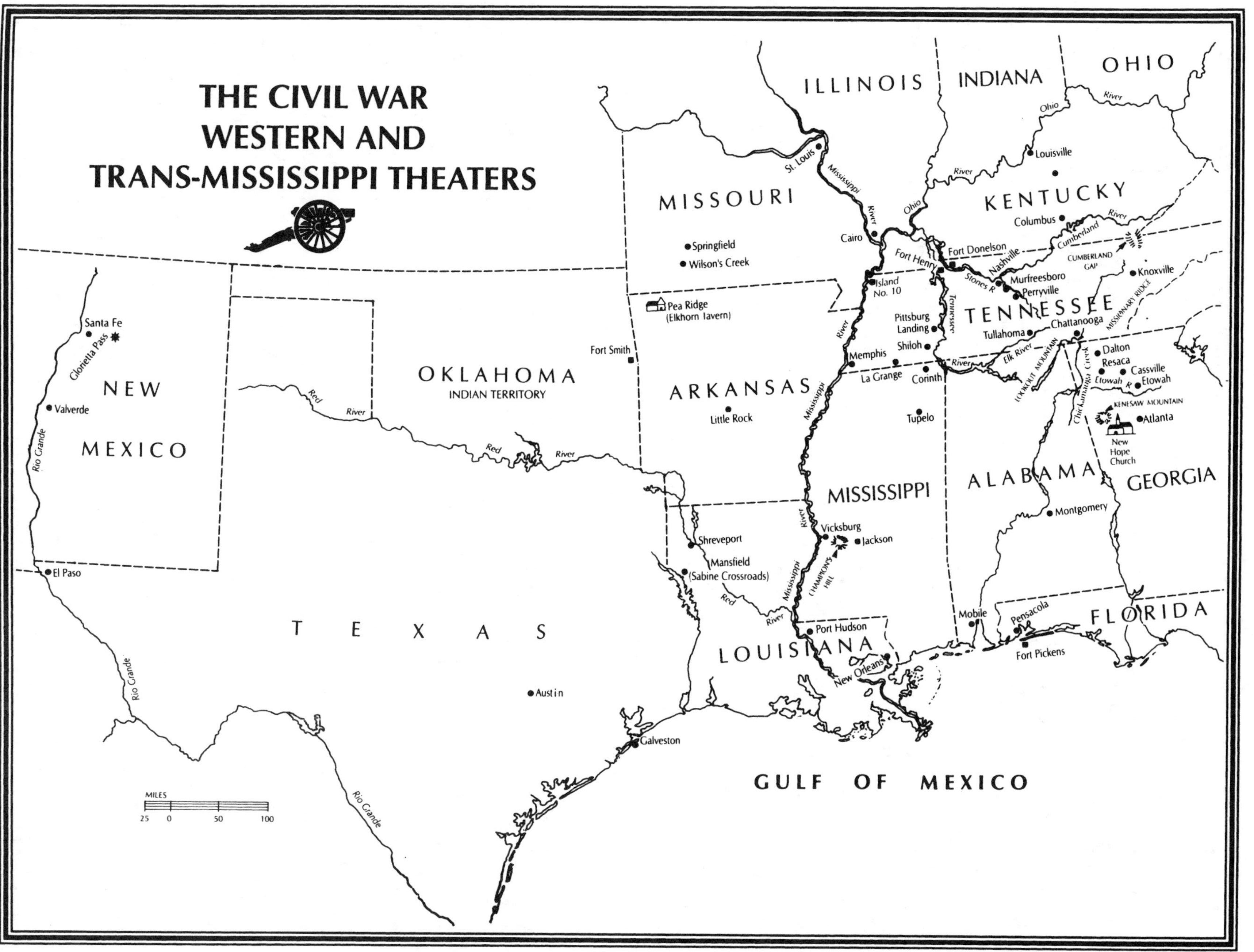

THE CIVIL WAR
WESTERN AND
TRANS-MISSISSIPPI THEATERS
ILLINOIS
INDIANA
OHIO
MISSOURI
KENTUCKY
TENNESSEE
ARKANSAS
OKLAHOMA
INDIAN TERRITORY
NEW
MEXICO
TEXAS
LOUISIANA
MISSISSIPPI
ALABAMA
GEORGIA
FLORIDA
GULF OF MEXICO
St. Louis
Cairo
Louisville
Columbus
Fort Donelson
Fort Henry
Nashville
Murfreesboro
Perryville
Island No. 10
Pittsburg Landing
Shiloh
Memphis
La Grange
Corinth
Tupelo
Tullahoma
Chattanooga
Knoxville
CUMBERLAND GAP
MISSIONARY RIDGE
LOOKOUT MOUNTAIN
Chickamauga Creek
Dalton
Resaca
Cassville
Etowah R.
Etowah
KENESAW MOUNTAIN
Atlanta
New Hope Church
Montgomery
Mobile
Pensacola
Fort Pickens
Vicksburg
Jackson
CHAMPION'S HILL
Port Hudson
New Orleans
Shreveport
Mansfield
(Sabine Crossroads)
Springfield
Wilson's Creek
Pea Ridge
(Elkhorn Tavern)
Little Rock
Fort Smith
Santa Fe
Glorieta Pass
Valverde
El Paso
Austin
Galveston
Ohio River
Mississippi River
Cumberland River
Tennessee River
Stones R.
Elk River
Red River
Rio Grande
MILES
25 0 50 100

point in the war. At that point, Confederate strength, saved for the moment, could be used decisively. Davis followed the plan throughout the war to far better advantage than allowed by critics.

Although things looked generally better in the North, Lincoln wallowed in worry that first winter. Bull Run continued to rankle, and, despite successes on the periphery, Confederates still kept the field and more sacrifice would be needed to end an insurrection that was growing into one of history's big wars.

To those concerned with war planning, it seemed clear that the conflict would be waged in four sectors—east, middle, west, and on the seas. Each sector seemed equally important, with special significance, in Lincoln's view, hinging on operations in and around northern Virginia. Many others, however, said the war would be decided along the Mississippi, that old river of commerce that seemed now to offer inroads of doom or opportunity to either side. What of Scott's Anaconda Plan? According to that scheme, each sector offered opportunities to use the North's superiority in men and materiel and chop the Confederacy up bit by bit. Not actively pushed by anyone, Scott's plan seemed to be working itself out. Christmas holidays in the North were frantic and tinged with dread in 1861, and the new year seemed clouded in an endless mist of carnage.

CONCENTRATION IN THE EAST, 1862

Scarcely one hundred miles separated the opposing national capitals, and the corridor between Washington and Richmond was to become America's most contested stretch of earth. Ground between the cities had military advantages for both sides. Rolling Virginia country was cut by myriad streams and rivers and much lay hidden by forests and scrub timberland, the right type of geography for breaking up big infantry formations and slicing cavalry brigades into small scouting groups. Each side sought the way to put northern Virginia to martial advantage, especially when armies grew wary of frontal assaults and tried increasingly the ancient art of field entrenchment.

After the Battle of Manassas, Johnston and Beauregard held the Bull Run line, collected additional men, and sought to strengthen their positions with fieldworks. Above them, again around Washington, the federals rebuilt their army and found the second in a long roll of generals to lead it back toward Richmond. George McClellan's ego matched the size of his new command, the Military Division of the Potomac, which came under his charge on 27 July 1861. He accepted the assignment of leader of the Army of the Potomac as homage for brilliance and then proceeded to collect McDowell's wretched troop remnants and whip them into a large, flashy army and to perfect Washington's defenses in case the rebels pressed their post-Bull Run advantage. As he gathered men and supplies and confidence, his dapper figure on an imposing charger was seen prancing around the capital daily. His posturing angered some, but McClellan collected men like flies, trained them zealously, and won a fervent loyalty with paternal care and flamboyance.

All indicators ran well for "Little Mac"—an affectionate sobriquet conferred by his men. His operations in western Virginia showed him to be a good organizer, sound planner, a competent strategist, and a tactician of promise. While McClellan's manner may have gone against the plain grain of the president, Lincoln liked his record and hoped for the best. McClellan had no doubt of success as he prepared to invade Virginia, determining to use the Union's growing strength to advantage. With that in mind, he proposed to bypass Confederate lines by transporting his army by water to Urbana on the Rappahannock, disembark, and march rapidly to Richmond before Johnston could cover the capital. Lincoln had qualms but welcomed an aggressive idea. When Winfield Scott took reluctant retirement in November 1861, McClellan took his place as general in chief of the army. If Lincoln had misgivings, Scott assuaged them with firmer warlike words. Still, Lincoln chafed at delays in fear of flagging northern zeal and of too much time presented to the enemy.

Carefully McClellan built his legions, consuming time and mountains of supplies. Success, he believed, would reward care, and when he moved he wanted overwhelming superiority in his favor. McClellan's slowness through the winter sorely tried Lincoln's patience. Aware that campaigning usually stopped for the winter, the president certainly expected the campaign of 1862 to begin as soon as roads dried and temperatures moderated. Still McClellan honed his army and fended demands to attack until spring had almost gone. The Confederate government, on the other hand, worked earnestly through the winter of 1861 to fill ranks thinning from expiring enlistments; to procure and distribute arms, munitions, and other supplies; and especially to forward men to Johnston's army north of Richmond.

There were interesting blends of similarities between Johnston, Beauregard, and McClellan; in fact, a combination of Johnston's and Beauregard's personalities nicely duplicated Little Mac's methodical conceit. As grayclads clustered along Bull Run through the fall and winter, both Johnston and Beauregard fussed in isolation and in some rivalry over who commanded the army. Davis detested the silly command arguments and solved them by sending Beauregard, known as the "Great Creole" to the west early in 1862 as Johnston's second in command. Davis matched Johnston's contentiousness until relations between them chilled with the season. Johnston did organize well and kept his army supplied, and Davis shared his worries about federal intentions. Whenever McClellan moved, it seemed likely to be too soon. Men and munitions came slowly to northern Virginia, and Richmond seemed increasingly exposed.

Southern planners were not unaware of invasion avenues open to McClellan. A flanking move southeast of the capital had logic, and the Bull Run positions were too far north to permit swift adjustment. Johnston wanted to retire closer to the capital. On 9 March he fell back behind the Rappahannock River and neatly negated McClellan's Urbana plan.

Another rebel general also intruded on McClellan's hopes—the strange, solemn, Presbyterian deacon "Stonewall" Jackson, whose winter operations had confused a good many people. Against all precedent, Jackson decided on a winter campaign west of the Shenandoah Valley. Sent to the valley after the Battle of Manassas, he had collected some militia forces, received a few reinforcements, and harassed federal troops in the lower (northern) end of what was known as the "granary of Virginia." As winter set in, however, he knew that Union forces dominated most of the state from the Ohio River to the Shenandoah Valley. How best to thwart them? A glance at a map showed that a Confederate force posted at Romney, across the Alleghenies in the South Branch (Potomac) Valley, would disrupt federal railroad and highway communications and dominate northwestern Virginia.

Winter marching in the mountains would be severe, but the chance to lure McClellan into attacking Johnston before the Union army had finished preparation and the chance to clear western Virginia of the enemy were opportunities too good to ignore—or so thought a general who measured risks against rewards. General Johnston, the department commander, and Secretary of War Judah P. Benjamin approved Jackson's scheme and sent him a few more men. On 1 January 1862, with eighty-five hundred men, Jackson marched on Romney. Some of his untrained militia and recently attached men suffered, but the campaign fuddled the federals and satisfied Jackson. Some of his subordinates complained directly to the War Department about hardship and Jackson's "lunatic" strategy. Benjamin and President Davis blundered badly by listening out of channels and especially in giving Jackson a direct order to bring some of his men back from Romney. Complying instantly with the order, he also offered his resignation in the face of such lack of confidence. Johnston urged charity in the midst of crisis, while the governor of Virginia and many of Jackson's clerical friends urged restraint as they tried to explain to the government the chaos inherent in so "ruinous" a policy. In time, Jackson withdrew his resignation, his important point about command channels amply made.

Jackson could take consolation in knowing that activity in the Shenandoah Valley did indeed disturb Union forces. The enemy sent nearly twenty-five thousand men against his forty-five hundred. The ratio pleased him because he was attracting attention. Johnston wanted Jackson's little band to guard his flank, to stay between him and the federals, delay them in the valley, and keep reinforcements away from McClellan. Jackson could attract more Yankees if he had more men but he agreed to do what he could. With news that the federals were leaving the valley, Jackson took the offensive. At Kernstown on 23 March, inadequate intelligence led him to attack a superior force and he lost, and Jackson never again neglected field intelligence.

Lincoln kept harassing McClellan, and at one point, with unvarnished irony, the president allegedly mused that if the general was not using the army, he would like to borrow it.

Although a defeat, the Battle of Kernstown had the strategic advantage of stopping the movement of federal troops toward McClellan and brought more men against Jackson. As Johnston withdrew closer to Richmond, Jackson received some reinforcements and made plans to engage the enemy and continue his Valley Campaign, a dazzling series of actions in which Jackson fought several groups of federal forces and beat them in detail, a campaign that gave Jackson lasting rank among the world's great captains.

While Jackson prepared, so did McClellan. Lincoln kept harassing McClellan, and at one point, with unvarnished irony, the president allegedly mused that if the general was not using the army, he would like to borrow it. Although keeping outward confidence in his boisterous general's new plan to embark his army for the Virginia Peninsula between the York and James rivers, Lincoln took the unusual step of constructing "President's General War Order No. 1," on 27 January, which declared "that the 22d of February 1862, be the day for a general movement of the Land and Naval forces of the United States against the insurgent forces." Lest McClellan missed the point, the president issued the "President's Special War Order No. 1" on 31 January, which directed McClellan's Army of the Potomac to move south of Manassas.

McClellan's plans were not all bad, but they were confounded by phantoms. Convinced he was opposed by no less than 100,000 rebels north of Richmond, McClellan wanted at least 250,000 men in his area. Although he counted nearly 150,000 by March, he felt insecure about advancing. Lincoln, concerned that the "Young Napoleon" had too much to do, relieved him of all but his army command on the 11th, and at last McClellan moved. On 17 March the leading elements of his army embarked at Alexandria. Lincoln insisted on troops being left to defend Washington, and pressures from other sectors induced the president to siphon a few men from McClellan, but a peremptory presidential order on 3 April retaining McDowell's fine corps of thirty thousand men to watch Stonewall Jackson enraged McClellan. He knew Washington's safety hinged on his own success, but he had more than 100,000 men and rebel defenses around Yorktown and Williamsburg seemed thinner than expected. As he moved glacially toward Richmond, his spirits rose with his rhetoric. He would have been less enthused if he had known of Stonewall Jackson's doings.

The little Army of the Valley had moved up the Shenandoah to camps near Mount Jackson. Reorganization and refitting proceeded, and General Jackson kept an eye on General Nathaniel P. Banks, who moved south from Winchester with about fifteen thousand men and counted on help from scattered Union units. Talks with General Lee, now commanding Confederate operations outside Richmond, brought Jackson encouragement and the temporary aid of General Richard S. Ewell's six-thousand-man brigade. Lee admired Jackson's dogged determination—despite rising odds, he wanted to pin all the Yankee forces west of the Blue Ridge (even west of the Alleghenies) in the mountain theater and keep them away from Richmond.

In a sense, Lee measured Jackson by his achievements with a small force. Not only was General Banks returning in strength to the valley, but General John C. Frémont was also inching eastward toward the Shenandoah from his Mountain Department. Lincoln, responding to Frémont's calls, detailed General Louis Blenker's division from the Army of the Potomac to Frémont's army. Later, because of rising concerns about Jackson's movements, which were shrouded in mystery, he kept McDowell's corps to guard the capital. Therefore, with a few more men Jackson could hope for large results, but Lee could not promise more, because Johnston needed all the reinforcements available around Richmond.

Patiently, Jackson fell back up the valley and made a close study of its geography and geometry. In the area north of his main base at Staunton, Virginia, the valley sat between the Blue Ridge and the Alleghenies, varied in width from ten to thirty miles, and ran northward nearly one hundred miles to the Potomac. The Shenandoah River also ran northward, and divided at the southern base of Massanutten Mountain, a fifty-mile-long north-south range that created two valleys, the one to the east named Luray. Roads were not too good, although the six-foot-wide Valley Pike, connecting Staunton and Winchester, was "metalled" (macadamized). A skein of other dirt roads and traces created a rough parallelogram around Massanutten Mountain and in the upper and lower valley, which gave some maneuvering room to creative strategists.

Jackson lacked skill in understanding ground, but his brilliant topographical engineer, Jedediah Hotchkiss, provided maps that spread the valley clearly before Jackson. All kinds of chances beckoned, but chances shifted as Banks moved south to the end of Massanutten and threatened Staunton. In an unexpected series of moves at the end of April 1862, Jackson apparently took part of his army toward Richmond and left Ewell in observation at a strategic Blue Ridge mountain pass, put his infantry on the "cars," and raced through Staunton toward McDowell, Virginia, where he joined forces with General Edward ("Allegheny") Johnson's army of two thousand. On 8 May, Jackson's ten thousand defeated General Robert H. Milroy's force of six thousand at McDowell and pursued them down the South Fork Valley, sealing mountain passes eastward as they went. On 12 May, Jackson moved back toward Bank's force near Harrisonburg.

Banks was in trouble. He had detached James Shields and his ten thousand men toward Fredericksburg; with scarcely nine thousand left he feared Jackson's movements. He withdrew slowly northward toward Strasburg, which he fortified, and sent a flanking force eastward to Front Royal in hopes of reserving a reinforcement route. Meanwhile, he lost Jackson and Turner Ashby's splendid Confederate cavalry thoroughly screened the valley army. Stonewall had crossed the Massanutten, moved swiftly north down the Luray Valley, and on 23 May struck and smashed Banks's outpost at Front Royal, then sent his rebels racing to cut off Banks's retreat toward Winchester. A running engagement took the federals into their works at Winchester, where Banks made a stand. Jackson wasted no time—his men stormed the fortifications on 25 May, and Yankee remnants streamed for Harpers Ferry with Jackson in pursuit. A romantic figure of speech had it that the Shenandoah Valley pointed like a rifle barrel at the heart of the Union, but the figure now took the shape of Stonewall Jackson. He lurked in that barrel as a seemingly unstoppable charge. As his worn and weary legions crowded toward the Potomac, the Shenandoah was clear of the enemy and, with Shields on his way back to Banks, no help had gone to McClellan.

While Union commanders fumed at Jackson's quick marching—he had set up a system of ten minutes rest each hour and steady pacing through a whole day—Lincoln saw a Euclidean solution to the valley problem. If Jackson's army was at Winchester, the apex of a triangle, and if Shields was coming into the valley at Front Royal at the right base angle, Frémont could approach the left base angle and the two could close the base line at Strasburg and cut Jackson off as he tried to escape southward. It was, Lincoln saw, "a question of legs," and he hoped that shorter angles would put his men ahead of Jackson's "foot cavalry." Not quite. Jackson escaped, moved to the upper valley, and engaged the two forces of Frémont and Shields at Cross Keys on 8 June and Port Republic on 9 June. A double victory numbed federal initiative in the valley and forced them back on Banks beyond Massanutten. Stonewall reported to Lee that "God blessed our arms with victory."

The Valley Campaign remains a military classic, one still studied as a matchless example of what sound strategy combined with mobility, surprise, logistical planning, and determination can accomplish. In a period of forty-eight marching days, Jackson's army covered more than 650 miles, fought five major battles and countless combats and skirmishes. His 16,500 men kept three enemy armies, numbering more than sixty thousand, separated and away from Richmond, captured hundreds of Union wagons with precious supplies, and revived the rebel victory spirit when it seemed buried in bad news. By the time the Army of the Valley went into Blue Ridge for a rest, it had become legendary to South and North alike. Jackson ranked as a new American hero. His men told affectionate jokes about him and said they expected any day to be ordered to march to the gates of Hell and take them by storm. A proud biblical parody captured a great deal about the general and his men:

Man that is born of woman,
And enlisteth in Jackson's Army,
Is of few days and short rations.

Jackson had kept an eye on operations around the capital during the valley fighting to protect Richmond. He knew that McClellan had landed a big army at Fort Monroe and had eased toward Yorktown. He knew, too, that Johnston had countered by moving the main Confederate army toward Richmond and sent some units to support Yorktown and Williamsburg.

By the second week of June, Jackson had learned that Johnston had been severely wounded in the Battle of Seven Pines (Fair Oaks), near Richmond, on 31 May, and that the fifty-five-year old Lee now commanded the main army, which pleased Jackson because he trusted Lee completely. Meanwhile, McClellan, moving with customary caution, inched up the peninsula between the York and James rivers. Because Johnston's attack at Seven Pines had failed, Lee reconcentrated and replanned the battle for Richmond and suggested that Jackson come at once, keeping an eye out for McDowell's corps, which might come to join McClellan from the north. Lee thought Jackson should hit the federal right, north of the Chickahominy River, cut communications, and pressure the flank while Lee's men attacked in front. Lee's call was discretionary and Jackson should decide. He went.

In a period of forty-eight marching days, Jackson's army covered more than 650 miles, fought five major battles and countless combats and skirmishes.

McClellan's amphibious movement to Fort Monroe was well planned, but he made the reckless assumption that the Union navy would be able to prevent interference from the CSS *Virginia* (formerly the USS *Merrimac*), which threatened Hampton Roads and help take Yorktown. As it happened, federal naval forces could only neutralize the *Virginia.* That unexpected deficiency slowed the campaign, but men and supplies did get to the proposed area of operations and McClellan had reason for some satisfaction. Army organization and management were his strengths and the movement to Virginia showed them to best advantage.

Strategy usually came in grandiose ways to McClellan, but peninsular geography and weather conditions focused his vision. Overflowing rivers and streams reduced maneuverability in the lowlands south of the Chickahominy River, which bisected the peninsula north of Williamsburg. Despite poor maps, McClellan saw he might get between Johnston and Richmond by concentrating between the Pamunkey and Chickahominy rivers, a route that would protect his base at West Point on the York River and leave an opening for McDowell, coming from the north. He wanted to work south of the Chickahominy, however, to attack Richmond's weaker defenses.

General J. E. B. Stuart's three-day cavalry ride around the Union army, 13–15 June, dismayed the northern public as well as some of McClellan's men, but, oddly enough, not the general. He thought that the raid had glamour but little military value other than reconnaissance, although it did alert him to his exposed communications and he prepared to change base. The raid also alerted Lee to the fact that the Yankee right could be turned, which helped bring Jackson to Richmond. Lee, suffering a drop in reputation because of the West Virginia defeats, planned a brilliant attack, but one that probably required too much sophistication on the part of inexperienced generals and staffs. He had noted McClellan's gradual shift south of the Chickahominy after the Battle of Seven Pines and noted particularly that one federal corps, General Fitz-John Porter's of thirty thousand men, remained virtually isolated north of that torrent. Assuming McClellan's caution, Lee schemed to hold the main Union force in place with twenty-five thousand men, put the bulk of his army, sixty-five thousand, north of the Chickahominy, crush Porter, and roll up the Union flank in what would have been sound examples of mass and economy of force.

Jackson was to hit Porter's right flank early on the morning of 26 June. As soon as he heard Jackson's guns, General A. P. Hill was to advance against Mechanicsville and Porter's Union line at Beaver Dam Creek. Generals D. H. Hill and James Longstreet were to bring their divisions through Mechanicsville, the former going to aid Jackson, the latter to support A. P. Hill. Generals John B. Magruder and Benjamin Huger, holding in front of Richmond, were to demonstrate heavily and convince McClellan that he dare not attack. Only the demonstrations went according to plan.

Jackson arrived late and got lost; an impatient A. P. Hill attacked Porter's entrenchments almost alone and was repulsed. While Lee pondered his next day's battle, McClellan overcame the aggressive urging of some of his generals and decided that he not only could not attack Richmond, he should hasten his change of base to the James River and consolidate his positions. Lee, on 27 June, again ordered a flank attack on Porter and again saw his plans delayed. A. P. Hill advanced at 2:00 A.M., but Jackson did not attack with his three divisions until 4:00 A.M. Porter's corps fought fiercely and skillfully but his line finally broke as darkness fell. His fine artillery and two brigades from General E. V. Sumner's corps covered Porter's crossing of the Chickahominy at 4:00 in the morning of 28 June.

McClellan's situation had advantages. He knew that only one of his five corps had been engaged and that it fought well. He knew, too, that a new army, consisting of the commands of McDowell, Banks, and Frémont, had been organized under Major General John Pope and was ordered to his support. If the intact federal army held where it was on 28 June, Lee would soon find himself facing strong enemy forces in his front and rear. McClellan decided to retreat to his new base at Harrison's Landing on the James. If that decision seemed inexplicable, it hardly surprised Lee, who counted on his opponent's caution. For the moment, however, McClellan's movements baffled the Confederate leader. Where was he going? That question paralyzed southern movements during 28 June. If the bulk of the Union army moved South toward the James, Lee could cross the Chickahominy and attack. If, on the other hand, McClellan moved his men toward Fort Monroe and crossed the river downstream, Lee would have problems recrossing. Stuart's cavalry was off raiding instead of scouting and not until late in the day did Lee decide where McClellan was. Longstreet and A. P. Hill were sent to hit the federals in flank and Jackson was ordered to press the enemy rear. Magruder and Huger's men were to push southeastward.

McClellan himself seems to have lost interest in the battle for a time, but at least his subordinates were untrammeled by his leadership during three large actions. The bulk of his force—the Second, Third, and Sixth corps—struggled on 29 June to find crossings through White Oak Swamp. Magruder, hoping for help from Jackson, hit the three enemy corps at Savage Station in the afternoon; his action allowed the federals to get through the swampy barrier. Again the question ran through Confederate ranks: What happened to Jackson? He apparently spent the day resting his men and rebuilding Grapevine Bridge while he could hear Magruder's battle in the distance. Why his atypical procrastination? The obvious explanation was slow bridge repair, but that would not excuse Jackson ignoring the sound of Magruder's fight. The real reason for the delay was an order from headquarters, signed by Lee's adjutant general, ordering Stuart's cavalry to guard bridges against enemy attempts to recross, and ordering Jackson to stay at the Grapevine crossing for the same reason—and to stay put until released. Jackson obeyed, telling one of Magruder's subordinates who asked for help that he had "other important duty to perform." While Jackson waited, federals retreated and fought with Magruder.

The next day, 30 June, after crossing the swamp, the Yankees kept moving toward the James. Lee hoped to get Jackson and Huger into action to press the enemy rear from the north, and have Magruder and Longstreet pick up the attack west of the federals as they bunched toward their base. Again Jackson delayed, this time in front of White Oak Swamp, despite the sound of battle in the near distance. Longstreet and A. P. Hill were in desperate combat at Frayser's Farm, but Jackson made no strong move to press on through the swamp. Instead, he dozed most of the day, apparently a victim of pent-up fatigue and short rations.

A sort of weirdness tinged 30 June, a Monday of errors and missed chances for the Confederates and hard fighting for the federals, who struggled to move their wagon trains and most of their army to Malvern Hill. This strong defensive position had height for Union cannon and the advantage of proximity to the base at Harrison's Landing. McClellan's men settled atop the hill under protection of artillery and bloodily repulsed another rebel attack on 1 July—an attack poorly organized and haphazardly delivered. McClellan retired that night to his base, ending his Peninsula Campaign against Richmond.

The casualties in the Seven Days' Battles were appalling to a people unprepared for a war of modern artillery and improved rifles. Lee had more than 20,000 (some 4,000 killed, 15,000 wounded, and 1,000 missing) out of a total of nearly 88,000 men engaged from an army of nearly 90,000 men. Union losses amounted to 16,000 (about 2,000 killed, 8,000 wounded, and 6,000 missing) out of a total of 83,000 engaged from an army of more than 115,000 men.

The casualties in the Seven Days' Battles were appalling to a people unprepared for a war of modern artillery and improved rifles.

Some reputations were casualties as well, especially that of McClellan. A storm of recrimination burst over him, but he continued preaching to President Lincoln on military as well as political matters. Lincoln visited the Army of the Potomac and tried to encourage the men. McClellan was through, however, despite his boast that he was still near Richmond and might resume the offensive in time. Jackson, too, suffered. So lately a national hero, he seemed almost a failure in some eyes. During the battles, Lee had scolded Jackson in his gentlemanly way but appeared to have no lingering ill feelings. President Davis seemed to have some doubts about the strange, dowdy-looking soldier, and so did some Richmond newspapers, which were remarkably fickle. A few days before they had cried for deliverance, and now that the enemy no longer thronged the gates, they carped. Far from savior, Lee was pictured as nearly a villain, blamed for badly planned battles, wasted opportunities, and heavy losses.

Lee and his generals, however, had no time for rebuttals. While McClellan floundered around the peninsula, General John Pope had collected Union troops and issued grandiloquent orders and proclamations, which irritated his army and angered Virginia civilians about to be subjected to illegal martial law. Originally created to help McClellan, Pope's Army of Virginia now had a new mission. When Pope moved east of the Blue Ridge in mid-July, he threatened the Gordonsville rail hub. Adhering to the basic strategy of the offensive-defensive, Lee sent Jackson to do something about Pope.

Lincoln had appointed Major General Henry W. Halleck to the revived post of general in chief of the Union armies on 11 July. Halleck had field experience in the west and the confidence of military men. "Old Brains" (Halleck's sobriquet) decided to bring McClellan's forlorn legions from the peninsula to strengthen Pope's army—a decision McClellan detested and one that Pope did not clearly understand. By the time McClellan's army began a move to Aquia Creek, Jackson had a new lease on glory.

On July 13, Jackson led his divisions toward Gordonsville. Reinforcements went to Jackson until he counted almost twenty-five thousand bayonets. He made good time on his march and beat Pope to Gordonsville. Rashly, Pope decided not to wait for McClellan's reinforcements and moved south. Unexpectedly, his advance under General Banks ran into Jackson's vanguard at Cedar Mountain on 9 August and a major battle developed. Badly managed on both sides, the battle ended in Banks's withdrawal, but Jackson did not pursue against all of Pope's army.

McClellan's men were arriving at Aquia by early August and were routed to Pope. Lee, knowing that Pope would be reinforced, wanted to beat him before all of McClellan's men joined. He devised a plan to fix Pope along the Rappahannock while Jackson secretly went around his right to occupy the large Union supply base at Manassas Junction—near the old battlefield. During 27 August, Jackson's men occupied Bristoe Station and Manassas Junction. Gorging on the mountainous Union supply dumps, Jackson's men filled ammunition wagons, packed four-days rations, and moved that night to a strong position in an unfinished railroad cut not too far from the Henry House hill.

Pope lost control of the situation, confused by conflicting reports, short of cavalry, and some of his men short of ammunition. By the afternoon of 28 August, he decided that Jackson was at Centreville and directed his various corps there. Late in the afternoon Jackson's men attacked a Union force crossing their front, because he wanted to bring Pope's army down on him so that Longstreet's divisions could hit the enemy on the left flank and perhaps achieve a double envelopment. Now certain of Jackson's location, Pope concentrated. Jackson's men stood off several attacks on the 29th and narrowly held the field at nightfall. Pope misconceived the situation and thought the Confederates were withdrawing; he ordered a pursuit that subjected Jackson's weary men to another series of attacks. At the crucial moment, Longstreet's artillery swept across the Union advancing front, and late in the afternoon his five divisions hit Pope's army on the left rear. Pope managed to extract his troops and retreated toward Centreville, toward which Jackson was also moving. Through a drenched 31 August, both armies groped to new positions, and on 1 September a pitched engagement at Chantilly produced only casualties. But Pope was beaten. Receiving permission to fall back into the Washington defenses, his sodden legions reached the capital on 2 September 1862.

During this Second Battle of Bull Run (Second Manassas), from 27 August through 2 September, Pope had a total of 16,000 casualties, Lee, a total of 9,500. The war had grown costlier with practice. If Confederates boasted fewer losses, they also faced a shrinking manpower pool—a cause of growing alarm in Richmond.

Alarm about dwindling numbers of men and enemy incursions around southern borders forced President Davis and the new secretary of war, George W. Randolph, to ask the Confederate congress to draft men for the armies. By March 1862, however, attempts to encourage reenlistments had increased morale problems in the army—liberal furlough policies had riddled the ranks and many on leave would not come back. Rebels had learned, like their stout enemies, that war was hard. Many of them resented the physical labor of digging trenches and latrines, and slaves were sometimes impressed into labor service. Both armies had learned that life in the field lacked glamour. There were proud, parading moments, but mostly things were dirty, wet, hot, or cold, and disease stalked camps with grim imparti-

Much fighting during the Civil war took place along the banks of the Rappahannock River in Virginia. This column of Union cavalry faced the Rappahannock waters in 1862. (National Archives)

ality. Both sides had recruiting problems after the first winter, but the Confederacy's armies seemed to be melting away as spring 1862 gave way to the dog days of summer and the Yankees appeared to be winning everywhere. The Confederate congress enacted the first draft law in American history on 16 April 1862, calling to the colors all white men between eighteen and thirty-five; a liberal exemption law watered down the effect, but the armies were saved for the moment. Union armies were saved, too, as Lincoln's repeated calls for men boosted enlistments in the Army of the Potomac. Lincoln pondered ways to defend Washington and kept a wary eye on Maryland, which might be a Confederate objective.

TROUBLES IN THE FAR WEST, 1861–1862

Both Lincoln and Davis looked on the middle border as a strategic area. Lincoln felt that losing Tennessee, Kentucky, and Missouri might be tantamount to losing the war. Davis knew that the Confederacy needed some of those states—preferably all—to solidify the northern border and Confederate national spirit.

Lincoln counted on a groundswell of unionism to hold the border, while Davis relied on sweeping southern nationalism. Both were right and wrong. There were divided loyalties in each of the border states. People in east Tennessee thought much like west Virginians, but prosecessionists prevailed and the state joined the Confederacy. Kentucky, with sentiments spread fairly evenly across the state and a secessionist governor, sought a neutral's profiteering status, which persisted until Confederates entered the state in September and triggered Union occupation. A rump Kentucky government joined the Confederacy in December. Missouri had a prosecessionist governor and majority in the legislature; St. Louis, however, claimed a pro-Union majority and was the state's power center. Federal troops held that city firmly for the Union. The state government, exiled to southwestern Missouri, joined the Confederacy late in November 1861.

A divided Arkansas became a Confederate state with modest difficulty in May 1861, which made easier friendly relations with the Five Civilized Tribes and some of the Plains Indians. Several treaties of Confederate alliance not only helped solidify the turbulent western frontier but also brought many good troops into rebel ranks. Military operations in the Far West began with secession and spread from the Mississippi to Arizona. With rare exceptions, operations in the Far West were peripheral and of slight effect.

One of the two most important western campaigns in the first year started in Texas. Confederate General Henry Hopkins Sibley led an expedition of twenty-five hundred men into New Mexico during February-April 1862, in an attempt to secure that area and to open routes to the far west; it was a confederate dream to hold all the southwest to California. At Valverde on 21 February 1862, his men skirmished with troops under Colonel E. R. S. Canby and marched on to Santa Fe. Sibley sent a probing column eastward toward Las Vegas, New Mexico, where it had an engagement on 28–29 March 1862 with federal troops moving toward Santa Fe. The Yankees retreated until part of their force got behind the rebel lines and burned their supply and ammunition wagons. With the withdrawal of this force, Sibley began a bitter winter retreat to Texas and the Confederate dream of a western empire faded. Scattered fights in Arizona that were aimed at political results were abortive.

The other important campaign centered in northwestern Arkansas and was a result of the union defeat at Wilson's Creek, near Springfield, Missouri, on 10 August 1861. A resultant federal buildup threatened Arkansas and induced President Davis to send the dashing, competent cavalry general, Earl Van Dorn to the trans-Mississippi. With an army of fourteen thousand, including a brigade of Indians, Van Dorn, who hoped to capture St. Louis, fought a confused, two-day battle against the army of twelve thousand under General S. R. Curtis at Pea Ridge (Elkhorn Tavern), Arkansas, 7–8 March 1862. Defeated, Van Dorn gave up hope of invading Missouri and was unable to help General Albert Sidney Johnston, then in northern Mississippi.

THE KENTUCKY-TENNESSEE LINE, 1861–1862

All through the winter of 1861, pressure steadily mounted against the thin Confederate defense lines in Kentucky and Tennessee. Unconsciously pushing the Anaconda Plan, Lincoln saw the war in geographical and geometrical terms, and he read maps with a strategist's eye. When he looked at a map of the middle of the country, he was instantly struck by the rivers. The Mississippi bisected the rebel states; if it could be forced, the trans-Mississippi Confederacy would be cut off, and Davis' eastern armies dealt with piecemeal. The Ohio River ran like the lifeline of the Union from western Pennsylvania to its junction with the Mississippi at Cairo, Illinois.

To Southerners, the Ohio seemed a natural northern border for the Confederacy. To Lincoln, some of its tributaries were open arteries to the rebel heartland. As increasing numbers of gunboats joined the Union naval inventory along the Mississippi, Lincoln envisioned amphibious operations on the Tennessee and Cumberland rivers and eventually along the "Father of Waters," but he had a familiar problem—aggressive commanders were hard to find. The president had approved General in Chief McClellan's suggestion that two departments be created in the west: the first, the Department of Missouri, including western Kentucky, should be commanded by Halleck; the second, the Department of the Ohio, encompassing the rest of Kentucky and Tennessee, should be under General Don Carlos Buell. A moment's pondering might have raised an important question in Lincoln's mind: Did McClellan pick generals like himself? If so, the new co-command structure would confound rather than coordinate.

To Southerners, the Ohio seemed a natural northern border for the Confederacy. To Lincoln, some of its tributaries were open arteries to the rebel heartland.

Jefferson Davis shared Lincoln's unease about activities in the west. Too many little actions persisted, conducted by too many disorganized units. Perceiving that the area west of the mountains offered great advantages as well as weaknesses to the South, Davis grasped the need for unified command in that key sector. He had, he thought, just the man for the job—Albert Sidney Johnston. A highly trusted friend of Davis, Johnston boasted illustrious careers in the armies of the United States and the Republic of Texas. He resigned his U.S. commission on 10 April 1861 and was appointed a full general in the Confederate regular army. Confident that Sidney Johnston could organize a cohesive defense of the Tennessee-Kentucky line, in September, Davis gave him command of all Confederate forces from Arkansas to the Cumberland Gap, some fifty thousand men.

Johnston knew that Halleck and Buell combined in their departments about 130,000 widely scattered men. Confederate advantages were few; the best was good lateral communications. The federals, however, now counted on heavy naval support on the rivers and could infiltrate swiftly. Johnston's position hinged on three key points—big Fort Donelson on the Cumberland River, the smaller Fort Henry on the Tennessee, and Columbus, Kentucky, on the Mississippi. He had small forces at each of these places and at several others, but delayed concentration as he pondered logistics and the moves of the army under General Ulysses S. Grant.

Halleck sent Grant against the two river forts, and after an opéra bouffe affair on 6 February at Fort Henry (which sat so close to the river that Union gunboats floated by and fired down into the works), Grant thoroughly dominated the timid commanders of Fort Donelson and took it on 16 February 1862, along with 11,500 men and forty cannon. With his center broken, his lateral communications cut, and an opportunity to defeat Grant's smaller force wasted, Johnston pondered a disaster created in part by his vacillation.

General Beauregard arrived to aid Johnston and soon convinced him to concentrate the scattered Confederate units to wrest the initiative from the federals. Johnston selected Corinth, Mississippi, as the junction point, and Beauregard departed to take command of all rebel troops between the Tennessee and Mississippi rivers. Beauregard used the telegraph to coerce reinforcements from across the Mississippi and urged help from the Deep South. He also saw the danger posed by Johnston's two main forces being separated by Grant and Buell, who had moved to Nashville. He urged Johnston to hasten the concentration at Corinth, and moved the Columbus force in that direction, leaving a garrison at Island No. 10 in the Mississippi to delay twenty-five thousand Union troops. Johnston, oddly enough, did not move with any special sense of urgency.

Command problems hampered federal efforts to take advantage of their inner lines. Halleck talked of attacking such strategic points as Memphis or Corinth and bragged about Grant's operations, but he squandered the splendid opportunity to destroy Johnston's forces in detail. Buell saw the chance and wanted to join Grant and attack before Johnston got his men together. Halleck sent Grant's force up the Tennessee to raid rebel rail lines. Lincoln solved the command tangle on 11 March 1862 by giving Halleck command of the central theater, and, once in charge, Halleck acted. He ordered Buell to join Grant's force near Pittsburg Landing (Shiloh), Tennessee, where the combined forces could threaten Memphis. Buell moved casually and took thirteen days to cover thirty-five miles to Columbus; a wrecked bridge there again delayed him considerably.

Fortunately for Sidney Johnston, he had Beauregard to goad him and Davis to plan for him. Davis, as much a student of war as vaunted "Old Brains" Halleck, saw the chance to hit Grant's army in its relatively isolated position near Shiloh. He began a strategic concentration of reinforcements using the latest military technology in a Napoleonic application of the offensive-defensive. Davis telegraphed for reinforcements from Charleston and New Orleans, released Bragg from Mobile with his ten thousand troops, and pushed them all forward by an innovative use of railroads and river steamers. By early April, Johnston had forty-thousand men at Corinth. Grant, unaware of enemy concentration, had encamped at Pittsburg Landing without bothering about security.

Johnston, hoping for surprise, moved his men forward under heavy security. A skirmish on 4 April 1862 seemed to have compromised the attack, but the Confederates pressed on. They found Grant's position circumscribed by the Tennessee to their right, with Owl and Snake creeks to their left. They would be attacking into a sack but both flanks were protected and the enemy had no place to run. An early morning attack on 6 April 1862 caught most of the federals unprepared.

Johnston wanted to turn the enemy left and cut them off from the river. Federal positions and terrain dictated a frontal assault, weighted to the right. Beauregard had overall command of the field and botched his tactical dispositions by deploying in two lines of division with a corps in reserve. As the battle progressed, bunching along the blazing battle lines confused organization. Beauregard fed in his reserves almost evenly across the front, so there were no tactical emergency forces available to exploit opportunities. Johnston had gone forward to encourage the front. Fatally wounded, he died about 2:30 A.M. Beauregard continued to manage the advance, which had been halted by several strong points of resistance. By nightfall, the Union left had been turned, but rebel troops were too scattered and too weary to exploit their advantage, especially against freshly massed Union cannon. During the night, Buell's men began arriving on the field. Grant counterattacked on 7 April and slowly drove the rebels back to the original Union positions. Beauregard retreated at the end of the day. Losses were appalling in what was the hardest fighting of the war—nearly fourteen thousand Union casualties, and eleven thousand Confederate.

Disaster threatened the Confederacy. Beauregard's strength was gone, Union troops controlled the Mississippi almost to Memphis, and Halleck, with a large army near Corinth, had decisive victory in his grasp—but it eluded him. Beauregard's optimism persisted and he collected reinforcements, many of them on the way, but too late for Shiloh. He soon commanded about 70,000 men at Corinth, but Halleck had also collected troops and was nearby with no fewer than 120,000. Beauregard wisely decided not to try holding heavily fortified Corinth, because he might simply find himself bottled up. Instead, he retired to Tupelo. Halleck, happy with having taken Corinth, left the enemy army alone. Davis was furious over the wasted opportunities in the west, and Beauregard resigned his command and took sick leave. Davis gave the Army of Tennessee to General Braxton Bragg on 27 June, as crises compounded for the South.

Even before the impact of the Battle of Shiloh could be fully felt, a decisive federal success crowned joint naval and land efforts at the southern end of the Mississippi. For months, the Confederate commander of New Orleans, General Mansfield Lovell, had called for reinforcements to strengthen the defenses of the South's largest city and most important port. Instead, he had been repeatedly ordered to send men to help Sidney Johnston. Lovell watched anxiously a buildup of Union ships, mortar boats and transports under Flag Officer David Glasgow Farragut and General Benjamin F. Butler. To defend the mouth of the Mississippi, the Confederates counted on two large brick forts on the river below New Orleans and on a barrier of hulks and chain across the river. A small rebel river fleet of wooden boats supporting the new ironclad ram *Manassas* was expected to hamper Union operations. At 2:00 A.M. on 24 April 1862, Farragut's fleet ran past the forts, broke through the barrier boom, fended off rebel fire rafts, and reached New Orleans's docks.

In moments of dark reflection, Davis might have pondered the qualities of his generals in the West.

A daring gamble had brought the biggest Union prize of the war. The fall of New Orleans not only had military and economic impact but heartened the Union. If the South could not protect so vital a city, it must be weak indeed. With efforts apparently succeeding to clear the Mississippi from both ends, Lincoln felt that soon the Confederacy would be cut in two. Once that was accomplished, it might be chopped up as envisioned by Winfield Scott. Davis became increasingly aware of the impossibility of defending every threatened point and sought a different strategy to make the offensive-defensive more effective.

In moments of dark reflection, Davis might also have pondered the qualities of his generals in the West. The Shiloh campaign showed good logistical planning on his own part and that of railroad and quartermaster officers. If Davis had been able to surmount his personal likes and dislikes, he would also have seen that Beauregard had sound strategic sense and certainly more energy than Sidney Johnston. Beauregard's mercurial nature sometimes undermined his tactical sense, but he had values worth using. Bragg's part in the battle had been commendable enough and his men fought well and shared no shame in defeat. Davis hoped that Bragg, "who had shown himself equal to the management of volunteers and at the same time commanded their love and respect," might somehow hold the sagging central front. The president would try to send men from the interior, but they were scarce and demands constant.

For the moment, the best southern defense came from federal inaction. Leaving two divisions to hold Grant in place, on 21 July, Bragg began to move thirty-five thousand men by rail from Tupelo, Mississippi, via Mobile to Chattanooga. Buell had been ordered there on 10 June, but his march on inner lines was slow and plagued by logistical troubles. Bragg reached Chattanooga before Buell and developed a plan to carry the war into Kentucky. While he gathered ammunition and other supplies, Lee cleared Virginia of federal troops.

With Lee victorious and Bragg planning boldly, President Davis enjoyed a rare opportunity to rise above daily war necessities to think strategically. He evolved a scheme for a major two-pronged Confederate offensive in the east and west. Lee, who wanted to invade Maryland, would do so; Bragg would march for Kentucky, aided by General Edmund Kirby Smith's force of ten thousand men at Knoxville. Davis promised to comb the Confederacy for men in the hope that a combined attack on the Union's right and left fronts would prevent constant shuttling of troops and tend to equalize numbers. Although risky, his plan had great potential for wresting the initiative from the Union, for clearing Tenneesee, and for shifting pressure into vital federal territory. Davis also added a political dimension to his planning—overtures would be made to the people of those states to induce them to join rebel ranks and to perhaps entice other states into the Confederacy. The invading generals would renew the southern call for peace, independence, and free trade and offer liberal terms of alliance. Such a bold program would commit every reserve of Confederate men and supplies into one venture. Failure in the west could lose the Mississippi Basin; failure in the east could uncover Richmond. Success, however, could change the strategic balance of the war.

Things looked good at the start for the Confederates. As Bragg moved north from Chattanooga at the end of August and Lee crossed into Maryland in early September, Union forces were abruply thrown on the defensive and faced depressing possibilities. Should Louisville fall, all of Indiana and Ohio would be threatened, the Baltimore and Ohio rail link would break, and Bragg might reach the Great Lakes. If Lee was not stopped, Washington might be captured and the war lost.

Lee would be bold enough, but what of Bragg? Union commanders who had met him knew his personal courage, his spit and polish discipline and his McClellan-like capacity to weld an army out of broken remnants. They also knew he had some kind of restless force in him, but a few surely guessed he lacked the essential fighter's spark. As he advanced from Chattanooga on 30 August 1862, he had the rhetoric for the moment. "This campaign," he said, "must be won by marching, not fighting." If this seemed a bravado's boast, Bragg at least tried to make it true. He maneuvered Buell almost back to the Ohio without fighting, but command problems and political realities negated Bragg's great venture. Kirby Smith, an independent commander, did not join Bragg. People were not flocking to rebel banners. Buell, who had admirably cooperated by caution, finally began to concentrate. A sharp engagement at Perryville, Kentucky, on 8–9 October bruised both armies indecisively, but Bragg lost heart, abandoned his campaign, and marched through the Cumberland Gap all the way to Murfreesboro. General William S. Rosecrans relieved Buell, and Halleck, now called to Washington as general in chief, pushed him to occupy east Tennessee.

Rosecrans moved against Bragg in late December and in the big, confused Battle of Stones River (Murfreesboro), 30 December 1862–2 January 1863, he won a victory of sorts. Each army suffered nearly ten thousand casualties and Bragg withdrew toward Tullahoma, Tennessee. Rosecrans had at least held middle Tennessee, but he did not advance for another six months.

In all of his campaigning, Bragg underused his cavalry. His mounted arm, under such able leaders as Joseph Wheeler and Nathan Bedford Forrest (probably the greatest natural soldier of the nineteenth century) could have done much better duty than allowed by Bragg's limited thinking. The left prong of Davis' joint offensive had been stopped and bent back. Bragg could boast of many supplies captured, of holding the initiative for months, and of not losing the Confederate center altogether, but the writ for 1862 in the west ran for the Union. What of the other prong of Davis' offensive?

EASTERN CAMPAIGNS AND COMMAND CHANGES, SEPTEMBER 1862–JULY 1863

Pope's army straggled into Washington in August 1862 and spilled through the city, ragged, demoralized veterans clotting the streets and shocking the populace. Lincoln also felt the shock. Pressure of northern public opinion burdened him now; how many more defeats would the country tolerate? McDowell had marched off to finish the rebels at Bull Run, McClellan to finish them at Richmond, Banks to smash Stonewall Jackson in the Shenandoah Valley, and Pope had taken his "headquarters in the saddle" into Virginia to help McClellan finish Lee. Now remnants of all those finishing schools were flotsam roaming through the capital. Things might look good in the west, but the main armies had been driven from Virginia and criticism mounted.

Although Pope had done a reasonably competent job, Lincoln knew he would have to go, but who could organize the wreckage of the Army of the Potomac and shove it into battle against Lee's victorious legions thronging along the Potomac, possibly about to invade the North? McClellan's organizational skills were acknowledged even by his enemies and the men in the ranks loved and trusted him. Lincoln now considered him a fine army builder but not a fighter. He could refit the army, prepare adequate defenses for the capital, but would probably be replaced when an offensive opportunity came. McClellan, ignorant of presidential misgivings, took the assignment while Lee pondered a new campaign.

Pressure of northern public opinion burdened Lincoln; how many more defeats would the country tolerate?

President Davis' military-political application of his offensive-defensive strategy clarified some of Lee's thinking. Logistical facts lent impetus to the idea of invading Maryland. Virginia had been scavenged mercilessly by all the armies and had little left worth taking. Food, forage, and other supplies awaited in abundance across the Potomac. A Confederate army in Maryland would give loyal Marylanders a chance to join the southern colors—as Davis firmly hoped. One possible negative was that the Confederacy had repeatedly said that all it wanted was to be left alone in independence, that it had no territorial interests outside its own boundaries. Would the joint invasions make mockery of that claim? Possibly, but it could be reasonably argued that Maryland, and Kentucky, were really part of the Confederacy and that gray legions would be operating within legitimate borders.

Lee really had no choice and wasted little time preparing for the Maryland incursion, which left several things dangling. He did not seem to have a clear objective save the vague possibility of moving on Harrisburg, Philadelphia, or Baltimore, cutting important Union rail communications and hitting targets of opportunity. In his hasty planning, Lee committed an unprofessional error in judgment. When he learned that McClellan again would be the opponent, he made the complacent assumption that his old foe would move with typical sloth. This time he was wrong.

Screened by Jeb Stuart's cavalry, Lee's men crossed the Potomac on 4 September 1862 and were near Frederick, Maryland, by the 7th. McClellan moved slowly northwestward with 85,000 men, but had overestimated Lee's 55,000 into 120,000. Lee divided his force. Jackson went to capture Harpers Ferry, possibly to secure the Shenandoah as a supply line, and Longstreet was sent to meet a threatened federal militia force. By 10 September, Lee had scattered his army in the face of the enemy. Why this dangerous gamble? Probably because Lee believed that McClellan could not bring himself to move quickly enough to make a difference. That was a likely assumption, but on 13 September, McClellan received a copy of Lee's Special Order No. 191, which outlined his whole plan of dispersal. For sixteen hours McClellan did not move and digested the information, but then he moved with unwonted speed.

Lee, quickly alerted to McClellan's intelligence coup, made hasty efforts to reconcentrate. He sent a force to block South Mountain and ordered concentration at Sharpsburg on Antietam Creek. McClellan struck Lee's men at South Mountain while Longstreet moved toward Sharpsburg. Jackson besieged Harpers Ferry, which fell to him on 15 September, and could not join immediately. When McClellan forced the mountain, Lee prepared to hold along Antietam in relatively weak positions unstrengthened by fieldworks and with scarcely twenty-thousand men on the field. McClellan arrived late on 15 September. Had he attacked vigorously on the 16th, Lee would probably have been crushed, but McClellan waited and planned himself into fragmentation. On the 17th, after Lee had been reinforced by Jackson's men from Harpers Ferry, McClellan watched as his army delivered a series of bold and tactically sound attacks from the right, to the center, and then on the left. McClellan took no personal part in coordinating his attacks and they went in piecemeal, nearly succeeded, and at length all were repulsed because Lee was allowed to shift men from attack to attack. Lee was saved almost at the moment of defeat by the arrival of reinforcements.

Both commanders mismanaged the Battle of Antietam (Sharpsburg). Lee's determination to stand with inferior numbers on weak ground seemed uncharacteristic and was certainly dangerous. McClellan's typical hesitancy confounded his subordinates, who were frequently frustrated in attempts to take advantage of Confederate weaknesses. Every battle seems to have its swaying moments of crisis and usually one of real decision, and Antietam had many moments of Confederate crises, several of real decision, and McClellan missed every one of those chances.

Against the advice of his subordinates, Lee held the field during 18 September, apparently hoping to lure McClellan into another attack, which probably would have eliminated the Army of Northern Virginia. Not only did McClellan have an unused corps available, he had received reinforcement, but he did not attack and Lee retired to Virginia during the night. Of about 39,000 Confederate men on the field, there were about 13,700 casualties; of 70,000 Union troops, there were about 12,500 casualties. On the threadbare victory at Antietam, Lincoln issued his Preliminary Emancipation Proclamation on 22 September and changed the nature of the war. Great Britain began to turn slowly to the northern side.

Now that the right prong of Davis' offensive had been clipped, what strategy could retain the initiative and somehow negate the rising tide of Union numbers? Davis learned from his double offensive. Unwilling to believe that Bragg had failed because of resolution, Davis fixed on faulty command arrangements as the cause of western problems. With Bragg and Kirby Smith coequal commanders, cooperation had been difficult and coordination from Richmond impossible. Davis, guided by the brilliant new War Secretary James A. Seddon, recognized that command arrangements for the Army of Northern Virginia needed no tinkering. The west, however, posed vast problems that caused the two war planners to consider a new concept in military delegation, one that indicated the president and the secretary were original organizational theorists. Because geographical departments had not solved issues of rank and seniority in the field, Davis began to think of what is now called a "theater command" in the west.

Despite the telegraph, distance still wrapped battlefields in the fog of war, the west in particular because of widely scattered forces. A deputy war leader was needed out there, a general of experience equal to the broadest authority. If he rose to his chance he would coordinate all rebel forces and all logistical efforts in his domain and intrude on state and local politics to military purpose. The right man would seize the heartland

On the threadbare victory at Antietam, Lincoln issued his Preliminary Emancipation Proclamation and changed the nature of the war. On 3 October 1862, President Lincoln visited General McClellan and his staff at the Antietam battlefield. (National Archives)

and rule it as his satrapy. Lee was in exactly the right niche; Bragg, Davis hated to admit, was marred by defeat; Beauregard—too flamboyant for the president's austerity—was back in Charleston doing brilliant work in defending the city, leaving only one man of proper experience, the man Seddon had in mind, Joseph E. Johnston. Davis had qualms and Johnston may have had some, but he wanted to be back in the field and accepted the assignment.

Lincoln also pondered command problems. He thought he had arrived at the right command structure with McClellan installed as general in chief, then he thought Halleck could do the job. McClellan's plans were obscurantist classics and Halleck wrapped himself in minutiae. Therefore, like it or not, Lincoln was still a practicing commander in chief, but he looked for some competent military man to run the war for him. It had not yet occurred to him that he was fast becoming a master strategist as he kept his eye fixed on the whole conflict and on the enemy's armies.

In November, Lincoln fired McClellan for the last time. Who could pick up the pieces after Antietam and get after Lee? Who had the sense to know that the North had more of everything, the sense to mobilize it, and overwhelm the rebels? Despairingly, he turned to a gentleman soldier, a fine corps commander in the Army of the Potomac, General Ambrose E. Burnside, whose tonsorial sweep gave a word to the English language, "sideburns." A rightfully humble man, Burnside said he was incompetent to command a large army and, lamentably, would prove his point. Taking command on 7 November 1862, he reorganized the Army of the Potomac and moved south toward Fredericksburg.

Lee hated losing the initiative and after Sharpsburg stayed close to the Potomac, hoping to lure McClellan into an attack. Reorganizing his army into two corps (Longstreet commanding the First Corps and Stonewall Jackson the Second Corps), Lee left Jackson in the valley, threatening the Union right flank, and went with Longstreet to Culpeper Court House, to confront the main enemy thrust.

Dividing the army had dangers, but McClellan would not likely take advantage of it, nor would Burnside. Burnside ranked as a competent corps commander but was hardly fervent. Lee might impose on him as he had his predecessor. Burnside, however, had a coherent plan of operations—not brilliant, but coherent. He wanted to concentrate near Warrenton, threaten a dash to the valley to cut off Jackson, and move the main army to Fredericksburg, where he would be between Lee and Richmond. Lee would have to come to him, and Burnside could either fight or take the enemy capital. Skeptical, Lincoln approved with the caveat that speed was essential. Burnside moved quickly to Falmouth, north of Fredericksburg, by 17 November and caught Lee out of position. General E. V. Sumner urged a swift river crossing, but Burnside called for pontoon bridges and Halleck failed to urge haste on supply officers. It was not until 25 November that the first bridges arrived, but by then Longstreet's men resisted Rappahannock crossings.

Who had the sense to know that the North had more of everything, the sense to mobilize it, and overwhelm the rebels?

Burnside might still have gotten between Lee's corps by a quick march up the river because Jackson could not arrive for several days. Like so many Civil War generals, Burnside focused on the wrong objective. His eye was fixed on Richmond, not on Lee's army, so he waited to control the river and cross closer to the enemy capital. That decision is indefensible on almost any ground—Longstreet's men were in front, and although the federals might well have overwhelmed them, the price would have been high. Waiting for more bridges simply gave Jackson time to reach the field. Obviously, the Union commander should have moved upriver and threatened both wings of Lee's army, or crossed the river and moved on Richmond via the Rapidan River and Gordonsville. As Burnside waited for more pontoons in front of Fredericksburg, Lee's lines grew stronger in men and entrenchments.

A kind of eerie fatalism hung over Burnside's headquarters while Lee's legions gathered and opportunities faded. The road to Richmond seemed to lead straight through the Army of Northern Virginia, which was perched mainly on high ground behind frowning earthworks. Burnside believed the erroneous reports of balloon observers that Lee had posted his army south of Fredericksburg, with his left resting opposite the town. Burnside skewed the strength of his three "grand divisions" to his right, arraying Hooker and Sumner against formidable Marye's Heights and General William B. Franklin on the left in open ground fronting Jackson's Second Corps. He counted on superb artillery support from the high ground across the river to sustain an attack against massed men and guns. The attack began on the cold morning of 13 December 1862. Repeated assaults on Marye's Heights and its grisly sunken road piled up Union casualties; Franklin's attack on the left made early progress but was finally driven back without result. By nightfall the attacks waned at a cost of nearly twelve thousand Union casualties to about five thousand Confederates killed, wounded, and a few missing.

In Washington an anxious president dogged the military telegraph and once more heard of high hopes dashed in gore—another defeat, another wasted campaign, and thousands more dead as winter seemed to freeze the nation's hope. In Richmond, a grateful President Davis congratulated a victorious general as he rested his legions and begged for food, firewood, and simple comforts for men suffering a Valley Forge–type winter on the Rappahannock. Lee hoped fighting had ended for the year, but Burnside, scorched to the high anger of a timid man, tried one more tilt for glory. Late in January 1863, he ordered a flanking movement upriver from Lee, only to endure a charade of his men losing the campaign to Virginia mud. Derisive comments from his subordinates nearly maddened Burnside, who lashed out with threats of dismissal. Sadly, Lincoln relieved the humble general on 25 January in favor of General Joseph Hooker, proudly known as "Fighting Joe." Lincoln hoped for truth in the sobriquet.

Hooker received an intriguing order of appointment, one filled with the president's personal brand of honest criticism, one aimed at bristling pride. Lincoln told him

> There are some things in regard to which, I am not quite satisfied with you. . . . You are ambitious, which, within reasonable limits, does good rather than harm. But I think that during General Burnside's command of the Army, you have taken counsel of your ambitions, and thwarted him as much as you could, in which you did a great wrong to the country, and to a most meritorious and honorable brother officer. I have heard . . . of your recently saying that both the Army and the Government needed a Dictator. Of course it was not for this, but in spite of it, that I have given you the command. Only those generals who gain successes can set up Dictators. What I now ask of you is military success, and I will risk the Dictatorship. . . . I much fear that the spirit which you have aided to infuse into the Army, of criticizing their Commander, and withholding confidence from him, will now turn upon you. I shall assist you as far as I can, to put it down. Neither you nor Napoleon if he were alive again, could get any good out of an Army, while such a spirit prevails in it. . . . And now, beware of rashness.—Beware of rashness, but with energy and sleepless vigilance, go forward, and give us victories.

Hooker overlooked this presidential homily in the fullness of fortune. With characteristic energy, he plotted Lee's destruction—and he plotted well. He would fix Lee in the Fredericksburg lines with part of his army, take the main body to an upriver crossing, swing around the Confederate left, and get between Lee and Richmond. Aware that much of Longstreet's corps had been detached to the south, Hooker determined to use his much larger numbers to force the rebels to fight on Yankee terms. He began his campaign swiftly in late April 1863 as spring greened the Rappahannock Valley, roads dried, and spirits rose.

Anticipating action from Hooker, Lee quickly grasped his strategy, and on 30 April ordered Jackson to intercept the enemy in or near the Wilderness of Virginia, a great, gloomy, wooded area stretching west and south from Fredericksburg. When Jackson's men moved into the Wilderness to catch Hooker before he cleared the woods, the Battle of Chancellorsville began—a battle that is now famous as a classic in maneuver and applied psychology.

Hooker's dispositions were excellent, and when he reached Chancellorsville, he might be able to get between Jackson's men and General Jubal Early's screening force at Fredericksburg. Greatly outnumbering both enemy forces, Hooker could beat them in detail. He squandered the opportunity as the dank, dripping woodland worked its alchemy of dread. Jackson's probe on 1 May stalled the Yankees; Hooker entrenched and yielded the initiative. Lee and Jackson sought ways to negate the heavy log works constructed by the Yankees. Could a way around Hooker's right be found? Yes. A fairly well-covered road led all the way around the Union army. Jackson received his most exciting orders from Lee—take twenty-eight thousand men and flank Hooker while Lee held the front with a scant sixteen thousand grayclads.

One of the great flank marches of military history began at 8:00 A.M. on 2 May 1863. The Second Corps of the Army of Northern Virginia marched fifteen miles across Hooker's front and around his army and hit it from behind. Security cracked several times during the march; some federal troops attacked the column and reported a mass of rebel infantry to Hooker, who, surprisingly, concluded that Lee was retreating to Richmond. When Jackson attacked at 5:15 A.M., the Union right crumbled and spilled into Hooker's rear area. He tried to rally an artillery defense, but the rebel attack rolled on remorselessly. At a critical point in the action, "Fighting Joe" was leaning against a column on the porch of his headquarters when it was struck by a rebel shell. Knocked senseless, Hooker recovered slowly but refused to yield command. Although competent subordinate leadership saved his army and provided an opportunity to attack, Hooker lost his nerve.

Jackson's attack stalled with night and he rode ahead of his lines to find enemy positions. Riding back to his troops, he was fired on by nervous infantry, wounded, and carried from the field. Command passed to Jeb Stuart as the senior general present. Stuart renewed the attack with morning, as did Lee. Hooker's men were now fortifying and fighting stubbornly. Hearing that Major General John Sedgwick's corps had driven Early out of the Fredericksburg lines, and convinced that Hooker had gone on the defensive, Lee left Stuart with twenty-five thousand men to hold the Wilderness and took twenty-one thousand to deal with Sedgwick. With speed and daring, a whole Union corps might be cut up and captured.

Battle weary, hungry, and working in hard ground, Lee and Early's men were slow and ragged in their attack on Union positions west of Fredericksburg. Sedgwick escaped, but Lee still hoped to finish Hooker and planned a final attack for 6 May—a rash idea because the entire federal line now was heavily entrenched. Hooker, however, recrossed the Rappahannock during the night of 5–6 May, and his great venture to Richmond cost seventeen thousand casualties to Lee's thirteen thousand.

How to assess the Battle of Chancellorsville? It crowned the cooperation between Lee and Jackson and stands as a signal southern victory. Hooker never used all his force and had lost his nerve; the knock on the head only addled an already broken psyche. When Lincoln heard the news he cried out in anguish: "My God! My God! What will the country say?" The North would rage, but the South would mourn the costliest victory

Wounded soldiers were tended in the field near Fredericksburg on 2 May 1863 after the Battle of Chancellorsville, a battle that crowned the cooperation between Lee and Jackson and stands as a signal southern victory. (National Archives)

of the war. On 10 May 1863, Stonewall Jackson, thirty-nine years old, died, having been shot by his own troops in the confusion of battle on 2 May.

On 10 May 1863, Stonewall Jackson, thirty-nine years old, died, having been shot by his own troops in the confusion of battle on 2 May.

Lincoln pondered a complex problem of morale versus failed men, failed opportunities, and failed ideas. The Army of the Potomac, beaten again, was made of firm stuff—its body battered but heart sound—and it would fight for a good leader. Some of the man wanted McClellan back, because he, at least, had stopped the rebs at Antietam. Some of the men wanted to go home, the war seeming hopeless. There were some who thought they could whip Lee, however, given a fighting chance. For a time after Chancellorsville, Hooker acted like a general. A thorough refitting and reorganization put his army in top shape and he kept a close watch on Lee. Hooker, Halleck, and Lincoln all thought Lee would do something aggressive, but what and where?

Those questions engaged President Davis, his cabinet, and senior military advisers while Lee recruited, refurbished, and reorganized the Army of Northern Virginia. Jackson's death left a chasm in command. Lee now divided his army into three corps: Longstreet kept his solid First; Jackson's famed Second went to his trusted lieutenant, Richard Stoddert Ewell; the new Third was given to A.P. Hill. Ranks swelled with conscripts and new units from the Deep South; supplies filled the depots—though rations were thin—and Stuart's horses were rejuvenated. What should this reinvigorated army do?

Longstreet, noting that the South still had interior lines, suggested that Bragg be reinforced to crush Rosecrans. That would surely call Grant from Vicksburg. Beauregard thought relief of General John C. Pemberton, besieged in Vicksburg, essential to defeat Grant and save the Mississippi. Lee saw logic in both schemes but kept his own focus on the Virginia theater and suggested that an invasion of Pennsylvania would relieve his army as well as Vicksburg by putting pressure on the sorest point of the Union—Washington. Lee's power prevailed and he prepared to move north.

Hooker understood strategy and sifted intelligence well, and by late May he suspected Lee planned to move down the Shenandoah, either to flank him back to Washington or to recross the Potomac. General Alfred Pleasonton's horsemen went in search of Lee and had an engagement with Stuart's full force at Brandy Station on 9 June. Brandy Station swirled into the biggest cavalry battle in American history. Confused, seesawing, and hectic, the battle engaged about ten thousand men on each side in shooting, hacking and charging until late in the day, when Stuart's men began to prevail, especially after some foot soldiers arrived to help. Pleasonton retired, encouraged by near victory, and gave Hooker the vital information that the rebels were in force near Culpeper and it looked as though Stuart was preparing to move.

Lee's vanguard crossed the Potomac in mid-June, headed for Chambersburg, Pennsylvania. Hooker, using his own inner lines, took his army toward Frederick, Maryland, which covered Washington and threatened Lee's communications. Hooker's reactions to Lee were sound, but Lincoln had lost confidence in him, and he was losing his grip on himself. Clearly, he was afraid to fight Lee. Like McClellan, he fantasized about enemies in Washington, felt hugely outnumbered, and resented interference with his army. In a fit of pique he asked to be relieved and Lincoln hastily complied. On 27 June 1863, the command went to General George Gordon Meade, a Pennsylvanian, veteran corps commander, and a competent, plodding soldier of nervous demeanor, fiery temper, and considerable personal fortitude. Surprised at the assignment, Meade took it on as a duty. Ordering the army north from Frederick, he hoped to catch Lee at a scattered disadvantage, which summed up Lee's situation fairly well.

Lee's army was spread across a big part of southern Pennsylvania, from Chambersburg to Carlisle to Harrisburg and York, and his troops were wallowing in the rich farmland's food and forage. They heard rumors of hats and shoes at Gettysburg, which stirred trouble. Rumors were curiously hard to check. Stuart, acting under Lee's usually permissive orders, had gone off on a wagon hunt in Maryland—probably trying to heal the scars of Brandy Station—and the cavalry that remained with the main army had been spread too thinly for sound reconnaisance.

Lee pulled his army toward Cashtown, which had strong defensive positions and sat on the flank of an advancing Union force, but some of A. P. Hill's men wandered on toward Gettysburg to "get those shoes." At about 8:00 A.M. on 1 July, Hill's men ran into strong resistance just northwest of Gettysburg. A Union cavalry division, carefully deployed with good artillery support, confronted the Confederates. Troops of both armies piled up around the town and a major battle began without either army commander's intent.

For three days a bitter, bloody battle raged around Gettysburg. Several times Lee attacked, several times he was repulsed—once in the bare nick of time. A fearsome, grueling testing of both armies finally culminated in one of gallantry's last great gestures—Pickett's Charge. George Edward Pickett led fifteen thousand men against Meade's well-entrenched center on 3 July. It was a splendid effort, one of flying banners, precision marching, storms of grape and canister sweeping over the attackers, of gaps and fallen, and a few men who broke through the blue lines, and of the shattered survivors who streamed back, shocked, torn, and maimed. It was America's greatest battle.

It was Lee's worst. Confederate casualties neared twenty-one thousand to the federals twenty-three thousand—almost a third of Lee's army had been killed, wounded, or captured. He escaped total destruction only because Meade failed to counterattack or to push the Confederate retreat, failure that grievously wounded President Lincoln. It seemed to be another Antietam, another great chance gone. Who could win a decisive battle?

Jefferson Davis rejected Lee's suggestion of relief—he had no greater general—but surely the Confederate president was troubled. What had gone wrong? Word had been received of a different Lee at Gettysburg, a petulant, stubborn man, heedless of Longstreet's proposal to flank Meade, an ill man the day that Pickett's men marched into death and history, a superior sharply demanding obedience to orders some found futile. When those broken five thousand came back down from Cemetery Ridge, the old Lee snapped back in tender, guilty anguish. "It is all my fault," he quietly confessed to those who still would follow him. Lee's return to normal loomed more vital now than ever. Not only did the South suffer Gettysburg that week, but also it suffered the loss of Vicksburg, Mississippi, and its thirty-thousand-man garrison. With that bastion went effective connection with the trans-Mississippi.

VITALITY AT VICKSBURG: WESTERN CAMPAIGNS, JANUARY–JULY 1863

Meade's failure put Lincoln in a deep gloom. He poured out furious anguish to Navy Secretary Gideon Welles, in the wake of Lee's escape after Gettysburg. "We had them within our grasp. We had only to stretch forth our hands and they were ours." He had expected this news, he despondently told Welles. "And that, my God, is the last of this Army of the Potomac! There is bad faith somewhere. . . . What does it mean, Mr. Welles? Great God! What does it mean?" In a familiar way of teaching and venting, Lincoln wrote a long letter to Meade, probably the toughest he ever wrote to a general. He filed it, unmailed, probably fearing it would do more harm than good to an earnest, willing soldier. The letter, however, showed that the president was advanced far beyond most military minds in a firm grasp of the war. Lincoln knew the first week of July was the turning point in the war—two rebel armies were exposed, and armies were the main objectives. Had Lee been smashed as Vicksburg fell, the stuffing would have gone out of the Confederacy. "As it is," Lincoln mourned, "the war will be prolonged indefinitely." He did not relieve Meade, but he had little faith that the Army of the Potomac could do more in Virginia than it had in Pennsylvania. He doubted Meade could win in an offensive battle with Lee.

Ulysses S. Grant had gumption.

When he fixed on an enemy, he stuck.

As Lincoln looked for consolation, he saw one bright sign. Ulysses S. Grant had gumption. When he fixed on an enemy, he stuck. A grizzled, disheveled soldier without grace or much couth, he chewed on his cold cigar as he chewed on the enemy and kept going forward. Once detached from Buell, Grant fixed on Vicksburg and tried various ways to capture it. A great Confederate bastion with heavy cannon dominating the Mississippi, combined with the smaller, no less vital, Port Hudson downriver, Vicksburg served to hinge the Trans-Mississippi Department to the eastern Confederacy. Vicksburg truly deserved all the attention both sides offered.

While Grant had his own schemes for taking this key site of the South, he had considerations other than military necessity working on him. Forced to react to political and journalistic carping, he tried four different approaches to the South's vital Mississippi bastion; all four failed, one to a daring cavalry raid by General Earl Van Dorn, but Grant kept at it. By late April his cooperating gunboat fleet had passed Vicksburg's batteries, and he moved a large force along the west bank of the Mississippi to find a promising crossing point where he would use his gunboats again. By 1 May, Grant had recrossed the Mississippi and turned north to get between General John C. Pemberton's defenders of Vicksburg and Joseph E. Johnston's small force at Jackson, Mississippi. In all of these operations, he had fuddled Confederate reactions by the unexpected. During late April, he had pushed a daring cavalry raid under General Benjamin H. Grierson, to damage rail communications with Vicksburg and to alarm and scatter Pemberton's thin mounted force all the way from La Grange, Tennessee, to Baton Rouge, Louisiana. Grant had produced.

Productive aggressiveness set him far apart from his colleagues. Lincoln always looked for generals who did well on their own and kept grinding on the rebels. If Grant took Vicksburg, he would achieve the greatest strategic victory since the fall of New Orleans in May 1862. It took a good deal of marching and some hot fighting, but he finally did it. He fought Pemberton in a pitched battle at Champion's Hill, won it, and invested the Confederate fortress city on 18 May. He made a quick, violent assault on Pemberton's formidable works on 19 May and was bloodily repulsed. Grant wanted to beat Pemberton quickly, not only so that he could hit Johnston before he was strengthened, but also so that he could swing south to aid General Nathaniel P. Banks in his siege of Port Hudson, the last Confederate fort commanding the Mississippi. A renewed attack on Vicksburg's strong works failed on 22 May, costing Grant thirty-two hundred casualties.

Grant now moved to get between Johnston's force and that of Pemberton. Johnston, trying to save the garrison, pondered how to relieve Vicksburg. Pushed out of Jackson, he gathered a thin force north of Mississippi's capital at the apex of a right-angle triangle with Jackson and Vicksburg the right and left anchors of the base line. About thirty-five miles from Pemberton's works, Johnston strove to build up his army and, on 17 May, ordered Pemberton to evacuate Vicksburg and save his army. A council of war and President Davis advised Pemberton to stay put—Vicksburg had strate-

From 1–3 July 1863, a bitter, bloody battle raged around Gettysburg, Pennsylvania. In the end nearly 3,000 Union soldiers and 4,000 Confederate soldiers were dead. Union and Confederate dead lay together on the Gettysburg field in this photograph taken shortly after the battle. (National Archives)

gic and morale importance far beyond its military potential. Johnston continued working to scavenge men from a War Department trying to help both Lee and Bragg.

Grant's siege ground on until 4 July, when Pemberton surrendered, hoping for generous terms on Independence Day. He got none save the paroling of himself and his army. On 9 July, the small, heroic garrison of Port Hudson surrendered to Banks. Johnston, moving toward Vicksburg with some thirty thousand men, retreated beyond Jackson.

Grant had determined to get Vicksburg, and he kept to the siege despite enemy and friendly distractions. Grant parried Confederate efforts to relieve the bastion with fortitude. Attacks from the northern press and the rumors that eddied congressional halls did more harm. Siege operations were too slow, carpers said, and Grant lost too many men to the joint fogs of war and of deep delta country. Lincoln ignored calls for Grant's removal. "I rather like the man," he said, because "he doesn't worry and bother me. He isn't shrieking for reinforcements all the time. He takes what troops we can safely give him . . . and does the best he can with what he has."

In the afterglow of success at Vicksburg, Lincoln wrote Grant one of the most graceful confessions ever made by a commander in chief. Writing a week after Vicksburg's surrender, Lincoln's letter said: "I write this . . . as a grateful acknowledgment for the almost inestimable service you have done the country." Grant must have seen how much he and the president thought alike about the war. Lincoln said he had watched Grant's operations with growing approval. He had thought Grant should go by river, march south, recross, and operate below Vicksburg, but he thought that then Grant should have turned south to help General Banks at Port Hudson. "I now wish to make the personal acknowledgment that you were right and I was wrong."

The Vicksburg campaign had opened the Mississippi at a relatively small cost. Since 1 May, Grant's casualties came to ninety-five hundred men. The Confederacy had not only lost control of the river but also a good field army. Combined with Lee's defeat at Gettysburg, in the first week of July the Confederacy, had lost some fifty thousand men and sixty-five thousand stands of arms, many of them fine British Enfield rifles. Men and arms were running out in the South. More than that, the Confederacy, now cut in twain, began a precarious dual existence, with Richmond's span of control clearly atrophying.

On Jefferson Davis' side of things, post-Gettysburg analyses were cold indeed. His great hopes for the Department of the West under Johnston had been dashed by the general's incapacity to rise to his powers. Instead of taking charge, ordering armies and supplies where he wanted, taking command of a field army when circumstances dictated, Johnston served more as a coordinator than commander. He knew the Army of Tennessee had lost faith in Bragg and should have removed him, but he felt unable to do that to so staunch a friend of the president—and he was probably right in his fears. Still, Johnston hewed to old fancies of his own—to him an army command was the highest post a general could have—and he wanted that more than some amorphous post as facilitator of bits and dribbles. Thus, he missed what was probably the greatest chance of the conflict.

Halleck and others, knowing Lincoln's views about the victorious Grant, schemed to get the command of new western hero Meade, but Grant, who wanted to keep moving on Mobile, dodged the eastern army. "Whilst I would disobey no order I should beg very hard to be excused before accepting that command," he confessed. The Army of the Potomac seemed to wallow in bad luck. Certainly it battled formidable odds and enemies.

General William Starke Rosecrans faced lesser obstacles but acted with greater timidity. It was not until 26 June 1863 that he finally moved his army from Murfreesboro. Halleck had prodded him restlessly since January. Bragg, his army starved for men as all aid went to Vicksburg, held on below Murfreesboro and kept pressure on the enemy by cavalry raids that earned little, and on one of those, the famed rebel raider John Hunt Morgan was captured. Rosecrans countered with equally fruitless mounted expeditions.

Bragg's main concern was Chattanooga—he had to hold that strategic city. A rail center that anchored one of the Confederacy's main east-west trunks, Chattanooga also anchored the mountain barrier to Alabama and Georgia. If the federals took it, they would have interior lines for advancing in almost any direction. When Rosecrans started, he moved with deceptive speed, and he ran Bragg's Kentucky campaign in reverse. Maneuvering instead of fighting, by 30 June he had forced the rebels back to Tullahoma, Tennessee. Again swift marches almost trapped Bragg north of Elk River. By 4 July, Bragg fell back on Chattanooga.

In the woeful news of those first July days, Jefferson Davis understood better than most the strategic portent of Bragg's failure but had little mourning time. Critical blows at Vicksburg and Gettysburg overshadowed the slow agony of the Army of Tennessee. With Vicksburg's garrison and important arms supplies gone, Bragg's beleaguered force propped the Confederacy's sagging left shoulder.

In a way, the fall of Vicksburg unburdened Confederate planning. Most of the time, Davis and Seddon had been forced to defend wrong objectives to satisfy local commands, but this time they were right to concentrate on saving a city. Chattanooga's logistical and morale value could not be exaggerated. Even Johnston acted like a theater commander when he sent Bragg some units he had collected near Jackson. He knew Bragg's scant forty-four thousand, including fourteen thousand cavalry, had to hold several possible Tennessee River crossings against Rosecrans' sixty-five thousand, which might be reinforced by Grant.

Only scattered bodies of men could be stripped from such places as Mobile. A strategic crisis faced Davis' government. Lee showed reluctance to take a western command. What could be done to sustain Bragg? The old idea of detaching Longstreet's corps from Lee's army reappeared. Longstreet was for it; he wanted an independent chance for glory. Lee reluctantly approved; the want of men made it about the only workable option, if Bragg was to be quickly strengthened. Bragg's recent call for S. B. Buckner's nine thousand-man corps from Knoxville yielded the main rail line from Richmond to Chattanooga. Longstreet's move would have to be made on roundabout rail routes. On 6 September, Longstreet received his coveted orders. He wanted Bragg's command; victory might win it, if the First Corps could arrive in time.

Bragg's situation had good and bad potential. By the end of August, he had virtually forted up in Chattanooga and deployed General Forrest's cavalry as a screening force along the east bank of the Tennessee, which all but eliminated any chance to discover enemy movements. Rosecrans began crossing on 20 August and aimed to sever Bragg's supply line below the city. Bragg's cavalry greatly outnumbered their mounted foes and brought Bragg copious intelligence of enemy moves through various mountain passes south of Chattanooga. News of "rats from so many holes" baffled him and not until 8 September did he realize the threat to his rear. He evacuated Chattanooga that night—outmaneuvered, he left without a fight, but he planned one.

Victorious and overconfident, Rosecrans stumbled into trouble. Part of it came from the terrain, the rest from unexpected rebels. Rosecrans knew that east of the Tennessee and below Chattanooga various mountains and ridges covered approaches to the city. Cut by various passes and defiles, the ridges were real and puzzling barriers. Bad maps and scarce cavalry left "Rosy" more ignorant of terrain than he guessed.

Bragg had sound strategic sense, once he found out what was happening. He plotted the destruction of the Army of the Cumberland. Rosecrans had split his force into three widely separated units. Bragg, suddenly seized with aggressiveness, concentrated to pick off these exposed units piecemeal. Everything went wrong with his proposed attack on 10 September. General Thomas C. Hindman failed to move speedily, other subordinates wallowed in timidity, and Rosecrans escaped during the next several days. Bragg nearly isolated several federal forces but lost them to slow obedience to good orders. He complicated his problem by not being close enough to the front personally to insist on quick action. He kept to the offensive, however, never yielding initiative to his opponent.

Longstreet's First Corps had moved with remarkable speed, despite the long circuit through the Deep South. His lead elements, under General John B. Hood, arrived early on 18 September, in time to join an attempt to turn the Union left, resting nearly ten miles south of Chattanooga, along Chickamauga Creek. Delays again frustrated rebel hopes, but more men arrived during the night, and Bragg planned to press on the next day. Bitter, confused, and uncertain fighting took up most of the 19th, with Bragg unaware of what happened. He stubbornly held to the attack. During the night Rosecrans strengthened his line and ordered fieldworks erected on the left. When the rebels lauched their drive at about 9:30 A.M. on 20 September, federal resistance slowed them from the start.

Bragg stuck to his flanking plan and ordered an echelon attack on a close timetable. Early rebel success against General George H. Thomas on the left prompted Rosecrans to send help from his right, but in sending it, he left a gap in his line that Longstreet exploited expertly late in the morning. Rosencrans' battle went to pieces, and some of his men bolted the field. Swept up in the confused retreat himself, Rosecrans did not know of the heroic stand on the left that earned Thomas his battle name, 'The Rock of Chickamauga." Thomas finally had to retreat becasue he was left virtually alone.

Bragg had won but he failed to pursue, much to Forrest's frustration. As Rosecrans pulled his remnants into Chattanooga, both sides counted Chickamauga's costs. Rosecrans sustained 16,170 casualties out of some 58,000 engaged, while Bragg, with about 66,000 engaged, lost 18,454—nearly 28 percent on both sides. Rosecrans lost more than men, of course; he had lost the initiative and huddled in Chattanooga's defenses. Bragg partially surrounded the town and cut federal supply lines down to one uncertain road. Rosecrans faced starvation as Bragg's men and cannon sat atop such surrounding heights as Missionary Ridge and Lookout Mountain. Neither command could boast about Chickamauga. True, Bragg won, but failure to reinforce his attack at crucial times on the 20th robbed him of the smashing victory he designed. Thomas had saved Rosecrans from the disaster his own tactical errors almost ensured.

Bragg still had the initiative. He could stay where he was and maintain the investment; he could cross the river and flank Rosecrans out of the city and force him to fight; or he could leave an observation force in front of Rosecrans and move quickly to beat Burnside's small force at Knoxville. His unwonted daring gone, he chose to sit and besiege.

Lincoln read dispatches from Chattanooga in mounting gloom. He thought that Rosecrans had acted "stunned like a duck hit on the head."

Lincoln read dispatches from Chattanooga in mounting gloom. He thought that Rosecrans had acted "stunned like a duck hit on the head." The president wanted Chattanooga held at all costs—he easily grasped its strategic value—and ordered reinforcements from Meade's idle army. In a sweeping reorganization, Lincoln put all western departments and armies under General Grant. Directing Grant to look at the Chattanooga situation, the president gave him full authority to do whatever seemed best. In effect, he copied Davis' theater command scheme. Grant replaced Rosencrans with Thomas.

Energy, audacity, and courage were Grant's contribution to his new post. Wasting no time, he organized several attacks on Bragg's lines, each time gaining an advantage. Bragg, apparently confident of his lofty lines, had detached Longstreet to take Knoxville and had to go on the defensive against Grant. In a dazzling series of attacks, Grant's army unexpectedly carried Bragg's at Lookout Mountain on 24 November and smashed through the main front along Missionary Ridge the next day. Grant failed to pursue. Bragg's army fled to the southeast, leaving sixty-six hundred casualties behind. Grant's losses amounted to fifty-eight hundred.

President Davis had reason to regret his earlier decision to overlook criticism by Bragg's generals and keep him in command after the Kentucky campaign. As the Army of Tennessee retreated into northwest Georgia, Davis accepted Bragg's resignation. Despite personal reservations, on 16 December 1863, Davis appointed Johnston to replace Bragg. It was Johnston's proudest moment.

Longstreet failed to take Knoxville. Grant, using the full logistical powers of his new command, sent help to Burnside, which forced the besiegers to abandon their task. Longstreet fell back to Greeneville, Tennessee, where he could either rejoin Lee or threaten Grant's left. His withdrawal signaled the end of the western campaign in 1863, a year that saw Grant win two of the Union's major objectives—control of the Mississippi and possession of Chatanooga—which ensured control of Tennessee and a good route to the heart of Dixie.

Out of the year's turmoil, Grant emerged and Bragg faded. The Union grew stronger in the west and the Confederacy's power ebbed as the Trans-Mississippi Department went into a kind of semi-independence. Lincoln stated the main import of the western year from the North's standpoint: "The Father of Waters again goes unvexed to the sea." Davis could point to nothing positive from the year in the west save the continued presence of the Army of Tennessee, an army of lost battles and opportunities, led by incompetents and sometimes by fools, that still survived and fought and stayed to its steadfast duty.

COMING THUNDER DRUMS: WINTER 1863–SUMMER 1864

As was the Army of Tennessee, the Union Army of the Potomac was labeled unlucky, badly officered, and slackly run, an army of wasted lives and chances and cast against the fates and Lee. Still, it stood bulwark to Washington. The ranks had almost abandoned hope of good leaders when they lost McClellan and events had not disabused such thoughts. Meade, however, had a kind of following, and after Gettysburg, like all of Lee's opponents, settled the army into rebuilding and refitting. The army liked that because "getting after Lee" had never been a winning game. Waiting to throw him back had always been best. Meade clearly agreed.

Halleck and Lincoln wanted something done in those post-battle days, with Longstreet absent and Lee's army licking its wounds, but Meade had the stubbornness of his predecessors. He needed men, supplies, and horses before he could move. Despairing of an offensive against Lee, Lincoln ordered the detachment of some of Meade's army to Rosecrans, and Lee tried to take advantage of a weakened opponent.

In early October 1863, the Army of Northern Virginia crossed the Rapidan, in a familiar try to get around Meade's right and move on Washington. Meade, despite the detachments, largely outnumbered Lee, but the old Napoleonic flanking threat made him retreat. Lee saw his chance: He would hit Meade's retreating columns at Bristoe Station, break them up, take their trains, and give battle on the old Manassas grounds. It did not happen. Lee's command structure had lost its nimbleness; orders went slowly and were even more slowly obeyed. The Army of Northern Virginia showed alarming signs of attrition at almost every level. None marked the import more clearly than Lee.

Both armies found no opportunity to strike a decisive blow and the rebels retired. Meade picked up the gauntlet, as good weather held in Virginia. Halleck and Lincoln hazed him into crossing the Rapidan with about eighty-five thousand men on 26 November 1863 in a campaign to turn Lee's right. Meade, much to Lincoln's chagrin, still aimed at Richmond, not at Lee's army. He hoped to maneuver Lee into a retreat to his capital. With slightly fewer than fifty thousand men—Longstreet had not yet returned—Lee move quickly to meet the enemy and occupied strong positions along the brook Mine Run. So strong were Lee's works that Meade found no point of attack and his campaign failed aborning.

Operations along Mine Run confirmed a new element that was shaping battles—field entrenchments. Wherever armies halted, they now threw up heavy works. It should have been done earlier, considering the engineering background of all West Pointers. For the early years, however, marching and stand-up fighting were the ways of American combat. Some students suggest that this passion for open formation attacks reflected the Celtic element in both armies. Whatever the cause, discretion overcame foolish valor. Improved weapons brought a fearsome growth in firepower. Massed rifles and vastly improved field artillery shattered old European attack formations. Immense slaughter forced entrenching. Fieldworks sprang up on western battlefields earlier than in Virginia, but by winter 1863, veteran troops were deft diggers.

They were also superior scavengers, especially Lee's men. Virginia had been picked clean for three years by various hordes. Fervent efforts by commissary and quartermaster agents to supply the Army of Northern Virginia during the cold winter of 1863–1864 produced starvation rations. The men foraged a bare landscape. Lee constantly requested supplies in letters increasingly like George Washington's missives from Valley Forge. Davis gave all he could, but scarcity crippled the logistical chain. By mid-1863 the effects of attrition were widespread across the Confederacy.

Attrition in the South affected not only manpower but also facilities and transportation. With repeated drives to fill ranks, some supply officers and men were shifted and often replaced by the less skilled and able-bodied. Shortages of shops and equipment retarded repair of war-worn trains and tracks. Rickety wagons, patched harness, and thinned horses and mules became standard equipment by mid-1863—all symptoms of scarcity. Sometimes these symptoms came from poor administration. Bad planning occasionally piled up supplies at one point, while starving another. Coordination came hard to a laissez-faire government. War pressure finally led Davis' government to limited nationalization of transportation, an essential policy, although damned as dictatorial.

Men were in shortest supply. The Confederacy's military population was running out. Various schemes were tried to fill the ranks—amnesty for deserters, bounties, special leave consideration—but as the war ground on morale sagged and even a slight wound became a discharge. Confederate congressmen had understood the manpower crisis and passed the first draft law in American history in April 1862. Approved by most state courts, often opposed by such ardent states' rights governors as Georgia's Joseph E. Brown and North Carolina's Zebulon B. Vance, the act produced too few men. Increasingly stiff draft acts were enacted, attacking the sacrosanct substitution system, expanding eligible years to from seventeen to fifty, and cutting exemptions. Slaves were enrolled for work on fortifications; too late in the war, they were accepted as soldiers, and a few actually donned the gray just at the end.

In the government's view, conscription's special value came from its control of the national manpower pool. Under War Department regulations, the war secretary could manage the talent of the Confederacy and put men where they could best serve the cause. Without the draft, however, rebel ranks would probably have disintegrated by the end of 1862. Modern estimates indicate about eighty-two thousand conscripts enrolled east of the Mississippi from 16 April 1862 until war's end.

Early glamour quickly tarnished; volunteers wrote brothers to avoid army camps as places of pestilence, vermin, and corruption.

Even with vast manpower superiority, the United States had difficulty in keeping up the armies. Early glamour quickly tarnished; volunteers wrote brothers to avoid camps as places of pestilence, vermin, and corruption. Religious youths were horrified at the army's coarse secular tone. Patriotism became a selective thing. After Lincoln's first call for volunteers, a visible drop in response prompted the so-called "draft of 1862." A mishmash of state and national programs, this early conscription effort kept responsibility at the state level;

where states had no laws drafting the militia, national orders were to prevail. Liberal exemptions and a general lack of enthusiasm vitiated these early efforts. It was not until 3 March 1863 that the U.S. Congress adopted conscription. Enforcement wallowed in problems. New York City—where Mayor Fernando Wood supported the South—writhed in draft riots, 13–15 July, and resistance sparked across the North.

As in the South, control of national manpower ranked as an important result of northern conscription. Additions to the ranks, however, were vital to the federal cause. Best estimates are that 249,259 men were drafted and that 86,724 paid to be exempted. Consequently 162,535 men actually were drafted. Federal numbers were swelled in July 1862 by the acceptance of blacks in the ranks. Some 179,000 served in many regiments during the war. Conscription's value to both sides came more from suasion than from force. Even though a draft law lurked in the background, volunteering and reenlistments continued.

As cold clamped on the armies' camps at the end of 1863, mere existence took precedence over war, and as a new campaign season approached, Lincoln reshaped his entire command structure. After years of groping, he recognized in Grant just the general to run the war. On 10 March 1864, the president promoted Grant, who was forty-one years old, to the revived rank of lieutenant general and made him general in chief of the Union armies. More than half a million men were in Grant's charge, and he could hardly handle the heavy minutiae of so many and happily accepted Lincoln's notion that Halleck be chief of staff to handle relations between the civilian president and his general and between the general and his various department commanders. This arrangement, as historian T. Harry Williams observed in *Lincoln and His Generals* (1952), marked the beginning of a modern command system.

Grant knew his headquarters had to be close to Washington but did not want to stay in the city. He went to the field with the Army of the Potomac. Meade remained in command, but Grant's tent always stood close by. This potentially volatile arrangement worked well because both generals cooperated. Grant gave overall strategic directions and left tactics to Meade. As a result, an aggressive spirit permeated the army as it began to believe in victory.

The new general in chief shared President Lincoln's understanding of power and pressure. He knew the United States had vastly more war resources than the Confederacy and worked to use that superiority. As Winfield Scott proposed much earlier and Lincoln often repeated, Grant wanted to put as many troops in the field as possible and press the Confederates everywhere—a program one modern student has called "Operation Crusher." Recognizing that uncoordinated federal operations permitted the enemy to shift troops from one army to another on inner lines, Grant intended to put all federal forces into some kind of action; those not fighting could menace by maneuver. Lincoln had a metaphor for that: "Those not skinning can hold a leg."

Grant projected three major offensives for the 1864 campaign. The Army of the Potomac under Meade (whom Grant came to admire greatly) would stick to Lee's army and not let go, while smaller forces would threaten Richmond from the James River side and the Shenandoah Valley. A big western army under one of Grant's favorites, William T. Sherman, would press the Army of Tennessee through north Georgia, into Atlanta. While pressing Johnston, Sherman would also destroy southern war resources in the state. As Sherman moved south, an army under General Banks would march from New Orleans to Mobile, where it might link with Sherman and at last secure one of Grant's pet objectives, the Chattanooga-Mobile line.

These good plans quickly skewed. Banks started an expedition of his own up the Red River in Louisiana in April. Using gunboats, he hoped to capture Shreveport, headquarters of the Trans-Mississippi Department and bring war to Texas. Everything went wrong. He lost the major Battle of Mansfield (Sabine Crossroads) on 8 April 1864, had to abandon his campaign, and was unable to make the Mobile move. An infuriated Grant wanted Banks removed, but Lincoln needed that general's considerable political support in the upcoming presidential election. He put Banks on the shelf at New Orleans.

Sherman continued to get his army of more than ninety thousand ready to move against Johnston, and Meade collected more than one hundred thousand to hurl against Lee. These coordinated offensives would stress the Confederacy at its weakest point—manpower. Unable to shift troops from one army to the other, Davis would have to scrape the barrel for men. This situation put a premium on killing in the coming campaigns, because the North had replacements aplenty while the South had few.

Anxious but not despondent, Davis also modified his command structure. He brought the unemployed Bragg to Richmond as his chief of staff—an absurdity in the eyes of Bragg's widening circle of critics—but Bragg had good strategic sense. Davis would have preferred advice from Lee on all Confederate fronts, but Lee's attention fixed on Meade. Bragg, at least, knew logistical fundamentals and the odd ways of rebel soldiers. After that key appointment, Davis rejoiced in Banks's failure and in the limited successes of Forrest at Okolona, Mississippi, and also of General Joseph Finnegan's victory over a federal expedition into Florida's interior (the Battle of Olustee) in late February 1864. Glad of some good news, the Confederate president had done valiantly in sending help to both Lee and Johnston. Despite the heavy threat hanging over the Confederacy, the new year had promise. If Sherman and Grant (Meade) could be checked, the coming Union election might change the character of the war; another Union stalemate might finally induce foreign recognition. There were reasons for hope as Johnston received men from Alabama and Mississippi and the coast until he counted nearly sixty thousand, and Lee, supported again by Longstreet's corps, counted almost seventy thousand.

Many bluecoats, seeing the awesome strength of Lee's trenches, wrote their names on slips of papers and pinned them on their uniforms to avoid being listed among the "unknown."

Meade advanced just after midnight on Wednesday, 4 May 1864, and began a desperate series of battles in the Virginia Wilderness, near the old Chancellorsville fields. Fearsome fighting on the 6th found Lee going forward to encourage his men and hearing them cry "Lee to the rear! General Lee to the rear!" Longstreet took a serious wound as carnage among the generals shook command. Opportunities came to both sides, were seized and missed, and light fieldworks proved their value. By the end of the day, opposing lines were stabilized. More than 100,000 federals were in the fight and 17,666 of them were casualties. Across from them, Lee lost 7,500 from his 60,000 engaged. Unlike his predecessors, Meade did not turn back to Washington. Grant, holding the strategic initiative, ordered continued pressure on the rebel right. Lee hurried troops to intercept the enemy at Spotsylvania Court House, an important road hub.

Running into unexpected rebel entrenchments at the court house on 8 May, Meade's men were repulsed and fighting faded. Grant ordered General Philip H. Sheridan to take the cavalry on a raid to hit Lee's communications and so divert Stuart's riders. Light encounters the next day underscored a general field readjustment and further entrenching. General John Sedgwick, one of Meade's corps commanders, fell. Meade ordered a morning attack.

A general assault on rebel works in late afternoon on 10 May was repulsed, but some dents were made at cost. Light skirmishing took up most of the next day, and Grant determined to exploit one of the dents in Lee's works by a major attack on 12 May. Furious assaults and counterattacks occupied the day. General Ewell's corps of Lee's army lost some four thousand prisoners in before-dawn fighting. The "bloody angle" consumed men for most of the afternoon and into the night. This day ranks as one of the costliest of the war—federal casualties ran to sixty-eight hundred, and five thousand Confederate troops were killed or wounded. All the rage and fury cost men and gained little, but attrition stalked Lee's ranks. Hard war resumed in the Wilderness on 18 May, when a series of Union attacks failed against strengthened rebel works. So strong were the enemy lines at Spotsylvania that Grant decided to shift the battle further to Lee's right. Actions around the court house cost more than 17,500 federal casualties out of 110,000 engaged. Confederate losses were much less (about 8,000) but not reliably counted. In both the Wilderness and Spotsylvania engagements, Meade lost 33,000 men—a terrible price for slow progress.

Lee guessed Grant's moves and also turned toward the southeast. Some good news came from the James River front. Beauregard, brought up to command in southern Virginia, had pretty well bottled up General Benjamin F. Butler's army at Bermuda Hundred neck. Richmond's situation need not worry Lee, for the moment, but he worried about Grant. Along the North Anna River, confused fighting won Lee a chance to hit a divided federal army. Lee was sick, subordinates confused, and the opportunity passed. By 26 May, Grant ordered another flank move, far to Lee's right, but rebels got to Cold Harbor first and began a maze of fortifications. On 1 and 2 June, Meade's men concentrated at Cold Harbor. Many bluecoats, seeing the awesome strength of Lee's trenches, wrote their names on slips of papers and pinned them on their uniforms to avoid being listed among the "unknown." Meade attacked on 3 June at 4:30 A.M. in a pell-mell rush to smash through Lee's lines. Three Union corps stormed toward rebel works and in little more than a half hour were repulsed at probably the highest cost of any day in the war. Numbers are disputed, but Unions losses are put at seven thousand to fifteen hundred Confederates. Lee remarked that the concentrated Confederate rifle fire sounded like wet sheets tearing in the wind.

Grant's stubborn campaign raised high criticism at home. One prominent Northerner rightly wrote that the Army of the Potomac "has literally marched in blood and agony from the Rapidan to the James." At last Grant halted. So strong were opposing entrenchments that neither side could attack. Grant was of different stuff than McClellan and the others and would not quit. What would he do and where?

Being closer to Richmond gave Lee logistical advantages. As he fell back on his base, he received some reinforcements and reorganized. Beauregard's situation grew bothersome, however, because Butler outnumbered him two to one. Nevertheless, Lee hoped Beauregard could put some men in front of Richmond, between the James and the Chickahominy.

Sticking to the scheme of pressing Lee from various quarters, Grant engineered several incursions into Virginia. One, led by General David Hunter, would probe the upper end of the Shenandoah, take Staunton, destroy crops and shops, pin down scattered Confederate forces and perhaps force Lee to detach forces to stop

General Grant (at left) studies a map over the shoulder of General Meade during a meeting to plan strategy on 21 May 1964 near Massaponax Church, Virginia. (National Archives)

him. Hunter's threat came after Lee had brought General John C. Breckinridge's small force from the Shenandoah Valley to help fill the Cold Harbor lines. With Sheridan's cavalry on the way to Hunter, Lee sent Breckinridge back, but his twenty-one hundred men seemed a hollow threat to Hunter's eighteen thousand. Breckinridge and Lee guessed Lynchburg would be Hunter's objective, a supply center vital to Lee. Something would have to be done about Hunter.

Desperately short of men and eager to avoid a siege of the capital or its consort city, Petersburg, some thirty miles south, Lee knew that any further detachments from his ranks would commit him to the heavy works ringing Richmond. He had to act, however, and sent Early to deal with Hunter. It seemed a good choice. Early commanded Jackson's Second Corps, including remnants of the Army of the Valley, had drive and gall, and liked fighting. Lee gave him wide discretion.

Early dealt with Hunter at Lynchburg, then moved boldly down the Shenandoah to threaten Harpers Ferry, crossed the Potomac, and moved directly on Washington. Only the stubborn defense of the Monacacy River in Maryland by General Lew Wallace on 9 July prevented Early's twelve thousand from possibly wandering the streets of Washington. Early's raid in June and July 1864 was in the best offensive-defensive tradition. Lee hoped it would force Grant to send troops to protect the Union capital; it did, but not enough to change the odds compounding at Richmond and Petersburg. At its high point, Early's campaign reached the outskirts of Washington—even fired on President Lincoln in a redoubt—and convinced some foreign observers that "the Confederacy is more formidable as an enemy than ever." The raid scared Lincoln and Halleck and cleared the valley of federals at a crucial time. Early remained a threat as Lee left him there to protect the granary of the army.

By the end of the first week in June, Lincoln and Grant were disappointed. Grant, who intended to fight on to Richmond if it took all summer, found that it would take that time and more. After all the carnage, his campaign had failed. True, he was seven miles from Richmond, but Lee's army remained intact. No good way seemed open to flank the rebels away from Richmond's formidable entrenchments. Grant told the president he intended to give up the direct approach, cross south of the James, and hit Richmond from its supposedly soft underbelly. He wanted to get Lee out in the open for a decisive blow. Lee would not come out of his lines to fight Grant's battle; hence, he magnified his numbers.

Grant, for once, however, fooled the wily rebel leader. He began crossing the James on 12 June and Lee lost him for several days. Expecting a move south of the James, Lee nevertheless lacked definite information of Grant's movements. A large part of the Army of the Potomac crossed beyond the river, and by 15 June, sixteen thousand Yankees attempted to attack Beauregard's three thousand men defending Petersburg. Bad maps, combined with botched orders and short rations, confused the advance, and Beauregard's brilliant countermeasures staved off ruin.

If Lee was confused about Grant's whereabouts and intentions, Beauregard was not—he kept reporting mounting Union numbers to Lee, and kept asking for help. Lee remained unconvinced of Grant's doings. Beauregard held against mounting numbers, contracted his lines, called for help, stripped his Bermuda Hundred line, and by 17 June had done about all he could to hold Petersburg. On that day Lee sent heavy reinforcements and saved the southern gateway to Richmond. The siege of Petersburg began on 18 June 1864. Over the next months Lee's lines would extend some thirty miles and be held by scarcely more than 60,000 men against Meade's 110,000. The four-day defense of Petersburg had been bloody—Meade lost about 8,000 killed and wounded. Confederate losses were less in number, more in portent.

ON TO HISTORY

Although many Northerners thought Grant's new strategy had failed, it was working. While Meade battled his way through northern Virginia, Sherman moved from Chattanooga against the Army of Tennessee. As both Lee and Johnston called for men, Davis and Seddon found fewer and fewer; the pool of eligible white males had about gone dry. Some brigades were scraped together in the spring and summer of 1864 from outlying posts and stations, usually from exposed coastal areas, and each shipment brought loud complaints from fearful governors.

Large sections of the southern heartland had no men left. Part of the manpower problem stemmed from the need to protect the armies' lines of communication against Union raiders, even against disaffected Southerners and organized deserters. When such hard war measures as conscription and impressment drained morale, trouble sprang up behind the lines, and Confederate troops were detached for rear-area security. As summer fighting ground on, casualties could not be replaced. Grant's suspension of prisoner exchanges hit the South harder than the North—there were more than 150,000 rebels in Union prisons who were badly needed in the ranks.

All of the logistical support network of the Confederacy wobbled under Grant's joint offensives. Ammunition and clothing could be had but distribution to the armies became problematical as federal cavalry wrecked railroads and bridges. Rations grew thinner as agricultural areas went to the enemy. An iron shortage crippled cannon production while scarcity of copper cut percussion cap manufacture. When would all these shortages coalesce into defeatism?

Hard campaigns vastly consumed Union manpower as well. As the staggering casualty lists filled northern papers, a great spasm of agony and anger racked the country. Lincoln, as well as Grant, was hotly criticized, so much so that Lincoln thought he might lose the election of 1864, might not even get the Republican nomination. He would stay the course, but his opponent might not. The cause might be lost by ballots. Signs of war weariness and apathy multiplied.

No signs of defeatism showed in the field. Hope and determination fired Sherman's one hundred thousand men, divided into three armies, as they began moving on 7 May 1864. Sherman launched a great raid, aimed at smashing Johnston's army and at cutting Georgia in two with a sixty-mile wide incursion to the sea. It became a surprisingly effective logistical campaign that threatened key Confederate arsenals, armories, and depots. The first rush stalled, however, because Johnston's lines were too strong. Johnston always had a good eye for holding ground, and he had entrenched his sixty thousand devoted men along a ridge near Dalton, Georgia. Sherman tried turning the Confederate left. Johnston began one of history's great retreats. Grudgingly, he backed down the Western and Atlantic Railroad toward Atlanta, entrenching where he could, standing when he had a chance to fight, slipping away from flankers with sure control of his men and superb sense of timing. The retreat became a kind of offense; Sherman repeatedly deployed, skirmished, flanked, only to see Johnston's rear guard still ahead. From 13 to 28 May, battles at Resaca, Cassville, the Etowah River, and New Hope Church each stalled Sherman's march. At Kenesaw Mountain, 27 June 1864, Johnston bloodily repulsed a major attack.

To a worried Lincoln, Sherman's operations offered vast potential. If Johnston's army was destroyed, Lee would be finished quickly and the war would end. By the end of June, however, Sherman seemed to be emulating Grant's tactics—pushing the enemy back on his base while extending federal supply lines. At last, Johnston fell back into Atlanta's strong defenses and awaited battle.

Through the weeks of Johnston's retreat President Davis watched in mounting frustration. How far would he go? When and where would he fight? These understandable presidential questions Johnston either ignored or parried with some excuse about security. Silence might have been prudent because Johnston would have had to say that the army took precedence over cities or ground and he would keep it between Sherman and the sea. Still, the president had a right to know what the commander of one of the South's main armies had in mind. When Johnston pulled his men into the Atlanta lines, Davis made a mistake. Unable to find out what his general planned, save retreat, the president replaced him with General John Bell Hood, one of Lee's best division leaders and a corps commander in the Army of Tennessee. The army seethed because the men loved "Old Joe" and many felt that Hood had undermined him and frustrated chances to attack Sherman. There was truth to the thought, but the deed stood, and fear chilled veterans so often pawns to ambition.

Davis had asked Lee's advice and heard cautionary words about leaving a good man in command, about Hood being a fighter but perhaps not quite of army command caliber. Hood knew that Davis wanted a fight for Atlanta. Two hard attacks, on 20 and 22 July failed, and Hood abandoned the city on 1 September 1864. This disaster crowned a grinding summer for the south. Atlanta's fall proved the value of Grant's "Operation Crusher." Sherman wasted no time as he prepared a march through the industrial heart of Georgia and on to the coast, finally on to Charleston, the "Cradle of Secession."

Rickety trains ran slower and more unreliably when winter dug the army deeper into its strange dirt warrens.

Hood made a good attempt to recoup his fortunes. Guessing that a march up Sherman's communications toward Nashville would force him to follow, Hood started for Tennessee in November. Sherman followed only a short way, left Hood to others, and on 14 November marched on to the sea. Hood wasted the flower of his army in a useless frontal attack on 30 November at Franklin, Tennessee, then limped on to clamp a partial siege on Nashville. General Thomas broke the siege on 15–16 December and also broke Hood's army. Bits and pieces of the army drifted back to Georgia, where Johnston tried to rebuild it as some kind of a buffer to Sherman. Out from Sherman's army had gone clouds of "bummers," who burned, pillaged, and degraded young and old as they carried freedom's flag. A gallant remnant of the Army of Tennessee later fought Sherman at Bentonville, North Carolina, on 19–21 March 1865, and surrendered at Durham Station, North Carolina, on 26 April 1865.

Lee hated the defensive. As siege lines snaked ever longer south and west along the Appomattox River early in 1865, as more of his men were confined in burgeoning labyrinths of trenches, he knew the initiative had firmly passed to Grant. Now the Army of Northern Virginia faced the daily routine of attrition—the slow death Lee had so fiercely fended. Petersburg had to be held because important rail lines joined there from the Deep South that sustained the army's thin rations and supplies. Federal cavalry raided the lines and others coming directly to Richmond, but Fitzhugh Lee, who took over from the dead Jeb Stuart, kept them at bay, even though his horsemen had to forage almost forty miles from the Confederate army. Supplies grew fewer as enemy thrusts into the logistical heart of the Confederacy sapped resources. Rickety trains ran slower and more unreliably when winter dug the army deeper into its strange dirt warrens.

From mid-June 1864 to 2 April 1865, the siege distracted Lee. Desperately, he wanted to maneuver, to get out and attack Grant with some chance of flanking him, turning him back toward the Potomac. Grimly, Grant stuck to his trenching, steadily extending westward to thin out Lee's defenders. These long months saw raids and frontal assaults, charges, skirmishes, and the endless, dreary burrowing. Occasionally the lines twitched. A Union attempt to blow up part of the rebel trenches east of Petersburg, the Battle of the Crater on 30 July 1864, changed the veteran feelings of respectful ani-

Union soldiers wait in trenches during the siege of Petersburg in 1865. The siege, which began in mid-June 1964, ended when Grant's troops broke the Confederate line on 2 April 1865 and Lee evacuated Petersburg. (National Archives)

mosity into one of real bitterness against black troops, who gallantly led the way into an inferno. Several times during the winter of 1864–1865, Lee tried to gain a strategic advantage along the trench lines, but heavy Union strength in men and guns usually prevailed.

Slowly Grant moved to his left, until Lee's forty-five thousand men were stretched to cover nearly thirty miles of line. Caught in the geometry of a closing circle, Lee, who had been made commander in chief of the Confederate armies in February 1865 by a congress angry at Davis, planned a desperate gamble. If, somehow, he could cripple Grant's army, he would leave a holding force at Petersburg and join Johnston to defeat Sherman. The combined Confederate armies would then return to deal with Grant. The plan had the forlorn logic of fantasy, but Lee tried. At 4 A.M. on 25 March 1865, he launched an attack on Fort Stedman at the north end of the Union lines, a costly failure—five thousand casualties. Grant followed that battle with a major effort on Lee's attenuated right, and on 2 April 1865 the Confederate line broke. Lee evacuated Petersburg and Richmond and began marching southwestward with the hope of finding rations and perhaps of joining Johnston.

On 9 April 1865, with federal columns front and rear, Lee went to the house of Wilmer McLean, who had moved when the first Battle of Bull Run overran his residence, and surrendered the Army of Northern Virginia. Terms were generous. Horsemen kept their horses, officers their side arms, the men got Union rations, and everyone was paroled on Grant's authority. With Lee's surrender the remaining Confederate fragments yielded everywhere, and by the end of May the first of the modern wars was over. The Confederacy went on to legend and the United States to world power.

President Lincoln toured a smoking, subdued Richmond on 5 April 1865. Crowds of cheering former slaves swirled around him. He visited the Confederate White House, listened to an old friend, former Supreme Court Justice John A. Campbell, suggest that the Virginia legislature might withdraw Virginia from the Confederacy—and approved the idea—then walked around a bit. Stopping at George Edward Pickett's house, he found he had missed his friend, who was with General Lee.

At Ford's Theater in Washington on the evening of 14 April 1865, the Lincolns were watching a performance of "Our American Cousin." During the performance, the actor John Wilkes Booth shot the president, who died at 7:22 A.M. the next day. Lincoln had lived to see victory. Problems of Reconstruction passed to President Andrew Johnson.

THE NAVAL WAR, 1861–1865

Lincoln's proclaimed blockade of the southern coasts on 19 April 1861 looked good on paper and nowhere else. The United States Navy had only forty-two ships in commission and many of those were in repair. Many of the warships were flung far around the globe. Lincoln expected more diplomatic than commercial results from his announced policy. Although the Declaration of Paris of 1856 held that blockades had to be effective to be honored, Lincoln had some hope that Great Britain and European nations might find it advantageous to respect his paper interdiction of the Confederacy. He was right. Great Britain, whose concern with maritime rights had helped cause the War of 1812, chose to honor the blockade. When Queen Victoria proclaimed neutrality soon after Lincoln's call for volunteers, she also enjoined her subjects not to defy the blockade. Many did, but the precedent had been set. There might come a time when Albion would want a paper cordon acknowledged by the Yankees.

Davis and his secretary of state, Robert A. Toombs, expecting support from signatories to the Declaration of Paris, took pains to compile statistics on the sieve-like nature of the blockade in the first months of application. Beyond that, the government strove to create a navy strong enough to keep the harbors open to the world's cotton trade. King Cotton would change everything. A shortage in British and European mills would force not only foreign recognition, but also foreign help in mocking Lincoln's empty prohibition.

Both sides raced to build a fleet. Although small, the mere existence of the Union navy carried great advantages. Dry docks and shipyards existed on the East Coast, which suggested a possibly easy conversion from commercial vessels to warships. Naval stores abounded in both North and South, but skilled builders clustered north of Mason and Dixon's Line. More than that, facilities for making marine engines capable of propelling giant wooden warships, or perhaps the heavy new ironclads, existed only in the North. Even with these advantages and a rich industrial base, the possible effectiveness of the Union navy depended on the skill and drive of its leaders.

President Lincoln selected Gideon Welles to be secretary of the Union navy. An unlikelier appointment could hardly have been fantasized. A former Democrat and a New England newspaper publisher, Welles had a doleful man's acerbic tongue and a look of melancholy. Welles brought surprising ability and zeal to his office and a captiousness reflected in the biting wit of his diary to Cabinet meetings. About ships and sailors he had little knowledge, perhaps less interest, but Lincoln saw in him a fine organizer and administrator who might learn. His challenges were fearsome, but he learned.

First among the problems was the blockade and how to enforce it. With more than thirty-five hundred miles of insurrectionary coastline to cover, the Union navy needed massive help. Welles ordered a blockade semblance immediately, and the steam frigate *Minnesota* and the sail frigate *Cumberland* anchored at Hampton Roads, which would become the main base for the North Atlantic Blockading Squadron. Two ships patrolled North Carolina waters in May 1861. Welles rushed a naval acquisition program that emphasized not only construction, but also purchase of all potentially useful vessels—from sailboats to tugs—and pushed production of naval ordnance. Slowly the Union ship inventory grew and more vessels deployed along the Atlantic seaboard. Welles went further. Major construction of big ships-of-the-line received attention, and unusual orders were entered for some of the new ironclads already in use in foreign navies. Recruiting also received attention from the top.

Welles and senior naval officers quickly grasped the new tactics of sea-land cooperation in attacking southern coastal areas, and specially designed gunboats were ordered to expand that effort. Marines usually participated, as amphibious operations became one of the most important and successful efforts of the Union navy. With so much of the south Atlantic coast protected by inland waterways, Confederate shipping, including potential runners of the nascent blockade, could sail inside the barrier islands until a clear inlet was found. A quick rush out would foil blockaders sitting around major harbors. Navy-army cooperation brought three important Union victories: the closure of Hatteras Inlet on 29 August 1861, the capture of Roanoke Island on 8 February 1862, and the signal victory at New Orleans in April 1862. These joint efforts not only foreclosed many options for the rebels, but also provided fine bases for blockading squadron operations. Similar cooperative efforts greatly helped Grant's Tennessee and Vicksburg campaigns. Indeed, without the ironclad gunboats bombarding Confederate fortifications, army efforts to take Forts Henry and Donelson or to storm Vicksburg would have been much costlier, if successful at all.

Experience tightened and improved all navy enterprises, particularly antiblockade activity. As more ships cruised the southern coasts, Confederate efforts to break the cordon intensified. Specially designed blockade runners—small, speedy, light-draught vessels painted to blend with the sea—plied the trade and were attacked by new or updated gunboats and cruisers. Lincoln and Welles understood the importance of shutting off foreign supplies to the beleaguered South. Blockade runners were never entirely stopped, but trade slackened gradually to a point of diminishing returns. When Fort Fisher, the formidable bastion guarding the entrance to Cape Fear River and hence to Wilmington, North Carolina, fell to amphibious attack on 15 January 1865 the Confederacy's last Atlantic port closed.

Mail deliveries were scarce, the food monotonous, men were cold in winter, stifled on summer station, and there were no women.

Officers and men on blockading service wallowed in the troughs of boredom. Weeks of uninterrupted sea duty, sometimes moving, sometimes not, galled the hottest patriots. Mail deliveries were scarce, the food monotonous, men were cold in winter, stifled on summer station, and there were no women. "Adventure! Bah!" complained one frustrated buccaneer. "The blockade is the wrong place for it."

Boredom might be relieved by capturing a blockade runner and sharing the prize money. Boredom could be totally conquered in the derring-do of such officers as Commander Charles Wilkes, whose capture of two Confederate diplomatic commissioners, James Mason and John Slidell, from the British mail steamer *Trent* almost caused a foreign war in November 1861. Reckless and finally humiliating to the United States, the venture caught northern enthusiasm and made Wilkes a passing hero. Opportunities abounded for thrill seekers. Various small excursions along the southern coasts involved volunteers in high danger, such as the small but spectacular expedition of Lieutenant William B. Cushing, 27–28 October 1864, in which he rammed and sank the feared rebel ironclad *Albemarle.* Standard naval doctrine expected navies to fight navies in big sprawling battles between heavy-gunned ships-of-the-line, a theory that narrowed some naval views in the early years of the war. Most Union operations were on blockading station or in combined river operations, but there were some real battles.

Secretary Welles contracted for some of the new ironclads shortly after he took office and that visionary gamble brought important results at Hampton Roads, where the first battle between ironclads occurred. When the Confederates captured Norfolk Navy Yard, they raised the *Merrimack,* encased it in armor, renamed it the CSS *Virginia,* and sent it to clear off coastal blockaders. On 8 March 1862, this giant, commanded by Captain Franklin Buchanan, steamed to attack the Union blockading squadron at Hampton Roads. Moving right into the large wooden ships, the *Virginia* rammed and shelled the USS *Cumberland,* sank it, and then destroyed the USS *Congress.* Apparently impervious to enemy fire, the *Virginia* became, for that day, queen of the Civil War at sea. One of the Union's ironclads appeared in Hampton Roads the next day. The *Monitor* was a small, low-lying craft with its flat deck almost awash and crowned with a round turret (it looked like a "cheese box on a raft" to some, to others like a "tin can on a shingle"). Almost unseaworthy, the *Monitor* nearly foundered on the way to Hampton Roads, but on 9 March it engaged the *Virginia* for several hours in a close-fought duel that resulted in both vessels withdrawing without real injury. The day of the iron warship had arrived—all wooden navies were suddenly obsolete.

Another classic encounter involved Admiral David G. Farragut in the Battle of Mobile Bay on 5 August 1864. During that battle against both rebel ironclads and mines (then called "torpedoes"), Farragut had himself lashed to his flagship's rigging and gave the famous attack order, "Damn the torpedoes! Full speed ahead."

Confederate cruisers posed one of the most difficult challenges to the Union navy. Buying some ships and ordering others abroad, the Confederate navy concentrated on commerce raiding. Some of the ships in this service were fine fighting vessels, often commanded by daring and resourceful captains. These cruisers usually avoided battle against heavier warships but not always. Various efforts were made to track them and trap them in neutral harbors and fight them when found. In one case, a raider was taken out of a Brazilian harbor, with diplomatic repercussions, and while these campaigns were exciting, they were also time-consuming and of limited value.

Diplomatic issues compounded some federal naval activities. Lincoln, and particularly Secretary of State Seward, wanted to deprive the Confederacy of any foreign aid. Doing so involved some high-tension clandestine activity in foreign capitals, where southern agents sought to buy blockade runners and warships. Occasionally, Union warships would lay off neutral ports to intercept Confederate vessels, or presumed Confederate vessels, often to the irritation of host countries. The practice, however, did often inhibit southern activities and showed considerable international deference to the U.S. Navy.

Welles deserves much credit for his evenhanded, progressive administration of the Navy Department. Organization and management were his strengths, and he created and ably led a huge bureaucratic structure with minimum confusion. Perhaps his amateur sailor's status helped; for him, there were no sacrosanct precedents and innovations held no terrors.

Audacity counted far more poignantly in Confederate navy leaders. As with the army, inferior numbers demanded vision and innovation. Jefferson Davis' choice of Stephen R. Mallory as navy secretary irritated some members of the Provisional Congress. Born in Trinidad, Mallory grew up in Key West and had been one of Florida's senators when the state seceded. As chairman of the U.S. Senate Committee on Naval Affairs, he had worked to modernize a service rusted in the past. Unfortunately, he had a look of slowness to him that bred more anxiety than faith. Many students of the Confederacy consign him to the usual middling rummage of Davis' cabinet. Viewed from the standpoint of the resources he commanded and the loom of his opponents, Mallory's achievements rank him among the best navy secretaries in American history.

Without shipbuilding facilities of consequence once Norfolk and New Orleans fell, without machine shops capable of making sound marine engines, with ample but scattered naval stores, and with most men wanting to join the army, Mallory's challenges dwarfed those facing Welles. Aware that the South could not compete with the United States in conventional ways, Mallory became one of the true naval innovators. He had a kind of restless intuition that sometimes led to outlandish things but mostly steered him to sound ideas and brilliant novelties.

Early in his tenure he said that "I regard the possession of an iron-armored ship as a matter of the first necessity," and when the *Merrimack* came into Confederate hands, he pressed its speedy conversion. Other ironclads received his money and attention, including the iconoclastic railroad ironclad *Arkansas,* until the small southern navy had a respectable number of the latest things in naval combat, albeit most of them lacked efficient engines. Naval ordnance also earned Mallory's early eye, and he stimulated development of the Torpedo Bureau, which produced numbers of mines that did deadly duty against many federal hulls. More ships were lost to these "infernal machines" than to regular combat.

Confronted with the fact that the South could not compete with the Union war fleet, Mallory supported President Davis' reliance on the old American practice of privateering. Because the United States had not agreed to banning privateers under the Declaration of Paris, the Confederacy legitimately inherited the right to use these "militia of the sea." Northern outrage against this "inhumane" practice merely cloaked irritation at its being used against the Union. Many would-be privateers signed up as soon as allowed in May 1861, and initial seizures were impressive; but the practice faded as coasts were interdicted and prizes could not be brought into the Confederacy.

Mallory tried to have the navy cooperate in resisting combined federal river operations. Some Confederate naval gunners served important land batteries, notably Drewry's Bluff near Richmond, and Confederate marines helped protect ships under construction from Union raiders. If the Confederacy could hit commercial shipping hard enough, federal ships might be diverted from the blockade to relieve the merchantmen. With that in view, and also with a view to unfurling the Confederate banner around the world, Mallory supported the construction and purchase abroad of commerce raiders. They were not unknown to war; their success depended on leadership, morale, and the stoutness of the ships. Many were commissioned and some reached the high seas. Famed far and wide were the *Sumter, Alabama, Florida, Shenandoah,* and *Stonewall.*

Their captains are inseparable from these fast, well-armed, rakish cruisers that accounted for many northern ships and millions in prizes. The *Sumter* and *Alabama* were commanded by Raphael Semmes, an officer of long and prosaic duty in the "old navy." Much like Stonewall Jackson, Semmes rested on arms for his moment, and when it came, he seized it and became one of the great sea raiders of history. He sailed in the *Sumter* for six months in the Atlantic and Caribbean, received honors from neutral ports, and captured eighteen

Captain John Winslow (3rd from left) and officers pose on board the U.S.S. Kearsarge in 1864 after sinking the Confederate ship Alabama. *(National Archives)*

ships. Trapped at Gibraltar, Semmes abandoned the *Sumter.* His great days were ahead.

President Davis had dispatched Captain James D. Bulloch to England in May 1861 to contract for warships, cruisers, and blockade runners. His surprisingly successful activities in the nether world of diplomatic infighting produced contracts for big and little warships and for myriad blockade runners from Liverpool and Glasgow. The Laird Rams, two double-turret ironclads ordered from John Laird and Sons, were his prime hope, frustrated when the United States frightened Great Britain into impounding them. His great success was a stray ship constructed in the Laird yards under its way number, *290.* Federal agents suspected the purpose of the *290* but could not prove it before it left on a shakedown cruise. A modern vessel, the *290* had every essential for a cruiser—1,000 tons, more than 200 feet long, and, most important, two 300-horsepower engines in addition to sail. Making quickly for the Azores, it received its armament and ammunition and a mixed crew (with many Yankees). On 24 August 1862, off the island of Terceira, its new captain, Semmes, took charge of the *290,* now the *Alabama.*

For two years Semmes and the *Alabama* scourged the high seas. He coursed the Atlantic, the Gulf of Mexico (where he sank the USS *Hatteras*), to Oriental waters, to Cape Town in Africa, and back to the Azores, and finally lost the ship in a fight with the USS *Kearsarge,* 19 June 1864, off Cherbourg, France. He might have been consoled by his record, as he and his men sought ways back to the Confederacy: one ironclad warship (100 tons heavier) sunk; sixty-two vessels captured.

Other cruisers did direct damage, too, but their real impact was on creating fear in the North. Insurance rates soared and a general "flight from the flag" took more than seven hundred American ships to the protection of the British ensign. These raiders set an important precedent that the Russian czar's navy tried to emulate before the First World War.

Blockade running posed a special problem for the Confederate navy. Nominally a private matter, in which great fortunes were often the order of one or two successful trips to and from Bermuda and Wilmington or Nassau and Wilmington, occasionally Havana to Mobile or Galveston, several government agencies became involved in running their own ships through the blockade. Control of free space on these vital runners intruded on the freedom of commerce, but a beleaguered Confederate Congress approved partial nationalization of space on incoming and outgoing ships in early 1864. When the Ordnance Department, under the remarkably able General Josiah Gorgas, bought several runners and ran them in conjunction with the Medical and Quartermaster departments of the War Department, Mallory worked to enhance their efforts. He encouraged the participation of Confederate naval officers in the blockade-running effort by granting official leaves. Several served as captains on harrowing voyages through the Union naval curtain. Not only were the trips important to sustaining a flow of essential supplies, but also in boosting the zest of participants. A careful organization underlay the blockade-running effort. Depots in Bermuda and Nassau received freight from England and the Continent, and the shipments were then transferred to blockade runners for the run to the Confederacy.

The high profits and higher risks of blockade running were run by a kind of shadow cast of captains and crews.

The high profits and higher risks of blockade running were run by a kind of shadow cast of captains and crews unknown save to sponsors and to daring. A successful run in and out might pay for the ship, several runs would indemnify disaster, and anyone whose blood ran high never got enough. Tom Taylor of the blockade runner *Banshee* recalled:

> The night proved dark, but dangerously clear and calm. No lights were allowed—not even a cigar; the engine-room hatchways were covered with tarpaulins, at the risk of suffocating the unfortunate engineers and stokers in the almost insufferable atmosphere below. But it was absolutely imperative that not a glimmer of light should appear. Even the binnacle was covered, and the steersman had to see as much of the compass as he could through a conical aperture carried almost up to his eyes. . . . We steamed on in silence except for the stroke of the engines and the beat of the paddle-floats, which in the calm of the night seemed distressingly loud; all hands were on deck, crouching behind the bulwarks; and we on the bridge, namely, the captain, the pilot, and I, were straining our eyes into the darkness. . . . And fortunate it was for us we so near. Daylight was already breaking, and before we were opposite the fort [Fisher] we could make out six or seven gunboats, which steamed rapidly towards us and angrily opened fire. Their shots were soon dropping close around us; an unpleasant sensation when you know you have several tons of gunpowder under your feet.

Such excitement roiled the blood and made addicts of even the careful men.

How important was blockade running? Ratios of successful runs are impressive: in 1861 blockaders caught one out of ten runners; in 1862, one out of eight; in 1863, one out of four; in 1864, one out of three; in 1865, after most Confederate Atlantic ports were gone, one out of two. Only estimates can be made, but they indicate it was one of the Confederacy's most successful ventures: 330,000 small arms imported for the government from 1861 to 1865; 624,000 pairs of boots; 378,000 blankets. During the one-year period from December 1863 to December 1864, blockade runners brought in 1,933,000 pounds of saltpeter, 1,507,000 pounds of lead, 8,632,000 pounds of meat, 520,000 pounds of coffee, plus much more uncategorized material. Some commercial freighters reached Matamoros, Mexico, which remained open throughout the war, and almost-direct shipments from there to Texas helped sustain the Confederate Trans-Mississippi Department. Quite simply, blockade running extended the Confederacy's life for at least two years.

Did Mallory's efforts fail? In the sense that they did not prevail over federal fleets, yes. An overall view shows that Mallory's innovative efforts, including the rudimentary submarine *Hunley,* which sank the Union corvette *Housatonic* in February 1864, changed the nature of naval war and opened the vision of navies around the world. If he did not secure Confederate independence, he did free naval minds from shackling inhibitions.

Important to the story of the Confederate navy is the fact that the last rebel banner flew on the *Shenandoah*'s

Union soldiers guard captured Confederate troops in a camp near Shenendoah Valley in May 1862. Prisoners-of-war faced extremely harsh conditions during the Civil War; thousands of soldiers, both Union and Confederate, died in prison camps. (National Archives)

mast. It ranged the Atlantic and Pacific beginning in September 1864, was second only to the *Alabama* in destruction, and struck its colors at Liverpool on 6 November 1865.

WHAT KIND OF WAR?

The Civil War began as an old-fashioned war of armies against armies and had evolved, as Bruce Catton observed, into a "war against"—against the enemy, against even civilians. Building its own momentum, it became a great rolling agent of change that freed the slaves; reworked social, economic and political seams in the North and South; and left America forever different.

It was a war of more than 10,500 fights. It was also the first war of the industrial revolution: of machinery and firepower and engineering beyond imaginings; of railroads and iron ships and submarines and rifled cannon; of telegraphs and rudimentary air observation; of massed firepower and the end of massed charges; of machines against gallantry. The costs were also commensurate with new machinery and with new ways of killing. Estimates vary, but adjusted statistics indicate on the Union side 110,100 killed and mortally wounded, 224,580 dead of disease, plus 275,175 wounded and 30,192 prisoner-of-war dead, for 642,427 total casualties of all causes. Confederate figures are more conjectural (no naval figures are available), but a fair assessment gives 94,000 Confederates killed or mortally wounded, 164,000 dead of disease, plus 194,026 wounded and from 26,000 to 31,000 prisoner-of-war dead, for 483,026 total casualties of all causes. Total Civil War deaths from all causes are estimated at least at 623,026, with minimum wounded totals at 471,427, and an overall war casualty figure of 1,125,453. More than 25 percent of the 1861 available manpower of the North and South became casualties of some kind.

Numbers alone do not tell the whole wages of the war. Vast areas of the South stood scorched, ravaged, pillaged, and wrecked by friendly and hostile armies. In both North and South the returning veterans were not the same men as before the war. A dread scythe of maiming and disfiguring passed across their ranks; whole men were hard to find. The lame, broken, and blind lingered as mutant hostages of conflict.

Numbers do offer interpretive aid in assessing the monetary costs of America's great war. Again, figures are disputed, but careful students estimate that northern costs ran to about $8.5 billion and that southern costs could hardly have been less than $6 billion. In addition, there were, of course, intangible horrors to count in hope, pride, courage, and faith that affected psyches, North and South, for generations to the present. In that terrible expense of blood and treasure and intangibles, Americans tested whether they had the courage of their convictions in democracy.

More than anything else, it had been a war about democracy, a war to test whether human freedom or political liberty were the main themes of the American Revolution. Out of the crucible of carnage came an iron decision—all men were forever free. That decision reforged old themes of brotherhood into a new and stronger America. There were scars and sorrows and anguish mixed in a strange, surging thirst for destiny. The Civil War was actually the war of American unification.

BIBLIOGRAPHY

Official Publications

Journal of the Congress of the Confederate States of America, 7 vols. (1904–1905).

Official Records of the Union and Confederate Navies in the War of the Rebellion, 31 vols. (1894–1927).

War of the Rebellion: A Compilation of the Official Records of the Union and Confederate Armies, 128 vols. (1881–1901).

Matthews, James M., ed. *The Statutes at Large of the Confederate States of America* (1862–1864).

———. *The Statutes at Large of the Provisional Government of the Confederate States of America* (1864).

Ramsdell, Charles W., ed. *Laws and Joint Resolutions of the Last Session of the Confederate Congress (November 7, 1864–March 18, 1865) Together with the Secret Acts of Previous Congresses* (1941).

Bibliographies and Atlases

Atlas to Accompany the Official Records of the Union and Confederate Armies (1891–1895, new ed. 1958).

Coletta, Paolo E. *A Bibliography of American Naval History* (1981).

Esposito, Vincent J., ed. *The West Point Atlas of American Wars,* 2 vols. (1959).

Kennedy, Frances H., ed. *The Civil War Battlefield Guide* (1990).

Mitchell, Joseph B. *Decisive Battles of the Civil War* (1955).

Nevins, Allan, Bell I. Wiley, and James I. Robertson. *Civil-War Books: A Critical Bibliography,* 2 vols. (1967–1969).

Steele, Matthew F. *American Campaigns,* 2 vols. (1909).

Photographic Collections

Davis, William C., ed. *The Image of War, 1861–1865,* 6 vols. (1981–1984).

———. *Touched by Fire: A Photographic Portrait of the Civil War,* 2 vols. (1985–1986).

Ketchum, Richard M., ed. *The American Heritage Picture History of the Civil War.* Text by Bruce Catton (1960).

Milhollen, Hirst D., and Milton Kaplan, eds. *Divided We Fought: A Pictorial History of the War, 1861–1865.* Narrative by David Donald (1956).

Miller, Francis T. *The Photographic History of the Civil War,* 10 vols. (1911).

Ward, Geoffrey C., Ric Burns, and Ken Burns. *The Civil War: An Illustrated History* (1990).

Biographies

Ambrose, Stephen E. *Halleck: Lincoln's Chief of Staff* (1962).

Bushong, Millard K. *Old Jube: A Biography of General Jubal A. Early* (1965).

Cleaves, Freeman. *Rock of Chickamauga: The Life of General George H. Thomas* (1948).
———. *Meade of Gettysburg* (1960).
Current, Richard N., ed. *Advance and Retreat: The Memoirs of John Bell Hood* (1959).
Davis, Varina Howell. *Jefferson Davis, Ex-President of the Confederate States of America: A Memoir by His Wife,* 2 vols. (1890).
Dodd, William E. *Jefferson Davis* (1907).
Dowdey, Clifford. *Lee* (1965).
Durkin, Joseph T. *Stephen R. Mallory: Confederate Navy Chief* (1954).
Dyer, John P. *The Gallant Hood* (1950).
Eaton, Clement. *Jefferson Davis* (1977).
Freeman, Douglas Southall. *R. E. Lee: A Biography,* 4 vols. (1934–1935).
———. *Lee's Lieutenants,* 3 vols. (1942–1944).
Fuller, J. F. C. *Grant and Lee: A Study in Personality and Generalship* (1938; rev. ed. 1982).
Gosnell, Harpur A. *Rebel Raider: Being an Account of Raphael Semmes' Cruise in the C.S.S. Sumter* (1948).
Govan, Gilbert, and J. W. Livingood. *A Different Valor: The Story of General Joseph E. Johnston, C.S.A.* (1956).
Grant, U. S. *Personal Memoirs of U. S. Grant,* 2 vols. (1885–1886).
Hart, B. H. Liddell. *Sherman: Soldier, Realist, American* (1929).
Hassler, Warren W. *General George B. McClellan: Shield of the Union* (1957).
Haupt, Herman. *Reminiscences* (1901).
Hebert, Walter H. *Fighting Joe Hooker* (1944).
Heleniak, Roman J., and Lawrence L. Hewitt, eds. *The Confederate High Command and Related Topics: The 1988 Deep Delta Civil War Symposium: Themes in Honor of T. Harry Williams* (1990).
Henderson, G. F. R. *Stonewall Jackson and the American Civil War,* 2 vols. (1919; rev. ed. 1936).
Lamers, William M. *The Edge of Glory: A Biograhy of General William S. Rosecrans* (1961).
Lewis, Lloyd. *Sherman, Fighting Prophet* (1932).
Luthin, Reinhard H. *The Real Abraham Lincoln* (1960).
McFeely, William S. *Grant: A Biography* (1981).
McMurry, Richard M. *John Bell Hood and the War for Southern Independence* (1982).
McWhiney, Grady. *Braxton Bragg and Confederate Defeat* (1969).
Maurice, Frederick. *Robert E. Lee, the Soldier* (1925).
Meade, George G. *The Life and Letters of George Gordon Meade, Major General United States Army,* 2 vols. (1913).
Merrill, J. M. *William Tecumseh Sherman* (1971).
Niven, John. *Gideon Welles: Lincoln's Secretary of the Navy* (1973).
Oates, Stephen B. *With Malice Toward None: The Life of Abraham Lincoln* (1977).
Parks, Joseph H. *General Edmund Kirby Smith, C.S.A.* (1954).
Piston, William G. *Lee's Tarnished Lieutenant: James Longstreet and His Place in Southern History* (1987).
Poore, Ben P. *The Life of Ambrose E. Burnside* (1882).
Randall, James G., and Richard Current. *Lincoln the President,* 4 vols. (1945–1955).
Roberts, W. Adolphe. *Semmes of the Alabama* (1938).
Robertson, James I., Jr. *General A. P. Hill: The Story of a Confederate Warrior* (1987).
Roland, Charles P. *Albert Sidney Johnston: Soldier of Three Republics* (1964).
Roman, Alfred. *The Military Operations of General Beauregard in the War Between the States, 1861–1865,* 2 vols. (1884).
Sandburg, Carl. *Abraham Lincoln: The Prairie Years,* 2 vols. (1926).
———. *Abraham Lincoln: The War Years,* 4 vols. (1939).
Sanger, D. B., and T. R. Hay. *James Longstreet* (1952).
Sears, Stephen W. *George B. McClellan: The Young Napoleon* (1988).
Seitz, Don. *Braxton Bragg: General of the Confederacy* (1924).
Sherman, William T. *Memoirs of William T. Sherman, Written by Himself,* 2 vols. (1875).
Strode, Hudson. *Jefferson Davis,* 3 vols. (1955–1964).
Tate, Allen. *Jefferson Davis: His Rise and Fall* (1929).
Thomas, Benjamin. *Abraham Lincoln: A Biography* (1952).
Thomas, Benjamin P., and Harold M. Hyman. *Stanton: The Life and Times of Lincoln's Secretary of War* (1962).
Thomas, Emory M. *Bold Dragoon: The Life of J. E. B. Stuart* (1986).
Vandiver, Frank E., *Mighty Stonewall* (1957).
Vandiver, Frank E., ed. *Narrative of Military Operations Directed During the Late War Between the States: The Memoirs of Joseph E. Johnston* (1959).
———. *War Memoirs: Autobiographical Sketch and Narrative of the War Between the States: The Memoirs of Jubal A. Early* (1960).
Warner, Ezra J. *Generals in Gray: Lives of the Confederate Commanders* (1959).
———. *Generals in Blue: Lives of the Union Commanders* (1964).
Weigley, Russell F. *Quartermaster-General of the Union Army: A Biography of Montgomery C. Meigs* (1959).
Welles, Gideon. *Diary of Gideon Welles: Secretary of the Navy Under Lincoln and Johnson,* 3 vols. (1911).
Williams, T. Harry. *P. G. T. Beauregard: Napoleon in Gray* (1955).

General Histories of the Civil War

Adams, Michael C. C. *Our Masters, the Rebels: A Speculation on Union Military Failure in the East, 1861–1865* (1978).
Boatner, Mark Mayo, III. *The Civil War Dictionary* (1959).
Catton, Bruce. *This Hallowed Ground* (1956).
———. *The Centennial History of the Civil War,* 3 vols. (1961–1965).
Commager, Henry Steele, ed. *The Blue and the Gray: The Story of the Civil War as Told by Participants,* 2 vols. (1950).
Dornbusch, C. E., comp. *Regimental Publications and Personal Narratives of the Civil War: A Checklist,* 2 vols. (1961–1971).
Dupuy, R. Ernest, and Trevor N. Dupuy. *The Compact History of the Civil War* (1960).
Dyer, Frederick. *A Compendium of the War of the Rebellion* (1959).
Foote, Shelby. *The Civil War: A Narrative,* 3 vols. (1958–1974).
Griess, Thomas E., ed. *The American Civil War* (1980).
Hattaway, Herman, and Archer Jones. *How the North Won: A Military History of the Civil War* (1986).
Long, E. B., and Barbara Long. *The Civil War Day by Day: An Almanac, 1861–1865* (1971).
Luraghi, Raimondo. *Storia della Guerra Civile Americana* (1966).
McPherson, James M. *Battle Cry of Freedom: The Civil War Era* (1988).
Nevins, Allan. *The War for the Union,* 4 vols. (1959–1971).
Randall, J. G., and David Herbert Donald. *The Civil War and Reconstruction,* 2nd ed. (1969).
Roland, Charles P. *An American Iliad: The Story of the Civil War* (1991).
Thomas, Emory M. *The Confederate Nation: 1861–1865* (1979).
Vandiver, Frank E. *Their Tattered Flags: The Epic of the Confederacy* (1970).
Wakelyn, Jon L., ed. *Biographical Dictionary of the Confederacy* (1977).

Campaigns and Battles

Barrett, John G. *Sherman's March Through the Carolinas* (1956).
Bigelow, John. *The Campaign of Chancellorsville* (1910).
Carter, Samuel, III. *The Final Fortress: The Campaign for Vicksburg* (1980).

Catton, Bruce. *A Stillness at Appomattox* (1953).
Coddington, Edwin B. *The Gettysburg Campaign: A Study in Command* (1968).
Connelly, Thomas L. *Army of the Heartland: The Army of Tennessee, 1861–1862* (1967).
———. *Autumn of Glory: The Army of Tennessee. 1862–1865* (1971).
Dowdey, Clifford. *The Seven Days* (1964).
Downey, Fairfax. *Storming the Gateway: Chattanooga, 1863* (1960).
Glatthaar, Joseph T. *The March to the Sea and Beyond: Sherman's Troops in the Savannah and Carolina Campaigns* (1987).
Haskell, Frank A. *The Battle of Gettysburg* (1908).
McDonough, James L. *Shiloh: In Hell Before Night* (1977).
———. *Stones River: Bloody Winter in Tennessee* (1980).
Miers, Earl Schenck. *Web of Victory: Grant at Vicksburg* (1955).
Murfin, J. V. *The Gleam of Bayonets: The Battle of Antietam and the Maryland Campaign of 1862* (1965).
Sears, S. W. *Landscape Turned Red: The Battle of Antietam* (1983).
Sommers, Richard. *Richmond Redeemed: The Siege at Petersburg* (1981).
Stewart, George R. *Pickett's Charge: A Microhistory of the Final Attack at Gettysburg* (1959).
Sword, Wiley. *Shiloh: Bloody April* (1974).
Walker, Peter F. *Vicksburg: A People at War* (1960).

Strategy, Tactics, and Theories of War

Connelly, T. L., and Archer Jones. *The Politics of Command: Factions and Ideas in Confederate Strategy* (1973).
Fuller, J. F. C. "The Place of the Civil War in the Evolution of War." *Army Quarterly* 26 (1933).
Hagerman, Edward. *The American Civil War and the Origins of Modern Warfare* (1988).
Jones, Archer. *Confederate Strategy from Shiloh to Vicksburg* (1961).
———. "Jomini and the Strategy of the American Civil War: A Reinterpretation." *Military Affairs* 34 (Winter 1970).
———. *The Art of War in the Western World* (1987).
McWhiney, Grady, and Perry D. Jamieson. *Attack and Die: Civil War Military Tactics and Southern Heritage* (1982).
Moore, John G. "Mobilization and Strategy in the Civil War." *Military Affairs* 24 (Summer 1960).

The Armies

Cook, Adrian. *The Armies of the Streets: The New York City Draft Riots of 1863* (1974).
Hernon, Joseph. *Celts, Catholics, and Copperheads* (1968).
Jimerson, Randall C. *The Private Civil War: Popular Thought During the Sectional Conflict* (1988).
Linderman, Gerald. *Embattled Courage: The Experience of Combat in the American Civil War* (1987).
Lonn, Ella. *Desertion During the Civil War* (1928).
Martin, Bessie. *Desertion of Alabama Troops from the Confederate Army* (1932).
Meneely, Alexander H. *The War Department, 1861* (1928).
Mitchell, Reid. *Civil War Soldiers: Their Expectations and Experiences* (1988).
Shannon, Fred A. *The Organization and Administration of the Union Army, 1861–1865,* 2 vols. (1928).
Robertson, James I., Jr. *Soldiers Blue and Gray* (1988).
Tatum, Georgia L. *Disloyalty in the Confederacy* (1934).
Wiley, Bell I. *The Life of Johnny Reb: The Common Soldier of the Confederacy* (1943).
———. *The Life of Billy Yank: The Common Soldier of the Union* (1952).

The Navies

Cochran, Hamilton. *Blockade Runners of the Confederacy* (1958).
Gosnell, H. A. *Guns on the Western Waters: The Story of River Gunboats in the Civil War* (1949).
Jones, Virgil C. *The Civil War at Sea,* 3 vols. (1960–1962).
Mahan, A. T. *The Gulf and Inland Waters* (1883).
Perry, Milton F. *Infernal Machines: The Story of Confederate Submarine and Mine Warfare* (1965).
Reed, Rowena. *Combined Operations in the Civil War* (1978).
Scharf, John T. *History of the Confederate States Navy* (1887).
Soley, James R. *The Blockade and the Cruisers* (1883).
Still, W. N. *Confederate Shipbuilding* (1969).
———. *Iron Afloat: The Story of the Confederate Armorclads* (1971).
Wells, Tom H. *The Confederate Navy: A Study in Organization* (1971).
Wise, Stephen R. *Lifeline of the Confederacy: Blockade Running During the War* (1988).
Vandiver, Frank E., ed. *Confederate Blockade Running Through Bermuda, 1861–1865; Letters and Cargo Manifests* (1947).

Black Troops and Slaves

Brewer, James H. *The Confederate Negro: Virginia's Craftsmen and Military Laborers, 1861–1865* (1969).
Cornish, Dudley T. *The Sable Arm: Negro Troops in the Union Army, 1861–1865* (1956).
Durden, Robert F. *The Gray and the Black: The Confederate Debate on Emancipation* (1972).
Genovese, Eugene. *Roll, Jordan, Roll: The World the Slaves Made* (1974).
Glatthaar, Joseph T. *Forged in Battle: The Civil War Alliance of Black Soldiers and White Officers* (1990).
McPherson, James M. *The Struggle for Equality: Abolitionists and the Civil War and Reconstruction* (1964).
———. *The Negro's Civil War: How American Negroes Felt and Acted During the War for Union* (1965).
McPherson, James M., et al. *Blacks in America* (1971).
Mohr, Clarence L. *On the Threshold of Freedom: Masters and Slaves in Civil War Georgia* (1986).
Quarles, Benjamin. *The Negro in the Civil War* (1953).
Wiley, Bell I. *Southern Negroes, 1861–1865* (1938).

Technology

Black, Robert C., III. *The Railroads of the Confederacy* (1952).
Broun, W. LeRoy. "The Red Artillery." *Southern Historical Society Papers* 26 (1898).
Fuller, Claude. *The Rifled Musket* (1958).
Goff, Richard D. *Confederate Supply* (1969).
Gorgas, Josiah. "Ordnance of the Confederacy, I, II." *Army Ordnance* 16 (1936).
Naisawald, L. Van Loan. *Grape and Canister: The Story of the Field Artillery of the Army of the Potomac, 1861–1865* (1960).
Nichols, James L. *The Confederate Quartermaster in the Trans-Mississippi* (1964).
Turner, George E. *Victory Rode the Rails: The Strategic Place of the Railroads in the Civil War* (1953).
Vandiver, Frank E. *Ploughshares into Swords: Josiah Gorgas and Confederate Ordnance* (1952).
Weber, Thomas. *The Northern Railroads in the Civil War, 1861–1865* (1952).
Wise, Jennings Cropper. *The Long Arm of Lee: The History of the Artillery of the Army of Northern Virginia* (1959).

— FRANK E. VANDIVER

Reconstruction and American Imperialism

In 1897 the United States Army operated on a limited budget and mustered only about twenty-eight thousand officers, noncommissioned officers, and enlisted men. Many of the senior officers had entered the army as volunteers in the Civil War thirty-five years earlier and were no longer fit for arduous field service. Five years earlier the army had adopted a new rifle, the Krag-Jörgensen, and gradually distributed the five-shot-magazine shoulder weapon modeled on a Danish design, but some soldiers considered the Krag to be inferior to the standard rifles of the Spanish and German armies. For an industrialized nation populated by 70 million people and having thousands of miles of vulnerable coastline, the U.S. Army was not very imposing.

Not surprisingly, when the German General Staff issued a report in 1897 covering modern military forces, it failed to include the U.S. Army. The report evaluated the armies of most Western countries—among them modest Portugal and little Montenegro—but the U.S. Army was absent from its pages. It would be illuminating to have the German evaluation of the U.S. Army on the eve of the War with Spain in 1898 and deployment to Cuba, Puerto Rico, and the Philippines, events that helped spur the United States to institute a series of military reforms that modernized the army. Some of those reforms had been debated for thirty years.

When the German General Staff issued a report in 1897 covering modern military forces, it failed to include the U.S. Army.

In contrast to the imperial adventures of 1898, during the 1870s, 1880s, and 1890s, the U.S. Army had fallen back on the varied duties it had fulfilled before the Civil War, including patrolling borders, guarding the coasts, exploring and mapping the West, and fighting Indians. In addition, the army took on new or less familiar responsibilities, such as operating military governments in the South and Alaska, suppressing wide-scale labor strikes, and conducting a social experiment of sorts—recruiting and maintaining regular regiments of African-American soldiers under the leadership of white officers. In other words, the army was a multipurpose organization that performed several jobs simultaneously, the nation's "obedient handyman," according to historian Samuel Huntington (1957).

Many army officers, however, wanted to be more than handymen and as early as the 1870s, reform-minded soldiers called for such measures as tripling the size of the army, developing new weapons, and creating a reliable reserve, steps that would prepare the army to conduct war against Europeans or other conventional adversaries. These calls came even before the campaigns against the trans-Mississippi Indian tribes drew to a close. Critics of these reforms—they might be termed "traditionalists"—harped on the high cost of reform and the low chance of such a conventional conflict. Where was the threatening enemy? Would the threat take the form of bombarding North America's coastal cities? The army's fortifications and U.S. Navy coastal defense ships could meet such threats. Might a potential crisis involve a significant deployment of U.S. Army units into a contested Latin American nation in defense of the Monroe Doctrine? Taking such action, the reformers argued, would overtax the military capabilities of the United States. They proposed that the army be designed to meet a conventional enemy, not just the scattered and uncoordinated Indian tribes.

For the last third of the nineteenth century the traditional advocates of a low-cost, multipurpose army had their way. They saw no need for the United States to maintain an up-to-date army commensurate with its economic strength. If a threat arose, they reckoned that the nation would have several months to respond and that thousands of volunteers would spring to the colors. In the meantime, a small, inexpensive army took orders from its civilian leaders—the president and the secretary of war. Claiming fiscal responsibility, and recognizing both historical American concerns over a large standing army and distrust of the officer corps as a military elite, the traditionalists merely sought to keep the kind of army expected by most Americans.

By 1897, however, the picture was changing. Colonial unrest in the Caribbean indicated an increasing possibility of war. As newsboys hawked tabloids on street corners, influential newspaper owners promoted the notion of war for nationalist and imperialist goals. The war they wanted led to the first major overseas deployment of the U.S. Army since Winfield Scott's invasion of Mexico in 1847. The experimental black units contributed to the war's major campaign. When a treaty ended the fighting, the army again operated postwar military governments. After years of functioning as a frontier constabulary and part-time internal police force, and amidst the controversy and confusion of island expeditions, the U.S. Army began to come of age.

RECONSTRUCTION

Postwar military occupations are seldom easy or popular, either with the soldiers on duty or the civilians whose land they occupy. Military forces often have occupied territory after a war using martial law—short-run suspensions of civil government—and sometimes by establishing military governments that supplant civil officials altogether for longer stretches of time. During much of their history, the British and Americans have displayed a deep distrust of standing armies as engines of tyranny. The English provided a specific example of military government at work following the English Civil Wars (1642–1646 and 1648–1651). After ordering the execution of King Charles in 1649, General Oliver Cromwell established a dictatorship, disbanded Parliament, and in 1655 divided the nation into eleven military districts, each administered by a general. Cromwell's protectorate was a short-lived aberration in England's heritage of constitutional government and civil law.

Two centuries later, northerners and southerners faced the daunting task of binding up the self-inflicted wounds resulting from the American Civil War. In contrast to the traumatic English example, U.S. civil gov-

Columbia, South Carolina, shown here in 1865, lay in ruins after the Civil War, as did much of the South. The soldiers of the Union Army were the logical force to carry out Reconstruction. (National Archives)

ernment continued to function on the national level. Congress met in regular sessions, and Vice President Andrew Johnson succeeded to the office of president, as called for in the U.S. Constitution, after the assassination of Abraham Lincoln. The southern situation was more chaotic. Confederate armies surrendered in the spring of 1865, and thousands of ex-Confederate soldiers began returning home. The war's campaigns had devastated some southern cities and parts of several states. Nearly 4 million African-Americans had discarded the shackles of slavery, but their new freedom was ill-defined. In Louisiana, Arkansas, and Tennessee, governments approved by Lincoln himself had been laboratories of Reconstruction, a contemporary term denoting the steps that would have to be taken to restore the Union. Elsewhere in the South, the collapse of the Confederacy had disrupted southern government and judicial process at the local and state levels.

Across the nation more than one million soldiers wore the blue uniform of the Union army, and they were the logical force to carry out Reconstruction. There were not enough U.S. marshals or agents of the Treasury Department to act either as temporary federal policemen or as administrators. In other words, under the pressures of the time, no existing federal agency other than the army possessed the size or strength to reconstruct the South.

Although the influence of the army over civil affairs was unique in U.S. history, it was not without precedent. After the Mexican War (1846–1848), U.S. Army units occupied parts of Mexico, including the capital, Mexico City. For several months they operated under martial law, supervising local elections, policing saloons and streets, and holding courts-martial to hear cases involving U.S. soldiers and Mexican nationals. When negotiators completed the Treaty of Guadalupe Hidalgo, the U.S. Army gladly left Mexico. Meanwhile, other army officers administered a territorial government in California, part of the land taken from Mexico in the war. Military governors there enforced the law, suppressed civil unrest, and drafted a constitution, paving the way for California statehood in 1850. No field manual was ever produced describing the successes and pitfalls of military administration in either Mexico or California. In retrospect this is not surprising, given the lack of attention to formal doctrine in the army during the nineteenth century.

Without written doctrine for guidance, Union army officers—often volunteers or political appointees, such as Benjamin F. Butler and Nathaniel P. Banks—undertook Reconstruction duties in Louisiana, Arkansas, and Tennessee before the end of the Civil War. The generals acted independently with little direction from Washington. As the need arose, they removed mayors and councilmen, jailed newspaper editors, cleaned city gutters to protect public health, and ordered units to patrol streets and roads. Moreover, the army issued thousands of its rations to the destitute, both black and white. Military officers in several southern states also operated banks and railroads, arranged for labor contracts between planters and the freedmen, supervised orphanages and almshouses, and licensed gaming establishments.

After Johnson took the oath as president, he moved quickly to take control of Reconstruction. A southerner, former slaveholder, and lifelong Democrat, Johnson acted without consulting Congress. On 29 May 1865 he issued his Proclamation of Pardon and Amnesty, designed to accomplish a speedy restoration of the Union. Accordingly, he recognized the Lincoln governments in Louisiana, Arkansas, and Tennessee, moved exiled Unionist Virginians from West Virginia to Richmond, and appointed provisional governors for the rest of the Confederate states. The president wanted the army to cooperate with the provisional governors while continuing to perform its ad hoc roles as part-time police force, occasional judge and jury, and short-term administrator for various banks and businesses.

Johnson needed the presence of the army in the South for his plan to work. He required the civil governors to act promptly in registering voters and ensuring that new state constitutions were drafted to abolish slavery, void Civil War debts, and nullify ordinances of secession. Statewide elections would then be held for all offices. His aim was to have all this done by the time Congress reconvened in the winter. In pushing for a quick Reconstruction, Johnson specified nothing for the former slaves and opposed the recently created Freedmen's Bureau as unnecessary and unconstitutional.

On the other hand, Johnson treated the Union's enemies leniently. The president gave a blanket pardon to most southerners who fought in the rebellion but excepted many high-ranking civil officials, senior rebel military officers (colonel and above), and anyone who, in his words, "voluntarily participated in said rebellion and the estimated value of whose taxable property was over $20,000." Johnson aimed this barb of his plan at rich southern planters, but there was a loophole. Anyone denied a pardon (and therefore denied participation in politics) was permitted to apply for a personal pardon from Johnson. In the next six months he gave out hundreds of pardons to ex-Confederate officials and planters, the very men who had favored secession or led the war to break up the Union. Thus, the president let slip the opportunity to temporarily exclude the economic, political, and military leadership of the Confederacy from the process of forming and operating new governments in the South. Johnson's indulgent pardoning scheme drew opposition from moderate Republicans in Congress, emboldened ex-Confederates, and made the soldiers' roles as policemen and managers of civil affairs more difficult.

Meanwhile, the army cooperated with the Bureau of Refugees, Freedmen, and Abandoned Lands, a federal agency established on 3 March 1865. Major General Oliver Otis Howard served as commissioner of the Freedmen's Bureau. Other army officers or former officers filled slots as state superintendents and local agents. The Freedmen's Bureau fulfilled many functions, including arranging employment for blacks and determining their wages, opening special courts to hear cases involving freedmen, operating schools, and handing out rations. Had the president supported the bureau, it no doubt would have accomplished even more than it did. Nevertheless, as an agency of the War Department, the Freedmen's Bureau was a remarkable experiment in social welfare.

A small, experimental agency was one thing, but even Republicans in Congress could not support retaining a one-million-man army now that the war was over. During the summer of 1865, the War Department began mustering out the Union army. Not even the short-lived prospect of war with France over its occupation of Mexico slowed the process. By Christmas of 1865 most of the volunteers who had marched under Ulysses S. Grant, George G. Meade, Philip H. Sheridan, and William T. Sherman were civilians again. In January 1866 only 123,000 soldiers remained in uniform.

Hundreds of black volunteers found soldiering to their liking and wanted to stay in the nation's service.

Many of the soldiers still on duty were African-Americans, who had made up more than 10 percent of Union forces. Hundreds of black volunteers found soldiering to their liking and wanted to stay in the nation's service. Subsequently (in July 1866), the War Department gained authorization from Congress to create the first black units in the regular army, four regiments of infantry and two of cavalry. These units represented an unusual social experiment. Although conservative politicians tried to have them disbanded, the segregated black regiments, under the command of white officers, remained a part of the army until the Korean War. In these regiments black citizens demonstrated their abilities as soldiers and were a visible reminder that blacks were no longer slaves.

In the meantime, relations between President Johnson and Congress grew tense and antagonistic. Congress exercised its prerogative to determine the validity of its own members, and in December 1865 rejected the southern representatives, including several notable former Confederates, elected under Johnson's state governments. Thus, Congress rejected the president's Reconstruction plan. Early the next year he vetoed both a civil rights bill and a bill to extend the Freedmen's Bureau. Congress later passed the two measures over the president's veto, but both moderate and radical Republicans had reason to be concerned.

Encouraged by Johnson's restricted view of federal power, the southern state legislatures separately enacted Black Codes, which restricted the rights of freedmen. Race riots occurred in Norfolk, Virginia (April), Memphis, Tennessee (May), and New Orleans, Louisiana (July), each with particular local causes but all sharing the themes of conflict between the races and white desperation at the thought of blacks holding offices or jobs that had been denied to them in the days of slavery. In each case, army commanders acted hesitantly and failed to head off the violence.

The race riots, Johnson's vetoes and lenient restoration plan, and the South's recalcitrant attitude—including passing the Black Codes, electing former Confederates, and rejecting the proposed Fourteenth Amendment—prompted Republicans in Congress to pass a series of laws that took the reins of Reconstruction from the president. On 2 March 1867 congressional Republicans passed over Johnson's veto the first Military Reconstruction Act, officially styled "An Act to Provide for the More Efficient Government of the Rebel States." Subsequent Military Reconstruction Acts clarified or added powers not well-defined in the first one. Collectively, these laws divided the former Confederate states into five military districts. (Tennessee, which had ratified the Fourteenth Amendment, was exempted.) Each of these districts would be commanded by an army general appointed by the president, but the civil governments cobbled together under Johnson's original plan would no longer have legal standing. Civilian officials and state judges would keep their posts only at the sufferance of the army and could be removed from office by the district commanders.

The Reconstruction Acts conferred considerable responsibility on the generals. Military courts could supplant civil courts if necessary, and the generals supervised the drafting of new state constitutions in

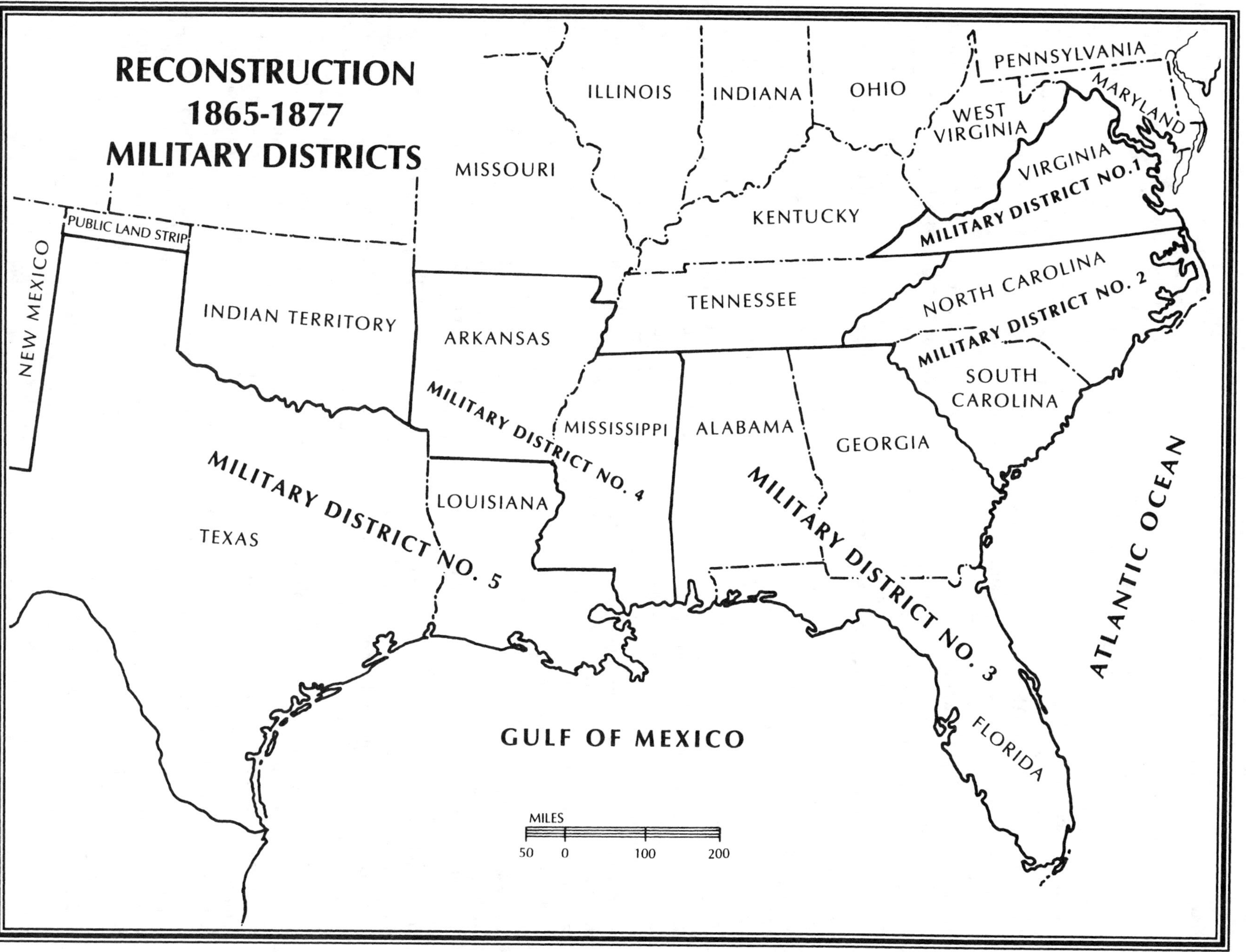
RECONSTRUCTION
1865-1877
MILITARY DISTRICTS
ILLINOIS
INDIANA
OHIO
PENNSYLVANIA
WEST VIRGINIA
MARYLAND
VIRGINIA
MILITARY DISTRICT NO. 1
MISSOURI
KENTUCKY
PUBLIC LAND STRIP
NEW MEXICO
INDIAN TERRITORY
ARKANSAS
TENNESSEE
NORTH CAROLINA
MILITARY DISTRICT NO. 2
SOUTH CAROLINA
MILITARY DISTRICT NO. 4
MISSISSIPPI
ALABAMA
GEORGIA
MILITARY DISTRICT NO. 5
LOUISIANA
TEXAS
MILITARY DISTRICT NO. 3
ATLANTIC OCEAN
FLORIDA
GULF OF MEXICO
MILES
50
0
100
200

conventions. All adult males (including blacks) would be able to vote for delegates to these conventions, except former Confederates temporarily denied the right to hold office under the terms of the proposed Fourteenth Amendment. Furthermore, the Reconstruction Acts required that the new state constitutions enfranchise the freedmen. After the delegates drafted the state's constitution, elections would take place for approving or rejecting the constitution and electing men to state offices and the U.S. Congress. The new state legislatures would have to ratify the Fourteenth Amendment before a state's congressional leaders would be eligible to assume their places in Washington. When Congress gave permission for southern congressmen and senators to take their seats, military reconstruction would end and the state's civil government could begin exercising its legal authority.

The use of the U.S. Army by Congress to implement Reconstruction's unusual political changes was a radical step in U.S. history. Certainly, it seemed that way to many nineteenth-century Americans, especially most white southerners and many northern Democrats. Congressional Reconstruction instituted political changes that carried significant social implications, requiring that state constitutions give certain types of persons (African-American men) the right to vote. Moreover, in order for a state's senators and congressmen to regain their voices, Congress demanded that state legislatures ratify a proposed amendment to the U.S. Constitution.

No doubt it would have been possible to make the process more radical. Congress could have included provisions banning top Confederates from voting and holding office for many years. Confiscated or federal lands might have been given to the freedmen, and a federally supported system of schools and colleges for blacks could have been provided. These steps, in addition to the radical ones that were taken, probably would have meant greater results for Reconstruction and, likewise, a longer involvement of the army in the South.

As it was, congressional leaders were unable to put their plan into effect without President Johnson. In his role as commander in chief, he chose the generals who supervised the military districts. General Grant exerted some influence on Johnson's choices, which included John M. Schofield for the First District (Virginia), Daniel E. Sickles for the Second District (North and South Carolina), John Pope for the Third District (Georgia, Florida, and Alabama), Edward O. C. Ord for the Fourth District (Mississippi and Arkansas), and Sheridan for the Fifth District (Louisiana and Texas).

These and other generals were divided in their attitudes toward Reconstruction. A conservative at heart, Schofield opposed black suffrage and doubted the propriety of the congressional acts, but he enforced them unflinchingly and removed pro-Confederate politicians, including a governor. Ord was moderate on the race issue but evolved into a stern administrator. Pope, Sickles, and Sheridan favored congressional Reconstruction. Sheridan removed the governors of both Texas and Louisiana. The radical trio enforced the acts of Congress in a scrupulous fashion and therefore ran afoul of Johnson in the coming months. General Sherman was uncomfortable with military Reconstruction but believed that ex-Confederates had failed to accommodate themselves to the outcome of the war. General Grant concluded that the Republicans, and not Johnson, had the right idea about the nation's needs during Reconstruction and acted in concert with the leaders of Lincoln's party. Other generals, such as Winfield Scott Hancock and Meade, either were Democrats or wished for a speedy and easy restoration.

During 1867 and into 1868, the generals pushed to complete the congressional plan. Showing their disgust for the Reconstruction Acts, various southern state and local officials resigned. The district commanders removed others, usually after they had obstructed federal laws, discriminated against blacks, or in some other way had been "impediments to Reconstruction," in the phrase used by the generals. Local and state offices of all kinds thus fell vacant, and the district commanders filled them with their appointees.

Johnson demonstrated his opposition to congressional Reconstruction by removing four of the district commanders. At the president's order, in August 1868, General Edward R. S. Canby stepped in for Sickles, and General Hancock, an outspoken conservative, took over for Sheridan. Reversing or watering down some of Sheridan's directives in the Fifth District, Hancock scored points with his Democratic supporters. Canby turned out to be one of the most evenhanded district commanders, but he enforced the letter of the law and southerners did not like him. In December, again at Johnson's order, Major General Meade, recognized as a moderate, replaced Pope, and Major General Alvin Gillem took Ord's place. To Johnson's surprise, and demonstrating how difficult it was to predict a general's actions, Meade deposed the governor of Georgia and made an army officer acting governor.

On top of his reassignments of Sheridan, Sickles, Pope, and Ord, Johnson removed Secretary of War Edwin M. Stanton in August and replaced him with temporary substitutes, including Generals Grant and Schofield. Stanton protested Johnson's actions, and the radicals in Congress had hoped to protect Stanton with the Tenure of Office Act, a law of dubious constitutionality passed over Johnson's veto on 2 March. As

Harold Hyman argues in a landmark essay (1960), with military forces in both the West and the South, Johnson was commander in chief of what were essentially two distinct armies, so different were their missions. The Republicans let the president control the Indian-fighting army but opposed him when he began interfering with the Reconstruction army.

The showdown resulted in Johnson's impeachment on 24 February 1868. According to the U.S. Constitution, impeachment proceedings could be applied to any federal officeholder for "treason, bribery, or other high crimes and misdemeanors." Two-thirds of the House of Representatives were needed to impeach (indict) an official and two-thirds of the Senate needed to convict and remove him. The impeachment power had been used sparingly since 1789. Eight of the eleven items on the Johnson bill of impeachment dealt in some way with the removal of Stanton. The ninth item concerned the president's supposed violation of another dubious law, passed on 2 March 1867, the Command of the Army Act, which supposedly required the president to send all orders to the army by way of General of the Army Grant. The two other items were poorly phrased or vaguely worded catchalls drawn up to snare the votes of senators who might not go along with the first nine. In May 1868, Johnson escaped conviction and removal by only one vote in the Senate, but the impeachment and trial combined to restrain the president. His personal political aspirations now curtailed, Johnson had slowed the process but failed to block the path of the nation's Reconstruction.

The army guided the southern states down that path, but violence marred the process prescribed by Congress. Shootings, assaults, and arson took place in numbers that indicated the army had too few soldiers to police the entire region. Former Confederates realized that they could commit these crimes with impunity. At the same time, while they prosecuted a form of guerrilla warfare, southern Democrats complained loudly about "bayonet rule" and "military despotism." By using such loaded terms, the Democrats were implying that the U.S. Army was acting illegally or improperly to carry out the Reconstruction Acts passed by Congress. If violence threatened or occurred, the army usually re-

After the Civil War, the U.S. Army was a familiar presence in cities and settlements west of the Mississippi. In this photograph, a company of infantry parades through Kearney, Nebraska, in 1888. (National Archives)

sponded as a *posse comitatus*. Marching or riding with local sheriffs or U.S. marshals who requested their aid, the soldiers assisted the civilian lawmen in making arrests. Sometimes the army acted on its own and arrested suspects without civilian officials present, although mayors, governors, or state attorneys-general could call for the army's assistance.

According to the U.S. Constitution, impeachment proceedings could be applied to the President for "treason, bribery, or other high crimes and misdemeanors."

In June 1868, seven former Confederate states had completed the requirements of the Military Reconstruction Acts. At one stroke Alabama, Arkansas, Florida, Georgia, Louisiana, North Carolina, and South Carolina all regained their representation in Congress and thereby were readmitted to the Union. Army units remained stationed in the South, not only garrisoning posts, forts, and arsenals that they had used in the antebellum years, but also occupying barracks in some of the region's larger cities.

In both the recently readmitted states and those that had not yet met the requirements, the army guarded the southern polls during the presidential election of 1868. The Republicans nominated General Grant, and former Governor Horatio Seymour of New York was the choice of the Democrats. In several states vigilante groups such as the Ku Klux Klan intimidated white Republicans and the newly enfranchised freedmen. The Klan and similar organizations, such as the Knights of the White Camelia in Louisiana, presented a significant challenge to the army. By the fall of 1868, fewer than eighteen thousand soldiers occupied the South, and they were unable to guard every ballot box, protect the life of each Republican, or patrol every highway. The Klan rode, day and night, threatening or shooting Republicans, burning houses and schools, escaping ahead of army patrols. Brigadier General Lovell H. Rousseau, one of Hancock's successors and President Johnson's political friend, commanded troops in Louisiana during the election. Rousseau's tardy actions were either inept or disingenuous, and despite a large black voting population, Louisiana and Georgia went for Seymour in his losing bid for the presidency.

After Grant's election, the army was still faced with the task of preparing the remaining southern states for readmission. Texas, by virtue of its size, frontier conditions, and confused political circumstances, was particularly troublesome. Military commanders had to worry about hostile Indians in the central and western parts of the state. Following Sheridan's departure, General Joseph J. Reynolds eventually commanded the troops in Texas, and although he devoted considerable time to the Indians and the frontier, he became involved in state politics as a Republican and sought election as U.S. senator from Texas. Reynolds ordered his troops to suppress Klanlike groups in east Texas. In some cases the lawless men were simply bandits, and the army assisted U.S. marshals in tracking them down. In a few cases politically motivated vigilantes directly confronted the army, but usually they dispersed or escaped before the soldiers arrived on the scene. Until Texas was readmitted in 1870, trials for some lawbreakers were held before military commissions.

Georgia was another difficult test for the army. The Georgia legislature balked at seating some elected black representatives, and in December 1869 the state went back under military control. The Freedmen's Bureau had documented more than three hundred cases of politically inspired assault in Georgia during 1868. In 1870, President Grant sent General Alfred H. Terry to replace Meade. Terry established a special three-officer board to hear the cases involving the disputed legislative seats. Eventually the Georgia legislature was reconstituted, and, after it ratified the Fifteenth Amendment, which prohibits the denial of suffrage on account of race, the state's congressmen and senators were reseated in 1870. Virginia also completed Reconstruction in 1870.

After the readmission of the southern states, the army's role in the South diminished, but it never was completely without influence, especially in South Carolina and Louisiana. The generals no longer operated military commissions, but Republican governors (and sometimes Democratic ones) called on the army to enforce civil law and keep the peace. During the 1870s the army continued to provide guards at polling places on election days, and occasionally soldiers acted as referees between rival claimants to gubernatorial offices in southern states.

During the 1870s the army's duties were made more difficult by the declining numbers of troops available for duty in the South. At the time of the Military Reconstruction Acts, more than twenty-thousand soldiers were in the southern states. One year later there were fewer than eighteen thousand, and by late 1869 there were only slightly more than eleven thousand troops occupying the territory of the old Confederacy. The number continued to decline in succeeding years for three reasons. First, and perhaps most important, was the need for more soldiers to fight the Indians on the Plains. The second reason was that the longer Reconstruction lasted, the less support it received from northerners and Congress as they turned their attention to the Indian wars, western settlement, and business expansion. The third reason for declining troop strength in support of Reconstruction also pertained to economics. The nineteenth-century Congress was much more tightfisted than the free-spending solons of the twentieth century. Politicians, especially Democrats, minutely scrutinized War Department budgets and often reduced them to the bare minimum to allow operations. Congress demanded reductions in the size of the regular army from sixty thousand in 1865 to about thirty thousand in 1871, and to about twenty-seven thousand in 1876. When all the former Confederate states gained readmission in 1870, there were fewer and fewer troops to go around.

Increasingly, officers avoided Reconstruction duty by taking extended leaves, going on recruiting duty, or accepting assignments away from their regiments. In letters or in testimony before congressional committees, they expressed their desire to be out of the South and serving instead on the frontier. Officers who later wrote memoirs described at length their experiences in the West, but often skipped over their service in the South altogether or mentioned it only briefly. After 1870 some army officers became impatient with escorting U.S. marshals, arresting moonshiners who refused to pay federal revenue taxes, or chasing down white-sheeted Klansmen in South Carolina. Such actions offered no opportunity for glory or advancement, and many officers thought it was duty without honor.

Despite these attitudes, however, officers and soldiers carried out their assigned tasks in the latter part of Reconstruction, rendering invaluable aid to black and white Republicans and supporting the legally elected state governments. Moreover, the officers in the South often had to act with very little guidance from their superiors in Washington. The secretary of war, the adjutant general, and President Grant all usually left important decisions to the officer on the scene.

For a time it appeared that organizations like the Ku Klux Klan would sweep the South and remove all the Republicans from their elected offices. General Terry suggested that the army pick one state and kill the Klan at the roots. Acting under Enforcement Acts passed by Congress in 1870–1871, to enforce the Fourteenth and Fifteenth Amendments, President Grant singled out South Carolina. The army went to work there with a vengeance against the Klan; army units also acted in other states. Several companies of the Seventh Cavalry were sent into nine South Carolina counties where the president had declared martial law. Patrols were constant and U.S. marshals with strong military escorts arrested hundreds of Klansmen. The Klansmen stood trial in regular federal courts and dozens were convicted. Others were set free, but at least for a time they had been incarcerated and out of circulation.

Army patrols and federal prosecutors broke the power of the Klan, but former Confederates switched tactics. They formed "gun clubs" that claimed to be "hunting" on election days when actually they were stalking their quarry near polling places. Other Democrats used economic threats against blacks—reduced wages, loss of jobs, or the like—to get them to vote for Democrats or to sit out elections. Despite Democratic sniping, murder, and arson, brave Republican precinct leaders (white and black), vocal newspaper editors, and courageous elected officials continued to hold out in several southern states. As historian George C. Rable emphasizes (1984), the Democrats fine-tuned their use of violence in order to bring down Republican administrations in the South.

As for election duty in the 1870s, the army's main job was to keep the peace. Commanders did not always wait for civil authorities to invite them to act. In the larger cities military commanders paraded their soldiers through the main streets to discourage violence. Troops watched voters in selected precincts or patrolled entire wards where violence was likely to occur. After the election was over, soldiers usually guarded the ballot boxes themselves to prevent tampering or fraud.

Former Confederates formed "gun clubs" that claimed to be "hunting" on election days when actually they were stalking quarry near polling places.

The General Amnesty Act of 1872 allowed more ex-Confederates to participate legally in politics once again. They registered to vote in great numbers, and, combined with their selective use of terror and intimidation, the Democrats won back control of southern state governments one by one. Furthermore, revelations of corruption in the Grant administration and a lessening in Republican radicalism resulted in what some historians later termed a "retreat from Reconstruction."

Rivalry between claimants to governorships involved the army in two states before the election turmoil of

1876–1877. Two Republicans in Arkansas, Joseph Brooks and Elisha Baxter, claimed to have been elected governor in 1872. Democrats supported Baxter, if only to divide the Arkansas Republican party. Baxter held office from 1872 until 1874, when he was ousted by Brooks. The commander of the army garrison at Little Rock, Captain Thomas E. Rose, believed at first that he could maintain order until the authorities in Washington decided which of the claimants deserved the office, but he had a difficult time keeping the militias of the two "governors" apart. Outside of Little Rock the two sides clashed in several bloody encounters and Rose was helpless. Finally, President Grant recognized Baxter and ordered both militias to disperse. Rose breathed a sigh of relief when the antagonists did as the president ordered.

In Louisiana the situation was even more complex, but in the final analysis both the army and the Grant administration supported the Republican claimants to office. Fearing a yellow-fever epidemic in 1874, the army garrisoned Louisiana with only a handful of soldiers. These few failed to stop the overthrow of the Republican governor, William Pitt Kellogg, in September 1874. Several thousand armed men attacked the state militia and took possession of the state capitol in New Orleans. Only one company (about forty soldiers) was in the city at the time, and they elected to remain out of the fighting, in which twenty-five men were killed and more than one hundred wounded.

In a matter of hours the telegraph lines were buzzing between Washington and General William Emory's temporary headquarters in Mississippi. Troops were sent from Mississippi to New Orleans, arriving within a matter of hours after the fighting. President Grant issued an executive proclamation demanding that the rebels disperse within five days or face the might of the U.S. Army. The Democrats who had engineered the coup denied that they were usurping the government and boldly asked for recognition from Grant. Two days after the takeover, General Emory arrived in New Orleans, and soon he was supported by more than seven hundred soldiers from three regiments. The Democrats reluctantly yielded possession of the capitol and other state buildings they had captured and occupied. Kellogg resumed his office a couple of days later, after army Colonel John R. Brooke had temporarily acted as military governor.

By 1876 only three southern states still had Republican governors—Louisiana, South Carolina, and Florida. Following the disputed presidential election of 1876—when Republicans successfully challenged the votes of four states accused of irregularities, leading to the election of their candidate Rutherford B. Hayes—soldiers protected the Republican claimants to the governorships of South Carolina and Louisiana until the new president decided to withdraw the army's support and allow the Democratic candidates to become governors of the two states. In each state before the election the Democrats had carried out programs of intimidation against black and white Republicans. The results of each election are shrouded in the fog of fraud and violence, and the debate will continue as to who would have won in a fair, open, and nonviolent contest. Hayes, however, allowed the Democrats to take office, and Reconstruction and the army's unique role in it finally came to an end in April 1877.

Reconstruction was the army's second significant experience with military government, but it lasted much longer than such duties after the Mexican War. During Reconstruction the army had to occupy some of the states of its own nation, contribute to rebuilding their economies, and support the creation of a new social order, imperfect as it was. A few officers, such as Sheridan and Pope, enforced the Military Reconstruction Acts to the letter, and a few others, such as Hancock and Rousseau, tried to circumvent the laws or sided with the Democrats. Most officers, however, tried to administer the extraordinary laws evenhandedly. The federal government's policies on Reconstruction changed from president to president and from year to year. After the ratification of the Fourteenth and Fifteenth Amendments and the readmission of the former Confederate states, many northerners and members of Congress lost interest in Reconstruction, leaving small army detachments to stand between resurgent ex-Confederates and vulnerable Republicans. All of that made Reconstruction the most difficult peacetime duty in the army's history.

THE INDIAN-FIGHTING ARMY

By 1870 the army had completed its legally mandated duties called for under the Military Reconstruction Acts, and senior military officers began turning their attention to other matters—a war in Europe, reform of the services, and Indian-fighting in the trans-Mississippi West. For its traditional, dangerous, and thankless task of fighting Indians, the army had developed no doctrine either before or after the Civil War. Having no set of accepted tactical guidelines for Indian wars, and no strategy for that matter, the burden again fell on individual commanders and resulted in haphazard application of military force.

As was the case with Reconstruction in the South, the army dealt regularly with civilians in the West. Southern duties brought the army into contact with the Freedmen's Bureau, its agents, teachers, and, of course,

Some Indians served as scouts for the U.S. Army. These Warm Spring scouts posed in 1873 in Lava Beds, California. Their leader, called Donald McKay, stands in the center. (National Archives)

the freedmen themselves. High-ranking officers met with members of Congress and the cabinet and eastern reformers who wanted to improve the lot of the freedmen. Soldiers interracted with southerners from all walks of life as well as with politicians of both parties. In a similar fashion, western duties called for the army to work with the agents of the Bureau of Indian Affairs (part of the Interior Department, not the War Department) and, of course, with the Indians themselves. In Washington, senior officers, especially Commanding General of the Army Sherman and the adjutant general, met with members of Congress and the cabinet and eastern philanthropic organizations who debated how to protect, educate, and "civilize" the Indians. Local, state, and territorial politicians in the West alternately condemned the army for its timidity or complimented its field campaigns. In most cases these same politicians sought to gain or keep forts or army depots in the area they represented. On many occasions soldiers came in contact with ranchers, settlers, businessmen, railroad workers, and miners between the Canadian and Mexican borders. Western expansion and settlement called for the army to build roads, map the country, guard railroads, purchase goods and services, deliver the mail, provide medical care to civilians, and protect Indian reservations. After the collapse of the wartime and immediate postwar treaties with several Indian tribes, the army demonstrated its flexibility in numerous ways in the West, even as some of its main units, such as the Seventh Cavalry, remained on duty in the South. As in the southern states, the army in the West had too few soldiers to accomplish everything that everyone wanted. The territory it covered was too vast and the demands too many.

The army approached Indian warfare by combining several factors. Soldiers built forts and depots and set up temporary cantonments to keep pace with the settlers and railroad construction. In fact, railroad resupply often helped maintain and move army units in the trans-Mississippi. The forts and supply depots provided bases from which expeditions took the field. Typical forts, unlike the ones in Hollywood films or television melodramas, were not surrounded by wooden palisades. Instead, rows of clapboard buildings clustered around a large parade ground. Usually garrisoned by a combination of infantry and cavalry units, most forts had a lifespan of ten or fifteen years before they were closed and their units consolidated at a larger post, often near a town or city.

When a crisis loomed or a clash occurred between Indians and whites, the soldiers, usually the cavalry but sometimes a joint column of horse and infantry units, sortied from the fort to restore order. They arrested whites who illegally crossed onto Indian lands and returned marauding Indians to their reservations. Routinely, small detachments of ten to twenty troopers went on patrols (called "scouts"), checking for signs of Indian raiders or wayward hunting parties, watching for white miners or settlers who trespassed on the reservations, and making maps of the region. Like modern police cars cruising sectors of urban terrain in order to deter or detect criminal activity, army units typically performed a police function rather than preparing for and conducting large-scale combat operations.

In the unusual event of a major campaign, the army's senior officer in the West outlined a plan of action for four or five heavy columns of soldiers. Lieutenant General Sheridan sketched out the opening movements of the multicolumn campaigns of 1874–1875 and 1876–1878, the two largest such efforts in the trans-Mississippi Indian wars. He left most of the details of the 1870s campaigns to the column commanders and their subordinates and declined to take the field in either case. Although Sheridan relied on multiple columns, the tactic had been suggested before the Civil War by Winfield Scott and Montgomery Meigs. When they caught Indians ensconced in a lightly guarded winter encampment (as happened in 1868 and 1874), soldiers inflicted devastating defeats on the tribes.

To patrol the West the army recruited volunteers, as was the standard practice in times without a major war. At any one time, perhaps 50 percent of U.S. soldiers were European-born immigrants recently arrived in eastern cities. The typical enlistment was for five years, and military service allowed the immigrant-soldiers, mostly Irish, to become acclimated to America, earn some money (about $13 a month for a private), and receive free transportation to the West.

In the months following the Civil War the army's Ordnance Department concluded that a new standard issue rifle was needed for the service—a breechloader rather than the old-style muzzleloader. Accordingly, after testing several weapons, the Ordnance Department adopted the Model 1873 Springfield rifle, originally a .50–.70 caliber. After additional experimenting, the caliber was changed to .45–.70 for the infantry version and .45–.55 for the shorter cavalry carbine. The Model 1873 possessed advantages over the standard issue infantry shoulder weapon of the Civil War, the .58-caliber Springfield Model 1855 (modified in 1861). The Model 1873 was breechloaded rather than muzzleloaded, and it accepted a centerfire copper cartridge rather than using a tear-open paper cartridge that contained the so-called minié ball. The cartridges for the Model 1873 still used heavy-grain black powder, however, rather than a fine-grain fast-burning powder, and, like the earlier Springfield rifles, was only single shot. A soldier fed one round at a time through a pop-up door in the top of the barrel, thus giving the Model 1873 its distinctive nickname, the "trapdoor" Springfield. Until the changeover was complete, some cavalry units still carried other carbine models, including the seven-shot Spencer.

Although the trapdoor Springfield had some advantages, there was a problem with its ejector mechanism. After a soldier fired ten or fifteen shots, the barrel became hot, sometimes causing the soft copper base of the cartridge to stick in the breech. The trooper needed a knife to pry out the spent shell before inserting a new round. Having to take such action in the midst of combat was, of course, both disconcerting and potentially dangerous. Nevertheless, the trapdoor Springfield became the army's standard shoulder weapon. The rifle possessed tremendous stopping power: When its large bullet hit either man or beast, the target came down. It provided the added advantage of uniformity of ammunition among infantry and cavalry units. The Ordnance Department expected the single-shot rifle to reduce ammunition expenditure and therefore cost less to use than an updated version of the seven-shot Spencer carbine, which had been issued to some Union cavalry regiments in the Civil War.

Not every soldier was satisfied with the trapdoor Springfield, but an overwhelming number responded favorably to the Ordnance Department's selection of other items. The .45-caliber 1872 Colt pistol became the standard-issue sidearm. Popular with civilians as well as soldiers, the "Peacemaker," as the pistol was called, had been issued to most units by 1874. Some troopers obtained canvas or leather cartridge belts on their own, but by 1876 such belts were general issue, replacing the old-style, flip-open cartridge boxes. In the years to come, the Ordnance and Quartermaster departments continued to make modifications in weapons, uniforms, and equipment.

Utilizing this equipment against the Sioux, Cheyenne, Comanche, Apache, or other tribes severely tested the army and its conventional, constabulary organization. When the army changed from police patrols to larger campaigns, it demonstrated spotty performance against the guerrillalike tribesmen. Although Indians seldom used prearranged battle plans, they naturally sought any advantage that terrain or weather provided and relied upon stealth, surprise, speed of movement, and deception. Combining such concepts or military principles sometimes produced victories for the Indians, especially against isolated or poorly led army detachments. At other times the Indians abandoned their villages and fought rearguard actions, using their tactics to stave off a severe defeat. From the point of view of the Indians, staying to fight in a disadvantageous circumstance only invited defeat in detail at the hands of the army. Dispersing and reassembling for another opportunity for combat was a typical Indian maneuver. Therefore, army officers, frustrated after numerous scouts produced nothing, concluded that locating a sizable force of warriors or an entire village was half the contest; bringing the warriors to battle or destroying the logistical resources contained in the village was the other half. Consequently, in major campaigns the army moved its conventional units in such strength that it focused on making contact, fighting the engagement, and pursuing the enemy, rather than showing concern about being outnumbered, cut off, or defeated.

The post–Civil War campaigns started badly for the army. At a time when many of the top officers were serving in the South, Captain William J. Fetterman brazenly proclaimed that he could lead two companies of soldiers into the heart of Sioux territory. Stationed at Fort Phil Kearny in Wyoming Territory in late 1866 to help guard the Bozeman Trail, Fetterman and other officers had opportunities to observe the Sioux in action. Colonel Henry B. Carrington, Fort Phil Kearny's senior officer, believed in acting cautiously away from the safety of the fort. Rather than studying the enemy's capabilities, however, Fetterman decided that other detachment commanders lacked élan. Using an attack on a wood-gathering detail from the fort as a decoy, the Sioux planned to ambush the force that sortied to rescue the workers. Itching to take a crack at the Sioux, Fetterman picked a detachment of mounted infantry (fifty men) and cavalry (twenty-eight men); two civilians also accompanied the impetuous officer. An unknown number of Sioux wiped out Fetterman's command on 21 December only a few miles from the fort. A combat officer with battlefield experience against Confederates in the Civil War, Fetterman underestimated and misjudged the Sioux. To commemorate the captain's aggressive spirit (but presumably not his faults), in 1867 the army named a new post in Wyoming Fort Fetterman.

In 1867 the army fought two other notable skirmishes on the North Plains, the so-called Hayfield Fight (1 August), near Fort C. F. Smith in Montana Territory, and the Wagon Box Fight (2 August), near Fort Phil Kearny. In both instances, large groups of Sioux or Cheyenne attacked isolated detachments less than half the size of Fetterman's but failed to defeat them. These fights seemed to indicate that determined soldiers armed with breechloaders could stand off hundreds of Indians and may have offset some of the negative consequences of the Fetterman defeat. Such defensive stand-offs, however, were not going to clear the northern Plains for the wave of white settlers, miners, ranchers, farmers, and railroaders.

In the same year, Major General Winfield Scott Hancock initiated a campaign against the Cheyenne and Kiowa in Kansas. Those Indians had been buying weapons from traders and had used them in response to Hancock's attack on the Indian village at Pawnee Fork in western Kansas. Commanding units from the Seventh Cavalry and the Thirty-seventh Infantry (about fourteen hundred soldiers altogether), Hancock and his officers chased the warriors from Fort Riley in central Kansas to Colorado Territory and back again. Hancock's top subordinate, Lieutenant Colonel George A. Custer, received his introduction to Indian warfare in Kansas. From April to July 1867, Custer rode far, skirmished occasionally, and accomplished little. Mostly the campaign created ill-will between the army on the one hand and the Indians and the Indian Bureau on the other. It also tarnished Hancock's lustrous military reputation. As one of the Union's heroes of the Battle of Gettysburg, Hancock's major generalcy was secure, but his fumbling behavior on the Plains demonstrated again that most army officers found it difficult to make the transition from conventional combat to Indian-fighting. Despite Hancock's efforts and the signing of the major treaty of Medicine Lodge at Barber County, Kansas, in October 1867, groups of Cheyenne and warriors from other tribes continued their attacks on settlers and ranchers.

Consequently, the following year the army mounted one of its most important post–Civil War campaigns, the South Plains campaign of 1868–1869. Sheridan conferred with Sherman and drew up a plan, which called for Sheridan himself (then commanding the Military Department of the Missouri) to take the field. In its destructive potential the plan bore a similarity to Sherman's march to the sea and Sheridan's Shenandoah Valley campaign. As the weather chilled, strong army columns set out from forts in Kansas, Colorado Territory, and New Mexico Territory, converging on the suspected locations of winter campsites of hostile bands. The soldiers were to engage the warriors and damage or destroy their villages—in other words, the Indians' logistics bases. If it was not total war, it was something close to it. The Indians could not survive the winter without tepees, blankets, stored food, weapons, and horses. Their alternatives were either to surrender, accept the government's rations, and be confined on restricted reservations, or to die—which some preferred to do. A plan on paper was one thing, but finding and defeating the Indians was another matter. Cold-weather campaigning strained the army's heavy-wagon supply system and ruined many of its grain-fed horses. In contrast to previous efforts, however, the South Plains campaign produced devastating results.

Custer ordered his men to kill more than eight hundred Indian horses, destroying the transportation and offensive capability of the Cheyenne.

On the snowy morning of 27 November, Custer and the Seventh Cavalry (about seven hundred soldiers) located and attacked the large Cheyenne village of Chief Black Kettle on the Washita River in Indian Territory (Oklahoma). As was his custom from Civil War days, Custer disdained much reconnaissance and struck precipitously. A brisk skirmish resulted, forcing most of the Cheyenne out of the camp. Finding evidence that some of the village's warriors had committed raids on settlements in Kansas, Custer ordered his soldiers to set fire to the village. Meanwhile, Major Joel H. Elliott and fifteen troopers had galloped off in pursuit of the fleeing

Cheyenne. When threatened by hundreds of warriors from other nearby Indian camps (who were closer than he realized), Custer ordered his men to kill more than eight hundred Indian horses, destroying the transportation and offensive capability of the Cheyenne. Custer thereupon abandoned the ruined camp (and Major Elliott), escaping with his regiment from a potential Indian trap. Elliott and his detachment were later found, all dead. Even a large rescue party might have met the same fate, but Elliott's death and Custer's refusal to send help to him inflamed animosities among officers in the Seventh Cavalry.

The Washita engagement and Custer's subsequent punitive patrols indicated the army's destructive power in this conflict between two cultures. It showed that the army could put two thousand soldiers in the field and sustain them under adverse weather conditions. The Plains Indians found it impossible to abide by Anglo-American notions of boundaries and restrictions. The army, for its part, often found itself attempting to prevent white encroachment on Indian lands at the same time it was seeking out Indian raiding parties. The unstoppable wave of white settlers—whether ranchers, European immigrants, railroad builders, or workers from eastern cities—had little regard for the Indians or the sanctity of their lands. This inexorable wave of settlement transformed the trans-Mississippi landscape and destroyed the buffalo, on which the Plains Indians depended for their livelihood. Hunters slaughtered the buffalo nearly to the point of extinction. If the Indians resisted, in their uncoordinated fashion, they suffered at the hands of the army and the settlers. When the Indians decided not to resist, they were shunted off to ever-smaller, less-desirable reservation lands.

Winter or summer, the army was determined to find and fight bands or whole tribes that rejected the white man's law or stood in the way of the expansion of the rival culture. As needed, the army shifted its forces to deal with particular tribes. For example, soldiers nearly wiped out the Piegan in a winter attack in Montana (1870), suppressed the Modoc on the West Coast (1872–1873), and several times pursued the Kiowa and Lipan-Apache across the border into Mexico (1873–1877).

To complete the subjugation of the South Plains tribes, the army conducted another multicolumn campaign, the Red River War of 1874–1875. Five powerful army expeditionary forces marched in Texas, New Mexico Territory, and Indian Territory. The most damage was inflicted by the column under Colonel Ranald S. Mackenzie, commander of the Fourth Cavalry, who developed into one of the army's most successful Indian fighters. In September 1874, Mackenzie's men rode into a large encampment of Comanche, Kiowa, Arapaho, and Cheyenne at Palo Duro Canyon in the Texas Panhandle. The Indians sustained only a handful of casualties before they escaped. Mackenzie took over the village and, like Custer at the Washita, destroyed the Indian supplies, food, weapons, blankets, and tepees and killed or captured one thousand horses. During the next six months, hundreds of tribesmen and their families surrendered themselves at army posts or Indian reservations. Subsequently, some of their main leaders were imprisoned in Florida. With the exception of scattered outbreaks of violence, the power of the South Plains tribes was broken.

On the North Plains, railroad builders and mining entrepreneurs coveted rights-of-way and access to tribal lands held sacred by the Sioux. Military exploring parties pointed out the best routes and confirmed rumors of gold in the Black Hills of the Dakotas. Intrusions on Indian lands and evident Anglo-American intent to acquire the lands in question pushed most of the Teton Sioux and Northern Cheyenne, as well as some Arapaho and other Sioux bands, to the brink of war in the winter of 1875–1876. Some left the reservations, and others, who had never come into the agencies, assembled along the Little Bighorn River.

In some ways this extraordinary gathering of Indians helped the army. Its size made it easier for civilian scouts or Indian auxiliaries to track and locate the enemy. Initially, Sheridan's outline of campaign called for another winter-weather success. Various problems, including severe weather, lack of cooperation among subordinate commanders, and strong Indian resistance, turned the army's main effort into a summer expedition. Sheridan allowed distractions to occupy his time and failed to coordinate the campaign.

Adhering to Sheridan's outline, three powerful columns, totaling about twenty-six hundred soldiers and Indian auxiliaries, aimed to crush the Plains tribes in Montana Territory. One column marched eastward from Fort Ellis, Montana, including several companies each from the Seventh Infantry and Second Cavalry (about five hundred soldiers), commanded by the doughty Brevet Major General John Gibbon, colonel of the Seventh Infantry Regiment. The second column moved northward from its base at Fort Fetterman, Wyoming Territory, and was led by Brevet Major General George Crook, holder of a controversial but productive record against the Apache in Arizona Territory. Crook's forces totaled eleven hundred soldiers and more than two hundred Indian auxiliaries. Brigadier General Alfred Terry, the senior field commander, led the third column, marching westward from Fort Abraham Lincoln, Dakota Territory. Terry's column contained all of

Custer's Seventh Cavalry (750 officers and men) plus units of the Sixth Infantry (one company), Seventeenth Infantry (two companies), Twentieth Infantry (a detachment of thirty-one men with Gatling guns), and Terry's headquarters (twelve soldiers), nearly nine hundred officers and men altogether. This was the largest and most capably led of all the army's post–Civil War Indian campaigns, although small when contrasted to Civil War armies. Lacking only Sheridan's central coordination, it became the most sustained conventional campaign of the Indian wars.

The number of Indian combatants assembled in the Yellowstone River–Little Bighorn vicinity remains in dispute. The estimates vary from around fifteen hundred to more than four thousand, or even perhaps six thousand. In any event, the Plains had never seen such a multitribal gathering before, and a reasonable estimate is approximately fifteen hundred warriors from the extraordinary Indian encampments. Furthermore, these Indians, the Sioux especially, planned to fight, not to hit and run or skirmish and withdraw.

Led by Crazy Horse, an exceptional warrior who used all of his influence to keep the warriors together, the Sioux already had defeated Crook's column in southern Montana along Rosebud Creek. On 17 June 1876, Crook's troopers fought for six hours (a remarkable engagement itself) and suffered more than twenty killed and fifty wounded before retreating all the way back to a base camp in Wyoming. The tenacity and unexpected belligerence of the Indians shook Crook's self-confidence, deflecting his column southward and out of the battle on the Little Bighorn, where his men were needed to complete the ring around the Indians. Had Crook resumed his march toward the Yellowstone River, at least word of his advance might have undermined the Indian alliance. At best, some of his troops could have contributed to the Battle of the Little Bighorn itself or been available to mount a proper pursuit. Instead, after taking less than 10 percent casualties among his soldiers, Crook abandoned the field, failed to inform Terry of his whereabouts, and left open the southern area of the campaign.

Bones cover the site of the Battle of Little Bighorn in the Montana Territory. In this battle, which occurred on 25 June 1876, Sioux and Cheyenne Indians killed Custer and 212 members of his regiment. (National Archives)

Receiving no word from Crook as to his decision to retreat, Terry, Gibbon, and Custer met on 21 June in the cabin of a steamboat to discuss the campaign. Terry authorized Custer to forge ahead, giving the Seventh Cavalry's field commander flexible orders to use his own discretion about engaging the enemy. Echoing Fetterman's boast, but elevating it to an epic scale, Custer reputedly stated that he could "whip all the Indians on the continent with the Seventh Cavalry." Minus the band and others on detached duty, the regiment mounted 647 men who rode toward the Little Bighorn.

On 25 June, more than twenty-four hours ahead of the forces of Gibbon and Terry, Custer found the huge Indian assemblage. Interpreting his orders to his own satisfaction, he decided to attack—in part, at least, because he was concerned that the Indians might flee before battle could be joined—but Custer made four decisions that compounded the problems in the battle before him. First, prior to riding ahead of the main column, Custer rejected Terry's offer of taking several companies of the Second Cavalry from Gibbon's command; Custer wanted the glory that awaited only for himself and the Seventh Regiment. Second, as was his habit, he had disdained much reconnaissance for fear of alerting the Indians and perhaps scaring them away. Third, in the face of a superior enemy force of unknown numbers, Custer divided his regiment into four parts; probably he became aware of the enemy's strength only after the battle was underway. Finally, by dividing his regiment, Custer kept with his battalion the officers who were his best and most dependable subordinates. If his brothers and friends, however, had been with the other battalions, an argument can be made that they would have responded to the sounds of heavy firing and to Custer's scribbled messages to come quickly and bring more ammunition. Custer and almost one-third of his regiment (212 officers and soldiers) were killed in the battle. The other battalions suffered losses totaling fifty-three killed and sixty wounded.

The Battle of the Little Bighorn marked the high point of Indian resistance to Anglo-American encroachment on their lands. It also prompted an exceptional response from the United States and its army. Grant, Sherman, and Sheridan all had been enjoying the festivities celebrating the nation's Centennial in Philadelphia. Custer's defeat forced them to turn some of their attention to the war at hand. Congress authorized an increase of twenty-five hundred soldiers for the regular army. Terry, Gibbon, Crook, and other officers reorganized their columns, and reinforcements arrived in the North Plains. The army's pursuit of the Indians who won at the Little Bighorn lasted for twenty-four months and drove the battle's victors onto reservations or across the Canadian border. Crazy Horse was killed on 7 September 1877 at Camp Robinson, Nebraska, and Sitting Bull fled into Canada. In addition, Colonel Nelson A. Miles and General O. O. Howard launched a campaign against the Nez Percé through Montana and into Idaho, forcing that tribe and its renowned leader, Chief Joseph, to surrender on 5 October 1877. Using conventional field forces, in winter and summer, by the end of 1879 the army had broken the power of the North Plains tribes.

Although soldiers fought occasional skirmishes and rode on dozens of patrols on the North Plains after 1879, the army began shifting its attention to the Southwest, where the Apache blocked white expansion. Under the leadership of Crook and Miles, the campaign to completely defeat the Apaches took seven more years. The Apache wars challenged the army with the most grueling guerrilla-style combat since the poorly conducted Second Seminole War in Florida (1835–1842).

From 1871 to 1875, Crook had built a creditable record in Arizona; he knew the terrain and the tribesmen intimately. Taken off this familiar ground and moved to the North Plains in 1876, he had failed to win the kind of glorious victory that might have earned him a major-generalcy and changed much else besides. Had Crook's column defeated Crazy Horse at the Rosebud, all that came after that battle might have been quite different. Following a defeat, Crazy Horse's leadership might have waned and the fragile Indian alliance might have weakened or fallen apart, thus affecting the outcome of the Battle of the Little Bighorn a few days later. Furthermore, speculation abounds about Custer's objectives in 1876: If he had scored a spectacular battlefield victory, he surely would have won promotion to brigadier general and perhaps would have sought the Democratic presidential nomination in 1880 (which went instead to Hancock).

In contrast to Custer, Crook was not a high-profile public figure, and a political career for him was unlikely. Crook's earlier success against the Apache had earned him respect from those Indians but no more than grudging acknowledgment from his fellow officers and little recognition from the public. Crook did not help his own cause. He was irascible, possessed of complete self-assurance that he was right and most other officers were wrong when it came to fighting Indians. Crook and his peers parted company over his consistent reliance on Indian auxiliaries and his use of mobile pack mules rather than heavy wagons to carry supplies. Furthermore, these and other professional differences had estranged Crook from Sheridan, his longtime friend and former West Point classmate. The two had had a falling out over allocation of credit for portions of Union victories in Sheridan's Shenandoah Valley campaign, in which Crook served as a valued corps commander. The Crook-Sheridan feud was one of several that undercut the harmony of the officer corps of the U.S. Army in the 1870s and 1880s. Such animosities often were connected to disagreements originating in the Civil War.

Crook called the Apache

"the tigers of the human race."

Therefore, when Crook resumed the fight against the Apache in September 1882 (after a stint in the Department of the Platte), he had something to prove. He aimed to refurbish his reputation and achieve promotion to major general by fighting the type of Indian warfare he knew best. Crook called the Apache "the tigers of the human race." Led by the warrior Geronimo, the Apache operated on both sides of the U.S.-Mexican border and played off the Mexican government, the U.S. Army, and the Indian Bureau against one another. Crook, however, may have led the army in patience as well as innovation, and Apache guerrilla tactics did not dismay him. Moreover, Crook wanted to conclude the wars leaving the Apache their self-respect and some of their traditional lands, views not shared by other senior officers, especially Sheridan, who was appointed commanding general of the army in 1883.

During 1883–1884, Crook and his subordinates, usually commanding units in the field at company strength (about fifty soldiers plus numerous Apache auxiliaries) suppressed an uprising in the Sierra Madre led by Chato, Nana, and Geronimo. Skirmish by skirmish, patrol after patrol, parley by parley, Crook's small mobile units pursued the enemy. These tactics temporarily persuaded many Apache bands to return to reservations under army supervision.

Another outbreak undermined Crook's reputation and again called his tactics into question. Warm Springs and Chiracahua Apache conducted several raids, killing more than thirty settlers. In the resulting Sierra Madre campaign of 1885–1886, Crook again employed his mule-pack trains, small mobile units, and helpful Apache auxiliaries. Sheridan, however, wanted a line of stationary posts along the border and, to resolve the issue, a plan to deport from the Southwest to confinement in the East all Apache, even those who had fought alongside the army. Crook had one more chance to end things his way.

Units composed mostly of Apache auxiliaries led by army captains and lieutenants fanned out into the mountains and across the border into Mexico. Captain Emmet Crawford, one of Crook's best field officers, and Lieutenant Britton Davis led the most effective counterstrikes. Although Crawford was killed in a skirmish, his efforts led to a conference between Geronimo and Crook in Mexico in March 1886. Crook promised to keep up the pursuit until the last hostile Apache was subdued—even "if it takes fifty years," he concluded. Giving in partly to Sheridan's wishes, Crook indicated that some Apache leaders would be locked up for several months in an eastern prison when they surrendered. Heeding Crook's words, Geronimo and other leaders pledged to surrender, but instead resumed fighting a few days later, after Crook had telegraphed Sheridan the news that the campaign had ended.

As far as Sheridan was concerned, Crook had lost his chance. The commanding general applied pressure and expressed doubts about Crook's methods and capabilities. Such pressure produced the result Sheridan desired—Crook requested that he be reassigned. Replacing him in Arizona was the ambitious and aggressive Miles, who had been one of Crook's strongest critics.

Ironically, once Miles had been in Arizona a few days, he saw the wisdom of most of Crook's unorthodox methods, including putting reinforced mobile companies in the field, operating on both sides of the border, and, especially, using Apache auxiliaries to track down the renegades. Miles, too, rejected Sheridan's notion of depending upon a line of fixed positions along the Mexican border. Four months after he took over, Miles forced Geronimo's surrender in September 1886. According to Sheridan's wishes, the most important Apache leaders and warriors went into exile in a Florida prison. The Apache wars were finished.

Often listed as the final battle of the trans-Mississippi wars, the confrontation at Wounded Knee, South Dakota, between reservation Sioux and elements of the Seventh Cavalry in December 1890 was not much more than a police assignment gone awry. In the process of disarming several potentially hostile Sioux, an altercation led to guns being fired on both sides, including four mountain howitzers that the cavalry had set up on a nearby hill. For several minutes the two sides exchanged shots. The soldiers killed 150 Indians and wounded 50 others. The cavalry lost 25 dead and 39 wounded. The mismatch gave the Seventh Cavalry a small measure of revenge for the Little Bighorn, and ended the army's Indian-fighting in a familiar, constabulary role. In the years to come—even into the early twentieth century, the army could not reject completely the possibility of another Indian war.

THE ARMY AND REFORM

By 1890 most officers had put aside Indian-fighting and turned their attention to other concerns. Indeed, twenty years before the tragic events at Wounded Knee, a handful of officers wanted to reject the traditional task of Indian-fighting as the army's primary function. Throughout the 1870s these reformers, mid-ranking officers as well as Sherman and other top generals, sought ways to increase professionalism within the service. Unfortunately for these reformers and their political allies in Congress, the active Indian campaigns of the 1870s, among other things, diluted or distracted the reform efforts. Even as late as the mid-1890s, on the eve of a war with Spain, the reformers could not agree on what needed to be done. Nevertheless, the army took incremental steps toward maturing into a force that would be capable of conducting conventional war in the twentieth century.

From the 1870s to the 1890s, as it considered and adopted some reforms, the army demonstrated a remarkable elasticity in its ability to fulfill multiple purposes. U.S. soldiers have never lacked jobs. Some of the tasks they undertook after Reconstruction were traditional, some were new, others were short-lived, and still others lasted longer than expected and were handed over to another federal agency. For example, the army operated a weather service from 1870 to 1890, at which point it was taken over by the newly established Department of Agriculture. Thus, for twenty years the army kept records on a variety of meteorological and climatological data across the nation. In 1867, President Johnson ordered Brevet Major General Rousseau to lead the official delegation that received Alaska from the

Russians. The army stayed on to administer and explore the territory for ten years before giving the duties to civilians. Beginning with Meriwether Lewis and William Clark in 1803, army explorers had gathered a variety of information about the trans-Mississippi. Many post–Civil War patrols acquired valuable geological, botanical, and geographical information while fulfilling their more immediate military orders. Notable among such efforts were those of Colonel William R. Shafter in his numerous scouts during the 1870s across the Llano Estacado (Staked Plain) in Texas and New Mexico.

Few outside the army knew of Shafter's patrols, but more controversial activities caught the public's attention. The Yellowstone expeditions of 1871, 1872, and 1873, the last one led by Colonel David S. Stanley, guarded surveying parties searching for the best railroad route through the Sioux country. The Black Hills expedition of 1874, promoted by Lieutenant Colonel Custer, confirmed the location of gold in the sacred Indian promontories, including the Black Hills, causing prospectors to flood the area and bringing on the Great Sioux War of 1876. On the other hand, scientific and geographical data were the goals of the Wheeler Survey and the Greely Arctic Expedition. Led by Lieutenant George M. Wheeler, a team of soldiers made fourteen field trips between 1871 and 1879 from the Great Plains to the Pacific. Wheeler went on to compile two large volumes describing these activities before the U.S. Geological Survey, a new civilian agency, took over the work. In 1881 Lieutenant Adolphus W. Greely volunteered to take charge of a twenty-five-man scientific group planning to set up a meteorological station in the Arctic. Severe conditions cut the scientists off from resupply. In 1884 a relief party led by a flamboyant naval officer, Commander Winfield Scott Schley, rescued Greely and five other desperate survivors. Two years later, the War Department ordered army officers to administer and protect the priceless handful of U.S. national parks. As the park system grew, the army maintained this responsibility until the nascent National Park Service stepped in in 1918.

Such diverse accomplishments called into question whether the army had a paramount purpose. An un-

The confrontation at Wounded Knee is often listed as the final battle of the trans-Mississippi wars. These army scouts, who fought at Wounded Knee, rode across the snow-covered plains to their camp after the battle in 1890. (National Archives)

sought adjunct to Indian-fighting and a follow-up to Reconstruction presented itself in the railroad strikes of 1877. In the closest thing that the United States has had to a general strike, thousands of workers walked off their jobs to protest working conditions and low wages. President Rutherford B. Hayes ordered several regiments, some from barracks or forts in the South, to relocate to the East, Midwest, and the trans-Mississippi, where they guarded railyards, locomotives, and rolling stock; they also allowed strikebreakers to cross the picket lines. The president's orders established a precedent. Although the army had been used to restore order in various domestic disturbances before and during the Civil War, for the next several years the army's strikebreaking duties complemented its constabulary duties against the Indians.

Had the army found its métier as a national police force? Several officers wrote articles in military journals indicating the need to maintain order across the country. Such articles also gave indications of the authors' support for the business community—which abhorred the disruptions and violence that the strikes engendered—and carried antilabor overtones. From 1877 to the mid-1890s, in railyards and coal mines from Pennsylvania to Coeur d'Alene, Idaho, and in Chicago's Pullman Strike of 1894, soldiers acted as strikebreakers, under orders from President Grover Cleveland. Throughout these deployments, the War Department developed no official doctrine for the army to use in labor disturbances. Most officers eventually concluded that their future did not lie with an army that acted as a national police force. Carrying out such duties later moved Colonel William A. Ganoe to label the 1870s as the army's "Dark Ages."

By the late 1870s, the commander of the Military Division of the Atlantic at Governors Island in New York City, General Hancock, had had his fill of Reconstruction and strikebreaking. Hancock and several subordinate officers began discussing the broader roles of the U.S. Army. They were familiar with Great Britain's Royal United Service Institution and knew, of course, that U.S. naval officers had established the U.S. Naval Institute in 1873. Encouraged by Sherman, in September 1878 Hancock helped to form the Military Service Institution (MSI) of the United States, an organization to improve army professionalism. Less than two years later, the MSI had enrolled 550 members (about one-fourth of the officer corps) and published the first issue of its *Journal of the Military Service Institution* (JMSI). Until World War I, *JMSI* was an unofficial but respected means for army officers to express ideas, arguments, and observations on a wide variety of political as well as military subjects. Another similar professional journal, *United Service,* began publication in April 1879.

These journals were the most sophisticated U.S. military periodicals of the nineteenth century and were the forerunners of such twentieth-century publications as *Army* and *Military Review. United Service* and *JSMI* included articles on topical matters, such as equipment and Indians, but other essays pointed toward the future. Officers wrote about such issues as field training, multiunit maneuvers, mandatory officer retirement, and developments in European armies.

The Franco-Prussian War of 1870, for example, attracted the attention of U.S. Army officers. During the short conflict General Sheridan obtained official permission to travel in Europe as an observer. Despite this expression of interest in European warfare, however, Sheridan never contributed significantly to army reforms in America. In sharp contrast to Sheridan, General Sherman set the example for army reformers in the post–Civil War era. By necessity he had to devote attention to the West and, like Sheridan, supported the construction of railroads there for military as well as civilian use. Unlike Sheridan, Sherman disapproved of Reconstruction and increasingly spent time trying to make the army a more professional organization and seeking ways to improve military education.

Following the Franco-Prussian War, Sherman and other officers made European tours, visiting several nations, including England, Russia, and Germany. When Sherman inspected the battlefields in France, he gained a favorable impression of Prussian military victories. Preceding Sherman to Europe, Colonel William B. Hazen wrote a book about his own tour entitled *The School of the Army in Germany and France* (1872). Sherman's protégé, Colonel Emory Upton, later made the most thorough inspection of Asian and European military forces by an American in the nineteenth century. Sherman did not endorse all of the suggestions Upton had to offer when he returned, but he did put some of them on the reform agenda.

Reform-minded, practical, but cautious, Sherman faced several political challenges as commanding general of the army from 1869 to 1883. A budget-conscious Congress reduced the army's authorized strength to 27,400 in 1876 and threatened further cuts. Sherman watched as Congress debated a series of bills that contained some "reform" features but which, if passed, might have crippled the army.

From 1876 to 1878 Congressman Henry Banning (a Democrat from Ohio) proposed a series of omnibus bills that provided for reducing the number of army officers, cutting the pay of officers (especially that of lieutenants), eliminating the black regiments, preventing soldiers from supervising elections, establishing examination boards for officer promotion, and setting compulsory retirement for officers at age sixty-five. The first version of the bill passed the House of Representatives in 1876 but failed in the Senate. Banning and other Democrats then salted the proposed legislation with enough features to make it appear that reform or thrift inspired them, when in actuality vindictiveness and racism motivated them to weaken the army and remove freedmen from the service. News of Custer's defeat at the Little Bighorn, however, turned another likely reduction of the service into a twenty-five-hundred-man increase.

According to Upton, German techniques had to be incorporated in the reformation of the U.S. Army.

In 1878, Senator Ambrose Burnside (a Republican from Rhode Island) chaired a congressional committee on army reorganization. Burnside was a West Point graduate and former Union general who took a serious interest in reforming the army. In 1879 the Burnside committee, which included Banning, issued a seven-hundred-page report. The resulting bill revealed the need to compromise with Banning and the Democrats in order to obtain some worthwhile changes. Among its many articles, the Burnside bill recommended reducing the number of officers by three hundred, consolidating and reducing some staff departments, setting officer retirement at age sixty-two, encouraging officer rotation from the staff to line units, requiring staff officers to report to the commanding general rather than the secretary of war, restructuring infantry regiments to allow for wartime expansion, increasing the pay for noncommissioned officers, and shrinking the army to a size that probably would have meant disbanding some or all of the black regiments. The Burnside bill split the army, with some line officers favoring and most staff officers opposing it. Sheridan was against it, but Sherman, Hancock, Upton, and Schofield all found provisions they liked well enough to justify their support. Because of these divisions, in 1879 the Burnside bill failed to pass in Congress. It probably tried to change too much in one stroke.

The multiple agendas behind the Banning and Burnside bills and the flagrant abuse of the army during these congressional debates (the service went unpaid during much of 1877) only deepened Sherman's conviction that most politicians were not trustworthy. Banning and Burnside each claimed the reform mantle, but some of the provisions of their bills could have had negative consequences for the army. Political leaders seemed to agree: With no foreign wars or invasions likely, the primary goal of reform was to reduce the strength of the army and the number of its officers. Military leaders winced at the prospect of further cutbacks because promotion in the army was difficult enough, limited as it was to vacancies by death or retirement in an officer's regiment. Accordingly, Sherman laid out a practical agenda to do what he could within the army's existing structure and budget to improve the service.

Sherman's reforms stressed military education, and he first looked to the existing specialty schools and sought to modernize them. The Artillery Schools at Fortress Monroe, Virginia, had operated from 1824 to 1860 and reopened in 1868. Sherman ordered improvements in the curriculum and sent Upton to serve on its staff. That same year the Signal School began holding classes at Fort Greble in Washington, D.C. Sherman hoped one day to have an advanced school covering practical and theoretical instruction for each of the army's branches, all crowned by a "war college."

Sherman's most important contribution to military education came in 1881 when he authorized the School of Application for Infantry and Cavalry at Fort Leavenworth, Kansas. The school opened the next year with an initial class of forty-two lieutenants who not only took courses in a variety of military subjects, but also studied mathematics and geography and brushed up on their grammar and reading. At the outset, Sherman expressed both public optimism and private skepticism about the Leavenworth school and what good it might accomplish; it was an experiment, the U.S. Army's first attempt at post–graduate education, as opposed to training, for its officers. Sherman wanted students to have the opportunity to study the higher art of war and to familiarize themselves with the responsibilities of various levels of command—captains as company commanders, colonels as regimental commanders, and brigadier generals as brigade commanders. Undergoing several name and curriculum changes in succeeding years, the school began to take root. Sherman had planted the seeds of what would eventually become known as the Command and General Staff College and in so doing filled a yawning gap in army professionalism. By 1914 the "Leavenworth experience" of studying strategy and staff duties created a pool of capable officers who provided leadership for millions of U.S. soldiers in World War I.

To accomplish all—and more—that Sherman expected of the new school, the army needed a handful of educated, intellectually gifted professors at Leavenworth in the 1880s and 1890s. Two officers in particular came forward and left a lasting impression on the experimental military school, Arthur L. Wagner and Eben Swift. Wagner joined the staff at Leavenworth in the fall of 1886, concerned about the deficiencies in the U.S. Army's size, training, and weapons when contrasted to several European armies. He provided the Leavenworth schools and the army at large with badly needed textbooks and other reference works, including *The Service of Security and Supply (1893), Organization and Tactics* (1894), and *Elements of Military Science* (1898). Wagner taught at Leavenworth from 1886 to 1898 and served there again when it resumed classes in 1902, after a break caused by the Spanish-American War. Swift served as an instructor at the Leavenworth schools from 1893 to 1898 and devised a series of challenging war games using maps and field exercises. He also developed the standardized five-paragraph field order that became uniform throughout the army and has been in use ever since. In 1902, Secretary of War Elihu Root reopened the school and renamed it the General Service and Staff College.

Sherman's other notable contribution was to advance the career and writings of Upton. A combat veteran of the Civil War, Upton detested Indian-fighting and saw no future in it. Defeating the western tribes simply added to the list of thankless duties that detracted from what he believed was the army's true calling—preparing for the next war with a conventional opponent. Upton's star burned white-hot in the 1870s. He served as commandant of cadets at West Point from 1870 to 1875. He wrote down his ideas at a feverish pace, publishing *Cavalry Tactics* in 1874 and *Artillery Tactics* in 1875 to supplement his earlier work, *A New System of Infantry Tactics* (1867). Recognizing the changes brought on by improved weapons, his tactics incorporated looser, more flexible formations, stronger skirmish lines, and allowed more responsibility for noncommissioned officers and the soldiers themselves. Returning as a reform zealot after his year abroad evaluating the armies of other countries, he published *The Armies of Asia and Europe* in 1878, emphasizing the accomplishments and techniques of the German army in particular.

According to Upton, German techniques had to be incorporated in the reformation of the U.S. Army. He supported the parts of the Burnside bill that provided for consolidating staff departments (a first step toward a more sophisticated, German-style general staff), setting an age or length of service for mandatory officer retirement, and redesigning regiments to allow for expanding them in wartime. Beyond these reasonable changes, he deplored America's past reliance on inadequate volunteers to round out the officer corps after a war began and urged the adoption of the German system of always maintaining a corps of well-educated officers on active duty to meet the needs of wartime mobilization. A modification of John C. Calhoun's "expansible army" plan (which itself relied on even earlier proposals), Upton's reform scheme was grandiose and seemed too dependent on a foreign model. He stridently promoted his reforms and insisted on their worth. He wanted them adopted as a package and the sooner the better. All of these factors combined to make Upton's scheme unacceptable to politicians of both parties and to a number of army officers as well.

Disappointed by the rejection of his ideas, Upton again turned to his writing, this time producing his magnum opus, *The Military Policy of the United States,* a book that was not published until 1904. In it he emphasized the mistakes of U.S. wartime civilian leadership and was especially critical of what he considered interference in military matters by President Lincoln. He also decried the traditional military unpreparedness of the United States, the error of relying on an inadequate militia, and the indiscipline of volunteer officers. Unfortunately for Upton, such disrespect for presidents and heroic volunteers negated much of his effort at reforming the army. Despite being Sherman's protégé, he failed to make flag rank in 1880; he was promoted to full colonel but did not receive the brigadier's star he thought he deserved. He grew despondent over the lack of congressional support for his sweeping reforms. Other officers, such as Hazen, favored some of what he wanted, but accepted the slow pace of such changes. Upton's health complicated these disappointments, and he committed suicide on 15 March 1881.

After persevering under trying circumstances, in 1877 Henry O. Flipper became the first black to graduate from West Point and earn a commission.

Upton's personality and impatience put off both reform-minded officers such as Hancock and traditionalists such as Sheridan. He rejected the concept of working gradually for his goals; in his opinion, everyone—officers, politicians, newspaper editors—should have seen the wisdom of what he proposed. Neither his sincerity nor his intensity overcame his failure to understand and to work within the U.S. political system. Consequently, his actions and the manner in which he proselytized on behalf of his reforms embittered civil-military relations in the years to come. Had he demonstrated more patient, sagacious leadership, he might have increased the chances of obtaining some of his goals.

Upton had found time to write two of his books while serving as commandant of cadets at the U.S. Military Academy, but neither he nor Sherman dwelt on reforming West Point. Overall, Sherman appeared to be satisfied with his alma mater. As commanding general, Sherman was lenient toward misbehaving cadets accused of hazing. He also declined to diversify the academy faculty by adding new civilian professors, and the curriculum remained much the same as it had been when Sherman graduated in 1840. Perhaps the most important academic change at West Point came in 1871, when Colonel Dennis Hart Mahan, who had taught at West Point for more than forty years and had made a personal impression on the army officer corps, was forced to retire.

Another significant change at West Point in the post–Civil War years was the admission in 1870 of the first African-American cadet, James W. Smith. After suffering through racist epithets, isolation, and other forms of mistreatment, Smith was dismissed for academic deficiencies in 1873. Tracing the lives of other black cadets at West Point and the few black officers in the period indicates how unwelcome they were in the army. Between 1870 and 1889 twenty-five blacks received appointments to the academy. Twelve passed the tests and gained admission, but only three graduated. After persevering under trying circumstances, in 1877 Henry O. Flipper became the first black to graduate from West Point and earn a commission. Flipper served with the Tenth Cavalry from 1877 to 1882, when he was hounded out of the army by Colonel William Shafter on charges of "conduct unbecoming an officer" stemming from misuse of military funds. The most deplorable case of mistreatment was that of Johnson C. Whittaker, a black cadet from South Carolina. Whittaker was found beaten and tied to his bunk, but the superintendent, General John M. Schofield, ruled that the bruises and cuts were self-inflicted and that Whittaker had roped himself to his bed. An academy review board dismissed Whittaker in 1882 for a failing grade. Two other African-Americans graduated from West Point and served with the Ninth Cavalry, John H. Alexander

In the late 1800s, the Army relied on mules and wagons to transport men and supplies to remote regions not served by railroads. In this photograph, Company B of the U.S. 10th Infantry crosses the Gila River near San Carlos in the Arizona Territory in 1885. (National Archives)

(class of 1887) and Charles Young (class of 1889), the last black graduate until Benjamin O. Davis, Jr., in 1936.

Despite the grim record of African-Americans who aspired to become officers, the fact that black enlisted men served in the regular army set a significant example for the future. The Reconstruction Congress established six units for them in 1866—the Ninth and Tenth Cavalry regiments, and the Thirty-eighth, Thirty-ninth, Fortieth, and Forty-first Infantry regiments. The four infantry regiments were consolidated in the army reduction of 1869 into the Twenty-fourth and Twenty-fifth regiments. These units made up about 10 percent of the army's enlisted strength, slightly less than the percentage of black troops in Union service in 1865. Commanded mostly by white officers (with the few exceptions noted above), the black units not only earned the distinction of having the lowest desertion rates in the army, but also boasted high reenlistment rates. They performed a variety of duties, including fighting Indians, breaking strikes, and garrisoning western outposts. These black regulars—nicknamed "buffalo soldiers" by the Indians—established a creditable record of more than thirty years of service by the time of the Spanish-American War. Although the buffalo soldiers and their white officers suffered indignities, insults, assaults, and discrimination, they paved the way for other African-Americans to serve in U.S. forces in the major wars of the twentieth century. These experimental army units therefore made an important contribution to civil rights for blacks in the United States.

There were several other positive developments in the service during the Gilded Age. A federal law set sixty-four as the standard retirement age for army officers in 1882. The Engineer School of Application at Willett's Point, Long Island, New York, opened in 1885, and the School of Cavalry and Light Artillery at Fort Riley, Kansas, was authorized in 1887. Several officers formed the U.S. Cavalry Association in 1885, which supported the publication of the *Cavalry Journal,* launched in 1888. Adjutant General Robert C. Drum supervised preparation of the *Soldier's Handbook* in 1884, a valuable reference covering a variety of duties and details pertaining to the lives of enlisted men. At the end of the 1880s, the army changed the traditional Sunday-morning inspections of enlisted men's barracks, uniforms, and bunks to Saturday morning, thus allowing soldiers some time for recreation and personal activities on the weekend.

In the late 1880s, a number of officers, including Miles, Crook, and Wesley Merritt, planned and conducted regimental field-training exercises, some of which were supplemented by soldiers from other infantry, cavalry, and artillery outfits. Following an example set by the navy when it established the Office of Naval Intelligence in 1882, the army established its own intelligence-gathering agency, the Bureau of Military Information, in 1885. Army attaches assigned to several U.S. embassies began sending data to this bureau, which changed its name to the Military Information Division in 1890. These modest reforms were carried out in the 1880s despite Sheridan's lack of interest. Schofield replaced Sheridan as commanding general in August 1888.

According to federal law, the commanding general held no direct control over either line units or staff bureaus, but he could attempt to use his influence or powers of persuasion to affect military legislation and, like Sherman, carry out special projects, such as establishing the Leavenworth schools. The background Schofield brought to this task was exceptional. In addition to holding standard departmental commands, Schofield had served as a special U.S. representative to negotiate the withdrawal of French forces in Mexico in 1866, a district commander during Reconstruction, interim secretary of war from June 1868 to March 1869, and superintendent of West Point in the late 1870s. Schofield also had traveled to Europe for a year (1881–1882). No other post–Civil War commanding general had such breadth of experience.

Although he was not an Uptonian, Schofield was acutely interested in army reform. In particular, he wanted to improve and standardize the working relationship between the secretary of war and the commanding general, which he believed should be a position more like that of a European chief of staff. Unlike Upton, Schofield understood the need to subordinate the U.S. military to its civilian leadership—the president and the secretary of war. In his memoirs, *Forty-six Years in the Army* (1897), Schofield concluded: "Nothing is more absolutely indispensable to a good soldier than perfect subordination and zealous service to him whom the national will may have made the official superior for the time being." Furthermore, he encouraged professionalism in the army and stressed that officers must keep abreast of technological changes in arms, munitions, and equipment.

As head of the army's Board of Ordnance and Fortification, Schofield had the duty of implementing some of the recommendations made by the joint army-navy Endicott Board on Fortifications. Chaired by Secretary of War William C. Endicott, the board included four army officers, two navy officers, and two civilians, and met several times in 1885. It issued a lengthy report in

January 1886 calling for elaborate coastal defenses. In coordination with the navy, these defenses would protect the twenty-seven primary U.S. harbors as well as points along the Great Lakes, employ hundreds of modern breechloading cannons, and cost more than $127 million, a huge expenditure for the time. Because of its cost, the Endicott defense system was never fully funded and construction progressed slowly, but the public tolerated these expenditures, whereas it might have blanched at spending the same money for new infantry or field artillery weapons and increasing the number of regiments in the army. Although the usefulness of the Endicott defense system was questionable, the army did not reject the money sent its way for the traditional role of coastal defense.

In the late nineteenth century, life at the army's coastal forts and interior posts gradually improved as the number of forts decreased. As the Indian wars drew to an end, the War Department closed posts throughout the trans-Mississippi. By 1890 the army maintained 103 posts across the nation, contrasted with 167 posts in 1870 and 130 in 1880. Garrisoning dozens of one-, two-, or three-company forts during Reconstruction and the Indian wars undercut regimental integrity and discouraged officers who wanted to turn their attention to broader questions of national defense. Nevertheless, the army never lost contact with civilians and civilian society. In the West, army doctors, libraries, stores, mail delivery, and social activities such as band concerts drew civilians and travelers to the forts. Even near the smaller

Nelson Appleton Miles was one of the army's most successful leaders during the Indian wars. In this photograph, Miles (center) and scout Buffalo Bill Cody (left) survey hostile Indian territory near Pine Ridge Agency in South Dakota in 1891. (National Archives)

forts, towns grew and developed symbiotic relationships with the posts. In the South, most forts were located near towns or cities. Seeking a break from routine, soldiers naturally gravitated to the shops, saloons, restaurants, and bordellos of nearby towns.

Based on the research of historian John M. Gates, students of the period must reconsider the interpretation advanced by Samuel P. Huntington in his valuable and influential *The Soldier and the State* (1957). Huntington argues that the army was isolated from civilian society in the late-nineteenth century. Gates shows that by 1891, however, 20 percent of the army's officers held assignments in or near eastern cities such as New York and Washington, D.C. Another 28 percent occupied billets in midwestern or western cities such as Chicago, Denver, Omaha, Portland, St. Paul, San Antonio, San Francisco, and Salt Lake City. The percentage of officers stationed in or near urban centers increased in the 1890s. These figures reinforce the conclusion that army officers were not isolated from society, and were aware of the progressive reforms under way in the late 1890s. Reform-minded officers, such as Colonel August V. Kautz, wanted to see steps taken to advance the army's professional standing much the same way that reformers in other areas of society advocated improved professional accreditation of physicians, attorneys, schoolteachers, civil-service employees, social workers, and policemen, among others.

The years 1890–1901 saw several beneficial changes for the army. In October 1890 a federal law changed the outmoded system of army-officer promotions. Thereafter, officers would be promoted within their branch of service (infantry, artillery, cavalry) rather than within their regiment. This modernizing step was one of the most important reforms of the late nineteenth century. In addition, the School for Cavalry and Light Artillery opened at Fort Riley in 1892 and the *Journal of United States Artillery* began publication that year. The following year officers formed the Infantry Society (which changed its name to the Infantry Association in 1904) and the *Infantry Journal* began publication in 1894. In the mid-1890s, about one hundred army officers served as instructors of tactics or military science at civilian colleges and universities around the nation. Overseas, the army stationed officers as attaches in sixteen U.S. embassies, including those in London, Berlin, Paris, Vienna, Rome, St. Petersburg, Brussels, Mexico City, and Tokyo.

The army accomplished another step toward modernization in the 1890s by adopting the new Krag-Jörgensen rifle. Picking a rifle based on a foreign (Danish) rather than a U.S. design caused opposition by Americans who pulled political strings to delay the Krag's manufacture. They hoped to rescind the choice and reopen testing. Therefore, although the Ordnance Department approved it in 1892, the Krag did not swing into production until 1894. By 1898 the arsenal at Springfield, Massachusetts, had turned out 53,000 rifles and 14,800 Krag carbines, more than enough to equip the regular army of 28,000. Nevertheless, Congress declined to appropriate money to begin issuing the new rifle to National Guard units, and guardsmen had to make do with the Model 1873 Springfield. Guard units carried the venerable trapdoor rifle into the Spanish-American War.

Desertion rates remained high, averaging almost 15 percent of the enlisted force per year, but in the 1870s it exceeded 30 percent.

There were still many aspects of the army that needed improvement. For example, the army required no standard medical examinations for senior officers to remain on active duty. There were no pension or retirement plans for noncommissioned officers or officers, so they remained in uniform for as long as possible. Other matters needed attention. Throughout the second half of the nineteenth century, desertion rates remained high, averaging almost 15 percent of the enlisted force per year, but in the 1870s it exceeded 30 percent in some years. By contrast, the desertion rate in the British army was only about 2 percent. Observers and critics offered numerous explanations for so many deserters—low pay, poor food, inadequate amenities at some posts, dangerous assignments, or lack of excitement. The adjutant general took some steps to better the enlisted men's lot, and desertion rates dipped to about 5 percent in the 1890s, a considerable improvement. Furthermore, training and military planning left much to be desired. The United States lacked a European-style general staff to draw up contingency plans, and there was no army-wide doctrine for field-training exercises. The War Department addressed some of these matters after the War with Spain.

In August 1899, Russell Alger resigned as secretary of war and President William McKinley replaced him with Elihu Root. An astute corporate attorney who brought to the post energy, progressive attitudes, and a willingness to consider changes for the War Department, Root was receptive to some army officers' ideas for reform. Reversing the post–Civil War trend, Root became a civilian reformer who sought an increase, rather than a reduction, in the size of the army. Deployments to China and the Philippines during Root's administration helped bolster his advocacy of a larger force. Root supported some Uptonian concepts and later authorized the publication of the colonel's *Military Policy of the United States.* Particularly important among Root's early steps was his call for the approval of the Army Reorganization Act, subsequently passed by Congress on 2 February 1901. This law limited the tour of duty for most army staff officers to four years, thus instituting a rotation between line units and staff bureaus that had been an ideal sought by reform-minded officers even before Upton's time. This important law nullified the earlier practice of some officers who had secured for themselves an entrenched staff billet in Washington away from regimental duties in garrison and field.

The Reorganization Act of 1901 indicated the direction that Root's later, more famous reforms would take. He began considering numerous other changes, such as establishing a war college, reforming the National Guard, improving the Leavenworth schools, and creating a new general staff. The latter would have a chief of staff similar to that found in European armies, but also like the one John Schofield, among other American officers, had recommended some years before. Thus, the Root reforms culminated years of debate among politicians and military officers by combining American and European ideas that led to a rejuvenated army.

THE U.S. NAVY: FROM "DARK AGE" TO "NEW NAVY"

For the U.S. Navy and its officer corps, fighting the Confederacy had been a professional challenge successfully met. Over the four years of the Civil War the navy increased the number of warships and other vessels in service from 42 in 1861 to about 700 by 1865. Personnel on duty grew accordingly, from 7,600 enlisted men and 1,300 officers in 1861 to 51,500 sailors and 7,000 officers by 1865. Many of the warships in service in 1865 were based on the innovative *Monitor.* Like their namesake, they sported modernistic turrets, low freeboard, armor protection, and were highly maneuverable. These design features would be incorporated into the major warships of all nations in years to come.

Furthermore, the U.S. Navy Department had grown to accommodate the demands of the service, managed by the capable Secretary of the Navy Gideon Welles and by a newly created office, assistant secretary of the navy, filled admirably by Gustavus Fox. This administrative tandem supervised the blockade of the enemy's coast, a traditional navy responsibility in wartime. The blockade had been one of several causes contributing to the Confederacy's demise. Moreover, the Union navy's river gunboats had worked with the army to defeat the South in the war's western theater. The navy had fallen short in only one category—failing to suppress the South's *guerre de course* ("war of the chase," or attacks on cargo ships), even though the most infamous Confederate commerce raider, the *Alabama,* had been destroyed by the USS *Kearsarge.* Indeed, the *Alabama* made such an impression on U.S. naval officers that some of the navy's cruisers in the postwar years would be prepared as commerce raiders, ready to prey upon the cargo ships of potential enemies. Altogether, then, by 1865 the U.S. Navy had reached a high point of strength, pride, and sense of accomplishment, and made the United States one of the world's major naval powers.

This elevated status could not last. Within eighteen months after the Civil War ended the government began selling off ships, some of which, after all, had been merchant vessels converted to wartime use. Innovative monitor-style ships, some with two turrets, demonstrated their greatest usefulness in harbors and rivers. Their postwar ocean voyages only proved the point. In other words, traditional wooden war steamers still formed the heart of the blue-water navy, and by the 1870s the navy had dropped to only one hundred warships and about fifteen support vessels of various kinds. This drastic reduction came as no surprise, but what really stung America's navalists was its speed. U.S. political leaders saw no external threats and therefore no need to continue funding an expensive modern navy to keep pace with European navies. The American sea service had entered its own "dark age."

Within a decade after the Civil War, the U.S. Navy was stigmatized for relying on ships and guns that Europeans considered obsolescent or obsolete. By the 1880s, American wooden-hulled warships mounting smoothbore, muzzleloading Dahlgren cannon looked like dinosaurs when they dropped anchor near new metal-hulled British or French ships carrying rifled, breechloading guns. Because of the shortage of overseas coaling stations and reduced funds for buying coal, archconservative Admiral David Porter opposed using steam power and issued orders requiring U.S. Navy ships to use their sails when on patrol. Porter also used his clout as a hero of the Civil War to oppose progress in steam engineering, maintaining a feud with Benjamin Franklin Isherwood, chief of the navy's Bureau of Steam Engineering. Although this bitter rivalry involved personality as well as professional ideology, it revealed the first of several postwar contests in the naval officer corps between progressives who wanted the United States to build a European-style navy and traditionalists willing to accept wooden ships and antique cannon as the best the U.S. Navy could get out of Congress in a time of stringent budgets.

For two decades after the Civil War, it appeared as if technology had left the U.S. Navy behind, but its ships still "showed the flag" at a number of distant stations around the world. In the mid-1870s ten wooden war steamers sailed in the North Atlantic Squadron (that is, off the East Coast), while only five patrolled in the European Squadron, based for part of the time at Villefranche, France. The navy assigned nine ships to the Asiatic Squadron and seven to the Pacific Ocean. A point to note in these squadron assignments is that while they varied slightly in number from year to year, the United States had approximately twice as many ships patrolling in foreign wars in the 1870s as it had in the 1840s, even if the ships were obsolescent. In other words, the nation, as represented by its navy, was somewhat more visible and involved around the world, although it was arguable how much respect was earned by the wooden ships.

As the years passed, the navy, like the army, remained top-heavy with officers who were Civil War veterans. During the 1880s and 1890s younger officers complained about slow promotion and called for regular medical examinations to determine the fitness of commanders, proposed that Congress pass a retirement pay plan to encourage geriatric leaders to retire, and wanted more ships added to the service, thus opening up command assignments and sea time for junior and mid-level officers. As new ships were commissioned this pressure for promotion eased somewhat, but overage, infirm officers still dotted the naval list by the time of the Great White Fleet in 1906.

Traditional ideas dominated strategic thinking among many of the older officers. Reflecting wisdom or fossilization, some senior commanders recognized that appropriations could be had for defense from a tight-fisted Congress skeptical of offensive schemes against imaginary foes. During 1885 the Endicott Board, including navy Commander William T. Sampson, met over a period of several months and then issued a report in January 1886. The lengthy report indicated, among several conclusions, that coastal defense would continue to be a joint army-navy responsibility. The army would garrison forts near major cities and the navy would guard the coasts and the merchant marine. Commander Sampson specified the variety of vessels that might be used in a comprehensive coastal defense plan, including gunboats and new, modern torpedo boats, as well as the employment of submarine mines in harbors. Furthermore, the Endicott Board called for U.S. industry to improve its capability to manufacture high quality steel needed for shipmaking and artillery production.

The Naval Appropriations Act of 1883 providing for the so-called "ABC" ships, three all-steel cruisers named for the cities of Atlanta, Boston, and Chicago.

While the Endicott Board report combined traditional themes and new ideas, changes already had begun that led the way to a "new navy." In 1881, Secretary of the Navy William H. Hunt picked several officers to serve on the unofficial Naval Advisory Board that gave advice to the secretary on a wide range of subjects. Hunt, who served only from March 1881 to April 1882, took the advice of the board and recommended that several new ships of steel be built, despite their high cost. Republican President Chester A. Arthur listened to Hunt and pressed Congress to allocate money for the ships. Congress failed to designate such funds in 1882 but passed the Naval Appropriations Act of 1883 providing for the so-called "ABC" ships, three all-steel cruisers named for the cities of Atlanta, Boston, and Chicago, and the dispatch boat *Dolphin.* Coal-burning steam engines powered the ships, which were capable of 17 knots, but they also had a full complement of masts and sails. The new cruisers also had "protected" steel decks designed for improved defense against plunging fire from enemy shells. The *Atlanta, Boston,* and *Chicago* did not have full armor defensive belts, however, and carried guns of smaller caliber in contrast to similar ships in European navies. Nevertheless, the ABC ships signified the turn from wood to steel for the U.S. Navy. As these new ships were commissioned, the U.S. Navy could be ranked above such nations as Chile and Bolivia.

Additional congressional appropriations during the rest of the 1880s permitted construction of other steel ships. Led by Secretary of the Navy William Whitney, under Democratic President Grover Cleveland, Congress funded nine more steel cruisers—six without sails—which carried stronger armor similar to the ships of European navies. Included in this group were the *Maine* and the *Texas.* The trend to a modern navy with bipartisan support was now unmistakable.

In addition to new ships, the 1880s saw other important steps in U.S. naval modernization. In 1882 Secretary Hunt got approval from Congress to establish the

Office of Naval Intelligence (ONI). Its duties involved collecting and studying information on foreign navies in order to assess their capabilities. To assist in the collection of data, attachés were sent to major European and Asian nations and reported their observations to Washington, D.C. By the 1890s, ONI maintained files on every major navy in the world and drew up contingency plans addressing the possibility for war between the United States and several countries, notably Great Britain and Spain. The Naval Institute, a private organization for naval officers and interested civilians, had been founded in 1873. By the mid-1880s the institute's journal, *Proceedings,* had been published for ten years, allowing navalists to offer ideas for discussion in an unofficial forum.

Yet another step in modernization began in 1884. A three-officer board, composed of Commodore Stephen B. Luce, Commander Sampson, and Lieutenant Commander Casper Goodrich, reported to Secretary of the Navy William E. Chandler, urging him to support a postgraduate college for naval officers. In their report, the three officers pointed out that in an age of new inventions and changing technology, military leaders needed to "bring to the investigation of the various problems of modern naval warfare the scientific methods adopted in other professions." Chandler approved the officers' recommendation and obtained funding for the Naval War College, which began its first classes in September 1885 at Newport, Rhode Island, with Luce serving as it first president.

Luce had maintained a long interest in naval education. An Annapolis graduate (class of 1849), Luce originally had gained his midshipman's papers in 1841 and served at sea before going to the Naval Academy. During his long career (1841 to 1889), he devoted attention to improving the training of enlisted men as well as the education of officers. He taught at the Naval Academy, commanded a training ship and a training squadron, and advocated programs for naval cadets at the state land-grant colleges where the Morrill Act authorized training army cadets. Becoming president of the Naval War College in 1885 was a capstone to his career, but he also held the position of president of the Naval Institute from 1887 to 1898, guiding the institute for a decade after his retirement. While in uniform Luce wrote many magazine articles calling for naval reform

The Naval Appropriations Act of 1883 provided for the building of three all-steel cruisers named for the cities of Atlanta, Boston, and Chicago. In this 1889 photograph, the flagship Chicago *leads a squadron that includes the* Yorktown, Boston, *and* Atlanta. *(National Archives)*

and professional education. Promoted to the rank of rear admiral in 1885, Luce was an unusual combination of intellectual and administrator. Subsequently, after retiring in 1889, he returned to active duty and served an exceptional ten-year stint on special assignment at the Naval War College.

One of Luce's first appointments to the college's faculty was also his most important. The admiral tapped Captain Alfred Thayer Mahan to teach naval history. He was the son of West Point professor Dennis Hart Mahan. From his Annapolis graduation in 1859 to 1883, Alfred Mahan's naval career combined patience and ennui. New horizons opened with the publication of his first book, *The Gulf and Inland Waters* (1883), a volume in the Scribner's History of the Civil War series. In 1885 Luce directed Mahan to prepare lectures in naval history and to begin delivering them in 1886. Mahan not only taught, he succeeded Luce as president of the college (1886–1888 and 1892–1893). He helped shape the study of naval history, not only in the United States but also in other nations, including Great Britain, Germany, and Japan, by the publication of his seminal work, *The Influence of Seapower upon History, 1660–1783* (1890), which book made Mahan the most important U.S. writer on military affairs.

Mahan remains an important author worthy of study. In his writings (especially in the long introductory section of *The Influence of Seapower upon History*) he proposed that nations may have a certain aptitude for the sea, based upon several factors, such as geographical area, length of coastline, number of ports, overseas outposts, resources applicable to maritime endeavors, and the maritime "character" of the population. Furthermore, he asserted that a nation pretending to international leadership must maintain modern naval forces in existence to protect its interests and gain "command of the sea" in wartime, precepts that became fundamentals of modern military thought. According to Mahan, navies existed for offensive capabilities beyond blockades, the *guerre de course,* and coastal defense. Naval forces should be prepared to seek out, engage, and destroy enemy navies in fleet action. Most of his writings on naval tactics, however, soon became outdated and his stress, along the lines of Antoine Henri Jomini, of concentrating entire national fleets no longer became applicable. Likewise, his dictum that the *guerre de course* (destroying an enemy nation's commerce-carrying ships) could never be decisive was severely tested by the German successes with submarines in the world wars of the twentieth century. This highlighted that Mahan limited his strategic view to one dimension—war on the sea—not in the air above it or in the water beneath the surface.

Mahan's writings described the maturation of the British Royal Navy and how Britain relied upon its navy to become a great imperial power. It was ironic that books by an American naval officer greatly enhanced the reputation of the Royal Navy. Mahan implied that for any nation to have similar imperial success, it must also possess a strong navy. Indeed, he showed that building a powerful navy was one of the prerequisites of being a great power. Mahan went on to produce a series of successful volumes, including *The Influence of Seapower upon the French Revolution and Empire* (2 vols., 1892), *Seapower in its Relation to the War of 1812* (2 vols., 1905), *The Major Operations of the Navies in the War of American Independence* (1913), as well as biographies of David G. Farragut (1892) and Horatio Nelson (1897) and a work titled *Naval Strategy* (1911).

A number of British military and political leaders delighted in Mahan's broad conclusions, emphasizing as they did the accomplishments of the Royal Navy. Mahan's writings could also be used to confirm the verisimilitude of a large navy of capital ships and lend credence to the European imperialistic system during another round of competition for colonies, this time in Africa and the Pacific Ocean. Accordingly, U.S. leaders came to see America's need for a modern navy if their nation was to join this imperialistic contest, and to give the United States an improved status among the Western nations.

Adding endeavors in journalism not only brought Mahan financial comfort but boosted his national standing. His essays on naval subjects, imperialism, and contemporary affairs were published in such widely circulated magazines as *Collier's, North American Review, Atlantic, Century, McClure's,* and *Harper's Monthly.* Political, military, business, and religious leaders were pleased to use Mahan's name and conclusions to bolster their own agenda, such as building a bigger navy, acquiring colonies, expanding U.S. trade abroad, or increasing Protestant missionary activities in foreign lands. Although Mahan had been skeptical of imperialistic ventures in the 1870s, he pushed for U.S. procurement and consolidation of colonial possessions from the 1890s to his death in 1914. The U.S. control of a canal in Panama became one of his pet projects. Theodore Roosevelt, Henry Cabot Lodge, and others had already been advocating a larger role for the United States in international affairs and they applauded Mahan and his writings.

Mahan, of course, favored regular forces, so an unusual aspect in naval activities began in 1888 when Congressman Washington C. Whitthorne (a Democrat from Tennessee) proposed to establish "the enrollment of a naval militia and the formation of a naval reserve in the several sea and lake board States." According to the *Report of the Secretary of the Navy* for 1889, Whitthorne's bill did not pass through Congress in 1888, but he brought it up again the next year. In the meantime, the legislatures of Massachusetts, Rhode Island, and New York passed state laws anticipating the approval of a national naval militia, which could be considered a complement to the army's National Guard. In 1889, Secretary of the Navy Benjamin F. Tracy supported the Whitthorne bill, but Congress disappointed Tracy again. Acting on his own, Tracy authorized the New York and Massachusetts state naval militiamen to conduct drills on a navy ship for a few days of summer training. He continued to lobby Congress for support of a bill that would provide surplus federal arms and equipment for the naval militias. Tracy concluded that hundreds of naval militia could be trained to supplement the active forces, which were limited by law to seventy-five hundred sailors. Some militiamen might serve in front-line ships in wartime, but in Tracy's view most would be involved in harbor defense.

Tracy's diligence was rewarded by the Naval Appropriations Act of 1891, which allocated $25,000 annually for the support of state naval militias, funds to be distributed by the secretary of the navy. State governors would make requisitions for arms and equipment from the Navy Department based on the number of naval militia enrolled. Based on the *Report of the Secretary of the Navy* for 1891, California led all states by enlisting 371 men into its naval militia, followed by New York (342), Massachusetts (238), North Carolina (101), Rhode Island (54), and Texas (43). In the next few years, other states initiated naval militia programs and eastern states expanded theirs. For example, in 1892 New York surpassed all states with 401 naval militiamen. California, Massachusetts, North Carolina, South Carolina, and Maryland tallied 376, 331, 296, 208, and 124, respectively. Pennsylvania and Illinois announced their intentions to recruit naval militia battalions, while Texas disbanded its company.

During the 1890s the naval militia program was not uniform from state to state. Secretary of the Navy Hilary A. Herbert placed Assistant Secretary of the Navy William G. McAdoo in charge of the Navy Department's relations with these new state organizations, which went by various names. The Naval Militia of the National Guard of California drilled haphazardly and usually without the benefit of an active duty navy ship. The Naval Brigade, Ohio National Guard was established in 1896 and enrolled 174 men in 1897. The Naval Militia of Illinois recruited most of its 448 men in the Chicago area in 1897 and was considered by the navy to be "a valuable naval auxiliary in time of war." The First Naval Battalion of the Louisiana State National Guard received an excellent rating for discipline and activity from the regular navy officer assigned to evaluate it in New Orleans in 1897. On the other hand, another officer rated the discipline of the Naval Force of the State of Pennsylvania only "as good as can be expected of such an organization." Other states dubbed their units variously, such as the Naval Reserve of New Jersey and the Michigan State Naval Brigade.

Putting the best face on his duties, in 1896 Assistant Secretary McAdoo found most naval militia he inspected to be patriotic, interested in their avocation, and enthusiastic about the naval service. McAdoo also found a need, however, for more weapons, equipment, and boats and noted that, although it differed state by state, between 50 percent and 85 percent of the militia in the states attended their summer drills, but not enough navy ships were available for all militiamen to see how things were done in an active duty vessel. Secretary Herbert concluded that most militiamen possessed "limited knowledge and experience" about the shipboard duties they could be asked to assume in wartime.

In 1897, on the eve of war with Spain, Assistant Secretary of the Navy Theodore Roosevelt called for more congressional appropriations for naval militia summer drills. Its enrollment had been increasing year by year, and in 1897 totaled 3,703 men in fifteen states, six in the Northeast (Massachusetts, Rhode Island, Connecticut, New York, New Jersey, and Pennsylvania), five in the South (Maryland, North Carolina, South Carolina, Georgia, and Louisiana), three in the Midwest (Illinois, Michigan, and Ohio), and California in the West. (At about this time the army enrolled some 105,000 citizens across the country in the National Guard.) Roosevelt personally visited naval militia units in New York and the three Midwest states and noted that there was "a great variety in the condition of efficiency reached by the different organizations." In the conflict with Spain some naval militiamen were brought on active duty, but the naval militia units provided proof to businessmen and politicians, especially on the eastern seaboard, that the navy was paying attention to their needs for local defense in time of war.

Far more important than the naval militia to the "new navy" were the modern warships commissioned in the 1890s. Secretary of the Navy Tracy served from 1889 to 1893 under Republican President Benjamin Harrison. When Tracy took office some European observers ranked the U.S. Navy twelfth in the world. Beginning with the Naval Appropriations Act of 1891, Tracy recommended construction of several new ships, including three battleships and supporting cruisers. He also expanded the Naval War College and developed a tactical training unit called the "squadron of evolution." Congress was still skeptical of so-called offensive weapons and therefore Tracy classified his largest new vessels as "coastal defense" battleships. Comparable in some respects to their European cousins, the coastal defense battleships displaced 10,000 tons, reached speeds up to 17 knots, menaced potential opponents with 13-inch guns, and were fully armored. The battleships (named for states) included the *Indiana, Oregon,* and *Massachusetts,* supplemented by the cruisers (named for cities) *Brooklyn* and *Minneapolis.* All of them served in the U.S. Navy's confrontation with Spanish forces near the end of the decade. Secretary of the Navy Herbert endorsed new construction for additional battleships during President Grover Cleveland's second term (1893–1897). Especially notable was the completion of the 11,000-ton battleship *Iowa* in 1897, but five other battleships were under construction by the time Cleveland left office.

Thus, in 1898 the U.S. Navy possessed sturdy new battleships and modern armored cruisers as well as older battleships and protected cruisers. Taken together with torpedo boats and other auxiliaries, they would not overawe such first-class navies as those of Great Britain or France, but they presented a formidable array against a second-class power, such as Spain. The U.S. Navy's ships had the advantage of newness, most having been commissioned during the years 1886–1897 and incor-

The U.S. Navy commissioned many modern warships in the 1890s. The 11,000-ton battleship Iowa, *shown here entering dry dock in 1898, was completed in 1897 during President Grover Cleveland's second term. (National Archives)*

porating some of the era's best technology, such as range finders, automated ammunition hoists, and sophisticated electrical systems. Some of these innovations had been invented or developed by an exceptional U.S. naval officer Bradley A. Fiske.

The world ranking of the U.S. Navy had moved up from twelfth in 1889 to around sixth or seventh in 1898.

While European opinions varied, and taking numerous factors into account, the ranking of the U.S. Navy had moved up from twelfth in 1889 to around sixth or seventh in 1898. It ranked behind the navies of Great Britain, France, Russia, Germany, and Italy and just above or below that of Spain. Whatever its international ranking, the navy certainly justified its traditional claim of being the nation's first line of defense. Based on such factors as gunnery, ammunition quality, serviceability of ships' engines, and general seaworthiness of the fleet, the U.S. Navy compared favorably with European navies. As events showed, in all of these specifics, the U.S. Navy proved to be ranked above the Spanish navy.

The U.S. Navy had made great strides in the 1880s and 1890s. On such comparable points as overall capability, level of training, and use of modern technology it surpassed the U.S. Army. Officers on the German General Staff could (and did) disregard the U.S. Army in their 1897 report on military forces in other nations, but the U.S. Navy deserved to be ranked as a high-quality military force.

BIBLIOGRAPHY

General Works

Coffman, Edward M. *The Old Army: A Portrait of the American Army in Peacetime, 1784–1898* (1986).

Dawson, Joseph G., III. *The Late 19th Century U.S. Army, 1865–1898: A Research Guide* (1990).

Ganoe, William A. *The History of the United States Army* (1924).

Hagan, Kenneth J., and William R. Roberts, eds., *Against All Enemies: Interpretations of American Military History from Colonial Times to the Present* (1986).

Millett, Allan R., and Peter Maslowski. *For the Common Defense: A Military History of the United States of America* (1984).

Spiller, Roger J., Joseph G. Dawson III, and T. Harry Williams, eds., *Dictionary of American Military Biography,* 3 vols. (1984).

Weigley, Russell F. *Towards an American Army: Military Thought from Washington to Marshall* (1962).

———. *History of the United States Army* (1967, rev. 1984).

Reconstruction

Clendenen, Clarence C. "President Hayes' 'Withdrawal' of the Troops—An Enduring Myth." *South Carolina Historical Magazine* (1969).

Coakley, Robert W. *The Role of Federal Military Forces in Domestic Disorders, 1789–1878* (1988).

Dawson, Joseph G., III. *Army Generals and Reconstruction: Louisiana, 1862–1877* (1982).

Hyman, Harold M. "Johnson, Stanton, and Grant: A Reconsideration of the Army's Role in the Events Leading to Impeachment." *American Historical Review* 66 (1960).

Rable, George C. *But There Was No Peace: The Role of Violence in the Politics of Reconstruction* (1984).

———. "William T. Sherman and the Conservative Critique of Radical Reconstruction." *Ohio History* 93 (1984).

Richter, William L. *The Army in Texas During Reconstruction, 1865–1870* (1987).

Sefton, James E. *The United States Army and Reconstruction, 1865–1877* (1967).

The Indian Wars

Ambrose, Stephen E. *Crazy Horse and Custer* (1975).

Athearn, Robert G. *William Tecumseh Sherman and the Settlement of the West* (1956).

Fowler, Arlen. *Black Infantry in the West, 1869–1891* (1971).

Gates, John M. "Indians and Insurrectos: The U.S. Army's Experience with Insurgency." *Parameters* 13 (1983).

Gray, John S. *Centennial Campaign: The Sioux War of 1876* (1976).

Haley, James L. *The Buffalo War: The History of the Red River Indian Uprising of 1874* (1976).

Hutton, Paul A. *Phil Sheridan and His Army* (1985).

Knight, Oliver. *Life and Manners in the Frontier Army* (1978).

Leckie, William H. *The Buffalo Soldiers: A Narrative of the Negro Cavalry in the West* (1967).

Rickey, Don, Jr. *Forty Miles a Day on Beans and Hay: The Enlisted Soldier Fighting the Indian Wars* (1963).

Stewart, Edgar I. *Custer's Luck* (1955).

Thrapp, Dan L. *The Conquest of Apacheria* (1967).

Tate, Michael L. "The Multi-Purpose Army on the Frontier: A Call for Further Research." In *The American West,* edited by Ronald Lora (1980).

Utley, Robert M. *Frontier Regulars: The United States Army and the Indian, 1866–1891* (1973).

———. *Cavalier in Buckskin: George Armstrong Custer and the Western Military Frontier* (1988).

Wooster, Robert. *Soldiers, Sutlers, and Settlers: Garrison Life on the Texas Frontier* (1987).

———. *The Military and United States Indian Policy, 1865–1903* (1988).

Army Reforms

Abrahamson, James L. *America Arms for a New Century: The Making of a Great Military Power* (1981).

Ambrose, Stephen E. *Upton and the Army* (1964).

Browning, Robert S., III. *Two if By Sea: The Development of American Coastal Defense Policy* (1983).

Coffman, Edward M. "The Long Shadow of *The Soldier and the State.*" *Journal of Military History* 55 (1991).

Cooper, Jerry M. *The Army and Civil Disorder: Federal Military Intervention in Labor Disputes, 1877–1900* (1980).

Cosmas, Graham A. *An Army for Empire: The United States Army in the Spanish-American War* (1971; rev. ed. 1993).

Foner, Jack D. *The United States Soldier Between Two Wars: Army Life and Reforms, 1865–1898* (1970).

Gates, John M. "The Alleged Isolation of U.S. Army Officers in the Late 19th Century." *Parameters* 10 (1980).

———. "The 'New' Military Professionalism." *Armed Forces and Society* 11 (1985).

Hacker, Barton C. "The United States Army as a National Police Force: The Federal Policing of Labor Disputes, 1877–1898." *Military Affairs* 33 (1969).

Hampton, Duane H. *How the U.S. Cavalry Saved Our National Parks* (1971).

Huntington, Samuel P. *The Soldier and the State: The Theory and Politics of Civil Military Relations* (1957).

Karsten, Peter. "Armed Progressives: The Military Reorganizes for the American Century." Peter Karsten, ed., *The Military in America* (1980).

Nenninger, Timonthy K. *The Leavenworth Schools and the Old Army: Education, Professionalism, and the Officer Corps of the United States Army, 1881–1918* (1978).

The U.S. Navy, 1865–1890s

Alden, John D. *The American Steel Navy* (1972).

Allin, Lawrence C. *The United States Naval Institute: Intellectual Forum of the New Navy, 1873–1889* (1978).

Bradford, James C. *Admirals of the New Steel Navy* (1990).

Buhl, Lance C. "Maintaining 'An American Navy,' 1865–1889." In *In Peace and War,* edited by Kenneth Hagan (1984).

———. "Mariners and Machines: Resistance to Technological Change in the American Navy, 1865–1869." *Journal of American History* 59 (December 1974).

Cooling, Benjamin F. *Benjamin Franklin Tracy: Father of the Modern American Fighting Navy* (1973).

———. *Gray Steel and Blue Water Navy: The Formative Years of America's Military-Industrial Complex, 1881–1917* (1979).

Dorwart, Jeffrey M. *The Office of Naval Intelligence: The Birth of America's First Intelligence Agency, 1865–1918* (1979).

Herrick, Walter B., Jr. *The American Naval Revolution* (1966).

Karsten, Peter. *The Naval Aristocracy: The Golden Age of Annapolis and the Emergence of Modern American Navalism* (1972).

Livezey, William E. *Mahan on Sea Power* (1947; rev. ed. 1980).

Ransom, Edward. "The Endicott Board of 1885–86 and the Coast Defenses." *Military Affairs* 31 (1967).

Seager, Robert, III. *Alfred Thayer Mahan: The Man and His Letters* (1977).

Spector, Ronald. *Admiral of the New Empire: The Life and Career of George Dewey* (1974).

———. *Professors of War: The Naval War College and the Development of the Naval Profession* (1977).

———. "The Triumph of Professional Ideology: The U.S. Navy in the 1890s." In *In Peace and War,* edited by Kenneth Hagan (1984).

Still, William N. *American Sea Power in the Old World: The United States Navy in European and Near Eastern Waters, 1865–1917* (1980).

— JOSEPH G. DAWSON III

The Spanish-American War and Its Aftermath

Although the briefest of American conflicts, the Spanish-American War of 1898, otherwise known as the War with Spain, was nevertheless of considerable significance. It began as a humanitarian enterprise, but it led to the acquisition of a measurable insular empire. Moreover, it marked the beginning of the nation's transformation from an isolated nation indifferent to events in Europe and Asia to an interventionist power implicated in developments throughout the world. Finally, the war led to a new mission for the armed forces, the administration and protection of the new empire.

ORIGINS OF THE WAR

The Spanish-American War stemmed from the failure of Spain to put down an insurgency in Cuba. This revolt, beginning in February 1895, constituted a resumption of the Ten Years War (1868–1878), an earlier uprising that ended unsuccessfully. A Cuban junta in New York augmented by others in Latin America raised funds to support the insurgents and attempted to run arms to them past Spanish naval vessels guarding the coast of Cuba. The principal Cuban rebel general, Máximo Gómez, adopted a scorched-earth strategy, seeking to disrupt the island's principal enterprise, the sugar industry, and force affluent Cubans to support the insurgency. Recognizing that he could not defeat the superior Spanish army by waging conventional war, he avoided pitched battles, preferring to make surprise raids on sugar plantations and then to seek refuge in heavily forested or mountainous locations. This partisan warfare was designed to wear out the opposition; the *insurrectos* hoped that Spain would eventually tire and give up the struggle. Gómez never had more than forty thousand lightly armed troops under his command at any one time. The Spanish army and its Cuban auxiliaries numbered about 230,000 troops. Tropical diseases—malaria, dysentery, and yellow fever—seriously impaired the efficiency of the Spanish organizations.

Having decided to pacify Cuba, the Spanish government sent the victor of the Ten Years War, General Arsenio Martínez de Campos, to lead the campaign against Gómez. His strategy was to construct a defensive line (*trocha*) from the northern coast of Cuba to the southern coast between Morón and Júcaro to isolate the eastern province of Oriente, stronghold of the insurgents. This essentially defensive scheme did not work. The insurgents easily penetrated the *trocha* and operated at will to the west.

A more vigorous commander, General Valeriano Weyler y Nicolau, soon replaced Martínez de Campos and immediately issued an order of reconcentration. This measure gathered all civilians (*reconcentrados*) into camps and halted movement in the countryside. Its chief objective was to deny arms and supplies to the enemy. Weyler then built another *trocha*, this one in the west from Mariel to Majana, isolating the province of Pinar del Río, which he planned to pacify and then move against Oriente. Unfortunately for Weyler, his measures proved no more successful than those of his predecessor. The insurgents remained free to operate at will throughout the Cuban countryside.

President Cleveland's policy called for some form of home rule or autonomy for Cuba.

Weyler's activities stimulated considerable criticism in the United States, imparting new impetus to the generally anti-Spanish sentiment of the public. The suffering of the *reconcentrados* aroused general sympathy. President Grover Cleveland at first ignored the insurgency, but, in response to congressional pressure, he eventually tendered his good offices to Spain. Madrid's answer defended Spanish policy in Cuba without reserve and rejected all proposals for reform. As his term ended, Cleveland adopted a more advanced policy, calling for some form of home rule or autonomy for Cuba and suggesting that Spain's failure to take action might lead to American intervention.

Like his predecessor, Republican President William McKinley, who took office in March 1897, did not want to involve himself in the struggle between Spain and Cuba, preferring to concentrate on a domestic agenda that included reform of the tariff and the currency. Growing public support for the Cuban revolutionaries, however, forced him to take action. He sent a new minister to Spain, General Stewart L. Woodford, to urge autonomy upon a new government in Madrid headed by the Liberal party leader, Práxedes Mateo Sagasta. McKinley indicated, as had Cleveland before him, that delay might lead to U.S. intervention on the side of the insurgents. The Liberals had agreed to autonomy for Cuba, but they were constrained by strong Spanish opinion favoring the retention of Cuba, the jewel of their decaying empire. Sagasta's conduct reflected his fear that any sign of undue weakness on his part might result in a powerful domestic reaction, perhaps a revolution that would overthrow the Restoration monarchy established in 1875. His policy was doomed to failure because it encouraged the insurgents to sustain their operations. Why accept autonomy when independence was within sight?

A great outburst of public opinion, fed by inflammatory yellow journalism in the American press, favored the expulsion of Spain from Cuba.

In February 1898 two events suddenly transformed the situation. One was the publication of a private letter written by Enrique Dupuy de Lôme, the Spanish minister in Washington, which included several derogatory comments about President McKinley. The Cuban junta in New York had stolen the letter and given it to the press, and the American public was instantly inflamed. Dupuy de Lôme admitted authorship and resigned, bringing to an end an embarrassing affair.

A few days later, however, on 15 February, the U.S. battleship *Maine*, lying at anchor in the harbor at Havana, blew up and sank, killing 266 crew members and wounding many others. The ship had been sent to Cuba to provide protection for U.S. citizens and their property. A U.S. investigation concluded that an explosion of external origin had caused the disaster, strengthening the instinctive public assumption that Spain had been at fault. A Spanish commission found that an internal explosion had occurred, which placed the responsibility with the Americans. Decades later, careful inquiry proved with near-certainty that the forward coal bunkers had caught fire and caused adjacent magazines to explode, but few Americans reached that conclusion in 1898.

Before 15 February, the Cuban question had been one of many important public issues in the United States, but the destruction of the *Maine* dwarfed all other matters. A great outburst of public opinion that favored the expulsion of Spain from Cuba, fed by inflammatory yellow journalism in the American press, found expression in insistent calls for action from Congress. McKinley, who hoped to find a peaceful solution, tried to obtain sufficient concessions from Madrid, working through Minister Woodford. To exert pressure on Sagasta, McKinley gained congressional authority on 9 March to expend $50 million for national defense. On 27 March, McKinley instructed Woodford to seek independence for Cuba, recognizing that he could no longer defy public opinion without grievously undermining his political position.

Sagasta proved unresponsive despite energetic efforts to move him from autonomy to independence. He retained the belief that a grant of independence to Cuba under U.S. pressure would lead to domestic revolution and the destruction of the Restoration monarchy. Ironically, both Sagasta and McKinley desired peace, but public opinion denied them the freedom of action necessary to produce such a result. Sagasta renewed efforts to obtain support for his position from other European states, but no help was forthcoming. Spain lacked claims on other nations, having followed a foreign policy of isolation for many years, and none of the great powers wished to alienate the United States.

On 11 April, having exhausted all his diplomatic options, President McKinley sent a message to Congress asking for authority to intervene in Cuba on the side of the insurgents, a step that soon led to war. He did not, however, call for recognition of the Cuban insurgent government, seeking to retain as much flexibility as possible. During the congressional debate, Senator Henry M. Teller, a Democrat from Colorado, offered an amendment that sought to establish the purity of U.S. motives. This self-denying ordinance disclaimed any intent to annex Cuba. On 19 April, Congress passed a joint resolution providing for intervention. McKinley signed the resolution on 20 April, and an ultimatum was then sent to Madrid, demanding that Spain act by noon on 23 April.

Spain had already determined its course. The Spanish minister in Washington was ordered home on 21 April and Spain declared war on 23 April. In Washington, on 25 April, the president asked congress for a declaration of war as of 21 April. This step reflected the need to legitimize certain acts of war that had already taken place, particularly the establishment on 22 April of a naval blockade against Havana.

WAR PLANS

It was evident to both countries long before the outbreak of hostilities that a Spanish-American conflict would turn largely on naval warfare. The Spanish minister of marine, Admiral Segismundo Bermejo y Merolo, envisioned dispatch of a naval squadron composed of six armored vessels—a battleship and five cruisers—to Cuban waters, where it would join eight lesser vessels stationed at Havana. After destroying the U.S. naval base at Key West, Florida, it would blockade the eastern seaboard. Rear Admiral Pascual Cervera y Topete, the commander of the proposed expedition, protested the plan, noting worriedly that some of his ships were under repair and that the vessels at Havana were useless. Economic difficulties at home had interfered with the growth and readiness of the navy. The U.S. naval forces were three times stronger than those of Spain, and Cervera had to assume a defensive posture. When further pressures for offensive action came from the Ministry of Marine, Cervera insisted that the United States would exercise command of the sea and that a sortie to the Caribbean Sea would "surely cause the total ruin of Spain."

Bermejo remained adamant and, like all too many in the Spanish government, underestimated the capabilities of the United States. He gave orders to locate one squadron near Cádiz in home waters and to send another to Cuba. Early in April he arranged to concentrate a squadron under Cervera in the Portuguese Cape Verde Islands. When all ships arrived at St. Vincent, the Spanish squadron consisted of four armored cruisers—*Cristóbal Colón, Infanta María Teresa, Vizcaya,* and *Almirante Oquendo*—and three destroyers. The *Cristóbal Colón* was potentially stronger than any armored cruiser in the U.S. North Atlantic Squadron, but the Spanish vessel lacked its main batteries of ten-inch guns and could not participate in a squadron engagement. Despite continuing protests from Cervera, who wanted to return to Spain, his squadron remained in the Cape Verdes prepared to depart for the Caribbean Sea.

Spain did not make plans to reinforce its land forces in Cuba, Puerto Rico, and the Philippines. The army in Cuba was much larger than any force the United States could hope to send for many months. A sizable army was also stationed in the Philippines, where Span-

The USS Maine *passes Morro Castle as it enters Havana Harbor 25 January 1898. Three weeks later, the* Maine *blew up and sank, killing 266 crew members. (National Archives)*

ish troops, numbering about twenty-six thousand, were augmented by fourteen thousand Filipino militia. Twenty-three thousand men were on the main island of Luzon, nine thousand of them assigned to the defense of Manila. For the moment, nothing was done to reinforce the weak Spanish naval squadron at Manila despite the pleas of Admiral Patricio Montojo, who feared that the U.S. Asiatic Squadron, then anchored at Hong Kong, would mount an early attack. Montojo had only two unprotected cruisers and five gunboats. These ships carried just thirty-seven modern guns, of which the largest were seven 6.3-inch rifles. Spain's insular possessions would have to make do with the land forces available at the start of hostilities. Madrid staked everything on the hope that it could prevent the United States from establishing command of the sea and interdicting communications between the insular empire and the homeland, an achievement that would prevent eventual reinforcement and resupply of the overseas forces and interrupt all maritime commerce.

Much more extensive planning took place in the United States. Officers at the Naval War College in Newport, Rhode Island, had interested themselves in a possible conflict with Spain as early as 1894, but the initial war plan was not prepared until 1896. Lieutenant William Warren Kimball, an intelligence officer assigned to the Naval War College, concocted a scheme that contemplated a naval war only. U.S. forces would seize control of the Straits of Florida and help the Cuban insurgents. If necessary, an army expedition would move against Havana. While operations unfolded in the main theater of war, secondary campaigns would develop, including a naval demonstration in Spanish waters to prevent the dispatch of reinforcements to the Caribbean and a naval strike against Manila to exert pressure on Spain to end the war. Later plans reflected the general ideas included in the early scenarios. Among them were a blockade of Cuba and Puerto Rico, an attack by land forces against Cuba, the occupation of Puerto Rico, a naval attack on Manila, and naval operations in Spanish home waters.

After the sinking of the *Maine,* actions were taken to put these ideas into effect. On 25 February 1898, Assistant Secretary of the Navy Theodore Roosevelt sent a message to Commodore George Dewey, commander of the Asiatic Squadron, ordering him to move his squadron from Japan to Hong Kong. If war came, he was to prevent the Spanish squadron from leaving Asiatic waters, an order that reflected prior planning. Dewey's movement to Manila Bay would provide a base for the Asiatic Squadron, which could not remain long in neutral ports during time of war, and preclude Spanish attacks on U.S. merchant shipping in the Pacific Ocean. The Navy Department then ordered the first-class battleship *Oregon,* stationed on the West Coast, to steam around Cape Horn and join the North Atlantic Squadron, a move intended to assure naval superiority in the principal theater of war. Also, the department began a strenuous search for suitable auxiliary vessels and launched an effort to purchase ships of war from various foreign powers.

During March 1898, the navy prepared to take action against Cuba. To guard against possible Spanish naval raids on eastern U.S. ports, a "flying squadron," able to move rapidly to threatened locations, was organized and stationed initially at Hampton Roads in Virginia. Commanded by Commodore Winfield S. Schley, it included three armored vessels, the battleships *Texas* and *Massachusetts* and the armored cruiser *Brooklyn.* Most of the vessels available in the Atlantic, however, were placed under Captain William T. Sampson, commander of the North Atlantic Squadron, whose orders were to blockade Cuba and Puerto Rico. His ships included the battleships Iowa, Indiana, and Oregon, the latter en route from the West Coast, and the armored cruiser *New York.* When combined, the seven armored ships in the Atlantic vastly outclassed the modern armored vessels available to Spain.

In March 1898, Secretary of the Navy John D. Long organized the Naval War Board, which directed naval intelligence and provided advice on important naval matters. One of its three members was Captain Alfred Thayer Mahan, the renowned naval historian, recalled to active duty during the emergency. Adopting a principle that would guide later activities, the board soon decided that the navy should concentrate on Spain's vulnerable insular possessions. Operations would take place in Spain's home waters only after victory had been assured in the Caribbean theater. Early naval operations would buy time for the army, which needed to mobilize a large volunteer force before it could undertake serious operations against the large Spanish force around Havana.

Meanwhile, Commodore Dewey prepared for operations against Montojo at Manila. Dewey's Asiatic Squadron included the protected cruisers *Olympia, Raleigh,* and *Baltimore,* the unprotected cruisers *Concord* and *Boston,* the gunboat *Petrel,* the revenue cutter *McCulloch,* and three auxiliary vessels. Although he did not have a modern armored ship, his squadron was much superior to the decrepit enemy force at Manila. He had fifty-three heavy guns, including ten 10-inch breechloading rifles that outranged all the Spanish naval guns.

The prewar planning and preparations of the U.S. Army reflected the general presumption that it would

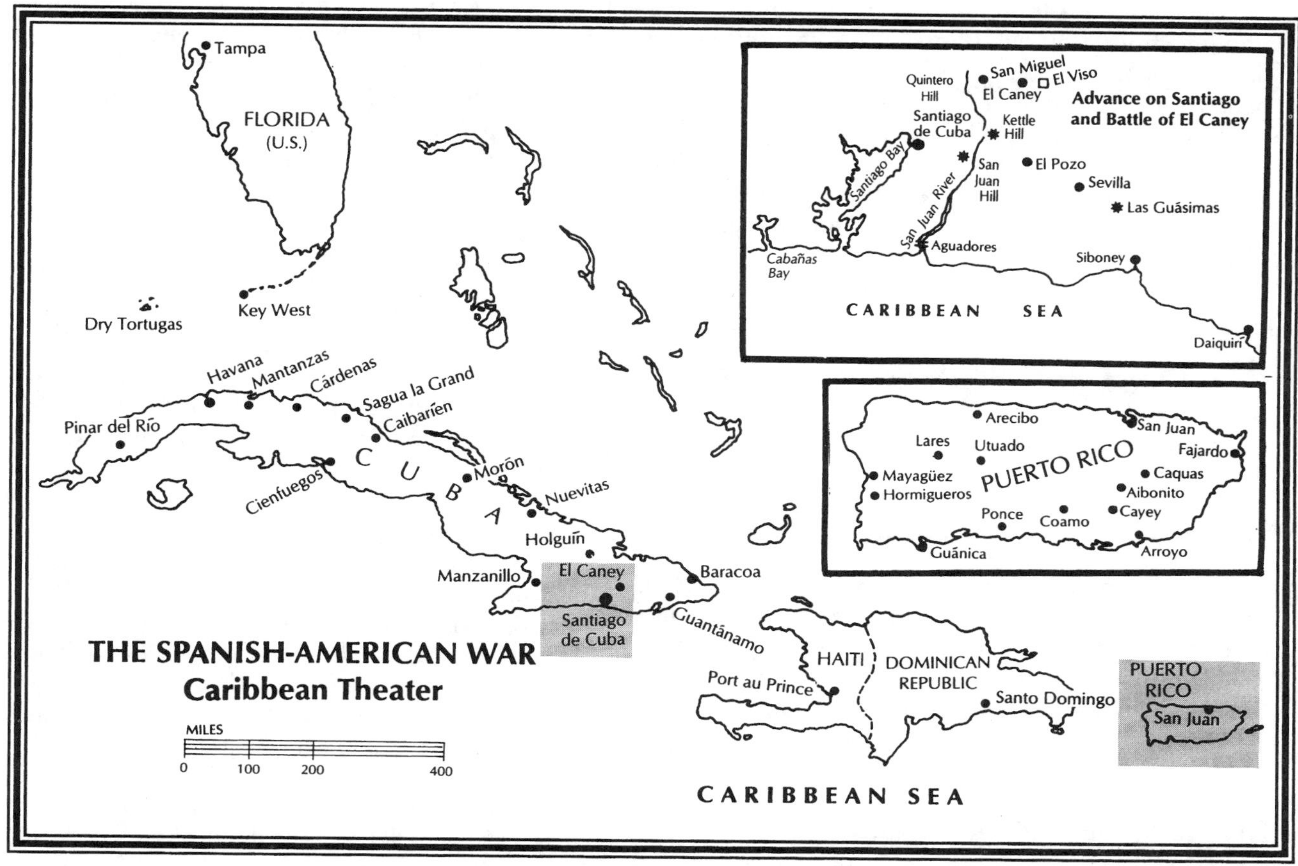

play a subordinate role in a war with Spain. It was assigned only $19 million from the $50 million appropriation voted by Congress in March, and the secretary of war, Russell Alger, decided that he could use the special fund only for defensive purposes, such as coast defense. When the War Department began to consider land operations in support of the navy, it contemplated small hit-and-run raids on the Cuban coast, recognizing the limitations that stemmed from the size of the regular army, only about twenty-eight thousand men. Ultimately, it would prepare a volunteer force of about a hundred thousand recruits from which, if necessary, it could draw men for a strike at strong enemy troop concentrations such as those around Havana.

These ideas guided decisions about the army's mobilization in 1898. The first step was to concentrate most of the regular army in the southeastern United States at three ports—New Orleans, Mobile, and Tampa. Other troops went to Camp Thomas at Chickamauga Park, Tennessee. Meanwhile, Congress passed legislation on 22 April that provided for the volunteer army. This measure reflected the considerable political influence of state-controlled militia units. An initial call for volunteers would be confined to members of the National Guard, who would enter the federal service, quotas being established for each state. Guard units could volunteer en masse and serve under their officers. The president was authorized to appoint staff officers and general officers, but state governors retained the right to select officers of lower rank. The act of 22 April also permitted recruitment of three thousand national volunteers, a provision that led to the formation of the First United States Volunteer Cavalry Regiment, better known as the Rough Riders, and several other similar organizations. The volunteer army would be formed into corps of three divisions, each of which included no more than three brigades. The brigades contained no more than three regiments.

In a flurry of activity the government soon completed preparations for the mobilization of the army. President McKinley immediately issued a call for 125,000 volunteers, approximately the strength of militia units. On 26 April, Congress agreed to expand the regular army to 65,000 men. On 11 May, Congress approved a plan calling for the organization of ten regiments of men immune from tropical disease; black men from the South supposedly would not contract diseases such as malaria and yellow fever, an assumption later proved unfounded. On 25 May, McKinley called for an additional 75,000 volunteers. Eventually about 200,000 volunteers entered the service, of whom only about 65,000 were sent overseas. Congress thus authorized a combined force of about 280,000 men, of whom 216,500 were volunteers and 65,700 regulars.

Congress approved a plan calling for the organization of ten regiments of men immune from tropical disease.

The tardy provisions for mobilization of a volunteer army ensured that the navy would have to bear the burden of early operations. Fortunately, the navy was prepared to take immediate action in the Caribbean Sea and in the South China Sea. If successful, the initial operations of the navy would prepare the way for army expeditions as troops became available.

INITIAL NAVAL OPERATIONS

On 27 April, Commodore Dewey left Mirs Bay, China, where he had anchored after leaving Hong Kong, following orders received on 25 April that directed him to attack the Spanish squadron at Manila. Having received intelligence that Admiral Montojo intended to make his defense at Subic Bay, outside the entrance to Manila Bay, Dewey and his squadron of five cruisers and a gunboat sailed in column across the South China Sea and arrived off Subic Bay on the afternoon of 30 April.

Meanwhile, Admiral Montojo maneuvered in preparation for the expected American onslaught. Believing that planned fortifications at Subic Bay had been carried out, Montojo had indeed intended to make his defense at Subic Bay, rejecting alternatives, such as the entrance to Manila Bay and the naval station at Cavite south of Manila, because neither place was appropriately fortified with artillery and mines. When he arrived at Subic Bay, however, he discovered that the fortifications had not been completed. With his options thus narrowed, he elected to fight at the Cavite naval station after all, where he could anchor in shallow water and gain at least some artillery assistance from a battery on Sangley Point. This decision reflected Montojo's belief in the superiority of the U.S. squadron. If his ships foundered in shallow water, his crews could hope to survive.

Theoretically, there were other options. Montojo might have accepted battle in the open sea, but this course would almost certainly have led to defeat. He also could have fled Manila and sent his ships to various widely separated ports, at least denying an early victory to the Americans. The governor-general at Manila, Basilio Augustín, vetoed this course, reflecting the wishes of the Spanish residents of Manila who thought that Montojo could overcome the U.S. squadron.

When Dewey ascertained that Montojo was not at Subic Bay, he immediately moved into Manila Bay. This operation required a dash past several artillery batteries at the entrance to the bay, some on the mainland and others on the islands of Corregidor and El Fraile. Although it seemed likely that the entrance was mined, Dewey discounted this as a serious obstacle. At midnight the U.S. squadron ran through Boca Grande, the entrance to the bay. Only three shots were fired from El Fraile. Apparently Dewey achieved surprise, the Spanish batteries assuming that he would attempt to enter in daylight. No mines were encountered.

After entering the bay, Dewey prepared for action. He arranged his ships in line—the four protected cruisers *Olympia, Baltimore, Raleigh,* and *Boston;* the unprotected cruiser *Concord;* and the gunboat *Petrel.* He first bore in on Manila, but then observed the Spanish squadron anchored to the south in a crescent-shaped line in Cañacao Bay. It consisted of two unprotected cruisers, *Reina Cristina* and *Castilla,* and five gunboats. Although the crew strengths of the two squadrons were roughly comparable, the U.S. ships were much heavier and were better protected, manned, and armed. Had Montojo anchored under the guns of Manila somewhat farther north, he would have enjoyed the support of powerful batteries, including four modern breech-loading 9.4-inch guns. He did not do so, hoping to avoid a U.S. bombardment of the city.

After closing to five thousand yards, Dewey opened fire on the enemy squadron at 5:40 A.M. on 1 May, beginning the Battle of Manila Bay. The U.S. squadron turned to the right and brought its port batteries into action. It then returned on a parallel line, employing its starboard batteries. At 7:00 A.M. the Spanish flagship *Reina Cristina* made a valiant attack, but it was soon driven back to its anchorage. Montojo was then forced to move to the gunboat *Isla de Cuba.* At 7:30 Dewey broke off the battle temporarily, fearing that he was about to exhaust his ammunition. A check showed that he had plenty of rounds available. Enemy fire had been ineffective; only minor damage had been inflicted on the U.S. ships, but the Spanish vessels were afire. During the lull in the battle, Montojo moved his stricken ships to the roadstead at Bacoor Bay. The Americans resumed the attack at 11:16, and a white flag was raised at Cavite about 12:15 A.M. By this time, the enemy squadron had been destroyed. The two unprotected cruisers and one of the gunboats had been sunk, and the remaining gunboats were set on fire. Three were later salvaged and refitted.

The casualty lists revealed the extent of Dewey's victory. He suffered only nine wounded and none killed. Montojo's ships endured 371 casualties, 161 killed and 210 wounded, most of them on the *Reina Cristina.* The outcome assured Dewey of a base and gave him control of Manila Bay. He anchored off Cavite and occupied that location. After being refused the right to use the Manila cable to Hong Kong, he cut it. Service was not restored until after the end of hostilities in August; Dewey communicated by dispatch boat to Hong Kong. The Spanish garrison was able to send messages to the Visayan Islands south of Luzon by another cable unknown to Dewey; from there, boats carried dispatches to a cable station off the coast of Borneo, which in turn sent them to Madrid. Messages returned from Madrid along the same route.

Unconfirmed news of Dewey's victory reached Washington on 3 May, but official dispatches did not arrive until 7 May. The dramatic victory stimulated wild celebrations across the United States, and Dewey, now the object of national adulation, was immediately promoted to admiral. Although Dewey could maintain himself safely in Manila Bay for an indefinite time, he could not move against Manila itself because he lacked troops for this purpose. Nevertheless he had fulfilled his orders. The victory at Manila Bay destroyed Spanish naval power in the Pacific Ocean, assuring the safety of U.S. maritime commerce and providing a refuge for the U.S. squadron. Most important, Dewey's triumph accorded fully with the U.S. need to confront Spain with instant and unrelenting pressure, a means of encouraging an early turn to peace negotiations. McKinley entered the war reluctantly, but once in, he hoped to bring the struggle to a conclusion at the earliest possible moment. Early and sustained indications of American resolve would help lead to this outcome.

As Dewey conducted his operations in Manila Bay, Sampson, now promoted to rear admiral, established a blockade of Cuba. The North Atlantic Squadron moved from Key West to Havana on 22 April and immediately sent vessels to cover Matanzas and Cárdenas to the east and Mariel and Cabañas to the west. Soon he also blockaded the important port of Cienfuegos on the south coast, but he could not immediately cover all the ports of eastern Cuba, including Nuevitas, Sagua la Grande, and Caibarién on the north coast and Santiago de Cuba and Guantánamo on the south coast. As the weeks passed, Sampson was able to strengthen the blockade and extend it to cover additional ports. It proved exceedingly effective—only two vessels exited past the blockading ships at Havana and only eight ships entered Cuban ports without detection. Some minor engagements with Spanish vessels or shore batteries occurred at various ports during the war. Spain could never prove its claim that the blockade was ineffective, which under international law would have rendered it illegal. The North Atlantic Squadron ensured that Spain could not reinforce or resupply its army in Cuba.

As Sampson perfected his blockade, Admiral Cervera finally steamed westward across the Atlantic from the Cape Verde Islands, leaving St. Vincent on 29 April bound for San Juan, Puerto Rico. He had four armored cruisers and three torpedo-boat destroyers. The cruiser *Vizcaya* had a fouled bottom and slowed the pace of the squadron. The new *Cristóbal Colón* proved of little use without its main battery of 10-inch guns. Captain French E. Chadwick, commander of the U.S. cruiser *New York,* aptly described the pathetic condition of the Spanish force: "Spain was without the primal necessities of a fleet—without guns, without ammunition, without engineers, without coal, and even with the ships short of bread." Had Cervera remained in European waters, the Spanish navy could have functioned as a "fleet-in-being," avoiding engagements and restricting the freedom of action of the opposing navy. By moving to the Caribbean, he surrendered these options and played directly into the hands of Sampson.

"Spain was without the primal necessities of a fleet—without guns, without ammunition, without engineers, without coal, and even with the ships short of bread."

When Sampson learned that Cervera had left the Cape Verdes, he took a strong detachment east to San Juan, assuming that the enemy was bound for that port. Not finding Cervera in the harbor at San Juan, he bombarded the city briefly on 12 May and returned to his station off Havana. Cervera wisely decided to avoid San Juan. He did not reach Martinique, his first port of call, until 10 May because of his slow steaming speed. He was forced to leave a damaged destroyer at Fort de France. Deciding against moving either to Santiago de Cuba, which had not been blockaded, or to Havana, where he would have to deal with Sampson, he proceeded instead to the Dutch island of Curaçao, hoping to find a collier there to refuel his vessels. This hope was dashed, and the Dutch governor allowed him only a few hundred tons of coal from local stocks, a decision following international law. He had to leave Curaçao, a neutral port, within twenty-four hours. Seeking to avoid contact with any U.S. vessels, Cervera now determined to go to Santiago de Cuba, a decision that largely decided the future course of the war. He arrived there on 19 May, one day after Sampson returned to Havana from San Juan. Sampson immediately learned of this landfall, and, on 22 May, Commodore Schley and the Flying Squadron, then on the way to blockade Cienfuegos, received orders to pen up Cervera in port. The bumbling Schley took eight days to establish the blockade, arriving off Santiago de Cuba on 26 May but failing to observe Cervera in the harbor. After moving westward, he finally returned to Santiago de Cuba and established a blockade on 28 May. Cervera was thus given an opportunity to escape, but he did not do so. Sampson was highly critical of Schley's decisions during this period. After the war a board of inquiry ruled that Schley had shown "vacillation, dilatoriness, and lack of enterprise."

When Sampson learned of the blockade, he left Havana for Santiago de Cuba with a force that included all his remaining armored ships. He was finally able to consolidate his principal vessels because he no longer had to worry about Spanish naval raids against either the U.S. East Coast or the blockading squadron in Cuba. Arriving at Santiago de Cuba on 1 June, he devoted himself to strengthening the close-in blockade of the harbor. He wished to storm the narrow entrance to the port and engage Cervera, but he feared electrical mines in the channel that could be triggered from the shore as well as five shore batteries. To prevent Cervera from attempting to run the blockade, he tried to sink a collier, the *Merrimac*, in the channel on the night of 3 June. Richmond Pearson Hobson, a naval constructor, undertook this mission. He managed to sink his ship, but it came to rest too far north to accomplish its purpose. Sampson then settled down to await land reinforcements from the United States, hoping that they would neutralize the defenses at the harbor entrance and allow him to attack Cervera. To secure a nearby protected anchorage where ships could coal, the First Marine Battalion landed at Guantánamo Bay on 10 June. It secured the eastern shore by 15 June, and Sampson's vessels were able to use the bay after that.

PREPARATIONS FOR ARMY OPERATIONS

Early U.S. planning for the employment of the army centered on the preparation of small expeditions to support the navy, it being recognized that no major operations could take place until the volunteer army had been mobilized, a matter of many months. Meanwhile, energetic but chaotic efforts were made to enroll volunteers and to send them to training camps. On 29 April, Major General William R. Shafter was ordered to prepare an expedition of six thousand men at Tampa, Florida, that would land on the south coast of Cuba to support the Cuban guerrillas, departing after a brief stay. This operation was dropped when news of Cervera's movement to the Caribbean reached the War Department, but Shafter continued to prepare for later unspecified operations.

On 2 May a council of war at the White House considered a plan to establish a base at Mariel and mount an attack on Havana, but no such operation was possible soon. This plan was cancelled when Cervera's arrival at Martinique became known, but Shafter continued to concentrate troops at Tampa. Also on 2 May, President McKinley directed the dispatch of troops to the Philippines to support Dewey. Major General Wesley Merritt was made commander of a force that eventually numbered twenty thousand men. Designated the Eighth Army Corps, Merritt's expedition was given the mission of conquering Manila. Troops for this purpose were gathered at San Francisco.

The complexity of affairs in the Philippines increased considerably because of the activities of the Filipino insurgent leader, Emilio Aguinaldo y Famy. He had been exiled to Hong Kong after the defeat of the Filipino insurgents in 1897 and had departed for Europe early in April 1898. When he stopped at Singapore, the American consul general there, E. Spencer Pratt, held conversations with him and arranged his return to Hong Kong. When Dewey was consulted, he urged this action, thinking that Aguinaldo might be of assistance at Manila. Aguinaldo reappeared in Hong Kong early in May, and at the insistence of his followers returned to the Philippines on 19 May, arriving on the dispatch boat *McCulloch*. Dewey then supplied some arms that Aguinaldo used to help equip an insurgent force near Manila. Aguinaldo later claimed that the Americans with whom he dealt in the Far East had offered Filipino independence in return for armed assistance. Evidence for this assertion is lacking; Washington specifically ruled out any such promise, adopting a wait-and-see policy concerning the future of the Philippines. Although increasingly concerned about the ultimate intentions of the Americans, Aguinaldo collaborated with Dewey because no other course seemed appropriate. The first task was to throw out the Spaniards; he would deal with the Americans later.

With considerable U.S. assistance, Aguinaldo obtained a store of arms and soon gained control of the area just outside Manila, but he lacked sufficient strength to storm the city, defended by nine thousand Spanish troops. On 12 June he proclaimed the independence of the Philippines, and on 23 June he formed a provisional government, which took the form of a military dictatorship. Such was the situation when the first contingent of U.S. troops arrived at the end of June.

Meanwhile, after Cervera arrived at Santiago de Cuba, important decisions were being made concerning future U.S. operations in Cuba. Plans for a strike at Havana were suspended. On 26 May a council of war approved not one but two expeditions to the Caribbean Sea. Shafter's troops at Tampa would move immediately to Santiago de Cuba, and another force would occupy Puerto Rico. Shafter's orders were to land near Santiago de Cuba with twenty-five thousand troops and cooperate with the navy in measures to capture Cervera and the garrison defending the city.

Like some naval leaders, the commanding general of the army, Major General Nelson A. Miles, wanted to seize Puerto Rico because it would provide a convenient base from which to interdict possible Spanish efforts to reinforce Cuba. He also envisioned limited operations in the interior of Cuba designed in part to support the insurgents. On 9 April, more than two weeks before the declaration of war, he had ordered Lieutenant Andrew S. Rowan to contact the insurgent General Calixto García Iñiguez in eastern Cuba. Rowan did so just after war was declared. Early in June arrangements were made for insurgent support of a landing at Santiago de Cuba. Soon, however, President McKinley rejected Miles' plans for operations in Cuba other than at Santiago de Cuba. After that the commanding general concentrated on preparations for the Puerto Rican expedition.

During the early days of June, a mad scramble followed at Tampa as Shafter attempted to load the troops concentrated there onto transports. Supplies were scattered along the rail line between Columbia, South Carolina, and Tampa, often in unmarked railroad cars. An attempt to leave about 7–8 June failed when false reports of Spanish naval vessels, the "ghost squadron," forced postponement. Finally, a convoy was formed outside Tampa Bay on 14 June, consisting of twenty-nine transports and six supporting vessels. Three naval vessels escorted the convoy to the Dry Tortugas, where other vessels, including the battleship *Indiana,* joined the covering force.

Shafter's troops, officially designated the Fifth Army Corps, numbered about seventeen thousand troops. Fewer than twenty-five hundred were volunteers, although subsequent reinforcements raised this number to about seventy-five hundred. The regular army dominated the expedition because its regiments were organized and ready for action. Among these were four black regiments, the Ninth and Tenth cavalries and the Twenty-fourth and Twenty-fifth infantries. The principal volunteer organization was the Rough Riders, commanded by Colonel Leonard Wood and his deputy, Lieutenant Colonel Theodore Roosevelt, who had left the Navy Department. Only four other volunteer units participated in the initial phases of the Cuban campaign—the Second Massachusetts, the Seventy-first New York, the Thirty-third Michigan, and one battalion of the Thirty-fourth Michigan. About twenty-three hundred horses and mules were taken along. Artillery being scarce, the force was equipped with only sixteen light field guns, eight field mortars, and a detachment of four Gatling guns.

EVOLUTION OF WAR AIMS

The United States began the war with but one political objective—independence for Cuba—but early successes led to additional demands. On 3 June, after confirmation that Cervera was bottled up at Santiago de Cuba, Secretary of State William R. Day communicated a list of war aims to the U.S. ambassador in London, John M. Hay. This information went through British channels to Vienna for transmission to Madrid. First, Spain must hand over Cuba to the United States, which would help the Cuban people establish a stable government. Second, Spain must cede Puerto Rico to the United States instead of a monetary indemnity to satisfy claims of U.S. citizens stemming from the war. Third, the Philippines would remain in Spanish hands with the exception of a port to be selected by the United States. Fourth, Spain must cede a port in the Mariana Islands with a harbor suitable for a coaling station. The acquisition of Puerto Rico would strengthen the ability of the United States to maintain command of the sea in the western Atlantic. A coaling station in the Marianas would improve maritime communications to East Asia. On 14 June, however, Hay modified the provision concerning the Philippines, noting that the Filipino in-

The most important development of the summer was the peaceful annexation of the independent Hawaiian Republic by joint resolution of Congress.

surgents had become a factor and that their situation must receive attention. "It is most difficult without further knowledge," he concluded, "to determine as to the disposition of the Philippine Islands."

Various considerations lay behind this secret diplomatic initiative to bring Spain to the peace table. The U.S. government hoped that Spain's honor had now been satisfied, its forces having offered resistance in the Caribbean Sea and in the Philippines. McKinley sought to end the war promptly with the least possible expenditure of blood and treasure. Recognizing the Spanish penchant for delay and obfuscation, Hay concluded his message with the warning that U.S. demands might expand, should Spain continue to fight. For the moment, Spain rejected negotiations on McKinley's terms. The Austrian foreign minister, Count Agenor Goluchowski, soon informed the British foreign secretary, Lord Salisbury, that the Spanish government was not ready to consider the U.S. terms. This result, which was made known to Ambassador Hay, meant that further operations would develop in the two theaters of war, the primary arena being the Caribbean Sea and the secondary one being the western Pacific Ocean.

The expansion of U.S. war aims did not yet suggest strong public or official desire for extensive territorial gains. In this respect, the most important development of the summer was the peaceful annexation of the independent Hawaiian Republic by joint resolution of Congress. Interest in absorbing the Hawaiian Islands had existed for many years, one motive being to deny the islands to Japan. A treaty of annexation proposed in 1897 had languished in the Senate until the need for improved communications to Asia became evident during the wartime summer of 1898. Broad public support for annexation developed, and large majorities in both the House of Representatives and the Senate voted for the joint resolution. The strategic argument for annexation had earlier emphasized the defensive value of the islands, which screened the West Coast, but events in 1898 drew attention to their utility as stepping stones across the broad Pacific to the Philippines. Thus, the war stimulated territorial ambitions that had not previously gained much support.

NAVAL EXPEDITION OF ADMIRAL CÁMARA

As the United States moved energetically against Cuba, Puerto Rico, and Manila, the Spanish government decided to send a naval squadron to the Philippines. Admiral Manuel de la Cámara was given command of this force. It included two armored vessels, the battleship *Pelayo* and the cruiser *Carlos V,* two auxiliary cruisers, two troop transports with four thousand men aboard, and four colliers. Cámara left Spain on 16 June, steaming eastward through the Mediterranean Sea to the Suez Canal. Once through the canal, he intended to go to Mindanao, where he would decide his later movements. Planning to leave the Suez area about 8 July, he could expect to arrive in the Philippines forty days later, around 17 August.

The departure of Cámara's squadron stimulated activity in the U.S. Navy Department. The initial response was to order two heavily armed seagoing monitors based on the West Coast, the *Monterey* and the *Monadnock,* to the Philippine Islands. These vessels, more than a match for Cámara's armored ships, were expected to reach Manila before the Spanish squadron. Another reaction was to begin preparation of an organization that became known as the Eastern Squadron. It was to include three armored vessels detached from Sampson's command (*Iowa, Oregon,* and *Brooklyn*) and four other vessels.

The mission of the Eastern Squadron was to operate in Spanish waters, should Cámara move beyond the Suez Canal, which would force Spain either to allow uncontested attacks on its coastal cities or to recall its expedition. Commodore John C. Watson was made commander of the Eastern Squadron. Admiral Sampson dragged his feet, loath to give up armored vessels as his responsibilities broadened in the Caribbean theater. This reaction raised an important question: Did the United States possess enough armored vessels to operate successfully in both the Caribbean Sea and Spanish waters? The Navy Department was never convinced that Cámara would move beyond the eastern Mediterranean Sea, but it pressed for the early designation of vessels for the Eastern Squadron as a prudent response to the Spanish naval initiative.

SANTIAGO DE CUBA CAMPAIGN

The Spanish force at Santiago de Cuba, commanded by General Arsenio Linares Pomba, was ill-prepared to make a stout defense against a determined enemy. Insurgent detachments had interdicted his land communications with Spanish forces, elsewhere in Cuba, especially at Havana, and the U.S. Navy had cut its maritime connections. Initially, Linares had only ninety-four hundred men, but a contingent of sailors from Cervera's squadron added another thousand. A third of the force was composed of Cuban militia, *voluntarios,* who were not deemed fully effective. Linares organized his small command into a division with two brigades, one under General of Brigade Joaquín Vara del Rey and the other under General of Division José Toral. About twenty-five thousand Spanish troops were located elsewhere in eastern Cuba, garrisoned at Sagua de Tánamo, Baracoa, Guantánamo, Holguín, and Manzanillo. The governor-general of Cuba, Don Ramón Blanco y Erenas, did not order these troops to concentrate at Santiago de Cuba for several compelling reasons. It would have been impossible to supply so many troops, concentration would have left all eastern Cuba to the insurgents, and an enlarged force would have been vulnerable to naval gunfire from Sampson's powerful squadron.

The location of Santiago de Cuba dictated the U.S. Army's plan of campaign. It lay at the western end of a valley that stretched for twenty miles and widened to seven miles near El Caney and San Miguel, two towns northeast of the city. The San Juan River ran in a southerly direction about two and one-half miles east of Santiago de Cuba below elevations known as the San Juan Heights. The harbor was about four miles in length. A narrow one-mile channel, commanded by the Punta Gorda Heights, connected the harbor to the sea. Two elevations of about two hundred feet, the Morro and the Socapa heights, rose at the mouth of the channel.

Both the channel and the city were fortified. Two lines of electrical mines, controlled from the shore, were laid in the channel.

Both the channel and the city were fortified. Two lines of electrical mines, controlled from the shore, were laid in the channel. Five artillery batteries were placed on the Socapa, Morro, and Punta Gorda heights to help deny entrance. If the batteries could be silenced, an attacking navy might force its way into the harbor, but only one ship could move through the channel at a time. General Linares constructed three lines of defense around the city. An outer screen was placed between Daiquirí and Siboney, where Linares anticipated a U.S. landing. The main line of fortifications ran close to the boundary of the city, passing southward through Ermitano, El Caney, San Miguel de Lajas, Quintero Hill, and the hills of Veguita and La Caridad. A line of blockhouses and forts about eight miles in length lay farther west, including strong points on the San Juan Heights. Linares spread his forces thinly, seeking not only to defend the city but to protect a rail connection that ran north to the Sierra Maestre and an aqueduct that supplied the city with water. He had to cover his entire perimeter because of the Cuban insurgents, although he expected the U.S. attack to come from the east.

The U.S. expedition arrived off Santiago de Cuba on 20 June, and General Shafter immediately contacted Cuban General Calixto García to plan his attack on the city. It was decided to land the Fifth Army Corps at Daiquirí on 22 June.

Contingents of insurgents would attack Cabañas to give the false impression that the Americans would land at that point. Meanwhile, Sampson's squadron would shell various other coastal locations, including Daiquirí.

Once ashore, Shafter planned to move against Santiago de Cuba by a route that would take his troops away from the shore, rejecting the navy's plan for an attack on the elevations at the entrance to the channel that would allow Sampson's squadron to enter the harbor. This interior route would deprive Shafter of support from the guns of the squadron. Sampson did not learn of this decision for several days. Shafter later insisted that he rejected the navy's suggestions because of delays that would result from movement through difficult terrain along the approach to the channel entrance. He felt compelled to move rapidly because of a historical precedent. In 1741 an English army had landed at Guantánamo and attempted to move overland against Santiago de Cuba, but before it could approach the city, it suffered more than two thousand deaths from tropical disease. Shafter's decision neglected the strength of the second line of fortifications around Santiago de Cuba, particularly those associated with the San Juan Heights.

There may have been another motive. Shafter's adjutant, Lieutenant Colonel Edward J. McClernand, reported later that the commander thought he could minimize casualties by investing the city and forcing its surrender rather than storming it. An attack on the heights at the channel entrance might have produced unacceptable losses. Still another concern may have influenced Shafter. The navy had monopolized the glory of the early campaigns. Shafter may have wished to seize Santiago de Cuba and Cervera's squadron by himself, denying the navy another opportunity to distinguish itself. In any event, Shafter's decision precluded effective coordination between the army and navy in a joint operation.

Shafter arranged with García to make use of the insurgent army. In addition to the Cuban troops around Santiago de Cuba, which helped to prevent Spanish troops from leaving or entering the city, large Cuban concentrations at other locations made certain that Spanish reinforcements at other locations, such as Guantánamo or Holguín, would be unable to move overland to Santiago de Cuba. Unfortunately, cooperation with García tended to break down because of growing U.S. dislike of the insurgents. Racial prejudice was part of the cause, as was distaste for the Cuban guerrilla tactics. On the Cuban side, concern developed that the United States might not honor its pledge of independence for Cuba.

A dramatic episode added to Cuban-American tensions. On 22 June, Spanish Colonel Federico Escario and thirty-seven hundred Spanish troops marched from Manzanillo to Santiago de Cuba, seeking to break through the Cuban cordon around the city and to reinforce the trapped garrison. This column had to traverse about 160 miles of difficult terrain, facing guerrilla harassment at every turn. The march turned into a remarkable achievement; the Spaniards fought as many as forty skirmishes with the Cuban insurgents along the route. On 2 July, the day after the battles of El Caney and the San Juan Heights, Escario entered Santiago de Cuba with thirty-three hundred men despite the attempts of García's troops to stop them. The Americans attributed this outcome to the inadequacies of the Cubans, but Shafter had vetoed García's proposal to reinforce the area of the perimeter through which Escario approached the city.

The Fifth Army Corps began its landing at Daiquirí on 22 June. Linares did not oppose the operation. When sufficient troops were ashore, they moved on Siboney. This coastal location was secured by 23 June, and elements of the Fifth Army Corps began coming ashore there. Shafter intended to concentrate his entire force at Siboney before moving forward, but Major General Joseph ("Fighting Joe") Wheeler, a former

The First U.S. Volunteer Cavalry, better know as the Rough Riders, fought in Cuba under the leadership of Leonard Wood and Theodore Roosevelt. The unit is pictured here with Roosevelt at center after its victorious charge up Kettle Hill, near San Juan Hill, on 1 July 1898. (National Archives)

Confederate cavalryman commanding the dismounted cavalry division composed of the First and Tenth cavalries and the Rough Riders, decided to attack a concentration of about fifteen hundred Spanish troops at Las Guásimas, a few miles to the northwest along the road to Santiago de Cuba. He overrode orders to another commander that would have precluded such an engagement.

The Spanish force at Las Guásimas, occupying a strong position, had orders to withdraw when attacked, but before it abandoned the position a sharp skirmish took place on 24 June. This confused engagement heightened morale in the Fifth Corps, but it created serious problems. It further committed Shafter to an advance in the interior against Santiago de Cuba, but the route passed through difficult terrain along a very poor road. To prevent Wheeler from undertaking any more unauthorized adventures, Shafter forbade further advance until he had his troops well in hand.

The Fifth Army Corps lingered in the area of Sevilla, a small town near Las Guásimas, while Shafter prepared to attack Santiago de Cuba. He wanted to move as quickly as possible, fearing outbreaks of tropical disease, but he needed several days to build up for a strong assault on the city. The army suffered from a dearth of docks, transportation, and good roads, circumstances that slowed preparation, and the hasty departure from Tampa also had an adverse effect. It proved difficult to locate and land the supplies deemed most critical for the impending attack. Although Shafter had brought some heavy artillery, he decided to rely solely on four batteries of light artillery and the Gatling-gun detachment, a concession to the difficulties of moving equipment along the road from Siboney that passed through Las Guásimas and Sevilla.

The delay around Sevilla allowed General Linares to strengthen his defensive arrangements. He gave special attention to the outer line of fortifications that ran through El Caney and the San Juan Heights and thence to the shore near Aguadores. About 4,760 troops occupied eleven strong points on this line, but they were divided into many small detachments. Only 520 men occupied El Caney, and on the crucial San Juan Heights there were but 137 men each on San Juan Hill and Kettle Hill. This force was later increased to 520 men. Linares used almost thirty-four hundred of the approximately ten thousand troops available to him to defend the western side of the bay.

Shafter decided to move quickly when he learned of Escario's approach. His intelligence was faulty, leading to the misapprehension that about eight thousand Spanish reinforcements were approaching Santiago de Cuba, more than twice the correct number. Shafter hastily reconnoitered the Spanish positions at El Caney and the San Juan Heights. El Caney lay about six miles to the northeast of Santiago de Cuba, where defenders manned six blockhouses and a stone fort known as El Viso. Troops could approach it by turning north off the main road to Santiago de Cuba at El Pozo. A road connected El Caney directly with Santiago de Cuba. About two miles east of the city, the San Juan Heights began their rise. Kettle Hill lay just to the north of the road from Sevilla and El Pozo. San Juan Hill, a higher point, was located about four hundred yards to the southwest.

The Spanish defenders suffered terribly, losing their commander, Vara del Rey, and all but about 100 of the 520 troops.

Shafter decided to make his main assault on the San Juan Heights on 1 July, organizing two secondary attacks in support. After moving across the heights, he intended to storm Santiago de Cuba, which meant that he would encounter the city's main defense lines about a thousand yards farther on. Worried about the threat to his right flank from the direction of El Caney, he decided to have a division under Brigadier General Henry W. Lawton clear that location before it moved into position on the right of the line that would sweep across the San Juan Heights. To deceive Linares into thinking that his main attack would come against the elevations at the entrance to the channel, he planned to move the Michigan Volunteers under Brigadier General Henry M. Duffield along a coastal rail line and demonstrate at Aguadores on the coast. Two divisions, one under Brigadier General Jacob F. Kent to the south of the road to Santiago de Cuba and the other the dismounted cavalry under General Wheeler to the north of the road, would assault the San Juan Heights. Lawton's division would come on line on the right next to Wheeler's troops after reducing El Caney.

ACTIONS AT AGUADORES AND EL CANEY

The Michigan Volunteers made the first move on 1 July, advancing by train to the railroad bridge just west of Aguadores. Upon arriving, they discovered that the Spanish defenders had destroyed the western end of the bridge, an act that precluded further action. This demonstration was supposed to prevent Linares from reinforcing the San Juan Heights, but only 275 Spanish defenders faced Duffield's force of twenty-five hundred men. The move against Aguadores did not influence the battle.

Meanwhile, General Lawton attacked El Caney. He expected to begin at 7:00 A.M. and to reach his objectives two hours later, a schedule that would allow him to join the force below the San Juan Heights by 10:00 A.M., the time set for the main action of the day. Lawton assaulted El Caney with two of his three brigades, one under Brigadier General William Ludlow on the left and another under Brigadier General Adna R. Chaffee on the right. He kept his other brigade, commanded by Colonel Evan Miles, in reserve. A battery of light artillery, consisting of four 3.2-inch guns, was positioned about twenty-three hundred yards south of El Caney. The Spanish defenders lacked artillery, which would have allowed Lawton to locate the guns much closer to El Caney. In any event, Lawton's artillery fire was ineffective for much of the battle.

Lawton attacked at 7:00 A.M. as planned, but the 520 Spanish defenders under General Vara del Rey, armed only with Mauser rifles, made a valiant defense based on the fort of El Viso. This delay upset the timetable for the attack on the San Juan Heights. The struggle at El Caney wore on through the morning. Lawton then committed his reserve brigade and the independent brigade under Brigadier General John C. Bates. Shortly after noon, Shafter decided to order Lawton to break off the engagement so that he could move to his position on the right of the line below the San Juan Heights. Lawton resisted this order, successfully requesting permission to complete his mission. He feared that withdrawal might be construed as defeat. Besides, his brigades were deeply engaged and therefore difficult to extract.

The Battle of El Caney continued into the afternoon. Finally, the artillery battery obtained the range on El Viso, which permitted the Twelfth Infantry, with help from other regiments, to overrun the fort at about 3:00 P.M. It took two more hours to mop up. The Spanish defenders suffered terribly, losing their commander, Vara del Rey, and all but about 100 of the 520 troops. Lawton lost 81 killed and 360 wounded.

The delay at El Caney kept Lawton's troops out of the main attack on the San Juan Heights. Critics of the operation argue that a small force could have held the Spanish garrison at El Caney in place, avoiding a frontal attack on a strong defensive position. Lawton could then have participated in the main attack, a contribution that might have led to the fall of Santiago de Cuba on 1 July. As it was, Secretary of War Russell Alger made the curious argument that the hand of Providence was at work. If Lawton had joined the rest of the Fifth Army Corps, he maintained, the assault on Santiago de Cuba might have been pressed to a conclusion, increasing the number of American casualties taken during the attack on the San Juan Heights for no good reason.

BATTLE OF THE SAN JUAN HEIGHTS

To defend the San Juan Heights, General Linares established a line about four thousand yards long anchored on San Juan Hill, the largest elevation in the area. He manned this position with about 1,700 men, of whom only 520 were on San Juan Hill and Kettle Hill In addition, a reserve of about 400 men with two artillery pieces, a 6.3-inch gun and a 4.7-inch gun, supported the troops on the two hills.

The division commanders, General Kent and General Sumner (who had replaced Wheeler as commander of the dismounted cavalry division), began their deployments at 7:00 A.M. A U.S. artillery battery of four 3.2-inch guns at El Pozo opened on the heights at 8:00 A.M. from a distance of twenty-six hundred yards. The black powder used by the Americans was clearly visible, and Spanish guns to the rear of the heights soon silenced the battery. This development meant that eight thousand attackers would have to move to their initial positions without benefit of artillery support along a single highly congested road.

Shafter made use of a hot-air balloon to provide observation, because he lacked good information about the terrain, not having conducted an adequate reconnaissance of the battlefield. The balloon was towed along the road and was visible above the trees, thus pinpointing the movement of the U.S. column and attracting enemy fire that caused many casualties.

Shafter made use of a hot-air balloon to provide observation, because he lacked good information about the terrain.

The approach march did not go well. Kent's infantry division, moving west along the road from El Pozo, was supposed to turn south of the main road below the heights and move against San Juan Hill. Sumner's dismounted cavalry division, proceeding along the same route, was to turn north and move across Kettle Hill before joining Kent on the main elevation. A lagoon lay between the two hills. Unfortunately, one of Kent's regiments, the Seventy-first New York Volunteers, broke in the face of heavy enemy fire as it moved toward its starting position. Kent and others managed to stop the flight of the Seventy-first New York, which was held in place while the two regular army regiments of the brigade, the Sixth and Sixteenth infantries, passed through them. Another of Kent's brigades, which included the Ninth, Thirteenth, and Twenty-fourth infantries, got into position on the left. Kent's third brigade, composed of the Second, Tenth, and Twenty-first infantries, came up just to the rear of the leading brigades. Meanwhile, the two brigades of Sumner's division, the first made up of the Third, Sixth, and Ninth cavalries and the second of the First and Tenth cavalries and the Rough Riders, moved into position below Kettle Hill.

At 1:00 P.M., three hours after the time set for the assault, Kent and Sumner began their movement against the San Juan Heights. Lieutenant John D. Miley, Shafter's aide, authorized the charge at the urging of General Sumner, although Lawton's troops had not arrived. As Kent's left brigade started up San Juan Hill, the most important event of the engagement took place. Second Lieutenant John H. Parker's Gatling-gun detachment opened on the Spanish positions at the summit, three weapons using .30-caliber ammunition at ranges between six hundred and eight hundred yards. Parker fired for about eight minutes, expending as many as thirty-six hundred rounds per minute, and his guns had an instant effect. The Spanish defenders fled down the opposite slope. Despite confusion, the Sixth and Sixteenth regiments, in the lead, occupied the abandoned hilltop, and the rest of Kent's division followed them into positions on the heights. Meanwhile, Sumner moved against Kettle Hill without benefit of supporting fire from artillery or Gatling guns. The Ninth Cavalry led the assault with the First Cavalry and the Rough Riders following. The defenders abandoned the crest before the Americans arrived, and the U.S. troops pressed on past the lagoon to the northern end of San Juan Hill.

After gaining control of the San Juan Heights, the two assault divisions halted and began to entrench, abandoning any thought of going on to Santiago de Cuba. Shafter feared a counterattack, but none happened, the enemy having retreated to the principal defensive positions of Santiago de Cuba. Although defeated, the Spanish defenders at El Caney, outnumbered twelve to one, and those at the San Juan Heights, outnumbered sixteen to one, made a brave defense. Only three thousand U.S. troops of the Fifth Corps reached the heights in the initial charge. Exhausted by their effort, these troops were in any event too few to continue toward Santiago de Cuba.

Both sides suffered many casualties. Shafter lost 205 men killed and 1,180 wounded at El Caney and the San Juan Heights. Including losses suffered during the two days immediately following the attack, about 10 percent of the Fifth Army Corps became casualties. The Spanish lost about 35 percent of the seventeen hundred men who defended the positions at El Caney and the San Juan Heights.

Shafter worked feverishly to reinforce the San Juan Heights, a confused effort because he had made no plans for it, having assumed that he would carry Santiago de Cuba in one grand leap. Some authorities do not think that Shafter intended to move on to Santiago de Cuba on 1 July, but the evidence clearly establishes this intention. After the battle, Shafter noted that the "hitch" in his operations, the cause of the failure to finish the assault, was Lawton's inability to reduce El Caney quickly. He concluded that "it was better as it was, for had he [Lawton] been on the right on the Caney road at 10 o'clock, we should have taken the city of Santiago that day, and would have had none of the territory or outside soldiers that we got later." As did Secretary Alger, he made a virtue out of Lawton's necessity.

Somehow the Fifth Army Corps occupied the heights in strength. Lawton's troops did not reach the front line until 2 July. As they marched along the road from El Caney to Santiago de Cuba during the evening of 1 July, the advance guard encountered enemy fire. Shafter's deputy, Colonel McClernand, then directed Lawton to return to El Pozo, greatly lengthening the distance that had to be covered. Meanwhile, the independent brigade under General Bates moved into the line at the extreme left next to Kent's division with Duffield's division of volunteers, which included the newly arrived Ninth Massachusetts. Some Cuban troops came into the line to the right of Lawton's brigade. Shafter also brought up the four light-artillery batteries and Parker's Gatling-gun detachment.

Many students of the battle have criticized both commanders. Linares did not concentrate sufficient troops and artillery at the probable point of attack, and when his troops were forced off the San Juan Heights, he did not order a counterattack. Shafter has been faulted for using too many men against El Caney, for failing to make a good reconnaissance of the battlefield, and for not making the most effective use of his few artillery pieces. He also did not call upon the guns of Admiral Sampson, which could easily have fired on the Spanish positions. Of course, Admiral Cervera also could have fired on the Americans.

The stubborn resistance of the Spanish garrison, largely unexpected, had adverse effects on the confidence of the Fifth Army Corps and its commander. Shafter, who was in poor health, greatly overestimated his difficulties and as grossly underestimated those of the enemy. General Linares had been wounded on 1 July, and his successor, General Toral, quickly reinforced the positions between the Americans and the city, placing about fifty-five hundred troops along a line of about six miles with another thousand in reserve. His troops were short of ammunition and ill-fed, a situation that grew worse because the attacks of 1 July had cut off access to the water supply and cultivated regions to the north. Meanwhile, the Fifth Army Corps was well-positioned to fire on the city from protected locations on the San Juan Heights, and Admiral Sampson's squadron also could bombard the city. Shafter, however, worried mostly about his difficulties—the possibility that reinforcements might appear to bolster Toral, that his miserable supply line from Siboney and Daiquirí might break down, that tropical weather might inhibit operations, and that disease might overwhelm his command.

Bearing these problems in mind, Shafter cast about for a course of action. He first considered the operation he had rejected earlier, an attack on the elevations at the entrance to the channel, but General Wheeler counseled successfully against this proposal because it might produce many casualties, precisely what the commander of the Fifth Army Corps wished to avoid. Shafter then contemplated a withdrawal, reporting to Washington by cable that many officers thought it "absolutely necessary for us to retreat in order to save ourselves from being enfiladed by the Spanish lines and cut off from our supplies, as an attack by the Spanish with a few fresh troops would result in our utter defeat."

Meanwhile, Shafter asked Sampson to move against the channel entrance. The admiral refused, noting that the electrical mines were the chief threat to his ships, not the batteries. An attack by land would be necessary to effect their neutralization, pending countermining operations. The Navy Department was anxious to avoid risking the loss of any armored ships, recognizing that they were all required to support operations elsewhere, perhaps against Puerto Rico or in Spanish waters. Secretary of the Navy Long also considered the possibility that Spain might gain naval support from some European power.

When President McKinley received word of Shafter's inclination to withdraw to more secure positions, he immediately headed off any such initiative. Noting the adverse effect on public opinion that would stem from a retreat, he urged Shafter to hold fast. Brigadier General Henry Clark Corbin, the adjutant general, promised immediate reinforcements. McKinley also considered replacing Shafter because of his illness. When Shafter learned of Washington's interest in his health, he moved to dispel concern. He and Admiral Sampson arranged to confer on the morning of 3 July. He also decided to act on an idea that he had mentioned to his adjutant, McClernand, while on the voyage to Santiago de Cuba. After placing his troops in sound positions around the city, he would demand the surrender of the city. Accordingly, a message was dispatched to the enemy, warning Toral that the Fifth Army Corps would begin bombardment of the city unless it was surrendered.

NAVAL BATTLE OF SANTIAGO DE CUBA

On Sunday morning, 3 July, Sampson's flagship, the cruiser *New York,* left the blockading squadron to go to Siboney; from there the admiral intended to go on to Shafter's headquarters for their planned meeting. After steaming east about seven miles, however, he spotted gunsmoke at the entrance to the channel. Admiral Cervera's squadron was attempting to flee. The *New York* immediately turned to rejoin its squadron, but it missed much of the ensuing action. Commodore Schley, in whom Sampson lacked confidence, was the senior officer present on the blockade.

"I have considered the squadron lost

ever since it left Cape Verde

for to think anything else seems madness to me."

Admiral Cervera had actually received authority to leave Santiago de Cuba back on 23 June, but he had expended considerable energy attempting to avoid any such sortie. He had an excellent reason for his view, being fully aware that the U.S. blockading squadron was much stronger than his command. He stated to Linares, "I have considered the squadron lost ever since it left Cape Verde for to think anything else seems madness to me, in view of the enormous disparity which exists between our own forces and those of the enemy." Unfortunately, the governor-general in Havana, Blanco, thought differently, arguing that the moral effect of surrendering without a fight would have terrible consequences in Spain. Naval authorities in Madrid urged Cervera to attempt escape at night, but the Spanish commander noted later that the U.S. blockaders moved close to the entrance during the evening hours, not only illuminating the channel, but making it impossible for exiting ships to avoid running aground or colliding with other vessels. Nevertheless, on 28 June, Blanco ordered Cervera to depart, but Cervera had trouble recovering the seamen who had become part of Linares' defense. These men participated in the battles of El Caney and the San Juan Heights on 1 July.

After the battles, however, Cervera had been forced to decide his course of action. The fall of Santiago de Cuba appeared imminent, and consideration was given to an early departure of the garrison, which might march north to join forces from Holguín or Manzanillo. Blanco again ordered Cervera to leave, informing Toral that the loss of the squadron would mean that "Spain will be morally defeated and must ask for peace at mercy of enemy."

Thus it was that late on 2 July, Cervera issued instructions for a sortie from the harbor at 9:00 A.M. on 3 July. The *Infanta María Teresa* would depart first, followed by the three armored cruisers. The two destroyers would come out last. The objective was escape; those vessels that could do so were to steam for Cienfuegos or Havana. Captain Víctor Concas y Palau, one of the Spanish ship commanders, noted the most harrowing aspect of the sortie. The narrow channel meant that Cervera's ships would have to exit one by one, allowing the U.S. squadron to concentrate its fire on each exiting vessel.

Spanish observations on the morning of 3 July revealed a gap in the western end of the U.S. blockade, a circumstance that led Cervera to order flight westward to Cienfuegos. Several U.S. vessels were absent. The battleship *Massachusetts,* two cruisers, and a converted tender had gone to Guantánamo to coal, and the armored cruiser *New York* with Sampson aboard and two small vessels had left for Siboney. Seven ships remained on station. At the east side of the semicircular formation was the converted yacht *Gloucester.* Next came the battleships *Indiana, Oregon, Iowa,* and *Texas* and the armored cruiser *Brooklyn,* Schley's flagship. At the western end was the converted yacht *Vixen.*

The U.S. squadron, as Cervera recognized, was much stronger than the Spanish force. Cervera's six vessels displaced less than thirty thousand tons and carried only forty-two big guns. Sampson's vessels displaced almost fifty thousand tons and carried seventy-six big guns. Only the crews were roughly similar in number. With Cervera's ships emerging one at a time, the U.S. advantage was all the more imposing.

At 9:35 A.M. the *Infanta María Teresa* came out with Admiral Cervera aboard, and the other ships followed at intervals of ten minutes, separated by eight hundred yards and moving at a speed of eight to ten knots. All turned west toward Cienfuegos, an act that Sampson later wrote "removed all tactical doubts or difficulties." When the Spanish flagship exited, it forced Commodore Schley on the *Brooklyn* into a serious error. Cervera hoped to engage the *Brooklyn* because it was the fastest of the U.S. ships. If it could be disabled, it might ease the escape of other ships. Faced with Cervera's approach, Schley ordered his ship to turn northeastward away from the onrushing Cervera, passing behind the *Iowa* and the *Texas,* which screened him temporarily. This "loop" was so unexpected that the *Texas* had to reverse its engine to avoid a crash. Despite Schley's error, the *Infanta María Teresa* did not survive for long. It turned westward, but, mortally wounded, it was driven on the shore at Punta Cabrera only an hour after it came out of the channel.

The next two Spanish ships to exit, the *Vizcaya* and the *Cristóbal Colón,* benefited from the attention paid to the Spanish flagship. The fourth ship to appear, the *Almirante Oquendo,* was next to be destroyed. It also was driven on the shore just west of the *Infanta María Teresa* at 10:40 A.M. The remaining destroyers, *Furor* and *Plutón,* drew fire from the four U.S. battleships present, but the *Gloucester,* commanded by Lieutenant Commander Richard Wainwright, a survivor of the *Maine* disaster, finished off both vessels. The Plutón struck the shore at 10:45 A.M. west of Cabañas, and the *Furor* foundered somewhat nearer Cabañas offshore.

After two hours of battle, only two Spanish ships remained afloat, the speedy *Cristóbal Colón* and the *Vizcaya.* Although the *Vizcaya* exited first, the faster vessel soon passed it, but the U.S. squadron first concentrated its fire on the *Vizcaya,* which was beached on a reef at 11:15 A.M. near Asseraderos. At this point, the *New York* reached the scene of the battle, and the U.S. flagship conducted the pursuit of the *Cristóbal Colón.* Sampson ordered the *Iowa* and the *Indiana* to return to the blockade, fearing that two Spanish ships remaining at Santiago de Cuba might attack noncombatant ships unloading at Siboney. Thus, the cruisers *New York* and *Brooklyn* and three battleships chased the *Cristóbal Colón.* At full speed, the Spanish ship was faster than its pursuers, but it ran out of good coal and had to make use of an inferior grade that it had taken on at Santiago de Cuba. When it slowed and came within range of the *Oregon,* its captain decided to drive his ship on the shore, which he did near the Turquino River fifty miles west of Santiago de Cuba at 1:15 P.M.

Few sea battles have ended more disastrously for the loser. Sampson's squadron lost one sailor killed and another wounded, and three ships sustained minor damage. The Spanish squadron may have lost 323 killed and 157 wounded, about one in five of the crew members, the figure reported by Captain Concas. A large number of prisoners of war, 1,720 officers and men, were later detained in the United States, the officers at Annapolis, Maryland, and the enlisted men at Portsmouth, New Hampshire. The critical difference between the performance of the two squadrons was gunnery. Cervera's four armored ships were struck no less than 123 times, the *Almirante Oquendo* taking fifty-seven shells. Spanish gunnery suffered from lack of practice and deficient ammunition. Nevertheless, as at Manila Bay, the percentage of U.S. hits was low, an outcome that stimulated efforts to improve gunnery methods after the war.

Schley's performance during the battle, especially his loop turn away from the *Infanta María Teresa,* further lowered his standing with Sampson, and it influenced the postwar inquiry into the commodore's actions, which criticized him severely. Although fate kept Sampson out of most of the action, he deserves high praise for having prepared his squadron very well for the action of 3 July. An unfortunate postwar dispute between Sampson and Schley over credit for the victory at Santiago de Cuba did not add to the reputation of either officer.

Sampson's victory produced an immediate result that eased the navy's concerns in both the Caribbean and the Pacific—the recall back to Spain of Admiral Cámara, whose squadron was then in the Red Sea. As his squadron proceeded eastward across the Mediterranean Sea to Egypt, the U.S. Navy Department tracked its progress carefully and from time to time adjusted the list of vessels to be assigned to the Eastern Squadron. Eventually the list included three armored vessels—the *Oregon, Iowa,* and *Brooklyn*—a development that worried Sampson. When word of Cervera's catastrophe reached Spain, however, Cámara was brought back to Spanish waters because, as Spanish Minister of Marine, Captain Ramón Auñón, later acknowledged, there was fear of a U.S. naval descent on the undefended Spanish coast. Sampson's concerns were thus allayed, and in the Philippines, Dewey no longer had to consider the possibility that he might have to face Cámara with only one armored vessel, the monitor *Monterey,* then en route to the Philippines and scheduled to arrive before the *Monadnock,* another monitor.

About 385 American servicemen were killed in action during the Spanish-American War; another 2,061 died from disease. Some of them were buried at this site in Cuba. (National Archives)

The Navy Department did not, however, immediately disband the Eastern Squadron. It considered sending naval reinforcements to Dewey via the Mediterranean Sea, seeking by this expedient to discourage other nations, especially Germany, that were thought to have an interest in acquiring the Philippines. Under this plan, Admiral Watson would take two armored ships to the Philippines. A powerful covering squadron would accompany him to Gibraltar, including all the remaining armored ships, and they would remain in the area until Watson had moved well to the east. This plan came to nothing, because the navy had to support operations against Puerto Rico, and in any case there were indications of an early end of the war.

SIEGE OF SANTIAGO DE CUBA

Sampson's naval triumph strengthened Shafter's preference for a siege, rather than an assault, of Santiago de Cuba. News that Spanish reinforcements were on the way added to the argument against storming the city. Shafter again demanded its surrender, but Toral did not respond favorably. The arrival of Escario's relief column in Santiago de Cuba heightened Shafter's interest in reinforcements and in the proposal for a naval attack on the channel entrance. Claiming that Escario's arrival had nearly doubled the strength of the enemy garrison, an exaggeration, he revealed a major concern to Sampson: "My present position has cost me 1,000 men, and I do not want to lose any more."

President McKinley and his advisers in Washington wanted action. Shafter received orders to plan an attack with the cooperation of the navy. The Navy Department and Sampson, however, opposed operations that might entail loss of armored vessels. The nation could replace troops, but it could not easily replace cruisers or battleships. Sampson wanted to use his marines to attack the western side of the channel while Shafter moved against the eastern side. Control of the elevations would permit removal of mines and other obstacles in the channel. In its final form, the plan of joint operations called for another demand for the surrender of Santiago de Cuba. If it was rejected, Sampson's ships would bombard the city. If the shelling did not produce results, an attack on the elevations at the entrance to the harbor would take place. This scheme again revealed Shafter's wish, to avoid further combat if possible.

Growing medical, logistical, and tactical complications reinforced Shafter's thinking. Although yellow fever did not appear, the troops began to contract malaria and dysentery. Adding to the difficulties of the Fifth Army Corps was the tenuous supply line between Siboney and the San Juan Heights and the shortage of transports to move personnel, equipment, and supplies from U.S. ports to Cuba. Finally, the War Department expressed concern about the failure to cover the flanks of the U.S. position adequately, to which observation Shafter responded with a plea for additional reinforcements.

As the U.S. grip on the city tightened, the two sides continued negotiations for the surrender of the city. On 8 July, Toral proposed to evacuate Santiago de Cuba in return for the right to march unmolested to Holguín. Shafter referred this deal to his superiors, correctly anticipating refusal. McKinley responded almost immediately, the adjutant general conveying his sentiments in unequivocal language: "You will accept nothing but unconditional surrender and should take extra precautions to prevent the enemy's escape." Meanwhile, however, Shafter had decided to recommend acceptance of Toral's proposition. It would convey the city to the Americans, minimize disruption of civil life, and allow the Fifth Army Corps to move elsewhere, presumably to Puerto Rico. The War Department replied to this proposal with a clear veto, insisting on an assault at the proper time in language that implied considerable criticism of Shafter's hesitancy.

"My present position has cost me 1,000 men, and I do not want to lose any more."

On 9 July, Shafter finally fell in with the instructions of the War Department and made the required dispositions. He notified Toral that he expected unconditional surrender. Otherwise, he would bombard the city. Reinforcements had arrived, which allowed the Fifth Army Corps to extend its right flank, a step intended to preclude Toral from breaking out to the north. Admiral Sampson was asked to bombard Santiago de Cuba, although Shafter enjoined him to make certain that his shells did not fall near the San Juan Heights, less than two miles from the town. The naval bombardment duly took place on 10–11 July. The navy destroyed some houses in the city, but many missiles appear to have missed their targets, a consequence of Sampson's endeavors to avoid hitting the U.S. positions. Shafter thought the bombardment ineffective, but it was not pressed to its limits. If the navy had used its larger armament extensively, the city could have been destroyed easily, but no further naval gunfire was ordered.

The bombardment nevertheless forced Toral into negotiations that led to the capitulation of Santiago de Cuba several days later. On 11 July, the War Department informed Shafter that should Toral accept unconditional surrender, the United States would bear the cost of transporting the Spanish garrison to Spain. At this point, General Nelson A. Miles arrived at Santiago de Cuba with the troops he had gathered to conduct an invasion of Puerto Rico. He did not supersede Shafter in command of the Fifth Army Corps but attempted to arrange for a joint army-navy attack on the channel entrance. Shafter disapproved of this initiative and Miles suspended it. Together the two generals again raised the idea of granting Toral safe conduct to Holguín, but President McKinley rejected this course, recognizing that it would likely elicit adverse public reaction at home and that Spain might interpret any such step as a sign of weakness.

In Madrid, Sagasta inclined strongly toward an end to the war. Spain had fought honorably, and could now negotiate a settlement acceptable to the public. Besides, the tactical situation at Santiago de Cuba appeared hopeless, and the U.S. Eastern Squadron might descend on the Canary Islands or the Balearic Islands. Governor-general Blanco urged continued resistance, but Sagasta ended the session of the Spanish parliament on 14 July and took steps to end the siege at Santiago de Cuba. When Blanco finally accepted McKinley's proposal to follow capitulation with repatriation of the Spanish garrisons, Toral acted immediately, proposing to Shafter the capitulation not only of the garrison at Santiago de Cuba but those located elsewhere in eastern Cuba.

Both sides appointed commissioners to negotiate the settlement and formal meetings began on 14 July. Various delays followed, and Shafter at one point considered allowing the Spanish troops to retain their arms, an initiative that elicited instant disapproval in Washington. Soon, however, Toral received formal permission to capitulate, and final arrangements were made on 16 July, including the surrender of the garrisons elsewhere in the region. Shafter later wrote that he had been "simply thunderstruck that of their own free will they should give me twelve thousand men that were absolutely beyond my reach." Shafter would not allow Admiral Sampson to sign the articles of capitulation, a further manifestation of the tension that had marked interservice relationships throughout the campaign.

The formal capitulation occurred on 17 July, an event that preceded the beginning of diplomatic attempts to end the war. On 18 July, the Duque de Almodóvar del Río, the Spanish foreign minister, moved through the French government to notify the United States of Spain's willingness to accept Cuban independence and to suspend hostilities. The Spanish government recognized that further delay might lead to more defeats because U.S. expeditions aimed at Puerto Rico and the Philippines were about to launch attacks. Delays postponed delivery of the Spanish proposal in Washington until 26 July, when French Ambassador Jules Cambon delivered it to the president. This development showed the importance of the naval and military victories at Santiago de Cuba. The action in southeastern Cuba fulfilled the president's wish for an early settlement, one that would come before much further expenditure of blood and treasure.

As the capitulation took place at Santiago de Cuba, the Fifth Army Corps experienced an alarming epidemic of tropical diseases. Despite various expedients, including frequent changes of campsites and rigorous sanitation measures, the number of men taken ill continued to rise. On 23 July, Shafter recommended the return of his command to the United States. On 24 July he reported 396 new illnesses and by 27 July a total of 3,770 on sick report. This number increased to 4,270 men on 28 July. When Shafter on 2 August warned of a likely outbreak of yellow fever, the War Department proposed that he move troops to high ground above the fever belt.

When Shafter warned of a likely outbreak of yellow fever, the War Department proposed that he move troops to high ground above the fever belt.

This action stimulated complaints from elements of the Fifth Army Corps that led to action. A round-robin letter signed by leading officers argued that the army must depart or suffer massive losses. Another letter signed by the surgeons at Santiago de Cuba expressed the same sentiments. Lieutenant Colonel Roosevelt wrote a private letter to Senator Henry Cabot Lodge in which he claimed that remaining in Cuba would "simply involve the destruction of thousands." When the round-robin and Roosevelt letters were leaked to the press, they generated a burst of public concern, but the War Department had already decided to act. Shafter received orders to return his command to the United States. Other troops would continue the occupation of Santiago de Cuba.

Arrangements were hurriedly made to construct a camp at Montauk Point on the eastern tip of Long Island, New York, a thinly populated location, where the Fifth Army Corps would recuperate after returning from Cuba. The first troops left Cuba on 7 August, and others followed when transportation became available. The hasty evacuation of Santiago de Cuba and the short warning at Montauk Point led to much confusion, but the Fifth Army Corps was saved from disaster. More than twenty thousand troops arrived at Camp Wikoff at Montauk, but only 257 died there compared with 514 deaths in Cuba. As soon as their health permitted, the men were released from service. On 3 October, the Fifth Army Corps was formally disbanded at Camp Wikoff.

PUERTO RICAN CAMPAIGN

Attention now turned to Puerto Rico and the expedition headed by General Miles that was organized to invade that island. The conquest of Puerto Rico would deprive Spain of a most useful base and provide an excellent eastern location from which to guard against Spanish naval or military movements to the Caribbean Sea. Perhaps more important, operations there would add to the pressure exerted upon Madrid to come to terms. Some military advisers, including Captain Alfred Thayer Mahan of the Naval War Board, had argued that Puerto Rico should come under attack before Cuba, but logistical considerations had doomed any such decision.

General Miles took a special interest in a Puerto Rican campaign, and he spearheaded preparations for an invasion of the island, an operation decided upon at the same time as the movement to Santiago de Cuba. Feverish preparations, particularly at Key West and Charleston, South Carolina, were made to prepare troops for the attack on Puerto Rico.

When difficulties developed at Santiago de Cuba, Miles was ordered to move the troops intended for Puerto Rico to that city, where he arrived on 11 July. While at Santiago de Cuba, Miles completed arrangements for his invasion of Puerto Rico. When arranging a naval escort, he said that he planned a landing at Fajardo, which was at the northeast corner of the island. From there he would move against San Juan. Miles sought a powerful naval escort for his transports, to which Sampson raised objections. President McKinley resolved this dispute summarily, evidently tired of interservice squabbling at Santiago de Cuba, asking Secretary of the Navy Long to assign sufficient ships—including a cruiser or battleship or both—to serve as Miles' escort. Sampson then designated the battleship *Massachusetts,* the auxiliary cruiser *Dixie,* and the armed yacht *Gloucester* to this duty.

Miles cleared Guantánamo Bay on 21 July with three transports carrying about thirty-four hundred men, expecting other troops to join him. Major General James H. Wilson left Charleston on 20 July with thirty-six hundred troops, and Brigadier General Theodore Schwan departed from Tampa four days later with another twenty-nine hundred men. Eight thousand troops awaited transports at Newport News, Virginia, and Tampa, so that Miles anticipated a total force of about eighteen thousand men. He expected to deal with a Spanish garrison of about seventeen thousand members, more than half of them unreliable Puerto Rican volunteers. While on his way to Fajardo, Miles abruptly changed his plan of campaign. He decided not to land at Fajardo, but to continue to steam around Puerto Rico until he reached Guánica on the southwestern coast. A landing at this point, which possessed an excellent harbor, would gain surprise. He would then seize nearby Ponce, the largest city in Puerto Rico, and after that move north against San Juan. The commander of the *Massachusetts,* Captain Francis J. Higginson, raised objections, arguing the advantages of a landing at Fajardo, which included easy landing operations and the availability of coal and communications at the adjacent island of St. Thomas. When Miles persisted, Higginson gave in. This change of plan meant that the army would have to operate all the way across the mountainous interior of Puerto Rico to reach objectives on the north coast, including San Juan. Miles must have thought that the advantages of surprise would outweigh the difficulties that would stem from landing far from the enemy center of resistance.

The Spanish governor-general, General Manuel Macías y Casado, was well-informed of Miles' intended invasion, and he disposed his forces to sustain resistance, a means of strengthening Spain's bargaining power in forthcoming peace negotiations. Instead of concentrating all his forces around San Juan, Macías sent strong detachments to Ponce and Mayagüez and another to Caguas, which lay on the road from Ponce to San Juan.

Miles conducted successful landing operations and then established himself in force at several important southern locations before launching columns northward. Troops went ashore at Guánica without resistance and soon secured the place. He then moved against Ponce, somewhat to the east, taking possession of the city on 27–28 July. Shortly after that, reinforcements arrived from the United States, swelling his force to more than fifteen thousand men. A contingent of five thousand men commanded by Major General John R. Brooke landed at Arroyo, another port on the southeast coast of Puerto Rico, on 3–5 August.

Miles' decision to begin his campaign on the south coast led to a scheme initiated by Commander Charles H. Davis—a naval operation to capture San Juan without the help of the army. Sampson fell in with this idea, perhaps smarting from previous setbacks in controversies with army leaders. He sought permission from Secretary Long to attack San Juan from the sea. It could "be destroyed from the water and may yield without much resistance to a proper show of naval strength." Unfortunately for the navy, Miles learned of this plan and managed to scotch it. Like the attack on Santiago de Cuba, the Puerto Rican campaign stimulated unseemly interservice controversy.

Miles began his northern movement during the first week of August, following a plan of campaign that called for several sweeps across the interior of Puerto Rico to the north coast, eventually converging on San Juan. General Schwan was ordered to lead his Independent Regular Brigade of 1,450 troops, mostly infantry with a cavalry troop and two batteries of light artillery, to Mayagüez and from there through Lares to Arecibo, conquering western Puerto Rico. On the right flank, General Brooke was ordered to move against Cayey, a strong point on the route to San Juan. Meanwhile, General Wilson would move from Ponce against Aibonito. These two forces would then move north to Caguas and San Juan. Brigadier General George H. Garretson was to move toward Utuado north of Ponce.

Only a few engagements took place before word arrived that a protocol providing for a cessation of hostilities had been signed in Washington. Wilson's troops outflanked a Spanish force at Coamo on 9 August and opened the route to Aibonito. On 10 August, Schwan routed a Spanish force at Hormigueros a few miles south of Mayagüez, permitting him to occupy the latter city on 11 August before starting his march on Lares. The most difficult engagement of the campaign seemed

Only a few engagements took place during the Puerto Rican campaign. One battle (shown above) occurred when American troops shelled a Spanish force at Coamo on 9 August 1898. (National Archives)

destined to take place at Aibonito, where thirteen hundred Spanish defenders occupied a strong position. The battle, which was to take place on 13 August, never happened because of the cessation of hostilities the previous day.

Miles insisted that he would have conquered all Puerto Rico in four days. Although it might have taken longer to overcome the defenses at Aibonito and San Juan, Macías could not have mounted a serious defense. U.S. casualties were only seven killed and thirty-six wounded. The Spanish losses were perhaps ten times that many. If Miles had landed at Fajardo, he might have conquered Puerto Rico before the protocol of peace was signed. His general opposition to frontal assaults was understandable, given the likelihood of extensive casualties and uncertain results, but the U.S. plan of operations should have been governed by the weak defenses of Puerto Rico, not by unwarranted caution. In any event, Spain did not conduct a successful defense of the island, an outcome that might have influenced the protocol of peace in its favor.

MANILA CAMPAIGN

After his victory of 1 May, Admiral Dewey settled down to await the arrival of troops. Although his naval guns dominated Manila Bay and the city, he lacked sufficient manpower to deal with about nine thousand Spanish troops ashore. The governor-general, Basilio Augustín, decided not to call in garrisons located elsewhere, about twenty-three thousand men, including Filipino volunteers, thinking that they could retain control of the countryside. This assumption proved erroneous; the insurgents of Aguinaldo rapidly defeated all but a courageous garrison at Baler, which managed to hold out for almost a year. Augustín attempted to retain control of Cavite province but proved unable to do so. Only the city of Manila remained in his hands, but he recognized that he needed additional troops and supplies from Spain to hold out indefinitely.

It was in response to Augustín's situation that Madrid dispatched Admiral Cámara eastward toward Manila with the goal of reinforcing and resupplying the city. When he was recalled to Spain after the debacle at Santiago de Cuba, however, the two U.S. seagoing monitors *Monterey* and *Monadnock*, which were sent across the Pacific to give Dewey vessels that could cope with the armored ships in Cámara's squadron, continued on to the Philippines. They did not arrive until August—the *Monterey* on 4 August and the *Monadnock* four days after the end of the war on 16 August. When word of Cámara's recall reached Manila, morale plummeted in the city. The fall of the city could only be a matter of time.

Dewey's principal preoccupation at Manila while awaiting the U.S. Army was the German navy. By 27 June the German squadron at Manila included two armored vessels and three other ships, displacing almost twenty-five thousand tons, a much stronger force than Dewey's. Germany sent the ships to Manila to take advantage of any opportunity that might present itself to occupy the islands—but only, the Germans asserted, if the Americans decided to leave. Nevertheless, U.S. suspicions grew after a debate developed over certain questions of international law. Although Germany did not intend to dispute U.S. control of the islands, the suspicion, although unfounded, still lingers in some quarters.

Germany sent the ships to Manila to take advantage of any opportunity that might present itself to occupy the islands.

When word of Dewey's victory reached the United States, President McKinley decided to send an army expedition to Manila. No evidence exists to support the view of some historians that this step was part of a conscious plan to annex the Philippine Islands. The U.S. motive was to fulfill a prime strategic purpose—maintenance of constant and growing pressure on Spain's insular possessions to encourage early peace negotiations. Sentiment for annexation began to build later in the United States, but none existed before the war or at its outset.

Major General Wesley Merritt, a veteran of the Civil War, was designated commander of the force that became the Eighth Army Corps, and he mounted an expedition of considerable strength. It included units from the regular army and several regiments of volunteers mostly from western states. Merritt assembled his troops at the Presidio in San Francisco, California, managing to avoid much of the confusion that had characterized the buildup at Tampa for the expedition to Cuba. Merritt's orders merely required him to complete "the reduction of Spanish power" at Manila and to provide security for the Philippines while in U.S. hands. No one from President McKinley on down had yet decided the long-term fate of the distant archipelago.

A small contingent of troops commanded by Brigadier General Thomas M. Anderson left San Francisco on 25 May bound for Manila Bay with the unprotected cruiser Charleston as an escort. Three transports

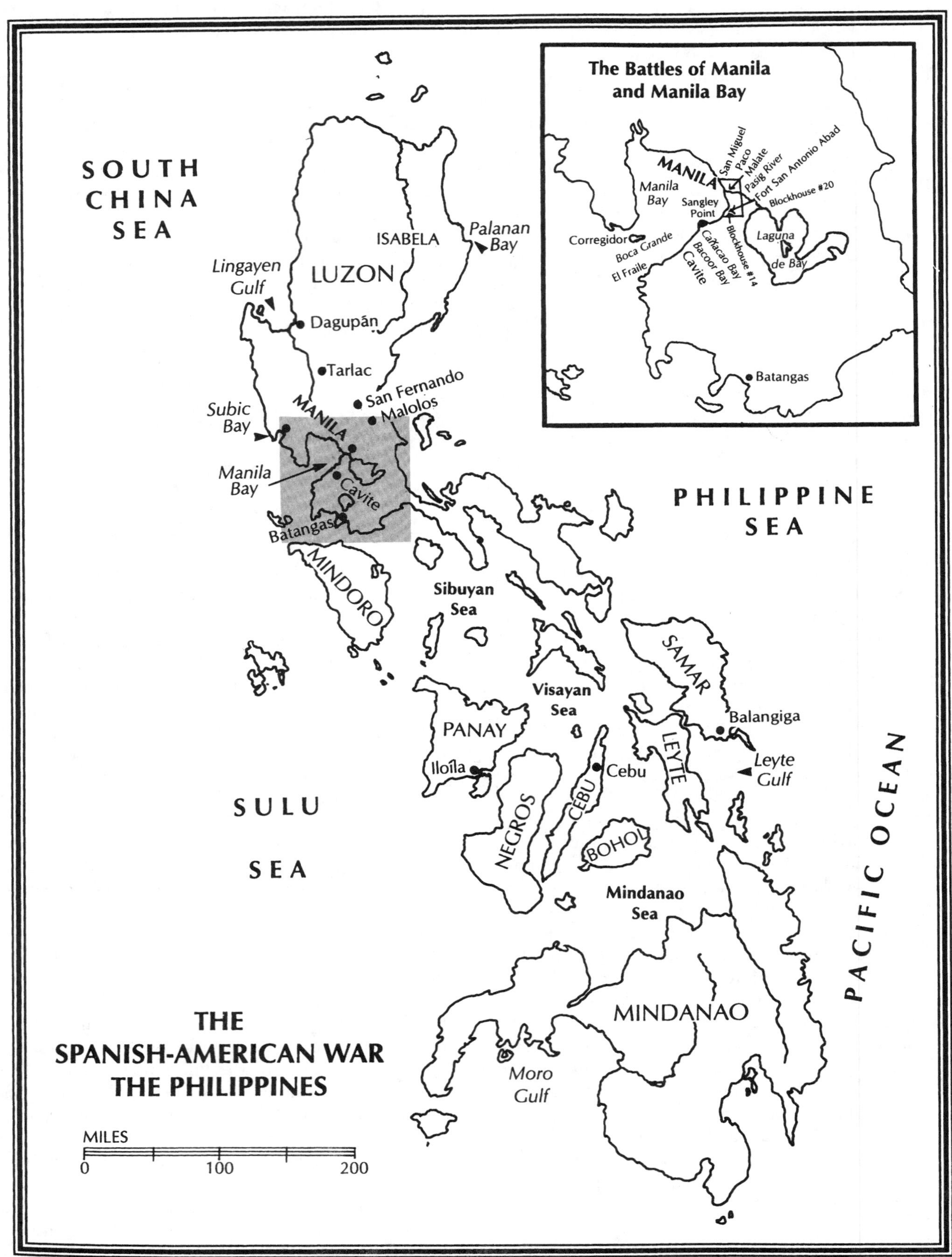
The Battles of Manila and Manila Bay
MANILA
San Miguel
Paco
Malate
Pasig River
Fort San Antonio Abad
Blockhouse #20
Manila Bay
Sangley Point
Corregidor
Boca Grande
El Fraile
Cañacao Bay
Bacoor Bay
Cavite
Blockhouse #14
Laguna de Bay
Batangas
SOUTH CHINA SEA
Lingayen Gulf
LUZON
ISABELA
Palanan Bay
Dagupan
Tarlac
San Fernando
Malolos
MANILA
Subic Bay
Manila Bay
Cavite
Batangas
MINDORO
PHILIPPINE SEA
Sibuyan Sea
SAMAR
Visayan Sea
PANAY
Balangiga
LEYTE
Leyte Gulf
Iloila
Cebu
NEGROS
CEBU
BOHOL
SULU SEA
PACIFIC OCEAN
Mindanao Sea
MINDANAO
Moro Gulf
THE SPANISH-AMERICAN WAR THE PHILIPPINES
MILES
0
100
200

carried about twenty-five hundred men—elements of the Fourteenth Infantry, the First California, and the Second Oregon. This force arrived at Manila on 30 June. The *Charleston* was assigned a special mission to discharge while on the way—to stop at and take possession of Guam, the southernmost island in the Marian group owned by Spain. This island lay about thirty-three hundred miles west of Honolulu and from thirteen hundred to eighteen hundred miles east of the principal east Asian ports of Yokohama, Shanghai, Canton, Hong Kong and Manila. On 20–22 June the *Charleston* accomplished its mission, encountering no resistance from the minuscule Spanish garrison of sixty troops. Thus, the United States easily gained an important link in its line of communications to the Philippines.

Two other contingents of troops sent from San Francisco eventually reached the Philippines, making a total of approximately eleven thousand officers and men. A group of about thirty-six hundred men on three transports departed on 15 June under the command of Brigadier General Francis V. Greene and arrived at Manila on 17 July. Some elements of two regular army units, the Eighteenth and Twenty-third infantries, and four volunteer units—the First Colorado, the First Nebraska, the Tenth Pennsylvania, and two batteries of Utah Artillery—made up the force. The third contingent of almost forty-nine hundred troops under Brigadier General Arthur MacArthur left San Francisco on seven transports between 25 and 29 June and reached Manila on 31 July. This group included the remaining elements of the regular regiments sent earlier, a company of regular army engineers, and more volunteers—the First Idaho, the Thirteenth Minnesota, the First North Dakota, and the First Wyoming. Like Shafter's troops, the Philippine expedition did not have much artillery support, depending on sixteen light field guns, six mountain guns, and a few rapid-fire weapons. When General Merritt arrived at Manila, he set about preparing to attack the city, a task that posed difficulties because Aguinaldo's troops occupied positions around Manila that lay between the city and the Eighth Army Corps. Merritt wanted to avoid any action that might be construed as recognizing the insurgent government, following a policy like that of Shafter toward the Cuban insurgents. Accordingly, he arranged for General Greene, a subordinate, to deal directly with the local Filipino commander. This procedure worked well. The insurgents agreed to abandon trenches to the north of the U.S. camp near a suburb called Malate, opening the way to Manila.

On 29 July, Merritt occupied these field fortifications and then built another line facing two Spanish strong points, Fort San Antonio Abad and Blockhouse No. 14, both parts of a line of blockhouses that covered the southern and eastern outskirts of Manila. This act spurred an exchange of fire with the Spanish defenders on the night of 31 July. Ten Americans were killed and thirty-three were wounded. Other firefights during the following days caused more U.S. casualties—five killed and twenty wounded. Meanwhile, the U.S. position was extended for a thousand yards so that its right flank ended at an impassable swamp.

Merritt wanted to move quickly against Manila, and sought supporting naval gunfire from Dewey, but the admiral temporized. He wanted to await the arrival of the *Monterey* and its powerful weapons, including two twelve-inch and two ten-inch guns. He also hoped to negotiate a surrender of the city that would eliminate the need for a serious engagement. Attempts to arrange a capitulation took place on two levels. Formal demands were made on the new governor-general, Don Fermín Jáudenes y Alvarez, who had replaced the despairing Augustín. This effort culminated on 9–10 August with Jáudenes asking for time to consult Madrid, but Merritt and Dewey rejected this request. Meanwhile, secret discussions were held through the Belgian consul in Manila, Edouard C. André. Also involved was the Roman Catholic archbishop of Manila, one of a group of civilians organized to help in the defense of the city. Eventually, Jáudenes made an intriguing proposal: He would capitulate provided the Americans agreed to a sham battle that would preserve the garrison's honor and that they pledged to keep Aguinaldo's troops from entering the city. Dewey agreed, proposing to shell Fort San Antonio Abad briefly and then signal a request for surrender. The Spanish garrison would then display a white flag.

Dewey's informal deal with Jáudenes did not cover land forces, but General Merritt, although skeptical of the plan, agreed to board one of Dewey's supply ships, the *Zafiro,* taking with him six companies of the Second Oregon, which would occupy the walled city after the surrender. To assure the capture of the city should the secret arrangement break down, Merritt made plans for an assault. He did not inform his subordinate commanders of the Jáudenes-Dewey agreement.

Merritt's plan of operations entailed a frontal attack by two brigades. General MacArthur, with about five thousand men, would move at the right of the U.S. line against Blockhouse No. 14. General Greene and about thirty-eight hundred men would move at the left of the line against Fort San Antonio Abad after Dewey finished his bombardment of that position. General Anderson was to arrange for the evacuation of insurgents in front of Blockhouse No. 14, but if the insurgents proved uncooperative, the Americans were not to force them out. Artillery was placed to avoid firing on insurgent positions.

On 13 August, Dewey's squadron took positions opposite the fortifications of Manila. Four ships moved off Fort San Antonio Abad and began to bombard it at 9:35 A.M., firing slowly for an hour. At 10:25 General Greene approached Fort San Antonio Abad, but no Spanish troops were found within. Some firing came from Malate, however, and Greene's force took a few casualties, one killed and fifty-four wounded. On the right, MacArthur advanced when he heard gunfire on the left, and his troops became engaged in a sharp fight. He took Blockhouse No. 14 and then assaulted Blockhouse No. 20 at Singalong, where resistance continued until 1:30 P.M. Taking casualties of five killed and thirty-eight wounded, MacArthur moved through Paco into the walled city.

As these operations unfolded on land, Dewey tested the planned surrender. At 11:00 A.M., after completing his bombardment of Fort San Antonio Abad, he moved off Manila and there discovered a white flag displayed from the south bastion of the city walls. U.S. officers went ashore to arrange the details of the surrender with Jáudenes and Admiral Montojo, which were completed by 2:30 P.M. The companies of the Second Oregon assigned the task of occupying the walled city went ashore and acted as a provost guard, disarming the Spanish garrison. The sham battle produced the desired result. Unfortunately, some U.S. casualties were incurred after the display of the white flag on the Manila bastion.

Merritt ensured that Aguinaldo's forces were kept out of Manila. On 11 August, General Anderson informed the insurgents that they were not to enter the city, and he reiterated this notice forcefully on the day of the battle. Nevertheless, about four thousand insurgents moved into suburban areas, portending future difficulties.

Unlike the campaign in Cuba, operations in the Philippines proceeded very smoothly. Merritt's orderly preparations placed his troops in position to move quickly after their arrival at Manila. Dewey's efforts to avoid unnecessary bloodshed helped greatly to obtain an early capitulation without extensive bloodletting. The interservice wrangling that occurred at Santiago de Cuba did not happen at Manila. Nothing comparable to the epidemic of tropical diseases that struck the Fifth Army Corps developed in the Philippines. In both instances, the navy's ability to establish command of the sea determined the outcome. Land operations proved successful because Spain could not reinforce and resupply its garrisons.

TREATY OF PARIS

While General Merritt in the Philippines and General Miles in Puerto Rico accomplished their missions, negotiations in Washington between President McKinley and French Ambassador Jules Cambon at length produced a protocol of peace that ended hostilities. Consultations in Washington led to the formulation of the U.S. demands. Three were quickly specified—independence for Cuba, the cession of Puerto Rico instead of an indemnity, and cession of an island in the Marianas, probably Guam. Only the disposition of the Philippines occasioned debate because opinion was divided. Some opposed any territorial acquisition, and others wanted a naval base or Luzon or the entire island group. McKinley eventually decided simply to demand the retention of Manila and Manila Bay for the moment, leaving the final settlement to a postwar peace conference. Despite vigorous efforts by Cambon, McKinley would not budge from these requirements. Sagasta finally accepted the U.S. terms, recognizing that further delay would lead only to further exactions. The protocol ending the war was signed in the White House on 12 August, President McKinley acting for the United States and Cambon for Spain.

President McKinley soon chose commissioners to represent the United States at the peace conference scheduled to convene in Paris during September. Secretary of State William R. Day was selected to head the delegation. John Hay, the U.S. ambassador in London, was brought back to Washington to take Day's place at the State Department. Three senators were named, recognizing that the U.S. Senate must give advice and consent to a treaty of peace by a two-thirds majority. One was Senator George Gray of Delaware, the ranking Democratic member of the Senate Foreign Relations Committee. The fifth member was Whitelaw Reid, publisher of the *New York Tribune,* a highly partisan Republican whose expansionist views balanced those of the antiexpansionist Gray. McKinley showed his political acumen by selecting a commission that represented different currents of opinion and that would follow wherever he wished to lead them.

Some Americans objected to the acquisition of a largely nonwhite and Roman Catholic populace.

The negotiations at Paris during October and November 1898 reflected the dominant bargaining position of the United States. The only question of great importance decided during the peace negotiations was the disposition of the Philippine Islands. Spanish diplomats labored mightily to influence the outcome, but President McKinley controlled the settlement. Although the United States entered the war with only one war aim, independence for Cuba, expansionist sentiment soon developed. Puerto Rico and Guam were taken principally for strategic reasons, to strengthen the U.S. position in the Caribbean Sea and in the Pacific Ocean. The same motive dictated the peaceful annexation of the independent Hawaiian Republic during the summer of 1898. Therefore, expansionist aspirations after the end of the war centered on the Philippine Islands.

A significant body of opinion opposed annexation of the Philippines, but over time a clear majority of the American people came to favor this step. Those who argued against annexation offered many compelling arguments, among them the claim that annexation of a noncontiguous area was unconstitutional and that it violated the democratic principle of self-determination. Another argument reflected racial and religious prejudices—some objected to the acquisition of a largely nonwhite and Roman Catholic populace. Most influential, however, were the claims that the annexation of the Philippines would assure U.S. access to the China market and that imperialism was the natural policy for a great power. Psychological elements also developed. The quick victory over Spain engendered great enthusiasm and confidence. In this mood, overseas expansion seemed fully justified.

President McKinley hesitated, recognizing the complications that might result from annexation of the Philippines, and he took several weeks to decide. In search of guidance, he consulted some experts, among them General Greene, who had returned from the Philippines. Most important, he undertook a speaking tour to the Middle West during the period 11–21 October, encountering extensive support for the retention of the Philippines and developing three interrelated arguments for annexation that ultimately guided his decision. First, he decided, there were humanitarian responsibilities. Second, the United States, having intervened in Philippine affairs, had a certain obligation to the inhabitants. Third, destiny seemed to exert its influence. These powerful justifications undergirded a message sent to Paris on 26 October that instructed the peace commission to negotiate the annexation of the entire Philippine archipelago.

The Spanish delegation strenuously resisted this demand, but it could not carry the day, and the final terms of the Treaty of Paris reflected the president's desires. To sweeten the bitter pill, the United States agreed to pay $20 million in compensation for the Philippines. The undertakings specified in the protocol of 12 August, including independence for Cuba and the annexation of Puerto Rico and Guam, were formalized in the peace treaty. Some U.S. interest in the Caroline Islands had surfaced during the conference, but nothing came of it. Earlier, in September, Spain had made a secret agreement with Germany to sell the Caroline, Mariana, and Palau island groups, a deal completed on 10 December. Not having obtained an island such as Kusaie in the Carolines that would have improved its line of communications across the Pacific Ocean, the United States occupied Wake Island to serve that purpose.

A lively debate took place in the U.S. Senate over the Treaty of Paris. Although the public clearly favored ratification of the treaty, a significant minority advanced the familiar arguments against this course. Given the requirement for a two-thirds majority of the Senate to give consent to treaties, the outcome appeared in doubt. Two developments provided sufficient votes to assure ratification. One was the influence of William Jennings Bryan, the Democratic candidate for the presidency in 1896 who wanted to run again in 1900. He argued that the Democratic party should support the treaty but after that seek independence for the Philippines. Another was the sudden outbreak of hostilities between the insurgents and U.S. forces near Manila on 4 February. McKinley recognized that this deed would agitate public opinion and strengthen his hand. On 6 February, the treaty received senatorial consent by a vote of fifty-seven to twenty-seven. Two more negative votes would have led to its defeat. In Spain, the treaty did not muster the necessary votes in the Cortes, but the Queen Regent decided to make use of her constitutional powers to override the legislature. The treaty was ratified on 19 March and proclaimed on 11 April 1899.

THE PHILIPPINE WAR

For approximately six months, while the Treaty of Paris was negotiated and discussed, relations between the U.S. occupation force and the Filipino insurgents continually worsened. The outcome of the postwar negotiations confirmed what the insurgents had suspected from the first, that the United States would take the Philippines. On 17 August 1898, the War Department had issued instructions to guide relations with the insurgents that would remain in force until February 1899. There was to be no joint occupation of Manila. The United States would preserve peace and protect the people and property within the zone of occupation, and the insurgents must respect this policy. General Merritt then reached an agreement with Aguinaldo that allowed the insurgents to remain in several suburbs around Manila while denying them access to the city. Admiral

Dewey was uneasy and requested reinforcements. The protocol of peace precluded any such measure, but the Navy Department decided to send the *Oregon* and the *Iowa* to Hawaii, from which point they could move quickly to Manila.

The outcome of the postwar negotiations confirmed what the Filipino insurgents had suspected from the first, that the United States would take the Philippines.

When General Merritt left to advise the peace commission at Paris, Major General Elwell S. Otis took command of the Eighth Army Corps. He had brought the last contingent of troops to Manila, landing on 21 August 1898, a force that included 172 officers and 4,610 enlisted men. An exceptionally hardworking officer, Otis found it difficult to delegate authority, leading one observer to note, "he lives in a valley and works with a microscope, while his proper place is on a hilltop with a spyglass." Otis remained in Manila throughout his tenure, a practice that annoyed troops in the field. Nevertheless, Otis was an efficient civil administrator who rapidly gained the respect of the Filipinos. Otis faced many problems during the early months of the occupation. One task was to force the withdrawal of insurgents to positions well outside Manila. Another was to provide effective security within the city itself. When possible, Otis, a lawyer, allowed local courts to hear civil cases and he set up military tribunals to hear criminal cases. Hoping to revive the economy, he resumed collection of the customs and established a fiscal system.

Meanwhile, Aguinaldo set up a capital at Malolos and strengthened his government and his armed forces. His authority was extended to much of Luzon, and he energized a junta in Hong Kong to conduct his foreign relations, which consisted of seeking aid for his regime. On 28 September, he named Antonio Luna director of war, and he soon designated other senior commanders. Luna, an Ilocoan *ilustrado* who had lived in Spain and undertaken a study of military affairs, set about creating a conventional army along European lines that would fight according to the strategy and tactics generally followed in the western world. His initial plans for war entailed conventional warfare in northern Luzon along the Manila-Dagupan railway. To prepare for these operations, he placed his troops on a line north of Manila that extended from Caloocan to Novaliches.

As the U.S. Army made its arrangements, factionalism within the insurgent camp led to a lively debate over the provisions of a constitution. The more conservative elements in the insurgency, including men such as Pedro Paterno and Felipe Buencamino, proved successful in frustrating the desires of a more radical faction led by Apolinario Mabini that advocated advanced social revolution. The Malolos constitution, promulgated on 31 January 1899, placed the executive and judicial branches largely under legislative control, frustrating the radical wish for a strong central administration that could act quickly and efficiently.

Although Aguinaldo gave many indications of his intention to resist U.S. authority, Otis hoped that a peaceful resolution could take place, making plans to maintain an army of occupation numbering about twenty-five thousand troops. He remained optimistic even after the terms of the Treaty of Paris became known.

On 21 December 1898 President McKinley issued a proclamation that established his policy for the future government of the Philippines. He ordered the extension of U.S. authority to all points in the Philippines, although the treaty was not yet ratified. The Americans would rule as friends and protectors rather than as invaders or conquerors. Municipal law would remain in force within the context of U.S. military authority. Public property would fall to the United States but private property would remain unaffected. The United States would collect taxes and ports would be opened to friendly nations. The president also ordered Otis to seek the support of the people by assuring them "that full measure of individual rights and liberties which is the heritage of free peoples." The mission of the United States was "benevolent assimilation, substituting the mild sway of justice and right for arbitrary rule." Otis was enjoined to conduct a "temperate administration" but nevertheless to use "the strong arm of authority to repress disturbance."

The optimism of Otis may have led to misapprehension in Washington of the difficulties that lay ahead. The Americans held only Manila and Cavite; Aguinaldo was in control elsewhere. Many Filipinos were prepared to take up arms rather than acquiesce to benevolent assimilation. Otis himself delayed issuing the president's proclamation for two weeks and then expurgated it, using the word "beneficent" rather than "benevolent" and the term "temporary administration" rather than "temperate administration." He also added a promise of Filipino representation in the government. Seeking to extend his authority to the Visayan Islands, Otis sent an expedition to occupy the important port of Iloílo on the island of Panay. Before these troops arrived, an in-

As the war with Spain ended, insurgent Filipinos challenged American authority in their country. These U.S. soldiers stand in a trench in the Philippines, ready for battle in 1899. (National Archives)

surgent force took control of the city, and Otis decided to avoid trouble by postponing a landing. He explained his action to the War Department as an attempt to arrange a settlement with the more moderate elements of the insurgent leadership. McKinley accepted this policy, hoping to avoid developments that might prejudice consideration of the Treaty of Paris, which was before the Senate. Otis then engaged in secret negotiations, but his effort came to nothing. This outcome showed that the two positions were irreconcilable. The Filipino wish for independence clashed hopelessly with the U.S. policy of annexation. Although Otis has been criticized for his rigid negotiating position, it was unlikely that more flexibility would have led to a peaceful outcome.

To provide assistance to Otis and Dewey in dealing with the insurgents, President McKinley formed a group that became known as the First Philippine Commission. Jacob Gould Schurman, the president of Cornell University, served as its chairman. It was ordered to "facilitate the most humane, pacific, and effective extension of authority . . . and to secure, with the least possible delay, the benefits of a wise and generous protection of life and property to the inhabitants." After studying conditions in the Philippines, the commission was to make recommendations for the governance of the islands. Meanwhile, military government would continue. Before the commission reached Manila, however, accumulating tensions led to a passage at arms.

Otis became increasingly worried about an insurgent attack on his troops, although he did not convey his suspicions fully to his superiors. To assure a sound defense of the city, he placed a division under General Anderson to the north and east of Manila and another under General MacArthur to the south and the east, forming a front of about sixteen miles. His army consisted of about twenty thousand enlisted men and fewer than a thousand officers, more than two thousand of whom had been sent to Iloílo. Others were ill or assigned to a provost guard, leaving only ten thousand men to man the line facing the insurgent army. In addition to making arrangements for defense of the city, Otis prepared plans for operations against the waterworks east of Manila and the insurgent capital of Malolos to the north.

The Filipino regular army at this time consisted of about fourteen thousand men, eight thousand of whom faced the U.S. troops at Manila. Militia and irregular troops raised the total Filipino force to somewhere between twenty thousand and thirty thousand. The troops at Manila were divided into two groups, one on each side of the Pasig River four miles east of Manila. Despite Luna's efforts, the insurgent army was poorly trained and equipped, and it lacked organized operational plans. If attacked, Luna planned to hold his defensive positions, to create an uproar in the city, and to attack targets of opportunity.

At 8:30 P.M. on the evening of 4 February, a Filipino patrol approached the American line, an act that started the Philippine War (also known as the Philippino Insurrection and the Filipino-American War). A guard from the First Nebraska Volunteers challenged the patrol which passed 150 yards beyond the midpoint between the two armies. After the third challenge, the guard opened fire, killing one insurgent. Another U.S. soldier wounded a second insurgent, and firefights followed during the night on both the north and south sides of the Pasig River. Meanwhile, the provost guard in Manila dealt effectively with an insurgent uprising.

General Otis later claimed that the insurgent action represented a premature beginning to a planned assault, but Filipino commentators dispute this view. According to the U.S. commander, the incident on 4 February came several days before the insurgents planned to attack, but their initiative could not have been delayed long because of the need to move before significant U.S. reinforcements could arrive. Filipino observers claim that the insurgents did not inaugurate the action. Luna lacked plans for operations at the time, and he and his principal subordinates were absent on the night of 4 February. It seems probable that neither side intended to attack the other, but, once an exchange of fire took place, it was impossible to suppress further action. Aguinaldo may have attempted to halt hostilities, but the Americans, once engaged, made no such effort. Otis merely informed Aguinaldo that he would receive an insurgent proposition for suspension of the fighting. The Filipino leader made no response.

It seems probable that neither side intended to attack the other, but, once an exchange of fire took place, it was impossible to suppress further action.

Otis reached his initial objectives without difficulty. He quickly seized the waterworks, and by 8 February had moved north to a line near Caloocan from which he planned to move on Malolos. To husband his available troops, Otis did not move farther south of Manila than the line Pasay–San Pedro Macatí.

Senator Henry Cabot Lodge of Massachusetts had called the Spanish-American War "a splendid little war," an apt characterization perhaps, but this description did not apply to the Philippine War, which lasted for more than three years. Of the more than 125,000 Americans who served in it, 4,224 died and 2,818 were wounded. The insurgent losses were much greater, perhaps sixteen thousand killed and wounded, and the civilian population may have endured as many as a hundred thousand fatalities from famine and disease.

CONVENTIONAL WARFARE IN 1899. General Otis faced the task of engaging a large Filipino force with few troops. He led more than twenty thousand men, of whom about fifteen thousand were volunteers. The latter troops were due for discharge shortly, having served a year. During the early months of the war, Otis was forced to exchange many of his units for others arriving from the United States. As the volunteer regiments departed, regular regiments came in, including the Third, Fourth, Seventeenth, Twentieth, and Twenty-second infantries by the end of March. The new troops were deployed immediately, but Otis rarely could place more than ten thousand men in the field at any one time. Although General Otis was by nature a cautious commander, his limited available manpower explains the deliberate and controlled character of his operations north of Manila during 1899.

His task was made easier because General Luna persisted in treating his army as a conventional force that could conduct operations along European lines. Aguinaldo apparently preferred guerrilla warfare from the beginning, but his views did not prevail until Luna's approach was fully tested and found wanting. Guerrilla operations might have narrowed the gap between the two armies, but conventional warfare played into the hands of the much more experienced, better-trained, and better-equipped U.S. troops.

During the initial phase of the conventional war, February–March 1899, the Eighth Army Corps pursued two interrelated objectives. Otis began to project forces into the Visayan Islands, hoping by this measure to prevent Aguinaldo from gaining full control of the region. Meanwhile he pursued an attack on the insurgent capital of Malolos. In the Visayans, an expedition moved on the port of Iloílo almost immediately and seized it. Soon after, the gunboat *Petrel* succeeded in taking Cebu City, the largest port on the island of Cebu. Early in March an army expedition took the island of Negros. The Americans were unable to take further action in the Visayans during 1899, but another army expedition occupied the island of Joló in the Sulu group. Although difficulties arose in Mindanao, the huge southern island of the archipelago, Otis lacked sufficient strength to undertake operations in that quarter.

Most of Otis' troops were employed north of Manila in a drive on Malolos that began on 25 March. Otis deployed two divisions, one under MacArthur on the right and the other under Brigadier General Henry Lawton on the left. His plan was to envelop and capture the entire insurgent army of between six thousand and eight thousand troops. The envelopment failed, but the insurgents were driven back easily, and Malolos fell on 26 March. Casualties were light, amounting to only 139 killed and 891 wounded as of 1 April.

During May, Otis pushed farther north but then ceased offensive operations. MacArthur reached San Fernando and Lawton in the Ildefonso–San Miguel–San Isidro region, short of the new insurgent capital at Tarlac. This delay reflected the necessity to exchange more volunteer regiments for units coming out from the United States and the difficulties of campaigning in the torrid, rainy summer. Otis had contained the insurgents to the south and east of Manila and defeated them to the north, but he was forced to await a more propitious moment to resume the attack. This pause contributed to growing irritation with Otis among his troops. The commander did not communicate his strategic and tactical intentions effectively to his force. Another source of discontent was his continuing policy of maintaining extraordinarily close command and control from his headquarters in Manila. He even managed to alienate the American journalists congregated in Manila by maintaining stringent censorship.

Although Otis incurred growing criticism at this time, perhaps his only serious error was his delay in requesting sufficient reinforcements to complete the campaign. Eventually he stated that a force of thirty thousand troops could quell the insurgency. On 2 March 1899, Congress passed legislation that made additional troops available in the Philippines. The regular army was increased to a level of sixty-five thousand men, and the War Department was authorized to recruit thirty-five thousand volunteers from the nation at large, to be organized into twenty-seven infantry regiments and three cavalry regiments. Strength reports during the summer and fall of 1899 reflect the increase in the size of Otis' army. Effectives at the end of August numbered about twenty-eight thousand, but this figure rose to about thirty-six thousand by the end of October. By the end of December, the total strength mounted to more than fifty thousand troops.

While the army awaited reinforcements and the end of the rainy season, opposition to the war began to develop rapidly in the United States, a recrudescence of the antiimperialist movement that had opposed the Treaty of Paris. Many arguments—ideological, humanitarian, economic, religious, racial, constitutional, and political in nature—emanated from a diverse coalition of antiimperialists who urged that the United States withdraw from the Philippines and grant some form of self-government. Pressure from the antiimperialists led President McKinley to defend his policy energetically. So did Secretary of War Elihu Root, who in vigorous language disputed the antiimperialist view that the insurgency in the Philippines had legitimate origins and that it represented the best interests of the Philippine people. This outspoken official support at home strengthened the position of General Otis as he prepared to resume active operations in October–November 1899.

During the summer, General Luna had come to a violent end. His relations with Aguinaldo had become increasingly strained, leading him to resign, a gesture that was refused. On 5 June, however, members of an insurgent unit from Kawit, Aguinaldo's home town, assassinated Luna. Many have suspected Aguinaldo of ordering this deed, but direct proof is lacking. Intense rivalries among the insurgent leadership adversely affected the operations of the Philippine army. The death of Luna made it possible for Aguinaldo to adopt a different military strategy. An alternative to conventional operations was to wage guerrilla war, a means of postponing defeat and playing for time. McKinley would be standing for reelection in 1900, and his Democratic rival, the antiimperialist William Jennings Bryan, might win the presidency and end the war.

In the autumn of 1899, General Otis launched an attack in northern Luzon intended to destroy the insurgent army. He anticipated no difficulty in defeating the insurgents in the central plain of Luzon. His principal problem was to prevent the defeated enemy from fleeing into the adjacent mountains of the north. Otis decided upon a complicated plan of operations. MacArthur's division was ordered to attack north from the San Fernando–Baliaug line, seizing both the insurgent capital at Tarlac and Dagupan at the end of the railroad. Lawton's division would move in a northeasterly direction up the Rio Grande at the northeastern edge of the central plain, seeking to close mountain passes leading eastward out of the plain. He would link with MacArthur at Dagupan. Brigadier General Lloyd Wheaton would make an amphibious landing near San Fabian on the Lingayen Gulf. After gaining control of the coastal road that ran to the northern end of Luzon, he would move eastward to a junction with Lawton's division. The insurgent army, fleeing from MacArthur, would be driven onto the forces of Lawton and Wheaton.

The operation itself proved successful, although it did not follow the script exactly. Lawton began his attack on 12 October, and by mid-November he had reached most of his objectives, although the Rio Grande proved difficult to use. MacArthur's frontal attack began on 5 November. He captured Tarlac on 12 November and reached Dagupan on 20 November. Wheaton landed at San Fabian on 7 November, but he was delayed. Otis dispersed the regular Philippine army, but Aguinaldo and many of his troops managed to escape into mountainous regions. Even so, Otis was convinced that he had practically ended the war. MacArthur was ordered to provide small garrisons at various locations to guard against depredations by *ladrones* and any insurgent forces that might conduct local operations. Otis resisted proposals to offer a general amnesty, hoping instead to quell all resistance. To this end, during the first four months of 1900, he attempted to pacify southern Luzon and the Visayan Islands.

Throughout his tenure, Otis believed the insurrection was largely the doing of the Tagalog tribesmen in Luzon. Failing to recognize the extent of disaffection among the general populace and the broad base of support for Aguinaldo that had developed throughout the Philippines, he assumed that when Tagalog resistance was ended, the insurgency would collapse. All that was needed after that, he thought, was the establishment of an effective constabulary to protect the citizenry against *ladrones* and small detachments of insurgent bitter enders. To support this effort, Otis established four administrative districts, the Department of Northern Luzon north of the Pasig River, the Department of Southern Luzon south of the Pasig River, the Department of the Visayas, and the Department of Mindanao and Joló. A military governor directed affairs in Manila.

In April 1900, Otis asked for relief and soon left for the United States, believing that his pacification efforts has been successful. His superiors in Washington accepted this estimate of the situation. President McKinley promptly formed a second Philippine Commission to help create an efficient civilian government in the islands. Its chairman was a respected judge, William Howard Taft. General MacArthur, named to succeed Otis as military commander, proceeded to organize small garrisons throughout the Philippines to assure stability.

GUERRILLA WARFARE, 1900–1902. On 12 November 1899, even as the U.S. forces were capturing the insurgent capital of Tarlac, Aguinaldo issued orders just before his flight to the mountains that inaugurated a new phase of the war. Troops in central Luzon were now to "maneuver in flying columns and guerrilla bands." Although insurgent organizations in Luzon would not begin serious guerrilla operations until the summer of 1900, after a period of rest and preparation, it was clear to Aguinaldo that guerrilla warfare was the only means available to prolong the war. If insurgent forces could remain in the field, antiimperialist sentiment in the United States, intensified because of continuing losses of blood and treasure in a protracted conflict, might eventually force changes in policy and lead to independence for the Philippines. Aguinaldo especially hoped for the overthrow of McKinley and the Republican party in the election of 1900. Various motives ranging from patriotism to profit energized the decentralized detachments of guerrillas that now prepared for an entirely new war, one that eventually would be fought throughout the Philippines.

Aguinaldo directed troops in central Luzon to "maneuver in flying columns and guerrilla bands."

In June 1900, MacArthur issued a proclamation of amnesty, assuming, as had Otis before him, that he had only to mop up the remaining resistance and to organize effective police protection. Only about five thousand insurgents took advantage of his offer, a disappointing result that led him to recommend retention of a substantial force. (By March 1901 that force would grow to forty-five thousand men.) Meanwhile, he emphasized construction of a road net to improve communications and created a constabulary made up of two thousand Filipinos to help police the archipelago.

By September 1900, MacArthur had established more than four hundred military stations, but by this time a much-diminished Filipino force held an enlarged number of U.S. troops in the field. The number of engagements with small groups of insurgents mounted rapidly as guerrilla leaders loyal to Aguinaldo, whose headquarters now moved from place to place, emerged in various locations and perfected their plans of operations. They benefited greatly from widespread assistance that came either voluntarily or by coercion from the civil population. Dual governments developed in some areas. Officials who worked for the Americans during the day served the guerrillas at night. Although the guerrilla bands fled into mountainous or jungle areas when necessary to avoid battle, they were usually based in towns, which kept them supplied.

Guerrilla operations greatly compromised the measures undertaken by the military to put benevolent assimilation into effect. These included education, road construction, sanitation, and other humanitarian enterprises. The military intent of these measures was to attenuate local support of guerrilla bands, but the insurgents used nationalist appeals and terrorism to thwart many of the army's efforts to pacify the islands.

At length General MacArthur decided to turn away from the garrison policy of Otis and resume aggressive operations against the insurgents. This decision brought him into conflict with the Second Philippine Commission headed by Taft, which had reached Manila in June 1900. The army disliked civilian interference, an attitude reflected in a line of doggerel poetry popular among the troops who rejected patronizing talk of brown brothers: "He may be a brother of Big Bill Taft, but he ain't no brother of mine." Taft naturally advocated an early resumption of civil government, and he pursued what became known as "the policy of attraction," adoption of civil measures designed to wean support from the insurgents. The army did not oppose "attraction," but they objected to steps that might interfere with effective military operations in the field.

President McKinley and Secretary of War Root supported a policy that emphasized both attraction and aggressive military operations. Theodore Roosevelt summarized very well the attitude of the home government: "By every consideration of honor and humanity we are bound to stay in the Philippines and put down the insurrection, establish order and then give a constantly increasing measure of liberty and self-government, while ruling with wisdom and justice. Whenever the islands can stand alone, I should be only too glad to withdraw." This general posture met with public approbation. Aguinaldo's hopes for the election of Bryan in

1900 were disappointed, McKinley winning by an impressive majority.

Nothing had developed in the Philippines to counter the McKinley administration's assertion that the insurgents were under great pressure and doomed to defeat. Aguinaldo did not provide effective leadership. Had he avoided the debacle of 1899, preventing Luna's disastrous experiment with conventional operations, and had he organized an effective system of command and control for the conduct of coordinated guerrilla operations, the insurgency might have fared far better. The inadequacies of the insurgent organization for guerrilla warfare played directly into the hands of the Americans. Its weakness prevented a clear demonstration that the insurgents could remain in the field indefinitely and exact a considerable cost in American lives and resources, a result that might have aroused considerable domestic opposition to the Philippine War. As it was, the antiimperialist movement in the United States, divided in purpose and leadership, never gained broad public support.

After the election of 1900, both Taft and MacArthur expanded their operations, the civilian emphasizing measures of political attraction and the soldier directing offensive operations in the field. Success in both areas would result in mutually reinforcing gains. Failure might encourage growing resistance.

MacArthur revised the initial U.S. assumptions about the proper means of ending the insurgency. He decided upon "an entirely new campaign . . . based on the central idea of detaching the towns from the immediate support of the guerrillas in the field, and thus also precluding . . . indirect support." On 20 December he issued a proclamation that showed his change of policy. The United States would no longer tolerate violations of the laws of war. Zones of military operations were placed under martial law. MacArthur's forces would protect citizens from guerrillas who would from now on be subject to condign punishment.

MacArthur also adopted a tactical innovation of great importance, an emphasis on untiring pursuit in the field. If the guerrillas could be denied support from towns, they would lack sufficient supplies and equipment. If kept constantly in flight, they would eventually be forced either to surrender or to leave the field. The tactics of untiring pursuit created a need for additional manpower, and it was forthcoming. After the U.S. force was built up to seventy thousand troops in 1901, MacArthur had sufficient strength both to protect civilians and maintain constant pressure on the guerrillas. To strengthen his intelligence, MacArthur developed a force of fifty-four hundred Philippine Scouts, an organization distinct from the Philippine Constabulary, and created the Division of Military Information to gather and distribute military intelligence. Perhaps the most striking evidence of MacArthur's willingness to press affairs to a conclusion was his experimentation with the concentration of civilians in camps, a means of depriving the guerrillas of support in the countryside. He sought to avoid the errors of Weyler in Cuba, arguing that concentration was "exclusively a military measure carried out without objectionable or offensive measures."

Although MacArthur advocated broad general changes in strategy and tactics, he allowed considerable freedom of action to local commanders, who adopted a variety of approaches, reacting to specific circumstances. In his 1989 study of the subject, Brian M. Linn shows conclusively that the counterinsurgency in Luzon, the critical arena, reflected regional variations rather than a centralized approach, although these measures were consistent with MacArthur's general directives. Decentralization reflected the regional character of the Filipino insurgency, which varied markedly from place to place.

U.S. troops, goaded by Filipino terrorism, resorted to torture, especially the "water cure," forcing water down a victim's throat.

MacArthur supplemented his counterinsurgency program with other measures designed to force an early end to Filipino resistance. He ordered a naval blockade of certain locations in the Visayas to prevent the insurgents from collecting levies on trading goods. He expedited the road-building program to improve his communications. He also authorized the banishment of captured insurgent leaders, among them Apolinario Mabini and Artemio Ricarte, who were detained on Guam. MacArthur's counterinsurgency operations occasionally led to U.S. violations of the laws of war. Antiimperialist opponents exaggerated the extent of these activities, but at times U.S. troops, goaded by Filipino terrorism, an unacceptable motivation, resorted to torture, especially the "water cure," forcing water down a victim's throat, and the "rope cure," which required the use of a garrote.

As the army put into effect the new military practices, Taft and the Philippine Commission strengthened the policy of attraction. Chief among its measures was support of a pro-American political organization, the Federal party. Its leaders were among the more circumspect, expediential, and politically conservative members of the Filipino opposition. It provided a workable means of exerting Filipino influence, and it gained strength as U.S. military operations systematically dealt with guerrilla bands. The policy of attraction received a considerable boost when the daring U.S. General Frederick Funston managed to capture Aguinaldo. When it was learned that Aguinaldo was settled at Palinan, in Isabela Province near the northeastern coast of Luzon, Funston organized a small expedition of eighty Macabebe scouts disguised as guerrillas. He and a few other Americans posed as prisoners. The navy ferried Funston and his men to the east coast about a hundred miles south of Palinan. He then marched northward, sending forged messages ahead announcing his approach. On 23 March 1901, he reached Palinan and surprised Aguinaldo and his small bodyguard of fifty men. Funston's romantic and improbable scheme had worked to perfection. Once in American hands, Aguinaldo took an oath of loyalty and called for an end of the insurgency.

By the summer of 1901, the army had all but quelled organized insurgent operations in Luzon except in Batangas and emphasis shifted to the Visayas. Mopping-up operations against specific guerrilla bands in a few salient locations took place during the last phase of the Philippine War from the summer of 1901 to July 1902, when the insurgency was officially declared at an end. Major General Adna R. Chaffee had succeeded MacArthur in July 1901, presiding over the last operations. One by one the Visayans were pacified, Panay by March 1901, Cebu by September 1901, and Bohol by December 1901.

The most serious resistance came in Samar, where Vicente Lukban took advantage of difficult terrain to remain active. On 28 September 1901, Lukban succeeded in wiping out a garrison of seventy-four men at Balangiga—only twenty-six soldiers survived the attack—but this success turned into disaster. Brigadier General Jacob H. Smith, nicknamed "Hell-Roaring Jake," was ordered to run Lukban into the ground, which he did by a thorough application of the tactical principles that had been applied effectively in Luzon. Lukban finally surrendered on 18 February 1902, ending the last resistance in the Visayas. Smith's enthusiastic campaign led to the most ruthless measures of the Philippine conflict, including some violations of the laws of war. One of Smith's subordinates accused him of ordering troops to turn Samar into a "howling wilderness." Smith was eventually court-martialed and officially admonished. Soon after, the disgraced general retired from the service.

While Smith pacified Samar, Brigadier General J. Franklin Bell moved against the guerrilla forces of Miguel Malvar in Batangas province, the last resistance of any consequence. Malvar was Aguinaldo's successor as titular head of the insurgents. The most distinctive aspect of this campaign was the systematic application of concentration; some 300,000 Filipinos were enclosed in "zones of protection," while four thousand troops ran the guerrillas into the ground. Bell was careful to avoid the errors of Weyler, and concentration soon deprived Malvar of essential resources. On 16 April 1902 he was forced to surrender.

Bell's operations, like those in Samar, produced some atrocities, and these came to the attention of a committee of the U.S. Senate organized to investigate complaints about the conduct of the Philippine War. The committee identified some war crimes, but its activities also publicized the rationale for the counterinsurgency. The successful end of the war and the passage of the Philippine Organic Act, defining the future civil government for the Philippines, worked to minimize public reactions.

While Chaffee's troops ended the last resistance, Taft and his colleagues managed a successful transition from military to civil government. Taft had become civil governor on 4 July 1901 and had soon organized executive departments. In September he appointed several Filipinos to the Philippine Commission, a good example of attraction. The Organic Act for the Philippines went into effect on 4 July 1902, the official end of the Philippine War. By October of the following year, the army in the Philippines had been reduced to a force of about fifteen thousand men.

The Philippine War was brought to a successful conclusion because the United States adopted a sound program of counterinsurgency and executed it effectively in a minimum of time. The ill-coordinated and often flawed resistance of the insurgents lessened the difficulty of the task. The insular situation of the Philippines precluded effective outside assistance and use of protected sanctuaries. Attraction played an important role in the outcome, but if military operations in the field had not produced prompt and decisive results, it could not have been so influential. Public opposition to the Philippine War in the United States never seriously interfered with the conduct of the struggle because of the efficient conduct of the counterinsurgency on all levels.

The successful outcome of the Spanish-American War and the Philippine War equipped the armed services of the United States with a modified mission to replace those of the latter nineteenth century. Before 1898 the U.S. Army had devoted itself principally to constabulary activity in the American West, and the U.S. Navy had provided protection for U.S. maritime commerce. After 1898, until the coming of World War I, the two services devoted themselves primarily to the protection and administration of the modest insular empire annexed in 1898 and to the construction of the Panama Canal, completed in 1914.

Considerable growth and modernization accompanied the acceptance of this new mission. Perhaps the most significant achievements were the creation of a general staff system for the army in 1903 and the construction of several huge new armored vessels for the navy in 1906 and after. These accomplishments did not represent a national embrace of defense policies that would create armed services designed to engage the great armies and navies of Europe on equal terms. The emphasis was on hemispheric defense, a much different proposition. Nevertheless, the reforms of the years between 1898 and 1917 provided a useful foundation for the extraordinary revolution in national defense policy, strategy, and operations that resulted from the onset of the Great War in Europe. The small wars of 1898–1902 brought the armed services into extensive operations in the Caribbean Sea and in the western Pacific Ocean, an outcome that no one expected before the sudden burst of war fever that accompanied the destruction of the *Maine* in February 1898. Many officers who gained their first experience of warfare at the turn of the century rose to positions of high command during the ensuing two decades, and they led the army and navy during World War I.

BIBLIOGRAPHY

The Spanish-American War

Alger, Russell A. *The Spanish-American War* (1901).

Braisted, William R. *The United States Navy in the Pacific, 1897–1909* (1958).

Chadwick, French E. *The Relations of the United States and Spain: The Spanish-American War,* 2 vols. (1911).

Concas y Palau, Victor. *The Squadron of Admiral Cervera* (1900).

Cosmas, Graham A. *An Army for Empire: The United States Army in the Spanish-American War* (1971).

Dewey, George. *Autobiography of George Dewey: Admiral of the Navy* (1913).

Leech, Margaret. *In the Days of McKinley* (1959).

Linderman, Gerald F. *The Mirror of War: American Society and the Spanish-American War* (1974).

Long, John D. *The New American Navy,* 2 vols. (1903).

Mahan, Alfred Thayer. *Lessons of the War with Spain, and Other Articles* (1899).

May, Ernest R. *Imperial Democracy: The Emergence of America as a Great Power* (1961).

Millis, Walter. *The Martial Spirit: A Study of Our War with Spain* (1931).

Morgan, Howard Wayne. *America's Road to Empire: The War with Spain and Overseas Expansion* (1965).

Rickover, Hyman G. *How the Battleship Maine Was Destroyed* (1976).

Sargent, Herbert H. *The Campaign of Santiago de Cuba,* 3 vols. (1907).

Sargent, Nathan. *Admiral Dewey and the Manila Campaign* (1947).

Spector, Ronald. *Admiral of the New Empire: The Life and Career of George Dewey* (1974).

Trask, David F. *The War with Spain in 1898* (1981).

Trask, David F., Michael C. Meyer, and Roger R. Trask, comps. *A Bibliography of United States–Latin American Relations Since 1810,* ch. 5 (1968).

Venzon, Anne Cipriano. *The Spanish-American War: An Annotated Bibliography* (1990).

Wagner, Arthur L. *Report of the Santiago Campaign,* 1898 (1908).

Wheeler, Joseph. *The Santiago Campaign* (1898).

The Philippine War

Agoncillo, Teodoro C. *Malolos: The Crisis of the Republic* (1960).

Gates, John M. *Schoolbooks and Krags: The United States Army in the Philippines, 1898–1902* (1973).

Linn, Brian M. *The U.S. Army and Counterinsurgency in the Philippine War, 1899–1902* (1989).

Miller, Stuart C. *"Benevolent Assimilation": The American Conquest of the Philippines, 1899–1903* (1982).

Salamanca, Bonifacio S. *The Filipino Reaction to American Rule, 1901–1913* (1984).

Sexton, William T. *Soldiers in the Sun: An Adventure in Imperialism* (1939).

Welch, Richard E. *Response to Imperialism: The United States and the Philippine-American War, 1899–1902* (1979).

Wolff, Leon. *Little Brown Brother: How the United States Purchased and Pacified the Philippine Islands at the Century's Turn* (1961).

Zaide, Gregorio. *The Philippine Revolution,* rev. ed. (1968).

— DAVID F. TRASK

The Mexican Border Campaign

Between 15 March 1916 and 5 February 1917, United States Army troops under the command of Brigadier General John J. Pershing conducted a punitive expedition into Mexico in pursuit of Francisco (Pancho) Villa, a charismatic revolutionary leader who was in rebellion against the constituted government of Mexico and whose men had attacked American border towns over a period of two months. Marching south of the Rio Grande with the grudging consent of the Mexican government, Pershing's forces not only skirmished with Villista bands but also encountered civilian hostility and, eventually, active opposition from the Mexican army. Pershing ultimately failed to capture Villa but secured the border region until the political situation stabilized and his troops could safely be recalled. Swiftly overshadowed by the mobilization for World War I a few months later, the Mexican Punitive Expedition and the entire border campaign revealed deficiencies in military organization, equipment, and training that provided many useful lessons for the U.S. Army as it entered the European war.

THE POLITICAL BACKGROUND

The political situation that led to Pershing's expedition into Mexico in 1916 had its roots in the years of rebellion, revolution, and unrest that followed the overthrow of Porfirio Díaz in 1911. Mexico had enjoyed a degree of stability under Díaz, president since 1877, albeit one enforced by dictatorial methods. Although he had increased Mexican prestige abroad and made material progress in commerce, industry, and internal communications, Díaz had also favored policies that set the stage for social and political revolution. His economic practices fostered the concentration of wealth in the hands of a few large landowners and financiers and created peonage. Likewise, his concessions to foreigners, while stimulating investment in Mexico, debilitated the middle and working classes. By 1910, few Mexicans actually participated in their government, and widespread frustration became open revolt. In May 1911, Francisco I. Madero deposed Díaz and became president.

Madero was no more successful in resolving Mexico's political crises, however, and was himself overthrown on 18 February 1913 by General Victoriano Huerta, whom the army and twenty-five of Mexico's twenty-seven states immediately recognized as president. Although many foreign nations extended recognition to the Huerta government, the United States was not among them, because U.S. officials believed Huerta was responsible for Madero's death. Tensions between the two countries increased with a series of incidents, the most serious at Tampico in April 1914. Local officials arrested a U.S. naval officer and seven sailors and marines on shore. Although city officials released them and apologized, subsequent discussions between Admiral Henry J. Mayo and the Huerta government exacerbated the situation. President Woodrow Wilson directed Mayo to demand a 21-gun salute to the U.S. flag. When Huerta's government demurred, U.S. troops under Brigadier General Frederick Funston occupied Veracruz on 21 April. Ill will continued to build, but the Huerta government collapsed in July, and U.S. troops were withdrawn.

By 1910, few Mexicans actually participated in their government, and widespread frustration became open revolt.

Refusal of the United States to recognize his government had made Huerta's situation almost impossible and encouraged his opponents. A movement headed by Venustiano Carranza, governor of Coahuila, had compelled Huerta's resignation, and one month later a Constitutionalist army under command of General Alvaro Obregón occupied Mexico City and made Carranza president, but he controlled only part of the country and found himself in the midst of a chaotic civil war in which major factions were led by Emiliano Zapata in the southwest and by Villa (once a supporter of Carranza), who virtually controlled the state of Chihuahua. Villa had held the capital for a short time in December, but was ousted by Obregón's troops on 27 January 1915.

Events in Mexico had early on persuaded President Wilson to adopt a wait-and-see policy in the matter of granting recognition to any government there. In the first quarter of 1915, General Hugh L. Scott, army chief of staff, had toured army garrisons in Texas and New

---

See The Mexican War map on page 159 for The Mexican Border Campaign geography.

General John J. Pershing, standing with an aide at his headquarters in Mexico in 1916, commanded the U.S. forces that entered Mexico in pursuit of Pancho Villa. (National Archives)

Mexico to inspect troops in the southwest and assess the situation along the border. In the course of his travels, Scott met with Villa and arranged the release of U.S. funds seized by the revolutionaries. The two men established a mutual respect that evidently led Villa to believe that the United States would eventually side with him. Events would prove otherwise.

With Carranza in firm possession of the government by midsummer, Mexican army troops began to show that they could defeat the rebels. Villa lost considerable prestige, and all hopes for the presidency, when General Obregon defeated him in a series of fights at Celaya, Leon, Agua Prieta, and Hermosillo. In August the diplomatic representatives of six Latin American countries met in Washington, D.C., to discuss the factional conflict in Mexico and took note of Carranza's strengthened position. They concluded that Carranza and his party represented the de facto government of the country and its best hope for stability. Accordingly, the United States recognized Carranza's government on 19 October, as did the Latin American powers. Diplomatic recognition led to some practical aid as well. The United States allowed Carranza to make use of American railroads in Arizona to move his troops during battles with Villa.

Angered by what he viewed as U.S. duplicity, Villa decided to provoke the United States into armed intervention in Mexico.

Angered by what he viewed as U.S. duplicity, Villa mustered his forces in western Chihuahua and decided to provoke the United States into armed intervention in Mexico. Broadly, his plan relied on pervasive anti-Americanism in the border state as a mobilizing sentiment that would make him the leader of the Mexican populace in a patriotic uprising against an invading American army. Having supplanted Carranza in popular opinion, Villa's thinking went, he would then be propelled to the presidency of Mexico. Villa began his two-pronged campaign against federal army forces under Carranza and against Americans in the opening months of 1916.

THE COLUMBUS RAID

A series of attacks on U.S. citizens and property—by Villistas and by Mexicans pursuing other political agendas—occurred in the opening months of 1916. On 10 January 1916, for example, some of Villa's troops halted a Mexican train at Santa Ysabel, just south of Chihuahua City, and forced off seventeen American mining engineers invited by Carranza's government to reopen mines in that area. The troops shot sixteen of the Americans, touching off a storm of outrage in the United States. Carranza offered apologies and promised to punish the criminals, a concession that allowed President Wilson to take no immediate action. Nor did cross-border forays that took place near Hachita, New Mexico (18 January), Fort Hancock, Texas (17 February), and Edinburg, Texas (7 March), among others, precipitate the American reaction Villa was seeking. What was needed, he decided, was a major raid into the United States.

Brigadier General Funston, commanding the Southern Department, which included the Mexican border from the Gulf of Mexico to the California state line, had the task of preventing or deflecting such raids and keeping order along the frontier. To do so, he divided his seventeen-hundred-mile-long area of responsibility into cavalry patrol districts, establishing camps and garrisons at intervals along the international border. One of those districts was centered on Columbus, New Mexico, where Colonel Herbert J. Slocum patrolled sixty-five miles of terrain with the five hundred men of the Thirteenth Cavalry. Early in March 1916, rumors of pending Villa actions prompted Slocum to reinforce his garrisons in the vicinity of Columbus and to engage the services of paid spies who periodically brought him information about Villa's movements. Because local rumors continued to place the rebel leader in the vicinity, Slocum led a large patrol along the border on the night of 7–8 March but received assurances from the commander of local Carranza forces that Villa was not in the area. In fact, Villa was at that moment poised to attack into the United States.

Villa descended upon the little town of Columbus in the predawn hours of 9 March with about four hundred men. Converging on the town in separate columns about 4:00 A.M., Villa's troops attacked both the town and the garrisons of the Thirteenth Cavalry. A scattered gunfight developed that lasted for a little more than an hour. As dawn broke, Villa's men retreated, having killed eight U.S. soldiers and eight civilians and wounded seven soldiers and three civilians. They also burned and looted several homes and stores. Major Frank Tompkins led a squadron of the Thirteenth Cavalry some fifteen or twenty miles into Mexico in pursuit, returning only when his ammunition was exhausted. Cavalrymen found sixty-seven Mexican dead around Columbus and estimated that seventy to one hundred were killed during the pursuit into Mexico.

Within hours of the Columbus attack, General Funston dispatched a telegram to General Hugh Scott at the War Department, asking permission to send his troops into Mexico after the raiders. It was clear, he thought, that there would be no security along the international frontier as long as Villa and similar bands of outlaws had freedom of action. Furthermore, he argued, the de facto government of Mexico lacked the ability to suppress the insurgents who were threatening American lives and property. He believed that further attacks were imminent. President Wilson quickly agreed, and on 10 March he directed Funston to send armed forces into Mexico to capture Villa and prevent further raids into the United States. Wilson cautioned Funston, however, to have a scrupulous regard for the sovereignty of Mexico. Secretary of War Newton Baker invited Funston to inform him of what the army needed to carry out the president's order.

Funston had appended to his telegram a plan for two columns of troops to enter Mexico from Columbus and Hachita, New Mexico, link up around Ascención, some sixty miles into Mexico, and then patrol to the south and west in search of Villa, whom Funston expected to draw back into his traditional stronghold of the mountains of Chihuahua. A general depot would be established at El Paso, Texas, and supplies forwarded to the troops by means of the Mexican Northwestern Railroad. Using the available four cavalry regiments, Funston intended to march a brigade of cavalry in each column and protect the line of the advance with a reinforced infantry brigade.

The next day the War Department approved the basic plan, but with several exceptions. Funston was not to assume that he could use Mexican railroads to transport and supply his forces and was not to permit his soldiers to enter Mexican towns or cities. The expedition was to leave Mexico as soon as it captured or broke up Villa's bands, or sooner if the Mexican government was able to relieve it of the task. General Scott and General Tasker H. Bliss recommended, and Secretary Baker approved, the appointment of Brigadier General John J. Pershing, at that time in El Paso in command of the Eighth Cavalry Brigade, to command the expedition. The War Department staff then turned to considering the problem of mobilizing the state militias, which would make up the greater part of any wartime army. While Scott prepared for war, diplomatic discussions continued.

While Funston was awaiting permission to enter Mexico, a note arrived in Washington from the Carranza government expressing its regret for the Columbus attack. The same note asked permission for Mexican troops to enter the United States in pursuit of Villa and granted similar privileges to the U.S. Army if there were any additional raids. In his reply to the Mexican proposal, President Wilson did not wait for another attack in the United States but agreed that the arrangement Carranza proposed was in force, and that he could exercise the privilege of sending U.S. forces across the border whenever he felt necessary. The War Department informed Pershing that the Mexican government would tolerate U.S. operations south of the Rio Grande, and two days later, on 17 March, Congress adopted a resolution approving Pershing's orders.

The situation in Mexico at that time was somewhat confused. Carranza's intention, obviously (and possibly deliberately) misunderstood by Wilson, was to allow U.S. troops to enter Mexico only when in hot pursuit of bandits. His subsequent actions make it clear that Carranza never meant to grant President Wilson carte blanche to mount a major expedition on Mexican soil. Conscious of the danger of misunderstandings, General Obregon, the Mexican secretary of war and navy, informed the governors of the northern states of the agreement into which the Mexican government had entered and asked them to advise commanders of Mexican army garrisons closer to the border. Conflicting instructions issued from Mexico City clouded the matter, however, and allowed Mexican officers to draw the conclusion that permission for U.S. troops to enter had not been granted after all. The matter continued to be a subject of discussion between the two governments as Pershing's troops began to move south. In any case, the control Carranza and Obregón exercised from the capital was tenuous at best, and they had some doubts about the essential loyalty of federal troops in Chihuahua. It began to seem possible that the appeal Villa had for the Mexican population at large was extending to the military as well.

THE U.S. ARMY IN 1916

With few exceptions, the last major ground battles U.S. troops had fought was in the Civil War, more than fifty years earlier. Over the intervening years of the Plains Indian wars, the army had become a frontier constabulary in which the largest tactical organization was typically the company, troop, or squadron. Only rarely did units as large as regiments or brigades come together, and there was little practical training in the art of commanding large bodies of troops. During the Spanish-American War in 1898, scattered units of the regular army, hastily mobilized militia units, and volunteers temporarily formed larger tactical organizations for the brief fighting in Cuba and the extended campaign in the Philippines. After that war, the service disbanded its volunteer units and returned the regular army to its peacetime garrisons. At the time of the Mexican revo-

THE PUNITIVE EXPEDITION FORCES

First Provisional Cavalry Brigade (Colonel James Lockett)	Thirteenth Cavalry (Negro) (less one troop) Eleventh Cavalry (Negro) Battery C, Sixth Field Artillery
Second Provisional Cavalry Brigade (Colonel George A. Dodd)	Seventh Cavalry Tenth Cavalry (Negro) Battery B, Sixth Field Artillery
First Provisional Infantry Brigade (Colonel John H. Beacom)	Sixth Infantry Sixteenth Infantry Company E, Second Engineer Battalion Company H, Second Engineer Battalion
Service Troops	Ambulance Company Number Seven Field Hospital Number Seven Signal Corps Detachments First Aero Squadron Wagon Company Number One Wagon Company Number Two

lution, the U.S. Army remained little changed in organizational terms from the days of the Indian wars.

Sharply increasing tensions along the U.S.-Mexico border in 1911 prompted Secretary of War Henry L. Stimson to make a show of strength in Texas. On 6 March 1911, he detailed Major General William H. Carter to command a "maneuver division" at San Antonio and issued orders to concentrate troops into three infantry brigades, a field artillery brigade, and an independent cavalry brigade, together with the necessary auxiliary service units and a brigade of coast artillery. The inevitable problems encountered in forming the maneuver division threw the inefficacy of a tactically efficient small-unit army into sharp relief. Funding constraints limited the duration of the experiment, and the division never managed to reach full strength before it was disbanded early in 1912. Inexperienced in mobilization planning, the War Department took several months, even using railroads, to get the last regiments to San Antonio. A failure in many ways, the maneuver division still offered army officers the chance to work with a modern-style division for the first time and to understand the complexities of maintaining and operating such a force. For the War Department, the maneuver division was a sobering experience in just how difficult mobilization could be. Because the division used nearly all of the units of the regular army then in the United States, it also graphically demonstrated the army's inability to confront any significant foreign armed force.

Border raids continued, however, and six cavalry regiments and other troops totaling about sixty-seven hundred men began patrolling the international border from Texas to Arizona and enforcing an embargo on shipments of arms and munitions to Mexico. By mid-1913, fighting between various Mexican factions in the northern territories had intensified to the point that the battles were spilling over into the United States. In response to the increased tension, the War Department ordered the creation of the Second Division at Texas City, under the command of General Carter. This time the organization of the division went smoothly, although it reached only a little more than half its planned strength. As with the maneuver division, the army soon disbanded the Second Division.

During the Veracruz expedition the following year, General Funston commanded brigade-size units in the field, thus further training his officers in the handling of larger units. At Veracruz, however, the army and marines were chiefly an occupation force, albeit one that conducted regular patrols into the hinterlands around the city. By the beginning of 1915 the army had returned to the Mexican border, where its mobile troops dispersed into patrol districts along the frontier.

By the middle of 1915, the army had gained a certain amount of experience in operating division-size units. The service had thirty-one infantry regiments, fifteen cavalry regiments, and six field-artillery regiments available for field duty. Nearly all of the mobile combat units then in the United States were assigned to what amounted to war duties along the frontier. Well-trained and of high quality at the small-unit level, the army was not well-prepared in a material sense. There were only seven hundred field guns in the entire army, including units overseas, and no more than fifty-eight hundred rounds of ammunition. Quartermaster returns showed that the entire army had only enough rifle ammunition to fight for four days. There were very few field-service units, among which were only three battalions of engineers and eight companies of the Signal corps. The army also had barely begun to make the transition to motor transport and had only just started to experiment with the organization of an air service. It was from this slowly modernizing army that Pershing was to form his expeditionary force.

ORGANIZATION OF THE EXPEDITION

Funston gave Pershing his orders on 11 March and directed him to comply with the basic plan approved by the War Department. Until Pershing reached and established an advanced base in Mexico, Funston would maintain the line of communications from Columbus. After that time, the logistics responsibility, like the responsibility for tactical command, would devolve on Pershing. Meanwhile, Funston placed the troops of the Southern Department at Pershing's disposal. Roughly ten thousand men were available to organize a provisional division to be known as the Punitive Expedition, U.S. Army. In organizing his expedition, Pershing could refer to the recent experiments with the maneuver division and Second Division, in which some of his subordinates had been involved.

The theater of operations influenced Pershing's organizational decisions. Chihuahua, a large and sparsely populated state, had both a rugged terrain and a forbidding climate. Some 80 percent of the land was a high desert plateau ranging from three thousand to six thousand feet in elevation. Good water was scarce, and the land supported little vegetation for forage at any time of the year. The ground varied from gravel to a fine silt, making travel difficult. The peaks of the trackless mountains of the Sierra Madre in the west sometimes reached ten thousand feet. Inaccessible except through hazardous rocky canyons, the Sierra Madre were the assumed refuge of Villa's bands. The area was extremely dry except in the midsummer months of late June through early August, when heavy rains were common. During the summer, Chihuahua was intensely hot during the day but often chillingly cold at night. In winter, temperatures plunged, with dust storms punctuated by ice and snowstorms. Most of the campaign took place on the plateau, a strip of plains and foothills fifty to one

Pancho Villa, standing third from left, was a charismatic revolutionary leader whose men attacked American border towns over a period of two months, prompting U.S. troops to enter Mexico in March 1916 to pursue him. (National Archives)

hundred miles wide and about five hundred miles long, bounded on the west by the mountains and on the east by the National and New Mexico Railroad.

On balance, a predominantly cavalry force seemed best to maneuver in such conditions, and Pershing organized his expedition around two provisional cavalry brigades that would enter Mexico in two columns. On east, the First Provisional Cavalry Brigade, would march from Columbus, New Mexico, while to the west, the Second Provisional Cavalry Brigade would enter from the town of Hachita. One company of engineers and the First Aero Squadron were to advance with the First Provisional Cavalry Brigade from Columbus, and the remaining service troops marched from Columbus with the First Provisional Infantry Brigade, charged with protecting the expedition's lines of communication.

Once it was clear that Pershing would not be able to use the Mexican railways to supply his troops, he had to find means to sustain the expedition overland. In Washington, General Scott directed the acting quartermaster general, Brigadier General Henry G. Sharpe, to purchase enough trucks for that purpose. General Sharpe worked quickly, soliciting bids and awarding a contract at 5:00 A.M. on 14 March. By 16 March, the first consignment of trucks was shipped by train from Wisconsin, arriving at Columbus on 18 March. The army employed civilian drivers, who arrived in New Mexico at the same time the trucks were delivered. Quickly organizing motor convoys, supporting troops in Columbus shipped the first consignments across the border to Pershing before his command exhausted the supplies they had carried with them. The first truck company was quickly followed by two others. By June the army had placed ten such companies in operation to support Pershing 588 trucks were in service on the lines of communication. Sharpe's department also established two auxiliary remount depots at El Paso and Fort Sam Houston to provide the expedition with animals to replace those that died or became unfit for service. For the moment, adequate supplies of food and other equipment were on hand. The quartermaster had earlier stocked depots at El Paso, Fort Sam Houston, Harlingen, Columbus, Nogales, and other towns against the possibility of trouble on the border.

Availability of supplies did not imply efficiency in their distribution. When Pershing arrived in Columbus from El Paso, the confusion he found there rivaled that at the Tampa, Florida, embarkation point during the Spanish-American War. There was no chief quartermaster or ordnance officer in Columbus, and the line officers detailed to duty in those departments had no experience and less knowledge of the complicated requisitioning and supply system. The quartermaster supplies, medical supplies, and ordnance matériel that arrived by train were unloaded and stored in no particular order. Wagons and trucks were also delivered promptly, but without instructions for their assembly. Through furious effort, Pershing and his staff imposed some order on the chaos, but the unsuitability of a supply system designed for small garrisons for an army in the field was already clearly apparent and became a gnawing problem as the expedition advanced into Mexico.

From the beginning, both motor trains and animal pack trains supplied Pershing's troops. The lack of good roads dictated the disposition of the logistical trains. The western column from Hachita, which Pershing expected to move most quickly, took with it only pack trains; the wagon transportation followed the eastern column from Columbus. Simultaneously, the two companies of engineers began to consider ways to improve the trails over which the truck trains would eventually have to drive. The problem was compounded by a lack of good maps of northern Chihuahua, and Pershing had to detail an engineer detachment to draw them, based on reports from scouts as the force advanced.

A variety of signal equipment sustained communications within the march columns and with the bases of supply. Lacking proper wire, Signal Corps troops improvised a telegraph line that paralleled the route of march. Radio sets with the marching cavalry columns were useful over short ranges, while the longer-range radios were mounted in wagons. Pershing planned to use Signal Corp airplanes both for scouting and for maintaining contact among his scattered forces.

Inaccessible except through hazardous rocky canyons, the Sierra Madre were the assumed refuge of Villa's bands.

Less than a week after the Columbus raid, General Pershing had completed preparations based on War Department and Southern Department orders and reported himself ready to cross into Mexico. In the interval, Funston had mustered remaining regular troops to replace the cavalry regiments along the border, and the War Department had acted to create a transportation service to replace the railroad that political considerations denied Pershing. It remained to be seen whether Villa could actually be caught.

THE CAMPAIGN IN MEXICO

There were six discernable stages of the campaign. In the first, Pershing's two columns marched to the Mormon colony of Colonia Dublán, in Chihuahua, where they met and established a base. Next, the general dispatched three independent cavalry columns from that base in search of Villa. In the third phase, four more independent cavalry detachments scoured the southern region of the state. Fourth, Pershing recalled his scattered troops to a central base. Fifth, having failed to find Villa, the U.S. troops began a policy of policing the northern part of Chihuahua by districts. The final stage, almost a year after the expedition began, was the evacuation of all troops to Columbus.

APPROACH MARCH TO COLONIA DUBLÁN. Despite the diplomatic discussions that had gone before, the reaction of the Mexican government to Pershing's march into Mexican territory was anything but certain. Nevertheless, Funston instructed Pershing to begin his operation no later than 6:00 A.M. on 15 March because he feared the effects of further delay. Among the other shortcomings of the expedition was a lack of definite information about the strength and intentions of the Mexican army in Chihuahua, estimated at around eight thousand men with additional militia forces available, and about the location and strength of Villa's forces, estimated at between five hundred and a thousand men.

Pershing had a letter from General Obregon that he could present to local authorities as authorization for his presence south of the frontier, but he still feared he might encounter opposition. He impressed on his men the need for calm and restraint in dealing with Mexican officials, especially during the border-crossing. Indeed, there very nearly was an incident when the commander of the garrison at Palomas, a few miles south of the border, objected to the intrusion. Explaining his intentions, Pershing managed to calm the belligerent Carranzista commander in part by hiring him as a guide for the expedition. Thus, the Columbus column entered Mexico a few minutes after noon on 15 March, camping that night at Las Palomas and arriving at Colonia Dublán on 20 March by way of Boca Grande, Ascensión, and Corralitos. The wagon trains that followed Colonel Lockett's Second Brigade could only travel twenty to forty miles per day and thus lagged behind.

Colonel Dodd's Second Provisional Cavalry Brigade marched from Culbertson's Ranch, about fifty miles west of Columbus, and crossed the border about 1:00 A.M. on 16 March. The brigade then marched 125 miles over the dusty alkali roads without incident in a column of twos, the Seventh Cavalry leading, and reached Colonia Dublán in the early evening of 17 March. Pershing established his advanced base about a mile north of the colony, adhering to War Department instructions to avoid towns or cities. With both brigades in camp, Pershing had a force of about forty-eight hundred men available and began to make detailed plans to pursue Villa.

The U.S. Army used both trucks and pack mules to carry supplies during the expedition into Mexico. These privates played with one of the sturdy animals at a camp in Mexico in 1916. (National Archives)

Pershing presumed that Villa and his men had begun retreating to the south of Chihuahua as soon as they had learned the U.S. Army was in pursuit. To capture him would require extremely fast-moving columns, unencumbered by slow baggage trains or excessive equipment. Believing that Villa was somewhere in the vicinity of San Miguel de Babicora, a village about fifty miles south, Pershing determined that the best plan was to send three parallel columns after him. By so doing, the Americans could keep Villa from escaping into Sonora to the west or across the Mexican National Railway to the east. If the cavalry troopers moved fast enough, they might even get ahead of Villa before he could reach the mountains at Guerrero.

To implement the plan, the general organized three detachments of cavalry. In the west, Major Ellwood W. Evans left Colonia Dublán by train on 19 March with the First Squadron, Tenth Cavalry. His objective was the village of Las Varas, near Madera, farthest to the south and not far from Guerrero. That same day, Colonel William C. Brown led the Second Squadron, Tenth Cavalry, to the San Miguel plateau in the center, taking the train as far as Rucio. The eastern column, comprising the Seventh Cavalry under Colonel James B. Erwin, left Colonia Dublán on the night of 17–18 March bound for the San Miguel plateau by way of Galeana and the region southwest of El Valle.

PURSUIT BY MAJOR COLUMNS. Erwin's Seventh Cavalry set out on horseback, but Pershing wanted the Tenth Cavalry columns to go at least part of the way by train. This was an attempt in part to gain time on Villa's forces, but an equally important consideration was the fatigue of animals that had already marched more than 250 miles in the past fortnight. Although Pershing could not resupply his men over the Mexican railways, he requested, and was granted permission, the use of the Mexican Northwestern Railway to move the Tenth Cavalry. When the train arrived at Colonia Dublán on the morning of the 19th, however, the dilapidated rail cars took so much time to repair that Colonel Brown and his men did not reach Rucio until the next morning. There he left the train and led his men over a mountain trail in the direction of the San Miguel plateau. Major Evans continued the rail journey but encountered worse fortune when the train wrecked, injuring eleven of his men. He also left the train and reached the vicinity of Las Varas on the 22nd.

Meanwhile Colonel Brown had arrived in the San Miguel area about noon on 21 March and found that intelligence reports were entirely wrong: Villa had not been there. Following a rumor (which subsequently proved false) that Carranzista troops had fought and had defeated Villa at Namiquipa, Brown continued southward to meet with Mexican Colonel Chico Cano there on 25 March. He learned that Villa was probably around El Oso or Santa Clara and proposed that if Cano could locate Villa, the Tenth Cavalry would attack. Cano agreed and promised to send out scouting parties. Brown remained in camp near Namiquipa, where, in response to Pershing's orders, Major Evans joined him with the First Squadron on 24 March. Within a few days, Brown concluded that Cano had no intention of making the promised reconnaissance, and he moved his regiment toward San Diego del Monte and Le Quemada, where rumors placed the bandit.

The other column had more success. Colonel Dodd, the brigade commander, joined Colonel Erwin's Seventh Cavalry on 21 March and assumed command of the column. After reaching El Valle on 22 March, he conferred with Mexican General Salas, who reported that contrary to the rumor that brought U.S. troops there, his men had in fact been defeated by Villa on the 19th at Namiquipa and had fallen back in a demoralized condition to El Valle, where they assumed defensive positions. Despite his defeat, Salas spurned any help from the Americans and disputed Dodd's right to be there, asserting that he had never heard of Obregon's proclamation. Salas declined to cooperate with Dodd in tracking Villa. Like Brown, Dodd determined to go on without assistance from the Mexican forces.

After a week of scouting over rough trails in the face of extremely cold weather, Dodd had virtually exhausted both forage and supplies. He reached the town of Bachiniva on the morning of 28 March and learned that a substantial force of Villistas was nearby at Guerrero. Dodd immediately marched his command in that direction, traveling all night with the hope of surprising the bandits at first light. He approached the town from the east with half his regiment, but placed Major Edward B. Winans with his Second Squadron to the west of the town to block the enemy's retreat.

Opening long-range rifle and machine-gun fire, the Seventh Cavalry began a four-hour running fight in which they killed thirty Villistas.

Early on the morning of 29 March, the Villistas spotted Dodd's column approaching from the bluffs to the east and immediately began to flee. Dodd had surprised approximately 230 men, apparently commanded by Elicio Hernandez, one of Villa's principal lieutenants. Opening long-range rifle and machine-gun fire, the Seventh Cavalry began a four-hour running fight in which they killed thirty Villistas and captured a number of weapons, horses, and other equipment. The remainder of the Villa troops broke into small detachments and scattered into the mountains, carrying their wounded away with them. Dodd could not pursue his demoralized enemy because the Seventh Cavalry's horses were exhausted, having marched seventeen hours out of the previous twenty-four.

In the first phase of his operations, Pershing had enjoyed only modest success. Inadequate intelligence had kept his columns largely occupied chasing rumors, aside from Dodd's encounter at Guerrero. Convinced that Villa would retreat into the mountains as a result of that skirmish, and believing that only carefully selected cavalry detachments could follow him there, Pershing decided on a change in tactics and in his own methods of command.

CHANGES IN COMMAND TECHNIQUES. Pershing knew that communications lay at the heart of command, but found that the available technology was not up to the task of controlling his far-flung cavalry columns. The regiments' pack-mounted radio sets proved so unreliable as to be useless. Radio sets carried on wagons worked better, but wagons could not keep up with the fast-marching cavalry, even when the horsemen kept to roads that the wagons could traverse. To direct his men, Pershing had to rely on mounted couriers and on the airplanes of the First Aero Squadron, under Captain Benjamin Foulois. Couriers, however, could move little faster than the columns they sought, and even then spent much precious time looking for the intended recipients of the messages. Airplanes, unfortunately, fared little better.

The First Aero Squadron took off from Columbus on 18 March with eight Curtiss JN-2 airplanes. One crashed en route to the advanced base and two others were forced down and arrived late. Eventually, seven reached the base at Casas Grandes near Colonia Dublán. During the first month of operations, the pilots kept busy carrying dispatches and messages to Columbus and among units of the expedition. On several occasions, pilots managed to find the scouting cavalry squadrons and deliver orders to them; just as often, they failed. Underpowered aircraft were not up to some of the missions. On 20 March, for example, two aircraft turned back just twenty-five miles into a reconnaissance flight because they could not climb over the foothills of the Sierra Madre. Dust storms and gales often grounded the machines, and rough terrain took its toll when pilots tried to land near cavalry columns on the march.

The squadron made seventy-nine flights between 26 March and 4 April, but by the end of the first full month of flying operations, five of the airplanes had been wrecked and another was so badly damaged that its crew abandoned it far from the base. The remaining two flew back to Columbus, where they were condemned as unfit for further use. The squadron's occasional successes in reconnaissance and liaison showed the potential that aircraft offered, but the fragile machines of the First Aero Squadron could not realize that potential. Pershing had to find other means of tactical control.

Precarious communications thus forced a difficult decision on the expedition's commander. Pershing decided to divide his headquarters. The majority of his staff remained at the advanced base at Colonia Dublán, where it functioned under the direction of the chief of staff, Lieutenant Colonel DeRosy C. Cabell, and performed the logistical and administrative tasks necessary to keep the regiments in the field. The real general headquarters became Pershing's automobile, which the commander adopted as the only feasible means of coordinating cavalry operations. Around the end of March, Pershing began the practice of moving forward in a convoy of three automobiles, which carried his aides de camp, a small armed escort, his cook, and a couple of press correspondents. The party lived under the stars, regardless of the weather, and generally on short rations. When necessary, Pershing dispatched one of his aides—George Patton, J. Lawton Collins, and Martin C. Shallenberger—with a car to carry messages either to Colonia Dublán or to one of his subordinate commanders. Pershing kept moving forward, at considerable personal risk, so that he could stay reasonably close to his columns, keep up with their reports, and issue timely and appropriate orders.

The drawback to Pershing's method of command was that he had no good means of communicating with General Funston at Southern Department headquarters in San Antonio. Throughout the campaign, he faced the dilemma that he could either control his deployed columns or maintain satisfactory contact with his own superior, but not both. The telegraph line his signal troops had laid ended at Colonia Dublán, where Colonel Cabell could sustain communications with Columbus and thence with the department headquarters in San Antonio. Pershing was isolated from such rapid communications and could only respond to Funston's queries by messenger to Colonia Dublán, where Colonel Cabell in turn forwarded his dispatches. The inherent delays frustrated Funston and periodically created misunderstandings in San Antonio and in Washington about what was actually happening in Mexico.

INDEPENDENT CAVALRY DETACHMENTS. While the Seventh and Tenth cavalries continued their search for Villa, Pershing moved his field headquarters to Namiquipa, where he would be better able to control the march columns to the south. Using the uncommitted portions of his two cavalry brigades, he organized four pursuit columns, each of approximately squadron strength. To enable them to move swiftly in the high country into which he expected Villa had fled, Pershing directed the soldiers to ride with minimum amounts of equipment. Pack-mule trains supported and supplied the columns, each of which also had a detachment of Apache Indian scouts for tracking and intelligence gathering. This happened to be the last time the army used an organized Indian scout unit in field operations.

Lieutenant Colonel Henry T. Allen and Major Robert L. Howze commanded provisional squadrons drawn from the Eleventh Cavalry. Major Frank Tompkins, who had pursued Villa into Mexico on the morning of the Columbus raid, commanded a provisional squadron of two troops each from the Tenth and Thirteenth cavalries. Major Elmer Lindsley led the Second Squadron, Thirteenth Cavalry. The first three columns left Colonia Dublán between 21 March and 29 March and all had arrived in Namiquipa by 2 April, where Pershing awaited them. Lindsley drew the task of screening the western flank from Namiquipa to Chuhuichupa to San Jose de Babicora to keep Villa's men from escaping over the mountain trails into the state of Sonora. Supplied with five days' rations for men and horses and 150 rounds of ammunition per man, his squadron rode out of the base on 20 March and was in San Jose de Babicora ten days later, having struggled through a driving snowstorm during the latter part of the march.

The farther south Pershing's expedition moved, the worse the problem of unreliable information became. As the squadrons concentrated at Namiquipa, the Americans received reports that placed Villa in several different places at the same time. It also seemed likely that Villa's forces had split up into many small detachments and were dispersing before the advancing American columns. Several sources indicated that Villa was somewhere to the west of Bachiniva. In response, Pershing ordered Tompkins to take his men there on a night march by way of Santa Ana, in the west, while Howze and his men scouted the mountains to the east. Taking his small personal staff, the general went directly to Bachiniva, where Tompkins and Howze met him on 1 April, reporting that they had found nothing.

Lacking more substantial information, Pershing then decided to resort once again to advance by parallel columns. After making certain that the passes to the north and west were guarded, he sent all of his men to the south, hoping to catch Villa before he crossed the line into Durango. Tompkins led the advance, with Brown's Tenth Cavalry a day's march behind him and to his left rear. Howze and his squadron occupied a similar position to Tompkins' right rear, and Allen's column followed about three days' march directly behind. The force was lightly equipped and carried minimal supplies, but Pershing adjudged it strong enough to fight any hostile force it encountered. The flexible organization allowed the columns to cover a great deal of territory and to reinforce quickly any column that ran into trouble.

Those precautions appeared wise. As the expedition marched deeper into Chihuahua, the likelihood increased that Carranzista forces would resist its movement. Although the two armies were ostensibly working toward the same goal of putting down the Villa rebellion and pacifying the border region, the Mexican troops had never displayed much enthusiasm for working with Pershing's forces. As March turned into April, the indifference that Brown and Dodd had encountered in their first meetings with their Mexican counterparts was deepening into active hostility. Soon there was little question that, to the Carranzistas, ejecting the foreigners from Mexico was more important than capturing Villa.

Although the two armies were ostensibly working toward the same goal, the Mexican troops had never displayed much enthusiasm for working with Pershing's forces.

During the month of April, Pershing's columns systematically searched the southern half of Chihuahua. As the four flying columns marched to the south, Colonel Dodd's column guarded the trails leading into the mountains to the west while Colonel Brown secured the eastern flank; gradually they would converge on a selected spot near the Chihuahua-Durango border. During those several weeks of hard riding in cold and difficult conditions, the Americans fought a series of skirmishes, but only a few were with Villa's men. Instead, their major battles were with units of the regular Mexican army.

Colonel Brown's Tenth Cavalry column, moving southward in a blizzard that interrupted communications both with Pershing and with Colonel Dodd, made the first contact. On 1 April, riding from San Diego del Monte toward Guerrero, Brown's men unexpectedly met a small band of Villistas near Agua Caliente, just across the Continental Divide. The troopers attacked under the overhead fire of machine guns (the first time the army had used that technique), killing two bandits and chasing the others out of the town. A pursuit over a half-dozen miles of timbered terrain ended at dusk. Major Evans, leading the remainder of the Tenth Cavalry, received orders to guard the country between Santa Clara and El Oso. His detachment, so occupied until early May, encountered no action.

Brown took the remainder of his regiment on to San Antonia de los Arenales on 3 April, where Mexican General Jose Cavazos threatened that any further American advance would be considered a hostile act and treated accordingly. Sidestepping the Mexican forces, Brown continued south. On 6 April an airplane found his column and delivered orders from Pershing to secure the eastern border of the territory and advance to Parral. On 9 April, Brown reached Tres Hermanos, where General Juan Garza, a Carranzista commander, agreed to cooperate and sent out scouts. Hearing nothing from the Mexican reconnaissance, Brown set out on 10 April toward Parral, this time with the assistance of a Mexican liaison officer. By the afternoon of 12 April, he was encamped about ten miles from his objective.

Following Villa's trail on a route that led them through Agua Caliente, San Antonio de los Arenales, and San Francisco de Borja, Major Tompkins and his column were also nearing Parral. Like Brown, Tompkins had been threatened by Cavazos, who told him that further pursuit was fruitless in any case, because Villa had been killed. Following his orders to avoid a clash with the Carranzistas, Tompkins withdrew north to Cienguita and then east to Santa Rosalia, whence he continued his march to the south on 7 April.

Adhering to Pershing's plan for mutually supporting columns, Howze resupplied his squadron and pushed out to the southwest, passing by the village of Cusihuiriachic along a track that Brown and Tompkins had followed earlier. He then pursued a rumor that Villa, only wounded, was heading along the mountains to Durango. Avoiding Cavazos' units, on 9 April Howze reached the village of San Jose del Sitio, where locals fired into his camp during the night. The next day he skirmished with a group of Villistas at La Joya de Herrera, killing its commander and reporting that he had dispersed the surviving bandits. Two days later, on 11 April, he surrounded Santa Cruz de Herrera and fought with another force believed to be Villistas, most of whom escaped. It later turned out that Villa had been encamped about a mile away at the time.

While those columns advanced, Dodd continued to watch the passes to the west, skirmishing frequently but inconclusively with small, armed parties. He moved part of his command to Miaca on 8 April to protect Howze's flank and to try to locate Villista bands re-

U.S. Company A, Sixth Infantry, en route from El Valle to Las Cruces, Mexico, on 10 April 1916, have encamped and dug emergency trenches in preparation for a Mexican attack. (National Archives)

ported in the area. As planned, Colonel Allen and his squadron trailed several days behind the advance columns. He left Namiquipa on 2 April, scouted El Oso, and joined the main body at San Geronimo Ranch. By 8 April, he had reached San Antonio de los Arenales and left there the following morning to scout the area for Villistas. After sixteen straight days in the saddle, Allen's men arrived at Satevo on 12 April, where Pershing had established a temporary command post and aerodrome.

Such was the disposition of forces when Tompkins' squadron approached Parral on 12 April. Tompkins knew that several thousand soldiers of the Mexican army were encamped in his vicinity and to his rear and had firm intelligence that some three hundred Villistas, including Villa and his staff, were scattered throughout the region. He was confident of rapid support, knowing that Howze was about three days' march behind him to one side, and Brown about a day and a half behind to the other side. Thus, he decided to go as far as Parral, where he intended to buy fodder and supplies, before striking farther south toward the Durango line.

Tompkins paused at the little town of Valle de Zaragosa on 10 April, where he was able to purchase clothing for his troopers, many of whom were literally in rags. While there, Tompkins met a Carranzista officer from the garrison at Parral, who agreed to deliver a message to the garrison commander, General Ismael Lozano, requesting a guide to a camp site and permission to purchase supplies. When the column reached Parral at noon on 12 April, Tompkins halted outside the town and then went to visit General Lozano at his headquarters. Suspicious that Lozano was directing his men into a camp site where they could easily be attacked that night, Tompkins instead planned to move away from the town. While inspecting the site, a belligerent mob gathered, and Carranzista soldiers evidently began firing into the American column. The situation rapidly deteriorated, and General Lozano lost control of his men, who numbered five to six hundred.

Tompkins attempted to get the Mexicans to cease fire and, failing that, began to withdraw to the north, pursued by Mexican troops and skirmishing with them from around 1:30 to 4:00 in the afternoon, when his men reached defensible terrain near Santa Cruz de Villegas. Several hundred Mexican soldiers directed a sporadic fusillade at the American positions, but Tompkins' men easily kept them at a distance by accurate long-range rifle fire. U.S. losses were two killed, one missing, and six—including Major Tompkins—wounded. An estimated forty Mexican soldiers were killed and an unknown number wounded.

A rider sent in search of Colonel Brown's column returned with detachments of the Tenth Cavalry around evening, at which point the Mexicans broke off the action and retired into Parral. Brown assumed command, demanded explanations from the Mexican general commanding the region, and dispatched reports to General Pershing, then in his new headquarters at Satevo, eighty miles to the northwest. By the next day, both provisional squadrons of the Eleventh Cavalry under Allen and Howze had arrived, which relieved Brown's concern about Mexican attacks but exacerbated an already severe supply problem. In an unsatisfactory exchange of notes, Mexican authorities denied any responsibility for the attack. For his part, Pershing praised Tompkins for his attempt to avoid trouble and his restraint in dealing with the crisis. Nevertheless, in the face of escalating Mexican opposition, Pershing decided to withdraw his men from southern Chihuahua. The columns left Santa Cruz de Villegas on 22 April.

While events were developing around Parral, Colonel Dodd's security forces continued to scout for Villistas in the western highlands of the state. On 18 April he and his men, accompanied by a detachment of Carranzista cavalry, followed up a rumor that a large Villista band was in the vicinity of Yoquivo. Early in the march, the U.S. and Mexican forces became separated, and when Dodd reached Yoquivo on 20 April, he found that the Carranzistas had already been there and that the bandits had fled farther west. Convinced that the commander of the Mexican detachment had warned Villa's men of his approach, Dodd pushed on toward Tomochic, where he ran into about 150 Villistas under Camdelario Cervantes on 22 April.

Dodd's men were fired on from the surrounding hills as they approached the village in the late afternoon. They found the bandits rapidly leaving the town and immediately opened fire. The cavalrymen quickly overcame the Villista rear guard and several scattered detachments in the hills around the village. The enemy main body was in the hills to the east. Because it was late in the day and there appeared to be no way to flank or get behind the enemy, Dodd ordered his men to attack frontally. By dark, they had driven the Villistas from their positions, killing or wounding some twenty-five of them, and the survivors fled. In Dodd's judgment, his attack had completely disintegrated the band.

He then returned with his men to Minaca, where he continued patrolling until early June, when Pershing ordered the column back to El Valle. In July, Dodd reached his sixty-fourth birthday, was promoted to brigadier general, and retired from the army. Brigadier General Eben Swift replaced him in command.

REASSEMBLY OF THE PUNITIVE EXPEDITION

The fight at Parral marked both the southernmost advance of U.S. troops into Mexico and a turning point in the campaign. With the bulk of his cavalry in the vicinity of Parral, Pershing would have been in a position to control the southern half of Chihuahua, where support for Villa appeared to be particularly strong. Serious logistical problems, however, far outweighed the desirable tactical advantages of remaining so far south.

The Mexican civilian population was unfriendly, and there was little hope that Pershing's columns could purchase food, fodder, clothing, and other supplies locally.

Relations between the governments of Mexico and the United States were increasingly strained, and the expeditionary force had no assurance that the hostility of the federal garrison at Parral would be an isolated occurrence. The civilian population was equally unfriendly, and there was little hope that his columns could purchase food, fodder, clothing, and other supplies locally. Pershing's own logistical system, rudimentary at best, was simply not up to the task of supplying two cavalry brigades that were 180 miles south of the advanced bases. Furthermore, such long lines of supply were extremely vulnerable to attack.

Although the expedition relied primarily on wagon and pack-mule train, which operated with customary, if slow, efficiency, motor trucks were also used for supply. This was a new experience, and the men assigned to the lines of communications had to improvise standard operating procedures. Skilled mechanics from the First Aero Squadron quickly overcame the initial muddle at Columbus when the trucks were delivered in parts and without instructions for assembly. Most of the personnel assigned to the truck trains were civilian drivers and mechanics, although some drivers were soldiers and each column had a detachment of infantry detailed for guard duty. Pershing ordered a maintenance shop set up at Columbus to inspect and overhaul trucks after each round trip, but it was soon evident that the rigors of the poor and nonexistent roads made it necessary for each truck train to carry along a good supply of repair parts.

Leaving the railhead at Columbus, the normal truck route extended due west to Gibson's Ranch, where it crossed the border, then led through Boca Grande, Espia, Ascension, and Corrialitos to the expeditionary base at Colonia Dublán. From that point, trucks struck out to the advanced bases at Galeana, El Valle, Las Cruces, and Namiquipa. The White, FWD, and Jeffrey Quad trucks followed a trail defined by wagon ruts and the telegraph wire laid by the Signal Corps troops between Colonia Dublán and Columbus. The steel and hard rubber wheels of the trucks soon churned the trails into an almost impassable morass of ruts and chuck holes. Consequently, wherever the land was reasonably flat, the drivers kept broadening the track until it was half a mile wide in some places. Once the rains began, those tracks became impassable. The expedition's two engineer companies were completely overwhelmed by the task of maintaining the primitive roads.

The daily cartage requirements were staggering. The expedition needed 223,000 pounds of forage, 120,000 pounds of fuel, 60,000 pounds of rations, 10,000 pounds of clothing and miscellaneous supplies, and 5,000 pounds of dry stores. Early in the campaign, Pershing's staff established an adequate rate of supply from the United States to the expedition's base at Colonia Dublán and made satisfactory arrangements for forwarding materiel to the advanced bases. The logistical system broke down, however, between the advanced bases and the marching cavalry columns, which rarely returned north to resupply. Pack and wagon trains could not keep up with the cavalry, and only periodically reached the squadrons. Supply difficulties multiplied the farther the cavalrymen rode. As a consequence, the scouting columns had to rely on the little they could carry with them and on foraging to supplement the meager quantities of food, fodder, and equipment provided by their pack trains. The barren countryside provided little for them in any case, even when the Mexican population did not recoil in hostility at their approach.

The usual foraging system relied on issuance of government receipts, which the seller presented to the army quartermaster for payment. Increasingly, Mexican civilians and businessmen were unwilling to accept such "scraps of paper" that could only be redeemed far in the north. Eventually, commanders found that only cash would produce the supplies their men needed, and some, lacking government funds, paid for the army's needs out of their own pockets. The experience of Colonel Brown, commanding the Tenth Cavalry, was typical. The day his men rode out of Colonia Dublán was the last on which they had government rations until 20 April. Brown paid out more than $1,600 of his own money over that month to buy what little food the country had to offer. By and large his men subsisted on corn and beans, rarely getting sugar, coffee, or fruit. Poor food debilitated their health, although they did not always eat all they received. Following the old cavalry dictum of "the horse, the saddle, the man," they reserved their corn for their animals whenever necessary. Horses accustomed to grass and oats fared poorly on dry hay and corn, however, and the animals quickly thinned down.

Equipment suffered correspondingly. Clothing wore out rapidly, and officers only occasionally were able to buy civilian trousers, shirts, and hats to replace it. Stirrup cups soon disappeared, as soldiers used them to resole light issue shoes worn out while leading their horses over difficult terrain. Pieces of shelter halves soon appeared as patches on riding breeches, and some of the men replaced their tattered campaign hats with ones made from the linings of their saddle bags. No column had a forge, and periodic stops at ranches to use local blacksmith shops barely sufficed to keep the horses shod. As it was, there developed a dangerous shortage of horseshoes, and commanders ordered their men to contribute all their spares to a common pool and to pick up any they saw along the trail. It was no wonder that Pershing was so shocked at the gaunt, ragged appearance of his men and their mounts when they finally rode back into camp after the fight at Parral.

With those limitations in mind, Pershing sent his chief of staff, Colonel Cabell, to Santa Cruz de Villegas to determine whether the troops could stay there. Brown pointed out that his men and their animals needed a minimum of one ton of food, six tons of hay, and four and a half tons of grain every day. Cabell found no way to sustain such a rate of supply and quickly concluded that all of Pershing's apprehensions were justified. Thus, on 21 April, Brown was ordered to begin withdrawing by way of Satevó to San Antonio de los Arenales. By 22 April, the last column was on the march to the north.

PATROL OF THE DISTRICTS. Pershing perceived the actions of the Carranzista troops as simple treachery and became convinced that Mexican officers did not want him to find Villa. In messages to Funston, he decried the fiction of Carranza's cooperation with the expedition and suggested investing sufficient military force to control all of Chihuahua. The attack on Tompkins and his men at Parral alarmed Washington, however, and President Wilson opted instead for further negotiations with the Mexican government. While those talks progressed, Pershing was to make every effort to avoid confrontation.

At first, the pause in operations was a welcome one. As his tattered and weary columns reported into the encampment at San Antonio de los Arenales, Pershing realized that rest and refitting were the first priority for the cavalry troops. Within a week, however the general had become impatient. Finding extended inactivity distasteful, he instituted a rigorous training program that kept the men occupied. While negotiations between Generals Scott and Obregón dragged on without result in Juárez, Pershing sought some way to continue his mission.

The campaign of the three columns and the subsequent operations of the four smaller columns had succeeded in catching a number of Villistas and, perhaps more important, dispersing and discouraging others. Villa was still at large in Chihuahua, however, and scattered bands of his supporters remained under arms. After withdrawing his troops from the southern part of the state and reestablishing his general headquarters at Namiquipa, Pershing decided on 29 April to adopt a system of patrol by district. The idea, strongly reminiscent of the methods successfully used by the British in policing the northwest frontier of India, was inspired by the work of Colonel Dodd's Seventh Cavalry. While busy securing the western passes, Dodd's men had remained essentially in the same area and had become familiar with both the terrain and the population. Such propinquity bred a mutual respect that allowed the cavalrymen to develop good sources of information about Villista bands. Dodd knew the reliability of his Carranzista counterpart and, well-informed about matters around Miñaca, had been able to sift probability from rumor. Diligently following up sound information had brought Dodd the success of Tomochic. Dodd's methods, Pershing reasoned, might bring similar successes to his other commanders.

As soon as his men were rested and reequipped, Pershing sent the cavalry regiments out to five patrol dis-

MEXICAN DISTRICT PATROLS

District	Regiment	Commander
Satevó	Fifth Cavalry	Colonel Wilbur E. Wilder
Guerrero	Seventh Cavalry	Colonel George A. Dodd
Namiquipa	Tenth Cavalry	Major Ellwood W. Evans
San Francisco de Borja	Eleventh Cavalry	Colonel James Lockett
Bustillos	Thirteenth Cavalry	Colonel Herbert J. Slocum

tricts that covered all of central Chihuahua from Galeana, just south of his original base at Colonia Dublán, to the region just north of Parral.

Pershing tried to assign each cavalry regiment to the district with which it was most familiar because of its service, although that obviously could not apply to the Fifth Cavalry, newly arrived from the United States. He also based much of his infantry and artillery forward in the districts to support the cavalry regiments when necessary. Pershing charged his commanders with organizing their own agents and services of information within their districts and taking independent action to pursue Villistas whenever the opportunity presented itself. Although civilians were to be treated with special consideration, he warned that U.S. troops were always in some danger of being attacked and ordered appropriate precautions to be taken. By 4 May, the regiments had moved into their districts.

Active patrolling quickly produced results. Reacting to a request from the local Carranzista commander for help, Major Howze rode with six troops of the Eleventh Cavalry to Ojos Azules, where approximately 120 Villistas under Julio Acosta, Cruz Dominguez, and Antonio Angel were still celebrating a victory over Mexican federal troops. After a long night march, Howze arrived at the town just after dawn on 5 May. Having achieved surprise, Howze ordered an immediate attack. His six troops of cavalry delivered a mounted pistol charge that broke the Villista resistance in little more than twenty minutes and rescued a group of Carranzista prisoners that the bandits had intended to execute. A two-hour fight followed, during which the Villistas separated into three groups and fled into the hills. Howze's men virtually wiped out one of the groups, killing sixty-two and capturing a large number of horses and mules. The Eleventh Cavalry suffered no casualties in an action that Pershing called "a brilliant piece of work" in his report to Funston.

In an action that newspaper reporters played up as an innovation in warfare, Patton and his men returned fire from their moving vehicles and killed several bandits.

Chance governed some of the encounters. Pershing's supernumerary aide de camp, Lieutenant George S. Patton, Jr., encountered a party of Villistas on 14 May while on an expedition to purchase corn. When Patton and his detachment of ten men from the Sixteenth Infantry drove up to the San Miguel Ranch near Rubio, a number of men ran out of the buildings and opened fire. In an action that newspaper reporters played up as an innovation in warfare, Patton and his men returned fire from their moving vehicles and killed several bandits, one of whom happened to be Julio Cárdenas, one of Villa's better commanders. In another brief fight near Las Cruces, Villistas ambushed a small U.S. detachment from the Seventeenth Infantry that was escorting a detail of engineers sketching roads. After the skirmish the patrol discovered that they had killed Candelario Cervantes, another of Villa's right-hand men. Slowly but surely, sustained pressure was eroding Villa's organization.

THE THREAT OF WAR. Measurable and satisfactory progress in Pershing's district scheme was not accompanied by similar progress in U.S.-Mexican relations. The failure of talks between Scott and Obregón and the increasing hostility of the Mexican government spurred a flurry of telegrams between Pershing, Funston, and the War Department, debating what the expedition ought to do. Fearing the outbreak of general war, Secretary of State Robert Lansing had already warned U.S. consuls in Mexico to be ready to advise Americans to leave the country. In Chihuahua, swelling numbers of Mexican federal troops worried both Funston and the War Department, causing them to urge Pershing to withdraw his scattered regiments and shorten his exposed lines of communication. Receiving no reports from his district commanders of threatening Mexican troop movements, Pershing calmly advised against any withdrawal. Secretary of War Baker firmly believed that Pershing had to stay as long as the danger to the border remained, but warned him not to provoke the Mexican authorities and advised him to be ready, in the event of attack, to fall back with his entire command in the direction of El Paso and the Fifth Infantry Brigade.

By the end of May, Carranzista patrols had become more aggressive, and U.S. and Mexican armed detachments had the dual task of pursuing Villa and keeping careful watch on each other. Concerned about the possibility of accidentally firing on Mexican federal troops, Pershing emphasized discretion and restraint in his instructions to his officers. Through the month, the threat of war loomed larger as additional Mexican units arrived in Chihuahua and deployed along Pershing's lines of communications. By 1 June, approximately thirty thousand men were encamped to the east and west of Pershing's expeditionary force. General J. B. Treviño wired Pershing on 16 June to inform him that the Mexican army would not permit movement of U.S. troops in any direction except north. Pershing defiantly replied the same day to the effect that he would follow the instructions originally issued by the United States government and conduct patrols to accomplish those instructions in accordance with his own best judgment. Thus, considerable anxiety attended the dispatch of more U.S. patrols in search of Villa. A few days later, a clash occurred, bringing the two nations to the brink of war.

In an attempt to keep tabs on the disposition of Mexican troops, Pershing ordered general reconnaissance, particularly to the east of the U.S. lines of communication. He had reports that Mexican troops were massing near Villa Ahumada, about eighty miles from Colonia Dublán. Troops C and K, Tenth Cavalry, marched out on 18 June with specific orders from Pershing to avoid trouble. Advancing along separate lines, the two troops met at Santo Domingo Ranch, where Captain Charles T. Boyd, as the senior of the two leaders, assumed overall command. For reasons that remain unclear, he decided to march directly through the town of Carrizal, which lay between the ranch and his objective of Villa Ahumada. Captain Lewis S. Morey argued against such a provocative move, because there were good roads around the town. Similarly, the American foreman of the ranch warned that there were Mexican troops in Carrizal who would surely oppose the U.S. troops. Boyd, however, insisted, and the hundred men of the two cavalry troops arrived at Carrizal about 6:30 A.M. on 21 June.

Boyd halted just short of the town and requested permission to march through. He consulted with General Felix Gomez, the garrison commander, who refused permission and emphasized General Trevino's orders that Americans were not to be permitted to move in any direction except toward the international border. As the two men talked, Mexican troops debouched from the town and took up positions along irrigation ditches and in front of the village. Boyd formed up his troops and dismounted to attack, believing that the Mexicans would not stand up to his men.

His estimate of the situation was incorrect. The Carranzistas opened fire and Captain Boyd was killed in the opening exchange. In the course of the next hour, Troop K fell back and the Mexicans turned the open flank of Troop C. In the ensuing debacle, seven Americans were killed, twelve wounded, twenty-four captured, and five reported as missing. The remainder of the two troops retired about one thousand yards to the west and then disengaged from the action and eventually reached a relieving column from the Eleventh Cavalry, led by Major Howze.

Captain Boyd had completely misjudged Mexican resolve and, expecting no resistance, had frittered away every tactical advantage by delaying action so long that the Mexicans had plenty of time to deploy in strong positions. Then, although he certainly observed the Mexican preparations, he ordered a frontal attack. Boyd's thoroughly bad judgment caused unnecessary casualties. Worse, it brought on a battle that Pershing wanted to avoid at all costs. Popular outrage over the Carrizal fight in the United States and the continued failure of talks between the United States and Mexico, both at the military and political levels, appeared to make open war inevitable.

Immediately, Chief of Staff Scott directed the War Department General Staff to frame plans for war with Mexico. In general, the plan envisioned an advance into the country by three major columns, to be commanded by Funston (eastern), Pershing (central), and General William H. Sage (western), then in Nogales. Overall command was to be vested in Leonard Wood. In Mexico, Pershing promptly fulfilled simultaneous War Department orders to concentrate his expeditionary division at Colonia Dublán and to prepare for offensive action. To provide the manpower for the other two columns, the War Department had nowhere to turn but to the states.

The previous month, Generals Scott and Funston had voiced concerns to the administration about the lack of security along the border. Despite the successes Pershing's men had enjoyed, periodic raids continued, although the evidence was far from clear that Villistas were always responsible for them. General Scott, having heard reports of extremist Mexican rhetoric about crushing the expeditionary force and riding into the United States far enough to "water their horses on the Potomac," was concerned that the Mexicans considered their long border with Texas to be undefended and therefore might be tempted to make an attack in force across it, thereby precipitating war. There were not enough regular army troops to guard against such an eventuality, and the two generals asked the president to call out the militia of the border states for additional protection. Scott did not pretend that the militia troops, whose standard of readiness and training was far below that of the regulars, could actually campaign against the Mexicans in the wastelands around the Rio Grande. He recognized, however, that the presence of a highly visible large group of uniformed armed men would serve as an effective deterrent. On 9 May 1916, President Wilson agreed and called the militias of Texas, New Mexico, and Arizona into federal service.

Those troops provided the nucleus for the second call-up of state troops and provided the bulk of the men to be assigned to Sage and Funston. The passage of the National Defense Act on 3 June made the process easier, because it clearly defined the relationship between the regular army and the state forces, now to be known as the National Guard. On 18 June, state forces were federalized and ordered to the Mexican border. Between then and the end of August, a total of 111,954 National Guardsmen from almost every state in the Union reached the Southwest, where they were stationed in large camps at El Paso, San Antonio, Brownsville, and Douglas, Arizona, in addition to smaller detachments all along the border.

Many units, overwhelmingly infantry, cavalry, and field artillery, reported for duty. Most were at far from full strength, however, and the National Guard mustered 155,971 fewer than called for by their tables of organization. Plans to employ the men in National Guard divisions and brigades foundered in the face of the same problems Pershing had already encountered in Mexico. There were not enough service troops—signal engineer, medical, transportation, and quartermaster—to allow commanders to create and use large formations. As a consequence, most of the National Guard units functioned as independent regiments or battalions under a garrison command. While newspapers played up citizen-soldier complaints that they had to travel to Texas in cramped railway cars, War Department officials were quietly delighted that their movement had been, although probably uncomfortable, a rapid and efficient one. Colonel Chauncey Baker of the Quartermaster Department had studied the problems in concentrating troops for the maneuver division in 1911 and resolved them through special arrangements with the railroads.

Once the National Guard troops arrived in the Southern Department, they could begin sharpening their military skills, and regular army commanders began planning for their eventual use in case of war with Mexico. Funston and Scott were satisfied that the martial display of so many troops along the border would impress, and thus deter, any Mexican forces that might be tempted to raid the United States on a large scale.

EVACUATION

While soldiers prepared for war, diplomats sought a settlement. Negotiations that began in May continued through June. At first the positions of the two countries appeared too far apart for any orderly resolution. Mexico properly emphasized its sovereignty, while the State Department stressed the right of the United States to guarantee the safety and security of its citizens. On 29 June, the Mexican government took a step to ease tensions when it released the prisoners from the Tenth Cavalry taken during the fight at Carrizal. Early in July, the two governments set up a joint commission to resolve the conflict. While talks were going on in New London, Philadelphia, New York, and Washington, confrontations between the two armies virtually ceased.

Villa had ceased to be a threat to the United States, lost most of his capable leaders, and found that his remaining supporters had been scattered by the U.S. cavalry.

By that time Pershing's command was concentrated at Colonia Dublán, where shorter supply lines improved the welfare and readiness of the troops. Villa had ceased to be a threat to the United States, lost most of his capable leaders, and found that his remaining supporters had been scattered by the diligent patrolling of the U.S. cavalry. His prestige, however, began to grow as soon as reports of a possible U.S. withdrawal began to be common knowledge. Villa again commenced limited operations against the Mexican federal troops farther south. Pershing dutifully reported those facts to Funston, along with his considered opinion that the Carranza government was incapable of managing the situation.

Expeditionary troops remained in Colonia Dublán over the next six months while the two governments painfully reached an accord, and Pershing spent the time developing his encampment into a regular military cantonment. After frustrating experiments, the Americans finally learned the art of making adobe bricks and built neat rows of huts, using their shelter halves for roofs. His staff laid out a logical arrangement of facilities that included a supply depot at the railhead, ordnance and engineering shops, truck parts, maneuver areas, baseball fields, and an airfield. With routine and relative comfort, however, came the boredom that can quickly blunt a soldier's readiness to fight. The remedy for that, Pershing knew, was training.

At Pershing's insistence, and with his close supervision, the expedition therefore filled the ensuing months in Mexico with an intensive and carefully thought-out training program that made those regulars among the most proficient men under arms in the nation's history. The campaign against Villa and its almost classical cavalry operations had nothing to do with modern warfare. It had toughened the men but not introduced them to, for example, the conditions under which men were even then fighting in France. Rigorous musketry courses were followed by machine-gun training, reflecting Pershing's ardent faith in marksmanship. Next were maneuver problems that stressed infantry tactics in open order, and the expeditionary force also learned to dig field fortifications and practiced fighting from trenches. Carefully planned exercises, followed by thoughtful critiques, drove the lessons home. By early winter, Pershing had a first-rate division at his disposal.

The need for retaining that division in Mexico, however, was fast disappearing. President Wilson worried that the United States might become involved in the war in France, and did not want the largest part of the regular army tied down on the Mexican border if that eventuality came to pass. While the U.S.-Mexican joint commission had reached no firm agreement, the U.S. members of the commission recommended to the president that Pershing's command be withdrawn from Mexico. Wilson agreed. Funston, acting on instructions from the War Department, directed Pershing on 18 January 1917 to return to the United States.

Funston left the exact date to Pershing, who organized his withdrawal in order to leave nothing behind. He began with the shipment of surplus equipment and supplies to Columbus, and followed on the night of 27–28 January 1917 with the evacuation of his men. Crews of soldiers demolished the orderly rows of huts and administrative buildings before leaving. The division marched north to Palomas, where the men halted on 5 February to clean up before reentering the United States. Pershing crossed the border first and reviewed his troops as they rode into Columbus, the last of them crossing out of Mexico at three o'clock in the afternoon.

SIGNIFICANCE OF THE CAMPAIGN

Withdrawal of the Punitive Expedition proved the final hurdle to normalizing relations between the United States and Mexico. In March, Carranza was elected president of Mexico, and in August, Wilson extended recognition of and reopened full diplomatic relations with Carranza's government. Even so, tensions between the two countries did not really abate until after World War I. During the war U.S. soldiers occasionally pursued Mexican raiders back across the international frontier. Villa remained a problem until July 1920, when he surrendered and, in return for retiring entirely from politics, was given vast estates in Chihuahua. He was assassinated in 1923.

Shortly after the return of the expedition, General Funston died of a heart attack, leaving Pershing commander of the Southern Department as of 20 February 1917. Summing up the successes and failures of the expeditionary force, Pershing regretted that he had failed to catch Villa, but concluded that, given the steadily growing opposition of all Mexicans to his operations, he had done well in dispersing Villista bands and returning a sense of security to the southern regions of Texas, New Mexico, and Arizona. Secretary of War Baker, noting that capturing Villa would have been desirable, shared Pershing's sentiments that the real purposes of the expedition in terms of U.S. security had been met. General Scott and senior officers in the War Department were as impressed with Pershing's restraint as with his military successes. They observed that he had accomplished his mission with very few casualties and had weathered numerous crises and provocations without allowing periodic clashes of arms to bring on war with Mexico.

The Punitive Expedition into Mexico was the United States Army's last great cavalry campaign, and cavalry supporters derived considerable satisfaction from the reliable and, at times, exciting performance of the mounted troopers. Some, such as Patton and Tompkins, saw the campaign as proof that the cavalry would continue to have a role in warfare and drew up careful lists of ways that the equipment and techniques of the arm could be improved. While the experience of World War I eventually proved supporters of the mounted arm wrong about their hopes for cavalry in general war, the Punitive Expedition continued to bear witness to the arm's utility in small-scale fighting, particularly over rough terrain. Throughout the 1920s and 1930s, U.S. war plans for defense of the Western Hemisphere continued to envisage such a role for the horse cavalry. The Cavalry School at Fort Riley, Kansas, was the legacy of the Punitive Expedition until World War II.

While the expedition suggested the continued utility of the horse cavalry, it also made clear that the days of fighting with saber and lance were past. Few of Pershing's cavalrymen bothered to carry the saber, which, despite the protestations of such vigorous supporters as Patton, clearly no longer had much use. Concerned about the loads their mounts had to carry and conscious that the saving of even a few ounces would significantly affect the endurance of their horses, troopers commonly preferred the more effective rifle and pistol. The doctrinal lesson of the Punitive Expedition was that the principal use of cavalry in the future would be as mounted rifles.

If it was the last great cavalry campaign, the Punitive Expedition was also the army's first modern campaign, presaging the mechanization of the service in the decades to come. Operations in Mexico forced doctrinal development in many areas, the most spectacular of which was the use of airplanes. Signal Corps airmen, observing the progress of the air war in Europe, believed that their airplanes should have been employed chiefly for reconnaissance and only incidentally for liaison. Foulois and his pilots saw that, given more reliable machines, they could have been invaluable to Pershing as scouts and that the information they provided would have multiplied many times over the value of the cavalry columns by directing them more efficiently. The thinking of the Air Service about the observation function of aircraft, founded in the experience in Mexico, developed dramatically over the next two years.

The brilliant small-unit actions fought by the cavalrymen could not, however, conceal the many shortcomings displayed by the army. Before the United States Army could fight a major war against a modern opponent, much thought would have to be given to reorganizing and expanding the administrative and logistical services. Quartermaster, signal, ordnance, and maintenance organizations demanded full-time, highly qualified specialists if combat soldiers equipped with modern weapons and machines were to be kept ready for battle. The army could not continue merely to detail line officers to organize logistical support, as had been tried at Columbus.

The expedition also served a useful purpose in testing airplanes, radios, machine guns, trucks, cars, and other equipment then entering the inventories of Western armies. U.S. soldiers learned many lessons about how much equipment suffers under the stress of constant use and quickly discovered which machines were too complicated, unreliable, or simply ill-suited for field service. Thus, the army replaced the JN-2 aircraft with more robust and powerful machines and discarded the Benet-Mercier machine gun that had failed as early as the night of Villa's raid on Columbus and never served satisfactorily thereafter. Pershing's command difficulties raised more serious problems, pointing to the need for more reliable field communications.

Service in Mexico was perhaps most valuable as a opportunity for hardening and training the regulars who would become the core of the national army a few months later. Pershing had the opportunity to train hard, without the usual distractions of garrison duty. Also, the campaign allowed many younger officers to lead large formations of troops for the first time in their careers and offered them the opportunity for independent action with the consequent difficult decisions such command implied. Many succeeded, others failed, and Pershing developed the system of merit by which he would award commands in France. In Mexico, Pershing concluded that modern war required young leaders—this despite the spectacular performances of men such

On 27 January 1817, Pershing and his men began their withdrawal from Mexico. They marched north to Polomas, crossed the border at Columbus, and reentered the United States on 5 February. (National Archives)

as Dodd and Brown, well into their sixties, and of many company commanders and field officers who were forty and older.

Controversies surrounding passage of the National Defense Act of 1916 and later difficulties in manning the National Guard regiments detailed for border duty convinced Scott, Pershing, and others that the nation could no longer rely solely on its militia in time of war. Conscription, they concluded, was the only way to guarantee enough men to field an appropriate fighting force. That decision—logical enough in view of the fact that less than half the National Guard's presumed strength ever appeared for duty—ignored the political clamor that selective service was certain to raise.

In Mexico, Pershing concluded that modern war required young leaders.

Although the National Guard did not serve in Mexico, the mobilization did reveal important deficiencies in its organization and training, as well as in its mobilization system. Inefficient leaders stood out, as did good ones. After he returned from Mexico, Pershing extended his training program in the Southern Department to include the National Guard until the regiments returned to state control. That training had important consequences after the United States declared war on Germany. The National Guard mobilization in 1916 was an important dress rehearsal that made the general national mobilization in 1917 a more successful and efficient procedure.

In sum, the Punitive Expedition into Mexico and the entire border campaign that began in 1911 helped to lay a sound foundation for the vast expansion of the U.S. Army in 1917. While the reforms of Secretary of War Elihu Root at the turn of the century improved the functioning of the War Department General Staff, the Punitive Expedition was the laboratory in which those reforms were worked out in practice.

The Punitive Expedition made Pershing the best and, perhaps, only choice to command the American Expeditionary Forces in France. By 1917 he had gained experience in handling large numbers of troops, which no one else in the army could claim. Further, he had the opportunity to think deeply about battle and, particularly in the period after June 1916, to experiment with various types of tactics. The confused political situation during the Punitive Expedition required him to deal tactfully with foreign officials and to consider the political implications of military actions. The entire experience was excellent training for a commander in chief of an army on foreign service. At the declaration of war, Pershing offered a combination of skill, experience, and proven ability unique in the officer corps.

BIBLIOGRAPHY

Blumenson, Martin, ed. *The Patton Papers, 1885–1940* (1972).

Braddy, Haldeen. *Pershing's Mission in Mexico* (1966).

Brimlow, George Francis. *Cavalryman Out of the West: Life of General William Carey Brown* (1944).

Campobello, Nellie. *Apuntes Sobre la Vida Militar de Francisco Villa* (1940).

Clendenen, Clarence C. *The United States and Pancho Villa: A Study in Unconventional Diplomacy.* (1961).

———. *Blood on the Border: The United States Army and the Mexican Irregulars* (1969).

Cramer, Stuart, Jr. "The Punitive Expedition from Boquillas." *Cavalry Journal* 27 (November 1916).

Dallam, Samuel F. "The Punitive Expedition of 1916." *Cavalry Journal* 36 (July 1927).

Elser, Frank B. "General Pershing's Mexican Campaign." *Century Magazine* (February 1920).

Evans, Ellwood W. "Cavalry Equipment in Mexico." *United States Cavalry Journal* 28 (November 1916).

Foulois, Benjamin. *From the Wright Brothers to the Astronauts* (1968).

Ganoe, William Addleman. *The History of the United States Army* (1942).

Greer, Thomas H. "Air Arm Doctrinal Roots, 1917–1918." *Military Affairs* 20 (Winter 1956).

Guzman, Martin Luis. *Memoirs of Pancho Villa,* translated by Virginia H. Taylor (1965).

Johnson, William Weber. *Heroic Mexico: The Violent Emergence of a Modern Nation* (1968).

Kreidberg, Marvin A., and Merton G. Henry. *History of Military Mobilization in the United States Army, 1775–1945* (1955).

Lister, Florence C., and Robert H. Lister. *Chihuahua: Storehouse of Storms* (1966).

Mason, Herbert Molloy, Jr. *The Great Pursuit* (1970).

Maurer, Maurer. *The U.S. Air Service in World War I,* 4 vols. (1978–1979).

Morey, Lewis S. "The Cavalry Fight at Carrizal." *Cavalry Journal* 27 (January 1917).

Page, Victor W. "Substituting Gasoline for Horseflesh: Work of Motor Trucks with the Army in Mexico." *Scientific American* (5 August 1916).

Palmer, Frederick. *Newton D. Baker, America at War* (1931).

Patton, George S., Jr. "Cavalry Work on the Punitive Expedition." *Cavalry Journal* 27 (January 1917).

Pickering, Abner. "The Battle of Agua Prieta." *United States Infantry Journal* 12 (January 1916).

Pool, William C. "Military Aviation in Texas, 1913–1917." *Texas Military History* 2 (February 1962).

Porter, John A. "The Punitive Expedition." *Quartermaster Review* 12 (January-February 1933).

Rippy, J. Fred. "Some Precedents of the Pershing Expedition into Mexico." *Southwestern Historical Quarterly* 24 (April 1921).

Scott, Hugh Lenox. *Some Memoirs of a Soldier* (1928).

Shunk, William A. "The Military Geography of Mexico." *United States Cavalry Journal* 6 (June 1893).

Smythe, Donald. *Pershing: General of the Armies* (1986).

Spaulding, Oliver Lyman. *The United States Army in War and Peace* (1937).

Swift, Eben, Jr. "Experiences in Mexico." *United States Cavalry Journal* 27 (November 1916).

Tompkins, Frank. *Chasing Villa: The Story Behind the Story of Pershing's Expedition into Mexico* (1934).

Toulmin, H. A., Jr. *With Pershing in Mexico* (1935).

Troxel, O. C. "The Tenth Cavalry in Mexico." *Cavalry Journal* 28 (October 1917).

Vandiver, Frank E. *Black Jack: The Life and Times of John J. Pershing*, 2 vols. (1977).

Weigley, Russell F. *History of the United States Army* (1967).

Weissheimer, J. W. "Field Ovens in Mexico." *United States Infantry Journal* 13 (February 1917).

Wharfield, H. B. "The Affair at Carrizal." *Montana, The Magazine of Western History* 18 (October 1968).

Williams, S. M. "The Cavalry Fight at Ojos Azules." *Cavalry Journal* 27 (January 1917).

– CHARLES E. KIRKPATRICK

World War I

AMERICA ON THE EVE OF ENTRY INTO THE GREAT WAR

On 9 January 1917, the German war leadership held a momentous meeting at the castle of Pless on the border of Poland. This crown council finalized a policy—unrestricted submarine warfare against Allied and neutral maritime commerce—that would have profound consequences for the outcome of World War I. Frustrated by the exhausting military stalemate and nervous over signs of growing unrest on the home front, which the Allied naval blockade had exacerbated, the German army and naval leadership had for some time favored an all-out campaign of undersea assault to shorten the war. Pressure from the neutral United States previously had forced Germany to stay its hand.

"We can take care of America," von Hindenburg blustered. "The opportunity for the U-boat war will never be as favorable again."

In addition to Germany's army and naval leaders, this council of war included Kaiser Wilhelm II and Chancellor Theobold von Bethmann-Hollweg. The leaders of Germany's armed forces exuded confidence. The admiralty had prepared a two-hundred-page memorandum, one that was sustained more by faith than by the questionable tables and charts that sought to bolster its conclusions that the British would be starved out of the war before another harvest. An equally misguided assumption by the military was that Germany had nothing to fear from forcing the United States into the war. When Bethmann-Hollweg spoke with the voice of caution, he was silenced by the confidence of the war lords. Having earlier assured victory through unrestricted submarine warfare, the chief of the Naval General Staff, Admiral Henning von Holtzendorff, was quick with another promise: "I guarantee on my word as a naval officer that no American will set foot on the Continent!" Field Marshal Paul von Hindenburg, the German supreme commander, was equally contemptuous of U.S. potential to influence the course of the global conflict. "We can take care of America," he blustered. "The opportunity for the U-boat war will never be as favorable again." The Kaiser, who in January was indifferent in word and deed toward the prospect of war with the United States, concluded the discussion by affixing his signature to a document: "I order that unrestricted submarine warfare be launched with the utmost vigor on the first of February."

German underestimation of the United States at first glance appears incredibly shortsighted, analogous to the Japanese decision to attack Pearl Harbor in December 1941. The United States had vast mineral and financial resources, with an industrial base on the verge of outproducing that of all the European states combined. With a population of about 100 million, the United States had the potential to provide more soldiers than either France or Great Britain. During the course of the war, almost 24 million Americans between the ages of eighteen and forty-five would register for the draft; by war's end the American Expeditionary Forces (AEF) in Europe would number just over 2 million. Supported by the U.S. Navy, with personnel numbering almost 500,000, and a Marine Corps of more than 60,000 men, the AEF would give the Allies clear military superiority.

It should be noted, however, that there is little agreement about the statistical data for the First World War. Figures vary considerably according to the sources consulted, official or otherwise. The figures given here for the AEF and its supporting forces are taken from Kreidberg and Henry (1955).

That the United States emerged in Europe by 1918 as a great military power was in truth a surprise for America's allies as well as for Germany. The British, who welcomed U.S. belligerency in April 1917 for the financial relief it provided, certainly did not initially expect U.S. arms to be an important factor in defeating the German army. The views of the British chief of the Imperial General Staff on U.S. military potential differed little from that of the German military authorities. General Sir William R. Robertson, whose sensible and down-to-earth military advice, strength of character, and force of personality had led to his elevation as the government's strategical adviser in late 1915, saw little direct military value in America's entry into the war. Two weeks after Berlin announced that it would resume unrestricted U-boat warfare, Robertson wrote a fellow general: "I do not think that it will make much difference whether America comes in or not. What we want

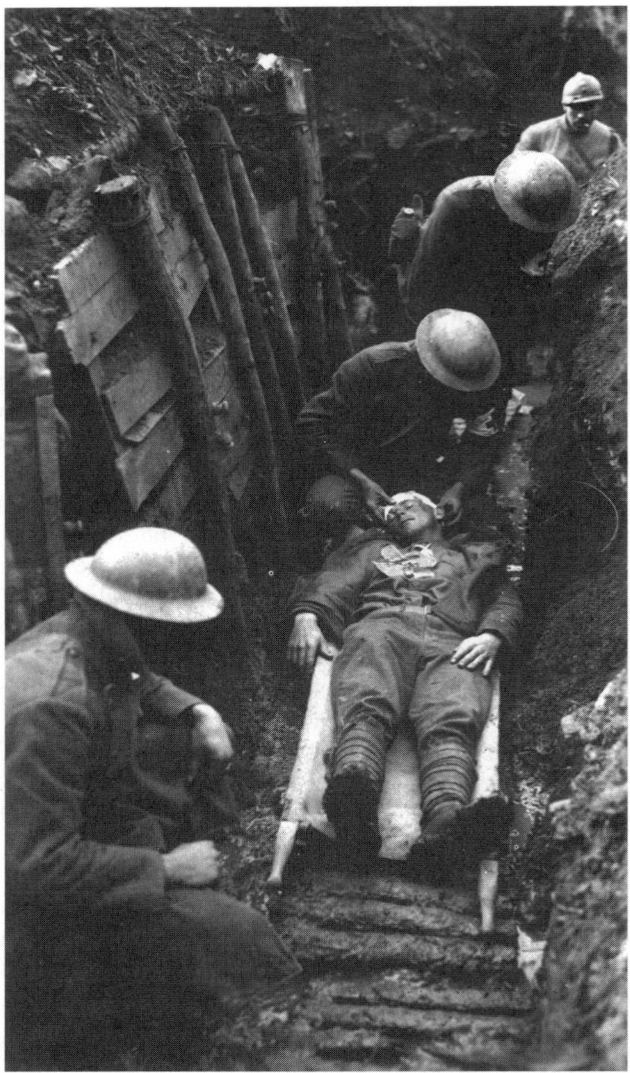

Trench warfare was adopted by both sides during World War I. Infantry dug ditches six to eight feet deep to protect themselves and their positions before attacking. This injured soldier lies in the trench near the front as he awaits evacuation in March 1918. (National Archives)

to do is to beat the German Armies, until we do that we shall not win the war. America will not help us much in that respect."

Robertson's typically blunt assessment of the inability of the United States to play an extracontinental role was not an offhand comment. On the contrary, it was based on the British General Staff's evaluation of the existing U.S. military establishment and its leadership from 1914 to the beginning of 1917. What were the Allies to think of the U.S. commander in chief, the scholar-president Woodrow Wilson, who earlier had been "too proud to fight" after the sinking of the *Lusitania* in 1915. One manifestation of Wilson's hatred of war was his tepid interest in military matters. He appeared bored with questions of defense and was uncomfortable in the presence of soldiers. Convinced that the authors of the U.S. Constitution intended the president to be a civilian, he had been angered by a wartime etching that showed him dressed in a military uniform as commander in chief. His secretaries of war and the navy, the diminutive Newton D. Baker and the North Carolina newspaperman Josephus Daniels, were pacifists; the army chief of staff, Major General Hugh L. Scott, a former Indian fighter now in the twilight years of his career, oversaw an army that was ranked seventeenth in the world. The army's armament was obsolete, its supply of munitions hopelessly inadequate. The U.S. Army had enough rounds for its field artillery to sustain a bombardment on the western front for only a few minutes. The army had no tanks, poison gas, flamethrowers, mortars, hand and rifle grenades, heavy field howitzers, or aircraft fit for combat. As the global conflict being waged in Europe, Mesopotamia, Palestine, East Africa, and elsewhere threatened to entangle the United States, the army remained, in the words of former Secretary of War Henry L. Stimson, "a profoundly peaceful army."

Some of the shortcomings of the U.S. military establishment were vividly demonstrated when President Wilson dispatched the Punitive Expedition into Mexico in response to Francisco "Pancho" Villa's raid in March 1916 on Columbus, New Mexico. This expedition, which at its maximum strength numbered about eleven thousand troops, advanced three hundred miles into Mexico in its futile effort to capture the elusive Mexican bandit. There were breakdowns in the mobilization of units of the regular army and especially of the National Guard, whose training was shown to be rudimentary at best. Munitions shortages, poor logistics (compounded by the shortage of trucks), and an insufficient supply of machine guns also plagued this limited military venture.

On 3 June 1916, while U.S. troops were engaged in Mexico, Wilson signed the National Defense Act, which represented the first attempt by Congress to establish a comprehensive system of national security. In addition to the regular army, which had its peacetime strength increased to 175,000 men over a five-year period, future U.S. land forces were to be composed of reserves, the National Guard, and a volunteer force raised in the event of war.

This act reflected the political realities of 1916. Americans overwhelmingly opposed U.S. involvement in the war. Hence, the provisions for the expansion of the army were totally inadequate for U.S. participation in the gigantic battles taking place in Europe. The National Guard, politically popular but incapable of providing the training to fight a modern war, was expected to grow to more than 400,000 officers and men. (In April 1917, however, it numbered only 174,008 officers and men.) The cornerstone of U.S. land warfare thus became the militia, a primitive fighting force by European standards. Refusing to follow the example of the European powers, Congress rejected conscription and kept the regular army relatively small. Equally detrimental to adequate military preparedness was the refusal of Congress to sanction the plans and machinery necessary for national mobilization. As former Assistant Secretary of War Henry Breckenridge put it, the act was "either a comedy or a tragedy." In his blunt assessment, "surely the mountain has labored and brought forth a mouse."

The preparedness campaign of 1916 clearly was not designed to prepare the United States for the European war. The focus, rather, of U.S. leaders was defensive—to protect the nation's vital interests against the victors of the war. There is no better example of this than the Naval Act of 1916, which appropriated money for a battleship-dominated fleet, which would prove to be ineffective in containing Germany's most formidable threat on the high seas, the submarine. Besides being designed for a war quite different from the one it would actually fight, the U.S. Navy was woefully unprepared in 1917, entering the conflict with nine out of its ten warships inadequately manned and two of three not materially fit.

President Wilson's antimilitary views contributed to the army's ineffectiveness. He helped thwart conscription in 1916, and his views on the duties of soldiers in peacetime served to undermine the efforts of military authorities to prepare for the war they were likely to fight. Artificially separating civil and military responsibilities, Wilson insisted that the soldiers had no role to play in the formulation of national policy prior to the outbreak of war. In 1915 he had exploded in rage when the *Baltimore Sun* erroneously reported that the General Staff was considering calling up a million men to fight against Germany. The U.S. General Staff was not then contemplating intervention in Europe, and the president's heated response to such a charge guaranteed that it would not do so as long as the United States remained neutral.

Congress, reflecting the strong neutralist and isolationist sentiment of the country, also crippled strategic planning by including in the National Defense Act the stipulation that the General Staff, which was responsible for the mobilization and strategic deployment of U.S. forces, be restricted to a chief of staff, two general officers of the line, ten colonels, ten lieutenant colonels, fifteen majors, and seventeen captains—a total of fifty-five officers. No more than half of these officers could be posted to or near the District of Columbia. When the United States entered the war, there were in fact only nineteen officers attached to the General Staff in the War Department, with only eleven assigned to intelligence and the strategic deployment of U.S. forces. The staff officers were warned to make no public statements about the war; civilian employees were under orders to not even discuss the war while at work. Advances in tactics and the impact of the new military technology went unexamined up close because the War Department did not send observers to the front, as it had done during the Russo-Japanese War (1904–1905). Wilson's instructions to his countrymen to be "impartial in thought as well as in action" served to impose an ostrichlike position upon the military professionals who would largely be held responsible for the success or failure of U.S. arms in the event of war.

That is not to say that many U.S. officers did not think seriously about their profession in the prewar years. Professionalism was in fact growing in the U.S. Army. The overwhelming majority of U.S. commanders (although not their chiefs of staff) who engaged the German army in 1917–1918 were West Pointers. The Leavenworth School, founded in 1881, also afforded both graduates and nongraduates of the U.S. Military Academy a chance to study seriously the art of war, with the cream of the class being given an additional year of study at the Staff College. The final stage of an officer's education was at the Army War College, established in 1903. The future AEF leaders received valuable instruction in organizing and leading large military units.

German U-boat warfare had killed Americans,

and war fever now swept the country.

The education of the U.S. military elite, however, did not prepare it for stalemated and industrialized trench warfare dominated by the machine gun and artillery. Through its concentration on the American Civil War, the Army War College reinforced an image of nineteenth-century warfare. As was the case with the European general staffs, the U.S. Army's officer corps emphasized offensive and maneuver warfare prior to the Great War. The new fire weapons, however, presented attacking forces with serious tactical problems. If U.S. officers had made a serious study of the killing fields of the western front from 1914 to 1916, they would have learned far more about modern warfare than they did from their extended studies of earlier wars or their tours of Civil War battlefields.

Given the strength of its adversary and the logistical difficulties of confronting an enemy some three thousand sea miles away, the United States found itself less prepared to fight on the eve of the Great War than it had been for the War of 1812 or even the American Revolution. The country had neither the plans, the army, the modern equipment, nor even the transport ships to wage a European campaign. The German and British professional soldiers can be forgiven for believing that the war would be over before any U.S. expeditionary force could play an important military role in Europe.

On 2 April 1917, President Wilson, escorted by a troop of cavalry, made his way from the White House to Capitol Hill to end his country's armed neutrality with a war message. British blockade measures had impinged on the freedom of U.S. overseas commerce, but unrestricted German U-boat warfare had killed Americans, and war fever now swept the country. Just prior to President Wilson's meeting with his cabinet on 20 March, to decide on a response to Germany's provocative acts, the American people were told that three U.S. merchant ships had been sunk, with the loss of fifteen Americans. German outrages also included the foolhardy attempt by German Foreign Secretary Arthur Zimmermann to enlist the support of Mexico and Japan against the United States. The headline of the *New York Times* on 1 March 1917 announced:

GERMANY SEEKS ALLIANCE AGAINST U.S.
ASKS JAPAN AND MEXICO TO JOIN HER

During Wilson's pivotal discussion with his cabinet on 20 March, Albert S. Burleson, a Texan who headed the Post Office Department, asserted that Germany "woke up a giant." He and the other cabinet members wanted to teach the Kaiser a lesson.

Although Wilson decided soon after this meeting that he had no choice but to make war, he apparently did not fully comprehend the consequences of U.S. belligerency. He told Congress that the United States would "exert all its power and employ all its resources to bring the government of the German empire to terms and end the war." He apparently believed at this time, however, that the war was nearing a conclusion because of the exhaustion of the warring states and that the U.S. role would be that of a maritime rather than a land power. He thought of fighting with the navy, industrial might, and finance. In these circumstances, there might be little difference between armed neutrality and belligerency.

The General Staff in the War Department did not share Wilson's view that the war was rushing to a conclusion. Immediately following Germany's resumption of unrestricted submarine warfare, General Hugh Lenox Scott had asked the War College Division, the section of the General Staff responsible for war planning and intelligence, to "submit without delay a statement of a plan of action that should be followed by the United States in case hostilities with Germany occur in the near future." Four days before the president's war message, the General Staff produced its first strategic appreciations (memorandums) of a war on European soil.

Allowed for the first time to consider seriously the consequences of a forward policy in Europe, the War College Division initially considered independent U.S. operations either in Holland (if that neutral country were forced into the war) or in the Balkans in Macedonia. Both of these plans were, to be blunt, daft. The suggestion that U.S. forces could play a decisive and independent role in the Balkans was amateurish; the advocacy of U.S. "surprise" attack on the unprotected German flank via Holland even more so. After reviewing these plans, the chief of the War College Division, Brigadier General Joseph E. Kuhn, concluded that it was "impossible" for the United States to launch military operations against Germany except in cooperation with the Triple Entente powers.

The initial considerations of sending an expeditionary force to European theaters served a useful purpose, by highlighting the enormous difficulties facing the U.S. military establishment. For the first time, the General Staff came to grips with such vital questions as the size of an expeditionary force, where that force might fight, and the time it would take to deliver that force to the chosen theater.

The General Staff realistically argued that the essential first step for U.S. involvement in the war was the acceptance of conscription without delay. Secretary of War Baker agreed and lobbied the president, who, although he had not yet decided to send Americans to Europe, accepted the necessity of the draft. His adroit handling of the controversial issue of compulsory service in Congress represented what was perhaps his finest hour in the military realm during the war. Without this prompt decision it would have been impossible to have a U.S. army of 2 million men in Western Europe by the armistice.

Although Congress gave the War Department the ability to conscript a mass army with passage of the Selective Service Act on 18 May 1917, the training and equipping of that force seemed months, perhaps even years, away. Starting essentially from scratch, the United States had neither the training camps, equipment, nor officers for the rapid expansion of the army. The British War Office believed that the U.S. War Department was incapable of calling more than 100,000 men at any one time. As British General Staff appreciation noted, "When this 'call' has entered the field another 100,000 could be handled perhaps in five months or slightly less, after the 'first call.' " The pessimistic British conclusion was that it would take a full year for the Americans to put 250,000 men into the field.

As U.S. officers studied the possibility that arms would be deployed in Europe, they encountered an even greater problem than the creation of an American army to fight on Germany's level—the transport of that force to Europe and its supply. The United States did not have a merchant marine to match its industrial might, while Great Britain in 1917 had a merchant marine that was eight times larger. When the General Staff examined the logistics for an expeditionary force in the Balkans, it discovered that it would take at least ten months to transport an army of 500,000 men to the eastern Mediterranean if fully half the U.S. merchant marine were diverted for this task.

The all-out campaign of undersea assault by the U-boats in April highlighted the problems of sea transport for both London and Washington. The month that America entered the war was the most successful month for the German submarine in World War I. The Allies lost a staggering 881,027 gross tons, of which the British share was 500,000 gross tons, a fivefold increase over January. One out of every four ships departing England was sunk. On the day that the United States went to war, London informed Washington that "the most vital thing for the Allies at present is the provision of shipping."

Beginning in about 1914, German submarines called Unterseeboote *or U-boats, such as this one seen surfacing in the Atlantic, sank many American merchant ships and even attacked passenger ships. Such attacks angered the American public and convinced U.S. officials to enter the war in 1917. (National Archives)*

The Allies, especially the French, also needed new recruits if they were to win what had become a war of attrition. The appeal of the marshal of France, Joseph Joffre, could not have been more direct: "We want men, men, men." Given its lack of military readiness, however, the United States seemed better prepared to build ships than to deploy large troop formations to Europe, especially if President Wilson followed the advice of his General Staff, which now advocated the creation of a large and modern army in the United States before sending it to Europe. The sea transport of an American army to Europe might take longer than its organization. Major General Tasker H. Bliss, the assistant chief of staff, concluded on the eve of U.S. belligerency that "the war must last practically two years longer before we can have other than naval and economic participation."

Several weeks after the passage of the war resolution on 6 April, British and French missions arrived in Washington with the intention of giving U.S. mobilization a sense of urgency. To enable American manpower to have an immediate impact on the war, the French and British made an extraordinary proposal: to feed American draftees and volunteers into British and French divisions, either as individuals or in small units. Americans, although serving under foreign flags, would then be able to fight in battle-tested armies, equipped with modern weapons of war and provided with sophisticated logistical and experienced staff support.

From a purely military point of view, this proposal had much to recommend it, but it asked much of a great nation. If amalgamation was accepted, there might never be an independent U.S. force with its own commander and sector of operations in Europe. More was at stake than national pride. President Wilson's efforts to create a new world order would be compromised if Americans fought in the armies of nations with annexationist objectives, and the president's voice in any peace settlement would be muffled if U.S. arms were given such a limited role in the war. Not surprisingly, this proposal, in the words of a British officer, had to be dropped "like a hot potato," but only for the moment. As the fortunes of the Allies declined in late 1917 and early 1918, the amalgamation issue resurfaced, creating serious friction between the United States and its war partners.

Wilson's desire to create a new world order decisively influenced his decision for war with Berlin. In order to achieve a liberal peace, he valued U.S. political and military independence just below the defeat of Germany. Determined to avoid any entanglement with Allied war objectives, he chose the designation of "associate" power rather than "ally." He also emphasized that he was fighting against Germany and not its allies. (On 7 December, however, the United States would declare war on Austria-Hungary.)

Despite his suspicion of the political objectives of his war partners, in early May President Wilson made another crucial military decision. Pressed by the British and French missions, who emphasized the political aspects of a symbolic show of U.S. arms in Europe, he told Marshal Joffre, the chief military representative of the French mission, "to take it for granted that such a force would be sent just as soon as we could send it." On 14 May, Baker and Joffre reached a formal agreement that called for U.S. military cooperation with the French army. The U.S. Navy was already moving to cooperate with the British Grand Fleet in European waters.

When Wilson learned that the British were concerned by this ambitious naval construction program, he asserted, "Let us build a navy bigger than hers and do what we please."

Even before the United States entered the war, Wilson had sought better communications with the British Admiralty. Secretary of Navy Daniels chose Vice Admiral William S. Sims, known for his forthrightness and independence of mind, as the U.S. Navy's man in London. When Congress declared war, Sims was en route to Great Britain. Soon the view in Washington was that the Canadian-born Sims, as commander of American Naval Forces in European Waters, did his job of coordinating the U.S. naval role with the British too well. Arguing that the United States should accept Britain's primacy on the high seas, Sims wanted the U.S. fleet to play a supportive naval role that emphasized the submarine threat to the Allies, especially Great Britain. On the other hand, Wilson, Daniels, and Admiral William S. Benson, chief of naval operations and responsible for advising the government on the strategic deployment of the navy, were reluctant to play second fiddle to the British Admiralty. The White House and Navy Department viewed the Royal Navy as an ally, but also as a future rival. "Don't let the British pull the wool over your eyes," Benson lectured Sims as the latter was about to depart for London. "It is none of our business pulling their chestnuts out of the fire. We would as soon fight the British as the Germans."

As late as 1889, the year before Alfred Thayer Mahan published his book on the importance of sea power, *The*

Influence of Sea Power upon History, 1660–1783, the U.S. Navy ranked twelfth in the world in number of warships, behind such countries as Norway, China, and Turkey. The Wilson administration, however, challenged Britain's naval supremacy, and in 1916 Congress approved the largest U.S. naval expansion program in history. When Wilson learned that the British were concerned by this ambitious naval construction program, 168 warships, he asserted, "Let us build a navy bigger than hers and do what we please."

Given the grave menace of German undersea assault, Benson belatedly accepted Sims's advice to concentrate U.S. destroyers in the eastern Atlantic to prevent the economic strangulation of Great Britain by U-boats. More than 70 percent of the navy's modern destroyers in 1917 were located at Queenstown, Ireland, where they cooperated with the Royal Navy on antisubmarine patrols.

By the end of 1917, U.S. cooperation with the Royal Navy on the maritime front in Europe included a fleet of thirty-six destroyers (a number that grew to sixty-eight by the end of the war) and the Sixth Battle Squadron, five coal-burning battleships commanded by Rear Admiral Hugh Rodman, which represented a degree of amalgamation never achieved by U.S. land forces with the British and French. Despite this joint effort, which inevitably assigned the Americans a secondary role in the eastern Atlantic and Mediterranean, there were serious underlying conflicts about naval strategy and priorities between the Navy Department and British Admiralty.

Possessing a love for the sea, the president, who had once hoped to attend Annapolis, took a stronger interest in the sea war than in the land war in Western Europe. If the German U-boat campaign succeeded, as appeared possible in the spring of 1917, the United States, of course, would be unable to play a decisive part in the land war in Western Europe. To clear a path for U.S. transports across the sub-infested North Atlantic, Wilson pressed the British to accept the convoy system, which the Admiralty hitherto had vetoed in favor of anti–U-boat patrols in the danger zone around the British Isles. Advocates of the convoy system, including British Prime Minister Lloyd George, however, argued that better use could be made of destroyers as escorts for convoys of cargo ships. A convoy of twenty or thirty ships was almost as difficult for a submarine to locate as a single ship in the vast ocean. The destroyer also had a much better chance of engaging and destroying a submarine when it was attempting to attack a convoy. Many anxious months lay ahead, but the adoption of the convoy system eventually provided the answer to the submarine threat.

In an attempt to play a leading role in the naval campaign, Benson, Daniels, and Wilson pressed the British to be more aggressive in waging war against the submarine. On 11 August 1917, the president, accompanied by Daniels, spoke to naval officers aboard the USS *Pennsylvania*, the flagship of the Atlantic Fleet: "We are hunting hornets all over the farm and letting the nest alone. None of us knows how to go to the nest and crush it, and yet I despair of hunting for hornets all over the sea when I know where the nest is, and know that the nest is breeding hornets as fast as I can find them." Believing that the war would be won if German U-boat bases were neutralized, Wilson professed a readiness to lose half the U.S. and British naval strength in an assault against the bases of the "hornets." In opposition to U.S. naval leadership, the British, perhaps influenced by the Royal Navy's failed attack operation in the Dardanelles in 1915, opposed employing their battleships against German-controlled ports.

The Admiralty did, however, accept the U.S. proposal to build a great mine barrier from Scotland across the North Sea to Norwegian waters. Begun in the spring of 1918, this largely American enterprise led to the planting of fifty-seven thousand U.S. and sixteen thousand British mines by the end of the war. The effectiveness of the hugely expensive ($80 million) North Sea Mine Barrage remains a subject of controversy. Only four subs were destroyed and perhaps four more were damaged. On the other hand, this mine barrier may have discouraged many U-boats from using this route.

The United States also employed 110-foot wooden subchasers that were modeled after the sturdy New England fishing boat against the submarine. By the armistice of 11 November 1918, the navy had 120 wooden subchasers deployed in European waters, sailing in groups of three. One group of subchasers was based on the island of Corfu to block the Strait of Otranto between Italy and Greece. This so-called Splinter Fleet employed depth charges and an acoustic sounding device, the forerunner of sonar, to locate the submarines.

Despite the offensive-minded stance of the U.S. administration on the European maritime front, the foremost priority of the U.S. Navy was the protection of American troops and supplies crossing the Atlantic to Europe. Less than 15 percent of the navy's personnel was in the eastern Atlantic and Mediterranean for other purposes. In the words of Benson's assistant, Captain William Veazie Pratt: "The impelling reason of the British was protection to food and war supplies in transit. Our basic reason was protection to our military forces in crossing the seas."

The reluctance of U.S. political and naval leadership to accept an auxiliary part in the naval campaign was also characteristic of the AEF's military role in the land war in Western Europe. To command the AEF, Baker, with the president's verbal approval, chose Major General (soon General) John J. Pershing, the commander of the Punitive Expedition, which had been withdrawn from Mexico in early February 1917. Pershing had never commanded more than eleven thousand men, but no U.S. general officer in active service had ever led a force that large. Given the questionable physical condition of Brigadier General Leonard Wood, Pershing's only serious rival for the command, Baker's choice was an easy one. Pershing had many qualities to recommend him. He had taught tactics at the U.S. Military Academy, and he had been tested by fire even before the Punitive Expedition—in skirmishes with Apaches, at San Juan Hill in the Spanish-American War, and during the pacification of the Moros in the Philippines. He was a thoroughgoing professional, recognized for his integrity, dedication, and force of personality. Although he was only five feet, nine inches tall, his ramrod-straight bearing led many to think him six feet or taller.

Pershing initially had doubts about Wilson's war leadership, and when Wilson made his "too proud to fight" statement after the *Lusitania* went down, the rugged Missourian had exclaimed, "Isn't that the damnedest rot you ever heard a sane person get off?" When Wilson responded firmly to the German resumption of U-boat warfare, however, Pershing changed his mind, expressing unconditional admiration for the president as a war leader. Wilson met Pershing only once during the war. On 24 May 1917, Baker had Pershing with him when he called on Wilson at the White House. Except for a cursory mention of the tonnage problem in transporting U.S. troops to Europe and the bloody bludgeoning in the trenches, the president had nothing else to say directly at this meeting about the U.S. role in the war. Pershing's instructions came later, when he visited Baker in the War Department just prior to his departure for Europe. "Here are your orders, General," Baker allegedly told him. "The president has just approved them." Baker also told Pershing: "If you do not make good, they [the American people] will probably hang us both on the first lamppost they can find."

Until an independent American army was a reality, Pershing's instructions were to "cooperate as a component" of the Allied armies. Alarmed by the obvious desire of the French and British to incorporate U.S. troops into their forces, Wilson and Baker made a point of emphasizing that Pershing was to maintain the American "identity" of his forces serving with the Allies. Pershing's civilian superiors also gave him the authority to expand or limit the cooperation of U.S. armed forces according to his reading of the military situation. These instructions granted Pershing virtual control over the extent of U.S. commitment to the war in Western Europe. No American field commander in history has been given a freer hand from civilian control to plan and execute military operations. These powers were all the more remarkable in light of the fact that the United States was involved in a coalition war and had the interests of its war partners to consider as well as its own. Inevitably, Pershing would have to deal with military matters marked by strong political overtones.

On 28 May, Pershing, with a small contingent of officers and enlisted men, sailed from New York on the transport *Baltic*. During their voyage across the Atlantic, Pershing and his staff attempted to take stock of the colossal struggle and to explore the role that America might play. Units forming the First Division in Europe began embarking the following month. Pershing's most important initial appointment was Major James G. Harbord as AEF chief of staff. The cool and self-possessed Harbord, who had risen through the ranks after enlisting as a private in 1889, soon justified his reputation as one of the army's most able officers.

EUROPE ENGULFED

On 28 June 1914, in the Bosnian capital of Sarajevo, a nineteen-year-old Bosnian assassinated Archduke Franz Ferdinand, the heir to the throne of Austria-Hungary. With considerable justification, the Austrian government blamed this terrorist act on Serb nationalism and decided to punish Serbia. Having gained Berlin's firm support, Vienna provoked a war with Serbia. Germany and Austria-Hungary hoped to confine this conflict to the Balkans and avoid triggering the alliance system that divided Europe between the Triple Alliance (Germany, Austria-Hungary, and Italy) and the Triple Entente (France, Great Britain, and Russia). This proved impossible when Russia chose to back Serbia by ordering general mobilization on 29 July. Germany's response to Russian mobilization was to declare war on Russia (1 August) and France (3 August) and invade Belgium. By 4 August, when Great Britain declared war on Germany, all of the great European powers save Italy had been drawn into this war.

The military stalemate facing Pershing in Western Europe had its roots in the first weeks of the conflict. The Great War had begun in the west in August 1914 with the French and German armies on the offensive. The French frontally assaulted the German southeastern flank in Alsace-Lorraine while Germany violated the neutrality of Belgium in an attempt to envelop the French army—the Schlieffen Plan. The German offensive through Belgium was far more successful than the reckless and easily repulsed French attack along the German frontier. The German army reached the Marne River and threatened Paris, but an Anglo-French counterattack, the First Battle of the Marne, saved the French capital. More important, it shattered German hopes for a quick victory over France and the illusion of a short war.

"The German Fleet has assaulted its jailor; but it is still in jail," was a New York newspaper's accurate assessment.

Following this German setback, each side attempted to outflank the other in what came to be called the "race to the sea." When the sea was reached and there were no more flanks to turn, the armies began to dig in. Siege warfare replaced the war of movement. For the next three years, neither side succeeded in moving its opponent's front for more than ten miles at any point, despite heavy and prolonged attacks that resulted in horrendous slaughter. The war at sea was also a standoff, which worked in favor of the British Grand Fleet. Operating a distant blockade from bases in Scotland at Scapa Flow and the village of Rosyth, the British fleet kept German surface ships from threatening the world's sea lanes. Only one great sea battle occurred during the war, the Battle of Jutland on 31 May 1916. In this clash between the Grand Fleet and the German High Seas Fleet, 259 warships were engaged. Following this indecisive sea battle, the High Seas Fleet remained bottled up for the remainder of the war. "The German Fleet has assaulted its jailor; but it is still in jail," was a New York newspaper's accurate assessment.

The war inexorably spread to other corners of the globe, drawing in other powers that included Italy, who joined the Allies, and Bulgaria and Turkey, who cast their lots with the Central Powers. With Turkey a belligerent, new theaters opened in Egypt-Palestine, Mesopotamia, and the Caucasus. Czarist Russia, beleaguered and virtually isolated, now fought on a front that stretched from the Baltic almost to the Caspian. Hoping to mobilize the Balkan states against the Central Powers and to open better communications with Russia, the British in 1915 attempted to force their way through the Dardanelles, first by an unsuccessful naval attack, then by an amphibious assault on Gallipoli. Following the failure of the Dardanelles and Gallipoli ventures, the Allies, in a quixotic attempt to save Serbia, established a base in Salonika, Greece, the beginnings of a major campaign in the Balkans.

Despite these military operations in the outlying theaters, most Anglo-French military leaders believed in 1915–1916 that the war was going to be won or lost on the western front. These "westerners," as they are popularly known, opposed any indirect approach to defeating the major enemy, Germany.

While the British expanded their small volunteer force to a mass army capable of measuring up to the Continental conscript armies, the French bore the brunt of the fighting in the west until the summer of 1916. In February 1916 the Germans, having made great gains in league with Austria-Hungary against Russia the previous year, abandoned their defensive stance in the west, concentrating on the French army. During the next ten months, the French and Germans stained the churned earth of northeastern France around the fortress town of Verdun with their blood, with casualties reaching 1 million. Fearing that the French were about to crack, the British launched a massive attack along the Somme River in July. When winter brought the inconclusive Battle of the Somme to a halt, the British had suffered almost 500,000 casualties, approximately the same number they would lose fighting Germany during all of World War II.

The year of Verdun and Somme ended with neither side enjoying a clear military advantage. The world had never witnessed such large-scale slaughter, with casualties surpassing 1.75 million for these two battles. Although the Germans maintained their forward positions in Belgium and France, they were in danger of losing the attrition war. Some 4 million French, British, and Belgain soldiers confronted approximately 2.5 million Germans on the western front. In the east, however, the Central Powers were in the ascendancy. They occupied Russian Poland, dominated southeastern Europe, and it seemed only a matter of time before the collapse of the Russian Romanov dynasty. Russia's decline, however, was roughly offset by growing war-weariness in Austria-Hungary, Allied military successes against Turkey, and the maintenance of a blockade that imposed severe hardships on the home fronts of the Central Powers. Allied plans for 1917 called for roughly simultaneous attacks on the Russian, western, and Italian fronts. Realistically, however, only the Allied forces in the west were capable of achieving a major strategical success. War-weary Italy and Russia were more likely to receive than to deliver a knockout punch.

A new French commander in chief, Robert Nivelle, rashly promised to end the military stalemate in the west with a breakthrough in twenty-four or forty-eight hours. His method was a sudden and violent attack, utilizing improved artillery tactics, especially the "rolling" or "creeping barrages," against the flanks of the huge Noyon bulge (the German-held salient in the French line). The British Expeditionary Force (BEF) was assigned the diversionary role of drawing off German reserves by an attack on Vimy Ridge. On 9 April 1917, three days after U.S. entry into the war, the BEF attacked along a broad front (the Battle of Arras). The resulting conquest of Vimy Ridge represented the greatest British success yet against the German army. The continuation of this battle into early May to assist the French, however, resulted in minor gains and heavy losses.

The world had never witnessed such large-scale slaughter.

When finally launched on 16 April, Nivelle's offensive (Second Battle of the Aisne) was a crushing disappointment, in part because of the unrealistic expectations raised by the French commander in chief. Surprise had been lost, with Parisian taxi drivers openly talking of the day the offensive was scheduled to begin. Moreover, the Germans had just eliminated their vulnerable flanks by withdrawing their forces (thereby shortening their front by some twenty-seven miles) to a much strengthened defensive system in depth, the Siegfried Position (a section of what the Allies called the Hindenburg Line). Nivelle's assault with 1.2 million troops cost him 120,000 dead, wounded, or captured. His violent artillery bombardment failed to destroy the German machine gunners, who had been spaced in depth to mow down the advancing French soldiers.

Nivelle's stubborn continuation of his offensive despite his failure to break through the German defenses demoralized his tired poilus, and a series of mutinies, beginning in late May, rocked the French army. Many soldiers, including some officers, put aside their arms and refused to advance to the front. At Missy-aux-Bois, an infantry regiment established an antiwar "government" during the first week of June. In one of the best-kept secrets of the war, however, the French were able to mask this widespread mutiny from their Allies and the Germans.

"OVER THERE"

Pershing and his staff, after a brief visit to London, arrived at Boulogne, France, on 13 June 1917. The arrival of this tiny U.S. contingent coincided with a serious downturn in Allied fortunes and growing uncertainty about the future. The fall of the Romanov dynasty had not slowed the decline of the Russian army. If anything, the March Revolution unleashed a whirlwind of change that accelerated its demise. Sir William Robertson told the British leadership that the Russian army, which had "fallen to pieces," was incapable of putting pressure on the Germans and Austrians in Europe or the Turks in Asia. As for Great Britain's other vital ally, France, that country was badly shaken by Nivelle's failure and was inclined to defer action until the Americans arrived in force. But when might that be? Could the Americans get to Europe in sufficient strength to turn the tide before it was too late?

The answer appeared to be in the negative. Major General Tom Bridges, who had accompanied the British mission to Washington in late April and May, in June told the British War Cabinet (the small inner committee created to direct the war effort when Lloyd George became prime minister) that the United States was likely to have no more than 120,000 to 150,000 men in Europe by 1 January 1918 and that the number would probably not rise beyond 500,000 by the end of the year. If Bridges' prediction proved correct, the United States would not be able to play a decisive role until 1919 at the earliest. No wonder therefore that Lord Curzon, a member of the War Cabinet lamented that this was the "most depressing statement that the cabinet had received for a long time."

Aboard the *Baltic,* Pershing and his fellow officers addressed fundamental questions about U.S. participation in the war. Among other matters, they discussed logistics and lines of supply, possible theaters of operations, the limits of cooperation with the Allies, and the timetable for introducing U.S. units into combat. The most urgent matter to be decided was the size of the AEF. Pershing's messages to the War Department were soon echoing Joffre's earlier appeal for "men, men, men." Initially, the leaders of the AEF thought in terms of an army of 1 million men, which considerably exceeded the initial U.S. draft. The AEF planners expected this force ultimately to grow to 3 million, but before the war ended Pershing was asking for 5 million soldiers, a mighty force that would have dwarfed all other armies on the western front.

The War Department, although sometimes taken aback by Pershing's accelerating manpower demands, accepted the necessity of creating a great army on foreign soil. By mid-July, when Pershing's appeal for a million men reached Washington, the General Staff had reached a similar conclusion. To project American power to Europe as quickly as possible, the General Staff had also abandoned any thought of creating an army in the United States and then shipping it intact

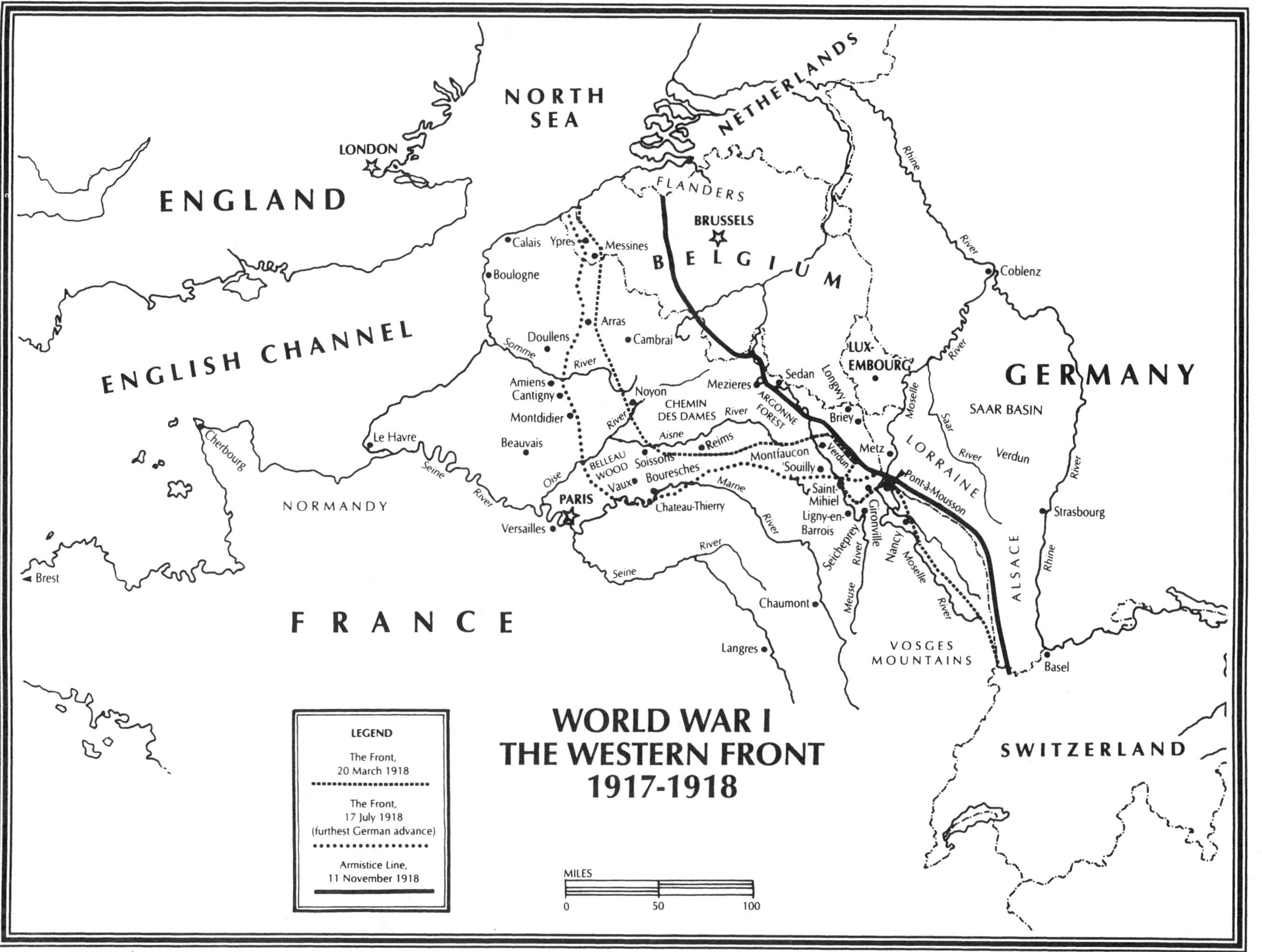

WORLD WAR I
THE WESTERN FRONT
1917-1918
ENGLAND
LONDON
NORTH SEA
ENGLISH CHANNEL
NETHERLANDS
FLANDERS
BRUSSELS
BELGIUM
GERMANY
LUX-EMBOURG
SAAR BASIN
LORRAINE
ALSACE
SWITZERLAND
FRANCE
NORMANDY
VOSGES MOUNTAINS
Calais
Ypres
Messines
Boulogne
Arras
Cambrai
Doullens
Somme
River
Amiens
Cantigny
Montdidier
Beauvais
Noyon
CHEMIN DES DAMES
Aisne
River
Le Havre
Cherbourg
Brest
Seine
River
Oise
PARIS
Versailles
BELLEAU WOOD
Vaux
Soissons
Bouresches
Chateau-Thierry
Marne
Reims
Mezieres
Sedan
ARGONNE FOREST
Longwy
Briey
Metz
Verdun
Montfaucon
Souilly
Saint-Mihiel
Ligny-en-Barrois
Seicheprey
Gironville
Pont-à-Mousson
Nancy
Moselle
Meuse
River
Chaumont
Langres
Coblenz
Rhine
River
Saar
Verdun
Strasbourg
Basel
LEGEND
The Front, 20 March 1918
The Front, 17 July 1918 (furthest German advance)
Armistice Line, 11 November 1918
MILES
0
50
100

to Europe. The tonnage shortage necessitated shipping U.S. forces piecemeal, in a continuous flow, with training on both sides of the Atlantic.

Although Pershing was a commander without an army for many months, he never thought small. His gaze remained firmly fixed on the time when he would have the military muscle to defeat the German army. His choice of a front was greatly influenced by his desire to play the decisive role in the outcome of the war. The British lobbied for an American zone at the northern end of the British front in Belgium or at the junction of the British and French armies. Pershing, however, ultimately selected Lorraine, the area between the Argonne Forest and Vosges Mountains, as the American sector. He rightly suspected the British of attempting to harness U.S. power to their own. Proximity to the BEF would increase the pressures and dangers of amalgamation with their Anglo-Saxon cousins. In addition, any U.S. force, even if operating under its own flag and commander, would inevitably be assigned a secondary role if it fought alongside the British on the seaward side of the western front or at the point where the British and French defenses joined.

Logistics also contributed to Pershing's choice of an American sector on the southern end of the western front. The war had rapidly become a war of railroads as well as of artillery. A front to the southeast of Paris enabled the AEF to utilize its own ports of supply along the southwestern French coast; a railway network, running south of Paris, promised to provide the Americans in Lorraine with less-congested although distant lines of supply.

At the beginning of September, Pershing and his fellow officers established in great secrecy ("somewhere in France") their headquarters at Chaumont, a small city in the rolling countryside of the headwaters of the Marne. While U.S. soldiers trickled across the Atlantic (the last elements of the First Division did not arrive in France until December), the Leavenworth-taught staff officers, occupying a four-story regimental barracks, turned their attention to the formulation of war-winning strategy (where to attack) and tactics (how to fight).

Pershing ordered his operations section to focus on German defenses running from Verdun to the Swiss frontier. The resulting memorandum, entitled "A Strategical Study on the Employment of the A.E.F. Against the Imperial German Government," dated 25 September 1917, decisively shaped the future U.S. role in the coalition war against Germany.

Pershing's operations staff, headed by the robust Colonel Fox Conner, was attracted to the strategic possibilities of an attack to the east and west of the fortress city of Metz. If the railway lines running laterally between the German right and left wings could be captured, the thinking went, the enemy's southern defenses would collapse, compelling the German army to retreat from northern France to eastern Belgium and perhaps even beyond the Rhine. A successful advance beyond Metz also would result in the capture of some of the enemy's important iron-ore deposits in Longwy-Briey and the coalfields of the Saar, which would cripple—or so it was believed—the German war economy.

As a prelude to this distant and extremely ambitious offensive, the operations section planned a minor offensive (with French assistance) that would take place in late 1918 to eliminate the pronounced salient of Saint-Mihiel, southwest of Metz. With the AEF's front shortened by the conquest of Saint-Mihiel and the threat of a German counterthrust from Metz neutralized, the next phase of the offensive would commence in 1919. In conjunction with other Allied attacks to the north to occupy German reserves, a massive war-winning assault by five U.S. corps (or 1,272,858 men when line of communications troops were included) would commence.

To spur his government to action, Pershing enlisted the support of the Allied commanders, and on 5 December 1917, a cablegram that reported the conclusions of an Allied military conference arrived at the War Department. The United States was asked as its minimum effort to send twenty-four divisions to France by the end of June. By autumn, if the required shipping tonnage was secured, the U.S. presence in Europe was expected to increase to thirty divisions, or five complete corps. This figure, not by chance, was precisely what Pershing's operations staff estimated would bring victory in 1919. With U.S. mobilization proceeding erratically and at a snail's pace, this request seemed unrealistic. "Is such a programme *possible*?" a shaken President Wilson asked Secretary of War Baker. Certainly the Allied generals, who had been prompted by Pershing to make their request, did not think it feasible. As late as January 1918, the French General Staff believed that it would be May 1919 before the AEF had sixteen trained divisions in Europe, with four or five of that number capable of holding a quiet sector of the front.

By European standards, U.S. divisions were unusual because of their size, approximately twice the size of German, British, and French divisions. Before the war, the U.S. Army had been built around regiments, and divisions existed only in theory or on paper. Hence, the leadership of the AEF had the freedom to experiment in the organization of the field army in Europe. Pershing's staff ultimately decided upon a large "square" division, commanded by a major general, consisting of four regiments of infantry, three regiments of artillery, fourteen machine-gun companies, one engineer regiment, one signal battalion, one troop of cavalry, and other auxiliary units. The total authorized strength, which included 17,666 rifles, was a little more than 28,000 men.

The revolution in firepower meant more emphasis on machine guns and artillery and less on infantry shock tactics.

In deciding upon these oversized divisions, the AEF planners were at odds with many German, British, and French political and military authorities who were either recommending or implementing the downsizing of their divisions. The accelerating manpower crisis of every European belligerent, of course, pressured military planners to reduce the size of divisions to maintain their number, but there was another justification for smaller divisions. The revolution in firepower meant more emphasis on machine guns and artillery and less on infantry shock tactics. The organization of the AEF, however, did not always take the increased lethality of the battlefield into consideration. The infantry-rich U.S. divisions, although approximately double the size of Allied divisions, had no greater artillery complement per division, which in effect meant that artillery was undervalued. The same could be said for machine guns.

Defenders of the large U.S. division argued that its size would enable it to sustain losses and remain in the line longer than a smaller division. Perhaps, but this did not fully take into account the morale factor. As was demonstrated later in the war, AEF divisions in heavy combat needed relief after a short time no matter what their size. Another justification was that large divisions would enable the AEF to better utilize its limited supply of regular army commanders and staff, glossing over the fact that one of the greatest weaknesses of the prewar officers corps was its lack of exposure to large military formations. It was by no means certain that doubling the responsibilities of the leadership of a division would further either its tactical or logistical effectiveness. To the contrary, the size of U.S. divisions, when combined with inexperienced officers, contributed to serious command and control breakdowns. Dubious communications and an understandable lack of faith in its inexperienced officers encouraged GHQ (General Headquarters) AEF to adopt rigid schemes of fire and maneuver at a time when the more experienced European general staffs were abandoning such rigidity and the consequent heavy loss of attacking forces.

The goal toward which the AEF leaders directed their tactics was the complete destruction of the German Imperial Army. Influenced by the American Civil War, the U.S. military elite of 1917–1918 believed in total victory—the strategy of annihilation as opposed to a limited or indirect strategy that sought a favorable peace through conquering territory or destroying enemy morale through attrition or blockade. Both the War Department General Staff and AEF planners believed in concentration and mass on the western front, which would force Germany to collect its forces there. "The contest will then narrow down to a tug-of-war like Grant had against Lee until, by means of our unlimited resources, we are enabled to force a favorable conclusion," wrote one General Staff officer in Washington in September 1917.

The U.S. war planners consequently looked with disfavor upon the "easterners," or the Allied leaders who advocated a peripheral (or "knocking away the props") strategy against Berlin. U.S. political and military leaders saw this indirect approach as being predominantly political. It might add imperial plums to the European states in the Middle East and elsewhere, but it also might prolong the war. Putting its faith in the superiority of its men and morale, the AEF leadership sought total victory through a massive assault to rupture the strongly fortified German positions. The cost in human terms was almost certain to be high if the AEF's advance across the pulverized and shell-pocked battlefields on the western front paralleled the experiences of previous Allied offensives.

In 1914 most Allied generals had begun the war with images of heroic warfare; the courage of individual soldiers was given priority over the technological revolution that dramatically altered warfare. Senior officers initially viewed battles as rigidly structured and tactically simple. Decisive results would largely be achieved through offensive spirit. Illustrative of this emphasis on the fighting qualities of the foot soldier is the following account by a British officer who observed the first day of the Battle of the Somme (1 July 1916), in which few British soldiers survived to reach the enemy trenches. British infantry, he reported to his superiors, had advanced in "admirable order" into the teeth of German artillery and machine guns. "Yet not a man wavered, broke the ranks, or attempted to come back." He had "never seen, indeed could never have imagined, such a magnificent display of gallantry, discipline and determination." As Tim Travers has astutely observed (1987): "What is striking about senior British army officers before and during the First World War was their ready acceptance of new weapons, but their emotional difficulty in coming to mental grips with the tactical and command changes implied by the new or improved technology." This emphasis on the psychological as opposed to the technical aspects of modern warfare contributed to the cult of the *offensive à l'outrance* ("offensive beyond anything else").

Before the United States entered the war, Allied generals launched repeated attacks against the much more sophisticated German defensive system. Foot soldiers were sent in waves across no-man's-land to occupy trenches that supposedly had been conquered by the artillery. The objective was to punch a hole or open a gap in the enemy defensive system. The horse soldier, which in reality had no place on a battlefield dominated by artillery, automatic weapons, and barbed wire, was expected to maintain the momentum of the advance to prevent the Germans from digging in once again. In 1914–1917, these offensives resulted in huge casualties and modest advances. The multiple German positions could not be fully penetrated and the decisive battle remained a chimera.

To end the stalemate, governments looked to scientists and engineers and mobilized the entire country for conducting war. New and vast quantities of war material were produced. High-explosive shells, rifle grenades, flamethrowers, poison gas, tanks, and airplanes, however, did not alone provide the solution to the deadlock. These weapons had to be applied intelligently. In 1917, the BEF, commanded by Sir Douglas Haig, launched four offensives—Arras, Messines, Ypres, and Cambrai—and the French one significant offensive, the disastrous Nivelle offensive on the Aisne. The results of these offensives had limited tactical success and failed to achieve their ultimate strategical goals. Nevertheless, lessons were learned. When success was achieved, it was primarily because of limited objectives for the infantry and the massive application of artillery to terrify the defenders and neutralize their machine guns and artillery. The artillery's success was not attributable to just the increased number of big guns and shells. Bombardments were now minutely orchestrated and delivered with timing and accuracy to provide cover for the advancing infantry. Robin Prior and Trevor Wilson (1992) explain how soldiers were learning to make artillery a part of a comprehensive system, with weapons ranging from heavy machine guns to poison gas to tanks. The stage was being set for victory in 1918. "This volume of weaponry," they argue, "and the development of an administrative structure capable of placing it on the battlefield in appropriate quantities and circumstances, served to produce a strike force against which the enemy ultimately could provide no effective resistance."

In their war planning, Pershing and his staff rejected the now cautious and increasingly technical Allied approach to fighting the German army. When a reporter challenged him at a press conference in the fall of 1917 as to whether he thought a breakthrough would be possible, he retorted: "Of course the western front can be broken. What are we here for?" Pershing's formula for ending the stalemate was to deploy fearless U.S. foot soldiers trained for open warfare. "An aggressive spirit must be developed until the soldier feels himself, as a bayonet fighter, invincible in battle," was the language he imposed on AEF training instructions.

Another consideration for Pershing was his fear that AEF acceptance of Allied tactics (which by necessity would give a leading role to foreign military instructors) would mean a loss of independence and a subordinate role in the fighting. In this he had the firm backing of Secretary Baker. When President Wilson's closest adviser, Colonel Edward House, expressed the fear that the AEF might repeat the costly blunders of the European generals, Baker responded by emphasizing the connection between U.S. pursuit of its own military doctrine and the maintenance of the AEF's separate "identity."

U.S. officers closer to the front proved much more adaptable to the realities of the new technology of warfare than their commander in chief. The Germans were not going to be driven from their sophisticated defensive systems by "bayonet fighters." The official doctrine of the AEF, however, never deviated from its reliance on riflemen and its advocacy of mobile warfare.

To help many U.S. officers overcome their lack of experience in modern large-scale warfare, Pershing sent them to school. At Langres, just south of this GHQ at Chaumont, he established the important General Staff College, under the direction of Brigadier General James W. ("Dad") MacAndrew, who eventually became his chief of staff. With some advice from French and British officers, the General Staff College did its best during the rapid buildup of U.S. forces in Western Europe to provide the AEF with competent staff officers.

Logistical problems as well as the handling of large bodies of troops were emphasized in the instruction of AEF officers at the school. Modern armies consumed an ever-increasing amount of war material. To distribute supplies, Pershing created a line of communications (LOC) headquarters (later called the Services of Supply, or SOS) under his direction. Almost one-third of Pershing's manpower was eventually delegated to the gigantic task of supplying the AEF with everything from tinned hash to cuspidors and condoms.

There were numerous breakdowns in the logistical support, especially during the summer of 1918. Many factors were to blame, including the insistence of the overburdened commander in chief to concern himself directly with both military and supply matters. Problems stemmed from lack of experience in logistical management as well as a rapid buildup of personnel that emphasized riflemen over stevedores and railwaymen. New leadership was also needed to head the Services of Supply. Pressed by the War Department in July to end the bottleneck of supplies, primarily at ports between Brest and Bordeaux, Pershing chose Harbord as chief of staff of the SOS.

"I am his man," Harbord had once noted about Pershing. "He can send me to hell if he wants to."

Harbord was selected in part for his loyalty. "I am his man," he had once noted about Pershing. "He can send me to hell if he wants to." Harbord reorganized the SOS, and his hands-on style improved the delivery of supplies from the ports to the trenches. During his first one hundred days, he spent fifty-five nights on a special train touring the AEF supply lifeline. Ports competed with each other in unloading cargo in a contest called the "Race to Berlin." Army bands played ragtime music to increase the tempo of the work of stevedore companies unloading ships. French ports were modernized, railway communications improved, and vast supply centers constructed. By the end of the war, 670,000 men were allocated to provisioning U.S. forces. Logistics improved, but the war ended before the SOS reached maturity and its full potential.

The Medical Department of the army had an important advantage over the SOS. Because most U.S. troops were not in combat until the last 110 days of the war, the Medical Department had time to provide for beds, evacuation trains, and operating facilities to care for the wounded. Working closely with the Red Cross and other civilian health agencies, the medical services were reasonably well prepared for the entry of the AEF into heavy combat during the last months of the war. The Medical Department's record in caring for the sick was also commendable. Compared with that of the Civil War, the mortality rate among Americans in World War I from disease was lowered from sixty-five to fifteen per thousand. The catastrophic influenza epidemic of 1918 that affected all armies, however, took a great toll of American lives. A soldier was almost as likely to die from disease as from gas, bullet, or shell. In the U.S. Army, influenza and pneumonia claimed almost as many victims (46,992) as combat with the Germans.

As Pershing and his staff at Chaumont made plans for the organization, training, and provision of an independent army capable of launching limited operations in late 1918 as the prelude for a major, war-winning campaign in Lorraine in 1919, the Allied position became extremely precarious. The war-weary French army, worn thin by more than three years of hard fighting, lost its offensive spirit. The Italian army, which had suffered heavy losses with little gain in eleven unsuccessful attacks in the mountainous terrain of Isonzo, was shattered by an Austro-German surprise attack (Battle of Caporetto) on 24 October 1917. French and British divisions had to be rushed south of the Alps to save Italy from being driven from the war.

More serious than either the setbacks to Italy and France was Russia's total collapse. On 7 November 1917 the Bolsheviks stormed the Winter Palace in Petrograd, overthrowing the democratic-minded Provisional Government. The triumph of communism in Russia and the subsequent demise of the eastern front dramatically altered the strategic landscape. Germany, by concentrating its forces in Western Europe, might achieve a numerical superiority on the western front for the first time since 1914. Conversely, Great Britain, which had become the cornerstone of the alliance after Nivelle's failed offensive, was nearing the end of its resources. The BEF offensives during the last half of 1917 had maintained pressure on the German army, but at a price that the British government believed it could no longer sustain. As winter led to a lull in the fighting, the strategic initiative passed into the hands of the Germans. U.S. participation perhaps offered hope for the future, but only if the flow of American manpower crossing the Atlantic substantially increased and if these fresh and unbloodied soldiers entered into the line as soon as possible.

Tasker H. Bliss, who in September had replaced Scott as chief of the General Staff in Washington, captured the increasingly desperate Allied mood and American predicament. "It is pitiful to see the undercurrent of feeling that the hopes of Europe have in the United States," he wrote his wife in a letter from London on 8 November, "pitiful because it will be so long before we can really do anything, although the very crisis seems to be at hand."

The AEF was not yet a factor in the war and would apparently not be for some time. After occupying a quiet section of French trenches near Nancy, elements of the First Division fired the first American shots of the war on 23 October 1917. In early November three

Americans, Corporal James Bethel Gresham, Private Thomas F. Enright, and Private Merle D. Hay, were killed in a German trench raid, a portent of the many thousands to follow.

Mobilization on the home front during the first months of the war paralleled the disappointing projection of U.S. power abroad. This was to be expected, given the enormity of the task of rapidly moving from a peace to a war economy and creating a great army from almost nothing. Raw draftees and volunteers flocked to hastily built camps and cantonments, where frequently they did not receive adequate training, equipment, or even uniforms. At Camp Funston, Kansas, recruits attired in blue overalls drilled with wooden rifles. The shortage of officers was especially acute. Some 200,000 officers were required to lead the U.S. Army, which grew to 4 million by the end of the war, but there were only 18,000 regular and National Guard officers available when the war began. Thousands of "ninety-day wonders" were soon turned out by officer-training camps, many of which were established in colleges and universities across the United States.

One training-camp poster warned,

"A German bullet is cleaner than a whore."

Particular attention was devoted to clean living for those about to embark on what Theodore Roosevelt had called the "great adventure." Secretary of the Navy Daniels argued that "men must live straight if they would shoot straight." The War Department closed down bars near military bases in an effort to create "sin-free zones." Storyville, the legally established district for prostitution in New Orleans, was closed on 12 November 1917 because of Daniels' concern for its influence on a nearby naval institution. Men in uniform were forbidden to buy a drink. Sex, as well as temperance, engaged the interest of those responsible for preparing Americans to fight in a foreign war. Sex education and prophylactics were provided the trainees. One training-camp poster warned, "A German bullet is cleaner than a whore."

As young Americans prepared for war, U.S. industry failed to provide them with modern weapons. Although thousands of tanks were ordered, virtually none of them reached the AEF by the armistice. The AEF manned 2,250 artillery pieces on the western front, only about 100 of U.S. manufacture. Similarly, aircraft production fell far short of expectations, with no U.S. combat airplanes arriving in Europe before the war's end. Even machine gun production was slow in developing. Eventually John M. Browning was responsible for a series of superior .30-caliber automatic weapons, the water-cooled heavy machine gun M1917, the air-cooled light machine gun M1919A1, and the Browning automatic rifle M1918, but none of these Brownings were available to the AEF at the front until September 1918. Most of the rapid-fire weapons of the AEF were of French production.

The breakdown in industrial mobilization with the most serious consequences, however, was the chaos in the U.S. shipbuilding program. The raising of an army received far more attention in Washington than its sea transport. "The United States shipbuilding programme had broken down very badly," British Prime Minister Lloyd George gravely informed his colleagues in early December 1917, "and it would be impossible to get the American troops over in American ships at the rate we had thought possible a short time ago." In Washington, Bliss was telling Baker the same thing. "The one all-absorbing necessity now," he told the administration in mid-December, "is soldiers with which to beat the enemy in the field, and ships to carry them." If U.S. arms were unable to play a vital role in the fighting in 1918, Bliss warned, there might be no campaign of 1919. Instead of a victory parade for the AEF, Pershing's forces might be incarcerated behind German barbed wire.

The U.S. desire to maintain the identity of its forces and play a decisive role in the defeat of the enemy created division within the anti-German coalition as 1917 came to an end. Frustrated over Pershing's program of building an independent U.S. army, and fearful that Germany might win the war in 1918, the Allies revived the amalgamation question, which the French and British missions in Washington had been forced to drop because of U.S. resistance in April and May. The French and especially the British (who had no U.S. forces in their sector) now made compelling arguments that the only practicable method of getting Americans into combat by the spring and summer (when the Germans were expected to make a bid for victory) was through "brigading," or amalgamation of U.S. units with French and British divisions.

Amalgamation remained anathema to Chaumont. Pressed by the Allies in December, however, the U.S. administration emphasized to Pershing on 18 December that the identity of U.S. forces was secondary to the utilization of U.S. troops to save the alliance from military defeat. At the same time, Wilson continued to give Pershing total control over the employment of U.S. military power in Western Europe. Pershing alone was responsible for interpreting whether a "critical" military situation existed and determining the manner of U.S. cooperation with the Anglo-French forces.

As events were soon to demonstrate, Pershing was prepared to see the British driven into the sea and Paris conquered before he allowed any military emergency to alter fundamentally his plans to create an independent force as soon as possible with its own zone of operations and strategic goals. When his staff reviewed their operations plans in response to Washington's 18 December note, it emphasized that the U.S. 1919 offensive in Lorraine offered the best opportunity to bring the war to a conclusion. The introduction of U.S. forces piecemeal into battle in 1918, on the other hand, would undermine the gathering of a powerful U.S. strike force. Moreover, if U.S. units smaller than a division cooperated with the British or French, the necessary development of higher U.S. commanders and staffs would be undermined as well.

The British, who had borne the brunt of the fighting during the second half of 1917, were especially anxious to have access to American manpower to keep Haig's forces up to strength. On 9 January, Robertson began direct negotiations with Pershing, trying to persuade him to place a U.S. infantry regiment (or three battalions) with British divisions for training. He used two main arguments. First, maximum use could be made of the scarce available tonnage if the Americans shipped only infantry battalions and machine gun companies instead of full divisions with their artillery, engineers, typists, cooks, and so on. Second, Americans could come to the rescue of the Allies sooner if they fought as part of mature Allied military organizations, with their experienced and well-organized logistical, artillery, and staff support. None of Pershing's generals had ever commanded even a brigade in action.

Robertson further contended that the Germans, who already had either crippled or defeated Italy, Russia, and France, would do the same to the BEF in 1918 if U.S. assistance was not immediately forthcoming. Pershing was unmoved by these arguments. He was, however, painfully aware that the United States did not have the ships to bring its forces to Europe. Robertson promised to find additional shipping for the transport of brigades (but not complete divisions). Without a substantial increase in British shipping, the AEF would never reach its goal of having 1 million men in Europe during the second half of 1918. Consequently, Pershing gave tentative support to Robertson's plan to transport 150 U.S. battalions of infantry and machine gunners in British bottoms, but he had no intention of allowing these Americans to be introduced into combat under the Union Jack.

Pershing's concession to Robertson could not have come at a worse time for the Wilson administration, which was under attack in Congress in January for the snail-like pace of mobilization. Employing U.S. troops in foreign divisions would offer dramatic proof of the charges that the U.S. war machine was sputtering badly. Wilson warned his military leaders abroad not to allow any shipping negotiations with the British to interfere with the building of an independent AEF.

Fortified by Wilson's suspicions of the British, Pershing backtracked. He told Robertson that he would accept only the transport of American divisions to be placed in the British sector for training. In tangled and heated discussions, Pershing got his way, and the British government reluctantly accepted a plan to transport six divisions instead of 150 battalions in British ships to train with the BEF.

The worrisome question remained of whether the United States could play a military role, independent or otherwise, before it was too late. The War Department's thirty-division program was far from being realized. Nine months after entering the war, the United States had 175,000 troops in France, the vast majority of them unprepared for combat. Only four divisions, in various stages of readiness, had been organized: the First Division (Major General Robert L. Bullard), Second Division (Major General Omar Bundy), Twenty-sixth Division (Major General Clarence R. Edwards), and Forty-second Division (Major General Charles T. Menoher).

Discouraged by his negotiations with Pershing, Robertson informed his government in January that "America's power to help us win the war—that is to help us to defeat the Germans in battle—is a very weak reed to lean upon at present, and will be so for a very long time to come unless she follows up her words with actions much more practical and energetic than any she has yet taken."

THE GERMAN BID FOR VICTORY

The immense cost to attacking armies had discouraged many Allied military and political leaders from thinking big; instead, emphasis was now being placed on the defense until the Americans arrived in great numbers. The U.S. presence in Europe also influenced German strategists, but in a quite different way. Although the Germans had launched only one major offensive (Verdun) in the west during the past two and a half years, their strategy in 1918 was directed toward an all-out offensive to win the war before the AEF became a factor. In 1914, Berlin had failed in its gamble to smash France before Russia could threaten in the east; now the German high command gambled again, committing the country's last reserves in the hope that it could defeat the British and French before the Yanks came to the rescue. General Erich von Ludendorff, the de facto commander of the German army, and the military party rejected any thought of seeking peace negotiations while the military situation favored Germany. Instead, Germany's leaders sought to guarantee their country's hegemony in Europe through victory in the west in 1918.

To succeed where others had failed, the Germans placed their faith in massive reinforcements (nearly a million men) from the moribund eastern front and on innovative tactics that had been developed in successful attacks in Russia at Riga and in Italy at Caporetto. Unlike Haig, who had embraced dazzling distant objectives in Flanders in 1917 without the tactical innovation to achieve them, the Germans placed primary emphasis on new methods to achieve a breakthrough.

These new tactics have been aptly described as infiltration tactics. As opposed to linear tactics with fixed objectives, German troops were trained for a more flexible and responsive form of warfare. To achieve a deep penetration and the disruption of enemy communications, emphasis was placed on surprise; short but violent preliminary bombardments in depth with a mix of high-explosive shells and mustard, chlorine, and phosgene gas; coordination of artillery and advancing infantry; and small-unit actions. Recognizing the dominance of rapid-fire weapons, riflemen were given a subordinate role, that of protecting the machine gun.

Ludendorff's war-winning strategy called for a series of blows against the Allies to achieve victory in the west. Strangely, the ultimate political and military objectives of his attack remain vague. Ludendorff sought to escape trench warfare, but his strategic goals were undefined. Rather, he aimed at shattering the spirit of the enemy, especially the British.

The superiority of German forces on the western front in early 1918 put the anti-German coalition in jeopardy. The British naturally thought of defending

During World War I, armies began using airplanes for attack as well as reconnaissance. These American pilots are preparing military biplanes in France in August 1918 for an aerial raid on German trenches and cities. (National Archives)

their escape and supply route, the English Channel ports; the French gave first priority to the defense of Paris. A unified command, especially the handling of Allied reserves, was more vital in defense than it had been when the Allies had the strategical initiative. In response to the Italian debacle at Caporetto, the Allies at Rapallo, Italy, had created the Supreme War Council (SWC) on 7 November 1917. Located at Versailles, the SWC, consisting of political representatives of the Allies who met periodically and assisted by a body of military advisers in permanent session, represented an attempt to unify Allied war policy. President Wilson and the U.S. military, who believed that the war would be won or lost on the western front, enthusiastically supported the principle of unity of command in Western Europe but withheld full cooperation. Wilson, determined to keep his political distance from the Allies, refused to appoint a permanent political representative, instead allowing Colonel House to represent him on occasion. Bliss was appointed the U.S. permanent military representative at Versailles.

Efforts to give the military representatives at Versailles control of the Allied reserves, however, broke down completely. An executive committee, chaired by French General Ferdinand Foch, was created, but the British and French field commanders argued that they had no spare reserves to delegate to this body. The Americans, they insisted, were the only effective Allied reserve. Pershing, of course, had already stated in unmistakable terms his opposition to using his men as replacements for the reduced French and British divisions. As the Allies squabbled, the Germans methodically advanced their preparations for a massive attack against the British Fifth and Third armies from the Somme to Cambrai.

On 21 March 1918 at 4:40 in the morning, the earth began to vibrate when some six-thousand German big guns unleashed a torrent of steel and poison gas against the British defenses. Under a dense morning fog, the German infantry broke into and through the British defenses of the Fifth Army. Within twenty-four hours, the Germans captured about 140 square miles. The Fifth Army began to disintegrate. On the first day of the German offensive, Haig requested three French divisions as reinforcement, and on the second day requested twenty. The French, however, fearing for the safety of Paris, refused to join the battle.

Elated by his success, Ludendorff attempted to drive a wedge between the British and French armies. Such a rupture would, in all likelihood, spell doom for the Allies. On 26 March, the British and French held a desperate council of war at the small town of Doullens. To provide for a unified response to the German attack, especially in the handling of reserves, Foch was given the authority to coordinate military operations on the western front. Although the Doullens agreement did not cover the AEF, Pershing went to Foch's headquarters on 28 March and made a dramatic pledge of immediate American support: "Infantry, artillery, aviation, all that we have are yours; use them as you wish. More will come, in numbers equal to requirements." A more concrete U.S. commitment to the Allied cause came several days later at the Beauvais Conference on 3 April 1918, when the AEF was officially placed under Foch's command. Pershing, with his course for an independent U.S. force firmly charted, wanted it that way. "I think this resolution should include the American Army," he insisted. "The arrangement is to be in force, as I understand it, from now on, and the American Army will soon be ready to function as such and should be included as an entity like the British and French armies."

Pershing stated in unmistakable terms his opposition to using his men as replacements for the reduced French and British divisions.

The Beauvais Agreement extended Foch's authority to control of inter-Allied strategy on the western front. The field commanders, however, were specifically given the right to appeal to their governments if they believed an order from Foch placed their forces in danger. Bliss, alarmed by the mischief-making potential of this condition, argued unsuccessfully against the right of appeal. Foch's powers after Beauvais should not be exaggerated. He was more persuader in chief than commander in chief. Certainly his position cannot be compared to that of General Dwight D. Eisenhower during World War II. There was no Allied joint chiefs of staff or supreme headquarters for Allied forces to coordinate strategy. Foch relied on his own staff, and future strategy was developed through personal diplomacy with Pershing, General Henri Philippe Pétain (who had replaced Nivelle), and Haig.

Pershing's "all that we have" pledge of 28 March initially had little practical effect. He had neither planes nor artillery of his own, only men. Aware of the seriousness of the situation, he had been prepared to put all four of his divisions in the line as a corps, which would be an important first step toward creating a separate army. General Pétain, however, argued that such an inexperienced force holding its own section of the line would serve as a magnet for the Germans, and he was right. Although the First Division was moved from Lorraine to Picardy, U.S. divisions were not committed to the battle. The only Americans to engage the enemy were two engineer companies, which found themselves in the path of the German advance while engaging in railway work behind the British Fifth Army. The Americans suffered seventy-eight casualties.

Meanwhile, the German advance slowed to a crawl, unable to maintain its momentum across the battle-scarred ground. The brilliant tactical success, a forty-mile advance in eight days, was not matched by a strategic victory as British and French resistance began to stiffen, but the German onslaught took its toll on Allied, especially British, manpower. The BEF lost 38,512 men (more than half of these taken prisoner) on 21 March, and casualties, excluding sick, reached 115,868 by the end of the first week in April. In sharp contrast, American combat deaths after one year in the war equalled 163. On 7 April, Haig reported to his government that "in the absence of reinforcements, which I understand do not exist, . . . the situation will, therefore, become critical unless American troops fit for immediate incorporation in my Divisions arrive in France in the meantime."

The War Office was more emotional in its request for assistance. Following the 21 March attack, the U.S. military attaché in London was told, "For God's sake get your men over!" Faced with the prospect that Germany might triumph on the Continent, the U.S. administration handsomely responded to these appeals. When the British diverted additional shipping through further sacrifices on their home front, Wilson agreed to send 120,000 infantry and machine gunners a month and actually did considerably better than that. The employment of these Americans, however, continued to provoke controversy.

The British and French expected these raw soldiers to be fed into their divisions for training. Pershing, however, skillfully (and not without guile) worked to keep any Americans training with the Allies organized as divisions, which would enable him to develop staff and command. He also sought to keep U.S. units from going into the line on any active front, partly because of the lack of training of many doughboys. In some cases, Americans were being rushed across the Atlantic only days after they had been inducted. Another consideration for Pershing was his fear that U.S. units, once they took their place in the line on an active Allied front, would be difficult to reclaim for the formation of an independent U.S. army.

Ludendorff continued to provide the British and French with their best argument for amalgamation. With its initial drive stalled, the German army shifted its attention to Ypres salient in the north of the British sector. On 9 April, twenty-seven German divisions tore a great gap in the British defenses and pushed forward three and a half miles on the first day. If anything, the British were more anxious than they had been three weeks earlier, because if this German advance carried as far as the one launched on 21 March, the channel ports would be endangered. In desperate fighting the BEF prevented the Germans from capturing their vital arteries, but it was a near thing. While the outcome of this great battle was still uncertain, Lloyd George cabled Washington: "We can do no more than we have done. It rests with America to win or lose the decisive battle of the war." The British insisted that the United States abandon its efforts to create an independent army in order to save the alliance from decisive defeat.

Under intense pressure, Pershing bent—but not by much. Opposed to feeding battalions into the Allied armies, he held out for shipping divisions of infantry and machine gun units, minus their artillery. He was prepared to place temporarily these disembarking divisions with Allied forces for training. Angered by Pershing's continued reluctance to fall in with Allied desires for amalgamation, Foch demanded to know at a 1 May meeting of the SWC whether the United States was prepared to see the French driven beyond the Loire. Pershing answered without hesitation, "Yes, I am willing to take the risk. Moreover, the time may come when the American Army will have to stand the brunt of this war, and it is not wise to fritter away our resources in this manner."

DRESS REHEARSAL: CANTIGNY, CHÂTEAU-THIERRY, AND BELLEAU WOOD

The Allies might take issue with Pershing's utilization of American manpower, but they had no complaints about the dramatically increased flow of U.S. troops across the Atlantic. The heightened German menace and increased British assistance in shipping coincided with new leadership for the General Staff in the War Department. In late January, Baker asked Pershing to send his chief of artillery, Peyton C. March, to serve as chief of the General Staff in Washington. March was a tough, no-nonsense soldier who made an immediate impact. The lights literally went on: Before March's arrival, General Staff officers normally did not work on Sunday or at night. March ordered that for the duration of the war the offices of the General Staff would be lit at all hours—and occupied by staff officers long into the evening. His reorganization of the army included the creation of an air service, tank corps, and chemical-warfare service. He attempted to eliminate tension between the regular army, National Guard, and national army (or draftees) by eliminating all distinctions between these forces.

March's most vital contribution to the war effort was increasing the flow of men to Europe. "I am going to get the men to France if they have to swim," he exclaimed. In April the monthly shipment of soldiers to Europe exceeded 100,000 for the first time, the beginning of a massive transport of troops that would number 1,788,488 while March was wartime chief of the General Staff. The carrying capacity of the transports was increased by putting tiers of bunks all the way to the ceiling; hammocks and slung bunks were placed in passageways and mess halls. They moved to Europe in convoys of packed transports, three men to a bunk, sleeping in shifts. Amazingly, not a single soldier was lost to a submarine attack during the eastward transatlantic voyage. The accelerated U.S. commitment to the western front, with the inevitable snafus because of haste, served to exaggerate the inexperience of the army's leadership. Divisions arrived without essential personnel to make them operational. Cooks and supply clerks might not kill Germans, but they were almost as essential to a modern army as riflemen and artillerymen. An additional problem was that the War Department rushed many raw soldiers across, men who had never fired a rifle or tried on a gas mask, much less experienced hostile fire.

"I am going to get the men to France if they have to swim," March exclaimed.

To demonstrate the validity of creating an independent U.S. force over all else, Pershing concentrated his energies on developing the First Division (the Big Red One) into a superior fighting organization. This was no easy task. Most of the U.S. soldiers knew little of modern war or life in the military. On 20 April 1918, the AEF commander had been dismayed when the Twenty-sixth (Yankee) Division, occupying a supposedly quiet section of the front on the Saint-Mihiel salient, suffered 669 casualties when attacked. This engagement at Seicheprey was the largest thus far for the Yanks, and the results raised questions about the competence of American leadership.

Seicheprey encouraged Pershing to redouble his efforts to make the first U.S. offensive of the war a clear success. "Our people today are hanging expectant upon your deeds," he told the officers of the First Division. "Our future part in this conflict depends upon your action. You are going forward and your conduct will be an example for succeeding units of our army." He selected Major General Robert L. Bullard, who had had combat experience in the Philippines, as the commander of the Big Red One. Seasoned by a winter in the trenches, the First Division was thought to be sound defensively. Given its inexperience in logistics and administration, however, its offensive ability remained in doubt. As April began, the First Division conducted its last exercise in open warfare. The division then marched to the front to join the French First Army. Its objective was Cantigny, a small village some five kilometers west of Montdidier, the site of the deepest penetration of the German 21 March attack.

Lieutenant Colonel George C. Marshall, Jr., an operations officer for the First Division, and Brigadier General Charles P. Summerall, the division's artillery commander, served as the primary planners for the assault, which was conceived as a limited, setpiece battle involving a reinforced U.S. regiment (about four thousand men). This operation was reminiscent of "bite and hold" operations favored by some Allied officers in 1916–1917, as opposed to ambitious attacks aimed at breakthrough and distant objectives.

The planners of the operation made meticulous preparations, building a model Cantigny behind the front and launching mock infantry attacks. Surprise and artillery domination were thought (correctly) to be the formula for success. About 200,000 shells were amassed. A short preliminary bombardment was scheduled to be at its most intense just before the Americans left their trenches. The infantry was taught to advance within fifty to seventy-five yards of the exploding shells of the creeping or rolling barrage as it preceded them across no-man's-land. The planners also emphasized counterbattery fire. No amount of training, of course, could truly prepare the members of the Twenty-eighth Regiment for the hellish conditions of trench warfare that they were about to experience first-hand.

H-hour was 6:40 A.M. on 28 May. Huddled in their jump-off trenches, the doughboys, all freshly shaved, were each equipped with 220 rounds, two hand grenades, one rifle grenade, two water canteens, chewing gum, and emergency rations. Their rifles and bayonets represented their only American-made weapons. The tanks, aircraft, flamethrowers, big guns, and trench mortars were foreign-made. Heartened by the massive artillery support and spurred on by their officers, the men of the Twenty-eighth Regiment easily took Cantigny. Then the major fight began as the Americans faced violent counterattacks and German artillery. The Americans lost fifty men in taking the village, a thousand in holding it.

Pershing was elated by the Cantigny success. The Americans, after repulsing six or seven German counterattacks, now held a village that the French previously had taken and lost twice. He wired the War Department: "It is my firm conviction that our troops are the best in Europe and our staffs the equal of any." The Americans had indeed fought hard and well. They had without question proven their courage in their first major test of wills with the Imperial German Army. Too much should not, however, be made of the first U.S. battle—and victory—of the war. Fourteen months after the United States entered the war, four thousand U.S. soldiers had captured a village in France. Meanwhile, battles of far greater magnitude and importance were taking place elsewhere on the western front in May and June. Much of the French artillery and air support in fact had been withdrawn from Cantigny after the first day to be utilized elsewhere.

One day before the battle for Cantigny began, the Germans launched their third great offensive of 1918. This time the German storm broke upon the French Sixth Army in the Chemin des Dames sector in Champagne. Ludendorff, having dealt two sledgehammer blows in March and April against the BEF, was becoming desperate. His forces had been depleted without decisive effect. Meanwhile, the War Department had sent 117,202 Americans to Europe in April and was in the process of sending 244,207 in May. Ludendorff planned to launch a diversionary attack against the French to weaken the BEF by drawing French reserves southward. Then he would once again seek to defeat the British in Flanders.

In its initial phase, the German attack proved to be the most successful offensive yet on the western front. On the first day, gray-clad troops covered an amazing thirteen miles in one giant leap. The situation quickly became extremely precarious for the Allies as the enemy marched across open country. Within a week the Germans were halfway to Paris, standing on the Marne, near Chateau-Thierry. Panic reigned among Parisians. Bliss requisitioned trucks and prepared to abandon his offices at Versailles if necessary, and Pershing issued secret orders to plan for the evacuation of his headquarters at Chaumont. Fortunately, although this was by no means clear at the time to the Allies, the German advance was grinding to a halt. Mesmerized by his dramatic success, Ludendorff had attempted to exploit the breakthrough with fresh reserves. His troops, supplied by only one railway line, however, were soon running out of supplies. His forty-mile advance served to exhaust his forces, leaving them in an exposed and indefensible salient.

The Supreme War Council met in a crisis atmosphere in Paris on 1 June. Despite the recent U.S. success at Cantigny, the Allied leaders emotionally pressed Pershing to abandon for the immediate future the creation of a separate army, but he proved to be as intractable as ever about amalgamation. When the British prime minister threatened to go over his head to President Wilson, Pershing retorted: "Refer it to the president and be damned. I know what the president will do. He will simply refer it back to me for recommendation and I will make to him the same recommendation as I have made here today." Pershing was, of course, eager to assist the Allies in their crisis, which ultimately threatened the destruction of his forces—but only on his own terms. He ordered forward the two U.S. divisions closest to the battle, the Second and Third, commanded respectively by Bundy and Joseph T. Dickman. Conveyed by trucks the first Americans, two companies of the Seventh Machine Gun Battalion, Third Division, reached the battlefield on 31 May, taking up a position to defend the bridges across the Marne at Château-Thierry. Infantry began to arrive the next day. The Third Division was soon dug in along a ten-mile front astride the Marne River.

Meanwhile, on 1 June, the Second Division (which included a marine brigade), took up a defensive position on the Metz-Paris highway, west of Château-Thierry. The German offensive had lost its momentum when the Yanks arrived, but this division was still the first unit to hold its ground against the German onslaught. The Americans not only stood against the advance units of Ludendorff's forces, they assumed the offensive. On 6 June, the marines began a twenty-day battle with a twin attack west of Belleau Wood (Hill 142) and the village of Bouresches, including a nearby section of the wood. Hampered by poor artillery support and linear tactics (advancing in waves), the marine brigade suffered heavy losses. The 1,087 casualties represented the bloodiest day in Marine Corps history until Tarawa twenty-five years later. The marines fought their way into Belleau Wood, an attacker's nightmare with its heavy woods, immense boulders, and dense undergrowth. Short of food and water, dirty, under constant gas and artillery attack, the Americans launched repeated attacks to dislodge the Germans. On 26 June the marines finally emerged on the other side of the wood. A terse message arrived at headquarters: "Woods now U.S. Marine Corps entirely."

The marine brigade (Second Division) had won the respect of the Germans as well as a piece of French real estate, later renamed "Bois de la Brigade de Marine," but the cost had been great—5,200 casualties, or more than half of the brigade's strength. The reality of war struck home, not just for the U.S. marines, but for the army brigade (Second Division) that had captured the village of Vaux and for their superior commander who had ordered them into the line—some to their death.

Pershing was moved by the sacrifice of his men. Visiting a surgical ward, he stopped by the bed of a young soldier recuperating from an operation. The soldier apologized for not saluting. Pershing, whose reputation as a martinet was well deserved, noticed that the soldier's right arm was missing. "No," he said, gently touching the young man, "It's I that should salute you."

Again, the U.S. role at this stage of the war should not be exaggerated. Of much greater consequence than the capture of the village of Vaux and Belleau Wood was the blunting of the fourth German offensive. The Germans had won three tactical victories in 1918, but at a cost of 600,000 casualties. Ludendorff now attempted to improve his vulnerable position in the Marne salient through an offensive along a twenty-mile front from Montdidier to Noyon. His attack on 9 June resulted in heavy losses and disappointing gains. On 13 June he called off the attack. He was fast running out of time. The arrival of the Americans signaled doom if he could not bring the war to a successful conclusion soon.

A year and two months after declaring war, the United States, at Cantigny, Château-Thierry, and Belleau Wood, was finally entering the fray with tens of thousands more soldiers moving toward the front. Pershing, elated by the success of U.S. forces, believed that future of the war belonged to the AEF. "The Allies are done for," he wrote House on 19 June, "and the only thing that will hold them (especially France) in the war will be the assurance that we have force enough to assume the initiative. To this end we must bend every possible energy, so that we may not only assume the offensive, but do so with sufficient force to end the war next year at the latest."

Believing that the future of the alliance was in his hands, Pershing began maneuvering to collect most of his divisions in one place to form an independent force. Because of his agreement with the British (which had provided him with the necessary tonnage to accelerate the transport of his forces), all of his divisions—except for one coming across in April, May, and early June—ten in all, were stationed behind the British front, where they were fed and equipped by the British. The only exception was the African-American Ninety-second Division. As Lord Milner, the British secretary for war, expressed it to Pershing, to avoid "a good deal of administrative trouble," the British War Office had asked Pershing and the War Department not to send them black soldiers. Hence, the Ninety-second was temporarily assigned to the French, who, unlike the British, had long employed soldiers such as the Moroccans from their African colonies in the line. When the United States entered the war, W. E. B. Du Bois, a leader of the NAACP, urged blacks to support their country. "If this is our country, then this is our war," he asserted. Almost 400,000 U.S. Afro-Americans participated in World War I "to make the world safe for democracy."

Most blacks who served in France had whites as superior officers and frequently were handed shovels instead of rifles.

Most blacks who served in France had whites as superior officers and frequently were handed shovels instead of rifles, serving as laborers behind the lines instead of as combat soldiers. The Ninety-second Division, however, played a role in the Meuse-Argonne offensive. Three of its four regiments fought well. The 368th Infantry Regiment did not, falling apart on the battlefield. The racial prejudice of the white officers of this regiment perhaps played the major role in the disintegration of part of this unit in the Argonne Forest. What is certain is that this incident unfairly brought into question the combat effectiveness of black men and their officers. Many blacks won the Croix de Guerre, but no black soldier received the U.S. Medal of Honor. An effort was made to right this wrong in 1991, when President George Bush awarded posthumously the Medal of Honor to corporal Freddie Stowers, a South Carolina farm worker, who was mortally wounded in an assault against a German position on 28 September 1918.

To an even greater extent than that of blacks, the role of women in the war was limited by the prevailing attitudes toward their proper role in society. Still, women had never before participated on so wide a scale in a U.S. conflict. Perhaps as many as a million women were employed in war work, but too frequently their employment proved to be restricted and for only as long as the war lasted. The Women's Committee of the Council of National Defense was created in 1917; women made bandages, served as hostesses at canteens, and provided similar types of volunteer work. Some women went overseas, for the most part as volunteers in France for such service organizations as the YMCA. A handful of women served with the AEF as telephone operators or nurses. The U.S. Navy enlisted eleven thousand women during the war.

Ironically, one of the few occasions when Pershing allowed true amalgamation was in the case of black soldiers. Four black regiments, who arrived without their brigade and divisional organizations and could not be formed as expected into the Ninety-third Division, fought as part of French divisions until the armistice. Pershing, however, was determined that this would be the exception rather than the general rule. Although Americans had thus far fought in small units and in limited engagements, Pershing was now in a hurry to form large military formations.

Pershing had the strong backing of his political superiors in Washington in his attempt to magnify the U.S. role in the war. On 7 July 1917, Baker wrote him a confidential and personal note that stressed two points: "1. I want the Germans beaten, hard and thoroughly—a military victory. 2. I want you to have the honor of doing it." President Wilson was equally determined that U.S. arms play a decisive role in the war. Without a prominent military role, he feared that he would not have the necessary leverage at the peace conference to impose his new world order upon his war partners.

On 10 July, before receiving Baker's personal letter, Pershing met with Foch. He made it clear that he expected soon to have his own army, front, and strategic objectives. Lorraine in the south was Pershing's first choice for a theater, but he was prepared to settle for establishing the nucleus of a U.S. force near the Marne salient, where the German threat was still great and where he already had his best divisions.

To give the AEF the means to victory, he continued to escalate his demands on Washington for men. He now asked for more than a threefold increase in the thirty division program he had requested at the end of 1917. He pressed the War Department to provide him with the impossible—one hundred divisions in Western Europe by 1919. The Allies, fearing a German victory during the first half of 1918, had also suggested this number, which could mean a force of as many as 5 million men if replacements for casualties and SOS troops were included. This would have meant the creation of a U.S. force the equal of two hundred Allied or German divisions at full strength. With most of the French, British, and German divisions much below their authorized strength, one hundred U.S. divisions would actually be comparable to three hundred or more divisions of the Allies or Germans. Suffice it to say that such an elephantine U.S. force would have trampled underfoot any German force in 1919, but such a massive force was difficult to raise and train and impossible to supply across the "bridge of ships."

March made every effort to give Pershing sufficient manpower for victory. He told the Senate Military Affairs Committee on 7 August that the military stalemate could only be broken through weight of numbers. He also proclaimed in August, "We are going to win the war if it takes every man in the United States." To give meaning to this sentiment, Congress extended the draft age down to eighteen and up to forty-five, although drafting eighteen-year-olds was not popular. The best that March thought that the War Department could actually achieve was an eighty-division program by 1919. Behind these cold numbers and fighting words and actions was an horrific thought. If Pershing's predictions of his manpower needs were proven correct by events, the result promised to be U.S. casualties unmatched by any of the country's prior conflicts.

The War Department's realism on the number of divisions that could be transported and supplied contributed to a growing gulf between the General Staff in Washington and GHQ AEF. Distance, differing perspectives, and personalities explain this friction to a degree, but the conflict also had its roots in an unresolved institutional question. Who was supreme—March as chief of the General Staff or Pershing as commander in chief of the AEF? This power struggle between the War Department and GHQ AEF was never satisfactorily resolved by the secretary of War or the president.

THE AISNE-MARNE COUNTEROFFENSIVE

As Pershing squabbled with March about the size of the AEF, the Germans made their fifth attempt to gain a victor's peace on the battlefields of France and Flanders. If Ludendorff failed this time in gambling his declining manpower for victory, he knew that he would not have another throw of the dice. His plan was to attack east and west of Rheims, hoping to encourage Foch to concentrate Allied strength there to defend Paris. After shifting his reserves north, he would then finish off the British.

On 15 July the Germans attacked with fifty-two divisions. Facing them were thirty-six divisions, twenty-three French, two British, two Italian, and nine American (equal to at least eighteen Allied divisions). Forewarned of this attack, the French, taking a chapter from German defensive doctrine, had skillfully prepared defenses in depth with a false front along part of their sector. This time the Germans quickly met their match. The Allied line bent only a little. The U.S. Third Division, serving with the French Sixth Army, was involved in an especially desperate struggle east of Château-Thierry along the Marne. Fighting off the Germans in three directions, front, left, and right, the Yanks held their ground, earning the nickname "Rock of the Marne." The fifth and last German offensive of 1918 ended almost as soon as it began. Ludendorff's offensives had now cost him more than 800,000 casualties. His exhausted and diminished troops lay exposed in vulnerable salients. A chagrined Ludendorff paid Hindenburg a visit. "What must we do?" he asked. "Do? Do?" Hindenburg exploded. "Make peace, you idiot!"

However the war may have looked to the German High Command at this juncture, victory did not appear likely in the near future in Allied cabinet offices and general staffs. It was rare to find a British or French leader who thought that the war could be ended before 1919, and many feared that the stalemate would continue into 1920. Foch, however, had longed to return to the offensive to wrest the strategical initiative from the Germans and regain the moral ascendancy. He got Pershing's enthusiastic support.

Foch's design was to eliminate the Marne salient with counterthrusts along its flanks. The focal point of the attack was the western face of the salient near Soissons. If the heights near Soissons could be secured, Allied artillery could disrupt German rail and highway communications and force a German withdrawal from the salient. The French Tenth Army's XX Corps, which included Pershing's best-trained divisions, the First and the Second, was assigned the task of securing the heights. Both of the U.S. divisions had new commanders: Major General Summerall led the First Division and Harbord commanded the Second.

On 18 July, in great secrecy, the Americans moved forward in darkness to the jump-off trenches just prior to H-hour, 4:35 A.M. Timing was essential because no preliminary bombardment was scheduled. Instead, the attack would open with a rolling barrage, one hundred meters every two minutes, which the infantry had to be in position to follow into the enemy trenches. Some units, at double-quick time, reached their designated positions just minutes before the artillery opened up. At H-hour the Americans and their French comrades surged forward, assisted by almost four hundred French tanks. Facing them were understrength German divisions fighting from hastily and poorly prepared defensive positions. On the first day, the First Division advanced almost three miles, the Second Division some four and one-half miles. During the next three days, the going became much harder as the infantry lost the element of surprise and outdistanced its artillery support. At the end of four days, the two U.S. divisions had advanced from six to seven miles, capturing 143 guns and sixty-five hundred POWs. Other U.S. divisions also participated in the Allied counteroffensive against the Marne salient—the Third, Fourth, Twenty-sixth, Twenty-eighth, Thirty-second, and Forty-second divisions.

The Allied counteroffensive of 18 July–6 August, officially known as the Aisne-Marne Counteroffensive, provided the AEF with its first opportunity at open warfare. The terrain over which the Americans advanced was mostly rolling countryside, dotted with villages and covered with fields of wheat. In sharp contrast to the war-weary French and British, the doughboys were especially impressive in their dash and aggressiveness. Conversely, their hell-for-leather advance cost them dearly. The First Division's Twenty-Sixth Infantry could muster only two hundred effectives out of the three thousand men who went over the top on 18 July. In securing the village of Sergy, the Forty-second (Rainbow) Division suffered catastrophic losses. Douglas MacArthur stumbled over the dead as he walked across the battlefield in darkness. "There must have been at least two thousand of those sprawled bodies. . . . The stench was suffocating. Not a tree was standing. The moans and cries of wounded men sounded everywhere," he later wrote in his *Reminiscences.*

"The stench was suffocating. Not a tree was standing. The moans and cries of wounded men sounded everywhere."

A postbattle evaluation by Pershing's staff revealed tactical weaknesses. The artillery fired by map rather than by direct observation; the coordination of other supporting arms, machine guns, mortars, and 37-mm cannon with infantry was lacking; and the advance, characterized by rigid planning, cost lives through its frontal assaults in waves of infantry and lack of flexibility. As had been demonstrated so often in past attacks on the western front, the rifle and bayonet, no matter how great the élan of the attackers, were no match for artillery and machine guns.

Despite the limits of GHQ AEF's open-warfare doctrine, Pershing had reason to be pleased with the results of the counteroffensive. Eight of his divisions, 270,000 troops, had participated, playing an important role in forcing the Germans to evacuate the Marne salient. While this battle was progressing, Pershing had met with his fellow commanders in chief and Foch on 24 July. The results of this meeting could hardly have been more satisfactory to the U.S. field commander. The European generals agreed with him that pressure must be maintained on the enemy for the rest of the year, and he secured his own theater of operations with permission to launch an attack to clear a salient in Lorraine, taking its name from the town of Saint-Mihiel. Pershing immediately issued a general order to establish an independent American army.

CREATION OF THE FIRST ARMY AND THE SAINT-MIHIEL OFFENSIVE

The First Army, with Pershing as commander, officially became a reality on 10 August. When his forces had been attached to the French army, he had received his orders from Foch through Pétain. Now, commanding a separate force, he was on equal grounds with Haig and Pétain. Pershing had a right to be proud of the creation of the First Army. In resisting amalgamation, in effect withholding the most viable assistance the United States could give in the near term, he had run the risk that the British and French might be beaten. There had been many anxious weeks, with hundreds of thousands of Parisians fleeing their city and the British contemplating withdrawal of the BEF from Europe, but the alliance had survived the three tactical victories achieved by the German attacks of March, April, and May. The last two German attacks in June and July had been nonstarters, with U.S. soldiers finally beginning to play an important role on the battlefield.

Pershing located First Army headquarters at Lignyen-Barrois, about twenty-five miles southeast of Saint-Mihiel, and began to collect his divisions on and behind the British and French fronts to man an all U.S. front just east of Verdun running south as far as Pont-à-Mousson. Developments on the battlefield and in inter-Allied strategy, however, threatened to undermine his plans. The BEF hoped to duplicate the Franco-American success in the Marne salient on their own front.

On 8 August two thousand big guns opened fire along a fifteen thousand-yard front in the Amiens sa-

The Saint-Mihiel offensive in France in the fall of 1918 was such an easy victory for Pershing's troops that some characterized the battle as "the stroll at Saint-Mihiel." This American machine-gun battalion rested in Saint Baussant on the way to the Saint-Mihiel front. (National Archives)

lient. In a dense early-morning fog, General Rawlinson's Fourth Army advanced against an outnumbered and poorly entrenched foe. Massed tanks and especially the successful bombardment that neutralized German artillery made this the best day of the war for the BEF. Within twelve hours most objectives had been gained and four hundred guns and twelve thousand German prisoners were taken. "August 8th was the black day of the German Army in the history of the war," Ludendorff later lamented.

Encouraged by his spectacular success at Amiens, Haig began to think that the war might be won in 1918. With considerable justification, he considered the forces he commanded the best army in the anti-German coalition. The French were exhausted after absorbing the latest blows of the German army, and the AEF had yet to prove itself as an independent force. Haig held in contempt the civilian and military authorities in London who—even after his Amiens success—continued to believe that the war might last until 1920. Haig's plan for defeating the German army was an assault against the formidable Hindenburg Line (in reality not a "line" but a series of well-designed redoubts and fortifications in depth) and the rupture of the lateral German rail communications, either through capture or placing them under artillery fire, which would force a German withdrawal.

The BEF commander in chief, however, needed support from the French and Americans to tie down German reserves. Rather than each army attacking separate German salients, he wanted the French and Americans to combine with the BEF, treating the front from Verdun almost to the North Sea as one gigantic salient, attacking it on its flanks or shoulders. The acceptance of Haig's plan would force Pershing to change the direction of his offensive. Instead of eliminating the Saint-Mihiel salient (which would take the AEF sixty miles south from where Haig wanted it to attack), he would have to join the French in a combined attack on the right shoulder of this bulge, driving northwest toward Mézières and Sedan.

Having fallen in with Haig's plan, Foch paid Pershing a visit at the First Army's headquarters on 30 August. Pershing was stunned at this turn of events, which threatened to fragment his forces once again and undermine his ultimate strategic goals. More was at stake than the Saint-Mihiel offensive. The unity of his forces and his long-planned drive in the direction of Metz were imperiled. "But Marshal Foch," he said with feeling, "here on the very day that you turn over a sector to the American army, and almost on the eve of an offensive, you ask me to reduce the operation so that you can take away several of my divisions and assign some to the French Second Army and use others to form an American army to operate on the Aisne in conjunction with the French Fourth Army, leaving me with little to do except hold what will become a quiet sector after the Saint-Mihiel offensive." When Foch bluntly asked him soldier-to-soldier if he wanted to "take part in the battle," Pershing warmly retorted, "Most assuredly, but as an American army and in no other way."

On 2 September, Pershing, Pétain, and Foch effected a compromise. Pershing's counterproposal was accepted. The AEF would launch a limited offensive to reduce the Saint-Mihiel salient, but as soon as this was accomplished, it had to extend its front to the Argonne Forest. With most of the U.S. forces in Europe under his command, Pershing would then cooperate with the converging Allied attacks with a massive attack of his own in late September in the Meuse-Argonne sector.

The timetable and mission that Pershing accepted asked a great deal of his green corps and army staffs. The creation of the U.S. I Corps under Major General Hunter Liggett, which had functioned as a part of the French Sixth Army during the Aisne-Marne counteroffensive, represented the first time since the Civil War that the U.S. Army had employed a corps organization in tactical command of troops. Was it realistic to expect the First Army to reduce the Saint-Mihiel salient, disengage, and then launch an even greater offensive sixty miles to the north in the direction of Sedan and Mézières? Moving the First Army, which would involve mountains of material, a vast force of men, machines, and animals, vital communications, and medical facilities, would normally take months of preparation by even the most experienced military organization. Now it might have to be done in weeks—for the most part with inexperienced staff organizations. Pershing's choice of the Meuse-Argonne area for his offensive has also been questioned. His actions can best be explained by his desire to keep his newly formed army intact.

The First Army now comprised three corps of fourteen divisions, total of 550,000 soldiers. As part of his bargain with Foch about limiting his operations in Lorraine, Pershing requested massive French support to ensure the success of the first operation by an independent U.S. force. He asked for and received the assistance of 110,000 French troops. None of his 3,010 guns or 267 tanks were of American make. Slightly more than 40 percent of the personnel for his tanks and guns were French. Breakdowns in U.S. industrial mobilization and the decision to ship infantry and machine-gun units without their artillery meant that Pershing was almost totally dependent upon the Allies for his firepower.

The AEF also had no combat airplanes of American manufacture. The chief of Air Service, AEF, was Mason

M. Patrick, the sixth man to hold that position, but Colonel William "Billy" Mitchell had the greatest influence on the development of American air power. He joined with Major General Sir Hugh Trenchard, the commander of the British Royal Air Force, in stressing the offensive potential of air power. On the eve of the Saint-Mihiel offensive, he commanded the First Army's combat air operations. The 1,481 planes under his command, which included a French air division and British independent bombing squadrons under Trenchard, constituted the largest air strike force yet amassed on the western front. Prior to U.S. entry into the war, neither the army nor Congress had paid much attention to the potential of air power. When the United States entered the war, the army's two flying fields had fifty-five obsolescent airplanes and only a handful of qualified pilots. A war-aroused Congress, attempting to make up for its previous neglect, appropriated millions for what some air advocates called the "winged cavalry." Baker promised "the greatest air fleet ever devised," a pledge the War Department could not fulfill prior to the armistice. The War Department first promised 20,000 airplanes, but the number dropped with each snafu in production, from 17,000 to 15,000 to 2,000. Meanwhile, the U.S. Navy developed its own air arm in Europe. Its Northern Bombing Group, operating from land bases, conducted bombing attacks against German submarine bases. Naval aviators also flew anti-U-boat patrols.

Despite the enthusiasm of advocates of mechanized warfare, the 1916–1918 tank was no war-winner, often breaking down on the battlefield.

The Army Air Service relied on Americans who had received combat experience prior to U.S. intervention in the war as volunteers in the British Royal Flying Corps or the Lafayette Escadrille (an American avation unit in the French Air Squadron). The most important training base in France, located at Issoudun, had as a member of its training staff Lieutenant Edward V. Rickenbacker, who became America's most famous ace, with twenty-two enemy airplanes and four balloons to his credit.

The Air Service's roles in the war included reconnaissance (including the use of balloons and their defense), bombing communications, the strafing of ground troops, and engaging the enemy for the control of the sky. By the armistice, the Air Service had grown to 20 pursuit squadrons, 18 observation squadrons, and 7 bombing squadrons. The British (97 squadrons) and the French (260 squadrons) played a considerably larger role in the air war. Still, a nucleus had been established for the phenomenal growth that would have taken place if the war had lasted into 1919 or 1920.

The Saint-Mihiel salient, twenty-five miles across and sixteen miles deep, had been formed during the autumn of 1914. Although a quiet sector, the salient posed a threat to Allied lines of communication and served as a barrier to any advance into Lorraine. The First Army had to overcome extensive fortifications in depth and miserable weather. Rain poured down as U.S. soldiers prepared for the offensive. Fortunately, the Germans had only eight and a half second- and third-rate divisions (about seventy-five thousand men) in these trenches. To ensure the success of this limited operation, Pershing employed his best divisions—the First, Second, Fourth, Twenty-sixth, and Forty-second. These veteran divisions were joined by four new divisions—the Fifth, Eighty-second, Eighty-ninth, and Ninetieth. Four French divisions also supported the attack.

In addition to air cover, tanks were given a role in the offensive. Despite continuing rain that made the ground extremely muddy, Brigadier General Samuel D. Rockenbach, AEF chief of Tank Corps, and Lieutenant Colonel George S. Patton, Jr., a tank brigade commander, were optimistic about the effectiveness of tanks. "You are going to have a walkover," Rockenbach promised Pershing. Despite the enthusiasm of advocates of mechanized warfare, however, the 1916–1918 tank was no war-winner, often breaking down on the battlefield.

Artillery was considered vital to success. Some members of Pershing's staff wanted a preliminary bombardment to soften the defenses. In order to gain the element of surprise, other officers favored keeping the big guns silent until the moment of attack. Pershing wavered until almost the last moment, then ordered a preliminary bombardment, four hours on the southern face and seven hours on the western. In addition to demoralizing the enemy, the artillery was expected to destroy the extensive barbed-wire entanglements if the tanks could not do this job for the infantry.

On the eve of the attack there was an air of great anticipation at the headquarters of the First Army. The AEF had made giant strides since its regiment-sized attack against the village of Cantigny in late May. Six carloads of war correspondents, including sixteen Americans, arrived during the evening of 11 September. They met with a U.S. intelligence officer, who, after using a map and pointer to describe the next day's action, told them: "Gentlemen, it is now midnight; in one hour our artillery begins and at five our infantry starts." The world would soon know whether the AEF was capable of planning and executing a large-scale, independent operation. Secretary of War Baker would not have to await the wire reports; he was present at the front for the debut of the First Army.

Pershing watched the awesome display of the power of artillery from the old Fort Gironville, which afforded him a commanding view of the battlefield from the south. Most of the shells fell on vacant trenches. Faced with overwhelming odds, the Germans had already begun to withdraw from the salient. Except for isolated machine-gun positions, U.S. troops, rifles often slung on their shoulders, advanced without any opposition. Following in the footsteps of the retreating Germans, the Americans made rapid progress. Sergeant Harry J. Adams of the Eighty-ninth Division chased a German into a dugout at Bouillonville, firing his last two shots from his pistol through the door. He then demanded that the German surrender. To his amazement, three hundred Germans, hands raised in surrender, filed through the door. Adams, his revolver still empty, then marched his captives to the rear.

Although local operations continued until 16 September, the salient was reduced and the battle over in about thirty hours. With the loss of only seven thousand casualties, the AEF liberated two hundred square miles of French territory and captured 450 guns and sixteen thousand prisoners. This victory had come with deceptive ease because of the First Army's overwhelming superiority in men and equipment and, even more important, because of its lucky timing. Some characterized the Battle of Saint-Mihiel as "the stroll at Saint-Mihiel" or as "the sector where the Americans relieved the Germans."

For his part, Pershing believed that the battle was one of lost opportunities. "Without doubt an immediate

Military tanks were first used during World War I and early mechanized warfare had many advocates. However, these 1916–1918 tanks were no war-winners; they were hard to maneuver and often broke down on the battlefield. (National Archives)

continuation of the advance would have carried us well beyond the Hindenburg line and possibly into Metz," he later wrote. MacArthur, a brigade commander in the Forty-second Division, also argued in his *Reminiscences* that the failure to continue the advance was "one of the great mistakes of the war." The continuation of the advance, of course, would have thrown a monkey wrench into the Meuse-Argonne offensive, but even if Pershing had had the freedom to expand this limited operation into an ambitious attempt to seize Metz and break the Hindenburg Line, it is doubtful that he would have succeeded.

From top to bottom, the First Army was still learning to fight. Much still had to be learned about handling large troop formations, command and control problems abounded, and monumental traffic jams occurred behind the front. Hunter Liggett, the I Corps commander at Saint-Mihiel and later commander of the First Army, was almost certainly correct when he wrote in his account of the war: "The possibility of taking Metz and the rest of it, had the battle been fought on the original plan, existed in my opinion, only on the supposition that our army was a well-oiled, fully coordinated machine, which it was not as yet."

In retrospect, the fact that the First Army existed in September and had won its first battle was just short of miraculous. Even after the United States had been in the war a full year, the military leaders of France and Great Britain believed that it was impossible for the AEF to conduct independent military operations in 1918. On the day the Saint-Mihiel offensive began, 12 September, 13 million Americans registered for the second selective draft. A confident—perhaps too confident—Pershing began to believe that the emergence of the United States as a land power in Europe might mean that none of these Americans would have to fight overseas.

THE MEUSE-ARGONNE OFFENSIVE

Pershing and his staff had no time to enjoy the results of the Saint-Mihiel offensive. Within two weeks, on 26 September, the First Army was expected to engage the Germans sixty miles to the north between the Argonne Forest and the Meuse River. The first hurdles that the First Army had to overcome were the monumental transportation and supply problems. Restricted to three roads in questionable condition leading to the Meuse-Argonne front, the First Army had to replace the French Second Army, which was defending this sector. In approximate terms 600,000 Americans had to move in while some 220,000 Frenchmen moved out. Moreover, the transfer had to take place at night to keep the approaching offensive secret.

Given the responsibility for moving the First Army into position, Colonel George C. Marshall, Jr., who earned the nickname "Wizard" for his work, has rightly received high praise. Nevertheless, there were many breakdowns between paper plans and their execution. A four-mile convoy of as many as one thousand trucks was required to move the personnel of a division. When the division's artillery, food, ammunition, and other baggage were included, transported by thousands of horses as well as by trucks, the movement of a division took up to twenty miles of roadway. Extensive preparation also had to be made to supply the First Army once it engaged the enemy. Almost 300,000 men eventually were assigned directly to its logistical support. Supply depots and a vast and complicated network of road and rails were established to feed the voracious appetite of a modern army in battle—food, fuel, weapons, munitions, medical stores, and other vital supplies. Twelve trains brought some forty thousand tons of ammunition to the front each day.

Another more serious hurdle facing Pershing and his planners was the rugged terrain of woods, steep hills, and ravines that favored the German defenders. Colonel Hugh Drum, the First Army chief of staff, thought that it was the "most ideal defensive terrain" he had ever witnessed. The Germans also had become better than anyone else on the western front in developing elastic defensive systems. They had constructed a sophisticated network of fortifications, which included pill boxes and miles of barbed wire. To reach its distant objective, the vital German rail communications at Sedan-Mézières, the First Army had to advance against a strong defensive position, both natural and man-made, along a narrow front of twenty miles between the Meuse River and the formidable Argonne Forest, coming under artillery fire from the Argonne Hills to the west and the Heights of the Meuse to the east. As Drum later expressed the problem, "There was no elbow room, we had to drive straight through."

The Americans had yet to encounter such formidable fortifications manned by determined defenders. Their narrow front and distant objectives made the goal of winning the war in 1918 an unlikely one unless their initial attack led to a breakthrough and rapid advance. The Anglo-French forces (with U.S. assistance) had won victories during the last half of July and August by attacking the Germans in the salients they had bludgeoned in the Allied front. Beyond the Hindenburg Line, the German army lay exposed with vulnerable flanks to defend. As the Germans retired to the strong defensive position they had held before 21 March, the Allied strategy from September onward focused on violent surprise attacks that led to tactical victories and the growing exhaustion of the German army through attrition. When German resistance stiffened and casualties mounted, however, the British and French would not continue pounding the same section of the front. Instead, they would shift their attention to another part of the line. These attacks were meticulously planned and supported by unprecedented artillery bombardment. In their 28–29 September attack on the Hindenburg Line, for example, the BEF expended 943,847 artillery rounds in one twenty-four hour period. In mid-September, Foch praised Haig and tried to explain this new approach to Lord Milner. "Instead of hammering away at a single point, [the British] made a series of successive attacks, all more or less surprises and all profitable."

Foch's motto was "Tout le monde a la bataille," which could be translated as "Everyone go to it." These simultaneous attacks along most of the front kept the Germans off-balance and prevented them from concentrating their reserves at one or more points. The danger for the AEF was that if its attack bogged down, attracting an increasing number of German reinforcements, it would be unable to switch off to other objectives as the British did during their "Hundred Days' Campaign " of 8 August to 11 November, when the BEF inflicted nine successive defeats upon the German army. On its narrow front the AEF would have nowhere to go but forward, and at a terrible cost in lives.

Operating from the new First Army Headquarters in the town hall of Souilly, Pershing and his staff devised a plan to achieve a breakthrough that emphasized numbers, surprise, and speed. The greatest asset of the AEF was its size and material superiority, with a three-to-one air superiority and an overwhelming advantage in artillery. Nine divisions, organized into three corps, I Corps (Liggett), V Corps (Major General George H. Cameron), and III Corps (Bullard), were crowded along the twenty-mile front. The order of battle from the Meuse River to the Argonne Forest was as follows: the Thirty-third, the Eightieth, the Fourth, the Seventy-ninth, the Thirty-seventh, the Ninety-first, the Thirty-fifth, the Twenty-eighth, and the Seventy-seventh divisions. Facing these nine double-strength U.S. divisions were five understrength German divisions. At the point of attack, with about 100,000 troops in jump-off trenches, the numerical superiority of the First Army was roughly four to one. Overall, the U.S. advantage in men may have been as great as eight to one. To ensure surprise, Americans dressed in French army uniforms inspected the front. Unfortunately, the Germans suspected an attack twenty-four hours before it started and began to bring up reinforcements.

The most questionable assumption of general headquarters concerned the speed of the advance. Perhaps deluded by the easy success at Saint-Mihiel and their great advantage in men and equipment, the planners hoped for deep penetrations on either side of the hogback ridge in the center of the German defenses, which contained the strong point of Montfaucon. Field Order No. 20 envisaged smashing through the first lines of the German defensive system and reaching the most formidable position, the Kriemhilde Position, part of the Hindenburg Line, by the afternoon of the first day. Drum hoped to breach this line on the next morning, before the anticipated German reinforcements could be brought forward. If the Kriemhilde Position were not taken quickly, Drum worried that the attempted breakthrough would become a slogging battle of attrition.

To succeed in this first and most vital stage of the Meuse-Argonne offensive, the First Army had to advance ten miles the first day, a distance no AEF division had ever covered in a single day. Also, it would almost certainly take a well-trained and -led army with combat experience to achieve such a blitzkrieg. This did not describe the First Army on 26 September. Some of Pershing's best divisions were still at Saint-Mihiel. Only four of the nine divisions in the initial attack had ever been in the line. More than half the troops in the first wave were recent draftees. Some had been rushed to France without receiving even rudimentary training on either side of the Atlantic. The Seventy-seventh, a division that had been in the line, had four thousand replacement troops who had been drafted in July. Some soldiers had never fired a rifle.

A lay preacher from the hills of Tennessee, Corporal Alvin C. York single-handedly smashed a German machine-gun battalion in the Argonne Forest.

On 25 September the opening bombardment began at 11:30 P.M., with nearly four thousand guns raining death upon the Germans in their dugouts. The offensive began the next day at dawn. After initial success, the advancing units began to lose their cohesion in the confusion of the battlefield and in the face of stiffening German resistance. After four days the offensive ground to a halt short of the Kriemhilde Position. The German high command had six fresh divisions at the front by 30 September and five more in reserve. The First Army's original plan of a breakthrough and rapid advance lay in ruins.

The exploits of Corporal Alvin C. York have provided the popular image of Americans at war during this forty-seven-day battle. A lay preacher from the hills of Tennessee, York single-handedly smashed a German machine-gun battalion in the Argonne Forest. He captured 132 Germans and 35 machine guns and may have killed 25 Germans. When asked by an officer how many Germans he had captured, America's most decorated combat soldier in the war is supposed to have answered: "Jesus, Lieutenant, I ain't had time to count them yet!"

The reality of the battlefield, however, was often quite different. The AEF repeated many of the tactical errors of earlier engagements, with poorly trained doughboys attacking in bunches and being mowed down. Serious breakdowns occurred in the chain of command. Corps headquarters could not even communicate with its divisions. Perhaps the greatest collapse came in logistics. Roads to the front were clogged with monumental traffic jams, the churned-up earth in the battle zone difficult to cross. Artillery, ammunition, food, and even water could not be brought forward; nor could wounded men be evacuated to the rear. Donald Smythe notes in his biography of Pershing (1986): "Whether because of incompetence or inexperience or both, the First Army was wallowing in an unbelievable logistical snarl. It was as if someone had taken the army's intestines out and dumped them all over the table."

On 4–5 October the First Army tried again in attacks that began to resemble the bloody and futile battles of attrition of the Somme and Verdun. The outcome of the battle depended more on the manpower superiority of the AEF than on skill and firepower. The Germans were surprised by the raw courage of the massed infantry attacks and the apparent disregard for the resulting heavy losses. As casualties mounted and his offensive remained mired in the mud, the strain began to tell on

Corporal Alvin C. York, a lay preacher from the hills of Tennessee, single-handedly smashed a German machine-gun battalion in the Argonne forest in 1918. York became one of America's most decorated combat soldiers of World War I. (National Archives)

Pershing. While driving to the front, he momentarily broke down. His head dropped to his hands, and he repeated his dead wife's name. Pershing's courage and great strength of character got him through this difficult period. He was constantly on the move, visiting his corps and division commanders, pushing his subordinates to drive their men forward.

The continuous fighting prevented GHQ AEF from retraining soldiers. Commanders who displeased Pershing, however, were removed. When Major General Adelbert Cronkhite of the Eightieth Division hesitated to launch an attack, he was bluntly informed by his corps commander: "Give it up and you're a goner; you'll lose your command in twenty-four hours." Four infantry brigade commanders, three division commanders, and a corps commander were sacked before the battle ended. Pershing also reorganized the AEF into two armies. The First Army had grown to an unwieldy force of 1,031,000 (when 135,000 French soldiers attached to Pershing's command were included). Liggett was appointed commander of the First Army on 16 October. A fat man, Liggett had initially made a poor impression on Pershing because of the latter's emphasis on physical fitness for his officers. Liggett, however, soon proved that he had "no fat above the neck." His able leadership of the I Corps made him an obvious successor to Pershing as the field commander of the First Army. Bullard commanded the new Second Army, which was activated on 12 October. The Second Army was given the responsibility for operations to the east of the Meuse River, from Fresnes-en-Woevre to the Moselle River, a front of approximately thirty-four miles. Pershing, as Army Group commander, established his headquarters at Ligny-en-Barrois.

On 14 October, the First Army resumed the attack to take the Kriemhilde Position. Although some of Pershing's best divisions spearheaded the attack, the going on the first day was slow and difficult. Three weeks after the Meuse-Argonne offensive had begun, the Thirty-second and Forty-second divisions finally breached the most formidable German defenses. The Thirty-second Division conquered Côte Dame Marie, the key redoubt of the Kriemhilde Position, and the Forty-second Division captured Côte de Chatillon, another vital position.

Although the German army fought a tenacious and skillful defensive battle in the Meuse-Argonne area, it was at the end of its tether by mid-October. The course of the war in Western Europe and elsewhere over the past month had been all Allied. One by one Germany's allies began to drop out of the war. In mid-September, the Allied army in the Balkans shattered the Bulgarian army, forcing that country to sign an armistice before the end of the month. Meanwhile, the Turks were dealt one of the most overwhelming defeats in history at Megiddo and signed an armistice before the end of October, beating Austria-Hungary out of the war by only a few days. As the Central Powers disintegrated, Foch kept unrelenting pressure on the war-weary German army along most of the western front. Germany's generals as well as its politicians knew that they had lost the war. As October began, Berlin appealed to President Wilson for an armistice based on his liberal Fourteen Points. There then ensued a peace dialogue that lasted more than a month, during which time there was uncertainty that Germany would accept armistice terms that reflected its defeat on the field of battle. The chances that they would were greatly increased by the greatest British victory of the war, the breaching of the final defenses of the Hindenburg Line. On October 5, the BEF (with the assistance of a U.S. corps of two divisions) concluded a nine-day drive that had torn a gap in Germany's primary defenses and resulted in the capture of 35,000 prisoners and 380 guns. During its Hundred Days' Campaign, Haig's forces captured a total of 188,700 prisoners and 2,840 guns.

A comparison of the AEF's progress with that of the French and especially the British armies was most unfavorable to Pershing. Many British and French leaders believed that the AEF's limited advance confirmed their frequently expressed view that the creation of an independent American army in 1918 was unwise from a military perspective. Pershing, who had resisted feeding American soldiers into Allied divisions or scattering U.S. divisions along the French and British sectors, became the focal point for biting criticism. Lloyd George characterized the AEF as an "amateur army" suffering enormous casualties because of poor leadership. If anything, the French political leadership was even more critical. Clemenceau commenting on the modest progress made by the AEF after 26 September, wrote Foch: "Nobody can maintain that these fine [American] troops are unusable; they are merely unused." The fierce-tempered premier wanted Pershing's head.

There was some validity to these harsh remarks. When Pershing handed over the First Army to Liggett, it was in some disarray. Immediately behind the front there may have been as many as 100,000 stragglers (Liggett's estimate). On the other hand, the casualties suffered by the AEF during forty-seven days of sustained fighting, approximately 120,000 (25,000 battle deaths) were not unusual for western-front offensives, especially if a breakthrough did not occur quickly. The BEF had suffered almost 60,000 casualties on the first day of the Battle of the Somme (1916), its first monster battle with the German army. During its attacks of August–September 1914, the French army had suffered almost 400,000 casualties. It can be argued that the AEF operationally was at least the equal of the French and British armies when it first engaged the German army in large-scale battles.

There really was no chance in October that President Wilson would accept these Allied criticisms of the performance of the AEF and appoint a new field commander. Pershing, whatever his liabilities as a strategist and tactician, had given strong support to Wilson's revolutionary diplomacy through his creation of an independent army with its own front and strategic objectives. Nevertheless, Pershing's reputation would have suffered if an armistice had been signed on 31 October. With the exception of the easy—some would say misleading—victory at Saint-Mihiel, the AEF had been fought to a standstill by the Germans in September and October. The AEF's greatest contribution to the Allied war-winning offensive had been to tie down German divisions on its front.

"No man is ever so tired that he cannot take one step forward. The best way to take machine guns is to go and take 'em! Press forward."

On 1 November, Liggett's First Army resumed the offensive. All of his divisions, both in the line and in reserve, were veteran divisions. This time preparations for the attack were carefully made; particular attention was given to the chain of command and the coordination of supporting arms with the infantry. The AEF had come of age, its operational skills forged in the fire of battle. Summerall, whose V Corps would lead the assault against the center of German defenses, visited his battalion commanders in late October. "There is no excuse for failure," he told them. "No man is ever so tired that he cannot take one step forward. The best way to take machine guns is to go and take 'em! Press forward."

At 5:30 A.M. the greatest U.S. force ever sent into battle left its trenches. In its most skillfully executed attack of the war the First Army pressed forward. The V Corps in the center penetrated German defenses almost six miles. The securing of the heights of Barricourt forced a general German withdrawal and assured the success of the operation. During the last week of the offensive, operating on both sides of the Meuse, the AEF advanced twenty-four miles. During its eleven-day advance, the AEF captured more territory than it had during the previous month. The AEF had the Germans—who, without reserves, were unable to establish a new defensive line—on the run. As the German front disintegrated, the Kaiser abdicated and revolution swept across Germany.

THE ARMISTICE AND INTERVENTION IN RUSSIA

At 6:30 A.M. on 11 November, First and Second Army headquarters learned that the Germans had signed an armistice that was to go into effect at 11:00 A.M. In some instances, however, U.S. soldiers continued to kill and be killed until the last minute of the war. Some units never received word of the end of the war, others were ordered forward. What some considered a senseless loss of life prompted a congressional investigation after the war.

Pershing, who had angered Wilson with his opposition to an armistice, believed that the war should have been fought on until unconditional surrender was imposed upon the enemy. "If they had given us another ten days we would have rounded up the entire German army, captured it, humiliated it," he said shortly after the war ended. "The German troops today are marching back into Germany announcing that they have never been defeated. . . . What I dread is that Germany doesn't know that she was licked. Had they given us another week, we'd have *taught* them."

These words were prophetic. Many Germans, with their forces everywhere still on conquered territory in November 1918, came to believe that they had not lost the war. It is extremely doubtful, however, that the Allies could have ended the war through military operations before the end of 1918. Germany was clearly defeated, but all of the armies on the western front were exhausted. The distant advances, which strained logistical systems to the breaking point, the approach of winter, and the heavy casualties combined to prevent an invasion of Germany without a pause to regroup. Logistics alone would have thwarted a continued U.S. advance. The shipping of riflemen and machine gunners had seriously dislocated the supply of the AEF. "We were long on bayonets, and short on stevedores, railroad operating men, engineers and the like," Harbord has written. "It is certain that if the armistice had not come when it did, there would have had to be a suspension of hostilities and movement until the supply and troop movement could be brought back into balance."

With the cannons silent on the western front, the U.S. War Department turned its attention to demobilization, which naturally went much faster than had mobilization, although not fast enough for many homesick soldiers. By June 1919, 2,700,000 of the army's

3,703,273 men had been discharged with a uniform, a pair of shoes, a coat, and a $60 bonus. Soldiers who had served abroad were also allowed to keep a helmet and a gas mask as war mementos. The return home for some soldiers in Western Europe was delayed. As part of the Allied effort to ensure that Germany would sign a peace treaty, U.S. forces occupied a bridgehead on the Rhine at Coblenz. Once peace was formally made, a small occupation force, called the American Forces in Germany, commanded by General Henry T. Allen, remained until January 1923. Other U.S. troops stayed in Europe, some for as long as a year after the armistice, to clean up after the AEF.

The armistice did not mean the end of combat for a few unlucky American soldiers. The collapse of the Romanov dynasty and the eventual triumph of communism in Russia created a confusing and complicated situation for U.S. policymakers. "I have been sweating blood," Wilson wrote to House in July 1918, "over the question what is right and feasible to do in Russia. It goes to pieces like quicksilver under my touch." The Communists, who made themselves the masters of the heart of the old czarist empire, holding such key cities as Moscow and Petrograd (formerly St. Petersburg), signed a peace treaty with the Central Powers in March 1918, the Treaty of Brest-Litovsk. This annexationist treaty gave Germany a dominant position in the east. London and Paris feared that their economic stranglehold over Germany might be broken if Berlin gained control of the wheat fields in the Ukraine and Russia's vast mineral resources. Meanwhile, a civil war erupted between the Communists (the Reds) and anti-Communists (the Whites).

The British and the French pressured a reluctant Wilson to support armed intervention on behalf of the Whites. The motives of the interventionists were varied and are still the subject of heated historical debate. To a considerable degree the advocates of sending soldiers into Russia during the first half of 1918 were motivated more by a fear of Germany (blocking its advance eastward and denying it the resources of Russia) than by fear and hatred of communism. Wilson and his chief military adviser, Chief of the General Staff March, however, remained unconvinced of the strategic arguments advanced in favor of intervention in Russia. They rightly viewed as unrealistic the desperate Anglo-French

In August 1918, fourteen thousand U.S. troops landed in Russia, where they became embroiled in conflict with both the Bolsheviks and the Japanese. This column of American soldiers marched in Vladivostok, in northeastern Russia. (National Archives)

plan to reestablish the eastern front with a Japanese force sent from Vladivostok along the Trans-Siberian Railway to European Russia. Nonetheless, Wilson eventually acquiesced to a limited U.S. military presence in both north Russia and Siberia.

In August, before the war ended, five thousand U.S. troops landed at Archangel in north Russia, serving under British command, and another nine thousand soldiers, under the command of Major General William S. Graves, landed at Vladivostok in Siberia. The U.S. North Russian Expeditionary Force had an especially miserable winter at the Artic Circle. Temperatures plunged to fifty degrees below zero; snow was waist-deep at times. As the AEF in France was being demobilized, the "Polar Bears" were at war with the Bolsheviks, or as the doughboys called them, Bolos. Before being withdrawn in June 1919, the North Russian Expeditionary Force lost 139 officers and men killed in action or dead from wounds. Embroiled in conflict with both the Bolsheviks and their allies, especially the Japanese, AEF-Siberia stayed almost another year in Russia. The last group of U.S. soldiers departed Vladivostok on 1 April 1920. A Japanese band gave them a send-off with Stephen Foster's "Hard Times Come Again No More." Thirty-five doughboys had lost their lives in battle in Asiatic Russia.

Pershing commanded the largest single army in American history when the war ended. The projection of U.S. power was all the more impressive because the U.S. Army was essentially a nineteenth-century force in April 1917. Twenty-nine (or 1.3 million men) of the forty-two divisions that reached Western Europe engaged the German army in battle. Seven of these divisions were regular army, eleven were National Guard, and eleven were national army. What the Germans and the Allies thought impossible by 1918, the United States had achieved. The most significant U.S. contribution to victory was that U.S. troops, despite their almost total unpreparedness for an extracontinental military role, got to Europe in time. Many of the breakdowns in the projection of U.S. power overseas can be explained by this rapid expansion to prevent Germany from gaining hegemony in Europe. As Ludendorff destroyed his divisions in attack after attack against the British and French, Americans poured across the Atlantic, arriving in July at the rate of ten thousand a day. The psychological consequences of the emergence of the United States as a land power in Europe on both the Allies and the Central Powers cannot be exaggerated. The rapidly expanding AEF assured an Allied military triumph, if not in 1918, then in 1919 or 1920.

Conversely, the actual military and naval role of the United States in Europe needs to be put in proper perspective. Numbers tell part of this story. U.S. ships transported only half of the AEF to Europe; ships controlled by the British carried the rest. The U.S. war industry, which had to retool for the production of modern weaponry, did not achieve its potential before the war ended. The AEF depended on the Allies for its modern weapons, including its artillery, high-explosive shells, automatic weapons (with the exception of the last few weeks of the war), tanks, and airplanes. According to Liggett, except for some fourteen-inch naval guns, none of the four-thousand artillery pieces of the First Army during the Meuse-Argonne offensive were American-made. Nor were any of the shells expended manufactured in the United States for the use of the AEF. In the air war, the U.S. Army Air Service constituted only 10 percent of the air power of the anti-German alignment. On the high seas, the Royal Navy dominated the antisubmarine war. Its escorts and U-boat patrols were responsible for most of the 132 U-boats destroyed in 1917–1918. U.S. destroyers, yachts, and subchasers could claim only four certain "kills." The U.S. Navy concentrated on protecting U.S. communications to Western Europe.

On land, most of the fighting and dying in 1918 was done by the British and French, not Pershing's forces.

On land, most of the fighting and dying in 1918 was done by the British and French, not Pershing's forces, which were in heavy fighting for only 110 days. The U.S. First Army fought its first battle at Saint-Mihiel on 12 September 1918, just two months before the war ended. In the final offensives of the war, the British, as well as the French, captured considerably more territory, guns, and prisoners than the AEF. The war had also taken a much greater toll of British and especially French manpower. The U.S. War Department reported in 1924 that 36,926 of its soldiers had been killed in action and another 13,628 had died of their battle wounds. Approximately 200,000 additional soldiers were wounded in action. France had mobilized 8,410,000 men and suffered 6,160,800 casualties. Great Britain and the Dominions had mobilized 8,904,467 men and suffered 3,190,235 casualties. For its part, Germany had mobilized 11,000,000 men and suffered 7,142,558 casualties. Expressed in crude form, the percentage of casualties to the total mobilized for France, Germany, the British Empire, and the United States was, respectively,

73.8 percent, 64.9 percent, 35.8 percent, and 8.2 percent.

These statistics should not be used to denigrate the U.S. effort. When the United States entered the war, the realistic timetable, widely accepted by both U.S. and European military authorities, for a decisive American role in the war was a minimum of two years. To prevent the western front from collapsing, the United States was forced to speed its buildup in Western Europe. As the war was ending, the AEF developed into a fighting force that had to be taken seriously by both friend and foe. If the war had continued into 1919, as was generally assumed as late as July-August 1918, Pershing's forces would have become without question the dominant factor in the European war. Meanwhile, the U.S. war industry was finally beginning to achieve its potential. Whatever its limitations in 1918, the AEF was the army of the future, making any continued resistance by the German army a futile effort.

BIBLIOGRAPHY

Reference Works

American Battle Monuments Commission. *American Armies and Battlefields in Europe* (1938).

Ayres, Leonard P. *The War with Germany: A Statistical Summary* (1919).

Banks, Arthur. *A Military Atlas of the First World War* (1975).

Herwig, Holger H., and Neil M. Heyman, comps. *Biographical Dictionary of World War I* (1982).

Higham, Robin, ed. *A Guide to the Sources of United States Military History* (1975).

Jessup, John E., and Robert W. Coakley, eds. *A Guide to the Study and Use of Military History* (1979).

Pappas, George S. ed. *United States Army Unit Histories* (1971).

Schaffer, Ronald, comp. *The United States in World War I: A Selected Bibliography* (1978).

Smith, Myron J., Jr., ed. *American Naval Bibliography,* vol. 4, *The American Navy, 1865–1918: A Bibliography* (1974).

———. *World War I in the Air: A Bibliography and Chronology* (1977).

Woodward, David E., and Robert Franklin Maddox, eds. *America and World War I: A Selected Annotated Bibliography of English-Language Sources* (1985).

The AEF

Army War College, Historical Section. *The Genesis of the American First Army* (1928).

Barbeau, Arthur E, and Florette Henri. *The Unknown Soldiers: Black American Troops in World War I* (1974).

Braim, Paul F. *The Test of Battle: The American Expeditionary Forces in the Meuse-Argonne Campaign* (1987).

Coffman, Edward M. *The War to End All Wars: The American Military Experience in World War I* (1968).

DeWeerd, Harvey A. *President Wilson Fights His War: World War I and the American Intervention* (1968).

Feidel, Frank. *Over There: The Story of America's First Great Overseas Crusade* (1964).

Hassler, Warren W., Jr. *With Shield and Sword: American Military Affairs, Colonial Times to the Present* (1982).

Kennedy, David M. *Over Here: The First World War and American Society* (1980)

Lonergan, Thomas Clement. *It Might Have Been Lost!* (1929).

Millett, Allan R. "Cantigny, 28–31 May 1918." in *America's First Battles 1776–1965,* edited by Charles E. Heller and William A. Stofft (1986).

Millett, Allan R., and Peter Maslowski. *For the Common Defense: A Military History of the United States of America* (1984).

Page, Arthur W. *Our 110 Days' Fighting* (1920).

Palmer, Frederick. *America in France: The Story of the Making of an Army* (1918).

Smythe, Donald ."St. Mihiel: The Birth of an American Army." *Parameters* 13 (1983): 47–57.

Stallings, Laurence. *The Doughboys: The Story of the A.E.F, 1917–1918* (1963).

Trask, David F. *The United States and the Supreme War Council: American War Aims and Inter-Allied Strategy, 1917–1918* (1961).

U.S. Army. *Order of Battle of United States Land Forces in the World War,* 3 vols. (1931–1949).

U.S. Department of the Army, Office of Military History. *The United States in the World War 1917–1918,* 17 vols. (1948).

Weigley, Russell F. *History of the United States Army* (1967).

———. *The American Way of War: A History of United States Military Strategy and Policy* (1973).

Williams, T. Harry. *The History of American Wars:. From Colonial Times to World War I* (1981).

Woodward, David R. *Trial by Friendship: Anglo-American Relations, 1917–1918* (1993).

General Surveys of the War

Baldwin, Hanson W. *World War I: An Outline History* (1962).

Cruttwell, C. R. M. F. *A History of the Great War 1914–1918* (1964).

Ellis, John. *Eye-Deep in Hell: Trench Warfare in World War I* (1976).

Esposito, Vincent J., ed. *A Concise History of World War I* (1964).

Falls, Cyril. *The Great War 1914–1918* (1959).

Liddell Hart, B. H. *The Real War, 1914–1918* (1930).

Marshall, S. L. A. *The American Heritage History of World War I* (1964).

Stokesbury, James L. *A Short History of World War I* (1981).

Terraine, John. *To Win a War: 1918, The Year of Victory* (1980).

Toland, John. *No Man's Land: 1918, The Last Year of the Great War* (1980).

Woodward, David R. *Lloyd George and the Generals* (1983).

The Air War

Flammer, Philip M. *The Vivid Air: The Lafayette Escadrille* (1981).

Hudson, James J. *Hostile Skies: A Combat History of the American Air Service in World War I* (1968).

Kennett, Lee. *The First Air War 1914–1918* (1991).

Mason, Herbert Molloy, Jr. *The United States Air Force: A Turbulent History, 1907–1975 (1976).*

Maurer, Maurer, ed. *The U.S. Air Service in World War I,* 4 vols. (1978–1979).

Sweetser, Arthur. *The American Air Service:. A Record of Its Problems, Its Difficulties, Its Failures, and Its Achievements* (1919).

The War at Sea

Allard, Dean C. "Anglo-American Naval Differences During World War I." *In Defense of the Republic,* edited by David Curtis Skaggs and Roberts S. Browning III (1991).

Belknap, Reginald R. *The Yankee Mining Squadron: Or, Laying the North Sea Mine Barrage* (1920).

Corbett, Sir Julian S., and Sir Henry Newboldt. *Official History of First World War, 1914–1918: Naval Operations,* 5 vols. (1920–1931).

Frothingham, Thomas G. *The Naval History of the World War,* 3 vols. (1924–1926).

Gray, Edwyn A. *The Killing Time: The U-Boat War 1914–1918* (1972).

Hagan, Kenneth J. *This People's Navy: The Making of American Sea Power* (1991).

Herwig, Holger H., and David F. Trask. "The Failure of Germany's Undersea Offensive Against World Shipping, February 1917–October 1918." *The Historian* 33 (1971): 611–636.

Trask, David F. *Captains and Cabinets: Anglo-American Naval Relations, 1917–1918* (1972).

———. "The American Navy in a World at War, 1914–1918." In *In Peace and War: Interpretations of American Naval History, 1775–1978,* edited by Kenneth J. Hagan (1978).

James, Henry J. *German Submarines in Yankee Waters: First World War* (1940).

Sprout, Harold and Margaret. *The Rise of American Naval Power, 1776–1918* (1939).

Military and Civilian Leadership

Alexander, Robert. *Memories of the World War, 1917–1918* (1931).

Allen, Henry T. *The Rhineland Occupation* (1927).

Beaver, Daniel R. *Newton D. Baker and the American War Effort, 1917–1919 (1966).*

Blake, Robert, ed. *The Private Papers of Douglas Haig 1914–1919* (1952).

Blumenson, Martin, ed. *The Patton Papers,* vol. 1: *1885–1940* (1972).

Bullard, Robert L. *Personalities and Reminiscences of the War* (1925).

Clements, Kendrick A. *Woodrow Wilson, World Statesman* (1987).

Coffman, Edward M. *The Hilt of the Sword: The Career of Peyton C. March* (1966).

Dickman, Joseph T. *The Great Crusade: A Narrative of the World War* (1927).

Ferrell, Robert H. *Woodrow Wilson and World War I, 1917–1921* (1985).

Graves, William S. *America's Siberian Adventure* (1941).

Harbord, James G. *The American Army in France, 1917–1918* (1936).

Hurley, Alfred F. *Billy Mitchell: Crusader for Air Power* (1964).

Lejeune, John A. *The Reminiscences of a Marine* (1930).

Liggett, Hunter. *Commanding an American Army: Recollections of the World War* (1925).

Link, Arthur S., ed. *The Papers of Woodrow Wilson,* vols. 41–51 (1983–1985).

MacArthur, Douglas. *Reminiscences* (1965).

March, Peyton C. *The Nation at War* (1932).

Marshall, George C. *Memoirs of My Service in the World War, 1917–1918* (1976).

May, Ernest R. *The Ultimate Decision: The President as Commander in Chief* (1960).

Millett, Allan R. *The General: Robert L. Bullard and Officership in the United States Army, 1881–1925* (1975).

Mitchell, William. *Memoirs of World War I: "From Start to Finish of Our Greatest War"* (1960).

Morrison, Elting E. *Admiral Sims and the Modern American Navy* (1942).

Palmer, Frederick. *Bliss, Peacemaker: The Life and Letters of General Tasker Howard Bliss* (1934).

———. *Newton D. Baker: America at War,* 2 vols. (1931).

Patrick, Mason, M. *The United States in the Air* (1928).

Pershing, John L. *My Experiences in the World War,* 2 vols. (1931).

Pogue, Forrest C. *George C. Marshall: Education of a General, 1880–1939* (1963).

Rickenbacker, Edward V. *Fighting the Flying Circus* (1919).

Rodman, Hugh. *Yarns of a Kentucky Admiral* (1928).

Sims, William S., and Burton J. Hendrick. *Victory at Sea* (1920).

Smythe, Donald. *Pershing: General of the Armies* (1986).

Vandiver, Frank E. *Black Jack: The Life and Times of John J. Pershing,* vol. 2 (1977).

Woodward, David R., ed. *The Military Correspondence of Field-Marshal Sir William Robertson: Chief Imperial General Staff December 1915–February 1918* (1989).

Industrialized Warfare, Strategy, and Doctrine

Bidwell, Shelford, and Dominick Graham. *Fire-power: British Army Weapons and Theories of War 1904–1945* (1982).

Coffman, Edward M. "The AEF Leaders' Education for War." In *The Great War, 1914–18: Essays on the Military, Political and Social History of the First World War,* edited by R. J. Q. Adams (1990).

Ellis, John. *The Social History of the Machine Gun* (1975).

Fuller, J. F. C. *Tanks in the Great War, 1914–1918* (1920).

Gilmore, Russell. "The 'New Courage' Rifles and Soldier Individualism, 1876–1918," *Military Affairs* 40 (1976).

Gudmundsson, Bruce I. *Stormtroop Tactics: Innovation in the German Army, 1914–1918* (1989).

Holley, I. B., Jr. *Ideas and Weapons: Exploitation of the Aerial Weapon by the United States in World War I* (1953).

Hunt, Barry, and Adrian Preston, eds. *War Aims and Strategic Policy in the Great War, 1914–1918* (1977).

Lupfer, Timothy T. *The Dynamics of Doctrine: The Changes in German Tactical Doctrine During the First World War* (1981).

Miller, Steven E., ed. *Military Strategy and the Origins of the First World War* (1985).

Millett, Allan R. "Over Where? The AEF and the American Strategy for Victory, 1917–1918." In *Against All Enemies: Interpretations of American Military History from Colonial Times to the Present,* edited by Kenneth J. Hagan and William R. Roberts (1986).

Nenninger, Timothy K. "The Development of American Armor, 1917–1940: The World War I Experience." *Armor* 78 (1969).

———. *The Leavenworth Schools and the Old Army: Education, Professionalism, and the Officers Corps of the United States Army, 1881–1918* (1978).

———. "American Military Effectiveness in the First World War." In *Military Effectiveness,* vol. 1: *The First World War,* edited by Allan R. Millett and Williamson Murray (1988).

Prior, Robin, and Trevor Wilson. *Command on the Western Front* (1992).

Rainey, James W. "Ambivalent Warfare: The Tacical Doctrine of the AEF in World War I." *Parameters* 13 (1983): 34–36.

Spector, Ronald. " 'You're Not Going to Send Soldiers Over There Are You!': The American Search for an Alternative to the Western Front 1916–1917." *Military Affairs* 36 (1972): 1–4.

Terraine, John. *The Smoke and the Fire: Myth and Anti-Myths of War, 1861–1945* (1980).

———. *White Heat: The New Warfare, 1914–1918* (1982).

Travers, Tim. *The Killing Ground: The British Army, the Western Front, and the Emergence of Modern Warfare, 1900–1918* (1987).

———. *How the War Was Won: Command and Technology in the British Army on the Western Front, 1917–1918* (1992).

Mobilization and Logistics

Chambers, John Whiteclay, II. *To Raise an Army: The Draft Comes to Modern America* (1987).

Clifford, John C. *The Citizen Soldiers: The Plattsburg Training Camp Movement, 1913–1920* (1972).

Finnegan, John P. *Against the Spector of a Dragon: The Campaign for American Military Preparedness, 1914–1917* (1974).

Frothingham, Thomas G. *The American Reinforcement in the World War* (1927).

Gleaves, Albert. *A History of the Transport Service: Adventures and Experiences of United States Transports and Cruisers in the World War* (1921).

Hagood, Johnson. *The Services of Supply: A Memoir of the Great War* (1927).

Hurley, Edward N. *The Bridge to France* (1927).

Huston, James A. *The Sinews of War: Army Logistics, 1775–1953* (1966).

Kreidberg Marvin A., and Merton G. Henry, *History of Military Mobilization in the United States Army 1775–1945* (1955).

U.S. General Staff, War Plans Division, Historical Branch. *Organization of the Services of Supply: American Expeditionary Forces* (1921).

Wilgus, William J. *Transporting the A.E.F. in Western Europe, 1917–1919* (1931).

— DAVID R. WOODWARD

World War II

BACKGROUND TO THE WAR

For the United States of America, World War II began with an attack upon its own territory. At 7:55 A.M. on 7 December 1941, Japanese aircraft struck the U.S. naval base at Pearl Harbor, Hawaii. Japanese bombers destroyed or seriously damaged eighteen U.S. warships, including eight battleships. The following day the United States Congress declared war against Japan. Three days later Nazi Germany and Fascist Italy declared war against the United States.

At 7:55 A.M. on 7 December 1941, Japanese aircraft struck the U.S. naval base at Pearl Harbor, Hawaii.

Although twenty-two years had elapsed since Germany signed the Treaty of Versailles in June 1919, the events of December 1941 can be traced directly back to that date. As artillery batteries saluted the signing of the treaty, one historian wrote, "The First World War was buried and the Second World War conceived . . . not because of its severity, nor because of the lack of wisdom, but because it violated the terms of the Armistice of 11 November 1918."

In October 1918, the Germans had replied favorably to President Woodrow Wilson's Fourteen Points and requested peace negotiations based upon them. Unfortunately, the Allies failed either to negotiate or to incorporate the Wilsonian peace proposals into the treaty, which enabled a generation of German politicians, among them Adolf Hitler, to reject the Versailles Treaty. Upon this rejection, Hitler was able to build a dictatorship and the Third Reich.

Taking advantage of postwar suffering caused by continuation of the Allied blockade, occupation of the Rhineland, catastrophic inflation, and worldwide depression, the Nazis built up sufficient national resentment of the perceived injustices of the Versailles Treaty to support a rearmament program in defiance of the Allied powers. On 1 September 1939 rearmament culminated in the invasion of Poland by the German armies, despite Anglo-French guarantees of Polish territory. With this act World War II began. Poland vanished under the onslaught of both German and Soviet armies. In 1940 the Netherlands, Belgium, Denmark, and Norway succumbed to German arms, and France surrendered to the Germans on 22 June in the same railway car at Compiègne, France, where the Germans had signed the armistice in November 1918. France was divided between an occupied area, including most of northern France, and a satellite government under Marshal Henri-Philippe Pétain with its capital in the resort town of Vichy. The elimination of France from the alliance left only Great Britain in the ranks of the unconquered enemies of Germany.

Ironically, as Hitler observed in his book *Mein Kampf,* written in 1923 while a prisoner in Landsberg for his participation in the Munich revolt, friendship with Great Britain was a prerequisite for a restored German empire in Europe that would, of necessity, be created upon the ruins of the Soviet Union. Great Britain was now at war with Germany, however, and, despite having been driven from the Continent, seemed determined to carry on the fight against Nazism, as Prime Minister Winston Churchill declared. Great Britain still had formidable resources, as Hitler was aware: seapower and a still viable Anglo-Saxon empire, including Canada, South Africa, India, Australia, New Zealand, and other smaller elements of the empire, all of whom had joined in war against Germany and, with the fall of France, Italy. As British Major General J. F. C. Fuller observed:

> The one enemy was England, as she had been the one enemy of Philip II, Louis XIV, Napoleon, and William II. Yet now in June 1940 the German leader found himself unable to "hit the common center of gravity of the whole war," because the momentum of his strategy of annihilation had been halted at the English Channel—twenty odd miles of water—and how to cross them had not figured in his strategical calculations. While gazing at the map of the British Empire, he [Hitler] had overlooked the Strait of Dover.

Both Churchill and Hitler at first believed that a seaborne invasion of Great Britain was not only possible but likely. From August until mid-October 1940, the Luftwaffe and the Royal Air Force had fought a battle for control of the skies above the channel and England itself. Thanks to the superiority of the British Spitfire fighter over the German Messerschmitt and Sir Robert

Watson-Watt's invention of radar, the British retained control of the air. Radar operators along the coast of Great Britain enabled the numerically inferior British fighter command to concentrate its strength where needed and thereby repulse the massive German air fleets. By mid-October the aerial offensive had failed, and Germany faced operations in the Balkans, North Africa, and the Soviet Union, with Great Britain unfallen and its power intact.

With the Italians attempting to expand their dominion in North Africa, and the British clinging desperately to footholds in the eastern Mediterranean, the Germans were drawn inexorably toward the Balkans and eventually into North Africa. Romania, Yugoslavia, Greece, and the island of Crete fell rapidly to German military power. British seapower, however, still controlled the Suez Canal and the Middle East, including Egypt, which denied the Germans the sea-lanes to Persia, Turkey, and southern Russia. Denied power over the eastern Mediterranean, Hitler turned his attention to the Soviet Union, in what turned out to be the critical strategic blunder of World War II. Once Germany invaded the Soviet Union, Hitler was doomed to a vast continental campaign with the Soviets, who were able to more than replace the manpower lost to Great Britain after the fall of France. On 22 June 1941, German troops crossed the Neman River, and the great campaign on the eastern front began. During the first months the Germans drove deep into European Russia, encircling entire armies and capturing thousands of prisoners.

Alarmed by Hitler's apparent success, President Franklin D. Roosevelt, supported by those in the United States who had long urged a policy of aid to Great Britain and intervention in the European war, took steps that eventually involved the United States in war.

U.S. PREPARATION AND PLANNING FOR WAR

Despite the dramatic events taking place in Europe and the Middle East, the attention of U.S. General Staff planners since the 1930s had focused on possible military operations in the Pacific area. Plan Orange (for war against Japan) had received increased attention as the Japanese invaded Manchuria in 1931 and launched a full-scale war with China in 1937. During the same decade, Italy conquered Ethiopia (1935); the Spanish Civil War broke out (1936), in which Italo-German military assistance confronted that from the Soviet Union; and Germany remilitarized the Rhineland. U.S. military planners reexamined Plan Orange with the thought that the United States might become involved eventually in a two-front war. Army and navy staffs developed an uneasy compromise in strategic planning; until it had been determined that the Atlantic flank had been secured, there were to be no offensive operations in the Pacific.

While German armies overran most of Europe, Americans watched with interest but no great concern. Economic depression and a national mood of isolationism had kept both the army and navy limited by modest congressional appropriations—in 1936, less than $578 million for the army and less than $489 million for the navy. The active army numbered fewer than 138,000 men and the navy 96,000. On 5 September 1939, Roosevelt declared U.S. neutrality, according to the provisions of the congressionally endorsed Neutrality Acts of 1936 and 1937, which placed an embargo on arms and munitions to the warring powers. Three days later, the president proclaimed a limited national emergency, under which he authorized small increases in the armed forces—fifty-eight thousand for the navy and seventeen thousand for the army. These increases brought the army up to a strength of 185,000, but none of its units had a full complement of men. In theory, the army had nine infantry divisions, but only three were organized as divisions, and these were at less than one-half strength. All of them lacked sufficient transport for field maneuvers. One mechanized cavalry brigade at half strength was all the armor the army had. The National Guard totaled 199,000 men but lacked enough equipment for its eighteen poorly trained divisions. As for the Army Air Corps, there were only seventeen thousand men organized in sixty-two understrength, ill-equipped squadrons.

Despite the obvious lack of military preparedness, the population of the United States felt reasonably secure behind the shield of the Neutrality Acts. Isolationism, a determination to remain aloof from the distant wars, characterized the nation. The first break in the national mood was dramatized on 10 June 1940 by President Roosevelt during a commencement speech at the University of Virginia, when he declared, upon learning that Italy had attacked France, that the hand that held the dagger had struck. For the first time the president declared publicly his and the nation's full support for the Allied powers: "We will extend to the opponents of force, the material resources of this nation." On 27 August 1940 Congress gave the president authority to call the National Guard and reserves to federal service, and on 16 September approved the Selective Training and Service Act (Burke-Wadsworth Bill). This legislation, however, the nation's first peacetime draft, placed a one-year limit on service, did not permit service outside the United States, and provided for equipment and reserves for 2 million men.

building (the Pentagon) to house the growing War Department.

As for the Pacific, on 26 July, Roosevelt nationalized the armed forces of the Philippines, placing them under the leadership of General Douglas MacArthur. In addition to the U.S. units under his command, MacArthur counted ten Philippine divisions of doubtful quality—a force totaling about 200,000 men and hardly capable of defeating the battle-hardened Japanese recently deployed from service in China. Confident that their fleet could keep the Americans in place, the Japanese armed forces planned a campaign into the East Indies, where the oil-fields of Indonesia could be expected to supply the oil denied them by the U.S. embargo. Japanese strategists did not believe that the United States could vigorously fight and win a war simultaneously on both the Atlantic and Pacific fronts. Despite the misgivings of Japanese Emperor Hirohito, the military commanders remained confident that they could achieve their goals. By November 1941, Roosevelt and his staff had concluded that the Japanese had resolved on war with the United States (U.S. cryptanalysts had broken the Japanese diplomatic code in late 1940), but the question until 7 December 1941 remained when and where.

Although after 7 December 1941 Japan was at war with the United States, Germany for a time demurred, because Japan had attacked the United States without consulting the Nazi government. Hitler had originally preferred to complete the conquest of the Soviet Union before taking on the Americans, but he had promised the Japanese to declare war against the United States even if Japan attacked first. He declared war against the United States on 11 December 1941, as did Italian dictator Benito Mussolini. There was now global war, with the United States, Great Britain, and the Soviet Union arrayed against Germany, Italy, and Japan around the world (although the Soviet Union did not enter the war against Japan until 1945).

Despite two years of gradual buildup, the day following Pearl Harbor found the U.S. Navy with only nine battle-worthy battleships, twenty-nine seaworthy cruisers, and six aircraft carriers. In manpower, the navy numbered about 325,000 men, plus 70,000 in the Marine Corps and 25,000 in the Coast Guard. Although the draft had increased the army to almost 1.75 million men, this was far short of the four million deemed necessary to defend just the Western Hemisphere. At the end of 1940, only one army division was fully trained and equipped for combat, with thirty-seven others in various stages of readiness, but there was not enough shipping to move them overseas. The Army Air Forces contained only 348,535 men, and Japanese operations against Hawaii and the Philippines had reduced the number of aircraft to a low point of 807, of which only 159 were four-engined bombers. The United States moved rapidly to remedy the situation. Aircraft plants employed more than 425,000 workers with a goal of almost three thousand planes off the assembly lines during the first months of 1942.

President Roosevelt reorganized the armed forces command structure. He eliminated the arrangement whereby the commander of the largest of the three navy fleets acted as overall fleet commander. The position of navy commander in chief became a separate post, with Admiral Ernest J. King, the former Atlantic Fleet commander, the first occupant of the post. The commander in chief had responsibility for plans and operations, while the chief of naval operations (CNO) retained responsibility for logistics, procurement, and housekeeping. The arrangement resembled the relationship between the army chief of staff and the GHQ head. To solve inherent conflicts and ambiguities, in March 1942, Roosevelt put King in both positions, while former CNO Admiral Stark went to Britain as commander of U.S. naval forces in Europe. Roosevelt rounded out his wartime operational command post with General Marshall as army chief of staff and General Arnold as chief of the Army Air Forces. He also enlisted bipartisan support by appointing Republicans Henry L. Stimson as secretary of war and Frank Knox as secretary of the navy. Secretary of State Cordell Hull had only a minor role to play, because Roosevelt preferred to be his own secretary of state. To this inner group was added Harry L. Hopkins, an obscure nonpolitical figure who had resided in the White House since 1940, a crony and confidant of the president.

The War Department completed its reorganization in March 1942 by eliminating the GHQ and putting in its place three separate arms: Army Air Forces, General Arnold; Army Ground Forces, General Lesley J. McNair; and Army Service Forces, General Brehon B. Somervell. Following reorganization of the army high command, provision was made for joint army-navy direction of the war, through the formation of the Joint Chiefs of Staff (JCS), made up of King, Marshall, and Arnold. In the summer of 1942, Fleet Admiral William D. Leahy, as the president's personal chief of staff, was added to the JCS. These four would work with their British opposite numbers—Field Marshal Sir Alan Brooke, chief of the Imperial General Staff; Admiral of the Fleet and First Sea Lord Sir Dudley Pound; and Sir Charles Portal, chief of the Air Staff—to form the Combined Chiefs of Staff (CCS). Since Washington, D.C. was to be the permanent seat of the staff, Churchill appointed Field Marshal Sir John Dill to represent the

British chiefs in the intervals between formal conferences.

In addition to the CCS, there were several combined civilian and paramilitary agencies, such as the Munitions Assignment Board, the Shipping Board, and the Production and Resources Board. These enabled the United States and Great Britain to fuse their war efforts in a manner unparalleled in the history of alliances and superior in central planning and direction to those on the Axis side. The Atlantic Charter was signed by Churchill and Roosevelt when they and the CCS met aboard ship in mid-August 1941. The first meeting after the United States entered the war, however, took place in Washington in late December 1941. Designated the Arcadia Conference, it set the pattern for subsequent top-level conferences.

Although there was considerable pressure to concentrate the war effort against Japan, the CCS, Roosevelt, and his advisers remained determined to concentrate on the defeat of Germany and Italy. Washington despaired of holding the Philippines and decided to concentrate on holding open the lines of communication through Hawaii to Australia, which left little shipping available for troop movements across the Atlantic.

Encouraged by recent victories that had carried the British from Egypt into Libya (November 1941–January 1942), Churchill raised the possibility of a British advance westward to the border of Tunisia. Vichy France might then agree to permit the Allies to enter Algeria and Morocco. With the British occupying Tunisia and Algeria, the Americans would have responsibility for Morocco. Roosevelt, eager for successful

The Ninety-Third Infantry Division was the first unit during World War II to include only African-American soldiers. In this photograph, the Ninety-Third Infantry trains in Arizona in May 1942. (National Archives)

operations, supported Churchill's idea. His advisers did not, citing a shortage of shipping, and the North African venture was shelved for the time being. Meanwhile, German submarines continued to roam the Atlantic, sinking 506 Allied vessels.

The navy had concentrated its rebuilding program on large battleships, cruisers, and aircraft carriers, leaving little resources for constructing smaller craft, such as destroyers, capable of combating U-boats. Only twenty-three large and forty-two small Coast Guard cutters, plus twenty-nine miscellaneous craft and twenty-two converted trawlers, the latter loaned by the Royal Navy, were available to reinforce against this menace. Despite loud protests from coastal communities, in April 1942 the navy managed to impose stringent restrictions on lighting in cities to make it difficult for enemy submarines to locate targets. Although many antisubmarine measures were devised during the war, the Allies did not check the U-boat menace until the establishment of the convoy system, with sufficient escort craft to protect shipping from Key West, Florida, to Norfolk, Virginia. In May the system was extended northward to join the main convoy routes from the major northern ports. Not a single ship was sunk off the Atlantic coast during the remaining months of 1942. Thus, the submarine was defeated in the Caribbean and U.S. coastal waters. In the north Atlantic the battle against the U-boats went on as they shifted their operations to the transatlantic routes.

As the Japanese broadened their control in the Pacific and East Asia, there was some pressure within the JCS for a shift of emphasis from Europe to the Pacific. Marshall and his chief of war plans, Major General Dwight D. Eisenhower, vigorously opposed this view, and in April 1942, Marshall presented a War Department plan for the invasion of Europe to President Roosevelt. The buildup in Great Britain for this plan was given the code name Bolero, and the invasion itself designated Round Up, which was to be carried out by forty-eight divisions supported by six thousand aircraft. Two-thirds of the divisions and more than 50 percent of the aircraft were to be American. Scheduled for April 1943, the operation might be launched earlier, under the code name Sledgehammer, if the Soviet Union gave indication of collapse. Roosevelt approved the plan immediately and General Marshall left for London to persuade the British staff to accept the plan. Anxious lest their U.S. colleagues shift their efforts to the Far East, the British readily accepted the proposal. At the same time, however, Churchill cautioned Roosevelt against a premature landing in Europe in 1942, but the Americans had assured visiting Soviet Foreign Minister V. M. Molotov that, if necessary, the Allies would open a second front somewhere on the continent in 1942. Nevertheless, Churchill flew to Moscow to tell Joseph Stalin that the Anglo-American Allies had not enough sea lift to launch an invasion. Stalin indicated that he understood, but this became the basis of a propaganda claim that the Allies planned to allow the Nazis to destroy the USSR.

THE CAMPAIGN IN NORTH AFRICA

In North Africa, British forces had been driven back into Egypt in May 1941, and by early 1942 there was a threat that the Germans and their Italian allies might reach the Suez Canal, gain control of the Middle East oil fields, and link up with Axis forces occupying the Balkans. This threat was the basis for Churchill's concept of opening another front in North Africa. He faced opposition from General Marshall, who believed the main issue to be rejection of anything that would delay Plan Bolero. In his eyes an Allied operation in North Africa would be expensive and ineffective, and he was so opposed to Churchill's idea that he proposed that the United States concentrate in the Pacific against Japan rather than accept the British plan for operations in North Africa. Roosevelt, however, was willing to accept the British proposal for North Africa, and on the evening of 30 June 1942, he announced his decision for U.S. forces to concentrate on Operation Torch, the code name for an Allied invasion of North Africa, which was to take precedence over all other operations.

The 1940 armistice with the Germans at Compiègne had left the French in control of their North African territories with a lightly equipped 135,000-man army made up mainly of indigenous territorials but with regular French army officers. An air force of some 350 older combat aircraft completed the military picture. What remained of the French navy patrolled the coastal waters of Morocco and Algeria. Although unimpressive, this force was loyal to Pétain, whom the Germans had placed in control of Vichy France. Because of poor relations between the British and the French, it was agreed that the invasion force should be under the command of an American. The British initially suggested Marshall, with Eisenhower as his deputy. Since late June 1942, Eisenhower had been stationed in London as commander of U.S. forces in the European theater of operations. Roosevelt was heavily dependent upon Marshall for advice and did not want Marshall to leave his side. Consequently, Eisenhower became his and Marshall's choice to command Operation Torch. Eisenhower's deputy, General Mark Wayne Clark, was also his deputy for Torch.

The British insisted upon a landing inside the Mediterranean basin at Oran, Algiers, and Bône. They wanted a landing close enough to Tunisia to enable their armor to strike rapidly overland to Bizerte and Tunis. The Americans wanted to land on the Atlantic coast of Morocco to ensure a line of communications to the United States. The CCS finally agreed that the Americans would land one force on the Atlantic coast to take Casablanca, another on the Mediterranean coast at Oran, and a third at Algiers, followed by British reinforcements landing at eastern Algerian ports to support a drive into Tunisia. Once North Africa had been secured, the Allies were to drive into Libya to strike Axis forces from the rear as the British launched a counteroffensive from Egypt. Thus, the Axis forces would be eliminated from North Africa and the western Mediterranean. This would clear shipping lanes for lend-lease supplies to the Soviet Union. A cross-channel operation planned for 1943 was postponed.

To command the landing of the Western Task Force's thirty-five thousand men on Morocco's Atlantic coast, Eisenhower selected an associate of long standing, Major General George S. Patton, Jr. Patton shared responsibility for the amphibious operation with Rear Admiral Henry Kent Hewitt. The Western Task Force was to sail from East Coast ports in the United States in 107 vessels and to land at three minor ports on the Moroccan coast and then drive five hundred miles to the east to link up with the Center Task Force at Oran, commanded by Major General Lloyd R. Fredendall. The Center Task Force was to land over the beaches near Oran and then move inland to capture the port. The Eastern Task Force, composed of ten thousand Americans and twenty-three thousand British, was under the command of British Lieutenant General Kenneth A. N. Anderson. Initially, Anderson was to remain at Gibraltar, while U.S. Major General Charles L. Ryder, commander of the Thirty-fourth Infantry Division, led an assault force at Algiers made up mainly of Amer-

British General Bernard Montgomery, who forced the German-Italian Army to retreat from North Africa in October 1942, monitors tank movements in North Africa in November of that year. (National Archives)

icans. Both the Center and Eastern task forces were moved from Great Britain in British transports; the naval commander was Admiral Sir Andrew Browne Cunningham. Air support for the Western Task Force was commanded by Brigadier General James H. Doolittle's newly created Twelfth Air Force, with 1,244 U.S. aircraft. The British supplied the Eastern Air Command made up of 454 Royal Air Force planes.

Most landing craft on the Atlantic coast were Higgins boats, thirty-six-foot plywood craft, many without landing ramps, and the men had to clamber over the sides to disembark. A few of the early models of a steel construction LCM (landing craft mechanized), capable of carrying a thirty-ton tank, were also used. For the Mediterranean half of the invasion force, there was a miscellaneous mixture of various craft, some converted to carry tanks, others resembling large lifeboats. (Sophisticated ship-to-shore vessels did not appear until later in the war.)

The major question facing the Anglo-American invasion force was the reaction of the French garrison in Algiers and Morocco. Allied intelligence believed that the French would most likely support General Henri Honoré Giraud, who at that time was residing in unoccupied France but was in contact with General Charles E. Mast, the anti-Vichy chief of staff of the French forces in Algiers who with four civilians comprised the anti-Vichy leadership in Algeria. The senior French official in North Africa, however, was Admiral Jean François Darlan, second in command to Pétain and commander in chief of the French forces in North Africa. The major Allied command problem was how to get Darlan to cooperate with Giraud and Mast. His support was necessary because he controlled what was left of the French fleet. The problem was the subject of a secret meeting between Generals Giraud, Mast, Robert D. Murphy, and Clark, whom Eisenhower had selected to command the army element in Operation Torch.

Clark arrived in a submarine at the meeting place, a seaside villa ninety miles west of Algiers. Murphy, the U.S. intelligence agent in Algiers who hosted the meeting, summoned the others to make plans for Franco-Allied cooperation during the forthcoming invasion. Although the meeting was dispersed by the unexpected arrival of French police, apparently nothing was compromised, thanks to Murphy's skill in reassuring the police. General Clark escaped undetected back to his submarine. Vichy officials had learned nothing, but the Germans remained suspicious that the Allies would strike somewhere in the Mediterranean during 1942. Axis forces, however, were in no position to take protective countermeasures, and as the year drew to a close, the Germans decided that there would be no Allied operation until 1943.

Suddenly, on 23 October the British Eighth Army, commanded by General Sir Bernard L. Montgomery, attacked Field Marshal Erwin Rommel's Italian-German army in the western desert in the vicinity of El Alamein in Egypt. Montgomery's attack was preceded by air and artillery bombardment against Axis supply lines. The Eighth Army attacked across a six-mile front, and on 26 October, Rommel launched a series of violent counterattacks. When the British held their front, on 4 November Rommel ordered his forces to retreat, after losing fifty-nine thousand killed, wounded, and taken prisoner, of whom thirty-four thousand were German. Five hundred tanks, four hundred guns, and thousands of vehicles were also lost. The British losses were 13,500 killed, wounded, and missing and 432 tanks lost. Thus ended the Battle of El Alamein, with a victorious British army in control of the western desert.

Field Marshal Rommel ordered his forces to retreat, after losing fifty-nine thousand killed, wounded, and taken prisoner.

The Eighth Army now took up full pursuit against Rommel's skilled withdrawal. Advancing westward across the desert, the British entered Tobruk on 13 November, Al-Gazala on the fourteenth, Benghazi on the twentieth, Sirte on 26 December, and Tripoli, Libya, on 24 January 1943. There was little fighting during the fourteen-hundred-mile advance, but significantly, Rommel gained in strength as he fell back. The Americans, advancing from the west, soon found this out.

During the night of 6 November, Eisenhower, from his headquarters at Gibraltar, ordered his invasion force to land, despite efforts of Giraud, recently arrived from France, to delay the action. Upon learning of the Allied landing on 8 November, Mast and a few hundred men seized control of the telephone service, police headquarters, substations, and Algiers radio, from which they broadcast an appeal in Giraud's name for all French troops to rally in support of the invasion. Mast's men also cut the telephone lines leading to naval headquarters and the big coastal batteries. After placing his superior General Louis Marie Koeltz in protective custody, Mast ordered the main body of French troops, the Algiers Division, to assist the Allied landings. Guides hurried to nearby beaches where they expected the Allied forces to land, while an army detachment seized control of a nearby airfield.

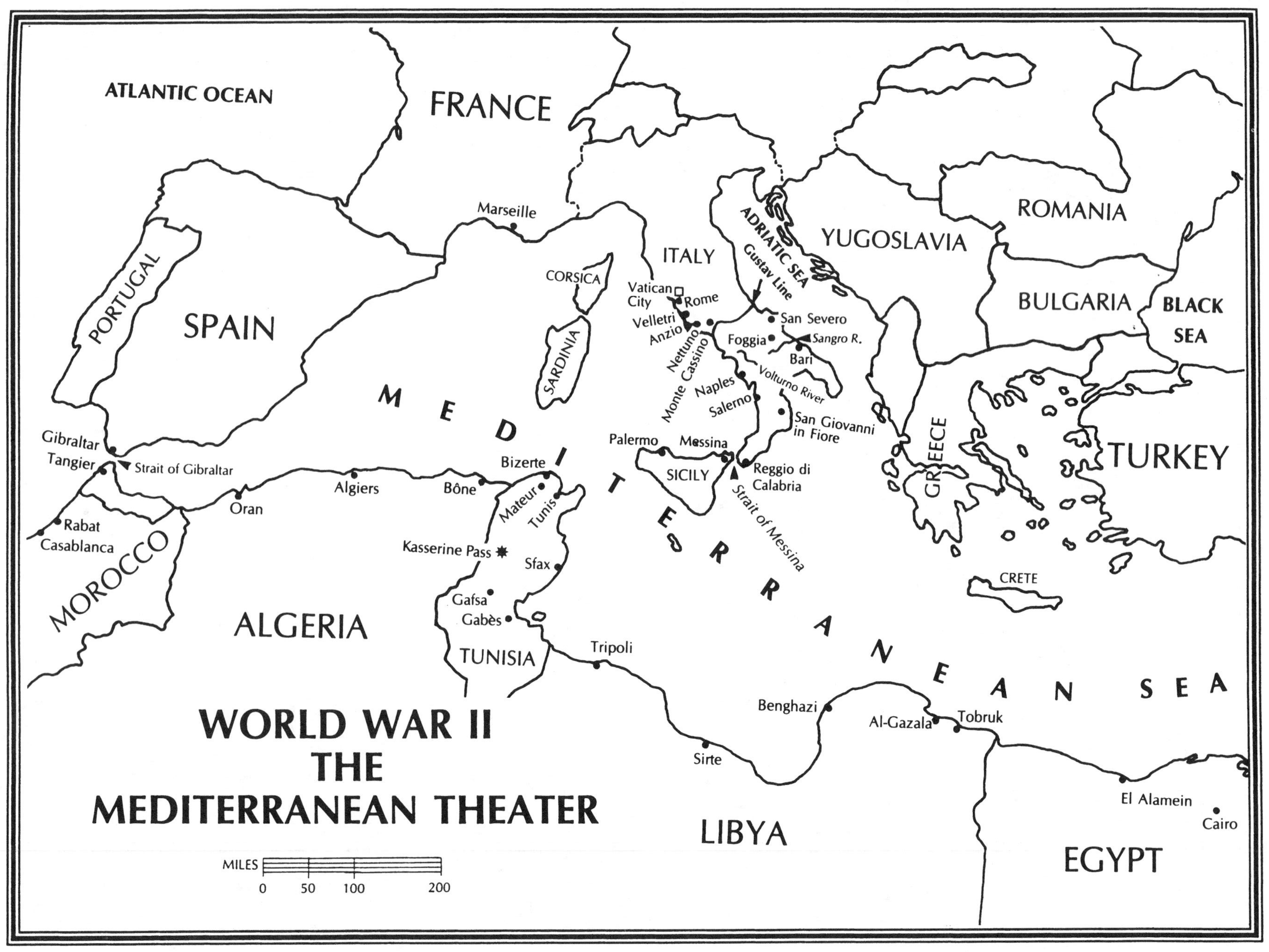
ATLANTIC OCEAN
FRANCE
Marseille
SPAIN
PORTUGAL
Gibraltar
Tangier
Strait of Gibraltar
Rabat
Casablanca
MOROCCO
Oran
Algiers
Bône
Bizerte
Mateur
Tunis
Kasserine Pass
Sfax
Gafsa
Gabès
TUNISIA
ALGERIA
CORSICA
SARDINIA
ITALY
Vatican City
Rome
Velletri
Anzio
Nettuno
Monte Cassino
Naples
Salerno
Foggia
San Severo
Sangro R.
Bari
Volturno River
San Giovanni in Fiore
Gustav Line
ADRIATIC SEA
Palermo
Messina
SICILY
Reggio di Calabria
Strait of Messina
YUGOSLAVIA
ROMANIA
BULGARIA
BLACK SEA
GREECE
TURKEY
CRETE
M E D I T E R R A N E A N SEA
Tripoli
Sirte
Benghazi
Al-Gazala
Tobruk
El Alamein
Cairo
LIBYA
EGYPT
WORLD WAR II
THE
MEDITERRANEAN THEATER
MILES
0
50
100
200

Meanwhile, Murphy hurried to the residence of the French army commander, General Alphonse Juin, to urge him to support the operation. Juin insisted that only Darlan could make this decision. Murphy sent for him, and upon Darlan's arrival, the Admiral found himself a prisoner of Mast's men. Meanwhile, in Morocco General Emile Bethouart had seized control of Rabat, the capital, and awaited the arrival of the invasion force.

Resistance was light almost everywhere except at Oran, where two British cutters ran into heavy fire from French naval units in the harbor. Fire from two French destroyers sank the cutters, killing 307 Allied navy and army men and wounding 350 more. Only forty-seven soldiers landed unhurt and they were quickly captured. Fighting ceased at Oran on 10 November.

Despite sporadic resistance and confusion among both the invasion force and the French defenders, the question of continued resistance was decided in Algiers, Rabat, and Vichy. After some hesitation, Darlan, who had returned to his headquarters in Algiers, decided that this was not just another raid but a major Allied effort. He ordered Juin to cease fire and to arrange for a cessation of hostilities in Algiers. A meeting between Juin and Giraud on 11 November produced an armistice by which Giraud would take command of all French forces in North Africa, with Juin as his deputy.

Thus far the invasion and subsequent combat in Algiers and Morocco had cost the Allies 1,181 men killed and missing, of which 584 were Americans. An additional 891 U.S. soldiers, sailors, and airmen were wounded. British wounded numbered 178, while the French lost more than 1,600 men (two-thirds of them naval personnel at Casablanca) and another 1,000 wounded. Political arrangements with Darlan, leaving him in command, enabled Eisenhower's force to gain time and to reach Tunisia, on 15 November, before the Germans and Italians. Nevertheless, the enemy managed to land reinforcements at Bizerte and Tunis.

Operations in North Africa turned into a vast pincers movement, with the British preparing to counterattack Rommel's forces from the east, while from the west, Allied forces under Eisenhower and Clark prepared to advance on Tunisia, the base from which the Axis armies operated, after consolidating their control over Algeria and Morocco.

German reaction to the Allied landings in Algeria and Morocco was to send reinforcements to Tunisia, where they encountered and quickly repulsed French units under General Georges Barre. This was the first French military commitment in North Africa against the Germans. Field Marshall Albert Kesselring, the German commander in chief, south, had poured German and Italian troops into Tunisia to provide depth and maneuvering room for a German beachhead and to check an Allied effort from Algeria. At the same time, he would be able to protect the rear of Rommel's Afrika Korps in Libya and secure Tunisian ports for resupply.

Although Rommel despaired of holding on to North Africa, Hitler ordered him to secure Libya while the newly arrived Axis forces prepared to push westward to drive the Allies from Algeria and to possibly draw Spain into intervention on the Axis side. Both Axis and Allied forces prepared to occupy Tunisia in strength—the Allies to cut off the Germans and the Axis to drive the Allies back into the sea or back into the desert. At first the Axis held on to Tunisia, and the Allies were forced by bad weather to halt their drive.

In mid-February 1943, the Germans, advancing from their Tunisian base against Major General Lloyd R. Fredendall's U.S. Second Corps, recaptured Faïd and Kassarine passes, Gafsa, and Sbeïtla from the hastily assembled Franco-American force that had recently captured them. The next month the newly reconstituted Second Corps, commanded now by Patton, counterattacked eastward to retake Gafsa and to establish supply depots for Montgomery's Eighth Army. After outflanking the Mareth Line, the Eighth Army moved into Tunisia. Meanwhile, U.S. Major General Omar Bradley, Patton's deputy, took over the U.S. Second Corps to enable Patton to concentrate on the forthcoming invasion of Sicily. Bradley now moved northward for a drive along the coast for an advance to Mateur and Bizerte. At the same time, the British broke the Mareth Line and captured Gabès on 30 March and Sfax on 10 April. On 7 May, Bradley captured Bizerte and Montgomery captured Tunis, and Pont du Fahs fell to the French. By 13 May, Axis resistance had ceased, and after General Jürgen von Arnim surrendered 150,000 men, the total number of Axis prisoners numbered 262,000. Additional Axis losses were 30,000 killed and 27,000 wounded. Total U.S. casualties for the North African campaign were 18,558—2,184 killed, 9,437 wounded, and 6,937 missing and prisoners of war. The principal burden of the Allied military effort in North Africa had been borne by the British First and Eighth armies.

THE ITALIAN CAMPAIGN, 1943–1944

In mid-January 1943, while the Axis still occupied Tunisia, Churchill and Roosevelt and their chiefs of staff met at Casablanca in Morocco to plan for an invasion of Sicily following a victory in North Africa. Despite Churchill's preference for an initial landing in Europe, ideally somewhere in the Balkans, the CCS agreed that plans be made for a cross-channel invasion of northern France in 1944. Lack of landing craft and a need to supply the Russians would prevent a cross-channel operation in 1943. Nevertheless, plans were made for an invasion of Sicily in 1943 (Operation Husky). At a press conference in Casablanca on 24 January, Roosevelt announced, with British concurrence, his policy of "unconditional surrender" as a prerequisite for peace with the Axis powers. The Allies were to negotiate on no other terms. The policy was the result of a carefully thought-out effort to reassure the Russians that the western Allies would not make a separate peace with Nazi Germany and use it as a possible bulwark against an advance by the Soviets into Central Europe, leaving them to face the Germans alone. Moreover, the Allies did not want to repeat the mistake of the armistice of 1918 and allow the German military to recreate the myth that their armies had not really been defeated. This time the German generals, not German civilians, would surrender. The demand for unconditional surrender, however, neither promised nor precluded a reasonably generous peace.

INVASION OF SICILY. As long as the Axis powers or nations friendly to them controlled the northern shore of the Mediterranean, the Allies had to make a twelve-thousand-mile detour around the Cape of Good Hope to reach Russia, India, and China. Control of the Mediterranean was the next logical step for the Allies, taken on 10 July 1943 with an amphibious assault on the island of Sicily. As in North Africa, General Eisenhower was in supreme command, with British General Sir Harold R. L. G. Alexander as his deputy commander of Allied ground forces. General Patton's Seventh Army—whose Second Corps, with Bradley in command, landed on Sicily's southern coast—pushed with an armored spearhead northwestward across the island to Palermo. For the first time, U.S. parachute troops of the Eighty-second Airborne Division participated in division strength in combat. After seizing Palermo on 24 July, Bradley moved eastward along the northern coast. Meanwhile, Montgomery's Eighth Army had landed in the southeast and advanced northward along the east coast. After thirty-nine days of combat, the two armies closed the pincers at Messina on 17 August.

Air power, although employed in significant numbers, appears not to have been decisive—a forecast of the later campaign in the Italian peninsula. Unfortunately, Allied naval antiaircraft shot down several troop-carrying craft with their cargo of parachutists from the Eighty-second Airborne. On 19 July, 272 heavy and 249 medium bombers of the U.S. Air Force bombed the San Lorenzo and Littoria railway marshalling yards in Rome and a nearby airfield. Churches and historical monuments had been clearly identified on the maps used by the air crews, and none were damaged. The attack, however, was sufficient to force Mussolini's resignation as premier on 25 July and dissolution of the Fascist party three days later.

During the campaign, however, the Germans, under cover of heavy antiaircraft fire, managed to extricate a considerable portion of their armored and airborne troops across the Strait of Messina to the Italian mainland. The campaign in Sicily cost the Germans 37,000 men and the Italians 137,000, most of whom were prisoners of war. Allied armies lost 31,158 killed, wounded, and missing.

INVASION OF ITALY. Following the German army's successful withdrawal across the Strait of Messina despite Allied air and naval superiority, the Canadian and British divisions of Montgomery's Eighth Army also crossed the strait and landed over the beaches near San Giovanni in Fiore and Reggio di Calabria on 3 September 1943, the first Allied foothold on the European continent. Italy accepted the terms of unconditional surrender on 8 September, and the next day Clark's U.S. Fifth Army, consisting of the U.S. Sixth Corps and the British Tenth Corps, came ashore at Salerno on Italy's west coast.

The Eighth Army met little resistance as it raced from the toe to the heel of the Italian boot. On 13 September, Bari, a major east coast port, had fallen to the British, whose patrols met those from the U.S. Fifth Army forty miles southeast of Salerno. By 16 September, the Allies held a front across the peninsula from the bay of Naples to the Adriatic.

In the Salerno area, however, the Germans, who had expected and prepared for an Allied landing in the vicinity of Genoa, held the high ground, from which they mounted strong defensive operations. Eight German divisions held in the north against a possible Allied landing remained there, but the light divisions stationed in the south were sufficient to limit the two Allied armies to a slow, grinding advance from the line held on 16 September to the so-called winter line of January 1944, which extended from the west coast along the Garigliano and Sangro rivers, across the Liri Valley south of Monte Cassino and the central mountains to the Adriatic. Italian forces, now part of the Allied coalition, forced the Germans from Sardinia on 20 September. On 27 September, Foggia and its vital airfields were captured by the British and Naples fell to Clark's army on 1 October. Kesselring, in command of the German armies in southern Italy since Hitler had made his decision to hold there rather than withdraw to the north, conducted a skillful withdrawal to the Volturno River, then later to the Garigliano and Sangro rivers.

Meanwhile, Allied shipping (300,000 tons) brought forward from North Africa vast quantities of matériel, machine shops, and warehouses to establish an Allied logistical base around Naples. On 1 November 1943 the Fifteenth Strategic Air Force, commanded by General Doolittle, who had led the first air raid against Japan, was activated at the ten airfields around Foggia. From this base Allied bombers could reach into Austria and the Balkans.

On 16 January 1944, General Eisenhower arrived in Great Britain to assume duties as supreme commander of the Allied Expeditionary Forces. His place as supreme Allied commander in the Mediterranean was taken by General Sir Henry Maitland Wilson. Air Marshal Sir Arthur W. Tedder took command of the British air fleets, and Alexander became commander of Allied armies in Italy. Lieutenant General Sir Oliver Leese took over command of the British Eighth Army from Montgomery, who returned to Great Britain as Eisenhower's deputy. Lieutenant General Ira C. Eaker became commander of the Mediterranean Allied air forces.

ANZIO AND CASSINO. Alexander, with Churchill's encouragement, decided to outflank the admittedly strong German line by landing U.S. General John Lucas' Sixth Corps in the Anzio-Nettuno area, thirty miles south of Rome. Once a beachhead had been established, the Anglo-American forces under Lucas were to capture Rome and cut off Kesselring's armies in the Liri Valley and along the Garigliano. Under the cover of darkness during the night of 17–18 January 1944, the Allies attacked in the south along the winter line. They crossed the river on the left, but the attack ground to a halt

Men of the 697th Field Artillery Battalion, during operations in Italy's Mignano region, prepare to fire a 240mm howitzer into German held territory in January 1944. (National Archives)

before the village of Castelforte, while on the right it failed completely. On 22 January the Sixth Corps, composed of fifty thousand U.S. and British troops, came ashore at Anzio at 2:00 A.M.

Allied aircraft dropped leaflets on Cassino's Benedictine abbey warning the monks to leave at once. The following day, 229 bombers dropped 453 tons of bombs on the abbey.

The Germans were completely surprised, having expected a landing closer to the Garigliano River. Fortunately for Kesselring, Lucas at first consolidated his beachhead instead of immediately pushing on to the Alban Hills, the high ground overlooking the beachhead south of Rome. The Germans, aware that their lines of communication were not in jeopardy, contained the Sixth Corps flanks and spearhead to build up a strong counterattacking force, which left the Sixth Corps immobilized at Anzio for four months. Along the Garigliano at the mouth of the Liri Valley, the proposed route to Rome, the Allies fought three desperate but fruitless battles for the town of Cassino. Believing the ancient Benedictine abbey overlooking the town to be the key to the enemy's defenses, the Allied command decided to bomb it. On 14 February 1944, Allied aircraft dropped leaflets on the abbey warning the monks and refugees known to be there to leave at once. The following day, 229 bombers dropped 453 tons of bombs on the abbey and destroyed the buildings. Another bombing attack followed on the 16th, but the infantry did not attack until early on the 18th, following a five-hour artillery barrage at the rate of ten thousand rounds per hour. In the meantime, the Germans, who heretofore had remained outside the abbey, moved into the massive ruins to set up defensive positions and forced the Allies to break off their attack on the 19th. The Allies intermittently bombed and shelled the abbey and the town of Cassino for eight days. It was not until 11 May that a second Battle of the Garigliano was launched, but this time Monte Cassino was bypassed, because the Germans evacuated the ruins and withdrew into the Liri Valley.

OPERATION DIADEM. In preparing for the spring offensive, code-named Operation Diadem, that was expected to carry the Allied armies to Rome and beyond, the inhospitable terrain before them left the commanders little choice in their selection of sites for major military operations. The western half of the peninsula, including the Liri Valley and its narrow coastal plain, offered the most favorable terrain and the best possibilities for employing Allied sea power in outflanking operations against enemy defenses. The western coastal plain extended northwestward one hundred miles from the mouth of the Garigliano to San Severo, a small port about twenty miles west of Rome. The Sixth Corps beachhead at Anzio-Nettuno lay in the Pontine Marshes at the foot of the Alban Hills. Crisscrossed with drainage ditches and irrigation canals, the terrain did not offer conditions for employment of armor on a wide front.

From its very inception, Generals Clark and Marshall had opposed the concept of the Anzio beachhead. Churchill and Alexander, however, had envisioned it as a base for a thrust northwest along the axis of Highway 6 into the Alban Hills and on to Rome, while the main Allied forces drove the enemy from the southern front up the Liri Valley into a trap to be formed by the Sixth Corps, now commanded by Lieutenant General Lucian K. Truscott, athwart enemy lines of communication around Rome. The Anzio concept was a British idea carried out in large part by Americans. It had much to do with the later Anglo-American disagreement over the ultimate role of the Allied forces.

Clark saw Truscott's corps as the potential spearhead of a Fifth Army drive on Rome. The Alban Hills and not Highway 6 had become, in Clark's opinion, the road to Rome. He believed that his forces should secure the Alban Hills before attempting to cut off the German Tenth Army's right wing at Valmontone. Alexander, on the other hand, viewed an attack from the beachhead as his most important weapon of opportunity, to be launched when the situation was fluid. If the operation went according to plan, he expected that the Sixth Corps thrust toward Valmontone on Highway 6 would possibly block the withdrawal for a large percentage of the German forces on the southern front. Although he was aware that Clark's views differed sharply from his own, he remained confident that Leese's Eighth Army, after breaking through the Gustav Line in the Liri Valley, would lead the way up Highway 6. Furthermore, the Allied commander believed that the projected French Expeditionary Corps attack (commanded by General Juin) over the Arunci Mountains on the Fifth Army's front would be a secondary and supporting effort to the main operation in the valley.

Instead, when Operation Diadem began on 11 May, the French colonial troops under Juin led the way through the Gustav Line over Monte Majo, the high ground overlooking the valley from the west. To the left of the French Expeditionary Corps, the U.S. Second

Corps advanced rapidly across Monte Petrella, the high ground overlooking the narrow coastal plain, on 15 May. With an overall Allied strength of twenty-five divisions as opposed to nineteen enemy divisions, superiority in both air and artillery, sufficient reserves, and the troops rested and ready, the Fifth Army made contact with Truscott's beachhead force by 25 May. Two weeks after the beginning of the offensive and 125 days after the landings at Anzio, the troops from the southern front had joined with those of the beachhead. There remained only for Operation Diadem to break out from the beachhead and for Rome to be captured.

As Truscott prepared the Sixth Corps for the breakout and final drive on Rome, Clark decided on his own initiative to modify the British concept for the landing—a drive on Valmontone and Highway 6 to cut off the enemy withdrawal from the south. From the beginning Clark had believed that there were too many alternate roads leading northward out of the Liri Valley that would enable Kesselring to bypass a trap at Valmontone.

Clark's decision was reinforced by intelligence reports that the German 362d Division had already withdrawn from the vicinity of Cisterna di Latina before the Second Corps' front into a sector between Velletri and Valmontone, and that Kesselring had moved the Hermann Goering Parachute Division into the Valmontone gap. Clark reasoned that even if Truscott managed to reach Valmontone, his lines of communication would be vulnerable to the enemy overlooking it from the Alban Hills. Accordingly, without consulting either Truscott or Alexander, Clark decided to turn the Sixth Corps—the Thirty-fourth and Forty-fifth infantry divisions and the First Armored Division—northwestward, directly into the Alban Hills. Only the Third Infantry Division would continue in the original direction toward Valmontone and Highway 6.

The Thirty-fourth and Forty-fifth divisions attacked on 26 May, while the two British divisions demonstrated west of the Anzio-Albano road in order to hold the Germans to that front. Despite the commitment of the First Armored Division on the 28th, the Germans continued to hold their front. By then Kesselring no longer believed the Third Infantry Division's thrust toward Valmontone to be the axis of the main Allied attack from the beachhead. Only after radio intercepts identified the First Armored Division as being on the Albano-Lanuvio front did he conclude that the offensive toward Valmontone was actually a secondary effort.

This news had come as no surprise to General August von Mackensen, commander of the German Fourteenth Army, who had assumed that the Anzio breakout would move toward his Caesar Line in the Alban Hills. Consequently, von Mackensen was not caught by surprise when, on the night of 30 May, the Sixth Corps turned toward the Alban Hills and halted the offensive.

As discouraging as this repulse was to both Clark and Truscott, a means to crack the line had been found. During the night of 27 May reconnaissance patrols from the Thirty-sixth Division, probing the slopes of Monte Artemisio in the Alban Hills, had discovered a four-mile-wide gap in the Caesar Line, and two regiments began moving through it during the night of 30 May. By the morning of 31 May, the regiments were in firm control of a four-mile-wide sector of the Caesar Line, and von Mackensen's defenses were in danger.

In the meantime, Lieutenant General Geoffrey Keyes's Second Corps had reached Valmontone and Highway 6. The Fifth Army's final drive on Rome was launched on 3 June across the Alban Hills by the Sixth Corps and Second Corps astride Highway 6. It soon developed into a race between the two corps as to which would be the first in Rome. Clark, aware of the imminent cross-channel invasion of Normandy, was anxious to capture the first of the Axis capitals before the world press focused on northwestern France. Faced with an assault on Rome, Kesselring had only two choices—to evacuate Rome or to defend the city street by street and house to house. The latter would be only a modest delaying action and would leave the city in ruins and arouse the condemnation of Christians worldwide.

Hitler declared that Rome,

"because of its status as a place of culture,

must not become the scene of combat operations."

It was not until late on 3 June, when advance detachments of the U.S. Fifth Army drew within sight of Rome, that Berlin authorized Kesselring to approach the Allies through the Vatican to obtain a joint agreement to declare Rome an open city. Although the Allied command had called upon the civilian populace to rise up and join the battle to oust the Germans from the city, German units were already desperately trying to reach the Tiber River to escape the advancing Americans, who had vowed to spare the city only if the Germans did not resist. As German units fought on in the southern outskirts of the city, Hitler declared that Rome, "because of its status as a place of culture, must not become the scene of combat operations." This order also spared Rome's historic bridges across the Tiber.

Operation Diadem, which had begun on 11 May, ended on 4 June with the liberation of Rome.

Although the British Eighth Army had originally been given the major role and a wider front, its casualties in the operation were less than those of the U.S. Fifth Army—11,639, as compared with U.S. losses of 17,931. If the losses of the attached French and British units are added to those of the Fifth Army, however, the disproportion becomes greater—28,566 for the entire Fifth Army, because the Eighth Army figures included Canadian and Polish forces as well as British. Total Allied losses amounted to 40,205 of all categories. For approximately the same period (10 May to 10 June), the two defending German armies had incurred a total of 38,024 casualties. The Allies claimed to have captured 15,606 prisoners.

The feelings of many on the Allied side were perhaps best summed up in the words of a British war correspondent: "Now, at last, the victory had arrived. It was good that it should come, for it had been bravely contested and, in the end, brilliantly achieved. But it had been a long journey, and everyone was very weary. And too many had died."

THE INVASION OF NORMANDY

The Anglo-American forces based in Great Britain had not been idle during the campaigns in North Africa and Italy. During the North African campaign, Allied navies so improved their antisubmarine tactics that by May 1943 U-boat losses rose to 30 to 50 percent of all U-boats at sea. From May onward the famed wolf packs were no longer safe from detection and attack. Before the end of the North African campaign, owing to the successful antisubmarine campaign, the Allies had transported to Europe and Africa more than two million men and their supplies without losing a loaded troop ship. Meanwhile, the accelerated Allied shipbuilding program had outpaced the German submarine building program. Not only had the war at sea taken a bad turn for the Axis, but the German homeland had come under increasing attack from Allied bombers, with major destruction visited upon cities and industrial centers. By mid-September 1943, one million civilians had been evacuated from Berlin. Europe was awash with bombed-out refugees. The Luftwaffe had lost the war in the air before Allied armies landed in France.

Since late December 1943, Eisenhower and his three senior commanders—Admiral Sir Bertram H. Ramsay, commander of the Allied naval forces; Air Chief Marshal Sir Troffard Leigh-Mallory, commander of the Allied air forces; and Field Marshal Montgomery, commanding general of the Allied land forces—had been planning for the invasion of the Continent. The land forces consisted of the U.S. First Army, including the Eighty-second and 101st Airborne Divisions, under General Bradley; and the Twenty-first Army Group, comprising the First Canadian Army (Lieutenant General H. D. G. Crearar), the British Second Army (Lieutenant General M. C. Dempsey), the Sixth Airborne Division (Lieutenant General F. A. M. Browning), and miscellaneous Allied contingents. On 21 January, Air Chief Tedder was named deputy supreme commander to Eisenhower.

Originally, Allied planners had thought that the initial landing on the Continent (Operation Overlord) might be accomplished with three divisions. This number was eventually deemed insufficient and the force increased to five divisions. D-Day moved from 1 May to 5 June. On 21 January 1944 the changes were agreed to by Eisenhower and his commanders, who also decided upon the Bay of the Seine at Normandy as the landing area. The decision was influenced by the fact that the Cotentin Peninsula provided some protection from the prevailing westerly winds and because destruction of the Seine and Loire bridges would isolate the northwestern quarter of France. Moreover, two large ports, Le Havre and Cherbourg, lay on the flanks. Since the latter lay on the Atlantic tip of the peninsula, once it was overrun, the port would be completely isolated. Frontage on the Bay of the Seine stretched from the town of Quinéville, south of Harfleur, to the estuary of the Orne River. The Americans were to land on the western half, the British on the eastern. The first day's objective was a sixty-mile line from the Orne to the beaches at Sainte-Mère Èglise and Carentan and the towns of Bayeux and Caen, the latter linked by a canal to the channel.

Eisenhower planned first to secure a lodgement area that embraced Caen, Cherbourg, and nearby airfields. Next, the armies were to advance on Brittany with the object of capturing the ports southward to Nantes on the Atlantic coast. The Allies would then turn eastward on the line of the Loire River in the direction of Paris and northward across the Seine River to destroy as many enemy forces as possible. Operation Anvil was to begin simultaneously, with a landing in southern France, followed by an advance up the Rhone Valley to meet the forces under Eisenhower. The landing was to be made by the U.S. Seventh Army under Major General Alexander M. Patch.

Opposing the Allied offensive north of the Loire were two of Germany's most distinguished generals—Field Marshal Karl von Rundstedt, commander in chief of the western front, and Field Marshal Rommel, commander of the armies in France. The two generals held diametrically opposing strategic views. Rundstedt believed German forces to be overextended and favored evacuating France and withdrawing to Germany's frontiers. Nevertheless, he had yielded to Hitler's demand that all of France be defended and agreed that the French Atlantic ports be held to the last man to deny their use to Allied shipping. Rommel planned to engage the Allies on the beaches and advocated strong garrisons along the coast with nearby reserves. Von Rundstedt was willing to allow the enemy to gain a landing and then counterattack before he had an opportunity to consolidate his beachhead. For this purpose, Von Rundstedt would keep the bulk of the German forces well to the rear of the coasts. These divergent views led, in the words of the British historian Major General J. F. C. Fuller, to a fatal compromise, the worst thing in war.

The Germans kept their infantry forward and the bulk of their armor in the rear, which denied them the benefit of coordination between the two arms when the crisis came. Furthermore, their coastal defenses were linear, in effect a Maginot Line with little depth. There were no secondary defensive positions. The Germans also incorrectly concluded that the Allies would make their main effort in the Pas de Calais area and concentrated their strength there. Allied aerial reconnaissance had revealed this concentration, and the Allied command encouraged the Germans to believe it to be the Allied intent. Eisenhower expected that the deception would pay enormous dividends when the cross-channel offensive began.

To support Operation Overlord, landing craft were drawn from operations in the Mediterranean, which meant that the projected landing on the Mediterranean coast of France could not coincide with the landing in Normandy as planned. A vast naval armada was assembled to cover the landings: 702 warships and twenty-five flotillas of minesweepers, eventually a total of five

On the night of 5 June 1944, thousands of ships and craft set out for the coast of Normandy in France. These American soldiers face heavy German machine gun fire as they leave the ramp of a landing boat for Normandy beach on 6 June 1944. (National Archives)

thousand ships and an additional four thousand ship-to-shore landing craft. All mechanized vehicles and tanks were waterproofed to permit them to be driven through deep water. To permit landings over open beaches, five sheltered harbors, code-named Gooseberries, were formed by sinking sixty blockships and two prefabricated ports, code-named Mulberries, were constructed and towed to sea in sections. An underwater pipeline, known as Pluto, was prepared to carry gasoline to the landing areas. The landings were to be covered by both tactical and strategic air power—the former to provide close air support to the landing forces and the latter to prevent reinforcements of German armor from coming forward. Guns from naval craft offshore were to provide additional support.

General Eisenhower's battle plan, in brief, was as follows: Airborne troops, employing 2,395 aircraft and 867 gliders, were to land at 2:00 A.M.; the aerial bombardment by 2,219 aircraft was to begin at 3:14 A.M. and be augmented at 5:50 A.M. by naval bombardment; the first wave of the five-division landing force, consisting of 4,266 ships and landing craft, were to come ashore at 6:30 A.M. The three airborne divisions—the British Sixth and U.S. Eighty-second and 101st—were to protect the flanks of the assault. Only the first managed to drop precisely on its objective along the estuary of the Orne. The two U.S. divisions were scattered over an area near Carentan that measured twenty-five by fifteen miles.

Prior to the invasion, during one of several Allied training exercises, two German E-boat (torpedo boat) flotillas attacked the convoy, destroying two LSTs (landing ship tanks) and damaging a third. About seven hundred men were lost during the action, reducing the Allied reserve of LSTs to none. The Germans failed to appreciate the potential damage they could inflict on the invasion fleet. Loading of the landing forces began on 30 May, with all on board by 3 June. They were divided into twelve convoys for the crossing of the English Channel, depending on their missions, assembly points, and speed. After several changes in the weather, meteorologists finally forecast a break in unfavorable weather on 4 June. Winds of 25 to 31 knots would moderate, and cloud conditions would permit heavy bombing on the night of 5 June and the morning of 6 June.

Eisenhower and his staff decided to go ahead on schedule, aware both that it was a gamble and of the hazards of delay. On the night of 5 June, five thousand ships and craft of the largest fleet ever assembled set out for the coast of Normandy. Despite several intercepted warnings to the French resistance, the Germans failed to change their state of defense readiness, which had existed throughout the spring.

The six parachute regiments of the two U.S. airborne divisions, together with organic supporting units, some of them seaborne, numbered more than thirteen thousand men. They were carried in 822 transport planes flying from nine airfields. The aircraft began taking off before midnight along routes designed to take them to the drop zones between 1:15 A.M. and 1:30 A.M. over the Cotentin Peninsula. At the same time, the British airborne began landing near Caen, and the main body of the invasion force began landing on the beaches of Normandy. After several hours of confused action by widely scattered units, the U.S. airborne divisions eventually managed to accomplish their missions and make contact with the infantry moving inland from the beaches. D-Day losses among the airborne were 1,259, including 156 known killed and 756 missing, presumed captured or killed.

Beach landing forces were greatly assisted by naval gunfire after H-hour (6:30 A.M.) that neutralized some of the enemy batteries and fortifications, broke up counterattacks, wore down the defenders, and dominated the assault areas. Early success and light casualties on Utah Beach contrasted sharply with difficulties experienced during the first hours at Omaha Beach. For most of the first day, the Germans believed that they had repulsed the Allied landing at Omaha Beach. Heavy seas helped the defenders, swamping considerable equipment before it reached the beach. Mist, mixed with the smoke and dust raised by the naval bombardment, obscured landmarks along the coast. Also, a strong lateral coastal current carried landing craft eastward of their touchdown points.

Most enemy batteries and fortifications were able to continue their fire as soon as the naval bombardment was forced to lift, as some units moved inland from the beach. The resulting heavy losses and disorganization of the first wave of troops had repercussions on each succeeding wave throughout the morning of D-Day. Nevertheless, the Germans were unable to prevent Allied lodgements on both beaches. Rommel's armor, in reserve, was too close to be mobile, being pinned down by naval gunfire and bombing, while Von Rundstedt's was too far away and was prevented from coming forward by Allied strafing and by fuel and ammunition shortages caused by a breakdown in transportation. German reserves did not arrive in time to prevent the establishment of beachheads or in sufficient strength to destroy them, as ordered by Hitler. Moving out from their beachheads, the Allies secured the Cotentin Peninsula by 18 June and captured the port of Cherbourg on 27 June, despite Hitler's orders that it be defended

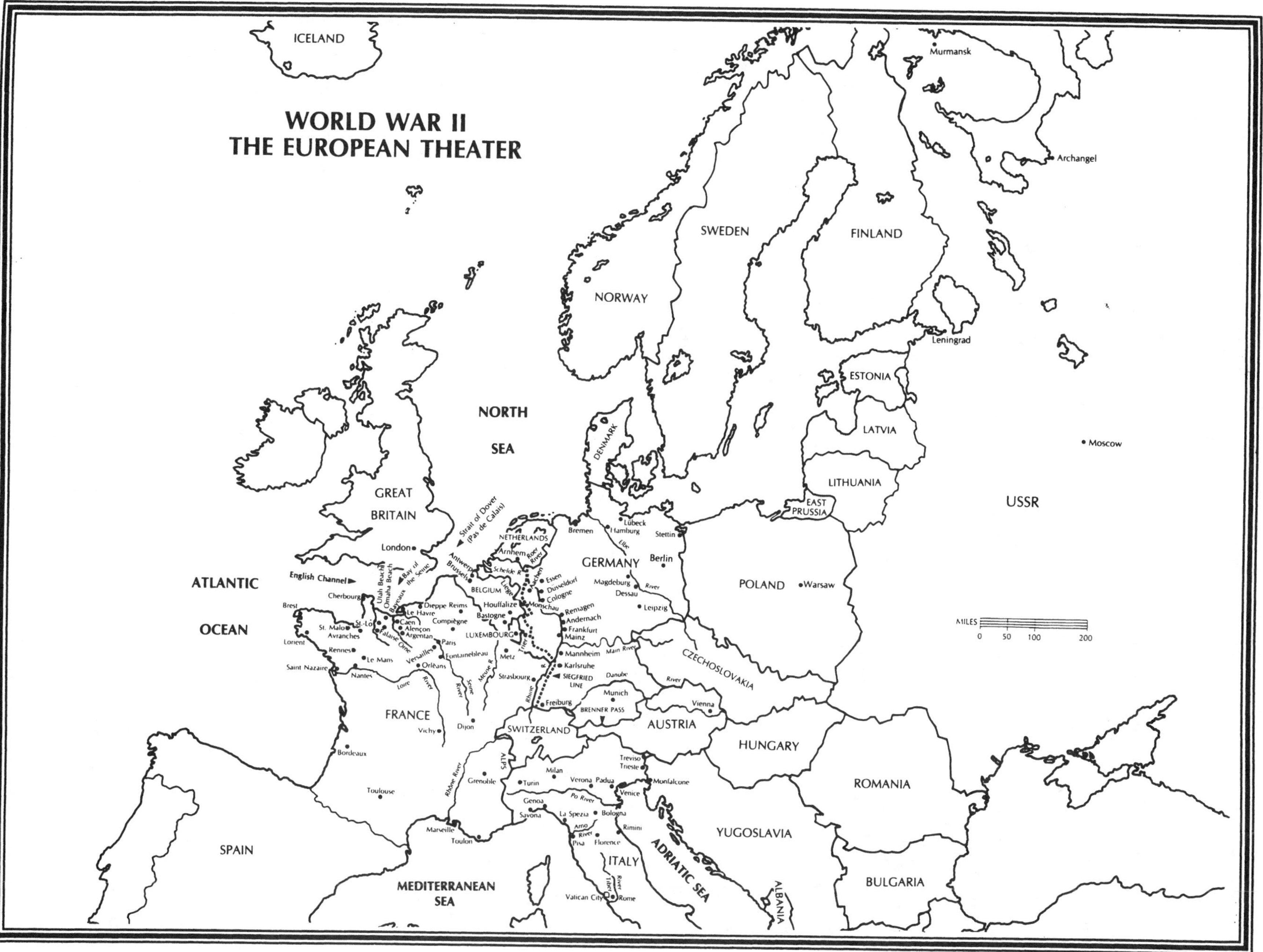
WORLD WAR II
THE EUROPEAN THEATER
ICELAND
NORWAY
SWEDEN
FINLAND
Murmansk
Archangel
Leningrad
ESTONIA
LATVIA
LITHUANIA
EAST PRUSSIA
Moscow
USSR
NORTH SEA
DENMARK
GREAT BRITAIN
London
ATLANTIC OCEAN
English Channel
Strait of Dover (Pas de Calais)
NETHERLANDS
BELGIUM
LUXEMBOURG
GERMANY
Berlin
POLAND
Warsaw
MILES
0 50 100 200
CZECHOSLOVAKIA
AUSTRIA
Vienna
HUNGARY
ROMANIA
YUGOSLAVIA
BULGARIA
ALBANIA
SWITZERLAND
FRANCE
Paris
ITALY
Rome
ADRIATIC SEA
SPAIN
MEDITERRANEAN SEA
SIEGFRIED LINE
BRENNER PASS
ALPS

to the last man. The Allies now had a firm grip in Normandy and were prepared to break out from their beachhead.

Although the Allies had secured a major landing in France by the end of June, they were still far behind the original timetable set by the planners. By that time they should have held all of Normandy, but they occupied an area only about one-fifth the size of the province. The question now arose whether a military stalemate had been reached with the possibility of trench warfare similar to that of World War I. To overcome this threat, the Allies ferried additional combat troops to the Continent at the expense of service units. The imbalance between combat and service formations was not serious, because the lines of communication were short, but when the Allies eventually broke out of their relatively modest lodgement area and overran a large area, the small number of service troops might make adequate logistical support difficult.

Hedges of hawthorne, brambles, vines, and trees one to three feet thick and three to fifteen feet tall checked the progress of the infantry.

As had been the case in Italy, local agricultural practices had compartmentalized the terrain, greatly restricting maneuvering and favoring the defense. Centuries-old hedgerows enclosed each plot of land, no matter how small. Half-earth and half-hedge, these fences had a dirt parapet at their base varying in thickness from one to four or more feet and from three to twelve feet high. Hedges of hawthorne, brambles, vines, and trees one to three feet thick and three to fifteen feet tall checked the progress of the infantry. Innumerable wagon trails wound among the hedgerows. Looking like sunken lanes, they formed a labyrinth where the hedgerows overarched the trails. For the next few weeks, this terrain determined the tactics of Allied efforts to break free of the Normandy lodgement.

Perhaps the greatest threat to the Allies, however, was the British failure to secure the port of Caen by 1 July. A vital communications center, Caen was the key to operations eastward to the Seine and southeastward to the Paris-Orléans gap. Although Cherbourg had been captured on 27 June, Montgomery deemed the capture of Caen too difficult to accomplish immediately. Eisenhower, denied access to the favorable terrain east of Caen and to the main approaches to the Seine and Paris, looked to Bradley's First Army for breakout leadership. Thus, in July U.S. troops had the difficult task of launching a major attack on the Cotentin Peninsula through terrain favoring the defense rather than over the more open terrain near Caen where, however, the Germans lay in wait for an Allied offensive.

THE BATTLE OF FRANCE

Despite the lack of a major port in France and frequent periods of bad weather that interrupted the flow of men and matériel through the artificial ports off the Normandy coast, by 25 July the Allies had assembled four armies for a breakout offensive. The Northern Army Group, commanded by Montgomery, consisted of the Canadian First Army under General Crearar and the British Second, commanded by Lieutenant General Sir M. C. Dempsey. The Second was to capture Caen and break into the Seine Valley. General Bradley was in command of the Central Army Group, which included Lieutenant General Courtney H. Hodges' U.S. First Army and (after 1 August) General Patton's Third Army.

On the Allied left wing, the Northern Army Group launched a massive holding attack on 15 July against the stronger enemy forces along the Orne River above Caen. At the same time, the First Army attacked and, under cover of heavy aerial bombardment, broke through at St. Lô (18 July) and Coutances (28 July). The Third Army took advantage of the breakthrough to advance southward by 31 July along the western side of the Cotentin Peninsula through Avranches, thence across the base of the Brittany peninsula through Rennes on 4 August. They reached Le Mans by 9 August and went to Nantes and eastward, up the right bank of the Loire to Angers, where they arrived the next day. The Eighth Corps of the Third Army had the task of overrunning Brittany and capturing Saint-Malo, Brest, Lorient, and Saint-Nazaire, all of which was held by seventy-five thousand German troops to deny the Americans use of these ports to support the invasion.

Meanwhile, the Germans under von Rundstedt's successor, Hans Günther von Kluge, saw an opportunity to attempt a counterattack through Avranches and thereby cut off the Third Army, which was supplied through the narrow Avranches corridor. On 7 August the Germans launched a heavy armored counterattack against the Americans and the British and Canadians. These counterattacks continued until 12 August, but the First Army managed to hold open the corridor.

The German defense around Mortain enabled an Allied pincer maneuver to entrap the German Fifth (Panzer) and Seventh armies. Against fierce resistance, the British and Canadians fought their way southeastward to reach Falaise by 17 August. In the meantime, elements of the Third Army turned northward from Le Mans through Alençon. By the evening of 12 August, they had reached the outskirts of Argentan. Despite a severe tank battle with German Panzers desperately seeking to hold open the Falaise-Argentan pocket in order to permit the escape of their Seventh and Fifth armies, which were recalled too late from Mortain, the Allies began to close the pocket on 18 August. Moving from the north and south, the Allies pressed forward rapidly to close the gap near Chambois on 20 August. Two days later the pocket was eliminated with the capture of 100,000 prisoners and several thousand other casualties. Although many Germans managed to escape to the east, resistance west of the Seine and north of the Loire had collapsed, and the way to Paris lay open.

The Third Army had meanwhile turned eastward to deny the Germans use of lines of communication between the Seine and the Loire. The Twelfth Corps reached Orléans on 17 August; three days later the Americans entered Fontainbleau, outside Paris. By the end of the month these advance units had passed south of Paris and moved east 140 miles to a point within 60 miles of the German frontier. Throughout this advance, fighter-bomber groups of the U.S. Ninth Air Force—attached to the ground force column—flew reconnaissance, bombed, and strafed in close support. The air force also guarded the long open southern flank of the Third Army along the line of the Loire. Allied forces took Versailles to threaten the encirclement of Paris from the south, a signal for an uprising in the city. The ten-thousand-man German garrison ignored Hitler's order to defend Paris or destroy its bridges. On 25 August, General Dietrich von Choltiz surrendered the city and its garrison to General Jacques Le Clerc of the French Second Armored Division.

On 25 August 1944, General Dietrich von Cholitz surrendered Paris to General Jacques Le Clerc of the French Second Armored Division. Allied troops soon swarmed the city; among them were these American soldiers who drove their tank past Paris's Arc de Triomph. (National Archives)

An important Allied shortfall remained—most French and Belgian ports had not been taken. Brest, Lorient, Saint-Nazaire, and Bordeaux remained in German hands, which prevented the Allied armies from resupplying their forces directly from the United States. The Allies were forced to rely upon the channel ports; Dieppe was captured on 31 August and in use by 7 September, and Le Havre fell on 11 September and was opened as a port on 9 October.

As the Allied armies advanced across France they had a daily requirement of approximately one million gallons of gasoline and needed various vehicles and other supplies to keep the offensive moving. Allied bombers had destroyed so many bridges, however, that the supply problem became critical in September and October. Eisenhower had to decide whether to give supply priority to Patton, who was moving rapidly toward Metz and the Rhine River, or to Montgomery's army group, which had liberated Brussels, Belgium, on 3 September and taken Antwerp the following day. Unfortunately, Montgomery still had to fight for two months to clear the lower Scheldt River in order to open the port of Antwerp to the sea and Allied shipping, and the port was not in operation until 27 November. In the meantime, trucks of the so-called Red Ball Express rolled day and night from the channel ports to forward depots. Pipelines were also laid from channel ports overland in the wake of the advancing armies. Advanced units were supplied frequently by airlift.

In the meantime, Operation Anvil (15 August to 15 September) had opened additional ports in southern France. Supported from the ports of Marseilles and Toulon, the Sixth Army Group, commanded by General Jacob Devers and consisting of General Patch's U.S. Seventh Army and the First French Army, commanded by General J.-M.-G. de Lattre de Tassigny, moved northward toward a planned junction with the U.S. Third Army. After landing on 15 August, the U.S. Seventh Army fanned out eastward, first to take Nice, then northward to take Grenoble on 22 August, and advance up the valley of the Rhone. On Patch's left the First French Army cleared the remaining Mediterranean ports before sending units toward Toulouse and Bordeaux, while other First Army units joined Patch in his advance up the Rhone. The Germans, harassed by French resistance forces, withdrew toward Orléans. On 16 September, about twenty thousand German troops, cut off from their retreat into Germany, surrendered to the Eighty-third Infantry Division southwest of Orléans. The First French Armored Division, attached to the U.S. Seventh Army, on 11 September met with the Second French Armored Division of the U.S. Third Army northwest of Dijon.

The Sixth Army Group continued to be supplied from bases in Italy through Marseilles and Toulon. Eventually fourteen more divisions passed through these ports. With the opening of the main rail lines through Lyons and Dijon connecting the Mediterranean ports with the interior, the Southern Army Group was supplied, as well as the Central Army Group until the approaches to Antwerp had been cleared.

As the first summer of an Allied presence on the Continent drew to an end, thirty-eight Allied divisions—twenty American, twelve British, three Canadian, two French, and one Polish—had been landed to liberate Europe from Germany. Awaiting in Great Britain for movement to the Continent were six more U.S. divisions; three of them airborne, of which two were veterans of the Normandy invasion. In addition, the Allies mustered 4,035 operational heavy bombers; 1,720 light, medium, and torpedo bombers; and 5,000 fighter aircraft. There were more than 2,000 transport aircraft in the air transport command. As for the British, they had strained themselves to the limit. They had no more divisions not already fully committed to the fight, and national service (the draft) was calling up men between the ages of sixteen and sixty-five and women between the ages of eighteen and fifty. The Germans, however, had been able to draw upon the labor of other nationalities. In 1944 they also extended the work week to sixty hours and began combing men out of nonessential occupations. German women had not yet been drafted for work.

THE BATTLE FOR GERMANY

German armed forces facing the Allies in the west had paid a heavy price since D-Day. Approximately one million men had been in action. Of these, nearly 500,000 had been lost, 250,000 of which had been captured—135,000 between the breakout at Saint-Lô and the liberation of Paris. Of the fifty German divisions in the field in June, only ten remained as combat-effective units. By the beginning of September the Allies had taken more than 350,000 prisoners. Hitler brought back the elderly von Rundstedt to command what was left of the German armed forces in France. Von Rundstedt was more intent on withdrawing the remnants of his armies to the frontier than on trying to keep French and Belgian territory. The only serious German resistance from September to December was along the waterways controlling the approaches to Antwerp and at Metz and Aachen.

Despite Allied bombing, the Germans were busily producing a jet-propelled fighter aircraft, potentially a serious threat. Another, more immediate threat were the vaunted V-2 heavy rockets, whose production had been increased from three hundred in August to seven hundred per month from September 1944 to March 1945. First launched from sites in the Netherlands on 7 September 1944 against England, they did extensive damage and caused numerous casualties, but in no way did they prove to be decisive war-ending weapons.

After September 1944, the Luftwaffe was hampered greatly by fuel shortages caused partly by the loss of Romanian oil fields and by Allied bombing of synthetic oil plants in Germany. Diesel fuel supplies were always sufficient for the submarine service, but Allied bombing hampered submarine production despite widely scattered prefabrication facilities. Of 290 new boats scheduled between July and December 1944, only 65 were delivered. The number of submarines in service declined from 181 in June 1944 to 140 in December.

The Allies had cleared the enemy from the area north of the Loire and west of the Seine in less than three months, but three more months were needed to close up to the frontiers of the Third Reich. The reasons for this delay in the Allied advance had been chronic logistical problems caused by a shortage of service units and parts. Realizing that without the port of Antwerp it would be impossible to mount a winter campaign, the Allied command decided to allocate to Montgomery's Northern Army Group the supplies and transport needed to establish a bridgehead across the lower Rhine near the city of Arnhem in the Netherlands, then to clear the Scheldt below Antwerp, Belgium, and close up to the lower Rhine. This would eventually open up a vital port for a winter campaign and supply an average of 25,000 tons of military supplies per day.

The Netherlands were filled with natural obstacles—broad streams and low-lying, often flooded, land. It was in this region on 17 September that the First Allied Airborne Army, based in Great Britain, dropped the Eighty-second Airborne Division near Eindhoven west of the Meuse, the 101st Airborne near Nijmegen between the Meuse and the Waal (an arm of the Rhine),

Troops of the 370th Infantry Regiment move up through Prato, Italy, on 9 April 1945, at the beginning of the Allied offensive against Italy. (National Archives)

and the British First Airborne Division at Arnhem east of the Rhine. Seizing roads and bridges, these units tried to clear the way for ground units that would follow to advance into northwest Germany. Bad weather, however, interfered with airborne resupply and reinforcement, which enabled the Germans to overwhelm the British airhead at Arnhem on 25 September. The Northern Army Group concentrated on clearing the Scheldt (9 October–9 November) so that Antwerp could be employed for resupply. Aachen fell to the U.S. First Army on 21 October, Metz to the Third Army on 22 November, and Strasbourg to the Seventh Army the following day. These advances at last brought the Allied armies up to the Siegfried Line (or Westwall). This defense was most formidable before the Saar but weakest above Karlsruhe and west of Aachen. The defense was costly: By the end of November, German losses since D-Day had risen to 750,000.

THE OFFENSIVE CONTINUES IN ITALY

Following the conquest of Rome on 4 June 1944 by the U.S. Fifth Army, the Allied effort in Italy lost much of its momentum. In June and July, the demands of Operation Anvil had stripped the Fifth Army of much of its strength. Seven of its veteran divisions—the Third, Thirty-sixth, and Forty-fifth infantry divisions, as well as one Algerian and three Moroccan mountain divisions—were withdrawn for operations in southern France. Nevertheless, both the U.S. Fifth and the British Eighth armies steadily pressed their advance toward the northern Apennines and the Po Valley. Their strategic goal was to maintain sufficient pressure against Kesselring to prevent withdrawal of German units from Italy to reinforce other fronts beyond the Alps. Despite determined enemy resistance along the Arno River, Florence fell to British units under Fifth Army command in early August, Pisa to the Fifth Army on 2 September, and Rimini, on the Adriatic flank of the Po Valley, to the Eighth Army on 21 September. Although this enabled the British to outflank the Po Line, for the balance of 1944 the Germans managed to hold on to much of their transpeninsular Gothic Line south of Bologna until the following spring melted the snows and opened the passes.

In December, Field Marshal Alexander assumed the position of supreme Allied commander in the Mediterranean area. General Clark became commander of the Allied armies in Italy, while General Truscott took command of the U.S. Fifth Army in Italy. At the beginning of 1945, three of the Eighth Army's combat divisions were moved to northern Europe. Another division was shifted to the eastern Mediterranean to take part in operations in Greece, and one remained in reserve. The three Italian combat groups assigned to the Eighth Army were unable to replace these units in terms of quality. The Allied Strategic Air Force, however, remained stronger than the German air force in Italy and continued to assist both in supply and in harassment of the enemy lines of communication.

The Allied spring offensive began on 9 April 1945, and Bologna fell to U.S. and Polish troops on 20 April. From 23 to 25 April, the British crossed the lower Po in force, while the Fifth Army seized the Ligurian naval base of La Spezia. South of the Po, most of the army of General Heinrich von Vietinghoff (Kesselring's successor after he was reassigned to command the western front north of the Alps) had been overrun and much of its equipment destroyed. Beyond the Po during the last week in April, the British Eighth Army swept across the plain to Padua, Venice, and Treviso, and the Fifth Army, after crossing the Po as well, moved on to Verona, Milan, Genoa, and Turin, and onto the approaches to the Brenner Pass and into the foothills of the Alps. Northwest of Trieste, the British contacted Yugoslav partisans at Montfalcone, and the Fifth Army met French forces beyond Savona near the Franco-Italian frontier. In their final sweep, the two Allied armies net-ted more than 160,000 prisoners. Von Vietinghoff, after protracted negotiations, agreed to surrender his army unconditionally on 2 May 1945.

THE FINAL WEEKS IN THE EAST

While the Allies advanced to the Rhine in the west and to the Alps in Italy, the Soviet army offensive, begun on 23 June 1944, had advanced by August to a line including southeastern Latvia and eastern Lithuania. The Soviets also reached the east bank of the Vistula River opposite Warsaw, Poland, where they deliberately paused while the Germans crushed an uprising in the city on 5 October, and thereby eliminated the remnants of Polish leadership. Meanwhile, on 21 August, the Red Army began another offensive, this time into the Balkans. Romania was the first to capitulate; King Michael surrendered unconditionally to the Russians on 23 August 1944. On 2 September Finland broke relations with Germany and on 10 September signed an armistice with the Soviet Union. The Russians thereby recovered territory lost since 1939, plus a promise from the Finns to pay reparations. Bulgaria, although never at war with the Soviets, had otherwise sided with the Germans. The Soviet Union nevertheless declared war on Bulgaria and occupied it by mid-September. An official armistice between Bulgaria, the Soviet Union, and the western Allies was signed in Moscow on 28 October. About the same time, the Allies announced the results of a conference held 21 August to 7 October 1944 at Dumbarton Oaks near Washington, D.C., to implement the Moscow (October) and Teheran (November) declarations of 1943, which indicated their intention to establish an international organization for maintaining world peace and security.

From positions in Romania and Yugoslavia, Red Army columns bypassed northwestern Hungary to menace Austria from the southeast. The Hungarians managed to delay the Red Army at Budapest, however, until 13 February 1945. Consequently, the Russians were unable to occupy Vienna until 13 April.

THE ARDENNES COUNTEROFFENSIVE

Like the French army command in the first year of the war, in late 1944 Eisenhower placed considerable reliance on the deterring power of the rugged terrain of the Ardennes Forest in Belgium and Luxembourg and the bordering Eifel mountain region. If his confidence was soundly based, he believed that he would be able to maintain the Central Army Group's offensive into the Saarland and thereby enable the Northern Army Group to cross the Rhine below Cologne and lay siege to the Ruhr Valley. Eisenhower backed his decision and his confidence by assigning four divisions, some of them recently arrived in Europe and lacking combat experience, to a front 75 miles wide between Monschau and Trier in the Rhineland.

Allied intelligence officers knew only that a new Panzer army, the Sixth, had been formed in the vicinity of Cologne, but they were uncertain as to its purpose. If it was to be employed in a counterattack, the time and place for such an operation was unknown. Consequently, on 16 December, when the Sixth Panzer Army began to move against the northern flank of the Central Army Group, the Allies were caught by surprise. Hitler and his staff planned to drive a wedge between the Central and Northern Army groups to reach the Meuse River within two days, then to take Namur and Liège and continue on to Brussels and the port of Antwerp within fourteen days. If this offensive succeeded, the Germans planned to deny the Allies the use of Antwerp and trap the Northern Army Group in the Netherlands. Hitler called upon von Rundstedt to command the new offensive. Von Rundstedt's force included the Sixth Army, commanded by SS General Sepp Dietrich; the Fifth (Wehrmacht) Army on its left; and the reconstituted Seventh Army, which was to hold the salient's southern shoulder against an anticipated counterattack by the Third Army, then facing the western border of the Saar.

Originally planned for 12 December, the offensive was postponed to await a period of bad weather that was expected to limit Allied air power. Four days later, when fog and heavy snow grounded Allied aircraft, von Rundstedt attacked with eight Panzer divisions across a forty-mile-wide front. Caught by surprise, many front-line U.S. units were overwhelmed, and the Germans made rapid progress on the first day, disrupting communications between the northern and southern Allied armies. Therefore, Eisenhower placed Montgomery in command of all forces north of the penetration, including the U.S. First and Ninth armies, while Bradley retained command of the forces to the south. The British Thirtieth Corps had the task of holding the line of the Meuse and the area around Liège.

The Allies managed to halt the Germans four miles east of the Meuse, largely because they held the shoulders of the German offensive and prevented the enemy from widening the base of its penetration. To the north, the Seventh Armored Division of the U.S. Ninth Army held the shoulder at Saint-Vith, and in the south the U.S. 101st Airborne Division rushed forward from a rest area near Reims and held at Bastogne, which had been surrounded by the Germans on 20 December. A change in the weather on 23 December enabled Allied aircraft to harass the stalled enemy columns. By Christmas Day the tide had turned, because the Allies attacked the flanks of the penetration from both north and south. By 2 January, von Rundstedt had decided to withdraw, but he did not receive permission to do so for a week. When the Allied pincers met at Houffalize on 16 January, the Battle of the Ardennes had been won by the Allies and the "bulge" in Allied lines was eliminated.

The failed offensive cost the Germans heavily—220,000 men, half of whom were prisoners; more than 1,400 tanks and the destruction of assault guns; and 6,000 other vehicles. Allied losses in the Ardennes were 77,000 men—8,000 killed, 48,000 wounded, 21,000 captured or missing, and 733 tanks or tank destroyers destroyed.

Although the Ardennes counteroffensive had delayed the resumption of the principal Allied advance toward the Rhine for about six weeks, it resumed at the end of January 1945 against a greatly diminished Wehrmacht (German armed forces). The Second British Army continued its advance at Sittard and drove ten miles into Germany, as far as the Roer River valley northeast of Aachen. Diversionary thrusts by the enemy southward from the Saar toward northern Alsace and Lorraine were checked. The Colmar pocket in south Alsace on 2 February was also eliminated, which brought the Allies to the west bank of the Rhine from Strasbourg to the Swiss frontier. The territory of the French Republic had now been restored to its 1939 boundaries.

THE LAST YEAR OF WAR IN EUROPE

On 12 January the Russians launched an offensive that would carry them into East Prussia. Tannenberg, site of

Two American soldiers from the 101st Infantry Regiment dash through a square on 14 April 1945 in Kronach, Germany, during the Rhineland campaign. (National Archives)

the great Russian defeat in World War I, fell on 21 January. By the end of the month, the Red Army was in East Prussia and held the east bank of the Oder River from the vicinity of Breslau to near Frankfurt on the Oder, within thirty miles of Berlin. On 20 January, as the American people inaugurated Franklin D. Roosevelt as president for a fourth term, a new provisional national government of Hungary signed an armistice with Russia, Great Britain, and the United States.

British and U.S. strategists were divided over the course to follow for the remainder of the war in 1945. In general, Churchill and his advisers favored a direct thrust, as soon as weather and terrain permitted, across northern Germany to Berlin. They believed that a military conquest of the capital of the Reich would lead to a quick collapse of the Nazi regime, and, furthermore, that the city would be a valuable pawn in postwar negotiations with the Soviets. Eisenhower believed that such a drive would leave the rest of the western front at a standstill for want of logistical support. Berlin was not, in the U.S. view, worth the price, inasmuch as the Russians were already within easy striking distance of the city. For Eisenhower, the destruction of the German armies as far to the west as possible and the capture of the Ruhr war industries were the primary objectives, followed by an advance across Germany on a broad front.

U.S. Chief of Staff Marshall, at a meeting of the Combined Chiefs of Staff at Malta in January, supported Eisenhower's strategy. His five-step plan was to:

1. Close up to the Rhine, destroying as much as possible of the enemy forces.
2. Cross the Rhine at several points.
3. Send a four-pronged offensive across Germany, north and south of the Ruhr.
4. Advance eastward toward Berlin and via the valley of the Main River toward Leipzig, after meeting east of the Ruhr, to meet the Red Army on or near the upper Elbe.
5. Advance to the upper Danube, then southward to the Brenner Pass and a junction with the U.S. Fifth Army moving northward from Italy, and eastward to a second meeting with the Red Army in Austria and Czechoslovakia.

Decisions, such as zoning boundaries, had already been made in London the previous September and were to be confirmed at a forthcoming conference at Yalta, but Eisenhower deemed these matters as purely political and of little strategic importance.

It was, however, of great importance to Roosevelt to ultimately persuade the Soviet Union to participate actively in the war against Japan as soon as hostilities against Germany had ceased. The president and his advisers believed at this time that the intervention of vast Russian manpower in the Far East was essential to the defeat of Japan. Neither Okinawa nor Iwo Jima had been taken yet, and the cumulative effect of the Allied war on Japanese shipping was not yet apparent. Costly campaigns in the Philippines and Ryukyus, followed by a costly invasion of the main Japanese islands, loomed large in Allied staff thinking. Furthermore, an expected final campaign on the mainland of China against the self-sufficient Kwantung army was possible only with the assistance of the Soviet Far Eastern Army. Air bases in southeastern Siberia were also needed. These concerns were to dominate Roosevelt's thinking at the Yalta Conference on 4–11 February 1945. Because the Soviet Union was not then at war with Japan, the Yalta agreements were kept secret until the Soviets entered the war in the Far East.

While defining the concept of unconditional surrender, the three conferees claimed supreme authority over defeated Germany, which included disarmament, demilitarization, and dismemberment of the country. Only Churchill expressed doubts as to the wisdom of these policies. The most difficult national and minority problems were deferred until the eventual peace conference. In their final declaration, the three powers, as Chester V. Easum, a distinguished American historian has written, "reaffirmed their faith in the principles of the Atlantic Charter, their pledge, as expressed in the Declaration of the United Nations, and their determination to build, in cooperation with other peace-loving nations, a world order under law, dedicated to peace, security and freedom, and the general well-being of all mankind."

Roosevelt was advised "that virtually no price would be too high to pay for Soviet assistance to speed the day of victory over Japan as well as Germany."

Although post-Yalta criticism of Allied decisions was severe, Roosevelt could not disregard the advice of his military advisers "that virtually no price would be too high to pay for Soviet assistance to speed the day of victory over Japan as well as Germany." Furthermore, he hoped to persuade the Russians to join the United Nations and to obtain their friendship. In his decisions at Yalta, the president undoubtedly had at that time the full support of the American public, who both believed in and desired a continuation of cooperation with the Soviet Union in the postwar period. Roosevelt died (12 April) before the full consequences of the conference were realized, but, in any case, the Russians did not obtain anything of significance at Yalta that their army had not already seized or would soon take.

THE RHINELAND CAMPAIGN. The western Allies had resumed their advance to the Rhine southeast of Nijmegen in the Netherlands on 8 February 1945. The Northern Army Group, including the Canadian First Army, the British Second Army, and the U.S. Ninth Army on the Allied northern wing, at first made slow progress because of the waterlogged terrain of the Roer River valley. The Germans destroyed the floodgates of the Schwammanuel Dam the day before the Allied offensive began. Nevertheless, Kleve fell on 12 February, on 23 February the Ninth Army crossed the Roer, and a week later the Ninth Army, commanded by General William N. Simpson, reached the Rhine opposite Düsseldorf. The U.S. First Army, commanded by General Hodges, also advanced on the southern or right wing, its Seventh Corps reaching Cologne on 5 March. Two days later a small advance unit of the Third Corps, Ninth U.S. Armored Division in the lead, crossed the unexpectedly intact Ludendorff Bridge at Remagen, north of Cologne.

Rapidly expanding their bridgehead from Remagen, the Allies pressed northward toward the Ruhr. In response, the Germans shifted troops northward, thereby thinning out their defenses between Mainz and Mannheim and enabling Patton's Third Army to move easily up to the Rhine in its sector. On 2 March, the Third Army captured Trier and within a week pulled up to the Rhine at Andernach, northwest of Koblenz. Thereafter, it swung southward toward a junction with the U.S. Seventh Army, which on 15 March attacked the Saar salient from the south. During the night of 22–23 March, the Fifth Division of the Third Army crossed the Rhine against slight resistance, establishing a second Allied bridgehead beyond the Rhine.

After intense artillery preparation, Montgomery's Northern Army Group also crossed the Rhine in four places. Some forty thousand airborne troops (parachutists and gliders) assisted in the crossing by dropping beyond enemy defenses along the river. The Ruhr was soon encircled. The British then turned northeastward toward Hamburg and Bremen, and the Canadians swung northward to seal off the Netherlands. The fourth and fifth major crossings of the Rhine were made by the Seventh Army below Mannheim, while the French First Army crossed near Freiburg in the south. After the Allies joined hands along the east bank from Switzerland to the North Sea, they were poised for the final phase of the war—a dash across the remnant of Germany to meet the Red Army along the Elbe. By 25 March the Rhineland campaign had been completed. The Germans had lost about ten thousand men daily, raising their losses since D-Day in the west to about two million men.

By 1 April the Ruhr had been surrounded by the U.S. Ninth Army on the north and by the U.S. First Army from the south. Over the next two weeks the Americans gradually squeezed the encircled garrison, and on 16–18 April the survivors of the garrison, 325,000 men, including thirty general officers, surrendered.

Elements of the U.S. First Army, released from the Ruhr operation, had entered the city of Dessau just west of the Elbe, and on 11 April the Second Armored Division of the U.S. Ninth Army established a small bridgehead east of the Elbe near Magdeburg but withdrew within a few days. Further south, the Eighty-Third Division also crossed the Elbe but also withdrew, inasmuch as earlier Allied agreements had established dividing lines between the Soviet and western Allied occupation zones. The interzonal boundary had been drawn earlier by Eisenhower in direct negotiations with the highest Red Army echelon in order to avoid mistaken confrontation deep within enemy territory.

On 25 April patrols from the U.S. forces and the Red Army met at Torgau, between Dresden and Magdeburg, on the Elbe. German armies north and south were now separated from one another, while the U.S. First and Third armies and the First French Army moved into Czechoslovakia, Austria, and Italy, respectively, and toward junctions with the Soviets, closing up to Vienna, Dresden, Berlin, and Stettin.

SURRENDER. On 24–25 April, through Swedish Count Folke Bernadotte, Heinrich Himmler, the German minister of the interior, national leader of the SS, and titular commander of the Home Front, sought to arrange for a separate surrender to the United States and Great Britain but insisted upon excluding the Russians. Harry S. Truman, who had succeeded to the presidency following Roosevelt's death, replied through Bernadotte that there could be no partial surrender. German armies in the east must surrender to the Russians at the same time as those in the west. After the Soviets had been informed, negotiations were dropped.

On 30 April, Hitler committed suicide in his command bunker in Berlin. Late on 1 May, Admiral Karl Doenitz, Hitler's successor, announced on Radio Hamburg that Hitler had died "a hero's death at the head of his troops in Berlin." On behalf of the Nazi government, Doenitz once again sought to divide the Allies by saying he would continue to fight the western Allies only insofar as they hindered him in the defense of eastern Germany against bolshevism. This too was rejected, and the following day Stalin announced the fall of Berlin to the Red Army.

Hitler's death released from their oaths those German generals who had sworn fealty to Hitler as long as he lived. The military collapse followed swiftly. In Italy on 29 April, SS General Karl Wolff and von Vietinghoff signed articles of surrender for the remaining one million Germans in Italy. Field Marshal Alexander accepted the final surrender in the presence of U.S. and Russian officers on 2 May at his headquarters in Caserta.

North of the Alps the British Second Army occupied Hamburg on 3 May and Lübeck on 4 May, while Admiral Hans von Friedburg, on behalf of Doenitz, offered to surrender to the western Allies three German armies on the eastern front, in order to avoid surrender to the Russians. Montgomery refused this offer as well. On 4 May, as earlier authorized by Eisenhower, Montgomery accepted the military surrender of all German troops in northwest Germany, the Netherlands, and Denmark. The following day, the German First and Nineteenth armies, composing Army Group B in western Austria, surrendered to General Devers, commanding an Allied Army Group made up of the U.S. Seventh and the French First armies. It was not, however, until early on 7 May at Eisenhower's headquarters in Reims, France, that Admiral Friedburg and Field Marshal Alfred Gustav Jodl signed for all German armed forces an instrument of unconditional surrender. All hostilities were to cease as of midnight on 8 May. Eisenhower ordered the German emissaries to appear at Red Army headquarters in Berlin on 9 May to sign a formal ratification of the surrender instrument of 7 May.

The human costs of the war against Germany were enormous. The United States suffered a total of 772,626 battle casualties in the European theater, of which 135,576 were combat deaths. Crossed rifles in the sand honor this American soldier who died at the barricades of Western Europe in 1944. (National Archives)

A SUMMING UP

The human costs of the war against Germany were enormous. The German armed forces alone lost in battle about 8 million men killed, captured, or permanently disabled. Allied bombing killed 500,000 German civilians and wounded 700,000 more. Thirty thousand of the original 38,000-man submarine force was lost. Italy, Germany's Axis partner, listed 760,000 military casualties. Of that number, 60,000 had been killed, 500,000 taken prisoner, and 200,000 were missing. From 8 September 1943 to 30 April 1945, as a cobelligerent with the Allies against Germany, Italy lost 48,078 men—17,494 killed, 9,353 wounded, 17,647 missing. The Italian navy lost 3,584 men.

British military losses, including those of the Commonwealth and Empire and those in other theaters of war, exceeded one million. British merchant seamen listed 30,184 of their service dead, 5,264 missing, 4,402 wounded, and 5,556 interned. In Great Britain, there were approximately 150,000 civilian casualties.

Norway, with a population of only 3 million, lost more than 10,000, including 900 members of naval and air forces, and 3,200 merchant seamen. Poland, the first Nazi military target, had 250,000 military casualties, and had a total loss of 5 million persons, including 3 million Jews. An additional 3 million other Jews were systematically killed and millions of others were exiled. Yugoslavia lost 1,685,000 soldiers and civilians, 75 percent of them in battle with the Germans.

The United States sent more than 3 million men to the European theater and employed in combat sixty of the sixty-one combat divisions shipped there; only the Thirteenth Airborne Division was not employed. With the dispatch of these units, there were no ready combat divisions left in the United States. A total of 772,626 battle casualties were incurred in Europe, of which 135,576 were combat deaths. The infantry, comprising 20.5 percent of total armed strength, suffered 70 percent of the casualties, the rate being slightly higher among officers than among enlisted men. Improvements in surgery and medical care, such as plasma, sulfa and penicillin drugs, however, reduced the death rate from wounds to less than half the 1918 rate, returning 58.8 percent of wounded men to duty.

THE OPENING OF WAR IN THE PACIFIC

Unlike the beginning of the war in Europe, in the Pacific, the United States and Great Britain were the direct objects of Japanese aggression. Japan's primary object was to achieve economic and strategic self-sufficiency by conquering what its leaders considered to be their southern resources area—the Malay Peninsula and the East Indies. Before they could embark on this venture, however, they had to eliminate any possible response from U.S. bases at Guam and the Philippines and to neutralize the striking power of the Pacific Fleet based at Pearl Harbor and the British base at Hong Kong. Consequently, the attack on Pearl Harbor on 7 December 1941 coincided with air attacks on Clark Field near Manila in the Philippines, Hong Kong, and Shanghai, as well as amphibious landings in Thailand and northern Malaya.

Bases for Japanese operations were available in the Pescadores Islands, at Cam Ranh Bay in Indochina, and on Palau, Saipan, and other mandated (former German) islands. Oil and gasoline depots were already in position. On 5 November 1941, Imperial Japanese Navy headquarters notified its combined fleet commanders that war was inevitable. On 21 November all forces were ordered to their rendezvous points. On 1 December the imperial government signaled their commanders that hostilities would begin on 8 December (7 December, Honolulu time).

Even though word of the impending air action against Clark Field reached General MacArthur eight or nine hours before the arrival of the first enemy planes, he chose to ignore it.

U.S. forces in the Philippines were caught unprepared at Clark Field, as were the forces at Pearl Harbor. Even though word of the impending air action against Clark Field reached General Douglas MacArthur eight or nine hours before the arrival of the first enemy planes, he chose to ignore it. The Japanese, however, were amazed to find U.S. aircraft at Clark Field lined up in a defensive attitude. The Japanese destroyed the only radar and radio transmitter in the first assault, and half of the heavy bomber strength of the U.S. Army's Far Eastern air force and a third of its fighter force were destroyed the first day. The Japanese quickly overran the Malay Peninsula. In a desperate attempt to intercept a Japanese amphibious force, British Admiral Sir Tom Phillips left Singapore on 8 December with a heavy battle cruiser, the *Repulse,* and a new battleship, the *Prince of Wales,* which had just arrived from European waters. With the fleet were four destroyers but no aircraft carrier and no cruisers. The Japanese attacked the fleet on 10 December. Both battleships were sunk, but two thousand of the nearly three thousand men on board were rescued by the accompanying destroyers. The two commanding officers went down with their ships.

Having gained control of the air, Japanese invasion forces assembled on Formosa (Taiwan) and Palau, moved on 22 December into Lingayen Gulf, southeastern Luzon at Legaspi, and southern Mindanao at Davao. On 10 December, Thailand had signed a ten-year treaty of alliance with Japan and on 25 January 1942 declared war on the United States and Great Britain. The United States responded on 5 February with a declaration of war against Thailand. Manila and the nearby Cavite naval base fell to the Japanese on 2 January, which enabled the Japanese Third Fleet to return to Formosa to refuel and then to participate in operations against Borneo and the Celebes.

U.S. and Filipino forces withdrew to Bataan Peninsula, across the bay from Manila. General MacArthur, under orders from President Roosevelt, broke through the Japanese blockade by patrol boat and escaped to Australia, which he reached on 17 March. General Jonathan M. Wainwright remained behind to defend Bataan until 9 April and the Manila Bay island fortress of Corregidor until 6 May, when he surrendered the remnants of his forces.

ORGANIZING FOR THE PACIFIC WAR

The U.S. Congress had passed the first War Powers Act on 18 December 1941. Empowered by this legislation, President Roosevelt established the War Production Board to stimulate and coordinate wartime production and appointed Donald M. Nelson as its chairman. The board's first task was to promote synthetic rubber production to make up for the supplies lost to the Japanese. One of the key agencies in waging total war, one of the primary purposes of the board was to deny essential war materials to the enemy by preemptive purchasing and supplying weapons and materials to the Allies and potential allies under the Lend-Lease Act. By 1942 war production in the United States equaled that of Germany, Italy, and Japan combined; in 1943 it increased by 50 percent; and by the end of 1944, production was twice what it had been in 1942.

The War Shipping Administration, established on 7 February, had control over all oceangoing shipping and added more than four thousand newly constructed ships. The United States also greatly improved its global repair, supply, and refueling facilities and techniques.

Early in 1942, Great Britain and the United States created the Pacific War Council, which included representatives from Australia, New Zealand, the Netherlands East Indies, and India. The Combined Raw Matériels Board was organized in Washington, and the Combined Shipping Adjustment Board was formed in London and Washington. On 5 May the Allied Supply Council was organized in Australia. Thus were created the foundations of what was to be a victorious alliance.

JAPANESE ADVANCES

The Japanese pressed forward from Davao in the Philippines against the Celebes and oil-rich Borneo, using air power from one forward base to another and to support amphibious landings at Tarakan Island, 10–12 January. By 10 February they captured Macassar, on the southwestern tip of the Celebes, which gave them control of the Macassar Strait, then proceeded to Dutch Timor and Bali. The fall of Singapore on 15 February opened the way for an attack on Java from the east and west. Similar conquests were made at Rabaul and Gasmato on New Britain, Kavieng on New Ireland, and Lae on New Guinea.

Throughout this early phase of the war the superiority of Japanese air power was the decisive factor. Dutch, British, and U.S. naval and air forces were heavily outgunned and outnumbered everywhere. The Japanese, notably superior in torpedo tactics and training, also had more dependable torpedoes. Damage to Allied ships and planes was especially serious because replacements were unavailable. Repair facilities, never adequate, rapidly diminished as Japanese air power made base after base untenable. On 19 February, an air attack from four aircraft carriers attached to Admiral Chuichi Nagumo's First Air Fleet, which had begun the war in the Pacific with the attack on Pearl Harbor, destroyed nearly every ship in the harbor at the port of Darwin in northern Australia.

In a final attempt to sink Japanese convoys, in the Battle of the Java Sea, a mixed force of five cruisers and ten destroyers—Dutch, British, Australian, and American—attacked the Japanese on 27 February. Two Allied cruisers and three destroyers were sunk, but no Japanese ships were lost to surface attack. After 1 March, when five more Allied cruisers were sunk while trying to escape from the Java Sea through enemy controlled exits, the Japanese poured into Java. The U.S. cruiser *Marblehead,* crippled in earlier action, escaped from Chirluchop on Java's south coast and reached Ceylon for repairs. Two modern U.S. destroyers, the *Whipple* and the *Parrot,* four old four-stacked destroyers of Division 58, and two U.S. gunboats survived the campaign. The Japanese lost only two destroyers to submarine attack, but none were sunk by Allied surface ships. The major instrument of these victories was Admiral Nagumo's carrier strike force, a combat unit built around a core of six aircraft carriers, two battleships, two heavy cruisers, one light cruiser, and nine destroyers. Without los-

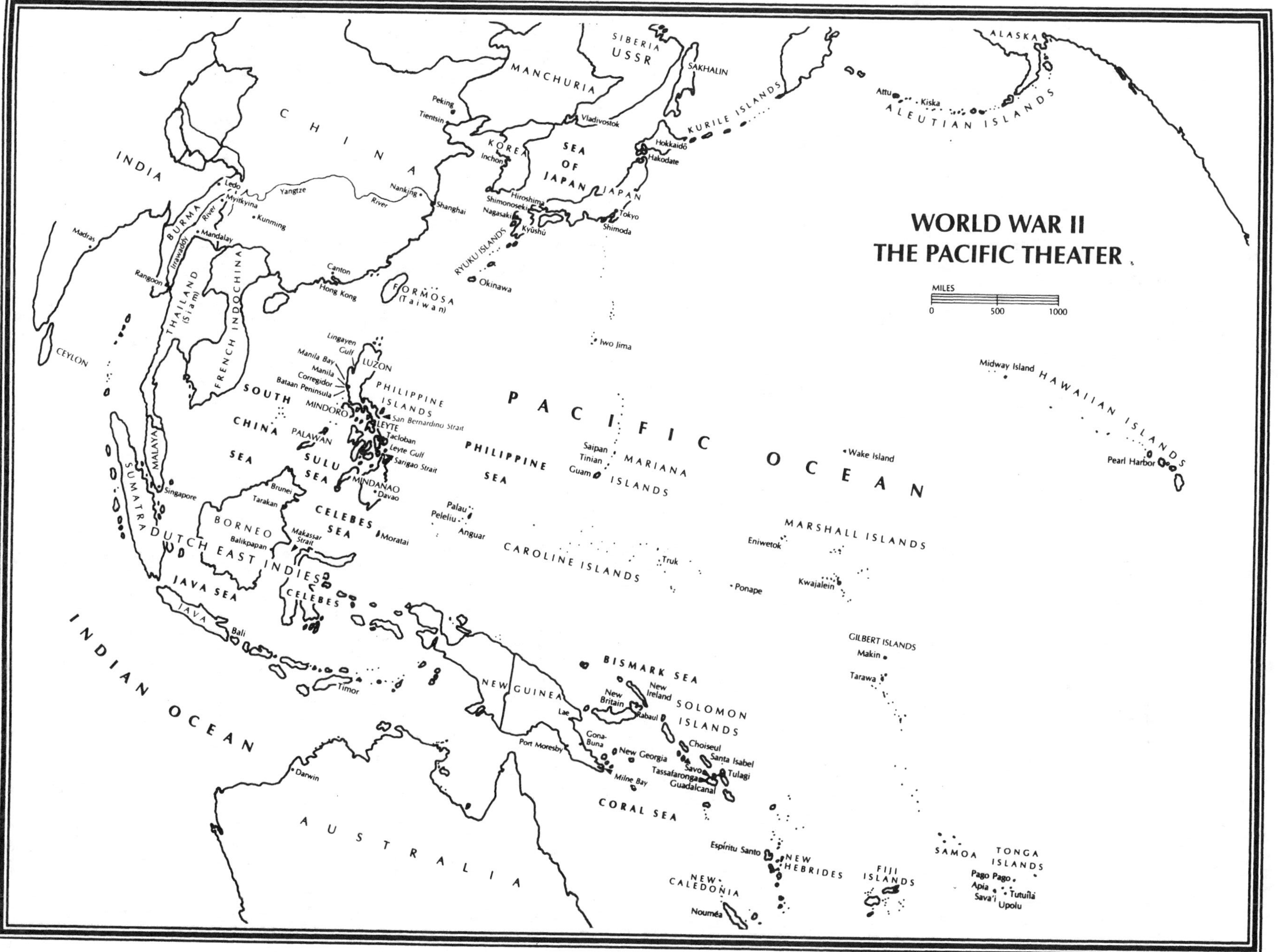

WORLD WAR II
THE PACIFIC THEATER
MILES
0
500
1000
ALASKA
ALEUTIAN ISLANDS
Attu
Kiska
SIBERIA
USSR
SAKHALIN
KURILE ISLANDS
MANCHURIA
Peking
Tientsin
Vladivostok
KOREA
Inchon
SEA OF JAPAN
JAPAN
Hokkaidō
Hakodate
Tokyo
Shimoda
Hiroshima
Shimonoseki
Nagasaki
Kyūshū
RYUKU ISLANDS
Okinawa
Iwo Jima
CHINA
INDIA
Ledo
Myitkyina
Yangtze
Nanking
River
Shanghai
Kunming
Mandalay
River
Irrawaddy
BURMA
Madras
Rangoon
Canton
Hong Kong
FORMOSA
(Taiwan)
THAILAND
(Siam)
FRENCH INDOCHINA
CEYLON
Lingayen Gulf
Manila Bay
Manila
Corregidor
Bataan Peninsula
LUZON
PHILIPPINE ISLANDS
MINDORO
San Bernardino Strait
LEYTE
Tacloban
Leyte Gulf
Surigao Strait
MINDANAO
Davao
PALAWAN
SOUTH CHINA SEA
SULU SEA
PHILIPPINE SEA
PACIFIC OCEAN
Saipan
Tinian
Guam
MARIANA ISLANDS
Wake Island
Midway Island
HAWAIIAN ISLANDS
Pearl Harbor
MALAYA
Singapore
SUMATRA
Brunei
Tarakan
BORNEO
Balikpapan
Makassar Strait
CELEBES SEA
Morotai
Palau
Peleliu
Anguar
CAROLINE ISLANDS
Truk
Ponape
MARSHALL ISLANDS
Eniwetok
Kwajalein
DUTCH EAST INDIES
CELEBES
JAVA SEA
JAVA
Bali
Timor
INDIAN OCEAN
NEW GUINEA
Lae
Port Moresby
Gona-Buna
Milne Bay
BISMARK SEA
New Britain
New Ireland
Rabaul
SOLOMON ISLANDS
Choiseul
Santa Isabel
New Georgia
Savo
Tulagi
Tassafaronga
Guadalcanal
CORAL SEA
GILBERT ISLANDS
Makin
Tarawa
Darwin
AUSTRALIA
Espíritu Santo
NEW HEBRIDES
NEW CALEDONIA
Nouméa
FIJI ISLANDS
SAMOA
TONGA ISLANDS
Pago Pago
Apia
Sava'i
Tutuila
Upolu

ing a ship or having one damaged by enemy action, it had been the clear victor in operations in the Java Sea and elsewhere.

Nagumo's carriers next ranged westward into the Indian Ocean. In early April their aircraft severely damaged naval installations and shipping in Ceylon and sank a British aircraft carrier, two cruisers, and a corvette in the Indian Ocean. During the week of 2–9 April, twenty-eight Allied merchant ships were lost in waters around India, twenty-three in the Bay of Bengal. During the long run of unbroken success, Nagumo's carrier force was rarely sighted or attacked; only its planes appeared. Its mission completed, in mid-April the fleet returned to Kure in the inland Sea of Japan to refit and to replenish its complement of aircraft and pilots.

BATTLES OF CORAL SEA AND MIDWAY

The first check to the Japanese advances came in the Battle of the Coral Sea (7–8 May). To set up a defense parameter and hold on to what they had seized, the Japanese sent a task force and convoy down from Truk in the mandated Caroline Islands, seized and occupied Tulagi in the Solomons on 3 May, then turned westward across the northern arm of the Coral Sea toward Port Moresby on the southeastern coast of New Guinea. Possession of this port would have given the Japanese control of New Guinea and brought them close to Australia. To intercept them, a U.S. task force built around the aircraft carriers *Lexington* and *Yorktown* entered the Coral Sea from the southeast. Early reconnaissance had been accomplished imperfectly by land-based B-17s. U.S. and Japanese forces sought to locate one another without being discovered by the other.

On the morning of 7 May, U.S. carrier planes discovered and attacked part of the Japanese transport force and sank its escorting light carrier, *Shoho.* The following day, aircraft from each force attacked, each finding its target inadequately protected, with fighter planes away on mission. The *Lexington* was sunk and the *Yorktown* badly damaged, and the destroyer *Sims* and the oiler *Neasho* lost. Two of Nagumo's carriers, *Shokaku* and *Zuikaku,* were heavily damaged, and the destroyer *Kikuzuki* was sunk. The Japanese inflicted more damage than they received, but the principal mission of the Coral Sea operation had been accomplished—halting the southward expansion of the Japanese-dominated area northeast of Australia. The Japanese abandoned the attempt to take Port Moresby by sea, and Milne Bay on the southeastern extremity of New Guinea was occupied by Japanese forces before the end of August.

By June 1942, the Japanese knew that their expansion east and southeastward had reached its limits. Nevertheless, they believed they required outposts to guard against inevitable Allied counterattacks. They planned, therefore, to capture the Fijis, New Caledonia, and possibly even New Zealand in the southwest Pacific, Midway in the central Pacific, and some of the Aleutians in the north Pacific, in order to cut off the United States. Thereafter, they would go onto the defensive and await whether the United States, so heavily involved in a major war in Europe, would make the necessary effort to win back what had been so quickly lost.

The Battle of Midway, a turning point of the war in the Pacific, began at dawn on 4 June 1942. Admiral Isoroku Yamamoto on the super battleship *Yamato* led a force of twelve battleships and six aircraft carriers, including Admiral Nagumo's First Air Fleet, and a full complement of cruisers, destroyers, and supply ships, escorted by submarines and followed by transports carrying an occupation force.

When the Japanese attacked Midway at 6:30 A.M., every U.S. plane capable of leaving the ground was airborne.

Although the U.S. naval staff, having access to the Japanese code, had anticipated the attack, it could send only three carriers—the *Enterprise, Hornet,* and *Yorktown*—with a complement of cruisers, destroyers, and twenty-nine submarines, commanded by Admirals Raymond A. Spruance, Thomas C. Kinkaid, Frank J. Fletcher, and Charles A. Lockwood. Their strategy was to hold their carriers to the north and northeast of Midway, anticipating a Japanese aerial assault against the islands. While the enemy was so engaged, the Americans planned to launch aircraft to attack the Japanese carriers in the absence of their fighters.

When the Japanese attacked Midway at 6:30 A.M., every U.S. plane capable of leaving the ground was airborne. When the attack ended twenty minutes later, seventeen Midway pilots were missing, but U.S. aircraft and antiaircraft had shot down one-third of the attack force. Meanwhile, the U.S. carrier planes had attacked as planned. By noon they had sunk three enemy carriers, and a fourth, badly damaged, sank the following morning. The cost of this operation was high. The *Enterprise* lost fourteen of its thirty-seven dive-bombers, ten of fourteen torpedo bombers, and a Wildcat fighter plane. The *Hornet* lost all of its torpedo bombers and twelve wildcats and the *Yorktown* all but one of its torpedo bombers, two dive-bombers, and three Wildcats.

A second enemy strike launched from other Japanese carriers caught the *Yorktown* with too many of its fighter planes away and so severely damaged it that it had to withdraw from action. On 7 June, while steaming toward Pearl Harbor, the *Yorktown* and its destroyer escort, the *Hammann,* were sunk by an enemy submarine.

Yamamoto withdrew westward, but as he did so two of his damaged cruisers were overtaken by dive-bombers from the *Enterprise* and *Hornet.* The cruiser *Mikama* was sunk, and the *Mogami* withdrew to Japan and remained for two years in drydock undergoing repairs. The Battle of Midway cost the Japanese four of the carriers that had attacked Pearl Harbor, a heavy cruiser, 253 aircraft, and thirty-five hundred men. The United States lost one carrier, a destroyer, 150 aircraft, and 307 men.

Although the carrier strength of the two forces was now numerically equal, Admiral Spruance's striking force had been seriously depleted and his surface complement was not comparable with his opponent's fleet. A Japanese task force of four carriers remained in the north Pacific and would have welcomed a carrier battle with the remaining two of Spruance's fleet. Against such odds, however, Admiral Chester W. Nimitz, commander in chief of the Pacific fleet, recalled Spruance and his fleet from the area.

The Battles of the Coral Sea and Midway confirmed the superiority of naval air warfare. While submarines played important roles, they were not decisive in the battle. Battleships, cruisers, and destroyers did not exchange gunfire, but without them the carriers could not have played their effective roles. Japanese sea power had been halted and forced to retreat. The enemy never regained the initiative, which henceforth remained in American hands.

On 12 June, the Japanese occupied Attu and Kiska in the Aleutians, but, under relentless shelling, the Japanese were gradually forced to withdraw from the Aleutians. They evacuated Kiska, their last outpost, at the end of July 1943, then fell back on their northernmost islands—the Kurils, Karafuto, and Hokkaido.

BATTLES FOR THE SOLOMONS

It was in the Solomon Islands in the western Pacific that the ground arm of the U.S. Navy—the Marine Corps—finally got its opportunity to engage the enemy. The Battle of Guadalcanal, Japan's farthest point of advance in the Solomons, was fought largely by the First U.S. Marine Division. On 7 August, the marines landed east of Lunga Point and quickly seized an unfinished airstrip, which they renamed Henderson Field. Located near the northern coast of the island, Henderson Field was surrounded on the west, south, and east by enemy-held territory and was the center around which fierce fighting raged for six months. Unable to drive the marines from the field with ground forces, the Japanese bombed heavily and frequently.

Rabaul on New Britain, with support from nearby islands, gave the Japanese a logistical advantage over the U.S. Navy, which was operating from faraway bases at Espíritu Santo and Nouméa. This advantage was seen during an engagement at Savo Island, northwest of Guadalcanal, on 9 August with seven enemy cruisers. The battle cost was three U.S. heavy cruisers (*Quincy, Vincennes,* and *Astoria*) and one Australian (*Canberra*) and caused major damage to the U.S. heavy cruiser *Chicago.* Allied losses in this engagement were 1,270 killed and 709 wounded. The Japanese lost one cruiser. The accompanying Japanese transports managed to unload their men on Guadalcanal and nearby Tulagi and withdrew unscathed.

The Japanese continued to reinforce their own forces on Guadalcanal. In waters northeast of the island, a U.S. carrier force commanded by Admiral Fletcher attempted to intercept them. On 24 August aircraft from the carrier force attacked the Japanese carrier *Ryujo* far out at sea and sank it, the destroyer *Matsuki,* and a transport, and shot down ninety Japanese planes. The U.S. task force lost twenty aircraft, and the *Enterprise* was slightly damaged by bombs. Two additional Japanese carriers and the U.S. carrier *Saratoga* also took part in the action, with the U.S. carrier *Wasp* in reserve. While serving with the *Hornet* as escort for the Marine Corps Seventh Regiment, which was being sent as reinforcement to Guadalcanal, the *Wasp* was sunk northwest of Espíritu Santo on 15 September. The battleship *North Carolina* and the destroyer *O'Brien* were also damaged by submarine attack. Fortunately, the *Hornet* recovered all but one of the *Wasp's* airborne planes. The *North Carolina* managed to reach Pearl Harbor, where it went into drydock for repairs, but the *O'Brien* sank on 19 October en route to Pearl Harbor. On 18 September the troop transport reached Guadalcanal, where within twelve hours it landed four thousand men with their equipment and supplies.

Heavy land and sea battles continued. On 28 September, sixty-two Japanese planes attacked Guadalcanal, and twenty-three bombers and a fighter were shot down without the loss of a single U.S. aircraft. Up to that time, more than two hundred Japanese aircraft had been lost during the battle for Guadalcanal as opposed to thirty-two American. From 16 to 25 October, antiaircraft fire destroyed ten enemy planes, while fighters dispersed 103. U.S. losses for the same period were fourteen.

On 15 October, the U.S. Army Americal Division landed four thousand troops on Guadalcanal to reinforce the four thousand marines landed earlier. By then, Japanese strength on the island had risen to about thirty thousand men. Undeterred by their defeat in the eastern Solomons, the Japanese used fast destroyers at night to continue to reinforce their forces on Guadalcanal. Steaming through what was known to the Americans as "the slot" between New Georgia, Choiseul, and Santa Isabel, the destroyers were referred to as the "Tokyo Express" by U.S. troops.

Japanese destroyers were referred to as the "Tokyo Express" by U.S. troops.

Early in October, a Japanese task force, composed of four heavy cruisers and a destroyer, headed toward Cape Esperance on Guadalcanal's western extremity. It was surprised and attacked in an engagement on 11–12 October off Javu Island by a U.S. force of four cruisers and five destroyers commanded by Rear Admiral Norman D. Scott. One U.S. destroyer, the *Duncan,* was lost, and the Japanese heavy cruiser *Furutaka* and a destroyer were sunk by gunfire. Two more enemy destroyers were sunk by aircraft from Henderson Field the next day. Nevertheless, the Japanese destroyers managed to land troops and heavy artillery at Tassafaronga, and on 14 October the Japanese shelled the Americans from the sea.

On 24 October, twenty-four Grumman fighters shot down twenty Japanese fighters and a bomber. The following day, marine pilots shot down seventeen enemy fighters and five bombers, but by 26 October, the marines had only twenty-three fighters, sixteen dive-bombers, and one torpedo plane left on Henderson Field. Naval efforts to resupply the marines eventually enabled them to survive the offshore enemy gunfire, mud, mosquitoes, malaria, and food shortages, and to hold the island and begin to roll back the Japanese invasion of the southwest Pacific area.

In the period 25–27 October, the Japanese sent from Truk and Rabaul the largest naval and air fleet they had assembled since Midway. Admiral Nagumo commanded the force, which included four battleships (*Hiei, Kirishima, Kingo,* and *Haruna*), four carriers, and cruisers, destroyers, and submarine scouts in proportion. Meanwhile, two U.S. carrier task forces formed around the *Hornet* and *Enterprise* and moved into the area west of Santa Cruz Island, east of San Cristoval, and southeast of Guadalcanal. On 26 October, Japanese dive-bombers and torpedo bombers from the *Shokaku* and *Zuikaku* took advantage of the absence of the *Hornet's* aircraft away on mission and so badly damaged the ship that it was abandoned and later sunk by U.S. destroyers. The U.S. force also lost seventy-four planes to antiaircraft and the destroyer *Porter* to a submarine in the Battle of Santa Cruz. The *Enterprise,* the battleship *South Dakota,* and the cruiser *San Juan* were damaged, leaving the *Saratoga* the only carrier in the area still fit for action. The Japanese, in turn, lost 100 aircraft and two destroyers, and eight other warships were damaged, including the carrier *Ziuho,* whose flight deck was badly damaged. The *Shokaku* was heavily damaged and knocked out of the war for nine months.

By mid-November 1942, the tide of battle had turned in the Solomons. Deeming destroyers ultimately unsatisfactory to support a force large enough to defeat the Americans on Guadalcanal, the Japanese assembled a fleet of heavy transports with ten thousand replacements and thirty-five hundred elite assault troops. During the night of 12–13 November, near Savo Island, Admirals D. J. Callaghan in the *San Francisco* and Norman Scott in the *Atlanta,* together with their destroyers, attacked head-on the battleships *Hiei* and *Kirishima* and fifteen destroyers. Although the Japanese guns were loaded, their ammunition was not armor-piercing, unlike their torpedoes.

U.S. cruisers concentrated close-range fire long enough to disable the *Hiei.* The following day, aircraft from Henderson Field so badly damaged the battleship that it was scuttled by its crew. The Japanese also lost two destroyers. Callaghan was killed aboard the *San Francisco,* which incurred major damage, and Scott was killed on the *Atlanta.* The new light antiaircraft cruiser *Juneau,* badly damaged, was torpedoed the next day as it attempted to reach Nouméa with the *Helena* and *San Francisco.* Four U.S. destroyers were also sunk. The next night Japanese cruisers shelled Henderson Field.

On 14 November, Japanese troop transports again approached the island. Eight were sunk, and four were beached at Tassafaronga under attack from marine aircraft operating from Henderson Field and from the *Enterprise,* which, after making emergency repairs, had returned to battle. During the night of 14–15 November, battleships fought one another with radar-directed 16-inch guns. Drawing most of the Japanese fire, the *South Dakota* enabled Admiral Willis A. Lee, in the new battleship *Washington,* to concentrate his fire and sink the *Kirishima* and an accompanying destroyer. The United States lost three more destroyers, the *Benham, Preston,* and *Walke.* Although the Japanese had sunk seven U.S. destroyers at a cost of only three of their own, the loss of two veteran battleships and thousands of troops on the transports discouraged the Japanese commanders.

Nevertheless, they attempted once again to reinforce at night with destroyer transports. They were frustrated but at a high price. The cruiser *Northampton* was sunk by torpedoes, and three other cruisers, the *Minneapolis, New Orleans,* and *Pensacola,* were severely damaged. In February 1943 the Japanese at last began to evacuate their forces from the island. In the first week of February, twelve thousand to thirteen thousand men were withdrawn. By 9 February, General Patch reported the island cleared of the enemy.

Of the sixty thousand marines and soldiers committed on Guadalcanal, 1,592 were killed in action and many more were incapacitated by wounds and disease. The Japanese had committed thirty-six thousand men, of which one thousand were taken prisoner and nine thousand died of disease. Twelve thousand or so were listed either as killed or missing.

The battles at sea for the Solomons cost the United States and the Japanese twenty-four ships each. Although greatly inconvenienced by the loss of thousands of troops, Japan was more affected by the loss of warships and their crews, which could not be replaced easily. The country was mortally wounded by the severe depletion of land and naval air strength. Moreover, its subsequent defensive efforts were weakened as the result of its losses. It no longer had enough aviation gasoline, training facilities, or time to train and to replace those pilots lost during 1942 in the Indian Ocean, at Midway, in the Coral Sea, and in the Solomons.

SUBMARINE WARFARE

Fortunately, the attack on Pearl Harbor had virtually ignored submarine base and repair facilities, and the U.S. Pacific submarine fleet immediately went on a counterattack. In addition to seventy-three submarines then under construction, the U.S. Navy had fifty-five large and eighteen medium submarines in the Pacific. Japan, which in 1930 had been given treaty right to submarine parity with Great Britain and the United States, had about sixty. As the war continued, the United States increased the number of its fleet of submarines, while Japan only maintained its number of fleet-type submarines and kept an average of forty to forty-five vessels continuously in operation, despite ultimately the almost total destruction of its surface navy. Midget submarines, built for coastal defense, were rarely used.

Neither Japanese nor U.S. submarines had adopted the German snorkel device that enabled the vessels to draw in air for their diesel engines and crews when submerged. Japanese submersibles were faster on the surface but slower when submerged than U.S. vessels, but they were also inferior in radar equipment, radio communications, and electronic search and sound gear that served as underwater eyes and ears. The only advantages the Japanese enjoyed were numerous bases near their operating areas and more reliable torpedoes. Although U.S. torpedoes improved somewhat toward the end of the war, they had many operational faults.

Submarines were to penetrate enemy defenses,

to injure where possible, to operate by stealth,

and to strike without warning.

In the first two years of the war, submarines usually operated independently, but in the last years frequently in groups of three. Communication between submarines was always at the risk of betraying one's position, and the boats usually remained silent while on mission. Missions were usually to penetrate enemy defenses, to injure where possible, to operate by stealth, and to strike without warning. Their most important service, however, was cutting the lifelines of Japan by sinking its cargo ships, tankers, and transports. The Japanese, in turn, used their submarines with their fleets of other warships against carriers and cruisers. They were not very effective, however, against U.S. convoys, transports, and naval tankers.

Although Allied submarines sank twenty-five Japanese and five German U-boats in the Pacific, submarines rarely fought their counterparts, but they remained effective throughout the war. The last major U.S. ship lost was the heavy cruiser *Indianapolis,* torpedoed east of Leyte on 29 July 1945 by the Japanese submarine I-58. The last Japanese ships sunk by a U.S. submarine were two coast defense frigates torpedoed in the Sea of Japan on 14 August 1945 by the *Torsk.*

It was merchant shipping, however, that held together the Japanese Empire. At the beginning of the war, Japan had approximately six million tons of merchant shipping. Although three million tons were needed by the civilian economy, more than two-thirds of all available shipping had been allocated immediately to the armed forces. Destruction of this shipping was the U.S. submarine fleet's primary mission. The highest total number of submarine cruising days spent on offensive patrol in operating areas in one month in 1942 by U.S. submersibles was 512 each in November and December; fifty-five ships were attacked in December, 159 torpedoes expended; in August 1943, 858 days,

105 ships attacked, 387 torpedoes expended; in September, 697 days, 112 ships attacked, 461 torpedoes; in October 1944, 1,306 days, 230 ships, 799 torpedoes; in June 1945, 1,067 days, 147 ships, 522 torpedoes. In July of 1945, the number of targets, military or other, diminished sharply. In August only fifty-nine ships were attacked.

New Japanese ship construction could not keep pace with this loss rate. Starting at 27 percent of losses from all causes in 1942, it reached its peak at 877,392 tons, 49 percent of losses from all causes in the first half of 1944. In the second quarter of 1945, it had fallen to 15 percent. The main islands of Japan were steadily being blockaded. The U.S. Navy paid a price for this success. Of the 288 submarines that saw active duty, 52 (just less than one in five) were lost—a number nearly equal to the number of the larger fleet type available in the Pacific at the beginning of the war. Thirteen percent of the enlisted men, or 3,505 men, and 16 percent of the officers were lost at sea. The Japanese lost 103 submarines and at war's end had only 58 left, many of them unfit for service. Germany lost 801 submarines with thirty thousand men; Italy lost 85 vessels.

THE PACIFIC WAR, 1943–1945

OPERATIONS IN NEW GUINEA. In July 1942 the Japanese had landed strong forces at Buna, Gona, and Sarnanda on the northeast coast of New Guinea and began to push southward overland toward Port Moresby. During the last week of August, they landed troops at Milne Bay but were driven off in September-October with heavy losses by Australian troops. Australian and U.S. troops of General MacArthur's Southwest Pacific Command, based in Australia, blocked the Japanese

The 165th Infantry assaults a beach on the Makin Atoll of Gilbert Islands on 20 November 1943. (National Archives)

overland advance toward Port Moresby and pushed them back toward Buna-Gona.

Lack of adequate overland routes on New Guinea compelled both the Allies and the Japanese to depend almost entirely on air and sea transport. Consequently, on 2–4 March 1943 the Japanese suffered heavy losses in the Battle of the Bismarck Sea, when more than three hundred land-based Australian and U.S. aircraft destroyed eight loaded cargo transports and four destroyers. Although 2,734 Japanese survivors were rescued by Allied destroyers and submarines, more than three thousand went down with their ships.

Although driven from Guadalcanal in February 1943, the Japanese continued to consolidate their airfields and bases to the northwest. The U.S. forces in the south Pacific therefore undertook the conquest of New Georgia. Losses in this operation included the light cruiser *Honolulu* and the destroyer *Gwinn,* as well as damage to the light cruiser *St. Louis.* On 5 August the Americans captured Munda and immediately placed it in operation as a base for future operations. By 9 October, New Georgia was completely occupied. MacArthur's combined forces began a long process of island-hopping and leap-frogging on 30 June along New Guinea's northern coast—a course that eventually carried them back to the Philippines.

CENTRAL PACIFIC, NOVEMBER 1943–NOVEMBER 1944. Captured by the Japanese in December 1941, Tarawa was the first of the Gilbert Islands to fall to the Second U.S. Marines, on 20–24 November 1943. The battle cost the marines 20 percent casualties among its fifteen thousand combat troops, but of the nearly five-thousand-man Japanese garrison, only 146 were taken prisoner. At the same time, Makin, also of the Gilberts, fell to the Twenty-seventh U.S. Army Division with significantly fewer casualties. Undefended Apamama Island was quickly taken on 21 November by troops landed from a submarine. These operations were all supported by nine hundred carrier-based aircraft. The escort carrier *Liscome Bay* fell victim to a submarine, but the light cruiser *Independence* survived a torpedo attack.

In December 1943, Rabaul, already partially neutralized by carrier-born air strikes, and with the seizure of neighboring islands, was isolated by the capture of Arawe (15 December) and Cape Gloucester (26 December), in southwestern and northwestern New Britain. After the Japanese withdrew their air strength from Rabaul, U.S. forces seized the Admiralty Islands on 1 March 1944.

From the Gilberts, the Allied offensive moved westward to the Japanese-mandated (formerly German) Marshall Islands. Once again a joint U.S. Army-Marine operation took place. The U.S. Seventh Infantry Division, which on 3 June 1943 had retaken Attu in the Aleutians, and the Fourth Marine Division landed on the Marshalls on 31 January 1944. By 4 February they had completed the conquest of Kwajalein and Majuro, each with atolls offering excellent anchorages.

While U.S. carrier planes raided Truk, Ponape, and the Marianas, the Eniwetok atoll was taken 17–22 February by the U.S. Seventh Division and a marine combat team sailing from Kwajalein. By 25 March all the Admiralty Islands were in U.S. hands, thus neutralizing the Japanese central and southwest Pacific base. In a carrier strike 16–17 February, 200,000 tons of merchant and naval shipping were destroyed. All major Japanese naval vessels abandoned the area and retired either to the Palaus or to their home islands. Except at Brunei Bay on the coast of Borneo and Singapore, the Japanese fleet was back where it had started the war and with far less strength. Moreover, the surviving portion of the Japanese First Air Fleet, found in the Marianas in February 1944, was destroyed.

The Fifth U.S. Marine Amphibious Corps, consisting of the Second and Fourth Marine Divisions, landed on Saipan on 15 June 1944, followed by the Twenty-seventh U.S. Army Division. One month of bitter fighting followed before the enemy garrison was destroyed. From 21 July to 9 August the Seventy-seventh Infantry Division and the Third Marine Division and a Marine Corps brigade fought to conquer Guam, but the conquest of Tinian took only nine days (24 July–1 August). While the fighting went on, engineers prepared runways for the B-29 Superfortresses to use as bases for long-range strategic bombing of Japan. The first major air strike took off on 24 November from Saipan, which had been declared secure on 9 July.

Japanese efforts to frustrate the operations in the Marianas failed. Three Japanese aircraft carriers and two tankers were sunk, two of the carriers by submarines. One carrier was the veteran *Shakaku,* sunk by the *Cavalla* on the submarine's first patrol. The submarine *Albacore* torpedoed the *Taiho,* Japan's newest and the world's largest (31,000 tons) battleship. Four other carriers, the battleship *Haruna,* and the cruiser *Mayu* were also sunk, which so decimated the Japanese naval air fleet that it was now nearly finished as a factor in the war. The U.S. battleships *Indiana* and *South Dakota* incurred some minor damage in the attack of 19 June.

The first U.S. Marine Corps Division, meanwhile, had landed on Pelelui in the Palau group of the western Carolines on 15 September 1944, and two days later the Eighty-first Infantry Division landed on Angaur, south of Peleliu. Except for a few snipers still hidden in caves, the conquest of both islands was completed on

13 October. On 21 September, Ulithi fell, where the U.S. command established an advance naval base that helped support later operations in the Philippines. As Peleliu fell, the southwest Pacific command's Thirty-first and Thirty-second army divisions seized Morotai, south of Mindanao in the Philippines.

BURMA-INDIA-CHINA THEATER. On 12–25 May 1943, the Anglo-American (Trident) Conference took place in Washington. Generals Joseph W. Stilwell, Claire L. Chennault, and Albert C. Wedemeyer, and a representative from China, argued over differing priorities for the Indo-Burma theater of operations. One of the decisions made was to increase the quantity of aviation gasoline being flown from India into China in order to increase the effectiveness of Allied airpower on mainland China. By January 1945, the Himalayan air route alone was carrying 46,000 tons of gasoline a month.

The Quebec (Quadrant) Conference took place on 11–24 August 1943 to establish the Southeast Asia Command, with Lord Louis Mountbatten as supreme commander with Stilwell as his deputy. He was replaced in the autumn of 1944 by Wedemeyer, who was preferred by Chinese commander Chiang Kai-Shek. The combined Royal and U.S. combat air forces, including the U.S. Tenth, were placed under the command of U.S. General George E. Stratemeyer. On 7 September, MacArthur, having moved his headquarters from Brisbane, Australia, to Hollandia, Indonesia, reorganized his ground forces as the Sixth and Eighth armies under Generals Walter Krueger and Robert L. Eichelberger, respectively.

In February 1944, in the Hukawng Valley in northern Burma, two Chinese divisions, reequipped and trained by General Stilwell in northeastern India, joined Merrill's Marauders, an all-volunteer force of three thousand men commanded by General Frank D. Merrill. On 17 May this combined force captured a Japanese airstrip at Myitkyina and the town on 3 August, while General Orde C. Wingate's British and Indian jungle troops blocked the Irrawaddy Valley. From then on the attempted Japanese invasion of northeastern India was halted, as the Allies steadily drove them from Burma.

The Stilwell Road, a 400-mile military highway from Ledo, India, that joined an existing 717-mile road to Burma from Kunming, China, was completed by 28 January 1945, and the first convoy of trucks carrying war matériel reached China from northeast India. Meanwhile, Japan's sea-lanes to Burma had been cut, while the British captured Mandalay on 21 March and Rangoon on 3 May. Lord Mountbatten estimated that the Burma campaign had cost the Japanese a total of 300,000 casualties, including 97,000 dead.

Until the Marianas base was opened in June 1945, U.S. B-29 Superfortresses flew bombing runs from Chinese bases to Japan. In May 1944 and April 1945, the Japanese launched their last major offensives of these years in a vain effort to make it impossible for the U.S. Air Force in China to join hands with those operating over the Philippines and the Ryukyus. General Stratemeyer's Tenth and Fourteenth air forces operated out of Linchow and Kunming. Living largely off the land, the Japanese continued to occupy most of China's most fruitful areas until ordered by their government to surrender in September 1945.

PHILIPPINES CAMPAIGN, 1944–1945. As the U.S. Navy closed in on the Philippines in September 1944, Admiral Halsey suggested that the date for the invasion of Leyte Island be advanced to 20 October from 20 December. The CCS, then in conference in Quebec, approved, and troops, already battle-loaded for other objectives, were diverted to join others in the main effort.

In a series of preliminary air strikes on Okinawa, Luzon, and Formosa beginning on 19 June, Task Force 38 encountered the most violent enemy air resistance east of Formosa. In the fiercest battle of the war to date between ship- and land-based aircraft, the Japanese lost 650 planes in the air and on the ground. Their repair shops, facilities, and bases also suffered major damage. During the two-day Battle of the Philippine Sea, Task Force 38 lost 76 aircraft in combat and operational accidents. The Japanese defeat in the battle helped significantly to determine the outcome of the later battles for Leyte Island and Leyte Gulf.

The United States had assembled 53 assault transports, 54 assault cargo ships, 151 tank landing craft, 72 infantry landing craft, 16 rocket launching ships, and 400 assorted amphibious craft to carry the U.S. Sixth Army to Leyte. Planes from 18 escort carriers provided an umbrella for the invasion fleet. Six battleships, with cruisers and destroyers, served as naval escort as the troops came ashore south of Tacloban on 20 October. The Americans needed Leyte as a base for future operations in the Philippines. The Japanese were aware of this and sought to reinforce their garrison through the west coast port of Ormoc. General Tomoyuki Yamashita came down from Manchuria to take charge of the defense of the Philippines. He brought with him one of the finest Japanese divisions from the Kwantung army. By the end of November, U.S. troops had reached Limon on the northern part of the Leyte Island. Ormoc fell on 11 December, following a landing by the

Seventy-seventh Division. Japanese resistance on Leyte ceased by the end of the year.

The Japanese High Command realized that holding the rest of the Philippines was vital for their survival, because if the Americans captured the islands, they could close the China Sea to Japanese shipping and cut off the oil of Sumatra and Borneo. Consequently, the High Command decided to commit their last line of naval defense, their battle fleet, to break up the defensive cordon of the U.S. Third and Seventh battle fleets around the Leyte area.

The U.S. Seventh Fleet, under Admiral Kinkaid, came up from the southwest Pacific with MacArthur, and the Third Fleet under Admiral Halsey came across the central Pacific under the general direction of Admiral Nimitz.

Vice Admiral Takeo Kurita, with a central attack force of four battleships, including the two giants *Musashi* and *Yamato,* eight cruisers, and eleven destroyers, was to push through the Sibuyan Sea and the San Bernardino Strait, then turn southward to Leyte Gulf, where a supporting attack force moving through the Surigao Strait under Admiral Shoji Nishimura was to join him.

During the battle on 23–25 October, Kurita's force lost two heavy cruisers, the *Maya* and the *Atago,* to the U.S. submarines *Dace* and *Darter.* A third cruiser, the *Takao,* was heavily damaged and returned to Brunei Bay with an escort of two destroyers. Kurita transferred with his staff to the *Yamato.* While passing through the Sibuyan Sea on 23 October, Kurita's fleet was attacked by U.S. carrier-based planes, which destroyed the *Musashi.*

The Fifth U.S. Marine Amphibious Corps landed on Saipan on 15 June 1944. One month of bitter fighting followed before the enemy garrison was destroyed. These reinforcements waded across the coral reef toward a Saipan beach soon after the initial landing. (National Archives)

Kurita flinched but then recovered, continued during the night through the San Bernardino Strait at high speed, and appeared in the morning off Samar. Nishimura's support force was attacked south of Leyte on the night of 24–25. The Japanese lost two battleships, a cruiser, and three destroyers, largely by gunfire, and approximately five thousand men.

Before dawn on 25 October, Kurita escaped through the San Bernardino Strait to attack a weak Seventh Fleet outpost of light escort carriers, destroyers, and a destroyer escort, all that stood between him and his quarry in the Leyte Gulf. He managed to destroy the U.S. carrier *Princeton,* two escort carriers, the *Gambier Bay* and *St. Lô,* and the destroyer escort. Three Japanese heavy cruisers were disabled by aircraft, another by a destroyer's torpedo. The superstructure of the *Yamato* was so badly damaged that the ship was virtually isolated from the rest of Kurita's fleet. Fearing a trap, he reversed his course and again retreated through the San Bernardino Strait.

Carrier- and land-based aircraft harassed the retreating Japanese through 26 October and brought Kurita's losses to three battleships, four carriers, including the *Zuikaku,* ten cruisers, nine destroyers, and a submarine—45 percent of the tonnage committed. The U.S. fleet lost only 2.8 percent of its total tonnage committed to the action.

The conquest of Leyte was completed in December 1944, and the U.S. Seventh Fleet's escort carriers entered the Sulu Sea in support of a two-regiment task force that landed on the south coast of Mindoro. Concerned about this new threat to their South China Sea lifeline, the Japanese had expected their base on Palawan to be the object of the next Allied attack. Consequently, they had only a small garrison on Mindoro, which fell quickly to the U.S. troops that quickly established a base on the island from which to cover an amphibious landing on Luzon. Feints were made to suggest that the next landing would take place on the south coast of Luzon.

In early January 1945, a U.S. Army assault force on transports passed east of Leyte through the Surigao Strait and the Mindanao and Sulu seas. When the landing force turned northward off the west coast of Luzon, it was attacked by land-based Japanese suicide bombers. Despite efforts from the U.S. fast carrier force to close down the Japanese airfields, sixteen ships were hit on 6 January, ten of them incurring serious damage. Nevertheless, sixty-eight thousand U.S. troops landed at Lingayen Gulf on 9 January and a deep beachhead was soon established. Although the Japanese had landed at the same site in 1941, they were apparently surprised by the move.

MacArthur first deployed a cover force to protect the beachhead from strong enemy forces known to be located in the hills to the north and east. He then sent, as the Japanese had done three years before, an armored spearhead southward to Clark Field and Manila. On 29 January a second landing was made at Subic Bay and quickly sealed off the Bataan Peninsula as its base. Two days later, the U.S. Eleventh Airborne Division made an amphibious landing on the west coast at Nasugbu, south of Manila. Within a week the First Cavalry and Eleventh Airborne reached the outskirts of Manila from the north and the south. On 16 February troops landed on Corregidor by parachute and from the sea. Manila was taken on 23 February, and Manila Bay was soon open. More than 4,215 Japanese were killed during the conquest of Corregidor while the United States lost 136 killed, 8 missing, and 513 wounded.

In late February and into March, under the cover of aircraft based on Palawan Island, landings were made against feeble resistance on Panay, Cebu, and Negros. Nevertheless, stubborn and prolonged fighting took place as the enemy retreated into the hilly interior of the islands. Fighting for Mindanao lasted from March until May. At that time in Borneo, Australian and Netherlands East Indies troops took Tarakan Island, Brunei Bay, and adjacent airfields on 10 June and Balikpapan in July.

Resistance continued on Luzon throughout the summer, while U.S. forces steadily expanded their control from Legaspi and Manila, pushing north and northeastward from the central Luzon plain. By 1 July the Cagayan Valley had been cleared. Japanese losses in the Philippines totaled 317,000 killed and 7,236 captured, as opposed to 60,628 U.S. troops killed, wounded, and missing.

With the Philippines in hand, U.S. and Allied forces had virtually cut off the Japanese from the South China Sea. On 11 January a fast U.S. carrier force had run the strait between Formosa and Luzon, then swept southward along the China coast to Hong Kong and Cam Ranh Bay in Indochina, sinking forty-six ships, including seven large tankers. Seven thousand Japanese aircraft and most of their surface fleet had now been lost. The Allies carried the war into the main islands of Japan through heavy aerial bombardment from bases in the Mariana Islands. Iwo Jima and Okinawa remained to be conquered to enable bombers to operate freely.

IWO JIMA AND OKINAWA. Iwo Jima, valued for its strategic location—less than eight hundred miles from Tokyo—was the first Japanese possession to be invaded in the war. It had two airfields and was defended by a garrison of more than twenty thousand men under the command of General Tadamishi Kuribayashi.

The Third, Fourth, and Fifth marine divisions had trained in the Hawaiian islands for the invasion of Iwo Jima. A fleet of 495 ships carried the assault force of 75,144 men and 36,164 garrison troops to Iwo, supported by seven old battleships, four heavy cruisers, and fifteen destroyers.

On the eve of the invasion, 16–17 February, a fast carrier force of 118 ships, including 8 battleships and 17 aircraft carriers with 1,120 planes, made the first carrier-based raids on the Japanese home islands.

Upon completion of this aerial bombardment, the marines landed on Iwo's southeastern shore on 19 February. Although the bombing had destroyed most surface installations, the island was honeycombed with well-concealed emplacements that had been dug in on the slopes of Mount Suribachi, a volcano that dominated the beach. Other emplacements on a hill at the other end of the beach had also survived. Marines took Mount Suribachi on 23 February, but several weeks of hard fighting followed before the enemy was burned or blasted out. The last Japanese sortie from an emplacement was made on 27 March, ten days after the island had been declared secured.

The defense of Iwo Jima had cost the Japanese an estimated total of 21,304 men, of whom 13,234 were counted and buried by U.S. forces. Two hundred and twelve were taken prisoner. U.S. casualties, not including naval losses, were 4,590 killed, 301 missing, and 15,954 wounded.

The first of the two airfields taken was quickly placed into operation, despite occasional enemy mortar fire from the high ground, saving many lives in emergency bomber landings. A submarine and seaplane lifesaving service was maintained between the island and Japan. A meteorological station was also established, and as long as the war lasted, and for several months thereafter, Iwo was the hub of airborne traffic over the western Pacific.

The U.S. strategic assault forces of the central Pacific next concentrated on forthcoming operations against Okinawa. The largest island in the Ryukyus, Okinawa was large enough to accommodate several large airfields and to serve as a staging area for troops assembled for the invasion of Japan. The island also offered excellent anchorages for naval installations. Most important, it lay athwart Japan's remaining sea and air routes to Asia and the South China Sea and was only 350 miles from the home islands. To prevent interference from the Japanese, carrier aircraft bombed installations in the Inland Sea on 19 and 24 March, then the nearby Kerama Islands were seized on 26 March by the U.S. Seventy-seventh Division to provide an anchorage and seaplane base.

The Okinawan campaign (1 April 1945–21 June 1945), while the last of the Pacific war, was one of the most difficult and costly. The battle for Okinawa was fought by an expeditionary force of 1,213 ships and 451,866 ground troops, covered and supported by a U.S. carrier force of eighty-two ships and a British carrier force of twenty-eight. The latter also bombed Formosa and other Japanese bases. On 1 April the combined ground forces landed with comparative ease on the southwestern coast of Okinawa. Marines and army troops advanced then separated, the marines turning to the north and the army divisions to the south, where they encountered the main enemy resistance in well-prepared positions. Within a week four divisions had landed and Wontan Airfield was prepared for operations. The northern part of the island was secured two weeks later, and the marines joined the army units in a final assault in the south. Despite fire support from battleships and carrier aircraft, organized resistance continued until 21 June.

More than 110,000 Japanese died in defending the island, and approximately 7,500 were taken prisoner. U.S. casualties were 7,213 killed and 31,081 wounded. The U.S. commanding general, Simon Buckner, was killed three days before all resistance collapsed.

At sea, Japan's last battleship, the *Yamato,* a light cruiser, and a destroyer escort were sunk. Suicide aircraft called kamikaze attacked relentlessly, destroying thirty-six ships, twenty-eight by air attack, of which twenty-six were victims of kamikaze. None larger than a destroyer, however, was lost. The Okinawa campaign cost the Japanese navy more than seventy-eight hundred aircraft, of which more than three thousand fell victim to U.S. naval and marine aircraft; 2,655 pilots were lost through operational losses caused by poor pilot training and careless ground crews; and 2,498 sailors went down with the *Yamato.* In addition to ships sunk, U.S. naval losses from 1 April to 1 July were 368 ships damaged, 763 planes lost, 4,907 men killed or missing, and 4,824 wounded. The cost of the battle for Okinawa was high, but a final staging base for the last offensive against the main Japanese islands was won.

On 19 March, 22 June, and 24 July, two thousand carrier-borne aircraft and those based on Okinawa completed the destruction of the Japanese navy in the Inland Sea, and U.S. submarines entered the Sea of Japan to destroy the remaining shipping to the Asiatic mainland. From the new airfields on Okinawa hundreds of heavy bombers and strafing fighter aircraft joined others from the Marianas and Iwo Jima in attacking the main Japanese home islands. Seven times in July and once in August, naval craft bombarded Japanese coastal areas. Two hundred fifty-eight Allied aircraft were destroyed by enemy antiaircraft and 104 in operational mishaps, while 1,386 Japanese planes were destroyed in the air and on the ground, and 1,980 were lost because of operational mishaps. Throughout July and August 1945, the Allies maintained a complete air and sea blockade of Japan.

BOMBING OF JAPAN. Although military resistance on the main islands had been substantially weakened, the Japanese still had five million men in eastern China, Manchuria, and Korea. The Allies had long assumed that large-scale landings on the main islands would be needed, and such landings, it was estimated, would result in one million casualties. Much, therefore, depended upon when the Russians would enter the war against Japan. Against the strategic background, the employment of the atomic bomb appeared as a means to make the Japanese realize the futility of further resistance. Commenting on the decision to bomb Hiroshima and Nagasaki, Secretary of War Henry L. Stimson wrote, "We had developed a weapon of such revolutionary character that its use against the enemy might well be expected to produce exactly the kind of shock on the Japanese ruling oligarchy which we desired, strengthening the position of those who wished peace, and weakening the military party."

The city and military base of Hiroshima was bombed with an atomic bomb on 6 August and the city and naval base Nagasaki with a similar weapon on 9 August. More than 100,000 people died as a result of these two attacks. Approximately the same number had perished in a series of firebomb attacks on Tokyo in 1945. On 8 August, the day before the attack on Nagasaki, the Soviet Union declared war on Japan and rapidly conquered Manchuria, southern Sakhalin, and the Kuril Islands. On 12 August the Red Army entered Korea.

JAPANESE SURRENDER

On 10 August the Japanese government offered to surrender militarily if the prerogative of the emperor as sovereign in Japan could be preserved. The Allies agreed but stated that from the moment of surrender his authority and that of his government were to be subject to the authority of MacArthur. The Potsdam Declaration of 26 July 1945 had already stated the Allied terms for Japan: limitation of Japan's sovereignty to its home islands; Allied occupation; liquidation of war industries; trial and punishment of war criminals; freedom of speech, thought, and religion; and removal of obstacles to the revival and strengthening of democratic tendencies among the population. These terms were similar to those already imposed upon Germany.

At midnight on 14 August 1945, President Truman and Prime Minister Clement Attlee announced that the surrender terms had been accepted by Japan. The next day Emperor Hirohito ordered a cease-fire. On 19 August, representatives of the Japanese armed forces received the instrument of surrender at MacArthur's headquarters. The famed Kwantung Army in Manchuria surrendered to the Red Army on 21 August. On 27 August, U.S. troops took over Atsugi Airfield near Tokyo and began the occupation of Japan.

The instrument of surrender was signed by representatives of the Imperial Japanese government aboard the battleship *Missouri* at anchor in Tokyo Bay on 2 September 1945. Scattered surrenders took place later in the southwest Pacific and in China, culminating in the surrender of Hong Kong on 16 September.

The war cost the Japanese more than five and a half million casualties, of whom more than half a million were civilians. Of Japan's 12 battleships, only one was left; of 22 carriers and escort carriers and 43 cruisers, none was operational; of 165 destroyers, 26 had been heavily damaged; and of 104 submarines, 26 (6 of them German) had survived. Japanese merchant shipping losses exceeded by one-third the tonnage with which Japan had started the war, and replacements by new construction were less than two-fifths of losses; 116,000 had been lost from the merchant marine; twenty-seven thousand were dead or missing.

The United States had sent 1.25 million men to the Pacific. Total casualties amounted to 170,596, of whom 41,322 had been killed.

OCCUPATION OF GERMANY AND JAPAN

With the cessation of hostilities, demobilization of the nation's armed forces proceeded rapidly. One-half of the army's remaining strength remained overseas, however, assigned to the occupation of Germany and Japan. A large force also remained in Korea, with a Soviet force sent into Korea to accept the surrender of Japanese troops stationed there.

At first, the Allied powers, under policies adopted at Yalta and Potsdam, assumed joint sovereign authority over Germany on 5 June 1945. The Allied Control Council, however, was unable to achieve the necessary unanimity. Consequently, each of the occupying powers—the United States, Great Britain, France, and the Soviet Union—developed its own policies and administration for its own zone. The result by September 1949 was a divided Germany, the Federal Republic of Germany comprising the area of the U.S., British, and French zones, and a communist government, the German Democratic Republic, came into existence in the Russian-occupied eastern zone.

Republican federalization of the U.S., British, and French zones was completed with the adoption of a federal constitution by a parliamentary council in Bonn on 8 May 1949. The basic law provided for a federal diet, or Bundestag, whose members would be directly elected for a four-year term, and a federal council, or Bundesrat, composed of State of Land governments. The constitution provided that the Bundestag choose a new chancellor by majority vote before it could, by a vote of no confidence, ask the president to dismiss the old one. This resulted in a more stable government than that of the former Weimar (prewar) constitution. U.S. forces continued to occupy Germany until 5 May 1955.

By mid-1947, the free election of a new diet and a thorough revision of the nation's constitution began Japan's transformation into a constitutional democracy.

The occupation of Japan, which began on 27 August 1945, developed differently, as a result of President Truman's insistence that the entire country be placed under U.S. control. The Far East Advisory Commission, representing the eleven nations that had fought against Japan, was headquartered in Washington, with a branch in Tokyo. Real power, however, rested with General MacArthur. Unlike Germany, Japan retained its government. By mid-1947, the free election of a new diet and a thorough revision of the nation's constitution began Japan's transformation into a constitutional democracy, with the emperor's role limited to that of a constitutional monarch. The way was thus opened for the ultimate restoration of Japanese sovereignty. A final peace treaty was signed by the United States and Japan on 8 September 1951.

BIBLIOGRAPHY

Grand Strategy

Butler, J. R. M., ed. *History of the Second World War: Grand Strategy,* 6 vols. (1956–1976).

Cline, Ray S. *Washington Command Post: The Operations Division* (1951).

Churchill, Winston. *The Second World War: The Grand Alliance,* 6 vols. (1948–1953).

Conn, Stetson, and Byron Fairchild. *The Framework of Hemisphere Defense* (1960).

Craven, Wesley F., and James L. Cate, eds. *The Army Air Forces in World War II,* 7 vols. (1948–1958).

Fuller, J. F. C. *The Second World War, 1939–1945: A Strategic and Tactical History* (1968).

Green, Constance M., Harry C. Thomson, and Peter C. Roots. *The Ordnance Department: Planning Munitions for War* (1955).

Millett, John D. *The Organization and Role of the Army Service Forces* (1954).

Morison, Samuel E. *United States Naval Operations in World War II,* 15 vols. (1947–1962).

Romanus, Charles F., and Riley Sunderland. *Stilwell's Mission to China* (1953).

The War Against Germany and Italy

Ambrose, Stephen E. *The Supreme Commander: The War Years of General Dwight D. Eisenhower* (1970).

Beckett, Ian F. W. *Great Campaigns of World War II* (1991).

Bennett, Ralph F. *Ultra in the West: The Normandy Campaign of 1944–1945* (1980).

Blumenson, Martin. *Anzio: The Gamble that Failed* (1963).

———. *Breakout and Pursuit* (1964).

Brereton, Lewis Hyde. *The Brereton Diaries* (1946).

Clark, Mark W. *Calculated Risk* (1950).

Cole, Hugh M. *The Lorraine Campaign* (1950).

———. *The Ardennes: The Battle of the Bulge* (1965).

Critchell, Laurence. *Four Stars of Hell: The 501st Parachute Infantry Regiment in World War II* (1947, 1987).

D'Este, Carlo. *World War II in the Mediterranean, 1942–1945* (1990).

Eisenhower, Dwight D. *Crusade in Europe* (1948).

Fisher, Ernest F. *Cassino to the Alps* (1989).

Garland, Albert N., and Howard McGaw Smyth. *Sicily and the Surrender of Italy* (1965).

Gelb, Norman. *Desperate Venture: The Story of Operation Torch, The Allied Invasion of North Africa* (1992).

Gibson, Hugh, ed. *The Ciano Diaries, 1939–1943* (1946).

Goebbels, Joseph. *The Goebbels Diaries* (1983).

Halder, Franz. *Hitler as War Lord* (1950).

Harrison, Gordon. *Cross-Channel Attack* (1951).

Hastings, Max. *Overlord: D-Day and the Battle for Normandy* (1984).

Howe, George F. *Northwest Africa: Seizing the Initiative in the West* (1957).

Kappe, Siegfried, and Charles T. Brusaw. *Soldat: Reflections of a German Soldier, 1936–1949* (1992).

Keegan, John, ed. *Churchill's Generals* (1991).

Kemp, Anthony. *The Unknown Battle: Metz, 1944* (1981).

MacDonald, Charles B. *The Mighty Endeavor: American Armed Forces in the European Theater in World War II* (1969).

———. *The Last Offensive* (1973, 1984).

———. *Company Commander* (1978).

———. *A Time for Trumpets: The Untold Story of the Battle of the Bulge* (1984, 1985).

Merriam, Robert. *Dark December* (1947).

Montgomery, Sir Bernard L. *El Alamein to the Sangro River* (1974).

———. *Normandy to the Baltic* (1974).

Paisley, Melvin. *Ace: Autobiography of a Fighter Pilot, World War II* (1992).

Plivier, Theodor. *Stalingrad.* Translated by Richard and Clara Winston (1983).

Pogue, Forrest C. *The Supreme Command,* 2 vols. (1959).

———. *George C. Marshall,* vols. 2 and 3 (1966, 1973).

Root, Waverly L. *Secret History of the War: Casablanca to Katyn* (1946).

Ruppenthal, Roland G. *Logistical Support of the Armies,* vols. 1 and 2 (1954).

Schlabrendorff, Fabian von. *The Secret War Against Hitler.* Translated by Hilda Simon (1965).

Sears, Stephen W., ed. *Eyewitness to World War II: The Best of American Heritage* (1991).

Smith, Bradley, F., and Elena Agrossi. *Operation Sunrise: The Secret Surrender* (1979).

Stettinius, Edward R. *Roosevelt and the Russians: The Yalta Conference* (1949, 1970).

Trevor-Roper, H. R. *The Last Days of Hitler* (1947).

Weigley, Russell F. *Eisenhower's Lieutenants: The Campaigns of France and Germany, 1944–1945* (1981).

Werth, Alexander. *Russia at War, 1941–1945* (1964).

Wheeler-Bennett, John. *Munich: Prologue to Tragedy* (1948, 1964).

Wilmot, Chester. *The Struggle for Europe* (1952).

Wood, Edward W., Jr. *On Being Wounded* (1991).

Young, Desmond. *Rommel, the Desert Fox* (1951).

The War Against Japan

Baker, Leonard. *Roosevelt and Pearl Harbor: The President in a Time of Crisis* (1970).

Belote, James, and William Belote. *Titans of the Sea: The Development and Operations of Japanese and American Carrier Task Forces During World War II* (1975).

Falk, Stanley. *Bataan: March of Death* (1962).

Feifer, George. *Tennozan: The Battle of Okinawa and the Atomic Bomb* (1992).

Griffith, Samuel B. *The Battle for Guadalcanal* (1979).

James, D. Clayton. *The Years of MacArthur, 1941–1945* (1975).

King, Ernest J. *The U.S. Navy at War, 1941–1945* (1946).

La Forte, Robert S., and Ronald E. Marcello, eds. *Remembering Pearl Harbor* (1991).

Layton, Edwin, with Roger Pineau and John Costello. *And I Was There* (1985).

Leahy, William D. *I Was There* (1950).

Marshall, S. L. A. *Island Victory* (1983).

Miller, John, Jr. *Guadalcanal: The First Offensive* (1949).

Morris, Samuel E. *United States Naval Operations in World War II*, 15 vols. (1947–1962).

Morton, Louis. *The Fall of the Philippines* (1953).

———. *Pacific Command: A Study in Interservice Relations* (1961).

———. *The War in the Pacific, Strategy and Command: The First Two Years* (1962).

Pelz, Stephen. *Race to Pearl Harbor: The Failure of the Second London Naval Conference and the Onset of World War II* (1974).

Prange, Gordon J. *At Dawn We Slept* (1981).

———. *Pearl Harbor: The Verdict of History* (1986).

———. *December 7, 1941: The Day the Japanese Attacked Pearl Harbor* (1987).

———. *God's Samurai: The Lead Pilot at Pearl Harbor* (1990).

Pratt, Fletcher. *The Marines' War* (1946).

Roscoe, Theodore. *United States Submarine Operations in World War II* (1949).

Smith, Robert Ross. *The Approach to the Philippines* (1953).

———. *Triumph in the Philippines* (1963).

Spector, Ronald. *Eagle Against the Sun: The American War with Japan* (1985).

Stimson, Henry L. "The Decision to Use the Atomic Bomb." *Harper's Magazine* (February 1947).

———. "The Nuremberg Trial: Landmark in Law." *Foreign Affairs* (January 1947).

Stockman, James R. *The First Marine Division on Okinawa, 1 April–30 June 1945* (1946).

Toland, John. *The Rising Sun: The Decline and Fall of the Japanese Empire* (1970).

Toynbee, Arnold J. *Civilization on Trial* (1960).

Tregaskis, Richard. *Guadalcanal Diary* (1955).

Van der Vat, Dan. *The Pacific Campaign: World War II and the U.S.-Japanese Naval War, 1941–1945* (1991).

Woodward, C. Van. *The Battle for Leyte Gulf* (1947).

— ERNEST F. FISHER

The Cold War

The cold war (1945–1990) was conceived in a curious union of victory and fear. Conquest over European and Asian fascism in World War II sent a thrill of accomplishment through the United States, Great Britain, and the Soviet Union, but it also raised deep anxiety over the shape of the future. World War II virtually destroyed two major regional powers—Germany and Japan—each with global aspirations. The removal of their strong military forces, each of which had played a critical role in the balance of power in its respective region, created a vacuum into which the war's most prominent winners might press—or be pulled. The price of victory for Great Britain was so high that it became, at least with respect to British overseas interests and colonies, nearly a Pyrrhic one. Similarly, in France, victory was a word more than a psychological fact, and internal recriminations would long preoccupy the French and limit their role in shaping postwar political structure in Europe, let alone beyond it. The impoverishment of nearly all of Europe, whether its countries had been victim or villain, weakened the economic base needed to sustain influential military force. The economic strength of the United States was one of the few remaining forces capable of extending influence far beyond its national borders, thus providing discipline and structure abroad. The military strength of the Soviet Union was, or at least seemed to be, another expansive force, extending itself into other countries. The cold war, conceived amid these tensions, was born when anxiety over the consequences of a global war overcame hope for the prospects of a simple peace.

In essence, the cold war supposed the necessity of competition between the political systems and power blocs led by the United States and the Soviet Union, but did not presume the inevitability of full-scale military conflict. In one sense, it was merely the ancient game of regional and world power cast in modern dress, a competition in which political, social, economic, and military power had always been intertwined to some extent. New conditions in the world after 1945, however, did make for a highly distinctive experience. The most important technological development was the invention of nuclear weapons, and the second most important one was the perfection of means to deliver them, notably by long-distance bomber aircraft and then long-range missiles. A key political and cultural problem was that U.S. and Soviet leaders saw one another's political, social, and economic systems not only as dangerous but as evil. This combination of the capacity to inflict swift mass destruction and a largely Manichean vision of world politics made the prospect of global annihilation seem real, and the perception arose among U.S. military and political leaders that they were dealing with problems of a wholly unprecedented nature. In this context, traditional military experience and advice lost status, while civilian strategists became both more numerous and more influential. Saving the United States and its allies from threat and attack in an era when nuclear weapons proliferated became the central task of these new planners and a focal preoccupation of U.S. political leaders.

Short of "hot lead" fired in open battle,

the conflict was a "cold" war.

In grand strategic terms, the cold war was marked by its comprehensiveness of scope, which included the entire world, and by the chilling majesty of its risks, which entailed increasingly the virtual destruction of the earth itself. In this sense, "total war" became a literal possibility and hence a vivid nightmare. In military terms, however, the cold war held curious parallels with warfare in the eighteenth century, when maneuvering sometimes led to battle but just as often served as a substitute. The buildup and deployment of forces was intended to achieve objectives by having the enemy rationally calculate that it would likely be defeated in the event of actual combat, thus affording one victory without fighting an all-out war. Deterring an adversary from an attack also suggested that military power was inseparably intertwined with all other elements of national strength. If war was the continuation of politics by other means, as Carl von Clausewitz has suggested, then politics was also the waging of war by means other than actual armed combat. Short of "hot lead" fired in open battle, the conflict was, therefore, a "cold" war.

Despite the often stated—and often erroneous—notion that Americans have frequently won a war and lost the subsequent peace, U.S. officials gave considerable attention to the shape they wished the future to take even while World War II was still under way. Soviet leaders appear to have done much the same, largely

Only two nuclear weapons have ever been used in war. The first was dropped on Hiroshima, Japan, on 6 August 1945. The second, dropped on Nagasaki three days later, produced this mushroom cloud. (National Archives)

within their own ideological framework. American military planners, obligated to foresee dangers before they had actually materialized, speculated on the identity of future potential adversaries even before the enemies of World War II had been defeated. Assuming that long-term restraints would be placed on both Germany and Japan, which was the case after 1945, military planners were seemingly left with no plausible enemy other than the Soviet Union. Economic and related foreign policy pressures were to be placed on Great Britain by the United States, aimed at breaking the "imperial preference" system in trade, which gave Commonwealth countries a tariff advantage that made U.S. goods less competitive. No one, however, saw Great Britain as a likely military opponent. Similarly, France and China lacked the economic strength and the political cohesiveness to pose credible military threats. Moreover, China had been a wartime ally and, under the major provisions of the new United Nations organization, was slated to serve as a major power, positively disposed toward Western democratic ideas. This forecast proved unduly sanguine, because Nationalist leader Chiang Kai-shek, favored by the United States, faltered before the Communist forces led by Mao Tse-tung in China's long civil war. The distress and disappointment of U.S. leaders were great when Mao consolidated his victory in mainland China and established the People's Republic of China in 1949. In 1945, however, China could not be—and was not—characterized as a likely threat and potential enemy.

It would be too much to say that the Soviet Union appeared as a potential adversary simply by default, because there were concrete differences in opinion between Harry Truman and Joseph Stalin over the future of the defeated enemies and the liberated peoples as well. It would, however, be too little to ignore how the element of accident—the removal of Germany and Japan, two traditional regional forces from the arena of international power—exaggerated and warped both the roles and images of the United States and the Soviet Union. Unlike Great Britain, whose colonial empire was entering a protracted period of dissolution, the United States retained and, indeed, expanded its informal empire of economic, political, and cultural influence. Unlike France, torn not only by defeat but by half a decade of collaboration with its conquerors, the United States gloried in a newly appreciated sense of itself as purposeful and capable in world affairs. China, a potential world power was treated as an actual one, thanks to Franklin D. Roosevelt's insistence and Stalin's acquiescence, fell back upon itself in its civil war, stripping it of the ability to exert monitoring influence over East Asia, notably Korea and Japan. Meanwhile, the Soviet Union, although physically devastated by German military campaigns and by a horrid occupation, emerged from the war with a measure of unity born of fighting a clear external enemy. Its "internal empire" was thus politically intact and poised to rebuild.

Despite their efforts to generate pro-Soviet sentiment in the United States during World War II, U.S. leaders had never been enthusiastic about the Soviet system or those who ruled it. Before Franklin Roosevelt, presidents had been clearly condemnatory of what the Soviet Union was and of what it did. President Woodrow Wilson had considered the Bolshevik Revolution a betrayal of Russia's chance for liberal democracy, and none of his three Republican successors—Warren Harding, Calvin Coolidge, and Herbert Hoover—chose to seek diplomatic relations with the Soviet Union. The underlying ideological objection of U.S. leaders to the Soviet Communist system never ceased, even when opinions varied about how Soviet ideology was to be countered. Deemed a victim during World War II, after the war the Soviet Union was soon seen not only as a predator but as evil.

With President Truman present,

Churchill spoke of an "Iron Curtain"

being drawn down through the heart of Europe.

In a world sensitized by revelations of the slaughter of millions of European Jews and others by the Nazis, state-sanctioned atrocities and even war itself took on a new aspect. The postulation of a new category of "crimes against humanity," such as at the trials of former Nazi leaders at Nuremberg, meant the insertion of a particular morality into world affairs and into the discourse of power politics. At the same time, the newly established United Nations, aimed at eradicating "the scourge of war" altogether, and condemning all intrusive exercise of force, provided a new forum for the expression of world opinion and cultivated the belief that ethical concerns must be embodied in the actions of even powerful states. Although the Soviet Union participated in the judgment of the indicted Nazis, it was subject to criticism itself for its own internal state terrorism, which had been an international scandal in the 1930s, and for expansionist military action against Finland and Poland at the start of World War II, bases that resembled the charges leveled against those in the dock.

Shortly after the end of World War II, President Truman and other key U.S. political leaders, as well as foreign leaders, such as Winston Churchill, viewed the Soviet Union as an evil force, advancing a doctrine as malicious and dangerous as nazism. Speaking in Fulton, Missouri, in March 1946 as a former prime minister and with President Truman present, Churchill spoke of an "Iron Curtain" being drawn down through the heart of Europe from north to south, portraying Soviet communism as "a peril to Christian civilization." Political passion increasingly joined religious rhetoric in the condemnation of the Soviet Union, most notably for its actions in Eastern Europe, where it ran roughshod over democratic processes and installed pro-Soviet governments in such countries as Poland, Hungary, Bulgaria, Romania, and Czechoslovakia. The transformation of Eastern Europe into a cordon of Soviet client states was depicted by many Americans not only as a political act but as the advance of "godless communism." Even worse, as an unlimited evil, communism could be expected to seek victims around the world. Such talk made the postwar contention between Eastern and Western blocs not only an exercise in *realpolitik* but an intense moral challenge in which compromise was death and neutrality a sin. Commonly, leaders spoke of unprecedented dangers, unique challenges, and the monstrous evils of the principal adversary, claiming that civilization itself had never been so endangered as it was in the cold war. The intense rhetoric of the cold war and the specific metaphors in which it was cast—with Christian civilization threatened by a communist antichrist—provided a favorable climate for greatly enlarged military spending in peacetime and greatly broadened military action as well.

Seen in the broad context of world history over the centuries rather than as some conceptually peculiar and chronologically isolated moment, the cold war emerged as a seemingly inevitable effort to fill great vacuums of power in different parts of the world. For this reason, the cold war may be said to have started in 1945, fast upon the conclusion of war in Europe and even before the conclusion of the war against Japan.

In July and August 1945, Truman, Churchill, and Stalin met at Potsdam, Germany, to deal with such questions as the political destiny of Germany and its wartime allies and victims, especially in Eastern Europe. The atmosphere of the meeting was less than cordial. For example, Truman had recently cancelled shipments of supplies to the Soviet Union that had been authorized under wartime lend-lease legislation. At the same time, he resisted various Soviet plans for extracting war reparations payments from Germany and other wartime enemies, such as Finland. For his part, Churchill aimed to revitalize Great Britain's battered global empire, an ambition philosophically and politically repugnant to both Stalin and Truman, albeit for fundamentally irreconcilable reasons. He also wished to reassert British interests in Greece and to preclude a future Soviet naval influence through the Dardanelles into the Mediterranean region. Stalin evidently intended to protect the Soviet Union from any prospect of future invasion by creating a buffer zone in Eastern Europe, an undertaking that was to challenge both U.S. and British interests. Therefore, a classic redistribution of power was under way even before Japan, the remaining member of the Axis powers that had not yet surrendered, had been defeated.

During the cold war, both the leaders of the Soviet Union and those of the Western bloc spoke as if their confrontation was without historical precedent. Instead of a unique clash of completely new forces and ideologies, however, the cold war embodied the basic elements of the traditional "balance of power" politics. Stalin himself hinted at this when, in discounting the Vatican's ideas about postwar Europe, he wryly asked how many armed divisions the pope had. Churchill also hinted at this same dynamic when he tried to quantify U.S., British, and Soviet influence in Eastern Europe and the Balkans with percentages that varied from one country to another. Ideology, whether communist or capitalist, was not irrelevant, but underlying shifts in the actual balance of world power were the base on which specific actions depended.

As natural and customary as such a reconfiguration of power was in the aftermath of a great war, it took place in a distinct historical moment whose features lent shape and tone to the cold war and were thus at the heart of the cold war's special identity. For one thing, Great Britain had been weakened badly as a world economic power as early as World War I, and its position eroded even more in World War II. Its economy and infrastructure had sustained great damage during the war, and it would be preoccupied for some two decades before the rebuilding could be called complete.

At the same time, Great Britain's military posture was weaker than it had been in peacetime for centuries. Its ground forces were swiftly returned to typically low peacetime levels on an all-volunteer basis, which was the standard British practice. The Royal Navy had declined in relative strength since the introduction of steel hulls and other technological advancements spawned by the industrial revolution of the nineteenth century. Although the Soviet navy remained small and limited in its capability, the U.S. Navy was the largest, strongest, and most versatile in the world. The Royal Navy had once aspired to a strength equal to that of all other navies combined and to a mission of dominance and control of the seas on a global scale. After World War

II, it was not only inferior to that of the United States, it was also most likely insufficient to service Great Britain's far-flung empire, too expensive to increase to meet those needs, and distinctly ill-suited to deal with anticolonialist protest and activism in such places as India. British naval construction had not given priority to carrier task forces, a fact born out of necessity in World War II, thus denying Great Britain much-needed flexibility to deal with its widely distributed imperial interests. The preponderance of its investment in military aircraft had been shot down during the war, and what remained was numerically and in many ways qualitatively inferior to the U.S. Army Air Forces (and, after 1947, to the U.S. Air Force).

The Soviet Union emerged from World War II as the country with by far the largest ground forces, although the numerical weight was not surprising when compared to Russian forces in World War I. On the other hand, Soviet forces were now present in Central Europe, and many Western leaders regarded this as a new problem. From a broader perspective, the Soviet expansion into Eastern Europe was a reassertion of age-old Russian imperial interests in Poland, Romania, Bulgaria, and elsewhere, based partly on the theory of Pan-Slavism, which supposed the unity of all Slavic peoples under Russian leadership. Although some experts on Russian and Soviet history, such as George Kennan, a key enunciator of the U.S. policy of containment of the USSR,

In February, 1945, American President Franklin D. Roosevelt, British Prime Minister Winston S. Churchill, and Soviet Premier Joseph Stalin met in Yalta in Crimea to discuss the problems facing the world at the close of World War II in Europe. The three leaders met again later that year in Potsdam, Germany. (National Archives)

understood this, no influential political leaders thought that Russia's long history of intervention in Eastern Europe justified a lasting Soviet military presence or political hegemony in the region.

Where Soviet forces would be deployed and for how long became a contentious issue and, for Western leaders, a highly disturbing one. Soviet participation in the occupation of Germany and Austria placed it far forward of its own boundaries. Although the Soviet Union had built numerous aircraft during the war, their primary purpose had been support of ground forces, making a Soviet bomber force only a potential threat in 1945. The Soviet aircraft industry, however, had proven its mettle in World War II and its potential might be realized rapidly. Soviet naval forces remained minimal by comparison to those of the United States and even to those of Great Britain.

Based on its forces, industrial capacity, economic vitality, scientific establishment, and the number and adaptability of its people, the United States stood at the end of World War II as the greatest and the most immediately capable military power in the world. The obvious superiorities of the United States were concentrated in higher technology rather than in sheer numbers, however, and U.S. military planners were never able to shake off a persistent fear of being outmanned. This fear had deep roots, dating back to such confrontations with American Indians during the colonial era as King Philip's War (1675–1676) and to occasions of manifest local inferiority, such as in the Battle of the Little Big Horn (1876). Taken as a practical matter, however, the great masses of Soviet troops in the heart of Europe inspired a search for means to offset this apparent advantage. Technology seemed to afford the answer. A substantial U.S. air force remained in Britain after World War II under special provisions, and U.S. forces acquired important forward bases for the projection of U.S. military power and its corresponding political influence, such as in Japan after its defeat. U.S. naval forces were not only large but diverse, and they enjoyed versatility as to mission so that they could be used in a wide range of possible conflict situations. These forces enjoyed wartime port visitation rights far from the United States, and they would win similar privileges in the postwar era in Italy, Japan, the Philippines, and elsewhere.

Pressure to return millions of draftees to civilian pursuits rose sharply at the war's end, and demobilization proceeded in due course, causing some inconvenience in the fulfillment of U.S. responsibilities in the occupations of Japan and Germany and in other duties. Nevertheless, the military draft was permitted to lapse and was not restored until 1948, in a time of growing tension with the Soviet Union. Destined to last for a quarter of a century, the selective peacetime conscription of citizens for long-term service in the armed forces violated the long-standing American opposition to a peacetime draft and also broke the long-held fear of a standing army.

At the end of World War II, the espoused political goals of the United States included freedom and self-determination on a global scale, while those of the Soviet Union included the hastening of worldwide revolution. In practice, however, the two superpowers settled into the old habits of spheres of influence, and their military forces and strategies conformed to the characteristics of their respective spheres. In a sense, the cause and effect may have been the other way around, because the force structure of each country dictated what strategy was practical at any given time. The land forces of the Soviet Union significantly outnumbered those of the United States, while U.S. air and sea forces were manifestly superior to those of the Soviet Union. It was a conflict, as Kennan suggested, between a dinosaur and a whale.

The most striking and immediately impressive complicating factor in the distribution of power was the emergence of nuclear weapons.

The peculiar quality of the distribution of power after World War II was sharpened by the determination to keep Japan and Germany militarily weak. On the face of it, this seemed an obvious solution to many at the time, such as Secretary of the Treasury Henry J. Morgenthau. Yet, even in the early years after the war, some keen observers, such as James V. Forrestal, the first U.S. secretary of defense, cautioned that limiting Japan and Germany to police forces deprived two important regions of counterweights to otherwise potentially dangerous elements. In Central and Eastern Europe, most evidently, Germany and Russia had offset each other for decades. The removal, or artificial control, of these states' military roles would necessitate the quick rigging of new schemes to compensate for them.

The most striking and immediately impressive complicating factor in the distribution of power was the emergence of nuclear weapons. In the early years of the cold war, this awesome and novel development was held solely by the United States, which successfully tested an atomic bomb in the New Mexico desert while Truman, Stalin, and Churchill were meeting at Potsdam. The dreadful scale of its power was evident in the devastation of two Japanese cities, Hiroshima and Nagasaki, soon after Potsdam, each by a single bomb. The novelty extended to how one calculated the relative strength of offense and defense, because the atomic bomb appeared as a great force multiplier, offsetting manpower and conventional forces by this release of unconventional power.

Truman thought that nuclear weapons would counterbalance Soviet manpower, and Forrestal, who became secretary of defense in 1947, referred to the atomic bomb as "the great equalizer," because few elements in an attacking force would need to penetrate enemy defenses to inflict a total defeat. While losses of 15 percent of an attacking bomber force, for example, were unsustainable with conventional forces and would ensure that the attacker would lose over a protracted period, a penetration rate of 15 percent of an air fleet armed with atomic weapons could probably deliver a knockout punch in a single attack. The enormity of the weapon's effects made it seem an awkwardly attractive necessity for any nation intending to stand as a world power after 1945. Therefore, the Soviet Union accelerated its nuclear research and development program, and Great Britain pressed forward with a separate nuclear weapons program when it was denied shared control of U.S. weapons produced with the help of British scientists. Even though Great Britain was an ally of the United States, the U.S. government first pursued a policy that would have required United Nations control of all atomic weapons with substantial U.S. oversight. When this plan, named for Bernard Baruch, its architect and chief proponent, failed to win Soviet agreement, the U.S. government aimed instead at preventing or at least limiting the proliferation of nuclear-capable nations.

The prospect of a sharp acceleration in the pace of change in military technology was just as awesome as nuclear weapons themselves. First, atomic bombs were not meaningful militarily if kept in depots in the United States, so the enhancement of delivery systems took on great importance. Long-range bombers were crucial, notably the B-29, which was modified for longer range as the B-50, and the B-36, originally designed to permit U.S. strikes against the Nazis if British bases became unavailable during World War II. Second, atomic weapons did not negate traditional principles of war, such as the advantages of speed and surprise. This encouraged the development of jet-powered bombers, first the intermediate-range B-47 and then the long-range, inflight refuelable B-52.

Meanwhile, there was no reason to assume that nuclear weapons had to be delivered by air or used only against industrial or urban targets, and a naval nuclear component, whether from aircraft carriers or submarines, became increasingly a topic of interest. Ground-based missiles also gained importance, although these were initially deemed to be a less realistic option because of the technological limits of bomb technology, where miniaturization of high-yield weapons posed a great challenge. To hold the kind of military superiority widely associated with meaningful defense against a nuclear attack appeared to require armed forces equipped with the most up-to-date and advanced weapons. The rapidity with which new weapons systems would become obsolete made keeping up with advancements in military technology extremely expensive. Obsolescence took on especially threatening implications for the United States, because the technological lead over the Soviet Union that constituted a force multiplier and offset Soviet manpower was ultimately not a long-lasting advantage in hardware but an uncertain and relatively brief advantage in time.

In addition, the swift pace of technological change required new institutional mechanisms for fostering advanced domestic military research and development to ensure that one was not surprised by a weapons breakthrough by an adversary. For example, organized operations research for the U.S. government dates from World War II programs assessing antisubmarine activity. In the immediate years after World War II, the Army Air Forces induced the formation of the civilian RAND Corporation to engage in operations and systems analysis on an ever-widening basis. Also, the federal government proved unwilling to risk relying on the pre–World War II practice of competitively testing weapons systems, such as aircraft, that had been researched and developed at the expense of private companies. Instead, it began to issue contracts covering the costs of more than one manufacturer during the research and development phases, partly because of the increasing sophistication and hence higher cost of weapons and their development, and also because of the government's wish to preserve a larger military industrial base.

In this and in other ways, the federal government contributed to the expansion and reshaping of the military-industrial complex in the United States, a phenomenon paralleled in the Soviet Union, albeit under a different general economic system, and in Great Britain, although within the limits of its strained postwar economy. The extreme sense of urgency felt among the leaders of the major powers strengthened the habit of classifying official information pertaining to policy, military hardware, and related issues for security purposes. Secrecy had always been an aspect of government, but the extent of security operations and the size of the security establishment both grew markedly after 1945, leading to expanded or even new agencies, most notably the Central Intelligence Agency (CIA).

What if the government were decapitated in a nuclear sneak attack, killing not only the president but the entire constitutionally specified line of succession?

All of this cost money and many of these new agencies and their procedures represented a challenge to customary political relationships within those countries participating in the hastening arms race. In the United States, while military expenditures were expected to drop from the levels sustained during World War II, the larger military program that seemed in the offing anticipated a higher level of peacetime expenditures for defense than had been sustained in any previous era of peace. This greater expenditure for the military signified that political relationships among the armed forces and between such institutions as Congress, the State Department, and the White House and the armed forces were apt to change. Even during World War II, some members of Congress and factions within the armed forces thought that change in military institutions was needed, but at the request of Secretary of War Henry L. Stimson and others, changes were deferred until after the war was won, lest protracted discussion of military reorganization interfere with the war effort.

Even the most basic political concepts and institutions, such as congressional power to declare war, were challenged. If war was waged swiftly and briefly with nuclear weapons, there might not be time for Congress to declare war. Theoretically, Washington, D.C., itself might be an irradiated ruin before the call had gone out to convene. Was a president to act without the constitutionally mandated act of Congress? And what if the government were decapitated in a nuclear sneak attack, killing not only the president but the entire constitutionally specified line of succession? Who then would lead the counterattack against the enemy? To an unprecedented degree a few changes in military technology were putting a heavy strain upon the fabric of American political beliefs. Similarly, if treachery among the citizenry contributed to an enemy's chances for success, the fabric of civil liberties might be strained, too. In the years after 1945, hypothetical military strategies, such as the projections of future wars by U.S. Defense Department planning staffs, and exaggerated subversive threats tended to be treated as clear and present dangers, actual and immediate, requiring expeditious countermeasures.

Many changes in military and political institutions that appeared in the United States in the years after World War II stemmed from the altered state of military technology, the impulse to fill vacuums of power in key regions of the world, and the sense of urgency derived from the attribution of demonic qualities to the adversary. For example, the advanced state of aviation technology led to the enhanced importance of aviation branches in the governance of the military, and U.S. concern over vacuums of power around the world led to a new structure of overseas bases and a complicated air and sea logistics system to support them. Most changes, however, were necessitated by the perception that the United States would soon be vulnerable to military attack in a way that was novel both qualitatively and quantitatively. With the exception of the War of 1812, the continental United States had been safe from external attack. Once the Soviet Union acquired a capability for penetration of U.S. air space, this security would end. While the surprise attack at Pearl Harbor was widely perceived as an avoidable lapse, an attack by the Soviet Union could, in theory, succeed even without the incompetence of fools or the collusion of traitors. It was a curious kind of powerlessness to govern its own destiny that seemed to face what was, quite ironically, militarily the most powerful country on earth.

Soon after the first atomic bombs were used against Japan, many U.S. policymakers, such as Forrestal and President Truman himself, concluded that the development of atomic bombs and advanced aircraft to deliver them meant the superiority of offensive systems over defensive ones for far into the future. Specifically, it appeared impossible to guarantee complete protection against a possible nuclear attack by a determined enemy, because the expected damage from even a small fraction of the nuclear weapons sent was enormous and, at the time, conceptually unacceptable. This led swiftly to the belief that deterring such an attack was the only available recourse. Assuring possible attackers that any assault on the United States would bring on a massive and devastating counterstrike, one far more sweeping and effective than their own, emerged as the very heart of strategic defense.

To deter a potential enemy, however, the United States could no longer rely on a gradual buildup of its forces during a time of crisis and before combat began. Because a nuclear attack might come as a surprise and would presumably come quickly and last briefly, a ready defense against an attack was essential. In short, potential force was irrelevant. Only a force actually in being and substantially invulnerable to destruction could provide a sufficient threat. A potential enemy was to be deterred from launching a nuclear attack by the sure fear of massive retaliatory strikes. In the initial strategic conception favored by U.S. leaders, air forces ensured the swiftness of response and nuclear weapons guaranteed that retaliation would be massive.

After 1948, with the passage of the Selective Service Act and the introduction of the peacetime military draft, it was clear that the "force in being" would include a large ground element as well. Persistent pressure within Congress and from special interest groups in industry and elsewhere led to the preservation of a significant naval element in the force in being and, eventually, to its significant expansion. In all, traditional concern over the consequences of maintaining a large standing armed force fell before the urgency of the perceived Soviet threat.

Therefore, air power and atomic weapons were seen as a cause of fear and danger and the means of allaying the fear and countering the danger. This internal tension, if not contradiction, lay at the heart of the psychology of the cold war. Safety appeared to depend on the very weapons that, in the hands of the enemy, would cause one's own ruin. The literally world-shattering power of atomic weapons seemed to many planners to be the only tools adequate to a global strategy.

President Truman also regarded them as the most economical tools, and, throughout the cold war, strategic weapons did prove to be cumulatively the least expensive element of force structure and defense as a whole. Containing defense expenditures within limits that the U.S. economy could support indefinitely, however, would have been an exercise in futility and the absurd if the forces sustained at those spending levels had failed to pay for a force sufficient to the military tasks at hand, such as deterrence of a prospective Soviet attack and support of regimes friendly to the United States around the rim of Soviet influence. Truman not only thought a strategy based on air forces and atomic weapons to be economical, he thought it militarily sufficient, a view that would have made no sense outside the narrow framework to which he subscribed of bipolar conflict between the free world and the Communist bloc. The division of the world into two camps and giving controlling power over the Communist bloc to the Soviet Union diminished the autonomy of third-party nations against whom the use of nuclear weapons would have seemed preposterously disproportionate if they were regarded as truly independent. For his part, Truman also believed that all the world was falling into one camp or the other, and at the end of that process there might be peace or war, depending on the final distribution of postwar power. Within such a scenario, a heave emphasis on air forces with nuclear weapons fit well.

Deterrence may have appeared to be an active strategy and, in terms of technical implementation, an offensive one, but it actually locked the strategic systems of the United States into a fundamentally reactive posture. The active element of the systems lay in the threat of their use, while actual use itself would have indicated that the nation's general policy of deterrence had failed. The initiative, such as in probes to find where the United States had "drawn a line in the sand" in Greece and elsewhere, lay with the nation's potential adversaries. At the same time, the evidence that deterrence had presumably worked lay in the inactivity of adversaries, which presupposed that they would otherwise have gone on the offensive. Such contrary-to-fact assertions were technically only speculations, and their persuasiveness depended partly on adhering to the most negative interpretation of official statements from the Soviet leadership. For example, when Stalin stated in 1946 that the Soviet people must be ready for a war with the Western nations, Truman and other leaders viewed it as a statement of intent to start one, likening it to a declaration of World War III. When a full-scale war did not develop, the state of relative peace was attributed to the effect of military deterrence.

A striking feature of early cold war strategy was that it was a reaction to fear, or, more specifically, to apprehension.

A striking feature of early cold war strategy was that it was a reaction to fear, or, more specifically, to apprehension. U.S. strategy took into account expected or feasible actions of the adversary, rather than actions already undertaken. Impressed by the devastation that might be caused by a nuclear attack, U.S. strategists relied less on calculations of the adversary's intentions and more on a prediction of its capabilities. Because the consequence of miscalculating intentions might be a defeat from which recovery would be impossible, there was a strong body of opinion, espoused almost uniformly by U.S. military leaders and by such influential congressmen as Carl Vinson, favoring policies based only on material capability. Some, such as Air Force Major General Orvil A. Anderson, even flirted with conducting a preemptive or preventive war against the

Soviet Union, depriving them of the military option of attack altogether. In the peculiar context of the immediate postwar world, it seemed to be the only logical alternative to deterrence.

President Truman sharply disciplined open advocates of preventive war within the military, but the option they advocated reveals much about deterrence itself. For example, deterrence presupposed that Soviet leaders were rational and that their logical assessment of likely risks and benefits would cause them to refrain from military adventurism and subversion. In this way, deterrence proved especially compatible with the view that Stalin was masterminding an elaborate conspiracy of global proportions. If the threat were not a conspiracy—that is, a logical design—then it could not be reliably countered by fears of massive retaliation, which required a conventional appreciation of the costs and benefits of actions. Advocates of preventive war, by contrast, refused to rely on the rationality of the enemy in a *reductio ad absurdum* of the contention that the Soviet Union embodied values fundamentally inimical to those of Western civilization, such as respect for human life. In this way, they departed from the traditionally stated purpose of affecting the enemy's will to resist. Preventive war was not about will but about capacity. Deterrence, on the other hand, was concerned about capacity in order to affect will. In this way, deterrence was political as well as military in nature from the very start.

Deterrence was also, in important ways, a highly theoretical strategy, inextricably dependent on the most physically powerful weapons ever created, yet lacking a base in military experience except for the two devastating examples of Hiroshima and Nagasaki. The conviction that atomic weapons had opened a new military world stripped respect away from traditional military knowledge. Atomic weapons also stripped authority from the military leaders who had been the guardians of military lore.

Civilian strategists rapidly rose in importance by articulating theories that took the new weapons into account. A notable example was the academic Bernard Brodie, who promptly grasped the implications of nuclear weapons on the balance of offense and defense. Brodie perceived that a perfect defense against a large nuclear attack could not be assured. Thus, the only fully successful defense was to prevent an attack from being launched in the first place. This strategic emphasis on deterrence, articulated within months after the bombing of Hiroshima, was nevertheless applicable at least until the early 1980s, when President Ronald Reagan reasserted the prospects of a strategic defense. For the remainder of the cold war, other civilian strategists, such as Herman Kahn, explored the theoretical diversity of ways in which a nuclear war might start and might be waged. Kahn exemplified the experts who worked on contract with the U.S. government in "think tanks," such as the RAND Corporation, which was established by the Army Air Forces in 1946, and the Hudson Institute. In such books as *On Thermonuclear War* (1960), Kahn explored dozens of possible nuclear war scenarios other than the all-out "spasm war" that had been the original expectation, thus also contributing the thought that some kinds of nuclear war could be fought and won.

The decline in importance of top-ranking military officers in the formation of strategy did not come about solely because the new class of civilian theorists proved so zealous and energetic. From the birth of the Republic and even from colonial times, Americans had been committed to the principle of the supremacy of the civilian political authority over the military. Effective control of the management of the armed forces had often been delegated for practical purposes to the uniformed officers in the first century and a half of the national experience, but warfare in the twentieth century had blurred the distinction between combatant and noncombatant and between soldier and civilian. Not only did technology emerge that could be indiscriminate in its applications, such as airplanes dropping bombs on cities, but theories also emerged, such as those of Italian military strategist Giulio Douhet, that made cities and their civilian occupants the preferred targets of the military forces. In the twentieth century, too, the concept of total national mobilization was realized on the home front, and if the home territories were truly an arsenal for the nation's war effort, then they were also a relevant target. During the nineteenth and twentieth centuries, moreover, the ratio of civilian to military deaths in war changed markedly, as the proportion of civilians killed rapidly expanded.

Military and civilian spheres had been growing more intertwined during the twentieth century, and atomic weapons simply brought the process to fulfillment.

In short, military and civilian spheres had been growing more intertwined during the twentieth century, and atomic weapons simply brought the process to fulfillment. If military and civilian spheres were inextricably bound, however, and if the military must not be permitted control over the civilian sphere, then the military could not be allowed substantial autonomy over the military sphere either. This, too, must be an immediate concern of civilian strategists and managers and of the civilian political leaders.

These events help to explain the greater direct participation of the president in military affairs in the cold war era. Under the provisions of the constitution, the president is commander in chief of the armed forces. Typically, however, presidents in office before the twentieth century involved themselves closely with strategy and the management of the armed forces only during war. James K. Polk and Abraham Lincoln exemplify the activist commander in chief who not only endorsed general plans but followed the details of their implementation. In the twentieth century, such activism became increasingly typical and, eventually, normative. When Truman succeeded to the presidency after the death of Roosevelt, the popular expectation that the president had the right to involve himself in the intimate details of military affairs was widely and well established. Roosevelt's use of military advisers on his own staff had also established the premise that the president could rightly be expected to make military judgments independent of the top-ranking officers of the military services. This premise of presidential independence was to be a guiding feature of postwar reorganization of the military services, and the persuasiveness of this premise was enhanced by the special threat represented in nuclear weapons and advanced systems for their delivery.

Throughout the cold war era, too, the term "strategic" was increasingly linked with "nuclear," and the terms were often used interchangeably. For many military planners, the next war was envisioned as nuclear, creating a conceptual lacuna in which even a major nonnuclear conflict of a traditional sort might be deemed not a real war at all or, at least, a new kind of war. In time, when war began in Korea in 1950, a traditional and conventional conflict was treated as if it were a historical anomaly, reflecting the compelling sway of the nuclear strategic paradigm. If real war was preconceived as nuclear, then no war had ever been fought that could serve as a referential example for the strategists of 1950.

The heightened sense of peril arising from a global competition in which nuclear weapons were a focusing dimension also contributed to the rise of political bipartisanship in foreign policy in the United States. This political formulation was new to the American scene, at least in peacetime. In the nineteenth century, for example, and even into the twentieth century, there was a presumption that loyalty to the nation required unanimity of opinion about overseas policies. This was true even in time of war. In the War of 1812, the Mexican War, and the Spanish-American War, Americans differed markedly not only as to method but as to the goals of policy. During the twentieth century, however, dissent from the stated policies of the executive branch during wartime became less practicable. In World War II, for example, Democratic President Roosevelt appointed Republicans Frank Knox and Henry Stimson as secretary of the navy and secretary of war, respectively, to build a bipartisan coalition for the U.S. war effort. During the early years of the cold war, Truman also cooperated with important Republicans, such as Senator Arthur Vandenberg of Michigan, who had once been deemed an isolationist, to build a reliable political base for extensive and open-ended U.S. military presence and involvements overseas. To the extent that dissent stopped at the water's edge, the president enjoyed a relative increase in actual power in foreign and military affairs.

The emphasis on global deterrence thus greatly affected American institutions by strengthening the authority of the president, compared to that of Congress, in setting U.S. overseas policy. For two decades, until political dissent against the war in Vietnam broke the bipartisan consensus, Democrats and Republicans in Congress alike assumed a clearly secondary role even in such areas as making war where Congress had a clear constitutional responsibility. It also gave basic shape to U.S. military force structure and greatly affected political and military relations with other countries. A credible threat to a distant enemy presupposed a highly capable offensive force whose weapons were high in yield and whose delivery systems enjoyed great power of penetration. Just as military and civilian spheres seemed to be inextricably linked within the United States, however, so were the interests and the resources of the United States and its allies perceived to be interactive and mutually supportive. The further European economic recovery from World War II progressed, the question of European contributions to regional defense became more relevant. In this way, despite its economic, political, and humanitarian motives, the program for European economic recovery under the Marshall Plan also had significant military implications. The resources of the United States were great but not infinite, and the question of appropriate balance of forces—air, sea, and land within the services, but also U.S. or allied in the free world as a whole—became a regular topic of discussion among allied leaders.

To wage its part in the cold war—or, as President Dwight D. Eisenhower later put it, to "wage peace"—the Truman administration greatly enlarged the military budget in order to fund a substantially greater peacetime defense establishment than had been customary for the United States. Compared to force levels and spending during World War II—$80.5 billion in 1945, for example—the Truman administration cut deeply into the military, but compared to pre–World War II spending, the military was rising to a previously unattained peacetime eminence. The share of the total federal budget devoted to the military was much larger, and the increase in real dollars was impressive. In 1938, for example, excluding veterans' benefits, the military budget amounted to about $1.25 billion. In 1948, it was nearly $12 billion. In 1949, the first budget reflecting the new independent status of the U.S. Air Force, the figure was about $14 billion. In 1953, at the end of the Korean War, the budget surpassed $44 billion, and for the remainder of the 1950s it stayed in the range of $35–$40 billion.

The rate at which the military budget grew far exceeded the growth rate of the entire federal budget. In 1938 the total federal budget was about $6.8 billion, and military spending accounted for about 18.4 percent. In 1948, the total budget was about $33 billion, and the $12 billion in military spending amounted to 36.4 percent. In 1956, when the federal budget ran to $66.5 billion, the military share was 54.1 percent. There are many ways to calculate the economic sustainability of such expenditures. For example, while the 1948 military budget took twice the share of the total federal budget than the 1938 military budget, the gross national product (GNP) had tripled in the same period. Also, while the 1956 military budget took three times more of the federal total than the 1938 budget, the GNP was five times greater. Military spending emerged as a major component of the federal budget and a focal preoccupation of the national leadership.

In 1945, and even as late as the Korean War, it was unclear how much the federal government could afford to spend on a long-term basis to provide for national defense and international security. Peacetime military spending before World War II had rarely approached $1 billion, but after the war the military budget, including supplementals, averaged about $15 billion after World War II obligations had been fulfilled. How much more could be spent without damaging the national economy, such as by contributing to the national debt, inflation, higher interest rates, or the imposition of governmental control of production and prices, was not known. It was a process of trial and error, as well as one of economic forecasting. Although actual U.S. military spending in peacetime rose to all-time highs, fear of overstraining the economy made Truman seek ways to restrain the growth of spending. This gave added impetus to the administration's efforts to restructure the U.S. defense establishment to be better suited for global competition with the Soviet Union.

The desire to save money contributed to calls for unification of the armed forces, but such calls also reflected a wish for coherence within the military so that it could respond promptly and purposefully to the will of the president. The organizational changes wanted by President Truman and such advisers as White House aide Clark Clifford, Secretary of War Robert Patterson, Army Chief of Staff General George C. Marshall, and Assistant Secretary of War for Air Stuart Symington (later the first secretary of the air force) presupposed a shift from a relatively simple notion of defense against specific attacks to a more complex idea of protecting national security. Although traces of this idea can be found in earlier eras, it achieved full force and currency after 1945, especially after the enactment of the National Security Act of 1947. This law created the National Military Establishment, amended to the Department of Defense in 1949, and created the position of secretary of defense. It separated the Army Air Forces from the army and turned them into an independent and coequal air force. In addition, it created the Joint Chiefs of Staff (JCS) and the position of chairman of the JCS. The principle behind the reorganization was to confine access to the president on military matters to a comparatively few individuals, ultimately, at least in theory, to only the secretary of defense. The prospect of centralized authority led many high-ranking officials to oppose the idea of unification and to weaken its implementation. Secretary of the Navy Forrestal, for example, advocated coordination of the services rather than centralized control, but as the first secretary of defense, he soon learned the weaknesses of his proposals. The history of defense reorganization in the next four decades was basically a quest to replace coordination with greater control.

The restructuring under the act of 1947 did not stop with the uniformed services. The comprehensive vision of what constituted national defense necessitated the creation of the National Security Council (NSC), which to some extent replaced the former meetings of the State, War, and Navy departments during World War II. In addition to the president and secretaries of state and defense, membership on the NSC included agency heads responsible for the national economy and national intelligence, the chairman of the National Security Resources Board (NSRB), and the director of the Central Intelligence Agency (CIA). The creation of the NSRB reflected the view that national strength and security depended on economic vitality, as well as recognizing the dependence of the United States on various critical strategic minerals. The CIA grew out of the wartime Office of Special Services (OSS), and it increasingly put attention on the gathering and assessment of information rather than limiting itself to special covert operations. Even so, the CIA had peculiar significance because it did undertake limited military and paramilitary operations outside traditional U.S. military channels and, consequently, without the customary and constitutionally mandated checks and balances. This legislation also established a niche for the creation of a purely appointed staff dealing with national security policy at the pleasure of the president and without and not subject to the Senate's right to advise and consent to major appointments, such as those of cabinet officers.

The CIA had peculiar significance because it undertook limited military and paramilitary operations without the customary and constitutionally mandated checks and balances.

While changes in the management of national security were being undertaken within the country, more significant changes were in progress in foreign relations. Notable was the extensive program for the acquisition of overseas military bases initiated by Truman and continued by his successors. The most ironic agreements were those with wartime enemies Italy, Germany (or at least its western part), and Japan, which became important allies of the United States in the cold war and all of which provided crucial facilities for a forward-basing policy aimed at the Soviet sphere from the Mediterranean and central and northern Europe to northeast Asia. Meanwhile, wartime allies, the Soviet Union and, after 1949, China, were regarded as adversaries. Having been granted independence by the United States in 1946, the Philippines also extended air and naval base rights to the United States.

Perhaps the single most illustrative base agreement was that between the United States and Spain. As late as 1946, the United States denounced the government of Generalissimo Francisco Franco as fascist and totalitarian, and it participated in a United Nations–sponsored recall of ambassadors from Madrid. In 1948, however, Secretary of Defense Forrestal called for U.S. naval bases in Spain, and air force officials sought bases the following year. By 1950 the United States began providing loans and gifts to Franco's regime, and in 1953 a treaty providing for U.S. military bases in Spain was negotiated and approved. Thus, it was clear that old ideological demons had yielded to new ones, and world power politics proved more pertinent in determining practical policy than ideological beliefs.

Antifascism was not the only political belief to be set aside for purposes of pursuing the cold war. Anticolonialism was, too. The most notable example was the shift of U.S. policy toward France in Southeast Asia, where Roosevelt and Truman had opposed the reestablishment of French colonial rule in Vietnam, Laos, and Cambodia. As fear of communism came to outweigh repugnance of colonialism, the United States increased economic and military aid to France, still urging political reform within Southeast Asia but tolerating French intransigence out of fear that the Communists posed an even greater danger. That Vietnamese Communists in particular could seem so threatening reflected the U.S. distress over the Chinese Communist consolidation of power in mainland China and the Truman administration's view that all unrest in Asia was ultimately keyed to the connivance of Mao's government in Beijing. Seen one way, then, this was a case of resistance to an alien philosophy, as was U.S. cooperation with Spain. Seen another way, however, both were examples of U.S. willingness to accommodate the distasteful political views of its allies out of concern over the power and regional influence of its new adversaries.

In the years after World War II, some military planners, especially within the air force, suggested that there was no military need for overseas bases. Even so, bases could serve a political role, especially if one thought that sufficient military force could be applied from great distances by air and sea forces. U.S. overseas bases could give encouragement to fragile political elements in Western Europe and elsewhere with pro-American sympathies. More significantly—and, as time passed, more durably—the crucial strategic significance of such deployments of U.S. forces overseas included the idea that they served as a tripwire. Let any Americans be killed overseas in an attack launched by an enemy, and the full weight of U.S. military might would be brought to bear upon that enemy from bases in the continental United States. For a strategic theory that was to depend on the threat of massive retaliation, even at the risk of devastation to one's own nation, deployment of U.S. troops at such overseas bases contributed to making nuclear deterrence seem credible.

This array of interlocking policies was designated containment, a term attributed to State Department official George Kennan. In 1946, while serving at the U.S. embassy in Moscow, Kennan, a specialist in Soviet studies, drafted a lengthy memorandum aimed at explaining what he termed "the sources of Soviet conduct." A modified version of Kennan's report was published anonymously in the July 1947 issue of *Foreign Affairs* and, now called the "X article," became a sensation overnight. According to Kennan, the Soviet Union had inherited the deep-seated suspicion of foreigners and their designs that dated back for centuries into Russian history. He likened Soviet energies to a windup toy, and if the United States resisted the momentum of the windup toy, it would gradually spend its energy and fall into stasis. Peace would be at hand, and aggression would have been contained.

The general belief that Soviet power had to be contained within a fixed perimeter existed before Kennan gave his special expression to the concept. His memo was read by several government agencies, whose reaction suggested that Kennan did no more than articulate what was already on the minds of many in Washington rather than persuade them to take a new position. Naval Intelligence, for example, assessed Kennan's analysis for Secretary of the Navy Forrestal, saying that it contained nothing new. It was regarded, however, as an especially lucid presentation of views widely held among high-ranking U.S. officials. Kennan was called back to Washington to lecture at the National War College and then to serve as head of the State Department's Policy Planning Staff, symbolically marking the dominance of containment in U.S. official thinking.

In 1947, Truman enunciated as U.S. policy an open-ended commitment to resist attack upon or subversion of any government by Communist factions.

The subtleties of Kennan's version of containment, which he insisted ought not to be narrowly or even fundamentally military, were soon overtaken by the events that the doctrine helped to shape and by other events that the doctrine was used to counter. In the aftermath of World War II, a bitter civil war had emerged in Greece. Although there was an indigenous Communist element in Greece, it was substantially supplied by the Soviet Union through Bulgaria. By 1947 the British government made clear to President Truman that it no longer had the ability to support the anti-Communist government and implied its willingness to accept whatever might happen after the end of their own aid program. On 12 March 1947, Truman spoke before Congress, enunciating as U.S. policy an open-ended commitment to resist attack upon or subversion of any government by Communist factions. The concept of containment, which had been historically particular in its original formulation, was now applied generally to the world as a whole. Truman regarded this as "the turning point in America's foreign policy."

Although the Truman Doctrine has sometimes been criticized for its universal extensiveness, it may have created more strain on the United States for the military obligations to which it committed the nation. Given the enfeebled economic condition of Great Britain and the weakness of Europe as a whole, any intervention in Greece to sustain the anti-Communist regime was inevitably destined to be an exclusively U.S. enterprise. Although it had genuine hopes for concerted allied effort against the Communists, the United States, for the most part, had to stay the course on its own. This tension between hopes for concerted effort and coordinated defense and the practical imperatives of resources and timing became a hallmark of Western defense efforts throughout the cold war. What began in 1947 as a recognition that European nations had little within their power to combat communism eventually became a concern that those nations were taking advantage of the U.S. military presence in Europe and also that they lacked political will.

It is striking that no Communist state recognized the "Government of Free Greece" proclaimed by the insurgents. Stalin told Nikos Zachariadis, political leader of the Greek Communists, that armed struggle in Greece should be avoided. Stalin even criticized Josip Broz Tito, the leader of Yugoslavia, for continuing to supply small arms to the Communist rebels from across his southern border within Greece. In fact, Stalin appears to have written off the Greek Communists and, by helping to cut off their supplies, contributed to their demise. If this had been aggression, it was perhaps more in the form of opportunism than ideological compulsion, as suggested by Stalin's recognition of British and U.S. interests in the Mediterranean. What was understood by U.S. military advisers, such as General James Van Fleet, but not given public attention was that the Greek Communists continued to sustain themselves in 1947 and 1948 largely on their own resources, replenishing their numbers from among the Greek peasantry. Not only did they not depend on Soviet aid, but the Greeks actually pursued a program that violated Soviet wishes. Had the indigenous nature of the Greek insurgency received greater attention, the notion that all troubles could be traced to Moscow (or, later, Beijing) would have been discredited and might in turn have impeached the application of containment policy worldwide.

At the same time, however, the pragmatic dimensions of U.S. policy that lay behind the inclusive sweep of the Truman Doctrine are also revealed in this incident and in the curious relationship with Tito and Yugoslavia that grew out of it. Despite Yugoslav support of the Greek Communists even after Stalin had abandoned them, the United States swiftly cooperated with Tito when the Yugoslav leader broke with Stalin in 1948, partly out of frustration over Stalin's behavior toward Greece. Again, the test of cooperation was practical rather than ideological. Tito was surely a Communist, hence deserving of the same hot rhetoric devoted to Stalin, but Tito's defection from the Soviet bloc won him economic and even military support in the West.

Overlapping the U.S. intervention in Greece was one of the early "signature" military operations of the cold war—the conflict between the two superpowers over the status of Germany and particularly over that of Berlin in 1948–1949. The Berlin crisis followed bitter disagreements over both the political and military status of Germany. The United States had never endorsed the extreme if understandable claims of the Soviet Union for war reparation payments from Germany and was thus distressed by the wholesale dismantling of German assets within the zone occupied by Soviet forces. As a part of its de-Nazification policy, the United States was more interested in reconstruction and the rapid introduction of democratic institutions in Germany, aims dating back to the war years when the occupation was being planned. By 1948, U.S. and British officials had come to administer their zones cooperatively, and they eventually persuaded the reluctant French to do the same. The Soviet Union resisted, however, not only for economic reasons but also out of concern over the possible military strength and likely political alignment of a reunited Germany. Seeking to disrupt the creation of a separate west German state out of the zones occupied by France, Great Britain, and the United States, the Soviet Union imposed a land blockade of the city of Berlin on 23 June 1948, isolating the sectors of the old German capital administered by the three Western nations.

President Truman appears never to have considered acquiescing to the consequences of the Soviet action. At the first cabinet meeting held after the initiation of the blockade, Secretary of Defense Forrestal began to list options, including the withdrawal of Western personnel, but Truman cut him short, indicating that whether to resist the blockade was not the issue but rather how to overcome it. General Lucius D. Clay, the U.S. high commissioner for Germany, recommended shooting through the blockade. Others, relying on the considerable American aviation assets in Europe, urged the creation of an "air bridge" to the city. This latter course became policy, and at the peak of airlift operations, planes brought in thirteen thousand tons of supplies every day, even including such cost-inefficient but crucial material as coal. After a year in which the U.S. air forces proved their ability to sustain West Berlin indefinitely, the Soviet Union ended the blockade on 12 May 1949, but the crisis allowed the issuance of an independent currency and the de facto creation of the state of East Germany. Germany was to remain thus divided until 1990, and in the interval its great military potential was split between the two great power blocs led by the United States and the Soviet Union.

In NATO, the United States assumed the leading role of what was basically an alliance aimed at the defense of Europe.

The successful defiance of the Berlin Blockade by the Western allies lent credence to claims that air power gave important new capabilities to those who possessed it. Even more, it appeared that air power cold actually substitute for land and sea forces, at least under some circumstances. This notion of substitution played a major role in U.S. strategic thought in the late 1940s and early 1950s, contributing to the rise to dominance of nuclear defense by demonstrating the capabilities of air delivery systems. The relief of Berlin also provided an imaginative precedent for a host of missions proposed or undertaken throughout the cold war that depended on the flexible application of air power, such as the proposed relief of Dien Bien Phu in North Vietnam (1954), the planned support of a Cuban anti-Communist invasion of their home island (1961), and the defense of the fire base at Khe Sanh in South Vietnam (1967–1968).

The success of the Berlin resistance also contributed weight to the argument for establishing a standing alliance among the Western powers, even as the initial Soviet action in staging the blockade suggested the need for such an alliance in the first place. The open split with the Soviet Union over the future of Germany even permitted the inclusion of West Germany into an alliance, provided concerns raised by the French were dealt with.

The alliance that eventually emerged was one of the most extraordinary departures in U.S. security policy in American history. In the North Atlantic Treaty Organization (NATO), the United States assumed the leading role of what was, on the face of it, basically an alliance aimed at the defense of Europe. Equally striking was the fact that the U.S. commitment was not only economic and short-term, for which there were many precedents, but military and open-ended, for which there was none, save perhaps America's agreement with France in 1778. On 4 April 1949, twelve nations signed the treaty—France, Great Britain, Belgium, Luxembourg, the Netherlands, Portugal, Italy, Denmark, Norway, Iceland, Canada, and the United States. By the end of 1949, U.S. officials were also calling for the formation of German military units, possibly to be included in NATO, a possibility that outraged the Soviet Union. Membership in NATO, however, with its profession that attacks on other member states would be treated as an attack on the United States, fit the definition of an "entangling alliance" very well. The description, in advance of how the U.S. government would interpret any such hypothetical attack, was to make NATO a powerful element in the general scheme of deterrence. By testing the limits of the constitutional provision that the Senate must advise and consent not only to treaties but to the decision to go to war, NATO also went further than previous U.S. overseas commitments. Moreover, the undertakings were of indefinite duration.

It was by no means clear to all responsible U.S. officials that NATO was even necessary. Kennan, for example, told Secretary of State Dean Acheson that NATO afforded "military defense against an attack no one is planning." John Foster Dulles, later secretary of state to President Eisenhower, claimed in Senate hearings that no "responsible high official, military or civilian," believed that the Soviet Union "plans conquest by open military aggression." Whatever may have been the ultimate rationale for NATO, it had the effect of letting the U.S. government construe its forces as part of an international military structure that provided balance overall, even if U.S. forces were heavily skewed to the strategic side. To fill out the overall force structure of NATO, especially to enable it to meet its requirements for troops, Secretary of State Dulles, beginning in 1953, pressed for West German membership in NATO, which was accomplished in May 1955.

That same month, Soviet officials led in forming the Warsaw Pact, comprising the Soviet Union and its various dependent Eastern European states, which East Germany joined early in 1956. It was not quite the formation of NATO that induced the creation of the Warsaw Pact but NATO's inclusion of West Germany. More than putting a public name on what had already been a private fact, the militarization of Germany—and, at the time, specifically of its two parts—was a genuinely troubling issue, because all the original member states of the Warsaw Pact could regard themselves in one way or another as Germany's recent victims. Still, it is not clear whether the Warsaw Pact may have been, in its early years, meant somewhat as a bargaining chip. Proposals emerged from Eastern Europe, notably from Poland, to dismantle both alliances and create, in essence, a militarily neutral buffer zone through central Europe. At nearly the same moment as Dulles accomplished the inclusion of West Germany within NATO, the Soviet Union had agreed to withdraw its occupation forces from Austria, and a key provision in the agreement was that the country would remain militarily neutral. The disparity between the Austrian agreement and the dispute over the destiny of Germany could scarcely have been greater.

The pursuit of a strong regional alliance in Western Europe, later followed by similar efforts in the Middle East (CENTO) and Southeast Asia (SEATO), reflected the view that a "division of labor" was desirable in global defense according to which each member would contribute according to its special abilities. The military forces of the various member states would thus not necessarily be structured proportionately. In NATO, for example, the importance of the U.S. nuclear shield clearly exceeded that of the direct, combat-ready capability of U.S. troop units stationed in Europe. Eisenhower observed that it cost ten times as much for the United States to field an infantryman as it cost Turkey, a new NATO member. At the same time, Turkey lacked the strategic delivery systems and nuclear weapons possessed by the United States. Each state would thus be wise—and most effective—to contribute according to its special strengths.

The kind of force structure envisioned for the United States and the anticipated role international alliances would play in world security grew out of evolving notions of what sort of war the next one, if it occurred, would be. Both popular and military professional literature of the late 1940s abounded with predictions that the next war would be an intense and absorbing third world war in which nuclear weapons would be used promptly and that, because of its brevity, would be fought with whatever forces and weapons were on hand. Later, the notion of an all-out and brief nuclear war acquired the description "spasm war," while the notion of fighting it with what was on hand was called a "come as you are" war. Both notions had tremendous consequence for strategy, force structure, and readiness.

The paradigm of "the next war" is apt to survive for some time even in the face of much anomalous experience. During the administration of President Eisenhower, for example, many officials appreciated that local and regional military problems, bearing such names as "limited war," "insurgency," and "wars of national liberation," might well be of indigenous origins. The problem was to define a meaningful and effective role for the United States when its force structure and its operational ethos were so heavily oriented toward strategic and even specifically nuclear issues. During the Truman years, one means of accommodation was to conceive of forces as having multiple purposes. Aircraft carriers and other surface vessels, for example, might be capable of a show of force or of a discrete mission in a regional problem, such as when the Seventh Fleet sailed into the straits between Taiwan and the Chinese mainland to secure Chiang Kai-shek at the outset of the Korean War. The fleet might also be used to intervene on behalf of supposedly pro-Western regimes. In 1957, Eisenhower ordered the Sixth Fleet into the eastern Mediterranean to protect Jordan's King Hussein against an attempted overthrow by forces favoring Gamal Abdel Nasser of Egypt, and in 1958 he ordered seven thousand marines to land in Lebanon to shore up the faltering government of Camille Chamoun.

On the evening of 25 June 1950, while on a visit to Missouri, Truman was informed of the North Korean invasion of South Korea.

Actual U.S. behavior, therefore, could be flexible, even if rhetoric concerning a single-sourced global conspiracy had to be stretched somewhat to fit the occasion. Indeed, the exploration of this discomforting diversity in the world was a more evidently pressing matter during the Eisenhower years than it had been under President Truman. The force structure and much of the strategic policy with which Eisenhower initially had to work were those of his predecessor, however, and it must be noted that Eisenhower had served Truman as a leading adviser on military and strategic policy until 1952.

Truman's concern over the prospect of a nuclear World War III meant that he did not give nearly so much attention or resources to the development of forces appropriate to undertaking limited and conventional expeditions in widely separated parts of the world. His political policy, as suggested in the Truman Doctrine, was global in scope, but the means available for its implementation were largely strategic in nature. Suitable as this was to the vision of bipolar competition, it was inadequate to the practical demands of regional and local military problems.

The continued importance of the U.S. strategic role was restated in 1950, just months before the North Korean attack that began the Korean War. After an extensive study of the world security situation, the National Security Council concluded that a massive buildup of U.S. and allied forces was essential to counter anticipated Soviet probes against the West long into the future. NSC memorandum 68 (NSC-68), a policy statement intertwining doctrine and strategy, gave an overall vision of world security problems and did not specifically discount the prospect of local military problems of indigenous origin, but it also did not put great priority on them. Given this emphasis on the general strategic picture as well as Truman's understandable preoccupation with problems in Europe and the Middle East, the emergence of war in Korea must be understood as a very special surprise for the Truman administration. Oddly, it was not an entirely unpleasant surprise and the fact that it was not, is itself an illustration of the transitions that had to be made to provide the United States a wider range of military options for the remaining decades of the cold war.

If the Berlin Blockade afforded a chance to test military systems important to the defense of the West, the war in Korea (1950–1953) tested the theory of deterrence itself and probed its nature. The North Korean attack was resisted in a scenario that revealed many problems and tensions in a cold war alliance in which the United States played a dominant role. On the evening of 25 June 1950, while on a visit to Missouri, Truman was informed of the North Korean invasion of South Korea. The president returned to Washington the next day, and soon after his arrival held a meeting on the crisis. The decision to resist the North Korean move was immediate, based less on consultation with other nations that might participate in military action in Korea, whether from NATO or from the United Nations, than on supposition as to how they ought to respond. The task for the U.S. government soon became turning a "U.S. into UN decision," as indicted in notes written by White House aide George Elsey. Thus, U.S. forces were committed prior to any United Nations action and before the U.S. government had obtained comparable commitments from its NATO allies.

The role of the United Nations during this period was itself a curious one. In its initial conception, the United Nations presupposed at least some measure of cooperation among the world's leading powers, represented by the five veto-holding members of the Security Council. The cold war conflict had frustrated that early purpose, and the emergence of two Chinese governments, the Nationalist remnant in Taipei and the triumphant Communist regime in Beijing, complicated the aim even more. Increasingly frustrated at the state of affairs within the United Nations, Truman flirted with seeking to transform the United Nations into a "Free World alliance." Nevertheless, the studied absence of the Soviet delegate from the Security Council vote authorizing the United Nations to use force to repel the North Korean forces permitted the world body to act. Apart from limited efforts at peacekeeping in the Middle East, this marked the first major use of force by the United Nations.

As the war progressed, however, an equitable commitment of forces by various allies within the United Nations was difficult, if not impossible, either to define or to obtain after the United States had already entered the fray. In a sense, the United States lost leverage by sending its own forces so promptly, even if such action was a military necessity. At a minimum, the commitment of U.S. land-based and naval air forces seemed essential to slowing the advance of North Korean units down the peninsula. Once U.S. forces were committed, however, the enterprise had become, practically if not formally, an American war rather than an allied or United Nations one. Thus, instead of seeing their roles in Korea as equal and comparable to that of the United States in support of a poorly armed people against aggression, other combatant nations, such as Great Britain, France, and Turkey, were just as apt to see themselves as helping out the Americans and might do so with no more than token forces. Cooperation with the United States in Korea reciprocated U.S. commitment to Europe in the NATO alliance, and in the case of France, it strengthened the U.S. commitment to support the French effort to hold Indochina against local insurgents. In the event, aside from Korean nationals, the United States provided some 90 percent of the troops fighting against the North Koreans and their allies, the Soviet Union and Communist China.

There were other lessons learned in this conflict. The Korean War was basically a conventional war in both political and military terms and the first significant one fought after the production and deployment of a substantial number of nuclear weapons. The principle of self-restraint and avoidance of first use of nuclear weapons also arose, less as a statement of U.S. policy than as a practical consequence of international political realities. It is not clear that President Truman had any personal distaste for using nuclear weapons in Korea, even though he chose not to do so, but leaders of allied states, such as Clement Atlee of Great Britain, made unmistakable their firm hostility to their use. This issue—when to "go nuclear," how, and under what provocations—became an important theme in discussions of U.S. strategic policy and even tactical military doctrine during the 1950s.

Although the U.S. and UN experience in Korea was often both confused and confusing, the war lent credibility to the sense of threat in other regions, notably in Europe. Difficult though it is to demonstrate concretely, the Korean War appears to have helped in transforming NATO from a paper alliance to a real, working multinational force. Even more, however, Truman believed that the Korean War proved the credibility of U.S. strategic forces and the effectiveness of its policy of deterrence. Truman believed that the Soviet Union was behind the various regional conflicts facing the United States, including Korea. In the case of Korea, however, this view had some plausibility, because the division of the peninsula into two political entities was essentially an extension of its division into two administrative units during the Soviet and U.S. transitional occupations of North and South respectively. By assuming that his adversary had contemplated an all-out war, Truman saw the war in Korea as it actually developed, limited geographically and fought without nuclear weapons, as a proof that deterrence had succeeded. To the American public, however, the Korean conflict seemed to be a long, drawn-out stalemate, and President Truman's popularity slumped.

Many other Americans failed to see the war as Truman did, but they shared the administration's view that the Korean conflict was a most peculiar sort of war. In some ways, this was so. Rhetorically, for example, the military action in Korea was called a "police action," an awkward and curious choice of terms, but to call it a "limited war" was not the view of Koreans, for whom this civil war abetted by outsiders was as intense an experience as they could manage. Only if one defined "war" as a conflict marked by all-out commitment of the full arsenal and forces of the United States and the Western allies could one construe the Korean War as fundamentally new and atypical. In essence, the reference points were World War II—with its talk of unconditional surrender and a relentless offensive—and the hypothetical nuclear World War III. Yet those might more fairly have been deemed exceptional. The United Nations was committed by its charter to eliminating the "scourge of war" from human experience, which helps to explain the use of rhetorical substitutes for the word "war." Avoiding the use of the word, however, also gave Truman a justification for refraining from calling upon Congress for a declaration of war. This contributed to the broadening of presidential discretion in foreign affairs, even including military action, in the cold war era.

The actual nature of the Korean War merits appreciation, because the Korean War soon became a model both for emulation and avoidance. The slogan that emerged in the presidential campaign of Eisenhower and continued as the Korean conflict came to an end in 1953 was that there must be "no more Koreas," but exactly what did that mean in real military and political terms? What it clearly did not mean was acquiescence to probes or provocations by members of the Communist bloc. One principle important to the new presidential administration of Eisenhower (1953–1961), was to place greater reliance on genuinely allied, cooperative action, achieving agreements for it in advance of committing U.S. troops and thus avoiding the risks and the practical costs of unilateral action. A second major principle was to retain the choice of weapons when an adversary challenged the "free world." Although circumspect on the subject while serving as the supreme allied commander in NATO (1950–1952), Eisenhower later criticized Truman for having limited the U.S. and UN response to the North Korean invasion of South Korea to weapons chosen by the North Korean government in Pyongyang. In fact, this criticism was not completely correct, because early in the war the United States had employed the long-range bombers of its Far East Air Force (FEAF), based in Japan, to destroy North Korean industry and other major facilities useful to a war effort. However indirectly, Eisenhower seemed to be making a point about the deployment of nuclear weapons. For him, there was no sense in denying in advance the use of any weapon in the arsenal.

The Korean War possessed an irony. How was it that so powerful a nation as the United States could be tied up so long by a third-rate military force?

Curiously, Eisenhower's approach echoed Truman's own manner at the very outset of the cold war when, as Secretary of War Stimson put it, Truman went to the Potsdam Conference (1945) with the wartime allies, notably Stalin, "wearing the atomic bomb ostentatiously on his hip." Given the fact that the United States would not move to accelerated production of atomic bombs until well into 1947, the ostentation was a pretense. The pretense, however, was not so different from that of Eisenhower when he pledged in 1952 that he would, if elected, "go to Korea." Go for what? To observe and to find a resolution of the stalemate, to be sure. But how? Nuclear weapons had taken their place as the inescapable background static of all undertakings in the early cold war.

Even though this was not the only meaning of "no more Koreas," it was the one that most closely matched the gut feeling of the early and mid-1950s. For many Americans, the Korean War possessed an irony. How was it that so powerful a nation as the United States could be tied up so long by a third-rate military force? Convinced that nuclear weapons could offset manpower and conventional forces, serving as what Forrestal had called the "great equalizer," Americans lapsed into the sense that military power was generic rather than specific.

Limits to violence and to the risk of nuclear war seemed essential, however, clearly so to President Eisenhower. There were several means of holding those limits and trimming those risks. One method was to deploy U.S. forces in Korea on an indefinite basis, thus discouraging a new North Korean attack and providing time for the South Korean regime to grow stronger politically and militarily. Talk of the need for allied cooperation notwithstanding, the Eisenhower administration, like other presidencies, was ultimately willing to commit U.S. forces and prestige on a purely bilateral basis.

Eisenhower was also genuinely interested in improving relations with Soviet leaders, even while pressing for significant strengthening of NATO forces and advancing new weapons programs in the United States, such as new jet-powered bomber forces, intercontinental ballistic missiles (ICBMs) armed with thermonuclear warheads, and nuclear-powered naval vessels and missile-carrying submarines. Eisenhower advocated "people to people" diplomacy for the average citizen, and his interest in "summit diplomacy"—free-ranging talks among the leaders of the world's greatest powers—established one of the devices eventually used as part of the apparatus for developing arms control programs.

Eisenhower also sought ways of making nuclear weapons more "useful." During his presidency, U.S. defense research focused on diversifying the nuclear arsenal, most notably on creating the "clean bomb." Producing low-radiation nuclear weapons would presumably make it easier to use them, especially in European battlefield conditions. Physical destruction would be great and would be produced economically, but the devastated areas could supposedly be reoccupied with relative promptness. Meanwhile, tests in the Nevada desert measured the effects on ground troops of operating near a nuclear explosion and of entering the area of devastation soon after the blast. All such efforts ultimately aimed at enhancing the credibility of the deterrent threat posed by NATO and by the United States. Even though such test programs concentrated on nuclear weapons, it was significant that the more traditionally conceived battlefield was returning to strategic importance. Also, the development of battlefield nuclear weapons eventually forced reexamination within the armed forces, notably the army, of unit organization, tactics, and strategy. This contributed to the doctrine of "flexible response," which embraced a broad spectrum of possible military options from which the United States might choose to react to hostile action. One critical element in flexible response was the concept of limited nuclear warfare, in which atomic weapons would be used in one theater, notably in Europe, without assuming that such a conflict would automatically escalate into global nuclear war. In future wars fought according to flexible response, the choice of weapons would be in the hands of the President of the United States.

Such strategic concepts as flexible response help to explain the real meaning of the statement "no more Koreas." What Eisenhower really opposed was not commitment to "small wars," but Truman's hesitancy over the use of nuclear weapons. Eisenhower and his military aids and advisers insisted that the wronged party had the right to choose the weapons most convenient to its defense. By making various nuclear and nonnuclear options seem more credible, deterrence was further enhanced.

While U.S. military policy included the search for "clean" atomic weapons, coupled with ever more exact targeting and delivery systems, the Soviet Union set about enhancing explosive yield without regard for the "dirt" of radiation. U.S. policy was a sign of its technological superiority over the Soviet Union. A comparatively precise targeting and delivery assured that a weapon yielding perhaps one megaton—the equivalent of one million tons of conventional explosives—could take out the designated enemy site. The inexactness of Soviet targeting and delivery argued in favor of using weapons of much greater megatonnage as insurance against inaccuracy. The larger the crater, the greater the likelihood of destroying the intended target, even if much else in collateral damage went along with it.

The slogan "better dead than red" won currency as an expression of popular anticommunism.

The impression that U.S. military policy was dominated by massive retaliation and the spirit of brinksmanship during the Eisenhower years owed something to the image of Dulles. Eisenhower's first secretary of state, Dulles was a fervent and religious man, whose open anticommunism reflected his passionate inner beliefs. As the slogan "better dead than red" won currency as an expression of popular anticommunism, Dulles seemed peculiarly likely to turn the slogan into policy and then, if necessary, into action. If some thought nuclear war disproportionate to the provocations the United States was likely to face, Dulles did not let on that he was among them. Indeed, his vigorous denunciations of communism as utter evil and neutralism as immorality permitted an argument in favor of nuclear war under traditional just war theory. In retrospect, however, it all took on an odd air of doublethink, because this was the same Dulles who in 1950 had doubted the military necessity of NATO. The war in Korea had contributed to his changed views but, still, by himself Dulles remains somewhat puzzling. As part of the Eisenhower administration, however, he was a key player in the elaborate, if not always fully conscious, foreign policy game of "good cop, bad cop."

As always, however, massive retaliation made sense only if the world truly was bipolar, divided neatly into two conflicting camps, with each regional faction taking orders from a central power. Nuclear war, however, could only make sense if there were many discrete levels and kinds of nuclear war, representing many different scenarios. As noted, Eisenhower sought not only to strengthen the U.S. strategic nuclear force but also to develop weapons usable on the battlefield. In this sense, he may be regarded as the presidential parent of tactical nuclear weapons. His advocacy of scaled-down yield and reduced radiation effects for nuclear weapons reflected his perception of the atomic bomb as a realistic part of the U.S. arsenal.

What purpose there might be for such weapons was suggested when, according to French officials, Eisenhower offered France two atomic bombs in 1954 to break the Viet Minh siege against the embattled French outpost at Dien Bien Phu in the far northwest of Vietnam. In the Eisenhower years, it was evident to the government that a policy of massive retaliation did not fit all situations and that it was singularly ill-suited to the anticolonial struggles in Asia and in Africa. Had there been time to train French air crews or a U.S. willingness to use U.S. air crews to deliver atomic bombs in the vicinity of Dien Bien Phu, the selective use of specialized nuclear weapons might have been tested.

The Eisenhower administration did other things to broaden the range of means by which the United States might intervene in widely separated and distinct trouble spots. As judged by the administration's stated aims, its efforts were not unsuccessful. In Guatemala, for example, a CIA operation in June 1954 overturned the reformist government of Jacobo Arbenz Guzmán, aided by the Guatemalan army's refusal to fight in defense of Arbenz's legitimately elected regime. Concerned that Arbenz was leading Guatemala to the political left and troubled by Guatemala's refusal to endorse the March 1953 resolution of the Organization of American States opposing communism, Eisenhower authorized CIA Director Allen Dulles to back exiled Guatemalan Colonel Carlos Castillo Armas with arms and aircraft. Starting with just two hundred men on 18 June 1954, Castillo gathered new volunteers as he advanced toward Guatemala City, but CIA broadcasts exaggerated their numbers. The Guatemalan army refused to support Arbenz, who ceded power to a provisional government that, in turn, yielded to another short-lived interim regime. After negotiations in which U.S. Ambassador John E. Peurifoy was prominent, Castillo became part of a ruling junta and eventually its head. U.S. air support of Castillo had been a crucial signal to the Guatemalan army to oppose Arbenz.

In the Philippines, on the other hand, the United States provided economic aid and substantial military assistance and advice to aid the government from its independence in 1946, notably through Defense Minister (later president) Ramón Magsaysay, in suppressing the Communist Hukbalahap (Huk) guerrillas. U.S. Air Force Colonel Edward G. Lansdale advocated a mixture of land reform, political rights, and armed resistance against the Huks, depriving them of support among the peasantry and so facilitating the demise of the rebels. In essence, to use the imagery of Mao Tse-tung, Lansdale sought to dry up the "sea of the people" in which the "guerrilla fish" swam, and, albeit temporarily, Magsaysay achieved that aim. It was a test case of counterinsurgency, although the term itself did not enjoy great vogue until the administration of John F. Kennedy (1961–1963).

In other places, however, great losses suffered by the colonial powers during World War II all but destroyed their chances of retaining control against insurgents in the years after the war. Notably, France faced a more intractable problem in the Southeast Asian states of Cambodia, Laos, and Vietnam. French Indochina, as the region had been known for a century, had experienced a generally exploitative colonial rule in which education, health care, and other components of social infrastructure had been neglected. On top of this, the French, who had administered Indochina on behalf of the Japanese during World War II, could expect great difficulty trying to reassert themselves as legitimate rulers of Indochina when the Japanese Empire fell in 1945. French collaboration with the Japanese had helped especially to spark Vietnamese national consciousness and, at the very least, Japan's successes in Southeast Asia in World War II proved that European powers—and presumably the French—could be beaten. By the time the United States became the major active outside influence in the region, from about 1956, the political context in which economic reform and military security would have to be accomplished had been fundamentally and, as it turned out, fatally compromised.

For all the professions of interest in the world as a whole, the preponderance of U.S. and free world forces was concentrated in a very few areas, most notably in NATO Europe. This fact alone necessitated that problems in other parts of the world be viewed in terms of their relationship to Europe and to the North Atlantic community in general. At the time of the Korean War, for example, Truman at first speculated that action on the Korean peninsula might be a diversionary move meant to give the Soviet Union a freer hand in the Middle East and Eastern Europe. Similarly, the change in U.S. policy from opposition to colonialism to support of the French in Indochina owed much to U.S. concern to stabilize a staunchly anti-Communist government in Paris. Time and again, U.S. and Soviet competition for the loyalties of developing nations was assessed for potentially destabilizing implications in Europe.

Hence, events touching upon Europe and the Mediterranean proved most powerful in determining the shape and character of the cold war. After 1953, for example, Korean affairs became an American rather than a NATO issue, and the same was substantially true of the U.S. venture in Vietnam in the 1960s. In fact, despite talk of a unified stance by the Western bloc, there were differences of perspective and of interest among Western nations, notably among Great Britain, France, and the United States. Great Britain and France sought to retain the vestiges of their empires, while the United States genuinely preferred and often promoted political self-determination. U.S. policy aimed at capitalizing on emerging Third World nationalism, provided it could be kept in traditional liberal-democratic political channels. France and Great Britain, however, sought to retain privileged interests, such as ownership and management of the Suez Canal, French domination of Algerian oil, and other practical benefits of empire.

Consequently, U.S. policies occasionally clashed with those of its formal allies. The unity of the Western bloc did not extend beyond opposition to the Soviet Union. Regional issues, such as access to oil, were shaped by national interests that were largely independent of the cold war with the Soviet Union. The tensions within the Western alliance, however, helped to shape the cold war conflict by limiting the measures the Western nations could take against the Eastern bloc.

Therefore, a sequence of events in Europe and the Mediterranean during the 1950s assumes an importance comparable in impact to the Korean War. One event was the Anglo-French conflict in 1956 with Egypt over the ownership of the Suez Canal, into which the Israelis injected themselves, largely in quest of their own national security interests. On 29 October, Israeli forces moved swiftly against Egyptian forces in the Sinai Peninsula, and within days French and British forces occupied the territory along the canal. Eisenhower was displeased at the neocolonialist tone of the operations, and he supported a UN resolution calling for a truce and a cutoff of oil to France and Great Britain, but the president was also angry at not having been consulted about the operation in advance. To the French and British, it was their own affair. To Eisenhower, it was part of the broad fabric of the cold war and a proper issue for consideration under the aegis of the North Atlantic alliance.

The Suez Crisis further exposed the anomalous place of Israel within the cold war. A creation of the United Nations, which authorized its founding in 1948, Israel became a focal point of tension between the superpowers, less because of specific Soviet concerns about Israel itself than because its existence so alienated neighboring Arab states whose anger might be exploited. The creation of Israel did much to help shape Arab consciousness and to give strength to the Arab nationalism and solidarity pursued by Egypt's Nasser. Culturally, the Israel of the 1950s was distinctly an outpost of European ideas and customs in the midst of an equally distinctly Arab region. Militarily, Israel was born in war and put a high percentage of its national income into defense. The country developed a domestic arms industry while also buying arms extensively abroad; it maintained a vigorous intelligence system and engaged in several wars and numerous preemptive strikes against its adversaries. Sympathy for the State of Israel within the United Nations owed a great deal to the revelations of the Holocaust in Europe during World War II, but continuing cooperation between the United States and Israel owed much, too, to U.S. interest in securing free communications in the eastern Mediterranean and free flow of oil from the Middle East. To confuse matters further, Israel was touted as an island of democracy in a sea of autocracy—at a time when U.S. officials wryly referred to the practice of human slavery in Saudi Arabia as an "idiosyncrasy." It is suggestive, therefore, that the U.S. anger over the Suez Crisis was aimed more at France and Britain than at Israel.

The Anglo-French action in Suez also blunted the criticism of the Soviet Union for its invasion of Hungary that same year, when the government of Imre Nagy announced its intention to withdraw from the Warsaw Pact. Secretary of State Dulles had spoken of the need for a rollback of communism and for liberation of the "captive nations," but Soviet Premier Nikita Khrushchev held on to Hungary at a cost of seven thousand Soviet and thirty thousand Hungarian dead. For the United States, the timing could scarcely have been worse. The Soviet action in Hungary began on 31 October 1956, just two days after the start of Israeli operations in the Sinai and immediately before the British and French joined the fight against Egypt. Sandwiched between these aggressive moves by U.S. allies, the Soviet assault on Hungary became less of a political liability for Moscow than might otherwise have been the case.

Despite its earlier calls for rollback of communism, the disquieting calm of the Eisenhower administration in the face of the Soviet attack in Hungary suggested a de facto recognition of Eastern Europe as a Soviet sphere of influence, although formal acceptance of the notion would have been repugnant to most Americans. Rhetoric aside, the confrontation between NATO and the Warsaw Pact was to be a static one—an indefinite face-off rather than a dynamic series of thrusts and parries. As some Europeans quipped, under Truman there had been "active containment," while under Eisenhower there was "passive liberation." Beneath the superstructure of change, therefore, was the substructural continuity of containment.

The U.S. intervention in Lebanon in 1958 further helped to set the terms of the cold war confrontation. Eisenhower was concerned over the future of the Middle East, particularly with the rise of Arab nationalism. In 1957, he watched the effort by pro-Nasser forces nearly unseat Jordan's King Hussein. In July 1958, the government of Iraq was overthrown in a coup, which was an especially distressing development because Iraq had been the only Arab member of the U.S.–sponsored Baghdad Pact, renamed the Central Treaty Organization (CENTO) when Iraq withdrew. Thus, when Lebanon's President Chamoun sought U.S. intervention in his country, largely to shore up the strength of his political faction against its principal rival, Eisenhower was already primed to accede to the request. On 14 July 1958, Eisenhower ordered U.S. marines into Lebanon to guard against what was termed "indirect aggression." The first marine units to land found tourists and sunbathers on the beaches rather than a hostile force. Fortunately for U.S. interests, Lebanese armed forces refrained from engaging the Americans, and while the situation gradually cooled, the incident suggested the limits of U.S. understanding of the Middle East.

The intervention in Lebanon was premised on the Eisenhower Doctrine, first articulated on 5 January 1957 in a special message to Congress. Eisenhower requested—and later received—a congressional resolution authorizing his use of force to save any friendly Middle Eastern regime from attack by "international communism." The president did not wish the "holy places of the Middle East" to come under the sway of "atheistic materialism," nor did he want two-thirds of the known oil reserves to be "dominated by alien forces hostile to freedom." Although Eisenhower failed to comply with his own professed intention of informing Congress in advance of the use of force, the U.S. action in Lebanon was greeted with almost no question or criticism, thus serving as a milestone in the gradual expansion of presidential power that was a feature of the cold war era.

Eisenhower did not wish the "holy places of the Middle East" to come under the sway of "atheistic materialism."

The emergence of a call for wars of national liberation forced the U.S. government to field questions on whether massive retaliation was a credible threat and hence a real deterrent in all cases. In practice, U.S. policy had proven itself to be relatively flexible for years prior to open debate on the subject in the later 1950s. The intervention in Lebanon proved this, as did the destabilization of the Arbenz government in Guatemala and the war in Korea. Conceivable as a response to a Soviet nuclear attack on the United States, U.S. nuclear retaliation strained belief when applied to anticolonial insurgencies in the "Third World."

What was new at the end of the 1950s was the elevated importance attached to the Third World as deserving of interest and of appropriate policy in its own right. Flexible response was first posed in the mid-1950s to revise strategic and theater nuclear war policies and was advocated prominently by Army Chief of Staff Maxwell Taylor. Flexible response allowed for the possibility of a general nuclear war, but it put greater emphasis on a tactical rather than strategic role for nuclear weapons. Moreover, it gave room for completely nonnuclear options, ranging down to counterinsurgency in conflicts given such terms as "brushfire wars" and "sublimited wars." Clearly, such an approach, if taken as national policy, inferred the need for major realignments of the U.S. military force structure.

How the desire to intervene flexibly in a regional or local conflict could affect force structure, deployments, and strategic thinking was well illustrated in the war in Vietnam, especially from 1956 to 1973. At various times, the war was fought as a counterinsurgency, as a conventional localized ground war, as a quasi-independent air war, as a civil insurrection, as a regional aggression, and as a proxy war within the global cold war context. Each view invited the use of different forces or required the use of weapons and forces in different ways. One extreme example was the use of B-52 strategic bombers in tactical support of ground forces in South Vietnam after 1966. Similarly, the demands of the Vietnam War accelerated development of the combat use of the helicopter gunship, which first seemed key in opposing insurgencies but was soon adapted to planning for possible conventional war in Europe. Although flexible response could provide new options, it also risked fostering confusion.

There were pressures building against the status quo in the cold war from the Soviet side as well. Under Premier Khrushchev, the Soviet Union had developed a significant capability in ICBMs, strengthening Khrushchev's resolve to increase Soviet political influence in areas of long-standing differences, such as Central Europe and in the Third World. From the perspective of public relations, this posed a dilemma for the Eisenhower administration and for the successor Kennedy administration. The need to meet the challenge of insurgency and sublimited war was clear, but the grand posturing of Khrushchev and his claims to superiority in intercontinental missiles seemed to call for rejoinder.

Much of Khrushchev's bluster was simply a matter of personal style, one that contrasted markedly with the reserve of Eisenhower and, later, with the sharply articulated sophistication of Kennedy. Khrushchev's brash manner was more than a personal idiosyncrasy, however, and he knowingly overstated Soviet military capability, hoping to bluff his way into diplomatic leverage that his actual military power did not justify. Although Eisenhower knew that Khrushchev was exaggerating Soviet military strength, he was reluctant to reveal the human and technical intelligence means that gave him evidence that Khrushchev's claims were false. As a result, Khrushchev's bluff contributed to the incorrect view that Soviet military forces and experimental military technology surpassed those of the United States.

Beneath mannerisms, too, lay serious issues, such as the dangers of an escalating arms race, the lethal dangers of atmospheric testing of nuclear weapons, the risks of miscalculation of the intentions of one's adversary, and more. Hoping to resolve such issues, British Prime Minister Harold Macmillan urgently called for a new summit meeting. The major parties agreed—the United States rather as a personal favor to Macmillan—and they were scheduled to meet on 16 May 1960 in Paris.

Shortly before the meeting was to convene, however, on 1 May a U.S. U-2 reconnaissance aircraft was shot down over the Soviet Union. Such overflights had been known to the Soviet leadership for some time. The U.S. government pretended that they were not taking place, and the Soviet Union, for fear of revealing its inability to shoot the aircraft down, had chosen not to complain. By 1960, however, Soviet air-to-ground missile technology had achieved the capability of taking down the high-flying U-2. First doubting that the Soviets could have shot the aircraft down and then believing that its pilot, Francis Gary Powers, would have killed himself, Eisenhower openly described the incident as an accidental straying of the U-2 off course. Unfortunately for Eisenhower—and for Macmillan's hopes for the Paris summit—Powers survived to confess that he had been on a spy mission for the CIA. President Eisenhower's embarrassment at being caught in a lie over the U-2 aerial reconnaissance program was great—made all the more so by Khrushchev's deliberate exploitation of the incident.

Khrushchev's belittling of Eisenhower at the Paris summit was a foretaste of his own loss of face during the Cuban Missile Crisis.

The failure of the Paris summit was curiously instructive. Whether he did so consciously or not, Khrushchev chose to capitalize on the political gaffe of Eisenhower, rather than restrain himself and strive for agreement on such issues as development and testing of nuclear weapons. It also suggested that, in the cold war the alleviation of an actual military problem through negotiation might be deemed less advantageous to a nation than the exploitation of the failings of one's adversary for the purposes of public relations. In short, image counted, sometimes it seemed even more than military dangers. Credibility also counted, as if the personal embarrassment of a president caught in a lie might reduce the strategic clout of the nation he represented. In this sense, Khrushchev's belittling of Eisenhower at the Paris summit was a foretaste of his own loss of face during the Cuban Missile Crisis (1962).

Shortly before leaving the presidency in 1961, Eisenhower delivered a "farewell address" to the American people that became his most famous and most enduringly influential speech. In this address, Eisenhower warned Americans to resist the rising influence of university elites and "think tanks," which had enormous impact on government policy despite having no electoral mandate. Above all, however, official and popular attention fastened upon Eisenhower's caution against unwarranted influence from the military–industrial complex. Because of its large place in the economy and its important role as an employer of both civilian workers and military personnel, the military–industrial complex could not escape having widespread impact on American society. Eisenhower saw this as a potential danger to the social, economic, and political system, even if it also seemed to be a necessary cost of waging the cold war. Observant though he was, Eisenhower could offer no concrete solution and no protection, other than lasting public vigilance.

The 1961 farewell address marked a culmination in early cold war thinking. Eisenhower's caution about a military–industrial complex would have been superfluous had it not been for the magnitude of that complex. Eisenhower, who as president had worried over the size of the federal budget in general and the military budget in particular, ironically presided over what was, compared to its share of the federal budget in peacetime years before 1940, the largest peacetime military budget in history. In addition, the increasing complexity and cost of developing new weapons systems had led to a closer intertwining of private contractors and government agencies, as more federal money went into research and development. The armed forces were not only greater in size but more grand in sweep and in mission than in the past.

Eisenhower worried over where it all would lead. He knew that the military forces he left to Kennedy in 1961 enjoyed overwhelming superiority over those of the Soviet Union, but he also knew that Soviet capabilities were growing. Negotiations seemed all the more important, but as his recent experience at Paris suggested, confrontation remained the rule of the day.

When Kennedy succeeded Eisenhower as president in January 1961, he made clear in his inaugural address that he would confront what he saw as a coordinated Communist challenge against the non-Communist periphery of the free world. This made the continuing problems in Southeast Asia, especially in Laos, a major source of concern to Kennedy. Even more galling was the presence of an avowedly Marxist government on the island of Cuba, scarcely seventy miles from the southernmost tip of Florida. The success of the Cuban revolution of 1959, led by Fidel Castro, established a Communist foothold in the Western Hemisphere, and both Eisenhower and Kennedy considered a Communist Cuba to be a violation of the spirit of the Monroe Doctrine and a challenge to the integrity of the Organization of American States. In secret, Eisenhower had authorized the CIA to plan the overthrow of the Castro regime.

In April 1961, Kennedy authorized the implementation of most parts of the CIA plan. He approved a limited invasion of Cuba by about fifteen hundred exiles who had fled their home island during the early phases of its rules under Castro, but Kennedy did not approve air support using U.S. aircraft and crews, a deficiency that contributed to the failure of the plan. Although the invasion had been planned during Eisenhower's tenure, the idea of intervening in a "flexible" way appealed to Kennedy. The landing, at the Bay of Pigs on 17 April, proved disastrous, and the Kennedy administration was soon bartering for the release of prisoners.

Weakened and embarrassed by his failure over the Bay of Pigs incident, Kennedy met with Nikita Khrushchev in Vienna (3–4 June). Evidently, Khrushchev was not impressed. Their key disagreement was over the status of Germany. Khrushchev sought de jure recognition of the boundary between East Germany and West Germany, part of an effort to stem the loss of skilled and educated East Germans to the West. Kennedy feared that any renegotiation of the *modus vivendi* in Germany would open a Pandora's box. Determined to show strength, Kennedy won an immediate multibillion dollar supplement to the military budget, called up reservists, increased draft calls, and otherwise sought to mobilize in the face of what he described as an attempt at the "neutralization of Western Europe." Disregarding the flurry of U.S. activity, on 13 August 1961,

In autumn of 1962, U.S. reconnaissance aircraft acquired firm evidence that bases were being built in Cuba for the deployment of Soviet intermediate range missiles. This photo shows the construction of a missile launch facility in the San Cristobal area of Cuba on 23 October 1962. (UPI/Corbis-Bettmann)

Khrushchev ordered the construction of a wall dividing East and West Berlin. For most of three decades, the Berlin Wall was a prominent symbol of the division of Europe in the cold war. Practically, however, it stemmed the exodus of talent through East Berlin that had been a cause of Soviet concern. In essence, Khrushchev had gotten his way.

The Cuban Missile Crisis (October 1962) brought the early phases of the cold war to a frightening culmination in a test of deterrence based on the risk of nuclear conflict. It also reflected the Kennedy administration's belief in crisis management, an approach that contributed to the manner in which the Berlin Crisis had been handled yet also fostered a fixation on one's credibility. The incident also required prompt response of the military to presidential directives, thus reflecting the ever deeper penetration of the president into the management of military operations as the cold war progressed. By establishing a special separate group known as ExCom to manage the crisis, Kennedy did something of an end run around some of the formal and standard mechanisms for defining and executing national security policy.

By early autumn 1962, U-2 reconnaissance aircraft had acquired firm evidence that bases were being built in Cuba for the deployment of Soviet intermediate-range missiles. By deploying a forward threat against targets in the eastern United States before having a sufficient number of intercontinental missiles, Khrushchev sought to leapfrog his own technology to accomplish the same strategic objective. Kennedy viewed such a deployment as a direct violation of the Monroe Doctrine as well as a serious threat to the physical security of the United States. On 22 October 1962, Kennedy informed the Soviet ambassador that he would insist that no missiles be deployed and, as he added in a television broadcast to the American public that same evening, that he would accept the risk of worldwide nuclear war.

Precisely how to persuade the Soviets to reverse their plans, and what methods to use to force the issue, was a subject of intense discussion. The president saw problems with air strikes at targets in Cuba. For one thing, their promptness—customarily seen as a positive attribute—made the decision to use them functionally irreversible. Similarly, for all the talk of precision in the execution of bombing runs, the word "precision" needed political definition. Was bombing "precise" and discriminate if, in destroying missile installations, Soviet technicians were also killed? Would that constitute an escalation in the face-off between the Soviet Union and the United States?

Kennedy thus gravitated toward a naval blockade, aimed at preventing missiles from the Soviet Union from actually reaching Cuba and thus averting the need for a direct attack on Cuban territory. Meanwhile, at sea, the threats raised by a blockade would force the Soviet Union to make yet another decision—whether to attempt to run the blockade—giving it a chance to back away from the challenge or, in the contrary case, raising anew the question of ultimate responsibility for the crisis. Naval blockades have traditionally been regarded as acts of war. Imposing one, therefore, would permit nationals affected by it to condemn the United States for "firing the first shot." Kennedy's solution to this last difficulty was rhetorical. Instead of imposing a blockade, Kennedy specified that it was to be a naval quarantine of the island. Despite specificity as to what cargo was to be interdicted, it amounted to the same thing, but the neologism was politically convenient, permitting friend and foe alike to pretend that the level of challenge was lower than was really the case and to act accordingly.

How was it that Soviet missiles in Cuba could be called offensive when comparable U.S. missiles based in Turkey were defensive?

The widespread tolerance of the Kennedy administration's concept of a naval quarantine was itself a commentary on the nature and state of the cold war at the time—Charles de Gaulle of France, considered Kennedy's actions necessary and statesmanlike, Great Britain's Prime Minister Macmillan loyally supported Kennedy, and there was widespread support in the United Nations, a body presumably dedicated to the preservation of international law. The compelling horror of a possible nuclear war induced nations to give new turns to traditional precepts of international law, affording some latitude to the nuclear-equipped powers by not holding them to the letter of the law. In fact, if not in formal rhetoric, the United States could make a "wartime" commitment without resorting to a full array of wartime measures. In the process, new pages in international law were written de facto. For example, how was it that one country, the Soviet Union, had no right to supply weapons to another, Cuba? How was it, too, that Soviet missiles in Cuba could be called clearly offensive when comparable U.S. missiles based in Turkey and targeted at the Soviet Union were clearly defensive? Both legal and technical argumentation swayed before the power of nuclear armaments. The outcome, however, was that Khrushchev "blinked," offering to remove the missiles in exchange for a U.S. guarantee against an invasion of Cuba. Kennedy agreed on 27 October, and later and much more quietly and in a manner that gave no prestige to the Soviet Union, U.S. missiles were withdrawn from Turkey.

In the Cuban Missile Crisis and other affairs, the Kennedy administration's national security team tended to perceive themselves as engaged in a largely if not wholly new approach to world military problems. They made much of the concept of crisis management, for example, and they relied extensively on new quantitative and conceptual tools in military management. Still, despite the difference in tone that Kennedy hoped to create, his emphasis on "crisis consciousness" in many ways extended the psychology of brinksmanship articulated by Eisenhower and Dulles. Like Eisenhower, Kennedy remained wedded to the pursuit of U.S. strategic superiority over the Soviet Union, which still required a commitment to the use of massive retaliation as the basis for deterrence. Without strategic superiority, what sort of outcome would have been possible in the Cuban Missile Crisis?

The Cuban Missile Crisis, therefore, was one of the most intense moments of the cold war and a culmination and a conclusion of its formative and early phases. The strategy of deterrence based on massive retaliation had been developed, implemented, and terrifyingly tested. The crisis wrought changes in temperament as well as in leadership in the Soviet Union and in the United States. In the Soviet Union, Khrushchev was soon displaced as premier and Communist party chairman, succeeded by Leonid Brezhnev, who set out on a military buildup aimed at achieving strategic military parity with the United States. Meanwhile, while continuing the modernization of its strategic forces in an ultimately vain effort to preserve strategic military superiority, the U.S. government increasingly pursued a capability for flexible response to international challenges. Having come so close to nuclear war encouraged the quest for nonnuclear alternatives. Events after 1962 thus led to a new formulation of the relationship between the superpowers and a new phase of the cold war.

The subsequent history of the cold war was long and tangled, but in the main it recapitulated and then resolved the several major problems that had been set out during its inception and first decades. For example, the quest for nuclear superiority that had been linked to the policy of massive retaliation yielded to a succession of policies that accommodated real, if unwelcome, developments. Under Brezhnev, the Soviet Union built more and larger missiles, modernized and expanded its air forces, and enlarged its naval forces. Despite the Minuteman ICBM deployments in the 1960s and the subsequent fitting of the Minuteman III missiles with multiple, independently targeted reentry vehicles (MIRVs), the Soviet Union persisted in the arms race until it enjoyed "essential equivalency" with the United States, albeit with a different distribution of weapons.

In this environment, each side was capable of punishing the other so severely in the event of an attack that they were said to have "mutually deterred" one another. After still further developments and deployments, the Soviet Union and the United States were also said to possess the capacity for mutual assured destruction (MAD). These arms buildups, nevertheless, gave added impetus to arms negotiations. From the 1963 treaty that limited nuclear testing through the Strategic Arms Limitation Treaty (SALT I) signed by President Richard Nixon and Leonid Brezhnev in May 1972 to the SALT II treaty signed by Brezhnev and President Jimmy Carter in June 1979, signs emerged that a modus vivendi might be not only necessary but possible. For the Soviet Union, the attainment of parity created a chance for negotiations. For the United States, the ever more evident complexity of the world, perhaps best exemplified by the gradual resumption of U.S. relations with China, beginning in 1969, suggested that much of the conceptual framework of the cold war might be discarded.

Perhaps no single phenomenon so transformed the U.S. perception of world affairs during the cold war era after 1962 as America's long involvement in Vietnam. From its origins in the 1950s and early 1960s, the Vietnam conflict was cast as a battle against China, as a test case in the vast brief of the cold war, and not primarily as an indigenous conflict and civil war. By the late 1960s and most assuredly by 1973, when the United States withdrew from Vietnam, the cold war consensus of bipartisanship within the United States had returned, along with a more traditional spirit of skepticism toward U.S. policies and policymakers. It is telling that the Nixon administration's steps toward normalization of relations with China, at first conceived as the master plan of the Vietnam conflict, were taken during the late throes of that very same war. The U.S. venture in Vietnam took down much of the architecture of cold war thinking along with it.

Tensions arose in many parts of the world in the 1970s, such as in sub-Saharan Africa, southeast Asia, and the Middle East, but U.S. leaders showed increasing sensitivity to the strength of local conditions as the determining force of political and military events, even if it was sometimes too difficult to accept the results that such local conditions by themselves might yield. It appeared that the United States and the Soviet Union were now distinctly third parties in regional conflicts; both were being used as much as they were using others. In 1973, for example, the start of the Yom Kippur War between various Arab states and Israel required neither Americans nor Soviets, but the risk of war between the superpowers rose because of their embroilment in what was, in its inception, the affairs of others. The slow recognition of this phenomenon helped U.S. and Soviet leaders to become more favorable to discussion of complicated regional security issues, the defusing of which would go far toward terminating the cold war.

One region in which a clearly different reality existed by 1990 than had prevailed in 1945 or 1950 was in northeast Asia. As Soviet policy changed under Mikhail Gorbachev, giving more opportunity for institutional change and free expression of ideas, the largely Stalinist regime of Kim Il-sung in North Korea was virtually isolated. South Korea, thriving economically, opened talks with North Korea aimed at eventual reunification of their peninsula. Meanwhile, Japan was being brought toward reexamination of its constitutional prohibition against maintaining an expeditionary military capability, a provision insisted on by the United States as part of the treaty arrangements with Japan executed in 1951 but now questioned by many U.S. leaders. So, too, China was officially acknowledged to be one country, although subtle mechanisms allowed the continuation of a non-Communist government on Taiwan, and it enjoyed its seat on the Security Council in the United Nations as well as diplomatic relations with the world at large. In all, the peculiar and artificial special arrangements concocted after World War II for the administration of east Asian affairs were yielding to relationships that seemed to grow naturally from the economic and social realities of the region.

Europe, however, was the region where perhaps the most significant change had been needed to hasten the end of the cold war. Each side had held to a particularly hard line in central and eastern Europe. The Eisenhower administration had called for a rollback of communism from the Eastern European countries, but

Soviet Communist Party leader Leonid Brezhnev met on several occasions with U.S. President Richard Nixon in attempts to ease tensions between the USSR and the United States during the Cold War. In June 1973, Brezhnev visited Nixon at his home in San Clemente, California. (National Archives/Corbis)

Khrushchev had sent troops and tank forces into Budapest to crush the independence-minded Hungarian government when it sought to pull out of the Warsaw Pact in 1956. When the government of Alexander Dubcek in Czechoslovakia pursued a course of reform that smacked too much of intellectual and political diversity, Brezhnev ordered Warsaw Pact forces into the capital city of Prague and throughout the country to reinstitute more repressive policies in August 1968. Worse, Brezhnev articulated his own doctrine, a mirror image of Truman's, claiming the right to intervene anywhere to save a Communist regime from enemies foreign or domestic.

Throughout this period, Europe remained virtually an armed camp, even if its western half and much of its center also enjoyed extraordinary economic vitality. In the late 1970s and throughout the 1980s, special technological efforts to meet the perceived security needs of NATO actually fostered reexamination of many aspects of the policies the technology was designed to implement. The proposal to build and deploy neutron bombs, for example—weapons that would have limited blast effect but had great radiation lethality—forced the issue of whether NATO was to defend people or structures. The deployment of cruise missiles, whose inexpensiveness made it possible to buy them in large numbers and whose low-altitude attack profile made defending against them extremely difficult, raised the ugly prospect of still new realms in the already dizzying arms race. By 1990 the sheer absence of war in Europe for several decades made NATO and the Warsaw Pact seem to be artifacts from a very different age, especially because the large majority of the European population had no first-hand experience of war at all.

Even so, President Ronald Reagan continued to see the Soviet Union as a threat, NATO as a necessity, and the cold war confrontation as a still vital reality. Swept into the presidency in 1980 by a strong majority, Reagan used his political strength effectively to expand and hasten a military buildup that had been started on a more modest basis by Jimmy Carter in the second half of his presidency (1977–1981). In essence, Reagan sought to make clear to Soviet leaders that the United States would not slacken in opposing Soviet efforts to expand its influence. Even more so, the U.S. rearmament program, including the new Peacekeeper ICBM, B-1 and B-2 bombers, and a navy of six hundred ships, would raise the cost of military competition to a level that could not be sustained by the Soviet economy.

While criticizing the Soviet Union as an "evil empire," Reagan also challenged Brezhnev to negotiate a sharp reduction in strategic arms levels. After Brezhnev's death, Constantin Chernenko served briefly, followed by the similarly short-lived rule of Yuri Andropov. Little could be achieved in U.S.-Soviet relations during that unstable period, which nevertheless whetted both the Soviet and the U.S. appetites for renewed efforts at negotiation. This appetite was to be sated when Mikhail Gorbachev came to power. Calling for *perestroika,* a restructuring of Soviet institutions, and *glasnost,* a new openness in Soviet society that seemed to promise the chance for liberal reforms, Gorbachev first warned that the Soviet Union would counter any weapons that the United States chose to deploy. U.S. Secretary of State George Schultz saw this as evidence that the U.S. arms buildup was having the desired effect of forcing the Soviet Union to negotiations, lest the moribund Soviet domestic economy have no prospect for improvement. In essence, *perestroika* seemed inconsistent with a perpetual arms race, and Gorbachev went to great pains to reassure America's NATO allies of his good intentions.

In 1983, Reagan proposed that the United States develop a space-based system to defend against ICBMs carrying nuclear warheads. Officially designated the Strategic Defense Initiative (SDI), the concept was soon given the satirical nickname "Star Wars," after a popular film blending science fiction and myth. Urged upon Reagan by influential scientist Edward Teller, SDI was debated primarily on three grounds. One was its feasibility, which Teller and retired Army Lieutenant General Daniel O. Graham, who promoted SDI under the rubric "High Frontier," insisted was within sight. A second was its effect on the cold war, since critics feared that SDI would open a whole new realm of arms competition. Those who saw space as a sanctuary to be kept free of weapons objected in principle. A third area of debate was SDI's morality, which Reagan, Teller, Graham, and other advocates insisted was unassailable.

President Ronald Reagan continued to see the Soviet Union as a threat, NATO as a necessity, and the cold war confrontation as a still vital reality.

The debate over these issues tended to overlook the extraordinary change in strategic conceptualization that Reagan was proposing. Ever since 1945, the primacy of the strategic offensive had been taken as unassailable truth, and preventing the attack by deterrence was the only means of avoiding devastation. Reagan proposed that the technology foreseeable in the 1980s and beyond would restore primacy to the strategic defensive. To the extent that the whole history of the cold war revolved around group risk in an era of inevitable vulnerability to strategic nuclear attack, Reagan was also pointing beyond the horizon of the cold war itself.

For Gorbachev, however, SDI was another threat to the internal reforms that he knew the Soviet Union needed desperately if it were to remain a world power. If a greater arms race over space were to join the existing arms race on the planet's surface, the economy of the Soviet Union would be strained even more severely. Worse, under immediate external pressures from the United States and NATO, Gorbachev would have no breathing room in which to execute internal reforms. The entire arms buildup, then, played a role in making success in strategic arms reduction talks (START) essential.

Reagan and Gorbachev also anticipated aspects of world politics after the cold war when they focused increasingly on regional security issues. A global perspective, which had stereotyped conflict as either part of a centrally organized Communist conspiracy or else a capitalist one, had been part and parcel of cold war thought. Viewing regional problems as having their own dynamics not only pointed beyond bipolar confrontation but also contributed to the eventual joining of the United States and the Soviet Union in common political cause during the Gulf War of 1991.

The "new world order" foreseen by President George Bush would include many problems that had originated before the cold war era and had survived it.

The relaxation of internal imperial sway over the Warsaw Pact countries by Gorbachev sharply accelerated the pace of change within Eastern Europe, where a succession of political revolutions took place at the end of the 1980s and culminated in 1990. One immediate consequence was the virtual negation of the internal cohesion of the Warsaw Pact as a military force. Effectively deprived of mechanisms of command and forces to control, the pact merely awaited official announcement of its demise toward the end of 1990. Another consequence was the rapid reunification of Germany with the leaders of its eastern and western parts scarcely concealing their comparative disinterest in the fate of NATO and the Warsaw Pact. By late 1990, symbols of the artificial divisions of the cold war such as the Berlin Wall had been torn down, and Germany, the architect of the conflict that had led to the cold war, had itself once again been made whole. Large arsenals and great armed forces remained in many countries and posed many risks, but such phenomena reflected the nature of conventional power politics more than any special ideology-bound conflict. World powers and the world community at large had substantially freed themselves of the clichés of the cold war, and for a while the tormenting union of victory and fear seemed to yield to a moment of accommodation and hope.

The clear end of the cold war came with the clear end of the Soviet Union and hence with the absolute destruction of the bipolar competition that had been under way since 1945. In August 1991 a group of Soviet officials opposed to Gorbachev's internal reforms and external policies as well attempted a coup. Resistance in Moscow formed rapidly, a reflection to some extent of the success of Gorbachev's *glasnost,* and Boris Yeltsin, president of the Russian Federation and alternately an ally and an opponent of Gorbachev, led the stand against the coup. Gorbachev was soon returned to office, but his power, already depleted as the strains of nationalist sympathy among the Soviet Union's constituent republics increased, continued to decline. By late 1991, little remained of the Soviet Union but a name, and in December 1991 the Chamber of People's Deputies officially voted the Soviet Union out of existence. The cold war was clearly at an end.

The military legacy of the cold war to the succeeding era included still massive arsenals of missiles, warheads, bomber aircraft, sea forces, and other assets, distributed among many of the former Soviet Union's constituent republics, which were now independent states. These arsenals also could be treated as warehouses for arms sales to other nations, whose own local and regional aspirations could no longer be restrained by reference to a global bipolar confrontation or by an authoritarian Communist regime. The political legacy of the cold war included an array of long-suppressed nationalist conflicts within the states of the former Soviet Union and within the Eastern European nations that had been under Soviet sway. The "new world order" foreseen by President George Bush would include many problems that had originated before the cold war era and had survived it.

BIBLIOGRAPHY

Borowski, Harry R. *A Hollow Threat: Strategic Air Power and Containment Before Korea* (1982).

Brodie, Bernard. *Strategy in the Missile Age* (1959).

Campbell, Thomas M. *Masquerade Peace: America's U.N. Policy, 1944–1945* (1973).

Canan, James W. *The Superwarriors: The Fantastic World of Pentagon Superweapons* (1975).

Chang, Gordon H. *Friends and Enemies: The United States, China, and the Soviet Union, 1948–1972* (1990).

Davis, Lynn E. *The Cold War Begins, Soviet-American Conflict over Eastern Europe* (1974).

Dobbs, Charles M. *The Unwanted Symbol: American Foreign Policy, the Cold War, and Korea, 1945–1950* (1981).

Eglin, James Meikle. *Air Defense in the Nuclear Age: The Post-War Development of American and Soviet Strategic Defense Systems* (1988).

Etzold, Thomas H. *Defense or Delusion?: America's Military in the 1980s* (1982).

Gaddis, John Lewis. *Strategies of Containment: A Critical Appraisal of Postwar American Security Policy* (1982).

Gardner, Lloyd C. *Architects of Illusion: Men and Ideas in American Foreign Policy, 1941–1949* (1970).

Halle, Louis J. *The Cold War as History* (1967).

Haynes, Richard F. *The Awesome Power: Harry S. Truman as Commander in Chief* (1973).

Herkin, Gregg. *The Winning Weapon: The Atomic Bomb in the Cold War, 1945–1950* (1980).

Hewes, James E., Jr. *From Root to McNamara: Army Organization and Administration, 1900–1963* (1975).

Kimball, John C. *Europe and North America: An Atlas-Almanac of Allies and Adversaries* (1986).

Kissinger, Henry. *Nuclear Weapons and Foreign Policy* (1957).

Kuniholm, Bruce Robellet. *The Origins of the Cold War in the Near East: Great Power Conflict and Diplomacy in Iran, Turkey, and Greece* (1980).

LaFeber, Walter. *America, Russia, and the Cold War, 1945–1980,* 4th ed. (1980).

Linenthal, Edward Tabor. *Symbolic Defense: The Cultural Significance of the Strategic Defense Initiative* (1989).

Lukacs, John. *A New History of the Cold War,* 3rd ed. (1966).

———. *1945, Year Zero* (1978).

Luttwak, Edward. *The Pentagon and the Art of War: The Question of Military Reform* (1984).

Nincic, Miroslav. *Anatomy of Hostility: The U.S.-Soviet Rivalry in Perspective* (1989).

Russett, Bruce M., and Alfred Stepan, eds. *Military Force and American Society* (1973).

Teller, Edward. *Better a Shield Than a Sword: Perspectives on Defense and Technology* (1987).

Treverton, Gregory F. *The Dollar Drain and American Forces in Germany: Managing the Political Economics of Alliance* (1978).

Wittner, Lawrence S. *Cold War America: From Hiroshima to Watergate* (1975).

———. *American Intervention in Greece, 1943–1949* (1982).

Yergin, Daniel. *Shattered Peace: The Origins of the Cold War and the National Security State* (1977).

York, Herbert. *Making Weapons, Talking Peace: A Physicist's Odyssey from Hiroshima to Geneva* (1987).

— DONALD J. MROZEK

The Korean War

On Sunday morning, 25 June 1950, the Communist government of North Korea launched its army in a full-scale offensive against the Republic of Korea to the south. In one sense the invasion marked the beginning of a civil war between segments of a strongly nationalistic people whose country had been divided politically, economically, and geographically in the aftermath of World War II. U.S. officials, however, saw the attack as an eruption in the cold war, the larger sequel to World War II in which, short of open warfare, the United States led efforts to contain attempts by the Soviet Union to extend the reach of its power and Communist ideology. In this view the North Korean attack was a Soviet move, through a puppet state, to bring all of Korea under Communist control. Out of this perception the United States immediately took steps against the venture. Set in motion by the North Korean invasion and the U.S. reaction to it was a multinational war lasting three years.

KOREA AND THE COLD WAR

To much of the world Korea was an unknown place at the time of the North Korean attack. The land had received some notice when the Allied victory over Japan in World War II freed Korea from forty years of Japanese rule. After U.S. and Soviet occupation forces entered the land, most people outside Asia gave scant heed to subsequent events in Korea and, consequently, knew little of the circumstances that set the stage for the North Korean invasion.

Shaped somewhat like the state of Florida, Korea is a peninsula measuring two hundred miles at its widest and reaching some six hundred miles southeastward from the central Asian mainland. Out of a mass of high, jumbled ridges in the far north, the main Taebaek Mountains run the length of the east coast. From this axial spine spur ranges spread southwestward across most of the peninsula. Predominant among these spurs is the Sobaek range in southern Korea, which stands between the drainage basins of the Han River in the north and the Naktong River in the south. The few existing lowlands, dotted by hills and surrounded by mountains, lie mainly along the west coast.

In the north, Korea borders on Manchuria and, for a few miles in the far northeast, on the Soviet Union. To the west the Yellow Sea separates Korea from north-central China. To the east the Sea of Japan stands between the peninsula and the islands of Japan. Less than one hundred fifty miles off the southeastern tip of Korea across the Korea and Tsushima straits lies Kyushu, Japan's southernmost main island.

For China and Russia,

Korea was a dagger pointed at Japan.

So located, Korea represented a strategic crossroads to its three stronger neighbors. For China and Russia, it was a dagger pointed at Japan; for Japan, it was a stepping stone to the Asian mainland. Rivalry over control of Korea among these nations ended at the turn of the twentieth century with Japan the victor, first in the Sino-Japanese War (1894–1895), then in the Russo-Japanese War (1904–1905). Japan initially handled Korea as a protectorate, then, in 1910, formally annexed the land as a colony in the Japanese empire. In the course of developing Allied strategy during World War II, President Franklin D. Roosevelt, Great Britain's Prime Minister Winston S. Churchill, and China's Generalissimo Chiang Kai-shek agreed during the Cairo Conference in November 1943 that Japan was to be stripped of all territories it had seized "by violence and greed." Addressing Korea specifically, they declared that "in due course Korea shall become free and independent." Following the surrender of Germany on 8 May 1945, Allied leaders reaffirmed the Declaration of Cairo as they set out terms for the surrender of Japan during the Potsdam Conference in July 1945. The Soviet Union subscribed to the declaration when it entered the war against Japan on 9 August 1945.

At the time of the Potsdam meeting, Allied planning for operations in the Far East rested on estimates that Japan could be defeated in about one year. The end came much sooner. On 6 August 1945, the United States dropped the world's first atomic bomb on the Japanese city of Hiroshima, and three days later—the same day that Soviet forces opened attacks on Japanese troops in Manchuria—delivered a second atomic bomb on the city of Nagasaki. The Japanese sued for peace on 10 August and accepted the Potsdam surrender terms four days later. As planned by U.S. officials, Korea was divided into two occupation zones delineated by the thirty-eighth parallel of north latitude crossing the peninsula at its waist. Soviet troops were to take the Japanese surrender north of the parallel, U.S. forces to the south. Soviet Premier Joseph V. Stalin accepted this plan on 16 August, by which date the Soviet Twenty-fifth Army, commanded by Colonel General Ivan Chistyakov, already had entered northern Korea. By the end of August, the Soviets interned Japanese military forces and members of the colonial government located in their zone and began transferring many of the captives to labor camps in the Soviet Union.

General Douglas MacArthur was charged by U.S. authorities to handle the occupation of southern Korea as well as all of Japan. He designated the U.S. Army Twenty–fourth Corps, commanded by Lieutenant General John R. Hodge, to accept the Japanese surrender below the thirty-eighth parallel. As commander of U.S. Army forces in Korea, General Hodge led his corps, consisting of the Sixth, Seventh, and Fortieth infantry divisions, into Korea on 8 September. On the following day, he received the surrender of Japanese troops and governmental officials in a ceremony at Seoul, Korea's capital city in the west-central area of the peninsula.

Upon the arrival of Soviet and U.S. forces, the Korean people clamored for full and immediate independence. One group, a Communist-dominated coalition of "people's committees" calling itself the People's Republic, declared itself to be the government of all of Korea. In southern Korea alone, some seventy political and social organizations sprang up, each claiming to be qualified to form a government, but none of these factions possessed a solid constituency or candidates of proven ability and experience. This inadequacy had

Much fighting during the Korean War occurred in and around the South Korean city Seoul. This U.S. marine plants a flag on the roof of the American consulate in Seoul in September 1950 while fighting rages around the compound. (National Archives)

been anticipated in the Declaration of Cairo, which legislated an independent Korea "in due course." First to be achieved under Allied guidance, at least in the U.S. view, was the regeneration of indigenous leadership, so completely denied by the Japanese, and the redirection and rehabilitation of the Korean economy, which had been geared to serve Japanese requirements and was now in chaos.

According to U.S. officials, the achievement of these goals would be a relatively short-term process. First, Japanese troops in all of Korea would be disarmed and repatriated to Japan, along with Japanese officials and civilians residing in the country. Next there would be a gradual transfer of governmental functions to Korean officials. Last, U.S. and Soviet forces would withdraw after the Korean people established a united and independent government of their own choosing.

In line with this view, General Hodge spread his divisions throughout southern Korea to disarm and evacuate the Japanese and to maintain order. On 12 September he established the United States Army Military Government in Korea with Major General Archibald V. Arnold, the commander of the Seventh Division, as military governor. General Arnold drew an immediate storm of protest from the Korean people when he retained experienced Japanese in key positions, including zonal police, to bridge the eventual transfer of functions to Korean officials. To the Koreans, retaining the hated Japanese in authority, even temporarily, was unthinkable. Arnold quickly corrected the matter. At top government levels, he replaced the Japanese with U.S. officers, assigning Koreans to them as advisers and apprentices. He also established, under U.S. supervision, the all-Korean Police Bureau. Over time places were nominally reversed. Koreans occupied the positions of authority and Americans assumed the roles of advisers, but the latter continued to exercise decisive influence on government activities.

Late in 1945, U.S. military government officials proposed to establish a South Korean army, navy, and air force, but Washington authorities disapproved any development of full-fledged defense forces lest doing so jeopardize forthcoming negotiations with the Soviet Union on the organization of a provisional government for the whole of Korea. The most allowed was the formation of a constabulary as a police reserve to assist in maintaining internal order, for which there was distinct need, and a coast guard to suppress the smuggling and piracy then prevalent in the coastal waters. Both forces took shape slowly. By December 1946 the constabulary numbered scarcely more than five thousand men, armed with Japanese rifles, a few Japanese machine guns, and a small amount of ammunition for each. Development of the coast guard was handicapped by a paucity of experienced Korean seamen and a shortage of ships.

The Soviets established no military government in northern Korea. Initially, they governed through the people's committees that had sprung up. They also brought back large numbers of Korean expatriates who had long resided in the Soviet Union. Under the guidance of a special political detachment from the headquarters of the Soviet army's First Far Eastern Front, the expatriates enlarged and took control of the people's committees. In October 1945, the Soviets placed expatriate Kim Il Sung in control of all Korean Communists, creating the North Korean Labor Party. Four months later, Kim was established as head of a central government called the Interim People's Committee, which was seated in the city of Pyongyang, 120 miles north of Seoul. Thus, behind a facade of native government, the Soviets, in rather short order, communized all of northern Korea.

Behind a facade of native government,

the Soviets, in rather short order,

communized all of northern Korea.

As had the Americans in the south, the Soviets formed native zonal police. They also organized two groups of military forces, the Border Constabulary and the Peace Preservation Army, drawing their core personnel from experienced Koreans brought back from the Soviet Union and reinforcing these with returning Koreans who had fought the Japanese in China during World War II. Most of the constabulary units eventually took position along the thirty-eighth parallel. The army, which reached a strength of twenty thousand by the end of 1946, trained for combat.

Meanwhile, General Hodge failed in his attempt to negotiate a unification of the economy and a central Korean administration with his counterpart in the north. General Chistyakov restricted movement into and out of northern Korea, limited telephone communications between zones, withdrew a Soviet liaison detachment established earlier in Seoul, and in mid-October 1945 notified Hodge that there would be no negotiations between them until decisions were made and relations established at the top political level. Following his only recourse, Hodge channeled a request to Washington for government action on the matter.

During the Potsdam Conference in July 1945, the Allied leaders had established a council of foreign ministers to guide the progress of postwar settlements, and to develop peace treaties with Italy, Germany, and the latter's European satellites. This process became one of lengthy debate and disagreement, especially between the United States and the Soviet Union. U.S. Secretary of State James F. Byrnes had more success, introducing the question of Korea's unification and eventual independence at a Moscow meeting of the council in December 1945. The ministers agreed that the U.S. and Soviet commands in Korea should establish a joint commission that, in consultation with Korean political and social organizations, would make recommendations for establishing a provisional government for all of Korea. These recommendations were to be submitted for consideration by the governments of the United States, Soviet Union, United Kingdom, and China in the joint development of a trusteeship under which these four powers would guide the provisional government for a maximum of five years.

The prospect of continued foreign control through trusteeship angered almost all Koreans, and most Korean organizations vehemently opposed the measure. Among the major groups only the Communists openly supported the plan. In meetings of the joint commission between January and May 1946, the Soviets insisted that the commission deal exclusively with the Koreans favoring trusteeship. The United States refused because doing so would pave the way for a provisional government dominated by Communists. Persistent Soviet demands to the same end met equally persistent American refusals when the commission reconvened in the spring and summer of 1947. Seeing no possibility that the joint commission could produce a satisfactory government for Korea, the United States submitted the matter to the United Nations for resolution. Addressing the body on 17 September 1947, Secretary of State George C. Marshall stated: "We do not wish to have the inability of two powers to reach agreement delay any further the urgent and rightful claim of the Korean people to independence."

More than the welfare of the Korean people lay behind U.S. efforts to prevent further delay in settling the issue. To begin with, Korea held a minor place among U.S. postwar foreign concerns. In addition to the occupation of Japan, U.S. concerns in Asia focused on China. Stimulated in large part by an abiding commercial and paternal interest developed over decades of trade and missionary work with the Chinese, the United States fostered the establishment of a peaceful, unified China that would help stabilize eastern Asia. Complicating the American effort was the long-standing civil war between the recognized Nationalist Government under Chiang Kai-shek and the Communists under Mao Tse-tung.

Begun in the late 1920s, then largely interrupted when the rival armies turned to fight invading Japanese forces in 1937, the civil war in China resumed soon after Japan's defeat in what amounted to a race for possession of territory that had been occupied by the Japanese. The United States favored and supported Chiang in this contest for control, providing his forces with military supplies and air and sea transportation. In addition, more than fifty thousand U.S. marines were placed in ports and other areas to prevent Mao's forces from occupying them.

At the same time, American diplomats attempted to end the civil war and unify China by promoting the development of a coalition government in which Chiang and his Kuomintang party, then in sole authority, would be dominant, but in which Mao's Communists and other, lesser political elements would have an effective voice. The Soviet Union, whose forces had occupied Manchuria in August 1945, agreed to support the unification of China under Chiang's leadership along the lines proposed by the United States. By late 1947, however, the U.S. diplomatic effort had failed and been discontinued. The civil war by that time centered in Manchuria, where, contrary to their vow to support Chiang, the Soviets had allowed Mao to establish a base of operations.

After confiscating most of Manchuria's well-developed industrial plant as war booty and shipping thousands of Japanese prisoners to Siberia as slave laborers, the Soviet occupation force had withdrawn from the region in the spring of 1946, leaving at Mao's disposal large stockpiles of Japanese military equipment and supplies. The United States continued to provide Chiang with military advisers, matériel, and money, but the outcome of the civil war was now in doubt. There appeared to be no way of ensuring a victory for Chiang short of committing U.S. troops in the conflict, an involvement far greater than could be justified by U.S. interest in China.

In any case, a steep and continuing decline in U.S. military strength precluded large troop commitments anywhere. Immediately after World War II, pressure from an articulate public, Congress, and the troops themselves to "bring the boys home" had led to a rapid, disorderly demobilization. By mid-1947 the strength of the U.S. armed forces dropped from a wartime peak of more than 12 million to just over 1.5 million. At the same time, President Harry S. Truman, out of determination to balance the federal budget and reduce the national debt, had sharply lowered military appropriations.

THE KOREAN WAR 1950-1953
USSR
MANCHURIA
CHINA
Chongjin
Yalu
River
UN COMMAND FRONT
25 NOVEMBER 1950
Kanggye
NORTH KOREA
Changjin Reservoir
Iwon
Chongchon River
Hungnam
SEA OF JAPAN
PYONGYANG
Yongdok
Wonsan
IRON TRIANGLE
ARMISTICE LINE
27 JULY 1953
Pyonggang
Imjin R
Kumhwa
Chorwon
Yangyang
38TH PARALLEL
ONGJIN PENINSULA
Kaesong
Panmunjom
Chunchon
Kimpo Airfield
Inchon
SEOUL
Suwon
Osan
Han River
TAEBAEK MTS.
SOUTH KOREA
SOBAEK MTS.
YELLOW SEA
Kum River
Taejon
Yondok
Taegu
Naktong River
PUSAN PERIMETER
15 SEPTEMBER 1950
CHIRI MTS.
Masan
Pusan
KOJE-DO ISLAND
KOREA STRAIT
TSUSHIMA
TSUSHIMA STRAIT
KYUSHU
JAPAN
MILES
5 10 20 30 40 50

The sharp manpower losses brought on by the hasty demobilization and budgetary restrictions prompted a close scrutiny of U.S. commitments overseas. By late 1947, U.S. authorities had begun to remove the marines stationed in China and intended to complete their withdrawal in 1948. As for Korea, because the United States had no interest in maintaining bases there, the forty-five thousand ground troops on the peninsula could well be used elsewhere. Until a Korean government had been established, however, these troops could not be withdrawn, a condition that further inspired U.S. action in the United Nations.

On 14 November 1947, over Soviet objections, the United Nations General Assembly established a commission to supervise the election of a legislative body for all of Korea, whose members were then to form a government. The commission consisted of representatives from Australia, Canada, China, El Salvador, France, India, the Philippines, and Syria. The Ukranian Soviet Socialist Republic was asked to furnish a member, but refused to do so. Soviet authorities responded by declaring the UN project illegal, and when the commission reached Korea in January 1948, blocked its entry into northern Korea. The commission proceeded to arrange an election in the southern zone. While arrangements for the election went forward, authorities in Washington established the basis for U.S. relations with the prospective regime. All occupation forces were to leave Korea by the end of 1948. During that time General Hodge was to enlarge the South Korean constabulary to fifty thousand, equip it with U.S. gear, and train it for border defense and internal security. After the troop withdrawal, the United States would provide both economic and military aid to the new nation and establish a diplomatic mission. Above all, as set out in a formal policy statement prepared by the National Security Council and approved by President Truman in April 1948, the United States was not to become "so irrevocably involved in the Korean situation that an action taken by any faction in Korea or by any other power in Korea could be considered a *casus belli* for the United States." The continuing low state of the military forces and increased tensions in Europe served to deepen U.S. resolve to avoid commitment in Korea or indeed anywhere on the Asian mainland.

In southern Korea the election was set to take place on 10 May 1948. Few South Koreans relished the prospect of a government whose authority reached only to the thirty-eighth parallel, and many political factions urged a boycott of the election. Pressing hardest for a boycott were the Communists, now organized as the South Korean Labor Party and affiliated with the labor party in the north. Despite the resulting propaganda, demonstrations, riots, and raids on voting places, the election established a national assembly of two hundred representatives for the twenty million people living in the south. One hundred seats were left vacant for representatives of the nine million people in the north, but appeals to the northerners to elect representatives and join in establishing a government proved fruitless. In July the assembly developed a constitution and elected as president Syngman Rhee, the assembly chairman and longtime champion of Korean independence. With the inauguration of Rhee, the government of the Republic of Korea (ROK) was established on 15 August 1948.

By the autumn of 1948, the thirty-eighth parallel represented a confirmed border between two hostile governments.

The Soviets reacted by creating a Communist government in the north. On 25 August northern Korea elected the Supreme People's Council from candidates chosen by the Interim People's Committee. On 9 September 1948, the council proclaimed the establishment of the Democratic People's Republic of Korea, with Kim Il Sung as premier. Thus, by the autumn of 1948, the thirty-eighth parallel represented a confirmed border between two hostile governments. Both claimed jurisdiction over all of Korea, and their leaders, Kim and Rhee, each vowed to reunite the land under his authority.

By the end of 1948, the Soviets withdrew all their troops from North Korea except for military advisers, who remained with the North Korean armed forces. Under Soviet supervision the Border Constabulary and, as it was now called, the North Korean People's Army (NKPA) grew substantially in the following year. Thousands of conscripts were gathered at training centers, Koreans who had served with Chinese Communist forces were brought home and inducted, and increasing numbers of men were sent to the Soviet Union for training in tank warfare and as pilots and aircraft mechanics. Tanks, heavy artillery, and aircraft began to arrive from the Soviet Union.

In South Korea the U.S. military government ended, and Special Representative John J. Muccio arrived on 26 August to establish a diplomatic mission. Under plans calling for the departure of all U.S. troops from Korea by the end of 1948, the first troops left in September. U.S. advisers meanwhile continued to train the South Korean constabulary and coast guard. As U.S.

forces began to withdraw, some constabulary units took station along the thirty-eighth parallel, where a third of each unit occupied strongpoints opposite North Korean border troops while the remainder engaged in training well away from the parallel. Other constabulary units trained in areas farther south and worked with the national police in maintaining internal security.

As the withdrawal continued, Rhee appealed to President Truman for the retention of a U.S. force in Korea. Fearful of a North Korean invasion, shaken by recent rebellions incited by Communist groups within two regiments of the constabulary, and disturbed by increasing disorder and guerrilla raids in much of the countryside, Rhee wanted U.S. troops to remain until his own forces had grown stronger. The most serious internal threat came from the South Korean Labor Party, which, although driven underground after its attempt to prevent the May election, remained a functioning organization firmly allied with the Communist regime in the north. With a membership exceeding 100,000, the party maintained cells in all provinces; in most counties, cities, and large towns; and in some constabulary units. The party organization also included about five thousand armed guerrillas, a force that was growing as those trained at a special school in North Korea worked their way south through the Taebaek Mountains. Almost all the guerrillas were concentrated in three mountain areas, some in the Taebaeks along the east coast, others in the Sobaeks near the center of South Korea, most in the Chiri Mountains in the southwest. Their raids were launched mainly against farms, villages, and police installations in and around their mountain bases and were designed to create doubt among the people that the Rhee government could protect them. Outside the guerrilla areas, party members provoked riots and strikes, committed widespread robbery and arson, and disrupted commercial communications. Emulating the Communist line being broadcast from North Korea, party propaganda blamed the government for all the troubles besetting the people, promised the redress of grievances, and called for a peninsula-wide election of a new legislature.

In response to the appeal from President Rhee, U.S. authorities kept troops in Korea beyond the planned withdrawal date. After a full review, however, and some modification of policy toward the new republic, all the forces were removed by the end of June 1949. By then General Douglas MacArthur, commander in chief of the Far East Command, was relieved of all responsibilities in Korea except for providing supplies to the military advisers and for evacuating U.S. personnel in an emergency. Designated as the United States Military Advisory Group to the Republic of Korea (KMAG), the advisers became part of the military section of the U.S. diplomatic mission, now raised to embassy level under Ambassador Muccio. The role of the advisers was to assist in developing a considerably larger constabulary and coast guard—since renamed the army and navy by the ROK government—and a small air force. Still, the air group was to receive no combat aircraft, the navy no ships of the line, and the army no tanks, heavy artillery, or other heavy equipment. As had been decided in 1948, the ROK military establishment was to be designed only for maintaining internal order and border security. The United States would supply matériel to sustain the enlarged forces and further economic aid to promote national stability, but it remained the U.S. goal to minimize involvement in Korea.

Because of further budget cuts, the withdrawal of troops from Korea scarcely improved the posture of U.S. armed forces. The ceiling placed on military expenditures for the fiscal year beginning 1 July 1949 not only would erase manpower increases allowed in 1948 but would compel further reductions in the army and navy. In effect, the continuing budgetary limitations largely restricted the defense of the United States and any NATO commitment to air power and the atomic bomb. For any circumstance in which use of the bomb would be excessive or otherwise inappropriate, military resources were decidedly limited.

During the last half of 1949, two events jarred U.S. leaders into new lines of action. The first was the explosion of an atomic bomb over Siberia by the Soviet Union. The loss of the atomic monopoly drew recommendations from Truman's advisers for a major expansion of conventional military power. Defense Department planners began to translate the recommendations into forces and costs, but whether President Truman would raise military appropriations to allow expansion remained in question, still unanswered by the time of North Korea's breach of the thirty-eighth parallel in June 1950. The second event was a Communist victory in China. With most of the Chinese mainland in his grasp by 1 October, Mao Tse-tung proclaimed establishment of the People's Republic. As Chiang Kai-shek, the Nationalist Government, and remnants of Chiang's armed forces withdrew offshore to Taiwan (Formosa) by the end of the year, Mao also claimed sovereignty over the island and vowed to capture it. At that point the United States applied its policy of containment to Asia. In January 1950, Secretary of State Dean G. Acheson announced that the United States would defend by force a line running south from the Aleutian Islands through Japan and the Ryukyu Islands to the Philippines. Both Taiwan and South Korea lay outside this perimeter. Amid harsh protests from the China Lobby, an American group of Chiang supporters and anti-Communists in and out of government, President Truman declared that U.S. armed forces would not help defend Taiwan and that Chiang would receive no more military supplies. South Korea, on the other hand, would continue to receive both economic and military aid. Otherwise, as Secretary Acheson stated with respect to areas outside the U.S. defense perimeter, "should an attack occur . . . initial reliance must be on the people attacked to resist it and then upon the commitments of the entire civilized world under the Charter of the United Nations."

From the time of Secretary Acheson's announcement until the invasion five months later, South Korea's ability to resist an attack from the north was a question given mixed answers by U.S. officials in Seoul, Tokyo, and Washington. In June they placed the strength of the NKPA near sixty-six thousand men, which made up, at most, six infantry divisions and an armored brigade equipped with sixty-five tanks. The north's border constabulary was rated as essentially a paramilitary police force and its navy as an insignificant collection of torpedo boats and patrol craft. Its air force, however, they considered a worthy group of one hundred fighters and seventy attack bombers. In judging the south's ability to withstand an attack, their main concern was the north's possession of tanks, combat aircraft, and medium and heavy artillery, while the South Koreans had no similar equipment.

The South Korean army (ROKA) totaled ninety-five thousand men in eight divisions, only half of which were at full strength, and six battalions of light artillery. Four divisions and a regiment stood along the thirty-eighth parallel. Remaining forces, some in the Seoul area but most farther south operating against guerrillas, constituted a reserve for counterattacks or reinforcement under long-established plans for defending the border. Despite the north's edge in armor, artillery, and air support, KMAG officials believed that the ROKA was otherwise superior and therefore could repel any invasion. Central Intelligence Agency analysts predicted that the NKPA superiority in tanks, artillery, and aircraft gave its armed forces the capability of attaining limited objectives, including the capture of Seoul, but doubted that they could overrun all of South Korea. Ambassador Muccio, on the other hand, stated flatly on 6 June, that the NKPA tanks, artillery, and planes would provide its forces with the margin of victory in any full-scale invasion of the republic.

Whatever their opinions on the relative military strength of North Korea, U.S. diplomatic and intelligence officials repeatedly reported during the first half of 1950 that South Korea was not in imminent danger of invasion. They forecast a continuance of the northern regime's efforts to undermine the Rhee government through propaganda, political pressure, and guerrilla raids, which had intensified after the last U.S. troops withdrew in mid-1949. North Korean border troops launched hundreds of forays into ROK territory. South Korean forces at the parallel held their ground, and even responded in kind, but the border clashes nevertheless further strained the southern republic. U.S. authorities concluded that the North Koreans saw promise of unifying Korea under their control by such efforts and thus would continue that course rather than resort to open warfare.

Although taken by surprise, the South Korean border garrisons fought stout delaying actions and brought the North Koreans to a full halt in two areas.

The U.S. estimates of North Korea's armed strength were close to the mark for its navy and air force but not for its ground strength. A concerted buildup during the first months of 1950 increased the NKPA by June to eight infantry divisions with full complements of light, medium, and heavy artillery; two divisions at half strength; an armored brigade with 120 Russian T-34 medium tanks; a separate armored regiment with thirty tanks; a separate infantry regiment; and a regiment of reconnaissance troops mounted on motorcycles. Also ready for field operations were the staffs and support elements of the Army Front Headquarters and two corps. These forces numbered almost 117,000 and, together with five infantry-trained constabulary brigades, placed the total North Korean ground strength at more than 135,000. Except for the South Korean navy, which equaled its northern counterpart, ROK armed forces were clearly outmatched in both numbers and guns.

The U.S. prediction of North Korean intentions was also wrong. On 15 June the North Korean high command had begun moving forces toward the thirty-eighth parallel, and by the evening of 24 June more than ninety thousand troops were deployed along their lines of departure for attack. Remarkably, their deployment was neither seen nor sensed from the south, providing the NKPA assault forces the added advantage of surprise when they struck the next morning.

INVASION

In deploying the invasion force, General Chai Ung Jun, commander in chief of the NKPA, distributed two corps across the breadth of the peninsula. In the west, the First Corps, with the First, Third, Fourth, and Sixth divisions and the 105th Armored Brigade was to clear the isolated Ongjin Peninsula on the far west coast and, in its main effort, converge on Seoul. The Second Corps was to launch secondary attacks in the center of the peninsula and along the east coast. In the central zone the Second and Seventh divisions with a regiment of tanks were to strike toward the towns of Chunchon and Hongchon. On the east coast the Fifth Division, 766th Independent Infantry Regiment, Twelfth Motorcycle Regiment, and a band of one thousand guerrillas were to combine an overland attack with amphibious landings well south of the thirty-eighth parallel. In every zone of attack, axial roads led to Pusan, South Korea's principal port at the southeastern tip of the peninsula, whose seizure was the final North Korean objective.

Behind early morning artillery and mortar barrages on 25 June, NKPA forces scored gains everywhere in their initial attacks. In support of the First Corps, North Korean fighter planes sporadically strafed Seoul and the nearby airfield at Kimpo. Although taken by surprise, the South Korean border garrisons fought stout delaying actions and brought the North Koreans to a full halt in two areas, along the Imjin River northwest of Seoul and at Chunchon. Major General Chae Byong Dok, the ROKA chief of staff, began moving the bulk of his reserve divisions north to reinforce the defense of

U.S. Marines take cover behind a tank while it fires on North Korean tanks ahead on 22 May 1951 in hills near the town of Hongchon. (National Archives)

Seoul. Of these divisions, the Second was to join the Seventh in counterattacks on the morning of the 26th against the greatest threat to the capital. Positioned due north of the city, this threat was posed by the North Korean Third and Fourth divisions and the bulk of the 105th Armored Brigade.

The Seventh Division launched its counterattack, but the Second arrived too late and the attempt failed. By evening of the 26th the North Koreans advanced within twenty miles of Seoul against what became increasingly uncoordinated defensive efforts by units of the South Korean Capital, Second, Third, Fifth, and Seventh divisions. Elsewhere, the Seventeenth Regiment of the Capital Division, after losing its forwardmost battalion on the Onjin Peninsula, had withdrawn by sea to the port of Inchon west of Seoul to assist in defending the capital area. On the east coast the Eighth Division had fallen back twenty miles and was preparing to withdraw inland to escape being trapped between the North Koreans advancing from the north and those that had come in by sea to the south. Northwest of Seoul the First Division maintained positions along the Imjin River but was in danger of being outflanked by the North Koreans driving on the capital from the north. In the central sector the Sixth Division still held Chunchon but the NKPA Second Corps commander was reinforcing his attack to take the town. South Korean ammunition stores were dwindling fast, although a resupply requested of General MacArthur by KMAG officials on the 25th, was en route by sea from Japan. Even so, with almost all South Korean forces now committed, it was becoming clear that they could do no more than slow the North Koreans.

As this picture developed, Ambassador Muccio ordered all dependents of U.S. government and military officials out of Korea. By 29 June about two thousand people were safely evacuated by sea and air to Japan, including other Americans, foreign nationals, and some KMAG officials.

INTERVENTION

The first reports from Seoul to Washington of multiple border attacks came from a United Press International representative; next the military attaché at the U.S. embassy, which also alerted General MacArthur's headquarters; and a cable from Ambassador Muccio, which stated that the North Korean attacks constituted "an all-out offensive against the Republic of Korea." Secretary of State Acheson immediately notified President Truman at his home in Independence, Missouri, and, with the president's approval, arranged a meeting of the United Nations Security Council to consider the North Korean aggression as a threat to world peace. The council immediately passed a resolution proposed by the U.S. representative, which demanded an immediate cessation of hostilities and a withdrawal of all North Korean forces to the thirty-eighth parallel. The resolution also called on all UN members "to render every assistance to the United Nations in the execution of this resolution." The swift action of the council was facilitated by the absence of the Soviet delegate, who had boycotted meetings since January 1950, when the council refused to replace the Chinese Nationalist representative with a Communist. Shortly after passage of the resolution, Acheson cabled Moscow, requesting that Soviet officials use their influence to persuade North Korean authorities to withdraw their forces. The Soviets replied that their government "adheres to the principle of the impermissibility of interference by foreign powers in the internal affairs of Korea."

That same evening, President Truman directed General MacArthur to continue supplying South Korean forces and determine how best to assist them further. The president also ordered the Seventh Fleet from Philippine and Ryukyu waters to Japan. The next day, in a broad interpretation of the UN request for support of the Security Council's resolution, Truman placed MacArthur in charge of all U.S. military activities in Korea and authorized him to use the planes and ships of his Far East air and naval forces against North Korean targets south of the thirty-eighth parallel. He also redirected part of the Seventh Fleet to Taiwan, where, by controlling the waters between the Chinese Communists on the mainland and the Nationalists on the island, naval air and surface forces could discourage either one from attacking the other and so prevent a widening of hostilities.

The U.S. commitment of forces reversed the earlier policy against fighting in Korea, but President Truman, convinced that the North Korean attack was an eruption in the cold war rather than an extension of a local dispute, concluded that the United States had to contest the invasion lest inaction invite armed aggression elsewhere.

North Korean authorities ignored the UN call for withdrawal. Attacking on all fronts on 27 June, General Chai's forces gained ground everywhere except at Chunchon. As the main force neared Seoul, which it reached at midnight, members of the ROK government, army headquarters, KMAG, and embassies left the capital, accompanied and followed by crowds of citizens and soldiers streaming over three railroad bridges and a highway bridge spanning the Han River at the south edge of the city. Previously prepared for demolition as the final feature of withdrawal should Seoul have to be surrendered, the bridges were ordered blown up by a panicky South Korean official long before the bulk of the city's defenders were pushed out of position at the northern outskirts. As the North Koreans drove through the city on the 28th, retreating South Korean troops, in growing disarray, abandoned nearly all their trucks, supplies, and heavy weapons and swam the Han or crossed on boats and rafts.

While the North Koreans regrouped after capturing Seoul, South Korean commanders struggled to reassemble forces in defenses at Inchon, the Kimpo airfield, and along the Han directly below and east of the capital. Further east, the Sixth Division lost Chunchon on the 28th, but withdrew in good order to positions fifteen miles south. The Eighth Division moved inland from the east coast to come alongside the Sixth, while a regiment of the Third Division took over defense of the coastal road. The ROKA estimated that it had so far lost almost half its men and more than half its weapons and equipment.

On 27 June the UN Security Council asked all UN members to provide military assistance to help South Korea repel the invasion. President Truman's first response was to extend U.S. air and naval attacks into North Korea and to allow ground troops to protect and operate the port of Pusan. After observing the ROKA weak defenses along the Han River, General MacArthur recommended that a U.S. infantry regiment be deployed in the Seoul area at once and that this force be enlarged to two divisions. Truman's reply on 30 June allowed MacArthur to commit all ground units available to him.

Infantry units in the Far East Command included the First Cavalry; Seventh, Twenty-fourth, and Twenty-fifth divisions under Lieutenant General Walton H. Walker's Eighth Army in Japan; and the Twenty-ninth Regimental Combat Team on Okinawa in the Ryukyus. The post–World War II reductions had affected all of them; each regiment except one had only two of the normal three battalions, most artillery battalions had just two of the normal three firing batteries, organic armor was generally lacking, and weapons and equipment on hand were largely worn leftovers from World War II. Nevertheless, MacArthur believed that two of his divisions, strengthened from other units at hand, could halt the North Koreans.

SOUTH TO THE NAKTONG

MacArthur would have no opportunity to deploy forces in the Seoul area because by the time he received approval to commit ground units, the main NKPA force had moved over the Han River. Crossing west of Seoul, the Sixth Division captured Kimpo Airfield and Inchon, while the Third and Fourth divisions crossed directly below the capital into its suburb, Yongdungpo. Pausing while engineers repaired a railroad bridge so that tanks could join the attack, the Fourth Division then pressed forward astride the main road and rail line that followed a gentle southeastward course all the way to Pusan. The division reached Suwon, twenty miles south of Seoul, on 4 July. With the secondary attacks at the center of the peninsula and down the east coast keeping pace, North Korean forces had now advanced some fifty miles into South Korea.

MacArthur still expected to stop the North Koreans with two divisions and, once done, intended to defeat them by sea-landing a third division behind them in concert with a counterattack from the south. In opening operations, however, the speed of the North Korean drive compelled him to trade space for time. His first order went to Major General William F. Dean's Twenty-fourth Division encamped in southwestern Japan nearest to Korea. Dean's division was to fight a delaying action against the main North Korean attack while MacArthur strengthened and shipped the Twenty-fifth Division to complete the blocking force and prepare the First Cavalry Division for the amphibious landing. General Dean was to begin with an "arrogant display of strength," as MacArthur called it, by airlifting an infantry task force to the peninsula and deploying it as far north as possible. As task force members expressed it, the North Koreans might "turn around and go back when they found out who they were fighting."

Forces and facilities eventually assembled within the unified command came from twenty UN members and one nonmember nation (Italy).

When finally organized, Task Force Smith, named after its commander, Lieutenant Colonel Charles B. Smith, included two rifle companies and supporting units of the Twenty-first Infantry, plus a five-piece battery of the Fifty-second Field Artillery Battalion. The 540-man force took position near Osan, ten miles south of Suwon, before dawn on 5 July. Coming out of Suwon in a heavy rain, the North Korean Fourth Division attacked the Americans around 8:30 A.M. In the ensuing battle the North Koreans lost four tanks, forty-two men killed, and eighty-five wounded. The U.S. force suffered larger losses. It lacked antitank mines, its recoilless rifles and 2.36-inch rocket launchers could not penetrate the armor of the T-34s, and its artillery had only a few rounds of antitank ammunition that did prove effective.

The rain cancelled air support, communications broke down, and, in any case, the task force was too small to prevent North Korean infantry from flowing around its flanks. By midafternoon Task Force Smith was in retreat with more than 150 casualties and the loss of all equipment save small arms.

Although given air support, delaying actions fought by larger forces of the Twenty-fourth Division over the next week had similar results. By 13 July the division was pressed back on Taejon, sixty miles south of Osan, where it took position along the Kum River above the town against the approach of the NKPA Third and Fourth divisions and 105th Armored Brigade. In central Korea, where the North Koreans had added the Fifteen Division to their attack, South Korean forces had backed off slowly. By 13 July they were defending three road corridors through the Sobaek Mountains. With the North Korean advance along the east coast still keeping pace, General Chai's forces now had overrun half of South Korea.

As General Dean's division and ROKA forces fell back, General MacArthur realized that he had far underestimated the NKPA. Putting aside his plan for an amphibious landing, he directed the First Cavalry Division to join the delaying action and requested substantial reinforcement from the United States, mainly in ground troops but also in air strength. His requests far exceeded the numbers and readiness of forces in the

These U.S. troops patrol the mountains 10 miles north of Seoul on 3 January 1951 in an attempt to locate enemy lines and positions. (National Archives)

United States, but by mid-July, Washington officials began a concerted buildup from forces available to strengthen MacArthur's command.

Meanwhile, fifty-three of the fifty-nine UN members signified support of the Security Council's 27 June resolution and twenty-nine made specific offers of assistance. As it became clear that the United States would be the major contributor of forces by far, the Security Council on 7 July asked the United States to form a field command into which all forces would be integrated. The evolving command structure placed President Truman in the role of executive agent for the UN Security Council, although he had no obligation to clear his decisions with that agency. Assisting him were the National Security Council and Joint Chiefs of Staff, which helped develop the strategic concepts of operations in Korea. In the strictly military channel, the joint chiefs issued instructions to the unified command in the field through its army member, General J. Lawton Collins. The unified command, designated the Unified Nations Command, was formally established on 24 July under General MacArthur, who superimposed its headquarters over that of his Far East Command in Tokyo.

Forces and facilities eventually assembled within the unified command came from twenty UN members and one nonmember nation (Italy). The United States, Great Britain, Australia, New Zealand, Canada, Turkey, Greece, France, Belgium, Luxembourg, the Netherlands, Thailand, the Philippines, Colombia, and Ethiopia furnished ground combat troops. The United States, Sweden, Norway, and Italy provided field hospitals and India an ambulance unit. Ground-based air units, including combat and transport formations, came from the United States, Australia, Great Britain, South Africa, Canada, Belgium, Greece, and Thailand. Naval forces, including carrier-based aircraft and hospital ships, arrived from the United States, Great Britain, Australia, New Zealand, Canada, Colombia, France, the Netherlands, Thailand, and Denmark.

As forces arrived in Korea, MacArthur assigned air units to the Far East Air Forces, commanded by Lieutenant General George E. Stratemeyer, who, in turn, placed them with his Fifth Air Force and Combat Cargo Command. With its ninety-nine B-29s, Stratemeyer's Bomber Command remained an entirely American-manned force. Incoming naval units joined Naval Forces, Far East, under Vice Admiral C. Turner Joy. All of them, along with the South Korean navy, eventually became part of a force blockading the Korean coast. General MacArthur assigned all ground units to the Eighth Army, which established headquarters in Korea on 13 July. Shortly after taking command of U.S. ground troops then on the peninsula, General Walker also assumed control of the ROKA at the offer of President Rhee.

As the United Nations Command was taking shape, the Twenty-fifth and First Cavalry divisions, strengthened by forces taken from the Seventh Division, entered Korea between 10 and 22 July. By then the battle for Taejon had opened. New 3.5-inch rocket launchers hurriedly airlifted from the United States proved effective against the T-34 tanks, but the Twenty-fourth Division lost Taejon after the NKPA Third and Fourth divisions established bridgeheads over the Kum River and encircled and then penetrated the town. In running enemy roadblocks during the withdrawal from Taejon, General Dean took a wrong turn and was captured a month later as he attempted to reach U.S. lines through mountains to the south. On 22 July the First Cavalry Division relieved the much-reduced Twenty-fourth Division in positions about twenty miles southeast of Taejon, and the Twenty-fifth Division backed up ROKA forces being steadily pushed back in the Sobaek Mountains passes. General MacArthur had meanwhile ordered two battalions of the Twenty-ninth Infantry from Okinawa to Korea, which reached the peninsula and reinforced the Twenty-fourth Division just as General Walker was obliged to recommit the damaged unit in the face of enlarged North Korean attacks.

In continuing their advance the North Koreans added two divisions, the Thirteenth and Eighth, the latter newly created by expanding a border constabulary brigade. Two divisions of the main force opened an enveloping maneuver, the Fourth moving fifty miles south out of Taejon and then pivoting east through undefended ground, the Sixth marching down the west coast to the tip of the peninsula and then turning east toward Pusan over the south coast road. Walker sent the Twenty-fourth Division back into the line to oppose these threats.

By 24 July, UN air forces had won control of the air, destroying almost all North Korean planes in the process and, with good effect, began concentrating attacks on the advancing North Koreans and their lengthening supply lines. In a single engagement naval warships had decimated the small North Korean navy, blockaded both coasts to prevent any movement of enemy troops or supplies by water, and were delivering punishing gunfire on the North Koreans moving down the east coast. Nevertheless, U.S. and ROKA forces steadily gave way and by 1 August held only a small portion of southeastern Korea.

Pressed by General MacArthur to stop further withdrawals, General Walker ordered a stand along a 150-

mile line running from the south coast town of Chindong-ni, thirty miles west of Pusan, north to a bend above the city of Taegu, then east to the coastal town of Yongdok, ninety miles north of Pusan. By 4 August, Walker placed his three U.S. divisions along the western segment of the line, basing most of their positions behind the Naktong River, and set ROKA forces, recently reorganized into two corps and five divisions, along the northern stretch.

The North Koreans raised additional units by converting constabulary brigades and conscripting large numbers of recruits, many from overrun regions of South Korea. During the six weeks of the Battle of the Pusan Perimeter (6 August–15 September), they committed thirteen infantry divisions, an armored division, and two tank regiments against Walker's line. The additional strength, however, failed to compensate for fifty-eight thousand trained men and the many tanks lost during their advance to the new line. Lieutenant General Kim Chaek, head of the North Korean Army Front Headquarters and now in charge of operations, also failed to mass his forces for a single decisive penetration. Instead, he dissipated his strength by attacking at several points along the Eighth Army line.

General Walker's defense hinged on shuttling his scarce reserves to block a gap, reinforce a position, or counterattack wherever needed. Timing was the key. With air support all along the front and naval gunfire support at the eastern anchor of the line, Walker's responses successfully contained enemy penetrations and inflicted telling losses that steadily drew off North Korean offensive power. His own strength meanwhile was growing. By mid-September he had more than five hundred medium tanks, and troop replacements came in a steady flow. Additional units also arrived, among them the Fifth Regimental Combat Team from Hawaii, the Second Infantry Division and First Provisional Marine Brigade from the United States, and the British Twenty-seventh Infantry Brigade from Hong Kong. As NKPA forces weakened, the Eighth Army acquired the men and means for offensive action.

ENVELOPMENT, BREAKOUT, AND PURSUIT

Meanwhile, General MacArthur returned to his concept of an amphibious landing behind the North Koreans combined with an overland attack from the south. He favored Inchon as the landing site because the landing force would have to move only twenty-five miles inland to recapture Seoul and cut the principal North Korean supply routes. Enemy troops retiring before the Eighth Army attack would be cut off by the amphibious force or be compelled to make adifficult withdrawal through the eastern mountains.

In shaping a landing force, MacArthur formed the headquarters of the Tenth Corps from members of his own staff, naming his chief of staff, Major General Edward M. Almond, as commander. The Seventh Division was rebuilt with incoming replacements and more than eight thousand ROKA recruits. He also acquired the bulk of the First Marine Division from the United States, which he filled out with the marines in the Pusan Perimeter. The Tenth Corps, operating as a separate force under MacArthur's direct command, swept into Inchon on 15 September against light resistance and pushed inland over the next two weeks. One arm struck south and seized Suwon, while the bulk of the corps cleared Kimpo Airfield, crossed the Han River, and fought through Seoul. In a dramatic ceremony, General MacArthur returned the capital city to President Rhee on 29 September.

General Walker's Eighth Army attacked out of the Pusan Perimeter on 16 September. For a week his forces could make only scant gains, but on 23 September the North Koreans broke in retreat. Reorganized into four corps—two American and two South Korean—the Eighth Army rolled forward in pursuit, linking with the Tenth Corps near Suwon on 26 September. Approximately thirty thousand NKPA troops escaped above the thirty-eighth parallel through the eastern mountains while several thousand hid out in South Korea, most of them in the Chiri Mountains, to fight as guerrillas. By the end of September the NKPA no longer existed as an organized force anywhere in the southern republic.

NORTH TOWARD THE YALU

Up to this point, President Truman had frequently described the U.S.-led operations in Korea as a "police action," a euphemism for war that produced both criticism and amusement, but he was reaching for perspective. Determined to halt the North Korean aggression, he was equally determined to limit hostilities to the peninsula and to avoid taking steps that might prompt Soviet or Chinese intervention. Thus, a case could be made for halting ground operations at the thirty-eighth parallel. In reestablishing the border, General MacArthur's forces had met the UN call for assistance in repelling the attack on South Korea, but failure to destroy the NKPA forces that had escaped above the parallel and the thousands more in northern training camps could leave South Korea at risk of another invasion. A complete victory, which appeared within easy grasp, also could set the scene for reunifying Korea under UN supervision. There had been warnings from Communist China against the entry of the United Nations Command into North Korea, but these were considered diplomatic blackmail rather than genuine threats to enter the war. On 27 September, President Truman authorized General MacArthur to send his forces north.

MacArthur's subsequent plan called for the Eighth Army to advance overland with its main attack aimed at Pyongyang, the North Korean capital, in the west, while the Tenth Corps made another amphibious landing, this time to capture Wonsan, North Korea's major seaport on the east coast. Earlier, General Walker, General Almond, and most of MacArthur's principal staff officers had assumed that MacArthur would assign the Tenth Corps to the Eighth Army after the two commands joined forces in the Seoul area. Doing so would follow the military principal that ground operations can be conducted most effectively under a single field commander. MacArthur, however, believed that Walker would have trouble controlling widely separated forces in the rough terrain of North Korea, where lateral communications were difficult, and maintained the Tenth Corps as a separate force. MacArthur reasoned that the Eighth Army and Tenth Corps, coordinated and supported from Japan, especially after gaining the Wonsan port facilities, could operate separately without impairing the effectiveness of either.

President Truman frequently described the operations in Korea as a "police action," a euphemism for war that produced both criticism and amusement.

On the east coast, the ROKA First Corps crossed the parallel on 1 October, and the ROKA Second Corps entered central North Korea on the 6th. The next day the UN General Assembly voted for the restoration of peace and security throughout Korea, thereby giving tacit approval to MacArthur's attack. On 2 October, Communist China's foreign minister, Chou En-lai, had passed word through diplomatic channels that if any forces other than those of South Korea crossed the parallel, China would enter the war, but this warning was dismissed. The U.S. First Corps crossed the parallel in the west on 9 October in an attack toward Pyongyang.

Two weeks later, the Eighth Army was deep in North Korea. In the west the U.S. First Corps cleared Pyongyang on the 19th. On the following day, the U.S. 187th Airborne Regimental Combat Team, which had arrived at Kimpo Airfield from the United States in late September, parachuted at two sites twenty-five miles beyond Pyongyang in an effort to trap North Korean government officials leaving the capital. These officials, however, had moved out of Pyongyang on 12 October and eventually established a new seat of government in the town of Kanggye, deep in the north-central mountains. The airborne landing nevertheless helped ease the advance. On 24 October, the First Corps reached the Chongchon River within sixty-five miles of Korea's Yalu River border with Manchuria, while the ROKA Second Corps veered northwest to come alongside. On the east coast on 10 October the ROKA First Corps captured Wonsan and over the next two weeks reached the town of Iwon, another hundred miles north. Meanwhile, under KMAG tutelage, the ROKA had formed three new divisions, for a total of eight, and activated the Third Corps. For the time being, the new corps and two of the new divisions operated in South Korea against bypassed enemy troops and guerrillas.

In the hope of ending operations before the onset of winter, General MacArthur ordered his ground commanders on 24 October to clear the remainder of North Korea as rapidly as possible. In the west the Eighth Army sent several freewheeling columns toward the Yalu. In the east the separate Tenth Corps came in by sea at Wonsan and Iwon and took control of the ROKA First Corps, sending columns up the coast and inland toward the Yalu River and the huge Changjin Reservoir atop the Taebaek Mountains. The forces on both coasts advanced easily, and reconnaissance troops of an interior South Korean column in the Eighth Army zone reached the Yalu.

Almost everywhere else the columns encountered stout resistance, and on 25 October discovered that they were being opposed by Chinese. Initially, General MacArthur's intelligence officer, Major General Charles A. Willoughby, and MacArthur himself discounted the appearance of Chinese troops in Korea as clear evidence that China had intervened in the war. As stated by General Willoughby on 28 October: "It would appear that the auspicious time for such intervention had long since passed; it is difficult to believe that such a move, if planned, would have been postponed to a time when remnant North Korean forces have been reduced to a low point of effectiveness." On 6 November, however, after receiving further intelligence reports from the field, MacArthur charged China with having "committed one of the most offensive acts of international lawlessness . . . by moving without any notice . . . Communist forces across the Yalu River into North Korea," and with massing possible reinforcements behind the sanctuary of the Manchurian border.

In the east, Chinese forces delayed General Almond's advance toward the Changjin Reservoir. In the west, stronger attacks compelled General Walker to pull the

Eighth Army back to the Chongchon River. In the air, Chinese pilots flying into Korea from Manchurian airfields challenged UN air forces with Russian-built MIG-15 jets. The MIGs were more maneuverable than the F-80 jets flown by Americans, but the Chinese pilots were less skilled and, more often than not, either disengaged or were shot out of the sky. Meanwhile, on the ground, the Chinese abruptly broke contact on 6 November.

As announced by the North Korean government and the Chinese ministry of foreign affairs on 7 and 11 November, all Chinese forces in Korea were "volunteers," an obvious ploy to reduce reprisals because of China's intervention, primarily to mitigate the American response. In fact, the forces constituted regular units of the People's Liberation Army led by its deputy commander, Peng Teh-huai, and were in Korea by government order. By 6 November intelligence agencies estimated these forces at three divisions in the Eighth Army sector and two divisions in the Tenth Corps area—altogether about fifty thousand men. In light of this estimate and with no sightings of additional troops entering Korea by aerial observers, General MacArthur believed that future Chinese operations would be defensive only and would not be strong enough to block a reinforced UN Command advance. Given assurances by MacArthur that his forces could defeat the Chinese and that his air power could prevent any substantial reinforcement from crossing the Yalu, U.S. authorities allowed him to resume his attack toward the border. There was, MacArthur said, no other way to obtain "an accurate measure of enemy strength."

MacArthur opened air attacks on Yalu River bridges on 8 November, restricting the bombing to the overwater spans on the Korean side of the river so as to not violate Manchurian territory. In northeastern Korea the Tenth Corps, now strengthened by the arrival of the Third Infantry Division from the United States, resumed its advance on the 11th. Along the east coast, South Korean units reached the city of Chongjin, about sixty-five miles short of Korea's border with the Soviet Union. Inland, the U.S. Seventh Division forces reached the Yalu on 26 November, and on the corps' west flank, U.S. marines and other Seventh Division units occupied the Changjin Reservoir area. Westward, the Eighth Army, strengthened by the U.S. Ninth Corps with the Second and Twenty-fifth divisions and a newly arrived brigade from Turkey, attacked on 24 November. Other new arrivals in the Eighth Army included the British Twenty-ninth Brigade and infantry battalions from the Philippines, Netherlands, Thailand, and Australia. Except for the last, which joined the British Twenty-seventh Brigade, these troops remained in reserve. Two more new divisions also raised the ROKA's total to ten.

For two days, General Walker's forces met little opposition as they drove west and north astride the Chongchon River. During the night of the 25th, however, strong Chinese attacks struck Walker's center and right, and on the 27th hit General Almond's units at the Changjin Reservoir. Continued assaults on the 28th began to carry the Chinese through the inland flank forces of both the Eighth Army and Tenth Corps. General MacArthur now had a truer measure of Chinese strength. The Thirteenth Army Group with six armies of eighteen divisions stood opposite the Eighth Army, and the Ninth Army Group with three armies of twelve divisions opposed the Tenth Corps in the Changjin Reservoir area. Altogether some 300,000 Chinese were in Korea. As General MacArthur reported to Washington on the 28th, the UN Command faced "an entirely new war."

THE NEW WAR

On 29 November, MacArthur instructed General Walker to withdraw as necessary to escape being enveloped by Chinese troops pushing deep through his eastern sector. General Almond was ordered to pull Tenth Corps forces into a beachhead around the port of Hungnam, north of Wonsan. In the Eighth Army's withdrawal from the Chongchon, a strong roadblock, set by Chinese attempting to envelop Walker's forces from the east, caught and severely punished the U.S. Second Division, last away from the river. Thereafter, at each report of approaching enemy forces, Walker ordered another withdrawal before any solid contact could be made. By 15 December the Eighth Army was completely out of contact with the Chinese and was back at the thirty-eighth parallel. There Walker began to develop coast-to-coast defenses.

On 23 December, General Walker was killed in a motor vehicle accident while traveling north from Seoul to the front.

In the withdrawal of the Tenth Corps to Hungnam, General Almond's central and rightmost forces had little difficulty reaching the port, but the First Marine Division and Seventh Division forces retiring from the Changjin Reservoir had to fight a costly battle through the Chinese rimming a long stretch of the road leading to the coast. By the time these forces reached Hungnam,

General MacArthur had ordered the Tenth Corps to withdraw by sea and proceed to South Korea where, at last, it was to become part of the Eighth Army. With little interference from enemy forces, the last of General Almond's forces left Hungnam on Christmas Eve. Under additional orders from MacArthur, the ROKA First Corps went ashore not far below the thirty-eighth parallel and took up east coast positions along the new Eighth Army front. The remainder of the Tenth Corps proceeded to Pusan and then into assembly areas nearby.

On 23 December, General Walker was killed in a motor vehicle accident while traveling north from Seoul to the front. Lieutenant General Matthew B. Ridgway was hurriedly flown in from Washington to take command of the Eighth Army. Earlier, in routine anticipation of casualties, General MacArthur had obtained chief of staff General Collins' agreement that Walker's replacement, should one be needed, would be General Ridgway. Ridgway's experience and strong leadership as commander of an airborne division and an airborne corps during World War II had MacArthur's high respect, and his service as the deputy chief of staff for operations and administration on the Department of Army staff, which had involved visits to MacArthur's headquarters, had kept him well informed of operations in Korea.

During his initial inspection of the front, General Ridgway found dispirited troops, the result of the hard Chinese attacks and successive withdrawals. He also found the defense line thin in the central and eastern sectors, manned only by the ROKA Third, Second, and First Corps. Having slowly followed the Eighth Army's withdrawal out of North Korea, the Chinese Thirteenth Army Group meanwhile was massing on the front of the U.S. First and Ninth corps in the west, while the NKPA Fifth and Second corps with twelve reconstituted divisions were concentrating in the east-central region.

Ridgway's first tactical move was to place the U.S. Second Division, still damaged but now reinforced by infantry battalions from the Netherlands and France, in a central position where it could oppose any North Korean penetration of the South Korean front. At the same time, he pressed General Almond to quicken preparation of the Tenth Corps, whose forces needed refurbishing before moving into the line. Judging that an enemy attack was likely before he could fully strengthen his defenses, Ridgway also ordered his western forces to organize a bridgehead above Seoul to cover a withdrawal over the Han River, should that become necessary.

Enemy forces opened attacks on New Years' Eve. As expected, the Chinese made the main effort toward Seoul while the North Koreans pressed south in the central and eastern sectors. As the offensive gained momentum, General Ridgway withdrew his western forces to the Seoul bridgehead, pulled the rest of the Eighth Army to positions roughly on line to the east, and strengthened the central sector with the Tenth Corps. Unable to hold the bridgehead, Ridgway ordered his forces back to a line across the peninsula anchored in the west at a point forty miles south of Seoul. The last troops left the capital on 4 January 1951, just as the Chinese entered the city from the north. Only light Chinese forces pushed south of the city and attacks in the west diminished. In the east-central sector, however, NKPA forces infiltrated South Korean lines and reached within a hundred miles of Pusan before they were defeated by Tenth Corps troops striking from the west and the First Marine Division blocking in the south.

By mid-January enemy pressure subsided all along the new Eighth Army line. As the front quieted, reconnaissance patrols searching north encountered only screening forces, and intelligence sources reported that most enemy units had withdrawn to refit. It became clear to General Ridgway that enemy forces operated under the limitations of a primitive logistical system. The Chinese troops in particular could conduct offensive operations for only a week or two before having to pause for replacements and new supplies, a pattern Ridgway intended to exploit. In coming Eighth Army operations ground gains and losses would have only incidental importance. Primarily, Ridgway's forces were to inflict maximum casualties on the enemy with minimum losses to themselves. "To do this," he instructed, "we must wage a war of maneuver—slashing at the enemy when he withdraws and fighting delaying actions when he attacks."

While Ridgway was certain his forces could achieve that objective, General MacArthur was far less optimistic. He had notified Washington earlier that the Chinese could drive the Eighth Army out of Korea unless it received major reinforcement. At the time, there was still only a slim reserve of combat units in the United States. National Guard divisions had been brought into federal service but only two of these, the Fortieth and Forty-fifth, were scheduled for the Far East—for duty in Japan, not Korea. The main concern in Washington was the possibility that the Chinese entry into Korea was only one part of a Soviet move toward global war, a concern great enough to lead President Truman to declare a state of national emergency on 15 December. Washington officials, for their part, considered Korea no place to become involved in a major war. For all these reasons, the U.S. Joint Chiefs of Staff (JCS) notified MacArthur that a major buildup of his forces was out of the question. MacArthur was to stay in Korea if he could but should the Chinese drive the Eighth Army back to a line along and eastward from the Kum River, the JCS would order a withdrawal to Japan.

Opposing the reasoning in Washington, MacArthur urged four retaliatory measures against the Chinese—blockade the China coast, destroy China's war industries through naval and air attacks, reinforce the troops in Korea with Chinese Nationalist forces, and allow diversionary operations by Nationalist forces against the China mainland. Although these proposals for escalation received serious study in Washington, they were discarded in favor of confining the fighting to Korea. Next, the issue of withdrawal from Korea was settled after General Collins visited Korea and saw that the Eighth Army was improving under Ridgway's leadership. He became as confident as Ridgway that the Chinese would be unable to drive the Eighth Army off the peninsula. "As of now," General Collins announced on 15 January, "we are going to stay and fight."

Ten days later, Ridgway opened a cautious offensive, beginning with attacks in the west and gradually widening them to the east. With naval gunfire support on both flanks and ample air support all along the front, the Eighth Army advanced methodically, wiping out each pocket of resistance before moving farther north. Enemy forces fought back vigorously and in February struck back in the central region. During that counterattack, the Twenty-third Regiment of the U.S. Second Division successfully defended the town of Chipyong-ni against a much larger Chinese force, a victory that symbolized to Ridgway the Eighth Army's recovery of its fighting spirit. After defeating the enemy's February effort, the Eighth Army again advanced steadily, reentered Seoul in mid-March, and by the first day of spring stood just below the thirty-eighth parallel. In the meantime, infantry battalions from Greece, Canada, and Belgium, including a detachment from Luxembourg, and an artillery battalion from New Zealand joined Ridgway's forces.

More Chinese forces also had entered Korea, the Nineteenth Army Group in February and the Third Army Group in March. The additions raised the Chinese total to four army groups, fourteen armies, and forty-two divisions. As sensed by intelligence agencies, the Chinese reinforcement was part of preparations for a new offensive. Aiming to spoil these preparations, Ridgway opened an attack on 5 April in which he pointed the main effort toward the Iron Triangle, a centrally located road and rail complex bounded by the towns of Pyongyang in the north and Chorwon and Kumhwa in the south. A unique center of communications, the complex was of obvious importance to the enemy high command's ability to move troops and supplies within the forward areas and to coordinate operations laterally. Ridgway's first concern was to occupy ground that would serve both as a base for continuing the attack toward the complex and as a defensive position. The ground he selected, Line Kansas, followed the Imjin River in the west, extended two to six miles north of the thirty-eighth parallel across the approaches to the Iron Triangle, then reached a depth of ten miles above the parallel before falling off southeastward to the town of Yangyang on the coast. On 11 April, as the Eighth Army closed on Line Kansas, Ridgway sent his central forces toward Line Wyoming, which traced the prominent heights commanding the Chorwon-Kumhwa base of the Iron Triangle. Evidence of an imminent enemy offensive mounted as these troops advanced, and as a precaution, on 12 April Ridgway issued plans for delaying actions to be fought when and if the enemy attacked.

Plans being written in Washington in March might well have kept the Eighth Army from moving above the thirty-eighth parallel. Since the Chinese intervention, the United States and other members of the UN coalition had gradually come to accept what they had not been ready for the past autumn—the clearance of enemy troops from South Korea as a suitable final result of their efforts. On 20 March the JCS notified General MacArthur of a forthcoming announcement by President Truman expressing his willingness to negotiate with the Chinese and North Koreans to make "satisfactory arrangements for concluding the fighting." The announcement would be issued "before any advance with major forces north of the thirty-eighth parallel." Before the president's announcement could be made, however, MacArthur issued his own offer to enemy commanders. More an ultimatum than an offer to discuss an end to the fighting, MacArthur placed the United Nations Command in the role of victor. "The enemy . . . must by now be painfully aware," MacArthur said in part, "that a decision of the United Nations to depart from its tolerant effort to contain the war to the area of Korea, through an expansion of our military operations to its coastal areas and interior bases, would doom Red China to the risk of imminent military collapse." President Truman considered the statement at cross-purposes with the one he planned to issue and so cancelled his own. Hoping the enemy might sue for an armistice if kept under pressure, he permitted the question of crossing the thirty-eighth parallel to be settled on the basis of tactical considerations, and thus it became Ridgway's decision.

On 5 April, Joseph W. Martin, Republican leader in the House of Representatives, read to the House MacArthur's response to a request for comments on Martin's proposal to use Nationalist Chinese forces to open a second front. MacArthur said he believed in "meeting force with maximum counterforce," and that the use of Nationalist forces fitted that belief. He added that there could be "no substitute for victory" in Korea. President Truman could not accept MacArthur's open challenge of national policy and concluded that MacArthur was "unable to give his wholehearted support to the policies of the United States government and of the United Nations in matters pertaining to his official duties." MacArthur was recalled on 11 April and General Ridgway was named his successor. MacArthur returned to the United States to receive the plaudits of a nation shocked by the relief of one of its military heroes. He defended his own views against those of the Truman administration before Congress and the American public. The controversy endured for many months, but the American people eventually accepted the fact that, whatever the merit of MacArthur's arguments, the president as commander in chief had a right to relieve him.

Before transferring to general headquarters in Tokyo, General Ridgway turned over the Eighth Army to Lieutenant General James A. Van Fleet on 14 April. Van Fleet was the personal choice of army Chief of Staff Collins, who considered him to be cast in the same leadership mold as Ridgway. Van Fleet had achieved wide acclaim as head of the U.S. military assistance group sent to Greece in 1948, where he was the mainstay in guiding Greek forces to victory over the Communist-led insurgency. As General Van Fleet assumed command, the Eighth Army was consolidating positions along Line Kansas while its west-central forces moved toward Line Wyoming. Until 21 April the units making the Wyoming advance and patrols searching elsewhere above Line Kansas encountered few Chinese or North Koreans and aerial observers sighted no enemy forces massing near the front. All this changed on the night of the 21st, when patrols ran into strong enemy positions; at daybreak on the 22nd, aerial reconnaissance disclosed the forward movement of large enemy formations from rear assembly areas. By evening Chinese and North Korean assault forces were massed at the front. Around 8:00 P.M. they launched their opening attacks.

The main objective of the enemy offensive was Seoul, whose capture Peng Teh-huai reportedly promised to Mao Tse-tung as a May Day gift. Peng planned to converge on the city with the newly arrived Nineteenth and Third Army groups from the northwest and north and the Ninth Army Group, now restored after losing heavily at the Changjin Reservoir, from the northeast. These three groups constituted a force of 270,000 men. Peng's plan included auxilliary attacks along each flank of the main effort—the NKPA First Corps on the west and the somewhat worn Thirteenth Army Group on the east. In what would be essentially a separate effort, the NKPA Third and Fifth corps were to attack in the east-central region.

The main objective of the enemy offensive was Seoul, whose capture Peng Teh-huai reportedly promised to Mao Tse-tung as a May Day gift.

Under an umbrella of strong support from both ground- and carrier-based aircraft and helped by 8-inch naval gunfire along the west flank, the Eighth Army fought hard defensive battles as it withdrew twenty to thirty miles through successive delaying positions. By 30 April, Van Fleet's forces had contained Peng's advance along a line reaching northeastward from positions a few miles above Seoul. Enormous casualties compelled Peng to pull his forces well to the north for refurbishing.

The high enemy losses notwithstanding, Van Fleet cautioned his forces that the Chinese and North Koreans had the men to attack again as hard as before or harder. He ordered the full length of the Eighth Army line fortified, counterattack plans developed, and provisions made for delivering lavish artillery fire wherever Peng's forces might attack. Although local advances to improve the line and deep patrolling produced little meaningful contact with the enemy, the composite of reports from aerial observers, agents, civilians, prisoners, and other intelligence sources made clear that some major Chinese units were shifting eastward from the area above Seoul. Expecting, therefore, that the enemy's next principal effort would come either in the west as before or on the central front, Van Fleet shifted forces to place most of his strength in those sectors.

Actually, Peng had shifted five armies of the Third and Ninth groups into the east-central area, where they and the NKPA Fifth Corps struck south during the evening of 16 May. Apparently realizing that his superior numbers of men could defeat an enemy superior in other respects only if the latter's superiority was not too great, Peng chose to attack through some of the most difficult ground on the front. Rugged ridges and a sparse road net would reduce to some degree the UN Command's advantage of superior mobility, firepower, and air power. His strategy nevertheless failed. Adjusting units to place more troops in the path of Peng's advance while his forces laid down tremendous amounts of artillery fire, Van Fleet halted the attack by 20 May after enemy forces had penetrated thirty miles. He immediately ordered the entire Eighth Army forward in counterattack. The Chinese and North Koreans resisted wherever their escape routes and supply installations were threatened, but elsewhere Van Fleet's forces advanced with almost surprising ease. By 31 May they were just short of Line Kansas, and on 1 June Van Fleet sent forces toward Line Wyoming. By mid-June the Eighth Army occupied both Line Kansas and the Wyoming bulge.

Because the Kansas-Wyoming line traced ground suitable for a strong defense, Washington decided to hold that line and wait for a bid for armistice negotiations from the Chinese and North Koreans. In line with this decision, General Van Fleet began to fortify his positions. Enemy forces used the respite from attack to recoup heavy losses and to develop their own defenses. The fighting lapsed into patrolling and small local clashes.

THE STATIC WAR

In an effort to encourage an offer to negotiate an armistice, Secretary of State Acheson enlisted the help of George F. Kennan, a State Department official with a solid background in U.S.-Soviet relations. On 31 May, Kennan met with Yakov A. Malik, Soviet delegate to the United Nations, to make sure that the Soviets were clearly aware of the U.S. desire for a cease-fire and to obtain Moscow's views and suggestions. At a second meeting on 5 June, Malik told Kennan that the Soviet government wanted a peaceful solution in Korea but could not appropriately take part in negotiations. His personal advice was that U.S. authorities should approach their Chinese and North Korean counterparts. In a speech broadcast on the United Nations "Price of Peace" program on 23 June, Malik, after blaming the United States for the war, announced that the Soviet Union believed the conflict could be settled. As a first step, he said, the belligerents should start discussions to arrange a cease-fire and an armistice that provided for the mutual withdrawal of forces from the thirty-eighth parallel. After China endorsed Malik's proposal over Peking radio on 26 June, President Truman authorized General Ridgway to arrange armistice talks with enemy commanders. Through an exchange of radio messages and a meeting of liaison officers, both sides agreed to begin negotiations on 10 July at the town of Kaesong in western no-man's-land, which would be designated a neutral area. General Ridgway appointed Admiral Joy to head a delegation that included four other officers of general or flag rank. The five-man Communist delegation was led by General Nam Il, chief of staff of the NKPA, but from the beginning, he appeared to be dominated by the ranking Chinese member, Hsieh Fang.

At the first conference the two delegations agreed that hostilities would continue until an armistice was signed. In a little more than two weeks of negotiations, they established the points to be settled: fixing a military demarcation line; organizing a supervisory body to carry out the terms of an armistice; arranging the disposition of prisoners of war; and developing recommendations to the governments of countries involved in the war. On the first point, negotiations to fix a military demarcation line, there was a complete impasse. General Nam insisted that the thirty-eighth parallel be the dividing line, while Admiral Joy, acting on instructions from Washington, pointed out that the parallel had no military significance and proposed that the division be located along the line of contact between opposing forces. After accusing the UN Command of dropping a napalm bomb in the conference area, a fraudulent charge, the Communist delegation broke off negotiations on 22 August.

At that juncture, General Van Fleet opened limited attacks, hoping that the pressure would help persuade enemy authorities to resume the armistice talks and drive enemy forces off positions that favored attacks on Line Kansas. UN Command naval surface forces also applied pressure by keeping enemy shore installations under bombardment, and air forces concentrated attacks on major road and rail lines, troops, vehicles, and supply dumps in enemy rear areas and on Pyongyang, which was again the seat of North Korean government. In air-to-air combat, the fighting was concentrated in the far northwest between the Chongchon and Yalu rivers, an area that became known as MIG Alley.

In east-central Korea, Van Fleet sent forces toward terrain objectives given the names Punchbowl, Bloody Ridge, and Heartbreak Ridge.

As Van Fleet began his attacks, the Eighth Army was strengthened by infantry battalions from Ethiopia and Colombia and the Canadian Twenty-fifth Infantry Brigade, which absorbed the Canadian battalion already in Korea. In July all British Commonwealth units were consolidated to form the First Commonwealth Division. Chinese forces had been reinforced by two armies from the Twentieth Army Group. On both sides these recent arrivals would be the last ground units to enter the war.

In east-central Korea, Van Fleet sent forces toward terrain objectives five to seven miles above Line Kansas, among them places given the names Punchbowl, Bloody

Ridge, and Heartbreak Ridge. Forces struck in the west on a wide front to secure a line three to four miles north. All objectives were taken by the last week of October. At that point the Comunist delegation agreed to return to the armistice conference table.

Negotiations resumed on 25 October, but this time, at General Ridgway's insistence, in Panmunjom, a small settlement seven miles southeast of Kaesong. Hopes for an early armistice grew on 27 November, when the two delegations agreed that the line of demarcation would be the existing line of contact, provided an armistice agreement was reached within thirty days. Hence, while both sides awaited the outcome of negotiations, the fighting during the remainder of 1951 tapered off to patrol clashes, raids, and small battles for possession of outposts. Discord over several issues, including the exchange of prisoners of war, prevented an armistice agreement within the stipulated thirty days. The prisoner of war quarrel heightened in January 1952, after UN Command delegates proposed to give captives a choice in repatriation proceedings, maintaining that those prisoners who did not wish to return to their homelands should be free to choose their own destinations. The Communist delegates protested vigorously. While the argument continued, both sides tacitly extended the 27 November provisions for a line of demarcation, which had the effect of holding battle action to the pattern of the thirty-day waiting period.

By May 1952 the two delegations worked out all armistice matters except the prisoner repatriation issue, on which they were completely deadlocked. On 7 May, inmates of United Nations Command Prison Camp Number 1 on Koje-do, an island off the southern coast, on orders smuggled to them from North Korea, enticed

The Korean War was the first war in which helicopters were widely used to rescue wounded soldiers on the ground and to carry troops into combat. This helicopter carried marines into hostile territory in South Korea on 20 September 1951. (National Archives)

the camp commander, Brigadier General Francis T. Dodd, to a compound gate, pulled him inside, and held him captive. The strategy, which became clear in subsequent prisoner demands, was to trade General Dodd's life for admission of inhumane treatment of captives, including alleged cruelties during the screenings of prisoners, during which large numbers of them declared their wishes not to be repatriated. The obvious objective was to discredit the repatriation stand taken by Admiral Joy's delegation. A new camp commander, Brigadier General Charles F. Colson, obtained Dodd's release but in the process signed a damaging statement admitting that "there have been instances of bloodshed where many prisoners of war have been killed and wounded by UN Forces." There was no change in the UN Command stand on repatriation, but the statement was widely exploited by the Communists at Panmunjom and elsewhere for its propaganda value.

During the Koje-do affair, General Ridgway received orders placing him in command of NATO forces in Europe. General Mark W. Clark became the new commander in the Far East on 12 May, with one less responsibility than MacArthur and Ridgway had carried. On 28 April a peace treaty with Japan had gone into effect, restoring Japan's sovereignty and ending the occupation. Faced immediately with the Koje-do matter, General Clark repudiated General Colson's statement. Moving swiftly, he placed Brigadier General Haydon L. Boatner in charge of the camp with instructions to move prisoners into smaller, more manageable compounds and to institute other measures that would eliminate the likelihood of another uprising. General Boatner completed the task on 10 June.

On 22 May, Major General William K. Harrison replaced Admiral Joy as chief delegate at Panmunjom, where arguments continued over repatriation. Meanwhile, action at the front held to a pattern of artillery duals, patrols, ambushes, raids, and bitter battles for outposts on oddly shaped land masses such as Sniper Ridge, Old Baldy, The Hook, T-Bone, and Pork Chop Hill. On the Eighth Army front, the National Guard Fortieth and Forty-fifth divisions had replaced the First Cavalry and Twenty-fourth divisions, which returned to Japan. Although costly fighting continued, the lines remained substantially unchanged at the end of 1952. In October the armistice conference went into an indefinite recess with the repatriation issue still unresolved.

There had been a great deal of popular discontent over the war in Korea among the American people, especially with the lack of progress toward an armistice. During the presidential campaign in 1952, Dwight D. Eisenhower pledged to "go to Korea," implying that if elected he would end the war quickly. Consequently, when the president-elect visited Korea in early December, there was some expectation of a dramatic change in the conduct of the war. General Clark even set out detailed estimates of measures needed to win a military victory. Eisenhower, however, like Truman before him, preferred to seek an armistice. Still, he let Communist authorities know that if satisfactory progress toward an armistice were not forthcoming, "we intended to move decisively without inhibition in our use of weapons, and would no longer be responsible for confining hostilities to the Korean peninsula." Immediately after taking office, he made sure these words reached Moscow, Peking, and Pyongyang.

In the hope of prompting a resumption of armistice negotiations, in February 1953 General Clark proposed to his enemy counterparts that the two sides exchange sick and wounded prisoners. His offer was ignored and by spring there was still no break in the deadlock at Panmunjom. At the front, where in February Lieutenant General Maxwell D. Taylor had replaced General Van Fleet as Eighth Army commander, the battle action continued in the mold of the previous year.

The break finally came near the end of March 1953, about three weeks after the death of Joseph Stalin, when enemy armistice delegates not only replied favorably to General Clark's proposal on the exchange of sick and wounded captives, but also suggested that this exchange perhaps could "lead to the smooth settlement of the entire question of prisoners of war." The armistice conference resumed in April and an exchange of sick and wounded prisoners was carried out that same month (Operation Little Switch). Enemy authorities returned 684 ailing prisoners, of whom 149 were American, while the UN Command returned 6,670 captives. The prisoner repatriation problem was finally settled by mid-June with an agreement offering each side an opportunity to persuade those captives refusing return to their homelands to change their minds.

The pace of battle meanwhile quickened in May when sizable Chinese forces attacked several outposts guarding the Eighth Army's main line in the west. A larger battle opened in the central sector on 10 June, when three Chinese divisions drove two miles through South Korean positions before being contained. Because the terms of an armistice by then were all but complete, that engagement could have been the last of the war. On 18 June, however, President Rhee, who had steadfastly objected to any armistice that left Korea divided, ordered the release of North Korean prisoners who had refused repatriation. Within a few days about twenty-seven thousand North Korean captives were allowed to escape and disappeared among a cooperative

South Korean populace. Because the prisoners had been guarded by South Korean troops, UN Command officials disclaimed responsibility for the break, but enemy armistice delegates denounced the action as a serious breach of faith. Another month of negotiations was required to repair the damage done by Rhee's attempt to disrupt the conclusion of the proceedings.

During the delay, enemy forces attacked on 13 July, driving a wedge eight miles deep in the Eighth Army's central sector. General Taylor deployed units to contain the attack and then sent them forward in counterattack. On 20 July he halted the attack force because the armistice delegations finally reached accord and needed only to work out a few details. Taylor's order ended the last major battle of the war.

After a week of dealing with administrative details, the senior delegates, Generals Harrison and Nam, signed the military armistice agreement at Panmunjom at 10 A.M. on 27 July. Shortly afterward, General Clark, Kim Il Sung, and Peng Teh-huai affixed their signatures at their respective headquarters. As agreed, all fighting stopped twelve hours after the first signing, at 10 P.M., 27 July 1953. By the terms of the armistice, the line of demarcation between North Korea and South Korea approximated the front line as it existed at the final hour. Three days after the signing, each opposing force withdrew two kilometers from the line to establish a demilitarized zone that was not to be trespassed. The new border differed only slightly from the prewar division of the country, slanting from a point on the west coast fifteen miles below the thirty-eighth parallel northeastward to an east coast anchor forty miles above the parallel.

Over the thirty-seven months of fighting, the total United Nations Command losses in dead and wounded numbered 385,274. The estimate of enemy dead and wounded was 1,467,000, of which 945,000 were Chinese and 522,000 North Koreans. South Korea had suffered 58,127 dead and 175,743 wounded, United Nations members other than the United States 3,194 dead and 11,297 wounded, and the United States 33,629 dead and 103,284 wounded. After the return of American prisoners in the repatriation proceedings, more than 8,100 men remained unaccounted for. Officially written off as "presumed dead," their true fate remains unknown.

To oversee enforcement of armistice terms and negotiate any violations, the Military Armistice Commission, composed of an equal number of officers from each side, was established, with Panmunjom as its meeting site. Assisting this body was the Neutral Nations Supervisory Commission, whose members were from Sweden, Switzerland, Czechoslovakia, and Poland. Representatives of these same countries, with India furnishing an umpire and custodial forces, formed the Neutral Nations Repatriation Commission to handle the disposition of prisoners refusing repatriation. Also, a provision of the armistice agreement recommended that the belligerent governments convene a political conference to negotiate a final settlement of Korea's future.

Prisoners of war described brutal treatment in enemy prison camps and brainwashing techniques designed to produce prisoner collaboration.

All prisoners wishing to be repatriated were exchanged by 6 September. UN Command authorities delivered 75,823 captives, of whom 70,183 were Chinese and 5,640 North Koreans. Returned from the north were 12,773 prisoners, of whom 7,862 were South Koreans, 3,597 Americans, and 1,314 from other countries. From these returnees came accounts of brutal treatment in enemy prison camps and of an extensive Communist indoctrination program, of brainwashing techniques designed to produce prisoner collaboration. Of several hundred American returnees investigated on charges of collaborating with the enemy, only fourteen were tried and, of these, eleven were convicted.

The transfer of nonrepatriates to the Neutral Nations Repatriation Commission came next. Few prisoners changed their minds when officials from both sides tried to convince former members of their commands to return. Of 22,604 Chinese and North Koreans delivered to the Repatriation Commission, 14,247 Chinese and 7,674 North Koreans returned to UN Command control. Most of the Chinese eventually were shipped to Taiwan. Of 325 South Koreans, twenty-three Americans, and one Britisher brought to the commission, just twelve changed their minds. Almost all of the twenty-one Americans who stayed with the Communists eventually returned to the United States. Because these men had already been dishonorably discharged from military service, no further action was taken against them. After releasing the last of the nonrepatriates, the Repatriation Commission dissolved itself on 1 February 1954.

The scene then shifted to Geneva, Switzerland, where the political conference recommended in the armistice agreement convened on 26 April. From the beginning there was a complete deadlock. Representatives of UN Command member countries wanted to reunify Korea through elections supervised by the United Nations; the Communist delegates refused to recognize UN authority to deal with the matter. The talks ended on 15 June 1954 with Korea still divided and with opposing forces still facing each other across the demilitarized zone.

Although the armistice agreement and the Geneva impasse left Korea divided essentially along the prewar line, the war had far more consequence than merely to restore its *status quo ante bellum.* In South Korea the ROKA, under an able chief of staff, Major General Chung Il Kwon, and with KMAG guidance, had grown into a well-developed and experienced force of sixteen divisions. Scheduled to raise four more divisions, it was a force that North Korea's resources would be strained to match. To further discourage any future North Korean aggression, substantial U.S. army combat troops were to remain in Korea. In addition, sixteen nations who had contributed forces to the UN Command, including the United States, declared on the day the armistice agreement was signed that they would resist any renewal of armed attack and that if Communist aggression reoccurred, "in all probability, it would not be possible to confine hostilities within the frontiers of Korea," a warning aimed not just at North Korea, but also at China.

The conflict also had a transforming impact on the course of international relations in both Asia and Europe. For the Communist East, the major result was the emerging of China as a great power. A steady improvement in the Chinese army and air force during the war gave China a more powerful military posture at war's end. Despite vast losses, its performance in Korea won China respect as a nation to be reckoned with not only in Asian but in world affairs. For Western nations, a primary result was a decided strengthening of the NATO alliance. Greece and Turkey were now members and, whereas before the war the total forces available to the organization included just twelve divisions, four hundred aircraft, and a small navy, by the end of the Korean War, NATO had grown to fifty-two divisions, four thousand aircraft, and substantial naval units.

As a direct consequence of the war, there was also a multiplication of U.S. political, economic, and military ties with non-Communist nations throughout the western Pacific. Between 1951 and 1953, the United States negotiated bilateral security ties with Korea, Japan, Taiwan, the Philippines, Australia, and New Zealand. The Communist armed aggression in Korea also inspired the United States to hedge a repetition in Southeast Asia, principally in Indochina. In 1954 it promoted and joined the Southeast Asia Treaty Organization (SEATO), a defense alliance whose members included Great Britain, France, Australia, New Zealand, Pakistan, Thailand, and the Philippines, and whose defense area included Laos, Cambodia, and South Vietnam.

The war also prompted a marked rise in U.S. military strength. By war's end, U.S. armed forces had increased by two million. The army alone numbered more than a million and a half and had twenty divisions, twice the prewar number. There would be a substantial postwar reduction of forces but no drastic dismantling as had followed World War II. The cold war obviously would continue and U.S. authorities intended that the United States would maintain ready forces fully capable of supporting the U.S. strategy of containment. In the process there would be added emphasis on nuclear power. The air force would increase its strategic bombing capability, the navy would concentrate on developing nuclear missiles that could be launched from submarines and other ships, and the army would seek to perfect tactical nuclear weapons. In January 1954, Secretary of State John Foster Dulles announced that in the future the United States would "depend primarily upon a great capacity to retaliate instantly, by means and at places of our choosing," a policy to become known as "massive retaliation" during Dwight Eisenhower's presidency. Indeed, the Korean War was a landmark in the rise of the United States as a superpower.

BIBLIOGRAPHY

Acheson, Dean. *Present at the Creation: My Years in the State Department* (1969).

Alexander, Bevin. *Korea: The First War We Lost* (1986).

Appleman, Roy E. *South to the Naktong, North to the Yalu: June–November 1950* (1961).

Barclay, C. N. *The First Commonwealth Division: The Story of British Commonwealth Land Forces in Korea, 1950–1953* (1954).

Biderman, Albert D. *The March to Calumny: The Story of American POW's in the Korean War* (1962).

Blair, Clay. *The Forgotten War: America in Korea, 1950–1953* (1987).

Bohlen, Charles E. *Witness to History, 1929–1969* (1973).

Bradley, Omar, N., and Clay Blair. *A General's Life: An Autobiography* (1983).

Cagle, Malcolm W., and Frank A. Manson. *The Sea War in Korea* (1957).

Cho, Soon Sung. *Korea in World Politics, 1940–1950: An Evaluation of American Responsibility* (1967).

Clark, Mark W. *From the Danube to the Yalu* (1954).

Collins, J. Lawton. *War in Peacetime: The History and Lessons of Korea* (1969).

Cowdry, Albert E. *The Medics' War* (1987).

Dean, William F. *General Dean's Story* (1954).

Deane, Philip. *I Was a Captive in Korea* (1953).

Eisenhower, Dwight D. *Mandate for Change: The White House Years, 1953–1956* (1963).

Farrar-Hockley, Anthony. *The Edge of the Sword* (1954).

Field, James A., Jr. *United States Naval Operations, Korea* (1962).

Futrell, Robert F. *United States Air Forces in Korea, 1950–1953* (1961).

George, Alexander L. *The Chinese Communist Army in Action* (1967).
Gittings, John. *The Role of the Chinese Army* (1967).
Goldberg, Alfred, ed. *A History of the United States Air Force, 1907–1957* (1957).
Goodrich, Leland M. *Korea: A Study of U.S. Policy in the United Nations* (1956).
Goulden, Joseph R. *Korea: The Untold Story of the War* (1982).
Griffith, Samuel B., II. *The Chinese People's Liberation Army* (1967).
Gugeler, Russell A. *Combat Actions in Korea* (1954).
Heinl, Robert D., Jr. *Victory at High Tide: The Seoul-Inchon Campaign* (1968).
Heller, Francis H., ed. *The Korean War: A 25-Year Perspective* (1977).
Hermes, Walter F. *Truce Tent and Fighting Front* (1966).
Higgins, Trumball. *Korea and the Fall of MacArthur: A Precis of Limited War* (1960).
James, D. Clayton. *The Years of MacArthur, Triumph and Disaster, 1945–1964* (1985).
Joy, C. Turner. *How Communists Negotiate* (1955).
Kinkead, Eugene. *In Every War but One* (1959).
Leckie, Robert. *Conflict: The History of the Korean War, 1950–1953* (1962).
MacArthur, Douglas. *Reminiscences* (1964).
McCune, George M., and Arthur L. Gray, Jr. *Korea Today* (1950).
Marshall, S. L. A. *The River and the Gauntlet* (1953).
———. *Pork Chop Hill: The American Fighting Man in Action, Korea, Spring 1953* (1956).
Meade, Edward Grant. *American Military Government in Korea* (1951).
Montross, Lynn, et al. *U.S. Marine Corps Operations in Korea, 1950–1953,* 5 vols. (1954–1972).
Mossman, Billy C. *Ebb and Flow: November 1950–July 1951* (1990).
Office of the Chief of Military History, Department of the Army, *Korea 1950* (1952).
———. *Korea 1951–1953* (1956).
Rees, David. *Korea: The Limited War* (1964).
Ridgway, Matthew B. *The Korean War* (1967).
Sawyer, Robert K. *Military Advisers in Korea: KMAG in Peace and War* (1962).
Schnabel, James F. *U.S. Army in the Korean War: Policy and Directions: The First Year* (1972).
Sebald, William. *With MacArthur in Japan: A Personal History of the Occupation* (1965).
Simmons, Robert R. *The Strained Alliance: Peking, P'y'ongyang, Moscow and the Politics of the Korean Civil War* (1975).
Taylor, Maxwell D. *The Uncertain Trumpet* (1960).
Truman, Harry S. *Memoirs: Years of Trial and Hope,* vol. 2 (1955).
Vatcher, William H., Jr. *Panmunjom: The Story of the Korean Military Armistice Negotiations* (1958).
Weigley, Russell F. *History of the United States Army* (1967).
Whiting, Allen S. *China Crosses the Yalu* (1960).
Wood, Herbert Fairlie. *Strange Battleground: The Operations in Korea and their Effects on the Defence Policy of Canada* (1966).

— BILLY C. MOSSMAN

The Vietnam Era

The tragic involvement of the United States in Vietnam began with little fanfare. Most Americans knew nothing of the limited contact U.S. servicemen had with Vietnamese anti-Japanese resistance fighters during World War II or paid much attention when President Harry S. Truman decided to aid the attempt by the French government to restore colonial rule after the war. That ignorance ended in the 1960s. Throughout the decade Vietnam was on nearly everyone's mind as the U.S. military commitment inexorably grew into a costly, inconclusive war that, before it ended in 1975, tore apart the American body politic. The Vietnam War raised questions about the fitness of the U.S. military and the role of military power in a political struggle. It also opened debate about priorities—whether domestic problems of poverty and racial discrimination had a higher claim on the purse and conscience of the nation than the expenditure of lives and money in an overseas crusade to preserve South Vietnam. A sideshow in World War II, the Vietnam War arguably became the dominant issue in U.S. history from the mid-1960s to the mid-1970s and divided the United States as no other conflict had since the Civil War.

The decisions of U.S. presidents and military leaders on how and when to fight directly influenced the course of the war. Throughout its involvement in Vietnam, the United States fought a limited war for limited objectives. The goal was not the destruction or surrender of its foe, North Vietnam, or the conquest of its territory, but the preservation of the U.S. ally, South Vietnam, as a sovereign, non-Communist nation. Successive administrations, hoping to keep costs at acceptable levels, placed limits on how the military employed air, sea, and ground power. To preserve its ally and deter its foe required the U.S. government to develop a sophisticated political/military strategy that precisely formulated ends and means and dealt with all aspects of the threat. That task proved difficult, as conventional military measures to defeat enemy forces could work at cross-purposes with political efforts to help the Saigon government establish a solid base of support. Differences arose between civilian and military leaders over priorities and procedures. The need to balance the political and military components of strategy for a limited war proved to be a vexing issue throughout the period of direct U.S. involvement.

BACKGROUND TO A U.S. WAR

The U.S. commitment to Vietnam evolved from the abortive attempt by France to retain its colonial holdings in Southeast Asia. Ambivalence characterized U.S. policy toward Indochina during World War II. On the one hand, the United States reassured France that it would get back its former possessions. On the other, President Franklin D. Roosevelt personally advocated independence for Indochina, and members of the Office of Strategic Services (OSS) fought alongside the League for the Independence of Vietnam—the Vietminh guerrillas—against the Japanese. Ultimately, military strategy and British intransigence on colonial policy determined U.S. policy. Concentrating its forces against Japan, the United States agreed that the British and Chinese would divide Indochina for purposes of occupation. With British cooperation, French military forces returned to Vietnam in September 1945.

After World War II, most European powers relinquished their Asian empires. The French were the exception.

After World War II, most European powers relinquished their Asian empires. The French were the exception. Great Britain granted independence to India, Pakistan, Burma, Ceylon, and Malaya, and Holland gave up control of Indonesia. The French opposed Vietnamese independence and sought to reassert dominion over Vietnam. France rejected the claim of the Vietminh to rule Vietnam. Under their leader, Ho Chi Minh, who was both an ardent nationalist and the leader of the Indochinese Communist party, the Vietminh in 1945 had sought to replace departing Japanese occupation forces, establishing in Hanoi the Democratic Republic of Vietnam (DRV). French authorities returned to Hanoi in March 1946, following an accord in which Ho acceded to their return in exchange for limited recognition of the DRV. In April the United States acknowledged French control. Relations between the French and the Vietminh quickly deteriorated, and in late 1946 war broke out. The Vietminh fought to end colonial rule and establish an independent Vietnam.

The involvement of the United States in Vietnam grew steadily. In 1950, in an international climate characterized by open hostilities in Korea and worldwide confrontation between Communist and non-Communist powers, President Truman began to increase military supplies to the French through the newly formed U.S. Military Assistance Advisory Group (MAAG), Indochina. Headquartered in Saigon, the MAAG grew from 65 men in 1950 to 342 in 1954. Linking the war against the Vietminh to the worldwide struggle to contain Communist expansion, the United States late in 1950 committed more than $133 million in aid to Indochina and ordered immediate delivery of large quantities of arms and ammunition, naval vessels, aircraft, and military vehicles. By 1952 the amount of aid exceeded $300 million.

US Marines on reconnaissance make their way stealthily through a jungle in Vietnam during the height of the war in 1969. (The Mariners Museum/Corbis)

The French had plenty of equipment, but they used it unwisely, trying to defeat the Vietminh in large battles. They neglected the village war, failing to protect the Vietnamese people from Vietminh guerrillas and political operatives. The decisive battle in 1954 at Dien Bien Phu, a remote village in the northwest, which led to the withdrawal of France, epitomized the folly of their strategy. Hoping to lure the Vietminh into a set-piece battle, French forces occupied Dien Bien Phu, a site far removed from coastal supply bases. Vietminh forces surrounded and slowly strangled the garrison. Antiaircraft fire made it difficult for the French to bring in supplies by air. General Paul Ely, French chief of staff, arrived in Washington on 20 March 1954 to ask for direct U.S. military intervention. Admiral Arthur Radford, chairman of the Joint Chiefs of Staff (JCS), proposed an air attack against Vietminh positions. President Dwight D. Eisenhower declined to provide air support or send U.S. forces to save the French. A bleak intelligence estimate, the difficulty of obtaining congressional support, and the warning of Army Chief of Staff General Matthew Ridgway and others who feared that the use of U.S. ground forces in an Asian land war would severely strain the army dissuaded Eisenhower from unilateral intervention.

Dien Bien Phu fell in May 1954 while the fate of Indochina was being negotiated in Geneva, Switzerland. Faced with political divisions at home, soaring war costs, and a decisive military defeat, the French ceded control of Indochina. The Geneva Accords of 1954 established Vietnam as an independent but divided country. Two newly recognized, distrustful regimes warily eyed each other across a common border, the seventeenth parallel. The Democratic Republic of Vietnam, the Communist regime in the north invoking Vietnamese nationalism, sought to unite Vietnam under its banner. The non-Communist State of Vietnam in the south was determined to resist unification under the Communists. Neither the United States nor South Vietnam signed the accords.

Following the withdrawal of France from Indochina in 1955, the Eisenhower administration, which, like its predecessor, was fearful of Communist expansion in Indochina, enlarged the U.S. role in Vietnam. The administration decided to give military aid directly to the newly formed South Vietnamese government in Saigon, headed by Ngo Dinh Diem, a Roman Catholic of mandarin background. Eisenhower also set up a collective defense organization, the Southeast Asia Treaty Organization, to provide for regional security.

To preserve its independence, the Diem regime needed to establish itself as the sole legitimate political authority in South Vietnam in place of the Vietminh and the departing French colonists, no easy task for a new political entity that lacked a unifying national identity. Regional, ethnic, and religious antagonism afflicted South Vietnam from its creation as a separate nation. Sizable ethnic minorities, principally Chinese, ethnic Cambodians (Khmers), and mountain tribes, called montagnards, living in the central highlands lived uneasily with the Vietnamese. Between 1954 and 1956, thousands of Roman Catholics fearing persecution left the north and settled in South Vietnam. The Catholic émigrés, a minority in a predominantly Buddhist country, filled many critical military and political leadership posts in the south as colonial authorities withdrew. Many Diem supporters, having cooperated with the French, had questionable credentials as nationalists. Most émigrés from the north had little knowledge of the problems that burdened the peasants. Opposition from the Communists as well as from the armed sects—the Cao Dai, the Hoa Hao, and the Binh Xuyen—made the early survival of the Diem regime uncertain. In 1954 the government of South Vietnam controlled only the cities and large towns. To govern, Diem had to extend his rule to the villages, where the bulk of the people lived, and gain their support. Pacification, the effort to provide security and improve economic conditions in the countryside, was thus a key government program from the inception of the government of South Vietnam.

By 1956, Diem had taken some promising steps toward building a political base. He had disarmed the sects and installed loyal province and district chiefs, establishing a degree of political stability many thought unattainable when he took power, and his government enacted a land reform statute in 1956. In consolidating his rule, however, Diem also turned against his political opponents and remnants of the Vietminh, many of whom were anti-Communist nationalists. As Diem became more authoritarian, a growing number of the politically disaffected joined the insurgent movement.

In Hanoi, Ho Chi Minh's Indochinese Communist party (renamed the Dang Lao Dong Vietnam or the Vietnam Workers Party) governed North Vietnam and led the battle for unification. The party issued guidance to the Vietminh cadres remaining in the south and trained in the techniques of revolutionary warfare some ninety thousand southern-based Vietminh who had moved north following the partition of the country. They later returned south and merged with the stay-behind cadres to form a new insurgent force, commonly known as the Vietcong.

In 1956 the Vietcong started building a political organization and forming local military units in Quang Ngai province, the U Minh forest, and the heavily populated farming regions around Saigon and in the Mekong River delta. The former Vietminh leaders rebuilt their base camps in the unsettled jungles close to the capital—War Zones C and D and the Iron Triangle, a base area with headquarters directing military and political activity around the capital. The key base area, War Zone D, forested and difficult to penetrate, was close to the Cambodian border but accessible to the lower delta and the central highlands. These remote bases allowed the nascent guerrilla forces to develop and operate in secret. By the following year, Vietcong forces numbered thirty-seven armed companies and began small-scale guerrilla operations. Vietcong strength grew from roughly five thousand at the beginning of 1959 to about 100,000 by the end of 1964. The growth resulted from the return of the Vietminh trained in the north, recruiting within South Vietnam, and the infiltration of native North Vietnamese soldiers into South Vietnam as replacements and reinforcements.

The Geneva Accords of 1954 established Vietnam as an independent but divided country.

Over time, Vietcong forces encompassed part-time hamlet and village guerrillas and full-time professional soldiers. Guerrillas gathered intelligence, propagandized, and recruited, and kept government officials away. The presence of guerrillas allowed the political cadres that comprised the infrastructure, or secret government, to impose taxes and run the village. Local force units consisted of full-time soldiers, who usually attacked isolated, weakly defended outposts or vulnerable government forces. Main force units, larger and more heavily armed, were formed into battalions, regiments, and even divisions. Each unit included a three-man political cell to impose party policy and military discipline. A political officer assigned missions to Vietcong units, often specifying which South Vietnamese unit to attack.

In the early years of his rule, the harsh attacks by Diem on the Vietcong movement, which relied on police sweeps, detention, and operations by the Army of the Republic of Vietnam, known as ARVN, put the Communists on the defensive. By 1957, Diem had so weakened the movement that its leaders feared for its survival. In 1959, Hanoi decided that it had to resume the armed struggle and began sending supplies and manpower southward. Under the new strategy, the insurgents stepped up attacks on villages and government outposts, aiming to undermine Saigon's ability to govern the countryside. Several hundred government officials were assassinated. The party enlarged the political struggle. To organize and lead the opposition to Diem's rule, in December 1960 Hanoi created the National Liberation Front of South Vietnam. Through a combined military and political struggle they hoped to hasten the disintegration of the Saigon government and gain adherents to their movement from the ranks of dissatisfied Vietnamese. Throughout 1959, the insurgency grew, forcing Saigon to move people into protected settlements, so-called *agrovilles,* from villages vulnerable to Communist political action.

MORE AID FOR VIETNAM

The burgeoning guerrilla war found the MAAG and ARVN ill-prepared to mount effective opposition. In the late 1950s, the United States, fearing another invasion of South Korea by a Communist army, viewed the regular forces of North Vietnam as the most significant threat to South Vietnam. Consequently, the MAAG, which had grown to 740 men by 1956, trained the South Vietnamese military to stop a conventional invading force. The MAAG emphasized the operations of large tactical military formations—regiments, divisions, and corps—and the gathering of conventional military order of battle information. U.S. funds covered some of the costs of Vietnamese military pay and allowances, training, construction, and medical services. The MAAG fixation on the threat of an invasion by conventional forces caused it to slight counterinsurgency doctrine, intelligence, and training. An insurgency, or a war of national liberation, as the Communists termed it, was as much a contest for political legitimacy as it was an armed struggle. Most army advisers assigned to Vietnam in the late 1950s and early 1960s were inadequately trained to help their counterparts deal with the political and social dimensions of insurgency. In a civil conflict between warring Vietnamese groups, the advisers were political and cultural outsiders. To quell the insurgency would require both the defeat of the guerrillas and the successful engagement of popular support for the government cause.

That the United States underestimated the danger from Communist guerrilla forces or political cadres was apparent in the counterinsurgency plan that Admiral Harry Felt, commander in chief of Pacific forces (CINCPAC), began to develop in March 1960. The plan emphasized preparations for conventional war and financed an increase of 20,000 men in the South Vietnamese army, bringing total strength to 170,000. It also supported a modest expansion of the paramilitary forces charged with providing local security to 68,000. Those security forces were already less well-trained and less well-armed than the ARVN. It was assumed that the Saigon government would make political reforms on its own to enhance its popular support.

Kennedy believed it important to stop the Communists in South Vietnam, which he called "the cornerstone of the Free World in Southeast Asia."

After President John F. Kennedy took office in 1961, he tried to change the direction of national security policy. Eschewing what his administration considered to be the rigidity of the Eisenhower New Look policy of relying on massive retaliation to protect U.S. national interests, Kennedy advocated flexible response, training, structuring, and equipping forces to fight across the spectrum of conflict from limited guerrilla campaigns to full-scale nuclear war. The new strategic framework was also intended to help his administration better handle insurgencies, such as the one in South Vietnam, which Soviet Premier Nikita Khrushchev had pledged to support. Kennedy believed it important to stop the Communists in South Vietnam, which he called "the cornerstone of the Free World in Southeast Asia." His administration hoped to sharpen the focus on counterinsurgency. U.S. Army Special Forces featured prominently in counterinsurgency thinking.

In the early 1960s, the U.S. Army did not embrace counterinsurgency as fervently as civilian disciples of the doctrine in the administration. Army Chief of Staff General George Decker allegedly told Kennedy that "any good soldier can handle guerrillas." Like much of the army staff, Decker was unenthusiastic about special training for insurgent warfare. He favored the development of "balanced" U.S. Army forces that could meet a range of threats rather than specialists trained in one kind of warfare. The army did little to alter its force structure to meet the requirements of counterinsurgency, which called for a simpler form of combat, lighter weaponry, and constant small-unit patrolling. The army simply added the counterinsurgency mission to combat divisions that were organized, trained, and equipped to fight as conventional units. Like the ARVN, U.S. divisions were better prepared to engage regular than irregular forces.

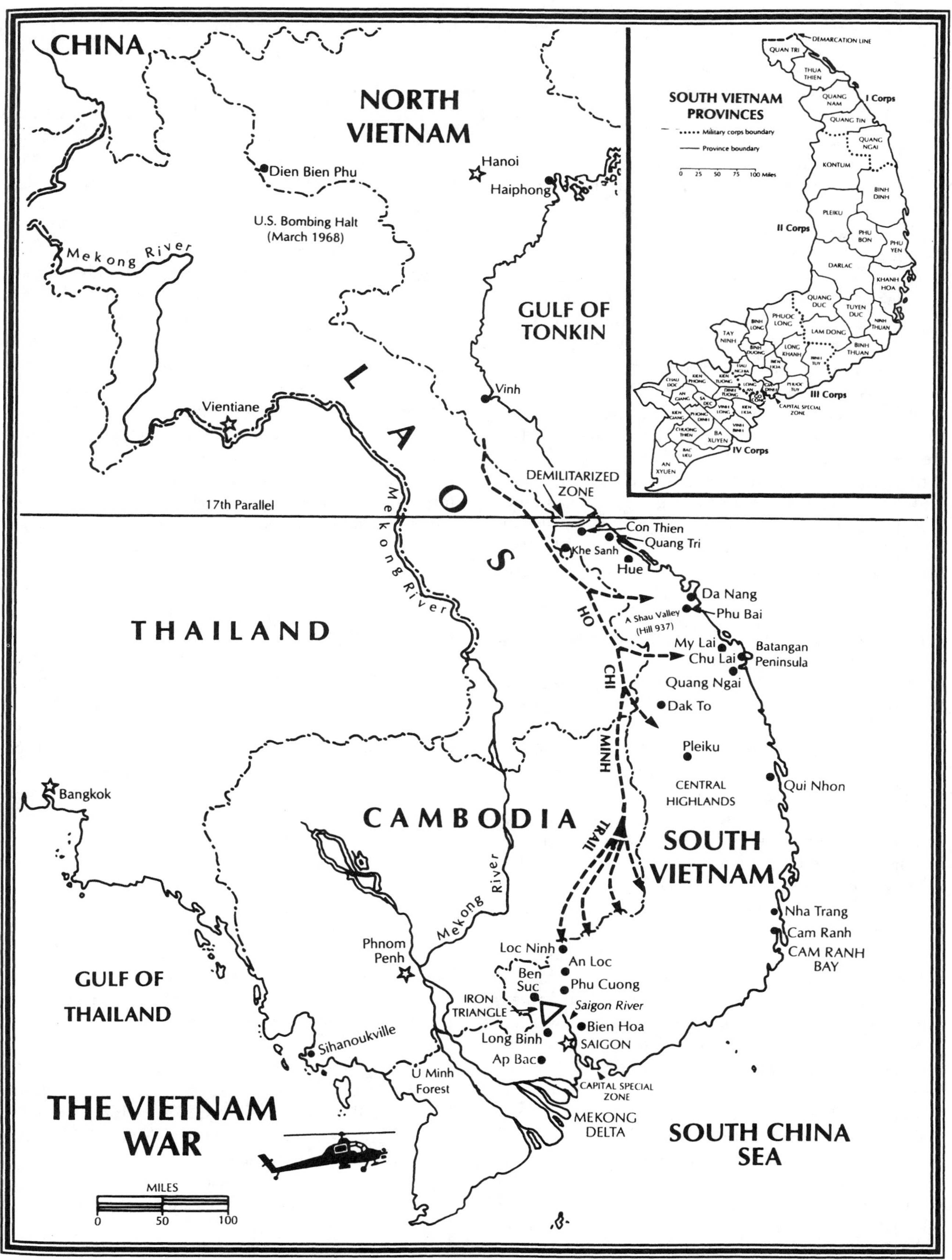

THE VIETNAM WAR
CHINA
NORTH VIETNAM
Dien Bien Phu
Hanoi
Haiphong
U.S. Bombing Halt (March 1968)
Mekong River
GULF OF TONKIN
LAOS
Vinh
Vientiane
DEMILITARIZED ZONE
17th Parallel
Con Thien
Quang Tri
Khe Sanh
Hue
Da Nang
Phu Bai
A Shau Valley (Hill 937)
HO CHI MINH TRAIL
My Lai
Chu Lai
Batangan Peninsula
Quang Ngai
Dak To
Pleiku
THAILAND
Bangkok
CENTRAL HIGHLANDS
Qui Nhon
CAMBODIA
SOUTH VIETNAM
Nha Trang
Cam Ranh
CAM RANH BAY
Phnom Penh
Loc Ninh
An Loc
Ben Suc
Phu Cuong
IRON TRIANGLE
Saigon River
Bien Hoa
Long Binh
SAIGON
Ap Bac
GULF OF THAILAND
Sihanoukville
U Minh Forest
CAPITAL SPECIAL ZONE
MEKONG DELTA
SOUTH CHINA SEA
MILES
0
50
100
SOUTH VIETNAM PROVINCES
Military corps boundary
Province boundary
0 25 50 75 100 Miles
DEMARCATION LINE
QUAN TRI
THUA THIEN
QUANG NAM
I Corps
QUANG TIN
QUANG NGAI
KONTUM
BINH DINH
PLEIKU
II Corps
PHU BON
PHU YEN
DARLAC
KHANH HOA
QUANG DUC
TUYEN DUC
PHUOC LONG
BINH LONG
TAY NINH
LAM DONG
NINH THUAN
BINH DUONG
LONG KHANH
BINH THUAN
BIEN HOA
CHAU DOC
KIEN PHONG
KIEN TUONG
LONG AN
DINH TUONG
PHUOC TUY
III Corps
AN GIANG
SA DEC
GO CONG
CAPITAL SPECIAL ZONE
KIEN GIANG
PHONG DINH
VINH LONG
KIEN HOA
CHUONG THIEN
VINH BINH
BA XUYEN
IV Corps
BAC LIEU
AN XYUEN

Even ostensible counterinsurgency measures gradually took on a conventional cast. In 1961, the Special Forces took over responsibility for advising the Civilian Irregular Defense Groups (CIDGs), a village self-defense and development program. Composed of montagnard tribesmen, the CIDGs soon were involved in border surveillance and control as well as village defense. Located in the sparsely populated provinces of the highlands, the camps and the Special Forces were far removed from the populous Mekong Delta and coastal regions, which were the primary targets of the Vietcong insurgency. Relatively isolated, the CIDG camps were also vulnerable to enemy attack, and by 1965, as the military situation worsened, many CIDG units changed their role and began to launch quasi-conventional operations.

By October 1961, Kennedy had to help the South Vietnamese counter growing Vietcong attacks and increases in enemy forces. Mounting political discontent with Diem inside South Vietnam promised to complicate U.S. initiatives to help Saigon. Any U.S. assistance that strengthened Diem's hand might also allow him to become more authoritarian. Kennedy sent a high-level delegation headed by General Maxwell Taylor, the president's military representative, and Walt Rostow, a White House adviser, on a fact-finding mission to Saigon. They discovered the plight of the Diem government to be more desperate than anticipated and recommended that the president send eight thousand troops and three companies of helicopters to Vietnam. Absent from their report was any consideration of how to invigorate Diem's fragile political base in the villages, which some members of the delegation feared made the regime vulnerable over the long term.

Kennedy ordered two helicopter companies to Vietnam and decided to assign U.S. Army advisers to South Vietnamese regiments, battalions, and provinces. He believed that the gradual dispersion of advisers to smaller Vietnamese units in the field would more directly help improve South Vietnamese military performance and give the U.S. command a new source of influence. The introduction of advisers to field units was a major change that Diem had resisted, in hopes of minimizing U.S. involvement in his affairs. Fewer than one hundred U.S. Army advisers had worked with the Vietnamese before, mostly at the command level and in ARVN training centers; it was hoped that their advice would filter down to units in the countryside. By early 1962, the army had stationed close to nine hundred advisers in Vietnam and had begun to train officers and noncommissioned officers (NCOs) at the Special Warfare Center at Fort Bragg, North Carolina. By early 1965, the army posted officers in all South Vietnamese corps and division headquarters, thirty-one regiments, three brigades, ninety-three battalions, forty-four provinces, and numerous districts.

Advising was an extremely difficult assignment. An adviser helped plan operations and train forces and served as a conduit between the U.S. command and the South Vietnamese, reporting to his superiors on local conditions and attempting to get his counterpart to heed his advice. He also tried to ensure that his South Vietnamese counterpart used U.S. funds and materials honestly and productively. In practice, the adviser could exercise little leverage over South Vietnamese officials, who might be senior in rank, age, and experience. The adviser had no authority to issue direct orders. Instead, his superiors encouraged him to work to establish rapport with his counterpart. It usually took an American several months to begin to understand the local military situation and the nuances of South Vietnamese military and civilian politics. Unfortunately, short tours of duty for advisers made it difficult to build rapport or develop more than a superficial acquaintance with the local scene. A military adviser would also need to coordinate his activities with those of the province representative, a civilian official of the Agency for International Development (AID), who administered U.S. support of nonmilitary programs, such as police training and economic development.

Army advisers were well-represented in nearly every aspect of South Vietnamese military activity, except territorial security, a critical element of pacification. Only 100 to 150 of 1,820 U.S. Army advisers were assigned to pacification-related duties at the end of June 1964. This figure represented something of an improvement; before 1963 only five advisers assisted the territorial security forces. Despite Kennedy's interest in stemming wars of national liberation, U.S. assistance from the counterinsurgency plan to the 1964 buildup of advisers concentrated on conventional forces.

To help ARVN cope with the Vietcong, Kennedy continually sent helicopters to Vietnam. First used to support ARVN corps and divisions, they soon became indispensable in carrying out other functions. The UH-1, or Huey, which was introduced in the early 1960s, transported men and supplies, reconnoitered, evacuated wounded, and provided command and control for ground operations. Advisers instructed ARVN in special air assault tactics that took advantage of the speed, mobility, and lift of the craft. Exercises in 1963 and 1964, encouraged by Defense Secretary Robert McNamara, validated new uses for helicopters. Armaments—first machine guns and later rockets—were added to suppress antiaircraft fire, "soften" landing zones, and furnish fire support to ground soldiers.

The Kennedy administration witnessed a dramatic growth in U.S. resources invested in the preservation of South Vietnam. Military strength went from fewer than eight hundred in the last year of the Eisenhower administration to about twenty-three thousand by the end of 1964. The army accounted for the bulk of these numbers, fifteen thousand, of whom about two thousand were advisers. In 1962 a provisional Special Forces Group was formed in Vietnam. Air force strength reached six thousand; the navy, 1,150; and the marines, 850. With a growing military presence in South Vietnam, the United States obviously committed its prestige. Less obvious at the time was how difficult it would be to withdraw or compel the Saigon regime to make basic reforms.

Changes in the command structure accompanied the growth in military personnel. In February 1962, the JCS established the United States Military Assistance Command, Vietnam (MACV), to oversee the U.S. military effort.The MACV commander, army General Paul Harkins, was the senior U.S. military official in Vietnam. Responsible for U.S. military policy, operations, and assistance, Harkins reported to Admiral Felt, CINCPAC, in Hawaii, but because of the growing interest in Vietnam he also enjoyed direct access to military and civilian leaders in Washington. Harkins was authorized to discuss military operations and assistance with President Diem and other Vietnamese leaders. Under Harkins, MACV also came to assume direction of the advisory effort from the MAAG, which was formally disestablished in 1964. In addition to managing the advisory effort, MACV commanded army support units. The U.S. Army Support Group, Vietnam, provided administrative and logistical support for army units. Harkins' responsibility also extended to U.S. forces in Thailand, where he exercised the same authority he did as commander of MACV.

The creation of MACV raised new organizational issues. After MACV was set up, the Pacific Air Forces Command (PACAF), which was part of the Pacific Command in Hawaii, established the Second Advanced Squadron in Vietnam. Originally formed as an air component command, the squadron evolved into the air component command headquarters. A separate naval component was thought unnecessary when MACV was established. The Naval Section of the MAAG and the Headquarters Support Activity, Saigon, a small navy logistical office under MACV, was assigned to develop a viable Vietnamese naval force. Some army officers pressed for a separate army component commander, but the air force opposed the idea, arguing that an army command already existed under MACV. In their view, Harkins favored the army in resolving joint issues, such as the respective aviation roles of the services. Interservice disagreements over command of aircraft continued through the war.

FUTILE EFFORTS

While Kennedy was president, the Diem government devised the Strategic Hamlet Program to defeat the Vietcong in the countryside. Launched late in 1961 by Diem and his brother, Ngo Dinh Nhu, the program sought to create thousands of new, fortified settlements that would isolate people from the Vietcong. The new residents, who frequently were moved from their homes involuntarily, were responsible for hamlet construction and defense. ARVN and paramilitary units provided security during construction. The government planned to carry out social, political, and economic reforms in the hamlets to preempt Vietcong promises of land ownership and economic improvement. The program directly imperiled insurgent ties with the rural population, which was the movement's base of support.

By 1963 the program met determined resistance from the Vietcong, who concentrated on its destruction. In too many instances, inhabitants had scant security from insurgent raids, and Vietcong agents easily entered hamlets, levying taxes and obtaining fresh recruits. With increased Communist pressure, rural security dropped. In late November 1963, Harkins, a constant purveyor of good news, reported that no strategic hamlets were under the control of the Vietcong, but the situation deteriorated dramatically. A U.S. and South Vietnamese survey undertaken in July 1964 judged that only thirty of the 219 strategic hamlets completed in Long An province, for example, still remained under government control.

When Buddhists mounted protests against the government in the summer, Diem used military force to suppress them.

Grandiose plans led to overexpansion, creating far more hamlets than Saigon's military forces could protect or its cadre administer. Too many strategic hamlets had been built too hastily. MACV was justifiably skeptical about how many viable hamlets existed, because the central government exerted strong pressure to show gains, and official reports from the field were generally unreliable. Some hamlets existed only on paper, lacking credible defenses and social programs. Many peasants resented the often harsh living conditions. Promised reforms did not materialize and the program failed to realize its potential.

Not all U.S. officials approved of the strategic hamlets. The head of the MAAG between September 1960 and July 1962, Lieutenant General Lionel McGarr, objected because the program downgraded the activities of conventional military forces. In his mind, defended hamlets connoted a defensive posture of ground forces tied down in static positions.

The MAAG effort to build ARVN as a competent fighting force, however, was having little success. New weapons and U.S. technical advice failed to compensate for deficient ARVN leadership and planning, unimaginative operations, and unwillingness at times to engage the foe. The widely publicized and embarrassing defeat of government forces at the village of Ap Bac in January 1963 pointedly demonstrated the skill of Vietcong forces in negating ARVN advantages in firepower and mobility. The defeat was an ominous sign that the Vietcong could challenge ARVN units of equal strength and step up the intensity of the fighting. If Ap Bac emboldened the Vietcong, it made ARVN more tentative. Government forces generally refrained from night operations and resorted to large sweeps that avoided known enemy base areas.

By the summer of 1963, Diem was in serious trouble. The war was going badly and the main pacification effort, strategic hamlets, was being subverted by the Vietcong and vitiated by the ham-handed management of the regime. When Buddhists mounted protests against the government in the summer, Diem used military force to suppress them, further weakening his political support. Some of his generals concluded that South Vietnam would go down to defeat if he remained in power. With U.S. encouragement, a group of ARVN generals overthrew Diem on 1 November. His ouster and murder prefaced a period not of reform but of political turmoil.

In the aftermath of the coup, no leader was able to unite the South Vietnamese political factions vying for power and reverse the losing trend of the war. The vestiges of central government authority in the countryside began to disappear. The new government replaced thirty-five of forty-one province chiefs, most of whom had been Diem loyalists. Almost all military commands changed hands. Vietcong forces took advantage, increasing their control over rural areas. By March 1964, Washington estimated that 40 percent of South Vietnamese territory was under Communist control. Leaders in Hanoi moved to intensify the armed struggle by training North Vietnamese army units possibly to intervene and by sending conscripts (replacements for the original members of the Vietminh) down the Ho Chi Minh trail, a complex network of trails and roads from North Vietnam through Laos and Cambodia to South Vietnam.

DIRECT U.S. INTERVENTION

The disintegration of the South Vietnamese government and armed forces and the undeniable enemy gains caused the United States to seek new ways to bolster its ally. The restricted U.S. role of providing advice and support had failed to strengthen its ally and had no impact in deterring the Communists. Lyndon B. Johnson, who became president in November 1963 upon the assassination of Kennedy, explored a number of options for limited military action before eventually authorizing direct intervention. He gradually escalated the commitment of U.S. armed forces, hoping with each step to deter North Vietnam and bolster South Vietnam. As one of his first initiatives, he approved OPLAN 34A, authorizing U.S. support for South Vietnamese covert operations against North Vietnam. It was hoped that the plan, which was implemented in February 1964, would increase military pressure on North Vietnam and signify U.S. support for the Saigon regime.

In effect, OPLAN 34A served as the preamble for a new statement of policy, National Security Action Memorandum (NSAM) 288 of March 1964, calling for an enlarged U.S. effort. Washington's new objective was to seek an independent, non-Communist South Vietnam that was free to accept outside assistance to maintain its security. This objective, which advanced no U.S. claims on South Vietnam, came to justify whatever steps were needed to prevent a Communist victory. As part of NSAM 288, the JCS developed a program of air attacks against military and industrial targets in North Vietnam. Air force planners and such presidential advisers as Rostow assumed that because the Vietcong relied heavily on backing from North Vietnam, harming the north would induce Hanoi to curtail its support. The bombing plan was temporarily shelved because the administration regarded the government of General Nguyen Khanh, then ruling Saigon, as so weak and unstable that it might collapse before the bombing could have any effect. Punishing North Vietnam by bombing was at the least an indirect, if not enigmatic, way to implement the policy of developing an independent, sovereign nation in the south. The bombing could in no way render the Saigon government more effective. The bombing also failed to acknowledge the self-sufficiency of a Vietcong movement that could carry out an insurgency with indigenous resources.

Pacification, the objectives of which were tantamount to the NSAM 288 goal of an independent non-Communist state, received comparatively less emphasis under the new policy. The ill-fated *Hop Tac* plan, an effort to secure the area around Saigon, became part of the NSAM. Poorly supported by ARVN, *Hop Tac* was a major disappointment, failing to improve security or shift the balance of power in the countryside around the capital. Alongside the planning for a bombing campaign and the initiation of covert operations (intelligence overflights, commando raids, and the infiltration of guerrilla units into North Vietnam), the new pacification plan was a minor step.

Johnson's graduated pressure had little effect. North Vietnam showed no inclination to back down and responded defiantly to U.S. warnings. In August, North Vietnamese torpedo boats attacked U.S. Navy destroyers engaged in electronic eavesdropping in the Gulf of Tonkin off the coast of North Vietnam. The episode was sufficient reason for President Johnson to approve retaliatory air strikes. Aircraft from the U.S. Navy carriers *Ticonderoga* and *Constellation,* stationed in the South China Sea, bombed North Vietnamese torpedo boat bases and oil storage dumps, destroying twenty-five boats and damaging the oil storage facility at Vinh. The president also used the incident to secure passage on 7 August, with only two dissenting votes, of a congressional resolution authorizing him to take "all necessary measures" to repel any armed attacks and prevent further aggression. It was analogous to a formal declaration of war and allowed Johnson to consider additional military efforts in Vietnam without prior congressional approval.

An Easter march against the war drew about twenty thousand mostly young persons to Washington.

The Tonkin Gulf Resolution also filled domestic political needs. It demonstrated that the nation was united. The show of force and appeal for national support permitted Johnson to disarm his Republican challenger, Senator Barry Goldwater, who had vigorously urged escalation of the war, but this apparent domestic benefit carried a hidden cost. In arguing for the resolution, the administration misled Congress and the public, portraying the attacks as deliberate and unprovoked aggression. The decision not to disclose the program of covert actions that the destroyers were carrying out later harmed the administration.

The retaliatory raids and the threat of further reprisals seemed to spur the Communists on rather than dissuade them. In November 1964 the Vietcong shelled the U.S. air base at Bien-hoa, killing four men. Later in the year, regular North Vietnamese Army (NVA) units began to move south and were poised to enter the central highlands. In February 1965, enemy forces struck U.S. installations in the highlands, first attacking an advisory compound in Pleiku and then sabotaging quarters in Qui Nhon.

The administration again looked to bombing to show U.S. resolve, promptly mounting retaliatory raids on military targets in North Vietnam. Individual raids gave way to a sustained bombing campaign of increasingly intense strikes against military and industrial targets in North Vietnam that began on 13 February 1965. Code named Rolling Thunder, the campaign was designed to harm the enemy and boost South Vietnamese morale by demonstrating the commitment of the United States to the defense of its ally. A parallel air war, identified as Operation Barrel Roll, had begun on a limited scale in December against military targets in the Laotian panhandle. From the beginning, Rolling Thunder proved controversial. It was viewed by the White House as a campaign for political objectives, and the president and his top civilian advisers established controls on bombing targets and the frequency of attacks, much to the annoyance of the military. The president's top civilian advisers—McGeorge Bundy, Rostow, McNamara and his deputy John McNaughton, and William Bundy, an assistant secretary of state—subscribed to the theory of limited war, and Rolling Thunder was carried out under its tenets. The underlying notion was to limit the U.S. military response to avoid a wider war or the involvement of other Communist powers, but to use enough force, coupled with the threat of greater punishment, to induce Hanoi to seek terms. The administration viewed bombing as a means of communicating resolve. Only Undersecretary of State George Ball vigorously objected to the bombing, and by late March 1965 other advisers had lost faith in its sufficiency and doubted that Rolling Thunder alone would quickly achieve the goal of deterring North Vietnam from fighting. At this time, the White House began to contemplate the use of U.S. ground forces in Vietnam as the primary way to win.

Even as some in the administration came to question the bombing, Rolling Thunder galvanized elements of the U.S. populace. Antiwar and radical political groups, which had started to coalesce at the beginning of the bombing, made it the focal point of their outcry. An Easter march against the war drew about twenty thousand mostly young persons to Washington. Teach-ins, protest lectures on the war, started at the University of Michigan in May 1965 and by the end of the school year had been held in more than 120 schools. At this point, public opinion polls indicated that most Americans supported the president and looked on the demonstrations as radical troublemaking.

Throughout the spring the Vietcong continued to disrupt pacification, making gains in the central coastal provinces and resisting government efforts in the delta and provinces around Saigon. The Communists pressed for a major military victory over the ARVN, attacking border posts and highland camps and hoping to draw government units away from populated areas. Strengthened by several NVA regiments that infiltrated into South Vietnam, Vietcong forces were decisively winning the war in most of the country. ARVN losses in the summer were the equivalent of nearly a battalion a week. By inflicting a series of defeats on government forces already suffering serious losses from casualties and desertions, the Communists hoped to force the Saigon government into negotiating a political settlement and the withdrawal of U.S. forces.

President Johnson did not wish to become embroiled in an Asian land war that would divert funds from his ambitious social and economic reform program, the Great Society, and he wanted to avoid a confrontation with Hanoi's Communist allies, Russia and China. He nevertheless realized he had to do more than bomb North Vietnam to prevent the almost certain defeat of South Vietnam. His desire to avoid a wider war and his concern with saving Vietnam persuaded him to commit a small number of ground forces. On 8 March 1965 the Third Battalion, Ninth Marine Regiment, and the First Battalion, Third Marine Regiment, landed on the beaches north of Danang, where the Americans had a sprawling air base. The mission was to protect the facility, but the force was barely adequate to do so. More marines followed, and the president modified their mission to allow them to conduct offensive operations close to their bases. To protect U.S. installations near the capital, Johnson sent the first army combat unit to South Vietnam and, to support the growing military presence, authorized the army to begin deploying twenty-five thousand logistical troops, the main body of the First Logistical Command. By May, U.S. military strength in Vietnam passed fifty thousand. Presidential

"The United States landed two battalions of Marines on the coastal city of Da Nang on March 8, 1965, beginning the U.S. commitment of ground forces in the Vietnam conflict. (UPI/Corbis)

caution about the domestic and international consequences of widening the war led to the incremental deployment of ground troops rather than sending at one time the number of soldiers necessary to preserve South Vietnam.

The president indicated he would go only so far in pursuing the war. The combat units he sent were regulars, and he had turned down a recommendation by McNamara to mobilize National Guard or reserve units, expecting the gradual escalation of the air and ground war to induce Hanoi to negotiate. His decision, however, had a serious impact on how the army, the only service that had to rely on the draft to fill its ranks, would sustain the buildup and manage its role in the war. The Department of the Army and the Continental Army Command in their contingency planning had assumed that a partial call-up of the reserves would offset the deployment of forces to Vietnam. Johnson's decision rendered these plans useless. To meet the need for additional combat forces, preserve the training base, and develop a pool of replacements for Vietnam, the army had to increase its active strength over a three-year period, relying on draft calls, volunteers, and the reassignment of experienced soldiers from units in Europe and South Korea. Combat units were pulled out of the strategic reserve, essentially a contingency force, and sent to Vietnam to help meet MACV force requirements. Significantly, no reserve units were called up to fill their places. At bottom, the decision against a call-up of reserve forces implied a lack of political will to support the national objective in Vietnam. The president decided to wage war in Vietnam and fight poverty at home, but he limited the military commitment in hopes of being able to win without compromising his domestic agenda.

The decision not to call up the reserves also required the army to organize additional combat units. In the second half of 1965, it activated three light infantry brigades, reactivated the Ninth Division (the first army division activated, organized, equipped, and trained for deployment to a combat theater in two decades), and alerted the Fourth and Twenty-fifth divisions for deployment. By the end of 1966, military strength in Vietnam reached 385,000 and the next year almost 490,000. Army personnel accounted for almost two-thirds of the total.

The arrival of North Vietnamese and U.S. combat forces in South Vietnam in the summer of 1965 transformed the nature of the war. It was no longer just a struggle to defeat Vietcong insurgents. A war between North Vietnamese conventional forces that had entered South Vietnam and U.S. ground forces, the main force war, was superimposed on the continuing political struggle for the countryside. The deployment of growing numbers of ground troops also represented the relative downgrading of pressure against North Vietnam in favor of more intensive activity in South Vietnam. Operation Rolling Thunder eventually assumed a secondary role, its main value as a bargaining chip to get Hanoi to begin talks. President Johnson periodically halted the bombing over the years to entice Ho's government into serious negotiations.

With the growth in military strength, the army tried to establish the U.S. Army, Vietnam (USARV) as the component command responsible for army operations, but General William Westmoreland, who had become MACV commander in June 1964, opposed this idea and prevailed. He remained unified commander of MACV as well as commander of USARV. USARV served exclusively in a logistical and administrative capacity but in the course of the buildup managed a massive support base. Westmoreland also established several army corps-level headquarters, called field forces, to oversee ground operations in various regions of Vietnam. Westmoreland perceived the conflict in the south as essentially a ground war, with air power playing a supporting role. Consequently, he resisted requests from the other services for high-level representation on the MACV staff. Throughout his tenure, indeed throughout the existence of MACV, the army dominated MACV headquarters in numbers of personnel and control of key slots.

Unity of command proved unachievable in other areas. Westmoreland had no command authority over South Vietnamese troops or of those of other countries—Korea, Australia, New Zealand, and Thailand—contributing combatants to defend Vietnam. He executed compacts with commanders of each national force (including the South Vietnamese) that ensured cooperation but fell short of giving him actual command over allied forces. The MACV commander did not have authority over the operations of other U.S. agencies, such as the Central Intelligence Agency (CIA), that in effect were running their own war in Vietnam.

Westmoreland viewed air power as a key weapon in supporting his effort to defeat enemy forces, but he exercised limited operational control of the air war. Much of the U.S. air and naval operations, including Rolling Thunder, fell outside his authority and were carried out by forces under the overall command of Admiral Ulysses Grant Sharp, CINCPAC, with the White House playing a role in target selection. Interservice rivalry stood in the way of establishing a single commander for the air war. The respective air and naval components of the Pacific Command, PACAF and PACFLT, directed the efforts of their respective services at Rolling Thunder. Navy and air force units divided North Vietnam into separate zones for aerial attacks, and navy and air force units vied for the highest sortie rate. Under PACAF, the Seventh Air Force located in Vietnam and an echelon of the Thirteenth Air Force operating from Thailand shared control. The Seventh Air Force served two masters, providing planes for Rolling Thunder under CINCPAC and supporting allied ground operations under General Westmoreland. Under the overall control of PACFLT, the commander of the Seventh Fleet mounted the naval portion of Rolling Thunder, tactical reconnaissance operations in North Vietnam and Laos, and ground support in South Vietnam. The large Marine Air Wing flew its missions under the operational control of III Marine Amphibious Force (III MAF), a corps-type headquarters at Danang. To further complicate the situation, the B-52 force, upon which MACV relied to break up enemy troop concentrations and strike base areas in South Vietnam, remained under the operational control of the Strategic Air Command, although MACV designated the targets.

Prosecuting the war suffered from divided command in another area—where military and pacification operations intersected. After the military intervention, the conduct of military operations and U.S. support of pacification were handled separately, with MACV tending to military issues and the civilian agencies tending to support pacification. In a war fought for the political goal of establishing a viable nation in South Vietnam, the failure to unify the political and military aspects of the struggle, as the Communists had, was a serious flaw. The patchwork of command arrangements, the division of the war into civil and military spheres, contributed to the absence of a unified strategy and the pursuit of parochial service interests. Westmoreland, the senior military officer in South Vietnam, lacked authority to devise an overall strategy or coordinate all military aspects of the war.

In addition, Westmoreland faced severe constraints in using the forces under his command. In the spring of 1965, although Johnson issued no directives to General Westmoreland on how U.S. troops should operate to sustain the independence of South Vietnam, he did limit options by prohibiting ground operations against Communist sanctuaries in Laos and Cambodia. He banned U.S. conventional ground operations inside North Vietnam, despite that country's role as a de facto belligerent. Restrictions on ground and air operations and the prospect of receiving more U.S. troops were the framework within which Westmoreland planned his ground strategy.

Westmoreland believed that the Communists had decided to start the climactic third stage of guerrilla warfare (mobile warfare by battalions, regiments, and divisions). As evidence he pointed to the North Vietnamese Army units coming into South Vietnam and the Vietcong strengthening of forces from village guerrillas to main force regiments. Because he could not pursue enemy units into their cross-border sanctuaries, Westmoreland hoped to find and destroy enemy formations inside South Vietnam before they could endanger population centers. Accordingly, he decided to station U.S. Army forces in base camps and firebases away from population centers and near probable infiltration routes so they could more readily engage enemy forces in remote areas. The mobility and firepower of the army made such a deployment feasible. Hueys, which arrived with the newly activated First Cavalry Division in the fall of 1965, provided air transport for combat troops and allowed U.S. commanders to concentrate quickly soldiers in scattered bases against an enemy unit.

At the end of July 1965, President Johnson announced plans to increase U.S. military strength in South Vietnam to 175,000 by the end of the year.

Westmoreland devised a three-phase concept of operations in which pacification had a distinctly subordinate role. His plan called first for averting the defeat of South Vietnam by using forty-four U.S. battalions (army and Marine Corps units), his initial increment of soldiers, primarily to clear logistical base areas and protect military installations for the arrival of subsequent units. Because he felt that the threat posed by North Vietnamese and Vietcong main force units was severe, he did not include support of ongoing pacification efforts in the first phase. His primary concern was to contain the enemy's spring-summer offensive of 1965 with the relatively small number of U.S. troops on hand. The offensive in the central highlands, led by at least three NVA regiments, overran border camps, besieged district towns, and, Westmoreland feared, threatened to cut the nation in two. In the second phase, beginning in 1966, Westmoreland expected, with the twenty-four additional battalions that would then be at his disposal, to go on the offensive and "resume and expand pacification operations" in priority areas—the capital region, certain delta provinces, most of I Corps, and Binh Dinh and Phu Yen provinces in II Corps. In the final phase, he envisioned victory at some unspecified time after 1968. By that point, the incremental attrition of enemy strength would make the war so costly the enemy would seek a negotiated settlement, an underlying rationale identical with that of the air campaign.

Not everyone agreed with Westmoreland's approach. Another school of thought believed that U.S. ground forces should focus on population security and pacification, concentrating their efforts in coastal enclaves around key urban centers and bases. U.S. forces would provide security so that the Vietnamese could expand pacified areas. This concept, reflecting the pattern of initial deployments, proved short-lived as more U.S. and regular North Vietnamese forces entered South Vietnam. At the end of July 1965, President Johnson announced plans to increase U.S. military strength in South Vietnam to 175,000 by the end of the year. By late summer, enemy combat strength reached an estimated 221,000, including fifty-five NVA battalions and 105 Vietcong battalions. Given the superior firepower and mobility of U.S. ground forces, Westmoreland rejected what he regarded as the defensive strategy of using U.S. soldiers to protect populated enclaves, a strategy suggested by Army Chief of Staff General Harold K. Johnson and embraced by Taylor, whom the president had named U.S. ambassador to Vietnam. Westmoreland regarded the enclave theory as "an inglorious, static use of U.S. forces in overpopulated areas" that would leave them positioned in vulnerable beachheads and allow the enemy to hold the initiative on the battlefield.

As part of his concept of operations, Westmoreland agreed with the South Vietnamese command that U.S. forces would concentrate on fighting the main force war against the NVA, while ARVN, which was disintegrating as a fighting force, would fix their efforts on the Vietcong. He focused on pursuing the enemy away from population centers, even though throughout the spring and summer guerrilla units seriously threatened the inhabited areas of the countryside. In large parts of the country, government control was restricted largely to areas surrounding district and province capitals and the major roads and waterways during daylight.

Not all U.S. forces subscribed to Westmoreland's emphasis on search-and-destroy and attrition. Stationed in I Corps, U.S. Marine Corps units under Lieutenant General Lewis Walt, III MAF commander, concentrated on providing security for the densely populated hamlets in their area of operations, which, Westmoreland complained, left the enemy free to recruit in areas the marines had not yet entered and to operate in nearby hills with impunity. Walt saw little advantage in having marines seek out enemy forces in remote areas when the real target of the war was political—control of the population. Marine Corps operations represented a clear alternative to Westmoreland's strategy and were frequently praised by critics of the so-called big-unit war.

GROUND OPERATIONS UNDER WESTMORELAND

South Vietnam's high command divided the nation into four corps (I, II, III, and IV) largely for purposes of organizing and controlling military operations. Westmoreland followed Vietnamese precedent and deployed his forces within existing corps boundaries, appointing an army or Marine Corps general as the senior U.S. military official in each. The corps consisted of several provinces, and owing to varying terrain, proximity to North Vietnam, population density, and the enemy strength and force structure, the nature of the ground war was different in each corps.

In III Corps, Westmoreland concentrated on the defense of Saigon, deploying his forces where they could protect the approaches and infiltration routes to the city. The first army unit in Vietnam, the 173d Airborne Brigade, deployed from Okinawa. It was initially assigned to protect the air base at Bien-hoa, northeast of the capital, and in June 1965 began operations in War Zone D. The First Infantry Division secured base camps north of Saigon and helped South Vietnamese forces clear the Chu Chi area of Hau Nghia province, which was west of the capital. After the spring of 1966, the Twenty-fifth Infantry and the Fourth Infantry divisions assisted in the defense of Saigon, completing an arc of U.S. deployments around the capital.

During the buildup of U.S. ground forces, most operations were devoted to base and area security and to clearing and rebuilding roads. In road-clearing operations, the army improvised a new technique, Rome plows (bulldozers with a modified sharpened front), to remove vegetation alongside roads that might provide cover for ambushes. Over time the army also used chemical defoliants to kill trees and plants along canals and to destroy crops and the natural cover in enemy-held areas. In Operation Ranch Hand the air force conducted aerial spraying of herbicides on South Vietnam jungles and mangrove forests between 1961 and 1971.

By the summer of 1966, Westmoreland believed his forces were strong and large enough to begin the second phase of his strategy, offensive operations to search out and destroy enemy main force units. Operation Attleboro represented this transition. It began in September, when the 196th Infantry Brigade and a brigade from the Fourth Division moved into Tay Ninh province against War Zone C, and grew into a multidivision battle. Despite the large U.S. force involved, most combat occurred at night at the platoon and company level. As the U.S. contingent swelled, the opposing Ninth Vietcong Division avoided contact and withdrew across the Cambodian border to fight again. The reaction of the Vietcong under fire was not unusual. The enemy preferred to mount small-scale attacks on isolated outposts containing few troops or poorly defended settlements, having little interest in allowing the Americans with their superior firepower to decimate them in a set piece battle. The enemy approach to combat was the perfect antidote to Westmoreland's strategy of attrition.

The army used chemical defoliants to kill trees and plants along canals and to destroy crops and the natural cover in enemy-held areas.

The U.S. Army launched another major operation, Cedar Falls, in January 1967. This time the target was the Iron Triangle, the base area near the capital. Westmoreland hoped to uproot enemy forces and dismantle the Vietcong infrastructure, which, in effect, governed many villages and hamlets. Operation Cedar Falls was a multidivision assault. Although sparsely populated, the Iron Triangle was strategically situated between the cross-border sanctuaries in Cambodia on one side and the population and rice crops of the capital region and delta on the other.

Expecting organized defense to come from the vicinity of Ben Suc, a settlement of about three thousand people thirty miles northwest of the capital on the Saigon River, Major General William E. DePuy, commander of the First Infantry Division, wanted to seize and evacuate the village before the Iron Triangle itself was encircled. That would allow him to use the division's firepower while minimizing the risk of inflicting civilian casualties. Relocating and assisting the villagers was the responsibility of South Vietnamese provincial officials and the Office of Civil Operations (OCO), a U.S. organization under Deputy Ambassador William Porter.

Fearing that Communist agents in the government and armed forces might compromise Operation Cedar Falls, the Americans closely held their plans. They informed South Vietnamese paramilitary forces, the ARVN Fifth Division commander, the U.S. civilian province representative, and the Binh Duong province chief after the operation was under way. The province chief had no time to plan for relocating refugees, even though it was his responsibility. John Paul Vann, director of OCO in III Corps and the only official of his agency to participate in the early planning, was expressly forbidden to coordinate with South Vietnamese authorities or to stockpile supplies at the site of the refugee center in the town of Phu Cuong in advance of the operation. Not surprisingly, the evacuation of Ben Suc was delayed. It took the province chief two days to obtain enough boats to move some twenty-eight hundred people, their personal belongings, and livestock. Then, the village was razed.

Attentive primarily to the enemy threat, military planners overlooked the political problems associated with the involuntary relocation of South Vietnamese civilians from their homes. Many of the new refugees complained about being removed from their land and put into poorly prepared camps that offered them little chance of earning a living. The necessity from the military perspective of having to relocate civilians, many of whom were already unsympathetic or even hostile to the government, gained no support for Saigon. Concerns over security exacerbated relations between civilian AID officials and the First Division. General DePuy wanted to run the refugee relocation and assistance effort, because he was convinced that Vann's agency and the South Vietnamese would be unable to handle the operation. Strained relations between the U.S. military and the Saigon government were an inauspicious outcome of Operation Cedar Falls. South Vietnamese authorities apparently had no voice in the decision to destroy and evacuate several villages—actions that clearly denigrated government sovereignty. The U.S. press publicized the relocation as a brutish action.

Besides the cost in adverse publicity, friction between U.S. civil and military agencies, and strained relations with the South Vietnamese government and people, Cedar Falls failed to achieve lasting military or political control of the Iron Triangle. According to Brigadier General (later general and chief of staff of the army) Bernard W. Rogers, assistant commander of the First Division, neither the South Vietnamese nor the Americans had sufficient forces to continue to operate in the Iron Triangle or prevent the enemy from returning.

The operation was significant for another reason—it clearly illustrated Westmoreland's operational priorities. Although he frequently preached about the importance of army operations in support of pacification, he devoted his energies to operations like Cedar Falls and not to clearing and holding the small hamlets and villages around Saigon. Despite the steady growth of U.S. personnel in 1965 and 1966, Westmoreland still lacked sufficient forces to conduct search-and-destroy missions and to provide security for Vietnamese settlements.

Operation Fairfax, a joint operation to improve security around Saigon, began about the time of Cedar Falls. U.S. units paired off with South Vietnamese Rangers in a year-long operation that ended in December 1967. Even though the operation lasted more than twelve months and combined military and police forces against the Vietcong, it failed to eliminate the infrastructure in the districts adjacent to the capital. This lack of success was evidence to U.S. and Vietnamese pacification officials of the need to devise a special program that joined Vietnamese police forces and intelligence agencies in an integrated effort to attack the Communist underground government.

In a war fought for political control, IV Corps, located south of Saigon, was critical. This heavily populated area contained the most fertile rice lands of the Mekong River delta. There the conflict was largely between the Vietcong and South Vietnamese regular and paramilitary forces. Besides army and navy advisory teams, only one major U.S. Army unit, the Second Brigade of the Ninth Division, was assigned to the delta, but it carried out an innovative campaign with the U.S. Navy reminiscent of river operations by Union forces in the western theater of the Civil War. Riverine operations sought to dislodge Vietcong forces, protect food-producing areas, and stem the movement of enemy supplies. The Vietcong used the thousands of miles of interconnecting inland waterways as their chief routes for transporting men and equipment. To patrol and fight in the marshlands and rice paddies, the Second Brigade was quartered on navy barracks ships, which transported infantry and artillery units to battle and provided fire support from monitors, heavily armed and armored river craft.

The Second Brigade began operations in May 1967. The riverine force proved its value by being able to move rapidly through difficult terrain to relieve beleaguered villages and pursue enemy forces. The force effectively integrated the capabilities of army and navy units and carried out wide-ranging operations into previously inaccessible or remote Vietcong territory. Mounting artillery on barges substantially increased effectiveness. Such mobility and fire support improved the security of the waterways for South Vietnamese citizens.

Riverine operations in the delta's waterways complemented the navy's task forces of Operations Game Warden and Market Time. Market Time had the mission of patrolling coastal areas to prevent the resupply of Vietcong forces by sea. Game Warden sought to interdict enemy lines of communication and assist government forces in repelling attacks on river outposts of the Regional and Popular Forces (RF/PF), Vietnamese paramilitary units that were responsible for providing local security.

II Corps, geographically the largest corps in Vietnam, posed a unique challenge for Westmoreland. The MACV commander had to stem the 1965 Communist offensive in the sparsely settled central highlands, which he feared was intended to cut South Vietnam in two, and also to protect the heavily populated coastal areas where the ports and logistical bases that supported the U.S. buildup were located. To deal with both contingencies, the First Cavalry Division, with more than four hundred helicopters, established its main base at An Khe, halfway between Qui Nhon and the highland city of Pleiku, allowing it to keep the main east-west road open and operate in the highlands or the coastal plain. In addition to the First Cavalry, South Korean forces and other U.S. units were deployed to II Corps in 1965 and 1966. Some of these units, along with the South Vietnamese forces, provided area security for the ports and supply facilities at Cam Ranh Bay, Nha Trang, and Qui Nhon.

In the fall of 1965, three battalions of the First Cavalry ran into elements of two NVA regiments in a series of engagements in the Ia Drang Valley, a mountainous region in the western part of Pleiku province. At Landing Zone X-Ray, a surrounded U.S. unit had to call on all available firepower—helicopter gunships, artillery bombardment, bombing and strafing by tactical aircraft, and heavy ordnance dropped by B-52 bombers flying from Guam—to hold off repeated NVA assaults. This fight cost six hundred enemy and seventy-nine American deaths.

Acclaimed as a major victory, Ia Drang was a costly and questionable success. The enemy did not leave the valley. At Landing Zone X-Ray and Landing Zone Albany, the enemy assaulted vulnerable U.S. units, which were saved by massive air and artillery support. This support required incredible logistical efforts to bring in fuel, spare parts, air support crews, pilots, and aircraft. The division's logistical resources proved insufficient. Prolonged operations consumed more fuel and ammunition than helicopters could supply, and air force tactical aircraft were pressed into resupply missions; divisional helicopters suffered from heavy use, heat, and humidity. Following the Ia Drang fighting, frequent North Vietnamese attacks on remote Special Forces camps signaled the enemy's intention to continue to infiltrate forces and fight in the highlands. Westmoreland felt compelled to deploy forces near the border in an effort to keep enemy main forces as far as possible from heavily populated areas.

It was part of Hanoi's strategy to keep U.S. forces off balance by posing simultaneous threats in the highlands and the coastal plain. The threat in the highlands siphoned friendly forces from supporting pacification programs in the more populous regions. Whenever guerrilla or local forces were endangered, Hanoi tried to draw U.S. units from the capital region in III Corps and the II Corps coastal plain to the less populous zones along the border. Ground operations took on an all too familiar pattern. Airmobile assaults, often in the wake of Arc Light air strikes of B-52 bombers flown from bases on Guam to bomb Vietcong bases, resulted in episodic contact with the Vietcong and withdrawal after a few days of extensive patrolling of enemy territory. Enemy forces generally chose when to stand and fight.

The goal of Operation Golden Fleece was to keep the crop out of Vietcong hands and allow farmers to sell their rice on the local market.

In I Corps, U.S. Marine forces operated under a different philosophy than army troops in II and III Corps. In their initial operations, the marines sought to provide security for the area around the air bases at Phu Bai, Chu Lai, and Da Nang. They gradually expanded the tactical area of operations within which they attempted to weed out the Vietcong. In the fall of 1965, the marines sought to protect the rice harvest in the agricultural areas south of Da Nang. The goal of Operation Golden Fleece was to keep the crop out of Vietcong hands and allow farmers to sell their rice on the local market. The operation targeted anyone trying to interfere with the harvest and protected farmers from Vietcong levies but did not provide continuous security.

The marines set up the Combined Action Platoon (CAP) program to do just that. A noteworthy innovation begun in August 1965, a CAP consisted of a marine rifle squad, a navy medical corpsman, and a Popular Forces (PF) platoon. The CAP would settle in a village, typically consisting of five hamlets spread out over four square kilometers and containing thirty-five hundred people, and help to protect the settlement from Vietcong raids. Although the number of CAPs grew, there were never enough to cover all the villages in I Corps, and, partly owing to Westmoreland's opposition, CAPs were not tried in other parts of Vietnam. Unfortunately, the program often induced a sense of dependency in the PF platoon, resulting in only transitory improvements. After a marine squad left a village, security usually deteriorated. In many cases, PF platoons had come to depend on outside assistance and frequently proved unable to cope with the local Vietcong on their own.

As the marines recognized, sustained local security was the critical component of pacification, providing a shield for the government cadre that carried out programs to improve conditions in poor villages that lacked schools, adequate sanitation, and water supply. If the government could not protect its people, it had little chance over the long term of holding their political support. Without effective security provided by paramilitary or regular forces, the Vietcong could assassinate or kidnap local officials, levy taxes, spread propaganda, and obtain recruits. In the absence of security, reforms and social welfare programs would prove ephemeral.

Westmoreland was critical of marine operations because of their relatively static deployment and primary focus on pacification. Rather than have them protect villages and rice harvests, he wanted the marines to deploy as mobile units actively seeking out Vietcong formations over a broad area. The marines objected to Westmoreland's determination to fight guerrillas by staging decisive battles, reflecting from the outset the strong disagreement within the military over his attrition strategy.

HELP FOR THE "OTHER WAR"

Despite the promise of innovations such as the CAP program and the humanitarian and medical projects of military civil affairs teams, the pacification program was in trouble. The Vietcong continued to consolidate their rule in the absence of an effective national pacification program. Although the Johnson administration called pacification the "other war," it regarded the political struggle as more than an adjunct to the fighting. Westmoreland's concept of operations and the tendency of U.S. forces to fight the war for the Vietnamese worried policymakers, who feared that pacification was being pushed deeper into the shadows as more U.S. soldiers arrived in South Vietnam. The White House was convinced that military actions alone could not accomplish the stated goal, expressed in NSAM 288, of developing an autonomous South Vietnam that could defend itself.

The imbalance between the "other war" and an expanding military conflict was troubling. Even at the start of the buildup in 1965, money for military assistance (hardware, gear and clothing, and ammunition for the Vietnamese), a total of $318 million, already outstripped economic aid of $290 million, and the amount spent for military assistance excluded the cost of U.S. military operations. As policymakers pondered how to improve pacification, they came over time to consider directly involving MACV, because it had the largest logistical structure and the most personnel in

Vietnam. In practical terms this meant formally recognizing that offensive operations by U.S. units to destroy the Vietcong were "but a part of the total pacification program," as one army officer described it.

The eclipse of pacification by the burgeoning ground war was only one aspect of pacification's troubles. U.S. support of the program was poorly organized. Although the ambassador was in charge of the country team and thus the nominal manager of U.S. support, the representatives of the separate agencies largely went their own way, taking direction from their respective headquarters in Washington. The absence of strong centralized management led to duplication of effort in the field and poor coordination among responsible U.S. agencies. It proved close to impossible to forge a pacification plan with common goals.

The efforts of civilian and military advisers in the provinces also were not coordinated. There was no clear delineation of military and nonmilitary responsibilities, and procedures to reconcile overlapping programs or conflicting priorities were inadequate. Advisers were not empowered to take charge. Without a single advisory coordinator at the province level, it was hard to develop a concerted policy on ways to influence South Vietnamese officials. Under their guidance, South Vietnamese cadre teams, police, and territorial forces carried out the economic and security programs that comprised pacification. Difficulty in coordinating civil and military programs extended to the district level. In the provinces and districts, two separate U.S. hierarchies—civilian and military—supported different aspects of pacification and advised the Vietnamese. With the relative ne-

U.S. Air Force jets, photographed from above, drop bombs over the southern panhandle of North Vietnam on 14 June 1966. (National Archives)

glect by the U.S. Army, poorly organized support, ineffective South Vietnamese management of its various programs, and a strong adversary in the Vietcong, pacification had little chance against a well-organized and entrenched Communist movement that controlled significant parts of the countryside.

A number of developments made reform of pacification possible. Growing numbers of U.S. Army forces, which exceeded 180,000 by the end of 1965, made unlikely the military defeat of South Vietnam. With that threat removed, the administration could seek to remedy pacification. The Saigon government itself, long vitiated by factional fighting, attained a measure of stability under the military rule of Premier Nguyen Cao Ky and Chief of State Nguyen Van Thieu, who came to power in June 1965. Thus, there was hope of establishing a program to bring security to the countryside on a secure political foundation.

The program's stagnation concerned President Johnson, who became directly involved in making reforms. At the Honolulu Conference with South Vietnamese leaders in February 1966, he sought to redress the imbalance of U.S. strategy, which he felt was skewed to military solutions, and the managerial weaknesses of U.S. nonmilitary programs. The conference resulted in two noteworthy appointments that the president hoped would lead to more effective use of U.S. resources for pacification. Johnson named Robert W. Komer, a member of the White House staff, as special assistant to the president for Vietnam, with a mandate to provide a Washington focal point for the other war. He was authorized to work directly with the secretaries of state, defense, and agriculture and the heads of AID and the CIA. He also had authority to direct, coordinate, and supervise the nonmilitary programs making up the other war and had direct access to the president, a privilege which enormously strengthened Komer's hand. On paper at least, the appointment of Komer remedied the absence of a single manager. The second appointment occurred in Saigon. The president placed Ambassador William Porter, deputy to Ambassador Henry Cabot Lodge, in charge of U.S. nonmilitary programs and assigned him the task of weaving together the civil and military strands of the pacification effort.

The two appointments foretold other organizational changes. In the fall of 1966, Ambassador Lodge tried an experimental "single manager" approach to pacification in Long An, a III Corps province directly south of Saigon. He appointed the province representative, U.S. Army Colonel Samuel Wilson, as leader of the entire provincial advisory team. The ambassador expected all civilian and military advisers to respond to Wilson's directions and the U.S. Army battalion commanders to consult with him on combat operations. Significantly, Wilson could call upon the assistance of U.S. Army battalions in the province to provide security and logistical support.

The single-manager experiment helped persuade President Johnson of the desirability of military involvement in pacification, an option vigorously advocated by Komer. In 1967 the president acted, putting Westmoreland in charge of all aspects of pacification. Johnson then appointed a single manager to serve as Westmoreland's deputy for U.S. support of pacification throughout South Vietnam. His decision made Westmoreland responsible for ensuring that pacification received adequate logistical and engineering support and that newly drafted plans eliminated overlapping and redundant military and civil efforts.

In 1967, Westmoreland requested 200,000 more troops to undertake ground operations in Laos to cut infiltration from the Ho Chi Minh trail.

Johnson's decision may be regarded as part of an administration effort to modify the ground strategy. In the spring of 1967, Westmoreland had requested 200,000 more troops to undertake ground operations in Laos to cut infiltration from the Ho Chi Minh trail. Civilian advisers in the White House and Pentagon, who had lost faith in Westmoreland's attrition strategy, opposed the request, arguing that the enemy could bring in more forces and offset any U.S. reinforcements. Fearing that additional soldiers in Vietnam might result in Americans taking over even more aspects of the war and higher casualties, the president chose to enhance support of pacification and improve the South Vietnamese armed forces.

A new agency, Civil Operations and Revolutionary (later Rural) Development Support (CORDS), was created within MACV to carry out the president's decision. Headed by Komer, who was given the rank of ambassador, CORDS was composed of both civilian and military (primarily army) personnel. Its key feature was the appointment of a single manager (either a military officer or a civilian official) for pacification support at each echelon—Saigon, corps, province, or district. The organization combined army officers and civilians from the State Department, AID, the U.S. Information Agency, the Department of Agriculture, and the intelligence agencies in such a way that civilians commanded army officers and officers civilians. Komer more than doubled the number of advisers who were assigned to CORDS from twenty-three hundred in 1967 to more than fifty-two hundred in 1968. About 95 percent of the military advisers assigned to CORDS came from the army. In addition, Komer had army civil affairs companies in Vietnam put under the operational control of CORDS. The new organization took on responsibility for many of the pacification programs formerly run by Ambassador Porter, such as Revolutionary Development Cadre (a CIA-run training program to develop a Vietnamese cadre to counteract Vietcong influence in the villages), refugees, police, and the *chieu hoi* ("open arms") program to encourage defections from the Vietcong. CORDS simplified command and control of U.S. support of pacification, even if divided control persisted in other areas, such as the air war, and the main force war and pacification remained as separate and sometimes conflicting efforts.

During the early 1960s, Washington policymakers had debated whether programs to win political allegiance or programs to protect people deserved precedence. CORDS settled that argument on pragmatic grounds, concluding that security was a prerequisite for development programs, although it worked to open roads and waterways in areas considered secure. It undertook two new major initiatives in 1967 to improve security. The first was the Phoenix program, which was designed to eliminate the Vietcong infrastructure by capturing key members. The program was supposed to collate current information on Vietcong leaders and cadre from U.S. and Vietnamese intelligence agencies so the Vietnamese authorities could arrest, interrogate, and try suspects and jail those convicted. Phoenix attempted to redress a fundamental weakness of earlier pacification efforts—the absence of a systematic effort designed specifically to dismantle the underground leadership that controlled guerrilla operations and provided political leadership in Communist-controlled areas. Despite pressure from the Americans, Thieu did not immediately put this program into operation.

In addition to devising a new program for attacking the infrastructure, Komer also worked to upgrade the combat effectiveness of the RF/PF. RF companies were lightly armed infantry forces that operated within a district or province; PF platoons were assigned to a specific village for local security. Komer won approval for a significant increase in the size of the RF/PF (they grew from 300,000 to more than 500,000 between 1967 and 1970), developed better training programs, and was successful in replacing the hand-me-down weapons of the territorials with new M-16s and other modern light weapons so the guerrillas would not outgun them in firefights.

By establishing a single-manager system for pacification, CORDS essentially solved the interrelated problems of poor interagency coordination and overlapping programs. By making more U.S. military assets available for the other war, logistical and security support had greatly improved. It would take longer, however, to achieve a comprehensive pacification strategy that integrated military operations with pacification campaigns and that counteracted all aspects of the Vietcong threat from guerrilla raids on villages to political subversion.

BEFORE THE STORM

During 1967, U.S. leaders in Saigon felt that the tide of battle was against the Communists. Allied military power had reached formidable levels, with 278 maneuver battalions, twenty-eight tactical fighter squadrons, three thousand helicopters, and twelve hundred monthly B-52 sorties available for combat. U.S. military strength reached 486,000 men during the year. Ground forces were well-armed, well-supplied, and well-trained. South Vietnamese armed forces also had increased in size during 1967. By the end of the year the total strength of the South Vietnamese military reached 643,000—an increase of 129,000 (about 25 percent) since the end of 1964.

The allies could point to evidence that the ground campaign had weakened the enemy. Thanks to their firepower and mobility, allied forces had mounted large operations inside formerly inviolate bases within South Vietnam and kept steady pressure on enemy units. These forays into base areas, which housed supplies, hospitals, headquarters, training centers, and rest areas, took the initiative from the Vietcong and made it more difficult for main forces to support guerrilla operations near populated areas. Operations like Cedar Falls convinced the Communist leadership that they could no longer use main force units near populated areas, forcing enemy units into increased reliance on the border sanctuaries. Even though body count statistics were notoriously inflated and need to be regarded skeptically, the enemy suffered a heavy cumulative casualty toll. Estimated enemy combat deaths went from seventeen thousand in 1964 to eighty-eight thousand in 1967. The Vietcong also had to contend with understrength units and recruiting difficulties in the delta. They suffered losses not merely from battlefield casualties but also from desertion, disease, and defections—more than twenty-seven thousand soldiers and political cadre in 1967—to the government. As the percentage of North Vietnamese fillers in Vietcong units grew, Westmoreland estimated that by the end of 1967 half the enemy combat battalions in the south came from the North

Vietnamese army. Vietcong tax revenues were also lower, because allied military operations had opened more roads to commerce, making it more difficult to tax goods in transit. Most important, captured enemy documents indicated a decline since 1965 in Vietcong-controlled population. An enemy cadre's notebook seized in January 1967 during Operation Cedar Falls estimated that the number of people living in areas under Vietcong authority had fallen by more than one million between mid-1965 and mid-1966. A loss of anything near that magnitude represented a significant reduction of the Communist manpower base.

In addition, prospects for pacification looked promising. Westmoreland had incorporated the notion of increased military support of pacification by U.S. forces into the 1967 Combined Campaign Plan. CORDS possessed more funds, personnel, and equipment and by sheer mass of resources seemed to be better equipped than its predecessor to wear down the insurgents. The South Vietnamese presidential and legislative elections of 1967 carried out under a new constitution promised an end, Washington hoped, to political instability and constituted the first step toward a broad-based popular government. Thieu, an ARVN general, was elected president but did not receive a clear majority in a race against several rival candidates.

Draft calls began to rise, causing many young men to regard the war not as an abstraction but as an event affecting them personally.

Restoration of elected government and continued allied military victories on the battlefield failed to assuage the American public's impatience with the war. In September 1967, an opinion poll showed for the first time that more Americans opposed than supported the war. Opposition was linked to U.S. casualties, which mounted the longer the war lasted. The number of Americans killed, wounded, or missing grew to eighty thousand in 1967. Draft calls began to rise, causing many young men to regard the war not as an abstraction but as an event affecting them personally. The president's request for a surtax to help pay for the war also proved unpopular. The ranks of those against the war began to include professionals and businessmen. To the argument voiced on college campuses that the war was immoral was added the damning verdict that the U.S. military effort was leading not to victory but to an inconclusive struggle at a higher level of cost in dollars and lives. Some questioned the worthiness of the cause, finding no compelling national interest at stake that justified defending a military regime halfway around the world against what many at the time concluded to be an independent nationalist movement, the Vietcong.

The president had little success in rallying opinion. A Gallup poll of June 1967 concluded that half of the Americans interviewed had no idea why the United States was fighting in Vietnam. Some mainstream newspapers began to express doubts about the war, feeling that misleading government claims about progress had created a credibility gap and that the president could no longer count on unquestioning support from Congress.

Dismayed that press and television accounts gave little sense of U.S. and Vietnamese progress in the war, President Johnson launched a public relations campaign to counteract what Rostow called the "stalemate doctrine." His reasons were largely political. During the coming year, Johnson was expected to seek reelection, and the campaign for the highest office could become a referendum on Vietnam. An antiwar wing took root in the Democratic party, and Senator Eugene McCarthy of Minnesota, a Democrat, decided in November to challenge the president for his party's nomination. As part of an effort to disprove the notion that the country was bogged down in a futile war, the president had Westmoreland and Ellsworth Bunker, ambassador to Saigon, return to Washington in November. They spoke before Congress and tried to reassure the public and the legislature that the allies were winning the war. These public reassurances would have unforeseen consequences in the months to come.

THE TET OFFENSIVE

In the latter part of 1967, the Johnson administration publicly expressed confidence about its prosecution of the war. At the same time, the Communists reappraised their strategy, aware that the sheer weight of U.S. arms was grinding down their military forces and weakening their ability to control the population. General Vo Nguyen Giap, head of North Vietnam's military forces, feared U.S. forces might invade North Vietnam, Laos, or Cambodia. The loss of these sanctuaries would be catastrophic to the Communist cause. The bombing was also a cause for alarm. The sortie rate over North Vietnam had risen from 2,401 in June 1965 to an average of eight thousand to nine thousand per month in late 1966 and early 1967, causing mounting destruction of roads, bridges, petroleum, oil, lubricant (POL) facilities, and heavy industry and unintended and incidental damage to homes, schools, office buildings, and other structures near military targets. In February 1967,

The Tet Offensive began on January 30, 1968, at the start of Tet, the Vietnamese New Year, when North Vietnam and the Viet Cong attacked major cities of South Vietnam, including Saigon, pictured here during Tet bombing. (National Archives)

the U.S. Navy began to mine internal waterways and coastal estuaries in North Vietnam below the twentieth parallel. Hanoi worried that the National Liberation Front (NLF), under increasing military pressure, might attempt to settle with the Saigon government.

If the leadership in Hanoi acknowledged its military vulnerabilities, it also knew the political weaknesses of its foe and hoped to exploit them. The Buddhist antigovernment protests of 1966, the so-called Struggle Movement, which Ky ended by dispatching one thousand Vietnamese marines to Da Nang, had revealed deep divisions in South Vietnam, and internecine intrigues continued among political factions in Saigon. Popular resentment of corruption and the lack of a strong popular base for the central government also helped persuade the Communists that enough people in South Vietnam were disaffected and could be induced to overthrow the Thieu government. Hanoi also believed that the South Vietnamese army was a political and military liability to the Saigon government. It was poorly led and equipped and split into factions. Morale was low and units lacked a strong commitment to the regime. Assessing its position, Hanoi decided to embark upon a new strategy to end the war. It would mount a general offensive throughout South Vietnam during the Tet holiday season coupled with a popular political uprising against the "puppet" government. By focusing attacks on South Vietnamese units and facilities, Hanoi sought to undermine the will and morale of the Saigon forces, subvert confidence in the ability of the government to provide security, further weaken support for the war in the United States, and force a political accommodation. Ho's government also took comfort in the antiwar movement within the United States, correlating the loss of political support with the traffic in coffins.

In December intelligence officers detected massive enemy troop movements throughout the country and along infiltration routes. Vietcong main forces moved toward Saigon, Da Nang, Hue (the former imperial capital of Vietnam), and a number of provincial capitals; the evidence pointed to an impending offensive. In mid-January 1968, two NVA divisions massed for an attack on the marine base at Khe Sanh, located in the northwest corner of South Vietnam, not far from Laos. The garrison at Khe Sanh could serve as a base for a potential corps-size operation into Laos to cut the Ho Chi Minh trail. Enemy attacks on Khe Sanh, beginning at the end of 1967, riveted the attention of Westmoreland, the president, and much of the press. Many commentators regarded Khe Sanh as Giap's play for a repetition of Dien Bien Phu. President Johnson insisted that the outpost be held, and the media carried daily reports of the action. To defend the outpost, B-52s carried out some of the heaviest air raids of the war, eventually dropping more than 100,000 tons of explosives on a five-square-mile battlefield.

The siege of Khe Sanh may have been part of a longstanding attempt to lure U.S. forces to the border regions. In the spring of 1967, heightened activity (artillery barrages and infiltrating NVA units) along the northern border drew marine units from southern I Corps to the demilitarized zone (DMZ). Army units from II and III Corps, making up Task Force Oregon, replaced the marines. (The task force was later reorganized as the Twenty-third Infantry Division, also known as Americal, the only army division to be formed in South Vietnam.) In September, the North Vietnamese regulars attacked the marine base at Con Thien just south of the DMZ. Supported by air power, naval gunfire, and artillery, the marines beat back the assault. In II Corps, North Vietnamese attacked the CIDG camp at Dak To in November 1967. Westmoreland sent the

Fourth Infantry Division and the 173d Airborne Brigade into the central highlands to reinforce the garrison.

The battle for Dak To, the longest and most violent in the highlands since the struggle for Ia Drang in 1965, was only won by grueling infantry assaults supported by artillery fire and B-52 air strikes. Elsewhere, U.S. forces confronted the enemy along the border. North Vietnamese forces moved against Loc Ninh and Song Be, district capitals in III Corps. Westmoreland sent reinforcements to drive back the enemy units, leaving U.S. forces dispersed. By the end of 1967, the First Infantry Division was concentrated near the Cambodian border and the Twenty-fifth Division had returned to War Zone C. The border battles opened the way for the Tet offensive by inducing Westmoreland into withdrawing forces from populated areas.

The border battles opened the way for the Tet offensive by inducing Westmoreland into withdrawing forces from populated areas.

While the enemy increased pressure against Khe Sanh, a force of eighty-five thousand men, mostly Vietcong units, reinforced with recruits and part-time guerrillas, prepared for the offensive. Arms, munitions, and trained bands of fighters were infiltrated into Saigon and other towns, mostly without being detected. Although the U.S. command had warnings of an impending attack and pulled some army units, such as the Twenty-fifth Infantry Division, closer to the capital, U.S. and Vietnamese forces were largely unprepared for what was to happen.

On 31 January fighting erupted throughout South Vietnam. Vietcong forces attacked thirty-six of forty-four provincial capitals and sixty-four of 242 district capitals, as well as five of South Vietnam's major cities, among them Saigon and Hue. The government moved a number of its ARVN and RF/PF units out of the countryside to defend beleaguered cities. Without security forces to protect them, the government pulled some Revolutionary Development (RD) cadre teams, which brought government economic and political programs to rural areas, from their assigned villages. The withdrawal of local security forces and cadre teams represented a setback for the pacification program.

Many Americans were involved in the fighting during Tet—advisers to ARVN units, isolated detachments, troops that intercepted enemy units, air force pilots, helicopter crews, and military police. Except at airfields used jointly by Americans and Vietnamese, such as that at Bien-hoa, the only major strike against a U.S. installation was made by a Vietcong regiment at the perimeter of the massive Long Binh compound. The 199th Infantry Brigade under Colonel Frederic Davison defeated the invading regiment. Davison's later promotion made him the first black general officer in the army since World War II. In most cities and towns, U.S. and South Vietnamese forces repelled the attacks and regained control after a few days of fighting. The exception was Hue, where it took U.S. Army and Marine Corps units and South Vietnamese forces three weeks of house-to-house fighting to drive out North Vietnamese regulars. Civilians rallied around the Thieu government, ignoring Communist calls for a general uprising.

With a strong push from CORDS, the government quickly embarked on a plan to rebuild war-ravaged cities and resettle families made homeless by the offensive. U.S. agencies provided funds and relief supplies, and army engineer and navy Seabee units helped rebuild damaged roads, bridges, and neighborhoods. President Thieu approved a number of measures over which his government had long temporized—general mobilization, an armed militia, and full implementation of the Phoenix program, the U.S. plan to attack the Vietcong infrastructure. The government finally issued operational guidance to the Vietnamese agencies involved in Phoenix and set up intelligence operations and coordination centers in the provinces and districts. The Police Special Branch, the National Police Field Forces, and the Provincial Reconnaissance Units (PRU) exercised the principal operational role. The PRUs were CIA-financed and CIA-controlled elite Vietnamese commando squads. The goal of the Phoenix program to capture known members of the infrastructure often proved difficult. Some suspects were killed resisting arrest, others died in the course of firefights, and an unknown number of others were likely eliminated in contravention of the program's regulations. The government's decision to promulgate standard operating procedures signified its readiness to attack the infrastructure. The Phoenix program would prove to be the one that the Communists most feared, because it targeted the control center of their organization in South Vietnam, and would also prove to be the most controversial program as well.

After the initial shock wore off, MACV realized that the offensive offered an opportunity. In targeting the cities, the Vietcong had suffered a major military defeat, losing thousands of seasoned fighters and veteran political cadres, seriously weakening their insurgent base. By March, Westmoreland concluded that the worst was over and urged his commanders to go on the offensive. The Tet offensive had hit the province and district towns, bypassing the rural villages. Komer judged that the government could make relatively easy gains in pacification simply by returning RF/PF units and the RD cadre teams to the countryside. In his estimation, the enemy was too weak to resist.

TET HITS HOME. On the battlefield, the Tet offensive turned out to be a bloody setback for the Vietcong, but the drama of the initial assaults on the U.S. embassy in Saigon and the other cities overwhelmed the media, creating an image of allied defeat. The offensive deeply shocked Americans, who witnessed on television the skirmish for the embassy in Saigon and heard respected newscasters conclude that the war could not be won. Coming after repeated claims of progress, the Tet attacks severely damaged the credibility of Johnson's war policy and Westmoreland's affirmations of success in wearing down the enemy. By early 1968 support for Johnson's war policy was already weak on Capitol Hill and fading in the press. Campus protests against the war and the draft were spreading and increasing in intensity. Tet hit Johnson when he was vulnerable and the country uneasy.

The request by the military for an additional 206,000 troops, which was leaked to the press in February, was the psychological knockout punch. Nearly half a million U.S. troops were already in Vietnam, and the call for such a large increase reinforced the erroneous, as it would turn out, public perception of a military defeat. Most of the additional forces were intended to reconstitute the U.S. strategic reserve that had been depleted by the Vietnam buildup. Westmoreland had asked for his share of the 206,000 additional soldiers not to stave off defeat but to operate inside Laos and cut the Ho Chi Minh trail.

By early 1968, the manpower requirements of the war had already attenuated the capability to meet other contingencies. More combat units for Vietnam meant that the army could deploy fewer forces to Europe or South Korea, where Communist forces posed an imposing and immediate threat. The army had already diverted units from Germany to Vietnam. The air force was using bombers from the Strategic Air Command in the Pacific to provide tactical support. Heightened international tensions following chronic crises in the Mideast and the seizure of the USS *Pueblo* by North Korea prior to the Tet offensive underscored the potential danger of further weakening forces deployed overseas and of not reconstituting the strategic reserve. In addition, the administration had to call on army units to quell civil disturbances in Newark and Detroit in 1967. Riots by blacks protesting racial discrimination and the lack of economic opportunity intensified antiwar sentiment, evoking calls for the administration to end the war so that more resources would be available to solve domestic problems. An antiwar march on the Pentagon in October 1967 also required the mobilization of federal troops.

Coming after repeated claims of progress, the Tet attacks severely damaged the credibility of Johnson's war policy and Westmoreland's affirmations of success.

Mounting demands on dwindling military resources, the shock of the Tet offensive, and growing public clamor against the war forced the Johnson administration in February and March to reassess its commitment to Vietnam. The new secretary of defense, Clark Clifford, took the lead, objecting to a strategy that devoured more and more resources in pursuit of an elusive victory in the indefinite future. The president decided to limit the U.S. commitment. As in 1967, Johnson vetoed a major infusion of soldiers, only sending two army brigades and calling up a small number of reserves, about forty thousand men, for service in Vietnam and South Korea. His decision clearly implied that the ARVN would have to shoulder a larger part of the fighting. Johnson also decided not to seek reelection, hoping his withdrawal would facilitate a settlement, and curtailed air strikes against North Vietnam. His moves led to the opening of peace talks in Paris between the United States, South Vietnam, North Vietnam, and the Vietcong.

Although Americans opposed to the war generally viewed Johnson's withdrawal and the start of talks as hopeful signs, other domestic crises intensified antiwar sentiment. On 4 April, civil rights leader Dr. Martin Luther King, Jr., was assassinated, a tragic event that provoked rioting in black neighborhoods in many cities. Federal troops were mobilized and National Guard units were called out to restore order in Washington, Chicago, and Baltimore. In all, major disturbances erupted in 125 cities in twenty-nine states. The murder of the nation's most influential black civil rights leader was particularly appalling to those who believed social programs had been sacrificed to help pay for the growing costs of an unpopular war. King had spoken out against the fighting, claiming that a disproportionate number of blacks were dying in the conflict.

THE ACCELERATED PACIFICATION CAMPAIGN

The Tet offensive raised sharp questions about the shortcomings of the South Vietnamese government and military. With increased U.S. casualties and heightened skepticism about progress, the criticism that the Saigon regime was corrupt, undemocratic, and unwilling to defend itself took on added virulence. Public sympathy for the goal of preserving South Vietnam noticeably declined. U.S. leaders in Vietnam—Komer, Ambassador Bunker, Westmoreland and his deputy General Creighton Abrams—realized that public alienation was likely to grow unless the government and ARVN were able to accomplish more on their own behalf. They concluded that demonstrable progress against the enemy was the only possible way to convince the American electorate that the war would not be lost or end in a stalemate. Restoring credibility, they hoped, would regenerate support at home.

The Americans made repeated efforts to galvanize the South Vietnamese in the spring. Westmoreland proposed that the commanders of the allied forces and General Vien, chief of the Joint General Staff, undertake a general counteroffensive before the enemy could recover. Komer wanted Thieu to send South Vietnamese territorial forces back to the villages from which they had withdrawn in February. He reasoned that if the government could quickly increase its hold on the countryside, it would limit Communist access to the rural population, promote the expansion of pacification programs into new areas, and strengthen Saigon's position at the bargaining table. A counteroffensive would also put the government in a stronger position in rural areas in case of a cease-fire that would fix opposing forces in the areas they controlled. Cautious by nature and lacking a strong political base, Thieu was fearful throughout 1968 of a repetition of Tet. He resisted Komer's calls for a counteroffensive until he was certain that the last wave of the enemy's 1968 offensive, which occurred in August, had failed. Only in October did he agree to carry out a counteroffensive.

Called the Accelerated Pacification Campaign (APC), the counteroffensive was a three-month crash effort that began on 1 November 1968. Its primary goal was to improve security in a thousand contested hamlets. The APC employed no new concepts of pacification but brought together all civil and military programs in a tightly integrated effort. It coordinated the upgrading of hamlet security by South Vietnamese paramilitary forces, police, and cadre teams with the other programs comprising pacification as well as with operations by U.S. and South Vietnamese ground forces. What was unprecedented was the degree of military involvement. The APC represented the first time that the military campaign was subordinated to the objectives of the pacification program. U.S. Army and Marine Corps operations provided a shield for government cadres and territorial forces. According to Pentagon statistics, an estimated 50 percent of U.S. ground operations during the APC supported pacification. The efforts of U.S. ground forces were concentrated for the first time on the struggle for control of the people. For most forces, the APC was a period of small unit actions—ambushes, surveillance, and mobile spoiling attacks.

General Abrams, who replaced Westmoreland in July, exhorted his commanders to support the campaign, which, in his view, would help establish a rural political base for the South Vietnamese government. If the RF/PF and the police could keep the Vietcong out of the villages and prevent them from assassinating government officials, thus allowing South Vietnamese villagers to manage their own affairs, then, Abrams believed, the government would stand for something.

In quantitative terms, the results of the APC were significant. By the end of the campaign, according to official statistics, more than eleven hundred contested hamlets had been brought under some degree of government control, and MACV estimated that Vietcong control had dropped from about 17 to 12 percent of the rural population. Nearly all newly secured hamlets had popularly elected or appointed officials, an important step toward establishing responsive local government. More than eight thousand Vietcong had defected and some seven thousand members of the infrastructure had been killed or captured.

Prior to the campaign, no pacification effort had significantly raised the degree of government control of the countryside. The success of the APC was attributable to the centralization of pacification support under the military, the development of an integrated military/pacification plan that set objectives for the Americans and South Vietnamese, the insistence of General Abrams on army and Marine Corps participation, and a severely weakened insurgent force. The campaign set the stage for the expansion of pacification in succeeding years.

Its success, however, was at best qualified. While it achieved its immediate statistical goals, it failed to realize its larger purpose of erasing public doubts about the war. The campaign's premise, that evidence of progress would dispel public skepticism, resembled the supposition behind President Johnson's effort to rebut the stalemate doctrine. That premise was flawed. After years of exposure to official claims of progress, the jolt of the Tet offensive decisively altered public perceptions of the war. Much of the public and media in the aftermath of the enemy attacks had come almost reflexively to dismiss official claims without consideration of their merits. The APC, like other aspects of the war, had relied on statistics to measure progress, and by 1968 the numbers emanating from MACV and the Pentagon had little popular credibility. Moreover, Thieu's slow start in launching the campaign, about nine months after the Tet offensive, hardly contributed to the image of a bold, resilient Saigon government. The APC, which began with the U.S. presidential election and ended with the inauguration of a new president, was little noticed in the larger debate over Vietnam. The campaign ended on 31 January 1969, twelve months after the start of the Tet offensive.

NIXON AND VIETNAMIZATION

The administration of Richard M. Nixon continued the policy of seeking an independent, non-Communist Vietnam but found its pursuit of that goal severely circumscribed. Nixon was elected president by a narrow margin in 1969 in part because he claimed to have a plan to end the war. He faced a restive population tired of a stalemate achieved at a high cost in casualties and dollars. He did not want to abandon Vietnam, but he realized that political pressure in the United States compelled him to pull out forces. His stragegy became known as what his secretary of defense, Melvin Laird, called "Vietnamization," or turning over the war to the South Vietnamese.

Nixon faced a restive population tired of a stalemate achieved at a high cost in casualties and dollars.

Initiated in the spring of 1969, Vietnamization had three interrelated components: gradual withdrawal of U.S. troops from South Vietnam; the buildup of South Vietnamese military capabilities (better equipment and weapons as well as greater numbers); and the assumption of greater combat responsibility by the South Vietnamese. In general, Vietnamization bought time for South Vietnam to prepare itself for the day when it would have to fight the war on its own. Vietnamization was part of the so-called Nixon Doctrine, the administration's basic foreign policy. Hoping to avoid U.S. involvement in limited wars unless the national interest was at stake, Nixon called on the country's allies to bear more of the burden of their own defense.

Ostensibly, U.S. troop withdrawals would be measured. The pace would be tied to success in pacification, improvements in South Vietnamese armed forces, and progress in the Paris peace talks. The departure of the first units from Vietnam in July 1969 increased domestic political pressure for additional redeployments, and it became impossible to slow, let alone reverse, the withdrawals whether or not the military situation warranted reductions in fighting strength. Antiwar moratoriums of 15 October and 15 November drew large and emotional crowds across the nation. Secretary of Defense Laird, a former congressman, believed that the political fate of the administration was tied to the withdrawals and became a catalyst within the administration for the steady, one-sided redeployment of forces. The pullout of U.S. troops was not contingent on the reciprocal departure of North Vietnamese forces.

ABRAMS IN COMMAND: ONE WAR

During the Nixon years, U.S. forces operated in an environment beset with contradictions. Early in his administration, the president decided that maintaining the greatest possible military pressure on the enemy would best serve U.S. negotiators, forcing the enemy to make concessions, but other presidential policies created difficulties for the MACV commander. Like President Johnson, Nixon held that Communist sanctuaries in Laos, Cambodia, and North Vietnam were off-limits to U.S. Army and Marine Corps ground forces, although small cross-border raids and reconnaissance patrols continued. The Nixon administration also wanted to keep U.S. casualties as low as possible. The political need to do so and the continuing ban on invading the sanctuaries limited General Abrams' military options.

By mid-1969, Abrams had to plan for the withdrawal of U.S. forces while carrying out military operations and keeping pressure on the enemy. Although he faithfully carried out Nixon's policy, he believed it unwise to remove U.S. troops precipitously before ARVN had matured as a fighting force. The need to scale down combat forces was a severe limitation in conducting the war not faced by his predecessor. The number of U.S. ground, air, and naval forces steadily declined, from 536,000 at the end of 1968 to 158,000 at the end of 1971. By the end of 1972 only 24,000 remained. Over the same period, Vietnamese force levels increased from about 850,000 to more than one million. Huge quantities of the newest weapons, including M-16 rifles, M-60 machine guns, M-79 grenade launchers, mortars, and howitzers, plus ships, planes, helicopters, and vehicles, were turned over to the Vietnamese as U.S. troops left the country.

Vietnamization made the advisory effort increasingly important. Abrams sought advisers who could work with the Vietnamese in the related areas of pacification and upgrading South Vietnamese armed forces. In light of the planned U.S. withdrawal, advisers from all branches of military service had to think in terms of working themselves out of a job. Management support programs were critical. Assistance was most needed in the areas of command and control, personnel, logistics, training, communications-electronics, intelligence, and local self-defense. Army and marine advisers had to prepare the Vietnamese to operate and maintain weapons, helicopters, and computers on their own. Air force advisers had to prepare pilots to fly and mechanics to maintain a large number of aircraft. The Vietnamese air force had to integrate many types of aircraft into their logistical system and take over several large air bases vacated by the U.S. Air Force. Likewise, U.S. Navy advisers needed to ready Vietnamese naval personnel to operate and maintain complex equipment. Specific problem areas such as overhaul scheduling, supply and parts requisition, and repair capabilities required attention. Unfortunately, Vietnamization also dictated the swift decline of the advisory structure. MACV staff advisory strength, province and district pacification advisers, combat assistance teams at the battalion and regimental level, and personnel assigned to Vietnamese training centers sharply declined through 1971 and 1972. The U.S. Air Force and naval advisory groups, mostly technical personnel, remained strong until the final departure.

Between October 1968 and 22 February 1969, enemy battle deaths averaged twenty-five hundred per week.

According to some accounts, Abrams had been long dissatisfied with Westmoreland's attrition strategy. To Abrams, all aspects of the struggle comprised "one war," adopting a phrase Ambassador Bunker had used in 1967 to describe his approach to the war. In his view, the pacification program was equal in importance to military operations against enemy main forces. He wanted the war of the battalions fused with the struggle to pacify the countryside.

Soon after assuming command of MACV, Abrams began to devise a framework for ground operations that would link them more directly to the ultimate goal of building a viable government and society in South Vietnam. He wanted to emphasize small-unit operations, extensive patrolling, and ambushes to reduce the enemy base of support among the population. A related objective was to wear down the enemy logistics system, crippling their ability to mount offensive operations and sustain their guerrilla forces. These steps represented more a change in emphasis than a radical break with the past. Abrams chose to focus on the Vietcong threat to Saigon's control of the countryside rather than the main forces of the enemy and to use U.S. forces to protect critical populated areas (especially the capital) so that the government could extend its hegemony to contested areas. In the summer and fall of 1968, Abrams redeployed three powerful units—the First Cavalry Division, the 101st Airborne Division, and the Third Brigade of the Eighty-second Airborne Division—from the northern provinces to the Saigon area.

The redeployments proved significant. In February 1969, the enemy launched another offensive during Tet. In contrast to the Tet attacks of the previous year, the Communists focused on U.S. forces and installations, hoping to inflict heavy casualties. Vietcong main and local forces supported by the North Vietnamese Army struck more than a hundred targets, but allied forces, aware of enemy intentions, repulsed all attacks, at a cost of more than eleven hundred Americans killed. The enemy was unable to hold any major objectives. Communist forces shelled Saigon but, unlike the previous year, failed to enter the city. The First Cavalry and the First and Twenty-fifth U.S. Infantry Divisions stopped the movement toward the capital of the First North Vietnamese Division and the Fifth Vietcong Division.

Not as intense as the offensive of the previous year, Tet 1969 further weakened the Vietcong and North Vietnamese, who suffered heavy personnel losses on top of the serious casualties of the previous months. Between October 1968 and 22 February 1969, enemy battle deaths, according to MACV data, averaged twenty-five hundred per week; between November and January defections averaged around 650 and infrastructure losses about 500 weekly. Unable to sustain continued heavy erosion of manpower, the enemy decided to forgo large countrywide assaults against strong allied positions and primarily emphasized sporadic, small-unit actions designed to reduce casualties. Communist attacks by units of battalion size and larger, for example, fell after the peak year of 1968, while the number of attacks by enemy units smaller than a battalion remained fairly constant. Tet 1969 was the last major enemy effort for several years.

After Tet 1969, it was easier for Abrams to focus on promoting population security because the Vietcong were weaker and main force units had tended to remain in sanctuaries for extended periods and avoid contact after Tet 1968. Moreover, the enemy was unable to operate as freely as before because allied ground operations had disrupted the enemy logistics system inside South Vietnam. Abrams consequently had less reason to stress the big-unit war, although like Westmoreland he still had to be prepared to cope with the entire spectrum of the Communist threat, from the assaults of North Vietnamese divisions and regiments to guerrilla attacks and terrorism. Abrams' preferences were clear, but he had to allow subordinate commanders flexibility to meet local contingencies. His guidance did not result in a universal change in the nature of ground operations.

ONE WAR: PACIFICATION

Between 1969 and 1972, the Americans and South Vietnamese continued the strategy used successfully in the Accelerated Pacification Campaign of moving territorial forces into contested or enemy-controlled hamlets. Security in the countryside steadily improved, as measured by official statistics and the movement of allied forces into previously contested or enemy-held villages. During this period, the Thieu government took steps to open the South Vietnamese political system to broader participation and to give more people an interest in supporting the Saigon government. The number of villages with elected local governments grew, and, through the Land to the Tiller Law, sweeping land reform legislation enacted in March 1970, unprecedented numbers of Vietnamese became landowners. By 1973 the government issued titles to more than a million hectares of redistributed land. Land tenancy fell and the new group of landowners were better off economically. These developments sparked optimism in CORDS, even if critics assailed the credibility of the official numbers and some officials in Washington doubted the ability of the South Vietnamese to translate the gains of these halcyon days into lasting political and security improvements.

Because the ultimate political goal of pacification, frequently expressed at the time as "winning hearts and minds," was largely intangible, it proved difficult to reach a clear verdict on what was accomplished by pacification. Improvements in rural economic conditions and limited local rule were no guarantee of popular allegiance. Moreover, the Thieu government proved inconsistent about building a democratic government. The 1971 election was a public relations disaster. Although Thieu won, the campaign procedures seemed

During the war, thousands of U.S. troops served in Saigon, and many Vietnamese moved there to escape fighting in the countryside. In this picture, a U.S. Army tank moves through a Saigon street on 12 March 1966 shortly after disembarking from a landing craft in Saigon harbor. (National Archives)

designed to eliminate rivals from the race. Some candidates boycotted the election, which confirmed the view of critics that the regime was authoritarian, lacked genuine political support, and sought to emasculate the anti-Communist opposition. Before and after reelection, Thieu suppressed political dissent and curtailed press freedoms and village elections.

In extending its writ in the countryside, Saigon depended on the sheer size of its growing military forces to protect the people living in areas under its control. Under Vietnamization, the RF/PF would take on the former role of ARVN in area security and the militia would become responsible for village and hamlet defense. To accommodate the added role, RF/PF grew in size until by 1971 they accounted for roughly half the South Vietnamese force structure of 1.1 million men.

As South Vietnamese territorial forces grew, their ability remained open to question. According to its own criteria (the Territorial Forces Evaluation System), CORDS deemed more than half the RF/PF units in the country in March 1971 to be unsatisfactory. The standards used for this evaluation took into account the number of men present for duty, the quality of their training and equipment, and their performance in the field. The large number of units rated as unsatisfactory in 1971 made it problematical that the RF/PF could sustain a high level of security over the long term and assume the role of ARVN.

The sheer size of the Saigon defense establishment, seemingly a sign of strength, was also a source of weakness. The government could not maintain more than a million men in its armed forces without continued, massive material support from the United States. That fact posed a serious problem for the Thieu regime, because in 1971 and 1972 the level of U.S. assistance began to decline, and the American political will to sustain the war had begun to wane even earlier. More than the war effort was dependent on U.S. funds and equipment. Economic and social programs for the peasantry also required continued U.S. support.

The effect of pacification on the Vietcong appeared clear in some respects. Between 1967 and 1971, more than 145,000 Vietcong or North Vietnamese defected to the government under the *chieu hoi* amnesty program. About 60 percent of the defectors were from military units, contributing to the difficulty the Communists had in stopping pacification cadres and territorial forces from gaining access to contested and enemy-controlled villages. The effect of the Phoenix program was harder to gauge. Although the infrastructure dropped from an estimated eight-five thousand in 1967 to sixty-six thousand in October 1971, much of that loss was suffered in the course of routine combat operations, not through the police arrest or capture of suspects. Most of those captured or sentenced under Phoenix were low-ranking officials and not hard-core leaders, suggesting that the party retained the nucleus for regenerating itself.

Phoenix suffered from a mismatch of U.S. managerial philosophy and South Vietnamese interests. Coordination of South Vietnamese intelligence and police units against the nerve center of their adversary was sensible by U.S. standards. For bureaucratic and political reasons, however, CORDS found it difficult to get the individual Vietnamese agencies to cooperate, share information, and contribute qualified personnel to a combined anti-infrastructure effort.

The program was flawed in other respects. A quota system was established to monitor results but led to false reporting. Among other problems were arbitrary sentencing and detention procedures, a shortage of detention facilities, bribery, political accommodation between government officials and the Vietcong, and the occasional use of the program to silence political opponents. Without question, the program's objective was essential to the defeat of the Communists, who with good reason feared its effects. Phoenix proved to be a two-edged sword. Although the program weakened the enemy, its negative image stemming from abuses and allegations of torture and assassination forced South Vietnamese and U.S. officials to prove that they were not engaged in crimes. Such adverse publicity did nothing to rekindle support for the war in the United States and only added to public disenchantment.

ONE WAR: GROUND OPERATIONS

During the period of Vietnamization many ground operations focused on support of pacification. Their underlying objective was to clear enemy forces from populated areas, providing an opportunity for the South Vietnamese government to strengthen itself without interference from its adversary. Small engagements for control of villages, mostly initiated by enemy forces, constituted the overwhelming majority of combat actions. Despite the prevalence of small operations, large-scale conventional fighting and the major bombing campaigns captured public attention. Ground operations, especially the large publicized ones, had significant political ramifications. Were they too costly in lives at a time of withdrawal? Major campaigns could also be regarded as tests of Vietnamization. Did they demonstrate growing military competence on the part of ARVN?

In view of the proximity of the Ho Chi Minh trail and the DMZ, it proved difficult in I Corps to ignore the big-unit war. The scene of heavy fighting, nearly 30 percent of friendly combat fatalities throughout the war occurred there. Throughout 1969, U.S. Army and Marine Corps units, ARVN, and South Korean troops drove deep into established enemy bases, inflicting heavy losses on main force units, seizing supplies, and destroying fortifications. The North Vietnamese and Vietcong were still able to mount attacks, especially in northern I Corps, but supply shortages and allied military pressure forced them to revert to harassing tactics, and the number of engagements with major enemy units steadily declined. Despite setbacks, Communist forces continued to contest the pacification program, especially as U.S. forces began to leave. Even in operations that directly supported pacification, it was hard to discern long-term gains.

Operation Meade River sought to clear the Vietcong from villages and hamlets so that cadre teams could restore local government.

Meade River, a Marine Corps operation lasting from September 1968 to January 1969, was launched to pacify the Dien Ban district in the eastern part of Quang Nam province. Long under enemy domination, Dien Ban had a heavy concentration of North Vietnamese forces and served as a staging area for numerous attacks against Da Nang and the provincial capital. Operation Meade River sought to clear the Vietcong from villages and hamlets so that cadre teams could restore local government and administer social and economic programs. The operation employed six U.S. Marine Corps battalions, three battalions of the Fifty-first ARVN regiment, and one battalion of South Korean marines to sweep the target area. In addition, National Police units and elements of the Special Police Branch were also involved, interrogating civilians and identifying members of the guerrillas. The operation opened with a U.S. Marine heliborne assault from ships of the U.S. Navy's Amphibious Task Force 76 and swept enemy forces from the area. Abrams and William Colby, who replaced Komer as head of CORDS, saw Operation Meade River as an example of the effective use of tactical units in support of pacification, but at the end of the operation security remained problematic. Continuous U.S. Marine patrolling, the use of free fire zones, sensors, and scanners were all needed to prevent the enemy from massing forces to attack isolated PF outposts in the district. Vietcong agents still circulated freely among the people and carried out assassinations. Meade River left unanswered questions about the permanence of any gains after the withdrawal of U.S. ground forces. A weakened but still viable Vietcong remained.

By June 1971, all Marine Corps units had left Quang Nam province, leaving the army's 196th Light Infantry Brigade as the remaining U.S. ground unit. The brigade had only brief firefights with small enemy detachments and suffered most of its casualties from booby traps. Guerrillas and local force units kept up a steady campaign of terrorism and small attacks by fire on South Vietnamese positions, eroding security. Security also declined in the neighboring provinces of Quang Tin and Quang Ngai.

Other I Corps operations seemed to set back progress toward the goal of building support for the government. Operation Russell Beach/Bold Mariner, which took place in the Vietcong stronghold of the Batangan Peninsula on the coastal plain of Quang Ngai province, was indistinguishable from those conducted during the days of the big-unit war under Westmoreland. Reversing a trend toward the more sparing use of force in inhabited areas, the operation was marked by practices that had characterized earlier sweeps, like Cedar Falls, through enemy-controlled populated areas. Its object was to further pacification, but it resulted in heavy property destruction and made refugees of area inhabitants. This occurred despite MACV policy, dating from the middle of 1968, of minimizing damage to homes and crops and making inhabited villages secure rather than moving people into secure zones or camps.

The coastal plain was an unforgiving area. Sweeps by U.S., South Vietnamese, and Korean forces in 1967 and 1968 had failed to clear out the Vietcong. The infamous My Lai massacre of South Vietnamese civilians occurred in this area in March 1968. A year after My Lai, allied forces still had made little headway against the Vietcong. Enemy forces attacked U.S. units, launched rocket attacks on the province capital, Quang Ngai city, and protected the infrastructure.

Operation Russell Beach/Bold Mariner began in January 1969 when two U.S. Marine Corps battalion landing teams stationed with the Seventh Fleet landed on the Batangan Peninsula. On the same day, the southern boundary was sealed off by Task Force Cooksey, composed of units from the U.S. Twenty-third Division; the Fifth Battalion, Forty-sixth Infantry Regiment; and the Fourth Battalion, Third Infantry Regiment. The U.S. battalions and two battalions of ARVN infantry forced the enemy toward the sea, killing more than two hundred and capturing more than one hundred. More than two hundred persons were identified as Vietcong cadre. The allied sweep displaced close to twelve thousand people, more than 40 percent of the population. They were evacuated by helicopter from their villages. Because their homes had been destroyed, the refugees were forced to live in camps. Poor security delayed resettlement. It was not until 1971 that the environment had improved enough to permit all refugees to leave the camps and rebuild their homes.

The marines considered Russell Beach/Bold Mariner a successful invasion of an enemy sanctuary, and the province adviser called it a symbol of the successful expansion of government control, but these judgments proved premature. Allied forces had temporarily occupied, but not eliminated, a Communist stronghold. Vietcong forces in the area continued to levy taxes and abduct local officials. The relocations bestowed no political advantage on the government. It was unlikely that the experience of the refugees, many of whom were already sympathetic to the Communists, kindled any allegiance to the Saigon government. Rather than a successful pacification operation, Russell Beach was a misguided failure.

Unwilling to cede control of the remote, mountainous western part of I Corps, the enemy built up logistic bases in the A Shau Valley near the Laotian border after the 1968 Tet offensive. Some U.S. ground operations in this area were little different than those conducted under Westmoreland's command. On 11 May 1969, a battalion of the 101st Division climbing a hill literally collided with the waiting Twenty-ninth North Vietnamese regiment. The division fought to capture Hamburger Hill (Hill 937), a remote mountain distant from any population centers. Supported by artillery and air strikes, the Americans had to root out the enemy regiment, engaging in hand-to-hand combat as they cleared out one entrenched position after another. After ten days of fighting, the 101st captured the hill, sacrificing seventy dead and 372 wounded. The costly operation achieved no lasting gains. The division abandoned the hill a few days later allowing the enemy to return and reestablish bases. To many the battle seemed to be a pointless use of men and equipment that did nothing to bring the allies closer to military victory. Critics regarded the engagement as epitomizing the futility of attrition, and Washington quietly reminded Abrams to hold down casualties. The 101st Division departed from the A Shau Valley in June. By the summer of 1970, strong pressure from NVA units forced abandonment of two outlying fire support bases, an ominous sign that Communist forces still sought to dominate the valleys leading to the coastal plain. Enemy moves forced the 101st Division and the marines to protect the coastal city of Hue until they left Vietnam in 1971, ironically as if it were an enclave.

Until redeployment, army units in the highlands of II Corps carried out several types of missions. They guarded the borders, protected population centers, and kept major roads open. Special Forces detachments were stationed in remote areas to detect the movement of enemy units across the border. A few Special Forces personnel and CIA personnel conducted clandestine operations outside Vietnam. Detachments also served as reinforcement and reaction forces for CIDG camps, called mobile strike (MIKE) forces. Composed of ethnic minorities under U.S. leadership, these units were better armed and trained than normal CIDG elements. Because of their proximity to infiltration routes and enemy strongholds, Special Forces camps continued to be lucrative targets for enemy attacks. The Fifth Special Forces Group left Vietnam in March 1971, by which time all CIDG units had been converted to Regional Force units or had been absorbed by the South Vietnamese Rangers.

The pacification effort received special attention in the II Corps province of Binh Dinh, where the Vietcong movement was deeply entrenched. In this critical province, however, even exemplary support of pacification failed to eradicate doubts about the ability of the central government to control the Vietcong over the long term. In furtherance of the one-war concept of Abrams, the 173d Airborne Brigade carried out Operation Washington Green, working closely with the South Vietnamese, to deny logistical support to local Vietcong units and keep them away from hamlets. The operation emphasized the continuous deployment of U.S. and South Vietnamese forces in hamlets long dominated by the Vietcong. It was an opportune time to strike. The operation began in April 1969, after the enemy main forces had pulled back to the Que Son mountains in the west to rest and refit, and generally avoided engagements with allied forces. When Washington Green formally ended in December, the 173d had disrupted enemy organization and restricted access to hamlets in the area of operation. The operation's methods were held up for emulation. Unfortunately for the South Vietnamese, the benefits were also short-lived. The infrastructure in this province had earlier bounced back after losses suffered during the Tet offensive of 1968 and did so again. The Vietcong began in early 1970 to step up their recruiting and proselytizing in order to build strength for the day when U.S. troops would be gone. The infrastructure in Binh Dinh began growing in 1971, jumping from nine thousand in September to about fifteen thousand in October. It was no surprise that security declined. Looked at over the long term, Washington Green offered little reason for optimism. Considered a model operation, it had achieved noteworthy gains, but the Vietcong, as determined as ever, were able to recoup their losses.

In III and IV Corps, U.S. units were involved in joint training operations with the South Vietnamese to protect the Cambodian border and the land and river approaches to Saigon. Over time, helping provide security became the predominant role for U.S. forces in this populous area. As in I Corps, the exceptions stand out. The operations of the Ninth Division during the first half of 1969 more closely resembled the war of attrition than they conformed to a pacification-oriented strategy.

The Ninth was the only U.S. division to mount ground operations in the fertile, populous Mekong delta. MACV sent the unit there originally because of poor ARVN performance and because another U.S. unit, the Twenty-fifth Division, had compiled a good pacification record in the deltalike provinces of Long An and Hau Nghia. The Twenty-fifth employed special rules of engagement to help prevent noncombatant casualties in highly populated areas. Operation Speedy Express, conducted from December 1968 to June 1969, concentrated on attacking the Vietcong in Dinh Tuong, Kien Hoa, and Go Cong provinces in the upper delta. The division's commander, Major General Julian Ewell, insisted on measuring performance with statistics, such as the body counts, which by this point in the war had earned a measure of public scorn. Because his approach was to wear down enemy forces by unrelenting military pressure, a favorable body count was proof of success. Relying on the relatively free use of air strikes, artillery, and helicopter gunships in the densely populated provinces, the Ninth Division claimed to kill 10,883 enemy while suffering only 267 combat deaths. The results of Speedy Express were hard to take at face value, especially when the division captured fewer than eight hundred enemy weapons. According to some accounts, it was likely that many noncombatants—Vietcong supporters and innocent bystanders—were killed in addition to enemy personnel bearing arms. It was also likely that operational statistics were inflated to satisfy the quest for high kill ratios. Operation Speedy Express left behind a weakened foe and a great deal of devastation. The Ninth Division had provided a security umbrella and thus aided pacification, but any positive effect was counterbalanced by civilian casualties. At the end of the operation, security in Dinh Tuong and Kien Hoa, longtime enemy strongholds, remained disappointing.

Vietnamization began first in IV Corps when two brigades of the U.S. Army Ninth Division left Vietnam in July 1969. Their departure ended the innovative riverine operations with the U.S. Navy and made the ARVN Seventh Division responsible for securing the southern approaches to Saigon. The Seventh, which had fought a defensive war, virtually collapsed under an ineffective commander after the departure of the U.S. division.

U.S. forces conducted search-and-destroy operations to ferret out enemy supplies and push guerrillas away from villages.

After the Fourth Division withdrew at the end of 1970, the remaining army combat units in III Corps—the First Cavalry Division, Twenty-fifth Infantry Division, and the Eleventh Armored Cavalry Regiment—concentrated on the defense of Saigon. Elements of the First and Twenty-fifth Divisions and other units also guarded the Cambodian border to cut enemy supply trails into the capital area. In the heavily populated lowlands, U.S. forces conducted search-and-destroy operations to ferret out enemy supplies and push guerrillas away from villages, but the sanctuaries in Cambodia remained a serious concern for Abrams, because they allowed the Communists to sustain operations by North Vietnamese and Vietcong units.

CROSS-BORDER OPERATIONS: CAMBODIA. With most U.S. combat units slated to leave Vietnam by the end of 1971, time was critical for the success of pacification and Vietnamization. Neither could thrive if the enemy could attack villages or challenge Saigon's forces from well-established cross-border sanctuaries, which provided haven and served as logistic bases. In March 1969, Nixon ordered intensive bombing attacks against North Vietnamese positions in Cambodia, an action that the Joint Chiefs of Staff had advocated for years, to curtail the North Vietnamese capacity to mount an offensive. Nixon also wanted to demonstrate that he would take measures avoided by Johnson, hoping the intensified military pressure would induce the Communists to settle on his terms. Over the next fifteen months, more than 100,000 tons of bombs were dropped on Cambodia in Operation Menu, which the administration concealed from the American public and from much of the government and military. The secrecy of the bombing mocked congressional oversight of the war and put the military in the position of deliberately concealing the existence of a major operation. In addition to its political liabilities, the bombing did not destroy the Cambodian bases. Their existence, which the neutralist leader of Cambodia, Prince Norodom Sihanouk, tolerated, posed a continuing threat to South Vietnam. The overthrow of the prince by a pro-

American clique under Prime Minister Lon Nol gave Nixon the opening for a ground assault on the Cambodian sanctuaries. Lon Nol closed the port of Sihanoukville to Communist shipping, sought U.S. aid, and was amenable to military action against the sanctuaries. In authorizing units of the First Cavalry Division, the Twenty-fifth Infantry Division, and the Eleventh Armored Cavalry Regiment to enter Cambodia in May 1970, Nixon expected to buy time for Vietnamization by destroying enemy supply bases and headquarters. He also hoped to prop up the feeble regime of Lon Nol.

Although the cross-border operation caused heavy losses of Communist manpower, weapons, ammunition, and supplies, the reaction in the United States was cataclysmic. The surprise expansion of the war during a period of withdrawal enraged those opposed to the war and provoked violent demonstrations on campuses across the nation. Students at Kent State University in Ohio and Jackson State College in Mississippi were killed in confrontations with National Guardsmen and police. More than 100,000 protesters gathered in Washington, D.C., in early May to protest the incursion and the killings at Kent State. An outraged Senate revoked the Tonkin Gulf Resolution of 1964 by an overwhelming vote. The Cambodian incursion, as the Pentagon termed it, was a major event in the alienation of the public. The later disclosure of the secret bombing campaign contributed to the erosion of credibility in the administration's Vietnam policy and the loss of public support.

CROSS-BORDER OPERATIONS: LAM SON 719. With the closing of Sihanoukville, the destruction of supply caches in Cambodia, and the effectiveness of Operations Market Garden and Game Warden, the Ho Chi Minh trail was the only available way for Hanoi to supply its forces in the south. Years of bombing the trail in Laos—Operation Commando Hunt, which used sensors to identify targets for U.S. gunships—had diminished but never completely halted the movement of supplies. Abrams believed a ground operation inside Laos to sever the trail physically could give Vietnamization another breathing spell. The Cooper-Church amendment, however, passed by Congress after the Cambodian incursion, prohibited U.S. ground forces or advisers from entering Laos or Cambodia. The U.S. role in any cross-border operation would thus be limited to strikes by airplane and helicopter pilots flying over Laos; artillery units firing from inside South Vietnam; logistic, combat, and engineering support for the South Vietnamese; and maintenance of fixed-wing aircraft and helicopters. ARVN would have to enter Laos on its own. Operation Lam Son 719, to sever the trail in Laos, began in February 1971. Compromised by security leaks, it was in trouble from the outset. ARVN units stalled inside Laos when they encountered strong resistance from North Vietnamese infantry, armor, and artillery. Thieu, fearing the loss of some of his elite troops, ordered his forces to withdraw. South Vietnamese units hastily pulled out while under heavy counterattack from North Vietnamese combined arms fire, leaving behind many dead and wounded. Although Thieu's concerns about excessive casualties hindered the operation, the performance of ARVN demonstrated the inadequacy of its leadership. Lam Son ended with renewed questions about the ability of the ARVN to stand by itself; it was an ominous test of Vietnamization.

The Americans contributed to the failings of Operation Lam Son 719. Planning was hasty and too closely held, allowing ARVN little time to train, and the ARVN military intelligence office had no part in the planning. The Americans kept their command post about eight miles from that of ARVN, complicating allied coordination. In addition, the U.S. Seventh Air Force and the U.S. XXIV Corps, the ground force headquarters, disagreed over the concept of air support and which headquarters should control assault and support operations. As it turned out, the Americans supported a major operation with inadequate planning, deficient coordination with ARVN, and major service differences over the concept and execution of the operation. At the bottom of these deficiencies lay a lack of unity of command. Nobody took charge of the operation and nobody coordinated it. In Operation Lam Son the allies paid a price for the long-unresolved issues of command and control.

THE EASTER OFFENSIVE, 1972

Operation Lam Son 719 had convinced the North Vietnamese that ARVN was vulnerable to attacks by tanks and heavy artillery. In May 1971, the political bureau in North Vietnam, hoping in the coming year to win the war militarily and hasten a negotiated settlement, elected to launch a major offensive against South Vietnamese forces. Hanoi timed the offensive to begin after U.S. ground combat elements had left the country. The Communist leadership expected that the Saigon government would have to redeploy large numbers of its forces to battle the invading divisions. In turn, the diversion of units would weaken local security, permitting Vietcong and North Vietnamese forces to return to their former strongholds and regain sources of manpower and supply.

On 30 March 1972, Hanoi launched the so-called Easter Offensive, a massive invasion by twenty North Vietnamese Army divisions. Making extensive use of armor and artillery fire, the NVA attacked across three fronts—the DMZ, the central highlands, and the III Corps border area west of Saigon. The enemy made dramatic gains on all three fronts. The task of stopping the ground offensive fell almost completely on South Vietnamese army and territorial forces. Total U.S. military strength had fallen to ninety-five thousand, of which only six thousand were combat troops. By March 1972, the air force had withdrawn most of its planes, leaving only seventy-six fighter and attack aircraft in Vietnam. Only two navy carriers, the *Hancock* and the *Coral Sea,* with a total of 180 aircraft, were stationed off the coast of Vietnam. Only eighty-three B-52s operated in theater.

In April, Nixon augmented U.S. Navy and Air Force personnel in Southeast Asia in an effort to halt the offensive. Air force fighter and attack planes soon totaled 409, and 171 B-52s were available at the end of May. The navy brought four additional carriers, one heavy cruiser, five cruisers, and forty-four destroyers to the South China Sea. With the added aircraft, there was a jump in the number of sorties that B-52s and fighter and attack planes flew against the invading divisions. In large measure, U.S. airpower was responsible for stopping the advance of the NVA in the northernmost province of Quang Tri, the central highlands, and the III Corps town of An Loc. The inexperience of the North Vietnamese Army in maneuvering tanks and infantry slowed their advance and made their forces more vulnerable to air strikes.

In addition, Nixon ordered the bombing of targets in North Vietnam, codenamed Linebacker. Between May and October 1972, air force and navy pilots struck

This wounded soldier is being treated by a medic as he awaits evacuation from the field in 1966. Access to sufficient supplies of drugs and whole blood enabled military doctors, nurses, and medics to save the lives of innumerable servicemen with the kinds of wounds that had proved fatal in earlier wars. (National Archives)

the cities of Vinh, Haiphong, and Hanoi with fighter-bombers and B-52s. North Vietnam had been a refuge from U.S. bombing since November 1968, when President Johnson had ended the Rolling Thunder program. Compared to Rolling Thunder, which largely served to restrict the movement of men and supplies from the north to support the guerrilla war in the south, the Linebacker bombing campaign proved more effective. It was directed at stopping a conventional military offensive that required large amounts of fuel, supplies, and ammunition. More sustained bomb tonnage was dropped between May and October than in any other comparable period. The bombing damaged lines of communications, destroyed oil storage facilities and a significant percentage of North Vietnam's power-generating capacity, and wrecked the ability of North Vietnam to conduct conventional offensive war. Nixon also ordered the navy to mine Haiphong harbor, closing off sea traffic to the country's primary port. His resolve in bringing air and naval power to bear provided the margin of victory.

The so-called Christmas bombing destroyed Hanoi's airport, major bus and train stations, and North Vietnam's largest hospital.

As a test of Vietnamization, the Easter Offensive was as discomfiting as Operation Lam Son 719. In addition to the inability of ARVN to stop invaders, territorial forces and militia proved no match for large conventional units. Pacification ceased when the North Vietnamese Army entered an area. The need to stop an invasion forced the government to spread its forces thinly, reducing the protection provided to the rural populace. The absence of U.S. units and advisers meant that the South Vietnamese had to deal with the Communists in provinces where they were traditionally strong and government control weak. In addition, North Vietnamese forces entered the delta between 1969 and 1973, compensating for Vietcong losses and reviving the insurgency. After the 1972 offensive, the Communists were in a strong position to continue the struggle to unify Vietnam under their banner.

The fighting of 1972 failed to break the stalemate. Although U.S. bombing and the South Vietnamese army had stopped North Vietnamese forces at heavy cost, Hanoi retained significant forces in the south. Both sides turned to negotiations, but when talks bogged down in the fall of 1972, Nixon resumed the air war, bombing North Vietnam in December in order to force Hanoi to conclude a treaty. The JCS conducted this air campaign without the restrictions on targets, sorties, and tonnage routinely imposed by the Johnson administration. The bombing was intensive and devastating. From 18 December to 29 December, B-52s and fighter bombers dropped more than twenty thousand tons of bombs, exceeding the tonnage that fell during 1969–1971. The so-called Christmas bombing (Linebacker II) destroyed Hanoi's airport, major bus and train stations, and North Vietnam's largest hospital, but at a considerable toll. Fifteen B-52s were lost to intense antiaircraft fire. Nixon's bombing provoked a fresh outcry on the part of congressional critics and war protesters. Many who had accepted the spring bombing as necessary to stop a blatant invasion questioned the necessity of the harsh Christmas attacks. Nixon's approval rating dropped to 39 percent.

In early 1973, the United States, North Vietnam, South Vietnam, and the Vietcong signed a peace agreement that promised a cease-fire and national reconciliation. Hanoi dropped an earlier demand for the removal of Thieu, but the United States agreed that Hanoi could keep its troops in the south, a concession that directly contributed to the final defeat of South Vietnam. Under the agreement, MACV was dissolved and remaining U.S. forces were withdrawn. U.S. military advisers, still the backbone of the ARVN command structure, were completely pulled out, although Nixon secretly promised Thieu he would take steps, such as bombing and continued matériel support, to preserve the independence of South Vietnam.

THE END OF A WAR

The defeat of South Vietnam in 1975 after a major invasion by North Vietnamese ground, armor, and artillery forces was a bitter end to a long struggle by the United States to preserve the sovereignty of South Vietnam. Ranging from advice and support for all components of South Vietnamese armed forces to direct participation in air, ground, and sea combat, which eventually involved nearly three million U.S. servicemen, the effort failed to prevent Hanoi from unifying Vietnam. The decisive defeat of Saigon tended to obscure the inability of the U.S. military undertaking to compensate for the regime's political shortcomings. For nearly two decades, from the hopeful days of Diem's rule to the ignominious collapse of Thieu's government, no South Vietnamese leader or group had succeeded in mobilizing that nation's political, social, and economic resources to build a base of support. The final role of the U.S. military was to use its helicopters to evacuate U.S., Vietnamese, and Cambodian citizens to the waiting ships of the Seventh Fleet as the capitals of Saigon and Phnompenh fell in April 1975.

The Americans operated again and again in the same areas and made infrequent contact with the enemy. Repeated fruitless operations built up frustration.

In assessing the defeat, the shortcomings of U.S. policy and strategy stand out in sharp relief. Political limitations on the conduct of the war obviously hampered the armed services. Restrictions on bombing, prohibitions against ground operations inside North Vietnam and the cross-border sanctuaries, and the application of graduated military pressure under the doctrine of limited war made it more difficult to wage war in Southeast Asia. The lack of a realizable, positive political/military objective, such as the defeat of North Vietnamese forces, was a more crucial failing. The U.S. goal expressed in NSAM 288 of seeking an independent South Vietnam was difficult to conceptualize in a military strategy that would be carried out on behalf of an ally. The chosen means of fighting were ill-suited to realize the U.S. objective. Bombing infiltration routes and industrial targets in North Vietnam might halt a conventional invasion but could not force Vietcong guerrillas to cease fighting. They enjoyed indigenous logistic and political support and sources of manpower inside South Vietnam. Search-and-destroy operations were all too frequently exercises in futility. The enemy, whenever possible, refused to stand and fight and tried to avoid being trapped and destroyed by superior allied firepower. U.S. generals conducted untold sweeps in a largely unavailing effort to find, fix, and destroy enemy units. The Americans operated again and again in the same areas and made infrequent contact with the enemy. Repeated fruitless operations built up frustration. Continuous sweeps also meant that U.S. forces were not well-deployed to provide sustained local security against Vietcong guerrillas and infrastructure. Enemy forces initiated most engagements throughout the period of U.S. involvement, choosing as a rule to strike U.S. and South Vietnamese forces where they appeared vulnerable or where the Communists could enhance their control in the countryside.

With the establishment of CORDS, the Accelerated Pacification Campaign, and Abrams' one-war approach, allied strategy was more sharply focused. This change, however, came too late to make a difference. By the time the APC demonstrated the potential of a comprehensive pacification program in defeating the insurgency, support for the war had sharply fallen and Nixon had decided to disengage from Vietnam.

The success or failure of pacification and Vietnamization ultimately rested on the ability of the government and armed forces of South Vietnam. Lacking authority to manage Vietnamese programs or command Vietnamese units, advisers had limited ability to influence their counterparts, let alone have them removed for incompetence or corruption. The goal of an independent, sovereign South Vietnam precluded the Americans from taking control of the war effort at the local or national level. Even with the advantages of Vietnamization—better weapons, equipment, and training and greater numbers—South Vietnamese forces on their own proved incapable of standing up to the North Vietnamese. Leadership remained politicized and weak. Government cadres generally lacked the fervor their adversary routinely displayed and inspired no outpouring of political enthusiasm in the countryside for the corrupt, authoritarian Thieu regime. It may not be too harsh to conclude that Vietnamization, which denied Abrams the chance to obtain military victory, served primarily to prolong the stalemate long enough for the Americans to depart.

THE IMPACT OF VIETNAM

The U.S. military paid dearly in a futile undertaking to preserve South Vietnam, suffering more than fifty-eight thousand deaths. Young, low-ranking enlisted men, of whom 13 percent were black, made up the majority of the fatalities. With the relative infrequency of large set-piece battles, it was not surprising that most soldiers died from small-arms fire. In a war of numerous small-unit actions, it was also no surprise that a significant proportion of the deaths, 30 percent, resulted from mines, booby traps, and grenades. Artillery, rockets, and bombs were responsible for only a small share of total casualties.

Save for the unprecedented medical care that the armed services provided in South Vietnam, the death toll would have been higher. The expert emergency care given by battlefield medics at great personal risk was the first link in the medical treatment system. Medical helicopters quickly evacuated the wounded to nearby army, Marine Corps, and navy hospitals and hospital ships, where they were relatively secure from attack. With access to up-to-date technology and sufficient supplies of drugs and whole blood, military doctors and nurses were able to save the lives of innumerable servicemen

About 58,000 American military personnel died in the Vietnam war. Their names are inscribed in the order they were killed on the Vietnam Veteran's Memorial in Washington D.C. The memorial was designed by Maya Lin and dedicated in 1982. (Department of Defense)

with the kinds of wounds that had proved fatal in earlier wars.

Exposure to herbicides that were sprayed to destroy crops and foliage in Communist-held areas harmed U.S. soldiers and sailors as well as Vietnamese. In many cases, the servicemen's suffering commenced after they returned home, because not all wounds were physical. Some who served in Vietnam suffered adverse psychological effects from combat, including post-traumatic stress syndrome, and required counseling and psychiatric help long after they returned to civilian life.

American prisoners of war endured long and harsh captivity at the hands of the Vietcong and North Vietnamese. Search-and-rescue missions saved some downed pilots and crews from capture, but not all were so fortunate. Air force and navy pilots were shot down by MIGs and surface-to-air missiles while bombing North Vietnam. Soldiers and helicopter pilots were captured in the south. POWs remained imprisoned, chiefly in Hanoi, until the cease-fire of 1973. Because war had not been formally declared, Hanoi chose not to observe the Geneva Conventions on the treatment of POWs. Most prisoners were physically and psychologically tortured by their captors, who extracted "confessions" of war crimes as part of a propaganda effort to weaken political support for U.S. policy.

The final reckoning of the human cost of the war may never be complete. More than a decade after the end of the war, about twenty-three hundred Americans remained unaccounted for. South Vietnamese military deaths exceeded 200,000, while war-related civilian deaths were close to half a million. Many others were wounded, maimed, or harmed by herbicides. Accurate estimates of enemy military casualties are especially difficult because of imprecise body counts, verification problems, and the uncertainty of distinguishing between civilians and combatants. Still, close to one million Vietcong and North Vietnamese soldiers probably perished in combat through 1975.

The costs of the war to the U.S. military were more than battle casualties. Defeat in Vietnam tarnished the image of the military and called its competence into question. Doubts centered on the air and ground strategy, the necessity and effectiveness of the bombing campaigns, and the soundness of the military's advice to its ally. Critics questioned the military's understanding of the nature of the war and the caliber of those in uniform.

The presence of less than ideally trained and disciplined soldiers in dangerous areas long sympathetic to the Communist cause led to tragic results on the coastal plain of southern I Corps. For years French forces had labored unsuccessfully to subdue insurgents in this area, which they termed "Street without Joy." The Americans had no better success. Operations against enemy units were slow, dangerous exercises in which snipers, mines, and booby traps caused most U.S. casualties. The line between combatants and civilians was blurred, especially in this area of Vietnam, where, as in other areas where the population sympathized with the Vietcong, old men, women, and children planted mines and booby traps. Operating in such a climate often raised anxiety and frustration to the breaking point. Self-protection became primary. In the hamlet of My Lai, soldiers of the U.S. Twenty-third Infantry Division killed about two hundred civilians in the spring of 1968. The incident came to light in 1969, prompting a major investigation, the dismissal of the commanding general of the division and other army officers, and the trial and conviction of one officer of war crimes.

The My Lai incident might have occurred in any other army unit in the late 1960s and early 1970s. The withdrawal of U.S. soldiers by a government and nation eager to escape the war and the lack of a clear military purpose in continuing to risk U.S. lives in an unpopular cause contributed to weakened discipline. Troop withdrawals and the emphasis on negotiated peace signified to servicemen that the United States was engaged in a no-win war. Criticism of the war and low public regard for the military services also served to degrade discipline and morale and contributed to a growing disenchantment with the war among soldiers in the field.

During the latter stages of its involvement in Vietnam, the U.S. Army, perhaps more than the other services, seemed to be coming apart. Although personnel problems afflicted all branches of the armed forces, the army, which had come to depend on draftees to fill its ranks, seemed to epitomize the array of serious problems besetting the military in Vietnam. Because of the policy of granting educational deferments to college students, draftees tended to be from less well-educated and lower socioeconomic groups. One-year tours in Vietnam exacerbated personnel turbulence and shortages of qualified leaders and technicians. The long inconclusive war and failures of leadership also contributed to the erosion of morale and discipline. The number of drug offenders in Vietnam jumped nearly sevenfold between 1970 and 1971, even as the number of U.S. troops in Vietnam fell. Drug use became so serious that mandatory drug testing of military personnel in Vietnam was imposed in 1971. As the fighting wound down, there was an increase in incidents of "fragging," attempts by enlisted personnel to scare or kill their commanding officers. Desertions and AWOLs in all services also climbed. The number of general and special courts-martial increased in 1970 and 1971, as did the most serious military offenses—insubordination, mutiny, and refusal to perform a lawful order. Racial tensions, mirroring those in U.S. society, also became a serious problem with troops stationed in support units, especially after the riots of the late 1960s and the assassination of Martin Luther King.

Although a generation of officers, including many of the future leaders of the armed services, gained combat experience in Vietnam, many regretted that the reputation of the military had been besmirched in a crusade that only marginally involved the national interest. The military had won battles on land, sea, and air yet lost the war. How to avert the mistakes of Vietnam became the central issue for the services as they examined doctrine and strategy after the war.

The end of the draft in 1972 and the transition to an all-volunteer army in 1973—a direct consequence of the war—meant that the nation would be unlikely to fight another major conflict with the flawed personnel policies of Vietnam. No longer would the draft and deferment system create "winners and losers" among the population of young adults. The all-volunteer military would be composed of persons who wanted to serve. Reliance on volunteers also meant that future administrations would have to mobilize reserve forces and in so doing tap the national will in fighting wars.

The military had won battles on land, sea, and air yet lost the war.

The War Powers Act of 1973 also made it unlikely that the Vietnam War would be repeated. The legislation required the president to inform Congress within forty-eight hours of the deployment of U.S. forces abroad and obligated him to withdraw them in sixty days in the absence of an explicit congressional endorsement. The act was intended to prevent a president from committing armed forces, as Lyndon Johnson had, in prolonged conflict without a formal declaration of war. The trauma of defeat manifested itself as a universal and deep-rooted desire to avoid another Vietnam.

BIBLIOGRAPHY

Reference Works

Olson, James S., ed. *Dictionary of the Vietnam War* (1988).

South Vietnam: U.S.-Communist Confrontation in Southeast Asia, 7 vols. (1973).

Summers, Harry G. *Vietnam War Almanac* (1985).

U.S. Pacific Command. *Report on the War in Vietnam (as of 30 June 1968),* Sec. I: *Report on Air and Naval Campaigns against North Vietnam and Pacific Command-wide Support of the War, June 1964–July 1968,* by U.S. Grant Sharp; Sec II: *Report on Operations in South Vietnam, January 1964–June 1968,* by W. C. Westmoreland (1969).

General Accounts

Andrews, Bruce. *Public Constraint and American Policy in Vietnam* (1976).

Baskir, Lawrence, and William A. Strauss. *Chance and Circumstance: The Draft, the War, and the Vietnam Generation* (1978).

Berman, Larry. *Planning a Tragedy: The Americanization of the War in Vietnam* (1982).

———. *Lyndon Johnson's War: The Road to Stalemate in Vietnam* (1989).

Blaufarb, Douglas S. *The Counterinsurgency Era: U.S. Doctrine and Performance, 1950 to the Present* (1977).

Braestrup, Peter. *Vietnam as History: Ten Years After the Paris Peace Accords* (1984).

Charlton, Michael, and Anthony Moncrieff. *Many Reasons Why: The American Involvement in Vietnam* (1978).

Colby, William, and James McCargar. *Lost Victory: A Firsthand Account of America's Sixteen-Year Involvement in Vietnam* (1989).

Cooper, Chester. *The Lost Crusade: America in Vietnam* (1970).

Davidson, Phillip B. *Vietnam at War: The History, 1946–1975* (1988).

DeBenedetti, Charles. *An American Ordeal: The Antiwar Movement of the Vietnam Era* (1990).

Ellsburg, Daniel. *Papers on the War* (1972).

Gelb, Leslie, and Richard Betts. *The Irony of Vietnam: The System Worked* (1979).

Herring, George. *America's Longest War: the United States and Vietnam, 1950–1975* (1979).

Herrington, Stuart. *Silence Was a Weapon: The Vietnam War in the Villages* (1982).

Johnson, Lyndon. *The Vantage Point: Perspectives of the Presidency, 1963–1969* (1971).

Karnow, Stanley. *Vietnam: A History* (1984).

Kinnard, Douglas. *The War Managers* (1977).

Kolko, Gabriel. *Anatomy of a War: Vietnam, the United States, and the Modern Historical Experience* (1985).

Kissinger, Henry. *White House Years* (1974).

———. *Years of Upheaval* (1982).

Komer, Robert. *Bureaucracy at War: U.S. Performance in the Vietnam Conflict* (1986).

Lewy, Guenter. *America in Vietnam* (1978).

McGarvey, Patrick J., ed. *Visions of Victory: Selected Vietnamese Communist Military Writings, 1964–1968* (1969).

Mueller, John. *War, Presidents, and Public Opinion* (1973).

Nixon, Richard. *RN: The Memoirs of Richard Nixon* (1978).

Pike, Douglas. *Viet Cong: The Organization and Techniques of the National Liberation Front of South Vietnam* (1966).

Schandler, Herbert. *The Unmaking of a President: Lyndon Johnson and Vietnam* (1977).

Shawcross, William. *Sideshow: Kissinger, Nixon, and the Destruction of Cambodia* (1979).

Summers, Harry G., Jr. *On Strategy: A Critical Analysis of the Vietnam War* (1982).

Thompson, Robert. *Defeating Communist Insurgency: The Lessons of Malaya and Vietnam* (1966).

Turley, William. *The Second Indochina War: A Short Political and Military History* (1986).

Vogelsang, Sandy. *The Long Dark of the American Soul: The American Intellectual Left and the Vietnam War* (1974).

Ground, Air, and Naval Operations

Andrews, William. *The Village War: Vietnamese Communist Revolutionary Activities in Dinh Tuong Province, 1960–1964* (1973).

Bergerud, Eric. *The Dynamics of Defeat: The Vietnam War in Hau Nghia Province* (1991).

Bonds, Ray, ed. *The Vietnam War: The Illustrated History of the Conflict in Southeast Asia* (1983).

Braestrup, Peter. *Big Story: How the American Press and Television Reported and Interpreted the Crisis of Tet 1968 in Vietnam and Washington* (1977).

Chandler, Robert. *War of Ideas: The U.S. Propaganda Campaign in Vietnam* (1981).

Clarke, Jeffrey. *Advice and Support: The Final Years, 1965–1973* (1988).

Clodfelter, Mark. *The Limits of Air Power: The American Bombing of North Vietnam* (1989).

Coleman, J. *Pleiku* (1988).

Cooper, Chester. *The American Experience with Pacification in Vietnam* (1972).

Cosmas, Graham, and Terrence Murray. *U.S. Marines in Vietnam, 1970–1971* (1986).

Croziat, Victor. *The Brown Water Navy: The River and Coastal War in Indochina and Vietnam, 1948–1972* (1984).

Demma, Vincent. "The U.S. Army in Vietnam." In *American Military History,* edited by William Stofft (1989).

Dorland, Peter, and James Nanney. *Dust Off: Army Aeromedical Evacuation in Vietnam* (1982).

Duiker, William. *The Communist Road to Power* (1981).

Hay, John. *Vietnam Studies: Tactical and Materiel Innovations* (1974).

Hooper, Edwin, Dean Allard, and Oscar Fitzgerald. *The United States Navy and the Vietnam Conflict* (1976).

Kelly, Francis. *U.S. Army Special Forces, 1961–1971* (1973).

Krepinevich, Andrew. *The Army and Vietnam* (1986).

Marolda, Edward, and Oscar Fitzgerald. *The United States Navy and the Vietnam Conflict,* Vol. 2 (1986).

Marolda, Edward, and G. Wesley Pryce III. *A Short History of the United States Navy and the Southeast Asian Conflict, 1950–1975* (1984).

McChristian, Joseph. *The Role of Military Intelligence, 1965–1967* (1975).

Meyerson, Harvey. *Vinh Long* (1970).

Meyerson, Joel. *Images of a Lengthy War* (1986).

Morrocco, John. *Rain of Fire: Air War, 1969–1973* (1985).

Palmer, Bruce. *The 25-Year War: America's Military Role in Vietnam* (1984).

Palmer, Dave. *Summons of the Trumpet: A History of the Vietnam War from a Military Man's Viewpoint* (1984).

Rogers, Bernard. *Cedar Falls–Junction City: A Turning Point* (1974).

Schlight, John. *The War in South Vietnam: The Years of the Offensive, 1965–1968* (1988).

Scoville, Thomas. *Reorganizing for Pacification Support* (1982).

Sheehan, Neil. *A Bright Shining Lie: John Paul Vann and America in Vietnam* (1988).

Shulimson, Jack. *U.S. Marines in Vietnam, 1965* (1978).

———. *U.S. Marines in Vietnam, 1966* (1982).

Spector, Ronald. *Advice and Support: The Early Years* (1983).

Stanton, Shelby. *The Rise and Fall of an American Army: U.S. Ground Forces in Vietnam, 1965–1973* (1985).

Thayer, Thomas. *War Without Fronts: The American Experience in Vietnam* (1985).

Thompson, James. *Rolling Thunder: Understanding Policy and Program Failure (1980).*

Thompson, W. Scott, and Donaldson D. Frizzell, eds. *The Lesson of Vietnam* (1977).

Turley, G. *The Easter Offensive, Vietnam 1972* (1985).

Tilford, Earl. *Search and Rescue in Southeast Asia, 1961–1975* (1981).

Walt, Lewis. *Strange War, Strange Strategy: A General's Report on Vietnam* (1970).

Westmoreland, William. *A Soldier Reports* (1976).

Zaffiri, Samuel. *Hamburger Hill* (1988).

– RICHARD A. HUNT

Gulf War of 1991

The invasion of Kuwait by 140,000 Iraqi troops and 1,800 tanks on Aug. 2, 1990, eventually led to U.S. involvement in war in the Persian Gulf region. Instead of repaying billions of dollars of loans received from Kuwait during the eight-year war between Iran and Iraq (1980–1988), Iraqi dictator Saddam Hussein resurrected old territorial claims and annexed Kuwait as his country's nineteenth province. President George Bush feared that Saddam might next invade Saudi Arabia and thus control 40 percent of the world's oil. Bush organized an international coalition of forty-three nations, thirty of which sent military or medical units to liberate Kuwait, and he personally lobbied United Nations Security Council members. By November the UN had imposed economic sanctions and passed twelve separate resolutions demanding that the Iraqis withdraw. Bush initially sent 200,000 U.S. troops as part of a multinational peacekeeping force to defend Saudi Arabia (Operation Desert Shield), describing the mission as "defensive." On November 8, Bush expanded the U.S. expeditionary force to more than 500,000 to "ensure that the coalition has an adequate offensive military option." Contingents from other allied countries brought the troop level to 675,000. UN Security Council Resolution 678 commanded Iraq to evacuate Kuwait by Jan. 15, 1991, or else face military attack.

What Saddam Hussein had hoped to contain as an isolated regional quarrel provoked an unprecedented alliance that included not only the United States and most members of the North Atlantic Treaty Organiza-

The Unites States and its allies quickly proved their superiority in the air with a spectacular five-week aerial bombardment of Iraq and Kuwait that began on 16 January 1991. This B-52G Stratofortress bomber was one of hundreds of bombers that took part in Operation Desert Storm. (Department of Defense/U.S. Air Force)

tion (NATO) but also Iraq's former military patron, the Soviet Union, and several Arab states, including Egypt and Syria. The Iraqi dictator must have found Washington's outraged reaction especially puzzling in view of recent efforts by the administrations of Presidents Ronald Reagan and Bush to befriend Iraq. Off-the-books U.S. arms transfers to Iraq were kept from Congress from 1982 to 1987, in violation of the law. Washington had supplied intelligence data to Baghdad during the Iran-Iraq war, and Bush had blocked congressional attempts to deny agricultural credits to Iraq because of human rights abuses. The Bush administration had also winked at secret and illegal bank loans that Iraq had used to purchase $5 billion in Western technology for its burgeoning nuclear and chemical weapons programs. Assistant Secretary of State John H. Kelly told Congress in early 1990 that Saddam Hussein acted as "a force of moderation" in the Middle East. Only a week before the invasion Ambassador April Glaspie informed Saddam Hussein that Washington had no "opinion on inter-Arab disputes such as your border dispute with Kuwait."

"Choose your target, decide on your objective, and try to crush it."

Bush and his advisers, without informing Congress or the American people, apparently decided early in August to use military force to expel Saddam Hussein from Kuwait. "It must be done as massively and decisively as possible," advised General Colin Powell, chairman of the Joint Chiefs of Staff. "Choose your target, decide on your objective, and try to crush it." The president, however, described the initial deployments as defensive, even after General H. Norman Schwarzkopf had begun to plan offensive operations. Bush did not announce the offensive buildup until after the November midterm elections, all the while expanding U.S. goals from defending Saudi Arabia, to liberating Kuwait, to crippling Iraq's war economy, even to stopping Saddam Hussein from acquiring nuclear weapons. UN sanctions cut off 90 percent of Iraq's imports and 97 percent of its exports. Secretary of State James Baker did meet with Iraqi Foreign Minister Tariq Azziz in early January 1991, but Iraq refused to consider withdrawal from Kuwait unless the United States forced Israel to relinquish its occupied territories. Bush and Baker vetoed this linkage, as well as any Arab solution whereby Iraq would retain parts of Kuwait. Iraq's aggression, which the president likened to Adolf Hitler's, should gain no reward.

Although Bush claimed he had the constitutional authority to order U.S. troops into combat under the UN resolution, he reluctantly requested congressional authorization, which was followed by a four-day debate. Senator Joseph R. Biden of Delaware declared that "none [of Iraq's] actions justify the deaths of our sons and daughters." Senator George Mitchell of Maine cited the risks: "An unknown number of casualties and deaths, billions of dollars spent, a greatly disrupted oil supply and oil price increases, a war possibly widened to Israel, Turkey or other allies, the possible long-term American occupation of Iraq, increased instability in the Persian Gulf region, long-lasting Arab enmity against the United States, a possible return to isolationism at home." Senator Robert Dole of Kansas scorned the critics, saying that Saddam Hussein "may think he's going to be rescued, maybe by Congress." On January 12, after Congress defeated a resolution to continue sanctions, a majority in both houses approved Bush's request to use force under UN auspices. Virtually every Republican voted for war; two-thirds of House Democrats and forty-five of fifty-six Democratic senators cast negative votes. Those few Democratic senators voting for war (among them Tennessee's Al Gore and Joseph Lieberman of Connecticut) provided the necessary margin.

Operation Desert Storm began with a spectacular aerial bombardment of Iraq and Kuwait on Jan. 16, 1991. For five weeks satellite television coverage via Cable News Network enabled Americans to watch "smart" bombs hitting Iraqi targets and U.S. Patriot missiles intercepting Iraqi Scud missiles. President Bush and Secretary Baker kept the coalition intact, persuading Israel not to retaliate after Iraqi Scud attacks on its territory and keeping Soviet Premier Mikhail Gorbachev advised as allied bombs devastated Russia's erstwhile client. On Feb. 24 General Schwarzkopf sent hundreds of thousands of allied troops into Kuwait and eastern Iraq. Notwithstanding Saddam's warning that Americans would sustain thousands of casualties in the "mother of all battles," Iraq's largely conscript army put up little resistance. By February 26 Iraqi forces had retreated from Kuwait, blowing up as many as 800 oil wells as they did so. Allied aircraft flew hundreds of sorties against what became known as the "highway of death," from Kuwait City to Basra. After only 100 hours of fighting on the ground, Iraq accepted a UN-imposed cease-fire. Iraq's military casualties numbered more than 25,000 dead and 300,000 wounded; U.S. forces suffered only 148 battle deaths (35 from friendly fire), 145 nonbattle deaths, and 467 wounded (out of a coalition total of 240 dead and 776 wounded). An exultant President Bush proclaimed, "By God, we've kicked the Vietnam syndrome."

The war itself initially cost $1 million per day for the first three months, not including the ongoing expense of keeping an encampment of 300,000 allied troops in Saudi Arabia, Iraq, and Kuwait. The overall cost of the war was estimated to be $54 billion; $7.3 billion paid by the United States, with another $11 billion from Germany and $13 billion from Japan, and the remainder ($23 billion) from Arab nations. For the first time in the twentieth century, the United States cold not afford to finance its own participation in a war.

Bush chose not to send U.S. forces to Baghdad to capture Saddam Hussein, despite his earlier designation of the Iraqi leader as public enemy number one. Attempts during the fighting to target Saddam had failed, and Bush undoubtedly hoped that the Iraqi military or disgruntled associates in the Ba'ath party would oust the Iraqi leader. When Kurds in northern Iraq and Shi'ites in the south rebelled, Bush did little to help. As General Powell stated: "If you want to go in and stop the killing of Shi'ites, that's a mission I understand. But to what purpose? If the Shi'ites continue to rise up, do we then support them for the overthrow of Baghdad and the partition of the country?" Powell opposed "trying to sort out two thousand years of Mesopotamian history." Bush, ever wary of a Mideast quagmire, backed away: "We are not going to permit this to drag on in terms of significant U.S. presence à la Korea." Saddam used his remaining tanks and helicopters to crush these domestic rebellions, sending streams of Kurdish refugees fleeing toward the Turkish border. Public pressure persuaded President Bush to send thousands of U.S. troops to northern Iraq, where the UN designated a security zone and set up makeshift tent cities. Saddam's survival left a sour taste in Washington, and created a situation that Lawrence Freedman and Efraim Karsh have compared to "an exasperating endgame in chess, when the winning player never seems to trap the other's king even though the final result is inevitable."

Under Security Council Resolution 687, Iraq had to accept the inviolability of the boundary with Kuwait (to be demarcated by an international commission), accept the presence of UN peacekeepers on its borders, disclose all chemical, biological, and nuclear weapons including missiles, and cooperate in their destruction. What allied

Beginning on 24 February 1991, hundred of thousands of allied troops, including the marines manning these two battle tanks, moved into Kuwait and eastern Iraq during the ground phase of Operation Desert Storm. (Department of Defense/U.S. Marine Corps)

bombs had missed, UN inspectors did not. Saddam Hussein's scientists and engineers had built more than twenty nuclear facilities linked to a large-scale Iraqi Manhattan Project. Air attacks had only inconvenienced efforts to build a bomb. Inspectors also found and destroyed more than a hundred Scud missiles, seventy tons of nerve gas, and 400 tons of mustard gas. By the fall of 1992 the head of the UN inspection team rated Iraq's capacity for mass destruction "zero."

An exultant President Bush proclaimed,

"By God, we've kicked the Vietnam syndrome."

Results from the war included the restoration of Kuwait, lower oil prices, resumption of peace negotiations between Israel and the Arabs, and at least a temporary revival of faith in the United Nations. Improved relations with Iran and Syria brought an end to Western hostage-taking in Beirut. Firefighters extinguished the last of the blazing oil wells ignited by the retreating Iraqis in November 1991, but only after the suffocating smoke had spread across an area twice the size of Alaska and caused long-term environmental damage. An estimated 200,000 civilians died, largely from disease and malnutrition. Millions of barrels of oil befouled the Persian Gulf, killing more than 30,000 sea birds.

BIBLIOGRAPHY

Atkinson, Rick. *Crusade* (Boston, 1993).

Freedman, Lawrence, and Efraim Karsh. *The Gulf Conflict, 1990–1991* (Princeton, N.J., 1993).

Jentleson, Bruce. *With Friends Like These: Reagan, Bush, and Saddam, 1982–1992* (New York, 1994).

Record, Jeffrey. *Hollow Victory* (New York, 1993).

Woodward, Bob. *The Commanders* (New York, 1991).

– J. GARRY CLIFFORD

Gunboat Diplomacy, 1776–1992

The term "gunboat diplomacy" may be defined as the use of warships in peacetime to further a nation's diplomatic and political aims. The focus of this essay, however, is not exclusively on gunboat diplomacy or even on the United States Navy. Instead, its concern is with

Gunboat diplomacy involves the use of military force to "preserve domestic tranquillity," to police occupied territory, or to combat unrest abroad.

the potential or actual use of military force in nonwar contexts. In continental North America, it may involve militia, volunteer forces, or regular army units on the frontier in a peacekeeping role. It also may involve naval units anywhere on the world's oceans, protecting commerce, ensuring the safety of American nationals whose lives or property may be threatened, and furthering the nation's interests abroad, however they are defined. It may involve the use of military force to "preserve domestic tranquillity," to police occupied territory, or to combat unrest or insurrection abroad.

THE EARLY NATIONAL PERIOD, 1783–1815

The end of the American Revolution understandably brought about a reduction in the military establishment. Both the Continental army (1784) and the Continental navy (1785) were largely dissolved, but even before the war's end, national leaders had begun to grapple with the problem of national security. The solution seemed deceptively simple. With Great Britain on the verge of admitting defeat, and with weak Spanish forces to the south and west unable to menace the Confederation, there was no need for a standing army. Downplaying the degree to which Spanish and French military assistance had contributed to the British defeat, national leaders assumed that the country could, as it had once before, create its own military establishment should any European power again threaten invasion. Reliance could be placed on state-raised and state-funded militia forces, which posed no threat to American liberties. As with most simple solutions, it also turned out to be wrong, although this would not be immediately apparent.

Requests to Congress for military assistance from the states of Pennsylvania and New York in the spring of 1783 prompted the formation of a congressional committee to grapple with the issue of security. As chair of the committee, Alexander Hamilton wrote to George Washington, the commander of the Continental army, for his advice. Washington, consulting first with his subordinates, worked their recommendations into a proposal titled "Sentiments on a Peace Establishment." Assuming that the government must occupy and police the trans-Allegheny region, Washington urged the establishment of a national army, a uniform nationally controlled militia force, federal arsenals, and the establishment of an institution for the study of war and military skills.

The army, as Washington envisioned it, would consist of four infantry regiments and one artillery regiment—more than twenty-six hundred officers and men. One detachment would guard the New England frontier and the Lake Champlain–Hudson River corridor; a second would be stationed along the Great Lakes frontier (Fort Oswego, Fort Niagara, Fort Detroit, Fort Michilimackinac); a third would occupy various posts in the Ohio River valley; and the fourth would patrol the frontier in the Carolinas and Georgia. Washington's proposal, revised but not significantly changed by Hamilton's committee, was rejected by Congress, which on 3 June 1784 established the seven hundred-man First American Regiment, comprised of militia from the states of Connecticut, New York, New Jersey, and Pennsylvania, under the command of Lieutenant Colonel Josiah Harmar. Its inadequacies soon were made manifest.

The occupation and control of the trans-Allegheny region was contingent upon relations with the Indian nations resident there. Those relations were not good. An expedition launched against the Shawnees in 1774 by the colony of Virginia, although successful, had been followed by Indian raids against the Kentucky territory settlements in 1777 and 1778. These in turn were a factor in the George Rogers Clark expedition that captured the British posts at Kaskaskia, Cahokia, and Vincennes. Raids along the northern frontier in 1778 at Wyoming Valley, German Flats, and Cherry Valley

For early frontier Indian fighting, see map on page 90. For Cuba and Puerto Rico, see also map on page 305. For interventions in the Pacific Ocean, see maps on pages 324 and 429.

prompted a retaliatory expedition in 1779 against the Iroquois. In addition, British aid and support to dissident native American tribes did not end after the revolutionary war. Great Britain's refusal to evacuate the posts held along the line of the Great Lakes and the Saint Lawrence River emboldened Indian resistance. The refusal to evacuate was based on American noncompliance with portions of the Treaty of Paris of 1783 and facilitated British control of the fur trade.

From 1784 to 1789 a series of military posts were established along the Ohio River and its tributaries. The garrisons—companies of the First American Regiment—were to provide escorts to those sent to treat with the Indians, evict squatters, and defend land surveyors and settlers. It was an impossible task. In 1786, Congress voted to increase the size of the army to 2,040, ostensibly to deal with the Indians but in reality to confront the menace of Daniel Shays's Rebellion (August 1786–February 1787) in Massachusetts. In the event, only two artillery companies assembled, and the rebellion was put down by Massachusetts militia.

The Constitution gave Congress the power to "provide and maintain a navy" and "raise and support armies," levying taxes for these purposes.

Based on recent experience, therefore, delegates to the Constitutional Convention in Philadelphia in 1787 could agree that the government's ability to enforce its will had been insufficient. There was some hesitation that any augmentation of military power, be it in terms of an army or a navy, to defend the nation against enemies foreign or domestic, carried the risk of oppression of both states' rights and individual citizens' rights. Thus, the Constitution gave Congress the power to "provide and maintain a navy" and "raise and support armies," levying taxes for these purposes. The Department of War was created in August 1789, the First American Regiment was adopted as a nucleus for a regular force, and four more companies were added within six months, bringing the total force to 1,216 officers and men. They were soon needed in the Ohio Valley.

The tribes that inhabited the Wabash, Maumee, and Sandusky valleys had never recognized any American right to their lands either by virtue of conquest or treaty cession. Westerners—4,200 whites in the Northwest Territory, another 1,820 west of the Mississippi in Spanish territory, and more than 61,000 in Kentucky—felt neglected and ignored by the federal government. They believed that the army detachments were inadequate and that peace on the frontier was unobtainable unless expeditions were undertaken against Indian settlements to destroy both them and their inhabitants. Federal leaders, who were predominantly easterners, preferred negotiation to war. Wars were costly, and the regular military establishment was insufficient to defeat the Indians, who could bring into the field from fifteen hundred to twenty-five hundred warriors. Furthermore, the militia was unreliable. The Washington administration, preferring peace, began to descend the slope to war. In the fall of 1789, Congress approved a measure authorizing the mobilization of a frontier militia, which allowed the president to wage war without applying to Congress. These preparations, in turn, threatened the success of a negotiated settlement; to the Indians, a punitive expedition, or even the threat of one, seemed little short of total war.

Kentuckians not only viewed the national government's Indian policy as misguided, but believed that the army's presence was designed to prevent them from mounting their own expeditions against the tribes north of the Ohio. To disregard Kentucky's concerns risked the establishment of a separate government, possibly allied with Spanish Louisiana. Finally, there also was the matter of the land companies: both Harmar (now a general) and Arthur St. Clair, governor of the Northwest Territory, were Ohio Company shareholders.

Early in June 1790, Secretary of War Henry Knox ordered an expedition against the Indians. In fact, a two-pronged expedition was planned: the western arm, consisting of three hundred militia and the garrison of Fort Knox (Vincennes, Indiana), under the command of Major John F. Hamtramck, would proceed up the Wabash; the eastern arm, consisting of twelve hundred Kentucky and Pennsylvania militia and three hundred regulars, commanded by General Harmar, would leave Fort Washington (Cincinnati) for the Maumee. The columns would be mutually supporting. After dealing with any opposition, a military garrison would be established on the upper Maumee, designed in part to sever the Indians from their British suppliers. The plan did not work out that way. The western prong of the expedition turned back before reaching its objective. Harmar's eastern prong destroyed some Indian settlements, but two detachments were ambushed, and by early November the force was back at Fort Washington, minus two hundred men.

The failure of Knox's expedition was attributed partly to Harmar, but even more to the inept performance of the militia. With the Indians emboldened rather than cowed, the administration would try again with a larger force composed of regulars. The only portion of the government's plans that were successful were negotiations with the Iroquois and the conclusion of a treaty with the Cherokees. Hostilities thus remained limited to the northwestern Ohio tribes.

Whatever could go wrong with the buildup of forces did in 1791. St. Clair's force of regulars, militia, and levies was an army in name only when it headed north in October. Five weeks later, on 4 November, a predawn attack by one thousand Indians led to the destruction of St. Clair's force, which suffered a 60 percent casualty rate—632 deaths and more than 300 wounded out of a force of 1,400. After this disaster the army was increased the following year from two regiments to five (more than five thousand men), reorganized into four legions of twelve hundred men each and comprised of infantry, cavalry, and artillery. There also was a new army commander, Major General Anthony Wayne. Before resorting to force, however, President Washington attempted to negotiate a settlement.

These diplomatic efforts, undertaken seriously in 1792 to assuage public opinion, and somewhat less so in 1793, amounted to very little. The Indian tribes wanted the removal of all whites north of the Ohio. The British, hoping for the establishment of an Indian buffer state between Upper and Lower Canada and the United States, supported the Indians in their refusal. Wayne, kept apprised of the state of negotiations, would have undertaken a campaign in 1793 were it not for the lateness of the season and illness among his forces. The establishment of a British fort at the Maumee Rapids (Toledo, Ohio) was the final straw. Wayne's campaign began in the early summer of 1794.

During the winter Wayne established Fort Recovery at the site of St. Clair's 1791 defeat. In June 1794 its garrison beat off a two-day assault by the Indians. On 28 July, Wayne's force (two thousand regulars and fifteen hundred Kentucky volunteers) left Fort Greenville and proceeded northward, establishing Fort Defiance at the junction of the Auglaize and Maumee rivers, then proceeded down the Maumee. The Battle of Fallen Timbers was fought 20 August 1794. It was a decisive Indian defeat, which, coupled with the failure of the British to continue previous levels of support, led to the Treaty of Greenville the next year. Most of the future state of Ohio was ceded to the United States and the British decided to evacuate the frontier posts they had held since 1783.

The Washington administration not only had to deal with the Indians along the Northwest frontier but also with domestic unrest sparked by an excise tax on whiskey. The so-called Whiskey Rebellion of 1794 came at an awkward time for President Washington, as the regular forces were fully committed on the frontier. Deciding that the need to preserve "domestic tranquillity" was overriding, the government called upon state militia. Ultimately a force of 12,500 was assembled to move against the rebels in the southwestern portion of Pennsylvania. The rebellion collapsed and the government appeared vindicated. In another sense, it succeeded too well.

The coalescing opposition to the Federalists in the Fourth Congress proposed a 60 percent reduction in the army. Legislation passed in 1796 provided for a force of two thousand men in four regiments of eight companies each, a thousand-man contingent of artillerists and engineers, and a small cavalry force. Even more important, this act marked the true establishment of a permanent peacetime army, in a form that was to exist well into the nineteenth century. The army's primary mission became the manning of frontier posts, overseeing Indian-white contacts, and keeping settlers out of Indian territory—in short, serving as a frontier constabulary to maintain peace along the nation's borders.

For the North African states of Morocco, Algiers, Tunis, and Tripoli, U.S. shipping vessels were easy prey.

The country possessed maritime frontiers as well as those on land. As colonists and part of the British empire, merchants and shipowners could look to the Royal Navy for protection. Naturally, the winning of independence saw the loss of this protection, felt most keenly in the eastern Atlantic and the Mediterranean. For the North African states of Morocco, Algiers, Tunis, and Tripoli, U.S. shipping vessels were easy prey. In 1783 six vessels fell to Moroccan and Algerian corsairs, and the toll continued in succeeding years. Options seemed few; the last Continental navy vessel was sold in 1785. With force unavailable, negotiation appeared the only alternative. A fifty-year treaty of amity and friendship was signed with Morocco in 1786. The situation improved only briefly.

The outbreak of war between the European powers in 1793 was followed by a British-inspired settlement between Portugal and Algiers, which allowed Algerian vessels into the Atlantic to harass neutral commerce. Eleven American vessels were captured that year, their crews held hostage. In January 1794 a House committee recommended the construction of four forty-four-gun and two twenty-four-gun vessels, and Congress approved the program on 27 March, with the proviso that it would be suspended if an agreement could be reached with Algiers. A September 1795 treaty with the Dey of Algiers provided for a payment of $21,600 annually in tribute in the form of naval stores, and the "gift" of a thirty-six-gun frigate (actually delivered to Algiers in 1798). Less costly settlements were reached with Tripoli in 1796 and Tunis in 1797.

Meanwhile, the improvement in relations with Great Britain signified by Senate ratification of Jay's Treaty in 1795 was followed swiftly by a deterioration in U.S. relations with France. The French viewed Jay's Treaty as a virtual Anglo-American alliance, and in retaliation began to seize American shipping. In 1797 President John Adams sent a commission to France to resolve differences between the two nations, but when faced with the prospect of a bribe to even begin negotiations, the commissioners balked. The subsequent uproar in the United States against France led to the Quasi-War (1798–1800). Congress appropriated funds to send three of the six frigates authorized in 1794 to sea and to build the remaining approved vessels. In 1798 it created a separate Department of the Navy, and authorized the reestablishment of the Marine Corps to provide ship's guards and when necessary to serve in shore landing parties. The end of the Quasi-War and the election of Thomas Jefferson as president in 1800 led to a significant reduction in naval strength. At this point, however, the Pasha of Tripoli declared war on the United States (May 1801).

Commodore Richard Dale, the first of a series of naval commanders in the Mediterranean, succeeded in immobilizing two Tripolitan vessels at Gibraltar. His forces also blockaded Tripoli for a time, but lacking authority to negotiate, Dale returned to the United States in April 1802. His successor, Commodore Richard Morris, did have authority to negotiate, but what he could offer was far from what was sought by the Tripolitan ruler. Morris himself was captured by the Bey of Tunis and had to be ransomed, an incident that led to his dismissal from the navy.

Commodore Edward Preble, who arrived in the Mediterranean in September 1803, enjoyed better fortune. He possessed both sufficient naval strength—four frigates and five sloops—and the will to use it. Learning that the emperor of Morocco had authorized attacks on U.S. merchantmen, Preble took his squadron to Tangier and forced the emperor to abide by the terms of the 1787 treaty. Meanwhile, unfortunately, the frigate *Philadelphia,* commanded by William Bainbridge, ran aground in the harbor of Tripoli, 31 October 1803, and its entire crew of 307 was taken prisoner. The following year, during a series of attacks launched by Preble against Tripoli, a contingent of volunteers under Lieutenant Stephen Decatur burned the captured *Philadelphia* (16 February). Negotiations were less successful; Preble was succeeded as naval commander by Samuel Barron.

Barron accomplished little, but General William Eaton, agent to the Barbary states, more than compensated for him. Leading a motley force of some 450 men westward from Egypt in March 1805, he succeeded in capturing the port of Derna. This assault posed a potential threat to Tripoli itself, but the hostages remained at risk. An agreement ending the conflict was signed 3 June 1805. U.S. merchantmen were to be immune from attack, and the United States was to be granted most-favored-nation treatment for its vessels. On the other hand, Derna had to be evacuated, the captives ransomed for $60,000, and payment of tribute resumed. John Rodgers, who succeeded Barron shortly before the conclusion of the agreement, overawed the Bey of Tunis into making a separate settlement later that year, and might well have had sufficient strength to capture Tripoli itself had he been given the opportunity. American commerce was free to sail the Mediterranean once more, although the Barbary states would be heard from in the future.

The regular army's primary role of peacekeeping along the frontiers of the United States had remained unchanged following the Treaty of Greenville in 1795. During Jefferson's second term in office, it became a domestic peacekeeping force, detachments being called upon to help enforce the embargo on trade with Great Britain passed in 1807, particularly along the Canadian boundary. The deterioration in relations with Great Britain, combined with renewed unrest among the Indians in the Northwest, led to an expedition mounted by the governor of Indiana Territory, William Henry Harrison, in 1811. This expedition grew out of opposition to the 1809 Treaty of Fort Wayne and was led by the Shawnee chief Tecumseh. Taking advantage of Tecumseh's absence from the area, Harrison moved against a Shawnee concentration on the upper Wabash with a force of one thousand men comprised of regular infantry, militia, and volunteers. The Indians attacked Harrison's force on 7 November 1811 but were repulsed after severe fighting. The Battle of Tippecanoe resolved nothing; discovery of British-supplied equipment nearby angered settlers and frontiersmen and brought closer a renewed struggle for control of both the Northwest and the Southwest—a struggle that would resume during the War of 1812.

A projected invasion of Upper Canada across the Detroit River in 1812 did not go well. In rapid succession that year, a British force captured Fort Michilimackinac, the garrison of Fort Dearborn (Chicago) was massacred as it retreated after evacuating the post, and General William Hull surrendered both his army and Detroit. An attempt to retrieve the situation during the winter of 1812–1813 miscarried as a portion of Harrison's relieving force was cut to pieces at the Battle of Frenchtown on the River Raisin. Much of the Northwest Territory thus passed from American control for the duration of the conflict. Oliver Hazard Perry's victory at the Battle of Lake Erie, 10 September 1813, led to the retreat of British forces from Detroit. Pursued by the Americans, they were brought to bay and defeated at the Battle of the Thames on 5 October. Tecumseh's death in this engagement was to break up the coalition of Northwest tribes.

In the Southwest an uprising of a portion of the Creek nation (the Upper Creek or Red Sticks) occurred in 1813. The massacre of the garrison of Fort Mims near Mobile, Alabama, on 30 August was followed by the raising of a force of twenty-five hundred Kentucky and Tennessee volunteers, led by Andrew Jackson. The Creek were defeated in the engagements of Tallishatchee and Talladega later that same year, and on 27 March 1814 the Battle of Horseshoe Bend effectively ended the conflict. Some of the Creek fled to Spanish East Florida, in retreat but hardly defeated.

The War of 1812 also led to renewed depredations against U.S. shipping by the Barbary states. In 1815 the U.S. Navy had the opportunity to retaliate. A squadron led by Commodore Stephen Decatur captured the Algerian frigate *Mashuda* off the coast of Spain on 17 June, and two days later took the *Estedio.* On 28 June, off the port of Algiers, Decatur compelled the dey to pay an indemnity for seized vessels and to renounce future demands for tribute. Tripoli and Tunis, which had permitted British warships to seize U.S. vessels in their harbors during the War of 1812, were also forced to pay indemnities. An Anglo-Dutch expedition against Algiers in 1816 ended the Barbary threat for good. The conclusion of the Napoleonic wars marked an end to the era when warfare in Europe more often than not had meant warfare in North America and the Caribbean. The United States was to remain aloof from European conflicts for the next century, allowing its armed forces to concentrate on the role of maintaining peace on both the land and maritime frontiers.

INDIAN REMOVAL AND THE BEGINNING OF EXPANSION, 1815–1861

The army was able to slip rather easily back into its constabulary role, extending or reestablishing the authority of the federal government, controlling Indian-white and Indian-Indian relations, and, on occasion, dealing with domestic disorder. Military posts were established in the upper Great Lakes area along the principal water routes from the Great Lakes to the Mississippi and less quickly on the western tributaries of that river. In the former instance, a primary purpose of the army was to control the routes by which British goods from Upper Canada could reach the northwestern tribes. An 1816 congressional prohibition against foreign traders helped to accomplish this. Except for a near uprising among the Winnebago in southern Minnesota Territory in 1827, the Northwest remained quiet. Not so the Southeast.

Spanish Florida was inhabited by Indians of the Muskhogean family, who, although sharing the Creek culture, were called Seminole—"wild people"—because they had broken away from the Georgia and Alabama Creek towns and migrated southward. Following Andrew Jackson's victory over the Red Stick Creeks in 1814, their numbers were augmented when about one thousand warriors and their families moved into Florida. The problems caused by their arrival were exacerbated by the presence of free blacks who had also chosen to settle near the Seminole. Spain lacked a strong military presence in Florida, and there were frequent raids and counterraids across the border. The destruction of Negro Fort on the Apalachicola River in 1816 was followed by an assault on the Seminole village of Fowltown in Georgia, which inaugurated the First Seminole War. In March 1818, Andrew Jackson led a force of five hundred regulars, one thousand militia, and two thousand Creek warriors across the Florida border against the Seminole, decisively weakening their power and forcing them further southward. Jackson went on to capture St. Marks and Pensacola from the Spanish, and the expedition contributed to the Spanish decision to transfer Florida to the United States in 1821. Two years later, with the Treaty of Moultrie Creek, the Seminole relinquished their territorial claims in northern Florida in return for reservation lands in the south central part of the state.

Efforts at law enforcement often brought lawsuits from outraged traders whose supplies of liquor were confiscated.

Peace on both the northern and southern frontiers brought with it congressional demands for a reduction in the size of the army. A 50 percent cut was effected in 1821, bringing the army to approximately six thousand officers and men, and was the last such reduction incurred by the antebellum army. On the eve of war with Mexico in 1846, its strength had risen to 8,349; in 1861 the total stood at 16,367.

Enforcement of trade and intercourse laws regulating relations with the Indians brought the army, more often than not, into conflict with white traders and settlers. The sympathies of military personnel often lay with the Indians, particularly as efforts at law enforcement often brought lawsuits from outraged traders whose supplies of liquor were confiscated, or from white settlers whose title to Indian lands was none too clear. The Indian Removal Act, to transplant eastern Indians west of the Mississippi, was passed in 1830, and removal reached its peak during Jackson's presidency (1833–1841) and inevitably led to army involvement as well. In some instances, such as with the Choctaw and Chickasaw, removal was accomplished without incident. In others there was resistance, as with the Creek (1836) and the Sac and Fox (Black Hawk War of 1832).

The removal issue lay at the heart of the Second Seminole War (1835–1842), which, like the Vietnam War in the twentieth century, was both protracted and unpopular because it was indecisive. It ultimately involved army, navy, and Marine Corps forces, caused 1,466 deaths in the army alone, and cost the government $30 million to $40 million. A series of commanders tried, usually without success, to force the elusive Seminole to stand and fight. The presence of so great a portion of the army in Florida also proved an embarrassment to the government when two rebellions occurred in Canada along the border in 1837–1838. The absence of available troops to calm the tempers of Americans who sided with the Canadian rebels threatened to widen the conflict. This crisis in Anglo-American relations eventually subsided. It also was fortunate that the trans-Mississippi area remained peaceful, although in 1845 the annexation of Texas would bring the United States closer to its conflict with Mexico (1846–1848).

The navy, like the army, had a responsibility to protect American citizens. In the latter case, this occurred within U.S. territory; in the former, it could occur anywhere on the globe. The expansion of overseas trade and commerce after the War of 1812 was accompanied—except in northern European waters—by a naval presence, which is best illustrated by the proliferation of squadrons based abroad. The earliest such squadron, the Mediterranean, was formally established in 1815. The Latin American Wars of Independence (1808–1829) provided a backdrop for the establishment of the West Indian Squadron (1822), the Pacific Squadron (1818), and the Brazil Squadron (1826). Last to appear were the East Indian (1835) and African (1843) squadrons.

Protection of U.S. commerce and those engaged in it was a complex endeavor. Naval officers could be involved in dealing with foreign officials and on occasion were called upon to negotiate commercial treaties. Officers might also be required to rescue American nationals afloat or ashore whose possessions or lives were threatened. These threats could be met with the actual or potential use of force.

In time of peace, any interference with U.S. trade afloat or ashore was considered an act of piracy, and the perpetrators were dealt with accordingly. In time of war, as was the case during the Latin American Wars of Independence, each of the contending parties attempted to ensure that its forces received necessary food, equipment, and military reinforcements while denying these same resources to the opposition. Denial took the form of a naval blockade of ports controlled by the opposition and the capture of all vessels trading with the enemy.

In time of peace, any interference with U.S. trade afloat or ashore was considered an act of piracy, and the perpetrators were dealt with accordingly.

These captures were made occasionally by naval vessels but more often by privateers licensed for the purpose. The U.S. government's desire to protect the right of its citizens to trade freely required naval officers enforcing this right to make certain that declared blockades actually were in existence and that they could effectively determine the nature of the seized property. Trading in goods of direct military applicability was considered contraband; all other goods were immune. Naval officers were often required to make decisions or take action without reference to the State or Navy departments in Washington, D.C. This was the case until the expansion of the Atlantic cable network late in the nineteenth century.

WEST INDIAN SQUADRON. The Caribbean became positively unsafe for U.S. merchant shipping as both the Spanish government and insurgent regimes in Venezuela and Colombia issued privateering licenses in carload lots in 1817. Not only did these vessels prey on any weaker ship, but the situation was worsened by the existence of pirates living ashore in uninhabited regions of the Caribbean, particularly portions of Cuba and Puerto Rico. These buccaneers would dash to sea in small craft, snap up their victims, and dispose of the loot ashore, often with the connivance of local officials. In 1819, Congress empowered the navy to convoy U.S.-

flag vessels and to capture any pirate vessel interfering with commerce, which was easier said than done. The formation of the West Indian Squadron in 1822 helped. Under the command, successively, of James Biddle (1822–1823), David Porter (1823–1824), and Lewis Warrington (1825–1826), the threat of piracy was finally eliminated, but the tide did not begin to turn until the squadron's vessels were downsized to beat the pirates at their own game, and Spanish authorities in Cuba and Puerto Rico extended permission for the pursuit of pirates ashore. The cooperation of the Royal Navy also helped.

PACIFIC SQUADRON. Life was equally difficult for successive naval commanders off the west coast of South America. The Spanish navy lacked sufficient ships to effectively blockade rebel Chilean ports, but U.S. vessels that chanced to be in any of these ports when a Spanish warship appeared were liable to seizure. The Chileans made strenuous efforts to establish a navy, and in due course succeeded in wresting control of the eastern Pacific from the Spanish.

In November 1819, Chilean Admiral Thomas Cochrane was sent in a cutting-out expedition to seize the Spanish frigate *Esmerelda* in the harbor of Callao, Peru. Spanish forces ashore, assuming U.S. naval complicity in the assault, fired upon the USS *Macedonian.* The vessel's tender, sent ashore for supplies, was also fired upon; two crewmen were killed and six were wounded. An American schooner, the *Rampart,* also came under fire and was abandoned by its crew. For a time it appeared that Americans ashore and in the nearby capital of Lima were in danger from loyalist mobs. Captain John Downes of the *Macedonian* entered a vigorous protest with the Spanish viceroy, who released the *Rampart* and promised to conduct a thorough investigation of the entire episode. The triumph of the insurgents in Peru and Bolivia made the task of U.S. naval officers much easier as the wars in Latin America drew to a close.

Mexico's proximity to the United States and its continuing political and social instability after independence from Spain was achieved in 1821 seemed to presage a significant level of involvement by the U.S. Navy. Such involvement as did take place occurred following the independence of Texas (1836), when Mexican efforts to institute a blockade of the Texas coast were vitiated by the navy's recognition of Texan belligerence. U.S. warships frequently escorted merchant vessels through the blockade. The seizure of the Mexican warship *General Urrea* by Commander William Mervine for having illegally detained two American merchantmen created a brief war scare in both countries.

The actions in October 1842 of Commodore Thomas ap Catesby Jones caused even greater damage to Mexican-American relations. Jones, the commander of the Pacific Squadron, received information from the

U.S. consul in Mazatlán that led him to believe that war between the two countries was imminent. He also had to deal with the reported sale of the province of California to Great Britain and the mysterious departure of British and French warships stationed in the eastern Pacific. With the *United States* and the *Cyane,* Jones sailed to Monterey, capital of Alta California. Hearing nothing that might cause him to change his intended course of action, Jones demanded the surrender of the port and took possession of Alta California in the name of the United States. Two days later, as information came to light proving that war was not imminent, he restored Monterey to the Mexican authorities and sailed away. He was recalled as squadron commander but was subject to no further disciplinary action at the government's hands.

SOUTH ATLANTIC SQUADRON. Brazil established its independence from Portugal in 1822 without undue violence, but soon after came into conflict with Argentina over the Banda Oriental (Uruguay). Brazil, which enjoyed command of the sea during much of its 1825–1828 war, established a blockade of the Rio de la Plata that affected American merchant shipping. Captain Jesse D. Elliott (*Cyane*) and Commodore Biddle (*Macedonian*) were involved in separate episodes, the former insisting that foreign shipping must have prior notification of the blockade, and the latter successfully protesting against the requirement that U.S. vessels purchase bonds from the Brazilian government. The bonds would be forfeit should such ships attempt to run the blockade. In December 1828, Commander Daniel Turner with the *Erie* cut out the Argentine privateer *Federal* in the harbor of Swedish St. Bartholomew. The Swedish authorities had refused Turner's demand for the *Federal*'s surrender because of the seizure of a U.S. vessel bound for Brazil. The seizure occurred after the end of the Argentine-Brazil conflict, a fact known to the privateer's captain. Some years later, Turner, back on the South Atlantic station, seized a U.S.-owned slave ship, the *Porpoise,* for violation of U.S. laws. In this instance his action was repudiated and apologies made to the Brazilian government.

A major crisis in U.S.-Argentine relations erupted in 1831–1832. The governor of the Falkland Islands seized several U.S. merchantmen that, he claimed, had engaged in illegal sealing among the islands. Their cargoes were seized and the crews imprisoned. Protests to mainland authorities proved unavailing. Commander Silas Duncan (*Lexington*), arriving off Puerto Soledad late in December 1831, forced the surrender of the port, dismantled its guns, liberated the captive American crewmen, and broke up the Argentine settlement there. The Argentine government subsequently severed diplomatic relations with the United States. Duncan's action was upheld by his government, even though he had exceeded his orders. The British government, which also claimed the Falklands, seized them soon after the *Lexington* departed, in part to preempt a possible takeover by the U.S. government.

Juan Manuel Rosas, president of Argentina, imposed an intermittent blockade of Uruguayan ports between 1843 and 1852. The governments of France and Great Britain opposed this action, and Rosas, hoping to enlist the sympathy and support of the United States, refrained from interfering with U.S. merchant vessels. In September 1844 a warship of the Uruguayan rebel movement that Rosas supported was pursuing a fishing vessel. In the course of its pursuit, a nearby U.S. merchantman was struck accidently by gunfire. Assuming the complicity of Argentine vessels on blockade duty, Captain Philip Voorhees (*Congress*) captured them all in rapid succession, which resulted in the raising of the blockade on Montevideo. Voorhees, however, was under orders to observe strict neutrality between the contending parties. Although he subsequently freed the Argentine warships, he made a bad situation worse by announcing his refusal to recognize a reimposed Argentine blockade. Voorhees's actions were overruled by Commodore Daniel Turner of the Brazilian squadron. Voorhees himself was recalled and court-martialed, but rather than being dismissed from the service, he received a five-year suspension of duty.

Improbably, in 1859 the U.S. government dispatched a major naval expedition to the Rio de la Plata. Under the command of Commodore William B. Shubrick, it consisted of nineteen warships, mounting an aggregate two hundred guns, and comprising twenty-five hundred officers and men. This expedition came about because of a variety of disputes with the Paraguayan dictator Carlos Antonio López. Equally capable was the American adventurer and former naval officer Edward A. Hopkins, who tried to throw his weight around; navy Lieutenant Thomas Jefferson Page, who in the course of exploring the rivers of the Paraguay-Paraná system exceeded his authority; and Lieutenant William N. Jeffries, whose vessel, the *Water Witch,* was fired upon by a Paraguayan fort after ignoring repeated requests to withdraw. Matters were amicably resolved, thanks largely to the efforts of commissioner James B. Bowlin, and U.S. merchant vessels were permitted to ply Paraguayan rivers. It was not the threat of force that gave López pause—most of the vessels of Shubrick's force could not ascend the river any distance—but rather the prospect of a U.S. blockade of the Rio de la Plata disposed all sides to conciliation.

WEST INDIAN SQUADRON. Growing interest in the acquisition of Cuba (President James K. Polk unsuccessfully offered Spain $100 million for it in 1848), particularly in the southern states, involved the navy in thwarting several filibustering episodes. Three such expeditions, led by a Cuban exile, Narciso López, were mounted from U.S. territory against Cuba. The first, in 1849, was broken up before it got started by order of President Zachary Taylor. The following year, López and five hundred American followers tried again. Leaving New Orleans in three vessels, they sailed to an island off the Yucatán peninsula, boarded one of the vessels, the *Creole,* and managed to elude patroling American and Spanish warships and land 18 May 1850 at Cárdenas, east of Havana. After clashing with Spanish troops, the filibusters reembarked and headed for Key West, Florida, hotly pursued by the Spanish warship *Pizarro.* Arriving just ahead of their pursuer, they avoided capture and possible execution because Lieutenant John Rodgers, commanding the USS *Petrel,* insisted that although the *Creole* and its crew had been guilty of piracy, he could not allow the seizure of vessel or crew in a U.S. port. Acquitted by a U.S. court, López and four hundred followers tried once again in 1851. Going ashore at Bahia Honda on 11 August, one detachment moved inland while the other remained to guard the expedition's supplies. The first group was attacked by converging Spanish forces, and all of López' force was captured. The leaders were subsequently executed in Havana.

Cornelius Vanderbilt's refusal to pay duties in 1851 led to his ship being fired upon by a British warship.

The navy was heavily involved in events in Nicaragua soon after. Nicaragua represented one of the two routes across the Central American isthmus—Panama was the other—utilized by those preferring a sea route to the California goldfields. New Yorker Cornelius Vanderbilt and other investors had established the Accessory Transit Company (ATC), with a major terminus at San Juan del Norte. This port near the mouth of the San Juan River, also called Greytown, lay within the British protectorate of Mosquitia. Greytown had been named a free port, with the right to levy its own harbor duties on goods landed there. Vanderbilt's refusal to pay duties in 1851 led to his ship being fired upon by a British warship. Refused harbor, the ship was compelled to return to the United States. Because the U.S. government did not recognize the protectorate, this episode had ominous overtones of a major crisis in Anglo-American relations. That it did not become so (despite the dispatch of U.S. warships to Greytown) was due to the efforts of the British naval commander in the Caribbean who repudiated the actions of his subordinate in firing upon Vanderbilt's vessel in the first place.

Two years later, some Greytown inhabitants sought to dismantle some ATC property at nearby Punta Arenas, but were stopped by Captain George N. Hollins in command of the *Cyane.* This was merely a curtain-raiser to an even more serious episode in 1854, triggered by the murder of a Greytown native by the captain of one of Vanderbilt's ships and the attempted arrest of a former U.S. consul who intervened on the captain's behalf. Word of this incident prompted the dispatch of the *Cyane* to Greytown once more; Hollins was ordered to uphold the authority of the United States and to show that its nationals could not be subject to arrest with impunity. Arriving on 11 July 1854, Hollins learned from a U.S. commercial agent for Central America that the inhabitants would not pay for destruction of ATC property nor apologize for the assault on the former consul. Hollins formally demanded restitution; if it was not forthcoming, he declared he would bombard the town the next day. He was as good as his word. His actions ultimately were upheld by the U.S. government in the face of a vigorous British protest on the ground that although he had stretched his orders, he had not exceeded them.

This was not the navy's last involvement in Nicaragua. In 1856 the country was taken over by filibusterer William Walker, who erred by cancelling the ATC's concession and becoming dependent for supplies upon rivals of Commodore Vanderbilt. The commodore struck back, helping to form a coalition of other Central American states against Walker and interdicting supplies and reinforcements ordered from New York. U.S. Navy Commander Charles H. Davis was sent to the Pacific coast of Central America with orders to protect American citizens and their property. Arriving at San Juan del Sur in February 1857, he was soon in contact with Walker. Davis was instrumental in working out an agreement between the beleaguered Walker and opposing Costa Rican forces, whereby Walker agreed to leave the country, unharmed, in return for surrendering his weapons.

Walker had no sooner returned to the United States than he planned another expedition to Nicaragua, which sailed from Mobile, Alabama, in mid-November 1857, landing near Greytown despite the presence of a U.S. warship. On 6 December, Commodore Hiram

Paulding appeared off Greytown and leveled the guns of the *Wabash, Saratoga,* and *Fulton* at Walker's camp; a landing party cordoned it off. Walker was captured and once again he and his men returned to the United States. Paulding received a reprimand and a brief suspension from duty for having exceeded his authority by seizing Walker in Nicaraguan territory.

The navy also became involved in two brief episodes in Panama at this time. The first intervention followed the so-called Watermelon Riot of April 1856; the second followed an outburst of unrest in September 1860. Naval forces went ashore at Panama City on both occasions to maintain or to restore order. Other occasions would arise for similar displays of force on the isthmus during the next half century.

EAST INDIAN SQUADRON. Across the Pacific, China posed a different set of problems. Commercial relations had begun in the eighteenth century through the southern port of Canton—the only one where westerners were permitted. The first U.S. naval vessel did not visit Chinese waters until 1819; the de facto establishment of the East Indian Squadron in 1835 signified a more regular naval presence, but formal relations between the United States and China had to await the Treaty of Wanghia in 1844. Ratifications were exchanged in 1846. Aside, however, from operations to suppress piracy along the south China coast, no U.S. warship used force or intervened ashore until the 1850s, during the internal convulsions brought on by the Taiping Rebellion, which began in 1849, and the Arrow War (1856–1858), in which Great Britain and France went to war against China.

The city of Shanghai had been occupied by Taiping rebels in the spring of 1854, and imperial troops attempted its recapture. When a U.S.-owned vessel was halted by imperial troops and its crew taken into custody, Commander John Kelly (USS *Plymouth*) compelled their return. Kelly and the *Plymouth*'s crew also took part on 4 April 1854 in an assault with British forces against imperial troops camped outside the city. Two years later, with the Arrow War under way, imperial forces in the barrier forts below Canton fired on two U.S. merchantmen. Unable to obtain assurances from Chinese authorities that similar incidents would not occur again, Commodore James Armstrong ordered Commander Andrew H. Foote, the new commander of the *Plymouth,* and the *Levant* into action. In an operation lasting from 16 to 22 November 1856, Foote's forces, at a cost of seven dead and twenty-nine wounded, successfully stormed four major forts and captured nearly two hundred guns from imperial troops. Armstrong refused to be drawn into the Sino-British conflict, having finally received assurances that U.S. vessels would not be harassed again.

Commodore Josiah Tattnall was less restrained three years later. Tattnall, in a chartered Chinese steamer, observed an Anglo-French assault on the Taku forts on 25 June 1859. The British commander, Admiral James Hope, had three flagships shot from under him; Tattnall had himself rowed to the fourth and, despite admonitions from the U.S. minister, John E. Ward, not to become involved, utilized his steamer to tow British reinforcements into range. He also authorized his men to man the guns on the fourth British flagship and later that day took ashore a British landing party that failed to storm the Great South Fort. Tattnall escaped a court-martial, probably because of the favorable British governmental reaction to his doings. Anglo-American relations were well served, even if Sino-American relations suffered.

Contacts with Japan were even more limited than those with China. It was not until 1846 that a U.S. warship visited Japanese waters, when Commodore Biddle entered Edo (Tokyo) Bay with the USS *Columbus* and *Vincennes* to inquire whether or not Japanese ports might be opened to American shipping. The Japanese refused, and Biddle sailed away. Three years later, Commander James Glynn (USS *Preble*) succeeded in obtaining the release of some U.S. sailors at Nagasaki. Neither experience promised much success to Commodore Matthew C. Perry on his expedition to "open" Japan to U.S. commerce. On his first visit in July 1853, the Japanese agreed to accept a letter from President Millard Fillmore outlining trade proposals. Perry returned to Edo Bay in February 1854, remaining in Japanese waters until late June. The Treaty of Kanagawa, signed on 31 March, provided that shipwrecked U.S. sailors would be cared for, and also authorized the opening of two ports—Hakodate and Shimoda—to American vessels for supplies and provisions.

The East Indian Squadron, as its name implied, had a greater area of responsibility than China and Japan. The Indian Ocean, Southeast Asia, and the Dutch East Indies also lay within its sphere. When the Malayan inhabitants of Kuala Batu, in northwestern Sumatra, seized and plundered a Salem, Massachusetts, vessel engaged in the pepper trade in 1831, the Jackson administration dispatched Captain John Downes to obtain an apology and redress. Downes, not stopping to negotiate, sent ashore a force of 282 sailors and marines, captured four forts, and killed nearly a hundred Malays. Although publicly defended by the administration, Downes was privately castigated for failing to enter into negotiations with the local inhabitants before resorting to force. His naval career was ruined.

Commodore George C. Read was dispatched on a commerce-protecting mission in 1838 with orders to stop in Sumatra to see if the Malays had been truly

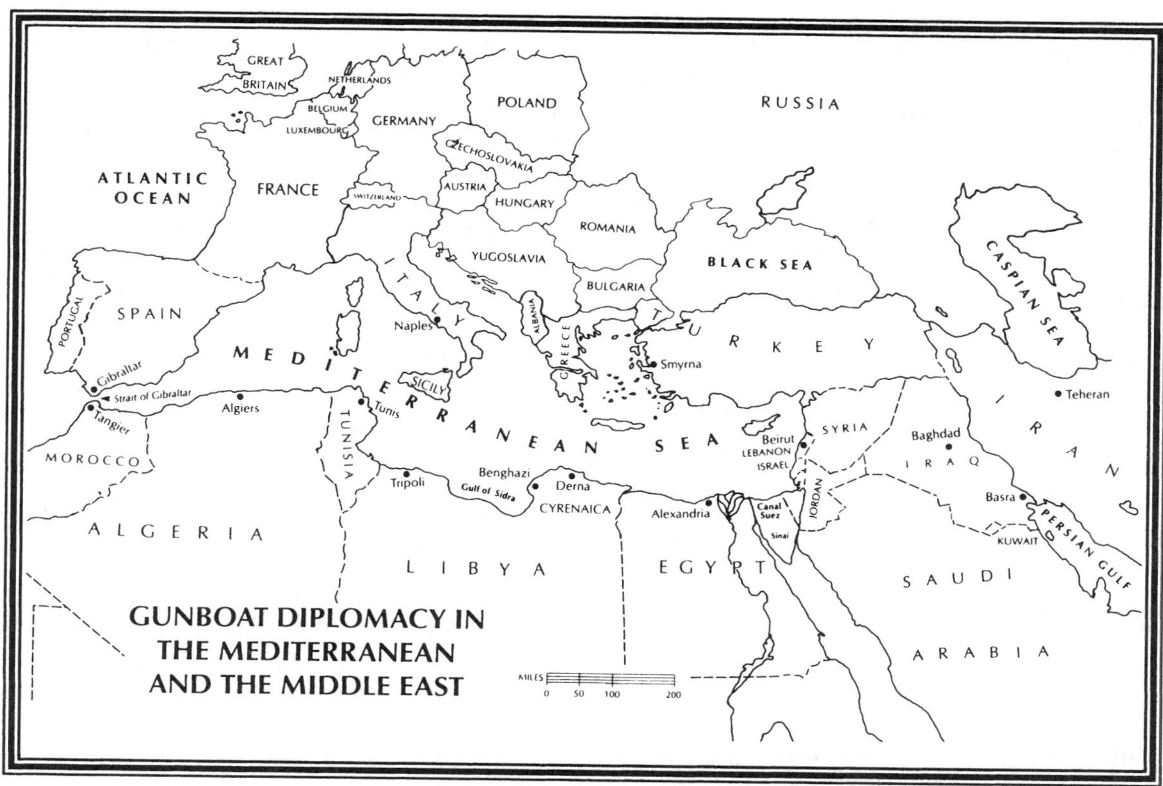

pacified. Learning in Ceylon of the plunder of another U.S. vessel, he arrived off Kuala Batu on 22 December 1838. Having requested and failed to receive either the guilty parties or restitution for the goods seized, he bombarded Kuala Batu on 25 December and nearby Muki 1 January 1839. Unlike Downes, Read followed his instructions. Neither officer's action, however, permanently altered Malay behavior.

PACIFIC SQUADRON. A growing U.S. presence in the Kingdom of Hawaii led to the appearance of the navy, the first warship arriving in 1826. Later that year Commander Thomas ap Catesby Jones of the USS *Peacock* negotiated an agreement with the Hawaiian monarchy that provided for peace between the two nations and granted most-favored-nation status to merchants of both countries. Although the treaty was never ratified, it nevertheless was observed by both countries for many years until superseded by an 1849 trade pact. The growing U.S. commercial presence, which achieved predominance by midcentury, neither foreshadowed annexation by the United States nor precluded it by other powers. When in 1843 a British naval officer unilaterally annexed the kingdom, Commodore Lawrence Kearny of the USS *Constellation* protested the action, which was soon nullified by the British admiral commanding the Pacific Squadron. The following year the governments of France, Great Britain, and the United States agreed to the continued independence of the islands.

A significant U.S. naval presence among the islands of Polynesia and Melanesia, south of the equator, dates from the time of the Charles Wilkes Exploring Expedition of 1838–1842. Agreements signed with Samoa and Fiji chiefs to protect the persons and property of Americans, although praiseworthy, could not be enforced. Less praiseworthy were punitive expeditions in 1840–1841 in Samoa, Fiji, and the Gilbert Islands, when the destruction of villages (and their inhabitants) by the U.S. Navy often exceeded the crimes committed. In 1855, Commander Edward B. Boutwell aboard the USS *John Adams* extorted an agreement from a Fiji chief recognizing vastly inflated U.S. claims for property damage. A second treaty inflicted upon Chief Thakombau in 1858 led him to offer Fiji to the British government if it would agree to assumption of the debt. The offer was refused; it was not until 1874 that Fiji was passed to British rule.

MEDITERRANEAN SQUADRON. There was proportionately less need for the protection of persons and property by the navy in European waters than in other portions of the globe, but on occasion a naval presence could be useful. One such instance occurred in 1832, when U.S. naval vessels at Naples in the Kingdom of the Two Sicilies lent weight to efforts to reach agreement on spoliation claims stemming from the Napoleonic wars. In the aftermath of the revolutions of 1848 in Hungary, Germany, France, and Italy, there was much showing of the flag, particularly in the Italian peninsula. These operations lessened as peace was restored.

A growing U.S. presence in the Kingdom of Hawaii led to the appearance of the navy, the first warship arriving in 1826.

The Hungarian uprising of 1848 against Austria, crushed the following year by a massive Russian intervention, incited considerable sympathy for the Hungarian revolutionaries by the American public. Lajos Kossuth and Martin Koszta, two revolutionaries who had fled to the Ottoman Empire, were offered passage by the United States minister to Turkey in an American warship. Captain John C. Long refused to compromise American neutrality, however, by permitting Kossuth to disembark at Marseilles when France refused him permission to transit the country. Kossuth eventually made his way to the United States, where he received a tumultuous welcome. Austro-American relations plunged accordingly.

A potentially more serious incident arose in 1853 when Koszta was abducted and confined aboard an Austrian warship in the harbor of Smyrna (˙Izmir) in Turkey. Commander Duncan N. Ingraham demanded Koszta's release and was refused. On 2 July 1853, he issued an ultimatum stating that he would release Koszta himself, using force if necessary. The Austrian captain finally agreed, and Ingraham's actions were upheld despite the fact that Koszta was not an American citizen.

AFRICAN SQUADRON. In 1824 the West Indian Squadron had West Africa added to its area of responsibility. The dispatch of individual vessels from time to time had done little to deter a thriving trade in slaves there, nor were British vessels on that station able to stop ships flying the U.S. flag. The Webster-Ashburton Treaty of 1842 provided for the establishment of a West African Squadron and promised a more effective assault against the slavers. Successive commodores, however, were hampered by orders to further U.S. commerce to West Africa as a first order of business. In addition, many U.S. warships were too deep draft to effectively interdict the inshore traffic. In 1862 an Anglo-American treaty gave the British navy the right to search U.S.-flag vessels suspected of carrying slaves.

Between 1815 and 1862, therefore, the navy's overseas squadrons increased from one to six, establishing a presence in most of the globe's oceans.

THE CIVIL WAR. In similar fashion, the army moved westward, from the upper Great Lakes–Mississippi region in 1817 to the fringe of the Great Plains, Texas, and, in the 1840s and 1850s, to the Southwest, California, and the Pacific Northwest. Within these larger maritime and territorial spheres, both services continued to perform increasingly traditional roles—protecting American settlers, traders, and nationals abroad; supporting trade and commercial expansion; and, on occasion (as in Kansas and Utah territories), responding to breakdowns in civil authority. The Civil War interrupted these operations as officers and men of the army returned to the East and vessels on foreign stations were called home. The Civil War did not, however, cause any fundamental change in the peacetime missions of either service.

Naval vessels from the disbanded overseas squadrons served on the Union blockade of the Atlantic and Gulf coasts or were employed to hunt down commerce raiders. The army's pacification of the trans-Mississippi and Far West perforce ended, but its role was taken up by settlers and militia. The conflict between North and South did not end Indian-white conflict, only the regular army's dominant role in such fighting. In some locales, regular forces were committed, such as the upper Mississippi region in 1863 and 1864.

RECONSTRUCTION AND THE BEGINNINGS OF IMPERIALISM, 1865–1885

The war's end in 1865 led to the shrinkage of both services to peacetime levels and a resumption of traditional peacekeeping roles. The navy's overseas squadrons were reconstituted, and the army resumed its role of frontier constabulary. Thus for both services the thirty-eight-year interval between the end of the Civil War and the outbreak of the Spanish-American War bore many similarities with the antebellum era. There were differences as well, particularly with the army.

The presence along the Texas-Mexican frontier of a force of fifty-two thousand troops under the command of General Philip Sheridan in June 1865 was especially helpful to the efforts of Andrew Johnson's administration to keep the civil war in Mexico from spreading northward. Their presence also led to the withdrawal of French forces from Mexico—a withdrawal that occurred within two years.

Another peacekeeping mission—more precisely, the maintenance of law and order in the South—proved less easy to accomplish. On average, one-third of the army was stationed in the military districts of the South from 1865 to 1869, and although the percentage fluctuated over the remaining years of Reconstruction, it never went below 13 percent. Neither the experiences of the Mexican War nor its service in the South during the Civil War had prepared the army for this postwar duty.

Nor did its antebellum experiences of peacekeeping prove helpful in its policing of labor disputes in 1877 and 1894. To many, the railroad strike of 1877 in Pittsburgh and West Virginia and the boycott by the American Railway Union of the Pullman Palace Car Company, which affected the western railroads in 1894, proved as distasteful as their duties during Reconstruction.

Peacekeeping and pacification in the West also had its low points. As had been true of the antebellum army, both officers and troops often showed greater sympathy toward the Indians than their civilian counterparts. Respect for the foe, however, was combined with a determination to force the Indians onto reservations and to keep them there, although the task was frequently unpleasant. The disappearance of the frontier in the 1890s and the simultaneous disappearance of the army's principal constabulary role potentially represented the greatest challenge to its continued existence since its establishment in the 1780s. If one purpose of the army in peacetime is to prepare for war, the question in the 1890s was, war against whom? The answer, surprisingly, was the Spanish empire.

The end of the Civil War enabled the navy to resume the squadron dispositions of the antebellum era. From 1865 to 1885 the occasions on which naval force was used or threatened were few; most occurred in the Caribbean or the Pacific Ocean and east Asia. Naval interest in obtaining a coaling station in the Caribbean indirectly contributed to an instance of "big stick" diplomacy. Efforts by the Johnson administration to acquire a lease of the Bay of Samaná in the Dominican Republic in 1868 having been unsuccessful, the incoming administration of Ulysses S. Grant raised its sights by concluding a treaty in 1869, which, if it had been approved, would have led to the annexation of the Dominican Republic. Opposition to the treaty surfaced both in the Dominican Republic and adjacent Haiti. The toppling of a pro-treaty Haitian president and his replacement by an opponent of annexation led Grant to order a massing of U.S. warships at Port-au-Prince in 1870. Admiral Charles H. Poor informed the Haitian regime that "any interference or attack therefore by vessels under the Haytien or any other Flag upon Dominicans . . . will be considered an act of hostility to the Flag of the United States, and will provoke hostility in return." In the short run, this declaration had the desired effect, but in the long run contributed to the failure of the treaty in the U.S. Senate.

Two years before, a rebellion broke out in Cuba against Spanish rule, which was to smolder for ten years. As would be the case in the 1890s, success for the insurrectionists was dependent in large part upon the attitude of the U.S. government. Secretary of State Hamilton Fish convinced President Grant that it would be unwise to recognize the belligerency of the rebels. This decision notwithstanding, the Spanish desire to halt the flow of arms and supplies from sympathizers in the United States to the rebels led to two incidents involving the U.S. Navy. The first, in 1869, followed the deaths of two Americans whose ship had been comandeered by Cuban rebels who landed the vessel near Santiago. Admiral Henry H. Hoff, commander of the North Atlantic Squadron, entered into discussions with Spanish authorities in Santiago in July 1869 and received assurances that such incidents would not reoccur.

There was in fact a much more serious recurrence four years later. The *Virginius,* a rebel vessel that had long been a thorn in the side of the Cuban authorities, was captured by a Spanish gunboat and taken into Santiago on 31 October 1873. Fifty-three passengers and crew, many of them Americans, were executed. A British naval officer stopped further retribution by threatening to bombard the town. His threat was echoed several days later by Commander William B. Cushing. The threat of war between Spain and the United States was averted, although not before a substantial concentration of warships was effected at Key West.

Such naval interventions as occurred in East Asian waters in this time period involved protection of merchant vessels and sailors. In 1863 the closure of the Shimonoseki Strait between the Japanese islands of Kyūshū and Honshū was followed in June and July by the firing upon an American steamship by the Choshu clan. Commander David McDougal and the USS *Wyoming* seriously damaged several Choshu vessels and bombarded shore batteries in retaliation, without however succeeding in reopening the strait to commercial use. In September a chartered American warship participated in an international seventeen-vessel assault on Shimonoseki and its forts on 5–6 September, which reopened the strait.

The misadventures of two U.S. merchantmen also led in due course to naval intervention. In 1866 the *General Sherman* ascended the Taedong River in Korea. Trapped in the river by the falling water level, the vessel fired upon a group of Koreans ashore. The local governor responded by ordering the ship and its crew destroyed. Efforts to investigate the affair in 1867 and 1868 proved abortive. Another two years passed before further efforts were made to obtain satisfaction for the destruction of the *General Sherman,* enter into arrangements with the Korean authorities for treatment of shipwrecked sailors, and perhaps conclude a trade treaty. To this end, in the spring of 1871 a fleet commanded by Rear Admiral John Rodgers, consisting of a frigate, two corvettes, and two gunboats (eighty-five guns, 1,240 men), assembled off Inchon. Korean forts on Kanghwa Island opened fire on the gunboats on 1 June. The fire was returned. An ultimatum demanding an apology was ignored, and Rodgers dispatched a landing force against the forts on 10–11 June. This operation was successful in capturing the positions but brought the Korean government no closer to agreement over a trade treaty. In early July the squadron left Korean waters and returned to China.

In March 1867 the American bark Rover *was driven ashore on the southern tip of Formosa by a storm.*

In March 1867 the American bark *Rover* was driven ashore on the southern tip of Formosa by a storm. The crew managed to get ashore but were killed by local tribesmen (Koaluts). The Asiatic Squadron commander, Admiral Henry H. Bell, ordered to investigate the deaths, took the bit in his teeth and sent a landing party ashore to punish the Koaluts. He, too, was unsuccessful. Later efforts mounted by the U.S. consul at Amoy, China, resulted in a treaty protecting shipwrecked seamen and, not long after, the extension of Chinese control over the area.

Elsewhere in the Pacific that same year, Captain Fabius Stanley aboard the USS *Tuscarora* threatened to bombard the capital of Fiji if the king failed to sign a treaty recognizing his indebtedness to several U.S. merchants. A final settlement was made two years later, and the islands were annexed to Great Britain in 1874. That same year, a joint Anglo-American force went ashore in Honolulu, Hawaii, to break up an attack on the courthouse by followers of a disappointed candidate for the Hawaiian throne.

The European Squadron's area of responsibility in the post–Civil War era included North Africa and western Africa as far south as Portuguese Angola. In 1875 the U.S. consul in Tripoli, Michel Vidal, managed to antagonize the pasha by his opposition to slavery and his outspoken advocacy of an expanded American commercial and naval presence in the province of Cyrenaica. A minor incident involving a Turkish sailor reached an impasse and led Vidal to ask the State Department for naval protection. The USS *Congress* (Captain Earl English), later joined by the *Hartford,* was dispatched to "exact ample reparations." The appearance of the vessels excited local opinion and resulted in the landing of a company of marines with a Gatling gun. Captain English presented what amounted to an ultimatum to the pasha by ordering both vessels to anchor with their guns trained on the shore fortifications. The pasha blinked first, going to the consulate in full uniform to abase himself. The episode did nothing for American prestige either in North Africa or Europe.

A somewhat better performance occurred in Alexandria, Egypt, in 1882. Growing foreign influence and Egyptian nationalism combined to produce riots that resulted in the death of a number of Europeans and rumors of anti-Christian massacres. Rear Admiral James W. A. Nicholson (USS *Lancaster*) commanded the European Squadron, which also included the *Galena, Nipsic,* and *Quinnebaug.* All four vessels converged on Alexandria, providing refuge to Americans and other foreign nationals. Nicholson received word on 9 July that the British intended to bombard the forts, which they did on 11–12 July, prompting Egyptian forces to evacuate both the forts and the city. Portions of Alexandria were set on fire and looting was widespread. Acting in response to a request from the U.S. consul, Nicholson sent ashore a landing party of 150 sailors and marines commanded by Lieutenant Commander Caspar F. Goodrich on 14 July. As contingents from other nations went ashore in subsequent days, the U.S. presence gradually was reduced. On 22 July the *Lancaster* and *Nipsic* sailed for Villefranche, France, leaving the other two vessels at Alexandria.

1885–1898

The apparently random, ad hoc interventions that had characterized the navy throughout much of its existence were about to change. The protection of shipwrecked sailors or American nationals threatened by a variety of perils abroad would become more and more the protection or furtherance of U.S. national interests abroad. Some Americans were beginning to look outward, in the process discovering that the European powers were moving to extend their control of Africa, Asia, the Middle East, and perhaps even Latin America—both economically and politically. Technological change in warship design and capability not only threatened to shrink the moats guarding the United States from overseas foes but to render obsolete the traditional reliance on coastal defenses and commerce raiding in time of war. Change began within the navy early in the decade of the 1880s, and the pace of change would accelerate throughout the remainder of the nineteenth century.

Continued concern over U.S. control of Central American isthmian transit routes is a case in point. Interest in the 1840s and 1850s had focused on Nicaragua and Panama. In the former instance, the signing of the Clayton-Bulwer Treaty of 1850 provided for joint Anglo-American control of a Nicaraguan canal. In the latter case the Bidlack-Mallarino Treaty with Colombia provided U.S. nationals freedom of transit of the isthmus on equal terms with Colombian nationals. For its part, the government of the United States undertook to guarantee the neutrality of the isthmus and ensure that freedom of transit was not interrupted. On a number of occasions, and always at the invitation of Colombian authorities, naval forces were employed ashore or afloat in times of domestic unrest or revolution, as in 1865, 1873, and 1879. The beginning of the Ferdinand de Lesseps Panama Canal venture in 1881 was answered by a U.S. governmental pronouncement that its policy was a canal under U.S. control. In 1884 the Frelinghuysen-Zavala Treaty with Nicaragua provided for a U.S.-controlled canal, but the Senate refused to approve it. Matters rested there when revolution in Colombia in 1885 was followed by interruption of isthmian transit and much destruction of property.

A cable dated 1 April 1885 from the U.S. consul in Colón, Panama, reported the burning of much of the town and threats of death to American nationals on the isthmus. The administration of Grover Cleveland authorized a full-scale intervention. At its height it comprised six vessels from the North Atlantic Squadron and two from the Pacific Squadron. Between them they put ashore a landing force of four hundred men—the largest number actually employed in an amphibious operation abroad between the Mexican War and the Spanish-American conflict. Rear Admiral James E. Jouett, the expedition's commander, was instructed to restore freedom of transit, protect American lives and property, but to "interfere in no respect" with Colombian authority. By late April the worst was over, and the landing force was withdrawn. Pressure for a permanent naval presence on or near the isthmus was rejected by Secretary of the Navy William C. Whitney, and normal operations were resumed by vessels of both squadrons, although care was taken to keep at least one naval ship at Colón and Panama City as frequently as possible.

Trouble of a different sort and in a different quarter greeted the Republican administration of President Benjamin Harrison in 1889. The governments of Great Britain, Germany, and the United States had supported commercial and strategic interests developed by their nationals in Samoa in the southwest Pacific. By 1880 all had concluded treaties with Samoan rulers; all desired coaling stations. These conflicting interests and aspirations had led to the dispatch of naval forces to the islands. In early March rumors of a clash between German and U.S. naval units were followed by a report from Rear Admiral L. A. Kimberly, commander of the Pacific Squadron, that a hurricane sweeping through the islands had destroyed or driven ashore three German warships, the *Eber, Adler,* and *Olga,* and three U.S. vessels, the *Trenton, Vandalia,* and *Nipsic.* Only HMS *Calliope* had been able to steam out to sea. Secretary of the Navy Benjamin F. Tracy concluded, not inaccurately, that the United States had almost no warships "worthy of the name" in the Pacific Ocean. Much might be made of this in encouraging Congress to loosen the purse strings for further construction of warships; in the meantime, the Samoan situation was resolved—or at any rate placed on hold—by an agreement between the contending nations to establish a tripartite rule of Samoa, an arrangement that would last until 1899.

Secretary of the Navy Benjamin F. Tracy concluded that the United States had no warships "worthy of the name" in the Pacific Ocean.

President Harrison in his inaugural address had called for an expansion of the navy and the acquisition of overseas bases for its use. The search for bases would assume growing urgency and lead to the use or threatened use of force both in the Western Hemisphere and the Pacific Ocean. The Môle Saint Nicolas affair was an example. The overthrow of the president of Haiti in 1888 led to a scramble for power among the generals who had deposed him. One, François Legitime, was elected president and recognized as such by the governments of France and Great Britain. Another, Florvil Hyppolite, sought and received assistance from the U.S. government, promising in return both commercial concessions and the lease of Môle Saint Nicolas on the Windward Passage to the navy. This latter promise was withdrawn, but Hyppolite's triumph in August 1889 raised expectations in Washington. Rear Admiral Bancroft Gherardi, commander of the North Atlantic Squadron, noting the strategic value of the island of Hispaniola, urged continued support of the Hyppolite regime "by the display of a naval force" at frequent intervals. In due course, the government might obtain possession of the desired base.

The granting of commercial privileges to the Clyde West India Steamship line in 1890 prompted William P. Clyde (a close friend of Secretary of the Navy Tracy) to request the Haitian government to grant use of Môle Saint Nicolas exclusively to his company—and the U.S. Navy. The request was refused by the Hyppolite regime but Admiral Gherardi, appointed as a special agent to negotiate the lease of Môle, tried again early the following year. Despite the presence at Port-au-Prince of his vessels and the navy's Squadron of Evolution, commanded by Rear Admiral John G. Walker, Gherardi failed to secure a lease for Môle. In the final analysis, the U.S. government was unwilling to seize Môle itself or to force the Haitian government to cede it. Lacking an enemy in the Caribbean at the time, there was no imperative either to acquire Caribbean bases or to deny their acquisition by a potential foe.

At this point events in Chile distracted the attention of the administration. In January 1891, civil war broke out between supporters of President José Manuel Balmaceda and his congressionalist opponents. Although proclaiming neutrality, the United States government continued to recognize the Balmaceda regime for a time, and raised the ire of the opposition by granting asylum to Balmacedistas in the U.S. embassy and aboard naval vessels in Valparaiso roadstead. The USS *Baltimore,* commanded by Captain Winfield S. Schley, carried a number of refugees to Peru in September, and against the wishes of the insurgents had also been involved in a cable-laying operation off Iquique. The pursuit and seizure of the insurgent vessel *Itata,* accused of having violated U.S. neutrality laws, earlier that summer also created a climate of opinion hostile toward the navy.

In any event, the triumph of the congressionalist faction and its recognition by the United States government early in the fall should have quieted matters but did not. Sailors from the *Baltimore,* which had remained at Valparaiso, were granted liberty on 16 October. A subsequent riot ashore by a Chilean mob left two American sailors dead and led to a full-blown crisis in U.S.-Chilean relations. The U.S. government subsequently demanded both an apology and reparations from the Chilean regime. The USS *Yorktown* (Commander Robley D. Evans) remained at Valparaiso through most of December 1891 and January 1892, figuratively daring the Chileans to do their worst. Perhaps fortunately, the *Yorktown* had sailed for Callao when a U.S. ultimatum arrived late in January 1892. The Chilean government apologized for the incident, paid $75,000 to the injured and survivors of the dead sailors, and war was averted.

In the Pacific, long-standing interest in the Hawaiian Islands led the Harrison administration in 1890 to propose the establishment of a U.S. protectorate over the islands. A feature of the proposal would have made the 1887 cession of Pearl Harbor to the navy both permanent and exclusive. The failure of the protectorate and the ending of commercial reciprocity led to a revolution in January 1893 by pro-American interests, which overthrew the government of Queen Liliuokalani. A timely landing of marines from the USS *Boston,* commanded by Captain Charles G. Wiltse, to protect U.S. property helped to consolidate the new regime's power. A treaty of annexation was concluded and submitted to the U.S. Senate in mid-February. Democratic opposition prevented its prompt ratification, and it was later withdrawn by the administration of Grover Cleveland. Hawaiian annexation did not occur for another five years.

A revolution in Brazil against the government of Floriano Peixoto late in 1893 claimed the attention of the Cleveland administration and Secretary of State Walter Q. Gresham. The insurgents, with tacit support from some of the European powers, were opposed to a recently concluded commercial reciprocity treaty with the United States. Gresham evolved a policy that required a U.S. naval presence at Rio de Janeiro, which necessitated denying the insurgents belligerency status (which would render an insurgent blockade of Rio illegal), thus frustrating their attempt to blockade Rio and impose a ban on imported goods, thereby starving the Peixoto regime of customs revenues. Gresham replaced two U.S. naval commanders who had pursued a policy of strict neutrality between the Brazilian government and the insurgents. A third, Rear Admiral Andrew E. K. Benham, aligned his South Atlantic Squadron forces behind Gresham's policy. Matters came to a head late in January 1894, when an insurgent vessel fired a blank across the bows of a U.S. merchant ship being escorted to its berth by the USS *Detroit.* The *Detroit* replied with a live shell into the side of the insurgent craft, warning that if they fired on merchant ships again they would be sunk. Further efforts by the insurgents to obtain belligerency status were denied by the U.S. government; this time the European nations followed the American lead. By April the insurrection had collapsed.

That same year the Nicaraguan government moved to establish its control over the Mosquito Indians who inhabited the Caribbean coast. The area had been a British protectorate since the 1850s, although within the past decade an increasing U.S. economic interest, attributable to the development of banana plantations, had become apparent. The British reaction to the Nicaraguan move was to dispatch a naval force to Bluefields and disarm the Nicaraguans. Gresham used the occasion to force the British to relinquish control of the protectorate (formal Nicaraguan sovereignty was recognized in December 1894) and at the same time ensure that President José Santos Zelaya would not infringe upon U.S. rights in the Mosquito reservation or disturb the Maritime Canal Company concession. Both policies ultimately were successful. A July uprising by the Mosquito authorities against Nicaraguan rule resulted in the landing of U.S. forces to restore order, an episode that marked the beginning of the British retreat in the Caribbean.

The first Venezuelan Crisis (1895–1896)—perhaps an exercise in gunboat diplomacy without the gunboats—was simultaneous with another one in Mediterranean waters. Turkish repression of Armenian nationalism, and the threat to sympathetic American missionaries and their property in the interior, led to an increased naval presence in the eastern Mediterranean from 1894 to 1897. This U.S. presence in Ottoman ports proved unable to aid the missionaries materially and was unsuccessful in obtaining redress for destroyed property. The only successful episode of gunboat diplomacy in the Mediterranean at this time occurred at Tangiers in 1897 when a naval presence reinforced the U.S. consul's demand for an apology and an indemnity growing out of the robbery of a servant of a naturalized American.

A crisis materialized in the Caribbean rather than the Mediterranean. A renewal of the Cuban rebellion against Spanish rule in 1895 overshadowed for a time a growing U.S.-German antagonism. This state of affairs had developed in 1897 with two episodes of German gunboat diplomacy in areas traditionally of interest to the United States. The first incident followed the murder of two German missionaries by Boxers in China, precipitating Germany's seizure of Kiaochow on the Shantung Peninsula. An insult by Haitian officials to a German merchant, Emil Luders, provided the occasion for the second when Germany threatened a bombardment of Port-au-Prince if an apology and indemnity were not forthcoming. Japanese-American relations also were briefly strained that same year by Japanese protests over the proposed U.S. annexation of Hawaii. Finally, if the dispatch of the USS *Maine* to Havana in January 1898 can be considered a form of gunboat diplomacy, it surely was one with unintended consequences. The vessel's destruction on 15 February was arguably the greatest single step on the road to war with Spain.

FROM WAR WITH SPAIN TO WORLD WAR I, 1898–1918

The Spanish-American War, undertaken to free Cuba from Spanish rule, had a number of unexpected consequences. High on the list was the decision to acquire the Philippines from Spain for $20 million. The other provisions of the Treaty of Paris of 10 December 1898 were clear-cut and understandable. The island of Guam in the Marianas, which surrendered to Captain Henry Glass of the USS *Charleston* 20 June 1898, was extracted from Spain for use as a coaling station and cable terminus. Puerto Rico, occupied in the latter stages of the war, was also retained by the United States. This acquisition, along with the right to establish a base or bases in Cuba through the Platt Amendment of 1901, significantly improved the navy's strategic position in the Caribbean on the approaches of the Central American isthmus. Independently of the war, but not coincidentally, Hawaii was acquired 7 July 1898 by a joint congressional resolution of annexation.

The death of the Samoan king in 1898 led to the appearance of rival candidates for the throne, one backed by Great Britain and the United States, the other by Germany.

As for the Philippines, the Asiatic Squadron, commanded by George Dewey, had been given the task of eliminating Spanish naval forces there. Once this was accomplished in early May 1898, an expeditionary force arrived to capture Manila and its environs. Once the United States gained control of the capital, the Philippines might be used as another bargaining chip in subsequent negotiations with Spain. It soon became apparent, however, that whatever the ultimate fate of the islands, independence was not a viable option. If the United States did not retain them, other powers—in particular Germany—would arrive. In retrospect, it is clear that insufficient consideration was given to the aspirations of the Filipinos themselves. The insurrection that had begun in 1896 against Spanish rule now spilled over into an assault on U.S. occupation forces.

Fighting began 4 February 1899, two days before the U.S. Senate approved the Treaty of Paris. The subsequent exercise in peacekeeping (or conquest) was to involve a substantial commitment both by the army and the navy. By the summer of 1900, seventy-thousand troops (approximately three quarters of the army) were in the Philippines. The six naval vessels on the Asiatic station in 1898 increased to thirty in 1899, thirty-five in 1900, and fifty-two in 1901. The conflict, officially declared at an end by President Theodore Roosevelt in

July 1902, cost the United States between $400 million and $600 million, 4,234 dead, and 2,818 wounded. Estimates of Filipino casualties run to 20,000 military deaths and perhaps 200,000 civilians. The naval side of the Philippine Insurrection included transporting and supplying U.S. troops, maintaining patrols throughout insular waters to sever insurgent communications, and intercepting the import of arms.

South of the Philippines trouble arose in another quarter. The death of the Samoan king in August 1898 led to the appearance of rival candidates for the throne, one backed by the governments of Great Britain and the United States, the other by Germany. A revolt by the German-supported candidate, Mataafa, broke out early in 1899, prompting the dispatch of the cruiser *Philadelphia,* commanded by Rear Admiral Albert Kautz, to Apia. When the ultimatum to the insurgents to return to their homes was ignored, the *Philadelphia* and two British cruisers bombarded the hinterland 15 March. A subsequent Anglo-American landing party was ambushed on 1 April by Mataafa's forces and lost eight men. At the suggestion of the German government, a tripartite commission was established to restore peace. Admiral Kautz left Samoan waters on 21 May. The commissioners recommended to their governments that Samoa should be ruled by one power. The accord worked out gave Upolu and Savai'i to Germany, Tutuila (with the harbor of Pago Pago) to the United States, and the Tonga Islands and most of the German Solomon Islands to Great Britain. The acquisition of Tutuila, along with uninhabited Wake Island that same year, rounded out U.S. acquisitions in the Pacific.

The significant military presence in the Philippines enabled the U.S. government to respond more forcefully to events in China than would otherwise have been the case. The Ch'ing dynasty, beset by internal foes and the imperial powers, attempted to capitalize on growing antiforeign sentiment within the kingdom to bolster its declining authority. The rise of the antiforeign secret society known as the Righteous Hand, or Boxers, particularly in north China, and increasing attacks on foreign interests prompted the ministers of the foreign powers in China to request an armed demonstration and an expanded military presence in the legation compound in Peking. Matters came to a head in the spring of 1900. At the request of U.S. Minister Edwin H. Conger, the USS *Newark,* flagship of Rear Admiral Louis Kempff, was ordered to Taku at the mouth of the Pei-ho River on 17 May. The vessel landed a force of fifty marines and sixty sailors on 29 May, and two days later, the marines proceeded to Peking by rail with a multinational contingent. They were subsequently involved in the defense of the legation compound during the fifty-five-day siege from 17 June to 14 August.

By 3 June no fewer than twenty foreign warships were off the mouth of the Pei-ho. The shallow-draft monitor *Monocacy,* commanded by Captain Frederick W. Wise, was ordered north from Shanghai. The severing of the Tientsin-Peking railway on 6 June prompted the formation of an international contingent that departed for Peking on 10–11 June. Bowman H. McCalla, captain of the *Newark,* commanded the Americans in the party. The *Monocacy* arrived 15 June and anchored in the Pei-ho above the Taku forts. When the demand for their surrender was refused, the imperial garrison opened fire on gunboats in the river 17 June. Although it did not return the fire, the *Monocacy* was forced to shift its anchorage. Chinese forces also attacked the foreign quarter of Tientsin, and Admiral Kempff received orders to act in unison with the other foreign contingents. Additional forces were ordered north from the Philippines, including the USS *Nashville* and the USS *Oregon,* as well as the Ninth Infantry Regiment (with other units to follow). The force that had set out from Tientsin on 10–11 June had been unable to reach Peking and was required to fight its way back downriver to Tientsin, which had been secured on 23 June.

While a larger force was being assembled, the siege of the legation quarter in Peking continued. On 8 July, Rear Admiral George C. Remey, commander of the Asiatic Squadron, arrived in the USS *Brooklyn.* The international relief expedition of fourteen thousand (including twenty-five hundred Americans commanded by Brigadier General Adna R. Chaffee) departed Tientsin for Peking on 5 August, arriving nine days later to lift the siege. Restoration of order in north China permitted a gradual reduction of U.S. naval and army forces during the fall.

The aftermath of the Spanish-American War proceeded much more smoothly in the Western Hemisphere than in Asia. The occupations of both Cuba and Puerto Rico proceeded without incident, and the Treaty of Paris provided for the annexation of the latter colony. The status of Cuba remained to be settled. Although the Teller Amendment of 1898 had forbidden the annexation of Cuba, it was by no means certain that U.S. occupation of the island would not result sooner or later in something very much like it. Events in the Philippines were to make the administration of William McKinley reluctant to risk something comparable occurring in Cuba. At the same time, certain broader needs vis-à-vis Cuba had to be met. The resulting Platt Amendment, which evolved early in 1901, was ultimately approved without change by the Cuban constitutional convention and the U.S. Senate. The amendment prohibited an independent Cuban government from making treaties with foreign governments that could impair its political or financial independence. The United States would have the right to naval bases in Cuba, and Cuba had to grant the United States "the right to intervene for the preservation of Cuban independence." Cuba thus became a U.S. protectorate, and the right of intervention was to be tested sooner than the U.S. government expected or wished.

Control of Cuba through the Platt Amendment and the acquisition of Puerto Rico—both fruits of the Spanish-American conflict—made U.S. hegemony feasible in the Caribbean. At the same time, it was becoming clear that the U.S. government was about to undertake construction of the long-deferred isthmian canal. The second Hay-Pauncefote Treaty (November 1901) removed fears that Great Britain, the only nation then deemed capable of blocking a canal controlled and fortified by the United States, might actually do so. British acquiescence in U.S. hegemony in the region was accompanied by a growing concern on the part of both naval and civilian policymakers that Germany was able and willing to contest such control. Political instability and the appearance of financial irresponsibility on the part of some of the nations in the area, added to the perceived threat of German intervention, led to the second Venezuelan crisis (1902–1903), the taking of Panama in November 1903, and an expanded U.S. presence in the Dominican Republic.

The Venezuelan crisis could be said to have begun in 1901, when Lieutenant Commander Nathan Sargent reported that the German gunboat *Vineta* had been making hydrographic surveys of the harbors on Margarita Island. It was clear to Sargent that the German government wanted a coaling station there, because German naval leaders had earlier "made a pretext of

These American soldiers, riding along the Great Wall near Beijing, were part of a contingent of troops sent to northern China in 1900 to help suppress the Boxer Rebellion. (National Archives)

hydrographic work to lay their plans for obtaining Kiaochow [in 1897]." His report caused considerable unease in Washington. Sargent was recalled for consultation with Navy Department officials and Secretary of State John Hay, Secretary of War Elihu Root, and Senator Henry Cabot Lodge. Despite subsequent denials by the German government, the damage had been done. The appearance in contemporary U.S. naval war plans of Margarita Island as the probable location of a German base in the Caribbean unquestionably stems from this incident.

Roosevelt declared that the Monroe Doctrine did "not guarantee any state against punishment if it misconducts itself."

The refusal of Venezuela's President Cipriano Castro to make payment on bonds worth more than $12.5 million finally exhausted the patience of Germany and Great Britain—never very great in any case when dealing with the Latin American republics. In his first annual message to Congress, President Theodore Roosevelt had declared that the Monroe Doctrine did "not guarantee any state against punishment if it misconducts itself, provided that punishment does not take the form of acquisition of territory by any non-American power." The German government, receiving—as was thought—a green light, decided to initiate a blockade of Venezuelan ports and seizure of gunboats to compel Castro to settle the outstanding debt. The British government, and later the Italian government, joined in the action. Castro asked the United States to arbitrate. In due course, the matter was submitted to the Permanent Court of International Justice at The Hague.

Years later, Roosevelt claimed that German reluctance to arbitrate had caused him to assemble the U.S. battle fleet at Culebra, a small island off the coast of Puerto Rico, for maneuvers. He further claimed to have informed the German ambassador that he would send the U.S. fleet into Venezuelan waters unless Germany agreed to arbitration. In fact, the fleet was sent to Culebra in mid-October 1902, long before the crisis erupted in December, to test some of the conclusions reached during the 1901 summer course at the Naval War College. The planning for these maneuvers had begun months earlier, and in this sense it was purely fortuitous that the U.S. warships were in the Caribbean. Naval officers with the fleet were aware that their presence might well strengthen Roosevelt's hand, preserve peace, and render U.S. diplomacy effective. The broader significance of this episode of muscle-flexing, whether or not an ultimatum was presented to Germany, was that it led to a hardening of naval and civilian attitudes towards the Kaiser's restive global ambitions.

The Venezuelan crisis, in turn, deepened official Washington's already profound apprehension that some European power might intervene in the Isthmus of Panama. Both in 1901 and in 1902, U.S. naval forces were dispatched to the isthmus, and forces landed in order to preserve the freedom of transit of the isthmus (guaranteed to American nationals under the terms of the Bidlack-Mallarino Treaty of 1846). American sailors had gone ashore on many previous occasions, but invariably only after the Colombian government expressly requested assistance in combating local disturbances. On these last two occasions, however, U.S. intervention either occurred before the Colombian authorities requested it or went well beyond the degree of assistance envisioned by Bogotá. At one stage U.S. naval officers denied Colombian forces the use of the Panama railroad until overruled by the U.S. State Department. Reports from these same officers reveal a hardening of attitude to the chronic disturbances on the isthmus. Their major concern was that instability would lead to intervention by other powers in an area of great strategic importance to the United States.

Roosevelt shared the apprehension. From the beginning of his administration, he moved to eliminate residual British influence in Central America and to obtain exclusive U.S. rights to build and fortify a canal. Convinced of the superiority of the Panama route, he directed Secretary of State Hay to conclude an agreement with Colombia. The resulting Hay-Herrán Treaty of 22 January 1903 involved the cession of canal rights to the United States for $10 million. The Colombian legislature insisted on a higher payment (presumably a portion of the $40 million the United States had agreed to pay the New Panama Canal Company for its assets), Roosevelt balked, and from mid-1903 on there was growing talk of the possibility of an uprising on the isthmus that would obtain U.S. support.

Well before the actual insurrection of 3 November 1903, the Navy Department (at Roosevelt's instruction) ordered ships in the Pacific and the Atlantic to steam southward to within easy range of the isthmus. On the eve of the revolution, the cruiser *Nashville* was dispatched from Jamaica to Colón, on the Caribbean side of Panama, with orders to prevent Colombian government troops from suppressing the insurrection. Those instructions miscarried, but the *Nashville* nonetheless arrived in time to lend moral support to the revolutionaries as they resourcefully kidnapped and bribed the senior Colombian officers. At noon on 4 November—the day after the revolution began—Secretary of State Hay bestowed formal recognition on the newly sovereign republic of Panama. A growing U.S. naval and military presence prevented Colombia from reversing the province's secession.

The ink was scarcely dry on the Hay-Bunau-Varilla Treaty of 18 November 1903, by which the United States acquired virtual sovereignty over Panamanian territory sufficient for construction of the canal, when the United States government moved to close another gap in the Caribbean defense perimeter. The object was the Dominican Republic. In this instance the initiative lay with the State and Navy departments, because Roosevelt, stung by public criticism of his role in the Panama affair, was reluctant to intervene. His hand, however, was forced to some extent by Assistant Secretary of State Francis B. Loomis and Rear Admiral Henry Clay Taylor. Furthermore, when The Hague, deliberating on the Venezuelan claims case, decided that the powers participating in the blockade—Great Britain, Germany, and Italy—were entitled to preferential treatment, an uncomfortable impetus to European intervention in the affairs of other Caribbean states was established.

The navy's General Board was convinced that German merchants were financing one of the insurgent groups active in the Dominican Republic. As a countermeasure, the board urged a course of action that would bring the Dominican Republic under U.S. control. A board memo stated that it would be easy "to develop a request for some sort of occupation by the United States, and this would virtually secure to us control of this most important strategic point in the Caribbean." In conjunction with the army, the navy also began to develop plans for the preemptive seizure of Hispaniola should the United States become involved in war with a European power.

U.S. Minister William F. Powell and Dominican President Carlos Morales drew up a request for a U.S. guarantee of Dominican independence and for military and financial aid against the insurgents, which was presented in February 1904. Roosevelt dispatched several General Board members, accompanied by Loomis, to investigate conditions in the Dominican Republic. On his return, Loomis reported that the country was "approaching—indeed, if it has not already reached—a state of anarchy." After noting that Morales wished to turn the customshouses over to U.S. officials as well as to give the navy a long-term lease of Samaná Bay, he suggested that the status quo could be maintained for the time being by maintaining a strong naval patrol in Dominican waters.

Rear Admiral Taylor recommended that the customshouses be taken over and administered by the U.S. government for at least three years. "It is quite possible," Taylor intoned, "that three years of enforced public order would make the whole country self-governing to the extent Cuba is now." A protectorate along Platt Amendment lines was never far from the mind of Loomis or Taylor. President Roosevelt proposed another solution. The Roosevelt Corollary to the Monroe Doctrine, first enunciated publicly in late May 1904, served notice that the United States was prepared to act as "an international police power" in the Caribbean. Roosevelt's avowed purpose was to forestall European intervention. "If we are willing to let Germany or England act as the policemen of the Caribbean," Roosevelt stated succinctly, "then we can afford not to intervene when gross wrongdoing occurs. But if we intend to say 'Hands off' to the powers of Europe, sooner or later we must keep order ourselves."

Despite continued professed reluctance to intervene, the Roosevelt administration was driven by the logic of the corollary and continued unrest in the Dominican Republic to propose a customs receivership, provided by an agreement of 8 February 1905. Despite difficulties in implementation, the agreement initiated a period of U.S. involvement in Dominican affairs that was to culminate a decade later in a full-fledged protectorate.

Cuba, despite the existence of the Platt Amendment, was finally a subject of military intervention in 1906. Trouble began the preceeding year, when the incumbent president, Tomás Estrada Palma, threw in with the Moderate faction against the Liberals headed by José Miguel Gomez. When the Moderates fraudulently controlled a September election, the Liberals boycotted the December presidential contest and planned a rebellion. The Liberals hoped that the United States would be forced to intervene and in due course oversee fair elections—elections that the Liberals felt they would be sure to win. The uprising occurred in August 1906. At the request of U.S. Consul General Frank Steinhart, warships were sent to Havana and Cienfuegos.

The Roosevelt administration, reluctant to intervene, was slow to realize that both factions were counting on U.S. intervention to uphold their respective positions. Estrada Palma, rather than compromise with the opposition, resigned in September, and Secretary of War William Howard Taft ordered the marines ashore on 29 September. The second occupation of Cuba lasted only until January 1909. There were to be no further interventions in the Caribbean–Central American region during the remainder of Roosevelt's presidency.

Although the intervention by European powers in Latin American affairs had led to the promulgation of the Roosevelt Corollary, the United States itself was not above resorting to similar interference elsewhere. In 1899, and again in 1901, Tangier was visited by U.S. warships whose captains were instructed to deliver an ultimatum to the authorities ashore where debts owed American nationals were unpaid. In both instances the Moroccan authorities paid up, and the ships' guns remained silent.

The kidnapping of a U.S. citizen, Ion Perdicaris, by the Moroccan chieftan Ahmed ibn-Muhammed Raisuli permitted the Roosevelt administration to flex its naval muscles.

In 1903 the Roosevelt administration was involved in an episode at the other end of the Mediterranean. Receiving word on 27 August that the U.S. vice-consul in Beirut, Lebanon, had been killed (it turned out that he had not), Roosevelt ordered several vessels of the European Squadron, commanded by Rear Admiral Charles S. Cotton, to Beirut. The ships arrived 3 August, and three days later rioting broke out in the city between Christians and Muslims. Requests from some of the local representatives of the European powers that a landing force be put ashore were turned down by Admiral Cotton. Calm ashore returned, but the fleet's continued presence there was utilized in an unsuccessful attempt to obtain a settlement of certain other U.S. claims against the Ottoman government. The warships left Beirut 1 February 1904.

The kidnapping of a naturalized U.S. citizen, Ion Perdicaris, by the Moroccan chieftan Ahmed ibn-Muhammed Raisuli on 18 May 1904 from his summer villa near Tangier not only provoked much discussion in the press concerning his release or recapture, but permitted the Roosevelt administration to flex its naval muscles. In the aftermath of Caribbean maneuvers, the South Atlantic Squadron, the European Squadron, and the battleships of the North Atlantic fleet all headed for European waters. The South Atlantic Squadron (Rear Admiral French E. Chadwick) and subsequently the European Squadron (Rear Admiral Theodore Jewell) were diverted to Tangier. The battleships (Rear Admiral Albert S. Barker) were in nearby Gibraltar. The 22 June cable from Secretary of State Hay to the U.S. consul-general in Tangier, Samuel Gummere, stated (for public consumption): "We want Perdicaris alive or Raisuli dead." No forces from the squadrons at Tangier went ashore, however, and when Perdicaris was released the ships departed. One by-product of the U.S. naval presence in the Mediterranean was the agreement on 12 August of the Ottoman government to many long-standing U.S. demands (such as proper treatment of missionaries and their property), coincidentally, just as the European Squadron arrived for a visit in Smyrna.

Amid the changes occurring in east Asia during Roosevelt's presidency, those brought about by the Russo-Japanese War of 1904–1905 were perhaps the most sweeping. Japan's goal was to make the island nation the foremost military power in the region and one with which the United States would have to reckon. Both Japan and China were to serve notice that the old relationships of dominant Western powers and subservient Asian states no longer would apply. China declared a boycott of U.S. goods entering through the treaty ports in late 1905, in part a protest against U.S. exclusion of Chinese laborers, which prompted an expanded U.S. naval presence in Asian ports. Roosevelt also authorized the preparation of an expeditionary force from the Philippines should the need arise. The waning of the boycott in 1906 obviated the use of military forces in China.

Similar discrimination against Japanese immigrants on the U.S. West Coast, such as segregation of Japanese schoolchildren in San Francisco, led to a momentary crisis in U.S.-Japanese relations in 1907. Its peaceful resolution through the "Gentlemen's Agreement" was followed by the decision to send the U.S. battleships from the Atlantic coast to the Pacific, and subsequently across the Pacific on what has become known as the cruise of the Great White Fleet. At first glance what appears as an exercise in gunboat diplomacy against Japan in fact was nothing of the kind. Far from threatening Japan, the cruise was designed to test the capability of moving the battleship fleet to the Pacific should the need arise. The success of the cruise in this respect was demonstrated when the fleet, which departed Hampton Roads, Virginia, in mid-December 1907, arrived at San Francisco in May 1908 on the first leg of the voyage.

Trouble, meanwhile, was brewing closer to home in the Caribbean, an area of traditional concern. The Taft administration had long been unhappy with Nicaragua's President Zelaya. In October 1909 a revolt broke out against Zelaya, centered upon the Caribbean port of Bluefields. The leader of the rebellion, Juan J. Estrada, received substantial financial support and encouragement from the local American community, which hoped to see Central America become independent of Nicaraguan control. Zelaya erred in ordering the execution of two American soldiers-of-fortune serving with the Estrada forces, thereby giving the Taft administration the opportunity to sever diplomatic relations on 1 December. Zelaya resigned two weeks later, turning the presidency over to José Madriz. The rebellion continued, and the United States refused to recognize Madriz's regime. A naval buildup began in Nicaraguan waters—the *Des Moines, Marietta, Tacoma,* and *Prairie* stationed on the Caribbean coast and the *Albany, Yorktown, Vicksburg,* and *Princeton* on the Pacific coast. Overall command of naval and marine forces rested with Rear Admiral William W. Kimball. He was ordered not to land any forces without authorization from Washington and (following Madriz's accession) to observe "strict neutrality" between the factions.

Kimball found himself in difficulty with the State Department for his apparent sympathies for Madriz and the Liberal faction. A major setback for the Estrada forces in late December led the admiral to recommend the recognition of the Madriz regime. His advice was ignored. Rather than relieving Kimball from command, as he requested, the naval units under his authority were withdrawn for other duty, and on 7 April 1910, the Nicaraguan Expeditionary Squadron was formally disbanded. Madriz now dispatched an expedition against Bluefields, whose capture effectively ended the rebellion.

Bluefields was invested by land and blockaded from the sea by the *Maximo Jerez.* At this point, Commander William W. Gilmer (USS *Paducah*) on his own initiative informed the belligerents that he would permit no fighting in the city, presumably to protect the lives and property of foreign nationals, but also clearly in favor of the Estrada contingent. Both the Navy Department and State Department tried unsuccessfully to find a precedent for Gilmer's action but supported the commander in any event. Gilmer was instructed to ignore the *Maximo Jerez*'s blockade of Bluefields on the grounds that it had violated U.S. neutrality statutes by claiming falsely that it was not going to undertake military operations when it sailed earlier from New Orleans. Gilmore was also instructed to ignore the capture of the Bluefields customshouse because the town itself remained under Estrada's control. Madriz' forces, baffled, retreated westward. Conservative opponents of the regime fomented new uprisings against the Liberal government, and on 20 August, Madriz resigned and followed Zelaya into exile.

The course of events in Nicaragua over the next two years substantiated the dictum that whatever can go wrong, will. The Estrada regime was in a perilous position from the beginning, having to fend off charges of subserviency to the United States, infighting among its leaders, and the continued hostility of the Liberal opposition. Attempting to curb his rivals, Estrada was ousted from power in May 1911, and succeeded by Vice President Adolfo Díaz. The Knox-Castrillo Convention, concluded in June 1911, provided that Nicaragua would receive a $15 million loan from a consortium of New York banks, repayment to be secured by customs revenues. The U.S. Senate failed to act on the treaty, and a stop-gap loan of $1.5 million was first rejected then approved by the Nicaraguan assembly, but the government's financial woes continued. With ever more stringent conditions being imposed by the bankers, Nicaraguans feared the country had been sold out to Wall Street interests. A visit by Secretary of State Philander Knox in the spring of 1912 did little to resolve the issues. Díaz, fearing an uprising by the Liberals, moved to arrest his political opponent, but the attempt backfired, and a new rebellion was launched with widespread Liberal support.

With Managua surrounded and bombarded by rebel forces, the U.S. minister, George T. Weitzel, successfully pressed Díaz to request U.S. forces in order to protect the lives and property of foreign nationals. An initial detachment of 100 sailors and marines arrived in Managua in mid-August, followed soon after by an additional 350 marines commanded by Major Smedley D. Butler. The rebels subsequently occupied both Granada and León, severing railroad communications between Corinto and Managua. Two additional marine battalions arrived on 4 September and entrained for Managua. Overall command of forces in Nicaragua, now approximately twelve hundred strong, was assumed by Rear Admiral William H. H. Southerland. Acting Secretary of State Huntington Wilson, comparing the situation in Nicaragua to the Boxer Rebellion in China in 1900, wanted army forces from the Panama garrison sent to Nicaragua, but was opposed by Secretary of War Henry Stimson, who believed the commitment of the army would have an adverse impact on world and regional opinion. Stimson also believed that the unrest in Nicaragua was less crucial to the United States than the revolution in Mexico. In any event, the orders to the Tenth Infantry were cancelled.

Admiral Southerland had hoped to quell the rebellion by denying the rebels the use of the railway to move troops and munitions, and in this respect largely succeeded. Secretary Wilson, fearing that Southerland was carrying neutrality to an extreme (government forces also had been denied railway use), prevailed upon Taft to revise the admiral's orders. Southerland also was told to clear the remaining forces, led by Liberal General Benjamin Zeledon, from their position near Masaya. Butler's assault force of three battalions stormed Coyotepe Hill on 4 October, routing Zeledon's force. León, a Liberal stronghold, was occupied by another marine battalion. With the exception of minor skirmishing in northern towns, the rebellion was over. The largest commitment up to that time of U.S. forces overseas in peacetime—2,350 sailors and marines—was withdrawn, except for a legation guard of one hundred marines. Díaz remained in power, at some cost to Nicaraguan autonomy.

The change of administrations in Washington in 1913, contrary to expectation, brought about little change in policy in the Caribbean–Central American region. No less than his predecessors, Woodrow Wilson desired stability in Latin America and in order to achieve it was prepared to countenance intervention in a variety of forms. The outbreak of revolution in Mexico in 1910 threatened substantial U.S. interests that had developed during the lengthy rule of Porfirio Díaz. The subsequent overthrow of popularly elected President Francisco Madero by one of his generals, Victoriano Huerta, in 1913 led Wilson to refuse to recognize the Huerta administration and to lift a U.S. arms embargo so that the Constitutionalist opposition could more easily obtain weapons. Wilson also undertook to build up a U.S. naval presence off the Gulf and Pacific coasts of Mexico.

The navy's presence off Veracruz and Tampico in Mexico created the possibility of an incident, as the Constitutionalist forces moved to invest the port of

In 1915, U.S. marines and sailors landed in Port-au-Prince, Haiti, to maintain order and protect American interests there. U.S. military forces remained in Haiti until 1934. In 1919, these troops helped suppress a peasant uprising that had began in 1918. (National Archives)

Tampico and its nearby oil fields. On 9 April 1914, a party of sailors from the USS *Dolphin* was apprehended and detained by Federalist forces as they were removing supplies of gasoline from a warehouse. Their release, together with an apology for their detention, soon followed, but Rear Admiral Henry T. Mayo, on his own authority, demanded a more formal apology and a salute of the U.S. flag. His demand was upheld by Wilson and Secretary of State William Jennings Bryan. The refusal of Huerto to acquiesce created the condition for a more significant military riposte, which occurred some miles up the Pánuco River, at nearby Veracruz. Orders to land sailors and marines from the force off Veracruz, commanded by Rear Admiral Frank F. Fletcher, went out from Washington 20 April. Contrary to expectations, the occupation of the town was not unopposed. It took two days—21 and 22 April—to complete occupation in the face of sporadic opposition and sniper fire. Within four days nearly twenty-four hundred marines and four hundred sailors were ashore, later joined by a brigade of army troops under the command of General Frederick Funston. At a cost of nineteen dead and forty-seven wounded, U.S. forces secured Veracruz. It soon became apparent that this would not be followed by a march on Mexico City, as had happened during the war with Mexico in the previous century. Huerta resigned and fled the country in July, but U.S. forces were not withdrawn until late November.

Trouble was also brewing on the strategically important island of Hispaniola. The customs receivership established by the Roosevelt administration in the Dominican Republic had briefly achieved economic and political stability. The assassination of President Rámon Cáceres in 1911, however, brought about renewed instability that invited foreign intervention. The U.S. stake in the Banque Nationale d'Haiti had also failed to lead to political stability—rather the reverse. Government succeeded government as efforts by the Wilson administration to bring about the election of a president it could support served only to undermine the Haitian leaders negotiating with the administration. Intervention by the United States seemed—not only in retrospect—increasingly probable. The fact that it occurred first in Haiti rather than the Dominican Republic was largely a matter of accident.

As Europe was sliding into war in July 1914, the U.S. government offered to support Haitian President Oreste Zamor in return for the establishment of a customs receivership similar to that in place in the Dominican Republic. Zamor temporized, and by the time he agreed it was too late for his regime. U.S. Marines sent to Port-au-Prince remained aboard ship. His successor, Davilmar Theodore, agreed to a similar arrangement, but opposition to the negotiations in the national assembly forced him to withdraw it. His government was replaced by yet another, led by Vilbrun Guillaume Sam. In return for protection against foes both internal and external and U.S. supervision of the country's finances, Sam and his regime were offered recognition and support by American commissioners in May 1915. This proposal also was rejected.

The outbreak of revolution in Mexico in 1910 threatened substantial U.S. interests that had developed during the lengthy rule of Porfirio Díaz.

An uprising in the north was followed by one in the capital itself. A number of political prisoners were executed, which led to Sam's taking refuge in the French legation. Admiral William B. Caperton (USS *Washington*), who had been off the north coast of Haiti, was ordered to Port-au-Prince to protect foreign life and property, but arrived too late to save Sam, who was taken from the legation by a mob and torn to pieces. A landing force of sailors and marines took control of Port-au-Prince on 28 July 1915. Reinforcements dispatched to Caperton enabled the Americans to extend their control to other ports. The Haitian national assembly chose as president Philippe Sudre Dartiguenave, who had promised to cooperate with the U.S. authorities. A treaty, signed in mid-September and ratified later that year, provided for U.S. control of customs and government finance, a national constabulary trained and officered by Americans, and automatic extension of the agreement should either side request it after ten years.

The task of pacification fell to the First Marine Brigade, commanded by Colonel L. W. T. Waller, and Major Butler. The opposition was led by Ronsalvo Bobo, drawing upon *caco* (guerrilla) bands of peasants in the northern mountains. A combination of selective offers of amnesty, the buying up of weapons, and assaults against the most militant groups gradually had its effect. In mid-November 1915 an operation led by Major Butler killed fifty-one Haitians in Fort Rivière. By 1916 dwindling opposition allowed the marines to settle into routine occupation duties.

Meanwhile, conditions in the neighboring Dominican Republic were leading the United States closer to direct intervention as well. The election of Juan Isidro Jiménez as president in 1914 might have led to the long-sought-for stability had the United States not insisted upon Jiménez's agreement to a series of controls that would have established a protectorate in fact as well as name. The minister of war, Desiderio Arias, went into open opposition against Jiménez in the spring of 1916. U.S. Marines went ashore, Jiménez resigned the presidency, and Admiral Caperton, who arrived 12 May at the capital of Santo Domingo, sent additional forces ashore to operate against Arias' forces. The capital was occupied on 13 May without opposition while Caperton called for more reinforcements, some of which were sent from Haiti, and began to occupy Dominican port towns. A campaign was mounted against Arias' forces in the Cibao Valley in the north, and succeeded against slight opposition in forcing their surrender by early July. Unable to find any Dominican leader willing to cooperate with the occupying forces, the State Department finally opted for direct military rule. In late November, Rear Admiral Harry S. Knapp was appointed military governor. The task of suppressing opposition and confiscating weapons was given to the Second Marine Brigade under Colonel Joseph Pendleton. By the fall of 1917, pacification on Hispaniola seemed well in hand.

In fact, it was not. A fresh *caco* uprising began in Haiti in 1918 and was not suppressed until 1920. In the Dominican Republic resistance flared in the eastern provinces at the same time and was not ended until 1922. These low-grade conflicts brought about changes in U.S. occupation policy in both countries, sparked by accounts of mistreatment and on occasion unauthorized executions of prisoners and civilians. A special Senate committee concluded that the initial interventions, although justified, had been characterized by poor administration. Preparations were made to bring the occupation of the Dominican Republic to a close; that of Haiti would continue for more than another decade. There would be a reduced marine presence in both countries, with the Haitian *gendarmerie* and Dominican *Guardia Naçional* taking on increasing responsibilities for peacekeeping.

Both in 1912 and 1917, uprisings in eastern Cuba (principally Oriente province) led to the commitment of U.S. marines. Their role was restricted to guarding U.S. property in the disaffected areas, thus permitting the Cuban government to concentrate on suppressing the dissidents. Admiral Caperton, who had taken charge of the initial occupations of the Dominican Republic and Haiti, believed it was time the United States tightened its grasp on the "wavering republics" of the Caribbean. The grasp had indeed been tightened; whether it was for good or ill remained to be seen. The United States was on the verge of entry into the First World War. All that could be foreseen at the time was that the world would be changed for both victors and vanquished.

BETWEEN THE WORLD WARS, 1919–1939

One of the consequences of World War I was the breakup of empires: Imperial Russia, Austria-Hungary, and the Ottoman Turkish empire. In Russia, convulsed by revolution as was Mexico, the U.S. government found itself committing military forces. In northwestern Russia, centering upon the ports of Murmansk and Archangel, approximately five thousand U.S. troops were sent in March 1918, ostensibly to protect U.S. and Allied supplies. These forces were withdrawn in June 1919.

The northern expedition was simplicity itself compared to the Siberian Expedition (1918–1920), centered on the port of Vladivostok. It was variously characterized as aiding Czechoslovakian forces along the trans-Siberian railway, protecting Allied and U.S. supplies, preserving order as various factions struggled for control of the maritime region, and keeping an eye on Japan, who had interests of its own in the region. The decision to send ten thousand troops from the Philippines early in August 1918, under the command of Major General William S. Graves, was based on an amalgam of all of these reasons. Following the armistice with Germany of 11 November 1918, the continued presence of U.S. forces in Vladivostok was increasingly viewed as supporting the regime of Admiral A. V. Kolchak's White forces against the Bolsheviks. The subsequent collapse of Kolchak the following year and the eastward advance of Bolshevik forces led to the decision to withdraw U.S. troops, which was completed by 1 April 1920. Thereafter the navy maintained a watching brief (continued observation) on the Japanese, who themselves finally withdrew in the fall of 1922.

Naval forces also appeared in the Black Sea. In May 1920, U.S. naval and relief personnel were withdrawn from the Caucasus region. A larger operation, consequent upon the collapse of Bolshevik opposition in southern Russia, was mounted in the Crimea in November that same year. From late 1921 to late 1922, naval vessels delivered supplies to various Russian Black Sea ports under the auspices of an arrangement worked out by the American Near East Relief Administration.

Rear Admiral Mark L. Bristol, senior naval officer in the Near East and subsequently U.S. high commissioner to Turkey, opposed the breakup of the Ottoman Empire and, in particular, the idea that the United States acquire a mandate in the area under League of Nations auspices. Turkish nationalists continued to oppose Allied designs in Anatolia, that is, the establishment of an Armenian state, and the Greek occupation of Smyrna, which came to an end in the fall of 1922 when Turkish forces recaptured the area. Several U.S.

destroyers under the command of Captain Arthur J. Hepburn were dispatched to the area to protect U.S. lives and property and became involved in the subsequent evacuation of more than 250,000 people from the area. Following the conclusion of a treaty between Turkey and the Allied powers in 1923, U.S. naval forces left Turkish waters and Bristol's command dissolved the following year.

During the interwar years the United States maintained a fleet of river gunboats based at Shanghai that patrolled the Yangtze River.

In China the position of the western powers also was steadily eroded. The outbreak of revolution against the Ch'ing dynasty in 1911, followed not long after by the outbreak of World War I, ushered in a lengthy period of instability in the country that, in some degree, was to last for nearly forty years. The U.S. Open Door policy of maintaining and supporting the administrative entity and territorial integrity of China complicated any straightforward attempt to protect U.S. lives and property. The U.S. presence was buttressed by the Legation Guard in Peking (initially soldiers but after 1905 comprised of marines), a battalion of the Fifteenth Infantry at Tientsin, and elements of the Asiatic fleet. During the interwar years the United States also maintained a fleet of river gunboats based at Shanghai that patrolled the Yangtze River and its main tributaries. In contrast to the Mexican revolution, which at its most chaotic never threatened the essential unity of the state, the overthrow of the Ch'ing dynasty led to a dissolution of central authority. North of the Yangtze competing warlords ruled, while south of the Yangtze the Chinese Nationalist Party (Kuomintang) gradually consolidated its position, and in the mid-1920's began to move northward.

Nationalist forces reached the Yangtze Valley in 1926. In September of that year, British naval forces ran into an ambush at Wanhsien in which they were roughly handled. Nor was it at all unusual for foreign-owned vessels—private or military—to be fired upon from shore.

In March 1927 matters came to a head. In Shanghai defeated warlord forces attempted to flee into the International Settlement on 21–24 March but were repulsed. U.S. marines came ashore to help man the defenses but were not involved in hostile action. At the same time, in Nanking, Nationalist forces entered the city and local mobs, in some cases aided by the soldiery, attacked foreign nationals. To protect one group of refugees ashore, the U.S. destroyers *Noa* and *Preston* opened fire to drive back the threatening soldiery. This was the most serious episode involving American nationals, because much of the antiforeign sentiment in the Yangtze Valley and in the south around Canton had been aimed at the British.

In response to the apparently deteriorating situation, reinforcements of marines and naval vessels were sent to China in the early part of 1927. A buildup of forces occurred in the Peking-Tientsin area in north China in late 1927, although most were withdrawn the following year as the Nationalists succeeded in establishing control of the region. Rear Admiral Bristol, commander of the Asiatic fleet from September 1927 to September 1929, recognized that the days of traditional gunboat diplomacy were numbered. If the need arose, American lives and property could best be preserved by evacuation rather than by force. Foreign concessionary areas, including those controlled by Americans, were increasingly reverting to Chinese control.

Perhaps more ominously, the Fourth Marine Regiment witnessed clashes between Japanese and Chinese forces in Shanghai in 1932. Five years later the Sino-Japanese War began. The Fourth Marines was reinforced by the Sixth, although the latter subsequently was withdrawn. The Fourth remained in Shanghai until its withdrawal in November 1941 to Corregidor in the Philippines. For the five hundred members of the regiment stationed in Peking and Tientsin, the withdrawal decision came too late. They were captured by the Japanese after Pearl Harbor and became prisoners of war for the duration.

The interwar years also brought change to the Caribbean and Central America. In Honduras, local U.S. interests supported the Conservative presidential candidate, Tiburcio Carías Andino, against his Liberal opponent, Rafael Lopez Gutiérrez, in the October 1923 election. Carías declared himself the winner, but the election was thrown into the national assembly. As the U.S. government withdrew its recognition of the Liberal regime, supporters of the respective candidates looted and shelled the capital of Tegucigalpa. Sailors and marines from the USS *Milwaukee* occupied the city. In the spring of 1924, a State Department representative, Sumner Welles, arrived to negotiate between the two factions. The Conservative candidate, Carías, finally withdrew from the contest after Welles persuaded United Fruit, a U.S. company, to halt loans to his faction.

In Nicaragua, the marine legation guard had been withdrawn in August 1925. In April of the following year, Emiliano Chamorro Vargas forced out of office the incumbent president and vice president. The United States, however, refused to recognize Chamorro as president; the Liberal opposition rose in revolt, assaulting Bluefields and seizing funds from the town's banks. These incidents prompted a landing by U.S. marines in Bluefields in early May. An American-sponsored conference between the contending groups settled little, although Chamorro did resign the presidency. The Nicaraguan assembly chose Adolfo Díaz as his successor. Juan Secasa, the deposed vice president, rose in open revolt against Díaz with the backing of the Mexican government. In December, marines again were sent ashore. An arms embargo was declared to stop the importation of weapons by the Liberals. The U.S. government, which in the meantime had recognized Díaz, landed 160 marines at Corinto from the USS *Galveston* in February 1927. These forces proceeded to Managua. Admiral Julian Latimer declared the Corinto-Managua railroad a neutral zone. In April 1927, Henry Stimson was appointed as a special mediator. The subsequent Convention of Tipitapa granted amnesty to the Liberals. Díaz for his part agreed to step down after the 1928 elections, which were to be supervised by the U.S. government.

Most Liberals ceased their hostilities; one, Augusto César Sandino, did not. General Logan Feland, marine Commander in Nicaragua, assigned Nicaraguan constabulary forces to track down Sandino's guerrilla bands. These efforts were not entirely successful. By January 1928 reinforcements had brought the number of marines in the country to fifteen hundred. The election was won by the Liberal candidate, José Maria Moncada. In 1929, U.S. marine forces, having reached a peak of

The U.S. Marine presence in Nicaragua reached a peak of 5,000 in 1929, after which the troops were gradually withdrawn. These marines posed with Sandino's flag in 1932, shortly before the last marine units left the country in 1933. (National Archives)

five thousand, were gradually withdrawn. Sandino, who had been in Mexico for a time, returned to Nicaragua in May. Again, Nicaraguan forces, with marine assistance, unsuccessfully attempted to bring him to bay. The insurrection continued, with Sandino's forces eluding capture and, in the spring of 1931, attacking Standard Fruit interests in the eastern lowlands. Stimson, now secretary of state, opposed further marine reinforcements. In the election of 1932, Juan Secasa became president, and the remaining marines were withdrawn the following year. Sandino entered Managua in February 1934 to discuss the disarmament of the last of his forces. A plot engineered by Anastasio Somoza, commander of the *Guardia Nacional,* resulted in the capture and execution of Sandino. Somoza would emerge as the ruling force in Nicaragua, and he and his family would remain in control until 1979.

THE EARLY COLD WAR, 1945–1960

The end of World War II in 1945 continued what some have called "the American century." The strength of its military, the possession of the atomic bomb, and an industrial capacity unravaged by war gave the United States the power, seemingly, to exert its influence anywhere on the globe. As had been the case after earlier wars, however, a massive demobilization, which affected all the services, soon reduced the capacity of the United States to intervene even if the will to do so had existed. The apparent threat posed by the Soviet Union, soon to harden into the cold war, was perceived initially as applying particularly to Europe. The threat was met initially with nuclear deterrence, economic aid to the Western European countries, and the North Atlantic Treaty Organization (NATO), established in 1949.

Another legacy of the war, although one not immediately perceived, was the decisive weakening of the will to empire of the European powers. The first effects were felt in east and south Asia. Burma, India, Malaya, the Netherlands East Indies, and the Philippines all achieved independence in the 1940s. France, attempting to retain control of Indochina, found itself involved in a guerrilla war with the Viet Minh. The U.S. government provided economic aid and, on occasion, military advisers. As long as the U.S. Navy controlled the Pacific, and Japan remained occupied and pacified, what happened elsewhere in Asia evoked little concern in Washington. The sole exception was China.

Fifty-five thousand marines from the Third Amphibious Corps were sent into northern China (Hopeh and Shantung provinces) in September-October 1945 to assist in the surrender and repatriation of Japanese troops and help maintain order. The first part of the mission was completed by mid-1946. The second portion became increasingly difficult outside the cities, as China slid into civil war between the Nationalist and Communist forces. Occasional clashes between marines and Communist irregulars resulted in casualties to both sides. By early 1947 the remnant of the marine forces, now numbering five thousand and designated Fleet Marine Force Western Pacific, was based at Tsingtao. As they had done in the 1920s, the marines helped evacuate American nationals caught in the conflict from north China and the Yangtze Valley. By 1949 the last marines left China.

As long as the U.S. Navy controlled the Pacific, and Japan remained occupied, what happened elsewhere in Asia evoked little concern in Washington.

The U.S. naval presence in east Asian waters was also significantly reduced. By 1950 the Seventh Fleet consisted of one heavy cruiser, eight destroyers, four submarines, and one aircraft carrier. The Naval Forces Far East Command, operating from Japanese ports, was even more modest.

In the Mediterranean there was also a slow awakening to new responsibilities. The British government told the administration of Harry S. Truman in 1947 that it would have to withdraw its forces from Greece. The near-simultaneous threat to Turkey from the Soviet Union over a revision of the Montreaux Convention governing passage of the Bosporus and Dardanelles not only gave rise to the Truman Doctrine but saw the establishment of a U.S. naval presence in the Mediterranean—the Sixth Fleet. Economic aid and military advisers were sent to the Greek government. This aid, coupled the following year with the withdrawal of Yugoslav aid to the Greek Communist insurgents, helped to bring victory to government forces. A U.S. naval presence in the Mediterranean seemed also sufficient to deter Soviet adventurism. For the near term, perhaps it did. In the long term, however, the Middle East would become an area of constant concern, as the United States assumed Great Britain's traditional role in the "great game" of blocking Soviet access to the Mediterranean, the Persian Gulf, and the Indian Ocean.

The relatively modest commitment of U.S. forces overseas was to change with the end of the U.S. nuclear monopoly in 1949, the establishment of NATO, and above all with the North Korean invasion of South Korea in June 1950, signaling not only an expansion of the cold war to Asia, but, during the presidency of

Dwight D. Eisenhower (1953–1961) to the Middle East, Africa, and Latin America.

Containment of communism in the Middle East took the form of supporting milder forms of nationalism in the area and simultaneously seeking to keep the Soviet Union from the region through the alliance of 1955 called the Baghdad Pact, consisting of Great Britain, Turkey, Iraq, Iran and Pakistan. The pact was one element that was to lead to the Suez Crisis the following year. In 1956, Egyptian President Gamal Abdel Nasser denounced the Baghdad Pact and sought to strengthen Egypt militarily. Failing to obtain aid from the West, he successfully sought it from the Communist bloc. His subsequent decision to recognize the People's Republic of China proved to be the last straw for U.S. Secretary of State John Foster Dulles, who in July abruptly reversed the decision to provide economic aid for the Egyptian Aswan High Dam project. Nasser, in turn, nationalized the Suez Canal, thereby bringing Great Britain, France, and Israel to a decision to attack Egypt.

The Israeli invasion of the Sinai Peninsula on 29 October 1956 was followed just days later by an Anglo-French invasion to "separate" the combatants and maintain freedom of transit of the canal. The U.S. Sixth Fleet was ordered to assist in the evacuation of U.S. citizens from the war zone. A marine battalion landing team went ashore at Alexandria on 1–2 November and assisted in the evacuation of more than fifteen hundred U.S. and other foreign nationals. Pressure by the U.S. government halted the Anglo-French invasion and ultimately led to the evacuation of allied forces from Egypt. In the aftermath of the crisis was the realization by Great Britain and France that their governments could no longer act without U.S. approval in the Middle East. The crisis also did not signal the end of Soviet involvement in the region.

In an effort to reassure the member states of the Baghdad Pact that the United States was committed to their security and integrity, the Eisenhower administration promulgated the Eisenhower doctrine, put forth in a special address to Congress on 5 January 1957 and which declared the Middle East vital to U.S. national interests. Even more important, Congress was requested to authorize the dispatch of military and economic aid to any country desiring it, plus the dispatch of military forces should they be necessary to prevent political subversion or to counter foreign invasion. Both the Senate and the House of Representatives passed the necessary legislation in March. The presence of the Sixth Fleet in the eastern Mediterranean enabled Jordan's King Hussein to weather a crisis that same year, but could not prevent the union of Syria and Egypt into the United Arab Republic early in 1958.

Civil war erupted in Lebanon in May 1958 between Christian and Muslim elements, leading to a strengthening of marines within the Sixth Fleet and contingency plans to put ashore two battalion landing teams in that country. The overthrow of the pro-Western Iraqi government on 14 July led to the decision by the Eisenhower administration to land forces in Lebanon lest Lebanon's government, too, be overthrown. Three marine battalion landing teams went ashore 15–16 July, secured control of the Beirut airport, and established a defensive perimeter around it. U.S. Army forces were flown in from Germany, landing on 19 July. At the end of the buildup phase on 5 August, nearly fifteen thousand personnel were in place. Although in the early stages the marines were subject to some harassing rifle fire, no casualties were incurred. A political settlement that called for the election of the Lebanese army commander, General Fuad Shehab, to the presidency enabled the withdrawal of U.S. forces to begin on 14 September 1958. The last military personnel left on 25 October. Clearly, U.S. military power could be projected into states along or near the Mediterranean littoral. Whether they could be committed without risk was yet to be determined.

Meanwhile, in the Caribbean, the United States had first isolated then destabilized the government of Guatemala. The president, Jacobo Arbenz Guzmán, was deemed to be Communist-leaning; his decision to purchase weapons from the Communist bloc helped to seal his fate in 1954. A U.S.-sponsored insurgency led by Carlos Castillo Armas and the defection of key Guatemalan military personnel led to the overthrow of Arbenz. No U.S. forces were involved; the closest the United States came to military intervention was the transfer of two P-51 aircraft via a third country to Castillo Armas' insurgents.

John F. Kennedy would test whether U.S. military power could be threatened or actually committed hemispherically at little or no cost.

In Panama, late in 1959, U.S. Army personnel stationed in the Canal Zone were called to the zonal borders to prevent the entrance of Panamanians determined to fly their country's flag in the zone as a symbol of ultimate sovereignty. The incoming administration of John F. Kennedy would test whether U.S. military power could be threatened or actually committed hemispherically at little or no cost. It seemed, initially, that it could.

The downfall of the Fulgencio Batista regime in Cuba in 1959 and the triumph of Fidel Castro was at first greeted with rejoicing or at least with equanimity. Disquieting signs soon appeared that this revolution promised to be different. Castro's predilection to export his revolution to other Caribbean countries, plus his inability or unwillingness to reach a modus vivendi with the United States that might compromise Cuban nationalism began a downward spiral that neither side could halt. The nationalization of the Cuban sugar industry in the fall of 1960 was followed by the severance of diplomatic relations by the United States on 4 January 1961.

THE 1960s

Vice President Richard M. Nixon had recommended as early as April 1959 that Cuban exiles be organized to overthrow Castro. President Eisenhower formally ordered such an operation in mid-March 1960. It was this plan, run by the Central Intelligence Agency, that was inherited by the incoming Kennedy administration. Kennedy, having charged Eisenhower with "losing" Cuba, was almost obliged to let the plan proceed. Essentially the CIA called for a conventional military operation, in which air cover was a key component. Kennedy specified there were to be no Americans involved in the actual landing. On the eve of the operation, he ordered the CIA's Richard Bissell to keep U.S. air support to a minimum.

On 15 April 1961, a raid was staged by several B-26 bombers on Cuban airfields. It failed in its attempt to knock out or cripple the Cuban air force. The invasion fleet carrying Brigade 2506, consisting of 1,453 men, had sailed from Puerto Cabezas, Nicaragua, and was off the southern Cuban coast in the early hours of 17 April. Landings were made at Playa Largo and Playa Giron in the Bay of Pigs (Cochinos Bay), and the brigade pushed inland against slight resistance. Cuban air attacks against the vessels that morning sunk one craft and knocked out nine others. Belatedly, a dozen B-26s arrived to provide air cover but five of them were shot down. The loss of the invasion force's supply and communication network, and the absence of any wide-scale uprising on the part of the Cubans themselves made failure a virtual certainty. The surviving 1,179 captives of Brigade 2506 were released by Castro in the fall of 1962 in exchange for $53 million in medical supplies and food.

The Guatemalan experience of 1954 had misguided the planning of the 1961 venture. Even worse, Soviet Premier Nikita Khrushchev drew certain conclusions regarding Kennedy's performance in the entire affair, which were to lead to a much more serious crisis in U.S.-Soviet relations eighteen months later. The Monroe Doctrine was seriously weakened by Castro's survival, and the United States incurred considerable obloquy both in the Western Hemisphere and elsewhere for having intervened in Cuba while simultaneously proclaiming the principle of nonintervention.

The Kennedy administration, for its part, saw the failure to commit U.S. forces as one of the reasons for the Bay of Pigs fiasco, and the Joint Chiefs of Staff were ordered to prepare for a direct intervention in Cuba should one be ordered. The planning involved all four services, and exercises undertaken in 1961 and 1962 in the Caribbean tested the readiness of some units. The threat of invasion in turn prompted a step-up in Soviet military aid to the Cuban government, although it does not by itself explain the decision to introduce intermediate range ballistic missiles and nuclear-capable medium bombers into Cuba. Given overwhelming U.S. preponderance in reliable nuclear weapon delivery systems at the time, no "quick fix" was possible for the Soviets. If Khrushchev believed Kennedy was prepared to acquiesce in the presence of missiles in Cuba, he seriously miscalculated. Not only would operational missiles pose a threat to U.S. cities, their presence would seriously threaten the administration's authority, hemispheric hegemony, and leadership of the NATO alliance.

In the course of forty-eight hours (20–22 October), U.S. armed forces went to a war footing that was both impressive and unprecedented since World War II. Troops from the Second Marine Expeditionary Force would have led the way ashore on beaches west of Havana had an invasion been ordered. One hundred thousand army troops, including armored and airborne units, would have been committed to the assault. The navy, for its part, not only was prepared to provide air cover for the invasion from the nuclear carriers *Enterprise* and *Independence,* but also the blockading ("quarantine") force to halt further importation of missiles into Cuba. The blockade went into effect on 24 October, and achieved its goals. On 28 October, Kennedy was informed by Khrushchev he was prepared to dismantle the missiles already in Cuba and return them to the Soviet Union. Khrushchev fell from power eighteen months later. The Soviet government nevertheless embarked on a massive program to strengthen both its nuclear capabilities and its navy, so that it would never, as one Soviet diplomat succinctly put it, be caught like that again. The United States decided that economic sanctions and hemispheric isolation would be sufficient against Cuba, but if not, the U.S. government was prepared to live with the Castro regime, so long as it was not duplicated elsewhere in the Caribbean.

The U.S. fear of Castro-inspired regimes contributed to right-wing military coups in Guatemala, Honduras, and the Dominican Republic in 1963. In the Dominican Republic, the democratically elected regime of Juan Bosch was overthrown. Bosch went into exile, but pro-Bosch elements, including some in the military, agitated for his return. This all came to a head when the regime of Donald Reid Cabral was toppled 25–26 April 1965 by pro-Bosch forces. The following day right-wing military forces under General Elias Wessin y Wessin attacked the Constitutionalist forces in Santo Domingo but were unable to crush them, which in turn led to U.S. military intervention. Marines from the USS *Boxer* went ashore early on 28 April and established a perimeter west of the city around the Hotel Embajador. Ostensibly this step was undertaken to protect and evacuate foreign nationals caught in the fighting. In fact, however, in a critical meeting of top U.S. officials in Washington on 29 April, it was decided that the intervention was to be a massive one; U.S. prestige was at stake. There would be no Castro-style regime in the Dominican Republic. An airlift of troops began into the San Isidro airport, and in the space of two weeks force levels were raised to more than twenty thousand. Support of the venture from the Organization of American States (OAS) and of the Johnson Doctrine (equated in some circles with the Roosevelt Corollary to the Monroe Doctrine) was less than fulsome. Much energy was expended in the search for a regime acceptable to the U.S. government. U.S. troops eventually withdrew in September 1966.

Other areas saw U.S. military interventions between 1961 and 1969. Army and marine forces were introduced into Thailand, March 1961, at the height of the Laotian crisis that year but were withdrawn by July. In November 1964, Belgian paratroopers were dropped from U.S. aircraft to rescue foreign nationals in the Congo trapped by rebel forces. Earlier that same year, army forces in the Canal Zone again were called upon to disperse Panamanian rioters. The U.S. Sixth Fleet stood by during the 1967 Arab-Israeli war although not, as in 1956, without casualties. On 5 June the USS *Liberty,* an electronic surveillance vessel, was attacked by Israeli warplanes and torpedo boats, resulting in 34 killed and 171 wounded. Overshadowing all these episodes was the growing U.S. presence in Vietnam, which reached its peak in 1968 and was to diminish slowly during the presidencies of Richard Nixon and Gerald Ford.

THE 1970s

It is surprising how few interventions involving U.S. forces occurred from 1969 to 1977. Seizure of the container ship *Mayaguez* in Cambodian waters by Khmer Rouge forces in May 1975 prompted a military operation mounted to retrieve the vessel and rescue its crew.

No longer the world's policeman, the United States would rely more and more on regional surrogates, such as Israel, Iran, and Brazil, to keep order.

The ship was retrieved on 15 May, but marine forces lifted by helicopter onto Koh Tang Island suffered severe casualties (fourteen dead or missing, forty-one wounded) in the effort to rescue the crew. They were later released unharmed into U.S. custody. This episode aside, the temper of the years of Nixon's and Gerald Ford's administration was anticipated in the 1969 Nixon Doctrine, which declared that the United States would continue to honor its commitments to the NATO alliance, Japan, and South Korea. Elsewhere, and particularly in Asia, Africa, and Latin America, the United States would perhaps provide air support, economic and technical aid, and weaponry—but the burden of resisting insurrection or outside aggression would fall upon the nations in which it was occurring. No longer the world's policeman, the United States would rely more and more on regional surrogates, such as South Vietnam, Israel, Iran, and Brazil, to keep order. Covert operations had also fallen from favor. The destabilization of the Salvatore Allende regime in Chile and its subsequent overthrow in 1973 by the Chilean military provoked such an outcry that Congress was prompted to pass legislation the following year severely limiting covert action. The decision by Congress to refuse further funding to support insurgency in Angola the following year led to the triumph of the Popular Movement for the Liberation of Angola in 1976. In neither the Jordanian crisis of 1970 nor the Yom Kippur War of 1973 did the United States intervene. The presence of the Sixth Fleet in both instances, however, was a deterrent to a widening of hostilities.

Jimmy Carter became president in 1977 determined to make changes in U.S. foreign policy as practiced during the Nixon-Ford years. U.S. defense budgets would be pared; forces abroad would be reduced; economic and military aid to right-wing regimes would be cut; and there would be no more Vietnams and no more

Chiles. This new *weltanschauung* (world view) helped to produce an historic settlement in the Middle East; the 1977 Camp David Accords brought peace between Egypt and Israel, and, as part of a United Nations peacekeeping detachment, U.S. forces into the Sinai region. The accords also contributed to the U.S.-Panamanian agreements that same year abrogating the Hay-Bunau-Varilla Treaty of 1903 and granting Panama increased revenues and greater administrative authority within the Canal Zone. The United States retained the right to defend the "neutrality" of the canal, and could intervene unilaterally should service through the canal be interrupted. The long rule of the Somoza family in Nicaragua ended in 1979 without interference from the United States.

On the other hand, one of the regional pillars of the United States in the Middle East toppled in 1979—the government of the shah of Iran. The successor regime was dominated by fundamentalist Iranian clerics led by the Ayatollah Khomeini. The decision later that year to permit the shah to receive medical attention in the United States was followed within weeks by the seizure of the U.S. embassy in Teheran by militants on 4 November. U.S. embassy personnel were held hostage. Late in November, President Carter ordered two carrier battle groups (the *Midway* and the *Kitty Hawk*) into the Indian Ocean. The *Kitty Hawk* and its escorts were relieved by the *Nimitz* in January 1980. Negotiations for the release of the hostages were unsuccessful, and in March the president decided to undertake a rescue mission.

The plan, dubbed Operation Eagle Claw, was devised by Air Force General David Jones, chairman of the Joint Chiefs of Staff. The two-day operation called for a nighttime rendezvous at a site (Desert One) two hundred miles southeast of Teheran. Six C-130 Hercules transports carrying the multiservice Delta Force commandos, fuel, and equipment would fly from an Egyptian airfield and be met by eight navy RH-53 Sea Stallion helicopters from the *Nimitz*. The refueled hel-

On 23 October 1983, terrorists detonated an explosives-laden truck near the headquarters of the Marine Battalion Landing Team in Beirut, destroying the building and killing 241 marines. The site is shown here after the explosion. (Department of Defense/U.S. Marines)

icopters would take the assault team to a location closer to Teheran (Desert Two) and take cover until the second night. The commandos would proceed by commandeered vehicles to the embassy compound and the Iranian Foreign Ministry building, free the hostages, then proceed to a nearby stadium, from which they would be transported by helicopter to an airfield south of Teheran, occupied that same evening by a U.S. military transport group. All personnel would then be flown out to safety.

The operation, which began on 24 April 1980, was unsuccessful. Two of the eight helicopters turned back en route to Desert One. A third developed a problem in its hydraulic system. Colonel Charles Beckwith, the commander of the operation, recommended that the mission be terminated at that point. President Carter concurred. During takeoff one of the remaining helicopters struck a C-130, and eight crewmen were killed. Abandoning the helicopters, the assault force flew out in the transports. The embassy hostages were ultimately released on 20 January 1981, after 444 days in captivity, in a deal brokered by Algerian government representatives. To add to the Carter administration's woes in this part of the world, the Soviet Union sent troops into Afghanistan in December 1979, and Iraq's Saddam Hussein attacked Iran in September 1980, beginning a conflict that would drag on for eight years and involve the United States naval forces in the Persian Gulf before it ended. Carter lost his bid for reelection in 1980 to Ronald Reagan in part because of his presumed weaknesses in the international realm.

THE REAGAN-BUSH YEARS, 1981–1993

Reagan came into office committed to strengthening the U.S. military, aiding foreign governments combating communism, and undermining those regimes (as in Angola and, closer to home, in Nicaragua) that were too leftist for comfort. He proclaimed that the United States was back, free of its post-Vietnam syndrome. The administration's resolve would be severely tested in Lebanon, which had gained the unenviable reputation as the snakepit of the Middle East.

Israeli forces moved into Lebanon in June 1982, driving northward to Beirut. Late in August, eight hundred U.S. marines went ashore, the Thirty-second Marine Amphibious Unit (MAU), but were withdrawn fifteen days later. The marines returned that fall as part of a multinational force to safeguard civilians and foreign nationals, with the task of protecting the Beirut international airport and its environs. The position of the Twenty-fourth MAU, 1,250 strong, which replaced the Thirty-second MAU in early November, was increasingly tenuous. Forbidden to fire unless directly fired upon and subject to sniper fire and artillery fire from the hills to the east, they were perceived as being in league with Lebanese Christian forces. Neither return fire by their own artillery, naval gunfire (including at one point the big guns of the battleship *New Jersey*), nor naval air assault seemed to help. In mid-April 1983 the bombing of the U.S. embassy in Beirut resulted in more than sixty deaths (including seventeen Americans). On 23 October an explosives-laden truck was driven into the marine headquarters building and detonated, killing 241 of the 300 marines asleep there. On 26 February 1984 the marines were withdrawn from Lebanon and the following month the U.S. government announced its formal withdrawal from the multinational police force.

On 3 July 1987, the Aegis missile cruiser Vincennes *mistakenly shot down an Iranian airliner, killing all 290 aboard.*

Even before the Lebanese venture, the U.S. military had encountered problems elsewhere in the Mediterranean. The ruler of Libya, Colonel Muammar Khadhaffi, claimed the Gulf of Sidra as part of Libya's territorial waters. During maneuvers by the Sixth Fleet in the gulf in August, two Libyan jets were shot down by naval fighters. Libya, as well as Syria and Iran, was seen as responsible for a number of terrorist-related acts in the Middle East and elsewhere during the 1980s. In 1982 the U.S. government embargoed Libyan oil. In January 1986 all trade with Libya was banned, and in March a further clash with naval forces in the Gulf of Sidra left two Libyan patrol boats sunk. Libyan shore missile batteries and radar installations also were attacked. In April the bombing of a West Berlin discotheque resulted in the death of a U.S. serviceman. This, too, was laid at Khadhaffi's door and resulted in an assault days later on Benghazi and Tripoli by carrier- and land-based planes. As an exercise in extreme power quickly applied and quickly withdrawn, it proved highly successful.

The Iran-Iraq conflict that had begun in 1980 also involved the U.S. military. With the war stalemated on the ground, Iraq turned increasingly to attacks on Iranian oil installations and the tankers using them. The Iranians replied in kind. The U.S. Navy became responsible for ensuring the safe passage of U.S.-flag or flag-of-convenience tankers through the Persian Gulf and the Strait of Hormuz. On 17 May 1987 the guided-missile frigate *Stark* was hit by two Exocet missiles fired from an Iraqi F-1 Mirage fighter. The attack was in error, but the vessel's commander was criticized for failing to take action (arming its own surface-to-air missiles), even though it had been warned that the approaching fighter's radar was locked on to the ship. On 14 April 1988 the frigate *Samuel B. Roberts* was badly damaged by a mine. Just days later A-6 Intruder attack bombers sank an Iranian frigate. The navy's mission was broadened to protect all friendly, neutral, and innocent shipping. In June 1988, two Iranian oil platforms utilized as bases for harassment of shipping were attacked and destroyed by naval and marine forces. On 3 July the Aegis missile cruiser *Vincennes,* during a clash with Iranian speedboats, mistakenly shot down an Iranian airliner, killing all 290 aboard.

During Ronald Reagan's presidency, the U.S. military did not intervene in Cuba, El Salvador, or Nicaragua. In the latter two cases, it proved to be a near-run thing. The triumph of the Sandinistas in 1979 and the outbreak of an insurrectionary movement in neighboring El Salvador the following year prompted the Reagan administration to send military aid and advisers to the El Salvador regime, and to undertake a policy of supporting *contra* opposition to the Nicaraguan government. This near-obsession with leftist forces in Central America supported by Cuba and the Soviet Union also figured in the 25–27 October 1983 invasion of Grenada. Since 1979, Grenada had been ruled by an avowed Marxist, Maurice Bishop. His overthrow by an even more radical faction in 1983, it was feared, would lead to even closer ties to Cuba. The extension of the island's airport by Cuban laborers also seemed suspicious. American nationals living there were thought to be at risk as hostages. Finally, the overthrow of the coup's leaders would send a strong message to the Cubans and the Sandinistas (not to mention those responsible for the bombing of the marine headquarters building in Lebanon days before). The invasion force of Operation Urgent Fury consisted of a marine amphibious battalion, two army Ranger battalions backed by fighter-bombers from the USS *Independence,* air force C-130 gunships, five M60 tanks and other armored fighting vehicles, helicopters, and two Eighty-second Airborne battalions flown in 26 October as reinforcements. It took three days to secure the island despite minimal Cuban-Grenadian resistance. At a cost of $75.5 million, it was shown that gunboat diplomacy still could succeed. U.S. forces were withdrawn in mid-December.

Panama strongman Manuel Antonio Noriega was a thorn in the side of both the Reagan and George Bush administrations. Allegations of corruption in 1987 by a former aide led to increasing calls for Noriega's resignation by Panamanians. U.S. foreign aid to Panama ceased early in 1988, and two Florida grand juries indicted Noriega for his involvement in the drug trade and for permitting the laundering of drug money by Panamanian banks, among other charges. Refusing all threats and blandishments, Noriega overturned an internationally supervised election in May 1989. Several months later he easily foiled a plot by elements of the Panamanian Defense Force to unseat him. Claiming that a state of war existed between Panama and the United States, Noriega remained impervious to all forms of economic coercion by the Bush administration. Clashes between Panamanian forces and U.S. military personnel in the zone claimed the life of one marine. Contingency planning for an invasion of Panama, begun early in 1989, turned into the real thing. Opera-

Two soldiers from the 5th Mechanized Infantry Division search for snipers in a building near the headquarters of the Panamanian Defense Force on 21 December 1989, the second day of Operation Just Cause. (Department of Defense/U.S. Navy)

tion Just Cause, launched early on 20 December 1989, involved 22,500 troops from the United States and the 13,500 in the Canal Zone. Panama City itself was devastated, 24 U.S. servicemen were killed, and more than 300 Panamanians also died. Noriega ultimately surrendered to the U.S. forces and was remanded to a jail in Florida. The invasion forces were withdrawn early in February 1990.

Panama City was devastated,

24 U.S. servicemen were killed,

and more than 300 Panamanians also died.

Six months later another invasion occurred, not in Latin America, but at the head of the Persian Gulf. Iraq's Saddam Hussein invaded and occupied Kuwait, ostensibly to restore to his country one of its lost provinces. Fearing a subsequent invasion and occupation of Saudi Arabia, President Bush ordered in more than 500,000 combat troops, several carrier task forces, and a number of air squadrons to help defend Saudi territory. Bush also orchestrated an international economic boycott of Iraq. The U.S. military contingent of Operation Desert Shield was in time joined by forces of other nations, including Great Britain, France, Egypt, and Syria. With the backing or neutrality of the international community, and the authority of the U.S. Senate to resort to military action, the allies went over to the offensive—Operation Desert Storm—in mid-January 1991. Following some days of air operations and missile attacks, General Norman Schwarzkopf's forces distracted Iraqi forces in Kuwait with a feigned seaborne assault near Kuwait City, sending instead his armored forces on a sweep west and north behind the prepared Iraqi defensive positions. In four days the Iraqi army was routed and Kuwait liberated.

To the extent that the cold war formed the backdrop to a number of U.S. interventions in the post–World War II era, the ending of the cold war and the breakup of the Soviet Union into its constituent parts presaged a new order indeed—although not precisely in the form envisioned by President Bush.

During the first century of its existence, the United States committed forces in peacetime with both a continental and a maritime dimension. The latter approached most closely gunboat diplomacy in its classic form, defined as the use of naval vessels to protect American lives and property abroad. The disappearance of the western frontier in the late nineteenth century ended the continental dimension, while the commitment of forces abroad increasingly was undertaken in furtherance of perceived national interests, such as the security of the Central American isthmian canal and the maritime approaches to it. The greatest incidence of force geographically occurred in the Western Hemisphere, east Asia, and the Pacific during the last decade of the nineteenth century and the first three decades of the twentieth. In the second half of the twentieth century, U.S. interests became global, encompassing not only the western Atlantic and the Pacific littoral but the Mediterranean and Indian oceans as well. Where forces have been committed, they increasingly have involved all of the armed services. Ideally, when military force is to be used during peacetime, the objective should be clear, the mission limited in scope and time, and the force itself proportionate to its task. More often than not, the reality has corresponded to the ideal.

[See also The Cold War; The Early National Period; Expansion and the Plains Indian Wars; Reconstruction and American Imperialism; The Spanish-American War and Its Aftermath; The Vietnam Era; and The War of 1812 and Postwar Expansion.]

BIBLIOGRAPHY

General Works

Asprey, Robert B. *War in the Shadows: The Guerrilla in History,* 2 vols. (1975).

Blechman, Barry, and Stephen S. Kaplan. *Force Without War* (1978).

Cable, James. *Gunboat Diplomacy* (1971).

Dupuy, R. E., and Trevor N. Dupuy. *Military Heritage of America* (1956).

Hagan, Kenneth J. *This People's Navy: The Making of American Sea Power* (1991).

Hagan, Kenneth J., ed. *In Peace and War: Interpretations of American Naval History, 1775–1984,* 2nd ed. (1984).

Hagan, Kenneth J., and William R. Roberts, eds. *Against All Enemies: Interpretations of American Military History from Colonial Times to the Present* (1986).

Hassler, Warren W. *With Shield and Sword: American Military Affairs: Colonial Times to the Present* (1982).

Heinl, Robert D. *Soldiers of the Sea: The United States Marine Corps, 1775–1962* (1962).

Howarth, Stephen. *To Shining Sea: A History of the United States Navy, 1775–1991* (1991).

Hoyt, Edwin P. *America's Wars and Military Excursions* (1987).

Millett, Allan R. *Semper Fidelis: The History of the United States Marine Corps* (1980).

Millett, Allan R., and Peter Maslowski. *For the Common Defense: A Military History of the United States of America* (1984).

Morris, James M. *America's Armed Forces: A History* (1991).

Perrett, Geoffrey. *A Country Made by War: From the Revolution to Vietnam* (1989).

Stern, Ellen P., ed. *The Limits of Military Intervention* (1977).

Weigley, Russell F. *History of the United States Army* (1967).

———. *The American Way of War: A History of the United States Military Strategy and Policy* (1973).

1783–1815

Bird, Harrison. *War for the West, 1790–1813* (1971).

Bradford, James C. *Command Under Sail: Makers of the American Naval Tradition, 1775–1850* (1985).

Coakley, Robert W. *The Role of Federal Military Forces in Domestic Disturbances, 1789–1878* (1989).

Coffman, Edward M. *The Old Army: A Portrait of the American Army in Peacetime, 1784–1898* (1986).

Field, James A., Jr. *America and the Mediterranean World, 1776–1882* (1969).

Fowler, W. M., Jr. *Jack Tars and Commodores: The American Navy, 1783–1815* (1984).

Guthman, William H. *March to Massacre* (1975).

Kohn, Richard H. *Eagle and Sword: The Federalists and the Creation of the Military Establishment in America, 1783–1802* (1975).

Long, David F. *Nothing too Daring: A Biography of Commodore David Porter, 1780–1843* (1970).

———. *Ready to Hazard: A Biography of Commodore William Bainbridge, 1774–1833* (1981).

———. *Sailor-Diplomat: A Biography of Commodore James Biddle, 1783–1848* (1983).

———. *Gold Braid and Foreign Relations: Diplomatic Activities of U.S. Naval Officers, 1798–1883* (1988).

Mahon, John K. *The American Militia: Decade of Decision, 1789–1800* (1960).

McKee, Christopher. *Edward Preble: A Naval Biography, 1761–1807* (1972).

Prucha, Francis P. *The Sword of the Republic: The United States Army on the Frontier, 1783–1840* (1969).

Remini, Robert V. *Andrew Jackson and the Course of American Empire* (1977).

Sword, Wiley. *President Washington's Indian War: The Struggle for the Old Northwest, 1790–1795* (1985).

Szatmary, David. *Shays' Rebellion: The Making of an Agrarian Insurrection* (1980).

Tucker, Glenn. *Dawn Like Thunder: The Barbary War and the Birth of the U.S. Navy* (1963).

1815–1861

Billingsley, E. B. *In Defense of Neutral Rights: The United States Navy and the Wars of Independence in Chile and Peru* (1967).

Bradford, James C., ed. *Captains of the Old Steam Navy: Makers of the American Naval Tradition, 1840–1880* (1986).

Buker, George E. *Swamp Sailors: Riverine Warfare in the Everglades, 1835–1842* (1975).

Eby, Cecil D. *"That Disgraceful Affair": The Black Hawk War* (1973).

Henson, Curtis T. *Commissioners and Commodores: The East India Squadron and American Diplomacy in China* (1982).

Johnson, Robert E. *Thence Round Cape Horn: The Story of the United States Naval Forces on the Pacific Station, 1818–1923* (1963).

———. *Rear Admiral John Rodgers, 1812–1882* (1967).

———. *Far China Station: The U.S. Navy in Asian Waters, 1800–1895* (1979).

Mahon, John K. *History of the Second Seminole War, 1835–1842* (1967).

Morison, Samuel Eliot. *"Old Bruin": Commodore Matthew C. Perry, 1794–1858* (1967).

Prucha, Francis P. *Broadax and Bayonet: The Role of the United States Army in the Development of the Northwest, 1815–1860* (1953).

Satz, Ronald N. *American Indian Policy in the Jacksonian Era* (1975).

Utley, Robert M. *Frontiersmen in Blue: The United States Army and the Indian, 1846–1865* (1967).

Wheeler, Richard. *In Pirate Waters* (1969).

1865–1898

Barrow, Clayton R., Jr., ed. *America Spreads Her Sails: U.S. Sea Power in the Nineteenth Century* (1973).

Bradford, James C., ed. *Admirals of the Steel Navy: Makers of the American Naval Tradition, 1880–1930* (1990).

Bradford, Richard H. *The Virginius Affair* (1980).

Coletta, Paolo E. *A Survey of U.S. Naval Affairs, 1865–1917* (1987).

Cooling, Benjamin Franklin. *Benjamin Franklin Tracy: Father of the American Fighting Navy* (1973).

Cooper, Jerry M. *The Army and Civil Disorder: Federal Military Intervention in American Labor Disputes, 1877–1900* (1980).

Drake, Frederick C. *The Empire of the Seas: A Biography of Rear Admiral Robert Wilson Shufeldt, USN* (1984).

Goldberg, Joyce S. *The "Baltimore" Affair* (1986).

Grenville, John A. S., and George B. Young. *Politics, Strategy, and American Diplomacy* (1966).

Hagan, Kenneth J. *American Gunboat Diplomacy and the Old Navy, 1877–1889* (1973).

Herwig, Holger H. *Politics of Frustration: The United States in German Naval Planning, 1889–1941* (1976).

Herrick, Walter R., Jr. *The American Naval Revolution* (1966).

LaFeber, Walter. *The New Empire* (1963).

Offut, Milton. *Protection of Citizens Abroad by the Armed Forces of the United States* (1928).

Plesur, Milton. *America's Outward Thrust* (1971).

Sefton, James E. *The United States Army and Reconstruction, 1865–1877* (1967).

Still, William N., Jr. *American Sea Power in the Old World: The United States Navy in European and Near Eastern Waters, 1865–1917* (1980).

Utley, Robert M. *Frontier Regulars: The United States Army and the Indian, 1866–1891* (1973).

1898–1917

Braisted, William R. *The United States Navy in the Pacific, 1897–1909* (1958).

———. *The United States Navy in the Pacific, 1909–1922* (1971).

Challener, Richard D. *Admirals, Generals, and American Foreign Policy, 1898–1914 (1973).*

Collin, Richard H. *Theodore Roosevelt's Caribbean: The Panama Canal, the Monroe Doctrine, and the Latin American Context* (1990).

Gates, John M. *Schoolbooks and Krags: The U.S. Army in the Philippines, 1898–1902* (1973).

Healy, David F. *The United States in Cuba, 1898–1902: Generals, Politicians, and the Search for Policy* (1963).

———. *Gunboat Diplomacy in the Wilson Era: The U.S. Navy in Haiti, 1915–1916* (1976).

———. *Drive to Hegemony: The United States in the Caribbean, 1889–1917* (1988).

Karnow, Stanley. *In Our Image: America's Empire in the Philippines* (1989).

Langley, Lester D. *The United States and the Caribbean in the Twentieth Century*, rev. ed. (1985).

Linn, Brian M. *The U.S. Army and Counterinsurgency in the Philippine War, 1899–1902* (1989).

Miller, Stuart C. *"Benevolent Assimilation": The American Conquest of the Philippines, 1899–1903* (1982).

Millett, Allan R. *The Politics of Intervention: The Military Occupation of Cuba, 1906–1909* (1968).

Munro, Dana Gardner. *Intervention and Dollar Diplomacy in the Caribbean, 1900–1921* (1964).

Musicant, Ivan. *The Banana Wars: A History of the United States Military Intervention in Latin America from the Spanish-American War to the Invasion of Panama* (1990).

Quirk, Robert E. *An Affair of Honor: Woodrow Wilson and the Occupation of Veracruz* (1962).

Reckner, James R. *Teddy Roosevelt's Great White Fleet* (1988).

Roth, Russell. *Muddy Glory: America's "Indian Wars" in the Philippines, 1899–1935* (1981).

Sweetman, Jack. *The Landing at Veracruz: 1914* (1968).

Welch, Richard E., Jr. *Response to Imperialism: The United States and the Philippine-American War, 1899–1902* (1979).

1919–1941

Lester H. Brune. *The Origins of American National Security Policy: Sea Power, Air Power, and Foreign Policy, 1900–1941* (1981).

Cole, Bernard D. *Gunboats and Marines: The United States Navy in China, 1925–1928* (1986).

Goldhurst, Richard. *The Midnight War: The American Intervention in Russia, 1918–1920* (1978).

Kennan, George F. *The Decision to Intervene* (1956–1958).

Macaulay, Neill. *The Sandino Affair* (1967).

Offner, Arnold A. *The Origins of the Second World War: American Foreign Policy and the Second World War: American Foreign Policy and World Politics, 1917–1941* (1975).

Unterberger, Betty Miller. *America's Siberian Expedition, 1918–1920* (1956).

Wheeler, Gerald E. *Prelude to Pearl Harbor: The United States Navy and the Far East, 1921–1931* (1963).

1945–1993

Allison, Graham T. *The Essence of Decision: Explaining the Cuban Missile Crisis* (1971).

Bryson, Thomas A. *Tars, Turks, and Tankers: The Role of the United States Navy in the Middle East, 1800–1979* (1980).

Cable, James. *Gunboat Diplomacy, 1919–1979: Political Applications of Limited Naval Force* (1981).

Cottrell, Alvin J. *Sea Power and Strategy in the Indian Ocean* (1981).

Etzold, Thomas H. *Defense or Delusion? America's Military in the 1980s* (1982).

Hammel, Eric M. *The Root: The Marines in Beirut: August 1982–February 1984* (1985).

Hosmer, Stephen T. *Constraints on U.S. Strategy in Third World Conflicts* (1987).

Howe, Jonathan T. *Multicrises: Sea Power and Global Politics in the Missile Age* (1971).

Johnson, Haynes B. *The Bay of Pigs* (1964).

Karsh, Efraim, et al. *The Iran-Iraq War: Impact and Implications* (1989).

Kupchan, Charles. *The Persian Gulf and the West: The Dilemmas of Security* (1987).

Lowenthal, Abraham F. *The Dominican Intervention* (1972).

Neff, Donald. *Warriors at Suez: Eisenhower Takes America into the Middle East* (1981).

Paul, Roland A. *American Military Commitments Abroad* (1973).

Ryan, Paul B. *The Iranian Rescue Mission: Why It Failed* (1985).

— RICHARD W. TURK

PART 2
THE ARMED FORCES

Introduction

In the Preamble to the U.S. Constitution, the role of the nation's armed forces is first identified in broad terms: to "provide for the common Defence." The document then makes a succession of declarations that expand the perception of the Constitution's framers of the function of the national military forces.

Article I, section 8, paragraph 11, states that Congress shall have the power "To declare War, grant Letters of Marque and Reprisal, and make Rules concerning Captures on Land and Water," thus acknowledging that the broad expression "the common defense" was intended to embrace both offensive and defensive operations.

In the Preamble to the U.S. Constitution, the role of the nation's armed forces is first identified in broad terms: to "provide for the common Defence."

Paragraph 12 of the same section allows Congress "To raise and support Armies, but no Appropriation of Money to that Use shall be for a longer Term than two Years," thus confirming the conviction that the existence of national armies would be a transitory matter and providing a fiscal provision to ensure that this principle would be observed.

Paragraph 13, "To provide and maintain a Navy," underscores the differentiation between soldiers, who could be called up or mustered out at will, and ships, which, once built, must be maintained and exercised.

The collection of import duties on maritime commerce, a critical matter for the young republic, gave rise, in 1790, to the creation of the Revenue Cutter Service within the Department of the Treasury. The role of the service grew slowly until 1915, when it was officially designated the U.S. Coast Guard and assigned additional duties related to contraband control, search and rescue, and, in time of war, assignment to combatant duties under the Department of the Navy.

The philosophy underlying how the armed forces of the United States were to come into being, and what, in general, they should be prepared to do, was not an original one. The drafters of the Constitution found their guidance in the laws and customs then prevailing in Europe and, most particularly, England. While France had abandoned the idea of volunteer citizen-soldiery after its defeat at Agincourt in 1415, the English continued to reject the idea of a conscripted standing army until the Restoration in 1660. They relied, in time of need, on county militia and on volunteers attracted by the promise of compensation or material reward, exactly as stated in Article I, section 8, paragraph 12.

Similarly, beginning in the Elizabethan period, the British Crown encouraged and authorized individual citizens to provide and man ships to serve the royal will. Fully a quarter of those ships that defeated the Spanish Armada in 1588 were of this category. The remainder were part of the Royal Navy and the complements were sworn members of that service. In addition, the Crown authorized semipiratical voyages by both the Royal Navy and civilians, establishing firm rules for the distribution of the consequent profits, which was the origin and pattern for "Letters of Marque and Reprisal" and "Rules concerning Captures on Land and Water."

In the United States, however, the military role of capturing enemy ships for profit was never carried to the extreme practiced in England, where prize money was a highly formalized consideration and persisted until after World War II, when the Prize Bill of 1948 ended the practice.

While the Constitution provides for the existence of armed forces, it also establishes a clear division of authority between the executive and legislative branches on the conduct of military affairs. Drafters of the Constitution were willing to allow the chief of state to command directly the armed forces of the nation, as was the custom in Europe. Article II, section 2, paragraph 1, states, "The President shall be Commander in Chief of the Army and Navy of the United States, and of the Militia of the several States, when called into the actual Service of the United States."

The drafters, however, were unwilling to follow the European pattern and accord the president, as commander in chief, unlimited power to decide exactly what the military forces should be, how large they should be, how they should be armed or compensated, and what the individual service roles should be or how they should relate to one another. These important decisions were reserved for the Congress, as indicated in Article I, section 8: "To provide for the common Defence"; "To declare War"; "To make Rules for the Government and Regulation of the land and naval Forces"; "To provide for calling forth the Militia to execute the Laws of the Union, suppress Insurrections and repel Invasions"; "To provide for organizing, arming, and disciplining, the Militia"; and "To make all Laws which shall be necessary and proper for carrying into Execution the foregoing Powers."

The distribution of powers between the chief of state and the legislature was not practiced anywhere else in the world at the time. It reflected a unique determination by the drafters of the Constitution that the people, through their elected representatives, would have a strong voice in what the military forces should be, what the individual services should do, and how they should be governed.

The almost universal lack of professional military competence in the new country had a direct effect on the internal workings of the executive branch itself in assigning roles and functions to the army and navy. At the outset, when the offices of the secretaries of war (1789) and navy (1798) were first established, instructions from the commander in chief assigning tasks to the military were usually transmitted through the appropriate departmental secretary. As warfare became more complex, however, the authoritarian relationship between the president and the fighting forces became less clear. Should the chain of military and administrative command go from the president through the secretary, a political appointee? Or were there two lines of authority emanating from the president—a political-administrative line to the secretary and a military line direct to the highest professional officer? The Constitution offers no clue as to how these relationships are

For many years, the division of roles and responsibilities amongst the branches of the U.S. military was not clearly defined. During World War II, aviation missions were carried out by the Navy and the Army. The U.S. Air Force was not formed until 1947. (National Archives)

to be handled, an omission that was highlighted in the controversy over post–World War II roles and missions, which were resolved in 1947.

Another reality affecting the assignment of military functions was the fact that until the middle of the nineteenth century the idea of a standing army was unacceptable to the American people, although the nature of ships and the technical requirements of sailing and fighting them made tolerable the existence of a barebones navy. Thus, according to the Constitution, raising and supporting armies is a sometime matter, responding to crisis and providing and maintaining a navy a continuing obligation.

Until the mid-nineteenth century there was little professionalism in the U.S. military.

As a consequence of the national repugnance for a standing army, until the mid-nineteenth century there was little professionalism in the U.S. military and little interest in how responsibilities should be apportioned between the services. As the public saw it, all that was needed were guards for arsenals and for ships in decommissioned status, and there was no call for a professional officer corps. Politicians and the great majority of military leaders were all cast in the same mold. President George Washington, for example, assigned the missions and led troops in the Whiskey Rebellion in 1794. James Madison, with no professional military background, had the same responsibilities with respect to service roles in the War of 1812, as did James Polk during the Mexican War. Abraham Lincoln determined the strategy of the Civil War, a conflict in which most of the officers on both sides were citizen-soldiers, in uniform only for the duration. In uniform or out, they spoke their minds on military matters, not as soldiers, but as citizens. Indeed, it was members of Congress, dissatisfied with the cautious strategy of General George McClellan, who pressed Lincoln to replace him.

Stirrings of professionalism began to appear in the U.S. military in the mid-1800s, in the wake of the experience of European nations that had acknowledged the growing influence of technology on warfare early in the century and had created the basis for a professional officer corps. The British founded the Royal Military College in 1802, and the Prussian Kriegsakademie was founded in 1810, both designed to develop a permanent officer corps and a professional staff to support the military high command as it determined who should do what and how. The professionalizing process was stimulated by the unsettled conditions in Europe in the eighteenth and early nineteenth centuries, and it was facilitated by the rise of democracy, in which the aristocrat who bought or inherited his commission was replaced, at least in part, by the career commoner-professional.

Neither of these stimuli was present in the United States, where, for the first hundred years of the country's existence, the military officer felt little pressure to broaden his technical knowledge and had little interest in enhancing the combat role of his service. He brought to the military a reflection of the cultural pattern of his society—only the knowledge of the marketplace, the farm, or his profession plus his personal patriotic motivation was deemed sufficient. Following the Civil War, however, it became clear that the matter of warmaking demanded officers with more than a reasonable general education. In 1875 General Emory Upton was sent to Europe by Secretary of War William W. Belknap to study and report on the professional development of European armies. Upton was greatly impressed, particularly by the French, and he returned with several revolutionary recommendations: that the source of officers should be only from formal military schools or by promotion from the ranks following a qualifying examination; that a high-level school be established to educate commanders and staff officers; that the overall general staff include only the highest quality officers; and that there be periodic formal professional reports rendered on the qualifications of all officers. Upton's recommendations were received favorably by the War Department and, in time, all became reality.

The growth of a professional officer corps gave rise to the concept that because officers are subordinate to the president as commander in chief, independent political activity on the part of an officer, whether related to service roles or other considerations, was inappropriate. There was, however, more than a half century of precedent of military leaders making their views known in the political arena. The sentiment remains strong today, fortified in fact by the availability of the National Guard, the National Guard Association, the service and retired officers associations, and the veterans organizations to represent and support the views of the professional military in Congress, a circumstance made critically plain in the post–World War II roles and missions debates.

Organization of and the assignment of roles to the fighting forces were not viewed as a major consideration in the earliest days of the Republic. Congress decided in 1789 that a single executive department, the Department of War, should handle all such military matters as might arise. Those matters were not of great moment since, at the time, the United States had no armed forces organization or any soldiers or seamen in its pay.

It was not until 1798 that Congress concluded that the administration and support of the military forces was sufficiently challenging to warrant creation of a separate department for governance of the navy. With the establishment of the Department of the Navy, administration of naval affairs was transferred from the secretary of war to the secretary of the navy.

During the better part of the next century, many laws were enacted providing for the support and administration of the armed forces. While there was little conflict at the national level concerning assignment or apportionment of roles or distribution of resources, Congress repeatedly exhibited its determination to control the assignment of functions to the armed forces. They did this by resolution as various crises arose, such as the Quasi-War with France, suppression of the slave trade, the Mexican War, the Barbary Wars, the elimination of piracy, and the Spanish-American War.

In reality, however, role assignment was an uncomplicated matter. As a matter of course, during most of the nineteenth century it was seen that the army would fight on land and the navy would fight at sea. Any coordination necessary between the two services was achieved by the use of joint boards, such as the Joint Board of the Army and Navy, the Army-Navy Munitions Board, and the Joint Economy Board, whose efforts in the apportionment of functions related less to combat roles than to the division of logistic responsibilities.

One operational area where joint boards were employed related to establishing service roles in coastal defense. The Bernard Board of 1816, the Endicott Board of 1885, and the Taft Board of 1905 all sought to isolate and solve conflicting service views as to their roles in the defense of the coastline. Emanuel Raymond Lewis (1970) states:

> Throughout the nineteenth century precisely what constituted the navy's coastal defense function varied with changes in materiel and tactics; at any given moment, its exact nature was imperfectly agreed upon not only by congressmen and the public but by military and naval professionals as well. Some saw the role of the fleet as a simple extension of the harbor defenses; others saw it as a means of covering the long, unfortified stretches of coast; still others, as a complete and possibly more economical substitute for fortifications. But whatever the view, there was agreement that the Navy was to perform the same general function as the fortifications, either as a parallel or an adjunctive agency, or as an alternative to them.

Apart from the coordination problems addressed mainly by joint boards, the history of U.S. armed forces discloses three major developments that had a significant impact on the comfortable and simple two service–two element environment.

By the end of WWI, many experts had become aware that the conduct of warfare would never again be a simple matter of fighting on the land and the sea.

The first development was the establishment of the Marine Corps. Although marines had been enlisted for service in naval vessels from the beginning of the Revolution, it was not until 1798 that a corps of marines was created by act of Congress. Neither seamen nor soldiers, the corps nevertheless found itself a useful niche and contributed significantly to the nation's affairs in the following years.

Problems with the navy and army over what exactly the marines should do were chronic and were usually resolved by congressional action. A pertinent example was the repeated determination by the navy near the beginning of the twentieth century to remove marines from service aboard men-of-war. This conflict resulted in Congress generating an act in 1909 requiring that marines remain in the shipboard role. Problems regarding what the marines should do in operational terms reached a climax in the 1946–1947 efforts to codify the roles of all the services.

The second, and by all measure the greatest, challenge to land-sea symmetry in assignment of combat roles was the advent of military aircraft. It was not long after the historic 120-foot flight at Kitty Hawk in 1903 that the U.S. military evinced an interest in the prospective capability of the heavier-than-air machine. Shortly after the Wright Brothers procured their patent in 1906, the Army Signal Corps, with extraordinary vision, concluded a contract (incidentally, only one page in length) for the construction of one of the craft for use in observation and communications.

In the years immediately preceding World War I, the army, navy, and Marine Corps were committed to the perfection of an aviation capability in their operating forces. By the end of that conflict, many men in the army and navy had become aware that the conduct of warfare would never again be a simple matter of fighting on the land and the sea, that what went on in the air above them would be significant.

Between the two world wars, as the capability of the airplane grew, so did the role of the aviation force within the U.S. Army and its evolution toward autonomy. First, the Army Signal Corps was assigned the roles of aerial communication, liaison, and observation. There followed the U.S. Army Air Corps, and then the Army Air Forces. The last enjoyed a largely autonomous existence within the War Department, where it had strategic, tactical, and logistical authority for air combat activity. The equal status of the Army Ground Forces, Army Air Forces, and Army Service Forces was formalized for the first time in 1942. The navy had moved aggressively after World War I into the arena of combat air operations, creating its first three aircraft carriers (*Langley, Lexington,* and *Saratoga*) and a budding air logistic arm. The Marine Corps likewise developed a fighter and fighter-bomber capability.

As World War II approached and as air capabilities increased, conflicts developed over the assignment of aerial operational roles among the services, although they were deferred by the exigencies of combat. At the end of the war, the Army Air Forces was reorganized under the War Department General Staff to include the Strategic Air Command, the Tactical Air Command, and the Air Defense Command.

The year immediately following the Japanese surrender saw a rapid intensification in service competition for operational roles. There was conflict between the Army Ground Forces and the Army Air Forces in the matter of who should have the responsibility for close air support of ground elements, between the Army Air Forces and the navy over the strategic air function, between the army and the Marine Corps in the area of amphibious warfare. Probably most intense was the disagreement over whether the Army Air Forces should acquire independent service status separate from the army.

The issues quickly found their way into Congress in an intensive two-year reexamination of all service roles and functions and were finally resolved in a single statute, the National Security Act of 1947. It created the National Military Establishment under a secretary of defense and three executive departments of the army, navy and air force, and it formalized the wartime Joint Chiefs of Staff. In addition, it created a National Se-

The Pentagon in Arlington, Virginia, serves as the headquarters for the Department of Defense, which includes the Departments of the Army, Navy, and Air Force. Construction of the massive five-sided building was completed in 1943. (Department of Defense)

curity Council, the Central Intelligence Agency, and the National Security Resources Board. Amplified by the Key West Agreement of 21 April 1948 and six subsequent statutory revisions, the National Security Act remains the seminal treatment of roles and missions allocation and the most comprehensive ever undertaken by the United States Government.

The third development that tended to upset the symmetry of service combat roles was the advent and development of nuclear weapons, along with the maturation of multistage rocketry. These immense technological breakthroughs, coupled with developments in inertial guidance and laser technology, introduced wide fields for competition among the services for new or modified combat roles and for corresponding funding.

As early as 1950, the Joint Chiefs of Staff undertook to achieve a resolution to the many existing responsibility problems affecting the development and use of new weapons through a comprehensive recommendation to the secretary of defense. The recommendation, which the secretary approved, covered all of the then-existing missile developments. A procession of subsequent executive decisions further refined the detailed relationship among the services for weapons development and employment.

Over a period of two centuries, U.S. history portrays a constant evolution in the assignment of service combat roles. While national policy and national aspirations might be expected to have been the prime determinant in allocation of roles, it turns out that assignments have derived less from policy and less from the elements in which the services fight than from changes in the character and quality of the mechanisms with which they do the fighting. Therefore, just as constant developments in technology have been a major engine driving the assignment of service roles and functions, that same dynamic evolutionary force is expected to persist. As such, the interrelationship between those roles will be an ever-changing phenomenon.

BIBLIOGRAPHY

Augustine, Norman. *Augustine's Laws* (1982).

Caraley, Demetrios. *The Politics of Military Unification* (1966).

Fowler, William M., Jr. *Rebels Under Sail: The American Navy during the Revolution* (1968).

Hammond, Paul Y. *Organizing for Defense: The American Military Establishment in the Twentieth Century* (1961, repr. 1977).

Huntington, Samuel P. *The Soldier and the State* (1957).

Johnson, Woolsey. *History of the Organization of the Navy Department* (1933).

Keiser, Gordon W. *The Politics of Survival* (1975).

Kolodziej, Edward A. *The Uncommon Defense and Congress, 1945–1963* (1966).

Krulak, Victor H. *First to Fight* (1984).

———. *Organization for National Security* (1984).

Lewis, Emanuel Raymond. *Seacoast Fortifications of the United States: An Introductory History* (1979).

Schratz, Paul R. *Evolution of the American Military Establishment Since World War II* (1978).

Turner, E. S. *Gallant Gentlemen, A Portrait of the British Officer* (1956).

Weigley, Russell F. *History of the United States Army* (1967).

Williams, T. Harry. "The Committee on the Conduct of the War, An Experiment in Civilian Control." *Journal of the American Military* (1949).

Wolf, Richard I. *Basic Documents on Roles and Missions* (1987).

– VICTOR H. KRULAK

The Army

The central role of the United States Army, conduct of military operations on land, has been defined and changed by the policies and traditions of military affairs that have shaped the history of the United States. The survival of the first colonial settlements in America depended upon the ability of the colonists to conduct land warfare. The British colonists, however, also brought with them an aversion to a standing army, from earlier experience with such armies used for political change in the English civil wars of the seventeenth century. Thus, a reliance upon militias of armed citizens dates from the earliest American settlements.

COLONIAL ARMIES

All the American colonies formed militias, which performed well in defending their settlements. Generally, their effectiveness declined as the distance of the conflicts from their dwellings increased. The militiaman was disinclined to fight to the death for a cause not directly related to his land and vital interests.

Initially, militias consisted of all able-bodied males, but later, certain conditions allowed exceptions from service and members of some professions were exempted. Colonial compacts and laws required attendance at musters, at which basic military training was given by appointed or elected officers. Colonial militias were subject to the command of the governors of each colony, but legislatures exercised fiscal control, primarily to prevent their use by governors in political disputes.

The Indians were stealthy in approach when raiding a fort or settlement and were especially deadly in ambush.

The militias were trained in the linear tactics of the musket-powered armies of Europe. Training was rudimentary and unsuited for fighting the primary foe, the native American Indians. These tribes refused to form for a decisive engagement in the manner of European armies. The Indians were more stealthy in approach when raiding a fort or settlement and were especially deadly in ambush. The American colonists, however, quickly became adept woodsmen and hunters and, despite the informality of their militia associations, were better organized than the Indians. Most of the male colonists possessed shoulder weapons, and about one in twenty carried a rifle. While rifles had longer-range killing power, they were heavy and time-consuming to load and were also expensive. Thus, they were not in general use among military forces of the period. In fighting the Indians, the colonists learned to engage them advantageously by attacking them in their villages at night and in the winter, when they were most vulnerable. Light infantry units were formed in some colonies, as part of the regular armies of the European powers in America, but were trained to fight like the Indians.

A number of volunteer military organizations came into being. These provided additional, high-spirited forces whose training was often poor. As the colonies matured and expanded, the militias in the eastern cities and towns were also less vigorously trained and tested, and their drills became more social affairs than instructional sessions. Exceptions to this general decline in combat readiness of militia were in the southern colonies, where the militias were more active and mobile, often employed to apprehend runaway slaves, and maintained in a high state of effectiveness as security against slave rebellions. Militias on the frontier remained active, as the Indian threat was reinforced by contesting regular military organizations of the European powers. By the middle of the eighteenth century, the older militias had become training depots and armories from which volunteers and "selectees" were sent to participate in military expeditions.

Forts were built at the sites of the early settlements to protect inhabitants against Indian attacks. As the immigrant population increased, forts were established inland, generally at river crossings, to extend control along transportation routes and over larger areas. When America became a theater of the European wars for empire, forts were also built along the coast and on seaward approaches of major rivers. These forts were manned initially by local militias and later by volunteers under a variety of military contracts.

Colonists were committed to the European wars for empire, both in militia and volunteer aggregations, with support and occasional command by the regular forces of the European power that ruled each colony. They were involved in extensions of the wars between Great Britain, France, and Spain. Most of the military cam-

James Montgomery Flagg created this famous image for a World War I army recruiting poster. Pictured above is a World War II-era version of the famous poster. (National Archives)

paigns were fought on inland frontiers. In British America, the militias were most decisively engaged in the American phase of the Seven Years' War, called the French and Indian War in America. Militias accompanied British expeditions to drive the French away from the Appalachian frontier and to conquer Canada. Although they lost some battles on the western frontier, the British, with American militia in assistance, finally defeated the French in Canada, the most decisive engagement being the capture of Quebec in 1759.

From their combined military experiences, the colonists gained a hearty dislike of the regular British military leaders, while the British reinforced their unfavorable opinions of the fighting abilities of the colonial militia. The militias were found to be poorly trained and lacking in discipline, disinclined to withstand the rigors of a long campaign, and unsteady in close combat. Nevertheless, the Americans gained considerable military experience in the wars for empire. They also developed a casual attitude toward military matters and an overweening self-confidence in military affairs, which is still a characteristic of Americans in war today.

To attribute the failings of colonial and revolutionary war militias to an antimilitary bias is to misread American history. In the same vein, the term "peace-loving" is misapplied to Americans. In their short history, the peoples of the United States have fought ten wars and hundreds of minor military engagements. Rather, it is better to describe Americans as relatively unmilitary in manner yet inclined to fight quickly when they feel their interests to be threatened. Such dispositions have affected the readiness and performance of the U.S. Army throughout its history.

THE ARMIES OF THE AMERICAN REVOLUTION

In 1774, the First Continental Congress urged the American colonies to strengthen their militia in recognition of the likelihood of some form of armed struggle with Great Britain. On 15 June 1775, the Second Continental Congress appointed George Washington commanding general of the Continental army, consisting of the militia of the northern colonies then besieging the British in Boston. Congress also authorized enlistment in the Continental army, increasing its strength authorizations as the war continued. This was the beginning of the United States Army.

Washington's mission was to preserve the liberties of the colonists by preventing British forces from imposing political controls. The relatively undisciplined forces he commanded in Boston were to contain the British in the harbor and lower town. They performed with increasing efficiency as their training and numbers improved, but the curse of militia, the proclivity to dribble away as a campaign extended in time or distance from its base, plagued Washington at and after Boston and for the entire war.

After the signing of the Declaration of Independence in 1776, the Second Continental Congress assumed the task of augmenting and sustaining the Continental army for the duration of the war. The Congress, forced to assume executive as well as legislative roles, could only request of the newly independent states that they furnish troops, munitions, and sustenance for the Continental army based upon demographic formulas that were much disputed and seldom followed. The Congress and Washington were forced to develop a strategy for the war in the same ad hoc fashion as they addressed their governing powers.

Initially, the role of the Continental army was to prevent the British from seizing control of any inland area of significant population. Following the abandonment of New York by Washington's defeated forces, the army was positioned to attempt to protect the Congress at Philadelphia. When the British occupied Philadelphia in September 1777 (and Congress moved to the interior of Pennsylvania), Washington's strategy consisted of preserving the Continental army by refusing decisive battle except on favorable terms and remaining inland of the head of navigation of the major rivers to avoid the concentrated might of the British army and navy.

While the British sought to isolate the rebellion and control the areas of major population, Washington and Congress attempted to sustain the Continental army, reinforce and train its troops, and count on time to erode the British position and give legitimacy to the American cause. The loss of Philadelphia was offset by the surrender of an entire British army to the Americans at Saratoga, New York, on 17 October 1777. That victory brought France, Spain, and Holland into war against the British and was the turning point in the American Revolution, although it was not so appreciated at that time.

The winter of 1777–1778 was the low point of the American army. As it suffered through a cold and hungry winter at Valley Forge, its strength fell to a low of three thousand and enlistments stopped, despite increases in bonuses, and greater enforcement of conscription only brought in a few undesirables. It was under these adverse circumstances, however, that the Continental army was forged into a fighting machine. Denied reinforcements, the British commander, Major General Sir Henry Clinton, withdrew his army to his base in New York, pursued by Washington and his hardened and trained Continental army.

Ever seeking a loyalist population upon which to restructure their American empire, the British launched major offensives in the South in 1779. British forces captured Savannah and later Charleston, where they found loyalist sympathies. Loyalist units were organized, and the British swept into the sparsely populated interior of South Carolina and Georgia. Some of the most severe fighting occurred in the backcountry of the South. Major General Nathanael Greene, who took command of the American forces in the South in 1780, employed regular columns and guerrilla forces in deft combinations to force the British out of the Carolinas.

As the external threat subsided, the idle Continental army erupted in demands for pay and pensions.

The British commander in the South, Lord Charles Cornwallis, established a base at Yorktown, Virginia, and moved the bulk of his forces there in 1781. Meanwhile, a French army and fleet had arrived in the United States. Washington moved the Continental army and the cooperating French force south and besieged Cornwallis in Yorktown. Victory of the French fleet over a British fleet off the Virginia Capes sealed the fate of Cornwallis, as his seaward line of communication was severed. Washington conducted a deliberate siege, moving his lines forward by considerable digging of trenches and some sharp fighting. U.S. and French forces numbered fifteen thousand; the besieged British had about eight thousand. Unable to reinforce or resupply his force, Cornwallis surrendered on 19 October 1781. Although British forces remained in America until conclusion of the Peace of Paris in 1783, the victory at Yorktown assured the Americans the freedom they sought.

As the external threat subsided, the fragile American Confederation shook with internal disputes long ignored. The idle Continental army erupted in demands for pay and pensions. Faced with these demonstrations of the political power of a standing army, many in the Congress called for dissolution of the military, while others called attention to the remaining threats from the Indians, the British on the Ohio frontier, and the admittedly less serious threat from the Spanish in Florida. In April 1783, Congress appointed a committee to determine a future military policy and an appropriate peacetime military force.

THE ARMY OF THE CONFEDERATION

At the request of Congress, Washington submitted his "Sentiments on a Peace Establishment" on 2 May 1783. A modest proposal, it called for a regular force of 2,630 soldiers to garrison the posts on the frontiers. The major feature of the plan was his call for a "well-organized militia," under national control, to respond to major threats. To support the small regular forces, a system of armories and a military academy were also recommended. After much dispute over the need for a peacetime army (as opposed to the dangers of the same), the Congress of the Confederation directed, on 2 June 1784, that the Continental army be disbanded. The act of disbandment was reinforced by the statement, "standing armies in time of peace are inconsistent with the principles of republican government." Almost as an afterthought, Congress authorized the retention of eighty artillerymen to guard the federal munitions and military stores. The next day, reflecting on its hasty decision for complete disarmament, Congress authorized the raising of a regiment of seven hundred militia, the First American Regiment, to garrison the western posts.

The postwar surge of population into the Ohio River frontier resulted in Indian retaliation and demands upon Congress for military action to protect the settlers. Because the states had ceded these western lands to the Confederation government, it was up to Congress to deal with the Indian problem. A further military challenge came in 1786, when Massachusetts farmers, under the leadership of Daniel Shays, revolted over tax-related foreclosures on farms and moved in armed offensive against the Massachusetts Assembly. Although militia forces defeated the rebels, the uprising revealed the weakness of the military forces of the Confederation to deal with challenges to its governmental responsibilities.

Military weakness was one of the problems of the Confederation that provoked the establishment of the Constitution of the United States in 1787. Under the new government, the president was designated commander in chief of the army and navy and of the militia of the states when called into national service. Only Congress could declare war, however, "raise and support Armies," and "provide and maintain a Navy." Congress was empowered to call "forth the Militia to execute the Laws of the Union, suppress Insurrections and repel Invasions." Congress was further empowered to establish regulations for "organizing, arming, and disciplining the Militia," and for governing the militia when in national service. Thus were established dualities in federal control of military forces between the president and Congress, and between federal and state governments with respect to control of militia.

To execute its military responsibilities, Congress carried over the War Department of the Confederation into the new government and reappointed (at President

Washington's nomination) Henry Knox as secretary of war. Resisting the proposal of Washington and the Federalists for a nationally controlled militia, Congress debated until 1792, when it passed the Uniform Militia Act. This act, which remained the basic militia law until the twentieth century, established universal military service by requiring enrollment in the militia of every able-bodied white man between eighteen and forty-five years of age. The act allowed for exemptions from service, which the states did establish.

This compromise between federal and state control of militias failed to provide for a national army. Congress moved slowly to strengthen the existing army as the Indian threat increased in the Northwest, supported by the British. Under pressure from Congress, the small active army, with the aid of badly organized militia and volunteers, launched two campaigns against the Indians in the Northwest Territory in 1790 that resulted in disastrous failures.

In reaction, Congress reopened negotiations with the Indians as a measure to prevent costly military campaigns. It also acted to strengthen the army. Knox organized the new army into the Legion of the United States. President Washington selected Anthony Wayne, of revolutionary war fame, to command the legion. Wayne, who insisted upon training his force before committing them to battle, launched a campaign in September 1793 with the legion, reinforced by militia from the Kentucky and frontier territories. At the Battle of Fallen Timbers on 20 August 1794, he decisively defeated and scattered an Indian band of five hundred braves. The defeat signaled the end of the Indian resistance in the Ohio Valley.

Simultaneously, the reinvigorated national government put down the Whisky Rebellion of frontiersmen in the western region of Pennsylvania. Jeffersonian Republicans in Congress, fearful of the power of the federal army, caused the abolition of the legion in 1796, but a reduced federal army remained for "pacification of the frontier." This task remained the major mission of the peacetime army for the next century.

THE ARMY OF THE REPUBLIC

Early in the nineteenth century, warring European powers began blockading each other's coasts and disrupting international commerce, which forced the United States to build a navy and to expand the army again. In 1798 war hysteria provoked the rapid increase of the U.S. army to more than ten thousand men, and plans were made to invade Canada and Florida and to repel anticipated invasions, alternately expected by forces of France and Great Britain. The war furor died, without land conflict, at the turn of the century. With the election of President Thomas Jefferson in 1801, army authorizations were rapidly reduced to the old peacetime numbers, and the army was redirected to the frontier. In the Military Peace Establishment Act of 1802, a "Republican" army was authorized, but it was to remain "out of the purview of civilized society." The act authorized the establishment of a military academy at West Point, New York, as a means of "republicanizing" the officer corps of the army and for the training of engineers to improve the nation's roads and waterways.

In 1798 war hysteria provoked the rapid increase of the U.S. army to more than ten thousand men.

The Republicans found the army useful in exploring and settling the frontier. After purchasing the Louisiana Territory in 1803, President Jefferson directed Captain Meriwether Lewis and Lieutenant William Clark to explore and map this uncharted wilderness. An army expedition departed from St. Louis, Missouri, in 1804, crossed the continent to the Pacific Ocean, sketched the route and recorded their travails, and returned east to report in 1806. Subsequently, the army established forts along the routes of the explorers, pioneers, trappers, and settlers, guided and protected caravans of immigrants, and both fought and protected the Indians in the territories as the burgeoning population of the nation expanded westward.

THE WAR OF 1812

The seizure by Great Britain of U.S. ships and seamen on the oceans and its support of Indian depredations along the western frontier of the Republic led to war between the United States and Great Britain. Unconcerned about the poor state of its military forces, the government of the United States declared war in 1812 and simultaneously voted to increase the army and navy. Regular army authorized strength was increased to thirty-five thousand; fifty thousand volunteers were called for; and a militia of one hundred thousand was to be activated. President James Madison appointed a number of revolutionary war veteran officers to command the augmented army forces and urged these leaders to invade Canada. U.S. offensives were launched around the Great Lakes from Detroit, Niagara, and up the Hudson to take Montreal. U.S. offensives and British counteroffensives in this theater resulted in no significant gains during the entire war.

The weaknesses of the informal U.S. military system were exemplified by the rout of forces defending Washington, D.C., and the subsequent burning of the capital by the British. The ability of Americans to fight when properly led, however, was exhibited in July 1814 at Lundy's Lane, near Niagara Falls, and at Baltimore and in 1815 in the final campaign at New Orleans. U.S. naval victories were bright spots in a war in which the United States won largely because of British struggles with France. An exception to the very bad leadership exhibited on both sides was the effective professional leadership of some of the younger regular officers, especially those from the U.S. Military Academy (USMA) at West Point.

THE ARMY IN WESTWARD EXPANSION

In 1815, Congress reduced the regular army to an authorized strength of ten thousand officers and men. The larger-than-usual peacetime figure resulted from recognition by Congress of the continuing Indian problem, of the need for coastal forts, and of the role of the army in improving the nation's transportation system. In conjunction with modernizing the navy as the "first line of national defense," the U.S. government allocated $800,000 to build a system of fifty coastal forts. Army engineers began the work, which grew in scope until after the Civil War, when development of rifled guns on ships made the forts obsolete.

As the industrial revolution increased the nation's power and mobility in the first half of the nineteenth century, the army slowly improved its weaponry. Eli Whitney's development of interchangeable parts allowed for better machining of weapons, and the development of the conoidal bullet increased the

The U.S. Military Academy was established in 1802 at West Point, New York. Robert E. Lee, Ulysses S. Grant, John J. Pershing, Douglas MacArthur, Dwight D. Eisenhower, George Patton, and Norman Schwarzkopf were all trained at West Point. (Department of Defense)

range and effectiveness of the soldier's individual weapon.

Since its earliest years, the Engineer Corps of the U.S. Army had a dual civil-military role. From their center at West Point, engineers joined the army to construct forts and military facilities. Army engineers were also assigned to build the transportation infrastructure that propelled the expansion of the nation across the West and to construct public buildings and roads. Many of the graduates of the academy left the service to lead in developing transportation and industrial facilities in the rapidly expanding economy. Among the major projects initiated by the army were the Chesapeake and Ohio Canal and the Baltimore and Ohio Railroad. Largely because of the infusion of USMA officer graduates, the officer corps of the regular army became more professional. In 1824 the army opened the Artillery School of Practice at Fortress Monroe, Virginia, the first post-graduate school for USMA cadets, commissioned primarily in the coast artillery.

The peacetime regular army was distributed in a great circle of small forts about four thousand miles in circumference—from the Atlantic and Gulf coasts up the Mississippi River to the Canadian border at Mackinac and Detroit, then east along the Great Lakes. The eastern and coastal posts were manned by artillery, the western by infantry. By 1820, foreign threats having subsided, Congress called on Secretary of War John Calhoun to reduce the regular army to about six thousand. Calhoun submitted a plan for an expansible army, with the small peacetime force heavy with officers and noncommissioned officers, but the plan was not accepted. The army was instead reduced to seven regiments of infantry; three general officers were authorized.

Following the pattern set by Lewis and Clark, army officers at posts west of the Mississippi were sent out to survey vast areas of the Great Plains and Rocky Mountains. These survey parties contacted Indian tribes and represented the federal government in negotiations. They also made trails and extended the lines of forts across the West. In 1824, Calhoun established the Bureau of Indian Affairs, which oversaw Indian removal and related matters until 1849, when it became an agency of the Department of the Interior.

Indian removal west of the Mississippi River and related fighting with Indian tribes that resisted removal was the major role assigned the peacetime army in the nineteenth century. Most of the eastern and midwestern tribes reluctantly moved west, their movements escorted and supported by detachments of soldiers.

The Seminole wars in Florida, beginning in 1816 and extending at least until 1842, involved army regular and militia units in waterborne raids and counterguerrilla campaigning deep into the swamps and jungles of interior Florida. The fighting was sporadic, the service enervating, and disease rampant. Runaway slaves joined the Seminole bands and war became associated with apprehension of slaves. The cession of Florida to the United States by Spain in 1819 removed foreign support for the Seminole. With the removal of resisting bands of Indians from the swamps to west of the Mississippi, the war was gradually reduced to occasional hostile contacts.

Army officers and units were directed to take action in domestic disturbances during this period. During the nullification controversy of 1830–1831 in South Carolina, President Andrew Jackson ordered army forces strengthened in the region. Major General Winfield Scott defused this political confrontation by the judicious movement of troops while he consulted with regional political and militia leaders. Scott was later dispatched to terminate the confrontation of militias and volunteers on both sides of the Canadian border in Maine during the Aroostock War (1838–1839). Again, Scott moved troops and negotiated to resolve the issues without fighting. In 1834, Jackson ordered federal troops to quell riots of workers on the Chesapeake and Ohio Canal—the first use of federal troops in a labor conflict. The militias of some of the southern states were also employed in quelling slave revolts, the most notorious being Nat Turner's insurrection in 1831 in Virginia.

THE MEXICAN WAR

The annexation of Texas by the United States in 1845 led to war with Mexico. At the onset of war, the U.S. Army totaled 7,365, and Mexico had approximately thirty-two thousand men under arms, but both armies were woefully unprepared for war. Upon rupture of negotiations with Mexico over the issue, President James Polk ordered Major General Zachary Taylor, commander of army units in the Southwest, to move his forces into an area along the Rio Grande, that river being in dispute as the southern boundary of Texas. U.S. forces were mostly untrained volunteers, leavened by a small regular army with good junior leadership. The first clashes, at Palo Alto and Resaca de la Palma in May 1846, resulted in surprising American victories and a U.S. declaration of war.

President Polk, in consultation with Secretary of War William Marcy and the commanding general of the army, Major General Winfield Scott, hastily drew up a campaign plan for commitment of the army into Mexico. Taylor was told to seize the sparsely populated provinces of northern Mexico. After much discussion and disagreement between Scott (a Whig) and the Democrat Polk, Scott launched a joint army-navy invasion of Mexico at Veracruz, then proceeded into the interior to capture Mexico City.

Regular, militia, and volunteer units were committed on long overland marches to reinforce Taylor in Mexico, while other units were deployed to assist in seizing California. These were challenging missions for the provincial military forces of the United States, requiring command, communications, and logistical support on a scope far beyond existing capabilities. Reinforced, Taylor's ragged force advanced into northern Mexico, defeating larger Mexican armies at Monterrey and Buena Vista in 1847.

The victory over Mexico convinced the American people that their militia and volunteers from civil society could meet all military challenges.

Scott's invasion of Mexico was a bold and optimistic operation for an army and navy that had no experience in working together or in conducting an amphibious landing on a hostile coast. Landing unopposed at Veracruz on 9 March, Scott's forces advanced into central Mexico, defeating larger Mexican armies at Cerro Gordo. Although victorious, Scott was also in a dilemma. His militia were leaving in droves, as their short terms of duty expired, and replacements were not in the offing. At his rear, cholera and malaria were rampant. Scott made a bold strategic decision and advanced his small force into the heart of Mexico, cutting his forces away from their line of communication and resupply. By audacious movement, sound tactics, and a lot of luck, Scott's forces assaulted and conquered Mexico City in September.

The victory over Mexico convinced those in authority, and the American people at large, that their militia and volunteers from civil society could meet all military challenges. In that frame of reference, the regular army was reduced in 1849 to eleven thousand and assigned primarily to border posts throughout the West. Army engineers were engaged in surveying the route for a railroad between the Mississippi and the western coast in the period immediately before the Civil War. Engineers also supervised the construction of the north and south wings of the nation's Capitol and the initiation of the Washington Aqueduct. In 1855, the army adopted the minié ball and began issuing rifled muskets. In 1857 the Utah expedition explored the Great Salt Lake area. In that same year, the army supervised elections in Kansas, which resulted in a free-state legislature. In 1859, army forces under Colonel Robert E. Lee retook the federal arsenal at Harpers Ferry from John Brown's group of militant abolitionists and captured Brown, who was later hanged.

THE ARMIES IN THE CIVIL WAR

At the beginning of the Civil War, the regular U.S. Army was at an approximate strength of sixteen thousand. President Abraham Lincoln initially called for seventy-five thousand militia to be brought into federal service for a three-month period. As the upper South joined the Confederacy, in the summer of 1861, Lincoln increased the regular army by eleven regiments and called for forty additional regiments of volunteers to be recruited for three years of service. The northern population of twenty-two million (including the border states) versus that of the Confederate states, nine million (including 3.5 million slaves), did not translate into a military advantage until late in the war. In July 1861 the Union had approximately 187,000 men under arms, while the Confederates had about 112,000. The Union strength advantage did not guarantee dominance of force on battlefields, however, because the Confederate militias were concentrated and positioned for their mission of defense while Northern forces were scattered.

The existing regular army being mostly in the West, it was necessary for the War Department to constitute a force to defend the capital and to take early offensive action to suppress the insurrection—a task that, it was initially estimated, would take only a few months. During the summer after the surrender of Fort Sumter in April 1861, fifty thousand federalized forces encamped around Washington under the command of Brigadier General Irvin McDowell. Directly opposing them were twenty-thousand Confederates under Brigadier General Pierre Beauregard. Under pressure from Congress and the media, Lincoln ordered the federal forces to advance on the Confederates. McDowell moved south and attacked at Bull Run stream, north of Manassas, Virginia, on 21 July 1861. Beauregard's troops, reinforced by nine thousand troops from the Shenandoah Valley, drove the Union forces from the field in mixed fighting. The victory gave a boost to Confederate morale and forced Lincoln and Union leaders to the understanding that a long struggle was in store.

Union strategy developed slowly as the scope of the war became apparent. The blockading of the Confederate coastline was an early action, which was effective, in the main, because of the reluctance of foreign nations to challenge it. The Union strategy took advantage of the rivers west of the Appalachian Mountains to drive into the heart of the Confederacy, while the rivers in the East, running across the federal line of advance, gave the Confederates a defensive advantage. As it was finally executed, Union strategy isolated the regions of the Confederacy. First, the Union gained control of the Mississippi, thus preventing reinforcement and supply of the war from the trans-Mississippi West. Second, the die-hard lower South was cut from the upper South by advance to the sea at Savannah. Finally, the eastern Confederate armies were destroyed by concentration from the north and south. Confederate strategy was simpler—to defend the territory of the states in rebellion, then gain legitimacy and support from foreign powers by playing the "cotton card." The Confederates also hoped that support for the war in the North, never strong, would erode with time.

The war in the West resulted in slow and bloody victory for the Union, as the Mississippi was cleared and Union armies ground their way south and east into the lower South. In the East, Confederate generalship stymied the Union power advantage for more than three years, until Confederate warmaking power was exhausted. By the spring of 1865, Union armies from the West reached the Atlantic and turned north. In the East, the Union strategy of attrition, which was carried out, at great cost in blood, by General Ulysses Grant against General Robert E. Lee's Army of Northern Virginia, caused the Confederacy to crumble. Lee's surrender at Appomattox Court House in Virginia on 9 April 1865 sounded the death knell.

THE ARMY IN THE DARK AGES

After a two-day victory march in Washington, the Army of the Potomac was demobilized in 1865. Of the one million volunteers who were in uniform at the end of the war, fifty-two thousand were sent to the Mexican border to threaten the French in control of Mexico. After swift French evacuation, these volunteers were also disbanded. In 1866, Congress, anticipating problems in restoring the nation, authorized a peacetime army of 54,302, but they did not provide funds for a force of that size. Despite commitments to Reconstruction and pacifying the Plains Indians, the army was progressively reduced to a strength of 27,442 by 1876. It remained at approximately that level until the Spanish-American War. The role of the regular army was, as before, primarily to provide for internal security. In the Civil War, Americans had verified the effectiveness of their emer-

For most of its history, the United States Army used pack mules and horses to carry troops and supplies. These government mules and packers were photographed near the Mexican border in 1883. (National Archives)

gency armies, and, again, in the absence of a postwar threat from beyond their borders, the United States refused to provide a standing army for future contingencies.

Reassigned to the small, dusty posts on the western Plains, the regular army in the last half of the nineteenth century fought and persuaded the Indians to accept the seizure of their lands by the encroaching settlers. Criticized for insensitivity to the Indians by humanitarians in the East, the army was equally condemned by settlers on the frontier for not striking them down. Led by a mixture of officers who hated Indians and others sympathetic with their plight, the army carried on a pacification campaign, which lessened the Indian threat by a combination of counterguerrilla operations and territorial control. The Battle of the Little Bighorn in 1876 called national attention to the Indian problem, but no better solution resulted than subjugation of the Indians and their cultures. In 1890, the Census Bureau announced that the frontier was no more. Slowly, the small, isolated army posts in the West were closed as the requirement declined for security for the surrounding regions.

The post–Civil War Congress, rejecting Lincoln's plan (which President Andrew Johnson attempted to execute) for reintegration of the Confederate states into the Union, directed the military occupation and government of the defeated Confederacy by passage of the Reconstruction Acts. The acts divided the South into five military districts, each commanded by an army general. The army was charged with not only securing the areas and the freed slaves therein, but also with registering voters and holding elections, appointing officials, conducting court trials, and approving state constitutions and legislation. Commanding General Grant opined that the army had "entire control over the civil governments." The defeated South did not accept the Republican governments, whose officers included freed slaves. Guerrilla warfare sponsored by the Ku Klux Klan spread across the occupied South. The army's operations against the Klan had little effect on its terrorism, and few army officers relished the occupational task. Criticized by northern and southern political leaders, the army was happy to be relieved of the duty in 1877.

Freed from occupation of the South, the regular army was quickly assigned another unpalatable task—strikebreaking. In 1877 a wave of strikes began on the railroads and in the mines and spread to urban labor. When state militiamen refused to move against some of the strikers, President Rutherford Hayes asked the army to restore order in the mines in Idaho. Thus began a period of military intervention in labor disputes, in which the regular army was the force of last resort, continuing into the twentieth century. These interventions led to the strengthening of state militias, increasingly called the National Guard. As labor troubles increased in the industrializing nation, National Guard units were called out frequently to restore order, and the regular army was gradually relieved of this task.

During these "dark ages" of service in isolated posts, the army leadership improved its professionalism. Leading the educational effort was General William T. Sherman, commanding general of the army from 1869 to 1883. Sherman established schools for officers and fostered military associations for the study of military affairs.

During the Alaska gold rush of 1898, the army established safety zones in the Yukon Territory.

After the purchase of Alaska in 1867, the army established a Department of Alaska and relieved Russia at posts in the Aleutians. In 1869, Captain Charles Raymond and a team of army engineers explored the northern coast of Alaska and the Yukon River. In 1881, Lieutenants Patrick Ray and Adolphus W. Greely led teams of soldiers on arctic expeditions for meteorological testing. The next year Lieutenant James Lockwood led a team exploring the northern coast of Greenland. In 1892 the army adopted the Krag-Jörgensen repeating rifle, which used smokeless powder cartridges. The artillery adopted breech-loading, rifled guns. During the Alaska gold rush of 1898, the army established safety zones in the Yukon Territory for the protection of civil life and property in the mining areas. The Signal Corps also established a communications system for the isolated settlements of Alaska.

AN ARMY FOR THE AMERICAN EMPIRE

On 20 April 1898, Congress declared Cuba to be free and independent and authorized President William McKinley to use military force to expel Spain from the island. Five days later, Congress declared that a state of war existed with Spain, and in May the president called for 125,000 volunteers. Naval battles in Manila Bay in the Philippines and Santiago de Cuba Bay were decisive victories for the United States over Spain, but the army expedition to free Cuba was an exemplar of unpreparedness in action.

The small and scattered regular army was ordered to expand, and, at the same time, it was to take command of and train a flood of volunteers arriving at camps in the Southeast. In haste, a badly organized, corps-sized force was dispatched to seize Santiago. The expedition of seventeen thousand, under Major General William R. Shafter, was outnumbered by Spanish forces in Santiago province. Shafter's forces landed twenty miles east of Santiago and began a disorganized march toward the Spanish defenses. With spirit and a great deal of luck, U.S. troops seized Kettle and San Juan hills and the defenses of El Caney, driving in the Spanish outer defenses. Fearful of imminent Spanish reinforcement, Shafter demanded surrender of Spanish forces in the city on 2 July. The following day, U.S. naval forces decisively defeated the Spanish fleet as it attempted to exit Santiago de Cuba Bay. Negotiations led to the surrender of Spanish forces in the province on 17 July. Puerto Rico was easily taken by an expedition of U.S. soldiers commanded by Lieutenant General Nelson Miles, who was the commanding general of the army at that time. The city of Manila fell to the Americans under Major General Wesley Merritt on 13 August 1898. Spain agreed to a peace treaty on 10 December that freed Cuba, ceded Puerto Rico and Guam to the United States, and granted the United States sovereignty over the Philippines for a payment of $20 million. The United States was now a world power, with overseas possessions in Latin America and across the Pacific in Asia.

Congressional and media criticism of poor management of the invasion led to reorganization of the War Department and improvements in staffing. The new secretary of war, Elihu Root, who took office in 1899, established the General Staff and attempted to place the semi-independent bureaus under the chief of staff. He also founded the Army War College. Root's success was marginal in modernizing the War Department, as he was fought by both long-term bureau chiefs and their friends in Congress. However, the staffing and planning system he established did improve the execution of future contingencies and the support of army forces later committed into battle. In 1903, Congress passed the Dick Act, establishing the National Guard as a federal military force and improving peacetime support of reserve forces.

Following the Spanish-American War, the U.S. Army governed and pacified the newly acquired possessions. Possession of the distant Philippine Islands, however, provoked a revolt against the U.S. occupying army. The Philippine Insurrection (1899–1902) was an early rejection of the U.S. policy of paternalistic hegemony. Convinced that Filipinos were not ready for independence, U.S. military and civil authorities employed a congeries of force and assistance. Major General Elwell Otis, military governor of the Philippines, launched an offensive that quickly defeated Filipino forces in conventional battles; fighting the Philippine guerrillas was a more difficult task for the U.S. Army. Nevertheless, pacification proceeded apace, with improvements in the economy, transportation, communications, health, education, and governmental services. The appointment of William Howard Taft as civil governor of the Philippines on 1 September 1900 began the civilianization of U.S. rule. U.S. Army personnel in the Philippines peaked at seventy-five thousand, half of whom were volunteers who enlisted for the campaign. As Philippine constabulary were recruited, U.S. forces were reduced, but army elements fought guerrillas on the southern islands for many years after 1902.

In July 1900, five thousand U.S. Army and Marine Corps troops were committed to Peking, China, as part of the China relief expedition during the Boxer Rebellion. Although the commitment was short, it was another indication of growing U.S. interest in the Pacific. This projection of power into the Pacific was mainly by naval ships and bases, but the U.S. Army established departments in Hawaii and the Philippines, and the Fifteenth Infantry Regiment remained in China.

On 18 April 1906, San Francisco, California, was struck by a strong earthquake. The army established law and security in the city, fed and sheltered the homeless, reestablished transportation and communications, and administered to the populace until the resumption of civil government. Also in 1906, at the request of the Cuban president, following the eruption of civil war, the Army of Cuban Pacification was committed to secure that island, institute sanitation projects, and cooperate with local officials in reestablishing civil government. U.S. Army troops were withdrawn from the island in early 1909.

At President Theodore Roosevelt's suggestion, the army undertook to study the use of airplanes. In 1907 the Signal Corps formed an Aeronautical Division to manage aerial activities, including balloons, airships, and airplanes. In 1909 the army purchased its first airplane, a Wright Flyer. Also in 1907, President Roosevelt turned over construction of the Panama Canal to the army, after civil engineers had failed to get the project underway. Lieutenant Colonel George Goethals headed the difficult construction project, which was completed in 1914. During medical experiments in Cuba in 1900, army surgeon Major Walter Reed discovered the cause and later the cure for yellow fever.

U.S. relations with Mexico deteriorated during the early twentieth century as revolutions within Mexico continued and incidents increased along the border. In 1911 a provisional division of U.S. troops was assembled along the Mexican border. In April 1914, after Mexican seizure of a naval launch occasioned a confrontation in Tampico, U.S. naval personnel and marines were put ashore at Veracruz and occupied the port, skirmishing with Mexican troops for several days. On 28 April, army troops under Major General Frederick Funston relieved the navy ashore and took command of army and marines at Veracruz. Funston established local military government but avoided offensive action from his enclave. With the overthrow of the Mexican government by a regime more friendly to the United States, forces were withdrawn.

Mexican civil war continued in 1915, resulting in an armed invasion of U.S. territory on 8–9 March 1916 by a rebel force of about five hundred led by Francisco "Pancho" Villa. The raiders struck the town of Columbus, New Mexico, and a garrison of U.S. cavalry. U.S. soldiers repulsed the attack, killing one hundred of the raiders; ten civilians and fourteen soldiers were killed. By order of President Woodrow Wilson, ten thousand U.S. troops under the command of Brigadier General John J. Pershing were committed to a "punitive expedition" into Mexico to kill or capture Villa and his band. The expedition moved in several columns and penetrated four hundred miles into Mexico. Some desultory contact was made with Villistas and with the forces of Mexican President Venustiano Carranza. After diplomatic exchanges, the U.S. expedition was withdrawn. Because of all its commitments from 1898 to 1917, active army (regular and activated militia/volunteer) strength remained at a high peacetime rate of eighty to ninety thousand until U.S. entry into World War I.

THE U.S. ARMY IN THE GREAT WAR

When the United States declared war on Germany on 6 April 1917, the War Department was unprepared for commitment of the army to a war zone. President Wil-

In 1865, the 26th U.S. Colored Volunteer Infantry paraded at Camp William Penn in Pennsylvania. Although African-Americans had served in previous wars, the Union army did not call blacks into service during the Civil War until faced with manpower shortages. (National Archives)

son, however, concluded that it would be necessary for the army to fight a decisive campaign in order for the United States to influence a subsequent peace settlement. The active army (including federalized National Guard) totaled 213,557. The government quickly enacted military conscription, and the army hastily planned for receiving, equipping, and training up to four million men. The War Department organized the divisions according to a "square" plan of four maneuver units in each organization up to the division. This made the U.S. divisions, at an authorized strength of twenty-eight thousand, as large as most corps of the warring armies. The War Department initially planned its training base in the United States to provide for the deployment of an army of one million in France. As requirements for the immediate shipment of combat units became more urgent, personnel and training plans and programs were revised and scrapped weekly; training camps and headquarters responded to the most urgent demands by stripping units and individuals in various stages of training to fill units being shipped overseas. The result was an uneven flow of personnel, neither trained nor programmed for combat. In 1917, the army grew to a strength of 421,000.

Pershing was instructed to "cooperate with the forces of the other countries employed against the enemy."

On 26 May 1917, Major General Pershing, recently returned from the Punitive Expedition in Mexico, was appointed commander of the American Expeditionary Forces (AEF), which comprised the land force sent to fight on the western front in France. Pershing was instructed by Secretary of War Newton D. Baker to "cooperate with the forces of the other countries employed against the enemy" but was also told that "the forces of the United States are a separate and distinct component." Pershing and a small planning staff arrived in France on 13 June 1917. In coordination with the Allies, the AEF established a U.S. sector in Lorraine, in northeastern France. The first U.S. fighting force, a contingent of the First Division, arrived in France on 26 June 1917.

The organizational task for the AEF headquarters was daunting—to create and position an administrative, training, and logistical support structure for a complete theater of war at the same time that great numbers of personnel were arriving. Ultimately, two million men were processed through this system, and fifteen million tons of equipment and supplies were forwarded to the fighting forces. Pershing directed a three-phase program of training integrated with combat experience. His emphasis upon marksmanship and "open warfare" tactics was somewhat inappropriate to the fortified, impacted French battlefields. To manage the administration and logistics for the U.S. theater in France, Pershing created the Services of Supply on 13 March 1918. By the end of 1917, the AEF had four combat divisions in France and two more en route from the United States.

By the end of 1917, the Central Powers (read Germans) had accomplished the first part of their plan—to defeat the Russians, then concentrate their forces on the western front before the Americans could intervene in sufficient numbers to stop their offensive. The Allies knew that the German attack was coming early in 1918, and on 21 March, the great German offensive struck in the Somme and Lys sectors of the western front. Led by specially trained assault troops, the offensive broke the three-year stalemate, and the leading elements of the Germans drove all the way to the Marne River. The Allied leaders appealed to Pershing, then directly to President Wilson, for U.S. combat troops to reinforce their armies. Pershing agreed to provide the trained U.S. divisions in France to the Allied armies to contain the German advance. The United States later agreed to send to France the combat units of six divisions, without their supporting and logistical units, to fight in Allied armies. Pershing got the Allies to agree that these divisions would be returned to his control after the German offensive was stopped. The U.S. divisions in France were flung into the fighting with little preparation or an opportunity to assess the situation into which they were committed, but the spirit and drive of fresh reinforcements strengthened the Allied defenses. The German drives halted on 17 July 1918.

By the summer of 1918, one million U.S. troops were in France and three hundred thousand were scheduled to arrive each month thereafter. As the Allies began planning for a general offensive, Pershing demanded, and achieved, the creation of an American army, rather than the assignment of all U.S. divisions in France to that army (excepting those with the British). The First U.S. Army was activated in Lorraine on 10 August 1918. The first offensive for this army was the elimination of the enemy salient in the Allied lines in the vicinity of St. Mihiel. The St. Mihiel offensive, which began on 12 September 1918, was a swift success, clearing the salient and capturing fifteen thousand enemies in two days.

The Allied supreme commander, Marshal Ferdinand Foch, directed the splitting of the U.S. forces for his upcoming general offensive. Pershing objected to the planned separation of his forces and, after acrimonious exchanges, the U.S. troops were given an offensive mission in the Meuse-Argonne sector. The Meuse-Argonne was a vital hinge of the German defenses on the western front, with strong fortifications covering German lines of communication into their Laon Bulge. Because the more experienced U.S. divisions were still involved in the St. Mihiel offensive when the buildup was initiated, most of the divisions committed were not well trained.

Moved into the area with little opportunity for reconaissance or preparation and given last-minute Allied artillery, tank, and air support, nine U.S. divisions attacked in the early morning hours of 26 September. Raked by well-laid defensive fires as the sun rose, they halted, became disorganized, and took heavy casualties. Under great pressure and criticism from Allied commanders, Pershing reorganized, moved his veteran divisions into the offensive, and continued the attack. They were halted several times by effective fires from the reinforced defenders. After a month of costly advances against dug-in weapons positions, the Americans broke into the German rear in early November and reached the heights south of the rail center of Sedan at the hour of the armistice, 11:00 A.M., 11 November 1918.

The United States also committed army units to the Allied Expeditionary Forces dispatched to Archangel-Murmansk and to Siberia in 1918. These forces remained in a quasi-occupational status, with the last units withdrawn in 1920. Following the armistice, Pershing created the Third U.S. Army to occupy the U.S. enclave on the Rhine. This army, designated the Army of Occupation, controlled a fifty-mile semicircular zone centered on the Rhine at Coblenz. The U.S. government withdrew the last of these forces from German occupation duty on 24 January 1923.

THE INTERWAR PERIOD

Committed to occupation duties in Germany and Russia, to constabulary duties on the Mexican border and in the Philippines, and to the thousands of tasks essential to the dissolution of the Army of the United States and the reconstitution of the regular army, the active army declined in number to 144,000 in 1922 and remained at that general strength until the late 1930s. The army has always found it difficult to close posts, because political pressures from local economic interests combine with military inertia to cause forces to remain in an area long past the requirement for their stationing. Thus, the peacetime army of the 1920s and 1930s remained well above that of the previous century. This strength did not, however, translate to increased combat readiness. Republican presidents and Congress were disinclined to purchase the relatively expensive airplanes and tanks being developed around the world. The army again returned to barracks, relatively isolated from the civilian populace, and most officers were reduced from their wartime ranks. Garrison duties were few, while many officers were detached to liaison duties with foreign armies, U.S. governmental boards, and civil agencies.

The senior officers of the postwar army had served much of their time in an animal-powered era, and most resisted new military developments, especially in armor and aviation. Air power enthusiasts, led in the United States by Colonel William "Billy" Mitchell, trumpeted a new age, in which air power would make all other weapons obsolete. They were supported by some members of Congress and by newspaper reporters. In 1924 the army sent four Douglas World Cruisers around the world. Although the trip took six months, and only three much-repaired aircraft made the entire trip, it gained much publicity. Earlier, in 1921, the army forced the navy to agree to a bombing test on a former German battleship, the sinking of which, arguably, proved their theories and forced a recalcitrant President Calvin Coolidge to establish studies and boards to determine the future role of air power in national defense. While the results of these studies did not provide a great boost to air power, the Army Air Corps was created in 1926 and given greater funding than the Air Service of previous years.

The solo flight across the Atlantic by army reserve Captain Charles Lindbergh in 1927 aroused the interest of the American public in air power and the need to build a fleet of military aircraft. The argument against aviation expenditures, other than the penurious state of the U.S. Treasury during the Great Depression, was the assertion by many strategists, particularly naval, that there was no threat that air power could address. As bomber aircraft increased their range and capacity, U.S. Army planners pointed to the threat of an offensive against the American hemisphere, which, they said, justified modest increases in appropriations.

In 1934, President Franklin D. Roosevelt directed the Army Air Corps to fly the airmail. During a four-month period, there was a series of aircraft crashes and deaths of military pilots, and it became apparent that the Air Corps was insufficiently skilled and instrumented to fly at night and in bad weather. By the end of the year, the army was relieved of the duty, and civilian contractors were returned to the routes.

In 1932, upon orders of President Herbert Hoover, the army, under the personal direction of the chief of staff, General Douglas MacArthur, drove out the Bonus Army who had remained in Washington, D.C., after the adjournment of Congress ensured that those veterans would not receive immediate payment of a bonus for World War I military service. While the operation was accomplished without any civilian deaths and with few injuries, the action reinforced a negative image of the army in the minds of many citizens. In 1933 the army joined in the reforestation and conservation efforts of the Civilian Conservation Corps (CCC). Support of a New Deal program was not accepted with enthusiasm by the army, but the experience of directing and supplying a dispersed corps of three hundred thousand youths gave the officer corps, including reserve officers called to active duty, experience in managing large units. It also gave CCC youth a modicum of experience in military discipline and order, which was valuable later in readying civilians to fight World War II.

In 1940 the president was given authority to call up reserve forces, and Congress subsequently inaugurated peacetime conscription.

After Europe went to war in 1939, the active army strength increased swiftly. On 8 September, President Roosevelt declared a limited national emergency. In 1940 the president was given authority to call up reserve forces for twelve months, and Congress subsequently inaugurated peacetime conscription. In March 1941, president Roosevelt declared an unlimited national emergency. In June, the Army Air Forces were established as a separate command, and in July U.S. forces were sent to secure Iceland and some of the bases in the Caribbean leased from Great Britain. In August, the Atlantic Charter was drawn up by the United States and Great Britain. In the same month, Congress authorized the extension of active service, and the peacetime active army increased rapidly to 1,462,000 as training camps opened around the nation.

In the fall of 1941, two large (although badly trained and organized) armies in Louisiana and the Carolinas attacked each other in free maneuvers, the first ever conducted by the U.S. Army. The tank corps, created in July 1940, was tested against antitank guns, much of the weaponry being simulated. The maneuvers were good training for all ranks and served as a screening for newly activated National Guard leaders, many of whom were either sent home or reassigned to administrative duties.

WORLD WAR II

The United States Army went to war as a result of the devastating Japanese attack on Pearl Harbor, Hawaii, on 7 December 1941. The attack, which sank much of the Pacific fleet, destroyed or disabled two hundred army aircraft, but army casualties were relatively light. On 8 December, the United States declared that a state of war existed with Japan, and on 11 December, Germany and Italy declared war on the United States. The wartime mission of the army, at home and abroad, was one of defense. The first priority was defense of the homeland, which became a very active role after the surprise Japanese attack. Army troops on the lookout for hostile submarines and aircraft manned coastal forts. On 19 February 1942, President Roosevelt authorized the exclusion of aliens from areas designated as restricted. Shortly thereafter, persons of Japanese ancestry living in California, Oregon, Washington, and Arizona were moved to camps in the Midwest. The army was responsible for the movement of these people and the management of the camps until the emergency regulation was lifted on 2 January 1945. Fearful of the possibility of invasion, the War Department shifted military units to vital areas on the Pacific Coast and tested alert procedures in coordination with the navy.

Beginning with the establishment of the Inter-American Defense Board in March 1942, the army was committed to cooperative actions with Latin American nations for hemispheric defense. U.S. Army units in Panama were strengthened, and air bases were established in Guatemala to further defend the Panama Canal. Army engineers constructed the Alaskan Highway in 1942–1943 and built bases in Alaska. In August 1942 the engineers initiated the secret development of the atomic bomb (the Manhattan Project).

In December 1941, British civil and military leaders, led by Prime Minister Winston Churchill, concluded a series of agreements with the United States in Washington at the Arcadia Conference. Overall priorities for conduct of the war were set, with first priority assigned to the defeat of Germany. A defensive strategy was adopted for the Pacific theater. The Combined (U.S.-British) Chiefs of Staff organization was established to jointly conduct the war. The U.S. service chiefs also formed a loose organization called the Joint Chiefs of Staff. To accomplish the huge training mission in the United States, the Army Ground Forces were organized to oversee combat forces training, the Army Air Forces for aviation-related training, and the Army Service Forces for noncombat service schooling and training.

Japanese forces captured Guam and Wake Island in December 1941, and their main forces invaded the Philippines on 22 December and captured that entire island chain from U.S. and Philippine defenders by 9 April 1942. On 16 March, U.S. Army units landed in Australia; General MacArthur arrived in Australia on

17 March and was designated supreme allied commander of Allied forces in the southwest Pacific. The naval Battle of Midway in June was a major U.S. victory, the result of poor command decisions on the part of the Japanese and considerable luck for the United States. After the defeat at Midway, the Japanese went on a strategic defensive in the Pacific, and the United States was on the offensive.

In June 1942, the U.S. Army established the European Theater of Operations (ETO), with Major General Dwight D. Eisenhower in command. Army ground and air units were deployed in great numbers to England to establish a base for the early invasion of Nazi-controlled Europe. Pressed by the beleaguered Russians to open a second front in the west, the British convinced U.S. planners that the first invasion should be in North Africa—to relieve their forces fighting the Germans and Italians in Egypt. The North African invasion (Operation Torch) was launched on 8 November 1942. Its purpose was to clear North Africa of Axis forces, protect the Suez Canal, and free the Mediterranean for Allied use. A combined U.S.-British force of 170,000 under General Eisenhower invaded the coasts of Morocco and Algeria. The Vichy French offered little resistance, but the Axis commander, German General Erwin Rommel, turned his reinforcements from confrontation with the British in Egypt and struck the Americans at Kasserine Pass in Tunisia. The poorly trained and poorly led Americans were badly beaten by Rommel. After reorganization, the Americans and their British allies were able to overwhelm the Axis forces in North Africa by May 1943. The campaign was a sobering lesson for the United States regarding the ineffectiveness of their armor against that of the Germans.

The Sicilian invasion (Operation Husky) on 10 July 1943 was a quick Allied victory, in which the Seventh Army, under Lieutenant General George S. Patton, was demonstrably more aggressive than the slow-moving British, under General Bernard Montgomery. The impending surrender of the Italian government provoked a hasty Allied invasion of Italy on 3 September 1943. The Italian surrender on 8 September was offset by swift German occupation of the peninsula. The result was a long and bitter struggle, with U.S. and British forces attacking across unfordable rivers and up well-defended mountain slopes.

Operation Overlord, the Allied invasion of France, was the greatest military operation conducted in modern history. Launched on 6 June 1944, the invasion forces landed in Normandy. Preceded by an airborne invasion by three divisions behind the beaches, 176,000 U.S. and British soldiers landed from four thousand landing craft, supported by five thousand ships and eleven thousand aircraft. With air superiority on the order of thirty-to-one over the Germans, the beachheads were seized after some heavy fighting (especially by the Americans at Omaha Beach), and the invasion forces secured a lodgment in France before the German forces launched effective counterattacks. By 1 July 1944, the Allies had one million men in France, over five hundred thousand tons of supplies, and 170,000 vehicles. The Allied armies advanced across France on a broad front, expanded by the landing of the U.S. Seventh Army in southern France on 15 August. U.S. and Allied forces under Eisenhower approached Germany's "West Wall" as winter set in.

The Allies were preparing for the final phase of the war in the west when Hitler launched a desperation counteroffensive at the juncture of the U.S. and British forces in Belgium on 16 December. In the ensuing Battle of the Bulge, conducted in adverse weather, the Germans were stopped short of their objective, the port of Antwerp. As the Allies concentrated their forces and the weather cleared, the bulge was eliminated, and the Allies approached the Rhine River with the Germans offering only isolated resistance. The western Allies met the Russians at the Elbe River on 25 April (the Russians having taken Berlin), and the Germans surrendered on 7 May 1945.

The Women's Army Auxiliary Corps was established on 14 May 1942.

By 1943 the U.S. government had organized its resources and expanded its productivity sufficiently to furnish men and weapons to conduct major offensive war in both the European and Pacific theaters. In addition, the organization and support of the scientific community gave the United States new and powerful weaponry, including the atomic bomb. The Women's Army Auxiliary Corps was established on 14 May 1942, and women were also recruited as civilian pilots for delivery of military aircraft and as administrative workers in army headquarters.

On 27 December 1943, the army took over the nation's railroads temporarily to prevent their closing during a strike, and on 16 June 1945, ten thousand troops were called to Chicago to preserve order during a strike by truckers. Army units transported German and Italian prisoners of war to the United States, erected stockades, and guarded these prisoners until the end of the war.

In the Pacific, from the first U.S. Army and Marine Corps offensive at Guadalcanal (August 1942–February

1943) until the final invasion and seizure of Okinawa (April–June 1945), the offensive never ceased, and the victory was not in doubt. In May 1945, the Joint Chiefs of Staff approved a plan for the invasion of the home islands of Japan on 1 November 1945. On 21 November 1944, Army Air Forces launched massive strategic bombings of Tokyo and other major Japanese cities. Atomic bombs were dropped on Hiroshima (6 August) and Nagasaki (9 August). On 14 August, the Japanese accepted unconditional surrender terms and on 2 September they signed instruments of surrender.

THE COLD WAR

The major mission of the army in the immediate post–World War II period was establishing comprehensive military governments, occupation of conquered areas, and control of defeated peoples. A major unspecified mission was the demobilization of nine million forces and the disposal of millions of weapons systems and related items of equipment. Many wartime staff activities continued, the army seeking and finding new duties in the developing environment of the cold war. Army units continued to support the atomic energy program, including providing assistance in conduct of tests of blast and radiation effects. Agencies of the army service branches were involved in the sale of excess military equipment and real property disposal.

In the U.S. Zone of Germany, under the command of General Lucius Clay, some divisions were reorganized as constabulary forces, with security duties extending the functions of military government. Remaining combat divisions worldwide were reduced in strength and given additional security and occupation-support duties. The four-power government in Berlin succumbed to the confrontational relationships of the cold war. After attempting to force the Allies to leave Berlin, the Russians blocked the roads and railroad from the western sector into Berlin beginning in March 1948. The U.S. Army and U.S. Air Force, in cooperation with the British and French, organized a massive airlift to feed the population of Berlin. Frustrated by the success of the airlift, the Communists suddenly lifted the land blockade in May 1949.

Under the Truman Doctrine in 1947, the U.S. Army was committed to provide military equipment to Greece and Turkey and to furnish military advisers to prevent Communist-supported insurgencies in those countries. U.S. Army officers cooperated with military leaders of the Western European nations to form the North Atlantic Treaty Organization (NATO) in 1949. NATO was organized for collective defense against the growing Soviet threat; Eisenhower was appointed its first supreme commander. The Seventh U.S. Army was "forward based" in Germany, ultimately consisting of two corps of five divisions with supporting tactical air power in West Germany. Total U.S. military strength in Germany rose to more than four hundred thousand at the height of the cold war.

In July 1948, President Harry Truman ordered the total integration of all races in the armed forces.

The requirement for international military cooperation in furtherance of forty-two mutual defense agreements executed worldwide by the United States called for an increasingly sophisticated military establishment in the immediate postwar period. To modernize and centralize the U.S. military command, the National Defense Act of 1947 created the Department of Defense. As extended by acts passed in 1949, the Defense Department was organized under a secretary of defense, who served as the president's chief civil officer directing the department and the U.S. armed forces. Civil secretaries were created for the Departments of the Army (replacing the secretary of war) and of the Navy and the newly independent Department of the Air Force. These departments were limited by law to organizing, equipping, and training land, sea, and air forces. Military forces were assigned to unified (two or more services) and specified (single-service) commands around the world, directed by the secretary of defense, with the assistance of the chairman of the Joint Chiefs of Staff. The National Security Council was also created to assist the president in establishing military policy and direction. Joint military and civil agencies were created by these acts. Most important were the Central Intelligence Agency and the National Security Agency. Army officers served in these agencies and provided support for their operations. Active army strength, despite these commitments, had declined to 593,000 by 1950.

In July 1948, President Harry Truman ordered the total integration of all races in the armed forces. The army led this societal change, although integration in army units was not completed until after the Korean War.

THE KOREAN WAR

The U.S. Army was committed to military government and occupation of defeated Japan in a pattern similar to that described for postwar Germany. General MacArthur's Far East Command became a unified (four-service) command. The southern half of Korea was occupied by U.S. Army forces in 1945. The division between U.S. and Soviet zones in Korea was established at the thirty-eighth parallel, a line that identified the two Koreas, as the Soviets refused to cooperate with the United States in developing a democratic government for the entire peninsula. The Republic of (South) Korea was established on 15 August 1948; thereafter, the U.S. Army established the Korean Military Assistance Group (KMAG) to equip and train the Republic of Korea Army (ROKA).

The North Koreans invaded South Korea on 25 June 1950. U.S. Army forces from Japan were committed to assist in the defense of South Korea on 27 June under the auspices of the United Nations. The UN Security Council (with the Soviets absent) approved military assistance to South Korea, and General MacArthur was designated commander in chief, United Nations Command. The UN military intervention was called a "police action." The United States, having instituted a peacetime draft in 1948, increased draft calls and recalled individuals and units of the army, air force, and navy reserves and the National Guard.

UN forces retreated to a 120-mile defensive perimeter in the southeast corner of Korea in early August. MacArthur withheld his gathering reserve and launched an invasion at Inchon on 15 September 1950—well in the rear of North Korean forces. The Inchon invasion, considered to be the most decisive turning movement in modern military history, destroyed the organization of the North Korean army.

The X Corps was moved by ship around the peninsula to land on the east near Wonsan, and all UN forces drove deep into North Korea. On 25 November two Chinese Communist field armies drove into central North Korea in a gap between the Eighth Army and X Corps. As UN forces retreated south of Seoul and reorganized, MacArthur declared that the fighting constituted a "new war". Despite MacArthur's criticisms on limitations, the Joint Chiefs of Staff, concerned that the Soviet Union might launch an offensive against Western Europe, concluded that the United Nations must keep the war limited to the territories of North Korea and South Korea.

On 25 January 1951, UN forces under the command of General Matthew Ridgway launched a counter-counteroffensive. In heavy fighting, the Chinese and North Koreans abandoned Seoul and withdrew slowly to the north, with UN forces in pursuit. On 11 April, President Truman relieved MacArthur and replaced him with Ridgway. A Chinese counteroffensive, seven hundred thousand strong, drove south again on 22 April. The UN forces, which now numbered 557,000, stopped the offensive after again losing Seoul. In mid-May, UN forces ground forward and the lines stiffened north of Seoul, from Munsan-ni northeast across the peninsula. Both sides dug in and erected fortifications. Despite heavy fighting during the next two years and local gains, the line remained impacted until the truce ended the fighting. For the U.S. Army, the major lesson learned from the Korean War was that it should be prepared for commitment in wars for limited and changing political purposes that might entail severe limitations upon military action.

The accession of Eisenhower to the presidency resulted in the announcement of the new military strategy of massive retaliation, which emphasized deterrence by strategic nuclear weaponry, delivered mainly by aircraft. The army had a small and declining role in this scheme. In 1953, and again in 1958, laws were passed giving the secretary of defense more command authority over the services. Meanwhile, the army searched for a mission and reorganized under a pentomic structure. At infantry division level, the new maneuver elements, called "battle groups," were light regiments of five rifle companies with appropriate support and communications. The pentomic army gained tactical nuclear missiles and artillery shells and trained for employment of nuclear weapons and survival in limited nuclear war. The bulk of the army in the late 1950s was involved in training for a conventional or tactical nuclear war in Europe, and at least one half of army combat strength was stationed in Europe, committed to this mission, under NATO.

Meanwhile, having pioneered the launching of rockets in the period before World War II, the army established the Ballistic Missile Agency at Redstone Arsenal, Alabama, in 1957. In the immediate aftermath of the Soviet launching of the first orbiting space satellite in 1957, army work on a system for launching objects into space was expedited. On 31 January 1958, the army successfully launched a thirty-pound satellite, the Explorer, into orbit around the earth. The Explorer began sending signals to earth concerning temperatures, cosmic rays, and meteoric particles to stations on earth. The army also led the development of surface-to-surface rockets, which could carry nuclear warheads, to support armies in the field in combat, and surface-to-air missiles, which could intercept supersonic aircraft.

As the second Eisenhower administration began, the inflexibility of reliance upon massive retaliation became apparent. Problems in the Middle East led to the announcement of the Eisenhower Doctrine of military support for governments under pressures from international communism. Camille Chamoun, the president of Lebanon, requested U.S. aid, leading to the commitment of forces in 1958. While the marines made the first landings (on a friendly beach at Beirut), the majority of the thirteen thousand combat and support troops sent to Lebanon were army units. The deployed forces were to promote stability through their presence. Although this was difficult to translate into specific missions for the troops, the U.S. presence did act to calm international tension, and the army and marine units were quickly withdrawn without engaging in combat.

U.S. assistance to the Republic of Vietnam began during the Eisenhower administration, with the commitment of a military equipment delivery team to South Vietnam. The mission of this team, largely of army personnel, was to facilitate delivery of weapons and equipment to the South Vietnamese and to conduct specialized training in operation and maintenance of these systems. The program grew into the Military Assistance Advisory Group (MAAG) by the end of the Eisenhower administration.

THE VIETNAM WAR

The administration of John F. Kennedy announced its military strategy under the title "flexible response." In line with Kennedy's announcement of U.S. readiness to "go anywhere, undertake any task" in support of freedom, this strategy involved the selective commitment of U.S. military forces in trouble spots. It gave the army greater roles to fill than had been assigned earlier. Vietnam was selected to receive major increases in U.S. military and civil assistance under a new program called nation building, defined at the time as a bold effort to "literally create a free and prosperous nation" of South Vietnam.

The military strategem to which U.S. Army commissioned and noncommissioned officers were committed was called counterinsurgency. The army, however, undertook to do what it knew best—to train the Army of the Republic of South Vietnam (ARVN) to fight, primarily, a conventional war. The Vietnamese military hierarchy was equipped with the weaponry and accoutrements of a conventional army. U.S. Army advisers were to accompany ARVN units into combat, to give Vietnamese leaders a sense of security and confidence in battle. It was in this arena that advisers encountered their greatest problem: The ARVN leaders, for a variety of personal and cultural reasons, did not want to engage the enemy. By the mid-1960s, U.S. Army personnel were advising Vietnamese military and paramilitary forces and military and civil leaders, from the highest governmental levels to those of small hamlets. President Kennedy became personally interested in the U.S. Army Special Forces and concluded that they would be an ideal agency to carry out the task of counterinsurgency in Vietnam. Special Forces were committed primarily to organize and train the mountain tribesmen of South Vietnam.

The first U.S. military units committed into Vietnam were U.S. Army helicopter companies, beginning in 1961. The helicopter gave conventional forces the mobility to trap guerrillas and to quickly reinforce units in combat. These units and the growing number of army, marine, air force, and navy advisers to South Vietnam were eventually targeted by the Vietcong. Reactions to attacks on Americans (after congressional passage in August 1964 of the Tonkin Gulf Resolution) led to commitment of marine and army combat units into Vietnam in 1965. Initially, these units were to defend U.S. bases, but to defend the bases, it was necessary to patrol, on ground and in the air. It was not long until U.S. forces were engaging in offensive operations throughout South Vietnam.

Members of the modern U.S. Army undergo rigorous and continuous training. These soldiers direct activities with a field radio during training exercises. (Department of Defense)

A newly organized airmobile division (the First Air Cavalry) went to Vietnam in September 1965. This division was organized around a revolutionary concept—the employment of squadrons of helicopters to move and support major combat elements directly into attack. This uniquely capable division swiftly defeated a much larger force of North Vietnamese in its first major offensive, the Ia Drang Valley campaign, in 1965. As other divisions were committed, they received sufficient helicopters to move and support sizable combat elements as well. By vigorous use of the helicopter as a combat maneuver and support vehicle, the U.S. Army literally "wrote the book" on airmobile operations while fighting.

Much like the nation it served, the U.S. Army returned from its Vietnam ordeal a weakened and disheartened service.

As U.S. military strength in Vietnam rose to 540,000 (mostly army), the region became a U.S. theater of war. U.S. army forces worldwide were drawn down in strength to provide personnel, and regulars found themselves rotating in and out of Vietnam. Because the United States did not declare war and U.S. presidents chose not to call up major reserve component organizations, the war was fought by a small, dwindling corps of regulars augmented by draftees and swiftly promoted volunteers. The twelve-month tour gutted unit effectiveness and esprit and led to short command tours by selected officers (a practice known as ticket punching). The seconding of U.S. advisers to the officers of ARVN and other services continued but took a definite lower priority to the U.S. combat role. Ever-younger U.S. officers were assigned as advisers to ever-older Vietnamese officers, the former having no combat experience and the latter many years of experience. The U.S. command came to rely on the advisers mostly to report on the Vietnamese leadership, and the ARVN officers used their advisers for the grubby staff work they were disinclined to do.

U.S. and South Vietnamese combat units swept across Vietnam, generally from east to west, and swiftly gained control in the air and on the land—in the daytime. Despite repeated operations through all areas in which enemy forces were known to be located, the United States and ARVN were seldom able to ensure control of the population, infiltrated as it was by enemy agents and supporters. The enemy, however, persuaded by its own propaganda that the people of South Vietnam were ready to revolt, launched the Tet Offensive in January 1968. This conventional attack struck all sizable settlements; its early military success was the result of total surprise. After the U.S. forces reacted and ARVN forces also took to the offensive, the enemy was decisively defeated, and the Vietcong political infrastructure, having "uncovered" its leadership, was destroyed. The war then became, essentially, a conventional operation between U.S.-ARVN forces and those of North Vietnam. By mid-1968, U.S. and ARVN forces had won the war on the ground in South Vietnam, but after President Lyndon Johnson's decision to stop Vietnam reinforcement and President Richard Nixon's subsequent decision to withdraw U.S. forces, the Communists knew they had only to wait out the United States.

Nixon's strategy of Vietnamization (turning the war gradually over to the Vietnamese) was certainly logical. Combined with bombing of North Vietnam, it may have brought a relatively positive solution to the war. The political fallout in Washington from the Watergate scandal, however, convinced the North Vietnamese leaders that the United States would take no action to stop a Communist victory. This was all the assurance they needed to win.

Much like the nation it served, the U.S. Army returned from its Vietnam ordeal a weakened and disheartened service. Political leaders, civil technocrats, and army leadership were all assigned blame for the failure. At the highest levels, military leaders had accepted conditions and limitations on military operations that ultimately caused the most powerful nation in the world to be humbled.

In 1971, Nixon ended the draft, and the army announced a new, all-volunteer force with the slogan, "The Army Wants to Join You!" It was a low point in the army's relationship to the people it served. It was, also, a very low state for the nation, as the societal revolution had brought a condition of disarray to U.S. leadership.

THE NADIR OF AMERICAN ARMS

As the bicentennial of America's founding approached in 1976, the mood of the American people was somewhat less than celebratory. The fall of South Vietnam was a recent memory, and the societal revolution at home, called by some observers "a national temper tantrum," was continuing, albeit at a diminished pace. The army, struggling to meet enlistment goals for its volunteer force, bore the brunt of criticism of military affairs, as, indeed, it had the brunt of damage, in all respects, from the war.

The general who withdrew most of the U.S. troops from Vietnam, Creighton W. Abrams, vowed, as chief of staff, never again to allow the army to be committed into war without the prior approval of the American people. To improve the relationship of the army to civilian society and to offset the declining strength of the active force, Abrams announced the "total army" concept, a series of steps to better integrate the reserve components with the active army. Some changes were made in priorities for equipment for the reserves, but the most significant improvement was the assignment of National Guard combat units to round out the strength of active divisions. While such assignments reduced the actual combat readiness of these divisions (as later commitments would reveal), the concept was more than cosmetic, and the result was an improvement in morale in the reserves. Still, army recruiting failed to meet goals, and strength declined during the 1970s to the point that the term "a hollow army" was often used to describe the force—strong in rank and weak in soldiers.

President Jimmy Carter's successes in propounding human rights and military deescalation, highlighted by the Camp David Accords between Israel and Egypt, were offset by Soviet aggression in Afghanistan and increases in military aid to nations of the Third World. In response, Carter reluctantly restored some major weapons systems. To facilitate his Middle East settlement, he created the Rapid Deployment Joint Task Force, a four-service contingency headquarters oriented primarily toward the Middle East and North Africa. Also under Carter's direction, the army led the way in completing the integration of minorities into all its ranks and activities and began to include women in its ranks and specialties as well.

Carter's greatest military failure was the attempt to rescue the fifty-two American hostages held in the U.S. embassy in Tehran, Iran. This four-service operation was a tragic fiasco. After the rescuers landed in an unpopulated area in Iran, their helicopters broke down; then a helicopter crashed into a fueling aircraft, and panic ensued. The rescue forces evacuated hastily, leaving behind their dead and, of course, the hostages.

THE ARMY TRIUMPHANT

Ronald Reagan's presidency began with the announcement of the foreign policy of "peace through strength." His defense budget increased military appropriations by 18 percent. The military bureaucracy seized this increment to build its strength and control, and a significant improvement in army force structure and readiness resulted. The Abrams tank and the Apache helicopter reached the troops, while improved artillery and medium-range missiles were deployed. Army training became more sophisticated (using simulators) and more realistic (at national training centers), and army readiness and morale climbed to a post-Vietnam high.

On 25 October 1983, a joint U.S. task force, whose major elements were from the Army's Eighteenth Airborne Corps, assaulted and seized Grenada, defeating Cubans and local resistance and evacuating Americans deemed to have been in danger. Despite poor interservice coordination and less than aggressive leadership at some high levels, the operation freed Grenada from Communist domination. Americans took satisfaction in the successful employment, for a change, of their military forces in their own interests.

President George Bush was pressed to cut as many as one million troops from the active forces.

Reagan's interest in Latin America was sparked by the surge of Communist guerrilla operations in Central America, emanating from and supported by Nicaragua and Cuba. The United States increased military assistance (primarily Army Special Forces and helicopter units) to the free nations in the area and achieved some success in its aid program to El Salvador, as that nation's forces regained ascendancy over Communist guerrilla rebels. Assistance was also rendered to Guatemala, and a major training mission was dispatched to Honduras to teach the forces of that nation counterguerrilla tactics and techniques. Reagan also supported—enthusiastically, and with increasing military supplies and assistance—internal armed resistance to the Sandinista government in Nicaragua; these resistance forces were called the "Contras" in the world press. As the second Reagan administration got under way in 1985, a Democratic-controlled U.S. Congress restricted funding and covert assistance to the Contras. Despite setbacks in financial support, the Contras seized and held border regions in Nicaragua.

To better define the military policy of the Reagan administration, U.S. Secretary of Defense Caspar Weinberger announced preconditions for use of U.S. military force. Such commitment, he stated, should:

- Be vital to the national interest.
- Be a wholehearted commitment to win.
- Have clear military objectives.
- Have force sufficient for the objectives.
- Have the support of the American people.
- Be entered upon as a last resort.

For some years, the commitment of U.S. forces to minor operations around the world had revealed command problems that resulted from inadequate coordination and cooperation among the military services. The relative impotence of the organization of the Joint Chiefs of Staff to direct the services was recognized by Congress. On 1 October 1986, Congress passed the Goldwater-Nichols Department of Defense Reorganization Act, which established the chairman of the JCS as the principal adviser to the president and the secretary of defense, able to make his own recommendations rather than following those agreed upon by the service chiefs. The bill also gave increased authority to the commanders of the unified commands.

The fall of the Berlin Wall in November 1989 signaled the beginning of the disintegration of the Soviet empire. By 1991, the Soviet Union no longer posed a threat of aggression outside its borders. The immediacy of any threat to NATO from the East having declined, U.S. and Western European leaders attempted to expand the NATO charter and to define its future. In Western Europe and the United States, opposition political leaders called for massive cuts in deployed forces (primarily army) and for a peace dividend to be applied to domestic problems. President George Bush was pressed to cut as many as one million troops from the active forces, and, in quick response, Defense Secretary Richard Cheney announced plans for a 25 percent reduction in all U.S. military forces. These cuts began in 1991, with plans for easing the force-out of volunteer career personnel even as Congress demanded more reduction.

Relations with Panama had worsened during the latter years of the Reagan administration, after the United States indicted Panamanian dictator Manuel Noriega for aiding the transshipment of drugs from Colombia through Panama to the United States. Shortly before Christmas 1989, the United States launched an invasion of Panama (Operation Just Cause) to seize Noriega and to return Panama to its elected rulers. U.S. forces swiftly occupied the capital and the countryside after crushing scattered but determined resistance.

In 1994 and 1995, U.S. Army troops were stationed in Haiti to maintain order during a period of unrest in the country. These soldiers are engaging in a weapons seizure operation while Haitian civilians look on. (Department of Defense)

A major domestic and international problem for the United States is the flow of drugs, principally cocaine, from Latin America. Most Latin American governments have cooperated in destroying crops and processing plants in their nations and have aided in capturing drug lords and in interdicting the transport of drugs. U.S. military forces (primarily Special Forces and helicopter units) have assisted this important mission.

On 2 August 1990, Iraq, under the leadership of dictator Saddam Hussein, invaded the small sultanate of Kuwait. The United Nations Security Council condemned the invasion, and the United States and some other UN member nations sent military forces to Saudi Arabia, others provided nonmilitary support, and some provided monetary assistance to defray the costs of maintaining forces in Saudi Arabia. The United States called this commitment Operation Desert Shield.

In a surprising show of unity, the UN Security Council (including the USSR) agreed to use "all measures including force" to remove the Iraqis from Kuwait. The U.S. government built up its forces in Saudi Arabia to a total of 440,000 by the end of January 1991. These forces included units and personnel from reserve components of all the U.S. military services. Western intelligence agencies estimated that Iraq had 550,000 troops in Kuwait and southwestern Iraq.

On 17 January, UN forces launched Operation Desert Storm to liberate Kuwait. U.S. air forces, augmented by other allied aircraft, struck military targets in Kuwait and Iraq. Most Iraqi aircraft remained hidden or fled to Iran, where they were impounded. By the third week in February, UN forces had launched over seventy thousand aircraft sorties.

The most effective offensive action of the Iraqis was the launching of Scud surface-to-surface missiles into Saudi Arabia and Israel (the latter not a combatant in the war). The Scuds inflicted very few casualties and had no significant military effect, but their political and psychological effects were considerable. On 24 February, the United Nations ground offensive to liberate Kuwait, Operation Desert Sabre, commenced. The main attack was a three hundred-mile turning movement by armored forces around the west flank of Iraqi forces in Kuwait and southern Iraq. UN forces reached the outskirts of Basra (the center of the vaunted Iraqi Republican Guard) by 25 February, while the eastern

ACTIVE U.S. ARMY PERSONNEL STRENGTH, 1789–1990 (in thousands)

Year	Strength	Year	Strength	Year	Strength	Year	Strength
1789	1	1848	47	1907	64	1940	269
1794	4	1849	11	1908	77	1941	1462
1795	3	1855	16	1909	85	1942	3076
1801	4	1858	18	1910	81	1943	6994
1803	2	1860	16	1911	84	1944	7995
1804	3	1861	187	1912	92	1945	8268
1808	6	1862	637	1913	93	1946	1891
1809	7	1863	918	1914	99	1947	991
1810	6	1864	971	1915	107	1948	554
1812	7	1865	1001	1916	108	1949	660
1813	19	1866	57	1917	421	1950	593
1814	38	1868	51	1918	2396	1951	1532
1815	33	1869	37	1919	852	1952	1596
1816	10	1871	29	1920	204	1953	1534
1817	8	1875	26	1921	231	1954	1405
1819	9	1876	29	1922	149	1955	1109
1820	11	1877	24	1923	133	1956	1026
1821	6	1878	26	1924	143	1957	998
1823	6	1879	27	1925	137	1960	871
1833	7	1889	28	1926	135	1965	967
1836	10	1891	27	1929	139	1969	1510
1837	12	1893	28	1931	141	1970	1320
1838	9	1898	210	1932	135	1975	781
1839	11	1899	81	1933	137	1980	772
1840	12	1900	102	1935	139	1984	776
1841	11	1901	86	1936	168	1987	770
1843	9	1902	81	1937	180	1988	764
1846	28	1903	70	1938	185	1989	760
1847	45	1905	68	1939	190	1990	746

drives reached Kuwait City. Iraqi forces were quickly and decisively defeated.

Without denigrating this great victory, it should be noted that it came against a force that was surrounded and did not fight, and it came only after a long period of preparation that would not likely be possible in future war.

In 1992, reductions in army forces were underway, as the United States began to base its military forces primarily within the country. Reductions in army strength were expected to exceed 25 percent, probably reaching 33 percent. This smaller army should be increasingly well-trained and equipped with high-tech weapons and communications and battlefield maneuver systems. There will likely be a light force for quick movement to trouble spots in contingencies, backed up by armor-heavy reinforcements. The army will have to limit its mission to training and equipping forces to fight in multiservice, unified commands.

The future appears to be bright for a denouement of military confrontations involving the U.S. Army, but there are still U.S. troops at the far frontiers of the free world, and it is likely that U.S. worldwide interests will require their deployment to distant battlefields in the future.

[See also Great American Military Leadership.]

BIBLIOGRAPHY

Abrahamson, James L. *American Arms for a New Century* (1981).

Ambrose, Stephen E. *Duty, Honor, Country: A History of West Point* (1966).

Bernardo, C. Joseph, and Eugene H. Bacon. *American Military Policy: Its Development Since 1775* (1977).

Braim, Paul F. *The Test of Battle: The American Expeditionary Forces in World War I* (1987).

Browning, Robert S., III. *Two If by Sea: The Development of American Coastal Defense Policy* (1983).

Colby, Elbridge. *The National Guard of the United States: A Half Century of Progress* (1977).

Downey, Fairfax. *Sound of the Guns: The Story of American Artillery from the Ancient and Honorable Company to the Atom Cannon and Guided Missile* (1955).

Dupuy, R. Ernest, and Trevor N. Dupuy. *American Military Heritage* (1984).

———. *The Evolution of Weapons and Warfare* (1980).

Ekirch, Arthur A., Jr. *The Civilian and the Military: A History of the American Antimilitarist Tradition* (1956).

Ganoe, William A. *A History of the United States Army*, rev. ed. (1942).

Goldberg, Alfred, ed. *A History of the United States Air Force, 1907–1957* (1957).

Gurney, Gene. *A Pictorial History of the United States Army* (1966).

Hassler, Warren W. *With Shield and Sword: American Military Affairs, Colonial Times to the Present* (1982).

Hewes, James E., Jr. *From Root to McNamara: Army Organization and Administration, 1900–1963* (1975).

Hicken, Victor. *The American Fighting Man* (1969).

Higham, Robin. *Bayonets in the Streets: The Use of Troops in Civil Disturbances* (1969).

Hill, Jim Dan. *The Minute Man in Peace and War: A History of the National Guard* (1964).

Holley, Irving. *Ideas and Weapons* (1953).

Huston, James A. *The Sinews of War: Army Logistics, 1775–1953* (1966).

Huzar, Elias. *The Purse and the Sword: Control of the Army by Congress Through Military Appropriations, 1933–1950* (1950, repr. 1971).

Jessup, John E., and Robert W. Coakley. *A Guide to the Study and Use of Military History* (1979).

Karsten, Peter, ed. *The Military in America from the Colonial Era to the Present* (1980).

Mahon, John K. *History of the Militia and the National Guard* (1983).

Mahon, John K., and Romana Danysh. *Infantry, Part I: Regular Army* (1972).

Merrill, James M. *Spurs to Glory: The Story of the United States Cavalry* (1966).

Millis, Walter. *Arms and Men: A Study in American Military History* (1956).

Nenninger, Timothy K. *The Leavenworth Schools and the Old Army: Education, Professionalism and the Officer Corps of the United States Army, 1881–1918* (1978).

Palmer, John McAuley. *America in Arms: The Experience of the United States with Military Organization* (1941).

Pappas, George. *Prudens Futuri: The War College, 1901–1967* (1967).

Peterson, Harold L. *Round Shot and Rammers* (1956).

Risch, Erna. *Quartermaster Support of the Army: A History of the Corps, 1775–1939* (1962).

Root, Elihu. *The Military and Colonial Policy of the United States* (1916).

Smith, Louis. *American Democracy and Military Power: A Study of Civil Control of Military Power in the United States* (1951).

Spaulding, Oliver L. *The United States Army in War and Peace* (1937).

Stubbs, Mary Lee, and Stanley Russell Connor. *Armor, Cavalry, Part I: Regular Army and Army Reserve* (1969).

———. *Armor, Cavalry, Part II: Army National Guard* (1972).

Weigley, Russell F. *Towards an American Army: Military Thought from Washington to Marshall* (1962).

———. *The American Way of War: A History of United States Military Strategy and Policy* (1973).

Williams, T. Harry. *Americans at War: The Development of the American Military System* (1960).

— PAUL F. BRAIM

The Navy

The United States is a nation with a long maritime heritage. Until the advent of air travel in the mid-twentieth century, all Americans of European, African, and Asian ancestry came to North America by ship. For colonial America, the North Atlantic was the umbilical cord that connected the colonies to the mother country, Great Britain. Once Americans broke their political ties with Great Britain, the Atlantic became a new frontier, such as those in the North, West, and South, that offered the opportunity for expansion and potential avenues for a foreign invader.

Not surprisingly, Americans early on chose to establish a navy; in fact, they did so nine months before they declared themselves politically independent. To Americans, a navy was a symbol of their sovereignty, their national maturity, and their determination to fight for control of their seaboard frontier. Throughout its history, the United States has had a navy for all but nine years. While historically there has been a broad consensus in the country to support a navy, the type and size of the naval service the nation required has often been the subject of contention. As early as 1775, Americans debated what have come to be termed "roles and missions." What role was a navy to play within a national scheme of defense? What missions would naval forces be called upon to conduct in support of American interests?

Americans chose to establish a navy nine months before they declared themselves politically independent.

Some comprehension of the changing nature of American national security policy since 1775 is necessary to understand the roles and missions assigned the U.S. Navy over the course of two centuries. Samuel P. Huntington, writing in the U.S. Naval Institute *Proceedings* in 1954, suggested that the history of the nation's defense policy could best be divided into three periods. Huntington identified the continental period, beginning in 1775 and lasting until the 1890s, as an era during which threats to American national security were narrowly defined and either originated or were dealt with in North America. A navy, accordingly, played a secondary role in national defense. The oceanic period began in the 1890s and lasted until 1945. Americans defined their national interests in somewhat broader terms and chose to prevent would-be threats from reaching the continental United States, or even the Western Hemisphere. As the nation began to draw its national security horizons in the mid-Pacific and western Atlantic, the U.S. Navy found itself playing a preeminent role, becoming the nation's first line of defense.

Since 1945 the United States has defined its national interests even more broadly and attempted to head off or confront threats to those interests along the periphery of the Eurasian landmass. Throughout this post–World War II transoceanic period, the U.S. Navy, frequently as part of an integrated, multiservice team, has been assigned missions that involved the projection of naval power ashore by means of aviation, amphibious, and missile—cruise and ballistic—assets.

THE CONTINENTAL PERIOD, 1775–1890

The North American colonies of Great Britain developed in the seventeenth and eighteenth centuries as parts of a powerful European maritime empire. Americans provided the mother country with a variety of export goods, among them naval stores, and even constructed ships. American sailors, some by choice, some as the result of the efforts of British press gangs, served in the men-of-war of the Royal Navy. Continental navy Captain Nicholas Biddle, for example, served as a youth in the Royal Navy alongside Horatio Nelson.

During the colonial wars of Great Britain with France and Spain, Americans took part not only in the campaigns fought in the west along the frontier but also in the North Atlantic and Caribbean. Americans, among them Lawrence Washington, the elder half-brother of George Washington, served in Admiral Edward Vernon's abortive Central American expedition (1739–1741). In 1745 New England sailors and troops landed on Cape Breton Island and besieged and captured the French fortress of Louisburg, which guarded the approaches to the Saint Lawrence River. American merchants armed scores of ships as privateers and operated them against the commerce of Great Britain's enemies.

Thus, in 1775, Americans were no strangers to the ways of the sea, either in peace or in war. In the years immediately before the outbreak of the rebellion, Americans demonstrated their growing disenchantment with British rule by taking action against ships collecting revenue or delivering tea in Boston Harbor. Once the revolution began, Americans recognized that events in the Atlantic Ocean theater would have a major, and potentially decisive, impact on the course of the war in North America. In the fall of 1775, Americans initiated a privateering campaign against British commerce, and on 13 October the Continental Congress, after some difficult political debate, also established a small naval force, hoping that even a diminutive navy would be able to offset to some extent what would otherwise be an uncontested exercise of British sea power.

The Continental Congress had a very limited role in mind for the navy. It was not expected to contest British control of the seas, but rather to wage a traditional *guerre de course* against British trade, in conjunction with the scores of privateers outfitting in American ports. The Continental navy's ships were to raid commerce and attack the transports that supplied British forces in North America. To carry out this mission, the Continental Congress began to build up, through purchase, conversion, and new construction, a cruiser navy of small ships—frigates, brigs, sloops, and schooners. For the most part, Continental navy ships cruised independently or in pairs in search of their prey, avoiding whenever possible fights with Royal Navy men-of-war.

McClelland Barclay designed this U.S. Navy recruiting poster in 1942 during World War II. (National Archives)

The record of the Continental navy was mixed during the revolutionary war. Its cruisers ranged far and wide and demonstrated that British commerce was nowhere safe, not even in British home waters. Few of the navy's larger ships ever put to sea, however, because most of the frigates Congress authorized to be built were either destroyed by British forces or burned by the Americans to prevent capture. There were occasional triumphs in single-ship engagements—for example, the capture by Captain John Paul Jones's *Ranger* of the British sloop of war *Drake* in April 1778. Jones gained international notoriety for his operations against the British in the North Sea and raided the coast of Great Britain itself. The navy was somewhat less successful in small-squadron actions. Its successes included the 1778 amphibious raid against New Providence in the Bahamas, but there were even more failures, most notably the ill-fated Penobscot expedition of 1779. While the Continental navy had its share of tactical triumphs, not once did its efforts cause the British an operational or strategic check.

Many of the failures of the Continental navy were directly attributable to the uneven and uncertain quality of the highly politicized officer corps. Mediocre officers vied for rank and privilege. Many commanders lacked drive, and others, while perhaps excellent seamen, were simply incompetent warriors. Even highly successful officers, such as Jones, labored under marked character deficiencies.

Nevertheless, whatever the shortcomings of the Continental navy, the course of the war demonstrated to Americans the importance of sea power. The control of the Atlantic by the Royal Navy allowed Great Britain to transport a large army to North America and to sustain it there. French sea power, allied with the American cause after 1778, enabled General George Washington to isolate and destroy the British army of Lord Charles Cornwallis at Yorktown in 1781. One of the decisive battles of the war, it ended Great Britain's hope of crushing the rebellion.

While sea power clearly had played an extremely important role in the Revolution, the years immediately following the war were difficult ones for the Continental navy. Under the Articles of Confederation, the Congress reserved for itself greater control over the nation's naval than its land forces, but this had less to do with a judgment of the importance of sea power than with the traditional Anglo-American fear of standing armies. The national government could be trusted with control of less politically dangerous, and more expensive, naval forces. Two years after the end of the war, the money-poor Congress sold off the last ship of the Continental navy, the frigate *Alliance*.

The failure of Congress to maintain a naval force was understandable. Navies were, and remain, expensive instruments of national power. Moreover, there were virtually no roles or missions that a small American navy could realistically be expected to play in the mid-1780s. The primary threats the new republic faced were to be found along the western frontier. In the Northwest, the native American tribes and the British, who refused to complete their withdrawal, challenged U.S. sovereignty and control of potentially valuable western lands. In the Southwest, the Spanish and their tribal allies held a lock on the lower Mississippi and disputed the southern boundary of the United States. Naval power could do little to change these balances of force.

A navy also could not remove the major impediments to the complete recovery of U.S. commerce. The problems the United States faced in its relations with Great Britain, Spain, and France were rooted in the philosophy of mercantilism and, as such, were more likely to be settled diplomatically than through the application of military force. Although a small effective navy might have been a source of national pride and an international display of nationhood, most congressmen were understandably less than eager, given the rather mixed record of the Continental navy, to embark on an expensive naval program.

Conditions began to change when the question of a proper response to aggressors became a national issue. In the Mediterranean, the corsairs of the Barbary states began to prey on U.S. merchant ships, no longer protected by the Royal Navy. Ships and cargoes were captured, and U.S. seamen were ransomed or sold into slavery. Although the number of ships and seamen actually lost were few, the psychological effect on Americans was marked. Among the possible responses that the United States debated were paying the Barbary states to spare U.S. commerce from attacks and building a small navy to protect trade.

The debate over naval policy was both economic and philosophical. Many Americans, among them Thomas Jefferson, later minister to the French court from 1785 to 1789, favored a naval response. Jefferson wrote in the fall of 1784: "We ought to begin a naval power, if we mean to carry on our commerce. Can we begin it on a more honorable occasion, or with a weaker foe?" Other Americans feared the establishment of a navy, which they viewed as an instrument that, while less politically dangerous than a standing army, nevertheless could lead the United States into innumerable foreign embroilments. Still others, such as John Adams, took the exceedingly practical position that the American people had had their fill of war and that a negotiated settlement—that is, payment for protection—was the best course to pursue. Moreover, given the fiscal weakness of the Confederation Congress, the United States lacked the resources to undertake the establishment of a navy. In fact, Congress lacked the funds to offer a negotiated settlement.

Jefferson wrote in 1784: "We ought to begin a naval power, if we mean to carry on our commerce."

While the Barbary depredations did not lead immediately to the resurrection of U.S. naval power, they did highlight the apparent helplessness of the country in the international arena and helped shape a consensus in the United States for the establishment of a stronger national government. In Philadelphia in 1787, delegates drew up a constitution, which was adopted in 1789. As part of that debate, the Federalists, the nationalists who supported the new scheme of government, envisioned a state powerful enough to maintain a navy capable of protecting U.S. commerce. Some Federalists went even further. Alexander Hamilton argued that while the United States could not challenge Europe's principal maritime powers on the seas, in the event of a European war pitting France against Great Britain, a small fleet of American battleships would allow the United States to play the makeweight in the balance of power in the Western Hemisphere. For Hamilton and his supporters, a navy could play a broad national role in pursuit of the interests of the United States, and not just a limited role protecting the ships and cargoes of U.S. merchants.

The U.S. Constitution gave the government the power to play such a role. In language that reflected the Anglo-American antiarmy tradition, Congress was given the right "to raise and support armies" but "to provide and maintain" a navy. Nevertheless, no consensus yet existed to support a large national navy. In fact, until the mid-1790s, the United States continued as it had under the Confederation Congress—without any naval force at all. Potential challenges to U.S. interests were many, but actual threats addressable by naval forces were few.

The outbreak of war in Europe in 1793 dramatically altered the equation. For Americans, European war presented the United States with opportunities. Both the French and the British began to rely heavily on U.S. shipping and, under the pressures of war, began to relax many mercantile commercial restrictions that had hindered the recovery of U.S. commerce. U.S. trade and the shipping industry expanded accordingly. Along with these opportunities, however, came great hazards. As more and more U.S. ships took to the seas, the possibility increased of depredations against them by the European powers. The British, for example, were more than happy to see U.S. ships plying the sea-lanes in service of the interests of Great Britain, but did not look kindly on Yankee vessels trading with France or its colonies.

The initial challenge to the rapid expansion of U.S. commerce, however, came not from London or Paris but from the corsairs of the Barbary coast. In the 1790s the Algerians again began to prey on U.S. commerce in the Mediterranean. Once again, Congress debated whether the nation ought to buy protection or establish a navy to safeguard shipping. In March 1794 Congress decided to respond with force and passed a naval act that called for the construction of a half-dozen frigates.

The United States again had a navy. The new frigates were to be well built and heavily armed, akin to twentieth-century battle cruisers—fast enough to run from European ships of the lines, powerful enough to overwhelm any European or Barbary cruiser in a single-ship duel. Work began on the forty-four-gun frigates *Constitution, United States,* and *President* and the thirty-six-gun frigates *Congress, Constellation,* and *Chesapeake.* Successful diplomacy, however, cut short the program. The demonstrated willingness of the United States to respond militarily helped American diplomats negotiate a more reasonable financial agreement with Algiers in 1796, and the naval building program was put on hold, its future uncertain. U.S. diplomats were likewise able to negotiate successful treaties with Spain and Great Britain that secured the Northwest and Southwest frontiers and temporarily ended British harassment of U.S. trade.

In 1797, however, the French, enraged by their former ally's agreement with Great Britain, retaliated by striking at U.S. commerce. Hundreds of ships and cargoes were seized worldwide, although most were taken in the Caribbean. The United States responded as it had in 1794 to the Algerian depredations, by offering to negotiate, while work resumed on the frigates already under construction. Since the bulk of the French navy was blockaded in its home ports by the Royal Navy, the prospect of a limited U.S. naval response to depredations primarily in the Caribbean appeared to be realistic. When the negotiations with the French collapsed, in what has become known as the XYZ Affair, Congress between 1798 and 1800 passed a series of bills expanding the navy to a force of more than thirty ships and, on 30 April 1798, passed an act that established the independent executive Department of the Navy.

Between 1798 and 1800, this new, jury-rigged navy fought the undeclared Quasi-War with France. For the United States, this was not another *guerre de course.* Because the Royal Navy had all but swept French commerce from the seas, there were few targets for U.S. privateers or navy cruisers. Instead, the navy found itself protecting U.S. ships from French corsairs. Operations were centered in the Caribbean, although during the course of the war U.S. Navy ships operated along the American coast, in the approaches to the Mediterranean, and in the Indian Ocean basin, cruising as far as the Sunda Strait.

The Quasi-War was a limited conflict. Congress, in an effort to protect U.S. commerce, allowed the navy to operate only against armed French ships on the high seas. Directed by its first civilian secretary, Benjamin Stoddert, the navy employed a variety of techniques to carry out its congressional mandate. Warships convoyed merchant vessels and patrolled the shipping lanes on the lookout for French privateers, but Stoddert also chose to employ his small force as offensively as possible. He dispensed with escorts for convoys and patrolling and, in a move that carried the war to the Caribbean, sent virtually the entire navy south, where French privateers operated, and eliminated the French threat along the coast.

Stoddert also excelled as a manager, weeding out many of the service's mediocre officers, among them more than a few Continental navy veterans, and establishing a pipeline of young midshipmen and lieutenants who made the navy their career and would become the future "ornaments" of the service. The U.S. Navy managed during the Quasi-War to do what the Continental navy had failed to do during the American Revolution, that is, to emerge from the conflict with an excellent reputation and broad political support. Stoddert and other U.S. navalists used wartime political backing in an attempt to build not only a small force to protect commerce but a larger battle fleet that would be able to play the broader national role envisioned by Hamilton. Congress initially supported Stoddert's ambitious programs, and in 1799 and 1800, construction began of six powerful ships of the line. In 1801, however, waning political support for a large navy, discontent over the high taxes necessary to complete the program, and a change in administration ended the effort.

If Stoddert's hopes of building a U.S. battle fleet were doomed by the election of President Thomas Jefferson in 1800, the future of the U.S. Navy was not in doubt. Jefferson took office in March 1801 as a crisis with Tripoli loomed on the horizon, and the U.S. Navy found its squadrons en route to the Mediterranean. Between 1801 and 1805, the U.S. Navy protected U.S. commerce from Tripolitan corsairs, but Jefferson did not limit the navy to patrolling and convoy escort. He used sea power in a forward, offensive manner, blockading and bombarding Tripoli, and supporting the march of an army of mercenaries in 1805 from Egypt to Derna in an effort to topple the dey of Tripoli from his throne or force him to negotiate.

The successful application of naval power during the Quasi-War and Barbary Wars by the Federalist administration of Adams and the Republican administration of Jefferson marked the political coming of age of the U.S. navy. By 1807 there existed in the United States a clear political consensus supporting a naval establishment. Its role was circumscribed, being restricted to protecting the nation's commerce and not the nation itself. Primary responsibility for coastal defense rested, and would continue to rest, primarily with the U.S. Army and its coastal fortifications and the state militias, although the navy's fleet of gunboats, principally the brainchild of Jefferson, were expected to play a supporting role. This was not by any means a witless policy, given the nature of the threat and the nature of the newly established federal government. While the small but powerful navy envisioned by Stoddert might have been able to play a role in national policy, perhaps even deterring Great Britain from harassing Americans on the seas during the years leading up to the War of 1812, the United States in 1800 possessed neither the fiscal resources nor the manpower necessary to provide and maintain such a force. Already saddled with an enormous debt from the Revolution, the country could not afford the additional cost of Stoddert's naval program. Nor could the nation, which at the time filled the ranks of its navy with volunteers, have found the thousands of seamen and officers necessary to man such a fleet. Ships were generally undermanned during the Quasi-War by about 10 percent, and the officer corps was barely up to the demands imposed by a small force.

The second war with Great Britain—the War of 1812—led to a resurrection of the naval debate in the United States. As it had during the wars with the French and the Tripolitans, the U.S. Navy found itself fighting a *guerre de course*, this time not to protect U.S. commerce but against British shipping. The frigates built in the 1790s, commanded by officers who had begun their professional careers under Stoddert, scored numerous successes. In 1812 the *Constitution*, commanded by Captain Isaac Hull, destroyed the Royal Navy frigate *Guerrière*. The *United States*, commanded by Captain Stephen Decatur, Jr., captured then scuttled the British frigate *Macedonian*. Late in the year, the *Constitution*, commanded by William Bainbridge, captured the *Java*. U.S. men-of-war won many other single-ship engagements, although several were also lost—for example, the *Chesapeake* was captured by the *Shannon* in June 1813.

Despite the brilliant victories, and despite the successes of the campaign waged by the U.S. Navy and hundreds of American privateers against British commerce, the costs to the United States because it lacked adequate naval power were quickly driven home. Great Britain was able to send numerous naval squadrons and several armies across the Atlantic. The United States found its ports blockaded and its trade all but destroyed. The British raided the coast at will. In the summer of 1814 a small British force captured Washington, the national capital, and burned many public buildings and facilities, including the navy yard and the White House.

Command of the sea also allowed Great Britain to build up powerful forces along the Great Lakes. During the campaigns fought along the lake frontier between 1812 and 1814, Americans struggled to keep pace with the British in naval building races that consumed enormous amounts of money, manpower, and resources. Dramatic U.S. victories on Lake Erie (September 1813) and Lake Champlain (September 1814), unfortunately, were not matched on Lake Ontario, the most important of the lakes, and there, at the end of the war, the Americans faced a difficult dilemma.

The prospect of a British, French, or Spanish invasion was nil, and the U.S. Navy did not need battleships to protect commerce from pirates.

When he resigned in late 1814, Secretary of the Navy William Jones informed President James Madison that Great Britain's ability to move resources, including partly disassembled ships, across the Atlantic to the lakes, principally to Lake Ontario, made loss of control by the United States inevitable. Jones suggested that the lakes be abandoned, the ships already constructed burned, and the frontier defended inland. Fortunately, Great Britain had no desire to continue the struggle and signed a treaty of peace late in the year.

For U.S. navalists, the course of the War of 1812 appeared to be a clear lesson of the importance of sea power. The commerce of the nation had been swept from the seas and its coast blockaded and subjected to raids and invasions, despite the presence of an enormous fleet of gunboats and an extensive, and expensive, network of fortifications. As the need for a seagoing battle fleet to keep the enemy at bay became increasingly obvious, navalists found themselves in the political ascendancy, with a national consensus to support the creation of a powerful battle fleet, much like that envisioned by Hamilton and Stoddert in the 1790s.

The crash naval building program that began in 1812 could not, of course, reach fruition before the end of the war, but this time the consensus for a strong navy survived the peace, and the program continued in the postwar years. Ironically, by the time the first of the ships took to sea, they were no longer needed. The century-long era of Anglo-French wars ended in 1815 with the Congress of Vienna and opened a new age of "free security" for the United States. The prospect of a British, French, or Spanish invasion of the United States was virtually nil, and the U.S. Navy did not need battleships to protect commerce from pirates or to suppress the slave trade.

Moreover, the United States, along with the rest of the industrializing world, had entered an era of rapid technological transformation that would shortly bring about enormous changes in warship-building technology that had heretofore been in a period of relative stasis for more than a century. For the most part, the powerful, beautiful, and expensive ships of the line constructed by the United States during and after the War of 1812 proved to be all but useless.

The major post–War of 1812 mission of the U.S. Navy remained commerce protection. Not long after the ink had dried ending the war with Great Britain, a squadron sailed for the Mediterranean, where it blockaded and bombarded Algiers (1815). In the decades after the War of 1812, the navy kept small squadrons in the Mediterranean, the Caribbean, off the west African coast, and in the Pacific. While its ships supported commerce and diplomacy in the far-flung corners of the world and suppressed piracy in the Caribbean and the

The U.S. Naval Academy at Annapolis, Maryland, was organized in 1845 in an effort to enhance what was already a well-established profession. The campus appears to the right in this aerial photograph. (Department of Defense/U.S. Navy)

slave trade off the African coast, as before, the navy was limited to support of the merchant class, and it was still not assigned any broad national roles during peacetime.

The U.S. Navy struggled during the decades following the War of 1812 to keep up with rapidly changing technology. While the navy was not in the forefront of technological change, it experimented with steam-powered propulsion systems, armor plating, breech-loaders, shell guns, and the telegraph. The service also organized an engineering-oriented naval academy in 1845 at Annapolis, Maryland, in an effort to enhance what was already a well-established professionalism.

During the Mexican War (1846–1848), the U.S. Navy again demonstrated the value of sea power and, for the first time, proved itself to be a national asset. Along the California coast and in the Gulf of Mexico, U.S. naval forces blockaded Mexican ports and supported operations ashore. When President James Polk found himself confronting a weak Mexican government unable to negotiate a peace settlement, he turned to sea power as part of the answer. At Polk's direction, Major General Winfield Scott's army in 1847 moved by sea to Veracruz, Mexico. From there it marched inland on the Mexican capital, Mexico City, ultimately forcing an end to the war.

The Civil War, which began in 1861, also highlighted for the United States the potential national virtues of sea power. The Union had a near monopoly on naval power during the war. Naval officers, more so than army officers, remained loyal to the Union. The majority of the U.S. Navy's men-of-war were in northern ports. The absence of Confederate oceangoing sea power initially gave the Union de facto control of the seas.

As the war progressed, the Confederacy managed to purchase several swift cruisers with auxiliary steam power that wreaked havoc on commercial shipping in the North, although the Confederates were never able to challenge northern control of the seas, and warships such as the CSS *Alabama* were eventually run down and destroyed by Union men-of-war. Union control of the sea allowed the North to blockade the coastal ports of the South. Historians continue to debate the effectiveness of the blockade, and many now doubt whether it was as decisive as initially believed. Innumerable Confederate blockade runners evaded capture and carried critically needed supplies into southern ports. Without doubt, however, the blockade handicapped the southern war effort and was yet another advantage enjoyed by the North in the secession struggle.

Control of the sea and possession of strong naval forces also allowed the North to apply military force against the entire coastline of the South. Confederate commanders had to maintain tens of thousands of troops to guard against Union forays from the sea, a burden that northern leaders did not share. As had Scott's army in 1847, Lieutenant General George B. McClellan's Army of the Potomac moved by sea in 1862 to the James River to strike directly, although unsuccessfully, against an enemy capital, in this case Richmond. Two years later, Lieutenant General Ulysses S. Grant directed the operations against Richmond of two Union armies, both supplied by sea.

The North also flexed its naval muscles along inland waters. Armor-clad gunboats fought their way south with army ground operations and safeguarded river routes that usually became major conduits for supply. In the critical battles fought along the Mississippi River, Union oceangoing and inland-water naval forces combined in a classic campaign to cut the Confederacy in two.

The victory of the North in the Civil War might have been expected to further cement the political position of pronaval forces in the United States. Union superiority on the seas had played a large role in assuring northern victory. Moreover, the quickening pace of technological change, epitomized in the May 1862 clash between the Confederate ironclad *Virginia* (actually the captured and rechristened Union *Merrimack*) and the Union ironbuilt *Monitor*, demonstrated that henceforth it would be increasingly difficult to create the jury-rigged naval forces that the United States had relied upon in its previous wars.

Nevertheless, after 1865 the U.S. Navy entered a generation-long period of decline. The reasons for the deterioration of the service were many. Americans, North and South, were tired of war and struggled to reconstruct the nation politically and socially. The Civil War had challenged the country's belief in preordained progress. Almost a generation would pass before Americans recovered from the conflict and began to shape a new national consensus.

There also were no obvious threats to the nation's security in the decades immediately following the Civil War. Once the French had been chased from Mexico, there existed no foreign peril. No European struggle threatened to spill across the Atlantic or onto the ocean that might endanger U.S. commerce. American merchants and missionaries continued their work abroad in an era of relative global security and order.

On distant stations the U.S. Navy recommenced its pre-1861 roles and missions—commerce protection and support for diplomacy, likewise aimed at expanding U.S. markets. U.S. naval forces returned to the Mediterranean, the Pacific, the Indian Ocean, and the Persian Gulf. The ships of the navy were aging and not always gracefully. In addition, as the pace of technological change accelerated, the service fell even further behind the navies of Europe. By the 1870s, the U.S. Navy was a collection of antiquated, obsolescent men-of-war, notable for their quaintness rather than their prowess as warships.

THE OCEANIC PERIOD, 1890–1945

In the 1880s, the United States entered an era of dynamic change. Their country reconstructed, Americans began once again to turn outward, imbued with a renewed sense of nationalism, mission, and purpose. Robert L. Beisner (1986) characterizes this period as a transition from an old paradigm of U.S. foreign affairs to a new paradigm of U.S. foreign policy. At home, Americans sought change through reform, broadened democracy, efficient bureaucracy, and professionalization, as evidenced by the steady ascent of progressive politicians in local and national government.

When Americans looked abroad, they saw a new global surge of imperialism. The products of the industrial revolution—the repeating rifle, the machine gun, the telegraph, and the railroad—allowed Europeans to expand their political and economic control from the periphery into the hearts of Africa and Eurasia. The United States, its own frontier closed, now saw its overseas economic frontiers threatening to close as well. The Ottoman and Chinese empires, for example, long the target of U.S. commercial and missionary interest, were under severe and steady pressure from the European powers and appeared at times to be on the verge of collapse. In the Western Hemisphere, the European powers became increasingly involved in the internal affairs of the states of Central America and South America.

Under such circumstances, the Monroe Doctrine of 1823 suddenly took on new meaning. In the Western Hemisphere, the industrial revolution had brought about a dramatic change in strategic geography. When distances had been measured in sailing days, because of prevailing winds and currents, much of the Caribbean basin and all of South America had been closer to Europe than to the United States. The advent of steam-powered fleets that measured distances in nautical miles meant that the Caribbean, Central America, and South America were, for the first time, truly in the backyard of the United States.

The U.S. Navy quickly found itself assigned new missions. During the Chilean crisis of 1891–1892, it supported a policy aimed not at preserving an existing market but at keeping open a potential market and preventing a possible penetration of the Western Hemisphere by Great Britain. The use of U.S. naval power as a tool of a national foreign policy during the Chilean crisis and battles over Samoa, Hawaii, Venezuela, and Cuba marked the beginning of a new era for the U.S. Navy. A renewed consensus supporting the development of naval power was an element within the new paradigm of U.S. policy. Among those who worked to shape the navy were civilian leaders, such as Presidents Benjamin Harrison, William McKinley, and Theodore Roosevelt; secretaries of the navy, such as William H. Hunt, Benjamin F. Tracy, and Hilary A. Herbert; and historians and propagandists, most notably former U.S. Navy Captain Alfred Thayer Mahan, who defined sea power for the world at the end of the century.

A strong navy would allow the United States to prevent European powers from threatening the United States or the Western Hemisphere.

The U.S. Navy would no longer serve only the interests of the commercial community but would protect the nation as a whole. A strong navy would allow the United States to command the oceanic approaches to the continent and prevent European powers from threatening the United States or the Western Hemisphere and would also allow the United States to play a more forceful role in the Far East, keeping open the door of commercial opportunity. U.S. policymakers saw commerce as the lifeblood of a modern industrializing nation.

The Spanish-American War helped define the new roles of the navy. As soon as conflict began in April 1898, the navy found itself in the forefront of operations in the Pacific and the Atlantic. As planned, in an effort to destroy the Spanish fleet in the Pacific, Rear Admiral George Dewey's Asiatic Squadron entered Manila Bay and annihilated the enemy force. In the Atlantic, other navy squadrons blockaded Spanish naval forces based in Cuba, while transports moved U.S. troops to the island. Ultimately, the navy destroyed Spanish naval power in the western Atlantic, sealing the fate of Spain's empire in the New World and demonstrating, once again, the value of sea power to the United States.

After the Spanish-American War, the United States continued to expand its naval forces. In 1907 and 1908, President Theodore Roosevelt sent the Great White Fleet of sixteen new battleships on a global cruise to demonstrate U.S. naval power to the world, and especially to Japan. Under the administrations of Roosevelt and William H. Taft, the United States continued to build battleships. The U.S. Navy had become the nation's first line of defense, defending a line drawn far from American shores.

By 1913, when Woodrow Wilson became president, support for a strong navy had become a bipartisan issue. Behind a shield provided by U.S. naval power, Wilson held the European powers at bay while naval and ground forces sought to preserve order in the Western Hemisphere. In 1914 U.S. marines and sailors returned to Veracruz. That same year, as the Panama Canal finally opened, allowing the Atlantic and Pacific fleets to become mutually reinforceable, World War I began in Europe.

The European war threatened U.S. freedom of the seas, as German submarines struck at Allied and neutral shipping indiscriminately. Great Britain exploited its control of the seas to the detriment of U.S. commerce. Wilson worked to maintain U.S. neutrality (which tended to favor the Allied powers) and to bring the belligerents to the bargaining table. In 1916, increasingly frustrated, Wilson and the U.S. Congress responded to the actions of Great Britain and Germany by launching a massive naval building program designed to make the U.S. Navy second to none. The following year, Wilson ended his three-year effort to keep the nation out of the conflict when the Germans rejected his efforts to broker a peace, resumed unrestricted submarine warfare in the waters around the British Isles, and tried to inveigle the Mexicans into a conflict with the United States. On 2 April 1917 Wilson went to Congress and asked for a declaration of war against Germany. He then sent the U.S. Navy and the American Expeditionary Forces across the Atlantic in a move that ensured Allied victory.

Despite this victory, by the end of the war the foundations that supported Mahanian concepts of sea power had been shaken. European battle fleets had fought few

Americans used submarines for military purposes during the Civil War, and submarines served extensively during World Wars I and II. The USS Ohio (pictured here) is a nuclear-powered strategic missile submarine. Such submarines play an essential role in modern warfare. (Department of Defense/U.S. Navy)

actions, and none of them, most notably at Jutland (1916), had been decisive. The advent of new instruments of warfare, such as the submarine and the airplane, had raised serious questions about the utility of the battleship and the worth of existing naval programs. Americans, along with their British allies, had discovered that large, expensive battleships were useless against the German *guerre de course.* To counter German U-boats, the Allies needed destroyers and other smaller warships.

These new realities, combined with a widespread desire to reduce military expenditures and to ensure that the Great War proved to be the war to end all wars, led inexorably to postwar naval disarmament. Throughout the 1920s, the United States and the other major naval powers of the world reduced the size of their navies. The series of naval treaties signed in Washington in 1923 ensured parity between Great Britain and the United States but also gave Japan, despite an inferior ratio of naval forces, veritable dominance in the western Pacific.

For a nation determined to avoid military entanglements overseas, a powerful navy was an unnecessary luxury. As a result, for more than a decade after World War I, the U.S. Navy struggled to maintain force levels at treaty limits, to keep pace with rapidly changing technology, and to remain the nation's first line of defense. During the 1920s the service also successfully warded off the first of many assaults by air power advocates who believed that airplanes had made navies obsolete. The U.S. Navy embraced the airplane, coopting air power in the form of the aircraft carrier. The service, with the benefit of knowledge gained from captured U-boats, also sought improved designs for submarines capable of coastal operations and fleet support in the vast Pacific.

Having operated for nearly a century and a half in the shadow of the Royal Navy, the U.S. Navy now secured for itself the mantle of naval leadership.

The navy faced yet another challenge with the beginning of the Great Depression, when construction of warships all but stopped. The global depression also undermined the stability of the existing order, and ultimately led to the growth of the navy, as Americans grew concerned about Japanese expansion in the Far East and the rise to power of the Nazis in Germany. President Franklin D. Roosevelt viewed military spending both as a means to meet these potential international threats and as a method to stimulate the U.S. economy.

Throughout the mid- and late 1930s, the United States began to build a two-ocean navy capable of meeting threats in both the Atlantic and the Pacific. The navy remained wedded to the battleship, the centerpiece of the U.S. Plan Orange strategy for a war with Japan that was to be won by a climactic and decisive engagement in the central Pacific. By 1939, however, the navy had also begun building long-range submarines—which, after 7 December 1941, would prove capable of conducting a *guerre de course* against Japanese commerce—and carriers armed with sea-based aircraft whose capabilities approximated those of land-based aircraft.

Between the German invasion of Poland in September 1939 and the Japanese attack on Pearl Harbor in December 1941, Roosevelt tried to use U.S. naval power to deter war. In the Pacific the fleet moved from the California coast to the Hawaiian islands in an attempt to discourage further Japanese expansion. In the North Atlantic, Roosevelt waged an undeclared naval war against German U-boats.

Despite these efforts, on 7 December 1941 Japanese carrier-based aircraft raided Pearl Harbor. The U.S. Pacific Fleet battleline was all but destroyed. On 11 December, Germany declared war on the United States. The country now faced a two-ocean war.

The initial phases of World War II went poorly for the United States, and especially the navy. In the Atlantic, U-boats torpedoed Allied tankers and freighters within sight of the eastern coast of the United States. Throughout 1942 the navy found itself relearning many of the lessons of the anti-U-boat campaign of 1917–1918.

Victory in what British Prime Minister Winston S. Churchill termed the Battle of the Atlantic was essential if the products of the U.S. arsenal of democracy were to be shipped from the new world to the old and brought to bear against the Axis. Although U-boats remained a menace throughout the war, by the middle of 1943 the Allies had largely controlled them through technological advances, codebreaking, and the productive capacity of U.S. shipyards and factories, which turned out new tankers, freighters, escorts, and patrol aircraft in great numbers.

Once the Atlantic shipping lanes were secured, the Allies brought to bear their land and air forces, supported by sea power, around the periphery of Adolf Hitler's empire. The Allies staged massive amphibious assaults that cracked Hitler's western wall and assured the defeat of Nazi Germany, including assaults in North Africa in November 1942, Sicily in July and Italy in

September 1943, Normandy, France, in June 1944, and the southern coast of France in August of that same year.

In the Pacific Ocean, the United States fought what was primarily a naval conflict. For the U.S. Navy the war against Japan marked the service's final coming of age. Having operated for nearly a century and a half in the shadow of the Royal Navy, the U.S. Navy now secured for itself the mantle of naval leadership. In the central Pacific it sought a modern-day Trafalgar—a decisive, annihilative battle against the Imperial Japanese Navy. No single battle or campaign proved decisive, but a series of carrier battles fought in 1942 in the Coral Sea, at Midway, and in support of operations in the Solomon Islands turned the seemingly inexorable tide of the Japanese advance. Large-scale amphibious operations, part of an island-hopping strategy, supported by carrier-borne aviation, carried the Americans back across the Pacific. In 1944 the Battles of the Philippine Sea—the Marianas Turkey Shoot—and Leyte Gulf virtually ended the threat posed by Japan.

By 1945 the United States and its allies were closing in on Japan. U.S. Navy submarines had devastated the Japanese merchant marine and isolated the home islands from the Asian mainland. Amphibious forces seized Iwo Jima and Okinawa, strategically placed islands guarding the approaches to Japan itself. From bases in the Marianas, U.S. Army Air Forces B-29 heavy bombers pounded fragile cities with massive incendiary raids. Strikes from U.S. Navy carriers, ranging along the eastern coast of Honshu, added to the destruction. Rather than acknowledge their defeat, the Japanese continued the struggle until the entry of the Soviet Union into the war and the dropping of atomic bombs on the cities of Hiroshima and Nagasaki shocked Japan into surrender.

Sailors in the modern U.S. Navy engage in extensive shipboard training that includes instruction in handing mooring lines. This sailors haul a mooring line onto a nuclear submarine as a tugboat pushes the submarine closer to the pier. (Department of Defense/U.S. Navy)

THE TRANSOCEANIC PERIOD, 1945–1992

Victory in World War II vindicated U.S. principles of sea power. The navy had proven wrong its interwar critics who had argued that naval power had become obsolescent. Naval forces had demonstrated tremendous mobility, sustainability, flexibility, and striking power, especially in the Pacific.

Nevertheless, with the end of the war, the future of U.S. naval power was once again in doubt. Political leaders expected the wartime Grand Alliance to continue to function smoothly in the postwar world. There remained no potential naval threat. Whatever the demonstrated shortcomings of strategic air power during the war, the advent of the atomic age appeared to make the air-delivered bomb the ultimate weapon. The trend toward integration of the services—jointness—threatened control of naval aviation and amphibious forces. Critics justifiably asked: What roles and missions could a postwar navy play that the other services could not perform just as well, if not better, and perhaps more cheaply?

Naval leaders—among them Admirals Chester W. Nimitz, Forrest P. Sherman, Robert B. Carney, Richard L. Conolly, and Arthur W. Radford—and civilians, most notably James V. Forrestal, secretary of the navy and later secretary of defense, guided the service through the postwar period. By 1947 the navy had developed a viable strategic concept, despite the intensity of intra- and interservice arguments. The battles with joint organizations—the Joint Chiefs of Staff and the newly created Department of Defense—and with the nation's civilian political leadership were at times vicious and would remain so for years to come, as demonstrated by the cancellation of the carrier *United States* and the subsequent refusal of many high-ranking naval officers to quietly accept Truman administration decisions regarding naval force structure—the revolt of the admirals—in 1949. The navy managed to survive, however, as a sizable, balanced force with a major role to play in U.S. national security policy, although it no longer could claim to be the nation's first line of defense.

Postwar naval strategy began to take shape within a fortnight of Japan's surrender. In September 1945 the Joint Chiefs of Staff identified the Soviet Union as the most likely enemy of the United States, helping to focus the efforts of military planners. At first it was unclear how sea power could be brought to bear against the Soviet Union, a land power without even a moderate-sized oceangoing navy that was not susceptible to a naval blockade or a *guerre de course* waged by U.S. submarines. The planners soon discovered, however, that there were naval tasks that would have to be performed in the event of a Soviet-American conflict. If war began with a Soviet ground offensive to drive U.S. and Allied armies from the Eurasian mainland, such forces would have to be evacuated by naval units. The scarcity of atomic weapons during the early postwar years meant that any strategic air campaign, viewed by most planners as the sine qua non of Allied victory, would be primarily conventional in nature and, until the advent in the 1950s of the intercontinental bombers, would also have to be conducted from forward bases in the British Isles, the Middle East, and Japan. U.S. naval forces operating in the Atlantic, the Mediterranean, and the Pacific would have to shield these bases. The Soviets, in possession of advanced U-boat technology, were likely to build up a force of submarines to threaten Allied sea lines of communication (SLOCs), which would have to be protected by naval forces.

The difficulties experienced by the Allies with German U-boats at the end of World War II led many British and U.S. naval strategists to favor forward, offensive operations against submarine bases. The experience of operating off the coast of Japan in the face of land-based air power had shown that strikes against Soviet submarine bases were feasible. As a result, the U.S. Navy and the Royal Navy formulated the notion of the use of sea power applied ashore along the Eurasian periphery, thus entering the transoceanic era. In 1949 this forward maritime strategy would also become accepted NATO doctrine and would remain the core of Allied conventional naval thinking throughout the cold war.

The new concept was fairly simple. In the event of war, Allied carriers would strike hard at enemy naval and air bases around the periphery of the Soviet Union. Amphibious units would reinforce threatened positions or retake lost ones, perhaps conducting raids or invasions against the Soviet Union itself. U.S. submarines, armed with advanced sonar and eventually powered by nuclear energy, would no longer stalk merchant ships but would hunt down Soviet submarines as they left their bases, before they could reach the SLOCs.

The shift from foreign policy to a national security policy in which diplomacy and military power were closely intertwined also provided the navy with yet another and related role. Forward-deployed, offensively capable naval forces, generally built around carrier battle groups, became symbols of the U.S. commitment to its allies, most notably those in the eastern Mediterranean and the western Pacific. The outbreak of war in the Korean peninsula in June 1950 further strengthened the hands of U.S. navalists. Most notably during the carrier-supported Inchon amphibious assault of September 1950, the United States demonstrated that naval power still had an important role to play in the atomic age.

The resurrection of the navy's carrier program, with construction of the first supercarrier, the *Forrestal*, in the early 1950s, not only indicated that the service had a relatively secure future but ensured that the navy would remain a partner, albeit a junior one, alongside the U.S. Air Force in strategic nuclear warfare.

During the mid-1950s, the pressures of service unification and the shift toward President Dwight D. Eisenhower's New Look policy (sufficient deterrence based on massive retaliation) at first seemed to threaten the roles and mission of the navy, but the shortcomings of the concept of massive retaliation soon became evident. Naval forces demonstrated their crisis response capability during troubles in the Far East and Lebanon. Missile guidance technology led to the development of mobile, stealthy, and therefore survivable submarines (SSBNs) capable of launching intercontinental ballistic missiles (Polaris). These factors, combined with the excellent leadership for six years of Admiral Arleigh Burke, chief of naval operations, ensured that the navy continued to play an important role in national security policy.

During the 1960s, the navy faced some new and some old challenges. President John F. Kennedy brought a team of specialists to Washington who were determined to root out military inefficiency, which they attributed in large part to insufficient centralization. Practical experience, such as the debacle over the operational problems with the F-111, tempered these ideas somewhat. Crises in the Caribbean, the Mediterranean, and the Pacific also demonstrated the value of naval forces. The navy also found itself playing a sizable role in the Vietnam War.

At the close of the 1960s, President Richard Nixon conducted "a retreat from empire," a major retrenchment for a country whose national security consensus had been shaken by the politically divisive war in Indochina. The Nixon Doctrine formalized the unwillingness of the United States to continue to "pay any price" or "bear any burden" in international affairs. It looked to local powers, such as Iran, to police the world's troubled regions and to provide the ground forces that might be necessary in a crisis, and, accordingly, it placed a premium on U.S. air and, especially, naval forces. While naval roles within Nixon's national security strategy were in many ways expanded, the force structure of the service was aging, the victim of neglect during the Vietnam War and reduced military spending in subsequent years. The mid-1970s and late 1970s were lean years for the navy and all the other services.

The United States faced a crisis in the Middle East when, in 1979, the foundations of the Nixon Doctrine collapsed with the fall of the shah of Iran. The Soviet invasion of Afghanistan and the beginning of the Iran-Iraq war in 1980 contributed to instability in the region.

During his final years in office, President Jimmy Carter took steps to restructure U.S. policy in the Middle East, although too late to save his political future. In his 1980 State of the Union address, the president outlined what became known as the Carter Doctrine, warning that the United States would not allow the Soviet Union to threaten the flow of oil from the Persian Gulf. A 1980 pledge by Secretary of State Edmund Muskie went even further, putting the gulf states on notice that the United States would not allow anyone to interfere with oil tanker traffic through the Strait of Hormuz. To add muscle to these pronouncements, the Carter administration began to build up the Rapid Deployment Force, what would eventually become Central Command. In the interim, the president relied heavily on naval power. Carter expanded the naval presence of the United States in the Persian Gulf and Indian Ocean, marking the beginning of what would turn out to be a decade of crisis and war in the region.

This redirection of U.S. national security policy was matched by an intellectual renaissance in the U.S. military. All the services began rethinking their strategy, operational concepts, tactics, and doctrine. By the early 1980s, the navy had developed what it termed the Maritime Strategy, a highly controversial concept even

A U.S. Navy task force of three aircraft carriers accompanied by seven destroyers and cruisers heads toward the Persian Gulf during Operation Desert Shield in 1991. (Department of Defense/U.S. Navy)

though it embraced the established post–World War II practices of forward, offensive operations by carrier, amphibious, and attack submarine forces, in order to seize the initiative from the Soviets in an initial, conventional stage of what the navy was certain would be a global war.

The administration of Ronald Reagan worked hard to rush these and many other Carter policies to maturity. To help support a three-ocean naval commitment, Secretary of the Navy John Lehman, the most active and effective secretary since Forrestal, became the administration advocate for a six hundred-ship navy, one element of a broad-based defense buildup. With its new strategy, a larger force structure, high retention rates, and capable platforms and weapons, the navy entered a period of expansion unmatched in the postwar era.

The Reagan administration made good use of naval capabilities. Trident-armed ballistic missile submarines patrolled the oceans as an increasingly critical element of the nuclear deterrent force, and the rejuvenated naval service continued to conduct its traditional postwar forward presence mission in the North Atlantic, the Mediterranean, and the western Pacific. The navy supported military operations conducted against Lebanon, Libya, Grenada, and Panama, and between July 1987 and August 1988, fought an undeclared naval war in the Persian Gulf and its approaches against Iran in an ultimately successful effort to prevent the escalation of the 1980–1988 Iran-Iraq War to the waters of the gulf. On 18 April 1988, during the course of these operations, the navy won its largest surface action (Praying Mantis) since World War II.

In the summer of 1990 a new crisis loomed in the Persian Gulf. On 2 August, Saddam Hussein sent Iraqi forces into Kuwait. The United States responded forcibly, initiating Operation Desert Shield to prevent Saddam from moving further south into the Arabian peninsula. The forward-deployed forces of the navy led the way. Carriers in the Gulf of Oman and the Red Sea covered the transfer of U.S. Air Force interceptors during their fly-in from bases in the United States, as well as the initial airlift of transports carrying U.S. Army airborne troopers to Saudi Arabia. Navy prepositioning ships rushed equipment and supplies for an entire marine brigade from Diego Garcia in the Indian Ocean to the gulf. The navy guarded the sea-lanes over which hundreds of ships during the next six months carried their cargoes to the gulf, while the United States and its allies built up a powerful force in the Arabian peninsula. The navy also began maritime intercept operations in support of a U.S.-led blockade and United Nations sanctions against Iraq.

On 17 January 1991, when it became clear that Saddam would not withdraw, Desert Shield became Desert Storm. The navy supported both the air and ground operations that ultimately forced the Iraqi army from Kuwait. During the subsequent months, as U.S. Air Force and U.S. Army assets withdrew, the U.S. Navy–Marine Corps team remained in the gulf, enforcing United Nations sanctions against Iraq in an effort to force Saddam to comply fully with the resolutions then in force. U.S. naval forces remained in the Persian Gulf and Indian Ocean as a symbol of the U.S. commitment to the security of the region.

For more than two centuries, the navy of the United States has served the nation well. It grew from a small force that performed a limited role, protecting U.S. commerce, into a large and powerful fleet that for most of the first half of the twentiety century was the first line of defense of the United States. During the cold war, while no longer the nation's premier service, it played critically important roles in support of U.S. na-

UNITED STATES NAVY* PERSONNEL STRENGTH, 1794–1990

Year	Strength
1794	1,856
1800	5,400
1810	5,149
1814	8,024
1820	3,988
1830	4,929
1840	8,017
1849	11,345
1850	8,794
1860	9,942
1865	58,296
1870	10,562
1880	9,361
1890	9,246
1898	22,492
1900	18,796
1910	48,533
1918	448,606
1920	121,845
1930	96,890
1940	160,997
1945	3,380,817
1950	381,538
1952	824,265
1960	617,984
1969	775,869
1970	692,660
1980	526,200
1990	604,562

* Excludes the Marine Corps.

tional interests. In fact, the victory of the western powers in the cold war was a victory of maritime states over land powers, of Mahan over the geopoliticians. Few strategists in 1992, U.S. or Russian, were to be heard heralding the intrinsic strength of the Eurasian heartland.

Trident-armed ballistic missile submarines patrolled the oceans as an increasingly critical element of the nuclear deterrent force.

Over the course of two centuries, the navy developed a strategic tradition of forward, offensive operations. During the Quasi-War with France, the Barbary wars, the Mexican War, the Civil War, the Spanish-American War, and World War II, such operations became its hallmark or "way of war," to quote historian Russell F. Weigley. The Maritime Strategy of the 1980s reflected not only the realities of the post–World War II era but also the service's well-developed strategic inheritance.

The effects on the navy of the end of the cold war and the collapse of the Soviet Union are unclear. It remains to be seen whether these events will usher in a fourth period in the history of U.S. national security and transform the country from one of the world's two superpowers to the globe's omnipower, and whether Americans will remain engaged internationally.

However the country chooses to act in the years ahead, the U.S. Navy will more than likely play an enhanced role in national security policy. Declining defense budgets will affect all the services, but less so the navy. Strategic deterrent forces will probably increasingly be sea-based. The absence of a Soviet threat will probably undermine the alliance system of the United States, resulting in the closing of overseas bases and increased reliance on naval air and amphibious forces. The possibility exists that by the year 2000, the navy might be, once again, the nation's first line of defense.

[See also The Air Force; The Coast Guard; Gunboat Diplomacy, 1776–1992; and The Marine Corps.]

BIBLIOGRAPHY

Allen, Gardner W. *A Naval History of the American Revolution,* 2 vols. (1913, repr. 1962).

———. *Our Navy and the Barbary Corsairs* (1905, repr. 1965).

Beisner, Robert L. *From the Old Diplomacy to the New* (1986).

Braisted, William R. *The United States Navy in the Pacific, 1897–1922,* 2 vols. (1958, 1971).

Challener, Richard D. *Admirals, Generals, and American Foreign Policy: 1898–1914* (1973).

Field, James A., Jr. *America and the Mediterranean World, 1776–1882* (1969).

———. *History of United States Naval Operations: Korea* (1962).

Grenville, John A. S., and George B. Young. *Politics, Strategy, and American Diplomacy: Studies in Foreign Policy, 1873–1917* (1966).

Hagan, Kenneth J. *This People's Navy: The Making of American Sea Power* (1991).

Hattendorf, John B. "The Evolution of the Maritime Strategy: 1977 to 1987." *Naval War College Review* 41 (1988).

Hewlett, Richard G., and Francis Duncan. *Nuclear Navy, 1946–1962* (1974).

Hooper, Edwin Bickford, Dean C. Allard, and Oscar P. Fitzgerald. *The United States Navy and the Vietnam Conflict,* Vol. 1, *The Setting of the Stage to 1959* (1976).

Howarth, Stephen. *To Shining Sea: A History of the United States Navy, 1775–1991* (1991).

Huntington, Samuel P. "National Policy and the Transoceanic Navy." U.S. Naval Institute *Proceedings* 80 (1954).

Knox, Dudley W. *The History of the United States Navy* (1948).

Long, David F. *Gold Braid and Foreign Relations: Diplomatic Activities of American Naval Officers, 1798–1883* (1988).

Love, Robert W., Jr. *History of the U.S. Navy,* Vol. 1, *1775–1941* (1992).

Mahan, Alfred Thayer. *The Influence of Sea Power upon History, 1660–1783* (1890).

Marolda, Edward J., and Oscar P. Fitzgerald. *The United States Navy and the Vietnam Conflict,* Vol. 2, *From Military Assistance to Combat, 1959–1965* (1986).

Morison, Samuel E. *History of United States Naval Operations in World War II,* 15 vols. (1947–1962).

Palmer, Michael A. *Stoddert's War: Naval Operations During the Quasi-War with France, 1798–1801* (1987).

———. *Origins of the Maritime Strategy: The Development of American Naval Strategy, 1945–1955* (1990).

———. *On Course to Desert Storm: The United States Navy and the Persian Gulf* (1992).

Reynolds, Clark G. *The Fast Carriers: The Forging of an Air Navy* (1968).

Roosevelt, Theodore. *The Naval War of 1812* (1882).

Schroeder, John. *Shaping a Maritime Empire: The Commercial and Diplomatic Role of the American Navy, 1829–1861* (1985).

Smelser, Marshall. *The Congress Founds the Navy, 1787–1798* (1959).

Sprout, Harold, and Margaret Sprout. *The Rise of American Naval Power, 1776–1918* (1939, 1967, repr. 1980).

———. *Toward a New Order of Sea Power* (1940, rev. 1943).

Still, William N., Jr. *American Sea Power in the Old World: The United States Navy in European and Near Eastern Waters, 1865–1917* (1980).

Symonds, Craig L. *Navalists and Antinavalists: The Naval Policy Debate in the United States, 1785–1827* (1980).

— MICHAEL A. PALMER

The Marine Corps

A federal judge once ruled that the United States Marine Corps was sui generis—in a class of its own. None of the numerous other marine corps in the world, many of which are modeled after the United States Marine Corps, has quite its status, which includes the paradoxical and sometimes controversial position of being an admired elite force in a determinedly egalitarian society.

The Marine Corps is the only U.S. armed service to have its specific organization spelled out in the law. Title 10, U.S. Code, 5063, states, "The Marine Corps, within the Department of the Navy, shall be so organized as to include not less than three combat divisions and three aircraft wings and such other land combat, aviation, and other services as may be organic therein." The same paragraph further states, "The Marine Corps will be organized, trained, and equipped to provide fleet marine forces of combined arms, together with supporting air components, for service with the fleet in the seizure or defense of advanced naval bases and for the prosecution of such land operations as may be essential to the prosecution of a naval campaign."

For the last half of the twentieth century the home-basing of the divisions and wings of the Marine Corps has been divided among the East and West coasts of the United States and the Far East. The home of the First Marine Division is Camp Pendleton, California; its aviation counterpart, the Third Marine Aircraft Wing, is at nearby El Toro. The Second Marine Division is at Camp Lejeune, North Carolina, and the Second Marine Aircraft Wing is at nearby Cherry Point. Since the end of the Korean War, the Third Marine Division and the First Marine Aircraft Wing have been largely home-based in Okinawa, Japan. The Marine Corps Reserve includes the Fourth Marine Division and the Fourth Marine Aircraft Wing, both headquartered in New Orleans, Louisiana. The active duty strength of the Marine Corps in the post-Vietnam period has averaged about 190,000 marines.

CONTINENTAL MARINES

The Marine Corps dates its beginning on 10 November 1775, when the Second Continental Congress passed a resolution in Philadelphia that two battalions of marines be raised. They were to be part of the Continental army, then besieging Boston, and were intended for an amphibious operation against Nova Scotia. George Washington, the commanding general of the Continental army, was not enthusiastic about the possible dilution of his force, and he discouraged both the expedition and the raising of the marines. The two battalions were never raised and there was no Nova Scotia expedition, but the equivalent of a battalion of marines, about three hundred men, was enlisted at Philadelphia in December 1775 and went with the first American naval squadron on a raid into the Bahamas.

They landed on 3 March 1776 under the command of Captain Samuel Nicholas on New Providence Island, took an undefended fort, then marched to Nassau and took another undefended fort. For the first time an American flag (presumably the Grand Union flag; the record is not clear) was raised over a captured foreign position.

Their uniform coats were green with white facings because green cloth seems to have been plentiful in Philadelphia.

Captain Nicholas returned to Philadelphia something of a hero, was promoted to major, and was directed to raise four companies of marines to provide the guards for the four frigates then being built in the Delaware River. Their uniform coats were green with white (or sometimes red) facings—not, as legend would have it, because they were riflemen (they were armed with muskets), but because green cloth seems to have been plentiful in Philadelphia.

By December 1776 the Continental army, down to three thousand men, had been pushed across New Jersey by Major General Lord Charles Cornwallis with eight thousand British regulars. Washington asked for reinforcement by the Pennsylvania militia. Three companies of Nicholas' marines (the fourth company was already on board the frigate *Randolph*), strength about 140, were brigaded with the militia. The brigade failed to cross the Delaware in time to join what Washington had planned as a Christmas night converging attack on Trenton but fought well at Princeton on 3 January 1777.

Major Nicholas never again took the field but remained in Philadelphia as a functionary of the Second Continental Congress. There was no further effort at centralized recruiting or training of the Continental marines. Instead ship's marine guards were raised locally, in the same way as the seamen of the ship's company, wherever the ship was being fitted out for sea.

Shipboard uses of marines were better understood than their expeditionary uses, although there was the expeditionary model of British marines to be followed. There had been American marines in the British service, most notably in the War of Jenkins' Ear (1739–1742), when an American regiment of thirty-six companies was recruited for service with the West Indies Squadron of Vice Admiral Edward Vernon. This regiment took part in the failed landing against the Spanish at Cartagena, Colombia, in 1741.

One Continental navy commander who did understand the uses of marines was Captain John Paul Jones. Early in the war he had participated in the New Providence raid in the Bahamas. Two years later, in April 1778, when he sailed the twenty-gun sloop of war *Ranger* into the Irish Sea, he used his marines for two raids, against Whitehaven and St. Mary's Isle. Later, he made the *Bonhomme Richard* into an amphibious command ship with extra berthing for a particularly large detachment of French-Irish marines.

While Jones was fitting out the *Bonhomme Richard* in France for his famous foray and victory over HMS *Serapis* off Flamborough Head on the east coast of England in September 1779, the Continental marines were taking part in an amphibious disaster. In June 1779 the British had come down from Halifax and established themselves in Penobscot Bay, Maine. In July an expedition of state ships and three Continental navy ships set out from Boston to eject them. The landing force consisted of about 850 militia to support 227 Continental and Massachusetts marines. Newly built Fort George (near present-day Castine, Maine) was assaulted on 28 July, with the marines leading the way. The impetus of the attack, however, was lost in bickering between the landing force commander, Brigadier General Solomon Lovell, and the naval commander, Commodore Dudley Saltonstall. Two weeks passed while the seven-hundred-man British garrison in the fort awaited the opportunity to surrender. A British relief squadron swept into the bay on 13 August, and all the American ships were lost. Most of the men (Lieutenant Colonel Paul Revere among them) found their way back to Boston, where there were recriminations and courts-martial. The United States would not attempt another large-scale amphibious assault for nearly three-quarters of a century.

Howard Chandler Christy designed this recruiting poster for the U.S. Marines during World War I. (National Archives)

THE ACT OF 11 JULY 1798

After the revolutionary war the Continental marines were disbanded, as was the Continental navy. The marines were reborn on 11 July 1798 by an act of Congress, signed by President John Adams, which created the Marine Corps, under a major commandant, with thirty-two captains and lieutenants, forty-eight sergeants and corporals, 720 privates, thirty-two fifers, and thirty-two drummers. (Active strength in these early years would seldom be more than half of authorized strength.) This new corps was to provide detachments for service in the armed vessels of the navy, most importantly the six new frigates. The marines could also serve ashore, such as guards for the navy yards or for other missions as the president might direct. Afloat the marines would be governed by naval regulations, ashore they would come under the Articles of War. They were accoutered by the War Department in blue uniforms with red facings, reportedly surplus from Major General Anthony Wayne's Legion. Thus began the tradition of Marine Corps "dress blues."

William Ward Burrows, originally of Charleston, South Carolina, but more recently a Philadelphia lawyer-merchant, and a strong Federalist, was the first major commandant and was soon promoted to lieutenant colonel commandant. The title "commandant" persisted, and the corps came to number its commandants; Samuel Nicholas is counted as the first commandant, although he never held the title.

There was immediate employment of marines in the Quasi-War with France. Captain Daniel Carmick, another Philadelphian, commanded the marine detachment on the frigate *Constitution* when it entered the harbor of Puerto Plata on the north coast of Santo Domingo on 12 May 1800 to cut out the French privateer *Sandwich.* It was the first of many marine landings on Hispaniola, the island shared by Haiti and the Dominican Republic.

On 31 March 1801, Burrows went out on horseback to look "for a proper place to fix the Marine Barracks on."

In June 1800 the national capital was moved from Philadelphia to the new federal District of Washington. Burrows brought his marines down from Philadelphia and set them up in a temporary camp near today's Lincoln Memorial. Determined to transform his fifers and drummers into a full-fledged military band, he assessed his officers ten dollars each to buy additional instruments. The Marine Band made its debut at the president's house on New Year's Day before President John Adams, played at President Thomas Jefferson's inauguration in March 1801, and has played at every inauguration since, becoming the "president's own" in 1805. To improve the quality of the band, and with Jefferson's encouragement, musicians were later recruited (not kidnapped, as legend would have it) in Italy by marine officers serving afloat in the Mediterranean.

On 31 March 1801, Burrows went out on horseback with the new president to look "for a proper place to fix the Marine Barracks on." They chose a double square in southeast Washington, bounded by G and I streets and Eighth and Ninth streets, because "it lay near the Navy Yard and was within easy marching distance of the Capitol." This was the beginning of the Marine Barracks at "Eighth and Eye." For nearly a century it would also serve as Headquarters Marine Corps and it still remains the ceremonial heart of the corps.

Ill health forced Burrows to resign early in 1804. He was followed as lieutenant colonel commandant by Franklin Wharton, a member of the prominent Philadelphia family. He approved new uniform regulations for the marines, still blue with red facings, but now also a tall shako and a cut influenced by the uniforms of the Napoleonic wars. He also pushed the construction of the commandant's house on G Street on the north side of the barracks. Since 1806 all commandants have lived in that house, the oldest official residence in Washington still used for its original purpose.

Early in 1804 Captain Carmick was sent with 122 marines to garrison New Orleans, newly American because of the Louisiana Purchase. Carmick fought pirates, slave insurrections, and yellow fever, and was in place, with a promotion to major, when the War of 1812 began with Great Britain.

TO THE SHORES OF TRIPOLI

Trouble with the Barbary pirates (as the corsairs from the North African states were bluntly called) had followed the war with France. In May 1801 the bey of Tripoli, irritated at not receiving his share of tribute for unmolested passage along North Africa's Barbary Coast, cut down the flagstaff in front of the U.S. consulate and declared war against the United States. Jefferson sent a navy squadron to the Mediterranean, but little happened until William Eaton, an Arabic scholar and one-time army captain, arrived on the scene with a secret plan approved by the president. He found the bey's deposed brother living with the warlike Mamelukes several hundred miles up the Nile and persuaded him to join an expedition against the bey. An "army" of perhaps four or five hundred persons, mostly Arabs, was recruited in Alexandria. The leavening professional element was Marine Lieutenant Presley O'Bannon, with a sergeant and six privates. Eaton's force marched across six hundred miles of Libyan desert and on 27 April 1805, with naval gunfire support coming from three ships of the Mediterranean squadron, successfully assaulted the walled city of Derna. O'Bannon raised the U.S. flag over the battlements and brought home a Mameluke sword given to him by the new bey.

THE SECOND WAR FOR INDEPENDENCE

The chief contribution of the Marine Corps to the War of 1812 was again service in the frigates. Of particular note was the service of Lieutenant John Marshall Gamble in the *Essex* during a long cruise to the South Pacific under the command of Captain David Porter, and of Captain Archibald Henderson on the *Constitution* (Commanded by Captain Charles Stewart) in its capture of the *Cyane* and *Levant* on 20 February 1815.

Inland the marines did their share of the fighting against British squadrons coming down from Canada on the Great Lakes. Ashore, 103 marines marched out to Bladensburg, Maryland, from Marine Barracks in

Washington on 24 August 1814 to join the militia and naval contingency, who were vainly trying to stop the British attack on Washington. Lieutenant Colonel Wharton elected not to lead them but to go instead with President Madison, who was fleeing the city.

Carmick's marines had taken their place in New Orleans in General Andrew Jackson's defensive line. Carmick was wounded in the first attack, on 28 December 1814, and eventually died of his wounds. His marines continued to hold staunchly in the second attack, the Battle of New Orleans, 8 January 1815, which saw the complete defeat of the British.

Such men as Captain Henderson did not view Wharton's failure to take the field at Bladensburg in August 1814 as appropriate. Charges were preferred and there was an army court-martial in 1817. Wharton was acquitted and, although ostracized, remained in office until his death the following year. By seniority, the new lieutenant colonel commandant was Irish-born Anthony Gale, who drank too much and had other bad habits. He fell afoul of the secretary of the navy, there was another army court-martial, and he was cashiered in 1820.

Gale's successor, Archibald Henderson, a Virginian, would be commandant for thirty-eight eventful years. In 1826 Henderson standardized the marine officer's sword on the Mameluke model brought home from the Mediterranean by O'Bannon and others, and so it remains to this day. During Henderson's first fifteen years there were operations against pirates in the Caribbean, antislave patrols off West Africa, and landings at such diverse places as the Falkland Islands and Sumatra.

Despite this global employment, President Andrew Jackson saw no reason for the continuance of the Marine Corps and in 1829 moved to have it absorbed into the army. Five years of contention followed, eventuating in the passage by Congress of the Act for the Better Organization of the Marine Corps on 30 June 1834. The act raised the rank of the Commandant to colonel. More important, it resolved some of the ambiguities of the 1798 act. It made clear that the Marine Corps, as part of the Navy Department, was subject to navy regulations, at sea and ashore, unless specifically ordered by the president to do duty with the army.

Almost immediately, President Jackson did exactly that, responding favorably to Henderson's offer in the spring of 1836 that he provide a regiment of marines for operations against the Seminole in Georgia and Florida. (In 1835, for the first time, the strength of the Marine Corps exceeded one thousand, with sixty-eight officers and 1,349 enlisted marines on the rolls.) Henderson formed the regiment in a week by stripping down Marine Barracks and the guards at the navy yards.

The first companies of American marines, organized in 1775, wore green uniforms with white (sometimes red) facings. Modern marines don formal dress blues for ceremonial occasions. (Department of Defense/U.S. Marine Corps)

Taking personal command, he moved his regiment to Florida by chartered steamer, railroad, and foot march. The marines were now, at President Jackson's order, in green uniform coats, a return to revolutionary war practice. The Army gave Henderson command of a brigade that included the marine regiment. His success in the Seminole War (1836–1842) gained him the brevet rank of brigadier general. After a year in the field, Henderson returned with most of his marines to Washington. The green uniform had faded badly in the Florida sun and in 1839 a return to a blue uniform was authorized.

THE MEXICAN WAR THROUGH THE CIVIL WAR

The Marine Corps next played a role in President James K. Polk's Manifest Destiny territorial ambitions. In the late fall of 1845, Polk dispatched First Lieutenant Archibald H. Gillespie on a spy mission into Mexico and then on to California to find Captain John C. Frémont, to whom he was to give memorized secret orders. Gillespie became Frémont's adjutant and later figured prominently in joint army-navy operations.

During the Mexican War (1846–1848), there were marine landings at such places as San Francisco, Monterey, Santa Barbara, San Pedro, Los Angeles, and San Diego, and later, to the south, on the west coast of Mexico, at Mazatlán, Guaymas, Muleje, San Blas, and San José, which demonstrated the strategic leverage of a small landing force in a geographically remote area against an unsophisticated defense.

The first great amphibious operation of U.S. military history was the landing by General Winfield Scott at Veracruz on 9 March 1847. In a highly efficient operation, Scott put twelve thousand men ashore, including only one battalion of marines. The landing and capture of Veracruz was a great turning movement that literally changed the direction of the Mexican War. There were other operations on Mexico's Gulf Coast, made by Commodore Matthew C. Perry, who had a remarkable grasp of amphibious techniques and possibilities. With a marine brigade, made up of his ships' detachment, he made landings up and down the Gulf Coast. The war had brought an increase in the size of the corps to seventy-five officers and 1,757 enlisted in 1847.

Perry took the East India Squadron to Japan in 1853 in the "black ship" visit. Included in the squadron were two hundred marines in stovepipe shakos, under the command of Major Jacob Zeilin, a Philadelphian who had done well in the conquest of California. The marines made a lasting impression on the Japanese.

In 1855 the marines landed at Montevideo, Uruguay. The following year they fought Indians near Seattle in the Washington Territory and in that same year took part with the British in the capture of the Barrier Forts on the Pearl River below Canton in China. In this same decade there were also landings at Panama, Nicaragua, Uruguay, and Paraguay (by way of the Paraná River).

Henderson died in office in January 1859 at the age of seventy-six. His replacement was John Harris, age sixty-nine and a Pennsylvanian. Harris had led a detachment of horse marines in Florida under Henderson and had been breveted a major for bravery. In the Mexican War he gained command of a battalion, but too late in the war for combat.

On 16 October 1859, abolitionist John Brown and his party of zealots took possession of the U.S. arsenal at Harpers Ferry, Virginia. Because there were no regular army troops at hand to put down the insurrection, a detachment of eighty-six marines was sent from the Washington barracks by rail to Harpers Ferry, where they came under the command of Lieutenant Colonel Robert E. Lee. The marines stormed the firehouse that Brown had fortified, Brown was captured and hanged in December, and events moved inexorably toward a civil war over the question of slavery.

The record of the U.S. Marine Corps, never much larger than four thousand men and officers, was not brilliant in the Civil War. Harris appeared content to provide marine ships' detachments and navy yard guards with occasional battalions for forays against the Gulf and Atlantic coasts of the Confederacy. He died in office in May 1864. Secretary of the Navy Gideon Welles, unimpressed by the superannuated officers of the corps, went down the list until he found Zeilin, still a major at age fifty-seven. He had commanded a company at the First Battle of Bull Run, where he was wounded. Welles jumped him from major to colonel commandant, and he was promoted to brigadier general in 1867.

The record of the U.S. Marine Corps, never much larger than four thousand men and officers, was not brilliant in the Civil War.

REFORMING THE CORPS

During his time as commandant, Zeilin adopted the army's new system of infantry tactics, rearmed his marines with a breech-loading rifle, and gave them a new emblem, the Eagle, Globe, and Anchor, and the motto Semper Fidelis ("Always Faithful"). A new marching song, "From the Halls of Montezuma to the Shores of Tripoli," was beginning to be heard, the lyrics written sometime after the Mexican War and the tune possibly taken from an Offenbach operetta, and in 1868 the somewhat wayward thirteen-year-old son of Antonio Sousa (who doubled at the Washington barracks as a carpenter and a trombone player) was enlisted as a music boy. John Philip Sousa would serve as such until age twenty-one, when his enlistment expired.

In 1872 Captain James Forney (brevet rank of lieutenant colonel for bravery in the Civil War) was sent to Europe to survey the marines or naval infantry of Great Britain, France, Spain, Portugal, Germany, Turkey, and Italy. In general, the continental marines defended naval bases, but England's Royal Marines had an expeditionary record. Forney found much in their training to admire and came back with a list of suggestions.

Zeilin retired in 1876 and was succeeded, as the eighth commandant, by Charles G. McCawley with the commandant's rank going back to colonel. McCawley was yet another Philadelphian and only forty-nine years old. He had served in the battalion that went with Scott to Mexico City in September 1847 and had done well in the amphibious probes of the Carolina coastline. Despite Zeilin's initiatives, however, the corps was still in disarray. McCawley improved training, introduced the typewriter for office use, and negotiated the assignment of Naval Academy graduates as Marine Corps second lieutenants. In 1880 he brought John Philip Sousa back into the Marine Band as its leader.

McCawley retired on his sixty-fourth birthday, and the new colonel commandant as of 30 June 1891 was Charles Heywood, age fifty-one and born in Maine. A marine since 1858, he had taken a battalion to Panama in 1885 and had been a brevet "boy lieutenant colonel" in the Civil War.

In these years after the Civil War, as the navy slowly and rather reluctantly converted from wooden ships and sail to steel ships and steam, there was little progress in amphibious or expeditionary techniques, but there were many, many landings. The United States was quick to put marines ashore to "protect American lives and property" and to revenge real or imagined insults to the flag, with repeated landings in such places as China, Formosa, Japan, Nicaragua, Uruguay, Mexico, Korea, Panama, Hawaii, Egypt, Haiti, Samoa, Argentina, Chile, and Colombia. These were very unsophisticated landings, and only in rare cases were there active hostilities. In 1891 marines patrolled the Bering Sea, protecting the fur seals from poachers. The strength of the corps hovered around two thousand. The phrase "The marines have landed and the situation is well in hand" was coined and the myth created that if the army had made such landings it was an act of war, but not so for the marines.

THE SPANISH-AMERICAN WAR

The Spanish-American War and the teachings of Admiral Alfred Thayer Mahan changed the nature of naval operations. The navy's brand-new steel ships required coal, which dictated coaling stations at advanced bases. War was declared on 25 April 1898. By the end of May, Rear Admiral William T. Sampson had bottled up the Spanish Atlantic fleet in Santiago de Cuba, but he needed an advance base nearby from which to coal his blockaders. A marine battalion was hastily put together and landed from a former banana boat named the *Panther* on 10 June at Guantánamo Bay, Cuba, against modest Spanish opposition. The U.S. Navy has maintained an advanced base, protected by marines, at Guantánamo ever since. The beginning date for modern amphibious operations can be put at 10 June 1898. The battalion that landed at Guantánamo was the direct forerunner of the battalion landing teams of World War II, the Korean War, and the Vietnam War.

In August 1900 a marine brigade marched as part of an international column that relieved the foreign legations in Peking, shouldering aside the Boxers, then returned to the Philippines for service against Emilio Aguinaldo's insurgents until 1902, when the Filipino-American War ended. With the expansion of the Marine Corps to more than six thousand officers and men and for his own good service, Heywood was promoted to brigadier general in 1899 and major general in 1902. He retired in 1903 at age sixty-four and was succeeded by George F. Elliott of Alabama, a marine officer since 1870, with the rank of brigadier general.

The lessons of the Spanish-American War were studied at the Naval War College in Newport, Rhode Island. Marines had begun to think about the uses of a battalion or regiment kept afloat in transports. Such a force in the Caribbean, for example, would be conveniently on hand to land at half a dozen or more potential trouble spots. Such landings took place at Panama in 1903, where Elliott took personal command, and 1904, which led to the digging of the Panama Canal; eight landings in Cuba from 1907 to 1917; and a landing in Nicaragua in 1912.

Elliott retired in 1911 and was succeeded by Philadelphian William P. Biddle, who had been commissioned in 1875, had been the marine officer with Admiral George Dewey on the *Olympia* at the Battle of Manila Bay, and had marched in Peking in the Boxer Rebellion. His greatest achievement as commandant was probably the activation in 1913 at Philadelphia of the Marine Advance Base Force, forerunner of the Fleet Marine Forces. A brigade of two small regiments, it also had an aviation detachment—two primitive flying boats.

AVIATION COMES TO THE MARINE CORPS

The first Marine Corps aviator was First Lieutenant Alfred A. Cunningham, who had tried to learn to fly in 1911 by renting a pusher-type contraption that thrashed around a field inside the Philadelphia Navy Yard. His enthusiasm was rewarded with orders to flight training, and the corps observes 22 May 1912, the day he reported to the new navy aviation camp at Annapolis, as the birth date of marine aviation.

Biddle was succeeded as commandant early in 1914 by George Barnett of Wisconsin, the first Naval Academy graduate (class of 1881) to become commandant. Almost immediately, the Advance Base Brigade had its first expeditionary testing, a landing at Veracruz in April. In command of the brigade was Colonel John A.

Lejeune of Louisiana. As a major, Lejeune had commanded the pivotal marine battalion that landed in Panama in 1903, and he came to be called "the greatest leatherneck of them all."

Colonel John A. Lejeune came to be called "the greatest leatherneck of them all."

Just prior to U.S. entry into World War I, the Marine Corps (with a strength that had grown to just under eleven thousand) was involved in lengthy interventions in Haiti, beginning in 1915, and in the Dominican Republic, beginning in 1916. Mostly their work consisted of bandit chasing, building public works, and the formation of a marine-officered native constabulary.

MARINES IN FRANCE AND BETWEEN THE WORLD WARS

Over the objections of Secretary of War Newton Baker, a marine regiment sailed with the first U.S. convoy to France after the United States entered the war in April 1917. Another regiment followed, and the two regiments were joined together as the Fourth Brigade of Marines. From June to November 1918, the brigade, as part of the U.S. Second Infantry Division, attracted international attention at Belleau Wood, and afterward fought exceedingly well at Soissons and Saint-Mihiel, and then, with Major General Lejeune in command of the Second Division, at Blanc Mont and in the Meuse-Argonne.

Cunningham, by then a captain, was sent to France in 1917 to find a mission for marine aviation, anticipating that it would be in support of ground marines. After a promotion to major, he took four squadrons of DH-4 DeHavillands to France in the late summer of 1918, but they were shunted off to the British sector of the western front, far from where the Fourth Marine Brigade was engaged. There, in the last days of the war, they shot down twelve German aircraft and flew fifty-seven bombing missions, at a cost of four dead.

The corps had peaked to a strength of 75,101 by the end of 1918. Casualties in World War I totaled 11,366, of whom 2,459 were killed or forever missing in action.

Lejeune succeeded Barnett as major general commandant in 1921. By then the strength of the corps had decreased to 22,990. Lejeune formally organized the Marine Corps schools at Quantico, Virginia, and consolidated officer training into three levels: basic course (for new lieutenants), company officers course (for captains), and field officers course (for majors and lieutenant colonels). This three-tiered system of officer schools, with various name changes, would be continued and now consists of the Basic School, the Amphibious Warfare School, and the Command and Staff College. Lejeune also firmly established 10 November 1775, the date of the Second Continental Congress resolution authorizing the first marine battalions, as the official birth date of the Marine Corps, with a message that is read annually. In 1922, Lejeune redesignated the Advance Base Force, its headquarters moved from Philadelphia to Quantico, as the East Coast Expeditionary Force. The West Coast Expeditionary Force was activated at San Diego.

Between the world wars, the Marine Corps sent small expeditionary brigades to Haiti, the Dominican Republic, Nicaragua, and China. In every case, these brigades had an organic aviation element. Marine and navy strategic planners of the period foresaw a war against the Japanese in which the United States would have to fight its way back across the Pacific. For the Marine Corps this would mean the assault in the central Pacific of heavily fortified islands held by the Japanese. A clear statement of this was found in Operation Plan 712, "Advanced Base Operations in Micronesia," written in 1921.

After nine years as commandant, Lejeune retired in 1929 at age sixty-two and in retirement became superintendent of the Virginia Military Institute. His successor as commandant was a long-time comrade in arms in the Caribbean and France, Wendell C. ("Buck") Neville, who died after serving a little more than a year.

The fifteenth commandant, appointed in August 1930, was Ben H. Fuller, whose quiet nature was reflected in his nickname, "Uncle Ben." His immediate assistant was Major General John H. Russell, Jr., a Californian who for nine years had been high commissioner in Haiti. In 1933, largely as the work of the energetic and highly competent Russell, the East Coast and West Coast Expeditionary Forces became the Fleet Marine Forces, with the First Marine Brigade based at Quantico and the Second Brigade based at San Diego, each with its own aircraft group.

Also during the years of Fuller and Russell's tenure, officers at the Marine Corps schools, having analyzed the British disaster at Gallipoli in 1915, were working out a viable amphibious doctrine through a combination of theoretical studies and fleet exercises. A good deal of emphasis was placed on the development of landing craft and amphibian vehicles. By 1938 all the basic types of landing craft and amphibian vehicles used in World War II were well along in their evolution. The problem of getting from ship to shore was on its way to solution and so were the related problems of command relationships, ship-to-shore communications, combat loading of troop transports, and air and naval gunfire support.

While this work progressed, Thomas Holcomb of Delaware succeeded Russell as commandant in 1936. Holcomb, a highly successful battalion commander in France and a long-time "China Marine," (a veteran of China service), had the further advantage of being a friend and confidant of President Franklin D. Roosevelt. In the pre–World War II years, the Marine Corps began to qualify its squadrons for operations from aircraft carriers. The practice continued and gave great flexibility to naval aviation—marine squadrons could serve from on board ship, and navy squadrons, in many cases, could fly from expeditionary airfields.

As the war approached, it became increasingly clear that initially the role of the Marine Corps would be defensive. In 1941 the First Marine Brigade became the First Marine Division, and the Second Marine Brigade became the Second Marine Division. Correspondingly, the East Coast and West Coast air groups became the First and Second Marine Aircraft Wings. In the summer of 1941 a provisional marine brigade was sent to garrison Iceland. Defense battalions—composite units with antiaircraft and sea coast artillery, infantry, and aviation—were sent to Iceland, and in the Pacific to Samoa, Midway, Wake, Johnston, and Palmyra islands.

WORLD WAR II

War came on 7 December 1941. For the first eight months of the struggle, the battles fought by the marines, chiefly the defense battalions, were indeed defensive—Pearl Harbor, Guam, Wake Island, Bataan, Corregidor, and Midway. The role of marine aviation at Wake and later at Midway was significant, in both fighter-interceptor and scout-bombing missions.

Early World War II Marine Corps deployments were in brigade strength. In January 1942, the Second Brigade was taken out of the Second Division and sent to American Samoa. Two months later the Third Brigade was stripped out of the First Marine Division and dispatched to Western Samoa. In 1940 Holcomb assumed a second four-year term as commandant, and in January 1942 he was promoted to the three-star grade of lieutenant general, the first marine to hold that rank.

The first U.S. offensive action in the Pacific began in August 1942 with the landing on Guadalcanal of the First Marine Division, under the command of Major General Alexander A. Vandegrift. Marine aviation followed ashore just as soon as marine and navy engineers could scrape airstrips into the coral. The marines had landed on 7 August; the first two marine squadrons—a fighter squadron and a scout-bomber squadron—arrived at Henderson Field on 20 August. Ashore at Guadalcanal, the marines had to hold against the full fury of the Japanese air, sea, and land counteroffensive. It was not until February 1943, after reinforcement, that the Japanese gave up their efforts to retake the island. It was a turning point in the Pacific war.

In the South Pacific, New Georgia (June 1943) followed Guadalcanal and Bougainville (November 1943) followed New Georgia, but it was in the central Pacific, as predicted, that the navy–Marine Corps amphibious doctrine received its most violent testing. That trial came with the assault of Betio in the Tarawa atoll in the Gilbert Islands on 20 November 1943. Marine aviation was of no help at Tarawa; there were no close-by land bases or available carrier decks from which to launch marine planes. Even so, the three days that followed were bloody proof (Japanese casualties, nearly 6,000 dead; marine casualties, 1,027 dead, 2,292 wounded) that an amphibious assault of a heavily fortified position could be successful.

In January 1944, Vandegrift, the hero of Guadalcanal and with a Medal of Honor, succeeded Holcomb (who became minister to South Africa) as commandant. The remaining twenty months of the war saw marines battling for Cape Gloucester, Kwajalein, Eniwetok, Saipan, Guam, Tinian, Peleliu, Iwo Jima, and Okinawa.

In the central Pacific, marine air tended to get separated from Marine ground and found itself relegated to the bombing of bypassed Japanese bases. Toward the war's end, however, marine air dramatically demonstrated what it could do in its close support of the army's reoccupation of the Philippines and, at Okinawa, came into its own in support of the Marine Third Amphibious Corps.

The Marine Corps reached a peak strength of 485,053 in World War II. Force structure had grown to two corps, with a total of six divisions and five aircraft wings. Total marine casualties in the war were 19,733 dead and 62,207 wounded.

Faced with the challenge that the atomic bomb had made amphibious operations obsolete, the Marine Corps began experimenting with helicopters.

After the war it was decided that there would be a Fleet Marine Force, Atlantic, and a Fleet Marine Force, Pacific, each with a division and a wing. The "Battle of Capitol Hill" was being fought over the issue of "unification" of the armed services. There were strong pressures, endorsed by President Harry S. Truman, for a single Department of War. What emerged under the National Security Act of 1947 was the Department of Defense, with the three subordinate Departments of the Army, Navy, and Air Force. The Marine Corps remained in the Department of the Navy, but its future was uncertain. Faced with the challenge that the atomic bomb had made amphibious operations obsolete, the Marine Corps began experimenting with helicopters as a future means for the critical ship-to-shore movement. The first marine helicopter squadron, HMX-1, was organized in 1947 and now flies the president's helicopters.

Clifton B. Cates of Tennessee, a hero as a platoon leader and company commander in France during World War I and a regimental and division commander in the Pacific, succeeded Vandegrift on 1 January 1948 as commandant, a position that now carried the grade of four-star general. With postwar demobilization and Truman administration economies, his force shrank by the summer of 1950 to 74,279 marines, barely enough to man the skeletons of two divisions and two aircraft wings.

THE KOREAN WAR

The Korean War began on 25 June 1950. Lieutenant General Lemuel C. Shepherd, Jr., the commanding general, Fleet Marine Force, Pacific, met with General Douglas MacArthur, the commander in chief of the Far East, in Tokyo on 10 July. MacArthur told Shepherd that if he could get the First Marine Division under his command he would land it at Inchon, behind the North Korean Army. Two days later, the First Marine Provisional Brigade, hurriedly stripped out of the First Marine Division, sailed from San Diego, not to land at Inchon but to take its place in the desperate fight to hold the Pusan perimeter. The brigade landed at Pusan on 2 August and, with the support of Marine Aircraft Group 33 flying the F-4U Corsair, had a great deal to do with the perimeter's successful defense. The brigade then rejoined, at sea, the remainder of the First Marine Division, brought up to strength mainly by gutting the Second Marine Division and calling up the reserves. The division landed at Inchon on 15 September, turning the flank of the enemy and making possible the breakout of the Eighth Army from Pusan.

After fighting its way to Seoul, the capital of South Korea, the First Marine Division reembarked to land at Wonsan, on Korea's east coast. Then came the march north almost to North Korea's northern boundary, the Yalu River; the Chinese entry into the war; the epic march back to the sea from Chosin Reservoir; and the amphibious withdrawal from Hungnam, the last a virtuoso achievement on the part of the U.S. Navy.

The First Marine Division and the First Marine Aircraft Wing remained in Korea for the remainder of the war and turned in a good performance, both in the air and on the ground, but not without some jurisdictional and doctrinal problems with the Fifth Air Force. Air force doctrine would have it that everything that flew should be under air force control; the Marine Corps argued that its air-ground units fought best as a combined arms team.

Much less controversial was the pioneering use by the Marine Corps of helicopters in Korea. Starting with reconnaissance and liaison use, it moved into medical evacuation and then into the tactical movement of marines and their supplies. During the Korean War the corps also changed over from propeller-driven fighter bombers to jets.

Cates was openly at odds with Truman during much of their mutual tenures. Shepherd, a courtly Virginian and, like Cates, a hero and proven leader in both of the world wars, became the twentieth commandant in January 1952. The political battle on Capitol Hill had continued. In January 1951, just after the withdrawal of the marines from the Chosin Reservoir, Senator Paul H. Douglas and Congressman Mike Mansfield (both former marines) introduced a bill that in its final form provided for the peacetime structure of three active marine divisions and three air wings, and coequal status for the commandant within the Joint Chiefs of Staff when matters of direct concern to the Marine Corps were being considered. Marine strength climbed to nearly 250,000 in 1953; casualties for the Korean War were 4,262 marines killed and 21,781 wounded, twice the totals of World War I.

POST-KOREA CHALLENGES

Randolph McC. Pate, a Virginian and, like Shepherd, a graduate of the Virginia Military Institute, succeeded Shepherd as commandant in January 1956. Pate's severest test came a short time later, after a drill instructor at Parris Island, South Carolina, took his recruit platoon on an unauthorized night march, during which six marines drowned in marshy Ribbon Creek. This brought marine recruit training methods under great criticism and searching scrutiny, and only yeoman efforts on the part of the corps and its supporters saved the traditional boot camp training, shoring it up with additional safeguards against abuses.

In the summer of 1958, after the assassination of pro-Western King Faisal II of Iraq upset the equilibrium of the Arab world, four battalion landing teams, combined into a brigade equivalent, the Second Provisional Marine Force, were landed in Lebanon as a peacekeeping force at the behest of President Camille Chamoun.

David M. Shoup of Indiana, holder of a Medal of Honor from Tarawa, was chosen by President Dwight Eisenhower to succeed General Pate as commandant in January 1960. Shoup, a tough and earthy marine, concentrated on returning the Marine Corps to what he considered its fundamentals.

The successful and bloodless 1958 Lebanon intervention marked the last use of the time-honored term "provisional" for a task-organized Marine Corps expeditionary force. By the late 1950s, the Marine Air-Ground Task Force concept and its new terminology were beginning to crystallize. As prescribed in a directive promulgated in 1962, marine air-ground task forces (more commonly known by the acronym "MAGTF, pronounced "Mag-taff"), would henceforth come, with an occasional exception, in three sizes, a marine expeditionary unit (MEU) being the smallest, a marine expeditionary brigade (MEB) being next in size, and a marine expeditionary force (MEF) being the largest. In structure MAGTFs all had four elements—command, ground combat, aviation combat, and combat service support. An MEU ordinarily would have a battalion landing team as its ground element, a reinforced helicopter squadron as its aviation element, a tailored service support group, and a colonel as its commander.

An MEB most frequently would have a regimental landing team, a "composite" (meaning both fixed-wing aircraft and helicopters) marine aircraft group, and a brigade service support group, with a brigadier or major general as its commander. No two MEBs were to be exactly alike in structure. The size of a brigade could easily vary from as few as seven thousand to seventeen thousand troops or more, mostly marines, but with a considerable number of navy men because corps medical support and its chaplains, plus some engineering help, came from the navy. An MEF most often would be a division, an aircraft wing, and a force service support group, with a major general or lieutenant general in command.

General Wallace M. Greene, Jr., a Vermonter who had been Shoup's chief of staff and who had signed the directive formalizing the MAGTF concept, succeeded Shoup as commandant on 1 January 1964. The Dominican intervention of April 1965 saw the employment initially of the Sixth Marine Expeditionary Unit and a buildup of the Fourth Marine Expeditionary Brigade.

THE VIETNAM WAR

The first substantial commitment of U.S. ground combat forces in Vietnam was on 8 March 1965, when the Ninth Marine Expeditionary Brigade landed at Da Nang. The Ninth MEB was followed on 7 May by the landing of the Third Marine Expeditionary Brigade at Chu Lai, some fifty-five miles to the south. Both brigades were then absorbed into the Third Marine Expeditionary Force, which quickly had its name changed to Third Marine Amphibious Force because it was presumed that the South Vietnamese had unhappy memories of the French expeditionary force.

Eventually the Third Marine Amphibious Force included two marine divisions, two additional marine regimental combat teams, the huge First Marine Aircraft Wing, and the equally large Force Logistics Command, but this took several years, with battalions and squadrons being fed into the country one at a time.

The strength of the Third Marine Amphibious Force peaked at 85,755 marines in 1968, more marines than had been ashore during World War II at Iwo Jima or Okinawa. The blurred fighting in Vietnam did not divide itself nicely into campaigns and battles, but there was the pacification effort against the Vietcong and the marine force war against the North Vietnamese, and some names and places to remember, such as Da Nang, Chu Lai, Hue, Phu Bai, the DMZ (demilitarized zone), Dong Ha, Con Thien, and Khe Sanh.

Greene's successor as commandant in January 1968 was General Leonard F. Chapman, Jr., a Floridian known for his managerial efficiency. His overriding task was to manage the systematic withdrawal of the marines from Vietnam. By the time General Robert E. Cushman, Jr., took over as commandant in January 1972, the marines were almost out of Vietnam. Cushman, holder of the Navy Cross, received as a battalion commander in World War II, and a commander of the Third Marine Amphibious Force in Vietnam, faced the formidable task of rebuilding a Marine Corps shaken by the Vietnam experience, which had been the longest and in some ways the most bitter war in Marine Corps history. By mid-1972 casualties had reached 12,926 marines killed and 88,755 wounded, about half of the latter hurt badly enough to require hospitalization. In size the corps had grown from a 1965 strength of 190,213 to a peak of 314,917 in 1969; it would slip back quickly to a plateau of just under 200,000.

There had been no World War II- or Inchon-style beach assaults. There were, however, many battalion-size special landing force operations, either as amphibious raids or as a reinforcement of an ongoing operation, at spots along the South Vietnam coast. Amphibious techniques were also used in the evacuations of Phnom Penh, Cambodia, and Saigon in April 1975, the first by the Thirty-first Marine Amphibious Unit and the second by the Ninth Marine Amphibious

Brigade. Again there had been jurisdictional and doctrinal problems over the use of tactical air, this time with the Seventh Air Force. The decision came down on the air force side, with the designation of the commander, Seventh Air Force, as the single manager for air.

REFINING THE MARINE AIR-GROUND TEAM

Cushman cut short his four-year tenure, retiring six months early in July 1975. The new commandant was Louis H. Wilson, a courtly Mississippian and the holder of the Medal of Honor from Guam. By adroit political maneuvering he succeeded in gaining for the Marine Corps full membership on the Joint Chiefs of Staff. He also reintroduced more realism in marine training and brought together more closely the ground and aviation elements by creating the Marine Air Ground Combat Training Center at the vast Marine Corps desert base at Twentynine Palms, California. The core of the training was the Combined Arms Exercises (CAX), which involved battalion landing teams with supporting air passing through Twentynine Palms at the rate of ten battalions per year.

Wilson's successor in July 1979 was his good friend Robert H. Barrow of Louisiana, chosen by President Jimmy Carter, then in his embattled last eighteen months of office. Barrow had distinguished himself in combat as a lieutenant with Chinese guerrillas in World War II, as a company commander in Korea, and as a regimental commander in Vietnam. As a general officer he had made his mark as an expert in manpower and training. Barrow inherited a Marine Corps in a high peacetime state of readiness but facing a budget-driven cut in manpower from 189,000 to 179,000. Barrow fought these cuts, making no secret that quality recruiting remained his top priority.

In November 1979 the U.S. Embassy in Tehran, Iran, was sacked and sixty Americans, including nine members of the marine security guard, were taken hostage. A frustrated administration began talking of forming a rapid deployment force to deal with such recalcitrants as Iran. The Rapid Deployment Joint Task Force (RDJTF), forerunner to the U.S. Central Command, was activated on 1 March 1980, with its headquarters at MacDill Air Force Base, Florida, but was no more than a skeleton headquarters when Operation Desert One, the botched hostage rescue attempt, in which the marines provided transport helicopter crews, was launched in April 1980.

The RDJTF focused on the Middle East, "from Marrakech to Bangladesh." Troops could be airlifted to these potential crisis spots, but supplies and equipment required sealift. The first RDJTF commander was Lieutenant General Paul X. Kelley, an ebullient Boston Irishman, who had been both a battalion and a regimental commander in Vietnam. To support marine forces earmarked for deployment to the Middle East and in the absence of sufficient amphibious shipping, a new program called Maritime Prepositioned Ships (MPS) came into being. Under MPS, squadrons of leased commercial ships, preloaded with the equivalent of a marine amphibious brigade's thirty-day requirement in equipment and supplies, would be positioned strategically around the globe. These ships would not need ports; they could off-load either at a pier or in the stream. They would need a benign environment, however, and they would not be a substitute for amphibious ships that had assault capability.

During the last three years of Barrow's tenure, the Marine Corps benefited, particularly in new weaponry, from the generous budgets of the Ronald Reagan administrations. This beneficence continued under the next commandant, General Kelley, who had moved up to the post of assistant commandant after commanding the RDJTF.

LEBANON, GRENADA, AND PANAMA

A tragic chapter in Marine Corps history would soon confront Kelley. In August 1982, eleven months before he became commandant, the Thirty-second Marine Amphibious Unit had landed at Beirut, Lebanon, along with French and Italian troops, as part of a multinational peacekeeping force. After overseeing the evacuation of Palestine Liberation Organization (PLO) guerrillas, the Thirty-second MAU reembarked and briefly departed, to return again in September after the assassination of President-elect Bashir Gemayel.

An estimated six tons of explosives was detonated, 241 U.S. servicemen (220 of them marines) were killed, and another 70 were wounded.

The Marine Corps presence in Lebanon continued, one MAU relieving another at roughly four-month intervals, with the marines holding a defensive position at the Beirut international airport. There were occasional casualties when the marines were caught in the cross fire of the warring factions. The tempo of the civil war increased, with more and more attacks directly against the Americans, French, and Italians. U.S. policy came around to open support of the Lebanese army, but the marines were limited to a quasi-combat posture with highly restrictive rules of engagement.

Early Sunday morning, 23 October 1983, a truck swept by the marine checkpoints on the airfield and into position under a building that housed the headquarters of BLT-1/8, the ground combat element of the Twenty-fourth MAU. An estimated six tons of explosives was detonated, 241 U.S. servicemen (220 of them marines) were killed, and another 70 were wounded. Recriminations abounded.

On 22 October, before the Beirut barracks tragedy, the Twenty-second MAU, at sea en route to a routine relief of Twenty-fourth MAU at Beirut, was ordered to head for Grenada. An intervention had been triggered by the murder of Grenada's leftist Prime Minister Maurice Bishop on 19 October and the subsequent installation of the Revolutionary Military Council headed by General Hudson Austin. On 25 October 1983, army rangers and a sizable part of the Eighty-second Airborne Division air-landed on the southwest corner of the island to seize Point Salines airfield, while Marine BLT-2/8, landing by helicopter, secured Pearls airfield at the northeast corner against negligible resistance. Two marine Cobra attack helicopters were subsequently lost in assisting the army in the rescue of the British governor-general from his mansion above St. George's. In two days the operation was essentially over. On 1 November the marines made a subsidiary landing on the neighboring islet of Carriacou and found no enemy. Of the total U.S. casualties of nineteen dead and 115 wounded, three of the dead and fifteen of the wounded were marines.

Subsequent to the Carriacou landing the Twenty-second MAU reembarked and continued on its way to the Mediterranean. In mid-November it relieved the battered Twenty-fourth MAU. It stayed in Lebanon, was intermittently involved in hostile actions, and reembarked at the end of February 1984. The total cost to the Marine Corps for its eighteen-month presence in war-torn Lebanon was 238 dead and 151 wounded.

Although he was not in the operational chain of command, the Beirut tragedy overshadowed Kelley's commandancy. He was succeeded in July 1987 by General Alfred M. Gray, previously the commanding general,

On Oct. 25, 1983, U.S. Marine Corps and Army troops invaded Grenada to rescue Americans and restore order after a coup. At the close of the operation, this marine waited in front of captured members of the Granada's revolutionary army. (Department of Defense/U.S. Marine Corps)

Fleet Marine Force, Atlantic, and before that the commanding general, Second Marine Division. Gray, from New Jersey and once a marine sergeant, came to Washington on a wave of publicity that he was bringing a new broom (or baseball bat) to clean out the headquarters. For the first two years of his tenure he rode the crest of generous Reagan administration budgets. Underlying his reforms was his basic concept of the marine as a "warrior." Among Gray's changes was the return in 1988 of the designation of MAGTFs as "expeditionary" rather than "amphibious" to reflect more accurately the Marine Corps strategic mobility. He also reorganized the Marine Corps Development and Education Command (MCDEC) at Quantico into the Marine Corps Combat Development Command (MCCDC), with five separate but functionally related centers: Marine Air-Ground Task Force Warfighting; Training and Education; Intelligence; Wargaming and Assessment; and Information Technology. The resident schools were grouped into the Marine Corps University. Another new organization was the Marine Corps Research, Development, and Acquisition Command (MCRDAC).

At the national level, the new buzzwords were "low intensity conflict," (LIC), a concept that carried with it the highly selective and constrained use of force. The ousting of General Manuel Noriega from his position as dictator of Panama in December 1989 provided a testing for the new strategy. Noriega had been indicted for drug-related activities by a U.S. grand jury in January 1988. Attempts by the nominal president, Arturo Delvalle, to unseat him had precipitated violent civil unrest. The Marine Corps had only a minor role to play. A reinforced Marine Corps Security Force company was sent to Panama in March. It was followed in April by a contingency Marine Air Ground Task Force designated as Marine Force, Panama, initially built around a reinforced rifle company and service support, but with no aviation combat element. The marines were assigned to the west bank of the old Panama Canal Zone; the operation was a base defense mission that called for protection of U.S. naval and military facilities. Marine Force, Panama, was subordinate to the Joint Task Force, Panama. JTF Panama's "enemy" was Noriega's paramilitary Panamanian Defense Force (PDF), totaling about thirteen thousand, of whom perhaps three thousand were truly combat capable. The PDF set about harassing U.S. security forces, including marines, as well as U.S. citizens living or traveling in Panama.

On arrival, the marine rifle company took up defensive positions at the Arraijan tank farm, the fuel source for all U.S. forces in Panama. Probing of their lines by mysterious nighttime assailants began almost immediately. Between April and September 1988 there were fourteen separate shooting incidents, and one marine was killed. In November the marines were ordered to raze their fixed defenses and to limit their patrolling. The situation remained relatively quiet for several months until, in May 1989, after his party was soundly beaten in national elections, Noriega annulled the results. This action caused the United States to take more aggressive steps. Marine Force, Panama, was reinforced by a light armored infantry company equipped with the LAV-25, a light armored wheeled vehicle. A series of exercises, called Sand Fleas, followed.

On 3 October 1989, a U.S.-supported coup attempt against Noriega failed. Tensions mounted, and on the night of 16 December an off-duty U.S. marine lieutenant was fatally wounded by Noriega thugs. This incident and the detention of a U.S. Navy officer and his wife caused President George Bush to activate the contingency plan, Operation Just Cause, designed to remove Noriega. Marines began the movement to their objectives—chiefly the tank farm, the reinforcement of Howard Air Force Base, and the Bridge of the Americas, the only fixed bridge spanning the canal—shortly after midnight, 20 December. Reinforced with an army light infantry battalion and a freshly arrived marine rifle company, Marine Force, Panama, with a total of about 650 marines (of a total U.S. force of 27,000), successfully played its role in what was essentially a much larger army operation.

The fighter attack aircraft of the Marine Corps in the early 1990s was the F/A-18 Hornet. The attack aircraft were the British-designed AV-8B Harrier, a true vertical takeoff and landing aircraft, and the A-6E Intruder. Also in the fixed-wing inventory were the KC-130 Hercules, which served as both an aerial refueler and a transport, and the EA-6B Prowler, an electronics countermeasures aircraft. The heavy helicopters of the corps were the CH-53D Sea Stallion and the CH-53E Super Stallion, the medium helicopter was the CH-46 Sea Knight, and the light helicopters were the AH-1W Super Cobra and the UH-1N, last in a long line of Hueys.

THE PERSIAN GULF

The Iraqi invasion of Kuwait on 2 August 1991 precipitated Operation Desert Shield, the massive movement of U.S. forces to the Persian Gulf. Marine deployments were made in terms of marine expeditionary brigades—the Seventh Marine Expeditionary Brigade from California and the First MEB from Hawaii, both airlifted. Then came the seaborne Thirteenth MEU, the Fourth MEB, and the Fifth MEB, making up the landing force of the amphibious task force in the Persian Gulf. Subsequently, most of the Second Marine Expeditionary

UNITED STATES MARINE CORPS PERSONNEL STRENGTH, 1798–1992

Year	Officers	Enlisted	Total
1798	25	58	83
1799	25	343	368
1800	38	487	525
1801	38	319	357
1802	29	330	359
1803	25	317	342
1804	25	364	389
1805	22	556	578
1806	11	307	318
1807	11	392	403
1808	11	861	872
1809	10	513	523
1810	9	440	449
1811	14	542	556
1812	10	483	493
1813	12	579	591
1814	11	637	648
1815	8	680	688
1816	21	451	472
1817	14	652	666
1818	24	536	560
1819	21	664	685
1820	19	552	571
1821	35	844	879
1822	23	708	731
1823	20	681	701
1824	50	890	940
1825	35	746	781
1826	39	796	835
1827	43	903	946
1828	40	892	932
1829	43	852	895
1830	37	854	891
1831	35	780	815
1832	38	860	898
1833	43	853	896
1834	46	869	915
1835	68	1,349	1,417
1836	43	1,298	1,341
1837	37	1,524	1,561
1838	28	1,067	1,095
1839	34	916	950
1840	46	1,223	1,269
1841	44	1,156	1,200
1842	46	1,243	1,289
1843	43	1,041	1,084
1844	40	1,046	1,086
1845	42	986	1,028
1846	41	1,126	1,167
1847	75	1,757	1,832
1848	42	1,709	1,751
1849	46	1,030	1,076
1850	46	1,055	1,101
1851	43	1,150	1,193
1852	47	1,121	1,168
1853	49	1,205	1,254
1854	49	1,312	1,361
1855	52	1,552	1,604
1856	57	1,414	1,471
1857	57	1,694	1,751
1858	52	1,555	1,607
1859	47	1,804	1,851
1860	46	1,755	1,801
1861	48	2,338	2,386
1862	51	2,355	2,406
1863	69	2,931	3,000
1864	64	3,075	3,139
1865	87	3,773	3,860
1866	79	3,258	3,337
1867	73	3,438	3,511
1868	81	2,997	3,078
1869	70	2,314	2,384
1870	77	2,469	2,546
1871	74	2,439	2,513
1872	77	2,126	2,203
1873	87	2,675	2,762
1874	85	2,184	2,269
1875	76	2,037	2,113
1876	76	1,904	1,980
1877	73	1,824	1,897
1878	77	2,257	2,334
1879	62	1,906	1,968
1880	69	1,870	1,939
1881	70	1,832	1,902
1882	63	1,806	1,869
1883	60	1,724	1,784
1884	66	1,822	1,888
1885	65	1,819	1,884
1886	66	1,934	2,000
1887	61	1,870	1,931
1888	72	1,829	1,901
1889	54	1,718	1,772
1890	61	1,986	2,047
1891	66	2,092	2,158
1892	66	1,973	2,039
1893	63	2,070	2,133
1894	67	2,309	2,376
1895	71	2,914	2,885
1896	72	2,145	2,217
1897	71	3,735	3,806
1898	98	3,481	3,579
1899	76	3,066	3,142
1900	174	5,240	5,414
1901	171	5,694	5,865
1902	191	6,031	6,222
1903	213	6,445	6,658
1904	255	7,329	7,584
1905	270	6,741	7,011
1906	278	7,940	8,218
1907	279	7,807	8,086
1908	283	8,953	9,236
1909	328	9,368	9,696
1910	328	9,232	9,560
1911	328	9,292	9,610
1912	337	9,359	9,696
1913	331	9,625	9,956
1914	336	10,050	10,386
1915	338	9,948	10,286

UNITED STATES MARINE CORPS PERSONNEL STRENGTH, 1798–1992 *continued*

Year	Officers	Enlisted	Total	Year	Officers	Enlisted	Total
1916	348	10,253	10,601	1955	18,417	186,753	205,170
1917	776	26,973	27,749	1956	17,809	182,971	200,780
1918	1,503	51,316	52,819	1957	17,434	183,427	200,861
1919	2,270	46,564	48,834	1958	16,471	172,754	189,495
1920	1,104	16,061	17,165	1959	16,065	159,506	175,571
1921	1,087	21,903	22,990	1960	16,203	154,418	170,621
1922	1,135	20,098	21,333	1961	16,132	160,777	176,909
1923	1,141	18,533	19,674	1962	16,861	174,101	190,962
1924	1,157	19,175	20,332	1963	16,737	172,946	189,683
1925	1,168	18,310	19,478	1964	16,843	172,934	189,777
1926	1,178	17,976	19,154	1965	17,258	172,955	190,213
1927	1,198	18,000	19,198	1966	20,512	241,204	261,716
1928	1,198	17,822	19,020	1967	23,592	261,677	285,269
1929	1,181	17,615	18,796	1968	24,555	282,697	307,252
1930	1,208	18,172	19,380	1969	25,698	284,073	309,771
1931	1,196	17,586	18,782	1970	24,941	234,796	259,737
1932	1,196	15,365	16,561	1971	21,765	190,604	212,369
1933	1,192	14,876	16,068	1972	19,843	178,395	198,238
1934	1,187	15,174	16,361	1973	19,282	176,816	196,098
1935	1,163	16,097	17,260	1974	18,740	170,062	188,802
1936	1,208	16,040	17,248	1975	18,591	177,360	195,951
1937	1,312	16,911	18,223	1976	18,882	173,517	192,399
1938	1,359	16,997	18,356	1977	18,650	173,057	191,707
1939	1,380	18,052	19,432	1978	18,388	172,427	190,815
1940	1,800	26,545	28,345	1979	18,229	167,021	185,250
1941	3,339	51,020	54,539	1980	18,198	170,271	188,469
1942	7,138	135,475	142,613	1981	18,363	172,257	190,620
1943	21,384	287,139	308,523	1982	18,975	173,405	192,380
1944	32,788	442,816	475,604	1983	19,983	174,106	194,089
1945	37,067	437,613	474,680	1984	20,366	175,848	196,214
1946	14,208	141,471	155,679	1985	20,175	177,850	198,025
1947	7,506	85,547	93,053	1986	20,199	178,615	198,814
1948	6,907	78,081	84,988	1987	20,047	179,478	199,525
1949	7,250	78,715	85,965	1988	20,079	177,271	197,350
1950	7,254	67,025	74,279	1989	20,099	176,857	196,956
1951	15,150	177,770	192,920	1990	19,958	176,694	196,652
1952	16,413	215,544	231,957	1991	19,753	174,287	194,040
1953	18,731	230,488	249,219	1992	19,065	168,935	188,000
1954	18,593	205,275	223,868				

Force was sent to the Middle East, its parts used for the heavy reinforcement of the First MEF.

The First and Seventh MEBs took virtually nothing with them but their individual arms and equipment. The Maritime Prepositioning Force, consisting of squadrons of commercial ships prepositioned at strategic locations, carried MEB combat equipment and about thirty days of supply. There were three MPS squadrons—in the Atlantic, the Indian Ocean, and the western Pacific, a total of thirteen modern ships with civilian crews. As it happened, port facilities in Saudi Arabia were superb. The MPS ships carried tanks, howitzers, amphibious assault vehicles, light armored vehicles, and other weapons, supplies, and equipment, which reached the Seventh and First MEBs by mid-August. Concurrently, the fully equipped Fourth MEB, embarked in amphibious shipping, was en route from North Carolina.

On 2 September, the First Marine Expeditionary Force, formed by compositing the elements of the Seventh and First MEBs, assumed operational control of all marine forces ashore in the U.S. Central Command's theater of operations. Within days the three major subordinate headquarters of the First MEF were in place: the First Marine Division, the Third Marine Aircraft Wing, and the First Force Service Support Group. Meanwhile, the thirteenth Marine Expeditionary Unit had arrived in the Gulf of Oman from the Philippines, soon to be joined by the Fourth Marine Expeditionary Brigade. These forces were kept afloat as a potential landing force.

By the first week of November, Phase I of the Desert Shield deployment was complete. Nearly forty-two thousand marines, close to one-quarter of the total active-duty marine strength, had been deployed. On 8 November, President Bush announced that U.S. forces in the Persian Gulf would be increased by an additional 200,000 troops.

The Marine Corps had completed the Phase I deployments without calling up the Marine Corps Reserve. On 13 November, for Phase II, the involuntary call-up of selected Marine Corps reserve units began, which were brought in from all over the United States from the widely dispersed Reserve Fourth Marine Division and Fourth Marine Aircraft Wing. The Fifth Marine Expeditionary Brigade sailed from San Diego on the first of December, scheduled to arrive in the Persian Gulf by 15 January. Most of the East Coast-based Second MEF, numbering thirty thousand marines and sailors and including the Second Marine Division, began its move on 9 December to the gulf by airlift.

Desert Shield, the deployment phase of the war in the Persian Gulf, ended on 15 January 1991. Desert Storm, actual hostilities, began the following day. By then the First MEF was structured very much like the Third Marine Amphibious Force in Vietnam—two divisions, a very large wing, and a substantial service support command. In addition there were two MEBs and a special-operations-capable marine expeditionary unit afloat, offering a powerful landing force for any contemplated amphibious operations.

The air campaign began on 16 January 1991. The Third Marine Aircraft Wing, with about one-quarter of the total U.S. fixed-wing aircraft in the theater, had a full role to play. Initially the targeting was strategic, but as the opening day of the ground campaign approached, the weight of the air offensive shifted to intensified strikes against Iraqi forward positions.

These Marines are searching for hidden weapons in Mogadishu. They were part of a U.S. lead coalition of military forces from several countries that entered Somalia in December 1992 during a period of major unrest, famine, and violence in the country. (Department of Defense/U.S. Marines)

The air campaign also masked the forward movement of the allied ground forces to their attack positions. The ground elements of the First MEF had the mission of breaching the vaunted Iraqi defense line at the Kuwait border and then advancing on Kuwait City. On the immediate right flank of the First Marine Division, between the main road leading north and the Persian Gulf, was the Joint Forces Command East, comprised of five Saudi, Kuwaiti, Omani, and United Arab Emirate mechanized brigades. On the First Marine Division's left flank was the newly arrived Second Marine Division, and to their left was the Joint Forces Command North, an Egyptian-Syrian force. Further west was the U.S. Army heavy Seventh Corps, and on the left flank of the Seventh Corps was the lighter U.S. Eighteenth Airborne Corps. There were well-publicized amphibious demonstrations by the Fourth and Fifth MEBs, and the Thirteenth MEU.

The ground campaign began on 24 February. At 0100, the sixteen-inch guns of the battleships *Wisconsin* and *Missouri* began thundering against the Kuwaiti coast as though to signal the beginning of an amphibious assault. Three hours later the allied forces began advancing in two giant arms separated by more than 200 kilometers. At 0400 the First Marine Division jumped off, punching its way with unexpected ease through the two belts of field fortifications that had seemed so formidable. The Second Marine Division crossed its line of departure at 0530 and met with equal success in breaching the Iraqi line.

At 0100, the sixteen-inch guns of the battleships Wisconsin *and* Missouri *began thundering against the Kuwaiti coast.*

When the shooting stopped on 28 February, the First MEF and marine forces afloat had a strength of 92,990 (of the 540,000 total U.S. force), making Desert Storm by far the largest Marine Corps operation in history. The marines claimed 1,040 enemy tanks, 608 armored personnel carriers, and 432 artillery pieces destroyed or captured, and at least twenty thousand prisoners taken. It was also learned that the amphibious demonstrations successfully held in place some six divisions or fifty thousand Iraqis along the Kuwait coast, prepared for the amphibious assault that never came. As a postscript to the war in the Persian Gulf, the Twenty-fourth MEU, launched from the Mediterranean Sea, was the first sizable U.S. force to take part in the Kurdish relief operations in southern Turkey and northern Iraq. Simultaneously, a marine-commanded joint task force aided typhoon-ravished Bangladesh.

THE POST-COLD WAR PERIOD

General Gray retired on 1 July 1991. His successor, the thirtieth commandant, was General Carl E. Mundy, Jr. A native of Georgia, Mundy was commissioned in the Marine Corps in 1957 after graduation from Auburn University. A decorated veteran of the Vietnam War, he had been commanding general of the Fleet Marine Force, Atlantic, and commanding general of the Second Marine Expeditionary Force.

Mundy took charge of a Marine Corps that had barely returned to its pre–Persian Gulf posture and that faced sizable budget-driven shrinkage. The best estimates were that the corps would go from an active strength of 193,735 in 1991 to 171,000 in 1995. Although events in Eastern Europe and the Soviet Union eased the once overshadowing threat of a general war between the superpowers, there were indications that the United States would continue to send the Marine Corps abroad on expeditionary services ranging from the evacuation of endangered U.S. embassies and humanitarian missions in Third World countries to possible regional wars of the magnitude of the Persian Gulf.

[See also The Coast Guard; Gunboat Diplomacy, 1776–1992; and The Navy.]

BIBLIOGRAPHY

General Works

Heinl, Robert D., Jr. *Soldiers of the Sea: The United States Marine Corps, 1775–1962* (1962).

Lewis, C. L. *Famous American Marines* (1950).

Millett, Allan R. *Semper Fidelis: The History of the United States Marine Corps* (1980).

Moran, John B. *Creating a Legend: The Complete Record of Writing about the United States Marine Corps* (1973).

Moskin, J. Robert. *The Marine Corps Story* (1977, rev. 1987).

Simmons, Edwin H. *The United States Marines: The First Two Hundred Years, 1775–1975* (1975).

Schuon, Karl. *Home of the Commandants* (1966, rev. 1974).

Eighteenth and Nineteenth Centuries

Bauer, K. Jack. *Surf Boats and Horse Marines* (1969).

Collum, R. S. *The History of the United States Marine Corps* (1903).

Smith, Charles R. *Marines in the Revolution: A History of the Continental Marines in the American Revolution, 1775–1783* (1975).

Twentieth Century

Clifford, Kenneth J. *Progress and Purpose: A Developmental History of the U.S. Marine Corps, 1900–1970* (1973).

Fleming, Charles A., et al. *Quantico: Crossroads of the Marine Corps* (1978).

Frank, Benis M. *U.S. Marines in Lebanon, 1982–1984* (1987).

Isely, Jeter A., and Philip A. Crowl. *The U.S. Marines and Amphibious War: Its Theory and Its Practice in the Pacific* (1951).
Langley, Lester D. *The Banana Wars: An Inner History of the American Empire, 1900–1934* (1983).
Lejeune, John A. *The Reminiscences of a Marine* (1930).
Musicant, Ivan. *The Banana Wars: A History of the United States Military Intervention in Latin America from the Spanish American War to the Invasion of Grenada* (1990).
Spector, Ronald A. *U.S. Marines in Grenada, 1983* (1987).
Thomas, Lowell. *Old Gimlet Eye: The Adventures of Smedley D. Butler* (1933).

World Wars I and II

Asprey, Robert B. *At Belleau Wood* (1965).
Griffith, Samuel B. *The Battle for Guadalcanal* (1963).
Harbord, James G. *Leaves from a War Diary* (1931).
History of Marine Corps Operations in World War II, 5 vols. (1958–1968).
Hough, Frank O. *The Island War* (1947).
Leckie, Robert. *Strong Men Armed: The United States Marines Against Japan* (1962).
Merillat, Herbert L. *Guadalcanal Remembered* (1982).
Newcomb, Richard G. *Iwo Jima* (1965).
Pratt, Fletcher. *The Marines' War* (1948).
Sherrod, Robert L. *Tarawa: The Story of a Battle* (1944).
———. *On to Westward: War in the Central Pacific* (1945).
Sledge, Eugene B. *With the Old Breed at Peleliu and Okinawa* (1981).
Stallings, Lawrence. *The Doughboys* (1963).
Thomason, John W. *Fix Bayonets* (1926).
Toland, John. *No Man's Land: 1918, the Last Year of the Great War* (1980).

Korean War

Goulden, Joseph C. *Korea: The Untold Story* (1982).
Heinl, Robert D., Jr. *Victory at High Tide* (1968).
Knox, Donald. *The Korean War: Pusan to Chosin, An Oral History* (1985).
Montross, Lynn. *Cavalry of the Sky* (1954).
Russ, Martin. *The Last Parallel: A Marine's War Journal* (1985).
U.S. Marine Corps Operations in Korea, 1950–1953, 5 vols. (1954–1972).

Vietnam War

Arnold, Curtis G., and Charles D. Melson. *The War that Would Not End, 1971–1973* (1991).
Cosmas, Graham A., and Terrence P. Murray. *Vietnamization and Redeployment, 1970–1971* (1986).
Dunham, George R., and David A. Quinlan. *The Bitter End, 1973–1975* (1990).
Shulimson, Jack. *An Expanding War, 1966* (1982).
Shulimson, Jack, and Charles M. Johnson. *The Landing and the Buildup, 1965* (1978).
Simmons, Edwin H. *Marines: The Illustrated History of the Vietnam War* (1987).
Solis, Gary D. *Marines and Military Law in Vietnam: Trial by Fire* (1989).
Smith, Charles R. *High Mobility and Standdown, 1969* (1988).
Telfer, Gary L., Lane Rogers, and V. Keith Fleming. *Fighting the North Vietnamese* (1984).
Whitlow, Robert H. *The Advisory and Combat Assistance Era, 1954–1964* (1977).

Marine Corps Aviation

Johnson, Edward C., and Graham A. Cosmas. *Marine Corps Aviation: The Early Years, 1912–1940* (1977).
Fails, William R. *Marines and Helicopters*, 1962–1973 (1978).
Mersky, Peter B. *U.S. Marine Corps Aviation, 1912 to the Present* (1983).
Rawlins, Eugene W. *Marines and Helicopters, 1946–1962* (1976).
Sherrod, Robert L. *History of Marine Corps Aviation in World War II* (1952).

— EDWIN H. SIMMONS

The Coast Guard

Congress established the United States Coast Guard on 28 January 1915 by uniting the U.S. Revenue Cutter Service and the U.S. Life-Saving Service. The former, founded in 1790, helped to build the United States Navy and then fought alongside it in the Quasi-War with France, the War of 1812, the war against piracy in the Caribbean, the Seminole wars, the Mexican War, the Civil War, and the Spanish-American War. It also served the maritime needs of the nation. It began by collecting revenue for the new nation, a task at which it quickly succeeded, thus establishing a measure of respect for the new constitutional government and its laws. Because of its success, the government turned to it to carry out other delicate operations, such as enforcing President Thomas Jefferson's embargo of 1807, upholding national sovereignty in the Nullification Controversy in 1830–1831, enforcing the nation's laws against the slave trade before the Civil War, and protecting seal herds in Alaskan waters after the United States purchased that territory from Russia following the Civil War. The Life-Saving Service, founded in 1848, had established an outstanding reputation for saving the lives of shipwrecked mariners.

The establishment of the Coast Guard followed three and a half years of administrative maneuvering that threatened the existence of the Revenue Cutter Service. In 1911 President William Howard Taft accepted a report from the Committee on Economy and Efficiency in Government, citing a great duplication of federal agencies in maritime affairs. The report claimed there was no need for the cutter service and called for its abolishment. The nation still had to suppress smuggling, but, the committee argued, the navy could do that job for $1 million less a year than that expended by the cutter service. The committee proposed saving an additional $100,000 a year by uniting the Life-Saving Service and the Lighthouse Service, which had been founded in 1789. They performed similar work, were usually located close to one another, and could be administered by one organization, thus saving administrative costs.

The commission's proposals were opposed by Captain Ellsworth P. Bertholf, the commandant of the Revenue Cutter Service; Sumner I. Kimball, the superintendent of the Life-Saving Service; and Franklin MacVeagh, the secretary of the Treasury. Bertholf argued that the proposed changes would cost the government money. Without the Revenue Cutter Service every federal agency needing the services of ships or boats would have to employ its own vessels, and the resultant duplication would be costly. In addition, Bertholf presented evidence that the navy spent 53.2 percent more money to run a gunboat for a year than the cutter service spent to run a cutter of equal size. Therefore, having the navy perform revenue cutter operations would cost more money.

The sinking of the British White Star liner Titanic *on 14 April 1912 played a role in saving the service.*

The sinking of the British White Star liner *Titanic* on 14 April 1912 with the loss of fifteen hundred persons of the twenty-two hundred on board played a role in saving the service. One important consequence of the disaster was the establishment of the International Ice Patrol to warn mariners when icebergs posed a danger to shipping in the North Atlantic. The U.S. Navy ran the patrol in 1912, but the Revenue Cutter Service took it over the following year. Captain Bertholf campaigned to have the cutter service operate the ice patrol because he wanted to add that important job to the service's duties while the service was under attack. He was successful, first, in convincing MacVeagh to give the job to the service, and second, in convincing him that the service had the authority to do the job. In 1914 fourteen nations agreed that countries using the service would pay for the patrol and that the Coast Guard would operate it, which it has done every year since except when the patrol was suspended during World War I and World War II.

MacVeagh suggested as an alternative to the commission's plan of uniting the Life-Saving Service and Lighthouse Service, the union of the Life-Saving Service and the Revenue Cutter Service into a United States Coast Guard. The sinking of the *Titanic* and the subsequent operation of the International Ice Patrol by the Revenue Cutter Service led to widespread acceptance of MacVeagh's proposal within President Woodrow Wilson's administration. Senator Oscar Underwood and Congressman William C. Adamson supported Mac-

Veagh's proposal, arguing that his reorganization was reasonable, would facilitate recruitment of good men, and would create a naval reserve at no additional expense to the government. In 1914 and 1915 these were telling arguments. On 20 January 1915 Congress passed the Act to Create the Coast Guard by a vote of 212 to 79. President Wilson signed the bill on the twenty-eighth, and the union occurred on the thirtieth.

On that day the Coast Guard consisted of 255 officers, 3,900 warrant officers and enlisted men, a headquarters, seventeen regional commands, four depots, an academy, twenty-five cruising cutters, twenty harbor cutters, and 280 lifeboat stations.

The new organization continued the traditions of its ancestors, beginning in World War I. Coast Guard cutters supplemented naval destroyers on escort duty in the Atlantic and Mediterranean. As captains of major U.S. ports, Coast Guardsmen supervised the shipment of munitions, stopping losses from sabotage and careless handling of explosives. As part of the U.S. Navy, Coast Guard officers helped to alleviate the shortage of experienced seagoing professionals. The work of saving lives in home waters became more important when German U-boats began to sink ships along the Atlantic coast in the summer of 1918.

The Coast Guard did all of this under the control of the U.S. Navy, for the bill that created the Coast Guard called for it to "operate as a part of the Navy, subject to the orders of the Secretary of the Navy, in time of war or when the President shall so direct." Thus, on 6 April 1917, the day President Wilson asked Congress to declare that a state of war existed with Germany, Coast Guard Headquarters sent the order "Plan One Acknowledge" to all units. This terse message transferred the Coast Guard to the navy. From then on Coast Guard units continued to carry out their duties, but under the command of the naval districts in which they operated. Coast Guard Headquarters retained control of a few units, including the Coast Guard Academy at New London, Connecticut, a depot, the old lifeboat stations, and the Bering Sea Patrol. The latter had been created in the late nineteenth century to protect seal herds in Alaskan waters from being hunted to extinction.

Following the outbreak of war in Europe in 1914, Germany shocked the world by using the U-boat as a commerce raider, ultimately instituting a policy of unrestricted submarine warfare in February 1917. Allied losses that month reached 540,000 tons and did not drop below that figure until September. The logical solution to this problem was to convoy merchant ships through danger zones using destroyers and other vessels capable of fighting U-boats. While Coast Guard cutters were not as fast or as heavily armed as destroyers, they had many of the same characteristics, and they were armed and sent into the fray.

Between August and September 1917, six cutters sailed for Gibraltar, where they became Squadron Two of Division Six of the Atlantic Fleet Patrol Force. Until late in October, they escorted vessels through the danger zone around Gibraltar itself. Thereafter they escorted freight convoys between Gibraltar and Great Britain.

The cutter *Seneca* deserves special mention for escort work. It started its wartime career on 10 August 1914, cruising in the neutrality patrol between Gay Head, Martha's Vineyard, and the Delaware Breakwater. For three years it alternated between the International Ice Patrol and the neutrality patrol. On 19 August 1917, it sailed for European waters. Like other cutters at Gibraltar, *Seneca* was manned by a small crew of professionals augmented by enthusiastic young men, many with college experience, seeking early action in the war. At the beginning of the war, cutters were armed with old, outdated small cannon, which were replaced in the summer of 1918 with four-inch fifty caliber cannon, and the *Ossippe* carried depth charges that were thrown overboard by hand.

The skipper of the *Seneca,* Captain William J. Wheeler, reported its convoy record as about average. It escorted thirty convoys and a total of 580 ships, losing only five ships under its protection. During its tenth convoy between Milford Haven, Wales, and Gibraltar, on 25 April 1918, the *Seneca* and the British sloop *Cowslip* were guarding the rear of the convoy when a German U-boat surfaced and fired a torpedo that exploded just abaft of the *Cowslip*'s midship, killing six officers and men. At the time, orders were for ships to scatter when attacked in order to protect the convoy, leaving ships under attack to their own devices. The traditions of the Coast Guard were strongly ingrained, however, and the *Seneca* went to the *Cowslip*'s rescue. Lieutenant (junior grade) Fletcher W. Brown handled the *Seneca*'s lifeboat while Boatswain Petter W. Patterson of the *Seneca* manned the *Cowslip*'s boat. Between them they made three trips to rescue eighty-one men, taking off the last survivors just before the *Cowslip* plunged to the bottom of the sea.

Not all of Brown's efforts were successful. While the *Seneca* was escorting a twenty-one-ship convoy between Milford Haven and Gibraltar, in the Bay of Biscay, on 18 September 1918 a torpedo ripped a hole in the forepeak of the British collier *Wellington.* Its crew quickly abandoned ship, but the captain sent a message that he thought the ship could be salvaged. Brown read the signal and asked permission to lead a salvage effort. Permission granted, Brown chose eighteen men from many volunteers. They were delivered to the stricken ship, where eleven of the *Wellington*'s officers and crew joined them. Within an hour and a half they had gotten up steam and were underway to Brest, France. The *Seneca* then rejoined the convoy.

During the night a gale overtook the *Wellington*, making it impossible to maneuver. The U.S. destroyer *Warrington*, dispatched to its aid, arrived on the scene at 3:00 A.M. Soon thereafter the weakened bulkhead gave way and the *Wellington* asked for immediate assistance. At 3:30 the ship made its fatal plunge. Some of the salvage crew got off in lifeboats while others had to jump into the sea. Until the ship sank, Brown stayed at the radio sending a signal to the destroyer. He was pulled from the water unconscious. He awoke aboard the *Warrington* to learn that eleven of the *Seneca*'s crew and five of the *Wellington*'s had been lost. Captain Wheeler singled out Brown for special praise, and he was subsequently offered the Navy Cross for his efforts, but he turned down the honor because the same offer was not made to his crew.

It was on its way across Bristol Channel to its home base at Milford Haven when the Tampa *disappeared with barely a trace.*

Upon their arrival at Gibraltar, the survivors of the disaster learned the more tragic fate of the Coast Guard cutter *Tampa*. Under the command of Captain Charles Satterlee, it had earned a reputation for trouble-free, successful escort work. During ten months in European waters, it escorted eighteen convoys made up of 350 ships with the loss of just two ships. Then, on the evening of 26 September 1918, the *Tampa* successfully escorted its last convoy from Gibraltar. It was on its way across Bristol Channel to its home base at Milford Haven when it disappeared with barely a trace, a victim of U-53, commanded by Captain Hans Rose. A total of 131 men were lost aboard the *Tampa*. With the exception of the collier *Cyclops*, which disappeared in the Caribbean with 309 persons aboard, the *Tampa* suffered the greatest single naval loss sustained by the United States in World War I, and the *Cyclops* may not have been sunk by the enemy.

The race for tonnage was also waged on the home front, where Coast Guard officers played an important role by contributing to the efficient operation of the nation's major ports. The Espionage Act of 15 June 1917 required the Treasury Department to assume control of the movement and anchorage of vessels in U.S. ports whenever the president determined that a threat existed to U.S. security. During World War I the department assigned these duties to Coast Guard officers, who were made captains of the major U.S ports, including New York, Philadelphia, and Hampton Roads, Virginia. From December 1917 to June 1919, when Coast Guard officers were in charge, 350,000 tons of explosives were loaded onto 1,698 ships without an explosion or loss of life.

Because of their training, seagoing experience, and military readiness, Coast Guard officers were used by the navy in many capacities. Of the 138 line officers, fifty-two commanded navy combat ships and five commanded large bases, including two air stations. In addition, seventy commissioned Coast Guard marine engineers helped to alleviate the navy's need for technically competent officers.

Coast Guardsmen at the lifesaving stations continued to make courageous rescues during the war, and some rendered assistance to victims of German U-boats that visited the U.S. East Coast. On 21 July 1918, a lookout at the East Orleans Coast Guard Station on Cape Cod, Massachusetts, spotted a U-boat turning its deck guns on the tug *Perth Amboy* and its tow of four barges. The keeper of the station, Robert F. Pierce, and most of his crew immediately headed for the tug in an unarmed motor surfboat. As the surfboat approached the tug, the U-boat stopped its shelling and dove for safety. Soon thereafter two seaplanes from the Chatham Naval Air Station, also on Cap Cod, arrived on the scene and exchanged fire with the U-boat, which had come to the surface again. It submerged yet again and departed the area. One of the planes was flown by Coast Guard Captain Philip B. Eaton, who commanded the station.

Another incident occurred on 14 August 1918, when U-117 strung out nine mines across the shipping lane off Wimble Shoals, North Carolina. Two days later the 6,679-ton British tanker *Mirlo* hit one of the mines. Surfman Leroy Midgett at the Chicamacomico Lifesaving Station witnessed the explosion and notified Chief John A. Midgett, the man in charge. Within three minutes the surfmen had launched the power lifeboat. Meanwhile a second explosion rocked the *Mirlo*, setting its cargo afire and causing Captain W. R. Williams to abandon ship. A third explosion broke the *Mirlo* in two, dumping burning gasoline upon the water. As Chief Midgett approached the scene of the disaster, the *Mirlo* sank below the surface of a sea swept by nearly gale-force winds. The lifesavers made three trips through the surf, saving forty-two of the *Mirlo*'s fifty-two-man crew.

The armistice ended World War I on 11 November 1918. Shortly thereafter the five surviving cutters of the

Gibraltar patrol sailed for home, but the Coast Guard did not automatically transfer back to the Treasury Department. Following the war, Secretary of the Navy Josephus Daniels tried to keep the Coast Guard in the navy. Congressman Guy E. Campbell introduced a bill to that effect in January 1919.

Secretary of the Treasury Carter Glass opposed the Campbell Bill by referring to the studies done before the war that proved that it cost more to operate a naval vessel than a Coast Guard cutter. He insisted that the bill would ruin morale in the service and asked Congress to return the service to the Treasury Department as soon as possible. Glass had enough influence in Congress to get his bill passed, but, preoccupied with peace negotiations, President Wilson failed to sign the bill.

This left the battle in the Coast Guard itself, where many, including several important captains, wanted to become a permanent part of the navy. They wanted to retain their wartime rank, appreciated the superior vessels operated by the navy, and resented the inferior ships they had used before the war as Coast Guard officers.

The Coast Guard rests on the idea of humanitarianism, the Navy rests on the idea of militarism.

The most important officer in the Coast Guard, Commandant Bertholf, however, strongly opposed any move to the navy. In a private letter cited by Robert Erwin Johnson in *Guardians of the Sea* (1987), Bertholf wrote that "the Coast Guard does not exist solely for the purpose of preparing for war." He added that "while peace time usefulness is a by-product of the Navy, it is the war time usefulness that is a by-product of the Coast Guard." The Coast Guard, he argued, could not exist as a separate service in the Navy Department. It was too much like the navy for that to be tolerated. He stressed that he and his fellow officers would "be lost among many thousands of officers" and each would be "an outsider and an interloper." Bertholf concluded his letter: "This is a day when humanitarianism is in the minds of most people, and the war being over, militarism is on the wane. The Coast Guard rests on the idea of humanitarianism, the Navy rests on the idea of militarism. To my mind, the best band-wagon is the former, and so I say the Coast Guard for mine and no Navy under any consideration."

Bertholf retired on 30 June 1919, but Glass continued the battle in the administration. Finally, on 28 August 1919, many months after the end of World War I, President Wilson signed an executive order directing that as of that date the Coast Guard would operate under the Treasury Department. Bertholf and Glass, two most competent professionals, had won their fight for an independent Coast Guard. The battle over the basic character of the Coast Guard would continue.

By the time the Coast Guard returned to the Treasury Department, Congress had passed the Eighteenth Amendment in December 1917, establishing prohibition as U.S. policy. Having expected little opposition from the U.S. public, Congress was surprised when many Americans took up rumrunning. The Coast Guard's role in the Rum War was a natural outgrowth of its heritage as a law enforcement agency within the Treasury Department. From its inception as the Revenue Cutter Service in 1790, the service had enforced the customs laws of the nation.

Interdicting liquor remained a low priority for the Coast Guard until 1922, when the government officially assigned it the task of stopping rumrunning. The next year Rear Admiral Frederick C. Billard, commandant of the Coast Guard, requested additional funds for the job, but it took a year for his request to bear fruit. In the meantime the service had too few cutters to effectively counter rumrunning. At the beginning of 1924 only twenty-nine steam cutters and the small boats at the old lifesaving stations were available. As a result the service was not very effective.

During the first five years of prohibition, rumrunners used a variety of methods to smuggle liquor into the United States, but there were common features to their operations. Initially they just sailed into port and offloaded the liquor. Then they discovered that they could lay outside the nation's three-mile-limit laden with liquor, and, as long as they bore foreign registration, the Coast Guard could not board them. Thus, Rum Row was born, a virtual city of ships anchored off U.S. population centers waiting for smaller contact boats to come alongside to purchase liquor they had brought from abroad. The heaviest concentration lay off New York and New Jersey, but rumrunners were found anyplace along the coast where contact boats were willing to run out to them for a purchase.

The establishment of Rum Row led smugglers to build fast contact boats. Once loaded, the contact boats ran the liquor into shore, usually to a deserted beach where trucks waited to haul it off to a warehouse. Speed was the rumrunners first line of defense, but they also employed smoke-generating equipment, phony distress calls, and armed force. Six Coast Guard officers were killed during the Rum War. Another six were crippled for life. When the Coast Guard stepped up its enforcement efforts, rumrunners put more resources into the fight, using radios and aircraft to keep track of cutters and their operations.

Prior to 1924 the Coast Guard did its best with inadequate resources to stop the flow of liquor. Given its disadvantages, it tried to extend the three-mile limit to twelve miles. In 1924, Great Britain allowed the United States to seize vessels registered in Great Britain as far from the U.S. coast as the seized vessel could run in an hour. Other nations followed Great Britain's lead, and the resulting treaties forced Rum Row further offshore and increased the Coast Guard's chances for success.

More important was the appropriation of substantial funding for the service in 1924 and the years thereafter, which allowed the Coast Guard to increase the size of its fleet and manpower. In 1924 and 1925, it built 203 new seventy-five-foot patrol boats and about 100 thirty-six-foot picket boats. Between 1924 and 1926 it rehabilitated twenty-five pre–World War I navy destroyers. In the years from 1925 to 1927, it launched ten 100-foot and thirty-three 125-foot patrol boats. Over the next four years, it launched ten 250-foot Lake-class cutters (named after U.S. lakes) and in the early 1930s it added eighteen 165-footers. Almost all of these vessels participated in the Rum War. During those same years, the Coast Guard added to its rolls more than 4,300 men, including 149 commissioned officers. Because the Coast Guard was not prepared to recruit and train large numbers of men, the navy recruited and trained about three-quarters of the above number for the Coast Guard. In August 1925, the U.S. controller general ruled that without congressional action, naval facilities could not be used to train Coast Guardsmen. Thereafter the Coast Guard recruited for itself and trained new recruits at New London, Connecticut.

With its greatly augmented fleet the Coast Guard initiated three layers of defense against the rumrunners. Rehabilitated navy destroyers operated furthest offshore, locating and identifying the smugglers. The patrol boats picketed each ship on Rum Row, watching it constantly, and the smaller boats patrolled closest to shore. The object of picketing was to discourage the contact boats from going alongside the ships on Rum Row to take on board a load of liquor. The mission of the smaller patrol boats was to intercept the contact boats after they had succeeded in making contact with the vessels on Rum Row but before they could land their cargo on shore. Picketing succeeded in breaking up Rum Row and greatly complicated the smuggler's lives. Finally, on 5 December 1933, with President Franklin D. Roosevelt's encouragement, Congress passed the Twenty-first Amendment repealing the Eighteenth Amendment and ending prohibition. Between 1919 and 1934 the Coast Guard seized 26,659 vessels for violating federal law.

Prohibition had an enormous impact on the Coast Guard. The service emerged from the Rum War with an expanded fleet, and many of the vessels built for the Rum War and the lessons learned in it proved of even greater importance to the United States in World War II. Another significant consequence of the Rum War was the building up of the Coast Guard Academy.

The academy began as the Revenue Cutter School of Instruction in 1876–1877. After the Civil War, when corruption, incompetence, and political influence were widespread in both the service and the Treasury Department, Sumner Kimball, civilian head of the service, issued new regulations to eliminate these weaknesses. He started the academy to train young men and to ensure a steady supply of competent professionals for the officer corps. These objectives led the service to reject congressional appointments to the academy and to rely instead on competitive examinations and personal interviews for admissions, a policy that continues at the academy.

The first academy was a training ship, the topsail schooner *Dobbin*, which along with its replacement, the *Salmon P. Chase,* sailed out of New Bedford, Massachusetts, between 1877 and 1890. The federal government closed the school for four years, from 1891 to 1894, assigning Naval Academy graduates to revenue cutter billets during those years. By 1894 the navy was expanding and needed all of its own graduates for its fleet, so the Revenue Cutter School of Instruction was reopened. Until 1900 the training ship had no home port, but in that year it put in at Curtis Bay, Maryland, which remained the site of the academy until 1910, when the school moved to Fort Trumbull, an old army base at New London, Connecticut.

At New Bedford the school essentially had a liberal arts curriculum. Cadets studied for two years, spending one half of each year training at sea on the school ship and the other half of each year studying on shore. After the school reopened in 1894, cadets trained at sea for their entire two years. In 1900, at Curtis Bay, the service restored the combination of education on shore and training at sea. Three years later a third year of instruction was added to the curriculum, in order to add courses in science and mathematics that were deemed essential because of the addition of motorized lifeboats, radio, and modern cutters to the fleet. Engineers first attended the academy for six months of training in 1906. Before that year all cadets were educated to take billets as line officers.

The academy had a small enrollment during the years before the Rum War, generally graduating from three to ten cadets a year at New Bedford, from two to twenty at Curtis Bay, and from three to thirty-three at Fort Trumbull.

During the Rum War, the academy was expanded, as it became necessary to increase the size of the officer corps because of the expansion of the cutter fleet. When new cutters began to join the fleet in 1924, the academy graduated the class of 1925 a year early to provide some of the officers needed to command them. Entering classes were increased to about fifty cadets per class. Expansion of the cadet corps emphasized once again the inadequacies of Fort Trumbull, and the service began to search for a new site. The town of New London, anxious to retain the academy, competed by purchasing forty acres of land on the Thames River from a private estate for $100,000 and turning it over to the Treasury Department. Ground was broken in 1931, and the academy opened its fall semester in 1932 at the new site.

The new academy was palatial when compared with its predecessors. The entire corps could be assembled in the quadrangle of Chase Hall. The cadet barracks, which, like the first training ship ever built as an academy training ship, was named after President Lincoln's Treasury secretary, Salmon P. Chase. Hamilton Hall, named after President George Washington's Treasury secretary, Alexander Hamilton, provided office space for the administration. McAlister Hall and Satterlee Hall, the former named after a Coast Guard chief engineering officer and the latter after the skipper of the *Tampa,* which was lost with all hands in World War I, provided classroom facilities. Yeaton Hall, named after Captain Hopley Yeaton, the Revenue Cutter Service's first officer and the first seagoing officer appointed by the new constitutional government under Washington, provided living space for enlisted men stationed at the academy. The area in front of Satterlee, Hamilton, and Chase halls was turned to grass for a parade ground. The mainmast from the old training ship *Alexander Hamilton* was erected as a flagpole, and a bandstand was erected at the north end.

The Treasury Department appointed an advisory committee for the academy in 1932. The presidents of Yale, Columbia, and Harvard universities and the Massachusetts Institute of Technology made up the first committee. They played a significant role in having a curriculum for the new school that was heavily weighted in mathematics, science, and engineering, but also included an introduction to the humanities. A fourth year of study was added to the curriculum in 1932. The academy received accreditation in 1937 and gave its first four-year degrees in 1941. Professional studies still constituted 35 percent of a cadet's course time, and all cadets went to sea for twenty-six weeks before graduating.

Between the outbreak of war in Europe in 1939 and the attack on Pearl Harbor on 7 December 1941, the Coast Guard increased its involvement in war-related operations. Following President Franklin D. Roosevelt's proclaiming a national emergency on 8 September 1939, the Coast Guard initiated a neutrality patrol off the entrance to major U.S. ports. In February 1940 it inaugurated a weather patrol in the Atlantic to gather weather information vital to the safety of newly established Pan American Airways transatlantic flights. Under the leadership of Rear Admiral Russell R. Waesche, the Coast Guard undertook a massive arming program in 1940, fitting out 147 cutters with heavy guns, antiaircraft weapons, and antisubmarine devices. When Germany overran Western Europe that spring, President Roosevelt directed Admiral Harold R. Stark, the chief of naval operations, to maintain a patrol off the coast of Greenland. Stark gave the job to Waesche, and Coast Guardsmen seized Greenland to prevent Germany from establishing weather stations there that could assist German military operations in Europe and U-boat operations in the Atlantic. Following the destroyers-for-bases deal with Great Britain in September 1940, Roosevelt turned over to Great Britain ten 250-foot Lake-class cutters. In June 1940 the Coast Guard had assumed responsibility for the safety of explosives shipped from U.S. ports. A beach patrol that grew out of the work of the lifeboat stations stopped German infiltration of the United States. On 13 June 1942 four German saboteurs were put ashore in a rubber raft launched from a U-boat. They landed at Amagansett, Long Island, in New York and were discovered shortly thereafter by Seaman Second Class John C. Cullen, who was on his regular patrol of the beach. The Germans first threatened Cullen, then offered him a bribe, which he pretended to accept. Once out of sight of the Germans, Cullen ran for the station to report his discovery. Coast Guardsmen returned to the landing site, where they found boxes of money and explosive devices, but no Germans. The FBI was called into the case and apprehended all of the saboteurs.

A beach patrol that grew out of the work of the lifeboat stations stopped German infiltration of the United States in 1942.

At its peak the beach patrol employed more than twenty-four thousand officers and men who kept nearly the entire U.S. coastline under surveillance. On 1 November 1941, more than a month before the Japanese attack on Pearl Harbor, the Coast Guard was transferred into the Navy Department, and on the tenth, the *Campbell* joined destroyers on escort duty in the North Atlantic.

The Coast Guard and navy discussed their relationship between the wars, and in June 1940 Admiral Stark took the initiative to develop a policy for the growing crisis. He appointed a naval committee headed by Captain Alexander Sharp that met with a Coast Guard committee appointed by Admiral Waesche, who appointed Captain William H. Shea, Captain Lloyd T. Chalker, and Commander Frank J. Gorman. The joint committee drew up plans for the transfer of the Coast Guard to the Navy Department. It gave much of the responsibility for detailed plans for the transfer to the commanders of the Coast Guard and navy districts. When the transfer occurred, the Coast Guard district commanders reported to and served under the navy district commanders, who thus gained command of all Coast Guard personnel and units. Coast Guard Headquarters remained in existence as an administrative staff under the chief of naval operations. Coast Guard committee members tried to make sure that Coast Guardsmen retained their separate identity while serving with the navy and that the Coast Guard in its entirety would be transferred back to the Treasury Department when the war ended.

The two seagoing services discussed the transfer early in 1941, but transfer of the entire Coast Guard was postponed until 1 November 1941. Concern that the transfer would imply that a war was imminent was probably most important. As a result, the Coast Guard transferred some units as it seemed advisable, and some Coast Guardsmen were already at war in the North Atlantic before the transfer of all units took place.

After war was declared, the Coast Guard became greatly involved in amphibious operations. Using its century of experience operating lifeboats in the surf, it established training centers at New River, North Carolina, Camp Edwards on Cape Cod, and Hampton Roads, where it passed on the fruits of its experience to tens of thousands of recruits who manned landing craft all over the world. In addition, Coast Guardsmen manned transports used in amphibious operations. At Guadalcanal, they helped to establish a beachhead, moved troops, ammunition, and supplies, and directed beach traffic. It was at Guadalcanal that Signalman First Class Douglass Munro won the Medal of Honor for evacuating marines from a beach under heavy enemy fire on 27 September 1942. Munro placed his boat between the marines and the Japanese, and lost his life as he pulled off the beach, after all others had left. Following their introduction in the invasion of Sicily, Coast Guardsmen manned landing ship, tanks (LSTs), and landing craft, infantry (LCIs), and participated in all subsequent European and Pacific amphibious actions.

The United States used the Coast Guard at sea to the fullest extent possible during the war. In all, Coast Guardsmen manned 1,444 ships of sixty-five feet or more. Of this number 349 were major naval vessels, 288 major army vessels, including seventy-six LSTs, twenty-eight LCIs, seventy-five patrol frigates, thirty destroyer escorts, and twenty-two tankers.

To provide personnel for these ships and to meet its other growing obligations, the Coast Guard increased its numbers during the war from 11,500 in 1939 to 25,000 in 1941, and to 176,000 by war's end. Regulars and regular reservists were freed for sea duty by temporary reservists, SPAR (women members of the Coast Guard), and the Coast Guard Auxiliary. As a result, nearly half of the regulars and regular reservists served afloat.

Six 327-foot Secretary-class cutters built on the model of the navy gunboats *Erie* and *Charleston* in the 1930s performed escort duty in the North Atlantic, half of them supporting operations from Iceland, the other half escorting convoys between Argentina, Newfoundland, and Londonderry, Northern Ireland. In these operations, the *Hamilton* was torpedoed and sunk off Iceland while the cutters *Bibb, Campbell, Duane, Ingham,* and *Spencer* compiled impressive records.

The *Spencer* and *Duane* destroyed a U-boat while escorting a fifty-seven-ship convoy eastbound across the Atlantic in April 1943. At 11:00 A.M. on 17 April, after a night of U-boat contacts, the *Spencer* picked up the submarine on its sound equipment. General quarters were sounded and battle stations taken. The *Spencer* turned toward the convoy and tracked the submarine down the center of two columns of merchant ships, dropping depth charges perilously close to the convoyed vessels. Suddenly, six hundred yards off the stern of the convoy, the U-boat surfaced. The *Spencer* fired a round from its three-inch forward gun, and its five-inch guns fore and aft joined in. The *Spencer* charged directly at the U-boat prepared to ram it, only to veer off at the last second as the U-boat was clearly sinking. A victory message to the convoy read "Scratch one hearse!" The cutters picked up forty-one survivors—the rest of the crew was lost when the sub, stern first, plunged to the bottom of the ocean.

In the spring of 1943 the Secretary-class cutters were assigned to escort work in the Mediterranean Sea. The next year they were converted to amphibious force flagships, and some of them participated in the invasions of France, the Philippines, Okinawa, and Borneo.

Nearly all of the Coast Guard 165-foot and 125-foot patrol boats built for the Rum War were assigned to the Greenland patrol or to sea frontiers on the East and West coasts, in Alaskan waters, off Hawaii, and in the Gulf of Mexico. The *Icarus,* a 165-footer built at Bath, Maine, sank two U-boats during the war. In one instance it was on its way from New York to Charleston, South Carolina, under the command of Lieutenant Commander Maurice Jester, a man with a good reputation as a seaman. It picked up U-352 on its echo equipment as it approached Cape Lookout, North Carolina. After a torpedo missed it, the *Icarus* dropped five depth charges, reversed direction, and dropped another barrage. The sub surfaced one thousand yards from the *Icarus,* which gave chase and opened fire with machine guns and one three-inch gun. U-352 sank about twenty-six miles southeast of Beaufort, North Carolina, with eleven men still aboard. The crew of the *Icarus* picked up thirty-three survivors, including the skipper.

By mid-1943, Coast Guard cutters had sunk six out of eleven U-boats sunk by U.S. ships. Before the war ended, the service sank six more U-boats. The Coast Guard lost seven cutters to enemy action in World War II, and 572 Coast Guardsmen lost their lives in combat. Significantly, the Coast Guard suffered the highest per capita casualty rate of any U.S. service during the war.

During the Normandy invasion on 6 June 1944, Coast Guard eighty-three-foot patrol boats performed

Coast Guard personnel on the deck of the Coast Guard cutter Spencer *watch the explosion of a depth charge that destroyed a German U-boat on 17 April 1943. (National Archives)*

rescue operations for those thrown into the water when their landing craft were sunk. The boats had been transported to Great Britain as deck cargo on merchant ships. Once there, they were organized into two rescue groups of thirty boats each. One group was assigned to the British invasion sector, the other to the American sector. During landing operations, they made 1,438 individual rescues. After the initial landings, they continued to rescue men from sinking boats offshore for three months. They were then shipped back to the United States, having compiled an impressive record of rescue under fire.

The regular duties of the Coast Guard expanded considerably during the war. The service tended aids to navigation in U.S. waters and wherever the nation's armed forces went. The Coast Guard had absorbed the U.S. Lighthouse Service in 1939, and in March 1942 it absorbed temporarily the Bureau of Marine Inspection and Navigation. The service helped to develop LORAN, a long-range navigational aid, and manned and operated a total of seventy-five LORAN stations throughout the world by the end of the war.

In addition, Waesche laid plans for and promoted the retention of jobs that the Coast Guard had performed before the war and of new jobs it had acquired during the war. He and other officers wrote a statement on the Coast Guard's missions, calling for the service to continue to enforce laws both on the high seas and in U.S. navigable waters; to regulate the construction, manning, and operation of U.S. flag vessels; to operate aids to navigation; to ensure the safety of vessels at sea; to provide search and rescue operations at sea; and to maintain the military readiness of the Coast Guard. Duties performed for the first time during World War II that Waesche campaigned to keep for the Coast Guard included operating the Bureau of Marine Inspection and Navigation, LORAN stations, and weather stations.

World War II stimulated further growth at the Coast Guard Academy. The demand for officers led the academy to graduate the class of 1942 six months early and the classes of 1943 through 1947 one year early. The traditional program could not meet the needs of the service during the war, however, so in 1942 the service started a candidate for reserve commission program. The first officer candidates were put up in tents on the football field and held classes in the Billard Hall gymnasium. The government then took over fifteen acres of land on the north side of the academy and erected a number of flat-topped wooden buildings to house the new school. At its peak, the school had one thousand officer candidates in training and graduated two hundred officers a month.

During the war the academy acquired the Danish sail training ship *Danmark*, which was sailing in U.S. waters when Germany overran Denmark. Its captain, Knud L. Hansen, sent a message to Washington offering to place himself, his officers and cadets, and the *Danmark* in the service of the United States. Washington accepted the offer and sent Hansen and his ship to New London to serve as the academy training ship. Between 1942 and 1945 thousands of cadets and candidates for reserve commissions received their first training at sea aboard the *Danmark*. Coast Guard officers were its nominal commanders, but Captain Hansen and other Danish officers remained aboard.

The first officer candidates were put up in tents on the football field and held classes in the Billard Hall gymnasium.

Following the war, the Coast Guard determined that it needed three thousand officers and thirty thousand enlisted men to perform all of its jobs, but Congress authorized just fifteen hundred officers and seventeen thousand men. Morale suffered because many who had served in the war had to leave the service, while others had to accept reductions in rank, which led to still more resignations.

During a difficult transition to peacetime service, the jobs of the Coast Guard were defined and expanded. In 1946 President Harry S. Truman made the transfer of the Bureau of Marine Inspection and Navigation permanent. Weather patrols, begun as a wartime service to the airlines, continued as ocean stations, and the president assigned that duty to the Coast Guard. LORAN stations were likewise continued after the war and became Coast Guard obligations.

The service had just about readjusted after World War II when the Korean War broke out in 1950. The Coast Guard did not participate in combat in Korea, but it resumed the same type of port security duties that it had performed in World War II. It manned and operated newly established LORAN stations in the Pacific and set up search and rescue operations in combat areas. Thus, when the Korean War ended, the Coast Guard was more active in the Pacific than it had been at the outset of the war.

Following the Korean War, the Coast Guard committed both men and equipment to its newly acquired duties. Many a young officer's first independent command was as the commanding officer of an isolated LO-

RAN station. Coast Guard personnel spent a great deal of time on ocean stations relaying weather information, providing navigational assistance to international airlines, and rescuing downed flyers, crews, and passengers from the ocean. In 1956 the U.S. government officially made the Coast Guard responsible for search and rescue operations on the contiguous high seas and U.S. territorial waters. Since its beginning as the Revenue Cutter Service, the Coast Guard had aided mariners in distress; now that was an official obligation, and the service made saving lives its first priority.

The tempo of change quickened in the 1960s. A force of thirty-five thousand, the service built a new fleet of 210-foot and 378-foot cutters. When it was transferred from the Treasury Department to the Transportation Department in 1966, it increased its role in marine safety and environmental protection. Aids to navigation were modernized and automated. Four big polar icebreakers were taken over from the navy, and big cutters continued to alternate between ocean station patrols and naval operations in Vietnam.

The navy called upon the Coast Guard for assistance interdicting arms shipments to South Vietnam by sea. As U.S. involvement in the Vietnam War expanded, so did Coast Guard involvement. It played a significant role in port security, the handling of explosives, aids to navigation, regulation of merchant shipping, and search and rescue operations. Between March 1965 and January 1972, the Coast Guard deployed to Vietnam twenty-six eighty-two-foot patrol boats, thirty high-

The Coast Guard participated in many amphibious actions during World War II. In this 1944 photograph, soldiers disembark from two Coast Guard manned landing ships/tanks (LSTs) on the beach of Leyte Island in the Philippines. (National Archives)

endurance cutters, four buoy tenders, one cargo vessel, and more than eight thousand Coast Guardsmen.

In March 1965 the U.S. Navy set up a coastal surveillance task force to stop the flow of arms into South Vietnam by sea—Operation Market Time, after the junks and sampans that plied Vietnam's coastal waters. A shortage of small navy boats to patrol rivers and inshore waters led Admiral Edwin J. Roland, commandant of the Coast Guard, to volunteer Coast Guard eighty-two-foot patrol boats for the job. He was concerned about retaining the Coast Guard's naval character, which he believed could be lost if the Coast Guard failed to gain a combat role in Vietnam. Late in April, seventeen of the cutters were loaded onto merchant ships as deck cargo and transported to Subic Bay in the Philippines. A month later Squadron One was commissioned at Alameda, California. When interdiction efforts in Vietnam expanded, nine additional eighty-two-footers were added to Squadron One. While in Vietnam, Squadron One and all-other Coast Guard units served under the commander in chief of the Pacific Fleet of the U.S. Navy.

Despite problems, the cutters in Squadron One got under way, and, aided by Squadron Three and the South Vietnamese navy, helped to block access to South Vietnam by sea, thus forcing reinforcements of men and supplies to travel the long, arduous Ho Chi Minh Trail.

This success was the result of hard work. During their first year in Vietnam, the patrol boats stayed at sea 70 percent of the time. During its first month of combat, Division Eleven alone made more than eleven hundred boardings and inspected more than four thousand Vietnamese junks and sampans. Between 27 May 1965 and 15 August 1970, the squadron sailed 4,215,116 miles, detected 838,299 ships, boarded 236,396 vessels, inspected 283,527 ships, damaged or destroyed 1,811 ships, and detained 10,286 persons. The naval blockade was strengthened by an outer barrier patrol, conducted at first by destroyer escorts, minesweepers, and landing ships, and was reinforced in 1967 by 165-foot navy gunboats and by high-endurance Coast Guard cutters.

Coast Guard Squadron Three had been organized at Pearl Harbor on 24 April 1967 to administer the five high-endurance cutters that participated in Operation Market Time at any one time. A total of thirty cutters sailed with Squadron Three, including 255-footers, 311-footers, the venerable 327-foot Secretary class, and the new 378-footers. Counting transit time, all rotated on ten-month deployments.

Five cutters and seven naval vessels combined into a single task force after October 1967 to carry out the outer barrier patrol of Operation Market Time. During their nearly five years in Vietnam, the high-endurance cutters of Squadron Three cruised 1.3 million miles, inspected fifty thousand vessels, and participated in more than thirteen hundred gunfire support missions. One of the major tasks of the cutters was to cooperate with the inner barrier patrol on Market Time, which kept the cutters under way about 75 percent of the time. On the whole, the task was a tedious one. Most contraband was carried into South Vietnam by junks, which were usually harmless, but occasionally the cutters confronted belligerent, armed opponents.

One of the major objectives of Operation Market Time was to stop trawlers from reaching the Vietcong with large caches of arms. During the Tet Offensive in February 1968, there was a great deal of trawler activity, which led to orders for cutters on the outer barrier patrol to trail trawlers and to commence challenging them at six and a half miles from shore. In four separate engagements on 29 February 1968, high-endurance cutters, often supported by patrol boats, confronted four trawlers trying to infiltrate weapons to the Vietcong. They sank three of the trawlers and drove one out to sea.

In addition to their major tasks, cutters performed a variety of missions in Vietnamese waters. The patrol boats of Squadron One and the high-endurance cutters of Squadron Three provided gunfire support for U.S. and Vietnamese forces under a variety of circumstances. They transported friendly forces into and out of combat. Medical evacuations of combatants from both sides and civilians were commonplace. Cutters charted Vietnamese waters, conducted hydrographic surveys of the coast, provided damage control services, and rescued seamen and downed airmen from the water. Because the Coast Guard has been called upon to protect U.S. ports and to assure the safe handling of munitions and explosives since World War I, understandably the nation turned to the Coast Guard for these services in Vietnam.

Simas Kudirka, a Lithuanian fisherman, tried to defect by jumping from the Soviet ship onto the U.S. Coast Guard cutter Vigilant.

Although there were never more than fifty Coast Guardsmen assigned to port security duties in Vietnam, they were highly effective in reducing losses. They supervised the handling of more than four million tons of explosives aboard more than five hundred ships a year, members of the explosive loading teams working twelve hours a day seven days a week.

As a result of the Vietnamization program of the Nixon administration, which was meant to expedite U.S. withdrawal from Vietnam without condemning South Vietnam to certain defeat, the Coast Guard turned over all of its twenty-six eighty-two-footers and four high-endurance cutters to South Vietnamese forces.

The 1970s began badly for the U.S. Coast Guard. On 23 November 1970, U.S. and Soviet officials met at sea off Martha's Vineyard, Massachusetts, to try to work out a dispute over the quantity of yellow-tail flounder taken in U.S. waters by the Soviet fishing fleet. During the meetings that took place on board the Soviet factory ship *Sovietskaya Litva,* Simas Kudirka, a Lithuanian fisherman, tried to defect by jumping from the Soviet ship onto the U.S. Coast Guard cutter *Vigilant,* which had transported the U.S. delegation to the meeting and was tied alongside the Soviet ship. The commanding officer of the *Vigilant,* Commander Ralph W. Eustis, allowed five Soviet crewmen to board the *Vigilant,* seize Kudirka, and return him to the Soviet ship. Because Kudirka refused to return with the crewmen, they used force, beating him in the process. This tragic affair marked one of the worst failures in the two-hundred-year history of the U.S. humanitarian seagoing service.

President Richard Nixon was outraged. Secretary of State William P. Rogers was astounded that a Coast Guard officer allowed Soviets to board his ship for such a purpose. Demonstrators in New York, Boston, Philadelphia, Cleveland, and Chicago protested Kudirka's return to the Soviets. Admiral Chester R. Bender, commandant of the Coast Guard, ordered an investigation, as did the Department of State and Congress. As a result of the investigations, Commander Eustis was given a letter of reprimand by the commandant for allowing Soviet crewmen to exercise authority over Kudirka on a U.S. naval vessel and was transferred to other duties ashore. Rear Admiral William B. Ellis and Captain Fletcher W. Brown, Jr., submitted letters of immediate retirement that were accepted by Transportation Secretary John A. Volpe. Ellis, although on sick leave from his job as district commander of the First Coast Guard District in Boston, was consulted by the acting district commander, Captain Brown, when the district learned from the *Vigilant* of Kurdirka's request for asylum. Ellis, although officially out of the chain of command, told Brown to return Kudirka to the Soviets. Brown in turn ordered Eustis to return the Lithuanian seaman. In retrospect the decision should have been left with the men on the ship, who knew all the details of the incident. Ellis and Brown were given letters of reprimand and retired from the Coast Guard on 31 January 1971.

One happy development in the affair was the return of Kudirka to the United States in 1974. With the help of several prominent congressmen and senators and the Lithuanian-American Community, the U.S. government arranged his release from a Soviet prison camp and an exit visa to the United States.

There was a significant change of emphasis in Coast Guard operations in the 1970s, a result, in part, of the termination of old missions. In 1972 the service ended ocean station operations, and the following year the last Coast Guard units left Vietnam. At least as important as the termination of old missions in the change of emphasis was the increasing role played by law enforcement in Coast Guard operations. The Magnuson Act of 1976 made the Coast Guard responsible for protecting a two-hundred-mile conservation zone off all U.S. coasts. Most important, drug interdiction grew tremendously between 1973 and 1990.

In the 1980s the drug problem reached crisis proportions in the United States. Illegal drugs came into the country from many places, but basically marijuana came from Colombia, Mexico, Belize, and Jamaica, and cocaine came from Colombia, Bolivia, and Peru. Drug smuggling has changed dramatically since 1973, when the Coast Guard deployed just six cutters in drug interdiction. Seizures of marijuana shipments escalated through 1982, then began to drop off as smugglers shifted to cocaine, which is more profitable and easier to conceal than marijuana. In 1982 the service seized 3.5 million pounds of marijuana and 2,000 pounds of cocaine; in 1987, 1.3 million pounds of marijuana was

UNITED STATES COAST GUARD PERSONNEL STRENGTH, 1915–1990

Year	Strength
1915	4,155
1920	3,705
1925	9,219
1930	12,131
1935	10,409
1940	13,756
1945	176,000
1950	22,894
1955	28,607
1960	30,616
1965	31,776
1970	37,689
1975	36,788
1980	39,381
1985	38,595
1990	37,087

seized along with 14,000 pounds of cocaine. In the 1990s heroin began to appear in large quantities.

Until the late 1980s, most of the cocaine was smuggled into southern Florida, the marketing and distribution center for the business, and most of it came into the United States by the shortest route from Latin America, via Colombia. By the late 1980s, the Coast Guard had improved its interdiction operations, which drove the smugglers ashore. In the early 1990s, most cocaine came into the United States over the Mexican border, and illegal drugs began to show up in container ships.

To interdict drug shipments, the Coast Guard depends on a defense in depth. First, it tries to stop drugs in the departure zone in the southern Caribbean, where it employs seven or eight cutters and where the U.S. Navy sails one thousand ship days per year in support of the drug interdiction effort. Because the navy is forbidden to perform law enforcement duties under the Mansfield Amendment, naval ships carry a Coast Guard Tactical Law Enforcement Team to conduct boardings. A Department of Defense regulation passed on 7 April 1982 authorized use of naval vessels and personnel to interdict drug shipments to the United States, but the navy accepts the historical ban on direct military contact with civilians and still uses Coast Guard boarding teams. Second, the Coast Guard tries to interdict drugs in the transit zone, the choke points in the Caribbean, employing six or seven cutters in the three principal Caribbean passages. Third, the Coast Guard tries to interdict drugs in the arrival zone, maintaining six to eight cutters off the coast of Florida. All cutters are supported by aerostat balloons, fixed radar sights, and aircraft that help by spotting air and maritime traffic.

The interdiction efforts of the Coast Guard require ships and methods of operation that are of military consequence. The ships and methods developed during the Rum War proved of value during World War II. As was the case with the Rum War, those cutters and methods developed during the drug war can be used to defend the United States today and in future conflicts. The most obvious example is the navy's use of Coast Guard boarding teams on naval vessels to board and inspect ships in the Persian Gulf during the 1990–1991 Iraqi crisis. The Coast Guard also provided port security in the United States and the gulf, inspected the vessels in the Ready Reserve Fleet before they went to sea, and supervised the loading of weapons onto ships in U.S. ports.

As a result of a 1984 agreement between the secretary of transportation and the secretary of the navy, Coast Guard area commanders on the East and West coasts were designated Maritime Defense Zone commanders. As such, those Coast Guard area commanders, under the direct command of the commander in chief, Atlantic Fleet, and commander in chief, Pacific Fleet, coordinate naval, Coast Guard, and police forces involved in the coastal defense of the United States; the security of U.S. ports, harbors, and navigable waterways; antisubmarine warfare in the coastal area; mine countermeasures; intelligence; surveillance; interdiction operations; the control and protection of shipping; and search and rescue operations. In addition to running specific training exercises to hone the warfare skills needed to fulfill these obligations, the Coast Guard carries out its normal peacetime duties, all of which foster the skills needed to perform these tasks.

John F. Kennedy noticed the absence of black cadets at his inaugural parade and pressed the service to integrate the cadet corps.

There is a major difference in the way the navy and Coast Guard employ women in their services. The navy prohibits women from serving in combat units, while the Coast Guard has no restrictions on women's duty assignments. The cutters *Morgenthau* and *Gallatin* each went to sea with two female officers and ten female enlisted crew members in September 1977. The next year Admiral John B. Hayes, commandant of the Coast Guard, removed all restrictions based on sex in the way the service employed its people. Thereafter, there were no restrictions in training, duty assignments, or career opportunities for women in the Coast Guard. In 1979 Lieutenant (junior grade) Beverly Kelly took command of the ninety-five-foot patrol boat *Newagen* and another female officer took command of an isolated Coast Guard unit ashore. Three years later Lieutenant Colleen Cain died when the HH52A helicopter that she copiloted crashed into a mountain during a search and rescue operation in severe weather. The difference in employment practices by the two services poses problems for future Coast Guard operations with the navy in wartime. Both services understand that women might be removed from Coast Guard units ordered to serve under the navy in combat, but women currently serve in key positions, including command, on many cutters, and there are no Coast Guard men readily available to take their place.

The modern Coast Guard has a myriad of duties and responsibilities, including, but not limited to, making oceanographic surveys, enforcing conservation laws, inspecting merchant ships, boating safety, pollution control, ice breaking, maintaining aids to navigation, licensing mariners, and regulating bridges over navigable waters.

The Coast Guard Academy has undergone many changes since World War II. Following the war, the Candidates for Reserve Commission School was cut back and moved to Yorktown, Virginia. As the Officers Candidate School, it now provides roughly half of the new ensigns for the service. The academy had educated and trained almost all of the officers between 1877 and 1942. Before 1961 fewer than a handful of black cadets had graduated from the academy. In that year President John F. Kennedy noticed the absence of black cadets at his inaugural parade and pressed the service to integrate the cadet corps. In 1976 the academy admitted its first female cadets, and four years later graduated its first female officers. In December 1990 women made up 15 percent of the corps.

The cadet corps has fluctuated in size since World War II. Enrollment dropped to just under three hundred following the war. It rose gradually to around six hundred in the early 1960s, and during the Vietnam War rose to more than twelve hundred in the late 1960s and the early to mid-1970s. Following the Vietnam War, the corps dropped back to about 750. Rear Admiral Richard P. Cueroni, the academy superintendent, believed correctly that it was impossible to plan the academy program without some stability in the size of the corps, and he convinced the commandant, Admiral Paul A. Yost, to stabilize it at around 900 to 950, which was done by admitting classes of about 300 to 320.

The academy underwent a building boom during the Vietnam War. It took over land on both the north and south ends of the reservation, expanded Chase Hall to accommodate twelve hundred cadets, and erected Munro Hall to house enlisted personnel, Leamy Hall as a recreation building, Roland Fieldhouse for athletic events, Dimick Hall for lectures, Waesche Hall for a new library, and Smith Hall for the sciences.

Postwar changes in Coast Guard operations and the changing size of the corps of cadets have affected the

This Coast Guard patrol boat, the USCGC Maui, monitored the Florida coast in 1990. The Coast Guard is often called on to interdict drug smugglers and illegal aliens who try to enter the United State by boat. (Department of Defense/U.S. Coast Guard)

academy curriculum and organization. Until 1966 all cadets majored in engineering, studied the same courses for four years, and attended classes in the same cadet section for those four years. In 1966 cadets were given the option of studying engineering or humanities. A few years later, ocean science was added as an option, and by the 1970s cadets enjoyed thirteen options. As the corps size dropped from its high during the Vietnam era, the options were changed to majors, and their numbers were reduced to nine and finally to seven in 1983. Those seven options are civil engineering, electrical engineering, naval architecture and marine engineering, marine science, mathematics and computer science, management, and government.

All cadets graduate with a bachelor of science degree in one of the majors, and all cadets must complete twenty-five core courses that are, as they were in 1932, heavily weighted in engineering, mathematics, and science. The remaining fifteen courses taken by cadets are determined by their choice of majors.

All cadets also receive a commission as ensigns in the Coast Guard. They take courses in nautical science each year at the academy. They go to sea for a total of twenty-three weeks, and they live under a military system in the Chase Hall barracks. Following World War II the *Danmark* sailed for home and was replaced by the barque *Eagle,* a war prize that first went to sea in 1936 as the *Horst Wessel* to train German cadets. Coast Guard academy cadets still enjoy their first seagoing experience under sail, on board the *Eagle* during their first summer in New London.

[See also The Navy.]

BIBLIOGRAPHY

Bell, Kensil. *"Always Ready!" The Story of the United States Coast Guard* (1943).

Capron, Walter C. *The U.S. Coast Guard* (1965).

Carse, Robert. *Rum Row* (1959).

Johnson, Robert Erwin. *Guardians of the Sea: History of the United States Coast Guard, 1915 to the Present* (1987).

King, Irving H. *The Coast Guard Under Sail: The U.S. Revenue Cutter Service, 1789–1865* (1989).

Pearcy, Arthur. *Record of Movements: Vessels of the United States Coast Guard,* 2 vols. (1933, rev. 1989).

———. *A History of U.S. Coast Guard Aviation* (1989).

Scheina, Robert L. *Study of Roles and Missions of the United States Coast Guard,* 2 vols. (1962).

———. *U.S. Coast Guard Cutters and Craft of World War II* (1982).

———. *U.S. Coast Guard Cutters and Craft, 1946–1990* (1990).

Tulich, Eugene N. *The United States Coast Guard in South East Asia During the Vietnam Conflict* (1975).

Waters, John M., Jr. *Rescue at Sea* (1966, rev. 1989).

Wheeler, William J. "Reminiscences of World War Convoy Work." *U.S. Naval Institute Proceedings* 55 (1929).

Willoughby, Malcolm F. *The U.S. Coast Guard in World War II,* (1957, rev. 1989).

———. *Rum War at Sea* (1964).

— IRVING H. KING

The Air Force

The U.S. Air Force did not come into existence as a separate service until 18 September 1947, two years after World War II, but its organizational roots can be found forty years earlier on 1 August 1907, when the Army Signal Corps established an aeronautical divison to take charge "of all matters pertaining to military ballooning, air machines, and all kindred subjects." Allotted to carry out these tasks were one captain, one corporal, and one private.

Military ballooning had its roots in the wars of the French Revolution as a reconnaissance tool.

Military ballooning had its roots in the wars of the French Revolution as a reconnaissance tool. A half-century later, in 1849, balloons were first used as a weapon when the Austrians attempted an aerial bombardment of Venice with small, time-fused bombs, each carried by a small unmanned balloon. At the outbreak of the U.S. Civil War in 1861, several adventurous aeronauts offered their services to the Union, and by the end of 1862 the federal forces had at least seven captive (or tethered) balloons in service. The aeronauts were not taken seriously, however, and were disbanded by the end of 1863. For almost three decades, the army continued to ignore the balloon, but in 1890 the chief signal officer, Brigadier General Adolphus W. Greely, revived interest. Greely sent an officer to France to survey developments there and to purchase a balloon, which was displayed to the public at the World Columbian Exposition in Chicago in 1893.

During the exposition several hundred ascensions were made and a telephone was used for the first time between the balloonist and the ground. In conjunction with the exposition, General Greely had also arranged a meeting of the International Engineering Congress, where British Major J. Fullerton of the Royal Engineers presented a remarkably farsighted paper, "Some Remarks on Aerial Warfare." Fullerton argued that the world was on the verge of "as great a revolution in the art of war as the discovery of gunpowder in the past." The threat of aerial bombardment, he declared, would revolutionize warfare. Future wars would start with a great air battle, whose winner would then carry out naval and ground attacks. "The arrival of the aerial fleet over the enemy capital will probably conclude the campaign." Ten years before the success of the Wright brothers, he argued that the speed of the coming airplane, which he favored over existing balloons and dirigibles, would require nations to prepare for "lightning wars" in which naval and land warfare would be possible only when "a nation has command of the air."

In 1898 General Greely convinced the War Department to award a $50,000 contract to Samuel Pierpont Langley, secretary of the Smithsonian Institution, to construct a heavier-than-air, man-carrying aircraft. Langley's five-year effort failed in the end, with unsuccessful flights on 7 October and 8 December 1903. Ironically, little more than a week later, Wilbur and Orville Wright, two obscure bicycle makers from Dayton, Ohio, without benefit of government subsidy or encouragement, succeeded at Kitty Hawk, North Carolina, in launching the first sustained, controlled, power-driven flight of a heavier-than-air machine.

The initial success of the Wrights on 17 December 1903 was not widely noticed at the time, and almost four years elapsed until the Signal Corps established its aeronautical division. Five months later, however, the War Department issued Specification No. 486, calling for bids on a "Heavier-than-air Flying Machine," capable of carrying two persons with sufficient fuel for a flight of 125 miles and of attaining a speed of forty miles an hour. "It will be sufficiently simple in construction and operation to permit an intelligent man to become proficient in its use within a reasonable length of time. The price to be quoted includes instruction of two men."

Three bidders responded, but only the highest (the Wright brothers at $25,000) within the 180-day deadline. Formal acceptance tests were carried out at Fort Myer, Virginia, between 3 and 17 September 1908. During the two weeks, several new endurance records were set, and on 9 September, Lieutenant Frank P. Lahm became the first army officer to fly as a passenger in an airplane. The final acceptance flight on 17 September ended in tragedy when Lieutenant Thomas E. Selfridge, flying as a passenger with Orville Wright, was killed in a crash from about 125 feet over the field. (Wright remained hospitalized for seven weeks.)

After further tests the following summer, Signal Corps Airplane No. 1 was formally accepted on 2 August 1909. Flight training for officers began in October, using an open field at College Park, near the Maryland Agricultural College (now University of Maryland). Lieutenant Lahm received the first lesson on 8 October, but Lieutenant Frederic E. Humphreys (who would leave the service the following year) made the first solo flight by a military pilot on 26 October. Flying training continued intermittently at College Park through 1911. Among the students were several who would come to play a large part in air force history, including Second Lieutenant Benjamin D. Foulois (chief of the Air Corps, 1931–1935); Second Lieutenant Henry H. ("Hap") Arnold (commanding general, Army Air Forces, 1941–1946); and Second Lieutenant Thomas DeWitt Milling (first commandant of the Air Service Tactical School at Langley Field, Virginia).

Between acceptance of the first military aircraft in 1909 and the outbreak of war in Europe in 1914, military aviation stagnated in the United States. Public interest was almost nil and reflected in congressional appropriations of not more than $125,000 a year from 1911 through 1914. These amounts could not begin to sustain an industry already frustrated by the determination of the Wrights to enforce their patents, a conflict over royalties that was not resolved until after the United States entered the European war in 1917. With the few planes made available, experiments were conducted involving telegraphy, bomb dropping, aerial mapping, photography, mounting a Lewis machine gun, and directing artillery fire, but all were exceptional, as were such achievements by naval aviators of the first landing on the deck of a ship and the first catapult-assisted takeoff from a ship.

The first military aircraft were balloons, which Union forces used during the Civil War for reconnaissance. In this photograph, Professor Thaddeus Lowe observes the Battle of Fair Oaks (Seven Pines) from his balloon Intrepid *in May 1862. (National Archives)*

When war erupted in Europe in August 1914, the United States had fallen well behind the European powers in all aspects of military aviation. It still had only one flying school, which had managed to wander from College Park to San Antonio, Texas, back to College Park to San Antonio, Texas, back to College Park and then to Augusta, Georgia, finally landing at North Island in San Diego, California. In July the Aeronautical Division was redesignated the Aviation Section of the Signal Corps and authorized a strength of sixty officers and 250 enlisted men. In early August 1914, however, the entire army had fewer than two hundred people (officers, enlisted men, and civilians) in its aviation establishment. Of the total of thirty airplanes that had been obtained between 1909 and 1914, one—the first—was already in the Smithsonian Institution, and twenty-one had been destroyed or condemned. When the Signal Corps requested $1 million for fiscal year 1915, the secretary of war reduced the amount to $300,000 and Congress cut out another $50,000.

The misadventures of the First Aero Squadron in the pursuit of Pancho Villa in the Mexican Border Campaign of 1916 demonstrated the inadequacy of the military aviation establishment. After the Mexican revolutionary raided Columbus, New Mexico, the squadron was sent to join the punitive expedition under Brigadier General John J. Pershing. Captain Foulois commanded the unit in its unsuccessful attempts to fly reconnaissance and provide courier service during the yearlong campaign. At a time when European aircraft attained speeds approaching 200 miles an hour and altitudes of 15,000 feet or more, the squadron of Curtiss Scouts in Mexico could neither buck strong headwinds nor climb high enough to cross the mountain ranges. (Because equipment shortcomings by themselves rendered the air portions of that adventure a fiasco, it was perhaps in the end not important that the secretary of war had specifically excluded, in advance, any attempt at offensive operations for the air arm.)

WORLD WAR I

When the United States declared war in April 1917, the French and British governments asked immediately for industrial help. In particular, Alexandre Ribot, the French premier in early 1917, sent a (later famous) telegram asking the Americans to build forty-five hundred combat aircraft in time for an offensive to take place the following year. He was encouraged to do so by a Signal Corps officer, Major William L. (Billy) Mitchell, recently converted to aviation, fluent in French, and unmatched in enthusiasm. Mitchell was one of only five army officers then in Paris, and the only one who knew anything about aviation.

Billy Mitchell functioned as a one-man war college.

The U.S. government responded to the Ribot telegram by appropriating the then stunning sum of $10.8 million for aircraft in May 1917, another $43.5 million in June, and in July another $640 million—ultimately $1.68 billion. A succession of missions were dispatched to France, the United Kingdom, Italy, and Canada in search of information on organizing, recruiting, training, equipping, and employing a vastly expanded air arm. One group, under Major Raynal C. Bolling, selected the specific kinds of foreign aircraft that U.S. industry would be asked to build; another, led by Major Foulois, went to Canada to arrange cooperative flying training programs. In Paris, Billy Mitchell functioned as a one-man war college as he sought to learn from Allied airmen the lessons of almost three years of fighting (and completed his own pilot training under a French instructor).

In the United States, McCook Field, near Dayton, Ohio, became the early center for aeronautical research and design, largely by default because the laboratories of the National Advisory Committee for Aeronautics (NACA, predecessor of NASA) at Langley Field were not yet ready. Its principal triumph was the Liberty engine, of which thirteen thousand were built. Starting from scratch, U.S. aircraft builders produced twelve thousand aircraft in all, but only thirty-five hundred were combat types, of which no more than twelve hundred reached France before the armistice.

Responsibility for recruiting, training, and production soon overwhelmed the Aviation Section to the Signal Corps. On 21 May 1918, the new Division of Military Aeronautics was established and combined eight days later with the Bureau of Aircraft Production to form the Air Service of the Army, reporting directly to the secretary of the army through a newly created assistant secretary of war for air. The Air Service recruited and trained more than 200,000 officers and men, one-fourth of whom served overseas.

The cutting edge of the U.S. air effort overseas was the Air Service of the American Expeditionary Forces (AEF), commanded by Major General Mason M. Patrick, an officer of the Corps of Engineers installed by General Pershing to institute some kind of order among his rambunctious airmen. A full year elapsed between Mitchell's early arrival in France and the first action fought by a U.S. air squadron in April 1918. In July, Mitchell, now a colonel, was appointed chief of Air Service, First (U.S.) Army, the top combat post, from which he organized and led the air aspects of the Aisne-Marne, Saint-Mihiel, and Meuse-Argonne campaigns. In September 1918, Mitchell, soon to be a brigadier general, was placed in overall command of the Allied air forces for the Saint-Mihiel offensive. Some fifteen hundred aircraft were involved altogether, of which only 609 were piloted by Americans. "We had three tasks to accomplish," Mitchell later wrote, "one, to provide accurate information for the infantry and adjustment of fire for the artillery of the ground troops; second, to hold off the enemy air forces from interfering with either our air or ground troops; and third, to bomb the back areas so as to stop the supplies from the enemy and hold up any movement along the roads."

When hostilities ceased on 11 November 1918, there were 45 U.S. squadrons, 767 pilots, 481 observers, and 23 aerial gunners—equipped with 740 airplanes. Of enemy aircraft, 781 had been downed, and 289 U.S. aircraft had been destroyed in battle, the latter figure dwarfed by the unknown but huge number lost in training and other accidents. General Patrick's *Final Report on the Air Service, AEF,* stated that, in round numbers, U.S. squadrons took part in 150 bombing raids, during which they dropped 275,000 pounds of explosives, flew thirty-five thousand hours over the lines, and took eighteen thousand photographs of enemy positions. Despite these numbers, it was only in the final two months of the war, from early September to early November of 1918, that the Air Service had any significant impact on the fighting. Plans had been drawn for much more significant air action in 1919, but the war ended before they could be set in motion.

THE ARMY AIR SERVICE AND ARMY AIR CORPS, 1919–1939

The army returned from France convinced of the importance of what some were coming to call air power, but exclusively as a necessary supporting arm for the ground forces—to thwart enemy air efforts, bomb and strafe the battlefield as necessary, and provide reconnaisance. The National Defense Act of 1920 reflected this view, incorporating the Air Service into the army, but now divorced from the Signal Corps. Appropriations and personnel strength withered. From 20,000 air officers and 164,000 enlisted men in November 1918, the Air Service at the end of 1919 had 1,000 officers and some 10,000 enlisted men. By the end of 1920, the service was down to 896 officers and 7,846 enlisted men.

A future vision limited to an auxiliary arm of the army did not satisfy those, like Mitchell, who believed that air power had the potential to dominate all future warfare, whether ashore or afloat. The vision of such men was well ahead of any real capability, but the strong-minded among them felt they had an absolute duty to stress the future, even, when necessary, at the expense of the past. Mitchell was not alone in his thinking; indeed, most of his ideas had in fact been borrowed from an international circle of aviation enthusiasts—most notably Air Marshal Hugh Trenchard of the Royal Air Force and the Italians Giulio Douhet and Gianni Caproni. In the Air Service itself, men like Colonel Edgar S. Gorrell and Lieutenant Colonel William C. Sherman shared Mitchell's vision, as did many younger but less eloquent spokesmen who prided themselves on being looked on as "Mitchell's boys."

Mitchell's most important role in the years from 1919 to his death in 1936 was as a crusader, a polemicist, and a heroic role model. He was at his weakest in the role most often ascribed to him today, that of a theorist of air power, one for which he was ill-suited temperamentally. Except for his bottom line—that predictable advances in aeronautics meant that the oceans could no longer be relied upon for defense, and that, hence, an air force on equal standing with the army and navy should be established—his views were too unsystematic to qualify for description as a coherent theory. His dramatic bombing tests off the Virginia coast in 1921, involving the sinking of captured German battleships, caught but could not hold public attention. His frustrations over the continuing decline of both the Air Service and the naval air arm led him in 1925 to publicly charge the leadership of the services with "almost treasonable administration of the National Defense." President Calvin Coolidge himself promptly referred court-martial charges and on 17 December 1925—the twenty-second anniversary of the Wright brothers' flight at Kitty Hawk—he was found guilty and resigned to take up his continuing crusade as a civilian.

As Mitchell careened toward the all but inevitable court-martial, President Coolidge called upon Dwight Morrow, a banker and close friend, to investigate the condition of aviation, both military and civilian, in the United States. The findings of the Morrow Board resulted during 1926 in the elevation of the Air Service to the status of the Air Corps, organizationally on a level with the army's other combat arms. The position of assistant secretary of war for air was reestablished, but the idea of establishing a separate federal department of aeronautics responsible for military, naval, and civil aviation—Mitchell's goal—was shelved.

The new Air Corps promptly launched a five-year program of modernization and expansion, which crashed shortly after takeoff, colliding head-on with the Great Depression. Except for some visionary thinking at the Air Corps Tactical School, most of the period between the world wars was taken up with just trying to keep the air service alive. Recruitment and technical training continued, as did flying training, but at low levels. Gradually, the surplus of obsolescent wartime aircraft was replaced, but always in small numbers. Experimentation focused on all-metal aircraft, increasing speed and altitude, instrument (or "blind") flying, and improved engines.

In the defense of the United States, the Air Corps could play a major part if its aircraft could be formed into a mobile striking force capable of destroying an approaching invasion fleet. To provide such a force, General Patrick and his successors as chief of the Air Corps, James E. Fechet and Foulois, proposed establishing a centrally controlled General Headquarters Air Force (GHQAF) to which air units normally assigned to army corps areas would respond in time of crisis. A series of maneuvers in the late 1920s and early 1930s proved the feasibility of this idea, which took on added significance in 1931, when the army chief of staff, Douglas MacArthur, and the chief of naval operations, William V. Pratt, agreed that the Air Corps should take over the mission of aerial coast defense.

The mail had to be delivered on a rigid schedule that required flying both at night and in bad weather.

A crisis delayed the massing of combat aircraft to form the GHQAF. After a Senate investigation revealed collusion in the award of federal airmail contracts in 1934, President Franklin D. Roosevelt canceled the agreements. Asked if his airmen could fly the mail, Foulois, now chief of the Air Corps, told the president they could. In a costly miscalculation, Foulois committed the air arm to a task for which it did not have training, experience, or equipment. The Air Corps was trained to fly and fight by day in good weather, but the mail had to be delivered on a rigid schedule that required flying both at night and in bad weather. The results were dismaying—delays, cancellations, and sixty-six crashes that claimed the lives of twelve airmen.

The airmail fiasco triggered two investigations during 1934. The first was convened by the War Department, headed by former Secretary of War Newton D. Baker, and focused on deficiencies in the Air Corps. The other, a presidential commission directed by Clark Howell, editor of the *Atlanta Constitution,* studied civil aviation. The two panels agreed that the general state of aviation in the United States—rather than the incompetence of the Air Corps—was the primary villain, but stopped short of recommending a separate department of aeronautics, as urged by Mitchell and his disciples. They also agreed that the GHQAF should have the opportunity to prove itself.

Circumstances soon provided the GHQAF with a bomber that had the range and carrying capacity to meet its needs. In 1935, the Air Corps staged a competition for a new bomber, assuming but not requiring that all entries would be twin-engine aircraft. The Boeing Aircraft Company gambled on the four-engine SB-17, which proved faster than most fighters. Despite the crash of the first prototype, the Air Corps decided to buy thirteen modified Y1B-17s for a squadron-size test. Contemporaneously, the new Norden Mark XV bombsight encouraged the visionaries.

The establishment of the Air Service in 1921 had allowed it to establish several schools, including its Tactical School at Langley Field, later redesignated the Air Corps Tactical School and moved to Maxwell Field outside Montgomery, Alabama, in September 1931. From the beginning, the Tactical School treated all four classes (or types) of military aviation: attack (support of ground forces); observation (or reconnaissance); pursuit (or air-to-air fighter); and bombardment (of fixed targets away from the battlefield). Beginning around 1926, but rapidly accelerating after the school moved to Maxwell Field, was the emphasis accorded to bombardment aviation.

The faculty took its cues from both aeronautical advances and the visionary views of Trenchard, Douhet, and Mitchell. In a future war, they argued, the enemy's armies and fleets could be overflown by bombardment aircraft sent to strike directly at the enemy's roots of power—its military-industrial base and transportation centers, in short the capacity and will of the enemy government and people. The Tactical School referred to this concept as "the strategic role of air power," at least in part because it implied that air power was entitled to be considered on its own in planning the nation's strategy for future war. The rest of the army remained unconvinced, arguing that the Air Corps should concentrate on the support of ground forces.

Depression-era fiscal realities required that a means be found to defeat an enemy with a relatively small force of aircraft, which led in turn to ever-increasing emphasis on precision techniques and scientific target selection. In a series of problems set for Tactical School students, the United States was taken as a test case. Studies were made to identify the degree of industrial concentration (mostly in the Northeast and Middle West), the component parts of various industries, the relative importance of each of the parts, and, finally, the vulnerability to air attack of what appeared to be the most critical elements. Through such theoretical studies, it was hoped, the means might be found in wartime to single out particular targets whose destruction would of itself bring to a halt an entire industry, or even series of industries. The ability of future bombers to penetrate enemy air defenses was largely assumed, as was the idea that sufficient intelligence would exist regarding the enemy's industrial structure.

While purely theoretical speculation was centered at the Tactical School, related technological developments affecting aircraft, bombsights, and navigational equipment were presided over by the Materiel Division located at Wright Field in Dayton. After 1 March 1935, day-to-day flying activities involving field testing of both theories and equipment became the responsibility of the GHQAF and its three bombardment groups, located at Langley Field, Barksdale Field in Louisiana, and March Field in California. In 1937 the Air Corps numbered less than twenty thousand men, of whom about fifteen hundred were flying officers.

AIR CORPS TO ARMY AIR FORCES, 1939–1942

Late in 1938, President Roosevelt decided that the airplane was a weapon that might impress Germany and Japan, which were on the march in Europe and China. In January 1939 he called for expanding the Air Corps from sixteen hundred aircraft to fifty-five hundred (against an original fiscal year 1940 plan to purchase 178). By 1939 he was thinking in terms of building ten thousand aircraft per year, and in May 1940 asked Congress to authorize a further increase to fifty thousand military aircraft per year. (Following the Lend-Lease Act of 1941, many of these would go to future U.S. allies—twenty-six thousand to the United Kingdom and British Commonwealth, eleven thousand to the Soviet Union, and almost fourteen hundred to China, along with an American Volunteer Group under retired Colonel Claire Chennault, later famous as the Flying Tigers.)

During the U.S.-British staff conferences of 1941, endorsed by the president and Prime Minister Winston Churchill, it was agreed that Germany would have priority over Japan should the United States become involved in a worldwide war. In August 1941 the president called on the army and navy to estimate the "overall production requirements required to defeat our potential enemies." A newly formed Air War Plans Division, composed primarily of former faculty of the Air Corps Tactical School, postulated that the newly named (June 1941) Army Air Forces (AAF) would need 239 combat groups, 63,467 planes of all types, and a force of 2.2 million men. Given an immediate start, such a force could be trained and equipped by April 1944, following which a six-month air campaign focusing on Germany's electric power system, transportation network, and petroleum production would destroy Germany's warmaking capability.

General George C. Marshall, army chief of staff, endorsed the initial plan, at least in part because he realized that at least two years would be required to recruit, train, equip, and transport an army to Europe. In the interim, the proposed strategic air campaign would serve to weaken Germany in the face of an eventual assault aimed at destroying the German army in the field. Before the plan could be presented to the president, Japan attacked at Pearl Harbor and Adolf Hitler declared war on the United States.

Led by General "Hap" Arnold, the AAF made the strategic bombing of Germany and later Japan the focal point of its efforts in World War II, beginning with the dispatch of a planning cadre in February 1942 to establish the Eighth Air Force in England.

WORLD WAR II

The strategic bomber started off poorly in World War II, many being destroyed on the ground in the Philippines and at Pearl Harbor. In the Pacific, vast distances protected the Japanese home islands, although Lieutenant Colonel James H. Doolittle led sixteen B-25s from the carrier *Hornet* on a nuisance raid against Tokyo on 18 April 1942. The buildup of the bomber forces in England took longer than hoped for, particularly when more than half the force was redeployed to North Africa

Pilots in today's Air Force are a select group of specially-trained men and women. This pilot is examining maintenance records with his ground crew in preparation for a flight in an F-16 Fighting Falcon. (Department of Defense/U.S. Air Force)

at the end of 1942 to support operations subsequent to the Allied landings there (Operation Torch). The limited number of B-17s and B-24s in England, the need for training in high-altitude combat, and the lack of a long-range escort fighter to protect the bombers against German interceptors restricted the Eighth Air Force throughout 1942 to targets in enemy-occupied Western Europe.

In North Africa in early 1943, overall air power doctrine—governing air superiority and tactical ground support—grew by leaps and bounds. Tactical air control techniques, largely borrowed from the RAF, were incorporated in War Department Field Masnual 100-20, *Command and Employment of Air Power,* which opened by declaring that "land power and air power are coequal and interdependent forces; neither is an auxiliary of the other." For the tactical forces in particular, the manual spelled out an explicit hierarchy of priorities:

1. Establish air superiority.
2. Isolate the battlefield by attacking enemy forces and supply.
3. Provide close-in air support of engaged forces on the ground.

Ground and air commanders should be colocated whenever possible, especially in the planning stages.

For the Eighth Air Force in England, 1943 was a trying year. The attempts to strike key targets deep in Germany, most famously the ball-bearing plants at Schweinfurt on 17 August and again on 14 October, led to severe losses, more than one hundred bombers, that could not be borne consistently. Experiments were conducted with radar-bombing techniques, but it took the availability of long-range escorts—P-47s and P-51s outfitted with belly tanks that could be dropped—to enable the bombers to carry on with acceptable loss rates. Late in 1943 the Eighth was joined by the new Fifteenth Air Force, composed of B-24s nd B-17s stationed at newly captured bases in Italy. The two air forces made up the U.S. Strategic Air Forces (USSTAF), under the overall control of Lieutenant General Carl A. Spaatz, General Dwight Eisenhower's senior U.S. airman in the Mediterranean who accompanied him to England, where planning for the invasion of the Continent was under way.

Newly organized and equipped, the strategic air campaign began in earnest in late February 1944, with the German aircraft industry the primary target. In one week (20–25 February) the scale of attack exceeded the total for all of 1943. Following another month of bad weather and reduced scale of attack, General Eisenhower, as overall commander for the planned invasion, took control of the bomber forces, which concentrated for the next six months (April through September) on preparing the way for the planned invasion and protecting the lodgement and subsequent breakout from the Normandy peninsula. On a half-dozen occasions in May, prior to the invasion of 6 June, Eisenhower released Spaatz's bombers to attack oil industry targets with devastating effect. When the Luftwaffe was unable to contest the landings at Normandy, it was clear that the battle for air superiority had been won, but equally clear that German forces were still capable of fierce resistance.

When the Luftwaffe was unable to contest the landings at Normandy, it was clear that the battle for air superiority had been won.

Coincident with the invasion, most of the fighters, fighter-bombers, and medium bombers were consolidated in the Ninth Air Force, which provided tactical support throughout the campaign in France and Germany. Indeed, they so dominated the skies that Hitler's counterattack in the Ardenes in December 1944 was timed explicitly to take advantage of the foul weather that grounded the Ninth for more than a week. Less successful than hoped for were other aspects of air power, for example, reconnaissance and the accurate placement of airborne paratroopers.

The combined Royal Air Force and USSTAF bomber offensive took much longer than hoped for to achieve dramatic effects, but it must be remembered that its full efforts against targets within Germany did not take place until after the invasion had succeeded. Indeed, fully 72 percent of the bombs that fell in Germany did so after 1 July 1944. The U.S. Strategic Bombing Survey, a presidential commission set up in 1944, concluded after the war that "Allied air power was decisive in the war in Western Europe," but could not determine how decisive, thereby leaving the question open to seemingly endless postwar debate.

The Army Air Forces in the Pacific fought a tactical air war between 1942 and 1944, one marked by improvisation and ingenuity with limited forces. Lieutenant General George C. Kenney's Fifth Air Force was in almost daily contact with the enemy along what his commander, General Douglas MacArthur, liked to call "the New Guinea-Mindanao axis" toward the Philippines. Among the more impressive early operations were the destruction of a Japanese convoy, twelve ships sunk out of sixteen, in the Battle of the Bismarck Sea, 2–4 March 1943, and the interception the following month of a bomber carrying Admiral Isoroku Yamamoto, architect of the attack on Pearl Harbor.

The air attack on the Japanese home islands began in June 1944 with the new, long-range B-29s, based in India and staging through bases in southern China. By November 1944 the B-29s were concentrated in the Mariana Islands (Guam, Tinian, Saipan), whence they operated against Japan at the limit of their attack radius. The Assault on the home islands intensified after January 1945 when Major General Curtis E. LeMay took command and shifted the emphasis from high-level precision attacks with high explosives to low-level, nighttime, incendiary attacks against industrial areas in March 1945. The B-29 offensive also included minelaying in Japanese coastal waters and tactical support of the amphibious assaults on Iwo Jima and Okinawa. The air war culminated in August 1945 with the dropping of atomic bombs on Hiroshima and Nagasaki, attacks that prodded Japan, by then already mortally wounded, into surrender.

A SEPARATE AIR FORCE

Ever since World War I, army aviators had been arguing on and off for autonomy. Convinced early on that a third dimension had been added to warfare, that all wars of the future would be dominated from the air, the airmen had long resented their inferior status within the army. The prominence of what the aviators were now calling "air power" in World War II was evident on all fronts—including the home front, where the sudden ending of the war following the dropping of two atomic bombs profoundly affected public opinion. In testimony before Congress in November 1945, the wartime AAF leaders began a two-year war of words about the future of the U.S. miliatry establishment.

The driving force behind their campaign for a separate air force on a par with the army and navy was the picture they had in their minds of the emerging postwar world and the likely nature of any foreseeable armed confrontation in which the country might find itself, wittingly or otherwise. That picture, or vision, blending elements of the past with some from the rapidly evolving future, was decidedly pessimistic, and in its starkest form might be labeled "the atomic Pearl Harbor scenario." To wit, given the advantages that surprise confers on an unprincipled aggressor, along with the potentially devastating decisiveness of atomic weaponry married to rapidly advancing technology in both jet and rocket vehicles, the United States had to guard against the possibility that some future potential enemy, whether from calculated design or out of desperation, might open a war with an atomic air attack against New York, Chicago, or Washington—or all three and conceivably more.

Such were the views presented by General Spaatz late in 1945, who argued that only a separate and unified air force could answer the new needs of an emerging air-atomic age. Early in 1946, Spaatz succeeded General Arnold as the commanding general of the AAF, shortly after General Eisenhower succeeded General George C. Marshall as the army's chief of staff. Much wrangling and compromising ensued, but almost exactly two years after V-J Day, the U.S. Air Force emerged from the National Security Act of 1947 as a separate service on a coequal level with the army and navy, the latter retaining control over its own air arm and the Marine Corps.

The National Security Act created a defense pyramid with the president at the apex. He would rely for advice on the new National Security Council, its subordinate Central Intelligence Agency, the National Security Resources Board, and the National Military Establishment, in 1949 redesignated the Department of Defense. Headed by a civilian secretary of defense, the defense hierarchy included the Joint Chiefs of Staff, who advised the secretary and president. Initially, the secretary of defense had few powers, being charged only to coordinate the activities and budgets of the army, navy, and air force, each headed by a civilian secretary.

The U.S. Air Force became independent of the army on 18 September 1947, when W. Stuart Symington took office as the first secretary of the air force. After two years, power began shifting from the services to the Office of the Secretary of Defense (OSD). In 1949 the

EVOLUTION OF THE UNITED STATES AIR FORCE

Designation	From	To
Aeronautical Division, U.S. Signal Corps	1 August 1907	18 July 1914
Aviation Section, U.S. Signal Corps	18 July 1914	20 May 1918
Air Service	20 May 1918	2 July 1926
Air Corps	2 July 1926	20 June 1941
Army Air Forces	20 June 1941	18 September 1947
U.S. Air Force	18 September 1947	—

individual service secretaries lost both membership on the National Security Council and the right of the direct appeal to the president if dissatisfied with decisions of the defense secretary. (These changes were made all but inevitable following severe interservice wrangling over the respective roles and missions, budget shares, and priorities—most notably at the failed Newport and Key West conferences of 1948 and during the navy–air force supercarrier versus B-36 hearings of 1949).

Another reorganization in 1953 established several unified commands, those with components from different services, and specified commands (for example, the Strategic Air Command), made up essentially from one service. In 1958 another overhaul formally removed the service secretaries from the line of command that now ran from the president through the secretary of defense and the Joint Chiefs of Staff to the unified and specified commands. Still another change in 1986 increased the authority of the chairman of the Joint Chiefs of Staff, a position originally established in 1949.

Upon breaking away from the army, the air force adopted a basic organizational structure that remained in place, essentially, for four decades. At the top was the secretary of the air force, a civilian, and the uniformed chief of staff, their assistants, and their advisers in the Office of the Secretary (OSAF) and the Air Staff. The major air commands (MAJCOMs), carried over from the Army Air Forces, included the Air Defense Command (ADC, which lost this status in 1979), the Strategic Air Command (SAC, a specified command), the Tactical Air Command (TAC, disestablished in 1992), the Air Training Command (ATC, for technical training, including flying training), the Air University (for professional military education), and other commands that shared responsibility for research and development, procurement, supply, logistics, and maintenance. In addition, the service maintained overseas components of joint theater commands (like the U.S. Air Forces in Europe—USAFE—and Pacific Air Forces—PACAF) and a varying number of agencies performing services required throughout the air force, such as personnel management, law, medicine, and communications security.

Worldwide airlift posed a special problem. Initially, the Tactical Air Command carried cargo and personnel within the operational theaters, while the Military Air Transport Service (or MATS, a unified command) operated a global airline. MATS became the Military Airlift Command (MAC) in 1966, and in 1974 took control of all airlift, including intratheater operations. (Meanwhile, naval participation in the airlift organization had ended in 1967, MAC in 1988 became the air force component of the new U.S. Transportation Command, or USTRANSCOM).

While these organizational arrangements proceeded, postwar demobilization continued apace. From a wartime strength of 2,372,292 in 1944, the air forces fell to 455,515 in 1946 and a postwar low of 305,827 in 1947. With severe restrictions governing the numbers of men, aircraft, and weapons being made available, the presumably most dangerous eventuality, however unlikely, had to be prepared for first. Therefore, almost from its establishment in March 1946, SAC was given priority over the Air Defense Command and Tactical Air Command, both of which were combined into the new Continental Air Command, (CONAC) in December 1948 and then hastily reconstituted following the outbreak of war in Korea in 1950.

The success of the Berlin Airlift served to reinforce arguments for a more balanced air force.

The new USAF was not well prepared in the summer of 1948, when it was ordered to join the Royal Air Force (RAF) in an attempt to supply West Berlin from the air, in response to the Soviet decision to blockade the surface routes into Berlin from the west. USAF Chief of Staff General Hoyt S. Vandenberg (who succeeded Spaatz in 1948) was initially skeptical, on the grounds that such long-range transports as he had available were already committed to the SAC emergency war plan. In those days unassembled atomic bombs and assembly teams were sent in C-54 aircraft to bases overseas, where the weapons were then assembled and loaded onto bomber aircraft, B-29s, that had deployed separately. Despite a hesitant start, the USAF and RAF, eventually joined by the French air foce, ran a successful airlift from June 1948 through September 1949, airlifting more than 2,325,000 tons of food, coal, and other supples.

The success of the Berlin Airlift served to reinforce arguments for a more balanced air force, but continuing budget cutbacks severely limited funds for airlift forces and doomed tactical aviation to virtual obscurity in the years before the Korean War. Seeing no other choice open to them, air force leaders argued that adequate preparation for the decisive (atomic) phase of any major conflict would also be capable of providing tactical operations in the exploitation phase. From there it was not very far to asserting that the forces necessary for major conflict would be appropriate to lesser conflicts as well.

The war that broke out in Korea in June 1950 came as a shock to airmen as well as politicians, perhaps even more so to the former when it became evident that the latter had reservations about committing the decisive phase forces. The situation in the opening weeks demanded the instant employment of all available combat aircraft in direct support of the engaged ground forces. Improvisation and flexibility proved successful if awkward, and before long Far East Air Forces (FEAF) Headquarters shifted its attention to classical strategic targets in North Korea, of which there proved to be few. Attention moved next to the interdiction mission, where many of the lessons of 1944–45 in Italy had to be learned all over again, which were, essentially, that for the aerial interdiction of the enemy's battlefield supplies to be successful, one's own surface forces had to be in control of the tactical initiative. Although air superiority was achieved, the interdiction and close air support missions generated continuing controversy and acrimony. In the end, the low priority given to tactical aviation and doctrine between 1945 and 1950 proved costly.

THE USAF DURING THE AGE OF SAC, 1954–1963

In the years following the Korean War, the tactical air forces went rapidly into decline once again. As early as the summer of 1951, the Joint Chiefs of Staff and civilian leaders had arrived at budget decisions that would result in the large-scale—indeed monumental—buildup of SAC over the coming decade. These decisions were confirmed, rather than set in motion, by the Eisenhower administration in 1953–1954 with its New Look policy that would concentrate efforts on "more bang for the buck over the long haul."

Captain Charles (Chuck) Yeager broke the sound barrier in 1947 in the Bell X-1.

Under President Eisenhower (1953–1961) the early talk of massive retaliation became moot over time and steps were taken to improve conventional (nonnuclear-armed) military forces of all the services. This trend was accelerated under the John F. Kennedy administration (1961–1963) with a flexible response policy, but another decision made at the same time was to build up the strategic nuclear forces to previously undreamed-of levels, primarily by switching the emphasis from bombers to land- and sea-launched ballistic missiles (SLBMs) of intercontinental range (ICBMs), consisting of one thousand Minuteman and fifty-four Titan ICBMs and a fleet of forty-one Polaris-type submarines armed with sixteen SLBMs each. For most of the 1950s, however, SAC, under General LeMay from 1948 to 1957, remained a force of bombers, which at first relied on overseas bases to reach the Soviet heartland.

Growing fears about the vulnerability of overseas bases led to increased emphasis on the aerial refueling (at first by prop-driven KC-97s, later jet KC-135s) of bombers based in the United States, although SAC's withdrawal from England, Spain, and Morocco was not complete until the early 1960s. Within the bomber force, the B-52 (more than seven hundred built) replaced the B-29, B-50, and B-36 beginning in 1955, but the shorter-range four-jet B-47 (more than one thousand built) served well into the 1960s. The supersonic B-58 was added in 1960, proved a disappointment, and was retired in 1970. Its place was taken in 1969 by the FB-111, a stretched tactical fighter, retired at the end of the 1980s. Over the years the B-52 became the workhorse of SAC, its most recent models (manufactured in the early 1960s) remaining in service when the B-1 was introduced in 1985 and the radar-evading B-2 was unveiled in 1988.

Despite the priority accorded SAC, aircraft for TAC and the overseas commands improved dramatically during the 1950s and 1960s. Captain Charles (Chuck) Yeager broke the sound barrier in 1947 in the Bell X-1, and the war in Korea marked the beginning of the age of all-jet air combat. The air force worked hard to create cross-ocean deployment capabilities and techniques for its jet fighters (F-84, F-86, and later F-100), along with their modification, beginning with the F-84G, to allow them to carry a nuclear weapon. Before long USAF fighter designs, as in the F-105, were optimized for high-speed nuclear weapons delivery, and armament with guns began to give way to radar-guided and heat-seeking missiles.

While aircraft developments moved quickly in the early years of the separate air force, progress in intercontinental missiles and rockets lagged behind. This changed rapidly after the Soviet Union launced Sputnik, the first artificial earth satellite, in October 1957. Congress responded with increased funding for the Atlas (1959) and Titan 1 (1960). The latter's replacement, Titan II, with a storable liquid propellant, served into the 1980s, and variants of the solid-fuel Minuteman ICBM stood ready in their silos when a new missile, the MX (Missile Experimental, later peacekeeper) joined the deterrent force in 1986. Besides the MX, the USAF developed and deployed air-launched and ground-launched cruise missiles as well, although the latter were subsequently withdrawn as a result of arms control agreements.

Besides providing impetus for a U.S. space program, formally placed outside the USAF in the National Air and Space Administration (NASA), the dramatic appearance of Sputnik brought about a revolution in air defense and warning. Before the Korean War ended, the USAF had begun deploying a radar barrier to detect and intercept approaching bombers. The Soviet explosion of an atomic bomb in 1949 and a hydrogen bomb in 1953, followed by the unveiling of long-range bombers in 1955, lent an air of urgency and led to a reorientation of the radar picket line from bomber defense to ballistic missile warning required a central headquarters linked to SAC and the National Military Command Center (NMCC). Such a command post, built deep inside Cheyenne Mountain in Colorado, opened in 1962. The Balistic Missile Early Warning system (BMEWS) reported to the joint U.S.-Canadian North American Air Defense Command (NORAD), which could process data and provide minimal warning time. (In 1982 the underground complex became the headquarters for the new Air Force Space Command, which also assumed responsibility for monitoring the ever-increasing satellite traffic.).

Throughout the 1950s and early 1960s, SAC and its deterrent mission consumed the majority of resources available to the USAF. By 1959 almost 60 percent of those in the USAF were assigned to SAC on more than sixty bases worldwide. TAC experimented with Composite Air Strike Forces (CASFs) for deployment in crisis situations (for example, to Turkey and Taiwan in 1958) as the aerial component of U.S. Strike Command (which evolved ultimately to U.S. Central Command and fought the Gulf War against Iraq in 1991). Improvements in aerial reconnaissance were also important, especially the high-flying U-2, which photographed the Soviet missiles in Cuba in 1962. Vastly improved variants of the U-2 operated into the 1990s, joined in 1965 by the supersonic SR-71, which eventually became prohibitively expensive to operate and was retired in January 1990.

THE VIETNAM ERA, 1964–1975

The huge, nuclear-capable deterrent forces of the USAF proved irrelevant to the emerging conflict in Laos and Vietnam, into which the U.S. government was slowly drawn in the early 1960s. At first, the role of the USAF

The United States Air Force Academy was established at Lowry Air Force Base in Colorado in 1955. Three years later the academy moved to its present location at Colorado Springs. (Department of Defense/U.S. Air Force)

in Vietnam was advisory and supporting, featuring minimally capable aircraft operated by the air commandos in psychological warfare, transport, and liaison roles. By early 1965, however, F-105 Thunderchiefs and F-4 Phantoms (originally a naval aircraft) were being launched sporadically against targets in North Vietnam (Operations Flaming Dart and Rolling Thunder). The initial goals, beyond retaliation for Vietcong terrorist attacks against U.S. personnel, were first, to bring pressure on the government in Hanoi to withdraw support from the insurgents in South Vietnam; second, to interrupt the flow of men and supplies to the south; and third, to encourage the government in South Vietnam by demonstrating the U.S. commitment to the struggle. These goals were not established by the airmen but were accepted by them, despite there being no precedent for expecting such results from bombing measured out in limited, sporadic doses.

The concern of President Lyndon B. Johnson that unintended escalation might cause problems with the Soviet Union and China led to severe restrictions from the outset regarding target selection, pace, timing, routing to target, and weight of attack. The airmen chafed under these restrictions but did not rebel. Frequently in South Vietnam (for example, at the siege of Khe Sanh in 1968) and on occasion over North Vietnam (for example, during Linebacker I and Linebacker II in 1972), air power proved crucial in the limited circumstances of the moment. On the whole, however, the Indochina experience, for all the experimentation with new tactics and weapons, such as air-sea rescue techniques, helicopter and fixed-wing gunships, defoliation, and precision-guided munitions, proved disappointing and frustrating for the air force. Aside from an unsullied record of valor, both in the air and for some in POW camps, the most important result for the USAF was its development of tactics and techniques applicable to the emerging era of electronic warfare.

The North Vietnamese deployed a formidable air defense system based on Soviet-made antiaircraft guns and surface-to-air missiles (SAMs). In response, the USAF and U.S. Navy mounted complex air strikes employing aircraft of multiple types and capabilities, organized in what were called force packages. One such operation might begin with F-4 Phantom IIs entering the target area first to drop clouds of radar-reflecting metallic fibers called chaff. These would be followed by F-105 Thunderchiefs modified into Wild Weasels by the addition of radar-homing and warning devices to jam enemy radars and locate others. The Wild Weasels would guide other F-105s armed with radar-homing missiles to destroy the radars and SAM sites, thereby clearing the target area for the following main strike force of fighter bombers or B-52s carrying more than twenty tons of ordnance.

In the end, the war's lessons—reinforced by the Arab-Israeli experience of the Yom Kippur War in October 1973—proved to be equivocal in all save one respect—that the early 1970s marked the point in time beyond which the overriding concerns of air planners shifted from aircraft and engines to microprocessors, from technology as previously understood to computerology, from air warfare as classically conceived to electronic warfare.

FROM INDOCHINA TO THE PERSIAN GULF

In the years immediately following its withdrawal from Vietnam, the air force turned its primary attention to increased performance in aircraft, electronic countermeasures (ECM), air-to-air missiles, and to the air superiority mission as the necessary precondition for waging air-land battles. This was nowhere more evident than in Europe, where with Indochina behind them, U.S. planners fostered a large buildup of NATO air power as a counter to the Warsaw Pact's superiority in the accoutrements of mechanized land warfare, as well as an alarming buildup of Soviet frontal and long-range aviation. The F-15 Eagle and F-16 Falcon, along with the navy's F-14s and F-18s, marked a quantum jump in capabilities and gave the United States an undisputed lead for at least a decade. By 1985 the problem was becoming more and more one of spiraling costs, with the USAF and navy tactical air accounts consuming close to one-half the total general purpose forces budget.

The problems associated with controlling the costs of weapon acquisition have been a major concern of the USAF since its founding. The organizational problem is that of balancing research and development, purchase and deployment, and follow-on logistic support. At first the Air Materiel Command oversaw all these functions. In 1950, to increase the emphasis on research and development, a separate Air Research and Development Command (ARDC) was created. In the belief that research, development, and acquisition had to be tied closely together, the air force in 1962 placed all three under the new Air Force Systems Command (AFSC), while the new Air Force Logistics Command took over maintenance and supply, including the stocking and distribution of spare parts.

Given the emphasis placed by the air force on maintaining a technological lead in aeronautics, AFSC grew rapidly, by the late 1980s having almost ten thousand assigned officers. Its range of responsibilities included aircraft, engines, ICBMs, electronics, precision-guided munitions, stealth (or low-observable) technology, and all air force programs contributing to the national space

In 1988, the U.S. Air Force unveiled the B-2 "stealth" bomber, which has special features that make it difficult to detect by radar. The Persian Gulf War marked the B-2's first extensive use in battle. (Department of Defense/U.S. Air Force)

program, such as the early Dynasoar spacecraft (canceled in favor of competing NASA programs) and the launching of military satellites. Although the AFSC record of successes exceeded its failures, budget reductions in 1991 led to a decision to merge it with Air Force Logistics Command in a new Air Force Materiel Command.

Absolute control over costs is not possible for the air force, which is often the only customer for products it needs quickly, sometimes in small numbers, and can acquire from a limited number of sources. By the late 1980s, per-copy costs of some aircraft (for example, the F-15 Strike Eagle) approached $30 million. Looming on the horizon were worrisome avionics bills for such items as the AMRAAM (advanced medium-range air-to-air missile) and LANTIRN (low-altitude navigation and targeting infrared system for night). These problems led critics outside the air force to question the service's emphasis on quality as opposed to quantity in its aircraft systems and weapons. Following demonstrations of many of the new systems in the air campaign over Iraq, many of the critics fell silent, at least for a season.

Following thirty-eight days of intensive air attack, coalition ground forces expelled the Iraqis from Kuwait.

When Iraq occupied Kuwait in August 1990, the United States positioned forces in Saudi Arabia to prevent any further Iraqi incursions. When the decision was made to expel Iraq from Kuwait, air force planners were ready with a four-phase air campaign strategy. Early on the morning of 17 January 1991, Apache helicopters and F-117 Stealth fighter-bombers struck enemy air defenses—primarily radar sites—and hundreds of coalition aircraft poured through the resulting gaps to strike targets in Iraq—airfields, telecommunications, command-and-control centers, air defense sites, and military headquarters. Within days the coalition air forces, centrally controlled by the Joint Force Air Component commander, Lieutenant General Charles Horner, had achieved air supremacy, thereby allowing air power to roam virtually at will and making incomparably easier the task of isolating and destroying the Iraqi army. Following thirty-eight days of intensive air attack, coalition ground forces expelled the Iraqis from Kuwait in a campaign halted by President George Bush after one hundred hours.

Hallmarks of the air campaign of 1991 were centralized control of coalition air assets under the overall supervision of the joint force commander; virtually complete success in all aspects of electronic air warfare; and the marriage of stealth technology and precision-guided munitions. The air force had worked long and hard to create such capabilities.

SIGNPOSTS

The fall of the Berlin Wall in 1989, followed by the disintegration first of the Warsaw Pact and then the Soviet Union, profoundly affected the air force. A white paper published by Secretary of the Air Force Donald B. Rice in early 1990 entitled *Global Reach, Global Power* captured in its title his goals for the future. Among those were the ability to maintain global situational awareness, to paralyze through air attack an enemy's fighting power, to retain access to air and sea lanes as well as space, to forward-deploy forces, and to defend against ballistic missile attack from whatever quarter. A continuing deterrent force must also be provided, as well as a defense industrial base.

To achieve such goals in the face of dramatic budget and force reductions required a thoroughgoing reorganization of the service, many elements of which were announced during 1991 and scheduled to take place beginning in 1992. Among the most startling for air members was the decision to disestablish SAC and TAC, combining their bombers and fighters in the new Air Combat Command, with SAC's aerial tankers shifting to the new Air Mobility Command (replacing MAC) and its ICBMs going to the new U.S. Strategic Command (USSTRATCOM), which will also oversee the navy's SLBM fleet.

Coincident with this major restructuring is another at base level, in which the Air Combat Command will include a number of composite wings, rather like prefabricated force packages of multiple aircraft types. One such relatively autonomous strike force will be the rapid air intervention wing at Mountain Home Air Force Base, Idaho, composed of F-16s, F-15Cs, F-15Es, E-3s, B-52s, and KC-135s. Another composite wing is scheduled for Pope Air Force Base in North Carolina, where it will train with the Eighty-second Airborne Division at nearby Fort Bragg. Taken together, the changes announced during 1991 "are the most significant organizational changes made since we became a separate service in 1947," in the words of USAF Chief of Staff General Merrill A. McPeak. As the service set out on its new path, its total strength passed below 500,000 toward 450,000 by fiscal year 1993, its lowest total since before the Korean War.

[See also The Army; Gunboat Diplomacy, 1776–1992; The Korean War; The Vietnam Era; World War I; and World War II.]

UNITED STATES AIR FORCE PERSONNEL STRENGTH, 1907–1992

Year	Strength	Year	Strength
1907	3	1950	411,277
1908	13	1951	788,381
1909	27	1952	973,474
1910	11	1953	977,593
1911	23	1954	947,918
1912	51	1955	959,946
1913	114	1956	909,958
1914	122	1957	919,835
1915	208	1958	871,156
1916	311	1959	840,028
1917	1,218	1960	814,213
1918	195,023	1961	820,490
1919	25,603	1962	883,330
1920	9,050	1963	868,444
1921	11,649	1964	855,802
1922	9,642	1965	823,633
1923	9,441	1966	886,350
1924	10,547	1967	897,426
1925	9,670	1968	904,759
1926	9,674	1969	862,062
1927	10,078	1970	791,078
1928	10,549	1971	755,107
1929	12,131	1972	725,635
1930	13,531	1973	690,999
1931	14,780	1974	643,795
1932	15,028	1975	612,551
1933	15,099	1976	585,207
1934	15,861	1977	570,479
1935	16,247	1978	569,491
1936	17,233	1979	559,450
1937	19,147	1980	557,969
1938	21,089	1981	570,302
1939	23,455	1982	582,845
1940	51,165	1983	592,044
1941	152,125	1984	597,125
1942	764,415	1985	601,515
1943	2,197,114	1986	608,199
1944	2,372,292	1987	607,035
1945	2,282,259	1988	576,446
1946	455,515	1989	570,880
1947	305,827	1990	535,233
1948	387,730	1991	508,558
1949	419,347	1992	486,819*

* Programmed strength.

BIBLIOGRAPHY

General Histories

Glines, Carrol V. *A Compact History of the United States Air Force* (1963).

Goldberg, Alfred, ed. *A History of the United States Air Force, 1907–1957* (1957).

Mason, Herbert Molloy Jr. *The United States Air Force: A Turbulent History* (1976).

Specialized Works

Arnold, H. H. *Global Mission* (1949).

Berger, Carl, ed. *The United States Air Force in Southeast Asia, 1961–1973: An Illustrated Account* (1977, rev. 1984).

Borowski, Harry R. *A Hollow Threat: Strategic Air Power and Containment Before Korea* (1982).

Bright, Charles D., ed. *Historical Dictionary of the U.S. Air Force* (1992).

Clodfelter, Mark. *The Limits of Air Power: The American Bombing of North Vietnam* (1989).

Copp, DeWitt S. *A Few Great Captains* (1980).

———. *Forged in Fire* (1982).

Craven, Wesley Frank, and James Lea Cate, eds. *The Army Air Forces in World War II*, 7 vols. (1948–1958, repr. 1984).

Frisbee, John L., ed. *Makers of the U.S. Air Force* (1987).

Futrell, Robert F. *The United States Air Force in Korea, 1950–1953* (1961, rev. 1983).

———. *Ideas, Concepts, Doctrine: Basic Thinking in the United States Air Force, 1907–1984*, 2 vols. (1989).

Futrell, Robert F., and Martin Blumenson. *The United States Air Force in Southeast Asia: The Advisory Years to 1965* (1981).

Gropman, Alan L. *The Air Force Integrates, 1945–1964* (1978).

Hallion, Richard P. *Strike from the Sky: A History of Battlefield Air Attack, 1911–1945* (1989).

Hansell, Haywood S., Jr. *The Air Plan that Defeated Hitler* (1972).

———. *The Strategic Air War against Germany and Japan* (1986).

Hennessy, Juliette A. *The United States Army Air Arm, April 1861 to April 1917* (1958, repr. 1985).

Holley, I. B., Jr. *Ideas and Weapons* (1953, repr, 1971, 1983).

———. *Buying Aircraft: Materiel Procurement for the Army Air Forces* (1964).

Hudson, James J. *Hostile Skies: A Combat History of the American Air Service in World War I* (1968).

Hurley, Alfred F. *Billy Mitchell: Crusader for Air Power* (1964, new edition, 1975).

Kennett, Lee. *A History of Strategic Bombing* (1982).

LeMay, Curtis E., and MacKinlay Kantor. *Mission with LeMay* (1965).

MacIsaac, David. "The Evolution of Air Power Since 1945." In *War in the Third Dimension: Essays in Contemporary Air Power* edited by R. A. Mason (1986).

———. "Voices from the Central Blue: The Air Power Theorists." In *Makers of Modern Strategy: From Machiavelli to the Nuclear Age*, edited by Peter Paret (1986).

Maurer, Maurer. *Aviation in the U.S. Army, 1919–1939* (1987).

Maurer, Maurer, ed. *The U.S. Air Service in World War I*, 4 vols (1978–1979).

Mets, David R. *Master of Air Power* (1988).

Mitchell, William. *Memoirs of World War I* (1960).

Neufeld, Jacob. *The Development of Ballistic Missiles in the United States Air Force, 1945–1960* (1990).

Osur, Alan. *Blacks in the Army Air Forces during World War II* (1977).

Parton, James L. *Air Force Spoken Here* (1986).

Schlight, John. *The United States Air Force in Southeast Asia; The War in South Vietnam: The Years of the Offensive, 1965–1968* (1988).

Sherry, Michael S. *The Rise of American Air Power* (1987).

Shiner, John F. *Foulois and the U.S. Army Air Corps, 1931–1935* (1983).

Wolk, Herman. *Planning and Organizing the Postwar Air Force, 1943–1947* (1984).

— DAVID MACISSAAC

PART 3

America's Military Leaders

Introduction: Great American Military Leadership

In more than two hundred years of war and peace, the United States of America has produced a number of exceptional military leaders. By the superiority of their abilities and accomplishments, historical and popular consensus has placed some of these leaders upon pedestals of greatness.

Some were distinguished icons of America's past whose prestige has withstood the passage of time and historical scrutiny; others have been honored for more recent military deeds. Some rose to prominence by capturing public attention, while others eschewed headlines, preferring to lead by influence and the high standards of personal excellence they set. Still others remain relatively nameless and faceless, known only to those whom they emboldened by their example. Collectively, they comprise the chosen few who occupy America's pantheon of military leadership, those whom a grateful nation honors with the deserved appellation "great."

Great American military leaders are expected to exemplify the virtues and qualities that their fellow citizens hold dear but rarely practice themselves.

Admittedly, determining greatness hardly results from a totally objective appraisal. Rating historical figures, from baseball players to violinists, always raises tempers over the yardstick employed and who was included or excluded. Traditionally, victory in war and battle has been a significant factor in determining whether the word "great" prefaced a military leader's name. As with all of their heroes, however, Americans have come to expect something more than victories alone.

Great American military leaders must not only succeed, but they also must be paragons and supermen. In their command and personal conduct, they are expected to exemplify the virtues and qualities that their fellow citizens hold dear but rarely practice themselves. Once they gain public attention, America's great military leaders quickly become national treasures, role models for youth, embodiments of the American ideal, and, as such, are perceived, rightly or wrongly, as being larger than life. This is a heavy burden and a tough gauge by which to measure anyone. Compared against such superhuman standards, any individual's flaws, however minor, stand out, and even America's great military leaders are not without their imperfections. Americans, however, as with most other peoples, prefer their heroes to be as flawless as possible. Therefore, just as the popular historical imagination bestows greatness, it also can airbrush away or ignore any unsightly character blemishes, except possibly those it envies.

Since its origins in colonial times, American military leadership has reflected the ever-evolving nature of its parent society. Technologically, attitudinally, socially, and in every other way, American military leaders and the leadership they provided the nation have mirrored changes in American society. On certain issues, such as integration, American military leadership actually prodded a cranky society forward, but even then, President Harry Truman's actions reflected growing societal demands for reform. It is this very uniqueness of American society and what the nation expects from its military in war and peace—the American way of war—that imparts the same quality to its leadership. How leaders adapted to the changing conditions society imposed upon them is one way to assess the greatness of their leadership.

Some of the names of these great leaders are readily identifiable to most readers. Others will be less well-known. Still others embody leadership types instead of actual individuals. To those who were strengthened by the often unsung leadership of these anonymous leaders, however, they rank among the greatest of the great. The roll call of great leaders herein is hardly comprehensive, nor is it meant to be. Rather, these leaders rank among the foremost representatives of greatness in American military leadership. The exclusion of any particular individual is not intended in any way as a slight.

THE FACE OF AMERICAN MILITARY LEADERSHIP

When considering who are America's great military leaders, some names instantly spring to mind. Ranking at the very top, naturally, are the war leaders—the admirals and generals and other top commanders who won honors leading armies and fleets, corps and air wings in wars waged around the globe. Taken as a whole, in fact, the exemplary leadership qualities exhibited by these officers form a mosaic of the popular conception of great American military leadership.

In such a composite, great American military leaders should be as willingly subordinate to the civilian leadership as was George Washington. They should be as diplomatic yet resolute as John J. Pershing and Dwight D. Eisenhower. They should be intelligent yet active like Nathanael Greene, William Tecumseh Sherman, and Ira Eaker, a World War II advocate of daylight bombing of Germany. To their subordinates, they should be firm but fair disciplinarians, as were Friedrich von Steuben, William ("Bull") Halsey, and Omar Bradley. In war, they should be as bold as Winfield Scott, George S. Patton, Douglas MacArthur, and H. Norman Schwarzkopf. In battle, they should demonstrate the pugnacious tenacity of Lewis ("Chesty") Puller, marine hero of the retreat from the "Frozen Chosin" in Korea; the personal courage of David Farragut, James Doolittle, and James Gavin, a general who was in the forefront of his paratroopers at Normandy; and seek decisive victories, as did Thomas J. ("Stonewall") Jackson and Curtis LeMay. Confronting overwhelming odds, they should show the type of disdain displayed by John Paul Jones and Anthony C. McAuliffe. If, however, after having fought the good fight, they still must surrender, they should do so with the aplomb of the stoic but human Jonathan Wainright or with the grace and dignity of Robert E. Lee. Likewise, in victory, they should always be as magnanimous as Ulysses S. Grant or Sherman.

By anyone's criteria, the officers whose superlative qualities made up this composite American military leader certainly do number among the nation's greats. In wars and battles fought on and above the land and sea, from Trenton to Mobile Bay to Tarawa to the Persian Gulf, the great leaders and many others have rightly

General George Washington was one of the earliest and greatest American military leaders. Among his many daring wartime exploits was the Battle of Trenton (pictured above), in which Washington led four columns of troops in an invasion of the city on 26 December 1776. (National Archives/engraving from painting by E. L. Henry)

won their nation's admiration and respect. High command in war and battle, however, profiles only one side of the face of leadership.

Commanders of armies and fleets may have the greatest visibility, but just as all commanders are not leaders, all leaders are not necessarily commanders. Military leadership is exercised on a variety of levels, and where leadership is exercised, the opportunity exists to achieve greatness. Some American military leaders who earned greatness in battle and war were daring junior-grade commissioned officers, such as Stephen Decatur in the Tripolitan War and Richard Bong (America's greatest flying ace of World War II), and noncommissioned officers (NCOs), such as Sergeants Alvin C. York and Samuel A. Woodfill in World War I. Some even came from the enlisted ranks, such as Nathan Bedford Forrest in the Civil War and Audie Murphy in World War II, or were hostilities-only volunteers—tough, savvy warriors such as Robert Rogers, Andrew Jackson, Davy Crockett, and Sam Houston. These were natural leaders rising to the fore and leading by dint of personal courage and example.

Greatness in military leadership, however, cannot be limited to war and the battlefield; military leadership, after all, includes managing the whole structure that makes victory possible. Performing unglamorous but extremely vital tasks were the behind-the-scenes leaders, both uniformed and civilian, who are generally ignored when enumerating America's greats. Waging a peacetime fight to ensure preparedness was a thankless task for some of the nation's greatest unsung military leaders, thankless that is until the next war began. Without the singular efforts of these generally uncelebrated leaders, the commanders of armies and fleets would not have had airplanes, divisions, and ships to lead to glory. Among these architects of victory are Union Quartermaster General Montgomery Meigs and two chairmen of the Joint Chiefs of Staff, George C. Marshall (World War II) and Colin Powell (Gulf War of 1991); Presidents Abraham Lincoln, Franklin D. Roosevelt, and Harry Truman, who created and maintained internal coalitions and external alliances; and Alfred Thayer Mahan, Elihu Root, James Forrestal, Benjamin O. Davis, Hyman G. Rickover, and William (Billy) Mitchell, who fought for peacetime doctrinal, social, and technological changes to prepare an often unwilling nation and military for war.

Most of these leaders were men, but some were women, such as Oveta Culp Hobby and Mildred MacAffee, who headed, respectively, the WACs and WAVES in World War II, and not all were white, including Benjamin O. Davis, Sr., and Samuel Gravely, Jr., respectively the army and navy's first African-American general and admiral. They came in all shapes and sizes, from the 300-pound Henry Knox to the 120-pound Philip Sheridan. Some wore uniforms, but some dressed in civilian clothing. Some were presidents, political appointees, and civilian service secretaries, but others were doctors (Walter Reed), educators (Sylvanus Thayer and Dennis Hart Mahan), and even explorers (Richard Byrd)—military people who rose to meet the leadership needs of the nation in war, and in peace. Some of the uncelebrated but nonetheless great military leaders will forever remain anonymous, unknown save to those who trained and served under them or who were encouraged and strengthened by their example, such as the square-jawed drill instructors, tattooed boatswain's mates, calm-voiced air controllers, and unflappable gunnery sergeants.

While some of America's great leaders wore stars and gold braid and others mufti or chevrons, these admirable military leaders seemingly had little in common. Some bent opposing battle leaders to their will, others defeated equally intransigent bureaucracies. Some were professionals, others amateurs, and while some led from the vanguard, others directed and managed from the rear. Some conquered beachheads, others diseases, and still others small minds. They came from all levels of society, differing in background, education, military and civilian experience, and every aspect of their lives, and were as varied as the deeds that gained their greatness, but commonalities exist among them.

They were all military leaders—no matter what their rank or level of leadership, they met the criteria for leadership known since ancient times.

First, they were all military leaders—no matter what their rank or level of leadership, they met the criteria for leadership known since ancient times. Second, whether native-born or immigrants, they understood the unique society they served. Thus, they had an intuitive grasp, sometimes enhanced by training and experience, of what leading Americans in war entailed, of American society's attitudes toward war and the military, and of the special conditions this society imposed on its armed forces and military leaders. Third, while some were already in positions of leadership, others were relatively unknown, but when their country called, they performed above and beyond the call of duty—

beyond, in fact, what most people, including themselves, believed them capable of doing. Fourth, they had what might best be described as a very practical nature. In both war and peace, they exhibited a disciplined flexibility in thought and action. They identified their objective, held to it unswervingly, but, in striving to reach it, adopted whatever means were at their disposal while adapting themselves to ever-changing conditions.

MILITARY LEADERSHIP

Military leadership is a subject much written about but little understood in all of its complexities and contradictions. It is a quality easy to recognize but difficult to define. Some equate leadership with command, and, to be sure, the tangible qualities—personal courage, intelligence, clear-headedness, and so on—that one seeks in a commander are found in leaders, sometimes to even greater degrees. While many commanders are willing to assume the mantle of leadership, however, few can wear it well.

At its heart, military leadership is an art, not a science. It involves individualistic unquantifiable attributes and talents that cannot be taught, abstract, ephemeral qualities that, as a whole, are almost mystical in nature and that even leaders themselves often neither can explain nor comprehend. A commander's authority comes from the state and involves regimentation, a formal chain of command, and following orders. Leadership, on the other hand, comes from within, as a spark of inspiration or genius that can transform even a mediocre commander into a leader. Foremost among America's great military leaders, for instance, were those who took chances and often broke the rules. For example, eighteenth-century military doctrine forbade winter attacks, and in December 1776 Trenton was well-defended by Hessian troops and the Delaware River was considered impassable, but Washington won a resounding victory that was a turning point in the Revolution. Despite the fact that B-25s were considered too large to fly from a carrier's deck and Japan seemed much too far away, in April 1942, Doolittle led an extraordinary bombing raid on Tokyo. Other commanders would have heeded the proscription that the tides at Inchon were too fierce for a successful amphibious landing, but in September 1950, MacArthur landed his forces there and established a firm beachhead. Washington, Doolittle, and MacArthur knew that circumstances demanded bold action and they took it. Leaders are bold, decisive, and know when risks should be taken; conversely, they know instinctively when discretion is called for, when not to be bold. George Armstrong Custer was not bold but incautious and a gloryhound to boot—the antithesis of a true leader—and as a result was killed along with most of his command at the Little Bighorn in June 1876.

Both command and leadership necessitate paying attention to small details, but their ability to see the whole, larger picture marks a great leader. Sherman, no slouch as leader himself, wrote in his memoirs that he could have carried off the Vicksburg campaign more effectively than his commander, Grant, but that, unlike Grant, he "could not have dared to think of it in the first place." In World War II, the British thought that Generals Henry ("Hap") Arnold and Eaker's daring plan for precision daylight bombing of Germany was pure lunacy. But Eaker, who flew as an observer on many early raids, prevailed, convincing none other than the leading doubter, Winston Churchill, of the plan's efficacy, and "bombing around the clock" helped win that war. (Because Churchill's mother was an American, it is tempting to describe him as an honorary great American military leader.)

A famous axiom suggests that generals are not born but made, which may be valid, but what Shakespeare wrote about greatness definitely holds true for leadership, that some men are born leaders, other achieve leadership, and others have leadership thrust upon them. Leaders are at once dynamic—inspiring men and women with pride and confidence and energizing them to rise above their fears to perform herculean tasks—and epicenters of calm when everything about them is swirling in a maelstrom of activity. The image of a ship's captain, known as the "old man" no matter what his age, standing imperturbably smoking his pipe while immense seas and gale-force winds buffet his destroyer escort, hides a man churning with anxiety, perhaps because he has experienced the power of nature before. When his anxious men turn wide-eyed toward him, they are reassured by his apparent nonchalant posture. As Shakespeare's King Henry V (act 4, prologue) walks among his men before battle:

Upon his royal face there is no note
How dread an army hath enrounded him;
Nor doth he dedicate one jot of colour
Unto the weary and all-watched night,
But freshly looks, and over-bears attaint
With cheerful semblance and sweet majesty;
That every wretch, pining and pale before,
Beholding him, plucks comfort from his looks.

Leadership means not only solving immediate problems but recognizing and planning for those that have not yet arisen. A commander's expertise at aligning his troops, ships, or aircraft for battle or creating a vast cross-oceanic logistical network results from training and experience; making them work—as army logistician General Gus Pagonis did in the Persian Gulf—is a function of leadership. Military authority and discipline, fear, and peer pressure from within the ranks ensure that a commander's orders are obeyed, and leadership means getting airmen, marines, sailors, and soldiers to work, to fight, and to advance into the face of certain death willingly.

To a large measure, this ability comes from a leader's internalized personal and motivational skills, his ability to gain the confidence of his men, and his knowledge and understanding of them. It explains why some common, seemingly everyday people became great military leaders and why some excellent commanders with both high rank and superb paper credentials did not. It was not lust for war or power, but duty, responsibility, honor, and even patriotism that turned ordinary people into bold, dynamic military leaders whose orders might result in thousands of deaths or vast sums of public monies spent, while winning great victories.

Amid the excitement, fear, noise, and confusion that roils about them, true leaders—of any rank—stand unperturbed.

On a stage where death was omnipresent, it was a shared mark of great military leaders that they came alive, which is true at any level of leadership. The "fire in a leader's eyes" in battle is a timeworn cliché, yet this accurately summarizes a very real transformation that is hardly limited to combat. Amid the excitement, fear, noise, and confusion that roils about them, true leaders—of any rank—stand unperturbed. Training and experience have much to do with this, but the value of training and experience has its limits. Like Frederick the Great's famous mule that carried a pack for ten campaigns and was "not a better tactician for it," some men, the Prussian monarch noted, "grow old in an otherwise respectable profession without making any greater progress than this mule." Ultimately, however, this internal fortitude comes from a strength of character that most men do not share, no matter what their rank. It is a measure of self and as such cannot be quantified.

THE AMERICAN WAY OF WAR

The American way of war is, as the term suggests, a manner of war making that is unique to American society. In general usage it means combining firepower and mobility with high technology, but that is a modern definition, focusing specifically on battlefield performance. The American way of war can also be defined as the system American society imposes on its military leaders in war and peace—the basic attitudes, ideas, myths, practices, and traditions regarding war, the military, and military leadership held by Americans since the colonial period.

Briefly summarized, the American way of war originated under three principal influences—geographic, philosophic, and religious. None was mutually exclusive; each had varying and unquantifiable effects upon the others. Geographically, the New World offered conditions and opponents unlike any faced in Europe, and the Atlantic and Pacific oceans served as giant moats. Unlike European nations—save island Great Britain—where mutual land borders demanded expensive fortifications and armies, any foreign invasion of America would have required huge amounts of men, matériel, shipping, and time—time enough for American volunteers to flock to the colors and time to outfit large numbers of privateers. Thus, to early Americans, expensive, potentially menacing, and wasteful regular (standing) armies and navies were unnecessary. America's geographically secluded position also led to isolationism, which has had a strong influence on American military policy—and, thus, leaders and leadership—since the end of the eighteenth century.

In part, isolationism dovetailed nicely with America's long-entrenched antimilitarism. For many philosophic (and religious) reasons, colonial Americans loathed anything resembling a regular army or navy. To the colonists these institutions menaced personal and collective liberty by being potential vehicles for one powerful man (Caesarism) or a small group of officers (Praetorianism) to create tyranny. Being practical and recognizing the need for self-preservation, however, colonists opted for self-defense forces composed of citizen-soldiers (militia) for home guards, short-term volunteers for campaigns, and, for a navy, relied upon hastily armed merchantmen or licensed raiders known as privateers. Commanders were elected democratically or appointed and were supervised by colonial, then state, assemblies, thus ensuring subordination to the state. Unlike Great Britain, for example, where officers came from the nobility, egalitarian, relatively classless America allowed natural talent to rise to the surface.

In peace, this system worked well; in war, it resulted in horrible butchery. Undisciplined, frightened citizen-soldiers; unskilled, elected officers; and tough native Americans trained from youth in warrior arts and woodscraft proved a volatile mixture. Stung repeatedly by ambushes and bloody Indian raids on colonial noncombatants, the frustrated colonists borrowed a page from the ruthless English subjugation of Ireland and savagely attacked Indian villages, "Cutteinge downe their Corne, burneinge their howses, and Sutch lyke," killing men, women, and children, as one early Virginia colonist wrote. Occasionally, a true leader emerged, such as early seventeenth-century New Englanders John Church and Lion Gardener, who fused Indian tactics and Indian allies with European firepower to defeat native warriors. These leaders, unfortunately, were as rare as the woodswise sharpshooters (Daniel Boone, Davy Crockett, and the fictional Natty Bumppo). For the most part, colonial commanders and militiamen were as fearful of forest hobgoblins as they were Indians. They were reluctant citizen-soldiers driven to war by fear, anger, revenge, and, not least, religious fervor.

Borrowing from the Hebrew invasion of Canaan in biblical times, colonial ministers (some of whom, along with modern chaplains, must rank as unsung military leaders) urged militiamen in their sermons to attack and to "save alive nothing that breatheth." The colonists gathered their collective courage and marched out as if on a crusade against the heathen foe with God, the ministers assured them, as their "Captain-General." As with a dependency upon a citizen-soldiery, the fears of professionalism and militarism, and the subordination of the military to civil authority, the concept of war as a crusade remains central to the American way of war, another aspect American military leaders must understand.

Traditionally, Americans have been quick to go to war, but only for well-understood reasons and usually to right some wrong, real or imagined; European balance-of-power wars and simple land grabs were anathema to them. Thus, Americans have crusaded for liberty, freedom, Manifest Destiny, abolitionism, free enterprise, and to make the world safe for democracy, and crusaded against tyranny, militarism, national socialism, and communism. To be sure, many of these

Military leadership has taken many forms in American history. Ethan Allen (center, meeting Captain de la Place at Fort Ticonderoga) was the leader of a group of Vermont soldiers called the Green Mountain Boys, who helped capture Fort Ticonderoga. (National Archives/engraving from a painting by Alonzo Chappel)

wars actually had more to do with power and exercising the same against weaker foes—thereby grabbing large parcels of land. Nevertheless, these linked attitudes, practices, myths and realities, and ideas endure as integral parts of the modern American society's way of war, as part of the heritage of America's military leaders and what they must deal with in leading. Put another way, just as Americans live under a fundamental law—the U.S. Constitution—written more than two hundred years ago, the legacies of the flintlock and tomahawk days continued to influence the American way of war into the nuclear age.

EARLY AMERICAN MILITARY LEADERS

The beginnings of American military leadership coincided with the earliest colonial settlements. Some of those first colonists, encumbered by body armor and heavy matchlock muskets, clanked onto Virginia's clay and New England's rocky beaches as full-time settlers and only part-time, emergency-only citizen-soldiers. Prominent among their military leaders were several veterans of England's Irish and continental wars, including Sir Thomas Dale, Baron de la Warr, and John Smith in Virginia, who were also numbered among the colony's leaders. In Plymouth, Captain Myles Standish advised the civilian leadership. These men may not have been great military leaders by modern criteria, but by their efforts, they ensured the survival of their colonies.

As colonial society matured and the frontier and coastline separated, the colonists by necessity became increasingly self-reliant. They had to make do with what they had or do without, whether it was food, clothing, nails, or self-defense. Self-reliance bred self-assurance and self-esteem as a people. The colonists developed their own way of doing things, from farming to how they managed their military affairs. When the English began playing an active role in colonial affairs in the late seventeenth century, they found a wholly unique colonial society that looked upon them as interlopers. Colonial military leaders such as Robert Rogers of Rogers' Rangers fame taught the British much—his New England rangers were the prototypes for Britain's light infantry—and colonists learned the art of European war serving alongside British regulars and the Royal Navy, although not all lessons were positive. Practical in military affairs as in all things, the Americans adapted what they could use and discarded the rest.

As with many other American institutions and ideas, American military leadership evolved from a European background, and vestiges of this continental heritage remain today. Likewise, practical American leaders have never been shy about borrowing ideas learned from military history and wartime experience, including opponents, and adapting this knowledge to the American system. For example, Washington, Greene, and Knox avidly read the writings of Marshal de Saxe of France and Prussia's Frederick the Great. During much of the nineteenth century, American military leaders tried incorporating the operational art of Napoleon and Horatio Nelson in their land and sea campaigns. In the 1920s the then-radical ideas of air theoretician Billy Mitchell were developed from those espoused by Hugh Trenchard of Great Britain and Giulio Douhet of Italy. In 1991 the AirLand Battle strategy perfected by army General Schwarzkopf and Air Force General Charles Horner in the Persian Gulf owed as much to Germany's World War II blitzkrieg strategy as their operational blueprint did to Comte Alfred von Schlieffen's "swinging door" plan (Schlieffen Plan) of World War I. Yet, because America's military leadership was initially formed and shaped by the special conditions of the New World and because its development evolved parallel to the maturation of its parent society, taken as a whole, American military leadership is unique in both form and practice.

At Valley Forge in 1778, for but one example, von Steuben quickly learned that his Prussian methods of discipline and training did not work with American soldiers. He complained that they always wanted to know "why" they had to do something before following an order. Unlike Prussia (or Japan, for example), the United States was never a militaristic society. Conformity might have been required in American communities, but the American ideal, even in 1778, was for independency of thought and action, the very antithesis of the blind obedience demanded by a militaristic society.

This democracy in action offended most European officers who crossed the Atlantic during the War for Independence to teach the American farmers how to fight. These officers were conditioned to receiving total obedience from their troops, and they viewed Americans as little more than an armed mob, but not the erstwhile Baron von Steuben (and a few others, such as the German Johann de Kalb, the French Marquis de Lafayette, and engineers such as Tadeusz Kościuszko from Poland and Louis DuPortail from France). Von Steuben knew that the Americans were fighters, because they had proven themselves in battle. His job was to make soldiers out of them, and he quickly adapted himself to American conditions in order to accomplish his mission. He answered questions, simplified the drill, and before long the men whom the British had called "rag, tag, and bobtail" were transformed into a relatively disciplined, well-ordered army.

Revolutionary-era Americans who became great military leaders intuitively understood the distinctive requirements entailed in leading Americans, what took von Steuben trial-and-error and many German expletives to learn. Based on the egalitarian pattern of colonial days, talent and natural leadership qualities ensured the rise of these men to positions of command and leadership. To be sure, some were drawn from the plantation-owner class, such as Washington and Henry ("Light-Horse Harry") Lee, or were well-to-do merchants, politicians, and shipowners, such as Philip Schuyler and Richard Caswell, but not all. Ranked high among the wartime military leadership were a former anchorsmith (Greene), a bookseller (Knox), a druggist (Benedict Arnold, who, despite his treachery, ranks as one of the finest combat commanders of the war—on both sides), farmers (Francis Marion and Andrew Pickens), a wagonmaster (rifleman Daniel Morgan), and a young surveyor (George Rogers Clark). Among leaders in the Continental navy were such former merchant captains as John Paul Jones, Esek Hopkins, John Barry (considered the "father of the U.S. Navy"), Joshua Barney, and Abraham Whipple, whose burning of the British tax cutter *Gaspée* in 1772 rallied many to the war effort. Even Arnold must be considered as a great naval leader, because his valiant but doomed gunboat action in October 1775 off Valcour Island in Lake Champlain counts as a sea battle. These men were rank amateurs in 1775, with only a few, such as Washington, having had any prior military experience; but while they learned war through war, they became, like their men, hardened veterans, as capable—if not more so—than any the British sent against them.

War in the age of Washington was closer to that of Julius Caesar than to that of Pershing and MacArthur.

With a few exceptions of Yankee ingenuity, technological advances had little effect upon revolutionary-era leadership. Considering the range of eighteenth-century weapons (fifty yards was the maximum effective killing range for an unrifled musket), war in the age of Washington was closer to that of Julius Caesar than to that of Pershing and MacArthur. Men still depended solely upon animal power, man power, and wind power, and in matters of communication and control, the message still arrived with the messenger as it had in Caesar's day. The difficult to load but deadly accurate rifled musket made itself felt among skirmishers (light infantry deployed ahead of regular lines and columns), but it had little battlefield use. Mechanical geniuses, such as David Bushnell, who invented the first operational submersible (or submarine), the "Turtle," in 1775, were harbingers of what war would soon become.

AMATEURS AND PROFESSIONALS

Following the revolutionary war years, as American society matured, becoming more specialized and professional, the evolution of American military leadership kept pace, although it still retained a strong amateur flavor. Technology took a great leap forward, but its full effect was not felt until the Civil War. The United States fought wars trying to acquire land from its northern and southern neighbors; the former failed, but the latter extended the United States to the Pacific Ocean. U.S. military leaders dealt with a variety of opponents, from North African pirates to hardened veterans of Europe's Napoleonic Wars to the native Indians of the south, northwest, and west. Other military leaders fought a penurious Congress, others explored and mapped out the new nation—men such as Meriwether Lewis, William Clark, Zebulon Pike, and John Charles Frémont—while naval officers explored the Antarctic (Charles Wilkes) and the seas (Matthew Fontaine Maury).

The first step in professionalizing U.S. military leadership came with the establishment of service academies, the U.S. Military Academy at West Point (1802) and the U.S. Naval Academy at Annapolis (1845). Engendered fears of a professional officer corps were diffused by widespread recognition that in the event of war, the nation needed trained officers. The generally poor performance of the army during the 1790s (fighting Indians in the Old Northwest was a disaster until revolutionary war veteran Anthony Wayne's victory at Fallen Timbers in 1794), reinforced in 1812, brought back sad memories of 1775–1776. The officer corps would be kept very small, and a primary field of study would be engineering, filling a crying need in expanding America.

Unlike civilian colleges of the time that catered to the sons of the well-to-do, service institutions provided an avenue for the youth of the nation's emerging middle class to gain both a college education and an increasingly more respectable career. Upon graduation these professionally trained officers, along with long-serving noncommissioned officers, would form the nucleus of a small regular army and navy. When war came, as it did with Mexico in 1846, these officers would be the professional skeleton that would be fleshed out—with the traditional American dependence upon a citizen-soldiery—by vast numbers of volunteers and political appointees, some of whom, it should be noted, became superb leaders. By the time of the Civil War, the Mexican War veterans and other service academy graduates would provide both the North and the South with their primary military leadership. Until these future leaders matriculated and matured, however, the United States would continue to depend upon its natural, amateur military leaders.

These natural leaders were kept busy from the late eighteenth century through 1818. Because Annapolis did not come into existence until 1845, naval officers learned their duties on-the-job, starting as midshipmen (or, for a few, on the lower decks) and rising by dint of natural talent and grit. Among those who earned great distinction as leaders commanding squadrons and single ships in the Quasi-War with France, against the Barbary pirates, in duels with the Royal Navy, and on the Great Lakes and at sea in the War of 1812 were Oliver Hazard Perry, hero of the Battle of Lake Erie; the bluff, hearty Isaac Hull; Edward Preble, mentor to many early American naval leaders; tough-fighting William Bainbridge; Thomas Macdonough, hero of the Battle of Lake Champlain; Stephen Decatur, who ably led sailors and marines in burning the captured *Philadelphia* on the "shores of Tripoli"; and John Rodgers, Sr., scion of a famous naval family. Their achievements were accomplished despite the policies of Thomas Jefferson and Secretary of the Treasury Albert Gallatin, which shunned costly oceangoing ships in favor of cheaply built but totally useless coastal gunboats. Luckily, a small number of fast-sailing, heavily armed frigates had been constructed during the John Adams administration; with these ships, including the *Constitution* ("Old Ironsides," still afloat in Boston Harbor) and some brave, bold leadership, the United States was, for the most part, able to hold its own at sea.

On land it was another matter, but several men of considerable natural-leadership ability gained national prominence during this period. Secretary of War John C. Calhoun literally brought the U.S. Army into the nineteenth century, reforming and streamlining an outdated establishment. Andrew Jackson, a self-made man and rough-hewn backcountry southerner (or "westerner," in the language of the time), was not a particularly good commander, but he was a superb natural leader. In battles against the Indians, such as Horseshoe Bend in 1814, and against British regulars at New Orleans in 1815, where he earned the sobriquet "hero of New Orleans," he proved his talent again and again. Along with several great American military heroes (Washington, Zachary Taylor, Grant, Theodore Roosevelt, and Eisenhower), a grateful nation rewarded Jackson with the presidency (physically as well as politically uncompromising, Jackson carried two pistol balls in his body into the White House, mementos of earlier duels). The marine Archibald Henderson fought for his organization in battle after battle on several congressional fronts to ensure the survival of the corps, a very near thing. Another army hero of 1812, also with presidential aspirations was Winfield Scott. Nicknamed "Old Fuss and Feathers," which belied his innate boldness, Scott was the greatest U.S. soldier from 1812 to the Civil War. Overshadowed in the popular press by Taylor's victory in 1847 at Buena Vista (in which future president of the Confederacy, Jefferson Davis displayed superior leadership), Scott's daring thrust to Mexico City from Veracruz was a model of leadership and command. From his handling of refractory subordinates to his bold strategic design, Scott's leadership had a great influence upon his junior officers. This would be readily apparent when those officers rose to positions of leadership in the Civil War.

Those officers were also among the first military leaders anywhere who had to come to grips with advances in technology. On land and particularly at sea, steam power altered warfare. Robert Fulton's "folly," the building of the *Clermont*, the first economically sound steamboat, proved the conventional wisdom wrong. No longer were humans dependent upon winds and tides. Steam-powered paddle-wheeled ships crisscrossed the Atlantic, and their flat-bottomed cousins traveled upriver with ease, forever changing the face of naval warfare and combined operations. The coming of the screw propeller in the 1840s was perhaps an even greater advance. The 1840s and 1850s saw development of a variety of advanced naval technology, including the rifled cannon of John Dahlgren (1851) and other improvements in weaponry and communications.

U.S. military leadership, however, and the military leadership of any nation for that matter, is generally very conservative when it comes to instituting broad, sweeping changes. Much of this comes from the nature of the services, tradition, bureaucratic inertia, and simple intransigence. It also is a result of budget-conscious leaders unwilling to fall prey to every technological fad that comes along; the overall military-funding pie, after all, could only be sliced so many ways. In peacetime, Congress generally ignored procurement, and until the late twentieth century, defense expenditures were always considered last. Therefore, technological improvements first had to be proven in numerous tests, then funded—no small matter—and then accepted by the end users—the officers and men who had to use the new devices. At the start of the Civil War, for example, despite the availability of a great deal of improved technology, the U.S. Navy remained primarily wind-powered and wooden. This would soon change in the spring of 1862, however, with the world's first confrontation between ironclad ships—screw-propeller inventor John Ericsson's *Monitor* and the CSS *Virginia* (formerly the USS *Merrimack*).

On land the advent of the railroad and telegraph played significant roles in the Civil War—provided one had the equipment and one knew how to use it effectively; in other words, as with advances in naval technology, without leadership technical progress meant little. On Civil War battlefields, for example, command, control, and communication were exercised as they had been for a thousand years or more—leaders learned about the battle and directed it by means of human messengers. Frantic young officers took hastily scribbled or verbal messages back and forth from commanders to battlefield leaders. Some orders were lost, others based on already-old information were useless, and verbal information was almost always garbled. Although the armies were larger than any ever commanded by Americans, leadership still retained a very human flavor. In fact, many leaders of the Civil War led by heroic command—just like Alexander the Great—as witness the extraordinary numbers of leaders killed in battle. Warfare was changing, however, and those truly great leaders understood this.

The railroad and the telegraph were welcomed additions by those leaders who knew how to use them, to move large numbers of troops quickly over great distances, to transport foodstuffs and munitions directly from the producer to the unit in the field, and to communicate with various headquarters. George B. McClellan, a man who exhibited all the qualities of great military leadership until he reached the battlefield,

General Dwight D. Eisenhower, pictured in February 1945 at his headquarter in the European theater of operations during World War II, was one of several wartime military leaders that Americans have rewarded with the presidency. (National Archives)

loved the telegraph because he could pester Washington with requests for reinforcements; he hated it because Lincoln constantly used it to urge his reluctant general onward. Confederate leaders certainly utilized the telegraph, but Union commanders, with the ability to run lines right up to the front, used it as a modern means of exercising command and leadership from a distance—a significant change. Until Sherman cut his lines and started foraging a swath through the Deep South, he was in constant communication with the War Department in Washington and with Grant, who was in the field in Virginia. Heretofore, Sherman would have had to send reports by either fast ship or human messenger; the telegraph enabled Grant to almost instantly coordinate movements a thousand miles apart.

Lincoln was the first president to receive almost-up-to-the-minute reports of fighting directly from the field. He was so enthralled with this device that during Union offensives he had a cot set up for napping in the telegraph office, similar to Lyndon Johnson's communications setup during the Vietnam War and Jimmy Carter's direct communication with U.S. commandos during the failed Iranian hostage rescue attempt.

The Civil War produced a number of great military leaders whose names are familiar to students of American history, such as Farragut, Grant, Jackson, Lee, and Sherman, but there were many others: George Thomas, the "Rock of Chickamauga," a Virginian who remained loyal to the Union; Confederate Secretary of the Navy Stephen R. Mallory and his Union counterpart, Gideon Welles, and his chief aide, Gustavus Fox; Samuel F. Du Pont, the builder of the Union blockade; and such gifted Confederate commerce raiders as Raphael Semmes of the *Alabama*; Andrew Foote, whose riverine operations in the Mississippi Basin helped Grant divide the South; David Dixon Porter, who ran Vicksburg's batteries with his fleet; the abrasive, ambitious, but effective Union Secretary of War Edwin Stanton; dashing Lewis Armistead, who led the forlorn hope of Pickett's charge at Gettysburg, hat balanced upon his sword until he fell amid a clump of trees; the cool Winfield Scott Hancock, Armistead's prewar friend, steadying the Pennsylvanians of the Iron Brigade; and Montgomery Meigs, who created a logistical network that fueled the federal armies; and Herman Haupt, whose railroad lines and bridges followed Union troops everywhere.

There were two men who stand representative of the great leaders who were volunteer, Civil War–only citizen-soldiers—civilians forged into great military leaders on the anvil of wartime necessity. One is the brave, scarred battle leader John Brown Gordon of Georgia. A former mining engineer who began the war as an elected company captain, he rose by sheer talent to corps command. At Appomattox, Gordon was selected by Lee to lead the weary, shrunken Confederate army in stacking their arms in formal surrender. Heads bowed, Gordon and his troops marched in despair. Then, in one of those dramatic moments only war conjures up, a Union general sang out a command, and the waiting federal troops snapped to attention in honor of the grayclads' bravery. Gordon and his men, heads now held high, returned this magnificent gesture. The Union general who saluted his opponent was another bullet-riddled veteran who rose from elected command and whose leadership was the stuff of legends, Joshua Chamberlain. A professor from Maine, Chamberlain won the Medal of Honor for his actions at Little Round Top in the Battle of Gettysburg (July 1863).

The litany of great military leaders of the Civil War runs on endlessly at all levels.

The litany of great military leaders of the Civil War runs on endlessly at all levels. There were those unknown Union soldiers who paused then advanced without orders up Missionary Ridge in 1863 to triumph; those tough Texans and Alabamans who fought their way up Little Round Top and came so close to victory, only to be turned back by equally hard men from Maine; and the many black Americans—quite a few of whom were former slaves—who proudly wore Union blue as a badge of freedom and manhood as they charged into hailstorms of canister. In a war where many more soldiers died from disease than from battle, women organized to work in hospitals, to promote cleanliness, and to do their share. Clara Barton and others have received well-deserved kudos, but there were many others, North and South, white and black—women who forced an unwilling male medical corps to let them do their part for the war effort.

As in all American military efforts, leadership devolved upon those who understood their fellow citizens. The Civil War was fought by volunteer armies and navies. The tiny prewar regular armed forces furnished some commanders, and quite a few leaders, particularly those of the land forces, were graduates of West Point. As battle wounds, disease, and removal for incompetence depleted the officer corps and the vast numbers of volunteers increased the demand for commanders, leadership devolved for the most part on volunteer leaders. West Point-trained leaders, such as Grant, Lee, Sherman, and Joseph Johnston, may have held top commands, but it was such men as Chamberlain and Gordon, hostilities-only volunteers, who furnished the bulk of the great military leaders of the Civil War.

TOWARD PROFESSIONAL LEADERS

The period from the Civil War through World War I witnessed the development of an increasingly professional military leadership. By the turn of the century, U.S. economic and industrial might made the country a player on the world stage, and military leaders saw this as an opportunity to remodel the armed forces. The navy forged ahead in reorganizing, but only serious problems brought to light during the Spanish-American War of 1898 provided impetus for reforming and modernizing the army. Thus, when Woodrow Wilson went before Congress in 1917 to ask for a declaration of war against Germany, U.S. armed forces were much better organized to handle the millions of hostilities-only volunteers who flocked to the colors.

Initially following the Civil War, military affairs fell into disregard. Along the western frontier, military policy toward the Indians remained little altered from colonial times—unable to pin down Indian warriors, cavalrymen and soldiers attacked villages. Some Indians proved exceptionally capable leaders. Nelson Miles was constantly outfoxed by Chief Joseph of the Nez Perce and Geronimo, a brilliant Apache guerrilla tactician—two great Indian military leaders in a line running from Pontiac and Tecumseh to, perhaps the greatest of all, Crazy Horse. The Indian wars saw considerable courage and great small-unit leadership—on both sides—in hundreds of actions between the Canadian and Mexican borders.

The almost instant demobilization that followed the surrender at Appomattox reduced the army and navy to little more than a constabulary, overseeing Reconstruction in the South and guarding America's frontier and coastline. A postwar reduction in force has been the American way of war since the seventeenth century. Citizen-soldiers returned home, leaving only a small regular military. Institutional memory is notoriously short. Forgotten was the unpreparedness of 1861 (as it had been before and would be again), and wartime calls for reform were lost to the friction of peace. The general attitude was that what worked once in the last war will surely work again in the next. Generally, the few truly great leaders emerging from this period were the reformers, those who fought long and hard to modernize the military. Those farseeing military leaders monitored changes in Europe, and what they saw made them hasten to institute changes at home.

The American military traditionally looked to its European counterparts as big brothers, and avidly copied innovations in European warfare, perhaps because of a lingering colonial lack of confidence, but more likely because Europe was rarely at peace, either on the Continent or around the world in its far-flung colonial empires. The increasing modernization of European armed forces made Americans rethink their own military organization, mission, and the means for carrying out the nation's directives. Theorists, educators, and historians such as Emory Upton, Alfred Thayer Mahan (author of the widely read *The Influence of Sea Power Upon History*), Peter Michie, Stephen Luce, William S. Sims, and Theodore Roosevelt were among the reform leaders. Continuing officer education was a key reform, and to that end the Naval Institute was established at Annapolis in 1873, the Naval War College was created at Newport, Rhode Island, in 1894, and a forerunner of the Army Command and Staff School was developed at Fort Leavenworth, Kansas, in 1873, a legacy of former college superintendent Sherman.

George Dewey sailed his fleet into Manila Harbor,

ordered his flagship's captain to

"fire when you are ready, Gridley,"

and destroyed an outdated Spanish fleet.

The 1890s witnessed the beginnings of true military reforms. By then, like it or not, the United States had achieved status as a major power. In order to be taken seriously, economic-industrial power notwithstanding, the United States had to have a military capable of extending national power around the globe—and it did not. In the Caribbean Basin, U.S. strategic interests were protected by various contingents of marines. In Central America and on joint foreign expeditions, such as the 1900 Chinese Boxer Rebellion, marine leaders such as Smedley Butler and, later, Puller displayed their leadership talents. This was low-intensity warfare, however, more like Indian fighting than the conventional, high-intensity war European militaries prepared to fight. Officers such as William T. Sampson, Sims, and Bradley Fiske displayed great courage and leadership in fighting entrenched, hidebound bureaucrats, congressmen, and myopic officers. Some of these leaders managed to survive the storms they created as they strove to modernize the navy, but others saw their careers founder on dangerous political shoals. Some of these reforms paid dividends in the Spanish-American War of 1898. In the Philippines, George Dewey sailed his fleet into Manila Harbor, ordered his flagship's captain

(Charles V. Gridley, a brave man who stood to arms despite a painful and terminal cancer), to "fire when you are ready, Gridley," and destroyed an outdated Spanish fleet.

Army reform was a bit slower, waiting until all of the organizational problems highlighted during the war with Spain were uncovered. The United States mobilized when the *Maine* exploded in Havana harbor, but the thousands of volunteers overwhelmed the outdated army system. Fighting in Cuba, many soldiers fought with Civil War–era black-powder weapons, while hundreds of others sickened from poorly packaged food and even more died from yellow fever and other mosquito-borne diseases. At great risk to themselves, army doctors such as Reed identified the mosquito carrier and set about to prevent yellow fever, which annually claimed thousands in the United States. Using political calls for reform as a springboard, Secretary of War Root and his disciples, such as Leonard Wood, increased military education, developed the General Staff system, professionalized training, and made a hundred other improvements. Root was backed in his reforms by President Theodore Roosevelt, whose Rough Riders exploits spurred him into the White House. It was under Roosevelt's leadership that the Panama Canal was begun by army engineers (notably George W. Goethals), the greatest engineering project since the construction of the pyramids. Influenced by Mahan's book, Roosevelt sent the Great White Fleet (sixteen U.S. battleships painted white) around the world as a means of showing the flag and U.S. power.

These reforms and reorganizations came at the most opportune moment, because by 1917 the U.S. military was confronted with an entirely new type of warfare that would be a true test of leadership. Briefly, World War I saw the marriage of the new internal combustion engine with warfare. To be sure, other weapons—the machine gun, for one—played significant roles, and the trench warfare of the western front, reminiscent of ancient sieges, might well have been avoided had the Germans, French, and English paid closer attention to Lee and Grant's Petersburg campaign. Within only a few years after 1900, however, warfare suddenly moved above the ground (airplanes) and under the sea (submarines). Balloons and submersibles had been employed earlier, including Bushnell's "Turtle" and Horace L. Hunley's Confederate submersible, which sank the Union ship *Housatonic* off Charleston, South Carolina, in 1864, but trucks, the newly invented tanks, airplanes, submarines, torpedoes, and many more technological advances, all began changing the face of war.

Several great American military leaders emerged from World War I. Foremost among them was Secretary of War Newton Baker, Secretary of the Navy Josephus Daniels, Army Chief of Staff Peyton March, and John J. ("Black Jack") Pershing, who brilliantly walked a tightrope between the need to learn quickly about warfare as a part of an alliance while maintaining U.S. forces as a separate army. For his actions "over there," Pershing would be named general of the armies. Admiral Sims also played a major role in London, as commander of U.S. naval forces in European waters, keeping Anglo-American relations on an even keel. On the battlefield, MacArthur and Charles P. Summerall won accolades, as did NCOs such as Sergeants York and Woodfill, and a number of marines. Among the Marine Corps commissioned and noncommissioned leaders were such men as Major Thomas Holcombs, Gunnery Sergeant Daniel Daly (who had already been awarded two Medals of Honor), and many men from the ranks who were honored for battlefield heroics. In the air war, where aerial dogfights won the public's attention, former racing car driver Edward (Eddie) Rickenbacker demonstrated the cool calm that leadership demanded, and Mitchell's success in massed tactical bombing led to the formulation of the concept of modern strategic bombing.

Inundated by millions of Americans—volunteers and those drafted—the organization created by the army and navy reformers worked surprisingly well. There were mixups and muddles, which is to be expected when a nation tries to go on a wartime footing literally overnight, but, for just one example, the National Guard units (an updated version of the community militia), performed with a high degree of efficiency. The success U.S. forces enjoyed during World War I, as in most other conflicts, may be traced directly to superior American military leadership, both during and especially before the war.

FROM GREAT LEADERS TO WAR MANAGERS

The superior individual leadership qualities of the great U.S. military leaders of World War II contrasted sharply with those who followed them. Management has always been an integral part of war and military affairs, and some of the greatest U.S. military leaders were those who managed huge war machines. Prior to the post–World War II period, however, personal leadership, not impersonal management, was the American military ideal. After World War II, as the armed forces demobilized and reorganized to handle the exigencies of the cold war, the nuclear age, and an era of low-intensity wars of national liberation, management came to dominate leadership. By the Vietnam War, many of those who filled positions normally occupied by leaders were, in fact, managers more concerned with careers, evaluation reports, and not making mistakes than they were with leadership and leading.

The small military that emerged from the post–World War I demobilization was highly professional. With few exceptions, the military leadership of the armed forces was dominated by service academy graduates. The usual between-war problems encountered by every peacetime American military leader—tightened budgets, constant calls for additional reductions in men and ships—were all present, exacerbated by the national economic woes of the Great Depression. Wartime doctrinal and technological advances were refined and updated, but at a more leisurely pace because it was peacetime and there were few funds available for much experimentation. Tank technology was improved, and the air wings of both services made great strides, although never fast enough for the airmen. A new type of ship, the aircraft carrier, was developed, but the navy remained dominated by big-gun battleship thinking. Likewise, the army began mechanizing some units, but cavalry in the 1930s still meant horses, not tanks.

When war erupted in Europe in 1939, however, leadership did not devolve upon the heroes of the last war. With few exceptions, the men who would become the great U.S. military leaders of World War II were the mid-level officers of World War I. Franklin Roosevelt was a great wartime president, possibly exceeded only by Lincoln, but his place in the American pantheon of great military leaders would have been ensured based solely on his appointment of George Marshall as chief

American Generals of World War II, gathered here in 1945, exhibited superior leader qualities. Seated left to right are: William Simpson, George Patton, Carl Spaatz, Dwight D. Eisenhower, Omar Bradley, Courtney Hodges, and Leonard Gerow; standing are Ralph Stearley, Hoyt Vandenberg, Walter Bedell Smith, Otto Weyland, and Richard Nugent. (National Archives)

of staff of the army, then head of the combined service chiefs. Marshall proved to be the hub for all U.S. armed forces and for the vast number of Allies joined in the crusade against German-Japanese militarism.

By the Vietnam War, many of those who filled positions normally occupied by leaders were, in fact, managers more concerned with careers and evaluation reports than with leadership and leading.

Marshall may have headed the list of great American military leaders in World War II, but he was only the first of many. The list of the great U.S. military leaders from World War II exceeds even those from the Civil War. Henry Stimson and Frank Knox, Roosevelt's secretaries of war and navy, respectively, were key figures in the war effort. From the army, including the Army Air Corps, to mention but a few of the war leaders, came Eisenhower, Arnold, MacArthur, Joseph ("Vinegar Joe") Stilwell, and their chief subordinates; Patton, Bradley, Mark Clark, Matthew Ridgway, Gavin, Robert Eichelberger, Carl Spaatz, Curtis LeMay, Eaker, and Doolittle. The navy added dozens of names to the hall of great leaders—Ernest J. King, Halsey, Chester Nimitz, Frank Jack Fletcher, Raymond Spruance, and Marc Mitscher. The marines also had a number of great leaders, including Alexander ("Sunny Jim") Vandegrift, Puller, Joseph J. Foss, and Holland M. ("Howlin' Mad") Smith.

For every admiral like Nimitz, however, there were dozens of leaders like Howard Gilmore, a submarine captain who clung wounded on the bridge but, thinking of his ship and men, heroically ordered "take her down." For every general like Eisenhower, there were dozens of nameless leaders—officers, NCOs, and enlisted men—who organized units shattered by the German onslaught at the Battle of the Bulge into strong defensive perimeters, men who were natural leaders like Church, Gardener, Rogers, and Marion of the early American period, and for every "Howlin' Mad" Smith, there was a tough gunnery sergeant such as John Basilone, who won a Medal of Honor at Guadalcanal, and died at Iwo Jima. Behind these battle leaders were those who trained, supplied, and cared for them, such as Leslie McNair, Brehon Somervell, and Leslie Groves, director of the supersecret Manhattan Project, who desperately wanted a field command, but who, like his chief, Marshall, sacrificed personal ambition to the overall war effort.

World War II certainly was not the end of great American military leadership, but it may have been its highwater mark. Leadership, even great leadership, was exercised on the battlefields of Korea and Vietnam, but it was generally anonymous leadership, save for old warhorses such as Puller. MacArthur's brilliant invasion at Inchon—which had been rejected by the newly created Joint Chiefs of Staff (whose chairman was supposed to be the president's principal military adviser but rarely was)—was marred by his subsequent decision to advance to the Yalu River and even more so by relief from command following his insubordination to President Truman. Civilian secretaries, such as James V. Forrestal (the first secretary of defense—a position that, in function, was overlord to all the services and, in name, echoed the conflict between self-preservation and antimilitarism inherent to the American way of war) earned well-deserved praise. In the navy the brilliant but caustic Hyman Rickover brought a reluctant service into the nuclear age. Other military leaders gained recognition for deeds on the edge of space and beyond, such pilots as Charles (Chuck) Yeager and astronauts such as John Glenn of the marines and Alan Shepherd of the navy. Many leaders from this period were academy graduates, including some from the new Air Force Academy, whose first class graduated in 1959, but the vast number of people in positions of leadership in the 1950s, 1960s, and 1970s were Reserve Officer Training Candidates (ROTC) who received their training in civilian colleges and were commissioned upon graduation.

Overall, however, the number of great leaders declined. Leadership may be found on any level, but leadership at the top is particularly important because it sets the tone for others, and the inflection emanating from the Pentagon during this period was a don't rock the boat, can-do attitude. It became more important to master management techniques learned in business schools than to study and practice leadership. Making mistakes and learning from them—the essence of the maturation process of a leader on any level—were frowned on; they could lead to a black mark on evaluation reports which, in turn, would reflect badly on a superior and end a career.

In Vietnam whole units were at first transported incountry led by officers and NCOs who had trained and lived with that unit, but this soon changed. In order to move up the career ladder, officers needed command experience in a wartime situation. Officers were shuttled into company and battalion commands, for example, leaving after six months for a staff assignment, and troops were replaced piecemeal, instead of by whole units. What worked fine in a business school course on franchises, failed miserably in Vietnam. The absence of leadership was sorely felt. To be sure, there were many men and women on all levels who would have duplicated the great military leadership during World War II, but the rules had changed and the system forbade it. Overall, the Vietnam War left a bad taste as the wrong war run the wrong way. It took the Gulf War of 1991 to restore the nation's self-image as a military power.

AMERICAN MILITARY LEADERS—PRESENT AND FUTURE

Great American military leadership encompasses much more than leading troops in battle. At its heart, being a great military leader involves strength of character that, for the most part, goes unnoticed. The first American general officer of African-American ancestry, Benjamin O. Davis, Sr., was a lieutenant of volunteers in the Spanish-American War and military attaché in Liberia, 1911–1912. He was a good officer, a fine commander, and, based on his war and peacetime commands, may even be considered a significant military leader. By his courage and abilities in Jim Crow America, however, he certainly demonstrated great military leadership by his power to make others earn the right to salute him. The fruits of the efforts of black military leaders may be shown by the appointment of General Colin Powell—the non–West Point son of Jamaican immigrants—as chairman of the Joint Chiefs of Staff, not because he was black but because he was demonstrably the best person for the position. Powell's subsequent leadership during the Persian Gulf crisis and war more than confirmed the decision of George Bush to appoint him chairman.

Most of the great American military leaders discussed are no longer living, and one wonders how sorely their leadership will be missed as America moves into the twenty-first century. With the exceptions of those generally unknown leaders who displayed heroic leadership on the battlefields of Korea and Vietnam and possibly Maxwell Taylor, chairman of the Joint Chiefs in the early 1960s and a solid although hardly outstanding leader, the great U.S. military leaders since 1945 are

General Norman Schwarzkopf, who led the Allied forces to victory in the Persian Gulf War, became a American military hero. He is shown here speaking to soldiers at a base camp in 1991 during Operation Desert Shield. (Department of Defense/U.S. Army)

largely cloaked in anonymity. Even among the junior officers and enlisted ranks, while great leadership continued to be exhibited on the battlefield, few names if any earned national acclaim. To be sure, the Persian Gulf crisis and war brought such leaders as Bush, Cheney, Powell, Schwarzkopf, and Horner to the fore, but they were elevated to greatness for leading Americans to a resounding wartime victory. Were they an aberration, their greatness a result of the happenstance of war? Is modern U.S. military leadership only a wartime phenomenon or will other leaders rise to the surface to lead America in the future? Will trust in technology lead to an increasingly automated, dehumanized style of command, relegating leadership to history?

Will trust in technology lead to an increasingly automated, dehumanized style of command, relegating leadership to history?

Managing U.S. military resources has never been easier. The establishment of the Joint Chiefs of Staff, the age of consensus, and joint commands have made for a much more efficient military, but while management is a part of command—and always has been—it has nothing to do with leadership. Management is a science in which people are dehumanized in order to better fit mathematically calculated equations. Leadership cannot be programmed into a computer, nor can it even be recognized until tested and retested under the daily wear and stress of life in peace and especially in war.

The insidious growth of management is leaching down the chain of command. In Vietnam, for example, it became more and more the norm to micromanage the battlefield. A lieutenant would lead his platoon into a hamlet—a fairly complex test of leadership, but one which this young leader would have to pass at this stage. Unlike in any other American war, however, above him would float his company commander, directing him from a helicopter. Above the company commander was the battalion commander, then the brigade commander, and so on—all of this brass ordering and countercommanding one lieutenant and his platoon. Why? If the lieutenant happened to get a chance to do something on his own and erred—which is part of the leadership learning process—it would reflect poorly on all of the above-mentioned officers and earn them a less than "outstanding" rating on their officer evaluation reports.

The Gulf War of 1991 rekindled hopes that active human military leadership may still have a place in U.S. military thinking. Many of the men and women who incessantly bombed the Iraqis into submission, who leapfrogged supplies deep into enemy territory so that all that tank drivers had to say was "fill it up" before resuming their fast-paced flanking movement, and who stormed through minefields and barricades, exhibited true leadership. In the initial euphoria emanating from the Gulf War, superior technology and its unsaid-but-understood analogue, management, were hailed as the keys to victory. Technology played an integral role in the speedy and decisive allied victory, but ultimately history will record this war as a triumph of individual leadership.

Just as none other than Napoleon Bonaparte studied and restudied the works of Alexander the Great, Julius Caesar, and Frederick the Great to gain insights from their genius, so, too, must the future American leaders look back into the American past to brush away the detritus of consensus and management to uncover America's great military leaders. Military leadership, unfortunately, is becoming a subject more of interest to historians than to those who must practice it. Until this cycle changes, the future of American military leaders and leadership remains an unknown quality.

It is from a combination of old traditions and ancient sources, foreign and domestic examples, and experience gained at great cost in blood and treasure, that military leadership of the United States has evolved, and continues to evolve, into a unique form wholly American in nature.

BIBLIOGRAPHY

General Works and Early American Period

Blumenson, Martin, and James L. Stokesbury. *Masters of the Art of Command* (1975).

Commager, Henry Steele. "Leadership in Eighteenth Century America and Today." *Daedalus* 90 (1961).

Cress, Lawrence Delbert. *Citizens in Arms: The Army and the Militia in American Society to the War of 1812* (1982).

Dederer, John Morgan. *War in America to 1775: Before Yankee Doodle* (1990).

Higginbotham, Don. *George Washington and the American Military Tradition* (1985).

———. "The Early American Way of War: Reconnaissance and Appraisal." *William and Mary Quarterly* 44 (1987).

Keegan, John. *The Face of Battle* (1976).

———. *The Mask of Command* (1987).

Leach, Douglas Edward. "The Military System of Plymouth Colony." *New England Quarterly* 24 (September 1951).

Linderman, Gerald F. "Military Leadership and the American Experience." *Military Review* (1990).

Morgan, Edmund S. *The Genius of George Washington* (1980).

Sharp, Morrison. "Leadership and Democracy in the Early New England System of Defense." *American Historical Review* 50 (1945).

Shy, John W. "The American Military Experience: History and Learning." *Journal of Interdisciplinary History* 1 (1971).
Van Creveld, Martin. *Command in War* (1985).
Wood, W. J. *Leaders and Battles: The Art of Military Leadership* (1984).

Toward Professional Leadership

Ambrose, Stephen E. *Crazy Horse and Custer: The Parallel Lives of Two American Warriors* (1975).
Dederer, John Morgan. "The Origins of Robert E. Lee's Bold Generalship: A Reinterpretation." *Military Affairs* 49 (July 1985).
Freeman, Douglas Southall. *R. E. Lee: A Biography*, 4 vols. (1934–1935).
Fuller, J. F. C. *Grant and Lee: A Study in Personality and Generalship* (1957, rev. 1982).
Glatthaar, Joseph T. *Forged in Battle: The Civil War Alliance of Black Soldiers and White Officers* (1990).
Henderson, G. F. R. *Stonewall Jackson and the American Civil War*, 2 vols. (1989).
Liddell Hart, B. H. *Sherman: Soldier, Realist, American* (1929).
Millis, Walter. *Arms and Men: A Study in American Military History* (1956, rev. 1984).
Sears, Stephen W. *George B. McClellan: The Young Napoleon* (1988).
Wilkes, Charles. *The Autobiography of Rear Admiral Charles Wilkes, U.S. Navy* (1978).
Williams, Frances Leigh. *Matthew Fontaine Maury, Scientist of the Sea* (1963).

Twentieth-Century Leadership

Anderson, Charles R. *The Grunts* (1976).
Blumenson, Martin. *Patton: The Man Behind the Legend, 1885–1945* (1987).
Broughton, Jack. *Thud Ridge* (1969).
———. *Going Downtown: The War Against Hanoi and Washington* (1988).
Byrd, Martha. *Chennault: Giving Wings to the Tiger* (1987).
Coffey, Thomas M. *Iron Eagle: The Turbulent Life of General Curtis LeMay* (1986).
Considine, Robert, ed. *General Wainwright's Story* (1946, 1970).
Cook, John L. *The Advisor* (1987).
Copp, DeWitt S. *A Few Great Captains: The Men and Events that Shaped the Development of U.S. Air Power* (1980).
Davis, Burke. *Marine: The Life of Chesty Puller* (1964).
———. *War Bird: The Life and Times of Elliot White Springs* (1987).
Drury, Richard S. *My Secret War* (1979).
Evans, Douglas K. *Sabre Jets Over Korea: A Firsthand Account* (1984).
Gavin, James M. *On to Berlin: Battles of an Airborne Commander 1943–1945* (1978).
Haines, William Wister. *Command Decision* (1946, repr. 1974).
Hill, Joe. *Some Early Birds: The Memoirs of a Naval Aviation Cadet* (1983).
Hurley, Alfred F. *Billy Mitchell: Crusader for Air Power* (1965, repr. 1975).
Karsten, Peter. *The Naval Aristocracy: The Golden Age of Annapolis* (1972).
King, Ernest J., and Walter Muir Whitehill. *Fleet Admiral King: A Naval Record* (1952, repr. 1976).
Layton, Edwin T. *And I Was There* (1985).
Leinbaugh, Harold P., and John D. Campbell. *The Men of Company K* (1985).
MacDonald, Charles B. *Company Commander* (1978).
Mauldin, Bill. *Up Front* (1945, repr. 1968).
Moskos, Charles C. *The American Enlisted Man* (1970).
Newton, Welsey Phillips, and Robert R. Rea. *Wings of Gold* (1987).
O'Kane, Richard H. *Clear the Bridge!: The War Patrols of the U.S.S. Tang* (1977).
Parton, James. *"Air Force Spoken Here": General Ira Eaker and the Command of the Air* (1986).
Pogue, Forrest C. *George C. Marshall*, 4 vols. (1963–1987).
Potter, E. B. *Nimitz* (1976).
———. *Bull Halsey* (1985).
———. *Admiral Arleigh Burke, A Biography* (1990).
Rodman, Hugh. *Yarns of a Kentucky Admiral* (1928).
Scott, Robert L., Jr. *God Is My Co-Pilot* (1943).
———. *God Is Still My Co-Pilot* (1967).
Simpson, Mitchell, III. *Harold R. Stark* (1989).
Smith, Ben, Jr. *Chick's Crew* (1978).
Stafford, Edward P. *Little Ship, Big War: The Saga of DE-343* (1984).
Stouffer, R., ed. *The American Soldier in Combat and After* (1949).
Straight, Michael. *A Very Small Remnant* (1963).
Webb, James. *Fields of Fire* (1979).
Weigley, Russell F. *Eisenhower's Lieutenants: The Campaigns of France and Germany, 1944–1945* (1981).
Yarmolinsky, Adam. *The Military Establishment: Its Impact on American Society* (1973).
Yeager, Charles, and Leo Janos. *Yeager* (1985).
Zumbro, Ralph. *Tank Sergeant* (1988).

– ROBIN HIGHAM
JOHN MORGAN DEDERER

Selected Biographies

BRADLEY, OMAR NELSON

Omar Nelson Bradley (1893–1981), American general. Born in Clark, Missouri, Omar Bradley overcame the disadvantages of a modest family background to enter the United States military academy at West Point. Upon graduation in 1915 he was commissioned a second lieutenant in the artillery corps but saw no action in World War I. Nonetheless he rose to the rank of major.

Between the world wars Bradley pursued a career as an instructor of mathematics and military science and tactics at several institutions, among them West Point. As commander of the Fort Benning Infantry School, in Georgia, he impressed General George C. Marshall with his capabilities and innovative approach. Marshall's patronage enabled Bradley to rise through the ranks.

In 1938, Bradley was appointed to the general staff in Washington, D.C., and therefore did not see active duty in World War II until 1943. As commander of the U.S. Army Second Corps under General Dwight D. Eisenhower, Bradley led his troops in the final stages of the campaign to drive the Germans out of North Africa. He then served as deputy commander to General George Patton in the invasion of Sicily.

Bradley's grasp of frontline combat and his well-proven talents as an officer and tactician prompted Eisenhower to give him a key role in planning D-Day. In June 1944 Bradley led the U.S. First Army across the English Channel to storm the Normandy beaches.

Having succeeded in securing a bridgehead on the continent, Bradley was placed in command of all U.S. forces (1,300,000 men) in northwestern Europe. It was the largest contingent of troops ever under the control of one American officer. The relationships he cultivated with soldiers in the field helped him understand the mentality of men such as "the rifleman who trudges into battle knowing that statistics are stacked against his survival." General Patton did not favor Bradley's cautious attitude in advancing his troops.

Breaking out from the Normandy salient, Bradley's army swept across France toward Paris, only to be met by a surprise German counteroffensive. Conflict arose in turn with General Eisenhower, who wanted to put some of Bradley's army under the command of British General Bernard Montgomery. These confrontations climaxed during the Battle of the Bulge, during which, although threatening resignation, Bradley held his own and led his forces across the Rhine into Germany. There his troops made the first Allied contact with advance units of the Red Army.

Shortly before the war ended in March 1945 Bradley's contribution to the Allies was recognized with his promotion to full general. After the war he carried out important work as administrator of veterans' affairs. In 1949 he became the first chairman of the Joint Chiefs of Staff—the highest position attainable in the U.S. defense establishment. In 1951 he opposed General Douglas MacArthur's extension of the Korean War to the Chinese border, saying that this was "the wrong war, at the wrong place, at the wrong time, and with the wrong enemy." That same year Bradley's wartime memoirs, *A Soldier's Story,* were published; they contained harsh criticism of his colleagues, particularly General Montgomery. After retirement from the army in 1953, Bradley turned to business.

BIBLIOGRAPHY

J. Jones, *World War Two,* 1975.

R. E. Merriam, *Dark December: Battle of the Bulge,* 1947.

CRAZY HORSE (SIOUX)

The Oglala Lakota war chief Crazy Horse (ca. 1840–1877) was born near Bear Butte, South Dakota. He defeated two of the army's best-known officers during the Great Sioux War of 1876. His father, also known as Crazy Horse, was a noted Oglala warrior and medicine man. His mother, Rattle Blanket Woman, was a Minneconjou Lakota.

Crazy Horse was a skilled warrior and leader who earned the admiration of his own people and of his foes.

By 1861, the young man had earned his adult name Crazy Horse. He was a skilled warrior and leader who earned the admiration of his own people and of his foes. During the Oglala leader Red Cloud's war against white incursions on Lakota lands in Wyoming and Montana in the mid-1860s, Crazy Horse led warriors in the Fetterman fight at Fort Phil Kearny in 1866, the Hayfield fight in 1867, and the Wagon Box fight in 1867.

Crazy Horse earned a considerable following among nontreaty Lakotas, who increasingly looked to him as a chief. In 1868, Lakota Sioux gathered in northeastern Wyoming where, one witness recalled, the "old men or leaders" selected four young warriors, including Crazy Horse as "head warriors [or 'shirt wearers'] of their people." The leaders told the four that they "represented in their commands and acts the entire power of the nation." Crazy Horse was a "shirt-wearer" until his participation in a violent controversy in 1870. A Lakota woman left her husband for Crazy Horse, and the husband shot Crazy Horse in the face with a pistol. His formal position as a "shirt-wearer" then ended.

By 1875, government officials and army officers acknowledged Crazy Horse as one of the conspicuous leaders of Lakota resistance. The issue before the Lakotas was the Black Hills of South Dakota and Lakota hunting grounds in the Yellowstone River basin, which were allocated to the Lakotas in an 1868 treaty. The government now desired the Black Hills because, in 1874, gold was discovered there. By 1875, Lakota leaders were furious about the increasing numbers of prospectors and miners in the Black Hills.

In December 1875, the government ordered the Lakotas and Cheyennes in the Yellowstone River and Powder River region to move to reservations in Nebraska or on the Missouri River within six weeks or face military action. The nontreaty Lakotas had no intention of moving their families and villages to the reservations during the harsh winter weather.

In March 1876, an army attack on a Northern Cheyenne village persuaded Crazy Horse and other Lakota and Northern Cheyenne chiefs to fight the army. Crazy Horse and Sitting Bull, a Hunkpapa Lakota, emerged as two of the great leaders of the Lakota-Cheyenne alliance.

Crazy Horse was central to two of the most significant battles of the Sioux War of 1876. On June 17, he led approximately fifteen hundred warriors against Brigadier General George Crook's thirteen-hundred-man military column. In the ensuing Battle of the Rosebud, Crazy Horse coordinated his warriors' attack and, in a strategic victory, stopped Crook's advance. Eight days later, Lieutenant Colonel George Armstrong Custer and units of the Seventh Cavalry attacked the Lakotas and Northern Cheyennes in the Battle of Little Bighorn. Crazy Horse played an important role in the counterattack, which annihilated Custer and his immediate command.

The army continued to strike the Lakotas and Cheyennes in the Yellowstone River country during the winter of 1876 to 1877. Crazy Horse realized that further fighting was useless, and he and his followers surrendered at Camp Robinson in Nebraska on May 7, 1877.

Government officials and army officers were eager to meet the warrior who had so adroitly fought them. Because of the attention to Crazy Horse, jealous Oglala and Sicangu chiefs spread rumors about him. Inexperienced junior army officers believed the gossip and reported it to their superiors. By September 1877, the rumors induced army officers to arrest Crazy Horse. On September 5, during an attempt to incarcerate Crazy Horse at Camp Robinson, a soldier mortally bayoneted him, and he died a few hours later.

BIBLIOGRAPHY

Sandoz, Mari. *Crazy Horse: The Strange Man of the Oglalas.* New York, 1942.

Hardorff, Richard G. *The Oglala Lakota Crazy Horse: A Preliminary Genealogical Study and an Annotated Listing of Primary Sources.* Mattiuck, N.Y., and Bryan, Tex., 1985.

CROCKETT, DAVID (DAVEY)

Frontiersman, congressman from Tennessee, defender of the Alamo, and folk hero, David (Davey) Crockett (1786–1836) was born near present-day Rogersville in East Tennessee. He was raised in the backwoods of the Appalachian Mountains and received a limited education. As a young man, he joined the Tennessee militia and fought with Andrew Jackson against the Creek Indians in Alabama from 1813 to 1814. After military service, he lived in Jefferson, Lincoln, Franklin, Lawrence, Carroll, and Gibson counties in Tennessee. After serving as a justice of the peace, he was elected to the Tennessee legislature in 1821 and served for two terms. In 1826, he was elected to the U.S. House of Representatives as a Democrat.

Even during his lifetime,

Crockett established himself as a folk hero.

Although he was an early supporter of the Jacksonian Democratic party, he later broke ties with Andrew Jackson. Crockett demonstrated a rare comprehension of and appreciation for governmental affairs and cared little for party views on issues. He voted instead on his own convictions. Unable to overcome President Jackson's immense political power, Crockett failed to win reelection in 1830, but two years later, he was returned to Congress on the Whig ticket.

Giving up politics after his defeat in 1835, Crockett moved to Texas. When he arrived at the Alamo, he was offered, but declined, command of the old mission. Although tradition holds that Crockett was killed within the walls of the Alamo, modern research has revealed that he may have been captured by the Mexican army and executed with several other defenders.

Even during his lifetime, Crockett established himself as a folk hero. Magazines and books of the period carried outlandish tales of his battles with wild beasts and human enemies. His death at the Alamo enlarged his bigger-than-life image. During the 1950s, several fanciful Hollywood movies about his exploits were released and starred Fess Parker. Coonskin caps, toy rifles, lunch boxes, and songs abounded during the revival and brought Crockett and his times once again to the forefront of the American imagination.

BIBLIOGRAPHY

Harper, Herbert L., ed. *Houston and Crockett: Heroes of Tennessee and Texas, An Anthology.* Nashville, Tenn., 1986.

Shackford, James A., ed. *David Crockett: The Man and the Myth.* Chapel Hill, N.C., 1956.

CROOK, GEORGE

An army officer whose career spanned from his graduation from the Military Academy at West Point in 1852 to his death, General George Crook (1828–1890) made his most noteworthy mark during the Indian wars in the West. Born in Taylorsville, Ohio, Crook graduated with a mediocre academic record but an excellent history of personal conduct. His lack of demerits may have been due to his quiet, even taciturn, personality. Yet he made some friends while at West Point, including classmate Philip H. Sheridan.

Crook's reputation as an unusually humane officer stands up only if one assumes most army officers shared an antipathy toward Indians.

After graduation, Crook was stationed in the Pacific Northwest where he soon became involved in conflicts with the Rogue River and Pit River Indians. By 1856, Oregon Volunteers and Army Regulars exiled the Indians to reservations. It was in the Northwest that Crook first confronted the difficulties, including the moral dilemmas, posed by Indian warfare. He understood that American aggression and expansion played a key role in provoking Indian wars. At the same time, he believed peace could be achieved only through force. He also expected Indians would have to embrace Euro-American culture. Crook's reputation as an unusually humane officer stands up only if one assumes most army officers shared an antipathy toward Indians and an inclination to exterminate them. In fact, Indian-fighting officers proved more complicated than that. Crook's attitude toward Indian people and his ambivalence about their conquest was actually fairly typical.

After the Civil War, Crook returned to the Northwest where he inaugurated several tactics that characterized his efforts in the Indian wars: the use of Indian scouts (including speedy enlistment for those who had recently surrendered) and the use of pack mules. The latter tactic allowed his troops to move beyond their supply base. The use of Indian scouts allowed him to take advantage of Indian familiarity with terrain and to demoralize Indians still fighting the army. In addition, Crook was known for his reluctance to disclose his plans during campaigns, a characteristic that frustrated officers under his command. These novel tactics brought Crook great success in 1872 during the Tonto Basin campaign, which resulted in the confinement of more than six thousand Apaches and Yavapais on reservations. However, his approach brought only mixed results during the Sioux War of 1876. The Sioux turned his troops back at the Battle of the Rosebud in June of that year. Yet in November, Crook's soldiers destroyed a Cheyenne village in the Bighorn Mountains, which probably hastened some Indian surrenders.

Crook was not the only officer to hire Indian scouts, but his experiences with them garnered much publicity. In 1886, Sheridan concluded Indians were not trustworthy in that role. Meanwhile, during the Geronimo campaign, Crook secured the Apache leader's surrender with the aid of Indian scouts. Sheridan urged President Grover Cleveland to refuse anything short of unconditional surrender, and when Geronimo, having second thoughts, slipped away, a disgusted and frustrated Crook resigned his command. Sheridan replaced him with rival Nelson Appleton Miles. When Geronimo finally surrendered, all the Chiricahuas—including the loyal scouts—were shipped to Florida. His friendship with Sheridan forever severed, Crook complained about this outrageous treatment and, for his remaining years, lobbied unsuccessfully for the scouts' return to Arizona.

BIBLIOGRAPHY

Bourke, John G. *On the Border with Crook.* New York, 1891.

Crook, George. *General George Crook: His Autobiography.* Edited by Martin F. Schmitt. Norman, Okla., 1960.

Greene, Jerome A. "George Crook." In *Soldiers West: Biographies from the Military Frontier.* Edited by Paul Andrew Hutton, Lincoln, Nebr., 1987.

CUSTER, GEORGE ARMSTRONG

Soldier, frontiersman, and Indian fighter who led the Seventh Cavalry at the Battle of Little Bighorn during the Sioux Wars, George Armstrong Custer (1839–1876) was born in New Rumley, Ohio, but spent part of his childhood with a half-sister in Monroe, Michigan. He attended West Point Military Academy and graduated at the bottom of his class on the eve of the Civil War. Although a poor student, he excelled in the combat arts, and during the war, he proved himself a superb field soldier. As a staff officer for General George B. McClellan and later General Alfred Pleasonton, Captain Custer demonstrated such potential that he was promoted to brigadier general and was given command of the Michigan cavalry brigade. Twenty-three years old, with long yellow hair and a gaudy uniform, he won instant fame. From Gettysburg to Appomattox, he was known for slashing cavalry charges that often proved decisive and for a personal fearlessness that earned the devotion of his men. By the end of the war, he was a major general commanding a full division.

George Armstrong Custer. (National Archives)

Garbed in fringed buckskin instead of black velvet and gold lace, he was the embodiment of the dashing Indian fighter, skilled plainsman, and hunter.

Custer returned to the postwar regular army as lieutenant colonel of the newly authorized Seventh Cavalry Regiment and made a new name for himself in the West. Garbed in fringed buckskin instead of black velvet and gold lace, he was the embodiment of the dashing Indian fighter, skilled plainsman, and hunter. In the frequent absence of the colonel, Custer usually commanded the Seventh, and in the popular perception, it was his regiment.

Custer's first experience with Indians, in Kansas in 1867, ended in embarrassing failure. Not only did he fail to defeat any Indians, but he was court-martialed and sentenced to a year's suspension of rank and pay. In 1868, however, he surprised and attacked Chief Black Kettle's Cheyenne village on the Washita River in present-day Oklahoma and laid the groundwork for his reputation as an Indian fighter. Guarding railroad surveyors on the Yellowstone River in 1873, he fought the Sioux in two battles that reinforced his Indian-fighting record.

Easterners viewed Custer as the army's foremost Indian fighter. In fact, he was no more successful than some of his peers. His regiment, moreover, was badly factionalized. Some of his troops worshiped him; others loathed him. But he wrote popular magazine articles and a book, *My Life on the Plains,* and always, he made good newspaper copy.

In 1874, Custer led the Seventh Cavalry out of his base at Fort Abraham Lincoln to explore the Black Hills of the Dakota Territory. Part of the Great Sioux Reservation, guaranteed to the Sioux by the Treaty of 1868, the Black Hills region had long been coveted by whites who thought its dark recesses held gold. Miners with the expedition found gold, and the news set off a gold rush.

Government attempts to buy the Black Hills and legalize the mining settlements failed. The aggression of the Sioux bands led by Sitting Bull and Crazy Horse against friendly Indians gave officials a pretext to wage a war that would solve the Black Hills problem by depriving the Sioux of their independence and their power to obstruct the sale.

The Great Sioux War of 1876 resulted. Custer and the Seventh rode with one of the armies that converged on the Indian country. On June 25, he attacked the village of Sitting Bull and Crazy Horse on Montana's Little Bighorn River. In a sequence of moves that will forever remain controversial, he and five companies were wiped out

"Custer's Last Stand" stunned and angered white Americans and led to the conquest of the Sioux and the acquisition of the Black Hills. But it also awarded its namesake an immortality that fit his dashing persona. His adoring wife Elizabeth, or Libbie, devoted the rest of her long life to defending and glorifying his name. She wrote three books that stirred her contemporaries and are still minor classics today. The controversy over Custer's military moves keeps the battle alive in American consciousness, and the image of "Long Hair," erect on his hilltop with troopers falling around him and shouting Sioux closing in for the kill, remains a shining icon in American folklore.

In recent years, American Indians have made Custer the scapegoat for the ill treatment and injustice inflicted by white Americans and their government on the native population. "Custer died for your sins" was the slogan in the 1970s. Historically, Custer hardly merited the distinction, but the legend was not difficult to bend to that purpose. Custer the villain, however, joins with Custer the hero to give George Armstrong Custer an even firmer grasp on the immortality he sought.

[See also The Civil War.]

BIBLIOGRAPHY

Dippie, Brian W. *Custer's Last Stand: The Anatomy of an American Myth.* Missoula, Mont., 1976.

Hutton, Paul A., ed. *The Custer Reader.* Lincoln, Nebr., 1992.

Merington, Marguerite, ed. *The Custer Story: The Life and Intimate Letters of General Custer and His Wife Elizabeth.* New York, 1950. Reprint. Lincoln, Nebr., 1987.

Monaghan, Jay. *Custer: The Life of General George Armstrong Custer.* Boston and Toronto, 1959.

Utley, Robert M. *Cavalier in Buckskin: George Armstrong Custer and the Western Military Frontier.* Norman, Okla., 1988.

DAVIS, BENJAMIN O., SR.

Benjamin O. Davis, Sr. (1880–1970), general. Benjamin O. Davis, Sr., was born in Washington, D.C. During his fifty years of duty as an enlisted man and officer in the United States Army, he strove to help others surmount the barrier of racism.

Davis, the youngest of three children, grew up in Washington, D.C. After graduating from high school, he volunteered for service in the Spanish-American War. The Army appointed him a second lieutenant in the Eighth United States Volunteer Infantry. After the unit was deactivated at the end of the war in 1899, Davis decided to continue his military career and joined the regular army. Two years later, he successfully passed a competitive examination and became an officer. On October 22, 1902, he married his childhood sweetheart, Elnora Dickerson. During the next few decades he served in a variety of positions, usually removed from active duty with his regiment. This included duty as military attaché to Liberia (1909–1911), teacher of military science at Wilberforce University (1906–1911, 1915–1917, 1929–1930, 1937–1938), instructor with the Ohio National Guard (1924–1928), and professor of military science at Tuskegee Institute (1921–1924, 1931–1937). In 1912 a son, Benjamin O. Davis, Jr., was born. The elder Davis's wife died in 1917 after the birth of their third child, and three years later he married Sadie Overton. In late October 1940, President Franklin D. Roosevelt appointed Davis as brigadier general, making him the first African American to reach that rank.

During World War II, Davis carried out a variety of assignments in Washington and Europe, all generally connected with racial issues. For much of the period he was assistant inspector general. He conducted investi-

Benjamin Davis, 1944. (National Archives)

gations of racial incidents, tried to encourage the advancement of African-American soldiers and officers, and made efforts to convince the Army to face the consequences of its policies of segregation and discrimination. As a member of the Committee on Negro Troop Policies, Davis quietly worked toward these ends. In 1942 and again in 1944–1945, he served in England and dealt with racial problems in the European theater of operations. One of his most notable contributions occurred as a result of the manpower shortage created by the German attack in the Ardennes in December 1944. He advanced a proposal for retraining black service troops as combat soldiers and inserting these men into white units on an individual basis. Though Gen. Dwight Eisenhower, the theater commander, found this unacceptable, he was forced to accept integration of African-American platoons into white units. It was a significant breakthrough in the wall of segregation.

Following the conclusion of the war, Davis served in a variety of positions before his retirement in 1948. He continued to stress the inequities of segregation and was pleased when President Harry Truman ordered its removal. In the next decade he worked for the government of the District of Columbia and the American Battle Monuments Commission. He resided in Washington with Sadie until her death in 1966, and spent the last years of his life with his younger daughter, Elnora McLendon, in her home in Chicago.

BIBLIOGRAPHY

Fletcher, Marvin E. *America's First Black General: Benjamin O. Davis, Sr., 1880–1970.* Lawrence, Kans., 1989.

Nalty, Bernard C. *Strength for the Fight: A History of Black Americans in the Military.* New York, 1986.

DECATUR, STEPHEN

Commodore Stephen Decatur was a daredevil naval officer who won his reputation and greatest victories in the Mediterranean fighting against the Barbary states. Decatur was born on January 5, 1779, in Sinepuxent, Maryland. Decatur entered the Navy as a midshipman under Commodore John Barry, and served in a variety of posts until he was assigned to the force attempting to punish the ruler and people of Tripoli for piracy against United States vessels.

The U.S. frigate *Philadelphia* was captured by the enemy when she ran aground near Tripoli. The Tripolitan navy intended to use the big American ship against the American fleet. Decatur led a boarding force that sailed into the harbor, surprised the crew of Tripolitans aboard the *Philadelphia,* and destroyed her by fire. This took place on February 16, 1804, and made Decatur a hero in the United States.

During the War of 1812, he served with some distinction as commander of the U.S. frigates *United States* and *President.* He once more returned to glory in the Mediterranean in 1815 when he headed a squadron that set out to punish Algiers for attempted piracy. In this campaign he captured the Algerian flagship and dictated peace terms to the Algerian government. He filled a number of other posts, including a post on the Board of Naval Commissioners. While there, he refused to return Captain James Barron (who had commanded the *Chesapeake* in 1807) to active duty. Barron challenged Decatur to a duel in which he killed him in 1820. Decatur is remembered not only for his naval career, but for his famous toast—"my country, right or wrong!"

DEWEY, GEORGE

George Dewey was born in Vermont in 1837, and trained as a naval officer at Annapolis. He graduated from the U.S. Naval Academy in 1858 and served during the Civil War under Admiral David Farragut. During the peacetime years after the Civil War, he was given a number of important naval assignments, especially when the new steel warships were being designed and developed during the late 1880s.

In 1898, he was assigned to command the Asiatic Squadron, which was cruising in the vicinity of China. He had his ships and crews trained to a high stage of efficiency. When the war broke out with Spain that year, he sailed to Manila Bay in the Philippines. He followed Farragut's old tactic of pushing right into an enemy harbor, caught the defending Spanish squadron in the bay, and destroyed it.

Dewey's victory insured that the United States could take the Philippines when U.S. Army troops could reach those islands. He was greeted on his return to the United States as the greatest hero of the war. Dewey continued in active naval service until his death, attaining the rank of Admiral of the Navy, a rank created for him by Congress. His total naval service, including time as a midshipman at Annapolis, was over sixty-two years. Dewey died in 1917.

EISENHOWER, DWIGHT DAVID

Dwight David Eisenhower, ("Ike,"; 1890–1969), thirty-fourth president of the United States and commander of the allied forces that conquered Germany in World

War II. He was born in Denison, Texas, and his family moved the following year to Abilene, Kansas. His father, David, never earned more than $100 per month, but he and his wife Ida raised six boys, each of whom achieved success as adults. The Eisenhowers grew almost all of their own food and earned additional cash by selling the surplus. All of the boys worked to earn their own spending money.

Although Eisenhower was only an average student, he was an outstanding athlete in grade school and high school. After graduating from Abilene High School in 1909, he worked in the local creamery, and part of his salary went to help an older brother through college. He took a competitive examination for the U.S. Naval Academy because of the possibility of a free education and the opportunity to play football. After passing the examination, he found he was too old to attend Annapolis, and instead he entered West Point Military Academy in 1911. Here too Eisenhower proved an excellent athlete and during his second year played halfback on the army football team. Sportswriters praised his All-American capabilities, but a twisted knee cut his football career short.

Eisenhower was not particularly well read and was never considered an intellect, but he had a sharp, orderly, analytical mind.

Eisenhower graduated from West Point in 1915 and was sent to Fort Sam Houston in San Antonio, Texas, as a second lieutenant. Two weeks after reporting for duty, he met his future wife, Mamie Geneva Doud, who came from a wealthy Denver family. They were married in 1916 in Denver, Colorado.

Eisenhower was not particularly well read and was never considered an intellect, but he had a sharp, orderly, analytical mind, with the ability to look at a problem, see what alternatives were available, and decide wisely. In 1917 he was promoted to captain just after the United States entered World War I; although he wanted to lead men in battle in France, he was stationed at Camp Colt, a tank training center in Gettysburg, Pennsylvania, where he spent the entire war. Nevertheless, he was awarded the Distinguished Service Medal for his services as an outstanding instructor and trainer. He was promoted to major in 1920 and the following year graduated from the Tank Training School at Camp Meade, Maryland.

In 1922 Eisenhower was transferred to the Panama Canal Zone as the executive officer for the Twentieth Infantry Brigade. There he met General Fox Connor, who spoke to the young officer at length about military history and international problems. Certain that there would be another world war and that George C. Marshall (then colonel) would command the American forces, Connor suggested that Eisenhower seek an assignment under Marshall.

In 1925 Eisenhower was sent to the Command and General Staff School in Leavenworth, Kansas, finishing first in a class of 275. In 1928 he graduated from the Army War College, gaining the reputation of an outstanding staff officer. From 1929 to 1933 he served as the assistant secretary of war, and in 1933 he was made assistant to the chief of staff (General Douglas MacArthur), in which capacity he spent the next four years in the Philippines.

In December 1941 General Marshall, now army chief of staff, brought Eisenhower to Washington and put him in charge of the war plans division for the Far East. He was promoted to major general in March 1942, serving as head of the operations division, and in June of the same year, Marshall put Eisenhower in charge of the U.S. forces in the European Theater of Operations (ETO).

On November 8, 1942, with Eisenhower in command, British and American forces successfully landed near Casablanca, Oran, and Algiers and drove the Germans out of North Africa. In July 1943 Eisenhower, now a four-star general, launched the invasion of Sicily and the subsequent invasion of Italy. In December, the combined chiefs of staff sent him to London to take command of the forces gathered for the invasion of France. When he took over Supreme Headquarters, Allied Expeditionary Force, he commanded the most powerful single military force ever assembled. On June 6, 1944, over 156,000 men invaded the beaches of Normandy. During the conquest of Europe, under Eisenhower's command, were General Omar N. Bradley, General George S. Patton, as well as British chief of staff Bernard L. Montgomery. The forces led by Eisenhower, now a five-star general, advanced through France but were help up in Belgium during the winter, until they finally smashed through to Germany in the spring.

The Germans signed an unconditional surrender on May 8, 1945, and Eisenhower headed the occupation forces for six months. He was then reassigned to Washington to succeed Marshall as army chief of staff. After completing the task of demobilizing the American army, he traveled, making speeches to promote national defense. His book *Crusade in Europe* (1948) was a best-seller, and he was urged by both the Democratic and

Dwight D. Eisenhower, 1945. (National Archives)

Republican parties to accept a presidential nomination, but declined. In June 1948 he became president of Columbia University, holding that position until January 1953 but on leave of absence from December 1950 when he was appointed by President Harry S. Truman to be the supreme commander of the North Atlantic Treaty Organization (NATO).

The two major political parties continued to press Eisenhower to accept the presidential nomination. In 1952 he declared himself a Republican and in June of that year resigned his position as NATO supreme commander, returned to the United States, and began a hectic five-week preconvention campaign. He beat Robert A. Taft by a narrow margin on the first ballot at the Republican national convention.

Basically conservative, Eisenhower advocated a reduction in government controls and taxes, and in the presidential election he received 6.5 million more votes than the liberal Democratic candidate, Governor Adlai E. Stevenson of Illinois (442 to 89 votes in the electoral college). Riding in on the coattails of Ike's popularity, the Republicans captured both houses of Congress. The new president fulfilled one of his campaign promises by halting the fighting in Korea—where South Korea had been invaded by North Korea in 1950—but the cease-fire led to an uneasy truce rather than a genuine peace.

Eisenhower had a talent for getting people of diverse backgrounds to work together toward a common objective. Although he now drew on this and other capabilities he had shown as a military man, he did not prove to be a strong president. Day-to-day management of the government was left to his staff and he placed foreign policy decisions in the hands of Secretary of State John Foster Dulles. Among the achievements of Eisenhower's administration were the end of the Korean war and the creation of the Southeast Asia Treaty Organization and of the International Atomic Energy Agency.

In 1954 the Republicans lost their majority in both houses of Congress. At first, Congress continued to support the president, but opposition soon grew, and when Senator Robert Taft died, Eisenhower lost his main support in Congress. His attempts to balance the budget took three years, but were reversed shortly thereafter because of mounting expenditures for foreign aid and defense. He tried to end the cold war with the Soviet Union, but despite years of effort was unsuccessful in building mutual trust between the two countries.

Eisenhower was reelected in 1956 by an even greater majority, but his personal popularity did not help the Republican party, which lost in both houses of Congress. During the 1956 Suez crisis Eisenhower and Dulles forced Britain and France to break off their attack on Nasser's Egypt. Subsequently the president proposed the Eisenhower Doctrine, which pledged military help to any Middle Eastern country facing a Communist threat. This policy was put into effect in 1968, when U.S. troops were sent to Lebanon. At home Eisenhower opposed racial segregation and sent federal troops to Little Rock, Arkansas, to enforce desegregation at a local school. In response to the 1957 Soviet launching of Sputnik, the first satellite, he created the National Aeronautics and Space Administration (NASA) in 1958. A planned meeting with the Soviet premier Nikita Kruschev in 1960 was cancelled by the latter after a U.S. spy plane was shot down over the USSR.

Eisenhower groomed Vice President Richard Nixon as his successor, but Nixon was defeated in the 1960 election. Upon retirement, Eisenhower was treated as a respected elder statesman. President John F. Kennedy frequently asked his opinions on international problems. In his later years, Ike suffered a series of heart attacks, and in August 1965 he ended his active participation in public affairs. He remained a very popular public figure and in the 1968 Gallup Poll topped the list of the Most Admired Americans.

BIBLIOGRAPHY

S. E. Ambrose, *Eisenhower*, 1990.

D. Eisenhower, *Eisenhower at War: 1943–1945*, 1986.

R. H. Ferrell, ed., *The Eisenhower Diaries,* 1981.
H. E. Stassen, *Eisenhower: Turning the World Toward Peace,* 1990.

FARRAGUT, DAVID GLASGOW

David Farragut was the most distinguished and successful U.S. Navy officer in the Civil War. He was the first American to hold the rank of Admiral, a rank especially created for him by Congress.

Farragut was born near Knoxville, Tennessee, on July 5, 1801. He was the adopted son of Commodore David Porter, a naval hero of the War of 1812. As was the custom in the 19th century, he went to sea when he was only nine, and began his long career under the command of his foster-father. Farragut worked his way up through the Navy ranks, serving on a number of ships and on a variety of stations. He was briefly a British prisoner of war; he picked up a fluent command of Spanish, Arabic, Italian, and French while on Mediterranean duty; and he served in the American flotilla operating to crush West Indies pirates in 1822–1824.

David Farragut. (National Archives)

The Mexican War found him out of favor with some of his superiors and he was assigned to routine blockade duties, which he disliked. After that war, a number of other more or less routine assignments were interrupted by the task of laying out and starting the now famous Mare Island Navy Yard on San Francisco Bay.

In 1861, the Tennessee-born Farragut and his Virginian wife were stationed at Norfolk, Mrs. Farragut's home town. When the crisis of secession arose in Virginia, he had to choose whether to stay in Virginia or remain loyal to the Union. When he expressed his loyalty to the Union and President Lincoln, he was told he could not live in Norfolk. His reply, "Well, then, I can live somewhere else," was followed by a move to New York, where he waited for orders for active naval duty.

After a period of desk duty, during which his naval superiors had doubts about how far to trust this officer with southern connections, Farragut was assigned to command the West Gulf Blockading Squadron in January 1862. This assignment gave him the responsibility to cut off sea communications to Confederate ports from Texas to Florida. In the middle of his area of command lay the greatest gulf port of all, New Orleans.

Farragut had devised a plan for naval vessels to reduce land forts. At New Orleans, he put his ideas into action. He ran several vessels past the forts defending New Orleans, caught and defeated Confederate warships there, and then turned his guns on the forts. On April 28, 1862, Farragut scored a knockout victory over the Confederate ships at New Orleans, providing the Union with its most dramatic victory of the war up to that time.

Rear Admiral Farragut (promoted to that rank for his victory at New Orleans) followed a very similar plan at Mobile Bay on August 5, 1864. The Alabama seaport was the last major gulf port supplying the armies in Alabama, Georgia, and the Carolinas. Farragut, commanding his squadron from the flagship *Hartford,* had himself tied to its mast so that he would not be either blown overboard in an explosion, or fall off due to one of the dizzy spells he often suffered. Then, he ordered his ships to move past the Confederate forts and through a passage that was heavily mined (sea mines were then called "torpedoes"). When the lead ship, ahead of *Hartford,* slowed down, Farragut added a line to the traditions of the U.S. Navy with his order—"Damn the torpedoes! Four bells! Captain Drayton, go ahead! Jouett, full speed!" The order passed into American tradition. Just as at New Orleans, Farragut's squadron wiped out a Confederate fleet, and assisted in taking Confederate forts that guarded the harbor.

"Damn the torpedoes! Four bells!

Captain Drayton, go ahead! Jouett, full speed!"

Farragut was promoted to the grade of Admiral on July 26, 1866. He was always a methodical and thorough officer, seeing to it that all details were taken care of. His own health, in spite of his long active career in the Navy, was never unusually good, but he was able to drive himself to success in an especially demanding profession. His career covered naval developments from the days of pirates and wooden sailing vessels to the days of ironclad steamships. Farragut was a man who was willing to take responsibility for important actions, and was brave enough to lead warships through channels directly under the enemy guns. He died in 1870.

GRANT, ULYSSES SIMPSON

Ulysses Simpson Grant, (1822–1885), soldier and eighteenth president of the United States (1869–1877). He was born in Point Pleasant, Ohio, but the year after his birth the family moved to Georgetown, Ohio. Grant showed little academic ability but was very good with horses and preferred to work on his father's farm rather than in his tannery. Against his will, his father sent him to the U.S. Military Academy in 1839. After a short time Grant decided that, "A military life has no charms for me." He graduated in 1843, ranking twenty-first in a class of thirty-nine, his main achievement being in horsemanship. He was commissioned a brevet second lieutenant and assigned to the Fourth U.S. Infantry, which was stationed at Jefferson Barracks near Saint Louis, Missouri.

After a short time at the U.S. Military Academy,

Grant decided that,

"A military life has no charms for me."

From 1846 to 1848 Grant served with distinction in the Mexican War, where he was promoted to a full second lieutenant under General Zachary Taylor. In later years Grant copied Taylor's informal dress and lack of military pretension. Grant's regiment was transferred to the army of Winfield Scott, under whom he was promoted, in battle, to first lieutenant and then to captain. For the next four years Grant was stationed in Sachets Harbor, New York, and Detroit, Michigan, but in 1852 he was transferred to the Pacific coast, where he spent two miserable years with an inadequate income and without his family. At that point he had to resign his commission and went to Missouri to try his hand at farming. This attempt proved unsuccessful and he went to work on his father's farm.

In August 1861 President Abraham Lincoln appointed Grant brigadier-general of volunteers. In January 1862, while in command of the Twenty-First Illinois Volunteers, he achieved the first major Union victory in the Civil War and subsequently participated in many battles as second in command. When his commander was called to Washington in July 1862, Grant led the forces to victory in several impressive battles. In October 1862 he was made commander of the Department of Tennessee and it was his aggressiveness, resilience, independence, and determination that made possible the final victory at Vicksburg, where he succeeded in cutting the Confederacy in half.

Ulysses S. Grant. (National Archives)

His successes brought him to Washington in 1864, where he received Lincoln's personal thanks and was voted a gold medal by Congress. He was promoted to lieutenant general and commander of all the armies of the United States. He then developed a plan of action for the armed forces which, together with their superior numbers, enabled them to defeat the Confederates and on April 9, 1865, General Robert E. Lee officially surrendered to Grant.

Late in 1865 Grant, who recommended a lenient Reconstruction policy, toured the South, where he was greeted with friendliness. In 1866 he was given the rank of general of the armies of the United States. He became a popular public figure and was the obvious candidate for the presidency, easily defeating Democrat Horatio Seymour; he assumed the presidency on March 4, 1869.

At the time of his election he was forty-six years old, the youngest man to achieve that office. He proved an inept politician; his cabinet consisted of friends, not strong leaders. He had formulated no policy and displayed no leadership in dealing with the Congress, and for the next eight years the country was run by his advisers, whose counsel was for the most part poor. During his second term in office, both his domestic and his foreign policies were in such disarray that the Republican party as a whole was discredited and he was defeated at the Republican convention in his attempt to run for a third term.

When he left the presidency Grant went on a world tour, during which he was received not as a discredited president but as the victor of the Civil War. He returned to the United States after two years of traveling and again tried for the presidential nomination. On the thirty-sixth ballot at the 1880 Republican national convention, James A. Garfield was nominated and Grant's political career came to an end.

In 1881 he moved to New York and became involved with an investment firm in which his son was a partner. He invested heavily and encouraged friends to do the same, but a swindle by Ferdinand Ward left him with a debt of sixteen million dollars and a clouded reputation. Grant attempted to recoup some of his losses by becoming a partner in a brokerage firm but like all of his other business ventures, it failed, and in 1884 he was forced into bankruptcy.

He began to write reminiscences of his various battles and to prepare his memoirs. Suffering from throat cancer, he composed in his sickroom in Saratoga, New York, two volumes of his recollections and they remain one of the great war commentaries of all time. These memoirs, published by Mark Twain, brought the Grant family $450,000 in royalties. In 1885, the family moved to the Adirondacks, where Grant died. His grandiose tomb on Riverside Drive is a well-known New York City landmark.

BIBLIOGRAPHY

M. E. Mantell, *Johnson, Grant, and the Politics of Reconstruction,* 1973.

W. S. McFeely, *Grant,* 1981.

J. Y. Simon, ed., *The Papers of Ulysses S. Grant,* 4 vols., 1967–1972.

GREENE, NATHANAEL

Nathanael Greene was born July 27, 1742, in Warwick, Rhode Island. He was a self-made soldier and military leader. He overcame a permanent injury that made him lame and turned away from his religious upbringing as a Quaker to become one of the most important Revolutionary War generals.

Greene commanded Rhode Island's troops at the siege of Boston in 1775–1776. Thereafter, as a Continental officer, he became one of Washington's most trusted advisers and division commanders in battle. As

Nathanael Greene. (National Archives)

Quartermaster-General for the years 1777–1780, he was responsible for securing and moving all army supplies. In 1780, Greene was assigned to command the army in the South. Lord Cornwallis had just defeated General Horatio Gates at the battle of Camden and Greene took over a skeleton army. For the remainder of the war he built up its strength while he hacked away at Cornwallis' supply lines in a series of small actions, never allowing himself to be tricked into a major engagement. Greene's base of supplies was in Virginia, and it was an attempt to destroy Greene's supplies that drew Cornwallis and the British into the campaign that led to Yorktown. While Cornwallis was engaged in Virginia, Greene pushed his own army around the British and liberated the Carolinas and Georgia. Greene died in 1786 on a plantation given him by the grateful legislature of Georgia. Greensboro, N.C. was named in his honor, for it is located at the site of his victory at Guilford Court House.

HOUSTON, SAMUEL

Sam Houston led the tiny army of Texas to the victory at San Jacinto which won independence for the Lone Star Republic in 1836. After five years as president of Texas, and twelve years as a U.S. Senator from Texas, Houston served briefly as governor of his state in 1860 and 1861. He was driven out of the governorship because he refused to assist in the secession of Texas from the United States.

Sam Houston. (Corbis/Bettmann)

Houston was born in 1793 in Rockbridge County, Virginia. He was the son of a Revolutionary war officer who made the U.S. Army his career. Sam Houston, Sr., died when his son was only thirteen, and the young Houston was left with his mother in Tennessee. He became very friendly with the Cherokee Indians and lived with them for three years, before joining Andrew Jackson's unit in 1813 to fight the Creeks and the British. Houston served well, was wounded at the battle of Horseshoe Bend in 1814, and stayed in the Army until 1817 on duty among the Cherokees. In 1817, he left the Army, established himself in Nashville, Tennessee, as one of Andrew Jackson's friends and followers, and began a political career. He was a fast-talking, hard-drinking frontiersman, with little formal schooling; still, he prepared himself for a lawyer's career and began making political speeches. He was so successful as a leader of men that he was elected District Attorney the same year he was admitted to practice law. In 1823, he was elected a Congressman from Tennessee. He served in Congress until 1827, when he won the governorship of the state. Two years later, Sam Houston was married, but he and his wife separated almost at once. When this happened, the broken-hearted Houston resigned as governor of Tennessee and headed out to live with the Cherokee Indians in their new homeland in Arkansas.

Houston lived among the Cherokees until 1833 and became a citizen of the Cherokee nation. In 1833 he went to Texas (then a Mexican province), representing President Jackson, to arrange a treaty between the United States and some Indian tribes. Houston remained in Texas and settled there. In 1835, he supported Stephen Austin's effort to make Texas a separate state under Mexican rule. Just as in Tennessee, Houston's leadership attracted Texans to support him and follow him. When the war for Texas independence broke out in 1835, his neighbors first made him a commander of local militia, then named him commander-in-chief of the Texas armed forces.

His title did not mean that Texas had much of an army. Less than a thousand men all told served the Lone

Star Republic. Some of these men chose to defend the Alamo, a post which Houston wanted abandoned so that the garrison could join his own small force. However, after the Mexicans captured the old mission, Houston paraded his seven hundred-odd soldiers and aroused them with a speech that ended with the words: "Remember the Alamo!" Then he led them against a Mexican force commanded by General Santa Anna. Houston's Texans attacked the larger Mexican force on April 21, 1836, near the banks of the San Jacinto River. The Texans won an overwhelming victory, with small loss in Texans dead or wounded. Santa Anna himself was captured. This victory gained independence for Texas from Mexico.

Houston paraded his seven hundred-odd soldiers and aroused them with a speech that ended with the words: "Remember the Alamo!"

In the first election of a Texas president, Houston won over Stephen Austin and served two years. His chief concern was winning diplomatic recognition from the United States and other countries. He served until 1838, and was reelected in 1841, serving until 1844. In 1840, Houston married Margaret Lea, an Alabama girl who provided him with a normal family life for the first time in almost thirty years. Shortly after Texas was admitted to the Union, Houston returned to Washington, D.C., as one of his State's first Senators.

Houston was always a Jacksonian Democrat at heart. He loved and honored the Union. he was the only southern Senator to oppose several of the moves that led to the crisis between North and South and he was the only southerner to vote for all the elements in the Compromise of 1850. His stand for the Union did not indicate that he favored abolition of slavery (he himself owned slaves) but that he felt it his duty in honor to uphold and continue the Constitution and the Union of the States. This attitude caused him to lose popularity in Texas, where many people began to be "southern" rather than "national" in the 1850s. In 1858, he was replaced as a Senator by the Texas legislature.

Houston's last dramatic action as a Texan—and American—statesman was to run for the governorship of his state in 1859. He campaigned as a Union Democrat and won the post. However, Texas passed a resolution of secession in 1861 and Houston found himself the only southern governor who opposed secession. Like many northern Democrats he also opposed the use of force to put down secession and he refused to use U.S. troops to regain his governorship after he was stripped of office on March 18, 1861. He died in enforced retirement in 1863, not far from the Alamo. A little town founded and named for him in the year of San Jacinto is today the largest city in Texas.

JACKSON, ANDREW

Frontier military commander and Indian fighter Andrew Jackson (1767–1845) became the first "Westerner" to be elected president of the United States. Born in the Waxhaw area, he was raised in the wilderness of this North Carolina–South Carolina border region. After serving in the Revolutionary War and squandering his modest inheritance, he studied law, gained admission to the North Carolina bar, and moved to Nashville, Tennessee, where, in 1791, he became attorney general for the Southwest Territory and, subsequently, circuit-riding solicitor in the area surrounding Nashville.

In 1791, Jackson married Rachel Donelson Robards; both he and Rachel believed that she and her first husband had been legally divorced. When that proved not to be the case, they remarried in 1794, but the incident dogged Jackson's private life and political career for many years.

Jackson served as a delegate to the Tennessee constitutional convention in 1796. After his election to Congress in 1796, he earned a reputation as a fierce opponent of the Washington administration's conciliatory stance toward Great Britain and the Indian tribes that had sided with the British during the Revolution. In 1797, Jackson was appointed to serve out the senatorial term of his political mentor, William Blount. Jackson's continual financial problems prompted him to leave the Senate in 1798. From 1798 to 1804, he served as a Tennessee superior court judge and then resigned to devote himself to recouping his fortune.

Commissioned major general of volunteers in the War of 1812, Jackson defeated the pro-British "Red Stick" Creek Indians at the Battle of Horseshoe Bend on March 27, 1814. Federal authorities then appointed him to command the defense of New Orleans. Jackson devised a brilliant strategy and on January 8, 1815, soundly defeated the British. By the time the Battle of New Orleans was fought, however, the warring nations had signed a peace treaty (in Ghent, Belgium, on December 24), but the news failed to reach the commanders in the field.

Beginning in 1817, Jackson fought the Seminole Indians and pursued them into Spanish Florida during

Andrew Jackson. (National Archives)

the spring of 1818. He was eager to interpret his mission as nothing less than the conquest of Spanish Florida, and he set about not only attacking Indians, but deposing Spanish authorities until passage of the Adams Onis Treaty of 1819, by which Spain formally ceded Florida to the United States.

Jackson resigned his army commission in 1821 to become provisional territorial governor of Florida. The following year, the Tennessee legislature nominated him for the presidency and then, in 1823, elected him to the U.S. Senate. In 1824, Jackson ran for president but lost the election to John Quincy Adams. During the Adams administration, Jackson worked to create the powerful popular movement that ensured his election in 1828. The movement became the nucleus of the Democratic party, which positioned Jackson as a critic of John Quincy Adams's support of a strong, centralized government at the expense of what was coming to be called "states' rights."

Jackson defeated Adams in his bid for a second term, but his inauguration was a bittersweet occasion, since it came after the death of his beloved wife. Jackson made sweeping changes in the government in order to make it more responsive to what he interpreted as the will of the people. One of his first actions was to introduce the principle of rotation in office, removing a number of long-term appointees from public office and instituting what his political foes called the "spoils system" in its stead. Another nod toward the common man was Jackson's program of internal improvements, especially in the West, where his administration authorized the construction of roads and canals.

Having been elected in part on a platform of states' rights, Jackson supported this principle only when it suited his program of general national expansion. When the Cherokee Indians of Georgia attacked that state's depredations against them by successfully pleading their case before the U.S. Supreme Court (in *Worcester* v. *State of Georgia*), Jackson refused to enforce the court's decision and claimed that the federal government was powerless to intervene in the internal affairs of a state. Two years earlier, Jackson had signed the Indian Removal Bill, which authorized the removal of Eastern tribes to the Indian Territory, and Georgia's actions suited the president's program. Yet during the nullification crisis of 1832, Jackson demonstrated a firm commitment to the central government. When South Carolina declared the tariffs of 1828 and 1832 null and void and prohibited the collection of tariffs in South Carolina, Jackson responded with his Nullification Proclamation of December 10, 1832, announcing his intention to enforce the law—although also pledging a compromise tariff. South Carolina backed down, and the dissolution of the Union was postponed for almost three more decades.

Jackson vehemently opposed the Second Bank of the United States, a private corporation established in 1816 but operating under a federal charter. He charged that it not only failed to provide a stable currency but consistently favored the privileged few at the expense of the common man. When Congress passed a measure to recharter the bank, Jackson vetoed it, and the issue became important in the presidential election of 1832. After Jackson soundly defeated Henry Clay (a supporter of the bank), he waged war against the bank for the next four years. He offered no suitable alternative to the bank, however, and thus contributed to a highly unstable currency situation, especially in the South and West, where state-chartered banks freely engaged in the speculative issuance of paper currency. That situation stimulated a land boom, in which the sale of federal lands wiped out the national debt and even created a substantial surplus. Alarmed by the degree of speculation and the prevalence of paper currency, the Jackson administration issued the Specie Circular of 1836, which forbade the purchase of federal land or payment of federal debts in any currency except federally issued coins. This action created an instant demand for specie that triggered a tidal wave of bank failures—especially in the West and South—and brought on the panic of 1837.

Jackson was personally sympathetic to the American-organized Texas Revolution against Mexico, yet he refused to take a decisive official stand in favor of Texas independence. He feared dividing the Democratic party over the expansion of slavery into a new territory (assuming the Republic of Texas were to be annexed to the United States), and despite his bellicose reputation, he did not relish the prospect of war with Mexico.

Jackson was a powerful symbol and cultural icon: the embodiment of a Westerner or of what is popularly meant by the frontiersman.

After his retirement to the Hermitage, Jackson, who was seriously ill, nevertheless remained a powerful force in the Democratic party. When he transferred his support from his successor, Martin Van Buren, to James K. Polk, the latter not only captured the Democratic nomination, but became president in 1844.

Relatively little that characterized the Age of Jackson—the national expansion westward, the elevation of the common man, the displacement of the Native American—was due solely to his actions and policies as president. Yet Jackson was a powerful symbol and cultural icon: the embodiment of a Westerner or of what is popularly meant by the frontiersman.

[See also The War of 1812 and Postwar Expansion.]

BIBLIOGRAPHY

Davis, Burke. *Old Hickory: A Life of Andrew Jackson.* New York, 1977.

James, Marquis. *Andrew Jackson: Portrait of a President.* Indianapolis, Ind., and New York, 1937.

Meyers, Marvin. *The Jacksonian Persuasion.* New York, 1957.

Remini, Robert V. *Andrew Jackson and the Course of American Democracy, 1833–1845.* New York, 1984.

———. *Andrew Jackson and the Course of American Empire, 1767–1821.* New York, 1977.

———. *Andrew Jackson and the Course of American Freedom, 1822–1832.* New York, 1981.

Rogin, Michael. *Fathers and Children: Andrew Jackson and the Subjugation of the American Indian.* New York, 1975.

Schlesinger, Arthur M. *The Age of Jackson.* Boston, 1945.

Sellers, Charles. *Andrew Jackson: A Profile.* New York, 1971.

Van Deusen, Glyndon G. *The Jacksonian Era.* New York, 1959.

JACKSON, THOMAS J. ("STONEWALL")

Thomas J. ("Stonewall") Jackson, (1824–1863), lieutenant general. Stonewall Jackson ranks among the most brilliant commanders in American history. Even though his field service in the Civil War lasted but two years, his movements continue to be studied at every major military academy in the world. Jackson's death at the midway point of the war was the greatest personal loss that the Confederacy suffered. Jackson was born January 21, 1824, at Clarksburg, deep in the mountains of what is now West Virginia.

Jackson went to the U.S. Military Academy in 1842.

War had already been declared with Mexico when Jackson entered the army as a lieutenant in the Third U.S. Artillery. He proceeded at once to Mexico. His battery saw no action for six months, and Jackson openly despaired of getting into battle. In March 1847, however, he participated in the assault on Vera Cruz;

Thomas "Stonewall" Jackson. (National Archives)

other engagements followed, with Jackson cited for gallantry at Contreras and Chapultepec. By the end of the war, Jackson held the rank of brevet major.

Jackson returned to the States and reported for duty at Fort Hamilton on Long Island, New York. His duties as assistant quartermaster and occasional member of courts-martial left Jackson free to pursue his fondness for reading. History was his favorite subject. Jackson also maintained a steady correspondence with his beloved sister, Laura, who was married and lived in Beverly, Virginia.

In December 1850, Jackson's company transferred to Fort Meade in the remote interior of Florida. The artillerist uncharacteristically became embroiled in arguments with his commanding officer, Maj. William H. French. Jackson was soon under arrest for accusing French of having an affair with his maid. Meanwhile, Jackson had received an offer to become professor of artillery tactics and optics at the Virginia Military Institute in Lexington, Virginia. The academy was small, having been in existence barely a dozen years; nevertheless, it offered Jackson both a challenge and a change of scenery. He resigned his army commission and reported to the institute on the eve of the 1851–1852 school year. "The Major" spent a fourth of his life at VMI.

Jackson displayed a number of qualities that impressed those who knew him well. Devotion, duty, and determination were his bywords. He was honest to a fault, extremely conscientious, and pleasant in the confines of small, private gatherings.

Thoughts of a possible civil war began with Jackson in December 1859, when he and part of the VMI cadet corps were among the witnesses at the execution of abolitionist John Brown. Jackson remained a strong Unionist until he thought Virginia threatened by Federal coercion. At the secession of his state, he dutifully offered his services to the Confederacy. He left Lexington on April 20, 1861, never again to see his adopted town.

When Jackson and a contingent of cadets arrived in Richmond to serve as drill instructors for thousands of recruits gathering for military service, the ex-professor hardly resembled an impressive soldier. It had been fourteen years since Jackson had last seen combat. He was then thirty-seven, five feet, ten inches tall, with extended forehead, sharp nose, thick beard, and high-pitched voice. Unusually large hands and feet were the extremities of a 170-pound frame. Jackson rode a horse awkwardly, body bent forward as if he were leaning into a stiff wind. His uniform for the first year of the war consisted of battered kepi cap pulled down almost to his nose, the well-worn blue coat of a VMI faculty member, and boots that reached above his knees. Appearance was deceiving. Jackson swept into war with cool professionalism and complete confidence in himself.

Appointed a colonel of infantry on April 27, 1861, Jackson's first orders were to return to the Shenandoah Valley and take command of gaudily dressed militia and inexperienced volunteers rendezvousing at Harper's Ferry. The new commander assumed his duties with a stern and heavy hand. On June 17, 1861, he was promoted to brigadier general and given a brigade of five infantry regiments from the Shenandoah Valley. His first duty as a general was to help destroy railroad property at nearby Martinsburg. On July 2, Jackson and one of his regiments easily repulsed a Federal probe near Falling Waters, Virginia.

The most famous nickname in American history came to Jackson and his brigade on July 21 at Manassas. When a Union army moved into Virginia to seize the railroads at Manassas Junction, the forces of Johnston and P. G. T. Beauregard combined to resist the advance. The all-day battle was actually a collision between two armed mobs seeking to become armies. Jackson's brigade was posted back of the crest of Henry House Hill, an eminence that commanded the Confederate left. In early afternoon Federals broke through the first lines of the defenders and swept up the hill in anticipation of victory. Jackson ordered his men to the hilltop. Gen. Barnard E. Bee, seeing the force in position, shouted to his faltering South Carolina troops: "Look, men! There stands Jackson like a stone wall! Rally behind the Virginians!"

Stonewall Jackson's line held fast in hours of vicious combat. A late-afternoon counterattack by fresh Confederate regiments sent exhausted Federals in retreat toward Washington. The South had gained a victory and found a hero.

In the next three months, Jackson and his Stonewall Brigade lay quietly encamped near Centreville. Promotion to major general (retroactive to August 7) came with orders in November for Jackson to take command of the defenses of the Shenandoah Valley. He established his headquarters at Winchester, organized his small force, and obtained the use of Gen. W. W. Loring's small Army of the Northwest. On New Year's Day, 1862, Jackson embarked on an expedition to clear Federals from nearby railroad stations and Potomac River crossings. Owing primarily to sleet storms and wretchedly cold weather, the ensuing Romney campaign achieved little but underscored Jackson's always-present determination to strike the enemy.

Jackson returned with his men to Winchester after ordering Loring's troops to remain in the field at Romney. Loring complained to the War Department. Secretary of War Judah P. Benjamin ordered Jackson to recall Loring. Jackson did so and then submitted his resignation from the army because of what he regarded as unwarranted interference with his authority. Governor John Letcher and other friends succeeded in persuading Jackson to remain in command. Secretary Benjamin yielded, and Loring was transferred elsewhere.

This affair demonstrated that like all mortals of unswerving purpose, Jackson was convinced of his own infallible judgment. His greatest achievement was the 1862 Shenandoah Valley campaign. That spring, Jackson's responsibilities were twofold: to block any Union advance into the valley, and to prevent Federals there and at Fredericksburg from reinforcing George B. McClellan's army moving on Richmond. When Jackson began his offensive, a Federal officer later commented, the Confederate general "began that succession of movements which ended in the complete derangement of the Union plans in Virginia."

Rebuffed at Kernstown on March 23, Jackson retired up the valley. He appeared suddenly at McDowell on May 8 and sent a Federal force in retreat. Then his "foot cavalry" marched rapidly northward down the valley. On May 23, Jackson overpowered the Federal garrison at Front Royal, drove the main Federal army from Winchester two days later, and then fell back when three Federal armies totaling 64,000 soldiers began converging on Jackson's 17,000 Confederates. On June 8 and 9, Jackson inflicted defeats on his pursuers at Cross Keys and Port Republic. He had thwarted every Union effort made against him. He did so through a combination of hard marches, knowledge of terrain, unexpected tactics, singleness of purpose, heavy attacks concentrated at one point, and self-confidence arising from the belief that God was on his side.

Jackson shifted his army to Richmond to assist Robert E. Lee in the counterattack against McClellan. "Old Jack's" role in the Seven Days' Battle was critical and became controversial. He failed to make his expected June 26 arrival at Mechanicsville and the battle that exploded there; he was also late the next day in reaching the field at Gaines' Mill. On June 30, whether from fatigue or lack of directives from Lee, Jackson remained inactive at White Oak Swamp while conflict raged a few miles away at Frayser's Farm. It was a less-than-sterling performance by the general who had brilliantly whipped Union armies in the Shenandoah Valley.

On August 9, at Cedar Mountain, Jackson defeated the vanguard of Gen. John Pope's army. Later that month, Jackson executed the flank movement for which he became both feared and famed. He swung his men almost sixty miles around Pope's right, captured the main Federal supply depot in the rear of Pope's army, launched an attack of his own at Groveton, and then held off Pope's army at Second Manassas until Lee's forces arrived and sent the Union forces reeling in defeat. In Lee's Maryland campaign the following month, Jackson's troops overwhelmed the large Federal garrison at Harper's Ferry before rejoining Lee's army for the Battle of Sharpsburg. Jackson successfully withstood heavy Federal assaults throughout that morning and gave affirmation to the nickname "Stonewall."

Reorganization of the Army of Northern Virginia came in the autumn. On October 10, 1862, Jackson was appointed lieutenant general and placed in command of half of Lee's forces. Jackson's forces repulsed with comparative ease a major Federal assault at the December Battle of Fredericksburg. Four months of inactivity followed, in which Jackson oversaw the preparation of his 1862 battle reports, worked hard at enkindling a deeper religious spirit in his soldiers, and knew genuine happiness when Anna Jackson visited her husband with the five-month-old daughter he had not seen.

Jackson was returning through thick woods to his own lines when Confederates mistook him and his staff for Union cavalry and opened fire.

Spring 1863 brought a new advance from the Federal army. In the tangled confusion of the Virginia Wilderness, Jackson performed his most spectacular flanking movement. A twelve-mile circuitous march brought Jackson and 28,000 men opposite Gen. Joseph Hooker's unprotected right. Late in the afternoon of May 2, Jackson unleashed his divisions in an attack that drove routed Federals some two miles before darkness brought the battle to a standstill. Jackson was anxious to continue pressing forward. For the only time in the Civil War, he rode out to make a personal reconnaissance of the enemy's position. He was returning through thick woods to his own lines when Confederates mistook the general and his staff for Union cavalry and opened fire.

Three bullets struck Jackson. One shattered the bone in his left arm below the shoulder. Following amputation of the limb, Jackson was taken to the railhead at Guiney's Station for possible transfer to a Richmond hospital. Pneumonia rapidly developed. Jackson had always expressed a desire to die on the Sabbath. Around 3:15 on Sunday afternoon, May 10, 1863, he passed away quietly after saying: "Let us cross over the river and rest under the shade of the trees."

The general is buried beneath his statue, the centerpiece in Stonewall Jackson Cemetery, Lexington, Virginia.

BIBLIOGRAPHY

Chambers, Lenoir. *Stonewall Jackson.* 2 vols. New York, 1959.

Henderson, G. F. R. *Stonewall Jackson and the American Civil War.* 2 vols. London, 1898.

Jackson, Mary Anna. *Memoirs of "Stonewall" Jackson, by His Widow.* New York, 1892. Reprint, Dayton, Ohio, 1976.

Robertson, James I., Jr. *The Stonewall Brigade.* Baton Rouge, La., 1963.

Vandiver, Frank E. *Mighty Stonewall.* New York, 1957. Reprint, Texas A & M University Military History Series, no. 9. College Station, Tex., 1988.

JONES, JOHN PAUL

John Paul Jones (1747–1792), American naval hero of the War of Independence, whose indomitable courage and brilliant seamanship won him the title of father of the U.S. Navy.

Jones was born John Paul, son of a gardener in Scotland, where he inherited the doggedness and cavalier attitude that were to serve him well at sea. After briefly attending school in the local parish, he was apprenticed to a shipowner out of Whitehaven, England. His first voyage, at the age of thirteen, was to Virginia, where his brother had established a tailoring business. In Virginia, Jones stayed with his brother for a short period, but eager to continue at sea, soon found a berth aboard a slaver. Taking jobs where he could find them, by the age of nineteen he had advanced to the rank of first mate.

John Paul Jones. (National Archives/ engraving by J. M. Moreau, Jr.)

Jones received his first command at the age of twenty-one, of a small merchant vessel, the *John,* in which he made several voyages to Tobago. On one such voyage he flogged the ship's carpenter for neglect of duty; several weeks later, after a bout of malaria, the man died while on board another ship. Jones was charged with murder and briefly imprisoned. Although he subsequently proved his innocence, he earned a reputation as a harsh master.

On a later command in 1773, Jones killed the ringleader of a mutiny. According to Jones, the man had rushed onto his sword. Advised by his friends to leave Tobago because of the hostility of the witnesses in the case, Jones traveled incognito to Virginia. At this time he attached "Jones" to his name. He passed the next two years in quiet obscurity, running the estates of a dead brother in Virginia.

The impending War of Independence was an opportunity for the young seaman to show his mettle. He traveled to Philadelphia and made the acquaintance of a number of eminent congressmen, who were impressed with this small, intense Scotsman. In 1775 he received his first commission as a lieutenant on the frigate *Alfred* the first ship to fly the continental flag. The following year he was given command of the *Providence,* with overall command of a small fleet and promotion to the rank of captain soon following. He quickly established an unrivaled reputation for skill and strategy, achieving several resounding victories for the fledgling U.S. Navy. However, his common background rankled the naval establishment and, despite his obvious talent, Congress ranked him low on the captains' list. However, in clear deference to his ability, he was given command of the *Ranger,* and ordered to head for France.

The *Ranger* itself was a rather insubstantial ship when compared to the British man-o'-wars. Nevertheless Jones was determined to inflict serious punishment on the enemy in its own waters. His first attack at Whitehaven, a port he knew well from his youth, was not the total success he had sought. The most notable event of his first cruise was the capture of the *Drake,* the first British naval ship captured by the Continental navy. After twenty-eight days Jones returned triumphantly to port in Brest. The British for their part were rightly alarmed by the presence of an obviously formidable raider near their own territory. Jones was dubbed a renegade Scot pirate and a price was offered for his capture.

"Sir, I have not yet begun to fight!"

Jones was eager to continue his adventures, hoping that after his early successes he would be given command of a more significant ship. What he received was an old and slow refitted merchantman, which he named the *Bonhomme Richard.* After several false starts, he set sail accompanied by a number of other smaller ships all under his command. Jones's squadron had captured seventeen small vessels around the coast of Great Britain when, in September 1779, they encountered the Baltic trade fleet of forty-two vessels being escorted by two British ships of war, the small *Countess of Scarborough* and the forty-four-gun *Serapis.* The *Scarborough* soon surrendered, leaving the *Richard* engaged in a tremendous battle with the *Serapis,* which carried more than twice its firepower. Hopelessly outclassed, Jones saw his only hope of victory in close quarters action. He skillfully maneuvered the *Richard* alongside the *Serapis* and lashed the two ships together. For hours the two crews savaged each other's vessel. The *Richard* was set on fire and began taking on water so badly that a British officer asked Jones if he would surrender, to which he made the famous retort "Sir, I have not yet begun to fight!" After some three hours of desperate skirmishing, the *Serapis* struck its colors. The unlikely victory of the *Richard* was credited wholly to Jones's valor and skill. The *Richard* sank the following day, its colors still flying.

Returning to Paris, Jones was feted as a national hero. He enjoyed his time ashore, plunging into French society wholeheartedly. This harsh seafarer even composed poetry for his lady friends, of whom there were many. Eventually, Jones set sail for America in 1781. There too he was paraded and lauded for his heroic efforts, yet still his rank was not raised, due to objections by other senior officers. By way of compensation, Jones was given command of the soon-to-be-completed ship of the line *America,* which conferred on him the *de facto* rank of rear admiral. However, before he took command, the vessel was given to the French government as a gift.

Jones marked his time, writing on naval warfare and observing the maneuvers of the French fleet. He traveled to Europe for a few years where he negotiated the return of the booty he had captured from Britain. Returning to America in 1787, he was awarded a gold medal by Congress for his valor and service, but still had no place in an America at peace. In 1788 he received an offer to command a fleet for the Russian navy against the Turks, which he accepted, hoping to keep his hand in for future service in America. However, from the first his position was untenable. The other Russian officers were not happy to have this adventurer in their midst, and despite some notable battles his successes were credited to others. Then a scurrilous rumor was circulated that he had violated a young girl, and he unceremoniously returned to France in 1789. His disappointment in Russia affected his health badly. He took up comfortable lodgings in Paris, keeping company with a few close friends, his heroic days over. In 1792 the U.S. government appointed him commissioner to Algiers, but before the letter detailing the appointment reached him, he died, prematurely aged by his years at sea.

He was buried in a lead coffin, filled with alcohol and ready for shipping, in the hope that he would be accorded a hero's burial in the United States. However, over the years the cemetery was closed and forgotten, Only in 1905, after an intense search, was the coffin discovered, opened, and Jones's body positively identified. It was taken for its final interment at the U.S. Naval Academy in Annapolis, Maryland.

BIBLIOGRAPHY

L. Lorenz, *John Paul Jones,* 1969.
Morison and Eliot, *John Paul Jones,* 1964.

KEARNY, STEPHEN WATTS

U.S. Army General Stephen Watts Kearny (1794–1848) played a pivotal role in the American conquest of New Mexico and California during the United States–Mexican War. Born in Newark, New Jersey, Kearny began his thirty-five-year military career in the War of 1812 where he exhibited gallantry in action and was later wounded and captured.

At the beginning of the United States–Mexican War in 1846, Colonel Kearny received orders to take possession of California and New Mexico. Leaving Fort Leavenworth, Kansas, in June 1846, Kearny's 1,600 troops, dubbed the "Army of the West," reached Santa Fe on August 18. New Mexico officials surrendered the capital without bloodshed. After establishing a civil government, Brigadier General Kearny (he had been promoted during his overland expedition) left Santa Fe on September 25 for California. A few days into the journey, Kearny received word that California had been conquered by Commodore Robert F. Stockton. Kearny returned 200 of his dragoons to Santa Fe to assist in the suppression of Indian raids. With only 120 men, Kearny continued the march to California.

On December 6, Kearny reached the village of San Pasqual, where he discovered that California remained unconquered. Californios (native-born Californians of Hispanic descent) under Andrés Pico attacked Kearny's column, and American casualties totaled one-third of his command. A few days later, sailors and marines from San Diego lifted the siege. Kearny then joined Stockton to march on Los Angeles. On January 8 and 9, 1847, Kearny and Stockton defeated the Californios at San Gabriel and La Mesa. These victories, combined with Lieutenant Colonel John Charles Frémont's victory over another Californio command on January 13, terminated Mexican armed resistance to the American takeover of California.

With the end of the war, Kearny and Frémont fought over who would lead the American occupation. After Frémont proclaimed himself the civil governor of California, Kearny arrested him and returned with him to Fort Leavenworth. Although the military court and President James K. Polk supported Kearny in the dispute, he became the enemy of Missouri's U.S. Senator Thomas Hart Benton, Frémont's father-in-law. In the spring of 1848, Kearny returned to active service. He spent three months in Mexico, first as military governor of Veracruz and later in a similar position in Mexico City. While in Mexico, he probably contracted yellow fever. Returning to the United States, Kearny received a brevet promotion to major general. He died on October 31, 1848, near St. Louis on the estate of Major Meriwether Lewis Clark.

BIBLIOGRAPHY

Clarke, Dwight L. *Stephen Watts Kearny: Soldier of the West.* Norman, Okla., 1961.

Nevins, Allan. *Frémont: The West's Greatest Adventurer.* Vol. 1. New York, 1928.

KNOX, HENRY

Henry Knox was born in Boston on July 25, 1750. He commanded the artillery in the Continental Army. He served as first Secretary of War, both under the Continental Congress and in the cabinet of President George Washington. His early years were spent in bookstore management in Boston. He supported his mother and earned a living for himself while he read virtually everything written on the subject of artillery design, tactics, and use. When fighting began, he offered his services to General George Washington at Cambridge. He was named Colonel and put in charge of the artillery, although at that time there was little artillery in the American camp.

Knox commanded the unit that moved the heavy guns from captured Fort Ticonderoga to Boston. These guns, mounted on Dorchester Heights, helped drive the British out of the city in March 1776. Discovering that he could move big guns overland about as rapidly as troops on the march would move, he helped form a more mobile field artillery service than had been thought possible. Knox made the artillery a major arm of the American forces. He organized the Springfield Arsenal in Massachusetts as an artillery supply center; he planned the gun positions at West Point; and he organized a training school for artillery officers which was part of the beginnings of the U.S. Military Academy.

After the Revolutionary War, Knox served as Secretary of War, in charge of both army and navy affairs, for the Congress. Named to head the War Department in the newly organized Federal government under President Washington, he held that post from 1789 to 1795. Knox was an extremely optimistic man, cheerful under the worst conditions. He was an active, driving officer in spite of his great size (he weighed close to three

Henry Knox. (National Archives/painting by Gilbert Stuart)

hundred pounds) and did work around the clock with little or no sleep during the dangerous years of the Revolution. Knox died in 1806.

LEE, ROBERT EDWARD

Robert Edward Lee, (1807–1870), general of the Confederate army in the American Civil War. Best known for his role as an almost–legendary Civil War general, Lee is one of the few military geniuses who gained fame mainly through his actions in defeat. He was born in Westmoreland County, Virginia, the son of a famous American Revolution cavalry officer, Henry "Lighthorse Harry" Lee. Lee was raised as a Southern gentleman, albeit in near poverty because his father had squandered his and both his wives' family fortunes, even spending some time in prison because of his debts. After his father's death when he was only eleven, Lee took over family responsibility, caring for his mother and sisters. He was a pious and honest man, never smoked or drank and was friendly and even-tempered, his private life untouched by any hint of scandal.

At the age of eighteen Lee entered West Point, where he graduated second in his class, never having received a single demerit. He entered the army's prestigious Corps of Engineers and distinguished himself through his service in Mexico in 1846. Meanwhile, in 1831 Lee had married Mary Anne Randolph Custis, the daughter of George Washington's adopted son. The couple had seven children; their three sons all later served as Confederate soldiers. In 1857 Mary's father died, and the Lee family took up residence at her family estate in Arlington, Virginia.

After the Mexican War, Lee took charge of the construction of Fort Carroll in Baltimore Harbor. Following this assignment, Lee became superintendent of West Point in 1852. He soon tired of academic life and, in 1855, transferred to the Second Cavalry Division, serving in Missouri, Kansas, and Texas, where the cavalry protected settlers from roving bands of Indians.

Home on leave in Arlington in 1859, Lee was appointed to lead the troops that put down abolitionist John Brown's raid on Harper's Ferry. He then went back to Texas, remaining until February 1861. On his return to Arlington, Lee realized that the growing tension between North and South meant that he would have to decide whether he owed greater loyalty to his country or to his native state. Lee disapproved of slavery and had freed his own slaves years before the war. He was deeply distressed by the thought of the dissolution of the Union, but nonetheless decided that his primary duty lay in loyalty to his home state. Therefore in April 1861, when Lee was offered field command of the United States Army, he declined the position and resigned his commission in the army. He intended to remain a private citizen and wrote to his brother that, "Save in defense of my native state, I have no desire ever again to draw my sword." Soon after the governor of Virginia offered him command of that state's army, which he accepted.

Robert E. Lee. (National Archives)

In the field, Lee eschewed the privileges generally taken by officers. Not wanting to displace civilians from their homes, he lived in a tent and kept a minimum of aides-de-camp and servants. Lee's first field test came in June 1862 when, after he took over command from the wounded General A. E. Johnston, the army of Northern Virginia forced General George B. McClellan's Union troops to withdraw from their siege of Richmond. In August of the same year Lee, aided by Generals Thomas J. "Stonewall" Jackson and James Longstreet, faced the Union's General John Pope at Second Bull Run. Lee devised a bold plan for his greatly outnumbered troops, dividing the army and sending Jackson, with three divisions, around Pope's army to a point twenty-four miles behind the line of battle. Lee's daring strategy gained him his first decisive field victory.

Lee then moved his troops into Maryland and attempted to gain Marylanders' support for the South; the response was less enthusiastic than he had hoped. In a further stroke of bad luck, Union soldiers found a copy of Lee's orders for the invasion of Maryland, giving McClellan a valuable edge in the upcoming confrontation at Antietam (Sharpsburg). Despite that setback, Lee swiftly and elegantly maneuvered his troops in what historians call his most brilliant performance ever. The Antietam campaign, which included "the bloodiest single day of the war," on which over twenty-three thousand soldiers were killed and wounded and over twenty-seven hundred were missing (on both sides), could have resulted in the destruction of the Confederate army and the end of the war. But Lee's brilliance, coupled with McClellan's indecisiveness, turned what could have been annihilation into a mere defeat, with Lee withdrawing to Virginia.

Lee is one of the few military geniuses who gained fame mainly through his actions in defeat.

His next two engagements, against General Ambrose E. Burnside at Fredericksburg in November and at Chancellorsville in May 1863, brought victories to the South. Lee then decided to invade the North and drove his troops up the Shenandoah Valley, through Maryland and into Pennsylvania, where his next major battle took place at Gettysburg in July 1863. Bad judgment and delays by Lee's subordinate officers in carrying out his orders cost him severely. The end of the first day's fighting saw a decided Confederate victory, with Union troops retreating in disarray and panic. It was here that the Confederacy could have won the battle and, possibly, the war. Lee saw that the Union troops were beaten and tired and he knew that they could not withstand another assault. He also understood that whoever controlled the hills would command the battle. Knowing this, he told General Richard Ewell to "take that hill if at all practicable," but Ewell had made the fateful decision to wait until morning, giving the Union army all night to receive reinforcements and build barricades. On the second day of the battle Lee tried to crack the Union flanks. By then, however, they were well anchored and fortified and the assaults failed. On the third and final day Lee, feeling that he had no alternative, took a big gamble, sending 15,000 men in a charge, (Pickett's Charge) against the Union center. The men broke through briefly but, to Lee's horror, the surviving gray troops soon came wearily down the hill and Lee conceded, "this is all my fault." The Southern forces retreated to Virginia to regroup, expecting a counterattack, which never came. Casualties at Gettysburg numbered more than one third of the Virginia army's troops. Lee accepted blame for the defeat and offered his resignation, which was refused.

Lee's troops were severely lacking in supplies and rations throughout the rest of 1863 and early 1864 but resumed fighting in May 1864, sparring with General Ulysses S. Grant in the battle of the Wilderness and forcing the Union troops to a standstill. The Petersburg campaign began in June and dragged on for months, wearing down the poorly fed and badly equipped Confederate troops. In February 1865, Lee became general-in-chief of all Confederate armies, by then an almost meaningless title. In April, as Federal troops closed in, Lee ordered the evacuation of Petersburg and Richmond. He remained in retreat until his surrender to Grant at Appomattox Court House.

Lee had lost his United States citizenship because he had served as a Confederate officer and, after the war, was indicted for treason, but the case was allowed to lapse. Lee urged his troops and all Southerners to accept the Union victory and help to rebuild their country. He applied for the restoration of his citizenship and swore a loyalty oath before a notary, but by accident his citizenship was not restored until an act of Congress in 1975 corrected the oversight.

After the war Lee accepted the presidency of Washington College (later renamed Washington and Lee University) in Lexington, Virginia. He rebuilt and revitalized the war-ravaged college and after his death on October 12, 1870, was buried in the university chapel.

BIBLIOGRAPHY

B. Davis, *Gray Fox: Robert E. Lee and the Civil War,* 1956.

P. Earle, *Robert E. Lee,* 1973.

F. Lee, *General Lee,* 1961.

R. Wheeler, *Lee's Terrible Swift Sword,* 1992.

MACARTHUR, DOUGLAS

Douglas MacArthur, (1880–1964), U.S. military leader, commander of the Allied Pacific Forces during World War II and the U.S. Army during the Korean War. His father, who had been awarded the Congressional Medal of Honor for exceptional bravery during the Civil War, constantly reminded his son that he received the award for an assault he led without having received an order to do so, and encouraged his son to take similar initiatives. MacArthur's mother saw her two older sons die prematurely, perhaps explaining the curious bond she maintained with MacArthur until her death. She even

Douglas MacArthur, 1944, at Leyte Island. (National Archives)

followed him to West Point Military Academy, keeping a hotel room near the campus to support her son's diligence and to remove any external distractions, notably women, that might interfere with his progress. His father, Arthur, was a haughty and often flamboyant commander who served in such prestigious military positions as military attaché to China and commander of the Philippines. Douglas MacArthur excelled at West Point, finishing with a record average. He graduated with the rank of second lieutenant and chose to serve in the Philippines to be close to his father.

He found the Philippines alluring and befriended many prominent local leaders, including Manuel Quezon, later first president of that country. On the family's return to the United States, Douglas MacArthur studied engineering. He distinguished himself in the Spanish-American War for several daring assignments. In one, according to his own account, he single-handedly killed seven enemy gunmen. He was startled to discover that his bravery would not be rewarded since there was no verification of his feat and that the story, if true, was dismissed as an "error in judgment." He later served as military adviser to President Theodore Roosevelt.

During World War I MacArthur reached the rank of colonel and got the opportunity to command the Rainbow Division, formed, at his instigation, of National Guardsmen. In his two years in Europe he was the recipient of numerous medals and decorations. His troops fought in eight major battles. Yet despite his acknowledged bravery, MacArthur was regarded as an eccentric. He refused to wear a gas mask or helmet and carried no weapon but his riding crop. After a mission, he returned to base one night leading a high-ranking German officer with his crop.

After returning to America MacArthur was appointed superintendent of West Point, but was soon removed. Officially, his dismissal was attributed to the radical changes he had made in that institution, but he always ascribed his removal to the mutual distrust between himself and the commander of the army, General John J. Pershing. MacArthur was returned to the Philippines with the rank of major general.

In 1930 he was appointed army chief of staff. The depression-era posting saw enormous cuts in the military budget, including a cut in military pensions. Disgruntled veterans marched on Washington but were dispersed with considerable violence by MacArthur. Presidential candidate Franklin Delano Roosevelt responded to the attack on unarmed veterans by calling MacArthur, "one of the most dangerous men in the country."

Rather than settle for a lesser post, MacArthur accepted the position of military adviser to his old friend Quezon, soon to be president of an independent Commonwealth of the Philippines.

In return for his encouraging Quezon to assert full independence for the Philippines, MacArthur was appointed field marshal of the Philippine army, a force whose creation had been the result of his own devoted efforts in the face of official American opposition. Roosevelt came to detest MacArthur who, in turn, took every opportunity to deride the president. In 1937, two years before his tour of duty in the Philippines was to end, MacArthur was finally convinced to retire from active service. He remained in the Philippines at the request of President Quezon, who continued to employ him as adviser, but the relationship between the two men degenerated and Quezon sought unsuccessfully to have MacArthur replaced by his rival and former aide, General Dwight D. Eisenhower. MacArthur was, however, still recognized as an authority on East Asia; with the rising threat of Japan to the region, Roosevelt requested MacArthur to remain in Manila.

Franklin Delano Roosevelt called MacArthur, "one of the most dangerous men in the country."

Following the Japanese occupation of French ports in Indochina, the new chief of staff, General George C. Marshall, persuaded Roosevelt to appoint MacArthur supreme commander of the armed forces in the Far East. MacArthur encouraged the American administration to abandon its original plan to defend only Manila and Subic Bay in favor of a comprehensive defense policy for the entire archipelago. The islands soon had the largest force of fighter planes outside the United States. When the Japanese invaded the Philippines in 1942, the local army crumbled in just two days. MacArthur evacuated Manila and moved his troops to the Bataan Peninsula and Corregidor Island. He defended the area for five months until, upon realizing that the Americans had chosen to abandon the front, he too made plans to retreat. His own press releases from the embattled island had already assured his entry into the pantheon of American heroes. After accepting a $500,000 gift from Quezon as a token of their friendship. MacArthur led his family and troops to Mindanao, where a plane took them to Australia. Arriving in Darwin, he issued his famous statement, "I shall return!"

Despite his growing fame among the masses, MacArthur's popularity waned in the administration. It was said that some would have preferred, "to see MacArthur lose a battle than America win the war." He differed with the administration over wartime priorities and questioned the emphasis placed on the European rather than the Pacific front, claiming that life under the Nazis would be "tolerable; after all, the Germans are a civilized people."

Shortly before the Allied assault on Japan, MacArthur was appointed general of the army, empowered to lead the ground assault on Japan. To his dismay, this opportunity was "stolen" from him after the nuclear attacks on Hiroshima and Nagasaki. He did, however, conclude the armistice treaty with Japan and served as military governor of the country, overseeing its transformation into a democratic society. He showed great respect for Emperor Hirohito, and rejected all attempts to try him as a war criminal. His new constitution for Japan, drawn up in just six days, rejected militarism and redefined the role of the emperor. Although he was their conqueror, MacArthur won the esteem of the local population. From Japan MacArthur ran an unsuccessful bid for the Republican presidential nomination in 1948, but was defeated in the first two primaries and abandoned the race.

The Korean War in 1950 returned MacArthur to the forefront of American life. It was MacArthur who encouraged President Harry S. Truman to place American troops in combat and who planned the successful invasion of the port of Inchon, behind enemy lines. MacArthur was skeptical of the Chinese threat to enter the war, and when three hundred thousand Chinese troops swept down against American advances, he attributed it to faulty intelligence and refused to assume responsibility. MacArthur's support of an invasion of Communist China ran contrary to the plans of the American administration. His threat to disobey orders and carry out his plan forced Truman to recall him to the United States. It was there he made his last important public appearance, a farewell address to Congress interrupted by thirty ovations.

Three years before his death he made a last visit to the Philippines as the guest of honor at Independence Day celebrations.

BIBLIOGRAPHY

D. MacArthur, *Reminiscences,* 1964.
W. Manchester, *American Caesar,* 1978.
M. Schaller, *Douglas MacArthur,* 1990

MARSHALL, GEORGE CATLETT

George Catlett Marshall, (1880–1959), U.S. general and statesman. He was born in Uniontown, Pennsylvania, to a family of Virginia settlers; by the time Marshall entered Virginia Military Institute in 1897, his father, a coal merchant, had lost most of his money. He graduated in 1901 and was commissioned a second lieutenant in the cavalry.

After graduation, Marshall was sent to the Philippines for a year and a half. Early in his military career,

George Catlett Marshall. (Library of Congress/Corbis)

he developed the habit of rigid self-discipline, and his attitude toward command soon won him the respect both of his soldiers and of civilians. His quiet self-confidence brought out the best in those under his command.

Marshall attended school at Fort Leavenworth, Kansas, at that time the center of the army's advanced educational program, and graduated first in his class. He then served there as an instructor from 1908 to 1910. In 1913 Marshall was sent back to the Philippines, where he remained until being called, in 1916, to serve in San Francisco and on Governor's Island in New York Harbor. During World War I Marshall was sent to France as the chief of operations. From 1919 to 1924 he was General John Pershing's senior aide, and then assistant commandant in charge of instruction at the infantry school.

Pershing felt that Marshall had not been promoted quickly enough and said of him, "He is the best goddamned officer in the U.S. Army."

Although Marshall was by then a lieutenant colonel, Pershing felt that he had not been promoted quickly enough and said of him, "He is the best goddamned officer in the U.S. Army." In 1933 Marshall was promoted to full colonel. He was made the senior instructor of the Illinois National Guard and served as a brigade commander in Vancouver Barracks for two years.

In 1938, Marshall moved to Washington and served as chief of war plans and then deputy chief of staff. President Franklin D. Roosevelt then nominated him as the head of the army and on September 1, 1939, the day the war began in Europe, Marshall took full command, a position he held for six years. Under Marshall's command, the army grew from two hundred thousand to almost eight and a half million. When President Harry S. Truman, considering an alternative to dropping the atomic bomb, was weighing the possibility of a blockade coupled with heavy bombing of Japan, Marshall pointed out that similar action in Germany had not brought about an end to the war in Europe.

Marshall attended all the great conferences and was deeply involved in directing Allied strategy during the invasion of Europe. Paying tribute to his efforts in planning, training, and supplying the Allied troops, Britain's Winston Churchill said, "General Marshall was the true organizer of victory."

Marshall resigned as chief of staff on November 21, 1945, and Truman appointed him ambassador to China, where he served from 1945 to 1947. Despite his lack of success in mediating the Chinese civil war, he had proved himself an able statesman and was appointed secretary of state in January 1947. In a speech delivered at Harvard in June of that year he outlined what came to be known as the Marshall Plan for the economic recovery of Europe, based on his belief that Russia was taking advantage of Europe's economic problems to control the area. During this period, representing the United States, he worked diligently in the United Nations and spent time in South America developing greater cooperation between Latin American countries and the United States. Marshall resigned as secretary of state in 1949 due to ill health.

Unwilling to let Marshall retire, Truman appointed him secretary of defense in 1950, when Marshall was almost seventy. This position gave Marshall the freedom to criticize General Douglas MacArthur's statements and actions. He opposed MacArthur in controversy between Truman and MacArthur.

The Korean War had begun. Marshall again enlarged the United States army and helped to develop the North Atlantic Treaty Organization (NATO). As secretary of defense, Marshall strove to stop the expansion of the Korean conflict. While he obviously favored a strong America, he still sought peaceful solutions in Asia. In December of 1953 he was awarded the Nobel Peace Prize, after which he returned to private life.

In recognition of his service to the American people, the George C. Marshall Library was dedicated in Lexington, Virginia, in 1964, five years after his death. President Lyndon B. Johnson and former president Dwight D. Eisenhower both spoke at the dedication ceremony.

BIBLIOGRAPHY

G. Catlett, *George C. Marshall,* 1982.

R. H. Terrell, *George C. Marshall,* 1966.

MC CLELLAN, GEORGE BRINTON

George B. McClellan was born on December 3, 1826 in Philadelphia, Pennsylvania. During 1861 and 1862, McClellan was the most important general in the Union Army. Trained at West Point, he had served as an engineer officer after his graduation in 1846 and was considered one of the Army's most promising officers. He was sent to Europe to study the tactics and techniques of foreign armies; he designed the basic cavalry saddle (the McClellan saddle is still used for horseback riding); and he had three years of civilian railroad experience behind him when the Civil War broke out.

McClellan headed a Union force that won victories in the West Virginia mountains in 1861. After the Confederate victory at the first battle of Bull Run, he was called to Washington and placed in command of the army of the Potomac. "Little Mac," as he was called, was a popular and efficient trainer of troops but he was cautious to the point of over-caution in committing them to battle. He soon became a thorn in Lincoln's side because of his slowness in bringing on battle with the Confederates. He commanded during the Peninsular Campaign which almost captured Richmond. Replaced by a less competent general, McClellan was recalled to command after the second battle of Bull Run and led the Union forces at Antietam, a victory that turned back R. E. Lee's first invasion of the North. Lincoln retired McClellan again for not moving against Lee's forces more rapidly after Antietam.

In 1864, he ran for President as a Democrat but was thoroughly defeated. He had a successful career in railroading after the war. He served as governor of New Jersey for three years from 1878 to 1881. Although overshadowed by the successes of Grant and Sherman later in the war, McClellan was listed by General Lee as the best Union commander to face him. McClellan died in 1885.

George McClellan. (National Archives)

MILES, NELSON APPLETON

Civil War hero and captor of Chief Joseph and Geronimo, Nelson Appleton Miles (1839–1925) was the last commanding general of the United States Army. Miles was born in the rural township of Westminster, Massachusetts. In October 1861, he raised a company of volunteers and joined the Union Army of the Potomac. He participated in every subsequent major battle on the eastern front except the second battle of Manassas and Gettysburg. Wounded four times, he won a series of promotions culminating in a brevet major generalship. With the collapse of the Confederacy, Miles was assigned command of the Military District of Fort Monroe, Virginia, where he was responsible for holding ex-Confederate President Jefferson Davis prisoner. In 1866, Miles was promoted to full colonel in the Fortieth Infantry Regiment; from late February 1867 through March 1869, he was engaged in Reconstruction duties in North Carolina.

> *Miles rejected tribal values and believed that Indians were inferior to "civilized" societies.*

After securing a transfer to the Fifth Infantry, Miles joined his new regiment in Kansas. In August 1874, he led a column south from Fort Dodge during the Red River War. A determined campaigner, Miles won a minor skirmish at Tule Canyon, Texas, and kept troops in the field through most of the winter. After the Battle of Little Bighorn, he and his regiment established the Tongue River Cantonment (later Fort Keogh) in Montana in the fall of 1876. Launching several campaigns that winter, his victories against Sitting Bull's coalition at Cedar Creek (from October 19 to 20, 1876), Crazy Horse and the Oglalas and Cheyennes at Wolf Mountains (January 8, 1877), and Lame Deer's Minneconjous at Muddy Creek (May 7, 1877) were instrumental in breaking the military power of the Northern Plains tribes. From the Tongue River Cantonment, Miles also joined the chase against Chief Joseph and caught the Nez Percés just short of the Canadian border in the Bear Paw Mountains. The bluecoats' initial assault having failed, Miles settled in for a siege; Chief Joseph and most of his followers surrendered in early October

Nelson Appleton Miles. (Medford Historical Society/Corbis)

1877. Miles also assisted in the following year's Bannock campaigns.

In 1881, Miles was appointed brigadier general. Following commands of the Departments of the Columbia and the Missouri, he was transferred in 1886 to the Department of Arizona, where he directed the campaigns resulting in Geronimo's surrender. After a two-year stint as head of the Division of the Pacific, Miles was awarded his second star and command of the Division of the Missouri in 1890. Directing military operations during the Ghost Dance outbreak, Miles angered civilian and military superiors by pressing for strong disciplinary action against Colonel James W. Forsyth, who had commanded troops at Wounded Knee.

In 1892, Miles received the Medal of Honor for his gallantry at the Battle of Chancellorsville during the Civil War. In October 1895, he was named commanding general of the United States Army. During the Spanish-American War, he led the invasion of Puerto Rico. Although his opposition to substantive army reforms and his propensity to speak too freely with the press antagonized Presidents William McKinley and Theodore Roosevelt, Miles was appointed lieutenant general in June 1900. He retired from the army at the age of sixty-four. In 1904, he unsuccessfully sought the Democratic presidential nomination.

Although Miles lacked a formal military education, he was a talented, brave combat leader whose tenacious pursuits made him one of the nation's finest Indian fighters. Ambitious, jealous of the success of others, and egotistical enough to publish two autobiographies and a booklength account of his 1897 military tour of Europe, he had many conflicts with civilian superiors and fellow officers. Miles criticized the corruption within the Bureau of Indian Affairs and supported that agency's transfer back to the War Department. He rejected tribal values and believed that Indians were inferior to "civilized" societies.

Miles married Mary Hoyt Sherman, niece of Senator John Sherman and General William Tecumseh Sherman, in 1878. While escorting his grandchildren to the circus, he died in Washington, D.C., of a heart attack and was buried at Arlington National Cemetery.

BIBLIOGRAPHY

Personal Recollections and Observations of General Nelson A. Miles. 2 vols. 1896. Reprint. Lincoln, Nebr., 1992.

Utley, Robert M. "Nelson A. Miles." In *Soldiers West: Biographies from the Military Frontier.* Edited by Paul Andrew Hutton. Lincoln, Nebr., 1987.

Wooster, Robert. *Nelson A. Miles and the Twilight of the Frontier Army.* Lincoln, Nebr., 1993.

MITCHELL, WILLIAM

"Billy" Mitchell, the spokesman for American air power in the years following World War I, was born in France in 1879 while his parents were living there temporarily. He was raised in the family home at Milwaukee. When the Spanish-American War broke out, he was a college student at George Washington University in Washington, D.C. He left college to join the Army as a private. He was assigned to the Signal Corps, served in Cuba and in the Philippines, and decided to stay in the Army when he was offered a regular commission as 2d Lieutenant in 1901.

In the Signal Corps, Mitchell was part of the group that first experimented with airplanes. He worked with all sorts of equipment, and was the youngest officer assigned to the General Staff in 1912. When World War I broke out in Europe, Mitchell studied reports of aerial combat and decided that the United States ought to have a strong air arm. He was allowed to take pilot training and for a brief time he commanded the Signal Corps' Aviation Section. When the United States entered World War I, Mitchell was assigned to the staff of the American Expeditionary Forces, and in that assignment he drew up plans for developing and using a powerful air arm.

Mitchell made an impressive record during World War I. He did excellent staff work, supervising training and organization of squadrons, and he was in command of strikes on German positions during the early fall of 1918. He viewed air power as capable of disrupting enemy communications and road movements, and of destroying enemy forces in the field.

Following World War I, American defense budgets were slashed. Very little money was available for aerial forces. Mitchell argued publicly that the defense budget allotted to surface ships in the Navy was unwise and he ran a series of tests in which his bombers destroyed target battleships—vessels that had been captured from the Germans. His public statements were embarrassing to the higher officers of both the Army and Navy and he was shifted from his post as Assistant Chief of the Air Service in 1925. However, he continued to criticize the commanding officers for being shortsighted and unwise. When a Navy dirigible, the *Shenandoah,* was lost in a severe storm, Mitchell once more publicly criticized higher commanders for "the incompetency, criminal negligence, and almost treasonable administration of the national defense."

This charge led inevitably to a court-martial. Mitchell used the public trial as a means of advertising his views that aircraft should be used as offensive weapons, directed and commanded by men versed in their use. The trial ended in a verdict of guilty. Mitchell was suspended from duty for five years. He resigned from the Army to continue his propaganda campaign as a civilian. Mitchell inspired great loyalty and faith among American airmen of his time. Men whom he trained became the commanders of the U.S. air forces in World War II. In 1946, Congress authorized a posthumous Medal of Honor for Mitchell and one year later established a separate U.S. Air Force. Mitchell died in 1936.

PATTON, GEORGE SMITH

George Smith Patton, (1885–1945), U.S. general. Born in San Gabriel, California, to a family steeped in military tradition, George Patton from a very early age showed a keen interest in history; papers that he wrote in grade school clearly express his desire to gain recognition, fame, and glory through heroic acts. Academic learning did not come easily to him, but he had a good sense of humor and a great love of the military. He worked conscientiously to improve himself in order to be accepted to military school.

To prepare himself for a military career, Patton first attended the Virginia Military Academy, where he proved himself an outstanding athlete. He set the school record in the 220-yard hurdles, won the 120-yard hurdles, and placed second in the 220-yard dash. He expressed his philosophy: "By perseverance, study, and eternal desire, any man can be great." When he left the military academy, he went on to West Point, graduating in 1909, forty-sixth in a class of one hundred and three. Commissioned a second lieutenant in the cavalry, he remained deeply interested in the battles and history of the American Civil War.

While visiting wounded soldiers in a military hospital, Patton struck a soldier who was suffering from battle fatigue because he felt that the man was malingering.

Patton's first assignment was at Fort Sheridan in Illinois. In 1911 he was transferred to Fort Meyer, Washington, D.C., and was selected to compete in the fifth Olympic Games, which were held in Sweden. He was entered in the modern pentathlon, which involved shooting, swimming, fencing, cross-country steeplechase, and cross-country running, and finished fifth. This was a remarkable achievement, as he had not participated in sports competitions for over two years prior to beginning his training for the pentathlon.

In 1913 Patton was assigned to Fort Riley, Kansas, where he remained for two years. He was then transferred to Fort Bliss, Texas, and while he was there, Pancho Villa raided Columbus, New Mexico. Under General John J. Pershing, Patton became involved and remained in Mexico until February 1917. In appraising Patton, Pershing said, "Lieutenant Patton is a capable, energetic officer, and would perform the duties of a field officer of volunteers with credit to himself and the government."

With the onset of World War I, General Pershing brought Patton to France, where he served with distinction and was promoted several times. Returning to the United States in 1919, he served at Camp Meade, Maryland, and in 1920 was transferred back to Fort Meyer but this time as the commander of the cavalry. In a letter to his father, Patton wrote, "Some day I will show them. I fear that I will never be a general."

Between World War I and World War II Patton served at forts Riley and Leavenworth, both in Kansas, in Boston, and in Hawaii. His field of expertise changed from cavalry training to tanks, and he went on to prove his genius in tank warfare.

With the threat of war imminent, Patton was assigned to the Second Armored Division at Fort Benning, Georgia, promoted to divisional commander, and commanded what became the army's toughest outfit. He then took command of the First Armored Corps, a much larger unit; he and his troops were sent to fight in the North African Campaign, and he was promoted to lieutenant general. Under General Dwight Eisenhower, Patton was placed in charge of the Tank Force Troops and commanded the Seventh Army during the invasion of Sicily in 1943, capturing Palermo the following year.

Known for his quick temper and impetuosity, Patton created an incident that was to mark a reversal in his career. While visiting wounded soldiers in a military hospital, Patton struck a soldier who was suffering from battle fatigue because he felt that the man was malingering. Reprimanded by General Eisenhower, Patton was forced to make a public apology. This action delayed his promotion, and he lost his command; it was not until August 1944 that he was promoted to major general.

In March 1944 Patton assumed command of the Third Army and prepared it for the invasion of Normandy, where his brilliant sweep across the base of the Breton peninsula led to the liberation of Metz. The Germans then launched their Ardennes counteroffensive, and Patton turned his forces quickly northward against the German southern flank and helped contain the enemy. General Omar N. Bradley said later, "Patton accomplished one of the most astonishing feats of generalship of our campaign in the West."

Patton, together with his troops, caused the breakthrough in the Battle of the Bulge and went on to speed across Germany, cutting the country in half. "Old Blood and Guts," as Patton was known, proved himself to be one of the great tactical commanders of all times. However, he got himself into trouble once more, this time as military governor of Bavaria, when he made statements criticizing the "denazification" policies; it was felt he was too lenient with Nazis and was removed from his command. Patton was then assigned a lesser post and toward the end of 1945, was involved in a fatal automobile accident.

BIBLIOGRAPHY

M. Blumenson, *The Patton Papers,* 1972.

L. Farego, *The Last Days of Patton,* 1981.

P. B. Williamson, *Patton's Principles,* 1984.

PERRY, MATTHEW CALBRAITH

Matthew Calbraith Perry was known to his men as "Old Bruin," and in many respects he acted as the first official representative of the United States to the Emperor of Japan, and his work there succeeded in opening Japanese ports to American ships and in beginning the modernization of Japan.

Perry was born on April 10, 1794, in Newport, Rhode Island. He had a distinguished naval career, although not so sensational as that of his older brother Oliver Hazard Perry, hero of the battle of Lake Erie. He rose to command of the fleet that blockaded the Mexican coast during the Mexican War, and he was the naval commander at the victorious siege of Vera Cruz. Other accomplishments included a survey on which lighthouse locations on the East Coast were based; operation of the first naval gunnery school; and organization of a separate naval engineering corps.

In 1852, Perry sailed for China in command of a major warship. There he organized a squadron of U.S. Navy vessels and sailed to Japan, carrying letters from President Millard Fillmore to the Emperor. His orders were to deliver the letters, to try to get peaceful agreement on opening a Japanese port for American trade, and to work out details for protection of American seamen who might be shipwrecked in Japan. Perry sailed his warships into Yedo Bay for a nine-day stay in July 1853. He left his documents with representatives of Japan and then sailed off, giving the Japanese time to consider the possibilities. In February 1854, he returned and secured a treaty by which two Japanese ports were opened to our trading ships. He died in 1858.

PERRY, OLIVER HAZARD

Oliver Hazard Perry was born on August 20, 1785, in South Kingstown, Rhode Island. He commanded the American fleet that defeated and captured a British fleet at the battle of Lake Erie on September 9, 1813. This most distinguished naval victory of the War of 1812 ended British influence on the lake itself, and gave the Americans opportunity for an amphibious campaign to recapture Detroit and invade Canada.

In the actual battle, Perry commanded a brig, named the *Lawrence* in honor of the dead captain of the U.S.S. *Chesapeake.* He used Lawrence's dying words, "Don't Give Up the Ship!" as his battle cry and on his battle flags. The *Lawrence* took the major part of the British gunners' attention and suffered most of the American casualties. When the ship could no longer function as a fighting vessel, Perry transferred his flag to the *Niagara,* a sister ship, and split the British squadron. When the British fleet commander surrendered, Perry reported the success in a brief message to General William Henry Harrison: "We have met the enemy, and they are ours."

Perry came from a seafaring family: his father, brothers, and brothers-in-law were naval officers. His career in the Navy began as a fifteen-year-old midshipman on his father's frigate, and it ended when he was struck with yellow fever while on a naval assignment to visit Venezuela in 1819.

PERSHING, JOHN JOSEPH

John Joseph Pershing, (1860–1948), U.S. general. John Pershing was born near Laclede, Missouri, to a family of modest means. While still in his teens, he taught in a country school. He won an appointment to the United States Military Academy after taking a competitive examination, and graduated in 1886. He then served in the cavalry, fighting in wars against the Indian chief Geronimo (1886) and the Sioux (1890–1891).

While a military instructor at the University of Nebraska, he earned a law degree. In 1897 he was a tactical officer at West Point and fought in the Spanish-American War, where he was awarded a Silver Star for gallantry in action.

While in Mexico, Pershing learned that his wife and three daughters had perished in a fire and only his son had survived.

Between 1901 and 1903 he fought in the Philippines and was commended by President Theodore Roosevelt for his leadership ability. In 1905 Pershing was sent to Manchuria as a military attaché during the Russo-Japanese War. In 1906 Roosevelt promoted him to brigadier general over the objection of eight hundred senior officers. He then had another tour of duty in the Philippines after which he was sent to Mexico (1916) to crush the band of Mexicans led by Pancho Villa, who had made a surprise raid on the U.S. Cavalry garrison in New Mexico.

While in Mexico, Pershing learned that his wife and three daughters had perished in a fire and only his son had survived. However, six days later, he led his troops into Mexico and dispersed Villa's guerrillas, although Villa himself was never captured.

When the United States declared war on Germany in 1917, Pershing was appointed commander of the American Expeditionary Forces and sent to France to review the situation. Upon his arrival in Europe, he was told that the Allies saw America's role as limited to supplying more troops for their depleted ranks. Pershing rejected this view and gained approval for his plan to build a large army in Europe. Within two months he completed plans for a full scale offensive against Germany. He frequently feuded with French, British, and Italian commanding officers, and at one heated session he pounded his fist on the table and shouted, "Gentlemen, I have thought this program over very deliberately and will not be coerced!" The Allied commanders continually requested that Pershing be replaced, but U.S. secretary of war Newton Baker had faith in him. His newly formed United States First Army was used very effectively in September 1918 in the Saint-Mihiel salient in which sixteen thousand prisoners were taken. On 25–26 September, Pershing launched his second offensive and in forty-seven days the American Expeditionary Force had broken through to the outskirts of Sedan. On 11 November, 1918, an armistice was signed, marking an end to the war.

In eighteen months Pershing had established himself as a great military leader, having assembled an army of two million men who in two hundred days played a large role in defeating a German army hardened by four years of fighting experience. President Harry Truman, who served under him in World War I, said, "He was a great general and the only one without political ambitions."

In 1919 Pershing was made general of the armies, a rank unheard of prior to that time, and served in that capacity until he retired from the army in 1924. The following year he was sent to South America to settle a dispute between Peru and Chile. Upon his return to the United States, Pershing spent the rest of his active life as the chairman of the American Battle Monuments Commission. He wrote his memoirs, *Final Report* (1919) and *My Experiences in the World War* (two volumes, 1931). In 1937 he headed the U.S. delegation to the coronation of King George VI.

BIBLIOGRAPHY

F. Palmer, *J. J. Pershing, General of the Armies*, 1948.

D. Smythe, *Guerrilla Warrior: The Early Life of John J. Pershing*, 1973.

F. E. Vandiver, *Black Jack: The Life and Times of John J. Pershing*, 1977.

POWELL, COLIN LUTHER

Colin Luther Powell, (April 5, 1937–), Army officer, chair of the Joint Chiefs of Staff. Born and raised in

New York City, Colin Powell grew up in a close-knit family of Jamaican immigrants in the Hunts Point section of the Bronx. After attending public schools, Powell graduated from the City College of New York (CCNY) in 1958. Although his grades were mediocre, he discovered an affinity for the military. Participating in CCNY's Reserve Officer Training Corps (ROTC) program, he finished as a cadet colonel, the highest rank attainable. Like all ROTC graduates, Powell was commissioned as a second lieutenant after completing college.

Powell served for two years in West Germany and two years in Massachusetts, where he met his wife, Alma. In 1962, already a captain, Powell received orders to report to Vietnam. He was one of the second wave of more than 15,000 military advisers sent by the United States to Vietnam and was posted with a South Vietnamese Army unit for most of his tenure. During his first tour of duty, from 1962 to 1963, he was decorated with the Purple Heart after being wounded by a Viet Cong booby trap near the Laotian border.

After returning to the United States, Powell spent almost four years at Fort Benning in Georgia, serving as, among other things, an instructor at Fort Benning's Army Infantry School. In 1967, now a major, he attended an officers' training course at the United States Army Command and General Staff College at Fort Leavenworth, Kans., finishing second in a class of more than twelve hundred. In the summer of 1968, Powell was ordered back to Vietnam. On his second tour, Powell primarily served as a liaison to Gen. Charles Gettys of the American Division and received the Soldier's Medal for his role in rescuing injured soldiers, including Gen. Gettys, from a downed helicopter.

Powell disagreed with Clinton's proposal to end the ban on homosexuals in the military and was instrumental in limiting the scope of the change.

Powell returned to the United States in mid-1969 and began moving between military field postings and political appointments, a process that would become characteristic of his career. In 1971, after working in the Pentagon for the assistant vice chief of the Army, he earned an M.B.A. from George Washington University in Washington, D.C. Shortly thereafter, Powell was accepted as a White House Fellow during the Nixon administration and was attached to the Office of Management and Budget (OMB), headed by Caspar Weinberger. In 1973, after a year at OMB, Powell received command of an infantry battalion in South Korea; his mission was to raise morale and restore order in a unit plagued by drug abuse and racial problems. He then attended a nine-month course at the National War College and was promoted to full colonel in February 1976, taking command of the 2nd Brigade, 101st Airborne Division, located at Fort Campbell, Ky.

Colin Powell. (Department of the Defense/U.S. Army)

In 1979 Powell was an aide to Secretary of Energy Charles Duncan during the crisis of the nuclear accident at Three Mile Island in Pennsylvania and the oil shortage caused by the overthrow of the shah of Iran. In June of that year, while working at the Department of Energy (DOE), he became a brigadier general. Powell returned to the field from 1981 until 1983, serving as assistant division commander of the Fourth Infantry (mechanized) in Colorado and then as the deputy commanding general of an Army research facility at Fort Leavenworth. In mid-1983, he became military assistant to Secretary of Defense Caspar Weinberger. In 1986, Powell, by then a lieutenant general, returned to the field as the commander of V Corps, a unit of 75,000 troops in West Germany. The following year, in the wake of the Iran-Contra scandal, he returned to serve as President Ronald Reagan's national security adviser. During the Intermediate Nuclear Forces (INF) arms-control negotiations with the Soviet Union, Powell was heralded as being a major factor in their success.

In July 1989, Powell, a newly promoted four-star general, was nominated by President George Bush to become the first black chairman of the Joint Chiefs of Staff, the highest military position in the armed forces. As chairman, Powell was responsible for overseeing Operation Desert Storm, the 1991 international response to the 1990 Iraqi invasion of Kuwait. Through his commanding and reassuring television presence during the successful Persian Gulf War, Powell became one of the most popular figures in the Bush administration. Reappointed chairman in 1991, he was the recipient of various military decorations as well as a Presidential Medal of Freedom from Bush. In the same year, the NAACP gave Powell the Spingarn Medal, its highest award for African-American achievement.

When Bill Clinton was elected president in 1992, he and Powell had differences over Clinton's plan to substantially reduce the defense budget. Powell also disagreed with Clinton's proposal to end the ban on homosexuals in the military and was instrumental in limiting the scope of the change. Powell retired from the Army in September 1993 at the end of his second term as chairman of the Joint Chiefs. Upon his departure, President Clinton awarded him his second Presidential Medal of Freedom.

BIBLIOGRAPHY

Means, Howard. *Colin Powell: Soldier/Statesman—Statesman/Soldier.* New York, 1992.

Powell, Colin, with Joseph E. Persico. *My American Journey.* New York, 1995.

Roberts, Steven V., with Bruce Auster and Gary Cohen. "What's Next, General Powell?" *U.S. News and World Report* (March 18, 1991): 50–53.

Rowan, Carl. "Called to Service: The Colin Powell Story." *Reader's Digest* (December 1989): 121–126.

RICKENBACKER, EDWARD VERNON

"Captain Eddie" Rickenbacker was the leading American fighter pilot of World War I. He was born on October 8, 1890, in Columbus, Ohio. He became a prominent airline executive in the peacetime years thereafter. Rickenbacker's father died when he was only eleven and he had to support himself. He was very much attracted to engines and automobiles. He began to race cars in 1910, and by 1917 he was one of the best known daredevil drivers in America. He joined the Army, learned to fly, and became a fighter pilot in the "Hat-in-the-Ring" Squadron. That fighter squadron used a picture of Uncle Sam's hat as its symbol, and it was one of the most active American units on the western front. Rickenbacker rose to command of the squadron. In his months of active fighting, he shot down 22 enemy planes and four balloons to lead all U.S. pilots in the war. He received the Congressional Medal of Honor and dozens of other American and foreign awards. He became president of Eastern Airlines in 1938, and retired as chairman of its board of directors in 1963. During World War II, he was involved in a narrow escape when a plane he was flying across the Pacific had a crash landing at sea. His book *Seven Came Through* (1943) tells the story. Rickenbacker died in 1973.

Edward Rickenbacker, 1918. (National Archives)

SCHWARZKOPF, NORMAN

Norman Schwarzkopf, four star General in the United States Army, led the coalition of international military forces that liberated Kuwait from Iraqi occupation in the Gulf War of 1991. As a result of his success in this war, Schwarzkopf, nicknamed "Stormin' Norman," became one of the most popular American military leaders since Dwight D. Eisenhower.

Schwarzkopf was born on August 22, 1934, in Trenton, New Jersey. His father was General Herbert Norman Schwarzkopf, who had attended West Point and served during World Wars I and II. The elder Schwarzkopf gained national prominence in the 1930s when, as head of the New Jersey State Police, he led the investigation of the kidnapping of Charles Lindberg's baby.

When Norman Schwarzkopf was a child, his family lived briefly in Iran, where his father had been sent to train Iran's police force. The family also lived in Switzerland, Germany, and Italy, where young Norman learned to speak French and German. Back in the United States, ten-year-old Norman enrolled in the Bordentown Military Institute. He later attended Valley Forge Military Academy. In 1952, Schwarzkopf began studies at the United States Military Academy at West Point. He graduated in 1956 with a bachelor of science degree in mechanical engineering. Upon graduation, he was commissioned a 2nd Lieutenant in the United States Army and was assigned as platoon leader and executive officer to the 2nd Airborne Battle Group at Fort Benning, Georgia. His next assignments were with the 101st Airborne in Kentucky and the 6th Infantry in West Germany.

In 1964 Schwarzkopf earned a master's degree in guided missile engineering from the University of Southern California. He returned to West Point the next year to teach engineering, but soon left for Vietnam on the first of two tours during the Vietnam War. In Vietnam, Schwarzkopf served as Task Force Advisor to a South Vietnamese Airborne Division. At the end of this tour, he returned to his teaching post at West Point. In 1968, Schwarzkopf was promoted to Lieutenant Colonel. That same year, he married Brenda Holsinger, with whom he later had three children.

Norman Schwarzkopf. (Department of Defense/U.S. Army)

Schwarzkopf was shocked at the degree of public hostility he encountered to the Vietnam War and toward the United States military.

Colonel Schwarzkopf left for a second tour in Vietnam in 1969, this time serving as a battalion commander. Before this tour ended, he had been wounded twice and had earned three Silver Stars. He returned to the United States in 1971, wearing a cast from his hip to his shoulder. Following his recovery, the Army directed Schwarzkopf to address civilian groups about the war in Vietnam. During these speaking engagements, Schwarzkopf was shocked at the degree of public hostility he encountered to the Vietnam War and toward the United States military. He was forced to reevaluate United States military strategy in Vietnam and he came to believe that public support and a clear strategy were essential to victory in any military operation.

During the 1970s and 1980s, Schwarzkopf rose steadily through the military ranks. During this period he served in administrative posts in Washington DC, and various command assignments with mechanized infantry divisions in the United States and in Germany. In 1982, he was awarded his first star and became a Brigadier General. The following year, a coup occurred in the tiny island nation of Grenada. Neighboring Caribbean countries voted to intervene militarily and appealed to the United States, Jamaica, and Barbados for support. Fearing that Grenadan revolutionaries would help supply rebels in Central America and that Americans living on the island would be taken hostage, President Ronald Reagan authorized the commitment of 6000 troops from the United States and an invasion was planned. Although the Grenada invasion was largely an amphibious naval operation, General Schwarzkopf was placed in command of ground forces. Troops landed on the island on October 15, and quickly rescued the Americans and restored order.

Schwarzkopf became a full four-star general in 1988 and was appointed Commander in Chief of the United States Army Central Command based in Tampa, Florida. In this post, he was responsible for military operations in the Horn of Africa, South Asia, and the Middle

East, including the Persian Gulf region. Early in 1990, Schwarzkopf and his staff had begun preparing a detailed plan for the defense of the Persian Gulf oil fields in the event of attack by Iraq. When 140,000 Iraqi troops and 1,800 tanks invaded the small Gulf country of Kuwait on 2 August 1990, Schwarzkopf was ready.

Between August 1990 and January 1991, General Schwarzkopf led an operation called Desert Shield, which aimed at forcing Iraqi forces out of Kuwait and protecting Saudi Arabia from Iraqi invasion. Schwarzkopf directed the mobilization of 765,000 troops from 28 countries, including 541,000 American troops, hundreds of ships, and thousands of planes and tanks. During this buildup period, prolonged negotiations and economic sanctions failed to dislodge Iraqi forces from Kuwait. As a result, Schwarzkopf was directed to implement Operation Desert Storm.

Beginning on 17 January 1991, Allied forces carried out a devastating 6-week aerial bombardment of Iraq to destroy Iraqi communications, supply lines, and infrastructure. Using high-tech weaponry that seriously outmatched the Iraqi military hardware, the air war quickly grounded the Iraqi air force. Schwarzkopf then began a massive land war on February 24. Allied troops advanced rapidly through Kuwait and into Iraq, moving to within 150 miles of Baghdad. The demoralized Iraqi soldiers put up little resistance and began to surrender in massive numbers. After only 100 hours of fighting on the ground, Iraq accepted a United Nations cease-fire, and the war was over. Total casualties of the U.S. forces were 148 killed in action (35 by friendly fire) and 467 wounded, out of a coalition total of 240 dead and 776 wounded. Iraq's military casualties were estimated to number more than 25,000 dead and 300,000 wounded.

After the war, Schwarzkopf and his troops returned to the United States national heroes. A jubilant public welcomed them with numerous victory parades. Schwarzkopf retired from the army in August 1991, and found himself in great demand as a public speaker. His autobiography, *It Doesn't Take a Hero,* was published in 1992.

SCOTT, WINFIELD

Born in Petersburg, Virginia, Winfield Scott (1786–1866) was a dominant figure in the U.S. Army for more than a half-century. He attended William and Mary and was admitted to the bar before joining the army as a captain of artillery in 1808 and starting service on the Louisiana frontier.

Winfield Scott. (National Archives)

During the War of 1812, Scott won fame at the battles of Chippewa and Lundy's Lane. He was commissioned a brigadier general and received brevet rank as major general, while being recognized with medals by both Congress and the state of Virginia. He remained in the army, studied tactics in Europe, and was appointed departmental commander while writing and publishing *Rules and Regulations for the Field Exercise and Maneuvers of Infantry,* which became a standard reference for the army until the Civil War. His emphasis on military formality and propriety earned him the nickname "Old Fuss and Feathers," but he was also one of the most effective officers in the army. In 1838, he supervised the removal of the Cherokee Indians from Georgia along the Trail of Tears. He was also active in the Seminole War.

In 1841, Scott was made commanding general of the army and organized the forces for the United States–Mexican War. Originally denied a field command because of his Whig politics, Scott was given command of the force that captured Veracruz in 1847. Scott's planning for the campaign had won over Democrats who had previously opposed giving him command. Among the innovations he developed for the campaign were the first amphibious landing craft and the use of rockets.

Scott's emphasis on military formality and propriety earned him the nickname "Old Fuss and Feathers."

During his campaign to capture Mexico City, Scott's troops were plagued by lack of transport. In addition, many of the troops, as short-term volunteers, left for the United States when their terms ended. Scott pushed his command inland and succeeded in capturing the Mexican capital, thus demonstrating a triumph of personal will that overcame all obstacles. During that campaign, his forces of eleven thousand were outnumbered almost three to one by the Mexican army.

Four years later, the Whigs nominated Scott for president, but he lost the election to Democrat Franklin Pierce.

With the coming of the Civil War, Scott attempted to organize the army to prevent secession. His "Anaconda Plan" relied on the occupation of the Mississippi and a blockade of the coast to force the South into submission. Scott called Robert E. Lee back from Texas in 1861 and attempted to persuade him to take command of the army. In November 1861, Scott retired to West Point, where he lived and wrote about his career until his death.

BIBLIOGRAPHY

Smith, Arthur D. Howden. *Old Fuss and Feathers: The Life and Exploits of Lieutenant General Winfield Scott.* New York, 1937.

SHERIDAN, PHILIP H.

In the Indian Wars of the 1870s, Philip H. Sheridan (1831–1888) was the officer to whom William Tecumseh Sherman, then commander of the U.S. Army's division of the Missouri, entrusted the execution of his "total-war" policy, developed during Sherman's March to Atlanta at the end of the Civil War. Born in New York and raised in Ohio, Sheridan entered West Point in 1848 but did not graduate until five years later because of a one-year suspension for fighting. He saw his first frontier duty in Texas and the Pacific Northwest, where he fought in the Yakima War. Sheridan then served the Union brilliantly in the Civil War, rose rapidly to the rank of major general, and became commander of the Army of the Potomac's cavalry division, which was instrumental in cutting off Robert E. Lee's Army of Northern Virginia and bringing about the surrender at Appomattox. After the war, Sheridan commanded the Division of the Gulf from 1865 to 1867 and was given command of the Fifth Military District, which encompassed Texas and Louisiana. He held this post for only six months before President Andrew Johnson, concluding that Sheridan applied the principles of Reconstruction too harshly, caused his transfer to the West, where he replaced General Winfield Scott Hancock as commander of the Department of the Missouri.

During the Indian Wars, Sheridan was guided by Sherman's notion of total war—combat directed not against military objectives alone, but at the civilian population of the enemy as well, in order to destroy a people's very will to make war. In fact, Sheridan took Sherman's concept to an extreme by conducting a series of winter campaigns against the Cheyennes, beginning in 1868, with the aim of attacking Indians when they were most vulnerable. It was common practice among Indians to avoid fighting during the winter when food was usually in short supply and their maneuverability was limited. "These Indians required to be soundly whipped," Sheridan announced, "and the ringleaders in

Phillip H. Sheridan. (National Archives)

the present trouble hung, their ponies killed and such destruction of their property as will make them very poor." What came to be called "Sheridan's Campaign" ended the Cheyenne warrior society, the Dog Soldiers, in western Kansas, and the Cheyenne "hostiles" retired to reservations after suffering losses to George Armstrong Custer at Sweetwater Creek in the Texas Panhandle and along the Powder River in the Dakotas. But outside the brash and ambitious Custer, Sheridan's officers came to argue that such ruthless campaigns were almost as hard on the soldiers as they were on the Indians, although both Sherman and Ulysses S. Grant were heartened by the campaign.

Sheridan was promoted to lieutenant general in 1869 and given command of the Division of the Missouri when Sherman replaced Grant as general-in-chief of the army. Grant, of course, had become president of the United States. After campaigning in the Black Hills of the Dakotas from 1873 to 1874, against the Comanches, Kiowas, Southern Cheyennes, and Southern Arapahos in the Red River War from 1874 to 1875, and again against the Sioux in the Sioux War for the Black Hills from 1866 to 1877, Sheridan replaced Sherman as general-in-chief of the army in 1883. He then directed General George Crook and, after him, Nelson Appleton Miles, in the long struggle against the Apaches under Geronimo. Sheridan was promoted to the rank of general of the army in 1888, the year in which he died.

BIBLIOGRAPHY

Axelrod, Alan. *Chronicle of the Indian Wars: From Colonial Times to Wounded Knee.* New York, 1993.

Hutton, Paul. *Phil Sheridan and His Army.* Lincoln, Nebr., 1985.

Utley, Robert M. *Frontier Regulars: The United States Army and the Indian, 1866–1890.* New York, 1973.

SHERMAN, WILLIAM TECUMSEH

William Tecumseh Sherman, (1820–1891), American army commander. Born in Lancaster, Ohio, Sherman was the eldest of eight children. He had been named Tecumseh by his father as a token of respect to the elder Sherman's friend, an Indian chief. Orphaned at the age of nine, he was adopted by Thomas Ewing, who was active in national politics; Ewing's wife insisted on changing the child's name to William.

Through Ewing's influence, Sherman was given an appointment at the U.S. Military Academy at West Point, and in 1840 he graduated sixth out of a class of forty-two. He served as a second lieutenant in Florida and New Orleans, but was not very happy with army life, eventually leaving the army in 1853. He then joined a St. Louis banking firm as manager of its San Francisco branch. The bank failed and he then tried his hand at being a lawyer, quickly discovering that he did not possess the necessary temperament.

William Tecumseh Sherman. (National Archives)

In 1859, Sherman was made superintendent of a new military college in Alexandria, Louisiana, a position he held until 1861. He proved an excellent teacher and developed the abilities and skills which were to endear him to his troops during the Civil War. For the first time in his life he found satisfaction in what he was doing, but was forced to resign his position when Louisiana seceded from the Union.

With the onset of the Civil War, Sherman rejoined the army and in May 1861 was appointed a colonel, leading his troops at the Battle of Bull Run. He was not satisfied with the results and questioned his own ability to command, but President Abraham Lincoln disagreed and promoted him to the rank of brigadier general. At this point, General Henry W. Halleck discovered Sherman's ability as a military planner and requested that he prepare the battle plans for General Ulysses S. Grant's campaign. Sherman served brilliantly as Grant's subordinate, and quickly became his devoted friend.

In 1862, under Grant's command, Sherman and several other generals were able to drive back the Confederates at the Battle of Shiloh. Shortly thereafter Sherman was promoted to major general and effectively engineered the Union victory at Vicksburg, strategically important to the Union forces because it was located on the eastern bank of the Mississippi.

Sherman brought the war home to civilians by the destruction of goods rather than life.

Sherman succeeded Grant as the commanding general in Tennessee. During the following year he led his troops to victory on the Missionary Bridge and in Knoxville, Tennessee. With Grant's promotion to commander of all the Union armies, Sherman was put in charge of the armies in the south. With one hundred and ten thousand troops under his command, Sherman advanced toward Atlanta, Georgia, in May 1864. His army far outnumbered the Confederates, causing them to retreat again and again. By July 1864 Sherman's troops had reached the outskirts of Atlanta and on September 1, 1864, he sent a telegram to Lincoln saying, "Atlanta is ours and fairly won." After completing the destruction of the city, Sherman led his troops to the sea and they went on to capture Savannah, Georgia. Congress gave a vote of thanks to Sherman for his accomplishments. During this period, Sherman received orders that he and his troops were to live off the countryside. To this end, he destroyed the war supplies, public buildings, railroad lines, and factories of the enemy. He brought the war home to civilians by the destruction of goods rather than life. Sherman then marched his troops through the Carolinas to join Grant in Virginia.

Sherman received the surrender of J. E. Johnston at Durham, North Carolina, on April 26, 1865. From 1865 to 1869 Sherman commanded the military in Mississippi and when Grant became president of the United States, Sherman was promoted to general in command of the army, remaining in that position until his retirement in 1884.

In 1883 his name was put before the Republican Convention as a presidential candidate. In typical fashion he responded, "If nominated I will not accept; if elected, I will not serve." He remained a very popular figure, even after his retirement, and was often called upon as a speaker, especially at functions of war veterans.

BIBLIOGRAPHY

R. Charles, *William T. Sherman: Military Leadership,* 1991.

J. T. Glatthaar, *The March to the Sea and Beyond.* 1985.

B. H. Liddell Hart, *Sherman: Soldier, Realist, American,* 1978.

J. F. Marzalek, *Sherman's Other War—The General and the Civil War Press,* 1981.

SITTING BULL (SIOUX)

Sitting Bull (Tatanka-Iyotanka, 1831?–1890), a Hunkpapa Lakota Sioux chief, was probably born on the Grand River in present-day South Dakota. He counted his first coup at the age of fourteen, and thereafter, in warfare with enemy tribes, he accumulated a superior record that led to his designation, in 1857, as a tribal war chief. At the same time, he acquired a notable reputation as a holy man and master of the sacred mysteries and ceremonies of the Lakotas. His entire life was characterized by a profound spirituality, and many times he performed the sacrificial rites of the Sun Dance. As he assumed a commanding position among his people, Sitting Bull came to exemplify the four cardinal virtues of the Lakotas: bravery, fortitude, generosity, and wisdom.

Sitting Bull, 1885. (National Archives)

His name, fame, and finally his influence spread from his own Hunkpapa group to the other six Lakota tribes.

From Sitting Bull's earliest years, his people traded with whites at posts on the Missouri River. Not until the 1850s, however, did whites threaten the Hunkpapa world. Following the Minnesota Sioux uprising of 1862 and the discovery of gold in western Montana, the threat grew serious and immediate. The Lakotas were drawn into war with the United States. From 1863 to 1864, Sitting Bull and his warriors fought Generals Henry Hastings Sibley and Alfred Sully in Dakota, and in 1865, they skirmished with columns of General Patrick E. Connor in the Powder River country. Sitting Bull directed special venom against the military posts of the upper Missouri River, especially Forts Rice and Buford. He led a direct assault on each and, for five years, from 1865 to 1870, kept up a deadly harassment of Fort Buford.

The federal government's agents and policies divided the Hunkpapa and other Lakota tribes into factions. Some advocated accommodation; others, resistance. The Treaty of 1868, creating the Great Sioux Reservation in western Dakota, deepened the tribal division. Portions of each Lakota tribe settled on the reservation, while others remained in the buffalo ranges of the Powder and Yellowstone valleys.

Sitting Bull was the leading chief of these "nontreaty" Lakotas, whom government officials soon labeled "hostiles." A staunch foe of all government programs, he wanted no part of treaties, agents, rations, or any course that would interfere with the old life of following the buffalo and warring against enemy tribes. He and his friends designated him head chief of all the nontreaty Lakotas. For eight years, with the firm support of the Oglala war chief Crazy Horse, he held together a coalition of Lakota and Northern Cheyenne tribes that followed the old life in the buffalo ranges west and north of the Great Sioux Reservation.

Sitting Bull was the leading chief of "nontreaty" Lakotas, whom government officials soon labeled "hostiles."

Two white incursions roused the bitter ire of Sitting Bull's nontreaty bands. The first was the Northern Pacific Railroad, whose surveying parties, accompanied by military escorts, had to fight off Lakota and Cheyenne warriors led by Sitting Bull himself. The second outrage was the military exploration of the Black Hills by the Custer Expedition of 1874. The discovery of gold set off a rush to the hills, part of the Great Sioux Reservation and thus off limits to all whites. The Indians rebuffed government attempts to buy the area.

From the Black Hills dilemma sprang the Great Sioux War of 1876. If forced by military action to settle on the reservation, Sitting Bull's bands could be deprived of their independence and coerced into dropping their opposition to the cession of the Black Hills. The pretext for war lay in their continuing aggression against tribes friendly to the United States and scattered depredations against whites on the upper Yellowstone River. Both violated the Treaty of 1868, which Sitting Bull and his comrades had not signed.

On March 17, 1876, a military force attacked a village on Powder River, and Sitting Bull knew that the whites had declared war. The scattered bands drew together for self-defense and, bolstered by accessions from the reservation, made ready to fight. At the Battle of the Rosebud on June 17, they routed an army under General George Crook. A week later, on June 25, they wiped out part of the Seventh Cavalry under Lieutenant Colonel George Armstrong Custer at the Battle of Little Bighorn.

"Custer's Last Stand" on the Little Bighorn stunned and roused white Americans, and the government flooded the Sioux country with soldiers. Other battles were fought, and relentless military pressure through the winter caused most of the fugitives to surrender in the spring of 1877. Sitting Bull and others sought refuge in Canada.

Sitting Bull remained in Canada for five years. He got along well with the Queen's redcoats—the North West Mounted Police. But the buffaloes were dwindling toward extinction, and food shortages led to hunger and finally even starvation. His ranks thinned by defections, on July 20, 1881, Sitting Bull surrendered at Fort Buford in the Dakota Territory.

After nearly two years as prisoners of war, Sitting Bull and his followers settled at Standing Rock Agency, Dakota Territory. There Agent James McLaughlin sought to transform them into imitation whites—farmers, Christians, and American patriots. Sitting Bull resisted, and the two contended for the allegiance of the Hunkpapas for seven years. Sitting Bull vigorously contested the land agreement of 1889, which broke up the Great Sioux Reservation and opened nearly half of it to homesteaders. When this and other afflictions created a climate favorable to the Ghost Dance religion, he emerged as the leading apostle of the doctrine at Standing Rock.

McLaughlin and the military authorities decided that Sitting Bull had to be removed from the reservation. On December 15, 1890, Indian police surrounded his cabin on the Grand River. His followers resisted, and in a bloody shootout, Sitting Bull and others were killed. His body was later buried in the military cemetery at Fort Yates, adjacent to Standing Rock Agency.

Today, Sitting Bull is remembered as one of the greatest of all Indian chieftains. He achieved distinction as a military, political, and spiritual leader as well as a man of great humanity. His inflexible resistance to the white advance, coupled with his refusal to compromise his principles, made him the most distinguished patriot of the Sioux but also eroded his power and led finally to his death.

BIBLIOGRAPHY

Utley, Robert M. *The Lance and the Shield: The Life and Times of Sitting Bull.* New York, 1993.

Vestal, Stanley. *Sitting Bull, Champion of the Sioux.* Norman, Okla., 1957.

SMITH, JOHN

A member of England's first permanent settlement in America, at Jamestown, Virginia, in 1607, John Smith almost singlehandedly saved the colony from starvation in its first difficult years. During this time he also managed to explore Chesapeake Bay, making a map that served sailors and colonists for over 100 years. Later in his life, he mapped the coast of New England and gave the region its name.

John Smith was born in 1850 in Willoughby, England. As a young man, Smith spent several years as a soldier and adventurer in Europe. His last engagement there was against the Turks; he later told numerous tales of adventure, including the time he was taken prisoner and sent to Constantinople as a gift to the Pasha's wife, who fell in love with him. Small wonder that he was not content with humdrum English domestic life when he returned in 1604.

Seeking further adventure, Smith signed on with the Virginia Company of London and claimed to have been actively involved in promoting and organizing its Jamestown venture. When the settlers arrived in Jamestown in April 1607, their most pressing need was food. Smith soon took on the task of trading for corn with the local Indians, a task which he performed successfully and sometimes aggressively in the face of Indian reluctance. On one such excursion he was captured by Chief Opechancanough of the Pamunkey tribe and managed to save his life only by showing the chief a compass and entertaining him in broken Algonquin with tales of the sun and stars. Opechancanough eventually took Smith to his brother, Chief Powhatan. As Smith later told the story, Powhatan debated with his counselors and then decided to kill Smith. But the chief's beloved twelve-year-old daughter, Pocahontas, placed her head on top of Smith's to prevent the warriors from clubbing him to death. He was then returned unharmed to Jamestown; the settlement's relations with Powhatan remained uneasy.

In January 1608 new settlers arrived in Jamestown; the same month a fire that started through carelessness burned down much of the settlement. In the spring Smith organized the rebuilding of the village and the planting of crops and then escaped the burden of managing a colony full of shirkers and schemers by going exploring. In the summer of 1608 he made two separate excursions around Chesapeake Bay. In the first, he encountered Indians on the eastern shore of the bay and then traveled a distance up the Potomac and Rappahannock rivers, where the Indians were more suspicious and potentially hostile. On his second expedition, he went to the head of Chesapeake Bay and discovered the mouth of the Susquehanna River, where he met the Susquehanna Iroquois, who offered him trade goods that they had gotten from the French farther north. Smith's summer explorations resulted in a map of the bay region that was considered valuable by mariners and colonists for more than 100 years.

Smith returned to Jamestown to find that he had been officially chosen the new leader of the colony. For the next year, he continued to be the colony's primary problem-solver, repeatedly pressuring food out of the Indians, who were becoming more wary as more settlers arrived. When seven ships with nearly 300 new settlers arrived from England in August 1609, Smith was overwhelmed by the prospect of feeding them all. Fortunately, responsibility was to be lifted from him, as a new governor was expected from England soon. But an ironic form of relief for Smith arrived even sooner. A quantity of gunpowder accidently discharged in Smith's canoe, and he was burned severely enough to warrant his immediate return to England in October 1609.

Smith returned to North America in 1614 at the behest of a group of London merchants who wanted him to map the coast of an area called North Virginia (present-day New England). He summered on Monhegan Island (off the coast of Maine). From Monhegan, Smith mapped the coast as far south as Cape Cod. His map included a harbor called Patuxet, which Prince Charles insisted on renaming Plymouth, being convinced that it would be easier to attract English settlers to places with English rather than Indian names. This Plymouth was soon to become the home of the Pilgrims.

Smith returned to England, where, in 1616, he published *A Description of New England,* which gave a name to the region and proclaimed its desirability as a location for a colony. The Pilgrims relied on Smith's map and book but had no interest in inviting him to join the colony. The later years of Smith's life were spent in writing numerous books, the last of which was *Advertisements for the Unexperienced Planters of New England, or Anywhere,* a work that contains valuable and sometimes amusing advice based on his personal experiences. Smith died in London in 1631.

John Smith was not only a daring and courageous explorer, willing to go anywhere and do anything, he was also a knowledgeable, responsible, and resourceful leader. The Jamestown colony, filled as it was with those who did not want to pull their own weight, would not have survived its first two years without him, and, without the use of his map and book, the Pilgrims would probably have had an even more difficult time settling in the New World than they did. John Smith therefore deserves much credit for the establishment and survival of the first two permanent English colonies in America.

TAYLOR, ZACHARY

Zachary Taylor (1784–1850), U.S. Army officer and twelfth president of the United States, was born near Montebello in Orange County, Virginia. Before the age of one, he moved with his family to Louisville, Kentucky. In 1806, with little formal education, Taylor embarked on a military career, which he pursued with few interruptions for the next forty-two years. During the War of 1812, he served under General William Henry Harrison and earned the U.S. Army's first brevet promotion (from captain to major).

Earning the sobriquet "Old Rough and Ready," Taylor spent two years attempting to force the Seminole War to a conclusion.

In 1832, Taylor participated in Black Hawk's War. During the Second Seminole War (from 1835 to 1842), he defeated the Seminoles at the Battle of Lake Okeechobee in 1837, a victory that garnered him another brevet promotion, this time to brigadier general. Earning the sobriquet "Old Rough and Ready," he spent the next two years attempting to force the Seminole War to a conclusion. Unsuccessful in his endeavors, Taylor asked for and received a reassignment and transfer to Baton Rouge. He purchased a plantation near Baton Rouge and another in Mississippi. In 1841, he commanded a military district with departmental headquarters at Fort Smith, Arkansas.

With the annexation of Texas by the United States in 1845, Taylor was ordered to protect American interests in the boundary dispute with Mexico. In March 1846, Taylor advanced from Corpus Christi to present-day Brownsville, Texas, where he erected Fort Texas across the Rio Grande from Mexican-held Matamoros. He won major victories over a numerically superior Mexican army at Palo Alto (on May 8, 1846) and Resaca de la Palma (on May 9, 1846), the first battles of the United States–Mexican War. In August, with thirty-five hundred men, Taylor began his campaign to capture Monterrey, Mexico. In a six-day battle (from September 19 to 24), Taylor assaulted the city from front and rear. On September 25, the Mexican forces at Monterrey surrendered. Taylor granted the Mexicans an eight-week armistice, which infuriated President James K. Polk, who thought the terms too lenient. By that time Taylor suspected political sabotage by both Polk and Secretary of War William L. Marcy. His suspicions proved true when General of the Army Winfield Scott directed Taylor to relinquish command of most of his U.S. regulars for use in Scott's Veracruz invasion.

In February 1847, Taylor won a stunning victory over Mexican President Antonio López de Santa Anna at the battle of Buena Vista. Outnumbered by a four to one margin, Taylor's troops held steady and forced Santa Anna to retreat, thus ending the fighting in Mexico's northern regions. By then a national hero, Taylor won the Whig party's nomination and the 1848 presidential election.

As president, Taylor became embroiled in disputes with members of Congress over the admission of California and New Mexico as free states. Taylor's most notable achievement during his term in office was the signing of the Clayton-Bulwer Treaty with England. The treaty provided for dual control of any canal constructed across Central America. Taylor's last weeks in office were rocked with scandals involving cabinet members. While attending ceremonies for the laying of the cornerstone of the Washington Monument on July 4, 1850, Taylor suddenly took ill; he died on July 9 and was buried in his family's plot near Louisville, Kentucky. While Taylor was not a brilliant military strategist, his unpretentious dress and manners won him the loyal support of his troops.

BIBLIOGRAPHY

Bauer, Jack K. *Zachary Taylor: Soldier, Planter, Statesman of the Old Southwest.* Baton Rouge, La., 1985.

Dyer, Brainerd. *Zachary Taylor.* New York, 1946.

Eisenhower, John S. D. *So Far from God. The U.S. War with Mexico 1846–1848.* New York, 1989.
Nichols, Edward J. *Zach Taylor's Little Army.* Garden City, N.Y., 1963.

WASHINGTON, GEORGE

George Washington, (1732–1799), commander-in-chief of the Army of Independence and first president of the United States (1789–1797). Of British ancestry, the eldest of five children of his father's second wife, Washington was born in a modest farmhouse (destroyed by fire in 1799) near Fredericksburg, Virginia. His education was limited—he was the only one of the first six presidents who did not go to college. The marriage of his beloved elder half-brother Lawrence into an aristocratic English family, the Fairfaxes, provided the young Washington with his first experience as a land surveyor.

In the early 1750s Britain and France both laid claim to the upper Ohio Valley. The Fairfax family recommended Washington to head a small expedition representing English interests, but tragedy resulted when Washington attacked a small French encampment, thinking they were spies. Ten men, including the diplomatic commander, were killed; the French claimed they were on a peace mission. The event exacerbated tensions that led to the French and Indian War. In 1755, although war had not been declared, Washington served as an aide to British general Edward Braddock in his campaign to capture Fort Duquesne at the Forks of the Ohio. The campaign ended in catastrophic defeat for the British, although Washington drew praise from the British commanders for his "courage and resolution."

George Washington. (National Archives/painting by C. W. Peale)

At twenty-two, Washington was elected commander of all Virginia forces, his main task that of protecting the Virginia border from Indian attacks. After the retreat of the French from Fort Duquesne the war ended, having engaged Washington from 1753 to 1759. Resigning from military life, he turned his energies to Mount Vernon, the plantation home he had rented from the widow of his half-brother, which would later become his permanent estate in Virginia. In 1759 he married Martha Dandridge Custis, a wealthy widow with two small children. The Washingtons were charitable landowners, believing that no needy person should be turned away from Mount Vernon "lest the deserving suffer." Though he employed slaves, Washington was greatly troubled by the institution of slavery all his life. In his will he granted all his slaves their freedom, the only Virginia founding father to do so.

In the mid–1760s Britain's policy of taxing its colonies precipitated the American Revolution. At first Washington hoped that armed rebellion could be avoided. As a member of Virginia's House of Burgesses he protested the Stamp Act, which imposed taxes on the colonies to support the British army, and the Townshend Revenue Act, a tax on tea and other staples. In 1774 Washington was a delegate to the First Continental Congress in Philadelphia, which agreed to ban all British goods. Not until after the battles of Lexington and Concord and the convening of the Second Continental Congress in May 1775 did it become clear that the colonies would have to take up arms.

In the year preceding the signing of the Declaration of Independence (July 4, 1776), Washington created a navy of six ships that were ordered to capture British vessels; initiated a campaign to arrest and detain British Tories; and encouraged leaders of the colonies to adopt independence.

With the exception of Washington's stunning success at Trenton on December 25–26, 1776, when he recrossed the Delaware and surprised the Hessian mercenaries, his army had suffered several defeats in New York, culminating in the misery of the hard winter at Valley Forge. The battle of Monmouth (June 28, 1778), when Washington took the initiative boldly and drove the British back to their strongholds in New York, was the critical breakthrough for the Continental Army. In September 1781 Washington's army, assisted by able French troops, defeated the British garrison at Yorktown, Virginia, thereby inducing Britain's war-weary withdrawal. Washington was lauded for his outstanding conduct of the war, personal courage, and his concern for the underfed and ill-equipped men of his army. His suffering with them in their harshest trials, and his leadership and organizational ability, were later recognized by Congress as indisputably qualifying him for the presidency. He was already being called "the father of his country."

Though he employed slaves, Washington was greatly troubled by the institution of slavery all his life.

A period of longed-for retirement from 1783 to 1787 ended when Washington was called on to attend the Philadelphia Convention in May 1787. Lack of foreign markets for American goods and Britain's prohibition of trade with the British West Indies had led to a shortage of money and mounting debts. Following a mass insurgency in Massachusetts in 1786 called Shays' Rebellion, in which farmers demanded liquidation of their debts, fears of anarchy led to the growing conviction that a strong federal government was necessary. Washington used his influence with all the delegates to draft the Constitution. Signed first by Washington, the proposed Constitution established a national government consisting of "a supreme legislative, executive, and judiciary." Washington wrote: "It is clear to my conception that no government before introduced among mankind ever contained so many checks and such efficacious restraints to prevent it from . . . oppression." By June 1788 ten of the thirteen states had ratified the Constitution and on April 30, 1789, after unanimous election by the Electoral College, Washington took the oath in New York City as first president of the United States.

The judicial system and executive departments (the latter later known as the cabinet) established by Washington during his presidency have remained American institutions to the present time. Describing Washington's selection of executive heads for the five departments established by Congress, John Adams, the vice president, wrote, "He seeks information from all quarters and judges more independently than any man I ever knew." Perhaps no two appointments had more repercussions for Washington's administration than the appointment of Alexander Hamilton as secretary of the treasury and Thomas Jefferson as secretary of state. Beginning in Washington's first term, Jefferson's opposition to Hamilton's economic and political philosophy eventually gave rise to two distinct parties: the Republican party (later to become the Democratic party) represented by Jefferson of Virginia, advocating an agrarian-based economy, and the Federalists, represented by Hamilton, whose proposal for the Bank of the United States and for increased industrialization anticipated the business interests of modern America.

Washington's foreign policy emphasized avoiding involvement in a European war, seeking treaties with Britain and Spain to open up the Ohio Valley to American settlement, and promoting the nation's import trade. On April 22, 1793, two days after his re-election, again unanimous, to a second term, and ten days after hearing of war between Britain and France, Washington voted for the Proclamation of Neutrality prohibiting Americans from sending war materials to either country.

Despite Washington's efforts to resolve the Indian problem on the western front peacefully, it proved necessary to send an army against the Northwestern Indians. General Wayne's victory at the battle of Fallen Timbers in 1794 led to the Treaty of Greenville in 1795. The Indians gave up nearly all their land in Ohio, enabling pioneers to establish a new state. The Treaty of San Lorenzo in 1795 with Spain granted Americans the right to trade on the Mississippi.

In his farewell address of September 17, 1796, Washington set forth his principles for the future well-being of the nation. He stressed the need for religion to guide public morality, warned against foreign entanglements and partisan politics, and enjoined Americans to respect the Constitution and cherish the Union. He retired to his Mount Vernon plantation and, three days before his death, drafted a long document planning the rotation of crops on his farm.

BIBLIOGRAPHY

J. R. Alden, *George Washington,* 1984.

N. Emery, *Washington: A Biography,* 1976.

B. Schwarz, *George Washington,* 1987.

C. C. Wall, *George Washington, Citizen-Soldier,* 1980.

WESTMORELAND, WILLIAM

William Westmoreland, (1914–), general, U.S. Army; commander, U.S. Military Assistance Command, Vietnam (COMUSMACV), 1964–1968; U.S. Army chief of staff, 1968–1972. William C. Westmoreland was first captain (in effect, commander of the Corps of Cadets) in the West Point class of 1936. Commissioned in the

General William Westmoreland, 1968, in Saigon. (UPI/Corbis-Bettmann)

field artillery, Westmoreland served with distinction in World War II, commanding an artillery battalion during the North African campaign and serving as chief of staff of the 9th Division in the final assault against Germany.

After holding many of the most visible and important positions in the U.S. Army, Westmoreland became superintendent of the U.S. Military Academy at West Point in 1960. As superintendent, he impressed President Kennedy and Vice President Johnson with his abilities, and was subsequently selected to replace Gen. Paul Harkins as COMUSMACV.

Taking command in Vietnam in June 1964 after six months as Harkin's deputy, Westmoreland began to lay the groundwork for an expanded U.S. role in Vietnam. In 1965, when North Vietnamese regulars threatened to cut through the country in the Central Highlands, President Johnson, acting upon the advice of Westmoreland and the Joint Chiefs of Staff (JCS), increased the level of U.S. combat forces in South Vietnam to more than 100,000.

From 1965 to 1967 U.S. and Army of the Republic of Vietnam (ARVN) soldiers waged a war of attrition against Viet Cong and North Vietnamese forces. During this period, Westmoreland was instrumental in raising the level of U.S. forces committed to South Vietnam and in developing the military strategy for the ground war. He has been faulted for undue reliance on U.S. combat forces, for excessive use of helicopters, and for lack of attention to counterinsurgency. Westmoreland believed, however, that U.S. forces were necessary to counter the forces of the People's Army of Vietnam (PAVN); that the mobility provided by helicopters compensated for the limits on numbers of U.S. forces committed and the difficulties of terrain, especially in the Central Highlands; and that the counterinsurgency mission properly belonged to the ARVN.

Partly from worries over successes of U.S. and ARVN forces in the south, North Vietnam launched the Tet Offensive in 1968. Westmoreland's command, although taken by surprise, reacted quickly and wrought devastating losses on the attackers. Interpreting his success as an opportunity, and encouraged by the chairman of the JCS, Gen. Earle Wheeler, Westmoreland proposed a new strategy that called for operations outside South Vietnam and for the commitment of an additional 200,000 troops. Opposed to a further widening of the war and the economic costs that such an expansion would entail, President Johnson refused the military's recommendations and recalled Westmoreland to be chief of staff of the U.S. Army.

As chief of staff, Westmoreland's major challenges dealt with the withdrawal of U.S. forces from Vietnam; restoring the army's readiness to function in other theaters (a capability that had dwindled during the war years); mitigating the army's racial tensions; bringing drug use in the army under control; and making the transition to a volunteer army—all in the climate of powerful antimilitary sentiment in U.S. politics and society. He was probably most successful at improving the army's readiness, and laying the foundation for his successors to solve the other problems.

Westmoreland retired in 1972 but remained a major figure in the debate over the Vietnam War. He vigorously defended his conduct of the war in his 1976 memoir, *A Soldier Reports,* and in public statements and appearances. In the mid 1980s he sued the Columbia Broadcasting System over a television program that alleged his participation in a conspiracy to manipulate estimates of the number of Viet Cong and North Vietnamese troops he faced. The suit was settled out of court, and both sides claimed victory.

Westmoreland has been called "the inevitable general" and his achievements before the Vietnam War were substantial. History will judge him, however, on the basis of that war. Westmoreland's strategy in the war was threefold: first, halt the losing trend of South Vietnamese forces by the end of 1965; second, conduct offensive operations to defeat major Viet Cong and PAVN units and restore pacification programs; and third, secure and destroy enemy base areas. Concurrently, he sought to modernize and improve the ARVN—important ingredients for what was later termed Vietnamization. Implicit in the defeat of enemy units and base areas was cutting logistic support of North Vietnam to the south, which Westmoreland intended to do when ground troops were available to operate against the Ho Chi Minh Trail in Laos and Cambodia.

A courtly southern gentleman—handsome, ramrod erect, immaculate, and somewhat aloof—Westmoreland often appeared at odds with the culture of the 1960s.

Some critics charge that Westmoreland's strategy could never have prevailed in Vietnam without far higher troop levels than President Johnson was willing to provide, and that Westmoreland knew this. Westmoreland repeatedly asked for more combat units than the administration was willing to give, and he consistently predicted that the war would go on for a longer time. It is possible that Westmoreland thought that in time the constraints on troop levels would be removed.

Some of Westmoreland's problems in the Vietnam War resulted from a flawed articulation of his policies. The operational concept dubbed "search and destroy" was never explained clearly to the American people. Although Westmoreland envisioned operations that would search for enemy units, base areas, and logistic support services to destroy them, images of soldiers burning thatched huts translated for many Americans into a policy of destroying Vietnam itself. From 1964 to 1967, Westmoreland's press coverage was positive to mixed; following the Tet Offensive, it was almost uniformly negative. A forceful public speaker, Westmoreland persisted in giving press conferences, seeming to believe that if he could explain his policies in enough detail, reporters would understand and approve of them. While this may have worked early in the U.S. involvement, the media's later hostility toward him and toward the war made his courting of the press counterproductive. Some facets of Westmoreland's personality undoubtedly contributed to his problems with the press and the public. A courtly southern gentleman—handsome, ramrod erect, immaculate, and somewhat aloof—he often appeared at odds with the culture of the 1960s.

Whether Westmoreland's strategy could ever have won the war will never be known. Certainly victory would probably have required many things he did not have—more troops, more time, more political will, and reform of the ARVN, to name a few. Additionally, Westmoreland operated under constraints that U.S. commanders had not experienced in either World War II or Korea: he did not control the air war against North Vietnam, and he did not exercise command over the military forces of the allied nation. The Tet Offensive proved a military defeat for Viet Cong and PAVN forces, yet a psychological coup for them on the American home front. In the aftermath of Tet, as key policymakers and the press concluded that the war could not be won at acceptable costs, political support for the strategy that had become identified with Westmoreland crumbled, and negotiations and withdrawal became U.S. policy.

BIBLIOGRAPHY

Davidson, Phillip B. *Vietnam at War: The History 1946–1975.* 1988.

Halberstam, David. *The Best and The Brightest.* 1972.

Johnson, Lyndon B. *The Vantage Point: Perspectives of the Presidency, 1963–1969.* 1971.

Westmoreland, William C. *A Soldier Reports.* 1976.

APPENDICES

Medal of Honor Recipients

Total medals awarded:

AIR FORCE	16
ARMY	2,342
COAST GUARD	1
MARINES	300
NAVY	744
UNKNOWN SOLDIERS	9
	3,412

Glossary

Adj.	Adjutant
Adm.	Admiral
BM	Boatswain's Mate
Brig. Gen.	Brigadier General
CB	Chief Boatswain's Mate
CWO	Chief Warrant Officer
Capt.	Captain
Cmdr.	Commander
Col.	Colonel
Comm.	Commissary
Cpl.	Corporal
GM	Gunner's Mate
Gen.	General
Gy. Sgt.	Gunnery Sergeant
LCpl.	Lance Corporal
Lman	Landsman
Lt.	Lieutenant
Lt. (j.g.)	Lieutenant (junior grade)
Maj.	Major
MSgt.	Master Sergeant
NOR	Place of action not on record
Ord. Sman	Ordinary Seaman
Pfc.	Private First Class
Pvt.	Private
QG	Quarter Gunner
QM	Quartermaster
Reg'tal	Regimental
SQM	Signal Quartermaster
SSgt.	Staff Sergeant
Sfc.	Sergeant First Class
Sgt.	Sergeant
Sman	Seaman
Sp4c/5c	Specialist Fourth Class/Fifth Class

*posthumous award
+second award (first award earned in earlier conflict)

The Civil War, 1861–1865

Number of medals:	1,520
ARMY:	1,196
MARINES:	17
NAVY:	307

ARMY

Adams, Pvt. James F. (Nineveh, Va)
Adams, 2d Lt. John G. B. (Fredericksburg, Va)
Alber, Pvt. Frederick (Spotsylvania, Va)
Albert, Pvt. Christian (Vicksburg, Miss)
Allen, Cpl. Abner P. (Petersburg, Va)

Nathaniel M. Allen, Corporal, Company B, 1st Massachusetts Infantry. Place and date: At Gettysburg, Pa., 2 July 1863. Entered service at: Boston, Mass. Birth: Boston, Mass. Date of issue: 29 March 1899. Citation: When his regiment was falling back, this soldier, bearing the national color, returned in the face of the enemy's fire, pulled the regimental flag from under the body of its bearer, who had fallen, saved the flag from capture, and brought both colors off the field.

Allen, Pvt. James (South Mountain, Md)
Allen, Cpl. Nathaniel M. (Gettysburg, Pa)
Ames, 1st Lt. Adelbert (Bull Run, Va)
Ammerman, Pvt. Robert W. (Spotsylvania, Va)
Anderson, Pvt. Bruce (Fort Fisher, NC)
Anderson, Pvt. Charles W. (Waynesboro, Va)
Anderson, Sgt. Everett W. (Crosby's Creek, Tenn)
Anderson, Pvt. Frederick C. (Weldon Railroad, Va)
Anderson, Capt. Marion T. (Nashville, Tenn)
Anderson, Pvt. Peter (Bentonville, NC)
Anderson, Cpl. Thomas (Appomattox Station, Va)
Apple, Cpl. Andrew O. (Petersburg, Va)
Appleton, 1st Lt. William H. (Petersburg & New Market Heights, Va)
Archer, 1st Lt. & Adj. James W. (Corinth, Miss)
*Archer, Sgt. Lester (Fort Harrison, Va)
Archinal, Cpl. William (Vicksburg, Miss)
Armstrong, Pvt. Clinton L. (Vicksburg, Miss)
Arnold, Capt. Abraham K. (Davenport Bridge, Va)
Avery, Lt. William B. (Tranter's Creek, NC)
Ayers, Sgt. David (Vicksburg, Miss)
Ayers, Pvt. John G. K. (Vicksburg, Miss)
Babcock, Sgt. William J. (Petersburg, Va)
*Bacon, Pvt. Elijah W. (Gettysburg, Pa)
Baird, Brig. Gen. Absalom (Jonesboro, Ga)
Baldwin, Capt. Frank D. (Peach Tree Creek, Ga)
Ballen, Pvt. Frederick (Vicksburg, Miss)
Banks, Sgt. George L. (Missionary Ridge, Tenn)
Barber, Cpl. James A. (Petersburg, Va)
Barker, Sgt. Nathaniel C. (Spotsylvania, Va)
Barnes, Pvt. William H. (Chapin's Farm, Va)
Barnum, Col. Henry A. (Chattanooga, Tenn)
Barrell, 1st Lt. Charles L. (Camden, SC)
Barrick, Cpl. Jesse T. (Duck River, Tenn)
Barringer, Pvt. William H. (Vicksburg, Miss)
Barry, Sgt. Maj. Augustus (NOR)
Batchelder, Lt. Col. & Chief QM Richard N. (Catlett-Fairfax Stations, Va)
Bates, Col. Delavan (Cemetery Hill, Va)
Bates, Sgt. Norman F. (Columbus, Ga)
Baybutt, Pvt. Philip (Luray, Va)
Beatty, Capt. Alexander M. (Cold Harbor, Va)
Beaty, 1st Sgt. Powhatan (Chapin's Farm, Va)
Beaufort, Cpl. Jean J. (Port Hudson, La)
Beaumont, Maj. & Asst. Adj. Gen. Eugene B. (Harpeth River, Tenn & Selma, Ala)
Bebb, Pvt. Edward J. (Columbus, Ga)
Beckwith, Pvt. Wallace A. (Fredericksburg, Va)
Beddows, Pvt. Richard (Spotsylvania, Va)

Richard N. Batchelder, Lieutenant Colonel and Chief Quartermaster, 2d Corps. Place and date: Between Catlett and Fairfax Stations, Va., 13–15 October 1863. Entered service at: Manchester, N.H. Born: 27 July 1832, Meredith, N.H. Date of issue: 20 May 1895. Citation: Being ordered to move his trains by a continuous day-and-night march, and without the usual military escort, armed his teamsters and personally commanded them, successfully fighting against heavy odds and bringing his trains through without the loss of a wagon.

Beebe, 1st Lt. William S. (Cane River Crossing, La)
Beech, Sgt. John P. (Spotsylvania Courthouse, Va)
*Begley, Sgt. Terrence (Cold Harbor, Va)
Belcher, Pvt. Thomas (Chapin's Farm, Va)
Bell, Sgt. James B. (Missionary Ridge, Tenn)
Benedict, 2d Lt. George G. (Gettysburg, Pa)
Benjamin, Cpl. John F. (Sayler's Creek, Va)
Benjamin, 1st Lt. Samuel N. (Bull Run-Spotsylvania, Va)
Bennett, Pvt. Orren (Sayler's Creek, Va)
Bennett, 1st Lt. Orson W. (Honey Hill, SC)
Bensinger, Pvt. William (Georgia)
Benyaurd, 1st Lt. William H. H. (Five Forks, Va)
Betts, Lt. Col. Charles M. (Greensboro, NC)
Beyer, 2d Lt. Hillary (Antietam, Md)
Bickford, Cpl. Henry H. (Waynesboro, Va)
Bickford, Cpl. Matthew (Vicksburg, Miss)
Bieger, Pvt. Charles (Ivy Farm, Miss)
Bingham, Capt. Henry H. (Wilderness, Va)
Birdsall, Sgt. Horatio L. (Columbus, Ga)
Bishop, Pvt. Francis A. (Spotsylvania, Va)
Black, Lt. Col. John C. (Prairie Grove, Ark)
Black, Capt. William P. (Pea Ridge, Ark)
Blackmar, Lt. Wilmon W. (Five Forks, Va)
Blackwood, Surgeon William R. D. (Petersburg, Va)
Blasdel, Pvt. Thomas A. (Vicksburg, Miss)
Blickensderfer, Cpl. Milton (Petersburg, Va)
Bliss, Capt. George N. (Waynesboro, Va)
Bliss, Col. Zenas R. (Fredericksburg, Va)
Blodgett, 1st Lt. Wells H. (Newtonia, Mo)
Blucher, Cpl. Charles (Fort Harrison, Va)
Blunt, 1st Lt. John W. (Cedar Creek, Va)
Boehm, 2d Lt. Peter M. (Dinwiddie Courthouse, Va)
Bonebrake, Lt. Henry G. (Five Forks, Va)
Bonnaffon, 1st Lt. Sylvester, Jr. (Boydton Plank Road, Va)
Boody, Cpl. Robert (Williamsburg & Chancellorsville, Va)
Boon, Capt. Hugh P. (Sayler's Creek, Va)
Boquet, Pvt. Nicholas (Wilson's Creek, Mo)
Boss, Cpl. Orlando (Cold Harbor, Va)
Bourke, Pvt. John G. (Stone River, Tenn)
Boury, Sgt. Richard (Charlottesville, Va)
Boutwell, Pvt. John W. (Petersburg, Va)
Bowen, Cpl. Chester B. (Winchester, Va)
Bowen, Pvt. Emmer (Vicksburg, Miss)
Box, Capt. Thomas J. (Resaca, Ga)
Boynton, Lt. Col. Henry V. (Missionary Ridge, Tenn)
Bradley, Sgt. Thomas W. (Chancellorsville, Va)
Brady, Pvt. James (Chapin's Farm, Va)
Brandle, Pvt. Joseph E. (Lenoire, Tenn)
Brannigan, Pvt. Felix (Chancellorsville, Va)
Brant, Lt. William (Petersburg, Va)
Bras, Sgt. Edgar A. (Spanish Fort, Ala)
Brest, Pvt. Lewis F. (Sayler's Creek, Va)
Brewer, Pvt. William J. (Appomattox, Va)
Breyer, Sgt. Charles (Rappahannock Station, Va)
Briggs, Cpl. Elijah A. (Petersburg, Va)
Bringle, Cpl. Andrew (Sayler's Creek, Va)
Bronner, Pvt. August F. (White Oak Swamp, Va)
Bronson, 1st Sgt. James H. (Chapin's Farm, Va)
Brosnan, Sgt. John (Petersburg, Va)
Brouse, Capt. Charles W. (Missionary Ridge, Tenn)
Brown, Sgt. Charles (Weldon Railroad, Va)
Brown, Cpl. Edward, Jr. (Fredericksburg & Salem Heights, Va)
Brown, Sgt. Henri L. (Wilderness, Va)
Brown, Capt. Jeremiah Z. (Petersburg, Va)
Brown, 1st Sgt. John H. (Vicksburg, Miss)
Brown, Capt. John H. (Franklin, Tenn)
*Brown, Capt. Morris, Jr. Gettysburg, Pa)
Brown, Pvt. Robert B. (Missionary Ridge, Tenn)
Brown, Pvt. Uriah (Vicksburg, Miss)
Brown, Pvt. Wilson W. (Georgia)
Brownell, Pvt. Francis E. (Alexandria, Va)
Bruner, Pvt. Louis J. (Walker's Ford, Tenn)
Brush, Lt. George W. (Ashepoo River, SC)
Bruton, Capt. Christopher C. (Waynesboro, Va)
Bryant, Sgt. Andrew S. (New Bern, NC)
*Buchanan, Pvt. George A. (Chapin's Farm, Va)
Buckingham, 1st Lt. David E. (Rowanty Creek, Va)
Buckles, Sgt. Abram J. (Wilderness, Va)
Buckley, Pvt. Denis (Peach Tree Creek, Ga)
Buckley, Sgt. John C. (Vicksburg, Miss)
Bucklyn, 1st Lt. John K. (Chancellorsville, Va)

Charles Breyer, Sergeant, Company I, 90th Pennsylvania Infantry. Place and date: At Rappahannock Station, Va., 23 August 1862. Entered service at: Philadelphia, Pa. Date of issue: 8 July 1896. Citation: Voluntarily, and at great personal risk, picked up an unexploded shell and threw it away, thus doubtless saving the life of a comrade whose arm had been taken off by the same shell.

Buffington, Sgt. John E. (Petersburg, Va)
Buffum, Pvt. Robert (Georgia)
Buhrman, Pvt. Henry G. (Vicksburg, Miss)
Bumgarner, Sgt. William (Vicksburg, Miss)
Burbank, Sgt. James H. (Blackwater, Va)
Burger, Pvt. Joseph (Nolensville, Tenn)
Burk, Pvt. E. Michael (Spotsylvania, Va)
Burk, Sgt. Thomas (Wilderness, Va)
Burke, 1st Sgt. Daniel W. (Shepherdstown Ford, Va)
Burke, Pvt. Thomas M. (Hanover Courthouse, Va)
Burns, Sgt. James M. (New Market, Va)
Burritt, Pvt. William W. (Vicksburg, Miss)
Butterfield, Brig. Gen. Daniel (Gaines's Mill, Va)
Butterfield, 1st Lt. Frank G. (Salem Heights, Va)
Cadwallader, Cpl. Abel G. (Hatcher's Run & Dabney's Mills, Va)
Cadwell, Sgt. Luman L. (Alabama Bayou, La)
Caldwell, Sgt. Daniel (Hatcher's Run, Va)
Calkin, 1st Sgt. Ivers S. (Sayler's Creek, Va)
Callahan, Pvt. John H. (Fort Blakely, Ala)
Camp, Pvt. Carlton N. (Petersburg, Va)
Campbell, Pvt. James A. (Woodstock & Amelia Courthouse, Va)
Campbell, Pvt. William (Vicksburg, Miss)
Capehart, Maj. Charles E. (Monterey Mountain, Pa)
Capehart, Col. Henry (Greenbrier River, W Va)
*Capron, Sgt. Horace, Jr. (Chickahominy & Ashland, Va)
Carey, Sgt. Hugh (Gettysburg, Pa)
Carey, Sgt. James L. (Appomattox Courthouse, Va)
Carlisle, Pvt. Casper R. (Gettysburg, Pa)
Carman, Pvt. Warren (Waynesboro, Va)
Carmin, Cpl. Isaac H. (Vicksburg, Miss)
Carney, Sgt. William H. (Fort Wagner, SC)
Carr, Col. Eugene A. (Pea Ridge, Ark)
Carr, Cpl. Franklin (Nashville, Tenn)
Carson, Musician William J. (Chickamauga, Ga)
Cart, Pvt. Jacob (Fredericksburg, Va)
Carter, 2d Lt. John J. (Antietam, Md)
Carter, Capt. Joseph F. (Fort Stedman, Va)
Caruana, Pvt. Orlando E. (New Bern, NC & S. Mountain, Md)
Casey, Pvt. David (Cold Harbor, Va)
Casey, Pvt. Henry (Vicksburg, Miss)
Catlin, Col. Isaac S. (Petersburg, Va)
Cayer, Sgt. Ovila (Weldon Railroad, Va)
Chamberlain, Col. Joshua L. (Gettysburg, Pa)
Chamberlain, 2d Lt. Orville T. (Chickamauga, Ga)
Chambers, Pvt. Joseph B. (Petersburg, Va)
Chandler, Sgt. Henry F. (Petersburg, Va)
Chandler, QM Sgt. Stephen E. (Amelia Springs, Va)
Chapin, Pvt. Alaric B. (Fort Fisher, NC)
Chapman, Pvt. John (Sayler's Creek, Va)

Chase, Pvt. John F. (Chancellorsville, Va)
Child, Cpl. Benjamin H. (Antietam, Md)
Chisman, Pvt. William W. (Vicksburg, Miss)
Christiancy, 1st Lt. James I. (Hawes's Shops, Pa)
Churchill, Cpl. Samuel J. (Nashville, Tenn)
Cilley, Capt. Clinton A. (Chickamauga, Ga)
Clancy, Sgt. James T. (Vaughn Road, Va)
Clapp, 1st Sgt. Albert A. (Sayler's Creek, Va)
Clark, Lt. & Adj. Charles A. (Brook's Ford, Va)
Clark, Cpl. Harrison (Gettysburg, Pa)
Clark, Pvt. James G. (Petersburg, Va)
Clark, 1st Lt. & Reg'tal QM John W. (Warrenton, Va)
Clark, Cpl. William A. (Nolensville, Tenn)
Clarke, Capt. Dayton P. (Spotsylvania, Va)
Clausen, 1st Lt. Charles H. (Spotsylvania, Va)
Clay, Capt. Cecil (Fort Harrison, Va)
Cleveland, Pvt. Charles F. (Antietam, Md)
Clopp, Pvt. John E. (Gettysburg, Pa)
Clute, Cpl. George W. (Bentonville, NC)
Coates, Sgt. Jefferson (Gettysburg, Pa)
Cockley, 1st Lt. David L. (Waynesboro, GA)
Coey, Maj. James (Hatcher's Run, Va)
Coffey, Sgt. Robert J. (Bank's Ford, Va)
Cohn, Sgt. Maj. Abraham (Wilderness, Va)
Colby, Sgt. Carlos W. (Vicksburg, Miss)
Cole, Cpl. Gabriel (Winchester, Va)
Collins, Cpl. Harrison (Richland Creek, Tenn)
Collins, Sgt. Thomas D. (Resaca, Ga)
Collis, Col. Charles H. T. (Fredericksburg, Va)
Colwell, 1st Lt. Oliver (Nashville, Tenn)
Compson, Maj. Hartwell B. (Waynesboro, Va)
Conaway, Pvt. John W. (Vicksburg, Miss)
Conboy, Sgt. Martin (Williamsburg, Va)
Connell, Cpl. Trustrim (Sayler's Creek, Va)
Conner, Pvt. Richard (Bull Run, Va)
Connors, Pvt. James (Fisher's Hill, Va)
Cook, Bugler John (Antietam, Md)
Cook, Sgt. John H. (Pleasant Hill, La)
Cooke, Capt. Walter H. (Bull Run, Va)
Copp, 2d Lt. Charles D. (Fredericksburg, Va)
Corcoran, Pvt. John (Petersburg, Va)
Corliss, Capt. George W. (Cedar Mountain, Va)
Corliss, 1st Lt. Stephen P. (South Side Railroad, Va)
Corson, Asst. Surgeon Joseph K. (Bristoe Station, Va)
Cosgriff, Pvt. Richard H. (Columbus, Ga)
Cosgrove, Pvt. Thomas (Drewry's Bluff, Va)
Coughlin, Lt. Col. John (Swift's Creek, Va)
Cox, Cpl. Robert M. (Vicksburg, Miss)
Coyne, Sgt. John H. (Williamsburg, Va)

Cranston, Pvt. William W. (Chancellorsville, Va)
Creed, Pvt. John (Fisher's Hill, Va)
Crocker, Capt. Henry H. (Cedar Creek, Va)
Crocker, Pvt. Ulric L. (Cedar Creek, Va)
Croft, Pvt. James E. (Allatoona, Ga)
Crosier, Sgt. William H. H. (Peach Tree Creek, Ga)
Cross, Cpl. James E. (Blackburn's Ford, Va)
Crowley, Pvt. Michael (Waynesboro, Va)
Cullen, Cpl. Thomas (Bristoe Station, Va)
Cummings, Sgt. Maj. Amos J. (Salem Heights, Va)
Cumpston, Pvt. James M. (Shenandoah Valley, Va)
Cunningham, 1st Sgt. Francis M. (Sayler's Creek, Va)
Cunningham, Pvt. James S. (Vicksburg, Miss)
Curran, Asst. Surgeon Richard (Antietam, Md)
Curtis, Sgt. Maj. John C. (Baton Rouge, La)
Curtis, 2d Lt. Josiah M. (Petersburg, Va)
Curtis, Brig. Gen. Newton M. (Fort Fisher, NC)
Custer, 2d Lt. Thomas W. (Namozine Church, Va)
Second award (Sayler's Creek, Va)
Cutcheon, Maj. Byron M. (Horseshoe Bend, Ky)
Cutts, Capt. James M. (Wilderness, Spotsylvania, & Petersburg, Va)
Darrough, Sgt. John S. (Eastport, Miss)
Davidsizer, Sgt. John A. (Paine's Crossroads, Va)
Davidson, Asst. Surgeon Andrew (Vicksburg, Miss)
Davidson, 1st Lt. Andrew (Petersburg, Va)
Davis, Maj. Charles C. (Shelbyville, Tenn)
Davis, Sgt. Freeman (Missionary Ridge, Tenn)
Davis, 1st Lt. George E. (Monocacy, Md)
Davis, Pvt. Harry (Atlanta, Ga)
Davis, Pvt. John (Culloden, Ga)
Davis, Cpl. Joseph (Franklin, Tenn)
Davis, Sgt. Martin K. (Vicksburg, Miss)
Davis, Pvt. Thomas (Sayler's Creek, Va)
Day, Pvt. Charles (Hatcher's Run, Va)
Day, Pvt. David F. (Vicksburg, Miss)
De Castro, Cpl. Joseph H. (Gettysburg, Pa)
De Lacey, 1st Sgt. Patrick (Wilderness, Va)
De Lavie, Sgt. Hiram H. (Five Forks, Va)
De Puy, 1st Sgt. Charles H. (Petersburg, Va)
De Witt, Cpl. Richard W. (Vicksburg, Miss)
Deane, Maj. John M. (Fort Stedman, Va)
Deland, Pvt. Frederick N. (Port Hudson, La)
Delaney, Sgt. John C. (Dabney's Mills, Va)
Di Cesnola, Col. Louis P. (Aldie, Va)

John F. Chase, Private, 5th Battery, Maine Light Artillery. Place and date: At Chancellorsville, Va., 3 May 1863. Entered service at: Augusta, Maine. Birth: Chelsea, Maine. Date of issue: 7 February 1888. Citation: Nearly all the officers and men of the battery having been killed or wounded, this soldier with a comrade continued to fire his gun after the guns had ceased. The piece was then dragged off by the two, the horses having been shot, and its capture by the enemy was prevented.

Michael Dougherty, Private, Company B, 13th Pennsylvania Cavalry. Place and date: At Jefferson, Va., 12 October 1863. Entered service at: Philadelphia, Pa. Born: 10 May 1844, Ireland. Date of issue: 23 January 1897. Citation: At the head of a detachment of his company dashed across an open field, exposed to a deadly fire from the enemy, and succeeded in dislodging them from an unoccupied house, which he and his comrades defended for several hours against repeated attacks, thus preventing the enemy from flanking the position of the Union forces.

Dickey, Capt. William D. (Petersburg, Va)
Dickie, Sgt. David (Vicksburg, Miss)
Dilger, Capt. Hubert (Chancellorsville, Va)
Dillon, Pvt. Michael A. (Williamsburg, Va)
Dockum, Pvt. Warren C. (Sayler's Creek, Va)
Dodd, Pvt. Robert F. (Petersburg, Va)
Dodds, Sgt. Edward E. (Ashby's Gap, Va)
Dolloff, Cpl. Charles W. (Petersburg, Va)
Donaldson, Sgt. John (Appomattox Courthouse, Va)
Donoghue, Pvt. Timothy (Fredericksburg, Va)
Doody, Cpl. Patrick (Cold Harbor, Va)
Dore, Sgt. George H. (Gettysburg, Pa)
Dorley, Pvt. August (Mount Pleasant, Ala)
Dorsey, Cpl. Daniel A. (Georgia)
Dorsey, Sgt. Decatur (Petersburg, Va)
Dougall, 1st Lt. & Adj. Allan H. (Bentonville, NC)
Dougherty, Pvt. Michael (Jefferson, Va)
Dow, Sgt. George P. (Richmond, Va)
Downey, Pvt. William (Ashepoo River, SC)
Downs, Sgt. Henry W. (Winchester, Va)
Drake, 2d Lt. James M. (Bermuda Hundred, Va)
Drury, Sgt. James (Weldon Railroad, Va)
Du Pont, Capt. Henry A. (Cedar Creek, Va)
Duffey, Pvt. John (Ashepoo River, SC)
Dunlavy, Pvt. James (Osage, Kans)
Dunne, Cpl. James (Vicksburg, Miss)
Durham, 2d Lt. James R. (Winchester, Va)
Durham, Sgt. John S. (Perryville, Ky)
Eckes, Pvt. John N. (Vicksburg, Miss)
Eddy, Pvt. Samuel E. (Sayler's Creek, Va)
Edgerton, Lt. & Adj. Nathan H. (Chapin's Farm, Va)
Edwards, Pvt. David (Five Forks, Va)
Elliott, Sgt. Alexander (Paine's Crossroads, Va)
Elliott, Sgt. Russell C. (Natchitoches, La)
Ellis, Pvt. Horace (Weldon Railroad, Va)
Ellis, 1st Sgt. William (Dardanelles, Ark)
Ellsworth, Capt. Thomas F. (Honey Hill, SC)
Elson, Sgt. James M. (Vicksburg, Miss)
Embler, Capt. Andrew H. (Boydton Plank Road, Va)
Enderlin, Musician Richard (Gettysburg, Pa)
Engle, Sgt. James E. (Bermuda Hundred, Va)
English, 1st Sgt. Edmund (Wilderness, Va)

Samuel E. Eddy, Private, Company D, 37th Massachusetts Infantry. Place and date: At Sailors Creek, Va., 6 April 1865. Entered service at: Chesterfield, Mass. Birth: Vermont. Date of issue: 10 September 1897. Citation: Saved the life of the adjutant of his regiment by voluntarily going beyond the line and there killing one of the enemy then in the act of firing upon the wounded officer. Was assailed by several of the enemy, run through the body with a bayonet, and pinned to the ground, but while so situated he shot and killed his assailant.

Ennis, Pvt. Charles D. (Petersburg, Va)
Estes, Capt. & Asst. Adj. Gen. Lewellyn G. (Flint River, Ga)
Evans, Pvt. Coron D. (Sayler's Creek, Va)
Evans, Capt. Ira H. (Hatcher's Run, Va)
Evans, Pvt. James R. (Wilderness, Va)
Evans, Pvt. Thomas (Piedmont, Va)
Everson, Pvt. Adelbert (Five Forks, Va)
Ewing, Pvt. John C. (Petersburg, Va)
Falconer, Cpl. John A. (Fort Sanders, Tenn)
Fall, Sgt. Charles S. (Spotsylvania Courthouse, Va)
Fallon, Pvt. Thomas T. (Williamsburg, Va)
*Falls, Color Sgt. Benjamin F. (Gettysburg, Pa)
Fanning, Pvt. Nicholas (Selma, Ala)
Farnsworth, Sgt. Maj. Herbert E. (Trevilian Station, Va)
Farquhar, Sgt. Maj. John M. (Stone River, Tenn)
Fasnacht, Sgt. Charles H. (Spotsylvania, Va)
Fassett, Capt. John B. (Gettysburg, Pa)
Fernald, 1st Lt. Albert E. (Five Forks, Va)
Ferrier, Sgt. Daniel T. (Varnell's Station, Ga)
Ferris, 1st Lt. & Adj. Eugene W. (Berryville, Va)
Fesq, Pvt. Frank (Petersburg, Va)
Finkenbiner, Pvt. Henry S. (Dingle's Mill, SC)
Fisher, 1st Lt. John H. (Vicksburg, Miss)
Fisher, Cpl. Joseph (Petersburg, Va)
Flanagan, Sgt. Augustin (Chapin's Farm, Va)
Flannigan, Pvt. James (Nolensville, Ten)
Fleetwood, Sgt. Maj. Christian A. (Chapin's Farm, Va)
Flynn, Cpl. Christopher (Gettysburg, Pa)
Flynn, Sgt. James E. (Vicksburg, Miss)
Follett, Sgt. Joseph L. (New Madrid, Mo & Stone River, Tenn)
Force, Brig. Gen. Manning F. (Atlanta, Ga)
Ford, 1st Lt. George W. (Sayler's Creek, Va)
Forman, Cpl. Alexander A. (Fair Oaks, Va)
Fout, 2d Lt. Frederick W. (Harper's Ferry, W Va)
Fox, Sgt. Henry (Jackson, Tenn)
Fox, Sgt. Henry M. (Winchester, Va)
Fox, Pvt. Nicholas (Port Hudson, La)
Fox, Pvt. William R. (Petersburg, Va)
Frantz, Pvt. Joseph (Vicksburg, Miss)
Fraser, Pvt. William W. (Vicksburg, Miss)
Freeman, Pvt. Archibald (Spotsylvania, Va)
Freeman, 1st Lt. Henry B. (Stone River, Tenn)
Freeman, Pvt. William H. (Fort Fisher, NC)
French, Pvt. Samuel S. (Fair Oaks, Va)
Frey, Cpl. Franz (Vicksburg, Miss)
Frick, Col. Jacob G. (Fredericksburg, Va)
Frizzell, Pvt. Henry F. (Vicksburg, Miss)
Fuger, Sgt. Frederick (Gettysburg, Pa)
Funk, Maj. West (Appomattox Courthouse, Va)
Furman, Cpl. Chester S. (Gettysburg, Pa)
Furness, Capt. Frank (Trevilian Station, Va)
Gage, Pvt. Richard J. (Elk River, Tenn)
Galloway, Pvt. George N. (Alsop's Farm, Va)
Galloway, Commissary Sgt. John (Farmville, Va)
Gardiner, Pvt. James (Chapin's Farm, Va)
Gardner, Pvt. Charles N. (Five Forks, Va)
Gardner, Sgt. Robert J. (Petersburg, Va)
Garrett, Sgt. William (Nashville, Tenn)
*Gasson, Sgt. Richard (Chapin's Farm, Va)
Gaunt, Pvt. John C. (Franklin, Tenn)
Gause, Cpl. Isaac (Berryville, Va)
Gaylord, Sgt. Levi B. (Fort Stedman, Va)
Gere, 1st Lt. & Adj. Thomas P. (Nashville, Tenn)
Geschwind, Capt. Nicholas (Vicksburg, Miss)
Gibbs, Sgt. Wesley (Petersburg, Va)
Gifford, Pvt. Benjamin (Sayler's Creek, VA)
Gifford, Pvt. David L. (Ashepoo River, SC)
Gillespie, 1st Lt. George L. (Bethesda Church, Va)
Gilligan, 1st Sgt. Edward L. (Gettysburg, Pa)
Gilmore, Maj. John C. (Salem Heights, Va)
Ginley, Pvt. Patrick J. (Reams's Station, Va)
Gion, Pvt. Joseph (Chancellorsville, Va)
Godley, 1st Sgt. Leonidas M. (Vicksburg, Miss)
Goettel, Pvt. Philip (Ringgold, Ga)
Goheen, 1st Sgt. Charles A. (Waynesboro, Va)
Goldsbery, Pvt. Andrew E. (Vicksburg, Miss)
Goodall, 1st Sgt. Francis H. (Fredericksburg, Va)
Goodman, 1st Lt. William E. (Chancellorsville, Va)
Goodrich, 1st Lt. Edwin (Cedar Creek, Va)
Gould, Capt. Charles G. (Petersburg, Va)
Gould, Pvt. Newton T. (Vicksburg, Miss)
Gouraud, Capt. & Aide-de-Camp George E. (Honey Hill, SC)
Grace, Sgt. Pter (Wilderness, Va)
Graham, 2d Lt. Thomas N. (Missionary Ridge, Tenn)
Grant, Surgeon Gabriel (Fair Oaks, Va)
Grant, Col. Lewis A. (Salem Heights, Va)
Graul, Cpl. William (Fort Harrison, Va)
Gray, Pvt. John (Port Republic, Va)
Gray, Sgt. Robert A. (Drewry's Bluff, Va)
Grebe, Capt. M. R. William (Jonesboro, Ga)
Green, Cpl. George (Missionary Ridge, Tenn)
Greenawalt, Pvt. Abraham (Franklin, Tenn)
Greene, Maj. & Asst. Adj. Gen. Oliver D. (Antietam, Md)
Gregg, Pvt. Joseph O. (Richmond & Petersburg Railway, Va)
Greig, 2d Lt. Theodore W. (Antietam, Md)
Gresser, Cpl. Ignatz (Antietam, Md)
Gribben, Lt. James H. (Sayler's Creek, Va)
Grimshaw, Pvt. Samuel (Atlanta, Ga)
Grindlay, Col. James G. (Five Forks, Va)
Grueb, Pvt. George (Chapin's Farm, Va)
Guerin, Pvt. Fitz W. (Grand Gulf, Miss)
Guinn, Pvt. Thomas (Vicksburg, Miss)
Gwynne, Pvt. Nathaniel (Petersburg, Va)
Hack, Pvt. John (Vicksburg, Miss)
Hack, Sgt. Lester G. (Petersburg, Va)
Hadley, Sgt. Cornelius M. (Knoxville, Tenn)
Hadley, Cpl. Osgood T. (Pegram House, Va)
Hagerty, Pvt. Asel (Sayler's Creek, Va)
Haight, Sgt. John H. (Williamsburg, Bristol Station & Manassas, Va)
Haight, Cpl. Sidney (Petersburg, Va)
Hall, Chaplain Francis B. (Salem Heights, Va)
Hall, 2d Lt. & Capt. Henry S. (Gaines's Mill & Rappahannock Station, Va)
Hall, Cpl. Newton H. (Franklin, Tenn)
Hallock, Pvt. Nathan M. (Bristoe Station, Va)
Hammel, Sgt. Henry A. (Grand Gulf, Miss)
Haney, Chaplain Milton L. (Atlanta, Ga)
Hanford, Pvt. Edward R. (Woodstock, Va)
Hanks, Pvt. Joseph (Vicksburg, Miss)
Hanna, Sgt. Marcus A. (Port Hudson, La)
Hanna, Cpl. Milton (Nolensville, Tenn)
Hanscom, Cpl. Moses C. (Bristoe Station, Va)
Hapeman, Lt. Col. Douglas (Peach Tree Creek, Ga)
Harbourne, Pvt. John H. (Petersburg, Va)
*Hardenbergh, Pvt. Henry M. (Deep Run, Va)
Haring, 1st Lt. Abram P. (Bachelor's Creek NC)
Harmon, Cpl. Amzi D. (Petersburg, Va)
Harrington, Sgt. Ephraim W. (Fredericksburg, Va)

Benjamin F. Hilliker, Musician, Company A, 8th Wisconsin Infantry. Place and date: At Mechanicsburg, Miss., 4 June 1863. Entered service at: Waupaca Township, Wis. Born: 23 May 1843, Golden, Erie County, N.Y. Date of issue: 17 December 1897. Citation: When men were needed to oppose a superior Confederate force he laid down his drum for a rifle and proceeded to the front of the skirmish line which was about 120 feet from the enemy. While on this volunteer mission and firing at the enemy he was hit in the head with a minie ball which passed through him. An order was given to "lay him in the shade; he won't last long." He recovered from this wound being left with an ugly scar.

Harris, Pvt. George W. (Spotsylvania, Va)
Harris, Sgt. James H. (New Market Heights, Va)
Harris, 1st Lt. Moses (Smithfield, Va)
Harris, Pvt. Sampson (Vicksburg, Miss)
Hart, Sgt. John W. (Gettysburg, Pa)
Hart, Pvt. William E. (Shenandoah Valley, Va)
Hartranft, Col. John F. (Bull Run, Va)
Harvey, Cpl. Harry (Waynesboro, Va)
Haskell, Sgt. Maj. Frank W. (Fair Oaks, Va)
Haskell, Sgt. Marcus M. (Antietam, Md)
Hastings, Capt. Smith H. (Newby's Crossroads, Va)
Hatch, Brig. Gen. John P. (South Mountain, Md)
Havron, Sgt. John H. (Petersburg, Va)
Hawkins, 1st Lt. Gardner C. (Petersburg, Va)
Hawkins, Cpl. Martin J. (Georgia)
Hawkins, Sgt. Maj. Thomas R. (Chapin's Farm, Va)
Hawthorne, Cpl. Harris S. (Sayler's Creek, Va)
Haynes, Cpl. Asbury F. (Sayler's Creek, Va)
Hays, Pvt. John H. (Columbus, Ga)
Healey, Pvt. George W. (Newnan, Ga)
Hedges, 1st Lt. Joseph (Harpeth River, Tenn)
Heermance, Capt. William L. (Chancellorsville, Va)
Heller, Sgt. Henry (Chancellorsville, Va)
Helms, Pvt. David H. (Vicksburg, Miss)
Henry, Col. Guy V. (Cold Harbor, Va)
Henry, Sgt. James (Vicksburg, Miss)
Henry, Col. William W. (Cedar Creek, Va)
Herington, Pvt. Pitt B. (Kenesaw Mountain, Ga)
Herron, Lt. Col. Francis J. (Pea Ridge, Ark)
Hesseltine, Col. Francis S. (Matagorda Bay, Tex)
Hibson, Pvt. Joseph C. (Fort Wagner, SC)
Hickey, Sgt. Dennis W. (Stony Creek Bridge, Va)
Hickok, Cpl. Nathan E. (Chapin's Farm, Va)
Higby, Pvt. Charles (Appomattox, Va)
Higgins, Pvt. Thomas J. (Vicksburg, Miss)
Highland, Cpl. Patrick (Petersburg, Va)
Hill, Capt. Edward (Cold Harbor, Va)
Hill, Cpl. Henry (Wilderness, Va)
Hill, 1st Lt. James (Champion Hill, Miss)
*Hill, Sgt. James (Petersburg, Va)
Hilliker, Musician Benjamin F. (Mechanicsburg, Miss)
Hills, Pvt. William G. (North Fork, Va)
*Hilton, Sgt. Alfred B. (Chapin's Farm, Va)
Hincks, Sgt. Maj. William B. (Gettysburg, Pa)
Hodges, Pvt. Addison J. (Vicksburg, Miss)
Hoffman, Cpl. Henry (Sayler's Creek, Va)
Hoffman, Capt. Thomas W. (Petersburg, Va)
Hogan, Cpl. Franklin (Petersburg, Va)
Hogarty, Pvt. William P. (Antietam, Md)
Holcomb, Pvt. Daniel I. (Brentwood Hills, Tenn)
Holehouse, Pvt. James (Marye's Heights, Va)
Holland, Capt. Lemuel F. (Elk River, Tenn)
Holland, Sgt. Maj. Milton M. (Chapin's Farm, Va)

Orion P. Howe, Musician, Company C, 55th Illinois Infantry. Place and date: at Vicksburg, Miss., 19 May 1863. Entered service at: Woken, Ill. Birth: Portage County, Ohio. Date of issue: 23 April 1896. Citation: A drummer boy, 14 years of age, and severely wounded and exposed to a heavy fire from the enemy, he persistently remained upon the field of battle until he had reported to Gen. W. T. Sherman the necessity of supplying cartridges for the use of troops under command of Colonel Malmborg.

Holmes, 1st Sgt. Lovilo N. (Nolensvillle, Tenn)
Holmes, Pvt. William T. (Sayler's Creek, Va)
Holton, 1st Sgt. Charles M. (Falling Waters, Va)
Holton, 1st Sgt. Edward A. (Lee's Mills, Va)
Homan, Color Sgt. Conrad (Petersburg, Va)
Hooker, 1st Lt. George W. (South Mountain, Md)
Hooper, Cpl. William B. (Chamberlain's Creek, Va)
Hopkins, Cpl. Charles F. (Gaines's Mill, Va)
Horan, Sgt. Thomas (Gettysburg, Pa)
Horne, Capt. Samuel B. (Fort Harrison, Va)
Horsfall, Drummer William H. (Corinth, Miss)
Hottenstine, Pvt. Solomon J. (Petersburg & Norfolk Railroad, Va)
Hough, Pvt. Ira (Cedar Creek, Va)
Houghton, Capt. Charles H. (Petersburg, Va)
Houghton, Pvt. George L. (Elk River, Tenn)
Houlton, Comm. Sgt. William (Sayler's Creek, Va)
Howard, Cpl. Henderson C. (Glendale, Va)
Howard, Pvt. Hiram R. (Missionary Ridge, Tenn)
Howard, Sgt. James (Battery Gregg, Va)
Howard, Brig. Gen. Oliver O. (Fair Oaks, Va)
Howard, 1st Sgt. Squire E. (Bayou Teche, La)
Howe, Musician Orion P. (Vicksburg, Miss)
Howe, Sgt. William H. (Fort Stedman, Va)
Hubbell, Capt. William S. (Fort Harrison, Va)
Hudson, Pvt. Aaron R. (Culloden, Ga)
Hughes, Cpl. Oliver (Weldon Railroad, Va)
Hughey, Cpl. John (Sayler's Creek, Va)
Huidekoper, Lt. Col. Henry S. (Gettysburg, Pa)
Hunt, Pvt. Louis T. (Vicksburg, Miss)
Hunter, Sgt. Charles A. (Petersburg, Va)
Hunterson, Pvt. John C. (Peninsula, Va)
Hyatt, 1st Sgt. Theodore (Vicksburg, Miss)
Hyde, Maj. Thomas W. (Antietam, Md)
Hymer, Capt. Samuel (Buzzard's Roost Gap, Ga)
Ilgenfritz, Sgt. Charles H. (Fort Sedgwick, Va)
Immell, Cpl. Lorenzo D. (Wilson's Creek, Mo)
Ingalls, Pvt. Lewis J. (Boutte Station, La)
Inscho, Cpl. Leonidas H. (South Mountain, Md)
Irsch, Capt. Francis (Gettysburg, Pa)
Irwin, 1st Sgt. Patrick (Jonesboro, Ga)
Jackson, 1st Sgt. Frederick R. (James Island, SC)
Jacobson, Sgt. Maj. Eugene P. (Chancellorsville, Va)
James, Pvt. Isaac (Petersburg, Va)
James, Cpl. Miles (Chapin's Farm, Va)
Jamieson, 1st Sgt. Walter (Petersburg, Va)
Jardine, Sgt. James (Vicksburg, Miss)
Jellison, Sgt. Benjamin H. (Gettysburg, Pa)
Jennings, Pvt. James T. (Weldon Railroad, Va)
Jewett, 1st Lt. Erastus W. (Newport Barracks, NC)
John, Pvt. William (Vicksburg, Miss)
Johndro, Pvt. Franklin (Chapin's Farm, Va)
Johns, Cpl. Elisha (Vicksburg, Miss)
Johns, Pvt. Henry T. (Port Hudson, La)
Johnson, Pvt. Andrew (Vicksburg, Miss)
Johnson, Cpl. Follett (New Hope Church, Ga)
Johnson, Pvt. John (Fredericksburg, Va)
Johnson, 1st Lt. Joseph E. (Fort Harrison, Va)
Johnson, Maj. Ruel M. (Chattanooga, Tenn)
Johnson, Pvt. Samuel (Antietam, Md)
Johnson, Sgt. Wallace W. (Gettysburg, Pa)
Johnston, Pvt. David (Vicksburg, Miss)
Johnston, Musician Willie (NOR)
Jones, Pvt. David (Vicksburg, Miss)
Jones, 1st Sgt. William (Spotsylvania, Va)
Jordan, Cpl. Absalom (Sayler's Creek, Va)
Josselyn, 1st Lt. Simeon T. (Missionary Ridge, Tenn)
Judge, 1st Sgt. Francis W. (Fort Sanders, Tenn)
Kaiser, Sgt. John (Richmond, Va)
Kaltenbach, Cpl. Luther (Nashville, Tenn)
Kane, Cpl. John (Petersburg, Va)
Kappesser, Pvt. Peter (Lookout Mountain, Tenn)
Karpeles, Sgt. Leopold (Wilderness, Va)
Kauss, Cpl. August (Five Forks, Va)
Keele, Sgt. Maj. Joseph (North Anna River, Va)

Simeon T. Josselyn, First Lieutenant, Company C, 13th Illinois Infantry. Place and date: At Missionary Ridge, Tenn., 25 November 1863. Entered service at: Amboy, Ill. Born: 14 January 1842, Buffalo, N.Y. Date of issue: 4 April 1898. Citation: While commanding his company, deployed as skirmishers, came upon a large body of the enemy, taking a number of them prisoner. Lt. Josselyn himself shot their color bearer, seized the colors and brought them back to his regiment.

Keen, Sgt. Joseph S. (Chattahoochee River, Ga)
Keene, Pvt. Joseph (Fredericksburg, Va)
Kelley, Pvt. Andrew J. (Knoxville, Tenn)
Kelley, Capt. George V. (Franklin, Tenn)
Kelley, Sgt. Leverett M. (Missionary Ridge, Tenn)
Kelly, 1st Sgt. Alexander (Chapin's Farm, Va)
Kelly, Sgt. Daniel A. (Waynesboro, Va)
Kelly, Pvt. Thomas (Front Royal, Va)
Kemp, 1st Sgt. Joseph (Wilderness, Va)
Kendall, 1st Sgt. William W. (Black River Bridge, Miss)
Kennedy, Pvt. John (Trevilian Station, Va)
Kenyon, Sgt. John S. (Trenton, NC)
Kenyon, Pvt. Samuel P. (Sayler's Creek, Va)
Keough, Cpl. John (Sayler's Creek, Va)
Kephart, Pvt. James (Vicksburg, Miss)
Kerr, Capt. Thomas R. (Moorfield, W Va)
Kiggins, Sgt. John (Lookout Mountain, Tenn)
Kimball, Pvt. Joseph (Sayler's Creek, Va)
Kindig, Cpl. John M. (Spotsylvania, Va)
King, Maj. & QM Horatio C. (Dinwiddie Courthouse, Va)
King, 1st Lt. Rufus, Jr. (White Oak Swamp Bridge, Va)
Kinsey, Cpl. John (Spotsylvania, Va)
Kirby, Maj. Dennis T. (Vicksburg, Miss)
Kirk, Capt. Jonathan C. (North Anna River, Va)
Kline, Pvt. Harry (Sayler's Creek, Va)
Kloth, Pvt. Charles H. (Vicksburg, Miss)
Knight, Cpl. Charles H. (Petersburg, Va)
Knight, Pvt. William J. (Georgia)
Knowles, Pvt. Abiather J. (Bull Run, Va)
Knox, 2d Lt. Edward M. (Gettysburg, Pa)
Koogle, 1st Lt. Jacob (Five Forks, Va)
Kountz, Musician John S. (Missionary Ridge, Tenn)
Kramer, Pvt. Theodore L. (Chapin's Farm, Va)
Kretsinger, Pvt. George (Vicksburg, Miss)
Kuder, 2d Lt. Andrew (Waynesboro, Va)
Kuder, Lt. Jeremiah (Jonesboro, Ga)
Labille, Pvt. Joseph S. (Vicksburg, Miss)
Ladd, Pvt. George (Waynesboro, Va)
*Laing, Sgt. William (Chapin's Farm, Va)
Landis, Chief Bugler James P. (Paine's Crossroads, Va)
Lane, Pvt. Momrgan D. (Jetersville, Va)

Dewitt Clinton Lewis, Captain, Company F, 97th Pennsylvania Infantry. Place and date: At Secessionville, S.C., 16 June 1862. Birth: West Chester, Pa. Date of issue: 23 April 1896. Citation: While retiring with his men before a heavy fire of canister shot at short range, returned in the face of the enemy's fire and rescued an exhausted private of his company who but for this timely action would have lost his life by drowning in the morass through which the troops were retiring.

Lanfare, 1st Lt. Aaron S. (Sayler's Creek, Va)
Langbein, Musician J. C. Julius (Camden, NC)
Larimer, Cpl. Smith (Sayler's Creek, Va)
Larrabee, Cpl. James W. (Vicksburg, Miss)
Lawson, 1st Sgt. Gaines (Minville, Tenn)
Lawton, Capt. Henry W. (Atlanta, Ga)
Leonard, Sgt. Edwin (Petersburg, Va)
Leonard, Pvt. William E. (Deep Bottom, Va)
Leslie, Pvt. Frank (Front Royal, Va)
Levy, Pvt. Benjamin (Glendale, Va)
Lewis, Capt. DeWitt C. (Secessionville, SC)
Lewis, Cpl. Henry (Vicksburg, Miss)
Lewis, Cpl. Samuel E. (Petersburg, Va)
Libaire, Capt. Adolphe (Antietam, Md)
Lilley, Pvt. John (Petersburg, Va)
Little, Sgt. Henry F. W. (Richmond, Va)
Littlefield, Cpl. George H. (Fort Fisher, NC)
Livingston, 1st Lt. & Adj. Josiah O. (Newport Barracks, NC)
Locke, Pvt. Lewis (Paine's Crossroads, Va)
Lonergan, Capt. John (Gettysburg, Pa)
Longshore, Pvt. William H. (Vicksburg, Miss)
Lonsway, Pvt. Joseph (Murfree's Station, Va)
Lord, Musician William (Drewry's Bluff, Va)
Lorish, Comm. Sgt. Andrew J. (Winchester, Va)
Love, Col. George M. (Cedar Creek, Va)
Lovering, 1st Sgt. George M. (Port Hudson, La)
Lower, Pvt. Cyrus B. (Wilderness, Va)
Lower, Pvt. Robert A. (Vicksburg, Miss)
Loyd, Pvt. George (Petersburg, Va)
Lucas, Pvt. George W. (Benton, Ark)
Luce, Sgt. Moses A. (Laurel Hill, Va)
Ludgate, Capt. William (Farmville, Va)
Ludwig, Pvt. Carl (Petersburg, Va)
Lunt, Sgt. Alphonso M. (Opequan Creek, Va)
Lutes, Cpl. Franklin W. (Petersburg, Va)
Luther, Pvt. James H. (Fredericksburg, Va)
Luty, Cpl. Gotlieb (Chancellorsville, Va)
Lyman, QM Sgt. Joel H. (Winchester, Va)
Lyon, Cpl. Frederick A. (Cedar Creek, Va)
McAdams, Cpl. Peter (Salem Heights, Va)
McAlwee, Sgt. Benjamin F. (Petersburg, Va)
McAnally, Lt. Charles (Spotsylvania, Va)
MacArthur, 1st Lt. & Adj. Arthur, Jr. (Missionary Ridge, Tenn)
McCammon, 1st Lt. William W. (Corinth, Miss)
McCarren, Pvt. Bernard (Gettysburg, Pa)
McCauslin, Pvt. Joseph (Petersburg, Va)
McCleary, 1st Lt. Charles H. (Nashville, Tenn)
McClelland, Pvt. James M. (Vicksburg, Miss)
McConnell, Capt. Samuel (Fort Blakely, Ala)
McCornack, Pvt. Andrew (Vicksburg, Miss)
McDonald, Pvt. George E. (Fort Stedman, Va)
McDonald, Pvt. John W. (Pittsburg Landing, Tenn)
McElhinny, Pvt. Samuel O. (Sayler's Creek, Va)
McEnroe, Sgt. Patrick H. (Winchester, Va)
McFall, Sgt. Daniel (Spotsylvania, Va)
McGinn, Pvt. Edward (Vicksburg, Miss)
McGonagle, Pvt. Wilson (Vicksburg, Miss)
McGonnigle, Capt. & Asst. QM Andrew J. (Cedar Creek, Va)
McGough, Cpl. Owen (Bull Run, Va)
McGraw, Sgt. Thomas (Petersburg, Va)
McGuire, Pvt. Patrick (Vicksburg, Miss)
McHale, Cpl. Alexander U. (Spotsylvania Courthouse, Va)
McKay, Sgt. Charles W. (Dug Gap, Ga)
McKee, Color Sgt. George (Petersburg, Va)
McKeen, 1st Lt. Nineveh S. (Stone River & Liberty Gap, Tenn)
McKeever, Pvt. Michael (Burnt Ordinary, Va)
McKown, Sgt. Nathaniel A. (Chapin's Farm, Va)
McMahon, Capt. & Aide-de-Camp Martin T. (White Oak Swamp, Va)
McMillen, Sgt. Francis M. (Petersburg, Va)
*McVeane, Cpl. John P. (Fredericksburg Heights, Va)
McWhorter, Comm. Sgt. Walter F. (Sayler's Creek, Va)
Madden, Pvt. Michael (Mason's Island, Md)
Madison, Sgt. James (Waynesboro, Va)
Magee, Drummer William (Murfreesboro, Tenn)
Mahoney, Sgt. Jeremiah (Fort Sanders, Tenn)
Mandy, 1st Sgt. Harry J. (Front Royal, Va)
Mangam, Pvt. Richard C. (Hatcher's Run, Va)
Manning, Pvt. Joseph S. (Fort Sanders, Tenn)
Marland, 1st Lt. William (Grand Coteau, La)
Marquette, Sgt. Charles (Petersburg, Va)
Marsh, Sgt. Albert (Spotsylvania, Va)
Marsh, Pvt. Charles H. (Back Creek Valley, Va)
Marsh, Sgt. George (Elk River, Tenn)
Martin, Lt. Sylvester H. (Weldon Railroad, Va)
Mason, Sgt. Elihu H. (Georgia)
Mathews, 1st Sgt. William H. (Petersburg, Va)
Matthews, Cpl. John C. (Petersburg, Va)
Matthews, Pvt. Milton (Petersburg, Va)
Mattingly, Pvt. Henry B. (Jonesboro, Ga)
Mattocks, Maj. Charles P. (Sayler's Creek, Va)
Maxham, Cpl. Lowell M. (Fredericksburg, Va)
May, Pvt. William (Nashville, Tenn)
Mayberry, Pvt. John B. (Gettysburg, Pa)
Mayes, Pvt. William B. (Kenesaw Mountain, Ga)
Maynard, Pvt. George H. (Fredericksburg, Va)
Meach, Farrier George E. (Winchester, Va)
Meagher, 1st Sgt. Thomas (Chapin's Farm, Va)
Mears, Sgt. George W. (Gettysburg, Pa)
Menter, Sgt. John W. (Sayler's Creek, Va)
Merriam, Lt. Col. Henry C. (Fort Blakely, Ala)
Merrifield, Cpl. James K. (Franklin, Tenn)
Merrill, Capt. Augustus (Petersburg, Va)
Merrill, Pvt. George (Fort Fisher, NC)
Merritt, Sgt. John G. (Bull Run, Va)
Meyer, Capt. Henry C. (Petersburg, Va)
Miles, Col. Nelson A. (Chancellorsville, Va)

William H. Mathews, First Sergeant, Company E, 2d Maryland Veteran Infantry. Place and date: At Petersburg, Va., 30 July 1864. Entered service at: Baltimore, Md. Birth: England. Date of issue: 10 July 1892. Citation: Finding himself among a squad of Confederates, he fired into them, killing 1, and was himself wounded, but succeeded in bringing in a sergeant and 2 men of the 17th South Carolina Regiment (C.S.A.) as prisoners. (Enlisted in 1861 at Baltimore, Md., under the name Henry Sivel, and original Medal of Honor issued under that name. A new medal was issued in 1900 under true name, William H. Mathews.)

Miller, Pvt. Frank (Sayler's Creek, Va)
Miller, Capt. Henry A. (Fort Blakely, Ala)
Miller, Pvt. Jacob C. (Vicksburg, Miss)
Miller, Pvt. James P. (Selma, Ala)
Miller, Cpl. John (Gettysburg, Pa)
Miller, Pvt. John (Waynesboro, Va)
Miller, Capt. William E. (Gettysburg, Pa)
Mills, Sgt. Frank W. (Sandy Cross Roads, NC)
Mindil, Capt. George W. (Williamsburg, Va)
Mitchell, 1st Lt. Alexander H. (Spotsylvania, Va)
Mitchell, Pvt. Theodore (Petersburg, Va)
Moffitt, Cpl. John H. (Gaines's Mill, Va)
Molbone, Sgt. Archibald (Petersburg, Va)
Monaghan, Cpl. Patrick (Petersburg, Va)
Moore, Cpl. Daniel B. (Fort Blakely, Ala)
Moore, Pvt. George G. (Fisher's Hill, Va)
Moore, Pvt. Wilbur F. (Nashville, Tenn)
Morey, Pvt. Delano (McDowell, Va)
Morford, Pvt. Jerome (Vicksburg, Miss)
*Morgan, Pvt. Lewis (Spotsylvania, Va)
Morgan, Cpl. Richard H. (Columbus, Ga)
Morrill, Capt. Walter G. (Rappahannock Station, Va)
Morris, Sgt. William (Sayler's Creek, Va)
Morrison, Pvt. Francis (Bermuda Hundred, Va)
Morse, Pvt. Benjamin (Spotsylvania, Va)
Morse, Sgt. Charles E. (Wilderness, Va)
Mostoller, Pvt. John W. (Lynchburg, Va)
Mulholland, Maj. St. Clair A. (Chancellorsville, Va)
Mundell Cpl. Walter L. (Sayler's Creek, Va)
Munsell, Sgt. Harvey M. (Gettysburg, Pa)
Murphy, 1st Lt. & QM Charles J. (Bull Run, Va)
Murphy, Sgt. Daniel J. (Hatcher's Run, Va)
Murphy, Sgt. Dennis J. F. (Corinth, Miss)
Murphy, Pvt. James T. (Petersburg, Va)
Murphy, Pvt. John P. (Antietam, Md)
Murphy, Lt. Col. Michael C. (North Anna River, Va)
Murphy, Musician Robinson B. (Atlanta, Ga)
Murphy, Cpl. Thomas (Chapin's Farm, Va)
Murphy, Cpl. Thomas C. (Vicksburg, Miss)
Murphy, 1st Sgt. Thomas J. (Five Forks, Va)
Myers, Pvt. George S. (Chickamauga, Ga)
Myers, Pvt. William H. (Appomattox Courthouse, Va)
Nash, Cpl. Henry H. (Vicksburg, Miss)
Neahr, Pvt. Zachariah C. (Fort Fisher, NC)
Neville, Capt. Edwin M. (Sayler's Creek, Va)
Newman, Pvt. Marcellus J. (Resaca, Ga)
Newman, Lt. William H. (Amelia Springs, Va)
Nichols, Capt. Henry C. (Fort Blakely, Ala)
Niven, 2d Lt. Robert (Waynesboro, Va)
Nolan, Sgt. John J. (Georgia Landing, La)
Noll, Sgt. Conrad (Spotsylvania, Va)
North, Pvt. Jasper N. (Vicksburg, Miss)
Norton, 2d Lt. Elliott M. (Sayler's Creek, Va)
Norton, Lt. John R. (Sayler's Creek, Va)
Norton, Sgt. Llewellyn P. (Sayler's Creek, Va)
Noyes, Pvt. William W. (Spotsylvania, Va)
Nutting, Capt. Lee (Todd's Tavern, Va)
O'Beirne, Capt. James R. (Fair Oaks, Va)
O'Brien, Cpl. Henry D. (Gettysburg, Pa)
O'Brien, Pvt. Peter (Waynesboro, Va)
O'Connor, Sgt. Albert (Gravelly Run, Va)
O'Connor, Pvt. Timothy (NOR)
O'Dea, Pvt. John (Vicksburg, Miss)
O'Donnell, 1st Lt. Menomen (Vicksburg, Miss)
Oliver, Sgt. Charles (Petersburg, Va)
Oliver, Capt. Paul A. (Resaca, Ga)
O'Neill, Cpl. Stephen (Chancellorsville, Va)
Opel, Pvt. John N. (Wilderness, Va)
Orbansky, Pvt. David (Shiloh, Tenn, & Vicksburg, Miss, etc.)
Orr, Pvt. Charles A. (Hatcher's Run, Va)
Orr, Maj. Robert L. (Petersburg, Va)
Orth, Cpl. Jacob G. (Antietam, Md)
Osborne, Pvt. William H. (Malvern Hill, Va)
Oss, Pvt. Albert (Chancellorsville, Va)
Overturf, Pvt. Jacob H. (Vicksburg, Miss)
Packard, Pvt. Loron F. (Raccoon Ford, Va)
Palmer, Musician George H. (Lexington, Mo)
Palmer, Cpl. John G. (Fredericksburg, Va)
Palmer, Col. William J. (Red Hill, Ala)
Parker, Cpl. Thomas (Petersburg & Sayler's Creek, Va)
Parks, Pvt. Henry J. (Cedar Creek, Va)
Parks, Cpl. James W. (Nashville, Tenn)
Parrott, Pvt. Jacob (Georgia)
Parsons, Pvt. Joel (Vicksburg, Miss)
Patterson, 1st Lt. John H. (Wilderness, Va)
Patterson, Principal Musician John T. (Winchester, Va)
Paul, Pvt. William H. (Antietam, Md)
Pay, Pvt. Byron E. (Nolensville, Tenn)
Payne, Cpl. Irvin C. (Sayler's Creek, Va)
Payne, 1st Lt. Thomas H. L. (Fort Blakely, Ala)
Pearsall, Cpl. Platt (Vicksburg, Miss)
Pearson, Col. Alfred L. (Lewis's Farm, Va)
Peck, Pvt. Cassius (Blackburn's Ford, Va)
Peck, 1st Lt. Theodore S. (Newport Barracks, NC)
Peirsol, Sgt. James K. (Paine's Crossroads, Va)
Pennypacker, Col. Galusha (Fort Fisher, NC)
Pentzer, Capt. Patrick H. (Blakely, Ala)
Pesch, Pvt. Joseph (Grand Gulf, Miss)
Peters, Pvt. Henry C. (Vicksburg, Miss)
Petty, Sgt. Philip (Fredericksburg, Va)
Phelps, Col. Charles E. (Laurel Hill, Va)
Phillips, Pvt. Josiah (Sutherland Station, Va)
Phisterer, 1st Lt. Frederick (Stone River, Tenn)
Pickle, Sgt. Alonzo H. (Deep Bottom, Va)
Pike, 1st Sgt. Edward M. (Cache River, Ark)
Pingree, Capt. Samuel E. (Lee's Mills, Va)
Pinkham, Sgt. Maj. Charles H. (Fort Stedman, Va)
Pinn, 1st Sgt. Robert (Chapin's Farm, Va)
Pipes, Capt. James (Gettysburg, Pa)
Pitman, Sgt. George J. (Sayler's Creek, Va)
Pittinger, Sgt. William (Georgia)
Plant, Cpl. Henry E. (Bentonville, NC)
Platt, Pvt. George C. (Fairfield, Pa)
Plimley, 1st Lt. William (Hatcher's Run, Va)
Plowman, Sgt. Maj. George H. (Petersburg, Va)
Plunkett, Sgt. Thomas (Fredericksburg, Va)
Pond, Pvt. George F. (Drywood, Kans)
Pond, 1st Lt. James B. (Baxter Springs, Kans)
Porter, Comm. Sgt. Ambrose (Tallahatchie River, Miss)
Porter, Capt. Horace (Chickamauga, Ga)
Porter, Pvt. John R. (Georgia)
Porter, Sgt. William (Sayler's Creek, Va)
Post, Col. Philip S. (Nashville, Tenn)
Postles, Capt. James P. (Gettysburg, Pa)
Potter, Pvt. George W. (Petersburg, Va)
Potter, 1st Sgt. Norman F. (Lookout Mountain, Tenn)
Powell, Maj. William H. (Sinking Creek Valley, Va)
Power, Pvt. Albert (Pea Ridge, Ark)
Powers, Cpl. Wesley J. (Oostanaula, Ga)
Prentice, Pvt. Joseph R. (Stone River, Tenn)
Preston, 1st Lt. & Comm. Noble D. (Trevilian Station, Va)
Purcell, Sgt. Hiram W. (Fair Oaks, Va)
Purman, Lt. James J. (Gettysburg, Pa)

Albert O'Connor, Sergeant, Company A, 7th Wisconsin Infantry. Place and date: At Gravelly Run, Va., 31 March and 1 April 1865. Entered service at: West Point Township, Columbia County, Wis. Birth: Canada. Date of issue: Unknown. Citation: On 31 March 1865, with a comrade, recaptured a Union officer from a detachment of 9 Confederates, capturing 3 of the detachment and dispersing the remainder, and on 1 April 1865, seized a stand of Confederate colors, killing a Confederate officer in a hand-to-hand contest over the colors and retaining the colors until surrounded by Confederates and compelled to relinquish them.

Putnam, Sgt. Edgar P. (Crump's Creek, Va)
Putnam, Cpl. Winthrop D. (Vicksburg, Miss)
Quay, Col. Matthew S. (Fredericksburg, Va)
Quinlan, Maj. James (Savage Station, Va)
Rafferty, Pvt. Peter (Malvern Hill, Va)
Ramsbottom, 1st Sgt. Alfred (Franklin, Tenn)
Rand, Pvt. Charles F. (Blackburn's Ford, Va)
Ranney, Asst. Surgeon George E. (Resaca, Ga)
Ranney, Pvt. Myron H. (Bull Run, Va)
Ratcliff, 1st Sgt. Edward (Chapin's Farm, Va)
Raub, Asst. Surgeon Jacob F. (Hatcher's Run, Va)
Raymond, Cpl. William H. (Gettysburg, Pa)
Read, Lt. Morton A. (Appomattox Station, Va)
Rebmann, Sgt. George F. (Fort Blakely, Ala)
Reddick, Cpl. William H. (Georgia)
Reed, Sgt. Axel H. (Chickamauga, Ga & Missionary Ridge, Tenn)
Reed, Bugler Charles W. (Gettysburg, Pa)
Reed, Pvt. George W. (Weldon Railroad, Va)
Reed, Pvt. William (Vicksburg, Miss)
Reeder, Pvt. Charles A. (Battery Gregg, Va)
Reid, Pvt. Robert A. (Petersburg, Va)
Reigle, Capt. Daniel P. (Cedar Creek, Va)
Reisinger, Cpl. J. Monroe (Gettysburg, Pa)
Renninger, Cpl. Louis (Vicksburg, Miss)
Reynolds, Pvt. George (Winchester, Va)
Rhodes, Pvt. Julius D. (Thoroughfare Gap & Bull Run, Va)
Rhodes, Sgt. Sylvester D. (Fisher's Hill, Va)
Rice, Maj. Edmond (Gettysburg, Pa)
Rich, 1st Sgt. Carlos H. (Wilderness, Va)
Richardson, Pvt. William R. (Sayler's Creek, Va)
Richey, Cpl. William E. (Chickamauga, Ga)
*Richmond, Pvt. James (Gettysburg, Pa)
Ricksecker, Pvt. John H. (Franklin, Tenn)
Riddell, Lt. Rudolph (Sayler's Creek, Va)
Riley, Pvt. Thomas (Fort Blakely, Ala)
Ripley, Lt. Col. William Y. W. (Malvern Hill, Va)
Robbins, 2d Lt. Augustus J. (Spotsylvania, Va)
Roberts, Sgt. Otis O. (Rappahannock Station, Va)
Robertson, 1st Lt. Robert S. (Corbins Bridge, Va)
*Robertson, Pvt. Samuel (Georgia)
Robie, Sgt. George F. (Richmond, Va)
Robinson, Pvt. Elbridge (Winchester, Va)
*Robinson, Pvt. James H. (Brownsville, Ark)
Robinson, Brig. Gen. John C. (Laurel Hill, Va)
Robinson, Pvt. John H. (Gettysburg, Pa)
Robinson, Pvt. Thomas (Spotsylvania, Va)
Rock, Pvt. Frederick (Vicksburg, Miss)
Rockefeller, Lt. Charles M. (Fort Blakely, Ala)
Rodenbough, Capt. Theophilus F. (Trevilian Station, Va)
Rohm, Chief Bugler Ferdinand F. (Reams's Station, Va)
Rood, Pvt. Oliver P. (Gettysburg, Pa)
Roosevelt, 1st Sgt. George W. (Bull Run, Va & Gettysburg, Pa)
*Ross, Sgt. Maj. Marion A. (Georgia)
Rossbach, Sgt. Valentine (Spotsylvania, Va)
Rought, Sgt. Stephen (Wilderness, Va)
Rounds, Pvt. Lewis A. (Spotsylvania, Va)
Roush, Cpl. J. Levi (Gettysburg, Pa)
Rowand, Pvt. Archibald H., Jr. (Virginia)
Rowe, Pvt. Henry W. (Petersburg, Va)
Rundle, Pvt. Charles W. (Vicksburg, Miss)
Russell, Cpl. Charles L. (Spotsylvania, Va)
Russell, Capt. Milton (Stone River, Tenn)
Rutherford, 1st Lt. John T. (Yellow Tavern & Hanovertown, Va)
Rutter, Sgt. James M. (Gettysburg, Pa)
Ryan, Pvt. Peter J. (Winchester, Va)
Sacriste, 1st Lt. Louis J. (Chancellorsville & Auburn, Va)
Sagelhurst, Sgt. John C. (Hatcher's Run, Va)
Sancrainte, Pvt. Charles F. (Atlanta, Ga)
Sands, 1st Sgt. William (Dabney's Mills, Va)
Sanford, Pvt. Jacob (Vicksburg, Miss)
Sargent, Sgt. Jackson (Petersburg, Va)
Sartwell, Sgt. Henry (Chancellorsville, Va)
*Savacool, Capt. Edwin F. (Sayler's Creek, Va)
Saxton, Brig. Gen. Rufus (Harper's Ferry, W Va)
Scanlan, Pvt. Patrick (Ashepoo River, SC)
Scheibner, Pvt. Martin E. (Mine Run, Va)
Schenck, Pvt. Benjamin W. (Vicksburg, Miss)
Schiller, Pvt. John (Chapin's Farm, Va)
Schlachter, Pvt. Philipp (Spotsylvania, Va)
Schmal, Blacksmith George W. (Paine's Crossroads, Va)
Schmauch, Pvt. Andrew (Vicksburg, Miss)
Schmidt, 1st Sgt. Conrad (Winchester, Va)
Schmidt, Pvt. William (Missionary Ridge, Tenn)
Schneider, Sgt. George (Petersburg, Va)
Schnell, Cpl. Christian (Vicksburg, Miss)
Schofield, Maj. John M. (Wilson's Creek, Mo)
Schoonmaker, Col. James M. (Winchester, Va)
Schorn, Chief Bugler Charles (Appomattox, Va)
Schubert, Pvt. Martin (Fredericksburg, Va)
Schwan, 1st Lt. Theodore (Peebles's Farm, Va)
Schwenk, Sgt. Martin (Millerstown, Pa)
Scofield, QM Sgt. David H. (Cedar Creek, Va)
Scott, Cpl. Alexander (Monocacy, Md)
*Scott, Sgt. John M. (Georgia)
Scott, Capt. John W. (Five Forks, Va)
Scott, Drummer Julian A. (Lee's Mills, Va)

Conrad Schmidt, First Sergeant, Company K, 2d U.S. Cavalry. Place and date: At Winchester, Va., 19 September 1864. Entered service at: ——. Birth: Germany. Date of issue: 16 March 1896. Citation: Went to the assistance of his regimental commander, whose horse had been killed under him in a charge, mounted the officer behind him, under a heavy fire from the enemy, and returned him to his command.

Seaman, Pvt. Elisha B. (Chancellorsville, Va)
Sears, 1st Lt. Cyrus (Iuka, Miss)
Seaver, Col. Thomas O. (Spotsylvania Courthouse, Va)
Seitzinger, Pvt. James M. (Cold Harbor, Va)
Sellers, Maj. Alfred J. (Gettysburg, Pa)
*Seston, Sgt. Charles H. (Winchester, Va)
Sewell, Col. William J. (Chancellorsville, Va)
Shafter, 1st Lt. William R. (Fair Oaks, Va)
Shahan, Cpl. Emisire (Sayler's Creek, Va)
Shaler, Col. Alexander (Marye's Heights, Va)
Shambaugh, Cpl. Charles (Charles City Crossroads, Va)
Shanes, Pvt. John (Carter's Farm, Va)
Shapland, Pvt. John (Elk River, Tenn)
Shea, Pvt. Joseph H. (Chapin's Farm, Va)
Shellenberger, Cpl. John S. (Deep Run, Va)
Shepard, Cpl. Irwin (Knoxville, Tenn)
Shepherd, Pvt. William (Sayler's Creek, Va)
Sherman, Pvt. Marshall (Gettysburg, Pa)
Shiel, Cpl. John (Fredericksburg, Va)
Shields, Pvt. Bernard (Appomattox, Va)
Shilling, 1st Sgt. John (Weldon Railroad, Va)
Shipley, Sgt. Robert F. (Five Forks, Va)
Shoemaker, Sgt. Levi (Nineveh, Va)
Shopp, Pvt. George J. (Five Forks, Va)
Shubert, Sgt. Frank (Petersburg, Va)
Sickles, Maj. Gen. Daniel E. (Gettysburg, Pa)
Sickles, Sgt. William H. (Gravelly Run, Va)
Sidman, Pvt. George E. (Gaines's Mill, Va)
Simmons, Pvt. John (Sayler's Creek, Va)
Simmons, Lt. William T. (Nashville, Tenn)
Simonds, Sgt. Maj. William E. (Irish Bend, La)
Simons, Sgt. Charles J. (Petersburg, Va)
Skellie, Cpl. Ebenezer (Chapin's Farm, Va)
Sladen, Pvt. Joseph A. (Resaca, Ga)
Slagle, Pvt. Oscar (Elk River, Tenn)
*Slavens, Pvt. Samuel (Georgia)
Sloan, Pvt. Andrew J. (Nashville, Tenn)
Slusher, Pvt. Henry C. (Moorefiled, W Va)
Smalley, Pvt. Reuben (Vicksburg, Miss)
Smalley, Pvt. Reuben S. (Elk River, Tenn)
Smith, Sgt. Alonzo (Hatcher's Run, Va)
Smith, Col. Charles H. (St. Mary's Church, Va)
Smith, Sgt. David L. (Warwick Courthouse, Va)
Smith, 1st Lt. & Adj. Francis M. (Dabney's Mills, Va)
Smith, 1st Lt. Henry I. (Black River, NC)
Smith, Pvt. James (Georgia)
Smith, Lt. Col. Joseph S. (Hatcher's Run, Va)
Smith, Pvt. Otis W. (Nashville, Tenn)
Smith, Pvt. Richard (Weldon Railroad, Va)
Smith, Capt. S. Rodmond (Rowanty Creek, Va)
Smith, Cpl. Thaddeus S. (Gettysburg, Pa)
Smith, Cpl. Wilson (Washington, NC)
Snedden, Musician James (Piedmont, Va)
Southard, Sgt. David (Sayler's Creek, Va)
Sova, Saddler Joseph E. (Appomattox, Va)
Sowers, Pvt. Michael (Stony Creek Station, Va)

William R. Shafter, Rank and organization: First Lieutenant, Company I, 7th Michigan Infantry. Place and date: At Fair Oaks, Va., 31 May 1862. Entered service at: Galesburg, Mich. Birth: Kalamazoo, Mich. Date of issue: 12 June 1895. Citation: Lt. Shafter was engaged in bridge construction and not being needed there returned with his men to engage the enemy participating in a charge across an open field that resulted in casualties to 18 of the 22 men. At the close of the battle his horse was shot from under him and he was severely flesh wounded. He remained on the field that day and stayed to fight the next day only by concealing his wounds. In order not to be sent home with the wounded he kept his wounds concealed for another 3 days until other wounded had left the area.

Spalding, Sgt. Edward B. (Pittsburg Landing, Tenn)
Sperry, Maj. William J. (Petersburg, Va)
Spillane, Pvt. Timothy (Hatcher's Run, Va)
Sprague Cpl. Benona (Vicksburg, Miss)
Sprague, Col. John W. (Decatur, Ga)
Spurling, Lt. Col. Andrew B. (Evergreen, Ala)
Stacey, Pvt. Charles (Gettysburg, Pa)
Stahel, Maj. Gen. Julius (Piedmont, Va)
Stanley, Maj. Gen. David S. (Franklin, Tenn)
Starkins, Sgt. John H. (Campbell Station, Tenn)
Steele, Maj. & Aide-de-Camp John W. (Spring Hill, Tenn)
Steinmetz, Pvt. William (Vicksburg, Miss)
Stephens, Pvt. William G. (Vicksburg, Miss)
Sterling, Pvt. John T. (Winchester, Va)
Stevens, Capt. & Asst. Adj. Gen. Hazard (Fort Huger, Va)
Stewart, 1st Sgt. George W. (Paine's Crossroads, Va)
Stewart Pvt. Joseph (Five Forks, Va)
Stickels, Sgt. Joseph (Fort Blakely, Ala)
Stockman, 1st Lt. George H. (Vicksburg, Miss)
Stokes, Pvt. George (Nashville, Tenn)
Stolz, Pvt. Frank (Vicksburg, Miss)
Storey, Sgt. John H. R. (Dallas, Ga)
*Strausbaugh, 1st Sgt. Bernard A. (Petersburg, Va)
Streile, Pvt. Christian (Paine's Crossroads, Va)
Strong, Sgt. James N. (Port Hudson, La)
Sturgeon, Pvt. James K. (Kenesaw Mountain, Ga)
Summers, Pvt. James C. (Vicksburg, Miss)
Surles, Pvt. William H. (Perryville, Ky)
Swan, Pvt. Charles A. (Selma, Ala)
Swap, Pvt. Jacob E. (Wilderness, Va)
Swayne, Lt. Col. Wager (Corinth, Miss)
Sweatt, Pvt. Joseph S. G. (Carrsville, Va)
Sweeney, Pvt. James (Cedar Creek, Va)
Swegheimer, Pvt. Jacob (Vicksburg, Miss)
Swift, Lt. Col. Frederic W. (Lenoire Station, Tenn)
Swift, 2d Lt. Harlan J. (Petersburg, Va)
Sype, Pvt. Peter (Vicksburg, Miss)
Tabor, Pvt. William L. S. (Port Hudson, La)
Taggart, Pvt. Charles A. (Sayler's Creek, Va)
Tanner, 2d Lt. Charles B. (Antietam, Md)
Taylor, 1st Lt. Anthony (Chickamauga, Ga)
Taylor, Capt. Forrester L. (Chancellorsville, Va)
Taylor, Sgt. Henry H. (Vicksburg, Miss)
Taylor, Pvt. Joseph (Weldon Railroad, Va)
Taylor, Pvt. Richard (Cedar Creek, Va)
Taylor, Sgt. William (Front Royal & Weldon Railroad, Va)
Terry, Sgt. John D. (New Bern, NC)
Thackrah, Pvt. Benjamin (Fort Gates, Fla)
Thatcher, Pvt. Charles M. (Petersburg, Va)
Thaxter, Maj. Sidney W. (Hatcher's Run, Va)
Thomas, Maj. Hampton S. (Amelia Springs, Va)
Thomas, Col. Stephen (Cedar Creek, Va)
Thompkins, Cpl. George W. (Petersburg, Va)
Thompson, Pvt. Allen (White Oak Road, Va)
Thompson, Sgt. Charles A. (Spotsylvania, Va)
Thompson, Cpl. Freeman C. (Petersburg, Va)
Thompson, Pvt. James (White Oak Road, Va)
Thompson, Surgeon J. Harry (New Bern, NC)
Thompson, Sgt. James B. (Gettysburg, Pa)
Thompson, Cpl. John (Hatcher's Run, Va)
Thompson, Sgt. Thomas (Chancellorsville, Va)
*Thompson, Sgt. William P. (Wilderness, Va)
Thomson, 1st Lt. Clifford (Chancellorsville, Va)
Thorn, 2d Lt. Walter (Dutch Gap Canal, Va)
Tibbets, Pvt. Andrew W. (Columbus, Ga)
Tilton, Sgt. William (Richmond, Va)
Tinkham, Cpl. Eugene M. (Cold Harbor, Va)
Titus, Sgt. Charles (Sayler's Creek, Va)
Toban, Sgt. James W. (Aiken, SC)
Tobie, Sgt. Maj. Edward P. (Appomattox, Va)
Tobin, 1st Lt. & Adj. John M. (Malvern Hill, Va)
Toffey, 1st Lt. John J. (Chattanooga, Tenn)
Tompkins, Sgt. Aaron B. (Sayler's Creek, Va)
Tompkins, 1st Lt. Charles H. (Fairfax, Va)
Toohey, Sgt. Thomas (Franklin, Tenn)
Toomer, Sgt. William (Vicksburg, Miss)
Torgler, Sgt. Ernst (Ezra Chapel, Ga)
Tozier, Sgt. Andrew J. (Gettysburg, Pa)
Tracy, Lt. Col. Amasa A. (Cedar Creek, Va)
Tracy, Col. Benjamin F. (Wilderness, Va)
Tracy, Sgt. Charles H. (Spotsylvania & Petersburg, Va)
Tracy, 2d Lt. William G. (Chancellorsville, Va)
Traynor, Cpl. Andrew (Mason's Hill, Va)
Treat, Sgt. Howell B. (Buzzard's Roost, Ga)
Tremain, Maj. & Aide-de-Camp Henry E. (Resaca, Ga)
Tribe, Pvt. John (Waterloo Bridge, Va)
Trogden, Pvt. Howell G. (Vicksburg, Miss)
Truell, Pvt. Edwin M. (Atlanta, Ga)
Tucker, Sgt. Allen (Petersburg, Va)
Tucker, Cpl. Jacob R. (Petersburg, Va)
Tweedale, Pvt. John (Stone River, Tenn)
Twombly, Cpl. Voltaire P. (Fort Donelson, Tenn)
Tyrrell, Cpl. George W. (Resaca, Ga)
Uhrl, Sgt. George (White Oak Swamp Bridge, Va)
Urell, Pvt. M. Emmet (Bristoe Station, Va)
Vale, Pvt. John (Nolensville, Tenn)
Vance, Pvt. Wilson (Stone River, Tenn)
Vanderslice, Pvt. John M. (Hatcher's Run, Va)
Van Matre, Pvt. Joseph (Petersburg, Va)
Van Winkle, Cpl. Edward (Chapin's Farm, Va)
Veal, Pvt. Charles (Chapin's Farm, Va)
Veale, Capt. Moses (Wauhatchie, Tenn)
Veazey, Col. Wheelock G. (Gettysburg, Pa)
Vernay, 2d Lt. James D. (Vicksburg, Miss)
Vifquain, Lt. Col. Victor (Fort Blakely, Ala)
Von Vegesack, Maj. & Aide-de-Camp Ernest (Gaines's Mill, Va)
Wageman, Pvt. John H. (Petersburg, Va)
Wagner, Cpl. John W. (Vicksburg, Miss)
Wainwright, 1st Lt. John (Fort Fisher, NC)
Walker, Pvt. James C. (Missionary Ridge, Tenn)
Walker, Contract Surgeon (Civilian) Mary (Bull Run, Va & Chattanooga, Tenn, etc.)
Wall, Pvt. Jerry (Gettysburg, Pa)
Waller, Cpl. Francis A. (Gettysburg, Pa)
Walling, Capt. William H. (Fort Fisher, NC)
Walsh, Cpl. John (Cedar Creek, Va)
Walton, Pvt. George W. (Petersburg, Va)
Wambsgan, Pvt. Martin (Cedar Creek, Va)
Ward, Pvt. Nelson W. (Staunton River Bridge, Va)
Ward, Pvt. Thomas J. (Vicksburg, Miss)
Ward, Capt. William H. (Vicksburg, Miss)
Warden, Cpl. John (Vicksburg, Miss)
Warfel, Pvt. Henry C. (Paine's Crossroads, Va)
Warren, Cpl. Francis E. (Port Hudson, La)
Webb, Brig. Gen. Alexander S. (Gettysburg, Pa)
Webb, Pvt. James (Bull Run, Va)

Charles H. Tracy, Sergeant, Company A, 37th Massachusetts Infantry. Place and date: At Spotsylvania, Va., 12 May 1864; At Petersburg, Va., 2 April 1865. Entered service at: Springfield, Mass. Birth: Jewett City, Conn. Date of issue: 19 November 1897. Citation: At the risk of his own life, at Spotsylvania, 12 May 1864, assisted in carrying to a place of safety a wounded and helpless officer. On 2 April 1865, advanced with the pioneers, and, under heavy fire, assisted in removing 2 lines of chevaux-de-frise; was twice wounded but advanced to the third line, where he was again severely wounded, losing a leg.

Andrew J. Tomlin, U.S. Marine Corps. Born: 1844, Goshen, N.J. Accredited to: New Jersey. G.O. No.: 59, 22 June 1865. Citation: As corporal of the guard on board the U.S.S. Wabash during the assault on Fort Fisher, on 15 January 1865. As 1 of 200 marines assembled to hold a line of entrenchments in the rear of the fort which the enemy threatened to attack in force following a retreat in panic by more than two-thirds of the assaulting ground forces, Cpl. Tomlin took position in line and remained until morning when relief troops arrived from the fort. When one of his comrades was struck down by enemy fire, he unhesitatingly advanced under a withering fire of musketry into an open plain close to the fort and assisted the wounded man to a place of safety.

Webber, Musician Alason P. (Kenesaw Mountain, Ga)
Weeks, Pvt. John H. (Spotsylvania, Va)
Weir, Capt. & Asst. Adj. Gen. Henry C. (St. Mary's Church, Va)
Welch, Pvt. George W. (Nashville, Tenn)
Welch, Cpl. Richard (Petersburg, Va)
Welch, Sgt. Stephen (Dug Gap, Ga)
*Wells, Pvt. Henry S. (Chapin's Farm, Va)
Wells, Chief Bugler Thomas M. (Cedar Creek, Va)
Wells, Maj. William (Gettysburg, Pa)
Welsh, Pvt. Edward (Vicksburg, Miss)
Welsh, Pvt. James (Petersburg, Va)
Westerhold, Sgt. William (Spotsylvania, Va)
Weston, Maj. John F. (Wetumpka, Ala)
Wheaton, Lt. Col. Loyd (Fort Blakely, Ala)
Wheeler, 1st Lt. Daniel D. (Salem Heights, Va)
Wheeler, Pvt. Henry W. (Bull Run, Va)
Wherry, 1st Lt. William M. (Wilson's Creek, Mo)
Whitaker, Capt. Edward W. (Reams's Station, Va)
White, Cpl. Adam (Hatcher's Run, Va)
White, Pvt. J. Henry (Rappahannock Station, Va)
White, Capt. Patrick H. (Vicksburg, Miss)
Whitehead, Chaplain John M. (Stone River, Tenn)
Whitman, Pvt. Frank M. (Antietam, Md & Spotsylvania, Va)
Whitmore, Pvt. John (Fort Blakely, Ala)
Whitney, Sgt. William G. (Chickamauga, Ga)
Whittier, 1st Lt. Edward N. (Fisher's Hill, Va)
Widick, Pvt. Andrew J. (Vicksburg, Miss)
Wilcox, Sgt. William H. (Spotsylvania, Va)
Wiley, Sgt. James (Gettysburg, Pa)
Wilhelm, Capt. George (Champion Hill, Miss)
Wilkins, Sgt. Leander A. (Petersburg, Va)
Willcox, Col. Orlando B. (Bull Run, Va)
Williams, Pvt. Elwood N. (Shiloh, Tenn)
Williams, QM Sgt. George C. (Gaines's Mill, Va)
Williams, Sgt. Le Roy (Cold Harbor, Va)
Williams, Pvt. William H. (Peach Tree Creek, Ga)
Williamson, Col. James A. (Chickasaw Bayou, Miss)
Williston, 1st Lt. Edward B. (Trevilian Station, Va)
Wilson, Sgt. Charles E. (Sayler's Creek, Va)
Wilson, Pvt. Christopher W. (Spotsylvania, Va)
Wilson, Cpl. Francis A. (Petersburg, Va)
Wilson, Sgt. John (Chamberlain's Creek, Va)
Wilson, Pvt. John A. (Georgia)
Wilson, 1st Lt. John M. (Malvern Hill, Va)
Winegar, Lt. William W. (Five Forks, Va)
Wisner, 1st Lt. Lewis S. (Spotsylvania, Va)
Withington, Capt. William H. (Bull Run, Va)
Wollam, Pvt. John (Georgia)
Wood, 1st Lt. H. Clay (Wilson's Creek, Mo)
Wood, Pvt. Mark (Georgia)
Wood, Capt. Richard H. (Vicksburg, Miss)
Woodbury, Sgt. Eri D. (Cedar Creek, Va)
Woodruff, Sgt. Alonzo (Hatcher's Run, Va)
Woodruff, 1st Lt. Carle A. (Newby's Crossroads, Va)
Woods, Pvt. Daniel A. (Sayler's Creek, Va)
Woodward, 1st Lt. & Adj. Evan M. (Fredericksburg, Va)
Wortick, Pvt. Joseph (Vicksburg, Miss)
Wray, Sgt. William J. (Fort Stevens, DC)
Wright, Capt. Albert D. (Petersburg, Va)
Wright, Pvt. Robert (Chapel House Farm, Va)
Wright, Cpl. Samuel (Nolensville, Tenn)
Wright, Pvt. Samuel C. (Antietam, Md)
Yeager, Pvt. Jacob F. (Buzzard's Roost, Ga)
Young, Sgt. Andrew J. (Paine's Crossroads, Va)
Young, Cpl. Benjamin F. (Petersburg, Va)
Young, Sgt. Calvary M. (Osage, Kans)
Young, Pvt. James M. (Wilderness, Va)
Younker, Pvt. John L. (Cedar Mountain, Va)

MARINES

Binder, Sgt. Richard (Fort Fisher, NC)
Denig, Sgt. J. Henry (Mobile Bay, Ala)
Fry, Orderly Sgt. Isaac N. (Fort Fisher, NC)
Hudson, Sgt. Michael (Mobile Bay, Ala)
Mackie, Cpl. John F. (Drewry's Bluff, Va)
Martin, Sgt. James (Mobile Bay, Ala)
Miller, Sgt. Andrew (Mobile Bay, Ala)
Nugent, Orderly Sgt. Christopher (Crystal River, Fla)
Oviatt, Cpl. Miles M. (Mobile Bay, Ala)
Rannahan, Cpl. John (Fort Fisher, NC)
Roantree, Sgt. James S. (Mobile Bay, Ala)
Shivers, Pvt. John (Fort Fisher, NC)
Smith, Cpl. Willard M. (Mobile Bay, Ala)
Sprowle, Orderly Sgt. David (Mobile Bay, Ala)
Thompson, Pvt. Henry A. (Fort Fisher, NC)
Tomlin, Cpl. Andrew J. (Fort Fisher, NC)
Vaughn, Sgt. Pinkerton R. (Port Hudson, La)

NAVY

Aheam, Paymaster's Steward Michael (Cherbourg, France)
Anderson, QM Robert (Various)
Angling, Cabin Boy John (Fort Fisher, NC)
Arther, SQM Matthew (Forts Henry & Donelson, Tenn)
Asten, QG Charles (Red River, Va)
Atkinson, Yeoman Thomas E. (Mobile Bay, Ala)
Avery, Sman James (Mobile Bay, Ala)
Baker, QG Charles (Mobile Bay, Ala)
Baldwin, Coal Heaver Charles (Roanoke River, NC)
Barnum, BM James (Fort Fisher, NC)
Barter, Lman Gurdon H. (Fort Fisher, NC)
Barton, Sman Thomas (Franklin, Va)
Bass, Sman David L. (Fort Fisher, NC)
Bazaar, Ord. Sman Philip (Fort Fisher, NC)
Bell, Capt. of the Afterguard George (Galveston Bay, Tex)
Betham, Coxswain Asa (Fort Fisher, NC)
Bibber, GM Charles J. (Fort Fisher, NC)
Bickford, Capt. of the Top John F. (Cherbourg, France)
Blagheen, Ship's Cook William (Mobile Bay, Ala)
Blair, BM Robert M. (Fort Fisher, NC)
Blake, Robert (Legareville, SC)
Bois, QM Frank (Vicksburg, Miss)
Bond, BM William (Cherbourg, France)
Bourne, Sman & Gun Capt. Thomas (Forts Jackson & St. Philip, La)
Bowman, QM Edward R. (Fort Fisher, NC)
Bradley, Lman Amos (Forts Jackson & St. Philip, La)
Bradley, BM Charles (NOR)
Brazell, QM John (Mobile Bay, Ala)
Breen, BM John (Franklin, Va)
Brennan, Sman Christopher (Forts Jackson & St. Philip, La)
Brinn, Sman Andrew (Port Hudson, La)
Brown, QM James (Red River, Tex)
Brown, Capt. of the Forecastle John (Mobile Bay, Ala)
Brown, Capt. of the Top Robert (Mobile Bay, Ala)
Brown, Lman William H. (Mobile Bay, Ala)
Brown, Lman Wilson (Mobile Bay, Ala)
Brownell, Coxswain William P. (Great Gulf Bay & Vicksburg, Miss)
Brutsche, Lman Henry (Plymouth, NC)
Buck, QM James (Forts Jackson & St. Philip, La)
Burns, Sman John M. (Mobile Bay, Ala)
Burton, Sman Albert (Fort Fisher, NC)
Butts, GM George (Red River, Tex)
Byrnes, BM James (NOR)
Campbell, BM William (Fort Fisher, NC)

Carr, Master-at-Arms William M. (Mobile Bay, Ala)
Cassidy, Lman Michael (Mobile Bay, Ala)
Chandler, Coxswain James B. (Mobile Bay, Ala)
Chaput, Lman Louis G. (Mobile Bay, Ala)
Clifford, Master-at-Arms Robert T. (Wilmington, NC)
Colbert, Coxswain Patrick (Plymouth, NC)
Conlan, Sman Dennis (Fort Fisher, NC)
Connor, Ord. Sman Thomas (Fort Fisher, NC)
Connor, BM William C. (Wilmington, NC)
Cooper, Coxswain John (Mobile Bay, Ala)
Corcoran, Lman Thomas E. (Vicksburg, Miss)
Cotton, Ord. Sman Peter (Yazoo River, Miss)
Crawford, Fireman Alexander (Roanoke River, NC)
Cripps, QM Thomas (Mobile Bay, Ala)
Cronin, Chief QM Cornelius (Mobile Bay, Ala)
Davis, QG John (Elizabeth City, NC)
Davis, Ord. Sman Samuel W. (Mobile Bay, Ala)
Deakin, BM Charles (Mobile Bay, Ala)
Dempster, Coxswain John (Fort Fisher, NC)
Denning, Lman Lorenzo (NOR)
Dennis, BM Richard (Mobile Bay, Ala)
Densmore, Chief BM William (Mobile Bay, Ala)
Diggins, Ord. Sman Bartholomew (Mobile Bay, Ala)
Ditzenback, QM John (Bell's Mills, Tenn)
Donnelly, Ord. Sman John (Mobile Bay, Ala)
Doolen, Coal Heaver William (Mobile Bay, Ala)
Dorman, Sman John (Various)
Dougherty, Lman Patrick (NOR)
Dow, BM Henry (Vicksburg, Miss)
Duncan, BM Adam (Mobile Bay, Ala)
Duncan, Ord. Sman James K. L. (Harrisonburg, La)
Dunn, QM William (Fort Fisher, NC)
Dunphy, Coal Heaver Richard D. (Mobile Bay, Ala)
Edwards, Capt. of the Top John (Mobile Bay, Ala)
English, Signal QM Thomas (Fort Fisher, NC)
Erickson, Capt. of the Forecastle John P. (Fort Fisher, NC)
Farley, BM William (Stono River, SC)
Farrell, QM Edward (Forts Jackson & St. Philip, La)
Ferrell, Pilot John H. (Bell's Mills, Tenn)
Fitzpatrick, Coxswain Thomas (Mobile Bay, Ala)
Flood, Boy Thomas (Forts Jackson & St. Philip, La)
Foy, Signal QM Charles H. (Fort Fisher, NC)
Franks, Sman William J. (Yazoo City, Miss)
Freeman, Pilot Martin (Mobile Bay, Ala)
Frisbee, GM John B. (Forts Jackson & St. Philip, La)
Gardner, Sman William (Mobile Bay, Ala)
Garrison, Coal Heaver James R. (Mobile Bay, Ala)
Garvin, Capt. of the Forecastle William (Fort Fisher, NC)
George, Ord. Sman Daniel G. (NOR)
Gile, Lman Frank S. (Charleston Harbor, SC)
Graham, Lman Robert (Plymouth, NC)
Greene, Capt of the Forecastle John (Forts Jackson & St. Philip, La)
Griffiths, Capt. of the Forecastle John (Fort Fisher, NC)
Griswold, Ord. Sman Luke M. (Cape Hatteras, NC)
Haffee, QG Edmund (Fort Fisher, NC)
Haley, Capt. of the Forecastle James (Cherbourg, France)
Halstead, Coxswain William (Mobile Bay, Ala)
Ham, Carpenter's Mate Mark G. (Cherbourg, France)
Hamilton, Coxswain Hugh (Mobile Bay, Ala)
Hamilton, Coal Heaver Richard (NOR)
Hamilton, QM Thomas W. (Vicksburg, Miss)
Hand, QM Allexander (Roanoke River, NC)
Harcourt, Ord. Sman Thomas (Fort Fisher, NC)
Harding, Capt. of the Forecastle Thomas (Beauford, NC)
Harley, Ord. Sman Bernard (NOR)
Harrington, Lman Daniel (NOR)
Harris, Capt. of the Forecastle John (Mobile Bay, Ala)
Harrison, Sman George H. (Cherbourg, France)
Hathaway, Sman Edward W. (Vicksburg, Miss)
Hawkins, Sman Charles (Fort Fisher, NC)
Hayden, QM Joseph B. (Fort Fisher, NC)
Hayes, Coxswain John (Cherbourg, France)
Hayes, Coxswain Thomas (Mobile Bay, Ala)
Hickman, 2d Class Fireman John (Port Hudson, La)

John Lawson, Landsman, U.S. Navy. Born: 1837, Pennsylvania. Accredited to: Pennsylvania. G.O. No.: 45, 31 December 1864. Citation: On board the flagship U.S.S. Hartford during successful attacks against Fort Morgan, rebel gunboats and the ram Tennessee in Mobile Bay on 5 August 1864. Wounded in the leg and thrown violently against the side of the ship when an enemy shell killed or wounded the 6-man crew as the shell whipped on the berth deck, Lawson, upon regaining his composure, promptly returned to his station and, although urged to go below for treatment, steadfastly continued his duties throughout the remainder of the action.

Hinnegan, 2d Class Fireman William (Fort Fisher, NC)
Hollat, 3d Class Boy George (Forts Jackson & St. Philip, La)
Horton, GM James (NOR)
Horton, Sman Lewis A. (Cape Hatteras, NC)
Houghton, Ord. Sman Edward J. (NOR)
Howard, Lman Martin (Plymouth, NC)
Howard, BM Peter (Port Hudson, La)
Huskey, Fireman Michael (Deer Creek, Miss)
Hyland, Sman John (Red River, Tex)
Irlam, Sman Joseph (Mobile Bay, Ala)
Irving, Coxswain John (Mobile Bay, Ala)
Irving, Coxswain Thomas (Charleston Harbor, SC)
Irwin, Sman Nicholas (Mobile Bay, Ala)
James, Capt. of the Top John H. (Mobile Bay, Ala)
Jenkins, Sman Thomas (Vicksburg, Miss)
Johnson, Sman Henry (Mobile Bay, Ala)
Johnston, Lman William P. (Harrisonburg, La)
Jones, Chief BM Andrew (Mobile Bay, Ala)
Jones, Lman John (Cape Hatteras, NC)
Jones, QM John E. (Mobile Bay, Ala)
Jones, Coxswain Thomas (Fort Fisher, NC)
Jones, Capt. of the Top William (Mobile Bay, Ala)
Jordan, Coxswain Robert (Nansemond River, Va)
Jordan, QM Thomas (Mobile Bay, Ala)
Kane, Capt. of the Hold Thomas (Fort Fisher, NC)
Kelley, 2d Class Fireman John (Roanoke River, NC)
Kendrick, Coxswain Thomas (Mobile Bay, Ala)
Kenna, QM Barnett (Mobile Bay, Ala)
Kenyon, Fireman Charles (Drewry's Bluff, Va)
King, Lman Robert H. (NOR)
Kinnaird, Lman Samuel W. (Mobile Bay, Ala)
Lafferty, Fireman John (Roanoke River, NC)
Laffey, Sman Bartlett (Yazoo City, Miss)
Lakin, Sman Daniel (Franklin, Va)
Lann, Lman John S. (St. Marks, Fla)
Lawson, Lman John (Mobile Bay, Ala)
Lear, QM Nicholas (Fort Fisher, NC)
Lee, Sman James H. (Cherbourg, France)
Leland, GM George W. (Charleston Harbor, SC)
Leon, Capt. of the Forecastle Pierre (Yazoo River, Miss)
Lloyd, Coal Heaver Benjamin (Roanoke River, NC)
Lloyd, Coxswain John W. (Roanoke River, NC)
*Logan, Capt. of the Afterguard Hugh (Cape Hatteras, NC)
Lyons, Sman Thomas (Forts Jackson & St. Philip, La)
McClelland, 1st Class Fireman Matthew (Port Hudson, La)
McCormick, BM Michael (Red River, Tex)
McCullock, Sman Adam (Mobile Bay, Ala)
McDonald, BM John (Yazoo River, Miss)

Auzella Savage, Ordinary Seaman, U.S. Navy. Born: 1846, Maine. Accredited to: Massachusetts. G.O. No.: 59, 22 June 1865. Citation: On board the U.S.S. Santiago de Cuba in the assault on Fort Fisher, 15 January 1865. When the landing party to which he was attached charged on the fort with a cheer, and the determination to plant the colors on the ramparts, Savage remained steadfast when more than two-thirds of the marines and sailors fell back in panic during the fight. When enemy fire shot away the flagstaff above his hand, he bravely seized the remainder of the staff and brought his colors safely off.

McFarland, Capt. of the Forecastle John (Mobile Bay, Ala)
McGowan, QM John (Forts Jackson & St. Philip, La)
Machon, Boy James (Mobile Bay, Ala)
McHugh, Sman Martin (Vicksburg, Miss)
McIntosh, Capt. of the Top James (Mobile Bay, Ala)
Mack, Capt. of the Top Alexander (Mobile Bay, Ala)
Mack, Sman John (St. Marks, Fla)
McKnight, Coxswain William (Forts Jackson & St. Philip, La)
McLeod, Capt. of the Foretop James (Forts Jackson & St. Philip, La)
McWilliams, Lman George W. (Fort Fisher, NC)
Madden, Coal Heaver William (Mobile Bay, Ala)
Martin, QM Edward S. (Mobile Bay, Ala)
Martin, BM William (Yazoo River, Miss)
Martin, Sman William (Forts Jackson & St. Philip, La)
Melville, Ord. Sman Charles (Mobile Bay, Ala)
Mifflin, Engineer's Cook James (Mobile Bay, Ala)
Miller, QM James (Legareville, SC)
Milliken, QG Daniel (Fort Fisher, NC)
Mills, Sman Charles (Fort Fisher, NC)
Molloy, Ord. Sman Hugh (Harrisonburg, La)
Montgomery, Capt. of the Afterguard Robert (Fort Fisher, NC)
Moore, Lman Charles (Legareville, SC)
Moore, Sman Charles (Cherbourg, France)
Moore, Sman George (Cape Hatteras, NC)
Moore, BM William (Haines's Bluff, Miss)
Morgan, Capt. of the Top James H. (Mobile Bay, Ala)
Morrison, Coxswain John G. (Yazoo River, Miss)
Morton, BM Charles W. (Yazoo River, Miss)
Mullen, BM Patrick (Mattox Creek, Va)
Murphy, BM Patrick (Mobile Bay, Ala)
Naylor, Lman David (Mobile Bay, Ala)
Neil, QG John (Fort Fisher, NC)
Newland, Ord. Sman William (Mobile Bay, Ala)
Nibbe, QM John H. (Yazoo River, Miss)
Nichols, QM William (Mobile Bay, Ala)
Noble, Lman Daniel (Mobile Bay, Ala)
O'Brien, Coxswain Oliver (Sullivan's Island Channel, SC)
O'Connell, Coal Heaver Thomas (Mobile Bay, Ala)
O'Donoghue, Sman Timothy (Red River, Tex)
Ortega, Sman John (NOR)
Parker, Capt. of the Afterguard William (Forts Jackson & St. Philip, La)
Parks, Capt. of the Forecastle George (Mobile Bay, Ala)
Pease, Sman Joachim (Cherbourg, France)
Peck, 2d Class Boy Oscar E. (Forts Jackson & St. Philip, La)
Pelham, Lman William (Mobile Bay, Ala)
Perry, BM Thomas (Cherbourg, France)
Peterson, Sman Alfred (Franklin, Va)
Phinney, BM William (Mobile Bay, Ala)
Poole, QM William B. (Cherbourg, France)
Prance, Capt. of the Main Top George (Fort Fisher, NC)
Preston, Lman John (Mobile Bay, Ala)
Price, Coxswain Edward (Mobile Bay, Ala)
Province, Ord. Sman George (Fort Fisher, NC)
Pyne, Sman George (St. Marks, Fla)
Read, Ord. Sman Charles (St. Marks, Fla)
Read, Coxswain Charles A. (Cherbourg, France)
Read, Sman George E. (Cherbourg, France)
Regan, QM Jeremiah (Drewry's Bluff, Va)
Rice, Coal Heaver Charles (Fort Fisher, NC)
Richards, QM Louis (Forts Jackson & St. Philip, La)
Ringold, Coxswain Edward (Pocataligo, SC)
Roberts, Sman James (Fort Fisher, NC)
Robinson, BM Alexander (Wilmington, NC)
Robinson, BM Charles (Yazoo River, Miss)
Rountry, 1st Class Fireman John (NOR)
Rush, 1st Class Fireman John (Port Hudson, La)
Sanderson, Lman Aaron (Mattox Creek, Va)
Saunders, QM James (Cherbourg, France)
Savage, Ord. Sman Auzella (Fort Fisher, NC)
Schutt, Coxswain George (St. Marks, Fla)
Seanor, Master-at-Arms James (Mobile Bay, Ala)
Seward, Paymaster's Steward Richard E. (Ship Island Sound, LA)
Sharp, Sman Hendrick (Mobile Bay, Ala)
Shepard, Ord. Sman Louis C. (Fort Fisher, NC)
Sheridan, QM James (Mobile Bay, Ala)
Shipman, Coxswain William (Fort Fisher, NC)
Shutes, Capt. of the Forecastle Henry (New Orleans, La, & Fort McAllister, Ga)
Simkins, Coxswain Lebbeus (Mobile Bay, Ala)
*Smith, Coxswain Charles H. (Mobile Bay, Ala)
Smith, Ord. Sman Edwin (Franklin, Va)
Smith, Capt. of the Forecastle James (Mobile Bay, Ala)
Smith, 2d Capt. of the Top John (Mobile Bay, Ala)
Smith, Capt. of the Forecastle John (Mobile Bay, Ala)
Smith, Coxswain Oloff (Mobile Bay, Ala)
Smith, Sman Thomas (St. Marks, Fla)
Smith, Ord. Sman Walter B. (Mobile Bay, Ala)
Smith, QM William (Cherbourg, France)
Stanley, Shell Man William A. (Mobile Bay, Ala)
Sterling, Coal Heaver James E. (Mobile Bay, Ala)
Stevens, QM Daniel D. (Fort Fisher, NC)
Stoddard, Sman James (Yazoo River, Miss)
Stout, Lman Richard (Stono River, SC)
Strahan, Capt. of the Top Robert (Cherbourg, France)
Sullivan, Ord. Sman James (Fort Fisher, NC)
Sullivan, Sman John (Wilmington, NC)
Sullivan, Coxswain Timothy (NOR)
Summers, Chief QM Robert (Fort Fisher, NC)
Swanson, Sman John (Fort Fisher, NC)
Swatton, Sman Edward (Fort Fisher, NC)
Swearer, Sman Benjamin (Fort Clark, Md)
Talbott, Capt. of the Forecastle William (Arkansas)
*Tallentine, QG James (Plymouth, NC)
Taylor, Armorer George (Mobile Bay, Ala)
Taylor, Coxswain Thomas (Mobile Bay, Ala)
Taylor, Capt. of the Forecastle William G. (Fort Fisher, NC)
Thielberg, Sman Henry (Nansemond River, Va)
Thompson, Signal QM William (Hilton Head, NC)
Todd, QM Samuel (Mobile Bay, Ala)
Tripp, Chief BM Othniel (Fort Fisher, NC)
Truett, Coxswain Alexander H. (Mobile Bay, Ala)
Vantine, 1st Class Fireman Joseph E. (Port Hudson, La)
Verney, Chief QM James W. (Fort Fisher, NC)
Wagg, Coxswain Maurice (Cape Hatteras, NC)
Ward, QG James (Mobile Bay, Ala)
Warren, Coxswain David (Wilmington, NC)
Webster, Lman Henry S. (Fort Fisher, NC)
Weeks, Capt. of the Foretop Charles H. (NOR)
Wells, QM William (Mobile Bay, Ala)
White, Capt. of the Gun Joseph (Fort Fisher, NC)
Whitfield, QM Daniel (Mobile Bay, Ala)
Wilcox, Ord. Sman Franklin L. (Fort Fisher, NC)
Wilkes, Lman Henry (NOR)
Wilkes, Pilot Perry (Red River, Tex)
Williams, Sailmaker's Mate Anthony (Fort Fisher, NC)

Williams, Sman Augustus (Fort Fisher, NC)
Williams, BM John (Hilton Head, NC)
Williams, Capt. of the Maintop John (Mathias Point, Va)
Williams, Sman John (Franklin, Va)
Williams Sman Peter (Hampton Roads, Va)
Williams, Signal QM Robert (Yazoo River, Miss)
Williams, Lman William (Charleston Harbor, SC)
Willis, Coxswain Richard (Fort Fisher, NC)
Wood, Coxswain Robert B. (Nansemond River, Va)
Woods, Sman Samuel (Nansemond River, Va)
Woon, BM John (Grand Gulf, Miss River)
Woram, Sman Charles B. (Mobile Bay, Ala)
Wright, QM Edward (Forts Jackson & St. Philip, La)
Wright, Yeoman William (Wilmington, NC)
Young, Coxswain Edward B. (Mobile Bay, Ala)
Young, Sman Horatio N. (Charleston Harbor, SC)
Young, BM William (Forts Jackson & St. Philip, La)

The Indian Campaigns, 1861–1898

Number of medals: 423

ARMY: 423

Albee, 1st Lt. George E. (Brazos River, Tex)
Alchesay, Sgt. (Arizona)
Allen, 1st Sgt. William (Turret Mountain, Ariz)
Anderson, Pvt. James (Wichita River, Tex)
Aston, Pvt. Edgar R. (San Carlos, Ariz)
Austin, Sgt. William G. (Wounded Knee Creek, S Dak)
Ayers, Pvt. James F. (Sappa Creek, Kans)
Babcock, 1st Lt. John B. (Spring Creek, Neb)
Bailey, Sgt. James E. (Arizona)
Baird, 1st Lt. & Adj. George W. (Bear Paw Mountain, Mont)
Baker, Musician John (Cedar Creek, Mont)
+Baldwin, 1st Lt. Frank D. (McClellan's Creek, Tex)
Bancroft, Pvt. Neil (Little Big Horn, Mont)
Barnes, Pfc. Will C. (Fort Apache, Ariz)
Barrett, 1st Sgt. Richard (Sycamore Canyon, Ariz)
Beauford, 1st Sgt. Clay (Arizona)
Bell, Pvt. James (Big Horn, Mont)
Bergerndahl, Pvt. Frederick (Staked Plains, Tex)
Bertram, Cpl. Heinrich (Arizona)
Bessey, Cpl. Charles A. (Elkhorn Creek, Wyo)
Bishop, Sgt. Daniel (Turret Mountain, Ariz)
Blair, 1st Sgt. James (Arizona)
Blanquet (Arizona)
Bowden, Cpl. Samuel (Wichita River, Tex)
Bowman, Sgt. Alonzo (Cibicue Creek, Ariz)
Boyne, Sgt. Thomas (Mimbres Mountains & Ojo Caliente, N Mex)
Bradbury, 1st Sgt. Sanford (Hell Canyon, Ariz)
Branagan, Pvt. Edward (Red River, Tex)
Brant, Pvt. Abram B. (Little Big Horn, Mont)
*Bratling, Cpl. Frank (Fort Selden, N Mex)
Brett, 2d Lt. Lloyd M. (O'Fallon's Creek, Mont)
Brogan, Sgt. James (Simon Valley, Ariz)
Brophy, Pvt. James (Arizona)
Brown, Sgt. Benjamin (Arizona)
Brown, Sgt. James (Davidson Canyon, Ariz)
Brown, Pvt. Lorenzo D. (Big Hole, Mont)
Bryan, Hospital Steward William C. (Powder River, Wyo)
Burkard, Pvt. Oscar (Leech Lake, Minn)
Burke, Farrier Patrick J. (Arizona)
Burke, Pvt. Richard (Cedar Creek, Mont)
Burnett, 2d Lt. George R. (Cuchillo Negro Mountains, N Mex)
Butler, Capt. Edmond (Wolf Mountain, Mont)
Byrne, Sgt. Denis (Cedar Creek, Mont)
Cable, Pvt. Joseph A. (Cedar Creek, Mont)
Callen, Pvt. Thomas J. (Little Big Horn, Mont)
Calvert, Pvt. James S. (Cedar Creek, Mont)
Canfield, Pvt. Heth (Little Blue, Neb)
Carpenter, Capt. Louis H. (Kansas & Colorado)
Carr, Pvt. John (Chiricahua Mountains, Ariz)
Carroll, Pvt. Thomas (Arizona)
Carter, Pvt. George (Arizona)
Carter, 1st Lt. Mason (Bear Paw Mountain, Mont)
Carter, 2d Lt. Robert G. (Brazos River, Tex)
Carter, 1st Lt. William H. (Cibicue, Ariz)
Casey, Capt. James S. (Wolf Mountain, Mont)
Cheever, 1st Lt. Benjamin H., Jr. (White River, S Dak)
Chiquito (Arizona)
Clancy, Musician John E. (Wounded Knee Creek, S Dak)

Edgar R. Aston, Private, Company L, 8th U.S. Cavalry. Place and date: At San Carlos, Ariz., 30 May 1868. Birth: Clermont County, Ohio. Date of issue: 28 July 1868. Citation: With 2 other men he volunteered to search for a wagon passage out of a 4,000-foot valley wherein an infantry column was immobile. This small group passed 6 miles among hostile Apache terrain finding the sought passage. On their return trip down the canyon they were attacked by Apaches who were successfully held at bay.

Clark, Pvt. Wilfred (Big Hole, Mont, & Camas Meadows, Idaho)
Clarke, 2d Lt. Powhatan H. (Sonora, Mex)
Comfort, Cpl. John W. (Staked Plaines, Tex)
Connor Cpl. John (Wichita River, Tex)
Coonrod, Sgt. Aquilla (Cedar Creek, Mont)
Corcoran, Cpl. Michael (Agua Fria River, Ariz)
Co-Rux-Te-Chod-Ish (Mad Bear). Sgt. (Republican River, Kans)
Craig, Sgt. Samuel H. (Santa Cruz Mountains, Mex)
Crandall, Pvt. Charles (Arizona)
Crist, Sgt. John (Arizona)
Criswell, Sgt. Banjamin C. (Little Big Horn River, Mont)
Cruse, 2d Lt. Thomas (Big Dry Fork, Ariz)
Cubberly, Pvt. William G. (San Carlos, Ariz)
Cunningham, Cpl. Charles (Little Big Horn River, Mont)
Daily, Pvt. Charles (Arizona)
Daniels, Sgt. James T. (Arizona)
Dawson, Trumpeter Michael (Sappa Creek, Kans)
Day, 2d Lt. Matthias W. (Las Animas Canyon, N Mex)
Day, 1st Sgt. William L. (Arizona)
*De Armond, Sgt. William (Upper Washita, Tex)
Deary, Sgt. George (Apache Creek, Ariz)
Deetline, Pvt. Frederick (Little Big Horn, Mont)
Denny, Sgt. John (Las Animas Canyon, N Mex)
Dickens, Cpl. Charles H. (Chiricahua Mountains, Ariz)
Dodge, Capt. Francis S. (White River Agency, Colo)
Donahue, Pvt. John L. (Chiricahua Mountains, Ariz)
Donavan, Sgt. Cornelius (Agua Fria River, Ariz)
Donelly, Pvt. John S. (Cedar Creek, Mont)
Dougherty, Blacksmith William (Arizona)
Dowling, Cpl. James (Arizona)
Edwards, 1st Sgt. Wiliam D. (Big Hole, Mont)
Eldrige, Sgt. George H. (Wichita River, Tex)

Robert Temple Emmet, Second Lieutenant, 9th U.S. Cavalry. Place and date: At Las Animas Canyon, N. Mex., 18 September 1879. Entered service at: New York, N.Y. Birth: New York, N.Y. Date of issue: 24 August 1899. Citation: Lt. Emmet was in G Troop which was sent to relieve a detachment of soldiers under attack by hostile Apaches. During a flank attack on the Indian camp, made to divert the hostiles, Lt. Emmet and 5 of his men became surrounded when the Indians returned to defend their camp. Finding that the Indians were making for a position from which they could direct their fire on the retreating troop, the Lieutenant held his point with his party until the soldiers reached the safety of a canyon. Lt. Emmet then continued to hold his position while his party recovered their horses. The enemy force consisted of approximately 200.

Elsatsoosu, Cpl. (Arizona)
Elwood, Pvt. Edwin L. (Chiricahua Mountains, Ariz)
Emmet, 2d Lt. Robert T. (Las Animas Canyon, N Mex)
Evans, Pvt. William (Big Horn, Mont)
Factor, Pvt. Pompey (Pecos River, Tex)
Falcott, Sgt. Henry (Arizona)
Farren, Pvt. Daniel (Arizona)
Feaster, Pvt. Mosheim (Wounded Knee Creek, S Dak)
Fegan, Sgt James (Plum Creek, Kans)
Ferrari, Cpl. George (Red Creek, Ariz)
Fichter, Pvt. Hermann (Whetstone Mountains, Ariz)
Foley, Sgt. John H. (Platte River, Neb)
Folly, Pvt. William H. (Arizona)
Foran, Pvt. Nicholas (Arizona)
Forsyth, 1st Sgt. Thomas H. (Powder River, Wyo)
Foster, Sgt. William (Red River, Tex)
Freemeyer, Pvt. Christopher (Cedar Creek, Mont)
Gardiner, Pvt. Peter W. (Sappa Creek, Kans)
Gardner, Pvt. Charles (Arizona)
Garland, Cpl. Harry (Little Muddy Creek, Mont & Camas Meadows, Idaho)
Garlington, 1st Lt. Ernest A. (Wounded Knee Creek, S Dak)
Gates, Bugler George (Picacho Mountain, Ariz)
Gay, Pvt. Thomas H. (Arizona)
Geiger, Sgt. George (Little Big Horn River, Mont)
Georgian, Pvt. John (Chiricahua Mountains, Ariz)
Gerber, Sgt. Maj. Frederick W. (Various)
*Given, Cpl. John J. (Wichita River, Tex)
Glavinski, Blacksmith Albert (Powder River, Mont)
Glover, Sgt. T. B. (Mizpah Creek & Pumpkin Creek, Mont)
Glynn, Pvt. Michael (Whetstone Mountains, Ariz)
Godfrey, Capt. Edward S. (Bear Paw Mountain, Mont)
Golden, Sgt. Patrick (Arizona)
Goldin, Pvt. Theodore W. (Little Big Horn, Mont)
Goodman, Pvt. David (Lyry Creek, Ariz)
Grant, Sgt. George (Fort Phil Kearny-Fort C. F. Smith, Dak Terr)
Greaves, Cpl. Clinton (Florida Mountains, N Mex)
Green, Sgt. Francis C. (Arizona)
Green, Maj. John (Lava Beds, Calif)
Gresham, 1st Lt. John C. (Wounded Knee Creek, S Dak)
Grimes, Sgt. Edward P. (Milk River, Colo)
Gunther, Cpl. Jacob (Arizona)
Haddoo, Cpl. John (Cedar Creek, Mont)
Hall, Pvt. John (Arizona)
Hall, 1st Lt. William P. (White River, Colo)
Hamilton, Pvt. Frank (Agua Fria River, Ariz)
Hamilton, Pvt. Mathew H. (Wounded Knee Creek, S Dak)
Hanley, Sgt. Richard P. (Little Big Horn River, Mont)
Harding, Blacksmith Mosher A. (Chiricahua Mountains, Ariz)
Harrington, Pvt. John (Wichita River, Tex)
Harris, Sgt. Charles D. (Red Creek, Ariz)
Harris, Pvt. David W. (Little Big Horn River, Mont)
Harris, Pvt. William M. (Little Big Horn River, Mont)
Hartzog, Pvt. Joshua B. (Wounded Knee Creek, S Dak)
Haupt, Cpl. Paul (Hell Canyon, Ariz)
Hawthorne, 2d Lt. Harry L. (Wounded Knee Creek, S Dak)
Hay, Sgt. Fred S. (Upper Wichita, Tex)
Heartery, Pvt. Richard (Cibicue, Ariz)
Heise, Pvt. Clamor (Arizona)
Herron, Cpl. Leander (Fort Dodge, Kans)
Heyl, 2d Lt. Charles H. (Fort Hartsuff, Neb)
Higgins, Pvt. Thomas P. (Arizona)
Hill, Sgt. Frank E. (Date Creek, Ariz)

Peter W. Gardiner, Private, Company H, 6th U.S. Cavalry. Place and date: At Sappa Creek, Kans., 23 April 1875. Birth: Carlisle, N.Y. Date of issue: 16 November 1876. Citation: With 5 other men he waded in mud and water up the creek to a position directly behind an entrenched Cheyenne position, who were using natural bank pits to good advantage against the main column. This surprise attack from the enemy rear broke their resistance.

Hill, 1st Sgt. James M. (Turret Mountain, Ariz)
Hillock, Pvt. Marvin C. (Wounded Knee Creek, S Dak)
Himmelsback, Pvt. Michael (Little Blue, Neb)
Hinemann, Sgt. Lehmann (Arizona)
Hobday, Pvt. George (Wounded Knee Creek, S Dak)
Hogan, 1st Sgt. Henry (Cedar Creek, Mont) Second award (Bear Paw Mountain, Mont)
Holden, Pvt. Henry (Little Big Horn River, Mont)
Holland, Cpl. David (Cedar Creek, Mont)
*Hooker, Pvt. George (Tonto Creek, Ariz)
Hoover, Bugler Samuel (Santa Maria Mountains, Ariz)
Hornaday, Pvt. Simpson (Sappa Creek, Kans)
Howze, 2d Lt. Robert L. (White River, S Dak)
Hubbard, Pvt. Thomas (Little Blue, Neb)
Huff, Pvt. James W. (Arizona)
Huggins, Capt. Eli L. (O'Fallon's Creek, Mont)
Humphrey, 1st Lt. Charles F. (Clearwater, Idaho)
Hunt, Pvt. Fred O. (Cedar Creek, Mont)
Hutchinson, Sgt. Rufus D. (Little Big Horn River, Mont)
Hyde, Sgt. Henry J. (Arizona)
Irwin, Asst. Surgeon Bernard J. D. (Apache Pass, Ariz)
Jackson, Capt. James (Camas Meadows, Idaho)
James, Cpl. John (Upper Wichita, Tex)
Jarvis, Sgt. Frederick (Chiricahua Mountains, Ariz)
Jetter, Sgt. Bernhard (South Dakota)
Jim, Sgt. (Arizona)
Johnson, Sgt. Henry (Milk River, Colo)
Johnston, Cpl. Edward (Cedar Creek, Mont)
Jones, Farrier William H. (Little Muddy Creek, Mont, & Camas Meadows, Idaho)
Jordan, Sgt. George (Fort Tularosa & Carrizo Canyon, N Mex)
Kay, Pvt. John (Arizona)
Keating, Cpl. Daniel (Wichita River, Tex)
Keenan, Trumpeter Bartholomew T. (Chiricahua Mountains, Ariz)
Keenan, Pvt. John (Arizona)
Kelley, Pvt. Charles (Chiricahua Mountains, Ariz)
Kelly, Cpl. John J. H. (Upper Wichita, Tex)
Kelly, Pvt. Thomas (Upper Wichita, Tex)
Kelsay (Arizona)
Kennedy, Pvt. Philip (Cedar Creek, Mont)
Kerr, Capt. John B. (White River, S Dak)
Kerrigan, Sgt. Thomas (Wichita River, Tex)
Kilmartin, Pvt. John (Whetstone Mountains, Ariz)
Kirk, 1st Sgt. John (Wichita River, Tex)
Kirkwood, Sgt. John A. (Slim Buttes, Dak Terr)
Kitchen, Sgt. George K. (Upper Wichita, Tex)
Knaak, Pvt. Albert (Arizona)
Knight, Sgt. Joseph F. (White River, S Dak)

John B. Kerr, Captain, 6th U.S. Cavalry. Place and date: At White River, S. Dak., 1 January 1891. Entered service at: Hutchison Station, Ky. Birth: Fayette County, Ky. Date of issue: 25 April 1891. Citation: For distinguished bravery while in command of his troop in action against hostile Sioux Indians on the north bank of the White River, near the mouth of Little Grass Creek, S. Dak., where he defeated a force of 300 Brule Sioux warriors, and turned the Sioux tribe, which was endeavoring to enter the Bad Lands, back into the Pine Ridge Agency.

Knox, Sgt. John W. (Upper Wichita, Tex)
Koelpin, Sgt. William (Upper Wichita, Tex)
Kosoha, (Arizona)
Kreher, 1st Sgt. Wendelin (Cedar Creek, Mont)
Kyle, Cpl. John (Republican River, Kans)
Larkin, Farrier David (Red River, Tex)
Lawrence, Pvt. James (Arizona)
Lawton, Sgt. John S. (Milk River, Colo)
Lenihan, Pvt. James (Clear Creek, Ariz)
Leonard, Sgt. Patrick (Little Blue, Neb)
Leonard, Cpl. Patrick T. (Fort Hartsuff, Neb)
Leonard, Pvt. William (Muddy Creek, Mont)
Lewis, Sgt. William B. (Bluff Station, Wyo)
Little, Bugler Thomas (Arizona)
Lohnes, Pvt. Francis W. (Gilman's Ranch, Neb)
Long, 2d Lt. Oscar F. (Bear Paw Mountain, Mont)
Lowthers, Pvt. James (Sappa Creek, Kans)
*Loyd, Sgt. George (Wounded Knee Creek, S Dak)
Lytle, Sgt. Leonidas S. (Fort Selden, N Mex)
Lytton, Cpl. Jeptha L. (Fort Hartsuff, Neb)
McBride, Pvt. Bernard (Arizona)
McBryar, Sgt. William (Arizona)
McCabe, Pvt. William (Red River, Tex)
*McCann Pvt. Bernard (Cedar Creek, Mont)
McCarthy, 1st Sgt. Michael (White Bird Canyon, Idaho)
McClernand, 2d Lt. Edward J. (Bear Paw Mountain, Mont)
McCormick, Pvt. Michael (Cedar Creek, Mont)
McDonald, Pvt. Franklin M. (Fort Griffin, Tex)
McDonald, Cpl. James (Arizona)
McDonald, 1st Lt. Robert (Wolf Mountain, Mont)
McGann, 1st Sgt. Michael A. (Rosebud River, Mont)
McGar, Pvt. Owen (Cedar Creek, Mont)
Machol, Pvt. (Arizona)
McHugh, Pvt. John (Cedar Creek, Mont)
McKinley, Pvt. Daniel (Arizona)
McLennon, Musician John (Big Hole, Mont)
McLoughlin, Sgt. Michael (Cedar Creek, Mont)
*McMasters, Cpl. Henry A. (Red River, Tex)
McMillan, Sgt. Albert W. (Wounded Knee Creek, S Dak)
McNally, 1st Sgt. James (Arizona)
McNamara, 1st Sgt. William (Red River, Tex)
McPhelan, Sgt. Robert (Cedar Creek, Mont)
McVeagh, Pvt. Charles H. (Arizona)
Mahers, Pvt. Herbert (Seneca Mountain, Ariz)
Mahoney, Pvt. Gregory (Red River, Tex)
Martin, Sgt. Patrick (Castle Dome & Santa Maria Mountains, Ariz)
Matthews, Cpl. David A. (Arizona)
Maus, 1st Lt. Marion P. (Sierra Madre Mountains, Mex)
May, Sgt. John (Wichita River, Tex)
Mays, Cpl. Isaiah (Arizona)
Meaher, Cpl. Nicholas (Chiricahua Mountains, Ariz)
Mechlin, Blacksmith Henry W. B. (Little Big Horn, Mont)
Merrill, Sgt. John (Milk River, Colo)
Miller, Pvt. Daniel H. (Whetstone Mountains, Ariz)
Miller, Cpl. George (Cedar Creek, Mont)
Miller, Pvt. George W. (Arizona)
Mitchell, 1st Sgt. John (Upper Washita, Tex)
Mitchell, Cpl. John J. (Hell Canyon, Ariz)
Montrose, Pvt. Charles H. (Cedar Creek, Mont)
Moquin, Cpl. George (Milk River, Colo)
Moran, Pvt. John (Seneca Mountain, Ariz)
Morgan, 2d Lt. George H. (Big Dry Fork, Ariz)
Moriarity, Sgt. John (Arizona)
Morris, 1st Sgt. James L. (Fort Selden, N Mex)
Morris, Cpl. William W. (Upper Washita, Tex)
Mott, Sgt. John (Whetstone Mountains, Ariz)
Moylan, Capt. Myles (Bear Paw Mountain, Mont)
Murphy, Pvt. Edward (Chiricahua Mountains, Ariz)
Murphy, Cpl. Edward F. (Milk River, Colo)
Murphy, Pvt. Jeremiah (Powder River, Mont)
Murphy, Cpl. Philip (Seneca Mountain, Ariz)
Murphy, Cpl. Thomas (Seneca Mountain, Ariz)
Murray, Sgt. Thomas (Little Big Horn, Mont)
Myers, Sgt. Fred (White River, S Dak)
Nannasaddie (Arizona)
Nantaje (Arizona)
Neal, Pvt. Solon D. (Wichita River, Tex)
Neder, Pvt. Adam (South Dakota)
Neilon, Sgt. Frederick S. (Upper Washita, Tex)
Newman, 1st Sgt. Henry (Whetstone Mountains, Ariz)
Nihill, Pvt. John (Whetstone Mountains, Ariz)
Nolan, Farrier Richard J. (White Clay Creek, S Dak)
O'Callaghan, Sgt. John (Arizona)
Oliver, 1st Sgt. Francis (Chiricahua Mountains, Ariz)
O'Neill, Cpl. William (Red River, Tex)
O'Regan, Pvt. Michael (Arizona)
Orr, Pvt. Moses (Arizona)
Osborne, Sgt. William (Arizona)
O'Sullivan, Pvt. John (Staked Plains, Tex)
Paine, Pvt. Adam (Red River, Tex)
Parnell, 1st Lt. William R. (White Bird Canyon, Idaho)
Payne, Trumpeter Isaac (Pecos River, Tex)
Pengally, Pvt. Edward (Chiricahua Mountains, Ariz)
Pennsyl, Sgt. Josiah (Upper Washita, Tex)
Phife, Sgt. Lewis (Arizona)
Philipsen, Blacksmith Wilhelm O. (Milk River, Colo)
Phillips, Pvt. Samuel D. (Muddy Creek, Mont)
Phoenix, Cpl. Edwin (Red River, Tex)
Platten, Sgt. Frederick (Sappa Creek, Kans)
Poppe, Sgt. John A. (Milk River, Colo)
Porter, Farrier Samuel (Wichita River, Tex)
Powers, Cpl. Thomas (Chiricahua Mountains, Ariz)
Pratt, Blacksmith James (Red River, Tex)
Pym, Pvt. James (Little Big Horn River, Mont)
Raerick, Pvt. John (Lyry Creek, Ariz)
Ragnar, 1st Sgt. Theodore (White Clay Creek, S Dak)
Rankin, Pvt. William (Red River, Tex)
Reed, Pvt. James C. (Arizona)
Richman, Pvt. Samuel (Arizona)
Roach, Cpl. Hampton M. (Milk River, Colo)
Robbins, Pvt. Marcus M. (Sappa Creek, Kans)
Robinson, 1st Sgt. Joseph (Rosebud River, Mont)
Roche, 1st Sgt. David (Cedar Creek, Mont)
Rodenburg, Pvt. Henry (Cedar Creek, Mont)
Rogan, Sgt. Patrick (Big Hole, Mont)
Romeyn, 1st Lt. Henry (Bear Paw Mountain, Mont)
Rooney, Pvt. Edward (Cedar Creek, Mont)
Roth, Pvt. Peter (Wichita River, Tex)

Michael McCarthy, First Sergeant, Troop H, 1st U.S. Cavalry. Place and date: At White Bird Canyon, Idaho, June 1876 to January 1877. Birth: St. Johns, Newfoundland. Date of issue: 20 November 1897. Citation: Was detailed with 6 men to hold a commanding position, and held it with great gallantry until the troops fell back. He then fought his way through the Indians, rejoined a portion of his command, and continued the fight in retreat. He had 2 horses shot from under him, and was captured, but escaped and reported for duty after 3 days' hiding and wandering in the mountains.

Rowalt, Pvt. John F. (Lyry Creek, Ariz)
Rowdy, Sgt. (Arizona)
Roy, Sgt. Stanislaus (Little Big Horn, Mont)
Russell, Pvt. James (Chiricahua Mountains, Ariz)
Ryan, Pvt. David (Cedar Creek, Mont)
Ryan, 1st Sgt. Dennis (Gageby Creek, Indian Terr)
Sale, Pvt. Albert (Santa Maria River, Ariz)
Schnitzer, Wagoner John (Horseshoe Canyon, N Mex)
Schou, Cpl. Julius (Dakota Territory)
Schroeter, Pvt. Charles (Chiricahua Mountains, Ariz)
Scott, Pvt. George D. (Little Big Horn, Mont)
Scott, Pvt. Robert B. (Chiricahua Mountains, Ariz)
Seward, Wagoner Griffin (Chiricahua Mountains, Ariz)
Shaffer, Pvt. William (Arizona)
Sharpless, Cpl. Edward C. (Upper Washita, Tex)
Shaw, Sgt. Thomas (Carrizo Canyon, N Mex)
Sheerin, Blacksmith John (Fort Selden, N Mex)
Sheppard, Pvt. Charles (Cedar Creek, Mont)
Shingle, 1st Sgt. John H. (Rosebud River, Mont)
Skinner, Contract Surgeon John O. (Lava Beds, Ore)
Smith, Sgt. Andrew J. (Chiricahua Mountains, Ariz)
Smith, Cpl. Charles E. (Wichita River, Tex)
Smith, Cpl. Cornelius C. (White River, S Dak)
*Smith, Pvt. George W. (Wichita River, Tex)
Smith, Pvt. Otto (Arizona)
Smith, Pvt. Robert (Slim Buttes, Mont)
Smith, Pvt. Theodore F. (Chiricahua Mountains, Ariz)
Smith, Pvt. Thomas (Chiricahua Mountains, Ariz)
Smith, Pvt. Thomas J. (Chiricahua Mountains, Ariz)
Smith, Pvt. William (Chiricahua Mountains, Ariz)
Smith, Pvt. William H. (Chiricahua Mountains, Ariz)
Snow, Trumpeter Elmer A. (Rosebud Creek, Mont)
Spence, Pvt. Orizoba (Chiricahua Mountains, Ariz)
Springer, Pvt. George (Chiricahua Mountains, Ariz)
Stance, Sgt. Emanuel (Kickapoo Springs, Tex)
Stanley, Pvt. Eben (Turret Mountain, Ariz)
Stanley, Cpl. Edward (Seneca Mountain, Ariz)
Stauffer, 1st Sgt. Rudolph (Camp Hualpai, Ariz)
Steiner, Saddler Christian (Chiricahua Mountains, Ariz)
Stewart, Pvt. Benjamin F. (Big Horn River, Mont)
Stickoffer, Saddler Julius H. (Cienaga Springs, Utah)
Stivers, Pvt. Thomas W. (Little Big Horn, Mont)
Stokes, 1st Sgt. Alonzo (Wichita River, Tex)
Strayer, Pvt. William H. (Platte River, Neb)
Strivson, Pvt. Benoni (Arizona)
Sullivan, Pvt. Thomas (Chiricahua Mountains, Ariz)
Sullivan, Pvt. Thomas (Wounded Knee Creek, S Dak)
Sumner, Pvt. James (Chiricahua Mountains, Ariz)
Sutherland, Cpl. John A. (Arizona)
Taylor, Sgt. Bernard (Sunset Pass, Ariz)
Taylor, 1st Sgt. Charles (Big Dry Wash, Ariz)
Taylor, Cpl. Wilbur N. (Arizona)
Tea, Sgt. Richard L. (Sappa Creek, Kans)
Thomas, Sgt. Charles L. (Dakota Territory)
Thompson, Pvt. George W. (Little Blue, Neb)
Thompson, Sgt. John (Chiricahua Mountains, Ariz)
Thompson, Pvt. Peter (Little Big Horn, Mont)
Tilton, Maj. & Surgeon Henry R. (Bear Paw Mountain, Mont)
Tolan, Pvt. Frank (Little Big Horn, Mont)
Toy, 1st Sgt. Frederick E. (Wounded Knee Creek, S Dak)
Tracy, Pvt. John (Chiricahua Mountains, Ariz)
Trautman, 1st Sgt. Jacob (Wounded Knee Creek, S Dak)
Turpin, 1st Sgt. James H. (Arizona)
Varnum, Capt. Charles A. (White Clay Creek, S Dak)
Veuve, Farrier Ernest (Staked Plains, Tex)
Voit, Saddler Otto (Little Big Horn, Mont)
Vokes, 1st Sgt. Leroy H. (Platte River, Neb)
Von Medem, Sgt. Rudolph (Arizona)
Walker, Pvt. Allen (Texas)
Walker, Pvt. John (Red Creek, Ariz)
Wallace, Sgt. William (Cedar Creek, Mont)
Walley, Pvt. Augustus (Cuchillo Negro Mountains, N Mex)
Ward, Pvt. Charles H. (Chiricahua Mountains, Ariz)
Ward, Sgt. James (Wounded Knee Creek, S Dak)

Peter Thompson, Private, Company C, 7th U.S. Cavalry. Place and date: At Little Big Horn, Mont., 25 June 1876. Entered service at: Pittsburgh, Pa. Birth: Scotland. Date of issue: 5 October 1878. Citation: After having voluntarily brought water to the wounded, in which effort he was shot through the head, he made two successful trips for the same purpose, notwithstanding remonstrances of his sergeant.

Leonard Wood, Assistant Surgeon, U.S. Army. Place and date: In Apache campaign, summer of 1886. Entered service at: Massachusetts. Birth: Winchester, N.H. Date of issue: 8 April 1898. Citation: Voluntarily carried dispatches through a region infested with hostile Indians, making a journey of 70 miles in one night and walking 30 miles the next day. Also for several weeks, while in close pursuit of Geronimo's band and constantly expecting an encounter, commanded a detachment of Infantry, which was then without an officer, and to the command of which he was assigned upon his own request.

Ward, Sgt. John (Pecos River, Tex)
Warrington, 1st Lt. Lewis (Muchague Valley, Tex)
Watson, Cpl. James C. (Wichita River, Tex)
Watson, Pvt. Joseph (Picacho Mountain, Ariz)
Weaher, Pvt. Andrew J. (Arizona)
Weinert, Cpl. Paul H. (Wounded Knee Creek, S Dak)
Weiss, Pvt. Enoch R. (Chiricahua Mountains, Ariz)
Welch, Sgt. Charles H. (Little Big Horn, Mont)
Welch, Sgt. Michael (Wichita River, Tex)
West, 1st Lt. Frank (Big Dry Wash, Ariz)
Whitehead, Pvt. Patton G. (Cedar Creek, Mont)
Widmer, 1st Sgt. Jacob (Milk River, Colo)
Wilder, 1st Lt. Wilber E. (Horseshoe Canyon, N Mex)
Wilkens, 1st Sgt. Henry (Little Muddy Creek, Mont)
Williams, 1st Sgt. Moses (Cuchillo Negro Mountains, N Mex)
Wills, Pvt. Henry (Fort Selden, N Mex)
Wilson, Pvt. Benjamin (Wichita River, Tex)
Wilson, Cpl. Charles (Cedar Creek, Mont)
Wilson, Sgt. Milden H. (Big Hole, Mont)
Wilson, Sgt. William (Colorado Valley, Tex) Second award (Red River, Tex)
Wilson, Cpl. William O. (South Dakota)
Windolph, Pvt. Charles (Little Big Horn, Mont)
Windus, Bugler Claron A. (Wichita River, Tex)
Winterbottom, Sgt. William (Wichita River, Tex)
Witcome, Pvt. Joseph (Arizona)
Wood, Asst. Surgeon Leonard (Arizona & Mexico)
Woodall, Sgt. Zachariah (Wichita River, Tex)
Woods, Sgt. Brent (New Mexico)
Wortman, Sgt. George G. (Arizona)
Yount, Pvt. John P. (Whetstone Mountains, Ariz)
Ziegner, Pvt. Hermann (Wounded Knee Creek & White Clay Creek, S Dak)

The Wars of American Expansion, 1871–1933

Korea, 1871

Number of medals: 15

MARINES: 6
NAVY: 9

MARINES

Brown, Cpl. Charles (Korea)
Coleman, Pvt. John (Korea)
Dougherty, Pvt. James (Korea)
McNamara, Pvt. Michael (Korea)
Owens, Pvt. Michael (Korea)
Purvis, Pvt. Hugh (Korea)

NAVY

Andrews, Ord. Sman John (Korea)
Franklin, QM Frederick (Korea)
Grace, Chief QM Patrick H. (Korea)
Hayden, Carpenter Cyrus (Korea)
Lukes, Lman William F. (Korea)
McKenzie, BM Alexander (Korea)
Merton, Lman James F. (Korea)
Rogers, QM Samuel F. (Korea)
Troy, Ord. Sman William (Korea)

The Spanish–American War, 1898

Number of medals: 109

ARMY: 30
MARINES: 15
NAVY: 64

ARMY

Baker, Sgt. Maj. Edward L., Jr. (Santiago, Cuba)
Bell, Pvt. Dennis (Tayabacoa, Cuba)
Berg, Pvt. George (El Caney, Cuba)
Brookin, Pvt. Oscar (El Caney, Cuba)
Buzzard, Cpl. Ulysses G. (El Caney, Cuba)
Cantrell, Pvt. Charles P. (Santiago, Cuba)
Church, Asst. Surgeon James R. (Las Guasimas, Cuba)
Cummins, Sgt. Andrew J. (Santiago, Cuba)
De Swan, Pvt. John F. (Santiago, Cuba)
Doherty, Cpl. Thomas M. (Santiago, Cuba)
Fournia, Pvt. Frank O. (Santiago, Cuba)
Graves, Pvt. Thomas J. (El Caney, Cuba)
Hardaway, 1st Lt. Benjamin F. (El Caney, Cuba)
Heard, 1st Lt. John W. (Manimani River, Cuba)
Keller, Pvt. William (Santiago, Cuba)
Kelly, Pvt. Thomas (Santiago, Cuba)
Lee, Pvt. Fitz (Tayabacoa, Cuba)
Mills, Capt. & Asst. Adj. Gen. Albert L. (Santiago, Cuba)
Nash, Pvt. James J. (Santiago, Cuba)
Nee, Pvt. George H. (Santiago, Cuba)
Pfisterer, Musician Herman (Santiago, Cuba)
Polond, Pvt. Alfred (Santiago, Cuba)
Quinn, Sgt. Alexander M. (Santiago, Cuba)
Ressler, Cpl. Norman W. (El Caney, Cuba)
Roberts, 2d Lt. Charles D. (El Caney, Cuba)
Shepherd, Cpl. Warren J. (El Caney, Cuba)
Thompkins, Pvt. William H. (Tayabacoa, Cuba)
Wanton, Pvt. George H. (Tayabacoa, Cuba)
Welborn, 2d Lt. Ira C. (Santiago, Cuba)
Wende, Pvt. Bruno (El Caney, Cuba)

MARINES

Campbell, Pvt. Daniel (Cienfuegos, Cuba)
Field, Pvt. Oscar W. (Cienfuegos, Cuba)
Fitzgerald, Pvt. John (Cuzco, Cuba)
Franklin, Pvt. Joseph J. (Cienfuegos, Cuba)
Gaughan, Sgt. Philip (Cienfuegos, Cuba)
Hill, Pvt. Frank (Cienfuegos, Cuba)
Kearney, Pvt. Michael (Cienfuegos, Cuba)
Kuchneister, Pvt. Hermann W. (Cienfuegos, Cuba)
MacNeal, Pvt. Harry L. (Santiago, Cuba)
Meredith, Pvt. James (Cienfuegos, Cuba)
Parker, Pvt. Pomeroy (Cienfuegos, Cuba)
Quick, Sgt. John H. (Cuzco, Cuba)
Scott, Pvt. Joseph F. (Cienfuegos, Cuba)
Sullivan, Pvt. Edward (Cienfuegos, Cuba)
West, Pvt. Walter S. (Cienfuegos, Cuba)

NAVY

Baker, Coxswain Benjamin F. (Cienfuegos, Cuba)
Barrow, Sman David D. (Cienfuegos, Cuba)
Bennet, Chief BM James H. (Cienfuegos, Cuba)
Beyer, Coxswain Albert (Cienfuegos, Cuba)
Blume, Sman Robert (Cienfuegos, Cuba)
Brady, Chief GM George F. (Cardenas, Cuba)
Bright, Coal Passer George W. (Cienfuegos, Cuba)
Carter, Blacksmith Joseph E. (Cienfuegos, Cuba)
Chadwick, Apprentice 1st Class Leonard (Cienfuegos, Cuba)
Charette, GM 1st Class George (Santiago, Cuba)
Clausen, Coxswain Claus K. (Santiago, Cuba)
Cooney, Chief Machinist Thomas C. (Cardenas, Cuba)
Crouse, Watertender William A. (Cavite, Philippines
Davis, GM 3d Class John (Cienfuegos, Cuba)
Deignan, Coxswain Osborn (Santiago, Cuba)
Doran, BM 2d Class John J. (Cienfuegos, Cuba)
Durney, Blacksmith Austin J. (Cienfuegos, Cuba)
Eglit, Sman John (Cienfuegos, Cuba)
Ehle, Fireman 1st Class John W. (Cavite, Philippines)
Erickson, Coxswain Nick (Cienfuegos, Cuba)
Foss, Sman Herbert L. (Cienfuegos, Cuba)
Gibbons, Oiler Michael (Cienfuegos, Cuba)
Gill, GM 1st Class Freeman (Cienfuegos, Cuba)
Hart, Machinist 1st Class William (Cienfuegos, Cuba)
Hendrickson, Sman Henry (Cienfuegos, Cuba)
Hoban, Coxswain Thomas (Cienfuegos, Cuba)
Hobson, Lt. Richmond P. (Santiago, Cuba)
Hull, Fireman 1st Class James L. (Cavite, Philippines)
Itrich, Chief Carpenter's Mate Franz A. (Manila, Philippines)
Johanson, Sman John P. (Cienfuegos, Cuba)
Johansson, Ord. Sman Johan J. (Cienfuegos, Cuba)
Johnsen, Chief Machinist Hans (Cardenas, Cuba)
Johnson, Fireman 1st Class Peter (NOR)
Keefer, Coppersmith Philip B. (Santiago, Cuba)
Kelly, Watertender Francis (Santiago, Cuba)
Kramer, Sman Franz (Cienfuegos, Cuba)
Krause, Coxswain Ernest (Cienfuegos, Cuba)
Levery, Apprentice 1st Class William (Cienfuegos, Cuba)
Mager, Apprentice 1st Class George F. (Cienfuegos, Cuba)

James Robb Church, Assistant Surgeon, 1st U.S. Volunteer Cavalry. Place and date: At Las Guasimas, Cuba, 24 June 1898. Entered service at: Washington, D.C. Birth: Chicago, Ill. Date of issue: 10 January 1906. Citation: In addition to performing gallantly the duties pertaining to his position, voluntarily and unaided carried several seriously wounded men from the firing line to a secure position in the rear, in each instance being subjected to a very heavy fire and great exposure and danger.

John W. Heard, First Lieutenant, 3d U.S. Cavalry. Place and date: At Mouth of Manimani River, west of Bahia Honda, Cuba, 23 July 1898. Entered service at: Mississippi. Birth: Mississippi. Date of issue: 21 June 1899. Citation: After 2 men had been shot down by Spaniards while transmitting orders to the engine-room on the Wanderer, the ship having become disabled, this officer took the position held by them and personally transmitted the orders, remaining at his post until the ship was out of danger.

Mahoney, Fireman 1st Class George (NOR)
Maxwell, Fireman 2d Class John (Cienfuegos, Cuba)
Meyer, Carpenter's Mate 3d Class Willliam (Cienfuegos, Cuba)
Miller, Sman Harry H. (Cienfuegos, Cuba)
Miller, Sman Willard (Cienfuegos, Cuba)
Montague, Chief Master-at-Arms Daniel (Santiago, Cuba)
Morin, BM 2d Class William H. (Caimanera, Cuba)
Muller, Mate Frederick (Manzanillo, Cuba)
Murphy, Coxswain John E. (Santiago, Cuba)
Nelson, Sailmaker's Mate Lauritz (Cienfuegos, Cuba)
Oakley, GM 2d Class William (Cienfuegos, Cuba)
Olsen, Ord. Sman Anton (Cienfuegos, Cuba)
Penn, Fireman 1st Class Robert (Santiago, Cuba)
Phillips, Machinist 1st Class George F. (Santiago, Cuba)
Rilley, Lman John P. (Cienfuegos, Cuba)
Russell, Lman Henry P. (Cienfuegos, Cuba)
Spicer, GM 1st Class William (Caimanera, Cuba)
Sundquist, Chief Carpenter's Mate Axel (Caimanera, Cuba)
Sundquist, Ord. Sman Gustave A. (Cienfuegos, Cuba)
Triplett, Ord. Sman Samuel (Caimanera, Cuba)
Vadas, Sman Albert (Cienfuegos, Cuba)
Van Etten, Sman Hudson (Cienfuegos, Cuba)
Volz, Sman Robert (Cienfuegos, Cuba)
Wilke, BM 1st Class Julius A. R. (Cienfuegos, Cuba)
Williams, Sman Frank (Cienfuegos, Cuba)

Philippines/Samoa, 1899–1913

Number of medals:	91
ARMY:	70
MARINES	9
NAVY:	12

ARMY

Anders, Cpl. Frank L. (San Miguel de Mayumo, Luzon)
Batson, 1st Lt. Matthew A. (Calamba, Luzon)
Bell, Capt. Harry (Porac, Luzon)
Bell, Col. J. Franklin (Porac, Luzon)
Bickham, 1st Lt. Charles G. (Bayong, Mindinao)
Biegler, Capt. George W. (Loac, Luzon)
Birkhimer, Capt. William E. (San Miguel de Mayumo, Luzon)
Boeh, Pvt. Otto (San Isidro, Luzon)
Byrne, Capt. Bernard A. (Bobong, Negros)
Carson, Cpl. Anthony J. (Catubig, Samar)
Cawetzka, Pvt. Charles (Sariaya, Luzon)
Cecil, 1st Lt. Josephus S. (Bud-Dajo, Jolo)
Condon, Sgt. Clarence M. (Calulut, Luzon)
Davis, Pvt. Charles P. (San Isidro, Luzon)
Downs, Pvt. Willis H. (San Miguel de Mayumo, Luzon)
Epps, Pvt. Joseph L. (Vigan, Luzon)
Ferguson, 1st Lt. Arthur M. (Porac, Luzon)
Funston, Col. Frederick (Rio Grande de la Pampanga, Luzon)
Galt, Artificer Sterling A. (Bamban, Luzon)
Gaujot, Cpl Antoine A. (San Mateo)
Gedeon, Pvt. Louis (Mount Amia, Cebu)
Gibson, Sgt. Edward H. (San Mateo)
Gillenwater, Cpl. James R. (Porac, Luzon)
Greer, 2d Lt. Allen J. (Majada, Laguna Province)
Grove, Lt. Col. William R. (Porac, Luzon)
Hayes, Lt. Col. Webb C. (Vigan, Luzon)
Henderson, Sgt. Joseph (Patian Island)
High, Pvt. Frank C. (San Isidro, Luzon)
Huntsman, Sgt. John A. (Bamban, Luzon)
Jensen, Pvt. Gotfred (San Miguel de Mayumo, Luzon)
Johnston, 1st Lt. Gordon (Mount Bud Dajo, Jolo)
Kennedy, 2d Lt. John T. (Patian Island)
Kilbourne, 1st Lt. Charles E. (Paco Bridge)
Kinne, Pvt. John B. (San Isidro, Luzon)
Leahy, Pvt. Cornelius J. (Porac, Luzon)
*Logan, Maj. John A. (San Jacinto)

Robert Penn, Fireman First Class, U.S. Navy. Born: 10 October 1872, City Point, Va. Accredited to: Virginia. G.O. No.: 501, 14 December 1898. Citation: On board the U.S.S. Iowa off Santiago de Cuba, 20 July 1898. Performing his duty at the risk of serious scalding at the time of the blowing out of the manhole gasket on board the vessel, Penn hauled the fire while standing on a board thrown across a coal bucket 1 foot above the boiling water which was still blowing from the boiler.

Longfellow, Pvt. Richard M. (San Isidro, Luzon)
Lyon, Pvt. Edward E. (San Miguel de Mayumo, Luzon)
McConnell, Pvt. James (Vigan, Luzon)
McGrath, Capt. Hugh J. (Calamba, Luzon)
Maclay, Pvt. William P. (Hilongas, Leyte)
Mathews, Asst. Surgeon George W. (Labo, Luzon)
Miller, 1st Lt. Archie (Patian Island)
Moran, Capt. John E. (Mabitac, Luzon)
Mosher, 2d Lt. Louis C. (Gagsak Mountain, Jolo)
Nisperos, Pvt. Jose B. (Lapurap, Basilan)
Nolan, Artificer Joseph A. (Labo, Luzon)
Parker, Lt. Col. James (Vigan, Luzon)
Pierce, Pvt. Charles H. (San Isidro, Luzon)
Quinn, Pvt. Peter H. (San Miguel de Mayumo, Luzon)
Ray, Sgt. Charles W. (San Isidro, Luzon)
Robertson, Pvt. Marcus W. (San Isidro, Luzon)
Ross, Pvt. Frank F. (San Isidro, Luzon)
Sage, Capt. William H. (Zapote River, Luzon)
Schroeder, Sgt. Henry F. (Carig, Leyte)
Shaw, 1st Lt. George C. (Fort Pitacus, Mindinao)
Shelton, Pvt. George M. (La Paz, Leyte)
Shiels, Surgeon George F. (Tuliahan River)
Sletteland, Pvt. Thomas (Paete, Luzon)
Stewart, 2d Lt. George E. (Passi, Panay)
Straub, Surgeon Paul F. (Alos, Luzon)
Trembley, Pvt. William B. (Calumpit, Luzon)
Van Schaick, 1st Lt. Louis J. (Nasugbu, Bartangas)
Walker, Pvt. Frank O. (Taal, Luzon)
Wallace, 2d Lt. George W. (Tinuba, Luzon)
Weaver, Sgt. Amos (Calubus-Malalong, Luzon)
Weld, Cpl. Seth L. (La Paz, Leyte)
Wetherby, Pvt. John C. (Imus, Luzon)
White, Pvt. Edward (Calumpit, Luzon)
Wilson, 2d Lt. Arthur H. (Patian Island)

MARINES

Bearss, Col. Hiram I. (Cadacan & Sohoton Rivers, Samar)
Buckley, Pvt. Howard M. (NOR)
Forsterer, Sgt. Bruno A. (Samoa)
Harvey, Sgt. Harry (Benictican)
Hulbert, Pvt. Henry L. (Samoa)
Leonard, Pvt. Joseph M. (NOR)
McNally, Sgt. Michael J. (Samoa)
Porter, Col. David D. (Cadacan & Sohoton Rivers, Samar)
Prendergast, Cpt. Thomas F. (NOR)

NAVY

Catherwood, Ord. Sman John H. (Basilan)
Fisher, GM 1st Class Frederick T. (Samoa)
Fitz, Ord. Sman Joseph (Mount Dajo, Jolo)
Forbeck, Sman Andrew P. (Katbalogan, Samar)

Hiram Iddings Bearss, Colonel, U.S. Marine Corps. Born: 13 April 1875, Peru, Ind. Appointed from: Indiana. Other Navy award: Distinguished Service Medal. Citation: For extraordinary heroism and eminent and conspicuous conduct in battle at the junction of the Cadacan and Sohoton Rivers, Samar, Philippine Islands, 17 November 1901. Col. Bearss (then Capt.), second in command of the columns upon their uniting ashore in the Sohoton River region, made a surprise attack on the fortified cliffs and completely routed the enemy, killing 30 and capturing and destroying the powder magazine, 40 lantacas (guns), rice, food and cuartels. Due to his courage, intelligence, discrimination and zeal, he successfully led his men up the cliffs by means of bamboo ladders to a height of 200 feet. The cliffs were of soft stone of volcanic origin, in the nature of pumice, and were honeycombed with caves. Tons of rocks were suspended in platforms held in position by vine cables (known as bejuco) in readiness to be precipitated upon people below. After driving the insurgents from their position which was almost impregnable, being covered with numerous trails lined with poison spears, pits, etc., he led his men across the river, scaled the cliffs on the opposite side, and destroyed the camps there. Col. Bearss and the men under his command overcame incredible difficulties and dangers in destroying positions which, according to reports from old prisoners, had taken 3 years to perfect, were held as a final rallying point, and were never before penetrated by white troops. Col. Bearss also rendered distinguished public service in the presence of the enemy at Quinapundan River, Samar, Philippine Islands, on 19 January 1902.

Galbraith, GM 3d Class Robert (El Pardo, Cebu)
Harrison, Sman Bolden R. (Basilan)
Henrechon, Machinist's Mate 2d Class George F. (Basilan)
McGuire, Hospital Apprentice Fred H. (Basilan)
Shanahan, Chief BM Patrick (NOR)
Stoltenberg, GM 2d Class Andrew V. (Katbalogan, Samar)
Thordsen, Coxswain William G. (Hilongas)
Volz, Carpenter's Mate 3d Class Jacob (Basilan)

The Boxer Rebellion, 1900

Number of medals: 59

ARMY: 4
MARINES: 33
NAVY: 22

ARMY

Brewster, Capt. Andre W. (Tientsin)
Lawton, 1st Lt. Louis B. (Tientsin)
Titus, Musician Calvin P. (Peking)
Von Schlick, Pvt. Robert H. (Tientsin)

MARINES

Adams, Sgt. John M. (Tientsin)
Adriance, Cpl. Harry C. (Tientsin)
Appleton, Cpl Edwin N. (Tientsin)
Boydston, Pvt. Erwin J. (Peking)
Burnes, Pvt. James (Tientsin)
Campbell, Pvt. Albert R. (Tientsin)
Carr, Pvt. William L. (Peking)
Cooney, Pvt. James (Tientsin)
Dahlgren, Cpl. John O. (Peking)
Daly, Pvt. Daniel J. (Peking)
*Fisher, Pvt. Harry (Peking)
Foley, Sgt. Alexander J. (Tientsin)
Francis, Pvt. Charles R. (Tientsin)
Gaiennie, Pvt. Louis R. (Peking)
Heisch, Pvt. Henry W. (Tientsin)
Horton, Pvt. William C. (Peking)
Hunt, Pvt. Martin (Peking)
Kates, Pvt. Thomas W. (Tientsin)
Mathias, Pvt. Clarence E. (Tientsin)
Moore, Pvt. Albert (Peking)
Murphy, Drummer John A. (Peking)
Murray, Pvt. William H. (Peking)
Orndoff, Pvt. Harry W. (NOR)
Phillips, Cpl. Reuben J. (NOR)
Preston, Pvt. Herbert I. (Peking)
Scannell, Pvt. David J. (Peking)
Silva, Pvt. France (Peking)
Stewart, Gy. Sgt. Peter (NOR)
Sutton, Sgt. Clarence E. (Tientsin)
Upham, Pvt. Oscar J. (Peking)
Walker, Sgt. Edward A. (Peking)
Young, Pvt. Frank A. (Peking)
Zion, Pvt. William (Peking)

NAVY

Allen, BM 1st Class Edward (NOR)
Chatham, GM 2d Class John P. (NOR)
Clancy, Chief BM Joseph (NOR)
Hamberger, Chief Carpenter's Mate William F. (NOR)
Hanford, Machinist 1st Class Burke (NOR)
Hansen, Sman Hans A. (NOR)
Holyoke, BM 1st Class William E. (NOR)
Killackey, Lman Joseph (NOR)
McAllister, Ord. Sman Samuel (Tientsin)
McCloy, Coxswain John (China)
Mitchell, GM 1st Class Joseph (Peking)
Petersen, Chief Machinist Carl E. (Peking)
Rose, Sman George (Peking)
Ryan, Coxswain Francis T. (NOR)
Seach, Ord. Sman William (NOR)
Smith, Oiler Frank E. (NOR)
Smith, Lman James (NOR)
Stanley, Hospital Apprentice Robert H. (Peking)
Thomas, Coxswain Karl (NOR)
Torgerson, GM 3d Class Martin T. (NOR)
Westermark, Sman Axel (Peking)
Williams, Coxswain Jay (China)

Veracruz, 1914

Number of medals: 55

MARINES: 9
NAVY: 46

MARINES

Berkeley, Maj. Randolph C. (Veracruz)
Butler, Maj. Smedley D. (Veracruz)
Catlin, Maj. Albertus W. (Veracruz)
Dyer, Capt. Jesse F. (Veracruz)
Fryer, Capt. Eli T. (Veracruz)
Hill, Capt. Walter N. (Veracruz)
Hughes, Capt. John A. (Veracruz)
Neville, Lt. Col. Wendell C. (Veracruz)
Reid, Maj. George C. (Veracruz)

William Seach, Ordinary Seaman, U.S. Navy. Place and date: China 13, 20, 21, and 22 June 1900. Entered service at: Massachusetts. Born: 23 May 1877, London, England. G.O. No.: 55, 19 July 1901. Citation: In action with the relief expedition of the Allied forces in China during the battles of 13, 20, 21 and 22 June 1900. June 13: Seach and 6 others were cited for their courage in repulsing an attack by 300 Chinese Imperialist soldiers and Boxer militants with a bayonet charge, thus thwarting a planned massive attack on the entire force. June 20: During a day-long battle, Seach ran across an open clearing, gained cover, and cleaned out nests of Chinese snipers. June 21: During a surprise sabre attack by Chinese cavalrymen, Seach was cited for defending gun emplacements. June 22: Seach and others breached the wall of a Chinese fort, fought their way to the enemy's guns, and turned the cannon upon the defenders of the fort. Throughout this period and in the presence of the enemy, Seach distinguished himself by meritorious conduct.

NAVY

Anderson, Capt. Edwin A. (Veracruz)
Badger, Ensign Oscar C. (Veracruz)
Beasley, Sman Harry C. (Veracruz)
Bishop, QM 2d Class Charles F. (Veracruz)
Bradley, Chief GM George (Veracruz)
Buchanan, Lt. Cmdr. Allen (Veracruz)
Castle, Lt. Guy W. S. (Veracruz)
Courts, Lt. (j.g.) George M. (Veracruz)
Cregan, Coxswain George (Veracruz)
Decker, BM 2d Class Percy A. (Veracruz)
DeSomer, Lt. Abraham (Veracruz)
Drustrup, Lt. Neils (Veracruz)
Elliott, Surgeon Middleton S. (Veracruz)
Fletcher, Rear Adm. Frank F. (Veracruz)
Fletcher, Lt. Frank J. (Veracruz)
Foster, Ensign Paul F. (Veracruz)
Frazer, Ensign Hugh C. (Veracruz)
Gisburne, Electrician 3d Class Edward A. (Veracruz)
Grady, Lt. John (Veracruz)
Harner, BM 2d Class Joseph G. (Veracruz)
Harrison, Cmdr. William K. (Veracruz)
Hartigan, Lt. Charles C. (Veracruz)
Huse, Capt. Henry M. P. (Veracruz)
Ingram, Lt. (j.g.) Jonas H. (Veracruz)
Jarrett, Sman Berrie H. (Veracruz)
Johnston, Lt. Cmdr. Rufus Z. (Veracruz)
Langhorne, Surgeon Cary D. (Veracruz)
Lannon, Lt. James P. (Veracruz)
Lowry, Ensign George M. (Veracruz)
+McCloy, Chief Boatswain John (Veracruz)
McDonnell, Ensign Edward O. (Veracruz)
McNair, Lt. Frederick V., Jr. (Veracruz)
Moffett, Cmdr. William A. (Veracruz)
Nickerson, BM 2d Class Henry N. (Veracruz)
Nordsiek, Ord. Sman Charles L. (Veracruz)
Rush, Capt. William R. (Veracruz)
Schnepel, Ord. Sman Fred J. (Veracruz)
Semple, Chief Gunner Robert (Veracruz)
Sinnett, Sman Lawrence C. (Veracruz)
Staton, Lt. Adolphus (Veracruz)
Stickney, Cmdr. Herman O. (Veracruz)
Townsend, Lt. Julius C. (Veracruz)
Wainwright, Lt. Richard, Jr. (Veracruz)
Walsh, Sman James A. (Veracruz)
Wilkinson, Ensign Theodore S., Jr. (Veracruz)
Zuiderveld, Hospital Apprentice 1st Class William (Veracruz)

Haiti, 1915

Number of medals: 6

MARINES: 6

+Butler, Maj. Smedley D. (Fort Rivière)
+Daly, Gy. Sgt. Daniel J. (Fort Liberté)
Gross, Pvt. Samuel (Fort Rivière)
Iams, Sgt. Ross L. (Fort Rivière)
Ostermann, 1st Lt. Edward A. (Fort Liberté)
Upshur, Capt. William P. (Fort Liberté)

Dominican Republic, 1916

Number of medals: 3

MARINES: 3

Glowin, Cpl. Joseph A. (Guayacanas)
Williams, 1st Lt. Ernest C. (San Francisco de Macoris)
Winans, 1st Sgt. Roswell (Guayacanas)

Haiti, 1919–1920

Number of medals: 2

MARINES: 2

Button, Cpl. William R. (Grande Rivière)
Hanneken, Sgt. Herman H. (Grande Rivière)

Nicaragua, 1927–1933

Number of medals: 2

MARINES: 2

Schilt, 1st Lt. Christian F. (Quilali)
Truesdell, Cpl. Donald L. (Constancia)

The Medal in Peacetime, 1865–1940

1865–1870

Number of medals: 12

NAVY: 12

Bates, Sman Richard (Eastport, Maine)
Brown, Capt. of the Afterguard John (Eastport, Maine)
Burke, Sman Thomas (Eastport, Maine)
Carey, Sman James (NOR)
+Cooper, QM John (Mobile, Ala)
Du Moulin, Apprentice Frank (New London, Conn)
Halford, Coxswain William (Sandwich Islands)
+Mullen, BM Patrick (NOR)
Robinson, Capt. of the Hold John (Pensacola, Fla)
Robinson, Capt. of the Afterguard Thomas (New Orleans, La)
Stacy, Sman William B. (Cape Haiten, Haiti)
Taylor, Sman John (New York, NY)

1871–1898

Number of medals: 103

MARINES: 2
NAVY: 101

MARINES

Morris, Cpl. John (Villefranche, France)
Stewart, Cpl. James A. (Villefranche, France)

NAVY

Ahearn, Watertender William (NOR)
Anderson, Coxswain William (NOR)
Atkins, Ship's Cook Daniel (NOR)
Auer, Ord. Sman Apprentice John F. (Marseille, France)
Barrett, 2d Class Fireman Edward (Callao Bay, Peru)
Belpitt, Capt. of the Afterguard W. H. (Foochow, China)
Benson, Sman James (NOR)
Bradley, Lman Alexander (Cowes, England)
Buchanan, Apprentice David M. (New York, NY)
Cavanaugh, Fireman 1st Class Thomas (Cat Island–Nassau)
Chandron, Sman Apprentice August (Alexandria, Egypt)
Connolly, Ord. Sman Michael (Halifax Harbor, Nova Scotia)
Corey, Lman WIlliam (New York, NY)
Costello, Ord. Sman John (Philadelphia, Pa)
Courtney, Sman Henry C. (Washington Navy Yard, DC)
Cramen, BM Thomas (Washington Navy Yard, DC)
Creelman, Lman William J. (NOR)
Cutter, Lman George W. (Norfolk, Va)
Davis, Ord. Sman John (Toulon, France)
Davis, Lman Joseph H. (Norfolk, Va)
Dempsey, Sman John (Shanghai, China)
Deneef, Capt. of the Top Michael (Para, Brazil)

John Hayden, Apprentice, U.S. Navy. Born: 1863, Washington, D.C. Accredited to: Washington, D.C. G.O. No.: 246, 22 July 1879. Citation: On board the U.S. Training Ship Saratoga. On the morning of 15 July 1879, while the Saratoga was anchored off the Battery, in New York Harbor, R. L. Robey, apprentice, fell overboard. As the tide was running strong ebb, the man, not being an expert swimmer, was in danger of drowning. David M. Buchanan, apprentice, instantly, without removing any of his clothing, jumped after him. Stripping himself, Hayden stood coolly watching the 2 in the water, and when he thought his services were required, made a dive from the rail and came up alongside them and rendered assistance until all 3 were picked up by a boat from the ship.

Denham, Sman Austin (Greytown, Nicaragua)
Eilers, GM Henry A. (Fort McHenry, Md)
Elmore, Lman Walter (Mediterranean Sea)
Enright, Lman John (Ensenada, Mexico)
Everetts, GM 3d Class John (NOR)
Fasseur, Ord. Sman Isaac L. (Callao, Peru)
Flannagan, BM John (Le Havre, France)
Fowler, QM Christopher (Point Zapotitlan, Mexico)
Gidding, Sman Charles (New York, NY)
Gillick, BM Matthew (Marseilles, France)
Handran, Sman John (Lisbon, Portugal)
Harrington, 1st Class Fireman David (NOR)
Hayden, Apprentice John (New York, NY)
Hill, Chief QG George (Greytown, Nicaragua)
Hill, Capt. of the Top William L. (Newport, RI)
Holt, QG George (Hamburg, Germany)
Horton, Capt. of the Top James (NOR)
Jardine, Fireman 1st Class Alexander (Cat Island–Nassau)
Johnson, Sman John (Greytown, Nicaragua)
Johnson, Cooper William (Mare Island, Calif)
Kersey, Ord. Sman Thomas (New York, NY)
King, Ord. Sman Hugh (Delaware River, NJ)
Kyle, Lman Patrick J. (Port Mahon, Minorca)
Lakin, Sman Thomas (Mare Island, Calif)
Laverty, 1st Class Fireman John (Callao, Peru)
Lejeune, Sman Emile (Port Royal, SC)
Low, Sman George (New Orleans, La)
Lucy, 2d Class Boy John (Castle Garden, NY)
McCarton, Ship's Printer John (Coaster's Harbor Island, RI)
Maddin, Ord. Sman Edward (Lisbon, Portugal)
Magee, 2d Class Fireman John W. (NOR)
Manning, QM Henry J. (Newport, RI)
Matthews, Capt. of the Top Joseph (NOR)
Miller, BM Hugh (Alexandria, Egypt)
Millmore, Ord. Sman John (Monrovia, Liberia)
Mitchell, Lman Thomas (Shanghai, China)
Moore, BM Francis (Washington Navy Yard, DC)
Moore, Sman Philip (Genoa, Italy)
Morse, Sman William (Rio de Janeiro, Brazil)
Noil, Sman Joseph B. (Norfolk, Va)
Norris, Lman J. W. (New York, NY)
O'Conner, Sman James F. (Norfolk, Va)
Ohmsen, Master-at-Arms August (NOR)
O'Neal, BM John (Greytown, Nicaragua)
Osborne, Sman John (Philadelphia, Pa)
Osepins, Sman Christian (Hampton Roads, Va)
Parker, BM Alexander (Mare Island, Calif)
Pile, Ord. Sman Richard (Greytown, Nicaragua)
Regan, Ord. Sman Patrick (Coquimbor, Chile)
Rouning, Ord. Sman Johannes (Hampton Roads, Va)
Russell, Sman John (Genoa, Italy)
Ryan, Ord. Sman Richard (Norfolk, Va)
Sadler, Capt. of the Top William (Coaster's Harbor Island, RI)
Sapp, Sman Isacc (Villefranche, France)
Simpson, 1st Class Fireman Henry (Monrovia, Liberia)
Smith, Sman James (Greytown, Nicaragua)
Smith, Sman John (Rio de Janeiro, Brazil)
Smith, Sman Thomas (Para, Brazil)
Sullivan, BM James F. (Newport, RI)
Sweeney, Ord. Sman Robert (Hampton Roads, Va)
  Second award (New York, NY)
Sweeney, Lman William (Norfolk, Va)
Taylor, QM Richard H. (Apia, Samoa)
Thayer, Ship's Cpl. James (Norfolk, Va)
Thompson, Sman Henry (Mare Island, Calif)
Thornton, Sman Michael (Boston, Mass)
Tobin, Lman Paul (Hamburg, Germany)
Trout, 2d Class Fireman James M. (Montevideo, Uruguay)
Troy, Chief BM Jeremiah (Newport, RI)
Turvelin, Sman Alexander H. (Toulon, France)
Weisbogel, Capt. of the Mizzen Top Albert (NOR)
  Second award (NOR)
Weissel, Ship's Cook Adam (Newport, RI)
Williams, Sman Antonio (NOR)
Williams, Carpenter's Mate Henry (NOR)
Williams, Capt. of the Hold Louis (Honolulu, Hawaii)
  Second award (Callao, Peru)
Willis, Coxswain George (Greenland)
Wilson, Boilermaker August (NOR)

1899–1911

Number of medals: 51

ARMY: 1
MARINES: 2
NAVY: 48

ARMY

Gaujot, Capt. Julien E. (Aqua Prieta, Mex)

MARINES

Helms, Sgt. John H. (Montevideo, Uruguay)
Pfeifer, Pvt. Louis F. (NOR)

NAVY

Behne, Fireman 1st Class Frederick (NOR)
Behnke, Sman 1st Class Heinrich (NOR)
Bjorkman, Ord. Sman Ernest H. (NOR)
Boers, Sman Edward W. (San Diego, Calif)
Bonney, Chief Watertender Robert E. (NOR)
Breeman, Sman George (NOR)
Bresnahan, Watertender Patrick F. (NOR)
Brock, Carpenter's Mate 2d Class George F. (San Diego, Calif)
Cahey, Sman Thomas (NOR)
Clary, Watertender Edward A. (NOR)
Clausey, Chief GM John J. (San Diego, Calif)
Corahorgi, Fireman 1st Class Demetri (NOR)
Cox, Chief GM Robert E. (Pensacola, Fla)
Cronan, BM Willie (San Diego, Calif)
Davis, QM 3d Class Raymond E. (San Diego, Calif)
Fadden, Coxswain Harry D. (NOR)
Floyd, Boilermaker Edward (NOR)
Fredericksen, Watertender Emil (San Diego, Calif)
Girandy, Sman Alphonse (NOR)
Gowan, BM William H. (Coquimbo, Chile)
Grbitch, Sman Rade (San Diego, Calif)
Halling, BM 1st Class Luovi (NOR)
Hill, Ship's Cook 1st Class Frank E. (San Diego, Calif)
Holtz, Chief Watertender August (NOR)
Johannessen, Chief Watertender Johannes J. (NOR)
King, Watertender John (NOR)
  Second award (NOR)
Klein, Chief Carpenter's Mate Robert (NOR)
Lipscomb, Watertender Harry (NOR)
Monssen, Chief GM Mons (NOR)
Mullin, Sman Hugh P. (Hampton Roads, Va)
Nelson, Machinist's Mate 1st Class Oscar F. (San Diego, Calif)
Nordstrom, Chief Boatswain Isidor (NOR)
Peters, BM 1st Class Alexander (NOR)
Quick, Coxswain Joseph (Yokohama, Japan)
Reid, Chief Watertender Patrick (NOR)
Roberts, Machinist's Mate 1st Class Charles C. (NOR)
Schepke, GM 1st Class Charles S. (NOR)
Schmidt Sman Otto D. (San Diego, Calif)

Telesforo Trinidad, Fireman Second Class, U.S. Navy. Born: 25 November 1890, New Washington Capig, Philippine Islands. Accredited to: Philippine Islands. G.O. No.: 142, 1 April 1915. Citation: For extraordinary heroism in the line of his profession at the time of the boiler explosion on board the U.S.S. San Diego, 21 January 1915. Trinidad was driven out of fireroom No. 2 by the explosion, but at once returned and picked up R.E. Daly, fireman, second class, whom he saw to be injured, and proceeded to bring him out. While coming into No. 4 fireroom, Trinidad was just in time to catch the explosion in No. 3 fireroom, but without consideration for his own safety, passed Daly on and then assisted in rescuing another injured man from No. 3 fireroom. Trinidad was himself burned about the face by the blast from the explosion in No. 3 fireroom.

Shacklette, Hospital Steward William S. (San Diego, Calif)
Snyder, Chief Electrician William E. (Hampton Roads, Va)
Stanton, Chief Machinist's Mate Thomas (NOR)
Stokes, Chief Master-at-Arms John (Jamaica)
Stupka, Fireman 1st Class Loddie (NOR)
Teytand, QM 3d Class August P. (NOR)
Walsh, Chief Machinist Michael (NOR)
Westa, Chief Machinist's Mate Karl (NOR)
Wheeler, Shipfitter 1st Class George H. (Coquimbo, Chile)

1915–1916

Number of medals: 8

NAVY: 8

Cary, Lt. Cmdr. Robert W. (NOR)
Crilley, Chief GM Frank W. (Honolulu, Hawaii)
Jones, Cmdr. Claud A. (Santo Domingo)
*Rud, Chief Machinist's Mate George W. (Santo Domingo)
Smith, Chief Watertender Eugene P. (NOR)
Smith, GM 1st Class Wilhelm (NOR)
Trinidad, Fireman 2d Class Telesforo (NOR)
Willey, Machinist Charles H. (Santo Domingo)

1920–1940

Number of medals: 18

ARMY: 2
MARINES: 1
NAVY: 15

ARMY

Greely, Maj. Gen. Adolphus W. (Various)
Lindbergh, Capt. Charles A. (New York City–Paris, France)

MARINES

Smith, Pvt. Albert J. (Pensacola, Fla)

NAVY

Badders, Chief Machinist's Mate William (Portsmouth, NH)
Bennett, Machinist Floyd (North Pole)
Breault, Torpedoman 2d Class Henry (NOR)
Byrd, Cmdr. Richard E., Jr. (North Pole)
*Cholister, BM 1st Class George R. (Off Virginia coast)
*Corry, Lt. Cmdr. William M., Jr. (Hartford, Conn)
Crandall, Chief BM Orson L. (Portsmouth, NH)
*Drexler, Ensign Henry C. (NOR)
Eadie, Chief GM Thomas (Provincetown, Mass)
Edwards, Lt. Cmdr. Walter A. (Sea of Marmara, Turkey)
Huber, Machinist's Mate William R. (Norfolk, Va)
*Hutchins, Lt. Carlton B. (Off California coast)
McDonald, Chief Metalsmith James H. (Portsmouth, NH)
Mihalowski, Torpedoman 1st Class John (Portsmouth, NH)
Ryan, Ensign Thomas J. (Yokohama, Japan)

World War I, 1914–1918

Number of medals: 123

ARMY: 95**
MARINES: 7
NAVY: 21

**Includes five marines who also received army medal and one marine who received army medal only.

ARMY

Adkinson, Sgt. Joseph G. (Bellicourt, France)
Allex, Cpl. Jake (Chipilly Ridge, France)
Allworth, Capt. Edward C. (Clery-le-Petit, France)
Anderson, 1st Sgt. Johannes S. (Consenvoye, France)
*Baesel, 2d Lt. Albert E. (Ivoiry, France)
Barger, Pvt. Charles D. (Bois-de-Bantheville, France)
*Barkeley, Pvt. David B. (Pouilly, France)
Barkley, Pfc. John L. (Cunel, France)
Bart, Pvt. Frank J. (Medeah Ferme, France)
*Blackwell, Pvt. Robert L. (St. Soupplets, France)
*Bleckley, 2d Lt. Erwin R. (Binarville, France)
Bronson, 1st Lt. Deming (Eclisfontaine, France)
Call, Cpl. Donald M. (Varennes, France)
*Chiles, Capt. Marcellus H. (Le Champy Bas, France)
*Colyer, Sgt. Wilbur E. (Verdun, France)
*Costin, Pvt. Henry G. (Bois-de-Consenvoye, France)
*Dilboy, Pfc. George (Belleau, France)
Donaldson, Sgt. Michael A. (Sommerance-Landres-et-St. Georges Road, France)
Donovan, Lt. Col. William J. (Landres-et-St. Georges, France)
Dozier, 1st Lt. James C. (Montbrehain, France)
*Dunn, Pvt. Parker F. (Grand-Pre, France)
Edwards, Pfc. Daniel R. (Soissons, France)
Eggers, Sgt. Alan L. (Le Catelet, France)
Ellis, Sgt. Michael B. (Exermont, France)
Forrest, Sgt. Arthur J. (Remonville, France)
Foster, Sgt. Gary E. (Montbrehain, France)
Funk, Pfc. Jesse N. (Bois-de-Bantheville, France)
Furlong, 1st Lt. Harold A. (Bantheville, France)
Gaffney, Pfc. Frank (Ronssoy, France)
*Goettler, 1st Lt. Harold E. (Binarville, France)

Gregory, Sgt. Earl D. (Bois-de-Consenvoye, France)
Gumpertz, 1st Sgt. Sydney G. (Bois-de-Forges, France)
*Hall, Sgt. Thomas L. (Montbrehain, France)
Hatler, Sgt. M. Waldo (Pouilly, France)
Hays, 1st Lt. George P. (Greves Farm, France)
*Heriot, Cpl. James D. (Vaux-Andigny, France)
Hill, Cpl. Ralyn M. (Donnevoux, France)
Hilton, Sgt. Richmond H. (Brancourt, France)
Holderman, Capt. Nelson M. (Binarville, France)
Johnston, Sgt. Harold I. (Pouilly, France)
Karnes, Sgt. James E. (Estrees, France)
Katz, Sgt. Phillip C. (Eclisfontaine, France)
Kaufman, 1st Sgt. Benjamin (Argonne Forest, France)
Latham, Sgt. John C. (Le Catelet, France)
*Lemert, 1st Sgt. Milo (Bellicourt, France)
Loman, Pvt. Berger (Consenvoye, France)
*Luke, 2d Lt. Frank, Jr. (Murvaux, France)
Mallon, Capt. George H. (Bois-de-Forges, France)
Manning, Cpl. Sidney E. (Breuvannes, France)
McMurtry, Capt. George G. (Charlevaux, France)
*Mestrovitch, Sgt. James I. (Fismette, France)
Miles, Capt. L. W. (Revillon, France)
*Miller, Maj. Oscar F. (Gesnes, France)
Morelock, Pvt. Sterling (Exermont, France)
Neibaur, Pvt. Thomas C. (Landres-et-St. Georges, France)
O'Neil, Sgt. Richard W. (Ourcq River, France)
*O'Shea, Cpl. Thomas E. (Le Catelet, France)
Parker, 2d Lt. Samuel I. (Soissons, France)
Peck, Pvt. Archie A. (Argonne Forest, France)
*Perkins, Pfc. Michael J. (Belieu Bois, France)
*Pike, Lt. Col. Emory J. (Vandières, France)
Pope, Cpl. Thomas A. (Hamel, France)
Regan, 2d Lt. Patrick (Bois-de-Consenvoye, France)
Rickenbacker, 1st Lt. Edward V. (Billy, France)
Robb, 1st Lt. George S. (Sechault, France)
*Roberts, Cpl. Harold W. (Montrebeau Woods, France)
Sampler, Cpl. Samuel M. (St. Etienne, France)
Sandlin, Sgt. Willie (Bois-de-Forges, France)
*Sawelson, Sgt. William (Grand-Pre, France)
Schaffner, 1st Lt. Dwite H. (Boureuilles, France)
Seibert, Sgt. Lloyd M. (Epinonville, France)
*Skinker, Capt. Alexander R. (Cheppy, France)
Slack, Pvt. Clayton K. (Consenvoye, France)
*Smith, Lt. Col. Fred E. (Binarville, France)
Talley, Sgt. Edward R. (Ponchaux, France)
Thompson, Maj. Joseph H. (Apremont, France)
Turner, Cpl. Harold L. (St. Etienne, France)
*Turner, 1st Lt. William B. (Ronssoy, France)
Valente, Pvt. Michael (Ronssoy, France)
Van Iersel, Sgt. Ludovicus M. (Mouzon, France)
Villepigue, Cpl. John C. (Vaux-Andigny, France)
Waaler, Sgt. Reidar (Ronssoy, France)
Ward, Pvt. Calvin J. (Estress, France)
West, 1st Sgt. Chester H. (Bois-de-Cheppy, France)
Whittlesey, Maj. Charles W. (Argonne Forest, France)
*Wickersham, 2d Lt. J. Hunter (Limey, France)
*Wold, Pvt. Nels (Cheppy, France)
Woodfill, 1st Lt. Samuel (Cunel, France)
York, Cpl. Alvin C. (Chatel-Chehery, France)

MARINES

†Cukela, Sgt. Louis (Villers-Cotterets, France)
†Janson, Gy. Sgt. Ernest A. (Château-Thierry, France)
†Kelly, Pvt. John J. (Blanc Mont Ridge, France)
*†Kocak, Sgt. Matej (Villers-Cotterets, France)
*†Pruitt, Cpl. John H. (Blanc Mont Ridge, France)
Robinson, Gy. Sgt. Robert G. (Pittham, Belgium)
*#Stockham, Gy. Sgt. Fred W. (Bois-de-Belleau, France)
*Talbot, 2d Lt. Ralph (France & Pittham, Belgium)

NAVY

Balch, Pharmacist's Mate 1st Class John H. (Vierzy & Somme-Py, France)
Boone, Lt. Joel T. (Vierzy, France)
Bradley, Cmdr. Willis W., Jr. (NOR)
Cann, Sman Tedford H. (NOR)
Covington, Ship's Cook 3d Class Jesse W. (NOR)
Graves, Sman Ora (NOR)
Hammann, Ensign Charles H. (Pola, Aegean Sea)
Hayden, Hospital Apprentice 1st Class David E. (Thiaucourt, France)
*Ingram, GM 1st Class Osmond K. (NOR)
Izac, Lt. Edouard V. M. (German submarine U-90)
Lyle, Lt. Cmdr. Alexander G. (French Front)
MacKenzie, Chief BM John (NOR)
Madison, Lt. Cmdr. James J. (NOR)
McGunigal, Shipfitter 1st Class Patrick (NOR)
Ormsbee, Chief Machinist's Mate Francis E., Jr. (Pensacola, Fla)
*Osborne, Lt.(j.g.) Weedon E. (Bouresche, France)
Petty, Lt. Orlando H. (Bois-de-Belleau, France)
Schmidt, Chief GM Oscar, Jr. (NOR)
Siegel, BM 2d Class John O. (NOR)
Sullivan, Ensign Daniel A. J. (NOR)
Upton, QM Frank M. (NOR)

†Also received army Medal of Honor for same action.
#Received army medal only.

Deming Bronson, First Lieutenant, U.S. Army, Company H, 364th Infantry, 91st Division. Place and date: Near Eclisfontaine, France, 26–27 September 1918. Entered service at: Seattle, Wash. Born: 8 July 1894, Rhinelander, Wis. G.O. No.: 12 W.D., 1929. Citation: For conspicuous gallantry and intrepidity above and beyond the call of duty in action with the enemy. On the morning of 26 September, during the advance of the 364th Infantry, 1st Lt. Bronson was struck by an exploding enemy handgrenade, receiving deep cuts on his face and the back of his head. He nevertheless participated in the action which resulted in the capture of an enemy dugout from which a great number of prisoners were taken. This was effected with difficulty and under extremely hazardous conditions because it was necessary to advance without the advantage of cover and, from an exposed position, throw handgrenades and phosphorous bombs to compel the enemy to surrender. On the afternoon of the same day he was painfully wounded in the left arm by an enemy rifle bullet, and after receiving first aid treatment he was directed to the rear. Disregarding these instructions, 1st Lt. Bronson remained on duty with his company through the night although suffering from severe pain and shock. On the morning of 27 September, his regiment resumed its attack, the object being the village of Eclisfontaine. Company H, to which 1st Lt. Bronson was assigned, was left in support of the attacking line, Company E being in the line. He gallantly joined that company in spite of his wounds and engaged with it in the capture of the village. After the capture he remained with Company E and participated with it in the capture of an enemy machinegun, he himself killing the enemy gunner. Shortly after this encounter the company was compelled to retire due to the heavy enemy artillery barrage. During this retirement 1st Lt. Bronson, who was the last man to leave the advanced position, was again wounded in both arms by an enemy high-explosive shell. He was then assisted to cover by another officer who applied first aid. Although bleeding profusely and faint from the loss of blood, 1st Lt. Bronson remained with the survivors of the company throughout the night of the second day, refusing to go to the rear for treatment. His conspicuous gallantry and spirit of self-sacrifice were a source of great inspiration to the members of the entire command.

World War II, 1939–1945

Number of medals: 433

ARMY:	294
COAST GUARD:	1
MARINES:	81
NAVY:	57

ARMY

Adams, SSgt. Lucian (St. Die, France)
Anderson, TSgt. Beaufort T. (Okinawa)
*Antolak, Sgt. Sylvester (Cisterna di Littoria, Italy)
Atkins, Pfc. Thomas E. (Villa Verde Trail, Philippines)
*Baker, Lt. Col. Addison E. (Ploesti, Rumania)
*Baker, Pvt. Thomas A. (Saipan, Mariana Islands)
Barfoot, TSgt. Van T. (Carano, Italy)
Barrett, Pvt. Carlton W. (St. Laurent-sur-Mer, France)
*Beaudoin, 1st Lt. Raymond O. (Hamelin, Germany)
Bell, TSgt. Bernard P. (Mittelwihr, France)
Bender, SSgt. Stanley (La Lande, France)
*Benjamin, Pfc. George, Jr. (Leyte, Philippines)
Bennett, Cpl. Edward A. (Heckhuscheid, Germany)
Bertoldo, MSgt. Vito R. (Hatten, France)
Beyer, Cpl. Arthur O. (Arloncourt, Belgium)
*Bianchi, 1st Lt. Willibald C. (Bagac, Philippines)
Biddle, Pfc. Melvin E. (Soy, Belgium)
Bjorkland, 1st Lt. Arnold L. (Altavilla, Italy)
Bloch, 1st Lt. Orville E. (Firenzuola, Italy)
Bolden, SSgt. Paul L. (Petit-Coo, Belgium)
Bolton, 1st Lt. Cecil H. (Mark River, Holland)
Bong, Maj. Richard I. (Borneo & Leyte, Philippines)
*Booker, Pvt. Robert D. (Fondouk, Tunisia)
*Boyce, 2d Lt. George W. G., Jr. (Afua, New Guinea)
Briles, SSgt. Herschel F. (Scherpenseel, Germany)
Britt, Lt. Maurice L. (Mignano, Italy)
*Brostrom, Pfc. Leonard C. (Dagami, Philippines)
Brown, Capt. Bobbie E. (Aachen, Germany)
Burke, 1st Lt. Francis X. (Nuremberg, Germany)
*Burr, 1st Sgt. Elmer J. (Buna, New Guinea)
Burr, SSgt. Herbert H. (Dorrmoschel, Germany)
Burt, Capt. James M. (Wurselen, Germany)
*Butts, 2d Lt. John E. (Normandy, France)
Calugas, Sgt. Jose (Culis, Philippines)
*Carey, SSgt. Alvin P. (Plougastel, France)
*Carey, TSgt. Charles F., Jr. (Rimling, France)
*Carswell, Maj. Horace S., Jr. (South China Sea)
*Castle, Brig. Gen. Frederick W. (Germany)
*Cheli, Maj. Ralph (Wewak, New Guinea)
Childers, 2d Lt. Ernest (Oliveto, Italy)
Choate, SSgt. Clyde L. (Bruyères, France)
*Christensen, 2d Lt. Dale E. (Driniumor River, New Guinea)
*Christian, Pvt. Herbert F. (Valmontone, Italy)
*Cicchetti, Pfc. Joseph J. (South Manila, Philippines)

Alvin P. Carey, Staff Sergeant, U.S. Army, 38th Infantry, 2-t Infantry Division. Place and date: Near Plougastel, Brittany, France, 23 August 1944. Entered service at: Laughlinstown, Pa. Born: 16 August 1916, Lycippus, Pa. G.O. No.: 37, 11 May 1945. Citation: For conspicuous gallantry and intrepidity at the risk of his life, above and beyond the call of duty, on 23 August 1944. S/Sgt. Carey, leader of a machinegun section, was advancing with his company in the attack on the strongly held enemy hill 154, near Plougastel, Brittany, France. The advance was held up when the attacking units were pinned down by intense enemy machinegun fire from a pillbox 200 yards up the hill. From his position covering the right flank, S/Sgt. Carey displaced his guns to an advanced position and then, upon his own initiative, armed himself with as many hand grenades as he could carry and without regard for his personal safety started alone up the hill toward the pillbox. Crawling forward under its withering fire, he proceeded 150 yards when he met a German rifleman whom he killed with his carbine. Continuing his steady forward movement until he reached grenade-throwing distance, he hurled his grenades at the pillbox opening in the face of intense enemy fire which wounded him mortally. Undaunted, he gathered his strength and continued his grenade attack until one entered and exploded within the pillbox, killing the occupants and putting their guns out of action. Inspired by S/Sgt. Carey's heroic act, the riflemen quickly occupied the position and overpowered the remaining enemy resistance in the vicinity.

Clark, TSgt. Francis J. (Kalborn, Luxembourg, & Sevenig, Germany)
Colalillo, Pfc. Mike (Untergriesheim, Germany)
*Cole, Lt. Col. Robert G. (Carentan, France)
Connor, Sgt. James P. (Cape Cavalaire, France)
Cooley, SSgt. Raymond H. (Lumboy, Philippines)
Coolidge, TSgt. Charles H. (Belmont-sur-Buttant, France)
*Cowan, Pfc. Richard E. (Krinkelter Wald, Belgium)
Craft, Pfc. Clarence B. (Okinawa)
*Craig, 2d Lt. Robert (Favoratta, Sicily)
*Crain, TSgt. Morris E. (Haguenau, France)
*Craw, Col. Demas T. (Port Lyautey, French Morocco)
Crawford, Pvt. William J. (Altavilla, Italy)
Crews, SSgt. John R. (Lobenbacherhof, Germany)
Currey, Sgt. Francis S. (Malmedy, Belgium)
Dahlgren, Sgt. Edward C. (Oberhoffen, France)
Dalessondro, TSgt. Peter J. (Kalterherberg, Germany)
Daly, Lt. Michael J. (Nuremberg, Germany)
Davis, Capt. Charles W. (Guadalcanal)
*DeFranzo, SSgt. Arthur F. (Vaubadon, France)
*DeGlopper, Pfc. Charles N. (La Fière, France)
*Deleau, Sgt. Emile, Jr. (Oberhoffen, France)
Dervishian, TSgt. Ernest H. (Cisterna, Italy)
*Diamond, Pfc. James H. (Mintal, Philippines)
*Dietz, SSgt. Robert H. (Kirchain, Germany)
Doolittle, Lt. Col. James H. (Over Japan)
Doss, Pfc. Desmond T. (Okinawa)
Drowley, SSgt. Jesse R. (Bougainville Island)
Dunham, TSgt. Russell E. (Kayserberg, France)
*Dutko, Pfc. John W. (Ponte Rotto, Italy)
Ehlers, SSgt. Walter D. (Goville, France)
*Endl, SSgt. Gerald L. (Anamo, New Guinea)
Erwin, SSgt. Henry E. (Koriyama, Japan)
*Eubanks, Sgt. Ray E. (Noemfoor Island, Dutch New Guinea)
Everhart, TSgt. Forrest E. (Kerling, France)
*Femoyer, 2d Lt. Robert E. (Merseburg, Germany)
Fields, 1st Lt. James H. (Rechicourt, France)
Fisher, 2d Lt. Almond E. (Grammont, France)
*Fournier, Sgt. William G. (Guadalcanal)
*Fowler, 2d Lt. Thomas W. (Carano, Italy)
*Fryar, Pvt. Elmer E. (Leyte, Philippines)
Funk, 1st Sgt. Leonard A., Jr. (Holzheim Belgium)
*Galt, Capt. William W. (Villa Crocetta, Italy)
*Gammon, SSgt. Archer T. (Bastogne, Belgium)
Garcia, SSgt. Marcario (Grosshau, Germany)
Garman, Pvt. Harold A. (Montereau, France)
Gerstung, TSgt. Robert E. (Berg, Germany)

Joe E. Mann, Private First Class, U.S. Army, Company H, 502d Parachute Infantry, 101st Airborne Division. Place and date: Best, Holland, 18 September 1944. Entered service at: Seattle, Wash. Birth: Rearden, Wash. G.O. No.: 73, 30 August 1945. Citation: He distinguished himself by conspicuous gallantry above and beyond the call of duty. On 18 September 1944, in the vicinity of Best, Holland, his platoon, attempting to seize the bridge across the Wilhelmina Canal, was surrounded and isolated by an enemy force greatly superior in personnel and firepower. Acting as lead scout, Pfc. Mann boldly crept to within rocket-launcher range of an enemy artillery position and, in the face of heavy enemy fire, destroyed an 88mm. gun and an ammunition dump. Completely disregarding the great danger involved, he remained in his exposed position, and, with his M-1 rifle, killed the enemy one by one until he was wounded 4 times. Taken to a covered position, he insisted on returning to a forward position to stand guard during the night. On the following morning the enemy launched a concerted attack and advanced to within a few yards of the position, throwing hand grenades as they approached. One of these landed within a few feet of Pfc. Mann. Unable to raise his arms, which were bandaged to his body, he yelled "grenade" and threw his body over the grenade, and as it exploded, died. His outstanding gallantry above and beyond the call of duty and his magnificent conduct were an everlasting inspiration to his comrades for whom he gave his life.

*Gibson, Technician 5th Grade Eric G. (Isola Bella, Italy)
*Gonzales, Pfc. David M. (Villa Verde Trail, Philippines)
*Gott, 1st Lt. Donald J. (Saarbrucken, Germany)
*Grabiarz, Pfc. William J. (Manila, Philippines)
Gregg, TSgt. Stephen R. (Montelimar, France)
*Gruennert, Sgt. Kenneth E. (Buna, New Guinea)
Hall, SSgt. George J. (Anzio, Italy)
*Hall, Technician 5th Grade Lewis (Guadalcanal)
*Hallman, SSgt. Sherwood H. (Brest, France)
Hamilton, Maj. Pierpont M. (Port Lyautey, French Morocco)
*Harmon, Sgt. Roy W. (Casaglia, Italy)
*Harr, Cpl. Harry R. (Maglamin, Philippines)
*Harris, 2d Lt. James L. (Vagney, France)
*Hastings, Pfc. Joe R. (Drabenderhohe, Germany)
Hawk, Sgt. John D. (Chambois, France)
Hawks, Pfc. Lloyd C. (Carano, Italy)
*Hedrick, TSgt. Clinton M. (Lembeck, Germany)
Hendrix, Pvt. James R. (Assenois, Belgium)
*Henry, Pvt. Robert T. (Luchem, Germany)
Herrera, Pfc. Silvestre S. (Mertzwiller, France)
Horner, SSgt. Freeman V. (Wurselen, Germany)
Howard, Lt. Col. James H. (Oschersleben, Germany)
Huff, Cpl. Paul B. (Carano, Italy)
*Hughes, 2d Lt. Lloyd H. (Ploesti, Rumania)
*Jachman, SSgt. Isadore S. (Flamièrge, Belgium)
*Jerstad, Maj. John L. (Ploesti, Rumania)
*Johnson, Pvt. Elden H. (Valmontone, Italy)
Johnson, Col. Leon W. (Ploesti, Rumania)
*Johnson, Sgt. Leroy (Limon, Philippines)
Johnson, Sgt. Oscar G. (Scarperia, Italy)
Johnston, Pfc. William J. (Padiglione, Italy)
*Kandle, 1st Lt. Victor L. (La Forge, France)
Kane, Col. John R. (Ploesti, Rumania)
Karaberis, Sgt. Christos H. (Guignola, Italy)
Kearby, Col. Neel E. (Wewak, New Guinea)
*Keathley, SSgt. George D. (Mt. Altuzzo, Italy)
*Kefurt, SSgt. Gus (Bennwihr, France)
*Kelley, SSgt. Jonah E. (Kesternich, Germany)
*Kelley, Pvt. Ova A. (Leyte, Philippines)
Kelly, Cpl. Charles E. (Altavilla, Italy)
*Kelly, Cpl. John D. (Fort du Roule, France)
Kelly, Cpl. Thomas J. (Alemert, Germany)
Kerstetter, Pfc. Dexter J. (Galiano, Philippines)
*Kessler, Pfc. Patrick L. (Ponte Rotto, Italy)
*Kimbro, Technician 4th Grade Truman (Rocherath, Belgium)
*Kiner, Pvt. Harold G. (Palenberg, Germany)
*Kingsley, 2d Lt. David R. (Ploesti, Rumania)
Kisters, Sgt. Gerry H. (Gagliano, Sicily)
Knappenberger, Pfc. Alton W. (Cisterna di Littoria, Italy)
*Knigth, 1st Lt. Jack L. (Loi-Kang, Burma)
*Knight, 1st Lt. Raymond L. (Northern Po Valley, Italy)
*Krotiak, Pfc. Anthony L. (Balete Pass, Philippines)
Lawley, 1st Lt. William R., Jr. (Over Europe)
Laws, SSgt. Robert E. (Pangasinan Province, Philippines)
Lee, 1st Lt. Daniel W. (Montreval, France)
*Leonard, 1st Lt. Turney W. (Kommerscheidt, Germany)
*Lindsey, Capt. Darrell R. (L'Isle Adam Bridge, France)
Lindsey, TSgt. Jake W. (Hamich, Germany)
*Lindstrom, Pfc. Floyd K. (Mignano, Italy)
*Lloyd, 1st Lt. Edgar H. (Pompey, France)
*Lobaugh, Pvt. Donald R. (Afua, New Guinea)
Logan, Sgt. James M. (Salerno, Italy)
Lopez, Sgt. Jose M. (Krinkelt, Belgium)
Mabry, Lt. Col. George L., Jr. (Hurtgen Forest, Germany)
MacArthur, Gen. Douglas (Bataan Peninsula, Philippines)
McCall, SSgt. Thomas E. (San Angelo, Italy)
McCarter, Pvt. Lloyd G. (Corregidor, Philippines)
McGaha, MSgt. Charles L. (Lupao, Philippines)
McGarity, TSgt. Vernon (Krinkelt, Belgium)
*McGee, Pvt. William D. (Mulheim, Germany)
*McGill, Sgt. Troy A. (Los Negros Islands)
MacGillivary, Sgt. Charles A. (Woelfling, France)
*McGraw, Pfc. Francis X. (Schevenhutte, Germany)
*McGuire, Maj. Thomas B., Jr. (Luzon, Philippines)
McKinney, Pvt. John R. (Tayabas Province, Philippines)
*McVeigh, Sgt. John J. (Brest, France)
*McWhorter, Pfc. William A. (Leyte, Philippines)
*Magrath, Pfc. John D. (Castel d'Aiano, Italy)
*Mann, Pfc. Joe E. (Best, Holland)
*Martinez, Pvt. Joe P. (Attu, Aleutian Islands)
*Mathies, Sgt. Archibald (Over Europe)
*Mathis, 1st Lt. Jack W. (Vegesack, Germany)
Maxwell, Technician 5th Grade Robert D. (Besancon, France)
*May, Pfc. Martin O. (Ie Shima, Ryukyu Islands)
Mayfield, Cpl. Melvin (Cordillera Mountains, Philippines)
Meagher, TSgt. John (Ozato, Okinawa)
Merli, Pfc. Gino J. (Sars la Bruyère, Belgium)
*Merrell, Pvt. Joseph F. (Lohe, Germany)
*Messerschmidt, Sgt. Harold O. (Radden, France)
*Metzger, 2d Lt. William E., Jr. (Saarbrucken, Germany)
Michael, 1st Lt. Edward S. (Over Germany)
*Michael, 2d Lt. Harry J. (Neiderzerf, Germany)
*Miller, SSgt. Andrew (Woippy, France–Kerprich Hemmersdorf, Germany)
Mills, Pvt. James H. (Cisterna di Littoria, Italy)
*Minick, SSgt. John W. (Hurtgen, Germany)
*Minue, Pvt. Nicholas (Medjez-el-Bab, Tunisia)
*Monteith, 1st Lt. Jimmie W., Jr. (Collesville-sur-Mer, France)
Montgomery, 1st Lt. Jack C. (Padiglione, Italy)
*Moon, Pvt. Harold H., Jr. (Pawig, Philippines)
Morgan, 2d Lt. John C. (Over Europe)
*Moskala, Pfc. Edward J. (Kakazu Ridge, Okinawa)
*Mower, Sgt. Charles E. (Capoocan, Philippines)
*Muller, Sgt. Joseph E. (Ishimmi, Okinawa)
*Munemori, Pfc. Sadao S. (Seravezza, Italy)
Murphy, 2d Lt. Audie L. (Holtzwihr, France)
*Murphy, Pfc. Frederick C. (Saarlautern, Germany)

Murray, 1st Lt. Charles P., Jr. (Kaysersberg, France)
*Nelson, Sgt. William L. (Djebel Dardys, Tunisia)
Neppel, Sgt. Ralph G. (Birgel, Germany)
Nett, Lt. Robert P. (Cognon, Philippines)
Newman, 1st Lt. Beryl R. (Cisterna, Italy)
*Nininger, 2d Lt. Alexander R., Jr. (Abucay, Philippines)
*O'Brien, Lt. Col. William J. (Saipan, Mariana Islands)
Ogden, 1st Lt. Carlos C. (Fort du Roule, France)
*Olson, Capt. Arlo L. (Volturno River, Italy)
*Olson, Sgt. Truman O. (Cisterna di Littoria, Italy)
Oresko, MSgt. Nicholas (Tettington, Germany)
*Parrish, Technician 4th Grade Laverne (Binalonan, Philippines)
*Pease, Capt. Harl, Jr. (Rabaul, New Britain)
*Peden, Technician 5th Grade Forrest E. (Biesheim, France)
*Pendleton, SSgt. Jack J. (Bardenberg, Germany)
*Peregory, TSgt. Frank D. (Grandcampe, France)
*Perez, Pfc. Manuel, Jr. (Fort William McKinley, Philippines)
*Peters, Pvt. George J. (Fluren, Germany)
*Peterson, SSgt. George (Eisern, Germany)
*Petrarca, Pfc. Frank J. (New Georgia, Solomon Islands)
*Pinder, Technician 5th Grade John J., Jr. (Colleville-sur-Mer, France)
Powers, Pfc. Leo J. (Cassino, Italy)
*Prussman, Pfc. Ernest W. (Les Coates, France)
*Pucket, 1st Lt. Donald D. (Ploesti, Rumania)
*Ray, 1st Lt. Bernard J. (Hurtgen Forest, Germany)
*Reese, Pvt. James W. (Mt. Vassillio, Sicily)
*Reese, Pfc. John N., Jr. (Manila, Philippines)
*Riordan, 2d Lt. Paul F. (Cassino, Italy)
*Robinson, 1st Lt. James E., Jr. (Untergriesheim, Germany)
Rodriguez, Pvt. Cleto (Manila, Philippines)
*Roeder, Capt. Robert E. (Mt. Battaglia, Italy)
*Roosevelt, Brig. Gen. Theodore, Jr. (Normandy, France)
Ross, Pvt. Wilburn K. (St. Jacques, France)
Rudolph, TSgt. Donald E. (Munoz, Philippines)
Ruiz, Pfc. Alejandro R. (Okinawa)
*Sadowski, Sgt. Jospeh J. (Valhey, France)
*Sarnoski, 2d Lt. Joseph R. (Buka Area, Solomon Islands)
*Sayers, Pfc. Foster J. (Thionville, France)
Schaefer, SSgt. Joseph E. (Stolberg, Germany)
Schauer, Pfc. Henry (Cisterna di Littoria, Italy)
Scott, Lt. Robert S. (New Georgia, Solomon Islands)
Shea, 2d Lt. Charles W. (Mt. Damiano, Italy)
*Sheridan, Pfc. Carl V. (Weisweiler, Germany)

Alfred L. Wilson, Technician Fifth Grade, U.S. Army, Medical Detachment, 328th Infantry, 26th Infantry Division. Place and date: Near Bezange la Petite, France, 8 November 1944. Entered service at: Fairchance, Pa. Birth: Fairchance, Pa. G.O. No.: 47, 18 June 1945. Citation: He volunteered to assist as an aid man a company other than his own, which was suffering casualties from constant artillery fire. He administered to the wounded and returned to his own company when a shellburst injured a number of its men.While treating his comrades he was seriously wounded, but refused to be evacuated by litter bearers sent to relieve him. In spite of great pain and loss of blood, he continued to administer first aid until he was too weak to stand. Crawling from 1 patient to another, he continued his work until excessive loss of blood prevented him from moving. He then verbally directed unskilled enlisted men in continuing the first aid for the wounded. Still refusing assistance himself, he remained to instruct others in dressing the wounds of his comrades until he was unable to speak above a whisper and finally lapsed into unconsciousness. The effects of his injury later caused his death. By steadfastly remaining at the scene without regard for his own safety, Cpl. Wilson through distinguished devotion to duty and personal sacrifice helped to save the lives of at least 10 wounded men.

*Shockley, Pfc. William R. (Villa Verde Trail, Philippines)
Shomo, Maj. William A. (Luzon, Philippines)
*Shoup, SSgt. Curtis F. (Tillet, Belgium)
Silk, 1st Lt. Edward A. (St. Pravel, France)
Siogren, SSgt. John C. (San José Hacienda, Philippines)
Slaton, Cpl. James D. (Oliveto, Italy)
*Smith, Pvt. Furman L. (Lanuvio, Italy)
Smith, Sgt. Maynard H. (Over Europe)
Soderman, Pfc. William A. (Rocherath, Belgium)
*Specker, Sgt. Joe C. (Mt. Porchia, Italy)
Spurrier, SSgt. Junior J. (Achain, France)
*Squires, Pfc. John C. (Padiglione, Italy)
*Stryker, Pfc. Stuart S. (Wesel, Germany)
*Terry, 1st Lt. Seymour W. (Okinawa)
*Thomas, Pfc. William H. (Zambales Mountains, Philippines)
Thompson, Sgt. Max (Haaren, Germany)
*Thorne, Cpl. Horace M. (Grufflingen, Belgium)
*Thorson, Pfc. John F. (Dagami, Philippines)
Tominac, 1st Lt. John J. (Saulx de Vesoul, France)
*Towle, Pvt. John R. (Oosterhout, Holland)
Treadwell, Capt. Jack L. (Nieder–Wurzbach, Germany)
*Truemper, 2d Lt. Walter E. (Over Europe)
*Turner, Sgt. Day G. (Dahl, Luxembourg)
Turner, Pfc. George B. (Philipsbourg, France)
Urban, Capt. Matt (Renouf & St. Lo, France, & Meuse River, Belgium)
*Valdez, Pfc. Jose F. (Rosenkrantz, France)
*Van Noy, Pvt. Junior (Finschafen, New Guinea)
*Vance, Lt. Col. Leon R., Jr. (Wimereaux, France)
*Viale, 2d Lt. Robert M. (Manila, Philippines)
*Villegas, SSgt. Ysmael R. (Villa Verde Trail, Philippines)
Vlug, Pfc. Dirk J. (Limon Philippines)
Vosler, TSgt. Forrest T. (Bremen, Germany)
Wainwright, Gen Jonathan M. (Philippines)
*Walker, Brig. Gen. Kenneth N. (Rabaul, New Britain)
*Wallace, Pfc. Herman C. (Prumzurley, Germany)
Ware, Lt. Col. Keith L. (Sigolsheim, France)
*Warner, Cpl. Henry F. (Dom Butgenbach, Belgium)
*Waugh, 1st Lt. Robert T. (Tremensucli, Italy)
Waybur, 1st Lt. David C. (Agrigento, Sicily)
*Weicht, Sgt. Ellis R. (St. Hippolyte, France)
*Wetzel, Pfc. Walter C. (Birken, Germany)
Whiteley, 1st Lt. Eli (Sigolsheim France)
Whittington, Sgt. Hulon B. (Grimesnil, France)
Wiedorfer, Pvt. Paul J. (Chaumont, Belgium)
*Wigle, 2d Lt. Thomas W. (Monte Frassino, Italy)
Wilbur, Col. William H. (Fedala, French Morocco)
*Wilkin, Cpl. Edward G. (Siegfried line, Germany)
*Wilkins, Maj. Raymond H. (Rabaul, New Britain)
*Will, 1st Lt. Walter J. (Eisern, Germany)
*Wilson, Technician 5th Grade Alfred L. (Bezange la Petite, France)
Wise, SSgt. Homer L. (Magliano, Italy)
*Woodford, SSgt. Howard E. (Tabio, Philippines)
*Young, Pvt. Rodger W. (New Georgia, Solomon Islands)
Zeamer, Capt. Jay, Jr. (Buka Area, Solomon Islands)
*Zussman, 2d Lt. Raymond (Noroy le Bourg, France)

COAST GUARD

*Munro, Signalman 1st Class Douglas A. (Point Cruz, Guadalcanal)

MARINES

*Agerholm, Pfc. Harold C. (Saipan, Mariana Islands)
*Anderson, Pfc. Richard B. (Roi Island, Marshall Islands)
*Bailey, Maj. Kenneth D. (Guadalcanal)
Basilone, Sgt. John (Guadalcanal)
*Bauer, Lt. Col. Harold W. (Solomon Islands Area)
*Bausell, Cpl. Lewis K. (Peleliu Island)
*Berry, Cpl. Charles J. (Iwo Jima)
*Bonnyman, 1st Lt. Alexander, Jr. (Tarawa)
*Bordelon, SSgt. William J. (Tarawa)
Boyington, Maj. Gregory (Central Solomons Area)
Bush, Cpl. Richard E. (Okinawa)
*Caddy, Pfc. William R. (Iwo Jima)
*Cannon, 1st Lt. George H. (Sand Island, Midway Islands)
Casamento, Cpl. Anthony (Guadalcanal)
Chambers, Lt. Col. Justice M. (Iwo Jima)
*Cole, Sgt. Darrell S. (Iwo Jima)
*Courtney, Maj. Henry A., Jr. (Okinawa Shima)
*Damato, Cpl. Anthony P. (Engebi Island, Marshall Islands)
DeBlanc, Capt. Jefferson J. (Kolombangara Island, Solomon Islands)
Dunlap, Capt. Robert H. (Iwo Jima)
*Dyess, Lt. Col. Aquilla J. (Namur Island, Marshall Islands)
Edson, Col. Merritt A. (Guadalcanal)
*Elrod, Capt. Henry T. (Wake Island)
*Epperson, Pfc. Harold G. (Saipan Island, Mariana Islands)
*Fardy, Cpl. John P. (Okinawa Shima)
*Fleming, Capt. Richard E. (Midway)
Foss, Capt. Joseph J. (Guadalcanal)
*Foster, Pfc. William A. (Okinawa Shima)
Galer, Maj. Robert E. (Solomon Islands Area)
*Gonsalves, Pfc. Harold (Okinawa Shima)
*Gray, Sgt. Ross F. (Iwo Jima)
*Gurke, Pfc. Henry (Bougainville Island)
*Hansen, Pvt. Dale M. (Okinawa Shima)
*Hanson, 1st Lt. Robert M. (Bougainville Island & New Britain Island)
Harrell, Sgt. William G. (Iwo Jima)
*Hauge, Cpl. Louis J., Jr. (Okinawa Shima)
*Hawkins, 1st Lt. William D. (Tarawa)
Jackson, Pfc. Arthur J. (Peleliu Island)
Jacobson, Pfc. Douglas T. (Iwo Jima)
*Julian, Sgt. Joseph R. (Iwo Jima)
*Kinser, Sgt. Elbert L. (Okinawa Shima)
*Kraus, Pfc. Richard E. (Peleliu Island)
*La Belle, Pfc. James D. (Iwo Jima)
Leims, 2d Lt. John H. (Iwo Jima)
Lucas, Pfc. Jacklyn H. (Iwo Jima)
*Lummus, 1st Lt. Jack (Iwo Jima)
*McCard, Gy. Sgt. Robert H. (Saipan, Mariana Islands)
McCarthy, Capt. Joseph J. (Iwo Jima)
*McTureous, Pvt. Robert M., Jr. (Okinawa)
*Martin, 1st Lt. Harry L. (Iwo Jima)
*Mason, Pfc. Leonard F. (Guam)
*New, Pfc. John D. (Peleliu Island)
*Owens, Sgt. Robert A. (Cape Torokina, Bougainville Island)
*Ozbourn Pvt. Joseph W. (Tinian Island, Mariana Islands)
Paige, Sgt. Mitchell (Guadalcanal)
*Phelps, Pvt. Wesley (Peleliu Island)
*Phillips, Pvt. George (Iwo Jima)
Pope, Capt. Everett P. (Peleliu Island)
*Power, 1st Lt. John V. (Namur Island, Marshall Islands)
*Roan, Pfc. Charles H. (Peleliu Island)
Rouh, 1st Lt. Carlton R. (Peleliu Island)
*Ruhl, Pfc. Donald J. (Iwo Jima)
*Schwab, Pfc. Albert E. (Okinawa Shima)
Shoup, Col. David M. (Betio Island, Tarawa)
Sigler, Pvt. Franklin E. (Iwo Jima)
Skaggs, Pfc. Luther, Jr. (Guam)
Smith, Maj. John L. (Solomon Islands Area)
Sorenson, Pvt. Richard K. (Namur Island, Marshall Islands)
*Stein, Cpl. Tony (Iwo Jima)
Swett, 1st Lt. James E. (Solomon Islands Area)
*Thomas, Sgt. Herbert J. (Koromokina River, Bougainville Island)
*Thomason, Sgt. Clyde (Makin Island)
*Timmerman, Sgt. Grant F. (Saipan, Mariana Islands)
Vandegrift, Maj. Gen. Alexander A. (Guadalcanal)
Walsh, 1st Lt. Kenneth A. (Solomon Islands Area)
*Walsh, Gy. Sgt. William G. (Iwo Jima)
Watson, Pvt. Wilson D. (Iwo Jima)
Williams, Cpl. Hershel W. (Iwo Jima)
Wilson, Capt. Louis H., Jr. (Fonte Hill, Guam)
*Wilson, Pfc. Robert L. (Tinian Island, Mariana Islands)
*Witek, Pfc. Frank P. (Guam)

NAVY

Antrim, Lt. Richard N. (Makassar, Netherlands East Indies)
*Bennion, Capt. Mervyn S. (Pearl Harbor, Hawaii)
*Bigelow, Watertender 1st Class Elmer C. (Corregidor Island, Philippines)
Bulkeley, Lt. Cmdr. John D. (Philippines)
Bush, Hospital Apprentice 1st Class Robert E. (Okinawa)
*Callaghan, Rear Adm. Daniel J. (Savo Island, Solomon Islands)
*Cromwell, Capt. John P. (Truk Island)
*David, Lt.(j.g.) Albert L. (French West Africa)
*Davis, Cmdr. George F. (Lingayen Gulf, Philippines)
*Dealey, Cmdr. Samuel D. (Sulu Sea, Borneo)
*Evans, Cmdr. Ernest E. (Samar, Philippines)
Finn, Lt. John W. (Kaneohe Bay, Hawaii)
*Flaherty, Ensign Francis C. (Pearl Harbor, Hawaii)
Fluckey, Cmdr. Eugene B. (Coast of China)
Fuqua, Capt. Samuel G. (Pearl Harbor, Hawaii)
Gary, Lt.(j.g.) Donald A. (Kobe, Japan)
*Gilmore, Cmdr. Howard W. (Southwest Pacific)
Gordon, Lt. Nathan G. (Bismarck Sea)
Hall, Lt.(j.g.) William E. (Coral Sea)
*Halyburton, Pharmacist's Mate 2d Class William D., Jr. (Okinawa Shima)

Hershel Woodrow Williams, Corporal, U.S. Marine Corps Reserve, 21st Marines, 3d Marine Division. Place and date: Iwo Jima, Volcano Islands, 23 February 1945. Entered service at: West Virginia. Born: 2 October 1923, Quiet Dell, W. Va. Citation: For conspicuous gallantry and intrepidity at the risk of his life above and beyond the call of duty as demolition sergeant serving with the 21st Marines, 3d Marine Division, in action against enemy Japanese forces on Iwo Jima, Volcano Islands, 23 February 1945. Quick to volunteer his services when our tanks were maneuvering vainly to open a lane for the infantry through the network of reinforced concrete pillboxes, buried mines, and black volcanic sands, Cpl. Williams daringly went forward alone to attempt the reduction of devastating machinegun fire from the unyielding positions. Covered only by 4 riflemen, he fought desperately for 4 hours under terrific enemy small-arms fire and repeatedly returned to his own lines to prepare demolition charges and obtain serviced flamethrowers, struggling back, frequently to the rear of hostile emplacements, to wipe out 1 position after another. On 1 occasion, he daringly mounted a pillbox to insert the nozzle of his flamethrower through the air vent, killing the occupants and silencing the gun; on another he grimly charged enemy riflemen who attempted to stop him with bayonets and destroyed them with a burst of flame from his weapon. His unyielding determination and extraordinary heroism in the face of ruthless enemy resistance were directly instrumental in neutralizing one of the most fanatically defended Japanese strong points encountered by his regiment and aided vitally in enabling his company to reach its objective. Cpl. Williams' aggressive fighting spirit and valiant devotion to duty throughout this fiercely contested action sustain and enhance the highest traditions of the U.S. Naval Service.

*Hammerberg, BM 2d Class Owen F. P. (Pearl Harbor, Hawaii)
Herring, Lt. Rufus G. (Iwo Jima)
*Hill, Chief Boatswain Edwin J. (Pearl Harbor, Hawaii)
*Hutchins, Sman 1st Class Johnnie D. (Lae, New Guinea)
*Jones, Ensign Herbert C. (Pearl Harbor, Hawaii)
*Keppler, BM 1st Class Reinhardt J. (Solomon Islands)
*Kidd, Rear Adm. Isaac C. (Pearl Harbor, Hawaii)
*Lester, Hospital Apprentice 1st Class Fred F. (Okinawa Shima)
McCampbell, Cmdr. David (Philippine Sea)
McCandless, Cmdr. Bruce (Savo Island, Solomon Islands)
McCool, Lt. Richard M., Jr. (Okinawa)
O'Callahan, Cmdr. Joseph T. (Kobe, Japan)
O'Hare, Lt. Edward H. (Raboul, New Britain)
O'Kane, Cmdr. Richard H. (Formosa Strait)
*Parle, Ensign John J. (Sicily, Italy)
*Peterson, Chief Watertender Oscar V. (NOR)
Pharris, Lt. Jackson C. (Pearl Harbor, Hawaii)
Pierce, Pharmacist's Mate 1st Class Francis J. (Iwo Jima)
*Powers, Lt. John J. (Coral Sea)
Preston, Lt. Arthur M. (Wasile Bay, Halmahera Island)
Ramage, Cmdr. Lawson P. (Pacific)
*Reeves, Radio Electrician Thomas J. (Pearl Harbor, Hawaii)
*Ricketts, Lt. Milton E. (Coral Sea)
*Rooks, Capt. Albert H. (Java, Indonesia)
Ross, Machinist Donald K. (Pearl Harbor, Hawaii)
Schonland, Lt. Cmdr. Herbert E. (Savo Island, Solomon Islands)
*Scott, Rear Adm. Norman (Savo Island, Solomon Islands)
*Scott, Machinist's Mate 1st Class Robert R. (Pearl Harbor, Hawaii)
Street, Cmdr. George L. III (Quelpart Island, Korea)
*Tomich, Chief Watertender Peter (Pearl Harbor, Hawaii)
*Van Valkenburgh, Capt. Franklin (Pearl Harbor, Hawaii)
*Van Voorhis, Lt. Cmdr. Bruce A. (Greenwich Island, Solomon Islands)
Wahlen, Pharmacist's Mate 2d Class George E. (Iwo Jima)
*Ward, Sman 1st Class James R. (Pearl Harbor, Hawaii)
*Williams, Pharmacist's Mate 3d Class Jack (Iwo Jima)
*Willis, Pharmacist's Mate 1st Class John H. (Iwo Jima)
Young, Cmdr. Cassin (Pearl Harbor, Hawaii)

The Korean War, 1950–1953

Number of medals:	131
AIR FORCE:	4
ARMY:	78
MARINES:	42
NAVY:	7

AIR FORCE

*Davis, Maj. George A., Jr. (Sinuiju-Yalu River Area)
*Loring, Maj. Charles J., Jr. (Sniper Ridge, N. Korea)
*Sebille, Maj. Louis J. (Hanchang)
*Walmsley, Capt. John S., Jr. (Yangdok)

ARMY

Adams, Sfc. Stanley T. (Sesim-ni)
*Barker, Pvt. Charles H. (Sokkogae)
*Bennett, Pfc. Emory L. (Sobangsan)
Bleak, Sgt. David B. (Minari-gol)
*Brittin, Sfc. Nelson V. (Yonggong-ni)
*Brown, Pfc. Melvin L. (Kasan)
Burke, 1st Lt. Lloyd L. (Chong-dong)
*Burris, Sfc. Tony K. (Mundung-ni)
*Charlton, Sgt. Cornelius H. (Chipo-ri)
*Collier, Cpl. Gilbert G. (Tutayon)
*Collier, Cpl. John W. (Chindong-ni)
*Coursen, 1st Lt. Samuel S. (Kaesong)
*Craig, Cpl. Gordon M. (Kasan)
Crump, Cpl. Jerry K. (Chorwon)
Dean, Maj. Gen. William F. (Taejon)
*Desiderio, Capt. Reginald B. (Ipsok)
Dodd, 2d Lt. Carl H. (Subuk)
*Duke, Sfc. Ray E. (Mugok)
*Edwards, Sfc. Junior D. (Changbong-ni)
*Essebagger, Cpl. John, Jr. (Popsudong)
*Faith, Lt. Col. Don C., Jr. (Hagaru-ri)
*George, Pfc. Charles (Songnae-dong)
*Gilliland, Pfc. Charles L. (Tongmang-ni)
*Goodblood, Cpl. Clair (Popsudong)
*Hammond, Cpl. Lester, Jr. (Kumwha)
*Handrich, MSgt. Melvin O. (Sobuk San Mountain)
*Hanson, Pfc. Jack G. (Pachi-dong)
*Hartell, 1st Lt. Lee R. (Kobangsan-ni)
Harvey, Capt. Raymond (Taemi-Dong)
*Henry, 1st Lt. Frederick F. (Am-Dong)
Hernandez, Cpl. Rodolfo P. (Wontong-ni)
Ingman, Cpl. Einar H., Jr. (Maltari)
*Jecelin, Sgt. William R. (Saga)
*Jordan, Pfc. Mack A. (Kumsong)
*Kanell, Pvt. Billie G. (Pyongyang)
*Kaufman, Sfc. Loren R. (Yongsan)
*Knight, Pfc. Noah O. (Kowang-San)
Kouma, Sfc. Ernest R. (Agok)
*Krzyzowski, Capt. Edward C. (Tondul)
*Kyle, 2d Lt. Darwin K. (Kamil-ni)
Lee, MSgt. Hubert L. (Ip-o-ri)
*Libby, Sgt. George D. (Taejon)
*Long, Sgt. Charles R. (Hoeng-song)
*Lyell, Cpl. William F. (Chup'a-ri)
*McGovern, 1st Lt. Robert M. (Kamyangjan-ni)
Martinez, Cpl. Benito (Satae-ri)
*Mendonca, Sgt. Leroy A. (Chich-on)
Millett, Capt. Lewis L. (Soam-Ni)
Miyamura, Cpl. Hiroshi H. (Taejon-ni)
Mize, Sgt. Ola L. (Surang-ni)
*Moyer, Sfc. Donald R. (Seoul)
*Ouellette, Pfc. Joseph R. (Yongsan)
*Page, Lt. Col. John U. D. (Chosin Reservoir)
*Pendleton, Cpl. Charles F. (Choo Gung-Dong)
*Pililaau, Pfc. Herbert K. (Pia-ri)
Pittman, Sgt. John A. (Kujang-dong)
*Pomeroy, Pfc. Ralph E. (Kumhwa)
*Porter, Sgt. Donn F. (Mundung-ni)
*Red Cloud, Cpl. Mitchell, Jr. (Chonghyon)
Rodriguez, Pfc. Joseph C. (Munye-ri)
Rosser, Cpl. Ronald E. (Ponggilli)
*Schoonover, Cpl. Dan D. (Sokkogae)
Schowalter, 1st Lt. Edward R., Jr. (Kumhwa)
*Shea, 1st Lt. Richard T., Jr. (Sokkogae)
*Sitman, Sfc. William S. (Chipyong-ni)
*Smith, Pfc David M. (Yongsan)
*Speicher, Cpl. Clifton T. (Minari-gol)
Stone, 1st Lt. James L. (Sokkogae)
*Story, Pfc. Luther H. (Agok)
*Sudut, 2d Lt. Jerome A. (Kumhwa)
*Thompson, Pfc. William (Haman)
*Turner, Sfc. Charles W. (Yongsan)
*Watkins, MSgt. Travis E. (Yongsan)
West, Pfc. Ernest E. (Sataeri)
Wilson, MSgt. Benjamin F. (Hwach'on-Myon)
*Wilson, Pfc. Richard G. (Opari)
*Womack, Pfc. Bryant H. (Sokso-ri)
*Young, Pfc. Robert H. (Kaesong)

MARINES

*Abrell, Cpl. Charles G. (Hangnyong)
Barber, Capt. William E. (Chosin Reservoir)
*Baugh, Pfc. William B. (Koto-ri to Hagaru-ri)

George Andrew Davis, Jr., Major, U.S. Air Force, CO, 334th Fighter Squadron, 4th Fighter Group, 5th Air Force. Place and date: Near Sinuiju-Yalu River area, Korea, 10 February 1952. Entered service at: Lubbock, Tex. Born: 1 December 1920, Dublin, Tex. Citation: Maj Davis distinguished himself by conspicuous gallantry and intrepidity at the risk of his life above and beyond the call of duty. While leading a flight of 4 F-86 Saberjets on a combat aerial patrol mission near the Manchurian border, Maj. Davis' element leader ran out of oxygen and was forced to retire from the flight with his wingman accompanying him. Maj. Davis and the remaining F-86's continued the mission and sighted a formation of approximately 12 enemy MIG-15 aircraft speeding southward toward an area where friendly fighter-bombers were conducting low level operations against the Communist lines of communications. With selfless disregard for the numerical superiority of the enemy, Maj. Davis positioned his 2 aircraft, then dove at the MIG formation. While speeding through the formation from the rear he singled out a MIG-15 and destroyed it with a concentrated burst of fire. Although he was now under continuous fire from the enemy fighters to his rear, Maj. Davis sustained his attack. He fired at another MIG-15 which, bursting into smoke and flames, went into a vertical dive. Rather than maintain his superior speed and evade the enemy fire being concentrated on him, he elected to reduce his speed and sought out still a third MIG-15. During this latest attack his aircraft sustained a direct hit, went out of control, then crashed into a mountain 30 miles south of the Yalu River. Maj. Davis' bold attack completely disrupted the enemy formation, permitting the friendly fighter-bombers to successfully complete their interdiction mission. Maj. Davis, by his indomitable fighting spirit, heroic aggressiveness, and superb courage in engaging the enemy against formidable odds exemplified valor at its highest.

Cafferata, Pvt. Hector A., Jr. (Chosin Reservoir)
*Champagne, Cpl. David B. (Korea)
*Christianson, Pfc. Stanley (Seoul)
Commiskey, 2d Lt. Henry A., Sr. (Yongdungp'o)
*Davenport, Cpl. Jack A. (Songnae-Dong)
Davis, Lt. Col. Raymond G. (Hagaru-ri)
Dewey, Cpl. Duane E. (Panmunjon)
*Garcia, Pfc. Fernando L. (Korea)
*Gomez, Pfc. Edward (Hill 749)
*Guillen, SSgt. Ambrosio (Songuch-on)
*Johnson, Sgt. James E. (Yudam-ni)
*Kelly, Pfc. John D. (Korea)
*Kelso, Pfc. Jack W. (Korea)
Kennemore, SSgt. Robert S. (Yudam-ni)
*Littleton, Pfc. Herbert A. (Chungchon)
*Lopez, 1st Lt. Baldomero (Inchon)
McLaughlin, Pfc. Alford L. (Korea)
*Matthews, Sgt. Daniel P. (Vegas Hill)
*Mausert, Sgt. Frederick W., III (Songnap-yong)
*Mitchell, 1st Lt. Frank N. (Hansan-ni)
*Monegan, Pfc. Walter C., Jr. (Sosa-ri)
*Moreland, Pfc. Whitt L. (Kwagch'i-Dong)
Murphy, 2d Lt. Raymond G. (Korea)
Myers, Maj. Reginald R. (Hagaru-ri)
*Obregon, Pfc. Eugene A. (Seoul)
O'Brien, 2d Lt. George H., Jr. (Korea)
*Phillips, Cpl. Lee H. (Korea)
*Poynter, Sgt. James I. (Sudong)
*Ramer, 2d Lt. George H. (Korea)
*Reem, 2d Lt. Robert D. (Chinhung-ni)
*Shuck, SSgt. William E., Jr. (Korea)
Simanek, Pfc. Robert E. (Korea)
Sitter, Capt. Carl L. (Hagaru-ri)
*Skinner, 2d Lt. Sherrod E., Jr. (Korea)
Van Winkle, SSgt. Archie (Sudong)
*Vittori, Cpl. Joseph (Hill 749)
*Watkins, SSgt. Lewis G. (Korea)
Wilson, TSgt. Harold E. (Korea)
*Windrich, SSgt. William G. (Yudam-ni)

NAVY

*Benford, Hospital Corpsman 3d Class Edward C. (Korea)
Charette, Hospital Corpsman 3d Class William R. (Korea)
*Dewert, Hospital Corpsman Richard D. (Korea)
*Hammond, Hospital Corpsman Francis C. (Korea)
Hudner, Lt.(j.g.) Thomas J., Jr. (Chosin Reservoir)
*Kilmer, Hospital Corpsman John E. (Korea)
*Koelsch, Lt.(j.g.) John K. (North Korea)

The Vietnam War, 1964–1973

Number of medals:	238
AIR FORCE:	12
ARMY:	155
MARINES:	57
NAVY:	14

AIR FORCE

*Bennett, Capt. Steven L. (Quang Tri)
Day, Maj. George E. (North Vietnam)
Dethlefsen, Capt. Merlyn H. (North Vietnam)
Fisher, Maj. Bernard F. (A Shau)
Fleming, 1st Lt. James P. (Duc Co)
Jackson, Lt. Col. Joe M. (Kham Duc)
*Jones, Lt. Col. William A. III (Dong Hoi, N. Vietnam)
Levitow, Airman 1st Class John L. (Long Binh)
*Sijan, Capt. Lance P. (North Vietnam)
Thorsness, Maj. Leo K. (North Vietnam)
*Wilbanks, Capt. Hilliard A. (Da Lat)
Young, Capt. Gerald O. (Khe Sanh)

ARMY

*Adams, Maj. William E. (Kontum Province)
*Albanese, Pfc. Lewis (Phu Muu-2)
Anderson, SSgt. Webster (Tam Ky)
*Ashley, Sfc. Eugene, Jr. (Lang Vei)
Baca, Sp4c. John P. (Phuoc Long Province)
Bacon, SSgt. Nicky D. (Tam Ky)
Baker, Pfc. John F., Jr. (South Vietnam)
*Barnes, Pfc. John A. III (Dak To)
Beikirch, Sgt. Gary B. (Kontum Province)
*Belcher, Sgt. Ted (Plei Jrang)
*Bellrichard, Pfc. Leslie A. (Kontum Province)
Benavidez, SSgt. Roy P. (Cambodia)
*Bennett, Cpl. Thomas W. (Pleiku Province)
*Blanchfield, Sp4c. Michael R. (Binh Dinh Province)
Bondsteel, SSgt. James L. (An Loc Province)
*Bowen, SSgt. Hammett L., Jr. (Binh Duong Province)
Brady, Maj. Patrick H. (Chu Lai)
*Bryant, Sfc. William M. (Long Khanh Province)
Bucha, Capt. Paul W. (Phuoc Vinh)
*Buker, Sgt. Brian L. (Chau Doc Province)
Cavaiani, SSgt. Jon R. (Quang Tri Province)
*Crescenz, Cpl. Michael J. (Hiep Duc Valley)

Patrick Henry Brady, Major, U.S. Army, Medical Service Corps, 54th Medical Detachment, 67th Medical Group, 44th Medical Brigade. Place and date: Near Chu Lai, Republic of Vietnam, 6 January 1968. Entered service at: Seattle, Wash. Born: 1 October 1936, Philip, S. Dak. Citation: For conspicuous gallantry and intrepidity in action at the risk of his life above and beyond the call of duty, Maj. Brady distinguished himself while serving in the Republic of Vietnam commanding a UH-1H ambulance helicopter, volunteered to rescue wounded men from a site in enemy held territory which was reported to be heavily defended and to be blanketed by fog. To reach the site he descended through heavy fog and smoke and hovered slowly along a valley trail, turning his ship sideward to blow away the fog with the backwash from his rotor blades. Despite the unchallenged, close-range enemy fire, he found the dangerously small site, where he successfully landed and evacuated 2 badly wounded South Vietnamese soldiers. He was then called to another area completely covered by dense fog where American casualties lay only 50 meters from the enemy. Two aircraft had previously been shot down and others had made unsuccessful attempts to reach this site earlier in the day. With unmatched skill and extraordinary courage, Maj. Brady made flights to this embattled landing zone and successfully rescued all the wounded. On his third mission of the day Maj. Brady once again landed at a site surrounded by the enemy. The friendly ground force, pinned down by enemy fire, had been unable to reach and secure the landing zone. Although his aircraft had been badly damaged and his controls partially shot away during his initial entry into this area, he returned minutes later and rescued the remaining injured. Shortly thereafter, obtaining a replacement aircraft, Maj. Brady was requested to land in an enemy minefield where a platoon of American soldiers was trapped. A mine detonated near his helicopter, wounding 2 crewmembers and damaging his ship. In spite of this, he managed to fly 6 severely injured patients to medical aid. Throughout that day Maj. Brady utilized 3 helicopters to evacuate a total of 51 seriously wounded men, many of whom would have perished without prompt medical treatment. Maj. Brady's bravery was in the highest traditions of the military service and reflects great credit upon himself and the U.S. Army.

*Cutinha, Sp4c. Nicholas J. (Gia Dinh)
*Dahl, Sp4c. Larry G. (An Khe)
Davis, Sgt. Sammy L. (Cai Lay)
*Devore, Sp4c. Edward A., Jr. (Saigon)
Dix, SSgt. Drew D. (Chau Doc Province)
*Doane, 1st Lt. Stephen H. (Hau Nghia Province)
Dolby, Sp4c. David C. (South Vietnam)
Donlon, Capt. Roger H. C. (Nam Dong)
Dunagan, Capt. Kern W. (Quang Tin Province)
*Durham, 2d Lt. Harold B., Jr. (South Vietnam)
*English, SSgt. Glenn H., Jr. (Phu My)
*Evans, Sp4c. Donald W., Jr. (Tri Tam)
*Evans, Sgt. Rodney J. (Tay Ninh Province)
Ferguson, CWO Frederick E. (Hue)
*Fernandez, Sp4c. Daniel (Cu Chi)
Fitzmaurice, Sp4c. Michael J. (Khe Sanh)
*Fleek, Sgt. Charles C. (Binh Duong Province)
Foley, Capt. Robert F. (Quan Dau Tieng)
*Folland, Cpl. Michael F. (Long Khanh)
*Fournet, 1st Lt. Douglas B. (A Shau Valley)
*Fous, Pfc. James W. (Kien Hoa Province)
*Fratellenico, Cpl. Frank R. (Quang Tri Province)
Fritz, Capt. Harold A. (Binh Long Province)
*Gardner, 1st Lt. James A. (My Canh)
*Gertsch, SSgt. John G. (A Shau Valley)
*Grandstaff, Sgt. Bruce A. (Pleiku Province)
*Grant, 1st Lt. Joseph X. (South Vietnam)
*Guenette, Sp4c. Peter M. (Quan Tan Uyen)
Hagemeister, Sp4c. Charles C. (Binh Dinh Province)
*Hagen, 1st Lt. Loren D. (South Vietnam)
*Hartsock, SSgt. Robert W. (Hau Nghia Province)
*Harvey, Sp4c. Carmel B., Jr. (Binh Dinh Province)
Herda, Pfc. Frank A. (Dak To)
*Hibbs, 2d Lt. Robert J. (Don Dien Lo Ke)
*Holcomb, Sgt. John N. (Quan Loi)
Hooper, Sgt. Joe R. (Hue)
*Hosking, MSgt. Charles E., Jr. (Phuoc Long Province)
Howard, Sfc. Robert L. (Laos)
*Ingalls, Sp4c. George A. (Duc Pho)
Jacobs, 1st Lt. Jack H. (Kien Phong Province)
Jenkins, Pfc. Don J. (Kien Phong Province)
Jennings, SSgt. Delbert O. (Kim Song Valley)
Joel, Sp5c. Lawrence (War Zone D)
Johnson, Sp5c. Dwight H. (Dak To)
*Johnston, Sp4c. Donald R. (Tay Ninh Province)
*Karopczyc, 1st Lt. Stephen E. (Kontum Province)
*Kawamura, Cpl. Terry T. (Camp Radcliff)
Kays, Pvt. Kenneth M. (Thua Thien Province)
*Kedenburg, Sp5c. John J. (Laos)
Keller, Sgt. Leonard B. (Ap Bac)
Kinsman, Pfc. Thomas J. (Vinh Long)
Lambers, Sgt. Paul R. (Tay Ninh Province)
Lang, Sp4c. George C. (Kien Hoa Province)
*Langhorn, Pfc. Garfield M. (Pleiku Province)
*LaPointe, Sp4c. Joseph G., Jr. (Quang Tin Province)
*Lauffer, Pfc. Billy L. (Bong Son)
*Law, Sp4c. Robert D. (Tinh Phuoc Thanh)
*Lee, Pfc. Milton A. (Phu Bai)
*Leisy, 2d Lt. Robert R. (Phuoc Long Province)
Lemon, Sp4c. Peter C. (Tay Ninh Province)
*Leonard, Sgt. Matthew (Suoi Da)
Liteky, Capt. Angelo J. (Phuoc Lac)
Littrell, Sfc. Gary L. (Kontum Province)
*Long, Sgt. Donald R. (South Vietnam)
*Lozada, Pfc. Carlos J. (Dak To)
*Lucas, Lt. Col. Andre C. (FSB Ripcord)
Lynch, Sp4c. Allen J. (My An-2)
McCleery, Sgt. Finnis D. (Quang Tin Province)
*McDonald, Pfc. Phill G. (Kontum City)
*McKibben, Sgt. Ray (Song Mao)
*McMahon, Sp4c. Thomas J. (Quang Tin Province)
McNerney, 1st Sgt. David H. (Polei Doc)
*McWethy, Sp5c. Edgar L., Jr. (Binh Dinh Province)
Marm, 2d Lt. Walter J., Jr. (Ia Drang Valley)
*Michael, Sp4c. Don L. (South Vietnam)
Miller, SSgt. Franklin D. (Kontum Province)
*Miller, 1st Lt. Gary L. (Binh Duong Province)
Molnar, SSgt. Frankie Z. (Kontum Province)
*Monroe, Pfc. James H. (Bong Son)
Morris, SSgt. Charles B. (South Vietnam)
*Murray, SSgt. Robert C. (Hiep Duc)
*Nash, Pfc. David P. (Giao Duc)
Novosel, CWO Michael J. (Kien Tuong Province)
*Olive, Pfc. Milton L. III (Phu Cuong)
*Olson, Sp4c. Kenneth L. (South Vietnam)
Patterson, Sgt. Robert M. (La Chu)
Penry, Sgt. Richard A. (Binh Tuy Province)
*Petersen, Sp4c. Danny J. (Tay Ninh Province)
*Pierce, Sgt. Larry South (Ben Cat)
*Pitts, Capt. Riley L. (Ap Dong)
*Port, Pfc. William D. (Que Son Valley)
*Poxon, 1st Lt. Robert L. (Tay Ninh Province)

*Pruden, SSgt. Robert J. (Quang Ngai Province)
*Rabel, SSgt. Laszlo (Binh Dinh Province)
Ray, 1st Lt. Ronald E. (Ia Drang Valley)
*Roark, Sgt. Anund C. (Kontum Province)
Roberts, Sp4c. Gordon R. (Thua Thien Province)
*Robinson, Sgt. James W., Jr. (South Vietnam)
Rocco, Sfc. Louis R. (Katum)
Rogers, Lt. Col. Charles C. (Fishhook, Cambodian border)
*Rubio, Capt. Euripides (Tay Ninh Province)
*Santiago-Colon, Sp4c. Hector (Quang Tri Province)
*Sargent, 1st Lt. Ruppert L. (Hau Nghia Province)
Sasser, Pfc. Clarence E. (Dinh Tuong Province)
*Seay, Sgt. William W. (Ap Nhi)
*Shea, Pfc. Daniel J. (Quang Tri Province)
*Sims, SSgt. Clifford C. (Hue)
*Sisler, 1st Lt. George K. (Laos)
*Skidgel, Sgt. Donald South (Song Be)
*Smith, SSgt. Elmelindo R. (South Vietnam)
Sprayberry, 1st Lt. James M. (South Vietnam)
*Steindam, 1st Lt. Russell A. (Tay Ninh Province)
*Stewart, SSgt. Jimmy G. (South Vietnam)
*Stone, Sgt. Lester R., Jr. (LZ Liz)
*Stout, Sgt. Mitchell W. (Khe Gio Bridge)
*Stryker, Sp4c. Robert F. (Loc Ninh)
Stumpf, Sp4c. Kenneth E. (Duc Pho)
Taylor, 1st Lt. James A. (Que Son)
Thacker, 1st Lt. Brian M. (Kontum Province)
*Warren, 1st Lt. John E., Jr. (Tay Ninh Province)
*Watters, Maj. Charles J. (Dak To)
*Wayrynen, Sp4c. Dale E. (Quang Ngai Province)
Wetzel, Pfc. Gary G. (Ap Dong An)
*Wickam, Cpl. Jerry W. (Loc Ninh)
*Willett, Pfc. Louis E. (Kontum Province)
Williams, 2d Lt. Charles Q. (Dong Xoai)
*Winder, Pfc. David F. (South Vietnam)
Wright, Sp4c. Raymond R. (Ap Bac)
*Yabes, 1st Sgt. Maximo (Phu Hoa Dong)
*Yano, Sfc. Rodney J. T. (Bien Hoa)
*Yntema, Sgt. Gordon D. (Thong Binh)
*Young, SSgt. Marvin R. (Ben Cui)
Zabitosky, SSgt. Fred W. (Laos)

MARINES

*Anderson, Pfc. James, Jr. (South Vietnam)
*Anderson, LCpl. Richard A. (Quang Tri Province)
*Austin, Pfc. Oscar P. (Da Nang)
*Barker, LCpl. Jedh C. (Con Thien)
Barnum, Lt. Harvey C., Jr. (Ky Phu)
*Bobo, 2d Lt. John P. (Quang Tri Province)
*Bruce, Pfc. Daniel D. (Quang Nam Province)
*Burke, Pfc. Robert C. (Quang Nam Province)
*Carter, Pfc. Bruce W. (Quang Tri Province)
Clausen, Pfc. Raymond M. (South Vietnam)
*Coker, Pfc. Ronald L. (Quang Tri Province)
*Connor, SSgt. Peter South (Quang Ngai Province)
*Cook, Capt. Donald G. (Phuoc Tuy Province)
*Creek, LCpl. Thomas E. (Cam Lo)
*Davis, Sgt. Rodney M. (Quang Nam Province)
*De La Garza, LCpl. Emilio A., Jr. (Da Nang)
*Dias, Pfc. Ralph E. (Que Son Mountains)
*Dickey, Pfc. Douglas E. (South Vietnam)
*Foster, Sgt. Paul H. (Con Thien)
Fox, 1st Lt. Wesley L. (Quang Tri Province)
*Gonzalez, Sgt. Alfredo (Hue)
*Graham, Capt. James A. (South Vietnam)
*Graves, 2d Lt. Terrence C. (Quang Tri Province)
Howard, SSgt. Jimmie E. (Nui Vu)
*Howe, LCpl. James D. (South Vietnam)
Ingram, Sp3c. Robert R. (Quang Ngai)
*Jenkins, Pfc. Robert H., Jr. (FSB Argonne)
*Jimenez, LCpl. Jose F. (Quang Nam Province)
*Johnson, Pfc. Ralph H. (Quan Duc Valley)
*Keith, LCpl. Miguel (Quang Ngai Province)
Kellogg, SSgt. Allan J., Jr. (Quang Nam Province)
Lee, Capt. Howard V. (Cam Lo)
Livingston, Capt. James E. (Dai Do)
McGinty, SSgt. John J. III (Song Ngam Valley)
*Martini, Pfc. Gary W. (Binh Son)
*Maxam, Cpl. Larry L. (Cam Lo)
Modrzejewski, Capt. Robert J. (Song Ngam Valley)
*Morgan, Cpl. William D. (Laos)
*Newlin, Pfc. Melvin E. (Quang Nam Province)
*Noonan, LCpl. Thomas P., Jr. (A Shau Valley)
O'Malley, Cpl. Robert E. (An Cu'ong-2)
*Paul, LCpl. Joe C. (Chu Lai)
*Perkins, Cpl. William T., Jr. (Quang Tri Province)
*Peters, Sgt. Lawrence D. (Quang Tin Province)
*Phipps, Pfc. Jimmy W. (An Hoa)
Pittman, LCpl. Richard A. (DMZ)
Pless, Capt. Stephen W. (Quang Ngai)
*Prom, LCpl. William R. (An Hoa)
*Reasoner, 1st Lt. Frank S. (Da Nang)

Finnis D. McCleery, Platoon Sergeant, U.S. Army, Company A, 1st Battalion, 6th U.S. Infantry. Place and date: Quang Tin province, Republic of Vietnam, 14 May 1968. Entered service at: San Angelo, Tex. Born: 25 December 1927, Stephenville, Tex. Citation: For conspicuous gallantry and intrepidity in action at the risk of his life above and beyond the call of duty. P/Sgt. McCleery, U.S. Army, distinguished himself while serving as platoon leader of the 1st platoon of Company A. A combined force was assigned the mission of assaulting a reinforced company of North Vietnamese Army regulars, well entrenched on Hill 352, 17 miles west of Tam Ky. As P/Sgt. McCleery led his men up the hill and across an open area to close with the enemy, his platoon and other friendly elements were pinned down by tremendously heavy fire coming from the fortified enemy positions. Realizing the severe damage that the enemy could inflict on the combined force in the event that their attack was completely halted, P/Sgt. McCleery rose from his sheltered position and began a 1-man assault on the bunker complex. With extraordinary courage, he moved across 60 meters of open ground as bullets struck all around him and rockets and grenades literally exploded at his feet. As he came within 30 meters of the key enemy bunker, P/Sgt. McCleery began firing furiously from the hip and throwing hand grenades. At this point in his assault, he was painfully wounded by shrapnel, but, with complete disregard for his wound, he continued his advance on the key bunker and killed all of its occupants. Having successfully and single-handedly breached the enemy perimeter, he climbed to the top of the bunker he had just captured and, in full view of the enemy, shouted encouragement to his men to follow his assault. As the friendly forces moved forward, P/Sgt. McCleery began a lateral assault on the enemy bunker line. He continued to expose himself to the intense enemy fire as he moved from bunker to bunker, destroying each in turn. He was wounded a second time by shrapnel as he destroyed and routed the enemy from the hill. P/Sgt. McCleery is personally credited with eliminating several key enemy positions and inspiring the assault that resulted in gaining control of Hill 352. His extraordinary heroism at the risk of his life, above and beyond the call of duty, was in keeping with the highest standards of the military service, and reflects great credit on him, the Americal Division, and the U.S. Army.

Joe C. Paul, Lance Corporal, U.S. Marine Corps, Company H, 2d Battalion, 4th Marines (Rein), 3d Marine Division (Rein). Place and date: near Chu Lai, Republic of Vietnam, 18 August 1965. Entered service at: Dayton, Ohio. Born: 23 April 1946, Williamsburg, Ky. Citation: For conspicuous gallantry and intrepidity at the risk of his life above and beyond the call of duty. In violent battle, L/Cpl. Paul's platoon sustained 5 casualties as it was temporarily pinned down, by devastating mortar, recoilless rifle, automatic weapons, and rifle fire delivered by insurgent communist (Viet Cong) forces in well entrenched positions. The wounded marines were unable to move from their perilously exposed positions forward of the remainder of their platoon, and were suddenly subjected to a barrage of white phosphorous rifle grenades. L/Cpl. Paul, fully aware that his tactics would almost certainly result in serious injury or death to himself, chose to disregard his safety and boldly dashed across the fire-swept rice paddies, placed himself between his wounded comrades and the enemy, and delivered effective suppressive fire with his automatic weapon in order to divert the attack long enough to allow the casualties to be evacuated. Although critically wounded during the course of the battle, he resolutely remained in his exposed position and continued to fire his rifle until he collapsed and was evacuated. By his fortitude and gallant spirit of self-sacrifice in the face of almost certain death, he saved the lives of several of his fellow marines. His heroic action served to inspire all who observed him and reflect the highest credit upon himself, the Marine Corps and the U.S. Naval Service. He gallantly gave his life in the cause of freedom.

*Singleton, Sgt. Walter K. (Gio Linh)
*Smedley, Cpl. Larry E. (Quang Nam Province)
*Taylor, SSgt. Karl G., Sr. (South Vietnam)
Vargas, Capt. Jay R. (Dai Do)
*Weber, LCpl. Lester W. (Quang Nam Province)
*Wheat, LCpl. Roy M. (Quang Nam Province)
*Williams, Pfc. Dewayne T. (Quang Nam Province)
*Wilson, Pfc. Alfred M. (Quang Tri Province)
*Worley, LCpl. Kenneth L. (Bo Ban)

NAVY

Ballard, Hospital Corpsman 2d Class Donald E. (Quang Tri Province)
*Capodanno, Lt. Vincent R. (Quang Tin Province)
*Caron, Hospital Corpsman 3d Class Wayne M. (Quang Nam Province)
*Estocin, Lt. Cmdr. Michael J. (Haiphong, N. Vietnam)
Kelley, Lt. Thomas G. (Kien Hoa Province)
Kerrey, Lt.(j.g.) Joseph R. (Nha Trang Bay)
Lassen, Lt.(j.g.) Clyde E. (North Vietnam)
‡McGonagle, Cmdr. William L. (Eastern Mediterranean)
Norris, Lt. Thomas R. (Quang Tri Province)
*Ouellet, Sman David G. (Mekong River)
*Ray, Hospital Corpsman 2d Class David R. (Quang Nam Province)
*Shields, Construction Mechanic 3rd Class Marvin G. (Dong Xoai)
Stockdale, Capt. James B. (Hanoi, N. Vietnam)
Thornton, Petty Officer Michael E. (South Vietnam)
Williams, BM 1st Class James E. (Mekong River)

‡Six Day War, 1967–not included in Vietnam total

Somalia

*Gordon, MSgt. Gary I. (Mogadishu)
*Shughart, Sfc. Randall D. (Mogadishu)

Source: Congressional Medal of Honor Society

Wartime Speeches and Documents

King George III's Proclamation for Suppression of Rebellion, 1775

Three months after actual fighting had begun (at Lexington and Concord), the Second Continental Congress addressed a final appeal directly to the King. This petition was never formally received by George III; indeed, he refused to accept it. Instead, on August 23, 1775, he issued the following royal proclamation "for suppressing rebellion and sedition".

Whereas many of our subjects in divers parts of our colonies and plantations in North America, misled by dangerous and ill-designing men, and forgetting the allegiance which they owe to the power that has protected and sustained them, after various disorderly acts committed in disturbance of the public peace, to the obstruction of lawful commerce and to the oppression of our loyal subjects carrying on the same, have at length proceeded to an open and avowed rebellion by arraying themselves in hostile manner to withstand the execution of the law, and traitorously preparing, ordering, and levying war against us; and whereas there is reason to apprehend that such rebellion hath been much promoted and encouraged by the traitorous correspondence counsels, and comfort of divers wicked and desperate persons within this realm; to the end therefore that none of our subjects may neglect or violate their duty through ignorance thereof, or through any doubt of the protection which the law will afford to their loyalty and zeal; we have thought fit, by and with the advice of our Privy Council, to issue this our royal proclamation, hereby declaring that not only all our officers, civil and military, are obliged to exert their utmost endeavours to suppress such rebellion and to bring the traitors to justice; but that all our subjects of this realm and the dominions thereunto belonging are bound by law to be aiding and assisting in the suppression of such rebellion, and to disclose and make known all traitorous conspiracies and attempts against us, our Crown, and dignity; and we do accordingly strictly charge and command all our officers, as well civil as military, and all other our obedient and loyal subjects, to use their utmost endeavours to withstand and suppress such rebellion, and to disclose and make known all treasons and traitorous conspiracies which they shall know to be against us, our Crown and dignity; and for that purpose, that they transmit to one of our principal secretaries of state, or other proper officer, due and full information of all persons who shall be found carrying on correspondence with, or in any manner or degree aiding or abetting the persons now in open arms and rebellion against our government within any of our colonies and plantations in North America, in order to bring to condign punishment the authors, perpetrators and abettors of such traitorous designs.

Given at our court at St. James the twenty-third day of August, one thousand seven hundred and seventy-five, in the fifteenth year of our reign.

Declaration of Independence, July 4, 1776

When in the course of human events, it becomes necessary for one people to dissolve the political bands which have connected them with another, and to assume among the powers of the earth, the separate and equal station to which the laws of nature and of nature's God entitle them, a decent respect to the opinions of mankind requires that they should declare the causes which impel them to the separation.

We hold these truths to be self-evident: That all men are created equal; that they are endowed by their Creator with certain unalienable rights; that among these are life, liberty, and the pursuit of happiness; that, to secure these rights, governments are instituted among men, deriving their just powers from the consent of the governed; that whenever any form of government becomes destructive of these ends, it is the right of the people to alter or to abolish it, and to institute new government, laying its foundation on such principles, and organizing its powers in such form, as to them shall seem most likely to effect their safety and happiness. Prudence, indeed, will dictate that governments long established should not be changed for light and transient causes; and accordingly all experience hath shown that mankind are more disposed to suffer, while evils are sufferable than to right themselves by abolishing the forms to which they are accustomed. But when a long train of abuses and usurpations, pursuing invariably the same object, evinces a design to reduce them under absolute despotism, it is their right, it is their duty, to throw off such government, and to provide new guards for their future security. Such has been the patient sufferance of these colonies; and such is now the necessity which constrains them to alter their former systems of government. The history of the present King of Great Britain is a history of repeated injuries and usurpations, all having in direct object the establishment of an absolute tyranny over these states. To prove this, let facts be submitted to a candid world.

He has refused his assent to laws, the most wholesome and necessary for the public good.

He has forbidden his governors to pass laws of immediate and pressing importance, unless suspended in their operation till his assent should be obtained; and, when so suspended, he has utterly neglected to attend to them.

He has refused to pass other laws for the accommodation of large districts of people, unless those people would relinquish the right of representation in the legislature, a right inestimable to them, and formidable to tyrants only.

He has called together legislative bodies at places unusual uncomfortable, and distant from the depository of their public records, for the sole purpose of fatiguing them into compliance with his measures.

He has dissolved representative houses repeatedly, for opposing, with manly firmness, his invasions on the rights of the people.

He has refused for a long time, after such dissolutions, to cause others to be elected; whereby the legislative powers, incapable of annihilation, have returned to the people at large for their exercise; the state remaining, in the mean time, exposed to all the dangers of invasions from without and convulsions within.

He has endeavored to prevent the population of these states; for that purpose obstructing the laws for naturalization of foreigners; refusing to pass others to encourage their migration hither, and raising the conditions of new appropriations of lands.

He has obstructed the administration of justice, by refusing his assent to laws for establishing judiciary powers.

He has made judges dependent on his will alone, for the tenure of their offices, and the amount and payment of their salaries.

He has erected a multitude of new offices, and sent hither swarms of officers to harass our people and eat out their substance.

He has kept among us, in times of peace, standing armies, without the consent of our legislatures.

He has affected to render the military independent of, and superior to, the civil power.

He has combined with others to subject us to a jurisdiction foreign to our Constitution and unacknowledged by our laws, giving his assent to their acts of pretended legislation:

For quartering large bodies of armed troops among us;

For protecting them, by a mock trial, from punishment for any murders which they should commit on the inhabitants of these states;

For cutting off our trade with all parts of the world;

For imposing taxes on us without our consent;

For depriving us, in many cases, of the benefits of trial by jury;

For transporting us beyond seas, to be tried for pretended offenses;

For abolishing the free system of English laws in a neighboring province, establishing therein an arbitrary government, and enlarging its boundaries, so as to render it at once an example and fit instrument for introducing the same absolute rule into these colonies;

For taking away our charters, abolishing our most valuable laws, and altering fundamentally the forms of our governments;

For suspending our own legislatures, and declaring themselves invested with power to legislate for us in all cases whatsoever.

He has abdicated government here, by declaring us out of his protection and waging war against us.

He has plundered our seas, ravaged our coasts, burned our towns, and destroyed the lives of our people.

He is at this time transporting large armies of foreign mercenaries to complete the works of death, desolation, and tyranny already begun with circumstances of cruelty and perfidy scarcely paralleled in the most barbarous ages, and totally unworthy the head of a civilized nation.

He has constrained our fellow-citizens, taken captive on the high seas, to bear arms against their country, to become the executioners of their friends and brethren, or to fall themselves by their hands.

He has excited domestic insurrection among us, and has endeavored to bring on the inhabitants of our frontiers the merciless Indian savages, whose known rule of warfare is an undistinguished destruction of all ages, sexes, and conditions.

In every stage of these oppressions we have petitioned for redress in the most humble terms; our repeated petitions have been answered only by repeated injury. A prince, whose character is thus marked by every act which may define a tyrant, is unfit to be the ruler of a free people.

Nor have we been wanting in our attentions to our British brethren. We have warned them, from time to time, of attempts by their legislature to extend an unwarrantable jurisdiction over us. We have reminded them of the circumstances of our emigration and settlement here. We have appealed to their native justice and magnanimity; and we have conjured them, by the ties of our common kindred, to disavow these usurpations which would inevitably interrupt our connections and correspondence. They too, have been deaf to the voice of justice and of consanguinity. We must, therefore, acquiesce in the necessity which denounces our separation, and hold them as we hold the rest of mankind, enemies in war, in peace friends.

We, therefore, the representatives of the United States of America, in General Congress assembled, appealing to the Supreme Judge of the world for the rectitude of our intentions, do, in the name and by the authority of the good people of these colonies solemnly publish and declare, That these United Colonies are, and of right ought to be, ***FREE AND INDEPENDENT STATES;*** that they are absolved from all allegiance to the British crown and that all political connection between them and the state of Great Britain is, and ought to be, totally dissolved; and that, as free and independent states, they have full power to levy war, conclude peace, contract alliances, establish commerce, and do all other acts and things which independent states may of right do. And for the support of this declaration, with a firm reliance on the protection of Divine Providence, we mutually pledge to each other our lives, our fortunes, and our sacred honor.

Black Hawk's Account of the Black Hawk War, 1832

Few Americans (except for some zealous religious missionaries) concerned themselves at all with the condition of the American Indians. To most Americans, the Indian was still a "red varmint" or a "red devil". The following account of the "Black Hawk War" of 1832, as described by Black Hawk himself, had little practical influence in securing justice for the dispossessed tribes.

After Black Hawk's defeat and capture, he dictated his life-story to Antoine Leclair, the U.S. government interpreter at the Sac and Fox Agency. It was translated into English and published in several places and at several times. Our quotation is taken from the edition entitled Life of . . . Black Hawk, *published at Boston in 1834.*

During our encampment at the Four Lakes, we were hard put to obtain enough to eat to support nature. Situate in a swampy, marshy country, (which had been selected in consequence of the great difficulty required to gain access thereto,) there was but little game of any sort to be found—and fish were equally scarce. The great distance to any settlement, and the impossibility of bringing supplies therefrom, if any could have been obtained, deterred our young men from making further attempts. We were forced to dig *roots* and *bark trees,* to obtain something to satisfy hunger and keep us alive! Several of our old people became so much reduced as actually to *die with hunger!* And, finding that the army had commenced moving, and fearing that they might come upon and surround our encampment, I concluded to remove my women and children across the Mississippi, that they might return to the Sac nation again. Accordingly, on the next day, we commenced moving, with five Winnebagoes acting as our guides, intending to descend the Ouisconsin (*Wisconsin*).

Ne-a-pope, with a party of twenty, remained in our rear, to watch for the enemy, whilst we were proceeding to the Ouisconsin, with our women and children. We arrived, and had commenced crossing them to an island, when we discovered a large body of the enemy coming towards us. We were now compelled to fight, or sacrifice our wives and children to the fury of the whites! I met them with fifty warriors, (having left the balance to assist our women and children in crossing,) about a mile from the river, when an attack immediately commenced. I was mounted on a fine horse, and was pleased to see my warriors so brave. I addressed them in a loud voice, telling them to stand their ground, and never yield it to the enemy. At this time I was on the rise of a hill, where I wished to form my warriors, that we might have some advantage over the whites. But the enemy succeeded in gaining this point, which compelled us to fall back into a deep ravine, from which we continued firing at them and they at us, until it began to grow dark. My horse having been wounded twice during this engagement, and fearing from his loss of blood, that he would soon give out—and finding that the enemy would not come near enough to receive our fire, in the dusk of the evening—and knowing that our women and children had had sufficient time to reach the island in the Ouisconsin, I ordered my warriors to return, in different routes, and meet me at the Ouisconsin—and were astonished to find that the enemy were not disposed to pursue us.

In this skirmish, with fifty braves, I defended and accomplished my passage over the Ouisconsin, with a loss of only six men; though opposed by a host of mounted militia. I would not have fought there, but to gain time for my women and children to cross to an island. A warrior will duly appreciate the embarrassments I labored under—and whatever may be the sentiments of the *white people,* in relation to this battle, my nation, though fallen, will award to me the reputation of a great brave, in conducting it.

The loss of the enemy could not be ascertained by our party; but I am of opinion, that it was much greater, in proportion, than mine. We returned to the Ouisconsin, and crossed over to our people.

Here some of my people left me, and descended the Ouisconsin, hoping to escape to the west side of the Mississippi, that they might return home. I had no objection to their leaving me, as my people were all in a desperate condition—being worn out with travelling, and starving from hunger. Our only hope to save ourselves, was to get across the Mississippi. But few of this party escaped. Unfortunately for them, a party of soldiers from Prairie du Chien, was stationed on the Ouisconsin, a short distance from its mouth, who fired upon our distressed people. Some were killed, others drowned, several taken prisoners, and the balance escaped to the woods and perished with hunger. Among this party were a great many women and children.

I was astonished to find the Ne-a-pope and his party of *spies* had not yet come in—they having been left in my rear to bring the news, if the enemy were discovered. It appeared, however, that the whites had come in a different direction, and intercepted our trail but a short distance from the place where we first saw them—leaving our spies considerably in the rear. Ne-a-pope, and one other, retired to the Winnebago village, and there remained during the war! The balance of his party, being *brave men,* and considering our interest as their own, returned, and joined our ranks.

Myself and band having no means to descend the Ouisconsin, I started, over a rugged country, to go to the Mississippi, intending to cross it, and return to my nation. Many of our people were compelled to go on foot, for want of horses, which, in consequence of their having had nothing to eat for a long time, caused our march to be very slow. At length we arrived at the Mississippi, having lost some of our old men and little children, who perished on the way with hunger.

We had been here but a little while, before we saw a steam boat (the "Warrior,") coming. I told my braves not to shoot, as I intended going on board, so that we might save our women and children. I knew the captain and was determined to give myself up to him. I then sent for my *white flag.* While the messenger was gone, I took a small piece of white cotton, and put it on a pole, and called to the captain of the boat, and told him to send his little canoe ashore, and let me come on board. The people on the boat asked whether we were Sacs or Winnebagoes. I told a Winnebago to tell them that we were Sacs, and wanted to give ourselves up! A Winnebago on the boat called to us "*to run and hide, that the whites were going to shoot!*" About this time one of my braves had jumped into the river, bearing a white flag to the boat—when another sprang in after him, and brought him to shore. The firing then commenced from the boat, which was returned by my braves, and continued for some time. Very few of my people were hurt after the first fire, having succeeded in getting behind old logs and trees, which shielded them from the enemy's fire.

The Winnebago, on the steam boat, must either have misunderstood what was told, or did not tell it to the captain correctly; because I am confident that he would not have fired upon us, if he had known my wishes. I have always considered him a good man, and too great a brave to fire upon an enemy when sueing for quarters.

After the boat left us, I told my people to cross, if they could, and wished: that I intended going into the Chippewa country. Some commenced crossing, and such as had determined to follow them, remained—only three lodges going with me. Next morning, at daybreak, a young man overtook me, and said that all my party had determined to cross the Mississippi—that a number had already got over safe, and that he had heard the white army last night within a few miles of them. I now began to fear that the whites would come up with my people, and kill them, before they could get across. I had determined to go and join the Chippewas; but reflecting that by this I could only save myself, I concluded to return, and die with my people, if the Great Spirit would not give us another victory! During our stay in the thicket, a party of whites came close by us, but passed on without discovering us!

Early in the morning a party of whites, being in advance of the army, came upon our people, who were attempting to cross the Mississippi. They tried to give themselves up—the whites paid no attention to their entreaties—but commenced *slaughtering them*! In a little while the whole army arrived. Our braves, but few in number, finding that the enemy paid no regard to age or sex, and seeing that they were murdering helpless women and little children, determined to *fight until they were killed!* As many women as could, commenced swimming the Mississippi, with their children on their backs. A number of them were drowned, and some shot, before they could reach the opposite shore.

One of my braves, who gave me this information, piled up some saddles before him, (when the fight commenced,) to shield himself from the enemy's fire, and killed three white men! But seeing that the whites were coming to close to him, he crawled to the bank of the river, without being perceived, and hid himself under it, until the enemy retired. He then came to me and told me what had been done. After hearing this sorrowful news, I started, with my little party, to the Winnebago village at Prairie La Cross. On my arrival there, I entered the lodge of one of the chiefs, and told him that I wished him to go with me to his father—that I intended to give myself up to the American war chief, and *die,* if the Great Spirit saw proper! He said he would go with me. I then took my *medicine bag,* and addressed the chief. I told him that it was "the soul of the Sac nation—that it never had been dishonored in any battle—take it, it is my life—dearer than life—and give it to the American chief!" He said he would keep it, and take care of it, and if I was suffered to live, he would send it to me.

During my stay at the village, the squaws made me a white dress of deer skin. I then started, with several Winnebagoes, and went to their agent, at Prairie du Chien, and gave myself up.

On my arrival there, I found to my sorrow, that a large body of Sioux had pursued, and killed, a number of our women and children, who had got safely across the Mississippi. The whites ought not to have permitted such conduct—and none but *cowards* would ever have been guilty of such cruelty—which has always been practised on our nation by the Sioux.

The massacre, which terminated the war, lasted about two hours. Our loss in killed, was about sixty, besides a number that were drowned. The loss of the enemy could not be ascertained by my braves, exactly; but they think that they killed about *sixteen,* during the action.

I was now given up by the agent to the commanding officer at fort Crawford, (the White Beaver having gone down the river.) We remained here a short time, and then started to Jefferson Barracks, in a steam boat, under the charge of a young war chief, [Lieut. Jefferson Davis] who treated us all with much kindness. He is a good and brave young chief, with whose conduct I was much pleased. On our way down, we called at Galena, and remained a short time. The people crowded to the boat to see us; but the war chief would not permit them to enter the apartment where we were—knowing, from what his own feelings would have been, if he had been placed in a similar situation, that we did not wish to have a gaping crowd around us.

We passed Rock Island, without stopping. The great war chief, [Gen. Scott,] who was then at fort Armstrong, came out in a small boat to see us; but the captain of the steam boat would not allow any body from the fort to come on board of his boat, in consequence of the cholera raging among his soldiers. I did think that the captain ought to have permitted the war chief to come on board to see me, because I could see no danger to be apprehended by it. The war chief looked well, and I have since heard, was constantly among his soldiers, who were sick and dying, administering to their wants, and had not caught the disease from them—and I thought it absurd to think that any of the people on the steam boat, could be afraid of catching the disease from a *well* man. But these people have not got bravery like war chiefs, who never fear any thing.

On our way down, I surveyed the country that had cost us so much trouble, anxiety, and blood, and that now caused me to be a prisoner of war. I reflected upon the ingratitude of the whites, when I saw their fine houses, rich harvests, and every thing desirable around them; and recollected that all this land had been ours, for which me and my people had never received a dollar, and that the whites were not satisfied until they took our village and our grave-yards from us, and removed us across the Mississippi.

On our arrival at Jefferson barracks, we met the great war chief (White Beaver) who had commanded the American army against my little band. I felt the humiliation of my situation: a little while before, I had been the leader of my braves, now I was a prisoner of war! but had surrendered myself. He received us kindly, and treated us well.

We were now confined to the barracks, and forced to wear the *ball and chain!* This was extremely mortifying, and altogether useless. Was the White Beaver afraid that I would break out of his barracks, and run away? Or was he ordered to inflict this punishment upon me? If I had taken him prisoner on the field of battle, I would not have wounded his feelings so much, by such treatment—knowing that a brave war chief would prefer death to dishonor! But I do not blame the White Beaver for the course he pursued—it is the custom among white soldiers, and I suppose, was a part of his duty.

Resolution to Admit Texas as a State, 1845

Shortly before Polk was sworn in as President in 1845, Congress passed a "Joint Resolution" to admit Texas as a State. The Resolution, which follows, quoted from the U.S. Statutes at Large, *included an agreement that four additional States might be formed from Texas territory in the future.*

Resolved, That Congress doth consent that the territory properly included within, and rightfully belonging to the Republic of Texas, may be erected into a new State, to be called the State of Texas, with a republican form of government, to be adopted by the people of said republic, by deputies in convention assembled, with the consent of the existing government, in order that the same may be admitted as one of the States of this Union.

2. That the foregoing consent of Congress is given upon the following conditions, and with the following guarantees, to wit: *First,* Said State to be formed, subject to the adjustment by this government of all questions of boundary that may arise with other governments; and the constitution thereof, with the proper evidence of its adoption by the people of said Republic of Texas, shall be transmitted to the President of the United States, to be laid before Congress for its final action, on or before the first day of January, one thousand eight hundred and forty-six. *Second,* Said State, when admitted into the Union, after ceding to the United States, all public edifices, fortifications, barracks, ports and harbors, navy and navy-yards, docks, magazines, arms, armaments, and all other property and means pertaining to the public defence belonging to said Republic of Texas, shall retain all the public funds, debts, taxes, and dues of every kind, which may belong to or be due and owing said republic; and shall also retain all the vacant and unappropriated lands lying within its limits, to be applied to the payment of the debts and liabilities of said Republic of Texas, and the residue of said lands, after discharging said debts and liabilities, to be disposed of as said State may direct; but in no event are said debts and liabilities to become a charge upon the Government of the United States. *Third.* New States, of convenient size, not exceeding four in number, in addition to said State of Texas, and having sufficient population, may hereafter, by the consent of said State, be formed out of the territory thereof, which shall be entitled to admission under the provisions of the federal constitution. And such States as may be formed out of that portion of said territory lying south of thirty-six degrees thirty minutes north latitude, commonly known as the Missouri compromise line, shall be admitted into the Union with or without slavery, as the people of each State asking admission may desire. And in such State or States as shall be formed out of said territory north of said Missouri compromise line, slavery, or involuntary servitude, (except for crime,) shall be prohibited.

3. That if the President of the United States shall in his judgment and discretion deem it most advisable, instead of proceeding to submit the foregoing resolution to the Republic of Texas, as an overture on the part of the United States for admission, to negotiate with that Republic; then.

Be it resolved, That a State, to be formed out of the present Republic of Texas, with suitable extent and boundaries, and with two representatives in Congress, until the next apportionment of representation, shall be admitted into the Union, by virtue of this act, on an equal footing with the existing States, as soon as the terms and conditions of the remaining Texan territory to the United States shall be agreed upon by the Governments of Texas and the United States: And that the sum of one hundred thousand dollars be, and the same is hereby, appropriated to defray the expenses of missions and negotiations, to agree upon the terms of said admission and cession, either by treaty to be submitted to the Senate, or by articles to be submitted to the two houses of Congress, as the President may direct.

President James Polk's Message to Congress, 1846

War with Mexico began with a relatively minor frontier skirmish, after which President Polk requested Congress for a formal declaration. His war message, dated May 11, 1846, presented reasons why the President sought permission to carry on a war against Mexico.

In my message at the commencement of the present session I informed you that upon the earnest appeal both of the Congress and convention of Texas I had ordered an efficient military force to take a position "between the Nueces and the Del Norte." This had become necessary to meet a threatened invasion of Texas by the Mexican forces, for which extensive military preparations had been made. The invasion was threatened solely because Texas had determined, in accordance with a solemn resolution of the Congress of the United States, to annex herself to our Union, and under these circumstances it was plainly our duty to extend our protection over her citizens and soil.

This force was concentrated at Corpus Christi, and remained there until after I had received such information from Mexico as rendered it probable, if not certain, that the Mexican Government would refuse to receive our envoy.

Meantime Texas, by the final action of our Congress, had become an integral part of our Union. The Congress of Texas, by its act of December 19, 1836, had declared the Rio del Norte to be the boundary of that Republic. Its jurisdiction had been extended and exercised beyond the Nueces. The country between that river and the Del Norte had been represented in the Congress and in the convention of Texas, has thus taken part in the act of annexation itself, and is now included within one of our Congressional districts. Our own Congress had moreover, with great unanimity, by the act approved December 31, 1845, recognized the country beyond the Nueces as a part of our territory by including it within our own revenue system, and a revenue officer to reside within that district has been appointed by and with the consent of the Senate. It became, therefore, of urgent necessity to provide for the defense of that portion of our country. Accordingly, on the 13th of January last instructions were issued to the general in command of these troops to occupy the left bank of the Del Norte. This river, which is the southwestern boundary of the State of Texas, is an exposed frontier. . . .

The movement of the troops to the Del Norte was made by the commanding general under positive instructions to abstain from all aggressive acts toward Mexico or Mexican citizens and to regard the relations between that Republic and the United States as peaceful unless she should declare war or commit acts of hostility indicative of a state of war. He was specially directed to protect private property and respect personal rights.

The Army moved from Corpus Christi on the 11th of March, and on the 28th of that month arrived on the left bank of the Del

Norte opposite to Matamoras, where it encamped on a commanding position, which has since been strengthened by the erection of field-works. . . .

The Mexican forces at Matamoras assumed a belligerent attitude, and on the 12th of April General Ampudia, then in command, notified General Taylor to break up his camp within twenty-four hours and to retire beyond the Nueces River, and in the event of his failure to comply with these demands announced that arms, and arms alone, must decide the question. But no open act of hostility was committed until the 24th of April. On that day General Arista, who had succeeded to the command of the Mexican forces, communicated to General Taylor that "he considered hostilities commenced and should prosecute them." A party of dragoons of 63 men and officers were on the same day dispatched from the American camp up the Rio del Norte, on its left bank, to ascertain whether the Mexican troops had crossed or were preparing to cross the river, "became engaged with a large body of these troops, and after a short affair, in which some 16 were killed and wounded, appear to have been surrounded and compelled to surrender."

The cup of forbearance had been exhausted even before the recent information from the frontier of the Del Norte. But now, after reiterated menaces, Mexico has passed the boundary of the United States, has invaded our territory and shed American blood upon the American soil. She has proclaimed that hostilities have commenced, and that the two nations are now at war.

As war exists, and, notwithstanding all our efforts to avoid it, exists by the act of Mexico herself, we are called upon by every consideration of duty and patriotism to vindicate with decision the honor, the rights, and the interests of our country. . . .

In further vindication of our rights and defense of our territory, I invoke the prompt action of Congress to recognize the existence of the war.

Jefferson Davis's Message to the Congress of the Confederacy, 1861

Many of Lincoln's critics, both North and South, charged that he had delayed too long in making his position clear before the inauguration, and that his call for volunteers had driven several States into the Confederacy. Some argued that he had acted on his own, without Congressional approval; others answered that he had simply moved to protect the Union. The leader of the Confederacy was President Jefferson Davis of Mississippi. He began his presidency by issuing policy orders to General P. G. T. Beauregard and others, and by inviting shipowners to apply for "letters of marque and reprisal" so that they could operate privateers against United States shipping. Davis called the Confederate Congress into special session, and requested that it declare war to establish southern independence. His message, delivered April 29, 1861, contained a summary history of southern complaints against Federal policies.

The declaration of war made against this Confederacy by Abraham Lincoln, the President of the United States, in his proclamation issued on the 15th day of the present month, rendered it necessary, in my judgment, that you should convene at the earliest practicable moment to devise the measures necessary for the defense of the country. The occasion is indeed an extraordinary one. It justifies me in a brief review of the relations heretofore existing between us and the States which now unite in warfare against us and in a succinct statement of the events which have resulted in this warfare, to the end that mankind may pass intelligent and impartial judgment on its motives and objects. During the war waged against Great Britain by her colonies on this continent a common danger impelled them to a close alliance and to the formation of a Confederation, by the terms of which the colonies, styling themselves States, entered '*severally* into a firm league of friendship with each other for their common defense, the security of their liberties, and their mutual and general welfare, binding themselves to assist each other against all force offered to or attacks made upon them, or any of them, on account of religion, sovereignty, trade, or any other pretense whatever'. In order to guard against any misconstruction of their compact, the several States made explicit declaration in a distinct article—that '*each* State *retains its* sovereignty, freedom, and independence, and every power, jurisdiction, and right which is not by this Confederation *expressly delegated* to the United States in Congress assembled'.

Under this contract of alliance, the war of the Revolution was successfully waged, and resulted in the treaty of peace with Great Britain in 1783, by the terms of which the several States were *each by name* recognized to be independent. The Articles of Confederation contained a clause whereby all alterations were prohibited unless confirmed by the Legislatures of *every State* after being agreed to by the Congress; and in obedience to this provision, under the resolution of Congress on the 21st of February 1787, the several States appointed delegates who attended a convention 'for the *sole and express purpose* of revising the Articles of Confederation and reporting to Congress and the several Legislatures such alterations and provisions therein as shall, when agreed to in Congress *and confirmed by the States,* render the Federal Constitution adequate to the exigencies of Government and the preservation of the Union'. It was by the delegates chosen by the *several States* under the resolution just quoted that the Constitution of the United States was framed in 1787 and submitted to the *several States* for ratification, as shown by the seventh article, which is in these words: 'The ratification of the *conventions of nine States* shall be sufficient for the establishment of this Constitution *between the States* so ratifying the same.' . . . The Constitution of 1787, having, however, omitted the clause already recited from the Articles of Confederation, which provided in explicit terms that each State *retained* its sovereignty and independence, some alarm was felt in the States, when invited to ratify the Constitution, lest this omission should be construed into an abandonment of their cherished principle, and they refused to be satisfied until amendments were added to the Constitution placing beyond any pretense of doubt the reservation by the States of all their sovereign rights and powers not expressly delegated to the United States by the Constitution.

Strange, indeed, must it appear to the impartial observer, but it is none the less true that all these carefully worded clauses proved unavailing to prevent the rise and growth in the Northern States of a political school which has persistently claimed that the government thus formed was not a compact *between* States, but was in effect a national government, set up *above* and *over* the States. An organization created by the States to secure the blessings of liberty and independence against *foreign* aggression has been gradually perverted into a machine for their control in their *domestic* affairs. The *creature* has been exalted above its *creators;* the *principals* have been made subordinate to the *agent* appointed by themselves. The people of the Southern States, whose almost exclusive occupation was agriculture, early perceived a tendency in the Northern States to render the common government subservient to their own purposes by imposing burdens on commerce as a protection to their manufacturing and shipping interests. . . .

By degrees, as the Northern States gained preponderance in the National Congress, self-interest taught their people to yield ready assent to any plausible advocacy of their right as a majority to govern the minorities without control. They learned to listen with impatience to the suggestion of any constitutional impediment to the exercise of their will, and so utterly have the principles of the Constitution been corrupted in the Northern mind that, in the Inaugural Address delivered by President Lincoln in March last, he asserts as an axiom, which he plainly deems to be undeniable, that the theory of the Constitution requires that in all cases the majority shall govern. . . .

In addition to the long-continued and deep-seated resentment felt by the Southern States at the persistent abuse of the powers they had delegated to the Congress, for the purpose of enriching the manufacturing and shipping classes of the North at the expense of the South, there has existed for nearly half a century another subject of discord, involving interests of such transcendent magnitude as at all times to create the apprehension in the minds of many devoted lovers of the Union that its permanence was impossible. When the several States delegated certain powers to the United States Congress, a large portion of the laboring population consisted of African slaves imported into the colonies by the mother country. In twelve out of the thirteen States negro slavery existed, and the right of property in slaves was protected by law. This property was recognized in the Constitution, and provision was made against its loss by the escape of the slave. The increase in the number of slaves by further importation from Africa was also secured by a clause forbidding Congress to prohibit the slave trade anterior to a certain date, and in no clause can there be found any delegation of power to the Congress authorizing it in any manner to legislate to the prejudice, detriment, or discouragement of the owners of that species of property, or excluding it from the protection of the Government.

The climate and soil of the Northern States soon proved unpropitious to the continuance of slave labor, whilst the converse was the case at the South. Under the unrestricted free intercourse between the two sections, the Northern States consulted their own interests by selling their slaves to the South and prohibiting slavery within their limits. The South were willing purchasers of property suitable to their wants, and paid the price of the acquisition without harboring a suspicion that their quiet possession was to be disturbed by those who were inhibited not only by want of constitutional authority, but by good faith as vendors, from disquieting a title emanating from themselves. As soon, however, as the Northern States that prohibited African slavery within their limits had reached a number sufficient to give their representation a controlling voice in the Congress, a persistent and organized system of hostile measures against the rights of the owners of slaves in the Southern States was inaugurated and gradually extended. . . . Senators and Representatives were sent to the common councils of the nation whose chief title to this distinction consisted in the display of a spirit of ultra-fanaticism, and whose business was not 'to promote the general welfare or insure domestic tranquillity', but to awaken the bitterest hatred against the citizens of sister States by violent denunciation of their institutions; the transaction of public affairs was impeded by repeated efforts to usurp powers not delegated by the Constitution, for the purpose of impairing the security of property in slaves, and reducing those States which held slaves to a condition of inferiority. Finally a great party was organized for the purpose of obtaining the administration of the Government, with the avowed object of using its power for the total exclusion of the slave States from all participation in the benefits of the public domain acquired by all the States in common, whether by conquest or purchase; of surrounding them entirely by States in which slavery should be prohibited; of thus rendering the property in slaves so insecure as to be comparatively worthless, and thereby annihilating in effect property worth thousands of millions of dollars. This party, thus organized, succeeded in the month of November last in the election of its candidate for the Presidency of the United States.

In the meantime, the African slaves had augmented in number from about 600,000, at the date of the adoption of the constitutional compact, to upward of 4,000,000. In moral and social condition they had been elevated from brutal savages into docile, intelligent, and civilized agricultural laborers, and supplied not only with bodily comforts but with careful religious instruction. Under the supervision of a superior race their labor had been so directed as not only to allow a gradual and marked amelioration of their own condition, but to convert hundreds of thousands of square miles of the wilderness into cultivated lands covered with a prosperous people; towns and cities had sprung into existence, and had rapidly increased in wealth and population under the social system of the South; the white population of the Southern slaveholding States had augmented from about 1,250,000 at the date of the adoption of the Constitution to more than 8,500,000 in 1860; and the productions in the South of cotton, rice, sugar, and tobacco, for the full development and continuance of which the labor of African slaves was and is indispensable, had swollen to an amount which formed nearly three-fourths of the exports of the whole United States and had become absolutely necessary to the wants of civilized man. With interests of such overwhelming magnitude imperilled, the people of the Southern States were driven by the conduct of the North to the adoption of some course of action to avert the danger with which they were openly menaced. With this view the Legislatures of the several States invited the people to select delegates to conventions to be held for the purpose of determining for themselves what measures were best. . . .

☆

President Abraham Lincoln's Gettysburg Address, 1863

"Fourscore and seven years ago our fathers brought forth on this continent a new nation, conceived in liberty and dedicated to the proposition that all men are created equal. Now we are engaged in a great civil war, testing whether that nation or any nation so conceived and so dedicated can long endure. We are met on a great battlefield of that war. We have come to dedicate a portion of that field as a final resting-place for those who here gave their lives that that nation might live. It is altogether fitting and proper that we should do this. But in a larger sense, we cannot dedicate, we cannot consecrate, we cannot hallow this ground. The brave men, living and dead who struggled here have consecrated it far above our poor power to add or detract. The world will little note nor long remember what we say here, but it can never forget what they did here. It is for us the living rather to be dedicated here to the unfinished work which they who fought here have thus far so nobly advanced. It is rather for us to be here dedicated to the great task remaining before us—that from these honored dead we take increased devotion to that cause for which they gave the last full measure of devotion—that we here highly resolve that these dead shall not have died in vain, that this nation under God shall have a new birth of freedom, and that government of the people, by the people, for the people shall not perish from the earth."

The Emancipation Proclamation, 1864

By the President of the United States of America:

Whereas on the 22nd day of September, A.D. 1862, a proclamation was issued by the President of the United States, containing, among other things, the following, to wit:

"That on the 1st day of January, A.D. 1863, all persons held as slaves within any State or designated part of a State the people whereof shall then be in rebellion against the United States shall be then, thenceforward, and forever free; and the executive government of the United States, including the military and naval authority thereof, will recognize and maintain the freedom of such persons and will do no act or acts to repress such persons, or any of them, in any efforts they may make for their actual freedom.

"That the executive will on the 1st day of January aforesaid, by proclamation, designate the States and parts of States, if any, in which the people thereof, respectively, shall then be in rebellion against the United States; and the fact that any State or the people thereof shall on that day be in good faith represented in the Congress of the United States by members chosen thereto at elections wherein a majority of the qualified voters of such States shall have participated shall, in the absence of strong countervailing testimony, be deemed conclusive evidence that such State and the people thereof are not then in rebellion against the United States."

Now, therefore, I, Abraham Lincoln, President of the United States, by virtue of the power in me vested as Commander-In-Chief of the Army and Navy of the United States in time of actual armed rebellion against the authority and government of the United States, and as a fit and necessary war measure for suppressing said rebellion, do, on this 1st day of January, A.D. 1863, and in accordance with my purpose so to do, publicly proclaimed for the full period of one hundred days from the first day above mentioned, order and designate as the States and parts of States wherein the people thereof, respectively, are this day in rebellion against the United States the following, to wit:

Arkansas, Texas, Louisiana (except the parishes of St. Bernard, Palquemines, Jefferson, St. John, St. Charles, St. James, Ascension, Assumption, Terrebone, Lafourche, St. Mary, St. Martin, and Orleans, including the city of New Orleans), Mississippi, Alabama, Florida, Georgia, South Carolina, North Carolina, and Virginia (except the forty-eight counties designated as West Virginia, and also the counties of Berkeley, Accomac, Northhampton, Elizabeth City, York, Princess Anne, and Norfolk, including the cities of Norfolk and Portsmouth), and which excepted parts are for the present left precisely as if this proclamation were not issued.

And by virtue of the power and for the purpose aforesaid, I do order and declare that all persons held as slaves within said designated States and parts of States are, and henceforward shall be, free; and that the Executive Government of the United States, including the military and naval authorities thereof, will recognize and maintain the freedom of said persons.

And I hereby enjoin upon the people so declared to be free to abstain from all violence, unless in necessary self-defence; and I recommend to them that, in all case when allowed, they labor faithfully for reasonable wages.

And I further declare and make known that such persons of suitable condition will be received into the armed service of the United States to garrison forts, positions, stations, and other places, and to man vessels of all sorts in said service.

And upon this act, sincerely believed to be an act of justice, warranted by the Constitution upon military necessity, I invoke the considerate judgment of mankind and the gracious favor of Almighty God.

President Abraham Lincoln's Second Inaugural Address, 1864

In November, 1864, President Lincoln was reelected. His Second Inaugural Address, delivered a few weeks before he was murdered, expressed in its final paragraph the President's high hopes and indicated what his future course would be.

Fellow-Countrymen: At this second appearing to take the oath of the Presidential office there is less occasion for an extended address than there was at the first. Then a statement somewhat in detail of a course to be pursued seemed fitting and proper. Now, at the expiration of four years, during which public declarations have been constantly called forth on every point and phase of the great contest which still absorbs the attention and engrosses the energies of the nation, little that is new could be presented. The progress of our arms, upon which all else chiefly depends, is as well known to the public as to myself, and it is, I trust, reasonably satisfactory and encouraging to all. With high hope for the future, no prediction in regard to it is ventured.

On the occasion corresponding to this four years ago all thoughts were anxiously directed to an impending civil war. All dreaded it; all sought to avert it. While the inaugural address was being delivered from this place, devoted altogether to *saving* the Union without war, insurgent agents were in the city seeking to *destroy* it without war—seeking to dissolve the Union and divide effects by negotiation. Both parties deprecated war, but one of them would *make* war rather than let the nation survive, and the other would *accept* war rather than let it perish, and the war came.

One-eighth of the whole population were colored slaves, not distributed generally over the Union, but localized in the southern part of it. These slaves constituted a peculiar and powerful interest. All knew that this interest was somehow the cause of the war. To strengthen, perpetuate, and extend this interest was the object for which the insurgents would rend the Union even by war, while the Government claimed no right to do more than to restrict the territorial enlargement of it. Neither party expected for the war the magnitude or the duration which it has already attained. Neither anticipated that the *cause* of the conflict might cease with or even before the conflict itself should cease. Each looked for an easier triumph, and a result less fundamental and astounding. Both read the same Bible and pray to the same God, and each invokes His aid against the other. It may seem strange that any men should dare to ask a just God's assistance in wringing their bread from the sweat of other men's faces, but let us judge not, that we be not judged. The prayers of both could not be answered. That of neither has been answered fully. The Almighty has His own purposes. "Woe unto the world because of offenses; for it must needs be that offenses come, but woe to that man by whom the offense cometh." If we shall suppose that American slavery is one of those offenses which, in the providence of God, must needs come, but which, having continued through His appointed time, He now wills to remove, and that He gives to both North and South this terrible war as the woe due to those by whom the offense came, shall we discern therein any departure from those divine attributes which the believers in a living God always ascribe to Him? Fondly do we hope, fervently do we pray, that this mighty scourge of war may speedily pass away. Yet, if God wills that it continue until all the wealth piled by the bondsman's two hundred and fifty years of unrequited toil shall be sunk, and until every drop of blood drawn with the lash shall be paid by another drawn with the sword, as was said three thousand years ago, so still it must be said "the judgments of the Lord are true and righteous altogether."

With malice toward none, with charity for all, with firmness in the right as God gives us to see the right, let us strive on to finish the work we are in, to bind up the nation's wounds, to care for him who shall have borne the battle and for his widow and his orphan, to do all which may achieve and cherish a just and lasting peace among ourselves and with all nations.

Nez Perce Chief Joseph's Speech Upon Surrender to the U.S. Army, 1877

In 1877, the Nez Perce Indians were ordered off their lands in the Oregon Territory to a reservation in Idaho. Nez Perce Chief Joseph and members of his tribe tried to escape to Canada. Along the way they fought several battles with the United States Army, to whom they finally surrendered on October 5, 1877. This is Chief Joseph's surrender speech.

Tell General Howard I know his heart. What he told me before, I have it in my heart. I am tired of fighting. Our Chiefs are killed; Looking Glass is dead, Ta Hool Hool Shute is dead. The old men are all dead. It is the young men who say yes or no. He who led on the young men is dead. It is cold, and we have no blankets; the little children are freezing to death. My people, some of them, have run away to the hills, and have no blankets, no food. No one knows where they are—perhaps freezing to death. I want to have time to look for my children, and see how many of them I can find. Maybe I shall find them among the dead. Hear me, my Chiefs! I am tired; my heart is sick and sad. From where the sun now stands I will fight no more forever.

President William McKinley's Message to Congress concerning War with Spain, 1898

On April 11, 1898, President William McKinley sent a message to Congress, requesting a declaration of war against Spain. Congress declared war on April 20.

A part of the President's message is quoted below. It had several purposes in view, in addition to the obvious one. It was designed to be read and studied by people in other countries as a justification of the fight with Spain. It was also intended to influence the American public to support the war by summing up the "case" against Spain.

To the Congress of the United States:

Obedient to that precept of the Constitution which commands the President to give from time to time to the Congress information of the state of the Union and to recommend to their consideration such measures as he shall judge necessary and expedient, it becomes my duty to now address your body with regard to the grave crisis that has arisen in the relations of the United States to Spain by reason of the warfare that for more than three years has raged in the neighboring island of Cuba. . . .

The present revolution is but the successor of other similar insurrections which have occurred in Cuba against the dominion of Spain, extending over a period of nearly half a century, each of which during its progress has subjected the United States to great effort and expense in enforcing its neutrality laws, caused enormous losses to American trade and commerce, caused irritation, annoyance, and disturbance among our citizens, and, by the exterior of cruel, barbarous, and uncivilized practices of warfare, shocked the sensibilities and offended the human sympathies of our people.

Our trade has suffered, the capital invested by our citizens in Cuba has been largely lost, and the temper and forbearance of our people have been so sorely tried as to beget a perilous unrest among our own citizens, which has inevitably found its expression from time to time in the National Legislature, so that issues wholly external to our own body politic engross attention and stand in the way of that close devotion to domestic advancement that becomes a self-contained commonwealth whose primal maxim has been the avoidance of all foreign entanglements. All this must needs awaken, and has, indeed, aroused, the utmost concern on the part of this Government, as well during my predecessor's term as in my own.

In April 1896, the evils from which our country suffered through the Cuban War became so onerous that my predecessor made an effort to bring about a peace through the mediation of this Government in any way that might tend to an honorable adjustment of the contest between Spain and her revolted colony, on the basis of some effective scheme of self-government for Cuba under the flag and sovereignty of Spain. It failed through the refusal of the Spanish government then in power to consider any form of mediation or, indeed, any plan of settlement which did not begin with the actual submission of the insurgents to the mother country, and then only on such terms as Spain herself might see fit to grant. . . .

The overtures of this Government made through its new envoy, General Woodford, and looking to an immediate and effective amelioration of the condition of the island, although not accepted to the extent of admitted mediation in any shape, were met by assurances that home rule in an advanced phase would be forthwith offered to Cuba, without waiting for the war to end, and that more humane methods should thenceforth prevail in the conduct of hostilities. Coincidentally with those declarations the new government of Spain continued and completed the policy, already begun by its predecessor, of testifying friendly regard for this nation by releasing American citizens held under one charge or another connected with the insurrection, so that by the end of November not a single person entitled in any way to our national protection remained in a Spanish prison. . . .

The war in Cuba is of such a nature that, short of subjugation or extermination, a final military victory for either side seems impracticable. The alternative lies in the physical exhaustion of the one or the other party, or perhaps of both. . . .

Realizing this, it appeared to be my duty, in a spirit of true friendliness, no less to Spain than to the Cubans, who have so much to lose by the prolongation of the struggle, to seek to bring about an immediate termination of the war. To this end I submitted on the 27th ultimo, as a result of much representation and correspondence, through the United States minister at Madrid, propositions to the Spanish Government looking to an armistice until 1 October for the negotiation of peace with the good offices of the President.

In addition I asked the immediate revocation of the order of reconcentration, so as to permit the people to return to their farms and the needy to be relieved with provisions and supplies from the United States, cooperating with the Spanish authorities, so as to afford full relief.

The reply of the Spanish Cabinet was received on the night of the 31st ultimo. It offered, as the means to bring about peace in Cuba, to confide the preparation thereof to the insular parliament, inasmuch as the concurrence of that body would be necessary to reach a final result, it being, however, understood that the powers reserved by the constitution to the central Government are not lessened or diminished. As the Cuban parliament does not meet until the 4th of May next, the Spanish Government would not object for its part to accept at once a suspension of hostilities if asked for by the insurgents from the general in chief, to whom it would pertain in such case to determine the duration and conditions of the armistice. . . .

With this last overture in the direction of immediate peace, and its disappointing reception by Spain, the Executive is brought to the end of his effort.

In my annual message of December last I said:

Of the untried measures there remain only: recognition of the insurgents as belligerents; recognition of the independence of Cuba; neutral intervention to end the war by imposing a rational compromise between the contestants, and intervention in favor of one or the other party. I speak not of forcible annexation, for that can not be thought of. That, by our code of morality, would be criminal aggression. . . .

There remain the alternative forms of intervention to end the war, either as an impartial neutral, by imposing a rational compromise between the contestants, or as the active ally of the one party or the other.

As to the first, it is not to be forgotten that during the last few months the relation of the United States has virtually been one of friendly intervention in many ways, each not of itself conclusive, but all tending to the pacific result, just and honorable to all interests concerned. The spirit of all our acts hitherto has been an earnest, unselfish desire for peace and prosperity in Cuba, untarnished by differences between us and Spain and unstained by the blood of American citizens.

The forcible intervention of the United States as a neutral to stop the war, according to the large dictates of humanity and following many historical precedents where neighbouring States have interfered to check the hopeless sacrifices of life by internecine conflicts beyond their borders, is justifiable on rational grounds. It involves, however hostile constraint upon both the parties to the contest, as well to enforce a truce as to guide the eventual settlement.

The grounds for such intervention may be briefly summarized as follows:

First. In the cause of humanity and to put an end to the barbarities, bloodshed, starvation, and horrible miseries now existing there, and which the parties to the conflict are either unable or unwilling to stop or mitigate. It is no answer to say this is all in another country, belonging to another nation, and is therefore none of our business. It is specially our duty, for it is right at our door.

Second. We owe it to our citizens in Cuba to afford them that protection and indemnity for life and property which no government there can or will afford, and to that end to terminate the conditions that deprive them of legal protection.

Third. The right to intervene may be justified by the very serious injury to the commerce, trade, and business of our people and by the wanton destruction of property and devastation of the island.

Fourth, and which is of the utmost importance. The present condition of affairs in Cuba is a constant menace to our peace and entails upon the Government an enormous expense. With such a conflict waged for years in an island so near us and with which our people have such trade and business relations; when the lives and liberty of our citizens are in constant danger and their property destroyed and themselves ruined; where our trading vessels are liable to seizure and are seized at our very door by war ships of a foreign nation; the expeditions of filibustering that we are powerless to prevent altogether, and the irritating questions and entanglements thus arising—all these and others that I need not mention, with the resulting strained relations, are a constant menace to our peace and compel us to keep on a semi-war footing with a nation with which we are at peace.

These elements of danger and disorder already pointed out have been strikingly illustrated by a tragic event which has deeply and justly moved the American people. I have already transmitted to Congress the report of the naval court of inquiry on the destruction of the battleship *Maine* in the harbor of Havana during the night of the 15th of February. The destruction of that noble vessel has filled the national heart with inexpressible horror. Two hundred and fifty-eight brave sailors and marines and two officers of our Navy, reposing in the fancied security of a friendly harbor, have been hurled to death, grief and want brought to their homes, and sorrow to the nation.

The naval court of inquiry, which, it is needless to say, commands the unqualified confidence of the Government, was unanimous in its conclusion that the destruction of the *Maine* was caused by an exterior explosion—that of a submarine mine. It did not assume to place the responsibility. That remains to be fixed.

In any event, the destruction of the *Maine,* by whatever exterior cause, is a patent and impressive proof of a state of things in Cuba that is intolerable. . . .

The long trial has proved that the object for which Spain has waged the war cannot be attained. The fire of insurrection may flame or may smolder with varying seasons, but it has not been and it is plain that it cannot be extinguished by present methods. The only hope of relief and repose from a condition which can no longer be endured is the enforced pacification of Cuba. In the name of humanity, in the name of civilization, in behalf of endangered American interests which give us the right and the duty to speak and to act, the war in Cuba must stop.

In view of these facts and of these considerations I ask the Congress to authorize and empower the President to take measures to secure a full and final termination of hostilities between the Government of Spain and the people of Cuba, and to secure in the island the establishment of a stable government, capable of maintaining order and observing its international obligations, insuring peace and tranquillity and the security of its citizens as well as our own, and to use the military and naval forces of the United States as may be necessary for these purposes. . . .

President Woodrow Wilson's Appeal for American Neutrality, 1914

When the "Great War" broke out in Europe in August, 1914, President Woodrow Wilson proclaimed American neutrality. In the first document that follows, he appealed to the people of the United States to be truly neutral. However, this appeal, and others that the President made to the belligerents, did not halt the war and the President was obliged to ask Congress for a declaration of war against the Central Powers (principally Germany and Austria-Hungary). His reasons will be found in the second document that follows.

Appeal for Neutrality, August 19, 1914

My Fellow Countrymen:

I suppose that every thoughtful man in America has asked himself, during these last troubled weeks, what influence the European war may exert upon the United States, and I take the liberty of addressing a few words to you in order to point out that it is entirely within our own choice what its effects upon us will be and to urge very earnestly upon you the sort of speech and conduct which will best safeguard the Nation against distress and disaster.

The effect of the war upon the United States will depend upon what American citizens say and do. Every man who really loves America will act and speak in the true spirit of neutrality, which is the spirit of impartiality and fairness and friendliness to all concerned. The spirit of the Nation in this critical matter will be determined largely by what individuals and society and those gathered in public meetings do and say, upon what newspapers and magazines contain, upon what ministers utter in their pulpits, and men proclaim as their opinions on the street.

The people of the United States are drawn from many nations, and chiefly from the nations now at war. It is natural and inevitable that there should be the utmost variety of sympathy and desire among them with regard to the issues and circumstances of the conflict. Some will wish one nation, others another, to succeed in the momentous struggle. It will be easy to excite passion and difficult to allay it. Those responsible for exciting it will assume a heavy responsibility, responsibility for no less a thing than that the people of the United States, whose love of their country and whose loyalty to its Government should unite them as Americans all, bound in honor and affection to think first of her and her interests, may be divided in camps of hostile opinion, hot against each other, involved in the war itself in impulse and opinion if not in action.

Such divisions among us would be fatal to our peace of mind and might seriously stand in the way of the proper performance of our duty as the one great nation at peace, the one people holding itself ready to play a part of impartial mediation and speak to counsels of peace and accommodation, not as a partisan, but as a friend.

I venture, therefore, my fellow countrymen, to speak a solemn word of warning to you against that deepest, most subtle, most essential breach of neutrality which may spring out of partisanship, out of passionately taking sides. The United States must be neutral in fact as well as in name during these days that are to try men's souls. We must be impartial in thought as well as in action, must put a curb upon our sentiments as well as upon every transaction that might be construed as a preference of one party to the struggle before another.

My thought is of America. I am speaking, I feel sure, the earnest wish and purpose of every thoughtful American that this great country of ours, which is, of course, the first in our thoughts and in our hearts, should show herself in this time of peculiar trial a Nation fit beyond others to exhibit the fine poise of undisturbed judgment, the dignity of self-control, the efficiency of dispassionate action; a Nation that neither sits in judgment upon others nor is disturbed in her own counsels and which keeps herself fit and free to do what is honest and disinterested and truly serviceable for the peace of the world.

Shall we not resolve to put upon ourselves the restraints which will bring to our people the happiness and the great and lasting influence for peace we covet for them?

President Woodrow Wilson's War Message to Congress, 1917

Gentlemen of the Congress: I have called the Congress into extraordinary session because there are serious, very serious, choices of policy to be made, and made immediately, which it was neither right nor constitutionally permissible that I should assume the responsibility of making.

On the 3d of February last I officially laid before you the extraordinary announcement of the Imperial German Government that on and after the 1st day of February it was its purpose to put aside all restraints of law or of humanity and use its submarines to sink every vessel that sought to approach either the ports of Great Britain and Ireland or the western coasts of Europe or any of the ports controlled by the enemies of Germany within the Mediterranean. That had seemed to be the object of the German submarine warfare earlier in the war, but since April of last year the Imperial Government had somewhat restrained the commanders of its undersea craft in conformity with its promise then given to us that passenger boats should not be sunk and that due warning would be given to all other vessels which its submarines might seek to destroy, when no resistance was offered or escape attempted, and care taken that their crews were given at least a fair chance to save their lives in their open boats. The precautions taken were meagre and haphazard enough, as was proved in distressing instance after instance in the progress of the cruel and unmanly business, but a certain degree of restraint was observed. The new policy has swept every restriction aside. Vessels of every kind, whatever their flag, their character, their cargo, their destination, their errand, have been ruthlessly sent to the bottom without warning and without thought of help or mercy for those on board, the vessels of friendly neutrals along with those of belligerents. Even hospital ships and ships carrying relief to the sorely bereaved and stricken people of Belgium, though the latter were provided with safe-conduct through the proscribed areas by the German Government itself and were distinguished by unmistakable marks of identity, have been sunk with the same reckless lack of compassion or of priciple.

It is a war against all nations. American ships have been sunk, American lives taken, in ways which it has stirred us very deeply to learn of, but the ships and people of other neutral and friendly nations have been sunk and overwhelmed in the waters in the same way. There has been no discrimination. The challenge is to all mankind. . . .

With a profound sense of the solemn and even tragical character of the step I am taking and of the grave responsibilities which it involves, but in unhesitating obedience to what I deem my constitutional duty, I advise that the Congress declare the recent course of the Imperial German Government to be in fact nothing less than war against the Government and people of the United States; that it formally accept the status of belligerent which has thus been thrust upon it; and that it take immediate steps not only to put the country in a more thorough state of defense but also to exert all its power and employ all its resources to bring the Government of the German Empire to terms and end the war. . . .

While we do these things, these deeply momentous things, let us be very clear, and make very clear to all the world what our motives and our object are. My own thought has not been driven from its habitual and normal course by the unhappy events of the last two months, and I do not believe that the thought of the nation has been altered or clouded by them. . . . Our object now, as then, is to vindicate the principles of peace and justice in the life of the world as against selfish and autocratic power and to set up amongst the really free and self-governed peoples of the world such a concert of purpose and of action as will henceforth ensure the observance of those principles. Neutrality is no longer feasible or desirable where the peace of the world is involved and the freedom of its peoples, and the menace to that peace and freedom lies in the existence of autocratic governments backed by organized force which is controlled wholly by their will, not by the will of their people. We have seen the last of neutrality in such circumstances. We are at the beginning of an age in which it will be insisted that the same standards of conduct and of responsibility for wrong done shall be observed among nations and their governments that are observed among the individual citizens of civilized states.

We have no quarrel with the German people. We have no feeling toward them but one of sympathy and friendship. It was not upon their impulse that their Government acted in entering this war. It was not with their previous knowledge or approval. It was a war determined upon as wars used to be determined upon in the old, unhappy days when peoples were nowhere consulted by their rulers and wars were provoked and waged in the interest of dynasties or of little groups of ambitious men who were accustomed to use their fellow men as pawns and tools. Self-governed nations do not fill their neighbour states with spies or set the course of intrigue to bring about some critical posture of affairs which will give them an opportunity to strike and make conquest. Such designs can be successfully worked out only under cover and where no one has the right to ask questions. Cunningly contrived plans of deception or aggression, carried, it may be, from generation to generation, can be worked out and kept from the light only within the privacy of courts or behind the carefully guarded confidences of a narrow and privileged class. They are happily impossible where public opinion commands and insists upon full information concerning all the nation's affairs.

A steadfast concert for peace can never be maintained except by a partnership of democratic nations. No autocratic government could be trusted to keep faith within it or observe its covenants. It must be a league of honour, a partnership of opinion. Intrigue would eat its vitals away; the plottings of inner circles who could plan what they would and render account to no one would be a curruption seated at its very heart. Only free peoples can hold their purpose and their honour steady to a common end and prefer the interests of mankind to any narrow interest of their own. . . .

One of the things that has served to convince us that the Prussian autocracy was not and could never be our friend is that from the very outset of the present war it has filled our unsuspecting communities and even our offices of government with spies and set criminal intrigues everywhere afoot against our national unity of counsel, our peace within and without, our industries and our commerce. . . .

We are accepting this challenge of hostile purpose because we know that in such a government, following such methods, we can never have a friend; and that in the presence of its organized power, always lying in wait to accomplish we know not what purpose, there can be no assured security for the democratic governments of the world. We are now about to accept gage of battle with this natural foe to liberty and shall, if necessary, spend the whole force of the nation to check and nullify its pretensions and its power. We are glad, now that we see the facts with no veil of false pretence about them, to fight thus for the ultimate peace of the world and for the liberation of its peoples, the German peoples included: for the rights of nations great and small and the privilege of men everywhere to choose their way of life and of obedience. The world must be made safe for democracy. Its peace must be planted upon the tested foundations of political liberty. We have no selfish ends to serve. We desire no conquest, no dominion. We seek no indemnities for ourselves, no material compensation for the sacrifices we shall freely make. We are but one of the champions of the rights of mankind. . . .

It is a distressing and oppressive duty, gentlemen of the Congress, which I have performed in thus addressing you. There are, it may be, many months of fiery trial and sacrifice ahead of us. It is a fearful thing to lead this great peaceful people into war, into the most terrible and disastrous of all wars, civilization itself seeming to be in the balance. But the right is more precious than peace, and we shall fight for the things which we have always carried nearest our hearts—for democracy, for the right of those who submit to authority to have a voice in their own governments for the rights and liberties of small nations, for a universal dominion of right by such a concert of free peoples as shall bring peace and safety to all nations and make the world itself at last free. To such a task we can dedicate our lives and our fortunes, everything that we are and everything that we have, with the pride of those who know that the day has come when America is privileged to spend her blood and her might for the principles that gave her birth and happiness and the peace which she has treasured. God helping her, she can do no other.

President Woodrow Wilson's Fourteen Points

Even though the war of 1914–1918 was the greatest bloodbath in history until that time, there were serious hopes and plans for peace after the fighting ended. President Wilson seized the imagination of all the countries in the war with his appeal for peace based on "Fourteen Points", which he set forth in a speech to Congress on January 8, 1918. The text of these famous "points"—the President's program for lasting peace—reads as follows.

I. Open covenants of peace, openly arrived at, after which there shall be no private international understandings of any kind but diplomacy shall proceed always frankly and in the public eye.

II. Absolute freedom of navigation upon the seas, outside territorial waters, alike in peace and in war, except as the seas may be closed in whole or in part by international action for the enforcement of international covenants.

III. The removal, so far as possible, of all economic barriers and the establishment of an equality of trade conditions among all the nations consenting to the peace and associating themselves for its maintenance.

IV. Adequate guarantees given and taken that national armaments will be reduced to the lowest point consistent with domestic safety.

V. A free, open-minded, and absolutely impartial adjustment of all colonial claims, based upon a strict observance of the principle that in determining all such questions of sovereignty the interests of the populations concerned must have equal weight with the equitable claims of the government whose title is to be determined.

VI. The evacuation of all Russian territory and such a settlement of all questions affecting Russia as will secure the best and freest coöperation of the other nations of the world in obtaining for her an unhampered and unembarrassed opportunity for the independent determination of her own political development and national policy and assure her of a sincere welcome into the society of free nations under institutions of her own choosing; and, more than a welcome, assistance also of every kind that she may need and may herself desire. The treatment accorded Russia by her sister nations in the months to come will be the acid test of their good will, of their comprehension of her needs as distinguished from their own interests, and of their intelligent and unselfish sympathy.

VII. Belgium, the whole world will agree, must be evacuated and restored, without any attempt to limit the sovereignty which she enjoys in common with all other free nations. No other single act will serve as this will serve to restore confidence among the nations in the laws which they have themselves set and determined for the government of their relations with one another. Without this healing act the whole structure and validity of international law is forever impaired.

VIII. All French territory should be freed and the invaded portions restored, and the wrong done to France by Prussia in 1871 in the matter of Alsace-Lorraine, which has unsettled the peace of the world for nearly fifty years, should be righted, in order that peace may once more be made secure in the interest of all.

IX. A readjustment of the frontiers of Italy should be affected along clearly recognizable lines of nationality.

X. The peoples of Austria-Hungary, whose place among the nations we wish to see safeguarded and assured, should be accorded the freest opportunity of autonomous development.

XI. Rumania, Serbia, and Montenegro should be evacuated; occupied territories restored; Serbia accorded free and secure access to the sea; and the relations of the several Balkan states to one another determined by friendly counsel along historically established lines of allegiance and nationality; and international guarantees of the political and economic independence and territorial integrity of the several Balkan states should be entered into.

XII. The Turkish portions of the present Ottoman Empire should be assured a secure sovereignty, but the other nationalities which are now under Turkish rule should be assured an undoubted security of life and an absolutely unmolested opportunity of autonomous development and the Dardanelles should be permanently opened as a free passage to the ships and commerce of all nations under international guarantees.

XIII. An independent Polish state should be erected which should include the territories inhabited by indisputably Polish populations, which should be assured a free and secure access to the sea, and whose political and economic independence and territorial integrity should be guaranteed by international covenant.

XIV. A general association of nations must be formed under specific covenants for the purpose of affording mutual guarantees of political independence and territorial integrity to great and small states alike.

Neutrality Act of 1937

At the start of this period in our history, most Americans could be called "isolationists". They wished no part in foreign wars, and saw little connection between events abroad and the well-being of the United States. When Civil War broke out in Spain in 1936, several European powers sent aid to one or another of the warring sides. Americans responded to the war threat by passing a strict new Neutrality Act in 1937. Important sections are quoted below. It was intended to eliminate the kind of problem that led the United States directly into World War I.

JOINT RESOLUTION.

To amend the joint resolution, approved 31 August 1935, as amended.

Resolved . . .

SEC 1. (*a*) Whenever the President shall find that there exists a state of war between, or among, two or more foreign States, the President shall proclaim such fact, and it shall thereafter be unlawful to export, or attempt to export, or cause to be exported, arms, ammunition, or implements of war from any place in the United States to any belligerent State named in such proclamation, or to any neutral State for transshipment to, or for the use of, any such belligerent State.

(*b*) The President shall, from time to time, by proclamation, extend such embargo upon the export of arms, ammunition, or implements of war to other States as and when they may become involved in such war.

(*c*) Whenever the President shall find that a state of civil strife exists in a foreign State and that such civil strife is of a magnitude or is being conducted under such conditions that the export of arms, ammunition, or implements of war from the United States to such foreign State would threaten or endanger the peace of the United States, the President shall proclaim such fact, and it shall thereafter be unlawful to export, or attempt to export, or cause to be exported, arms, ammunition, or implements of war from any place in the United States to such foreign State, or to any neutral State for transshipment to, or for the use of, such foreign State.

(*d*) The President shall, from time to time by proclamation, definitely enumerate the arms, ammunition, and implements of war, the export of which is prohibited by this section.

SEC. 2. (*a*) Whenever the President shall have issued a proclamation under the authority of section 1 of this Act and he shall thereafter find that the placing of restrictions on the shipment of certain articles or materials in addition to arms, ammunition, and implements of war from the United States to belligerent States, or to a State wherein civil strife exists, is necessary to promote the security or preserve the peace of the United States or to protect the lives of citizens of the United States, he shall so proclaim, and it shall thereafter be unlawful, for any American vessel to carry such articles or materials to any belligerent State, or to a State wherein civil strife exists, named in such proclamation issued under the authority of section 1 of this Act, or to any neutral State for transshipment to, or for the use of, any such belligerent State or any such State wherein civil strife exists. The President shall by proclamation from time to time definitely enumerate the articles and materials which it shall be unlawful for American vessels to so transport. . . .

(*c*) The President shall from time to time by proclamation extend such restrictions as are imposed under the authority of this section to other States as and when they may be declared to become belligerent States under proclamations issued under the authority of section 1 of this Act. . . .

SEC. 3. (*a*) Whenever the President shall have issued a proclamation under the authority of section 1 of this Act, it shall thereafter be unlawful for any person within the United States to purchase, sell, or exchange bonds, securities, or other obligations of the government of any belligerent State, or of any State wherein civil strife exists, named in such proclamation, or of any political subdivision of any such State, or of any person acting for or on behalf of the government of any such State, or of any faction or asserted government within any such State wherein civil strife exists, or of any person acting for or on behalf of any faction or asserted government within any such State wherein civil strife exists, issued after the date of such proclamation, or to make any loan or extend any credit to any such government, political subdivision, faction, asserted government, or person, or to solicit or receive any contribution for any such government, political subdivision, faction, asserted government, or person: *Provided,* That if the President shall find that such action will serve to protect the commercial or other interests of the United States or its citizens, he may, in his discretion, and to such extent and under such regulations as he may prescribe, except from the operation of this section ordinary commercial credits and short-time obligations in aid of legal transactions and of a character customarily used in normal peacetime commercial transactions. Nothing in this subsection shall be construed to prohibit the solicitation or collection of funds to be used for medical aid and assistance, or for food and clothing to relieve human suffering, when such solicitation or collection of funds is made on behalf of and for use by any person or organization which is not acting for or on behalf of any such government, political subdivision, faction, or asserted government, but all such solicitations and collections of funds shall be subject to the approval of the President and shall be made under such rules and regulations as he shall prescribe. . . .

SEC. 4. This Act shall not apply to an American republic or republics engaged in war against a non-American State or States, provided the American republic is not co-operating with a non-American State or States in such war.

SEC. 5. (*a*) There is hereby established a National Munitions Control Board (hereinafter referred to as the "Board") to carry out the provisions of this Act. The Board shall consist of the Secretary of State, who shall be chairman and executive officer of the Board, the Secretary of the Treasury, the Secretary of War, the Secretary of the Navy, and the Secretary of Commerce. Except as otherwise provided in this Act, or by other law, the administration of this Act is vested in the Department of State. The Secretary of State shall promulgate such rules and regulations with regard to the enforcement of this section as he may deem necessary to carry out its provisions. The Board shall be convened by the chairman and shall hold at least one meeting a year.

(*b*) Every person who engages in the business of manufacturing, exporting, or importing any of the arms, ammunition, or implements of war referred to in this Act, whether as an exporter, importer, manufacturer, or dealer, shall register with the Secretary of State his name, or business name, principal place of business, and places of business in the United States, and a list of the arms, ammunition, and implements of war which he manufactures, imports, or exports.

(*c*) Every person required to register under this section shall notify the Secretary of State of any change in the arms, ammunition, or implements of war which he exports, imports, or manufactures; . . .

(*d*) It shall be unlawful for any person to export, or attempt to export, from the United States to any other State, any of the arms, ammunition, or implements of war referred to in this Act, or to import, or attempt to import, to the United States from any other State, any of the arms, ammunition, or implements of war referred to in this Act, without first having obtained a license therefor. . . .

(*k*) The President is hereby authorized to proclaim upon recommendation of the Board from time to time a list of articles which shall be considered arms, ammunition, and implements of war for the purposes of this section.

SEC. 6. (*a*) Whenever the President shall have issued a proclamation under the authority of section 1 of this Act, it shall thereafter be unlawful, until such proclamation is revoked, for any American vessel to carry any arms, ammunition, or implements of war to any belligerent State, or to any State wherein civil strife exists, named in such proclamation, or to any neutral State for transshipment to, or for the use of, any such belligerent State or any such State wherein civil strife exists. . . .

SEC. 7. (*a*) Whenever, during any war in which the United States is neutral, the President, or any person thereunto authorized by him, shall have cause to believe that any vessel, domestic or foreign, whether requiring clearance or not, is about to carry out of a port of the United States, fuel, men, arms, ammunition, implements of war, or other supplies to any warship, tender, or supply ship of a belligerent State, but the evidence is not deemed sufficient to justify forbidding the departure of the vessel as provided for by section 1, title V, chapter 30, of the Act approved 15 June 1917, and if, in the President's judgment, such action will serve to maintain peace between the United States and foreign States, or to protect the commercial interests of the United States and its citizens, or to promote the security or neutrality of the United States, he shall have the power and it shall be his duty to require the owner, master, or person in command thereof, before departing from a port of the United States, to give a bond to the United States, with sufficient sureties, in such amount as he shall deem proper, conditioned that the vessel will not deliver the men, or any part of the cargo, to any warship, tender, or supply ship of a belligerent State.

(*b*) If the President, or any person thereunto authorized by him, shall find that a vessel, domestic or foreign, in a port of the United States, has previously cleared from a port of the United States during such war and delivered its cargo or any part thereof to a warship, tender, or supply ship of belligerent State, he may prohibit the departure of such vessel during the duration of the war.

SEC. 8. Whenever, during any war in which the United States is neutral, the President shall find that special restrictions placed on the use of the ports and territorial waters of the United States by the submarines or armed merchant vessels of a foreign State, will serve to maintain peace between the United States and foreign States, or to protect the commercial interests of the United States and its citizens, or to promote the security of the United States, and shall make proclamation therefore, it shall thereafter be unlawful for any such submarine or armed merchant vessel to enter a port or the territorial waters of the United States or to depart therefrom, except under such conditions and subject to such limitations as the President may prescribe. Whenever, in his judgment, the conditions which have caused him to issue his proclamation have ceased to exist, he shall revoke his proclamation, and the provisions of this section shall thereupon cease to apply.

SEC. 9. Whenever the President shall have issued a proclamation under the authority of section 1 of this Act it shall thereafter be unlawful for any citizen of the President to travel on any vessel of the State or States named in such proclamation, except in accordance with such rules and regulations as the President shall prescribe: . . .

SEC. 10. Whenever the President shall have issued a proclamation under the authority of section 1, it shall thereafter be unlawful, until such proclamation is revoked, for any American vessel engaged in commerce with any belligerent State, or any State wherein civil strife exists, named in such proclamation, to be armed or to carry any armament, arms, ammunition, or implements of war, except small arms and ammunition therefor which the President may deem necessary and shall publicly designate for the preservation of discipline aboard such vessels. . . .

President Franklin D. Roosevelt's Message to Congress concerning WWII, 1941

During the late months of 1941, the United States drifted closer to full-scale war. In the Atlantic, American destroyers escorted merchant ships past German submarines; in the Pacific, American and Japanese interests also clashed. The opening guns of actual war were fired over Hawaii, when a Japanese naval task force struck Pearl Harbor, December 7, 1941. This surprise attack, which was highly successful, led to a declaration of war. President Roosevelt's brief talk to Congress, requesting the declaration, follows.

Yesterday, December 7, 1941—a date which will live in infamy—the United States of America was suddenly and deliberately attacked by naval and air forces of the empire of Japan.

The United States was at peace with that nation and, at the solicitation of Japan, was still in conversation with its government and its emperor looking toward the maintenance of peace in the Pacific.

Indeed, one hour after Japanese air squadrons had commenced bombing in the American Island of Oahu the Japanese Ambassador to the United States and his colleague delivered to our Secretary of State a formal reply to a recent American message. And, while this reply stated that it seemed useless to continue the existing diplomatic negotiations, it contained no threat or hint of war or of armed attack.

It will be recorded that the distance of Hawaii from Japan makes it obvious that the attack was deliberately planned many days or even weeks ago. During the intervening time the Japanese Government has deliberately sought to deceive the United States by false statements and expressions of hope for continued peace.

The attack yesterday on the Hawaiian Islands has caused severe damage to American naval and military forces. I regret to tell you that very many American lives have been lost. In addition American ships have been reported torpedoed on the high seas between San Francisco and Honolulu.

Yesterday the Japanese Government also launched an attack against Malaya.

Last night Japanese forces attacked Hong Kong.

Last night Japanese forces attacked Guam.

Last night Japanese forces attacked the Philippine Islands.

Last night the Japanese attacked Wake Island.

And this morning the Japanese attacked Midway Island.

Japan has therefore undertaken a surprise offensive extending throughout the Pacific area. The facts of yesterday and today speak for themselves. The people of the United States have already formed their opinions and well understand the implications to the very life and safety of our nation.

As Commander in Chief of the Army and Navy I have directed that all measures be taken for our defense.

Always will our whole nation remember the character of the onslaught against us.

No matter how long it may take us to overcome this premeditated invasion, the American people, in their righteous might, will win through to absolute victory.

I believe that I interpret the will of the Congress and of the people when I assert that we will not only defend ourselves to the uttermost but will make it very certain that this form of treachery shall never again endanger us.

Hostilities exist. There is no blinking at the fact that our people, our territory and our interests are in grave danger.

With confidence in our armed forces, with the unbounding determination of our people, we will gain the inevitable triumph. So help us God.

I ask that the Congress declare that since the unprovoked and dastardly attack by Japan on Sunday, Dec. 7, 1941, a state of war has existed between the United States and the Japanese Empire.

Cairo Conference Report, 1 December 1943

The several military missions have agreed upon future military operations against Japan. The Three Great Allies expressed their resolve to bring unrelenting pressure against their brutal enemies by sea, land, and air. This pressure is already mounting.

The Three Great Allies are fighting this war to restrain and punish the aggression of Japan. They covet no gain for themselves and have no thought of territorial expansion.

It is their purpose that Japan shall be stripped of all the islands in the Pacific which she has seized or occupied since the beginning of the first World War in 1914, and that all the territories Japan has stolen from the Chinese, such as Manchuria, Formosa, and the Pescadores, shall be restored to the Republic of China.

Japan will also be expelled from all other territories which she has taken by violence and greed. The aforesaid three great powers, mindful of the enslavement of the people of Korea, are determined that in due course Korea shall become free and independent.

With these objects in view the three Allies, in harmony with those of the United Nations at war with Japan, will continue to persevere in the serious and prolonged operations necessary to procure the unconditional surrender of Japan.

Agreements at Yalta, 1945 (excerpts)

The military plans for World War II were developed in a series of conferences. President Roosevelt himself attended some, and many other conferences were conducted at lower levels of command. A major problem lay in the differences among the Allied powers, and conferences at the highest level ("Summit") were provided for to prevent such differences from blocking the war effort. A parallel problem was to find a way of preventing international differences from threatening peace after World War II would end. One of the key conferences was held at Yalta, in the Soviet Union. In the following selection, passages from the published Yalta agreements are provided.

I. WORLD ORGANIZATION

1. That a United Nations Conference on the proposed world organization should be summoned for Wednesday, 25 April, 1945, and should be held in the United States of America.

2. The nations to be invited to this conference should be:

(*a*) the United Nations as they existed on the 8 February, 1945, and

(*b*) such of the Associated Nations as have declared war on the common enemy by 1 March, 1945. (For this purpose by the term "Associated Nation" was meant the eight Associated Nations and Turkey.) When the Conference on World Organization is held, the delegates of the United Kingdom and United States of America will support a proposal to admit to original membership two Soviet Socialist republics, *i.e.*, the Ukraine and White Russia.

3. That the United States government on behalf of the Three Powers should consult the government of China and the French Provisional Government in regard to the decisions taken at the present conference concerning the proposed world organization.

4. That the text of the invitation to be issued to all the nations which would take part in the United Nations Conference should be as follows:

The government of the United States of America, on behalf of itself and of the governments of the United Kingdom, the Union of Soviet Socialist Republics, and the Republic of China and of the Provisional Government of the French Republic, invite the government of ——— to send representatives to a Conference of the United Nations to be held on 25 April, 1945, or soon thereafter, at San Francisco in the United States of America to prepare a charter for a general international organization for the maintenance of international peace and security.

The above-named governments suggest that the conference consider as affording a basis for such a charter the proposals for the establishment of a general international organization which were made public last October as a result of the Dumbarton Oaks Conference, and which have now been supplemented by the following provisions for Section C of Chapter VI:

1. Each member of the Security Council should have one vote.

2. Decisions of the Security Council on procedural matters should be made by an affirmative vote of seven members.

3. Decisions of the Security Council on all other matters should be made by an affirmative vote of seven members, including the concurring votes of the permanent members; provided that, in decisions under Chapter VIII, Section A, and under the second sentence of paragraph 1 of Chapter VIII, Section C, a party to a dispute should abstain from voting.

Further information as to arrangements will be transmitted subsequently.

In the event that the government of ——— desires in advance of the conference to present views or comments concerning the proposals, the government of the United States of America will be pleased to transmit such views and comments to the other participating governments.

It was agreed that the five nations which will have permanent seats on the Security Council should consult each other prior to the United Nations Conference on the question of territorial trusteeship.

The acceptance of this recommendation is subject to its being made clear that territorial trusteeship will only apply to (*a*) existing mandates of the League of Nations; (*b*) territories detached from the enemy as a result of the present war; (*c*) any other territory which might voluntarily be placed under trusteeship; and (*d*) no discussion of actual territories is contemplated at the forthcoming United Nations Conference or in the preliminary consultations, and it will be a matter for subsequent agreement which territories within the above categories will be placed under trusteeship.

II. DECLARATION ON LIBERATED EUROPE

The following declaration has been approved:

The Premier of the Union of Soviet Socialist Republics, the Prime Minister of the United Kingdom, and the President of the United States of America have consulted with each other in the common interest of the peoples of their countries and those of liberated Europe. They jointly declare their mutual agreement to concert during the temporary period of instability in liberated Europe the policies of their three governments in assisting the peoples liberated from the domination of Nazi Germany and the peoples of the former Axis satellite states of Europe to solve by democratic means their pressing political and economic problems.

The establishment of order in Europe and the rebuilding of national economic life must be achieved by processes which will enable the liberated peoples to destroy the last vestiges of Nazism and Fascism and to create democratic institutions of their own choice. This is a principle of the Atlantic Charter—the right of all peoples to choose the form of government under which they will live—the restoration of sovereign rights and self-government to those peoples who have been forcibly deprived of them by the aggressor nations.

To foster the conditions in which the liberated peoples may exercise these rights, the three governments will jointly assist the people in any European liberated state or former Axis satellite state in Europe where in their judgment conditions require (*a*) to establish conditions of internal peace; (*b*) to carry out emergency measures for the relief of distressed peoples; (*c*) to form interim governmental authorities broadly representative of all democratic elements in the population and pledged to the earliest possible establishment through free elections of governments responsive to the will of the people; and (*d*) to facilitate where necessary the holding of such elections.

The three governments will consult the other United Nations and provisional authorities or other governments in Europe when matters of direct interest to them are under consideration.

When, in the opinion of the three governments, conditions in any European liberated state or any former Axis satellite state in Europe make such action necessary, they will immediately consult together on the measures necessary to discharge the joint responsibilities set forth in this declaration.

By this declaration we reaffirm our faith in the principles of the Atlantic Charter, our pledge in the Declaration by the United Nations, and our determination to build in cooperation with other peace-loving nations world order under law, dedicated to peace, security, freedom, and general well-being of all mankind.

In issuing this declaration, the Three Powers express the hope that the Provisional Government of the French Republic may be associated with them in the procedure suggested.

III. DISMEMBERMENT OF GERMANY

It was agreed that Article 12 (*a*) of the Surrender Terms for Germany should be amended to read as follows:

> The United Kingdom, the United States of America, and the Union of Soviet Socialist Republics shall possess supreme authority with respect to Germany. In the exercise of such authority they will take such steps, including the complete disarmament, demilitarization, and the dismemberment of Germany as they deem requisite for future peace and security.

The study of the procedure for the dismemberment of Germany was referred to a committee consisting of Mr. Eden (chairman), Mr. Winant, and Mr. Gousev. This body would consider the desirability of associating with it a French representative.

IV. ZONE OF OCCUPATION FOR THE FRENCH AND CONTROL COUNCIL FOR GERMANY

It was agreed that a zone in Germany, to be occupied by the French forces, should be allocated to France. This zone would be formed out of the British and American zones and its extent would be settled by the British and Americans in consultation with the French Provisional Government.

It was also agreed that the French Provisional Government should be invited to become a member of the Allied Control Council for Germany.

V. REPARATION

The following protocol has been approved:

1. Germany must pay in kind for the losses caused by her to the Allied Nations in the course of the war. Reparations are to be received in the first instance by those countries which have borne the main burden of the war; have suffered the heaviest losses, and have organized victory over the enemy.

2. Reparation in kind is to be exacted from Germany in the three following forms.

(*a*) Removals within two years from the surrender of Germany or the cessation of organized resistance from the national wealth of Germany located on the territory of Germany herself, as well as outside her territory (equipment, machine tools, ships, rolling stock, German investments abroad, shares of industrial transport, and other enterprises in Germany, etc.), these removals to be carried out chiefly for purpose of destroying the war potential of Germany.

(*b*) Annual deliveries of goods from current production for a period to be fixed.

(*c*) Use of German labor.

3. For the working out on the above principles of a detailed plan for exaction of reparation from Germany, an Allied Reparation Commission will be set up in Moscow. It will consist of three representatives—one from the Union of Soviet Socialist Republics, one from the United Kingdom, and one from the United States of America.

4. With regard to the fixing of the total sum of the reparation as well as the distribution of it among the countries which suffered from the German aggression, the Soviet and American delegations agreed as follows:

> The Moscow Reparation Commission should take in its initial studies as a basis for discussion the suggestion of the Soviet government that the total sum of the reparation in accordance with the points (*a*) and (*b*) of the paragraph 2 should be $20 billion and that 50 percent of it should go to the Union of Soviet Socialist Republics.

The British delegation was of the opinion that pending consideration of the reparation question by the Moscow Reparation Commission no figures of reparation should be mentioned.

The above Soviet-American proposal has been passed to the Moscow Reparation Commission as one of the proposals to be considered by the Commission.

VI. MAJOR WAR CRIMINALS

The Conference agreed that the question of the major war criminals should be the subject of inquiry by the three foreign secretaries for report in due course after the close of the conference.

VII. POLAND

The following Declaration on Poland was agreed by the conference:

A new situation has been created in Poland as a result of her complete liberation by the Red Army. This calls for the establishment of a Polish Provisional Government which can be more broadly based than was possible before the recent liberation of the western part of Poland. The Provisional Government which is now functioning in Poland should therefore be reorganized on a broader democratic basis with the inclusion of democratic leaders from Poland itself and from Poles abroad. This new government should then be called the Polish Provisional Government of National Unity.

M. Molotov, Mr. Harriman, and Sir A. Clark Kerr are authorized as a commission to consult in the first instance in Moscow with members of the present Provisional Government and with other Polish democratic leaders from within Poland and from abroad, with a view to the reorganization of the present government along the above lines. This Polish Provisional Government of National Unity shall be pledged to the holding of free and unfettered elections as soon as possible on the basis of universal suffrage and secret ballot. In these elections all democratic and anti-Nazi parties shall have the right to take part and to put forward candidates.

When a Polish Provisional Government of National Unity has been properly formed in conformity with the above, the government of the U.S.S.R., which now maintains diplomatic relations with the present Provisional Government of Poland, and the government of the United Kingdom and the government of the U.S.A. will establish diplomatic relations with the new Polish Provisional Government of National Unity, and will exchange ambassadors by whose report the respective governments will be kept informed about the situation in Poland.

The three heads of government consider that the eastern frontier of Poland should follow the Curzon Line, with digressions from it in some regions of five to eight kilometers in favor of Poland. They recognize that Poland must receive substantial accessions of territory in the north and west. They feel that the opinion of the new Polish

Provisional Government of National Unity should be sought in due course on the extent of these accessions and that the final delimitation of the western frontier of Poland should thereafter await the Peace Conference.

VIII. YUGOSLAVIA

It was agreed to recommend to Marshal Tito and to Dr. Subasic:

1. That the Tito-Subasic Agreement should immediately be put into effect and a new government formed on the basis of the agreement.

2. That as soon as the new government has been formed it should declare:

(*a*) that the Anti-Fascist Assembly of National Liberation (AUNOJ) will be extended to include members of the last Yugoslav Skupstina who have not compromised themselves by collaboration with the enemy, thus forming a body to be known as a temporary parliament and

(*b*) that legislative acts passed by the Anti-Fascist Assembly of National Liberation (AUNOJ) will be subject to subsequent ratification by a constituent assembly. And that this statement should be published in the communique of the conference.

IX. ITALO-YUGOSLAVIA FRONTIER; ITALO-AUSTRIA FRONTIER

Notes on these subjects were put in by the British delegation and the American and Soviet delegations agreed to consider them and give their views later.

X. YUGOSLAV-BULGARIAN RELATIONS

There was an exchange of views between the foreign secretaries on the question of the desirability of a Yugoslav-Bulgarian pact of alliance. The question at issue was whether a state still under an armistice regime could be allowed to enter into a treaty with another state. Mr. Eden suggested that the Bulgarian and Yugoslav governments should be informed that this could not be approved. Mr. Stettinius suggested that the British and American ambassadors should discuss the matter further with M. Molotov in Moscow. M. Molotov agreed with the proposal of Mr. Stettinius.

XI. SOUTHEASTERN EUROPE

The British delegation put in notes for the consideration of their colleagues on the following subjects:

(*a*) the Control Commission in Bulgaria

(*b*) Greek claims upon Bulgaria, more particularly with reference to reparations.

(*c*) Oil equipment in Rumania.

XII. IRAN

Mr. Eden, Mr. Stettinius, and M. Molotov exchanged views on the situation in Iran. It was agreed that this matter should be pursued through the diplomatic channel.

XIII. MEETINGS OF THE THREE FOREIGN SECRETARIES

The conference agreed that the permanent machinery should be set up for consultation between the three foreign secretaries, they should meet as often as necessary, probably about every three or four months. These meetings will be held in rotation in the three capitals, the first meeting being held in London.

XIV. THE MONTREUX CONVENTION AND THE STRAITS

It was agreed that at the next meeting of the three foreign secretaries to be held in London they should consider proposals which it was understood the Soviet government would put forward in relation to the Montreux Convention and report to their governments. The Turkish government should be informed at the appropriate moment.

The United Nations Charter, 1945 (excerpts)

The United Nations Organization, begun during the fighting, became a permanent, international, peace-keeping agency with the writing and adoption of its Charter in 1945. Americans reacted to the United Nations far more favorably than they had to the League of Nations a quarter-century earlier. In fact, by the end of World War II, most Americans seemed convinced that the surest way to maintain peace was through some international organization. The United Nations Charter (of which important Chapters are quoted below) was speedily adopted by the United States Senate.

We, The Peoples Of The United Nations, Determined

> to save succeeding generations from the scourge of war, which twice in our lifetime has brought untold sorrow to mankind, and to reaffirm faith in fundamental human rights, in the dignity and worth of the human person, in the equal rights of men and women and of nations large and small, and to establish conditions under which justice and respect for the obligations arising from treaties and other sources of international law can be maintained, and to promote social progress and better standards of life in larger freedom.

And For These Ends

> to practice tolerance and live together in peace with one another as good neighbors, and to unite our strength to maintain international peace and security, and to ensure, by the acceptance of principles and the institution of methods, that armed force shall not be used, save in the common interest, and to employ international machinery for the promotion of the economic and social advancement of all peoples,

Have Resolved To Combine Our Efforts To Accomplish These Aims.

Accordingly, our respective Governments, through representatives assembled in the city of San Francisco, who have exhibited their full powers found to be in good and due form, have agreed to the present Charter of the United Nations and do hereby establish an international organization to be known as the United Nations.

CHAPTER I

PURPOSES AND PRINCIPLES

ARTICLE I

The Purposes of the United Nations are:

1. To maintain international peace and security, and to that end to take effective collective measures for the prevention and removal of threats to the peace, and for the suppression of acts of aggression or other breaches of the peace, and to bring about by peaceful means, and in conformity with the principles of justice and international law, adjustment or settlement of international disputes or situations which might lead to a breach of the peace;

2. To develop friendly relations among nations based on respect for the principle of equal rights and self-determination of peoples, and to take other appropriate measures to strengthen universal peace;

3. To achieve international cooperation in solving international problems of an economic, social, cultural, or humanitarian character, and in promoting and encouraging respect for human rights and for fundamental freedoms for all without distinction as to race, sex, language, or religion; and

4. To be a center for harmonizing the actions of nations in the attainment of these common ends.

ARTICLE 2

The Organization and its Members, in pursuit of the Purposes stated in Article 1, shall act in accordance with the following Principles.

1. The Organization is based on the principles of the sovereign equality of all its Members.

2. All Members, in order to ensure to all of them the rights and benefits resulting from membership, shall fulfill in good faith the obligations assumed by them in accordance with the present Charter.

3. All Members shall settle their international disputes by peaceful means in such a manner that international peace and security, and justice, are not endangered.

4. All Members shall refrain in their international relations from the threat or use of force against the territorial integrity or political independence of any state, or in any other manner inconsistent with the Purposes of the United Nations.

5. All Members shall give the United Nations every assistance in any action it takes in accordance with the present Charter, and shall refrain from giving assistance to any state against which the United Nations is taking preventive or enforcement action.

6. The Organization shall ensure that states which are not Members of the United Nations act in accordance with these Principles so far as may be necessary for the maintenance of international peace and security.

7. Nothing contained in the present Charter shall authorize the United Nations to intervene in matters which are essentially within the domestic jurisdiction of any state or shall require the Members to submit such matters to settlement under the present Charter; but this principle shall not prejudice the application of enforcement measure under Chapter VII.

CHAPTER II

MEMBERSHIP

ARTICLE 3

The original Members of the United Nations shall be the states which, having participated in the United Nations Conference on International Organization at San Francisco, or having previously signed the Declaration by United Nations of January 1, 1942, sign the present Charter and ratify it in accordance with Article 110.

ARTICLE 4

1. Membership in the United Nations is open to all other peace-loving states which accept the obligations contained in the present Charter and, in the judgment of the Organization, are able and willing to carry out these obligations.

2. The admission of any such state to membership in the United Nations will be effected by a decision of the General Assembly upon the recommendation of the Security Council.

ARTICLE 5

A Member of the United Nations against which preventive or enforcement action has been taken by the Security Council may be suspended from the exercise of the rights and privileges of membership by the General Assembly upon the recommendation of the Security Council. The exercise of these rights and privileges may be restored by the Security Council.

ARTICLE 6

A Member of the United Nations which has persistently violated the Principles contained in the present Charter may be expelled from the Organization by the General Assembly upon the recommendation of the Security Council.

CHAPTER III

ORGANS

ARTICLE 7

1. There are established as the principal organs of the United Nations a General Assembly, a Security Council, a Trusteeship Council, an International Court of Justice, and a Secretariat.

2. Such subsidiary organs as may be found necessary may be established in accordance with the present Charter.

ARTICLE 8

The United Nations shall place no restrictions on the eligibility of men and women to participate in any capacity and under conditions of equality in its principal and subsidiary organs.

CHAPTER IV

THE GENERAL ASSEMBLY

Composition

ARTICLE 9

1. The General Assembly shall consist of all the Members of the United Nations.

2. Each Member shall have not more than five representatives in the General Assembly.

Functions and Powers

ARTICLE 10

The General Assembly may discuss any questions or any matters within the scope of the present Charter or relating to the powers and functions of any organs provided for in the present Charter, and, except as provided in Article 12, may make recommendations to the Members of the United Nations or to the Security Council or to both on any such questions or matters.

ARTICLE 11

1. The General Assembly may consider the general principles of cooperation in the maintenance of international peace and security, including the principles governing disarmament and the regulation of armaments, and may make recommendations with regard to such principles to the Members or to the Security Council or to both.

2. The General Assembly may discuss any questions relating to the maintenance of international peace and security brought before it by any Member of the United Nations, or by the Security Council, or by a state which is not a Member of the United Nations in

accordance with Article 35, paragraph 2, and, except as provided in Article 12, may make recommendations with regard to any such question to the state or states concerned or to the Security Council or to both. Any such question on which action is necessary shall be referred to the Security Council by the General Assembly either before or after discussion.

3. The General Assembly may call the attention of the Security Council to situations which are likely to endanger international peace and security. . . .

Voting

ARTICLE 18

1. Each member of the General Assembly shall have one vote.

2. Decisions of the General Assembly on important questions shall be made by a two-thirds majority of the members present and voting. These questions shall include: recommendations with respect to the maintenance of international peace and security, the election of the non-permanent members of the Security Council, the election of the members of the Economic and Social Council, the election of members of the Trusteeship Council in accordance with paragraph 1(c) of Article 86, the admission of new Members to the United Nations, the suspension of the rights and privileges of membership, the expulsion of Members, questions relating to the operation of the trusteeship system, and budgetary questions.

3. Decisions on other questions, including the determination of additional categories of questions to be decided by a two-thirds majority, shall be made by a majority of the members present and voting.

ARTICLE 19

A Member of the United Nations which is in arrears in the payment of its financial contributions to the Organization shall have no vote in the General Assembly if the amount of its arrears equals or exceeds the amount of the contributions due from it for the preceding two full years. The General Assembly may, nevertheless, permit such a Member to vote if it is satisfied that the failure to pay is due to conditions beyond the control of the Member. . . .

CHAPTER V

THE SECURITY COUNCIL

Composition

ARTICLE 23

1. The Security Council shall consist of eleven Members of the United Nations. The Republic of China, France, the Union of Soviet Socialist Republics, the United Kingdom of Great Britain and Northern Ireland, and the United States of America shall be permanent members of the Security Council. The General Assembly shall elect six other members of the United Nations to be non-permanent members of the Security Council, due regard being specially paid, in the first instance to the contribution of Members of the United Nations to the maintenance of international peace and security and to the other purposes of the Organization, and also to equitable geographical distribution.

2. The non-permanent members of the Security Council shall be elected for a term of two years. In the first election of the non-permanent members, however, three shall be chosen for a term of one year. A retiring member shall not be eligible for immediate reelection.

3. Each member of the Security Council shall have one representative.

Functions and Powers

ARTICLE 24

1. In order to ensure prompt and effective action by the United Nations, its Members confer on the Security Council primary responsibility for the maintenance of international peace and security, and agree that in carrying out its duties under this responsibility the Security Council acts on their behalf.

2. In discharging these duties the Security Council shall act in accordance with the Purposes and Principles of the United Nations. The specific powers granted to the Security Council for the discharge of these duties are laid down in Chapters VI, VII, VIII, and XII.

3. The Security Council shall submit annual and, when necessary, special reports to the General Assembly for its consideration.

ARTICLE 25

The Members of the United Nations agree to accept and carry out the decisions of the Security Council in accordance with the present Charter.

ARTICLE 26

In order to promote the establishment and maintenance of international peace and security with the least diversion for armaments of the world's human and economic resources, the Security Council shall be responsible for formulating, with the assistance of the Military Staff Committee referred to in Article 47, plans to be submitted to the Members of the United Nations for the establishment of a system for the regulation of armaments.

Voting

ARTICLE 27

1. Each member of the Security Council shall have one vote.

2. Decisions of the Security Council on procedural matters shall be made by an affirmative vote of seven members.

3. Decisions of the Security Council on all other matters shall be made by an affirmative vote of seven members including the concurring votes of the permanent members; provided that, in decisions under Chapter VI, and under paragraph 3 of Article 52, a party to a dispute shall abstain from voting. . . .

CHAPTER VI

PACIFIC SETTLEMENT OF DISPUTES

ARTICLE 33

1. The parties to any dispute, the continuance of which is likely to endanger the maintenance of international peace and security, shall, first of all, seek a solution by negotiation, enquiry, mediation, conciliation, arbitration, judicial settlement, resort to regional agencies or arrangements, or other peaceful means of their own choice.

2. The Security Council shall, when it deems necessary, call upon the parties to settle their dispute by such means.

ARTICLE 34

The Security Council may investigate any dispute, or any situation which might lead to international friction or give rise to a dispute, in order to determine whether the continuance of the dispute or situation is likely to endanger the maintenance of international peace and security.

ARTICLE 35

1. Any Member of the United Nations may bring any dispute, or any situation of the nature referred to in Article 34, to the attention of the Security Council or of the General Assembly.

2. A state which is not a Member of the United Nations may bring to the attention of the Security Council or of the General Assembly any dispute to which it is a party if it accepts in advance, for the purposes of the dispute the obligations of pacific settlement provided in the present Charter. . . .

CHAPTER VII

ACTION WITH RESPECT TO THREATS TO THE PEACE, ETC.

ARTICLE 39

The Security Council shall determine the existence of any threat to the peace, breach of the peace, or act of aggression and shall make recommendations, or decide what measures shall be taken in accordance with Articles 41 and 42, to maintain or restore international peace and security.

ARTICLE 40

In order to prevent an aggravation of the situation, the Security Council may, before making the recommendations or deciding upon the measures provided for in Article 39, call upon the parties concerned to comply with such provisional measures as it deems necessary or desirable. Such provisional measures shall be without prejudice to the rights, claims, or position of the parties concerned. The Security Council shall duly take account of failure to comply with such provisional measures.

ARTICLE 41

The Security Council may decide what measures not involving the use of armed force are to be employed to give effect to its decisions, and it may call upon the Members of the United Nations to apply such measures. These may include complete or partial interruption of economic relations and of rail, sea, air, postal, telegraphic, radio, and other means of communication, and the severance of diplomatic relations.

ARTICLE 42

Should the Security Council consider that measures provided for in Article 41 would be inadequate or have proved to be inadequate, it may take such action by air, sea, or land forces as may be necessary to maintain or restore international peace and security. Such action may include demonstrations, blockade, and other operations by air, sea, or land forces of Members of the United Nations.

ARTICLE 43

1. All Members of the United Nations, in order to contribute to the maintenance of international peace and security, undertake to make available to the Security Council, on its call and in accordance with a special agreement or agreements, armed forces, assistance, and facilities, including rights of passage, necessary for the purpose of maintaining international peace and security. . . .

ARTICLE 51

Nothing in the present Charter shall impair the inherent right of individual or collective self-defense if an armed attack occurs against a Member of the United Nations, until the Security Council has taken measures necessary to maintain international peace and security. Measures taken by Members in the exercise of this right of self-defense shall be immediately reported to the Security Council and shall not in any way affect the authority and responsibility of the Security Council under the present Charter to take at any time such action as it deems necessary in order to maintain or restore international peace and security.

CHAPTER VIII

REGIONAL ARRANGEMENTS

ARTICLE 52

1. Nothing in the present Charter precludes the existence of regional arrangements or agencies for dealing with such matters relating to the maintenance of international peace and security as are appropriate for regional action, provided that such arrangements or agencies and their activities are consistent with the Purposes and Principles of the United Nations.

2. The Members of the United Nations entering into such arrangements or constituting such agencies shall make every effort to achieve pacific settlement of local disputes through such regional arrangements or by such regional agencies before referring them to the Security Council. . . .

ARTICLE 54

The Security Council shall at all times be kept fully informed of activities undertaken or in contemplation under regional arrangements or by regional agencies for the maintenance of international peace and security.

CHAPTER IX

INTERNATIONAL ECONOMIC AND SOCIAL COOPERATION

ARTICLE 55

With a view to the creation of conditions of stability and well-being which are necessary for peaceful and friendly relations among nations based on respect for the principle of equal rights and self-determination of peoples, the United Nations shall promote:

a. higher standards of living, full employment, and conditions of economic and social progress and development;

b. solutions of international economic, social, health, and related problems; and international cultural and educational cooperation; and

c. universal respect for, and observance of, human rights and fundamental freedoms for all without distinction. . . .

CHAPTER XI

DECLARATION REGARDING NON-SELF-GOVERNING TERRITORIES

ARTICLE 73

Members of the United Nations which have or assume responsibilities for the administration of territories whose peoples have not yet attained a full measure of self-government recognize the principle that the interests of the inhabitants of these territories are paramount, and accept as a sacred trust the obligation to promote to the utmost, within the system of international peace and security established by the present Charter, the well-being of the inhabitants of these territories, and, to this end:

a. to ensure, with due respect for the culture of the peoples concerned, their political, economic, social, and educational advancement, their just treatment, and their protection against abuses;

b. to develop self-government, to take due account of the political aspirations of the peoples, and to assist them in the progressive development of their free political institutions, according to the particular circumstances of each territory and its peoples and their varying stages of advancement:

c. to further international peace and security;

d. to promote constructive measures of development, to encourage research, and to cooperate with one another and, when and where appropriate, with specialized international bodies with a view to the practical achievement of the social, economic, and scientific purposes set forth in this Article; and

e. to transmit regularly to the Secretary-General for information purposes, subject to such limitation as security and constitutional considerations may require, statistical and other information of a technical nature relating to economic, social, and educational conditions in the territories for which they are respectively responsible other than those territories to which Chapters XII and XIII apply.

ARTICLE 74

Member of the United Nations also agree that their policy in respect of the territories to which this Chapter applies, no less than in respect of their metropolitan areas, must be based on the general principle of good-neighborliness, due account being taken of the interests and well-being of the rest of the world, in social, economic, and commercial matters.

CHAPTER XII
INTERNATIONAL TRUSTEESHIP SYSTEM
ARTICLE 75

The United Nations shall establish under its authority an international trusteeship system for the administration and supervision of such territories as may be placed thereunder by subsequent individual agreements. These territories are hereinafter referred to as trust territories.

ARTICLE 76

The basic objectives of the trusteeship system, in accordance with the Purposes of the United Nations laid down in Article I of the present Charter, shall be:

a. to further international peace and security;

b. to promote the political, economic, social, and educational advancement of the inhabitants of the trust territories, and their progressive development towards self-government or independence as may be appropriate to the particular circumstances of each territory and its peoples and the freely expressed wishes of the peoples concerned, and as may be provided by the terms of each trusteeship agreement:

c. to encourage respect for human rights and for fundamental freedoms for all without distinction as to race, sex, language, or religion, and to encourage recognition of the interdependence of the peoples of the world; and

d. to ensure equal treatment in social, economic, and commercial matters for all Members of the United Nations and their nationals, and also equal treatment for the latter in the administration of justice, without prejudice to the attainment of the foregoing objectives and, subject to the provisions of Article 80.

ARTICLE 77

1. The trusteeship system shall apply to such territories in the following categories as may be placed thereunder by means of trusteeship agreements:

a. territories now held under mandate;

b. territories which may be detached from enemy states as a result of the Second World War; and

c. territories voluntarily placed under the system by states responsible for their administration.

2. It will be a matter for subsequent agreement as to which territories in the foregoing categories will be brought under the trusteeship system and upon what terms. . . .

CHAPTER XIV
THE INTERNATIONAL COURT OF JUSTICE
ARTICLE 92

The International Court of Justice shall be the principal judicial organ of the United Nations. It shall function in accordance with the annexed Statute, which is based upon the Statute of the Permanent Court of International Justice and forms an integral part of the present Charter.

ARTICLE 93

1. All Members of the United Nations are *ipso facto* parties to the Statute of the International Code of Justice.

2. A state which is not a Member of the United Nations may become a party to the Statute of the International Court of Justice on condition to be determined in each case by the General Assembly upon the recommendation of the Security Council.

ARTICLE 94

1. Each Member of the United Nations undertakes to comply with the decision of the International Court of Justice in any case to which it is a party.

2. If any party to a case fails to perform the obligations incumbent upon it under a judgment rendered by the Court, the other party may have recourse to the Security Council, which may, if it deems necessary, make recommendations. . . .

CHAPTER XV
THE SECRETARIAT
ARTICLE 97

The Secretariat shall comprise a Secretary-General and such staff as the Organization may require. The Secretary-General shall be appointed by the General Assembly upon the recommendation of the Security Council. He shall be the chief administrative officer of the Organization.

ARTICLE 98

The Secretary-General shall act in that capacity in all meetings of the General Assembly, of the Security Council, of the Economic and Social Council, and of the Trusteeship Council, and shall perform such other functions as are entrusted to him by these organs. The Secretary-General shall make an annual report to the General Assembly on the work of the Organization.

ARTICLE 99

The Secretary-General may bring to the attention of the Security Council any matter which in his opinion may threaten the maintenance of international peace. . . .

ARTICLE 100

1. In the performance of their duties the Secretary-General and the staff shall not seek to receive instruction from any government or from any other authority external to the Organization. They shall

refrain from any action which might reflect on their position as international officials responsible only to the Organization.

2. Each Member of the United Nations undertakes to respect the exclusively international character of the responsibilities of the Secretary-General and the staff. . . .

CHAPTER XVII
TRANSITIONAL SECURITY ARRANGEMENTS
ARTICLE 106

Pending the coming into force of such special agreements referred to in Article 43 as in the opinion of the Security Council enable it to begin the exercise of its responsibilities under Article 42, the parties to the Four-Nation Declaration, signed at Moscow, October 30, 1943, and France, shall, in accordance with the provisions of paragraph 5 of that Declaration, consult with one another and as occasion requires with other Members of the United Nations with a view to such joint action on behalf of the Organization as may be necessary for the purpose of maintaining international peace and security. . . .

The Truman Doctrine, 1947

The shift in American policy from the neutrality of the early 1930s was dramatized after World War II ended. The United States undertook to help other countries rebuild their cities and industries, as a means of encouraging them to live peacefully. President Harry S. Truman announced his "Truman Doctrine"—that American military aid would go to countries trying to maintain themselves free from Communist control. In the spring of 1947, American military equipment was shipped to Greece and Turkey. A few months later, that same year, Secretary of State George C. Marshall announced a plan to provide supplies for civilian rebuilding of war damage in Europe, open to both eastern and western countries. Significant parts of the Truman Doctrine (as stated in the President's message to Congress) and of the Marshall Plan are quoted below.

The gravity of the situation which confronts the world today necessitates my appearance before a joint session of the Congress. The foreign policy and the national security of the country are involved.

One aspect of the present situation, which I wish to present to you at this time for your consideration and decision, concerns Greece and Turkey.

The United States has received from the Greek Government an urgent appeal for financial and economic assistance. Preliminary reports from the American Economic Mission now in Greece and reports from the American Ambassador in Greece corroborate the statement of the Greek Government that assistance is imperative if Greece is to survive as a free nation. . . .

The very existence of the Greek state is today threatened by the terrorist activities of several thousand armed men, led by Communists, who defy the Government's authority at a number of points, particularly along the northern boundaries. A commission appointed by the United Nations Security Council is at present investigating disturbed conditions in Northern Greece and alleged border violations along the frontier between Greece on the one hand and Albania, Bulgaria and Yugoslavia on the other.

Meanwhile, the Greek Government is unable to cope with the situation. The Greek Army is small and poorly equipped. It needs supplies and equipment if it is to restore the authority to the Government throughout Greek territory.

Greece must have assistance if it is to become a self-supporting and self-respecting democracy. The United States must supply this assistance. We have already extended to Greece certain type of relief and economic aid but these are inadequate. There is no other country to which democratic Greece can turn. No other nation is willing and able to provide the necessary support for a democratic Greek government.

The British Government, which has been helping Greece, can give no further financial or economic aid after March 31. Great Britain finds itself under the necessity of reducing or liquidating its commitments in several parts of the world, including Greece.

We have considered how the United Nations might assist in this crisis. But the situation is an urgent one requiring immediate action, and the United Nations and its related organizations are not in a position to extend help of the kind that is required. . . .

Greece's neighbor, Turkey, also deserves our attention. The future of Turkey as an independent and economically sound state is clearly no less important to the freedom-loving peoples of the world than the future of Greece. The circumstances in which Turkey finds itself today are considerably different from those of Greece. Turkey has been spared the disasters that have beset Greece. And during the war, the United States and Great Britain furnished Turkey with material aid.

Nevertheless, Turkey now needs our support.

Since the war Turkey has sought financial assistance from Great Britain and the United States for the purpose of effecting that modernization necessary for the maintenance of its national integrity.

That integrity is essential to the preservation of order in the Middle East.

The British Government has informed us that, owing to its own difficulties, it can no longer extend financial or economic aid to Turkey. As in the case of Greece, if Turkey is to have the assistance it needs, the United States must supply it. We are the only country able to provide that help.

I am fully aware of the broad implications involved if the United States extends assistance to Greece and Turkey, and I shall discuss these implications with you at this time.

One of the primary objectives of the foreign policy of the United States is the creation of conditions in which we and other nations will be able to work out a way of life free from coercion. . . .

The peoples of a number of countries of the world have recently had totalitarian regimes forced upon them against their will. The Government of the United States has made frequent protests against coercion and intimidation, in violation of the Yalta Agreement, in Poland, Rumania, and Bulgaria. I must also state that in a number of other countries there have been similar developments.

At the present moment in world history nearly every nation must choose between alternative ways of life. The choice is too often not a free one.

The North Atlantic Treaty, 1949

The years immediately following World War II were marked by the start of the so-called Cold War—a series of rivalries between the United States and its allies on one side, and the Soviet Union and its Communist-managed states on the other. After it became clear that the Cold War would continue for some time, the western European countries and the United States signed a treaty of alliance in 1949. The treaty established the North Atlantic Treaty Organization.

PREAMBLE. The parties to this treaty reaffirm their faith in the purposes and principles of the Charter of the United Nations and their desire to live in peace with all peoples and all governments.

They are determined to safeguard the freedom, common heritage and civilization of their peoples, founded on the principles of democracy, individual liberty and the rule of law.

They seek to promote stability and well-being in the North Atlantic Area.

They are resolved to unite their efforts for collective defense and for the preservation of peace and security.

They therefore agree to this North Atlantic Treaty:

ARTICLE 1. The parties undertake, as set forth in the Charter of the United Nations, to settle any international disputes in which they may be involved by peaceful means in such a manner that international peace and security, and justice, are not endangered, and to refrain in their international relations from the threat or use of force in any manner inconsistent with the purposes of the United Nations.

ARTICLE 2. The parties will continue toward the further development of peaceful and friendly international relations by strengthening their free institutions, by bringing about a better understanding of the principles upon which these institutions are founded, and by promoting conditions of stability and well-being. They will seek to eliminate conflict in their international economic policies and will encourage economic collaboration between any or all of them.

ARTICLE 3. In order more effectively to achieve the objectives of this treaty, the parties, separately and jointly, by means of continuous and effective self-help and mutual aid, will maintain and develop their individual and collective capacity to resist armed attack.

ARTICLE 4. The parties will consult together whenever, in the opinion of any of them, the territorial integrity, political independence or security of any of the parties is threatened.

ARTICLE 5. The parties agree that an armed attack against one or more of them in Europe or North America shall be considered an attack against them all; and consequently they agree that, if such an armed attack occurs, each of them, in exercise of the right of individual or collective self-defense recognized by Article 51 of the Charter of the United Nations, will assist the party or parties so attacked by taking forthwith, individually and in concert with the other parties, such action as it deems necessary including the use of armed force, to restore and maintain the security of the North Atlantic Area.

Any such armed attack and all measures taken as a result thereof shall immediately be reported to the Security Council. Such measures shall be terminated when the Security Council has taken the measures necessary to restore and maintain international peace and security.

ARTICLE 6. For the purpose of Article 5 an armed attack on one or more of the parties is deemed to include an armed attack on the territory of any of the parties in Europe or North America, on the Algerian Departments of France, on the occupation forces of any party in Europe, on the islands under the jurisdiction of any party in the North Atlantic Area north of the Tropic of Cancer or on the vessels or aircraft in this area of any of the parties.

ARTICLE 7. This treaty does not affect, and shall not be interpreted as affecting, in any way the rights and obligations under the Charter of the parties which are members of the United Nations, or the primary responsibility of the Security Council for the maintenance of international peace and security.

ARTICLE 8. Each party declares that none of the international engagements now in force between it and any other of the parties or any third state is in conflict with the provisions of this treaty, and undertakes not to enter into any international engagement in conflict with this treaty.

ARTICLE 9. The parties hereby establish a Council, on which each of them shall be represented, to consider matters concerning the implementation of this treaty. The Council shall be so organized as to be able to meet promptly at any time. The Council shall set up such subsidiary bodies as may be necessary; in particular it shall establish immediately a Defense Committee which shall recommend measures for the implementation of Articles 3 and 5.

ARTICLE 10. The parties may, by unanimous agreement, invite any other European state in a position to further the principles of this treaty and to contribute to the security of the North Atlantic Area to accede to this treaty. Any state so invited may become a party to the treaty by depositing its instrument of accession with the Government of the United States of America. The Government of the United States of America will inform each of the parties of the deposit of each such instrument of accession.

ARTICLE 11. This treaty shall be ratified and its provisions carried out by the parties in accordance with their respective constitutional processes. The instruments of ratification shall be deposited as soon as possible with the Government of the United States of America, which will notify all the other signatories of each deposit. The treaty shall enter into force between the states which have ratified it as soon as the ratifications of Belgium, Canada, France, Luxemburg, the Netherlands, the United Kingdom and the United States, have been deposited and shall come into effect with respect to other states on the date of the deposit of their ratification.

ARTICLE 12. After the treaty has been in force for ten years, or at any time thereafter, the parties shall, if any of them so request, consult together for the purpose of reviewing the treaty, having regard for the factors then affecting peace and security in the North Atlantic Area, including the development of universal as well as regional arrangements under the Charter of the United Nations for the maintenance of international peace and security.

ARTICLE 13. After the treaty has been in force for twenty years, any party may cease to be a party one year after its notice of denunciation has been given to the Government of the United States of America, which will inform the governments of the other parties of the deposit of each notice of denunciation.

ARTICLE 14. This treaty, of which the English and French texts are equally authentic, shall be deposited in the archives of the Government of the United States of America. Duly certified copies thereof will be transmitted by that government to the government of the other signatories.

In witness whereof, the undersigned plenipotentiaries have signed this treaty.

President Harry S. Truman's Statements on the War in Korea, 1950

In 1950, large-scale fighting broke out in Korea. An American-supported government in South Korea was attacked by North Korean troops, under the orders of a Communist government. President Harry S. Truman ordered that troops and supplies be furnished to aid South Korea in this situation. Troops were sent first from Japan, where they were on duty as an army of occupation. President Truman appealed to the United Nations for approval of his acts to repel aggression in Korea, and he received this approval. The following statements were released to the public by President Truman:

Statement of June 26, 1950

I conferred Sunday evening with the Secretaries of State and Defense, their senior advisers, and the Joint Chiefs of Staff about the situation in the Far East created by unprovoked aggression against the Republic of Korea.

The Government of the United States is pleased with the speed and determination with which the United Nations Security Council acted to order a withdrawal of the invading forces to position north of the 38th parallel. In accordance with the resolution of the Security Council, the United States will vigorously support the effort of the Council to terminate this serious breach of the peace.

Our concern over the lawless action taken by the forces from North Korea, and our sympathy and support for the people of Korea in this situation, are being demonstrated by the cooperative action of American personnel in Korea, as well as by steps taken to expedite and augment assistance of the type being furnished under the Mutual Defense Assistance Program.

Those responsible for this act of aggression must realize how seriously the Government of the United States views such threats to the peace of the world. Willful disregard of the obligation to keep the peace cannot be tolerated by nations that support the United Nations Charter.

Statement of June 27, 1950

In Korea the Government forces, which were armed to prevent border raids and to preserve internal security, were attacked by invading forces from North Korea. The Security Council of the United Nations called upon the invading troops to cease hostilities and to withdraw to the 38th parallel. This they have not done, but on the contrary have pressed the attack. The Security Council called upon all members of the United Nations to render every assistance to the United Nations in the execution of this resolution. In these circumstances I have ordered United States air and sea forces to give the Korean Government troops cover and support.

The attack upon Korea makes it plain beyond all doubt that communism has passed beyond the use of subversion to conquer independent nations and will now use armed invasion and war. It has defied the orders of the Security Council of the United Nations issued to preserve international peace and security. In these circumstances the occupation of Formosa by Communist forces would be a direct threat to the security of the Pacific area and to United States forces performing their lawful and necessary functions in that area.

Accordingly I have ordered the 7th Fleet to prevent any attack on Formosa. As a corollary of this action I am calling upon the Chinese Government on Formosa to cease all air and sea operations against the mainland. The 7th Fleet will see that this is done. The determination of the future status of Formosa must await the restoration of security in the Pacific, a peace settlement with Japan, or consideration by the United Nations.

I have also directed that United States Forces in the Philippines be strengthened and that military assistance to the Philippine Government be accelerated.

I have similarly directed acceleration in the furnishing of military assistance to the forces of France and the Associated States in Indochina and the dispatch of a military mission to provide close working relations with those forces.

I know that all members of the United Nations will consider carefully the consequences of this latest aggression in Korea in defiance of the Charter of the United Nations. A return to the rule of force in international affairs would have far-reaching effects. The United States will continue to uphold the rule of law.

I have instructed Ambassador Austin, as the representative of the United States to the Security Council, to report these steps to the Council.

General Douglas MacArthur's Speech before Congress, 1951 (excerpts)

The overall command in Korea was held by General Douglas MacArthur. As the war went on, MacArthur and President Truman differed with each other on strategy and worldwide plans. MacArthur apparently wished to attack supply centers of the North Koreans which were located in China. Truman ordered that the fighting be restricted to Korea alone. After the two leaders had met, and continued to differ, President Truman dismissed MacArthur and relieved him of military command. The incident led to sharp debates in the United States over the proper relationship between professional military men and their civilian superiors. MacArthur, returning to the United States for the first time since World War II, received a warm welcome. Invited to address Congress, he spoke (in part) as follows on April 19, 1951.

While I was not consulted prior to the President's decision to intervene in support of the Republic of Korea, that decision, from a military standpoint, proved a sound one. As I say, it proved a sound one, as we hurled back the invader and decimated his forces. Our victory was complete, and our objectives within reach, when Red China intervened with numerically superior ground forces.

This created a new war and an entirely new situation, a situation not contemplated when our forces were committed against the North Korean invaders; a situation which called for new decisions in the diplomatic sphere to permit the realistic adjustment of military strategy. Such decisions have not been forthcoming.

While no man in his right mind would advocate sending our ground forces into continental China, and such was never given a thought, the new situation did urgently demand a drastic revision of strategic planning if our political aim was to defeat this new enemy as we had defeated the old.

Apart from the military need, as I saw it, to neutralize sanctuary protection given the enemy north of the Yalu, I felt that military necessity in the conduct of the war made necessary—

1. The intensification of our economic blockade against China.
2. The imposition of a naval blockade against the China coast.
3. Removal of restriction on air reconnaissance of China's coastal areas and of Manchuria.
4. Removal of restrictions on the forces of the Republic of China on Formosa, with logistical support to contribute to their effective operations against the Chinese mainland.

For entertaining these views, all professionally designed to support our forces committed to Korea and bring hostilities to an end with the least possible delay and at a saving of countless American and Allied lives, I have been severely criticized in lay circles, principally abroad, despite any understanding that from a military standpoint the above views have been fully shared in the past by practically every military leader concerned with the Korean campaign, including our own Joint Chiefs of Staff.

I called for reinforcements, but was informed that reinforcements were not available. I made clear that if not permitted to destroy the enemy built-up bases north of the Yalu, if not permitted to utilize the friendly Chinese force of some 600,000 men on Formosa, if not permitted to blockade the China coast to prevent the Chinese Reds from getting succor from without, and if there were to be no hope of major reinforcements, the position of the command from the military standpoint forbade victory.

We could hold in Korea by constant maneuver and at an approximate area where our supply line advantages were in balance with the supply line disadvantages of the enemy, but we could hope at best for only an indecisive campaign with its terrible and constant attrition upon our forces if the enemy utilized his full military potential.

I have constantly called for the new political decisions essential to a solution.

Efforts have been made to distort my position. It has been said in effect that I was a warmonger. Nothing could be further from the truth.

I know war as few other men now living know it, and nothing to me is more revolting. I have long advocated its complete abolition, as its very destructiveness on both friend and foe has rendered it useless as a means of settling international disputes. . . .

But once forced upon us, there is no other alternative than to apply every available means to bring it to a swift end. War's very object is victory, not prolonged indecision. In war there can be no substitute for victory.

There are some who for varying reasons would appease Red China. They are blind to history's clear lesson, for history teaches with unmistakable emphasis that appeasement but begets new and bloodier war. It points to no single instance where the end has justified that means, where appeasement has led to more than a sham peace. Like blackmail, it lays the basis for new and successively greater demands until, as in blackmail, violence becomes the only other alternative. Why, my soldiers asked of me, surrender military advantages to an enemy in the field? I could not answer.

Some may say to avoid spread of the conflict into an all-out war with China. Others, to avoid Soviet intervention. Neither explanation seems valid, for China is already engaging with the maximum power it can commit, and the Soviet will not necessarily mesh its actions with our moves. Like a cobra, any new enemy will more likely strike whenever it feels that the relativity in military or other potential is in its favor on a world-wide basis.

The tragedy of Korea is further heightened by the fact that its military action is confined to its territorial limits. It condemns that nation, which it is our purpose to save, to suffer the devastating impact of full naval and air bombardment while the enemy's sanctuaries are fully protected from such attack and devastation.

Of the nations of the world, Korea alone, up to now, is the sole one which has risked its all against communism. The magnificence of the courage and fortitude of the Korean people defies description. They have chosen to risk death rather than slavery. Their last words to me were: "Don't scuttle the Pacific." . . .

President John F. Kennedy's Proclamation on the Missile Crisis, 1962

Other critical situations developed during the period. None appeared to be a greater threat to world peace than the "Missile Crisis" in Cuba in 1962. Soviet-made missiles were observed to be emplaced in Cuba. Additional weapons were expected to be sent there, and, since the United States and the Castro government of Cuba were on hostile terms, these weapons seemed to be a threat to the United States. It appeared that the Soviet Union was supporting Cuba (if not acting directly itself) in the crisis. President John F. Kennedy issued the following proclamation on October 23, as a statement of United States policy for the area. The "quarantine" plan worked, and a shooting war was avoided.

Whereas the peace of the world and the security of the United States and of all American states are endangered by reason of the establishment by the Sino-Soviet powers of an offensive military capability in Cuba, including bases for ballistic missiles with a potential range covering most of North and South America:

Whereas by a joint resolution passed by the Congress of the United States and approved on Oct. 3, 1962, it was declared that the United States is determined to prevent by whatever means be necessary, including the use of arms, the Marxist-Leninist regime in Cuba from extending, by force or the threat of force, its aggressive or subversive activities to any part of this hemisphere, and to prevent in Cuba the creation or use of an externally supported military capability endangering the security of the United States; and

Whereas the Organ of Consultation of the American republics meeting in Washington on Oct. 23, 1962, recommended that the member states, in accordance with Articles 6 and 8 of the Inter-American Treaty of Reciprocal Assistance, take all measures, individually and collectively, including the use of armed force, which they may deem necessary to insure that the Government of Cuba cannot continue to receive from the Sino-Soviet powers military material and related supplies which may threaten the peace and security of the continent and to prevent the missiles in Cuba with offensive capability from ever becoming an active threat to the peace and security of the continent:

Now, Therefore, I, John F. Kennedy, President of the United States of America, acting under and by virtue of the authority conferred upon me by the Constitution and statutes of the United States, in accordance with the aforementioned resolutions of the United States Congress and of the Organ of Consultation of the American Republics, and to defend the security of the United States, do hereby proclaim that the forces under my command are ordered, beginning at 2:00 P.M. Greenwich time Oct. 24, 1962, to interdict, subject to the instructions herein contained, the delivery of offensive weapons and associated material to Cuba.

For the purposes of this proclamation, the following are declared to be prohibited material:

Surface-to-surface missiles; bomber aircraft; bombs; air-to-surface rockets and guided missiles; warheads for any of the above weapons; mechanical or electronic equipment to support or operate the above items; and any other classes of material hereafter designated by the Secretary of Defense for the purpose of effectuating this proclamation.

To enforce this order, the Secretary of Defense shall take appropriate measures to prevent the delivery of prohibited material to

Cuba, employing the land, sea and air forces of the United States in cooperation with any forces that may be made available by other American states.

The Secretary of Defense may make such regulations and issue such directives as he deems necessary to ensure the effectiveness of this order, including the designation, within a reasonable distance of Cuba, of prohibited or restricted zones and of prescribed routes.

Any vessel or craft which may be proceeding toward Cuba may be intercepted and may be directed to identify itself, its cargo, equipment and stores and its ports of call, to stop, to lie to, to submit to visit and search, or to proceed as directed. Any vessel or craft which fails or refuses to respond to or comply with directions shall be subjected to being taken into custody. Any vessel or craft which is believed en route to Cuba and may be carrying prohibited material or may itself constitute such material shall, wherever possible, be directed to proceed to another destination of its own choice and shall be taken into custody if it fails or refuses to obey such directions. All vessels or craft taken into custody shall be sent into a port of the United States for appropriate disposition.

In carrying out this order, force shall not be used except in case of failure or refusal to comply with directions, or with regulations or directives of the Secretary of Defense issued hereunder, after reasonable efforts have been made to communicate them to the vessel or craft, or in case of self-defense. In any case, force shall be used only to the extent necessary.

IN WITNESS WHEREOF, I have hereunto set my hand and caused the seal of the United States of America to be affixed.

Done in the city of Washington this 23d day of October in the year of Our Lord, 1962, and of the independence of the United States of America the 187th.

— JOHN F. KENNEDY

President Lyndon B. Johnson's Statement on the Gulf of Tonkin Incident, 1964

The foreign war in which the forces of the United States were engaged for the longest period of time was the war in Vietnam. American participation in the war in Southeast Asia began with the sending of specialists to help the South Vietnamese troops with advice. Covert air raids and other actions were undertaken during early 1964 in support of the efforts of the South Vietnamese to defend themselves (this was revealed by the unauthorized publication of the so-called Pentagon Papers in 1971). After a reported attack by the North Vietnamese on U.S. Navy vessels in the Gulf of Tonkin, and the presentation of this information to Congress by President Lyndon Johnson on August 5, 1964, Congress responded with a joint resolution (called the "Gulf of Tonkin" resolution) which pledged the fullest support to the President in his declared policy. In part, President Johnson said:

Last night I announced to the American people that the North Vietnamese regime had conducted further deliberate attacks against U.S. naval vessels operating in international waters, and that I had therefore directed air action against gunboats and supporting facilities used in these hostile operations. This air action has now been carried out with substantial damage to the boats and facilities. Two U.S. aircraft were lost in the action.

After consultation with the leaders of both parties in the Congress, I further announced a decision to ask the Congress for a resolution expressing the unity and determination of the United States in supporting freedom and in protecting peace in southeast Asia.

These latest actions of the North Vietnamese regime have given a new and grave turn to the already serious situation in southeast Asia. Our commitments in that area are well known to the Congress. They were first made in 1954 by President Eisenhower. They were further defined in the Southeast Asia Collective Defense Treaty approved by the Senate in February 1955.

This treaty with its accompanying protocol obligates the United States and other members to act in accordance with their constitutional processes to meet Communist aggression against any of the parties or protocol states.

Our policy in southeast Asia has been consistent and unchanged since 1954. I summarized it on June 2 in four simple propositions:

1. *America keeps her word.* Here as elsewhere, we must and shall honor our commitments.

2. *The issue is the future of southeast Asia as a whole.* A threat to any nation in that region is a threat to all, and a threat to us.

3. *Our purpose is peace.* We have no military, political, or territorial ambition in the area.

4. *This is not just a jungle war, but a struggle for freedom on every front of human activity.* Our military and economic assistance to South Vietnam and Laos in particular has the purpose of helping these countries to repel aggression and strengthen their independence.

The threat to the free nations of southeast Asia has long been clear. The North Vietnamese regime has constantly sought to take over South Vietnam and Laos. This Communist regime has violated the Geneva accords for Vietnam. It has systematically conducted a campaign of subversion, which includes the direction, training, and supply of personnel and arms for the conduct of guerrilla warfare in South Vietnamese territory. In Laos, the North Vietnamese regime has maintained military forces, used Laotian territory for infiltration into South Vietnam, and most recently carried out combat operations—all in direct violation of the Geneva agreements of 1962.

In recent months, the actions of the North Vietnamese regime have become steadily more threatening. . . .

As President of the United States I have concluded that I should now ask the Congress, on its part, to join in affirming the national determination that all such attacks will be met, and that the United States will continue in its basic policy of assisting the free nations of the area to defend their freedom.

As I have repeatedly made clear, the United States intends no rashness, and seeks no wider war. We must make it clear to all that the United States is united in its determination to bring about the end of Communist subversion and aggression in the area.

The Gulf of Tonkin Resolution, 1964

Joint Resolution

To promote the maintenance of international peace and security in southeast Asia.

Whereas naval units of the Communist regime in [North] Vietnam, in violation of the principles of the Charter of the United Nations and of international law, have deliberately and repeatedly attacked United States naval vessels lawfully present in international waters, and have thereby created a serious threat to international peace; and

Whereas these attacks are part of a deliberate and systematic campaign of aggression that the Communist regime in North Vietnam has been waging against its neighbors and the nations joined with them in the collective defense of their freedom; and

Whereas the United States is assisting the peoples of southeast Asia to protect their freedom and has no territorial, military or political ambitions in that area, but desires only that these peoples should be left in peace to work out their own destinies in their own way: Now, therefore, be it

Resolved by the Senate and House of Representatives of the United States of America in Congress assembled,

That the Congress approves and supports the determination of the President, as Commander in Chief, to take all necessary measures to repel any armed attack against the forces of the United States and to prevent further aggression.

Sec. 2. The United States regards as vital to its national interest and to world peace the maintenance of international peace and security in southeast Asia. Consonant with the Constitution of the United States and the Charter of the United Nations and in accordance with its obligations under the Southeast Asia Collective Defense Treaty, the United States is, therefore, prepared, as the President determines, to take all necessary steps, including the use of armed force, to assist any member or protocol state of the Southeast Asia Collective Defense Treaty requesting assistance in defense of its freedom.

Sec. 3. This resolution shall expire when the President shall determine that the peace and security of the area is reasonably assured by international conditions created by action of the United Nations or otherwise, except that it may be terminated earlier by concurrent resolution of the Congress.

Approved August 10, 1964.

President Richard Nixon's Announcement of the Agreement to End the Vietnam War, 1973

Years went by in negotiation and discussion, while U.S. servicemen were involved in greater and greater numbers in Vietnam. At last, in January 1973, a truce was arranged. President Richard M. Nixon announced the news in an address to the nation on January 23.

Good evening. I have asked for this radio and television time tonight for the purpose of announcing that we today have concluded an agreement to end the war and bring peace with honor in Viet-Nam and in Southeast Asia.

The following statement is being issued at this moment in Washington and Hanoi:

"At 12:30 Paris time today, January 23, 1973, the Agreement on Ending the War and Restoring Peace in Vietnam was initiated by Dr. Henry Kissinger on behalf of the United States, and Special Advisor Le Duc Tho on behalf of the Democratic Republic of Vietnam.

"The agreement will be formally signed by the parties participating in the Paris Conference on Vietnam on January 27, 1973, at the International Conference Center in Paris.

"The cease-fire will take effect at 2400 Greenwich Mean Time, January 27, 1973. The United States and the Democratic Republic of Vietnam express the hope that this agreement will insure stable peace in Vietnam and contribute to the preservation of lasting peace in Indochina and Southeast Asia."

That concludes the formal statement.

Throughout the years of negotiations, we have insisted on peace with honor. In my addresses to the Nation from this room of January 25 and May 8, I set forth the goals that we considered essential for peace with honor.

In the settlement that has now been agreed to, all the conditions that I laid down then have been met. A cease-fire, internationally supervised, will begin at 7 p.m. this Saturday, January 27, Washington time. Within 60 days from this Saturday, all Americans held prisoners of war throughout Indochina will be released. There will be the fullest possible accounting for all of those who are missing in action.

During the same 60-day period, all American forces will be withdrawn from South Viet-Nam.

The people of South Viet-Nam have been guaranteed the right to determine their own future without outside interference.

By joint agreement, the full text of the agreement and the protocols to carry it out will be issued tomorrow.

Throughout these negotiations we have been in the closest consultation with President Thieu and other representatives of the Republic of Viet-Nam. This settlement meets the goals and has the full support of President Thieu and the Government of the Republic of Viet-Nam, as well as that of our other allies who are affected.

The United States will continue to recognize the Government of the Republic of Viet-Nam as the sole legitimate government of South Viet-Nam.

We shall continue to aid South Viet-Nam within the terms of the agreement, and we shall support efforts by the people of South Viet-Nam to settle their problems peacefully among themselves.

We must recognize that ending the war is only the first step toward building the peace. All parties must now see to it that this is a peace that lasts, and also a peace that heals, and a peace that not only ends the war in Southeast Asia but contributes to the prospects of peace in the whole world.

This will mean that the terms of the agreement must be scrupulously adhered to. We shall do everything the agreement requires of us, and we shall expect the other parties to do everything it requires of them. We shall also expect other interested nations to help insure that the agreement is carried out and peace is maintained.

As this long and very difficult war ends, I would like to address a few special words to each of those who have been parties in the conflict.

First, to the people and the Government of South Viet-Nam: By your courage, by your sacrifice, you have won the precious right to determine your own future, and you have developed the strength to defend that right. We look forward to working with you in the future, friends in peace as we have been allies in war.

To the leaders of North Viet-Nam: As we have ended the war through negotiations, let us now build a peace of reconciliation. For our part, we are prepared to make a major effort to help achieve that goal; but just as reciprocity was needed to end the war, so, too, will it be needed to build and strengthen the peace.

To the other major powers that have been involved, even indirectly: Now is the time for mutual restraint so that the peace we have achieved can last.

And finally, to all of you who are listening, the American people: Your steadfastness in supporting our insistence on peace with honor has made peace with honor possible. I know that you would not have wanted that peace jeopardized. With our secret negotiations at the sensitive stage they were in during this recent period, for me to have discussed publicly our efforts to secure peace would not only have violated our understanding with North Viet-Nam; it would have seriously harmed and possibly destroyed the chances for peace. Therefore, I know that you now can understand why during these past several weeks I have not made any public statements about those efforts.

The important thing was not to talk about peace, but to get peace and to get the right kind of peace. This we have done.

Now that we have achieved an honorable agreement, let us be proud that America did not settle for a peace that would have betrayed our allies, that would have abandoned our prisoners of war, or that would have ended the war for us but would have continued the war for the 50 million people of Indochina. Let us be proud of the 2½ million young Americans who served in Viet-Nam, who served with honor and distinction in one of the most selfless enterprises in the history of nations. And let us be proud of those who sacrificed, who gave their lives so that the people of South Viet-Nam might live in freedom and so that the world might live in peace.

In particular, I would like to say a word to some of the bravest people I have ever met—the wives, the children, the families, of our prisoners of war and the missing in action. When others called on us to settle on any terms, you had the courage to stand for the right kind of peace so that those who died and those who suffered would not have died and suffered in vain and so that where this generation knew war the next generation would know peace. Nothing means more to me at this moment than the fact that your long vigil is coming to an end.

Just yesterday, a great American who once occupied this office died. In his life President Johnson endured the vilification of those who sought to portray him as a man of war. But there was nothing he cared about more deeply than achieving a lasting peace in the world.

I remember the last time I talked with him. It was just the day after New Year's. He spoke then of his concern with bringing peace, with making it the right kind of peace, and I was grateful that he once again expressed his support for my efforts to gain such a peace. No one would have welcomed this peace more than he.

And I know he would join me in asking for those who died and for those who live: Let us consecrate this moment by resolving together to make the peace we have achieved a peace that will last.

Thank you and good evening.

Peace Treaties

Paris Peace Treaty between Great Britain and the United States, 1783

The siege and surrender of Yorktown was the last important engagement of the Revolutionary War. In London and Paris, the politicians and diplomats now took over. After a great deal of intrigue, a Definitive Treaty of Peace was worked out between Great Britain and the now-recognized "United States of America".

The text of the Treaty is given here from Volume 2 of Treaties and Other International Acts of the United States, *edited by Hunter Miller (Washington, D.C., 1931).*

The original in English of the Definitive Treaty of Peace, signed at Paris September 3, 1783. Ratified by the United States January 14, 1784. Ratified by Great Britain April 9, 1784. Ratifications exchanged at Paris May 12, 1784. Proclaimed January 14, 1784.

In the Name of the most Holy & undivided Trinity.

It having pleased the divine Providence to dispose the Hearts of the most Serene and most Potent Prince George the third, by the Grace of God, King of Great Britain, France & Ireland, Defender of the Faith, Duke of Brunswick and Lunebourg, Arch Treasurer, and Prince Elector of the Holy Roman Empire &c., and of the United States of America, to forget all past Misunderstandings and Differences that have unhappily interrupted the good Correspondence and Friendship which they mutually wish to restore; and to establish such a beneficial and satisfactory Intercourse between the two Countries upon the Ground of reciprocal Advantages and mutual Convenience as may promote and secure to both perpetual Peace & Harmony, and having for this desirable End already laid the Foundation of Peace & Reconciliation by the Provisional Articles signed at Paris on the 30th of November, 1782, by the Commissioners empower'd on each Part, which Articles were agreed to be inserted in and to constitute the Treaty of Peace proposed to be concluded between the Crown of Great Britain and the said United States, but which Treaty was not to be concluded until Terms of Peace should be agreed upon between Great Britain & France, and his Britannic Majesty should be ready to conclude such Treaty accordingly: and the Treaty between Great Britain & France having since been concluded, His Britannic Majesty & the United States of America, in Order to carry into full Effect the Provisional Articles abovementioned, according to the Tenor thereof, have constituted & appointed, that is to say His Britannic Majesty on his Part, David Hartley Esq., Member of the Parliament of Great Britain; and the said United States on their Part, John Adams Esq., late a Commissioner of the United States of America at the Court of Versailles, late Delegate in Congress from the State of Massachusetts and Chief Justice of the said State, and Minister Plenipotentiary of the said United States to their High Mightinesses the States General of the United Netherlands; Benjamin Franklin Esq., late Delegate in Congress from the State of Pennsylvania, President of the Convention of the said State, and Minister Plenipotentiary from the United States of America at the Court of Versailles; John Jay Esq., late President of Congress, and Chief Justice of the State of New-York, and Minister Plenipotentiary from the United States of America at the Court of Madrid; to be the Plenipotentiaries for the concluding and signing the Present Definitive Treaty; who after having reciprocally communicated their respective full Powers have agreed upon and confirmed the following Articles.

ARTICLE 1ST His Britannic Majesty acknowledges the said United States, viz. New-Hampshire Massachusetts Bay, Rhode-Island & Providence Plantations, Connecticut, New York, New Jersey, Pennsylvania, Delaware, Maryland, Virginia, North Carolina, South Carolina & Georgia, to be free sovereign & Independent States; that he treats with them as such, and for himself his Heirs & Successors, relinquishes all Claims to the Government Propriety & Territorial Rights of the same & every part thereof.

ARTICLE 2D And that all Disputes which might arise in future on the Subject of the Boundaries of the said United States, may be prevented, it is hereby agreed and declared, that the following are and shall be their Boundaries, Viz. From the North West Angle of Nova Scotia, viz. That Angle which is formed by a Line drawn due North from the Source of Saint Croix River to the Highlands along the said Highlands which divide those Rivers that empty themselves into the River St. Lawrence, from those which fall into the Atlantic Ocean, to the Northwestern-most Head of Connecticut River: Thence down along the middle of that River to the forty fifth Degree of North Latitude; From thence by a Line due West on said Latitude until it strikes the River Iroquois or Cataraquy; Thence along the middle of said River into Lake Ontario; through the Middle of said Lake until it strikes the Communication by Water between that Lake & Lake Erie; Thence along the middle of said Communication into Lake Erie; through the middle of said Lake, until it arrives at the Water Communication between that Lake & Lake Huron; Thence along the middle of said Water-Communication into the Lake Huron, thence through the middle of said Lake to the Water Communication between that Lake & Lake Superior, thence through Lake Superior Northward of the Isles Royal & Phelipeaux to the Long Lake; Thence through the Middle of said Long-Lake, and the Water Communication between it & the Lake of the Woods, to the said Lake of the Woods; Thence through the said Lake to the most Northwestern Point thereof, and from thence on a due West Course to the River Mississippi, Thence by a Line to be drawn along the

Middle of the said River Mississippi until it shall intersect the Northernmost Part of the thirty first Degree of North Latitude. South, by a Line to be drawn due East from the Determination of the Line last mentioned, in the Latitude of thirty one Degrees North of the Equator to the middle of the River Apalachicola or Catahouche. Thence along the middle thereof to its Junction with the Flint River; Thence strait to the Head of St. Mary's River, and thence down along the middle of St. Mary's River to the Atlantic Ocean. East, by a Line to be drawn along the Middle of the River St. Croix, from its Mouth in the Bay of Fundy to its Source; and from its Source directly North to the aforesaid Highlands, which divide the Rivers that fall into the Atlantic Ocean, from those which fall into the River St. Lawrence; comprehending all Islands within twenty Leagues of any part of the Shores of the United States, & lying between Lines to be drawn due East from the Points where the aforesaid Boundaries between Nova Scotia on the one Part and East Florida on the other, shall respectively touch the Bay of Fundy and the Atlantic Ocean, excepting such Islands as now are or heretofore have been within the Limits of the said Province of Nova Scotia.

ARTICLE 3D It is agreed that the People of the United States shall continue to enjoy unmolested the Right to take Fish of every kind on the Grand Bank and on all the other Banks of New-foundland, also in the Gulph of St. Lawrence, and at all other Places in the Sea where the Inhabitants of both Countries used at any time heretofore to fish. And also that the Inhabitants of the United States shall have Liberty to take Fish of every Kind on such Part of the Coast of New-foundland as British fishermen shall use, (but not to dry or cure the same on that Island) And also on the Coasts Bays & Creeks of all other of his Britannic Majesty's Dominions in America, and that the American Fishermen shall have Liberty to dry and cure Fish in any of the unsettled Bays Harbours and Creeks of Nova Scotia, Magdalen Islands, and Labrador, so long as the same shall remain unsettled but so soon as the same or either of them shall be settled, it shall not be lawful for the said Fishermen to dry or cure Fish at such Settlement, without a previous Agreement for that purpose with the Inhabitants, Proprietors or Possessors of the Ground.

ARTICLE 4TH It is agreed that Creditors on either Side shall meet with no lawful Impediment to the Recovery of the full Value in Sterling Money of all bona fide Debts heretofore contracted.

ARTICLE 5TH It is agreed that the Congress shall earnestly recommend it to the Legislatures of the respective States to provide for the Restitution of all Estates, Rights and Properties which have been confiscated belonging to real British Subjects; and also of the Estates Rights and Properties of Persons resident in Districts in the Possession of his Majesty's Arms, and who have not borne arms against the said United States. And that Persons of any other Description shall have free Liberty to go to any Part or Parts of any of the thirteen United States and therein to remain twelve Months unmolested in their Endeavours to obtain the Restitution of such of their Estates Rights & Properties as may have been confiscated. And that Congress shall also earnestly recommend to the several States, a Reconsideration and Revision of all Acts or Laws regarding the Premises, so as to render the said Laws or Acts perfectly consistent, not only with Justice and Equity, but with that Spirit of Conciliation, which, on the Return of the Blessings of Peace should universally prevail. And that Congress shall also earnestly recommend to the several States, that the Estates, Rights and Properties of such last mentioned Persons shall be restored to them, they refunding to any Persons who may be now in Possession, the Bonâ fide Price (where any has been given) which such Persons may have paid on purchasing any of the said Lands, Rights or Properties, since the Confiscation.

And it is agreed that all Persons who have any Interest in confiscated Lands, either by Debts, Marriage Settlements, or otherwise, shall meet with no lawful Impediment in the Prosecution of their just Rights.

ARTICLE 6TH That there shall be no future Confiscations made nor any Prosecutions commenc'd against any Person or Persons for or by Reason of the Part, which he or they may have taken in the present War, and that no Person shall on that Account suffer any future Loss or Damage, either in his Person Liberty or Property; and that those who may be in Confinement on such Charges at the Time of the Ratification of the Treaty in America shall be immediately set at Liberty, and the Prosecutions so commenced be discontinued.

ARTICLE 7TH There shall be a firm and perpetual Peace between his Britannic Majesty and the said States and between the Subjects of the one, and the Citizens of the other, wherefore all Hostilities both by Sea and Land shall from henceforth cease: All Prisoners on both Sides shall be set at Liberty, and his Britannic Majesty shall with all convenient speed, and without causing any Destruction, or carrying away any Negroes or other Property of the American Inhabitants, withdraw all his Armies, Garrisons & Fleets from the said United States, and from every Port, Place and Harbour within the same; leaving in all Fortifications the American Artillery that may be therein: And shall also Order & cause all Archives, Records, Deeds & Papers belonging to any of the said States, or their Citizens, which in the Course of the War may have fallen into the Hands of his Officers, to be forthwith restored and deliver'd to the proper States and Persons to whom they belong.

ARTICLE 8TH The Navigation of the River Mississippi, from its source to the Ocean shall for ever remain free and open to the Subjects of Great Britain and the Citizens of the United States.

ARTICLE 9TH In Case it should so happen that any Place or Territory belonging to great Britain or to the United States should have been conquer'd by the Arms of either from the other before the Arrival of the said Provisional Articles in America it is agreed that the same shall be restored without Difficulty and without requiring any Compensation.

ARTICLE 10TH The solemn Ratifications of the present Treaty expedited in good & due Form shall be exchanged between the contracting Parties in the Space of Six Months or sooner if possible to be computed from the Day of Signature of the present Treaty. In Witness whereof we the undersigned their Ministers Plenipotentiary have in their Name and in Virtue of our Full Powers signed with our Hands the present Definitive Treaty, and caused the Seals of our Arms to be affix'd thereto.

Done at Paris, this third Day of September, In the Year of our Lord one thousand seven hundred & eighty three.

D Hartley	John Adams	B Franklin	John Jay
[Seal]	[Seal]	[Seal]	[Seal]

Treaty with the Six Nations, 1784

Articles concluded at Fort Stanwix, on the twenty-second day of October, one thousand seven hundred and eighty-four, between Oliver Wolcott, Richard Butler, and Arthur Lee, Commissioners Plenipotentiary from the United States, in Congress assembled, on the one Part, and the Sachems and Warriors of the Six Nations, on the other.

The United States of America give peace to the Senecas, Mohawks, Onondagas and Cayugas, and receive them into their protection upon the following conditions:

ARTICLE I. Six hostages shall be immediately delivered to the commissioners by the said nations, to remain in possession of the United States, till all the prisoners, white and black, which were taken by the said Senecas, Mohawks, Onondagas and Cayugas, or by any of them, in the late war, from among the people of the United States, shall be delivered up.

ARTICLE II. The Oneida and Tuscarora nations shall be secured in the possession of the lands on which they are settled.

ARTICLE III. A line shall be drawn, beginning at the mouth of a creek about four miles east of Niagara, called Oyonwavea, or Johnston's Landing-Place, upon the lake named by the Indians Oswego, and by us Ontario; from thence southerly in a direction always four miles east of the carrying-path, between Lake Erie and Ontario, to the mouth of Tehoseroron or Buffaloe Creek on Lake Erie; thence south to the north boundary of the state of Pennsylvania; thence west to the end of the said north boundary; thence south along the west boundary of the said state, to the river Ohio; the said line from the mouth of the Oyonwayea to the Ohio, shall be the western boundary of the lands of the Six Nations, so that the Six Nations shall and do yield to the United States, all claims to the country west of the said boundary, and then they shall be secured in the peaceful possession of the lands they inhabit east and north of the same, reserving only six miles square round the fort of Oswego, to the United States, for the support of the same.

ARTICLE IV. The Commissioners of the United States, in consideration of the present circumstances of the Six Nations, and in execution of the humane and liberal views of the United States upon the signing of the above articles, will order goods to be delivered to the said Six Nations for their use and comfort.

Treaty of Greenville, 1795

A treaty of peace between the United States of America, and the tribes of Indians called the Wyandots, Delawares, Shawanees, Ottawas, Chippewas, Pattawatimas, Miamis, Eel Rivers, Weas, Kickapoos, Piankeshaws, and Kaskaskias.

To put an end to a destructive war, to settle all controversies, and to restore harmony and friendly intercourse between the said United States and Indian tribes, Anthony Wayne, major general commanding the army of the United States, and sole commissioner for the good purposes above mentioned, and the said tribes of Indians, by their sachems, chiefs, and warriors, met together at Greenville, the head quarters of the said army, have agreed on the following articles, which, when ratified by the President, with the advice and consent of the Senate of the United States, shall be binding on them and the said Indian tribes.

ART. 1: Henceforth all hostilities shall cease; peace is hereby established, and shall be perpetual; and a friendly intercourse shall take place between the said United States and Indian tribes.

ART. 2: All prisoners shall, on both sides, be restored. The Indians, prisoners to the United States, shall be immediately set at liberty. The people of the United States, still remaining prisoners among the Indians, shall be delivered up in ninety days from the date hereof, to the general or commanding officer at Greenville, fort Wayne, or fort Defiance; and ten chiefs of the said tribes shall remain at Greenville as hostages, until the delivery of the prisoners shall be effected.

ART. 3: The general boundary line between the lands of the United States and the lands of the said Indian tribes, shall begin at the mouth of Cayahoga river, and run thence up the same to the portage, between that and the Tuscarawas branch of the Muskingum, thence down that branch to the crossing place above fort Lawrence, thence westerly to a fork of that branch of the Great Miami river, running into the Ohio, at or near which fork stood Loromie's store, and where commences the portage between the Miami of the Ohio, and St. Mary's river, which is a branch of the Miami which runs into lake Erie; thence a westerly course to fort Recovery, which stands on a branch of the Wabash; thence southwesterly in a direct line to the Ohio, so as to intersect that river opposite the mouth of Kentucke or Cuttawa river. And in consideration of the peace now established; of the goods formerly received from the United States; of those now to be delivered; and of the yearly delivery of goods now stipulated to be made hereafter; and to indemnify the United States for the injuries and expenses they have sustained during the war, the said Indian tribes do hereby cede and relinquish forever, all their claims to the lands lying eastwardly and southwardly of the general boundary line now described: and these lands, or any part of them, shall never hereafter be made a cause or pretence, on the part of the said tribes, or any of them, of war or injury to the United States, or any of the people thereof.

And for the same considerations, and as an evidence of the returning friendship of the said Indian tribes, of their confidence in the United States, and desire to provide for their accommodations, and for that convenient intercourse which will be beneficial to both parties, the said Indian tribes do also cede to the United States the following pieces of land, to wit:

1) One piece of land six miles square, at or near Loromie's store, before mentioned.

2) One piece two miles square, at the head of the navigable water or landing, on the St. Mary's river, near Girty's town.

3) One piece six miles square, at the head of the navigable water of the Auglaize river.

4) One piece six miles square, at the confluence of the Auglaize and Miami rivers, where fort Defiance now stands.

5) One piece six miles square, at or near the confluence of the rivers St. Mary's and St. Joseph's, where fort Wayne now stands, or near it.

6) One piece two miles square, on the Wabash river, at the end of the portage from the Miami of the lake, and about eight miles westward from fort Wayne.

7) One piece six miles square, at the Ouatanon, or Old Wea towns, on the Wabash river.

8) One piece twelve miles square, at the British fort on the Miami of the lake, at the foot of the rapids.

9) One piece six miles square, at the mouth of the said river, where it empties into the lake.

10) One piece six miles square, upon Sandusky lake, where a fort formerly stood.

11) One piece two miles square, at the lower rapids of Sandusky river.

12) The post of Detroit, and all the land to the north, the west and the south of it, of which the Indian title has been

extinguished by gifts or grants to the French or English governments: and so much more land to be annexed to the district of Detroit, as shall be comprehended between the river Rosine, on the south, lake St. Clair on the north, and a line, the general course whereof shall be six miles distant from the west end of lake Erie and Detroit river.

13) The post of Michilimackinac, and all the land on the island on which that post stands, and the main land adjacent, of which the Indian title has been extinguished by gifts or grants to the French or English governments; and a piece of land on the main to the north of the island, to measure six miles, on lake Huron, or the strait between lakes Huron and Michigan, and to extend three miles back from the water of the lake or strait; and also, the Island De Bois Blane, being an extra and voluntary gift of the Chippewa nation.

14) One piece of land six miles square, at the mouth of Chikago river, emptying into the southwest end of lake Michigan, where a fort formerly stood.

15) One piece twelve miles square, at or near the mouth of the Illinois river, emptying into the Mississippi.

16) One piece six miles square, at the old Piorias fort and village near the south end of the Illinois lake, on said Illinois river. And whenever the United States shall think proper to survey and mark the boundaries of the lands hereby ceded to them, they shall give timely notice thereof to the said tribes of Indians, that they may appoint some of their wise chiefs to attend and see that the lines are run according to the terms of this treaty.

And the said Indian tribes will allow to the people of the United States a free passage by land and by water, as one and the other shall be found convenient, through their country, along the chain of posts hereinbefore mentioned; that is to say, from the commencement of the portage aforesaid, at or near Loromie's store, thence along said portage to the St. Mary's, and down the same to fort Wayne, and then down the Miami, to lake Erie; again, from the commencement of the portage at or near Loromie's store along the portage from thence to the river Auglaize, and down the same to its junction with the Miami at fort Defiance; again, from the commencement of the portage aforesaid, to Sandusky river, and down the same to Sandusky bay and lake Erie, and from Sandusky to the post which shall be taken at or near the foot of the Rapids of the Miami of the lake; and from thence to Detroit. Again, from the mouth of Chikago, to the commencement of the portage, between that river and the Illinois, and down the Illinois river to the Mississippi; also, from fort Wayne, along the portage aforesaid, which leads to the Wabash, and then down the Wabash to the Ohio. And the said Indian tribes will also allow to the people of the United States, the free use of the harbors and mouths of rivers along the lakes adjoining the Indian lands, for sheltering vessels and boats, and liberty to land their cargoes where necessary for their safety.

ART. 4: In consideration of the peace now established, and of the cessions and relinquishments of lands made in the preceding article by the said tribes of Indians, and to manifest the liberality of the United States, as the great means of rendering this peace strong and perpetual, the United States relinquish their claims to all other Indian lands northward of the river Ohio, eastward of the Mississippi, and westward and southward of the Great Lakes and the waters, uniting them, according to the boundary line agreed on by the United States and the King of Great Britain, in the treaty of peace made between them in the year 1783. But from this relinquishment by the United States, the following tracts of land are explicitly excepted:

1st. The tract on one hundred and fifty thousand acres near the rapids of the river Ohio, which has been assigned to General Clark, for the use of himself and his warriors.

2nd. The post of St. Vincennes, on the River Wabash, and the lands adjacent, of which the Indian title has been extinguished.

3rd. The lands at all other places in possession of the French people and other white settlers among them, of which the Indian title has been extinguished as mentioned in the 3d article; and

4th. The post of fort Massac towards the mouth of the Ohio. To which several parcels of land so excepted, the said tribes relinquish all the title and claim which they or any of them may have.

And for the same considerations and with the same views as above mentioned, the United States now deliver to the said Indian tribes a quantity of goods to the value of twenty thousand dollars, the receipt whereof they do hereby acknowledge; and henceforward every year, forever, the United States will deliver, at some convenient place northward of the river Ohio, like useful goods, suited to the circumstances of the Indians, of the value of nine thousand five hundred dollars; reckoning that value at the first cost of the goods in the city or place in the United States where they shall be procured. The tribes to which those goods are to be annually delivered, and the proportions in which they are to be delivered, are the following:

1st. To the Wyandots, the amount of one thousand dollars.

2nd. To the Delawares, the amount of one thousand dollars.

3rd. To the Shawanees, the amount of one thousand dollars.

4th. To the Miamis, the amount of one thousand dollars.

5th. To the Ottawas, the amount of one thousand dollars.

6th. To the Chippewas, the amount of one thousand dollars.

7th. To the Pattawatimas, the amount of one thousand dollars, and

8th. To the Kickapoo, Wea, Eel River, Piankeshaw, and Kaskaskia tribes, the amount of five hundred dollars each.

Provided, that if either of the said tribes shall hereafter, at an annual delivery of their share of the goods aforesaid, desire that a part of their annuity should be furnished in domestic animals, implements of husbandry, and other utensils convenient for them, and in compensation to useful artificers who may reside with or near them, and be employed for their benefit, the same shall, at the subsequent annual deliveries, be furnished accordingly.

ART. 5: To prevent any misunderstanding about the Indian lands relinquished by the United States in the fourth article, it is now explicitly declared, that the meaning of that relinquishment is this: the Indian tribes who have a right to those lands, are quietly to enjoy them, hunting, planting, and dwelling thereon, so long as they please, without any molestation from the United States; but when those tribes, or any of them, shall be disposed to sell their lands, or any part of them, they are to be sold only to the United

States; and until such sale, the United States will protect all the said Indian tribes in the quiet enjoyment of their lands against all citizens of the United States, and against all other white persons who intrude upon the same. And the said Indian tribes again acknowledge themselves to be under the protection of the said United States, and no other power whatever.

ART. 6: If any citizen of the United States, or any other white person or persons, shall presume to settle upon the lands now relinquished by the United States, such citizen or other person shall be out of the protection of the United States; and the Indian tribe, on whose land the settlement shall be made, may drive off the settler, or punish him in such manner as they shall think fit; and because such settlements, made without the consent of the United States, will be injurious to them as well as to the Indians, the United States shall be at liberty to break them up, and remove and punish the settlers as they shall think proper, and so effect that protection of the Indian lands herein before stipulated.

ART. 7: The said tribes of Indians, parties to this treaty, shall be at liberty to hunt within the territory and lands which they have now ceded to the United States, without hindrance or molestation, so long as they demean themselves peaceably, and offer no injury to the people of the United States.

ART. 8: Trade shall be opened with the said Indian tribes; and they do hereby respectively engage to afford protection to such persons, with their property, as shall be duly licensed to reside among them for the purpose of trade; and to their agents and servants; but no person shall be permitted to reside among them for the purpose of trade; and to their agents and servants; but no person shall be permitted to reside at any of their towns or hunting camps, as a trader, who is not furnished with a license for that purpose, under the hand and seal of the superintendent of the department northwest of the Ohio, or such other person as the President of the United States shall authorize to grant such licenses; to the end, that the said Indians may not be imposed on in their trade.* And if any licensed trader shall abuse his privilege by unfair dealing, upon complaint and proof thereof, his license shall be taken from him, and he shall be further punished according to the laws of the United States. And if any person shall intrude himself as a trader, without such license, the said Indians shall take and bring him before the superintendent, or his deputy, to be dealt with according to law. And to prevent impositions by forged licenses, the said Indians shall, at least once a year, give information to the superintendent, or his deputies, on the names of the traders residing among them.

ART. 9: Lest the firm peace and friendship now established, should be interrupted by the misconduct of individuals, the United States, and the said Indian tribes agree, that for injuries done by individuals on either side, no private revenge or retaliation shall take place; but instead thereof, complaint shall be made by the party injured, to the other: by the said Indian tribes or any of them, to the President of the United States, or the superintendent by him appointed; and by the superintendent or other person appointed by the President , to the principal chiefs of the said Indian tribes, or of the tribe to which the offender belongs; and such prudent measures shall then be taken as shall be necessary to preserve the said peace and friendship unbroken, until the legislature (or great council) of the United States, shall make other equitable provision in the case, to the satisfaction of both parties. Should any Indian tribes meditate a war against the United States, or either of them, and the same shall come to the knowledge of the before mentioned tribes, or either of them, they do hereby engage to give immediate notice thereof to the general, or officer commanding the troops of the United States, at the nearest post.

And should any tribe, with hostile intentions against the United States, or either of them, attempt to pass through their country, they will endeavor to prevent the same, and in like manner give information of such attempt, to the general, or officer commanding, as soon as possible, that all causes of mistrust and suspicion may be avoided between them and the United States. In like manner, the United States shall give notice to the said Indian tribes of any harm that may be meditated against them, or either of them, that shall come to their knowledge; and do all in their power to hinder and prevent the same, that the friendship between them may be uninterrupted.

ART. 10: All other treaties heretofore made between the United States, and the said Indian tribes, or any of them, since the treaty of 1783, between the United States and Great Britain, that come within the purview of this treaty, shall henceforth cease and become void.

In testimony whereof, the said Anthony Wayne, and the sachems and war chiefs of the before mentioned nations and tribes of Indians, have hereunto set their hands and affixed their seals. Done at Greenville, in the territory of the United States northwest of the river Ohio, on the third day of August, one thousand seven hundred and ninety five.

The Treaty of Ghent, 1814 (excerpts)

Treaty of Peace and Amity, signed at Ghent December 24, 1814.

Submitted to the Senate February 15, 1815. Resolution of advice and consent February 16, 1815. Ratified by the United States February 17, 1815. Ratified by Great Britain December 31, 1814. Ratifications exchanged at Washington February 17, 1815. Proclaimed February 18, 1815.

His Britannic Majesty and the United States of America desirous of terminating the war which has unhappily subsisted between the two Countries, and of restoring upon principles of perfect reciprocity, Peace, Friendship, and good Understanding between them, have for that purpose appointed their respective Plenipotentiaries, that is to say, His Britannic Majesty on His part has appointed the Right Honourable James Lord Gambier, late Admiral of the White now Admiral of the Red Squadron of His Majesty's Fleet; Henry Goulburn Esquire, a Member of the Imperial Parliament and Under Secretary of State; and William Adams Esquire, Doctor of Civil Laws: And the President of the United States, by and with the advice and consent of the Senate thereof, has appointed John Quincy Adams, James A. Bayard, Henry Clay, Jonathan Russell, and Albert Gallatin, Citizens of the United States; who, after a reciprocal communication of their respective Full Powers, have agreed upon the following Articles.

ARTICLE THE FIRST. There shall be a firm and universal Peace between His Britannic Majesty and the United States, and between their respective Countries, Territories, Cities, Towns, and People of every degree without exception of places or persons. All hostilities both by sea and land shall cease as soon as this Treaty shall have been ratified by both parties as hereinafter mentioned. All territory, places, and possessions whatsoever taken by either party from the other during the war, or which may be taken after the signing of this Treaty, excepting only the Islands hereinafter mentioned, shall be restored without delay and without causing any destruction or carrying away any of the Artillery or other public property originally captured in the said forts or places, and which shall remain therein upon the Exchange of the Ratifications of this Treaty, or any Slaves or other private property; And all Archives, Records, Deeds, and Papers, either of a public nature or belonging to private persons which in the course of the war may have fallen into the hands of the Officers of either party, shall be, as far as may be practicable, forthwith restored and delivered to the proper authorities and persons to whom they respectively belong. Such of the Islands in the Bay of Passamaquoddy as are claimed by both parties shall remain in the possession of the party in whose occupation they may be at the time of the Exchange of the Ratifications of this Treaty until the decision respecting the title to the said Islands shall have been made in conformity with the fourth Article of this Treaty. No disposition made by this Treaty as to such possession of the Islands and territories claimed by both parties shall in any manner whatever be construed to affect the right of either.

ARTICLE THE SECOND. Immediately after the ratifications of this Treaty by both parties as hereinafter mentioned, orders shall be sent to the Armies, Squadrons, Officers, Subjects, and Citizens of the two Powers to cease from all hostilities: and to prevent all causes of complaint which might arise on account of the prizes which may be taken at sea after the said Ratifications of this Treaty, it is reciprocally agreed that all vessels and effects which may be taken after the space of twelve days from the said Ratifications upon all parts of the Coast of North America from the Latitude of twenty three degrees North to the Latitude of fifty degrees North, and as far Eastward in the Atlantic Ocean as the thirty sixth degree of West Longitude from the Meridian of Greenwich, shall be restored on each side:—that the time shall be thirty days in all other parts of the Atlantic Ocean North of the Equinoctial Line or Equator:—and the same time for the British and Irish Channels, for the Gulf of Mexico, and all parts of the West Indies:—forty days for the North Seas for the Baltic, and for all parts of the Mediterranean:—sixty days for the Atlantic Ocean South of the Equator as far as the Latitude of the Cape of Good Hope:—ninety days for every other part of the world South of the Equator, and one hundred and twenty days for all other parts of the world without exception.

ARTICLE THE THIRD. All Prisoners of war taken on either side as well by land as by sea shall be restored as soon as practicable after the Ratifications of this Treaty as hereinafter mentioned on their paying the debts which they may have contracted during their captivity. The two Contracting Parties respectively engage to discharge in specie the advances which may have been made by the other for the sustenance and maintenance of such prisoners.

ARTICLE THE FOURTH. Whereas it was stipulated by the second Article in the Treaty of Peace of one thousand seven hundred and eighty three between His Britannic Majesty and the United States of America that the boundary of the United States should comprehend "all Islands within twenty leagues of any part of the shores of the United States and lying between lines to be drawn due East from the points where the aforesaid boundaries between Nova Scotia on the one part and East Florida on the other shall respectively touch the Bay of Fundy and the Atlantic Ocean, excepting such Islands as now are or heretofore have been within the limits of Nova Scotia," and, whereas the several Islands in the Bay of Passamaquoddy, which is part of the Bay of Fundy, and the Island of Grand Menan in the said Bay of Fundy, are claimed by the United States as being comprehended within their aforesaid boundaries, which said Islands are claimed as belonging to His Britannic Majesty as having been at the time of and previous to the aforesaid Treaty of one thousand seven hundred and eighty three within the limits of the Province of Nova Scotia . . .

ARTICLE THE FIFTH. Whereas neither that point of the Highlands lying due North from the source of the River St. Croix, and designated in the former Treaty of Peace between the two Powers as the North West Angle of Nova Scotia, nor the North Westernmost head of Connecticut River has yet been ascertained; and whereas that part of the boundary line between the Dominions of the two Powers which extends from the source of the River St. Croix directly North to the abovementioned North West Angle of Nova Scotia, thence along the said Highlands which divide those Rivers that empty themselves into the River St. Lawrence from those which fall into the Atlantic Ocean to the North Westernmost head of Connecticut River, thence down along the middle of that River to the forty fifth degree of North Latitude, thence by a line due West on said latitude until it strikes the River Iroquois or Cataraquy, has not yet been surveyed: it is agreed that for these several purposes two Commissioners shall be appointed, sworn, and authorized to act exactly in the manner directed with respect to those mentioned in the next preceding Article unless otherwise specified in the present Article. The said Commissioners shall meet at St. Andrews in the Province of New Brunswick, and shall have power to adjourn to such other place or places as they shall think fit. The said Commissioners shall have power to ascertain and determine the points above mentioned in conformity with the provisions of the said Treaty of Peace of one thousand seven hundred and eighty three, and shall cause the boundary aforesaid from the source of the River St. Croix to the River Iroquois or Cataraquy to be surveyed and marked according to the said provisions. The said Commissioners shall make a map of the said boundary, and annex to it a declaration under their hands and seals certifying it to be the true Map of the said boundary, and particularizing the latitude and longitude of the North West Angle of Nova Scotia, of the North Westernmost head of Connecticut River, and of such other points of the said boundary as they may deem proper. And both parties agree to consider such map and declaration as finally and conclusively fixing the said boundary. And in the event of the said two Commissioners differing, or both, or either of them refusing, declining, or wilfully omitting to act, such reports, declarations, or statements shall be made by them or either of them, and such reference to a friendly Sovereign or State shall be made in all respects as in the latter part of the fourth Article is contained, and in as full a manner as if the same was herein repeated.

ARTICLE THE SIXTH. Whereas by the former Treaty of Peace that portion of the boundary of the United States from the point where the forty fifth degree of North Latitude strikes the River Iroquois or Cataraquy to the Lake Superior was declared to be "along the middle of said River into Lake Ontario, through the middle of said Lake until it strikes the communication by water between that Lake and Lake Erie, thence along the middle of said communication into Lake Erie, through the middle of said Lake until it arrives at the water communication into the Lake Huron; thence through the middle of said Lake to the water communication between that Lake and Lake Superior:" and whereas doubts have arisen what was the middle of the said River, Lakes, and water communications, and whether certain Islands lying in the same were within the Dominions of His Britannic Majesty or of the United States: In order therefore finally to decide these doubts, they shall be referred to two Commissioners to be appointed, sworn, and authorized to act exactly in the manner directed with respect to those mentioned in the next preceding Article unless otherwise specified in this present Article. The said Commissioners shall meet in the first instance at Albany in the State of New York, and shall have power to adjourn to such other place or places as they shall think fit. The said Commissioners shall by a Report or Declaration under their hands and seals, designate the boundary through the said River, Lakes, and water communications, and decide to which of the two Contracting parties the several Islands lying within the said Rivers, Lakes, and water communications, do respectively belong in conformity with the true intent of the said Treaty of one thousand seven hundred and eighty three. And both parties agree to consider such designation and decision as final and conclusive. And in the event of the said two Commissioners differing or both or either of them refusing, declining, or wilfully omitting to act, such reports, declarations, or statements shall be made by them or either of them, and such reference to a friendly Sovereign or State shall be made in all respects as in the latter part of the fourth Article is contained, and in as full a manner as if the same herein repeated.

ARTICLE THE NINTH. The United States of America engage to put an end immediately after the Ratification of the present Treaty to hostilities with all the Tribes or Nations of Indians with whom they may be at war at the time of such Ratification, and forthwith to restore to such Tribes or Nations respectively all the possessions, rights, and privileges which they may have enjoyed or been entitled to in one thousand eight hundred and eleven previous to such hostilities. Provided always that such Tribes or Nations shall agree to desist from all hostilities against the United States of America, their Citizens, and Subjects upon the Ratification of the present Treaty being notified to such Tribes or Nations, and shall so desist accordingly. And His Britannic Majesty engages on his part to put an end immediately after the Ratification of the present Treaty to hostilities with all the Tribes or Nations of Indians with whom He may be at war at the time of such Ratification, and forthwith to restore to such Tribes or Nations respectively all the possessions, rights, and privileges, which they may have enjoyed or been entitled to in one thousand eight hundred and eleven previous to such hostilities. Provided always that such Tribes or Nations shall agree to desist from all hostilities against His Britannic Majesty and His Subjects upon the Ratification of the present Treaty being notified to such Tribes or Nations, and shall so desist accordingly.

ARTICLE THE TENTH. Whereas the Traffic in Slaves is irreconcilable with the principles of humanity and Justice, and whereas both His Majesty and the United States are desirous of continuing their efforts to promote its entire abolition, it is hereby agreed that both the contracting parties shall use their best endeavours to accomplish so desirable an object.

ARTICLE THE ELEVENTH. This Treaty when the same shall have been ratified on both sides without alteration by either of the contracting parties, and the Ratifications mutually exchanged, shall be binding on both parties, and the Ratifications shall be exchanged at Washington in the space of four months from this day or sooner if practicable.

In faith whereof, We the respective Plenipotentiaries have signed this Treaty, and have thereunto affixed our Seals.

Done in triplicate at Ghent the twenty fourth day of December one thousand eight hundred and fourteen.

Treaty of Guadalupe Hidalgo, 1848 (excerpts)

Treary of peace, friendship, limits, and settlement between the United States of America and the United Mexican States concluded at Guadalupe Hidalgo, February 2, 1848; Ratification advised by Senate, with amendments, March 10, 1848; Ratified by President, March 16, 1848; Ratifications exchanged at Queretaro, May 30, 1848; Proclaimed, July 4, 1848.

IN THE NAME OF ALMIGHTY GOD The United States of America and the United Mexican States animated by a sincere desire to put an end to the calamities of the war which unhappily exists between the two Republics and to establish upon a solid basis relations of peace and friendship, which shall confer reciprocal benefits upon the citizens of both, and assure the concord, harmony, and mutual confidence wherein the two people should live, as good neighbors have for that purpose appointed their respective plenipotentiaries, that is to say: The President of the United States has appointed Nicholas P. Trist, a citizen of the United States, and the President of the Mexican Republic has appointed Don Luis Gonzaga Cuevas, Don Bernardo Couto, and Don Miguel Atristain, citizens of the said Republic; Who, after a reciprocal communication of their respective full powers, have, under the protection of Almighty God, the author of peace, arranged, agreed upon, and signed the following:

Treaty of Peace, Friendship, Limits, and Settlement between the United States of America and the Mexican Republic.

ARTICLE I There shall be firm and universal peace between the United States of America and the Mexican Republic, and between their respective countries, territories, cities, towns, and people, without exception of places or persons.

ARTICLE II Immediately upon the signature of this treaty, a convention shall be entered into between a commissioner or commissioners appointed by the General-in-Chief of the forces of the United States, and such as may be appointed by the Mexican Government, to the end that a provisional suspension of hostilities shall take place, and that, in the places occupied by the said forces, constitutional order may be reestablished, as regards the political, administrative, and judicial branches, so far as this shall be permitted by the circumstances of military occupation.

ARTICLE III Immediately upon the ratification of the present treaty by the Government of the United States, orders shall be transmitted to the commanders of their land and naval forces, requiring the latter (provided this treaty shall then have been ratified by the Government of the Mexican Republic, and the ratifications exchanged) immediately to desist from blockading any Mexican ports and requiring the former (under the same condition) to commence, at the earliest moment practicable, withdrawing all troops of the United States then in the interior of the Mexican Republic, to points that shall be selected by common agreement, at a distance from the seaports not exceeding thirty leagues; and such evacuation of the interior of the Republic shall be completed with the least possible delay; the Mexican Government hereby binding itself to afford every facility in its power for rendering the same convenient to the troops, on their march and in their new positions, and for promoting a good understanding between them and the inhabitants. In like manner orders shall be despatched to the persons in charge of the custom houses at all ports occupied by the forces of the United States, requiring them (under the same condition) immediately to deliver possession of the same to the persons authorized by the Mexican Government to receive it, together with all bonds and evidences of debt for duties on importations and on exportations, not yet fallen due. Moreover, a faithful and exact account shall be made out, showing the entire amount of all duties on imports and on exports, collected at such custom-houses, or elsewhere in Mexico, by authority of the United States, from and after the day of ratification of this treaty by the Government of the Mexican Republic; and also an account of the cost of collection; and such entire amount, deducting only the cost of collection, shall be delivered to the Mexican Government, at the city of Mexico, within three months after the exchange of ratifications.

The evacuation of the capital of the Mexican Republic by the troops of the United States, in virtue of the above stipulation, shall be completed in one month after the orders there stipulated for shall have been received by the commander of said troops, or sooner if possible.

ARTICLE IV Immediately after the exchange of ratifications of the present treaty all castles, forts, territories, places, and possessions, which have been taken or occupied by the forces of the United States during the present war, within the limits of the Mexican Republic, as about to be established by the following article, shall be definitely restored to the said Republic, together with all the artillery, arms, apparatus of war, munitions, and other public property, which were in the said castles and forts when captured, and which shall remain there at the time when this treaty shall be duly ratified by the Government of the Mexican Republic. To this end, immediately upon the signature of this treaty, orders shall be despatched to the American officers commanding such castles and forts, securing against the removal or destruction of any such artillery, arms, apparatus of war, munitions, or other public property. The city of Mexico, within the inner line of intrenchments surrounding the said city, is comprehended in the above stipulation, as regards the restoration of artillery, apparatus of war, & c.

The final evacuation of the territory of the Mexican Republic, by the forces of the United States, shall be completed in three months from the said exchange of ratifications, or sooner if possible; the Mexican Government hereby engaging, as in the foregoing article to use all means in its power for facilitating such evacuation, and rendering it convenient to the troops, and for promoting a good understanding between them and the inhabitants.

If, however, the ratification of this treaty by both parties should not take place in time to allow the embarcation of the troops of the United States to be completed before the commencement of the sickly season, at the Mexican ports on the Gulf of Mexico, in such case a friendly arrangement shall be entered into between the General-in-Chief of the said troops and the Mexican Government, whereby healthy and otherwise suitable places, at a distance from the ports not exceeding thirty leagues, shall be designated for the residence of such troops as may not yet have embarked, until the return of the healthy season. And the space of time here referred to as, comprehending the sickly season shall be understood to extend from the first day of May to the first day of November.

All prisoners of war taken on either side, on land or on sea, shall be restored as soon as practicable after the exchange of ratifications of this treaty. It is also agreed that if any Mexicans should now be held as captives by any savage tribe within the limits of the United States, as about to be established by the following article, the Government of the said United States will exact the release of such captives and cause them to be restored to their country.

ARTICLE V The boundary line between the two Republics shall commence in the Gulf of Mexico, three leagues from land, opposite the mouth of the Rio Grande, otherwise called Rio Bravo del Norte, or Opposite the mouth of its deepest branch, if it should have more than one branch emptying directly into the sea; from thence up the middle of that river, following the deepest channel, where it has more than one, to the point where it strikes the southern boundary of New Mexico; thence, westwardly, along the whole southern boundary of New Mexico (which runs north of the town called Paso) to its western termination; thence, northward, along the western line of New Mexico, until it intersects the first branch of the river Gila; (or if it should not intersect any branch of that river, then to the point on the said line nearest to such branch, and thence in a direct line to the same); thence down the middle of the said branch and of the said river, until it empties into the Rio Colorado; thence across the Rio Colorado, following the division line between Upper and Lower California, to the Pacific Ocean.

The southern and western limits of New Mexico, mentioned in the article, are those laid down in the map entitled "Map of the United Mexican States, as organized and defined by various acts of the Congress of said republic, and constructed according to the best authorities. Revised edition. Published at New York, in 1847, by J. Disturnell," of which map a copy is added to this treaty, bearing the signatures and seals of the undersigned Plenipotentiaries. And, in order to preclude all difficulty in tracing upon the ground the limit separating Upper from Lower California, it is agreed that the said limit shall consist of a straight line drawn from the middle of the Rio Gila, where it unites with the Colorado, to a point on the coast of the Pacific Ocean, distant one marine league due south of the southernmost point of the port of San Diego, according to the plan of said port made in the year 1782 by Don Juan Pantoja, second sailing-master of the Spanish fleet, and published at Madrid in the year 1802, in the atlas to the voyage of the schooners Sutil and Mexicana; of which plan a copy is hereunto added, signed and sealed by the respective Plenipotentiaries.

In order to designate the boundary line with due precision, upon authoritative maps, and to establish upon the ground land-marks which shall show the limits of both republics, as described in the present article, the two Governments shall each appoint a commissioner and a surveyor, who, before the expiration of one year from the date of the exchange of ratifications of this treaty, shall meet at the port of San Diego, and proceed to run and mark the said boundary on its whole course to the mouth of the Rio Bravo del Norte. They shall keep journals and make out plans of their operations; and the result agreed upon by them shall be deemed a part of this treaty, and shall have the same force as if it were inserted therein. The two Governments will amicably agree regarding what may be necessary to these persons, and also as to their respective escorts, should such be necessary.

The boundary line established by this article shall be religiously respected by each of the two republics, and no change shall ever be made therein, except by the express and free consent of both nations, lawfully given by the General Government of each, in conformity with its own constitution.

ARTICLE VI The vessels and citizens of the United States shall, in all time, have a free and uninterrupted passage by the Gulf of California, and by the river Colorado below its confluence with the Gila, to and from their possessions situated north of the boundary line defined in the preceding article; it being understood that this passage is to be by navigating the Gulf of California and the river Colorado, and not by land, without the express consent of the Mexican Government.

If, by the examinations which may be made, it should be ascertained to be practicable and advantageous to construct a road, canal, or railway, which should in whole or in part run upon the river Gila, or upon its right or its left bank, within the space of one marine league from either margin of the river, the Governments of both republics will form an agreement regarding its construction, in order that it may serve equally for the use and advantage of both countries.

ARTICLE VII The river Gila, and the part of the Rio Bravo del Norte lying below the southern boundary of New Mexico, being, agreeably to the fifth article, divided in the middle between the two republics, the navigation of the Gila and of the Bravo below said boundary shall be free and common to the vessels and citizens of both countries; and neither shall, without the consent of the other, construct any work that may impede or interrupt, in whole or in part, the exercise of this right; not even for the purpose of favoring new methods of navigation. Nor shall any tax or contribution, under any denomination or title, be levied upon vessels or persons navigating the same or upon merchandise or effects transported thereon, except in the case of landing upon one of their shores. If, for the purpose of making the said rivers navigable, or for maintaining them in such state, it should be necessary or advantageous to establish any tax or contribution, this shall not be done without the consent of both Governments.

The stipulations contained in the present article shall not impair the territorial rights of either republic within its established limits.

ARTICLE VIII Mexicans now established in territories previously belonging to Mexico, and which remain for the future within the limits of the United States, as defined by the present treaty, shall be free to continue where they now reside, or to remove at any time to the Mexican Republic, retaining the property which they possess in the said territories, or disposing thereof, and removing the proceeds wherever they please, without their being subjected, on this account, to any contribution, tax, or charge whatever.

Those who shall prefer to remain in the said territories may either retain the title and rights of Mexican citizens, or acquire those of citizens of the United States. But they shall be under the obligation to make their election within one year from the date of the exchange of ratifications of this treaty; and those who shall remain in the said territories after the expiration of that year, without having declared their intention to retain the character of Mexicans, shall be considered to have elected to become citizens of the United States.

In the said territories, property of every kind, now belonging to Mexicans not established there, shall be inviolably respected. The present owners, the heirs of these, and all Mexicans who may hereafter acquire said property by contract, shall enjoy with respect to it guarantees equally ample as if the same belonged to citizens of the United States.

ARTICLE IX The Mexicans who, in the territories aforesaid, shall not preserve the character of citizens of the Mexican Republic, conformably with what is stipulated in the preceding article, shall be incorporated into the Union of the United States and be admitted at the proper time (to be judged of by the Congress of the United States) to the enjoyment of all the rights of citizens of the United States, according to the principles of the Constitution; and in the mean time, shall be maintained and protected in the free enjoyment of their liberty and property, and secured in the free exercise of their religion without restriction.

ARTICLE XI Considering that a great part of the territories, which, by the present treaty, are to be comprehended for the future within the limits of the United States, is now occupied by savage tribes, who will hereafter be under the exclusive control of the Government of the United States, and whose incursions within the territory of Mexico would be prejudicial in the extreme, it is solemnly agreed that all such incursions shall be forcibly restrained by the Government of the United States whensoever this may be necessary; and that when they cannot be prevented, they shall be punished by the said Government, and satisfaction for the same shall be exacted all in the same way, and with equal diligence and energy, as if the same incursions were meditated or committed within its own territory, against its own citizens.

It shall not be lawful, under any pretext whatever, for any inhabitant of the United States to purchase or acquire any Mexican, or any foreigner residing in Mexico, who may have been captured by Indians inhabiting the territory of either of the two republics; nor to purchase or acquire horses, mules, cattle, or property of any kind, stolen within Mexican territory by such Indians.

And in the event of any person or persons, captured within Mexican territory by Indians, being carried into the territory of the United States, the Government of the latter engages and binds itself, in the most solemn manner, so soon as it shall know of such captives being within its territory, and shall be able so to do, through the faithful exercise of its influence and power, to rescue them and return them to their country or deliver them to the agent or representative of the Mexican Government. The Mexican authorities will, as far as practicable, give to the Government of the United States notice of such captures; and its agents shall pay the expenses incurred in the maintenance and transmission of the rescued captives; who, in the mean time, shall be treated with the utmost hospitality by the American authorities at the place where they may be. But if the Government of the United States, before receiving such notice from Mexico, should obtain intelligence, through any other channel, of the existence of Mexican captives within its territory, it will proceed forthwith to effect their release and delivery to the Mexican agent, as above stipulated.

For the purpose of giving to these stipulations the fullest possible efficacy, thereby affording the security and redress demanded by their true spirit and intent, the Government of the United States will now and hereafter pass, without unnecessary delay, and always vigilantly enforce, such laws as the nature of the subject may require. And, finally, the sacredness of this obligation shall never be lost sight of by the said Government, when providing for the removal of the Indians from any portion of the said territories, or for its being settled by citizens of the United States; but, on the contrary, special care shall then be taken not to place its Indian occupants under the necessity of seeking new homes, by committing those invasions which the United States have solemnly obliged themselves to restrain.

ARTICLE XII In consideration of the extension acquired by the boundaries of the United States, as defined in the fifth article of the present treaty, the Government of the United States engages to pay to that of the Mexican Republic the sum of fifteen millions of dollars.

Immediately after the treaty shall have been duly ratified by the Government of the Mexican Republic, the sum of three millions of dollars shall be paid to the said Government by that of the United States, at the city of Mexico, in the gold or silver coin of Mexico. The remaining twelve millions of dollars shall be paid at the same place, and in the same coin, in annual installments of three millions of dollars each, together with interest on the same at the rate of six per centum per annum. This interest shall begin to run upon the whole sum of twelve millions from the day of the ratification of the present treaty by the Mexican Government, and the first of the installments shall be paid at the expiration of one year from the same day. Together with each annual installment, as it falls due, the whole interest accruing on such installment from the beginning shall also be paid.

ARTICLE XXIII This treaty shall be ratified by the President of the United States of America, by and with the advice and consent of the Senate thereof; and by the President of the Mexican Republic, with the previous approbation of its general Congress; and the ratifications shall be exchanged in the City of Washington, or at the seat of Government of Mexico, in four months from the date of the signature hereof, or sooner if practicable. In faith whereof we, the respective Plenipotentiaries, have signed this treaty of peace, friendship, limits, and settlement, and have hereunto affixed our seals respectively. Done in quintuplicate, at the city of Guadalupe Hidalgo, on the second day of February, in the year of our Lord one thousand eight hundred and forty-eight.

Treaty with the Apache, 1852

Articles of a treaty made and entered into at Santa Fe, New Mexico, on the first day of July in the year of our Lord one thousand eight hundred and fifty-two, by and between Col. E. V. Sumner, U.S.A., commanding the 9th Department and in charge of the executive office of New Mexico, and John Greiner, Indian agent in and for the Territory of New Mexico, and acting superintendent of Indian affairs of said Territory, representing the United States, and Cuentas, Azules, Blancito, Negrito, Capitan Simon, Capitan Vuelta, and Mangus Colorado, chiefs, acting on the part of the Apache Nation of Indians, situate and living within the limits of the United States.

ARTICLE 1. Said nation or tribe of Indians through their authorized Chiefs aforesaid do hereby acknowledge and declare that they are lawfully and exclusively under the laws, jurisdiction, and government of the United States of America, and to its power and authority they do hereby submit.

ARTICLE 2. From and after the signing of this Treaty hostilities between the contracting parties shall forever cease, and perpetual peace and amity shall forever exist between said Indians and the Government and people of the United States; the said nation, or tribe of Indians, hereby binding themselves most solemnly never to associate with or give countenance or aid to any tribe or band of Indians, or other persons or powers, who may be at any time at war or enmity with the government or people of said United States.

ARTICLE 3. Said nation, or tribe of Indians, do hereby bind themselves for all future time to treat honestly and humanely all citizens of the United States, with whom they have intercourse, as well as all persons and powers, at peace with the said United States, who may be lawfully among them, or with whom they may have any lawful intercourse.

ARTICLE 4. All said nation, or tribe of Indians, hereby bind themselves to refer all cases of aggression against themselves or their property and territory, to the government of the United States for adjustment, and to conform in all things to the laws, rules, and regulations of said government in regard to the Indian tribes.

ARTICLE 5. Said nation, or tribe of Indians, do hereby bind themselves for all future time to desist and refrain from making any "incursions within the Territory of Mexico" of a hostile or predatory character; and that they will for the future refrain from taking and conveying into captivity any of the people or citizens of Mexico, or the animals or property of the people or government of Mexico; and that they will, as soon as possible after the signing of this treaty, surrender to their agent all captives now in their possession.

ARTICLE 6. Should any citizen of the United States, or other person or persons subject to the laws of the United States, murder, rob, or otherwise maltreat any Apache Indian or Indians, he or they shall be arrested and tried, and upon conviction, shall be subject to all the penalties provided by law for the protection of the persons and property of the people of the said States.

ARTICLE 7. The people of the United States of America shall have free and safe passage through the territory of the aforesaid Indians, under such rules and regulations as may be adopted by authority of the said States.

ARTICLE 8. In order to preserve tranquility and to afford protection to all the people and interests of the contracting parties, the government of the United States of America will establish such military posts and agencies, and authorize such trading houses at such times and places as the said government may designate.

ARTICLE 9. Relying confidently upon the justice and the liberality of the aforesaid government, and anxious to remove every possible cause that might disturb their peace and quiet, it is agreed by the aforesaid Apache's that the government of the United States shall at its earliest convenience designate, settle, and adjust their territorial boundaries, and pass and execute in their territory such laws as may be deemed conducive to the prosperity and happiness of said Indians.

ARTICLE 10. For and in consideration of the faithful performance of all the stipulations herein contained, by the said Apache's Indians, the government of the United States will grant to said Indians such donations, presents, and implements, and adopt such other liberal and humane measures as said government may deem meet and proper.

ARTICLE 11. This Treaty shall be binding upon the contracting parties from and after the signing of the same, subject only to such modifications and amendments as may be adopted by the government of the United States; and, finally, this treaty is to receive a liberal construction, at all times and in all places, to the end that the said Apache Indians shall not be held responsible for the conduct of others, and that the government of the United States shall so legislate and act as to secure the permanent prosperity and happiness of said Indians.

In faith whereof we the undersigned have signed this Treaty, and affixed thereunto our seals, at the City of Santa Fe, this the first day of July in the year of our Lord one thousand eight hundred and fifty-two.

Fort Laramie Treaty, 1868

ARTICLES OF A TREATY MADE AND CONCLUDED BY AND BETWEEN

Lieutenant General William T. Sherman, General William S. Harney, General Alfred H. Terry, General O. O. Augur, J. B. Henderson, Nathaniel G. Taylor, John G. Sanborn, and Samuel F. Tappan, duly appointed commissioners on the part of the United States, and the different bands of the Sioux Nation of Indians, by their chiefs and headmen, whose names are hereto subscribed, they being duly authorized to act in the premises.

ARTICLE I. From this day forward all war between the parties to this agreement shall for ever cease. The government of the United States desires peace, and its honor is hereby pledged to keep it. The Indians desire peace, and they now pledge their honor to maintain it.

If bad men among the whites, or among other people subject to the authority of the United States, shall commit any wrong upon the person or property of the Indians, the United States will, upon proof made to the agent, and forwarded to the Commissioner of Indian Affairs at Washington city, proceed at once to cause the offender to be arrested and punished according to the laws of the United States, and also reimburse the injured person for the loss sustained.

If bad men among the Indians shall commit a wrong or depredation upon the person or property of nay one, white, black, or Indian, subject to the authority of the United States, and at peace therewith, the Indians herein named solemnly agree that they will, upon proof made to their agent, and notice by him, deliver up the wrongdoer to the United States, to be tried and punished according to its laws, and, in case they willfully refuse so to do, the person injured shall be reimbursed for his loss from the annuities, or other moneys due or to become due to them under this or other treaties made with the United States; and the President, on advising with the Commissioner of Indian Affairs, shall prescribe such rules and regulations for ascertaining damages under the provisions of this article as in his judgment may be proper, but no one sustaining loss while violating the provisions of this treaty, or the laws of the United States, shall be reimbursed therefor.

ARTICLE II. The United States agrees that the following district of country, to wit, viz: commencing on the east bank of the Missouri river where the 46th parallel of north latitude crosses the same, thence along low-water mark down said east bank to a point opposite where the northern line of the State of Nebraska strikes the river, thence west across said river, and along the northern line of Nebraska to the 104th degree of river, thence west across said river, and along the northern line of Nebraska to the 104th degree of longitude west from Greenwich, thence north on said meridian to a point where the 46th parallel of north latitude intercepts the same, thence due east along said parallel to the place of beginning; and in addition thereto, all existing reservations of the east back of said river, shall be and the same is, set apart for the absolute and undisturbed use and occupation of the Indians herein named, and for such other friendly tribes or individual Indians as from time to time they may be willing, with the consent of the United States, to admit amongst them; and the United States now solemnly agrees that no persons, except those herein designated and authorized so to do, and except such officers, agents, and employees of the government as may be authorized to enter upon Indian reservations in discharge of duties enjoined by law, shall ever be permitted to pass over, settle upon, or reside in the territory described in this article, or in such territory as may be added to this reservation for the use of said Indians, and henceforth they will and do hereby relinquish all claims or right in and to any portion of the United States or Territories, except such as is embraced within the limits aforesaid, and except as hereinafter provided.

ARTICLE III. If it should appear from actual survey or other satisfactory examination of said tract of land that it contains less than 160 acres of tillable land for each person who, at the time, may be authorized to reside on it under the provisions of this treaty, and a very considerable number of such persons shall be disposed to commence cultivating the soil as farmers, the United States agrees to set apart, for the use of said Indians, as herein provided, such additional quantity of arable land, adjoining to said reservation, or as near to the same as it can be obtained, as may be required to provide the necessary amount.

ARTICLE IV. The United States agrees, at its own proper expense, to construct, at some place on the Missouri river, near the centre of said reservation where timber and water may be convenient, the following buildings, to wit, a warehouse, a store-room for the use of the agent in storing goods belonging to the Indians, to cost not less than $2,500; an agency building, for the residence of the agent, to cost not exceeding $3,000; a residence for the physician, to cost not more than $3,000; and five other buildings, for a carpenter, farmer, blacksmith, miller, and engineer-each to cost not exceeding $2,000; also, a school-house, or mission building, so soon as a sufficient number of children can be induced by the agent to attend school, which shall not cost exceeding $5,000.

The United States agrees further to cause to be erected on said reservation, near the other buildings herein authorized, a good steam circular saw-mill, with a grist-mill and shingle machine attached to the same, to cost not exceeding $8,000.

ARTICLE V. The United States agrees that the agent for said Indians shall in the future make his home at the agency building; that he shall reside among them, and keep an office open at all times for the purpose of prompt and diligent inquiry into such matters of complaint by and against the Indians as may be presented for investigation under the provisions of their treaty stipulations, as also for the faithful discharge of other duties enjoined on him by law. In all cases of depredation on person or property he shall cause the evidence to be taken in writing and forwarded, together with his findings, to the Commissioner of Indian Affairs, whose decision, subject to the revision of the Secretary of the Interior, shall be binding on the parties to this treaty.

ARTICLE VI. If any individual belonging to said tribes of Indians, or legally incorporated with them, being the head of a family, shall desire to commence farming, he shall have the privilege to select, in the presence and with the assistance of the agent then in charge, a tract of land within said reservation, not exceeding three hundred and twenty acres in extent, which tract, when so selected, certified, and recorded in the "Land Book" as herein directed, shall cease to be held in common, but the same may be occupied and held in the exclusive possession of the person selecting it, and of his family, so long as he or they may continue to cultivate it.

Any person over eighteen years of age, not being the head of a family, may in like manner select and cause to be certified to him or her, for purposes of cultivation, a quantity of land, not exceeding eighty acres in extent, and thereupon be entitled to the exclusive possession of the same as above directed.

For each tract of land so selected a certificate, containing a description thereof and the name of the person selecting it, with a certificate endorsed thereon that the same has been recorded, shall be delivered to the party entitled to it, by the agent, after the same shall have been recorded by him in a book to be kept in his office, subject to inspection, which said book shall be known as the "Sioux Land Book."

The President may, at any time, order a survey of the reservation, and, when so surveyed, Congress shall provide for protecting the rights of said settlers in their improvements, and may fix the character of the title held by each. The United States may pass such laws on the subject of alienation and descent of property between the Indians and their descendants as may be thought proper. And it is further stipulated that any male Indians over eighteen years of age, of any band or tribe that is or shall hereafter become a party to this treaty, who now is or who shall hereafter become a resident or occupant of any reservation or territory not included in the tract of country designated and described in this treaty for the permanent home of the Indians, which is not mineral land, nor reserved by the United States for special purposes other than Indian occupation, and who shall have made improvements thereon of the value of two hundred dollars or more, and continuously occupied the same as a homestead for the term of three years, shall be entitled to receive from the United States a patent for one hundred and sixty acres of land including his said improvements, the same to be in the form of the legal subdivisions of the surveys of the public lands. Upon application in writing, sustained by the proof of two disinterested witnesses, made to the register of the local land office when the land sought to be entered is within a land district, and when the tract sought to be entered is not in any land district, then upon said application and proof being made to the Commissioner of the General Land Office, and the right of such Indian or Indians to enter such tract or tracts of land shall accrue and be perfect from the date of his first improvements thereon, and shall continue as long as he continues his residence and improvements and no longer. And any Indian or Indians receiving a patent for land under the foregoing provisions shall thereby and from thenceforth become and be a citizen of the United States and be entitled to all the privileges and immunities of such citizens, and shall, at the same time, retain all his rights to benefits accruing to Indians under this treaty.

ARTICLE VII. In order to insure the civilization of the Indians entering into this treaty, the necessity of education is admitted, especially of such of them as are or may be settled on said agricultural reservations, and they, therefore, pledge themselves to compel their children, male and female, between the ages of six and sixteen years, to attend school, and it is hereby made the duty of the agent for said Indians to see that this stipulation is strictly complied with; and the United States agrees that for every thirty children between said ages, who can be induced or compelled to attend school, a house shall be provided, and a teacher competent to teach the elementary branches of an English education shall be furnished, who will reside among said Indians and faithfully discharge his or her duties as a teacher. The provisions of this article to continue for not less than twenty years.

ARTICLE VIII. When the head of a family or lodge shall have selected lands and received his certificate as above directed, and the agent shall be satisfied that he intends in good faith to commence cultivating the soil for a living, he shall be entitled to receive seeds and agricultural implements for the first year, not exceeding in value one hundred dollars, and for each succeeding year he shall continue to farm, for a period of three years more, he shall be entitled to receive seeds and implements as aforesaid, not exceeding in value twenty-five dollars. And it is further stipulated that such persons as commence farming shall receive instruction from the farmer herein provided for, and whenever more than one hundred persons shall enter upon the cultivation of the soil, a second blacksmith shall be provided, with such iron, steel, and other material as may be needed.

ARTICLE IX. At any time after ten years of the making of this treaty, the United States shall have the privilege of withdrawing the physician, farmer, blacksmith, carpenter, engineer, and miller herein provided for, but in case of such withdrawal, an additional sum thereafter of ten thousand dollars per annum shall be devoted to the education of said Indians, and the Commissioner of Indian Affairs shall, upon careful inquiry into their condition, make such rules and regulations for the expenditure of said sums as will best promote the education and moral improvement of said tribes.

ARTICLE X. In lieu of all sums of money or other annuities provided to be paid to the Indians herein named under any treaty or treaties heretofore made, the United States agrees to deliver at the agency house on the reservation herein named, on or before the first day of August of each year, for thirty years, the following articles, to wit:

For each male person over 14 years of age, a suit of good substantial woollen clothing, consisting of coat, pantaloons, flannel shirt, hat, and a pair of home-made socks.

For each female over 12 years of age, a flannel shirt, or the goods necessary to make it, a pair of woollen hose, 12 yards of calico, and 12 yards of cotton domestics.

For the boys and girls under the ages named, such flannel and cotton goods as may be needed to make each a suit as aforesaid, together with a pair of woollen hose for each.

And in order that the Commissioner of Indian Affairs may be able to estimate properly for the articles herein named, it shall be the duty of the agent each year to forward to him a full and exact census of the Indians, on which the estimate from year to year can be based.

And in addition to the clothing herein named, the sum of $10 for each person entitled to the beneficial effects of this treaty shall be annually appropriated for a period of 30 years, while such persons roam and hunt, and $20 for each person who engages in farming, to be used by the Secretary of the Interior in the purchase of such articles as from time to time the condition and necessities of the Indians may indicate to be proper. And if within the 30 years, at any time, it shall appear that the amount of money needed for clothing, under this article, can be appropriated to better uses for the Indians named herein, Congress may, by law, change the appropriation to other purposes, but in no event shall the amount of the appropriation be withdrawn or discontinued for the period named. And the President shall annually detail an officer of the army to be present and attest the delivery of all the goods herein named, to the Indians, and he shall inspect and report on the quantity and quality of the goods and the manner of their delivery. And it is hereby expressly stipulated that each Indian over the age of four years, who shall have removed to and settled permanently upon said reservation, one pound of meat and one pound of flour per day, provided the Indians cannot furnish their own subsistence at an earlier date. And it is further stipulated that the United States will furnish and deliver to each lodge of Indians or family of persons legally incorporated with them, who shall remove to the reservation herein described and commence farming, one good American cow, and one good well-broken pair of American oxen within 60 days after such lodge or family shall have so settled upon said reservation.

ARTICLE XI. In consideration of the advantages and benefits conferred by this treaty and the many pledges of friendship by the United States, the tribes who are parties to this agreement hereby stipulate that they will relinquish all right to occupy permanently the territory outside their reservations as herein defined, but yet reserve the right to hunt on any lands north of North Platte, and on the Republican Fork of the Smoky Hill river, so long as the buffalo may range thereon in such numbers as to justify the chase. And they, the said Indians, further expressly agree:

1st. That they will withdraw all opposition to the construction of the railroads now being built on the plains.

2nd. That they will permit the peaceful construction of any railroad not passing over their reservation as herein defined.

3rd. That they will not attack any persons at home, or travelling, nor molest or disturb any wagon trains, coaches, mules, or cattle belonging to the people of the United States, or to persons friendly therewith.

4th. They will never capture, or carry off from the settlements, white women or children.

5th. They will never kill or scalp white men, nor attempt to do them harm.

6th. They withdraw all pretence of opposition to the construction of the railroad now being built along the Platte river and westward to the Pacific ocean, and they will not in future object to the construction of railroads, wagon roads, mail stations, or other works of utility or necessity, which may be ordered or permitted by the laws of the United States. But should such roads or other works be constructed on the lands of their reservation, the government will pay the tribe whatever amount of damage may be assessed by three disinterested commissioners to be appointed by the President for that purpose, one of the said commissioners to be a chief or headman of the tribe.

7th. They agree to withdraw all opposition to the military posts or roads now established south of the North Platte river, or that may be established, not in violation of treaties heretofore made or hereafter to be made with any of the Indian tribes.

ARTICLE XII. No treaty for the cession of any portion or part of the reservation herein described which may be held in common, shall be of any validity or force as against the said Indians unless executed and signed by at least three-fourths of all the adult male Indians occupying or interested in the same, and no cession by the tribe shall be understood or construed in such manner as to deprive, without his consent, any individual member of the tribe of his rights to any tract of land selected by him as provided in Article VI of this treaty.

ARTICLE XIII. The United States hereby agrees to furnish annually to the Indians the physician, teachers, carpenter, miller, engineer, farmer, and blacksmiths, as herein contemplated, and that such appropriations shall be made from time to time, on the estimate of the Secretary of the Interior, as will be sufficient to employ such persons.

ARTICLE XIV. It is agreed that the sum of five hundred dollars annually for three years from date shall be expended in presents to the ten persons of said tribe who in the judgment of the agent may grow the most valuable crops for the respective year.

ARTICLE XV. The Indians herein named agree that when the agency house and other buildings shall be constructed on the reservation named, they will regard said reservation their permanent home, and they will make no permanent settlement elsewhere; but they shall have the right, subject to the conditions and modifications of this treaty, to hunt, as stipulated in Article XI hereof.

ARTICLE XVI. The United States hereby agrees and stipulates that the country north of the North Platte river and east of the summits of the Big Horn mountains shall be held and considered to be unceded Indian territory, and also stipulates and agrees that no white person or persons shall be permitted to settle upon or occupy any portion of the same; or without the consent of the Indians, first had and obtained, to pass through the same; and it is further agreed by the United States, that within ninety days after the conclusion of peace with all the bands of the Sioux nation, the military posts now established in the territory in this article named shall be abandoned, and that the road leading to them and by them to the settlements in the Territory of Montana shall be closed.

ARTICLE XVII. It is hereby expressly understood and agreed by and between the respective parties to this treaty that the execution of this treaty and its ratification by the United States Senate shall have the effect, and shall be construed as abrogating and annulling all treaties and agreements heretofore entered into between the respective parties hereto, so far as such treaties and agreements obligate the United States to furnish and provide money, clothing, or other articles of property to such Indians and bands of Indians as become parties to this treaty, but no further.

In testimony of all which, we, the said commissioners, and we, the chiefs and headmen of the Brule band of the Sioux nation, have hereunto set our hands and seals at Fort Laramie, Dakota Territory, this twenty-ninth day of April, in the year one thousand eight hundred and sixty-eight.

Treaty of Paris between Spain and the United States, 1898

At the end of the War with Spain, the United States found itself holding a number of islands which it had not previously claimed. The Philippines and Puerto Rico, once Spanish possessions, were under the Stars and Stripes by the end of 1898. The Treaty of Paris, signed in December of that year, brought peace. It also provided the start of an American "empire" over these islands. As an international treaty, it carried serious obligations for the United States. Significant sections of the Treaty are here given.

ARTICLE I. Spain relinquishes all claim of sovereignty over and title to Cuba.

And as the island is, upon its evacuation by Spain, to be occupied by the United States, the United States will, so long as such occupation shall last, assume and discharge the obligations that may under international law result from the fact of its occupation, for the protection of life and property.

ARTICLE II. Spain cedes to the United States the island of Porto Rico and other islands now under Spanish sovereignty in the West Indies, and the island of Guam in the Marianas or Ladrones.

ARTICLE III. Spain cedes to the United States the archipelago known as the Philippine Islands, and comprehending the islands lying within the following line:

A line running from west to east along or near the twentieth parallel of north latitude, and through the middle of the navigable channel of Bachi, from the one hundred and eighteenth (118th) to the one hundred and twenty seventh (127th) degree meridian of longitude east of Greenwich, thence along the one hundred and twenty seventh (127th) degree meridian of longitude east of Greenwich to the parallel of four degrees and forty five minutes (4° 45′) north latitude, thence along the parallel of four degrees and forty five minutes (4° 45′) north latitude to its intersection with the meridian of longitude one hundred and nineteen degrees and thirty five minutes (119° 35′) east of Greenwich, thence along the meridian of longitude one hundred and nineteen degrees and thirty five minutes (119° 35′) east of Greenwich to the parallel of latitude seven degrees and forty minutes (7° 40′) north, thence along the parallel of latitude seven degrees and forty minutes (7° 40′) north to its intersection with the one hundred and sixteenth (116th) degree meridian of longitude east of Greenwich, thence by a direct line to the intersection of the tenth (10th) degree parallel of north latitude with the one hundred and eighteenth (118th) degree meridian of longitude east of Greenwich, and thence along the one hundred and eighteenth (118th) degree meridian of longitude east of Greenwich to the point of beginning.

The United States will pay to Spain the sum of twenty million dollars ($20,000,000) within three months after the exchange of the ratifications of the present treaty.

ARTICLE IV. The United States will, for the term of ten years from the date of the exchange of the ratifications of the present treaty, admit Spanish ships and merchandise to the ports of the Philippine Islands on the same terms as ships and merchandise of the United States.

ARTICLE V. The United States will, upon the signature of the present treaty, send back to Spain, at its own cost, the Spanish soldiers taken as prisoners of war on the capture of Manila by the American forces. The arms of the soldiers in question shall be restored to them.

Spain will, upon the exchange of the ratifications of the present treaty, proceed to evacuate the Philippines, as well as the island of Guam, on terms similar to those agreed upon by the Commissioners appointed to arrange for the evacuation of Porto Rico and other islands in the West Indies, under the Protocol of August 12, 1898, which is to continue in force till its provisions are completely executed. . . .

ARTICLE VI. Spain will, upon the signature of the present treaty, release all prisoners of war, and all persons detained or imprisoned for political offences, in connection with the insurrections in Cuba and the Philippines and the war with the United States.

Reciprocally, the United States will release all persons made prisoners of war by the American forces, and will undertake to obtain the release of all Spanish prisoners in the hands of the insurgents in Cuba and the Philippines.

The Government of the United States will at its own cost return to Spain and the Government of Spain will at its own cost return to the United States, Cuba, Porto Rico, and the Philippines, according to the situation of their respective homes, prisoners released or caused to be released by them, respectively, under this article.

ARTICLE VII. The United States and Spain mutually relinquish all claims for indemnity, national and individual, of every kind, of either Government, or of its citizens or subjects, against the other Government, that may have arisen since the beginning of the late insurrection in Cuba and prior to the exchange of ratifications of the present treaty, including all claims for indemnity for the cost of the war.

The United States will adjudicate and settle the claims of its citizens against Spain relinquished in this article.

ARTICLE VIII. In conformity with the provisions of Articles I, II, and III of this treaty, Spain relinquishes in Cuba, and cedes in Porto Rico and other islands in the West Indies, in the island of Guam, and in the Philippine Archipelago, all the buildings, wharves, barracks, forts, structures, public highways and other immovable property which, in conformity with law, belong to the public domain, and as such belong to the Crown of Spain.

And it is hereby declared that the relinquishment or cession, as the case may be, to which the preceding paragraph refers, cannot in any respect impair the property or rights which by law belong to the peaceful possession of property of all kinds, of provinces, municipalities, public or private establishments, ecclesiastical or civic bodies, or any other associations having legal capacity to acquire and possess property in the aforesaid territories renounced or ceded, or of private individuals, of whatsoever nationality such individuals may be.

The aforesaid relinquishment or cession, as the case may be, includes all documents exclusively referring to the sovereignty relinquished or ceded that may exist in the archives of the Peninsula. Where any document in such archives only in part relates to said sovereignty, a copy of such part will be furnished wherever it shall be requested. Like rules shall be reciprocally observed in favor of Spain in respect of documents in the archives of the islands above referred to.

In the aforesaid relinquishment or cession, as the case may be, are also included such rights as the Crown of Spain and its authorities possess in respect of the official archives and records, executive as well as judicial, in the islands above referred to, which relate to said islands or the rights and property of their inhabitants. Such archives and records shall be carefully preserved, and private persons shall without distinction have the right to require, in accordance with law, authenticated copies of the contracts, wills and other instruments forming part of notarial protocols or files, or which may be contained in the executive or judicial archives, be the latter in Spain or in the islands aforesaid.

ARTICLE IX. Spanish subjects, natives of the Peninsula, residing in the territory over which Spain by the present treaty relinquishes or cedes her sovereignty, may remain in such territory or may remove therefrom, retaining in either event all their rights of property, including the right to sell or dispose of such property or of its proceeds; and they shall also have the right to carry on their industry, commerce and professions, being subject in respect thereof to such laws as are applicable to other foreigners. In case they remain in the territory they may preserve their allegiance to the Crown of Spain by making, before a court of record, within a year from the date of the exchange of ratifications of this treaty, a declaration of their decision to preserve such allegiance; in default of which declaration they shall be held to have renounced it and to have adopted the nationality of the territory in which they may reside.

The civil rights and political status of the native inhabitants of the territories hereby ceded to the United States shall be determined by the Congress.

ARTICLE X. The inhabitants of the territories over which Spain relinquishes or cedes her sovereignty shall be secured in the free exercise of their religion.

ARTICLE XI. The Spaniards residing in the territories over which Spain by this treaty cedes or relinquishes her sovereignty shall be subject in matters civil as well as criminal to the jurisdiction of the courts of the country wherein they reside, pursuant to the ordinary laws governing the same; and they shall have the right to appear before such courts, and to pursue the same course as citizens of the country to which the courts belong.

ARTICLE XII. Judicial proceedings pending at the time of the exchange of ratifications of this treaty in the territories over which Spain relinquishes or cedes her sovereignty shall be determined according to the following rules:

1. Judgments rendered either in civil suits between private individuals, or in criminal matters, before the date mentioned, and with respect to which there is no recourse or right of review under the Spanish law, shall be deemed to be final, and shall be executed in the form by competent authority in the territory within which such judgments should be carried out.

2. Civil suits between private individuals which may on the date mentioned be undetermined shall be prosecuted to judgment before the court in which they may then be pending or in the court that may be substituted therefor.

3. Criminal actions pending on the date mentioned before the Supreme Court of Spain against citizens of the territory which by this treaty ceases to be Spanish shall continue under its jurisdiction until final judgment; but, such judgment having been rendered, the execution thereof shall be committed to the competent authority of the place in which the case arose.

ARTICLE XIII. The rights of property secured by copyrights and patents acquired by Spaniards in the Island of Cuba, and in Porto Rico, the Philippines and other ceded territories, at the time of the exchange of the ratifications of this treaty, shall continue to be respected. Spanish scientific, literary and artistic works, not subversive of public order in the territories in question, shall continue to be admitted free of duty into such territories, for the period of ten years, to be reckoned from the date of the exchange of the ratifications of this treaty.

ARTICLE XIV. Spain shall have the power to establish consular officers in the ports and places of the territories, the sovereignty over which has been either relinquished or ceded by the present treaty.

ARTICLE XV. The Government of each country will, for the term of ten years, accord to the merchant vessels of the other country the same treatment in respect of all port charges, including entrance and clearance dues, light dues, and tonnage duties, as it accords to its own merchant vessels, not engaged in the coastwise trade.

This article may at any time be terminated on six months' notice given by either Government to the other.

ARTICLE XVI. It is understood that any obligations assumed in this treaty by the United States with respect to Cuba are limited to the time of its occupancy thereof; but it will upon the termination of such occupancy advise any Government established in the island to assume the same obligations.

Treaty of Versailles: Treaty of Peace between the Allied and Associated Powers and Germany, 1919 (excerpts)

THE COVENANT OF THE LEAGUE OF NATIONS.

THE HIGH CONTRACTING PARTIES, in order to promote international co-operation and to achieve international peace and security by the acceptance of obligations not to resort to war by the prescription of open, just and honourable relations between nations by the firm establishment of the understandings of international law as the actual rule of conduct among Governments, and by the maintenance of justice and a scrupulous respect for all treaty obligations in the dealings of organised peoples with one another Agree to this Covenant of the League of Nations.

ARTICLE 1. The original Members of the League of Nations shall be those of the Signatories which are named in the Annex to this Covenant and also such of those other States named in the Annex as shall accede without reservation to this Covenant. Such accession shall be effected by a Declaration deposited with the Secretariat within two months of the coming into force of the Covenant Notice thereof shall be sent to all other Members of the League. Any fully self-governing State, Dominion, or Colony not named in the Annex may become a Member of the League if its admission is agreed to by two-thirds of the Assembly provided that it shall give effective guarantees of its sincere intention to observe its international obligations, and shall accept such regulations as may be prescribed by the League in regard to its military, naval, and air forces and armaments. Any Member of the League may, after two years' notice of its intention so to do, withdraw from the League, provided that all its international obligations and all its obligations under this Covenant shall have been fulfilled at the time of its withdrawal.

ARTICLE 10. The Members of the League undertake to respect and preserve as against external aggression the territorial integrity and existing political independence of all Members of the League. In case of any such aggression or in case of any threat or danger of such aggression the Council shall advise upon the means by which this obligation shall be fulfilled.

ARTICLE 11. Any war or threat of war, whether immediately affecting any of the Members of the League or not, is hereby declared a matter of concern to the whole League, and the League shall take any action that may be deemed wise and effectual to safeguard the peace of nations. In case any such emergency should arise the Secretary General shall on the request of any Member of the League forthwith summon a meeting of the Council. It is also declared to be the friendly right of each Member of the League to bring to the attention of the Assembly or of the Council any circumstance whatever affecting international relations which threatens to disturb international peace or the good understanding between nations upon which peace depends.

ARTICLE 12. The Members of the League agree that if there should arise between them any dispute likely to lead to a rupture, they will submit the matter either to arbitration or to inquiry by the Council, and they agree in no case to resort to war until three months after the award by the arbitrators or the report by the Council. In any case under this Article the award of the arbitrators shall be made within a reasonable time, and the report of the Council shall be made within six months after the submission of the dispute.

ARTICLE 13. The Members of the League agree that whenever any dispute shall arise between them which they recognise to be suitable for submission to arbitration and which cannot be satisfactorily settled by diplomacy, they will submit the whole subject-matter to arbitration. Disputes as to the interpretation of a treaty, as to any question of international law, as to the existence of any fact which if established would constitute a breach of any international obligation, or as to the extent and nature of the reparation to be made or any such breach, are declared to be among those which are generally suitable for submission to arbitration. For the consideration of any such dispute the court of arbitration to which the case is referred shall be the Court agreed on by the parties to the dispute or stipulated in any convention existing between them. The Members of the League agree that they will carry out in full good faith any award that may be rendered, and that they will not resort to war against a Member of the League which complies therewith. In the event of any failure to carry out such an award, the Council shall propose what steps should be taken to give effect thereto.

ARTICLE 16. Should any Member of the League resort to war in disregard of its covenants under Articles 12, 13, or 15, it shall ipso facto be deemed to have committed an act of war against all other Members of the League, which hereby undertake immediately to subject it to the severance of all trade or financial relations, the prohibition of all intercourse between their nations and the nationals of the covenant-breaking State, and the prevention of all financial, commercial, or personal intercourse between the nationals of the covenant-breaking State and the nationals of any other State, whether a Member of the League or not. It shall be the duty of the Council in such case to recommend to the several Governments concerned what effective military, naval, or air force the Members of the League shall severally contribute to the armed forces to be used to protect the covenants of the League. The Members of the League agree, further, that they will mutually support one another in the financial and economic measures which are taken under this Article, in order to minimise the loss and inconvenience resulting from the above measures, and that they will mutually support one another in resisting any special measures aimed at one of their number by the covenant-breaking State, and that they will take the necessary steps to afford passage through their territory to the forces of any of the Members of the League which are co-operating to protect the covenants of the League. Any Member of the League which has violated any covenant of the League may be declared to be no longer a Member of the League by a vote of the Council concurred in by the Representatives of all the other Members of the League represented thereon.

PART IV. GERMAN RIGHTS AND INTERESTS OUTSIDE GERMANY

ARTICLE 118. In territory outside her European frontiers as fixed by the present Treaty, Germany renounces all rights, titles and privileges what ever in or over territory which belonged to her or to her allies, and all rights, titles and privileges whatever their origin which she held as against the Allied and Associated Powers.

Germany hereby undertakes to recognise and to conform to the measures which may be taken now or in the future by the Principal Allied and Associated Powers, in agreement where necessary with third Powers, in order to carry the above stipulation into effect.

PART VIII. REPARATION. SECTION I. GENERAL PROVISIONS.

ARTICLE 231. The Allied and Associated Governments affirm and Germany accepts the responsibility of Germany and her allies for causing all the loss and damage to which the Allied and Associated Governments and their nationals have been subjected as a consequence of the war imposed upon them by the aggression of Germany and her allies.

ARTICLE 232. The Allied and Associated Governments recognise that the resources of Germany are not adequate, after taking into account permanent diminutions of such resources which will result from other provisions of the present Treaty, to make complete reparation for all such loss and damage.

The Allied and Associated Governments, however, require, and Germany undertakes, that she will make compensation for all damage done to the civilian population of the Allied and Associated Powers and to their property during the period of the belligerency of each as an Allied or Associated Power against Germany by such aggression by land, by sea and from the air, and in general all damage as defined in Annex 1 hereto.

Treaty of Peace with Japan, 1951

Whereas the Allied Powers and Japan are resolved that henceforth their relations shall be those of nations which, as sovereign equals, cooperate in friendly association to promote their common welfare and to maintain international peace and security, and are therefore desirous of concluding a Treaty of Peace which will settle questions still outstanding as a result of the existence of a state of war between them;

Whereas Japan for its part declares its intention to apply for membership in the United Nations and in all circumstances to conform to the principles of the Charter of the United Nations; to strive to realize the objectives of the Universal Declaration of Human Rights; to seek to create within Japan conditions of stability and well-being as defined in Articles 55 and 56 of the Charter of the United Nations and already initiated by post-surrender Japanese legislation; and in public and private trade and commerce to conform to internationally accepted fair practices;

Whereas the Allied Powers welcome the intentions of Japan set out in the foregoing paragraph;

The Allied Powers and Japan have therefore determined to conclude the present Treaty of Peace, and have accordingly appointed the undersigned plenipotentiaries, who, after presentation of their full powers, found in good and due form, have agreed on the following provisions:

CHAPTER I: PEACE

ARTICLE 1. (a) The state of war between Japan and each of the Allied Powers is terminated as from the date on which the present Treaty comes into force between Japan and the Allied Power concerned as provided for in Article 23.

(b) The Allied Powers recognize the full sovereignty of the Japanese people over Japan and its territorial waters.

CHAPTER II: TERRITORY

ARTICLE 2. (a) Japan, recognizing the independence of Korea, renounces all right, title and claim to Korea, including the islands of Quelpart, Port Hamilton and Dagelet.

(b) Japan renounces all right, title and claim to Formosa and the Pescadores.

(c) Japan renounces all rights, title and claim to the Kurile islands, and to that portion of Sakhalin and the islands adjacent to it over which Japan acquired sovereignty as a consequence of the Treaty of Portsmouth of September 5, 1905.

(d) Japan renounces all right, title and claim in connection with the League of Nations Mandate System, and accepts the action of the United Nations Security Council of April 2, 1947, extending the trusteeship system to the Pacific islands formerly under mandate to Japan.

(e) Japan renounces all claim to any right or title to or interest in connection with any part of the Antarctic area, whether deriving from the activities of Japanese nationals or otherwise.

(f) Japan renounces all right, title and claim to the Spratly islands and to the Paracel islands.

. . .

CHAPTER III: SECURITY

ARTICLE 5. (a) Japan accepts the obligations set forth in Article 2 of the Charter of the United Nations, and in particular the obligations

(i) to settle its international disputes by peaceful means in such a manner that international peace and security, and justice, are not endangered;

(ii) to refrain in its international relations from the threat or use of force against the territorial integrity or political independence of any State or in any other manner inconsistent with the Purposes of the United Nations;

(iii) to give the United Nations every assistance in any action it takes in accordance with the Charter and to refrain from giving assistance to any State against which the United Nations may take preventive or enforcement action.

(b) The Allied Powers confirm that they will be guided by the principles of Article 2 of the Charter of the United Nations in their relations with Japan.

(c) The Allied Powers for their part recognize that Japan as a sovereign nation possesses the inherent right of individual or collective self-defense referred to in Article 51 of the Charter of the United Nations and that Japan may voluntarily enter into collective security arrangements.

ARTICLE 6. (a) All occupation forces of the Allied Powers shall be withdrawn from Japan as soon as possible after the coming into force of the present Treaty, and in any case not later than ninety days thereafter. Nothing in this provision shall, however, prevent the stationing or retention of foreign armed forces in Japanese territory under or in consequence of any bilateral or multilateral agreements which have been or may be made between one or more of the Allied Powers, on the one hand, and Japan on the other.

(b) The provisions of Article 9 of the Potsdam Proclamation of July 26, 1945, dealing with the return of Japanese military forces to their homes, to the extent not already completed, will be carried out.

. . .

CHAPTER IV: POLITICAL AND ECONOMIC CLAUSES

. . .

ARTICLE 10. Japan renounces all special rights and interests in China, including all benefits and privileges resulting from the provisions of the final Protocol signed at Peking on September 7, 1901, and all annexes, notes and documents supplementary thereto, and agrees to the abrogation in respect to Japan of the said Protocol, annexes, notes and documents.

ARTICLE 11. Japan accepts the judgements of the International Military Tribunal for the Far East and of other Allied War Crimes Courts both within and outside Japan, and will carry out the sentences imposed thereby upon Japanese nationals imprisoned in Japan. The power to grant clemency, to reduce sentences and to parole with respect to such prisoners may not be exercised except on the decision of the Government or Governments which imposed the sentence in each instance, and on the recommendation of Japan. In the case of persons sentenced by the International Military Tribunal for the Far East, such power may not be exercised except on the decision of a majority of the Governments represented on the Tribunal, and on the recommendation of Japan.

ARTICLE 12. [Trade arrangements] . . . (c) In respect to any matter, however, Japan shall be obliged to accord to an Allied Power national treatment, or most-favored-nation treatment, only to the extent that the Allied Power concerned accords Japan national treatment or most-favored-nation treatment, as the case may be, in respect of the same matter.

. . .

CHAPTER V: CLAIMS AND PROPERTY

ARTICLE 14. (a) It is recognized that Japan should pay reparations to the Allied Powers for the damage and suffering caused by it during the war. Nevertheless it is also recognized that the resources of Japan are not presently sufficient, if it is to maintain a viable economy, to make complete reparation for all such damage and suffering and at the same time meet its other obligations.

Therefore,

(i) Japan will promptly enter into negotiations with Allied Powers so desiring, whose present territories were occupied by Japanese forces and damaged by Japan, with a view to assisting to compensate those countries for the cost of repairing the damage done, by making available the services of the Japanese people in production, salvaging and other work for the Allied Powers in question. Such arrangements shall avoid the imposition of additional liabilities on other Allied Powers, and, where the manufacturing of raw materials is called for, they shall be supplied by the Allied Powers in question, so as not to throw any foreign exchange burden upon Japan. . . .

(b) Except as otherwise provided in the present Treaty, the Allied Powers waive all reparations claims of the Allied Powers, other claims of the Allied Powers and their nationals arising out of any actions taken by Japan and its nationals in the course of the prosecution of the war, and claims of the Allied Powers for direct military costs of occupation.

. . .

ARTICLE 16. As an expression of its desire to indemnify those members of the armed forces of the Allied Powers who suffered undue hardships while prisoners of war of Japan, Japan will transfer its assets and those of its nationals in countries which were neutral during the war, or which were at war with any of the Allied Powers, or, at its option, the equivalent of such assets, to the International Committee of the Red Cross which shall liquidate such assets and distribute the resultant fund to appropriate national agencies, for the benefit of former prisoners of war and their families on such basis as it may determine to be equitable. . . .

CHAPTER VII: FINAL CLAUSES

ARTICLE 23. (a) The present Treaty shall be ratified by the States which sign it, including Japan, and will come into force for all the States which have then ratified it, when instruments of ratification have been deposited by Japan and by a majority, including the United States of America as the principal occupying Power. . . .

ARTICLE 26. Japan will be prepared to conclude with any State which signed or adhered to the United Nations Declaration of January 1, 1942, and which is at war with Japan, or with any State which previously formed a part of the territory of a State named in Article 23, which is not a signatory of the present Treaty, a bilateral treaty of peace on the same or substantially the same terms as are provided for in the present Treaty, but this obligation on the part of Japan will expire three years after the first coming into force of the present Treaty. Should Japan make a peace settlement or war claims settlement with any State granting that State greater advantages than those provided by the present Treaty, those same advantages shall be extended to the parties to the present Treaty.

The Vietnam Peace Agreement (Paris Peace Accords), 1973

The Parties participating in the Paris Conference on Vietnam,

With a view to ending the war and restoring peace in Vietnam on the basis of respect for the Vietnamese people's fundamental national rights and the South Vietnamese people's right to self-determination, and to contributing to the consolidation of peace in Asia and the world,

Have agreed on the following provisions and undertake to respect and to implement them:

CHAPTER I
THE VIETNAMESE PEOPLE'S FUNDAMENTAL NATIONAL RIGHTS

ARTICLE 1 The United States and all other countries respect the independence, sovereignty, unity, and territorial integrity of Vietnam as recognized by the 1954 Geneva Agreements on Vietnam.

CHAPTER II
CESSATION OF HOSTILITIES—WITHDRAWAL OF TROOPS

ARTICLE 2 A cease-fire shall be observed throughout South Vietnam as of 2400 hours G.M.T., on January 27, 1973.

At the same hour, the United States will stop all its military activities against the territory of the Democratic Republic of Vietnam by ground, air and naval forces, wherever they may be based, and end the mining of the territorial waters, ports, harbors, and waterways of the Democratic Republic of Vietnam. The United States will remove, permanently deactivate or destroy all the mines in the territorial waters, ports, harbors, and waterways of North Vietnam as soon as this Agreement goes into effect.

The complete cessation of hostilities mentioned in this Article shall be durable and without limit of time.

ARTICLE 3 The parties undertake to maintain the cease-fire and to ensure a lasting and stable peace.

As soon as the cease-fire goes into effect:

(a) The United States forces and those of the other foreign countries allied with the United States and the Republic of Vietnam shall remain in-place pending the implementation of the plan of troop withdrawal. The Four-Party Joint Military Commission described in Article 16 shall determine the modalities.

(b) The armed forces of the two South Vietnamese parties shall remain in-place. The Two-Party Joint Military Commission described in Article 17 shall determine the areas controlled by each party and the modalities of stationing.

(c) The regular forces of all services and arms and the irregular forces of the parties in South Vietnam shall stop all offensive activities against each other and shall strictly abide by the following stipulations:

—All acts of force on the ground, in the air, and on the sea shall be prohibited;

—All hostile acts, terrorism and reprisals by both sides will be banned.

ARTICLE 4 The United States will not continue its military involvement or intervene in the general affairs of South Vietnam.

ARTICLE 5 Within sixty days of the signing of this Agreement, there will be a total withdrawal from South Vietnam of troops, military advisers, and military personnel, including technical military personnel and military personnel associated with the pacification program, armaments, munitions, and war material of the United States and those of the other foreign countries mentioned in Article 3 (a). Advisers from the above-mentioned countries to all paramilitary organizations and the police force will also be withdrawn within the same period of time.

ARTICLE 6 The dismantlement of all military bases in South Vietnam of the United States and of the other foreign countries mentioned in Article 3 (a) shall be completed within sixty days of the signing of this Agreement.

ARTICLE 7 From the enforcement of the cease-fire to the formation of the government provided for in Articles 9 (b) and 14 of this Agreement, the two South Vietnamese parties shall not accept the introduction of troops, military advisers, and military personnel including technical military personnel, armaments, munitions, and war material into South Vietnam.

The two South Vietnamese parties shall be permitted to make periodic replacement of armaments, munitions and war material which have been destroyed, damaged, worn out or used up after the cease-fire, on the basis of piece-for-piece, of the same characteristics and properties, under the supervision of the International Commission of Control and Supervision.

CHAPTER III
THE RETURN OF CAPTURED MILITARY PERSONNEL AND FOREIGN CIVILIANS, AND CAPTURED AND DETAINED VIETNAMESE CIVILIAN PERSONNEL

ARTICLE 8 (a) The return of captured military personnel and foreign civilians of the parties shall be carried out simultaneously with and completed not later than the same day as the troop withdrawal mentioned in Article 5. The parties shall exchange complete lists of the above-mentioned captured military personnel and foreign civilians on the day of the signing of this Agreement.

(b) The parties shall help each other to get information about those military personnel and foreign civilians of the parties missing in action, to determine the location and take care of the graves of the dead so as to facilitate the exhumation and repatriation of the remains, and to take any such other measures as may be required to get information about those still considered missing in action.

(c) The question of the return of Vietnamese civilian personnel captured and detained in South Vietnam will be resolved by the two South Vietnamese parties on the basis of the principles of Article 21 (b) of the Agreement on the Cessation of Hostilities in Vietnam of July 20, 1954. The two South Vietnamese parties will do so in a spirit of national reconciliation and concord, with a view to ending hatred and enmity, in order to ease suffering and to reunite families. The two South Vietnamese parties will do their utmost to resolve this question within ninety days after the cease-fire comes into effect.

CHAPTER IV
THE EXERCISE OF THE SOUTH VIETNAMESE PEOPLE'S RIGHT TO SELF-DETERMINATION

ARTICLE 9 The Government of the United States of America and the Government of the Democratic Republic of Vietnam undertake to respect the following principles for the exercise of the South Vietnamese people's right to self-determination:

(a) The South Vietnamese people's right to self-determination is sacred, inalienable, and shall be respected by all countries.

(b) The South Vietnamese people shall decide themselves the political future of South Vietnam through genuinely free and democratic general elections under international supervision.

(c) Foreign countries shall not impose any political tendency or personality on the South Vietnamese people.

ARTICLE 10 The two South Vietnamese parties undertake to respect the cease-fire and maintain peace in South Vietnam, settle all matters of contention through negotiations, and avoid all armed conflict.

ARTICLE 11 Immediately after the cease-fire, the two South Vietnamese parties will:

—achieve national reconciliation and concord, end hatred and enmity, prohibit all acts of reprisal and discrimination against individuals or organizations that have collaborated with one side or the other;

—ensure the democratic liberties of the people: personal freedom, freedom of speech, freedom of the press, freedom of meeting, freedom of organization, freedom of political activities, freedom of belief, freedom of movement, freedom of residence, freedom of work, right to property ownership, and right to free enterprise.

ARTICLE 12 (a) Immediately after the cease-fire, the two South Vietnamese parties shall hold consultation in a spirit of national reconciliation and concord, mutual respect, and mutual non-elimination to set up a National Council of National Reconciliation and Concord of three equal segments. The council shall operate on the principle of unanimity. After the National Council of National Reconciliation and Concord has assumed its functions, the two South Vietnamese parties will consult about the formation of councils at lower levels. The two South Vietnamese parties shall sign an agreement on the internal matters of South Vietnam as soon as possible and do their utmost to accomplish this within ninety days after the cease-fire comes into effect, in keeping with the South Vietnamese people's aspirations for peace, independence and democracy.

(b) The National Council of National Reconciliation and Concord shall have the task of promoting the two South Vietnamese parties' implementation of this Agreement, achievement of national reconciliation and concord and ensurance of democratic liberties. The National Council of National Reconciliation and Concord will organize the free and democratic general elections provided for in Article 9 (b) and decide the procedures and modalities of these general elections. The institutions for which the general elections are to be held will be agreed upon through consultations between the two South Vietnamese parties. The National Council of National Reconciliation and Concord will also decide the procedures and modalities of such local elections as the two South Vietnamese parties agree upon.

ARTICLE 13 The question of Vietnamese armed forces in South Vietnam shall be settled by the two South Vietnamese parties in a spirit of national reconciliation and concord, equality and mutual respect, without foreign interference, in accordance with the postwar situation. Among the questions to be discussed by the two South Vietnamese parties are steps to reduce their military effectiveness and to demobilize the troops being reduced. The two South Vietnamese parties will accomplish this as soon as possible.

ARTICLE 14 South Vietnam will pursue a foreign policy of peace and independence. It will be prepared to establish relations with all countries irrespective of their political and social systems on the basis of mutual respect for independence and sovereignty and accept economic and technical aid from any country with no political conditions attached. The acceptance of military aid by South Vietnam in the future shall come under the authority of the government set up after the general elections in South Vietnam provided for in Article 9 (b).

CHAPTER V
THE REUNIFICATION OF VIETNAM AND THE RELATIONSHIP BETWEEN NORTH AND SOUTH VIETNAM

ARTICLE 15 The reunification of Vietnam shall be carried out step by step through peaceful means on the basis of discussions and agreements between North and South Vietnam, without coercion or annexation by either party, and without foreign interference. The time for reunification will be agreed upon by North and South Vietnam.

Pending reunification:

(a) The military demarcation line between the two zones at the 17th parallel is only provisional and not a political or territorial boundary, as provided for in paragraph 6 of the Final Declaration of the 1954 Geneva Conference.

(b) North and South Vietnam shall respect the Demilitarized Zone on either side of the Provisional Military Demarcation Line.

(c) North and South Vietnam shall promptly start negotiations with a view to reestablishing normal relations in various fields. Among the questions to be negotiated are the modalities of civilian movement across the Provisional Military Demarcation Line.

(d) North and South Vietnam shall not join any military alliance or military bloc and shall not allow foreign powers to maintain military bases, troops, military advisers, and military personnel on their respective territories, as stipulated in the 1954 Geneva Agreements on Vietnam.

CHAPTER VII
REGARDING CAMBODIA AND LAOS

ARTICLE 20 (a) The parties participating in the Paris Conference on Vietnam shall strictly respect the 1954 Geneva Agreements on Cambodia and the 1962 Geneva Agreements on Laos, which recognized the Cambodian and the Lao peoples' fundamental national rights, i.e., the independence, sovereignty, unity, and territorial integrity of these countries. The parties shall respect the neutrality of Cambodia and Laos.

The parties participating in the Paris Conference on Vietnam undertake to refrain from using the territory of Cambodia and the territory of Laos to encroach on the sovereignty and security of one another and of other countries.

(b) Foreign countries shall put an end to all military activities in Cambodia and Laos, totally withdraw from and refrain from reintroducing into these two countries troops, military advisers and military personnel, armaments, munitions and war material.

(c) The internal affairs of Cambodia and Laos shall be settled by the people of each of these countries without foreign interference.

(d) The problems existing between the Indochinese countries shall be settled by the Indochinese parties on the basis of respect for each other's independence, sovereignty, and territorial integrity, and non-interference in each other's internal affairs.

CHAPTER VIII
THE RELATIONSHIP BETWEEN THE UNITED STATES AND THE DEMOCRATIC REPUBLIC OF VIETNAM

ARTICLE 21 The United States anticipates that this Agreement will usher in an era of reconciliation with the Democratic Republic of Vietnam as with all the peoples of Indochina. In pursuance of its traditional policy, the United States will contribute to healing the wounds of war and to postwar reconstruction of the Democratic Republic of Vietnam and throughout Indochina.

ARTICLE 22 The ending of the war, the restoration of peace in Vietnam, and the strict implementation of this Agreement will create conditions for establishing a new, equal and mutually beneficial relationship between the United States and the Democratic Republic of Vietnam on the basis of respect for each other's independence and sovereignty, and non-interference in each other's internal affairs. At the same time this will ensure stable peace in Vietnam and contribute to the preservation of lasting peace in Indochina and Southeast Asia.

CHAPTER IX
OTHER PROVISIONS

ARTICLE 23 This Agreement shall enter into force upon signature by plenipotentiary representatives of the parties participating in the Paris Conference on Vietnam. All the parties concerned shall strictly implement this Agreement and its Protocols.

Done in Paris this twenty-seventh day of January, One Thousand Nine Hundred and Seventy-Three in Vietnamese and English. The Vietnamese and English texts are official and equally authentic.

(There then follows a very long series of "Protocols," or precise agreements on specific points.)

Index

I

T